AGE, WEIGHT

For use wit

Distance	Age	Mar.	Apr.							
5f	4	10–0	10–0							
	3	9–0	9–2							
	2	6–8	6–13							
6f	4	9–13	10–0	10–0	10–0	10–0	10–0	10–0	10–0	10–0
	3	8–11	9–0	9–2	9–4	9–6	9–8	9–10	9–11	9–12
	2			6–13	7–3	7–7	7–11	8–1	8–5	8–8
7f	4	9–12	9–13	10–0	10–0	10–0	10–0	10–0	10–0	10–0
	3	8–8	8–11	9–0	9–2	9–4	9–6	9–8	9–10	9–11
	2					7–4	7–8	7–12	8–2	8–5
1m	4	9–11	9–12	9–13	10–0	10–0	10–0	10–0	10–0	10–0
	3	8–6	8–9	8–12	9–1	9–3	9–5	9–7	9–9	9–10
	2							7–9	7–13	8–2
9f	4	9–11	9–12	9–13	9–13	10–0	10–0	10–0	10–0	10–0
	3	8–4	8–7	8–10	8–13	9–2	9–4	9–6	9–8	9–9
1¼m	4	9–10	9–11	9–12	9–13	10–0	10–0	10–0	10–0	10–0
	3	8–2	8–5	8–8	8–11	9–0	9–3	9–5	9–7	9–8
11f	4	9–9	9–11	9–12	9–13	9–13	10–0	10–0	10–0	10–0
	3	8–0	8–4	8–7	8–10	8–13	9–2	9–4	9–6	9–7
1½m	4	9–9	9–10	9–11	9–12	9–13	10–0	10–0	10–0	10–0
	3	7–12	8–2	8–5	8–8	8–11	9–0	9–3	9–5	9–7
13f	4	9–8	9–10	9–11	9–12	9–13	9–13	10–0	10–0	10–0
	3	7–11	8–1	8–4	8–7	8–10	8–13	9–2	9–4	9–6
1¾m	4	9–7	9–9	9–10	9–12	9–13	9–13	10–0	10–0	10–0
	3	7–9	7–13	8–3	8–6	8–9	8–12	9–1	9–3	9–5
15f	4	9–6	9–8	9–10	9–11	9–12	9–13	10–0	10–0	10–0
	3	7–8	7–12	8–2	8–5	8–8	8–11	9–0	9–2	9–4
2m	4	9–6	9–8	9–10	9–11	9–12	9–13	10–0	10–0	10–0
	3	7–7	7–11	8–1	8–5	8–8	8–11	9–0	9–2	9–4
2¼m	4	9–6	9–8	9–9	9–11	9–12	9–13	10–0	10–0	10–0
	3	7–6	7–10	8–0	8–4	8–7	8–10	8–13	9–1	9–3
2½m	4	9–5	9–7	9–9	9–10	9–11	9–12	9–13	10–0	10–0
	3	7–5	7–9	7–13	8–3	8–6	8–9	8–12	9–1	9–3

For 5-y-o's and older, use 10-0 in all cases.

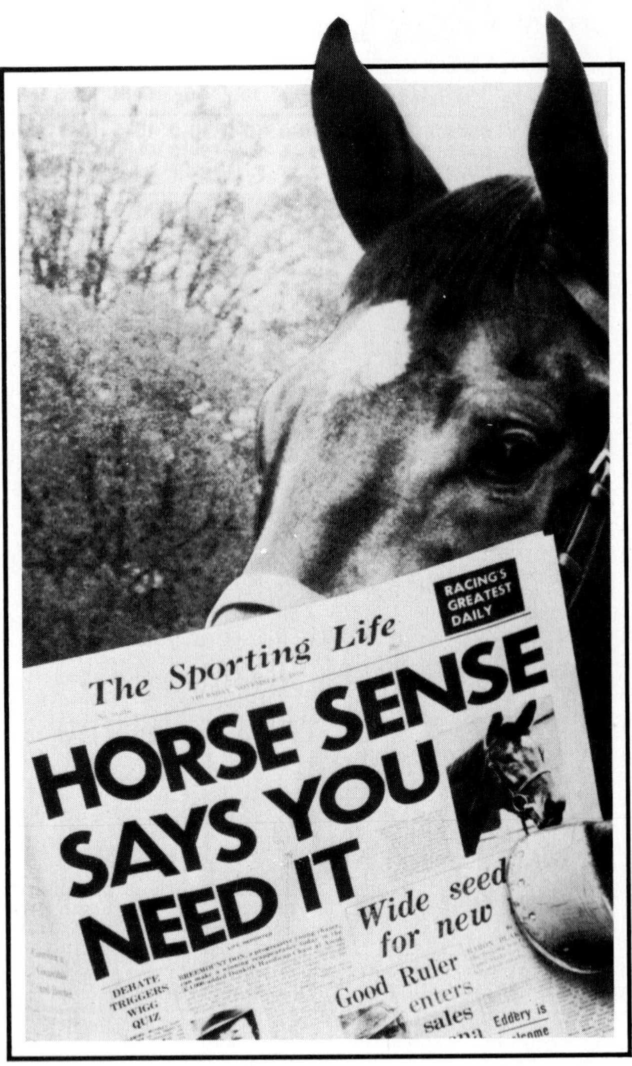
RACING'S GREATEST DAILY
The Sporting Life
HORSE SENSE SAYS YOU NEED IT
Wide seed for new
DEBATE TRIGGERS WIGG QUIZ
Good Ruler enters sales
Eddery is

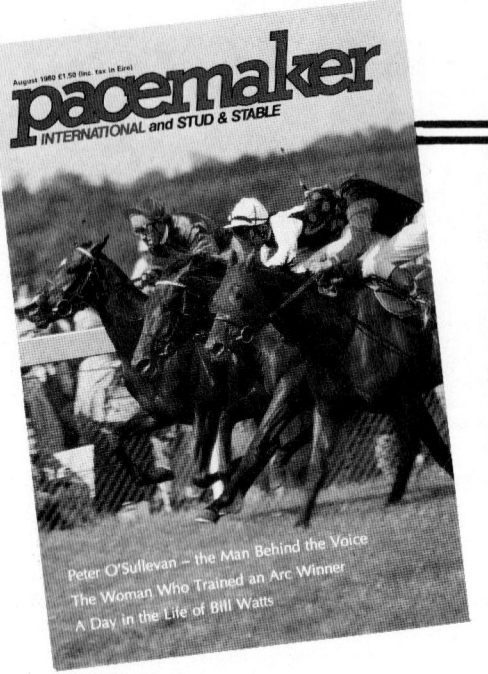

Airlie....for the best selection of stallions in Europe and the best care that money can buy

The five studs under the control of Captain A. D. D. Rogers comprise over 2,000 acres of fenced and watered lands. There is a permanent staff of over 100 including three veterinary surgeons and a resident farrier. The vets are immediately contactable around the clock by telephone or shortwave radio.
For the convenience of overseas patrons we can offer accommodation for mares prior to the start of the covering season. This enables mares visiting the stallions **ACAMAS, ARTAIUS, ASHMORE, DOUBLE FORM, ELA-MANA-MOU, HABITAT, MANADO, NONOALCO, NORTHERN BABY, STRADAVINSKY** and **TUMBLE WIND** to settle in their new surroundings.

Under the management of Captain A. D. D. Rogers

Airlie Stud
Lucan, Co. Dublin

Simmonstown Stud
Celbridge, Co. Kildare

Grangewilliam Stud
Maynooth, Co. Kildare

Ballyowen Stud
used solely for Yearlings

Williamstown Stud
for southern hemisphere stock

Loughmore Stud
used solely for Yearlings

RACEHORSES OF 1980

A Timeform Publication Price £30.00

A Timeform Publication

Compiled and Produced under the direction of
Phil Bull, B.Sc., and Reg Griffin

by members of the Timeform Organisation

G. Greetham, B.A. (Deputy Managing Director), J. G. Clarke (Director), G. F. Walton, Dip.A.D. (Director), J. D. Newton, B.A. (Editor), D. P. Adams, A. M. Caulfield, G. C. J. Dench, B.A., J. P. Early, B.A., J. C. McGrath and C. S. Williams.

Published by Portway Press Limited, Timeform House, Halifax, Yorkshire, and Printed by Walter Pearce & Co., Brentford, Middlesex.

ISBN 0 900599 31 6

CONTENTS

1 Age, Weight and Distance Table

21 Foreword

25 Index to Photographs

37 Explanatory Notes

41 The Form Summaries and Rating Symbols

43 Racehorses of 1980

900 Timeform Horse of the Year 1980

901 Timeform Champions of 1980

902 1980 Statistics

905 The Free Handicaps

919 Racing Abroad

946 Index to Racing Abroad

952 Trainers

960 Jockeys

963 Apprentices

968 Characteristics of Racecourses

981 Stallion Section

1034 Index to Advertisements

Foreword

"Racehorses of 1980" deals individually, in alphabetical sequence, with every horse that ran under Jockey Club Rules in 1980, plus a number of foreign-trained horses that did not race here. For each of these horses is given (1) its age, colour and sex, (2) its breeding, (3) a form summary giving details of all its performances during the past two seasons, (4) a rating of its merit, (5) a commentary upon its racing or general characteristics as a racehorse, with some suggestions, perhaps, regarding its potentialities in 1981, and (6) the name of the trainer in whose charge it was on the last occasion it ran.

The book is published with a twofold purpose. Firstly, it is designed to provide the betting man with data for practical use in analysing the racing programmes from day to day, and instructions as to its use in this capacity will be found in the Explanatory Notes which follow this Foreword; and secondly, the book is intended to have some permanent value as a review of the exploits and achievements of the more notable of our thoroughbreds in 1980. Thus, while the commentaries upon the vast majority of the horses are, of necessity, in note form, the best horses are more critically examined, and the short essays upon them are illustrated by half-tone portraits and photographs of the finishes of some of the races in which they were successful.

The attention of foreign buyers of British bloodstock, and others who are concerned with Timeform Ratings as a measure of absolute racing class in terms of a standard scale, is drawn to the section headed "The Level of the Ratings" in the Explanatory Notes on page 37.

February, 1981.

INDEX TO PHOTOGRAPHS

PORTRAITS & SNAPSHOTS

Horse		*Breeding*	*Copyright*	*Page*
Admiral's Heir (USA)	2 b.c.	Crafty Khale–Triggs'z (Successor)	*Fiona Vigors*	46
Angelo Salvini ..	4 br.g.	Relko–Sweet Sauce (Fr) (Hard Sauce)	*Timeform*	62
Anifa (USA) ..	4 b.f.	Herbager–Flail (Bagdad)	*E. G. Byrne*	65
Arctique Royale	2 b.f.	Royal and Regal–Arctic Melody (Arctic Slave)	*Jacqueline O'Brien*	73
Ardross	4 b.c.	Run The Gantlet–Le Melody (Levmoss)	*Jacqueline O'Brien*	76
Argument (Fr) ..	3 b.c.	Kautokeino–Arantelle (Tapioca)	*E. G. Byrne*	79
Balinger	4 b.c.	Welsh Pageant–Ripeck (Ribot)	*Fiona Vigors*	90
Band Practice (USA)	2 b.c.	Stop The Music–Fleet Empress (Young Emperor)	*Jacqueline O'Brien*	93
Bel Bolide (USA)	2 ch.c.	Bold Bidder–Lady Graustark	*W. W. Rouch & Co.*	102
Benefice (USA) ..	2 b.c.	Damascus–Shuvee (Nashua)	*Jacqueline O'Brien*	108
Bireme	3 ch.f.	Grundy–Ripeck (Ribot)	*W. W. Rouch & Co.*	119
Bold Raider (Fr)	2 ch.c.	Bold Lad (USA)–Kalise (Kashmir II)	*Fiona Vigors*	129
Bonnie Charlie ..	2 br.c.	Mummy's Pet–Aberdonia (Alycidon)	*W. W. Rouch & Co.*	131
Brentex	2 gr.c.	Birdbrook–Black Mink (Gratitude)	*Fiona Vigors*	137
Cairn Rouge ..	3 b.f.	Pitcairn–Little Hills (Candy Cane)	*Jacqueline O'Brien*	150
Calandra (USA)	3 br.f.	Sir Ivor–Intrepid Lady (Bold Ruler)	*Jacqueline O'Brien*	151
Chirk Castle ..	2 ch.c.	Welsh Pageant–Helcia (Habitat)	*Fiona Vigors*	172
Church Parade ..	2 b.c.	Queen's Hussar–Christchurch (So Blessed)	*Fiona Vigors*	175
Clear Verdict (USA)	2 b.c.	Judger–Ideal Day (Buckpasser)	*Fiona Vigors*	179
Cracking Form	3 b.c.	Habitat–Miss Petard (Petingo)	*Fiona Vigors*	194
Critique (USA) ..	2 br.c.	Roberto–Cambrienne (Sicambre)	*Jacqueline O'Brien*	200
Crofter (USA) ..	3 ch.c.	Habitat–Marie Curie (Exbury)	*Jacqueline O'Brien*	202
Cut Throat ..	2 br.c.	Sharpen Up–Zantedeschia (Zimone)	*W. W. Rouch & Co.*	207
Dance Bid (USA)	2 b.c.	Northern Dancer–Highest Trump (Bold Bidder)	*Jacqueline O'Brien*	210
Detroit (Fr) ..	3 br.f.	Riverman–Derna II (Sunny Boy III)	*George Selwyn*	222
Doc Marten ..	2 b.c.	Hotfoot–Rockney (Roan Rocket)	*W. W. Rouch & Co.*	227
Dukedom ..	3 ch.c.	Connaught–Albany (Pall Mall)	*Fiona Vigors*	235
Dunphy	2 b.c.	Riverman–Dourdan (Prudent II)	*P. Bertrand*	238
Ela-Mana-Mou	4 b.c.	Pitcairn–Rose Bertin (High Hat)	*W. W. Rouch & Co.*	248

Enchantment ..	3 b.c.	Habitat–Lady of Chalon (Young Emperor)	*W. W. Rouch & Co.* 252
Euclid	2 b. or br.c.	Lyphard–Lucky For Me (Appiani II)	*Jacqueline O'Brien* 256
Fairy Footsteps	2 b.f.	Mill Reef–Glass Slipper (Relko)	*E. G. Byrne* 263
Final Straw ..	3 ch.c.	Thatch–Last Call (Klairon)	*W. W. Rouch & Co.* 270
Fine Sun	3 ch.g.	Fine Blade–All Sunshine (Miralgo)	*Timeform* 272
Flower	3 br.f.	So Blessed–Sunflower (Paveh)	*Timeform* 279
Geoffrey's Sister	4 ch.f.	Sparkler–Eilan Aigas (Counsel)	*Timeform* 293
Giannutri ..	2 b.f.	Wolver Hollow–Cesarea (Raeburn II)	*Fiona Vigors* 295
Glint Of Gold ..	2 b.c.	Mill Reef–Crown Treasure (Graustark)	*Fiona Vigors* 302
Golden Bowl (USA)	2 b.f.	Vaguely Noble–Rose Bowl (Habitat)	*W. W. Rouch & Co.* 305
Gonzales (USA)	3 b.c.	Vaguely Noble–Gazala (Dark Star)	*Jacqueline O'Brien* 311
Goodbye Starter	2 ch.c.	Owen Dudley–Curfew (Midsummer Night II)	*Sporting Pictures (UK)* 313
Good Thyne (USA)	3 b.c.	Herbager–Foreseer (Round Table)	*Jacqueline O'Brien* 314
Grandiose ..	3 ch.c.	Grundy–Secret Session (Court Martial)	*Fiona Vigors* 317
Gregorian (USA)	4 br.c.	Graustark–Natashka (Dedicate)	*Jacqueline O'Brien* 323
Hello Gorgeous (USA)	3 ch.c.	Mr Prospector–Bonny Jet (Jet Jewel)	*J. Crofts* 344
Huguenot (USA)	3 ch.c.	Forli–Captain's Mate (Turn-to)	*Jacqueline O'Brien* 364
Icelandic ..	5 b.h.	Rarity–Arctic Walk (Arctic Slave)	*Jacqueline O'Brien* 367
In Fijar (USA) ..	3 b.c.	Bold Commander–Apache Queen (Marshal At Arms)	*P. Bertrand* 372
Kalaglow ..	2 gr.c.	Kalamoun–Aglow (Crepello)	*W. W. Rouch & Co.* 391
Kampala ..	4 br.c.	Kalamoun–State Pension (Only for Life)	*Fiona Vigors* 394
Karamita ..	3 b.f.	Shantung–Shahinaaz (Venture VII)	*George Selwyn* 396
Kilijaro	4 br.f.	African Sky–Manfilia (Mandamus)	*P. Bertrand* 403
Kings Lake (USA)	2 b.c.	Nijinsky–Fish Bar (Baldric II)	*Jacqueline O'Brien* 407
Kittyhawk ..	2 b.f.	Bustino–Sky Fever (Skymaster)	*Fiona Vigors* 411
Known Fact (USA)	3 b.c.	In Reality–Tamerett (Tim Tam)	*W. W. Rouch & Co.* 416
Kris	4 ch.c.	Sharpen Up–Doubly Sure (Reliance II)	*W. W. Rouch & Co.* 418
Last Fandango ..	3 ch.c.	Gay Fandango–Welsh Game (Pall Mall)	*Fiona Vigors* 429
Last Light (Fr) ..	2 b.c.	Round Table–Lighted Glory (Nijinsky)	*Jacqueline O'Brien* 430
Lawmaker (USA)	2 b.c.	Round Table–Greek Victress (Victoria Park)	*Jacqueline O'Brien* 433
Leap Lively (USA)	2 ch.f.	Nijinsky–Quilloquick (Graustark)	*W. W. Rouch & Co.* 435
Le Marmot (Fr)	4 b.c.	Amarko–Molina (Molvedo)	*P. Bertrand* 439

Le Moss	5 ch.h.	Le Levanstell–Feemoss (Ballymoss)	*J. Crofts*	444
Light Cavalry ..	3 b.c.	Brigadier Gerard–Glass Slipper (Relko)	*W. W. Rouch & Co.*	450
Little Bonny ..	3 gr.f.	Bonne Noel–Little Fuss (Sovereign Path)	*Sporting Pictures (UK)*	454
Main Reef ..	4 ch.c.	Mill Reef–Lovely Light (Henry the Seventh)	*J. Crofts*	470
Marwell	2 b.f.	Habitat–Lady Seymour (Tudor Melody)	*W. W. Rouch & Co.*	484
Masked Marvel	4 b.c.	Hard to Beat–Mosstown (Mossborough)	*J. Crofts*	486
Master Willie ..	3 ch.c.	High Line–Fair Winter (Set Fair)	*W. W. Rouch & Co.*	489
Monroe (USA) ..	3 b.f.	Sir Ivor–Best in Show (Traffic Judge)	*Jacqueline O'Brien*	513
Monteverdi ..	3 ch.c.	Lyphard–Janina II (Match III)	*Jacqueline O'Brien*	516
Moomba Masquerade ..	3 b.c.	Gay Fandango–Pampered Dancer (Pampered King)	*Press Association Photos*	517
Moorestyle ..	3 b.c.	Manacle–Guiding Star (Reliance II)	*P. Bertrand*	523
Mrs Penny (USA)	3 ch.f.	Great Nephew–Tananarive (Le Fabuleux)	*Fiona Vigors*	534
Muscovite (USA)	3 b.c.	Nijinsky–Alyne Que (Raise A Native)	*Jacqueline O'Brien*	537
Nadjar (Fr) ..	4 gr.c.	Zeddaan–Nuclea (Orsini)	*P. Bertrand*	542
Nasseem (Fr) ..	2 gr.f.	Zeddaan–Noureen (Astec)	*Fiona Vigors*	544
Night Alert (USA)	3 b.c.	Nijinsky–Moment of Truth (Matador)	*Jacqueline O'Brien*	553
Nikoli	3 b.c.	Great Nephew–Aliceva (Alcide)	*Jacqueline O'Brien*	557
Niniski (USA) ..	4 b.c.	Nijinsky–Virginia Hills (Tom Rolfe)	*Fiona Vigors*	559
Northern Baby (Can)	4 b.c.	Northern Dancer–Two Rings (Round Table)	*P. Bertrand*	567
Nureyev (USA) ..	3 b.c.	Northern Dancer–Special (Forli)	*George Selwyn*	573
Olympic Glory ..	2 ch.c.	Hittite Glory–Nalindele (Miralgo)	*W. W. Rouch & Co.*	578
One Fleet Street	3 b.c.	Habitat–The Creditor (Crepello)	*Fiona Vigors*	579
Palumba ..	2 b.f.	Derring-Do–Dove (Sea Hawk II)	*W. W. Rouch & Co.*	588
Parkdale ..	2 ch.c.	Swing Easy–Miss McWorden (Worden II)	*Timeform*	591
Pentaquod (USA)	3 gr.c.	London Company–Enamor (Drone)	*J. Crofts*	599
Piaffer (USA) ..	5 b.h.	Nijinsky–Strong Drink (Sound Track)	*J. Crofts*	605
Policeman (Fr) ..	3 b.c.	Riverman–Indianapolis (Barbare II)	*P. Bertrand*	614
Posse (USA) ..	3 ch.c.	Forli–In Hot Pursuit (Bold Ruler)	*Sporting Pictures (UK)*	621
Prince Bee ..	3 b.c.	Sun Prince–Honerko (Tanerko)	*Fiona Vigors*	628
Prince Roland ..	3 b.c.	Prince Regent–Aunt Audrey (Aureole)	*Fiona Vigors*	634

Name	Age/Sex	Breeding	Owner	No.
Pushy	2 ch.f.	Sharpen Up–Mrs Moss (Reform)	*J. Crofts*	641
Quick As Lightning (USA)	3 b.f.	Buckpasser–Clear Ceiling (Bold Ruler)	*W. W. Rouch & Co.*	648
Ramian	3 b.c.	Mount Hagen–Chevy Chase (Raise You Ten)	*Jacqueline O'Brien*	653
Rankin (Fr) ..	3 ch.c.	Owen Dudley–Cup Cake (Dan Cupid)	*W. W. Rouch & Co.*	654
Reçitation (USA)	2 b.c.	Elocutionist–Irish Party (Irish Lancer)	*W. W. Rouch & Co.*	660
Robellino (USA)	2 b.c.	Roberto–Isobelline (Pronto)	*Fiona Vigors*	677
Rule Britannia ..	3 ch.f.	English Prince–Sea Music (Atan)	*Fiona Vigors*	690
Saint Jonathon ..	3 b.c.	Welsh Saint–Climbing Rose (Pirate King)	*Fiona Vigors*	696
Saison (USA) ..	3 b.f.	L'Enjoleur–Singing Bird (T. V. Lark)	*J. Crofts*	698
Salt of the Earth	3 b.f.	Sterling Bay–Pinch of Salt (Super Sam)	*Fiona Vigors*	700
Saviour	3 b.c.	Blakeney–Set Free (Worden II)	*W. W. Rouch & Co.*	707
Sayyaf	3 b.c.	Habitat–Pavello (Crepello)	*W. W. Rouch & Co.*	709
Scarrowmanwick	2 b.c.	Tickled Pink–Almadena (Dairialatan)	*Fiona Vigors*	710
Sea Chimes ..	4 ch.c.	Gulf Pearl–Canterbury Belle (St Alphage)	*W. W. Rouch & Co.*	716
Sea Pigeon (USA)	10 br.g.	Sea-Bird II–Around The Roses (Round Table)	*George Selwyn*	719
Shafaraz (Fr) ..	6 b.h.	Levmoss–Asharaz (Sicambre)	*P. Bertrand*	725
Sharpo	3 ch.c.	Sharpen Up–Moiety Bird (Falcon)	*W. W. Rouch & Co.*	731
Shoot A Line ..	3 b.f.	High Line–Death Ray (Tamerlane)	*W. W. Rouch & Co.*	742
Silken Knot ..	2 ch.f.	Nonoalco–Silken Way (Shantung)	*Fiona Vigors*	747
Skyliner ..	5 b.h.	African Sky–Keep Going (Hard Sauce)	*Fiona Vigors*	755
Snow	3 gr.f.	Young Emperor–Arctic Walk (Arctic Slave)	*Fiona Vigors*	760
Storm Bird (Can)	2 b.c.	Northern Dancer–South Ocean (New Providence)	*Jacqueline O'Brien*	788
Sula Bula ..	2 b.c.	Midsummer Night II–Blue Ann (Road House II)	*Timeform*	794
Super Asset (USA)	3 b.c.	Sir Ivor–Sunday Purchase (T. V. Lark)	*J. Crofts*	798
Tahitian King ..	4 b.c.	Luthier–Ten Double (Decathlon)	*J. Crofts*	809
Tarvie	3 ch.f.	Swing Easy–Tamergene (Tamerlane)	*Fiona Vigors*	813
Taufan (USA) ..	3 b.c.	Stop the Music–Stolen Date (Sadair)	*Fiona Vigors*	814
Tina's Pet ..	2 b.c.	Mummy's Pet–Merry Weather (Will Somers)	*E. G. Byrne*	832
To-Agori-Mou ..	2 br.c.	Tudor Music–Sarah Van Fleet (Cracksman)	*W. W. Rouch & Co.*	836

Tolmi	2 b.f.	Great Nephew–Stilvi (Derring-Do)	*E. G. Byrne*	838
Try Sandicliffe	3 ch.c.	Star Appeal–Peral Five (Will Somers)	*Fiona Vigors*	850
Tyrnavos ..	3 b.c.	Blakeney–Stilvi (Derring-Do)	*W. W. Rouch & Co.*	858
Vielle	3 b.f.	Ribero–Hurdy-Gurdy (Espresso)	*W. W. Rouch & Co.*	869
Water Mill ..	3 b.c.	Mill Reef–Heavenly Thought (St Paddy)	*Fiona Vigors*	876
Wicked Will ..	2 b.c.	Mill Reef–Green Glade (Correspondent)	*Fiona Vigors*	886

RACE PHOTOGRAPHS

Race and Meeting	*Copyright*	*Page*
Airlie/Coolmore Irish Two Thousand Guineas (The Curragh)	*E. G. Byrne*	556
Alycidon Stakes (Goodwood)	*E. G. Byrne*	875
Andy Capp Handicap (Redcar)	*A. Russell*	503
Ascot Stakes	*George Selwyn*	341
Ballymore Plate (York)	*A. Russell*	518
Basil Samuel Plate (York)	*A. Russell*	524
Benson and Hedges Gold Cup (York)	*Sporting Pictures (UK)*	488
Bessborough Stakes (Ascot)	*A. Russell*	94
Bloodstock and General Insurance Stakes Nursery Handicap (Newmarket)	*A. Russell*	399
Blue Seal Stakes (Ascot)	*George Selwyn*	603
Bretby Handicap (Newmarket)	*A. Russell*	155
Cecil Frail Handicap (Haydock)	*A. Russell*	321
Champion Stakes (Newmarket)	*E. G. Byrne*	149
Cherry Hinton Stakes (Newmarket)	*George Selwyn*	544
Chesham Stakes (Ascot)	*A. Russell*	409
Chester Vase	*Press Association Photos*	346
Chivas Regal Sprint (Sandown)	*Sporting Pictures (UK)*	761
Clerical, Medical Greenham Stakes (Newbury)	*W. Everitt*	269
Coral Autumn Cup (Newbury)	*George Selwyn*	161
Coral Eclipse Stakes (Sandown)	*E. G. Byrne*	246
Coral Northumberland Plate (Newcastle)	*A. Russell*	514
Coral Racing Champion Sprint (York)	*A. Russell*	691
Cordwainers Stakes (York)	*A. Russell*	135
Cork and Orrery Stakes (Ascot)	*Press Association Photos*	399
Coronation Cup (Epsom)	*Sport and General*	715
Coronation Stakes (Ascot)	*Sport and General*	149
Coventry Stakes (Ascot)	*Sport and General*	659
Crathorne Stakes (Thirsk)	*A. Russell*	774
Criterium de Maisons-Laffitte	*P. Bertrand*	197
Criterium de Saint-Cloud	*P. Bertrand*	826
Crown Plus Two Apprentice Championship Final (York)	*A. Russell*	816
Cumberland Lodge Stakes (Ascot)	*Sport and General*	273
Dance In Time Plate (Doncaster)	*A. Russell*	255
Daniel Prenn Handicap (Newmarket)	*Sport and General*	893
Daniel Prenn Plate (York)	*A. Russell*	633
Derby Stakes (Epsom)	*Press Association Photos*	347
Derby Stakes (Epsom)	*A. Russell*	349
Diadem Stakes (Ascot)	*E. G. Byrne*	768
Diomed Stakes (Epsom)	*A. Russell*	334
Doncaster Cup	*A. Russell*	443
Duke of Edinburgh Stakes (Ascot)	*Press Association Photos*	732
Duke of York Stakes (York)	*A. Russell*	276

Race	Photograph	Page
Earl of Sefton Stakes (Newmarket)	*Sport and General*	243
Ebbisham Stakes (Epsom)	*Sport and General*	593
Extel Stakes (Goodwood)	*Sport and General*	395
Firth of Clyde Stakes (Ayr)	*A. Russell*	780
Flying Childers Stakes (Doncaster)	*Sport and General*	483
Fortnum and Mason Handicap (Ascot)	*Press Association Photos*	866
Foxhall Maiden Stakes (Goodwood)	*E. G. Byrne*	834
Fred Darling Stakes (Newbury)	*Sporting Pictures (UK)*	500
Furniture Factors Sprint Handicap (Doncaster)	*A. Russell*	197
Galtres Stakes (York)	*A. Russell*	214
Garrowby Stakes (York)	*A. Russell*	778
Geoffrey Freer Stakes (Newbury)	*George Selwyn*	551
Gilbey Champion Racehorse Futurity (York)	*A. Russell*	792
Gimcrack Stakes (York)	*Sporting Pictures (UK)*	101
Gladness Stakes (The Curragh)	*Ruth Rogers and Associates*	552
Glasgow Stakes (York)	*A. Russell*	597
Goffs Irish One Thousand Guineas (The Curragh)	*Ruth Rogers and Associates*	148
Gold Cup (Ascot)	*A. Russell*	440
Goodwood Cup	*George Selwyn*	442
Goodwood Stakes	*E. G. Byrne*	341
Grand Criterium (Longchamp)	*P. Bertrand*	659
Grand Prix de Paris (Longchamp)	*P. Bertrand*	864
Grand Prix de Saint-Cloud	*P. Bertrand*	727
Grand Prix d'Evry	*P. Bertrand*	712
Great Voltigeur Stakes (York)	*A. Russell*	626
Gus Demmy Memorial Stakes (Haydock)	*A. Russell*	708
Hardwicke Stakes (Ascot)	*George Selwyn*	713
Harewood Handicap (York)	*A. Russell*	703
Heathorn Stakes (Newmarket)	*A. Russell*	687
Henry II Stakes (Sandown)	*Sport and General*	115
Hoover Fillies Mile (Ascot)	*Sport and General*	434
Horris Hill Stakes (Newbury)	*E. G. Byrne*	390
Houghton Stakes (Newmarket)	*A. Russell*	797
Hungerford Stakes (Newbury)	*George Selwyn*	393
Intercraft Solario Stakes (Sandown)	*Sport and General*	835
Irish Guinness Oaks (The Curragh)	*E. G. Byrne*	740
Irish St Leger (The Curragh)	*Ruth Rogers and Associates*	310
Irish Sweeps Derby (The Curragh)	*E. G. Byrne*	857
Jersey Stakes (Ascot)	*Sport and General*	333
Jockey Club Cup (Newmarket)	*A. Russell*	74
Joe McGrath Memorial Stakes (Leopardstown)	*Ruth Rogers and Associates*	322
Johnnie Walker Oaks Trial Stakes (Lingfield)	*E. G. Byrne*	297
John Smith's Magnet Cup (York)	*A. Russell*	271
King Edward VII Stakes (Ascot)	*George Selwyn*	448
King George VI and Queen Elizabeth Diamond Stakes (Ascot)	*W. Everitt*	247
King's Stand Stakes (Ascot)	*A. Russell*	50
Kiveton Park Steel Stakes (Doncaster)	*A. Russell*	414
Kris Plate (Newbury)	*Press Association Photos*	736
Ladbroke Blue Riband Trial Stakes (Epsom)	*Sporting Pictures (UK)*	428
Ladbroke Chester Cup	*E. G. Byrne*	70
Ladbroke Derby Trial Stakes (Lingfield)	*Sport and General*	299
Ladbrokes Abernant Stakes (Newmarket)	*A. Russell*	327
Ladbrokes Ayr Gold Cup Handicap	*A. Russell*	771
Ladbrokes Craven Stakes (Newmarket)	*A. Russell*	856
Ladbrokes Nell Gwyn Stakes (Newmarket)	*A. Russell*	258
Lancashire Oaks (Haydock)	*A. Russell*	868

Race	Photographer	Page
Laurent Perrier Champagne Stakes (Doncaster)	*A. Russell*	296
Lowther Stakes (York)	*A. Russell*	410
Marston Moor Stakes (York)	*A. Russell*	772
May Hill Stakes (Doncaster)	*E. G. Byrne*	259
McCairn's Trial Stakes (Phoenix Park)	*E. G. Byrne*	555
Mecca-Dante Stakes (York)	*A. Russell*	343
Mill Reef Stakes (Newbury)	*E. G. Byrne*	804
Molecomb Stakes (Goodwood)	*E. G. Byrne*	482
Mornington Stakes (Ascot)	*George Selwyn*	164
Moyglare Stud Stakes (The Curragh)	*Ruth Rogers and Associates*	72
Musidora Stakes (York)	*A. Russell*	117
Nassau Stakes (Goodwood)	*Press Association Photos*	868
National Stakes (Sandown)	*Sport and General*	598
National Stakes (The Curragh)	*E. G. Byrne*	786
New Stand Stakes (Goodwood)	*E. G. Byrne*	846
Norfolk Stakes (Ascot)	*A. Russell*	174
Oaks Stakes (Epsom)	*A. Russell*	117
Oldbawn Maiden Plate (Leopardstown)	*Ruth Rogers and Associates*	199
Old Newton Cup (Haydock)	*A. Russell*	724
One Thousand Guineas Stakes (Newmarket)	*A. Russell*	647
Ormonde Stakes (Chester)	*E. G. Byrne*	559
Palace House Stakes (Newmarket)	*George Selwyn*	863
Park Hill Stakes (Doncaster)	*A. Russell*	741
Playboy Bookmakers' Newbury Spring Cup	*E. G. Byrne*	569
Poule d'Essai des Poulains (Longchamp)	*P. Bertrand*	371
Poule d'Essai des Pouliches (Longchamp)	*P. Bertrand*	81
Prince of Wales' Nursery (Doncaster)	*A. Russell*	734
Prince of Wales's Stakes (Ascot)	*Sport and General*	244
Princess Elizabeth Stakes (Epsom)	*Sport and General*	98
Princess Margaret Stakes (Ascot)	*A. Russell*	837
Princess of Wales's Stakes (Newmarket)	*George Selwyn*	550
Prix d'Arenberg (Chantilly)	*P. Bertrand*	321
Prix de Diane de Revlon (Chantilly)	*P. Bertrand*	532
Prix de l'Abbaye de Longchamp	*P. Bertrand*	522
Prix de la Cote Normande (Deauville)	*P. Bertrand*	301
Prix de la Foret (Longchamp)	*P. Bertrand*	522
Prix de la Nonette (Deauville)	*P. Bertrand*	220
Prix de la Porte Maillot (Longchamp)	*P. Bertrand*	463
Prix de l'Arc de Triomphe (Longchamp)	*P. Bertrand*	221
Prix de Meautry (Deauville)	*P. Bertrand*	402
Prix de la Salamandre (Longchamp)	*P. Bertrand*	511
Prix de Saint-Georges (Longchamp)	*P. Bertrand*	47
Prix des Chenes (Longchamp)	*P. Bertrand*	238
Prix d'Harcourt (Longchamp)	*P. Bertrand*	829
Prix d'Ispahan (Longchamp)	*P. Bertrand*	541
Prix Djebel (Maisons-Laffitte)	*P. Bertrand*	571
Prix Dollar (Longchamp)	*P. Bertrand*	566
Prix du Cadran (Longchamp)	*P. Bertrand*	725
Prix du Gros Chene (Chantilly)	*P. Bertrand*	48
Prix du Jockey-Club (Chantilly)	*P. Bertrand*	613
Prix du Moulin de Longchamp	*P. Bertrand*	403
Prix du Palais Royal (Longchamp)	*P. Bertrand*	95
Prix du Prince d'Orange (Longchamp)	*P. Bertrand*	236
Prix Eclipse (Saint-Cloud)	*P. Bertrand*	604
Prix Fille de l'Air (Saint-Cloud)	*P. Bertrand*	220
Prix Ganay (Longchamp)	*P. Bertrand*	438
Prix Gladiateur (Longchamp)	*P. Bertrand*	64
Prix Greffulhe (Longchamp)	*P. Bertrand*	638
Prix Jacques le Marois (Deauville)	*P. Bertrand*	542
Prix Jean Prat (Chantilly)	*P. Bertrand*	553
Prix Lupin (Longchamp)	*P. Bertrand*	107
Prix Marcel Boussac (Longchamp)	*P. Bertrand*	849
Prix Maurice de Gheest (Deauville)	*P. Bertrand*	127

Race	Photograph	Page
Prix Morny (Deauville)	*P. Bertrand*	60
Prix Niel (Longchamp)	*P. Bertrand*	627
Prix Perth (Saint-Cloud)	*P. Bertrand*	355
Prix Robert Papin (Maisons-Laffitte)	*P. Bertrand*	377
Prix Royal-Oak (Longchamp)	*P. Bertrand*	308
Prix Saint-Alary (Longchamp)	*P. Bertrand*	590
Prix Saint-Roman (Longchamp)	*P. Bertrand*	477
Prix Thomas Bryon (Saint-Cloud)	*P. Bertrand*	113
Prix Vermeille (Longchamp)	*P. Bertrand*	533
Queen Anne Stakes (Ascot)	*A. Russell*	125
Queen Elizabeth II Stakes (Ascot)	*George Selwyn*	415
Queen Mary Stakes (Ascot)	*George Selwyn*	640
Queen's Vase (Ascot)	*A. Russell*	841
Ribblesdale Stakes (Ascot)	*George Selwyn*	739
Richmond Stakes (Goodwood)	*W. Everitt*	67
Rose of York Handicap (York)	*A. Russell*	501
Rous Nursery Handicap (Doncaster)	*A. Russell*	609
Royal Hunt Cup Handicap (Ascot)	*Sport and General*	817
Royal Lodge Stakes (Ascot)	*George Selwyn*	676
Sagaro Stakes (Ascot)	*E. G. Byrne*	623
Sancton Stakes (York)	*A. Russell*	145
Sean Graham Stakes (Kempton)	*E. G. Byrne*	211
Sidney Thompson Memorial Stakes (Brighton)	*Press Association Photos*	130
Sir Charles Clore Memorial Stakes (Newbury)	*Sport and General*	821
Spillers Stewards' Cup (Goodwood)	*E. G. Byrne*	667
Sporting Chronicle Handicap (Haydock)	*A. Russell*	185
Sporting Chronicle Spring Handicap (Doncaster)	*A. Russell*	714
St James's Palace Stakes (Ascot)	*George Selwyn*	619
St Leger Stakes (Doncaster)	*Sport and General*	449
Strensall Stakes (York)	*A. Russell*	464
St Simon Stakes (Newbury)	*George Selwyn*	737
Sun Chariot Stakes (Newmarket)	*A. Russell*	759
Sunday Sun Handicap (Newcastle)	*A. Russell*	460
Sussex Stakes (Goodwood)	*Press Association Photos*	620
Tattersall Nursery Handicap (Newmarket)	*A. Russell*	309
Thirsk Hall Stakes (Thirsk)	*A. Russell*	382
Timeform Charity Day Selling Plate (York)	*A. Russell*	535
Timeform Race Card Stakes (Redcar)	*A. Russell*	796
Timeform Race Card Stakes (Thirsk)	*A. Russell*	696
Tote Cesarewitch Handicap (Newmarket)	*A. Russell*	617
Tote Charity Stakes Handicap (Ascot)	*Sporting Pictures (UK)*	505
Tote-Ebor Handicap (York)	*A. Russell*	726
Tote Free Handicap (Newmarket)	*Sport and General*	519
Tote Lockinge Stakes (Newbury)	*Sport and General*	417
Troy Stakes (York)	*A. Russell*	563
Two Thousand Guineas Stakes (Newmarket)	*George Selwyn*	412
Tyros Stakes (The Curragh)	*E. G. Byrne*	629
Ultramar Jubilee Stakes (Kempton)	*Sport and General*	124
Vaux Breweries Gold Tankard (Redcar)	*A. Russell*	718
Vernons Fillies Plate (York)	*A. Russell*	352
Vernons Sprint Cup (Haydock)	*A. Russell*	521
Ward Hill Bunbury Cup Handicap (Newmarket)	*E. G. Byrne*	783
Washington D.C. International (Laurel)	*Laurel Racecourse Inc.*	78
Washington Singer Stakes (Newbury)	*George Selwyn*	612
Waterford Crystal Mile (Goodwood)	*E. G. Byrne*	413
William Hill Cambridgeshire Handicap (Newmarket)	*A. Russell*	97

William Hill Cheveley Park Stakes (Newmarket)	*Sport and General*	484
William Hill Dewhurst Stakes (Newmarket)	*A. Russell*	787
William Hill Futurity (Doncaster)	*A. Russell*	104
William Hill Gold Cup (Redcar)	*A. Russell*	159
William Hill July Cup (Newmarket)	*Sporting Pictures (UK)*	520
William Hill Lincoln Handicap (Doncaster)	*Press Association Photos*	408
William Hill Middle Park Stakes (Newmarket)	*A. Russell*	491
William Hill November Handicap (Doncaster)	*A. Russell*	593
William Hill Portland Handicap (Doncaster)	*A. Russell*	807
William Hill Sprint Championship (York) ..	*A. Russell*	730
William Hill Trophy (York)	*A. Russell*	581
Windsor Castle Stakes (Ascot)	*E. G. Byrne*	187
Wokingham Stakes (Ascot)	*Sport and General*	645
Yorkshire Cup (York)	*A. Russell*	562
Yorkshire Oaks (York)	*A. Russell*	741

EXPLANATORY NOTES

TO assess the prospects of any horse in a race it is necessary to know two things about him: first, how good he is; and second, what sort of horse he is. In this book the merit of each horse is expressed in the form of a *rating* (printed on the right); and the *racing character* of the horse given in the commentary.

TIMEFORM RATINGS

The Timeform Rating of a horse is simply the merit of the horse expressed in pounds. More precisely, it is *the number of pounds which, in our opinion, the horse would be entitled to receive in an average Free Handicap*. Thus, a horse which we regard as worth 9 st 7 lb in an average Free Handicap, i.e., 133 lb, would receive a rating of 133: and one regarded as worth 8 st (112 lb) would receive a rating of 112; and so on.

This explains what the ratings are; but of course individual ratings are not actually allocated in this way, merely by "inspection." The rating of any horse is a result of careful examination of its running against other horses. We maintain a "running" handicap of all horses in training throughout the season, or, to be strictly accurate, two handicaps, one for horses aged three years and over, and one for two-year-olds.

THE LEVEL OF THE RATINGS

At the close of each season all the horses that have raced are re-handicapped from scratch, and each horse's rating is revised. It is also necessary to adjust the general level of the handicap, so that the mean of all the ratings is kept at the same standard level from year to year. Left to itself, the general level of the ratings, in each succeeding issue of Timeform, tends to rise steadily. For technical reasons it is desirable to allow it to do so during the season: but, in the winter, when the complete re-handicap is done, the ratings must, of course, be put back on their proper level again.

This explains why, in this book, the ratings are, in general, different from those in the final issue of the 1980 Timeform series.

RATINGS AND WEIGHT-FOR-AGE

These matters, however, are by the way. What concerns the reader is that he has, in the ratings in this book, a universal handicap embracing all the horses in training it is possible to weigh up, ranging from tip-top classic performers, with ratings from 130 to 145, down to the meanest selling platers, rated around the 40 or 50 mark. And what we now have to explain is the practical use of these ratings in the business of weighing up a race.

Before doing so, it is important to mention that all ratings are at weight-for-age, so that equal ratings mean horses of equal merit: perhaps it would be clearer if we said that the universal rating handicap is really not a single handicap, but four handicaps side by side: one for 2-y-o's, one for 3-y-o's, one for 4-y-o's and one for older horses. Thus, a 3-y-o rated, for argument's sake, at 117 is deemed to be identical in point of "merit" with a 4-y-o also rated at 117: but for them to have equal chances in, say, a mile race in June, the 3-y-o would need to be receiving 13 lb from the 4-y-o, which is the weight difference specified in the Age, Weight and Distance Table on the page facing the front cover. However, let us to cases!

USING THE RATINGS

In using Timeform Ratings with a view to discovering which horses in any race have the best chances at the weights, we have two distinct cases, according to whether the horses taking part are of the same age or of different ages. Here is the procedure in each case:—

A. Horses of the Same Age

If the horses all carry the same weight there are no adjustments to be made, and the horses with the highest ratings have the best chances. If the horses carry different weights, jot down their ratings, and to the rating of each horse add one point for every pound the horse is set to carry less than 10 st, or subtract one point for every pound he has to carry more than 10 st. When the ratings have been adjusted in this way the highest resultant figure indicates the horse with the best chance at the weights.

Example (any distance: any month of the season)

2 Good Girl (9-6)	.. Rating 119	add 8	127
2 Paulinus (9-4)	.. Rating 113	add 10	123
2 Abilene (8-11)	.. Rating 107	add 17	124
2 Bob's Joy (8-7)	.. Rating 108	add 21	129
2 Time Warp (8-2)	.. Rating 100	add 26	126
2 Eagle Eye (7-7)	.. Rating 92	add 35	127

Bob's Joy (129) has the best chance; Good Girl (127) and Eagle Eye (127) are next best.

B. Horses of Different Ages

Take no notice of the weight any horse receives from any other. Instead, consult the Age, Weight and Distance Table on the page facing the front cover. Treat each horse separately, and compare the weight it has to carry with the weight prescribed for it in the table, according to the age of the horse, the distance of the race and the month of the year. Then, add one point to the rating for each pound the horse has to carry less than the weight given in the table: or, subtract one point from the rating for every pound he has to carry more than the weight prescribed by the table. The highest resultant figure indicates the horse most favoured by the weights.

Example ($1\frac{1}{2}$ **miles in July**)

(Table Weights: 5-y-o 10-0; 4-y-o 9-13; 3-y-o 8-11)

6 Nimitz (9-12)	.. Rating 115	.... add 2	 117
4 Red Devil (9-9)	.. Rating 114	.... add 4	 118
6 Sweet Cindy (9-5)	.. Rating 115	.... add 9	 124
3 Jailhouse (8-12)	.. Rating 120	subtract 1	 119
4 Haakon (8-11)	.. Rating 101	.... add 16	 117
3 Fine Strike (8-7)	.. Rating 112	.... add 4	 116

Sweet Cindy (124) has the best chance at the weights, with 5 lb in hand of Jailhouse.

JOCKEYSHIP AND APPRENTICE ALLOWANCES

There is just one further point that arises in evaluating the chances of the horses on the basis of their ratings: the question of jockeyship in general, and apprentice allowances in particular. The allowance which may be claimed by an apprentice is given to enable apprentices to obtain race-riding experience against experienced jockeys. For the purposes of rating calculations it should, in general, be assumed that the allowance the apprentice is able to claim (3 lb, 5 lb, or 7 lb) is nullified by the boy's inexperience. Therefore, the *weight adjustments to the ratings should be calculated on the weight allotted by the handicapper, or determined by the conditions of the race*, and no extra addition should be made to a rating because the horse's rider claims an apprentice allowance.

The above is the general routine procedure. But of course there is no reason why the quality of jockeyship should not be taken into account in assessing the chances of horses in a race. Quite the contrary. Nobody would question that the jockeyship of a first-class rider is worth a pound or two, and occasionally an apprentice comes along who is riding quite as well as the average jockey long before he loses the right to claim. There is no reason whatever why, after the age and weight adjustments have been made to the ratings, small additional allowances should not be made for these matters of jockeyship. This, however, is a matter which must be left to the discretion of the reader.

WEIGHING UP A RACE

It having been discovered, by means of the ratings, which horses in a particular race are most favoured by the weights, complete analysis demands that the racing character of each horse, as set out in the commentary upon it, shall be checked to see if there is any reason why the horse might be expected not to run up to his rating. It counts for little that a horse is thrown in at the weights if he has no pretensions whatever to staying the distance, or is unable to act on the prevailing going.

These two matters, suitability of distance and going, are, no doubt, the most important points to be considered. But there are others. For example, the ability of a horse to accommodate himself to the conformation of the track. Then there is the matter of pace versus stamina: as between two stayers of equal merit, racing over a distance suitable to both, firm going, or a small field with the prospect of a slowly-run race, would favour the one with the better pace and acceleration, whereas dead or soft going, or a big field with the prospect of a strong gallop throughout the race, would favour the sounder stayer. There is also the matter of temperament and behaviour at the start: nobody would be in a hurry to take a short price about a horse with whom it is always an even chance whether he will consent to race or not.

A few minutes spent checking up on these matters in the commentaries upon the horses concerned will sometimes put a very different complexion on a race from that which is put upon it by the ratings alone. We repeat, therefore, that the correct way to use Timeform, or this annual volume, in the analysis of individual races is, first to use the ratings to discover which horses are most favoured by the weights, and second, to check through the comments on the horse to discover what factors other than weight might also affect the outcome of the race.

Incidentally, in setting out the various characteristics, requirements and peculiarities of each horse in the commentary upon him, we have always expressed ourselves in as critical a manner as possible, endeavouring to say just as much, and no whit more than the facts seem to warrant. Where there are clear indications, and definite conclusions can be drawn with fair certainty, we have drawn them: if it is a matter of probability or possibility we have put it that way, being careful not to say the one when we mean the other; and where real conclusions are not to be drawn, we have been content to state the facts. Furthermore, when we say that a horse *may not* be suited by hard going, we do not expect the reader to treat it as though we had said that the horse is *not* suited by hard going. In short, both in our thinking and in the setting out of our views we have aimed at precision.

THE FORM SUMMARIES

The form summary enclosed in the round brackets shows for each individual horse the distance, the state of the going and where the horse finished in each of its races on the flat during the previous two seasons. Performances are in chronological sequence, the earliest being given first.

The distance of each race is given in furlongs, fractional distances being expressed in the decimal notation to the nearest tenth of a furlong.

The going is symbolised as follows: h=hard or very firm; f=firm; fg=fairly good, or on the firm side of good; g=good; d=dead, or on the soft side of good; s=soft, sticky or holding; v=heavy, very heavy or very holding.

Placings are indicated, up to fourth place, by the use of superior figures, an asterisk being used to denote a win.

Thus, 1979 10s* 12f^{3} 11.7g signifies that the horse ran three times in 1979, winning over ten furlongs on soft going first time out, finishing third over twelve furlongs on firm going next time out, and then unplaced, not in the first four, over 11.7 furlongs on good going. NR means that the horse did not race.

Included in the pedigree details are the highest Timeform Annual ratings during their racing careers of the sires, dams and sires of dams of all horses where the information is available.

Where sale prices are given F denotes the price in guineas sold as a foal, Y the price in guineas sold as a yearling.

THE RATING SYMBOLS

The following symbols, attached to the ratings, are to be interpreted as stated:—

p the horse is likely to make more than normal progress and to improve on his rating.

P there is convincing evidence, or, to say the least, a very strong presumption that the horse is capable of form much better than he has so far displayed.

\+ the horse may be rather better than we have rated him.

d the horse appears to have deteriorated, and might no longer be capable of running to the rating given.

§ a horse who is somewhat ungenerous, faint-hearted or a bit of a coward; one who may give his running on occasions, but cannot be relied upon to do so.

§§ an arrant rogue or a thorough jade; so temperamentally unsatisfactory as to be not worth a rating.

? if used in conjunction with a rating this symbol implies that the rating is based upon inadequate or unsatisfactory data, upon form which it is impossible to assess with confidence. The use of a query without a rating implies that although the horse has form, his merit cannot be assessed on the data at present available.

RACEHORSES OF 1980

Horse *Commentary* *Rating*

ABALIGHT 2 gr.g. Abwah 118–Moonlight 101 (Djebe) (1980 5s 5d^2 5fg 6fg 7fg^2 7g^3) Apr 18; small gelding; half-brother to a minor winner; dam 2-y-o 5f winner; put up best performances on last 2 starts, finishing 6 lengths second of 17 to Ardrox Pioneer in maiden race at Warwick in July and third, beaten a head and 5 lengths, to Salon Privee in nursery at Redcar the following month; stays 7f. *T. Molony.* **72**

ABBEYDALE 4 ch.f. Huntercombe 133–Lucky Maid 85 (Acropolis 132) (1979 8g^2 8g^2 10.5g^4 8fg 10s* 10f^4 8d 1980 11s 10f) rangy filly; ran very well early in 1979, finishing second to One In A Million in 1,000 Guineas at Newmarket, but became disappointing and gained her only success when scrambling home in Virginia Stakes at Newcastle; not seen out until September in 1980 having been to stud and apparently didn't train on; finished behind in Doonside Cup at Ayr (sixth to Sea Pigeon) and Sun Chariot Stakes at Newmarket (blinkered, finished last of 7 to Snow); stays 1¼m; acts on any going. *J. W. Watts.* –

ABBEY GRANGE 9 ch.g. Stype Grange 92–Plutarch 93 (Above Suspicion 127) (1979 NR 1980 13d) of little account. *M. James.* –

ABBOTS PASS 4 b.g. Songedor 116–After the Seventh (Galivanter 131) (1979 7g 1980 11d) plater at 2 yrs; very lightly raced and no form since. *S. Holland.* –

ABDU 4 b.c. Balidar 133–Makura (Pampered King 121) (1979 6g^4 5g^3 6d* 6s* 5fg^4 6f 5d^2 5d^2 5fg^2 6fg^2 5d 1980 5fg* 5fg^3 5f^2 5fg^3 5g^3) neat colt; very smart sprinter; won Field Marshal Stakes at Haydock in April by 1½ lengths from Epsom Imp; placed on all his subsequent starts, finishing good second to Sharpo in Temple Stakes at Sandown and third in Palace House Stakes at Newmarket (to Valeriga), King's Stand Stakes at Royal Ascot (to African Song) and William Hill Sprint Championship at York (to Sharpo); acts on any going and on any track; blinkered third and fourth outings; thoroughly genuine and consistent; sold privately after his final start. *W. O'Gorman.* **114**

ABDUCTRESS 2 ch.f. Crowned Prince 128–Bold Bird (Bold Lad, Ire 133) (1980 6fg^4) Mar 9; 3,000Y; second foal; dam, who never ran, is from same family as Ambergris; second favourite when 5¾ lengths fourth of 14 to Piece of the Realm in newcomers race at Chepstow in August; will stay 1m; should improve. *C. Nelson.* – p

ABEER (USA) 3 ch.f. Dewan–Flame Tamer (Court Martial) (1979 5g* 5fg* 6f^2 6d^4 5f* 6f^3 5g^4 1980 7f 5fg) $50,000Y; lengthy, very attractive filly; very good mover; half-sister to winners by Stage Door Johnny and Ribot; dam won over 6f at 3 yrs; smart performer (rated 115) at 2 yrs when her wins included Queen Mary Stakes at Royal Ascot and Flying Childers Stakes at Doncaster; lightly raced in 1980, finishing in rear in Ladbrokes Nell Gwyn Stakes at Newmarket in April and King's Stand Stakes at Royal Ascot (showed early speed); doesn't stay 7f; acts well on firm going. *J. Tree.* –

ABELARD 2 gr.c. Abwah 118–Bala Girl 89 (Welsh Saint 126) (1980 5s 5fg 5fg 8.2d 6g 6f 5d) May 29; small colt; second foal; dam sprinter; plater; not sure to stay beyond sprint distances; sold 680 gns Doncaster November Sales. *M. Tompkins.* –

ABERFIELD 3 ch.c. Northfields–Abergara (Abernant 142) (1979 6d 7f 1980 8fg 10f^2 10d^3 12fg^3 12g^3 14d^4) leggy, narrow colt; placed in maiden and minor races; stays 1½m; acts on firm going; blinkered fifth outing; didn't negotiate hill at Epsom at all well on second start. *C. Brittain.* **64**

ABERCORN FLYER 2 b.f. Silly Season 127–Miss Casanova 84 (Galivanter 131) (1980 5f^2 5f^4 5d 6fg 6fg 5g 8g) Mar 21; lightly-made filly; third live foal; half-sister to 2 middle-distance winners, namely Chenotte (by Midsummer Night II) and 3-y-o Morality Stone (by Ragstone); dam 2-y-o 6f winner; in frame in maiden races at Windsor in May; stays 6f and will get further (had stiff task and finished in rear when tried over 1m); acts on firm going. *W. Musson.* **63**

ABERDARE 2 ch.c. Welsh Pageant 132–Overspent 85 (Busted 134) (1980 5g 7d 7.2d 8d) Mar 18; 8,600Y; lengthy, good sort; excellent walker; second living foal; dam won over 6f at 2 yrs on only start; beaten about 7 lengths when fifth of 15 to John Clare in 7f maiden race at Newbury in August, second outing and best effort; will stay middle distances; moved badly to start third appearance; sold 2,600 gns Newmarket Autumn Sales. *H. Candy.* **77**

ABERDARON 2 gr.f. Saritamer 130–Abergrove 103 (Abernant 142) (1980 5f 5.1fg 7g) Apr 13; small filly; half-sister to 2 winners, including fairly useful stayer Marzook (by Blakeney); dam best at 6f; towards rear in maiden races at Lingfield and Yarmouth (backed from 10/1 to 5/1) in August; reared in stalls and was withdrawn, under orders, at Yarmouth the following month. *H. Collingridge.* **–**

ABERDEEN ROSE 2 b.f. Crozier 117–Aberdeen Lassie 102 (Aberdeen 109) (1980 5s 5fg 5f 5.8fg) May 14; fair sort; first foal; dam won from 5f to 7f at 2 yrs; in rear in maiden and minor events. *J. Haine.* **–**

ABIELLE 4 b.f. Abwah 118–Cut and Thrust 78 (Pardal 130) (1979 7d^4 7g 7f^4 8fg 10s^3 11.5g* 12fg^2 12f* 12d^2 12d^2 1980 15fg^2 14fg 14f^3 14g^4 14fg^2 15.8g^3 14fg^2 14g) unfurnished filly; not disgraced most outings, but ran moderately on final start; stays well; acts on any going; suitable mount for an inexperienced rider. *G. Huffer.* **66**

ABINGTON 3 b.c. Jukebox 120–Silky 112 (Nijinsky 138) (1979 6f* 1980 8f 6fg 7g 8fg 8f 7s) strong, good-bodied, most attractive colt; very good mover; easily won Granville Stakes at Ascot at 2 yrs; usually faced stiff tasks in 1980 but wasn't disgraced when $4\frac{3}{4}$ lengths fifth to Tyrnavos in Ladbrokes Craven Stakes at Newmarket in April on first outing or when seventh to Hard Fought in Jersey Stakes at Royal Ascot on third; stays 1m; acts on firm going; sweated up badly third and fourth starts. *H. Wragg.* **91**

ABO ACE 2 ch.c. Hotfoot 126–Linum 81 (Takawalk II 125) (1980 5fg 6fg 7d 7g 6fg 7f 8g) May 18; 1,500Y; big, well-made colt; good walker; fourth foal; dam won twice over 6f; no worthwhile form, including in a Leicester seller; blinkered fifth outing. *M. Ryan.* **–**

ABORDAGE 3 ch.f. Luthier 126–Almyre (Wild Risk) (1979 NR 1980 10s 12d 14fg^4 14g*) well-made, attractive filly; sister to high-class middle-distance stayer Ashmore, and half-sister to 4 other winners, notably very smart middle-distance filly Acoma (by Rheffic); dam very useful winner at up to 13f; won 9-runner maiden event at Yarmouth in September; will stay beyond $1\frac{3}{4}$m; sold 54,000 gns Newmarket December Sales. *H. Cecil.* **79**

ABOUT TURN 3 b.g. Will Somers 114 § –Golden Darling 86 (Darling Boy 124) (1979 6g 7s^3 1980 6v 6d 6d 7fg^2 7.2fg* 7.2g^3 7g^2 8d 7f 7fg 7g 6s^2 7g*) compact gelding; plater; attracted no bid after winning at Haydock in May and Newcastle in October; stays 7f well; seems to act on any going; usually wears blinkers; suitable mount for a boy; sold 2,600 gns Newmarket Autumn Sales. *J. W. Watts.* **70**

ABROVIAN ROSE 2 br.f. Blue Cashmere 129–Saucy Jane 82 (Hard Sauce 131) (1980 5v 6g 5fg 5f* 5f 8s) Feb 26; 6,000Y; lengthy filly; half-sister to fair stayer C'est Afrique (by Behistoun); dam a sprinter; showed greatly improved form when backed from 25/1 to 10/1 in valuable 16-runner seller at York in September, winning comfortably by 2 lengths from Mountain Record; cost 7,800 gns to buy in; ran respectably next time out; well beaten in her other races (weak second favourite on first start and attracted very little market support on second, third and final appearances); should stay 6f; acts well on firm going. *M. W. Easterby.* **82**

ABU TORKEY 3 gr.c. Majority Blue 126– Nantgarw (Abernant 142) (1979 5g 7fg 1980 7f) tall, good sort; has shown a little ability in maiden and minor races; not certain to stay beyond 7f; sold 5,600 gns Doncaster September Sales. *R. Price.* **–**

ABWACADABWA 2 br.f. Abwah 118–Jetwitch 56 (Lear Jet 123) (1980 7f^3 7f^4 6d^2 7d 8f^4 7s^3 8d^4) Mar 16; 2,500 2-y-o; neat filly; first foal; dam, plater, stayed at least 1m; in frame in varied company, coming closest to success when $\frac{1}{2}$-length second to Moto in seller at Haydock in August; not disgraced when 5 lengths third to Countess Olivia in maiden race at Ayr the following month; probably stays 1m; seems to act on any going. *R. D. Peacock.* **67**

ACAPULCO GOLD 4 ch.c. Gulf Pearl 117–Capsville (Cyane) (1979 12d 10d* 10g 10g^4 12fg^2 10fg* 11g 10fg 10f 9f 6s 1980 12d 10g 10f 11f^3 10fg 8fg^3 10d^4 10.6d 12g 10g* 10f^3 10g^3) strong, well-made colt; good mover; beat Queen's **74**

Royale by 2 lengths in handicap at Folkestone in August; stays 1½m; seems to act on any going; blinkered fourth and fifth outings; trained by M. Francis until after eleventh start. *A. Pitt.*

ACCESSION 2 b.c. Crowned Prince 128–Sapphire Spray (Floribunda 136) (1980 7s³) Mar 24; 17,500Y; half-brother to several winners here and abroad, including smart Warmington (by Home Guard), successful at up to 1¼m; dam Irish 6f winner; second favourite, put up a pleasing first effort when 6 lengths third of 19 to Lord Never in maiden race at the Curragh in September; will stay 1m; sure to win races. *M. O'Toole, Ireland.* **83** p

ACCIARINO (ITY) 3 b.c. Viani–Andromeda (Claude) (1979 NR 1980 11fg 12f 14d) close-coupled Italian-bred colt; well beaten in maiden and minor events. *N. Vigors.* –

ACCLAIMED 2 b.f. Luthier 126–Acoma 121 (Rheffic 129) (1980 7.3d 7g³) Apr 6; big, strong filly; first foal; dam, very smart winner of 2 of her 3 starts, over 1¼m and 1½m, is half-sister to high-class middle-distance stayer Ashmore (by Luthier); apprentice ridden, showed promise behind Boathouse in £5,000 event at Newbury and Full of Reason in 26-runner maiden race at Newmarket in October, running on well both times, at Newmarket finishing third, beaten just over 1½ lengths; has plenty of scope and is likely to make a useful filly over middle distances at 3 yrs. *H. Cecil.* **81** p

ACCOUNTABILITY 2 br.g. Jukebox 120–Fiji Express (Exbury 138) (1980 5d 5f 5f 5fg⁴ 5g 7s 8g 8.2g 8d 7g) Jan 21; 4,300F, 6,500Y; useful-looking gelding; first foal; dam won over 7f and 1¼m in Ireland; only poor form, including in a selling nursery; stays 1m. *R. Hollinshead.* **56**

ACE POT 4 ch.g. Adropejo 114–Noonace (Space King 115) (1979 NR 1980 8g 8d) of little account. *R. Whiston.* –

ACTON WOOD 3 b.f. Sallust 134–Princess Ivor (Sir Ivor 135) (1979 5v 5d⁴ 5v* 5fg 6fg 7.2fg 8fg 8g 1980 7s 9fg 8g) workmanlike filly; only plating class; should stay at least 1m. *W. Marshall.* –

ACTON WOOD LAUREL 2 b.f. Sassafras 135–Moana (Zucchero 133 §) (1980 5d 6d 7d) Apr 11; 5,000Y; leggy, unfurnished filly; half-sister to 2 winners, including useful stayer Firefright (by Firestreak); dam half-sister to Sodium; behind in minor event at Doncaster and maiden races at Carlisle and Wolverhampton early in season. *W. Marshall.* –

ACT PROMPTLY 3 ch.f. Midsummer Night II 117–Impromptu 88 (My Swanee 122) (1979 5fg 6g 5f 1980 6f 8g 10fg 10f 10d* 10s) lightly-made filly; plater; bought in 800 gns after winning at Leicester in October; stays 1¼m; acts on a soft surface; trained by C. Bewicke first 2 starts. *J. Gifford.* **53**

ACUSHLA MACREE 3 ch.f. Mansingh 120–Cannie Cassie 70 (Canisbay 120) (1979 5f⁴ 5fg³ 6g 1980 7s 8f 10f 10.2fg³ 10g 11fg 10.1g 10fg⁴ 10g 9d 10s 10g) neat filly; stays 1¼m; best form on a firm surface; blinkered nowadays; sometimes bandaged behind; ran badly seventh outing. *F. J. Houghton.* **57**

ADAM CRAIG 2 b.c. Connaught 130–Karenina 95 (Silver Shark 129) (1980 8.2s 7d³) Feb 13; 8,000Y; strong, good sort; half-brother to 2 winners, including smart 1976 staying 2-y-o Sultan's Ruby (by Royal Palace); dam won twice from 4 starts at 2 yrs; 25/1 and still bit on burly side, in front rank throughout when 2½ lengths third of 20 to Soldan in minor event at Doncaster in October; will stay at least 1¼m; sure to win races if not tried too highly. *J. Hanson.* **78**

ADDY'S PET 3 br.f. Swing Easy 126–Ravenshead (Charlottown 127) (1979 NR 1980 8fg 9s) leggy filly; seems useless; blinkered second start. *J. Mulhall.* –

ADELA 3 gr.f. Kalamoun 129–Classic Tune (Ribero 126) (1979 5f⁴ 6f² 6f 5fg 6d³ 6g 6fg⁴ 7d 1980 9f 8fg 8fg⁴ 8f 8fg 7.6d⁴ 5f 8g⁴ 7d) small, light-framed filly; in frame in maiden races; will be suited by 1¼m; acts on firm going; has run respectably for an apprentice. *G. Huffer.* **59**

ADEPT 2 b.c. Mount Hagen 127–Tabatha (Soderini 123) (1980 6g 7d 8g 10s) neat, attractive colt; very good mover; fourth foal; half-brother to 1976 2-y-o 6f seller winner The Nadi Cat (by My Swanee); dam Irish 2-y-o 7f winner; showed ability, although beaten some way, when sixth to New Years Day in Granville Stakes at Ascot in July and to Cocaine in Acomb Stakes at York in August on first 2 starts; well behind in maiden races at Goodwood and Nottingham (sweating) subsequently; should stay at least 1m. *P. Walwyn.* –

ADMINISTRATOR 3 b.g. Gay Fandango 132–Maureen's Slipper (Gratitude 130) (1979 5.1g* 6fg 5.1fg⁴ 1980 6fg* 6fg 6v) useful-looking ex-Irish gelding; – §

has ability, as he showed when winning minor event at Naas in July, but is thoroughly unreliable and ran atrociously final start at 2yrs and in 1980 (£4,000 race at Doncaster); stays 6f; acts on a firm surface; one to be wary of; sold out of J. Hassett's stable 1,400 gns Ballsbridge September Sales after second outing. *H. O'Neill.*

ADMIRAL BIMBO 3 ch.c. Simbir 130–Daniela (Le Levanstell 122) (1979 NR 1980 14g 14.6d) 1,600F; big, long-backed colt; second foal; dam poor Irish maiden; unquoted when in rear in maiden races at Yarmouth (bandaged off-fore) and Doncaster in the autumn. *R. Boss.* –

ADMIRAL BLAKE 4 b.g. Blakeney 126–Bedeni 100 (Parthia 132) (1979 12g* 12fg^{3} 1980 13.3f 12s 12fg 14g 12fg) lengthy gelding; won minor event at Salisbury in 1979; had stiff tasks in 1980 but wasn't entirely disgraced on second and fourth starts; will stay well; blinkered third outing (tailed off). *G. Beeson.* –

ADMIRAL FLEET 2 b.g. Simbir 130–Send The Fleet (Bold Hour) (1980 7g 6fg 7f 7g 8fg) Mar 22; 2,300Y; strong gelding; bad plater. *M. W. Easterby.* –

ADMIRAL GRENVILLE 4 b.g. Sweet Revenge 129–Soverena 98 (Sovereign Lord 120) (1979 8d 10g 8fg 8fg 8g 8g 8fg^{4} 1980 8d 8s 10f 11.7fg 10d 12s* 10g^{4} 12f^{2} 12f^{4} 12g* 12f* 12fg* 12f*) big, rangy gelding; reportedly took a very long time to recover from being gelded at the end of his 2-y-o season but was in tremendous form in second half of 1980; won at Lingfield (twice), Folkestone, Salisbury (apprentices) and Ascot, beating Jam gamely by a short head after making most of running on last-named course; suited by $1\frac{1}{2}$m; acts on any going; blinkered second outing; runs well for apprentice A. Clark. *G. Harwood.* 82

ADMIRAL'S BARGE 3 ch.c. Brigadier Gerard 144–Pirogue 99 (Reliance II 137) (1979 7fg^{4} 1980 8d 8s 10fg^{3} 10g 10.1f 11.7h^{3} 14d* 12fg) neat, lightly-made colt; won 14-runner maiden race at Haydock in September; suited by $1\frac{3}{4}$m; probably acts on any going; sweated up fourth start; has run creditably for an apprentice; ran moderately final outing. *W. Wightman.* 72

ADMIRAL'S HEIR (USA) 2 b.c. Crafty Khale–Triggs'z (Successor) (1980 6fg 6fg^{4} 6g* 7g* 7d* 7f* 7g 7.6g* 8d) Mar 4; $12,000Y; quite attractive, com- 111

Mr W. H. Ponsonby's "Admiral's Heir"

pact colt; good mover; fourth foal; half-brother to a winner by I'm For More; dam won over 6f; sire stakes winner of 15 races from 6f to 13f; proved a bargain, winning maiden race at Brighton, minor events at Chester and Wolverhampton and 2 races at Lingfield; gained his successes at Lingfield in a nursery (odds on) and £4,300 event, being driven clear in final furlong to score by 2 lengths from Welham Green in latter race in September; met his last 2 defeats in pattern races at Doncaster, finishing 4½ lengths eighth of 9 finishers behind Gielgud in Laurent Perrier Champagne Stakes and 9 lengths fifth of 7 to Beldale Flutter in William Hill Futurity; will stay middle distances; acts on any going; consistent. *P. Cole.*

ADORATION (FR) 4 br.f. Dancer's Image–Angkor Vat (Vienna 127) (1979 12g³ 12.5g 10.5g 9d³ 9s³ 8g 1980 8fg 8g 11d³ 8g³ 9fg 10fg 10d) ex-French filly; third in maiden races at Hamilton in June and Beverley in July; effective at 1m and stays 1⅜m; acts on soft going; well beaten when blinkered penultimate outing; has a tendency to hang. *J. Mason.* **60**

ADRAAN 3 gr.c. Zeddaan 130–Adara (Le Haar 126) (1979 5fg³ 5g* 5g* 5.5fg 5d* 5d 1980 8g 5fg* 5s* 5f⁴) **124**

More often than not when a horse fails to stay anywhere near so far as might be expected on its breeding this can be ascribed to one of three reasons—training methods, temperamental peculiarities or the presence of some physical infirmity. By a sire who won a top-class race over nine furlongs by eight lengths, out of a mare who won once over seven furlongs and twice at a mile and a half, Adraan is bred to stay a mile. Such is his temperament, however, that breeding considerations don't come into it: he's a sprinter by nature, and a good one too.

Adraan's two-year-old career had seen him racing only at around five furlongs, but although he put up a very smart performance in the Prix d'Arenberg at Chantilly on his penultimate start, winning by two lengths from Manjam, on balance his form was a little patchy. His preliminary outing in 1980 in the Prix de Fontainebleau at Longchamp proved effectively that a mile was beyond him, for after going well within himself for much of the journey he went out like a light in the closing stages and eventually came in seventh of nine behind Nice Havrais. Henceforth Adraan raced only over the minimum trip, using his speed to good effect in two of France's most important sprints, the Prix de Saint-Georges at Longchamp in May and the Prix du Gros Chene at Chantilly in June. In each he put up a scintillating display, to all intents and purposes winning the race in the first furlong by bursting from the stalls and setting up too big a lead for his opponents to pull back. On paper the field for the Prix de Saint-Georges looked good, with such as Kilijaro, Greenland Park and Trio Boy also taking part, but in fact Kilijaro needed further than five furlongs to be seen to best advantage as a four-year-old while Greenland Park and Trio Boy were not so good as in the previous year. Thus Adraan's achievement in breaking the course record and giving weight and a three-length beating to Miliar (who had won his only other start) with Greenland Park third and Trio Boy fourth was not so good as it seemed at the time. Still, he won impressively, and it was no surprise that in the Prix du Gros Chene Adraan started at odds on

Prix de Saint-Georges, Longchamp—Adraan streaks home to a course-record win from Miliar and English challenger Greenland Park

Prix du Gros Chene, Chantilly—Adraan again finishes well clear of Miliar

to beat Miliar and Trio Boy again on worse terms. This he did, winning easily by four lengths from Miliar with Trio Boy third.

These wins encouraged French racegoers to believe that over his right distance Adraan could beat Moorestyle and company in the Prix de l'Abbaye de Longchamp in October on his final outing. He started at 5/4 with Moorestyle at 17/10. In the event Adraan was found wanting, for despite displaying his usual tremendous pace he was never able to draw clear of this top-class field and was caught not long after halfway. Once Moorestyle passed him it was noticeable that Adraan didn't show much fight, and he was well held by the first two the rest of the way home. Eventually he finished fourth of the nine runners, beaten just over four lengths. He came out best of the French horses—those behind him included the Prix Robert Papin winner Irish Playboy and Greenway, successful in the Prix d'Arenberg and subsequently in the Prix du Petit Couvert—but he was no match for the best English sprinters.

Adraan (gr.c. 1977)	Zeddaan (gr 1965)	Grey Sovereign (gr 1948)	Nasrullah
			Kong
		Vareta (gr 1953)	Vilmorin
			Veronique
	Adara (ch 1967)	Le Haar (ch 1954)	Vieux Manoir
			Mince Pie
		Paola (b 1957)	Palestine
			Tayeh

Adraan is only the second live foal out of Adara, who was singularly unproductive in the early years of her stud career, being barren twice to Tanerko, slipping to Djakao and producing a dead foal by Faristan. From her 1975 mating, again to Faristan, Adara produced Anafa, who showed useful winning form over a mile and nine furlongs in 1979. Adara was just a fair handicapper herself but, like so many of the Aga Khan's broodmares, she comes from a fine family, being a half-sister to three winners including Sharapour, who showed high-class form at up to a mile and a half, winning the Prix Dollar among other races. The grandam, Paola, stayed a mile but was effective at shorter distances and finished second in her time in the corresponding races Adraan won twenty years later. She was a daughter of the Molecomb winner Tayeh, also the dam of the 1959 One Thousand Guineas third Paraguana, and a granddaughter of the brilliantly fast Rivaz who produced numerous winners at stud, notably Palariva and Spicy Living, the latter one of the best three-year-old fillies in America in 1963.

Rivaz in fact was a sister to Nasrullah, who is the grandsire of Zeddaan, Adraan's sire. Despite siring such as Kalamoun, Nishapour and Nadjar, Zeddaan, now in Japan, has come in for some criticism as a stallion, with many of his runners accused of being inconsistent or ungenuine. Adraan was certainly excitable and as a result reportedly a bad traveller, and a question mark hung over his courage as well, since he caved in very quickly when tackled on his fourth start in 1979 besides looking irresolute in the Prix de l'Abbaye. Ironically Nasrullah was genuine only as long as he wasn't in front; with Adraan the reverse may well have been the case. Adraan, a strong, good-quartered colt, a sprint-type in appearance, acted on any going but put up his best performances on a soft surface. He has been retired to stud in Australia. *F. Mathet, France.*

ADVERTRACK 2 ch.f. Arch Sculptor 123–St Pet (St Chad 120) (1980 5fg 5fg 5d 5g* 5s^4) May 15; 4,100Y; half-sister to 1977 2-y-o 5f seller winner Portinaix (by Pontifex); dam never ran; backed from 12/1 to 7/1, won 19-runner maiden race at Folkestone in October by a neck from Welsh Cygnet, just holding on in a very tight finish indeed; not sure to stay 6f. *G. Hunter.* **77**

AEGEAN SEAMAN 3 b.g. Averof 123–Abadora (Abernant 142) (1979 5g 6d 6fg 7f^4 6f^4 6s 7.2g 7fg^3 5s 7d^4 6g 1980 6d 6v 6d 5g^2 6f 5g* 5g^3 5fg^4 5.6fg^3 6f 6s 7g) tall, lightly-made gelding; plater; ridden by 5-lb claimer when successful at Redcar in June (bought in 1,550 gns); placed in better company on 3 other occasions; effective from 5f to 7f; acts on any going; often wears blinkers but didn't when successful; sold 360 gns Doncaster November Sales. *S. Nesbitt.* **59**

AERIE 2 br.c. Royal Palace 131–Corriefeol 102 (Jaipur) (1980 7s 7f 7g 7.2s) Apr 11; first foal; dam useful sprinting 2-y-o; only poor form in maiden races and a selling nursery; blinkered third outing; sold to German International Bloodstock 520 gns Newmarket Autumn Sales. *Sir Mark Prescott.* –

AETHELFLAED 3 ch.f. Realm 129–Tegleaze 81 (Galivanter 131) (1979 5d 5fg 5g 5f 5fg 5fg 1980 8s) neat filly; only plating class. *R. Hannon.* –

AFOVOS 4 b.g. Averof 123–Abadora (Abernant 142) (1979 8g 8s^4 7fg 8fg 10f^3 8g 8fg^2 7fg 10f^3 10fg^4 9f 8d^2 1980 10g 8d) plater; best form at up to 1m; seems to act on any going; has worn blinkers; none too genuine. *F. Yardley.* –

AFRICAN EXPORT 2 br.f. African Sky 124–Space Princess 85 (Space King 115) (1980 5f 5fg^4 5fg 5fg 7.2s) Jan 24; 4,000Y; neat filly; third foal; half-sister to 2 winners, including 1m winner Furstin (by Furry Glen); dam won over 6f and 1½m; only plating class; probably needs further than 5f and should stay 7f+; off course nearly 3 months before fourth appearance; trained by S. Wainwright first 3 outings; sold 550 gns Doncaster November Sales. *G. Toft.* **60**

AFRICAN GUY 2 b.c. African Sky 124–Tinterne (Tin King 126) (1980 5f 6g 5g^2 5g 5g 6v 5d) May 20; 1,150Y; strong, compact colt; half-brother to 2 winners, including 1979 2-y-o 5f winner Lupaka (by Red Alert); dam poor maiden; ran easily best race when short-head second of 5 to Cooliney Prince in Emily Persse Cup at Phoenix Park in June; outpaced all way when 12 lengths fifth of 6 to Chummy's Special in Norfolk Stakes at Royal Ascot on next outing and finished last in all 3 of his subsequent starts in Ireland. *W. Fennin, Ireland.* **79**

AFRICAN HOPE (FR) 5 b.h. African Sky 124–Manfilia 95 (Mandamus 120) (1979 12s* 9.7fg^3 12s* 12g* 13d* 12g^3 11g^3 13.5s^3 12g^4 12g 1980 12g^4 15.5g 20fg 13.5g^2) French horse; smart performer at his best; not seen out after finishing 1½ lengths second to Armistice Day in Grand Prix de Marseille-Vivaux in June; ran respectably earlier, finishing 6 lengths fourth of 7 to Scorpio in Prix d'Hedouville, about 2½ lengths fifth of 9 to Hard To Sing in Prix Jean Prat and about 8½ lengths fifth to Shafaraz in Prix du Cadran, all at Longchamp; effective at middle distances and stays well; acts on soft going and is probably unsuited by a firm surface. *M. Zilber, France.* **116**

AFRICANOS 3 b.g. African Sky 124–Welshpool 75 (Henry the Seventh 125) (1979 5f 6g^4 5fg 5fg^2 6fg 5s 5s 1980 5fg 5f 6g 8d* 8.2s^2 9.4g^4 8.2g* 7d* 8fg* 8g^2 8s^2 8f 8fg^3 8s^4) strong gelding; had a good year, winning maiden race at Ayr and handicaps at Hamilton, Ayr again and Newcastle; beat Kithairon 3 lengths on last-named in July; effective at 7f and stays 9f; probably acts on any going; blinkered first start; sometimes sweats up; sometimes wears a tongue strap; ridden by apprentice N. Carlisle for 3 of his wins. *H. Bell.* **87**

AFRICAN PEARL 2 b.c. African Sky 124–Stickpin 74 (Gulf Pearl 117) (1980 5fg 5f^3 6d* 6g) Jan 3; 14,500Y; quite attractive colt; third foal; dam placed over 5f and 7f at 2 yrs; sweated up when odds on for 11-runner maiden race at Newmarket in July but ran on gamely to win by a length from Satin Grange; creditable sixth of 28 to Cavalry Twill in minor event at Windsor the following month; will stay at least 7f; seems to act on any going. *G. Pritchard-Gordon.* **86**

AFRICAN RHYTHM 4 b.g. African Sky 124–Velour (Golden Cloud) (1979 10v 10f^3 8g* 10d* 10s 1980 10g* 10d^3 10g 10g 10d 9f 10fg* 10d^3 10.2d) big, good-looking gelding; useful handicapper; won narrowly at Sandown in June (shade cleverly from Borderline) and Lingfield in October (apprentice event, from Constant Rose): not particularly consistent however; stays 1¼m; possibly unsuited by very soft going; sold to M. Pipe 5,800 gns Newmarket Autumn Sales. *G. Harwood.* **94**

King's Stand Stakes, Ascot—African Song is not extended to beat Runnett and Abdu

AFRICAN SONG 3 b.c. African Sky 124–Goldwyn Princess 72 (Native Prince) **121**
(1979 NR 1980 6f^3 5f* 6f^3 5fg* 5g)

It was regrettable that African Song ran only once after winning one of England's most important five-furlong races, the King's Stand Stakes at Royal Ascot. He came to Royal Ascot the winner of one of his three starts, having followed up a promising run in a maiden event at Newmarket, where he was backed almost to the exclusion of everything else but faded in the final furlong to finish third, by making all to win a similar race over five furlongs at Sandown with considerable ease from twenty opponents. After his Sandown success he ventured into pattern-race company for the first time in the six-furlong Duke of York Stakes and acquitted himself well, travelling strongly for the first half of the race, being driven along to join issue in the last furlong and a half and only giving best to Flash N Thunder and Gypsy Dancer inside the distance, coming home third of the seven runners, beaten three lengths.

On the evidence of his performances at both Newmarket and York the possibility existed that African Song would be well suited by a return to a shorter trip, and with the going remaining on the firm side he was not without some support in the market, starting at 10/1 in a substandard field of fourteen which included Abdu, second in the race the previous year, Greenland Park, who had shown good form at sprint distances in both 1978 and 1979, Runnett, a creditable second to Sayyaf at Haydock on his previous appearance, and Abeer, the winner of the 1979 Queen Mary Stakes and Flying Childers Stakes. African Song blinded his rivals for speed, soon going clear as he raced up the centre of the course and always having the legs of them, in the end winning without being extended by a length and a half from Runnett with Abdu a length away third.

African Song (b.c. 1977)	African Sky (b 1970)	Sing Sing (b 1957)	Tudor Minstrel
			Agin the Law
		Sweet Caroline (b 1954)	Nimbus
			Lackaday
	Goldwyn Princess (b 1970)	Native Prince (b 1964)	Native Dancer
			Sungari
		Goldwyn Girl (ch 1953)	Court Martial
			Zolotaia

Neither African Song nor those that finished behind him did anything to advertise the form of the King's Stand subsequently, managing to pick up only two more races between them by the end of the year. African Song's career after Royal Ascot was very much an anti-climax. Sent to Goodwood—a track that would have suited him admirably—for the King George Stakes, he was found to be lame at the start and was withdrawn without coming under orders. His next target was the William Hill Sprint Championship at York which saw leading sprinters who had not contested the King's Stand, such as Sharpo and Valeriga, taking part. It was to be anticipated that this race would help clarify the sprinting picture, but it did nothing to help assess the merit of African Song. He moved none too well to post, and after showing his usual good speed started to drop back from halfway, in the end passing the post a sorry last, many lengths behind the winner Sharpo. The reason for his sudden collapse was in all probability physical—he was reported to have finished with a ricked pastern joint—and he didn't race again. In September came the news that he had been sold to stand alongside Lithiot and Sea Break at the Haras du Theil-en-Auge, near Deauville.

African Song may well appeal to French breeders as a stallion since elements of his pedigree, in which there isn't a great deal of stamina, will be familiar to them. His sire African Sky showed good form at up to a mile in France and kept his name in the headlines in 1980 through Kilijaro's performances in the top races at six furlongs to a mile. On the distaff side, the dam Goldwyn Princess is a half-sister to Broadway Melody, who showed smart form at up to a mile and is the dam of the six-length winner of the 1974 Prix Morny, Broadway Dancer. Goldwyn Princess is a half-sister to several winners besides Broadway Melody, the best of them the latter's brother Lad's Love, a useful winner over sprint distances; but her own racecourse record, like that of the next two dams, was virtually non-existent. The three of them managed to run only a total of three times, the best effort being Goldwyn Princess' third place in a maiden race at Carlisle from two starts over five furlongs as a two-year-old before injury curtailed her career. Injury seems, indeed, to have dogged the family, and given that African Song was probably none too easy to train—he didn't run as a two-year-old and was difficult to keep sound in 1980—trainer Kelleway did well to win a race like the King's Stand with him. African Song, a strong colt, and a good walker, cost 7,400 guineas at the 1978 Newmarket October Sales. He was evidently best at five furlongs and acted well on firm ground. *P. Kelleway.*

AFRICAN STAR 2 b.g. Starbush 99–African Lily (Hanover) (1980 5g 8d) Feb 17; fifth foal; half-brother to a winning point-to-pointer; dam never ran; in rear in maiden races at Bath and Warwick in the autumn and looks of no account. *W. R. Williams.* —

AFROMOSIA 3 b.f. Queen's Hussar 124–Muninga 108 (St Alphage 119) (1979 5f 5fg 5g 1980 6fg 6h 6fg 8g) neat filly; poor form, including in sellers; blinkered third start at 2 yrs. *M. Tompkins.* —

AFTERNOON DELIGHT 3 ch.f. Rambah 67–Indaca (Pinza 137) (1979 8f 1980 10fg 12fg 14fg 16.1d) lengthy filly; poor form in varied company. *M. Francis.* —

AFTER SHAVE 4 b.c. Sallust 134–Blue Fragrance (Blue Prince 123) (1979 8s 8s* 8v 8fg 1980 10.2d 7v 7f 8f 10f 10fg 10g) strong colt; ran poorly in 1980; stays 1m; probably acts on any going; often wears blinkers; moved badly to post last 3 starts. *K. Stone.* —

AGAPOULA 3 b.f. Averof 123–Hannah Darling 108 (Match III 135) (1979 6f 1980 8fg 8f 5f) neat, strong filly; seems only plating class; will stay 1¼m; blinkered third start; sold 500 gns Newmarket Autumn Sales. *C. Brittain.* —

AGE OF REASON 2 b.g. Red Alert 127–Pampered Belle (Pampered King 121) (1980 5f 5fg² 6d* 7s⁴ 7f 6s) Feb 15; 20,000Y; strong, well-made gelding; half-brother to several winners here and abroad; dam won at up to 13f in Ireland; stayed on most gamely to win sponsored maiden race at Newcastle in June by a length from Steel Pass; ran best race afterwards on final outing when seventh of 19 to Hiz in nursery at Nottingham in October (blinkered); should stay 7f. *Denys Smith.* **81**

AGE QUOD AGIS (USA) 2 gr.c. Al Hattab–Alps (Pavot) (1980 5fg 6f* 6g* 6s* 5.5g³ 6g) May 31; $60,000Y; leggy colt; has rather a round action; half-brother to several winners in USA; dam very useful stakes winner at up to 1m; successful in maiden race at Yarmouth (by 4 lengths from Show-A-Leg), well-contested minor event at Doncaster (beat Dissipated Dollar same margin) and 3-runner July Stakes at Newmarket; made all, quickened when asked approaching final 2f and ran on strongly to beat long odds-on Recitation by 2½ lengths in last-named event, with Grain Race ¾ length away third; beaten subsequently in Prix Robert Papin at Maisons-Laffitte (seemed to find trip on short side when 2½ lengths third of 10 to Irish Playboy) and Gimcrack Stakes at York (odds on, had every chance but couldn't quicken when 6 lengths fifth of 9 to Bel Bolide); will be suited by 1m; appears to act on any going. *H. Cecil.* **113**

AGNI 3 b.f. Lyphard 132–Distinctiveness (Distinctive) (1979 6g 5.8g 5f 1980 6fg) small, sturdy filly; poor form in maiden races. *A. Breasley.* —

AIDANJAMES 3 ch.g. Sallust 134–Tarara 117 (Tamerlane 128) (1979 5fg 5fg⁴ 5fg 5fg 1980 7fg 5f 6g) workmanlike gelding; has shown little form since second start at 2 yrs and was well beaten in seller on final outing; blinkered last 3 outings in 1979; sweated up second appearance. *N. Vigors.* —

AILEEN'S GIFT 5 ch.m. Divine Gift 127–Gusty Girl 71 (Darling Boy 124) (1979 5.8g 5fg² 5f* 5.8h⁴ 6g 5fg 5.8fg 5fg 6g 1980 5fg 7h 6g 6fg 5f 7f⁴ 7g) plater nowadays; stays 7f; acts on firm going; occasionally wears blinkers; sometimes sweats up; suitable mount for an apprentice; retained by trainer 700 gns Ascot October Sales. *M. McCourt.* —

AINARA 2 gr.f. No Mercy 126–Kerkithalis 98 (Acropolis 132) (1980 7g⁴ 7g 6f³ 6v) Mar 12; 5,200Y; small, lengthy filly; half-sister to several winners, including fairly useful Willie Ormond (by Blakeney), a winner at up to 1½m; dam, daughter of top 2-y-o Sarcelle, won twice over 5f at 2 yrs; 1½ lengths third of 17 to Flash 'N' Fire in minor event at Redcar in September, best effort; possibly better suited by 6f than 7f; acts on firm going; dwelt when blinkered final outing but nonetheless ran badly. *B. Hobbs.* **75**

AIR DE DANSE (FR) 3 b.f. Gay Fandango 132–Satellite (Exbury 138) (1979 NR 1980 7s 8fg) lightly-made filly; first foal; dam once-raced daughter of top-class La Sega; well beaten in maiden race at Leicester in March and minor event at Pontefract (last of 18 finishers) following month; sold 900 gns Goffs November Sales. *F. J. Houghton.* —

AIR POWER 3 gr.g. Supreme Sovereign 119–Queen Of The Winds (Borealis) (1979 6g 5fg 1980 9v) small, fair sort; no sign of ability in maiden and minor events. *Mrs A. Cousins.* —

AIRSHIP 2 br.c. Manado 130–High Sphere (St Paddy 133) (1980 5f* 5f² 5f 6fg* 6fg² 7g) Apr 30; 13,000Y; rather lightly-made colt; half-brother to 1979 Irish 6f winner Buckles (by Targowice) and a winner in Italy; dam never ran; winner of maiden race at Warwick in April and £3,700 nursery at Kempton in September, getting up close home to win by a head from Scarrowmanwick in latter when having first race for over 3 months; unlucky when strong-finishing second of 12 in nursery at Ascot later in September, failing by only a head to catch Steelinctive after having to be switched at least twice; best form at 6f but wasn't disgraced over 7f and may well get 1m at 3 yrs; acts well on firm ground. *F. J. Houghton.* **96**

AIRSLEE 2 gr.c. Town Crier 119–Tavaro (Gustav 121) (1980 5fg 6g 6fg 5fg⁴ 8.2g 6g 6f³ 7s⁴ 6s) May 11; 5,000Y; useful sort; good walker; second foal; dam won in Norway; in frame in varied company, best effort on seventh outing when 2¼ lengths third of 18 to Kathred in seller at Newmarket in October; best form at 6f; acts on firm going; blinkered last 3 starts. *Mrs R. Lomax.* **71**

AIRSTREAM 2 br.c. Saritamer 130–Midsummertime (Midsummer Night II 117) (1980 6d) Feb 6; fourth foal; half-brother to Park Hill winner Idle Waters (by Mill Reef); dam never ran; 6/1 when last of 8 to Veleso in maiden race at Lingfield in July. *F. J. Houghton.* —

AJIMURA (USA) 2 b.c. Wajima–Clover Princess 110 (Right Tack 131) (1980 6d⁴) May 5; $70,000Y; lightly-built colt; first foal; dam, winner twice over 7f, finished second in Irish 1,000 Guineas; second favourite and pretty fit, came under pressure to no avail after racing in front rank for 5f in maiden race at Newmarket in October and was then eased, finishing 7¾ lengths fourth of 17 to Gabitat; didn't move well to start here; will stay 1¼m; hasn't a lot of scope but should win a race at 3 yrs. *H. Cecil.* **74** p

AKRAM 2 ch.c. Sandford Lad 133–La Marne (Nashua) (1980 5s 5f* 5f⁴ 6g³ 7.2d² 7g³ 7fg 8d* 7v) May 3; 13,500Y; sturdy colt; good mover; half-brother to a winner in Italy and 1979 Irish 2-y-o 9f winner Anna Livia (by Northfields); dam lightly-raced half-sister to leading 2-y-o fillies Crimea II and Bravery; winner of minor events at Newmarket in April and Leicester in October, putting up a thoroughly genuine display when battling on to hold off Whistling Tower by a head in latter; suited by 1m; seems to act on any going except, perhaps, heavy; sometimes sweats up but is genuine and consistent. *W. O'Gorman.* **89**

ALABAMA 2 gr.f. Warpath 113–Montana (Mossborough 126) (1980 8fg 10d* 10.2s) Feb 12; strong, deep-girthed, sturdy filly; first foal; dam poor maiden on flat and over hurdles; improved greatly on previous outing and landed a gamble when trotting up in 18-runner seller at Leicester in October, coming home 8 lengths clear of Malseedy despite being eased; sold out of C. Thornton's stable 4,100 gns afterwards; had stiffish task next time out; stays very well; suited by a soft surface. *D. Wilson.* **80**

ALADYAT 3 b. or br.f. Home Guard 129–Moon Cake (Red God 128§) (1979 6f 7g 7s 1980 10.2fg 10.1g 10.1s 11.5g 8.2s 8d) light-framed filly; seems only plating class; not certain to stay 1½m; sold 900 gns Newmarket Autumn Sales. *R. Armstrong.* —

AL-ALLAM 2 ch.c. Sun Prince 128–Ladys View 109 (Tin Whistle 128) (1980 5fg 6g 5g 7v) Apr 4; 17,000Y; sturdy, well-made colt; particularly good walker; half-brother to a winner in Denmark; dam speedy 2-y-o; prominent in maiden races in September on second and third starts, finishing 7 lengths sixth of 13 to Brummer in £3,200 race at Doncaster and 4 lengths fifth of 18 behind Portogon at Bath; well beaten in nursery (20/1) on final appearance; should stay 7f; retained 6,600 gns Newmarket Autumn Sales. *B. Hills.* **72**

AL-AMAL 4 ch.f. Green God 128–Maureen's Slipper (Gratitude 130) (1979 6v* 6s 5fg 6fg 6f 1980 6d 6f^{2} 6fg 5f^{4} 8s) useful performer at her best; 4 lengths second to Jebb Lane in Thirsk Hall Stakes in April; wore blinkers and didn't seem to find a great deal penultimate outing; stays 6f (had stiff task when tried over 1m on final outing in July); acts on any going; sweated first 2 starts. *W. O'Gorman.* **88**

ALANGROVE SOUND (USA) 2 gr.c. Champagne Charlie–De Soto Queen (Fleet Nasrullah) (1980 6g^{3} 8fg^{3} 8g^{3} 10s) May 1; $8,000Y; third foal; half-brother to a minor winner in USA; dam won at up to 1m, including claiming races; third in maiden races at Hamilton in July, Beverley in September and Edinburgh in October; stays 1m well (weakened in closing stages over 1$\frac{1}{4}$m). *B. Hanbury.* **74**

ALANOOD 3 ch.f. Northfields–Fast Motion 86 (Midsummer Night II 117) (1979 NR 1980 8f 12d* 12fg 14s) small, compact filly; second foal; dam won over 6f at 2 yrs; 50/1 when beating Karamita by 8 lengths in 21-runner minor race at Wolverhampton in June; beaten a long way in small race at Ripon and handicap at Sandown afterwards; stays 1$\frac{1}{2}$m; acts on a soft surface. *W. O'Gorman.* **85**

ALANYA 3 b.f. Streetfighter 120–Eurythme (Acropolis 132) (1979 5.8g 8fg 1980 8f 10fg 8g 10.1d) compact filly; bad plater; sold 540 gns Ascot November Sales. *S. James.* **–**

ALAUNA 3 br.f. Most Secret 119–Crook O'Lune 89 (Fury Royal 108) (1979 5s 6g 6s 6s* 1980 7.2fg 6fg 7fg* 7g^{2} 6g) compact filly; plater; attracted no bid after winning at Catterick in June; ran creditably in better company next time (apprentice ridden); stays 7f; seems to act on any going; sweated up second start. *M. H. Easterby.* **60**

ALBANY VICTOR 4 ch.g. Mount Hagen 127–Aswellas 93 (Le Levanstell 122) (1979 8.2s 7s* 7g 7d 7fg 8fg^{3} 8.3fg^{2} 8fg^{4} 10fg^{2} 10d 1980 7.6d) big, good-looking gelding; winner of maiden race at Epsom in 1979; well behind in apprentice handicap on only outing of 1980 (July); stays 1$\frac{1}{4}$m; acts on any going; wears blinkers; changed hands 2,500 gns Newmarket May Sales. *G. Fletcher.* **–**

ALBERT HALL (FR) 5 br.h. High Top 131–Silly Symphony 100 (Silly Season 127) (1979 8d 10g 8g 10.2fg 10f^{4} 8fg 9f 1980 8g 8.3fg 8h^{2} 8g 8g) small horse; finished strongly when head second to Traditional Miss in handicap at Bath in August; behind under 10-0 in valuable seller at Doncaster following month; stays 1$\frac{1}{4}$m; acts well on a firm surface; not particularly consistent. *R. Boss.* **88**

ALBOSAGGIA (ITY) 2 b.f. Swing Easy 126–Acireale (Veronese) (1980 5f 6d 8.2g) small, lightly-made filly; half-sister to winning Italian 3-y-o Altdorf (by Tudor Music) and Italian winner Aketi (by Weimar); dam won 3 times in Italy; behind in maiden races and a seller. *E. Weymes.* **–**

ALBRIZZI (USA) 3 b.c. Cannonade–Table (Round Table) (1979 NR 1980 5fg 8g 6d 8f* 8d^{3} 10s) $40,000Y; 3,800 gns 2-y-o; compact colt; not a good mover in his slower paces; plater; attracted no bid after winning at Redcar in September; should stay beyond 1m; probably acts on any going; blinkered final start. *I. Walker.* **55**

ALDEBURGH FESTIVAL 4 ch.c. Club House 110–Minor Chord 88 (Major Portion 129) (1979 7s 8fg^{3} 7fg 8g^{3} 7d 7f 1980 8fg 7.6f^{4} 8.5f^{2} 8g 8fg^{3} 10f* 8fg^{3} 10g 8s) good-looking, well-made colt; useful handicapper on his day; looked very well when winning by 2$\frac{1}{2}$ lengths from subsequently-disqualified Radigo at Epsom in August; ran easily best subsequent race on next start; stays 1$\frac{1}{4}$m; best on a firm surface. *D. Whelan.* **89**

ALDENHAM (USA) 2 ch.c. His Majesty–Mama's Silver (Silver King 119) (1980 7g^{2} 7d 6fg^{3} 7g) Mar 28; $50,000Y; smallish, fair sort; excellent mover; half-brother to several winners, 2 of them stakes winners, including I'm For Mama (by I'm For More), a winner of $212,000 at up to 1m; dam ran twice unplaced; placed in maiden races at Salisbury, going down by 1$\frac{1}{2}$ lengths to Price of Peace in July and finishing $\frac{3}{4}$-length third to Von Erlach when favourite **72**

for 16-runner race in September; had stiff task in nursery final start; will stay 1m. *G. Balding.*

ALEDA ROSE 3 b.f. Charlottown 127–Urugano 101 (Buisson Ardent 129) (1979 5s 1980 11fg 8fg 7.2fg4 7fg 7d* 7g4 8fg* 9g 8s 12f 8f 8.2s) leggy, unfurnished filly; plater; apprentice ridden when winning at Ayr in June (no bid) and July (bought in 3,000 gns); best form at up to 1m though is bred to stay middle distances; acts on a firm and a soft surface; sweated up eleventh start. *J. Wilson.* **56**

ALEOS (FR) 3 b.g. Faunus–Aphytis (Crepello 136) (1979 8fg3 1980 12f4 10f* 10fg* 10.1g 10fg3 10g3 10fg*) workmanlike gelding; successful in maiden race at Redcar in May, minor event at Ripon in June and handicap at Yarmouth in August; stays 1¼m; yet to race on a soft surface; sweated up, misbehaved in paddock and looked ungenuine when blinkered on sixth outing; sold to J. Old 9,200 gns Ascot August Sales. *M. Stoute.* **93**

ALERT 4 b.c. Red Alert 127–Dash On 93 (Klairon 131) (1979 7g3 7d4 8.5g 8g3 7fg* 8g3 7.3g4 (dis) 7fg3 8fg 1980 7fg 8f 7.2fg3 6g 7g 7g3 8g 8g 7.3d 7g4 6d2 7fg 7g) tall colt; has enlarged off-fore joint; good walker and mover; very useful performer; often faced with stiff tasks in 1980 and didn't win, but usually acquitted himself well; placed 3 times, finishing third in John of Gaunt Stakes (beaten just over 2 lengths by Hard Fought) at Haydock in June and minor event (2½ lengths behind Tahitian King) at York in July and second to comfortable winner Pace Jean in £2,000 event at Brighton in September; stays 1m; acts on any going; usually wears blinkers. *C. Brittain.* **110**

ALETHE 2 br.f. Derring-Do 131–Argitone (Aureole 132) (1980 6d) Mar 19; quite a well-made filly; sister to 1m winner Entebbe, and half-sister to useful 1974 2-y-o Sassari (by Sassafras); dam unraced daughter of Park Hill winner Collyria; unquoted when behind in 25-runner maiden race won by Little Wolf at Newbury in October. *J. Douglas-Home.* **–**

ALEXANDER NEVSKY 2 b.c. Furry Glen 121–Levanstell Queen (Le Levanstell 122) (1980 6g 6s) Mar 18; 1,400F, 3,000Y; rangy, useful-looking colt; brother to 1979 2-y-o 1¼m seller winner Levandene; dam never ran; unquoted when behind in sizeable fields of maidens at Nottingham in the summer. *M. Blanshard.* **–**

ALEXANDRA PARK 3 b.c. Cavo Doro 124–Paddy's Rose 81 (St Chad 120) (1979 5d 1980 8g 12g) small colt; bad plater; has worn blinkers; sold 290 gns Doncaster November Sales. *C. Crossley.* **–**

ALEX FLYER 2 gr.g. Hot Spark 126–Miss Rosy (Quorum 126) (1980 5fg 5fg3 5f* 5g 6g2 6g4) Apr 10; 6,000Y; compact gelding; fourth foal; half-brother to 3-y-o 1½m winner Eight Roses (by Pieces of Eight) and a winner in Holland; dam showed no form; favourite when winning 9-runner maiden race at Hamilton in June by 1½ lengths from Saulann; ran creditably afterwards; suited by 6f; exported to Hong Kong. *B. Hanbury.* **88**

ALEY 2 ch.f. Mount Hagen 127–Alsaga 86 (Alcide 136) (1980 6fg 6fg4 7d3) Feb 18; rather unfurnished filly; half-sister to 3-y-o 1m and 9f winner Alpaga (by On Your Mark) and winning stayer Albeni (by Great Nephew); dam won twice over 2m; in frame in minor event at Lingfield and maiden race at Leicester in October; will be suited by middle distances. *J. Dunlop.* **78**

ALFIE DICKINS 2 ro.c. Spanish Gold 101–Vila Real 76 (Town Crier 119) (1980 7d 6g) May 24; robust colt; first reported foal; dam won 4 sellers over 7f and 1m; unquoted and backward when behind in large fields for maiden races at Leicester (started slowly) and Newmarket in October. *R. Hollinshead.* **–**

ALFRED MILNER 3 gr.c. Roan Rocket 128–French Music (French Beige 127) (1979 5f 5f3 5.1g3 7s 1980 8fg3 8fg 10f 8.2f3 8fg 8g 10f* 10s2) small colt; blinkered and dropped in class when winning seller at Pontefract in September (retained 1,450 gns); again blinkered when running creditably in better company on final start; suited by 1¼m; acts on any going; sold out of J. Winter's stable 1,050 gns Doncaster August Sales after fifth outing. *W. Stubbs.* **77**

ALICE TOWN (USA) 2 b.f. Prince Dantan–South Bimini (Sir Ribot) (1980 8g 7s 7g) Apr 20; $22,000 2-y-o; lengthy, useful-looking filly; second foal; dam won at up to 1m in USA; sire at his best at 4 yrs when smart winner at up to 1¼m; behind in end-of-season maiden and minor events. *W. Hastings-Bass.* **–**

ALICUM (FR) 3 b. or br.c. Kashmir II 125–Alisma II (Alizier 131) (1979 6f4 5.8h2 7g 5fg 5fg 1980 8fg 5.8g 6s 6g) in frame in maiden races at 2 yrs; in **–**

rear in varied company, including selling, in 1980; should stay 1m; ran badly in blinkers final start. *P. Cole.*

ALISON NICOLA 2 b.f. Streak 119–Nicola Jane 90 (River Chanter 121) (1980 5s 5s 5g³ 5f² 5fg 5f³ 6fg 5d² 5g⁴) Mar 21; 1,850Y; small, lightly-made filly; half-sister to 2 winners; dam stayed 1m; plater; below form when tried at 6f; seems to act on any going; blinkered fourth and fifth outings. *T. Fairhurst.* **49**

AL KHASHAB 3 ch.g. Habat 127–Parlais 101 (Pardao 120) (1979 5s 5g 6d 6f 7s⁴ 1980 8v 8h 9g³ 8g³ 8f 9s² 8d 10d) workmanlike gelding; plating-class maiden; probably stays 9f; acts on soft going. *R. Hollinshead.* **61**

AL KUWAIT 4 br.c. Blakeney 126–Camenae 72 (Vimy 132) (1979 10s 11f³ 12g* 1980 12d² 12fg² 14g² 16.1d* 12f⁴ 18d) strong, good-bodied colt; favourite, quickened in final furlong and ran on well to beat Heighlin by 2 lengths in handicap at Newmarket in July; galloped on strongly in closing stages and ran easily better subsequent race when about 2 lengths fourth behind subsequently-disqualified Morvetta in similar race at Newmarket in October (no chance in last ½m when favourite for Tote-Cesarewitch on same course later in month); suited by further than 1½m and stays well; acts on any going, but is suited by some give in the ground; hung right in final furlong when narrowly beaten on second and third starts and wore blinkers afterwards. *J. Sutcliffe.* **86**

ALLEGRETTA 2 ch.f. Lombard 126–Anatevka (Espresso 122) (1980 8fg* 9d* 10g²) Mar 10; tall, lightly-made filly; half-sister to winners in Germany by Gulf Pearl, Alpenkonig and Charlottown; dam good winner in Germany, numbering 5f Versuchsrennen der Stuten and 6.7f Trial-Stakes among her successes; winner at Leicester and Wolverhampton in the autumn, scoring by 2½ lengths from Silver Snow in maiden race on former and beating More Stones 3 lengths in 12-runner minor event on latter; stayed on well, despite hanging right under pressure, when 1½ lengths second of 9 to Krug in Zetland Stakes at Newmarket in late-October; will stay 1½m; useful. *M. Stoute.* **101**

ALL EVEN 6 ch.g. Crisp and Even 116–Mistress Alcide (Alcide 136) (1979 NR 1980 20.4g) won 2m maiden race at Thirsk at 3 yrs; tailed off only outing of 1980 (July); quite a moderate hurdler. *W. A. Stephenson.* **–**

ALLEZ BRITAIN 7 ch.g. Double-U-Jay 120–Incendo (Ionian 128) (1979 NR 1980 6g 5.3d 6g 6d 5.8f) fair sprinter in 1977; lightly raced and well beaten since; best form on top-of-the-ground; bandaged both outings in 1978; sold 675 gns Ascot August Sales. *B. Swift.* **–**

ALLIED BEAUMEL 2 ch.f. Jimmy Reppin 131–Tarmandy (Black Tarquin 136) (1980 5s 6fg 6s 7d 6g) June 4; 3,000Y; compact filly; fourth reported living foal; dam won a selling hurdle and a point-to-point; beaten some way in maiden races and seems of little account; bandaged off-hind third start. *S. Harris.* **–**

ALLIED CARDIFF 2 b.f. Import 127–Monday Morning (Royal Record II) (1980 5f 5fg 5f 6f² 6g 6fg 6fg³ 6f 6s* 6fg 8d) Apr 25; 1,100F, 700Y; compact filly; fourth produce; half-sister to 1¼m seller winner Allied Oldham (by Goldhill); dam ran only at 2 yrs; put up easily best effort when racing on soft ground for first time, winning 20-runner seller at Nottingham in August by 2 lengths from Seymour Lady; changed hands 1,000 gns afterwards; had stiffish tasks in nurseries subsequently; may stay 1m; wears blinkers. *G. Blum.* **60**

ALLIED OLDHAM 3 b.f. Goldhill 125–Monday Morning (Royal Record II) (1979 5v 5d 5h 5f³ 6fg 6fg 6f 1980 6s 7f 6f 6fg 7g 10d 10d 10d*) compact filly; plater; won at Leicester in November (sold 1,700 gns); stays 1¼m; probably acts on any going. *G. Blum.* **47**

ALLIED SEFENITE 4 b.g. Crooner 119–Wharfequeen (Supreme Sovereign 119) (1979 12s 1980 7fg 6f 9.6f² 10d² 10g) plater; runner-up at Folkestone and Nottingham in June; stays 1¼m; probably acts on any going. *S. Harris.* **45**

ALL IN 2 ch.c. Lauso–Summer Rain (Palestine 133) (1980 7f 8d⁴ 10s) small, narrow colt; third foal; dam tailed off both outings; unquoted, kept on gamely when narrowly-beaten fourth of 16 to Jade and Diamond in maiden race at Warwick in October; stays 1m and should get further; well beaten final outing. *D. Sasse.* **76**

ALLI-RECO 2 ch.g. Record Run 127–Alli-Bee 57 (Violon d'Ingres) (1980 6d 6g 7g 7d) Jan 27; 2,600F; strong gelding; third produce; dam 2-y-o 5f seller winner; seems of little account; sold 500 gns Doncaster November Sales. *R. Ward.* **–**

ALL MOSS 2 b.f. Prince Tenderfoot 126–All Beige (Ballyciptic 122) (1980 7d 7g) Mar 27; neat, strong filly; first foal; dam unraced daughter of Yorkshire **–**

Oaks winner Feevagh and half-sister to dam of Levmoss, Sweet Mimosa and Le Moss; well beaten in maiden races at Leicester (20/1) and Newmarket (unquoted) in October. *B. Hobbs.*

ALL OUR YESTERDAYS 3 b.f. Jimsun 121–Metis 55 (Be Friendly 130) (1979 5g 7g 7fg 1980 10.8v 10.8s) little worthwhile form in maiden races. *M. Salaman.* —

ALL SUMMER 2 ch.f. Sun Prince 128–Right Now 100 (Right Royal V 135) (1980 7.2s) Mar 2; 27,000Y; unfurnished filly; half-sister to French 3-y-o 9f winner Northright (by Northfields) and 2 other winners, including useful hurdler Exalted (by King Emperor); dam 1½m winner and half-sister to Mon Fils and Son of Silver; 10/1 and in need of the outing, always behind when well-beaten fifth of 6 to Stats Emmar in Rose of Lancaster Stakes at Haydock in July. *M. Jarvis.* —

ALMIGHTY ZEUS 3 ch.g. High Line 125–Zeus Girl 75 (Zeus Boy 121) (1979 NR 1980 11fg4 16f 12g 16g) plain sort; first reported foal; dam stayed well on flat and won over fences; promising fourth in maiden race at Newbury in April but subsequently looked one paced when well beaten in similar events and a handicap; will stay long distances. *H. Candy.* —

ALMITRA 2 br.f. Targowice 130–Donna Cressida 116 (Don II 123) (1980 5d) Apr 28; second foal; dam smart winner from 7f to 1¼m in Ireland; well-backed second favourite when never-dangerous seventh of 17 to Corn Street in maiden race at Wolverhampton in October; will do better over 7f+. *J. Tree.* — p

ALMOND VALLEY 3 ch.f. Jimmy Reppin 131–Videmanette (High Perch 126) (1979 NR 1980 11fg2 12.2d* 12fg* 14g3) useful sort; good walker; half-sister to very useful stayer Mountain Cross (by French Beige); dam quite useful hurdler; favourite when winning maiden race at Newcastle in June and small race at Ripon in July; creditable 2 lengths third to Grandiose in Melrose Handicap at York in August; will stay beyond 1¾m; acts on a firm and a soft surface; ridden by 5-lb claimer at Ripon. *J. W. Watts.* **91**

ALMUNICAR 3 b.f. Sharpen Up 127–Zorelia (Chingacgook 128) (1979 5.1fg* 5f2 6f2 6fg2 7g 1980 8f 6g 6g) leggy, unfurnished filly; fairly useful (rated 93) at 2 yrs; well beaten in varied company in 1980; should stay 7f+; acts well on firm going; sweated up second outing. *R. Boss.* —

AL NASR 2 b.c. Green Dancer 132–Padrona 103 (St Paddy 133) (1980 8g) May 16; 156,000Y; rangy, good-looking colt; half-brother to Derby fourth Pelerin (by Sir Gaylord) and 7f and 1m winner Fair Melys (by Welsh Pageant); dam, half-sister to numerous winners, won over 5f and 6f at 2 yrs; weak in market, very much in need of race and very green, moved badly to start prior to finishing tailed-off last of 6 to Clear Verdict in minor event at Goodwood in September, only outing. *J. Dunlop.* —

AL NASR (FR) 2 b.c. Lyphard 132–Caretta (Caro 133) (1980 8g*) Feb 11; 550,000 francs Y (approx £58,000); first foal; dam, minor winner over 9.5f and 11f in France, is half-sister to smart French animals Kebah and L'Ensorceleur and to very speedy Klaizia, herself dam of smart miler Lypheor (by Lyphard); justified favouritism in 19-runner newcomers race at Saint-Cloud in October, racing in front rank throughout and running on gamely to hold off Mourtazam by a head; will stay 1¼m; bound to go on to better things at 3 yrs. *A. Fabre, France.* ?

ALNASR ASHAMALI 4 b.c. Lorenzaccio 130–High Powered 113 (Hugh Lupus 132) (1979 12s3 10f* 10.1fg4 11g4 12g 1980 12.2v 10f 10.7g 11.7s 16fg) good sort; well beaten in handicaps in 1980; best form at 1¼m; acts on firm going; blinkered final start at 3 yrs. *J. Benstead.* —

ALPAGA 3 b.g. On Your Mark 125–Alsaga 86 (Alcide 136) (1979 6f 1980 8d* 7g2 9f* 8g 10s4) rangy, useful-looking gelding; successful in maiden race at Salisbury in August and modest minor event at Wolverhampton (sweated up) in September; stays 1¼m; acts on any going; saddle slipped and unseated rider fourth start; sold 8,000 gns Newmarket Autumn Sales. *J. Dunlop.* **84**

ALPHA CENTAURI 3 gr.f. Grey Mirage 128–Pamsam 67 (Constable 119) (1979 5s 5g 5fg 6f 6h* 6s 6s 6g 7s 1980 8v4 6f 8f 8f 6d 5f) small filly; bad plater; has worn blinkers; sold 580 gns Doncaster August Sales. *J. Bingham.* —

ALPHA TOR 3 b.f. Great Nephew 126–Mahele 56 (Hawaii) (1979 6f4 6fg 5f4 8.2g 7f 1980 10.1fg) leggy filly; poor form, including in sellers. *D. Marks.* —

ALPINE DAMSEL 3 ch.f. Mountain Call 125–Lady R. B. (Gun Shot) (1979 5v 5s 6g 5g 5f 7fg 6fg 6f 8fg 1980 8d 8v 6d 11fg4) neat filly; poor plater; —

seemed to find 11f too far on fourth outing; has worn blinkers; sold 1,000 gns Newmarket May Sales. *K. Ivory.*

ALPINE MISS 2 b.f. Inclination 96–Confrontation (Combat 123) (1980 5g 5d 5fg 5d) Apr 11; sister to winning sprint plater Wrenaldo; dam never ran; poor plater. *A. Potts.* —

ALPINE ROCKET 3 ch.g. Shiny Tenth 120–Dusty Bluebell (Sky Gipsy 117) (1979 5g 5fg4 5.8f4 6g 6g 6f2 1980 6s 7d 6fg* 6f* 6fg* 6g* 5.8fg 6d3 6g2 6g 6g 6fg 6fg 6d) lengthy, useful sort; moderate handicapper; successful at Salisbury (apprentice race), Windsor, Haydock and Newbury in first half of season; best at 6f on a sound surface; wears blinkers; sweated up slightly eighth start; dwelt tenth outing; suitable mount for a boy. *G. Balding.* **82**

ALSKLING 2 b.f. Mummy's Pet 125–Frondia 76 (Parthia 132) (1980 5fg 5fg 5fg 7d3 7fg 7s 8d 6g) Feb 8; lengthy, attractive filly; good mover; half-sister to good continental stayer Duky (by Midsummer Night II) and useful French 5f and 1¼m winner Prince Dias (by So Blessed); dam, winner over 1½m, is half-sister to Gold Cup winner Shangamuzo; poor maiden; will probably stay 1¼m+; form only on a soft surface; sometimes sweats up. *J. Bethell.* **63**

ALTEZA REAL 3 ch.f. Mansingh 120–Princely Maid 71 (King's Troop 118) (1979 5fg4 5h* 5f* 5g 5f 1980 5.1g3 5g3 5f2 5d* 5d 6g2) lightly-built filly; sprint handicapper; won decisively at Pontefract in August; stays 6f; probably acts on any going; blinkered fourth and fifth starts. *M. Stoute.* **84**

ALUWHITE VENTURE 3 ch.c. Reliance II 137–Fierte (Relic) (1979 NR 1980 10g 14.6d) 2,700F, 4,000 2-y-o, 6,200 3-y-o, resold 960 3-y-o; leggy colt; half-brother to 3 winners, including fairly useful 1978 2-y-o 6f winner Paul Stuart (by Runnymede); dam half-sister to top-class French stayer Zamazaan; in rear in minor event at Nottingham and maiden race at Doncaster in the autumn. *A. Goodwill.* —

ALWAYS EIRLYS 2 ch.f. Toujours Pret 121–Eirlys 90 (Elopement 125) (1980 7g 5d) rangy filly; good walker; half-sister to 3 winners, including 1m and 1½m winner Piggy Malone (by Shiny Tenth); dam ran only twice; 12/1 when eighth of 19 to Universal Penny in valuable seller at Sandown in August, second outing; bred to stay middle distances. *N. Callaghan.* —

ALWAYS LINPAC 4 ch.g. Sandford Lad 133–Semper Fi (Above Suspicion 127) (1979 6v 5d 7fg 8fg 8h 9s 1980 12.2fg) poor maiden; usually blinkered at 3 yrs. *W. Elsey.* —

ALWAYS SANDICLIFFE 3 ch.f. Home Guard 129–Golden Glimpse (Gallant Man) (1979 7fg 1980 7f 10s 10s3 10d 12s2) lengthy filly; quite moderate; stays 1½m; acts well on soft going. *B. Hills.* **70**

ALWAYS THERE 2 b.c. Continuation 120–Majestic Gift (Majetta 115) (1980 5g 5f 5f) Apr 7; 500F; workmanlike colt; on burly side when last but one on all outings, final start a Catterick seller (July). *M. W. Easterby.* —

ALWAYS VIGILANT 4 ch.f. Dubassoff–La Presidente 69 (Primera 131) (1979 9s 12g4 12fg2 12f 12f 10h 1980 10v 11fg4 12fg3 12g) middle-distance maiden; in frame in varied company, including in a seller at 3 yrs; acts on a firm surface; blinkered once at 3 yrs; sold out of J. Fitzgerald's stable 3,500 gns Doncaster May Sales after third start. *M. Ryan.* —

AMAL NAJI 2 b.c. Rheingold 137–Nothing On (St Chad 120) (1980 7f 7d 8g3 10.2s) Mar 29; 10,000Y; leggy colt; first foal; dam unraced half-sister to 1,000 Guineas winner Nocturnal Spree; 25/1, prominent throughout when 2¾ lengths third of 16 to Uppety in minor event at Newmarket in October; well beaten next time out; should be suited by 1¼m+; blinkered last 2 outings. *W. O'Gorman.* **82**

AMANDA MARY 2 b.f. Wishing Star 117–Marchpane (Parthia 132) (1980 5v 5v 5g3 5d 5g 5f4 5g 5g3 5g 5f 5d 5g4 5d) May 26; 1,500F, 4,200Y; lengthy filly; half-sister to fairly useful 5f performer Ackabarrow (by Laser Light) and a winner in Sweden; dam never ran; in frame in maiden and minor events at Edinburgh (2) and Catterick (2); bred to stay much further than 5f; best form on a sound surface; wears blinkers. *W. Stubbs.* **67**

AMARETTO 2 ch.f. Continuation 120–Polly Bellino 56 (Dadda Bert 95) (1980 5fg) Mar 28; fourth living foal; half-sister to successful plater and hurdler Archetto (by Arcticeelagh); dam won at 1¼m; 16/1 when last of 17 to Gold Breeze in maiden race at Catterick in June; sold to D. Chapman 270 gns Doncaster October Sales. *J. Hardy.* —

AMAZING GRETTS 3 b.f. Pitskelly 122–King's Victress (King's Bench 132) (1979 8fg 1980 11.7fg 10fg 9g 10s) small filly; little worthwhile form in maiden races; ran badly in blinkers third start. *C. Nelson.* —

AMBASSADOR BOY 4 b.g. The Go-Between 129–Prefer (Preciptic 122) (1979 6g 6d 8g^4 8fg 1980 8f 8d 9g) strong gelding; poor maiden. *Mrs A. Cousins.* –

AMBER DANCER 2 ch.f. Can Can–Carmarthen-By-Pass (Marine Corps) (1980 7f 7g 5f) June 26; compact, rather lightly-made filly; first foal; dam never ran; soundly beaten in sellers. *G. Lockerbie.* –

AMBER PALACE 2 ch.f. Sallust 134–Breide's Wood (Le Levanstell 122) (1980 5f 5fg^4 5.8fg^4 5g^4) Mar 24; 8,000Y; attractive filly; half-sister to 5f winner Out of Depth (by Deep Diver); dam won over 6f in Ireland; only quite moderate; runs as though 5f is her trip at present. *G. Hunter.* **71**

AMBERSEA 3 ch.g. Amber Rama 133–Dame Aux Bijoux 71 (Charlottown 127) (1979 NR 1980 6d 7d 8fg 7f 8d 13g 14g 11.5fg 12g 12g 13.8fg 13.8d) workmanlike gelding; bad plater; has worn blinkers; trained by J. Etherington first 4 starts. *J. Harris.* –

AMBER VALE 3 gr.f. Warpath 113–Jackies Joy (Skymaster 126) (1979 7fg 8g^2 1980 10.5f 11fg* 11d* 9.4g* 12g 11s^2 10.6s 11fg^2 10.2d* 10g 12v) tall, unfurnished filly; successful in maiden race at Ayr, small race at Carlisle and handicaps at Ayr again and Doncaster; beat Ski's Double $\frac{3}{4}$ length on last-named in October; good second to Pulse Rate in Ladbrokes Ayrshire Handicap at Ayr on sixth start; should stay 1$\frac{1}{2}$m; probably acts on any going; ran moderately in amateur riders race seventh start. *J. Hanson.* **98**

AMBER VALLEY 7 b.g. Forlorn River 124–Jackies Joy (Skymaster 126) (1979 12d* 12d^3 12f^3 12.3f^4 14s 12fg 1980 12.3d 13fg^4 13d^4) fairly useful handicapper at his best; was suited by 1$\frac{1}{2}$m but seemed not to get 1$\frac{3}{4}$m; won on a firm surface, but revelled in the mud; was suited by forcing tactics and needed strong handling; dead. *J. Hanson.* –

AMBLER 4 b.c. Simbir 130–Am Stretchin (Ambiorix 130) (1979 10d^2 10g^2 11fg^4 11s^2 11.7fg^2 12fg^3 12g^3 10g^2 1980 12d 12g^2 16.1f^4 14g^4 12g^2 12g* 16.1d 11.7d 12fg 12g 12fg^4 12g* 12s^3) attractive, well-made colt; fair handicapper; successful in apprentice handicap at Doncaster in June and in amateur riders event at Brighton in October, winning quite comfortably both times; also won in Jersey; didn't seem to put much heart into his effort when second twice earlier; best form at up to 1$\frac{1}{2}$m and appears not to stay 2m; acts on any going; usually wears blinkers (didn't last 3 starts however). *G. Balding.* **81**

AMBRECA (FR) 3 b.f. Satingo 129–Ambrefine (Fine Top 125) (1979 NR 1980 8fg 8f 10.2g 10g 10g) neat filly; little worthwhile form, including in sellers; sold 400 gns Doncaster October Sales. *M. Camacho.* –

AMERICAN DANCER 2 gr.f. No Mercy 126–Quickmatch 89 (Match III 135) (1980 7s 7g) Feb 22; 2,200F; useful-looking filly; half-sister to 2 winners abroad; dam best at 1m; unquoted when behind in minor event at Sandown and maiden race at Newmarket in October. *P. Ashworth.* –

AMERICAN PRINCE 4 b.c. Prince Tenderfoot 126–Dogana (Zank) (1979 9g^4 10s^2 7.5v* 8g* 8g* 8fg* 8f* 8g* 1980 7g 8d* 8v 8g^3 8d) ex-Irish colt; half-brother to 3 winners, including high-class miler Don (by Yellow God); dam won over 9.5f in Ireland; didn't race so often as he had in 1979 and was nowhere near so successful, but gained another quite important success when beating Hilal by $\frac{1}{2}$ length in Prix du Muguet at Saint-Cloud in May; ran three times afterwards, best effort when good third of 4 to Muscovite in Ballychorus Stakes at Leopardstown in July; best form at 1m; acts on any going; genuine and consistent; sold out of S. Murless' stable 620,000 francs (approx £61,700) at Arc de Triomphe Sales; sent to U.S.A. *J. Pease, France.* **117**

AME TO KILL 2 b.c. Gay Fandango 132–Towards 69 (Worden II 129) (1980 5.1g^3) May 6; 11,000Y; narrow, neat colt; half-brother to 2 winners, including fairly useful 1975 2-y-o 5f performer Pert Princess (by Realm); dam placed over 1$\frac{1}{2}$m; 9/4, slow into stride and then ran green in final 2f when 2 lengths third of 7 to Lacework in maiden race at Yarmouth in August, only outing. *L. Cumani.* **77** p

AMIGO RAAPHORST 2 b.c. Swing Easy 126–Kazviney (Romney II) (1980 5d 6s 5g^3) Apr 23; wiry colt; first reported foal in this country; dam traces to Oaks winner Toboggan; unquoted when behind in maiden race at Wolverhampton and minor event at Windsor in June; just over 4 lengths third of 11 to Marmorera at Duindigt, Holland, the following month. *N. Guest.* ?

AMINA 2 b.f. Brigadier Gerard 144–Nedda 113 (Alcide 136) (1980 7fg^3) May 7; smallish, attractive filly; sister to Princess Eboli, winner of both Cheshire and **80** p

Lancashire Oaks, and half-sister to 3 other winners, including 3-y-o Canio (by Welsh Pageant), a very useful performer in 1979; dam stayed 1½m; third favourite, shaped well when 4½ lengths third of 22 to Clear Verdict in maiden race at Newmarket, running on in good style in final 2f without being subjected to a hard race; sure to improve and win races over middle distances at 3 yrs. *B. Hobbs.*

AMINA (USA) 3 ch.f. Arts and Letters–Garden Walk (Traffic Judge) (1979 NR 1980 12g 12g^4 13s^4 12g) $29,000Y; leggy, quite attractive sort; half-sister to 2 winners in USA; dam won twice at up to 6f at 4 yrs; fourth in maiden races at Lingfield in June and Nottingham in July; stays 1½m. *F. J. Houghton.* —

AMINTA 2 b. or br.f. Silly Season 127–Blue Book 101 (Majority Blue 126) (1980 6g) May 7; 3,300F; neat filly; half-sister to 4 winners, all successful at 2 yrs, including useful La Voleuse (by Burglar) and fairly useful Blues Swinger (by Swing Easy); dam, winner twice over 5f at 2 yrs, stayed 1m; unquoted, running on in closing stages when seventh of 14 to Musical Minx in maiden race at Nottingham in July, only outing. *W. Elsey.* —

AMIRS DRUM 3 b.c. Meldrum 112–Take a Chance 107 (Rockefella) (1979 6fg 8.2g 5fg^3 5d 6g^3 1980 10.6g) useful-looking colt; fair (rated 85) at 2 yrs; needed run only outing in 1980 (June); should stay 1m+; bought out of B. Hanbury's stable 6,000 gns Newmarket May Sales. *C. Tinkler.* —

AMODORO 3 b.f. Cavo Doro 124–Amorchow (Chou-Chin-Chow 99) (1979 NR 1980 14d) fifth reported foal; dam winning hurdler; 20/1 when soon pushed along and tailed off in maiden race at Haydock in September. *W. Wharton.* —

AMORAK 3 b.f. Wolver Hollow 126–Mary Murphy 85 (Aureole 132) (1979 7fg 1980 12fg^2 12fg 12g 10.2fg 9d^2 8g*) leggy ex-English filly; won maiden race at Navan in September; had earlier finished second in minor event at Salisbury and maiden race at Wolverhampton; pulled very hard and didn't look resolute in latter; stays 1½m; acts on a firm and a soft surface; often blinkered but wasn't when successful; sweated up third start; trained by F. J. Houghton first 5 outings. *K. Prendergast, Ireland.* 74

AMOROSAMENTE 2 b.f. Lyphard 132–Bel Paese (Forli) (1980 7fg^3 6g^3) Mar 24; 68,000Y; compact, leggy filly; fourth foal; dam, granddaughter of brilliantly speedy Careless Nora, won twice over 9f in French Provinces; third in August in maiden race at Yarmouth and minor event at Ripon (lost several lengths at start but stayed on to finish 4½ lengths behind Holdall); dead. *C. Brittain.* 85

AMOROUS 2 b.g. Mummy's Pet 125–Maxims 88 (Major Portion 129) (1980 5f* 5fg^3 5f^2 5.1fg^3 5g^3 5fg 6f^2 6g* 6g) Apr 23; 20,000Y; lightly-made, leggy, useful-looking gelding; half-brother to 6 winners, including useful miler Deadly Nightshade (by Floribunda); dam 2-y-o 5f winner; won maiden race at Newmarket in April and well-contested nursery on same course in October, running on strongly in lead from 1½f out to beat Ardoony decisively by 1½ lengths under top weight on latter occasion; placed in most of his races in between, putting up a particularly noteworthy performance when ¾-length second to Scarrowmanwick, again under top weight, in valuable 6f nursery at Newmarket; suited by 6f and may get further as a 3-y-o; acts well on firm going and has yet to race on a soft surface; genuine and consistent although was a little below his best when apprentice ridden on final start (had stiffish task). *J. Hindley.* 111

AMSAM 2 b. or br.f. Prince de Galles 125–Lovage (Linacre 133) (1980 5fg 5fg 5fg* 6fg 5g^3 7g 7g^2 6g) Mar 28; 1,000Y; narrow, light-framed filly; poor mover; half-sister to speedy filly Chain Lady (by Manacle); dam of little account; heavily-backed favourite when winning poor seller at Carlisle in May; ran wide into straight when 1½ lengths second of 12 to High Class Builder in another seller at Catterick in August; will probably stay 1¼m. *A. Smith.* 54

AMURANDA 3 b.f. Andrea Mantegna–Namur (Amber Rama 133) (1979 5v 5d 1980 9f 6fg^2 7fg 5g 5.8g 6s^3 6fg^2 7g 5f 6g^2 7f 5g 5fg) small filly; plater; best at 6f; probably acts on any going; has run creditably for an apprentice. *C. Wildman.* 52

ANARCHIST 2 ch.c. Upper Case–Miss Twights (Hopeful Venture 125) (1980 5g 6s 6g 8s) Mar 29; 1,900Y; workmanlike colt; second foal; dam twice-raced half-sister to smart miler Miracle; poor form in maiden auction events and a valuable seller; sold 750 gns Ascot November Sales. *K. Ivory.* —

ANASCEND 2 b.f. Ascendant 96–Anasayra (Sayajirao 132) (1980 5fg^2 5d^2 6d 8.2g 7.2s 8d) May 1; unfurnished filly; good mover; half-sister to 2 winning 59 platers; a plater herself; will stay middle distances; twice reared over backwards when withdrawn on intended fourth outing; trained by R. Hobson first 3 outings. *F. Dever.*

ANCHOR LADY 3 b.f. The Brianstan 128–Lazarette (Welsh Saint 126) (1979 NR 1980 10g 10g 15.5g) smallish, useful-looking filly; first foal; dam won over 9f in Ireland; behind in maiden races in the summer; unlikely to stay 2m. *P. Kelleway.* —

ANCIENT REGIME (USA) 2 gr.f. Olden Times–Caterina 124 (Princely Gift 137) (1980 5.5g* 5g4 5.5g2 6fg* 7g) **123**

Considering that two-year-old racing in France is nowadays dominated by fast-maturing American breds, it seems amazing that until Ancient Regime came over for the Queen Mary Stakes in 1980 there had been no French-trained challenger for any of the two-year-old prizes at Royal Ascot since Khairunissa, Kalamoun's dam, ran in the Queen Mary in 1962. The absence of the French is hard to understand, particularly since their first race of comparable value and importance, the Prix Robert Papin, doesn't take place until the end of July. A look at some of the more recent winners of the Coventry Stakes, such as Doleswood, Cawston's Clown, Lake City and Varingo, shows that a top-class two-year-old is not always required to win this valuable and prestigious race. A few runners from France can only add to the race's competitiveness and interest and hopefully more French trainers will show some initiative in 1981.

Ancient Regime's trip to England didn't result in a win but she emerged from her race with credit. Like thirteen others in the seventeen-strong field she was a previous winner and like Nasseem, Pushy and Welshwyn, the three preferred to her in the betting, she was unbeaten; at Evry the previous month she had run out an impressive winner of a newcomers race, drawing away from the distance for a four-length success. Another victory looked on the cards at Ascot as Ancient Regime came with a strong run approaching the final furlong but as soon as she got in touch with Pushy and Welshwyn, both of whom were racing towards the centre of the course, she started to edge away from the rails. By the time her jockey straightened her it was too late to make any further impression on the leaders and Nasseem got up to deprive her of third place close home. Pushy beat her two and a half lengths.

After her return to France Ancient Regime had three more outings, all against colts in Group 1 races, and twice put up splendid efforts. In the Robert Papin at Maisons-Laffitte she showed excellent pace, after being slightly hampered leaving the stalls, to take the lead off the July Stakes winner Age Quod Agis with two furlongs to run. Perhaps she made too quick a recovery from her mishap because her stride shortened in the closing stages and she failed by two lengths to hold off Irish Playboy. Few could have fancied Ancient Regime to turn the tables on the Papin winner over half a furlong further in the Prix Morny at Deauville the following month. The betting also suggested that she would have difficulty in coping with Miswaki, a most impressive winner of the Prix Yacowlef earlier in the Deauville meeting, and with Prince Mab, a much improved colt in blinkers and the winner in good style of his last three races. However, Ancient Regime was ridden much more patiently than she'd been at Maisons-Laffitte. Prince Mab held a narrow lead early on, setting a tremendous

Prix Morny, Deauville—Ancient Regime wins from Miswaki, Prince Mab and Watchdog

gallop, but by halfway both Irish Playboy and Miswaki had passed him. Irish Playboy was the first to weaken, leaving Miswaki in front, but by this time Ancient Regime had started a run up the rails which took her to the front in the closing stages. Her winning margin was three quarters of a length with Prince Mab a further two lengths behind, just in front of Watchdog, a colt who later showed up well in three important races in the autumn.

Only five turned out for the Prix de la Salamandre at Longchamp in September and, although there was a doubt whether seven furlongs would suit her, Ancient Regime was made a short-priced favourite to confirm her superiority over Miswaki and Prince Mab. Ancient Regime put up her only poor effort, trailing in last, over seven lengths behind Miswaki, and her trainer reported that she was so distressed after the race that he was having his vet inspect her. The inspection revealed a fracture of a small bone in her left knee and that the displaced bone had trapped a nerve.

Ancient Regime (USA) (gr.f. Apr 4, 1978)	Olden Times (b 1958)	Relic (bl 1945)	War Relic
			Bridal Colors
		Djenne (b 1950)	Djebel
			Teza
	Caterina (gr 1963)	Princely Gift (b 1951)	Nasrullah
			Blue Gem
		Radiopye (gr 1954)	Bright News
			Silversol

We understand that Ancient Regime is recovering well from her injury and that she remains in training. It's likely that she will be tried over a mile but she isn't certain to stay that far. Her sire Olden Times won the San Juan Capistrano Handicap over a mile and three quarters as a four-year-old but as a six-year-old he did all his winning at six furlongs to a mile, setting a new track record over seven furlongs at Churchill Downs. To a previous mating with Caterina he sired the very useful filly Olden, whose three stakes wins were over distances from four and a half furlongs to six furlongs. Caterina has spent all her time at stud in the USA since her racing career with Sam Armstrong came to an end. A half-sister to the high-class middle-distance colt Scottish Rifle, Caterina was a five-furlong performer. Her blistering speed made her very difficult to catch and she led throughout when winning the Nunthorpe Stakes from Lucasland at three years, having failed only narrowly to land the same race as a two-year-old. Of her other foals two have won, notably the Warfare colt Mug Punter who won two stakes at around a mile in California, and her yearling of 1980, a filly by Far North, was sold for 160,000 dollars at the Fasig-Tipton Sales.

Provided Ancient Regime makes a complete recovery from her accident her prospects must be quite bright. She has already proved herself capable of taking on and beating the colts and there are no sprinters of exceptional merit around in France. Should she stay a mile she must have an excellent chance in the Poule d'Essai des Pouliches. She's a compact filly; she has the unusual record for a French-trained animal of a season's experience of never having raced on a soft surface. *J. Fellows, France.*

ANDREA'S PET 2 ch.f. Sharp Edge 123–Warm Slipper (King's Company 124) **77**
(1980 5f 5g 7f 7g 7f^3 8fg^3 8d* 8s^2 7g) May 6; lengthy, fair sort; first foal; dam tailed off only start; attracted no bid after winning 11-runner selling nursery at Redcar in October by $\frac{1}{2}$ length from Faridella; carried overweight when running creditably in better-class events subsequently; suited by 1m; acts on any going but has shown her best form on a soft surface; good mount for an apprentice. *P. Wigham.*

ANDREW MARK 3 b.g. Rapid River 127–Lucy 83 (Sheshoon 132) (1979 5s^3 **–**
5d^4 6fg 7f^3 8g 7d 1980 10s 10.6d^4 10.8s 8.2g) quite moderate (rated 79) at 2 yrs; ran poorly in varied company in 1980; blinkered final outing (June). *N. Adam.*

'ANDSOME 4 br.g. Some Hand 119–March Stone 84 (March Past 124) (1979 **–**
10.2g 10f* 10.2f* 10fg^4 10.8fg* 10g^2 11.7fg 1980 10s^2) compact gelding; winner of seller and 2 apprentice handicaps in 1979; had no chance with winner but nevertheless ran creditably when 8 lengths second to Ringgit in handicap at Leicester in March on only outing of 1980; best form at $1\frac{1}{4}$m; acts on soft going, but is well suited by firm; good mount for a boy. *M. Pipe.*

ANDY LOU 2 b.g. Be Friendly 130–Ribara (Barbare II 128) (1980 5v^2 5d* 5h^2 **67**
5fg 5g^4 5g 5d 5fg) Jan 18; 2,100F, 1,500Y; well-grown gelding; poor mover in his slower paces; third foal; half-brother to a minor winner; dam won over 7f at 2

yrs in Ireland; made all to win 4-runner minor event at Newcastle in April by 2 lengths from General Times; ran well in small races at Stockton and Beverley afterwards; will stay 6f; gives strong impression he needs some give in the ground; off course 2 months after sixth outing and was well beaten in nurseries on his return. *G. Toft.*

ANDY REW 7 b.h. Lear Jet 123–Chantel-Gold 74 (Chantelsey 130) (1979 8g* 8g* 8f* 8f 8f 8fg 1980 8f 8.5f 8g 8g2 8fg4 8g 8g4 8s) useful handicapper at his best; favourite when runner-up to easy winner Galaxy Capricorn at Brighton in August; found nothing under pressure when fourth to Grand Conde at Salisbury following month; stays 1¼m; well suited by a sound surface; has been tried in blinkers; suitable mount for an apprentice; sold 5,000 gns Newmarket Autumn Sales. *P. Cole.* **88**

ANEX (FR) 3 b.c. Exbury 138–Nantana (Le Mesnil 133) (1979 7f 7fg 1980 12f 12.5h 16f 14d4 14g4 16s* 14fg) strong, plain colt; favourite when winning 10-runner maiden race at Lingfield in July; suited by a test of stamina; suited by some give in the ground; sold 5,600 gns Newmarket Autumn Sales. *F. Durr.* **73**

ANFIELD LADY 2 b. or br.f. Averof 123–Graceful Scot (Aberdeen 109) (1980 5v 5f) Feb 28; 3,100Y; leggy filly; poor mover; fourth foal; half-sister to winning sprinter Isthatchew (by Burglar); dam never ran; whipped round and took no part when backed from 7/1 to 9/2 in minor race at Ayr in May, second outing; started slowly on debut. *W. H. H. Williams.* –

ANGE GARDIEN (FR) 4 b.f. Home Guard 129–Laurelina (Sassafras 135) (1979 10s 8f 8fg 12f4 14.7f3 12fg 1980 8fg 10f 12d 12.2f3 15.8f 14.7d) slow maiden; behind in seller on second outing. *W. Bentley.* –

ANGELO SALVINI 4 br.g. Relko 136–Sweet Sauce (Fr) (Hard Sauce 131) (1979 NR 1980 12h2 13.8fg* 12.1fg* 12g* 18.4g3 13d* 14.7g 16d3 16f4 17.4s* 18d) narrow, rather sparely-made gelding; fairly useful performer; ridden by 5-lb claimer when putting up fine effort to win Eglinton and Winton Memorial Handicap at Ayr in September by ½ length from Nation Wide (pair clear), making **88**

Phil Bull's "Angelo Salvini"

all and refusing to be denied when challenged in last furlong; successful earlier in maiden race at Catterick, amateur riders events on same course and at Redcar and £2,500 event again at Ayr; also hacked up in NH Flat race at Stockton; rather disappointing in Tote Cesarewitch won by Popsi's Joy at Newmarket in October, fading steadily in last ¾m and finishing well behind; suited by a test of stamina; acts on any going but is well suited by soft; most game and genuine. *M. H. Easterby.*

ANGEL SONG (USA) 2 ch.f. Graustark–Primonetta (Swaps) (1980 6s) big, rangy filly; sister to smart Irish 6f to 1¼m winner Grenfall and to Maud Muller, a very smart stakes winner at up to 9f, and half-sister to high-class stakes winners by Hail to Reason, namely Prince Thou Art, successful at up to 9f, and Cum Laude Laurie, winner at up to 1¼m; dam, sister to Kentucky Derby winner Chateaugay, was a top-class winner at up to 1¼m; well-backed second favourite but looking in need of race, in touch till halfway and wasn't knocked about once chance had gone when 10 lengths eighth of 21 to Tolmi in maiden event at Newmarket in July, only outing; sure to do better. *R. Hern.* — p

ANGEVIN 2 b.f. English Prince 129–Paddyflower 88 (St Paddy 133) (1980 7.3d) Apr 18; big filly; half-sister to Fastpad (by Hotfoot), a useful winner from 6f to 11f in England and France; dam 2-y-o 5f winner; unquoted and backward when last of 12 to Boathouse in £5,000 event at Newbury in October; the type to make a better 3-y-o. *P. Walwyn.* —

ANGLE FIRE (USA) 2 b.c. Angle Light–Mary Biz (T.V. Lark) (1980 6fg² 7g³ 7d 6fg³ 8.2s²) Mar 9; $80,000Y; strong, lengthy colt; carries plenty of condition; second foal; dam, unplaced 4 times, is half-sister to smart Terrible Tiger, a winner at up to 8.5f; placed in maiden and minor events, easily best effort on final start when ½-length second of 20 to Irish Heart in maiden race at Haydock in October (might well have won had he not hung quite badly left under pressure inside final furlong); will stay 1¼m; sure to win races if not tried too highly. *S. Norton.* **86**

ANGLEPOISE (USA) 3 b.c. Angle Light–Burns' Babe (Fleet Nasrullah) (1979 6f* 7g² 8d* 1980 8f³ 8f 8.2g 8s³ 8g* 8g* 10g) compact colt; came back to his useful best in the autumn, winning 5-runner handicap at Ayr by ½ length from Lingdale and £2,500 event at York by a head from Saher, making all and battling on well each time; should stay 1¼m; suited by some give in the ground; blinkered at Ayr; genuine. *S. Norton.* **101**

ANGLESEY BOY 3 br.c. Home Guard 129–Haut Lafite (Tamerlane 128) (1979 8g 1980 8f 8fg 10fg) lightly-made colt; poor plater; blinkered last 2 starts. *D. Sasse.* —

ANGLO GREEK 3 b.g. English Prince 129–Orange Sensation 69 (Floribunda 136) (1979 8f² 1980 6f⁴ 6f* 6fg 5d) attractive, well-made gelding; odds on when readily winning maiden race at Redcar in May; will be suited by a return to 1m; acts on firm going; sold 600 gns Newmarket Autumn Sales. *C. Brittain.* **72**

ANGOR 3 ch.f. Lorenzaccio 130–Fanghorn 117 (Crocket 130) (1979 NR 1980 7f 10fg³ 8fg 8g² 8f² 8d² 9d*) tall, leggy filly; sister to very useful Gradiva, successful from 5f to 1m, and half-sister to top-class sprinter Double Form (by Habitat) and fairly useful 1978 2-y-o 5f performer Galka (by Deep Diver); dam placed in French 1,000 Guineas; won 15-runner maiden race at Wolverhampton in October; stays 1¼m; probably acts on any going; blinkered nowadays; raced with head in air sixth start. *F. J. Houghton.* **73**

ANICK 5 b.h. Prince Regent 129–April Twelfth (King's Leap 111) (1979 6g* 7s² 1980 6fg 7fg 6g 6g³ 5d² 6g 6g*) strong, good sort; poor mover; blinkered when winning handicap at Salisbury in July by 2½ lengths from Roman Scribe; stays 7f; acts on soft going; bandaged first 2 outings; had tongue tied down at Salisbury; sold only 440 gns Ascot September Sales. *D. Elsworth.* **76**

ANIECE 2 br.c. Ballymoss 136–Gay Maria (Tacitus 124) (1980 7fg 10s² 10.2s) Apr 27; 5,000F; good-topped colt; second live produce; half-brother to useful 7f performer Jenny Splendid (by John Splendid); dam never ran; 25/1 when 1½ lengths second of 17 to Spin of a Coin in maiden race at Nottingham in October; well beaten next time out; backward and very coltish first outing; will stay 1½m+. *R. Boss.* **81**

ANIFA (USA) 4 b.f. Herbager 136–Flail (Bagdad) (1979 10.5v³ 10.5g* 10.5g² 10fg 12d³ 12d* 13.5fg³ 12fg 12.5s 15.5s² 1980 10s² 15.5g 10.5d 12d* 12.5s 15g⁴ 13.5g⁴ 12f² 20d* 12v* 12f) **123**

It is very much to be hoped that Anifa can be saved after fracturing her off-fore cannon when racing among the leaders with half a mile or so to go in

Prix Gladiateur, Longchamp—Anifa wins this marathon from Le Moss and Kelbomec

the Washington International at Laurel in November; a very smart, extremely well-bred racemare and a notably tough and versatile one, she will be extremely valuable at stud. Racehorses with similar injuries have been saved with increasing frequency since Mill Reef's celebrated recovery in 1972, particularly in the United States, and Anifa is no doubt in excellent hands. After having her leg put in a cast she was taken to the University of Pennsylvania Veterinary Hospital.

Given easier ground Anifa would have had a good chance of winning the Washington International, for at Aqueduct a fortnight earlier over the same distance and on a similar track she had scored a resounding victory in the 300,000-dollar Turf Classic. High winds and heavy rain jeopardised racing that day and conditions were so bad that after the first two races had been run it was decided to cancel the third and fourth and wait hopefully for the predicted abatement in the storm. Had not the meeting been scheduled for beaming live via satellite to a London hotel, to promote interest in the live televising of American racing in England, it might well have been abandoned. Fortunately for Anifa's connections racing resumed after a ninety-minute delay. Owing to local racegoers' ignorance of her ability as well as to the strength of the opposition Anifa, who had beaten Le Moss in the Prix Gladiateur at Longchamp a month previously, started at odds of more than 40/1 in a field of eight. Her principal opponents seemed to be her compatriot Three Troikas, fourth in the Prix de l'Arc de Triomphe on her previous start, the five-year-old gelding John Henry, a consistent grass specialist, and the three-year-old Temperence Hill, already the winner of more than a million dollars in prize money in 1980. After breaking well Anifa settled down in second place behind John Henry and had no difficulty in going the pace in the muddy conditions. She passed John Henry readily at the bottom of the back straight and turned for home with a clear advantage. She stayed on resolutely, never seeming likely to be caught, and passed the post three lengths clear of the strong-finishing Golden Act who had a further five lengths to spare over third-placed John Henry.

Anifa (USA) (b.f. 1976)	Herbager (b 1956)	Vandale (b 1943)	Plassy
			Vanille
		Flagette (ch 1951)	Escamillo
			Fidgette
	Flail (b 1968)	Bagdad (br 1956)	Double Jay
			Bazura
		Batteur (ch 1960)	Bold Ruler
			Bayou

Anifa had a sound record in France. She didn't race as a two-year-old but did well at three, winning at Saint-Cloud and Evry and finishing second to Niniski when facing her stiffest test of stamina in the Prix Royal-Oak at Longchamp. She finished second to Kamaridaan in the Prix Exbury at Saint-Cloud in March on her reappearance, and after her campaign was interrupted by an injury sustained when falling on her third start she returned to win the Prix de la Porte de Passy at Longchamp towards the end of June. Her best efforts however were her second to Le Marmot in the Prix Foy at Longchamp and her win over Le Moss in the Prix Gladiateur on the same course, both in September. She impressed us as a grand type of animal in the former event where she made the running and looked all over a winner until Le Marmot produced a remarkable burst to snatch the race near the line. Even allowing for the 9 lb she received from Le Marmot hers was a good performance, especially as the going was unusually firm by Longchamp standards. In the Gladiateur she met Le Moss on the same terms as she had met Le Marmot, but had the benefit of dead ground. She was never far off the pace in a race that didn't seem to be particularly strongly run, and in the closing stages she had the better speed. She took the advantage early in the straight and withheld Le Moss's renewed challenge by half a length.

An attractive, good-bodied filly by the outstanding French middle-distance colt Herbager, Anifa cost 62,000 dollars as a yearling at the Keeneland Sales. She springs from an exceptionally successful family and one that has produced an unusually high proportion of good fillies. Her dam Flail won over six furlongs as a three-year-old and all Flail's three foals to race before Anifa were successful, the prolific winner Bask and the filly Surf, both by Hawaii, winning stakes races. Flail is a half-sister to the smart stakes winner Flag Officer. The next dam Batteur won twelve races and nearly 200,000 dollars. She in turn is a half-sister to Alluvial, the dam of the Belmont Stakes winner Coastal, and their dam Bayou was rated the best three-year-old filly of 1957. Bayou is a sister to the high-class filly Levee (dam of the brilliant racemare Shuvee and Royal Gunner) and a half-sister to Delta who won sixteen races and is the dam of Dike. With such a family tradition, it would be a great shame if Anifa is prevented from taking her place at stud. *M. Saliba, France.*

ANIKONERI 5 br.m. Yukon Eric–Sayarani 96 (Hard Tack 111 §) (1979 6g 6fg3 5f 5fg4 6f2 5f 5f2 5g 7d 5s 6s 1980 5f4 5fg4 5fg 6f4 6g 6d 6g4 5g 6f 8g 7fg 8.2s 6fg) sprint handicapper; didn't run up to her best, including in valuable seller on eleventh start; well suited by fast ground; suitable mount for an apprentice. *W. H. H. Williams.* **48**

ANIRAMSKY 5 br.g. African Sky 124–Villa Marina 96 (Tudor Melody 129) (1979 7f 6g 5fg 1980 11.7fg) plater; stays 7f; blinkered once at 2 yrs. *M. Bradley.* **–**

ANITA'S CHOICE 4 ch.f. Shantung 132–Solway Bay (Tamerlane 128) (1979 10f 12g 12g 12f 1980 12fg* 12f 12d) fair sort; won apprentice handicap at Leicester in May; refused to race final start; stays 1½m; blinkered final outing at 3 yrs; not one to trust. *G. Fletcher.* **45**

Mr M. Fustok's "Anifa" (A. Gibert)

ANITA'S MARC 2 b.f. Saulingo 122–Born Friendly (Takawalk II 125) (1980 5g 5fg 6g 6d 5d* 5f) Jan 10; 2,800F, 3,000Y; strong filly; half-sister to Irish 7f and 1m winner Matagouri (by Welsh Saint) and 1978 2-y-o 5f winner Salbob (by Deep Diver); dam ran 3 times; put up best effort when heavily gambled on in 9-runner seller at Wolverhampton in August, being hard ridden to win by 3 lengths from Portique; bought in 2,000 gns afterwards; possibly doesn't stay 6f; acts on a soft surface; exported to Barbados. *P. Rohan.* **64**

ANKUS 4 b.g. Fine Blade 121–Persuader 118 (Petition 130) (1979 7fg 10g 11.5fg^{2} 12f^{4} 1980 10.2d 12fg* 16fg^{3} 14f* 14.6g^{3} 14g^{3} 14fg* 14fg*) big gelding; reportedly split a pastern at 2 yrs; did well in 1980 and won maiden race at Haydock and 3 handicaps at Yarmouth; put up a remarkable performance when gaining second of his wins at Yarmouth, getting up close home to score by ½ length from Withy Copse after twice attempting to run out in first ½m when in the lead; stays well; acts on firm going. *B. Hobbs.* **76**

ANNA BATIC 3 ro.f. Sharp Edge 123–Elakonee Wind 110 (Restless Wind) (1979 6g 6fg^{3} 5f* 6g^{3} 1980 5fg* 6f^{2} 5.1f 5s*) small, fair sort; poor mover in her slower paces; won handicaps at Sandown in April and Warwick in July; stays 6f; acts on any going. *R. Armstrong.* **78**

ANNABELLA 3 ch.f. Habitat 134–Sovereign 129 (Pardao 120) (1979 5fg 5g* 6f^{3} 6f 1980 6f 6fg 8fg^{3} 8g^{4} 8g 7fg 8g 8g 8d) strong, well-made filly; good mover; quite a moderate handicapper; suited by 1m; acts on firm going; ran moderately in blinkers last 2 starts. *H. Wragg.* **71**

ANNARISE 3 b.f. Starch Reduced 112–Malarise 60 (Pall Mall 132) (1979 6fg 7fg 1980 10fg 9f 9.6f^{4} 7d 10fg) lengthy, lightly-made filly; seems only plating class; appears to stay 1¼m. *A. Pitt.* –

ANNA'S PET 3 br.f. Mummy's Pet 125–Anna Boleyna 84 (Right Royal V 135) (1979 6s 7g 7fg 7g 1980 16g) big, strong filly; no sign of ability in varied company; swerved at start and unseated rider third start at 2 yrs. *D. Jermy.* –

ANNDORA 2 br.f. Murrayfield 119–Hedonist 74 (Mandamus 120) (1980 5s 5f^{4} 5s^{3} 5.3fg 5g) June 4; 1,200Y; first produce; dam sprint plater; plater; will stay 7f; not seen out after August. *J. Holt.* **47**

ANNE BONNY (FR) 3 b.f. Roi Lear 126–Amante (Cadmus 124) (1979 7fg 8fg 10s^{2} 1980 10g 14g 13g 12d) quite attractive, useful-looking filly; has shown no form since final outing at 2 yrs; should stay 1½m+; suited by soft going; blinkered second outing; sold 2,000 gns Newmarket December Sales. *G. Balding.* –

ANNE ROCKETTE 3 gr.f. Roan Rocket 128–Arak 74 (Rustam 127) (1979 5g^{2} 6fg 6d^{4} 8g 1980 8f 8f 11fg 13d 8g) strong, lengthy filly; plating-class maiden; not certain to stay 11f; often blinkered. *T. Fairhurst.* –

ANNIE HILL 2 gr.f. Dragonara Palace 115–Tudor Velvet (Tudor Music 131) (1980 5g 5f^{3} 5s) Apr 23; leggy filly; first foal; dam poor daughter of 1962 Queen Mary Stakes winner Shot Silk; 5¼ lengths third of 8 to Gandoorah in minor race at Pontefract in April; didn't race again until October when in rear in a maiden event at Hamilton (blinkered); has twice had to be withdrawn (unseated rider once and bolted on other occasion) and is temperamental. *J. Berry.* **65 §**

ANNIE PANNY 2 b.f. Take A Reef 127–Honaria 75 (Honeyway 125) (1980 5g 5fg^{3} 5f* 6d 5.8f^{4} 7h 8g 8g) Apr 21; 2,000Y; short-coupled filly; bad walker; half-sister to several winners, including very useful 1971 Irish 2-y-o All Spirit (by Le Levanstell); dam won over 5f at 2 yrs; hampered when ¾-length second of 7 to Suburban Sue in seller at Bath in May and was awarded race by stewards; sold out of C. Nelson's stable 1,250 gns afterwards; probably stays 1m; hit rails and unseated rider seventh outing. *I. Wardle.* **51**

ANOINTED 4 b.c. Crowned Prince 128–Saint Agata (Wild Risk) (1979 12d 13v^{4} 16d^{2} 14f 16fg^{3}(dis) 16fg^{2} 15.8f* 14.6f^{2} 15.8d^{2} 16s 1980 15.8d) big, strong colt; stays well; best form on top-of-the-ground. *G. Richards.* –

ANOTHER BLUES 3 b.g. Majority Blue 126–Native Love 77 (Native Prince) (1979 5s 5g 5f 5.1g 7fg 5fg 7fg 6g 1980 8d 8v 7f 6f 6fg 5fg 5f 7g) poor plater; ran as though 7f was too far for him on third start; usually blinkered nowadays. *W. Marshall.* –

ANOTHER DECISION 4 gr.f. High Top 131–Field Mouse 108 (Grey Sovereign 128 §) (1979 NR 1980 8f^{4} 10fg) smallish, lengthy filly; plating-class maiden; should stay 1¼m. *J. Winter.* –

ANOTHER EAGLE (USA) 3 b.c. L'Aiglon–Rit-N-Rough (Rough 'n Tumble) (1979 NR 1980 8fg 7.6f^2 8g^3 8s) $25,000 2-y-o; quite attractive, lengthy colt; brother to Rough Eagle, a stakes-placed winner at up to 7f, and half-brother to 3 winners; dam stakes-placed winner at up to 6f; placed in maiden events at Lingfield in June and Newbury in July; runs as though he will stay beyond 1m; acts on firm going. *A. Pitt.* **67**

ANOTHER FIDDLER 9 ch.g. Burglar 128–Izeste (Lavandin 128) (1979 5g 6fg 7g 6fg 5f 6d 1980 6g 5fg 7g 8.3f 7f 7g) plater; stays 7f; acts on any going; used to wear blinkers; good mount for an apprentice. *G. Balding.* —

ANOTHER GANTLET 3 ch.f. Run The Gantlet–Another Daughter 106 (Crepello 136) (1979 7g^4 1980 10d) workmanlike filly; fourth in maiden race at Yarmouth in 1979; didn't impress in paddock when well beaten only start at 3 yrs in April; will stay 1½m. *N. Adam.* —

ANOTHER GENERATION 3 ch.c. Fine Blade 121–Brig O'Doon (Shantung 132) (1979 7fg 1980 10s^3 12s* 12.3f^4 15h* 16f* 20d 14g* 16f^2 14g 16fg* 18d) big, quite attractive colt; useful performer; had a fine season, winning maiden race at Kempton and handicaps at Folkestone, Chepstow, Goodwood and Newmarket; beat Double Florin impressively on last-named in October (apprentice ridden); suited by a test of stamina; acts on any going. *G. Harwood.* **104**

ANOTHER MOVE 4 ch.f. Farm Walk 111–Darling Do (Derring-Do 131) (1979 8s 15.8g 9.4f 9.4f 12g^3 12.3s^4 11d^2 15.8fg 12f^2(dis) 12s^3 12.5g 10s^2 1980 10v 12d 12fg* 11g 12f^2 12.2fg 12fg^3 12g* 12v^4 15d) neat, lightly-made filly; won minor event at Pontefract in July and handicap at Edinburgh in October, latter by 4 lengths from Pittencrieff; suited by 1½m (well beaten over further); acts on any going, except possibly heavy; has raced with her tongue tied down; sometimes inclined to hang under pressure. *J. Calvert.* **56**

ANOTHER REALM 2 gr.c. Realm 129–Tiara III (Persian Gulf) (1980 5f^2 5fg^2 5fg* 5f* 6d^4 6d* 5g^3 6g* 6fg) Feb 26; 15,200Y; strong, well-made colt; good walker; brother to fair 1975 2-y-o 5f winner Landed Lady, and half-brother to several winners; dam ran only once; trained on very well despite a busy campaign and won at Windsor, Newmarket, Newcastle (Chesters Stakes by a neck from Sausolito, rec 13lb) and Goodwood; rallied strongly to regain lead from Bel Bolide when winning Group 2 Richmond Stakes at Goodwood in July on eighth outing; favourite for Mill Reef Stakes at Newbury in September but was very much on his toes beforehand and didn't reproduce that form, finishing only 7½ lengths fifth of 7 to Sweet Monday, racing in rear throughout; will stay 7f, and may get 1m; seems to act on any going. *F. Durr.* **111**

Richmond Stakes, Goodwood—Another Realm (left) regains the lead from Bel Bolide

ANOTHER RUMBO 2 ch.g. Royben 125–Fiord (Mountain Call 125) (1980 5fg* 5f2 5h* 5f* 6fg2 5fg 5s2 5g2 5d) Apr 18; 4,400Y; workmanlike gelding; third foal; half-brother to quite useful sprinter Tirpitz (by Sweet Revenge) and to a winner in Austria; dam never ran; successful in maiden race at Wolverhampton and minor events at Brighton and Windsor before end of May; second afterwards in minor events at Catterick and Windsor and 3-runner Star Stakes at Sandown, proving no match for odds-on Mattaboy in last-named in July; stays 6f; acts on any going; off course 3 months before final start (had little chance at weights and was badly drawn when last in nursery); sold 5,000 gns Newmarket Autumn Sales. *G. Hunter.* **94**

ANOTHER SAM 3 b. or br.c. Comedy Star 121–Balandra Star 92 (Blast 125) (1979 6d 6g2 7g3 7fg4 7fg3 1980 7f 8fg 11f 10f 16g* 16fg4 14fg 16.5fg* 16f2 16.1g4 16fg4 16d* 14g) leggy, narrow colt; successful in handicaps at Chepstow, Folkestone and Warwick; suited by a test of stamina; probably acts on any going; suitable mount for an inexperienced rider. *R. Hannon.* **83**

ANOTHER SIGNCENTRE 3 br.g. Pitskelly 122–Route Royale (Roi Soleil 125) (1979 5g 5fg 6f* 6fg 6g3 6f 7f 1980 6s 6f 6fg 6f 7g 7d3 7g 6fg4) fair sort; inconsistent handicapper; suited by 7f; probably acts on any going; blinkered final 2 outings at 2 yrs; has run respectably for an apprentice; not one to trust. *J. Sutcliffe.* **– §**

ANOTHER VENTURE 3 b.g. Roan Rocket 128–Myna Tyna 85 (Blast 125) (1979 5g* 6f 1980 5d 6v 6fg 5.8g3 6g 6g 6g4 6g2) strong, useful-looking gelding; moderate handicapper; stays 6f; sometimes gives trouble at start; sold to R. Atkins 2,000 gns Newmarket Autumn Sales. *R. Hollinshead.* **85**

ANSUMDUS 3 b.c. Wolver Hollow 126–Misty Cat (Misty Flight) (1979 7fg 1980 11fg 11.7fg3 12fg3 12g 11.7f 12.2g) fair sort; third in Southern maiden races; stays 1½m; yet to race on a soft surface; ran moderately in blinkers last 2 starts; sold 6,200 gns Newmarket Autumn Sales. *I. Balding.* **62**

ANTERES 2 b.f. Andrea Mantegna–The Lady Brianstan (Signa Infesta 114) (1980 9d) May 31; 700Y; half-sister to 1977 2-y-o 5f winner Ladyracer (by Manacle); dam twice-raced half-sister to good sprinter The Brianstan; 16/1 when eleventh of 12 in minor event won by Allegretta at Wolverhampton in October. *H. Collingridge.* **–**

ANTIQUE BLOOM 4 ch.f. Sterling Bay–Hiatus 87 (High Treason 126) (1979 7fg 6s 5fg 5d 5s 5fg 5fg 5f 5g 7fg 7g 5fg3 6s 6s 1980 5d 6g 5g 5fg 6fg 6d 7f) leggy, unfurnished filly; quite a moderate handicapper nowadays; well backed but was never on terms in seller final outing; best form at 5f; acts well on a firm surface; occasionally wears blinkers; started very slowly sixth start; changed hands 1,800 gns Newmarket December Sales. *P. Kelleway.* **–**

ANTIQUE SEEKER 5 ch.m. Status Seeker–Julia Too 93 (Golden Horus 123) (1979 8s 10fg3 1980 11fg 10.8f 10f 8s 12d2 12d 10s3 11.5g3 11.5fg 10fg3 10fg) poor handicapper; stays 1½m; possibly unsuited by hard ground but seems to act on any other; blinkered second and third outings; suitable mount for an inexperienced rider. *M. Ryan.* **48**

ANTONY PETER 2 b.c. Roman Warrior 132–Braida (Tissot 131) (1980 6fg 6d 7g4 6fg 8g 8fg 7fg 8d) Apr 24; 5,400F, 7,600Y; fair sort; has a rather round action; twice showed ability in maiden and minor events but was well beaten in sellers last 2 starts; stays 1m; blinkered third, fourth and seventh outings; virtually pulled up in nursery fifth appearance; sold 1,500 gns Doncaster November Sales. *J. Etherington.* **64**

ANVIL INN 2 b.g. Roi Soleil 125–Floor Show 78 (Galivanter 131) (1980 8.2s 8.2s) May 31; second foal; dam middle-distance winner; tailed off in maiden race at Haydock and minor event at Hamilton in October. *T. Craig.* **–**

ANVIL LARK 2 b.g. Sir Lark 101–Douraine (Doubtless II 111) (1980 7d 6fg 8g 8.2s4 10s) 2,000 2-y-o; small, stocky gelding; of little account. *M. Reddan.* **–**

APACHEE LOVE 2 ch.f. Apalachee 137–Collatteral (Jim J) (1980 5f 5g) Apr 25; 17,500Y; attractive filly; third foal; dam, half-sister to Irish Guinness Oaks third Queen To Conquer, won over 6f in USA; second favourite, ruined chance by starting slowly when behind in 19-runner maiden event won by Sharp Venita at Newbury in April; out of first 14 of 26 to Nasseem in similar race at Salisbury in June but still looked as though run would do her good and was badly drawn. *B. Hills.* **–**

APACHE KID (FR) 3 ch.g. Jim French–Chillick (Royal Palace 131) (1979 5s 1980 14fg 14.6d) strong-topped gelding; behind in maiden races. *D. Morley.* **–**

APAPA PORT 2 ch.f. My Swanee 122–Cotton Town (Takawalk II 125) (1980 5d^4 5v^4 5v 5g 5fg^3 5fg^4 5fg 5f 5f 5f 5d^3 5d 5d^4 5s^2 5s*) Mar 9; 3,000Y; strong, leggy filly; second foal; sister to a winner in South Africa; dam unraced half-sister to 3 successful broodmares; in frame in varied races, including a seller, prior to winning 14-runner minor event at Stockton in November by 1½ lengths from Lady Arpege; will stay 6f; revels in the mud; effective with or without blinkers; formerly trained by S. Wainwright. *K. Stone.* **80**

APERITIVO 2 ro.c. Sharp Edge 123–Feasting (Sayajirao 132) (1980 5f 6d^4 7g 7.6f 8g*) Mar 18; 6,200Y; lengthy colt; half-brother to numerous winners, including quite useful stayer Beechway (by Primera); dam won at 1¼m and 11f in Ireland; backed from 12/1 to 13/2, ran by far his best race when winning £4,800 nursery at Brighton in October by ¾ length from Wicked Will; will stay middle distances; possibly needs an easy surface. *R. Price.* **93**

APERTURE 3 ch.f. Hotfoot 126–Opencast 97 (Mossborough 126) (1979 7fg^3 7g^2 7d 1980 7v 8v^3 7g 12g* 9f^4 14g 12s 12g* 14g 12d 14s 10f 12g) rather lightly-made ex-English filly; won maiden race at Clonmel in April and sponsored handicap at Killarney in July; tailed off in Lancashire Oaks at Haydock on seventh outing; suited by 1½m and should stay 1¾m; probably acts on any going; sold 29,000 gns Newmarket December Sales. *H. de Bromhead, Ireland.* **77**

APOCALYPSE 2 b.f. Auction Ring 123–Miss Stephen (Stephen Paul 131) (1980 5g^4 5f 5g 5d) June 2; neat filly; sister to 3-y-o 6f winner Zephyros, and half-sister to numerous winners, including top sprinter Deep Diver (by Gulf Pearl) and Irish 2,000 Guineas winner King's Company (by King's Troop); dam never ran; eighth of 22 to Copt Hall Realm in maiden race at Lingfield in September, third outing and best effort. *J. Douglas-Home.* –

APOLLO CREED 2 ch.c. Decoy Boy 129–Loppy Luv 67 (Soueida 111) (1980 6g 6fg 6g^2) Apr 3; 2,800F, 6,500Y; strong colt; fourth produce; dam won twice over 1m; odds on and dropped in class, failed by 2 lengths to hold off Floridian Dawn in 16-runner seller at Yarmouth in September; claimed afterwards. *P. Haslam.* **65**

APPALOOSA 2 b.c. Bay Express 132–Fivepenny Piece 78 (Fortino II 120) (1980 5fg^2 5g* 6g* 6fg) Apr 25; 4,000F, 15,000Y; neat colt; good mover; sixth foal; half-brother to a winner in Cyprus; dam won over 1m; made all and held on by short head from Prison Payment in £2,000 event at Sandown in July; bettered that effort when running on gamely to win nursery at Goodwood the following month by a neck from Tinjar; creditable 7½ lengths fifth of 7 to Cut Throat in hotly-contested Sirenia Stakes at Kempton in September; will stay 7f. *R. Price.* **95**

APPARENT 2 ro.c. Grey Mirage 128–Kingsley Girl § (Faberge II 121) (1980 5f 5f 5fg 7s 7fg 8fg) May 25; small, lengthy colt; soundly beaten in maiden races and a seller. *S. Holland.* –

APPELLE 2 b.f. Relko 136–Appellanda 92 (Reform 132) (1980 6d 6g 7f 7g 8d) May 14; small, well-made filly; third foal; half-sister to quite useful 3-y-o middle-distance winner Double High (by High Top); dam won over 5f and 6f at 2 yrs and stayed 1½m; showed a little ability in maiden races on last 3 starts and is likely to do better over middle distances at 3 yrs; dwelt fourth outing. *R. Smyth.* **71**

APPLEBY PARK 3 b.f. Bay Express 132–Pall Nan 86 (Pall Mall 132) (1979 7fg* 7fg* 8fg 1980 7fg) rangy filly; won £3,100 maiden race at Sandown (made all) and 4-runner nursery at Yarmouth at 2 yrs; behind in handicap at Newmarket in May, only start in 1980; not certain to stay 1m. *P. Cole.* –

APPLEMINT (USA) 2 b.f. Sir Ivor 135–Eltisley 82 (Grey Sovereign 128§) (1980 6g^3) compact filly; second foal; half-sister to useful sprinter Dare Me (by Derring-Do); dam 2-y-o 5f winner; ran very well against 2 more-experienced animals when odds on for 5-runner minor event at Windsor in August, leading at distance and keeping on so well that she was beaten only short head and ½ length by Saba Nejd and Buffavento; a promising filly who should prove useful at around 1m at 3 yrs. *R. Hern.* **81** p

APPLE WINE 3 ch.g. Ribston 104–Ruffino 99 (Como 120) (1979 6fg 6g 6g 5d 7s 1980 8v* 9g^4 8f 8f 9g 8fg^2 7f 8g 9g 8.2d 8s*) workmanlike gelding; 20/1 when winning maiden race at Stockton in March and apprentice handicap on same course in October (made all); stays 1m; probably acts on any going but revels in the mud; blinkered last 2 starts in 1979; sweated up badly fifth start; suitable mount for a boy; ran moderately eighth to tenth outings, moving poorly to post on second occasion. *M. W. Easterby.* **74**

APRIL BOUQUET 3 ch.g. Silly Season 127–Floral Gift 84 (Princely Gift 137) (1979 5fg 1980 8f 8fg^2 8.2fg 8fg* 8d^2 8fg) strong, well-made, good-looking **99**

Ladbroke Chester Cup—Arapahos wins in good style from Pollardstown and Taffy

gelding; slaughtered his field in Britannia Stakes (Handicap) at Royal Ascot, leading running into last furlong and storming clear to beat Windy Hill by 4 lengths; ran respectably next time; may stay 1¼m; acts on a firm and a soft surface; sold to J. Sutcliffe 12,000 gns Newmarket Autumn Sales. *R. Hern.*

APRIL LUCKY 7 b.g. St Alphage 119–Susceptible 86 (Supreme Court 135) **64**
(1979 6v 6d 6g^3 6g 6f^3 6f* 7g 6fg^3 6d 6d^4 6g^4 6g^2 1980 6g 6d^2 6f 6h^3 6f 6g* 6d^3 6g* 7fg^3 6g^4 7f 6s) leggy gelding; has won 7 times at Hamilton and won handicaps there in June and July (apprentice event); stays 7f; acts on any going; blinkered twice at 3 yrs; sometimes sweats up; good mount for an inexperienced rider; reportedly broke blood vessel once in 1979. *C. Crossley.*

APT DECISION 3 b.f. Abwah 118–Kerkithalis 98 (Acropolis 132) (1979 5.1fg —
6f 6f 1980 7fg 7d 10g) leggy, unfurnished filly; behind in maiden and minor races. *J. Winter.*

AQAB (USA) 3 br.c. Accipiter–De Soto Queen (Fleet Nasrullah) (1979 6f^4 6g —
1980 8d 9d) medium-sized, quite attractive colt; showed ability in maiden races at 2 yrs; well beaten in similar events in 1980; will stay 1¼m; blinkered second outing (pulled very hard) *J. Dunlop.*

AQUABELLE 2 b.f. Park Lane–Rockfire 65 (Epaulette 125) (1980 5g 5fg 5g **47**
6fg 5f 5g 7f 5d 5s) Mar 19; 500F, 800Y; small filly; bad plater; blinkered fourth start; sold 290 gns Doncaster November Sales. *S. Nesbitt.*

AQUA BLUE 3 ch.f. Blue Cashmere 129–Aquanimba (Acropolis 132) (1979 **51**
7.2g 7s 8.2g 1980 8fg 8f 7d^4 7.2d 6g* 6g 6d 6f 7d 7g^4 7s) lightly-made filly; plater; attracted no bid after winning at Redcar in July; stays 7f; blinkered sixth start. *P. Asquith.*

ARAB MERCHANT 4 b.g. Busted 134–Sardinia (Romulus 129) (1979 14g 12f —
1980 12.3s) fair sort; lightly raced and only poor form; looked unsuited by firm ground final outing at 3 yrs. *J. Hanson.*

ARAK FOR EVER 5 ch.m. Never Say Die 137–Arak 74 (Rustam 127) (1979 —
12s 7.6d 8s 8f 7fg^3 8fg 9fg 7.6f 1980 10v 9g 6g 10.6fg 10f 10d 7f 6g 7g 8s) poor plater; stays 1m; possibly needs a firm surface; blinkered final outing at 4 yrs and fourth start. *R. Ward.*

ARAMOSS 3 ch.g. Ballymoss 136–Mel Samara (Blason 109) (1979 NR 1980 —
10s 12fg) brother to a poor animal, and half-brother to fair 1973 2-y-o 5f winner Sweet Suspense (by Tenterhooks); dam never ran; in rear in maiden races at Lingfield and Brighton in the summer. *N. Gaselee.*

ARANDAR 2 gr.c. Royal and Regal–Sister Supreme 64 (Runnymede 123) **64**
(1980 5fg 6d 6g 6g^3 5d 8g 5s^2 8.2s 6v) Mar 15; 4,000Y; leggy, unfurnished colt;

second foal; dam won 6f seller; 1½ lengths second of 10 to Crosby Triangle in apprentice nursery at Ayr in September; in rear most of his other starts and is one to leave alone; acts well on soft going. *W. H. H. Williams.*

ARAPAHOS (FR) 5 ch.h. Gyr 131–Athenia II 74 § (Acropolis 132) (1979 14d 16s3 20fg3 16fg 21d2 14s 18fg2 20fg4 1980 16fg* 18.4f* 16.1fg2 20g 16d) strong, useful sort; half-brother to 3 minor winners in France; dam disappointing half-sister to Sunny Way and to Crepello's dam, Crepuscule; had his best season in 1978, when winning 5 times and finishing second in Goodwood Cup; came up against Le Moss regularly in the Cup races in 1979 and didn't win, but ran several good races; made a successful reappearance in small race at Newmarket in May, trouncing Olympios, and followed up by beating Pollardstown by 1½ lengths in Ladbroke Chester Cup (Handicap) later in month, quickening in good style; given plenty to do when 1½ lengths second to Balinger in slowly-run Lymm Stakes at Haydock later in May, best subsequent effort; behind afterwards in Gold Cup at Royal Ascot and Coral Northumberland Plate at Newcastle, both in June; stayed extremely well; acted on any going; genuine; ran moderately when tried in blinkers; standing at Ballyvolane Stud, Bruff, Co. Limerick. *B. Hills.* **112**

ARARAT 3 gr.f. Young Emperor 133–Alta-Vista (Skymaster 126) (1979 6f* 6f3 5g 1980 7f 8fg 8fg4 7.2fg 7fg) big, rangy filly; half-sister to four winners, notably smart Fabvista (by Faberge II), successful at up to 7f; dam unraced half-sister to very useful 1970 2-y-o Windstorm; good 3½ lengths fourth of 18 to Cairn Rouge in Goffs Irish 1000 Guineas at the Curragh in May; also ran creditably in 1000 Guineas at Newmarket on second start (5½ lengths eighth to Quick As Lightning) and John of Gaunt Stakes at Haydock in June on fourth outing (3¼ lengths fifth to Hard Fought); stays 1m; acts on firm going. *G. Hunter.* **106**

ARAVANIA 3 b.f. Rarity 129–Lady Sylvania (Hornbeam 130) (1979 NR 1980 7d 10s 10g) big, strong, attractive filly; half-sister to 2 winners in France, including 1m and 9f winner Temuco (by Red God); dam of little account; ran promisingly in maiden race at Salisbury on first outing but performed poorly in similar events subsequently; should stay 1¼m+. *R. Price.* **—**

ARAX 2 b.c. Auction Ring 123–Inner Guard (King's Bench 132) (1980 6g 7g) Apr 22; 16,000Y; well-grown colt; good mover; half-brother to numerous winners, including useful sprinter Tin Guard (by Tin Whistle) and useful French 3-y-o 4f to 9f winner Inner Pearl (by Gulf Pearl); dam of little account; last in newcomers event at Ascot in July and minor race at Brighton (slowly away) in October. *G. Hunter.* **—**

ARC D'OR (USA) 2 b.c. Ack Ack–Arme d'Or (Armistice 131) (1980 6.5d2 7.5g* 8g4 9fg2 10s) Feb 11; half-brother to several winners, including smart French middle-distance colts Caron (by Caro) and Oreste (by Luthier) and good North American stakes winner Morold (by Sir Gaylord); dam smart at around 1½m; won maiden race at Deauville in August by ¾ length; in frame in valuable events on next 2 starts, finishing only 1½ lengths behind The Wonder when fourth in Prix des Foals on same course and going down by only a short neck to Mariacho in Group 3 Prix Saint-Roman at Longchamp; ran below his best over 1¼m but should stay that far; acts on a firm surface and is possibly unsuited by soft going. *J. Cunnington, jnr, France.* **118**

ARCHIMBOLDO 2 b.c. Midsummer Night II 117–Quenilda 101 (Fair Copy) (1980 5fg2 6d3 5fg2 5g4 5g) May 6; 3,700F, 9,000Y; lightly-built, useful-looking colt; brother to smart 5f and 7f performer Quy and half-brother to numerous winners; dam a sprinter; placed in maiden races, notably on third outing when ¾-length third of 16 to subsequently-disqualified Holmbury Lad at Newbury in September (disputed lead throughout); didn't reproduce that form next time out, and had stiff task in a nursery on final start; should stay 7f. *M. Masson.* **83**

ARCH MELODY 2 b.c. Arch Sculptor 123–Prophetic Melody (Tudor Melody 129) (1980 5v 5f*(dis) 5fg*(dis) 5d 5g2 5g* 5g2 5d) Apr 25; fourth foal; half-brother to Irish 6f and 7f winner Michael's Tower (by Tower Walk) and a winner in Holland; dam placed over 5f at 2 yrs in Ireland; made all to win maiden race at Naas in April and minor event at Leopardstown in May but was disqualified from both wins after failing dope tests; gained compensation in another maiden race at Leopardstown in August, soon taking clear lead and holding on by ¾ length from Real Torque, and ran creditably when length second to Brooklyn Prince in nursery at the Curragh later in month; speedy and isn't sure to stay 6f; acts on firm going; wears blinkers. *K. Kerr, Ireland.* **100**

ARCH SCULPTRESS 2 b.f. Arch Sculptor 123–Effervescence II (Charlottesville 135) (1980 5fg 6s2 5d* 5fg 6fg 6g) Mar 29; strong, sturdy filly; half-sister to 3 winners, including fairly useful 3-y-o 5f performer Clicquot (by Bold Lad Ire) **85**

and smart French middle-distance colt El Famoso (by Ragusa); dam won twice over 1¼m in France and is half-sister to Zeddaan; quickened clear to win 8-runner maiden race at Lingfield in July by 5 lengths from Pencil Point; not disgraced in nurseries afterwards; stays 6f; acts well on soft ground. *J. Holt.*

ARC PRINCE 5 b.g. Prince Regent 129–Larch (Busted 134) (1979 NR 1980 12fg 12d) quite a moderate maiden; not seen out until September and was still on burly side on final start; will probably stay well. *W. Wharton.* —

ARCTIC RASCAL 9 b.g. Arctic Kanda 111–Sally Ann III (Port Corsair 98) (1979 11.7g 9s 16.9s 1980 10d 12d 13.8d 13s) poor handicapper; effective at 1¼m and stays 2m well; acts on any going; suitable mount for an inexperienced rider; usually wears bandages; blinkered final start (well beaten). *M. Bradley.* —

ARCTIC SPARK 2 ch.c. Hot Spark 126–Blue Wings (Majority Blue 126) (1980 7f) June 10; lengthy colt; second foal; dam apparently of little account; unquoted and in need of race when behind in 18-runner maiden race won by Blackfoot at Newmarket in October. *J. Hudson.* —

ARCTIC TRIBUNE 6 ch.g. Sallust 134–Arctrullah (Great Captain) (1979 7f 8s 8v 8fg 8.2fg 8h³ 8h 8.3fg 8fg 1980 7v² 8f 8f 7f³ 8s 7f 8fg² 8f⁴ 8g³ 7fg³ 8g 8.2s² 7d⁴ 8s) moderate handicapper, placed several times in 1980, including in a valuable seller; stays 1m well; acts on any going; often sweats up; has been tried in blinkers; none too reliable. *Miss S. Hall.* **69**

ARCTIQUE ROYALE 2 b.f. Royal and Regal–Arctic Melody 113 (Arctic Slave 116) (1980 5fg* 6s*) **102** p

The outstanding success enjoyed by the late Paddy Prendergast during his long training career was due in no small part to the patience he exercised with his horses. Arctique Royale, a very promising filly bred by Prendergast, has been handled with similar restraint by his successor, Paddy's son. Arctique Royale ran only twice, establishing herself as one of the best young fillies in Ireland, and before the end of August her trainer stated that she was unlikely to run again as a two-year-old as he thought she needed more time. Consequently she missed the chance of proving herself against the other leading fillies in the major autumnal events and she is almost certainly better than we have been able to rate her.

Both Arctique Royale's appearances were at the Curragh, the first coming as early as mid-May. Then, at odds on in an eleven-runner maiden race, she drew away in the final one and a half furlongs to come home two and a half lengths clear of Hear A Rhapsody. Her task on her other outing, in the Group 2 Moyglare Stud Stakes three months later, was naturally much stiffer with seven other previous winners among her thirteen rivals. Despite the greater strength of the opposition Arctique Royale, at 5/4, was the only one seriously

Moyglare Stud Stakes, the Curragh—Arctique Royale (centre) beats a useful field

backed and she ran out an impressive winner, finding a useful turn of foot in the final furlong to win by a length. Lady Tiffany, Lady Nightingale and Passion Wagon, all winners of their previous race, followed her home; and back in sixth place, beaten six lengths, came Lone Bidder, winner next time out of another of Ireland's top races for two-year-old fillies, the Park Stakes. Incidentally the ground was on the firm side for her first outing and soft for her second, so she seems to act on any going.

Arctique Royale (b.f. Apr 22, 1978)	Royal and Regal (b 1970)	Vaguely Noble (b 1965)	Vienna
			Noble Lassie
		Native Street (gr 1963)	Native Dancer
			Beaver Street
	Arctic Melody (b 1962)	Arctic Slave (b 1950)	Arctic Star
			Roman Galley
		Bell Bird (ch 1954)	Mustang
			Belpatrick

Arctique Royale's connections should certainly reap the rewards of their patience when she has the chance of running over distances of a mile or more at three. She is potentially the best daughter of Royal and Regal, a son of Vaguely Noble and winner of the Florida Derby. Although he has sired the very smart miler Hilal and the very useful Noble Shamus and Odeon, Royal and Regal has generally met with only modest success, particularly for a stallion whose fee was as high as 3,000 guineas when he retired to stud back in 1974. The average winning distance of his progeny is close to a mile and a quarter.

Arctic Melody, the dam of Arctique Royale, gained her most important success over the longest distance she was asked to tackle, beating that exceptional filly Aunt Edith in the Musidora Stakes over ten and a half furlongs. She is proving a splendid broodmare, perhaps surprisingly so as a daughter of Arctic Slave, a stallion who made his name largely as a sire of such fine chasers as Titus Oates, The Benign Bishop, Arctic Sunset and Arcturus. In addition to Arctique Royale Arctic Melody has produced five winners, including the three-

The Exors of the late Mr P. J. Prendergast's "Arctique Royale"

year-old Racquette (by Ballymore), second in the Pretty Polly Stakes and third in the Irish Guinness Oaks. Remarkably all six of her winners are fillies and two of her daughters have already produced notable offspring: Pollerton, winner of several good races including the Gordon Stakes and the Princess of Wales's Stakes, is out of the Relko mare Nilie; and that top-class out-and-out stayer Ardross is out of the Levmoss mare Le Melody. Arctique Royale has already shown she possesses speed and, if she also possesses the stamina suggested by her pedigree, she should make a formidable three-year-old. *K. Prendergast, Ireland.*

ARDAR 2 b.c. Relko 136–Adayra (Le Haar 126) (1980 6d3) Apr 28; tall, attractive colt; third foal; half-brother to 1979 2-y-o 1m winner Ayyabaan (by Sun Prince); dam, placed over 10.5f in France, is half-sister to high-class 7f to 1¼m winner Sharapour; took the eye in paddock when 7/1 for 15-runner maiden race at Newmarket in July and performed with credit, racing with leaders throughout and finishing 3¼ lengths third to Church Parade; a promising first effort by a stoutly-bred colt. *F. J. Houghton.* **83** p

ARDGOUR 2 b.c. Nonoalco 131–Hecla 117 (Henry the Seventh 125) (1980 5fg3 7s) May 1; attractive, well-made colt; half-brother to 3 winners, including useful miler Be Better (by Busted); dam, smart over 6f at 2 yrs, is half-sister to very speedy fillies Mange Tout and Rose Dubarry; well beaten in minor events at Ascot (very green) in September and Chepstow the following month. *P. Walwyn.* –

ARDOONY 2 b.c. Ardoon 124–Linbel (Linacre 133) (1980 5f4 5g 6fg 5g3 5d* 6g2 6d) Mar 25; 1,500Y, 4,700 2-y-o; neat colt; second foal; half-brother to 1½m seller winner Miss Poppy (by Lord Gayle); dam Irish 9f winner; much improved in the autumn and won 17-runner nursery at Wolverhampton by 4 lengths from Royal Duty; apprentice ridden, had a bad run but finished strongly when 1½ lengths second of 17 to Amorous in similar race at Newmarket on next outing, easily better subsequent effort (ran poorly final start); will stay 1m; possibly needs an easy surface; sweated up both at Wolverhampton and Newmarket. *R. Hollinshead.* **85**

ARDROSS 4 b.c. Run The Gantlet–Le Melody 102 (Levmoss 133) (1979 10s 12s* 12fg 1980 10v 16fg* 20g2 21fg2 18g2 16f* 15.5v3) **131**

The line that divides the champion from the also-ran in the public estimation is often fine-drawn; most big-race runners-up are soon forgotten, no matter how

Jockey Club Cup, Newmarket—a well-deserved success for Ardross who wins from More Light. French-trained Tin Soldier is a distant third

meritorious their performances or how narrow the margin of their defeats. But few who followed Le Moss's epic struggle with Ardross for the so-called stayers' triple crown are likely to forget either horse in a hurry; their stupendous rivalry was one of the features of the racing year. At Royal Ascot, Goodwood and Doncaster, Le Moss and Ardross did the much-maligned Cup races a power of good, putting on a superb exhibition on each occasion and providing further evidence, if any were needed, of the magnificent entertainment value of races between top-class stayers.

Ardross is a very good out-and-out stayer, better than some Gold Cup winners we could name, and but for the intervention of Le Moss he would have won the four major Cup races in the British Calendar, the Gold Cup, the Goodwood Cup, the Doncaster Cup and the Jockey Club Cup. But Le Moss proved an insuperable stumbling-block and Ardross ended the season with only the Jockey Club Cup. But there is still a chance for Ardross to be enrolled in racing's 'Hall of Fame': he remains in training and, with Le Moss retired, seems at this stage to be the one they all have to beat in the Cup races in 1981. Provided he retains his form, he has nothing to fear from the established out-and-out stayers and it is going to take a very good four-year-old to lower his colours. Ardross is a thorough stayer, as he showed in each of his races against Le Moss, and in the falsely-run Jockey Club Cup he demonstrated that his stamina is supplemented by a useful turn of finishing speed. Add to these attributes the fact that Ardross can handle all types of going, is an amenable ride and is one of the most game and genuine racehorses in training and you have a formidable Cup horse.

Like many a true stayer Ardross was slow to mature and did not reach his best until after three years of age. He was unraced at two and had only three races as a three-year-old, gaining his only success—at 50/1—in the Gallinule Stakes over a mile and a half at the Curragh in May. The Gallinule Stakes was poorly contested for a Group 2 pattern race but Ardross' success meant that he had to give 7 lb all round in the King Edward VII Stakes at Royal Ascot on his final outing; not surprisingly he was well beaten behind Ela-Mana-Mou who had finished fourth in the Derby. While Le Moss, who completed the Cup treble in 1979, wasn't seen out in 1980 until Royal Ascot, Ardross had two races in Ireland before being sent over for the Gold Cup. In the second of them, the Saval Beg Stakes at Leopardstown in May, he showed himself well suited by a distance of ground, starting favourite and winning by six lengths from the useful Croghan Hill. On the strength of this performance he started at 6/1 for the Gold Cup, fifth of the eight runners in the betting.

After the enthralling Gold Cups of recent years, which included Sagaro's wins in 1975, 1976 and 1977 and Le Moss's victory over his distinguished stable-companion Buckskin in 1979, it was difficult to imagine the race producing anything better in 1980. Yet the Gold Cup again proved vibrantly exciting and was all that a sporting occasion should be. Le Moss was in the lead, forcing the pace from the start. Approaching the home turn Ardross was not far behind in fourth place, but his jockey was already riding vigorously with hands and heels. Le Moss's strong, relentless gallop proved too much for all his rivals except Ardross. Ardross got to Le Moss just inside the two-furlong marker and kept up with him practically all the way to the line. Both seemed to be galloping more and more strongly as they ran home, but the harder Ardross tried to pass, the more Le Moss seemed to be spurred on. In the closing yards Ardross was clearly being held, although he refused to throw in the sponge, and the winning distance was three quarters of a length. It was a memorable finish; seldom have we seen two horses galloping so resolutely at the end of a truly-run Cup race. The six other runners didn't seem to count as first and second made their way to the unsaddling enclosure; for the record, Vincent, runner-up in the Jockey Club Cup as a three-year-old, came home ahead of the rest, six lengths behind Ardross and five ahead of the fourth Billion.

If Ardross' experience at Royal Ascot had left its mark on him it wouldn't have been altogether surprising; he had a very hard race and it could well have been discouraging for him to find Le Moss responding so indomitably to his sustained challenge. Yet six weeks later he was returned to England as fresh as paint for the Goodwood Cup, in which he met Le Moss on terms 2 lb better than at Royal Ascot. There were only three other runners—none of those that took on Le Moss and Ardross in the Gold Cup was in the field—and the race was virtually a match. Ardross began to close on the front-running Le Moss with half a mile to go and the pair were both flat out with three furlongs left. Ardross was almost level with Le Moss at the two-furlong marker and there followed another neck-and-neck battle to the line; as bravely as Ardross fought he

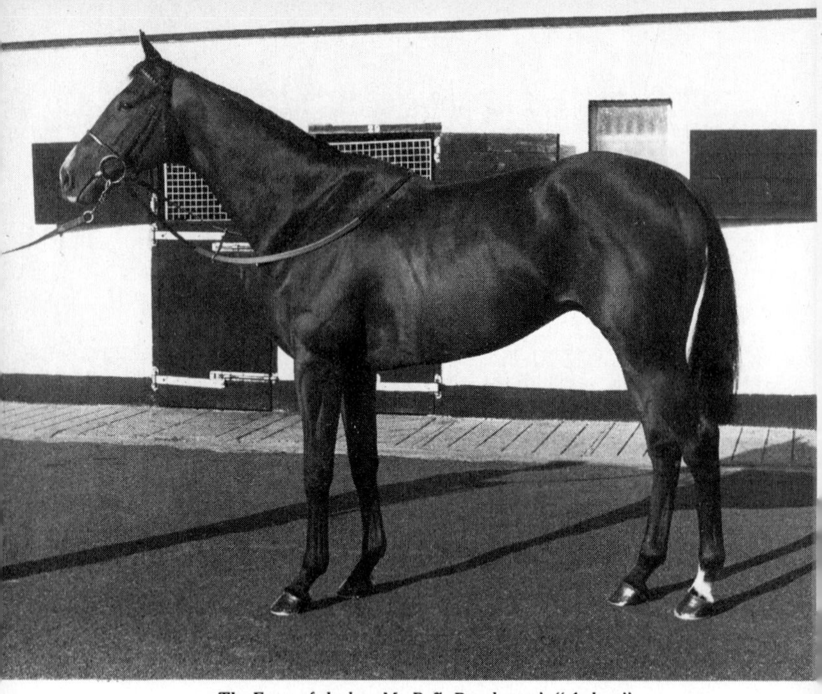

The Exors of the late Mr P. J. Prendergast's "Ardross"

couldn't get in front and there was a neck in it at the post. Ardross' connections, no doubt aware that the two and a quarter miles of the Doncaster Cup was the minimum trip for Le Moss in good company, decided to take him on again; the terms at Doncaster were identical to those at Goodwood with Ardross receiving 2 lb from Le Moss. Again it was virtually a two-horse race: 4/6 Le Moss, 13/8 Ardross, 14/1 bar. The shorter trip failed to tilt the balance in favour of Ardross. He made his challenge over the final quarter of a mile, again giving everything he had, but Le Moss would not be beaten; Ardross was still a neck behind at the finish and no longer getting any closer. After almost seven and a half miles of competition, the total margin between Le Moss and Ardross was little more than a length.

After Doncaster one could not help but wonder again how Ardross' defeats at the hands of Le Moss would affect his enthusiasm. However, Ardross' principal rival in the Jockey Club Cup at Newmarket in October, the Jockey Club Stakes winner More Light, provided Ardross with a plenty strong enough test of ability and character—and he came through it with flying colours. There was no gallop for much of the way and Ardross at first failed to respond when More Light's rider suddenly sharpened the pace and went for home with about three furlongs left. Ardross was soon three lengths adrift and, running into the Dip, More Light appeared in complete control. But, ridden very hard indeed, Ardross buckled down to an apparently hopeless task in great style and passed More Light on the final hill to win going away by a length and a half. No victory was ever more deserved! After the Doncaster Cup there had been talk of Ardross' crossing the Atlantic for the Canadian International Championship and, possibly, the Washington International. But the programme decided upon—the Jockey Club Cup followed by the Prix Royal-Oak—seemed, in truth, a much more sensible one, in view of Ardross' exertions. The Prix Royal-Oak, formerly the French equivalent of the St Leger, is now open to horses above the age of three. Some of those who oppose the idea of a similar change in the conditions of the St Leger were quick to sneer when the Prix Royal-Oak attracted only two older horses, neither of them outstanding, when the race was opened up in 1979 for the first time. But the latest Royal-Oak was certainly a more interesting and informative race with the likes of Ardross, Niniski and Vincent in the field than it would have been had only three-year-olds been eligible. The race went to the three-year-old filly Gold River, who had finished fourth in the Prix Vermeille; the French four-year-old Monsieur Marcel pipped Ardross for second place, three lengths behind Gold River. Ardross looked tremendously well, showing no outward sign of his hard races earlier in the year, but it's possible that he was a little past his best for the year. Nevertheless, the probability is that Gold River is a very good filly over two miles and if she proves as effective at two and a half, Ardross will have at least one worthy opponent if the pair meet in the Gold Cup.

Ardross (b.c. 1976)	Run The Gantlet (b 1968)	Tom Rolfe (b 1962)	Ribot
			Pocahontas II
		First Feather (ch 1963)	First Landing
			Quill
	Le Melody (ch 1971)	Levmoss (b 1965)	Le Levanstell
			Feemoss
		Arctic Melody (b 1962)	Arctic Slave
			Bell Bird

Ardross' sire Run The Gantlet, who was a top-class racehorse, winner of the Man o'War Stakes and the Washington International as a three-year-old, spent eight seasons at stud in Ireland before being sold back to North America; he has been resyndicated and will stand at Sunset Hill Farm, Kentucky, in 1981. Run The Gantlet has turned out to be an influence for stamina; his best progeny include the St Leger third Classic Example and the Prix du Jockey-Club third Providential. Ardross is the first foal of a daughter of Le Moss's brother Levmoss, himself a winner of the Gold Cup; Le Melody won her only starts, one at seven furlongs as a two-year-old and the other at a mile and a quarter at three. Ardross' grandam Arctic Melody won the Musidora Stakes in 1965. Ardross is a tall, attractive colt. *K. Prendergast, Ireland.*

ARDROX PIONEER 2 b.g. Wishing Star 117–Via Latina (Lauso) (1980 **90**
5fg^{3} 5f^{4} 6f^{3} 7s^{2} 7d 7fg* 7fg*) May 11; 1,300F, 7,600Y; leggy, close-coupled gelding; good mover; half-brother to 2 winners in Ireland, including miler Fickle City (by Continuation); dam won over 9f and 1¼m in Ireland; quickened clear when winning maiden race at Warwick in July and 6-runner nursery at Yarmouth following month; beat Hot Wind 2½ lengths on latter course; will stay 1¼m; acts on any going; ran moderately fifth outing; gelded after final outing; sent to Hong Kong. *P. Cole.*

ARDTULLY LASS 5 b.m. Cavo Doro 124–Lucky Jean (Counsel 118) (1979 **39**
8s 10.8d 8s 7d^{2} 10.6g 8f 8fg 1980 9.6fg 10.1fg* 10g 10g 8.3f 10fg 8g) quite a modest plater; bought in 1,080 gns after winning at Windsor in May; stays 1¼m; acts on any going; tried in blinkers at 3 yrs; sometimes sweats up. *C. Wildman.*

ARGENTINA BOUND 4 b.f. Amber Rama 133–Gold Poulet 84 (Goldhill 125) **82**
(1979 6g^{2} 6f 1980 6v 5f 6f^{3} 6fg 6f 6d^{4}) sprint handicapper; close third to Moybrook at Ayr in May, easily best effort of season; acts on firm going; sold 1,700 gns Newmarket December Sales. *W. H. H. Williams.*

ARGENTINO 2 gr.g. Rugantino 97–The Silver Darling 75 (John Splendid 116) **—**
(1980 5.8fg 5s) Apr 16; first foal; dam second in this country before winning at 2 yrs in Belgium; unquoted when in rear in maiden races at Bath in June and Warwick in July; sold 1,100 gns Ascot July Sales. *D. Nicholson.*

ARGIVE 5 ch.g. Homeric 133–Dana II (Orsenigo) (1979 NR 1980 10fg 12h^{3} **53**
12d 14.6fg^{2} 16g^{3}) strong, rangy gelding; placed in minor event at Pontefract and handicaps at Doncaster and Thirsk; stays 2m; acts on hard going; sold 820 gns Newmarket Autumn Sales. *Sir Mark Prescott.*

ARGUMENT (FR) 3 b.c. Kautokeino–Arantelle (Tapioca 123) (1979 6g* 8s^{2} **133**
8fg^{4} 1980 8s* 8g^{3} 10.5fg^{2} 12fg 11s* 10d^{2} 12g 12f^{2} 12f*)

Outsider Argument, beaten half a length into second place behind Detroit, was the unluckiest horse in the Prix de l'Arc de Triomphe. Too much was asked of him. After being held up right at the back of the field he seemed in a hopeless position turning for home with only two behind him, but he made up all of fifteen lengths on Ela-Mana-Mou from that point to the line and finished so strongly under vigorous riding that he would have won with a bit further to travel. His jockey Desaint, who rode waiting races on Comtesse de Loir and Gay Mecene in previous Arcs, was very fortunate in such a well-contested event as this to enjoy a trouble-free run in the straight.

Argument deserved to start at shorter odds than 74/1 for the Arc. He had often run well in good company, consistently well apart from one unaccountably modest performance behind Policeman in the French Derby, and had improved a lot since the time he had been rated 10 lb below top in the 1979 Handicap Libre after three outings as a two-year-old: he had earned place money in the French Two Thousand Guineas, the Prix Lupin and the Prix de la Cote Normande. In the last-named, at Deauville in August, he had gone down by only a head to Glenorum giving him 9 lb; Glenorum started at 12/1 for the Arc. Argument's wins during the season had come in the Prix Mary, a relatively minor race over a mile at Saint-Cloud in the spring, and the Grand Prix Prince Rose, a valuable race in the international calendar run over eleven furlongs at Ostend in July. He won by two lengths from the very useful French three-year-old Dhausli at Ostend, beating a field of pattern-race standards. On his only appearance between Deauville and the Arc Argument had finished fifth of ten to Nebos in the Grosser Preis von Baden, beaten just over two lengths by the winner and losing fourth place to Nicholas Bill by a nose. Argument was one of those involved in scrimmaging in this slowly-run contest, and afterwards Desaint received a fine from the stewards.

Argument was sold three weeks after the Arc and left the stable of J. Cunnington jnr to be trained by Zilber, retaining, nevertheless, the objective of the Washington International at Laurel in November. It is doubtful whether Europe could have provided a more worthy candidate for the International if every top horse had been available, instead of hardly any as is usual at this time of year. Argument, ridden by Piggott, represented France in the nine-runner field along with Anifa and the Prix Maurice de Nieuil winner Buckpoint, both of whom had been running in North America. For the third year in a row there was no representative from England in the race or, on Cairn Rouge's late withdrawal, from Ireland either. Argument gained some compensation for his most unfortunate Arc defeat, winning well from the tough American mare The Very One and the ex-French colt Yvonand; he showed a good turn of foot once again, without anywhere near as much being asked of him by his jockey. Moved up through the field on the last bend, he went ahead a furlong out after a short struggle with the eventual second and third, and drew almost two lengths clear by the line. Buckpoint finished sixth, but Anifa unfortunately broke a leg when up with the leaders about half a mile out.

Argument (Fr) (b.c. 1977)	Kautokeino (b 1967)	Relko (b 1960)	Tanerko
			Relance III
		Cranberry (b 1957)	Aureole
			Big Berry
	Arantelle (ch 1966)	Tapioca (b 1953)	Vandale
			Semoule d'Or
		Neptune's Doll (ch 1960)	Neptune II
			Dzena

By Kautokeino out of a Tapioca mare, Argument could hardly be said to be fashionably bred, but though he's easily his sire's best runner he's by no means his only winner in France; and the dam won races at around ten furlongs at Saint-Cloud and Deauville. The sire, a well-bred horse, won the Prix Juigne and finished third in the Prix la Force on his two racecourse appearances,

Washington D. C. International, Laurel—Argument beats The Very One

Mr B. McNall and Mr B. Gordy's "Argument" (J-C. Desaint)

sustaining an injury in the latter which ended his career. The Prix la Force, incidentally, was won by Sassafras, and the four behind Kautokeino that day were Roll of Honour, Armos, Jefferson and Dictus. Argument's dam bred the one-mile and nine-furlong winner Akena from a previous mating with Kautokeino and three minor winners by other stallions; she has a two-year-old by Kautokeino called Arad who has shown promise in France. The next dam Neptune's Doll was a surprise winner from Relko of the Criterium de Maisons-Laffitte in 1962; she was placed in the French One Thousand Guineas the following year before she trained off. The next dam Dzena, unraced, was out of the 1948 French Oaks second Doria II, a half-sister to the dam of the 1954 French Oaks winner Tahiti II.

Argument is a good horse at a mile and a quarter and a very good one at a mile and a half. He acts on any going, but seems particularly well suited by firm. *M. Zilber, France.*

ARIDJE 2 b.f. Mummy's Pet 125–Derrede (Derring-Do 131) (1980 5fg* 5g 6g 5g³) Apr 20; 19,500Y; lightly-made filly; half-sister to a winning 2-y-o plater; dam unraced half-sister to very speedy Singing Bede; came with a strong run from below distance when winning 15-runner maiden race at Kempton in May by 2 lengths from Little Starchy; soundly beaten in much better company subsequently although wasn't disgraced on 2 occasions; form only at 5f; looked very light indeed on final appearance (July), possesses little scope and is far from certain to train on. *R. Boss.* **79**

ARIEL 3 ch.f. The Go-Between 129–Valentina Rose 85 (Red God 128 **§**) (1979 5fg 5f 6f 6fg 5.1g* 5.1f* 1980 6fg 5fg³ 5d 5.8g 5fg 6g 5g) plain filly; plater; seems better suited by 5f than 6f; acts on firm going; trained by D. Elsworth first 6 starts. *G. Cottrell.* **45**

ARIOS 2 b.g. Manacle 123–Blue Bird 84 (Majority Blue 126) (1980 8s) May 15; big, strong gelding; brother to 1978 2-y-o 7f winner Clewiston, and half-brother to 2 winners, including successful middle-distance stayer Sockburn (by My Swallow); dam stayed 1¼m; 33/1 and in need of race when finishing down the field in 19-runner minor event at Stockton in October; nonetheless showed a little ability, has plenty of scope and should improve at 3 yrs. *M. Camacho.* **– p**

ARJUN (USA) 4 br.g. Bold Favourite–General Note (Royal Note) (1979 6d 55
7g 5g 6g 8f 8fg 10d 5.8fg 6d 1980 6h 5.8fg^2 6g 7d^3 6d 5.8f 8g 8h 8.3fg 6g 8g) strong, compact gelding; ridden by 7-lb claimer when placed in handicaps at Bath (beaten a head by Rama Tibodi) and Brighton, both in June; should stay 1m; acts on a firm and an easy surface; sometimes blinkered and also wore a hood on final outing at 3 yrs; occasionally sweats up; sold 740 gns Newmarket Autumn Sales. *A. Breasley.*

ARKAN 2 b.c. Prince Tenderfoot 126–Adamantos 92 (Yellow God 129) (1980 76
7f 8d^4 10g) May 23; $45,000Y; strong, good sort; third foal; half-brother to a winner in Belgium; dam, winner over 7f at 2 yrs, is half-sister to top 1960 2-y-o colt Typhoon; backed from 10/1 to 15/2 when 3½ lengths fourth of 16 to Rosie Black in maiden race at Warwick in October; not certain to stay beyond 1m (had stiffish task when tried over further). *J. Hindley.*

ARMATEX 3 b. or br.c. Kambalda 108–Marina (Supreme Court 135) (1979 —
7fg 1980 9f 12s^4 10.1s^3 15.5s 10.1g 12f^3) strong colt; only plating class; should stay well; acts on soft going. *M. Bolton.*

ARMISTICE DAY 4 b. or br.c. Rheingold 137–Peace 113 (Klairon 131) (1979 115
12d^2 12.3d 8fg 9s* 11.5g* 1980 12g^2 12g^3 11g* 12.5g^2 11.5g* 13.5g* 12g 10s* 11g^3 10g*) ex-English colt; had a very successful season and won 5 times, putting up a particularly good effort when beating Hilal by a length in Prix Gontaut-Biron at Deauville in August on eighth start; also won small race at Lyon, handicap at Avignon, Grand Prix de Marseille-Vivaux (by a length from African Hope) and Grand Prix de Marseille (from P'tite Tete); creditable 4½ lengths third of 8 to Marmolada in Premio Federico Tesio at Milan on penultimate start; suited by middle distances; acts well on soft going; blinkered third outing at 3 yrs; suitable mount for an amateur. *C. de Watrigant, France.*

ARMORIAL 4 b.g. Crowned Prince 128–Netherside 73 (Alcide 136) (1979 —
10v* 10s* 12.2g^3 11.7g^4 1980 10s 10f) robust, well-made gelding; moderate handicapper; had stiff tasks when behind in 1980 (not seen out after May); stays 1¼m; goes well in the mud; wore blinkers at 2 yrs; sold to A. Ingham 1,800 gns Newmarket Autumn Sales. *P. Makin.*

ARM THE LAW 3 b.f. Royal Palace 131–Escape 93 (Gilles de Retz 132) (1979 —
NR 1980 7.2d 12.2g) small filly; half-sister to smart performer Escapologist (by Derring-Do), successful at up to 1¼m, and good hurdler Within The Law (by Sharpen Up); dam won over 6f at 2 yrs; tailed off in maiden events at Haydock and Catterick in the summer. *K. Stapleton.*

ARMY SCOUT (USA) 3 b.c. Tom Rolfe–Bold Consort (Bold Ruler) (1979 69
8g 1980 12s 11d 11.7g 12d^3 12s 15s) big, rangy colt; best run at 1½m on a soft surface; sold 6,800 gns Newmarket Autumn Sales. *J. Dunlop.*

ARNALDO 2 b.g. Upper Case–Flower Petals (Busted 134) (1980 6g 6s 7d 8fg^4) 57
Apr 27; 5,000Y; neat gelding; first foal; dam, Irish 1¼m winner, is sister to smart middle-distance performer Bog Road; plater; beaten only 1¾ lengths when fourth of 14 to Blue Garter in seller at Carlisle in September, best effort; will probably stay 1½m. *N. Callaghan.*

ARNDEAN 2 b.c. Auction Ring 123–Dolly-Longlegs 74 (Majority Blue 126) 96
(1980 5f 5fg* 5f^2 5g* 6g^3 6s* 6d* 6fg^2 6fg 6d^2 6d) Mar 22; 3,100F, 3,000Y; neat colt; good mover; third produce; half-brother to a winner in Italy by Gulf Pearl; dam won 6f claiming race at 2 yrs; picked up quite a valuable prize when running on strongly to beat Parkdale ½ length in 5-runner Strathclyde Stakes at Ayr in July; had earlier won maiden race at Leicester in May and minor events at Windsor in June and July, gaining an easy 5-length success from Emphasis in last of them; ran another good race when apprentice ridden in £3,400 nursery at Haydock in October on tenth outing, failing by only a length to hold off Mrs Palmer; will stay 7f; has won on a firm surface but seems best with some give in the ground; blinkered last 2 starts; genuine and consistent. *H. T. Jones.*

ARROWHEAD 2 b.c. Steel Heart 128–First Round 97 (Primera 131) (1980 83
5g^2 5g^3) May 12; well-made, attractive colt; closely related to very useful 5f to 7f winner Glenturret (by Habitat) and half-brother to 2 winners, including very useful 1979 2-y-o sprinter Rollahead (by Tower Walk); dam won at up to 1½m; well-backed favourite when placed twice behind Sanu in August, going down by 2½ lengths at Salisbury and finishing 2¼ lengths third of 8 when meeting him on 7-lb better terms at Goodwood; will be suited by 6f+. *R. Price.*

ART BIDDER 3 b.f. Auction Ring 123–Pallet (Pall Mall 132) (1979 5g* 5fg^3 6fg^2 6g* 6f 5f^4 1980 7f 7fg 7g 7f 7fg) lightly-made filly; moderate handicapper; may stay 7f; yet to race on a soft surface. *N. Vigors.* 77

ARTIPIAR 3 ch.f. Tyrant–Persian Coach (Parthia 132) (1979 5s* 5fg^2 5s* 5fg* 5fg* 6fg* 6f 6fg^2 6f^2 6d^3 5fg^2 6d^2 6f 1980 8fg 5f 5f 5g^3(dis) 5g^3 6fg 5d^3 6g 5f^3 5.6g 5fg^2 5s^2) fair sort; good mover; useful performer, placed in varied company, including when creditable third in valuable handicaps won by Oh Simmie at Newcastle (didn't have best of runs and was disqualified), by Balvima at Sandown, by Swelter at Haydock and by Westacombe at York; finds 5f on sharp side and should stay 7f; acts on any going; usually blinkered nowadays; started very slowly final outing; genuine and consistent. *W. O'Gorman.* 106

ARTISTRY 2 gr. or ro.f. Gold Form 108–Palmural 111 (Palestine 133) (1980 5g 5d* 5fg^2 5g) Apr 14; compact filly; not a good mover in her slower paces; half-sister to 3 winners, including top-class German sprinter Pentathlon (by Ennis); dam very useful over 5f and 6f at 2 yrs; beat 7 newcomers in maiden race at Newbury in July, holding on by a head from Fine Honey; creditable second of 8 to Star of Enzo in nursery at Chepstow the following month; not sure to stay 6f; acts on a firm and a soft surface. *Mrs R. Lomax.* 82

ARTS AND SPARKS (USA) 4 ch.g. Arts and Letters–Sparkalark (Cornish Prince) (1979 8v* 9g^2 10s^3 8v^4 8g 8f 1980 8fg 10f 11.1fg 12f 12fg 8d) lengthy ex-Irish gelding; showed useful form at 3 yrs in Ireland when trained by D. Weld; well beaten in 1980 but had stiffish tasks; stays 1$\frac{1}{4}$m; best form with some give in the ground. *R. Atkins.* —

ARTSUM 5 ch.g. Midsummer Night II 117–Grecian Artiste 76 (Acropolis 132) (1979 NR 1980 11f) bad plater; blinkered on only outing of 1980. *R. Allan.* —

ARUSE 2 ch.f. Sharpen Up 127–Wind Break 81 (Borealis) (1980 5f 5f^3 6s^2 6g 7d^2 6g) Apr 10; 19,000Y; unfurnished filly; good mover; sister to Ron's Sign Centre, winner of two 7f sellers, and half-sister to several winners; dam 2-y-o 7f winner; placed in maiden races at Wolverhampton, Stockton and Brighton, going down by 2$\frac{1}{2}$ lengths to Lady Westleigh on last-named course in July; will probably stay 1m. *R. Boss.* 71

ARWA 3 b.f. Hot Spark 126–Secondhand Rose 102 (Hethersett 134) (1979 NR 1980 8f^2 10.2fg 8g^3 10fg^4 8f* 10.6d 10g^4) 3,400Y; sturdy filly; half-sister to 2 winners, including winning stayer More or Less (by Morston); dam stayed 1$\frac{1}{4}$m; won 15-runner maiden race at Beverley in August; best form at 1m; acts well on firm going. *R. Boss.* 69

ARYENNE (FR) 3 br.f. Green Dancer 132–Americaine (Cambremont 121) (1979 8s* 8d* 1980 8fg* 8d* 10fg^4 10.5g^2 12f) 125

Aryenne enjoyed a much more satisfactory second season than the only filly rated above her in the 1979 Handicap Libre, Princesse Lida. She beat Princesse Lida in the Prix de la Grotte and the Poule d'Essai des Pouliches at Longchamp in the spring; and, although meeting the first defeat of her career next time out in the Prix Saint-Alary on the same course, she went on to run the race of her life against Mrs Penny in the Prix de Diane de Revlon at Chantilly in June. She wore bandages when a creditable seventh to Mrs Penny in the Prix Vermeille at Longchamp in the autumn on her only subsequent appearance but reportedly stays in training, presumably with the idea of giving her the crack at the Prix de l'Arc de Triomphe she missed because of a mouth abscess in 1980.

It says much for Aryenne that her worst performance in the top company

Poule d'Essai des Pouliches, Longchamp—Aryenne gets up in the final strides to beat Safita. Princesse Lida short heads Teacher's Pet (obscured) for third place

is her fourth to Paranete in the Prix Saint-Alary: she was beaten no more than a length. She's a consistent and genuine animal with a turn of foot, and has been a tough opponent for the other good fillies throughout her career. Mrs Penny certainly found her very difficult to get the better of in the Diane, the French Oaks. The pair made their efforts at about the same time, Aryenne two or three places behind Mrs Penny to begin with; they started to draw away from the others going into the final furlong and had a good battle right to the line where, despite all Piggott's efforts, the winner had only a short head to spare over Aryenne, who beat Paranete by three lengths for second place. Aryenne finished about three lengths behind Mrs Penny in the Vermeille, on that occasion racing in touch from the start, turning for home in second place and staying on well to the end of what was, without any doubt, the most strongly-contested race for fillies run in Europe during the season. On this form she deserved a shot at the Arc, although it's doubtful whether she would have been good enough to trouble the best of the colts, let alone Detroit.

Aryenne's victories, like her defeats, were narrow ones. She was ridden for speed in her two early-season races at a mile, whereas she was ridden for stamina in the Vermeille, and on both occasions she got up on the post, by a neck from Princesse Lida in the Group 3 Prix de la Grotte and by a short head and a length and a half from Safita and Princesse Lida in the Poule d'Essai des Pouliches, the French One Thousand Guineas. Had she not prevailed in the Pouliches Aryenne would have been desperately unlucky. She was given plenty to do from the home turn and then, absurdly in a six-runner field on this magnificent track, looked in some danger of failing to obtain a clear run before, late on, she squeezed through to pull the race out of the fire.

Aryenne (Fr) (br.f. 1977)	Green Dancer (b 1972)	Nijinsky (b 1967)	Northern Dancer Flaming Page
		Green Valley (br 1967)	Val de Loir Sly Pola
	Americaine (ch 1968)	Cambremont (br 1962)	Sicambre Djebellica
		Alora (ch 1954)	Ballyogan Agnes

Aryenne is an attractive, compact filly by the same sire as the Oaks third The Dancer. Their sire, a good racehorse who started 6/4 favourite in Grundy's Derby, has made a flying start at stud with those two fillies in his first crop and another who may be their equal in his second in the Prix Marcel Boussac runner-up Coral Dance. A Green Dancer yearling half-brother to Detroit fetched 530,000 guineas at the latest Houghton Sales; and all in all, as we feared twelve months earlier, it can surely be only a matter of time before Green Dancer ends up at stud in the USA. Aryenne's dam Americaine bred two winners from three previous foals, easily the better the very useful Apachee (by Sir Gaylord). She was a winner herself, a half-sister to the French Two Thousand Guineas winner Adamastor, too, and has the same great grandam as that outstanding filly Roseliere, their respective grandams Agnes and La Paix being half-sisters.

Aryenne stays a mile and a half. She seems to act on any going but the fact that she wore bandages last time out could well mean that connections will be reluctant to risk her on ground as firm as it was in the Prix Vermeille; the more reluctant they become, the more remote must become the prospects of seeing her in England in one of the top middle-distance events. *J. Fellows, France.*

ASANIA (FR) 2 b.f. Ace of Aces 126–Aurinette (Sheshoon 132) (1980 6.5g 7.5d^3 8v*) Feb 23; 360,000 francs Y (approx £38,000); second foal; dam smart French winner at around 1½m; developed into a useful filly and won maiden race at Longchamp in October, making all and holding on by 2 lengths from Kazadancoa; had previously finished close-up third in similar event won by Marie Noelle at Saint-Cloud; will stay 1¼m; likely to make a better 3-y-o. *J. Cunnington, jnr, France.* **109**

ASANTE 3 br.f. Murrayfield 119–Gracia 103 (Matador 131) (1979 6fg 7fg^3 6fg^2 1980 6fg^3 7d^3 8g^4 7g 7g^4 6d) big, rangy filly; in frame in varied company; stays 7f; acts on a firm and a soft surface; has run respectably for an apprentice; sold out of W. Hastings-Bass's stable 7,800 gns Newmarket July Sales after second start. *P. K. Mitchell.* **68**

ASCENDANTS DREAM 3 ch.g. Ascendant 96–Impossible Dream 56 (Will Somers 114§) (1979 5d 5s 6d 5f 7f 5f^3 5fg^2 5s^2 5g 6g 8h 1980 9f) small gelding; poor plater; best at 5f; acts on any going; usually wears blinkers. *F. Dever.* —

ASCENDING STAR 2 b.c. Ballymore 123–Domination (Luthier 126) (1980 7g^2 6s*) Mar 28; 12,000Y; third foal; dam unraced daughter of sister to Match III and Reliance II; came out best in tight finish to 14-runner maiden race at the Curragh in August, beating Noble Monk a head; had earlier shown promise when 2 lengths second of 6 to Last Light in maiden race at Leopardstown; likely to make a useful middle-distance performer. *K. Prendergast, Ireland.* **89** p

ASCOT AGAIN 4 gr.g. Track Spare 125–Petite Path 106 (Sovereign Path 125) (1979 8s 8.2d 8fg 8g 10g^3 10f 10d^2 10g 10f 10.2fg 1980 12.2s 12fg 12fg 12fg^4 10.6fg 10s 12g^2 12d^2 11fg^2 11d^4 12fg 10.4d 10.6s 10.8d^2 12d) workmanlike gelding; behind in sellers on occasions, but was second 4 times in better company in 1980; stays $1\frac{1}{2}$m; acts on any going. *R. Mason.* **56**

ASCOT BLUE 7 b.g. Majority Blue 126–Pebble Ridge 107 (Big Game) (1979 6s^4 5v 5s 5.8g* 5g* 5fg 6fg 5g^3 5g 5fg* 5g 5.8fg^2 5fg 5fg 6d^3 6s 1980 5s^3 5g* 6g 5f 5f 5.8fg 5g 5fg 5d^4 5g 5g^3 5fg^2 5d^4 5f^3 6g 5.8g 5d* 5d^4 5d 6s) sprint handicapper; won narrowly at Beverley in April (from Cudgel) and Wolverhampton in October (from Broon's Secret); acts on any going; suitable mount for an amateur rider; blinkered last 2 outings in 1978. *M. Bradley.* **67**

ASCOT ROYALE 9 gr.g. Track Spare 125–Petite Path 106 (Sovereign Path 125) (1979 13v 12s 14.7f 12f 12f 12f 11g 11d 11g 1980 15s) middle-distance handicapper; appears to act on any going; has been tried in blinkers; often apprentice ridden; unreliable at start; often refuses to race and is one to leave alone. *J. Wilson.* **§§**

ASHBRITTLE 2 ch.f. Great Nephew 126–Solar 120 (Hotfoot 126) (1980 5fg^4 5fg* 5f* 5g 5fg^4 5fg* 6fg) Feb 26; good-bodied, workmanlike filly; very good mover; first foal; dam, half-sister to smart sprinters Walk By and Smarten Up, was one of leading 2-y-o fillies in 1975 and stayed $1\frac{1}{4}$m; won maiden race at Salisbury in May, Uplands Park Acorn Stakes at Epsom the following month (finished strongly to beat Rising Tide $\frac{3}{4}$ length) and minor event at Windsor in September (had more in hand than length margin over Hello Susie Greene suggests); not up to taking on the very best of her sex and was beaten $6\frac{1}{2}$ lengths when fourth to Marwell in Molecomb Stakes at Goodwood in July and 6 lengths by same filly when sixth of 8 in William Hill Cheveley Park Stakes at Newmarket in October; will stay 1m; acts well on firm going. *W. Wightman.* **101**

ASHBURNHAM 2 b.c. Averof 123–Greek Gift (Acropolis 132) (1980 6f 7d 7g 6f) Feb 5; strong, compact, useful sort; half-brother to 1m winner St Anthony (by Upper Case) and a winner in Belgium; only poor form, including in a seller; retained 1,000 gns Newmarket Autumn Sales. *D. Whelan.* –

ASH GAYLE 4 b.f. Lord Gayle 124–September Girl (French Beige 127) (1979 7s 7v 7fg 8.2d 8g 10f 1980 8s 11fg* 14fg 12fg 14g) plater; attracted no bid after winning apprentice handicap at Wolverhampton in April by 4 lengths; behind in better company afterwards; stays 11f; acts on a firm surface. *R. Hannon.* **49**

ASHLEIGH BOY 3 gr.c. Habat 127–Vimy Line (Vimy 132) (1979 5s 5v* 5s 5g 5fg 1980 7f 10.8g 7fg 10fg 8.2s 8.3g^3 8fg) small colt; poor handicapper; stays 1m; suited by some give in the ground; blinkered final outing at 2 yrs. *C. Wildman.* –

ASHORE 2 ch.g. Ashmore 125–Ornella (Princely Gift 137) (1980 5fg 6s 7g 7fg) May 5; 3,600F, 5,200Y; fair sort; fourth foal; dam won over 7f at 2 yrs in France; little worthwhile form in maiden races; retained 840 gns Newmarket Autumn Sales. *H. Candy.* –

ASHWATTHAMA (USA) 4 b.g. Bold and Brave–Tie It Up (Hitting Away) (1979 5s 5d 6g 7g^4 7f 8.3f 7g 7fg 7fg 1980 6fg 6g 7fg 7d^2 6g 6g 5.8f 8h 8.3fg^3 7f 8g) neat gelding; quite a moderate handicapper; stays 1m; acts on a firm and an easy surface; sold 720 gns Newmarket Autumn Sales. *A. Breasley.* **65**

AS I WISH 4 b.f. Red Alert 127–Ballydust (Bally Joy 112) (1979 8v 8g 6g 6d 7f 8.2g 1980 10v 10fg 10h 12fg) of little account. *Mrs A. Harvey.* –

ASPHODEL 4 ch.f. Busted 134–Ash 102 (Hornbeam 130) (1979 12g 12s 12s 16fg^4 16f 15.5fg 15.5fg 1980 10f 10fg 12d* 16g^4 12f 12fg) light-framed filly; 33/1 and apprentice ridden when beating Fumarella a neck in maiden race at Brighton in June, best effort; probably stays 2m; acts on a firm and a soft surface; has been tried in blinkers but is better without; sold 4,800 gns Newmarket December Sales. *M. Masson.* **55**

ASSITA (FR) 2 gr.f. Caro 133–Agila (Sicambre 135) (1980 8.5g*) Feb 7; 195,000 francs Y (approx £21,000); half-sister to 3-y-o Acquisition (by Caracolero) and 2 winners, including middle-distance winner Kheron (by St Paddy); **?**

dam, winner twice at around 1¼m, is granddaughter of high-class 1m to 1¼m filly Arbele II; favourite when winning 9-runner newcomers race by ¾ length from Flossa at Longchamp in October; will stay 1¼m; promising. *M. Zilber, France.*

ASTONISHED 3 b.f. Connaught 130–Amazer (Mincio 127) (1979 7fg 7fg^3 1980 8fg* 10.1g* 10fg^4 10f^4 12d) well-made filly; really good mover; successful in minor events at Goodwood and Windsor in August, showing a good turn of foot to beat Staying Alive ¾ length on former and easily landing the odds by ½ length from Vartkez on latter; respectable fourth afterwards in Sean Graham Fillies Stakes at Kempton (to Dancing Shadow) and Sun Chariot Stakes at Newmarket (stayed on well behind Snow), beaten just over 4 lengths each time; should stay 1½m; probably unsuited by soft ground. *J. Dunlop.* **111**

ASTRAL PRINCESS 2 b.f. Space King 115–Seven Sisters 88 (Supreme Court 135) (1980 5fg 6fg 7f 7g 8d 8d 8d) Jan 15; 1,500F, 2,500Y, 4,000 2-y-o; neat filly; sister to 3 winners, and half-sister to several more; dam won at 1¼m; well beaten all races, final one a Leicester seller (blinkered). *D. Elsworth.* –

ASTRAMAN 2 br.g. Workboy 123–Pronuba (Sica Boy 132) (1980 5g 5d 5g^4 5d 5g 5d 6g) Feb 3; 8,400Y; stocky gelding; half-brother to a winning plater and to 2 winners abroad; dam placed over 1¼m in Ireland; 3½ lengths fourth of 13 to Appaloosa in £2,000 event at Sandown in July, only worthwhile form; should be suited by 6f; blinkered last 3 outings; one to leave alone; sold to BBA 400 gns Newmarket Autumn Sales. *A. Bailey.* – §

ASTRANTIA 3 b.f. Gay Fandango 132–Amazing Maid 104 (Amazing) (1979 5d^2 1980 5fg^4 5f^3 5fg 8g^3 8fg^4 8fg^4 8fg 10.4d* 10.1fg^3 10s) compact filly; won 9-runner maiden race at Chester in August; stays 1¼m well; probably acts on any going; sweated up badly and got very worked up when blinkered third start. *G. Pritchard-Gordon.* **72**

ASWAD 3 br.c. Royal and Regal–Sayorette (Sayajirao 132) (1979 6s 7fg 7f^2 8.2g^3 7f^4 8s 1980 12fg 12h^3 12fg* 10d 10d 12f 12fg* 12g) neat, quite attractive colt; good mover; successful in maiden race at Brighton in May and handicap on same course in August; suited by 1½m and will stay further; probably unsuited by soft going; needs strong handling. *J. Dunlop.* **79**

AS YOU DESIRE ME 3 gr.f. Kalamoun 129–Royal Saint 117 (Saint Crespin III 132) (1979 7g^3 7.5g* 1980 7.5d* 8fg* 10.5fg^2 8s^4 10d) half-sister to several winners, including Irish Sweeps Derby and St Leger third Classic Example (by Run The Gantlet) and smart middle-distance performer Illustrious Prince (by Le Levanstell); dam smart miler and sister to Altesse Royale; won Prix Montenica at Maisons-Laffitte and Prix de Bagatelle at Longchamp, latter by a length from Wild Idea, early in year; subsequently ran creditably in 3 pattern races, going down by ½ length to Luth Music (rec 3 lb) in Prix de Royaumont at Chantilly, finishing 6 lengths fourth to Moon Ingraver in Prix d'Astarte at Deauville and being beaten just over 2½ lengths into fifth behind Sovereign Dona in Prix de Psyche at Deauville again; stays 1¼m well; probably acts on any going. *F. Mathet, France.* **112**

ATHFORD 4 b.g. High Line 125–Centro 86 (Vienna 127) (1979 14fg^2 13f* 14.6fg* 14d^3 16fg^4 16fg 1980 16fg^2 14fg^4 16fg^4 16fg 20d 16s* 19g^2 16d^2 16g 19g* 18d^3) tall, rather narrow gelding; won stayers' handicaps at Lingfield in July (made all) and Goodwood in September, beating Lex by 2 lengths in 3-runner event on latter course; runner-up to clever winner Heighlin at Goodwood and York in between and ran another honest race when 8½ lengths third of 27 behind Popsi's Joy in Tote Cesarewitch at Newmarket in October; acts on any going; genuine; one-paced. *H. Candy.* **84**

ATHOLL HOUSE 3 b.g. Jimsun 121–Chiltern Miss 85 (Hook Money 124) (1979 NR 1980 9.4g 10d 10fg 12s) 3,700Y; big, rangy gelding; half-brother to 2 minor winners; dam won over 1m; behind in maiden and minor events; looks slow. *M. H. Easterby.* –

ATILLA THE HEN 2 b.f. Hot Spark 126–Matloch 70 (Matador 131) (1980 5g^3 5f^2 5g* 5f 5d 5d) Jan 30; 10,500F; compact filly; half-sister to smart 1973 2-y-o 5f performer Eveneca and useful sprinter Elegante (both by Frankincense); dam sister to useful sprinter Spanish Sail; won 6-runner maiden race at Edinburgh in June by 1½ lengths from Millingdale; beaten in 3 nurseries subsequently, once running creditably; not sure to stay beyond 5f. *Sir Mark Prescott.* **64**

ATKINSON GRIMSHAW 2 b.c. Martinmas 128–Melba Sauce (Sing Sing 134) (1980 6g 6fg 7d) Apr 11; 3,300Y, 3,000 2-y-o; good mover; second foal in Ireland; dam, sister to very smart sprinter Saulingo and closely related to smart –

5f colt Music Maestro, ran twice at 2 yrs in England and reportedly won in
Jamaica; little worthwhile form in maiden and minor events; retained 1,050 gns
Newmarket Autumn Sales. *W. Wightman.*

ATLANTA CONNECTION (USA) 4 b.f. Noholme II–Amber Fields (Am- —
biorix 130) (1979 10.1f 11.5fg 9g 1980 10f 10g 12d) workmanlike filly;
poor maiden. *R. Boss.*

ATLANTA LADY 2 b.f. Run The Gantlet–Roman Twilight (Romulus 129) —
(1980 7g) Mar 17; 3,300Y; half-sister to 2 winning sprinters and to a winner in
Italy; dam placed at 2 yrs in Ireland; unquoted, moved badly on way to start
prior to finishing in rear in 19-runner minor event won by Grand March at
Salisbury in August. *J. Bethell.*

ATLANTIC BOY 3 b.c. Busted 134–Coming About 99 (Right Tack 131) **102**
(1979 7fg 7f* 8fg^2 1980 8f* 8.2fg 7g^4 8g* 8fg* 8g^3 8d* 8fg 9f) compact colt;
useful handicapper; had a good year, winning at Sandown (Esher Cup), Beverley,
Doncaster and Newcastle; quickened nicely to beat King James by 1½ lengths
in Northern Goldsmiths' Handicap on last-named in August; seems to stay 9f;
acts on firm going and a soft surface; moved poorly to post but ran respectably
final appearance; pulled hard second start; genuine and consistent. *M. Stoute.*

ATLANTIC CITY 3 b.c. Tudor Rhythm 112–Swannery 94 (My Swanee 122) **87**
(1979 6g^2 6g^2 6fg* 1980 7v 8f^2 7fg 8f^3 8fg 6d^3 6fg^4) small, compact colt;
fair performer; stays 1m; probably acts on any going; takes a good hold. *R.
Sheather.*

ATLANTIC MONARCH 4 b.g. Track Spare 125–Newstead Belle 74 (Chamier —
128) (1979 10.2g 7f 8f^3 8.3f 8g 8fg 8fg 12s^4 1980 8fg 10f) strong, lengthy
gelding; quite a moderate maiden; probably stays 1½m. *P. Cole.*

ATLANTIC SUPREME 2 b.c. Manacle 123–Atlantic Princess 69 (Four **63**
Burrow 91) (1980 5d 5.8f 5g^2) Apr 12; rather unfurnished colt; first foal;
dam won from 1m to 1½m; ran on when 4 lengths second of 14 to Crosby Triangle
in seller at Windsor in August, best effort; will stay 7f+. *P. Cole.*

ATLANTIC TRAVELLER (USA) 3 b.c. Noholme II–Mlle Quille (On-and-On) **84**
(1979 8fg 7d 1980 12f 12.3f^3 12fg^3 16g* 16.9d^3 16f^2 18f^3 16.1s) useful-looking
colt; battled on gamely when winning 10-runner maiden race at York in June;
suited by a test of stamina; acts on firm going. *J. W. Watts.*

ATRAMO 6 ch.g. Silly Season 127–Gold Cypher 76 (Pardao 120) (1979 12g^4 —
12h 15d^4 12s 13s 1980 16.1s 15d) strong gelding; showed ability in amateur
riders event and a handicap in the North in 1979; burly both outings of 1980
and showed a hint of temperament on final start; stays 15f. *P. Felgate.*

ATROBES 5 b.h. Tribal Chief 125–Miss Jack 97 (Pampered King 121) (1979 **39**
10s 11.1d 10f 9f^4 10g 10.2fg 1980 8s 9.6fg^2 8fg 10.1fg^2 10f 8fg 7f) short-
coupled horse; plater; stays 1¼m; probably acts on any going; sometimes wears
blinkers; has worn a tongue strap; sold 360 gns Ascot October Sales. *D. Hanley.*

ATTIVO 10 b.g. Appiani II 128–El Galgo 64 (Miralgo 130) (1979 NR 1980 —
16f^4) one-time useful stayer, winner of Chester Cup and Northumberland Plate
in 1974; lightly raced on flat afterwards but wasn't disgraced when fourth of 10
behind Shaab at Lingfield in May on only outing of 1980; broke down in October
and has reportedly been retired; acted on any going; was tried in blinkers but
was a notably game and genuine performer in his prime; was a suitable mount
for an apprentice. *P. Mitchell.*

A TUNEFUL SONG 4 b.g. Silly Season 127–Tuneful 81 (Reliance II 137) **63**
(1979 12d 9g 9f^2 1980 10fg 8g 10d 8h 7fg^3 8d 6d) small ex-Irish gelding;
ridden by 7-lb claimer, clear 2f out but weakened to finish 2 lengths third of 16
behind Sky Jump in handicap at Salisbury in September; needs further than 6f
and stays 9f; acts on firm going. *H. Blagrave.*

AUDACITY 3 gr.f. Zeddaan 130–Wide Of The Mark 91 (Gulf Pearl 117) (1979 **70**
5f^2 5d 5f^4 6d^4 1980 6f*) light-framed filly; good walker and mover; pushed
along most of way when narrowly winning maiden race at Pontefract in May;
will be suited by 7f+; probably acts on any going; sold 2,800 gns Newmarket
December Sales. *W. Hastings-Bass.*

AUDIT 2 ch.c. Henry the Seventh 125–Red Again (Red God 128§) (1980 5h **61**
5fg 5d^4 6g 6fg 7g 8.2d^2 8fg^2 8.2s*) Apr 28; 260F, 900Y; small, stocky plater;
first living produce; dam never ran; improved over 1m and won 13-runner event
at Hamilton in September by 2½ lengths from Plain Stalker; will stay 1¼m;
seems to act on any going; has run well both with and without blinkers but
didn't wear them when successful. *J. Etherington.*

AUDLEY END (USA) 3 b.c. Nijinsky 138–Favoletta 115 (Baldric II 131) **85** (1979 7fg^{3} 1980 12fg 11f 10.2fg 12g 10s^{3} 12d* 10g* 11d 11.1g^{4}) strong, rangy colt; good mover; successful in 2 handicaps at Newmarket in the summer; stays 1½m; evidently suited by some give in the ground; looked none too keen fourth start and ran badly eighth outing; not one to rely on. *H. Wragg.*

AULD MUNG 2 gr.g. Scallywag 127–Linton Spring 84 (Khalkis 127) (1980 – 5fg 7fg 8d) Mar 26; 3,700F, 3,300Y; half-brother to a winner in Denmark; dam stayed 9f; in rear in maiden races in Scotland. *Denys Smith.*

AUNTIE EVE 3 b.f. Forlorn River 124–Bouncey 85 (Bounteous 125) (1979 NR – 1980 8fg 8d 8g) 740F, 680Y, 400 2-y-o; no sign of ability in sellers and a claiming race; sold 420 gns Ascot August Sales. *R. Hannon.*

AUNT JOBISKA (USA) 2 br.f. What Luck–Aunt Aurilla (Tinsley) (1980 6f) – Apr 21; $35,000Y; strong, compact filly; closely related to minor winners by Master Hand and Raja Baba and half-sister to stakes-placed winner Go For Two (by Tudor Grey); dam unraced half-sister to 2 minor stakes winners; 25/1 and in need of race, moved badly to start when behind in 19-runner maiden race won by Long Legend at Newmarket in October. *W. Hastings-Bass.*

AUNTY MAY 2 br.f. Maystreak 118–Rosemarkie 75 (Goldhill 125) (1980 5f^{4} **63** 5fg^{4} 5f 6s 6d 6d^{2} 6fg*) Apr 2; leggy, lengthy filly; fourth foal; half-sister to moderate 5f winner Lana's Secret (by Most Secret); dam won over 13f; won 14-runner seller at Ripon in July (sold 2,400 gns afterwards); subsequently raced in Belgium and won over 7f in October; sweated up third and fourth starts; blinkered last 2 outings in this country. *M. H. Easterby.*

AUREUS 3 br.c. Cavo Doro 124–Rosaura 105 (Court Martial) (1979 8f 1980 – 12g 11d 12f 13g 12d) small, quite attractive colt; only plating class; didn't look too enthusiastic third start; blinkered last 2 outings; sold 500 gns Newmarket Autumn Sales. *H. Candy.*

AURORA'S HARBINGER 3 ch.f. Sallust 134–Rixensart 77 (Credo 123) – (1979 5d 5g^{3} 5s* 1980 8fg 6fg 6f^{2} 6fg^{3} 7d 6fg 7g 6g 7g) strong, well-made filly; quite a moderate handicapper at her best; bred to stay 1m but seems best at sprint distances; acts on any going; blinkered final outing; very troublesome at stalls in 1979 but behaved well enough at 3 yrs; ran moderately sixth start; sold 5,000 gns Newmarket December Sales. *S. Woodman.*

AUSTRALIA FAIR (AUS) 2 b.f. Without Fear 128–Chulgin Princess – Ruantallan 120) (1980 5f) Feb 4; Australian-bred filly; first produce; dam useful winner at up to 1¾m in Australia and was third in Group 3 Oaks Stakes at Ascot (1½m) and second in Group 3 Belmont Park Cup (also 1½m); 6/1 when behind in 17-runner maiden race won by Sodina at Lingfield in October; has reportedly been retired. *W. Hastings-Bass.*

AUSWAY (USA) 2 br.f. Impressive–Dell Holme (Noholme II) (1980 7g) – $15,000Y; neat, strong filly; sister to US winner Press for Holme; dam, unplaced 7 times, is sister to very smart stakes winner Noholme Jr.; 50/1 and very much in need of the outing, showed signs of inexperience before start of 14-runner minor event at York in October and came back tailed-off last behind Golden Bowl. *J. Douglas-Home.*

AUTODROME HULL 2 br.f. Most Secret 119–Playful 56 (Right Boy 137) – (1980 6fg 6s 6g 7.2d 10d) Apr 3; unfurnished filly; bad plater. *G. Toft.*

AUTOLUX 2 ch.g. Simbir 130–Autella (Aureole 132) (1980 5v 5s^{2} 5g^{3} 5fg 6g **55** 8fg 8.2s^{3} 10d 10d 8g) Mar 2; 2,800F, 2,400Y; compact gelding; half-brother to fairly useful 1977 2-y-o 7f winner Iapetus (by Jukebox); plater; stays 1m and should get at least 1¼m; acts on soft going; blinkered final start; trained by S. Wainwright first 5 outings. *R. Hobson.*

AUTUMN RUNNING 3 b.f. Ribero 126–Spring Running 91 (Nearula 132) – (1979 8f^{2} 8fg 1980 10fg 12fg 12fg^{3} 12.2fg 13.8f^{4} 14d^{4} 13.3fg 16fg 9s) big, rangy filly; in frame in handicaps and a maiden race; stays 1¾m; seems to act on any going; blinkered first start and behaved fractiously on second; sweated up and took charge of her apprentice rider on seventh outing; looked reluctant to struggle fifth appearance. *R. Boss.*

AUTUMN SUN 3 ch.c. Amber Rama 133–Rainswept (Charlottesville 135) – (1979 6g 7f 1980 7f 7f 10g 10s^{3} 10g 12fg 15.5g) fair sort; stays 1¼m (well beaten over further); evidently suited by soft ground; sold to D. Elsworth 1,050 gns Newmarket Autumn Sales. *M. Masson.*

AVEC L'AMOUR 2 ch.f. Realm 129–Hasta (Skymaster 126) (1980 5fg^{4}) Apr **75** p 28; 30,000Y; second foal; dam unraced half-sister to very useful animals Harken and High Powered; 20/1, ran creditably for a newcomer when beaten only 1¾ lengths into fourth-of-21 position behind Doubtwash Girl, after being hampered early on, in minor event at Catterick in September; will stay 6f. *Sir Mark Prescott.*

AVENGE 4 b.c. Mummy's Pet 125–B.S.R. 68 (March Past 124) (1979 6v^4 6s^3 8s 7fg 1980 7fg 7fg^4 6g 7g 6d 7.6d 8fg 8h* 8g^3) neat colt; plater; bought in 1,750 gns after winning at Bath in August; stays 1m; seems to act on any going; often wears blinkers (didn't at Bath). *P. Cole.* 56

AVENGED 4 ch.c. Sweet Revenge 129–Tortola § (Narrator 127) (1979 6s^2 6s* 6g^3 7s* 7d^2 8.2s 7fg 7g 7d^2 7.2g 7fg 1980 8d 7s 6fg 7.2fg 7g) strong, good-bodied colt; fairly useful handicapper at 3 yrs (rated 98); well beaten in 1980, including when blinkered second outing, and is possibly no longer genuine; best form at up to 7f but should stay 1m; ideally suited by soft going; off course nearly 5 months before final start. *M. Jarvis.* —

AVENTURA 2 gr.c. No Mercy 126–Queens To Open 75 (Darius 129) (1980 5fg) Apr 3; 10,500Y; lengthy, useful-looking colt; brother to No Cards, a useful winner from 5f to 1m, and half-brother to 3 other winners; dam won at 1m; 16/1, made no show in 16-runner maiden race awarded to Swinging Rhythm at Newbury in September. *H. Candy.* —

AVEREEN 3 b.f. Averof 123–Pirate Queen 77 (Pirate King 129) (1979 6fg 7f 7f 1980 8.5f 12d) leggy, unfurnished filly; in rear in varied company; sweated up badly first start; pulled up 1f out second outing; sold 3,100 gns Newmarket December Sales. *D. Whelan.* —

AVERSUN 4 b.g. Averof 123–Pirate Queen 77 (Pirate King 129) (1979 NR 1980 12.2fg^4 16g^4) plating-class staying maiden. *W. Haigh.* —

AVONA 2 b.f. My Swallow 134–Ratlings (Turn-to) (1980 6fg) Apr 10; well-made filly; third reported foal; half-sister to a winner in Italy; dam unraced half-sister to Bald Eagle; moved badly on way to start of minor event at Epsom in August and was tailed off throughout. *A. Breasley.* —

AVONDALE PRINCESS 2 b.f. The Brianstan 128–Roseanne 68 (St Paddy 133) (1980 5fg^4 5fg 5fg 6s 5d 7g 7f 7g^3 6g 6s^3 6s 6g) May 5; 3,500Y; sturdy filly; first foal; dam won over 1½m and is half-sister to Derby third Mount Athos and smart sprinter John Splendid; 7 lengths third of 16 behind More Stones in maiden race at Chepstow in September; beaten slightly further when third of 23 to Reconquest in seller at Haydock in October; suited by 7f and will probably stay 1m. *J. Haine.* 69

AVON SALMON 5 b.g. Forlorn River 124–Misylda 100 (Faubourg II 127) (1979 10s 12d 14v 12f 16fg 12d 1980 14fg 12f 10.6fg) plater; stays 1½m; acts on firm going. *D. Wintle.* —

AWARD FOR EXPORT 2 b.f. Abwah 118–Chequered Flag 70 (King's Troop 118) (1980 5v 5fg 5fg 6s 8d) Mar 25; 8,000Y; compact filly; half-sister to three 2-y-o winners; dam won over 5f at 2 yrs; in rear in moderate maiden company and in a selling nursery; trained by S. Wainwright first 3 outings; sold 340 gns Doncaster November Sales. *R. Hobson.* —

AWEL-HAF 2 b.f. Persian Breeze 121–Gold Pension 76 (Compensation 127) (1980 5f 5f 5g 5g^2 5d 6s 5s) May 1; fair sort; second foal; half-sister to 3-y-o 6f winner Phil Bennett (by Mountain Call); dam best at 5f; ran very green but put up best effort when neck second of 6 to Quality Road in seller at Ayr in July; not sure to stay 6f; blinkered fifth and seventh outings; had stiff tasks last 2 starts. *W. H. H. Williams.* 57

AYTIDEFS 7 br.g. Lear Jet 123–Will o' the Wisp 98 (Hornbeam 130) (1979 NR 1980 10.6fg 10.6fg 11g) middle-distance plater nowadays; acts on any going; usually bandaged in front. *D. Ringer.* —

AYYABAAN 3 b.c. Sun Prince 128–Adayra (Le Haar 126) (1979 5g 5fg 5g 6fg^3 7f^3 8fg* 7fg^3 1980 10.6d^3 12f^4 12f^2 10.1g 12f 12g^4 12fg) well-made, attractive colt; excellent mover; in frame in minor races at Haydock and Thirsk in April and handicap at Newbury in May; generally disappointing subsequently though ran respectably on sixth outing; stays 1½m; acts on firm going; blinkered third start in 1979; trained by F. J. Houghton first 3 outings. *J. Jenkins.* 83

AZAAM 2 b.c. Mummy's Pet 125–Emperor Star (King Emperor) (1980 5d* 6d^3) Mar 26; 12,000Y; useful-looking colt; first foal; dam of little account; ran on to lead close home when winning 14-runner maiden race at Wolverhampton in October by short head from Rawlinson End; 8½ lengths third of 9 to Cliff Bank in minor event at Leicester later in month; stays 6f. *W. O'Gorman.* 79

AZD 5 ch.g. Be Friendly 130–Portden (Worden II 129) (1979 12d^4 10s 12d —
10fg^2 10fg^4 10fg 10g* 10g^2 1980 12g) won amateur riders race at Lingfield at 4 yrs; stays 1¾m; probably acts on any going; wears blinkers. *M. Masson.*

AZERILA 4 br.g. Prince Regent 129–Red Solitaire 76 (Red God 128§) (1979 86
8d^3 8s 7fg* 6f^2 8.2fg^2 7fg* 7.2g^3 7.6f* 7d^3 7.2g 7g 1980 7d 7f* 7.6f^4 7f^2 7g^2 7f 7g 7s 7g^4 7g^4) compact gelding; good walker; quickened clear in final furlong to beat Moybrook by 1½ lengths in handicap at Thirsk in April; runner-up on same course in May and York in June; ideally suited by 7f on top-of-the-ground; acts on any track; consistent; suitable mount for an apprentice; has a tendency to hang left; sold 5,000 gns Newmarket Autumn Sales and is to be trained by J. Gifford. *Denys Smith.*

B

BAAS 2 b.c. Dancer's Image–Snobby Kate (Snob 130) (1980 7d 7d^2 7fg^3 99
8.2g* 8g* 10g) Mar 1; 38,000Y; lengthy, useful sort; third foal; half-brother to a winner in USA by Search for Gold; dam, half-sister to Godswalk (by Dancer's Image), won once from 20 starts in USA; improved over 1m, winning nurseries at Nottingham in August (by 1½ lengths from Principal Dancer) and Yarmouth in September (made all under top weight to beat Joint Command 1½ lengths); runs as though 1¼m should suit him (having first race for 6 weeks and always behind when tried at trip). *J. Hindley.*

BABAS BALLY 2 gr.c. Ballynockan 112–Clare Blue 83 (Blue Streak 106) §§
(1980 5f 5fg^3 5fg^2 5g 5f 5s^3 5d* 6fg 5fg 6s) Apr 28: leggy colt; first reported foal; dam won over 5.8f; placed in sellers and a nursery prior to winning 11-runner nursery at Hamilton in September by ½ length from Be Sharp; ran badly last 2 outings and is one to leave alone; best form at 5f on an easy surface; blinkered fourth outing; trained by D. Ancil first 3 starts. *Peter Taylor.*

BABBINGTON 2 b.c. Gay Fandango 132–Skipton (Breton 130) (1980 —
6d 7d 6g) Mar 2; 3,800Y; neat, strong colt; first foal; dam never ran; unquoted and backward when in rear in maiden and minor events at Newmarket and Doncaster in October. *R. Armstrong.*

BABBINSWOOD 3 b. or br.f. St Paddy 133–Wall Street 82 (Cash and —
and Courage 116) (1979 NR 1980 10.2d 10s 11v) small filly; seems useless. *W. Stubbs.*

BABS BAY 2 b.f. Bay Express 132–Babington Fats (Varano) (1980 5f 68
5g 5f 5d) Mar 13; third foal; half-sister to a winner in Malaya; dam never ran; showed ability on fourth outing when 5 lengths fifth of 17 finishers behind Fairgreen in maiden race at Warwick in October; will be better suited by 6f+. *A. Breasley.*

BABY BEN 6 b.m. Royben 125–Dorbe 80 (Tudor Melody 129) (1979 ran —
14 times winning twice 1980 8g 8fg 6s 7s) ex-Dutch mare; won handicaps over 9f and 10f at Duindigt in 1979; well beaten over here, on first occasion in valuable seller at Doncaster in September; blinkered final outing. *R. Whitaker.*

BABY CLAIR 3 ch.f. Gulf Pearl 117–Fortunes Lady 93 (Fortino II 120) (1979 61
5v^3 6g* 6f^3 5f^2 7s 7f 6d 8.2d 1980 8.2g 8.5g^2 8fg 10s^4 8.2d) lengthy, lightly-made filly; poor mover; did not handle track too well when respectable second in handicap at Epsom in April, easily best effort in 1980; stays 1m well; acts on any going; ran poorly third start (off course 3 months afterwards). *W. H. H. Williams.*

BACCHANTINA 2 ch.f. Gulf Pearl 117–Miss Maverick 76 (Vilmorin) (1980 —
5f 7g 6g 6fg 7g 7g 8fg) Apr 19; 1,300F, 2,200Y; small, useful-looking filly; sister to 3 minor winners, and half-sister to several winners, including useful 1968 2-y-o Mistral (by Whistling Wind) but is only a poor plater herself; blinkered last 2 outings. *R. Hannon.*

BADSWORTH GIRL 2 b.f. Arch Sculptor 123–Falcade (Falcon 131) (1980 72
5g^3 5d 8fg 6g^3 6fg^2 6d) Apr 6; 4,400Y; big, rangy filly; third produce; half-sister to 2 winners, including fairly useful 1977 2-y-o 6f and 7f winner Badsworth Boy (by Will Hays); dam ran only at 2 yrs; placed in maiden races, final occasion when going down by 2 lengths to Penshiel at Redcar in October; not bred to stay 1m; trained by S. Wainwright first 2 outings. *G. Toft.*

BAFFIN 2 b.c. Busted 134–Ocean 112 (Petition 130) (1980 7d^4) Mar 8; 82p
strong, useful-looking colt; half-brother to 2 winners, including useful 1½m

winner Baltic (by Ribero); dam won Coronation Stakes; 8/1 and backward, took some time to get going but was staying on really well when 3½ lengths fourth of 14 to Sunley Builds in Houghton Stakes at Newmarket in October; a well-bred colt who looks sure to make a useful middle-distance 3-y-o. *R. Hern.*

BAFFIN BAY 9 b.g. Derring-Do 131–Polar Way 104 (Borealis) (1979 NR — 1980 16g 12g) moderate hurdler at his best; does little racing on flat nowadays; wears bandages. *J. Cann.*

BAGIBA (ITY) 3 ch.g. Astese–Ciacolada (Rio Marin) (1979 7fg 7f 8fg 1980 — 10fg 12fg) compact gelding; poor maiden. *T. Molony.*

BAHAMAS BANK 3 br.f. Welsh Pageant 132–Piccadilly Lil 92 (Pall Mall 65 132) (1979 NR 1980 7fg^{2} 8f 8d 7g 8.2g) 30,000Y; lengthy, light-framed filly; fifth foal; dam 6f 2-y-o winner; showed promise when second in maiden race at Chepstow in July but was well beaten in similar races and a £2,900 event subsequently; should stay 1m; blinkered last 2 starts. *M. Smyly.*

BAHATI 3 b. or br.f. Royal Palace 131–Every Blessing 110 (Parthia 132) 59 (1979 7fg 8g 1980 10fg 12fg 12g 12d^{3} 15fg^{2} 14.7d^{2} 13.8g 14.7f 16g) quite a moderate maiden; stays well; acts on a firm and a soft surface; blinkered nowadays; sometimes sweats up; sold 5,000 gns Newmarket December Sales. *W. Elsey.*

BAJAN DANCER 4 b.c. Sharpen Up 127–Buff Beauty 92 (Mossborough — 126) (1979 10fg 12s 12s 1980 10fg 7h 8fg 8g 10g 8fg) plating-class maiden; blinkered penultimate start. *B. Palling.*

BAKER AND OVEN 3 gr.f. Roan Rocket 128–Glengarry 72 (High Hat 131) — (1979 5s 6f 1980 6fg 6fg 6h^{4} 6fg 7d) well-made filly; only plating class; will stay 1m. *B. Swift.*

BAKER'S COMPANY 3 ch.f. King's Company 124–Lepe 65 (Exbury 138) — (1979 NR 1980 9fg 10f 12g) 920F; lengthy filly; half-sister to a winner in Italy and 2 winning jumpers; dam needed at least 1½m; behind in newcomers event and maiden races; sweated up final start; sold 900 gns Doncaster August Sales. *M. Cousins.*

BAKER'S QUARTER 2 ch.c. Sheshoon 132–Right View 75 (Right Tack 131) — (1980 6g) Mar 20; 3,500Y; compact colt; first foal; dam won over 5f early at 2yrs; 25/1 and in need of race when twelfth of 13 to Lord Clarence in minor event at Salisbury in August; dead. *B. Swift.*

BAKER STREET 4 b.g. Polyfoto 124–Angelique II (Fast Fox 123) (1979 8g 8g — 8g 7fg^{4} 8f^{4} 8fg^{2} 8h 10d 12f^{4} 9d^{3} 12g 12s^{2} 10g 10d^{2} 10s^{3} 1980 13.8fg 10fg 8fg 8g 10.2g 8g 12.2f 10fg 13.8g 8f 8.2s 6d) compact gelding; good mover; inconsistent maiden; stays 1½m; acts on any going; finds little off bridle; sweated up second start; has been tried in blinkers (ran too freely on first occasion). *G. Toft.*

BALACCO 5 ch.m. Balidar 133–Cigarette 61 (Miralgo 130) (1979 11.7g 10s 10fg — 10d^{2} 10f 12fg 10fg 10d 12d 1980 12.2v 15fg) poor handicapper; stays 1¼m; appears to act on any going. *S. Woodman.*

BALAINE (GER) 2 b.f. Balidar 133–Donine (Soleil II 133) (1980 5fg 5g 6fg 5g) — Apr 11; 8,800Y; neat filly; half-sister to 2 winners, including middle-distance performer Rapide (by Gulf Pearl); dam unraced half-sister to smart 1½m filly Nanticious; no better than plating-class on form so far; sweated up badly fourth outing *S. Woodman.*

BALARAM (USA) 4 b.g. Blade–Yes Love (Double Jay) (1979 6g 5s 6g^{3} 6d* 5s 62 6f^{3} 7.6f 6fg 6g 1980 5.8fg 5fg 7g 7fg^{2} 7fg 5.8g^{3} 6fg) strong gelding; stays 7f; acts on firm going and an easy surface; usually wears blinkers; sold 720 gns Newmarket Autumn Sales. *A. Breasley.*

BALATINA 2 ch.f. Balidar 133–Toccatina 79 (Bleep-Bleep 134) (1980 6s 6g 5fg 85 5f^{2} 5fg^{3} 5.3g^{4} 5d* 6d^{4}) Mar 20; fair sort; half-sister to winning plater Townsong (by Town Crier); dam sprinter; ran best races in the autumn and won 13-runner nursery at Warwick in October readily by 2½ lengths from May Go Twice; best form at 5f; probably acts on any going; apprentice ridden when successful; bandaged off-hind last two starts. *A. Dalton.*

BALBOA 6 b.h. Bold Lad (Ire) 133–Sadair's Bouquet (Sadair) (1979 NR — 1980 5fg 6d) tall, rangy Irish-bred ex-Austrian horse; an outstanding horse in Austria, where he finished leading 2-y-o in 1976 (unbeaten in 4 races at up to 6.5f); won 3 races at up to 7f and finished in frame in Austrian 2,000 Guineas and Derby from 5 starts in 1977 and won once and was placed twice from 3 outings the following year; tried against leading European sprinters at 4 yrs also and won Goldene Peitsche at Baden-Baden and finished second to King of Macedon in

Prix de Meautry at Deauville; bandaged both outings of 1980, finishing respectable eighth of 14 behind African Song in King's Stand Stakes at Royal Ascot in June and in rear in William Hill July Cup won by Moorestyle at Newmarket in July; standing at Bensons Stud, Colchester £450 n.f.n.f. *R. Sheather.*

BALDA 2 br.f. Relko 136–Basilia Dea (Habitat 134) (1980 8g 8g) Apr 10; 3,300Y; tall filly; half-sister to 3-y-o Gagliardo Umbro (by Green Dancer), a smart winner over 1m at 2 yrs; dam placed in Italy; unquoted when well behind in end-of-season maiden and minor events at Newmarket. *W. Hastings-Bass.* —

BALDINGSTONE BOY 2 b.c. Seaepic 100–Vivyiki (Kirtonian 88) (1980 5fg 5fg 5fg 5.1f 5fg 5f 6g 7.2s 10.2s) May 7; 1,200Y; compact, narrow colt; well beaten, including in sellers. *A. Balding.* —

BALI GEORGE 2 b.c. Balidar 133–Ballyarctic (Arcticeelagh 119) (1980 7fg 6g³ 6g 7fg 7.6f⁴ 7f² 8.2s 8d) Apr 23; 3,300Y; workmanlike colt; second foal; dam won over hurdles in Ireland; quite a moderate maiden; stays 7f but ran moderately over 1m; acts on firm going and is probably unsuited by soft ground; often wears a tongue strap. *S. Mellor.* 83

BALI HYATT 2 b.c. Steel Heart 128–Maid of Iron (Crozier USA) (1980 6fg) Mar 11; 104,000Y; useful-looking colt; half-brother to 5 winners, including speedy 1974 2-y-o Amazing Maid (by Amazing) and useful 6f to 1m winner Iron Lad (by Petingo); dam never ran; 20/1 and in need of a race when well-beaten ninth of 12 to Douschkina in minor event at Newmarket in August. *C. Brittain.* —

BALILYCA 2 b.f. Balidar 133–Polycarpa (Polyfoto 124) (1980 5f 5g 5g 5fg 5g) Feb 20; 700F, 3,000Y; neat filly; first foal; dam unraced twin; only plating class *M. Francis.* —

BALIMAR 2 ch.f. Balidar 133–Sea-Hit 85 (Bleep-Bleep 134) (1980 5g 5d 5s 5d) Apr 1; 1,300Y; quite a useful sort; half-sister to 3 minor winners; dam sprinter; fifth in maiden races on first 3 outings, on second beaten 3½ lengths by Trytravelscene at Pontefract in August; gives impression a sharp 5f will suit her. *C. Booth.* 60

BALINGER 4 b.c. Welsh Pageant 132–Ripeck 90 (Ribot 142) (1979 11g³ 10s⁴ 10fg* 10.1f* 10.1fg* 12fg* 10g* 14d* 13.3g⁴ 1980 14f 16fg* 13.3f* 16.1fg* 22.2fg*) big, very attractive colt; half-brother to several winners, notably 116

Mr R. D. Hollingsworth's "Balinger"

Oaks winner Bireme (by Grundy), very good middle-distance stayer Buoy (by Aureole) and smart sprinter Fluke (by Grey Sovereign); dam stayed 1½m; developed into a very useful stayer and won his last 4 races; very much took the eye in paddock and put up a splendid performance under top weight to win Queen Alexandra Stakes at Royal Ascot in June by 1½ lengths from Donegal Prince (pair long way clear), leading 6f out and getting on top close home after a long-drawn-out battle; had a setback the following month and wasn't seen out again; had earlier won handicap at Newmarket, Lymm Stakes (beat Arapahos by 1½ lengths) at Haydock and Aston Park Stakes (got home by ½ length from Barley Hill) at Newbury; stayed extremely well; acted on any going except perhaps very soft; game, genuine and consistent; standing at Conduit Farm Stud, Churchill, Oxon, £75+ £225 (Oct 1st). *R. Hern.*

BALIROMA 2 ch.f. Balidar 133–Romany 87 (King's Bench 132) (1980 5.1fg⁴) Mar 12; small filly; sister to winning sprinter Aboma and half-sister to 3 winners, including useful 3-y-o 1m and 1½m winner John O'Groats (by Welsh Pageant); dam best at sprint distances; co-favourite, had every chance at distance when 1½ lengths fourth of 11 to Garnish Island in maiden race at Yarmouth in August, only outing. *J. Winter.* **68** p

BALLACOREY 4 b.c. Sallust 134–Broad River 75 (Chieftain) (1979 8s 8g⁴ 8f² 1980 10s 12fg 10f³ 10fg 11.1fg 8fg) lightly-made colt; quite a moderate handicapper; stays 1¼m (well beaten over further); acts on firm going. *T. Marshall.* **53**

BALLAQUINE 3 b.f. Martinmas 128–La Concha (Le Levanstell 122) (1979 5g 6f⁴ 6fg 7fg 5f 6f 6f 5g 1980 8d 10fg⁴ 10h* 10g) neat filly; plater; won at Pontefract in May (retained 950 gns); stays 1¼m; acts on hard going. *R. Hollinshead.* **52**

BALLINROBE 2 b.c. Connaught 130–Shallow Stream 100 (Reliance II 137) (1980 5f) Feb 6; small colt; first foal; dam, 1¼m 2-y-o winner, is daughter of half-sister to Cantelo; 20/1 when seventh of 19 to Airship in maiden race at Warwick in April; dead. *T. Waugh.* –

BALLIPAL 3 br.f. Balliol 125–Pal Greta 76 (Palestine 133) (1979 5g 5g 7d 1980 7fg 7g 12g) no sign of ability, including in a seller; slipped up third start; sold 580 gns Doncaster September Sales. *Denys Smith.* –

BALLROOM 3 b.g. Huntercombe 133–Lyceum 66 (Ballyciptic 122) (1979 NR 1980 8g) big gelding; third living foal; dam won sellers over 5f and 1m; unquoted and backward when tailed-off last in minor event at Thirsk in September. *W. A. Stephenson.* –

BALLYLINGO 2 b.f. Saulingo 122–Bally Keys 72 (Bally Russe 113) (1980 5fg 5fg* 5g³ 5g 5f⁴ 5fg² 5g³ 5fg⁴ 5d) Feb 21; 3,700Y; strong filly; first living foal; dam plating class; made all to win 9-runner maiden race at Folkestone in June by 2½ lengths from Archimboldo; ran well in nurseries afterwards; will be suited by 6f; acts on firm going (poorly drawn on only outing on a soft surface). *G. Lewis.* **85**

BALLYORAN 3 b.c. Ragapan 118–Mother 88 (Whistler 129) (1979 NR 1980 9fg 8fg⁴ 12f³ 15.5g 12s) useful sort; half-brother to 3 winners, including top-class North Stoke (by Northfields) and fairly useful middle-distance performer Balimar (by Ballymoss); dam won over 5f at 2 yrs; in frame in maiden races early in year; off course 4 months after third start and was well beaten on his return; not certain to stay 2m; sold 1,100 gns Ascot November Sales. *J. Dunlop.* –

BALLY SEAL 5 b.m. Privy Seal 108–Ballysally (Arctic Slave 116) (1979 12d 1980 12f) plating-class maiden on flat; dead. *H. Westbrook.* –

BALLYSEEDY HERO 2 gr.g. Supreme Sovereign 119–Knocknagrena (Worden II 129) (1980 6fg 6g 7fg) Apr 18; 9,600Y; tall, lengthy gelding; brother to smart 1976 Irish 6f and 7f winner Sovereign Dice, and half-brother to several winners; dam placed at up to 1¼m in Ireland; unquoted when behind in large fields for maiden and minor events. *D. Whelan.* –

BALLYTOP 3 b.c. High Top 131–Ballydowa 90 (Ballymoss 136) (1979 6f 1980 8s² 8fg⁴ 10.1s* 10d² 10.1g* 12g² 12g* 13s²) rangy colt; good mover; successful in 2 minor events at Windsor in the summer and ladies race at Chepstow in September; also ran well when second to very easy winner Spanish Dancer in minor event at Newbury on fourth start and to Blakes Beacon (pair well clear) in Royal Caledonian Hunt Cup at Ayr in September on final appearance; stays 13f; acts well on soft ground; to be trained by I. Balding. *F. J. Houghton.* **93**

BALMUICK BOY 4 b.g. Tumble Wind–Petit Chapeau 84 (High Hat 131) (1979 8s 8d 10g 8fg 8fg 8g⁴ 8f* 8.2fg³ 10s⁴ 8.2g 8d² 8fg 11g⁴ 8d 8g³ 1980 10.2d –

10v 11fg 8.2g 8f 8f) quite a useful-looking gelding; ran badly in 1980 (pulled up third start); best form at up to 1m; appears to act on any going; suitable mount for a claimer; sold 1,600 gns Doncaster May Sales, resold 600 gns Ascot December Sales. *T. Craig.*

BALRANALD 8 b.h. Burglar 128–Margaret Ann 83 (Persian Gulf) (1979 9s 8s 8.2g 8fg 10f 12f 8f 8g 8g 8g 10g 12d 1980 10.4d) strong horse; stays 1¼m; acts on any going; sometimes wears blinkers; has worn bandages; good mount for an inexperienced rider. *F. Durr.* —

BALTIC LOVE 8 b.g. Current Coin 118–Arctic Villa (Arctic Star) (1979 NR 1980 10d^3 16s 18fg) poor staying handicapper; acts on soft going. *G. Blum.* —

BALU 4 ch.c. Ballymore 123–Amablai (Levmoss 133) (1979 10v* 1980 10g 16g 12d^2 12s^3 9fg^3 10g^3 13s 12d) rather lightly-made Irish colt; placed in Royal Whip Stakes (3 lengths second to My Hollow) and Blandford Stakes, both at the Curragh, Whitehall Stakes (3 lengths third to Muscovite) at Phoenix Park and valuable handicap again at the Curragh; behind in Queen's Vase at Royal Ascot and Royal Caledonian Hunt Cup at Ayr (didn't impress in paddock) on his 2 outings over here; stays 1½m; seems to act on any going. *K. Prendergast, Ireland.* **100** d

BALVIMA 4 b.c. Balidar 133–Sevima 59 (Sovereign Lord 120) (1979 5v 5s 5s 5.1g* 5fg^4 5.1f^3 5fg^4 5.6fg 5s 5g^3 5g^3 5f* 5s 1980 5d 5s^2 5g^3 5f* 5f^2 5s 5g* 5g^2 5fg) compact colt; won handicaps at Haydock in May (decisively) and Sandown in July, beating Go Total by 1½ lengths in valuable Happy Valley Handicap on latter course; creditable second to Mi Favorita in Tilcon Trophy at York on penultimate outing; speedy and best at 5f; acts on any going; blinkered twice at 2 yrs; genuine; good mount for a boy and goes well for B. Crossley. *A. Dalton.* **86**

BAMBERAMA 2 b.f. Amber Rama 133–Bajour 89 (Forlorn River 124) (1980 5g) Apr 20; first reported live foal; dam, half-sister to smart Pugnacity, won from 5f to 7f; 50/1 when behind in 22-runner maiden race won by Copt Hall Realm at Lingfield in September. *N. Gaselee.* —

BAM EXPRESS 2 b.c. Bay Express 132–Beguiling 66 (Tower Walk 130) (1980 5g) May 20; second foal; half-brother to 1979 2-y-o 5f seller winner Enchante (by Manacle); last of 14 to stable-companion Crosby Triangle in seller at Windsor in August; sold 300 gns Doncaster September Sales. *P. Haslam.* —

BAMP 4 ro.g. Supreme Sovereign 119–Light Jumper 100 (Red God 128 **§**) (1979 8s 9s^3 9.4v* 11g^4 9.4f^2 8f 9fg^3 8s^3 8.2g* 8.2g^2 8g* 8.2s* 8.2s^2 8s 1980 7f 8s 8.2s^2 8.2s) fairly useful handicapper in 1979, winner 4 times; seemed to be returning to form when 1½ lengths second to Maryam at Hamilton in September but ran poorly at Haydock the following month; backward both previous outings; best form at around 1m, and doesn't stay 11f; acts on any going but is well suited by the mud; blinkered sometimes at 3 yrs, but not when successful; useful hurdler. *M. H. Easterby.* **84**

BANBURY CROSS 2 b.c. Tower Walk 130–Hark Hark 75 (Sing Sing 134) (1980 5d 5s 5f 5g 5d^4 5g 7fg^4 6g^4 7fg^3 6d^3 6s*) Mar 2; 17,000Y; useful sort; half-brother to 1m winner Yonder He Goes (by Gulf Pearl); dam disappointing; won 22-runner maiden race at Doncaster in November by ¾ length from Record Surprise; stays 7f; probably acts on any going. *W. Wightman.* **83**

BANCO 5 b.h. Shoolerville 121–Coup 106 (Hook Money 124) (1979 8d 8d 7s^4 7s* 7.6s 7f 7.2g* 1980 7fg 7fg 7.6f^4 7d 7d 6g^2 7fg 6d) close-coupled, useful-looking horse; didn't do so well as in 1979 but ran creditably on occasions, notably when head second to Enchantment in handicap at Goodwood in August, disputing lead from start until caught by winner in very last stride; effective at 6f but is ideally suited by 7f; appears to act on any going. *F. J. Houghton.* **96**

B AND K EMPEROR 3 ro.g. Young Emperor 133–Fiery Clare (Firestreak 125) (1979 5g 5s^4 6f 7g 7fg 1980 9.4d 8g 8fg 10g 10fg) leggy gelding; plating-class maiden; stays 1m; probably needs some give in the ground; blinkered final start at 2 yrs and on fourth outing. *M. W. Easterby.* **62**

BAND PRACTICE (USA) 2 b.c. Stop The Music–Fleet Empress (Young Emperor 133) (1980 5f* 5g^2 7g^2 6f^4) Apr 15; $260,000Y; neat, attractive, full-quartered colt; fourth foal; half-brother to a minor winner by Advocator; dam, minor winner over 6f, is half-sister to very smart Fleet Victress, successful at up to 9f, and smart Flit-To, a winner at up to 13f; left the rest standing in final furlong when winning maiden race at the Curragh in May by 10 lengths from Welsh Reel; in frame in important races on subsequent starts, failing by a head to catch Swan Princess in Gallaghouse Phoenix Stakes at Phoenix Park in August, going down by 4 lengths to odds-on Storm Bird (gave 7 lb) in Larkspur Stakes **109**

Mr J. L. Allbritton's "Band Practice"

at Leopardstown the following month and showing up throughout when 4½ lengths fourth of 9 to Mattaboy in William Hill Middle Park Stakes at Newmarket in October; bred to stay 1m but has shown best form at up to 6f; yet to race on a soft surface. *D. Weld, Ireland.*

BANDWAGON (USA) 2 ch.c. Secretariat–Show Stopper (Native Dancer) (1980 7fg² 7d*) Feb 22; $300,000Y; half-brother to a minor winner in USA; dam stakes-placed sister to leading American stallion Raise A Native; easy in market, came from a long way back when promising length second of 17 to Bustineto in maiden race at Leopardstown in August; got home by only a short head from Erins Isle when 9/4 on for 17-runner maiden event at Phoenix Park in October; will stay 1¼m. *V. O'Brien, Ireland.* **86**

BANK LAW 4 ch.g. Levmoss 133–Hidden Key 110 (Sing Sing 134) (1979 8.2s 10.1fg³ 10.8g³ 13fg 16.1s³ 12d 1980 16.1s) lengthy gelding; plating-class maiden; stays well. *W. Wightman.* **–**

BANK RUN 5 br.g. Gilded Leader 75–Seminole Squaw 66 (Seminole II) (1979 10d 10.6s 10.2d³ 12s³ 1980 12f* 12fg² 8fg 12g* 16d) won minor event at Pontefract in April and handicap on same course in June, latter by 1½ lengths from Sir Michael; blinkered when tailed off in Coral Northumberland Plate at Newcastle on final outing (had very stiff task); stays 1½m; acts on any going. *B. McMahon.* **64**

BANNOCKBURN 4 b.g. Scottish Rifle 127–Scattering 69 (Busted 134) (1979 12fg 8fg 5f 5s 6d 1980 12d 12g) fair sort; poor maiden. *J. Spearing.* **–**

BANNONWARD 4 b.f. Forlorn River 124–Double Bank 80 (Double Jump 131) (1979 5fg 5fg 5fg 5h² 5fg 1980 6f 5g³ 5g² 5fg 5fg 5fg) neat filly; short-running plater; acts on hard going; tried in blinkers at 2 yrs; has worn bandages. *T. Taylor.* **37**

BANOCO 2 b.c. Nonoalco 131–Denaneer 78 (Green God 128) (1980 5g² 5d) Mar 16; 29,000Y; useful-looking colt; good mover; first foal; dam 1¼m winner; **72**

Bessborough Stakes, Ascot—Barley Hill defeats Get Stoned and the blinkered Laska Floko

ran on without being knocked about when 5 lengths second of 8 to Sandon Buoy in maiden race at Sandown in July; looked very well when next seen out, in another maiden race at Sandown in October, but was under pressure before halfway and finished last of 20 to Little Starchy; almost certainly finds 5f too short and will stay 1m. *R. Price.*

BAPTISM 4 ch.c. Northfields–Bap 77 (Current Coin 118) (1979 10v* 10.4v³ 10fg⁴ 8g* 8g³ 8d² 8f⁴ 1980 8f 7d* 8d 7s) quite attractive, rather lightly-made colt; very smart performer; won Queen Anne Stakes at Royal Ascot as a 3-y-o; ran only 4 times in 1980, putting up by far his best performance when beating Kilijaro by 3 lengths in Prix du Palais Royal at Longchamp in June; showed signs of temperament and was disappointing in Queen Anne Stakes at Royal Ascot (9 lengths fifth to Blue Refrain) and Prix de la Porte Maillot at Longchamp (eighth of 10 behind subsequently-disqualified Ya Zaman) later in month, on latter course being tried in blinkers and having to be led part of way to start; stayed 1¼m but gave us impression shorter distances suited him better; acted on firm going but was probably better on an easy surface; standing at Rathbarry Stud, Cork, fee IR£1,750 (Oct 1st terms). *J. Tree.* **119**

BARAM PRINCESS 2 b.f. Furry Glen 121–Summer's Lease (Soderini 123) (1980 5fg 7fg 6g 8g) neat filly; half-sister to useful 1977 2-y-o 5f performer Pingat Mas (by Polyfoto); dam Irish 1½m winner; eighth of 23 in 1m maiden race at Goodwood in September, best effort; will stay 1¼m. *J. Holt.* **—**

BARBARA ALLEN 2 b.f. Song 132–Brave Ballard (Derring-Do 131) (1980 5f 5.8h²) Apr 20; first foal; dam unraced half-sister to very smart middle-distance colt Norfolk Air; 4 lengths second of 12 to Shalwa in maiden race at Bath in August; runs as though she'll stay 7f. *J. Bethell.* **59**

BARBOTTE (FR) 2 b.f. Direct Flight–Barbotine (Tanerko 134) (1980 8g*) May 7; second foal; half-sister to French 3-y-o 9f winner Millibar (by Misti IV); dam, daughter of half-sister to French Oaks winner Barquette, won over 9f; 26/1, had some very well-bred fillies behind when winning 19-runner newcomers event at Maisons-Laffitte in October by ¾ length from Mover; will stay at least 1¼m; should make a very useful 3-y-o. *G. Bridgland, France.* **?**

BARCHAM BRIDE 3 b.f. Henry the Seventh 125–County Court 98 (Grey Sovereign 128§) (1979 7d³ 7fg 1980 12f 14fg 14fg* 14.7f) neat filly; ridden by 5-lb claimer to win poor 4-runner maiden race at Yarmouth in August; **62**

stays 1¾m; acts on a firm surface; saddle slipped second start; slipped on turn at Redcar final outing. *R. Sheather.*

BARDENAC (FR) 2 b.c. Riverman 131–Barbaranne (Dapper Dan) (1980 **118**
6d 6d² 7f* 7.5g) May 1; 800,000 francs Y (approx £84,000); strong, lengthy colt; second foal; half-brother to 3-y-o Bartholin (by Targowice); dam, winner over 6f and 7f, is half-sister to smart sprinter River Rose (by Riverman); odds on, made strong headway on bridle in straight and drew right away to win 7-runner minor event at Longchamp in September impressively by 4 lengths from Tyranesque; seemed to have difficulty negotiating bend when 5/1 for Prix Thomas Bryon at Saint-Cloud in November and was beaten about 4½ lengths into fifth place behind Big John; will stay 1m; impressed us at Longchamp and is probably better than his run at Saint-Cloud suggests. *F. Boutin, France.*

BARGAIN DAY 8 ch.g. Hill Clown–Blue Mark 92 (Blue Train 114) (1979 —
10f 8fg 10.6g 1980 10s 10d) winner over hurdles and fences, but does little racing on flat. *D. Marks.*

BARGAIN LINE 3 b.f. Porto Bello 118–Bonsella 68 (Carlemont 132) (1979 **57**
5g 5g 7fg 7fg 8f* 8g 1980 9fg 8fg 7fg 8fg² 8d 8g 8.3d) strong, fair sort; won seller at Leicester at 2 yrs; respectable second in better company at Brighton in May, best effort in 1980; stays 1m; acts on firm going; often blinkered. *R. Hannon.*

BARIDI 3 ch.f. Ribero 126–Nelion 102 (Grey Sovereign 128§) (1979 6f³ **55**
1980 10fg 12f 13.8g 12f³ 9.4fg) lightly-built filly; stays 1½m; acts on firm going; one paced; trained by H. Cecil first 2 starts; sold 6,200 gns Newmarket December Sales. *W. Elsey.*

BAR JESTER 5 b.g. Bargello–Gay Tricks 57 (Vulgan 123) (1979 NR 1980 —
16fg) half-brother to several jumping winners; dam won over hurdles; brought down in amateur riders race at Newbury in September on first outing on flat. *A. Arnold.*

BARLEYCROFT STAR 8 b.g. Forlorn River 124–Lucker Jewel (Lord of —
Verona 120) (1979 8s 1980 8f) plater; stays 1¼m; acts on firm going; wears blinkers; sometimes wears bandages. *D. Yeoman.*

BARLEY HILL 4 b.c. Simbir 130–Pixie Hill (Goldhill 125) (1979 12g* 12g* **115**
12s³ 12fg² 11.7f² 12f⁴ 12d* 12g² 1980 12d³ 13.3f² 12g* 16g*) attractive, rangy colt; good mover; ran well on all his 4 outings and developed into a smart handicapper; placed at Kempton (third to Beau Reef) and Newbury (½-length second to Balinger in Aston Park Stakes) prior to winning twice at Ascot; kept on well after being kicked clear 3½f out in Bessborough Stakes in June and won by a length from Get Stoned; had to be shaken up to beat Rainfall by 1½ lengths in Brown Jack Stakes the following month after looking likely to trot up; suffered a setback afterwards and wasn't seen out again; stays 2m; acts on any going; consistent. *B. Hobbs.*

BARNET HEIR 2 ch.c. Great Nephew 126–Right as Rain 96 (King's Bench **100**
132) (1980 5d 5s* 5g* 5f⁴ 5g 5fg* 5f⁴ 5fg) Mar 19; 8,800F, 16,000Y; small, sturdy, very attractive colt; good mover; half-brother to several winners, including very useful sprinter As Friendly (by Be Friendly); dam won over 5f at 2 yrs; soon clear when successful twice in April, winning easing up by 4 lengths in 22-runner maiden race at Kempton and by 5 lengths in Hyde Park Stakes at Epsom; ran badly next 2 starts but came right back to form after a 3-month absence when winning valuable nursery at Newbury in September by a head from Brentex; also ran well next time out when apprentice ridden at Newmarket in October; very speedy and is unlikely to stay 6f; acts on any going. *B. Swift.*

Prix du Palais Royal, Longchamp—a smart performance from Baptism who wins from Kilijaro and Vox Populi

BARNLOUGH 2 br.f. Blue Cashmere 129–Stick 'Em Up (Burglar 128) (1980 5fg) Mar 2; 6,000Y; compact filly; second foal; dam never ran; unquoted and sweating when eleventh of 17 behind Pariscene in maiden race at Wolverhampton in August; refused to enter stalls on intended debut. *P. Haslam.* –

BARON BLAKENEY 3 gr.c. Blakeney 126–Teleflora 89 (Princely Gift 137) (1979 5s^{4} 5g 6g 6fg 8g 8.2fg 10.6d^{4} 10s^{2} 10g 1980 12s* 12g^{3} 12f 12fg 13s 14fg^{3} 16f 14g 16fg 14g^{4} 16s) neat colt; won minor race at Leicester in March; fair third in 2 handicaps subsequently; should stay well; best form on an easy surface; suited by strong handling; ran badly seventh and final starts, wearing blinkers on latter; sold 7,800 gns Newmarket Autumn Sales. *W. Marshall.* 78

BARONET 8 b.g. Huntercombe 133–Chagrin Falls 101 (Polic 126) (1979 10d 8d^{2} 8g^{2} 8g* 8fg 8f^{4} 8f^{3} 8g 8f^{4} 8fg 9f 10g^{2} 1980 10s* 10f 8f 8g^{4} 8g 8d 8g^{4} 10.2g 8fg* 9f*) 117

When beating Dromefs in a thrilling finish to the William Hill Cambridgeshire at Newmarket in October game old Baronet joined Hackler's Pride, Christmas Daisy, Sterope and Prince de Galles as the only horses to have won the Cambridgeshire twice since its inception in 1839. He also shares with The Widow, who won in 1847, the distinction of being the race's oldest winner. At the age of eight, when the vast majority of flat racers are well past their prime, and with over fifty races behind him including eight over hurdles, he was recording the best performance of his life, very clearly better than any of his three previous runs in the Cambridgeshire which had seen him a three quarter-length second to Sin Timon in 1977, a neck winner from Claudio Nicolai in 1978 and close sixth to Smartset in 1979. Baronet's short-head defeat of Dromefs brought him his third win of the season from ten starts, for he had beaten the Cambridgeshire favourite Tender Heart by a short head in the two-runner Swinley Forest Handicap at Ascot on his previous outing and had won the Rosebery Handicap at Kempton on his reappearance by a length and a half from Son Fils. He had also finished a fine fourth behind Tender Heart under 10-0 in the Royal Hunt Cup.

Baronet (b.g. 1972)	Huntercombe (b 1967)	Derring-Do (br 1961)	Darius
			Sipsey Bridge
		Ergina (br 1957)	Fair Trial
			Ballechin
	Chagrin Falls (br 1967)	Polic (br 1953)	Relic
			Polaire
		Brabantia (br 1953)	Honeyway
			Porthaven

Baronet was quite an expensive yearling in his day and he began his racing career with Lady Beaverbrook for whom he won twice as a three-year-old when trained by Dick Hern. He is the second foal of Chagrin Falls, a sister to Polyfoto and a useful five-furlong winner as a two-year-old, who has since bred several winners in the United States. Baronet may well continue to run well for another season or two and he will very probably be aimed for a third win in the Cambridgeshire. He is very well suited by the course and by the strong pace at which the race is invariably run. A lengthy, attractive gelding who acts on any going, Baronet is usually held up and has a good turn of foot. He is a credit to his trainer. *J. Benstead.*

BARQ 3 ch.f. Red Alert 127–Super Lyn (Supreme Sovereign 119) (1979 NR 1980 7d^{4} 8f 8fg 10.2fg 10g) 6,000Y; big, rangy filly; first foal; dam never ran; well beaten in newcomers event and maiden races. *A. Johnson.* –

BARRATT OAK 3 b.f. Daring Display 129–Wood Grouse 56 (Celtic Ash) (1979 5d 6g 7fg 8h 7d 1980 10fg 12.2fg^{4} 12g) small, lengthy, unfurnished filly; bad plater; has worn blinkers; sold 900 gns Newmarket July Sales. *P. Rohan.* –

BARRON JOHN 2 ch.c. Steel Heart 128–Sumintra 82 (El Gallo 122) (1980 6s 6g 7fg 7f 5d) Jan 25; 20,000F, 29,000Y; compact colt; half-brother to 2 winners, including quite useful Irish sprinter Concordia (by Realm); dam sprint maiden; eighth of 20 to Little Starchy in 5f maiden race at Sandown in October, best effort; blinkered fourth and fifth outings; sold to Susan Piggott Bloodstock 2,500 gns Newmarket Autumn Sales. *J. Dunlop.* –

BAR ROOM GIRL 2 b.f. Streetfighter 120–Sister Dear (Polyfoto 124) (1980 5fg 6fg* 5g 5.8f 8fg 8d) May 5; 400Y; small filly; sold out of A. Johnson's stable 750 gns after winning 13-runner seller at Warwick in June by ½ length from Gold Guinea; ran best subsequent race on first outing over 1m; dwelt and tailed off when blinkered first outing. *R. Hannon.* 56

William Hill Cambridgeshire Handicap, Newmarket—about three lengths covers the first eight. Baronet wins by a short head from Dromefs with Pulse Rate (No 7) third

BARSALOI 7 br.g. Lorenzaccio 130–Mara River 116 (Gratitude 131) (1979 7v 8s 8fg 8.2s 1980 8s) plater; stays 1m; acts on a soft surface; suitable mount for a boy; usually bandaged nowadays. *K. Bridgwater.* —

BARTELLA 3 b.g. Sterling Bay–Soopah (Paveh 126) (1979 5fg 6fg 8fg 1980 6f 8.5f 10g 10f) neat gelding; bad plater; sold 420 gns Ascot November Sales. *G. Hunter.* —

BARTERED BOY 2 b.c. The Brianstan 128–Royal Barter 94 (King's Bench 132) (1980 5d) Apr 4; strong, compact colt; half-brother to 3 winners, including useful 1971 2-y-o Floroyal (by Floribunda) and 1m winner Royal Bride (by Queen's Hussar), subsequently a good winner in South Africa; dam won her first 2 races at 2 yrs; second favourite but very burly, prominent until lack of fitness told after 3½f when 9½ lengths sixth of 18 behind Southern Frontier in maiden race at Salisbury in June, only outing. *R. Price.* — p

BARTRA 2 b.g. Mandamus 120–Pandomyne 71 (Pandofell 132) (1980 5fg* 5fg 6s 6g³ 6d 6g 8fg 8.2g⁴ 8.2s²) Mar 26; 4,600F; compact gelding; half-brother to 2 winners, including 1979 2-y-o 6f winner Inzera (by Decoy Boy); dam 1¾m winner; 25/1-winner of seller at Redcar in May (bought in 2,800 gns); ran respectably on most of his subsequent starts; will stay 1¼m+; seems to act on any going; sometimes dwells at start (did so when successful). *W. Wharton.* **65**

BARWIN (USA) 2 ch.g. Barachois–Winning Rosy (Winning Hit) (1980 6d³) Mar 20; $15,000F, $35,000Y; robust gelding; first produce; dam, placed at 3 yrs, is daughter of sister to champion filly Bed O'Roses; sire very smart at up to 1¼m in Canada; 6/1, kept on well to finish 4½ lengths third of 17 to Shark Song in maiden race at Newmarket in October; will stay 1¼m; should benefit from this experience. *H. Cecil.* **80** p

BASH STREET KID 5 b.g. Mummy's Pet 125–Bashi 73 (Zarathustra 131) (1979 10d⁴ 10.1fg 8fg 8fg⁴ 1980 9.6h) poor plater; stays 1m. *R. Hoad.* —

BATIK 2 ch.f. On Your Mark 125–Taffeta 72 (Shantung 132) (1980 5fg 6fg 6fg 6g) Apr 18; 5,400Y; lengthy filly; second foal; dam 1½m winner; only plating-class form so far; will stay 1m+. *D. Sasse.* **60**

BATTLEMENT 8 b.h. Tower Walk 130–Aspasie (Milesian 125) (1979 12.3v 13v 11d 12g 12s² 12.5g 12d⁴ 12s 1980 10.2d) quite a moderate handicapper; best form at up to 13f; acts on any going; used to wear blinkers; a difficult ride who needs to be held up and has won only for J. Lowe on flat in last 5 seasons. *C. Thornton.* —

BATTLEWIND (USA) 3 ch.f. Restless Wind–Battle Princess (Yorktown) (1979 7fg³ 7g 1980 7v* 7f⁴ 8fg 8g 10s⁴ 10fg⁴) attractive, well-made filly; second reported foal; dam won 2 of her 30 starts in USA; put up a good performance in 9-runner Salisbury 1000 Guineas Trial in March, leading over 1f out and staying on strongly to beat Lead The Floor 8 lengths; ran respectably in good company afterwards, including when fourth in Ladbrokes Nell Gwyn Stakes at Newmarket, Prix de Malleret at Longchamp and Nassau Stakes at Goodwood; stays 1¼m; acts on any going; sweated up final start. *R. Sheather.* **113**

BAUDELAIRE 6 ch.h. Klairon 131–Pinchbeck (Chanteur II 135) (1979 6.5s 8s 8d 8v* 10s* 8g³ 8g³ 8g² 7.2g³ 8d 1980 6v³ 7g 7fg 7g 7f 7fg 7s 8d 8.2s 7d⁴) strong, good-bodied horse; useful performer at his best; ran creditably over trip on sharp side for him when third to easy winner Kampala in handicap at Salisbury in March; little subsequent form but wasn't disgraced on final start when blinkered first time; stays 1¼m; acts on any going. *D. Sasse.* **83**

BAWDSEY 3 ch.g. Red Alert 127–Tribal Lass (Tribal Chief 125) (1979 5f 6f 6fg 1980 6v⁴ 6f 5.8f 5h) good sort; little better than plating class on balance of form; will stay 7f; blinkered final outing (May). *N. Callaghan.* **–**

BAY BETTY 3 b.f. Bay Express 132–Park Top 131 (Kalydon 122) (1979 NR 1980 8f 7.2d 6g) lengthy, quite attractive filly; third living foal; half-sister to 1m winner Uppark (by Sharpen Up); dam top-class winner at up to 13f; well beaten in maiden races; didn't look too genuine final start. *M. Stoute.* **–**

BAY FOULARD 2 b.f. Shantung 132–Vardo 92 (Crepello 136) (1980 6g 7g 7fg 8d) Apr 17; quite well-made filly; half-sister to 2 winners, including Irish middle-distance winner Great Decision (by Huntercombe); dam stayed 1m; well behind in maiden races and selling nursery. *R. Hollinshead.* **–**

BAY ROBIN 9 ch.g. Weathercock 96–dam unknown (1979 12.2g 14.6fg 1980 13d 8f 8f 10fg) useless. *T. Kersey.* **–**

BAY SONG 2 b.c. Song 132–Exquisite 80 (Exbury 138) (1980 5s 6s 7.2d 6s 8d 8g) May 3; 4,500F, 7,200Y; neat colt; first produce; dam suited by a test of stamina; plater; best run at 7f but will probably stay further (badly hampered first occasion over 1m); blinkered last 2 starts; sold 620 gns Doncaster November Sales. *J. Etherington.* **–**

BAY STREET 3 b.f. Grundy 137–Gliding 94 (Tudor Melody 129) (1979 7g* 7g² 1980 8d² 8.5g* 10.5f 12f 10s) 34,000Y; lightly-made filly; first foal; dam, winning sprinter, is half-sister to very smart 1973 2-y-o Splashing; runner-up to Star **103**

Princess Elizabeth Stakes, Epsom—stable companions Bay Street and Missed Blessing (No. 4) fight out the finish

Chamber in Masaka Stakes at Kempton prior to leading 2f out and keeping on strongly to beat stable-companion Missed Blessing a neck after lengthy battle in Princess Elizabeth Stakes at Epsom in April; well beaten afterwards in Musidora Stakes at York, Oaks and Pretty Polly Stakes at the Curragh (blinkered); stayed 1m well; best form on an easy surface; reportedly visits Alleged. *F. J. Houghton.*

BAZ BOMBATI 2 ch.c. Sun Prince 128–Salsafy 81 (Tudor Melody 129) (1980 7fg* 7.2d² 7fg* 7g 8g²) Jan 22; 8,000Y; well-made, useful-looking colt; good walker and mover; first foal; dam won over 12.2f; winner of maiden race at Yarmouth in July and 6-runner Fitzroy House Stakes at Newmarket the following month, in latter staying on strongly to beat odds-on The Thatcher a short head; beaten only 4 lengths when seventh of 9 finishers behind Gielgud in Laurent Perrier Champagne Stakes at Doncaster in September and had rest well strung out when 2 lengths second of 12 to Kalaglow (gave 5 lb) in £3,100 event at Goodwood later same month; will stay middle distances; genuine and consistent. *G. Pritchard-Gordon.* **112**

B. B. OIL 2 b.c. Netherkelly 122–Blue Mountain (Mountain Call 125) (1980 5fg 5s 6s 8.2s) Feb 18; small, lightly-made colt; poor plater. *B. Richmond.* –

BEACON HEIGHTS 3 b.g. Guillaume Tell 121–Moana (Zucchero 133§) (1979 5s 8fg 10s 1980 10fg) tall, lengthy gelding; well beaten in minor and maiden events; blinkered second outing at 2 yrs. *W. Marshall.* –

BEARWOOD BELLE 2 ch.f. Shiny Tenth 120–Flight Feathers (Ribocco 129) (1980 5d 5d) May 26; sister to poor plater; dam, unplaced 5 times in France, is half-sister to champion American mare Old Hat; unquoted when behind in maiden races at Bath and Wolverhampton in October. *D. Marks.* –

BEAU CHAT 3 ch.c. Morston 125–Kitten 102 (Pardal 130) (1979 NR 1980 7.6f 10d 8g 10g) small, quite attractive colt; no sign of ability in maiden and minor events. *A. Breasley.* –

BEAUCOUP D'ARGENT 2 b.c. Streak 119–Mona's Own (Entanglement 118) (1980 8g 8g) Mar 24; 4,000Y; small, lengthy colt; half-brother to a winning plater; dam never ran; well beaten in end-of-season maiden and minor races at Newmarket. *E. Eldin.* –

BEAUFORT STAR 4 b.f. Great Nephew 126–Fallen Star (Busted 134) (1979 8d 6s* 6f² 5fg 6fg* 6fg* 6d⁴ 5.6fg 6f² 6f³ 1980 6fg 6fg⁴ 6fg⁴ 6fg 6g⁴ 5f³ 6g³ 5d 5f 6g 7g 7d) strong, useful-looking filly; sprint handicapper; has very good early pace; acts on any going; suitable mount for an apprentice; sometimes bandaged in front; occasionally sweats up. *H. Collingridge.* **75**

BEAUFORT STREET 9 gr.g. Right Boy 137–Toccata (Kythnos 126) (1979 6s 6v 8g 6f 6fg 5f 1980 5g 5fg) plater nowadays; stays 7f; acts on any going; sometimes wears blinkers; often reluctant to race and is best left alone. *A. Dalton.* –

BEAUMAINS (USA) 2 b.g. Advocator–Firstboam (First Landing) (1980 6f 7fg) Apr 20; half-brother to several winners, including 2 very useful stakes winners by Tobin Bronze and 3-y-o stakes winner Stiff Diamond (by Delta Judge), a very useful winner at up to 8.5f; dam stakes-placed winner over 5f at 2 yrs; unquoted when behind in sizeable fields in maiden and minor events at Lingfield in the autumn. *J. Sutcliffe.* –

BEAU REEF 4 gr. or ro.c. Mill Reef 141–La Speroana 68 (Roan Rocket 128) (1979 8d 8d 11g² 12g² 13.3s* 12fg* 12fg² 13s² 12f² 14.6g* 1980 12d* 12f 16fg* 16d 12f* 14s*) well-made colt; improved and developed into a smart handicapper; put up excellent performances when making all at Kempton in April (kept on strongly to beat Al Kuwait a length) and May (never in danger when scoring by 2½ lengths from Heighlin); ran disappointingly when favourite for Coral Northumberland Plate at Newcastle in June but was in fine form on his return, winning at Newmarket (on disqualification of Morvetta, who beat him a head) and York, both in October; stayed on dourly to beat Path of Peace by 2 lengths in Sam Hall Memorial Trophy on latter course after Sea Pigeon had fallen when going easily 2f out; stays well; acts on any going; genuine; well suited by strong handling and was ridden by W. Carson when successful in 1980. *J. Dunlop.* **116**

BEAUX ARTS (FR) 2 ch.c. Luthier 126–Bon Appetit 107 (Major Portion 129) (1980 8g²) June 1; tall colt; brother to French 3-y-o 11f winner Blithe Spirit, and half-brother to French 1½m winner Battledress (by Run The Gantlet); dam, useful at up to 1¼m in France, is daughter of 1,000 Guineas and Oaks winner Sweet Solera; 12/1 for 17-runner minor event at Newmarket in November and **83** p showed plenty of promise, making up ground hand-over-fist up hill to take second place, 2½ lengths behind longer-priced stable-companion Video Tape; will stay 1½m; has scope and can win races at 3 yrs. *H. Cecil.*

BE BETTER 5 b.h. Busted 134–Hecla 117 (Henry the Seventh 125) (1979 8d² 8s² 7d 8d* 8g 8d 8g* 8f* 8f 8d* 8d² 1980 8s³ 8d 7fg 7f 8.5f⁴ 8d 8g* 8g⁴ 8fg² 8d³ 7.6d² 8g⁴ 8s³ 8d 8d) lengthy horse; good walker; useful handicapper; made all when winning Courage Brighton Challenge Cup in July by 5 lengths from Haddfan; in frame on most of his other starts, notably when third to King's Ride in William Hill Lincoln at Doncaster in March on reappearance and to My Hollow in Desmond Stakes at the Curragh in September on thirteenth start; best form at up to 1m; acted on any going; usually most consistent, although didn't run up to his best last 2 starts (possibly feeling effects of his long season); often gave trouble entering stalls but raced most genuinely; sold 40,000 gns Newmarket December Sales; stud in Cyprus. *I. Balding.* **100**

BECALMED 4 b.f. Right Tack 131–Motionless 109 (Midsummer Night II 117) (1979 8g 7s 8d 12fg 1980 7h 5d) useful sort; plating-class maiden; not bred to stay 1½m. *W. Wightman.* **—**

BEDFORD (USA) 2 b.c. Nijinsky 138–Drumtop (Round Table) (1980 7f 7d²) useful-looking colt; good mover; brother to American 1¼m winner Kyra's Slipper, closely related to very useful USA sprinter Topsider (by Northern Dancer) and half-brother to 2 winners, including smart 1979 2-y-o stakes winner War of Words (by Arts and Letters); dam top-class American middle-distance filly; ran on strongly under hard driving but failed by ¾ length to catch Sunley Builds in 14-runner Houghton Stakes at Newmarket in October; will be suited by middle distances; sure to win races at 3 yrs. *I. Balding.* **88**

BEDLAM HILL 6 b.g. Mummy's Pet 125–Acton Sattalite 79 (Gilles de Retz 132) (1979 5g 5f 6g 6fg⁴ 6h 6f 1980 10s 10g) one-time useful handicapper; best form at 6f on a sound surface and is not certain to stay 1¼m; has been tried in blinkers; winning hurdler. *J. W. Watts.* **—**

BEECH DALE 2 b.f. The Go-Between 129–Wasdale 97 (Psidium 130) (1980 5fg 5fg 5g) Apr 15; 680F, 1,650Y; light-framed filly; half-sister to 2 winners, including 1½m winner Caspardale (by Frankincense); dam won 5 races at 5f and 6f; behind in maiden and minor events; off course over 2 months after second outing; trained first 2 starts by J. Hardy. *F. Dever.* **—**

BEECHWOOD CON 4 ch.g. Siliconn 121–Look Out 84 (Vimy 132) (1979 12g 8s³ 8f* 8f* 10g⁴ 1980 8.2s) plater; stays 1m (well beaten when tried at further); acts well on firm going; wore bandages final outing in 1979. *R. E. Peacock.* **—**

BEECHWOOD SEEKER 2 b.g. Status Seeker–Julie's Gi-Gi (Brave Invader) (1980 6s 6s 7g 7fg* 7d 8.2s² 8g² 8.2v³ 8s) Apr 20; 500F, 1,000Y; workmanlike gelding; good walker; brother to a winner in Norway, and half-brother to a winning hurdler; dam poor Irish maiden; attracted no bid after getting up close home to beat Norman's Boy a neck in seller at Newcastle in July; second subsequently in nurseries at Hamilton and York (2½ lengths behind Stormy Jim in October); will stay 1¼m; seems to act on any going; ran well in blinkers eighth start and moderately without them on final appearance. *K. Stone.* **68**

BEELEIGH 2 b.g. Sallust 134–Mythical Lady 86 (Track Spare 125) (1980 6d 7fg 7g² 6fg²) Apr 7; 14,000Y; workmanlike gelding; second foal; half-brother to French 3-y-o 5f winner Casimir (by Blue Cashmere); dam won from 5.3f to 1¼m; found one too good for him when well-backed favourite for 2 maiden races, going down by ½ length to Golden Brigadier, after being clear into straight at Chester in August and failing by a length to hold off Miss St James's at Carlisle the following month; seems barely to stay 7f. *N. Callaghan.* **82**

BE FRIENDLY TOO 3 ch.f. Be Friendly 130–Cann-Tack 90 (Sound Track 132) (1979 5s 5.8s 6s⁴ 6d 5.9g 7s 1980 8.2g 12.2f 7g 12.5s²) sharp sort; ex-Irish; half-sister to Irish 5f winner Attuned (by Faberge II) and a winner in Greece; dam won twice over 5f at 2 yrs; second in amateur riders race at Stockton in October, easily best effort; stays 1½m; acts on soft going; sometimes wears blinkers. *W. Wright.* **45**

BEGGAR'S BRIDGE 5 br.h. Linacre 133–Monsel (Hook Money 124) (1979 10fg 10d³ 10.5s* 10.2f³ 10fg² 9f 12s³ 1980 10s 10s³ 12f 10.4f 12g 10g* 10.5g 12f* 10.5g* 12s² 10g 12d⁴ 10g) strong, good-looking horse; very useful performer; made all when unchallenged winner of Falmouth Handicap at York in August, beating Tolstoy by 7 lengths; successful earlier at Sandown (beat Mirror Boy by 3 lengths in Hong Kong Handicap) and Ascot (very leniently treated owing to handicapping error when getting home by ¾ length from Shaftesbury); ran easily best subsequent races when ½-length second to Nicke **115**

in Stockholm Cup at Taby in September and when 4 lengths fourth to Shining Finish in St Simon Stakes at Newbury in October; says 1½m; acts on any going but is well suited by some give in the ground. *R. Laing.*

BEGGAR'S BUSH (USA) 2 gr.g. Al Hattab–Sailly Le Sec (Yorky) (1980 5f 5d² 6d² 5.8f² 7d² 7h⁴ 8d³ 8d²) May 21; $19,000Y; small, lightly-made gelding; second living foal; dam won 9 races at up to 1¼m from 3 yrs to 7 yrs; second in maiden races and nurseries, running best race when beaten 2 lengths by Piping Queen at Wolverhampton in October on final occasion; will stay 1¼m; seems to act on any going. *H. Candy.* **80**

BEHAVE (FR) 3 b.f. Brigadier Gerard 144–Broadway Dancer 131 (Northern Dancer) (1979 NR 1980 8g³ 8.2g) smallish, quite well-made filly; first foal; dam won Prix Morny by 6 lengths; ran well for a newcomer to be 5½ lengths third of 7 to Etching (gave 9 lb) in £3,200 event at Doncaster in September; didn't fulfil promise of that run when well beaten in maiden race at Nottingham on only subsequent start (odds on); may stay beyond 1m; sold 61,000 gns Newmarket December Sales. *H. Cecil.* **94**

BE IN TOUCH 2 b.f. Windjammer (USA)–Claddie (Karabas 132) (1980 6s) Mar 21; 4,600Y; rather lightly-made filly; first foal; dam unraced half-sister to numerous winners; 33/1 and apprentice ridden at overweight, missed break and was always behind in 12-runner minor event won by Miss Menton at Stockton in October. *P. Rohan.* —

BEIRUT 3 ch.c. Northfields–Shelby (Pall Mall 132) (1979 8fg* 1980 10d² 10g 12f* 12g² 12f³ 10.2g 8s⁴ 10d 10.2v) good sort; won 3-runner event at Beverley in July; ran best other race on first outing (neck second to Dragon's Head in valuable handicap at Sandown) though wasn't disgraced on seventh start; stays 1½m; acts on any going; sweats up nowadays; blinkered sixth (pulled hard), eighth and ninth starts, running badly on last occasion; inconsistent. *W. O'Gorman.* **104** d

BEL BOLIDE (USA) 2 ch.c. Bold Bidder–Lady Graustark (Graustark) (1980 5fg* 6d³ 6g* 6g² 6g* 6f²) **119**

Izaak Walton's assertion that 'there is no good horse of a bad colour'

Gimcrack Stakes, York—Bel Bolide has a length to spare over Parkdale (left). Poldhu is third and Brooklyn Prince fourth

received further support from the exploits of Bel Bolide. This colt's flashy colouring—chesnut with blaze and four long white socks, one of which reaches above the knee—is just the sort often held to denote softness and unreliability, but few two-year-olds of 1980 ran more consistently than he. Most of Bel Bolide's efforts were distinguished by his enthusiasm, none more than when he gained his most important success in the Gimcrack Stakes at York's August meeting. For a race worth over £27,000 to the winner the field there was a modest one: of the nine runners only two, the odds-on Age Quod Agis and the National Stakes winner Penmarric, had previously won a pattern race and both of these had been beaten when tackling the French two-year-olds in the Prix Robert Papin. Bel Bolide had no trouble in taking an early lead in the Gimcrack and was clearly travelling very smoothly as he set the pace ahead of Age Quod Agis and the Irish colt Brooklyn Prince. Quickening from two furlongs out, he had his two pursuers beaten off by the distance only to face new challenges from the Northern colt Parkdale, who was running on strongly under hard riding from Piggott, and Poldhu. Neither quite managed to reach Bel Bolide who kept on to score by a length from Parkdale.

The general opinion was that Poldhu would have given Bel Bolide a lot to do had he not had to be checked and switched about a furlong out. However, when Bel Bolide and Poldhu met again in the William Hill Middle Park Stakes at Newmarket in October, Bel Bolide started favourite and beat him by two lengths, half a length further than at York. He didn't win though. Again he broke very fast and was soon striding along in the lead but with a furlong to run he was being hotly pressed by Mattaboy. Despite running on most gallantly Bel Bolide couldn't quite match the finishing speed of his sprint-bred rival and he went down by half a length. A smart effort nonetheless.

Bel Bolide's record prior to the Gimcrack had shown him to be an improving colt but also rather a green one. He had won a maiden race at Kempton in May on his debut, making his task more difficult by jumping a path early on and losing his action, and he'd had no difficulty in disposing of his two opponents in the Black Duck Stakes at York. He had also been placed in the Coventry Stakes at Royal Ascot and in the Richmond Stakes at Goodwood, the latter of which he should have won. After most of the ten runners came to the final

Mr K. Abdulla's "Bel Bolide"

two furlongs in the Richmond Stakes holding every chance, Bel Bolide and the 16/1-shot Another Realm started to draw away. Bel Bolide, pushed along by Carson, held a narrow advantage and looked the likely winner until he ducked slightly left away from the whip and became a shade unbalanced with about seventy-five yards to run, giving his rival the advantage. Quickly straightened, he rallied gamely but the post came too soon and Another Realm held him off by a head.

Bel Bolide (USA) (ch.c. Feb 5, 1978)	Bold Bidder (b 1962)	Bold Ruler (b 1954)	Nasrullah
			Miss Disco
		High Bid (b 1956)	To Market
			Stepping Stone
	Lady Graustark (ch 1969)	Graustark (ch 1963)	Ribot
			Flower Bowl
		Inyala (ch 1963)	My Babu
			Roman Rhonda

Bel Bolide, a rangy, quite attractive colt, cost 310,000 dollars as a yearling, the second highest price of the twenty-three Bold Bidder yearlings sold in the USA in 1979. Although, in our opinion, he's a little way removed from the top class he's already recouped about £57,000 towards his purchase price and is just the type to go on improving as a three-year-old. Bold Bidder, unraced as a two-year-old, has sired some excellent juveniles, such as Spectacular Bid, Auction Ring and Highest Trump, but most of his stock is at least as effective later on. Bel Bolide's dam, Lady Graustark, won twice at up to six furlongs at two years and has got off to a fine start at stud, producing a winner in Holland and two winners in the USA from her three previous foals. Easily best of the three, none of whom won at two years, was the Nijinsky filly Excitable who showed very useful form at around a mile both as a three- and four-year-old. Lady Graustark's fifth foal, a filly by Gallant Romeo, fetched 350,000 dollars at the 1980 Keeneland Selected Yearling Sale. The grandam, Inyala, was a very useful winner over sprint distances and has bred three winners besides Lady Graustark, most notably the filly Inyala's Goody, a stakes winner in 1980.

Bel Bolide's pedigree suggests that he'll be well suited by seven furlongs and a mile at three years. It's not out of the question that he will stay even further but he was a free-running sort at two years and he'll need to settle more to do so. An excellent mover with a long stride, he acts well on firm going; his one run on a soft surface wasn't nearly conclusive enough to say whether or not he acted on it. A galloping course will always suit him best. *J. Tree.*

BELDALE FLUTTER (USA) 2 b.c. Accipiter–Flitter Flutter (Cohoes) **127**
(1980 6fg^4 7.2d* 7f* 8fg^4 8d*)

Two-year-olds in training sales may be a novelty in England (and an unwelcome one, too, judged by the results of the Doncaster Sales over the last four years) but they are well established in the United States. The Florida Sales, the pioneers of this type of event, have long been successfully patronised by European trainers—the 1979 Prix Robert Papin winner Choucri was a Hialeah purchase—and in recent years the California Thoroughbred Breeders Association sales have attracted similar attention. Although the exploits of Alleged, who topped the 1976 sale at Hollywood Park, have fostered the interest now being shown by European buyers, Alleged is not the only big winner to have emerged from the Californian sales—Bold 'N Determined, an outstanding three-year-old filly who won both the Coaching Club American Oaks and the Acorn Stakes, was bought there for 70,000 dollars in 1979 and Beldale Flutter was bought there only seven months before his win in the William Hill Futurity Stakes.

Theoretically it should be much easier to separate the wheat from the chaff at these sales: by and large the animals look much more the finished product than those sold at the yearling sales, especially with having the benefit of a warm climate; and, perhaps more importantly, potential buyers have the opportunity of seeing the two-year-olds worked on the track beforehand. In practice, though, it seems that it's just as easy to make a big mistake at this type of sale as at any other—when Beldale Flutter, who had already changed hands for 32,000 dollars as a foal and for 20,000 dollars as a yearling, went through the ring he attracted so little attention that he was knocked down again for a mere 20,000 dollars, a figure over 30,000 dollars short of the average for the 'preferred' part of the sale and 385,000 dollars less than the top-priced colt.

Beldale Flutter's win in the Futurity at Doncaster in October came as a surprise to most people. He had gained his two successes by only narrow

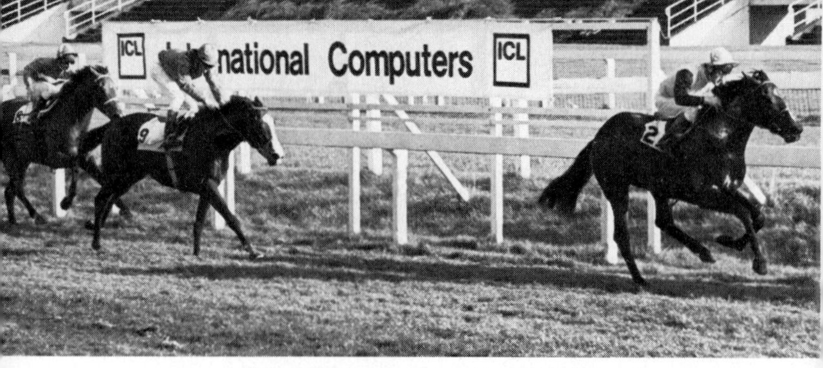

William Hill Futurity, Doncaster—Beldale Flutter wins from Shergar and Sheer Grit

margins, having half a length to spare over Baz Bombati in a small race at Haydock in August and little more in hand when landing the valuable Grand Criterium International d'Ostende from Wicked Will later in the month. And though clearly improving with every race he had found three too good for him, admittedly all previous pattern-race winners, when a 25/1-shot for the Royal Lodge Stakes at Ascot in September on his last appearance. Beldale Flutter put up a very bold display in the Royal Lodge, taking up the running turning into the straight and then battling on so well, despite showing a tendency to wander on the firmish ground, that Robellino, Recitation and Gielgud had to struggle hard to go past in the final furlong.

Considering that Robellino and Recitation beat Beldale Flutter by only one and three quarter lengths and one and a quarter lengths respectively at Ascot, it was perhaps a little surprising that when the three met again at Doncaster they should start at 2/1 and 9/4 while Beldale Flutter was easy to back at 14/1, particularly since Beldale Flutter's trainer made it clear that he expected an improved display on the dead ground. An improved display he got! As another outsider, the progressive Busted colt Sheer Grit, set out to make the running at a fast pace, Beldale Flutter was soon giving chase. It became clear early in the straight that the favourite Robellino wasn't going to take a hand in the finish, and, as Beldale Flutter went into a narrow lead from the pace-maker with a quarter of a mile to run, Recitation too started to weaken. Beldale Flutter took the best part of a furlong to shake off Sheer Grit, by which time Piggott had worked the well-fancied Shergar into a challenging position. That however was as close as Shergar was to get, and Beldale Flutter forged on under pressure in the final furlong to beat him by two and a half lengths, Sheer Grit holding on to third place a further two lengths behind.

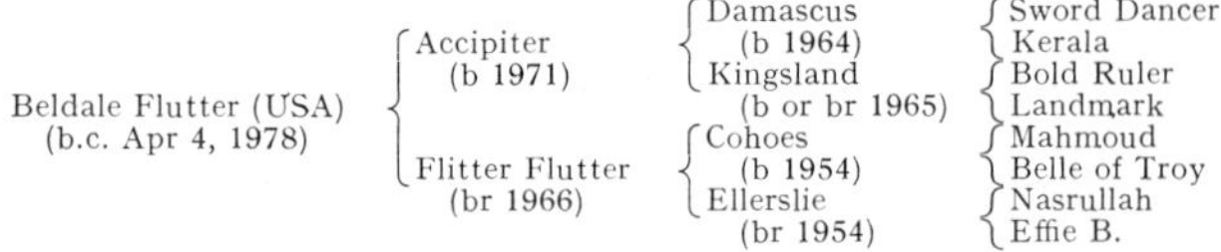

Beldale Flutter (USA) (b.c. Apr 4, 1978)	Accipiter (b 1971)	Damascus (b 1964)	Sword Dancer
			Kerala
		Kingsland (b or br 1965)	Bold Ruler
			Landmark
	Flitter Flutter (br 1966)	Cohoes (b 1954)	Mahmoud
			Belle of Troy
		Ellerslie (br 1954)	Nasrullah
			Effie B.

The post-race reaction to Beldale Flutter's win seemed unduly critical, with most journalists discounting his classic prospects and odds as long as 25/1 being freely available about his chance in the Two Thousand Guineas. Certainly Robellino and Recitation ran too far below form to base any assessment of Beldale Flutter on them—Recitation had most probably not recovered from his trip to France thirteen days before when he'd won the Grand Criterium—but there are grounds for thinking that Beldale Flutter put up a high-class performance at Doncaster. For one thing the time was very fast in the conditions; for another, while Shergar and Sheer Grit are very much unknown quantities they are well-bred, highly-regarded colts who had done little wrong between them, winning three of their four previous races; and then Beldale

Flutter had over nine lengths in hand of the fifth horse, the consistent Admiral's Heir who had won five of his last six races and been beaten little more than four lengths by Gielgud when eighth in the Laurent Perrier Champagne Stakes. We take the view that Beldale Flutter simply left his previous form behind, as he'd been doing all season. Should the ground be on the soft side for the Guineas his chance at this stage looks as good as that of any of the other established English colts with the exception of To-Agori-Mou.

Michael Jarvis has expressed the opinion that Beldale Flutter, a shapely colt, is more a Guineas than a Derby candidate. This opinion is supported by Beldale Flutter's pedigree. Neither Accipiter, his sire, nor Flitter Flutter, his dam, won over further than a mile and the furthest any of his five winning half-brothers and half-sisters has won over is ten and a half furlongs. Easily the best of Flitter Flutter's previous winners was the smart 1976 two-year-old Our Jimmy, who showed all his best form over six furlongs although he was by the Ribot horse Tom Rolfe. Neither of Flitter Flutter's wins came in events of any importance but she is half-sister to the smart Low Son, winner of the seven-furlong World's Playground Stakes as a two-year-old, and to Short Fall, winner of a stakes race over a mile; another half-sister, the unraced Candy's Best, is the dam of Candy Eclair, the joint-top two-year-old filly in the USA in 1978 and a very good winner both in 1979 and 1980.

Accipiter had a remarkably arduous time even by American standards for a horse of his class as a three-year-old, running no less than twenty-six times for seven wins, including successes in two stakes races over a mile, the Withers and the Saranac. His efforts evidently took their toll since he managed only three more outings, none of them successful, over the next two seasons before retiring to stud. His first runners, which appeared in 1979, included Accipiter's Dream, a speedy filly who was rated only 6 lb behind the top two-year-old filly in the USA. Accipiter is one of several promising young stallions by Damascus, a horse of outstanding ability and versatility who won over distances from six furlongs to two miles. With Damascus and Cohoes as his grandsires, the latter a winner of stakes races at up to nine and a half furlongs, Beldale Flutter must have reasonable prospects of staying a mile and a quarter. It's worth stressing that although he has won on firm going he seems best suited by some give in the ground. *M. Jarvis.*

BELDALE GUNFLINT (USA) 3 br.c. Gunflint–Irish Sister (Needles) (1979 6f^2 6g^4 7s* 7f 8f^2 8g 1980 10fg^3 7fg^2 8g^2 7g 8g^3 8fg) lengthy, attractive colt; good walker and mover; smart (rated 118) at 2 yrs; didn't run up to his best in 1980 although placed 4 times in varied company, including when runner-up to runaway winner Dalsaan in £3,200 race at Kempton in May and to Millbank (USA), beaten 4 lengths, in £2,800 event at Newbury following month; should stay 1¼m; acts on any going. *M. Jarvis.* **84**

BELDALE HILARITY (USA) 2 br.c. Fast Hilarious–Jamie's Court (Assagai) (1980 7d 7g 7d^3 8g 8.2s^3) Apr 13; $40,000 2-y-o; well-made, attractive colt; second foal; dam won twice at up to 1m at 3 yrs, including a claiming race; third in maiden races at Ayr in August and Hamilton (4¾ lengths behind Sage King) in September; will stay 1¼m+; yet to race on a firm surface; sold to German International Bloodstock 6,200 gns Newmarket Autumn Sales. *M. Jarvis* **82**

BELDALE LEADER (USA) 2 b.c. Mr Leader–Aptobe Fleet (Fleet Nasrullah) (1980 7g 7g 8.2s) May 4; $35,500 2-y-o; very good-looking colt; very good mover; half-brother to 3 winners, including stakes-placed Pirate Fleet (by Envoy); dam won at up to 1m; made running to distance when seventh of 15 to Kalaglow in minor event at Sandown in August, second outing; well backed, going well 3f out but found little and eventually finished eighth of 20 to Irish Heart in maiden race at Haydock in October; will stay 1¼m; probably unsuited by soft going. *M. Jarvis.* **74**

BELDALE QUEEN 3 b.f. African Sky 124–Quite a Storm 87 (Quorum 126) (1979 NR 1980 6d 7f 8s 7.2d 7fg 5fg) 1,300F, 9,000Y, 680 2-y-o; strong, compact filly; half-sister to 1978 2-y-o 5f winner Bay Tempest (by Swing Easy) and a winner in Norway; dam best at up to 1m; well beaten in varied company, including selling; trained first outing by M. Jarvis. *M. Camacho.* —

BELDALE ROBBER (USA) 2 b.c. No Robbery–Rock Diamond (Princely Gift 137) (1980 6g 7fg 7s^3) Mar 31; $18,000Y, $37,000 2-y-o; compact colt; half-brother to numerous winners, including French 1m and 9f winner Radetzky March and 1976 2-y-o 5f winner Aroche (both by Forli); dam won at 2 yrs and 3 yrs in USA; 8 lengths third of 14 to Royal Heritage in minor event at Chepstow in **64**

October; in rear in good-class races at Doncaster and Ascot previously; will stay 1¼m. *M. Jarvis.*

BELFORT (FR) 3 gr.c. Tyrant–Belle de Retz 104 (Gilles de Retz 132) (1979 6d 7.5g 1980 5s 6g* 7g 5g 5.8g^{2} (dis) 5g 5d^{2} 5d 5v) 170,000 francs Y (approx £20,000); small, quite well-made ex-French colt; half-brother to 3 winners in France, notably smart 1969 2-y-o 4.5f and 6.5f winner Belmont (by Cambremont); dam won 3 races over 5f at 2 yrs in this country and subsequently won at up to 1m in France; won 20-runner maiden race at Brighton in August; twice ran creditably in handicaps subsequently; stays 6f; yet to race on a firm surface; blinkered final outing; trained by P. Read first start. *A. Breasley.* **65**

BELGIO (FR) 3 b.c. Djakao 124–Tosta (Timour 112) (1979 6fg^{2} 6.5g* 8g 7.5g^{2} 7.5s^{3} 10v^{2} 1980 11g 12fg^{3} 10.5fg* 12fg 12.5d) first living foal; dam minor 2-y-o 5f winner; 16/1, kept on strongly to win 13-runner Prix Lupin at Longchamp in May by ½ length from Argument with In Fijar a short head away third; ran best other race in Prix Hocquart on same course a week earlier (2½ lengths third to Mot D'Or); well beaten in Prix du Jockey-Club at Chantilly (reportedly knocked a knee) and Grand Prix de Saint-Cloud on his last 2 outings; stays 1½m; seems to act on any going. *J. Cunnington, jnr, France.* **122**

BELLA PASQUA 8 b.m. Chebs Lad 120–Aristocratic Lady (Florus 110) (1979 NR 1980 12d) lightly raced and of no account. *R. Allan.* –

BELLA TRAVAILLE 2 b.f. Workboy 123–Thorganby Bella (Porto Bello 118) (1980 5g* 5f 5f^{3} 5fg^{2} 5f 5g 5fg^{2} 5g* 5f 5g 5f 5f 5d) Mar 13; lengthy filly; first foal; dam ran twice; won maiden race at Hamilton in April and nursery at Redcar in August, making all in latter to beat Mementa Mia a length; speedy and is unlikely to stay 6f; acts on firm going; genuine; sweated up when blinkered eleventh outing. *R. Hobson.* **82**

BELLCO 2 b.f. Comedy Star 121–Vectis 75 (Quorum 126) (1980 6g) Feb 13; first foal; dam, half-sister to Cesarewitch winner Centurion, won over 13f; 33/1, backward and ridden by 7-lb claimer, always behind in 20-runner maiden race at Leicester in November won by Nello. *A. Pitt.* –

BELLEAIR DREAM 2 b.f. Tower Walk 130–Dowerless (Busted 134) (1980 5fg^{4}) Apr 24; 5,200F; lengthy filly; first produce; dam once-raced half-sister to very smart 6f to 1m winner Mark Anthony; easy in market and on backward side, showed promise when running on to finish 7½ lengths fourth of 16 to Bel Bolide in maiden race at Kempton in May, only outing. *F. Durr.* –

BELLE CHAT 5 ch.m. Caliban 123–Kitten 102 (Pardal 130) (1979 8g 8fg 6f 10fg 12s 1980 10.2d) plating-class maiden; has worn blinkers. *W. Musson.* –

BELLE MELANIE (FR) 4 br.f. Roi Lear 126–Belle Margot (Counsel 118) (1979 8v 8s 10s 8g^{4} 8g^{3} 9g 8s^{3} 8d 8g 9s 8g 8g^{4} 8d 7g 10.5s 1980 9g 10g^{2} 8fg 8g^{4} 9g^{4} 10s 11.7g^{4} 10g 10.8d) ex-French filly; fourth foal; dam won at 1½m in France; in frame in handicaps at Maisons-Laffitte in April, Saint-Cloud in May and Chantilly in June when trained by H. van de Poele and in minor event at Windsor in September; stays 1¼m; wore blinkers in France; well beaten last 2 starts. *R. Akehurst.* –

BELLE SOUK 2 ch.f. Native Bazaar 122–Belle Bergere 104 (Faberge II 121) (1980 8fg 8d 10d^{4}) leggy, lightly-made filly; first reported foal; dam won at up to 1½m; well-beaten fourth of 18 behind very easy winner Alabama in seller at Leicester in October; probably stays 1¼m. *P. Cole.* –

BELLE VUE 7 b.g. Track Spare 125–Royal Camp 91 (Sovereign Path 125) (1979 10s 9s 8s^{4} 7s^{3} 8.2g 9fg^{2} 8.2fg^{2} 8.2f^{2} 8d* 8f 9fg^{4} 8.2g^{2} 8g 9g 8fg 8.2s 8.2s 7d 1980 8s 7g 8fg 8s 9g 8fg^{4} 8.2g* 8fg^{4} 8s^{4} 8f 8g* 9g 8d^{3} 8.2s^{3}) neat gelding; won handicap at Hamilton in July, and valuable seller (no bid) at Doncaster in September, latter by 4 lengths from Wise Man; stays 9f; acts on any going; used to wear blinkers; occasionally sweats up; suitable mount for an inexperienced rider. *R. Mason.* **63**

BELL HOP 4 b.g. Connaught 130–Haybells (Klairon 131) (1979 8s^{2} 1980 12s) smallish, compact gelding; second in maiden race at Warwick early in 1979; having first subsequent outing on flat when behind in apprentice event at Chepstow in October; won over hurdles in between. *P. Mitchell.* –

BELLICOSA 2 ch.f. Porto Bello 118–Tavira (Prince Tenderfoot 126) (1980 5fg* 5f^{3} 5fg^{3} 5fg 6fg^{3} 5g 5f^{2} 6fg 6fg^{2} 5d 6d 6g 7v) Apr 26; 1,300Y; leggy filly; first foal; dam unraced granddaughter of 1,000 Guineas and Oaks runner-up Spree; won maiden auction event at Salisbury in May by 4 lengths from Lady Acquiesce; ran creditably on several of her subsequent outings, twice finishing **76**

Prix Lupin, Longchamp—Belgio wins this valuable prize in a close finish with Argument and In Fijar (hidden). The first three are followed by Saint Jonathon, Corvaro and Blast Off

second in nurseries, but made little show from a moderate draw in valuable seller on eleventh start; suited by 6f (had stiffish task over 7f); probably needs a sound surface; wears blinkers; sold 3,000 gns Newmarket December Sales. *Mrs J. Reavey.*

BELLINO 3 b.f. Andrea Mantegna–Idle Spell 83 (Galivanter 131) (1979 5s 1980 8s 11fg4 12fg 13s 16g4 16.1d 10s 16s 16fg 16d 16s) plating-class maiden; suited by a test of stamina. *W. Musson.* —

BELLOC 2 b.c. Wollow 132–Fly For Home 78 (Habitat 134) (1980 7g4 7f* 8d2 7d*) May 3; 8,200Y; lengthy, lightly-made colt; second foal; dam, 1½m winner, is half-sister to very smart out-and-out stayer Biskrah; made a lot of running when odds on for small races at Lingfield in October (won by ¾ length from Doc Marten, gave 12 lb) and Leicester the following month (had to struggle to get home by a length from Odin's Raven); failed by only a short head to catch Golden Flak in nursery at Newbury in between; will stay 1½m; seems to act on any going; still looks weak and may make a better 3-y-o. *R. Price.* **103**

BELL-TENT 9 b.g. Bivouac 114–Chilcombe Belle 75 (Robert Barker 125) (1979 10d 10g 11fg 10s2 10fg2 10fg4 10g2 10g4 10fg2 10f 1980 10fg 10h3 10fg 10fg2 10g 10g 8f 10f2 10f 10d) useful handicapper in his day but is on the downgrade; placed at Brighton (twice) and Epsom (didn't have best of runs) but ran poorly on occasions; ideally suited by 1¼m on top-of-the-ground; acts on any track; usually held up; a difficult ride who needs strong handling and has done most of his winning when ridden by P. Eddery. *W. Wightman.* **81** d

BELMONT BAY 3 b.c. Auction Ring 123–Royal Escape 94 (King's Bench 132) (1979 6s* 6f3 6fg 7g* 7g* 1980 7f3 8fg 8d* 8d* 8g 10d) useful sort; very useful performer; 1½-length winner of 2 valuable handicaps at Newmarket in July, beating April Bouquet on first occasion and dead-heaters Parlour Game and Star Way in authoritative fashion in Food Broker's Trophy on second; had earlier finished creditable 3½ lengths third of 13 to Moorestyle in Tote Free Handicap at Newmarket in April; stays 1m (out of his depth in Champion Stakes at Newmarket over 1¼m); acts on any going but is well suited by some give in the ground; to be trained by H. Cecil. *I. Walker.* **111**

BELMONT BLUE 3 br.f. Kashmir II 125–Joie de France (Reliance II 137) (1979 NR 1980 8f 12fg 10s 8f 10s 10s*) 11,000Y; neat filly; closely related to good Mexican winner French Pageant (by Welsh Pageant); dam won over 1½m in Ireland; 25/1 and blinkered when showing much improved form to win 22-runner maiden race at Nottingham in October; stays 1¼m; acts on soft going; sold 7,000 gns Newmarket Autumn Sales. *I. Walker.* **75**

BELOPERONE 3 b.f. Porto Bello 118–Miss Bubbly 78 (Track Spare 125) (1979 NR 1980 7f 6f 7d) useful-looking filly; no sign of ability in newcomers and maiden events; sold 675 gns Ascot October Sales. *W. Wightman.* —

BELVOIR ROSE 2 b.f. Dubassoff–Rothwell Rose (Henry the Seventh 125) (1980 5d 6g 6g 7fg 7.2d 8fg) Apr 8; lengthy filly; third foal; dam ran only at 2 yrs; poor maiden. *Miss A. Hill-Wood.* —

BELVOIR VALE 2 b.c. Ribero 126–Plumtree Plain (Primera 131) (1980 6fg) May 26; 920F, 4,400Y; fifth foal; half-brother to 3-y-o 11f winner Rock Concert (by Star Appeal); dam 9f French winner; 20/1, in need of race and green, prominent 3f when last of 14 to Welham Green in maiden race at Salisbury in September; may do better over 1½m at 3 yrs. *B. Hills.* —

BE MY SWEET 4 br.f. Galivanter 131–Sweet Councillor (Privy Councillor 125) (1979 8g3 8d4 8f3 8h* 8f 10.2fg4 10fg 1980 8fg 9g2 10g2 9fg4 10d3 10f2 10fg*) compact filly; beat Haverhill Lad by a length in handicap at Beverley **66**

in September; second on same course (twice) and at Ripon (apprentices) earlier; stays 1¼m; acts well on firm going and has yet to race on really soft ground; blinkered last 3 outings. *J. W. Watts.*

BENDING MOMENT (USA) 3 ch.c. Graustark–Curvature (Gallant Man) (1979 NR 1980 10fg 11f) $52,000Y; strong, compact colt; second foal; dam unraced sister to Gentleman's Word and Draft Card, very useful stakes winners at up to 9f; very unfit when out of first 9 in large fields of maidens at Salisbury and Newbury in May. *N. Gaselee.* —

BENDOLUS 3 br.g. Bend A Bow–Last Rose (Don't Look 107) (1979 NR 1980 8fg 13s 12g 15.5fg) tall gelding; first foal; dam never ran; no sign of ability in maiden races; blinkered fourth start. *H. Westbrook.* —

BENEFACTOR (USA) 3 b. or br.c. Bold Bidder–Princess Pout (Prince John) (1979 NR 1980 10g 10g 12fg*) $700,000Y; third living foal; half-brother to dual Prix de l'Arc de Triomphe winner Alleged (by Hoist the Flag); dam won 13 races in USA, most of them at 4 yrs and 5 yrs, and showed high-class form at up to 9f on grass; not raced after landing odds in 10-runner maiden race at Naas in July by 8 lengths from Mr Representer; suited by 1½m; acts well on firm ground; racing in USA. *V. O'Brien, Ireland.* ?

BENEFICE (USA) 2 b.c. Damascus–Shuvee (Nashua) (1980 8s*) **109** p

As so often these days the O'Brien stable houses not only the champion Irish two-year-old but also a very strong back-up team. Supporting Storm Bird, the ante-post favourite for the Two Thousand Guineas and Derby, are Critique, beaten only a short head in the Grand Criterium, the promising Nijinsky colt Kings Lake, the once-raced winner Last Light and pattern race winners Benefice, Euclid and Lawmaker, as well as several beautifully-bred colts who have yet to race. One of the most promising of the stable's two-year-

Mr Daniel Schwartz's "Benefice"

olds after Storm Bird and Critique is Benefice, winner of the Ashford Castle Stakes at the Curragh in September on his only start.

Although the field for the Ashford Castle wasn't outstanding, all seven of the other runners had won at least once and Benefice had a very stiff task; he received no more than 4 lb from any of the others and met some at level weights. Benefice started favourite, punters no doubt taking account of the fact that the O'Brien stable had provided the last five winners of the race. One opponent that Benefice met at level weights was Master Thatch, the colt who had chased home Storm Bird at a distance of four lengths in the National Stakes, and it was Master Thatch who proved his main rival. Benefice quickly moved into second place as Master Thatch made the running, and stayed there until coming through to dispute the lead inside the final quarter mile. By this stage the only other source of danger was the English challenger Wicked Will, who'd been runner-up to Beldale Flutter and Sheer Grit on his last two starts, but his run petered out inside the last furlong and Benefice wore down the pacemaker to win by three quarters of a length. Although Benefice's form falls some way short of top class, he achieved much more than the vast majority of animals do on their first outing.

Benefice (USA) (b.c. Apr 17, 1978)	Damascus (b 1964)	Sword Dancer (ch 1956)	Sunglow
			Highland Fling
		Kerala (b 1958)	My Babu
			Blade of Time
	Shuvee (ch 1966)	Nashua (b 1952)	Nasrullah
			Segula
		Levee (ch 1953)	Hill Prince
			Bourtai

Like nearly all the O'Brien horses, Benefice is extremely well bred. Damascus, voted the Horse of the Year as a three-year-old, won twenty-one races including the two-mile Jockey Club Gold Cup, a race won twice by Benefice's dam Shuvee. Shuvee was not only top-class but versatile and durable as well. After being rated the joint-top two-year-old filly in 1968, when she ran thirteen times, she stayed in training until the end of her five-year-old days, winning the Coaching Club American Oaks at three, as did her dam Levee, and being voted champion handicap mare both at four and five. In all she won sixteen times. Benefice is her fifth winner from five foals and the third of note, following the Key To The Mint filly Shukey, a very useful winner at up to a mile at three years, and the Tom Rolfe horse Tom Swift, who didn't come to himself until he was five when he won the thirteen-furlong Seneca Handicap. Shuvee herself is a sister to Nalee, a smart racemare whose numerous good offspring include Meneval, winner of both the Irish St Leger and the Hardwicke Stakes when trained by O'Brien.

There's more stamina in Benefice's make-up than in that of many American breds and he could well develop into a fancied Derby candidate. The 325,000 dollars he cost as a yearling looks money well spent. *V. O'Brien, Ireland.*

BENETTE 2 ch.f. Royben 125–Pretty Mall 86 (Pall Mall 132) (1980 5fg 5d) — Jan 23; 1,550Y; strong filly; half-sister to useful 1973 2-y-o Rupert Bear (by Runnymede) and a winner in Brazil; dam placed over 6f; in rear in maiden races at Wolverhampton in April and Bath in October. *J. Hill.*

BENEVOLENCE (USA) 7 b.g. Never Bend–Amicable 117 (Doutelle 128) — (1979 12f 1980 12fg^3 14.7f^2 12h 16d 12fg 13g) poor handicapper; sometimes wears blinkers; not one to rely on. *W. Clay.*

BENICIA 3 b.f. Lyphard 132–Bashi (Stupendous) (1979 8fg* 8g^2 1980 9.5g^2 **116** 10fg^3 10.5g 10s^2 10d^4 8fg^3 10g* 9.2f^4 10.5g* 10g) strong, good-bodied filly; first foal; dam won from 6.5f to 9.5f in France and is daughter of half-sister to French Derby second Beaugency; raced most consistently and showed smart form in a busy season, winning Prix de Liancourt at Longchamp and Prix de Flore at Saint-Cloud in the autumn; won easily by 1½ lengths from Good To Beat (gave 3 lb) in latter; twice finished only a head behind Luth de Saron in important races at Longchamp, namely Prix Vanteaux and Prix de Malleret, and also ran well when third to Paranete in Prix Saint-Alary at Longchamp again on second start; none too lucky in running when fourth to Hortensia, beaten less than 2 lengths, in Prix de l'Opera at Longchamp on eighth outing (badly hampered 1f out); stays 1¼m well; acts on any going; genuine and consistent. *Mme C. Head, France.*

BENIFORM 2 ch.f. Gold Form 108–Benign 67 (King's Bench 132) (1980 5f 5s) — Mar 6; 120Y; bad walker; half-sister to 4 winners here and abroad, including

Jaffa Speed (by Pall Mall), a useful performer at around 7f in France; dam won 8.5f seller; bandaged in front when always behind in sellers at Ripon in August and Stockton in October (sweating). *J. Wilson.*

BENNY LYNCH 3 b.c. Streetfighter 120–Brighton Girl 96 (Right Boy 137) (1979 5g 6g 6g 5f² 5fg 6s 1980 6s 5v⁴ 6s 5fg 5g 5s 6d 6g² 6g 7fg⁴ 5g 8g 7g 8g 8.2s) well-made colt; plater; suited by 7f; probably acts on any going; sometimes blinkered; has run creditably for a boy. *R. Hannon.* **54**

BENTOP 3 b.g. Kibenka 119–Serena Kate 67 (Ron 103) (1979 NR 1980 14f 10.1s⁴ 8g 7g) plain gelding; poor plater; not certain to stay 1½m; sold 420 gns Ascot October Sales. *D. Dale.* **—**

BEOCAN (FR) 2 ch.g. Cavan–Beobie (Cernobbio 123) (1980 7d 7fg 7f³ 7d* 8g³) Mar 9; small, compact gelding; fifth foal; half-brother to French middle-distance winner Beyaca (by A Tempo) and to a winning stayer in Belgium; dam won at up to 1m; favourite when beating Pearlaway by a neck in 10-runner minor event at Brighton in September; bettered that effort when 3¾ lengths third of 11 to Aperitivo in £4,800 nursery on same course the following month; will stay 1½m; seems to act on any going; sent to Hong Kong. *D. Morley.* **93**

BE PATIENT 2 b.g. Dubassoff–Fighting Winnie (Fighting Charlie 127) (1980 6fg 8.2s 8g) Apr 14; 700Y; third foal; dam never ran; little worthwhile form in maiden races in the North but started slowly first and third outings. *Denys Smith.* **—**

BEPEEN 2 br.g. Green Shoon 102–Little Big Mover (Hot Brandy 119) (1980 5h 5f 5fg³ 10s) third foal; brother to Irish 11f to 2m winner Hamers Flame; dam never ran; 7½ lengths third of 7 to Rathmoy's Sparkle in maiden race at Carlisle in May; gelded subsequently and didn't race again until late-October; should stay 1¼m+. *F. Durr.* **47**

BERNICA (FR) 2 gr.f. Caro 133–Bernicia 81 (Native Prince) (1980 6d* 7g* 8f⁴) Apr 13; attractive, good-bodied filly; third foal; half-sister to French 3-y-o Berfan (by Gay Fandango), a winner from 1m to 1¼m; dam won over 5f at 2yrs and is granddaughter of Oaks winner Masaka; created a very favourable impression when winning first 2 races, justifying favouritism by a length in newcomers event at Chantilly in July and inflicting Phydilla's only defeat on her when beating her ¾ length in Group 3 Prix du Calvados at Deauville the following month; seemed to be given plenty to do when 6/4 favourite for Prix Marcel Boussac (formerly Criterium des Pouliches) at Longchamp in October and was beaten 2¼ lengths into fourth-of-10 position behind Tropicaro; not sure to stay beyond 1m. *F. Boutin, France.* **114**

BERNINI 2 b.c. Balliol 125–Night Fire (Night and Day II) (1980 5g 8d 8d 10d) half-brother to a good winner in Malaya by Welsh Saint; dam won over hurdles in Ireland; only a poor plater. *D. Wintle.* **—**

BERRY ISLAND 3 ch.f. Thatch 136–Home Glo (Globemaster) (1979 NR 1980 6d* 7fg³ 6d 6g) 44,000Y; lightly-made filly; half-sister to 2 winners in USA and one in Italy; dam, twice a winner at up to 6f at 2 yrs in USA, is half-sister to high-class sprinters Home Guard and Boone's Cabin; cantered home in 20-runner maiden race at Nottingham in April; well beaten in varied company afterwards; best run at 6f on a soft surface; ran poorly in blinkers final start. *F. J. Houghton.* **94**

BERTIDA 2 b.f. Porto Bello 118–Miss Bubbly 78 (Track Spare 125) (1980 5d 7g⁴ 6g 7d) Apr 22; useful sort; fourth foal; half-sister to a winning plater; dam 1¼m winner; plater; probably stays 7f. *P. Cole.* **66**

BERTIE ME BOY 5 b.g. Philip of Spain 126–Well Scored 104 (Final Score 113) (1979 8d 8d* 10.2d² 8g 8fg³ 8d 9fg 8d 8.2s 1980 8d 8d 8.2s 8.2s) fairly useful handicapper at his best, but has become disappointing; off course for 6 months before third start; stays 1¼m; seems to act on any going but goes well on a soft surface; usually ridden up with the pace; usually blinkered in 1980. *M. H. Easterby.* **—**

BERTRAM PERSONNEL 3 ch.c. Saintly Song 128–Lady in Trouble 112 (High Treason 126) (1979 5s 7fg 7g⁴ 7fg⁴ 8fg³ 8s² 8fg² 1980 10f⁴ 12.5fg* 12f* 12g² 11g³ 12.3fg* 16f³ 11d 12d 13.8d³ 12.5s³ 12v) leggy, quite useful sort; quite a moderate handicapper; successful at Stockton and Beverley in June and at Newcastle in July; appears not to stay 2m; acts on any going. *J. Etherington.* **82**

BERYL'S GIFT 3 b.f. Sayfar 116–Flying Nun 66 (Welsh Abbot 131) (1979 5v³ 5v 5v⁴ 5s 5g 6fg 7f² 7g³ 6g³ 7fg² 7g 1980 8f 7fg² 7fg 7g⁴ 6g 10g 12d 15.8fg³ **65**

12.2d4 15s) plain, workmanlike filly; seems to stay 15.8f; probably acts on any going; trained by Sir Mark Prescott first 7 outings. *N. Tinkler.*

BE SHARP 2 b.f. Sharpen Up 127–Natasha 87 (Native Prince) (1980 5fg 5fg* 5f 5d 5fg 5f3 5d2 5f 6d) Jan 29; 5,800F; rather leggy, fair sort; half-sister to fairly useful 1978 2-y-o winner Sindys Flame (by Sharp Edge); dam won 3 times over 5f at 2 yrs; made all, despite wandering about, to win 8-runner maiden race at Ayr in May by 2½ lengths from Age of Reason; ran well in nurseries on several occasions subsequently; probably doesn't stay 6f; seems to act on any going; blinkered fourth outing. *J. Berry.* **85**

BESIEGED (USA) 2 b.c. Cannonade–Regal Royal (Swoon's Son) (1980 7d) Apr 9; $80,000Y; fourth foal; half-brother to winners by Canonero and Bold Bidder; dam unraced half-sister to 2 stakes winners; 16/1, blinkered and backward, showed up for long way when 8½ lengths ninth of 14 to Sunley Builds in Houghton Stakes at Newmarket in October; should do better in 1981. *R. Hern.* **— p**

BESOFFEN 5 b.g. Twilight Alley 133–Seldom Sober 58 (Vimy 132) (1979 NR 1980 13.3f 16g) lightly raced and has shown only a little ability; bred to stay long distances. *G. Beeson.* **—**

BEST ALWAYS (USA) 3 ch.c. Vaguely Noble 140–Big Mistake (Barbizon) (1979 NR 1980 8g 8d4) $40,000 2-y-o; quite attractive, well-made colt; half-brother to 3 winners, including French middle-distance winner Maginot (by Jim French); dam stakes-placed winner at up to 1m; moved badly to post when staying-on fourth of 11 to Summer Soldier in maiden race at Salisbury in June, better effort; will be suited by 1¼m+; sold 1,200 gns Newmarket December Sales. *P. Walwyn.* **—**

BEST PORTION 5 ch.g. Major Portion 129–Grass Skirt 77 (Native Prince) (1979 7s 8s 7d 7.6v 7g4 7f4 7f3 7g 8g 8g 7.6fg 1980 8fg) strong, well-made gelding; plater; best form at around 7f; has twice been tried in blinkers; often wears bandages; sold 580 gns Ascot August Sales. *R. Atkins.* **—**

BEST TRADITION 3 b.c. Laser Light 118–Glorious Light 53 (Alcide 136) (1979 5g 5.3f4 5.8h 1980 8fg 7fg3 8.3g 7f 7f 7g) good-topped colt; ran creditably in handicap at Salisbury on second start in May; off course 3 months afterwards and was well beaten on his return; should stay 1m; acts on a firm surface; blinkered final outing; sold 725 gns Ascot November Sales. *C. Nelson.* **61**

BETA GOLD 3 ch.f. Beatic–Fewston Gold 73 (Goldhill 125) (1979 5s 6s 7fg 7g 1980 8f 10.6fg 8g 10.8s 7fg 6s 10fg) strong filly; poor maiden; has been tried in blinkers; sweated up fifth start. *R. Hollinshead.* **—**

BETSY RED 3 ch.f. Mount Hagen 127–My Sierra Leone (Relko 136) (1979 5s 5g 5g 5f3 5f* 5fg4 5d3 6fg3 6f2 6fg3 7d3 1980 6s 6fg* 7f2 6fg* 6g* 7g2 6fg) compact filly; useful handicapper; successful at Brighton (twice) and at Ripon; held on well to beat Denmore a head in Great St Wilfrid Handicap on latter course in August; stays 7f; goes well on top-of-the-ground; genuine and consistent; sold 41,000 gns Newmarket December Sales. *F. Durr.* **99**

BETTER BLESSED 6 br.h. So Blessed 130–Ribetta (Ribocco 129) (1979 6.5v4 6.5s2 8d 10d2 10d4 8g 10d2 10fg 10d 12d 1980 9.5g* 10g3 10s 9g 8d) quite a useful handicapper at his best; won 18-runner 25,000 francs race at Cagnes-sur-Mer in February; ran poorly third and last starts and was brought down in between; stays 1¼m; acts on any going; has run well for an apprentice; none too reliable; blind in one eye. *W. Hastings-Bass.* **—**

BETTYKNOWES 2 b.g. Satingo 129–Djimbaran Bay (Le Levanstell 122) (1980 6g 8d4) Mar 29; strong gelding; third foal; dam won at up to 1½m in France; put in best work in closing stages when 3¾ lengths fourth of 21 to Obrovac in maiden race at Sandown in October; will stay 1½m. *J. Tree.* **80**

BETTY'S BID 2 b.f. Auction Ring 123–Galway Gate (Laser Light 118) (1980 5f 6d 7g 5fg 5d) Apr 9; 520F, 550Y; small filly; first produce; dam unraced half-sister to Royal Hunt Cup winner Picture Boy; poor maiden; blinkered fourth outing. *S. Norton.* **—**

BETTY'S SECRET 3 ch.f. Most Secret 119–Royal Abbess 74 (Fury Royal 108) (1979 5s* 5fg3 6g 6s 5g 1980 5f3 7f 5f 7s 7d 13.8f 12fg) small filly; plater; unlikely to stay 1¾m; acts on any going; often blinkered. *J. Carr.* **41**

BEULAH LAND 2 ch.c. Targowice 130–Angel Chile (Herbager 136) (1980 5fg 5fg 5f3 5fg2 6g* 6s* 7.2d4) Apr 19; 4,000Y; neat, attractive colt; half-brother to 3 winners, including French 3-y-o 1¼m winner Wild Surf (by Mill Reef) and Irish 5f to 7f winner Ballymacarney (by Habitat); dam placed half-sister to high-class 1971 American 2-y-o Tarboosh; favourite when winning **95**

£4,200 Eagle Development Group Stakes at York (beat McCarthy going away by 3 lengths) in June and minor event at Windsor (came home 4 lengths in front of The Cliftonian, pair clear) later in month; most disappointing when 7 lengths last of 4 to Paulager in Cock of the North Stakes at Haydock in July (came under pressure 3f out and was soon beaten), only subsequent start; will stay 1m; acts well on soft going; exported to Trinidad. *R. Armstrong.*

BEVERLEY BOY 8 b.h. Chebs Lad 120–Painful Details (Shantung 132) (1979 $12v^2$ $13s^3$ $12d^3$ 12g* $12fg^4$ 12f $12.2d^3$ 1980 12s 12.2s 12f 12f 14fg 12.2g) middle-distance handicapper; has been hobdayed; revels in the mud; good mount for an apprentice. *G. Huffer.* —

BEWICK 5 b.g. Blakeney 126–Eringa 101 (Saint Crespin III 132) (1979 13s 12d 1980 12d* 12d $12fg^2$) small, compact gelding; fairly useful handicapper; ran on well to beat Bunce Boy by 3 lengths in Operatic Society Challenge Cup at Brighton in June, first outing for more than a year; went down by ¾ length to Aswad on same course in August; will probably stay beyond 1½m; acts on any going except perhaps very soft; retained 2,000 gns Newmarket Autumn Sales. *B. Hobbs.* 93

BEWITCHED 3 br.f. African Sky 124–Pavlova (Fidalgo 129) (1979 NR 1980 $7d^4$ $8g^4$ 12d 8g 9s 8s 10g) 18,000Y; light-framed filly; half-sister to 6 winners, notably high-class Lucky Wednesday (by Roi Soleil), a winner at up to 1¼m; dam Irish 1¼m winner; apprentice ridden when fourth in Southern maiden races in the summer; not certain to stay 1½m. *W. Wightman.* 63

BE YOUR AGE 3 ch.c. Galivanter 131–School Girl (St Chad 120) (1979 $7fg^2$ 7fg $7f^2$ $7s^4$ 1980 7s $7f^4$ $8fg^4$ $7d^3$ 7g 8fg) neat colt; quite a moderate handicapper; probably stays 1m; appears to acts on any going; blinkered nowadays; bandaged off-fore second outing; ran poorly final start. *W. O'Gorman.* 70

BEZIQUE 3 ch.f. Simbir 130–Tell The Bees (Narrator 127) (1979 $6g^2$ 1980 $6s^3$ 6d 8f* $8.5f^3$ 8fg $10g^2$ 10g 10g* 8g 10s) tall, useful sort; won maiden race at Chepstow in May and minor event at Nottingham in September; also ran well when third in valuable handicap at Epsom on fourth start; suited by 1¼m; probably acts on any going. *M. Smyly.* 88

BIAS 4 ch.f. Royal Prerogative 119–Brie 105 (Meldrum 112) (1979 7v $8g^3$ $8g^2$ 8fg* 10f 7.2fg 7g* 7g* 10.4f* 10.2fg* 1980 10.5f 9g 10.2g 9g $8g^2$ 8s $8f^2$ 8.2g) well-made filly; well-backed favourite and carrying 2-lb overweight when runner-up to Crown Witness in Ripon Rowels Handicap in August, running on strongly in last 200 yards and going down by only a short head; had earlier finished creditable second to Cracking Form in 17-runner ladies race at Ascot; broke blood vessel and was pulled up final outing; stays 1¼m well; suited by top-of-the-ground conditions; genuine; an ideal mount for an inexperienced rider. *M. W. Easterby.* 90

BIBBLYOTHECA 2 ch.f Keren 100–Miss Peebles (Twilight Alley 133) (1980 5fg 5fg 6fg 6g 6fg 7f $7g^3$ 8fg) Apr 11; 500 2-y-o (privately); small, light-framed filly; plater; best run at 7f; formerly trained by K. Ivory. *J. Czerpak.* 43

BICESTER GIRL 2 b.f. Easter Island 101–Film Fan (Fast Fox 123) (1980 5fg 5fg 6g 6s 5s 5d 6g) May 19; small, light-framed filly; poor mover; useless plater; has worn blinkers. *K. Bridgwater.* —

BICTON 3 ch.f. Decoy Boy 129–Dominica 71 (Tyrone 130) (1979 6d $7s^3$ 1980 7f $10.1s^4$ $11g^4$) lengthy, quite attractive filly; good walker; fair (rated 84) at 2 yrs; well beaten in 1980; not certain to stay 1¼m; acts on soft going. *J. Hindley.* —

BIDDER'S DREAM 3 b.f. Auction Ring 123–Metrovision (Golden Vision 105) (1979 NR 1980 7f 6g 7f 8.5f 5.8g $5d^3$ $6g^4$ 6fg 5g $5f^4$ 8g) 4,200Y; strong, well-made filly; half-sister to several winners by Gulf Pearl, including Ebor winner Anji; dam poor middle-distance maiden; in frame in Southern maiden races but is only plating class; best form at sprint distances though is bred to stay further; probably acts on any going. *R. Smyth.* —

BIG BELLA 3 ch.f. Joshua 129–Bun (Never Say Die 137) (1979 NR 1980 16f 12fg 12g) big filly; first foal; dam never ran; well beaten in maiden races. *M. Francis.* —

BIG BERTIE 3 ch.g. Tumble Wind–Anfitrite (High Hat 131) (1979 5s 5f $5fg^4$ 5.1g 6f $5s^4$ 1980 8g $8h^4$ $8.2fg^2$ 8fg 11d 12fg 8.2d $10f^4$ $7d^4$ 9s) small, strong gelding; poor plater: best form at up to 8.2f; acts on firm and a soft surface; sometimes blinkered; looked ungenuine fifth start; trained by J. Hardy first 4 outings; sold 1,050 gns Ascot October Sales. *G. Richards.* 38

BIGGLES 2 br.g. Derring-Do 131–Progress (March Past 124) (1980 5fg 6s 7g) Feb 24; 10,500Y; sturdy gelding; fourth foal; dam poor maiden on flat but won a point-to-point; prominent in large fields of maidens at Windsor and Leicester in July on second and third starts, wearing blinkers when 10 lengths sixth of 21 to Show-A-Leg on latter course; will probably stay 1¼m. *G. Harwood.* **64**

BIG JASPER 5 b.h. Sit In The Corner–Bebe Mine (Bleep-Bleep 134) (1979 8fg 10h* 1980 10g) plater; bandaged when tailed off on only outing of 1980 (August); stays 1¼m; acts on hard going; usually wears blinkers. *J. Doyle.* **—**

BIG JOHN (FR) 2 br.c. Gift Card 124–Trelex (Exbury 138) (1980 7d* 8d³ 7.5g*) **125**

If there's a champion among the French two-year-olds of 1980 it hasn't yet shown its true worth. The best French two-year-old race, the Grand Criterium, was dominated by the foreign-trained Recitation and Critique, and only Greenway and The Wonder managed to win more than one of the twenty-one pattern races open to two-year-olds in France.

When the Grand Criterium has passed by and there's still no clear-cut leader among the French-trained colts, the remaining pattern events become of even greater interest. Among these events the Prix Thomas Bryon at Saint-Cloud is perhaps the most significant nowadays. Although it takes place as late as November, by which time many two-year-olds have been put away for the season, it more often than not throws up a really good colt: Targowice beat Kalamoun in the 1972 race before topping the Handicap Optional, the 1975 winner Arctic Tern had Empery back in third place, the high-class milers Kenmare and Bellypha won in 1977 and 1978 respectively and Nureyev trotted up in 1979. Big John, the 1980 winner, has some improvement to make if he's to fare as well as most of those but he has to be regarded as one of the more promising French colts.

All ten of the runners in the Thomas Bryon had won at least once and several had already figured prominently in pattern races: the favourite, Lou Piguet, had followed up his impressive Deauville win with a close-up fourth to Mariacho in the Group 3 Prix Saint-Roman; the Brigadier Gerard filly Marie Noelle had gone down by only a short head to Votre Altesse in another Group 3 event, the Prix des Reservoirs, on her latest start; and Watchdog had been beaten only about three lengths in two Group 1 races, when fourth to Ancient Regime in the Prix Morny and sixth to Recitation in the Grand Criterium. Big John, a 13/1-shot, had also run in a pattern race. Despite his winning debut in a small race at Evry early in September, he'd been one of the least

Prix Thomas Bryon, Saint-Cloud—Big John finishes well to go clear of Watchdog and Lou Piguet

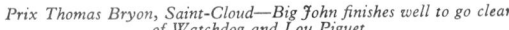

fancied candidates for the Prix des Chenes at Longchamp, a race in which Watchdog started favourite. On that occasion Big John had come out narrowly the worse of the pair as they filled the minor placings behind the length-and-a-half winner Dunphy. He'd looked particularly dangerous halfway up the straight but his run rather fizzled out and he was afterwards found to have swallowed his tongue.

With his tongue tied down in the Thomas Bryon, Big John comfortably turned the tables on Watchdog. Held up in the middle of the field as the useful English colt Blackfoot made the running, he was then forced wide by Bardenac as the field swung into the straight. Blackfoot was in trouble before the final furlong, leaving Watchdog in the lead and looking the likely winner. However Big John had by then started to stretch out in fine style and so well did he finish that he won by two lengths from Watchdog, even though he didn't hit the front until a hundred and fifty yards from the line. Lou Piguet, giving weight to first and second, stayed on to finish third just behind Watchdog, with Blackfoot beaten just over seven lengths into seventh place.

Big John (Fr) (br.c. Feb 16, 1978)	Gift Card (b 1969)	Dan Cupid (ch 1956)	Native Dancer
			Vixenette
		Gracious Gift (b 1958)	Princely Gift
			Malmaison
	Trelex (ch 1971)	Exbury (ch 1959)	Le Haar
			Greensward
		Dentrelic (ch 1965)	Prudent II
			Relict

Big John, who cost 145,000 francs or approximately £15,000 as a yearling, is the second pattern race winner for his sire and the first winner of any kind for his dam, the unraced Trelex. One of her two previous foals, the three-year-old Timonier (by Satingo), has shown only plating-class form in England. Although Big John's grandam, the eleven-furlong winner Dentrelic, died after producing only four foals she made her mark at stud. Her first foal, Worlica, won and became the dam of the St Leger third World Leader, her second is Trelex and her third is Dandy Lute, a very smart colt in France in the mid-'seventies when he won several important races in addition to finishing second in the Prix de la Foret and third in the Poule d'Essai des Poulains.

Gift Card is probably best remembered in England for his defeat of Scottish Rifle and Warpath in the Prince of Wales's Stakes at the 1973 Royal Ascot meeting. He stayed a mile and a quarter well and Big John should stay at least that far. Big John's turn of foot should stand him in good stead and more good races seem sure to come his way. He has yet to race on a firm surface. *E. Chevalier du Fau, France.*

BIG OIL (USA) 3 b. or br.f. Permian–Little Amazon (Intentionally) (1979 NR 1980 10f 8d 8s 12s^{3}) $10,000 2-y-o; quite well-made filly; half-sister to 3 winners in USA; dam ran twice; third in maiden race at Doncaster in November, easily best effort; evidently suited by 1½m on soft going. *A. Breasley.* **63**

BIG PAL 5 gr.g. Pals Passage 115–Queen's Honey (Tudor Treasure 119) (1979 8g 10.2d* 1980 10g 12g^{2} 10d^{3} 12d*) big gelding; made all and went clear in straight when beating Ski's Double by 3 lengths in handicap at Leicester in November; spoilt his chance by hanging when placed at Folkestone and Sandown the previous month; stays 1½m; acts on a soft surface. *G. Harwood.* **79**

BIHAS BOUNTY 4 br.g. Sahib 114–Unclaimed Treasure 61 (Nice Guy 123) (1979 7s 7g 6fg^{4} 6f 6fg 6g 7fg^{2} 8fg 6fg 1980 7fg* 7h^{4} 7fg 7g 7.6d 7fg) good-bodied gelding; fair plater; bought in 3,100 gns after winning at Brighton in April; ran creditably in handicap next time; stays 7f; acts on hard going; usually blinkered in 1980. *A. Pitt.* **53**

BILA SHAKA 2 ch.g. No Mercy 126–Powderhall 81 (Murrayfield 119) (1980 6d 6g) May 25: lightly-made gelding; first foal; dam won 4 races at up to 10.6f; unquoted when behind in maiden races at Newmarket in October. *W. Hastings-Bass.* **—**

BILBAO 5 b.m. Capistrano 120–Astronette (Skymaster 126) (1979 7.6d 5s^{4} 7d^{4} 5f 7.6f 6d^{3} 5g 6fg 6d 8g 6s 1980 5fg 7.6f 6fg^{4} 6fg* 7g^{4} 6g 6g 7f 7.6d) plater; bought in 725 gns after winning at Catterick in June; stays 7f; acts on any going; has worn a hood and often wears blinkers (did so at Catterick); temperamental. *L. Barratt.* **43**

BILLANELL 3 b. or br.c. Meldrum 112–Sew and Sew 96 (Hard Tack 111 §) (1979 NR 1980 8.2g 12g 12g) lightly-made colt; first living foal; dam won twice over 5f at 2 yrs; no sign of ability in maiden races. *M. James.* —

BILLBROKER 4 br.g. Lombard 126–Eastern Blue 84 (Majority Blue 126) **103**
(1979 11d^2 12g* 12s^2 11s* 12fg* 11.1f^4 14.6f 1980 12fg^4 14f^4 16g 16d) big, strong gelding; won 3 races as a 3-y-o, including valuable handicap at Newbury and Churchill Stakes at Ascot; didn't win in 1980 but ran creditably on first 3 outings, finishing fourth to More Light in Jockey Club Stakes at Newmarket and to Noble Saint in Yorkshire Cup at York and less than 3 lengths fifth to Toondra in Queen's Vase at Royal Ascot (weakened final furlong after making running); not seen out after running moderately in Coral Northumberland Plate at Newcastle late in June; stays 2m but is probably better over shorter distances; acts on any going; sometimes sweats up before his races but is genuine and consistent. *G. Pritchard-Gordon.*

BILL GIBB 3 ch.c. Cavo Doro 124–Fair Helen (Hopeful Venture 125) (1979 7fg 7fg 7g 7fg 8fg 1980 12s 12d 12d 12.2d 11d^3) neat colt; blinkered when third in seller at Wolverhampton in October; should stay 1½m; sold 875 gns Ascot November Sales. *Mrs J. Reavey.* —

BILLIE GIBB 2 ch.f. Cavo Doro 124–Fair Helen (Hopeful Venture 125) **73**
(1980 7f 7g 7g 8.2g^2 10d^2 10s^3 10.2s) Jan 21; 1,000Y; small, lightly-made filly; third foal; dam never ran; plater; also ran well in better company, notably on final start when sixth of 21 to Irish Heart in minor event at Doncaster in November; will be suited by 1½m; acts on soft going; wears blinkers. *Mrs J. Reavey.*

BILLIE JEAN 3 ch.f. Sweet Revenge 129–Volley (Ratification 129) (1979 **73**
5s 6fg 7f^4 7g 7fg 1980 8s^2 7s^2 8.5f 7d 7fg^4 8fg) tall, sparely-made filly; second in maiden race at Leicester and handicap at Warwick early in year; blinkered when well beaten in seller on final start in July; stays 1m; acts on soft going and didn't move well to post on firm third start; doesn't always impress in paddock; sold 1,500 gns Ascot August Sales; resold same venue in October 925 gns. *N. Vigors.*

BILLION (USA) 6 ch.h. Restless Wind–Festiva (Espace Vital) (1979 12d **113**
16s 16d* 22.2fg^2 18.4f* 19g 16g* 16fg* 16f^3 16d 1980 16f* 20g^4 18.4g^2 14.7g

Henry II Stakes, Sandown—the moody Billion wins from Buttress. The other horse in the picture is Halyudh who finished fifth

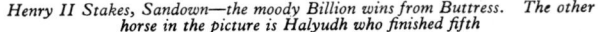

16d) well-made, attractive horse; smart stayer when in the mood; put up a fine effort when winning Henry II Stakes at Sandown in May, finishing strongly to beat Buttress by a neck; never on terms when about 12 lengths fourth of 8 to Le Moss in Gold Cup at Royal Ascot following month and never reached winner when 2 lengths second to Majestic Maharaj (rec 10 lb) in Chester Summer Handicap in July; skulked in rear throughout at Redcar and York on last 2 outings; needed a test of stamina; acted on any going; blinkered 3 times in 1977; a difficult ride who took time to get going and was suited by a strong gallop; standing at Helshaw Grange Stud, Market Drayton, Shropshire; £400 n.f.n.f. *J. Dunlop.*

BILLY KIP 3 b.g. Shoolerville 121–Shall Do (Passenger 122 or Derring-Do — 131) (1979 5g 5v 5fg 5f^{2} 5f 6g 6g 6g 1980 9.4g 8f 8f 5g) well-grown gelding; has shown no form since 2 yrs, including in a seller; not certain to stay 9f; acts on firm going. *T. Barron.*

BINCLEAVES 2 ch.c. Tumble Wind–Pink Doll (Palestine 133) (1980 5fg 79 5fg* 6g^{3}) Apr 6; 5,600F, 14,500Y; close-coupled, quite attractive colt; not a good mover in his slower paces; half-brother to 2 minor winners and a winner in USA; dam placed over 5f and 6f in Ireland; quickened clear up hill when winning 9-runner maiden race at Newmarket in May easily by 4 lengths from Joint Command; fair third to Tumbledownhill in minor event at Haydock the following month after being carried wide entering straight, only subsequent start; stays 6f. *M. McCormack.*

BINT AFRICA 3 b.f. African Sky 124–Kals Angel 68 (Kalydon 122) (1979 71 5fg 5fg 1980 7f 7fg^{2} 7d* 7d 7s 8.3g) quite a moderate performer; won 15-runner maiden race at Salisbury in June; stays 7f; acts on a firm and a soft surface; blinkered sixth outing; swerved badly under pressure second start. *R. Smyth.*

BIRD'S CUSTARD 4 gr.f. Birdbrook 110–Dairy Queen 76 (Queen's Hussar 62 124) (1979 5v 7s 10.2g 7d 7fg^{4} 7f^{3} 7g^{2} 7g* 7fg^{3} 7f^{3} 8fg^{3} 1980 7v 7g^{4} 7f) lengthy filly; ran respectably in handicaps on second and third outings, but wasn't seen out after May; stays 1m; acts on firm going; suitable mount for an apprentice. *R. Smyth.*

BIRD STREAM 4 gr.f. Birdbrook 110–Bream Bridge (Manicou) (1979 59 10.2d 10g 1980 12fg^{2}(dis) 10fg^{3} 12fg^{3} 12g 12fg^{2} 11.7s^{4} 12fg^{2} 10.6d^{4} 9d^{3}) leggy, lengthy filly; has a round action; in frame in maiden races and handicaps but is probably none too resolute in a finish; stays 1½m; appears to act on any going; blinkered sixth outing. *D. Gandolfo.*

BIREME 3 ch.f. Grundy 137–Ripeck 90 (Ribot 142) (1979 7f* 7fg^{3} 1980 127 10.5f* 12f*)

Of the depressingly large number of horses who failed to put in a full season, Grundy's first classic winner Bireme was undoubtedly one of the best; her absence, therefore, was one of the most regrettable, particularly as she could reasonably have been expected to have gone on to even greater things. She was a good Oaks winner who might well have succeeded in improving on her half-brother Buoy's second place in the St Leger. Injuries sustained when she got loose on the road at home shortly after Epsom led to her retirement to stud without a further race, and she made only four appearances all told, winning on her only other start as a three-year-old in the Musidora Stakes at York.

Bireme's stable became the first to win the Derby and Oaks in the same year since Warren Place sent out Crepello and Carrozza in 1957, stable-jockey Carson choosing correctly between Henbit and Water Mill for his mount in the Derby and between Bireme, Shoot A Line and The Dancer in the Oaks. Public form suggests the choice in both instances might have been very difficult to make. So far as the Oaks was concerned, all three fillies were well worth their place in the field. Like Bireme the other two had won their only race in 1980, Shoot A Line the Cheshire Oaks by five lengths and The Dancer the Sir Charles Clore Memorial Stakes at Newbury by seven. There were no doubts about the distance with any of them; as to the ground, which was firm on the day, all three had shown the ability to act on firm; Shoot A Line certainly acted on soft, too, but The Dancer had disappointed on soft. Probably The Dancer, blind in her near-eye and not certain to obtain the front-running rails position at Epsom she apparently needed, was the first to be rejected by Carson.

Bireme, a very well-bred filly from a family noted for producing late developers, went to Epsom with just one defeat in three runs—when, woolly

Musidora Stakes, York—Bireme shows great courage to beat Gift Wrapped. Our Home is third

in her coat, she had finished third of eight behind the colts Night Alert and Posse, giving each 4 lb, in the Houghton Stakes at Newmarket in the autumn. At the previous Newmarket meeting she had outstayed a big field of maidens over the same distance. The task facing her on her reappearance in the Musidora Stakes in May was more formidable than that faced by her two stable-companions in their respective trials: Our Home and Rapids, second and fifth in the One Thousand Guineas, were in the field, and so were the Lingfield Oaks Trial winner Gift Wrapped (seventh in the Guineas) and the Princess Elizabeth Stakes

Oaks Stakes, Epsom—another game performance from Bireme, who beats Vielle and The Dancer (blinkered). The fourth horse is Quick As Lightning

winner Bay Street. Although Bireme's lack of an outing just showed in the paddock she went down to the start very impressively indeed, outshining the others; she was one of the best movers we saw all season. She put up a tremendously game performance in the race, for she was asked to set the gallop, to make her stamina count, and then had to fight off Our Home and Gift Wrapped in the straight, being hard ridden fully two furlongs out and going half a length down to Gift Wrapped running into the final furlong before she finally prevailed by a length.

Surely more in hope than expectation of turning the tables over the longer distance, Gift Wrapped, Bay Street and another Musidora runner, Jem Jen, reopposed Bireme in the Oaks. Bireme started joint-second favourite with the Lupe Stakes winner Vielle at 9/2 behind the Guineas winner Quick As Lightning, who hadn't raced beyond a mile. None of the three Oaks runners still to be mentioned, Forlene, Rule Britannia and Pieces of Gold, had an obvious chance in the race, though Forlene's dam Arkadina had been placed in the Oaks in 1972. Contrary to many expectations The Dancer handled the course well; she jumped off quickly and tacked over to set a good pace on the rails, followed by Bireme, Bay Street, Gift Wrapped and the rest of the field closely grouped. Despite the strength of the pace all except Forlene managed to keep in touch with The Dancer on the run to Tattenham Corner, Forlene dropping right out down the hill as though there was something wrong with her; but as they came up the straight the race began to develop into a three-horse contest between The Dancer, Bireme and Vielle. Having been among the front-runners from the start, Bay Street, Rule Britannia and Gift Wrapped began to fade; Shoot A Line seemed outpaced, while Quick As Lightning was making only steady progress after being waited with; the rest didn't count. For a time it looked as though The Dancer might hold on. Then, as Bireme began to wear her down under vigorous riding and took a slight lead inside the two-furlong marker, Vielle seemed the most likely to succeed. However, Vielle hung in left behind Bireme instead of holding her ground on the outside, and only just managed to get the better of The Dancer over the final furlong as Bireme, gamely and gradually, in the style of a stayer, established a two-length winning lead. The first three finished well clear of Quick As Lightning, in turn well clear of the remainder led by Shoot A Line. The official time for the race, 2-34.33, improved on the record for the Oaks held by the 1927 winner Beam. Carson had now ridden his third classic winner of the English season; the next day tactics even more enterprising than on Bireme brought him success on the rank outsider Policeman in the French Derby. Later he won the Irish Guinness Oaks on Shoot A Line.

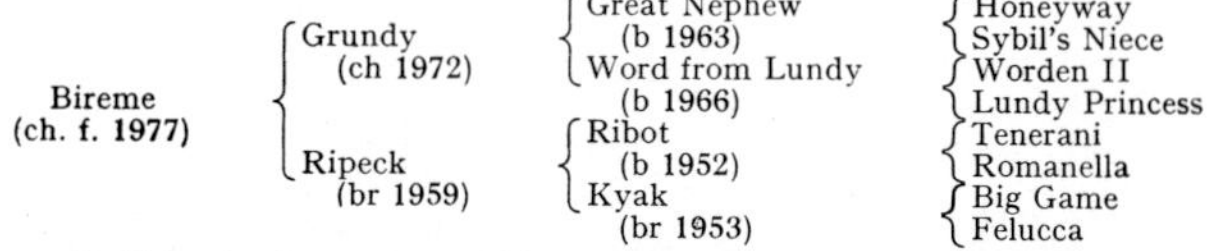

Bireme (ch. f. 1977)	Grundy (ch 1972)	Great Nephew (b 1963)	Honeyway
			Sybil's Niece
		Word from Lundy (b 1966)	Worden II
			Lundy Princess
	Ripeck (br 1959)	Ribot (b 1952)	Tenerani
			Romanella
		Kyak (br 1953)	Big Game
			Felucca

In Bireme's absence the stable could hardly have had a better filly than Shoot A Line to fall back on for the big staying races. Shoot A Line wasn't beaten again, and went on to win the Ribblesdale Stakes, Yorkshire Oaks and Park Hill Stakes besides the Irish Guinness Oaks. Whether Bireme, whose objective was said to be the St Leger, would have kept ahead in the second half of the season is impossible to tell but her breeding and the fact she'd raced only four times certainly suggested further improvement. Bireme's family is a very well known one, having achieved much in racing over the past twenty-five years or so—the period in which the half-sisters Ark Royal, Kyak and Cutter each won the Park Hill Stakes and then became broodmares. A large proportion of the family's runners have been fairly slow developers, better three-year-olds than two-year-olds with some, including Buoy, still better four-year-olds. Bireme's dam Ripeck, out of Kyak, ran once unplaced at two; at three she took on the classic fillies without success, finishing a good fourth in the Lingfield Oaks Trial on one occasion, before she finally accounted for modest opposition in a maiden plate at Newmarket. She has been much more valuable at stud than on the racecourse, and when the two-year-old Boathouse won at Newbury in October her record improved to eight winners from nine foals. Stake Boat (by St Paddy) let the side down. All Ripeck's winners before Bireme apart from the filly Helm (by Royal Palace) have been

Mr R. D. Hollingsworth's "Bireme" (W. Carson)

more than useful. Her first foal Kedge (by Petition) put up probably his best performance in finishing third to Reform in the St James Stakes at Epsom; her second, Anchor (by Major Portion), won the Nell Gwyn Stakes at Newmarket and started favourite for the One Thousand Guineas in 1969; her third, Fluke (by Grey Sovereign), won the Duke of York Stakes and the Jersey Stakes in 1970; then there came the good middle-distance stayer Buoy (by Aureole) who won the 1974 Coronation Cup, Stake Boat, Helm and the out-and-out stayer Balinger (by Welsh Pageant), whose very promising career was ended by injury at around the same time as Bireme's.

Physically Bireme is not so imposing as some of her dam's foals, and when last we saw her she was still on the leg. She was though, as we said, an excellent mover who acted very well on firm going. She visits Kris. *R. Hern.*

BIRKHOLM (USA) 6 b.g. Mickey McGuire–To My Lady (Amber Morn) (1979 8v 9s⁴ 9f 1980 8d) fair performer at 4 yrs; well beaten on flat since; acts on a firm surface. *D. Kent.* —

BIRWOOD LAD 4 b.g. Mummy's Pet 125–Madame Birwood (Constable 119) (1979 6g 6f 8fg 7fg 6g 1980 7fg 6fg 6g³ 6fg 7g 8fg 8.2s*) tall gelding; useful performer as a 2-y-o; mainly disappointing since and was running in a seller for first time when winning narrowly at Haydock in October (sold to S. Holland 3,800 gns); stays 1m; acts on any going; pulled very hard going to post fifth outing; wears blinkers nowadays. *G. Balding.* 77

BISCAYNE BAY 2 b.c. Welsh Saint 126–Silk Gown (High Hat 131) (1980 6g 6s 7g 5f 6g 5d) Apr 20; 3,300F, 8,200Y; compact colt; first foal; dam placed at up to 9f in Ireland; poor maiden; will stay 1m. *R. Hannon.* 62

BISKERYL 3 b. or br.f. Biskrah 121–Keryl 106 (Infatuation 129) (1979 7fg⁴ 7g⁴ 7g 8g 1980 11.7fg 12g 16.9d* 16fg²) moderate performer; won modest 80 maiden race at Wolverhampton in July; ran creditably in handicap only subsequent start; suited by a test of stamina; acts on a firm and a soft surface. *H. Candy.*

BITING WIT (USA) 2 br.f. Vitriolic–Lakewoods 83 (Hyperion) (1980 6f) — p
strong, good-bodied filly; closely related to 2 winners, notably 1,000 Guineas winner Waterloo (by Bold Lad, Ire), and half-sister to 2 more; dam placed at up to 1¼m; easy in market but looking well and fairly fit, wasn't knocked about after showing speed 4f when 9 lengths ninth of 19 to Long Legend in maiden race at Newmarket in October; should do better over 1m+ at 3 yrs. *J. Hindley.*

BIT SWEET 3 b.f. The Brianstan 128–Lady Honey 75 (Taste of Honey 92) —
(1979 5g 5fg 5f 1980 8s 7fg 11.7f 12f 8f 8d 8s) sturdy, plain filly; poor plater. *K. Bridgwater.*

BITTERMINT (USA) 3 b.f. Bold Bidder–Chocolate Beau (Beau Max) (1979 —
6f^3 7fg^4 7g* 1980 8.5g 8f) strong filly; landed the odds in maiden race at Leicester at 2 yrs; lightly raced in 1980, running moderately in handicaps at Epsom and York early in year; should be suited by 1m. *H. Cecil.*

BITTER SPARE 6 b.m. Track Spare 125–Shady Walk 72 (Gratitude 130) —
(1979 NR 1980 8.2fg 8fg 8g) of no account. *R. Ward.*

B. J. ALERT 3 ch.f. Red Alert 127–Pacquita (Matador 131) (1979 NR 1980 —
7d 7.6f) 5,600Y; big, strong filly; half-sister to useful 1974 Irish 2-y-o Birucina (by Majetta) and to a winner in Venezuela; dam half-sister to smart sprinter Poplin; well beaten in newcomers race at Doncaster in March and maiden race at Chester (sweating) in May; sold 1,000 gns Newmarket July Sales. *M. Jarvis.*

BLACKBROOK MELODY 3 ch.f. Jukebox 120–Naranja 81 (Roan Rocket 128) **58**
(1979 5f 6fg^4 1980 8v 8.5g^3 8fg 6fg 5.8g 5.8f^4 6fg* 6fg 5.8g^2 6fg) small, lightly-made filly; sprint handicapper; won at Folkestone in August; ran very well two outings later; stays 6f; acts on a firm surface. *M. Francis.*

BLACK CHARMER 2 br.c. Virginia Boy 106–Cygnets Charm (My Swanee **85**
122) (1980 5v 5g* 5fg* 5fg^4 6g 5d^2 5g 5f 5f^4 6d 6s 6d) May 15; 1,000Y; neat colt; first foal; dam Irish 1½m winner; successful in auction event at Ripon and minor race at Redcar in the spring, beating odds-on Royal Bid ½ length in latter; ran well on several occasions afterwards; will stay at least 1m; seems to act on any going. *G. Richards.*

BLACKCURRANT SONG 3 br.g. Master Sing 109–Ishka 58 (Tribal Chief —
125) (1979 NR 1980 8fg 6g 9f) no sign of ability in maiden races and a seller; sold 490 gns Doncaster November Sales. *R. Cambidge.*

BLACK EARL 3 br.c. So Blessed 130–La Presidente (Primera 131) (1979 **76**
6f 6fg 5f^3 7g^2 7d* 7fg 1980 7d^3 8.2d^3 8f^3 8g 10s) leggy colt; quite a moderate handicapper; stays 1m but appeared to find 1¼m beyond him on final outing; probably acts on any going; blinkered fourth start; sold to T. Hallett 2,600 gns Ascot October Sales. *P. Asquith.*

BLACKER 2 b.c. Arch Sculptor 123–Party Love (Parthia 132) (1980 5g 6g) —
Feb 26; 6,000Y; half-brother to 2 winners, including 6f winner Royal Love (by Green God); dam ran once in France; 9½ lengths sixth of 8 to Spanish Hind in minor event at Lingfield in June; not seen out again until October when behind in 14-runner minor event at Brighton. *G. Hunter.*

BLACKFOOT (USA) 2 bl.c. Charles Elliott–Augusta J (Lenso) (1980 7g **108**
7f* 7d^3 7.5g) Mar 22; fair sort; second foal; half-brother to 3-y-o Spook Too (by Plenty Old), a winner at up to 6f at 2 yrs in USA; dam won 3 races at up to 1m at 4 yrs, including a claiming event; heavily-backed second favourite, improved greatly on first effort when winning 18-runner maiden race at Newmarket in October by 2½ lengths from Madison Style; ridden by apprentice unable to claim his 5-lb allowance when length third of 14 to Sunley Builds in Houghton Stakes on same course later in month; not disgraced in Prix Thomas Bryon at Saint-Cloud in November, finishing 7¼ lengths seventh of 10 to Big John; will stay 1¼m; acts on any going; useful. *R. Sheather.*

BLACKMANSHIP (FR) 2 br.c. Brinkmanship 125–Balaklava (Fric 128) (1980 **74**
5s 5fg 5fg^3 6d^4 6s^3 6g* 7f) Apr 9; 38,000 francs Y (approx £4,500); neat colt; half-brother to minor 1976 2-y-o 1¼m winner Amberley (by Chaparral) and 2 winners over jumps; dam won over 5.5f at 2 yrs; sold 6,200 gns after winning valuable 20-runner seller at York in July by 2½ lengths from Maybehandy; subsequently raced abroad, including when 8¼ lengths fifth of 12 to Beldale Flutter (gave 6 lb) in Grand Criterium International d'Ostende the following month; stays 7f; acts on any going. *A. Johnson.*

BLACK MIKE 5 b.h. Hardicanute 130–Sariette (Barbare II 128) (1979 raced abroad, winning 3 times in Belgium 1980 7f2 12f 11.7g4 8fg 7.2d 7d2) smallish, strong sort of horse; useful performer at up to 1¼m in France at 3 yrs and won 3 times in Belgium in 1979; second in apprentice event at Catterick and 25-runner handicap at Doncaster in 1980, beaten ½ length by Willow Red in latter event in October; out of his depth when raced at 1½m on second and third starts; seems to act on any going. *P. Haslam.* **72**

BLACK MINSTREL 6 b.h. Luthier 126–Innocent Air 75 (Court Martial) (1979 7v2 8d* 7d* 7.6d* 7.6v2 7.2s4 8.2g 7.3g 7.2g 7d 8s2 1980 8d4 7s* 6fg 7g 8d 7.2d 7s* 8s3 7s) fairly useful handicapper; quickened clear in final furlong when winning McEwan's Lager Handicap at Newcastle in April by 5 lengths from Sabir; driven right out when beating Murillo by 1½ lengths in Portal Developments Handicap at York in October, best subsequent effort; best at up to 1m; revels in the mud; has been tried in blinkers; suitable mount for an apprentice; often bandaged in front. *D. Sasse.* **93**

BLACK OAK 3 bl.f. Seaepic 100–Hanaline (Hanassi 102) (1979 6f 1980 8v 8f 13.8g) tall, lightly-made filly; poor form in varied company, including selling; blinkered final outing; sweated up badly first start; trained by C. Gray first 2 starts. *N. Tinkler.* –

BLACK OUT (FR) 4 ch.f. Ragstone 128–Curfew 76 (Midsummer Night II 117) (1979 NR 1980 12.3d) small, lightly-made filly; first foal; dam, placed over 6f at 2 yrs, is half-sister to very smart French middle-distance winner Balompie; 100/1 and in need of race when behind in minor event at Newcastle in August, first outing. *I. Jordon.* –

BLACK PIRATE 3 bl.g. Barbary Pirate 91–Fire Fairy 70 (Firestreak 125) (1979 5s 6s3 6g3 6fg3 7f2 7f 10g 1980 10s3 10fg* 9fg 11fg3 9g 12g2 12fg 11d 11s) neat, lightly-built gelding; plater; wide-margin winner at Pontefract in April (sold out of R. Sturdy's stable 1,200 gns); stays 1½m; acts on firm going; blinkered at 2 yrs and on reappearance; has run respectably for a boy. *A. W. Jones.* **57**

BLACK ROD 3 gr.c. Bustino 136–Strip The Willow 79 (Native Dancer) (1979 8g 1980 10.8s 10fg 8d4 9.4g) robust colt; seems only plating class; will be suited by 1½m; sold to F. Winter 3,000 gns Ascot August Sales. *W. Hastings-Bass.* –

BLACK SUNSET (FR) 2 b. or br.f. Scottish Rifle 127–Rosie Bacardi (Ballymoss 136) (1980 6d) neat filly; half-sister to 2 winners; dam French 1¼m winner; 50/1 when behind in 18-runner maiden race won by Camisite at Doncaster in October. *M. Ryan.* –

BLACK SYMPHONY 5 gr.m. Grisaille 115–Gold Bloom 72 (Klondyke Bill 125) (1979 7f 8f 5f4 6fg* 6g 5f 1980 5f4 5g 5d 5f 5fg) plater; best at sprint distances; has worn blinkers; wears bandages; suitable mount for an apprentice. *R. E. Peacock.* **43**

BLADNOCH BOY 2 ch.g. Ellkar 87–Bonnie Bladnoch (Lord of Verona 120) (1980 8g 8.2s) Apr 23; 1,500 2-y-o; brother to a poor animal and half-brother to very useful staying hurdler Garliestown and leading point-to-pointer Glasserton (both by Sea Wolf); dam poor stayer; well behind in maiden and minor events in Scotland in October. *G. Richards.* –

BLAKE (FR) 3 b.c. Sir Gaylord–Blanche Hardy (Ribot 142) (1979 NR 1980 10s 10.5d 10d 12.5g 12s2 14d) strong, well-made ex-French colt; first foal; dam won over 1½m in Italy; stayed on strongly when second to wide-margin winner Wonderful Surprise in 20-runner maiden race at Haydock in October, easily best effort; should stay 1¾m; acts on soft going; blinkered first, fifth and sixth outings; trained by J. R. Lyon first 4 starts. *P. Walwyn.* –

BLAKENEY POINT 2 b.c. Blakeney 126–Lichen Lady 70 (Pardao 120) (1980 7g 7d 7fg 7fg) Feb 24; neat, attractive colt; typical of his sire; first foal; dam, winner over 1½m, is half-sister to the dam of very smart middle-distance colt Norfolk Air (by Blakeney); showed only a modicum of ability in maiden races but probably needs a stiff test of stamina; sold 4,000 gns Newmarket Autumn Sales. *J. Bethell.* –

BLAKES BEACON 3 b.c. Blakeney 126–Lighted Lamp (Sir Gaylord) (1979 NR 1980 12fg2 14f 13.3fg* 16g 14g* 13.3d 13s* 14g) 162,000Y; neat, strong colt; seventh foal; half-brother to 6 winners, including smart middle-distance stayer Torus (by Ribero); dam half-sister to Crocket; successful in maiden race at Newbury in June, small event at Yarmouth in July and Royal Caledonian Hunt Cup at Ayr in September; made most and held on well to beat Ballytop a neck in last-named; 6/4 when last of 6 to Lotar in St Leger Italiano at Milan later **94**

in September; stays 1¾m (well beaten in Queen's Vase at Royal Ascot over 2m); probably acts on any going; blinkered nowadays; ran moderately second start. *P. Walwyn.*

BLARE 2 b.c. Bustino 136–Swift Harmony 107 (Elopement 125) (1980 7d2) Mar 9; big colt; half-brother to 3 winners here and abroad, including Harmonise (by Reliance II), very useful performer at up to 1½m; dam middle-distance handicapper; 14/1 but looking well, showed plenty of promise when running on extremely well to finish 4 lengths second of 15 to John Clare in maiden race at Newbury in August; will stay 1½m; sure to win races at 3 yrs. *R. Hern.* **85** p

BLAST OFF (USA) 3 b.c. Graustark–Gris Vitesse (Amerigo 116 §) (1979 8fg4 8d 8s2 8s* 1980 10.5v3 8s 10.5fg2 11d* 10.5fg 12f 10s) strong, workmanlike colt; half-brother to Guarantor (by Indian Chief), successful over 1m in France and USA; dam won Prix Jacques le Marois; placed in 60,000 francs event at Maisons-Laffitte and Prix Greffulhe at Longchamp (went down by 1½ lengths to Providential) prior to getting up close home to win 10-runner Prix de Suresnes on latter course in May by a head from First of the Line; respectable sixth of 13 to Belgio in Prix Lupin, again at Longchamp, later in month (hampered early in straight); in rear afterwards in Derby (led for a long way) and Prix Eugene Adam at Saint-Cloud in July; probably finds 1m on sharp side and should stay 1½m; seems to act on any going; wears blinkers. *J. Fellows, France.* **115**

BLAZE OF GLORY 3 b.f. Queen's Hussar 124–Highlight 107 (Borealis) (1979 6g 7g 1980 10f4 13.3fg4 12d* 14g2 12f2 14.6g4) big, rangy filly; favourite when winning 16-runner maiden race at Haydock in August; very good ½-length second to Grandiose in Melrose Handicap at York later in month (made much of running and kept on well when headed); suited by 1¾m; acts on a soft surface; didn't look happy in blinkers final start (Park Hill Stakes). *R. Hern.* **92**

BLAZING 2 b.c. Streak 119–Sailing 109 (Doutelle 128) (1980 6fg 7fg) June 8; closely related to 2 plating-class animals by Runnymede, and half-brother to several winners, including fairly useful 6f and 1m winner Commander Bond (by Good Bond); dam stayed at least 1m; in mid-division in newcomers event at Chepstow in August and maiden race at Lingfield in October. *T. Marshall.* –

BLEACH 3 ch.f. Sun Prince 128–Brilliantine 109 (Stage Door Johnny) (1979 NR 1980 12g 12s) 12,000 2-y-o; rangy filly; first foal; dam, winner over 7f and 1¼m, is half-sister to very smart performers Bright Finish and Shining Finish; well beaten in maiden races at Salisbury in June and Doncaster in November. *R. Boss.* –

BLENHEIM PRINCE 3 b.c. Bigivor–Ulador (Sovereign Lord 120) (1979 6f 5fg 1980 5fg 5f 6fg 7f 7s* 8g 8g 8g 8d2 8d2) workmanlike colt; plater; successful at Stockton in June (bought in 1,750 gns); will stay beyond 1m; suited by some give in the ground; blinkered second and third starts. *J. Spearing.* **59**

BLESSED BLUE 2 b.c. So Blessed 130–The Danstan 66 (The Brianstan 128) (1980 5fg 5g4 6fg2 6g* 6d) Feb 15; 6,200Y; small, compact colt; first foal; dam won 5f seller at 2 yrs; made all and held on by a head from Water of Life to win seller at Ripon in August (pair clear); bought in 1,500 gns afterwards; ran moderately in selling handicap at Brighton following month; stays 6f; blinkered last 3 starts. *P. Haslam.* **65**

BLESSED DAMSEL 3 b.f. So Blessed 130–All Fours 84 (St Paddy 133) (1979 5g3 5g* 5g* 6f 6g* 7f* 7fg 1980 7fg 8f 8g) neat, attractive filly; fairly useful (rated 99) at 2 yrs; didn't grow much over the winter and failed to find her form in handicaps in 1980; should stay 1m; yet to race on a soft surface. *G. Pritchard-Gordon.* –

BLESSED PALM 3 ch.f. St Paddy 133–Planta Genista 89 (Princely Gift 137) (1979 NR 1980 12.2f 12d2 12s 10s 12s) neat filly; half-sister to several winners here and in Italy, including 1977 2-y-o 6f winner Plant at Dusk (by Crepello); dam won over 5f at 2 yrs; runner-up to Blaze Of Glory in maiden race at Haydock in August, easily best effort; stays 1½m; acts on a soft surface; ran freely in blinkers final start. *L. Cumani.* **76**

BLEU NUIT (FR) 5 br.h. Verkade–Mini Skirt (Kythnos 126) (1979 10v* 11d* 12s 12s3 12.5fg4 12d 13g 11.5s 11.5d 1980 9f 12fg 22.2fg4 20.2g2 16f 16.9f 16s 12g3 14fg4 16g* 16g) sturdy ex-French horse; 25/1-winner of handicap at Thirsk in September, beating Migelitto by 2½ lengths; broke down at Nottingham later in month; stayed well; appeared to act on any going; needed to be held up and was suited by strong handling; refused to race sixth outing (ridden by 7-lb claimer); dead. *A. Jarvis.* **68**

BLOAK MOSS 2 b.g. Cavo Doro 124–Tabasheer (Indian Chief) (1980 6fg 6d 70
6g 7fg) Mar 17; 9,000Y; neat, good-topped gelding; third foal; half-brother to 2 winners by Mummy's Pet, including fairly useful sprinter Tremellick; dam never ran; showed ability in maiden and minor events, on final outing finishing 4 lengths fifth of 19 to Oklahoma Star at Warwick in August; will stay 1m; gelded after fourth start. *Sir Mark Prescott.*

BLOCHAIRN SKOLAR 2 ch.f. Most Secret 119–Olibanum 61 (Frankincense —
120) (1980 5d 5f 5fg 5g) Apr 21; compact filly; first foal; dam plater; in rear in maiden and minor events. *V. Mitchell.*

BLOOD FOOL (USA) 3 b.f. Blood Royal 129–Fleet Fool (Model Fool) (1979 72
NR 1980 9f^4 10fg* 12.2fg^2 12.2fg 10d 13g 10.1g 13g 13.8d 16s^4) first foal; dam unplaced 8 times in USA; ran on gamely to win 15-runner maiden race at Brighton in May; ran creditably next start (apprentice ridden); seems to stay 2m; probably acts on any going; bandaged in front eighth outing (moved badly to post). *B. Hanbury.*

BLOOD ORANGE 5 ch.g. Warpath 113–Sunflower 96 (Paveh 126) (1979 —
13.8g 12s 12.3fg 16f 1980 18d 13.8f) poor maiden; stays 1¾m; sometimes has his tongue tied down; inconsistent. *J. Bingham.*

BLUE BRAID 6 gr.m. No Mercy 126–Braida (Tissot 131) (1979 NR 1980 —
10d) of no account. *A. Davison.*

BLUE BRIDGE 4 ch.c. Majority Blue 126–Awaken (Narrator 127) (1979 7f 92
6s 8d* 8fg 10fg 8f 8fg* 8.2s^4 8s* 8s 1980 8d^2 8d^3 8f 8g 8d 8g^2 8f 8g) leggy colt; fairly useful handicapper; caught on post by King's Ride in William Hill Lincoln Handicap at Doncaster in March; ran best subsequent races when third to New Berry at Kempton in April and close second to Grand Conde at Kempton in July; best at up to 1m; seems to act on any going except very firm; blinkered last 2 starts; suitable mount for an apprentice; sold 6,000 gns Newmarket Autumn Sales. *F. Durr.*

BLUE DAHLIA 3 ch.f. Warpath 113–Delphinium 93 (Tin King 126) (1979 —
6g 8.2s* 1980 10.6f 10s) poor performer; had stiff tasks when tailed off in handicaps in 1980; didn't impress in paddock on reappearance. *C. Thornton.*

BLUE EMPRESS 2 b.f. Blue Cashmere 129–Emperor's Treasure (King Emp- —
eror) (1980 5f 5fg) Apr 5; 3,800Y; light-framed filly; first foal; dam never ran; bandaged when behind in maiden races at Windsor in May and Warwick in June. *M. Francis.*

BLUE GARTER 2 ch.f. Targowice 130–Blue Rag 70 (Ragusa 137) (1980 5s 6s 70
7fg 7g 8fg* 8fg^2 6g^3 8d* 8d^3 7g) Feb 9; 3,400Y, 6,000Y; compact filly; first foal; dam won over 9f; fairly useful in selling company and won at Carlisle in September and Warwick in October, being bought in 2,600 gns after winning latter by 2½ lengths from Star Rhythm; will stay 1¼m; yet to show she acts on extremes of going; wears blinkers; consistent; sold to Curragh Bloodstock Agency 3,000 gns Newmarket Autumn Sales. *P. Mitchell.*

BLUE JANE 3 b.f. Blue Cashmere 129–Westmorland Jane 76 (Vimy 132) 72
(1979 5v 5g 6g* 6f^4 7f 6g* 6fg^4 1980 7d 7v 6fg^3 6fg 11.7s 8f^2 10g 8g^3 5d 7g) quite attractive, compact, good-quartered filly; quite a moderate handicapper; stays 1m; acts on firm going; sometimes blinkered but does at least as well without; has run respectably for inexperienced riders but unseated her amateur rider 3 times before going down to start on ninth outing. *P. Haslam.*

BLUE LASS 2 ch.f. Blue Cashmere 129–Gay Donna (Tudor Jinks 121) (1980 93
5f* 5fg^2 5.3g* 5d^2) Feb 22; small, lengthy, quite attractive filly; good walker and mover; sister to 3-y-o Kashmir Blue, a winner at up to 1m, and half-sister to two 2-y-o 5f winners, including useful Happy Donna (by Huntercombe); dam of little account; won 18-runner maiden race at Folkestone and minor event at Brighton in the autumn, landing the odds by 2 lengths from La Belle Sorciere in latter; second on both other outings, having rest well strung out when length behind Red Gold in 15-runner apprentice nursery at Sandown in October on fourth; will be suited by 6f; seems to act on any going; sold to Curragh Bloodstock Agency 11,000 gns Newmarket Autumn Sales. *M. Stoute.*

BLUE MORIN 3 ch.c. Porto Bello 118–Copper Corn 79 (Vilmorin) (1979 6d —
6fg 5d 1980 5h 5fg 7g 7g 6fg 5g 6g) strong colt; little worthwhile form in varied company, including selling; blinkered last 2 starts. *T. Fairhurst.*

BLUE OPAL 4 ch.f. Grisaille 115–Tisane (Crepello 136) (1979 8fg 1980 7g —
9d 8d) small, lightly-made filly; only poor form, including in sellers; looks temperamental. *R. Akehurst.*

BLUE PATROL 4 br.g. Queen's Hussar 124–Silk Stocking 109 (Pardao 120) **85**
(1979 8d^2 8d* 10f 8f^4 8.2g 7g 1980 7v* 8s^2 8fg 10fg^2 8.5f^3 10d 8g^4 8.3s 11.7d^4 8g 8g^4) big, tall gelding; fair handicapper; made all to win by 8 lengths at Warwick in March; in frame six times afterwards, on final outing looking well and finishing good fourth to Princes Gate in amateur riders race at Goodwood in September; best form at up to $1\frac{1}{4}$m; acts on any going; blinkered final start at 3 yrs; sold out of W. Hastings-Bass's stable 9,000 gns Newmarket May Sales after third outing. *D. Elsworth.*

BLUE PERSIAN 3 ch.f. Majority Blue 126–Gulf Bird 71 (Gulf Pearl 117) **111**
(1979 5s^4 5f* 5g* 5d^2 5f^3 5f^3 1980 5g 5f^4 5.6g 5fg* 5s^2) small, compact filly; first foal; dam won over $1\frac{1}{2}$m; didn't impress in paddock in 1980 but showed smart form, winning 3-runner minor race at Newbury in September by $\frac{1}{2}$ length from Hanu and going down by $1\frac{1}{2}$ lengths to Greenway in Group 3 Prix du Petit Couvert at Longchamp in October; had earlier finished creditable fourth to Westacombe in valuable handicap at York; acted on any going but was particularly well suited by top-of-the-ground; genuine and consistent; chipped bone in leg in October, and has been retired. *B. Hanbury.*

BLUE REFRAIN 4 ch.c. Majority Blue 126–Refrain (Crocket 130) (1979 7g^4 **121**
8g 7d^3 7d^2 7fg* 7.3g 8f* 1980 7fg^2 8f* 8d* 7fg^2 8g^4 10d)

Blue Refrain was some way behind the likes of Kris, Known Fact and Posse among the leading milers on the balance of his form, but he was a thoroughly genuine sort and for the third successive year his efforts were rewarded by a win at Royal Ascot. He added the Queen Anne Stakes to his wins in the Windsor Castle Stakes at two years and the Jersey Stakes at three, thus establishing a Royal Ascot record similar to that of the 1973 Queen Anne Stakes winner Sun Prince, who had won the Coventry Stakes and the St James's Palace Stakes previously.

Blue Refrain reportedly nearly missed the Queen Anne. He coughed for a fortnight after landing the Ultramar Jubilee Stakes at Kempton under fortuitous circumstances the previous month—House Guard beat him on merit but was disqualified for interfering with the third-placed Piaffer—and it was touch and go whether he could be prepared in time. He had to miss the Lockinge Stakes, in which he'd have met Kris, but he reportedly responded well to the administration of a well-known brand of cough medicine and duly took his place in the eleven-strong field. In the absence of Kris the Queen Anne had a fairly open look about it and Blue Refrain started at fourth favourite. Preferred in the betting were the O'Brien-trained Habituate, second to Kris at Haydock on his previous start, the 1979 Queen Anne winner Baptism and New Berry who was fancied to reverse

Ultramar Jubilee Stakes, Kempton—Blue Refrain gets this valuable prize on the disqualification of House Guard (rails). *Piaffer is promoted to second place*

Queen Anne Stakes, Ascot—third successive Royal Ascot win for Blue Refrain who beats New Berry and Foveros

the Diomed Stakes form with Hardgreen. In the event neither Habituate nor Baptism ran to form and Blue Refrain won in good style from New Berry. Held up towards the rear early on, he moved smoothly through the field to challenge for the lead two furlongs out and was well in command by the furlong pole. He was driven out to win decisively by three lengths, with Foveros two lengths further away in third.

After Ascot Blue Refrain's principal remaining target was the Waterford Crystal Mile at Goodwood but on the way he ran in the Beeswing Stakes at Newcastle. For the second time he found the task of conceding weight to Kampala beyond him and he went down by half a length, giving 4 lb. His trainer blamed the slow early pace for his defeat but he ran close enough to his form in the Autobar Victoria Cup at Ascot earlier in the year (where Kampala beat him a neck when in receipt of 2 lb) to suggest that he gave his running. At Goodwood four weeks later he was pitched in against some of the season's best three-year-old milers, notably Known Fact, Hard Fought and Night Alert, and even on terms more favourable than weight-for-age he simply wasn't good enough. He joined issue in the straight and ran on in his usual game fashion into fourth place, about a length and three quarters behind the winner Known Fact. He made his only subsequent appearance in the Champion Stakes, another tough race for him, and in all probability failed to stay the distance of a mile and a quarter. He rather surprisingly raced up with the leaders from the start, was still there with a chance at the two-furlong marker, then steadily lost his place and finished eighth behind Cairn Rouge, beaten about nine lengths.

Blue Refrain (ch.c. 1976)	Majority Blue (ch 1961)	Major Portion (ch 1955)	Court Martial
			Better Half
		Gorm Abu (b 1954)	My Babu
			Cnoc Gorm
	Refrain (ch 1966)	Crocket (ch 1960)	King of the Tudors
			Chandelier
		Lavella (b 1955)	Le Lavandou
			Lilting Lullaby

Blue Refrain is easily the best of three winners foaled by Refrain; the dam has since produced a filly Gay Refrain (by Furry Glen) who has run once. Refrain won over five furlongs in Ireland on her first outing as a three-year-old but showed little worthwhile form afterwards over longer distances, including in the Irish One Thousand Guineas. She is a half-sister to several winners, most notably the 1978 Diadem Stakes winner Creetown.

Blue Refrain will stand alongside Patch and Rusticaro at the Raffin Stud Farm, Castletown, County Meath, in 1981 at a fee of IR£2,000 with the October 1st concession. A tall, compact colt who seemed to act on any going, he was an admirable racehorse. He was at his best at seven furlongs or a mile. *J. Benstead.*

BLUE RHAPSODY 2 ch.c. Sandford Lad 133–Sovereign Court 87 (Sovereign Path 125) (1980 5f 5fg 6s* 6fg 7g 8.2g 7fg 7.2s) June 9: 2,600Y; strong, useful sort; half-brother to several winners here and abroad, including quite useful 3-y-o miler Hill's Northern (by Northfields); dam 7f 2-y-o winner; blinkered first time, led inside final furlong when winning 18-runner maiden auction event at Nottingham in June by a neck from Diamond Horseshoe: also blinkered when well beaten subsequently, including in a selling nursery; should stay 7f; acts on soft going; one to leave alone. *A. Goodwill.* **81** d

BLUE ROAD 3 b.c. Royal Palace 131–Blue Ray 82 (Royal Record II) (1979 6fg 7d 6fg 10s 8d 1980 8d 8.2s 12fg 10f 11.7s 10g 8.3s 7g 16g 16fg) small colt; bad plater; has worn blinkers; sold 300 gns Ascot October Sales. *C. Austin.* —

BLUES 3 b.c. Song 132–Lyrical 110 (Gratitude 130) (1979 5d 6fg² 1980 6s 6d 7g 6g 7g³ 6g 6g² 7fg 6d 6g³ 5fg 5d 6d 5s²) strong, compact colt; quite a moderate maiden; stays 7f: probably acts on any going: suitable mount for a boy. *N. Guest.* **62**

BLUE SINGH 2 ch.g. Mansingh 120–Great Blue White 73 (Great Nephew 126) (1980 5f 6fg* 6d 6g 7fg 8g 6g³) Apr 4; 7,200Y; fair sort; third foal; dam closely related to Cheveley Park winner Lalibela; ran on to win 16-runner maiden race at Haydock in June by a length from Katysue; finished strongly, after being outpaced, when 3¼ lengths third of 14 to Steel Pass in £3,500 nursery at Newmarket in October, best subsequent effort; best form at 6f but wasn't disgraced over 7f (not certain to stay further). *R. Boss.* **83**

BLUES SWINGER 3 ch.c. Swing Easy 126–Blue Book 101 (Majority Blue 126) (1979 5d 5f 5fg 7fg⁴ 6g* 1980 7d 8.2d 7f 6h² 6f 6fg 6fg 6fg² 6fg⁴ 6g⁴ 6d) lengthy colt; quite a moderate handicapper; stayed 7f; suited by top-of-the-ground and acted on hard going; moved poorly to post ninth start; retained 4,400 gns Newmarket July Sales; dead. *W. Marshall.* **67**

BLUE WIND 2 ch.f. Lord Gayle 124–Azurine 108 (Chamossaire) (1980 6s 7g² 7.5s* 8g* 8f) May 3; 5,600Y; neat filly; sister to Irish 9.5f and 1½m winner Callernish, and half-sister to several winners; dam third in Irish 1,000 Guineas; improved with distance and became one of best 2-y-o fillies in Ireland, winning maiden race at Gowran Park in August by 5 lengths and justifying favouritism by 2½ lengths from Overplay in Group 3 Silken Glider Stakes at Leopardstown in September; far from disgraced when 11/1-shot for Prix Marcel Boussac at Longchamp in October, dead-heating for sixth place only 2½ lengths behind Tropicaro; will stay 1½m; acts on any going; sold 180,000 gns Goffs November Sales and will be trained by D. Weld. *P. Prendergast, jnr, Ireland.* **110**

BLUSHING CHICQUITA 3 b.f. Upper Case–Sharivari 81 (Hugh Lupus 132) (1979 5f 6g 6d 5s² 6d⁴ 1980 7g 8g 10f 9.4fg³ 12f⁴ 8g 8.2v 8d) light-framed filly; plater; stays 1¼m; probably acts on any going. *W. A. Stephenson.* **57**

BLYTHSMERE 2 b.g. Blue Cashmere 129–Blesseen 71 (So Blessed 130) (1980 5g 5d⁴ 5f 5g) Apr 2; 6,200Y; leggy, light-framed gelding; second foal; dam raced only at sprint distances; taken down early to start when co-favourite for valuable seller at Sandown in August and was bit slow into stride, eventually running on strongly to finish 2½ lengths fourth of 19 to Universal Penny; will stay 6f; sold to M. Pipe 1,500 gns Newmarket Autumn Sales. *G. Harwood.* **63**

B.M.C. SPECIAL 5 gr.h. Supreme Sovereign 119–Agapimou (Great White Way) (1979 8s 8f² 8f³ 8.2f 8h 9g 1980 9fg 7fg 8fg 8s 8d 9d 8fg* 7fg 8g⁴) quite a moderate handicapper; ridden by 7-lb claimer, attracted no bid after winning seller at Yarmouth in August; suited by 1m on fast ground; blinkered once at 3 yrs; bandaged nowadays; trained until after fourth outing by N. Adam. *J. Gilbert.* **55**

BOARDMANS SPECIAL 6 b.g. Silly Season 127–Shenvallie 87 (Crepello 136) (1979 NR 1980 14g³) useful hurdler; well-backed second favourite and having first outing on flat since 1977 when length third to Seajan in amateur riders maiden race at Yarmouth in July; joined A. Jarvis afterwards; stays 1¾m. *W. Stephenson.* **54**

BOATHOUSE 2 b.f. Habitat 134–Ripeck 90 (Ribot 142) (1980 7.3d*) May 14; rangy filly; half-sister to several winners, including Oaks winner Bireme (by Grundy), very good middle-distance stayer Buoy (by Aureole), smart sprinter Fluke (by Grey Sovereign) and very useful stayer Balinger (by Welsh Pageant); dam stayed 1½m; 4/1, put up a very pleasing first effort when winning 12-runner Radley Stakes at Newbury in October, coming from rear of field in straight to lead about 1f out and then keeping on well, despite looking very green under **85** P

Prix Maurice de Gheest, Deauville—at this point Moorestyle leads from Kilijaro, but Boitron (rails) finishes strongly and heads the pair in the last strides

pressure, to score by 1½ lengths from Seasurf; will stay middle distances; has considerable improvement in her and could develop into a very good 3-y-o. *R. Hern.*

BODNANT 2 b.f. Welsh Pageant 132–Pot Pourri 97 (Busted 134) (1980 7.3d) Apr 21; fourth foal; half-sister to 1¼m winner Potshot (by Roan Rocket); dam a stayer and half-sister to very smart Almiranta; 12/1 and in need of race when never-dangerous ninth of 12 to Boathouse in £5,000 event at Newbury in October; should do better over middle distances at 3 yrs. *P. Walwyn.* —

BODY BLOW (USA) 6 b.g. What A Pleasure–Roman Meadow (Roman) (1979 10g 10s 10g 11.7fg 12f³ 11.7f* 12g 12g⁴ 12f 1980 12fg 12fg 11.7fg 11.7s 11.7g) poor middle-distance handicapper; probably acts on any going; tailed off when blinkered once in 1979. *D. Underwood.* —

BOGANACH 2 gr.c. Town Crier 119–Oudalia 107 (Gala Performance) (1980 5v 5d² 5f³ 5fg* 5d⁴ 6g 6g 5g⁴ 5fg 7s 5d⁴) May 5; 4,600Y; small colt; first foal; dam best at sprint distances; got up close home to win 7-runner maiden race at Hamilton in May by a neck from Silver Bill; best form at 5f; sold 1,550 gns Ascot December Sales. *T. Craig.* **69**

BOHEMIAN RHAPSODY 2 b.f. On Your Mark 125–Schull (Yorick II 127) (1980 5d² 5v* 5f² 5h* 5f* 5f 6s⁴ 6g⁴ 5f² 5d² 5g) Feb 27; 5,600Y; compact filly; half-sister to several winners, including very useful 6f to 7f performer Step Ahead (by Continuation); dam never ran; successful in 2 small races at Stockton and in another at Windsor in the spring, on latter course making all to beat odds-on Dissipated Dollar 2½ lengths; ran best races afterwards when second in nurseries at Lingfield and Newcastle (length behind Southern Swanee) in August; seems best at 5f; probably acts on any going; usually blinkered and ran below form without them final start. *P. Haslam.* **86**

BOITRON (FR) 4 b.c. Faraway Son 130–Barbentane (Prudent II 133) (1979 8d* 8g⁴ 9g³ 8g³ 8g⁴ 6.5d* 6g³ 8fg³ 7s 1980 8g² 8d 6.5d* 8d⁴ 8g⁴ 6d² 6v⁴) very smart French colt; won Prix Maurice de Gheest at Deauville in August for second time, getting up on line in a desperate finish from Moorestyle (gave 13 lb more than w.f.a.), Kilijaro and Manjam; ran well on other occasions, particularly when ¾-length second to Nadjar in Prix de Ris-Orangis at Evry **125**

in April and 1½ lengths second to Kilijaro in Prix de Seine-et-Oise at Maisons-Laffitte and when fourth to Nadjar in Prix Jacques le Marois at Deauville in between; effective at 6f and stays 9f; probably acts on any going except heavy; ran badly second outing (off course 3 months afterwards); blinkered once at 3 yrs; usually held up; sent to race in United States. *F. Boutin, France.*

BOKARAH IN SHALLAH 3 b.g. Forlorn River 124–My Worry 72 (March Past 124) (1979 NR 1980 5s4 6s 6g* 7fg 5fg3 6d 6d) sixth foal; dam placed over 5f at 2 yrs; 20/1-winner of 20-runner maiden race at Nottingham in July; stays 6f; possibly unsuited by very soft going; has run creditably for an apprentice. *Peter Taylor.* **65**

BOLD EAGLE 2 b.c. Legal Eagle 126–Vacation 102 (Remainder 106) (1980 6d 6g 7f) Jan 18; lengthy colt; half-brother to 1977 2-y-o 5f winner Cosmic Dancer (by Communication); dam 2-y-o 5f winner; only poor form in maiden races but finished seventh of 25 on final start. *T. Fairhurst.* **–**

BOLD FLAWLESS (USA) 2 b.f. Bold Bidder–Hardliner (Buckpasser) (1980 5f3 5fg2 5g4 5fg) Apr 13; $160,000Y; compact filly; good mover; first foal; dam unraced granddaughter of outstanding broodmare Cosmah; beaten favourite in maiden races at Chester, Doncaster and Edinburgh on first 3 outings, coming closest to success when ½-length second to Jiva at Doncaster in May; blinkered when last of 14 in similar event at Folkestone in August and looks expensive; will probably stay 1m. *B. Hills.* **67**

BOLD IKE 2 b.c. The Brianstan 128–Carina 98 (Tamerlane 128) (1980 5d 6fg 7g 8fg) Apr 14; 2,500Y; small colt; bad plater; sold 300 gns Ascot November Sales. *P. Haslam.* **–**

BOLD ILLUSION 2 ch.g. Grey Mirage 128–Savette (Frigid Aire) (1980 5fg 5f4 5f 5f4 6g 7fg 7d 7fg4 8.2s 7.2s 8d) May 5; sturdy sort; third foal; dam never ran; only poor form, including in sellers; should stay 1m. *A. W. Jones.* **49**

BOLD IMAGE 3 b. or br.c. Balidar 133–Darinda (Darius 129) (1979 5s2 5fg* 6f* 6f 6g3 1980 7f 6fg* 5f 5f 6fg) useful-looking colt; shows quite a bit of knee action; tracked leaders until pouncing entering final furlong when beating Ferriby Hall 1½ lengths in handicap at Newmarket in May; in rear in Temple Stakes at Sandown and handicaps at York and Newmarket afterwards; better suited by 6f than 5f and should stay 7f; seems to act on any going. *J. Winter.* **104**

BOLD L'AIGLON (USA) 3 b.g. L'Aiglon–Native Art (Tiziano) (1979 5s 5f 5fg 7fg 7fg3 1980 5h 6fg 7.2g) well-made gelding; has shown no form since final outing at 2 yrs; will probably stay 1m; coltish and sweating badly first outing. *P. Read, Isle of Man.* **–**

BOLDLY GO 2 b.c. Realm 129–Kilcarn Lass 74 (Bold Lad, Ire 133) (1980 5d 6d) Feb 1; 3,600Y; workmanlike colt; first foal; dam 6f winner; little worthwhile form in end-of-season maiden races at Warwick and Newbury. *R. Akehurst.* **–**

BOLDNESS 3 br.g. Bold Lad (Ire) 133–Dazzling Light 116 (Silly Season 127) (1979 NR 1980 8fg 10g 5s) poor form in maiden and minor events. *B. Palling.* **–**

BOLD OWL 4 b.c. Bold Lad (Ire) 133–Tawny Owl 123 (Faberge II 121) (1979 8d 8s4 8d* 8.2s* 8g3 8f2 8d3 1980 8f 8g 8d 8g) very attractive colt; useful handicapper as a 3-y-o; looked extremely well in 1980 but was disappointing, finishing behind in 4 valuable events, including when blinkered in Julio Mariner Handicap at Doncaster in September on final outing; stays 1m; acts on any going. *H. Wragg.* **–**

BOLD POLLY 3 b.f. Bold Lad (Ire) 133–Pipeline 85 (Gulf Pearl 117) (1979 5f 5g 1980 8h 8fg4 8.2g 8f 8g 5d3 5d 5d2 6d) neat filly; sprint handicapper; evidently best at 5f on a soft surface; trained by N. Callaghan first 4 starts. *J. Spearing.* **61**

BOLD RAIDER (FR) 2 ch.c. Bold Lad (USA)–Kalise 107 (Kashmir II 125) (1980 6fg 7d4 7g2) big, rangy, quite attractive colt; half-brother to 3 winners, including very useful French fillies Chere Alise and Cenerentola (both by Caro), successful at up to 10.5f and 1m respectively; dam very useful at up to 9f in France after winning over 6f in England at 2 yrs; put up easily best effort in 4-runner Intercraft Solario Stakes at Sandown in August, coming through to finish 2 lengths second to comfortable winner To-Agori-Mou after taking long time to find his stride; will be well suited by 1m+; sure to win races at 3 yrs. *R. Hern.* **111**

BOLD REPLY (USA) 3 b.c. Bold Reason–Pattee Canyon (Gallant Man) (1979 6g 1980 8f 8fg 8fg 10.8s3 12g) strong, compact colt; showed only a **–**

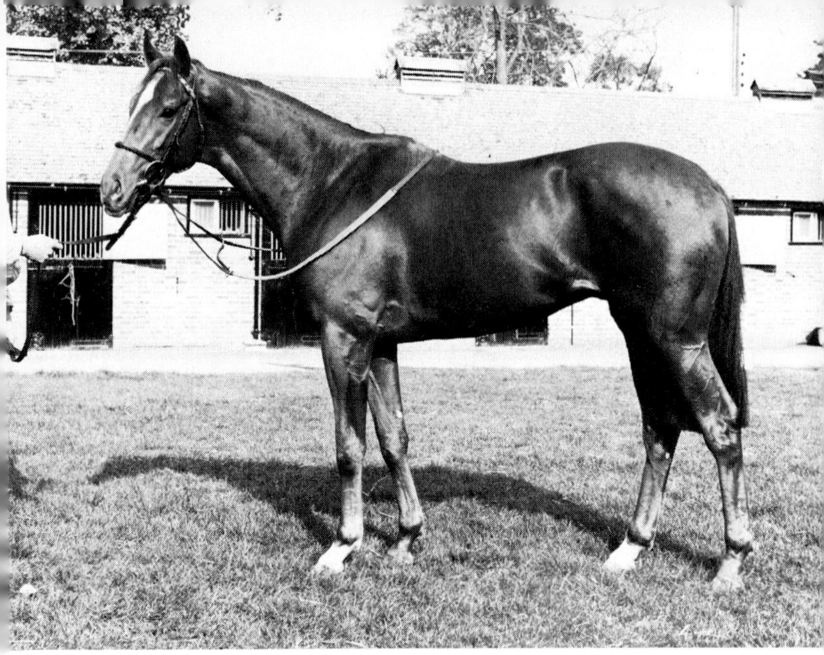

Sir Michael Sobell's "Bold Raider"

little ability in maiden races; should stay middle distances; sold 22,000 francs (approx £2,200) Chantilly October Sales. *B. Hills.*

BOLD ROBIN 4 b.g. Realm 129–Ragwort 68 (Ragusa 137) (1979 11.5g 16f 13.8fg³ 13s 12s 1980 13s 10fg 10g⁴ 10.2g 10g 10s) big, strong gelding; plating-class maiden; probably doesn't stay 2m; sold 750 gns Doncaster October Sales. *H. Collingridge.* —

BOLD SCUFFLE 2 b.c Bold Lad (Ire) 133–Cloe (Shantung 132) (1980 5f 5s² 6g⁴ 6g 6d⁴ 5g*) Mar 21; 4,000F, 6,800Y; useful-looking colt; half-brother to 2 winners in Italy; dam won at 2 yrs and 3 yrs in Italy; didn't stride out on way to start prior to winning modest maiden race at York in October by 2 lengths from Rehoboam, best effort; should be suited by 6f+. *R. Hollinshead.* **82**

BOLD THEME 4 gr.c. Bold Lad (Ire) 133–Leit Motif 95 (Fortino II 120) (1979 7v 6s 8fg 7g 6g² 8fg* 9f² 7g² 8g³ 7d⁴ 8fg 7fg⁴(dis) 10g³ 8d 7g 1980 7g 10g⁴ 10fg³ 9fg 10d 8g⁴ 7s⁴ 7f 9fg) Irish colt; 50/1 when 3¾ lengths fourth of 10 to Noelino in Sean Graham Ballymoss Stakes at the Curragh in April, on second start; had stiff tasks on occasions afterwards, including when tailed off in Prince of Wales's Stakes at Royal Ascot on fifth start, but ran creditably at times; suited by 1¼m; appears to act on any going; often blinkered, but didn't wear them on last 4 starts; sold 13,000 gns Ballsbridge September Sales. *W. Robinson, Ireland.* **80**

BOLDWIN 2 ch.c. Song 132–Final Game 83 (Pardao 120) (1980 5s 5d 6s 7d⁴ 5.3fg 6s 8fg 5d) Apr 4; 1,500Y; neat, strong colt; turns his front feet in; plater; stays 7f; slowly away first 2 outings and wore blinkers in most of his subsequent races; trained by A. Davison first 7 outings. *R. Ward.* **49**

BOLD WOOD 2 b.f. Bold Lad (Ire) 133–Stunog Wood 98 (Falcon 131) (1980 5f* 5f* 5f 5g 6g) Feb 22; neat, attractive filly; good mover; half-sister to 2 winners, including fairly useful Irish middle-distance performer St Domingo (by Connaught); dam, twice a winner over 5f at 2 yrs, is half-sister to good French stayer A Chara; justified favouritism in maiden race at Newmarket in April and **90**

£2,100 event at Chester the following month, in latter holding off Another Rumbo by a length; only eighth of 14 in nursery at Nottingham in September on final start (first outing for over 3 months); not certain to stay 6f; lacks scope. *J. Hindley.*

BOLTINGO 5 gr.g. Bold Lad (Ire) 133–Bundling (Petingo 135) (1979 NR 1980 10.6fg* 12fg) 20/1 and having first outing on flat for 2 seasons when winning seller at Haydock (no bid) in June by short head from Soie Grise; blinkered when behind in handicap at Chepstow following month; stays 10.6f; acts on a firm and a soft surface. *G. Beeson.* 51

BOMBALINI 4 b.g. Ribero 126–Villarrica (Dan Cupid 132) (1979 10.1fg 10.1fg 15.5fg 1980 12fg 16f) poor maiden *A. Ingham.* —

BOMBY ROLL (USA) 2 b.f. Droll Role–Bombycid (Shantung 132) (1980 7g 8fg) Jan 31; $6,500Y; neat filly; third foal; half-sister to a winner in USA; dam, unplaced 3 times, is half-sister to smart In Command and Icena; wasn't given a hard time once chance had gone in maiden races at Leicester, on first outing finishing seventh of 19 to Canaille in August. *P. Cole.* —

BONARD 4 ch.g. Realm 129–Miss Holborn (Pall Mall 132) (1979 6s 6v 8s 7v 6f 6g 6s 7f 1980 11fg 10fg 10.1fg) bad plater; sometimes wears blinkers. *K. Bridgwater.* —

BOND DEALER 3 ro.g. Habat 127–Sounion 69 (Vimy 132) (1979 7fg 7f 1980 8d³ 8.2s* 10d⁴ 10f³ 10fg 10f 8.3d 11.7g) good-looking gelding; made all to win maiden race at Nottingham in March; ran respectably next 2 starts but was well beaten subsequently; stays 1¼m; acts on any going. *B. Swift.* 75

BONDOR 4 b.g. Good Bond 122–Floradora Do 85 (Derring-Do 131) (1979 NR 1980 10.6fg 7.6g 8g 6g 9d) plater; not entirely disgraced in better company final start (sweating). *L. Barratt.* —

BOND'S BEST 6 ch.m. Good Bond 122–Izeste (Lavandin 128) (1979 12s⁴ 12fg 12d⁴ 12s⁴ 12.5g 12d 1980 16s² 15fg* 16f 15h 16fg) poor handicapper; made all at Folkestone in April and won by 5 lengths from stable-companion Abielle; ran poorly afterwards; stays well; acts on any going; suitable mount for a boy; inconsistent. *G.Huffer.* 50

BON-ET-VITE 3 b.g. Le Johnstan 123–Dobella (Sovereign Lord 120) (1979 5s 6s 6fg 7f⁴ 7f 7g 7g 7f 1980 10.8v 12fg 12f 14g) well-made gelding; only plating class; not certain to stay middle distances; blinkered final 3 starts at 2 yrs; sold 2,000 gns Ascot September Sales. *P. Mitchell.* —

BONITASS 5 b.m. Shiny Tenth 120–Tassel (Ragusa 137) (1979 7d 7f 8f 7f⁴ 6g 8.2g² 8fg 10h 8.2g⁴ 1980 8.2fg) poor plater; stays 1m; seems to act on any going; blinkered final start at 3 yrs; sold 820 gns Doncaster September Sales. *C. Gray.* —

Sidney Thompson Memorial Stakes, Brighton—Bonnie Isle is ridden with great dash by Willie Carson for an all-the-way win from Chukaroo and Tahitian King

BONITO 3 ch.c. Bonne Noel 115–Meadow Rhapsody (Ragusa 137) (1979 NR 1980 10f 10s 8fg 8g⁴ 6s 8d 8d) 750 3-y-o; leggy, close-coupled colt; half-brother to 3 winners, including Irish 7f and 1m winner Elegy (by Prince Tenderfoot); dam won over 6f and is half-sister to Meadow Court; plating-class maiden; will stay well; retained 1,750 gns Ascot November Sales. *K. Bailey.* —

BONNIE CHARLIE 2 br.c. Mummy's Pet 125–Aberdonia 71 (Alycidon 138) (1980 5fg³ 6fg² 6d* 6g³) Apr 13; 9,800Y; tall, good-bodied colt; half-brother to 2 winners, including very useful Level Par (by Hallez), a winner at up to 9f in this country; dam won at up to 1m; won 11-runner Piper Champagne Stakes at Salisbury in June by 1½ lengths from Glyndebourne; came up against useful colts on all other outings, running well when just over 4 lengths third of 10 to Another Realm in Group 2 Richmond Stakes at Goodwood the following month; may well stay further than 6f; acts on a firm and a soft surface. *G. Harwood.* **96**

Mrs D. Abbott's "Bonnie Charlie"

BONNIE ISLE 4 b.f. Pitcairn 126–Ruddy Duck 84 (Dicta Drake 126) (1979 8.5d³ 12v² 12d² 8f* 10f³ 10f² 10fg 12s² 1980 8fg* 8.5f³ 10d³ 8s 10fg² 10g 12d² 12d) big, well-made filly; good mover; smart performer on her day; runner-up to Scintillate in 1979 Oaks; made all and beat Chukaroo by 2 lengths in minor event at Brighton in April on reappearance; went through rest of season without a win although was placed in Diomed Stakes at Epsom (third to Hardgreen), Prince of Wales's Stakes at Royal Ascot (third to Ela-Mana-Mou), Nassau Stakes at Goodwood (second to Vielle) and Princess Royal Stakes at Ascot (second to Karamita); beaten comfortably in last 2 races; ran disappointingly on her other 3 starts; effective at 1m and stayed 1½m; acted on any going; stud in USA. *J. Dunlop.* **112**

BONNY BLINK 2 gr.f. Jimsun 121–Patel 101 (Constable 119) (1980 5f 8fg 5s) Feb 26; poor mover; half-sister to 2 winning platers; dam sprinter; soundly beaten in maiden races and a seller in the North; blinkered third outing. *Hbt Jones.* —

BONNYBRIDGE 2 br.f. Home Guard 129–Marypark 93 (Charlottown 127) (1980 6fg 7d⁴) Apr 22; quite a useful sort; half-sister to fairly useful stayer **72**

Halba (by Habat) and successful Scandinavian horse Coulstry (by High Top); dam well suited by long distances; had every chance 2f out when 4 lengths fourth of 20 to Soldan in minor event at Doncaster in October; should do better over $1\frac{1}{2}$m+ at 3 yrs. *B. Hobbs.*

BONNY GOLD 2 br.c. Goldhill 125–Politely 55 (Polic 126) (1980 5f 6g 6s^3 7g 7f 7fg* 7g 8f^4 8.2g 8d* 8.2s^4 7v) Feb 20; 1,300Y; strong colt who carries plenty of condition; good walker; fourth foal; half-brother to a winner in Malaysia; dam, poor plater, won over 1m; winner of maiden auction event at Doncaster in July and nursery at Pontefract in October, staying on gamely to win by 2 lengths from Rocket Song in latter; stays 1m well; acts on any going; genuine. *K. Stone.* **76**

BONOL 3 b.c. Ridan–Lynda's Own 94 (Schapiro 99) (1979 6f 6fg* 1980 7d* 7d* 8f^4) strong, good-bodied colt; good walker; useful performer; won £5,000 handicap at Doncaster and Northern Free Handicap at Newcastle early in year; odds on, drew clear inside final furlong to beat Joyous $2\frac{1}{2}$ lengths in latter event; moved short on way to start and had every chance from 2f out when $4\frac{3}{4}$ lengths fourth of 9 to Tyrnavos in Ladbrokes Craven Stakes at Newmarket in April; stays 1m; suited by some give in the ground; reportedly cracked a bone in one of his hind legs in June. *M. H. Easterby.* **109**

BON VOYAGE 3 b.f. Good Bond 122–My Gipsy Moth 81 (Aggressor 130) (1979 5fg 5fg^4 6g^3 6g^3 1980 8s^3 8g^2 8f 8f 8d* 7s* 8f^4 7g) neat filly; won claiming race at Brighton and handicap at Folkestone (apprentice ridden) in the summer; stays 1m; needs some give in the ground. *I. Balding.* **66**

BOOBY TRAP 2 gr. or br.g. Decoy Boy 129–Sue's Dolly (Quorum 126) (1980 5fg 5f 5fg^4 5f^3 6d^4 5.8fg 5.3fg^3 5g^2) Mar 1; 3,000F, 6,600Y; fair sort; third produce; brother to a winner in Malaya; dam never ran; in frame in varied company, including selling; stays 6f; seems to act on any going; blinkered fourth to seventh outings. *A. Johnson.* **65**

BOON 3 b.c. Great Nephew 126–Pavillon 88 (French Beige 127) (1979 8h* 7d^2 1980 9fg^3 13s^2 12g* 12g 12fg^3 14g) well-made colt; fairly useful handicapper; won 2-runner race at Beverley in July; had earlier run well when second at Nottingham; best form at up to 13f (pulled hard early on when tried at $1\frac{3}{4}$m); acts on any going. *B. Hobbs.* **96**

BOOST 3 b.g. Busted 134–Grandpa's Legacy 102 (Zeus Boy 121) (1979 NR 1980 11f 12g 13.3fg^2 12g 12g^4 14g*) rangy gelding; brother to minor French 11f winner Giulio Cesare, and half-brother to very smart 7f to 13.3f winner Consol (by Reliance II); dam stayed $1\frac{1}{2}$m; dead-heated with Homeson in maiden race at Sandown in July; suited by a test of stamina; didn't move well to post and looked a difficult ride on fifth start; dead. *N. Vigors.* **78**

BORDER BROOK 3 b.g. Forlorn River 124–Kelso Girl (Royal Palm 131) (1979 5fg 5f^4 6s 5f 7.2g* 8.2fg 1980 7v* 10s^2 10g 8fg^3 8f* 8g^2 8fg^4) plain, workmanlike gelding; moderate handicapper; won at Stockton in March and Beverley (apprentice ridden) in June: stays $1\frac{1}{4}$m; acts on any going; dwelt third start; game and genuine. *W. C. Watts.* **81**

BORDER KNIGHT 5 br.g. Targowice 130–Bruntlaw 94 (Bounteous 125) (1979 12.3v 12d 10f 10fg^2 11g^2 12fg^4 10.2fg 1980 12f^2 10.5f^4 10fg^2 11g* 12fg* 10fg^2 12g 12.2fg 12g 11fg^4) middle-distance handicapper; ridden by 7-lb claimer when successful at Hamilton in June and Edinburgh in July; acts on any going; usually blinkered nowadays; sometimes sweats up. *Denys Smith.* **74**

BORDERLINE 4 b.c. Silly Season 127–Near The Line 88 (Nearula 132) (1979 7g^4 8g 10s 10fg* 10fg^2 10.5f^4 10s^4 12g 10f 9f 1980 10g 10f 11f 10fg^3 10g^2 10.2g^2 10.6d 10fg*) well-made, attractive colt; ridden by 7-lb claimer and looked very well when beating Dasman by $\frac{3}{4}$ length in Chesterfield Cup at Goodwood in August; narrowly beaten in handicaps at Sandown (by African Rhythm) and Doncaster (by Fine Blue) earlier; suited by $1\frac{1}{4}$m on top-of-the-ground; blinkered fourth and fifth starts; usually ridden up with pace; sold 8,200 gns Newmarket December Sales. *I. Balding.* **88**

BORDER SPOIL 2 b.g. Mummy's Pet 125–Kelso Girl (Royal Palm 131) (1980 5fg 6d 6g 6fg^2 6g 7d^4 6g 8g) Apr 26; well-grown, useful-looking gelding; has a round action; half-brother to several winners, including fairly useful 1976 2-y-o 5f winner Forlorn Scot (by Forlorn River); dam never ran; in frame in minor event at Redcar in July (short-headed by Solway Winds) and maiden race at Chester the following month (kept on to finish $2\frac{3}{4}$ lengths fourth of 12 to Patchinia); probably stays 1m; acts on a firm and a soft surface. *W. C. Watts.* **74**

BOREAS 5 br.g. Boreen (Fr) 123–Great Aunt 74 (Great Nephew 126) (1979 **37**
8g 8s^{2} 8.2g* 8g 9fg 10f^{3} 13.8f* 12f 10fg 16g 16fg 18fg 12.2fg 12g 12.5g 15s 1980 12d 12h 12fg 16fg 12g 13.8f^{3} 16g 15.8g^{4} 15.8d 15d) plater; stays 1¾m; acts on any going; wears blinkers. *S. Nesbitt.*

BORISOV (USA) 2 b.c. Icecapade–Chance For Reign (Majestic Prince) (1980 **91**
5f^{2} 6f* 6g* 6g^{2} 6fg^{3}) Apr 7; $80,000Y; strong, compact, good sort; good mover; third foal; dam unraced half-sister to smart stakes winners Sailor Princess and Swift Lady; successful in minor events at Leicester and Newcastle in June; led 1f out and was well on top at finish when beating Sheba's Glory 1½ lengths on latter course; ran well on both subsequent starts; would have stayed 1¼m; acted on firm going; dead. *H. Cecil.*

BORLANDHILLS 3 bl.f. Goldhill 125–Phydorine (Vilmorin) (1979 5s 5d 5g **—**
5fg 5g 5f 5g 1980 5g 5f 7f 8d 6g) neat, strong filly; of no account. *T. Craig.*

BORN TO LOSE 3 gr.f. Rupert Bear 105–Cipticera (Ballyciptic 122) (1979 **—**
5g 5s^{3} 6fg^{4} 5f^{2} 5fg^{3} 5g 6fg 5h 1980 8s 8fg 8.3f 6fg) small, light-framed filly; has a round action; poor plater; best run at 5f on firm going; blinkered final 2 starts in 1979. *M. Salaman.*

BOSSALL 4 br.g. Warpath 113–Miss Barbara 87 (Le Dieu d'Or 119) (1979 **64**
NR 1980 10f 10fg 11g^{4} 12d* 11fg 14.6fg^{3} 16g* 16.1s 18d) lengthy, useful sort of gelding; good walker; half-brother to Lochnager (by Dumbarnie); quickened in final furlong when winning handicap at Haydock in July by 1½ lengths from Ascot Again; got home by a head from Broadsword after a ding-dong battle in last 2f when successful at Newcastle following month; stays well; acts on a firm and an easy surface; wears blinkers; sold out of C. Crossley's stable 7,100 gns Doncaster September Sales after seventh start. *S. Holland.*

BOTANIST 7 ch.g. Ballymoss 136–Larkspur's Love (Larkspur 128) (1979 **70**
12s 14g 13.1g 17.1g 14fg 12fg* 12f* 17.1h^{3} 14f* 12fg 13.1g 1980 11f 12f* 13.1fg^{3} 12fg^{2} 14g^{3} 12d^{4} 12fg 14g 12fg^{3} 12fg^{3} 14fg 12f* 16g* 12g* 17.1d* 16.1s 18s) staying handicapper; had an excellent season and was gaining his fifth success when beating Cecconi by 2½ lengths in 23-runner event at Bath in October; successful earlier at Chepstow, Wolverhampton (apprentices), Lingfield and Brighton; acts on a soft surface, but has done most of his winning on a firm one; good mount for an apprentice; trained until after seventh outing by J. Old. *G. Balding.*

BOTTISHAM 2 ch.c. Moulton 128–Relkalim 102 (Relko 136) (1980 6d 7.6g 8d) **79**
Feb 3; robust, short-legged colt; fifth foal; half-brother to a winner in Norway; dam, useful at up to 1¼m, is half-sister to Sovereign; 25/1 when 7 lengths fifth of 8 to Admiral's Heir in £4,300 event at Lingfield in September, second outing and best effort; unquoted and apprentice ridden next time out; will stay 1½m. *H. Wragg.*

BOTTLE TOP 2 b.c. High Top 131–Bananaquit 103 (Prove It) (1980 7f 6d) **—**
Mar 3; lengthy colt; third living foal; half-brother to 2 winners, including middle-distance performer Bicentennial (by Blakeney); dam won twice over 5f at 2 yrs; showed a little ability in large fields for maiden races at Newmarket in October, fading in final 2f both times; should stay 7f. *H. T. Jones.*

BOUNTY SEEKER 3 br.f. Pitcairn 126–Miss Lomond 74 (Preciptic 122) **—**
(1979 NR 1980 8fg) 4,500Y; half-sister to a minor winner; dam won at up to 1½m; unquoted, dwelt at flag start and was always behind in 7-runner maiden race won by Just Abroad at Warwick in August. *W. Holden.*

BOURIENNE 2 b.f. Bolkonski 134–Blanche Hardy (Ribot 142) (1980 5d 5g **58**
5.8f^{3} 6s 7g^{3} 8d^{3} 8d^{4}) Apr 26; small, lightly-made filly; dam won over 1½m in Italy; plater; will stay 1¼m; sold out of P. Walwyn's stable 880 gns Ascot September Sales after fifth start. *D. H. Jones.*

BOURNE'S CHAMPION 3 b.c. Sovereign Path 125–Yellow Ribbon (Shooting **—**
Chant) (1979 NR 1980 7d 8d) 5,000F, 8,000Y; strong, compact colt; first foal; dam won over 7f and 1m in Ireland; on burly side when behind in newcomers race at Doncaster in March and maiden event at Salisbury in June. *B. Swift.*

BOUZY ROSE 2 b.f. Roi Soleil 125–Scoop (Bleep-Bleep 134) (1980 5g 8g 6d) **—**
Feb 19; 2,500Y; fair sort; half-sister to a winning plater and 2 winners abroad; dam never ran; well behind in maiden and minor events. *J. Hudson.*

BOVEY BELLS 2 b.f. Supreme Sovereign 119–Canteen Katie (King's Troop **—**
118) (1980 5.8fg 5.8f) Feb 2; 560Y; half-sister to 3 winners in Italy; started none too well when in rear in maiden race and seller at Bath in July. *J. Cann.*

BOW LANE 2 b.f. Idiot's Delight 115–Highway Holiday (Jimmy Reppin 131) –
(1980 7fg 7.2d) Apr 22; compact non-thoroughbred filly; first foal; dam never
ran; in rear in maiden race at Leicester (very slowly away) and seller at Haydock
in October. *C. V. Miller.*

BOXBERGER CAPRI (HOL) 2 ch.f. Cadmus 124–Crepella (Crepello 136) –
(1980 7fg 7fg 6.5g 9g) Feb 23; workmanlike filly; half-sister to middle-distance
winners in France by Charlottown and Blue Tom; dam unraced daughter of
smart Toscanella; behind in sizeable fields of maidens at Warwick and Yarmouth
in the summer prior to finishing towards rear in 2 races in Holland. *A. Hide.*

BOXBERGER PRINS 5 b.g. The Brianstan 128–Queen's Ring (Royal Record **70**
II) (1979 8d 12.5s* 10g* 11fg* 10f* 10f* 10f* 11.5fg* 11.7fg^2 10d 10fg* 10f^3
12.5fg 10fg 1980 11.7s 11.5g 11.7f 10s 10fg 10f 10g^3 10fg^3 10g 12g^4 12g^4 11d 8s)
strong, compact gelding; won 8 races in 1979 but was mainly disappointing in
1980; suited by middle distances; acts on any going but is well suited by fast
ground; has often worn blinkers; used to have a good turn of foot. *M. Ryan.*

BOXBERGER RELKO (HOL) 2 br.c. Filandre–Head High 92 (Star Gazer **?**
123) (1980 7g 6.5g 9g^4) Dutch-bred colt; dam won over 7f at 2 yrs; unquoted
and very backward, unseated rider going on to course and galloped riderless to
start prior to finishing last of 15 to McCarthy in maiden race at Newmarket in
August; subsequently raced in Holland, finishing 6½ lengths fourth of 10 to
Marmorera in Dutch Criterium in September. *A. Hide.*

BOXBERGER RIBIO (HOL) 3 b.f. Sir Ribot–Tabitha (Watteau) (1979 8f –
1980 10g 13.3fg) leggy filly; in rear in maiden races; didn't impress in paddock
final start (June). *C. Nelson.*

BOXBERGER ROSE (HOL) 2 br.f. Cadmus 124–Moon Rose (Basalt) (1980 –
7g 8.2d 8f 6g 7.2s) lengthy filly; first foal; dam won over 1¼m at 2 yrs in France;
of little account; sold 300 gns Doncaster November Sales. *R. E. Peacock.*

BOXLAW 2 b.c. Jukebox 120–April Twelfth (King's Leap 111) (1980 5fg 6s 6s –
7fg 8d 7d) Apr 2; 820Y; tall, leggy colt; half-brother to 3 winners, including
3-y-o 5f winner Champ D'Avril (by Northfields); dam, 2-y-o 5f winner, is half-
sister to Music Boy; no sign of ability in maiden races, including an auction
event; blinkered fifth outing. *H. O'Neill.*

BOYLE EXPRESS 3 br.f. Furry Glen 121–Erica (Ballyciptic 122) (1979 5d^4 –
5fg^3 5f 5g^4 5g^3 6s 8fg 7s 1980 6f 7fg^2 8s 7fg 8f) light-framed filly; little worthwhile form in varied company, including selling; best run at 7f on a firm surface;
has worn bandages. *C. Gray.*

BOY MARVEL 7 b.g. Richboy 117–Miss Marvel 59 (Palestine 133) (1979 10d –
10.5d^3 1980 10f 10g) plain gelding; improved in 1978 and was unbeaten in 5
handicaps; lightly-raced since; stays 1¼m well; acts on any going; has been tried
in blinkers; bandaged in 1980; genuine; excellent mount for an apprentice.
G. Huffer.

BOYNE HILL 4 b. or br.f. Baroque 128–Swing On (Sheshoon 132) (1979 NR –
1980 9g 12fg 10fg 8g^3 10d) small filly; 50/1, ran easily best race when 4 lengths
third of 24 to Countess Virginia in amateur riders event at Warwick in June;
top weight when behind in selling handicap at Nottingham later in month.
D. Nicholson.

BOYNE VALLEY 4 ch.c. St Chad 120–My Valley 86 (Midas) (1979 8g^2 8f^3 –
7fg* 8f* 8fg^2 8f 8g^2 8fg^2 7fg^3 11.5d* 1980 12f) Irish colt; useful performer
at 3 yrs; stays 11.5f; seems to act on any going. *L. Greene, Ireland.*

BOZOVICI 3 br.c. Queen's Hussar 124–Doushiska 78 (Hornbeam 130) (1979 **113**
7fg^2 7f* 7s^2 7fg* 1980 12fg^4 12f 12fg^4 12f^3 10.5g* 12f) rangy colt; good walker;
brother to French 13f winner Romanova and half-brother to 3 winners, including
Serge Lifar (by Lyphard), very useful at up to 13f; dam won at 1½m; did well
physically from 2 yrs to 3 yrs and showed smart form on his fifth start, putting
up a game display to win 9-runner Cordwainers Stakes at York in August by 2
lengths from Fingal's Cave (gave 5 lb); in frame earlier in Predominate Stakes at
Kempton, Alycidon Stakes at Goodwood and £3,700 race at Lingfield; stays
1½m; acts on any going but needs an easy surface to show to best advantage. *R.
Price.*

BRACADALE 2 b.c. The Brianstan 128–Can't Wait (Eudaemon 129) (1980 6g **?**
6s 6fg^2 6g 5.1g^4) Feb 3; 9,800Y; neat, good-quartered colt; good mover; half-
brother to 3 winners, including 6f and 7f winner Steady Hand (by Some Hand);
dam of little account; ran easily best race when going down by 1½ lengths to
Sweet Monday in 19-runner Selsey Stakes at Goodwood in July; produced nothing
like that form subsequently, starting odds on for similar event at Yarmouth

in September on final start but finishing only 11 lengths fourth of 11 to Directorate; form only at 6f on a firm surface. *R. Armstrong.*

BRACKEN GILL 2 gr.c. Ribston 102–Gill Breeze (Farm Walk 111) (1980 5f 5f³ 5f* 6fg 5fg⁴ 5d³ 5f² 5d) Apr 13; 800Y; brother to 6f seller winner Pippin Gill, and half-brother to 3 winners; dam never ran; ½-length winner from Spurstow in 6-runner maiden race at Hamilton in May; also ran well when 2 lengths second to Water of Life in nursery at Ripon in August; should stay 6f; best form on a sound surface and goes well on firm going; trained by W. H. H. Williams first 4 outings; ran badly final start. *J. Wilson.* **73**

BRACONDA 3 b.f. So Blessed 130–Brilliant Reay 74 (Ribero 126) (1979 5d⁴ 5s* 5fg 5f 5g² 6fg* 6fg⁴ 1980 7fg⁴ 6f⁴ 6fg 6fg 6fg² 6fg 6g) leggy filly; quite moderate handicapper; stays 7f; acts on any going. *R. Armstrong* **74**

BRADAMANTE 4 ch.c. Royal Prerogative 119–Cracker 103 (Court Harwell 130) (1979 8d* 10v 8.2s⁴ 8g⁴ 10f 8g* 8fg 8d 1980 8d² 10g 10.4f² 8f² 10f 8d⁴ 8d 8d* 8g 8f³ 8g 8.2s) tall, leggy colt; quite a useful handicapper on his day; made all when scoring by 2½ lengths from Pinkerton's Man at Ayr in July; good third to Crown Witness in Ripon Rowels Handicap following month, but ran poorly on fifth and seventh starts; stays 1¼m; possibly not at his best on really soft going; not particularly consistent. *Denys Smith.* **89**

BRADETTE 3 b.f. Great Nephew 126–Dashing Diana (Silver Shark 129) (1979 5d³ 5s² 5g³ 6fg⁴ 7.2fg⁴ 6fg 7fg 6fg 1980 11fg 7f* 7fg 7f 8.3g 11.7d 12s) good sort; narrowly won handicap at Warwick in April; well beaten afterwards; not certain to stay 1½m; acts on any going; usually blinkered nowadays. *J. Hill.* **70**

BRAGGADOCCIO 5 b.h. Blast 125–Rhodia (Parthia 132) (1979 10f⁴ 12fg² 10fg* 12g⁴ 12fg* 12fg⁴ 12fg 1980 11.7fg) middle-distance handicapper; not disgraced only outing of 1980 (May); acts on firm going; blinkered twice at 3 yrs; suitable mount for an apprentice; sold 800 gns Newmarket Autumn Sales. *P. Makin.* —

BRAHMS AND LISZT 4 b.g. Will Somers 114 §–Fancy Pants 80 (Galivanter 131) (1979 8d 10g 5g 7fg* 6h 6f 6fg 6g 7d³ 7f 9f 1980 7f 7fg) neat gelding; modest plater; probably stays 9f; has been tried in blinkers and a hood. *A. Balding.* —

BRALANTA 3 ch.f. Green God 128–Hedgerow (Hornbeam 130) (1979 6g 7fg 6fg 7fg 1980 8fg 8.3fg 8g 7g) narrow filly; quite a moderate maiden at 2 yrs; well —

Cordwainers Stakes, York—Bozovici beats the favourite Fingal's Cave

beaten in handicaps in 1980; should stay 1m; blinkered third start (ran badly). *R. Armstrong.*

BRANCASTER 6 b.h. Huntercombe 133–Cigarette Case 89 (Faberge II 121) (1979 16.9s 12f 12f 12fg 14f^{2} 8g 12fg^{3} 16f 16f 1980 17.1f 12s) poor handicapper; stays 2m, but is better at middle distances; acts on firm going; used to wear blinkers. *J. Cann.* –

BRANDING IRON 3 ch.g. Hotfoot 126–Caesar's Love 85 (Above Suspicion 127) (1979 NR 1980 11fg) 7,400Y; lengthy gelding; brother to very useful 1974 2-y-o 1m winner Caesar's Flame; dam placed over 1½m on only start; unquoted, ran on in closing stages when 9 lengths fifth of 20 to Saviour in maiden race at Newbury in April; not seen out again. *I. Balding.* –

BRANDO 3 ch.c. Busted 134–Cafe au Lait 97 (Espresso 122) (1979 6d 7f^{3} 7f^{2} 7fg^{3} 8d^{2} 1980 12s 12fg 16f* 16f^{2} 16g^{4} 14d^{3} 14g 16d) leggy, lightly-made colt; stayed on well to win maiden race at York in May; ran well on fifth outing when 2½ lengths fourth to Toondra in Queen's Vase at Royal Ascot; suited by a test of stamina; probably acts on any going. *F. Durr.* 97

BRASS CHANGE 2 gr.c. Town Crier 119–Brass Finisher 93 (Cash and Courage 116) (1980 6d) Mar 25; 11,000Y; half-brother to very useful 1977 2-y-o 5f performer Emboss (by Tribal Chief) and 3-y-o 1¼m winner Groovy Girl (by Averof); dam, sister to very smart Sol 'Argent, won at up to 1¼m and also over hurdles; unquoted but fairly fit when behind in 17-runner maiden race won by Gabitat at Newmarket in October. *A. Bailey.* –

BRASSY 2 b.f. Bold Lad (Ire) 133–Monaco Melody 103 (Tudor Melody 129) (1980 5fg^{2} 5f^{3} 5f^{4} 6g^{4} 6g) Apr 17; 17,000Y; lengthy filly; first foal; dam useful 6f winner at 2 yrs and 3 yrs; placed in maiden races in the spring, finishing head second to Sybaris at Sandown and length third of 11 to Labista at York; fourth in June in £4,000 race at Beverley (favourite when beaten 4¼ lengths by Gandoorah) and maiden event at Doncaster (behind 10-length winner Her Grace); stays 6f; yet to race on a soft surface; blinkered fourth outing. *H. T. Jones.* 76

BRAUGHING 3 b.c. Martinmas 128–Lucasta (High Hat 131) (1979 6f 6fg^{2} 6g* 6d^{3} 6f^{3} 6fg^{3} 1980 7f 8.5f^{4} 8fg 12f 8d 8s 8f^{2} 10g 8d*) strong, round-barrelled colt; very useful (rated 114) at 2 yrs; returned to something like his best when making all to beat Carriage Way 2 lengths in handicap at Sandown in October; had run best previous races when fourth to Last Fandango in Ladbroke Blue Riband Trial at Epsom and second to Maintop in minor event at Newmarket (didn't look too enthusiastic); out of his depth in 2000 Guineas at Newmarket (blinkered), Derby and St James's Palace Stakes at Royal Ascot on third, fourth and fifth starts; should stay beyond 1m; probably acts on any going; sometimes sweats up; dwelt eighth appearance; ran badly sixth outing. *C. Brittain.* 111

BRAVE EFFORT 5 gr.g. Blakeney 126–Princess Caroline 68 (Sovereign Path 125) (1979 10.2s^{4} 10s 10fg 8g 1980 10.2d 16.1d 12.5s 18s) big gelding; staying maiden; wears bandages; suitable mount for an amateur. *P. Feilden.* –

BRAVE FELLOW 6 b.g. Giolla Mear 117–Mirastar (Miralgo 130) (1979 NR 1980 12.3s* 12.3f^{2} 12f 16d 13g^{3}) won maiden race at Newcastle in April comfortably; placed in minor event on same course later in month (didn't find a great deal off bridle) and handicap at Nottingham in July (didn't impress in paddock but finished creditable third to Jam); stays 13f well; acts on any going. *J. Fitzgerald.* 73

BRAVE GEM 2 b.c. Sparkler 130–Fearless 77 (Derring-Do 131) (1980 6d) Mar 4; lengthy colt; half-brother to 7f and 1m winner Gibbon (by Swing Easy); dam, winner over 7f, is half-sister to More Light and Shoot A Line; unquoted and on backward side, stayed on well final 2f when 6 lengths eighth of 19 to Imperial Measure in maiden race at Salisbury in June, only outing. *P. Cundell.* – p

BRAVE HUSSAR 2 ch.c. Brigadier Gerard 144–Tirana 101 (Ragusa 137) (1980 8g) Mar 14; half-brother to winning middle-distance stayer Scutari (by St Paddy); dam won over 6f and 7f at 2 yrs; easy in market and in need of race when behind in minor event won by Uppety at Newmarket in October. *H. Cecil.* –

BRAVE MAN 2 br.c. Manado 130–Miss Atalanta 83 (Hethersett 134) (1980 6fg 7f) May 14; 13,500Y; neat colt; half-brother to several winners, including 3-y-o 6f winner Going Strait and 7f winner Fettercairn (both by Manacle); dam placed over 7f at 2 yrs; no sign of ability in maiden races at Salisbury in September and Newmarket in October (missed break and jockey didn't persevere in final 1½f). *J. Dunlop.* –

BRAVE THE REEF (USA) 3 ch.c. Mill Reef 141–Gallina 120 (Raise A Native) (1979 6s 7f^{3} 8f^{3} 1980 12s^{2} 12f^{2} 16f 12.3s^{4} 12.3d* 12g^{4} 11.7d*) small, lengthy, 85

attractive colt; successful in minor event at Newcastle in August and handicap at Bath in October; runs as if he will be suited by 1¾m (well beaten when tried over 2m); acts on any going; suitable mount for a boy; genuine; changed hands 15,500 gns Newmarket Autumn Sales. *I. Balding.*

BRAVISSIMO 2 b.f. Roman Warrior 132–Gimima 54 (Narrator 127) (1980 6s 6s 6d 7fg) Apr 6; 7,400Y; compact gelding; half-brother to winners here and abroad, including 1978 2-y-o 5f winner Galleypot Girl (by Philip of Spain); dam won 1m seller; no worthwhile form in maiden and minor events. *D. Morley.* —

BRAVO 5 ch.g. Connaught 130–Country Path 101 (Mossborough 126) (1979 13s 14g 18.4d 10.8fg^2 12g 11d* 1980 12.2s 11.7fg 14fg 11f 20d 12d) good-bodied gelding; stays well; seems to act on any going; sometimes wears blinkers; suitable mount for an amateur rider; sold 1,600 gns Ascot July Sales. *D. Elsworth.* —

BREATHING EXERCISE 7 ch.g. Pall Mall 132–Karen Chase 82 (Will Somers 114 §) (1979 6s^4 7s 7v 7s 8d 6g* 7g 6s 1980 7d 7fg 6fg 7fg 6s 6d 6g 7.3fg 6fg 6d 7d) well-made gelding; quite a moderate handicapper; best form at 6f and 7f; acts on any going; has been tried in blinkers; occasionally sweats up; good mount for an apprentice; inconsistent. *J. O'Donoghue.* —

BRECQUOU CHIEF 2 b.c. Roi Soleil 125–Miss Vanadium (Helmar) (1980 5fg 6g 8.2s 8d) Mar 28; second foal; dam ran once in USA; poor plater. *J. Toller.* 50

BRENDAN 5 br.g. Saintly Song 128–Tigerlee 57 (Tiger 125) (1979 5v 5d* 5s 5s 5f 5fg 6fg^3 6f 6d 5fg 5g 5s 5d 1980 5v^4 5s 5g 5f 6fg 5fg 6g) small gelding; sprint handicapper; suited by an easy surface; sometimes wears blinkers but does better without; often wears a tongue strap; suitable mount for a boy; inconsistent and was well beaten in a seller on sixth start. *S. Nesbitt.* —

BRENTEX 2 gr.c. Birdbrook 110–Black Mink 83 (Gratitude 130) (1980 5g^4 5fg^3 5s^3 6fg 5.8f^4 5d^3 5f^4 5fg^2 5f^2 5d* 5g^4) Apr. 22; 8,600Y; neat colt; half-brother to fairly useful 1975 2-y-o 5f winner Hiliarchos (by Burglar); dam won 95

Mr S. Mason's "Brentex"

twice over 5f at 2 yrs; gained a well-deserved success when winning 19-runner maiden race at Warwick in October by 1½ lengths from Camisite; in frame in varied races on most of his other starts, including Windsor Castle Stakes at Royal Ascot on second outing and valuable nurseries at Newbury and Newmarket (2) on eighth, ninth and eleventh; best form at 5f but gave impression on final appearance that a return to 6f will suit him; appears to act on any going; blinkered sixth and seventh starts; suited by waiting tactics. *N. Vigors.*

BRETON BANQUET 2 gr.c. Brittany–Nosh (Court Martial) (1980 5fg 5fg 6f 7d 7fg 6s 6g 5.1fg 6d^4 6fg 6g^3 8fg 8.2g 8d) Apr 11; 1,150F, 4,900Y; compact colt; poor mover; moderate plater; form only at 6f; usually blinkered. *W. Marshall.* **61**

BRETTON PARK 2 b.c. Mummy's Pet 125–Trickster 92 (Major Portion 129) (1980 5s^4 6fg^4 6g 5g^2 5d^2 6v* 6s^2) Apr 30; strong, fair sort; third foal; half-brother to 2 winners, including useful 3-y-o sprinter Jebb Lane (by The Brianstan); dam sprinter; won 5-runner maiden race at Hamilton in October easing up by 5 lengths from Time-Table; creditable second of 12 to Marking Time in 12-runner minor event at Stockton the following month, the pair finishing clear; stays 6f well; acts on heavy going; blinkered fourth, sixth and seventh outings. *S. Norton.* **90**

BREWER'S GREEN 2 br.f. Dragonara Palace 115–Samia 73 (Galivanter 131) (1980 5f 6g 5d^3 5.8f) Feb 8; 2,500F, 2,300Y; strong, good-bodied filly but is only a bad plater; sold 440 gns Ascot September Sales. *A. Ingham.* **47**

BREWMASTER 7 br.h. John Splendid 116–Ronelda (Tyrone 130) (1979 NR 1980 8.2d 9d 10fg) short-backed horse; poor plater; stays 1¼m; acts on any going; blinkered once at 3 yrs; often apprentice ridden. *J. Mulhall.* **—**

BRIAN 3 b.c. The Brianstan 128–Aberside (Abernant 142) (1979 5s^4 5d 5d 6f 6fg^4 5g 5f 6fg 1980 5s 7d 7fg^3 7f^3 7f* 8d^3 7s 8.3d 8d 8s 6g) fair sort; plater; successful at Newmarket in May (bought in 2,400 gns); possibly stays 1m; suited by firm going and isn't at his best on soft; wears blinkers and has worn a hood in addition. *J. Benstead.* **71** d

BRIANKA 3 b.f. The Brianstan 128–Slightly Saucy 74 (Galivanter 131) (1979 NR 1980 7d 8v 8f 7fg 8fg 10.1g^3 10g^2 12.2g^3 12g 10s 10g) 780 2-y-o; fair sort; first living foal; dam stayed well; placed in maiden and minor races; suited by middle distances; wandered quite badly under pressure when apprentice ridden on seventh outing; blinkered final start; has worn bandages; sometimes has her tongue tied down; sold 620 gns Ascot November Sales. *M. McCormack.* **61**

BRIAN'S LADY 2 b.f. Dawn Review 105–Ickworth Lady 69 (Fleece 114) (1980 5fg 5fg 5fg 6f* 6g 6fg 5.1fg) Feb 16; 820Y; second foal; won 8-runner seller at Yarmouth in June by ½ length from Allied Cardiff; ran poorly afterwards, including in blinkers on final start. *M. Ryan.* **48**

BRIANS STAR 5 br.h. The Brianstan 128–Claral Star 71 (Top Star 96) (1979 5d 5d 5fg^4 5g* 5fg 5f* 5fg 5f 5fg^3 5f^3 5g 5d 5f 5f^3 5h 5s 1980 5s 5fg 5f^2 5g 5.1f^3 5fg 5fg 5g^4 5g^3 5f 5d 5d) workmanlike horse; quite a moderate handicapper; best form at 5f on a sound surface; wears blinkers; good mount for an apprentice. *A. Balding.* **56**

BRIANSTANWAY 3 br.c. The Brianstan 128–Carina 98 (Tamerlane 128) (1979 5s 5g 6f 6fg 5s 1980 6s* 6fg^2 6fg 6fg* 6g 6g 6s* 5g^3 6d 6s 6d^4) small, compact sort; fair performer; won modest maiden race at Leicester in March and handicaps at Windsor in May and June; stays 6f; seems to act on any going, but goes well in the mud. *D. Nicholson.* **84**

BRIANS VENTURE 5 b.h. Sallust 134–Lavarna (Le Levanstell 122) (1979 6s^2 6v^3 8d* 7s 8d* 7fg* 8g 8g^3 8f 8s 1980 10s 8f 8.2g) useful-looking horse; useful handicapper in 1979, winner of good prizes at Newbury, Sandown and York; lightly raced and didn't run up to his form in 1980, but was off course over 3 months before final start (needed race); stays 1¼m; appears to act on any going; sold 4,800 gns Newmarket December Sales. *F. Rimell.* **96**

BRIAR 2 b.f. Brigadier Gerard 144–Conciliation 98 (St Paddy 133) (1980 5f 7f* 8d) Jan 6; strong, good-quartered filly; first foal; dam, half-sister to smart middle-distance horse Colum, won over 6f and 7f at 2 yrs; put up a fair effort after a 3 months absence when winning 20-runner maiden race at Chepstow in August by 2½ lengths from Norfolk Queen; had plenty to do under top weight in 6-runner nursery at Newbury in October and weakened quickly in final 2f to finish 10 lengths fifth to Golden Flak; should be suited by 1m; acts on firm going. *R. Hern.* **87**

BRI-EDEN 6 b.h. The Brianstan 128–Dainty Eden 53 (Orbit 106) (1979 5s2 5s3 5fg3 5fg 5f 5fg 5g 5fg 5d 5d 1980 5f2 5fg2 5fg* 5g3 6d 5fg* 5g3 5fg* 5d 5f 5d4) fairly useful handicapper; has reportedly been operated on for soft palate; made all when successful at Carlisle, Edinbugh and Thirsk; stuck on gamely when scoring by 1½ lengths from Hyperion Chief on last-named course in August; speedy and is best at 5f; acts on any going; has won for an amateur rider; broke down on final start in September. *J. Berry.* **88**

BRIERKRETE BELL 3 gr.g. Runnymede 123–Dilwyn 84 (Immortality) (1979 5s 5v2 5d 5s 6g 6fg 6fg 5f 5h 8.2s 1980 8d 8v2 8.2fg 8f 8f 8.2fg) neat gelding; poor plater; stays 1m; suited by heavy ground; has worn blinkers; sold 420 gns Doncaster October Sales. *J. Berry.* **58** d

BRIGADIER GREEN 3 b.c. Brigadier Gerard 144–Queen's Parole (Worden II 129) (1979 NR 1980 10.2d* 9g 12g 14f2 12f 12g 16g3 16s4 14.6fg 13g4 13.8d) 5,000Y, 4,000 2-y-o; neat colt; half-brother to fairly useful 7f winner Pas de Probleme (by Sir Gaylord); dam, useful winner at 2 yrs in France, is half-sister to Rock Roi; made most of running to win modest newcomers race at Doncaster in March; placed in handicaps subsequently; stays well; probably acts on any going; ran badly in blinkers final start; sold to W. H. H. Williams 4,700 gns Newmarket Autumn Sales. *P. Kelleway.* **68**

BRIGADIER HAWK 2 b.c. Brigadier Gerard 144–Flibbertigibbet 97 (Klairon 131) (1980 6g 7fg) Jan 21; 32,000F, 12,000Y; compact, good-bodied colt; half-brother to several winners, including very useful middle-distance handicapper Funny Man (by Jolly Jet); dam won at up to 1½m; always struggling when behind in fairly valuable races won by Norman Style at Doncaster and Centurius at Ascot in September. *C. Brittain.* –

BRIGHT EDGE 2 b.g. Sharp Edge 123–Gold Of The Day 72 (Bing II) (1980 5d 7d) June 14; fourth foal; half-brother to 1978 2-y-o 5f winner Ergo (by Song) and a winner in Italy; dam won at up to 1m; unquoted when in rear in 14-runner maiden races won by Azaam at Wolverhampton and by Norfolk Realm at Leicester in October. *Mrs N. Kennedy.* –

BRIGHT FIRE 12 b.g. Firestreak 125–Light Case 107 (Borealis) (1979 12s2 12f 12fg3 14g* 12fg 1980 12fg 12g 17.1d) a grand old campaigner but is on the downgrade and finished behind all outings of 1980; stays 1¾m; acts on any going; often loses ground at start; usually apprentice ridden; blinkered once in 1978. *H. Blagrave.* –

BRIGHT LANDING 2 ch.f. Sun Prince 128–Land Ho (Primera 131) (1980 5f4 5g 5d2 5fg4 5g2 6d) Mar 13; quite attractive, lengthy filly; good mover; half-sister to 2 winners by Swing Easy, including very useful 1976 2-y-o 5f winner Easy Landing; dam daughter of very smart sprinter Lucasland; second in maiden event at Salisbury in June (1½ lengths behind Supine) and small race at Goodwood in September (chased home 10-length winner Labista); should be suited by 6f (blinkered when tried at trip). *J. Tree.* **78**

BRIGHT MARK 3 b.f. High Line 125–Funabashi (Venture VII 129) (1979 5v 5g 5.8v4 7f 7fg 7g3 7g 6fg2 8h 1980 12.2fg* 12fg 13.8g4 13.8d) compact filly; plater; successful at Catterick in May (bought in 1,350 gns); possibly stays 1¾m; acts on a firm surface; usually wears blinkers; bandaged second start; suitable mount for a boy; ran absymally final outing; sold 3,600 gns Newmarket December Sales. *P. Haslam.* **65**

BRIGHT PROMISE 2 gr.f. Balidar 133–Aabora (Don II 123) (1980 5d 5g 6fg4 6g* 6g 6d 7s) Feb 27; well-made, attractive filly; second foal; sister to 3-y-o Powder 'n Patch, successful at up to 7f in England and France; dam well beaten all outings; won 14-runner maiden race at Folkestone in August by 2½ lenghts from Fair Rosalind; behind in nurseries subsequently, finishing last of 17 on penultimate outing; should stay 7f; evidently none too reliable. *J. Dunlop.* **86**

BRIG ISLAND 2 gr. or ro.f. Sharp Edge 123–Sunny Sovereign 85 (Lucky Sovereign) (1980 5fg) May 28; second foal; dam 5f sprinter; last of 16 in maiden race won by Dressedtokill at Leicester in May; sold 280 gns Doncaster August Sales. *D. Leslie.* –

BRIGITTA 3 b.f. Brigadier Gerard 144–Gambola 105 (Exbury 138) (1979 5.1g 6f 5fg2 5g 5fg 5f 1980 11f 10.2fg) small, compact filly; has shown no form since third outing at 2 yrs and is unreliable (whipped round at start and virtually took no part second outing); trained by J. W. Watts first start; best left alone. *R. Akehurst.* **§§**

BRIGSTONE 3 b.g. Brigadier Gerard 144–Gem of Gems 106 (Grey Sovereign 128§) (1979 NR 1980 12fg 14f* 16.9d 14fg 14fg^4) 11,000Y; tall, rangy sort; half-brother to 3 winners, including fairly useful miler Cacique (by Derring-Do); dam winner at up to 1½m; narrowly won 8-runner maiden race at Yarmouth in June; stays 1¾m; possibly unsuited by soft ground; races with head in air. *J. Hindley.* 73

BRI-GYLL 3 b.g. The Brianstan 128–Aequanimitas (Infatuation 129) (1979 5d^4 5v^3 5g 5g 5d 1980 10fg 7s) useful-looking gelding; only plating class; best form at 5f on soft ground; blinkered fourth start at 2 yrs. *J. Berry.* —

BRILLIANT FELLOW 3 b.c. Sparkler 130–Flora Day 92 (Floribunda 136) (1979 5f 5s 6f 6f^3 1980 7f^4 8fg^4 8fg^2) good-topped colt; particularly good mover; not seen out after going down by only a neck to Cracking Form in 16-runner maiden race at Kempton in May; will stay beyond 1m; acts on firm going; sold only 2,000 gns Ascot July Sales. *B. Hobbs.* 84

BRIMBLECOMBE 5 b.g. Sir Lark 101–Semona (Seminole II) (1979 NR 1980 8g) first foal; dam winning chaser; unquoted and backward, didn't move well to post and finished tailed off in maiden race at Beverley in July, first outing. *O. Brennan.* —

BRIMPS 5 br.h. Hotfoot 126–Floricelle 92 (Derring-Do 131) (1979 8s 8d* 9s 10s 9.4g 10f 10.1f^2 10s 8fg 1980 8.2s) plater; probably stayed 1¼m; appeared to act on any going; sometimes blinkered; dead. *T. Hallett.* —

BRINKBERO (FR) 2 b.c. Brinkmanship 125–Tuberosa (Snob 130) (1980 8g* 8d 10s^2 10v^3) Mar 18; 120,000 francs Y (approx £12,700); half-brother to several winners in France, including 7f and 1m winner Laurel Boy (by Rose Laurel); dam, daughter of Spanish Derby winner Tacora, won at 10.5f in France; won 10-runner maiden race at Deauville in August by 1½ lengths; subsequently ran creditably in pattern races, finishing 3¾ lengths fifth of 8 to Dunphy in Prix des Chenes, being moved up to second place by stewards after finishing 1¾ lengths third of 8 to The Wonder in Prix de Conde and looking to have been given too much to do when length third to The Wonder in Criterium de Saint-Cloud; will stay 1½m; yet to race on a firm surface. *F. Boutin, France.* 117

BRINKLEY 3 ch.c. Moulton 128–Lauretta 111 (Relko 136) (1979 6f 7fg^3 7g^2 7fg^3 1980 12f 11d^2 10f*) strong colt; made all to beat Sand Hawk 3 lengths in valuable maiden race at Ascot in July; will stay beyond 1½m; probably acts on any going; sold 2,900 gns Newmarket Autumn Sales. *H. Wragg.* 94

BRISBANE 2 ch.g. Welsh Pageant 132–Pavello 94 (Crepello 136) (1980 7f 8g 10s) Apr 8; 28,000Y; compact, good-bodied gelding; good mover; second foal; half-brother to very smart 3-y-o sprinter Sayyaf (by Habitat); dam 1m winner and half-sister to smart Rymer; showed ability in maiden races at Newmarket (2) and Nottingham; just over 7 lengths fifth of 17 to Spin of a Coin on latter in October on third start; one paced and looks the type to be suited by 1½m+ at 3yrs. *J. Hindley.* 72

BRISTOL BLUE 3 b.g. Mon Fils 124–La Libertad (Sea Hawk II 131) (1979 5g 1980 8fg 7fg 8.3f^2 10s^3 10f^2) narrow gelding; plater; stays 1¼m; acts on any going; not at all impressive in paddock second start. *M. Pipe.* 49

BRITISH CROWN 4 ch.g. English Prince 129–Chapeau Bleue (High Hat 131) (1979 10.6v^4 8s^3 8fg^2 8f* 8fg^2 11.7f 9f 8.2g 1980 10g 10.2g^2) strong gelding; not seen out until September, easily better effort when ¾-length second to China Royal in handicap at Bath; stays 1¼m; possibly unsuited by heavy going. *D. Elsworth.* 66

BRITISH GUNNER (USA) 2 b.c. Ack Ack–Favia (Bold Ruler) (1980 6g 6g* 6s^3 7g 7g) Feb 9; $42,000Y; third foal; brother to a minor winner; dam, granddaughter of Prix de l'Arc de Triomphe winner La Sorellina, won over 6f; favourite when winning 5-runner maiden race at Navan in June by a length from Southern Music; good third of 18, a length behind Prince Echo, in Tyros Stakes at the Curragh 8 days later, easily best subsequent effort; should be suited by 7f+; acts on soft going. *A. Maxwell, Ireland.* 95

BRITWELL LAD (USA) 2 b.c. Son Ange–Hurricane Helen (Etonian) (1980 7fg 8g^4) Mar 6; $27,000Y; small, sturdy colt; good walker; fifth foal; half-brother to 3 winners, including stakes-placed Fiddle Miss (by Fiddle Isle); dam won claiming races at up to 1m; sire stakes-winning son of Raise A Native; 20/1 when about 4 lengths fourth of 15 to Riberetto in maiden race at Newmarket in October; will stay 1¼m. *P. Cole.* 76

BROAD PRINCIPLE 3 b.g. Bustino 136–Hazy Idea 118 (Hethersett 134) (1979 5s^4 6fg 7f^2 8.2g* 8f 1980 10d* 12f^3 10.6fg 10s 13g 11.5fg^4) strong, 89 close-coupled gelding; excellent mover; fair handicapper; won at Kempton in April; suited by 1½m and should stay further; probably acts on any going; pulled very hard early on and hung under pressure fifth outing. *M. Stoute.*

BROADSWORD (USA) 3 b.c. Ack Ack–Cutting (Bold Ruler) (1979 NR **104**
1980 12f 12fg 14fg* 12s^3 16fg^2 14g^2 16g^2) big, strong colt; half-brother to Operating (by Dr Fager), a stakes winner at up to 1m; dam, twice a winner at up to 5f at 2 yrs, is sister to best 1967 American 2-y-o Vitriolic; ran on strongly to win maiden race at Haydock in June; ran well afterwards, putting up a particularly good effort to be beaten only a head by Bossall in handicap at Newcastle on final start in August; suited by a test of stamina; seems to act on any going; genuine and consistent; useful young hurdler. *J. Dunlop.*

BROCKLEY 3 ch.g. St Alphage 119–Jukay (Galivanter 131) (1979 6f 5f –
6fg 6f 1980 8f 8f 6fg 7f) lightly-made, unfurnished gelding; seems of little account. *R. Hollinshead.*

BROCKLEY WOOD 2 ch.f. Sharp Edge 123–Hot Number 75 (Firestreak –
125) (1980 6fg 6d 7g 6g 6s) Mar 20; 650Y; neat, strong filly; bad plater; blinkered third and fourth starts; saddle slipped after 1f fourth outing. *R. Ward.*

BROKEN BONDS 3 b.g. Bustino 136–Betty Burke 95 (Prince Chevalier) –
(1979 NR 1980 10g) strong, good sort; half-brother to several winners, including very useful miler Stirling Castle (by Royal Palace) and very useful stayer Arisaig (by Acropolis); dam won at 5f and 6f; in need of race and apprentice ridden, didn't move too well to post when behind in maiden event at Nottingham in April. *H. Cecil.*

BROKEN FLIGHT 3 b.c. Busted 134–Shortwood 90 (Skymaster 126) (1979 **94**
NR 1980 12fg*) lengthy, stocky colt; half-brother to 3 winners, including smart middle-distance handicapper Royal Match (by Sovereign Path) and very useful Tranos (by Caliban); dam sprinter; second favourite, moved poorly to post but came back much better when staying on strongly to win 13-runner maiden race at Doncaster in May from Merciless King; not seen out again; will stay 1¾m; sold 2,200 gns Newmarket Autumn Sales. *H. Cecil.*

BROKEN LACE 2 ch.g. Redundant 120–Brocette (Brocade Slipper 116) –
(1980 5.8fg) Apr 20; 1,000Y; half-brother to 1975 2-y-o 1m winner Stilton (by Blue Streak); dam of little account; 50/1, started slowly when eleventh of 12 in maiden race won by Maryland Cookie at Bath in July. *Mrs N. Kennedy.*

BRONTOLINO 3 ch.c. Sandford Lad 133–Living Free 81 (Never Say Die 137) **68**
(1979 5f 5fg 1980 6s 7f 8h^3 8f 10.2g 16fg^2 16s^3 16f^2 15.8fg^4 17.1d 16d^3 14.6d) small, strong colt; good mover; staying maiden; acts on any going; blinkered nowadays; usually sweats up. *F. J. Houghton.*

BRONZAMER 3 gr.f. Saritamer 130–Palmitin 68 (Crepello 136) (1979 6f* 7fg **70**
7d 6s 1980 7v^3 7d^3 6fg^3 8f 8f^2 8fg 8fg 9g 8.2g 8f 8f 8fg) small, lightly-made filly; fair (rated 86) at 2 yrs; didn't run up to her best in handicaps in 1980 though wasn't entirely disgraced in first part of season; stays 1m; probably acts on any going. *P. Asquith.*

BRONZE GOD 4 ch.g. Green God 128–Sweet Success 81 (Privy Councillor 125) –
(1979 8s 10.1g 12g 10f^4 12f 9f^3 10g^3 1980 8s) plater; stays 1¼m; acts on firm going; blinkered on reappearance in March; sold 900 gns Ascot October Sales. *G. Kindersley.*

BRONZE MEDAL 2 ch.g. Jimmy Reppin 131–Maroon 92 (Roan Rocket 128) – p
(1980 6d) Apr 2; rangy, quite attractive gelding; first foal; dam, daughter of smart stayer Mulberry Harbour, won over 1½m and 2m; 6/1, chased along throughout and made some late progress to finish seventh of 17 to Shark Song in maiden race at Newmarket in October; will do better over further at 3 yrs. *R. Hern.*

BROOKLANDS BABY 3 gr.g. Owen Anthony 102–Bromhead (Sovereign Path –
125) (1979 6g 1980 9f 12h 12fg 14fg) strong gelding; bad plater; blinkered second and third starts; sold out of W. Wharton's stable 950 gns Doncaster June Sales after third outing. *M. Chapman.*

BROOKLYN PRINCE 2 b.c. Prince Tenderfoot 126–Buenaventura II (Celtic **107**
Ash) (1980 5g* 6s 5d^2 6g^4 5g* 5g) Apr 8; 11,000Y; strong, useful sort; good mover; half-brother to winners here and in Italy, including 3-y-o middle-distance winner Sirena (by Red Alert); dam placed at up to 1¼m in France; in frame in 2 Group races, going down a length to Crimson Heather after having none too clear a run in Curragh Stakes in July and showing plenty of speed 5f when 3 lengths fourth of 9 to Bel Bolide in Gimcrack Stakes at York the following month;

successful twice in lesser company, winning maiden race at Phoenix Park in June and taking advantage of a lenient weight in a nursery at the Curragh in August (beat Arch Melody a length); stays 6f; sweated up a bit and ran poorly sixth outing. *M. Fogarty, Ireland.*

BROOK NO ARGUMENT 3 br.g. Birdbrook 110–Lady Councillor (Privy — Councillor 125) (1979 NR 1980 9.4g 10d 8g 10s 8.2s) 2,800F, 9,000Y; leggy, sparely-made gelding; beaten some way in maiden and minor races; dwelt third start. *W. H. H. Williams.*

BROOMSTICK CORNER (USA) 3 b. or br.f. Bustino 136–Flashy 107 (Sir **104** Ivor 135) (1979 5f 1980 7.6f^2 9f^2 10.2g^4 10.4g^3 10fg^4 12f* 10g* 12f* 14.6g^2 12g* 12d) lengthy filly; much improved once fitted with blinkers, winning 4 of her last 6 starts, namely maiden race and £3,300 event at Lingfield, minor event at Goodwood and 4-runner race at York; beat 5-y-o Morse Code by a length at Lingfield in September for final success; creditable second to Shoot A Line in Park Hill Stakes at Doncaster on ninth start; stays $1\frac{3}{4}$m; possibly unsuited by soft ground. *H. Wragg.*

BROON'S SECRET 6 b.g. Most Secret 119–Vaudaville 77 (Vigo 130) (1979 6g **67** 6d* 6d 6g 5d^3 1980 6f 5fg 5g 6d 6f 5d^2 6d^2 5v) strong gelding; ridden by claimer when second in handicaps at Wolverhampton (to Ascot Blue) and Newbury (to Winter Wind) in October, best efforts; best form at up to 6f; acts on any going; blinkered twice at 3 yrs; slowly away third outing; sold out of J. Czerpak's stable 3,000 gns Doncaster June Sales. *A. Jarvis.*

BROONS SURPRISE 2 ch.f. Most Secret 119–Kinegar (Attractive 72) (1980 — 5fg 7f) Feb 7; workmanlike filly; second reported foal; dam placed over hurdles; last to finish in maiden races at Warwick in June (slowly away) and Catterick in July. *J. Czerpak.*

BROWN'S BABU 3 b.f. Top Hat 106–Irish Pearl (Gulf Pearl 117) (1979 NR — 1980 9.4fg) third foal; dam moderate Irish maiden; unquoted and apprentice ridden when in rear in maiden event at Carlisle in May. *Denys Smith.*

BRUMMER (USA) 2 b.c. Bold Hour–Rainwater (Rainy Lake) (1980 7g 6g*) **92** p Mar 3; $65,000Y; rangy colt; third foal; half-brother to Palm Hut (by Jungle Savage), a leading 2-y-o filly in 1978 when winner at up to 6f; dam 6f winner; second favourite, disputed lead throughout and battled on splendidly when strongly challenged by 3 others in final furlong to win £3,200 maiden race at Doncaster in September by a head from Montclair; will stay 1m. *R. Price.*

BRUNATTI 3 ch.g. Hasty Word 84–Como Star 63 (Como 120) (1979 7f 8g — 1980 10s 10.8s 12fg) workmanlike gelding; behind in maiden races and a handicap. *S. Holland.*

BRUSH DOWN 2 b.c. The Brianstan 128–Tacoma 89 (Hard Tack 111§) (1980 **52** 5f 5f 6d 7g^4 7fg 7g 8.2d) Feb 13; 4,000F, 3,800Y; compact colt; good mover; poor plater; evidently suited by 7f; blinkered seventh outing; exported to Malaysia. *P. Rohan.*

BUCHANAN (USA) 5 gr.g. Dancer's Image–Fiery Diplomat 120 (Diplomat — Way) (1979 8fg 12fg 12.2s 1980 14g) of little account on flat nowadays; has been tried in blinkers; wears a tongue strap. *M. Chapman.*

BUCKENHAM BELLE 3 b.f. Royben 125–Dux Girl 99 (Bewildered 102) **39** (1979 5fg 6f 7f^4 7.2d 1980 8.3f 10fg^3 8d 8s^3 8.3s^4 9d^3 10.8g^3 8.3f 10f 10g) lengthy filly; poor plater; stays $1\frac{1}{4}$m; acts on any going; often wears blinkers; suitable mount for a boy. *C. Wildman.*

BUCKEYE 2 b. or br.c. Royalty 130–No Saint 118 (Narrator 127) (1980 — 6fg) Apr 27; lightly-made, fair sort; half-brother to several winners, including useful stayer Reformed Character (by Reliance II) and very useful 1965 2-y-o Conjuror (by Crepello); dam smart stayer; 8/1, made little show when behind in maiden race won by Intercontinental at Newbury in June; dead. *R. Hern.*

BUCKLOW HILL 3 b.g. Rheingold 137–Parmassia (Pampered King 121) **70** (1979 7g^3 7d 1980 10fg^2 12.2d^3 10.2d 12v) tall gelding; quite a moderate maiden; will stay beyond $1\frac{1}{2}$m; acts on a firm surface; had very stiff tasks final 2 starts. *J. Fitzgerald.*

BUCKPOINT (FR) 4 b.c. Buckpasser–Pointilleuse (Le Fabuleux 133) (1979 **117** 10v^2 10.5g* 12s 12g 12g* 12d 10.5s^2 12s^2 1980 10.5g* 9.2fg^4 12g^3 12g^4 12.5s* 10.5d 11f^4 13f^2 12v 12f 8.5g*) second foal; dam very useful middle-distance filly and half-sister to $228,000-earner Point du Jour; very smart middle-distance performer, winner twice at Saint-Cloud, scoring by 6 lengths from Aiymann in well-contested minor event in April and by 3 lengths from Proustille in valuable Prix Maurice de Nieuil in July; struggling from 3f out when seventh of 12 to Master Willie in Benson and Hedges Gold Cup at York in August; sent to race in USA afterwards, probably best effort when 2½ lengths second to Great Neck in Canadian International Championship at Woodbine in October; won at Calder in December; says 1½m well; appears to act on any going but goes well in the mud; formerly trained by B. Secly. *J. B. Sonnier, USA.*

BUDDA 3 b.f. Club House 110–Never Seen (Ennis 128) (1979 NR 1980 10f 15.5s) half-sister to several minor winners; dam of no account; well beaten in Southern maiden races. *G. Harwood.* —

BUDDING RECRUIT 3 b.f. Dawn Review 105–Poinsettia 80 (Pinturischio 116) (1979 NR 1980 10fg) 940Y; compact filly; second foal; dam won at 1¾m; 16/1 and backward, broke a leg 3f out in maiden race at Yarmouth in August and was destroyed. *G. Pritchard-Gordon.* —

BUFFAVENTO 2 b.c. Connaught 130–Duke Street (Lorenzaccio 130) (1980 5f4 6g 6g* 7g2 6g2 6fg2) Mar 10; 11,000Y; neat colt; first foal; dam won small races over 7f and 1m in France; quickened in fine style to lead at distance when winning 13-runner maiden race at Newbury in July by 4 lengths from Junta; second subsequently in minor events at Newmarket and Windsor and in 7-runner Clarence House Stakes at Ascot, in last-named going down by 2½ lengths to Doc Marten; will probably stay 1¼m; yet to race on soft surface. *G. Pritchard-Gordon.* 91

BUFFOON 5 ch.g. Silly Season 127–Paphos 99 (Vilmorin) (1979 7g 10g 10.3f 8fg 8fg 1980 11.7g 10g 10f2 8d2 12.3g4 11.7d2 11.7g 16.9f3) quite a moderate handicapper; suited by middle distances and seems to stay 2m; acts on any going; carries his head on one side and is no great battler. *D. Elsworth.* 59

BUGATTI 2 ch.g. Arch Sculptor 123–Mandetta (Mandamus 120) (1980 5fg4 6g 6s* 6s 6g 6g) Apr 11; 9,200Y; strong, good sort; half-brother to 11f winner Maningo (by Saulingo) and a winner in Belgium; dam plater on flat and over hurdles; made all and held off Steel Pass by a neck in 18-runner minor event at Nottingham in July; ran poorly next time out and subsequently finished well down field in nurseries; stays 6f well; acts on soft going; gelded at end of season. *M. Jarvis.* 80

BUGLE 2 gr. or ro.f. Warpath 113–Golden Jewel (Aureole 132) (1980 8d) Mar 13; 3,200F; leggy, lightly-made filly; half-sister to several winners here and abroad; dam unraced sister to Hotroy; tailed-off last of 15 in maiden race at Leicester in November won by Rollrights; refused to enter stalls and was withdrawn on intended debut. *G. Balding.* —

BUGLE SOUND 3 b.f. Bustino 136–Melodina 118 (Tudor Melody 129) (1979 7g3 7g3 1980 10fg* 12.3f 14d4 12d3 12g) lightly-made filly; good walker; stayed on to win 21-runner maiden race at Sandown in April; looked one paced afterwards when in frame in handicaps; stays 1¾m; acts on a firm and a soft surface; blinkered last 2 outings, running poorly on second occasion; seemed unsuited by Chester track second start; sold 35,000 gns Newmarket December Sales. *J. Hindley.* 83

BULLDOZER 2 b.c. Busted 134–Woodwind 103 (Whistling Wind 123) (1980 8d) Feb 22; 33,000F; tall, useful-looking colt; has scope; first produce; dam, half-sister to very smart sprinter Le Johnstan, won twice over 6f at 2 yrs from 4 starts; 8/1 and in need of race, fell after 2f in 14-runner maiden race won by Sha'lan at Leicester in November. *P. Walwyn.* —

BULMER 3 ch.g. Some Hand 119–Klontina (Klondyke Bill 125) (1979 6d 5f 6fg 7f 6g 5fg 8.2g 1980 8f) strong, compact gelding; moderate plater; wasn't certain to have stayed 7f; dead. *M. W. Easterby.* —

BUNCE BOY 4 b.g. King Emperor–All Hail 112 (Alcide 136) (1979 10v 12.3s4 8s 8fg 10f* 12g2 10s4 10.1fg 11.7fg* 1980 11.7f2 12fg* 12d2 11.7s 12fg2 12f3 12fg* 12fg3 12fg 14g) useful sort; battled on well to beat Botanist by short head in handicap at Lingfield in June; made all and was never seriously challenged when scoring by 4 lengths from Virgin Soldier in similar event at Epsom in August; stays 1½m (had plenty to do when well beaten over 1¾m); seems to act on any going but goes well on firm; suited by forcing tactics; blinkered fourth start at 3 yrs; suitable mount for an apprentice. *A. Hide.* 67

BUNRATTY GIRL 3 b.f. Brave Invader–Viennese Puppet (Tudor Melody 129) (1979 7fg 6g 1980 10fg 12fg 12f 10.1f) neat filly; well beaten in maiden and minor events; blinkered final start. *P. Mitchell.* —

BURGENSTOCK 3 b.f. Mountain Call 125–Cloudari (Pindari 124) (1979 5d* –
5d^{3} 5s* 6g 5fg 5fg^{4} 5fg 5fg 6g^{4} 1980 5d 5v 6fg 6f) sturdy filly; quite a moderate handicapper; will probably stay 7f; probably acts on any going; blinkered last 2 appearances; apprentice ridden when successful at 2 yrs. *G. Hunter.*

BURGHCLERE 3 b.f. Busted 134–Highclere 129 (Queen's Hussar 124) (1979 **80**
7g 1980 10fg^{4} 12d^{4} 14g* 12d 14g) big, rangy filly; good mover; landed odds very comfortably in 12-runner maiden race at Sandown in July; had earlier run respectably when fourth in Playboy Pretty Polly Stakes at Newmarket and Ribblesdale Stakes at Royal Ascot; suited by $1\frac{3}{4}$m; acts on a firm and a soft surface; out of her depth fourth start and ran badly on final appearance. *W. Hastings-Bass.*

BURGLARS BOY 6 ch.g. Burglar 128–Tilt Guard 75 (Crepello 136) (1979 5s **58**
5v^{2} 5d 5d 5fg* 5fg 6f 5f^{2} 5fg 5g 5fg 5s 1980 5d 5g 5f 5f 6fg 5g^{4} 5fg^{3} 5d 6f) sprint handicapper; acts on any going; sometimes wears blinkers; ocassionally sweats up; has a tendency to hang left; has given trouble at start. *L. Barratt.*

BURGLAR'S MINK 3 ch.f. Burglar 128–Minkala (Master Rocky 106) (1979 –
5g 6d 6fg* 6g^{2} 5d 1980 10s 8fg 6f 6fg^{3} 8g^{4} 8fg 6g^{4} 7f) small filly; poor plater; not certain to stay $1\frac{1}{4}$m; acts on a firm surface. *T. Taylor.*

BURGLAR TIP 3 b.f. Burglar 128–Chatter 67 (Songedor 116) (1979 6g 6fg 7g^{3} **67**
6s^{2} 5fg* 6f 6fg^{4} 5d 1980 6s 6g 5g* 6h 5h 5f 7g 6g 7d 7fg) neat, lightly-made filly; ridden by 7-lb claimer when winning handicap at Hamilton in April; ran moderately afterwards; best form at sprint distances; acts on any going; blinkered sixth start at 2 yrs; unseated rider on way to start first outing. *G. Wallace.*

BURKE'S FOLLY 3 ch.g. Shiny Tenth 120–Miss Sousa (March Past 124) (1979 **45**
8g 1980 8f 7fg 7s^{3} 8s* 10.8fg^{2} 8fg 9f 8d 8d 10d) lightly-made gelding; plater; won at Warwick in July (sold out of W. Wharton's stable 2,200 gns); probably stays $1\frac{1}{4}$m; suited by soft going; suitable mount for a boy; ran poorly sixth start. *K. Bridgwater.*

BURLEIGH 8 ch.g. Charlottown 127–Running Blue 115 (Blue Peter) (1979 **67**
12fg^{2} 12s* 10s 14v 12d^{2} 14g^{4} 10g 12fg 10fg 1980 10fg 13.1fg^{2} 10g^{2} 12d^{4} 12g 10g^{4} 14g^{2} 10d) modest handicapper nowadays; used by stable for educating its apprentices; runner-up at Bath, Chepstow and Goodwood; carried 11 lb overweight when beaten $1\frac{1}{2}$ lengths by Port Aransas on last-named course in September; gives impression he needs at least $1\frac{1}{2}$m nowadays and stays $1\frac{3}{4}$m; acts on any going; sometimes starts slowly; used to wear blinkers; sometimes sweats up; has won 4 times at Goodwood. *R. Hern.*

BURLINGTON PORT 4 b.g. Sahib 114–The Maid (Milesian 125) (1979 8s 12g –
9fg^{2} 10f* 13.8f^{2} 12fg 1980 10g 12.2g 12d) unfurnished gelding; plater; evidently stays $1\frac{3}{4}$m; acts on firm going; sold to T. Hallett 900 gns Doncaster October Sales. *E. Carter.*

BURMA PINK 7 gr.g. Gulf Pearl 117–Magna 107 (Runnymede 123) (1979 7s^{4} –
7g 7fg^{2} 7f^{2} 7fg^{4} 7s* 7g* 7.2g 7.3g^{3} 7.2g 7.6fg^{3} 1980 8d) useful handicapper at his best; stays 1m; acts on any going; used to wear blinkers; needs strong handling and ran abysmally for an apprentice on only outing of 1980 (March); usually held up. *T. Fairhurst.*

BURNS NIGHT 3 ch.f. Midsummer Night II 117–Poosie Nansie (Combat 123) –
(1979 NR 1980 10g 10g 10.1fg) 1,200F; fair sort; half-sister to a winner in Greece and to 3 successful jumpers; dam of little account; beaten a long way in maiden and minor events. *J. Powney.*

BURST OF SONG 2 b.c. Reform 132–Sea Singer 104 (Sea-Bird II 145) (1980 **75** p
8g) Apr 9; strong, lengthy, quite attractive colt; second foal; brother to disappointing 1979 3-y-o Fleet Order; dam won over $1\frac{1}{4}$m; co-third favourite and reasonably fit, faded going into the Dip, after racing prominently, to finish about 5 lengths sixth of 17 to Video Tape in minor event at Newmarket in October; sure to do better over middle distances in 1981. *R. Hern.*

BURSTON LAD 4 br.g. Decoy Boy 129–Second String 95 (Tudor Minstrel 144) –
(1979 NR 1980 16.9d) unquoted when tailed off in maiden race at Wolverhampton in July, first outing; sold 1,100 gns Ascot August Sales. *M. Tate.*

BUSHWHACKER 4 ro.c No Mercy 126–My Bushbaby 100 (Hul a Hul 124) –
(1979 NR 1980 7d 5fg 6g 5s 6fg 7g) strong, lengthy colt; poor performer nowadays; stays 6f; acts on any going with possible exception of very soft; wears bandages; sold 500 gns Doncaster October Sales. *R. D. Peacock.*

BUSIRIS 6 b.g. Busted 134–Tudor Gal 106 (Henry the Seventh 125) (1979 11.7g 12s4 1980 17.1f2 17.1fg 12fg*) attractive gelding; won handicap at Chepstow in July; stays well; acts on any going; one paced. *L. Kennard.* **66**

BUSTELLINA 2 b.f. Busted 134–Naughty Party (Parthia 132) (1980 7.2s4 6f 8s 6s2) Feb 15; 6,000Y; tall, leggy filly; third foal; dam, 7f winner in Ireland, is half-sister to Whistling Wind; ½-length second of 8 to Monza Lady in nursery at Hamilton in October, easily best effort; bred to stay at least 1m (ran poorly over trip). *R. Hollinshead.* **81**

BUSTIKI 3 b.c. Bustino 136–Supreme Lady 86 (Grey Sovereign 128 §) (1979 NR 1980 12g4) 114,000Y; strong, good-bodied colt; half-brother to several winners, notably Irish St Leger winner M-Lolshan (by Levmoss); dam 2-y-o 5f performer; favourite, nearest at finish when 9 lengths fourth of 17 to Quiet Cannon in maiden race at Salisbury in June; not seen out again; will stay 1¾m. *R. Hern.* **–**

BUSTING 6 b.h. Busted 134–Yasseen (Charlottesville 135) (1979 14g 13v2 12s 14v 14fg3 13g 14d* 16g3 14f* 14fg* 16fg* 16d* 1980 13s2 12fg*) fair staying handicapper; confirmed promise of first run of season when winning apprentice handicap at Ascot in April by 1½ lengths from Rafael Molina (pair well clear); not seen out again; acts on any going; good mount for a claimer; genuine and consistent. *R. Turnell.* **78**

BUSTOMI 2 b.c. Bustino 136–Mineown 85 (Roan Rocket 128) (1980 6g 7g2 7f* 7fg2) Jan 24; lengthy, attractive colt; good mover; third foal; dam, placed over 5f and 6f, is half-sister to top Italian horse Weimar; made all to win by 3 lengths from Royal Heritage when favourite for 11-runner Sancton Stakes at York in September; far from disgraced when length second of 16 to Centurius in £3,900 race at Ascot later in month; will stay 1½m; a progressive individual. *R. Hern.* **105**

BUT BEAUTIFUL 2 b.f. Moulton 128–Alisarda (Aureole 132) (1980 6g 6fg 8fg 7d) Apr 17; 1,500Y; rather unfurnished filly; fourth living foal; dam never ran; unquoted when in rear in maiden and minor events; sold 400 gns Newmarket Autumn Sales. *R. Armstrong.* **–**

Sancton Stakes, York—Bustomi makes it all to win from Royal Heritage and Beocan

BUTOSKY 3 b.f. Busted 134–Patosky 94 (Skymaster 126) (1979 NR 1980 10fg 7d 10.1f 12f 10.1g4 11.7h 12f 13g2 12g3 12d) third living foal; half-sister to useful sprinter Crews Hill (by High Top); dam suited by 7f and 1m; quite a moderate maiden; stays 13f; blinkered first 2 starts, moving badly to post on second occasion; hung in closing stages when apprentice ridden on eighth outing. *A. Breasley.* **71**

BUTTON TOP 2 b.f. Jimmy Reppin 131–Red Lupus (Red God 128 §) (1980 7g 6f 6d3 7d* 7g* 7v4) Apr 13; 5,200Y; rangy filly; good walker; first foal; dam poor maiden; beat Green Memory, all out, by a head in 13-runner maiden race at Leicester in October, and Claudius Secundus 1½ lengths in £2,300 event at Newmarket later in month; creditable fourth of 20 to Supreme Fjord in nursery at Doncaster in November; will stay 1m; probably acts on any going; suitable mount for an apprentice. *N. Callaghan.* **86**

BUTTRESS 4 ch.c. Busted 134–Albany 120 (Pall Mall 132) (1979 11d 10.2g* 10v2 11fg* 16fg* 15g2 12s2 1980 16fg3 14f2 16f2 20g 14g 14.6g2) rangy colt; won 3 races as a 3-y-o, notably Queen's Vase at Royal Ascot; confirmed himself a smart stayer in 1980 but didn't manage to win; second 3 times, beaten 1½ lengths by Noble Saint in Yorkshire Cup at York and a neck by Billion in Henry II Stakes at Sandown, both in May, and beaten 4 lengths by facile winner Castle Keep in Rockingham Handicap at Doncaster in September; seventh of 8 behind Le Moss in Gold Cup at Royal Ascot on fourth start; acts on any going; wears blinkers nowadays; sold 20,000 gns Newmarket December Sales. *R. Hern.* **111**

BUTTY 5 br.h. Welsh Pageant 132–Kyak 111 § (Big Game) (1979 11s 12v* 16d 12s 1980 10.2d 10s 12d 12fg) leggy, tall horse; stays 1½m; acts well in the mud; blinkered final outing; wears bandages; front runner. *S. Harris.* **–**

BUXTON ROAD 3 b.c. Murrayfield 119–Necora 79 (Royal Record II) (1979 5g* 5g 5f4 1980 5fg 5d) compact colt; won maiden race at Ayr at 2 yrs; not seen out until September in 1980 and was well beaten both starts; will be suited by 6f+. *I. Vickers.* **–**

BUZUKI 4 b.g. Cavo Doro 124–Akebia (Abernant 142) (1979 NR 1980 10.1fg 10fg 10g) sturdy gelding; first foal; dam third in small French 10.5f race on only start; behind in maiden race at Windsor in August and apprentice event at Leicester and minor event at Nottingham in September. *B. Palling.* **–**

BUZZARDS BAY 2 b.c. Joshua 129–Grande Merci 82 (Gratitude 130) (1980 6d 7g 7fg 7.2d2 7g) May 28; 840F, 880Y; strong-topped, good sort; half-brother to a winning 2-y-o plater; dam, half-sister to very smart sprinter Jukebox, stayed 1m; stayed on strongly under pressure to be nearest at finish when 1½ lengths second of 19 to Craigour in maiden race at Haydock in September, easily best effort; will stay 1m; seems suited by some give in the ground; dwelt final start. *H. Collingridge.* **81**

BYCLOUGH BOY 3 br.g. The Brianstan 128–Corcyra Beach 60 (Behistoun 131) (1979 5g 6d 5g 5fg 6fg 6s 5s 6s 5f4 5d 5g 1980 5f 8f 7f 5h 7f 6fg 5g 8d) compact gelding; poor plater; probably better suited by 5f than longer distances; sometimes wears blinkers; ran deplorably fifth outing; trained part of season by S. Nesbitt. *A. Gillam.* **–**

BYCLOUGH GAL 2 b.f. Runnymede 123–Liberty Light 82 (Henry the Seventh 125) (1980 5fg) Apr 2; 300Y; small filly; first foal; dam, winner at up to 1m, is half-sister to speedy Canton Silk (by Runnymede); burly when last of 20 to Onward Gal in seller at Ripon in May (moved poorly to start). *S. Nesbitt.* **–**

BYCLOUGH PRIDE 2 ch.c. Native Bazaar 122–High Moor 104 (Sayajirao 132) (1980 5f) May 17; 980Y; leggy colt; half-brother to 2 winning platers; dam miler; unquoted and in need of race when fifteenth of 16 to Donatella in maiden auction event at Beverley in April. *S. Nesbitt.* **–**

BYE APPEAL 4 ch.g. Busted 134–One Extra 85 (Abernant 142) (1979 11d 12g 12fg4 12g3 14f2 14f2 15.5fg* 14.7g* 1980 15f3 14g 16g 16.5g* 16.5fg3 14fg) rangy gelding; made all when unchallenged winner of handicap at Folkestone in July; tailed off final start; stays well; acts on firm going and wasn't disgraced on only outing on a soft surface; wears bandages. *J. Winter.* **66**

BYROC BOY 3 b.g. Runnymede 123–Royal Pat 80 (King's Troop 118) (1979 5d 5g 5.8g 5f3 5f3 5f 5f 1980 7d 7fg 5f 5fg2 7f 6d 5s) small gelding; poor form, including in a seller; best at 5f; acts on firm going; sometimes blinkered; sold 330 gns Ascot November Sales. *D. Jermy.* **51**

C

CABALETTA 5 ch.m. Double Jump 131–Toccata (Kythnos 126) (1979 NR 1980 9d 8f) lightly raced and only poor form. *E. Weymes.* —

CABANA 3 br.c. Mill Reef 141–Siliciana 113 (Silly Season 127) (1979 6fg^4 7g^4 7f* 1980 8v^3 10d 12fg 12f 8g 8.5fg 13g 12d^3) lightly-made, quite attractive colt; third in handicaps at Salisbury in March and Doncaster (selling) in October; ran moderately in between; stays 1½m; acts on any going; suitable mount for an apprentice; blinkered fifth start; sold 2,700 gns Newmarket Autumn Sales. *I. Balding.* 69

CABBAGE MAN 2 b.c. Song 132–Star Trophy 63 (Umberto 118) (1980 6fg 6d^2 6g^2 8fg) Mar 23; 11,500Y; small, useful-looking colt; half-brother to several winners, notably Ribblesdale Stakes winner Star Ship (by Dicta Drake) and a good winner in Mexico; dam won 7f seller; second in maiden races at Haydock in August and Nottingham in September, going down by 2½ lengths to Melon Patch on latter; didn't reproduce that form on final outing; best form at 6f. *H. Candy.* 84

CADES 4 br.f. Wolver Hollow 126–Cenerentola 93 (Prince Chevalier) (1979 10s* 10.6s* 10.2g^2 12d^2 12fg^2 12fg 13.3g^2 12g^3 1980 12fg 12f 11.5g) neat filly; won handicaps at Beverley and Haydock at 3 yrs; well beaten in 1980 (not seen out after July); stays 13f; acts on firm going, but seems well suited by some give in the ground; goes well for apprentice M. Rimmer. *G. Pritchard-Gordon.* —

CAERNARVON BAY 4 b.g. Right Tack 131–Ever Swinging 104 (Immortality) (1979 9v 10.8s 8d 10g 10s 8s* 8f^3 8.2fg 12.2d 1980 8g 7d^3) plater; stays 1m; acts on any going. *W. Stubbs.* 52

CAIRNIE 4 ro.g. No Mercy 126–Tartlet 83 (Primera 131) (1979 8fg 9d 1980 7d 16fg) strong gelding; poor maiden; off course for 6 months before trying 2m (not certain to stay trip); has run well in blinkers. *P. Felgate.* —

CAIRN ROUGE 3 b.f. Pitcairn 126–Little Hills (Candy Cane 125) (1979 8g 8.5g* 7fg* 1980 7v 7s* 8fg* 8g* 10.5d^2 12f 10d*) 127

Fillies contributed much to the good of the season, Cairn Rouge more than most. She proved wonderfully tough and consistent, a credit to the so-called weaker sex as well as to her trainer, winning four of the six races she took part in and finishing close up in the other two following a run on very bad ground as early as March 17th. All the six were pattern races, the last of them the Champion Stakes run on October 18th in which she became the sixth filly to succeed in the last eleven years. Such was her standing by then that her success in the Champion Stakes, in sharp contrast to Flossy's, Hurry Harriet's and Swiss Maid's, caused no surprise whatever. She was undoubtedly one of the best of either sex around so it's very good news that she, like Detroit, Mrs Penny and Shoot A Line, stays in training; the reason for her withdrawal from the Washington International after she'd been sent to America was, apparently, nothing more serious than a high temperature.

Cairn Rouge soon established herself as one of the best fillies in Ireland, took very little longer to establish herself as one of the best in Europe too, and by the York August meeting showed herself well up to taking on the top colts. We must admit we didn't expect Cairn Rouge to go so far when we saw her beating Miss Taymore and Louise Moulton in the Malton Stakes at York in 1979 or when next we saw her winning the Mulcahy Stakes at Phoenix Park in April by the flattering margin of three lengths from Monroe. On the latter occasion the members of the field looked more like hairy dogs than classic horses, the runner-up seemingly not having grown through the winter. Seven weeks later, though, Cairn Rouge put up a performance of unmistakably high quality in the Goffs Irish One Thousand Guineas at the Curragh, a race boosted in value to over £50,000 to the winner with the help of sponsorship and a late-entry clause (late entrants, incidentally, paid £800 for the privilege and another £130 to run). She beat that eminently consistent pair Millingdale Lillie and Mrs Penny much more decisively than Quick As Lightning and Our Home did in the One Thousand Guineas, winning by two and a half lengths and a head after quickening clear of her seventeen opponents in an impressively short distance around the two-furlong pole. Next time out Cairn Rouge accounted for Quick As Lightning and Our Home, in the Coronation Stakes at Royal Ascot. The short-priced favourite, she was produced with a run up the rails as at the Curragh and burst

Goffs Irish One Thousand Guineas, the Curragh—home-trained Cairn Rouge routs the English fillies Millingdale Lillie (spotted cap), Mrs Penny (blaze) and the grey Ararat

through, fortunate to get an opening, to lead well inside the final furlong and touch off Quick As Lightning by a neck. Our Home, receiving 4 lb from the other two, finished third. The winning margin might well have been bigger in different circumstances, for the winner didn't enjoy the smoothest of runs in the straight.

Cairn Rouge (b.f. 1977)	Pitcairn (b 1971)	Petingo (b 1965)	Petition
			Alcazar
		Border Bounty (b 1965)	Bounteous
			B Flat
	Little Hills (b or br 1971)	Candy Cane (b 1965)	Crepello
			Candy Gift
		Ballyogan Queen (br 1956)	Ballyogan
			Stone Crop

Cairn Rouge and Mrs Penny disputed favouritism in the Benson and Hedges Gold Cup at York in August. It was Cairn Rouge's first time at the distance, her first time against top colts too, whereas Mrs Penny since their last meeting had won the French Oaks and finished within a length of Ela-Mana-Mou in the King George VI and Queen Elizabeth Diamond Stakes. Cairn Rouge ran a great race. She got the lead with less than two furlongs to go and held on until Master Willie caught her in the last hundred yards and went half a length up. The way she ran suggested that although she stayed ten and a half furlongs she might have difficulty staying a mile and a half, or at any rate have difficulty in reproducing her best form. The evidence provided by two more outings, in the Prix Vermeille and the Champion Stakes, without being conclusive is strong enough to discourage backing her at a mile and a half at present. Four beat her in the Prix Vermeille—Mrs Penny, Little Bonny, Detroit and Gold River—and she didn't run up to her best although only two and a half lengths behind the

Coronation Stakes, Ascot—another big race for Cairn Rouge who beats Quick As Lightning and Our Home

winner; to complicate matters, she might not be ideally suited by ground as firm as it was that day. Our guess is that given the chance as a four-year-old she'll prove best at up to a mile and a quarter.

Cairn Rouge will certainly do well to improve on her performance in the Champion Stakes: on the same terms as at York she decisively turned the tables on Master Willie, beating him by three parts of a length with the top-class French

Champion Stakes, Newmarket—Cairn Rouge takes the lead from Master Willie inside the last furlong. The grey Nadjar finishes strongly to beat Rankin (rails) for third place

Mr D. Brady's "Cairn Rouge"

four-year-old colt Nadjar third and the Derby third Rankin in fourth. Significantly, she was asked for her effort later than at York, not moving ahead until well onto the rising ground; she could be named the winner, barring accidents, running into the Dip.

Cairn Rouge's dam Little Hills stayed a mile and a half really well: she won a fifteen-runner maiden race over the distance in the mud at Galway by ten lengths. Soon after, she won a juvenile hurdle over a mile and three quarters at Navan in similar conditions. Pitcairn, a fairly stoutly-bred miler who was retired to stud only in 1975, has sired good horses who stayed a mile and a half in Ela-Mana-Mou and Bonnie Isle. The family on the dam's side has produced all types in recent generations. The third dam Stone Crop was a half-sister to Zarathustra and to the dam of Althrey Don. Not of much account on the racecourse herself, she produced the Sweeps Hurdle winner Normandy and Cairn Rouge's grandam, the 1959 Irish Cambridgeshire second Ballyogan Queen who seemed best at up to a mile. Ballyogan Queen produced five winners all told, two of them—the fairly useful miler Queen's Messenger (by Babur) and the useful middle-distance performer Countermarch (by Hard Ridden)—better than Little Hills.

Apparently Cairn Rouge nearly died of tetanus as a yearling; at that age she was retained for only 3,000 guineas at the sales. She is an unprepossessing type for a top performer, on the small side (conforming to the popular misconception of a first foal, for first foal she is) and unimpressive in her slower paces, with a round action that suggests, misleadingly, she would be ideally suited by soft going. However, to use the old cliche, handsome is as handsome does. She reminds us strongly of another Irish horse, the Champion Hurdler Monksfield, never looking the part until the contest itself brings out her qualities, very

Mr R. E. Sangster's "Calandra"

important among them a zest for racing. Cairn Rouge seems to act on any going, though she might not be at her very best on extremes. She has a better turn of finishing speed than most of her contemporaries and seems sure to win more good races if she progresses satisfactorily from three to four. *M. Cunningham, Ireland.*

CAJOLERY 4 br.c. Pall Mall 132–Do Please (I Say 125) (1979 8s 8g 7d 7f* 7fg 1980 7f 7.2fg4 7fg* 7g 7fg* 7fg 7g 7g 7d*) lightly-made colt; won handicaps at Lingfield in June, Doncaster in July (beat Steeple Bell in good style) and Leicester in November; best at 7f; seems to act on any going. *I. Walker.* **80**

CALA GALERA 4 b.f. Mummy's Pet 125–Never in Tune 63 (Never Say Die 137) (1979 6g 7d 6f3 5.6fg 5g 5h4 5fg4 6s3 1980 8h 8fg 6g 6s) compact filly; poor plater; stays 6f; acts on any going; blinkered final start (looked none too enthusiastic). *R. Hoad.* —

CALANDRA (USA) 3 br.f. Sir Ivor 135–Intrepid Lady (Bold Ruler) (1979 NR 1980 8g 7f2 10fg* 10s* 12d4 8g*) strong filly; second foal; closely related to Irish 1m winner Fonthill Abbey (by Habitat); dam, winner over 1½m in France at 3 yrs, is sister to very smart 1968 American 2-y-o filly Big Advance; successful at the Curragh in Kildare Fillies Stakes, Pretty Polly Stakes (moved short to post but came back much better when making all to beat Racquette unchallenged by a length) and Gilltown Stud Stakes; beat My Hollow a length in last-named in September; weakened in straight when 7¼ lengths fourth of 8 to Shoot A Line in Irish Guinness Oaks on same course in between; best at distances short of 1½m; probably acts on any going; smart. *V. O'Brien, Ireland.* **114**

CALA RATJADA 3 gr.f. Dancer's Image–Canning Place (Never Say Die 137) (1979 NR 1980 11.5f2 12.2f* 12f2 16fg 13.3d) good-topped filly; good mover; half-sister to 2 winners, including very smart 1975 French 2-y-o Bynoderm (by Faraway Son), subsequently a stakes winner at up to 1m in USA; dam placed in **89**

poor 1½m event; landed odds in maiden race at Catterick in July; ran respectably on next 2 starts but moderately on final outing (pulled up very sore); probably stays 2m; acts on firm going; sold 20,000 gns Newmarket December Sales. *H. Cecil.*

CALEDONIAN 4 b.c. Philip of Spain 126–Blasllyn 88 (Blast 125) (1979 6g^{2} 5g 6f^{3} 5f^{2} 6g 5g 6d^{4} 6d 6s^{2} 5f 7g 6d^{3} 1980 7f^{4} 6f^{3} 6h* 5f^{2} 5fg 6d 6fg 5d^{2} 5f 6g 5s 5d 5d^{4}) tall colt; sprint handicapper; neck winner at Pontefract in May; probably stays 7f; acts on any going; wears blinkers nowadays. *J. Calvert.* **63**

CALIBUNDA 5 b.g. Caliban 123–Fairabunda 59 (Floribunda 136) (1979 9f 7g 8fg 12d 12d^{3} 15d 13g^{3} 12fg 12g 1980 10v 11d* 8f 14.7f 9f 11g 9fg 15s) poor handicapper; won apprentice handicap at Hamilton in April; stays 13f; suited by a soft surface; sold 400 gns Newmarket Autumn Sales. *W. H. H. Williams.* **39**

CALIDORE 2 br.f. Scottish Rifle 127–Callidice 77 (Worden II 129) (1980 6g) May 10; half-sister to several winners, including useful Athelstan (by Derring-Do), successful here and in France at up to 9f; dam disappointing; 25/1 when behind in 20-runner maiden race at Leicester in November won by Nello. *T. Marshall.* –

CALL BEC 3 ch.c. Upper Case–Mountain Of Mourne 87 (Mountain Call 125) (1979 6fg 7g 8fg 1980 7s 8fg 10.fg 10f 7g 8.3s^{2} 8fg 10f^{4} 10d^{4} 10d) compact colt; plater; stays 1¼m; acts on soft going; blinkered fifth start; has worn bandages; has run respectably for an apprentice. *R. Akehurst.* **54**

CALL BIRD 3 ch.f. Le Johnstan 123–Shrubbery 86 (Ballymoss 136) (1979 5v 5s^{2} 5s 5d* 5s^{4} 5f 6fg 1980 5fg^{3} 5.8f 5fg 5fg 5.8g 6g 5g 6g) plater; best at 5f; probably acts on any going. *C. Wildman.* –

CALL ME CANDY 2 ch.f. Roman Warrior 132–Tit-Bit 61 (Hornbeam 130) (1980 5g 5g 5g 5g 5g 5d) May 10; useful-looking filly; third foal; half-sister to 3-y-o Good Larker (by Some Hand), a winner over 7f and 1m; dam poor maiden; plating-class maiden. *W. Wightman.* **60**

CALMACUTTER 3 br.g. Murrayfield 119–Snow Leap 66 (King's Leap 111) (1979 6g 6d^{4} 7f 6g 7fg 1980 6v 6fg 6f 7f 8fg 8f 8.2s) quite a useful sort; poor maiden; sometimes wears blinkers. *A. W. Jones.* –

CALVANIST (FR) 3 b.g. Reform 132–Calve 117 (Bold Ruler) (1979 6fg 1980 8g) strong, compact ex-Irish gelding; beaten some way in maiden races. *G. Lewis.* –

CALVOCORESSI (USA) 3 br.c. Cornish Prince–Wire Chief (Gallant Man) (1979 6fg* 1980 8g 10d^{4}) lengthy colt; won maiden race at Newmarket at 2 yrs; lightly raced and well beaten in 1980; should stay 1¼m; acts on a firm surface. *R. Price.* –

CALYPSO JOE 4 ch.g. Sovereign Gleam 117–Sarah Gee (Goldhill 125) (1979 12d 12g 13.3s^{4} 16fg* 16.9fg^{2} 16f 16fg 14g 1980 18d 16s 16s 14g) big, strong gelding; had stiff tasks and was well beaten as a 4-y-o; stays well; seems to act on any going. *B. Swift.* –

CAMACHO (USA) 5 b.g. Mickey McGuire–To My Lady (Amber Morn) (1979 8d 10g 8f 9fg^{3} 8g 8g 8f 1980 6g 8g^{2} 8fg 8f^{3} 8g 8h^{3} 10g* 10.2g 10.2d* 10d^{2} 11d) won handicap at Chepstow in September (ridden by 5-lb claimer) and apprentice event at Bath in October, making much of running both times and beating Mr Argentina by 5 lengths on latter course; good second to Dunderave in handicap at Sandown later in October; stays 1¼m; appears to act on any going. *G. Cottrell.* **76**

CAMBRAY LAD 2 b.c. Streetfighter 120–Dreamland (Atlas 126) (1980 5d 6g^{3} 5.8f 7d 7s) 460Y; leggy colt; half-brother to minor sprint winners by Silver Kumar and Royal Grey; dam ran only twice; only plating class; sweated up fourth start. *M. Bradley.* **55**

CAMBRO BOY 4 b.g. Mandamus 120–Palmette 103 (Premonition 130) (1979 13g 14.6fg^{4} 16d 18g 12f 12fg 13.8s* 16s 1980 18d) workmanlike gelding; plater; stays 1¾m; acts on soft going; dwelt when tried in blinkers on final outing in 1978. *R. Hobson.* –

CAMERONIAN LADY 3 br.f. Scottish Rifle 127–The Lady Brianstan (Signa Infesta 114) (1979 NR 1980 8s 10.8s 12fg) lengthy filly; of little account; sold out of Mrs R. Lomax's stable 460 gns Ascot July Sales. *M. Hinchliffe.* –

CAMESETA 5 b.g. Shantung 132–Camisole 94 (Psidium 130) (1979 NR 1980 8.3g) poor staying maiden at 3 yrs; bandaged when tailed off in seller on only outing of 1980; has worn blinkers. *A. Davison.* –

CAMISITE 2 ch.c. Hittite Glory 125–Camisole 94 (Psidium 130) (1980 6g 5d^{2} 5d* 6s^{3}) Apr 27; 2,700Y; leggy colt; half-brother to minor winners here and abroad; dam 2-y-o 6f winner; ran on under pressure when winning 18- **85**

runner maiden race at Doncaster in October by ½ length from Hit Record; well-backed favourite for 12-runner minor event at Stockton the following month but moved badly to post and finished only 6¾ lengths third to Marking Time; will probably stay 7f; yet to race on a firm surface. *W. O'Gorman.*

CAMPTON 2 b.g. Sharp Edge 123–Gretel (Grey Sovereign 128 §) (1980 5s 7g² 7f² 7fg 8d 8s³ 8.2s 8g) Apr 6; 2,800F, 4,600Y; workmanlike gelding; half-brother to 2 minor winners; dam an unraced twin; second in minor events, coming from long way back when failing by a neck to catch Principal Dancer at Sandown in July and going down by 2 lengths to very easy winner To-Agori-Mou at Lingfield the following month; subsequently descended to sellers, best effort when 3 lengths third of 21 to Santella Ascot at Newmarket in October; stays 1m; acts on any going; ran poorly last 2 outings, wearing blinkers on final appearance; one to be wary of. *J. Sutcliffe.* **71 §**

CAMWAY 5 b.g. Hot Brandy 119–Little Mohee (Border Chief 101) (1979 NR 1980 10fg 10fg 10h 8f 10g) leggy, light-framed gelding; useless. *A. Dalton.* **–**

CANAILLE 2 b.f. African Sky 124–Canning Place (Never Say Die 137) (1980 6s 7g 7g*) Feb 19; quite attractive, rangy filly; half-sister to 3 winners, including 3-y-o 1½m winner Cala Ratjada (by Dancer's Image) and very smart 1975 French 2-y-o Bynoderm (by Faraway Son), subsequently a stakes winner at up to 1m in USA; dam placed in poor 1½m event; improved with her races and was ridden by 7-lb claimer when winning 19-runner maiden race at Leicester in August pushed out by 3 lengths from Run Record Run after travelling well throughout; will stay 1¼m; has scope. *H. Cecil.* **84** p

CANDAULES 2 b.c. Supreme Sovereign 119–Sweet and Naughty 76 (Connaught 130) (1980 5.8fg² 5.8g² 7g⁴ 6fg 7h³ 7g*) Mar 11; 2,400F, 5,400Y; strong, quite attractive colt; first foal; dam ran only at 2 yrs when winner at 5f; well backed when winning 9-runner minor event at Brighton in October by ½ length from Gifford; will stay 1m+; acts on hard going; blinkered last 2 outings. *C. James.* **80**

CANDID PEAL 2 gr.f. Town Crier 119–Angelica (Hornbeam 130) (1980 5g 6d 6f 5g 8fg) May 7; 2,100Y; small, lengthy filly; bad plater. *P. Asquith.* **–**

CAN-DO-MORE 3 gr.c. Dancer's Image–Macha's Jewel (Majestic Prince) (1979 5g 5g 6fg 6f² 7f* 7g² 7f 8fg⁴ 7fg 1980 8d 7f² 7fg 7f 7.2g) useful-looking colt; quite a moderate handicapper; seems to stay 1m; acts on firm going; blinkered nowadays; sold 2,600 gns Doncaster September Sales. *N. Callaghan.* **68**

CAN-DO-MOST 3 b.c. Caliban 123–Amorce 81 (Le Levanstell 122) (1979 7d* 1980 10f⁴ 12.3f³ 10g 10fg 12d) quite attractive, well-made colt; quite a moderate handicapper at his best; off course 3 months after second start and ran as though something was wrong with him on his return; stays 1½m; probably acts on any going. *N. Callaghan.* **78**

CANDY COASTER 5 b.m. Candy Cane 125–Insouciante 71 (No Worry 105) (1979 10.8d 10.1fg 15.5fg 12g 16f 18fg 1980 12h) of little account. *R. Akehurst.* **–**

CANDY STREET 2 b.f. Streetfighter 120–Sweet Boronia 96 (Mandamus 120) (1980 5g 5fg 5d 5s 5fg 5g 6g 6fg) May 10; sturdy filly; useless; has worn blinkers; virtually refused to race final outing. *W. Charles.* **–**

CANE SPIRIT 3 b.f. Jimsun 121–Ibis 96 (Tamerlane 128) (1979 5d 5s 6g 7fg 8h 1980 9g 8h 10.6d) strong filly; has shown only a modicum of ability in maiden events; should be suited by 1m+. *M. W. Easterby.* **–**

CANIO 3 b.g. Welsh Pageant 132–Nedda 113 (Alcide 136) (1979 5d 6fg² 7fg* 7fg³ 1980 8f 10.4f 10g 8g 8d 8f⁴) lightly-made gelding; very useful at 2 yrs, winning Donnington Castle Stakes at Newbury and finishing excellent 1¼ lengths third of 9 to Final Straw in Laurent Perrier Champagne Stakes at Doncaster; below form in 1980, running his 2 best races at Newmarket when fifth to World Leader in valuable handicap in June on third start and fourth in minor event in October; well beaten in varied company on his other starts; needs further than 1m and will probably stay 1½m; blinkered fifth outing. *T. Waugh.* **114** d

CANNON HALL 3 b.c. Singing Bede 122–Glebe 83 (Tacitus 124) (1979 5fg 5fg 5g⁴ 1980 7s² 7d⁴ 10f³ 8fg³ 7f* 7g* 7fg² 7g 8d² 8fg 7d) strong colt; successful in maiden race at Redcar in May and minor event at Edinburgh (apprentice ridden) in June; best at up to 1m; acts on any going; sold 7,000 gns Newmarket Autumn Sales. *J. Hardy.* **78**

CANNON KING 4 b.c. Owen Anthony 102–Primmy 56 (Primera 131) (1979 6s^2 8.2s^2 9v^3 7d* 7s 8v^4 7f 8.2g^3 8g* 8g* 8s* 1980 8d 8fg 8fg* 8d 10g^3 10fg^3 10g^2 9fg* 9f 8.2s 10g^3) smallish colt; quite a useful handicapper; clever winner at Beverley in June and was driven out when scoring by 2 lengths from On Edge at Wolverhampton in August; excellent third of 19 to Spanish Dancer in Irish Sweeps Autumn Handicap at Newmarket in November; stays 1¼m; acts on any going; good mount for an apprentice. *J. Dunlop.* **95**

CANNY YATTON 5 br.g. John Splendid 116–Doubtful Request (Cheveley Lad 105) (1979 5s 5fg^3 5f 6g 6g^2 6s^3 8g^3 10h 8.2g 1980 6f 6h) plater; stays 1m; acts on any going; started slowly eighth outing (sweated up) at 4 yrs. *W. Stubbs.* –

CANOODLE 2 ch.f. Warpath 113–Turtle Dove (Gyr 131) (1980 7d 8s) Apr 25; small, lightly-made filly; third foal; sister to winning 3-y-o stayer Road to Mandalay and fairly useful middle-distance handicapper Path of Peace; dam ran only once; well beaten in end-of-season maiden and minor events; likely to need 1½m+. *C. Thornton.* –

CAN RUN 7 ch.g. Deep Run 119–Decalogue (Democratic 124) (1979 7s 7.2v* 7g* 7f^2 8g 7fg 8f^2 8fg^2 7g^3 8d 8f* 8fg^4 7g 8s 1980 7.6f 7.2fg^2 8fg 7g^4 7g 8fg^2 8fg^3 8d 7fg^2 8g^4) quite a moderate handicapper; stayed 1m; acted on any going; sometimes sweated up; often wore blinkers; dead. *D. Gandolfo.* **74** d

CANTANKEROUS (USA) 3 b.f. Raja Baba–Elizabeth C. G. (Windy Sea) (1979 NR 1980 5g 6g 10s) $62,000Y; fair sort; not a good mover in her slower paces; fourth foal; half-sister to 2 minor winners in USA; dam unraced sister to high-class performers Windy's Daughter and Miss Lady Bug; well beaten in maiden and minor races; sold 21,000 gns Newmarket December Sales. *B. Hanbury.* –

CANTELUPE 5 ch.m. Brioche 108–Robbi Tobbi (Rapace 130) (1979 14.6fg^3 14g^4 16fg 12fg 15.5f 1980 12d^3 13d 12h 12d) poor maiden; stays well; blinkered final start (sweated up); suitable mount for an amateur rider. *N. Tinkler.* –

CANTILEVER 4 b.g. Crooner 119–Span (Pan II 130) (1979 12g 12s^3 14f^2 12g^4 14g* 16.9fg^3 16f^2 1980 16s^4 15f 16g^3 16.5g^2 15.5fg) one-paced staying handicapper; acted on any going, but went well on firm; raced with his tongue tied down; dead. *B. Hobbs.* **69**

CANTON LIGHTNING 2 ro.f. Rheingold 137–Canton Silk 108 (Runnymede 123) (1980 7g^2 8f^2) Mar 12; 10,000Y; leggy filly; third foal; half-sister to very useful 5f to 8.5f winner Royal Pinnacle and a winner in Hong Kong (both by High Top); dam 5f performer; disputed lead throughout when second in £2,600 event at Redcar in August (short-headed by Sunion) and 10-runner maiden race at Wolverhampton the following month (favourite, went down by 1½ lengths to Cinderwench); likely to stay 1¼m; wears blinkers; lacks pace. *B. Hills.* **80**

CANTYCROON 4 b.g. Crooner 119–Canty Day 87 (Canadel II 126) (1979 8s 11.7f 12s 14g 16.9fg 12f 16.1s 16s 1980 13g* 15f^2 15.8d^4 12fg 16.1s) won maiden race at Hamilton in April; stays well; acts on firm going. *G. Richards.* **55**

CANUSA 2 b.c. Dubassoff–Houbichka (Swoon's Son) (1980 6d 6s) Mar 16; 4,500Y; half-brother to Irish middle-distance winner Migrator (by My Swallow) and a winner in Malaya; dam lightly-raced half-sister to smart miler Zingari; in rear in maiden races at Salisbury in June and Nottingham (last of 16) in August. *A. Johnson.* –

CAPABILITY 3 ch.f. Mount Hagen 127–Askalot (Javelot 124) (1979 NR 1980 6g) 2,500Y; half-sister to 2 winners; dam won over 1½m in Ireland; 20/1 when behind in 20-runner maiden race won by Bokarah In Shallah at Nottingham in July; sold 6,800 gns Newmarket December Sales. *R. Hollinshead.* –

CAPE CHESTNUT 3 ch.f. Bustino 136–Boswellia 109 (Frankincense 120) (1979 7fg^2 1980 8f^2 8f 7g^3 8f* 7fg 7.2g 8f 8g^4) lengthy filly; good walker and mover; odds on, settled better than previously when easily winning maiden race at Thirsk in August; ran creditably final start; often pulls hard and is unlikely to stay beyond 1m; yet to race on a soft surface. *W. Hastings-Bass.* **79**

CAPE HATTERAS 5 b.g. Cavo Doro 124–Hannah Darling 108 (Match III 135) (1979 NR 1980 11fg) selling hurdler; lightly raced and poor form on flat; has worn blinkers. *B. Forsey.* –

CAPELLI 2 bl.c. Lord Nelson 107–Lady Courageous (Cash and Courage 116) (1980 7s) Apr 2; fourth reported foal; dam sold for 90 gns at 2 yrs; unquoted –

when last of 15 in maiden race won by Principal Dancer at Warwick in July. *G. Wallace.*

CAPRICORN LINE 2 ch.c. High Line 125–Floradora Do 85 (Derring-Do 131) (1980 7fg² 7fg³) Apr 26; 2,200F, 13,500Y; good sort; dam won at up to 7f; placed in maiden and minor races at Yarmouth, going down by 1½ lengths to Baz Bombati in July and finishing 5½ lengths third of 9 to The Thatcher when co-favourite in August; will stay 1¼m. *L. Cumani.* **77**

CAPRILI (FR) 2 gr.f. Caro 133–Vivarella (Cambremont 121) (1980 6fg 6g) Mar 26; 160,000 francs Y (approx £18,800); small, fair sort; half-sister to minor French winners by Dike and Crowned Prince; dam very useful 2-y-o 5.5f winner; ran better race on second outing when 7¾ lengths fifth of 10 to Shasavaan in Duke of Edinburgh Stakes at Ascot in October; may do better over 1m+ at 3 yrs. *G. Balding.* **72**

CAPSTAN 2 b.c. Welsh Pageant 132–Packet 96 (Royal Palace 131) (1980 6g²) May 27; strong, compact, good sort; second foal; dam, half-sister to smart stayer Mariner, won at up to 1¾m; 5/4 favourite but just in need of race, failed by a head to hold off Norman Style in £5,900 event at Doncaster in September but wasn't given an unduly hard time and finished clear of 9 others; likely to improve considerably over middle distances in 1981. *R. Hern.* **80** P

CAPTAIN BRASSBOUND 3 b.g. Brigadier Gerard 144–Hardware 86 (Hard Sauce 131) (1979 5s 7g 6g 1980 10s 8g* 7f⁴ 8fg 11g 12.3fg⁴ 10s 8s⁴ 8d) fair sort; showed improved form to win maiden race at Beverley in April; possibly stays 1½m; seems to act on any going; sweated up first start and pulled hard on fifth; sold out of E. Weymes's stable 4,900 gns Doncaster May Sales. *R. McDonald.* **71** d

CAPTAIN NICK 4 b.c. Sharpen Up 127–Centime 82 (Double Jump 131) (1979 6d 6f* 6fg³ 6g 6s 5.6fg 7g 6fg² 6g 1980 6f 6f³ 6fg* 6fg 6fg 6fg⁴ 7g* 6s 7g² 7g³ 7fg³ 7g) quite a useful-looking colt; very useful performer; put up a fine performance when winning valuable Sir Noel Murless Stakes at Newmarket in June by ½ length from Premier Rose, getting on top in final furlong after being well behind in early stages; had also finished strongly when winning handicap **113**

Bretby Handicap, Newmarket—Captain Nick's strong run takes him into the lead inside the final furlong

at Newmarket the previous month by 1½ lengths from Hurworth House; ran well on most other outings, including when 3 lengths second of 4 to Known Fact in Kiveton Park Steel Stakes at Doncaster and third in well-contested handicaps on same course and at Ascot, all in September; suited by 7f; acts very well on firm ground and is possibly unsuited by soft; blinkered sixth outing at 3 yrs and on second start; suitable mount for an apprentice; best on a galloping track. *J. Hindley.*

CAPTAIN'S PLEASURE 5 b.g. Captain's Gig–Palmetta (Pall Mall 132) (1979 12fg 1980 16s 12g 12d) strong gelding; poor maiden; sold 500 gns Ascot November Sales. *R. Head.* —

CAPTAIN STEED (USA) 2 br.c. Chieftain–Barge (Curandero) (1980 6g 7fg[4] 8d 8d[3]) Apr 22; $50,000Y; compact colt; half-brother to numerous winners, including stakes winners Air Boat (by Open View) and Dominant Star (by Pia Star); dam won at 2 yrs; in frame in maiden race at Yarmouth in August and nursery at Pontefract in October, beaten 3½ lengths by Bonny Gold when blinkered in latter; will stay 1¼m; acts on a firm surface; sold 5,200 gns Newmarket Autumn Sales. *M. Stoute.* **68**

CAPTAIN WHITE 2 gr.c. The Go-Between 129–My Diana 94 (Sovereign Path 125) (1980 5f 5h* 5fg 5fg[3] 6fg 5f 5d 5f) Mar 22; 1,400F; big, lengthy colt; not a good mover; half-brother to 2 minor winners and 2 winners abroad; dam sprinter; justified favouritism in 12-runner maiden race at Thirsk in May by 3 lengths from Quality Road; ran respectably on next 3 outings but subsequently put up moderate displays, including in a valuable seller; stays 6f; blinkered sixth outing; sold 1,300 gns Doncaster October Sales. *M. H. Easterby.* **77**

CAPTIVE LIGHT 2 b. or br.g. Manacle 123–Acre Light (Linacre 133) (1980 5d 5f 5fg[4] 5fg 5fg 7g) Apr 10; neat, light-framed gelding; bad plater; blinkered fifth outing. *W. C. Watts.* —

CAPTIVE MAIDEN 2 b.f. Manacle 123–Sally Ann III (Port Corsair 98) (1980 5g 5d[4] 5fg 5g 5g 7d) May 4; workmanlike non-thoroughbred filly; reportedly half-sister to 1¼m to 2m winner Arctic Rascal (by Arctic Kanda) and to a winning jumper; dam never ran; poor maiden; sweated up last 2 outings. *M. Bradley.* **59**

CAP TOO 4 b.g. Continuation 120–Merry Thought (Pindari 124) (1979 6fg 8fg 8h 8f* 8g 1980 8.2d[3]) small, strong gelding; plater; stays 1m; acts on firm going. *G. Richards.* —

CAPTURED AGAIN 6 gr.g. Manacle 123–Moselle Mist 64 (Sovereign Path 125) (1979 5f 6fg 5fg 5s[2] 1980 5fg 5g 7f 5fg[2] 5s) plater; best form at 5f; sometimes wears blinkers. *B. McMahon.* **45**

CAPVISTA 5 b.g. Captain's Gig–Alta-Vista (Skymaster 126) (1979 NR 1980 8g) novice hurdler; started slowly and was always behind in maiden race won by Lotus Water Boy at Edinburgh in October, first outing on flat. *J. Spearing.* —

CARACOLERO'S GIRL (FR) 3 ch.f. Caracolero 131–Sally's Wish (Sensitivo) (1979 NR 1980 10fg 10fg) 50,000 francs Y (approx. £5,900); big, lengthy filly; half-sister to 2 winners, notably very smart middle-distance performer Lyphard's Wish (by Lyphard); dam ran 4 times; soundly beaten in maiden races at Sandown and Salisbury early in year; sent to USA. *P. Walwyn.* —

CARALIA 2 b.f. Caracolero 131–Mortefontaine (Polic 126) (1980 7g 7.2d[3] 8fg[3]) Feb 13; 11,500F; big, well-made filly; second produce; half-sister to Polifontaine (by Bold Lad, Ire), quite a useful winner in France over 6f and 7.5f at 2 yrs; dam, sister to very smart Polyfoto, won over 1m in France; lacked finishing speed when length third to Beldale Flutter in minor event at Haydock in August and when 3 lengths third to 24 to Allegretta in maiden race at Leicester in September; will be suited by middle distances; should win a maiden race in 1981. *R. Hern.* **77**

CARALIST 4 ch.g. Traditionalist–Hy Carol (High Hat 131) (1979 8s 8f 8f[2] 8h[4] 9.4f* 9fg[2] 8f[4] 12h[3] 12f* 10fg[3] 1980 10fg 12.2d) strong, attractive gelding; not seen out until September and was well beaten; stays 1½m; acts on hard going and is probably unsuited by soft; races with his head high. *M. Delahooke.* —

CARAVILLA 5 b.g. Communication 119–Weewanda 94 (Cagire II 122) (1979 NR 1980 10f 6fg) novice hurdler; of no account on flat. *H. O'Neill.* —

CARBURY'S PRINCESS 2 b.f. The Brianstan 128–Paveh Princess 75 (Paveh 126) (1980 5fg 5fg 6d 9d 8d 10d) May 19; 2,000Y; third foal; dam placed at up to 6f; well beaten, including in sellers; sold out of N. Gaselee's stable 620 gns Doncaster August Sales after third outing. *M. Delahooke.* —

CARDIE GIRL 2 ch.f. Sharpen Up 127–Gold Cypher 76 (Pardao 120) (1980 6f² 7g²) Mar 20; 8,000Y; well-grown, leggy filly; good walker and mover; half-sister to several winners, including middle-distance winner Laen (by Yellow River); dam ran only at 2 yrs; 9/1 and very fit, put up an excellent effort for a newcomer when 2½ lengths second of 13 to Star Pastures in Crathorne Stakes at York in September; short-priced favourite for 14-runner Malton Stakes on same course the following month but came up against a much-improved animal in Golden Bowl and went down by a length after hanging badly when in front 3f out; will stay 1m; certain to win a maiden race. *W. Hastings-Bass.* **104**

CARDIFF 3 ch.c. Appiani II 128–Christiana 106 (Double Jump 131) (1979 NR 1980 10d* 12f 9.6f 9fg³ 11.7s³ 10fg⁴) lightly-made colt; half-brother to 3 winners, including very useful 7f and 1m winner Chalet (by Luthier); dam won over 5f at 2 yrs and is half-sister to very smart Calpurnius; won minor event at Nottingham in April despite hanging badly left; not disgraced in handicaps on last 2 starts; stays 1½m; suited by some give in the ground; sold out of J. Hindley's stable 8,000 gns Newmarket May Sales. *R. Hoad.* **81**

CARDINAL FLOWER 3 ch.c. Sharpen Up 127–Ixia 91 (I Say 125) (1979 7f 1980 8fg² 8fg* 10.5d² 10s 10g* 9fg⁴ 9f) good sort; good mover; useful performer; won maiden race at Kempton in May; put up a supremely game performance when holding off stable-companion Roysia by a head in handicap at Yarmouth in August; stays 1¼m; acts on a firm and a soft surface; ran rather freely early on final start. *G. Pritchard-Gordon.* **101**

CARDINALS WALK 2 ch.g. Red Alert 127–Stay Nice 85 (Nice Guy 123) (1980 6fg 6d 8fg 8d⁴) Jan 31; 10,000Y; attractive, shapely gelding; half-brother to 2 winners and closely related to useful middle-distance performer Humdoleila (by Green God); dam won at 1m; 7½ lengths fourth of 14 to Nimblemoss in maiden race at Bath in October, first sign of ability; runs as though he'll stay 1¼m; gelded at end of season. *R. Hannon.* –

CARDOON 3 b.g. Some Hand 119–Lunawood 71 (Blast 125) (1979 6fg 8g 8fg 8d 1980 10.1g 8fg² 8g³ 8fg 8fg³ 10fg) quite well-made gelding; stays 1m; one paced; blinkered sixth start. *J. Powney.* **68**

CARD PALMER 4 ch.c. Malicious–Pardilly 71 (Pardao 120) (1979 8s³ 8f⁴ 14g⁴ 12fg 14f 12fg 12g 10f⁴ 1980 16f* 16f 15h³ 12f⁴ 15f 14.6g) won handicap at Warwick in April by 6 lengths but is only plating-class; suited by a test of stamina; acts on any going. *C. Wildman.* **47**

CAREFREE 3 gr.f. Birdbrook 110–Lena's Girl (Never Say Die 137) (1979 NR 1980 8fg 10fg) lengthy, lightly-made filly; first foal; dam ran only twice; in rear in 2 maiden races at Kempton in May. *B. Swift.* –

CAREY'S CHOICE 5 b.g. Reliance II 137–Piave (Alcide 136) (1979 10d 10d 10.2fg 10d 1980 10g 10g 11.7s 10g* 10g 10.2g 10g) strong gelding; disputed lead from start and ran on well to win handicap at Salisbury in August by 2 lengths from Cannon King; ran moderately afterwards; stays 1½m; acts on firm going; suitable mount for an apprentice; usually wears blinkers; sold to W. Elsey 4,000 gns Ascot November Sales. *H. Blagrave.* **73**

CARFLAX (USA) 2 ch.c. Prove Out–Sewing Circle (Round Table) (1980 5s 5f 6d 7s) Mar 14; 8,000Y; neat colt; half-brother to several winners in USA, including stakes winner Giggling Girl (by Laugh Aloud), and a winner in Algeria; dam ran only once; behind in large fields of maidens at Kempton, Warwick (2) and Salisbury but was still backward on third outing; quite stoutly bred. *D. Ancil.* –

CARIBBEAN BLUE 2 b. or br.f. Blue Cashmere 129–Dido's Granddaughter (By Thunder! 122) (1980 6s) Feb 28; half-sister to several winners, including fairly useful sprinter Heartbeat (by Burglar); dam never ran; 25/1 and on burly side, missed break and always behind in 21-runner maiden race won by Tolmi at Newmarket in July, only outing. *J. Winter.* –

CARIBBEAN BREEZE 2 b.f. Windjammer (USA)–Striped Shirt (Dunce) (1980 5f³ 5fg 5fg* 5g³ 6d 7d) Mar 26; leggy filly; poor mover; half-sister to Irish 1¼m winner Chard (by Ridan) and a winner in Belgium; dam won 6f claiming race in USA at 2 yrs; ridden by 7-lb claimer, showed good speed throughout to win 9-runner maiden race at Pontefract in June by ½ length from Linmill; stayed on strongly when very good third behind Katysue in minor event at Beverley the following month; form only at 5f but should stay further; acts on a firm surface. *B. Hanbury.* **83**

CARIBBEAN SUN 2 ch.c. Midsummer Night II 117–Sleepy (Hereward the Wake 75) (1980 10d) May 4; 700Y; third foal; dam poor hurdler; very backward when always tailed off in seller at Pontefract in October. *T. Kersey.* –

CARIBLUE 3 b.g. My Swallow 134–Double Powered (Double Jump 131) (1979 –
5d 5g 6s 1980 7g 8d 6g) lengthy gelding; good mover; well beaten, including in sellers; has worn bandages. *A. Davison.*

CARISSIMO 6 b.g. Ribero 126–Fortunes Darling 122 (Fair Trial) (1979 –
12.2g 7fg 8f 11f 16f 12fg 14fg 16fg 8fg 1980 8g 12.2f) of no account; has been tried in blinkers; sold 920 gns Doncaster August Sales, resold 410 gns Ascot December Sales. *R. Page.*

CARLTON HALL 3 b.g. Club House 110–Donna Lollo 102 (Donatello II) 75
(1979 5d^{2} 5s^{2} 5v* 5g^{3} 5d^{3} 5s* 5s^{2} 5s* 6g* 6f^{4} 6f^{4} 7g^{3} 6g^{3} 7fg 1980 10f^{4} 8f^{2} 8f 8fg 9.4g^{3} 8fg 8d* 9g 10s 10.6s) workmanlike gelding; quite a moderate handicapper; won at Redcar in August (ladies event); should stay 1$\frac{1}{4}$m; acts on any going and on any track; stumbled and nearly fell third outing; good mount for an inexperienced rider. *Denys Smith.*

CARLTON LADY 2 b.f. Redundant 120–Gala Honey 66 (Honeyway 125) –
(1980 5fg 5g) Feb 20; 850F, 700Y; half-sister to 3 winners, including 7f and 1$\frac{3}{4}$m winner Mac Kelly (by Irish Ball); dam stayed 1$\frac{1}{4}$m; well behind in minor event at Ripon in May and maiden race at Edinburgh in June; sold 480 gns Doncaster September Sales. *Denys Smith.*

CARLTON PRIDE 3 b.c. Bustino 136–Hors Serie 103 (Vaguely Noble 140) –
(1979 6f 7fg 1980 8d 5f 9f^{3} 7fg 12h^{4} 12.2fg 16g 9g) leggy, lightly-made colt; poor plater; seems to stay 1$\frac{1}{2}$m; acts on firm going; sold 500 gns Ascot October Sales. *A. Smith.*

CARLYLE 3 gr.c. Wolver Hollow 126–Sunblast 108 (Roan Rocket 128) (1979 90
7fg 1980 7fg* 8fg 7f* 8g^{3} 8g) leggy, quite attractive colt; successful in maiden race at Leicester in April (odds on) and apprentice handicap at Yarmouth in June; should stay at least 1m; acts on firm going; needs to be ridden up with pace; ran poorly final start (found to be running a high temperature afterwards); sold only 1,550 gns Newmarket Autumn Sales. *H. Cecil.*

CARMINA BURANA 2 b.f. Forlorn River 124–Sinzinbra 112 (Royal Palace –
131) (1980 5f 5g 6fg 6fg 6s 8fg) Apr 19; 3,400Y; small, lightly-made filly; poor plater; blinkered sixth outing; dead. *W. Bentley.*

CARNATION 2 ch.f. Runnymede 123–Natural Flora (Floribunda 136) (1980 64
5fg 5fg^{3} 5g^{2} 5g^{3} 5g 5f 5g 5s^{4} 6s) Apr 28; 3,300F, 4,400Y; fair sort; sister to quite useful 1976 Irish 2-y-o 6f winner Fairhaven Lady and half-sister to 2 other winners here and abroad; dam unraced; placed in maiden races at Pontefact (2) and Redcar in the summer but is little better than a plater; ran moderately last 4 starts; best form at 5f; blinkered fifth outing. *E. Weymes.*

CAROLINE LAMB 3 gr.f. Hotfoot 126–Young Lamb (Sea Hawk II 131) 71
(1979 5v^{4} 5s^{2} 6g 1980 8g 8fg* 9g^{2} 8d 10.6d 10fg 10d 10s) compact filly; quite a moderate handicapper; led in last strides when winning at Ripon in July; stays 1$\frac{1}{4}$m; probably acts on any going; pulled hard early on fifth outing; started slowly sixth and seventh starts. *Miss S. Hall.*

CAROLING 3 gr.f. Caro 133–Sapientia (Prudent II 133) (1979 NR 1980 62
9fg^{4} 12fg 12fg 16.9d^{2}) 460,000 francs Y (approx £54,700); big, strong filly; half-sister to Tende (by Dike), a winner at up to 1$\frac{1}{2}$m in France; dam won at up to 1$\frac{1}{4}$m in France, and comes from Great Nephew family; blinkered when second in maiden race at Wolverhampton in July; stays well; acts on a soft surface. *J. Tree.*

CAROUSER 3 b.g. Warpath 113–Brandy (Busted 134) (1979 NR 1980 65
12.3f 12fg^{3} 11fg^{4} 8g 9.4g^{2} 10d^{3} 9s 12g* 12g^{3} 12.2d^{2} 12d^{2} 12d^{2}) lightly-made, lean gelding; plater; bought in 3,100 gns after winning at Thirsk in September; placed in better company on several other occasions; suited by 1$\frac{1}{2}$m; acts on a firm and a soft surface; has run creditably for a boy; sold 3,700 gns Doncaster November Sales. *C. Thornton.*

CARP 2 b. or br.c. Heres 81–Native Alone (Indigenous 121) (1980 5g 6fg –
7g 8fg 8d 10d 8g) May 17; neat, quite attractive non-thoroughbred colt; soundly beaten in sellers; blinkered final outing. *C. Wildman.*

CARPENTER'S BOY 2 b.c. Steel Heart 128–Grandee Ann (Cyane) (1980 –
6g) Feb 15; 8,200Y; strong colt; half-brother to 3-y-o 1m winner Maris Quest (by Windjammer); dam won 6 times at up to 7f in USA; 20/1 and backward, moved badly to start and finished last of 11 to Norman Style in £5,900 event at Doncaster in September but ran better than placing suggests, showing speed until lack of fitness told at halfway. *Denys Smith.*

CARPET GENERAL 4 b.c. Sallust 134–Red Val 101 (Red God 128§) (1979 105
5f 7fg* 8fg 6s^{2} 6d^{2} 1980 6s^{2} 7.2d* 7f* 8f* 7fg 8g*) strong colt; much improved

William Hill Gold Cup, Redcar—fourth and most important win of the season for Carpet General who beats Miner's Lamp

and developed into a useful handicapper; put up an excellent performance to win William Hill Gold Cup at Redcar in August by 1½ lengths from Miner's Lamp, quickening to lead 1f out and running on extremely well; successful on same course on fourth outing and had earlier won at Haydock and Newcastle; stays 1m well; acts on any going; genuine and consistent; suitable mount for an apprentice; sweated at Haydock; joined Sir Mark Prescott after Redcar. *T. Molony.*

CARRIAGE WAY 6 br.h Track Spare 125–Polyandrist 92 (Polic 126) (1979 7s 8s4 8d 8d 8s2 8g2 8d 7fg 8fg 8d2 8.2s3 1980 8g 7.5g2 8g 8g 8d3 8fg* 8f4 8f 8fg* 8d3 7d 8g 8g 8g 8fg 8d 8d2) modest handicapper nowadays; top weight when winning apprentice handicaps at Kempton in May and Newbury in June; best form at around 1m; acts on any going; blinkered second start in 1979; none too reliable; sold 3,500 gns Doncaster October Sales. *N. Callaghan.* **97** d

CARRIED ALONG 4 ch.g. Mansingh 120–Drifting Along (Farm Walk 111) (1979 6g 7fg 8g 8fg* 8fg 10g 1980 8.2s) small gelding; won maiden race at Beverley in 1979, despite hanging left; well beaten in seller on only outing of 1980; not certain to stay 1¼m. *Miss S. Hall.* –

CARRONADE 4 br.g. Scottish Rifle 127–Negroni 103 (Quorum 126) (1979 12f 12.3fg 13f4 14.7g3 14.7g2 12.2d2 1980 17.1d) workmanlike gelding; stays 1¾m; blinkered first 2 starts at 3 yrs. *L. Kennard.* –

CARROWMORE BOY 4 b.c. Sharpen Up 127–Primanda 90 (Mandamus 120) (1979 8g2 8g 10.2d 1980 8fg 8d4 8f) plating-class maiden; stays 1m; sweating on reappearance; has run well for an apprentice and a lady rider. *W. Haigh.* –

CARRYMITA 4 b.f. Henry the Seventh 125–Miss McLairon 96 (Klairon 131) (1979 11g 11.7g 12s4 12fg 13f3 12g 11.1g 1980 15fg) strong, short-legged filly; probably stays 13f; acts on firm going; blinkered third to sixth starts at 3 yrs; has worn bandages. *J. Benstead.* –

CARRY ON AGAIN 2 ch.g. Swing Easy 126–Hi-Conkers 86 (Sica Boy 132) (1980 5s4 5f4 5f* 5fg2 5f3 6f 6g 6fg 7fg) Jan 23; 6,000F, 8,000Y; rangy gelding; brother to very useful 5f to 7f winner Swinging Sam, and half-brother to a winner; dam 2-y-o 5f winner; won 19-runner maiden race at Sandown in April by short head from Cut Throat; good third of 6, beaten 2½ lengths by Pontin Lad, in minor event at Lingfield the following month; gelded after sixth start and showed little form subsequently; not sure to stay 7f (eased once chance had gone when tried at trip); looked temperamental when blinkered fourth outing. *R. Armstrong.* **88** d

CARRY OVER 2 b.g. Some Hand 119–Hardella 60 (Hard Ridden 131) (1980 6g 7fg 6g) Mar 19; 600F, 1,150Y; sixth produce; dam won 1m amateur riders race; behind in newcomers race and valuable sellers; slowly away third outing. *G. Balding.* **57**

CARTON QUEEN 3 b.f. Tickled Pink 114–Kings Wench 61 (Kibenka 119) (1979 NR 1980 8fg 8g 8.3g) compact filly; third foal; dam won 1¼m seller; well beaten in maiden race and 2 sellers; trained by S. Matthews first 2 starts. *D. Wintle.* **—**

CARVERS CORAH 6 br.m. Easter Island 101–Marieran (Pappatea 114) (1979 12v 16v 12f 12f* 12fg* 12f^{3} 16.9g^{3} 15.8d 12fg 12fg^{2} 12f* 16f 12f 12d 12d 1980 12.2v 10.8f^{3} 12fg 12f^{3} 12f^{3} 12fg 12.2s^{4} 12fg 12d^{3} 11.5g 12g* 12.2g^{2} 12g^{2} 13.1h 12g 12g^{2} 18d 12d) quite a moderate handicapper; always going well when scoring by ¾ length from Sakeena at Ripon in August; best at around 1½m; acts on any going except heavy; good mount for an inexperienced rider; needs to be held up and doesn't find much off bridle. *D. Leslie.* **54**

CASABUCK 5 br.g. Master Buck–Casacello (Punchinello 97) (1979 NR 1980 16fg) first foal; dam won on flat and over hurdles; third in N.H. Flat race at Hereford in 1979; tailed off after leading 9f in amateur riders race at Ascot in September. *G. Balding.* **—**

CASA ESQUILLINA (USA) 2 b.c. Key To The Kingdom–Missile Miss (Cyclotron) (1980 6d 7fg^{2} 6d^{2}) May 20; $80,000Y; workmanlike colt with a round action; half-brother to numerous winners, 3 of them stakes winners, including very useful Nalees Miss (by Nalees Man); dam won 9 times, including claiming events; ran very well, especially since he'd been off course over 3 months, when length second of 19 to Jalabad in maiden race at Lingfield in October; came out best of stand-side group when 1½ lengths second of 25 to Little Wolf in similar race at Newbury later in month; will stay 1¼m; sure to win races. *P. Cole.* **84**

CASBAR LADY 5 b.m. Native Bazaar 122–So Unlikely 60 (Blast 125) (1979 5s^{3} 5fg* 5f* 5fg 5h 1980 5f 5g 5s^{2} 5g 5g 5f) light-framed mare; sprint handicapper; 3 lengths second of 6 to Mi Favorita at Haydock in July, best effort; acts on any going; suitable mount for an apprentice. *D. Leslie.* **55**

CASE HISTORY 2 gr.c. Track Spare 125–Petite Path 106 (Sovereign Path 125) (1980 5fg 5g 5f 6f 5d^{2}) Feb 8; 3,100Y; brother to 2 winners, including fair 1m to 1¼m winner Ascot Royale; dam won Queen Mary Stakes and Ayr Gold Cup; ¾-length second of 20 to Sedona in seller at Catterick in October, easily best effort; best form at 5f but wasn't disgraced over 6f and should stay further; possibly needs soft surface. *M. McCormack.* **71**

CASE THE JOINT 2 b.f. Upper Case–Ribo Pride 77 (Ribero 126) (1980 7g) Apr 14; first foal; dam won over 1½m; unquoted when behind in 22-runner maiden race won by Ring Moylan at Chepstow in September. *D. Elsworth.* **—**

CASH LIMIT 3 b.f. High Top 131–Overspent 85 (Busted 134) (1979 NR 1980 7f^{4} 7fg^{4} 8fg 6g) small, lightly-made filly; first living foal; dam won over 6f at 2 yrs on only start; fourth in newcomers race at Newbury in April and maiden event at Chepstow in July; needs further than 6f and will stay 1¼m; didn't impress in paddock first start. *H. Candy.* **62**

CASHMERE GIRL 3 b.f. Blue Cashmere 129–Lagoon Girl (First Landing) (1979 5v 5s 5f 5d 1980 6f 6fg* 6f 6h 6fg 7g 5fg 6fg 6g 6g 6g 6fg) compact filly; poor mover; well backed when showing improved form to win maiden race at Folkestone in April; didn't run up to that form afterwards; stays 6f; acts on a firm surface; blinkered ninth and final starts. *M. Ryan.* **69**

CASHMOOR 2 b.c. Ashmore 125–Go Friendly (Be Friendly 130) (1980 7d^{3} 8g) Mar 16; 4,800F, 13,500Y; third foal; half-brother to Garozzo (by Dancer's Image), a useful winner over 1m in Italy; dam poor half-sister to useful stayer Attivo; looked to have done plenty of work but went down badly to start prior to finishing 5½ lengths third of 20 in maiden race won by John Willoughby at Leicester in October; well beaten in minor event at Newmarket later in month; will stay 1½m. *R. Baker.* **79**

CASHWELL 3 b. or br.g. Blue Cashmere 129–Well Matched 79 (Niccolo Dell' Arca) (1979 5g 6f 6fg 10g 1980 12g 10g) lengthy gelding; plating-class maiden. *Hbt Jones.* **—**

CASS ARTE 3 ch.c. Bay Express 132–Last Report 86 (Democratic 124) (1979 NR 1980 7f 7.6f 8d 11d 8g 8.2g 8g) 14,000Y; useful-looking colt; half-brother to 6f winner Jantu (by Deep Diver); dam 6f to 1m handicapper; well beaten in maiden races and a handicap; blinkered fifth and sixth starts. *M. Smyly.* **—**

CASSINA 3 b.f. Habitat 134–Cesarea 108 (Raeburn II) (1979 NR 1980 7d* 7d 7d^{2} 7f 8s) lengthy filly; good mover; third foal; dam game winner of **91**

5 races from 5f to 1½m; won 18-runner maiden race at Sandown in June; went down by a short head to Charming Native in handicap at Newbury in August; ran moderately on her other starts; should stay 1m+; possibly unsuited by very firm ground. *P. Walwyn.*

CASTELNAU (USA) 2 b.c. Irish Castle–Bay of Lundy (Portsmouth) (1980 7fg[2] 8g[2] 10g[3]) Mar 21; strong, good sort; second foal; dam, stakes-placed winner at up to 1m, is sister to Brindabella, a very useful stakes winner at up to 1¼m; second in large fields of maidens at Brighton in August and Goodwood in September, going down by 3 lengths to Jungle Jim, when apprentice ridden, on latter; stayed on well when 3 lengths third of 9 to Krug in Zetland Stakes at Newmarket the following month; stays 1¼m and will get 1½m; capable of winning races. *P. Cole.* **97**

CASTLE DANCER 3 gr.f. Dancer's Image–Courting (Quorum 126) (1979 5g 5f* 6f 1980 7s 7f[3] 7fg) neat, strong filly; quite a moderate handicapper; not raced after May; stays 7f; possibly unsuited by soft going. *B. Hills.* **76**

CASTLE KEEP 3 b.c. Kalamoun 129–Fotheringay 101 (Right Royal V 135) (1979 7.6f 8g[2] 8d* 1980 10fg* 12f[3] 13.3d* 12fg* 14.6g* 13.3fg*) **121**

Castle Keep should make a good four-year-old, good enough to win a pattern race. He reminds us of his half-brother Ragstone and his stable's Sea Chimes at the same stage of their careers, an improving horse who looks ready for better races than handicaps. Although Castle Keep stays, he probably wouldn't be so well suited by really long distances as Ragstone was, and is likely to be kept at a mile and a half to a mile and three quarters to start with. If he comes to hand early enough he should go well in races such as the John Porter Stakes, Ormonde Stakes or Yorkshire Cup.

Castle Keep was raced only in handicap company as a three-year-old, and lost only once in six starts. He first showed significant improvement in the Trundle Handicap at Goodwood in August, by which time he had won narrowly at Salisbury and Newbury (the Morland Brewery Trophy) and had been decisively beaten behind Vaguely Tender and Lakin at Epsom. His performance in the Trundle Handicap was extraordinary. Carson rode the cheekiest of races on him to win by a neck from Bunce Boy, giving the leaders ten lengths start with half a mile to go, moving up very easily alongside the leader Bunce Boy two furlongs out and then allowing him just enough rein to take and hold the advantage. The horse had an immense amount in hand, as also he had next time out in the Rockingham Handicap at the Doncaster St Leger meeting. The way he simply laughed at Buttress there, beating him on a tight rein by four lengths over the Leger course, gave cause for regret that he wasn't in the big race on the Saturday instead. Castle Keep was an intended starter in the Irish St Leger the following month but missed it because

Coral Autumn Cup, Newbury—Castle Keep puts up a top-class performance to win this valuable handicap from Shady Nook, Le Soleil (not in picture) and Laska Floko

of the very testing ground. He must have gone close had he run, judging by his performance at Doncaster and another very fine one in the Coral Autumn Cup at Newbury later in September. Penalized 7 lb, Castle Keep carried top weight at Newbury in what is an important handicap, taking on some older horses as at Doncaster. After being given a lot to do from four furlongs out once again, he made his ground steadily (pushed along this time) to deprive Laska Floko of the lead entering the final furlong, and he ran on strongly under typical Carson driving to beat Shady Nook decisively by a length and a half. Not many of the season's staying three-year-olds could have improved on this.

Castle Keep (b.c. 1977)	Kalamoun (gr 1970)	Zeddaan (gr 1965)	Grey Sovereign
			Vareta
		Khairunissa (gr 1960)	Prince Bio
			Palariva
	Fotheringay (b 1964)	Right Royal V (br 1958)	Owen Tudor
			Bastia
		La Fresnes (ch 1953)	Court Martial
			Pin Stripe

The Gold Cup winner Ragstone, now dead, was by Ragusa, a sire who is a stronger influence for stamina than Kalamoun. However, there's no reason for doubting that Castle Keep will get two miles; his full sister Castle Moon stayed the distance. Castle Moon is one of her dam's four winners, the one not mentioned so far being another modest filly Forsaken (by Bold Lad, Ire), successful at a mile and having form up to a mile and a half. The dam was a miler out of the very smart sprinter La Fresnes. Castle Keep is a neat, strong colt. He has yet to show his form on extremes and has not raced on really soft going; it would seem that both his trainer and Carson regard very soft as likely to be against him. *J. Dunlop.*

CASTLESIZE 2 ch.g. Status Seeker–Unharmed (Breakspear II) (1980 6g 6s 6g 5d 6s^4) May 5; 1,400Y; rangy gelding; half-brother to a winner in Belgium by Linacre; dam never ran; no worthwhile form in a variety of races. *J. Leigh.* —

CAST PEARLS (USA) 3 ch.f. Cutlass–My Girl Pearl (Carry Back) (1979 5d 5fg 5g 5f 5fg^2 6d^2 1980 5h 7f 5d* 5g 6s^3 6fg 6fg^3 5g 5.8g 6fg* 6d* 6d* 5v^4) small, compact filly; good mover; sprint handicapper; successful at Sandown, Lingfield and Leicester (2); stays 6f; probably acts on any going; started slowly second outing; sweated up seventh start; apprentice ridden for her last 3 successes; trained by P. Read first 5 starts. *A. Breasley.* 79

CASUAL AFFAIR 4 ch.f. Grisaille 115–St Mary's Square 84 (Acropolis 132) (1979 5f 1980 8.3f) little worthwhile form, including in a seller. *A. Jarvis.* —

CASWEN 3 ch.f. Malicious–Hurricane Lady (Abernant 142) (1979 NR 1980 9fg 8fg 11.7f 8f 7fg 13g 8.2g) small filly; of no account. *K. Bridgwater.* —

CATHERINE BLAKE 4 b.f. Blakeney 126–Belinda Ann 86 (High Treason 126) (1979 12s 10.6g 12.3fg 12f 8.2d 10.6g 12d 1980 11.7fg 14fg 12f 10.7g 16.9d) rangy filly; poor maiden; has been tried in blinkers. *K. Lewis.* —

CATHERINE HOWARD 3 ch.f. Tower Walk 130–Righteous Girl 93 (Right Boy 137) (1979 5fg^4 1980 10f^3 10.8s 8g^4 8f) unfurnished filly; seems only plating class; best run at 1¼m on firm going; sold 2,600 gns Newmarket December Sales. *H. Candy.* 56

CAUGHT IN CAPETOWN 2 ch.f. Manacle 123–Caught Speeding (Psidium 130) (1980 5g 6fg) Mar 7; 3,300F, 5,400Y; third produce; dam half-sister to smart miler Miletus; 33/1 when behind in large fields for maiden race at Windsor in July and minor event at Lingfield in October; sold 3,200 gns Newmarket December Sales. *G. Hunter.* —

CAVALIER 3 b.g. Moulton 128–Reload 119 (Relko 136) (1979 NR 1980 10.1g 10g 14d 14g 14.6d) strong gelding; third foal; brother to useful 1977 2-y-o 1m winner War Whoop and half-brother to 1¼m winner Pine Grove (by Brigadier Gerard); dam, half-sister to Full Dress II, won Park Hill Stakes; well beaten in maiden and minor races; blinkered fourth start; looks slow; sold 1,600 gns Newmarket Autumn Sales. *H. Wragg.* —

CAVALIER SERVENTE 2 gr.c. Barbaro–Quoro Star (Quorum 126) (1980 6fg 7g 6f 7d^4 6d) May 6; compact colt; third foal; dam never ran; about 6 lengths fourth of 10 to Paltango in maiden race at Catterick in October, easily best effort; will probably stay 1¼m+; bandaged third outing. *P. Wigham.* 67

CAVALINGO 2 b.f. Rustingo 94–Cavalry Cloak (Queen's Hussar 124) (1980 5f 5g 6g 5fg 5g) Jan 26; first foal; dam never ran; only plating class; blinkered fifth start; trained first 3 outings by D. Wintle. *G. Price.* —

CAVALRY TWILL 2 b.c. Queen's Hussar 124–Coming About 99 (Right Tack 100
131) (1980 5fg^4 6g^2 6s* 6g* 7f* 6f* 6fg) Mar 30; 30,000Y; compact, fair sort; second foal; half-brother to useful 3-y-o miler Atlantic Boy (by Busted); dam won twice over 5f at 2 yrs; always going well when beating Spindrifter (gave 3 lb) by ½ length in small race at Pontefract in September (pair well clear); successful the previous month in maiden and minor events at Nottingham, Windsor and Epsom; will stay 1m; acts on any going; sweated up badly and ran poorly final outing. *M. Stoute.*

CAVENDISH 2 b.f. Kalamoun 129–Golden Gorse (Crepello 136) (1980 5fg —
8d 8d) May 3; half-sister to winning Irish stayer Quarter Bridge (by Thatch); dam, winner over 1¼m in Ireland, is half-sister to Derby fourth Royal Sword; well beaten in maiden races. *P. Bailey.*

CAVORT 2 b.f. Cavo Doro 124–Astraline 97 (Skymaster 126) (1980 6d 6g 7fg 71
7g 8fg^4) Apr 28; well-made filly; second foal; sister to 3-y-o 9f winner Fast Green; dam sprinter; quite a modest maiden; will stay 1¼m. *G. Pritchard-Gordon.*

CAVO VARKA 3 ch.f. Cavo Doro 124–Treasure Boat 54 (Hook Money 124) 79
(1979 6f 6g 6fg^4 8f 1980 9f 10d 8d^2 10g^4 8fg* 8fg 8.2g^3 8.2d) quite attractive, well-made filly; enterprisingly ridden when making all to win maiden race at Doncaster in July; had stiffish tasks in handicaps afterwards, running well on penultimate start; stays 1m well; acts on a firm and a soft surface. *C. Brittain.*

CECCONI 3 b.c. High Top 131–Stardom 75 (Hornbeam 130) (1979 NR 1980 82
8f 12.3f 12fg^4 13d^2 13.4g^2 16.9d* 16f^4 16f* 15.5f^2 17.1d^2 15.8d* 12.5s*) 23,000F, 86,000Y; workmanlike colt; good walker; half-brother to quite useful middle-distance performer Tolstoy (by Reform) and 2 winners in France; dam, half-sister to Irish Oaks winner Discorea, won over 13f; successful in maiden race at Wolverhampton, amateur riders events at Beverley and Stockton and handicap at Catterick; stays well; acts on any going; blinkered fourth start; good mount for an inexperienced rider; sold 19,000 gns Newmarket Autumn Sales. *J. Hindley.*

CEE BEAUTY 4 ch.f. Ribero 126–Sweet Reproach 94 (Relic) (1979 10.8s —
13v^3 11.7g 12.3d^4 10.2d^3 10.6v* 12fg* 12.2fg 12f^4 10.6g 1980 16s) fair sort; stays 1½m; acts on any going; suitable mount for an apprentice; often makes running. *E. Reavey.*

CEILE 5 br.m. Galivanter 131–Paddyflower 88 (St Paddy 133) (1979 NR —
1980 10.1s 12d 8fg) of little account. *S. Kernick.*

CELESTIAL ANN 2 br.f. Royalty 130–Dake (Floribunda 136) (1980 5s 66
5.3d 5.8g 5s^2 5fg 5g 5f 5g) May 21; 1,450Y; small, lightly-made filly; only plating class; bred to stay middle distances. *S. Matthews.*

CELESTIAL GEM 6 ch.g. Gulf Pearl 117–Purple Goddess 69 (Red God 128§) 69
(1979 8s* 7v 8s* 8s 8f* 8f* 8f^2 7f 10d* 8f 1980 8d 8d^4 10.6fg 10fg 10.2fg 10fg 9g 10.6d^4 9g 9fg* 10fg^3 10g^2 12g^4 10d^2 10fg 10g 9g 10.5s 10d) fair handicapper at his best; winner at Newcastle (apprentices) in July; stays 1½m, but races mainly at shorter distances; acts on any going; blinkered twice in 1978; has worn a muzzle in paddock; excellent mount for an apprentice; sometimes makes running; slipped up sixteenth start; sold 3,500 gns Newmarket Autumn Sales. *R. Hollinshead.*

CELIA'S HALO 3 b.f. Mountain Call 125–Aurelia 68 (Aureole 132) (1979 51
6fg 5d 6g 1980 8.2d 10.8f 10.2fg 10.6fg 10d^2 10g) strong, compact, well-made filly; plater; stays 1¼m; acts on a soft surface; blinkered last 2 starts. *W. Holden.*

CELLINE 2 ch.f. London Company–Like For Like (What A Pleasure) (1980 —
5.8h 5g 6g) Feb 15; 2,400Y; first foal; dam, placed at 3 yrs in USA, is daughter of very smart stakes winner Swoon's Flower; well behind in maiden races in second half of season. *W. Musson.*

CELTIC DANCER 3 b.f. Weavers' Hall 122–Celtic Twilight 111 (Varano) —
(1979 5fg 5f 1980 6fg 6f 6fg^4 7fg 6fg 8g) neat filly: poor maiden. *A. Pitt.*

CELTIC HALO 4 b.c. Welsh Saint 126–Levanswood 74 (Le Levanstell 122) 100
(1979 6fg 6v 6d 6d 7.2g^3 6f^4 5fg 6f* 8f 6g 8.2g^3 5f 7d 6f^4 6fg 6d 1980 7.2fg 7g^3 6fg 6d 6fg 6g^3 6s 7fg* 6d^3 8g^3 6fg 7g 6d* 6s) neat colt; useful handicapper; put up a game performance under 10-0 when scoring by 1½ lengths from Tower Joy at Yarmouth in August; beat Town Sky decisively by 2 lengths at Redcar in October; ran well when placed twice in between; effective at 6f and stays

1m; acts on any going; suited by strong handling; successful with blinkers and without (wore them at Redcar); sweated up second outing. *A. Jarvis.*

CELTIC ISLE 4 b.g. Celtic Cone 116–Jo (Jock Scot) (1979 NR 1980 16.1s2) fifth live foal; dam poor staying chaser; fair performer over hurdles; collared close home by Mi Dad after looking to have race won nearly all way up straight in amateur riders event at Haydock in October, first outing on flat (well backed). *F. Rimell.* **70**

CELTIC PRIDE 2 ch.f. Celtic Cone 116–Second Glance (Prince Hansel 118) (1980 5f 6s 6g 6s 5d) Mar 31; small, lightly-made non-thoroughbred filly; first foal; dam tailed off in 4 hurdle races; probably of no account but is bred to need long distances. *G. Wallace.* **–**

CELTIC TARA 4 b.f. Welsh Saint 126–La Sarmate (Hard Sauce 131) (1979 8f 10.4fg3 12f3 12fg 12d2 12.5g 1980 13g) neat filly; plating-class maiden; stays 1½m; acts on firm going and a soft surface. *C. Booth.* **–**

CENTURION 5 ch.g. Connaught 130–Calleva (Worden II 129) (1979 NR 1980 16fg) very useful and improving young stayer (rated 113) at 3 yrs, when he won 5 of his 6 races, notably Tote Cesarewitch; backward and bandaged, broke down in 3-runner Newmarket Challenge Whip in May, first outing since that event. *I. Balding.* **–**

CENTURIUS 2 ch.c. Great Nephew 126–Word from Lundy 93 (Worden II 129) (1980 7g2 7fg* 7s) Feb 17; 270,000Y; rangy, attractive colt; good walker; brother to Derby winner Grundy, and half-brother to 2 winners; dam stayed 2m; put up a very smooth performance when winning 16-runner Mornington Stakes at Ascot in September, travelling easily throughout and quickening really well, with the minimum of urging from his rider, to score by a length from Bustomi; had earlier acquitted himself very well when 2 lengths second of 15 to odds-on Kalaglow in minor event at Sandown in August but disappointed us in William Hill Dewhurst Stakes at Newmarket in October; looked to be going well 3f out in latter but found nothing when let down and came home distant last of 5 behind Storm Bird; will stay 1¼m+; evidently unsuited by soft going and must be given another chance on better ground to confirm the very favourable impression he created at Ascot. *M. Stoute.* **106** p

CERAMIC 3 b.c. Cavo Doro 124–Nimble Gate 84 (Nimbus 130) (1979 6fg4 6fg 7g 7g4 8fg2 7.3g3 8f4 7g 1980 8d 10fg* 10fg4 12f4 10fg 11.7s 10fg 10f2 10g 16d) compact colt; good mover; ridden by 5-lb claimer when winning handicap at Epsom in April despite swerving violently left; not certain to stay 2m; acts on firm going and is probably unsuited by soft; trained by S. Harris first 7 starts. *T. M. Jones.* **65**

CEREMONIOUS 2 ch.f. Queen's Hussar 124–Queen's Keys 84 (Right Royal V 135) (1980 5d 5s 5g 5d 6g3 7g 7f4 6g4 8g 8g 8g) Mar 24; small, unfurnished filly; plater; will stay 1¼m; sold out of E. Weymes's stable 900 gns Doncaster May Sales after third start. *R. Whitaker.* **59**

Mornington Stakes, Ascot—an impressive performance by Centurius who is barely off the bridle to beat Bustomi and Kings General

CERUA (USA) 6 b.g. Nashua–Cerisette (My Babu 136) (1979 NR 1980 15fg) poor performer on flat nowadays; bandaged only outing of 1980; has won over hurdles. *T. Hallett.* —

CHABRIAS (FR) 5 b.h. Bold Lad (Ire) 133–Almerilla (Abdos 134) (1979 7s 1980 9f 12fg 8fg 11fg^3) fair sort; ex-French horse; ran best race for a long time when third to Rafael Molina in handicap at Ayr in July; stays 11f; acts on any going. *A. Jarvis.* 59

CHADS GAMBLE 5 ch.g. St Chad 120–Another Flutter 75 (Credo 123) (1979 7d 8g 7g^2 8d^3 7f* 7f^3 6fg 7f^2 7g^2 7.2g 7.3g 1980 7fg 7f 7h^2 8fg^2 7d 7f^2 8g^3 7f^2 7fg* 7f) won handicap at Brighton in August by a short head from Balaram; ran well most other outings; suited by 7f or 1m; appears to act on any going but is suited by a sound surface; blinkered last 3 outings in 1978 and last 2 starts in 1980. *J. Bethell.* 70

CHAIN OF REASONING (USA) 6 b.g. Hail To Reason–Daisy Chain 103 (Darius 129) (1979 NR 1980 15f 17.1fg^2 16g 16g 17.1fg) lightly-raced staying handicapper nowadays; ran best race when second to Skyline Drive at Bath in June; acts on a firm surface; used to wear blinkers; often bandaged. *S. Harris.* 57

CHALET (FR) 4 br.c. Luthier 126–Christiana 106 (Double Jump 131) (1979 7g* 10f 7.6f* 8fg* 1980 7s 8f 7fg 7f 7g 7.2d 9g) smart handicapper at 3 yrs; well beaten in 1980 (doesn't impress in paddock these days) and is probably no longer genuine; tried in blinkers sixth start; best left alone. *A. Smith.* —

CHALK DOWN 3 gr.f. Saritamer 130–Chantal 74 (Charlottesville 135) (1979 5s 6f 8g 1980 10.1f 10d^4 10s) lengthy filly; only plating class; not certain to stay 1¼m; sold 1,000 gns Newmarket December Sales. *N. Henderson.* —

CHALKE VALLEY 3 b.f. Ragstone 128–Last Portion (Major Portion 129) (1979 7fg 1980 10v 10fg 12g 14g 10d^3 8fg^4 12f^2 15.5g 12s) useful-looking filly; plating-class maiden; stays 1½m; acts on firm going; blinkered sixth start. *W. Wightman.* —

CHALUMET 3 b.f. Bay Express 132–Life Story 65 (Only for Life 126) (1979 6fg 6g^4 1980 8fg 7fg 6g 7g 7fg 8.3f) lengthy filly; poor plater nowadays; should stay at least 7f; blinkered third and fifth starts; sold 1,000 gns Newmarket December Sales. *A. Bailey.* —

CHAMPAGNE CHARLIE 3 br.c. Charlottown 127–The Guzzler 69 (Behistoun 131) (1979 6fg 7fg 7g 7g 8g 1980 10.8s^2 11.7fg^2 11.7f^2 12g^4 11fg^2 12g 13.1g 14g* 13.3d 14g 16f* 14fg 16fg^4 16g 13.3d) compact colt; narrowly won 15-runner maiden race at Salisbury in July and trotted up in amateur riders handicap at Chepstow in August; suited by a test of stamina; appears to act on any going; suitable mount for an inexperienced rider; not particularly consistent. *P. M. Taylor.* 89

CHAMP D'AVRIL 3 b.f. Northfields–April Twelfth (King's Leap 111) (1979 5d* 6g 5g 1980 5s* 5f^2 5f^4 6s 6fg^2 6g 5d^3 6s) neat filly; fairly useful handicapper; successful at Nottingham in April; ran creditably several starts afterwards; stays 6f; acts on any going; suitable mount for a claimer; sold 19,000 gns Newmarket December Sales. *Sir Mark Prescott.* 89

CHAMPERELLE 2 ch.f. On Your Mark 125–Pretty Asset 100 (Galivanter 131) (1980 5f 6g 5fg 5g^3 5fg 6g 5s) May 25; 2,500F, 2,200Y; compact filly; half-sister to 3 winners, including 1¼m winner Nosebob (by Reform); dam miler; 7 lengths third of 5 in weakly-contested maiden race won by Fire Mountain at Chester in August; will be more at home in sellers. *R. Hollinshead.* 46

CHAMPERS CLUB 3 ch.f. Run The Gantlet–Vein (Kalydon 122) (1979 5s 6fg 8d 1980 8f 10.1s 10.1d^2 12g 10d 10d) fair sort; plater; stays 1¼m; acts on a soft surface. *D. Weeden.* —

CHAMPS ELYSE 3 ch.f. Goldhill 125–Whitestake 74 (Compensation 127) (1979 5v 5f 5fg 6s 1980 6d 5f 7f^4 6fg 7s 6d 8fg 9s) compact filly; poor plater; probably stays 7f; swerved start when blinkered final outing at 2 yrs; sold 600 gns Doncaster October Sales. *J. Berry.* —

CHANCE FLIGHT 4 b.g. Floriana 106–Super Phoenix 73 (Pandofell 132) (1979 NR 1980 10.1g 12fg) big, strong gelding; unquoted when in rear in minor event at Windsor and maiden race at Brighton in the summer. *W. Musson.* —

CHANCE MATCH 2 ch.f. Royal Match 117–Fallen Lady (Busted 134) (1980 5g 5d 7d) May 17; 1,800Y; good sort; second foal; dam last on only outing; unquoted when 3¼ lengths fifth of 19 to Voting Day in maiden race at Bath in October, second outing and best effort; should be well suited by 7f+. *A. Breasley.* 73

CHANCER'S LAST 4 b.f. Foggy Bell 108–Chancer 78 (Chamier 128) (1979 NR 1980 12.5v 12.3f 16.9d) poor maiden; trained until after second outing by J. W. Watts. *K. Lewis.* –

CHANDHEER 4 b.g. Swing Easy 126–Babucon 90 (My Babu 136) (1979 7fg 64
8d 10g^{2} 10s 10f^{3} 12fg^{4} 10h 10fg 10fg 14f* 16f 1980 12d 18f^{4} 14.7f^{2} 12.2fg^{4} 12g 12d 10s 10f^{2} 10fg^{2} 15.5f^{4} 8g^{3}) fair sort; usually owner ridden at around 11-7 in amateur riders races nowadays; ran creditably over 1m on final start and stays well; acts on firm going; used to wear blinkers; inconsistent; trained part of season by G. Hunter. *R. Smyth.*

CHANDOR 2 gr.f. The Go-Between 129–Go Baby Go 81 (Takawalk II 125) 49
(1980 5fg 5.8h 5f 6g) Feb 9; small filly; first foal; dam winning hurdler; in mid-division in maiden and minor events and a seller. *N. Vigors.*

CHANEY 2 b.g. Sparkler 130–Anippe 102 (Aggressor 130) (1980 6d) May –
15; 4,100F, 7,600Y; strong, compact gelding; half-brother to 3 winners, including very useful 7f to 1¼m winner Siliciana (by Silly Season); dam stayed 1½m; unquoted and very backward, moved badly to start and was always well behind, after being hampered leaving stalls, in maiden race won by Shark Song at Newmarket in October. *R. Armstrong.*

CHANGABANG 3 b.c. Touch Paper 113–Good Reliance (Good Bond 122) 99
(1979 5v 5s^{3} 5d* 6fg 6f^{2} 6h^{2} 7fg^{3} 6h* 6fg^{4} 8fg 6h* 8f 8g 1980 8d^{2} 7d 8fg^{2} 8.2f^{3} 8h* 8fg 8fg 8fg^{3} 7.2s^{3} 8d 9g 8d 8.2g^{2} 8g*) rangy colt; useful handicapper; won Thirsk Hunt Cup in May by ¾ length from Top O' Th' Lane and £6,000 race at Doncaster in September by a neck from Glowing Tan; also ran very well when short-head second to Geoffrey's Sister at Haydock earlier in September; stays 1m well; acts on any going but goes well on hard ground; suited by a strong gallop; sometimes gives trouble at start; ran moderately second outing; sold 11,000 gns Newmarket Autumn Sales. *R. Hollinshead.*

CHANSON D'OR 5 b.m. Gold Rod 129–Dundry Hill 95 (High Perch 126) –
(1979 NR 1980 8g) novice hurdler; 50/1 when well behind in amateur riders race at Warwick in June, first outing on flat. *J. H. Peacock.*

CHANSON DU NUIT 2 ch.c. Song 132–Mathilde 84 (Whistler 129) (1980 80
5f^{4} 5f^{4} 5fg^{3} 5f^{2} 5fg* 5fg^{4} 5g 5f) Mar 9; 6,600Y; short-backed, robust colt; brother to Material, winner of first 5 starts over 5f at 2 yrs, and half-brother to several winners, 3 of them fairly useful; dam at her best early on as a 2-y-o; made all to win 11-runner minor event at Bath in June by ½ length from Royal Blood; disappointing afterwards, finishing only seventh of 16 to Abrovian Rose when favourite for valuable seller at York in September on final start; barely stays 5f; yet to race on a soft surface; blinkered sixth outing. *P. Cole.*

CHANT 3 ch.c. Habat 127–Heavenly Sound 115 (Sound Track 132) (1979 5fg 97
1980 6d* 7v^{4} 7f* 8f^{2} 8fg 7g^{4} 8g^{3} 7g) strong, good sort; fairly useful performer; won maiden race at Doncaster in March and handicap at Newmarket in April; ran creditably in minor race at Warwick on next start and was far from disgraced when fourth to Sunfield in City of York Stakes in August; stays 1m; seems to act on any going; sold 14,000 gns Newmarket Autumn Sales, reportedly to race in California. *G. Harwood.*

CHANTAL see My Chantal.

CHANTERS LANE 2 b.c. Deep Diver 134–Anglesea Market (Sea Hawk II –
131) (1980 5f 5fg) May 3; 1,000Y (privately), resold 1,550Y; second foal; half-brother to Irish 3-y-o 1¾m winner Anglesea Lace (by Royal Palace); dam placed at up to 1½m in Ireland; behind in maiden races at Wolverhampton (May) and Windsor (August). *J. Hill.*

CHANTIC 4 b.f. Beatic–Crazy Legs (Chanteur II 135) (1979 8d^{3} 12.2s^{3} 7g^{4} –
8f 8fg 9g^{2} 1980 8g 8.2d 7f 8f) poor plater; probably does not stay 1½m; blinkered fourth start at 3 yrs. *W. Haigh.*

CHANTRY BRIDGE 2 ch.c. Porto Bello 118–Prime Thought 69 (Primera 131) 88
(1980 5fg 6d^{2} 6fg*) Apr 1; strong, useful-looking colt; fourth foal; dam comes from a good family; landed the odds by 2 lengths from Angle Light in 11-runner maiden race at Doncaster in July; had previously made much of running when 3 lengths second of 16 to Moores Miracle in maiden race at York in June; will probably stay 7f; acts on a firm and a soft surface. *J. W. Watts.*

CHANTRY LAD 4 b.c. Calpurnius 122–Merella 81 (Primera 131) (1979 10g –
12g 14.6fg^{4} 1980 14.7f 12fg) poor maiden; dead. *B. Wilkinson.*

CHAPEAU VERT 7 ch.g. Green God 128–Mon Chapeau (High Hat 131) (1979 53
NR 1980 10.2g 8g^{2} 8s^{4}) poor handicapper on flat; gambled on when failing

by a head to peg back Notiki in seller at Brighton in October; stays 1m; probably acts on any going; sometimes sweats up; suitable mount for an apprentice. *G. Balding.*

CHAPEL ASH 2 b.c. Derring-Do 131–Angel Beam 115 (Hornbeam 130) (1980 6fg⁴ 6fg 5d 5d³ 5s) Apr 23; well-made colt; good walker and mover; second living foal; half-brother to fairly useful 1976 2-y-o 5f performer Angelos (by Town Crier); dam, smart winner over 5f and 6f at 2 yrs, needed 1¼m+ at 3 yrs; quite moderate form in maiden races; bred to stay at least 1m; ran poorly final start. *P. Walwyn.* **80**

CHAPEL BREAK 3 ch.g. Reform 132–Bally's Gift 83 (So Blessed 130) (1979 5d 5s 5d 5s 5fg 6g 5g⁴ 1980 8f 7g) small gelding; of little account; has been tried in blinkers. *Mrs A. Harvey.* **–**

CHAPERON 4 b.f. Sit In The Corner–Kissing Grove (Midsummer Night II 117) (1979 12fg 7f 12g 8fg 8g 1980 8s² 12.5s) plater: second at Leicester in March; stays 1m; acts on soft going; blinkered last 3 starts in 1979. *J. Harris.* **42**

CHAPLINS NIGHTCLUB 3 b.c. St Chad 120–Olivia Staypleton 88 (Road House II) (1979 5g 5d 6d 6fg 7s⁴ 7d 8.2g³ 6f⁴ 1980 8s* 8f² 10f 10.4f⁴ 8h⁴ 8g 10g 8g⁴ 11d 8fg 8g² 8fg 10.4d* 10g⁴ 10.6s³) big, workmanlike colt; won maiden race at Warwick in April and ladies race at Chester in August; also ran well at Chester on fourth outing when fourth to Playboy Jubilee in Dee Stakes; stays 1¼m well; acts on any going but has done his winning on a soft surface; suitable mount for an inexperienced rider. *N. Guest.* **86**

CHARACTER BUILDER 3 b.f. African Sky 124–Dorrit 98 (Zucchero 133§) (1979 5d* 6g* 6f² 6fg³ 7g* 1980 8fg 7f⁴ 7g 8.2d² 8d⁴ 8.2s) quite a useful sort; not a good mover in her slower paces; stays 1m well; suited by some give in the ground; has run respectably for a boy; didn't impress in paddock second start; sold 7,000 gns Newmarket December Sales. *Sir Mark Prescott.* **70**

CHARIOT 4 ch.c. Northfields–Aura 92 (Aureole 132) (1979 8s 10v 8g 10.8s* 12s⁴ 12d 13.1h⁴ 12f* 16f⁴ 16.1g² 16fg³ 1980 20d) won maiden race at Warwick and apprentice event at Chepstow as a 3-y-o when trained by P. Walwyn; blinkered, didn't impress in paddock when tailed off in Ascot Stakes at Royal Ascot, only outing of 1980; stays well; probably acts on any going. *D. Barons.* **–**

CHARITY BAZZAR 3 b.f. Native Bazaar 122–Dualvi 91 (Dual 117) (1979 6s 6d 8.2s² 1980 11v 12d⁴ 10fg 8.5f 7g 6s) leggy filly; poor plater; has been tried in blinkers; trained by W. H. H. Williams first 3 starts; sold 460 gns Ascot July Sales. *R. Smyth.* **–**

CHARLES STREET 3 ch.c. Huntercombe 133–Limerick Queen (Whistling Wind 123) (1979 5v 5g² 5s² 5fg⁴ 5g* 5g³ 5f 5f⁴ 5d 5s² 5s 1980 5d 6f³ 5fg 6f 7f 5f 5s² 6g 6g 5s 5g 5d) neat colt; not a good mover in his slower paces; sprint handicapper; stays 6f; acts on any going but is well suited by some give in the ground; often blinkered; sold 4,700 gns Newmarket Autumn Sales. *C. Brittain.* **81** d

CHARLES WHO 3 br.g. Dragonara Palace 115–Daughter of Song 73 (Song 132) (1979 6fg 6fg⁴ 6g 7s 1980 7f 7d 10fg 10s) neat, strong gelding; poor plater. *C. Booth.* **–**

CHARLIE DAN 2 ch.c. Sandford Lad 133–Sensitive Touch (Sensitivo) (1980 7d) Apr 6; 5,000Y; big, rangy colt; first foal; dam ran only once and comes from a good Argentinian family; unquoted, ran on to finish 6¾ lengths sixth of 14 behind Sunley Builds after dwelling at start in Houghton Stakes at Newmarket in October; will probably stay 1¼m; should improve considerably at 3 yrs. *G. Harwood.* **74** P

CHARLIE'S GAMBLE 3 b.c. Sunotra 86–Desert Rose (Arabian Sky 101) (1979 NR 1980 9g 10fg 8fg 7g) first reported foal; dam never ran; poor form in maiden and minor races. *J. Berry.* **–**

CHARLIE'S INCENTIVE 6 b.g. Bribe 89–Charlies Double (Fighting Charlie 127) (1979 16.1g 1980 16fg) novice hurdler; in rear in maiden event at Haydock in 1979 (saddle slipped) and amateur riders race at Ascot in September. *A. Arnold.* **–**

CHARLIE'S SONG 2 b.f. Song 132–Sound Venture (Hopeful Venture 125) (1980 5g⁴ 5d 5s 5fg⁴ 6fg²) May 30; 1,250F, 2,400Y; workmanlike filly; second produce; dam poor maiden; in frame in maiden races, failing by only ½ length to catch Von Erlach at Salisbury in September; suited by 6f and will stay further. *J. Holt.* **70**

CHARLIE'S SUNSHINE 3 b.f. Jimsun 121–Dracaena 62 (Double Jump 131) 77
(1979 NR 1980 $7g^{3}$ 7.6d* 7s 8fg 8s 10.2v) small filly; first foal; dam won 7f seller at 2 yrs; won modest 12-runner maiden race at Chester in August; well beaten in varied company afterwards; should stay at least 1m; acts on a soft surface; sweated up third start. *J. Leigh.*

CHARLIE THEODORE 3 ch.g. Sheshoon 132–Theodora Courage (Cash and —
Courage 116) (1979 7f 6fg 8h 8g 1980 8f 12.5h 16d 12.2g 16f 12s 12.5s) neat gelding; poor maiden; blinkered fourth and fifth starts. *J. Calvert.*

CHARMING NATIVE (USA) 3 ch.c. Princely Native–Fair Charmer (Jet 98
Action) (1979 5g* 6fg* 6fg* 6f 1980 7v 7f 7d 6fg 7d*) neat, attractive colt; has a slightly rounded action; useful performer; 20/1 and apprentice ridden when returning to form in handicap at Newbury in August, holding off Cassina by a short head; not seen out again; stays 7f; acts on a firm and a soft surface. *J. Tree.*

CHARM TO SPARE (USA) 2 b.c. Gallant Romeo–Fabled (Illustrious) (1980 82
$6fg^{4}$ $6f^{2}$ $7f^{4}$) Mar 6; $27,000F, 72,000 gnsY; neat, quite attractive colt; second produce; dam unraced half-sister to top American colts Never Bend and Bold Reason; caught close home and beaten a neck by Scarrowmanwick in 18-runner minor race at Lingfield in September; second favourite when 5½ lengths fourth of 19 to King's Glory in maiden race at Newmarket the following month; will stay 1m. *M. Jarvis.*

CHARTER PLEA 2 gr.c. Runnymede 123–Impassioned Plea 91 (Counsel 118) —
(1980 8d) June 11; fair sort; half-brother to 1m winner Ball and Chain (by Manacle); dam won from 7f to 1½m; unquoted when tailed off after 3f in 16-runner maiden race won by Rosie Black at Warwick in October. *H. Collingridge.*

CHASE THE RAINBOW 2 b.c. Saritamer 130–Fiery Kiss 82 (Floribunda 136) 79
(1980 $7d^{4}$ 7g 7g 7f 8s 8d 8g*) Apr 16; 4,400Y; useful-looking but rather narrow colt; half-brother to fair 1979 2-y-o 1m winner Swift Kiss (by Sparkler) and a winner in Holland; dam won over 6f; sold to K. Ivory 850 gns after winning 24-runner seller at Leicester in November by a neck from Pansing (pair clear); stayed 1m; had worn blinkers, including at Leicester; dead. *C. Brittain.*

CHASTITY BELT 3 b.g. So Blessed 130–Queen's Keys 84 (Right Royal V 135) —
(1979 $7f^{4}$ $7fg^{3}$ 1980 11v 12d 12d) workmanlike gelding; poor maiden; sold out of E. Weymes's stable 3,900 gns Doncaster May Sales. *R. Allan.*

CHATEAU DANCER (USA) 2 ch.f. Giacometti 130–Delray Dancer (Chateau- 104
gay) (1980 $5f^{2}$ $5g^{2}$ 6fg* $6d^{4}$ 6g* $8g^{3}$) rangy, attractive filly; half-sister to winners here and in USA, including very useful 3-y-o 1¼m winner Stanislavsky (by Sir Ivor) and leading American jumper Zaccio (by Lorenzaccio); dam unraced granddaughter of champion American filly Parlo; successful in 2 quite valuable races, beating Golden Bowl a length in Kingsclere Stakes at Newbury in June and giving at least 9 lb to her 6 opponents when winning John Courage Stakes in fine style by 3 lengths from Marston Magna at York the following month; ran as though needing the race after a 2-month absence when 5½ lengths third of 8 to Exclusively Raised in May Hill Stakes at Doncaster in September, looking to be going as well as winner 3f out but failing to quicken when let down; will be suited by middle distances; probably acts on any going. *R. Price.*

CHATEAU ROYAL 5 br.h. Royal and Regal–Hot Coral (The Phoenix) (1979 91
12d $16s^{4}$ 14d 16fg $18.4f^{3}$ 14s $18fg^{2}$ 17.4s 14g 1980 17.4s $12d^{2}$ $18d^{4}$) fairly useful on his day; stayed on strongly over a trip on sharp side when 3 lengths second to Earl's Court in handicap at Haydock in October, only second outing of season; went down badly to start in Tote Cesarewitch at Newmarket later in month but nevertheless ran well, staying on to finish 10 lengths fourth of 27 behind Popsi's Joy; needs a test of stamina; acts on any going. *J. Hanson.*

CHATRAM (USA) 2 b.g. Time Tested–Nubbin Nugget (Bandit) (1980 5fg 85
$5fg^{2}$ $5fg^{3}$ $5g^{2}$) Mar 23; $8,000F, 10,000Y; small, useful sort; brother to two 6f winners in USA and half-brother to 4 other winners; dam never ran; placed in maiden and minor events, putting up easily best effort when head second of 17 to Arndean at Windsor in June on fourth start; should stay 6f; ran moderately at Catterick on third outing and was possibly unsuited by course; exported to Hong Kong. *M. Jarvis.*

CHATRU 2 b.g. Realm 129–Kaiserin (Carapalida) (1980 5s 5d $7f^{4}$ 8g 7g) Mar 64
20; 10,000Y; small, good-quartered gelding; half-brother to 3 winners, including useful 1977 2-y-o 6f winner Kayseri (by Brigadier Gerard); dam won 5 times in Argentina and was placed in Argentinian 1,000 Guineas; no better than plating class; stays 7f. *R. Smyth.*

CHATTY DOLLY 2 gr.f. The Go-Between 129–Cloister Rose 70 (Track Spare 125) (1980 5g) Mar 14; 4,500Y; first foal; dam stayed 1½m; 16/1, finished behind in 19-runner maiden race won by Advertrack at Folkestone in October. *G. Lewis.* —

CHAUD ET FROID 2 b.c. Tennyson 124–Belle Promesse 110 (Right Royal V 135) (1980 9g*) June 7; second foal; half-brother to 3-y-o Thunder Bold (by Northern Dancer); dam, winner twice at around 1m in France, is sister to French 1,000 Guineas winner Right Away and half-sister to top 1964 French 2-y-o Grey Dawn; a very late foal who put up a creditable effort to win 15-runner maiden race at Evry in October by a head from Fol Herbage; a well-related colt who's sure to do well over middle distances. *F. Mathet, France.* **105** p

CHAUVINIST 3 b. or br.c. Derring-Do 131–Oubliette 68 (Crepello 136) (1979 NR 1980 8.2s 9g^2 9.4d 8fg* 8.2g^4 8.2s 8d 7d) 7,000F, 23,000Y; big, useful sort; good walker; poor mover; first living foal; dam 1¼m winner; won modest 9-runner maiden race at Edinburgh in July; will stay 1¼m; unsuited by very soft ground; sold 4,900 gns Newmarket Autumn Sales. *Sir Mark Prescott.* **70**

CHAWLEIGH QUEEN 4 ch.f. Sir Lark 101–Tornadora (Typhoon 125) (1979 NR 1980 10.1d) small, light-framed filly; first foal; dam won a selling hurdle; tailed off on debut in seller at Windsor in July and looks useless. *R. Keenor.* —

CHECK SIGNAL 4 b.f. Manacle 123–Flashing Light (Sky Gipsy 117) (1979 7s 8.2g 1980 7s) lengthy, unfurnished filly; little worthwhile form, including in a seller (dwelt); sold 470 gns Doncaster August Sales. *R. D. Peacock.* —

CHEF MARCEL (USA) 2 b.c. Personality–Raise A Big Peach (Raise A Native) (1980 7f) lengthy colt; second foal; dam won 6f claiming race at 4 yrs; 33/1 and looking as though race would do him good when behind in 19-runner maiden event won by King's Glory at Newmarket in October. *J. Hindley.* —

CHEKA (USA) 4 b.g. Russian Bank 110–Sweet Seventeen (County Delight) (1979 12.3s^4 11.7g^3 12f^2 16.1s 1980 13g* 16f^4 14fg 16fg* 16.1s) strong gelding; staying handicapper; won convincingly at Nottingham in April and Beverley in September, on latter course beating Musketeer's Motto by 3 lengths; seems to act on any going. *I. Balding.* **71**

CHEMIN 2 ch.f. Steel Heart 128–Supreme Lady 86 (Grey Sovereign 128 §) (1980 6g* 6d^3 7g) Apr 23; 132,000Y; strong, workmanlike filly; half-sister to several winners, notably Irish St Leger winner M-Lolshan (by Levmoss); dam 2-y-o 5f performer; put up a very creditable first effort to win 12-runner £4,400 event at Newmarket in June by a length from Doobie Do (gave 9 lb); took on very useful fillies afterwards, running on strongly to finish length third of 11 to Nasseem in Cherry Hinton Stakes at Newmarket in July and not being disgraced when never-dangerous 7 lengths sixth of 10 to Fairy Footsteps in Waterford Candelabra Stakes at Goodwood the following month; stays 7f; yet to race on a firm surface. *J. Hindley.* **109**

CHEMIN DE GUERRE 3 gr. or ro.f. Warpath 113–Flying Florrie 74 (I Say 125) (1979 NR 1980 9s 14.6d^2 12s) workmanlike filly; first live foal; dam successful hurdler; caught close home when second to Tentwort in maiden race at Doncaster in October; favourite, went lame and was pulled up only subsequent start; stays 1¾m. *M. H. Easterby.* **78**

CHENNEL LANE 6 b.h. Caerdeon 98–Glebe 83 (Tacitus 124) (1979 NR 1980 11fg 12fg^4 13f^4) middle-distance handicapper; acts on any going but goes well in the mud; suitable mount for an apprentice. *T. Barron.* —

CHENSTONE 2 ch.c. Royben 125–On Remand 83 (Reform 132) (1980 5v 5f 5fg 5.8f^2 6g 6fg 7g^2 8d^2 7.2s* 8d) Apr 21; 2,900Y; compact colt; first foal; dam won over 1½m; won 19-runner selling nursery at Haydock in October ridden out by a head from Eskview Lad; bought in 1,750 gns at the auction; ran poorly under a penalty next time out; needs at least 7f; best form on an easy surface. *J. Hill.* **62**

CHERCHEZ LA FEMME 4 b.f. Mon Fils 124–Angele 98 (Match III 135) (1979 10.2g 10fg 1980 14d 12g 8d^3 8d 10s) quite useful sort; 6 lengths third of 22 behind Claudius Secundus in minor event at Warwick in October; well beaten on her other starts, including in 2 amateur events; should stay beyond 1m; bolted and had to be withdrawn once. *M. Pipe.* —

CHERRY CORNER 2 br.g. Sit In The Corner–Tudor Gus 64 (Gustav 121) (1980 5fg* 8.2d 7f 8fg* 8s) Apr 29; 500F; leggy gelding; third produce; brother to a poor animal; dam won 7f seller; sold out of Hbt Jones's stable 2,500 gns **76 ?**

after winning 10-runner seller at Beverley in June; came back to form when blinkered in another seller at Redcar in October, winning readily by 1½ lengths from Keelby Kavalier (no bid); stays 1m; acts on a firm surface and ran abysmally on soft ground on final start (again blinkered). *M. W. Easterby.*

CHESNEY 4 b.g. Comedy Star 121–Gold Ribbon 106 (Blast 125) (1979 6v 6v 7d 8d 7f³ 8.3d⁴ 8d 8g 10.1fg³ 1980 10f 10d 8d) poor plater; probably stays 1¼m; usually wears blinkers; sold 400 gns Doncaster October Sales. *T. Kersey.* —

CHESTNUT LODGE 4 b.g. Pontifex (USA)–Feijoa (Floribunda 136) (1979 7s 7d 1980 8s 8g 8.3s 7g⁴ 8g 8d) plater; stays 7f; acts on soft going; sold 420 gns Ascot November Sales. *M. McCourt.* 37

CHETINKAYA 4 b.c. Ragstone 128–Satina 83 (Pall Mall 132) (1979 12d² 12s 12v⁴ 12g 12fg 16fg 12f³ 14fg* 12g 12d 1980 12fg³ 14g* 14.6f 12g 12g) sturdy, lengthy colt; beat Sharp Fiddle 1½ lengths in handicap at Haydock in June; ran moderately fourth start but had stiff task and wasn't disgraced on fifth; stays 1¾m well (well beaten over 2m); acts on any going; has worn blinkers; suitable mount for an apprentice. *G. Balding.* 63

CHEVINGTON 3 b.c. Moulton 128–Joey 110 (Salvo 129) (1979 NR 1980 8f 10g* 8g* 10g³ 10.5g 9g 10.2d) strong, attractive, deep-bodied colt; second foal; dam, winner over 5f and 7.6f, stayed 1¼m; successful in 17-runner maiden race at Sandown and minor event at Doncaster in June; third in handicap at Sandown in July, best subsequent effort (ran as though something was wrong with him fifth start); stays 1¼m; blinkered final outing; sold to J. Gifford 19,500 gns Newmarket Autumn Sales. *H. Wragg.* 91

CHICBURY (FR) 3 b.c. Exbury 138–Chicoree (Lavandin 128) (1979 NR 1980 8.5g 10g² 10g² 12g³ 12g⁴ 15d*) 105,000 francs Y (approx. £12,500); brother to Chexbury, successful from 7f to 1½m and also over hurdles in France, and half-brother to a minor French winner by Saint Crespin III; dam useful at up to 13f in France; not seen out after showing himself well suited by a test of stamina and putting up a smart performance to win Group 3 Prix de l'Esperance at Longchamp in June by 2 lengths from Hortensio with Valiant Heart a short head away third; placed earlier in maiden and minor events at Cagnes-sur-Mer (twice) and Longchamp; stays well; acts on a soft surface. *C. Milbank, France.* 115

CHICKEN AGAIN 3 b.c. Royalty 130–Dust Sheet (Silly Season 127) (1979 6fg* 7.2g 6g 7fg 1980 8.2d 10.6f 9g 8.2d 7d² 7fg⁴ 6f 6s 6g* 6s* 7s 6d) tall colt; in good form in October, winning handicaps at Newcastle (apprentices) and Haydock; best at up to 7f; probably acts on any going; sometimes sweats up; often blinkered but wasn't at Haydock. *C. Crossley.* 72

CHIEF ADMIRAL (USA) 2 b. or br.c. Chieftain–Robadan (Prince John) (1980 5d² 5fg² 6g* 6s² 7f 6f) May 4; $19,000Y; big, useful sort; half-brother to several winners in USA; dam very useful stakes winner at up to 1m at 2 yrs; started on terms for first time when easily landing the odds by 4 lengths from Crockfords Green in maiden race at Hamilton in July; excellent second, 2 lengths behind Lady Lorelei, in minor event at Newcastle the following month; suited by 6f and should stay at least 1m (out of first 6 of 12 behind Beldale Flutter in valuable race at Ostend on only attempt at 7f); seems to act on any going except perhaps very firm (didn't move particularly well to post and ran poorly final outing). *S. Norton.* 90

CHIEF EXECUTIVE 6 br.g. Tribal Chief 125–Solly Graham 82 (Romulus 129) (1979 NR 1980 12fg) useless; dead. *D. Yeoman.* —

CHIEF MOORE 2 b.c. Bold Lad (Ire) 133–Nadjina 76 (Petition 130) (1980 5d) May 6; 6,800Y; brother to a winner in South Africa and half-brother to several winners, mainly abroad; dam sister to top-class sprinter French Plea; unquoted when behind in 17-runner maiden race won by Corn Street at Wolverhampton in October. *S. Woodman.* —

CHIEF SPEAKER 2 b.c. Nonoalco 131–Anice (Crepello 136) (1980 6g 7.2d³ 8fg² 7.3d) Mar 6; 8,800Y; tall colt; sixth foal; half-brother to a winner in Italy by Lorenzaccio; dam, half-sister to Italian St Leger winner Alcamo, won in Italy; improved with distance and ran well when 2½ lengths second of 23 to Shergar in minor event at Newbury in September; 33/1 when remote sixth of 10 to Kalaglow in Horris Hill Stakes on same course the following month; will stay 1¼m; capable of winning races if not tried too highly. *R. Sheather.* 95

CHILBLAINS 2 b.f. Hotfoot 126–Chiltern Red (Red God 128§) (1980 5fg 6s* 6fg^3 7fg^4 7d^4 8g* 8v) Feb 13; compact filly; first foal; dam poor sister to Red Alert; successful in 20-runner maiden race at Lingfield in June and nursery at Bath in September, running on gamely to win by a neck and a head respectively; subsequently sent to race in Italy; stays 1m; seems to act on any going; sweated up and ran a bit below best fifth outing; has won for an apprentice. *P. Cundell.* **83**

CHILLY MISS 3 b. or br.f. Frigid Aire–Miss Christine 103 (Pall Mall 132) (1979 5g 5s 5.8g 1980 5f 5h 5.8g) behind in varied company, including selling. *J. Hill.* —

CHILSTON 2 b.c. Tower Walk 130–Formula 72 (Reform 132) (1980 5g 5s 5d^3 6d 6s) May 19; 7,400Y; narrow colt; first foal; dam 1m winner; 33/1 and sweating when 2 lengths third of 19 to Universal Penny in £3,400 seller at Sandown in August, third outing and best effort; should be suited by 6f (dwelt on first attempt at trip). *T. Marshall.* **65**

CHILTERN LAD 2 b.c. Derring-Do 131–Chiltern Lass 100 (High Hat 131) (1980 6g 7fg 7d 8fg) May 4; neat colt; third foal; half-brother to 3-y-o Withy Copse (by Blakeney), a winner from 1½m to 1¾m; dam game middle-distance performer; quite a moderate maiden; bred to stay 1¼m+; swerved left start second outing; sold to NBA 1,000 gns Newmarket Autumn Sales. *M. Stoute.* **71**

CHILTERN STREET 3 b.f. Shiny Tenth 120–Tweetie Pie (Falcon 131) (1979 5d 5v 7fg 5fg 1980 8d 8.2s 8f) small, unimpressive-looking filly; little worthwhile form; sold 420 gns Ascot November Sales. *D. Marks.* —

CHIMAERA 3 gr.f Averof 123–Galeeny 72 (Grey Sovereign 128§) (1979 6fg 6d 1980 6d 5f 5h 5fg 5g 6g) strong, useful sort; poor maiden. *Sir Mark Prescott.* —

CHINAFIELD 3 ch.f Northfields–Belleek (Never Say Die 137) (1979 5d 5d 7f 6g 1980 9.6f 10g) small, hollow-backed filly; only plating class. *C. Dingwall.* —

CHINA GOD 7 b.g. Cumshaw 111–White Goddess 65 (Red God 128§) (1979 NR 1980 10fg 12d 13.8d) poor handicapper nowadays; stays 11f well; probably acts on any going; suitable mount for an amateur. *D. Francis.* —

CHINA ROYAL 3 ch.c Sovereign Path 125–King's Mate 91 (King's Bench 132) (1979 NR 1980 8fg* 8g^3 11g* 8.2g 10.2g* 12d 12s^4) 17,000Y; lightly-made, quite attractive colt; half-brother to three winners, including useful 5f to 7f performer Welsh Mate (by Welsh Saint) and useful Irish 7f to 1¼m winner Frankly Yours (by Frankincense); dam a sprinter; successful in maiden race at Warwick in June, minor race at Hamilton in July and 18-runner handicap at Bath in September; ran creditably in handicaps on last 2 outings; stays 1½m; probably acts on any going; possibly needs strong handling; ran poorly fourth start. *B. Hills.* **82**

CHINA RUN 2 ch.c. Chingnu 99–Gay Runner (Clear Run 109) (1980 7d 5f 5d) Apr 11; small colt; third foal; dam never ran; only poor form, including in a seller. *F. Yardley.* —

CHINCOTEAGUE 3 b.g. Gulf Pearl 117–Sheila's Pearl (Javelot 124) (1979 6fg 7fg 1980 10fg 16d* 16.9d^4 19f^2 16s* 16g 18.1g) neat, attractive gelding; good walker; won maiden race at Newcastle in June and handicap at Nottingham in August (had very hard race); stays well; acts on any going; usually sweats up. *M. Stoute.* **81**

CHINESE CHEROKEE 2 gr.f Warpath 113–Pekin Duck 73 (Tamerlane 128) (1980 6g 6g* 6g 8.2d) June 23; small filly; sister to a poor animal and half-sister to a winning hurdler; dam stayed 9f; attracted no bid after winning poor seller at Hamilton in July; best form at 6f but is bred to stay at least 1¼m; sold 370 gns Ascot November Sales. *W. A. Stephenson.* **50**

CHINESE KUNG FU 4 ch.c Roan Rocket 128–Gerfalcon 105 (Falcon 131) (1979 6v 6d* 6g^2 5d 5d* 6g^3 5.3fg 6f 5.3d^4 7f 1980 6d 6g 6s 6g 7.6d) really powerful colt; won 2 handicaps at Brighton in 1979; well beaten in 1980, including when blinkered on final start; should stay 7f; acts on any going; unreliable; sold out of R. Supple's stable 1,600 gns Ascot January Sales. *A. Davison.* —

CHINON 3 gr. or ro.f. Abwah 118–Vauchellor 72 (Honeyway 125) (1979 5g 7s 1980 10g 12fg 16f^3 16d 16s 18f^2 14.7f^3 15.5g) small filly; staying maiden; acts well on firm going and is probably unsuited by soft; suitable mount for a boy. *F. Durr.* **54**

Lord Howard de Walden's "Chirk Castle"

CHINTA CRISTA 4 b.f. Sun Prince 128–Marvedo 76 (Molvedo 137) (1979 10f 13f 10d 12fg² 1980 16f 9g 8fg 8g) neat filly; poor performer nowadays (well beaten in valuable seller final start); yet to show she stays further than 1¼m; often wears blinkers. *I. Walker.* —

CHIPPENHAM 3 b.g. Brigadier Gerard 144–Fardo 86 (Tudor Melody 129) (1979 6f 1980 8fg 9f⁴) attractive gelding; not seen out after finishing respectable fourth in minor event at Lingfield in May; stays 9f. *H. Wragg.* **79**

CHIQUITITA 3 b.f. Reliance II 137–Marcida 85 (Alcide 136) (1979 8f 8g 8d 1980 10fg* 9g 10d 10.8fg) neat filly; plater; narrowly won at Leicester in May (bought in 1,300 gns); stays 1¼m; suited by fast ground; tailed off last 2 starts. *P. Cole.* **44**

CHIRK CASTLE 2 ch.c. Welsh Pageant 132–Helcia 86 (Habitat 134) (1980 5fg 6d 6s* 6g² 7fg² 7g³) Feb 8; strong, well-made, attractive colt; first foal; dam, runner-up 5 times from 6f to 11.5f, is daughter of half-sister to top-class filly Bella Paola; won 8-runner maiden race at Haydock in July comfortably by 3 lengths from Scarlet Town; placed in good-class events afterwards, putting up best effort when making odds-on Church Parade fight hard to get home by a head in 6-runner Lanson Champagne Stakes at Goodwood in July on fifth outing; bandaged near-hind when 7 lengths third to To-Agori-Mou in Intercraft Solario Stakes at Sandown the following month; will stay 1¼m; seems to act on any going; useful; sent to USA. *P. Walwyn.* **104**

CHOCOLATE BISCUIT 3 br.f. Biskrah 121–Coconut 75 (Tesco Boy 121) (1979 NR 1980 13.8fg 16g 12.2d 12d⁴ 15fg) 900Y; workmanlike filly; half-sister to 2 minor middle-distance winners; dam stayed 1m; poor maiden. *T. Fairhurst.* —

CHOP GATE 5 ch.g. Connaught 130–Caergwrle 115 (Crepello 136) (1979 10g² 10g⁴ 10.2fg 1980 12fg) tall, lengthy gelding; best form at 1¼m but has run respectably over 1½m. *B. Palling.* —

CHORUS LINE 5 b.h. Maystreak 118–Damgol (Goldhill 125) (1979 10v 11.7g 10s 8d 10f 10fg 11.7fg3 8g 10g 10.4f 1980 12fg 12fg3 10fg* 12fg* 10.7g* 10s 10s 10s4 11.7fg 12g 12f 10g3 10fg4) middle-distance handicapper; won apprentice events at Kempton and Brighton in May and trotted up by 10 lengths at Warwick in June; ran respectably last 2 starts; acts on a firm and an easy surface; usually wears blinkers; good mount for a boy. *R. Akehurst.* **56**

CHOW 3 gr.f. Warpath 113–Full of Flavour (Romulus 129) (1979 6g 7s 7fg 1980 8v 10f 8f4 10fg 10.6d) neat filly; only plating class; possibly stays 1¼m; blinkered second and third starts. *C. Thornton.* —

CHRISANTHY 3 b.f. So Blessed 130–The Ambion 113 (Henry the Seventh 125) (1979 5v2 5d2 5d2 5d4 5d3 6g 6g 5fg* 1980 6fg 5f4 5.1f 5s 6fg 5f 5g 5d) light-framed filly; won maiden race at Folkestone at 2 yrs; didn't find her form in handicaps in 1980; should stay 6f; probably acts on any going; sometimes sweats up; has shown signs of temperament; sold only 500 gns Newmarket Autumn Sales. *H. Collingridge.* —

CHRISTINES FOLLY 2 b.f. Communication 119–Road Star (Road House II) (1980 5fg 6s 5g 5d 5g 5d 5f3 5fg 5f 5g2 5d3 5s4) May 15; 460 2-y-o; leggy, unfurnished filly; placed in valuable seller at York in September and in minor races at Edinburgh and Catterick in October; form only at 5f; best form on a sound surface; sweating final start. *S. Nesbitt.* **74**

CHRISTMAS COTTAGE 2 br.g. Lochnager 132–Nelski 83 (Skymaster 126) (1980 5g 5g4 5s) Apr 14; strong gelding; third foal; half-brother to 2 winners by Most Secret, including 1979 2-y-o 5f winner Miss Nelski; dam best at up to 7f; 6 lengths fourth of 6 to Bold Scuffle in modest maiden race at York in October; still looked in need of race on same course later in week (dwelt); should stay 6f. *J. Mason.* **65**

CHRISTMAS GREETING 2 ch.g. Bonne Noel 115–Princess Mea (Meadow Court 129) (1980 7g 7fg 7f 8fg 8.2s) Apr 21; 6,200Y; strong, well-grown gelding; half-brother to Irish 9f winner Prince Rarity (by Rarity); dam unraced half-sister to top 1965 2-y-o Young Emperor; soundly beaten in maiden and minor events; will stay middle distances; blinkered fourth outing; gelded at end of season. *M. H. Easterby.* —

CHRISTMAS VISIT 6 br.g. Daring Display 129–Aya Sofia (Milesian 125) (1979 12d 12.5d 11.5g2 13g* 11.5g* 1980 13.3g 12.2s 12g3 11.7g2 11.7f3 11.7f2) ex-French gelding; runner-up in handicaps at Windsor in July (had poor run when beaten neck by Zoro) and August (went down by 1½ lengths to Telsmoss); stays 13f; appears to act on any going; showed signs of temperament at 3 yrs (trained by B. Hills). *P. Makin.* **69**

CHROME MAG 2 br.f. Prince de Galles 125–Pat 98 (Ennis 128) (1980 6g 6fg) Mar 27; tall, useful-looking filly; half-sister to 1974 2 y-o 5f winner Royal Pat (by King's Troop) and to winners in Jersey and Belgium; dam 5f sprinter; 20/1 and still on backward side when 8 lengths fifth of 11 to Tumble Whirl in seller at Doncaster in July, second outing. *W. Bentley.* —

CHRYSIPPOS (USA) 3 ch.c. Damascus–Better Begin (Buckpasser) (1979 5s* 6fg2 5fg2 1980 6fg4 7g 6g 7d 8g 8f3 8g 6d) big, rangy, attractive colt; had stiff tasks when in frame in handicap at Kempton in May and minor event at Newmarket in October; not disgraced when 10 lengths sixth of 13 to Hard Fought in Jersey Stakes at Royal Ascot on second start; well beaten on his other outings; stays 1m; probably acts on any going; often sweats up; sold 1,950 gns Newmarket Autumn Sales. *G. Harwood.* **99**

CHUCK'S SONG 3 ch.g. King's Leap 111–Game Laura (Relic) (1979 5g 6f2 7fg4 7fg 6g 1980 11.7fg 10fg 9d* 9f 10d) rather lightly-made gelding; 33/1 when winning modest 21-runner maiden race at Wolverhampton in August; stays 9f; probably acts on any going. *R. Laing.* **63**

CHUKAROO 8 b.h. Kibenka 119–Wild Words 76 (Galivanter 131) (1979 8d 8g 7.6s 8g4 8f3 8f2 7fg 8g3 8d 8.3f3 7.3g4 1980 8fg2 8f4 10h* 10fg4 10fg) won apprentice event at Brighton in May (odds on) and finished creditable fifth to Sacrilege in Daily Mirror Handicap at Epsom in June, but is on the downgrade; stays 1¼m; best suited by top-of-the-ground; suitable mount for an apprentice; sometimes sweats up; blinkered last 2 starts in 1979. *R. Laing.* **84**

CHUMMY'S BEST 2 b.c. Tower Walk 130–Bright Diadem (Pall Mall 132) (1980 6fg 6d 6d) Mar 6; 11,000Y; useful-looking colt; good mover; half-brother to 3 winners, including Irish 1m winner Topless Dancer (by Northfields); dam —

never ran; behind in Newmarket maiden races in August and October, and in similar race at Newbury later in October, *G. Hunter*.

CHUMMY'S SPECIAL 2 b.c. Mummy's Pet 125–Go Too 78 (Goldhill 125) (1980 5f* 5fg^2 5g* 6g 5g) Mar 11; 8,600Y; shapely, attractive colt; second foal; dam sprinter; made all to win maiden race at Haydock in May by a length from Motavato and held on well, although strongly pressed by Tax Haven in final furlong, when winning 6-runner Norfolk Stakes at Royal Ascot the following month by ½ length; never promised to get on terms when poor sixth of 10 to Another Realm in Richmond Stakes at Goodwood in July or when eighth of 11 to Sharpo in all-aged William Hill Sprint Championship at York (25/1) the following month; by no means sure to stay 6f. *G. Hunter*. **101**

CHUMWAR 2 b.c. So Blessed 130–Lynwood Sovereign 102 (Connaught 130) (1980 5fg 6d 6f 6fg 5fg* 5fg*) Apr 9; 4,000Y; sturdy colt; first foal; dam stayed well; ridden with more restraint than previously when winning maiden race at Newcastle in July and £2,600 event at Thirsk in August, latter by 1½ lengths from Southern Swanee; gave impression on both occasions a return to 6f would suit him and is bred to stay at least 1m; acts on a firm surface. *D. Thom*. **93**

CHUPAH 2 b.c. Virginia Boy 106–Winning Wave (Victory Morn) (1980 5f 5g 6g^4 7fg 5f) Feb 6; 8,600Y; strong, short-legged colt; brother to fairly useful 5f and 7f winner Intercraft Boy, and half-brother to a winner in USA; dam won 6 times at up to 9f in USA; 4 lengths fourth of 8 to Admiral's Heir in maiden event at Brighton in July, best effort; should stay 7f. *R. Smyth*. **69**

CHURCH MOUNTAIN 2 b.f. Furry Glen 121–Milly Whiteway 112 (Great White Way) 1980 6s^2 6s* 7d 7v) May 5; lengthy, unfurnished filly; second foal; closely related to fairly useful 1978 Irish 2-y-o 6f and 1m winner Saylers Creek (by Wolver Hollow); dam very useful over 5f and 6f at 2 yrs in Ireland; rallied well to land the odds by ½ length from That's Magic in maiden race at Hamilton in September; favourite, missed break and was reportedly bumped on turn, when seventh of 10 to Supreme Fjord in small race at Catterick the following month; should be suited by 7f; has raced only on a soft surface. *W. H. H. Williams*. **83**

Norfolk Stakes, Ascot—Chummy's Special has half a length to spare over Tax Haven. Pontin Lad is third

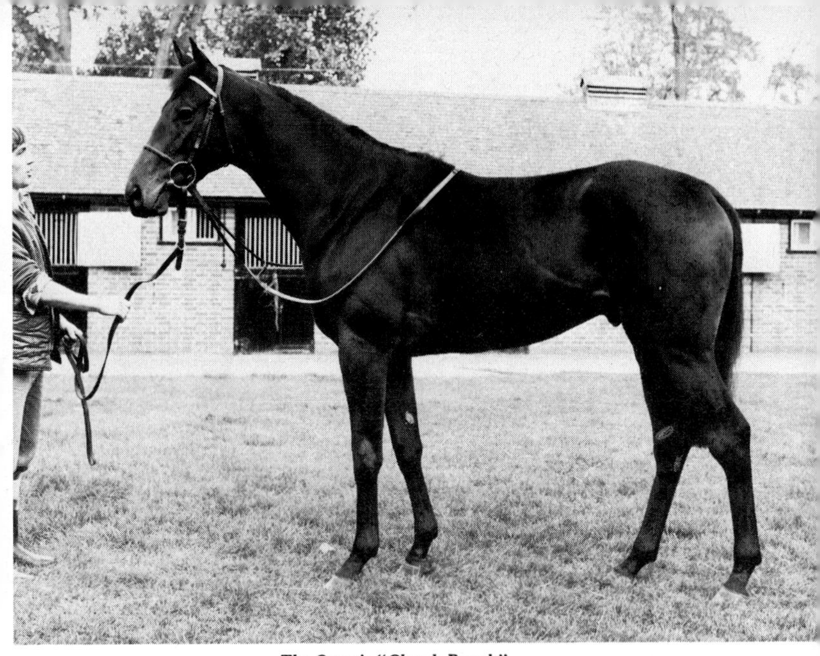

The Queen's "Church Parade"

CHURCH PARADE 2 b.c. Queen's Hussar 124–Christchurch 88 (So Blessed 130) **119**
(1980 6d* 7fg* 7g^3)

Since its inception in 1975 the Lanson Champagne Stakes at the main Goodwood meeting has been contested by five horses trained by Dick Hern, and their record is impressive. Four—Riboboy, Sky Ship, Troy and, in 1980, Church Parade—won the race, all of them starting favourite and all but Troy at odds on, while the fifth, One No Trump, finished second. Church Parade made a promising debut in a fifteen-runner maiden race at Newmarket in July where he started a well-backed second favourite and beat the sympathetically-handled To-Agori-Mou by three quarters of a length. This display, allied to the form his stable was in, resulted in his being backed down to 13/8 on at Goodwood three weeks later. His five opponents included two other winners from the Newmarket July meeting, Rahway and Scintillating Air, and Chirk Castle, successful in a maiden event at Haydock prior to proving no match for Bel Bolide at York.

Church Parade (b.c. Mar 4, 1978)	Queen's Hussar (b 1960)	March Past (br 1950)	Petition
			Marcelette
		Jojo (gr 1950)	Vilmorin
			Mary Jane
	Christchurch (b 1973)	So Blessed (br 1965)	Princely Gift
			Lavant
		Highlight (b 1958)	Borealis
			Hypericum

Church Parade duly landed the odds but he had to pull out all the stops to do so. Taking up the running two furlongs out he showed distinct signs of greenness in front and needed to be firmly ridden in the closing stages to hold off Chirk Castle by a head. Neither Chirk Castle nor the third, Scintillating Air, is better than useful, so Church Parade's performance left room for improvement which, given his lack of experience, could be anticipated from him. He did improve on his final start. Up against better horses than he had faced at Goodwood, Church Parade was third in the market for the Laurent Perrier Champagne Stakes at Doncaster in September behind Kirtling and Prince Echo. He didn't enjoy the best of runs but still finished a good third, tracking the pace-setting Parkdale for much of the race, being switched to challenge over a furlong out and keeping on strongly to be beaten only a neck and the same by Gielgud and Prince Echo in a driving finish. After this smart effort he was put by for the season.

Church Parade gave the impression at Doncaster that he would be suited by further than seven furlongs, and a look at his pedigree lends encouragement to this view. He is the first foal of Christchurch, who has subsequently produced a filly by Grundy and a colt by Blakeney before going back to Queen's Hussar in 1980. Christchurch ran only as a three-year-old, and though by the sprinter So Blessed, she stayed well enough to win a mile-and-a-half maiden race at Wolverhampton and wasn't disgraced when tried over fifteen furlongs. She is related to a number of good performers, being a half-sister to the One Thousand Guineas and Prix de Diane winner Highclere, the Yorkshire Oaks second Light Duty (both, like Church Parade, by Queen's Hussar) and the mile- to mile-and-a-half horse Gloss. Highclere is the dam of the smart middle-distance winner Milford. Highlight, Christchurch's dam, won at one and a half miles and is a half-sister to Restoration out of the 1946 One Thousand Guineas winner Hypericum. This is the family of Aureole, Above Board (dam of Doutelle and Above Suspicion) and Round Table among others.

There is no reason why Church Parade shouldn't stay a mile and a half, and while it is to be doubted whether he will be in the highest class, he has further improvement in him and should be able to win a nice prize or two at up to that distance in 1981. A well-made, attractive colt, who has an enlarged near-hind hock, he acts on a firm and a soft surface. *R. Hern.*

CIDER MAN 2 b.c. Manacle 123–Appleshaw (St Alphage 119) (1980 5fg 5fg 5f* 6fg 6d* 8f 8fg 6g) May 14; 4,000Y; good sort; second foal; dam unraced half-sister to Grand Prix de Paris winner Pleben; won maiden race at Thirsk in May by 4 lengths and seller at Newcastle the following month; bought in 8,400 gns after getting up close home to beat Maybehandy in latter event; stays 6f well and wasn't disgraced on second attempt over 1m; seems to act on any going; blinkered at Newcastle and in his subsequent races. *B. Hanbury.* **75**

CIFONELLI (USA) 2 ch.g. Timeless Moment–Real Pertly (In Reality) (1980 6fg^3 6d 7g^3 7d* 8g) Feb 19; $25,000Y; quite attractive gelding; first foal; dam placed at 3 yrs; sire smart winner of 10 races at up to 7f; just held off late rally of Restless Captain when odds on for 11-runner £2,500 event at Newcastle in August; third previously in maiden race at Newbury in June (2¾ lengths behind Robellino) and in £2,600 event at Salisbury in August; seems to find 7f his limit; best form on a sound surface; gelded after fifth outing. *R. Price.* **81**

CILIUM 3 br.c. So Blessed 130–Collyria 127 (Arctic Prince 135) (1979 6f* 1980 8g^3 10s^4 8s* 8d 8fg 8g^4) lengthy, workmanlike colt; short-priced favourite when winning minor race at Newcastle in August in good style; in frame in varied company on several other occasions; runs as if a return to 1¼m will suit him; acts on any going but is well suited by soft. *H. Cecil.* **95**

CILLA'S SECRET 2 ch.f. Most Secret 119–Lemoncilla (Philemon 119) (1980 5g 5h^3 5fg 5fg^2 6fg^4 5fg^3 5g^3 5d^2 5g 5f^3 6f^3 5g 5f^3 5d 5fg 8d) Apr 16; small, strong filly; second foal; dam never ran; placed in sellers on most of her outings, coming closest to success when going down by short head to Good Sweep at Hamilton in June on eighth start; stays 6f but ran poorly over 1m; seems to act on any going; wears blinkers; consistent. *K. Stone.* **54**

CIMA 2 br.c. High Top 131–Lemon Blossom 83 (Acropolis 132) (1980 5f 5f 6fg^4 7d^4 7g^2 8g 8g^4) Mar 13; 7,000Y; quite well-made colt; good mover; fourth foal; half-brother to a winner in Austria; dam won over 11f; in frame in maiden races and a nursery; will stay 1½m. *J. Old.* **82**

CIMARRON 2 ch.f. Carnival Dancer 113–Duresme 76 (Starry Halo 122) (1980 5s 5s 8d) Apr 13; leggy filly; third foal; dam third twice over 7f at 2 yrs; only plating class; none too well away first 2 appearances; trained by T. Molony first 2 outings. *R. Mason.* **—**

CIMON 2 br.c. Sallust 134–Fortlin 95 (Fortino II 120) (1980 8g 8s*) Mar 17; 105,000Y; brother to top-class French and American filly Sanedtki, successful at up to 9f, and half-brother to 2 winners, including French 9f and 11f winner Mrs Hippy (by Tudor Music); dam, winner of 4 races at 2 yrs, stayed 7f; 10/1, **92** p won 11-runner maiden race at the Curragh in November in impressive fashion, not being extended to score by 3 lengths from Pagan Love; stays 1m well; should make a good 3-y-o. *A. Maxwell, Ireland.*

CINDERWENCH 2 b.f. Crooner 119–Burning Deck 56 (Fighting Ship 121) 83
(1980 7f 8f* 9d*) May 10; leggy filly; second reported foal; half-sister to Flameproof (by Prince de Galles), a winner over 11f in Germany and a fair hurdler here; dam poor half-sister to 4 smart animals, including Bivouac; ridden by apprentice M. Malham when winning maiden and minor events at Wolverhampton in the autumn, running on to lead well inside final furlong when beating On Her Own a length in latter; will probably stay 1¼m; seems to act on any going. *P. Cole.*

CINDRUM 2 ch.c. Meldrum 112–Jacine Tudor (Henry the Seventh 125) (1980 –
7f) June 7; small, compact colt; first foal; dam, who never ran, comes from a good family; 50/1 and very backward when tailed off in 18-runner seller won by Rocket Venture at Redcar in September. *D. Yeoman.*

CIRCUIT BREAKER 2 br.f. Sovereign Bill 105–Longwings 75 (Vimy 132) –
(1980 5s 8.2d) May 21; 750Y; half-sister to a winning hurdler; dam winning stayer on flat and quite a useful staying hurdler; in rear in maiden race at Newcastle in August and seller at Hamilton in September. *R. Allan.*

CIRCUIT JUDGE 3 b.c. Tumble Wind–The Wig 81 (Counsel 118) (1979 65
5s 5.3fg^{3} 6fg^{2} 6fg^{2} 6g^{4} 6fg 6fg^{3} 6fg^{3} 7g^{3} 6g^{4} 1980 7f 7f 8.5f^{3} 10g 8fg^{2} 9d 9f 10fg 10f 9v) neat colt; third in valuable seller at Epsom in June; runner-up in much better company at Newmarket in August but is inconsistent and unreliable; stays 1m; acts on firm going and is possibly unsuited by soft ground; sometimes blinkered; sold 2,000 gns Newmarket Autumn Sales. *F. Durr.*

CISTO (FR) 5 b.h. Presto–Cypris (Devon III 125) (1979 12g^{2} 11g^{4} 10.5g^{3} 69
13.5g* 15g* 12g* 11g 12g 12.5g^{3} 12g 15g 12g 1980 14f 14.7f*(dis) 12fg^{4} 22.2fg 14g 15s) strong ex-French horse; favourite, won amateur riders event at Redcar in May by 1½ lengths from Scholar's Ring but was later disqualified on technical grounds; creditable fourth to Prince Rheingold in Watt Memorial Stakes at Beverley following month, best subsequent effort; effective at 1¼m and stays well; acts on firm going and seemed unsuited by soft final outing (sweating badly). *G. Huffer.*

CITISSIMA 2 ch.f. Simbir 130–Airgead Beo (Hook Money 124) (1980 8g 9d* 96
8s^{3}) May 14; third living foal; half-sister to 3-y-o El Cito (by Ridan), third in Irish St Leger, and successful Irish stayer La Cita (by Le Levanstell); dam never ran; led before halfway when winning 13-runner maiden race at Gowran Park in October by 2 lengths from Ilen, the pair clear; far from disgraced when 33/1 for Group 2 Beresford Stakes at the Curragh in October, running on to finish 6 lengths third of 8 to Euclid; will stay well; yet to race on a firm surface. *P. Needham, Ireland.*

CITY LINK EXPRESS 3 ch.g Dubassoff–Chaddy (St Chad 120) (1979 5v^{4} 54
5g 6fg 5fg^{4} 7g 7f^{3} 7g 7d 1980 10s 7f 7f 10.1s 8.3s^{3} 7g^{3} 8.3g^{4} 8.3f^{3} 8g 8g^{4} 10fg 10f 10g) leggy gelding; plater; best at around 1m; acts on any going; sometimes wears blinkers; has run creditably for a boy. *P. Ashworth.*

CITY LINK LAD 4 ch.g. Jimmy Reppin 131–Aleta 71 (Montaval 129) (1979 61
NR 1980 7.6f 10fg 13.3g 8g 8f 8g 7f 8fg* 8g 10d 8s) big, strong gelding; showed first form for a long time when 33/1-winner of apprentice handicap at Ascot in September, beating Monte Acuto by ¾ length; had stiffish tasks afterwards; stays 1m; acts on a firm surface; blinkered third, fourth and sixth outings. *P. Ashworth.*

CITY LINK STAR 2 ch.g. My Swallow 134–Come on Girl (Sheshoon 132) –
(1980 7g 7d^{4} 7fg) Feb 19; rangy gelding; half-brother to fairly useful 2-y-o sprint winners City Link Lass and Daikoku (both by Double Jump); dam never ran; well beaten all outings, finishing last of 22 in maiden race on third. *P. Ashworth.*

CITY PARADE 6 b.m. Decoy Boy 129–Rapacity (Rapace 130) (1979 NR –
1980 12g) half-sister to fair staying chaser Rapallo (by Straight Lad) and fairly useful point-to-pointer Vilacity (by Vilmoray); unquoted when well beaten in ladies race at Chepstow in September, first outing; sold 1,000 gns Ascot October Sales. *M. Scudamore.*

CLANDESTINA (USA) 2 b.f. Secretariat–My Charmer (Poker) (1980 5g^{2}) 94p
Apr 20; $750,000Y; fourth foal; half-sister to brilliant American triple crown winner Seattle Slew (by Bold Reasoning); dam minor stakes winner at up to 1m; 2/1, made good progress but failed by a head to catch Crimson Heather in minor

event at Phoenix Park in June; looked promising but wasn't seen out again. *V. O'Brien, Ireland.*

CLARABELLE 2 b.f. Flashback 102–Headliner (Pampered King 121) (1980 5s 5fg 5fg 5g² 5fg² 6g⁴ 5d 5s²) Apr 3; compact filly; fifth foal; dam ran only once; second in sellers at Salisbury, Lingfield and Folkestone in the summer, beaten 4 lengths by Woodhall on last-named course; yet to prove she stays 6f; wears blinkers. *Mrs R. Lomax.* 48

CLAREMONT PRINCE 3 b.g. Biskrah 121–Claremont Queen 80 (Galivanter 131) (1979 NR 1980 10.1g 10.1s 8g) good-topped, useful-looking gelding; first foal; dam best at 5f; in rear in maiden and minor events in the South; sold 510 gns Ascot December Sales. *B. Swift.* —

CLARENDON 3 gr.g. Brigadier Gerard 144–France (Milesian 125) (1979 5fg 1980 8d² 8g* 8fg 8.3g) compact, deep-girthed gelding; landed odds in workmanlike fashion in maiden race at Kempton in July; well beaten afterwards; will stay 1¼m; possibly needs some give in the ground; sold 4,700 gns Newmarket Autumn Sales. *R. Hern.* 79

CLARISTA (USA) 2 b.f. Riva Ridge–Furioso 116 (Ballymoss 136) (1980 7d) Feb 27; lengthy filly; third foal; half-sister to 3-y-o middle-distance winner Palmella (by Grundy) and very smart Topsy (by Habitat), successful at up to 1¼m; dam, half-sister to Irish 1,000 Guineas winner Favoletta, finished second in Oaks; unquoted and ridden by apprentice unable to claim his 5-lb allowance, dwelt and soon got well behind in Houghton Stakes at Newmarket in October but finished very strongly to come home seventh of 14, 7 lengths behind Sunley Builds; a very pleasing first effort by a filly who should make a very useful 3-y-o over middle distances. *H. Wragg.* — P

CLASSIC ATHENA 4 ch.f. Silly Season 127–Pardina 98 (Pardao 120) (1979 9s 8f 10g² 12g 10g³ 10g² 10h* 1980 12fg 14f⁴ 12g 14fg³ 12fg⁴ 12f 10g⁴ 10.8d) well-grown filly; stays 1¾m; seems to need a sound surface; ran badly when tried in blinkers once; has run well for an apprentice. *G. Huffer.* 61

CLASSIC ROCK 3 b.f. Charlottown 127–Cilerna Rock (Coliseum 116) (1979 7fg 7g 1980 12h 13.8fg⁴ 15fg 16f 12fg) tall, narrow filly; well beaten in varied company, including selling. *J. Powney.* —

CLASSIC TALENT (USA) 3 b.c. Master Hand–Miss Lynnfield (Errard King) (1979 5f 6g 1980 8f 10f 13s) good-looking colt; not a good mover in his slower paces; in rear in maiden races; blinkered final start; sold to J. Baker 1,100 gns Ascot July Sales. *G. Hunter.* —

CLASSIFICATION 2 ch.f. Sassafras 135–Cecilka (Porterhouse) (1980 7d 7g) Feb 18; 5,000Y; half-sister to winners in France, Denmark and Belgium; dam won 17f bumpers event; well beaten in maiden race at Brighton in July and minor event at Chepstow in September; likely to need long distances. *N. Gaselee.* —

CLAUDIUS SECUNDUS 3 b.g. Idiot's Delight 115–Versailles 93 (Never Say Die 137) (1979 NR 1980 9fg* 10g 10g 8.3f 8.2d 8d* 7g²) 300F, 2,100Y; big gelding; half-brother to Hungarian Derby winner Sky VII (by Skymaster); dam 1½m winner; won newcomers event at Wolverhampton in April and minor event at Warwick in October; ran well in £2,300 race at Newmarket on final start; best at up to 9f; acts on a firm and a soft surface. *M. Jarvis.* 79

CLAVERTON 2 b.f. Gold Form 108–Sea Baby (Babur 126) (1980 5f 5f³ 5fg³ 5d 5g) Apr 22; 950Y; sister to 1977 2-y-o 5f winner Gold Frame, and half-sister to 2 winners; dam won at up to 9f in Ireland; plater; third at Chepstow in May and Lingfield (7 lengths behind Superb Music) in June. *C. Wildman.* 36

CLAYMORE 3 ch.c. Murrayfield 119–Koko-Nor 56 (Crocket 130) (1979 5s 1980 13.6f⁴ 10g 12.2f 15s) stocky ex-Irish colt; poor maiden; blinkered final outing; trained by D. Weld first start. *W. Wright.* —

CLEAN WINNER 2 b.f. Record Run 127–Frothy 83 (Watergate 117) (1980 5fg 6g³ 7g 6g* 7f⁴ 7d³ 7.2s 8.2s) Apr 14; useful-looking filly; second reported foal; dam won twice over 7f at 2 yrs; bought in 950 gns after winning 10-runner seller at Leicester in July by ¾ length from Star Rhythm; creditable third of 17 to Show-A-Leg in nursery at Wolverhampton the following month; stays 7f and should get 1m; suited by some give in the ground; sold 540 gns Newmarket Autumn Sales. *Mrs J. Reavey.* 58

CLEAR MELODY 9 b.g. Highland Melody 112–Cape Clear 63 (Fastnet Rock 123) (1979 6g 5d 1980 5g 5d 5g) poor sprint handicapper nowadays; acts on any going; used to wear blinkers; suitable mount for an apprentice. *S. Nesbitt.* —

CLEAR VERDICT (USA) 2 b.c. Judger–Ideal Day (Buckpasser) (1980 7g^2 7fg* 8g*) **110** p

At the end of a season which saw the emergence of two outstanding two-year-old colts in Storm Bird and To-Agori-Mou and other two-year-olds as good as Beldale Flutter, Kalaglow and Recitation, and which saw English-trained youngsters win leading races in Belgium, France, Ireland and Italy, not everybody would consider the Cecil-trained Clear Verdict a serious contender for big-race honours in 1981. This is understandable, for Clear Verdict didn't run in any of the major two-year-old events—he won two of his three races, a maiden event at Newmarket and a minor contest at Goodwood. Nevertheless take care not to underrate his prospects: he's a progressive individual, and an imposing one too, altogether the type to do much better over middle distances as a three-year-old. Clear Verdict, who began his career by chasing home To-Agori-Mou in the Foxhall Stakes over seven furlongs at Goodwood in July, put up his most significant display in the one-mile Westhampnett Stakes on the same course nearly seven weeks later. That day, clearly suited by the longer distance, he stayed on strongly in the closing stages to floor the odds laid on Recitation by a neck. Recitation wasn't in anything like the form that brought him success in the Grand Criterium in October but the pair finished ten lengths clear of their rivals and it would be unfair not to give Clear Verdict credit for a useful performance.

Clear Verdict (USA) (b.c. May 4, 1978)	Judger (b 1971)	Damascus (b 1964)	Sword Dancer
			Kerala
		Face the Facts (ch 1961)	Court Martial
			Vashti
	Ideal Day (b 1969)	Buckpasser (b 1963)	Tom Fool
			Busanda
		Beautiful Day (ch 1961)	Bold Ruler
			Misty Morn

Clear Verdict's pedigree is one of a horse who will stay further. His sire Judger was one of the best three-year-olds in America in 1974, winning three races at up to nine furlongs. Judger, by Damascus, is out of Face the Facts, a

Lord Howard de Walden's "Clear Verdict"

Court Martial mare who raced for three seasons winning nine races at up to nine furlongs. Clear Verdict's dam Ideal Day is from one of the best American families. She is a daughter of Beautiful Day, a smart winner of seven races and a full sister to three stakes winners, including the champion two-year-old colts Bold Lad (USA) and Successor. Their dam, Misty Morn, also a top-class performer on the track, is a half-sister by Princequillo to Clear Ceiling, the dam of Quick As Lightning. Ideal Day didn't add significantly to her family's fine racing record. From eight starts she collected prize money on only one occasion, when winning a maiden race over seven furlongs as a juvenile. At stud her results are better. Her first foal Idealisme (by Bold Reason), gained a place three times in France as a three-year-old in 1979, and her second, Nawaf (by Apalachee), did better than that, winning over a mile and a mile and a quarter in 1980 and showing himself a useful animal.

An attractive, well-made colt and a good walker and mover, Clear Verdict cost 100,000 dollars as a yearling; he is one of the few animals bought at public auction by successful owner Lord Howard de Walden. *H. Cecil.*

CLEAT 2 b.f. Take a Reef 127–Elm Park (Aberdeen 109) (1980 5d^3 5s^2 5f* 5f^2 5fg 5fg 6d* 6g* 6fg* 7g) Feb 21; 460F; sharp, active sort; half-sister to winning sprinter Another Nickel (by Jukebox); dam never ran; did extremely well in nurseries after winning maiden race at Newcastle, scoring at Haydock and Windsor in August and again at Windsor in September; gained all her nursery successes by a neck, beating Cumulus on final occasion; better suited by 6f than 5f but ran below her best over 7f; acts on any going; suitable mount for an apprentice; has shown a tendency to hang but is genuine and consistent. *G. Pritchard-Gordon.* **91**

CLELAND 5 ro.h. Tower Walk 130–Thames Valley 64 (Runnymede 123) (1979 10.8fg 5fg 5g 5fg 5.8fg 1980 5f 5.8fg 5.8fg) neat horse; poor handicapper; best form at 5f; acts on any going; suitable mount for an apprentice; blinkered last 2 outings at 4 yrs; sold 300 gns Ascot August Sales. *D. H. Jones.* –

CLERE LIGHT 2 b.f. Idiot's Delight 115–Mistress Clare 95 (Prince de Galles 125) (1980 7.3d) Feb 28; lengthy filly; first foal; dam won from 7f to 2m; unquoted, backward and ridden by apprentice unable to claim when tenth of 12 to Boathouse in £5,000 event at Newbury in October. *I. Balding.* –

CLEVELAND 4 ch.g. Sallust 134–Proud Girl 99 (Premonition 130) (1979 12.3fg^4 10g^4 10fg* 10.6g^4 10s^3 8fg 10s 1980 8fg 15.8fg^3 15g* 12d^4 16g 15.8f^3 16s^4 15.8g 15d) strong gelding; has a round action; got home by short head from Wild Rosie in handicap at Edinburgh in June; ran poorly last 2 starts; effective at 1½m and stays well; acts on any going; sweating fifth start. *J. Mason.* **65**

CLEWISTON 4 b.g. Manacle 123–Blue Bird 84 (Majority Blue 126) (1979 9g 8.2fg^3 8f^2 9s 8fg^4 8.2g 6d 1980 8f 8fg 6fg 7d) useful-looking gelding; didn't run up to his best in 1980, but caught our eye when seventh of 14 behind subsequently-disqualified Tralee Falcon at Redcar in October on third start; stays 1m; possibly unsuited by soft going; sometimes sweats up. *M. Camacho.* –

CLICKHAM LAD 2 ch.g. Keren 100–Native Queen (Native Prince) (1980 6f^3 7g 7g 6g) Mar 15; sturdy gelding; third foal; dam well beaten in 4 races; well behind in maiden and minor events; blinkered, swerved left coming out of stalls and took no part final outing. *N. Chamberlain.* –

CLICQUOT 3 b.f. Bold Lad (Ire) 133–Effervescence II (Charlottesville 135) (1979 5fg* 5fg* 5.3fg* 1980 5fg 5fg^3 5g 5g* 5fg^3 5f 5fg^4 5g^4) strong, compact, good sort; fairly useful sprint handicapper; beat Mississipi Shuffle a head at Wolverhampton in July; ran respectably several times afterwards; gives impression she will be suited by 6f; yet to race on a soft surface. *Sir Mark Prescott.* **86**

CLIFF BANK 2 b.c. Take a Reef 127–Villa Marina 96 (Tudor Melody 129) (1980 5fg 5f 5s^3 6g^3 6fg* 6g^4 6g 6g^3 6g^2 6d*) Apr 21; 9,000Y; useful-looking colt; said by trainer to have a very poor mouth; half-brother to several winners, including fairly useful 5f to 7f winner Overseas Admirer (by High Top); dam sprinter; improved after winning a maiden race at Pontefract in July and put up a useful effort when winning minor event at Leicester in October going away by 2½ lengths from odds-on Montclair; will stay 1m; probably acts an any going but seems well suited by some give in the ground; blinkered first outing. *B. Hobbs.* **102**

CLINTWOOD 8 gr.g. Lauso–Evelina 99 (Floribunda 136) (1979 6fg 6f^4 7f^3 8d 6fg 1980 6h* 7f 5fg 6d^3 6g 7f 7f^3 6fg 7g 7f 6g 6f 6g) won apprentice handicap at Thirsk in May; ran well on occasions afterwards; stays 7f; acts on any going; used to wear blinkers. *J. Fitzgerald.* **68**

CLIPHOME 2 gr.c. Sandford Lad 133–Seamyside (Sea Hawk II 131) (1980 5f 6g 7fg 8g³ 8fg* 7s⁴) May 4; 3,400Y; useful-looking colt; second foal; dam, Irish 1¼m winner, is out of sister to Approval; improved steadily, justifying favouritism by 1½ lengths from Go My Love in 13-runner maiden race at Beverley in September; creditable fourth of 17 to easy winner Go Leasing in nursery at Newmarket the following month; will stay 1¼m; probably acts on any going. *G. Pritchard-Gordon.* **85**

CLO CLO (HOL) 2 ch.f. Pantheon–Gipsy Queen (Dark Tiger) (1980 5s 6g 5g² 6.5g³ 9g³) small Dutch-bred filly; dam poor half-sister to high-class 1972 French staying 2-y-o Ben Trovato; unquoted when behind in maiden races at Nottingham in June and Yarmouth in July; subsequently placed behind stable-companion Marmorera in 3 races at Duindigt, Holland; stays 9f. *M. Ryan.* **68 ?**

CLONEY BOY 2 gr.c. Sovereign Path 125–Moorland Chant (Double Jump 131) (1980 6f⁴ 6s 6fg) Mar 29; 11,500Y; strong, useful sort; third foal; half-brother to very useful Nedsatki (by Realm), successful at up to 7f in France; dam won over 9f in France; a good sort but showed only a modicum of ability, on final start finishing 5¼ lengths fifth of 6 in maiden race won by Penshiel at Redcar in October; bred to stay 1m. *Denys Smith.* **67**

CLOONAWILLIN 2 b.g. Tudor Music 131–Miss Milesian 74 (Martial 131) (1980 7.5fg 5d* 6s³ 7d* 6s*) Apr 2; fourth foal; half-brother to a winner in Italy by Green God; dam ran only 3 times; improved after winning maiden race at Limerick Junction in August by short head, gaining further successes in minor events at Down Royal (beat Top Pac 1½ lengths) and Punchestown (had same margin to spare over Can't Touch); also ran well when 2 lengths second of 13 to Euclid in small race at the Curragh in September but was moved down to third by stewards; will probably stay 1m; acts very well on soft ground. *L. Greene, Ireland.* **107**

CLOUDWALKER 2 gr.c. Dragonara Palace 115–Misfired 101 (Blast 125) (1980 5d 6d⁴ 6s³) Mar 31; 7,200Y; half-brother to 1978 2-y-o 6f winner Speedy Pet (by Mummy's Pet); dam won 4 races over 5f at 2 yrs; prominent in maiden races, on final outing keeping on well to finish 2½ lengths third of 22 behind Banbury Cross at Doncaster in November; suited by 6f. *G. Balding.* **77**

CLOVER BOY 5 br.g. Lord Gayle 124–Audsam (Le Dieu d'Or 119) (1979 10g 12s 10g⁴ 12f 10f 12f 1980 12fg⁴ 12.2fg 12fg⁴ 11g 11s 12.2d) workmanlike ex-Irish gelding; not disgraced when fourth in lady riders race at Ripon in June and minor event (bandaged) at Pontefract following month; stays 1½m; acts on any going; trained first 4 outings by S. Norton. *J. Spearing.* **—**

CLUED UP 12 ch.g. Smartie 102–Sage Warbler (Le Sage 128) (1979 NR 1980 12d) poor handicapper; lightly raced nowadays. *R. Mason.* **—**

CLWYD 6 ch.h. Crepello 136–Caerphilly 129 (Abernant 142) (1979 11v* 8g 9d³ 8.2g² 9g* 9fg⁴ 5f 8.2fg² 8fg³ 8.2g³ 11.5g 10.4f³ 8.2g⁴ 10.6g 8.2s 8g 1980 8d 8.2g³ 8fg³ 8g 8s* 9g⁴ 8.2g 10.4d⁴ 8fg 8.2s³) quite a moderate handicapper; got home by a short head from Ski Run at Stockton in June; stays 11f; probably acts on any going but is well suited by some give in the ground; has been tried in blinkers; suitable mount for an inexperienced rider. *Denys Smith.* **58**

COAL BUNKER 2 ch.c. On Your Mark 125–Powder Box (Faberge II 121) 1980 5s³ 5s 5s 5f 5h³ 6f³ 6s 6d³ 6d 6f³ 7h² 7g² 8fg* 8d) Apr 7; 4,000F, 2,000Y; short-backed colt; third foal; half-brother to 3-y-o Peppery (by Red God), a fairly useful winner at up to 1¼m; dam Irish stayer; placed in varied company, including selling early in season; subsequently ran well in 3 nurseries, getting up close home to win Rowley Mile Nursery at Newmarket in October by ½ length from Grain Race when apprentice ridden; will stay 1¼m+; best form on a sound surface; blinkered third outing. *R. Hannon.* **76**

COASTING BREEZE 2 br.c. Windjammer (USA)–Etoile Freda (Florescence 120) (1980 5fg) Apr 29; 2,000Y, 2,000 2-y-o; half-brother to Irish 6f winner Superb (by Roi Soleil); dam never ran; 33/1 when behind in 24-runner maiden race won by Trina's Girl at Windsor in August. *J. Bosley.* **—**

COBBLER SMITH 2 b.c. Crowned Prince 128–Galloping Nell 68 (Worden II 129) (1980 6d 6fg 6g 5fg³ 6s 6s³ 7g³) Feb 26; 6,200F; big, strong colt; fifth produce; dam ran only twice; ran well last 2 outings, finishing third to Miss Menton in minor event at Stockton in October and to Go Leasing in 17-runner nursery at Leicester in November; will be suited by middle distances; probably acts on any going. *T. Fairhurst.* **85**

COCAINE 2 ch.c. High Line 125–Golden Thoughts 86 (Golden Cloud) (1980 7d* **104**
8fg) Mar 22; 2,600F, 18,500Y; leggy, rather unfurnished colt; brother to successful Italian filly Cupina, and half-brother to several winners, including fairly useful miler Dream Town (by Town Crier); dam won over 5f at 2 yrs; soon prominent after losing 3 lengths at start of 11-runner Acomb Stakes at York in August and strode out in fine style in final 2f to win by 3 lengths from Glint of Gold; 7/1, dropped out very quickly after leading to straight when 10$\frac{3}{4}$ lengths sixth of 8 to Robellino in Royal Lodge Stakes at Ascot the following month; will be suited by middle distances. *J. Hindley.*

COCOA 4 b.g. Lord Gayle 124–Firey Ann 80 (Firestreak 125) (1979 10v 10v* **80**
12v* 12s* 12fg^3 16fg 14fg^2 16g* 16.3s 16g 14d^4 1980 12s 12d 14d^4 10d* 12fg 10s 10s) Irish gelding; won minor event at Phoenix Park in August; ran moderately afterwards, on first occasion in Moet and Chandon Silver Magnum (gentlemen riders) won by No Bombs at Epsom later in month; stays 2m; goes well in the mud. *M. Kauntze, Ireland.*

CODEOX 2 gr.f. Broxted 120–Decode 62 (Tangle 121) (1980 5g 5d 5g^4 5fg) –
Mar 12; strong, compact filly; third reported foal; dam 2m chaser; in rear in maiden and minor events; sold 500 gns Doncaster October Sales. *D. Francis.*

COFFEE DAY 2 b.f. Broxted 120–Palmette 103 (Premonition 130) (1980 5v 5f^4 **47**
5fg 6fg 8.2d 8fg 6s 5s) Mar 21; 2,900F, 1,100Y; plain filly; half-sister to winners here and in Sweden; dam won at up to 1$\frac{3}{4}$m; poor plater; will stay middle distances; blinkered eighth start (sweating). *J. Berry.*

COFFEE HOUSE 5 br.g. Silly Season 127–Village Gossip 69 (Narrator 127) **66**
(1979 10s 12.2s^4 10d^3 8s 11g^4 11fg^2 11d 8g* 8fg 10f* 10f 10.2fg^2 10fg* 10d^4 1980 8d 11fg^2 12fg^3 10fg 8fg 10g^2 10g^4 10g) middle-distance handicapper; not disgraced most outings, but ran moderately final start (July); acts on any going; blinkered sixth outing at 4 yrs; goes well for claimer S. Payne. *I. Balding.*

COJ 2 b.g. Copte–Warm Spring 67 § (Mid-day Sun) (1980 5fg 6s) Apr 26; –
small gelding; half-brother to 1$\frac{1}{4}$m winner Artesian (by Articulate) and to a winning chaser; dam stayer; well behind in minor race at Pontefract in April and seller at Nottingham in August. *D. Leslie.*

COLADA 2 ch.f. Manado 130–Yellow Temptress (Yellow God 129) (1980 6g 6fg –
5d) Mar 14; 3,600Y; lengthy filly; second foal; dam never ran; in rear in maiden and minor events. *A. Bailey.*

COLARO 2 b.f. Tennyson 124–Montcall (Mountain Call 125) (1980 6g 7d 7g 7fg –
7fg) Jan 31; 2,300F; compact, rather plain filly; second foal; dam unraced half-sister to French Champion Hurdle winner Hardatit; poor maiden. *A. Bailey.*

COLD BLOOD 4 gr.g. Great Nephew 126–Ice Ballet 87 (Ballymoss 136) (1979 –
13.3s^3 16fg* 13s^3 1980 16fg 14f 15f 11d^4 13.8f 16g) lengthy, useful-looking gelding; well beaten in handicaps in 1980; stays well; seems to act on any going; blinkered third to fifth starts; sold out of J. Hindley's stable 3,000 gns Ascot July Sales after fifth outing. *O. O'Neill.*

COLLECTOR'S ITEM 3 b.f. Run The Gantlet–Regal Splendour 76 (Sovereign **96**
Path 125) (1979 5g* 5v^4 6s^4 6g^3 5fg^2 5f^3 5f^4 5fg^3 1980 9f 7g 10f 9f 9g 8g* 8g* 8.5d* 8g 10.6s^4 10d) 4,400Y; useful-looking ex-Irish filly; second foal; half-sister to All Glorious (by Crowned Prince), successful at up to 1m; dam 3-y-o 6f winner; a reformed character once fitted with blinkers on sixth start and won handicaps at Bellewstown, Killarney and Galway in July, making all on first 2 courses; didn't wear blinkers last 3 starts, putting up best effort when staying-on fourth to Lonely Signorita in £2,400 race at Haydock in October; stays 1$\frac{1}{4}$m; appears to act on any going; trained by M. Kauntze first 8 outings. *M. H. Easterby.*

COLLEGE DON 3 br.g. Balliol 125–Impartial 91 (Big Game) (1979 7f 6g 5g –
1980 9.4fg 12g 12.2f) strong gelding; well beaten in varied company, including selling. *W. A. Stephenson.*

COLONEL CREOLE 4 ch.g. Major Portion 129–Creolina 72 (Quorum 126) –
(1979 9.4f 10f 1980 10fg) workmanlike gelding; plater; stays 1m; has given trouble at start; ran poorly in blinkers final outing at 2 yrs; sold 2,600 gns Ascot June Sales. *W. A. Stephenson.*

COLONIAL LINE (USA) 2 ch.f. Plenty Old–Es Cabalistica (Eslavo) (1980 **75**
6g 6g^3 5s 5s) Mar 8; 12,000Y; well-grown, good sort; half-sister to 2 winners in USA by Charles Elliott; dam won in Argentina and up to 1m in USA; gambled on from 12/1 to 5/2 when 2$\frac{1}{2}$ lengths third of 13 to Pieta in maiden race at Brighton in August; well beaten subsequently; finds 5f too sharp and will stay at least 1m. *G. Pritchard-Gordon.*

COLONIAL PRINCE 4 b.g. Martinmas 128–Liberdad 61 (Matador 131) (1979 –
NR 1980 10d 14g) lengthy gelding; tailed off in amateur riders races at
Newmarket and Yarmouth in July. *J. Powney.*

COLOR SPECTRUM 2 ch.f. Queen's Hussar 124–Gymnast (Red God 128§) –
(1980 6d 6g) Jan 17; 16,000F; neat filly; second reported produce; dam,
winner over 6f at 2 yrs in Ireland, is half-sister to smart 6f to 1$\frac{3}{4}$m winner Marquis
de Sade; well beaten in end-of-season maiden races at Newmarket and Leicester.
W. Hastings-Bass.

COLUMBIUM 3 ch.c. St Columbus 98–Lucky Janie 87 (Dual 117) (1979 5g **73**
6s 6fg 7fg 7g 8fg^2 1980 12s^2 10s^2 10fg^2 10f 14fg^4 16s* 16fg^3 15.5s) lengthy
colt; good mover; easily won maiden race at Lingfield in June; stays well; acts
well on soft going. *G. Beeson.*

COLUMNIST 3 b.c. Swing Easy 126–Namecaller 83 (Malicious) (1979 6s^2 **104**
6fg* 6fg^4 7d 6f^4 1980 6s 6fg^3 6d 6g^2 6g^3) lengthy colt; good mover; useful
performer; ran well when third to Queen's Pride in Wokingham Stakes at Royal
Ascot, second to Great Eastern in £2,800 race at Newbury (hung left) and third
to Pavahra in £4,000 handicap at York in the summer; runs as though a return
to 7f will suit him well; best form on a sound surface; wears blinkers. *J. Tree.*

COLWAY BOY 6 b.g. Faraway Son 130–Crassula (Canisbay 120) (1979 –
16s^3 15.5d^2 18.8g* 17.1g 15.5f* 16f 16.1g^4 16f^2 18fg* 16fg 17.1fg 14f^4 14g^4 1980
18.8g^2 14g 16.5fg) quite a moderate staying handicapper; appears to act on
any going; retained 3,300 gns Ascot November Sales. *R. Akehurst.*

COMBINE HARVESTER 4 ch.c. English Prince 129–Sea Music 108 (Atan) **98**
(1979 8v* 10v^4 9d 8g 10d* 10v 1980 10v 8g 8fg^2 8g* 9f 10g) Irish colt; third
foal; brother to useful 3-y-o 9f winner Rule Britannia and half-brother to fairly
useful sprinter Whenby (by Prevailing); dam won 8 races up to 6f at 2 yrs;
very useful performer; ran well when 3 lengths second to Gods Mark (rec 14 lb)
in Sean Graham Handicap at the Curragh in May; beat North Pole by 2 lengths
in 8-runner Kilruddery Stakes at Leopardstown later in month; stays 1$\frac{1}{4}$m;
probably acts on any going except perhaps firm; off course more than 3 months
before being pulled up in Joe McGrath Memorial Stakes on final outing. *C.
Collins, Ireland.*

COMEDIAN 2 b.g. Comedy Star 121–Ruetina 74 (Rugantino 97) (1980 6g **77**
6d 7fg^2) Apr 10; small, quite attractive gelding; second foal; half-brother to
fairly useful 1978 staying 2-y-o Faringdon Bell (by Mandamus); dam ran 3
times; ran on gamely when 2 lengths second of 16 to Sunion in maiden race at
Warwick in July; likely to stay 1$\frac{1}{4}$m; gelded after third outing. *J. Dunlop.*

COMEDY CROFT 3 b.g. Comedy Star 121–Twyford Ridge (Schapiro 99) **77**
(1979 5d 5g 5g* 6f 7.3g 8fg^4 8f 8s^2 1980 8f 10fg 10f^2 12f 11fg^4 11.7g 10fg^3 11.5g^2
12g* 14fg 16fg 12fg* 12g) compact, good sort; quite a moderate handicapper;
winner at Brighton in August and Leicester in September; doesn't stay 2m;
probably acts on any going; sometimes wears blinkers, but didn't when successful.
R. Hannon.

COME ON CHICKEN 2 gr.f. Abwah 118–Dialice 81 (King's Troop 118) –
(1980 5g 5f 5g 5d 5d) Apr 28; 1,900Y; neat filly; bad plater; blinkered fourth
outing; sold 420 gns Doncaster October Sales. *J. Doyle.*

COME ON FLOWER 4 b.f. Warpath 113–Creek Alley 91 (Klairon 131) (1979 –
NR 1980 8fg 11f) bad plater; blinkered first outing; sold 520 gns Newmarket
May Sales. *J. Berry.*

COME ON TAFFY 3 ch.c. Welsh Pageant 132–Come On Honey 94 (Never **80**
Say Die 137) (1979 7f 8fg 1980 10s 14g* 13.8g* 12.3d) robust, deep-girthed
colt; odds on when winning maiden race at Yarmouth despite running green
and minor event at Catterick in August; suited by 1$\frac{3}{4}$m and will stay further;
sold to I. Wardle 9,400 gns Newmarket Autumn Sales. *H. Cecil.*

COME PLAY WITH ME 5 b.g. Jukebox 120–Compatriot (Pindari 124) –
(1979 11.7fg 1980 10fg 10g 7fg 7d 8g) poor handicapper; stays 1$\frac{1}{4}$m; acts on
any going; suitable mount for a boy; has been tried in blinkers. *R. Atkins.*

COME WHAT MAY 3 b. or br.f. Derring-Do 131–Sincerity 91 (Soderini 123) –
(1979 5g 6fg* 6d^4 1980 7f 6h 7f 6d 8.3d) neat, strong filly; won maiden race
at Epsom at 2 yrs; didn't find her form in handicaps in 1980; should stay 1m+;
blinkered fourth start. *B. Swift.*

COMIC STRIP 3 b.f. Kalamoun 129–Joking 81 (Ribero 126) (1979 NR 1980 –
7g 8g) lightly-made filly; first foal; dam, winner over 1$\frac{1}{2}$m, is half-sister to
Queen's Hussar; unimpressive in paddock when behind in maiden races at
Leicester and Salisbury in the summer. *I. Balding.*

COMMANDER BOND 5 ch.g. Good Bond 122–Sailing 109 (Doutelle 128) –
(1979 8v^3 7f 8f 7s^3 6fg^2 7d 8fg* 1980 7d 9g) rated 89 in 1979; well beaten in 1980, but was off course almost 7 months between outings; stays 1m; appears to act on any going; suitable mount for an apprentice; sometimes wears blinkers. *A. Smith.*

COMMODORE BLAKE 3 br.c. Blakeney 126–Ribamba 82 (Ribocco 129) –
(1979 NR 1980 12s^4) 30,000Y; neat, quite attractive colt; second foal; dam half-sister to Bruni; not seen out after finishing promising fourth to runaway winner Wonderful Surprise in 20-runner maiden race at Haydock in October (well-backed favourite); will stay 1$\frac{3}{4}$m. *M. Stoute.*

COMMONTY (USA) 2 b.c. Empery 128–Duke's Little Gal (Duke of Dublin) **87** p
(1980 8d^2) $17,000Y; well-made, quite attractive colt; fourth foal; closely related to French 3-y-o middle-distance winner Platinum (by Vaguely Noble); dam won 9 races, including 7f Santa Paula Handicap; 33/1 but pick of paddock, ran promisingly in 14-runner maiden race won by Majorian at Leicester in November, running on strongly over the last 2f, without being punished unduly, to finish 4 lengths second; has scope and should improve over middle distances at 3 yrs. *J. Bethell.*

COMMUNITY STAR 2 b.c. Manado 130–Destinee (Roan Rocket 128) (1980 –
6fg) Mar 1; 13,000Y; third foal; half-brother to 1977 2-y-o 5f winner Treasure Seeker (by Deep Diver) and a winner in Malaya; dam won twice in Germany; 11/1, dwelt when distant last of 7 to No-U-Turn in minor event at Windsor in August *B. Swift.*

COMOR 3 ch.c Amber Rama 133–La Coquina (Le Fabuleux 133) (1979 6fg^4 **68**
5fg 1980 8g* 8g 10g^3 8f 8.2g 8.3g 10g) neat, strong colt; good mover; won modest maiden race at Pontefract in June; stays 1$\frac{1}{4}$m; sold 2,500 gns Doncaster September Sales. *R. Price.*

COMOROGUE 3 b.f. Crowned Prince 128–Lucybird (Sea-Bird II 145) (1979 **44**
NR 1980 8d 8.2s 6f^2) plain filly; second in seller at Pontefract in April; should stay beyond 6f. *W. Holden.*

COMPANIONSHIP 3 br.g. Kalamoun 129–Cupid's Delight 84 (St Paddy 133) (1979 –
NR 1980 7f 8fg 10fg) strong, shapely gelding; third foal; half-brother to Norfolk Arrow (by Blakeney), successful over 2m; dam, twice a winner over 1$\frac{1}{2}$m from 3 starts, is half-sister to good stayer Rangong; well beaten in maiden races and an amateur riders event. *P. Walwyn.*

COMPLETE PACKAGE 3 b.g. Manacle 123–Facade 99 (Double Jump 131) **58**
(1979 5s 5d^3 5g^3 5g 1980 5s 6s 5fg 6s^2 6g 7g) small, light-framed gelding; plater; stays 6f; acts on soft going; has run creditably for a boy; sold 850 gns Ascot September Sales. *A. Pitt.*

COMPOSER 2 ch.c Music Boy 124–Contadina (Memling) (1980 6d^2 6g*) **92** p
May 5; 7,600Y; big, lengthy, useful-looking colt; turns his front feet in; half-brother to very useful 3-y-o 7f performer Conbrian (by The Brianstan) and 2 other winners, including very useful and tough sprinter Manor Farm Boy (by Mansingh); dam never ran; short-priced favourite following a promising debut, quickened well up hill to win 25-runner maiden race at Newmarket in October by 2 lengths from Dynaboy; will probably stay 7f; has scope and could make a very useful 3-y-o. *W. Hastings-Bass.*

COMPOUND 6 b.g. Siliconn 121–Compose 94 (Compensation 127) (1979 7g 7f **52** §
7fg 10.2fg 1980 6f 6h^3 8f^2 6g^3 8fg 7f^2 7g^4 7f 6g^4 6fg 6fg) plater; ran well in better company on several occasions, including when blinkered for first time on tenth start; well beaten without blinkers only subsequent outing; stays 1m; acts on firm going; suitable mount for a boy; sometimes starts slowly. *Mrs N. Kennedy.*

COMPUTERCALL 4 b.c. Good Bond 122–Mercilla 94 (Welsh Abbot 131) **78** d
(1979 10v 8s* 8s^3 8fg 10f^3 8fg* 8fg* 8fg 8f 8.2g^2 8d* 8g 1980 8fg 8s 10d 8fg 8.3fg* 10fg 8f 8.3fg 8fg) strong, robust colt; ran best race when beating Hadera by a head in handicap at Windsor in August (well backed); best form at around 1m; acts on any going; blinkered seventh outing at 2 yrs; good mount for an apprentice; suited by forcing tactics; sold 3,700 gns Newmarket Autumn Sales. *G. Huffer.*

COMTEC 6 b.g. Communication 119–Tecllyn 97 (Technion 96) (1979 6v 6v –
6d^4 5f 5s* 5fg 6g 6fg4 5f 1980 6s 5d 5d 6d 6g 5d 5d 6s) sprint handicapper; acts on any going; usually wears a hood and blinkers. *K. Bridgwater.*

CONA 2 br.c. Connaught 130–Lowna 120 (Princely Gift 137) (1980 7fg 7d^4 6g) **72**
Mar 22; well-grown, useful sort; half-brother to several winners, including Gospill

Hill (by Crepello), a smart performer at up to 1¼m, and 1974 2-y-o 6f winner The Hobman (by Tudor Melody); dam won Molecomb Stakes; 3¾ lengths fourth to Cifonelli in £2,500 event at Newcastle in August, travelling well on bridle until 2f out but then hanging left when ridden; 16/1, again faded in final 2f when seventh of 13 to Brummer in £3,200 maiden event at Doncaster the following month; should be suited by a return to 7f. *Denys Smith.*

CONACRE 4 b.g. Connaught 130–Mrs Pankhurst 78 (Reform 132) (1979 8f 8h 8f 8fg 10.6g 1980 8v 6v 6f 7f) of little account. *A. W. Jones.* —

CONAN DOYLE 3 b.c. Derring-Do 131–Shot Gold (Vimy 132) (1979 6fg4 6f* 1980 10f 7.3f 7fg 7f4 6fg3 6s2 7s 6fg2 7.3fg* 7g) compact, good-looking sort; fairly useful handicapper; very much on toes prior to making all to beat Tower Joy 1½ lengths at Newbury in September; bred to stay middle distances but is headstrong and is unlikely to stay that far; acts on any going; sometimes wears blinkers; has run creditably for a boy; ran badly seventh start; sold 20,000 gns Newmarket Autumn Sales, reportedly to race in California. *P. Cole.* 92

CONBRIAN 3 b.c. The Brianstan 128–Contadina (Memling) (1979 5fg2 6s2 6f4 1980 7f2 7f* 8fg3 7.2s* 7fg* 7fg*) lengthy colt; third foal; half-brother to 2 winners, including very useful and tough sprinter Manor Farm Boy (by Mansingh); dam never ran; had a good year and developed into a very useful performer in the summer, winning minor event at Epsom and handicaps at Haydock (beat Jester's Boy comfortably in Sporting Chronicle Handicap), Goodwood (from Sandford Boy) and Newmarket; beat State Trooper a shade comfortably by 1½ lengths on last-named; best at 7f; acts on any going; sweated up slightly first 2 starts; genuine and consistent. *M. Smyly.* 113

CONCERT HALL 4 ch.c. Connaught 130–Hello Honey 105 (Crepello 136) (1979 8d3 10g* 10.2s 12d* 12fg2 12g4 14d4 1980 12d* 12d) well-made, good sort; second favourite and looking fit and well, won handicap at Doncaster in March by 2½ lengths from Path of Peace (pair clear); ran poorly at Kempton the following month and wasn't seen out again; stays 1¾m; acts on a firm and a soft surface. *G. Lewis.* 90

CONCORDE GIRL 5 ch.m. Jolly Jet 111–Gallopera 81 (El Gallo 122) (1979 8g3 8g 1980 10fg3 8fg 7fg 6g4 6d2 7g3 8d 8h) rangy mare; went down by short head to Quiet Touch in maiden race at Brighton in July; running-on third to Tugoflove in handicap at Newmarket following month, easily best subsequent effort; effective at 6f and seems to stay 1¼m; best form with some give in the ground. *N. Gaselee.* 52

CONDERIAN 8 b.g. Connaught 130–Dereta 92 (Aggressor 130) (1979 13v2 16g 12g 12d 14fg 12.2s 1980 12.2fg) poor perfomer; stays 13f; acts on heavy ground; wears bandages; suitable mount for an amateur; pulled up lame only outing of 1980. *P. Feilden.* —

CONDOMINIUM 2 b.c. Roan Rocket 128–Without Reproach 102 (Above Suspicion 127) (1980 5fg 5f 6d 7d4 8f 8s) Feb 1; 11,000Y; rangy colt; half-brother to several winners, including stayer Hikari (by Petingo); dam won 75

Sporting Chronicle Handicap, Haydock—Conbrian finishes clear of Jester's Boy

Lancashire Oaks; slow maiden; runs as though needing a thorough test of stamina; form only on a soft surface. *M. H. Easterby.*

CONFLICT 4 ch.c. Tyrant–Make A Pass (Prominer 125) (1979 8g 8d 8.2s^4 86 d
8.2g* 10g* 10s* 1980 10s^4 8.2s* 8fg 8g 8.2s^3 8.2g 8s) workmanlike colt; favourite when beating Copper Tinsell decisively by 3 lengths in handicap at Hamilton in April; stays 1¼m; acts on soft going; usually wears blinkers (ran creditably without fifth start). *I. Walker.*

CONGO 3 b.g. Goldhill 125–Connaught Girl (Connaught 130) (1979 NR 1980 —
12d) 10,000Y; 4,100 3-y-o; compact gelding; has a round action; first foal; dam never ran; unquoted, moved badly to post when distant sixth of 10 to Whitehall Bridge in maiden race at Newbury in October. *G. Kindersley.*

CON-MAN 4 b.g. Burglar 128–Calm Sea 83 (Set Fair 129) (1979 7v 6v 5fg —
6f^2 5f* 5f^2 5g^2 5s 5f 5h 5fg 1980 5d 5s 5fg 5f 6s 5d 6s 5v) neat gelding; sprint handicapper; acts on any going except perhaps heavy; sometimes wears blinkers. *J. Tierney.*

CONNAUGHT AMAZON 2 ch.f. Connaught 130–Herbary (Herbager 136) —
(1980 7fg) Mar 14; smallish, well-made filly; first foal; dam never ran; very backward when behind in 16-runner maiden race won by Ganimede at Yarmouth in August (difficult on way to start); unseated rider on way to start when withdrawn on same course earlier in month. *D. Ringer.*

CONNAUGHT NYMPH 2 b.f. Connaught 130–Constant Nymph 85 (Venture 71
VII 129) (1980 5fg^4 7g^4 6s^3 8d 8s^4) Mar 6; 16,000Y; compact filly; fourth reported living foal; half-sister to winners in Belgium and Austria; dam, sister to useful miler Loose Cover, stayed at least 7f; quite moderate form in maiden and minor events and a nursery; stays 1m and may well get 1¼m. *R. Hollinshead.*

CONNI-MIST 3 b.f. Connaught 130–Misoptimist 111 (Blakeney 126) (1979 72
NR 1980 10.2fg^3 12.3f 10f^2 10d^4) 15,000Y; compact, fair sort; first foal; dam won over 6f and 1¼m; quite a moderate maiden; bred to stay 1½m (out of her depth when tried at trip); acted on firm going; pulled hard and ran moderately final start; dead. *B. Hills.*

CONNORS 6 ch.g. Bold Lad (Ire) 133–Arenaria 102 (Aureole 132) (1979 —
11.7g 1980 11fg) poor handicapper nowadays; stays 1¼m but has done his winning at 1m; appears to act on any going. *J. S. E. Turner.*

CONSENT 2 br.f. Connaught 130–Truly Yours 93 (So Blessed 130) (1980 62
5fg^2 5g 5g^3 6d* 5d 6s 8fg^4 8.2v^2) Feb 25; lightly-made filly; first foal; dam, winner twice over 5f at 2 yrs, appeared to stay 1¼m; sold out of C. Thornton's stable 1,400 gns after making all to win 6-runner seller at Ayr in August by ½ length from First Child; creditable second of 6 in nursery won by The Small Miracle at Hamilton in October; will stay 1¼m; probably acts on any going. *T. Craig.*

CONSENTING (USA) 2 b. or br.c. Judger–Queen of the Sky (Bold Ruler) 83
(1980 8g 8g^4) Mar 11; $140,000Y; lengthy, quite attractive colt; half-brother to several winners in USA, including stakes-placed winners Halcyon Queen (by Hail to Reason) and Foreign Missile (by Damascus); dam unraced sister to champion American 2-y-o's Bold Lad (USA) and Successor; 12/1, prominent throughout when about 3½ lengths fourth to Uppety in minor race at Newmarket in November; gives impression he may need at least 1½m at 3 yrs. *J. Hindley.*

CONSISTENT QUEEN 2 b.f. Queen's Hussar 124–Consistent 90 (Connaught 55
130) (1980 5fg 5fg^3 6g 5d 5fg 5fg 5d^4 5s) Jan 31; 1,100Y; small, compact filly; first foal; dam won over 5f on first outing; placed in a maiden race at Catterick but is only a plater; should stay at least 6f; blinkered last 2 starts. *E. Weymes.*

CONSORTIUM 3 b.c. Targowice 130–Annerbelle 108 (Aureole 132) (1979 84 d
5d* 5s^3 6f 1980 8v^4 6fg 10fg 10s^4 10.2g^2 10.8fg^4 12g^4 12d^4 10.2d^4 8d) strong colt; good walker; runner-up in apprentice handicap at Bath in July; stays 1¼m (well beaten over further); suited by some give in the ground; blinkered eighth start; moved badly to post final outing; sold 4,000 gns Newmarket Autumn Sales. *P. Cole.*

CONSTANT ROSE 4 br.f. Confusion 118–Maizenrose 89 (Rustam 127) (1979 78
10g^3 8f^2 8f^2 10f^4 1980 10fg^3 10fg* 10f 10.6g 10g* 10g* 10g* 10fg 10g 10fg^2) leggy, rather sparely-made filly; had a good year and won maiden race at Redcar and handicaps at Pontefract, Leicester and Folkestone, beating Zoro readily by 2½ lengths on last-named course in July; ran easily best subsequent race when ½-length second to African Rhythm in apprentice handicap at Lingfield

in October; ran as though an extended 1¼m was too far for her on fourth outing; yet to race on soft ground; usually held up; goes well for P. Robinson; sold to J. Harris 5,000 gns Newmarket December Sales. *F. Durr.*

CONTENTION 2 b.f. Connaught 130–Mitigation 91 (Milesian 125) (1980 5g 7g 7f) Mar 2; smallish filly; half-sister to several winners, including smart middle-distance performer Colum (by Santa Claus); dam won at up to 1m; fairly prominent in maiden races, on third outing running on to finish 6¼ lengths sixth of 20 to stable-companion Briar when 33/1 at Chepstow in August; will stay middle distances. *R. Hern.* **72**

CONTE SANTI 5 b.h. Sassafras 135–Gloomy Portal 103 (Mossborough 126) (1979 8f* 10g^{3} 9fg 1980 8d) well-made, quite attractive horse; good mover; very smart at 3 yrs; only lightly raced since, and was well beaten at Kempton in April on only outing of 1980 (showed up for a long way); best form at up to 1¼m; acts on any going. *R. Price.* **—**

CONTOSA 2 ch.f. Condorcet–La Casita (Ballyciptic 122) (1980 7d 8d) Apr 29; 2,500F, 1,300Y; tall, lengthy filly; second produce; half-sister to 6f and 1m winner Countess Virginia (by Virginia Boy); dam fairly useful winner over 6f at 2 yrs in Ireland and stayed at least 7f; tailed-off last in maiden races at Leicester in October and November. *P. K. Mitchell.* **—**

CONWAY BAY 3 b.f. Saritamer 130–Menai 100 (Abernant 142) (1979 5d 5fg 5g 5f^{3} 5fg 5fg^{3} 5d^{3} 5fg 5s^{2} 5d 5d 1980 5f 5h 5fg 5s 7g 7f 12g 10f 5fg) compact filly; quite moderate (rated 74) at 2 yrs; poor plater nowadays; not certain to stay 7f; acts on any going; sometimes wears blinkers; didn't move well to post sixth start. *Hbt Jones.* **—**

COOLEEN JACK 2 b.c. Targowice 130–Polyxo (Polyfoto 124) (1980 6d 5g 5g* 5g 5g* 5g* 5s^{4}) May 13; 3,800F, 7,600Y; second produce; dam won over 5f and 7f in Ireland; favourite when successful in maiden race at Mallow in August, nursery under top weight at Tralee in September and Goffs Stakes at the Curragh, also in September; beat some fairly useful winners in last-named race, disputing lead all way and running on to get the better of Lady Blackfoot by ½ length; second favourite, faded after holding every chance 1½f out when 4¼ lengths fourth of 7 to Martinova in Waterford Testimonial Stakes at the Curragh in October; should stay beyond 5f. *E. O'Grady, Ireland.* **106**

COOLINEY PRINCE 2 gr.c. Tumble Wind–Aquaria (Double-U-Jay 120) (1980 5f 5f* 6fg* 5g* 5fg* 6f) Apr 18; 2,750Y (privately); strong colt; half- **104**

Windsor Castle Stakes, Ascot—at the post Cooliney Prince is clear of Parkdale (No. 9) and Brentex (No. 21)

brother to fairly useful 1¼m winner Killer Shark (by Tyrant) and a winner abroad; dam ran once; proved a very shrewd purchase and collected a valuable prize when blinkered first time in 13-runner Windsor Castle Stakes at Royal Ascot in June, quickening clear in final furlong to win by 3 lengths from Parkdale; had previously won maiden auction event at Phoenix Park, 7-runner race at the Curragh and Emily Persse Cup, also at the Curragh, last-named by short head from African Guy when 9/4 on; co-second favourite and again blinkered in William Hill Middle Park Stakes in October but never really got into race and finished 6½ lengths sixth of 9 to Mattaboy; should stay 1m; yet to race on a soft surface. *P. Prendergast, jnr, Ireland.*

COOL JADE 3 b.f. Furzebreck 62–Fiery Wade (Green God 128) (1979 NR 1980 8fg 7fg 8fg) very small filly; seems of little account. *R. Morris.* –

COPPER BEECHES 3 b.g. Owen Anthony 102–Primmy 56 (Primera 131) (1979 5s 5g4 5g 6s 5f2 5fg4 5d* 6g 1980 5fg2 5fg 6g 5s2 6fg3 7d 7g) quite attractive, lightly-made gelding; moderate handicapper; stays 6f; acts on any going; bandaged near-fore second start. *J. Holt.* 79

COPPER CLOUD 4 ch.f. Foggy Bell 108–Game Gypsy (Game Rights 91) (1979 NR 1980 14g 14g) novice hurdler; unquoted when behind in maiden races at Sandown in July. *S. James.* –

COPPER PRINCE 2 ch.g. Ampney Prince 96–Wandering Rose (Tudor Minstrel 144) (1980 6fg 6fg 5fg 8d 7s) Mar 9; rangy gelding; half-brother to middle-distance winner Tudor Wynk (by Wynkell); dam of little account; plating-class maiden; may stay 1m. *S. Mellor.* –

COPPER TINSELL 4 ch.f. Crooner 119–Camisole 94 (Psidium 130) (1979 8d 8g2 7fg 10f3 9.4f3 8.2d2 8fg3 8.2g2 8fg4 8.2fg 8fg* 1980 7v 8.2g2 8f 8fg 8s 8fg 8.2d3 8.2s 8.2v2 10s4) compact filly; placed at Hamilton (twice) and Haydock, on last 2 occasions in sellers; stays 1¼m; seems to act on any going; sometimes wears blinkers; sold to T. Barnes 1,750 gns Doncaster November Sales. *C. Thornton.* 47

COPSALE BRIDGE 3 b.g. Owen Anthony 102–Paddygrino (St Paddy 133) (1979 6f 6g 1980 10.8s 10.1fg) little worthwhile form in maiden races and a seller; blinkered in 1980. *P. Feilden.* –

COPT AGAIN 2 ch.f. Copte–Annie 65 (Damremont 121) (1980 6fg 7s 7g 8d 8d) Mar 4; compact filly; half-sister to modest 5f and 1m winner Huntley Wood (by Spanish Gold); dam sister to smart middle-distance handicapper Damredub; plating-class maiden. *R. Hollinshead.* –

COPT HALL PRINCESS 2 b.f. Crowned Prince 128–Gwendolyn (Bagdad) (1980 6g 6f) Feb 28; 5,200F; quite attractive filly; second foal; half-sister to Rosenbloom (by Simbir), successful in Belgium; dam, placed 3 times in USA, comes from a good family; 50/1 and having first race for 3 months, led her group to halfway when 6¾ lengths sixth of 19 to Long Legend in maiden race at Newmarket in October, second outing; has scope and may do better over 1m at 3 yrs. *J. Winter.* 70

COPT HALL REALM 2 ch.f. Realm 129–Darinda (Darius 129) (1980 6g3 5g*) Mar 31; 14,500Y; smallish, well-made filly; half-sister to very useful sprinter Bold Image (by Balidar) and to a winner in Italy; dam well bred but showed only poor form; having first race for 3 months but favourite, won 22-runner maiden event at Lingfield in September comfortably by a length from Sodina; had previously disputed lead 4f and kept on well when length third of 12 to Chemin in £4,400 event at Newmarket; will be suited by a return to 6f. *J. Winter.* 85

COPT HALL ROYALE 3 b.f. Right Tack 131–Sauce Royale (Royal Palace 131) (1979 7fg 7g 1980 8fg* 12f4 8.5f 8fg 10fg 8s 11d) tall, lightly-made filly; beat Magnificent Lady a neck in £4,400 fillies race at Ascot in April; didn't seem suited by track when just over 2½ lengths fifth to Parlour Game in valuable handicap at Epsom in June, third start and best effort afterwards; appears not to stay 1½m; acts on a firm surface; had stiff tasks fifth and sixth starts. *J. Winter.* 87

COPY WRITER 2 b.c. Copte–Story Writer 67 (Sweet Story 122) (1980 6g 7d 6g) strong, useful sort; first foal; dam 11f winner; well beaten in maiden and minor events, including 2 at Carlisle. *W. Haigh.* –

CORAL DANCE (FR) 2 b.f. Green Dancer 132–Carvinia (Diatome 132) (1980 7.5s3 8g* 8g3 8f2) Apr 6; 220,000 francs Y (approx £23,000); lengthy filly; good walker; second foal; half-sister to a winner over jumps; dam useful middle-distance winner and half-sister to high-class middle-distance stayer 111

Carvin; won 12-runner maiden race at Deauville in August by 1½ lengths from Alik; subsequently acquitted herself very well in 2 important races, finishing 1¼ lengths third of 9 to Ukraine Girl in Group 3 Prix d'Aumale at Chantilly and failing by 2 lengths to hold off Tropicaro after making much of running in 10-runner Prix Marcel Boussac (formerly Criterium des Pouliches) at Long-champ; will stay 1½m; genuine. *G. Bonnaventure, France.*

CORAL LEISURE 3 b.c. Welsh Saint 126–Bessborough (Mossborough 126) (1979 6f 7fg 6fg 1980 7s 8fg^2 8fg* 10f 10g^4 8d^3 8g^2 8g*) lengthy, good sort; fair performer; won handicap at Redcar in May (odds on) and amateur riders race at Goodwood in September; best form at 1m; acts on a firm and a soft surface; blinkered last 2 starts; sold 9,200 gns Newmarket Autumn Sales. *H. T. Jones.* **80**

CORBIE LYNN 2 b.g. Supreme Sovereign 119–Sarum Lady 97 (Floribunda 136) (1980 7f) Feb 8; 8,300F, 8,800Y; fourth foal; half-brother to 1976 3-y-o 6f winner Monymusk (by Sky Gipsy), subsequently successful abroad; dam a sprinter; unquoted and in need of race when last of 11 to Bustomi in minor event at York in September; gelded at end of season. *J. Etherington.* –

CORDUROY 4 ch.c. Hotfoot 126–Twill 89 (Crocket 130) (1979 8d^4 8s 8.2d* 8v* 9fg* 10.6g 10g 1980 8.2g^4 8fg 10g^2 8d^3 10g^3 10g* 11g* 10d 11s*) rangy colt; won handicaps at Beverley and Hamilton in July (made virtually all both times) and at Hamilton again in September; ran poorly eighth start; stays 11f; acts on any going; needs strong handling. *Sir Mark Prescott.* **66**

CORIACE 6 b.m. Prince Consort 121–Sound Recordo 95 (Sound Track 132) (1979 10g^3 10s^2 12.3f^2 10.2fg 12.2fg 12g 11g* 12.5g 1980 10v^4 11fg^3 12f^3 13f^2 12f^2 12.2fg^2 12g* 12f^4 12g* 11fg^2 10d^4 10d* 12.3d 12d 11fg) middle-distance handicapper; won at Carlisle (twice) in July and at Newcastle in August, winning in good style on last 2 occasions; tailed off 2 of her last 3 races; acts on any going; suitable mount for an apprentice; suited by waiting tactics. *G. Richards.* **78**

CORINNE'S GOLD 2 b.f. Gold Rod 129–Beaute Royal (Duc de Gueldre 129) (1980 5fg 5d 5g 5f) May 1; 210Y; small filly; half-sister to 2 winners in France, including middle-distance winner Proud Mary (by Fast Dip); dam ran twice; little worthwhile form, including in a valuable seller; bred to stay 1¼m. *R. Hoad.* –

CORINTHIAN BLUE 3 b.c. Mummy's Pet 125–Macadamia 87 (Martial 131) (1979 NR 1980 9fg) 9,000Y; big, rangy colt; half-brother to two winners, including useful 1974 2-y-o 5f and 6f winner Dashing Hussar (by Queen's Hussar); dam won over 5f at 2 yrs; in need of run when tailed off in 10-runner newcomers race at Wolverhampton in April. *N. Adam.* –

CORNISH BLUE 2 b.c. Blue Cashmere 129–Donzella 82 (Fidalgo 129) (1980 6g 7fg) May 2; 8,000Y, 900 2-y-o; tall, lengthy colt; half-brother to several winners, including fairly useful middle-distance winners O Mandado and Zellaman (by Mandamus); dam won at 1½m; seventh of 19 to Six Mile Bottom in maiden race at Lingfield in October, second outing and better effort; likely to stay 1¼m. *T. Marshall.* –

CORNISH EXPRESS 2 b.f. Sweet Revenge 129–Luckhurst (Busted 134) (1980 6fg 6fg 6d) Mar 1; 9,000Y; small, lengthy filly; third foal; half-sister to 2 winners by Owen Anthony, notably 3-y-o Stumped, a smart winner at up to 1m; dam unraced daughter of very smart sprinter Lucasland; towards rear in maiden company; moved badly to start third outing. *Mrs R. Lomax.* –

CORNISH GRANITE 2 gr.c. Ragstone 128–Pasty 122 (Raffingora 130) (1980 6g) May 30; small colt; first foal; dam best English 2-y-o filly of 1975; 16/1, dropped right out in final 2f when last of 10 to Shasavaan in Duke of Edinburgh Stakes at Ascot in October. *P. Walwyn.* –

CORNISH LULLABY 2 ch.f. Crooner 119–Long Valley 71 (Ribero 126) (1980 6fg 6d 6g) Apr 29; 1,300F; neat filly; second produce; half-sister to 1979 2-y-o 5f seller winner Lost Valley (by Perdu); dam showed a little ability at 2 yrs; showed a little ability in maiden races in second half of season; will stay 1m+; dwelt first outing, moved badly to post second and looked lean in paddock on third. *F. Durr.* **68**

CORNISHMAN 2 ch.c. Connaught 130–Alley Cat 100 (Alycidon 138) (1980 8.2s 7d) Apr 7; 13,000F, 21,000Y; strong colt; half-brother to numerous winners, including very useful animals Doleswood (by Double Jump) and Ma-Shema (by High Treason); dam won over 6f at 2 yrs; very backward, ran well to finish fifth of 20 behind Irish Heart, beaten 11 lengths, in maiden race at **66**

Haydock in October; had every chance over 2f out in 20-runner minor event at Doncaster later in month but dropped out rapidly and finished out of first 9 behind Soldan; the type to do better when fitter at 3 yrs. *R. Hollinshead.*

CORNISH SCOT 4 gr.c. Rupert Bear 105–Flying in Space (Bleep-Bleep 134) (1979 7d 6fg 1980 8s*) rangy colt; plater; retained 2,500 gns after winning at Leicester in March; stays 1m; acts on soft going; sometimes wears bandages. *M. McCourt.* **48**

CORN STREET 2 ch.c. Decoy Boy 129–Diamond Talk (Counsel 118) (1980 5g 5g 5d⁴ 5d* 7v) Apr 30; workmanlike colt; half-brother to 2 winners, including Pusey Street (by Native Bazaar), successful over 5f in 1979; dam never ran; improved late in season and won 17-runner maiden race at Wolverhampton in October by ½ length from Marmagoa, the pair finishing clear; will probably stay 6f but isn't certain to get further (had stiff task over 7f); acts on a soft surface. *J. Bosley.* **82**

COROMUS 3 br.f. Sit In The Corner–To Rome (Romulus 129) (1979 NR 1980 7fg 8s 8g³ 9s 7f) neat filly; poor plater; possibly stays 1m; sweated up second start; sold 400 gns Doncaster September Sales. *E. Weymes.* –

CORRAL'S BOND (HOL) 4 ch.c. Good Bond 122–Darling Caroline (Ilix) (1979 8.2s 9v 10.2g 9s² 10fg 12g* 10g 10fg* 12fg* 11.1fg⁴ 12.5fg⁴ 1980 10s 13.4f 12fg² 14d³ 11.7s 11.7f 11g² 11f 12.5g* 10.7g*) strong colt; won 2 valuable races at Duindigt in September; placed earlier at Doncaster (ran well when 2 lengths second to Majestic Maharaj), York (weakened final furlong when 5 lengths third behind No Bombs in valuable Troy Handicap) and Ostend; seemed to stay 1¾m; acted well on a firm surface; blinkered occasionally at 2 yrs; reportedly retired to stud in Holland. *N. Guest.* **76**

CORTIAN 5 b.m. Martinmas 128–Barrettstown Belle (Twilight Alley 133) (1979 NR 1980 10.1fg) poor maiden at 3 yrs; well beaten in seller in May. *H. O'Neill.* –

CORVARO (USA) 3 b.c. Vaguely Noble 140–Delmora 124 (Sir Gaylord) (1979 8s² 9d* 10d* 1980 9.7g² 10.5fg 12g² 10s* 10g⁴ 10d) good-looking colt; showed a bit of knee action; first foal; dam very smart performer at up to 1m; put up a very smart performance to win Group 2 Prix Eugene Adam at Saint-Cloud by 5 lengths from Dom D'Albignac in July; ran creditably most other starts, notably when in frame in Prix de Guiche at Longchamp (2 lengths behind Shakapour), Prix du Lys at Chantilly (beaten a neck by Lancastrian) and Joe McGrath Memorial Stakes at Leopardstown (didn't have a clear run when under 2 lengths fourth to Gregorian); well beaten in Champion Stakes at Newmarket on final outing; stayed 1½m; acted on a firm surface but went particularly well on soft ground; has been retired to Ardenode Stud, Co. Kildare. *F. Boutin, France.* **122**

CORVEN 3 b. or br.g. Owen Anthony 102–Cameo 114 (Como 120) (1979 5s³ 5f³ 5f 5fg 5f 6fg 6fg 6f² 6fg 1980 7s 7f 5fg 5g 5g⁴) useful-looking gelding; inconsistent handicapper; stays 6f; acts on firm going; sometimes blinkered. *W. Wightman.* –

CORVILLIA 2 b.f. Forlorn River 124–Irresistable (Siliconn 121) (1980 5s) Mar 24; 4,000Y; first foal; dam twice-raced half-sister to useful 7f and 1m performer Chukaroo; unquoted when behind in 21-runner maiden event won by Manita at Windsor in June. *G. Balding.* –

COSSET 2 br.f. Comedy Star 121–Sue Set 99 (Set Fair 129) (1980 5g 5.8h⁴ 6fg) Mar 16; neat, good-quartered filly; half-sister to useful sprinter Raffia Set (by Raffingora); dam won 5 times at up to 1m; beaten less than 6 lengths in maiden races won by Shalwa at Bath in August and by Von Erlach at Salisbury in September, second and third outings; will stay 1m. *H. Candy.* **56**

COSTAPLENTY 2 ch.f. Ribston 104–Forlorn Leap (Forlorn River 124) (1980 5fg 6g 7g) Mar 27; lengthy filly; third foal; half-sister to sprint winners High Voltage (by Electrify) and Mindblowing (by Pongee); dam never ran; behind in maiden races, including 2 at Catterick; trained first outing by N. Adam. *M. Blanshard.* –

COTTAM ROCKET 4 ro.g. Roan Rocket 128–Delinquent 88 (High Treason 126) (1979 5s³ 7v 5d* 6d⁴ 6s* 6f² 5fg² 6f³ 6d 6d* 6s 6g 5s 1980 5d 5s* 5g 5f 5s 5g² 5g) strong, useful-looking gelding; poor mover; beat Friendly Fun by 2½ lengths in handicap at Newcastle in April; 2 lengths runner-up to Oh Simmie in Gosforth Park Cup on same course in June; stayed 6f; acted on any going but was very well suited by some give in the ground; blinkered twice as a 2-y-o; dead. *M. W. Easterby.* **89**

COUNSEL'S VERDICT 3 b.f. Firestreak 125–Counsel's Opinion 83 (Counsel 118) (1979 NR 1980 6g 8g 7fg 6fg) small, well-made filly; half-sister to several winners, including fairly useful stayer Panco (by Panaslipper); dam effective at 6f to 1m; behind in maiden races and a handicap in the South. *A. Breasley.* –

COUNT CARLOS 4 b.g. Connaught 130–Token Girl 116 (Bolinas Boy) (1979 7s 8d 7.3g 10v 7fg² 8fg⁴ 8fg³ 7g 7fg⁴ 8fg* 1980 8fg 8fg 8fg 10g 8g 10fg⁴) strong, workmanlike gelding; had a disappointing season, best effort on final start when fourth to Galaxy Capricorn in handicap at Brighton in August; probably stays 1¼m; acts on firm going and is not at his best on soft; blinkered seventh and ninth starts in 1979; sold 1,600 gns Newmarket Autumn Sales. *W. Wightman.* –

COUNTESSA ARABELLA 3 b.f. Wolver Hollow 126–Scintillation 55 (Ballyciptic 122) (1979 5f 6g³ 7g* 1980 10.5f 8fg 8g) leggy, rather unfurnished filly; fair (rated 87) at 2 yrs; lightly raced in 1980, finishing last in Musidora Stakes at York in May and 2 handicaps at Ripon in June; should stay 1m+; sold 1,600 gns Newmarket December Sales. *J. Hanson.* –

COUNTESS OLIVIA 2 b.f. Prince Tenderfoot 126–Coralivia (Le Levanstell 122) (1980 6fg³ 7s*) Feb 25; half-sister to 6f and 1½m winner Bold Front (by Daring Display); dam won over 1½m in Ireland, and is half-sister to very smart Ballyhot; favourite and pick of paddock, ran green once in front and got home by only a short head from Minsden's Image in maiden race at Ayr in September; will be suited by middle distances; seems to act on any going. *G. Pritchard-Gordon.* **80**

COUNTESS VIRGINIA 5 ch.m. Virginia Boy 106–La Casita (Ballyciptic 122) (1979 7s 7d⁴ 6g² 8d² 7fg 8g* 7g 6fg² 8f 8fg 8g⁴ 7g³ 7d 1980 7g 8fg⁴ 8fg⁴ 7f 8g* 7g³ 7g² 7d 7fg 7g 8.3fg) leggy mare; good mount for an inexperienced rider and won amateur riders race at Warwick in June; ran moderately last 4 outings; stays 1m; appears to act on any going; blinkered tenth outing; sometimes sweats up. *R. Hannon.* **68**

COUNTESS WALEWSKI 3 b.f. Brigadier Gerard 144–Gingerale (Golden Horus 123) (1979 NR 1980 8g* 8g*) lengthy, lightly-made filly; third foal; sister to moderate 1978 2-y-o Byrrh; dam useful at up to 9.5f in France; winner of both her starts, maiden race at Newbury in July and minor event at Newmarket in August (pushed out when accounting for Lydia Rose by 2 lengths); runs as if she will be suited by 1¼m. *H. Cecil.* **85**

COUNT FERNANDO 3 b.g. Connaught 130–Ankole 85 (Crepello 136) (1979 6fg 7f 1980 8h 10.5f 12g² 12.2d 11g* 10g) smallish, lengthy gelding; stayed on strongly to win handicap at Ayr in July; stays 1½m; possibly unsuited by soft ground; sweated up and gave trouble at start fourth outing; moved very poorly to post and ran badly final start. *J. Hanson.* **77**

COUNT ON ME 4 gr.f. No Mercy 126–Rose Blanche 89 (French Beige 127) (1979 12fg 16fg² 14.7g* 13.8d 12fg 16s 1980 14fg 15f 11.7s 13s) rather lightly-made filly; poor form in 1980, including in a seller; stays well; acts on a firm and a soft surface. *S. Harris.* –

COUNT ROSTOV 2 b.g. Bold Lad (Ire) 133–Royal Sensation 103 (Prince Regent 129) (1980 6d⁴ 6fg 6s⁴ 8.2g 8g) Mar 3; neat, attractive gelding; good mover; second foal; dam stayed 1¼m; fourth in maiden races at Lingfield and Nottingham in the summer, in latter beaten 9¼ lengths by Cavalry Twill after dwelling and having plenty to do at halfway; should stay 1m; hung badly right and looked a difficult ride on fourth outing and wore blinkers when last on fifth; not one to trust; sold to M. Pipe 1,250 gns Newmarket Autumn Sales. *P. Walwyn.* **68 §**

COUNTRY SQUIRE 3 b.g. Galivanter 131–Esquire Maid 86 (Aureole 132) (1979 NR 1980 8fg 10s 8f 8g 6s) small gelding; half-brother to several minor winners here and abroad; dam won at 1¼m; well beaten, including in a seller. *E. Carter.* –

COUNTRY WALK 5 ch.h. Warpath 113–Country Ramble 93 (Kribi 110) (1979 NR 1980 10fg 12g⁴ 12d) has been fired; fairly useful handicapper (rated 96) at up to 1½m in 1978; lightly raced and no form since; acts on any going; invariably sweats up. *Miss S. Hall.* –

COUNT TOLSTOY 3 ch.g. Sir Ivor 135–Vaguely Mine 90 (Silly Season 127) (1979 NR 1980 10f) rangy gelding; third foal; half-brother to 2 winners, –

including fairly useful 1m to 1¼m winner Vaguely (by Bold Lad, Ire); dam, half-sister to St Leger winner Provoke, won at up to 1½m; remote eighth of 11 to Brinkley in valuable maiden race at Ascot in July; will stay 1½m; sold to W. Stubbs 1,300 gns Newmarket Autumn Sales. *R. Hern.*

COUNTY DOWN (USA) 6 br.g. Irish Castle–Bekky's Star (Dark Star) (1979 7f^4 10g^2 1980 8fg 9.6h* 10.6fg^2 10.6fg) ex-French gelding; plater; successful at Folkestone (no bid) in May; stays 10.6f; acts on any going; wears blinkers. *C. James.* **47**

COURAGEOUS BUZBY 4 b.g. Communication 119–Courageous Chic 75 (Cash and Courage 116) (1979 NR 1980 5fg 8g^4 6g^3 8fg 7g 6f 6fg 5d 5d) workmanlike gelding; backed from 100/1 to 25/1 and sweating, ran a remarkable race when very close third to Great Eastern in Hackwood Stakes at Newbury in July; didn't stay trip next time and was well beaten subsequently; best form at 6f with some give in the ground. *B. McMahon.* **–**

COURCHEVEL 2 ch.c. Reliance II 137–Christiana 106 (Double Jump 131) (1980 7g^4 8g) Feb 7; 13,500Y; attractive, robust colt; half-brother to 4 winners, including smart 7f and 1m winner Chalet (by Luthier) and 3-y-o 1¼m winner Cardiff (by Appiani II); dam, half-sister to very smart 1m and 1¼m performer Calpurnius, won over 5f at 2 yrs; prominent until weakened in final furlong and wasn't knocked about when 8½ lengths fourth of 10 to Sunley Builds in Hyperion Stakes at Ascot in October; had every chance 3f out in 17-runner minor event at Newmarket later in month but finished only tenth to Video Tape; will stay middle distances. *B. Hills.* **68**

COURREGES 2 b.f. Manado 130–Silk and Satin 108 (Charlottown 127) (1980 5fg^4 6g^4 5g 5g^2 5f^2 6f^2 6d) Mar 2; lengthy, lightly-made filly; first foal; dam won 4 races from 6f to 1m; second in maiden and minor events, on final occasion going down by 1½ lengths to Flash 'N' Fire in 17-runner race at Redcar in September; will stay 1m; ran moderately final outing and is possibly unsuited by a soft surface. *H. T. Jones.* **75**

COURT CAVALIER 3 ch.g. Simbir 130–Rosenkavalier 89 (Vienna 127) (1979 NR 1980 12f^4) 4,700F, 12,500Y; good-topped gelding; half-brother to fair 1974 2-y-o 7f winner Rofrano (by Wolver Hollow); dam, daughter of Irish 1,000 Guineas winner Northern Gleam, won at 1½m in Ireland; not seen out after showing promise in 9-runner maiden race at Ripon in August; will stay 1¾m. *D. Kent.* **–**

COURTEOUS LADY 3 b. or br.f. Birdbrook 110–Avonteous 60 (Rockavon 120) (1979 5g 5s^3 5f 5f^3 1980 5f 6f) leggy, unfurnished filly; bad plater; has been tried in blinkers. *A. Smith.* **–**

COURTESY WAY (USA) 2 b.g. Angle Light–Ribot Babe (Sir Ribot) (1980 7f 7d) Feb 24; $35,000Y; leggy, fair sort; half-brother to 2 winners, including stakes winner Indigo Star (by Star Envoy); dam, from good family, placed twice from 10 starts; in rear in maiden race and Houghton Stakes, both at Newmarket in October; sent to Singapore. *E. Eldin.* **–**

COURT GREEN 3 b.c. Bold Lad (Ire) 133–Knocknagrena (Worden II 129) (1979 5g 1980 8g 8fg 9f^4 12g 9d 10.2v) neat colt; only plating class; should stay middle distances; blinkered fifth and sixth starts; sold 1,450 gns Ascot November Sales. *I. Walker.* **–**

COURT HOUSE 6 ch.h. My Swanee 122–Windy Rush (Whistling Wind 123) (1979 10.2s 12v 13v 12s* 12s* 14v^3 16fg 12fg 12h^4 12fg 12g 12d 1980 12fg^4 12f 12d 12d 13.8f 12.2g 14fg 12d) poor handicapper; often reluctant to race nowadays and is one to leave alone; stays 1¾m; acts on soft going; sometimes wears blinkers; often ridden in spurs. *J. Harris.* **–**

COURT LEET 5 ch.g. Upper Case–Arbitrate 107 (Arbar 135) (1979 12v 12d^2 12.2g^2 12f 12d 12g 1980 16fg 12g) middle-distance maiden; acts on soft going; has been tried in blinkers. *V. Thompson.* **–**

COURT QUEEN 2 br.f. Hotfoot 126–Virginia Wade 116 (Virginia Boy 106) (1980 5g 5.3d* 5g^2 5f) Mar 28; small filly; first foal; dam won five times over 5f; went from 8/1 to 20/1 before making all to win 11-runner maiden race at Brighton in June by a head from Endless Moment; 5 lengths second of 7 to Olympic Glory in minor event at Salisbury the following month; ran poorly when apprentice ridden fourth outing; speedy and may prove best at 5f. *B. Swift.* **81**

COVENANT 3 ch.f. Good Bond 122–Concession Day 79 (Will Somers 114§) (1979 5s 5f 7fg 7d^4 7s* 8g 6d 1980 8f 8fg 7g 10f^3 10.2g 12d 10d 12.5s^4 12d 10.2v) neat filly; quite moderate (rated 75) at 2 yrs; seems only plating class **–**

nowadays; stays 1½m; acts on any going but goes particularly well on soft; blinkered final start. *Hbt Jones.*

COVENT GARDEN (USA) 2 ch.g. Stage Door Johnny–Rock Garden 86 **84**
(Roan Rocket 128) (1980 8d^3 8d) strong, well-made gelding; excellent mover; half-brother to a winner in Scandinavia; dam 1m winner, and half-sister to very smart Glen Strae; 33/1 and on backward side, ran on strongly to finish just over 2 lengths third of 21 to Obrovac in maiden event at Sandown in October; second favourite for similar race at Leicester the following month but finished only eighth to Rollrights; will stay 1¼m. *J. Tree.*

COVERGIRLS CHOICE 3 b.c. Red Alert 127–Singe (Tudor Music 131) **72**
(1979 NR 1980 5fg 5g^3 6g 5d 6s^3 5v*) 21,000Y; slightly hollow-backed colt; poor mover; second foal; half-brother to 1000 Guineas winner One In A Million (by Rarity); dam unraced half-sister to leading Irish 1968 2-y-o and Irish St Leger second Deep Run; 20/1 when winning handicap at Doncaster in November; stays 6f; revels in the mud; suitable mount for a boy. *N. Callaghan.*

COVER GIRL'S SON 3 b.g. Ragstone 128–Clouded Lamp 99 (Nimbus 130) —
(1979 NR 1980 9d 9.4fg 15.8fg 12.2d) 800F; little worthwhile form in maiden and minor races. *M. W. Easterby.*

COWDENBEATH (USA) 3 b.c. Buffalo Lark–Intervene (Prince John) (1979 **81**
6d 7g^4 1980 10fg 10g^3 12fg^4 12s^4 11d 10.1f^3 12d* 12fg^3 12.2d^2 12g^2) good-bodied, attractive colt; good mover; favourite when comfortably winning 11-runner maiden race at Brighton in September, ran well when blinkered in handicap at Newmarket on final start; stays 1½m; probably acts on any going; sold to R. Hollinshead 7,400 gns Doncaster November Sales. *R. Price.*

COWHILL 3 b.f. Habat 127–Mecca II 90 (Exbury 138) (1979 6g* 5g^2 6f^4 **94**
6g^2 7.2g^3 1980 6s 7f^3 7fg 6f 6d* 6fg^4 7.6g^3 7d^3 6g*) strong, compact filly; fairly useful handicapper; won at Carlisle and Hamilton in the summer; stays 7f; probably acts on any going; has run creditably for an apprentice; consistent. *B. Hanbury.*

CRACAVAL 4 ch.c. Mount Hagen 127–Priddy Maid 111 (Acropolis 132) (1979 **119**
11.7g^2 12.3d* 12g 11.1f* 14.6f 1980 9f^3 12fg^3 10fg^3 10g 12f^2 10.5d^3 12g 10g 10d) very smart performer; good mover; blinkered first time, put up an excellent effort when 1½ lengths third to Master Willie and Cairn Rouge in Benson and Hedges Gold Cup at York in August on sixth start, racing with leaders from start and keeping on well in closing stages; ran a long way below his York form when blinkered again in Grosser Preis Von Baden at Baden-Baden (eighth of 10 behind Nebos) and in Joe McGrath Memorial Stakes at Leopardstown (ninth of 11 behind Gregorian) in September, but wasn't entirely disgraced when sixth to Cairn Rouge in Champion Stakes at Newmarket in October (didn't wear blinkers); third 3 times earlier, to Ela-Mana-Mou in Earl of Sefton Stakes and to More Light in Jockey Club Stakes, both at Newmarket, and to Sea Chimes in Clive Graham Stakes at Kempton; also placed at Lingfield, finishing 2 lengths second to Masked Marvel; stays 1½m; probably acts on any going; not entirely reliable nowadays. *B. Hills.*

CRACKAWAY 2 b.c. Auction Ring 123–Milonia (Tambourine II 133) (1980 **78**
6g 6g 7fg^2 8fg^2 8.2s) Mar 21; 240F, 4,100Y; strong, well-made colt; half-brother to 4 winners, including very useful 1975 2-y-o 5f to 1m winner Allez Allostock (by Welsh Saint) and quite useful 1978 staying 2-y-o Sterlonia (by Sterling Bay); dam ran once; nearest at finish when second in maiden races at Warwick in August (½ length behind Oklahoma Star) and Beverley in September (beaten 3 lengths by Gifford); will probably stay 1¼m; gave trouble at start and ran moderately on fifth outing (possibly unsuited by soft going). *W. Wharton.*

CRACKERJILL 3 b.f. Sparkler 130–Token Girl 116 (Bolinas Boy) (1979 —
6fg 1980 7h^4 5g 6g 6fg) leggy, lightly-made filly; poor maiden; will stay 1m; yet to race on a soft surface. *W. Wightman.*

CRACKING FORM 3 b.c. H bitat 134–Miss Petard 113 (Petingo 135) (1979 **109**
NR 1980 8fg* 9fg* 10d 8g^2 8g* 7g^3) 154,000Y; big, strong, rangy colt; second living foal; half-brother to very useful middle-distance stayer Meistersinger (by Rheingold); dam, very useful at 2 yrs and 3 yrs, won at up to 1¼m; useful performer; won maiden race at Kempton, 3-runner event at Lingfield and ladies race at Ascot; never seriously challenged when beating Bias 3 lengths in last-named in July; also ran well when length second to Tahitian King in £3,100 race

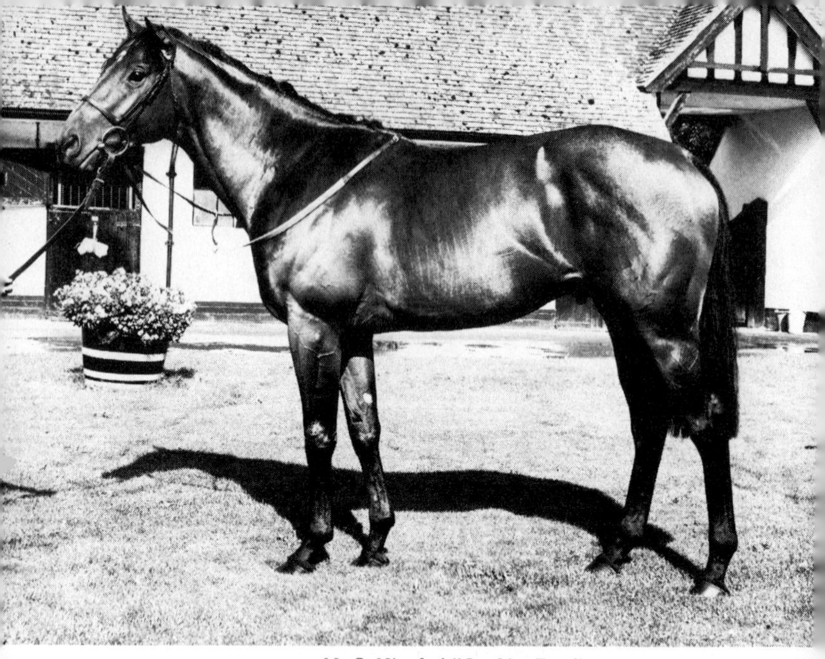

Mr S. Niarchos' "Cracking Form"

at York; finds 7f too sharp and should stay 1¼m (had stiff task when tried at trip); acts on a firm surface. *P. Walwyn.*

CRACKLING LAD 2 ch.g. Tarboosh–Xmas Cracker 66 (Roan Rocket 128) (1980 6fg 8d 8d) Apr 3; 2,000F, 2,800Y; resold 4,400Y; compact gelding; fourth produce; dam stayed 7f; in rear in maiden races and looks of no account; has worn blinkers; sold to Susan Piggott BA 900 gns Newmarket Autumn Sales. *J. Hudson.* —

CRACKLING ROSIE 3 ch.f. Smokey Rockett 107–Silicola (Pinicola 113) (1979 5d 1980 7g 8g 6g 6fg 7fg) strong, short-legged filly; of little account. *H. Collingridge.* —

CRAGADOR 3 b.c. Hoist the Flag–Croda Rossa (Grey Sovereign 128 §) (1979 5fg* 6g³ 1980 8.2fg⁴ 8d 7fg) very attractive colt; excellent mover; far from disgraced when 7¾ lengths fourth of 13 to Greenwood Star in Cecil Frail Handicap at Haydock in May; ran better subsequent race when blinkered and nearly 5 lengths fifth of 7 to Kampala in Beeswing Stakes at Newcastle in July on final outing; will stay 1¼m. *H. Wragg.* **107**

CRAIGOUR 2 br.c. Mill Reef 141–Sudden Glory 98 (Luthier 126) (1980 6g 7fg³ 7.2d* 8fg) Feb 7; 1,050,000 francs Y (approx £111,000); small, attractive colt; good mover; first foal; dam won over 6.5f and 1m in France; won 19-runner maiden race at Haydock in September going away by 1½ lengths from Buzzards Bay; 33/1, beaten early in straight and was eased afterwards when seventh of 8 to Robellino in Royal Lodge Stakes at Ascot later in month; will stay at least 1¼m. *P. Walwyn.* **96+**

CRAZYFOOT 3 b.f. Luthier 126–Great Guns 109 (Busted 134) (1979 NR 1980 10fg 11.7fg² 12.2fg² 14g³) useful sort; first foal; dam prolific winner from 1¼m to 2m; quite a moderate maiden; should stay 1¾m; yet to race on a soft surface though her action suggests one will suit her; sweated up and didn't impress in paddock final start. *P. Walwyn.* **76**

CRAZY HORSE 8 b.g. Jukebox 120–French Doll (Worden II 129) (1979 6fg 8fg 8.2g 1980 8g 10d 10g 10g 8.2d) poor plater; best at up to 1m; acts on any going; usually wears blinkers and a hood. *J. Mulhall.* —

CREAMY 2 ch.c. Double-U-Jay 120–Pot de Creme 68 (Candy Spots) (1980 5g* 5h³ 6g 5f 7f* 6d³ 6g² 8d) Apr 28; 1,000Y; lengthy colt; fourth foal; half-brother to Apace, a winner over 5.9f in Ireland at 2 yrs; dam stayed well; bought in 1,850 gns after winning seller at Beverley in April by 5 lengths and acquitted himself well in better company subsequently, beating El Strad 1½ lengths in £2,600 nursery at Thirsk in August; will stay 1¼m; seems to act on any going; badly hampered final outing. *Hbt Jones.* **74**

CREATIVE STAR 2 b.g. Wishing Star 117–Rag Flowers (Tarqogan 125) (1980 5f 5f 6g 8g⁴ 8d) Apr 21; 4,100Y; big gelding; poor walker; half-brother to 2 winners in Ireland, including 1976 2-y-o 7.5f winner Flower Grange (by Allangrange); quite moderate form in varied races, including seller; will stay middle distances. *J. Fitzgerald.* **62**

CREDIT CENTRE 3 gr.g. Tudor Music 131–Whispering Breeze (Caliban 123) (1979 8.2g 1980 10s³ 12.3f* 12f³ 12.5fg² 13s³ 12g²) strong gelding; good walker; won small race at Newcastle in April; creditable second in handicaps at Stockton and Carlisle subsequently; probably stays 13f; acts on any going; gives impression he will be suited by waiting tactics. *M. Jarvis.* **91**

CREE BREEZE 2 b. or br.c. Persian Breeze 121–Kalyanda 77 (Kalydon 122) (1980 5d 7d 5d) Mar 15; half-brother to 3-y-o Fine Point (by Sharpen Up), successful at up to 9f; dam 2-y-o 5f winner; last in £3,100 event and maiden races in Scotland. *W. H. H. Williams.* —

CREEPIN SUZIE 2 ch.f. Red Alert 127–Perceptive (Ballyciptic 122) (1980 5f³ 6f 5fg⁴ 5g² 5g 5g 5g) May 2; 2,700Y; second foal; half-sister to 1¾m winner Fra Mau (by Wolver Hollow); dam unplaced 5 times in Ireland; in frame in maiden races and a nursery, in latter going down by a length to Heart 'N' Soul at Leopardstown in July, but finished last of 14 in a maiden event at Tralee in September on sixth outing and in rear in maiden race at Folkestone in October on seventh; trained by R. McCormick in Ireland first 6 starts. *T. Gosling.* **79** d

CREESHA 3 ch.f. Mansingh 120–Cereum 84 (Tudor Grey 119) (1979 5f 6s 5d 1980 5f⁴ 6f 7g 6g 7f) small, light-framed filly; bad plater; sold 310 gns Doncaster October Sales. *C. Gray.* —

CREE SONG 4 b.c. Song 132–Gentle Gael 97 (Celtic Ash) (1979 5d² 6g² 6g* 6s* 5g* 6s⁴ 5g² 1980 5fg⁴ 5f³ 6fg³ 5g* 6fg 5d³ 5g 5.6g 6s 6d 5v) strong, sprint type; poor mover in his slower paces; reportedly broke a bone in his knee at 2 yrs; won handicap under 10-0 at Ayr in July a shade cleverly by a length from Firbeck, running on well to lead in final furlong after being off bridle from start in a strongly-run race; blinkered on 3 of his subsequent starts, putting up easily best effort on first occasion when fifth to Sharpo in William Hill Sprint Championship at York; stays 6f; acts on firm going but is particularly well suited by some give in the ground; dwelt at York; apparently not the most genuine of horses these days. *W. H. H. Williams.* **99**

CREME DE LA CREME 2 gr.f. Saritamer 130–Dairy Queen 76 (Queen's Hussar 124) (1980 5fg 5g³) Jan 31; well-made filly; third living foal; half-sister to 2 winners by Birdbrook, including 3-y-o Parlour Game, a very useful winner at up to 8.5f; dam placed from 6f to 13.8f; bit backward when soundly beaten in minor event at Folkestone and 4-runner maiden race at Epsom in April. *R. Smyth.* —

CRESTA RIDER (USA) 2 br.c. Northern Dancer–Thoroly Blue (Blue Prince 123) (1980 6d* 7g* 8d⁴) **124** p

That wonderful stallion Northern Dancer sired not only the champion English and Irish two-year-old Storm Bird in 1980 but also one of the very best French juveniles, Cresta Rider. Although Storm Bird had undoubtedly the better form in their first season, the strong, powerful, good-bodied Cresta Rider is the more imposing individual and there may well be much less between the pair at three.

Cresta Rider's first season consisted of only three races, of which he won the first two impressively. After making all to land the odds by a length and a half in a newcomers race at Deauville's August meeting, he started at 5/2 on when opposed by four useful previous winners in the Criterium de Maisons-Laffitte, a Group 2 event which his stable had won with Viteric and Crowned Music in the previous two seasons. Although Cresta Rider won by a length and a half from Diamond Prospect it wasn't so much what he achieved but how he achieved it that was so impressive; after settling at the back of the field for a long way he produced a turn of foot which cut down the rest in a matter of strides and wasn't pressed to win.

The Grand Criterium at Longchamp in October nearly always represents the best two-year-old form in France, so much so that since 1967, when the Irish-trained winner Sir Ivor was omitted from the handicap, only Satingo of the Grand Criterium winners has failed to head the French Free Handicap. However in 1980 all four of the season's previous two-year-old Group 1 winners, Irish Playboy, Ancient Regime, Miswaki and Tropicaro, were missing from the field. Left to dispute favouritism were Cresta Rider and the impressive Prix des Chenes winner Dunphy. Although neither was successful both ran well, with Cresta Rider putting up a bold show before finishing fourth. He could soon be seen travelling extremely well as his pacemaker Gilgit led into the straight and then made smooth progress to take the lead off Great Substence inside the final quarter mile. Hardly had he done so than the foreign challengers Recitation and Critique swept past on the outside, but he kept on well and it was only on the line that he lost third place by a short head to the strong-finishing Dunphy. Recitation beat him by little more than a length. Both Cresta Rider's trainer and jockey subsequently passed the opinion that he had been ill-at-ease on the ground and had consequently tended to become unbalanced. While in our opinion there is no evidence to suggest that Cresta Rider isn't effective on a soft surface he strikes us as the type who will be very well suited by top-of-the-ground conditions.

Cresta Rider (USA) (br.c. Feb 4, 1978)	Northern Dancer (b 1961)	Nearctic (br 1954)	Nearco
			Lady Angela
		Natalma (b 1957)	Native Dancer
			Almahmoud
	Thoroly Blue (b 1967)	Blue Prince (b 1951)	Princequillo
			Blue Denim
		Ambwithor (b 1954)	Ambiorix
			With Honor

Impressive-looking sons of Northern Dancer are highly sought-after commodities and Cresta Rider cost 475,000 dollars as a yearling. He's the second winner bred by Thoroly Blue, following the TV Lark filly Mitzi who won only a small race as a four-year-old. Thoroly Blue, one of the best American three-year-old fillies of 1970, gained both her stakes victories on turf, taking the eight-and-half-furlong Princess Stakes and a division of the nine-furlong Del Mar Oaks. She is one of ten winners bred by the unraced Ambwithor and she's a sister to another good grass performer, the very useful Blue Thor whose fifteen wins included a stakes success over nine and a half furlongs. Both Thoroly Blue and Blue Thor stayed fairly well by American standards, no doubt deriving a degree of stamina from their sire, the Gold Cup runner-up Blue Prince, and middle distances will suit Cresta Rider. He impressed us so much as an individual at Longchamp that we are sure he'll improve a good deal. A very interesting prospect! *F. Boutin, France.*

CRESTED CRANE 2 b.c. Royal Palace 131–Bird in the Hand 82 (Major Portion 129) (1980 7d 7d) Mar 20; 10,500Y; tall, lengthy colt; half-brother to 2 winners, including fairly useful stayer and hurdler Taffy (by Prince de Galles); dam won over 7f; behind in maiden races at Newmarket and Newbury in the summer; sold 640 gns Ascot September Sales. *H. Candy.* —

CRESTED GREBE 5 b.g. Blakeney 126–Palmavista 120 (Royal Palm 131) (1979 12s* 12d 11.7fg* 1980 10s) well-made gelding; useful handicapper in 1979 when trained by B. Hobbs; blinkered and very backward when last on only outing of 1980 (April). *D. Gandolfo.* —

CRESTED LARK 4 ch.c. Crowned Prince 128–Bird of Dawning (Sea-Bird II 145) (1979 8fg^4 7d^2 1980 8fg 8g 10.1f 10g^3 8g 10g 12g* 11d) big, rangy ex-Irish colt; made all and held off Big Pal by ¾ length in handicap at Folkestone in October; ran moderately only subsequent start; suited by middle distances. *M. Smyly.* 63

CRESTED WREN 3 ch.f. Major Portion 129–Pinwave 82 (Pinza 137) (1979 6f 7g 7fg 7fg 8h^2 7g^4 8g 1980 8f^2 10.2fg 10fg 10fg^2 10s 8g^2 9g^4) quite a moderate maiden; stays 1¼m; acts on firm going and is possibly unsuited by soft; sold 2,600 gns Doncaster November Sales. *Miss S. Hall.* 70

CRESWELL 5 b.m. Green God 128–Royal Solitude (Royal Challenger 129) (1979 8g 12.2g 16f 1980 12d) of little account; blinkered last two outings at 3 yrs. *P. Wigham.* —

Criterium de Maisons-Laffitte—the handsome Cresta Rider beats Diamond Prospect and Shoen

CREVER 5 b.h. Crepello 136–Forever 68 (Never Say Die 137) (1979 NR 1980 8fg^4 7f 6fg 7g 7fg^4) well-made horse; plater nowadays; bred to stay middle distances; occasionally blinkered. *G. Beeson.* —

CREWS HILL 4 b.g. High Top 131–Patosky 94 (Skymaster 126) (1979 7d 6g 7fg 1980 7v 5g^4 5f* 5fg* 5f* 5f* 5g 5g 5g 5f^2 6g 5.6g 5g^3) big, strong, good-topped gelding; not a good mover in his slower paces; much improved and put up excellent performances when winning David Dixon Sprint Trophy (Handicap) at York from Susarma and Northern Sprint Handicap at Redcar from King's Offering, both in May; had earlier been successful in handicaps at Carlisle and Doncaster, beating Sayyaf on latter course; also ran well when second to Dafydd at Epsom in August and when third to Ferryman at Ascot in October; best form at 5f, but has won over 6f and is bred to stay 1m; acts well on firm going; suitable mount for an apprentice; wore a boot on near-hind last 3 starts. *F. Durr.* **105**

Furniture Factors Sprint Handicap, Doncaster—apprentice-ridden Crews Hill beats Sayyaf

CRICKETERS CLUB 3 gr.c. Touch Paper 113–Mairi's Love (His Highness) – (1979 5g^4 5fg 6fg 5.1f^4 5.3fg 6s 1980 5fg 7f 6g 6g 5g 5g) small colt; poor maiden; sold 525 gns Ascot November Sales. *D. Weeden.*

CRIMSON ADVOCATE 2 ch.f. Red God 128§–The Wig 81 (Counsel 118) **75** (1980 6g 7g*) Feb 17; 35,000Y; neat filly: sister to fairly useful 1972 2-y-o 5f and 6f winner Reddish, and half-sister to several winners; dam, winner at 1¼m and 11f, is half-sister to high-class 6f to 1m performer Joshua; landed the odds by only a neck from Star Heading in maiden race at Ayr in July; will stay at least 1m. *J. Hindley.*

CRIMSON FLASH (USA) 2 ch.c. Crimson Streak–Anthesis (Big Game) – (1980 7fg 7g 8d 8fg) small, stocky colt; brother to a minor winner and half-brother to another; dam never ran; soundly beaten in maiden races; blinkered third and fourth starts. *S. Norton.*

CRIMSON HEATHER 2 gr.f. Red Alert 127–Georgie Girl 96 (Crocket 130) **103** (1980 5f^4 5f^2 5f 5g* 5g* 5d* 6g 5g) Jan 16; smallish, full-quartered filly; good walker; half-sister to 1977 2-y-o 6f winner Durcott House (by Gold Rod) and successful Italian horse Win the Wind (by Windjammer); dam best at 5f; gained narrow wins in minor events at Phoenix Park and Leopardstown prior to winning Group 3 Curragh Stakes in July; disputed lead throughout and stayed on well when beating Brooklyn Prince a length in last-named; put up better effort in this country when 6½ lengths fifth of 6 to Marwell in Flying Childers Stakes at Doncaster in September, coming to have a chance at distance only to weaken; best at 5f; suited by some give in the ground; unseated rider at start third outing. *L. Browne, Ireland.*

CRIMSON SATIN 4 ch.f. Porto Bello 118–La Muleta (Matador 131) (1979 – 6s 5g 8g^3 8fg 7fg 8g 6d^3 7d 1980 8.2fg 7fg 5g 6s 8g 8g 8g 8.2s 8d 10d) unfurnished filly; plater; stays 1m; sometimes blinkered. *R. Mason.*

CRIMSON SILK 6 ch.g. Counsel 118–La Muleta (Matador 131) (1979 6s **72** 6d 6s 6fg 6f 6g 6g^4 6d 6s^4 6s 7.2g 6g 1980 6d 6fg 6f 6fg 6fg 6d^4 6fg 8d 6d 6g 5.6g 6d 7d 6s 7d) sprint handicapper; fourth of 18 behind Hurworth House in valuable Home Ales Gold Tankard Handicap at Nottingham in June, best effort; appears to act on any going; used to wear blinkers. *R. Mason.*

CRINGLEFORD 3 b.c. Sterling Bay–Paludamentum (Royal Palm 131) (1979 **70** 7s 1980 7f 7.6f^4 8g 8g* 8d 7d) workmanlike colt; 20/1 when showing improved form to win 10-runner maiden event at Yarmouth in September; stays 1m; possibly needs some give in the ground; moved poorly to post third start; ran badly final outing. *D. Weeden.*

CRISPIN 3 b.c. Welsh Pageant 132–Syrona 113 (Salvo 129) (1979 7g 8g **90** 7d^3 1980 12f 11fg 12d^4 12s^2 13g 12g* 12.3d^2 11.7g*(dis) 12g^2 14.7f^2 16g* 14s^3) attractive colt; comfortably won maiden race at Redcar in August and accounted for Dawn Johnny by 2 lengths in handicap at Ascot in October; also first past post in minor event at Windsor but was disqualified for interfering with runner-up; stays well; acts on any going; ran respectably for a lady rider on ninth start but has sometimes tended to hang under pressure. *J. Dunlop.*

CRISPY LOBSTER 3 b.f. Crisp and Even 116–Lobster Pot 64 (Silver Shark – 129) (1979 NR 1980 10.1s) first foal; dam, poor handicapper, stayed 1½m; unquoted when behind in minor event won by Ballytop at Windsor in June. *K. Ivory.*

CRISTINA TIMES 2 b. or br.f. Will Somers 114§–Reina Cristina 84 (Tamerlane **50** 128) (1980 5f 5fg 5g 5fg 7g 7fg^4 7f^2 7fg 7g^4 6g 8.2d 7f 8.2s) May 19; 1,700Y; lightly-made filly; poor plater; stays 7f; acts on firm going; wears blinkers nowadays; sold 310 gns Doncaster November Sales. *W. Stubbs.*

CRITICAL TIMES 3 br.g. Abwah 118–Miss Pink (Marshal Pil 108) (1979 5d – 5g 1980 7fg 8fg) fair sort; well beaten in maiden races and a handicap. *W. Stephenson.*

CRITIQUE (USA) 2 br.c. Roberto 131–Cambrienne 95 (Sicambre 135) (1980 **126** 6s 8g* 8d^2)

For the superstitious who believe everything happens in threes, Critique is one to back for the Derby. As only the third runner from the O'Brien stable in

Oldbawn Maiden Plate, Leopardstown—Critique strides clear for a ten-length win

the top French two-year-old race, the Grand Criterium, Critique followed in the footsteps of Sir Ivor, winner of the race in 1967 and successful in the following year's Derby, and Roberto, only fourth at odds on in the 1971 Criterium but also winner of the Derby. Critique also deserves consideration as a potential Derby winner on rational grounds: he's trained by the man with the best modern record in the Derby, he's bred well enough to win any race, and, most relevantly, his form at two years placed him well up among the best of his age.

Both Sir Ivor and Roberto went to France with a more obvious chance than did Critique. Whereas they were impressive winners of the National Stakes, one of Ireland's most competitive two-year-old races, Critique had taken part in only two maiden races, putting up strikingly disparate performances. At 50/1 on his debut at the Curragh in August he'd run on to finish seventh, beaten six and a half lengths by the winner Ascending Star and about four lengths by his odds-on stable-mate Sailor King. At 5/4 at Leopardstown five weeks later he had slammed his fifteen opponents, storming away in the last one and a half furlongs to win by ten lengths. Both the second and third in the latter race had already shown ability—Harveysfield had been beaten only a short head by the fairly useful Miltown Eagle on his last appearance and Silver Creek, beaten over twelve lengths by Critique, had finished just eight lengths behind Storm Bird when third in the National Stakes three weeks earlier—and those behind were to make the form look increasingly good as the season wore on. Erins Isle, the fourth home, went down by only a short head to Bandwagon, another O'Brien colt, soon afterwards; the sixth, Tellurano, ran the highly-regarded

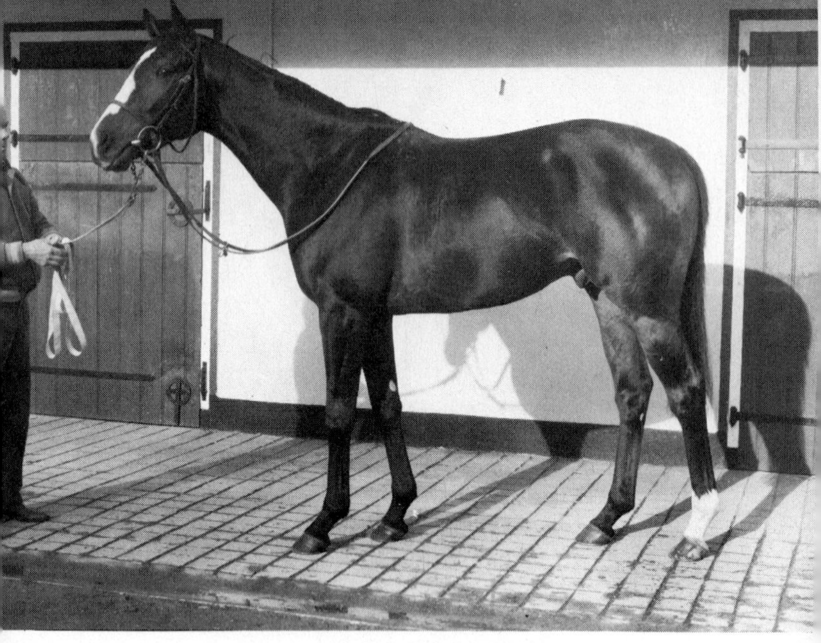

Mr J. A. Mulcahy's "Critique"

Kings Lake close at Naas; and Goldspun, Cimon and Gamble Hall, respectively fifth, seventh and eighth, each won their next race by a clear-cut margin.

If there was no doubting the merit of Critique's victory there was some doubt about his temperament. The fact that he wore blinkers wasn't in itself worrying, but it was alongside his actions in cutting sharply in front of Silver Creek as he took the lead and ducking sharply towards the stable entrance as he was being pulled up, hitting the rails and breaking his jockey Tommy Murphy's ankle. But when the blinkers were left off at Longchamp he comported himself in exemplary fashion. Eddery held him up in seventh-of-eleven position in the early stages, as Cresta Rider's pacemaker made the running. As the pacemaker weakened early in the straight, Critique and several others started to make their challenges with Pink Prism, Great Substence and Cresta Rider in turn taking the lead narrowly. Critique himself, only inches in front of the English colt Recitation, took over with a furlong to race but despite running on most gamely under Piggott-style driving from Eddery he failed by a short head to hold off Recitation.

Critique (USA) (br.c. Apr 3, 1978)	Roberto (b 1969)	Hail to Reason (br 1958)	Turn-to
			Nothirdchance
		Bramalea (b 1959)	Nashua
			Rarelea
	Cambrienne (br 1969)	Sicambre (br 1948)	Prince Bio
			Sif
		Torbella III (br 1955)	Tornado
			Djebellica

Critique, a neat colt, is a product of a mating between two former inmates of his stable. Whereas his sire Roberto was brilliant on his day, his dam Cambrienne had a disappointing racecourse career; she gained her solitary success in a small seven-furlong race at two years, ran only four times in all and recouped a mere £824 towards her large purchase price. Cambrienne's sale as a yearling provides a striking example of how bloodstock prices have soared over the last ten years. When sent up by the Haras d'Etreham to the 1970 Houghton Sales she fetched a new British and European record of 65,000 guineas, a far cry from the 625,000 guineas the same stud received for Ghadeer at the corresponding sale in 1979 and from the 530,000 guineas paid for its Green Dancer colt Dilligham in 1980.

Until Critique's emergence, Cambrienne's record at stud was as disappointing as her racecourse career. Although mated to some of the best stallions in the world she had produced only a winner in Holland Brehon Law (by Nijinsky), a winner of a maiden plate at Gowran Park, Cambretta (by Roberto), and a winner in Malaysia, Cambrensis (by Forli). As is to be expected with a record-priced yearling, Cambrienne comes from a top-class family. Her grandam Djebellica won the Irish Oaks and, as well as producing the French Two Thousand Guineas winner Cambremont, became the dam of two excellent broodmares in Djebel Idra, the dam of the Arc winner Bon Mot III, and Cambrienne's dam Torbella III. Torbella, who finished second in the Irish Oaks the year after winning the Dewhurst Stakes, is also the dam of Sussex Stakes winner Carlemont and the very smart French mile- and mile-and-a-quarter performer Avaray. This is also the family of the Grand Prix de Paris winner Tennyson and the top French two-year-old filly of 1979, Princesse Lida. *V. O'Brien, Ireland.*

CROAGH PATRICK 4 b.g. Connaught 130–Rustling Waters 72 (Ballymoss 136) (1979 12s 11.7d 10fg 14f^{2} 11.7fg^{2} 16g* 18.1g^{3} 12d 1980 16f^{2}) robust, good sort; fairly useful handicapper; ran well when 3 lengths second to Shaab at Lingfield in May; stayed well; appeared to act on any going; dead. *T. Waugh.* **89**

CROCKFORD LAD 3 b.c. Klairon 131–War Lass 100 (Whistler 129) (1979 5fg^{2} 6fg* 6d 1980 7fg^{2} 8fg 8fg^{3} 7g^{4} 8fg* 8fg^{4} 8fg 8.2d 8s) quite attractive, well-made colt; good mover; quite a useful handicapper; heavily-backed favourite when scoring at Yarmouth in August (hung left in last 2f); stays 1m; goes well on top-of-the-ground and isn't at his best on soft; sold 8,000 gns Newmarket Autumn Sales. *H. T. Jones.* **90**

CROCKFORDS GREEN 2 gr.f. Roan Rocket 128–Consister 89 (Burglar 128) (1980 5fg 5fg^{3} 6fg 5g^{4} 5g^{4} 6g^{2} 6d^{4} 6g 6fg^{4} 7f) May 26; lengthy filly; first foal; dam, fair 5f performer at 2 yrs, is half-sister to 2 very useful 2-y-o's; quite moderate form in varied company; stays 6f but isn't sure to stay 7f; wears blinkers. *J. Etherington.* **73**

CROFTER (USA) 3 ch.c. Habitat 134–Marie Curie 96 (Exbury 138) (1979 NR 1980 8fg* 7g* 8d* 7v^{2} 8d^{2}) **124**

For most of the year Crofter's light lay hidden under a bushel, and it wasn't until his last two outings that he showed the form of which he is capable. Unraced as a two-year-old, he made his debut in a twelve-runner maiden event at the Curragh in May, starting at odds on and winning by six lengths. Crofter was odds on for his next two starts as well and justified the confidence by three quarters of a length each time, accounting for Night Nurse's half-sister Frisky Matron in a £1,400 race at the Curragh in June and beating Kizzy rather cleverly in the Youghal Stakes at Phoenix Park in October.

Crofter was a lightly-raced colt who could be expected to improve, but even so he looked to have only a modest chance of extending his winning sequence in the Prix de la Foret at Longchamp later in October. The field was a strong one, very much stronger than any he'd met before, with Moorestyle and Luck Of The Draw from England and Kilijaro, Safita, Ya Zaman and the Prix Marcel Boussac winner Tropicaro heading the French challenge. Crofter, starting at 14/1, ran a very fine race and improved considerably on his previous form. Well behind in the early stages as Moorestyle set the pace, he began to make progress in the straight and ran on well under hard riding in the final furlong to take second place, only a length behind Moorestyle, who was all out at the end, and half a length ahead of the top-class filly Kilijaro.

The heavy ground on which the Prix de la Foret was run suited Crofter very well; when he returned to France for the Prix Perth at Saint-Cloud in November the going was on the soft side but nothing like so testing. The race conditions presented Crofter with an excellent chance of winning his first pattern event. A warm order in the market, he ran creditably without coming up to his Longchamp form, failing by three quarters of a length to peg back Hilal from whom he was receiving 3 lb more than weight-for-age.

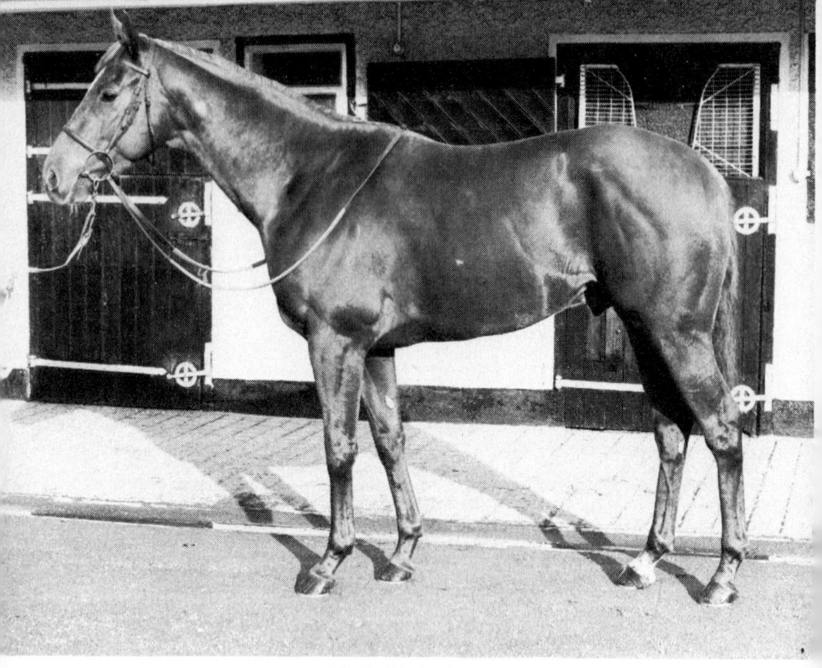

Mr D. McCarthy's "Crofter"

Crofter (USA) (ch.c. 1977)	Habitat (b 1966)	Sir Gaylord (b 1959)	Turn-to
			Somethingroyal
		Little Hut (b 1952)	Occupy
			Savage Beauty
	Marie Curie (ch 1970)	Exbury (ch 1959)	Le Haar
			Greensward
		Ela Marita (ch 1961)	Red God
			Fantan II

Though foaled in America Crofter was bred in Europe. He is the third foal of Marie Curie, the other two being the French mile- to mile-and-a-quarter winner Cooperation (by Be Friendly) and a successful English plater by Nonoalco. Marie Curie ran twice as a two-year-old in Ireland, winning a six-furlong race at the Curragh and finishing third in the Beresford Stakes over a mile. She is a half-sister to numerous winners, most notably the very smart, genuine and consistent Mariel, who won the Pretty Polly Stakes at the Curragh, finished in the frame in three classics and went on to produce Sarah Siddons, successful in the Irish One Thousand Guineas and the Yorkshire Oaks. Ela Marita, bought for a song as a yearling for 500 guineas, won the Fred Darling Stakes and Musidora Stakes from only four starts. The best of Fantan II's six winners was Ragusa; two of the others, Ribot's Fantasy and Hilo Girl, have respectively produced better than average performers at stud in Bold Fantasy, who showed smart form from six furlongs to a mile, and Princess Ivor, a stakes winner in America. Since foaling Crofter, Marie Curie has had colts by Vaguely Noble and Secretariat. The latter sold for 92,000 guineas at the 1980 Houghton Sales whereas Crofter fetched 20,000 guineas at the same venue two years earlier. Considering his pedigree, Crofter was bought very cheaply—his price was nearly

40,000 guineas below the average for Habitat's yearlings in 1978. A neat colt who stayed a mile and acted particularly well on heavy going, he has been retired to the Castle Hyde Stud, Co Cork, at a fee of Ir 4,000 guineas, no foal no fee. *V. O'Brien, Ireland.*

CROFTHALL 3 ch.c. Native Bazaar 122–Woodland Promise 76 (Philemon 119) (1979 5fg 1980 6d* 7fg* 7.2g^{4} 7f^{2} 7g^{3} 6s 7d^{4} 7fg* 7g^{4} 7g^{4} 7.2d) compact colt; well backed when winning sellers at Haydock in April and Doncaster (sold out of P. Cole's stable 4,600 gns) in May; showed himself better than a plater subsequently, and won handicap at Redcar in July; suited by 7f; acts well on firm ground; suitable mount for a boy; genuine. *A. Balding.* **71**

CROGHAN HILL 5 b.h. Lord Gayle 124–Good Report (Golden Cloud) (1979 9v^{2} 12v* 12v* 13fg* 13d 11.5d^{2} 1980 9v 10v*(dis) 10g^{2} 16fg^{2} 13g^{3} 22.2fg^{3} 12s 12d^{2}) Irish horse; very useful performer; put up an excellent performance to win Rank Cup at Phoenix Park in March by $\frac{3}{4}$ length from Icelandic; subsequently disqualified after failing a routine dope test; good second to Noelino in Sean Graham Ballymoss Stakes at the Curragh the following month and to Ardross in Saval Beg Stakes at Leopardstown in May; also second in Trigo Stakes at Leopardstown in October, beaten 3 lengths by Keshcorran; effective at around $1\frac{1}{4}$m and stays 2m (didn't get trip when remote third to Balinger in $2\frac{3}{4}$m Queen Alexandra Stakes at Royal Ascot); acts on any going; genuine and consistent. *D. Weld, Ireland.* **105**

CROQUE MONSIEUR (FR) 6 b.h. Sheshoon 132–Manush (Tanerko 134) (1979 14s^{2} 15.5s 16.5g 18g^{2} 20g^{2} 13.5d^{3} 18g* 15.5fg 20fg^{2} 15.5s 1980 15.5g 15.5g 20fg^{4} 20g 13.5s^{4} 18s 20d) big horse; out-and-out stayer; fourth in Prix du Cadran at Longchamp in May and handicap at Deauville (top weight) in August, putting up better effort in former event when 8 lengths behind Shafaraz; disputed lead until weakening 6f out and came back tailed off behind Le Moss in Gold Cup at Royal Ascot on fourth start; appears to act on any going; has been tried in blinkers. *E. Bartholomew, France.* **111**

CROSBY TRIANGLE 2 b.f. Windjammer (USA)–Cool Mistress 59 (Skymaster 126) (1980 5s 5g* 5f* 5s* 5f^{3} 6g* 5fg) May 19; 800F, 1,050Y; strong, compact filly; sister to a winner in Italy and half-sister to 1975 Irish 2-y-o 5f winner Simoon (by Prevailing); dam poor maiden; comfortable winner of sellers at Windsor and Ripon in August, costing 2,800 gns and 5,000 gns respectively to buy in; followed up with wins in nurseries at Ayr (apprentice race) and Nottingham (by $\frac{1}{2}$ length from Cliff Bank) the following month; made all when gaining 3 of her victories; stays 6f; acts on any going; genuine and consistent. *P. Haslam.* **72**

CROUTON 4 ch.g. Cornuto 111–Golden Stork 93 (Golden Cloud) (1979 9v^{4} 8d 8s* 9s* 10f 12g^{4} 12g 12g^{4} 11s^{3} 1980 12g^{4} 12fg) strong gelding; won twice in 1979; not seen out until August in 1980 and was weak in market both starts; stays $1\frac{1}{2}$m; acts on any going. *R. Price.* –

CROWDOWN 2 ch.c. Morston 125–Barlassina (Taine 131) (1980 8g 7g 8d) May 5; 6,600F, 8,000Y; big, rangy colt; third foal; half-brother to 1m and 11f winner Massena (by Our Mirage); dam won at 2 yrs and 3 yrs in Italy; beaten $8\frac{1}{2}$ lengths when fifth of 14 to Sha'lan in maiden race at Leicester in November, third outing; will stay $1\frac{1}{2}$m. *D. Sasse.* **68**

CROWEBRASS 2 ch.f. Crowned Prince 128–Sapientia (Prudent II 133) (1980 5fg 5fg 8d) Apr 26; 3,600F; leggy filly; half-sister to Tende (by Dike), a winner at up to $1\frac{1}{2}$m in France; dam won at up to $1\frac{1}{4}$m and comes from Great Nephew's family; in rear in maiden races; missed break first outing, unseated rider and bolted on second and was off course 4 months before third. *R. Hollinshead.* –

CROWEBRONZE 2 ch.f. Huntercombe 133–Frances Louise 88 (Saint Crespin III 132) (1980 5d 5f 5f) Mar 2; 3,700F; compact filly; sixth produce; dam won over 6f and $1\frac{1}{4}$m; ran best race on third outing when 6 lengths sixth of 16 to Sweet Spark in maiden event at Wolverhampton in August; will stay 1m. *R. Hollinshead.* **54**

CROWNING KHALID 3 b.c. No Mercy 126–Vanity (Vimy 132) (1979 NR 1980 6f^{4} 8g 6f) 6,600F, 9,600Y; quite attractive, rangy colt; brother to Irish 1977 2-y-o 7f winner No Risk and 3 winners in Belgium; dam never ran; seems only plating class; best run at 6f on firm going. *M. Haynes.* –

CROWNING MOMENT 5 br.g. Royalty 130–Moment Supreme 102 (Supreme Court 135) (1979 11.1d 12fg 11d 10g* 12fg^{4} 10fg 12.2g* 10d^{2} 12d 1980 12.3s^{3} 12fg^{3} 11.7f^{4} 11.1fg^{2} 10s 12.2s 12g 10fg 10g* 10g^{4} 12d) won handicap at Goodwood in September, starting at 20/1 and running on strongly under pressure **69**

to win by ½ length from Wearmouth; stays 1½m; seems to act on any going; suitable mount for an apprentice; fell seventh outing. *J. Bethell.*

CROWN JULES 2 gr.f. Abwah 118–Charville 73 (Town Crier 119) (1980 6g 7g 6g) Apr 12; first foal; neat filly; dam won 7 times from 1m to 1½m; behind in maiden races and a seller. *P. Cundell.* –

CROWN PAGEANT 4 b.g. Welsh Pageant 132–High Rise (Ballymoss 136) (1979 8d 8.5d 8g 8.5s³ 8fg 10.2fg 8h 7fg 8fg 1980 16f² 16fg³) plating-class maiden; placed in amateur riders races at Lingfield and Newbury in September; stays 2m; seems to act on any going; blinkered sixth start at 3 yrs. *P. Cundell.* 53

CROWN WITNESS 4 b.f. Crowned Prince 128–Melodramatic 112 (Tudor Melody 129) (1979 8d² 8.2g* 8.2g* 8d* 1980 8d 8fg 8d* 8g* 8.3s² 8d 8f* 8s² 7s³ 8g) useful sort; had another successful year and was gaining her third win when holding off Bias all out by a short head after making all in Ripon Rowels Handicap in August (ridden by 5-lb claimer); had earlier won at Newcastle (again made all in Dobson Peacock Handicap) and Sandown; placed in valuable handicaps won by Geoffrey's Sister and Peek-A-Boo at Ayr in September; stays 1m; acts on any going; genuine and consistent, although ran moderately final start. *W. Hastings-Bass.* 95

CRUEL PASSION 4 b.f. Some Hand 119–Artway 82 (Articulate 121) (1979 7fg 5fg 5fg 5f 5g 5g 5s 1980 10g 8g) bad maiden; has worn blinkers. *P. Feilden.* –

CRUISE MISSILE 4 b.c. Bend A Bow–Polaris Missile (Woodcut 114) (1979 11.7g 12f 1980 16.1s) good sort; well beaten in maiden races and an amateur riders event but is a useful performer over hurdles; needed race only outing of 1980 (October). *N. Henderson.* –

CRUSADER'S DREAM 3 b.f. St Paddy 133–Ragirl (Ragusa 137) (1979 6fg* 7g 1980 7f 7f 10f) well-made, quite attractive filly; fair (rated 88) at 2 yrs; didn't find her form in handicaps in 1980; should be suited by middle distances; sweated up second start; highly-strung; didn't keep a straight course either start in 1979; usually ridden by Eileen McGuffie. *M. Stoute.* –

CRUSTY PIE 2 b.f. Wishing Star 117–Cap A Pie 69 (High Hat 131) (1980 7fg 7.2d 8f 10d 8g) Apr 23; 600Y; neat filly; first living foal; dam 15f winner; plater; bred to stay well; blinkered final start; sold 340 gns Ascot November Sales. *I. Walker.* –

CRY NO MORE 7 b.h. Weepers Boy 124–Balfour Lass 81 (My Smokey 125) (1979 6v⁴ 6d* 7s 7.2s 6g 7.6s 7f 8f 8g 1980 6d 6fg 6g 6g 7d 6g) hollow-backed horse; fairly useful performer at his best but was mainly disappointing in 1980 (not seen out in second half of season); best at up to 7f; acts on any going but has done all his winning on an easy surface; sometimes wears blinkers. *J. Douglas-Home.* 69

CRYSTAL FOUNTAIN 3 b.f. Great Nephew 126–Crystal Palace 121 (Solar Slipper 131) (1979 NR 1980 8g) quite attractive filly; half-sister to several winners, notably Royal Palace (by Ballymoss), Prince Consort (by Right Royal V) and Selhurst (by Charlottesville); dam smart at 7f to 1¼m; backward, didn't stride out at all well to post when eighth of 14 finishers to Logan in maiden race at Sandown in July; not seen out again. *H. Cecil.* –

CRYSTAL GAEL 2 b.f. Sparkler 130–Gentle Gael 97 (Celtic Ash) (1980 6s 6g 7g 7g 8fg*) Mar 12; quite attractive filly; half-sister to useful sprinter Cree Song (by Song) and winners in Belgium and Italy; dam, sister to high-class Italian colt Hoche, won from 5f to 1m; improved with distance and ran on strongly to win 13-runner maiden race at Beverley in September by a length from Narnia's Princess; likely to stay 1¼m; acts on a firm surface. *J. Dunlop.* 79

'C' TOP 3 b.f. Swing Easy 126–Comotose 75 (Como 120) (1979 5d 5g 6f 5fg⁴ 6g 1980 8d* 8f³ 9f 12fg 8d* 10g* 8g 10g* 9s³ 10fg³ 11s³) leggy, lightly-made filly; plater; successful at Doncaster in March (no bid), Carlisle (bought in 1,660 gns) and Beverley (bought in 1,500 gns) in June and Redcar in August (no bid); seems to stay 11f; suited by some give in the ground; sweated up fourth start; doesn't always impress in paddock; tends to get behind early on. *P. Rohan.* 58

CUDGEL 7 br.g. The Brianstan 128–Pelta (Border Chief 101) (1979 7s⁴ 6s³ 7.6d⁴ 8.2g 7f² 8f 8fg 7g³ 7.6f⁴ 6h² 6f* 7fg² 6g² 1980 5d 5g² 6g⁴ 6f² 7.2fg 6d 6g 6fg* 6fg 7f 6f* 7g*) fairly useful handicapper, who retains his form well; goes well at Redcar and won narrowly there in July (from Moybrook) and September (from Primula Boy); beat Star Flare by ¾ length at York in October; stays 1m 96 but has done all his winning at shorter distances; acts on any going; ideal mount for an inexperienced rider. *P. Rohan.*

CUMNOCK SCOUSE 7 bl.g. Bluerullah 115–Sweet Morning Breeze (Vic Day 126) (1979 7fg 7f* 7g 7fg 7g4 7d2 7f 7.6f3 6d* 7fg 6d 7g3 6d2 7g 7g 1980 7f 7.6f 7.2fg 7f) modest handicapper; finished lame final start (May); gives impression he finds 6f on sharp side nowadays and stays 7f; acts on any going; suitable mount for an apprentice; genuine. *G. Richards.* **67**

CUMULUS 2 br.c. Relko 136–Nuageuse (Prince Regent 129) (1980 6f 7g2 7s 5g4 6fg2 6g2 6g) Mar 23; 6,600Y; strong, good-topped colt; second foal; dam won 4 times over 5f at 3 yrs in Ireland; second in minor event at Yarmouth in July and nurseries at Windsor and Lingfield in September; apprentice ridden when beaten a neck by Cleat and ¾ length by Salamina in nurseries; stays 7f and may get further at 3 yrs; seemed unsuited by soft ground on third start. *H.T. Jones.* **79**

CUNARD 5 gr.h. Crooner 119–Emerald Flag 77 (St Paddy 133) (1979 12g3 12s2 12f2 12f 12h* 10f3 10f 1980 10fg3) lengthy horse; very useful middle-distance performer; creditable third of 8 to Ringgit in Sandown Cup Handicap in April, only outing of 1980; acts on any going but is best suited by top-of-the-ground conditions. *B. Hobbs.* **99**

CURALE 3 ch.g. Le Johnstan 123–Last Sensation (Compensation 127) (1979 5s 5f 5f 6h 5fg 5g 1980 5fg 5s) hollow-backed gelding; looks and runs like a poor animal; has worn blinkers. *R. Ward.* –

CURLEEN 2 bl.f. Mansingh 120–Top Of The Tree 66 (Lorenzaccio 130) (1980 5g 5g) Mar 21; very small filly; first foal; dam daughter of smart filly Top of the Milk; 11 lengths sixth of 12 to Lady Lorelei in maiden race at Kempton in July, second outing. *J. Winter.* –

CURLEW CLIPPER 3 ch.f. Lombard 126–Darksome (Goldhill 125) (1979 5s* 5d 6f 1980 8f 8fg 6fg) lengthy filly; quite moderate (rated 77) at 2 yrs; in rear in Northern handicaps in 1980; best run at 5f on soft going; dead. *M. H. Easterby.* –

CURLY BIRD 6 gr.m. Quayside 124–Risky Miss 51 (Pinturischio 116) (1979 NR 1980 10.1g 16fg) tall, rangy mare; of no account over hurdles; behind in minor event at Windsor and amateur riders race at Ascot (last of 25 finishers) in September. *J. Scallan.* –

CURRENT CHARGE (USA) 3 b.c. Little Current–Midway Island (Turn-to) (1979 7s4 1980 6f 7g* 8f 12s 7g) $170,000Y; strong, well-made colt; half-brother to 3 winners, including very useful American performer Very Special Lady (by Buckpasser); dam unraced half-sister to Prix de l'Arc de Triomphe winner San San; 33/1, showed much improved form to win 9-runner Group 3 Tetrarch Stakes at the Curragh in April by ½ length from Cobblers Cove; well beaten afterwards in Airlie/Coolmore Irish 2000 Guineas and Irish Sweeps Derby (last of 13 behind Tyrnavos) at the Curragh and City Of York Stakes won by Sunfield in August; should be suited by middle distances. *C. Grassick Ireland.* **103** d

CURTSEY 2 b.f. Royal and Regal–Time To Be Careful (Olden Times) (1980 7g) Mar 29; useful-looking filly; half-sister to 1m winner Ivan Ivanovic (by Boldnesian); dam, daughter of half-sister to Sir Ivor, won small 6f race; unquoted and in need of race when last of 17 behind Golden Bowl in maiden event at Salisbury in August; has scope and should do better over further in 1981. *W. Wightman.* –

CURZON HOUSE 3 ch.f. Green God 128–Laburnum Grove 70 (Pall Mall 132) (1979 5f 5s 5fg3 5f4 1980 6fg4 6fg 8s 5g 6fg 5f 5d) short-coupled filly; sprint handicapper; stays 6f; acts on a firm and a soft surface; blinkered nowadays; sold 540 gns Newmarket Autumn Sales. *H. T. Jones.* –

CUT ABOVE 2 b.c. High Top 131–Cutle 86 (Saint Crespin III 132) (1980 7g3 7.3d2) **119**

Which are the odd two out among the following leading three-year-olds trained by Dick Hern in the period 1970-1980: Highest Hopes, Brigadier Gerard, Royalty, Homeric, Sallust, Sun Prince, Boldboy, Buoy, Sharp Edge, Bustino, Highclere, Sea Anchor, Smuggler, Relkino, Dunfermline, Homing, Cistus, Troy, Niniski, Henbit, Prince Bee, Water Mill, Bireme and Shoot A Line? The possible solutions are many, one of the most significant being Sallust and Sun Prince who were the only ones in that impressive list to run as many as five races as two-year-olds. Hern has won several of the big races for two-year-olds but his training methods are geared largely to producing top second- and third-season horses.

He showed his customary patience with his two-year-olds in 1980 and while there was no outstanding winner among them, several showed plenty of promise.

Cut Above was one of the most promising of the two-year-olds and he looks sure to make the grade at three. He had the misfortune to come up against Kalaglow on both his appearances in his first season. In the Viewsport Stakes at Sandown in August he put up an encouraging display, taking third place behind Kalaglow and Grundy's brother Centurius after racing in the front rank throughout. Carson wasn't at all hard on him here but he spared nothing when Cut Above ran in the Group 3 Horris Hill Stakes at Newbury nearly two months later. After turning into the straight in third place behind Noalto and Chief Speaker, Cut Above made steady progress to hit the front about a furlong and a half out. Although joined soon afterwards by Kalaglow he held grimly on to his lead for a while, showing great determination under strenuous driving; only close home was he outgunned. Cut Above, receiving 5 lb from the three-quarter-length winner, proved markedly superior to the eight other runners, seven of them good-class winners.

Cut Above (b.c. Apr 19, 1978)	High Top (br 1969)	Derring-Do (br 1961)	Darius
			Sipsey Bridge
		Camenae (b 1961)	Vimy
			Madrilene
	Cutle (ch 1963)	Saint Crespin III (ch 1956)	Aureole
			Neocracy
		Cutter (b 1955)	Donatello II
			Felucca

Cut Above is a half-brother to one of the animals mentioned earlier, the Irish Two Thousand Guineas and Prix Jean Prat winner Sharp Edge (by Silver Shark). Sharp Edge stayed a mile and a quarter as did another half-brother, the useful So Blessed colt So Sharp, and Cut Above will stay at least that distance. Their dam Cutle won at up to thirteen furlongs and is a daughter of the Park Hill Stakes and Yorkshire Cup winner Cutter. The family is a consistent source of high-class winners with Buoy, Sea Anchor and Bireme among the most recent, and it looks likely to provide plenty more for the stable which houses other excellent prospects in Baffin, Boathouse and Capstan, who, together with Cut Above, share Felucca as their great-grandam. *R. Hern.*

CUTLER HEIGHTS 3 ch.f. Galivanter 131–Lucky Deal 93 (Floribunda 136) **48**
(1979 5s 5d 5fg 5f 5fg 6f 6f 6s^4 5d 5d 1980 6d 6f 8f^3 8f^3 8.2fg 8fg^3 9g 10g^4 12d* 13.8g* 12g 11s) sturdy filly; plater; won at Pontefract (bought in 1,250 gns) and Catterick (no bid) in August; stays 1¾m; probably acts on any going; sometimes sweats up; ridden by 5-lb claimer when successful; ran badly final start. *J. Doyle.*

CUT THE RIBBON 3 gr.f. Sharp Edge 123–Rosy Ribbon 83 (Donore 119) —
(1979 5s 6g 1980 8fg 8f 8fg) narrow filly; well beaten in varied company. *G. Balding.*

CUT THROAT 2 br.c. Sharpen Up 127–Zantedeschia 91 (Zimone) (1980 **118**
5f^2 5fg* 5fg* 5g* 6d 6fg* 6f^2 6fg*)

For a two-year-old who didn't even gain a place in a pattern race let alone win one, Cut Throat collected the very worthwhile sum of £19,851 in prize money. He was one of the toughest and most genuine youngsters seen out in 1980 and a smart one too judged on his performance in the Sirenia Stakes at Kempton in September. Unfortunately he hadn't been entered in any of the big autumn races and his season ended just as he was hitting peak form.

Cut Throat came to Kempton the winner of four races, including the Salisbury Stakes, the Berkshire Stakes at Newbury and the New Ham Stakes at Goodwood. However, his limitations seemed to have been exposed in both the Coventry Stakes at Royal Ascot, in which he'd finished only tenth of thirteen, and in the Champion Two Yrs Old Trophy at Ripon, where he'd been completely outpointed by Noalto, and he started at 10/1 at Kempton behind the Cherry Hinton winner Nasseem and the Queen Mary winner Pushy. As the two fillies disputed the lead with Appaloosa, Cut Throat was tucked in a couple of lengths behind. Appaloosa was done with soon after halfway but anyone who thought it a two-horse race was in for a shock; Cut Throat loomed alongside the pair coming to the final furlong and stayed on the best to win by a length and a half from Pushy. Some discount the value of Cut Throat's performance on the grounds that the fillies had exhausted each other in their struggle for the lead but we don't. Sweet Monday, beaten five and a half lengths into fourth place, won the Mill Reef Stakes from Mattaboy next time out and Arndean, beaten a further four lengths, showed fairly useful form both before and after.

Cut Throat (br.c. Apr 5, 1978)	Sharpen Up (ch 1969)	Atan (ch 1961)	Native Dancer
			Mixed Marriage
		Rocchetta (ch 1961)	Rockefella
			Chambiges
	Zantedeschia (br 1963)	Zimone (br 1953)	Persian Gulf
			Lady Mary Rose
		Propitious (b 1956)	Propitiation
			Marsh Marigold

Cut Throat's display at Kempton was typical of him. Although he has an excellent, flowing action, he frequently takes a little time to find his full stride and he usually does all his best work in the closing stages. His connections tried him in blinkers in the Coventry Stakes, no doubt to sharpen him up, but they didn't seem to suit him and he ran his only poor race of the season. Perhaps the softish ground at Royal Ascot was a contributory factor to his modest display; certainly all his form is on fast going and he moves like a top-of-the-ground performer.

Good though Cut Throat's form was as a two-year-old, it still leaves him some way below classic standard. Neither his appearance—he's only neat—nor his pedigree suggests he'll make more than normal improvement, and his future is probably at the mercy of the handicapper. Each of the dams on the bottom line of Cut Throat's pedigree, Zantedeschia, Propitious and Marsh Marigold, won at least three times but none of them has met with much success at stud. Zantedeschia's two previous winners were the modest middle-distance winner Ortolano (by Lauso) and the fair 1977 two-year-old six-furlong winner Hemlock Cup (by Sweet Revenge). Zantedeschia was a fairly useful miler and Cut Throat will be well suited by seven furlongs and a mile at three years. He deserves to win more races. *H. Candy.*

Captain M.M.C. Clark's "Cut Throat"

CUTTING COMMENT 5 b.g. Sharpen Up 127–Mrs Hauksbee 102 (Pindari 124) (1979 10.2s 10s4 12d 12.2s 1980 10g 7.6g 8.2g 11g2 11g4 12fg 15.8d) disappointing and ungenuine handicapper; stays 11f; probably acts on any going; usually wears blinkers (didn't last 4 starts however). *M. James.* — §

CWM RHONDDA 4 ch.f. Celtic Cone 116–Golden Vase (Montaval 129) (1979 NR 1980 11.7f 16fg4 16fg) second foal; dam fair chaser; novice hurdler; 50/1 when 7 lengths fourth behind Mountain Man in amateur riders race at Newbury in September, only second outing on flat. *R. Akehurst.* —

CWMYREITHIN 4 b.f. Roxy–Whitney (Venture VII 129) (1979 12fg 1980 9.4g 16.9d 11.7f4 14.6fg* 16fg3 15.8d 16g* 17.1d 18s) staying handicapper; apprentice ridden when winning at Doncaster in July (maiden race) and Nottingham in September, beating Tholt E Will by 4 lengths on latter course; acts on firm going; pulled up (saddle slipped) second outing. *M. Tate.* 63

CYBRANDIAN 2 b.g. Prince Regent 129–Lavenham Rose 85 (Floribunda 136) (1980 6g 7g 8.2s) Mar 24; 10,500Y; big gelding; half-brother to 2 winners, including 9f winner Summer Sheets (by Levmoss); dam won at 1m; showed a modicum of ability in maiden races; will stay 1¼m; gelded after third outing. *M. H. Easterby.* 71

CYCLADIC 5 gr.g. Polacca 117–Pink Inn (Lavandin 128) (1979 8v 8s 8g 8fg 5h 1980 8g) poor plater; blinkered in 1979. *S. Wiles.* —

CYCLONIC 2 ch.c. Tumble Wind–Misacriolla (Runnymede 123) (1980 5s2 5d* 5g3 5fg4 7g 6fg 8.2d 6f4 6s4) Apr 5; 3,500F, 4,500Y; workmanlike, narrow colt; half-brother to fair 1978 2-y-o Silver Bazaar (by Lord Gayle), a winner over 5.3f; dam won over 9f in France; went down by 4 lengths to Scarlet Town in maiden race at Haydock in April but was awarded race; subsequently descended to sellers, running respectably when fourth in big fields over 6f at Newmarket and Haydock in October; stays 7f but seems not to get 1m; acts on any going. *T. Marshall.* 71

CYMBAL 3 b.f. Ribero 126–Zither 72 (Vienna 127) (1979 NR 1980 12fg 10.6d* 12g* 10f* 10.1fg2) lightly-made, quite attractive filly; closely related to smart middle-distance winner Zimbalon (by Ragusa), and half-sister to 3 winners; dam won at 1¼m; in good form in August, winning maiden race at Haydock and minor events at Leicester and Chepstow, starting favourite each time; will stay beyond 1½m; probably acts on any going. *R. Hern.* 80

CYPO (FR) 6 ch.g. Presto–Cypris (Devon III 125) (1979 10.5v 9v 8d4 8g3 8g 9.2fg 8g 8g 8g 10d 10fg 8d* 10d 9.7s2 12v2 1980 8v* 8s* 12fg 22.2fg 10fg 8g 8g) plain ex-French gelding; brother to winning stayer Cisto, also successful over jumps; won handicaps at Saint-Cloud early in season when trained by A. Bates; well beaten over here, but had stiff tasks; effective at 1m and stays 1½m; acts on any going; wears blinkers. *A. Jarvis.* —

CYPRUS SKY 3 ch.c. Redundant 120–Palestra 92 (Palestine 133) (1979 6g4 6fg3 6fg3 7g* 7g* 7fg3 7.6f2 8s 1980 7v2 7f 12f 10f4 12fg 8g3 8g3 8.5fg 8g2 8g4 10d) tall, close-coupled colt; runner-up in Salisbury 2,000 Guineas Trial in March (2 lengths behind Poyle Crusher) and 5-runner gentleman riders event at Goodwood in September; best at up to 1m; acts on any going; ran moderately tenth start. *F. Durr.* 97

CYPRUS SUN 3 b.c. My Swallow 134–Shirwani 77 (Major Portion 129) (1979 5s3 5s 6g 8f 8.2fg 8d 1980 10fg 12fg 14fg 12g 12g3 12fg4 14fg 14fg4 12fg2) fair sort; plating-class maiden; stays 1½m; blinkered third start; sold 2,700 gns Newmarket Autumn Sales. *F. Durr.* 62

CZERNIN 3 b.g. Forli–Nonsensical 99 (Silly Season 127) (1979 5s 6g 7.2fg 7f 1980 9f 7h2 7.2g 7g 9s 7fg 8g) narrow, quite attractive gelding; has shown ability but is none too consistent and was well beaten in sellers on last 3 starts; should stay at least 9f; suited by top-of-the-ground; blinkered fourth outing; sold 3,600 gns Doncaster September Sales. *C. Brittain.* —

D

DAFYDD 4 b.c. Welsh Saint 126–Fire Bell 93 (Firestreak 125) (1979 7s 6v 5d 5.3fg 5h 6fg4 6g* 5f 5.8f 5fg 1980 5f* 5fg4 5d3 5fg* 5fg4 5d 5f* 5g 5d) small colt; good walker and mover; has been hobdayed and has had a soft palate operation; sprint handicapper; put up a good performance when beating Crews Hill by 2 lengths at Epsom in August; successful earlier at Wolverhampton 81 (made all) and Ripon; acts on an easy surface, but is best suited by a sound one; good mount for an apprentice. *S. Norton.*

DAGGERS DRAWN 4 gr.g. Sharp Edge 123–Admonish 101 (Palestine 133) (1979 NR 1980 10.1g 12g) big gelding; half-brother to several winners, notably high-class Remand (by Alcide); dam stayed 1½m; tailed off in minor event won by Purple Flag at Windsor in June and £3,000 event won by Broomstick Corner at Lingfield in September; sold 1,100 gns Doncaster October Sales. *J. Douglas-Home.* —

DAIKOKU 3 ch.c. Double Jump 131–Come On Girl (Sheshoon 132) (1979 5d² 5d* 5g² 6d² 6f* 6fg³ 7s 6f 1980 7fg 6fg 8fg 7s² 6g 7g 8f) strong, sprint type; excellent mover; quite moderate; stays 7f; acts on any going; blinkered fourth and fifth starts; sold 1,600 gns Newmarket Autumn Sales. *M. Jarvis.* **67**

DAI'S BOY 2 b.g. Jimmy Reppin 131–Pinochle 61 (Matador 131) (1980 5d 7s) May 9; half-brother to useful sprint handicapper Pericet (by Atan); dam ran only at 2 yrs; unquoted when behind in maiden race at Wolverhampton and minor event at Chepstow in the autumn. *M. Bradley.* —

DALBY LODGE 2 b.g. Workboy 123–Dutch May 109 (Maystreak 118) (1980 5f⁴ 5g 5f 6fg) Mar 24; light-framed gelding; useless plater. *M. W. Easterby.* —

DALEGARTH 2 ch.g. Laser Light 118–Inkflash (Hul a Hul 124) (1980 5d² 5s 5g* 5f⁴ 5g³ 5g 5s 5.1g³ 5fg 5g³ 5.1fg² 5g* 5f⁴ 5fg) Apr 8; 3,000Y; compact, sturdy gelding; good mover; third foal; half-brother to 1979 2-y-o winner Rox (by Wishing Star); dam ran twice in Ireland; used to be a difficult ride but did nothing wrong in latter half of season and showed improved form, putting up a fairly useful effort when making all to win 13-runner nursery at Windsor in September; had earlier won 4-runner maiden race at Epsom; very speedy and unlikely to stay beyond 5f; possibly not at his best on very soft ground; blinkered ninth outing; goes well for apprentice R. Cochrane; consistent, and thrived physically despite his busy season. *K. Ivory.* **95**

DALESIDE HEATHER 3 ch.f. St Alphage 119–French Oyster (Gulf Pearl 117) (1979 5g 5g 5d 5fg 5fg 1980 5f 6g 5g 5g) leggy filly; poor form, including in sellers; blinkered final outing at 2 yrs. *T. Fairhurst.* —

DALSAAN 3 b.c. Habitat 134–Dumka 117 (Kashmir II 125) (1979 6f² 6g* 1980 7fg* 8d⁴) attractive, well-made colt; second foal; half-brother to French 4-y-o Dayzaan (by Riverman), successful at 1m and 10.5f; dam won French 1,000 Guineas; only lightly raced but has shown himself a very smart performer; landed odds very impressively in 6-runner £3,200 race at Kempton in May, leading on bridle over 2f out and sprinting away without being asked a serious question to beat Beldale Gunflint 20 lengths despite being eased inside last furlong; again odds on, led soon after entering straight but was quickly headed and weakened in last furlong to finish 3¾ lengths fourth to Posse in St James's Palace Stakes at Royal Ascot; not seen out again; stays 1m; acts well on fast ground; bandaged near-hind second start at 2 yrs; should win more races as a 4-y-o. *M. Stoute.* **122**

DAME SUE 4 b.f. Mandamus 120–Catherine Rose 59 (Floribunda 136) (1979 NR 1980 8f³ 10fg⁴ 8g⁴ 10d 8fg³ 8g³ 12f³ 12s² 12.5s) strong filly; modest maiden; stays 1½m; acts on any going; sweating fourth start (took strong hold); not particularly genuine and wore blinkers final start. *S. Mellor.* **54**

DAMPIER (ITY) 3 b.c. Prince Regent 129–Dorothy Sil (Silnet 131) (1979 NR 1980 11d 10.1f 12s⁴) strong, good sort; half-brother to several winners in Italy, including prolific Dominator (by Pall Mall); dam won 5 races in Italy and finished third in Oaks d'Italia; showed some ability in maiden race at Newbury in July, first start and best effort; should stay 1½m+; sold 4,200 gns Newmarket Autumn Sales. *L. Cumani.* —

DAN-AIR 3 ch.c. Ridan–Masandra 100 (Whistling Wind 123) (1979 5s 5g 6g⁴ 5f 5s³ 1980 8fg⁴ 8.2g 6d 6d 6s² 6s 5g) compact colt; plater; possibly stays 1m; acts on soft going; has worn blinkers. *W. H. H. Williams.* **44**

DANALCO (FR) 2 b.c. Nonoalco 131–Dancing Lass (King Emperor) (1980 7f 8d 10.2s) lengthy, good sort; dam won in Italy at 3 yrs; well behind in end-of-season maiden and minor events. *R. Armstrong.* —

DANCE BID (USA) 2 b.c. Northern Dancer–Highest Trump 112 (Bold Bidder) (1980 7g 7d*) reportedly syndicated for $600,000 as a foal; first produce; dam won Queen Mary Stakes and stayed 1m; had several subsequent winners behind when winning 19-runner maiden race at the Curragh in September by 1½ lengths **94** p

Mr J. B. Crook's "Dance Bid"

from newcomer Euclid; had previously finished 12 lengths seventh of 10 to Storm Bird when 33/1 for National Stakes on same course; will stay 1¼m; the type to make a very useful 3-y-o. *D. Weld, Ireland.*

DANCE LITTLE LADY 3 b.f. Moulton 128–Socialite 96 (Sica Boy 132) (1979 59
NR 1980 8s^4 7.2d^4 12d 10.4d^4 9.4fg 10.6d^3 10.2d) lengthy filly; half-sister to 3 minor winners here and abroad; dam won twice over 5f at 2 yrs; in frame in maiden races in the North; should stay 1½m (looked hard trained when tried at trip); suited by some give in the ground; blinkered fifth outing; sweated up final appearance; sold out of W. Hastings-Bass's stable 5,000 gns Newmarket July Sales after second start. *J. Fitzgerald.*

DANCIN' 2 b.f. Hotfoot 126–Miss Mandy 92 (Mandamus 120) (1980 6s 7g 8fg —
9d) April 15; 7,000Y; big, strong, good sort; half-sister to 2 winners, including useful 1974 2-y-o Le Chat (by Burglar); dam stayed 1¼m; little worthwhile form in maiden and minor events; blinkered fourth outing; sold 1,700 gns Doncaster November Sales. *P. Walwyn.*

DANCING BEAR 2 gr.f. Rupert Bear 105–Midnight Dance (Doudance 99) —
(1980 6f 5.1g^3) Apr 30; very small, light-framed filly; blinkered when 8 lengths third of 4 behind Silver Samantha in seller at Yarmouth in July; sold 380 gns Ascot October Sales. *D. Dale.*

DANCING KATE 5 ch.m. Jukebox 120–Epee (Cranach) (1979 10s 8g^4 8g 58
1980 12.5v 9g 9fg 8fg 12f^2 8fg 10g 14.6fg^2 10.6d^2 12f^4 12d 12s 12d) plating-class maiden; second at Wolverhampton (handicap), Doncaster and Haydock; stays well; acts on firm going and an easy surface; used to wear blinkers; suitable mount for an apprentice. *A. Arnold.*

DANCING MELBA 3 b.f. Gay Fandango 132–La Melba 99 (Chanteur II 135) —
(1979 5g 5f 5fg 1980 6fg 7.6f) behind in varied company. *D. Whelan.*

DANCING SALLY 2 ch.f. Sallust 134–Dance All Night 106 (Double-U-Jay 120) 84
(1980 6g* 6g 7.3d) Mar 12; quite attractive filly; second foal; half-sister to

3-y-o 9.4f winner Sporting Covergirl (by Luthier); dam won from 5f to 9f; ridden out only with hands and heels to win 19-runner newcomers race at Goodwood in September by ¾ length from Perlesse, the pair clear; 5½ lengths fifth of 11 to Boathouse in £5,000 event over 7.3f at Newbury in October, easily better subsequent effort; will stay 1m. *J. Dunlop.*

DANCING SHADOW 3 b.f. Dancer's Image–Sunny Valley (Val de Loir 133) (1979 7.3s3 1980 8f* 10.5g 8s 10fg3 10g3 10fg*) lengthy, quite attractive filly; first foal; dam won at up to 1½m in France; very useful filly who won £3,500 race at Sandown in May and 7-runner Sean Graham Fillies Stakes at Kempton in September; ran on gamely to beat Karamita (gave 3 lb) by a neck in latter; far from disgraced when third to Vielle in Nassau Stakes at Goodwood and to Little Bonny in Virginia Stakes at Newcastle in August; well beaten in Prix de Diane de Revlon at Chantilly and Child Stakes at Newmarket on her other starts; stays 1¼m; best form on a firm surface; genuine. *R. Hern.* **117**

DANCING SPRING 2 b.g. Carnival Dancer 113–Cathro (Appiani II 128) (1980 8.2d 6s) Mar 21; third foal; dam bad plater; well behind in 19-runner seller at Haydock in September (dwelt) and 22-runner maiden race at Doncaster the following month. *R. E. Peacock.* **—**

DANEHURST 3 b.c. Crowned Prince 128–Angel Falls (Sir Gaylord) (1979 6fg 7fg 8g 1980 7f 8g 8g 8d) compact colt; no sign of ability, including in a seller; sold 280 gns Ascot November Sales. *R. Akehurst.* **—**

DANE NIGHT 4 b.f. Midsummer Night II 117–Danica 56 (Floribunda 136) (1979 NR 1980 10.1s) second foal; sister to a poor animal; dam poor maiden; unquoted when behind in minor event at Windsor in June, first outing. *M. Bradley.* **—**

DANESTA (USA) 3 b.f. Majestic Prince–Dana II (Dan Cupid 132) (1979 NR 1980 8d 8g) narrow filly; sister to very useful 1976 3-y-o Danestic and half-sister to fair 1m winner Dana's Return (by Turn-to); dam never ran; on burly side when well beaten in maiden races at York in June and Salisbury in September; will stay 1¼m. *L. Cumani.* **—**

DANGAR DANCER 2 ch.f. Sword Dancer 97–Protest Marcher (March Past 124) (1980 5s 5f) May 15; third reported foal; dam placed over fences; beaten long way in sellers in the spring. *H. Willis.* **—**

DANLIFAR (FR) 2 b.c. Lyphard 132–Lady Dan (Dan Cupid 132) (1980 7g 7fg 7d2) neat colt; good mover; fifth foal; half-brother to French middle-distance winners Lithidan and Lit Up (both by Lithiot); dam ran once; ran on strongly after being outpaced early on when 4 lengths second of 20 to John Willoughby **82**

Sean Graham Fillies Stakes, Kempton—Dancing Shadow responds well to Carson's driving and beats Karamita

in maiden race at Leicester in October, best effort; will be well suited by middle distances. *J. Tree.*

DANNY BIDDER 4 b.g. Mount Hagen 127–Pensodoro 71 (Roan Rocket 128) (1979 8s 8f 8f 10f[2] 10g[2] 8s* 8h 8.2g 8g 1980 10v 8fg 8fg 8f 11g[3] 10f 10fg 12d) neat gelding; didn't run up to his best, including in a valuable seller on final start (blinkered); stays 1¼m; acts on any going except perhaps hard; often sweats up. *M. Camacho.* —

DANNY LA RUE 3 ch.g. Sharpen Up 127–Oceania (Aureole 132) (1979 NR 1980 7d 5d 8f) no sign of ability in varied company though has yet to race in a seller. *I. Walker.* —

DANNY PARK 2 b.c. Double-U-Jay 120–Plain Chant (Song 132) (1980 5fg* 5fg 5d 7d) May 23; 2,500Y; rangy colt; second foal; dam ran 6 times unplaced in Ireland; quickly into stride from a favourable draw and made all to win 16-runner newcomers race at Kempton in May by a head from Madison Style; third favourite when about 5 lengths seventh of 13 to Cooliney Prince in Windsor Castle Stakes at Royal Ascot, second outing and easily best subsequent effort; should stay 7f; possibly unsuited by a soft surface; off course over 2 months after third start. *R. Armstrong.* **80**

DANSACHA (USA) 2 ch.c. What Luck–Bellywhopper (First Landing) (1980 5d 5s[3]) Apr 7; $47,000Y; well-made colt; first foal; dam unraced daughter of Show Off, a smart winner at up to 1m; showed early speed both starts, on second keeping on to finish 4 lengths third of 11 to Pettistree in minor event at York in October; bred to stay 1m. *L. Cumani.* **84**

DANZIG 3 b.c. Wolver Hollow 126–None-So-Pretty (Never Say Die 137) (1979 7g 7s[4] 7f 1980 8d 8.2s 12g[4] 11.7f[4] 11.7f[3] 8.3fg 8g 10g) compact colt; quite moderate; stays 1½m; acts on firm going. *D. Sasse.* **68**

DAPHNE'S FAVOUR 2 ch.f. Martinmas 128–Martianess 101 (Red God 128**§**) (1980 5d 5fg[3] 5g 5.1fg* 5fg 5d) Mar 15; sturdy filly; poor walker; half-sister to a minor winner in USA; dam speedy sister to high-class 5f to 7f winner Red Alert; sold out of P. Cole's stable 2,200 gns after winning 9-runner seller at Yarmouth in August comfortably by 1½ lengths from Mount Eliza; will stay 6f; sold to Mrs G. Forbes 2,700 gns Newmarket Autumn Sales. *P. Haslam.* **64**

DARBY GREEN 4 br.g. Floriana 106–Fiona Green (Sing Sing 134) (1979 NR 1980 6f 6f 8d 6s) leggy gelding; plater; seems to stay 1m; probably acts on any going. *C. James.* **39**

DARING KNIGHT 3 ch.g. Daring Display 129–Sabotage 96 (High Treason 126) (1979 5g 5d[4] 7f 7f[4] 10.6d 1980 16f 12s[4] 10d 10g 10g) compact gelding; poor form in varied company, including in sellers; unreliable and virtually refused to race fourth start; probably stays 1½m; sometimes wears blinkers. *C. Brittain.* **64**

DARK HOPE 3 gr. or br.g. Meldrum 112–Coy Lady (Damremont 120) (1979 5s 8g 10s 8d 1980 12g 12f 12.3f 11.7g 12.2d 12d) quite a useful sort; quite a moderate handicapper at his best but ran badly last 3 starts, including in a selling handicap; stays 1½m; possibly unsuited by very firm going; blinkered third and final outings. *P. Kelleway.* —

DARK MONARCH 2 b.c. Scottish Rifle 127–Outward Bound 79 (Sing Sing 134) (1980 6fg[3] 7g[3] 7g[2] 7fg[4]) Feb 19; 5,000F, 10,000Y; neat colt; half-brother to several winners, including useful 3-y-o miler Morayshire (by Royal Palace); dam placed over 5f; had some useful previous winners well beaten off when 2 lengths second of 11 to Junta in minor event at Goodwood in September, best effort; 5/4 favourite, led 6f when 1¾ lengths fourth of 19 to Six Mile Bottom in maiden race at Lingfield the following month; will stay 1m. *J. Dunlop.* **95 ?**

DARKNESS VISIBLE 4 gr.f. Decoy Boy 129–Veejlee 101 (Vilmorin) (1979 6v[3] 5v 5d 5s 5g 1980 5d 5s[3] 5fg[4] 7f 6g 5d 5fg 6fg 5fg) neat filly; sprint maiden; suited by some give in the ground; blinkered seventh outing. *B. Richmond.* **42**

DARK PROPOSAL (USA) 2 b.c. Blood Royal 129–Lady Gertrude (Mr Leader) (1980 7v[4]) compact colt; second foal; dam won twice at up to 6f at 2 yrs; 20/1, last at halfway but ran on to finish about 8 lengths behind Sula Bula, in fourth place, in 9-runner Steel Plate Autumn Stakes at Doncaster in November; likely to stay 1¼m+; should improve. *B. Hanbury.* **79** p

DARLINSKI 2 b.f. Swing Easy 126–Sweet Reproach 94 (Relic) (1980 5g 6g) May 12; 11,500Y; big filly; half-sister to middle-distance winner Cee Beauty (by Ribero); dam 2-y-o 6f and 1m winner; last in maiden races at Redcar in June (dwelt) and Carlisle in July (blinkered but again started slowly); sold 575 gns Ascot August Sales. *M. H. Easterby.* —

DARTMOUTH 5 b.g. Captain's Gig–Nine Lessons 101 (Santa Claus 133) (1979 10d 8f^4 7f* 8f 8fg^3 7g* 8d^4 7.6f 7g* 1980 7g 7f 8fg 7d 7s^3) leggy gelding; fairly useful handicapper at his best; third of 26 behind Secret Gill at Doncaster in November, easily best effort of 1980; has won over 1m but is best at 7f; acts on any going; blinkered seventh and eighth starts at 4 yrs. *M. H. Easterby.* **79**

DARWOOD 4 b.c. Sallust 134–Hasten Slowly (Mark-Ye-Well) (1979 6d^3 6s* 6g^3 6f^4 5fg^2 6f 5fg 6f* 8fg^2 8g* 8d 1980 8d 8f^3 7.6f^3 8f^4 8g 8d 8d^2 8g^2 8.2g^3 7g) strong, good-looking colt; not a good mover in his slower paces; didn't manage to win but was placed 5 times, including in Playboy Bookmakers' Newbury Spring Cup (third to Northleach), Rose of York Handicap (short-head second to Miner's Lamp when ridden by 5-lb claimer), Playtex Trophy at Sandown (second to Seven Hearts) and Morecambe Handicap at Haydock (very close third to Geoffrey's Sister); didn't run up to his best final outing; stays 1m; acts on any going; blinkered fourth and seventh starts in 1979. *N. Callaghan.* **107**

DARYMOSS 3 b.f. Ballymoss 136–Darlinda 85 (Darius 129) (1979 5g 6f 5.8h^4 7fg 7f^3 1980 8fg 8f^4 8fg 7d 7g 8g 8fg^2 10fg 8.2g 8s) light-framed filly; quite a moderate maiden at her best; best run at 1m on a firm surface; sweated up eighth outing; has run creditably for a 5-lb claimer; pulled up when saddle slipped sixth start. *R. Turnell.* **73**

DASMAN 5 ch.g. Tower Walk 130–A Deux 80 (Crepello 136) (1979 8d^3 8g 7.6s* 8fg^4 8f^4 8f^4 8g 10fg 9f 8d^4 8s^2 10g 1980 7fg 10f^2 10g^3 10g 10fg^2 12g* 12fg 12v) fairly useful handicapper at his best; ridden by 7-lb claimer when winning valuable New Zealand-Great Britain Handicap at Newmarket in August by neck from Highway; good second earlier in Daily Mirror Handicap at Epsom (to Sacrilege) and Chesterfield Cup at Goodwood (to Borderline); stays 1½m; acts on any going; wears blinkers nowadays; suitable mount for an apprentice; usually held up. *J. Sutcliffe.* **86**

DASSEERA 2 b.g. Prince Regent 129–Red Laser 95 (Red God 128**§**) (1980 6fg 5g 6g) Feb 10; 10,500Y; robust, good sort; brother to useful 1976 2-y-o sprinter Regal Ray and fairly useful 3-y-o sprinter Gamblers Dream; dam 5f sprinter and closely related to very speedy Ruby Laser; backward and outpaced when behind in maiden races at Salisbury and Nottingham in September and at Newmarket the following month; gelded at end of season. *J. Sutcliffe.* **–**

DAUMONT (FR) 2 b.c. Viceregal–Miritis (Abdos 134) (1980 8.5fg* 10d*) Jan 19; 56,000 francs Y (approx £5,900); half-brother to French 1½m winner Pensee Sauvage (by Hard to Beat); dam, daughter of Prix Vermeille winner Astola, won over 11f; won both his starts in style of a very useful colt, coming through from rear to beat Scribe a short neck in 11-runner newcomers race at Longchamp in October and giving weight all round when winning fairly valuable Prix Isonomy at Evry the following month by a short neck from Singing Boy; will stay 1½m. *J. Audon, France.* **111**

DAVENPORT BOY 4 br.c. Workboy 123–Sea Tycoon 80 (Tycoon II) (1979 7s^3 6g* 6s^2 6fg* 6f^2 6g^4 6s^3 1980 6g* 6f^3 6f* 6fg 6fg) strong colt; looked well when comfortably winning handicaps at Epsom in April (beat Gusty's Gift by 2 lengths) and June (quickened in final furlong to score by 2½ lengths from Pink Blues); best form at 6f but has run creditably over 7f; acts on any going; genuine and consistent. *A. Pitt.* **96**

DAVIDGALAXY AFFAIR 3 b.c. Tower Walk 130–Lady's Walk (Pall Mall 132) (1979 5s^3 5s* 5s* 5g* 5d* 5s* 5g* 6g^3 6g 5g^3 5g 1980 6fg 6d 5g 7d 7fg 7.2d^3 6s 7d^3 8s) strong, good sort; fairly useful at his best; apprentice ridden when creditable third in handicaps at Haydock and Wolverhampton in October; stays 7f; acts well on soft ground; blinkered third start; trained by J. Etherington first 5 outings. *F. Yardley.* **91**

DAVINIA 3 br.f. Gold Form 108–Diascia (Dike) (1979 5d* 5g^2 6s 5fg^3 1980 5d^4 5v 5f 5fg 5g^4 5f) light-framed filly; sprint handicapper; ran badly when tried over 6f; possibly not at her best on very soft ground; didn't impress in paddock at all second start; none too consistent. *M. Masson.* **78**

DAWN HAIL 3 b.f. Derring-Do 131–All Hail 112 (Alcide 136) (1979 NR 1980 7f 7f^2 10fg 8s 12g 10.2fg^4 12f^4 14fg 14g^2 15.5g^2 16s*) 18,500Y; small filly; half-sister to 4 winners, including middle-distance winners Geminiani (by Lorenzaccio) and Bunce Boy (by King Emperor); dam staying daughter of St Leger second None Nicer; runner-up in maiden races prior to winning handicap at Nottingham in October decisively; suited by a test of stamina; acts on any going. *J. Winter.* **74**

Galtres Stakes, York—third in a row for Deadly Serious who wins from Old Kate

DAWN JOHNNY (USA) 3 gr.c. Grey Dawn II 132–Door Star (Stage Door Johnny) (1979 NR 1980 10fg 8d 8g* $9g^2$ $10f^3$ $10fg^2$ 14g* $16g^2$ 14g) $75,000Y; well-made colt; third foal; half-brother to winners in USA by Forward Pass and Olden Times; dam unraced half-sister to smart stakes winner Strong Strong; won maiden race at Beverley in July and handicap at Yarmouth in September; ran well next time but moderately on final start; stays 2m; acts on firm going; blinkered nowadays. *M. Stoute.* **90**

DAWN REDWOOD 2 b.f. Mummy's Pet 125–Brazilian Beauty (Busted 134) (1980 5g $5g^4$ 5d 5g 5fg) Mar 14; 9,200Y; leggy, unfurnished filly; none too good a mover; third foal; dam sister to useful Colourful and closely related to smart stayer Pink Gem; 2½ lengths fourth of 10 to Love For Money in maiden race at Redcar in July, best effort; last but one in nursery final outing. *T. Fairhurst.* **63**

DAWN'S DELIGHT 2 b.g. Dawn Review 105–Bird of Passage (Falcon 131) (1980 $5fg^4$ $5fg^3$ $6f^4$ 7fg 8s) May 15; 500Y; lightly-made gelding; second live foal; brother to a poor animal; dam won selling hurdle; in frame in sellers and a maiden auction event; had stiff tasks when tried over 7f and 1m; blinkered fifth outing. *K. Ivory.* **48**

DAY AFTER 4 b.g. High Top 131–Bisley (Polic 126 or Punchinello 97) (1979 $10.8s^2$ $11fg^2$ $12f^3$ 12g* 12.3s $11.7f^3$ $10f^3$ 10.6g 10fg 1980 12g $16g^4$ $12g^2$ 16.5g) good-looking gelding; went down by ½ length to Red Jay in handicap at Salisbury in July; best form at up to 1½m; appears to act on any going; usually wears blinkers. *S. Mellor.* **67**

DAY DREAM BELIEVER 2 ch.f. Wishing Star 117–Tackienne (Hard Tack 111§) (1980 $5f^4$ $5h^2$ $6g^4$ $5.8f^4$ 5d $5fg^3$ 7g $5g^4$ 5d) Mar 31; 660F; half-sister to winners here and abroad, including 1974 1m 2-y-o winner Ballyhardtack (by Ballyciptic); dam Irish 2-y-o 5f winner; in frame in maiden and minor events and a nursery; best form at 5f but should stay further; acts on hard going; retained 500 gns Newmarket Autumn Sales. *K. Lewis.* **66**

DAYLAY QUEEN 2 ch.f. Cili Smoker–Conkers Princess (Autre Prince 125) — (1980 5fg 6g 6g 7g) Jan 13; sturdy filly; first foal; dam never ran; little worthwhile form in maiden races. *F. Durr.*

DAYPORT 2 ch.g. Porto Bello 118–Long Days 92 (Bleep-Bleep 134) (1980 — 5g 5g 5d) May 19; smallish, sturdy gelding; in rear in August in maiden race and sellers; blinkered third outing. *J. Old.*

DAY OUT 3 b.c. Reliance II 137–Ming Vase 84 (Princely Gift 137) (1979 6g — 1980 8fg 7f 8.2g 8fg 8fg 6d 6s 8f 9.4fg) small, strong colt; plating-class maiden; best run at 6f on soft going; sold out of R. Hannon's stable 1,600 gns Ascot July Sales after seventh start. *S. Holland.*

DAZZLIN' DOLL 2 b.f. Sparkler 130–Karmala (Tanerko 134) (1980 7fg^4 8d^3 **76** 7g) Jan 21; lightly-made filly; third foal; dam placed at up to 12.5f in French Provinces; in frame in minor event at Newbury in September and maiden race at Warwick in October, finishing strongly each time; given too much to do on latter course and did well to finish 3 lengths third of 16 to Rosie Black; likely to stay 1$\frac{1}{4}$m+. *J. Tree.*

DEADLY SERIOUS (USA) 3 b.f. Queen's Hussar 124–Joking Apart 120 **113** (Jimmy Reppin 131) (1979 NR 1980 8fg 10g^4 12d* 10.1d* 12g*) good-bodied filly; first foal; dam very smart at up to 1m; put up a very useful performance to win Galtres Stakes at York in August, staying on strongly to beat Old Kate by 1$\frac{1}{2}$ lengths going away; had earlier won minor events at Wolverhampton and Windsor (odds on) in July; stays 1$\frac{1}{2}$m well; acts on a soft surface; genuine and consistent. *R. Hern.*

DEADLY VENTURE 3 b.f. Deadly Nightshade 107–Hope Baggot (Hopeful — Venture 125) (1979 NR 1980 12.2fg 7.2d) 360Y; first foal; dam never ran; last in maiden races at Catterick and Haydock in the summer. *A. Watson.*

DEAD STRAIT 2 b.c. Welsh Saint 126–Shade 87 (Gratitude 130) (1980 6fg **83** 7g 6g* 6fg 5fg 6d) Apr 2; 6,800F; robust, good-quartered colt; half-brother to several winners, including Bodelle (by Falcon), a winner at up to 13f in Ireland; dam stayed 13f; 25/1, improved greatly on previous efforts when making all to win 9-runner maiden race at Brighton in August by $\frac{1}{2}$ length from Sanu; ran well in a nursery next time out; will stay 1m. *R. Smyth.*

DEAN'S GUY 5 b.g. Double Jump 131–Misylda (Faubourg II 127) (1979 8g — 12fg 12.2s 1980 16s) of little account. *T. Taylor.*

DEAR ALICIA 2 gr.f. Runnymede 123–Dibby's Cousin (Be Friendly 130) **70** (1980 5d 5fg 5g^3 6fg) May 22; compact filly; second foal; dam never ran; quite a moderate maiden; 3$\frac{3}{4}$ lengths third of 18 to Portogon at Bath in September, best effort; yet to show she stays 6f. *W. Wightman.*

DEAR DENIZE 2 ch.f. Deep Diver 134–Hakoah (Palestine 133) (1980 5fg **64** 5fg 5s^4 5g 7g 5d) May 16; 17,000Y; lengthy, lightly-made, quite attractive filly; sister to useful 1976 2-y-o 5f performer Royal Diver, and half-sister to several winners; dam French 9f winner; no better than a plater and looks expensive; blinkered third and fourth outings. *H. Candy.*

DEAREST DOROTHY 3 gr.f. Sun Prince 128–Ivory Gull 70 (Sea Hawk II 131) **55** (1979 5d^4 5g^4 6s^3 7fg 1980 7f 8fg 9f 8d^4 12d^3 10d 10g 12f 15.5g) rangy filly; plating-class maiden; stays 1$\frac{1}{2}$m; suited by some give in the ground; out of her depth second start; ran badly in blinkers sixth outing. *R. Akehurst.*

DEAR JEM 2 b. or br.f. Dragonara Palace 115–Czar's Diamond 66 (Queen's **78** Hussar 124) (1980 5s 5fg^2 5f 5fg* 7.2g 6g 6fg^2 6g 6g 5fg 5d 5d^4) Apr 9; 4,800Y; lightly-made filly; half-sister to a winning plater and a prolific winner in Italy; dam plater; hard ridden when winning 14-runner maiden race at Warwick in May by $\frac{3}{4}$ length from Rosy Cottage; in frame in nurseries at Windsor and Warwick afterwards; stays 6f; acts on a firm and a soft surface; usually apprentice ridden; inconsistent. *A. Bailey.*

DEAR OCTOPUS 4 br.g. Pieces of Eight 128–Larkspur's Love (Larkspur 128) — (1979 10g 12s^4 12.2g* 14f 14f 12fg 12h^3 12fg* 13.8s* 12d 10d 1980 12.2v 16s 18f 12.3f) small gelding; ran poorly in 1980 and finished tailed off last 2 starts; stays 1$\frac{3}{4}$m; acts on any going; good mount for an apprentice. *M. Tate.*

DEBBIE MARY 3 b.f. Yellow River 114–Proper True (Right Tack 131) (1979 — NR 1980 12g 16fg 12g) 500F, 1,400Y; first foal; dam ran only once; well beaten in maiden race at Lingfield and small event at Chepstow in the summer, first 2 outings; slipped up final start. *A. Pitt.*

DEBBIE'S GIRL 3 b.f. Amber Rama 133–Treasure Ship (Sovereign Lord 120) – (1979 5d 5s 6f 7fg 1980 10s 8s) lengthy filly; poor form, including in a seller; wears blinkers. *W. Turner.*

DEBJEN-CLI-VAN 4 br.f. Dawn Review 105–Verona 91 (Quorum 126) (1979 – 6g 6fg 8g* 8.3fg 12f 1980 11fg 12f) lightly-made filly; modest plater at her best; best form at 1m. *D. Wintle.*

DECORATIVE 3 b.c. Martinmas 128–War Ribbon (Anwar 120) (1979 5g^4 **82** 6d 6fg^2 1980 8fg 8fg^3 8.2s* 8d 10d*) compact, attractive colt; successful in maiden race at Haydock and minor event at Leicester in the autumn; will stay beyond $1\frac{1}{4}$m; probably acts on any going. *D. Kent.*

DECOY DANCER 3 b.f. Decoy Boy 129–Second String 95 (Tudor Minstrel 144) **47** (1979 5f 6d 6f 8g 5d 1980 7f 5f 6s 6d^2 6d 8d) fair sort; plater; not certain to stay 1m; acts on a soft surface; sold 540 gns Ascot November Sales. *W. A. Stephenson.*

DEEANDEMMTIP 2 b.f. Gulf Pearl 117–Long Shadow 77 (Royal Palm 131) – (1980 5s 6s 6s 7g 9d 10s 10.2s) Apr 26; 460F, 1,300Y; neat filly; of little account. *G. Blum.*

DEEP BLUE SEA 3 ch.f. Gulf Pearl 117–Canterbury Belle (St Alphage 119) – (1979 5g 5d 6s 1980 8s 8f 10fg) big, well-made filly; sister to very smart middle-distance performer Sea Chimes but has shown little worthwhile form herself in varied company. *J. Benstead.*

DEEP DIG 2 b.g. Ancient Monro 89–Sea Sound 69 (Sea Hawk II 131) (1980 – 8fg) Apr 27; third reported foal; dam placed at up to $1\frac{1}{4}$m; last of 13 in maiden race won by Cliphome at Beverley in September. *S. Nesbitt.*

DEEP RIVER 8 b.h. Tudor Melody 129–Lucky Stream 99 (Persian Gulf) (1979 – 12d 12g* 12s^2 1980 12f 11s 12d 12v) useful handicapper at his best; lightly raced nowadays and showed no form in 1980; stays $1\frac{1}{2}$m; acts on any going; suitable mount for an apprentice; has been tried in blinkers; has won 4 times at Haydock; retained 3,100 gns Ascot December Sales. *I. Walker.*

DEEPSET 3 b.g. Deep Diver 134–Smart Sheila 113 (King's Leap 111) (1979 **93** 5d 5s* 5g^2 5d* 5s 5fg^2 5d 1980 5d^3 5g^4 5g 6g 5g^4) lengthy gelding; fairly useful sprint handicapper; creditable third at Doncaster in March; not disgraced on final start in July; doesn't stay 6f; probably acts on any going; very fast starter; sold 4,300 gns Ascot September Sales. *P. Cundell.*

DEIRA 3 ch.f. Bold Lad (Ire) 133–Royal Sensation 103 (Prince Regent 129) – (1979 6g 1980 7f 8h 8g) well-made filly; well beaten in maiden races; bandaged second start. *H. T. Jones.*

DELICIOUS MISS 3 b.f. Malicious–Haybells (Klairon 131) (1979 6f 7f 1980 – 10g 11.7fg 12d 11.7s 17.1fg 16.5g 10s) strong, compact filly; poor form, including in a seller; sometimes blinkered; sold 520 gns Ascot August Sales. *T. Gosling.*

DELLEAR (FR) 3 b.f. Roi Lear 126–Dellie Douglass (Mongo) (1979 5.5g^3 7g* **103** 8d 6.5g* 7g 1980 7d^3 8fg 6g^4 7g^3 6.5g^3 6.5d 6.5d 8d) 110,000 francs Y (approx £13,000); leggy filly; half-sister to smart Diligo (by Petingo), successful at up to 7.5f in France; dam, daughter of Secret Step, won over 6f at 4 yrs in USA; won minor events at Evry and Deauville at 2 yrs; $3\frac{1}{2}$ lengths third of 8 behind Firyal in Prix Imprudence at Maisons-Laffitte in April, first outing and probably best effort in 1980; sweated up when in rear in 1,000 Guineas won by Quick As Lightning at Newmarket on second start; will stay $1\frac{1}{4}$m; acts on a soft surface; sold 27,000 gns Newmarket December Sales. *P. Lallie, France.*

DEL SARTO (USA) 3 b.c. Bold Bidder–Queen Sucree (Ribot 142) (1979 8fg^4 **105** 8d* 1980 10g* 10g 10fg^4) \$250,000Y; blind in right eye; brother to Kentucky Derby winner Cannonade and high-class 1974 2-y-o Circle Home, and half-brother to 3 other winners; dam, half-sister to Champion filly Tosmah, was sold for \$1,000,000 when carrying this colt; landed odds in The Minstrel Stakes at Leopardstown in April by $2\frac{1}{2}$ lengths from Tie Anchor (gave 3 lb); favourite when fifth, $4\frac{1}{4}$ lengths behind Noelino, in Sean Graham Ballymoss Stakes at the Curragh later in month and when $1\frac{1}{2}$ lengths fourth of 8 to Ramian in BMW Nijinsky Stakes at Leopardstown in May; not raced again; will stay $1\frac{1}{2}$m; acts well on soft ground; wears blinkers; exported to South Africa by BBA. *V. O'Brien, Ireland.*

DELTA DIGGER (USA) 4 bl.g. Delta Judge–Sucha Snob (Dedicate) (1979 7fg **65** 8s^2 8d^2 7d^2 8s 8f 8fg 1980 8fg 12fg 8d^3 10s) rangy gelding; inconsistent maiden; favourite when third in seller at Warwick in October; stays 1m; acts on soft going; occasionally blinkered. *G. Lewis.*

DELTA'S PRIDE 4 b.g. Mummy's Pet 125–Alexandria 71 (Primera 131) (1979 5d3 5s4 5v2 6d3 5fg* 5g* 5fg 6fg4 6g 6d 5g 1980 5d 5v* 5fg 5f4 5fg 5s 6d 5fg3 5fg 5d 6g 6g 6g 5fg) leggy gelding; sprint handicapper; won apprentice event at Stockton in March comfortably but became rather disappointing; stays 6f; seems to act on any going; sometimes wears blinkers; suitable mount for a boy; sold out of T. Craig's stable 2,500 gns Newmarket July Stakes. *K. Ivory.* **68** d

DEMI FEU 4 b.g. Firestreak 125–Moiety Bird (Falcon 131) (1979 8s3 8d2 10s2 9fg* 10.1fg* 10f2 10s* 9g 1980 10s 8d 10s 10g 10d 12.3g 11.7fg) lengthy, quite attractive gelding; will stay 1½m; acts on any going; often starts slowly nowadays and refused to race last 2 starts; has been tried in blinkers; one to leave alone. *N. Callaghan.* **§§**

DEMMY OF THE NORTH 3 b.c. Roi Soleil 125–Miss Cervinia 72 (Memling) (1979 5s 7f 6d 10.6d 1980 12.5v4 12.3s2 12d3 16f) strong, good-quartered colt; plating-class maiden; not raced after May; stays 1½m (tailed off over 2m); acts on soft going; sold 760 gns Newmarket Autumn Sales. *R. Hollinshead.* **61**

DEMO'S LADY 2 ch.f. Status Seeker–Milesian Lady 85 (Milesian 125) (1980 5s 5.8h 5d) May 14; useful-looking filly; good mover; half-sister to 2 winners over hurdles; dam stayed 7f; 4¾ lengths sixth of 15 to Mementa Mia in maiden race at Warwick in April; not seen out again until August when in rear in similar race at Bath and valuable seller at Sandown (not well drawn). *R. Hannon.* –

DENIM JEAN 2 br.c. Lord Nelson 107–Talgita 72 (Talgo 130) (1980 6s) Apr 1; sixth foal; dam 1m winner; very green when last of 20 in seller at Nottingham in August. *J. Czerpak.* –

DENISE MARY 3 b.f. Tyrant–Veuve Joyeuse 60 (Vienna 127) (1979 5g 1980 11.7fg 7d 7fg 7f) poor form in maiden races and a handicap; swerved left at start third outing; sold 520 gns Ascot August Sales. *S. Pattemore.* –

DENMORE 4 ch.c. Moulton 128–Dugo 90 (Dumbarnie 125) (1979 8d 8g3 10d 7f 7g 10.2fg 11.7fg4 1980 8fg 7fg2 7f2 6fg* 6g* 6d3 6fg 6fg2 6g2 6g* 6s) sturdy, good-bodied colt; raced over shorter distances than in 1979 and returned to his fairly useful 2-y-o form; won handicaps at Brighton, Salisbury and Newcastle, beating Jebb Lane a neck in valuable Top Rank Club Handicap on last-named course in August; best form at 6f and 7f; acts on any going; blinkered twice at 2 yrs and fourth start in 1979; genuine and consistent. *C. Nelson.* **87**

DENNY STREET 5 b.g. Little Buskins 119–Santimwen (Cassim 120) (1979 NR 1980 16fg) ex-Irish gelding; first foal; dam winning Irish hurdler; behind in bumpers event at Leopardstown in 1979 and in amateur riders race at Ascot in September; novice hurdler. *G. Balding.* –

DENSOME BELLE 3 b.f. Perdu 121–Rock Dandy (Master Rocky 106) (1979 NR 1980 5f) non-thoroughbred filly; half-sister to two 2-y-o winners; dam ran twice over hurdles; unquoted when thirteenth of 14 to Kiss The Clowns in maiden race at Lingfield in September. *J. Bethell.* –

DENSTON 3 b.c. Moulton 128–Peaceful 95 (Crepello 136) (1979 7fg 1980 9f 8h4 11.5f 12g* 10g4 10.1s 12d* 10g2 10.6d 10s*) big, strong colt; won maiden race at Redcar (apprentice ridden) and handicaps at Wolverhampton and Stockton; will stay 1¾m; acts well on soft going; sold to D. Underwood 27,000 gns Newmarket Autumn Sales. *H. Wragg.* **89**

DEPICT 3 b.f. Derring-Do 131–Picture Palace 83 (Princely Gift 137) (1979 5s 6g* 6fg2 7.3g 1980 8.5g 8fg4 6fg2 7g* 7fg3 8.2s2 8fg3 8d) neat filly; quite a moderate handicapper; won in good style at Doncaster in June; ran creditably most starts afterwards; stays 1m well; probably acts on any going; has run well for an apprentice; ran poorly on final start at 2 yrs and on reappearance but is consistent enough nowadays. *I. Balding.* **76**

DEPUTY 3 b.g. Deep Diver 134–Lindera 71 (Linacre 133) (1979 NR 1980 6v* 5f3 8fg 6d 7f 10.6d 7fg 7g 7d2 7s3 6d2) 3,000Y; tall gelding; good walker; half-brother to Iron Ruler (by Lyphard), a very useful winner at up to 7.5f in France and Germany; dam stayed 1¾m; won maiden race at Stockton in March; finished only fifth in seller on eighth outing but ran creditably in handicaps on last 3 starts; stays 7f; suited by some give in the ground. *J. Fitzgerald.* **74**

DERGRET 3 b.c. Great Nephew 126–Dereta 92 (Aggressor 130) (1979 NR 1980 12fg 12fg 12.3s) strong colt; half-brother to 3 minor winners; dam a stayer; –

no sign of ability in Northern maiden and minor events; blinkered final start. *M. Camacho.*

DERLY (FR) 2 b.f. Lyphard 132–Derna II (Sunny Boy III) (1980 8g^4 8s*) ?
Mar 27; sister to top 1976 2-y-o filly Durtal, successful at up to 7.3f, and half-sister to several winners, notably Prix de l'Arc de Triomphe winner Detroit (by Riverman); dam placed from 1¼m to 13f in France; evens favourite when winning 17-runner maiden race at Maisons-Laffitte in November by a short neck; likely to do much better over middle distances. *Mme C. Head, France.*

DERRY DAUGHTER 2 br.f. Derring-Do 131–Lyndy Sue 70 (Major Portion 129) –
(1980 5g 6fg 7fg) Feb 22; tall, good-topped filly; half-sister to 3 winners, including quite useful 1m to 1¼m handicapper Kildoon (by Kalydon); dam disappointing; behind in maiden and minor events; sold 2,800 gns Newmarket Autumn Sales. *D. Whelan.*

DERRY DOE 2 b.f. Derring-Do 131–Salmorin 91 (Salvo 129) (1980 5d 8.2s 8d) –
Apr 18; 5,200Y; lightly-made filly; third foal; sister to useful Bold Shot, successful at up to 1m, and closely related to 1977 2-y-o 6f winner Leto (by High Top); dam won twice over 1½m; seventh in sizeable fields of maidens over 1m at Haydock and Redcar in October; trained by E. Reavey first outing. *D. Garraton.*

DESERT FALCON 3 b.c. Dancer's Image–Cenerentola 93 (Prince Chevalier) –
(1979 NR 1980 10d 10.2fg^4 12g 10.2g) 16,000Y; well-made colt; half-brother to several winners, including top 1969 French 2-y-o staying filly Vela (by Sheshoon) and very smart French middle-distance stayer Leading Man (by Above Suspicion); dam won at up to 1½m; showed only sign of ability on second outing; should stay 1½m; unseated rider shortly after leaving stalls on final start; sold 760 gns Newmarket Autumn Sales. *R. Boss.*

DESERT PRINCE 4 b.g. Sun Prince 128–Little Girl 67 (Le Mesnil 133) (1979 **42**
8.2s 6v 6v 6s 6s^3 7f 8fg 6f 6fg^4 6fg^4 7g 6g^2 6fg 7fg 8fg 7fg 1980 8s 7fg^4 8h 8.3f^2) poor plater; stays 1m; seems to act on any going; suitable mount for an apprentice. *W. Musson.*

DESERT STAR 3 ch.c. Hot Spark 126–Ice Ballet 87 (Ballymoss 136) (1979 **63**
NR 1980 8fg 10fg 11g* 10s 10fg 10fg) 15,000Y; attractive, well-made colt; half-brother to 3 winners, including fairly useful 1¼m winner Tanara (by Romulus); dam a stayer; landed odds in modest maiden race at Edinburgh in June; stays 11f; possibly unsuited by soft ground; blinkered and bandaged final outing; sold to R. Akehurst 840 gns Newmarket Autumn Sales. *R. Boss.*

DESERT VALLEY 2 ch.g. Abwah 118–Sand Valley 61 (Arabian) (1980 5f –
6d 7.2d) Apr 9; 4,300F, 8,600Y; well-made gelding; fourth living foal; half-brother to a minor winner in USA; dam won 3 sellers at around 1¼m; plating-class maiden. *P. Rohan.*

DESERT WARRIOR 6 b.g. Realm 129–Dorrit 98 (Zucchero 133§) (1979 5fg –
5fg^4 5fg 5d 5fg 5s 5d 1980 5v 6g) poor sprinter; has been tried in blinkers. *S. Wiles.*

DESIGN FOR LIVING 4 b.c. Habitat 134–Oserian 109 (Court Martial) (1979 –
8g 8d 6d 6s^4 5.6fg^3 6g 6s* 6d 1980 6s 6d 6g 6d 6g 6s 6s 6v) sprint handicapper; no form in 1980; acts on any going; wears blinkers. *I. Walker.*

DESPATCH 3 gr.f. Roan Rocket 128–Manipulation 90 (Appiani II 128) (1979 –
NR 1980 8f 13s 14g 13g 12fg 12g^3 13.8fg) strong filly; poor plater; stays 1½m; sold 1,200 gns Newmarket Autumn Sales. *Sir Mark Prescott.*

DESTINY HILL (USA) 9 b.g. Power of Destiny–Scotts Hill (Colonel O'F) –
(1979 16f^4 12f^4 16f^3 19f^2 1980 16fg) strong gelding; suited by a good test of stamina; appears to act on any going; sometimes wears blinkers; suitable mount for an apprentice; moderate hurdler. *S. Holland.*

DETENTION 3 b.f. Brigadier Gerard 144–Parolee 88 (Sing Sing 134) (1979 –
6g^2 6f* 6fg 7f 7d 1980 7f^4 7s 7f 7g) neat, well-made filly; respectable fourth in handicap at Epsom in April; off course almost 3 months afterwards and was well beaten on her return; will stay 1m; acts on firm going and is possibly unsuited by soft; sold 20,000 gns Newmarket December Sales. *J. Dunlop.*

DETONATE 4 b.f. Derring-Do 131–Shot Gold (Vimy 132) (1979 8d 10d 10s **50**
8f 10.2h^2 10g* 11g^3 12f^3 1980 10s 10.8f^4 10.5f 10g 11.5g) useful-looking filly; stays 1½m; possibly requires a sound surface; blinkered third and fourth starts in 1979; didn't impress going to post final start (July). *W. Hastings-Bass.*

DETROIT (FR) 3 br.f. Riverman 131–Derna II (Sunny Boy III) (1979 NR 1980 10.5s* 10.5d* 9d* 10g* 12f³ 12f*) **131**

Not since Topyo's year has the Prix de l'Arc de Triomphe, Europe's most important weight-for-age race, produced a blanket finish to match that of 1980. It was a finish that any handicapper would have envied; less than a length separated the winner Detroit from the fourth Three Troikas, and Detroit would undoubtedly have been beaten with a little further to go by Argument, a 74/1 outsider who had won only two of his seven races in the current season. When the principals in a top race come home one on top of the other the first reaction, a logical one which is also borne out by experience, is to write them all off as moderate by top classic standard. Such a reaction is not always the right one but we are satisfied that the form of the Arc in 1980 was a little below the standard of some recent years; not since 1967 when Topyo scrambled home from the English-trained pair Salvo and Ribocco, with Roi Dagobert and Heath Rose breathing down their necks, have we rated an Arc winner less highly.

Let us hasten to add that the Prix de l'Arc is never won by a bad horse. Detroit had against her the strongest field assembled for a middle-distance race in Europe all season. Although none of those that had contested the Derby at Epsom or the Curragh was in the field, the French-trained classic colts (who, incidentally, as a group, haven't produced an Arc winner since 1970) were represented, among others, by Policeman, winner of the Prix du Jockey-Club, Providential, third in that race, the Grand Prix de Deauville winner Glenorum, and Argument, who had finished out of the first ten in the Jockey-Club but had subsequently won Belgium's most important race, the Grand Prix Prince Rose. The four-year-olds seemed to have a very strong hand and included in their number: Ela-Mana-Mou, unbeaten in his last four races, the most recent of them the King George VI and Queen Elizabeth Diamond Stakes, Britain's most important weight-for-age race; Le Marmot, second in the 1979 Arc and winner of the Prix Ganay in the current season; Dunette, winner of the Prix de Diane as a three-year-old and runner of a dead-heat with the Prix du Jockey-Club second Shakapour in the Grand Prix de Saint-Cloud; Nebos, one of the best middle-distance horses trained in Germany for years; and Three Troikas, winner of the Arc in 1979 but unfortunately side-lined for much of 1980 with a broken bone in her off-fore foot. In contrast to the leading staying colts of the classic generation who, long before the Arc, were being labelled an ordinary bunch, the season's top three-year-old staying fillies seemed a near-vintage collection and, not for the first time in recent years, the Prix Vermeille, a race which is run over the Prix de l'Arc course in September and almost always attracts the cream of the French staying fillies, proved a good guide to the Arc. The Vermeille was won by an English-trained filly, Mrs Penny, who earlier had won the Prix de Diane de Revlon (French Oaks) and finished a highly creditable second to Ela-Mana-Mou in the King George VI and Queen Elizabeth Diamond Stakes. Mrs Penny and the Vermeille runner-up, the Irish-trained Little Bonny, both took the field for the Prix de l'Arc but more attention was focussed on the Vermeille third Detroit.

The Prix Vermeille was the first race of international importance in which Detroit had taken part. She didn't see a racecourse until the spring of her three-year-old days and she arrived at the Vermeille unbeaten in four races, starting with a newcomers race at Saint-Cloud in May, which she won by five lengths, and progressing through three Group 3 pattern events, the Prix Fille de l'Air at Saint-Cloud in June, the Prix Chloe at Evry in July and the Prix de la Nonette at Deauville in August. Such was the impression created by Detroit's victories that she started favourite for the Prix Vermeille, in which, in the absence of her stable's jockey Lequeux who was under suspension, she was ridden for the first time by Eddery. It was Eddery's first ride for owner Robert Sangster since the announcement that Eddery would be taking over from Piggott in 1981 as the number-one rider for the formidable Sangster-O'Brien team. It was an inauspicious start for Eddery to his association with Mr Sangster: Detroit encountered considerable difficulty getting an opening in the straight and by the time Eddery had extricated her there wasn't time to catch Mrs Penny and Little Bonny. Detroit was beaten half a length and three quarters but almost everyone who saw the race, including ourselves, forecast that Detroit would turn the tables on the first two in the Prix de l'Arc; she looked a very unlucky loser. Detroit started at 67/10 on Arc day, behind only Ela-Mana-Mou and Le Marmot (who were coupled for betting purposes) and Three Troikas; Mrs Penny was 12/1 and Little Bonny 41/1. Eddery retained the mount on Detroit, while Lequeux rode her stable-companion Providential who started at almost five times the odds of Detroit.

Prix Fille de l'Air, Saint-Cloud—Detroit shows herself to be a smart filly, beating Gold River and Indigene

The going on Prix de l'Arc day was very firm, a rarity for Longchamp in October, and the use of pacemakers for Policeman and for Ela-Mana-Mou's stable-companion Niniski ensured that the race was truly run from start to finish; in fact it was run in record time, a point of interest though not, on its own, a point of significance. Policeman was the first of the good horses to go on after the pacemakers had done their job and Ela-Mana-Mou, Mrs Penny, Glenorum, Providential, Dunette and Three Troikas were all well placed turning for home; Detroit wasn't much further behind but Argument was some way adrift after being last of twenty on the downhill run to the entrance to the final straight. Ela-Mana-Mou set sail for home early in the straight and was soon being strongly challenged by Three Troikas. Detroit was switched to the outside and began her run about two furlongs out. She made up ground in eye-catching style and, strongly ridden, caught Ela-Mana-Mou and Three Troikas with about a hundred yards to go. Argument's flourish came all too late and Detroit had half a length to spare at the post; Ela-Mana-Mou finished a short head behind Argument with Three Troikas a neck away in fourth place. Next came Nebos, followed by the English-trained five-year-old Nicholas Bill, Dunette and, in eighth place, Le Marmot; Le Marmot was less than five lengths behind Detroit. There were the usual hard-luck stories from some of the losers: the rider of Nebos, who made very good late progress, claimed that his mount had been bumped and hampered before the straight; Le Marmot and Glenorum were said to have finished lame.

Detroit's success in the Prix de l'Arc de Triomphe maintained the magnificent recent record of fillies in the race. Indeed, the emergence of an unusually large number of fillies capable of beating the best of the opposite sex at the regulation 3 lb allowance has been a feature of European flat racing in the period since the

Prix de la Nonette, Deauville—another success for Detroit, this time at the expense of India Song and Luth de Saron

early 'seventies. Nowhere has it been more evident than in the results of the Arc. In the first twenty-three runnings of the race from 1949, when its value was raised sharply to make it a race of world-wide importance, Coronation V and La Sorellina were the only fillies to win and only a small number of fillies managed to gain a place. The victory of San San in 1972, the first by a filly for nineteen years, was followed by those of Allez France, Ivanjica and Three Troikas; in contrast to the 'sixties when only three fillies—Monade, La Bamba and Park Top—gained a place in the Arc, the 'seventies saw Miss Dan, Pistol Packer, Cambrizzia, Rescousse, Comtesse de Loir, Trillion and Dancing Maid also achieve that distinction. History clearly shows that very few top fillies are good enough to hold their own against the best colts and more than one observer has questioned whether such an unusually high rate of success can be accounted for by coincidence. The 'seventies also saw Dahlia, Pawneese, Rose Bowl, Lianga, Flying Water, Sanedtki, Dunfermline and several other very good fillies achieve notable victories over top-class colts in major races. The fact that most of these so-called 'super-fillies' were trained in France has led to speculation about the methods used in France to condition fillies. There seems no justification for suggestions that the French successes can be attributed to better feeding or superior training methods: the leading French-trained fillies of the 'seventies were certainly better as a group than their Anglo-Irish counterparts but the reverse is true of the top colts. Where were the French-trained colts to rank, as a group, with Brigadier Gerard, Mill Reef, Nijinsky, Alleged, Rheingold, Grundy, Thatch, Troy and Bustino at their best? We are unaware of any factual justification for the rumour that has been spread that many of the French-trained fillies of the past decade owed their exceptional performance to the use of non-normal nutrients; such claims have never been proven and seem to us to be entirely uncalled for. Evidently, an anti-French feeling, which showed itself so clearly at the time of the Trepan dope cases in 1976, is very strong among some people in British racing. The most obvious conclusion to be drawn from the recent run of successes of the top fillies is that the 'seventies produced three or four vintage crops of fillies, some of which coincided with crops of colts which were moderate by comparison with those of most other years. If this conclusion is accepted the need to find more sinister explanations is avoided.

Until the big-race successes of Detroit and the two-year-old Storm Bird, the European flat-racing season was a modest one for Robert Sangster and his associates by their previous standards. Since 1975, syndicates in which Sangster has been involved have been among the biggest spenders at the world's principal yearling sales, sometimes paying record prices for some of the best-looking and most fashionably-bred yearling colts; the annual outlay, most of it in the United States, is currently running at between eight and nine million dollars (between £3.3m and £3.7m at 1980 exchange rates). Sangster and his associates are in business first and foremost 'to make stallions', as they put it: The Minstrel was among those purchased at the 1975 yearling sales and his syndication value as a stallion was nine million dollars. The yearlings

Prix de l'Arc de Triomphe, Longchamp—Detroit wins from Argument, Ela-Mana-Mou (far rails) and Three Troikas. Nebos is fifth, ahead of Nicholas Bill, Dunette, Le Marmot and Ruscelli

Mr R. E. Sangster's "Detroit" (P. Eddery)

bought in 1976 and 1977 to race in Europe were not so spectacularly successful as those of that first year but Sangster's conviction that fashionably-bred, good-looking colts would appreciate in value provided they met with some sort of racecourse success has been borne out by the substantial sums the Sangster syndicates have obtained, particularly in the United States, for some of their lesser-lights. The scale of the Sangster operation, incidentally, is breathtaking: at the time of Detroit's success in the Prix de l'Arc there were, spread over six countries and thirty-six trainers, two hundred and seventy-nine horses in training which he owned or in which he had shares; the mares, stallions, foals and yearlings that completed his portfolio numbered another four hundred or more. The annual running costs of the whole operation for Mr Sangster and his partners is currently estimated at around two million pounds; in 1977, their best racing year so far, the horses trained for the syndicates by O'Brien won seven Group 1 pattern races (the Derby, the Irish Sweeps Derby, the King George VI, the Prix de l'Arc, the King's Stand, the Irish One Thousand Guineas and the Dewhurst) but even then the total prize money did not cover the expenses of the animals in training in Europe. The success of the venture depends on the syndication of the best colts for stud.

Detroit (Fr) (br.f. 1977)	Riverman (b 1969)	Never Bend (b 1960)	Nasrullah
			Lalun
		River Lady (b 1963)	Prince John
			Nile Lily
	Derna II (b 1961)	Sunny Boy III (b 1944)	Jock II
			Fille de Soleil
		Miss Barberie (b 1950)	Norseman
			Vaneuse

Although Mr Sangster has concentrated on buying yearlings with stallion potential, he has also acquired an impressive collection of mares in recent years. Among those which he owns or has shares in is Detroit's half-sister Durtal (by Lyphard), winner of the William Hill Cheveley Park Stakes, who had to be withdrawn when favourite for the Oaks in 1977 after parting company with her rider and gashing herself on the way to the start. The genuine Detroit will not be retired to the paddocks for at least another year. She stays in training in

France and is said to be a probable for the inaugural running of the Arlington Million at Arlington Park, Illinois, at the end of August. The Arlington Million, billed as the most valuable race in the world and the world championship over ten furlongs on turf, will have a guaranteed first prize of 600,000 dollars (about £250,000 at 1980 values). Detroit's form at a mile and a half is considerably better than her form at shorter distances but Mr Sangster has everything to gain and little to lose by letting her take her chance in so prestigious an event; she acts on any going but is evidently very well suited by firm.

Detroit, an attractive filly, was bought privately as a foal for a sum reported to be about £100,000. Her dam Derna II didn't win but was placed from a mile and a quarter to thirteen furlongs in France; all told Derna bred five winners before Detroit, including the useful middle-distance fillies Darcounette (by Dapper Dan) and Valderna (by Val de Loir). A yearling half-brother to Detroit called Dilligham (by Green Dancer) fetched the top individual price of 530,000 guineas at the Newmarket Houghton Sales; the colt was knocked down to Detroit's trainer acting on behalf of Serge Fradkoff. Detroit's sire Riverman has followed his distinguished contemporary Lyphard, sire of the 1979 Arc winner Three Troikas, to the United States; Riverman will stand alongside Lyphard at Gainesway Farm, Kentucky, in 1981, having been syndicated for eighteen million dollars. *O. Douieb, France.*

DEUTZIA 2 br.f. Derring-Do 131–Peach Blossom (Blakeney 126) (1980 5.8h 6fg) May 8; small, lightly-made filly; first foal; dam lightly-raced half-sister to 2,000 Guineas third Dominion (by Derring-Do), subsequently a good winner in USA, and 3 good-class performers; 16/1, stayed on strongly when $7\frac{3}{4}$ lengths fifth of 16 to Down The Hatch in maiden race at Salisbury in September, second outing; may improve over middle distances at 3 yrs. *I. Balding.* —

DEUX ETOILES 3 b.f. Bay Express 132–Alezan Dore 82 (Mountain Call 125) (1979 5d 5g* 5s 5g 5fg^3 5fg* 1980 5fg^4 5fg 5f 5fg 5g) good-bodied filly; shows traces of stringhalt; fair (rated 86) at 2 yrs; creditable fourth in handicap at Newbury in April, best effort in 1980; possibly unsuited by soft going; wore bandages at 2 yrs. *N. Vigors.* **71**

DEVIL MAY CARE 3 b.g. Galivanter 131–Taffimai (Never Say Die 137) (1979 5g 6g^4 1980 8fg 8fg 10fg^3 8.2s^2 8s^4 7g^3) strong, good sort; quite a moderate maiden; stays 1m well; acts on soft going; sweated up third start. *W. Hastings-Bass.* **74**

DEVIL ROCK 2 br.c. Arch Sculptor 123–Charity Concert 80 (Vimy 132) (1980 6g 6s) May 31; good-bodied, attractive colt; half-brother to numerous winners, including useful miler Wild Root (by Tudor Melody) and 5f to 1m winner Kensington High (by Be Friendly); dam won over $1\frac{1}{4}$m, and is half-sister to fastest 1956 2-y-o Skindles Hotel; 16/1, ran on steadily to finish $6\frac{3}{4}$ lengths fifth of 22 to Banbury Cross in maiden race at Doncaster in November; the type to do better at 3 yrs. *J. Dunlop.* — p

DEVIL TO PLAY 4 b.c. Knave To Play 79–Pretty Gritty (Grit 95) (1979 NR 1980 10fg 16d^2 16.9d 16f) strong colt; stuck on well when $\frac{1}{2}$-length second of 20 to Chincoteague in maiden race at Newcastle in June, best effort; suited by a test of stamina; possibly needs some give in the ground. *R. Hollinshead.* **55**

DEVON BELLS 2 br.f. So Blessed 130–Plymouth Sound 89 (Tudor Melody 129) (1980 5.1fg^2 5.1fg^2 7g^2 6d) Feb 21; very tall, leggy, lightly-made filly; half-sister to fairly useful stayer Spanish Armada (by Levmoss); dam, winner at $1\frac{1}{4}$m, is daughter of smart stayer Seascape; second in maiden races won by Garnish Island, Lacework and Park Place at Yarmouth, putting up best effort when going down by $\frac{1}{2}$ length to last-named in 18-runner event in September; ran moderately at Pontefract in October; will be suited by middle distances; genuine; sold to BBA 7,400 gns Newmarket Autumn Sales. *T. Waugh.* **84**

DEVORGILLA (USA) 3 b.f. Majestic Prince–Darrynane (St Paddy 133) (1979 NR 1980 10fg 10.6d^4 12s 10.2d 10g^3) rangy filly; half-sister to several winners, including minor stakes winner Mikeydike (by Duel); dam never ran; in frame in maiden races at Haydock and Newmarket in the autumn; should stay $1\frac{1}{2}$m; sold 9,400 gns Newmarket December Sales. *R. Sheather.* **62**

DEWBERRY 2 b.f. Bay Express 132–Rosaberry 94 (Rockefella) (1980 6d 6g 5d 6s^4) Apr 13; 3,500F, 8,000Y; compact, well-made filly; good mover; sister to plating-class 1979 2-y-o Dormer Cottage and half-sister to 2 winners; dam placed over 7f at 2 yrs; seemed well thought of on first 3 outings but was well beaten at Hamilton on final start. *C. Nelson.* **64**

DHAUBIX (FR) 3 br.c. Dhaudevi 127–Bobasix (Bobar 127) (1979 8v4 1980 10s 10.5g2 12g* 15d* 15s 15g4 12s 15.5v) good-bodied colt; brother to Dhaubasix, smart winner at 1m to 1½m, and to Dhaubobi, successful at 1½m and 13f, and half-brother to 2 winners; dam won from 6.5f to 12.5f in France; won minor event at Evry in May and Prix Berteux at Chantilly in June, beating Balibest by 2½ lengths in latter; ran best subsequent race on sixth outing when short-neck second to What A Joy (rec 3 lb) in Prix de Lutece at Longchamp in September (moved down to fourth by stewards for hampering third horse); didn't run up to his best in Grand Prix de Paris at Longchamp in June or when blinkered in Prix du Conseil de Paris and Prix Royal-Oak on same course in October; suited by a test of stamina; yet to race on a firm surface. *R. Corme, France.* **118**

DHAUSLI (FR) 3 b.c. Dhaudevi 127–Leslie (Tanerko 134) (1979 7.5s 10v3 1980 10s* 10.5fg 12d2 15d 11g* 11s2 12f 12d2) fifth living produce; brother to French 1½m winner Dhaulesly and half-brother to 3 winners in France, notably very useful middle-distance performer Tajeslie (by Taj Dewan); dam placed at 8.5f from 2 starts at 3 yrs in France; smart performer; won small race at Evry early in year and Grand Prix de Lyon in June; also ran well when 2 lengths second to Argument in Grand Prix Prince Rose at Ostend in July and to Pawiment in Preis von Europa at Cologne in October and when sixth to Prince Bee, beaten 3 lengths, in Prix Niel at Longchamp in September; stays 1½m; acts on any going; consistent. *R. Corme, France.* **114**

DHUARD 3 br.c. Perdu 121–High Fidelyty (Hautain 128) (1979 NR 1980 6f 5g4 6s 5g2 5fg 5d 6g 5s) 6,200Y; good-topped colt; half-brother to useful but disappointing 1978 2-y-o Moulin (by Mill Reef), subsequently successful over 1¼m in France, and 2 other winners; dam won in Italy; sweated up when second in maiden race at Nottingham in July; well beaten in seller on seventh outing; should stay 6f; ran moderately fifth start; retained 525 gns Ascot November Sales. *D. Hanley.* **61**

DIAMANTE 5 ch.m. Sparkler 130–Feova 83 (Faberge II 121) (1979 8s 8s 8d4 8s2 8s 8g 8fg 8.2s4 8s 1980 8g) poor handicapper; moved very short to post when behind in seller on only outing of 1980; stays 1m; acts on any going; good mount for an apprentice. *J. Harris.* **–**

DIAMOND GALLERY 2 ch.f. Record Token 128–Stroppy Lou (Shantung 132) (1980 6s 7fg) May 14; 2,600Y; unfurnished filly; half-sister to 5f to 10.6f winner Bright Charlie (by Saintly Song); dam never ran; behind in maiden races at Nottingham in June (auction event) and Yarmouth in August. *R. Boss.* **–**

DIAMOND HORSESHOE 2 b.g. Some Hand 119–Hammerwood (Combat 123) (1980 5f 6f 6s2 6fg 6g 6fg 6d 5g) May 5; 2,100Y; lengthy gelding; half-brother to 1979 2-y-o 6f to 1m winner Silver Horseshoe (by Songedor) and 2 winners in Belgium; ridden by 7-lb claimer, gave impression he would have won with stronger handling when 2½ lengths second to Blue Rhapsody in 18-runner maiden auction event at Nottingham in June; beaten in nurseries subsequently, twice running respectably; will stay 7f; well suited by soft going (moved poorly to post on firm ground on second start); seems best in blinkers. *R. Akehurst.* **77**

DIAMOND PROSPECT (USA) 2 b.c. Mr Prospector–Sociable Angel (Social Climber) (1980 5g2 5s2 5.5g 6d* 7g2) Apr 11; $120,000 2-y-o; half-brother to several winners, including minor 1974 2-y-o stakes winner Track Fiddler (by Stevward); dam stakes-placed sprint winner at 2 yrs; won only a maiden race at Deauville in August but was second in 3 other races, 2 of them fairly important events; went down by only ½ length to Twig Prince in Prix du Bois at Longchamp in June on second start and by 1½ lengths to Cresta Rider in Group 2 Criterium de Maisons-Laffitte in September on fifth; will probably stay 1m; yet to race on a firm surface. *M. Saliba, France.* **114**

DIBBINSDALE LAD 4 ch.g. Sandford Lad 133–Travelling Fair 95 (Vienna 127) (1979 8s2 7v 8.2s2 8.2s3 10.6g* 10f 11g3 9fg 12d3 10.6g 10.5fg 11s 12g4 14fg 1980 10.4f) fair sort; quite useful handicapper; never-dangerous fifth of 7 to Masked Marvel at Chester in May on only outing of 1980; stays 1½m; acts on any going; usually blinkered at 2 yrs (and wore them once in 1979); often hangs but has run well for an apprentice. *M. H. Easterby.* **–**

DIBBINSDALE LASS 2 ch.f. Amber Rama 133–Bella Canto 82 (Crooner 119) (1980 6s 7d 7s 6s) Mar 28; 3,300Y; leggy, unfurnished filly; first foal; dam won over 1m and 1¼m; beaten some way in maiden races and in a nursery at Hamilton. *C. Crossley.* **64**

DIDAPPER 4 br.g. Seaepic 100–Golden Dove (Cracksman 111) (1979 NR 1980 8g 16.9d) probably of little account; sold 1,200 gns Ascot August Sales. *D. Ancil.* **–**

DIKEMAN 4 ch.g. Dike–Harambee 64 (Doutelle 128) (1979 6v 12s 16f 12g 1980 10v 8g 12fg) only poor form, but showed a little ability in sellers on last 2 starts; sold 390 gns Ascot November Sales. *P. Rohan.* —

DIKERY 4 b.g. Dike–Rum Butter 94 (Hard Sauce 131) (1979 8s* 12f^4 12g* 11.1fg* 13fg 13.3g* 1980 12d 16fg^4 16fg^2 16f^4) neat, attractive gelding; ran well when 2½ lengths second to Balinger in handicap at Newmarket in May but disappointed on his only subsequent outing (August); stays well; possibly unsuited by very firm going; usually held up. *J. Dunlop.* **96**

DIME A DANCE 4 b.f. No Mercy 126–Evening Shoe 111 (Panaslipper 130) (1979 7g 6d 8s 7fg 7f^2 7g 7.6f 6d* 8d 1980 8g^2 8fg^2 7f^4 7f* 6h^3 7g 6d 6g* 7f 6g 6s 6g 8d 6g^2) lightly-made filly; attracted no bid after winning sellers at Redcar in May and Ayr in July; good second of 30 to Hot Money in claiming handicap at Newmarket in October; stays 1m; acts on any going; blinkered seventh outing at 3 yrs; suitable mount for an apprentice. *G. Richards.* **58**

DINKUM CHIEF 6 gr.g. Tribal Chief 125–Sara Lady 81 (Roan Rocket 128) (1979 6v 6s 6g^3 6d^3 6fg 6fg^3 6f 5g 6d^4 5g 6fg^2 6f 6g 6g 6s 1980 7fg 6h 8g 6s 5d^3 6d^3 5g 6g 6f^3 5d) small gelding; stays 7f; probably acts on any going; good mount for an inexperienced rider; sold 500 gns Doncaster November Sales. *R. Cambidge.* **53**

DIOKLIS 2 ch.c. Busted 134–Honeysuckle Rose 105 (Honeyway 125) (1980 6s) Feb 27; half-brother to several winners, notably smart sprinter Rambling Rose (by Silly Season) and very smart French 7f to 1¼m winner Rose Laurel (by Klairon); dam won at 1¼m; 16/1 and in need of the outing, dwelt and was always struggling in 22-runner maiden race at Doncaster in November won by Banbury Cross. *H. T. Jones.* —

DIOR PRINCESS 2 b. or br.f. Manacle 123–Dior 80 (Dionisio 126) (1980 9d 7d) May 21; 1,500Y; sister to 2 fairly useful 2-y-o winners, including 1977 5f to 1m performer Dior Queen, and half-sister to several winners; dam, placed at up to 1½m, won over hurdles; in rear in minor events at Wolverhampton and Doncaster (last of 20) in October. *J. Tierney.* —

DIRECTED (USA) 3 br.f. Bagdad–Repoise (Ambiopoise) (1979 NR 1980 9fg 10fg 10s 10.1s^2 10s^4 12g 10fg 12g^4) tall filly; third foal; half-sister to a minor winner by Herbager; dam, very useful at 2 yrs, won at up to 7f; in frame in varied company; stays 1½m; needs some give in the ground; sold 30,000 dollars at Lexington in November. *J. Dunlop.* **70**

DIRECTORATE 2 ch.c. Gay Fandango 132–Gentle Way 74 (Gentle Art 121) (1980 5s 5.1g* 5s) Apr 18; 25,000Y; strong colt; brother to 3-y-o 6f winner Hawali and half-brother to good Belgian winner Arpad (by Connaught); dam half-sister to Sovereign Path; quickened well when winning 11-runner maiden race at Yarmouth in September by 3 lengths from Hayato; soon struggling in minor event at York the following month and came home last of 11 to Pettistree; will stay 6f; clearly unsuited by soft going. *M. Stoute.* **88**

DIRTY GERTIE 2 ch.f. Sharpen Up 127–Living Legend 88 (Derring-Do 131) (1980 5.3d 5g 6fg 7g 7g 6fg) June 4; close-coupled filly; first foal; dam won twice over 1m; no worthwhile form in maiden and minor events; sold 1,500 gns Newmarket Autumn Sales. *D. Whelan.* —

DISCO 2 ch.c. Jukebox 120–Only A Game (Whistling Wind 123) (1980 6d 6g^3) Apr 8; 14,100Y; neat, strong colt; half-brother to several winners, including useful Irish 3-y-o sprinter Saintly Game (by Welsh Saint); dam quite useful Irish sprinter; 13/2 for 25-runner maiden race at Newmarket in October and ran well, going on strongly over last 2f after having been behind, to finish 4 lengths third to Composer; took the eye in paddock here, wasn't punished unduly when it was clear he couldn't win and looks sure to win sprint races in 1981. *P. Walwyn.* **82** p

DISCO BEAT 3 gr.f. No Mercy 126–Evening Shoe 111 (Panaslipper 130) (1979 NR 1980 8fg^4 10fg 8s* 12d 7s 7fg 8.2g) 9,000Y; leggy filly; sister to 6f and 7f winner Dime a Dance, and half-sister to 3 winners; dam third in Irish 1,000 Guineas; won 15-runner maiden race at Stockton in June; well beaten in a minor event and handicaps afterwards; not certain to stay 1¼m; acts on soft going; sold 6,600 gns Newmarket December Sales. *B. Hanbury.* **70**

DISCO DANCING 2 ch.f. Record Token 128–Fire Dance (Habitat 134) (1980 5fg^3 5f^3 5g* 5g* 6g^3 5g^4 5fg) Apr 7; 6,400Y; small, strong filly; first foal; dam never ran; won 17-runner maiden race at Warwick in June and 7-runner minor event at Newcastle later in month; ran on strongly to beat Jade Girl 2 lengths **84**

on latter course; not disgraced on 2 of her subsequent starts; stays 6f; suited by some give in the ground; wears blinkers; sold 9,200 gns Newmarket December Sales. *P. Walwyn.*

DISCO FEVER 2 br.f. Workboy 123–Gin A Go Go 72 (Cash and Courage 116) (1980 5g 5f 5d* 5s 5fg 5s^3) May 20; strong, compact filly; half-sister to 2 minor 2-y-o winners and a winner abroad; dam won 6f seller at 2 yrs; backed from 12/1 to 6/1, put up best effort when winning 20-runner seller at Ripon in August by a length from Spurstow; will probably stay 6f. *J. Mason.* **65**

DISCO KING 2 b.c. Green Dancer 132–Glamorous (Snob 130) (1980 8fg 8g) Jan 16; 31,000Y; tall, close-coupled, rather narrow colt; second reported foal; dam won 9f apprentice race in French Provinces and is sister to high-class middle-distance filly Glaneuse; dropped out over 2f out when behind in 23-runner minor event won by Shergar at Newbury in September and 17-runner maiden event at Newmarket in October (7/1). *I. Balding.* **–**

DISCO LASS 2 b.f. Record Token 128–Pladda (Reliance II 137) (1980 5d 7g) Apr 11; 1,700Y; tall, close-coupled filly; half-sister to 1979 2-y-o 5f winner Lady Ember (by Hot Spark) and a winner in Italy; dam won 3 times over $1\frac{1}{2}$m in Ireland; unquoted when ninth of 19 behind Raja Sculptor in seller at Chepstow in September; blinkered and didn't move well to start on first appearance. *S. Matthews.* **–**

DISCRETION (FR) 4 ch.c. Bold Lad (USA)–Wordless 74 (Worden II 129) (1979 11d 12s 9g 10g^4 10g 10g^3 10.5d* 10.5s* 1980 11g 9.2d^4 9.7d* 8g^3 8g^2 10s 10g^4 10g*) French colt; won handicap at Longchamp in May and La Coupe de Maisons-Laffitte in September, latter by $\frac{1}{2}$ length from Speed Bus; placed in between in Prix du Chemin de Fer du Nord at Chantilly (third to Rostov) and Prix Messidor at Maisons-Laffitte (neck second to Tassmoun); best at up to 10.5f; probably acts on any going; blinkered third start at 3 yrs; sold to M. Fustok 70,000 gns Newmarket December Sales. *J. Cunnington, jnr, France.* **117**

DISMANTLER 4 ch.g. Laser Light 118–Ballydell (Pall Mall 132) (1979 8s^2 10s* 9v 8s* 8g^2 9d^2 8g^4 10f^4 12g^3 11g* 12g^2 10.6g 10g 10.2s 1980 11fg 8f 12.2fg 10g 8fg) short-coupled, good-bodied gelding; stays $1\frac{1}{2}$m; seems to act on any going, except perhaps heavy; blinkered once at 2 yrs; probably has his own ideas about the game nowadays; sold 2,600 gns Doncaster August Sales. *S. Norton.* **–**

DISSIPATED DOLLAR 2 b.c. My Swallow 134–Dissipation 83 (Disciplinarian) (1980 5f 5f* 5fg* 5f^2 6g^2) Feb 9; leggy, quite useful sort; half-brother to 2 winners, including 5f to 7f winner The Sampson Girls (by Double Jump); dam won over 5f at 2 yrs; easy winner of maiden race at Carlisle and minor event at Doncaster in the space of 4 days in May; runner-up in minor events at Windsor and Doncaster afterwards, final outing when 4 lengths behind Age Quod Agis in June; will stay 1m; yet to race on a soft surface; sent to USA. *F. Durr.* **86**

DITTON WOOD 3 b.c. Moulton 128–Fortezza 108 (Botticelli 129) (1979 NR 1980 12fg 13.3fg^3 12g* 13.3d 12fg^2 12d^2) big, strong colt; half-brother to 3 winners, including very useful 1m winner Royal Emblem (by Reform); dam a miler; landed odds in apprentice maiden race at Newmarket in June; ran creditably in apprentice event on same course and handicap at Ripon on last 2 starts; will stay well; acts on a firm and a soft surface; suitable mount for a boy. *H. Wragg.* **86**

DIVETTA 3 ch.f. Ribero 126–Star Story 117 (Red God 128 §) (1979 5d 6d 6s* 7f^4 7g^4 6g 5d 6s^3 6s 1980 8f 10f 8f^3 11f^3 8fg* 8fg 10d^2 10s^2 11fg^4 11g 8.2s 8.2s 10d 10s) neat filly; poor mover; quite a moderate handicapper at her best; won at Carlisle in May; ran creditably seventh and eighth outings but poorly subsequently; stays 11f; acts on any going; blinkered final outing at 2 yrs and on penultimate start. *T. Fairhurst.* **61**

DIVINO SANTI (USA) 3 ch.c. Jungle Savage–Concha Marina (Forli) (1979 6g^2 6g* 1980 6fg^4 5f 6fg 8g^4 8fg^4 10g* 11d^2 10g) very attractive, rangy colt; beat Intinto a short head in minor event at Brighton in October; second in handicap at Newbury later in month; suited by middle distances; acts on a firm and a soft surface; sold 6,800 gns Doncaster November Sales. *R. Price.* **91**

DIWALI 2 b.c. Great Nephew 126–Upanishad 85 (Amber Rama 133) (1980 6fg 7g) Feb 16; 28,000Y; small, lengthy colt; first foal; dam, $1\frac{1}{4}$m winner, is half-sister to smart Bas Bleu and very useful Primerello; not fully fit when last in well-contested race at Kempton and £3,000 event at Goodwood (disputed lead 4f) in September; to be trained by G. Lewis. *J. Sutcliffe.* **–**

DIXIELANDER 2 ch.c. Son of Silver 123–Warmspun 86 (Specific 103) (1980 5g 7f^3 8fg 8.2g 10d) leggy, narrow colt; only a bad plater and was well beaten when favourite at Pontefract on fifth start. *P. Rohan.* **45**

DIZZY HEIGHTS 2 b.f. Daring Display 129–Balholm 61 (Le Levanstell 122) 68
(1980 5g 5g^4 5f^2(dis) 7d 5.1fg 5.1fg^3 5.1fg 6fg 8fg* 10d 8.2s*) Feb 27; 1,500Y; small, lengthy filly; half-sister to 3-y-o $1\frac{1}{4}$m seller winner Mr Petit (by Zeddaan); sold out of D. Thom's stable 1,400 gns after winning selling nursery at Beverley in September; attracted no bid when winning at Nottingham in October, holding off Bartra by $1\frac{1}{2}$ lengths; suited by 1m but isn't sure to stay $1\frac{1}{4}$m; acts on any going; blinkered seventh and eighth outings. *H. Fleming.*

D'LO 2 b.c. Sovereign Path 125–Blaskette 99 (Blast 125) (1980 7.2d 8d) Apr —
14; 33,000Y; well-grown, quite attractive colt; first foal; dam successful middle-distance handicapper; well beaten in minor event at Haydock in August and maiden race at Leicester in November. *J. Bethell.*

DOBRINA (FR) 3 b.f. Our Mirage 123–Demonia (Phil Drake 132) (1979 NR —
1980 8g 10fg 8.2g^4 10s 12s) 25,000 francs Y (approx £3,000); neat filly; half-sister to French $1\frac{1}{2}$m winner Baraka Du Diable (by Bel Baraka); dam placed over 9.5f in French Provinces; little better than plating class; should stay $1\frac{1}{2}$m. *A. Breasley.*

DOBSON'S CHOICE 2 gr.c. Birdbrook 110–Dualvi 91 (Dual 117) (1980 7f) —
Mar 13; tall, narrow colt; second foal; dam won over 7f at 2 yrs; 12/1 and backward when behind in 18-runner maiden race won by Blackfoot at Newmarket in October. *H. T. Jones.*

DOCKLANDS 3 gr.f. On Your Mark 125–Persuader 118 (Petition 130) (1979 —
5s^3 5g^4 5fg^4 6f 1980 8fg 8.5f 8g 8.2g 9s^4 10g) fair sort; quite a moderate maiden; had very stiff task third start but wasn't disgraced in finishing last of 8 to Cairn Rouge in Coronation Stakes at Royal Ascot; should stay $1\frac{1}{4}$m; acts on any going; ran poorly fourth outing. *C. Brittain.*

DOC MARTEN 2 b.c. Hotfoot 126–Rockney 84 (Roan Rocket 128) (1980 102
6g^3 5d^2 6g* 5g^4 6fg* 7f^2 5s* 7v^3) Apr 19; 6,400F, 19,000Y; compact, quite useful sort; half-brother to 2 winners, including useful 1978 2-y-o 6f winner Funky Angel (by Sassafras); dam 2-y-o 5f winner; won 20-runner maiden race

R. Griggs & Co Ltd's "Doc Marten"

at Nottingham in July, Clarence House Stakes at Ascot in September (beat Buffavento by 2½ lengths with something to spare) and minor event at Stockton in October (just held off Spindrifter); also in frame in 2 races won by Marwell, finishing 4 lengths second in Chesterfield Stakes at Newmarket and 5¾ lengths fourth of six in Flying Childers Stakes at Doncaster, and was giving 12 lb to odds-on Belloc when ¾-length second in small race at Lingfield; effective at 5f to 7f; acts on any going except, perhaps, heavy (a little below his best final start); often bandaged behind; genuine and consistent. *W. O'Gorman.*

DOCTOR ATTY 3 b.g. Martinmas 128–Balabukha (Sayajirao 132) (1979 7f 6fg 1980 8.2s 8g⁴ 10g) rather leggy, attractive gelding; good walker; stays 1m (well beaten over further); whipped round and took no part in both his races at 2 yrs and is best left alone; sold to W. Clay 950 gns Doncaster October Sales. *R. Armstrong.* **§§**

DOCTOR FAUSTUS 2 gr.c. Martinmas 128–Pampatamy 75 (Immortality) (1980 5f³ 5fg 6fg 8s) Jan 31; 3,700F, 2,800Y; small colt; half-brother to 1976 2-y-o 1m winner Padovanna (by Allangrange); dam placed at up to 1m; kept on well when beaten 2 necks by Sweet Spark in maiden race at Wolverhampton in August, easily best effort; should stay 1m (behind in valuable seller when tried at trip); acts on firm going; whipped round and unseated rider at start third outing. *P. Cole.* **72**

DOCTOR SORBET 2 ch.f. Sweet Revenge 129–Beau Fleece (Fleece 114) (1980 6d 5s 5g 6fg 7fg) May 28; bad plater. *R. Hoad.* –

DOGBERRY 2 ch.c. Sassafras 135–Ombra Del Sol (Ballymoss 136) (1980 6fg 6g) Mar 30; 6,000F; quite well-made colt; half-brother to a winner in Italy by Prince Regent; dam won in Italy, including 1m Premio Royal Mares; apprentice ridden when in rear in maiden races at Doncaster and Newmarket in the summer; likely to need a test of stamina. *H. Wragg.* –

DOGWALK 4 b.g. Ribero 126–Country Path 101 (Mossborough 126) (1979 9v 10g 10fg 12d* 12fg 13d² 12f* 1980 10.6fg 12f³ 13.3g³ 12s⁴ 14.7g³) strong, good-bodied gelding; good mover; looked and ran well when 2½ lengths fourth of 10 to Shady Nook in Old Newton Cup at Haydock in July; not seen out after finishing third to Try Sandicliffe in £3,700 event at Redcar later in month; stays well; acts on any going. *H. Wragg.* **84**

DOIKAS 2 b.c. Condorcet–Rullabelle (Bluerullah 115) (1980 6d 7d 7fg³ 7fg 6s) May 4; 1,900Y; smallish, lengthy, rather lightly-made colt; first foal; dam never ran; prominent in 7f races in July, finishing 3 lengths fifth of 14 to Scintillating Air in maiden race at Newmarket and 1¾ lengths third of 13 to Bonny Gold when favourite for maiden auction event at Doncaster; behind in nurseries last 2 starts (moved moderately to post); will stay 1¼m. *I. Walker.* **71**

DOLBEARE LAD 2 b.g. Gambling Debt 98–Charm Spirit (Money Business 84) (1980 5fg 6g 5.8fg 5g) Apr 30; first foal; dam ran once over hurdles; in rear in maiden and minor events. *J. Cann.* –

DOLLARERINA 2 b. or br.f. Sit In The Corner–Goldwis 94 (Golden Cloud) (1980 5fg 6fg 6s 6fg² 7f 6g) Mar 15; neat filly; poor mover; sister to 2 winners, including dual 1977 2-y-o 5f winner Dollar-A-Corner; dam won from 5f to 7f; plater; neck second to Just Archy in 10-runner race at Pontefract in July, best effort; seems not to stay 7f; ran poorly in blinkers final outing. *K. Stone.* **49**

DOLLARHIDE 2 b.c. Busted 134–Pennycuick 101 (Celtic Ash) (1980 7s) May 6; 144,000Y; third living foal; half-brother to 3-y-o 11.7f winner Supreme Coin (by Great Nephew) and very useful 1978 2-y-o 5f winner Penny Blessing (by So Blessed); dam sprinting half-sister to Mummy's Pet, Arch Sculptor and Parsimony; 10/1, ran with promise when about 12 lengths sixth of 19 to Lord Never in maiden race at the Curragh in September, weakening only from distance after being left alone on far side over 2f out; sure to do better. *D. Weld, Ireland.* – p

DOLLAR POCKET (USA) 2 ch.c. Full Pocket–Stew Zoo (Sunrise Flight) (1980 5s 5fg⁴ 5fg⁴ 5f 7d 5f 5fg³ 5fg*(dis) 6f 5d) Feb 6; $70,000Y; compact colt; fourth foal; half-brother to 3 winners, including Pepysian (by Reflected Glory), a winner of over $100,000 at up to 9f; dam won 9 times at up to 6f; put up easily best efforts in September and looked outstandingly pick of paddock when winning 5-runner £3,100 event at Ascot by 1½ lengths from odds-on Queen of Prussia; failed a dope test afterwards and was disqualified; had previously run well when apprentice ridden in valuable nursery at Newbury in September, making up a tremendous amount of ground in final furlong and failing by only **93**

a head and a neck to catch Barnet Heir; best form at 5f on top-of-the-ground; blinkered fourth and sixth starts; none too consistent. *R. Simpson.*

DOLLYFUL 2 b. or br.f. Track Spare 125–Ever Joyful (Aureole 132) (1980 6fg 5fg) Feb 5; 8,000F, 16,000Y; sister to fair 5f and 7f winner Be Cross and half-sister to a winner; dam unraced half-sister to smart miler Patris; soundly beaten in minor events at Newmarket in August and Windsor in September. *R. Armstrong.* —

DOLLYMIXTURE BOY 2 b.c. Connaught 130–Country Niece (Great Nephew 126) (1980 6d 7g 7fg 8g 8g) Mar 27; 6,000Y; small, lengthy colt; good walker and mover; second foal; half-brother to French 3-y-o Balibest (by Ballymore), a winner over 10.5f; dam ran 3 times; had stiff tasks in good-class maiden and minor events, on last 2 outings showing some ability; will be suited by middle distances. *R. Armstrong.* **69**

DOLLY'S BADGE 4 ch.c. Tyrant–Snooty Girl (High Hat 131) (1979 8.5d 10.1g 12g 1980 15f 16s 14g) poor maiden; dead. *A. Pitt.* —

DOM ALDO (FR) 3 b.c. Hard to Beat 132–Aldonza (Exbury 138) (1979 NR 1980 8g 10g* 10g* 11g^2 12fg^4 12.5s) 75,000 francs Y (approx £8,900); third foal; half-brother to a winner in Italy; dam, winner once over 1½m from 2 starts at 3 yrs, is daughter of Oaks runner-up La Bamba; ran well in good company on fourth and fifth starts, going down by a neck to Julius Caesar in Prix Noailles at Longchamp in April and being beaten 6 lengths into fourth behind Policeman in Prix du Jockey-Club at Chantilly in June; had earlier won 2 small races at Cagnes-sur-Mer; should stay beyond 1½m; ran poorly in Prix Maurice de Nieuil at Saint-Cloud on final outing in July and is possibly unsuited by soft going. *C. Milbank, France.* **114**

DOM D'ALBIGNAC 3 b.c. Luthier 126–Primula (Petingo 135) (1979 NR 1980 10g^4 9g* 10d^2 10.5d* 9d* 10s^2 10d^4 10g* 12f 10g) strong, quite attractive colt; first foal; dam very useful winner over 1m in France; won small races at Evry and Saint-Cloud, Prix Ardan at Evry and Prix Ridgway at Deauville; beat Strong Gale by 1½ lengths in last-named in August; also ran well when 5 lengths second to Corvaro (rec 4 lb) in Prix Eugene Adam at Saint-Cloud, ½-length fourth to Glenorum in Prix de la Cote Normande at Deauville and 2¾ lengths fifth to Prince Bee (gave 4 lb) in Prix Niel at Longchamp; stays 1½m; acts on any going; usually blinkered; consistent. *O. Douieb, France.* **118**

DOMITIAN 2 b.f. Young Emperor 133–Schloss 87 (Busted 134) (1980 6fg 7f 7g 5f) Mar 17; first foal; dam, 1¼m performer, is sister to dam of Gimcrack winner Stanford; poor form in maiden races, best effort on final start; should stay 7f. *P. Cole.* —

DOM PERIGNON 5 b.g. Sparkler 130–Breathalyser (Alcide 136) (1979 12.2s 12d^2 12d^4 12s* 12f 12f^2 12g^2 12fg^3 12g 12f 12fg^3 10d 1980 12g 12d 12.3g* 13g^4 12fg 10.6s) middle-distance handicapper; made virtually all when unchallenged winner of ladies race at Newcastle in August, beating Seajan 5 lengths; not disgraced under a penalty next time; acts on any going. *W. Elsey.* **74**

DONALLAN 2 gr.f. No Mercy 126–Wait Now 90 (Vimy 132) (1980 6d 6s 8g 8.2s) Mar 29; 2,500F, 1,500Y; half-sister to several winners, including useful stayer Blind Harbour (by Star Moss) and useful 1m to 1¼m handicapper Delayed Tip (by Gratitude); dam won at 1½m; well beaten in Scottish maiden and minor events. *T. Craig.* —

DON AMIGO 6 br.g. Relko 136–Donna Lydia 110 (Hyperion) (1979 NR 1980 14d) quite a moderate staying handicapper; heavily bandaged when tailed off on only outing of 1980; suited by top-of-the-ground conditions; sold 330 gns Ascot September Sales. *W. Wright.* —

DONATELLA 2 b.f. Arch Sculptor 123–Raglin (Ragusa 137) (1980 5f* 5fg 6f^2 5f*) Apr 17; 3,600Y; compact, rather plain filly; second living foal; half-sister to Pot Hunter (by Mountain Call), successful over 6f; dam never ran; winner twice at Beverley, beating Ziparib a neck in maiden auction race in April and getting home by ¾ length from Queen's Token in nursery in July; stays 6f and may well get further; yet to race on an easy surface; goes well for an apprentice. *W. Wharton.* **80**

DONEGAL PRINCE 4 b.c. Prince de Galles 125–Serena Rose 76 (Hethersett 134) (1979 10s^3 16fg 12f^2 12.3s* 14s^2 12d 12s 1980 16.1d^3 8fg 12f^4 12fg^4 22.2fg^2 18.4g^4 21fg^4 14.7g 14g) quite attractive colt; ran very well and finished long way clear of remainder when going down by 1½ lengths to Balinger after a sustained battle in Queen Alexandra Stakes at Royal Ascot in June; kept on when creditable fifth to Sea Pigeon in Vaux Breweries Gold Tankard at Redcar **93**

in August, but dropped right out in straight when behind in Tote-Ebor at York later in month; needs a thorough test of stamina; acts on any going but is suited by some give in the ground; blinkered last 5 starts; suitable mount for an apprentice. *P. Kelleway.*

DONNA'S ROSE (HOL) 2 br.f. Cadmus 124–Donna Maria (Don Carlos) (1980 6s 7g 8fg 9d) Dutch-bred filly; dam well beaten in this country but won 5 times in Holland; unquoted when 3½ lengths fifth of 19 to Raja Sculptor in seller at Chepstow in September, second outing and best effort; should be suited by 1m. *J. Harris.* —

DON'T CRY FOR ME 3 b. or br.f. Hotfoot 126–Gold Poulet 84 (Goldhill 125) (1979 5s^4 1980 6f^4 7f 6g) leggy filly; plating-class maiden; best run at 6f on firm going. *W. H. H. Williams.* —

DONZEL 6 gr.g. Don II 123–Say Gwen (Never Say Die 137) (1979 16d^3 12f 19f 1980 9.6f*) plater nowadays; sold 2,050 gns after winning at Folkestone in April; effective at around 1m and evidently stays 2m; acts on any going; used to wear blinkers. *R. Carter.* **40**

DOOBIE DO 2 b.f. Derring-Do 131–Tortola§ (Narrator 127) (1980 5g* 6g^2 6d^2 6g 7g^3 8fg^4) Jan 30; 46,000Y well-made filly; half-sister to 3 winners, including fairly useful 6f to 7f winner Avenged (by Sweet Revenge); dam half-sister to high-class stayer Almeria; quickened to lead inside final furlong when beating Fast Friend ½ length in 17-runner maiden event at Sandown in June; subsequently ran very well when second in 2 races at Newmarket, notably when running Nasseem to ¾ length in 11-runner Cherry Hinton Stakes in July on third outing, but was soundly beaten by Tolmi on fourth outing and by Leap Lively on sixth; best form at 6f but should stay further; acts well on a soft surface. *M. Stoute.* **106**

DOOGALI 6 ch.m. Doon 124–Rogali 80 (Royal Avenue 123) (1979 8d 10d* 10.2d 12d^3 10g^3 10fg* 10d^4 10s^4 11s 9f 1980 8d* 10g 8f 11fg 11d^2 11s 11fg 10.2d) lengthy mare; won strongly-run handicap at Newcastle in April going away by 1½ lengths from Bradamante; ran easily best subsequent race when second to Prince at Ayr in August; best form at up to 11f; acts on any going; good mount for an apprentice; sometimes sweats up. *W. H. H. Williams.* **83**

DOONALLY 4 b.g. Gold Rod 129–Bust 93 (Tenerani 135) (1979 8fg 8fg 10g 8fg 1980 15.5fg^4 15.5fg^4 16f^3) small, stocky gelding; staying maiden on flat; behind in seller on final start at 3 yrs; has been tried in blinkers; winning hurdler. *C. James.* —

DOON SILVER 6 gr. or ro.m. Doon 124–Silver Pin (Pindari 124) (1979 10fg 8g 1980 10g 8fg^3) poor plater; wears bandages. *A. Davison.* —

DO OR DIE 3 b.g. Warpath 113–Shenandoah 88 (Mossborough 126) (1979 NR 1980 12g 12g 14.6fg 12s. 15s) strong, good sort; good walker; slow maiden. *C. Thornton.* —

DORA VACA 3 br.f. Cavo Doro 124–Guernavaca 46 (Klairon 131) (1979 5s^4 6fg 6s^4 8fg 8h^2 8.2d* 1980 12f 11d 10d 12.2f 8fg 12fg^3 12g 13.8fg 9s^4) fair sort; quite moderate (rated 78) at 2 yrs; poor plater nowadays; probably stays 1½m; acts on any going except very soft; blinkered fifth start; sometimes sweats up; sold to W. Clay 660 gns Doncaster October Sales. *J. Etherington.* —

D'ORLEANS 3 b.f. Duc D'Orleans 76–What A Performance (Gala Performance) (1979 6f 8f 8g 1980 8s 8s) well-grown filly; probably of little account. *B. Richmond.* —

DOROTHY KATE 3 ch.f. Pee Mai 107–Aderf (Pendragon) (1979 NR 1980 16.1s) strong filly; third foal; dam won over hurdles; unquoted and backward when tailed off in amateur riders maiden race at Haydock in October. *S. Norton.* —

DOTY 3 b.c. High Top 131–Luscinia 73 (Sing Sing 134) (1979 NR 1980 8g^2 8g 9d 10s) 20,000Y; strong, attractive colt; good walker; half-brother to 2 winners, including 5f and 6f winner Nariz (by Brigadier Gerard); dam won over 1m; second in maiden race at Kempton in July, easily best effort; stays 1m; ran badly last 2 starts; sold out of R. Price's stable 3,600 gns Doncaster September Sales. *M. Bradley.* **72**

DOUBLE DUCHESS 2 ch.f. Connaught 130–Double Vitesse (Double Jump 131) (1980 5f 5fg 5g 5g 6g 6fg 8fg) May 11; compact filly; third foal; half-sister to French middle-distance winner Cosworth (by Moulton); dam won at up to 1m at 2 yrs in France; only poor form in maiden races; blinkered seventh outing. *W. Elsey.* **55**

DOUBLE FLORIN (USA) 3 b.c. His Majesty–Stamp and Cash (Roi Rouge) **89** (1979 7g 7fg 8g 8g^3 1980 9fg 12fg* 11.7f* 14f* 12fg^2 12s 14g 16.5fg^2 16f 14g 16fg^2) small colt; good mover; fair handicapper; successful at Warwick, Windsor and Sandown in May; stays well; acts on firm going and is possibly unsuited by very soft; needs strong handling. *J. Dunlop.*

DOUBLE-HEADER 5 b.g. Double-U-Jay 120–Hi Tess 65 (Supreme Court 135) – (1979 17.1g 10f 10g 12fg 12f 1980 12d) poor plater; stays 1¼m; wears blinkers; good mount for a boy. *D. Jermy.*

DOUBLE HIGH 3 b.g. High Top 131–Appellanda 92 (Reform 132) (1979 **92** 6g 6d^2 8.2g^2 1980 10.8s* 12.3f* 12h* 12fg* 12f^4 10g) compact, well-made gelding; favourite when winning maiden race at Warwick in April and handicaps at Chester, Brighton and Ripon in May; landed odds with ridiculous ease by a length from Karlinsky on last-named; stays 1½m; acts on any going; exported to Hong Kong. *M. Stoute.*

DOUBLE MEANING 4 gr.g. High Top 131–Pseudonym 110 (Acropolis 132) **95** (1979 8fg* 8fg^2 8f* 1980 8d 8d 8f 10fg 8g 7d 8g 8h^4 9f^4 8g* 8d) rather unfurnished gelding; has reportedly been pin-fired; made nearly all and beat Monte Acuto decisively by 4 lengths in apprentice event at Ascot in October; ran creditably on other occasions, notably when close fourth of 19 behind Baronet in William Hill Cambridgeshire at Newmarket earlier in month; should stay beyond 9f; acts well on a sound surface. *A. Bailey.*

DOUBLE MIRAGE 5 ch.g. Our Mirage 123–Marilyns Mirage 75 (Skymaster **45** 126) (1979 12d^3 16fg 10.6g 1980 13d 12d 16.1d^3 16g 12g^4) poor staying handicapper nowadays; third to Lenygon in amateur riders event at Haydock in July; suited by a test of stamina; best form on a soft surface. *W. Charles.*

DOUBLE SHARP 2 gr.c. Sharp Edge 123–Florintina 104 (Floribunda 136) **84** p (1980 8d^2) Mar 16; tall, useful-looking colt; brother to very useful 3-y-o Premier Rose and useful 5f to 1m winner Shapina, and half-brother to a winner; dam won at 7f and 1m; 20/1, showed promise when 4 lengths second of 15 to Rollrights in maiden race at Leicester in November, showing up prominently throughout, despite running green under pressure; stays 1m; should improve. *P. Cole.*

DOUBLE STAR 8 ch.g. Star Moss 122–Corypha (Royal Palm 131) (1979 NR – 1980 12d 13d 14g) of little account; wears bandages. *D. Ringer.*

DOUBLE STRETCH 4 ch.f. Double-U-Jay 120–Robert's Carol 69 (Sing Sing – 134) (1979 NR 1980 6f 7fg 9.6f) bad plater. *J. Long.*

DOUBLE TOPS 2 ch.f. Paddy's Progress 113–Peg Top 93 (Star Moss 122) – (1980 5s 5fg 7g 8d 10s) Jan 31; strong filly; fourth reported foal; dam won over 1½m and over fences; only poor form. *D. Dale.*

DOUBTFUL FRIEND 2 ch.c. Be Friendly 130–Sunny Polly (Sunny Way 120) **57** (1980 5s 5s 6fg^2 6g^3 7f^2 7fg^4 8.2d) Apr 15; 850F, 750Y; leggy colt; half-brother to 2 minor winners in Ireland; dam never ran; second in sellers at Stockton and Beverley in the summer; best form at up to 7f; acts on firm going. *J. Hardy.*

DOUBTFUL PORTION 2 gr.c. Grey Mirage 128–Uproar 62 (Major Portion – 129) (1980 6fg^4 6g 6fg) Mar 5; 8,400Y; neat colt; second living foal; half-brother to 7f and 1m seller winner Lady Alinba (by Sharpen Up); dam showed little worthwhile form; emulating his dam so far. *J. Hill.*

DOUBTFUL SUN 5 b.g. Dieu Soleil 111–Doubtful Nelly (Doubtless II 111) – (1979 NR 1980 12.5s) lightly raced and no form in maiden and minor events on flat; unruly on only outing of 1980. *I. Jordon.*

DOUBTWASH GIRL 2 b.f. Hot Spark 126–Arodstown Alice (Sahib 114) **80** (1980 5f^4 5g 5f^3 5g 5g^2 5fg* 5g^3) Feb 20; 2,300F; small filly; third produce; dam ran only 3 times; made all to win 21-runner minor event at Catterick in September by a neck from unlucky-in-running Blue Lass; may stay 6f. *M. W. Easterby.*

DOUSCHKINA 2 b.f. Dubassoff–Marbella II 64 (Match III 135) (1980 6fg*) **86** p Feb 18; compact, quite useful sort; half-sister to 2 minor winners, including 1½m winner Missed (by Salvo); dam from same family as Miralgo and Parnell; third favourite, stayed on well when winning 12-runner minor event at Newmarket in August by 2 lengths from Holiday Club; could make a useful filly over middle distances at 3 yrs. *B. Hobbs.*

DOVETAIL 2 br.f. Brigadier Gerard 144–Duboff 120 (So Blessed 130) (1980 – p 7g) Mar 26; well-made, attractive filly; first foal; dam won 11 races, including

Sun Chariot Stakes and Child Stakes; 12/1, showed signs of inexperience on way to start of 26-runner maiden race at Newmarket in October and finished in rear behind Full of Reason; looks capable of better. *P. Walwyn.*

DOWNBEAT 3 b.f. Busted 134–Land of Song 82 (Sing Sing 134) (1979 7s^3 1980 8s^4 8g^3 8.2g^3) unfurnished filly; quite a moderate maiden; will stay 1¼m; yet to race on a firm surface. *W. Hastings-Bass.* **61**

DOWN THE HATCH 2 b.c. Relko 136–Swallow (Forli) (1980 6g 6fg* 7.6g) Apr 19; 14,000Y; tall, quite attractive colt; second foal; dam ran 3 times; drew clear from 1½f out when winning 16-runner maiden race at Salisbury in September by 2½ lengths from Serpina; had much stiffer task in £4,300 event at Lingfield later in month and finished only sixth, 10 lengths behind Admiral's Heir; will stay 1¼m. *F. Durr.* **76**

DOWN TO DARKIE 5 ch.g. Shantung 132–Nutting Grove 95 (Crepello 136) (1979 10.2s 13s^4 16d^2 12d^4 14fg 16f 14.6fg 1980 16fg* 16f 15f^2 14f 12g 16.5g 16.1fg) staying handicapper; made all and beat Athford by 6 lengths at Newbury in April; inconsistent afterwards; acts on any going; suitable mount for a lady rider; sweating fourth start; sold to M. Haynes 1,900 gns Newmarket Autumn Sales. *F. Durr.* **62**

DOWNTOWN AGENT 3 b.f. Rheingold 137–Bundling Board (Pretense) (1979 7g 1980 10v* 10f 12d 11.7s 8fg 8fg) big, well-made filly; stayed on really well to win maiden race at Salisbury in March; in rear in varied company afterwards; should stay 1½m+; acts on heavy going; out of her depth second and third starts. *C. Brittain.* **85**

DRAGOMAN 4 b.g. Dragonara Palace 115–Evendo 83 (Derring-Do 131) (1979 5f 8fg 5d 6s 1980 10fg 8s 6fg 7fg 8d) leggy, narrow gelding; blind in right eye; plating-class maiden; best form at sprint distances; possibly unsuited by soft ground; has been tried in blinkers; wears an eye shield. *K. Stone.* **–**

DRAGON (FR) 3 gr.c. Phaeton 123–Drogue (Dan Cupid 132) (1979 5.5g* 6g^4 7g^2 8fg^2 8s^4 6.5d^3 8s* 1980 11g 8g 12fg 9.2s 8d 7d 12d*) first foal; dam French 2-y-o 1m winner; put up a much-improved and high-class performance on final start at 2 yrs, making all to beat Nice Havrais by 2 lengths in Grand Criterium at Longchamp; didn't run up to that form in 1980, managing to win only £5,600 event at Saint-Cloud in November; put up best other efforts behind stable-companions at Longchamp on second and fifth outings, finishing under 6 lengths seventh to In Fijar in Poule d'Essai des Poulains in May on first occasion and about 6½ lengths sixth to Hilal in Prix du Rond-Point in September on second; well beaten on his other starts, including in Prix du Jockey-Club at Chantilly: stays 1½m; acts well on soft going. *M. Saliba, France.* **112**

DRAGONARA LADY 4 gr.f. Dragonara Palace 115–Broadside 72 (Fighting Ship 121) (1979 8v 8s 8s 8.5d 7d 1980 8.2d^4 7fg) poor plater; probably unsuited by soft ground; sold 520 gns Ascot May Sales. *H. O'Neill.* **–**

DRAGONARA MALTA 3 ch.f. Dragonara Palace 115–St Gay 77 (St Chad 120) (1979 5f 5fg^2 5g^3 5d^2 1980 5d 6g 6g 7f 8g 9d) compact, fair sort; moderate (rated 80) at 2 yrs; showed no form in 1980; bred to stay 1m; blinkered third and fifth starts; sold 660 gns Newmarket Autumn Sales. *J. Dunlop.* **–**

DRAGONIGHT 3 b.g. Dragonara Palace 115–Justerina (Aureole 132) (1979 5d 5d 5s 7fg 1980 10v 10.8s 7fg 7f 8g) workmanlike gelding; little worthwhile form in varied company, including selling. *J. Hardy.* **–**

DRAGONIST 2 b.f. Dragonara Palace 115–Tzu-Hsi 66 (Songedor 116) (1980 5g^4 5fg^2 5s* 5g^4 5d* 6d^4 5fg^4 5s^4) Mar 1; 3,500F; well-grown filly; second produce; dam 6f winner; made most and kept on well to win maiden race at Nottingham in June and 4-runner minor event at Ayr the following month, latter by 1½ lengths from Royal Duty; fourth in minor event and nurseries subsequently; seemed not to stay when tried over 6f; probably acts on any going but clearly goes well on soft ground; sweated up and gave impression she was past her best on final start. *J. Bethell.* **82**

DRAGON PALACE (USA) 2 ch.c. Le Fabuleux 133–Barbara Longhi (Ribot 142) (1980 7f 8g* 10.2s) May 7; $37,000Y; compact colt; fourth foal; half-brother to winners in Italy and USA; dam, winner twice in Italy, is half-sister to Italian St Leger winner Ben Marshall; 20/1 and looking still in need of race, showed a good turn of foot to lead 100 yds out and win 17-runner maiden race at Newmarket in October by a length from Nepentha; well beaten next time out; bred to stay at least 1½m; possibly unsuited by soft ground. *M. Jarvis.* **83**

DRAGON'S HEAD 3 b.g. Star Appeal 133–Royal Rosette 66 (Pardao 120) **97**
(1979 6fg^3 7f* 7f^3 1980 8s^2 8.2fg 10d* 10g) strong, well-made gelding; good walker; kept on well to beat Beirut a neck in Trafalgar House Handicap at Sandown in June; suited by 1¼m and will stay further; probably acts on any going; pulled hard second start; exported to Hong Kong. *R. Price.*

DRAKES COURT 3 ch.g. Marechal Drake 101–Amery Court (Malfaiteur) –
(1979 NR 1980 9fg 11.7f 12fg 12d) workmanlike gelding; second foal; dam poor maiden hurdler; no sign of ability in newcomers event and maiden races; sometimes sweats up. *C. V. Miller.*

DRAKE'S REST 2 b.c. Porto Bello 118–Crackle 74 (Nelcius 133) (1980 7g) –
Mar 9; 4,100Y; first foal; dam placed twice over 1m; seventh of 18 to Price of Peace in maiden race at Salisbury in July; dead. *G. Beeson.*

DRAS LASS 4 bl.f. Don Carlos–Lantern (Relic) (1979 10g 12d 10s^4 11s 8fg –
9fg^2 9g* 9s^2 9g^4 10s^3 10fg^4 10g 1980 8fg 8s^2 8.2d 8g 10.6s 8s 8s) lightly-made filly; mainly disappointing (behind in valuable seller fourth start), running best race when second to easy winner Cilium in minor event at Newcastle in August; stays 1¼m; seems to act on any going; blinkered sixth start. *N. Tinkler.*

DRAW SWORDS 4 ch.g. Queen's Hussar 124–Acute 79 (St Paddy 133) (1979 –
8d 8f 11.5fg 12f 9f^4 1980 10.1s 8d 10.1d^4 8.3g) temperamental plater; stays 9f; acts on firm going. *D. Wintle.*

DRAYPARCS 2 b.c. Will Somers 114§–Speckled Leinster (Prefairy 99) (1980 –
6fg 8fg 8d) May 20; 600F, 300Y; neat colt; first produce; dam, who won twice over hurdles in Ireland, is half-sister to dam of Balidar and Balliol (by Will Somers); in rear in maiden races at Salisbury, Beverley and Warwick, running very badly on last-named; sold 525 gns Ascot November Sales. *S. Mellor.*

DRAYTON STAR 3 b.g. Mountain Call 125–Malvina 82 (Fidalgo 129) (1979 **59**
5d 5fg 6f 5g 6f 1980 5h 7f* 11d 9.4g^4 8fg^2) workmanlike gelding; plater; attracted no bid after winning at Redcar in May; isn't certain to stay 11f; acts on firm going; sweated up badly but ran respectably fourth start; claimed by A. Jarvis after fifth outing. *M. H. Easterby.*

DREAM RACER 5 ch.m. Carrick Lodge 88–Fezattie (Fez 107) (1979 NR –
1980 13d^4 13s) first foal; dam never ran; unquoted when tailed off in minor events at Ayr in July and August. *T. Craig.*

DRED SCOTT (USA) 8 b.g. Tom Rolfe–Free Model (Phideas) (1979 13g –
16f 16fg 12g 1980 18d 12.2v 16s 8g 12g 12g) poor handicapper nowadays; stays 1¾m; acts on any going; wears blinkers; sold out of K. Ivory's stable 1,000 gns Ascot May Sales. *J. Old.*

DRESSEDTOKILL 2 b.f. Sharpen Up 127–Boudoir 95 (Klairon 131) (1980 **75**
5fg^3 5fg*) Feb 15; leggy, narrow filly; second foal; half-sister to fairly useful Lady's Slipper (by Hotfoot), winner over 6f at 2 yrs; dam stayed 1¼m; odds on following a promising third to Pushy at Newmarket, made all despite veering left 2f out when winning 16-runner maiden race at Leicester in May by short head from Time for Thought; not seen out again. *B. Hobbs.*

DR HACKENBUSH 3 ch.c. Communication 119–Belle Ann (Our Babu 131) –
(1979 7fg 8f 1980 8fg 8d 8.3s) leggy, narrow colt; bad plater; has been tried in blinkers; sold 270 gns Ascot August Sales. *C. Dingwall.*

DRILL 3 gr.f. No Mercy 126–Geology 74 (Rockavon 120) (1979 5f 6g^4 7g^4 6fg^2 –
1980 7f^4 7f 8s 6g 6s^4) lengthy filly; quite modest (rated 75) at 2 yrs; below form in 1980, including when blinkered in a seller on final start; probably stays 7f; best form on a sound surface; sold 680 gns Newmarket Autumn Sales. *G. Pritchard-Gordon.*

DRINK DEEP 2 ch.g. Record Run 127–Penny Wise (Hook Money 124) (1980 –
5d 5s 7g 6fg) Apr 20; 2,700Y; leggy, lengthy gelding; no sign of ability in maiden races and a seller. *W. Wharton.*

DROMEFS 5 b.g. Hotfoot 126–Grecian Palm 78 (Royal Palm 131) (1979 8d 10d **94**
8fg 8g 8fg^4 8fg 8g 7d^4 10.2f^4 8fg^3 9f^3 10d^4 8d^3 1980 8f^4 8fg* 8f 8f^4 7f^3 8g 8g^4 8g* 10g 8g 9f^2) quite attractive, useful-looking gelding; fairly useful handicapper on his day; placed in William Hill Cambridgeshire at Newmarket for second successive year in October, finishing very strongly and failing by only a short head to catch Baronet; had won two handicaps at Newmarket earlier, beating Tower Joy comfortably in May (apprentice event) and Royaber by a length in August; best form at up to 9f; acts on any going except perhaps soft; has run well in blinkers; goes well on a straight course. *G. Pritchard-Gordon.*

DRONACHARYA (USA) 4 br.c. Nijinsky 138–Belle de Nuit (Warfare) (1979 –
6s 8s 10.1fg 10f^4 8f 1980 6g 8d 8fg 10.1g 8g 10fg 8g 10.8d) good-bodied ex-American colt; disappointing maiden; looked none too genuine fourth start; should stay at least 1¼m; blinkered sixth outing; sold 820 gns Newmarket Autumn Sales. *A. Breasley.*

DROPSHOT 5 br.g. Town Crier 119–Lunawood 71 (Blast 125) (1979 12v –
12d 12s 13.8g 12f 12f 1980 12f) plater; stays 1¼m; has been tried in blinkers; inconsistent. *G. Balding.*

DR STEVE 2 ch.c. Wishing Star 117–Tabankula (Selko) (1980 5fg 6fg 6g 6g **75**
6g^3 7fg^3) Apr 29; 1,500F, 8,600Y; second produce; dam Irish 7f and 1½m winner; improved in August and was nearest at finish when 3¼ lengths third of 16 to Ganimede in 7f maiden event at Yarmouth; will be suited by middle distances. *R. Sheather.*

DRUMMER JESS 2 b.f. Rapid River 127–Jet Princess (Jolly Jet 111) (1980 **54**
5g 5.8fg 5g^4 5s 5g 5f 5f 5d) Mar 23; 1,050Y; useful-looking filly; not a good mover; second foal; dam apparently of little account; only poor form in varied races; sold 310 gns Ascot November Sales. *J. Douglas-Home.*

DUBAI CREEK 3 ch.c. Grundy 137–Be Noble (Vaguely Noble 140) (1979 NR **64**
1980 10s 10s 8fg 9.4fg 11.7d^2) 40,000Y; neat colt; second foal; dam, pulled up through injury on only outing, is daughter of high-class 1958 2-y-o Be Careful; 33/1 and apprentice ridden when showing first worthwhile form to be second in handicap at Bath in October; evidently suited by 1½m; acts on a soft surface; has worn bandages. *H. T. Jones.*

DUBANA 3 b.g. Dubassoff–Maimana (Charlottesville 135) (1979 8.2g 10.6d –
8g 1980 12.3s 8fg 12fg) tall, leggy gelding; poor maiden. *W. C. Watts.*

DUCHESS OF HOWFEN 2 b. or br.f. Steel Heart 128–Ballymaglasson **66**
(Ballyciptic 122) (1980 5f 7g 8fg 7d^4) Apr 7; 7,400Y; small filly; first foal; dam, half-sister to successful broodmares Messene and Indian Maid, won over 1½m in Ireland; only modest form, best effort when fourth of 10 to Supreme Fjord, beaten about 4½ lengths, in small race at Catterick in October; will stay 1m. *W. Hastings-Bass.*

DUC'S SPIRIT 3 ch.g. Duc D'Orleans 76–Spirit of Ecstasy 70 (Pardao 120) –
(1979 NR 1980 10fg) small, lengthy gelding; first foal; dam winning plater; dwelt, soon behind and finished tailed off in maiden race at Beverley in September. *B. Richmond.*

DUGALD 3 b.g. Six O'Clock–Toys (Sammy Davis 129) (1979 NR 1980 12.2g **58**
12.2g 10f^2 10fg 12.5s^4) 1,050Y; useful sort; second foal; dam never ran; best run at 1¼m on firm going; has run respectably for a 5-lb claimer. *J. Fitzgerald.*

DUKA 5 ch.g. Native Bazaar 122–Sultry One (Tropique 128) (1979 NR 1980 –
9fg) smallish, well-made gelding; poor maiden on flat; effective at 1m and does not stay long distances. *N. Gaselee*

DUKEDOM 3 ch.c. Connaught 130–Albany 120 (Pall Mall 132) (1979 NR **117**
1980 8f^3 10fg* 10.5f 12g 12fg^2 12v) strong, deep-bodied colt; half-brother to smart stayer Buttress (by Busted), very useful 1976 2-y-o 5f and 7f winner Card Player (by Crepello) and very useful middle-distance performer English Harbour (by Mill Reef); dam, daughter of high-class stayer Almeria, was smart at 1¼m; ran two very good races at Ascot, winning White Rose Stakes in April by 6 lengths (made all) and finishing 2 lengths second to Fingal's Cave in Cumberland Lodge Stakes in September (made most, and stayed on very gamely when headed); put up best other effort when 5 lengths fifth of 8 to Hello Gorgeous in Mecca-Dante Stakes at York on third outing; well beaten in Great Voltigeur Stakes at York (reportedly pulled a muscle in his back) on fourth start and Gran Premio del Jockey Club at Milan on final appearance; stays 1½m; acts well on firm ground and is probably unsuited by heavy. *I. Balding.*

DUKE OF BRITTANY 2 gr.c. Saritamer 130–Belle Bretonne 90 (Celtic Ash) **73**
(1980 5.8fg 6fg 5.8g 7d 8g 8d^4 7d 10s^4) Feb 22; 3,700Y; compact colt; first foal; dam needed at least 2m; quite a moderate maiden; will stay 1½m+; probably needs some give in the ground. *S. Woodman.*

DUKE OF CONNAUGHT 3 b.g. Connaught 130–Paul-Mary 107 (Pardao 120) –
(1979 7fg 7s 8.2g 1980 8f 9.4fg 12.2d) strong gelding; behind in maiden and minor events; sweated up first start. *M. W. Easterby.*

DUKE OF YORK (NZ) 9 b.g. Darnley–Belle York (Isaac of York) (1979 NR –
1980 8fg 10fg^4 12h 11.7fg) compact New Zealand-bred gelding; winner at

The Queen's "Dukedom"

least 4 times on flat in his native country; 10 lengths fourth of 14 to Playful Paddy in minor event at Leicester in April, easily best effort over here; bandaged third start; sold 350 gns Ascot November Sales. *K. Ivory.*

DUKESBAY 3 ch.g. King's Company 124–Rockspray 77 (Roan Rocket 128) (1979 6s 6g 8g 8fg 8g 10g 1980 11.7f 12g 10.1s) strong gelding; poor plater; sometimes blinkered; sold 440 gns Ascot November Sales. *T. Marshall.* —

DUKES GOLD 3 b.g. Goldhill 125–Tuwin (Tudor Treasure 119) (1979 NR 1980 9.4fg 8.2s) second reported foal; dam winning point-to-pointer; tailed-off last in Northern maiden races. *G. Richards.* —

DULLINGHAM LAD 2 gr.c. Saulingo 122–Ambient 68 (Amber Rama 133) (1980 5d4 6s4) Apr 9; 5,200Y; second foal; half-brother to useful 3-y-o sprinter Westacombe (by Huntercombe); dam lightly raced; ran better race on first start when about $1\frac{1}{4}$ lengths fourth of 14 to Azaam in maiden event at Wolverhampton in October; started slowly and ran wide next time out; probably stays 6f. *H. Collingridge.* **76**

DULWICH VILLAGE 2 ch.c. Reform 132–Dinah Do 77 (Derring-Do 131) (1980 5fg 6fg 6g 6f4 6fg) quite well-made colt; third foal; dam won over 1m; $5\frac{1}{2}$ lengths fifth of 13 to Top of the Mark in maiden race at Epsom in August (moved up to fourth on disqualification of third horse), best effort; will be suited by 7f+; blinkered fourth and fifth outings; sold 2,800 gns Newmarket Autumn Sales. *D. Whelan.* **65**

DUMPER 3 b.g. Moulton 128–Boulette 114 (Nasram II 125) (1979 NR 1980 8fg 10fg 10fg 12g 12s3 12fg4 12.3s* 12g4 14g 16d2) big, strong gelding; half-brother to fairly useful 11f to $1\frac{3}{4}$m winner Rampage (by Busted); dam staying half-sister to 1,000 Guineas winner Full Dress II; stayed on to win modest maiden race at Newcastle in August, despite racing with head in air and hanging quite **74**

sharply left; ran respectably in handicap on final outing; stays well; suited by soft ground; blinkered eighth start; sold 13,500 gns Newmarket Autumn Sales. *H. Wragg.*

DUMPLINO 3 b.c. Bustino 136–Boule de Suif 88 (Major Portion 129) **(1979** NR 1980 9f 12fg* 12g 12g³ 12d² 12g* 12d³) 8,200Y; attractive, well-made colt; fourth foal; half-brother to 2 winners in Italy, including sprinter Dari' (by Amber Rama); dam stayed 1m, and is half-sister to 3 good animals; successful in maiden race at Haydock in May and handicap at Goodwood in September, battling on well under top weight in latter; will stay 1¾m; acts on a firm and a soft surface; blinkered fifth and sixth starts; sometimes coltish in paddock; ran badly third outing; sold 8,200 gns Newmarket Autumn Sales. *P. Walwyn.* **95**

DUNDERAVE 3 b.c. Owen Anthony 102–Lavant 101 (Le Lavandou 111) (1979 6fg⁴ 6s² 6g² 1980 6f 6f⁴ 7f 8g 8g 8g³ 10.8d* 10d* 10s* 12d) strong, compact, good-looking colt; good mover; in good form in October, easily winning minor event at Warwick and scoring in handicaps at Sandown and Chepstow; suited by 1¼m but appeared to find 1½m too far for him final outing; needs some give in the ground; lost rider third start. *R. Price.* **88**

DUNETTE (FR) 4 b.f. Hard to Beat 132–Pram (Fine Top 125) (1979 9.5d² 10fg 10.5g* 12fg⁴ 1980 12g³ 12d 12.5d* 12g⁴ 10g* 12f) **122**

Dunette, the first horse to beat Three Troikas when winning the Prix de Diane de Revlon in 1979, justified the decision to keep her in training even though she failed to reach a place in her two main objectives, the King George VI and Queen Elizabeth Diamond Stakes and the Prix de l'Arc de Triomphe. She won two more races, including the Grand Prix de Saint-Cloud in which she dead-heated with Shakapour.

The Grand Prix de Saint-Cloud invariably attracts a strong field and Dunette was only the fifth filly to win it since its institution in 1904 as the Prix du President de la Republique. Dunette had made a satisfactory reappearance behind Scorpio and Gain in the Grand Prix d'Evry but more recently had finished a disappointing fifth when odds on for La Coupe at Chantilly. She faced a difficult task at Saint-Cloud, opposed once more by Scorpio and Gain, the former of whom had in the meantime won the Hardwicke Stakes, as well as Noble Saint, Two of Diamonds and a three-year-old challenge which included the first two in the Prix du Jockey-Club, Policeman and Shakapour, and the improving Lancastrian. Dunette, looking particularly well, was always well placed as first Two of Diamonds and then Policeman made the running. She challenged Policeman early in the straight and had shaken him off by the distance, but she was unable to beat off the challenge of Shakapour who pressed her all the way to the line. Neither Dunette's jockey Doleuze nor Shakapour's Saint-Martin distinguished himself on this occasion; Doleuze threw up his arm in premature celebration of victory passing the post, just as he had done when narrowly getting the better of Three Troikas in the Prix de Diane, and Saint-Martin dropped his whip a furlong from home but for which he felt he'd have won.

Dunette was a shade disappointing in the King George on her next start, although in finishing fourth she certainly wasn't disgraced. She wasn't in a good position as the field turned into the straight—she had pulled very hard

Prix du Prince d'Orange, Longchamp—Dunette beats Three Troikas and Northern Baby

early on and had then been left behind as the leaders quickened—and she never held out any threat to Ela-Mana-Mou or Mrs Penny. She failed by half a length to catch Gregorian in third. She missed the Prix Foy at Longchamp in September because of colic and instead had her preparatory race for the Arc in the Prix du Prince d'Orange on the same course a week later, a race also chosen for Three Troikas, and the race which Alleged had won in 1978 before his second win in the Arc. Three Troikas, odds on despite a three-and-a-half-month lay off with a leg injury, clearly wasn't at her best and Dunette beat her by half a length, with Northern Baby back in third. Dunette was unable to confirm her form with Three Troikas in the Arc itself but both fillies ran most creditably. Dunette was well placed from the start and held a chance of a place up to the closing stages. She finished seventh, about three lengths behind Three Troikas who was bang on the heels of Detroit, Argument and Ela-Mana-Mou. Dunette was subsequently invited to take part in the Washington International at the end of the season but unfortunately she injured herself just beforehand and couldn't run.

Dunette (Fr) (b.f. 1976)	Hard to Beat (b 1969)	Hardicanute (br 1962)	Hard Ridden
			Harvest Maid
		Virtuous (b 1962)	Above Suspicion
			Rose of India
	Pram (br 1969)	Fine Top (br 1949)	Fine Art
			Toupie
		Gourabe (b 1950)	Admiral Drake
			Godille

Dunette is one of three winning fillies produced by Pram from five foals that have raced. The other two are Paddle (by Jim French) who was a smart filly on her day and was fourth in the 1978 Prix de Diane and the two-year-old Godille (by Bolkonski) who won at Chantilly in September. Godille, incidentally, shares her name with her great grandam. Pram won over nine furlongs at Longchamp and is a half-sister to at least seven winners, including the useful handicapper Romancero and the Prix Chloe winner Felouque. Their dam Gourabe was a smart filly as well as a notably successful broodmare; she won the Prix de la Nonette and finished second in the Prix Vermeille.

Dunette visits Top Ville at stud in 1981. A rather nervous type who spoilt her appearance by sweating before the Arc and was reportedly a bad traveller, she was nevertheless a genuine filly and a high-class one too. She was just as effective at a mile and a quarter as at a mile and a half, needing a strong pace at both distances to give her the chance to settle. She probably acted on any going. *E. Chevalier du Fau, France.*

DUNGEON GHYL 2 ch.f. Roman Warrior 132–Birdcage 78 (Manacle 123) 68
(1980 5d $5g^{4}$ 6f) May 4; big, well-made filly; third foal; half-sister to 9f winner Klondike Kaptive (by Goldhill); dam seemed to need at least 6f at 2 yrs; showed ability on all starts; having first race for 2 months, wasn't knocked about when $6\frac{1}{4}$ lengths fourth of 8 to Sanu in minor event at Goodwood in August; will probably stay 7f. *D. Gandolfo.*

DUNHAM PARK 3 b.g. Manacle 123–Sweet Reproach 94 (Relic) (1979 6fg 80
$5s^{2}$ $6g^{2}$ $6fg^{2}$ $7g^{4}$ $7g^{2}$ $6d^{3}$ 1980 7d $8fg^{2}$ $8.2s^{4}$ 8s 10.2v) tall, useful sort; moderate maiden; stays 1m; probably acts on any going; blinkered final 2 starts at 2 yrs; sweated up badly second outing; trained by M. W. Easterby for first start. *P. Rohan.*

DUNNE WRONG 3 b.g. Welsh Saint 126–Shopping Wise (Floribunda 136) —
(1979 NR 1980 12g 15.5g) brother to Saintly Purchase, a fair performer at up to $1\frac{1}{2}$m, and half-brother to 2 winners, including Lynconlou (by Lord Gayle), useful winner at up to 9f; dam Irish 6f winner; unquoted when behind in two maiden races at Folkestone in the summer; not certain to stay 2m. *D. Morley.*

DUNPHY 2 b.c. Riverman 131–Dourdan (Prudent II 133) (1980 8fg* 8d* $8d^{3}$) **124**

Although Madame Alec Head had an outstandingly successful time as an owner during the 'seventies, racing such exceptional fillies as Pistol Packer, Realty, Riverqueen, Sigy and Three Troikas, her only good colt during that period was Fabulous Dancer, a disappointment when seventh in the Irish Sweeps Derby on his only run in a classic. However, in Dunphy, Madame Head now owns a potentially high-class three-year-old.

Dunphy's record in his first season was good. His first two runs, both in September, resulted in a narrow success in a newcomers race at Evry and an impressive win in the Group 3 Prix des Chenes at Longchamp; and on his third

Prix des Chenes, Longchamp—Dunphy finishes in front of Watchdog (noseband) and Big John

outing, when co-favourite for the Grand Criterium at Longchamp, he came out best of the home-trained colts. Dunphy put up similar displays on both his appearances at Longchamp in that he turned into the straight in last place and then showed splendid acceleration when put under pressure. In the Prix des Chenes his powerful late run took him to the front close home and so fast did he finish that he won by a length and a half and a head from Watchdog and Big John, the pair who later finished second and first respectively in the Prix Thomas Bryon. His effort in the Grand Criterium came too late though, and despite making up three or four lengths on the leaders over the last two furlongs he was still a length behind Recitation and Critique at the line.

Riverman became leading sire in France for the first time in 1980, thanks largely to the three-year-olds Detroit, Policeman and Gold River and the pattern-race winning two-year-olds Dunphy and Votre Altesse. Needless to say, his best season followed his exportation to the USA in January, 1980. Since his best son, Irish River, has also been sent to Gainesway Farm and Policeman has been sent to stud in New York State, Dunphy has only to win another good race or

Mme A. Head's "Dunphy" (F. Head)

two to become a very valuable stallion prospect. Perhaps he'll eventually take Riverman's place at the Haras du Quesnay.

Dunphy (b.c. Mar 29, 1978)	Riverman (b 1969)	Never Bend (b 1960)	Nasrullah
			Lalun
		River Lady (b 1963)	Prince John
			Nile Lily
	Dourdan (b 1964)	Prudent II (ch 1959)	My Babu
			Providence
		Denisy (b 1954)	Pan II
			Sainte Mesme

Both Dunphy's style of racing and his pedigree lend support to the view that he'll make a very good middle-distance performer. His sire made his name largely as a three-year-old, when a top-class colt from a mile to a mile and a half, and both Dunphy's dam Dourdan and grandam Denisy improved from two to three. Dourdan, winner of the Prix Cleopatre over ten and a half furlongs, has bred five winners from her first five runners, with the very useful French three-year-old middle-distance winner Doux Lord (by Sir Gaylord) easily the best after Dunphy. Although a useful filly, Dourdan wasn't nearly so good a racehorse as her half-brother Le Potelet, who was placed in such races as the Prix du Conseil Municipal, the Prix Dollar and the Prix Eugene Adam, or her dam. Denisy was a top-class filly, rated the best French three-year-old filly of her year. Among her most notable efforts were her seconds to Oroso in the 1957 Prix de l'Arc de Triomphe and to Tanerko in the 1958 Grand Prix de Saint-Cloud. Perhaps her grandson will prove good enough to run in those races in 1981. *Mme C. Head, France.*

DURANDAL 3 br.c. Bay Express 132–High Ransom 88 (High Treason 126) **104**
(1979 5fg^{2} 5f* 5f* 6fg^{4} 5g 1980 5fg^{3} 5f 6fg^{4} 6g 6d 5fg) strong, good sort; excellent mover; useful performer; in frame in Field Marshal Stakes at Haydock in April (2½ lengths third to Abdu) and £4,700 event at Lingfield in June (fourth to The Pug); creditable 6 lengths sixth of 20 to Kearney in Cork and Orrery Stakes at Royal Ascot on fourth outing; suited by 6f; acts well on firm ground and is possibly unsuited by soft; not seen out after July. *R. Boss.*

DUSKY TIGRESS 6 b.m. Dark Tiger–Desila (Silex II 125) (1979 NR 1980 —
10d 8g) French-bred mare; poor maiden. *B. Wise.*

DUSTY PATH 2 gr.g. Warpath 113–The Squeeze 85 (Bing II) (1980 7f 7fg 7g **73**
8s^{4} 7f 8s) May 11; small, leggy gelding; third foal; dam won 8 times from 5f to 1½m; showed first sign of ability when 8¼ lengths fourth of 8 to Rhein Bridge in maiden race at Ayr in September, leading 2f out after being scrubbed along in last place early on; very slowly away next start; will stay 1½m; wears blinkers. *W. Bentley.*

DUSTY PURPLE 3 b.f. Royalty 130–Feather Duster 80 (Tickler 106) (1979 —
5g 6d 1980 8fg 10s 10g 7f 7g 7g) bad plater. *D. Weeden.*

DUTCH CHALLENGER 3 b.g. Saintly Song 128–J'Accuse (I Say 125) (1979 **69**
6fg 1980 8h^{4} 10fg^{2} 10g^{3} 12s 12g 10fg^{2} 10g) quite a moderate maiden; best at 1¼m; suited by firm ground; trained by J. Fitzgerald until after second start. *D. Morley.*

DUTCH DOLL 3 ch.f. Goldhill 125–Rise 68 (Fury Royal 108) (1979 NR 1980 —
8f 8fg 10.8s 10s) strong, compact filly; seems of little account; trained part of year by J. Czerpak. *B. McMahon.*

DUTCH GIRL 3 b.f. Workboy 123–Dutch Gold 117 (Goldhill 125) (1979 5f 5f **65**
5g 6fg 6fg 5fg 1980 8f 5f* 6f 5h^{3} 5f^{4} 5fg* 5fg^{2} 5fg^{2} 5.6fg^{2} 5d^{4} 5fg 5d) compact filly; won maiden race at Beverley in April and handicap at Catterick in June; ran creditably most subsequent outings; stays 5.6f; goes well on fast ground; has run well for an apprentice. *M. W. Easterby.*

DUTCH MAID 2 b.f. Souvran 98–Moonstream 62 (Forlorn River 124) (1980 5f) —
Apr 29; fourth foal; dam plater; 10/1 and apprentice ridden when last of 17 to Sodina in maiden race at Lingfield in October. *B. Swift.*

DUTCH TREAT 7 b.h. Le Levanstell 122–Northern Beauty (Borealis) (1979 **87**
10g^{4} 10v^{2} 12g 12v^{2} 12d 10g* 12d* 10fg 12g 12fg^{2} 12fg 12fg 1980 12d 12s 12g^{3} 12f 12fg^{3} 12g*) middle-distance performer; ridden by 5-lb claimer, stayed on well and beat Lochranza by 1½ lengths after getting well behind early on in Great Yorkshire Handicap at York in August; acts on any going but has done nearly all his winning on an easy surface. *R. Price.*

DYK-A-TAK 5 ch.g. Dike–Takawin 109 (Takawalk II 125) (1979 12.2s 12v 8f 10g 10.1fg² 10d 10.1fg⁴ 10.1fg³ 10.1fg² 10f* 12f³ 10fg 10d 1980 12f² 12fg² 10.7g² 10s³ 10d* 10s 12fg 10g³ 10fg² 10g 10d 10fg) middle-distance handicapper; ridden by 7-lb claimer when beating Traquair by ½ length at Brighton in June; behind on last 3 starts; acts on any going; wears blinkers; good mount for an inexperienced rider. *J. Benstead.* **55**

DYNABOY 2 b.c. Jukebox 120–Wood Grouse 56 (Celtic Ash) (1980 6g² 6s) Feb 21; 8,600F, 11,500Y; lengthy colt; half-brother to 2 winners, including Great Sound (by Meadow Mint), successful at up to 7f at 2 yrs in Ireland and subsequently a very useful stakes winner in USA; dam, half-sister to Pitskelly, stayed 13f; 25/1 and looking as though race would do him good, ran on well over last 2f to finish 2 lengths second of 25 to Composer in maiden race at Newmarket in October; odds on for 22-runner event at Doncaster the following month but was never going well after a slow start and finished well beaten behind Banbury Cross; bandaged near-fore both starts. *J. Dunlop.* **87 ?**

DYNAPAK 3 b.g. Lear Jet 123–Derring Maid (Derring-Do 131) (1979 8fg 8d³ 1980 7fg 7.2g³ 9g³ 8fg⁴ 10g² 10fg 10f 12.5s³) plater; seems to stay 1½m; acts on any going. *F. Durr.* **56**

E

EAGLE BOY 4 ch.g. Huntercombe 133–Island Princess (Raise A Native) (1979 6s* 6s² 6f* 5fg² 6g 6g³ 6s 7g 6g 1980 7f 6fg³ 6fg³ 7g 6fg 6fg⁴ 7f* 6fg² 6s 6g⁴ 6g* 6s³ 7s 6d) compact, rather lightly-made gelding; won apprentice event at Catterick in July and handicap at Thirsk in September, putting up an excellent performance under top weight when beating Relative Ease very narrowly on latter course; also ran very well when short-head second to Repetitious in Spillers Stewards' Cup at Goodwood in between and when 2 lengths third to Sparkling Boy in Ladbrokes Ayr Gold Cup in September; well beaten when reappearing a day after latter event and again on final start; stays 7f; acts on any going; suitable mount for an apprentice; taken early to post on one occasion. *W. Bentley.* **98**

EAGLESFIELD 3 ch.c. Mountain Call 125–Rubella (Buisson Ardent 129) (1979 NR 1980 5fg 5d³ 6g 5g² 5s* 5.3fg* 5fg⁴ 5f 6s) 7,800Y; good mover; brother to speedy 1975 2-y-o Alacriter and half-brother to several winners; dam ran once; won maiden race at Nottingham in July (made all) and handicap at Brighton in August; best at around 5f; probably acts on any going. *C. Nelson.* **92**

EAGLE'S QUEST 2 b.f. Legal Eagle 126–My Cervantes (Hill Clown or Nulli Secundus 89) (1980 5g 5g) Apr 29; leggy, unfurnished filly; second foal; half-sister to modest 1979 2-y-o 5f winner Murrayflower (by Murrayfield); dam poor half-sister to smart miler Maystreak; showed a little ability when eighth of 10 to Goody Goody in minor event at Goodwood in September on second start; bred to stay 1m. *J. Holt.* **–**

EARL'S COURT 4 ch.c. Lord Gayle 124–Paddy's Rose 81 (St Chad 120) (1979 6s 6d 8.2d² 8d 8g² 9.4f² 10.4f² 10f* 10f³ 10s² 10.4f 10s 1980 10fg³ 9g 10.6d 9f 10fg⁴ 12.3d² 12d* 13.8d 12d) small colt; quite a moderate handicapper; enterprisingly ridden when beating Chateau Royal decisively by 3 lengths at Haydock in October; stays 1½m (well beaten over further on penultimate start); acts on any going; suitable mount for a boy. *C. Crossley.* **59**

EARMARK 3 ch.c. Hot Spark 126–Golden Ears 94 (Gratitude 131) (1979 5f* 5fg⁴ 5g 1980 5d 6f⁴ 5fg 6f 7f 7fg) neat, strong, full-quartered colt; useful (rated 108) at 2 yrs; fair fourth to Shaarid in handicap at Newmarket in April, best effort in 1980; ran moderately last 4 outings; stays 6f; possibly unsuited by a soft surface; blinkered second, third and fourth starts. *J. Bethell.* **–**

EASTER CANDLE 4 b. or br.f. So Blessed 130–Palmitin 68 (Crepello 136) (1979 6g 7g 8f 7fg 7s 1980 8s 10fg 10fg 8fg 11.7f 13.1h) quite well-made filly: poor maiden on flat; blinkered second outing; has won over hurdles. *J. Edmunds.* **–**

EASTERLY WIND 2 b.f. Windjammer (USA)–Lucky Plum (Lucky Guy 121) (1980 5g³ 7s³ 6g* 6fg* 6f) Mar 14; 900F; lengthy, good sort; half-sister to 7f and 1m winner Monetary Star (by Current Coin); dam won over 5f; successful in small races at Hamilton and Windsor in the summer, in latter making all to beat odds-on Arndean 2 lengths; didn't move well to start when tailed-off last of 6 to Noalto in £4,600 event at Ripon in August; stays 7f; possibly unsuited by very firm going but seems to act on any other. *C. Nelson.* **94**

EASTERN AIR 2 ch.f. Levanter 121–Wheal Harmony (Song 132) (1980 5.8g^4 6g 7fg 6g) Feb 28; first foal; dam never ran; beaten about 7 lengths in maiden races at Bath and Brighton on first 2 outings; had very stiff task in nursery on final start. *H. Candy.* **65**

EASTERN ISLE 3 b.f. Gulf Pearl 117–Fellow's Eyot (Roan Rocket 128) (1979 NR 1980 7f 8fg 7.6f^3 8fg 7s 7g 7.6d 5g^4 6g^4 6fg 8.2g 9d^2 10g^4 10.2v^4) 3,000Y; second foal; small, quite attractive filly; dam unraced half-sister to smart performers Piccadilly and Fast Colour; quite a moderate maiden; stays 1¼m; probably acts on any going; blinkered fifth and seventh starts; sold 2,500 gns Newmarket December Sales. *H. Candy.* **63**

EASTERN PALACE 6 gr.g. Habitat 134–Al-Burak 103 (Silver Shark 129) (1979 8d^4 7g^3 8s 10s 10g 10fg* 8f 8f* 10fg 10.2fg 12fg 8g 1980 8fg 10fg 10fg 10.6g 12d 8fg 8g 10g^4 12f) lengthy gelding; stays 1¼m (well beaten over 1½m); acts on firm going and has run poorly in the mud; best in blinkers; suitable mount for an apprentice; inconsistent and often starts slowly nowadays. *G. Beeson.* –

EASTERN PALM 3 br.f. Palm Track 122–Eastern Lullaby (Zulu 94) (1979 NR 1980 15.5g) first foal; dam placed over hurdles; pulled up 6f out in maiden race at Folkestone in October; dead. *W. Musson.* –

EASTERN SPRING 6 br.g. Queen's Hussar 124–Arawak 109 (Seminole II) (1979 12s^3 16fg 14g^4 14fg* 13.3fg 12fg 1980 12g 12g^3) big gelding; winner at Yarmouth in 1979 (rated 87); ran only twice in 1980 and was still not 100 per cent wound up when remote third to Golden River in amateur riders race at Beverley in July; effective from 1½m to 2m; acts on any going; suitable mount for an amateur or apprentice; genuine. *L. Cumani.* –

EASTER SUN 3 b.c. Bustino 136–Magical 95 (Aggressor 130) (1979 6f 7f^3 8fg 1980 10fg 10f* 10fg^2 10g^2 10g^3 9f 8s^4) compact, useful sort; useful handicapper; ran on strongly to beat Nocino 3 lengths at Newmarket in May; placed afterwards at Leicester, Newmarket (good head second to World Leader in £5,800 event) and Sandown and wasn't disgraced on last 2 starts in October; will stay beyond 1¼m; acts well on firm ground. *M. Jarvis.* **102**

EASTER WATERS 2 b.f. Rapid River 127–Fair Ellender (Sailing Light 119) (1980 7f) Mar 24; small, light-framed filly; third reported live foal; dam well beaten on flat and over hurdles; unquoted and apprentice ridden when in rear in 18-runner seller won by Rocket Venture at Redcar in September. *T. Fairhurst.* –

EATON CLOWN 3 b.f. Tycoon II–Comic Song 81 (Hill Clown) (1979 5v 5g 5fg^2 5.1f* 5fg 7g 5.1fg 5g^2 5s^4 5g^3 1980 5f 5f 5fg 5fg 5g 5fg) neat filly; not a good mover in her slower paces; fair performer (rated 88) at 2 yrs; well beaten in Northern handicaps in 1980; a free-running filly who isn't sure to stay 7f; acts on firm going; wears blinkers; sweated up first start; has worn bandages; sold 740 gns Newmarket July Sales. *T. Molony.* –

EBISU 2 br.g. Saulingo 122–Jemake 85 (High Treason 126) (1980 5f 5d 5d) Mar 16; 5,200Y; tall gelding; half-brother to fairly useful 5f to 1¼m winner Court Lane (by Mandamus); dam stayed 7f; in rear in maiden and minor events; sold 480 gns Newmarket Autumn Sales. *S. Cole.* –

ECCHINSWELL OAK 3 gr.c. Sharp Edge 123–Lutescens (Skymaster 126) (1979 5f 6f 1980 6f 6fg^4 7g 6g* 7f^3 8d^2 7fg 8.2d^2 8f^4 8.2s^4 8g^3 8s) neat colt; won seller at Yarmouth in July (bought in 1,100 gns); ran creditably in better company most subsequent starts; stays 1m well; probably acts on any going; good mount for an inexperienced rider. *N. Guest.* **58**

ECHENIOR 3 gr.f. Pongee 106–Miss Peebles (Twilight Alley 133) (1979 5g 6fg 7d* 8fg 8h 7.2d 10g^2 8d^2 1980 12s 10.1fg 12h^2) leggy filly; plater; stays 1½m; probably acts on any going; retained 1,350 gns Newmarket May Sales; trained part of year by K. Ivory. *P. Allingham.* **48**

ECHO SUMMIT (USA) 8 b.g. Hill Rise 127–Jib (Gulf Stream 120) (1979 18s 18.8g 20g 1980 16f) hobdayed gelding; does little racing on flat nowadays; stays well. *B. Palling.* –

ECONOMY PEP 4 ch.f. Jimmy Reppin 131–Pepperita 79 (Nelcius 133) (1979 8fg 8f 10.4f^4 12fg^4 10fg 14.6fg^2 12g* 14fg^4 1980 10g 14.6fg 16s 12f 16fg) big, strong filly; behind in 1980; stays well; seems to act on any going; sometimes sweats up badly. *P. Felgate.* –

EDEC 2 b.f. Comedy Star 121–Miss Taurus 79 (Bullrush 106) (1980 5fg 6g 8fg) Jan 22; useless plater; sold 290 gns Ascot October Sales. *A. Ingham.* –

EDGEDALE 2 gr. or ro.c. Sharp Edge 123–Queen's Penny (Queen's Hussar 124) (1980 5fg 5g^3 5d 6d) fair sort; half-brother to several winners, including 3-y-o 7f winner Habadale (by Habat) and smart 5f to 7f winner Hillandale (by Crossing The T); dam unraced; only quite moderate; should be suited by 6f+. *P. Cole.* **72**

EDGED GOLD 3 b.g. Sharp Edge 123–Gold of the Day 72 (Bing II) (1979 7f 1980 8fg 12g) well-grown gelding; no sign of ability in minor and maiden races. *P. Wigham.* –

ED'S FANCY 4 ch.c. Supreme Red 93–Dracula's Daughter (Hook Money 124) (1979 NR 1980 10.1s 8g) seems of no account. *C. Wildman.* –

EDWARD LADELL 2 ch.g. Sweet Revenge 129–Princess Lorna 63 (Royal Palm 131) (1980 7f 7d 6d) Apr 29; 3,800Y; strong gelding; half-brother to several winners, notably very smart Irish sprinter Sandy Row (by Blast) and useful sprinter Ginnies Pet (by Compensation); dam won at 1m; plating-class maiden. *Miss S. Hall.* –

EFFECT 4 b.c. Martinmas 128–Sweet Sharlie 77 (Fighting Charlie 127) (1979 6d 5fg 5f 5g 6d^4 8f 7g 1980 6g 6fg 6h 7g 8.3fg 6g 6fg^4 6g) well-made colt; good sort; has rather a round action; ran creditably in handicaps on last 3 starts, on first 2 occasions not having best of luck in running; should stay 1m (had stiff tasks when tried at trip); acts on firm going and an easy surface; changed hands 1,600 gns Ascot November Sales. *N. Callaghan.* **59**

E FOR EASY 2 gr. or ro.g. Birdbrook 110–Nonsuch Anne 58 (Tudor Melody 129) (1980 5.8fg 6g 5.8g 5.8f* 6d) Apr 15; 2,700Y; well-grown gelding; half-brother to a winner in Scandinavia; dam stayed 1½m; backed from 20/1 to 10/1, showed improved form when making all to win 14-runner seller at Bath in July by 4 lengths from Chenstone; bought in 1,850 gns afterwards; will stay 1m+; acts very well on firm going. *J. Holt.* **65**

EGERIA (USA) 3 b.f. Bold Hitter–Judy B (Perambulator 91) (1979 6f 6g 1980 8fg 10fg) lengthy filly; behind in maiden events; sold 23,000 dollars at Lexington in November. *J. Dunlop.* –

EGGINGTON 2 ch.g. Baragoi 115–Primeapple (Primera 131) (1980 5f 5f^4 5fg 6s 7g 7f 7d) Feb 24; 2,300Y; fair sort; brother to winning 3-y-o stayer Our Bara Boy and half-brother to a winning plater; plating-class maiden; will be suited by middle distances; blinkered final outing. *S. Mellor.* –

EGGNCHIPS 2 b.c. My Swallow 134–La Mariposa (T.V. Lark) (1980 7d 7fg^3 8fg 10d) May 6; 300Y; plain colt; half-brother to a winner in Hungary; dam placed at around 1m in France; poor plater; stays 7f; has worn bandages. *A. Davison.* **53**

EIGHT BALL 3 ch.g. Jukebox 120–Hillberry Corner 70 (Atan) (1979 5s 6fg 6fg 5h^4 6g^3 6g 7f 7.2g 7.2d^3 1980 6d) light-framed gelding; plater; stays 7f; blinkered eighth outing at 2 yrs; sometimes sweats up. *G. W. Richards.* –

EIGHT DIMES 3 ch.c. Pieces of Eight 128–Phaedima 76 (Darius 129) (1979 5g 5g 6s 7fg^4 1980 13.3fg 12s 12d 13.8g) workmanlike colt; little worthwhile form in varied company, including selling; blinkered last 2 starts; sold 950 gns Ascot August Sales. *E. Reavey.* –

EIGHT ROSES 3 ch.f. Pieces of Eight 128–Miss Rosy (Quorum 126) (1979 7g^2 8f^3 8g^2 1980 11.7fg 8fg^3 8fg^3 10fg 12fg* 10f 12d^4) small, narrow filly; plater; won weakly-contested claiming race at Leicester in September; will stay beyond 1½m; acts on a firm and a soft surface; often sweats up. *P. Cole.* **62**

ELA-MANA-MOU 4 b.c. Pitcairn 126–Rose Bertin 76 (High Hat 131) (1979 9fg* 12g^4 12fg* 12.5g^2 12f^3 10fg 1980 9f* 10d* 10g* 12g* 12f^3) **132**

We saw Ela-Mana-Mou make his debut at Newbury on June 15th 1978. At that stage all we knew of his value was that he cost 4,500 guineas as a yearling. In that first race, a maiden event, Ela-Mana-Mou showed himself to be a useful racehorse in the making, quickening clear of his fifteen rivals when asked to go about his business at the distance; he had quite a lot of scope and we marked him down as one who should win again. By the end of his two-year-old days Ela-Mana-Mou had chalked up four wins from five races, his defeat of Troy in the Royal Lodge Stakes earning him joint-second place to Tromos on the Free Handicap. His form at two left him, by our assessment, about 7 lb behind classic-winning standard and his record as a three-year-old, in which he won the King Edward VII Stakes at Royal Ascot and finished in the frame in the Derby, the Grand Prix de Saint-Cloud and the King George, confirmed him as a good horse a few pounds short of the highest class. In the winter he changed

Earl of Sefton Stakes, Newmarket—a close finish between Ela-Mana-Mou, the blinkered Haul Knight, Cracaval (rails) and Welsh Chanter

stables after a partnership consisting of Tim Rogers, the owner of the Airlie Stud complex, and members of the Weinstock family had bought him for £500,000. Ela-Mana-Mou looked to have plenty to do to recoup the outlay but the improvement that he made as a four-year-old was remarkable and his trainer, and those who worked with him at West Ilsley, can take great credit from his performances. He won successively the Earl of Sefton Stakes, the Prince of Wales's Stakes at Royal Ascot, the Coral Eclipse Stakes and the King George VI and Queen Elizabeth Diamond Stakes; he wasn't defeated until October when he went down in a photo-finish to the three-year-olds Detroit and Argument in the Prix de l'Arc de Triomphe. He was offered for syndication as a stallion at the end of the season with a valuation on him of £3,200,000, more than six times his market value a year earlier and more than six hundred times his value before he first set foot on a racecourse.

There were no fireworks in Ela-Mana-Mou's first two races for his new stable. He reappeared in the Earl of Sefton Stakes at Newmarket in April, which attracted three of the best of the previous season's middle-distance three-year-olds still in training—Ela-Mana-Mou, Cracaval and Haul Knight. None of them had been able to hold a candle to Troy or Dickens Hill the previous year and there was no sign in the Earl of Sefton that any of them had made abnormal improvement over the winter. With odds laid on him, Ela-Mana-Mou had to pull out all the stops to hold off Haul Knight and Cracaval by a neck and the same with Welsh Chanter, winner of the Britannia Handicap at Royal Ascot under 8-7, only a short head away fourth. Ela-Mana-Mou's performance wasn't so stylish as that of his stable companion Niniski in the John Porter Stakes, which was run at Newbury three days after the Earl of Sefton Stakes; it was Niniski who represented Hern at Epsom in the Coronation Cup. Ela-Mana-Mou wasn't seen out again until Royal Ascot, where he had nine opponents in the Prince of Wales's Stakes over a mile and a quarter, including Moomba Masquerade who had finished eleventh in the Derby, almost a dozen lengths behind Henbit. Moomba Masquerade met Ela-Mana-Mou on terms 8 lb better than weight-for-age and Ela-Mana-Mou beat him by two lengths with two four-year-olds, the filly Bonnie Isle and Haul Knight, in third and fourth. Again Ela-Mana-Mou had to work hard for victory and we saw nothing in this performance to suggest that he would prove up to beating the best of the classic three-year-olds if he were to meet any of them.

As a three-year-old, Ela-Mana-Mou had given the impression that a mile and a quarter might be his optimum trip; Ela-Mana-Mou evidently convinced his new stable from an early date that the Eclipse represented his best opportunity of a big-race win as a four-year-old. Once it had been decided that Niniski would represent the stable in the Coronation Cup, Ela-Mana-Mou had his programme mapped out with the Coral Eclipse Stakes at Sandown in July very much in mind. Ela-Mana-Mou arrived at Sandown looking trained to the minute; we couldn't remember seeing a horse more ready to race. The Coral Eclipse was worth £79,428 to the winner, easily the most valuable prize in the history of the race. Dickens Hill had earned £42,468 when successful in 1979, a year in which the Derby third Northern Baby had also taken the field. The three-year-olds were not so strongly represented in 1980, a factor which must have disappointed the sponsors and the racecourse executive. The Eclipse provides one of the first major opportunities to test the relative strength of the classic three-year-olds and the best of the older generation that have remained in training. Unfortunately, the race sometimes lacks an outstanding representative from the current crop of three-year-olds: the Irish Sweeps Derby takes place only a week earlier and its rise to international prominence since the early 'sixties has been an important factor in making the Eclipse something of a benefit for the older horses. The principals in the Derby at Epsom and the Curragh tend to by-pass the Eclipse and wait for the King George VI and Queen Elizabeth Diamond Stakes. Mill Reef, who didn't contest the Sweeps Derby, was the last Epsom or Sweeps Derby winner to run in the Eclipse; Artaius and Dickens Hill are the only three-year-olds that have finished in front in the race since Mill Reef's year, although Wollow got first place on the disqualification of Trepan in 1976. There were two three-year-olds in the six-horse line-up in 1980: Hello Gorgeous, who had narrowly defeated the Derby runner-up Master Willie in the Mecca-Dante Stakes at York before finishing sixth, finding the trip a little too far, at Epsom; and Last Fandango, runner-up in the Irish Two Thousand Guineas and no certainty, on what had been seen of him, to get the Eclipse distance.

Four-year-olds dominated the betting on the Eclipse: Ela-Mana-Mou, whose trainer and jockey were enjoying a purple patch, started favourite at 85/40 but there was also plenty of confidence behind the Irish-trained Gregorian, who had already won over the course and distance in the current season in the Westbury Stakes and the Brigadier Gerard Stakes. There was a good deal of support too for Sea Chimes, who had graduated from handicap company to take the Coronation Cup, his eighth consecutive victory. Ela-Mana-Mou gave a doggedly courageous performance; he may not have been a spectacular winner but he did what was needed, running on strongly to pass the front-running Gregorian halfway up the straight and holding on grimly when tackled thereafter by Hello Gorgeous. Ela-Mana-Mou went by the post a decisive winner by three quarters of a length from Hello Gorgeous with Gregorian a

Prince of Wales's Stakes, Ascot—Ela-Mana-Mou disposes of Moomba Masquerade and Bonnie Isle

length and a half away third and Sea Chimes another two lengths further back in fourth. The form looked very good: allowing that Hello Gorgeous was almost certainly a better horse at a mile and a quarter than a mile and a half, it seemed probable that Ela-Mana-Mou was by now little, if anything, behind the leading middle-distance three-year-olds.

Before Ela-Mana-Mou's Eclipse victory, it was plain that Hern's stable housed a very strong team of middle-distance three-year-olds: Henbit had won the Derby, Bireme the Oaks with The Dancer in third place, and Prince Bee had finished second in the Irish Sweeps Derby. But for Henbit's tragic injury at Epsom, it's probable that he would have been the stable's principal hope for the King George VI and Queen Elizabeth Diamond Stakes at Ascot in July. However, Ela-Mana-Mou's belated improvement gave the Hern yard a very live hope for Ascot. Four of the Eclipse winners in the 'seventies had gone on to contest the King George VI and Queen Elizabeth Stakes—Mill Reef and Brigadier Gerard completed the double, while Scottish Rifle and Star Appeal failed to finish in the first six at Ascot. Only four horses before Mill Reef—Tulyar, Ballymoss, Busted and Royal Palace—had completed the Eclipse-King George double in the same year since the King George was inaugurated as the King George VI and Queen Elizabeth Festival of Britain Stakes in 1951. Few Eclipse winners went on to Ascot in the 'fifties and 'sixties. For most of the period, the races were too close together for the good of either: Tulyar, Ballymoss and Busted had only a week between Sandown and Ascot and it wasn't until Royal Palace's year that the period between the races was lengthened to three weeks, a gap that has been maintained in most years since, although Brigadier Gerard had only two weeks between.

The field that Ela-Mana-Mou met at Ascot was a little below strength for a King George. Of the ten runners, the Irish Sweeps Derby winner Tyrnavos and the Epsom Derby fourth Pelerin (who had finished sixth at the Curragh) were the only representatives of the leading colts of the classic generation, a group which had provided six winners of the race in the 'seventies. The Epsom Derby form had been turned inside out at the Curragh, where Tyrnavos, twelfth at Epsom, also had the Derby second and third Master Willie and Rankin among those behind; the leading three-year-old middle-distance colts were being compared most unfavourably with their predecessors before the King George and neither Tyrnavos nor Pelerin put the classic form in a good light with their performances at Ascot. The only other three-year-old in the field was the filly Mrs Penny, winner of the Prix de Diane de Revlon (French Oaks) on her previous outing; Piggott's retainer to ride for O'Brien, who saddled Gregorian, was waived by mutual consent to allow him to ride Mrs Penny. The French were represented by two of their best four-year-olds: Le Marmot, who had finished second in the 1979 Prix de l'Arc but had not been seen out since winning the Prix Ganay in May; and Dunette, winner of the Prix de Diane in 1979 and runner of a dead-heat with the Prix du Jockey-Club runner-up Shakapour in the Grand Prix de Saint-Cloud on her most recent outing. Without underestimating Ela-Mana-Mou's performance in the Eclipse, the form-book seemed to suggest that he would be hard pressed to cope with a top-form Le Marmot. But for the fact that Le Marmot hadn't been seen on a racecourse for almost three months, and that rumours were circulating to his detriment, it is probable that he would have started at odds shorter than the 7/4 offered about him; Ela-Mana-Mou was second favourite at 11/4 with Tyrnavos (7/1) and Mrs Penny (9/1) the only others to start at less than 12/1.

The King George produced a magnificent finish between Ela-Mana-Mou and Mrs Penny, a finish that revived memories of Grundy's epic struggle with Bustino five years earlier. As in Grundy's year, the two principals drew out from the rest in the final stages and the issue remained in the balance until close home. Carson rode some brilliant races in 1980 on the way to his fourth jockeys' championship but we didn't see him ride a better one than that on Ela-Mana-Mou at Ascot. Despite his many virtues, Ela-Mana-Mou had an important shortcoming in his make-up: in the highest company he lacked that dash of top-class finishing pace. It may seem paradoxical to suggest of a horse who had just won one of the most important races in the Calendar at a mile and a quarter, and had not been raced at a longer distance for a year, that he should be ridden for stamina against good opposition at a mile and a half. But both Hern and Carson knew Ela-Mana-Mou's requirements and he was ridden perfectly at Ascot: Carson moved him up quickly to join the leaders soon after halfway and set him alight with half a mile to go, sharpening the pace markedly, a manoeuvre which soon had most of the field floundering, including Le Marmot and Dunette. Rounding the turn into the short straight Ela-Mana-Mou led from his stable-companion More Light, Tyrnavos, Mrs Penny, Main Reef and Gregorian with the others detached. It soon came down to a challenge between Ela-Mana-Mou and Mrs Penny. Two furlongs out, with Carson riding for all he was worth and Piggott sitting virtually motionless alongside, it looked all Robert Sangster's yearlings to a Shetland pony against Ela-Mana-Mou. But with Ela-Mana-Mou's determination matched by that of his jockey, Ela-Mana-Mou got on top in the closing stages to win by three quarters of a length, Mrs Penny herself having responded magnificently under the whip in the final furlong. Gregorian came home in third place, five lengths behind Mrs Penny, with Dunette and Le Marmot not far behind him. In terms of merit, there have been many better King George winners than Ela-Mana-Mou but no-one can say that there has been a more courageous one.

Ela-Mana-Mou's victory at Ascot took his earnings for the season to £236,332 and put his trainer within easy reach of a trainers' record for first-prize money won in an English season. No-one could touch Dick Hern in the trainers' list in 1980; he ended the season with earnings of £831,964, almost £150,000 more than the record set by Henry Cecil in 1979; Cecil himself had another fine season and finished in second place, more than £370,000 behind Hern. In addition, Hern won £86,775 abroad through the exploits of Shoot A Line, who won the Irish Guinness Oaks, and Prince Bee and Luck Of The Draw who picked up useful prizes in France. Not since the heyday of Sir Noel Murless has a trainer so dominated an English season. Hern's season ranks close behind that enjoyed by Murless in 1967, when he topped the list with earnings of £256,899, a staggering sum for those days, more than £100,000 above the existing record, which Murless himself had set in 1959, and four times that of his nearest rival in 1967, Sir Gordon Richards. In 1967 the Murless stable came close to monopolising the major English races for three-year-olds and upwards: Royal Palace won the Two Thousand Guineas and the Derby, Busted the Eclipse and the King George, and Fleet the One Thousand Guineas; Sucaryl, Hopeful Venture, St Chad, Pink Gem, Cranberry Sauce and Sun Rock were among others in the yard who won good races. Murless' prize-money record stood until 1975 when it was surpassed by Peter Walwyn whose stable won 121 races worth £382,527; the record went again in 1977 when Vincent O'Brien was leading trainer with earnings of £439,124. Hern's career as a trainer, which began in 1958, when he was appointed private trainer to Major L. B. Holliday, reached at least one other notable landmark in 1980: Shoot A Line's win in the Irish Guinness Oaks enabled him to equal O'Brien's hitherto-unique achievement of having saddled a winner in each of the English and Irish classics.

Hern's two previous winners of the King George VI and Queen Elizabeth Diamond Stakes, Brigadier Gerard and Troy, had next contested the Benson and Hedges Gold Cup at York's August meeting but, after some deliberation,

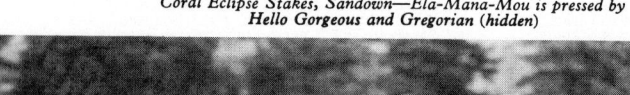

Coral Eclipse Stakes, Sandown—Ela-Mana-Mou is pressed by Hello Gorgeous and Gregorian (hidden)

King George VI and Queen Elizabeth Diamond Stakes, Ascot—Ela-Mana-Mou is a game winner from Mrs Penny and Gregorian (rails)

it was decided to rest Ela-Mana-Mou until the autumn when he would tackle either the Prix de l'Arc de Triomphe or the Champion Stakes. Only Ribot, Ballymoss and Mill Reef have won the King George and the Prix de l'Arc in the same year and several King George winners have failed at Longchamp to do as well as Ela-Mana-Mou, the most recent being Troy, although it must be said that Troy ran below his best and that the Arc took more winning in his year than it did in 1980. In the week before the Arc, Ela-Mana-Mou was backed down to 5/2 favourite in the English ante-post market on the race and, on the day, he shared favouritism on the French Tote with Le Marmot, with whom he was coupled for betting purposes because Tim Rogers was a shareholder in both horses. The going on Arc day was very firm, so firm in fact that it was thought necessary to have felt pads fitted under Ela-Mana-Mou's racing plates. Ela-Mana-Mou looked marvellous—well nigh as good as he had looked before the Eclipse—and he went to post in fine style. Carson was again seen at his best: he had Ela-Mana-Mou in the front rank from the start in a strongly-run race and set sail for home soon after rounding the final turn. Ela-Mana-Mou was in front until about a hundred yards from the post where Detroit caught him; Argument also finished strongly and at the post Ela-Mana-Mou was in third place, beaten half a length and a short head. It was the closest an English-trained horse had come to winning the Arc since Rheingold's success seven years earlier; only two other English-trained horses, Balmerino and Troy, had reached a place in the race in the intervening period. Ela-Mana-Mou seemed to get over his exertions at Longchamp very quickly and was soon giving evidence at home that he was in good spirits. However, plans to saddle him for the Champion Stakes had to be abandoned when he was found cast in his box a week before the race.

Ela-Mana-Mou, a rangy, useful looking colt, has been retired to Ireland

Mr S. Weinstock's "Ela-Mana-Mou" (W. Carson)

where he will stand in 1981 at the Simmonstown Stud, which is part of the Airlie Stud complex. His grandsires, Petingo and High Hat, both stood at Airlie. Of that pair, Ela-Mana-Mou bears a closer resemblance in racing character to High Hat than to Petingo. Petingo was a top-class racehorse at two, when he topped the Free Handicap, and trained on into a top-class miler as a three-year-old; he had a turn of foot. High Hat, on the other hand, was unraced at two and didn't reach the top class until he was four, at which age his victories, none of them gained at a distance shorter than a mile and a half, included a memorable one over Petite Etoile; High Hat, who ran fourth in the Arc on his final appearance, lacked finishing speed and he beat top-class opponents by outgalloping them, by wearing them down with pillar-to-post tactics. If Ela-Mana-Mou makes as good a start to his stud career as did High Hat—he sired two classic winners from his first crop—those who paid £80,000 for a share in him (£40,000 payable on November 1st 1980 with the balance due twelve months later) should be well satisfied. Ela-Mana-Mou's sire Pitcairn is now in Japan: Ela-Mana-Mou and Cairn Rouge were largely responsible for putting him at the top of the list of sires in 1980, in which High Line, a son of High Hat, finished in second place. Ela-Mana-Mou showed himself to be a better racehorse than his sire, who didn't race after the age of three: Pitcairn, who was from a stout family on his dam's side, was a good-class two-year-old, runner-up in the Middle Park and the Dewhurst, and showed better form at three, winning high-class races at around a mile and finishing second in the Irish Two Thousand Guineas. As we have pointed out in previous editions of *Racehorses*, all the mares shown in the bottom line of Ela-Mana-Mou's pedigree are first foals, as is Ela-Mana-Mou himself. The dam Rose Bertin won a maiden event at Wolverhampton over a mile and a half as a three-year-old; the grandam Wide Awake won the Ebbisham Stakes over a mile at Epsom; and the third dam Wake Island, who was out of a very useful staying daughter of the One Thousand Guineas winner Belle of All, was a useful but unreliable sprint winner, at her best as a two-year-old. No racehorse approaching Ela-Mana-Mou's merit has been produced by the family for some time.

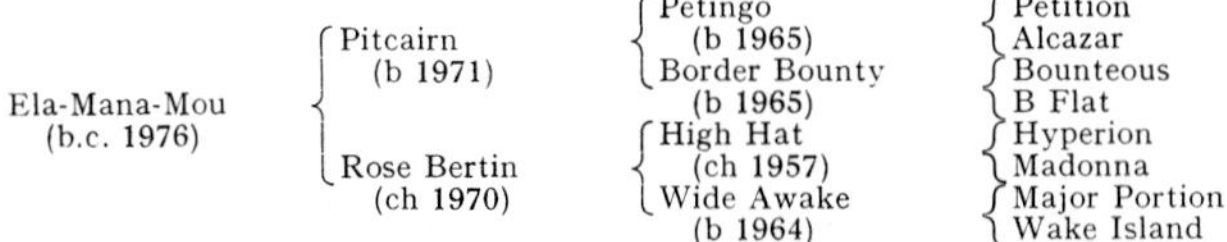

Ela-Mana-Mou stayed a mile and a half very well; he did most of his racing on a sound surface and never ran on very soft going. His record is hard to fault: he won ten of his sixteen races, earning £286,581 in first-place money and was only once out of the frame (in the Champion Stakes as a three-year-old). Although he was, for our money, the best middle-distance horse trained in England in 1980, Ela-Mana-Mou will undoubtedly be remembered first and foremost as a determined battler, a horse who stuck to his job in truly grand style; one would have to go a long way to find a more genuine and consistent racehorse. *R. Hern.*

EL CUBANO 2 b.c. Pitskelly 122–Aurorian (Rise 'N Shine II) (1980 6fg 6fg 8g 8g 8g) Mar 23; 5,000Y; workmanlike colt; third foal; dam poor Irish maiden; no worthwhile form in maiden and minor races, wearing blinkers on final start. *A. Demetriou.* —

ELDERBERRY 4 b.c. Shoolerville 121–Caprice 90 (King's Leap 111) (1979 5f* 5f* 5fg^{3} 5f* 5.6fg 5f^{4} 6fg 1980 6h 5f 5fg 5g 6g 6d) workmanlike colt; little form in 1980 and ran badly in blinkers third start; best form at 5f; acts on firm going; suitable mount for an apprentice. *W. Haigh.* —

ELEGANT DANCER 2 ch.f. Wollow 132–Omentello 91 (Elopement 125) (1980 7fg 6f 7d^{4}) Apr 9: leggy, useful-looking filly; half-sister to numerous winners, including useful Lyric Dance (by Lyphard), successful over 6f and 7f, and smart 7f performer Tudor Mill (by Derring-Do); dam won over 13f; put in best work in closing stages when 3 lengths fourth of 21 to Melissa Jane in maiden race at Leicester in October; will stay middle distances. *R. Laing.* 76

ELEGIDA 3 b.f. Habitat 134–Merta (Jaipur) (1979 5f^{3} 6g^{3} 5fg* 5g^{2} 5f* 5f 1980 7.3f 6fg^{4} 6fg^{3} 6fg* 6g* 6fg) small, leggy filly; didn't grow much from 2yrs to 3yrs; fairly useful handicapper; successful at Yarmouth in August and Goodwood (apprentice race) in September; should stay 7f; yet to race on a soft surface; suitable mount for an apprentice; seldom impresses in paddock. *G. Pritchard-Gordon.* 93

EL GRINGO (FR) 3 b.c. Riverman 131–Belle Margot (Counsel 118) (1979 NR 1980 10g 10.5g 12g^{3} 16f) strong, lengthy ex-French colt; fifth foal; dam won over 1½m in France; third in amateur riders race at Newmarket in August, best effort; wore bandages and finished sore only subsequent outing; stays 1½m; trained by H. Van de Poele first 2 starts. *R. Akehurst.* —

EL INGLES 2 b.c. Averof 123–Baby Elli (Diplomat Way) (1980 5f 6f 6g) Mar 26; 4,000Y; leggy, sparely-made colt; first foal; dam ran twice; only poor form; ran badly in seller when blinkered third outing. *N. Vigors.* —

ELISHEBA 3 ch.f. Nonoalco 131–Ivory Lady 87 (Sir Ivor 135) (1979 6f^{2} 6fg* 1980 8.5g^{4} 7f) attractive, sturdy filly; won 20-runner Crathorne Stakes at York in 1979; lightly raced at 3yrs, finishing nearly 8 lengths fourth of 8 to Bay Street in Princess Elizabeth Stakes at Epsom in April and remote sixth to Luck Of The Draw in 8-runner Strensall Stakes at York in September (sweated up); should stay 1m. *H. Cecil.* —

ELITE PETITE 2 b.f. Welsh Saint 126–Super Amber (Yellow God 129) (1980 6g) Apr 12; 1,200Y; unfurnished filly; first foal; dam never ran; unquoted when behind in 19-runner newcomers event won by Dancing Sally at Goodwood in September. *M. Haynes.* —

ELIZABETH HOWARD 2 ch.f. Sharpen Up 127–Molly Flo (Paveh 126) (1980 6g 7d 7fg 7.2d^{4} 7fg 8d^{3}) Apr 18; 5,000F, 6,200Y; strong, fair sort; fourth foal; dam never ran; beaten only 3 lengths, despite having had none too clear a run, when fourth to 19 to Craigour in maiden race at Haydock in September, best effort; stays 1m; blinkered second start. *I. Walker.* 74

ELIZABETH JANE 5 br.m. Andrea Mantegna–The Perch 109 (King's Bench 132) (1979 12s 1980 12.2fg 16g^2 16d) strong mare; sweating when ½-length second to Tshainik in poor maiden race at Beverley in June; stays well. *J. Powney.* 35

ELIZA DE RICH 3 b.f. Spanish Gold 101–Dumb Kathy (Dumbarnie 125) (1979 NR 1980 6d 7fg 6fg^3 8.2f 6g^2 7d 8g 8d 7d 6d) lightly-made filly; only plating class; best form at 6f on top-of-the-ground; sweated up fifth start. *R. Hollinshead.* 57

EL JACKO (USA) 2 ch.g. Bold Commander–Latin Fling (Around Two Turns) (1980 6d) Mar 19; $6,000F, $20,000Y; big, strong gelding; second foal; dam won 3 times at up to 6f at 2 yrs; unquoted and in need of race when tailed off in 15-runner maiden race won by Church Parade at Newmarket in July; gelded subsequently. *G. Harwood.* –

EL KABIR 3 b.c. Green God 128–Sweet Serenade 93 (High Perch 126) (1979 5g^2 6d 5.1g 6g 1980 8d 10g^3 10.6f^2 12fg* 12.2fg 12d) big colt; placed in handicaps prior to winning maiden race at Hamilton in May; stays 1½m; acts on firm going; not raced after June. *J. Hardy.* 73

ELKIE 3 b.f. Habat 127–Natasha 87 (Native Prince) (1979 5d 5g 5.3g 5f^2 5g 5g 5.1g^4 5.1f^2 1980 5fg 6f 5h 5fg 7g 5f 8.3f 6fg^3 8fg^3 6g 7g^2 5fg^3 7g) small, sturdy filly; plater; stays 7f; acts on firm going; has been tried in blinkers; has run respectably for a boy; sold 400 gns Newmarket Autumn Sales. *K. Ivory.* 42

ELLARON 2 gr.f. Abwah 118–Smartie Pants 68 (Galivanter 131) (1980 5f 5fg 6f^4 7d^4 8fg 8.2g) Apr 19; lengthy filly; second foal; dam plater; showed only a little ability in maiden races; best run at 7f but wasn't disgraced over 1m; will do better in sellers. *F. Durr.* 60

ELLERBURN 2 ch.c. Cavo Doro 124–Amorchow (Chou-Chin-Chow 99) (1980 6d) Feb 10; sixth reported foal; dam winning hurdler; 33/1, in need of race and coltish in paddock, soon behind when tailed-off last of 10 behind Age of Reason in sponsored maiden race at Newcastle in June. *D. Garraton.* –

EL-PEZ-ESPADA 2 b.f. Windjammer (USA)–Miss Peseta 95 (Sovereign Path 125) (1980 5d 6g) Apr 6; 500Y; resold 1,500Y; half-sister to 2 winners, including Irish 9f and 1½m winner Racy Lady (by Continuation); dam won over 5f at 2 yrs; behind in end-of-season maiden races at Wolverhampton and Leicester. *R. Morris.* –

EL PRESIDENTE 2 b.c. Bold Lad (Ire) 133–Inquisitive Girl 97 (Crepello 136) (1980 5fg* 5f^3 6g 5g 5d 6d 5g) Jan 27; 16,500F, 15,000Y; strong, good sort; not a good mover in his slower paces; half-brother to several winners, including 1976 2-y-o 1m winner Harriet Air (by Hardicanute); dam stayed 1m; finished strongly to win 10-runner maiden race at Newmarket in May by a neck from Sheba's Glory; had stiff tasks subsequently but wasn't disgraced when eighth of 20 in nursery sixth start; will stay 1m; blinkered fifth start. *A. Bailey.* 74

ELSA CLARA 4 br.f. Sahib 114–Persian Snow 68 (Tehran) (1979 8v^3 8.2s 10v 8f 8fg 7f 7fg* 7fg^2 6d 8g 7fg 1980 8s 8g 7f 8f 8.2fg^4 7s 8g) compact filly; plater; stays 1m; acts on any going; often wears blinkers. *G. Lockerbie.* –

EL SANTO 3 ch.g. Laser Light 118–Frontier Princess 86 (Crocket 130) (1979 5fg^3 5.3f 5.8h^3 5fg^3 5g 6f 5fg 5fg 5d^4 6g 1980 6d 6v^3 6d^3 7fg) small gelding; third in £1,500 race at Ayr and seller at Haydock early in year; stays 6f; probably acts on any going; blinkered fifth and sixth outings at 2 yrs; not seen out after April. *C. Bewicke.* 55

EL STRAD 2 br.c. Home Guard 129–Nas Dara (Aggressor 130) (1980 5f 5fg 5fg 6f* 6s 7f^2 7fg 7d^4 8f 7fg^2 8s^4) May 7; 4,000Y; neat, good-bodied colt; good mover; half-brother to very useful sprinter Irish Love (by Bold Lad, Ire); improved greatly on previous efforts when winning 11-runner maiden auction event at Epsom in June by a head from Hammering; ran creditably in good-class sellers at Newmarket in October on last 2 outings, on final one finishing 3 lengths fourth of 21 to Santella Ascot; stays 1m; acts on any going; often blinkered but is effective without. *J. Hindley.* 79

ELTHAM 6 b.g. Royal Palace 131–Electric Blue 91 (Sing Sing 134) (1979 NR 1980 12d) poor plater; has been tried in blinkers. *J. Old.* –

ELVIS RAAPHORST 2 b.c. Go Marching–Hidden Scene (Faberge II 121) (1980 5d 5s) close-coupled colt; half-brother to a winner in Holland by Saulingo; dam never ran; behind in maiden races at Wolverhampton (backward) and Windsor (last of 21) in June. *N. Guest.* –

ELWORTH 3 ch.c. Elvis 96–Fairworth 74§ (Fair Seller 126) (1979 5f 8h 10g 1980 10fg 9f 10g 13.8f*) leggy colt; plater; attracted no bid after winning at Catterick in July; evidently suited by $1\frac{3}{4}$m; acts on firm going. *T. Kersey.* **48**

EMBASSEN 3 gr.f. My Swallow 134–Rocket Crystal 84 (Roan Rocket 128) (1979 9fg 1980 13.8fg) of no account; sold 470 gns Ascot November Sales. *K. Ivory.* —

EMBLAZON 2 br.f. Wolver Hollow 126–Slip Stitch 120 (Parthia 132) (1980 8d* 8.2s* 8s) Mar 26; useful sort; good walker; half-sister to 3 winners, including fairly useful 1974 2-y-o 6f and 7f winner Moss Stitch (by Star Moss); dam good staying 2-y-o; winner twice in October, beating Harlew $2\frac{1}{2}$ lengths in 17-runner maiden race at Warwick and odds-on Sage King 2 lengths in minor event at Hamilton; not disgraced final start; will be suited by $1\frac{1}{4}$m; yet to race on a sound surface. *Sir Mark Prescott.* **91**

EMBUSTERA 2 ch.f. Sparkler 130–Mecca II 90 (Exbury 138) (1980 6d 6g) Mar 23; 10,500Y; lightly-made filly; half-sister to 3 winners, including fairly useful 3-y-o 6f winner Cowhill (by Habat) and good Spanish horse El Senor (by Taj Dewan); dam won at $1\frac{1}{4}$m; 20/1, still in need of race when $5\frac{1}{2}$ lengths fifth of 20 to Nello in maiden race at Leicester in November; will stay 1m; likely to do better at 3 yrs. *G. Pritchard-Gordon.* **71** p

EMERALD EMPEROR 6 b.g. Ribero 126–Frangipani 77 (Crepello 136) (1979 15d 12g 14.6g 15s 1980 12fg^{2} 16f 12f^{4} 12g 12g^{2} 15fg^{3} 13.8f) lengthy, useful sort; runner-up in handicaps at Pontefract in April and Ripon in June, on latter course looking none too keen; stays well; best form on a sound surface; blinkered penultimate start; joined M. Naughton after final start. *J. Hanson.* **51**

EMERGLEN 2 b.f. Furry Glen 121–Grass Emerald (Alcide 136) (1980 7g 6fg 7g) Apr 23; 4,900F, 9,600Y; lengthy filly; third foal; half-sister to fairly useful stayer The Bedford (by English Prince); dam from same family as Royal Palace; little worthwhile form in maiden races. *N. Vigors.* —

EMMA CHIZZET 3 br.f. High Top 131–Miss Lollypop (St Paddy 133) (1979 6g 8f^{4} 1980 9f 12f^{4} 12g^{4} 10g* 11.1g) neat filly; won claiming event at Brighton in August; stays $1\frac{1}{2}$m. *G. Harwood.* **59**

EMPEROR MARK 2 br.c. Young Emperor 133–Chinchilla II (Sicambre 135) (1980 5v 5f 6f) poor plater. *I. Vickers.* —

EMPEROR NAPOLEON 3 gr.g. Young Emperor 133–Polly Charlot (Charlottown 127) (1979 5d^{2} 5v^{2} 6g^{3} 7f^{3} 6f^{2} 7g^{4} 1980 8d 10g 12fg) tall gelding; in frame in maiden races in 1979; well beaten at 3 yrs; stays 7f; acts on any going; not seen out after May. *P. Rohan.* —

EMPEROR'S SHADOW 5 ch.h. Some Hand 119–Umbrage (Umberto 118) (1979 5s 5v^{2} 7s 6d 6s 6fg 6f 6fg 6d 5g 5fg 6s 6f* 5d^{4} 6d 5s 1980 5d 6v 7s 6fg^{4} 6f^{4} 6fg 6fg 6fg 7d 6d 8f 6s* 6fg^{4} 7f 7g 6fg) compact horse; 25/1 and ridden by 7-lb claimer when winning Nottingham Stewards Cup in August by short head from Overtrick; effective at 5f but is better at 6f; acts on any going; sometimes wears blinkers; good mount for an apprentice; inconsistent. *R. Hollinshead.* **81**

EMPHASIS 2 ch.c. On Your Mark 125–Grey Mink 86 (Double Jump 131) (1980 6s^{2} 6g 6f 7g^{2} 7d^{3}) Apr 13; compact colt; second foal; half-brother to moderate 1979 2-y-o 6f winner Ravens Tower (by Tower Walk); dam, half-sister to fast filly Flying By, won over 5f and 6f; second in minor event at Windsor and 17-runner nursery at Ascot, running easily best race when beaten $1\frac{1}{2}$ lengths by Remouleur in latter; evidently well suited by 7f. *J. Dunlop.* **91**

EMPRESS CARLOTTA 2 b.f. Derring-Do 131–Deodar 88 (Hopeful Venture 125) (1980 7fg^{2} 7g^{4} 7d^{4} 7v) Feb 11; compact, rather lightly-made filly; good mover; second foal; dam won over 7f and 1m; $\frac{3}{4}$-length second of 16 to Ganimede in maiden race at Yarmouth in August; didn't reproduce that form, including when blinkered in a nursery on final start; will stay 1m; best run on a firm surface. *M. Stoute.* **78**

EMPRESS CLEMENTINA 3 ch.f. Star Appeal 133–Failing Light 70 (Ballymoss 136) (1979 7s 1980 8fg 13s 10.6d 12s 14.6d 12.5s 12s) leggy filly; soundly beaten in varied company; sold 1,000 gns Doncaster November Sales. *J. Hanson.* —

EMPRESS JEANNIE 3 b.f. Young Emperor 133–Jean Armour 88 (Delirium 126) (1979 6s 1980 6f 10.1d 11.5g^{3} 11fg^{3} 10g) 380Y; workmanlike ex-Irish filly; half-sister to 9f and $1\frac{1}{4}$m winner Sovereign's Escort (by Supreme Sovereign) and 2 winners abroad; dam middle-distance winner; seems only plating class; may stay $1\frac{1}{2}$m; trained by L. Browne first start. *H. Collingridge.* **63**

EMPRESS MARIA 3 gr.f. Young Emperor 133–Maria Muldoon (Ballyciptic 122) (1979 6d 1980 7g) seems of little account; sold 400 gns Newmarket Autumn Sales. *B. Hills.* —

EN AVANT 3 ch.f. Sallust 134–Such Moor 77 (Santa Claus 133) (1979 6f* 6fg* 7g^4 1980 6f 6f^4 6fg 5g 6fg* 5d). neat filly; dead-heated with Hurricane Hill in minor event at Brighton in August; stays 6f; acts well on firm going and wasn't disgraced only outing on soft; sold 9,200 gns Newmarket December Sales. *Sir Mark Prescott.* 78

EN CALCAT (FR) 4 b.c. Margouillat 133–Rescousse 130 (Emerson) (1979 10s 10.5g 10g^3 12.5g 12.5fg^3 12.5g 12g* 11g* 12g 1980 10.5g* 12g* 12g^2 12g^4 12.5g^2 13.2g^3 10.5d* 12s*) French colt; half-brother to smart French 1m winner Reine Imperiale (by King Emperor); dam won Prix de Diane and was second in Prix de l'Arc de Triomphe in 1972; rather disappointing as a 3-y-o when trained by J. Cunnington, jnr, but did quite well after being sold to race in Provinces; won twice late in 1979 and was successful again at Toulouse and Cagnes-sur-Mer early in 1980 for P. Jean; returned to his original trainer in late summer and was successful twice more, in handicap at Maisons-Laffitte in September and Group 2 Prix du Conseil de Paris at Longchamp in October; put up a very good performance in latter event, leading inside last furlong and staying on to beat Lancastrian (gave 8 lb more than w.f.a.) by ½ length; stays 13f; probably best with some give in the ground; usually blinkered when racing in Provinces. *J. Cunnington, jnr, France.* 112

ENCAMPMENT 3 b.g. Bivouac 114–Sambell 71 (Sammy Davis 129) (1979 5v^4 5s 6fg 1980 5f) small gelding; little worthwhile form, including in a seller. *D. Garraton.* —

ENCHANTMENT 3 b.c. Habitat 134–Lady of Chalon (Young Emperor 133) (1979 5f 1980 6s 8f^3 7.2f^2 7f* 6g^3 6g* 6g 6g^2 6g* 6fg^3 6d*) strong, good sort; good mover; fairly useful performer; successful in maiden race at Sandown and handicaps at Newmarket (2) and Goodwood; put up a resolute performance at Newmarket on final outing in October, rallying gamely to beat Gamblers Dream a neck after being headed over 1f out; best at 6f and 7f; probably acts on any going; blinkered nowadays; ran moderately at Chester seventh start. *J. Tree.* 100

Mr K. Abdulla's "Enchantment"

ENDLESS MOMENT (USA) 2 b.f. Timeless Moment–Go On And On (On-and-On) (1980 5g 5g 5.3d² 6g 6fg⁴ 6g³ 6f² 6fg³ 6g³ 6g* 6g*) Apr 17; $30,000Y; strong, well-made, attractive filly; half-sister to 2 winners in USA, including Go Lucky Go (by Time Tested), a winner at up to 7f; dam won 4 races at up to 6f; improved in the autumn and won maiden race at Nottingham by 5 lengths and minor event at Brighton by a length from Good Offices; will stay 7f; seems to act on any going; blinkered seventh to ninth outings; sold 17,500 gns Newmarket December Sales. *B. Swift.* **87**

END OF WAR (USA) 3 b. or br.c. Bustino 136–Peace 113 (Klairon 131) (1979 7fg⁴ 1980 12g 11d* 12g² 11d³ 10g) well-made colt; got up in last strides to win 11-runner maiden race at Newbury in July; placed in small race at Salisbury and handicap at Newbury afterwards and ran creditably in Irish Sweeps Autumn Handicap at Newmarket on final outing; will stay beyond 1½m; acts on a firm and a soft surface. *J. Tree.* **104**

ENDORSMENT 7 b.g. Falcon 131–Traffic Offence 61 (Traffic Judge) (1979 NR 1980 7g 10d 9g 8.2d) poor plater; stays 1m; acts on hard going; wears blinkers; bandaged nowadays. *L. Barratt.* –

ENERGY PLUS 5 b.h. Tyrant–Reformed Maid (Reform 132) (1979 7s 6s* 6s 6v 6g 6fg 6h³ 6f 6fg 6fg 6f 6g 1980 6g 6g 6f 6fg 6fg² 6f 6g 6d⁴ 6g 6d⁴ 7g 5f 6fg) neat, strong horse; stays 6f; acts on any going; has been tried in blinkers; moved badly to post last 2 starts. *W. Bentley.* **49**

ENGLISH KING 3 b. or br.c. English Prince 129–Aunt Charlotte 85 (Charlottown 127) (1979 NR 1980 11fg 16d) tall, workmanlike colt; third foal; half-brother to 1¼m winner Chuzenji (by Filiberto); dam stayed really well; in rear in maiden races at Newbury in April and Nottingham (tailed-off last) in June. *H. O'Neill.* –

ENGLISH MAID 2 b.f. English Prince 129–Naval Artiste (Captain's Gig) (1980 5fg 5d 7d 6s 7fg 6f 7.2s) Feb 13; 2,600Y; plain filly; second foal; dam Irish 2-y-o 5f winner; no worthwhile form until finishing sixth of 17 to Flash 'N' Fire in minor event at Redcar in September on sixth start; had stiff task in selling nursery next time out. *A. Jarvis.* **58**

ENGULF 2 b.c. Gulf Pearl 117–Primrose 86 (Primera 131) (1980 5fg³ 6g³ 7d* 7s* 7g) Mar 18; 8,200Y; strong, compact, deep-girthed colt; good walker and mover; fourth living foal; half-brother to 1m seller winner Sporting Boy (by Prince Tenderfoot); dam 2-y-o 5f winner; successful in maiden race and 4-runner Heronslea Stakes, both at Ayr in the summer, quickening away impressively in final 2 furlongs to win by 8 lengths from Sula Bula in latter; brought down below distance when 6/1-shot for 10-runner Laurent Perrier Champagne Stakes at Doncaster in September (began to struggle when pace quickened over 2f out); will stay 1¼m; revels in the mud. *J. W. Watts.* **108**

ENID MAY 5 b.m. Communication 119–Corlipat (Flying Bee 94) (1979 NR 1980 8.2d) of little account. *F. Yardley.* –

ENIGMA (FR) 2 b.f. Habitat 134–Edelliette (Edellic 124) (1980 5.5s* 5d*) Mar 28; half-sister to several winners, including French 3-y-o 1¼m winner Evgenia (by Green Dancer) and very useful middle-distance performer Eddystone (by Barbare); dam won over 1¼m and 1½m in French Provinces; successful in newcomers race at Chantilly in June and fairly valuable Prix de la Vallee d'Auge at Deauville in August; second favourite in 6-strong field, disputed lead most of way when winning latter by ½ length from Sharmada with 3 other previous winners behind; bred to stay 1m; should make a very useful filly. *F. Boutin, France.* **110**

ENTEBBE 5 b.g. Derring-Do 131–Argitone (Aureole 132) (1979 7s 7s 7g⁴ 7g 7g² 7s 8g 7fg³ 8fg 8d 1980 7v 12f 16fg 16.1s⁴ 12.5s² 12d) fair sort; good walker; neck second to York Cottage in handicap at Stockton in October; evidently stays 2m; acts on any going; used to wear blinkers; successful hurdler. *F. Yardley.* **63**

ENTERPRISE EXPRESS 2 br.g. New Chairman–Smart Shoes (Langton Heath 97) (1980 7d) Apr 29; first foal; dam poor hurdler; unquoted when last of 15 in maiden race won by Hollow Laughter at Brighton in July. *G. Beeson.* –

ENTRE FANCY 3 b.c. Entrechat–Becassine (El Gallo 122) (1979 5v 5v* 5v* 5g* 5v 5d² 6g 5f 5f 6d² 5d 6d 1980 5v 6v³ 7g 5fg⁴ 6f³ 5g² 7g 6g 6.3s 5fg 6fg 5g 5g 6s) lengthy colt; placed in varied company, notably when 4 lengths second to Monroe in Ballyogan Stakes at Leopardstown in May; eleventh of 20 to Kearney in Cork and Orrery Stakes at Royal Ascot on eighth outing; best at sprint distances; acts on any going. *W. Fennin, Ireland.* **93**

EPSOM IMP 7 br.g. St Alphage 119–Sarah Jane 80 (Pardao 120) (1979 6g⁴ 5g⁴ 5fg³ 5d 5fg 5fg 5fg* 1980 5fg² 5fg 5f³ 5g 6fg 5f 5g³ 5fg) useful sprinter; good **107**

second to Abdu in Field Marshal Stakes at Haydock in April; third subsequently in handicap at Epsom and Scarbrough Stakes at Doncaster; beaten just over 4 lengths by Sayyaf in latter event in September; acts on any going; blinkered final outing at 2 yrs; good mount for an apprentice. *J. Holt.*

ERIC STUART 8 br.g. Precipice Wood 123–Hot Seat 73 (Sing Sing 134) –
(1979 16s 17.1g^3 16fg 14fg^3 15.5f 16f 16.5g 16g 16f 17.1fg 1980 18.8g 17.1fg 16.1d 16g 14fg 16g) poor stayer; acts on any going; suitable mount for an amateur rider; used to wear blinkers. *J. Holt.*

ERINBRIDGE 4 br.g. On Your Mark 125–Roman Rocket 84 (Aggressor 130) –
(1979 7d^4 6s 5g 6d 8fg 10.7fg 8fg^4 9fg* 10.8fg* 10f 1980 8g) plater; stays 1¼m well; blinkered fourth outing at 3 yrs; suitable mount for a boy. *J. Leigh.*

ERMAC 2 br.c. Balidar 133–Sateen 63 (High Treason 126) (1980 5h 6fg 6d^2 6d 97
6g* 7s* 7d 7g^2 8g 8g^4 7v) Mar 18; 1,700F, 7,100Y; useful-looking colt; half-brother to 3 winners, including useful sprinter Joy For The Boys (by Sovereign Lord); dam 2-y-o 6f winner; clear-cut winner of 16-runner maiden race at Carlisle and of nursery at Newcastle in the summer, coming home 3 lengths clear of Lady Ever-So-Sure under a 6-lb penalty in latter; creditable ¾-length second of 7 to Royal Realm in minor event at Newcastle in August (pair clear); best form at 7f; acts very well on soft going; suited by courses with an uphill finish. *E. Weymes.*

ERNEL 6 ch.g. Sassafras 135–Belaying Pin (Iron Peg §§) (1979 15.5d 15.5g^3 34
16.9s 15.5g 17.1g^2 14fg 15.5f^4 16f 16.5fg^3 16.1g^3 16.5g^3 16f 17.1fg 1980 17.1fg 12d 17.1fg^3 16.5fg 17.1d) poor staying handicapper; well suited by top-of-the-ground conditions; suitable mount for an amateur. *J. Benstead.*

ERRANTRY 5 br.g. Sterling Bay–Burletta (Derring-Do 131) (1979 10s 8s 10f –
10f 10fg 10g 16f 12d 1980 12d 13d 12fg 8g 10fg 10g 8g^3 10fg 12d) compact gelding; creditable third to Princes Gate in lady riders race at Salisbury in August; seems to stay 1¼m but not 1½m; best form on a sound surface; blinkered final outing at 2 yrs. *J. Benstead.*

ERROLL'S ELITE 2 b.f. Saulingo 122–Silly Sue 55 (Great Nephew 126) (1980 –
5f 5fg 6s 5s 6g 5f 6d) May 31; leggy filly; not a good mover; only plating class; blinkered sixth outing. *M. W. Easterby.*

ERROLLSTON 3 ch.c. Bay Express 132–Brave Sally (Sallymount 125) (1979 –
5d 5g^4 5s^3 5g 5g 5f 5f* 5f^3 5g 5d^4 5f 5g^4 5g^3 1980 5f 6fg 5fg^4 5s) strong, sprint type; fair fourth in handicap at Stockton in June; should stay 6f; acts on any going with exception of very soft. *M. W. Easterby.*

ERROLL'S WAY 2 ch.g. Sandford Lad 133–Picnic Dancer 71 (Hul a Hul 124) –
(1980 6g 5g 6fg 6g 6d) Mar 7; strong gelding; brother to 1978 2-y-o winner Sand Dancer; dam placed over 5f at 2 yrs; behind in maiden and minor events in the North; blinkered fourth outing. *M. W. Easterby.*

ESAL BOY 3 ch.g. Lorenzaccio 130–Idiot's Delight (USA) (Bold Ruler) (1979 –
6fg 6fg 1980 8f 8fg 8fg) small, strong gelding; behind in maiden and minor events. *J. Sutcliffe.*

ESCARLA 2 b.f. Averof 123–O'Shaunessy (Charlottesville 135) (1980 5s 5g 45
5g^4 5fg^3 5fg 8g 8fg 10d^4 8d) Mar 22; 1,150F, 900Y; quite a useful-looking filly; bad plater; stays 1¼m; blinkered fourth start; sold out of J. Hardy's stable 640 gns Doncaster May Sales after fifth outing. *J. Calvert.*

ESCOVITCH 4 ch.g. Shiny Tenth 120–Shusheta (Martial 131) (1979 6g 5fg 108
5g* 5fg^3 5fg 5g^3 5g^2 5fg 1980 6v 6f* 6fg* 6fg 6d 6fg 6s 6g^3 6s 7g 6d) big, good sort; useful handicapper; held on well to beat Right of Light by ½ length at Newbury in May and picked up a valuable prize when neck winner from Primula Boy in Amoco Handicap at Doncaster later in month; not disgraced most subsequent outings and finished close third to Enchantment at Goodwood in August; stays 6f; acts on firm going and is probably unsuited by soft or heavy; good mount for an apprentice. *G. Balding.*

ESCULTURA 2 br.f. Home Guard 129–Final Bridge (Welsh Abbot 131) (1980 –
6s 6f) May 19; 14,000Y; strong, sturdy filly; half-sister to 3 winners, including very useful miler Pontam (by Tamerlane); dam of little account; unquoted when behind in large fields of maidens at Newmarket in July and October. *B. Hanbury.*

ESKVIEW LAD 2 br.g. Abwah 118–Safe Anchorage 63 (Quayside 124) (1980 66
5g 6d 6g 5g^3 6g^3 7s^3 8d 8.2s 7g^2 7.2s^2 8.2v) Mar 22; small gelding; first foal; dam, plater, placed from 7f to 1¼m; plater; stays 1m and may get further; yet to race on a firm surface. *T. Craig.*

Dance In Time Plate, Doncaster—Etching challenges wide of the field and is soon clear of Our Home

ESPADRILLE 3 ch.f. Hotfoot 126–Tanara 93 (Romulus 129) (1979 5f 6f 6g 7g² 1980 10s³ 10fg 8.2g 10g 10s 8fg² 8g) neat, strong filly; placed in maiden races at Nottingham and Yarmouth; stays 1¼m; probably acts on any going; has run respectably for a boy. *B. Hobbs.* **64**

ESSENWOOD 3 b.f. Relko 136–Blue Wings (Majority Blue 126) (1979 NR 1980 12d 16s) lengthy, lightly-made filly; first foal; dam apparently of little account; apprentice ridden when well beaten in minor race at Wolverhampton in June and maiden race at Lingfield in July. *G. Hunter.* —

ESSEX 5 b.g. Tudor Melody 129–Fashion Model 100 (Road House II) (1979 10f 12f 10f² 12fg* 12s* 12d⁴ 1980 12d) middle-distance performer; well beaten only outing of 1980 (March) and was subsequently gelded; acts on any going. *D. McCain.* —

ETCHING 3 b.f. Auction Ring 123–Etta (Umberto 118) (1979 5g 5g 6g² 6fg³ 7fg⁴ 8fg 7fg* 6g 7s² 1980 7f 6fg 6fg 8.5f 8fg 10g 9g⁴ 10fg* 10g* 10.2g² 8g* 10fg* 8fg²) compact filly; improved into a very useful performer in second half of season, winning amateur riders race at Brighton, minor event at Nottingham, £3,200 race at Doncaster (from Our Home) and Peter Hastings Stakes (Handicap) at Newbury; favourite, got up by a short head from Telsmoss at Newbury, hanging for a long way in straight but finishing so well that she made up 2 lengths over last furlong; suited by 1¼m; seems to act on any going; sometimes sweats up and becomes upset in paddock; ran badly sixth start; genuine; sold 98,000 gns Newmarket December Sales. *F. Durr.* **109**

ETESIAN 2 b.f. Tumble Wind–Mansfield (Star Gazer 123) (1980 5f³ 5fg* 5fg²(dis) 5f* 5h³) Apr 10; 3,500F, 5,000Y; strong, attractive filly; good walker; sister to useful Irish 5f and 6f winner Tundra Wind, and half-sister to a winner; dam won at up to 1½m in Ireland; odds-on winner of maiden and minor events at Wolverhampton and Pontefract in the spring, coming home 7 lengths clear of Miss Chessy on latter track despite being eased right up in closing stages (could have won by 15 lengths); turned out again 3 days after Pontefract in minor event on same course but could finish only 3 lengths third to Spindrifter; will stay 6f. *C. Nelson.* **86**

ETOILE DE PARIS 3 b.f. Crowned Prince 128–Place d'Etoile 93 (Kythnos 126) (1979 NR 1980 7v³ 7g² 7g* 8fg 8fg 7g³ 7d³ 6fg 6d* 6fg) useful sort; fifth foal; half-sister to several winners, notably high-class 1m to 1½m performer Northern Treasure (by Northfields); dam won at up to 1¼m and is half-sister to smart stayer Irvine; won Group 3 Athasi Stakes at the Curragh in April by 2½ lengths from Olinda and Carna Fillies Stakes by ½ length from Nazwa on same course in September; ran creditably most other outings, including when second in April Fillies Stakes, again at the Curragh, and when third in Jersey Stakes at Royal Ascot (1¼ lengths behind Hard Fought) and handicap at Newmarket in July (beaten 5 lengths by Parlour Game); stays 1m; suited by some give in the ground. *M. Kauntze, Ireland.* **116**

ETONIAN 5 ch.h. Majority Blue 126–Gilded Egg (Faberge II 121) (1979 7d 7g 6g 6f² 6fg⁴ 6d 1980 5fg 7f 6fg 6s) quite a moderate handicapper; stays 7f; probably acts on any going; trained in Ireland by W. Robinson final start in 1979 and first outing of 1980. *M. Smyly.* —

EUCLID 2 b. or br.c. Lyphard 132–Lucky For Me 116 (Appiani II 128) (1980 **111** p 7d2 6s* 8s*)

Lyphard's progeny dominated the 1979 European yearling sales to such an extent that his thirteen offspring, including a pair of twins, averaged approximately 141,000 guineas. The highest-priced colt and filly at the Houghton Sales and the top-priced yearling sold in France were all by him. None of these three, now respectively named Ghadeer, Sangue and Willis, won a race as a two-year-old but Euclid, another son of Lyphard who fetched the second-highest price of 240,000 guineas at Goffs, won one of Ireland's most important races, the Beresford Stakes.

The Beresford was the last of Euclid's three races, all run at the Curragh within the space of four weeks in the autumn. Although he justified favouritism he didn't win like an odds-on shot. After racing in second place behind Master Thatch he took up the running with over two furlongs to run but couldn't shake off the determined Lord Never, an improving colt who'd had his eighteen opponents well strung out in a maiden race at the Curragh the previous month. Euclid's jockey had to ride him very powerfully to keep him a short head in front on the line. The six other runners, headed by the filly Citissima, were left well behind.

Euclid had also started at odds on on his previous appearances. Lack of experience contributed to his defeat in a nineteen-runner maiden race on his debut, when he went down by a length and a half to the beautifully-bred Dance Bid after looking the likely winner a furlong out. He made no mistake in a minor event eleven days later, putting in all his best work in the closing stages to win by two lengths and five lengths from Cloonawillin and Solo Star, whose placings were reversed by the stewards. Both placed horses were previous winners and both won on their subsequent starts, Cloonawillin in well-contested events at Down Royal and Punchestown, Solo Star with ease in one of Ireland's best nurseries, the Birdcatcher.

Euclid can't so far be considered in the same class as his stable-companions Storm Bird and Critique. However, he's a grand-looking colt, just the type to

Mr R. E. Sangster's "Euclid"

make more than normal progress. Improvement is also possible when he's tried on a sound surface; so far he has raced only on soft ground and, while he certainly can't be said to be unsuited by it, he tended to become unbalanced close home on his first appearance and seemed to roll under pressure in the Beresford.

Euclid (b. or br.c. Feb 10, 1978)	Lyphard (b 1969)	Northern Dancer (b 1961)	Nearctic
			Natalma
		Goofed (ch 1960)	Court Martial
			Barra II
	Lucky For Me (b 1972)	Appiani II (b 1963)	Herbager
			Angela Rucellai
		Lucky Day (ch 1958)	Vic Day
			Something Win

Distances of a mile and a quarter or more should also bring out improvement in Euclid. He's fairly stoutly bred, the second foal and first winner of the smart Irish middle-distance filly Lucky For Me, whose wins included the Galtres Stakes and the Trigo Stakes. His grandam Lucky Day did extremely well at stud although by the unfashionable Vic Day, a stayer whose best runner was the Champion Hurdle winner Anzio. From only four living foals she produced Lucky For Me and three other winners, most notably the very useful Lucky Drake, third in the 1971 Irish St Leger, and the smart Nor, who finished fourth in Nijinsky's Irish Sweeps Derby in addition to winning the valuable San Luis Rey Handicap in California. *V. O'Brien, Ireland.*

EVA ANNIE 2 ch.f. Galivanter 131–Amba Princess (Amber Rama 133) (1980 6fg 5d) Mar 18; 2,000Y; first foal, dam placed over 1m; in rear in maiden races at Salisbury in September and Bath in October; sold to Susan Piggott Bloodstock 400 gns Newmarket Autumn Sales. *D. Sasse.* —

EVADNE 2 b.f. Bold Lad (Ire) 133–War Lass 100 (Whistler 129) (1980 5fg) Mar 4; 22,000Y; neat, strong filly; half-sister to several winners, including useful Tamariscifolia (by Ridan) and 3-y-o Crockford Lad (by Klairon), latter successful at up to 1m; dam won twice over 5f at 2 yrs; weak 9/1-shot, didn't stride out particularly well on way to start and made no show when seventh of 8 to Fine Honey in maiden race at Goodwood in August; looks capable of better. *R. Price.* —

EVER-SO-SURE 2 ch.g. No Mercy 126–Monet Royal 79 (Monet 127) (1980 7fg 7f) Apr 5; 3,100F, 8,600Y; rangy gelding; walks well; half-brother to 3 winners, including fairly useful middle-distance performer Kentucky Fair (by Crocket); dam won twice over 6.5f in Ireland at 3 yrs; in rear in minor events at Doncaster in July and York in September. *J. Etherington.* —

EVERYBODYS FRIEND 2 b.g. So Blessed 130–Attitude 116 (Gratitude 130) (1980 5fg^3 5f 5fg 5.3d^4 6s) Mar 23; 6,200F, 10,500Y; neat gelding; half-brother to 3 winners, including very useful 1970 2-y-o 6f winner Outlook (by Ballymoss) and fairly useful 7f and 1m winner Rectitude (by Runnymede); dam appeared best at 5f and 6f; poor form in maiden and minor races; should stay 6f; disappointing and is not to be trusted. *N. Callaghan.* 55 §

EVITA 3 b.f. Reform 132–Pampas Flower 80 (Pampered King 121) (1979 6f* 1980 7f* 8fg 8s) 106

After winning the 1979 Blue Seal Stakes at Ascot in fine style Evita was widely expected to develop into a good filly at three. In the event she had a rather unsatisfactory year. She came through her seasonal debut in the Ladbrokes Nell Gwyn Stakes at Newmarket with flying colours, buckling down well to lead near the finish to beat Mother Earth by a length and a half, and she started a firm second favourite for the One Thousand Guineas behind her stable-companion Saison. Evita moved moderately to post, pulled a muscle in her back during the race and finished a remote fourteenth to Quick As Lightning. Worse followed in the Child Stakes at Newmarket in July. Close up early on, she came under pressure three furlongs out and steadily faded to last of nine behind Stumped. Possibly Evita had not fully recovered from her injury, for she didn't run again; alternatively the soft going might have been against her, it was the first time she had encountered such testing conditions.

Pampas Flower has produced three winners besides Evita, the 1975 staying two-year-old Queluz (by Royal Palace), La Pampa (by Crepello), successful over middle distances, and the one-mile winner Shepherd's Glass (by Blakeney).

Ladbrokes Nell Gwyn Stakes, Newmarket—Evita wins in good style from Mother Earth (extreme left) and Scigueta (centre)

Pampas Flower won at a mile and is a half-sister to a number of winners, notably Pharsalia, Gratitude and Highest Hopes. Evita would have stayed a mile and a quarter. A quite attractive, smallish, lengthy filly, she will be at stud in 1981. *H. Cecil.*

EXAGGERATION 2 b.f. Welsh Saint 126–Full Stretch 103 (Sing Sing 134) (1980 5f 5g 5d 5f) Apr 3; 3,100F, 4,800Y; quite attractive filly; half-sister to Irish 7f to 1¼m winner Parole (by Don II); dam won twice over 6f at 2 yrs from 3 starts; co-favourite, blinkered and dropped in class, soon under whip when poor fifth of 13 to Thai Anna in seller at Catterick in July on fourth outing; one to leave alone. *G. Hunter.* — §

EXCELSIOR 6 b.g. Aglojo 119–Honeymoon (Honeyway 125) (1979 10s⁴ 12fg 1980 12fg 10fg 12g) poor maiden; stays 2m; acts on any going. *H. O'Neill.* —

EXCLUSIVELY RAISED (USA) 2 gr.f. Exclusive Native–The Rarest 105 (Rarity 129) (1980 6s² 7g* 7g⁴ 8g* 8fg²) **116**

Few stallions can have established a more flourishing dynasty or enjoyed more far-reaching success during their lifetime than Raise A Native, the champion American two-year-old of 1963. Admittedly he had a head start over the majority of other stallions in that he covered his first mares at the unusually early age of three, but at the age of eighteen in 1979 he featured as the paternal great grandsire of the champion American two-year-old Rockhill Native. In the same year his son Alydar was one of the very best four-year-old colts in America while his other sons Majestic Prince, Exclusive Native, Marshua's Dancer and Mr Prospector all sired top winners, with the cumulative earnings of their offspring coming to the remarkable total of over 6,700,000 dollars for the season. Perhaps the best of his sons is Exclusive Native, one of his small first crop. Exclusive Native was a good two-year-old, rated only 6 lb below the best of his age, but he wasn't so successful at three and started his stud career in 1969 at the fee of 1,500 dollars. He has proved a stallion of the highest class, siring numerous stakes winners including Affirmed, winner of the American triple crown in 1978, and Genuine Risk, who in 1980 became the first filly to win the Kentucky Derby since Regret did so in 1915. Not surprisingly his fee in 1980 was the more substantial figure of 75,000 dollars. Despite his success in the USA, or maybe because of it, Exclusive Native has been only sparsely represented in England and when Exclusively Raised won the Sweet Solera Stakes at Newmarket in August, she became only his second winner here.

The turn of foot Exclusively Raised showed in beating Fairy Footsteps by a length and a half at Newmarket suggested that she was well above average; and so she proved against the best staying two-year-old fillies in her three remaining races. Weight beat her in the Waterford Candelabra Stakes at Goodwood later in August where she finished fourth of ten behind the four-length winner Fairy Footsteps, who was in receipt of 8 lb. We felt at Goodwood that Exclusively Raised could have held on to second place ahead of Madam Gay and Silken Knot had Piggott been harder on her and, when she and Silken Knot renewed rivalry in the May Hill Stakes at Doncaster, Exclusively Raised turned the tables decisively. Again her excellent turn of foot was in evidence; she made rapid headway from last place approaching the final quarter mile and then cut down the front-running Silken Knot to score by a length and a half. A further victory looked on the cards in the Hoover Fillies Mile at Ascot later in September when the odds-on Exclusively Raised moved up smoothly to head Leap Lively at the distance. However, the pace had been extremely fast and Exclusively Raised weakened into second place, eventually going down by a length and a half to Leap Lively. Considering that she was giving weight all round, including 4 lb to the winner, she can be said to have shared the honours.

Exclusively Raised (USA) (gr.f. Feb 3, 1978)	Exclusive Native (ch 1965)	Raise A Native (ch 1961)	Native Dancer
			Raise You
		Exclusive (ch 1953)	Shut Out
			Good Example
	The Rarest (gr 1973)	Rarity (b 1967)	Hethersett
			Who Can Tell
		Ashling (gr 1962)	Nashua
			No Strings

Although both her dam The Rarest and her grandam Ashling raced in Ireland, Exclusively Raised was bred in America, where she was sold as a yearling for 100,000 dollars. Her third dam, the stakes winner No Strings, was also American. She did extremely well at stud, producing Ashling's sister Featheredge who was second in the Diadem Stakes; Globemaster, a leading three-year-old in the USA in 1961; Nail, one of the best American two-year-olds of 1955; and the lightly-raced Mito who has sired the winners of over 4,000,000 dollars. Ashling too was lightly raced, running only three times, but she was a fairly useful winner over seven furlongs. Among her four winners were the Jersey Stakes winner Ashleigh and The Rarest, a five-furlong winner at three years who put up her best effort on her sole start the previous season when second in the National Stakes at the Curragh. Exclusively Raised is The Rarest's first foal.

Exclusively Raised, a lengthy, useful sort, has been entered in the Oaks and Irish Guinness Oaks but there must be a serious doubt about her staying beyond a mile. She must have a reasonable chance in the Guineas, though. *M. Stoute.*

May Hill Stakes, Doncaster—Exclusively Raised produces a bright turn of foot to win going away from Silken Knot

EXPEDIER 2 b.c. Sharpen Up 127–Be Serious (Laugh Aloud) (1980 6fg 7fg) May 12; 3,300F, 3,000Y; rangy colt; third foal; dam twice-raced daughter of half-sister to Tambourine II and Nasram II; well beaten in maiden race at Goodwood in July (sweating and coltish and finished tailed off) and in maiden race at Lingfield in October (ridden by 7-lb claimer). *R. Akehurst.* —

EXPONENTIA 3 ch.f. Manacle 123–Ponente (Hornbeam 130) (1979 5fg 1980 6f 8h 8.2d 7fg) leggy filly; well beaten in varied company, including selling; sold 480 gns Ascot August Sales. *J. W. Watts.* —

EXQUISE 2 b.f. Hittite Glory 125–Esquinade 84 (Silly Season 127) (1980 6d 7d) Apr 29; small filly; first foal; dam 2-y-o 6f winner; unquoted when well beaten in minor event at Pontefract and maiden race at Leicester (seventh of 13) in October; sold 400 gns Newmarket Autumn Sales. *B. Hanbury.* —

EXTRA STEEP 2 ch.f. Exbury 138–Directissima (Devon III 125) (1980 5g 5fg 6g² 7f³ 7g) Feb 8; neat, rather lightly-made filly; first reported foal; dam won over 1¼m in France at 2 yrs; placed in maiden races at Brighton (2 lengths second to Pieta) and Chepstow (3¼ lengths third of 20 behind Briar) in August; will be suited by middle distances; sold to G. Lewis 1,200 gns Newmarket Autumn Sales. *P. Walwyn.* 79

EXTRAVAGANT NATIVE (USA) 2 br.f. Full Pocket–Native Glow (Exclusive Native) (1980 5g 6g 7g 7fg 7fg 7g 8fg) Mar 12; $20,000Y; narrow, lengthy filly; good mover; third foal; dam unraced half-sister to Burning On, a smart winner at up to 1¼m; no better than plating class; blinkered fifth outing. *G. Pritchard-Gordon.* 63

EXTROVERT (FR) 8 b.g. Bon Mot III 132–Exhibition 109 (Nearula 132) (1979 NR 1980 16g 16.5g) selling hurdler; of little account on flat. *D. Jermy.* —

EYELIGHT 3 gr.g. Roan Rocket 128–Pie Eye 88 (Exbury 138) (1979 5g³ 6f 6f 7fg² 7g 7fg⁴ 1980 7.6f 8fg⁴ 10fg² 8fg 12g 10d 8fg 8d⁴ 8g⁴ 9f³ 9d 8.2s) robust, short-legged gelding; in frame in varied company, including in a ladies race; stays 1¼m; acts on a firm and a soft surface; usually wears blinkers; a front runner; has shown signs of being none too keen on occasions; trained by F. J. Houghton first 5 starts. *R. Hollinshead.* 64

F

FABULOUS DUNCE (USA) 2 b.c. Le Fabuleux 133–Dulia (Dunce) (1980 7f) Feb 11; $100,000Y; rangy colt; half-brother to several winners, including Canadian Derby winner Pampas Host (by Right Combination or Tinte) and Truchas (by Lt Stevens), a smart winner at up to 1m; dam won at up to 5f at 2 yrs; weak in market and in need of race, dropped right out after showing up for 5f when behind in 19-runner maiden race won by King's Glory at Newmarket in October; likely to stay 1¼m; not given a hard time here and will do better in 1981. *M. Stoute.* — p

FAINTING LIGHT 3 gr.f. Habat 127–Penumbra 99 (Wolver Hollow 126) (1979 NR 1980 7fg 5d² 5g⁴ 6fg 6g) 10,000Y; lightly-made filly; second foal; dam a sprinter; in frame in maiden races at Lingfield and Nottingham in July but seems only plating class; best at 5f; suited by some give in the ground; sold 3,100 gns Newmarket December Sales. *L. Cumani.* 55

FAIR AND FREE 2 b.f. Reliance II 137–Matala 65 (Misti IV 132) (1980 7g 8d 8d 8d) May 8; light-framed filly; dam winning hurdler; little worthwhile form in maiden races; likely to need at least 1½m. *Mrs R. Lomax.* —

FAIR ARTIST 2 ch.f. Fair Decision 93 §–Melpo 73 (Hook Money 124) (1980 5fg 5.3g) May 22; 560Y; second live foal; dam 2-y-o 7f winner; in rear in minor events at Folkestone in April and Brighton in October. *B. Wise.* —

FAIR CITY 3 b.c. Charlottown 127–Fair Amanda 105 § (Firestreak 125) (1979 6g 7g* 8s 7f 1980 10v³ 10.6f 9g 11d² 13g³) leggy colt; quite moderate; will stay 1¾m; suited by some give in the ground; has run creditably for a boy. *W. H. H. Williams.* 76

FAIRDALE 2 gr. or ro.c. Roan Rocket 128–Catalonia 97 (Abernant 142) (1980 5d 5d) Mar 29; 2,400Y; small, stocky colt; half-brother to 3 winners here and abroad, including 1979 2-y-o 5f winner St Benedict (by So Blessed); dam, half-sister to Philip of Spain, won 4 times over 5f; unquoted and still on backward —

side when about 11 lengths sixth of 20 in maiden race won by Little Starchy at
Sandown in October. *G. Cottrell.*

FAIR DINO 5 b.m. Thatch 136–Dino 82 (Vienna 127) (1979 8g^2 9s 8g 10s —
10f 8g 8g^3 10s 10s 1980 10v 8f 8fg) poor maiden; stays 1m; sometimes wears
blinkers; often wears bandages. *W. Wharton.*

FAIR DUEL 3 b.c. Status Seeker–Double Irish (Dual 117) (1979 6fg 6f 1980 **69**
6s 10.1fg 11.7s 10s^4 10.1f^2 10.1f^4 10.1g 10fg 10f 8s) strong, well-made colt;
runner-up in maiden race at Windsor in August; well beaten in seller ninth
outing; stays 1¼m; acts on any going; blinkered first and final starts; ran badly
seventh outing. *P. Makin.*

FAIR FIGHT 2 br.f. Fine Blade 121–Nortia 123 (Narrator 127) (1980 6fg **75**
7g 8f^4) May 2; close-coupled, good sort; sister to fair 1½m performer Fine
Tale, and half-sister to several winners, including quite useful middle-distance
performers Klemperer and Huzoor (both by Hethersett); dam very smart at
around 1¼m; running-on 6 lengths sixth of 15 to Kalaglow in minor event at
Sandown in August, second outing; again running on when 3¾ lengths fourth to
Cinderwench in 10-runner maiden race at Wolverhampton the following month;
will be suited by middle distances. *H. Candy.*

FAIR GLORY 2 ch.f. Hittite Glory 125–Travelling Fair 95 (Vienna 127) (1980 **57**
5f 5d 5.8fg^4 5g 5fg 5g 8d) Apr 23; 3,500F, 8,400Y; compact filly; half-sister
to 3 winners, including fairly useful 1m and 1¼m winner Dibbinsdale Lad (by
Sandford Lad); dam best at around 1m; 5 lengths fourth of 12 to Maryland
Cookie in maiden race at Bath in July; better suited by 6f than 5f, but ran as
though she didn't stay in 1m seller at Warwick in October; blinkered sixth
outing; sold 650 gns Ascot November Sales. *A. Ingham.*

FAIRGREEN 2 b.c. Music Boy 124–Sunny Bloom 71 (Forlorn River 124) **85**
(1980 6g 5fg 6f 6g^4 5d* 5g^3) Mar 7; big colt; bad walker; first foal; dam sprint
maiden; improved with his races and won 18-runner maiden event at Warwick
in October by 1½ lengths from Bretton Park after racing wide throughout;
didn't help his chance by wandering in the Dip when 1½ lengths third of 16 to
Fire Mountain in nursery at Newmarket later in month; possibly better suited
by 5f than 6f; acts on a soft surface. *H. Westbrook.*

FAIR HUNTER 6 br.h. Huntercombe 133–Selina Fair 94 (Hugh Lupus 132) ?
(1979 won twice at around 1¼m from 11 starts 1980 12f 7fg 13.4f 12.5f* 10s
10g 10.7g* 10g 9.5s 12.5g 8d) sturdy ex-Dutch horse; brother to Radetzky,
a very smart performer at up to 1¼m; winner of handicaps at Duindigt in May
and July; little other form in 1980; stayed 1½m; acted on firm going; sold 2,800
gns Newmarket Autumn Sales; stud in Devon. *M. Ryan.*

FAIRMAN 7 ch.h. Manacle 123–Fairabunda 59 (Floribunda 136) (1979 —
18s 12f^4 12f^3 10fg 1980 8g 10g) poor handicapper; stays 13f; acts on any
going; sometimes wears blinkers. *D. Jermy.*

FAIRMILE LAD 3 b.g. Starch Reduced 112–Anthela 76 (Acropolis 132) **78** d
(1979 5d 5d 6g* 6fg^4 6f 1980 6fg 6fg^2 6g^4 6d* 6s 6d 6g 6g) small gelding;
quite a moderate handicapper; won at Brighton in June; stays 6f; acts on
a firm and a soft surface; sweated up final start; suitable mount for a boy. *A.
Pitt.*

FAIRNESS 3 b.c. Run The Gantlet–Fair Arabella (Chateaugay) (1979 **69**
NR 1980 10.7v^2 16fg* 13s^3 17.1d) 30,000Y; long-backed colt; half-brother
to Oaks winner Fair Salinia (by Petingo) and very useful Italian colt Francis
Bacon (by Sovereign Path); dam won at up to 1m in USA and is half-sister
to top-class French miler Faraway Son; all out when winning 11-runner maiden
race at Warwick in July; soundly beaten on his other starts; stays 2m; acts
on a firm surface; sold 4,100 gns Newmarket Autumn Sales. *B. Hills.*

FAIR OF FACE 2 ch.f. Grundy 137–Golden Treasure 106 (Crepello 136) — p
(1980 6g) Feb 20; lightly-made, useful-looking filly; third foal; dam, unbeaten
in 3 races over 5f and 6f at 2 yrs, stayed 1¼m; 20/1 but looking as though she
had done a fair bit of work, made headway to finish first on far side of course
when about 7 lengths fifth of 25 to Composer in maiden race at Newmarket
in October; sure to win races over middle distances in 1981 . *H. Candy.*

FAIR ROSALIND 2 b.f. Mummy's Pet 125–Sweet Success 81 (Privy Councillor **88**
125) (1980 5d 5f^2 5g^3 5fg 6g^2 5.8h^2 6g* 6fg) Mar 25; 6,800Y; lengthy, lightly-
made filly; half-sister to a winning hurdler; dam won 6f seller at 2 yrs; second
in maiden races prior to winning 8-runner nursery at Salisbury in September
in good style by 3 lengths from That's Magic; stays 6f; acts on hard going;
ran poorly final outing. *N. Vigors.*

FAIR SARA 2 br.f. McIndoe 97–Fairstar 86 (Star Moss 122) (1980 6d 6fg 6g 7fg 8.2d^2 8fg^4 9d^4 7.2s^4) . May 4; leggy filly; sister to winning Belgian 3-y-o Bianca Girl; dam stayed at least 1m; in frame in varied company, including selling; will stay 1¼m; seems to act on any going: can win a seller. *K. Ivory.* **65**

FAIRSTEAD (USA) 2 b.c. Plenty Old–Bayadera (Venerador) (1980 6g) rangy colt; fourth foal; brother to Mama's Grey, a winner over 1m in USA, and half-brother to another winner; dam placed twice from 20 starts; 25/1, backward and green, finished well down field in 25-runner maiden race won by Composer at Newmarket in October. *R. Sheather.* **–**

FAIR SUE 3 b.f. Workboy 123–Dialice 61 (King's Troop 118) (1979 5s 5g* 5f^4 5f 5f 7.2g 5s^2 6f 1980 5s 5f 5f^3 5h 6g) small, unfurnished filly; plater; not sure to stay 7f; acts on any going; sweated up and ran poorly second start; often looks most unimpressive in paddock; moved badly to post fourth outing. *C. Gray.* **53**

FAIR TOUCH 2 ch.f. Touch Paper 113–Fair Appreciation 77 (Gratitude 130) (1980 5g 5g* 5f 6d 6g 6f) May 10; 1,800Y; tall, rather narrow filly; half-sister to fair 1974 2-y-o 5f winner Jaqray (by Polyfoto); dam 2-y-o 5f winner; favourite when winning 10-runner maiden auction race at Pontefract in June by ¾ length from Matilda Cave; backed at long odds and blinkered, ran best race afterwards when 4¼ lengths fifth of 18 to Kathred in £2,000 seller at Newmarket in October; stays 6f. *P. Rohan.* **67**

FAIR TRACK 2 ch.f. Track Spare 125–Fair Samela 108 (Constable 119) (1980 6s 6f^4 6fg 5f) Mar 8; lightly-made filly; half-sister to useful sprinter Fair Sarita (by King's Troop) and a winner in Italy; dam very game 6f and 7f performer; no worthwhile form in varied company; blinkered fourth outing. *Denys Smith.* **–**

FAIRY FISHERMAN 6 b.h. Captain's Gig–Pixie Jet 105 (Polly's Jet) (1979 10.2s 8d 12g 9fg 8g 8f* 8f^2 8d^2 8.2fg* 8fg 7d 8s 1980 8d 8f 10f^2 10f 10.7g^4 10g^4 8fg 8fg) quite a moderate handicapper nowadays; stays 1¼m; appears to act on any going but is well suited by top-of-the-ground; sometimes wears blinkers; sold 850 gns Doncaster October Sales. *J. Bingham.* **70**

FAIRY FOOTSTEPS 2 b.f. Mill Reef 141–Glass Slipper 100 (Relko 136) (1980 7g^4 7g^2 7g*) **118** p

The overwhelming significance of 1977 to many thoroughbred breeders will surely be that it was the year Contagious Equine Metritis (CEM) struck down several studs, most notably the National Stud which had to end its breeding season early in May. The National Stud's production, and most importantly that of the three Derby winners it houses, was drastically reduced. Blakeney, whose fertility had been as high as 95% three years earlier, sired only fifteen foals; Grundy's fertility, which had been 82.75% in his first year at stud, slumped to 51.52% in his second; and, most dramatically, Mill Reef achieved a fertility percentage of only 26.47%, compared to 89.18% and 94.11% in the two preceding seasons. Thankfully the precautionary measures taken by the National Stud in subsequent years—which unfortunately included closing the stud to the public—have met with great success. There were no cases of CEM at the stud during the 1979 breeding season during which Blakeney, Grundy and Mill Reef respectively got 93.18%, 100% and 88.64% of their mares in foal—outstanding figures.

Since Blakeney, Grundy and Mill Reef have cumulatively sired the winners of a Derby, two Irish Derbys, a French Derby, two Oaks, one Irish Guinness Oaks and a St Leger, the longer classic races in 1981 will do well to escape being the poorer for the lack of their representatives. But we know of one very live classic hope sired by Mill Reef: although there were only nine reported foals by him in 1978 one of them, Fairy Footsteps, looks to have all the makings of an Oaks winner. Her performance in the Waterford Candelabra Stakes at Goodwood in August on the last of her three starts at two years was most impressive. She had shown plenty of promise on her previous outings, coming from last place on the turn to finish fourth of sixteen to Seasurf in a maiden race at Sandown in July before running Exclusively Raised to a length and a half, without her jockey touching her with the whip, in the Sweet Solera Stakes at Newmarket. Although Fairy Footsteps was clearly very much on the upgrade and was 8 lb better off with Exclusively Raised at Goodwood, she was only third choice in the betting behind Exclusively Raised and the Virginia Water Stakes winner Silken Knot. Eddery, taking the mount on Fairy Footsteps for the first time, employed new tactics, sending her to the

Mr H. J. Joel's "Fairy Footsteps" (P. Eddery)

front from the start. She ran rings round the opposition, taking a clear lead three furlongs out and keeping on so strongly that none of the others could ever get in a blow. Exclusively Raised looked likely to take second place when coming to challenge at the distance but she wasn't given a hard time once pursuit was hopeless and Madam Gay and Silken Knot passed her close home. Fairy Footsteps won by four lengths and a length.

Cecil soon announced that Fairy Footsteps had been put away for the rest of the season. She therefore missed the two other top races for two-year-old staying fillies, the May Hill Stakes at Doncaster and the Hoover Fillies Mile at Ascot. The results of both races lend support to the view that Fairy Footsteps was the best young staying filly in England: Exclusively Raised and Silken Knot dominated the finish of the May Hill and the Ascot race went to the much-improved Leap Lively, who had finished only fifth at Goodwood, with the places going to Exclusively Raised and Fiesta Fun, respectively fourth and ninth in the Waterford Candelabra.

Fairy Footsteps (b.f. Jan 15, 1978)	Mill Reef (b 1968)	Never Bend (b 1960)	Nasrullah
			Lalun
		Milan Mill (b 1962)	Princequillo
			Virginia Water
	Glass Slipper (br 1969)	Relko (b 1960)	Tanerko
			Relance III
		Crystal Palace (b 1956)	Solar Slipper
			Queen of Light

Besides having the form of a high-class filly Fairy Footsteps also has the looks and pedigree of one. A good sort, well-made and robust, she's the third winner from the first three foals bred by Glass Slipper, a useful staying filly who finished in the frame in both the Musidora Stakes and the Ribblesdale Stakes. The first two were the Exbury colt Crystal Coach, a fairly useful stayer, and the Brigadier Gerard colt Light Cavalry, winner of the St Leger. Since Fairy Footsteps, Glass Slipper has produced the yearling filly Love's Dream (by Rheingold) and the colt foal Stage Coach (by Luthier). She visited

Sharpen Up in 1980. Perhaps Glass Slipper will become as celebrated a broodmare as her dam and grandam. Crystal Palace, who was put down at the age of twenty-four in 1980, produced three top colts in Royal Palace, Prince Consort and Selhurst; and Queen of Light, in addition to Crystal Palace, produced three other excellent broodmares in Picture Light, Chandelier and Lovely Light.

Fairy Footsteps looks sure to stay well and the Oaks looks her best chance of classic success. Should she win the Oaks she will complete a remarkable achievement for her veteran owner-breeder Jim Joel who has already won the Two Thousand Guineas, One Thousand Guineas, Derby and St Leger with Picture Play, Royal Palace and Light Cavalry, all descendants of Fairy Footsteps' fifth dam Amuse. *H. Cecil.*

FAIZ 2 b.c. Prince Tenderfoot 126–Grazia 90 (Aureole 132) (1980 5d2 5f2 6g* 6d2 5fg3 6d*) Mar 14; 22,000Y; well-made, quite attractive colt; half-brother to 7f and 9f winner Gracious Consent (by Prince Regent); dam won over 6f at 2 yrs; successful in maiden race at Newcastle in August and nursery at Leicester in October, scoring by 2½ lengths from Ramwadash in latter; will stay 1m; seems to act on any going; started slowly second outing. *J. Dunlop.* **95**

FALCON FOAM 2 b.g. Mr Mainwaring–Tartar Ash 89 (Celtic Ash) (1980 6g 7fg 6g 8d 10g) May 19; small, narrow gelding; second foal; brother to fair 1979 2-y-o staying maiden Falcon's Tartar; dam needed a test of stamina; little better than plating class; should be suited by 7f+. *T. Waugh.* **–**

FALCON'S REVENGE 3 b. or br.g. Sweet Revenge 129–Grey Falcon (Falcon 131) (1979 5f4 6g2 6f3 1980 7d3 7fg 8g 8.2s3 6g) plain gelding; plater; stays 1m well; acts on any going; blinkered final start. *W. Hastings-Bass.* **58**

FALCON'S TARTAR 3 b.g. Mr Mainwaring–Tartar Ash 89 (Celtic Ash) (1979 5s 5g 5.1g 7f4 7fg 8.2g 8g2 1980 8f 10.1fg 11.5f) neat, narrow gelding; fair (rated 85) at 2 yrs; ran moderately in 1980 and wasn't seen out after June; will stay well. *T. Waugh.* **–**

FALDOR 3 ch.g. Falaise–Little Dora (Bounteous 125) (1979 5s 5v2 5f 6fg 7f 7g 8.2d 8d 1980 12g 12g2 13.8f 10g 12g 13.8fg3 13.8d 11s* 8d) plain gelding; plater; attracted no bid after winning at Hamilton in October (apprentice ridden); probably stays 13.8f; acts on soft going; sometimes blinkered but wasn't when successful. *J. Calvert.* **51**

FALKELLY 4 b. or br.f. Pitskelly 122–Falcade (Falcon 131) (1979 10fg4 12d 16.1g 10.6g* 10g2 1980 12d2) tall, leggy filly; favourite, although unimpressive in paddock, when short-head second to all-the-way winner West Mon in amateur riders event at Doncaster in March; best form at distances shorter than 2m; dead. *M. H. Easterby.* **65**

FALKLAND PALACE 3 b.g. Royal Palace 131–Festival Night 115 (Midsummer Night II 117) (1979 NR 1980 9fg2 11.7fg 13.3fg 16d4) big, leggy, unfurnished gelding; first foal; dam won from 6f to 1½m; seems only plating class; appeared not to stay 2m on fourth start (sweated up). *H. Candy.* **71** d

FALLIG SCHNELL 4 ch.g. King's Leap 111–Sea Melody 79 (Tudor Minstrel 144) (1979 NR 1980 6f 9fg 7f 7d) workmanlike gelding; plater; showed a little ability final start (springer in market); bandaged second and third outings; sweating first start. *S. Wiles.* **–**

FALNAMA 3 b.f. Queen's Hussar 124–Falassa (Relko 136) (1979 5f4 1980 9f2 10fg4 12d* 12.2f4) lightly-made filly; won modest maiden race at Carlisle in July; suited by 1½m; probably acts an any going; sold 5,400 gns Newmarket December Sales. *F. J. Houghton.* **70**

FANADIX 4 ch.g. Dubassoff–My Dream 119 (King of the Tudors 129) (1979 14f3 10f 16.9fg3 16d 14g 1980 15fg 13g 10fg 16f 12g) poor maiden; trained until after second outing by R. Carter. *G. Pritchard-Gordon.* **–**

FANDANGLE 2 ch.c. Gay Fandango 132–Sandra II (Le Haar 126) (1980 6g4 8g2) Apr 12; 31,000Y; medium-sized, robust colt; half-brother to Prodigal Son (by Faraway Son), winner over 9f and 1½m in France; dam placed over 1m at 2 yrs in France; co-favourite following a promising debut at Salisbury in August, had every chance (led 1½f out but was caught near finish) when head second of 15 to Riberetto in maiden race at Newmarket in October; will stay 1¼m; sure to win a race. *J. Tree.* **85**

FANDANGO TIME 2 ch.c. Gay Fandango 132–Sapho 59 (Raeburn II) (1980 7f4) Apr 6; 30,000Y; lengthy, rather lightly-made colt; fifth foal; dam ran only 3 times at 2 yrs; 8/1, well clear of remainder when promising 3¼ lengths fourth of 11 to Glint of Gold in Sandwich Stakes at Ascot in July, running on **86** p nicely without being at all hard ridden; not seen out afterwards; will stay 1¼m. *B. Hills.*

FANNY KEYSER 5 ch.m. Majority Blue 126–Mega Fawn 87 (Sound Track 132) (1979 6s 7f 7fg 6g 5h 6s 5d 1980 6g) poor plater; often wears blinkers and a hood. *J. Mulhall.* –

FAR AWAY 3 b.f. Reliance II 137–Distant Horizon 92 (Nimbus 130) (1979 6s^2 1980 8fg 10f 7d 7d) workmanlike ex-Irish filly; second in maiden race at Punchestown at 2 yrs; behind in varied company in 1980; needs further than 7f and will stay 1½m; blinkered final start. *H. Blagrave.* –

FARCROFT 6 br.m. Country Retreat 91–Dunwen (Dumbarnie 125) (1979 NR 1980 10.6fg 8g 8g 10d) poor plater; has been tried in blinkers. *B. Shaw.* –

FARDANI 2 ch.c. Mount Hagen 127–Falassa (Relko 136) (1980 5f 5.8f 6s 7d) Mar 13; second foal; half-brother to 3-y-o 1½m winner Falnama (by Queen's Hussar); dam, placed at up to 1¼m in France, is half-sister to top-class Silver Shark; only poor form in maiden races but started favourite on first 2 outings; possibly needs a test of stamina; blinkered third appearance; sold 1,100 gns Newmarket Autumn Sales. *F. J. Houghton.* –

FAREWELL PARADE 4 b.f. March Past 124–Eringa 101 (Saint Crespin III 132) (1979 7s 7fg 1980 8f 7fg 10d 8g) fair sort; plating-class maiden; blinkered final start. *J. Bethell.* –

FARIDELLA 2 gr.f. Silly Season 127–Fair Fabiola 94 (Acropolis 132) (1980 5f 6fg^4 6g^4 7g^3 7s^4 8g^3 8d^2 8d^4) Apr 30; 2,900Y; lightly-made filly; second foal; dam won three 5f races at 2 yrs; in frame in maiden races and nurseries; will stay middle distances; acts on a soft surface; effective with or without blinkers. *I. Walker.* 75

FARLEIGH 2 b.f. Sandford Lad 133–Get Ready 91 (On Your Mark 125) (1980 5fg 5d 6g 8d) Mar 26; 4,600Y; neat filly; bad mover; useless plater; has worn blinkers; sold 380 gns Ascot November Sales. *J. Douglas-Home.* –

FARSOUND 2 b.f. Wolver Hollow 126–Farfisa 86 (Sassafras 135) (1980 7g) Mar 12; leggy filly; first foal; dam won 4 times over 1¼m; 50/1 when never-dangerous eighth of 18 to Park Place in maiden race at Yarmouth in September; may do better over further at 3 yrs. *M. Stoute.* –

FARTHING 6 b.m. Maystreak 118–Clouds of Gold (Goldhill 125) (1979 16.9s 12s^2 13.1g 12s 12fg 1980 10d 11.7d) poor middle-distance plater; seems to act on any going; good mount for an apprentice. *D. Wintle.* –

FASCADALE 6 br.g. Frankincense 120–Straight Off 88 (Straight Deal) (1979 10d^2 10f 12f^2 12f* 11g* 12d^3 11s* 10.5g^2 12s^4 1980 10v* 10.6fg 12fg* 12f* 12g^4 12g^3 12d* 11s 10.5s^4 12v) middle-distance handicapper; put up a good performance when getting home by neck from Ditton Wood at Ripon in August; successful earlier at Ayr (apprentice event) and Redcar (twice); ran poorly eighth start; acts on any going; genuine and consistent; sometimes sweats up; needs to be held up. *J. W. Watts.* 90

FASHION BOY 2 b.c. Go Marching–Telstop (Fine Top 125) (1980 7g 8g) Mar 20; 6,800F, 66,000Y; attractive, well-made colt; brother to a poor animal, and half-brother to 1½m winner Locksley (by Tennyson); dam, winner of small 11f race in France, is half-sister to dam of Le Marmot; in rear in minor event at Kempton and maiden race at Goodwood; to be trained by G. Lewis. *J. Sutcliffe.* –

FAST COLOUR 5 b.h. Red God 128§–Catchmenot 100 (Cagire II 122) (1979 6s 6s 6fg 5.3g^4 6fg^3 6h 6h^4 1980 6g^2 6g 6fg^2) sprint handicapper; good second at Ripon (apprentice event) and Kempton (to King of Spain) early in the year; best at 6f; appears to act on any going; wears blinkers. *H. T. Jones.* 71

FAST EDDY 3 ch.c. Jukebox 120–French Twist 79 (Crocket 130) (1979 NR 1980 7d 5f 7fg) 16,500Y; big colt; in rear in varied company, including selling; dead. *N. Callaghan.* –

FAST FRIEND 2 ch.f. Be Friendly 130–Hastily 99 (Hornbeam 130) (1980 5f 5g^2 5fg 6s^3 6d* 6g 6fg 7d) May 1; 2,200F, 4,100Y; rather leggy filly; sister to winners in Jersey, Germany and South Africa, and half-sister to a winner in France; dam 2-y-o 5f winner; won 11-runner minor event at Windsor in July by 1½ lengths from Think Ahead; best form at 6f; possibly needs some give in the ground and acts on soft going. *P. Kelleway.* 85

FAST GREEN 3 b.c. Cavo Doro 124–Astraline 97 (Skymaster 126) (1979 8fg^3 1980 8.2s 9g* 10.2fg 10fg 10g 10s 10g 10fg 11s^4) neat, good sort; narrowly won modest 11-runner maiden event at Hamilton in April; possibly stays 1¼m; best 70 d form on an easy surface; often wears blinkers; sold 3,000 gns Ascot November Sales. *C. Nelson.*

FASTNET ISLAND 3 b.g. Young Emperor 133–Long Shadow 77 (Royal Palm 131) (1979 8f 8d2 1980 8f 9f 12s 12d) tall, lengthy gelding; runner-up in maiden race at Leicester in 1979; showed no form in similar events at 3 yrs; not certain to stay 1½m; blinkered final start. *P. Kelleway.* –

FAST RECOIL 3 ch.c. Roan Rocket 128–Time Bomb (Supreme Court 135) (1979 6f2 6fg 1980 10.2fg2 10.4f 10.1f2 11.7fg* 12g 10d 10.1g 8d2 8d 8s) quite attractive, neat colt; won 18-runner maiden race at Bath in June; creditable second in handicap on same course in October; needs further than 1m and stays 1½m; probably acts on any going; ran poorly ninth start; sold 10,500 gns Newmarket Autumn Sales. *J. Bethell.* **80**

FATA MORGANA 5 gr.g. Grey Mirage 128–Monica Rose (Forlorn River 124) (1979 14.6s2 15.8g2 15fg4 14.6fg3 16.1f4 16g 14g 16g4 18.1g4 1980 18d2 16s 16f) poor staying handicapper; acts on any going; suitable mount for an apprentice. *D. Weeden.* –

FATH-EL-KEIR 2 ch.f. Record Token 128–Gorse Bush (Hallez 131) (1980 7g 6g* 6g) Mar 20; 920Y; first foal; dam won twice over 1¼m in Ireland; 33/1, dwelt in maiden auction event at Folkestone in July but ran on so well from halfway she got up to win by a neck from Unit Tent; 33/1 when behind in minor race won by Cavalry Twill at Windsor the following month; will stay 1m. *M. Blanshard.* **66**

FAVOURITE NIECE 2 b.f. Busted 134–Ashaireez (Abernant 142) (1980 7.2d) Feb 6; 20,000F; tall, lengthy filly; half-sister to 3 winners, including 1975 2-y-o 6f winner Taiseera (by Northfields) and a winner in Brazil; dam twice-raced daughter of Irish Oaks winner Amante; 12/1 and fit enough, made a little late headway after getting well behind when out of first 9 of 19 to Craigour in maiden race at Haydock in September. *F. J. Houghton.* –

FEARLESS FLIGHT 3 ch.c. Golden Mallard 103–Fear Not 106 (Faubourg II 127) (1979 NR 1980 8fg 8.2f 10f 11fg 10.5d 10.2g 6g2 6g4 7fg) big, strong colt; second reported live produce; dam won at up to 1m; showed first worthwhile form when second in 20-runner maiden race at Nottingham in July; not certain to stay 1m. *W. Elsey.* –

FEARLESS SEAL 3 b.g. Andrea Mantegna–Fearless Lady 92 (Privy Councillor 125) (1979 6g 7fg 5fg 1980 8.2s 8fg3 8fg 8g 7s 10.2v) workmanlike gelding; best run at 1m on a firm surface. *R. Hollinshead.* **69**

FEAR NO MORE 3 b.f. Morston 125–Fearless 77 (Derring-Do 131) (1979 NR 1980 10.1f) fourth foal; half-sister to Gibbon (by Swing Easy), successful over 7.2f and 1m; dam, winner over 7f, is half-sister to very smart More Light (by Morston) and high-class Shoot A Line; unquoted when out of first 10 in 24-runner maiden race at Windsor in August. *J. Hudson.* –

FEAST (NZ) 6 gr.g. Coeur Volant II–Whence (The Summit) (1979 unplaced in New Zealand 1980 8fg) wiry New-Zealand-bred gelding; 20/1 when remote sixth to Repetitious in apprentice event at Kempton in May. *D. Kent.* –

FEAST-RITE 2 b.f. Reform 132–Tribal Feast 100 (Tribal Chief 125) (1980 5fg) May 15; 4,000Y; second foal; dam speedy early-season 2-y-o; 20/1, out of first 9 of 21 behind Doubtwash Girl in minor event at Catterick in September but made late progress; may do better at 3 yrs. *K. Stone.* –

FEATHERSTONE FLYER 4 br.g. Goldhill 125–La Saane (Hard Sauce 131) (1979 NR 1980 8g 12.2f) seems of little account. *G. Lockerbie.* –

FEE 2 gr.f. Mandamus 120–Currency (Crepello 136) (1980 5d 5d4 6s2 6g* 6fg3 6d2 7g*) Feb 2; leggy filly; good walker and mover; first foal; dam never ran; hard held when landing the odds by ¾ length from Eskview Lad in nursery at Edinburgh in October; placed in varied company earlier, being awarded first place after finishing ¾-length second to Hexgreave Star (who failed a dope test) in Tolly Cobbold Nursery at Newmarket in July on fourth outing; will stay middle distances; seems to act on any going. *B. Hobbs.* **79**

FEELINGS (FR) 3 b.c. Green Dancer 132–Fast Iron (Iron Peg §§) (1979 8v 1980 12d 12fg4 12fg3 10.2g 10.2g 10s* 12g4 14.7d2 15d) well-made, quite attractive ex-French colt; second foal; dam, winner over 9f in France, is half-sister to 1971 American Horse of the Year Ack Ack; won small race at Ayr in September; not disgraced on penultimate start; stays well; acts on soft going; blinkered last 2 outings; trained by Mme C. Head first 2 starts. *J. Hanson.* **81**

FELICO 2 b. or br.f. Wolver Hollow 126–Palinda 117 (Palestine 133) (1980 –
5f 6g 7fg) Apr 30; 3,200Y; leggy filly; half-sister to 2 winners; dam second
in Cheveley Park and won at up to 1m; unquoted when remote sixth of 15
to Harp Strings in maiden race at Nottingham in July, second outing and only
glimmer of ability; sold to BBA 900 gns Newmarket Autumn Sales. *P. Rohan.*

FELTWELL (USA) 2 b.c. Habitat 134–Reload 119 (Relko 136) (1980 8g –
7d 8g) neat, quite attractive colt; fourth foal; half-brother to 2 winners,
including useful 1977 2-y-o 1m winner War Whoop (by Moulton); dam won
Park Hill Stakes and is half-sister to Full Dress II; behind in end-of-season
maiden and minor events at Newmarket (2) and Doncaster but was backward
on first 2 outings. *H. Wragg.*

FENNEY MILL 3 b.f. Levmoss 133–Pidget 120 (Fortino II 120) (1979 7g^4 99
1980 10fg* 12d^3) 32,000Y; very attractive filly; third foal; half-sister to
Irish 9f winner Palagonian (by Habitat); dam won Irish 1,000 Guineas and
St Leger; co-favourite when winning small race at Phoenix Park in May by
a length from Welsh Daylight; always close up but had no chance with winner
in straight when $6\frac{3}{4}$ lengths third to Shoot A Line in Ribblesdale Stakes at Royal
Ascot; not seen out again; will stay $1\frac{3}{4}$m; acts on a firm and a soft surface.
S. Murless, Ireland.

FERNARO 3 ch.g. Sharpen Up 127–Sea Fern (Klondyke Bill 125) (1979 83
5g^4 5s* 6g 5s^4 7g 6g 7g* 8fg 7.3g* 1980 8v 8fg 7fg* 8h* 8f 7g^3 7d^3 8g 7g^3 7d^4
7g* 10.2g 8fg 8g) useful-looking gelding; fair handicapper; successful at
Salisbury and Brighton in May and Sandown in August; best at up to 1m;
acts on any going; blinkered eighth start; genuine. *R. Hannon.*

FERRIBY HALL 3 ch.c. Malicious–Gallic Law 91 (Galivanter 131) (1979 89
6f 5d^2 5s 5g^4 5f* 5f 5g* 5g^2 1980 5d^2 5g 6fg* 6fg^2 6f^3 6f 6g^3 6g 5f 6s 6d^2 7s
5s^3 6d^3) strong colt; quite a useful handicapper; made all and battled on
gamely to beat Brianstanway a short head at Haydock in April; ran well on
several subsequent starts; stays 6f; acts on any going; sweated up slightly
when running moderately sixth outing; blinkered nowadays; has run well
for an apprentice. *T. Fairhurst.*

FERRYMAN 4 b.g. Forlorn River 124–La Miranda 80 (Miralgo 130) (1979 86
7s 6d^2 6v^4 5s 6fg 7g 7fg 5fg* 5.8fg* 6fg 1980 5g^2 6fg^2 5.8fg 5fg* 5d^2 5f 5g^2
5d^2 5g* 5d) small gelding; fair handicapper; successful at Windsor in August
and at Ascot in October, on latter course just holding on from Marching On
in valuable Bovis Handicap after going clear before halfway; runner-up in
between at Haydock, Salisbury and Goodwood; stays 6f and ran respectably
over 7f at 3 yrs; probably acts on any going; sometimes sweats up. *D. Elsworth.*

FETTERED 6 b.g. Manacle 123–Anatevka (Privy Councillor 125) (1979 63
NR 1980 8fg* 7f 8f^2 8fg 7.6d 8g^2 8g^4 8fg) quite a moderate handicapper;
ridden by 7-lb claimer and having first outing for 18 months after reportedly
breaking down, when beating Prince of Spain by $1\frac{1}{2}$ lengths at Warwick in
May; runner-up in 2 apprentice events afterwards; stays 1m; acts on any going
except hard; used to wear blinkers. *N. Vigors.*

FETTER LANE 4 b.c. Manacle 123–La Colline 97 (Acropolis 132) (1979 59
8g 9s 8fg^3 8fg^2 8fg^2 8.2g^2 12s^3 10s^2 12s 1980 11.7fg^3 12f^2 12f 12g^4 12.2s^2 12d
16.9d^2) unfurnished colt; plating-class maiden; one paced and seems to stay 2m;
acts on any going; sometimes wears blinkers. *B. Palling.*

FFINNANT FELLA 8 gr.h. Maestoso 94–Sister Jane (Pluchino 106) (1979 –
NR 1980 12fg 12g) very lightly-raced maiden. *R. Morris.*

FICKLE FIGHTER 2 br.g. Mummy's Pet 125–Breathalyser (Alcide 136) (1980 –
5f 7f 6d) Mar 31; 5,800F, 1,600Y; well-grown gelding; half-brother to 3 winners,
including smart middle-distance stayer Major Green (by Double-U-Jay); dam
showed only poor form; in rear in minor and maiden events. *W. Bentley.*

FIDATO 4 br.g. Reliance II 137–Sealed Order (Aureole 132) (1979 NR 1980 –
8g 10.1d 11.7f) temperamental and of little account; blinkered final outing.
B. Palling.

FIDDLER 3 b.g. Song 132–Silent Swindler 59 (Tacitus 124) (1979 5fg 5f 6s 6fg 66
5f 5d^3 1980 5v* 5fg* 5f* 5fg^4 5fg^3 5d 5g 5.8f 5d^4 5d 5d* 6d) sturdy gelding;
sprint handicapper; had a good year, winning at Warwick, Wolverhampton
(twice) and Beverley; best at 5f; acts on any going; blinkered fourth and fifth
outings at 2 yrs; started slowly sixth appearance and ran moderately on seventh.
C. Austin.

FIDDLERS BEE 3 b.f. Idiot's Delight 115–Drink Time 77 (Forlorn River 124) (1979 6fg⁴ 1980 8s) unfurnished filly; beaten some way in newcomers event and maiden race. *C. V. Miller.* —

FIDIBUS (FR) 4 b.c. Northfields–Flat (Bold Lad, Ire 133) (1979 10.2g³ 10.4d³ 8s* 8.2s² 8fg 10.2fg³ 7g⁴ 1980 8d 7v 14fg 8f 8fg 6g⁴ 7f* 7fg 7g 8.3fg) medium-sized colt; mainly disappointing in 1980, but won handicap at Catterick in July by a length from Compound; stays 1¼m; acts on any going; often blinkered nowadays; ridden by 7-lb claimer at Catterick; sold to B.B.A. Italia 5,000 gns Newmarket Autumn Sales. *B. Hills.* **65**

FIELD DAY 3 ch.f. Northfields–Royal News 74 (Sovereign Path 125) (1979 NR 1980 8fg 10h 10.1s 10fg* 12d* 10fg* 12f² 13.8d² 14g³) 20,000F; neat, attractive filly; sister to 3 winners, including 1m and 1¼m winner Life At Last, and half-sister to 2 winners, including very useful Less Ice (by Scottish Rifle); dam, winner over 1¼m, is sister to Irish 2,000 Guineas third Sovereign Edition; improved in second half of season, winning maiden race at Folkestone, minor event at Hamilton and 19-runner apprentice event at Leicester; ran creditably in handicaps afterwards; stays 1¾m; acts on a firm and a soft surface. *J. Dunlop.* **87**

FIELD GAME 5 ch.g. Northfields–Only A Game (Whistling Wind 123) (1979 7s 8s 7d 8f 1980 12s 10g) robust, attractive gelding; stays 1m; acts well on a sound surface; has twice worn blinkers; has on several occasions unseated his rider and started slowly; one to leave severely alone. *P. K. Mitchell.* **§§**

FIESTA FUN 2 br.f. Welsh Pageant 132–Antigua 100 (Hyperion) (1980 6f 7g 7g² 8fg³) Feb 2; workmanlike filly; sister to a poor filly, and half-sister to several winners including smart 6f and 7f winner Derrylin (by Derring-Do); dam won at 1½m; received weight from first 2 but nonetheless ran very well when staying on strongly to finish 4 lengths third of 7 to Leap Lively in Hoover Fillies Mile at Ascot in September; missed break but recovered to lead on stands side after 3f when length second of 17 to Golden Bowl in maiden event at Salisbury earlier in month; will be suited by 1¼m; sure to win races if not tried too highly. *P. Cole.* **102**

FIGUREHEAD 3 b.f. Seaepic 100–No Saint 118 (Narrator 127) (1979 5d 8g 1980 10s 10g) well-made filly; quite moderate; stays 1¼m; blinkered final start. *R. Hern.* —

FILEY BRIG 3 b.g. Blind Harbour 96–Bonkers 86 (Sallymount 125) (1979 NR 1980 12f 16f 16d) sturdy gelding; half-brother to 2m winner Mulberry Fool (by Shantung) and a winner in Italy; dam won over 2m; little worthwhile form in maiden races; sold 750 gns Ascot July Sales. *J. W. Watts.* —

FINAL CALL 2 gr.f. Town Crier 119–Last Case 109 (Firestreak 125) (1980 5g* 5g² 6g) Apr 15; compact filly; half-sister to 2 winners, including useful 6f to 1¼m winner Court Clown (by Silly Season); dam won 9 times at up to 1m; favourite and fit, ran on to lead inside final furlong when winning 11-runner maiden race at Nottingham in April by 1½ lengths from Katysue, pair clear; 1½ lengths second of 8 to Spanish Hind in minor event at Lingfield in June; not seen out again until September and seemed to have stiffish task when seventh of 8 behind Fair Rosalind in nursery at Salisbury (didn't have a clear run 2f out); should be suited by 6f. *H. Candy.* **79**

FINAL REQUEST 4 br.f. Sharp Edge 123–Bar Gold 80 (Lucky Brief 128) (1979 7v 8s⁴ 8d 9.4s 8h 10fg* 9fg 10s 12fg* 12.2d 1980 12f 10g 12fg² 12g⁴ 12d 12fg³ 12fg⁴ 12g 13.8d) narrow filly; plater; placed in minor event at Pontefract and handicap at Carlisle; stays 1½m; best form on a sound surface. *P. Asquith.* **47**

FINAL STRAW 3 ch.c. Thatch 136–Last Call 74 (Klairon 131) (1979 5g² 5g* 6g³ 7.2fg 6f* 7s* 7fg* 7fg 1980 7f* 8fg 8f³ 8d² 8g² 8d² 8g) **127**

Several of the runners in the Clerical, Medical Greenham Stakes at Newbury in April were to gain distinction before the season was out. The Greenham, which carries Group 3 pattern status, attracted the winners of the previous season's three Group 1 two-year-old races in England open to colts. Monteverdi, winner of the Dewhurst and Ireland's big winter hope for the classics, was sent to Newbury, as were Known Fact, the Middle Park winner, and the William Hill Futurity winner Hello Gorgeous. As a trial for the Two Thousand Guineas the Greenham seemed sure to prove highly informative. But in the event, the race raised as many questions as it answered. The winner Final Straw had been some way below top class as a two-year-old, although he had had an excellent season winning four races including the July Stakes at Newmarket, the Seaton Delaval Stakes at Newcastle and the Laurent Perrier Champagne Stakes at

Doncaster. Final Straw, who had finished last in the Dewhurst on his final appearance at two, looked in need of the race before the Greenham, and his half-length victory over the strongly-ridden Monteverdi seemed to indicate that he had made a good deal of progress over the winter. But more attention was focussed on Monteverdi, whose defeat was the first major shock of the season; and there were also promising performances to talk about by the third and fourth, Posse and Known Fact, who were both putting in good work in the closing stages. The lightly-raced Posse, who was only a neck behind Monteverdi at the line, convinced many observers that he would turn the tables on Final Straw and Monteverdi in the Guineas, while Carson was adamant that Known Fact would beat the lot of them at Newmarket.

Final Straw (ch.c. 1977)	Thatch (b 1970)	Forli (ch 1963)	Aristophanes
			Trevisa
		Thong (b 1964)	Nantallah
			Rough Shod
	Last Call (b 1964)	Klairon (b 1952)	Clarion III
			Kalmia
		Stage Fright (ch 1954)	Big Game
			Bashful

If Final Straw didn't get all the credit at the time that his Greenham win deserved, he certainly provided plenty of evidence later in the season that he was much improved as a three-year-old, a high-class miler in a year in which the leading three-year-old milers trained in England were well up to standard. He was raced in the best company all season and the only occasions on which he failed to finish in the first three in seven starts were in the Two Thousand Guineas, in which he had a rough passage in the second half of the race, and in the Prix du Moulin de Longchamp in September, when he ran as if past his peak. If examples of Final Straw at his best and most typical are required the reader need only refer to the races for the Airlie/Coolmore Irish Two Thousand Guineas in May and the Sussex Stakes in July. Final Straw wasn't quite good enough to win either but he is an admirably tough, game and genuine colt and on each occasion he battled on resolutely; Nikoli and Last Fandango beat him by a short head and half a length at the Curragh, and Posse by a head at Goodwood. Posse beat him easily by a length and a half when the pair met in the St James's Palace Stakes at Royal Ascot but, as at the Curragh and Goodwood, Final Straw did himself proud. At the start of the season, even after his Greenham victory, he was less highly regarded at home than some others in his trainer's string; and one of his stable-companions, Dalsaan, started odds on for the St James's Palace. Final Straw's career is a good example of the fact that home gallops do not always tell the whole truth: as a two-year-old he upset the odds laid on his

Clerical, Medical Greenham Stakes, Newbury—a great finish between Final Straw, Monteverdi and Posse

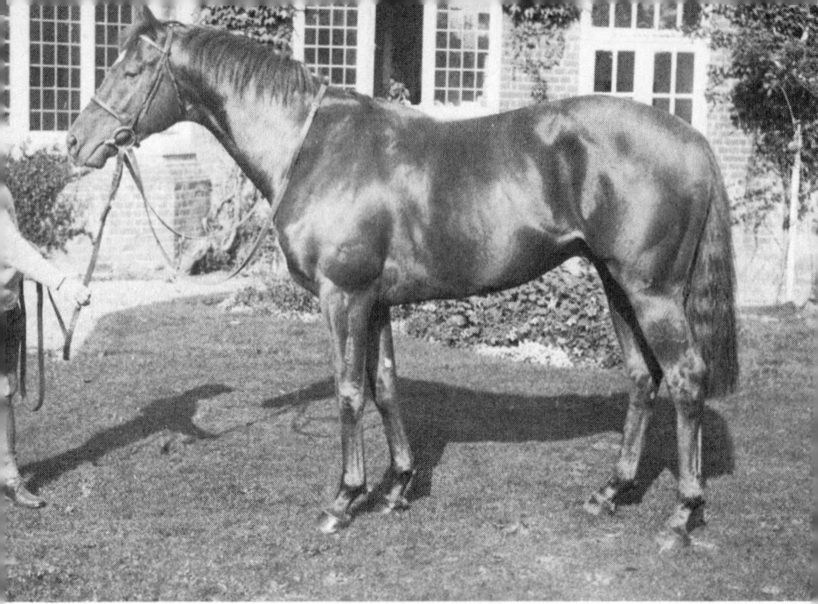

Mr James Wigan's "Final Straw"

stable-mate Lord Seymour in the July Stakes and after a protracted battle with Dalsaan in the Ascot straight it was Dalsaan who cracked and weakened into fourth place, two places behind Final Straw who held off Last Fandango by three quarters of a length. Final Straw's only other race was in the Prix Jacques le Marois at Deauville in August; he failed by a neck to beat Nadjar, the best four-year-old miler in France, with Known Fact, having his first race after an illness, back in fifth place.

Between Royal Ascot and Goodwood the Levy Board invested £375,000 in Final Straw's future as a stallion, purchasing fifteen shares. The other shares on offer were quickly snapped up and those who secured them may well turn out to have made a sound investment. As a stallion Final Straw is a good commercial proposition: in addition to his impressive racing record, he was an early-maturing horse who trained on, a highly desirable combination in a commercial stallion, one which suggests he is certain to sire horses capable of winning as two-year-olds; he is also a good-looking colt and an excellent mover and showed himself to be thoroughly sound; and he has a good pedigree—his sire was an outstanding sprinter-miler and has made a good start at stud, and his dam, a winning half-sister to the Cheshire Oaks winner Hardiesse, has bred four other winners including the smart mile- and mile-and-a-quarter performer Final Chord (by Tudor Melody) and the very useful mile-and-a-half filly Curtains (by Busted). A yearling brother to Final Straw made 162,000 guineas at the Newmarket Houghton Sales. A mile was the limit of Final Straw's stamina and he acted on any going. He has been retired to the Egerton Stud, Newmarket, where he will replace the disappointing Royal Palace who will be standing in the North in 1981. *M. Stoute.*

FIND THE SUN 3 ch.f. Galivanter 131–Sunshine Holyday 96 (Three Wishes 114) (1979 7f 7f 7d* 7d^3 8g 8g^2 1980 10f 10f 13.8fg^2 12d 13.8f 13.8g 10fg 12s^3 12d) leggy filly; placed in handicaps in the North; seventh in valuable selling handicap on final start; stays 1¾m; probably acts on any going. *C. Gray.* **63**

FINE BLUE 7 br.h. French Vine 111–Devon Card (Devon Prince 99) (1979 9s 10.5d 10d* 8fg 9f* 10g 10.5s 10.2f* 10fg^3 9f^4 1980 10fg^3 8g 10.2g* 10fg 10g **96**

John Smith's Magnet Cup, York—Fine Sun beats the hard-ridden Tender Heart. The favourite Masked Marvel (left of winner) is third

10fg^4 9f 10g^3 10d^4 10g) strong horse; returned to form when winning handicap at Doncaster in June, catching Borderline on post; ran creditably on occasions afterwards, notably when about 2 lengths sixth behind Baronet in William Hill Cambridgeshire at Newmarket in October; stayed 1$\frac{1}{4}$m well; acted on any going; game and genuine but needed strong handling; didn't move to post well fourth outing; stud. *P. Makin.*

FINE HOME 4 b.f. Fine Blade 121–Homecomings (Primera 131) (1979 8s 12fg 12f 16f 14f* 16g 13.8d 12f 1980 11f) workmanlike filly; fair plater at her best; ran badly on only outing of 1980; stays 1$\frac{3}{4}$m well; acts on firm going; usually wears blinkers. *J. Fitzgerald.* —

FINE HONEY (USA) 2 b.f. Drone–She's Sofine (Bold Hour) (1980 5d^2 5fg* 6fg^3) Mar 31; $140,000Y; lengthy, attractive filly; first foal; dam, minor stakes winner at up to 1m, is half-sister to Super Asset's dam and to 2 very smart animals; odds on and pick of paddock, quickened smoothly to lead below distance when winning 8-runner maiden race at Goodwood in August by $\frac{3}{4}$ length from Pipperetta; bettered that effort when tried over 6f, finishing 3$\frac{1}{4}$ lengths third of 12 to Steelinctive in nursery at Ascot the following month; will stay 1m. *J. Tree.* 90

FINE MARBLE 2 b.g. Mansingh 120–Upbeat 68 (Hopeful Venture 125) (1980 5fg 5fg 5f) Feb 16; 6,600Y; lengthy gelding; second living foal; dam slow half-sister to smart sprinter Porto Bello; behind in maiden races in April and May. *C. Bewicke.* —

FINE POINT 3 b.c. Sharpen Up 127–Kalyanda 77 (Kalydon 122) (1979 5d 5fg^3 5s 5d* 6d 6g 1980 5d 5v^4 8f* 9f^2 9fg* 8d 8f 8d 10s 8f) neat, strong colt; fair performer at his best; won handicap at Carlisle and slowly-run 3-runner minor race at Hamilton in May; stays 9f; appears to act on any going; ran poorly last 4 starts. *W. H. H. Williams.* 75

FINE SEASON 4 ch.c. Silly Season 127–Floral Palm 69 (Floribunda 136) (1979 5g 6d 5s 5fg 5f^3 8f 6d* 8fg^3 8fg 1980 5fg 5fg) quite a moderate handicapper; stays 1m; appears to act on any going; sometimes wears blinkers (did so last 3 starts in 1979). *Hbt Jones.* —

FINE SPUN 2 b.f. Mummy's Pet 125–Regal Silk (Henry the Seventh 125) (1980 5f 6g 5f 5fg 5d^3 5s) Apr 19; 3,000Y; smallish, lengthy filly; third foal; dam poor hurdler; 1$\frac{1}{2}$ lengths third of 20 to Sedona in seller at Catterick in October, easily best effort; blinkered last 3 starts; sold 440 gns Doncaster November Sales. *J. Etherington.* 66

FINE SUN 3 ch.g. Fine Blade 121–All Sunshine (Miralgo 130) (1979 6fg^2 7g^3 7fg 8d* 10.6d^2 1980 12f^3 10f* 10.6fg 10g^2 10g^3 10.5g* 14g 11s^3 12fg* 10g^2 **110**

Mr Bill Hobson's "Fine Sun"

12v) fair sort; very useful handicapper; successful in 2 valuable races, XYZ Handicap at Newcastle in April (beat Kahaila in good style by 7 lengths) and John Smith's Magnet Cup at York in July; ridden by 5-lb claimer when holding off Tender Heart by ½ length in latter; had little to beat for his third victory, in small race at Beverley in September; ran well most other outings, notably when second to Mirror Boy in Andy Capp Handicap at Redcar and to Spanish Dancer in Irish Sweeps Autumn Handicap at Newmarket; stays 1½m; probably acts on any going; often sweats up; thoroughly genuine and consistent and a credit to his trainer. *Miss S. Hall.*

FINE TALE 4 br.g. Fine Blade 121–Nortia 123 (Narrator 127) (1979 12s 10.6g² 12f* 12f⁴(dis) 13d 12f* 12fg* 12.5g* 12s 1980 12fg² 14g 14g 16.1g 12f³ 12fg 12f³) neat gelding; placed at Folkestone in August, Lingfield in September and Newmarket in October; ran moderately on his other starts; suited by 1½m; seems to need a sound surface; usually blinkered in 1978 and wore them again fourth to sixth starts; sold to M. Blackshaw 6,000 gns Newmarket Autumn Sales. *F. Durr.* **87**

FINGAL'S CAVE 3 b.c. Ragstone 128–Blue Echoes 105 (Mountain Call 125) (1979 7.6f⁴ 1980 9f² 12fg* 12s 12fg² 10.5g² 10d³ 12fg* 10d) **121**

When everything is right for Fingal's Cave he looks a very good horse indeed. He impressed enormously when beating small fields in two races run over a mile and a half on firmish ground at Ascot during the season, the Churchill Stakes in June and the Cumberland Lodge Stakes in September. On both occasions he was held up with considerable confidence, he had pace to spare to avoid trouble as he made his run in the straight, then quickened clear in great style in the last furlong; he was particularly impressive the second time, meeting better opposition. He won the Churchill Stakes by three lengths from Prince Roland and the Cumberland Lodge by two from Dukedom.

These are the only races Fingal's Cave has won. He never looked so good in defeat as a three-year-old though he put up smart performances at Goodwood in the Gordon Stakes and the Valdoe Stakes, the better one, significantly, in dividing Prince Bee and Light Cavalry in the Gordon Stakes the time conditions most closely resembled those at Ascot. He ran a poor race on soft going in the Irish Sweeps Derby (last but one), and another on dead over the daunting straight ten furlongs of the Champion Stakes (last of all) on his final outing. From what's been seen of him so far Fingal's Cave has more need for things to go right for him than many horses and needs more things right, too. He may not be easy to place as a four-year-old but a dry summer would help considerably.

Fingal's Cave (b.c. 1977)	Ragstone (b 1970)	Ragusa (b 1960)	Ribot
			Fantan II
		Fotheringay (b 1964)	Right Royal V
			La Fresnes
	Blue Echoes (b 1972)	Mountain Call (ch 1965)	Whistler
			Cloudy Walk
		Red Favourite (b 1964)	Floribunda
			Maiden Speech

Fingal's Cave, a neat colt and a good walker and mover, is the first foal of the speedy but lightly-raced Blue Echoes who was placed in the Windsor Castle Stakes in 1974. His grandam, a sprinter, a useful one at two years, was a half-sister to the middle-distance horses New Member (by Alcide) and Dubrava (by Ragusa) both of whom finished a respectable sixth in the Irish Sweeps Derby in their time. *J. Dunlop.*

FINGERLING (FR) 3 b.c. Yours 125–Lady Cowley (Alizier 131) (1979 6d 6f 8d 1980 10.1fg 11f 8d) strong colt; seems only plating class; sold 3,200 gns Ascot July Sales. *C. Bewicke.* —

Cumberland Lodge Stakes, Ascot—Fingal's Cave quickens in great style to beat Dukedom (noseband) and Sea Pigeon

FINLANDIA (FR) 3 b.f. Faraway Son 130–Musical (Prince Chevalier) (1979 6f 7.2g 1980 8.5g 11.7f 11fg 10.1fg 8g) quite well-made filly; poor walker; well bred but has shown little sign of ability; should stay at least 1¼m; blinkered last 2 starts; sometimes sweats up; sold 15,000 gns Newmarket December Sales. *D. Sasse.* —

FIONA (HOL) 2 gr.f. Vesins–Lovely (Royal Unity 106) (1980 6s 6.5g^{4} 9g) Apr 5; sister to Zilverster, a winner in Holland including once over 1¾m; dam Dutch; well behind in maiden race at Nottingham in August; beaten in races won by Marmorera at Duindigt, Holland, subsequently. *A. Hide.* —

FIRBECK 4 ch.f. Veiled Wonder–Highview Jill 73 (Proud Chieftain 122) (1979 5g 5s 5d 5fg^{3} 5g^{3}(dis) 5fg 5fg* 5g^{3} 6fg 5.6fg* 5g^{4} 5s 5.6fg 5f^{2} 1980 5s 6f 5f^{4} 5fg 5d* 5g^{2} 5fg 5fg^{3} 5d^{2} 5s 5g 5s) big, strong filly; sprint handicapper; successful at Wolverhampton in June; good second to Cree Song at Ayr and to Sandra's Secret in Harewood Handicap at York afterwards; acts on any going except perhaps very soft; usually wears blinkers; ran poorly tenth start. *A. Balding.* **73**

FIRE CHIEFTAIN 2 b.c. Owen Anthony 102–Fire Hawk 70 (Firestreak 125) (1980 6g) Apr 24; compact colt; third foal; dam, placed over 6f at 2 yrs, is daughter of smart 1959 2-y-o Laminate; unquoted when behind in 19-runner newcomers event won by Dancing Sally at Goodwood in September. *P. Feilden.* —

FIRE DRILL 5 ch.g. Firestreak 125–Free and Easy (Fr) 81 (Net 116) (1979 11.7g 12g* 10f 1980 10.2d) winning hurdler; lightly raced on flat; stays 1½m. *P. Cundell.* —

FIRE MOUNTAIN 2 gr.f. Dragonara Palace 115–Rosalina 71 (Porto Bello 118) (1980 5fg 5fg^{4} 5fg^{4} 6g^{4} 5g* 5d^{3} 5d^{3} 5d 5g*) Mar 25; 2,900F; light-framed filly; first produce; dam won over 7f and 1m; won modest 5-runner maiden race at Chester in August; subsequently ran well in nurseries and beat Red Gold ½ length in well-contested event at Newmarket in October; stays 6f; best form on an easy surface; good mount for an apprentice; trained first outing by P. Calver. *R. Hannon.* **87**

FIREPLACE 2 b.f. Thatch 136–Gaia 116 (Charlottesville 135) (1980 7d^{3} 7d^{2} 6v*) Apr 9; sister to a modest animal and half-sister to useful stayer Sir Daniel (by Sir Ivor) and very useful 1m and 1½m filly Galletto (by Nijinsky); dam won 1969 Irish Guinness Oaks; odds on and blinkered when winning small race at Fairyhouse in October by 5 lengths from Tea and Roses; had also started favourite when placed previously in maiden races at the Curragh (2¾ lengths third of 20 to Condessa) and Phoenix Park (went down by 2 lengths to Van Lingen); should stay 1¼m; yet to race on a sound surface. *V. O'Brien, Ireland.* **90**

FIRM CONVICTION 3 gr.f. Scottish Rifle 127–Kinharvie 63 (Abernant 142) (1979 NR 1980 10.1d 10.1g) 800Y, resold 1,000Y, 680 3-y-o; unfurnished filly; second living foal; half-sister to useful 1¼m winner Lanarkland (by Ragstone); dam placed twice over 1m; tailed off in 2 minor events at Windsor in July *T. Hallett.* —

FIRM FOUNDATIONS 3 br.g. Pieces of Eight 128–Streetcar 87 (Crocket 130) (1979 7f 8d 1980 8fg 11fg 8d^{3} 10g 13.8f^{4} 12g* 12fg* 12g^{4}) leggy gelding; plater; successful twice at Newmarket in August, attracting no bid on first occasion and being bought in 1,600 gns on second; best form at 1½m; acts on a firm and a soft surface. *Sir Mark Prescott.* **59**

FIRST ANNIVERSARY 5 gr.g. Grisaille 115–Westmoor 71 (Good Light 92) (1979 NR 1980 8.3f) bad plater. *H. O'Neill.* —

FIRST AWARD 2 ch.f. New Member 119–Cash Award (Cash and Courage 116) (1980 5f 5h 8fg 7d 10s) May 24; 300Y; compact filly; ninth foal; dam never ran; in rear in minor and maiden events. *H. Fleming.* —

FIRST CHILD 2 br.f. Keren 100–Only Child 68 (Foggy Bell 108) (1980 5fg 6s 5f 5f 6f^{4} 6d^{2} 6s) Apr 25; neat filly; first foal; dam 6f winner; plater; improved over 6f and went down by only ½ length to Consent at Ayr in August; had stiffer task next time out; will stay 1m; probably acts on any going; has run well for an apprentice. *Denys Smith.* **59**

FIRST CONTACT 2 ch.f. Simbir 130–Willow Bird 74 (Weepers Boy 124) (1980 6d^{4}) Apr 18; 3,000Y; leggy filly; fourth foal; half-sister to 2 winners including Willow Red (by Red Alert), successful at up to 1m; dam stayed 1m; unquoted, showed up well when 3 lengths fourth of 25 to Little Wolf in maiden race at Newbury in October; will stay 1¼m; should improve. *M. Smyly.* **77 p**

FIRST LIFT 5 ch.g. Pieces of Eight 128–Billingsgate 82 (High Perch 126) (1979 NR 1980 12d 11fg 10h 13fg* 12f³ 12.3g² 12fg² 12g² 11fg) middle-distance handicapper; winner at Hamilton in May; acts well on a firm surface; has twice worn blinkers. *T. Fairhurst.* **59**

FIRST MOVEMENT 2 b.c. Music Boy 124–Lunar Princess 109 (King's Bench 132) (1980 6g 6fg* 5g² 6s⁴) Apr 1; neat, fair sort; half-brother to several winners, including fairly useful miler Lunariver (by Forlorn River); dam best at up to 7f; came through strongly to lead 1f out in 15-runner maiden race at Newmarket in August but then wandered badly and held on by only a neck from newcomer Gielgud, the pair clear; bettered that effort when going down by a head to Princess Gayle in £4,000 event at Thirsk the following month (would have won had his apprentice rider been able to claim his 5-lb allowance); possibly better suited by 5f than 6f; possibly not at his best on soft going; again wandered under pressure fourth outing (bandaged near-hind). *G. Huffer.* **101**

FIRST NIGHT FLIGHT 2 b.c. Tumble Wind–Aracara (Prince Tenderfoot 126) (1980 5g⁴ 5fg 5s 6fg 6d 7g) Feb 17; 4,000Y; compact colt; first foal; dam placed at up to 1½m in Ireland; soundly beaten in maiden races and nurseries. *D. Whelan.* **–**

FIRYAL 3 ch.f. Nonoalco 131–Neriad (Princequillo) (1979 6d* 6fg³ 7g 8d⁴ 1980 7d* 8fg 10fg 8s 8d) 1,500,000 francs Y (approx £178,000); attractive filly; sister to useful Irish 1m winner Delaneige, and half-sister to several winners, notably top-class 1½m filly Comtesse de Loir (by Val de Loir) and smart middle-distance performer Zein (by Zeddaan); dam never ran: outclassed 7 opponents in Prix Imprudence at Maisons-Laffitte in April, beating Licara 3 lengths; ran best other race when creditable 3 lengths fifth to Paranete in Prix Saint-Alary at Longchamp on third start; never promised to take hand when tenth of 23 behind Quick As Lightning in 1,000 Guineas at Newmarket on second outing; stays 1¼m; acts on a firm and a soft surface; blinkered final appearance. *F. Boutin, France.* **111**

FISH EAGLE 2 b.c. Wollow 132–Lovely Lark (Larkspur 128) (1980 7f 6g 8.2s³ 7v) May 16; big colt; half-brother to 3 winners, including fairly useful 7f handicapper Tudor Rhapsody (by Tudor Melody) and Matsufuji Ehsu (by So Blessed), the top-rated 2-y-o in Japan in 1974; dam Irish 7f winner; ran well last 2 starts, finishing length third of 20 to Irish Heart in maiden race at Haydock in October and fifth of 20 to Supreme Fjord in nursery at Doncaster in November; suited by 1m and will probably stay further. *W. Hastings-Bass.* **85**

FITZ ITCHING 2 b.g. Tickled Pink 114–King's Wench 61 (Kibenka 119) (1980 6fg 5g 6g 8g) Feb 14; neat gelding; fourth foal; dam won 1¼m seller; plater; poor form in maiden races and sellers; blinkered fourth outing. *D. Elsworth.* **–**

FIVE ACES 3 ch.g. Some Hand 119–Doubtful Request (Cheveley Lad 105) (1979 5v* 5s⁴ 5s³ 5s⁴ 5g⁴ 6g⁴ 6s 6g 1980 5s³ 5v* 5fg² 5g⁴ 5f) workmanlike gelding; sprint handicapper; successful at Ayr in March; form only at 5f; seemed to act on any going; dead. *J. Berry.* **54**

FIVE SPARKS 2 b.g. Hot Spark 126–Sylvan Path 69 (Sovereign Path 125) (1980 5d) Jan 30; 5,000F, 4,000Y; big, strong gelding; half-brother to 2 winning platers; dam stayer; 33/1, totally outpaced when last of 13 in maiden race won by Supper's Ready at Windsor in July; sold 575 gns Ascot October Sales. *G. Lewis.* **–**

FIZZIE LIZZIE 2 br.f. Persian Breeze 121–Counteswells (Behistoun 131) (1980 6d 5g³ 7f⁴ 7fg 6g 7g 7f 10d) Mar 5; leggy filly; first foal; dam never ran; in frame in sellers at Hamilton and Beverley in the summer; stays 7f; sold out of W. H. H. Williams' stable 610 gns Doncaster Sales after second start. *S. Nesbitt.* **46**

FLAMEGUARD 2 ch.f. Hot Spark 126–Street Vendor 60 (High Perch 126) (1980 5fg 5fg 5s 6g 6f 7g) Mar 23; 4,000Y; small filly; half-sister to 6f winner Star Venture (by Swing Easy) and 2 winners abroad; dam won 5f seller at 2 yrs and also won over hurdles; showed ability in maiden and minor races in second half of season; stays 7f. *R. Armstrong.* **68**

FLAMING EAGLE 6 ch.g. Green God 128–Double Eagle 71 (Goldhill 125) (1979 5v 6v⁴ 9d 6s 6g⁴ 6s 7g* 1980 12d 8f 7fg 8f⁴ 10.6fg⁴ 11d 8.2d 8.2d 8fg 8.2s) strong ex-Irish gelding; plater nowadays; best form at up to 7f; acts on any going; blinkered seventh to ninth starts (gave mulish display on way to post on last occasion); sold 560 gns Doncaster October Sales and resold 480 gns Doncaster November Sales. *M. Naughton.* **48**

FLAMTEX LAD 3 ch.c. Ribero 126–Island Lore 100 (Court Martial) (1979 6d 8h 1980 10s 12s 12d 10g) short-coupled colt; no signs of ability in maiden and minor events; has been tried in blinkers. *H. T. Jones.* —

FLANDERS FLAME 3 b.f. Busted 134–Francoise 109 (French Beige 127) (1979 7f 1980 11fg³) unfurnished filly; favourite, ran very freely in early stages when third in 7-runner maiden race at Wolverhampton in April; not seen out again; will stay 1½m if she learns to settle. *B. Hobbs.* —

FLASH CONNECTION 3 b.c. Hot Spark 126–Carcosa 103 (Sovereign Lord 120) (1979 6g 5.1g² 5f² 1980 5g* 5g* 6s 6fg) strong, useful sort; decisive winner of 2 races at Cagnes-sur-Mer early in year; respectable fifth of 19 in handicap at Windsor on final start in May; stays 6f; acts on firm going; sweated up final start at 2 yrs. *W. Hastings-Bass.* —

FLASH GORDON 2 ch.c. Streak 119–Pibroch III (Specific 103) (1980 5fg* 5fg⁴ 6g 6s⁴ 5s⁴ 5f⁴ 5fg⁴ 5g 6fg 8s) Apr 6; compact non-thoroughbred colt; dam never ran; won 19-runner maiden event at Salisbury in May by 1½ lengths from Ringal; in frame several times, on sixth and seventh starts finishing creditable fourth in nurseries at Beverley and Goodwood; best form at 5f and is unlikely to stay 1m (always behind in valuable seller when tried at trip); seems to act on any going; trained first 3 outings by C. Nelson. *T. Marshall.* **81**

FLASH 'N' FIRE (USA) 2 ch.f. Charles Elliott–Thundering Streak (Craigwood) (1980 6f* 6fg² 7.3d⁴) workmanlike filly; sister to Quicker than Lite, a stakes-placed winner over sprint distances, and half-sister to very useful 3-y-o sprinter Flash N Thunder (by Key To The Kingdom); dam won over 4f at 2 yrs; put up a fair first effort when winning 17-runner minor event at Redcar in September by 1½ lengths from Courreges; in frame in minor event at Lingfield (beaten 1½ lengths by Sea Aura, giving weight all round) and £5,000 race at Newbury (ran on to finish 2½ lengths fourth of 11 to Boathouse) afterwards; will stay 1m; appears to act on any going. *R. Sheather.* **87**

FLASH N THUNDER (USA) 3 b. or br.c. Key To The Kingdom–Thundering Streak (Craigwood) (1979 5f* 6.5d² 1980 8f 6f* 6fg 6g⁴ 5fg² 5g) strong, compact colt; beat Gypsy Dancer 1½ lengths in Duke of York Stakes in May; subsequently finished creditable fourth to Kearney in Cork and Orrery Stakes at Royal Ascot and 2½ lengths second to Valeriga in King George Stakes at Goodwood in July; ran moderately at Haydock third start (didn't take sharp bend at all well) and in William Hill Sprint Championship at York in August on **115**

Duke of York Stakes, York—Flash N Thunder wins from Gypsy Dancer and African Song

final appearance; bred to stay 1m but pulled hard and was best at sprint distances; probably acted on any going; used to get very stirred up in preliminaries; stud in Greece. *B. Hills.*

FLASHRAY 2 ch.c. Flashback 102–Dumette 89 (Dumbarnie 125) (1980 5d 7d) Apr 30; first foal; dam won over 7f and also won over hurdles; tailed off in maiden race at Windsor in July and in minor event at Leicester in November. *A. Davison.* —

FLASHY GAYLE 4 ch.c. Lord Gayle 124–Fun of the Fair (Skymaster 126) (1979 8.5g 9f 12f 1980 12f) small ex-Irish colt; poor maiden; has been tried in blinkers; cost 700 gns at Ascot May Sales and ran only once on flat before being sold 350 gns at same venue in November. *F. Yardley.* —

FLECHA 5 ch.g. Duke of Ragusa 120–Zabbotina (Welsh Abbot 131) (1979 NR 1980 14g) poor maiden; has worn blinkers; bandaged in front on only outing of 1980. *M. Haynes.* —

FLEDGE 3 ch.c. Sharp Edge 123–Flotsam 67 (Rustam 127) (1979 5g 1980 12g^4 12d* 13g^2(dis) 12d) big, strong colt; stayed on resolutely to win 14-runner maiden race at Goodwood in September; ran creditably next time; promises to stay further than 13f; yet to race on a firm surface. *G. Harwood.* **81**

FLEMISH GIANT 4 ch.g. Salvo 129–Star Royal (Royal Tara 123) (1979 10s 14.6fg 15.8fg 15g^2 1980 12.5v 12fg) staying maiden; saddle slipped on second outing; dead. *G. Richards.* —

FLEUR DE GALLES 2 br.f. Prince de Galles 125–Reine d'Etat 53 (High Hat 131) (1980 5g^4 5f* 5fg 5d) Feb 27; 3,000Y; lightly-made filly; sister to 1¼m winner Le Pretendant and to a winner in Norway; dam placed over 1½m; favourite, finished strongly to win 10-runner maiden auction event at Epsom in April by 2 lengths from Dizzy Heights; always struggling on subsequent outings, in May and October; bred to stay at least 1¼m; trained by P. Feilden first 3 outings. *C. Nelson.* **66**

FLEURS (NZ) 3 gr.f. Namnan 102–Kiraye 76 (Crozier 117) (1979 5.8g 6fg 6g 1980 5fg 6fg^4 6fg 6g* 5g^3 6d 6g) small filly; plater; bought in 920 gns after winning at Windsor in September; will stay beyond 6f; has sometimes given impression she has her own ideas about the game; sold 520 gns Newmarket Autumn Sales. *D. Kent.* **58**

FLICKERING 3 b.f. Sparkler 130–Wold Lass 77 (Vilmorin) (1979 5d 5s 7g^3 1980 8.2s 8f 10.8s 10.1fg 10fg 9s^2 10g 12s) well-made filly; good walker; quite a moderate maiden at her best; stays 9f; acts on soft going. *I. Balding.* **66**

FLIGHT CONTROL 3 ch.f. Roan Rocket 128–Header 78 (High Hat 131) (1979 7g 1980 8f 10f^3 12d^4 10g 10fg^3 9s 10s^2) lengthy filly; quite a modest maiden; stays 1¼m; acts on any going; often blinkered; ran moderately fourth start; sold 5,200 gns Newmarket December Sales. *I. Balding.* **72**

FLIGHTING 2 b.f. Pitcairn 126–Ruddy Duck 84 (Dicta Drake 126) (1980 6f^4 7fg* 8g^2) May 20; well-made filly; good mover; sister to Oaks runner-up Bonnie Isle, and half-sister to several winners, including useful middle-distance filly Falls of Lora (by Scottish Rifle); dam, sister to very useful stayer Chinatown, needed at least 1½m; driven out to beat Murmansk (USA) 1½ lengths when 7/4 on for 9-runner maiden race at Brighton in August; in frame at Ascot and Goodwood on other outings; easily outpaced when 3 lengths second of 7 to Leap Lively in minor event on latter course in September; will be suited by middle distances. *J. Dunlop.* **105**

FLIGHT SHEET (USA) 4 b.g. Pago Pago–Jet To Market (Farm To Market) (1979 12d 10g 12f^3 12g 14g 14s 1980 12.5v 12fg 12f^2 12.5h 15f^3 15.8fg 16fg^4 16d) strong ex-Irish gelding; plating-class maiden; stays well; acts on firm going; one paced. *K. Stone.* **47**

FLING 2 ch.f. Red Alert 127–Beauty Time (Arctic Time 127) (1980 5g 6g 7fg^4 6d^3 7g 7fg 7g 6f 6d 5d) May 17; 4,200Y; strong, lengthy filly; half-sister to several winners, including Digitalis (by Divine Gift), a useful performer from 5f to 1¼m; dam never ran; ran best race when 2 lengths third of 11 to Paradise Bird in maiden race at Redcar in August; probably stays 7f; sold to BBA 1,800 gns Newmarket Autumn Sales. *D. Thom.* **74**

FLINT 4 ro.c. Sharp Edge 123–Yorkshire Gal 85 (Whistler 129) (1979 6v 6g 7d 6fg^2 6d 6g 7.6f* 7f 6g 1980 6s 6g^2 7g^2 7.6g 7g 7fg 7.3fg 6s) robust colt; runner-up in handicaps at Salisbury and Lingfield in June; stays 7.6f; best form **51**

on firm going but wasn't disgraced on soft on final outing; had stiffish task when well beaten in blinkers on seventh start; sold 3,200 gns Newmarket Autumn Sales; exported. *M. Smyly.*

FLIPPER 11 b.g. Little Buskins 119–Sea Sonnet (Ossian II) (1979 12h³ 1980 12fg) quite a moderate staying hurdler; does little racing on flat; sold 700 gns Doncaster October Sales. *J. Bingham.* —

FLOATING CHARGE 2 ch.c. Hotfoot 126–Loweswater 74 (Saint Crespin III 132) (1980 7g³ 7g) Jan 23; 5,000Y; tall colt; half-brother to winning stayer Village Swan (by My Swanee); dam won over 1½m; took some time to get the hang of things but ran on to finish 4 lengths third of 11 to Sheer Grit in maiden race at Kempton in July; never got into race when 20/1 for £3,900 maiden event at Goodwood later in month, finishing twelfth of 16 to To-Agori-Mou; will be suited by middle distances. *N. Vigors.* **75**

FLORAL DANCE 2 br.f. Record Token 128–Floral 82 (Floribunda 136) (1980 6d) May 6; 4,800Y; lengthy filly; good walker; half-sister to Sheer Elegance (by Runnymede), winner of 5f seller at 2 yrs and subsequently successful in Trinidad; dam 2-y-o 7f winner; 20/1, prominent long way and wasn't knocked about unnecessarily when out of first 9 of 25 behind Little Wolf in maiden race at Newbury in October; should stay 7f; will do better at 3 yrs. *H. Candy.* —

FLORAL HILL 2 b.f. Floriana 106–Mezel Hill (Tarqogan 125) (1980 6g 6g⁴ 7f) Apr 25; small, light-framed filly; first foal; dam last on only outing; poor plater. *R. Akehurst.* —

FLORENCE 4 b.f. Farm Walk 111–Wandering On (Klairon 131) (1979 8g⁴ 10h 10fg 13.8s² 10g² 8s² 1980 10f) plater; stays 1¾m; acts on soft going; sometimes wears blinkers; bandaged on only outing of 1980; doesn't always go through with her effort. *D. Garraton.* —

FLORIDIAN DAWN 2 br.f. Forlorn River 124–Donnabimba 83 (Don II 123) (1980 5d 5fg 5fg⁴ 5f* 5g³ 6g⁴ 6fg 5g³ 5fg 6fg 6g* 8g 6s 6s) Apr 1; small filly; second foal; dam placed at up to 1m; successful in sellers at Thirsk in May and Yarmouth in September; bought in 1,000 gns after coming through to win by 2 lengths from Apollo Creed on latter; suited by 6f but probably doesn't stay 1m; yet to race on really soft going but acts on any other; blinkered fourth to ninth outings; sold 2,200 gns Newmarket Autumn Sales. *K. Ivory.* **69**

FLOTTY 3 b.f. Tyrant–Flotilla 64 (Alcide 136) (1979 5fg 5g 1980 7f⁴ 9.4d 9.4fg 10s 11s² 10s 10d) plater; stays 11f; acts on soft going; often blinkered. *W. Elsey.* **47**

FLOWALONG 3 b.f. Beatic–Elsie Tanner (Buckhound 117) (1979 NR 1980 8f 8.2f 12d) unfurnished filly; ninth reported living foal; dam ran only once; behind in maiden races. *G. Richards.* —

FLOWER 3 br.f. So Blessed 130–Sunflower 96 (Paveh 126) (1979 5fg³ 5s* 5d* 1980 6fg 5g 6s* 5f 6s 7s 6d³ 6d³ 6d) quite a useful-looking filly; fairly useful handicapper; returned to form when beating Westacombe ½ length (pair clear) in Northumberland Sprint Trophy at Newcastle in August; good third at Newmarket (behind Enchantment) and Doncaster (to Nocturnal Boy) in October; suited by 6f and should stay further (didn't have too clear a run when tried at 7f); acts well on soft going. *C. Thornton.* **93**

FLOWER MEADOW 3 b.f. Runnymede 123–Flora Leigh 94 (Floribunda 136) (1979 6f 6fg³ 5.1g³ 1980 6d⁴ 7fg 6s) lengthy, attractive filly; good walker; quite moderate; stays 6f (well beaten over further); acts on a firm and a soft surface; blinkered final outing at 2 yrs (looked none too keen) and in 1980 (hung right); has run respectably for a boy. *J. Hindley.* **73**

FLUELLEN 7 b.g. Welsh Pageant 132–Ya Ya 84 (Primera 131) (1979 10d 10s 10.2d* 10d 10g 10g 1980 10fg 10d 11.1fg 12fg 12d 10g) tall, useful-looking gelding; very useful on his day but is completely unreliable and none too generous in a finish; often had stiff tasks in 1980 and wasn't placed; stays 1½m; acts on any going; often wears blinkers. *H. Wragg.* **105 §**

FLURRY KNOX 5 b.g. Irish Ball 127–Pardina 98 (Pardao 120) (1979 14f 1980 12g³) lightly-raced gelding; creditable third to Ambler in amateur riders race at Brighton in October; best form at up to 1½m; seems to act on any going except perhaps firm; usually wears blinkers but didn't at Brighton; winning hurdler/chaser. *J. Old.* **59**

FLY BIRD FLY 3 ch.f. My Swallow 134–Sardara 106 (Alcide 136) (1979 7s 8d 1980 9g⁴ 10f 12fg) lengthy, unfurnished filly; little worthwhile form in maiden —

races; not certain to stay 1½m; not raced after May; sold 460 gns Doncaster October Sales. *W. H. H. Williams.*

FLYING BID 3 b.f. Auction Ring 123–Skyway 76 (Skymaster 126) (1979 5g³ 5g 5d 5fg 5f² 5f⁴ 5.8h 6f 5fg 8.2s⁴ 1980 8s 10h² 10f 14g³ 11fg² 14fg) well-made filly; good mover; placed in maiden races but seems only plating class; stays 1¾m; acts on any going; got very upset in stalls and ran badly third outing. *S. Woodman.* **65**

FLYING COLOURS 7 b.m. King's Company 124–Dior 80 (Dionisio 126) (1979 NR 1980 10.2d) won over 7f at 2 yrs but has been lightly raced and shown little form since; seems to act on any going. *G. Cottrell.* **–**

FLYING DOLPHIN 3 ch.c. Deep Diver 134–Willow Bird 74 (Weepers Boy 124) (1979 5fg⁴ 5g* 1980 6s 7f 7f 7g⁴ 6g) strong colt; good mover; fair handicapper; stays 7f; blinkered final start. *J. Hudson.* **84**

FLYING DREAMER 2 b.c. My Swallow 134–Forgotten Dreams 82 (Shoemaker 121) (1980 5fg⁴ 5.8fg⁴ 7s 8.2g 8d*) Apr 17; leggy colt; first foal; dam won 3 times over 2m; ran best race for some time when winning 15-runner maiden race at Bath in October by ½ length from Whistling Tower; will stay 1½m; acts on a firm and a soft surface; sweated up fourth outing; sold 6,400 gns Newmarket Autumn Sales. *H. Candy.* **81**

FLYING GEORDIE 3 br.g. Scottish Rifle 127–Ninesprings (Chamier 128) (1979 NR 1980 10.2d 12s) sixth living foal; half-brother to quite moderate NH stayer Sea Drake (by Dicta Drake); dam never ran; beaten a long way in apprentice races at Bath and Chepstow in October. *M. Pipe.* **–**

FLYING GOLD 4 ch.c. Shiny Tenth 120–Quick Aim (Pardal 130) (1979 8fg³ 10f³ 10f 10s 1980 10.2g 10fg² 10fg³) big, strong colt; very good mover; placed behind easy winners Sashka and Miss Neustrie in maiden races at Yarmouth in August; stays 1¼m; possibly not at his best on soft ground. *G. Huffer.* **69**

Mr Guy Reed's "Flower"

FLYING LYNDSAY 4 b.f. Majority Blue 126–Kitty Wake (Milesian 125) (1979 8f 8f^{4} 8fg 8fg^{4} 1980 12fg 10h) poor plater; blinkered final start. *J. Jenkins.* –

FLYING MILLY 3 ch.f. Mill Reef 141–Shoshoni 72 (Ballymoss 136) (1979 6fg 1980 10f^{3} 12.2fg 13d^{3} 15fg 12f) lightly-made filly; good mover; little worthwhile form in varied company; should be suited by $1\frac{1}{2}$m+; ran badly final start. *C. Thornton.* –

FLYING OCTOPUS 3 b.c. Welsh Saint 126–Gang Plank 84 (Tower Walk 130) (1979 7fg 5fg 5.3fg 5f 1980 6f 5f 6fg 5fg 8.5f 7s 6fg 7g) small, close-coupled colt; poor plater; not sure to stay 1m; sold 775 gns Ascot September Sales. *A. Breasley.* –

FLYING OFFICER 3 b.g. Warpath 113–Rosie Wings 102 (Telegram II 120) (1979 NR 1980 10.2g 12fg 12f 15.8fg* 14.7f* 16g* 14.7d* 16s) neat, rather lightly-made gelding; good walker; brother to winning stayer Wild Rosie and half-brother to several winners, notably Derby third Mount Athos (by Sunny Way) and smart sprinter John Splendid (by Sing Sing); dam a stayer; showed improved form once given a test of stamina in the autumn, winning maiden race at Catterick, handicaps at Redcar and Newcastle and a 4-runner minor event at Redcar again; stays well; probably unsuited by very soft going. *C. Thornton.* 86

FLYING OPTICIAN 5 ch.h. Divine Gift 127–Game Coach (Big Game) (1979 8d 7d 7g^{3} 8d^{3} 7fg^{3} 7fg^{4} 8h^{4} 8g 7fg 8fg^{2} 8fg 1980 10.2g 12d 8.2s 7d) quite a moderate handicapper; well beaten in 1980 (not seen out until September); stays 1m; best form on a sound surface; ran respectably when blinkered once. *M. Bradley.* –

FLYING PHOENIX 3 b. or br.f. John Splendid 116–Jendean 68 (Florescence 120) (1979 6s 5fg 1980 6d 6fg^{3} 6s) leggy, lightly-made filly; poor maiden; pulled up 1f out in seller on final outing; dead. *W. H. H. Williams.* –

FLYING PIZZA AGAIN 2 gr.c. Lord Nelson 107–Nanalla 58 (Le Dieu d'Or 119) (1980 5s 5fg 5fg^{4} 6fg) bad plater; finished lame fourth outing. *S. Nesbitt.* –

FLYING PORTION 4 ch.f. Major Portion 129–Flying Escape 74 (Hook Money 124) (1979 6d 6g 7d 6g^{2} 5.3fg 6f 6fg 1980 6fg 6g 6d) lengthy, useful-looking filly; behind in 1980; best form at 6f (well beaten in seller when tried over further in 1979); often blinkered at 3 yrs. *J. Benstead.* –

FLYING RAGS 4 b.f. Ragstone 128–Sybilla (Relic) (1979 7.6d 7f 1980 8.3f 10fg 9.6f 6g 8.3s 8.3f 8d) poor plater. *H. O'Neill.* –

FLYING SAPPORO 4 gr.f. Mummy's Pet 125–Pall Nan 86 (Pall Mall 132) (1979 6g 6g 5g 1980 5g 5fg 5f 8d) lengthy, lightly-made filly; sprint maiden; acts on firm going; has been tried in blinkers. *Mrs R. Lomax.* –

FLYING SISTER 2 b.f. St Paddy 133–Quick Aim (Pardal 130) (1980 7s) Mar 19; tall, lightly-made filly; seventh foal; dam poor daughter of Oaks winner Steady Aim; unquoted when behind in 18-runner minor event won by Warily at Sandown in October. *C. Read.* –

FLYING SWALLOW 6 b.g. My Swallow 134–Senna (Sica Boy 132) (1979 NR 1980 12d 13s) poor maiden; best run at $1\frac{1}{4}$m on heavy ground (in 1977). *K. Bridgwater.* –

FOCHINE (FR) 3 b. or br.f. Derring-Do 131–Homeville (Blue Prince 123) (1979 6s 6f 1980 7f 10g 10s 7.6d) robust, good sort; poor maiden *C. Brittain.* –

FOG 2 b.f. English Prince 129–Heat Haze 102 (Nimbus 130) (1980 8s*) Apr 17; half-sister to several winners, including useful stayer Miss Dawn (by Chanteur II); dam useful winner at 2 yrs; easy in market, looked out of race after a slow start in maiden race at Leopardstown in October but made steady headway to lead well inside final furlong and won by $1\frac{1}{2}$ lengths from Loren's Pet; will stay $1\frac{1}{2}$m; a useful filly in the making. *A. Maxwell, Ireland.* 87 p

FOLK HERO 4 b. or br.g. Levanter 121–Faerie Rose 59 (March Past 124) (1979 8s* 7s^{2} 8s* 7s 7s^{2} 10v 8s^{3} 8g 8.5g 8d 1980 9v^{3} 8g* 8f 7s^{2} 7f 8g 7d* 8s 8g 6s) Irish gelding; 16/1 when winning Irish Lincolnshire Handicap at the Curragh in April by $\frac{1}{2}$ length from Slaney Idol; beat Curragh Express by $2\frac{1}{2}$ lengths in handicap on same course in September; not disgraced when fifth to House Guard in Hambleton Stakes (Limited Handicap) at York on third start; stays 9f; acts on any going but revels in the mud; usually wears blinkers. *R. McCormick, Ireland.* 86

FOLKLAW 2 ch.g. Song 132–Judiciary 74 (Above Suspicion 127) (1980 6d 6s 8fg) May 7; 6,600Y; big gelding; closely related to 3 winners, notably very smart –

miler Legal Eagle (by Manacle), and half-brother to 3 others; dam stayed middle distances; towards rear in maiden and minor events; not sure to stay 1m; has the scope to do better at 3 yrs. *Miss S. Hall.*

FOLLOW ME HOME 2 b.f. Welsh Saint 126–Redolence (Red God 128§) (1980 5g 7g 7d) Jan 28; 10,000Y; strong, quite attractive filly; first foal; dam ran only once; behind in maiden races. *J. Douglas-Home.* –

FOLLY LANE 3 b.f. Pompous 118–Amber Anne (Amber X 133) (1979 5d 5d 6g 6h 6f^4 7g 1980 8s 8f 8fg 7f 8g 10g 10.6d) fair sort; plater; stays 1m; trained part of year by J. Hardy. *R. E. Peacock.* –

FONTAINBLEAU 4 b.g. Royal Palace 131–Fille de Joie 106 (Midsummer Night II 117) (1979 13v* 12d 1980 12.2d) rangy gelding; won maiden race at Nottingham early in 1979; ran well for a long way when fifth to La Piccolina in handicap at Warwick in October, only second subsequent outing; suited by a test of stamina. *W. Hastings-Bass.* –

FONTANA 3 ch.f. Thatch 136–Artist and Model (Ribot 142) (1979 7fg 7.5s^2 1980 7f 8fg 9.4d) 37,000Y; neat ex-Irish filly; good mover; second living foal; half-sister to Irish and American winner Le Militaire (by Le Levanstell); dam unraced half-sister to smart middle-distance stakes winner Landscaper; second in maiden race at Gowran Park at 2 yrs; showed little worthwhile form in maiden and minor races in 1980; sent to USA. *M. Stoute.* –

FONTANA DI TREVI 2 ch.f. Roan Rocket 128–Campagna (Romulus 129) (1980 6g^2 6fg 6g) Feb 7; small filly; half-sister to 3 winners, including miler Druimfada (by No Mercy); dam won over $1\frac{1}{4}$m in France; disputed lead all way when length second of 9 to Sones in maiden race at Yarmouth in September; well beaten in similar events at Redcar (odds on, finished last) and Leicester subsequently; will stay 1m. *M. Stoute.* **72**

FOODBROKER LADY 3 b.f. Prince Regent 129–Who Can Tell 109 (Worden II 129) (1979 6fg 7f 7s 9fg^4 1980 11.1f) well-made filly; quite moderate (rated 75) in 1979; had stiffish task in handicap only start at 3 yrs in May; should stay 11f; sold 6,200 gns Newmarket December Sales. *J. Bethell.* –

FOOLISH PET 3 ch.f. Silly Season 127–Petocracy 102 (Petingo 135) (1979 5f 1980 8d^3 10s^2 8fg^3 8fg^3 10fg 8s^3 10s) workmanlike filly; quite a moderate maiden; suited by $1\frac{1}{4}$m; probably acts on any going; blinkered fifth start; sweated up final outing. *F. J. Houghton.* **65**

FOOL ON THE HILL 3 ch.g. Goldhill 125–Silk Willoughby (Pirate King 129) (1979 5f 8fg 1980 8s 7fg 7f 7.2fg 6s 5fg) plain gelding; bad plater *T. Marshall.* –

FOOL'S TESTIMONY 3 ch.g. High Line 125–Lady Advocate 116 (King's Bench 132) (1979 7f 8fg^2 8fg 1980 10fg 7fg 8d) well-made, good sort; runner-up in minor event at Doncaster at 2 yrs; behind in maiden races and a £3,200 event in 1980; finds 7f too sharp and will be suited by $1\frac{1}{2}$m. *N. Vigors.* –

FOOTBALL 2 br.c. Hotfoot 126–Born Free 105 (Alycidon 138) (1980 6g^4 6fg) May 25; strong, well-grown, attractive colt; brother to high-class miler Free State, and half-brother to several winners; dam won at up to 1m; showed promise when running on to finish $9\frac{1}{4}$ lengths fourth of 19 to Dancing Sally in newcomers race at Goodwood in September; 4/1 for Clarence House Stakes at Ascot later in month but never got into race after being a bit slow into stride and finished last of 7 to Doc Marten; will be suited by 1m; may bo better in 1981. *P. Walwyn.* – p

FOOTREST 2 b.f. Hotfoot 126–Restive 96 (Relic) (1980 5fg 5g) May 22; good-topped filly; fourth foal; half-sister to Irish 3-y-o 5f winner Restless Dancer (by Saritamer); dam suited by 6f; behind in maiden races at Kempton and Sandown (25/1, showed early speed) in the summer; sold to BBA Ireland 9,600 gns Newmarket Autumn Sales. *B. Hobbs.* –

FOOTSHORE 2 br.f. Prince Tenderfoot 126–Sea Horse 98 (Sea-Bird II 145) (1980 5d^2 5g 5g* 5g^2 5g 5fg^3 5fg 5d) Apr 29; 11,500Y; neat, quite attractive filly; third foal; half-sister to 2 winners in Italy, including very useful 1977 2-y-o African Horse (by African Sky); dam won over 7f and $1\frac{1}{4}$m in Ireland; made virtually all to win 21-runner maiden race at Windsor in July a shade comfortably by a neck from Nomadic Pleasure; put up some good efforts in nurseries afterwards but made little show from a poor draw when co-favourite on final outing; should stay 6f+. *G. Harwood.* **88**

FORCE OF ACTION 2 ch.f. Galivanter 131–Delayed Action 113 (Jolly Jet 111) (1980 5g* 5f 5f^2 5f^2 5fg^2 5f 5d^3 5g 5fg* 6d^2 6g* 5d 5f 6s^3) May 7; workmanlike filly; first foal; dam won seven 5f races, six of them at 2 yrs; won minor event at **90**

Ripon in April and nurseries at Redcar and Catterick in the summer; all out to beat Creamy a length under a 5-lb penalty on last-named course; suited by 6f; probably acts on any going; genuine and consistent until running moderately on eleventh and twelfth starts; usually apprentice ridden. *G. Toft.*

FORDIGAYLE 2 ch.f. Lord Gayle 124–Ragusalina 84 (Ragusa 137) (1980 6d 7d) Apr 27; 5,800Y; neat filly; half-sister to Irish 1½m winner Treechka (by Reform); dam won over 1½m, and is half-sister to 2,000 Guineas fourth Pinturischio; 25/1 when remote seventh of 16 to Quest in maiden race at Wolverhampton in July, second outing. *I. Walker.* —

FORESTERS BOY 3 br.g. Swinging Junior 118–Wilden (Will Somers 114 §) (1979 6d 7f^3 7fg* 7d^4 7fg 1980 7v 7d 10f^4 8fg^3 8fg 9g 7f 8d 8.2d 8fg) leggy, lop-eared gelding; only plating class; not certain to stay 1¼m; probably acts on any going; blinkered on reappearance (pulled hard) and on sixth outing; ran moderately last 4 starts; trained by S. Wainwright for part of season. *W. Haigh.* **64**

FORESTERS LAD 2 gr.c. Porto Bello 118–Raffinata (Raffingora 130) (1980 5fg^4 5fg 6d* 6d^4 6d 6d^3 6g) Apr 9; 960Y, 3,000 2-y-o; leggy colt; first foal; dam never ran; 50/1 when showing much improved form to win 10-runner maiden race at Haydock in August by 1½ lengths from Cabbage Man; ran well in nurseries last 3 outings; suited by 6f; acts well on a soft surface; wore bandages when fourth in a seller on first outing (subsequently claimed out of S. Wainwright's stable). *W. Haigh.* **90**

FOREST GROVE 3 ch.g. Jim French–Fusil 105 (Fidalgo 129) (1979 7f 7f 1980 8h 10f 10s 10g 10g 11.5g^2 12.5s) well-made, attractive gelding; slow maiden; should stay 1½m+; blinkered last 2 starts; sold 4,500 gns Newmarket Autumn Sales. *H. Wragg.* **62**

FOREST WALK 5 br.g. Tower Walk 130–Sylvan Wood (Red God 128 §) (1979 6v^4 5f 6g 10.4f 1980 5fg) poor plater. *W. H. H. Williams.* —

FORLENE 3 b.f. Forli–Arkadina 121 (Ribot 142) (1979 7fg* 7d^3 8g* 1980 7g^4 7g^3 12f) 162,000Y; third foal; half-sister to smart Irish middle-distance winner Encyclopedia (by Reviewer); dam, placed in 3 classics, is sister to high-class stayer Blood Royal; in frame in April Fillies Stakes (3 lengths fourth to Racquette, rec 8 lb) and Athasi Stakes (third, beaten 3¼ lengths by Etoile de Paris), both at the Curragh in April; dismal tailed-off last in Oaks in June, only subsequent start; should have stayed 1½m; stud. *V. O'Brien, Ireland.* **100**

FORM SETT 5 b.g. Pretty Form 97–Miss Atalanta 83 (Hethersett 134) (1979 5d* 5fg 5fg 1980 6fg 5g^3 5d 5g 6g 8d) plater; best form at 5f; probably acts on any going; sometimes wears blinkers; bandaged in 1980. *L. Barratt.* **43**

FORNELLY 3 b.c. Saritamer 130–Streak of Honour 102 (Firestreak 125) (1979 5v 6f 7f^3 7g 1980 8v 9g 10fg^4 10f 12h 12fg 11d 13.8f) quite a useful sort; poor plater; brought down fifth outing; finished lame final start; dead. *G. Richards.* —

FORRUNA 3 br.g. Forlorn River 124–Lunar Princess 109 (King's Bench 132) (1979 5v 5g 5f 5f 6fg 7fg* 7g^2 6g 7g 7f 1980 8d 7v^4 7f 7f 7fg 7g 6f) robust gelding; inconsistent handicapper; much better suited by 7f than shorter distances and should stay 1m (ran badly when tried at trip); wears blinkers; has shown signs of temperament; sold 900 gns Doncaster September Sales. *W. Wharton.* **— §**

FOR THE FLAG (USA) 2 b.f. Forli–In The Offing (Hoist the Flag) (1980 7.3d 7g) Mar 27; $170,000Y; quite attractive filly; first foal; dam, winner at up to 9f, is half-sister to smart American horses Dancing Champ, Sweet Alliance and Whydidju; behind in £5,000 event at Newbury won by Boathouse (very green and started slowly) and in 26-runner maiden race at Newmarket won by Full of Reason (showed up to past halfway) in October. *I. Balding.* —

FORTIFIED 2 ch.c. Sparkler 130–Andrew's Girl 84 (Quorum 126) (1980 5.8fg 6g^2 5f 6g 6g) Mar 2; leggy colt; poor walker; half-brother to a winner in Malaya by Polyfoto; dam won over 6f at 2 yrs; went down by 2 lengths to My Morton in 10-runner maiden race at Chepstow in June; off course over 2 months subsequently and was well beaten on return, including when badly drawn in valuable seller; stays 6f; sold 2,600 gns Newmarket Autumn Sales. *I. Balding.* **68**

FORTUNE'S FANCY 3 br.f. Workboy 123–Polly Peachum 123 (Singing Strand) (1979 5s 5fg 5f 1980 5d 6g 5f 8g 5f 5f) strong filly; showed only sign of ability on second start at 2 yrs; unlikely to stay 1m; blinkered fifth outing; sweated up first start. *M. W. Easterby.* —

FORTUNY (USA) 4 b.c. Reviewer–Plausible (Nashua) (1979 8s^4 8d^2 8d 8f* 8fg* 8g^3 8fg 8f* 1980 8f 8d 8d 8.2s^4 8g 10g 8.2s 10s) strong, attractive, good-bodied colt; had a disappointing season, best effort when fourth to Malvan in handicap at Nottingham in July (blinkered); stays 1m; appears to act on any going; good mount for an inexperienced rider. *G. Hunter.* —

FORTYANNA 3 b.f. Morston 125–Singing Witch 71 (Sing Sing 134) (1979 NR 1980 7f 6g 7fg 7d 10fg 10g) 16,000Y; lengthy, lightly-made filly; little worthwhile form in varied company, including selling; sold out of B. Swift's stable 720 gns Newmarket July Sales after fourth start; resold 725 gns Ascot October Sales. *W. Musson.* —

FOUND GOLD (USA) 2 b.c. Mr Prospector–Smart Dancing (Smart) (1980 5.1f^2 7s 7g) May 9; $33,000Y; leggy colt; fourth foal; half-brother to minor winners by Icecapade and Mississipian; dam half-sister to 3 minor US stakes winners and top Puerto Rican horse Ray Jeter; ran green but came to have every chance from distance when short-head second of 9 to Steelinctive in maiden race at Yarmouth in June; well behind both subsequent outings (off course 2 months in between them); should be suited by 6f+; acts on firm going; sent to France. *H. Cecil.* **89**

FOUNDRYMAN 3 b.c. Silly Season 127–Game Girl 85 (Abernant 142) (1979 5v^4 5s^3 5.1f^3 6fg^2 6g 6d^3 6fg 1980 5h 6fg 5d 5fg* 6s 5f^4 7d) neat colt; won apprentice race at Edinburgh in July; stays 6f; probably acts on any going; moved and ran poorly on fifth start in 1979; trained by T. Molony first 5 outings. *W. Haigh.* **52**

FOUR OF A KIND 4 b.c. Levmoss 133–Alauda (Shantung 132) (1979 12g 13v^2 16d^3 12s 14g^3 15.5f 14fg^4 16fg 1980 12g) big, strong, lengthy colt; staying maiden; best form with some give in the ground; sometimes wears blinkers. *W. Musson.* —

FOVEROS 4 b.c. Averof 123–Camina Bay 109 (Whistling Wind 123) (1979 8s 7g^3 8.5s* 8g 8.5g 8g^4 12f 8fg^3 10s^3 8g^3 8f^2 10fg 1980 7fg* 7.2f^3 8f^2 8d^3 9.2s^2 10.5d 8g 11s) useful-looking colt; a very smart and genuine racehorse at his best; beat Skyliner 1½ lengths in Philip Cornes Trophy at Leicester in April; placed on his next 4 starts, finishing 3 lengths third of 4 behind Kris in Cold Shield Windows Trophy at Haydock, ¾-length second to Kris in Tote Lockinge Stakes at Newbury, 5 lengths third to Blue Refrain in Queen Anne Stakes at Royal Ascot and the same distance second to Nadjar in Prix d'Ispahan at Longchamp; well beaten last 3 starts, and ran abysmally in Doonside Cup at Ayr on final start when tried in blinkers; best form at up to 1¼m; acts on any going; sold to race in South Africa. *C. Brittain.* **120**

FOXBURY 6 ch.m. Healaugh Fox–Sunny Fort (Fortina) (1979 NR 1980 16g 14g 13.4g 14.6fg) half-sister to quite useful chaser Oedipus Rex (by Tangle); dam won over fences; poor maiden. *G. Price.* —

FOXLEY MEL 4 b.f. Owen Anthony 102–Westerlands Prism (Primera 131) (1979 10.1g^4 8.3d 1980 11fg 8h 8.3f 8fg^4) poor plater; stays 1¼m. *S. Matthews.* —

FOXY FELLOW 2 ch.c. Porto Bello 118–Phlox 101 (Floriana 106) (1980 5s 5.8fg^3 5.8f^3 6g 6g) Mar 19; small colt; first foal; dam won 4 times over 5f; third in maiden races at Bath in July, beaten 6 lengths by Nature's Way and 4 lengths by Steel Pass; in rear in nurseries afterwards; stays 6f. *R. Akehurst.* **68**

FOXY LADY 3 b.f. Tudor Rhythm 112–Boston Lights (Fantastic Light 119) (1979 8f 8fg 1980 11.7fg 16g 16s) very plain, unfurnished filly; looks and runs as though she is of little account. *J. Douglas-Home.* —

FRAASH 7 ch.g. Frankincense 120–Desert Ash (Celtic Ash) (1979 12s^4 13s* 12.3v* 12s^3 12g^4 13fg^4 14g^3 12fg 14g 13d^4 16.1g^3 16d^4 16.1d^3 13s^3 12d 15s^4 1980 12s 13s^3) quite a moderate handicapper; stays well; well suited by some give in the ground; has been tried in blinkers; usually wears bandages; suitable mount for an apprentice. *C. Gray.* **67**

FRABWAH 2 b.f. Abwah 118–Frau 60 (Frankincense 120) (1980 5fg 6d 6g) June 10; small, lengthy filly; first living foal; dam placed in 1m seller; in rear in maiden and minor events at Catterick, Pontefract and Leicester in the autumn. *B. Richmond.* —

FRANCESCO 4 b.c. Royal and Regal–Rising Lark (Ballymoss 136) (1979 14f^3 13.8s* 15.8g* 14f* 14.8f^2 14fg* 14g^2 14s 18fg 16fg^3 16f 1980 14f^4 16fg 12fg 12fg^2 14.7g^2 14fg* 14g^3 14g^3) strong, deep-girthed, round-barrelled colt; fairly useful handicapper; ridden by 7-lb claimer when beating Abielle by 4 **91**

lengths at Yarmouth in August; runner-up earlier in lady riders race at Ripon and £3,700 event (went down by 2½ lengths to Try Sandicliffe) at Redcar; stays well; acts on any going; sweated up fourth and fifth starts. *H. Cecil.*

FRANCISCUS 3 br.c. Lord Gayle 124–Frances Jordan 102 (Prince Regent 86
129) (1979 7d 1980 12g* 12g 12f^{4} 11.7g^{3} 11.1g^{2} 12g* 13.3d^{3}) 16,000Y; neat ex-Irish colt; first foal; dam won over 7f and 1m at 2 yrs in Ireland; favourite when winning maiden race at Roscommon in June by a wide margin and minor event at York in October all out by a neck from Tentwort; creditable second in handicap at Kempton in between; stays 1½m; suited by some give in the ground; trained by K. Prendergast first start; sold 15,000 gns Newmarket Autumn Sales. *R. Armstrong.*

FRANK BERRY 2 ch.c. Lorenzaccio 130–Bora Bora 91 (Hethersett 134) 76
(1980 6g 7f 6g 7d^{4} 7g 8d) Apr 20; lengthy, attractive colt; good walker; second living foal; brother to very useful 1975 staying 2-y-o Cappuccilli; dam won over 1m; 5 lengths fourth of 10 behind Beocan in minor event at Brighton in September; bred to stay at least 1¼m (ran badly when tried at 1m); had stiff tasks second and fifth starts. *G. Lewis.*

FRANKIAN JON 4 b.c. Saulingo 122–Beauty Time (Arctic Time 127) (1979 –
5v^{3} 6g 6g 5fg 5g^{3} 5fg 5g 5d 1980 5s 6f 6f 5g) big colt; sprint plater; needs some give in the ground; sweated up and started slowly when blinkered once at 3 yrs; bandaged second start. *P. Haslam.*

FRANKNESS 4 br.g. Frankincense 120–Twice Shy (Lord of Verona 120) (1979 –
10g^{4} 11d^{3} 8v^{2} 10.6g^{3} 12fg^{3} 9.4f 13g^{4} 16fg^{3} 14.7g 1980 12.3d 10g^{4} 15d 12g^{4} 12d) fair sort; seems to stay 2m; probably acts on any going; sometimes races with his tongue tied down; behind in a valuable seller on final start. *G. Richards.*

FRANK STEWART 3 ch.g. Grey Mirage 128–Bontet (Bounteous 125) (1979 41
5v 5v 5d 5s 5fg 7f 6f 6h 1980 8v* 10fg 8d 13.8fg) compact gelding; poor plater; won at Stockton in March (no bid); should stay 1¼m; suited by some give in the ground; has worn blinkers; bandaged second start. *R. Ward.*

FRANTIC FRIDAY (USA) 3 ch.g. Champagne Charlie–Emquilla (Young 65
Emperor 133) (1979 5s 7.6f 8fg 7fg 1980 8s 6fg^{2} 6h* 6fg 7fg) useful sort; won 11-runner maiden race at Brighton in May; should stay 7f+; acts on hard going and is possibly unsuited by soft; blinkered final outing at 2 yrs; suitable mount for a boy; sold 3,000 gns Newmarket Autumn Sales. *H. Candy.*

FRANWIN 14 b.g. Fidalgo 129–Brunhilde 84 (Combat 123) (1979 NR 1980 –
12d) of little account nowadays. *A. Davison.*

FRASASS 3 b.g. Sassafras 135–Desert Flame 96 (Baldric II 131) (1979 6d 7f^{4} 86
7d 8.2s 1980 12fg 12f 12d^{3} 10d^{3} 12fg* 14d^{2} 15.8d* 16g 16.1s) strong, compact gelding; fair handicapper; successful at Doncaster (amateur riders) in July and Chester in August; scored in very good style on latter; stays well; acts on a firm and a soft surface; a front runner who used to pull very hard but is more tractable nowadays; pulled up when saddle slipped second start; ran out eighth outing; doubtful temperamentally. *M. H. Easterby.*

FREDA FLOCKTON 2 br.f. Arch Sculptor 123–Nearumba 73 (Quorum 126) –
(1980 5s 6g) Mar 7; 1,500F, 2,400Y; sturdy filly; fifth produce; dam won from 6f to 1¼m; unquoted when behind in seller at Stockton in October and maiden race at Leicester the following month. *S. Wiles.*

FREDDIE BEE 3 b.g. Welsh Saint 126–Linguist 90 (Mossborough 126) (1979 –
7fg 7fg 1980 7f 6fg 8g^{4} 8fg 12d) tall, lengthy gelding; only plating class; not certain to stay 1½m; sold 620 gns Newmarket Autumn Sales. *D. Whelan.*

FREDDY FLOCKTON 3 b. or br.c. Caliban 123–Court Royal 94 (Court Martial) –
(1979 8g 8g 7s 1980 12.2fg 10s 10fg) behind in maiden and minor races; blinkered last 2 starts; sold 1,500 gns Doncaster October Sales. *S. Wiles.*

FREE FORESTER (USA) 2 ch.c. Bold Bidder–Forest Friend (Linacre 133) 87
(1980 6g 7g^{3} 7g* 8d^{3}) Apr 6; strong sort; half-brother to several winners, including smart Irish stayer Moss Trooper (by Levmoss) and useful 1m and 1¼m winner Forest Lodge (by Executioner); dam, lightly raced, is half-sister to Vaguely Noble's dam; had to be hard driven to get on top over 1f out when 3/1 on for maiden race at Catterick in August but then drew away to win by 3 lengths from Paltango; creditable third of 6, apprentice ridden, in nursery won by Golden Flak at Newbury in October; will stay 1¼m; yet to race on a firm surface. *H. Cecil.*

FREEZE FRAME 3 b.f. Averof 123–Snowfield 69 (Meadow Court 129) (1979 7d 1980 10f 12g 12d 12s 12.5s 10d) well beaten in maiden and minor races; sometimes sweats up; pulled up second outing. *M. Camacho.* —

FRENCH COOKING 4 b.f. Royal and Regal–Costmary 108 (Grey Sovereign 128§) (1979 11g 12g 16fg² 16fg* 17.1fg 1980 12f) well-made filly; well beaten when blinkered final start at 3 yrs and on only outing of 1980; stays well; yet to race on soft ground. *W. Clay.* —

FRENCH HIGHWAY 3 br.f. Duc D'Orleans 76–Highway Jane (Royal Highway 117) (1979 5g 7d 7g 1980 8fg) big, strong filly; of no account. *J. Czerpak.* —

FRENCH KNOT 2 b.g. Take a Reef 127–Merette 63 (Runnymede 123) (1980 6fg 6g 7f 7g 8.2s⁴ 8d³) Apr 10; 6,200Y; neat gelding; first foal; dam second twice over 1m; in frame in nurseries, one of them a seller; suited by 1m; acts on soft going; wears blinkers. *J. W. Watts.* **68**

FRENCH SALVO (USA) 3 b.f. Cannonade–Sleep Till Noon (Ambiorix 130) (1979 NR 1980 7fg 5g 10fg) $29,000 2-y-o; lightly-made filly; third foal; dam unraced half-sister to Irish Sweeps Derby winner Malacate; in rear in maiden races in the South. *A. Breasley.* —

FRENCH STRATA (USA) 3 b.f. Permian–Pour Vous (Hill Prince) (1979 5.1fg 6g 5f 5f² 5fg⁴ 5d 1980 7f 8.5f 7d 5g) fair sort; runner-up in maiden race at Lingfield at 2 yrs; showed no form in 1980; should be well suited by 7f+. *P. Read, Isle of Man.* —

FRENCH TOUCH 3 ch.f. Dieu Soleil 111–Fabric 77 (Sheshoon 132) (1979 5v 5s³ 5d² 5s* 5fg 5fg² 5f 5h 6s 5d⁴ 1980 5f 7fg 5f* 6fg 5fg 5fg³ 5g 5g 6d 6g 5g³ 5d) neat filly; plater; made all at Ayr in May (bought in 2,000 gns); should stay at least 6f; acts on any going; sold 1,000 gns Doncaster November Sales. *A. Balding.* **51**

FRESA 3 gr.f. Lorenzaccio 130–Chokeberry (Crepello 136) (1979 NR 1980 8f⁴ 8fg 7g 10fg 10g 8s) small filly; first foal; dam unraced sister to smart 1¼m filly Cranberry Sauce; soundly beaten in maiden races and a handicap; trained part of year by P. Feilden. *A. Moore.* —

FRIARS WALK 2 b.c. African Sky 124–Arcticmars (Arctic Chevalier) (1980 6v*) Apr 13; third reported live foal; half-brother to bumpers winner Arctic Gull (by Roll of Honour); dam ran only once; put up a pleasing first effort when leading 1½f out to win 11-runner maiden race at the Curragh in November by 2½ lengths from Wet Bob; will be suited by 1m. *C. Collins, Ireland.* **92** p

FRIARS WELL 2 b.c. Song 132–Davina (Darius 129) (1980 5f 7g) Jan 20; 9,000F; dipped-backed colt; half-brother to winners in Hungary and Italy; dam never ran; made no show in large fields of maidens at York in May (12/1) and Leicester in July (20/1); sold 300 gns Ascot August Sales. *B. Hobbs.* —

FRIAR TUCK 4 b.g. Derring-Do 131–Wasdale 97 (Psidium 130) (1979 NR 1980 10.1fg 7f) poor plater; blinkered final outing. *J. Cann.* —

FRIENDLY ECHO 2 ch.f. Reliance II 137–Misty Echo 58 (Mountain Call 125) (1980 5.3d⁴ 5s 5g 6fg 7fg) Mar 30; 1,050Y; small, fair sort; first foal; dam ran only at 2 yrs; plating-class maiden; should be suited by 6f+ (had stiffish tasks last 2 starts). *M. Haynes.* **61**

FRIENDLY FALCON 2 ch.g. Be Friendly 130–Little Nell (Falcon 131) (1980 5f 5fg 6fg* 7d*) Apr 3; 650Y; small, lightly-made gelding; second foal; dam in frame over 5f at 2 yrs in Ireland; a fair performer in plating company; won at Pontefract in June (bought in 850 gns) and Newmarket in July (cost 3,200 gns to buy in after winning £2,200 event by a length from Sideline); suited by 7f; acts on a firm and a soft surface; exported to Hong Kong. *P. Rohan.* **67**

FRIENDLY FUN 5 ro.g. Be Friendly 130–Primerva (Primera 131) (1979 5s 5d* 5d* 5s⁴ 5fg 5fg* 5g 5d⁴ 5s² 5d 5s 1980 5d 5s² 5fg 5f³ 5f 5s 5g 5fg 5fg 5d 5d² 5.6g 6s 5g³ 5s³ 5v²) sprint handicapper; second at Newcastle, Haydock and Doncaster during a busy season, beaten a length by Covergirls Choice on last-named course on final day; had stiff task and also ran well when third to Lightning Label at Haydock on penultimate start; best at 5f; acts on any going, but is well suited by some give in the ground; effective with blinkers and without (usually wears them nowadays). *N. Crump.* **87**

FRIENDLY SOLO 3 ch.c. Be Friendly 130–Maryfield (Hul a Hul 124) (1979 5f 5f 5h 5fg⁴ 6s 5d 1980 6d 5fg³ 6g 6d 5fg) compact colt; poor plater; should **43**

stay 6f; has run respectably for a boy; sold 340 gns Doncaster October Sales. *A. Balding.*

FRIENDLY SOVEREIGN 2 b.c. Hard Fact 74–Friendly Queen 73 (Be Friendly 130) (1980 6fg 8d 7s) May 9; plain colt; first foal; dam, best at 5f on flat, stayed 2½m over hurdles; plating-class maiden. *R. Atkins.* —

FRIENDSHIP BAY 4 b.c. Mill Reef 141–Honey Portion 107 (Major Portion 129) (1979 12g 14fg 16f^{2} 15.5fg 16fg 1980 12d 13d^{4} 16f 16f 16s^{3} 17.1fg 16.5g 16f 16g) poor staying maiden; appears to act on any going; usually wears blinkers; suitable mount for an inexperienced rider. *M. Haynes.* —

FRIESLAND LASS 3 b.f. Warpath 113–Elche 107 (Flush Royal 127) (1979 7d 7fg 7fg 6f 6fg 1980 8d 8v 10s 12fg 12d) lightly-made filly; useless plater; has worn blinkers; trained first 3 outings by W. Wright. *J. H. Peacock.* —

FRIMLEY PRINCESS 3 gr.f. Sovereign Path 125–Nisette (Black Tarquin 136) (1979 NR 1980 10.1s 10g) 1,000 3-y-o; small, compact filly; sister to middle-distance winners Regal Ride and Royal Set and half-sister to 2 winners; dam won over 1¼m and 13f in Ireland; tailed off in maiden races at Windsor and Newmarket; trained by P. Arthur first start. *V. Soane.* —

FRIMLEY'S ALANA 4 b.f. Lear Jet 123–Olympus Girl 65 (Zeus Boy 121) (1979 5v^{4} 5s 5d 6d 5g 6g 6f^{4} 6fg 5f 5fg 5d 1980 6s 5fg 5g 6g) small, lengthy filly; stays 6f and should get further; has run well for an apprentice; has worn blinkers. *P. Arthur.* —

FRIMLEY'S JUNIC 6 br.m. Mandamus 120–True Pardal (Pardal 130) (1979 NR 1980 13s) of no account. *P. Arthur.* —

FRIMLEY TOWN 4 gr.c. Town Crier 119–Reigning Grace 108 (Roan Rocket 128) (1979 8s 8d 10.1g 1980 10.7g) lightly-made colt; poor maiden. *P. Arthur.* —

FRITHS FOLLY 3 ch.f. Good Bond 122–Drinka Pinta 101 (Court Feathers 123) (1979 5v 5v 5g^{2} 5f 6fg 7fg^{3} 7g^{3} 6s 6f^{4} 6f 7.2d^{4} 6s 1980 6v 5f 7f 9g^{4} 12g^{3} 10d 12f^{3} 12fg 12fg 12g 10d) not a good mover in his slower paces; plater; stays 1½m; acts on a firm surface and is probably unsuited by really soft ground; often blinkered; has worn bandages; sometimes sweats up; ran poorly last 3 starts. *R. Hobson.* **49**

FRIVOLOUS RELATION (USA) 2 b. or br.f. Buckpasser–Aunt Edith 128 (Primera 131) (1980 7d) attractive filly; half-sister to several winners, including smart French middle-distance performer My Great Aunt (by Bold Ruler) and smart stakes winner Critical Cousin (by Reviewer), successful at up to 1m; dam won Yorkshire Oaks, Prix Vermeille and King George VI and Queen Elizabeth Stakes; 20/1 and fit (although backward in coat), made no show when behind in 14-runner Houghton Stakes won by Sunley Builds at Newmarket in October; a well-related filly who should do much better at 3 yrs. *J. Dunlop.* — p

FROGTOWN (USA) 2 b.g. One For All–Ave Valeque (Bold Ruler) (1980 5fg 8g) Jan 22; well-made, attractive gelding; half-brother to several winners in USA and France, including Ciao (by Silent Screen), a very useful stakes winner at up to 7f at 2 yrs; dam stakes-placed winner at up to 6f; showed promise when never-dangerous 7 lengths ninth of 19 to Flash Gordon in maiden race at Salisbury in May; 13/2, looked very well when next seen out in maiden race at Newmarket in October, but could make no impression under pressure 1f out and eventually finished ninth of 17 to Dragon Palace; gelded subsequently; should be suited by 1m. *G. Harwood.* —

FROME (USA) 2 ch.c. Gentleman's Game–Happy Donna (Prince Blessed) (1980 5f 6fg 6d^{2} 7fg^{3} 7d^{3}) Jan 10; $10,000F; lengthy colt; good walker; half-brother to several winners in USA, including stakes-placed Happy to Go (by Ready Say Go); dam won claiming races at up to 6f at 2 yrs; sire stakes-placed winner from 5f to 1m; placed in maiden races at Salisbury (short head behind Imperial Measure) and Brighton and minor event on latter course (2 lengths third of 10 to Beocan in September); will probably stay 1m. *R. Smyth.* **83**

FRONT DESK 3 b.g. Shiny Tenth 120–Roblietta (Track Spare 125) (1979 NR 1980 7fg) 2,800F; first foal; dam never ran; stayed on strongly when sixth of 15 to The Trader in maiden event at Leicester in April; not seen out again. *H. Candy.* —

FRUITION 2 b.f. Rheingold 137–Welsh Flame 106 (Welsh Pageant 132) (1980 8g^{4}) Feb 19; 12,500Y; workmanlike filly; first foal; dam won 4 times over 1m; 12/1, beaten 14 lengths when fourth of 7 to Leap Lively in minor event at Goodwood in September but wasn't entirely disgraced; will stay 1¼m; should improve in 1981. *P. Kelleway.* **76** p

FRYSE HILL 4 b.c. My Swallow 134–True Course II (Sea Charger 129) (1979 NR 1980 12f 12.5h 16.1fg 16g 16f 12g) useful sort; ran respectably in an amateur riders race on final start, only sign of ability; changed hands 1,900 gns Newmarket July Sales. *M. Francis.* —

FTATATEETA 3 ch.f. Brigadier Gerard 144–Dorabella 88 (Rockefella) (1979 8fg 8d 1980 12g 15fg^4) neat filly; plating-class maiden; not certain to stay 15f; wears blinkers; sold 3,000 gns Newmarket December Sales. *B. Hills.* —

FUGACIOUS 2 ch.c. Sallust 134–Phantasmagoria 65 (Le Haar 126) (1980 6g 6fg^3 8d 6v^2 7g) Mar 7; small colt; third live foal; half-brother to a winner in Malaya; dam placed over 1½m; placed in maiden races at Salisbury (2 lengths third to Welham Green) and Hamilton (3 lengths second to Moonlight Sonata) in the autumn; should stay 1m; seems to act on any going; retained 4,000 gns Newmarket Autumn Sales. *D. Sasse.* **73**

FULL OF REASON (USA) 2 br.f. Bold Reason–Tasteful (Ribot 142) (1980 7g*) Feb 27; $16,000Y, resold 30,000 gns Y; half-sister to winners in USA by Viceregal and Personality; dam unraced sister to Kentucky Derby second Dapper Dan; 20/1 and looking as though race would do her good, finished well to win 26-runner maiden event at Newmarket in October by 1½ lengths from Murmansk (USA); will stay 1¼m; a good first effort by a filly who should do even better at 3 yrs. *L. Cumani.* **86** p

FULL VALUE 9 br.g. Relko 136–How Far 107 (Hethersett 134) (1979 8g^4 10.8fg^4 10g 1980 8f) fair hurdler; does little racing on flat; stays 1¼m; acts on a firm surface; bandaged only outing of 1980. *D. Ringer.* —

FUMARELLA 3 gr.f. Zeddaan 130–Wordless 74 (Worden II 129) (1979 7d 7fg^3 8f^3 1980 10fg 10.2f^4 10fg^2 12d^2 15.5fg^2 10f^4 12f) fair sort; quite a modest maiden; stays well; probably acts on any going; sold 20,000 gns Newmarket December Sales. *R. Smyth.* **69**

FUND MANAGER 3 ch.c. Connaught 130–Queensferry 81 (Pindari 124) (1979 NR 1980 10fg) 4,200Y; big, long-backed colt; has been tubed; closely related to 10.6f winner Ferrybridge (by St Paddy) and half-brother to 2 winners, including Buckland (by Busted), successful at up to 1½m; dam, from same family as Ribocco, Ribero, etc., won over 1¼m; 33/1 when tailed off after 4f in maiden race at Yarmouth in August. *C. Brittain.* —

FUNKY ANGEL 4 br.c. Sassafras 135–Rockney 84 (Roan Rocket 128) (1979 6d 5.6fg 1980 16fg 14fg) fair performer in 1978; very lightly raced since; will stay 1m (had stiff tasks and pulled hard when well beaten over long distances in 1980); acts on a firm and a soft surface; sometimes sweats up and has given trouble at stalls. *N. Adam.* —

FUNNY HAT 6 b.m. Will Hays–Tiny Toque (High Hat 131) (1979 NR 1980 12g) headstrong plater at 3 yrs; behind in amateur riders race at Kempton in September, only outing since. *M. Tompkins.* —

FUNNY SPRING 5 b.g. Rheingold 137–Lotus 79 (Aureole 132) (1979 10f 10.2fg^4 10f^4 10fg^3 10g* 12s 1980 10s 10fg^4 9g 10g 10g 10g*) stocky gelding, carries a lot of condition; took time to reach full fitness and was running easily his best race when staying on strongly to beat Red Rufus by ½ length in James Lane Handicap at Ascot in October (well backed); best form at up to 1¼m; acts on any going; genuine but needs strong handling and seems to do best for W. Carson; sold 15,000 gns Newmarket Autumn Sales. *L. Cumani.* **85**

FUTAN 4 b.g. St Chad 120–Andara (Hugh Lupus 132) (1979 6g 5s 7v^4 8d^4 8fg 10g 10fg* 10.6g^4 10f^2 10.6g 12g* 12g^3 1980 12s 11.7d 14.6fg 16.5fg 12fg 12d^2 12d 12d) useful-looking gelding; ran best race of season when second to easy winner Grafty Green in apprentice handicap at Pontefract in October; well suited by 1½m; probably acts on any going; often wears blinkers; suitable mount for an apprentice; behind in a valuable seller on final start. *D. Gandolfo.* **47**

FUTURE FOREST 7 ch.h. Continuation 120–Sylvan Wood (Red God 128§) (1979 8d 6g 6g^2 5s* 6d 5d^4 6fg 6f^3 6f 6s 5d 5s 1980 6v 5fg 6f 6fg 5g 5s 5v) smart sprinter in his prime; showed little form in 1980 and is best left alone; acts on any going but revels in the mud; has worn blinkers; has been to stud for a short while; sometimes bandaged nowadays; sweated up badly fourth start; trained until latter event by N. Adam. *D. Leslie.* —

FUTURE UNSEEN 2 b. or br.f. Prince de Galles 125–Fulfilment (David Jack 125) (1980 6g 7g 7fg 6g) Feb 13; sparely-made filly; third foal; half-sister to fairly useful 3-y-o Stephen's Day (by Bonne Noel), successful at up to 1½m, and quite useful 1¼m winner Westminster Abbey (by Royalty); dam ran only twice; only plating-class form, including in a nursery; will stay 1¼m. *W. Holden.* **61**

FYGHAME 3 ch.g. Sheshoon 132–Collateral 99 (Compensation 127) (1979 7g 8.2g 1980 14g 12.3d 12d 10.8d⁴ 8s) strong, good sort; seems only plating class; may stay 1¾m; blinkered nowadays; sold 3,800 gns Newmarket Autumn Sales. *G. Harwood.* —

FYLDON 3 ch.g. Sir Lark 101–Avoca Vale 100 (Golestan 127§) (1979 NR 1980 12g) workmanlike gelding; half-brother to 1965 Irish 2-y-o 5f winner Pavoca (by Polly's Jet); dam won from 5f to 1½m; in need of race when behind in minor event at Leicester in August. *O. Brennan.* —

G

GABITAT 2 ch.c. Arch Sculptor 123–Golden Hostess (Kythnos 126) (1980 5s 5.8f 6g³ 6g 6d* 6d³ 7v) Mar 9; 1,200F, 5,300Y; useful-looking colt; half-brother to 2 winners by Virginia Boy, notably fairly useful 1975 2-y-o 5f winner Hotcakes; dam placed over 5f at 2 yrs in Ireland; ran easily best race when winning 17-runner maiden race at Newmarket in October by ¾ length from newcomer Composer; creditable third of 9 to Man of Song in £4,200 nursery at Newbury later in month; stays 6f (well beaten over further); acts on a soft surface but is possibly unsuited by heavy ground; blinkered last 3 outings. *B. Gubby.* **96**

GAIN (USA) 4 b.c. Mississipian 131–Miss Ribot (Sir Ribot) (1979 8s² 7.5s³ 8d² 10.5g* 10s* 12g 11g* 12.5fg³ 10g 10g 10g⁴ 13s³ 12f 1980 10g² 10.5d⁴ 12g² 12g 12g 11g³ 12.5d 12d* 9d* 12.5d² 12v 12f³ 10s² 13f 11s) French colt; blind in near eye; successful in minor events at Saint-Cloud in July and Clairefontaine in August; also ran well when chasing home Three Troikas in Prix d'Harcourt at Longchamp on reappearance, when failing by only a short neck to beat Scorpio (gave 10 lb) in Grand Prix d'Evry on third start and when ½-length third of 4 to Le Marmot in Prix Foy at Longchamp; sent to race in North America in the autumn and finished 1¾ lengths second to Overskate in Jockey Club Cup at Woodbine after reportedly losing ground at start on first appearance there; stays 13f; appears to act on any going; wears a blinker; inconsistent. *M. Zilber, France.* **116**

GALASHIELS 3 gr.f. Grey Steel 90–Monkey Flight 59 (Flyover 109) (1979 5f⁴ 5fg 5g³ 1980 6s 6d 6fg 5g 5f) bad plater; best run at 5f; has been tried in blinkers; sold 680 gns Doncaster September Sales. *M. Cousins.* —

GALATCH 3 b.c. Thatch 136–Galicia 105 (Great Nephew 126) (1979 7fg 6f 7f* 7fg² 1980 8.2d² 8f 7f 8fg 8g 8fg³ 8d 7g) strong colt; good walker and mover; quite a moderate handicapper; suited by 1m and will stay further; probably acts on any going; usually blinkered nowadays; ran moderately last 2 starts. *M. H. Easterby.* **81**

GALAXINE (FR) 3 ch.f. Habat 127–Torre Blanca (Sailor) (1979 6d 1980 8fg 8h 8g 7.2d 8d) fair sort; behind in varied company; didn't move well to start first outing. *R. Hollinshead.* —

GALAXY CAPRICORN 4 ch.c. Red Alert 127–Lauso Girl 67 (Lauso) (1979 6d 6s 6g 7fg 6f 6d 1980 8f 7fg 10g 10g⁴ 8d* 10d² 8fg³ 10fg* 8g* 10fg* 10g 8.2g⁴ 10d² 10g 10d⁴ 10s) quite attractive colt; poor walker; has a high knee action; fair handicapper; won twice at Brighton in space of 3 days in August; successful earlier on same course (apprentice race) and at Yarmouth; ran moderately last 2 starts; stays 1¼m; acts on any going except perhaps very firm; wears blinkers nowadays; usually held up; sold 11,000 gns Newmarket Autumn Sales; to race in Italy. *R. Hannon.* **82**

GALAXY GEMINI 4 br.c. So Blessed 130–Riddels Bay (Primera 131) (1979 8.2v 6s⁴ 6fg 6f⁴ 7s² 6g 1980 6s 7f 6g 7d 6g 7s) strong, compact colt; fair handicapper at his best; well beaten in 1980; should stay 1m; acts on any going except perhaps heavy; ran moderately when blinkered final outing at 3 yrs; bandaged second start. *I. Walker.* —

GALAXY LEO 4 ch.c. Habitat 134–A.1 76 (Abernant 142) (1979 7v 6d² 5fg³ 6fg 7f² 5g³ 5d 6fg 6s 6s⁴ 1980 6f* 5fg³ 7g⁴ 6fg) big, well-made, handsome ex-Irish colt; kept on well to win minor event at York in May by ½ length from Leader Of The Pack; in frame at Ayr (amateur riders race) and York afterwards; stayed 7f but gave impression shorter distances suited him better; probably acted on any going; blinkered occasionally at 3 yrs; stud in New Zealand. *D. Thom.* **73**

GALIBIER (USA) 2 b.c. Marshua's Dancer–Bojon (Beau Max) (1980 8g) Apr 7; $25,000 2-y-o; strong, good sort; second foal; dam, winner of 6f claiming race at 4 yrs, is half-sister to good Australian filly But Beautiful; 20/1 and in need of the outing, finished tailed off in 16-runner minor event won by Uppety at Newmarket in October. *L. Cumani.* —

GALLANT LASS 3 ch.f. Galivanter 131–Broadway Lass 70 (March Past 124) (1979 5.1fg 5f 5.1f 6fg 6fg 7d^2 6s 1980 7f^4 7f 7g 8fg^4 7fg 8g 7f) light-framed filly; poor plater; possibly stays 1m; probably acts on any going; has been tried in blinkers; sometimes sweats up. *G. Blum.* —

GALLARATE (USA) 3 b.f. Pretense–Zatullah (Fleet Nasrullah) (1979 NR 1980 8fg^4 10s) $22,500Y; tall, lengthy, narrow filly; sister to False Claim, a minor winner at up to 1m, and half-sister to several winners; dam stakes-placed winner at up to 7f; creditable fourth in maiden race at Newmarket in May, better effort; should stay beyond 1m. *L. Cumani.* **78**

GALLEA 2 b.c. Prince de Galles 125–Russellia (Red God 128§) (1980 7fg) Feb 26; leggy, lengthy colt; third live foal; half-brother to 1978 2-y-o 6f winner Super Sirocco (by Tumble Wind); dam placed at up to 10.5f in France; 16/1 and backward when last of 10 to Baz Bombati in maiden race at Yarmouth in July. *M. Ryan.* —

GALLIC PRIDE (USA) 2 b.f. Key To The Kingdom–Gallina 120 (Raise A Native) (1980 7d 7g) Apr 25; well-made, quite attractive filly; second foal; half-sister to 3-y-o middle-distance winner Brave The Reef (by Mill Reef); dam won Ribblesdale Stakes; unquoted when behind in maiden races at Leicester and Newmarket in October. *I. Balding.* —

GALLIC-SAINT 3 ch.g. Galivanter 131–Saint-Cyr 73 (Set Fair 129) (1979 5g 6fg 5f 7fg^2 1980 8h 8fg 8g* 9.4g 9g 7g 8f) sturdy gelding; put up an improved performance to win maiden race at Pontefract in June despite hanging left; well beaten afterwards; stays 1m; blinkered sixth start; often sweats up. *Miss S. Hall.* **57**

GALLY 2 b.g. Comedy Star 121–Galliphanto (Galivanter 131) (1980 5fg^4 5fg 5.8fg 6g 7g 6d) Apr 21; compact gelding; third foal; dam of no account; soundly beaten in minor and maiden events and a nursery; unseated rider at start second outing. *R. Hollinshead.* —

GALVESTON 3 b.c. Sir Ivor 135–Happy Music 84 (Hethersett 134) (1979 5s^4 6fg 1980 7g 10.5g 10g* 10g* 11s* 12fg* 10g^4 12v) big, strong colt; well placed to win maiden race at Sandown and minor events at Yarmouth, Hamilton and Redcar in second half of season; landed odds on last 2 courses; ran very well in Irish Sweeps Autumn Handicap at Newmarket on penultimate outing, keeping on gamely to be $\frac{1}{2}$-length fourth to Spanish Dancer; stays $1\frac{1}{2}$m; suited by some give in the ground. *W. Hastings-Bass.* **104**

GAMBLE HALL 2 b.c. Martinmas 128–Ebnal Hour (Tacitus 124) (1980 8g 7.5v*) May 6; 4,000Y; third produce; dam won a selling hurdle; looked fairly useful when winning 16-runner maiden race at Gowran Park in October by 4 lengths from Maradona; will stay $1\frac{1}{4}$m; acts on heavy going. *P. Prendergast, jnr, Ireland.* **93**

GAMBLERS DREAM 3 b. or br.g. Prince Regent 129–Red Laser 95 (Red God 128§) (1979 5f^4 5s* 6fg 5f^2 5.1fg* 6fg^2 6fg^2 1980 6s* 6f^2 6f 6g 7d^4 6fg 7g 6s 6fg 5g 6d^2 5s^2) strong, attractive gelding; good mover; fairly useful handicapper; beat Shaarid $\frac{3}{4}$ length at Kempton in April; runner-up at Newmarket (twice) and Sandown subsequently; stays 7f; acts on any going; usually wears blinkers; ran moderately third start; trained by H. T. Jones first 4 outings. *D. Wilson.* **92**

GAMBLING WREN 4 br.f. Knave To Play 79–Parade 97 (March Past 124) (1979 8g 10s 1980 13.8fg 16g 16d 16.9d 14.6fg 12g 12fg* 12.2fg^4 14.7f^2 12.2d 13s 12d) 33/1 and ridden by 7-lb claimer, showed improved form when winning handicap at Carlisle in September by $1\frac{1}{2}$ lengths from Ski's Double; improved again when $1\frac{1}{2}$ lengths second to The Professor in minor event at Redcar later in month; stays well; best form on a sound surface. *W. Elsey.* **53**

GAMMA 2 b.c. Dragonara Palace 115–Aspiration 53 (Roan Rocket 128) (1980 5d* 5f* 5f^4 5fg 5g^4 6g^2 7d 7.2g 6g) Mar 29; tall, leggy, useful-looking colt; second foal; brother to 1m and $1\frac{1}{4}$m winner Jota; dam of little account; successful in 16-runner Brocklesby Stakes at Doncaster in March and £2,700 event at Thirsk (beating Melody Box 2 lengths) the following month; creditable $4\frac{1}{2}$ lengths third of 12 to Hexgreave Star in £4,000 nursery at Newmarket in August (subsequently moved up a place on disqualification of winner, who failed a dope test) but ran moderately in similar events later on; should stay 7f; seems to act on any going; sold 4,000 gns Newmarket Autumn Sales. *W. Wharton.* **81**

GANDOORAH 2 ch.f. Record Token 128–Coaster 61 (Right Tack 131) (1980 5s^4 5fg* 5f* 5fg^2 5fg^3 5f* 5g 6g 5f 6d) Apr 6; 15,000Y; useful-looking filly; **90**

second foal; dam, half-sister to top-class sprinter Roman Warrior, won over 1m; won maiden race at Haydock and minor event at Pontefract in April and 8-runner Hilary Needler Trophy at Beverley in June; put up a game effort under top weight in last-named race, getting up to win by ¾ length from Gorgeous Girl after struggling to go pace from start; faced stiffish tasks subsequently and was well beaten; should be very well suited by 6f; acts on firm going; usually wears blinkers. *W. O'Gorman.*

GANIMEDE 2 ch.c. Red God 128§–Gone Gay 86 (Crepello 136) (1980 7fg* 7fg) Apr 24; 16,000Y; well-made, most attractive colt; good mover; brother to winning hurdler Ruby Wine, and half-brother to 1¼m winner Mister Rushton (by Queen's Hussar); dam stayed 1½m; put up a very pleasing first effort when winning 16-runner maiden race at Yarmouth in August, coming home ¾ length ahead of Empress Carlotta; had much stiffer task when third favourite for £3,900 event at Ascot the following month and wasn't disgraced in finishing just over 4 lengths fifth of 16 to Centurius; will stay 1m. *L. Cumani.* **94**

GAP OF DUNLOE (FR) 2 b.c. Sassafras 135–Absaretch (Dancer's Image) (1980 8d 8g) Feb 21; 20,000Y; well-made, attractive colt; half-brother to Mossy Plume (by Levmoss), successful over 1m in France, and to a winner in USA by Targowice; dam won 7f maiden race at 2 yrs in USA; in mid-division in maiden race at Sandown (very slow into stride) and minor event at Newmarket (not knocked about behind Uppety) in October; likely to do better over middle distances in 1981. *J. Dunlop.* **– p**

GARAMOND (USA) 2 br.c. Sham–Sari's Flash (Y Flash) (1980 7fg 7fg 6d) May 28; $28,000Y; compact, quite attractive colt; third foal; half-brother to 2 winners, including minor stakes winner Sari's Tobin (by Tobin Bronze); dam, placed at 3 yrs, is half-sister to high-class 6f to 9f winner Singh; ran on to finish 6¾ lengths fifth of 19 to Six Mile Bottom in maiden race at Lingfield in October, second outing; showed excellent speed when blinkered in similar event at Newbury later in month but faded from distance to finish ninth of 25 to Little Wolf; will be suited by a return to 7f+; sold 5,200 gns Newmarket Autumn Sales. *G. Harwood.* **69**

GARDEN SWING (USA) 3 ch.f. Stage Door Johnny–Rock Garden 86 (Roan Rocket 128) (1979 7fg² 7g 7g² 1980 8d) neat, attractive filly; particularly good mover; second in maiden races at 2 yrs; blinkered when well beaten in similar event at Salisbury in August, only outing in 1980; should stay at least 1m; sold only 700 gns Newmarket Autumn Sales. *J. Tree.* **–**

GARNISH ISLAND 2 gr.f. Ardoon 124–Tarpon Springs (Grey Sovereign 128§) (1980 5.1fg* 5g) Jan 30; compact, sharp sort; good mover; half-sister to several winners, including fair 1979 2-y-o winner I'm Grand (by Martinmas); dam closely related to No Mercy; quickened well to lead at distance and was eased before post when winning moderate maiden race at Yarmouth in August by a length from Devon Bells; only seventh of 10 to Goody Goody in £2,800 event at Goodwood the following month; will be suited by 6f+. *G. Pritchard-Gordon.* **78**

GARRIDO (ITY) 3 ch.c. Mannsfeld 125–Gabrielle Lebaudy (Murrayfield 119) (1979 8d* 1980 10.5fg 11d⁴ 12g* 12f 12s⁴ 12f⁴ 12v 12f) attractive, full-quartered colt; first foal; dam won 3 times in Italy; odds on, won Derby Italiano at Rome in May by 2½ lengths from Pian Del Lupo; ran creditably most other starts, notably when 2¾ lengths fifth to Henbit in 24-runner Derby, 5½ lengths fourth to Tyrnavos in Irish Sweeps Derby at the Curragh and 2 lengths fourth of 9 to Prince Bee in Prix Niel at Longchamp in September (pulled hard in early stages but kept on well in straight); subsequently sent to USA, finishing well beaten in Turf Classic at Aqueduct and Oak Tree Invitational Stakes at Santa Anita (trained by J. Gosden); stays 1½m; appears to act on any going. *F. Boutin, France.* **126**

GARTER STAR 2 b.c. Star Appeal 133–Visite Royale (Dapper Dan) (1980 7s) Mar 24; third foal; half-brother to 1m winner Royal Performance (by Klairon) and a winner in Algeria; dam ran only twice; 20/1 when 11½ lengths fifth of 13 to John Willoughby in minor event at Chepstow in October. *Sir Mark Prescott.* **–**

GARTHDALE 3 b.f. Rapid River 127–Shoobabu (Shooting Chant) (1979 NR 1980 7f 7fg 7g 6g 7g 6s 6s) small filly; first living foal; dam of little account; poor maiden; best at 6f. *S. Nesbitt.* **48**

GAWNMYSUN 2 br.c. Furry Glen 121–Fair Colleen (King Emperor) (1980 5d³ 6d 7g) Apr 16; 28,000Y; neat colt; first foal; dam unraced half-sister to Double Jump and Royalty; took a while to get going but ran on to finish 5½ lengths third of 7 to Tax Haven in £2,700 event at Sandown in June; didn't fulfil the promise of that run and looks very expensive; should be suited by 6f+. *M. Francis.* **67**

GAY BELLO 2 b.f. Porto Bello 118–Bonsella 68 (Carlemont 132) (1980 5g 5f 6f 5s) Mar 21; compact, good-bodied filly; sister to 1979 2-y-o 1m seller winner Bargain Line, and half-sister to a winner in Belgium; dam placed at up to 1¼m; no worthwhile form in maiden races. *R. Hollinshead.* —

GAY BONNET 3 b.f. Malicious–Gay Ribbon (Ribero 126) (1979 5f 5fg 6d 7g 6d 1980 11g 9g 11d 11d 16f 10.6s 10.1s 12.5s) fair sort; no worthwhile form in varied company, including selling; often blinkered; sold out of W. Elsey's stable 650 gns Ascot July Sales after fourth start. *W. Clay.* —

GAY CHERIE 3 b.f. Pompous 118–Eve Darlin 50 (Arcticeelagh 119) (1979 5v 5v^4 5s^4 5g 6f 7fg 8h 6f 1980 8d^4 8.2fg 7f 12fg 8fg) lengthy filly; poor plater; stays 1m; best form on a soft surface; sold 460 gns Doncaster October Sales. *J. Hardy.* —

GAY GEORGE 4 br.c. Prince Regent 129–Kazanlik 116 (Ommeyad 120) (1979 12fg* 12g* 12fg^2 14d 1980 11.7g^2 12fg^3) nice, compact ex-Irish colt; quite a useful performer; ran well when beaten short head and a head by No Bombs and Lumen in Moet and Chandon Silver Magnum (gentleman riders) at Epsom in August; runner-up to easy winner Masked Marvel in minor event at Windsor on previous outing; probably stays 1¾m; seems to act on any going, usually ridden up with the pace; has done very well over hurdles. *F. Walwyn.* ?

GAY GRANGE 3 ch.f. Take a Reef 127–Godetia (Be Friendly 130) (1979 5d^4 5s^4 6fg 7f 8h 8.2g 5s^3 1980 8f 8f 12.2fg 9g 8fg 8d) lightly-made filly; poor plater; sold 330 gns Doncaster November Sales. *C. Gray.* —

GAYLES BAMBINA 3 b.f. Lord Gayle 124–Hasten Slowly (Mark-Ye-Well) (1979 5f^4 1980 6fg^3 8fg^2 10.1fg^4 11.7g 10fg*) strong filly; favourite when winning 11-runner maiden race at Salisbury in September in good style; promises to stay 1½m (had a very poor run when tried at trip); acts on firm going. *D. Kent.* 75

GAY MILLY (FR) 3 b.f. Mill Reef 141–Gaily 121 (Sir Gaylord) (1979 5g^4 6.5g 7.5fg^4 8d^4 8.5g 1980 8g* 8fg) well-made, quite attractive ex-French filly; second foal; dam won Irish 1000 Guineas; beat Maiden's Walk comfortably by 1½ lengths in 18-runner maiden race at Salisbury in September; ran respectably in much better race won by Glowing Tan at Newbury later in month but gave impression that 1¼m would suit her better. *R. Hern.* 74

GAY MINSTREL 2 br.c. Tudor Music 131–Belen (Milesian 125) (1980 5f 6f) May 24; 1,500Y; half-brother to 3 winners in Ireland and one in Italy; dam ran once; behind in 18-runner maiden and minor events at Folkestone and Lingfield in September. *G. Lewis.* —

GAY NOCTURNE 2 gr. or br.f. Lord Gayle 124–Pianissimo 113 (Fortino II 120) (1980 5fg 5g) Apr 10; nice filly; good walker; half-sister to 2 Irish winners, including speedy Coalminer (by Welsh Saint); dam very useful sprinter; second favourite when 2 lengths fifth to Caribbean Breeze in 9-runner maiden race at Pontefract in June; poorly drawn only subsequent start (July). *H. T. Jones.* 63

GAY SEASON 7 b.g. Silly Season 127–Lonely Leopardess 80 (Pardal 130) (1979 8s 1980 9.6h^2) plater; stays 1¼m; acts on hard going; sold 350 gns Ascot September Sales. *H. O'Neill.* 40

GAYTHORN 2 b.f. Laser Light 118–Olivia Staypleton 88 (Road House II) (1980 5s 5g 6g^2 6g 5g) May 5; 1,900Y; plain sort; third reported foal; half-sister to 3-y-o 1m and 1¼m winner Chaplins Nightclub (by St Chad); dam best at up to 1¼m; dropped in class when 6 lengths second of 10 to Job Bag in seller at Windsor in June; ran moderately in a seller next time out; will stay 1m. *A. Davison.* 55

GAY TROOP 3 ch.g. King's Company 124–Gayness (Merry Boy) (1979 6s 7f 7g 7d 1980 10v 12fg 16f 15s) tall, leggy gelding; poor maiden; unlikely to stay 2m; changed hands 560 gns Newmarket July Sales. *J. Berry.* —

GAY WALK 4 ch.f. Farm Walk 111–Gay Breeze (Con Brio 121) (1979 12.2fg^4 12g 10g 12f 10s^2 1980 12fg 16g 12d^3 12g 12fg 12.2fg 12f) smallish filly; plater; stays 1½m; acts on soft going; sold 1,950 gns Doncaster October Sales, shortly after winning over hurdles. *Miss S. Hall.* 50

GAY WHISTLER 2 b.c. Gay Fandango 132–Tin Saint 99 (Tin Whistle 128) (1980 6g 5g 7fg) May 6; 840Y; smallish, lengthy colt; fifth foal; half-brother to a winner in Trinidad; dam winning sprinter; plating-class maiden. *J. Powney.* —

GAZAAN 2 ch.c. Margouillat 133–Goldena (Relko 136) (1980 7f^4 8d) May 9; half-brother to 2 winners in France; dam, daughter of very smart French filly Golden Girl III, won 4 middle-distance races; 33/1 when about 12 lengths fourth —

of 6 to Belloc in small race at Lingfield in October; well beaten in similar event at Leicester won by same horse the following month; needs time; may do better over middle distances in 1981. *M. Stoute.*

GEARY'S FOR STEEL 2 ch.c. Realm 129–Vita (Roan Rocket 128) (1980 5f 5f* 5g³ 5fg 5s 5fg) Apr 11; 8,200F, 1,400Y; compact colt; second foal; dam, second over 7f in France, is half-sister to smart sprinter Glen Strae; favourite, improved greatly on first effort when winning maiden auction event at Redcar in May by short head from Miss Chessy; creditable third to Supertramp in small race at Ripon the following month but was subsequently well beaten; will stay 6f; acts on firm going. *T. Fairhurst.* **66**

GEARY'S FOR STRIP 4 b.c. Mansingh 120–Sociable (Be Friendly 130) (1979 6g⁴ 6g³ 5g* 6fg 5g⁴ 5f* 5d 5h² 5fg² 5g² 1980 5d 5v² 5s 5f* 5fg 5f 6fg 5g 5d 5fg 5f 5d 5.6g) big, strong, good-looking colt; disappointing after beating Wedding Vows in handicap at Beverley in April (made all); stays 6f; acts on any going; has worn blinkers but seems better without; finished lame third start. *T. Fairhurst.* **79** d

GEARY'S STEEL STOCK 2 gr.c. Sovereign Path 125–Beautician (Barron's Court) (1980 5d 5f* 6g 5fg) Mar 26; 7,000Y; quite a useful-looking colt; second foal; half-brother to 3-y-o Roysia (by Tumble Wind), a winner at up to 1¼m; dam won over 9.5f in Ireland; made all to win 10-runner maiden race at Redcar in May by ¾ length from Sovereign Landing; well beaten in minor event at Haydock (ran wide into straight) and nursery at Redcar (bit burly after 8 weeks absence) afterwards; should stay at least 6f. *T. Fairhurst.* **72**

GELIGNITE 3 b.f. St Paddy 133–Aberangell 96 (Abernant 142) (1979 NR 1980 9fg³ 10fg*) fair sort; half-sister to several winners, including 5f to 7f winner Hedingham Boy (by Amber Rama); dam won over 5f at 2 yrs; not seen out after decisively winning 18-runner maiden race at Salisbury in May; will stay 1½m. *H. Candy.* **84**

GELLIFAWR 4 gr.f. Saulingo 122–Lune Royale 77 (Sovereign Path 125) (1979 5v 5v 5s 5s³ 5.1g³ 5fg² 5f³ 5fg* 5g 1980 5d 6fg 5f 6fg 6fg 6s) sprint handicapper; well beaten in 1980; best at 5f; acts on any going; wore blinkers occasionally at 2 yrs. *V. Soane.* **–**

GEMA ROSS 3 gr.f. Town Crier 119–Popover (Dumbarnie 125) (1979 5s³ 5s 5s 6f³ 6fg 6fg³ 1980 8fg 7g 6fg 7g 9.4g 9fg 8fg 8fg⁴ 6g 6d) leggy, unfurnished filly; showed some ability at 2 yrs; well beaten in varied company, including selling, in 1980; should stay 1m; sometimes sweats up; blinkered fourth and seventh starts. *F. Durr.* **–**

GEMSBOK 2 br.g. Redundant 120–Duiker 81 (Sovereign Lord 120) (1980 5s³ 5v² 5s²) May 3; leggy gelding; second foal; dam won over 5f at 2 yrs; not raced after finishing second in maiden races at Warwick in the spring, going down by a head to Through the Valley after swerving badly and by 1½ lengths to Red Russett. *C. V. Miller.* **72**

GENEALOGY 3 b.g. Great Nephew 126–Golden Ivy 97 (Sir Ivor 135) (1979 8fg 1980 8f 10.2fg 10g 12d) strong, well-made gelding; well beaten in maiden and minor events; sold out of R. Hern's stable 3,200 gns Ascot June Sales after second start. *C. Read.* **–**

GENERAL BREYFAX 2 ch.c. Sweet Revenge 129–Perbury 88 (Grisaille 115) (1980 5fg 5g 6d³ 6s* 7.3fg 8d) Apr 13; 3,300Y; strong, workmanlike colt; first produce; dam 2-y-o 7f winner; won 25-runner maiden race at Windsor in July by 4 lengths from Sitex; had quite a lot to do at weights when in rear in nurseries subsequently (well-backed favourite final start); not sure to stay beyond sprint distances; acts on soft going. *M. McCourt.* **73**

GENERAL PATTERNS 6 b.g. Meldrum 112–Tre-Ami 70 (High Treason 126) (1979 8g 8fg 8f 11f⁴ 12fg³ 12g 1980 14g) poor maiden; stays 1½m; changed hands 390 gns Ascot March Sales. *R. Page.* **–**

GENERAL SUPREME 4 ch.c. Green God 128–Harbrook 95 (Le Haar 126) (1979 NR 1980 12h 14f 16g 12g 10g) rangy, attractive colt; plating-class maiden; tailed off final outing. *J. Powney.* **–**

GENERAL TIMES 2 ro.g. Dragonara Palace 115–Caught-At-It 77 (Poaching 115) (1980 5d³ 5v³ 5d² 5fg 5d 5fg 6d) Apr 1; 5,000Y; compact gelding; brother to 1978 2-y-o 5f winner Ego, and half-brother to 3 winners, including fairly useful 5f performer Panglima (by Tribal Chief); dam best at 7f to 1m; placed in early-season events; gelded after running badly in seller at York on **61**

fifth outing and put up a moderate effort when next seen out, over 2 months later; blinkered fourth and seventh outings; trained by P. Rohan first 5 appearances; sold to Mrs G. Forbes 500 gns Newmarket Autumn Sales. *W. O'Gorman.*

GENERAL WADE 5 br.h. Bold Lad (Ire) 133–Zerbinetta 96 (Henry the Seventh 125) (1979 5d 5.1g 5fg³ 5fg 5g 5g² 5f⁴ 5fg 1980 5g⁴ 5.3d² 5d 5g⁴ 5d 5v) strong, good sort; runner-up at Brighton in June; best form at 5f; acts on any going; wears blinkers; ran moderately last 2 starts but had been off course 2 months both times. *P. Makin.* **85**

GENEROSO 2 ch.g. Gay Fandango 132–Magnanimous 65 (Runnymede 123) (1980 7f) Feb 22; 5,000Y; third foal; half-brother to a winner in Belgium; dam ran only over 5f at 2 yrs; 14/1 and in need of run, never got into race and wasn't given a hard time when remote sixth of 11 to Bustomi in minor event at York in September; gelded subsequently. *J. W. Watts.* –

GENEROUS BID (USA) 3 b.g. Ward McAllister–Maraude II (Vandale) (1979 NR 1980 9fg³ 10.2fg 10s 12.2f 12g 14.7g) $15,000Y; big gelding; half-brother to 2 winners in USA; dam placed in France; third in newcomers race at Wolverhampton in April but seems only plating class; should stay 1¼m+; blinkered fourth start (pulled very hard); sold 2,100 gns Ascot August Sales. *E. Eldin.* –

GENTIAN PRINCE 4 b.g. King Emperor–Fragrant Morn 79 (Mourne 126) (1979 7s 8s 8g 8g 6f* 7g 7fg³ 6fg² 1980 5fg 7fg) strong, compact gelding; plater; best form at 6f; acts on firm going; blinkered nowadays. *T. Marshall.* –

GENUINE MING (FR) 2 b.f. Reliance II 137–Ming Vase 84 (Princely Gift 137) (1980 5fg 5f 5g 5d 5d) Mar 16; 3,200Y; neat filly; half-sister to minor winners here and abroad; dam 5f 2-y-o winner; poor form in maiden races and a seller; will need much further to show whatever ability she may possess; blinkered last 2 outings; sold 280 gns Ascot July Sales after fifth start. *J. Haine.* –

GEOFFREY'S SISTER 4 ch.f. Sparkler 130–Eilan Aigas 93 (Counsel 118) (1979 8d 8fg³ 8fg* 9d* 8.2g* 9d² 1980 8f 8f² 10f 8d* 8g* 8s* 8f⁴ 8.2g* 8s* 8v⁴) **102**

Mr R. M. West's "Geoffrey's Sister"

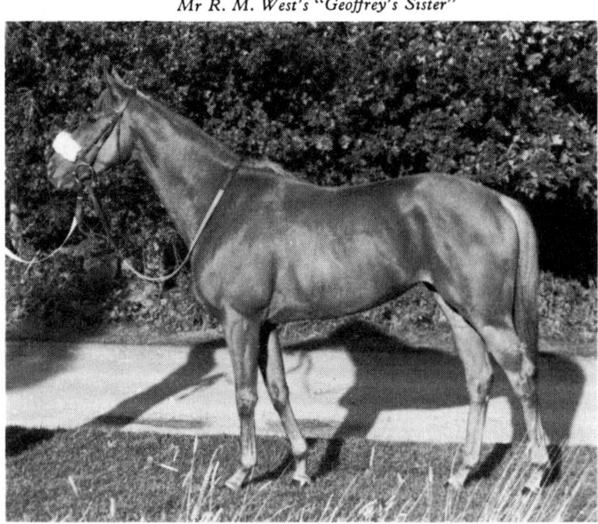

useful handicapper and a notably genuine and consistent performer; had a tremendous season and was gaining her fifth success when beating Crown Witness in good style by 5 lengths in Royal Caledonian Hunt Handicap at Ayr in September; had earlier won at Ayr (Long John Scotch Whisky Handicap), York (beat Seven Hearts by neck in Harp Lager Handicap), Ayr again and Haydock; fourth behind Isopach in Group 2 Premio Vittorio Di Capua in Milan in October; best form at up to 9f; acted on any going, but seemed particularly well suited by some give in the ground; stud. *C. Thornton.*

GEORGIAN LADY 3 ch.f. Dragonara Palace 115–Coral Flower (Quorum 126) – (1979 5d 5s^2 5.3g 7f^2 7f^3 6fg^4 1980 8.5g 8fg 12f 11.7g 6g) compact, quite attractive filly; runner-up in maiden races at Epsom and Brighton in 1979; showed no form at 3 yrs; should stay 1m; acts on any going; blinkered fourth start; sweats up badly nowadays. *R. Smyth.*

GEORGINA GIRL 2 gr.f. Owen Anthony 102–Bromhead (Sovereign Path 125) 60 (1980 5fg 5fg 6g 6f^2 6d^3 6g 6g) May 23; neat filly; sister to 3 poor animals; dam never ran; plater; will stay 7f; appears to act an any going. *M. Ryan.*

GEORGINA PARK 3 b.f. Silly Season 127–Glamorous Girl (Caliban 123) – (1979 5d 7fg* 7f* 7g^2 1980 10.1g 8fg) unfurnished filly; won maiden race at Wolverhampton and minor event at Sandown at 2 yrs; well beaten in handicaps in 1980; will probably stay beyond 1¼m; acts on firm going. *P. Cole.*

GERALD MARTIN 4 b.c. Martinmas 128–Willowy (Mourne 126) (1979 – 5v* 6v* 7v* 7s* 8v 1980 8f) lengthy, useful-looking colt; has been pin-fired; won 4 races at 3 yrs, including McCairns Vauxhall Trial at Phoenix Park and Tetrarch Stakes at the Curragh, but wasn't seen out after running dismally when odds on in Airlie/Coolmore Irish 2,000 Guineas won by Dickens Hill; last of 7 behind Kris in Lockinge Stakes at Newbury in May on only outing of 1980; should stay at least 1m; revels in the mud. *L. Browne, Ireland.*

GERONTAS (FR) 3 b.c. Sir Gaylord–Gun Princess (Gun Bow) (1979 7d^4 81 10g^4 1980 12s 10g 12fg 8.2f* 8g* 8g 8.3s^4 8fg^4 10.6d^3 10s^4 10f^4) useful-looking colt; has a round action; slaughtered his fields in maiden race at Hamilton and handicap at Doncaster in June; stays 1¼m well; seems unsuited by very soft going but acts on any other; sweated up eighth start; bandaged in front eighth and ninth outings; ran moderately sixth start. *B. Hanbury.*

GERRARD'S CROSS 6 b.g. Brigadier Gerard 144–Queen's Keys 84 (Right – Royal V 135) (1979 16v 16d 15.5d 17.1g 18s^4 18.8g 15.5f^3 16f^3 15.5fg 16g 1980 16s 16f 16.1d 15.5fg) poor staying maiden; acts on any going; used to wear blinkers; often sweats up; sold 580 gns Ascot November Sales. *J. Haine.*

GETAWAY GIRL 6 gr.m. Capistrano 120–Battling Bessie (Typhoon 125) 60 (1979 14.7f 12f^4 10fg^2 8g^3 10f^2 10.6g* 1980 10.2d* 10s 10.6fg^4 10h^4 12f^3 9f^4 13g^3 10g) middle-distance handicapper; comfortable winner from Neparree at Doncaster in March; off course nearly 3 months before finishing close third to Jam at Nottingham in September on penultimate start; stays 13f; probably acts on any going; sold 2,500 gns Doncaster November Sales. *P. Rohan.*

GET INVOLVED 6 b.m. Shiny Tenth 120–Shoulder Flash 89 (Epaulette 125) 70 (1979 6s* 6d* 5f^4 6d^4 5.8g^3 6f 6f 5fg* 5g^4 5.6fg 6f^4 5fg 1980 5d* 6v 5s^4 5g) sprint handicapper; a grand racemare who made a successful reappearance at Doncaster in March, beating Heywood Hardy a length; not seen out after mid-April and reportedly visited Bay Express; acted on any going; genuine and consistent; suitable mount for an apprentice; won 5 times at Warwick. *D. Marks.*

GET ME OUT 5 b.h. Habitat 134–Fleet Wahine 121 (Fleet Nasrullah) (1979 – 8g 10.1g 12fg 12f 1980 8fg 10h) poor maiden; sometimes blinkered; broke blood vessel and was pulled up final outing; dead. *A. Moore.*

GET STONED 4 ch.c. Home Guard 129–Romp Home 89 (Chanteur II 135) 94 (1979 7fg 10f^4 10f^3 10s* 12fg* 12g^2 1980 10fg^4 12g^2 12s^3 14g^4 12g* 18d 12v) big, rather leggy colt; looked a bit lean and light when beating Le Soleil by neck in £3,200 handicap at Doncaster in September; in frame in Bessborough Stakes at Royal Ascot, Old Newton Cup at Haydock and Tote-Ebor at York on his 3 previous outings, beaten ¾ length by Barley Hill in first-named event; stays 1¾m (well beaten over further in Tote Cesarewitch on penultimate start); acts on any going; consistent; usually sweats up. *L. Cumani.*

GETTING WARMER 4 b.f. Hotfoot 126–Shirwani 77 (Major Portion 129) – (1979 NR 1980 10g) plater nowadays; should stay 1m. *H. O'Neill.*

Mrs D. McCalmont's "Giannutri"

GHADEER (FR) 2 b.c. Lyphard 132–Swanilda (Habitat 134) (1980 6g³) Feb 4; 625,000Y (easily most expensive yearling sold at auction in Great Britain or Ireland to end of 1979); third foal; dam won over 1m in France and is half-sister to Super Dan, a very useful winner at up to 13f; third favourite, showed definite signs of greenness in Duke of Edinburgh Stakes at Ascot in October but kept on very well under strong driving to finish just over a length third of 10 to Shasavaan; will stay at least 1m; should do a lot better in 1981. *H. T. Jones.* **93** P

GHAZAL 4 br.g. Averof 123–Vilswitch 93 (Vilmorin) (1979 7g 8g 10.5g 6s 6f 8f 8fg 8d 1980 7v³ 12f⁴) useful-looking, dipped-backed gelding; stays 7f and wasn't entirely disgraced over 1½m on final outing; acts on any going; blinkered final start at 3 yrs. *J. Hardy.* **57**

GHIDALGO 2 b.c. Music Boy 124–First Court 82 (Primera 131) (1980 5fg 5fg 5.1g³ 6g 6fg 5f 5d 5d) Jan 24; 400Y; big colt; poor walker and bad mover; fifth foal; dam 1½m winner; 3½ lengths third of 6 to Lady Acquiesce in maiden auction event at Yarmouth in July, best effort; possibly doesn't stay 6f; will be more at home in sellers. *G. Blum.* **55**

GIANNUTRI 2 b.f. Wolver Hollow 126–Cesarea 108 (Raeburn II) (1980 6f 7fg*) Feb 25; lengthy, quite attractive filly; good walker; fourth foal; half-sister to 3-y-o 7f winner Cassina (by Habitat); dam game winner from 5f to 1½m; soon close up and ran on under strong driving when winning 11-runner minor event at Newbury in September by a neck from Train of Thought; will stay 1¼m; likely to make a useful 3-y-o. *P. Walwyn.* **76** p

GIBBON 4 br.g. Swing Easy 126–Fearless 77 (Derring-Do 131) (1979 6g 7d³ 6g³ 5f⁴ 7fg² 8f⁴ 8g* 7.2g* 7f³ 8fg² 1980 8d 7.2d 7f 8s 8d 9f² 9fg 10.2g) strong, good-bodied gelding; put head in air when shaken up and refused to do his best when runner-up to Graf Metternich in handicap at Wolverhampton in August; stays 9f; acts on any going except perhaps soft; blinkered fourth start at 3 yrs; faint-hearted; trained by M. W. Easterby until after fifth start. *J. Fitzgerald.* **77** §

GIBBS GARDEN 3 b.f. Palm Track 122–Enniris Wood (Precipice Wood 123) (1979 NR 1980 12s 15s) lengthy filly; first foal; dam never ran; looks of little account though has yet to run in a seller. *J. Wilson.* –

GIBRALTAR 4 b.c. Philip of Spain 126–Nasira 94 (Persian Gulf) (1979 5d^4 5s 6g^2 6d^2 6f 6fg 6d 6g^3 6d 1980 7d 6v* 6g 8.2s) neat colt; favourite, apprentice ridden and dropped to selling company when scoring at Ayr in March (bought in 4,000 gns); dwelt next time out and was subsequently off course for 6 months; best form at 6f; seems to need some give in the ground; occasionally blinkered; trained by P. Haslam until after third start. *S. Wiles.* **58**

GIDIAN 3 ch.c. Brigadier Gerard 144–Jovian 88 (Hardicanute 130) (1979 NR 1980 8.2s^3 8fg^2 7f^2 8f^3 8.2s 9v^2 10d) strong colt; third foal; dam won twice over 5f at 2 yrs; runner-up in maiden and minor events; stays 9f; acts on any going. *M. Camacho.* **72**

GIELGUD (USA) 2 ch.c. Sir Ivor 135–Best in Show (Traffic Judge) (1980 6fg^2 7g* 8fg^3 7.3d) **125**

Ivanjica, Godetia, Cloonlara, Optimistic Gal, Realty and Miss Toshiba are among those who make Sir Ivor's fillies, as a group, seem stronger than the colts. Sir Ivor does sire some very able colts though—such as Cavo Doro, second in the Derby, Imperial Prince, second in both the Derby and Irish Sweeps Derby and Sir Penfro, third in the Irish Sweeps Derby—and in Gielgud he has one of the best English two-year-old colts of 1980.

Gielgud's ability, looks and pedigree would normally have encouraged us to regard him as a fine prospect for 1981, but our enthusiasm for him was diminished by his display on his final outing when favourite for the Horris Hill Stakes at Newbury in October. He ran dismally. After being niggled at early in the straight, Gielgud made progress to get within striking distance of the leaders with two furlongs to run; hardly had he done so than he was beaten and he eventually came home a distant seventh of ten behind Kalaglow after being eased in the final furlong. The most obvious explanation for his poor showing is that he's completely unsuited by a soft surface.

Gielgud had done nothing wrong on his previous starts. Indeed he had done extremely well for such an inexperienced colt when winning the Laurent Perrier Champagne Stakes at Doncaster in September on only his second outing. None of the ten runners in that race had previously won a pattern race and Gielgud, a promising neck second to First Movement at Newmarket the previous month, was gambled on from 10/1 to 11/2, ending up fourth favourite behind the

Laurent Perrier Champagne Stakes, Doncaster—Gielgud in a driving finish with Prince Echo and Church Parade

Tyros Stakes winner Prince Echo, who had run extremely well behind Storm Bird in the Anglesey Stakes, the Chesham Stakes winner Kirtling and the Lanson Champagne Stakes winner Church Parade. The modest early gallop led to the whole field's being still tightly grouped as they came to the final quarter mile. Gielgud was still back in eighth place then, but he quickened impressively when switched to the outside soon afterwards, avoiding the trouble caused by Engulf's fall below the distance, and maintained his run in fine style to cut down Prince Echo and Church Parade well inside the final furlong. He won by a neck and the same with little over four lengths covering the first eight home. Gielgud also put up an excellent effort, although a beaten favourite, in the Royal Lodge Stakes at Ascot later in September. When Piggott brought him through to get his head narrowly in front inside the final furlong it looked as though he'd timed Gielgud's run to perfection. However Gielgud cracked in the last hundred yards, giving way to Robellino and Recitation who beat him by half a length and the same.

Gielgud (USA) (ch.c. May 1, 1978)	Sir Ivor (b 1965)	Sir Gaylord (b 1959)	Turn-to
			Somethingroyal
		Attica (ch 1953)	Mr Trouble
			Athenia
	Best in Show (ch 1965)	Traffic Judge (ch 1952)	Alibhai
			Traffic Court
		Stolen Hour (ch 1953)	Mr Busher
			Late Date

Gielgud's American breeding is now very familiar to British and Irish race-goers: he's the fifth of Best in Show's first nine foals to have raced over here and a sixth, Try My Best's dam Sex Appeal, is also a familiar name. Three of Best in Show's other runners here were also by Sir Ivor. All three won and two of them, the Ladbroke Craven Stakes winner Malinowski and the Ballyogan Stakes winner Monroe, were also successful in pattern races. None of the three won over further than a mile and Gielgud's display in the Royal Lodge suggests that a mile may also mark the limit of his stamina. He's a handsome, well-made colt, one of the most impressive-looking two-year-olds of 1980, and it's not surprising he cost 235,000 dollars as a yearling. *H. Cecil.*

GIFFORD 2 b.g. Joshua 129–Mayfell 107 (Rockefella) (1980 6d 7g 8g 8fg* 7g^2 7s 8g) May 3; 4,200Y; compact gelding; half-brother to minor 1976 2-y-o 6f winner Lindsell (by Charlottown) and a winner in Belgium; dam, half-sister to Be Hopeful and Mabel, won at up to $1\frac{1}{2}$m; showed improved form when making all to win 13-runner maiden race at Beverley in September by 3 lengths from Crack-away; again ran well when $\frac{1}{2}$-length second of 9 to Candaules in minor event at Brighton the following month; will stay $1\frac{1}{4}$m; acts on a firm surface; blinkered nowadays. *D. Morley.* **83**

GIFT WRAPPED 3 b.f. Wolver Hollow 126–Doc Nan (Francis S) (1979 6d 5f^2 5fg* 6f 1980 8d 8fg 12f* 10.5f^2 12f 10d 8fg^3 10f^3) big filly; good mover; half-sister to 4 winners, including quite useful Irish 5f and 7f winner Blue Doc (by **116**

Johnnie Walker Oaks Trial Stakes, Lingfield—Gift Wrapped has her opponents well strung out, her nearest pursuer being Port Aransas

Majority Blue); dam stakes-placed winner at up to 9f in USA; favourite, ridden with confidence to beat Port Aransas easily by 3 lengths in Johnnie Walker Oaks Trial at Lingfield in May; ran well afterwards to be placed in Musidora Stakes at York (went down by a length to Bireme) and Queen Elizabeth II Stakes at Ascot (just over 6 lengths third of 7 to Known Fact); didn't run up to her best when 4 lengths third to Snow in Sun Chariot Stakes at Newmarket on final start in October; best at up to 1¼m; acts well on firm ground and is probably unsuited by soft; sold 116,000 gns Newmarket December Sales. *F. Durr.*

GIGGLESWICK 4 b.f. Dieu Soleil 111–Fabric 77 (Sheshoon 132) (1979 8fg 12fg **41**
8g 8d 8s^3 1980 8f 7f 8f 8g^3 8g 10g^3 10g 10g 10s 10g 10g^3 10d) poor plater; stays 1¼m; suited by some give in the ground; occasionally blinkered. *K. Stone.*

GILDED CRESCENT 2 b.f. Gilded Leader 75–Rosemary Road (The Dane or –
Fair Map) (1980 6s) May 13; half-sister to 2 winners over jumps, including very useful hurdler and winning chaser Ronson Avenue (by Ron), a winner over 5f at 2 yrs; dam probably of little account over hurdles; 50/1 when well behind in 18-runner maiden race won by Will of Victory at Nottingham in August. *B. McMahon.*

GILDED VANITY 3 b.f. Run The Gantlet–Sunset Temple (Golden Horus 123) **83**
(1979 7fg 8.5g 9.5g^2 1980 9f^3 10.2fg* 8fg^4 11.1fg 12fg*) lengthy ex-Irish filly; second foal; dam won over 1m and 1¼m in Ireland; successful in maiden race at Bath in July (backed from 33/1 to 7/1) and minor event at Lingfield in October; decisively beat Paleor by 3 lengths in latter; stays 1½m; yet to race on a soft surface; wears a bandage on her off-hind; trained by B. Harrison Burcombe first start. *G. Beeson.*

GILLSON 3 b.c. High Top 131–Foiled Again 110 (Bold Lad, Ire 133) (1979 **104**
NR 1980 10f^2 10g^2 10s* 12g* 12g* 11g) 36,000Y; big, rangy colt; good mover; first foal; dam won from 6f to 1¼m; in good form in the summer, winning maiden race at Newmarket and small 5-runner races at Kempton (from New Jerusalem) and Salisbury; galloped on relentlessly to beat End of War a length (pair 8 lengths clear) on last-named; favourite when just over 5 lengths fifth to Ludovico in Group 3 Furstenberg-Rennen at Baden-Baden in August; will stay 1¾m; acts on any going; gives impression he will always do best on a galloping track. *P. Walwyn.*

GILLYMINT 4 b.f. Precipice Wood 123–Do Something 77 (Pardao 120) (1979 –
12d 10g 12fg^4 8g 12f 13g 13f 16fg^3 15.5fg 10s 11.1g 16f 12fg^3 16fg 15g 12s 1980 12d 12h 14.7f 10.6g 16f 10fg) poor maiden; best run at 1½m. *W. Charles.*

GIMRI 7 ch.g. Quayside 124–Conita 94 (Constable 119) (1979 7s 7s^4 7s* 7fg^3 **65**
7fg* 7fg^3 8g^4 7g 7d^4 1980 7v 7fg 7g 7g 7fg 7fg^3 8fg^2 7g 7g* 7.6d* 7d* 8g^4 8g 7fg 7.3fg 7g 8d) workmanlike gelding; successful in handicaps at Sandown, Lingfield (apprentices) and Newbury in July, winning by 7 lengths from Lucky Man on last-named course; stays 1m; acts on any going, but seems particularly well suited by some give in the ground; excellent mount for an apprentice. *J. Benstead.*

GIN AND LIME 5 ch.m. Warpath 113–Whisky Lima 82 (Midsummer Night –
II 117) (1979 16s^4 13g 15g^2 1980 15f) useful-looking mare; suited by a test of stamina; acts on any going; sold 1,100 gns Newmarket July Sales. *S. Leadbetter.*

GINA SAVINI 2 br.f. Ardoon 124–Repose (Relko 136) (1980 5g 6g 6fg 7g –
8.2s) Mar 14; 1,200Y; bad plater. *C. Nelson.*

GIN GAME 3 b.g. Red Alert 127–Watermark 83 (Henry the Seventh 125) **84**
(1979 5g^3 5fg 5g 1980 6g 7d^4 6s* 6g 6g^2 6g* 6s 6d 6d) neat, strong, attractive gelding; fair handicapper at his best but is none too consistent; won at Nottingham and Salisbury in the summer, scoring with ridiculous ease from Enchantment on latter; stays 7f; acts on soft going; blinkered final start; started slowly seventh outing and was reluctant to go to post on eighth. *W. Hastings-Bass.*

GINGER PUDDING 3 ch.f. Shiny Tenth 120–Shusheta (Martial 131) (1979 –
5d 6f 5g 5fg 5fg 1980 6f 5fg 5g 6s) compact, lightly-made filly; well beaten in varied company. *D. Marks.*

GINISTRELLI 3 b.g. Furry Glen 121–Humble Prayer (Shooting Chant) (1979 –
5g 5.1g 6fg 6fg^4 7d 1980 6g) neat gelding; little worthwhile form, including in a seller; should stay 7f+; blinkered final 2 starts at 2 yrs; sold 925 gns Ascot September Sales. *J. Winter.*

Ladbroke Derby Trial Stakes, Lingfield—Ginistrelli (USA) wins from Ribo Charter and Rontino

GINISTRELLI (USA) 3 b.c. Hoist the Flag–Friendly Circle (Round Table) (1979 6fg* 7g* 1980 10f3 12f* 12fg3) $370,000Y; attractive, rangy colt; did well physically over the winter; first foal; dam, smart stakes winner at 2 yrs, won at up to 9f; creditable 2½ lengths third to Henbit in Classic Trial Stakes at Sandown in April; quickened nicely to lead 1f out and stayed on strongly to hold off Ribo Charter (rec 5 lb) by a length in Ladbroke Derby Trial Stakes at Lingfield in May; didn't stride out too well on way to start and ran as though something was wrong with him when 7¾ lengths third to Prince Bee in Predominate Stakes at Kempton later in May; not seen out again; stayed 1½m; acted on firm going: stud in USA. *H. Cecil.* **117**

GINNIES PAL 3 gr.f. Sterling Bay or Pals Passage 115–Fainne Nua (Paddy's Birthday 110) (1979 5g 7fg 5fg 6fg 6f 1980 8d 10.1fg) unfurnished filly; poor plater; should stay 1m; has worn blinkers; ran poorly first outing. *T. Marshall.* —

GIN N' LIME 6 ch.g. Divine Gift 127–Fruit Cup 72 (Silver Shark 129) (1979 13.4f 14fg 1980 14g) poor maiden on flat; has been tried in blinkers; successful hurdler. *C. V. Miller.* —

GIOVANNA (USA) 3 b.f. Giacometti 130–Star Ship 115 (Dicta Drake 126) (1979 NR 1980 7d 7d3 10s 10g3 10s3) lengthy filly; third foal; dam won Ribblesdale Stakes and Lancashire Oaks; third in maiden races at Salisbury and Nottingham (2); will be well suited by 1½m; yet to race on a firm surface. *R. Price.* **63**

GIPSY PRINCE 5 ch.g. Sky Gipsy 117–Orseniga 97 (Privy Councillor 125) (1979 10.2s 10s 10.4f 1980 10.2d 10v 8f2 8d 8fg 9f 11.5fg) fair sort; stays 1m but probably not 1¼m; acts on firm going; started slowly fourth outing; has given us impression he is none too genuine. *R. Hollinshead.* **47 §**

GIRTON 4 b.f. Balidar 133–Miss Dorothy 87 (Major Portion 129) (1979 7f 5f^{3} 5g^{3} 5s* 6g* 6fg^{3} 1980 6s 5fg^{3} 5g^{2} 5.1f^{2} 5fg^{2} 5.1g 5d 5fg^{2} 5fg) good-topped filly; should stay further than 6f; acts on any going; blinkered final outing. *T. Waugh.* **66**

GIVEN 8 ch.g. Jolly Jet 111–Gift Token 107 (Firestreak 125) (1979 18s 17.1g 16fg 16f* 1980 17.1fg 16.5g) staying handicapper; acts on firm going. *J. Jenkins.* –

GLACIER BAY 2 b.c. Decoy Boy 129–Polar Cloud (Crisp and Even 116) (1980 5g 7fg 5d 5d) June 2; 360 2-y-o; first foal; dam never ran; behind in maiden races, twice finishing last. *R. Hannon.* –

GLAMOUR SHOW 4 b.g. Welsh Pageant 132–Maladie d'Amour 98 (Fidalgo 129) (1979 10s 14f^{3} 1980 16fg) compact gelding; lightly-raced maiden on flat; probably stays 2m. *J. Gifford.* –

GLASGOW CENTRAL 3 b.c. Roan Rocket 128–Nettlebed 84 (Hethersett 134) (1979 NR 1980 8fg 10s* 10.1s^{2} 12d^{4} 10.1s* 10f^{3}) compact, good sort; good mover; brother to Gairloch, a very smart performer at up to 1½m, and to smart miler Whistlefield; dam won at 7f and placed at up to 1½m; successful in minor events at Nottingham and Windsor in the summer; should stay 1½m; needs some give in the ground. *R. Price.* **84**

GLASGOWS PET 3 b.f. Mummy's Pet 125–Gold Bloom 72 (Klondyke Bill 125) (1979 5d 5v^{2} 5d^{3} 5v 5g^{2} 5fg* 5g^{4} 5fg^{3} 7fg 5g 1980 7v 5g 6h 6fg 6fg) leggy filly; won maiden race at Edinburgh at 2 yrs; didn't find her form in handicaps in 1980; not certain to stay 7f; probably acts on any going. *T. Fairhurst.* –

GLAZEPTA REWORK 6 br.g. Caliban 123–Benedetta da Castello (St Paddy 133) (1979 NR 1980 12.2s 13g 10fg 11.7fg 8f 10g) of little account nowadays. *K. Bridgwater.* –

GLEAMING WAVE 6 b.h. Sovereign Gleam 117–Sapphire Spray (Floribunda 136) (1979 12.2s^{2} 11.7g* 12fg* 12.2fg* 11g 11.5fg^{3} 12fg 12f 12.2fg^{3} 1980 12d 11.7fg 12f^{3} 12f* 12g 11.7g^{4} 11.7fg 12f 12.2fg 11s^{3} 12d 12d) middle-distance handicapper; got home by a neck from Mount Temple at Leicester in June; acts on any going; suitable mount for a boy. *G. Huffer.* **74**

GLEDSTONE 3 b.c. Royal Duet–Daughter of Rome (Lauso) (1979 5d 1980 12g) small colt; in rear in maiden races; sweated up only outing at 2 yrs. *A. Watson.* –

GLEEMING LADY 4 br.f. Pieces of Eight 128–Nonsuch Anne 58 (Tudor Melody 129) (1979 9g 8g 1980 8g) fair sort; plater; stays 1¼m; acts on any going except perhaps very firm; sometimes wears blinkers but does as well without; inconsistent. *R. Ward.* –

GLEN AIR 2 b.g. Furry Glen 121–Mountain Air 74 (Tudor Melody 129) (1980 6s 7fg 8fg 8d 8s^{3}) May 1; 1,600Y; neat gelding; second foal; dam placed over 1m and 1¼m; improved steadily, on final start finishing third, beaten 2 lengths and a neck, to Irish Heart in 19-runner minor event at Stockton in October; will stay 1¼m; acts on soft going. *G. Pritchard-Gordon.* **83**

GLENBANK LASS 2 ch.f. Patch 129–Pamaloo 93 (Pall Mall 132) (1980 5g 6fg* 8g*) Mar 25; 2,300Y; small filly; half-sister to a minor winner and a winner in Belgium; dam won from 6f to 1¼m; won 11-runner maiden auction event at Redcar in July and nursery at Thirsk in September, in latter running on strongly to score by 2½ lengths from Silver Leo after giving trouble at start; will be suited by middle distances. *H. Wharton.* **80**

GLENBURNIE 4 gr.f. Green God 128–Central Casting (Young Emperor 133) (1979 6d* 7fg 6fg 6d^{2} 6g 6fg* 6f 6fg^{3} 6s 1980 6fg^{3} 6g 6g^{2} 6fg* 6fg^{3} 7f) tall, unfurnished filly; led 2f out and ran on well when beating Russian Winter by 1½ lengths in handicap at Newmarket in August; stays 7f; acts on a firm and a soft surface; started rather slowly last 2 outings. *D. Ringer.* **79**

GLEN DANCER 3 b.f. Furry Glen 121–Fiddle Dancer 72 (Fidalgo 129) (1979 6f 7fg^{2} 7g 7s^{2} 7fg^{2} 7g* 1980 10fg^{3} 8g^{2} 8fg 8g 8g 8g 10s) rangy filly; placed in Lupe Stakes at Kempton in May (6½ lengths third to Vielle) and £3,400 handicap at Salisbury in June (went down by 2 lengths to Herons Hollow); below form in varied company afterwards; stays 1¼m; acts on any going; blinkered final start; sometimes sweats up. *M. Jarvis.* **94**

Prix de la Cote Normande, Deauville—Glenorum gets the verdict by a head from Argument. Un Reitre and Dom D'Albignac are third and fourth, followed by Opachisco and Fabulous Prince

GLEN GORSE 3 b.g. Forlorn River 124–Green Chartreuse 91 (French Beige 127) **62**
(1979 6f 1980 7f 5s 6g^2 6s^3 5f* 5d) useful sort; placed in seller prior to winning handicap at Wolverhampton in September (apprentice ridden); stayed 6f; acted on any going; sometimes bandaged in front; pulled up lame and was destroyed final start. *W. Wharton.*

GLENHAWK 4 b.g. Furry Glen 121–Genazzano (Shantung 132) (1979 8s* **84**
10d^2 10.6g^4 10fg^2 12d^4 10g^3 10f^3 8f^3 10d^4 1980 12f* 11f 14s) strong, rangy gelding; good walker and mover; made all when clear-cut winner of handicap at Lingfield in May; gelded after running moderately at Newbury the following month and wasn't seen out again until October (never dangerous); stays 1$\frac{1}{2}$m; acts on any going, but is possibly best served by a sound surface. *R. Price.*

GLENORUM (CAN) 3 b.c. Prove Out–Cailey Jane (Right Combination) (1979 **122**
7.5s^2 10s^4 1980 8v* 8s^2 9.2fg* 8.5d^4 10fg^3 10d* 13.5g* 12f) second foal; dam stakes-placed half-sister to prolific Canadian winner All Canadian; successful in 2 important races at Deauville in August, namely Group 3 Prix de la Cote Normande (got home by a head from Argument, gave 9 lb) and Group 2 Grand Prix de Deauville (led 1f out and kept on strongly to beat Perrault by 3 lengths); had earlier won maiden race at Saint-Cloud and valuable handicap at Longchamp and finished creditable third to Nemr (rec 3 lb), beaten just over $\frac{1}{2}$ length, in Prix la Force, also at Longchamp; reportedly finished lame in Prix de l'Arc de Triomphe at Longchamp in October; effective at 1$\frac{1}{4}$m and stays 1$\frac{3}{4}$m; seems to act on any going. *D. Smaga, France.*

GLEN O' THE DOWNES 3 b.g. Reformed Character 107–Coral Wreath **–**
(Chamossaire) (1979 6g 6fg 7g 8.2g 1980 12f 12f^3 12fg^4 12.2fg 13d^4 13d) big gelding; plating-class maiden; will stay 1$\frac{3}{4}$m; sold 1,150 gns Doncaster September Sales. *Denys Smith.*

GLENTANAR 2 b.f. Lochnager 132–Pink Standard 81 (Tudor Melody 129) **–**
(1980 5fg 6s 5f) seemingly useless. *M. W. Easterby.*

GLENVARA 3 b.g. Furry Glen 121–Varamette (Varano) (1979 7f 7s^4 8d **72**
1980 12.3f 10fg 12fg 10g^4 13d* 12.3fg^2 13.8g^3 15s 16g^3 15.8d^2 15d) useful-looking gelding; won maiden race at Ayr in July; ran respectably in handicaps several times afterwards; stays 2m; acts on a firm and a soft surface; has run creditably for a boy. *R. D. Peacock.*

GLEN WISE 4 b.f. Fair Decision 93§–Glen Paveh (Paveh 126) (1979 NR **–**
1980 12d) third foal; dam of little account; unquoted when well beaten in maiden race at Brighton in July, first outing. *B. Wise.*

GLIDE PATH 2 b.f. Sovereign Path 125–Falcon Bess (Falcon 131) (1980 7g) **–**
June 17; third foal; half-sister to fairly useful 1977 2-y-o 6f winner Beldale Ball (by Sharpen Up); dam useful winner over 7f and 1$\frac{1}{2}$m in Ireland; 50/1 when in rear in 18-runner maiden race won by Park Place at Yarmouth in September. *J. Winter.*

GLINT OF GOLD 2 b.c. Mill Reef 141–Crown Treasure (Graustark) (1980 **100**
7f* 7d^2 8s*) Apr 5; well-grown, rangy colt; excellent mover; first foal; dam very useful at 2 yrs in USA when winner over 5f, and is half-sister to smart filly

Mr Paul Mellon's "Glint of Gold"

Diomedia; winner of 2 good-class races, getting up on line to win 11-runner Sandwich Stakes at Ascot in July by a neck from Super Service and starting favourite when winning Group 1 Gran Criterium in Milan in October comfortably by 3½ lengths from Bold Brigadier; evens favourite for 11-runner Acomb Stakes at York in between but was never going well and stayed on at one pace to finish 3 lengths second to Cocaine; will stay middle distances; acts on any going. *I Balding.*

GLISSEEN 3 b.f. Shiny Tenth 120–Blesseen 71 (So Blessed 130) (1979 5s 1980 5f 7.6f 7g 10s 10d 9s² 7g 6g³ 10.1fg 12d 10fg 10s 9s 11s 8.2v) fair sort; plater; stays 9f; acts on soft going; wears blinkers. *F. Durr.* **46**

GLITTERTIND 2 b.c. Royal and Regal–Vesper Bell (Larkspur 128) (1980 8g² 7.5d 8d 7v* 7.5g) Mar 11; 22,000Y; tall, useful sort; third produce; half-brother to fairly useful 7f to 1½m winner Carnlea House (by Reindeer); dam ran once; won maiden race at Maisons-Laffitte in October by 2 lengths from Terrific Jim; also ran well when ½-length second to In Tissar in Prix de Fontenoy at Longchamp in September and when 4¾ lengths sixth of 10 to Big John in Prix Thomas Bryon at Saint-Cloud in November; will be suited by 1¼m+; acts on heavy going and has yet to race on a firm surface: unseated rider at start third outing. *A. Paus, France.* **113**

GLORIAMA 2 br.f. Targowice 130–Maria de Gloria (St Chad 120) (1980 5fg 6s⁴ 5f² 5d²) Apr 21; leggy, narrow filly; second foal; half-sister to winning Italian 3-y-o Marfisa (by Green God); dam never ran; creditable second in maiden races at Catterick in July and Pontefract (½ length behind odds-on Trytravelscene in moderate event) in August, on both occasions running as though a return to 6f will suit her well. *E. Weymes.* **68**

GLORINO 2 b.f. Bustino 136–Gloria Romana (Galivanter 131) (1980 6s 6fg⁴ 6d 5d) Feb 14; 18,000F; small, quite well-made filly; half-sister to 2-y-o winners **74**

in Italy by King Emperor and Prince Regent; dam useful winner over 5f and 1m in Italy; showed up well for a long way when 6¾ lengths fourth to Doc Marten in 7-runner Clarence House Stakes at Ascot in September; always outpaced when fifth of 18 behind Perlesse in minor event at Pontefract the following month; finds 5f inadequate and should stay at least 1m. *W. Hastings-Bass.*

GLORIOUS 2 ch.g. Hittite Glory 125–Cathays Park (Reliance II 137) (1980 6fg 6d 5g 5d 6d 6g4 6s) Mar 3; 8,000Y; strong gelding; fourth foal; half-brother to 2 winners, including Irish 1m winner Wendela (by Manacle); favourite when 8¼ lengths fourth of 23 to Hurtwood Lass in valuable seller at Doncaster in September; will stay 1m. *M. W. Easterby.* **65**

GLORIOUS IDEA 2 ro.c. Hittite Glory 125–Taurette (Major Portion 129) (1980 5g 7d 5g4 8.2d 6g 7fg) Apr 7; 6,600Y; neat colt; bad plater; not sure to stay 1m; sold to Mrs G. Forbes 640 gns Newmarket Autumn Sales. *P. Haslam.* **53**

GLOWING TAN (USA) 3 b.c. Plenty Old–Serving Wench (Mister Black) (1979 7fg 1980 7d* 10.4f3 8fg2 8fg2 12d2 10g2 10g2 10g4 11f 8g2 8fg*) workmanlike colt; won maiden race at Newcastle in May and £2,500 race at Newbury in September; sweated up and didn't impress in paddock on latter occasion but gave a genuine performance to beat Intinto by ½ length; effective at 1m and stays 1½m; acts on firm going and a soft surface; ran a bit freely in blinkers eighth outing; consistent. *R. Sheather.* **89**

GLUTTON 5 b.g. Major Portion 129–Field Daisy (White Fire III) (1979 NR 1980 10s 15.5g) of little account. *A. Davison.* **–**

GLYNDEBOURNE (USA) 2 ch.c. Annihilate 'Em–Worthy Charm (Boldnesian) (1980 5fg 5f3 6d2 6g*) Apr 5; $17,000Y; robust, useful sort; third foal; half-brother to a winner by Aljamin; dam won 6f claiming race at 2 yrs; not extended when winning £2,700 event at Leicester in July by 1½ lengths from Red Gloves; had previously run well when 1½ lengths second of 11 to Bonnie Charlie in Piper Champagne Stakes at Salisbury; will probably stay 1m. *G. Balding.* **89**

GNOS 6 b.g. Song 132–No Recall 85 (Tutankhamen) (1979 6d 7d 6fg 6h 7fg 7g 6g 7f2 8d 7fg 1980 6g 5f 7fg 6f 8s) strong gelding; stays 1m; acts on any going; usually wears blinkers; suitable mount for an apprentice; sometimes sweats up; has worn a tongue strap; inconsistent; bandaged in 1980. *P. Wigham.* **–**

GOBLIN 5 ch.h. Sun Prince 128–Rocelle 101 (Sodium 128) (1979 10d 10s 11fg 10d 12fg 12fg3 12g2 12fg* 12fg 13fg 12f2 12f* 10d 1980 12f) big, strong, workmanlike horse; good mover; useful handicapper when trained by W. Wightman; very burly only outing of 1980 (pulled hard); suited by 1½m; needs a sound surface; sold 1,700 gns Doncaster October Sales. *J. Douglas-Home.* **–**

GO COPPER 2 ch.c. The Go-Between 129–Copper Gold (Democratic 124) (1980 5fg 6g 5fg 5d) May 13; 2,200Y; plain colt; no sign of ability, including in a seller; blinkered fourth outing; sold 1,000 gns Ascot October Sales. *M. Tompkins.* **–**

GO DIANA 3 gr. or ro.f. The Go-Between 129–My Diana 94 (Sovereign Path 125) (1979 5v 5f 1980 6fg 5fg 6f 6fg 6fg 6s 7g 7fg 7g 7g) leggy filly; poor plater; stays 7f; blinkered last 4 starts, sweating up on first occasion; sold 675 gns Ascot October Sales. *W. Musson.* **–**

GODS MARK (USA) 4 ch.c. Little Current–Director (Swaps) (1979 6g 6fg3 7f* 1980 8g 10g 8fg* 7.2fg2 6fg* 8fg 7v) well-made, quite attractive colt; beat Combine Harvester 3 lengths in Sean Graham Handicap at the Curragh in May and Thousandfold a short head in Matt Gallagher Sprint Stakes at Phoenix Park in July; ran well when 2 lengths second of 8 to Hard Fought in John of Gaunt Stakes at Haydock in between; having first outing for 2 months when about 10 lengths fifth of 7 behind Known Fact in Queen Elizabeth II Stakes at Ascot in September; tailed-off last of 9 behind Moorestyle in Prix de la Foret at Longchamp the following month; stays 1m; acts on firm going; consistent. *C. Grassick, Ireland.* **108**

GODWIT 4 b.g. Birdbook 110–French Parade 113 (March Past 124) (1979 5v 5s3 7v 5g2 6fg 1980 8s 5f 5fg 6f 8fg* 10g 8g) compact gelding; fair plater; sold out of C. James's stable 1,500 gns after winning easily at Brighton in May; suited by 1m (well beaten over 1¼m); seems to act on any going; sometimes wears blinkers and did so on last 3 starts. *A. Moore.* **50**

GO GO BUST 4 br.f. Bog Road 119–Lady Gregory (Manacle 123) (1979 NR 1980 8f 6f) lightly-made filly; bad mover; probably useless. *K. Bridgwater.* **–**

GO GREEN 3 b.f. Saulingo 122–Red Over Amber (Amber Rama 133) (1979 6f 5g 5d 1980 5g) ex-Irish filly; first foal; dam never ran; in rear in maiden and minor events; sold 420 gns Ascot July Sales; resold same venue 420 gns in September. *C. James.* —

GOING STRAIT 3 b.g. Manacle 123–Miss Atalanta 83 (Hethersett 134) (1979 5d 6fg³ 7g³ 7g² 1980 7v 8s 5f³ 6f* 6g 5fg 6g 7g⁴ 7g⁴ 7g 10d⁴ 12g) good-bodied gelding; won 23-runner maiden race at Newbury in May by 2 lengths from Shady Spring; ran respectably in handicaps on several occasions afterwards; stays 1¼m; acts well on firm going; blinkered final start. *R. Smyth.* 79

GO-IT-ALONE 3 br.f. Linacre 133–Leuze (Vimy 132) (1979 5v 5d² 5d* 6d 6f 6fg⁴ 7f 1980 10s 10f 8f 10.6fg 9fg³) strong filly; only plating class; should stay 1¼m; blinkered final outing at 2 yrs (ran very wide into straight). *J. Berry.* —

GOLDBORN DAVID 2 b.g. Wabash 99–Panyana 88 (Pandemonium 118) (1980 6g 8.2s) May 4; lightly-made non-thoroughbred gelding; half-brother to fairly useful middle-distance performer Goodison (by Good Light) and 6f to 1¼m winner Mister Chicken (by Sermoney); dam won over 5f at 2 yrs; blinkered when well behind in sellers at Newcastle and Hamilton in second half of season. *C. Crossley.* —

GOLD BREEZE 2 b. or br.f. Persian Breeze 121–Gold Poulet 84 (Goldhill 125) (1980 5f 5fg* 5d³ 5fg 5d 5d 5f) May 1; strong filly; half-sister to fairly useful 1978 2-y-o 5f winner Argentina Bound (by Amber Rama); dam ran only at 5f; led well inside final furlong to win 17-runner maiden race at Catterick in June by a neck from Oxton Anne; put up best subsequent effort when eighth to Think Ahead in nursery at Redcar in September on final appearance; unlikely to stay 6f; ran deplorably in blinkers fifth and sixth starts; sold to P. Calver 540 gns Doncaster October Sales. *W. H. H. Williams.* 66

GOLD CLAIM 8 ch.h. Lucky Brief 128–Gold Cypher 76 (Pardao 120) (1979 10v 12.2s 12d 11.7d 8f 22.2fg 12.2fg 16g³ 1980 18f 12fg 10fg 17.1fg² 19f 16.5fg 16fg 16g 17.1d 18d) compact horse; stays 2m but has done all his winning at middle distances; particularly well suited by soft ground; has worn blinkers; suitable mount for an apprentice; slipped and unseated rider on first outing of 1980; trained most of season by M. Salaman. *V. Soane.* 32

GOLDEN ALRAY 2 br.f. Ballynockan 112–Mollie (I Say 125) (1980 6d 6g 7d³) small, leggy filly; third reported foal; half-sister to a winning 2-y-o plater; dam poor maiden; 5/1 when 4½ lengths third of 16 to Quest in maiden race at Wolverhampton in July; stays 7f. *B. McMahon.* 62

GOLDEN BABY 2 ch.f. Sharpen Up 127–Obedience (Reliance II 137) (1980 5f 6fg 5d⁴ 5d 5fg 6g 5d 6s) May 23; 5,000Y; small, compact filly; half-sister to a winning plater; will stay 1m; sweating and tailed off final outing. *A. W. Jones.* 52

GOLDEN BOWL (USA) 2 b.f. Vaguely Noble 140–Rose Bowl 133 (Habitat 134) (1980 6fg² 7g 6fg² 7g* 7g*) 111

Leap Lively and the exceptionally well-bred Golden Bowl are two excellent prospects from the same stable for the top three-year-old fillies middle-distance races in 1981. Leap Lively, successful in the Group 3 Hoover Fillies Mile at Ascot, did more as a two-year-old but Golden Bowl's performance in winning the Malton Stakes over seven furlongs at York in October on her final outing suggests that she's very little behind. Both Golden Bowl's sire and dam improved late in their two-year-old careers before developing into outstanding racehorses the following year. Although it's expecting too much for Golden Bowl to turn out as good as either of them there's no reason why she shouldn't train on and make a smart three-year-old.

Golden Bowl lined up at York the only previous winner in a field of fourteen. In September she had justified favouritism in a seventeen-runner maiden race at Salisbury, running on gamely under hard driving to hold off Fiesta Fun and Norfolk Queen. However, that performance wasn't good enough to make her favourite again in the Malton Stakes; she started second favourite, with a 5-lb penalty, to Cardie Girl who five weeks earlier in the Crathorne Stakes on the same course had finished an excellent second on her debut to the very useful Star Pastures. As the betting suggested they might, Cardie Girl and Golden Bowl dominated the race. Cardie Girl, breaking smartly, was soon up with the leaders and when going clear three furlongs from home looked the likely winner. Golden Bowl by this stage had improved her position from the middle of the field to take second place. Approaching the two-furlong marker Cardie Girl began to hang to her left and shortly afterwards Golden Bowl, switched to her outside, moved alongside. Taking the lead below the distance Golden Bowl ran on strongly to hold off Cardie Girl's renewed effort by a length; the third horse, Red Lady, was fully fifteen lengths behind. There seems little reason to doubt that Golden Bowl showed considerable improvement. The Malton Stakes was truly run and the subsequent performance of Red Lady was creditable—two weeks later she went down by one and a half lengths to Segos in a fourteen-runner maiden race at Redcar.

Golden Bowl (USA) (b.f. May 19, 1978)	Vaguely Noble (b 1965)	Vienna (ch 1957)	Aureole
			Turkish Blood
		Noble Lassie (b 1956)	Nearco
			Belle Sauvage
	Rose Bowl (b 1972)	Habitat (b 1966)	Sir Gaylord
			Little Hut
		Roseliere (br 1965)	Misti IV
			Peace Rose

Golden Bowl is a lightly-made, attractive filly. She was being carried by Rose Bowl when the latter was purchased by Paul Mellon in March 1978, along with Roseliere, in a deal that wound up the Engelhard family's notable involvement in racehorse ownership. Rose Bowl's second foal is a filly by Nijinsky, and she is due to foal to him again in 1981. Rose Bowl won six races from five furlongs to a mile and a quarter, including the Queen Elizabeth II Stakes (twice) and the Champion Stakes. In sixteen outings she failed to make the frame on only two occasions, the second of those when attempting a mile and a half in the Washington International on her final appearance. Like almost all the representatives of the miler Habitat, Rose Bowl found the distance beyond her. However, there's little doubt that Golden Bowl will stay the trip. Roseliere won over it and so did Rose Bowl's half-brother Ile de Bourbon (by Nijinsky), while her sire, Vaguely Noble, winner of the 1968 Prix de l'Arc de Triomphe, has got plenty of top-class winners over a mile and a half and, in Dahlia, Exceller and Duke of Marmalade, some that have won good races over further as well. *I. Balding.*

Mr Paul Mellon's "Golden Bowl"

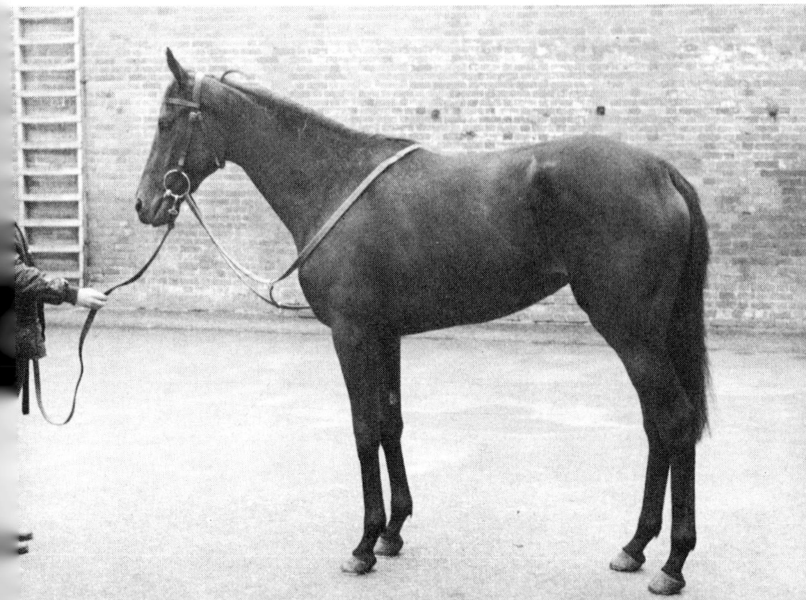

GOLDEN BRIGADIER 2 b.c. Brigadier Gerard 144–Golden Fez (Aureole 132) (1980 7s² 7f 7g³ 7g* 7.6f) Mar 14; 25,500F, 25,000Y; strong colt; half-brother to useful French middle-distance stayer Marriageable (by Great Nephew); dam, French middle-distance winner, is daughter of 1,000 Guineas winner Zabara; stayed on very strongly to catch weakening Beeleigh when winning 12-runner maiden race at Chester in August by ½ length; will be well suited by middle distances; probably needs some give in the ground; blinkered last 2 outings. *C. Brittain.* **83**

GOLDEN CAGE 3 b.f. Rheingold 137–Criminelle (Crepello 136) (1979 NR 1980 7f 11fg 8.2d) well-made filly; second foal; dam lightly-raced sister to 2 winners; in rear in varied company, including selling; started slowly last 2 starts; sold out of J. Dunlop's stable 1,000 gns Newmarket July Sales after second outing. *J. Fitzgerald.* –

GOLDEN COBWEB 4 ch.f. Midsummer Night II 117–Golden Shot 73 (Miralgo 130) (1979 10d 8f 1980 10.1g) bad maiden. *G. Balding.* –

GOLDEN ELDER 5 gr.h. High Top 131–Silver Birch 122 (Silver Shark 129) (1979 8d³ 6g² 7f³ 10g³ 8fg 6f* 7fg 7g* 7.2g³ 7.3g² 1980 8d 7fg 7.6f* 7.6f 8g 7d⁴ 8fg* 8f 8g³ 7fg⁴ 8d*) big, lengthy horse; useful handicapper; won comfortably at Lingfield in May (from Haddfan) and Goodwood in July (from Be Better) and gamely at Ascot in October (from Royaber); also ran well on other occasions, including when close third to Changabang in Julio Mariner Handicap at Doncaster; very well suited by a mile nowadays and stays 1¼m; acts on any going but goes particularly well on top-of-the-ground; consistent; a hard puller who needs strong handling and has won only for J. Mercer since his 2-y-o days. *T. Waugh.* **106**

GOLDEN FLAK (USA) 2 b.c. Ack Ack–Faith in Gold (Nashua) (1980 6g 6fg 6fg⁴ 7.6f* 8fg³ 8d* 8d⁴) Mar 28; $38,000Y; neat, strong colt; brother to a minor winner and half-brother to winning hurdler Gold T.V. (by T.V. Lark); dam half-sister to $309,000 earner Seaneen; found his form in the autumn, winning nurseries at Lingfield and Newbury, latter by short head from Belloc; took on better company on final start, finishing 12 lengths fourth of 9 to Panjandrum in Premio Tevere at Rome in November; will stay middle distances; probably acts on any going. *M. Jarvis.* **101**

GOLDEN GAYLE 8 ch.g. Lord Gayle 124–Golden Samantha 88 (Sammy Davis 129) (1979 10d 12f 11g² 12f³ 10f 11g³ 12g⁴ 10.2fg 12g 10fg 1980 10g 12fg 12fg* 12d³ 12fg) middle-distance handicapper; always going well when winning claiming event at Newmarket in August by 3 lengths from Malza; acts on any going; good mount for an amateur or apprentice rider; unseated rider when blinkered in 1979. *P. Rohan.* **56**

GOLDEN GLADE 5 ro.g. Precipice Wood 123–Hanina 83 (Darling Boy 124) (1979 16v 16g 16s 18s 12fg 15fg 16fg 12f⁴ 12g 1980 12f) poor plater; stays well; sometimes wears blinkers; sold 800 gns Doncaster August Sales. *R. Page.* –

GOLDEN HOLLY 2 ch.c. Golden Mallard 103–Holly Doon (Doon 124) (1980 6f) first foal; leggy colt; dam poor plater; 100/1, wasn't well away when tenth of 11 in small race won by Cavalry Twill at Pontefract in September. *J. Carr.* –

GOLDEN HORSESHOE 3 b.g. Tarboosh–Christmas Gift (Princely Gift 137) (1979 6g 8g 1980 10.8v 10fg 12f 16g 12fg) close-coupled gelding; poor maiden. *R. Akehurst.* –

GOLDEN KARMA 2 b.f. Condorcet–Eternal Youth (Continuation 120) (1980 5fg 5g 5fg) Apr 27; 880F, 3,000Y; small filly; half-sister to Irish 5f winner Trendy Youth (by Be Friendly); dam Irish 7f and 7.5f winner; poor maiden; bred to stay at least 1m; sold 310 gns Ascot November Sales. *D. Kent.* –

GOLDEN LEICESTER 4 br.c. Workboy 123–Snow Rum (Quorum 126) (1979 7g 1980 6f 8f 7f⁴ 7g⁴ 8f 10d 7f 8d) strong colt; stays 7f (well beaten over further); acts on any going; blinkered last 2 starts; sometimes sweats up; has worn bandages. *P. Wigham.* **71** d

GOLDEN LIBRA 5 b.h. Goldhill 125–Lush Pool 70 (Dumbarnie 125) (1979 6s 6d 6s 1980 5d 5s 6g) strong horse; has been hobdayed; very useful 2-y-o; poor performer nowadays; stays 6f; probably acts on any going. *D. Kent.* –

GOLDEN MATCH 2 ch.g. Royal Match 117–Hunea (Hornbeam 130) (1980 6g³ 7fg) Feb 19; 6,200F, 15,500Y; half-brother to minor winners here and in Belgium; dam lightly raced; 8/1 when 3 lengths third of 9 to Sones in maiden race at Yarmouth in September; well beaten in similar event at Lingfield the following month; likely to need 1¼m+ at 3 yrs. *G. Pritchard-Gordon.* **70**

GOLDEN REEF 3 b.rig. Mill Reef 141–Photo Flash 119 (Match III 135) (1979 NR 1980 10g^{2} 14f^{4}) well-made, attractive sort; half-brother to very useful stayer Golden River (by Rheingold) and fairly useful Lucky Shot (by Reform), a winner at up to 1$\frac{3}{4}$m; dam second in 1,000 Guineas and half-sister to Welsh Pageant; in frame in maiden races at Nottingham and Newmarket early in year; will stay well; sold 1,600 gns Newmarket Autumn Sales. *H. Cecil.* **68**

GOLDEN RIVER 4 b.g. Rheingold 137–Photo Flash 119 (Match III 135) (1979 9fg 13.3f^{2} 12g^{4} 13.3g 12g^{2} 15s* 12h* 16fg* (w.o.) 1980 13.3f^{3} 16.1fg^{4} 12fg^{2} 12g*) lengthy gelding; very useful performer; enterprisingly ridden and stole race when beating Sea Pigeon by 6 lengths in amateur riders race at Beverley in July; runner-up to clever winner Prince Rheingold in Watt Memorial Stakes on same course the previous month; stays well; acts on any going; ran moderately in blinkers fourth outing in 1979; gelded after last outing and is hurdling with R. Turnell. *H. Cecil.* **107**

GOLDEN ROYALTY 3 b.f. Royalty 130–Golden Wonder (Golden Cloud) (1979 5s 5s 6f 7g 8g 1980 10f 12g 12.2f^{2} 13.8g 14.6d^{4} 15.8fg 12.2d) unfurnished filly; only plating class; best run at 1$\frac{1}{2}$m on firm going; has worn blinkers; sometimes sweats up. *J. Calvert.* –

GOLDEN TULCHAN 2 b.g. Golden Dipper 119–Tulchan 95 (Tudor Melody 129) (1980 5s 5f 5fg 7s 7g 7d 6fg) Feb 5; 2,500Y; neat gelding; useless plater; wears blinkers; sold, presumably for export, 350 gns Doncaster November Sales. *W. Marshall.* –

GOLDEN VIRGINIAN 5 ch.g. Virginia Boy 106–Golden Hostess (Kythnos 126) (1979 7f 8f 7f 8.2g^{2} 1980 8.2fg) poor plater; stays 1m; acts on a firm surface; has been tried in blinkers. *J. Mulhall.* –

GOLDEN VOW 6 b.g. Good Bond 122–Sunsaly 75 (Sallymount 125) (1979 8s^{2} 10f 8fg 10g* 10s* 12f 10f 1980 12g 10fg) fair handicapper at his best; no form in 1980 (not seen out until September and needed race on reappearance); stays 1$\frac{1}{4}$m; acts on any going; suitable mount for an inexperienced rider; useful hurdler. *R. Hartop.* –

GOLD FLOOR 3 b.c. Goldhill 125–Floor Show 78 (Galivanter 131) (1979 5s 5g 5g 7fg 7g 1980 8fg 10.8s 8g 9.4g) small colt; little sign of ability in maiden and minor events. *M. Bradley.* –

GOLD GIFT 5 ch.m. Gold Rod 129–Wood Anemone 83 (Tangle 121) (1979 10.1fg 10.1fg 10.1fg 12f 1980 10.1fg^{4} 12f^{2} 10fg 12d) poor plater; stays 1$\frac{1}{2}$m; acts on firm going. *I. Dudgeon.* **36**

GOLD GUINEA 2 b.f. Golden Dipper 119–Brief Note 92 (Counsel 118) (1980 5g 5fg 5fg 6s^{4} 6fg^{2} 6s 6s 5s 5g 5s) Feb 12; 800F, 860Y; small filly; half-sister to 6f winner Piercing Note (by Bleep-Bleep); dam needed at least 1$\frac{1}{4}$m; plater; went down by only $\frac{1}{2}$ length to Bar Room Girl when apprentice ridden at Warwick in June; will stay 7f; probably acts on any going; blinkered final outing. *W. Musson.* **50**

GOLDLINER ABBEY 2 b. or br.g. Abwah 118–Bright and Early (Rise 'N Shine II) (1980 5v 5d^{3} 5f 7g* 7fg^{2} 7g) Mar 28; 1,450F (privately), 1,400Y; fair sort; half-brother to 2 winners here and abroad; dam never ran; won 11-runner seller at Beverley in June by 2$\frac{1}{2}$ lengths from Normans Boy; went down by a short head to Smuggle in similar race at Redcar the following month but would probably have won if jockey hadn't stopped riding when clear 1f out; suited by 7f; possibly not at his best on very firm going; blinkered last 3 outings; ran best races for apprentice A. Proud. *J. Hardy.* **62**

GOLDLINER GAME 3 ch.g. King's Leap 111–Hasten Up (Galivanter 131) (1979 5s 5g 6g^{4} 6f* 7f* 7.2g 7fg^{2} 7f^{2} 8fg^{4} 7fg 7g^{3} 1980 7d 7d 7f 7fg^{2} 7f^{4} 7fg^{3} 7.2g 8fg^{2} 8.2d^{4} 7g) big, rangy gelding; quite a moderate handicapper; stays 1m; suited by firm ground; suitable mount for an apprentice. *J. Hardy.* **86**

GOLDLINER IMP 2 b.g. Import 127–Strathclair (Klairon 131) (1980 5g 5fg 5g 6g^{4} 6d^{4} 7f^{2} 7g) May 28; 3,000Y; strong, useful sort; half-brother to a winner in South Africa; dam placed at up to 7f in Ireland and half-sister to good sprinter Right Strath; in frame in maiden company, finishing 1$\frac{1}{2}$ lengths second of 15 to Violino Fandango at Catterick in July; suited by 6f and 7f; ran poorly in nursery final start. *J. Hardy.* **74**

GOLD MEASURE 3 br.c. Goldhill 125–Fair Measure (Quorum 126) (1979 7d 8d 1980 11fg 8fg 10.1fg 8fg 8s 9.4fg) lengthy colt; poor form in varied company, including selling; sold out of P. M. Taylor's stable 1,800 gns Ascot July Sales after fifth start. *S. Holland.* –

GOLD PROSPECTOR 5 b.g. Gold Rod 129–Prairie Girl (Crocket 130) (1979 6v 5.1g 6f 6fg 5g 6f* 6g 6d 1980 5f 5g 6g 6fg) good-bodied gelding; no form in 1980 but still looked in need of race final outing; best form at 6f; acts on any going; has worn blinkers; inconsistent. *R. Armstrong.* —

GOLDRIDGE 3 ch.g. Gold Rod 129–Catherine Rose 59 (Floribunda 136) (1979 5f 6fg 7g 1980 9.4fg 10fg) strong, compact gelding; well beaten in maiden and minor events. *S. Mellor.* —

GOLD RIVER (FR) 3 ch.f. Riverman 131–Glaneuse 118 (Snob 130) (1979 NR 1980 10g* 10d* 10.5d^{2} 12d^{3} 13.5g* 12f^{4} 12.5d^{2} 15.5v*) **125**

How well the forthcoming Cup races survive the retirement of Le Moss remains to be seen. If owners can't be persuaded to run their best horses Ardross may have things pretty much his own way, and any races without Ardross must be in danger of becoming as insignificant if not as dull as most of those in France over the past two seasons. But that's looking on the black side. There are several interesting staying prospects around, one of the best among them the French filly Gold River, who may well be trained for long distances even though she is capable of high-class form over a mile and a half.

Gold River ran out a most impressive winner of the Prix Royal-Oak, the French St Leger, at Longchamp in October on her eighth and final outing of the season, preventing a clean sweep by the older horses (four-year-olds and upwards have been allowed in since 1979). Well behind in next to last place for most of the way and still at the rear on the home turn, she came storming up the straight to go clear a furlong out and win by three lengths and a short head from Monsieur Marcel and the favourite Ardross. Shafaraz, Vincent and the previous year's winner Niniski were the only others in the field of thirteen still in reasonable touch at the finish; the two best-known of the three-year-old colts, the Grand Prix de Paris winner Valiant Heart and second What A Joy, ran very disappointingly. Ardross' failure to shake off the relatively-unknown Monsieur Marcel and old Shafaraz suggests he might not have been at his best and that he may give Gold River more to do another time, over a longer distance on better ground perhaps. That, also, remains to be seen. There's not much doubt on her running in the Royal-Oak that Gold River will stay further, for the race provided a thorough test of stamina thanks to Niniski's pacemaker Lindoro's setting a strong gallop on the heavy going; and there's not much doubt, either, that Gold River acts on any going, although she's reportedly ideally suited by an easy surface.

Gold River ran fourth on firm going in the Prix Vermeille two outings earlier, beating Cairn Rouge, Mariella and Aryenne among others; the winner Mrs Penny beat her under two lengths. In between, Gold River finished a close second to Sagaro's half-sister Mariella in the Prix de Royallieu at Longchamp on terms 3 lb worse than in the Vermeille. Those two performances, especially the former, are plenty good enough to justify running her again at middle distances as a four-year-old but, having seen her in the Royal-Oak, we can well believe the report that her trainer has his eye on the Cup races.

Gold River (Fr) (ch.f. 1977)	Riverman (b 1969)	Never Bend (b 1960)	Nasrullah
			Lalun
		River Lady (b 1963)	Prince John
			Nile Lily
	Glaneuse (b 1966)	Snob (b 1959)	Mourne
			Senones
		Glamour (br 1960)	Djebe
			Tudor Gleam

Gold River's record is one of improvement. Unraced at two because of a

Prix Royal-Oak, Longchamp—Gold River wins most impressively from Monsieur Marcel, Ardross (far side) and Shafaraz. Vincent (No. 5) and Niniski are the next to finish

setback, she made her first two appearances winning appearances, picking up small races over a mile and a quarter at Longchamp in May and June. Thereafter she moved up to fillies pattern races, and was beaten at around a mile and a quarter in the Prix Fille de l'Air at Saint-Cloud (by Detroit) and at a mile and a half in the Prix de Minerve at Evry (third to Great Verdict) before winning the Prix de Pomone over a distance just short of a mile and three quarters at Deauville. She was most impressive at Deauville, coming from behind in a slowly-run race and beating Mariella virtually on the bridle by three lengths; the Pomone is open to older animals, and Anifa took fourth place.

Gold River's dam Glaneuse made a steady start to her stud career after a spectacular one on the racecourse, producing three minor winners in France—her only foals in the six years prior to Gold River's arrival. Gracious (by Habitat), who has since become the dam of the good French two-year-old Greenway, was her first winner, followed by Glena and Sir Godfrey, neither of which appeared to stay anywhere near so well as its full sister Gold River. Glaneuse had a magnificent season at middle distances as a three-year-old, crowning it with a win in the Gran Premio del Jockey Club at Milan; in France she finished third to Saraca in the Prix Vermeille besides winning the Prix Chloe and the Prix de Malleret. She is a half-sister to the 1970 One Thousand Guineas runner-up Gleam out of a winning half-sister to the Royal Hunt Cup winner Regal Light. The family was in the public eye in England recently as a result of the success of the hurdler Gleason, a son of Gleam.

One has to say that Gold River's pedigree is not that of an out-and-out stayer by any means: neither her sire nor dam raced beyond a mile and a half, and her maternal grandsire Snob, fourth in the Prix de l'Arc de Triomphe in 1962, was probably best at a mile and a half. So until she's run in a Cup race there's bound to be a doubt about her at extreme distances, however small that doubt after her performance in the Royal-Oak. Gold River, an attractive filly, is genuine and consistent. For one who stays as well as she does, she has a formidable turn of finishing speed. *A. Head, France.*

GOLD SONG 5 b.h. Song 132–Wardress 93 (Anwar 120) (1979 5v* 6d 6d 5fg 5fg* 5f2 5d 5fg2 1980 5fg4 6g 5fg 5f 5f2 5s 6fg 5d 5.6g) very useful handicapper at his best; finished well when length second of 15 to Susarma at Epsom in June, best effort in 1980; best form at up to 6f; acts on any going; wears blinkers; retained 1,700 gns Newmarket Autumn Sales. *N. Guest.* **104** d

GOLDSPUN 2 b.c. Weavers' Hall 122–Albigold 87 (Above Suspicion 127) (1980 8g 7.9v*) May 25; 3,000Y; fifth living foal; half-brother to Irish 3-y-o 1½m winner Chamorro (by Northfields); dam won from 7f to 2m; won 9-runner maiden race at Dundalk in October by 2½ lengths from Manilla Bay; should make a fairly useful stayer. *J. M. Oxx, Ireland.* **93**

GOLD T.V. (USA) 6 ch.h. T.V. Lark–Faith in Gold (Nashua) (1979 16f 1980 12.2fg 16.1d) of little account on flat. *W. Clay.* —

GO LEASING 2 ch.f. Star Appeal 133–Grand Velvet 83 (Grand Roi 118) (1980 6fg* 6g4 6d 7g 7d 7g 7s* 7g*) Feb 19; 5,000F; compact, sharp sort; half-sister to a winner in Belgium; dam stayed well; won 16-runner maiden race at Lingfield in June by 1½ lengths from Hunston; put up a much improved display when racing on soft ground for first time, striding clear in tremendous style up hill to win 17-runner nursery at Newmarket in October by 5 lengths from Master Golfer; defied a penalty at Leicester the following month, finishing strongly to beat Minmax a neck; proved incapable of beating very useful fillies on third and fourth starts; will be suited by middle distances; acts on **111**

Tattersall Nursery Handicap, Newmarket—Go Leasing runs away from Master Golfer and Singalong Joe

a firm surface but clearly revels in the mud; a very useful filly who should win more races when conditions are in her favour in 1981. *G. Harwood.*

GO LIGHTLY 3 b.f. Galivanter 131–Rosia Steps 98 (Red Pins 114) (1979 5fg 6g² 7g 6fg 5f 1980 6d 5fg 6fg 7fg 8d 8fg) leggy filly; has shown no form since 2 yrs; stays 6f; unseated rider coming out of paddock and started slowly when blinkered fourth appearance. *R. Price.* —

GO LISSAVA 2 gr. or ro.c. The Go-Between 129–Lissava Queen (Our Babu 131) (1980 5f 5h 5fg⁴ 6fg⁴ 5d³ 6fg³ 6g 5d 5fg) Mar 15; 720F, 1,050Y; small colt; third produce; dam never ran; in frame in sellers, final occasion when going down by 2 necks to Just Archy at Pontefract in July; better suited by 6f than 5f, and may stay 7f; blinkered second outing; sold to D. Chapman 650 gns Doncaster October Sales. *J. Hardy.* **51**

GO MARTELL 3 b.g. Golden Mallard 103–Ruritania (Pampered King 121) (1979 5s 5s 6f 6fg⁴ 7fg 7fg⁴ 7f 8fg 8g* 8g⁴ 8.2s* 7d⁴ 1980 10g 10f 10s* 11g) compact gelding; won handicap at Nottingham in June (apprentice ridden); stays 1¼m; revels in soft going; has been tried in blinkers but seems better without. *J. Doyle.* **64**

GO MAYS 3 b.f. Realm 129–How Much (Palestine 133) (1979 5f 5f 1980 7f 5f 5fg) tall, lengthy filly; well beaten in varied company. *R. Akehurst.* —

GO MY LOVE 2 b.c. Pitcairn 126–Star Set (Sunny Way 120) (1980 6d 7fg 8g³ 8fg² 8d² 8.2s³) Mar 7; 7,000F, 21,000Y; neat, well-made colt; half-brother to 1979 2-y-o 5f and 6f winner Rosette (by Red Alert) and 2 winners in Ireland; dam never ran; placed in maiden and minor events, including when going down by 1½ lengths to Cliphome at Beverley in September and by a short head to Rosie Black at Warwick in October (led 2f out and was caught on post); stays 1m; probably acts on any going. *J. Dunlop.* **83**

Irish St Leger, the Curragh—an easy win for Gonzales who is chased home by Good Thyne

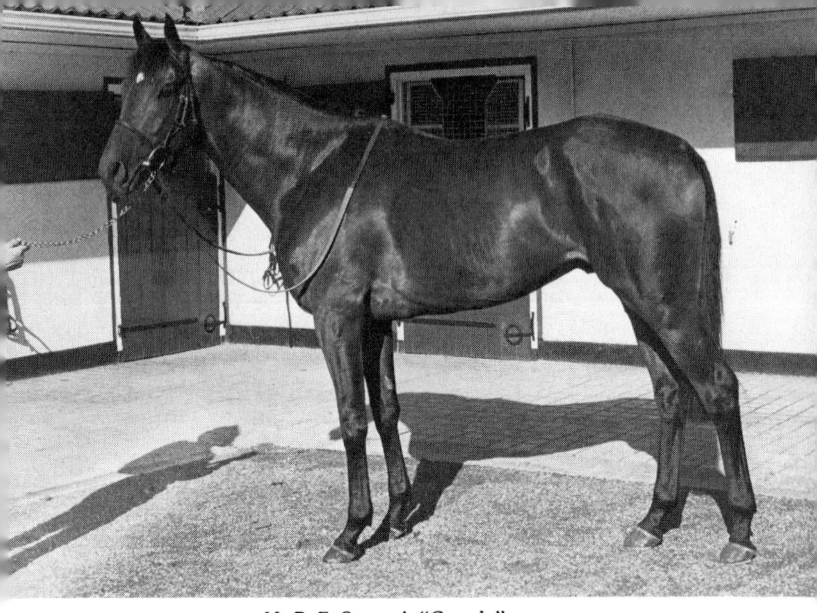

Mr R. E. Sangster's "Gonzales"

GONZALES (USA) 3 b.c. Vaguely Noble 140–Gazala 124 (Dark Star) (1979 NR 1980 10g* 12fg* 12fg 12s* 10g 14s*) **120**

Though it has been won by some very good horses in the past decade the Irish St Leger at the Curragh is all too often contested by fields whose overall quality is mediocre by classic standards. The 1980 race was no exception, only two of the eight runners, Gonzales and the Irish Sweeps Derby third Ramian, having form worthy of a Group 1 event. With Ramian running moderately Gonzales had a relatively simple task and he duly landed the odds easily, providing his trainer with a seventh success in the race in the process. Always close up, he led half a mile out, soon went clear and was in no danger in the last two furlongs, winning unchallenged by five lengths from Good Thyne with El Cito, beaten a long way in handicaps on his three previous starts and beaten in another on his only subsequent one, three lengths away third.

Prior to the Irish St Leger Gonzales had won three of his five outings, starting favourite each time and twice at odds on; he had been found out in his two sternest tests, the Prix du Jockey-Club and the Joe McGrath Memorial Stakes. He arrived for the former race at Chantilly in June with quite a reputation, having won a £1,900 event at Leopardstown by six lengths and the Gallinule Stakes at the Curragh comfortably by three from Good Thyne. In 1980, horses trained outside France started favourite in eleven French pattern races, more than usual, and Gonzales headed the market for the Prix du Jockey-Club from Providential, Mot D'Or and Shakapour, each of whom had won a well-contested classic trial previously. Gonzales ran creditably without justifying the confidence placed in him. Behind early on, he made progress from halfway to look a threat two and a half furlongs out but was unable to sustain his effort, and came home fifth, just over six lengths behind Policeman.

Gonzales returned to winning form with a hard-gained neck victory over My Hollow on terms 13 lb worse than weight-for-age in the Blandford Stakes at the Curragh, but in the Joe McGrath Memorial Stakes at Leopardstown he found a mile and a quarter on the sharp side against good horses and was outpaced in the closing stages, finishing fifth to his stable-companion Gregorian. Gonzales wasn't seen out after the Irish St Leger. Among the four-day acceptors for the Prix de l'Arc de Triomphe, he was withdrawn overnight. It was unlikely that he would have distinguished himself in such company.

Gonzales (USA) (b.c. 1977)	Vaguely Noble (b 1965)	Vienna (ch 1957)	Aureole
			Turkish Blood
		Noble Lassie (b 1956)	Nearco
			Belle Sauvage
	Gazala (b 1964)	Dark Star (br 1950)	Royal Gem
			Isolde
		Belle Angevine (br 1957)	L'Amiral
			Bella II

At 750,000 dollars Gonzales was the joint fourth-highest priced yearling sold at public auction in America in 1978. He is the fifth Vaguely Noble foal out of his dam and the third to have won; best of them was Mississipian, the top French two-year-old of 1973 who showed high-class form at up to one and a half miles the following year. Gazala has produced two winners by other stallions, the top-class middle-distance performer Youth (by Ack Ack) and the two-year-old Silky Baby (by What A Pleasure), who won over seven and a half furlongs in France in 1980. Gazala was a very smart filly with an excellent turn of foot which she used to good effect to win the Poule d'Essai des Pouliches and the Prix de Diane. Dark Star, her sire, won the Kentucky Derby; her dam and grandam both won in France, Belle Angevine at thirteen furlongs and Bella II at around a mile. Belle Angevine had only five foals, Gazala being her lone winner, but Bella II was more productive, her twelve foals including ten winners, notably Burgos, who dead-heated in the Grand Prix de Saint-Cloud, and Bell Hop, a stakes winner in America.

Gonzales didn't run as a two-year-old but by all accounts he was well thought of, and the fact that he wasn't one of the eight colts from his stable entered in the Derby suggests there might have been doubts about his acting on the Epsom course, particularly on the fast conditions that frequently prevail there in June. Gonzales is a big colt, one likely to be seen to best advantage on a galloping track, and although he seems to act on any going his action is of the type suited by some give in the ground. He stays a mile and three quarters and is consistent. *V. O'Brien, Ireland.*

GOOD-BYE GIRL 3 ch.f. Lorenzaccio 130–Knightside (Graustark) (1979 NR 1980 7g) 8,000Y; small filly; half-sister to middle-distance winner Justin Thyme (by Rheingold); dam won over 6f at 3 yrs in USA; never-dangerous sixth of 9 to Button Top in £2,300 race at Newmarket in October; sold 3,100 gns Newmarket December Sales. *L. Cumani.* —

GOODBYE STARTER 2 ch.c. Owen Dudley 121–Curfew 76 (Midsummer Night II 117) (1980 5f* 6f) Feb 5; well-made colt; second reported foal; dam ran only at 2 yrs when placed over 6f; justified favouritism in good style in 11-runner maiden race at Newmarket in May, drawing clear from halfway and running on strongly to score by 6 lengths from Rehoboam; had a chance 2f out when 9/2-shot for William Hill Middle Park Stakes on same course over 4 months later but couldn't quicken and finished 6 lengths fifth of 9 to Mattaboy; will stay 1m; evidently highly regarded. *H. Cecil.* 105

GOOD COVERT 2 b.f. Mummy's Pet 125–Miss Frenchy (Exbury 138) (1980 5g 5fg 6g) May 3; lightly-made filly; first foal; dam poor maiden; soundly beaten in maiden races at Nottingham and Folkestone (2); trained first 2 outings by T. Waugh. *R. Smyth.* —

GOOD GIRL TESS 2 ch.f. Jimmy Reppin 131–Anturia 87 (Aureole 132) (1980 5v^3 5g 6f) Mar 27; 1,400Y; small, light-framed filly; bad plater; has worn blinkers. *P. Haslam.* —

GOOD HABIT 2 ch.g. Habat 127–Parlais 101 (Pardao 120) (1980 5f 5f 6d 6g 8g 8d) Feb 1; 9,000Y; small, fair sort; half-brother to useful 5f winner Mi Favorita (by Mummy's Pet); dam sprinter; unquoted when in rear in varied company. *G. Beeson.* —

GOOD INFORMATION 3 ch.g. Sheshoon 132–Inside Job (Burglar 128) (1979 6fg 7fg 7g 7fg 8fg 8f 1980 10s^4 10s 12f* 12fg^4 12fg^2 14f^4 12fg) strong gelding; carries plenty of condition; 33/1, showed much improved form to win minor race at Thirsk in April; fair second in handicap at Doncaster following month; appears not to stay $1\frac{3}{4}$m; acts on firm going; sweating on second outing; not raced after June. *N. Guest.* 65

GOOD LARKER 3 ch.f. Some Hand 119–Tit-Bit 61 (Hornbeam 130) (1979 5d 5fg 5fg^4 5.1g^4 7f* 1980 13.8fg 12f 8g^3 8g* 8.2s* 8.3g 8.5fg^2) fair sort; poor 70 mover; plater at 2 yrs; showed improved form in 1980, winning handicaps at Pontefract (apprentice event) and Nottingham in August; unlikely to stay 1½m; acts on any going; suitable mount for a boy; sold 1,800 gns Newmarket Autumn Sales. *P. Haslam.*

GOOD LASSIE 3 b.f. Moulton 128–Violetta III 110 (Pinza 137) (1979 5fg4 6f 6f* 7g 1980 8d4 10fg 10f3 10fg 10.6fg 7.6g4 8fg) strong, attractive filly; in frame in 6-runner Masaka Stakes won by Star Chamber at Kempton in April, Sir Charles Clore Memorial Stakes at Newbury following month (third to The Dancer) and handicap at Chester in July; found 7.6f all too sharp for her on last-named and is bred to stay 1½m; acts on firm going; sold 84,000 gns Newmarket December Sales. *H. Wragg.* **83**

GOOD OFFICES 2 br.c. Murrayfield 119–Sun Queen 76 (Lucky Sovereign) (1980 6g 6fg3 6fg4 6s 6g2 6g) Apr 1; compact, attractive colt; third foal; half-brother to successful sprinter Swelter (by Tickled Pink); dam sprinter; ran well when blinkered in 14-runner minor event at Brighton in October, running on to finish length second to Endless Moment; again blinkered, had plenty to do at weights in nursery on next outing; will stay 7f; acts on a firm surface. *F. Durr.* **82**

GOOD ON YOU 3 br.f. Virginia Boy 106–Mini Skirt (Bald Eagle 119) (1979 NR 1980 8s 8fg 8g* 10.2g 9g* 12d 8.2s) half-sister to a poor animal in USA; dam won claiming races at up to 6f; successful in sellers at Edinburgh in June (bought in 2,200 gns) and Hamilton in July (sold out of C. Nelson's stable 2,100 gns); stays 9f. *R. Johnson.* **59**

GOOD SWEEP 2 b.c. Arch Sculptor 123–Jane Merryn (Above Suspicion 127) (1980 5g2 5d* 5g 5fg 6s) Mar 29; 1,600Y; compact colt; half-brother to winners here and abroad; dam never ran; 2/1-on when getting home by a short head from Cilla's Secret in 3-runner seller at Hamilton in June; went to post rather freely when blinkered at Ayr on next outing and finished last; should be suited by 6f; exported to Malaysia. *P. Rohan.* **55**

Mr Louis Freedman's "Goodbye Starter" (J. Mercer)

Mr J. Allbritton's "Good Thyne"

GOOD THYNE (USA) 3 b.c. Herbager 136–Foreseer (Round Table) (1979 8f² 8g³ 1980 10fg 10fg⁴ 12fg² 16g² 15s 12g* 15s* 14s²) $320,000Y; big, well-made colt; second foal; half-brother to Palmistry (by Forli), a stakes winner at 8.5f; dam, stakes-placed winner at up to 1m, is sister to top-class American middle-distance winner Royal Glint; successful in maiden race at Roscommon (long odds on) in August and Sam Hall Stakes at Ayr (beat Running Game) in September; also ran creditably to be runner-up in Gallinule Stakes at the Curragh (behind Gonzales), Queen's Vase at Royal Ascot (went down by a length to Toondra) and Irish St Leger, also at the Curragh; no match for Gonzales in last-named in October, being beaten 5 lengths; stays well; seems to act on any going; blinkered third, seventh and eighth outings. *D. Weld, Ireland.* **96**

GOOD TO BEAT (FR) 3 b.f. Hard to Beat 132–Good Fortune (Neptunus 132) (1979 8s 8s* 1980 10.5v* 9.5g⁴ 10.5g²) second foal; half-sister to a minor middle-distance winner by Blue Tom; dam won over 1¼m and is daughter of half-sister to high-class stayer Fontarabal; only lightly raced but is a smart performer; won Prix Penelope at Saint-Cloud in March by ½ length from Proustille; in frame subsequently in Prix Vanteaux at Longchamp in April (just over a length fourth to Luth de Saron) and Prix de Flore at Saint-Cloud in October (1½ lengths second to easy winner Benicia, rec 3 lb); will stay 1½m; acts well on soft going. *H. d'Aillieres, France.* **114**

GOODY GOODY 2 b.f. Mummy's Pet 125–Righteous Girl 93 (Right Boy 137) (1980 5g* 5fg) Mar 24; workmanlike filly; very good walker and extravagant mover; half-sister to numerous winners; dam 2-y-o 5f and 6f winner; came through to win 10-runner minor event at Goodwood in September by 1½ lengths **84**

from Tin Tessa despite running green when challenging; modest sixth of 21 to Doubtwash Girl after being outpaced early on in small race at Catterick later in month; will probably stay 6f. *F. J. Houghton.*

GORDON'S LAD 6 b.g. Connaught 130–Promotion Year 81 (Damremont 121) –
(1979 NR 1980 16.1s 12.5s 18s) little worthwhile form on flat. *J. Wilson.*

GORGEOUS GIRL 2 ch.f. Dragonara Palace 115–Daughter of Song 73 (Song **81**
132) (1980 5f* 5fg^3 5f^2 6g 6g^3 5f 6g 6d 5fg 6d) Feb 17; 5,000Y; neat, well-made filly; second foal; dam won 5f seller; stayed on to win 11-runner minor event at Thirsk in April by ¾ length from Force of Action; ran very well when 25/1 for Hilary Needler Trophy at Beverley in June, going down by ¾ length to Gandoorah (gave 7 lb); well beaten in nurseries last 5 starts; probably stays 6f; acts on firm going. *K. Stone.*

GORSKY 4 b.g. Dubassoff–Artistically (Ribot 142) (1979 12s 12d 8d 7d 8s^4 **49**
8f^3 8g^3 8.3g 8g^4 10fg 8fg 8d 1980 12fg^2 12f^2 12f 14f 11g 16d^3 15fg^2 20.4g 16fg^4 16.1s) small gelding; good mover; inconsistent maiden; stays 2m; seems to act on any going; used to wear blinkers; not resolute. *B. Richmond.*

GO TOTAL 4 br.c. Philip of Spain 126–Lazy Time (Linacre 133) (1979 5d^2 **100**
5g 5d^2 5fg 5fg 5f^2 5g 5.3g^3 5fg 5.6fg 1980 5f 6fg 5s^2 5g^2 5g^4 5fg 5.3g^3 5f^4 5d* 5fg 5g 5d^2 5v) robust, short-coupled colt; led 2f out and ran on well to beat Ferryman by a length (pair clear) in handicap at Goodwood in September; also runner-up at Lingfield, Sandown and Newbury, being very narrowly beaten by Marching On on last-named course in October; should stay 6f; acts on any going; blinkered occasionally at 3 yrs. *R. Boss.*

GOVERNOR'S CAMP 3 b.c. Blakeney 126–Fiddlededee 94 (Acropolis 132) **80**
(1979 7fg 8fg 1980 10.1fg 13s 14g 12g^4 12fg^2 11.7h^4 12.2d^3 12.5s*) small, well-made colt; wide-margin winner of moderate 18-runner maiden race at Stockton in October; will stay well; acts on any going; sold to G. Richards 20,000 gns Newmarket Autumn Sales. *J. Dunlop.*

GRACEFUL BOY 5 b.g. Prince de Galles 125–Only By Chance (Golden Cloud) **55**
(1979 NR 1980 7fg 6g* 6fg 6g 6s 6g^3) sprint handicapper; has been fired; made all at Nottingham in April; ran easily best subsequent race on final start; used to wear blinkers; wears bandages. *D. H. Jones.*

GRACEFUL DIVER 4 b.f. Deep Diver 134–True Time (Arctic Time 127) –
(1979 7d 6d 5g^3 5f 5fg 5f 1980 12fg) big, rangy filly; plating-class maiden; not bred to stay and was tailed off when tried at 1½m on only outing of 1980. *G. Beeson.*

GRACEFUL KELLY 3 gr.f. Saritamer 130–Irish Elegance 60 (French Beige –
127) (1979 5f 7g 1980 8d 8fg 8fg) rangy filly; poor maiden; dwelt final outing (flag start). *R. Mason.*

GRACIOUS FOLLY 3 b.f. Idiots Delight 115–Savette (Frigid Aire) (1979 –
NR 1980 8f 12d 10.8s 8f) second foal; dam never ran; well beaten in maiden and minor races; trained by M. Scudamore first 3 starts. *A. W. Jones.*

GRADE WELL 5 b.m. Derring-Do 131–Authors Correction 69 (Narrator 127) **57**
(1979 7fg^2 10f^3 10.1fg 9fg* 11.5fg* 10s^4 10g* 10f* 10f 8g 10.5g 1980 11fg 12fg 10f^3 11.7s^3 12d* 11.7d 11.7fg 10g 12d^2 12.2d^4 12d 12d^4) middle-distance handicapper; winner at Leicester in July; ran creditably on occasions afterwards; acts on any going; suitable mount for an apprentice; genuine; has won 3 times at Yarmouth. *G. Blum.*

GRAF METTERNICH 5 b.h. High Top 131–All Shy 64 (Alcide 136) (1979 **71**
12v 10v^4 11s 10g* 10v^4 11.7g 9s^3 10.5d 10s^2 10.7g* 11g^4 11g^4 10g^4 12fg 10f 10f 1980 10s 11fg* 10.7fg^4 10f 11f^4 10h^3 10.7g 10s 12fg 9f* 11.7fg 12d 12.2d 13s 12d) shapely horse; won handicaps at Wolverhampton in April and August; best at up to 11f; acts on any going; has worn blinkers; has run respectably for a boy; needs to be held up; trained by J. Haine until after ninth outing. *Mrs. J. Pitman.*

GRAF TRAUN 2 b.c. Huntercombe 133–Golden Lania 78 (Sea Hawk II 131) –
(1980 6g 7fg 7fg 7fg 8d) Apr 25; 10,000Y; strong colt; first foal; dam placed from 7f to 1½m; in rear in maiden and minor events; sold 2,600 gns Newmarket Autumn Sales. *C. Brittain.*

GRAFTY GREEN 5 ch.g. Traditionalist–Crusheen (Typhoon 125) (1979 8f^3 **56**
10f* 10f 8fg 10fg^2 10f 10h^4 12s 1980 10g^2 10g 8fg 11.7fg 10fg^2 10fg^3 8g 10fg 12d* 8d 10s 12d) won apprentice handicap at Pontefract in October by 8 lengths from Futan, being kicked clear ½m out and coming home unchallenged; stays

1½m; probably acts on any going; blinkered when successful in 1979 and fourth outing (well beaten). *D. Dale.*

GRAIN RACE 2 br.c. Windjammer (USA)–Crimson Velvet 89 (Above Suspicion 127) (1980 5fg* 5fg* 5f* 6s^3 6fg^4 7s 8fg^2 8.2s^3) Apr 25; 8,200Y; well-made, useful-looking colt; good mover; brother to 1m winner Windle, and half-brother to 2 winners, including Redfern (by Red God), quite a useful performer at up to 1¼m; dam stayer; narrow winner of his first 3 starts, maiden race at Newbury, 5-runner Garter Stakes at Ascot (shade cleverly by a neck from Another Realm) and 4-runner Tattersall's Yorkshire Stakes at York; subsequently proved not up to taking on pattern-race company but ran well in nurseries at Newmarket and Nottingham in October on last 2 starts; may well stay 1¼m; acts on any going. *B. Hobbs.* **103**

GRANDAK (FR) 3 gr.c. Tennyson 124–Mathoura (Sea Hawk II 131) (1979 6d^2 5.5g^2 1980 10g* 11g^3 10.5fg 12fg 13.5g 14.6g) 34,000 francs Y (approx £4,000); lengthy, useful sort; fourth living foal; brother to Jamma, successful at around 11f in France, and half-brother to successful French middle-distance stayer Dolina (by Timmy My Boy); dam never ran; won 8-runner maiden race at Longchamp in April by short head from Mot D'Or; 2 lengths fourth (promoted to third) behind Julius Caesar in Prix Noailles on same course later in month; not entirely disgraced when 5 lengths eighth of 13 to Belgio in Prix Lupin, again at Longchamp, in May; well beaten afterwards in Prix du Jockey-Club at Chantilly, Grand Prix de Deauville and St Leger at Doncaster (last of 7 to Light Cavalry); won over hurdles late in year; should stay 1¾m; trained first 2 starts by N. Pelat. *M. Zilber, France.* **112**

GRAND ALLIANCE 3 b.c. Sweet Revenge 129–Lima 105 (Abernant 142) (1979 6g 7fg 6fg 1980 10v 9g 7g 8f 7g 8g) strong, lengthy colt; poor form in varied company; not certain to stay middle distances; sweated up final start. *M. Camacho.* —

GRAND CONDE (FR) 5 b.h. Sun Prince 128–Contestation (Abdos 134) (1979 8d^2 7.6v 8v 8fg 8.3fg^4 8fg^3 7g^2 8.3fg 8fg* 8.3f^4 7.3g* 8fg* 8d 8f^2 8s 1980 7g 7fg^3 7h 7f^3 8.5f* 7.6f^3 8d^3 8g 8d^2 8g* 8fg^4 8.3fg 10g 8g 8fg* 7.3fg 8g 8d) fair handicapper; successful at Epsom in June, Kempton in July and Salisbury in September; came with a late run when beating Seven Hearts going away by a length on last-named; stays 1¼m but does most of his racing at around 1m; probably acts on any going but is very well suited by top-of-the-ground; often gets behind in early stages; prone to breaking blood vessels; sold 3,000 gns Newmarket Autumn Sales. *A. Breasley.* **85**

GRANDEPIC 3 b.c. Seaepic 100–Grandaire 65 (Grand Roi 118) (1979 NR 1980 5s) second foal; dam won 5.9f seller at 2 yrs; tailed off in 25-runner maiden race at Nottingham in July. *K. Bridgwater.* —

GRANDIOSE 3 ch.c. Grundy 137–Secret Session 108 (Court Martial) (1979 NR 1980 9f 12fg^3 12g 12d* 13.1g* 12fg^4 14g* 13.3fg 14g) strong, rangy colt; half-brother to several winners, including top-class stayer Rock Roi (by Mourne) and very smart French middle-distance performer Millenium (by Aureole); dam won twice at 1m; developed into a useful handicapper, scoring at Salisbury, Bath and York; beat Blaze of Glory by ½ length in Melrose Handicap on last-named in August; suited by 1¾m and will stay further; suited by some give in the ground; genuine; sold to D. Elsworth 31,000 gns Newmarket Autumn Sales. *P. Walwyn.* **95**

GRAND LEGACY 2 ch.f. Relko 136–Grandpa's Legacy 102 (Zeus Boy 121) (1980 8d) Feb 6; useful-looking filly; half-sister to 3 winners, including very smart 7f to 13.3f winner Consol (by Reliance II); dam stayed 1½m; 12/1 and green when behind in 14-runner maiden race at Leicester in November won by Majorian; may do better when given a test of stamina in 1981. *H. Candy.* —

GRAND MANOR 2 b.c. Great Nephew 126–Town House 91 (Pall Mall 132) (1980 7g) Apr 9; 30,000Y; small, quite attractive colt; half-brother to 2 minor winners; dam, sister to Reform, won at up to 9f; unquoted, made no show when tenth of 14 to Rasa Penang in minor event at Kempton in September. *F. Durr.* —

GRAND MARCH 2 b.g. Song 132–Calleva (Worden II 129) (1980 7g* 8.2g^2 8g^4) Feb 9; strong, well-made, quite attractive gelding; good walker and mover; brother to very useful 1975 2-y-o 7f winner Piper, and half-brother to several winners, including Cesarewitch winner Centurion (by Connaught); dam of little account; kept on strongly to win 19-runner £2,600 event at Salisbury in August by a head from the unlucky-in-running Bustomi; couldn't match **91**

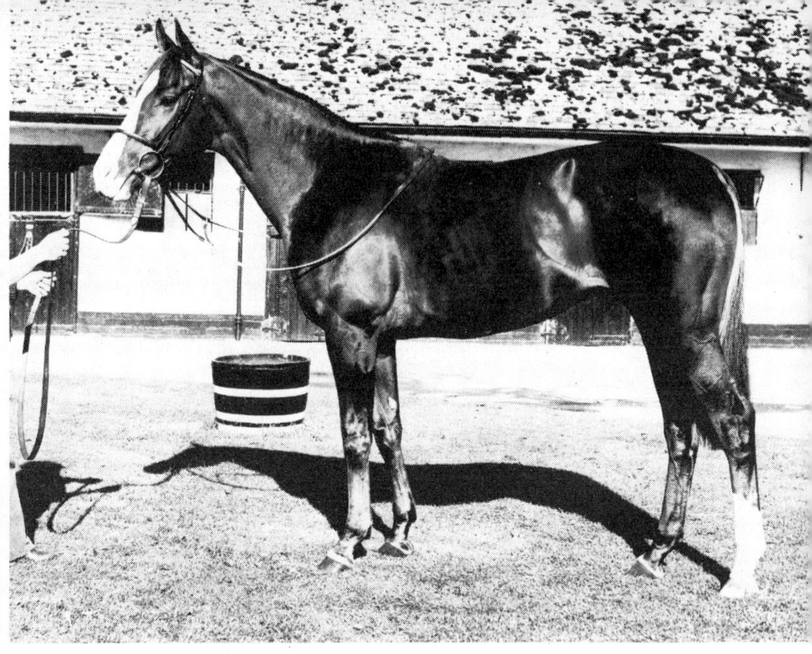

Col F. R. Hue-Williams' "Grandiose"

Pellegrini's pace and went down by 1½ lengths in £4,100 race at Haydock the following month; runs as though middle distances will suit him. *I. Balding.*

GRAND OEUVRE (FR) 3 b.g. Sir Gaylord–Contestation (Abdos 134) (1979 8fg 1980 12g) compact, well-made, attractive gelding; behind in maiden races; blinkered only start at 3 yrs (June). *B. Hills.* –

GRANDO KING 11 br.g. Negotiation–Yellow Streak (Shantung 132) (1979 18s4 16.9s* 18s3 18.8g4 16fg 16.9fg 1980 18f 18.8g) staying handicapper; suited by some give in the ground; apprentice ridden; saddle slipped first outing of 1980. *M. Tate.* –

GRANDOLA (GER) 3 br.f. Star Appeal 133–Gundula (Mercurius) (1979 including 7v2 7g4 6v2 7g2 8g2 7s 1980 7.3fg 8fg 8g* 9g4 8s 8g3 6g* 9g3 8v 8d) rangy, deep-girthed German filly; trained by F. Durr first 2 starts when in rear in Fred Darling Stakes at Newbury in April and 1,000 Guineas at Newmarket in May; showed good speed 5f when tailed off behind Quick As Lightning on latter course; returned to Germany afterwards and won races at Cologne later in May and Neuss in August; stays at least 1m. *T. Grieper, Germany.* ?

GRAND OPERA 3 ch.f. Great Nephew 126–Sheet Music 91 (Monet 127) (1979 6f 6f2 7d* 8g3 1980 8g) compact filly; quite useful (rated 92) at 2 yrs; needed run only outing in 1980 in July; seems to stay 1m; probably acts on any going; sold 4,000 gns Newmarket December Sales. *M. Stoute.* –

GRAND PROMENADE (FR) 3 b. or br.c. Prominer 125–Still Playing (Tambourine II 133) (1979 8g 8s 1980 11fg 16fg 16d 15s 16g 12d) strong colt; well beaten, including in a valuable selling handicap; didn't move to post well third start. *J. Hanson.* –

GRANGETOWN LADY 3 b.f. Charlottown 127–Gitana III (Alhambra) (1979 5v 5v4 7f 1980 12h 13.8fg) of no account; has worn blinkers. *I. Vickers.* –

GRANPARK 2 b.g. Huntercombe 129–Solandri (Resurgent) (1980 6fg³ 5d³ 6d 5s 5d 5s³ 6s) June 1; strong, deep-girthed gelding; fourth living foal; dam won 4 times in New Zealand; plater; best form at 5f; acts on soft going; blinkered final outing. *J. Wilson.* **66**

GRAPHICS SOLAR 2 b.c. Royal Palace 131–Tina Fort (Fortina) (1980 8d 7d) May 4; 8,000Y; leggy colt; sixth foal; half-brother to a winning jumper; dam winning chaser; unquoted when never-dangerous eighth of 20 behind Soldan in 7f minor event at Doncaster in October, second outing; will stay well. *B. McMahon.* **–**

GRASSHOPPER LADY 4 ch.f. Mountain Call 125–Right Abella 74 (Right Boy 137) (1979 5d 6s 5d 6d 6f² 6f² 6s³ 6s 6d 5s 5s 1980 5f 6f) poor sprint plater; stays 6f; acts on any going; sold 400 gns Doncaster June Sales. *S. Nesbitt.* **–**

GRAVAD LAX 3 bl.f. Home Guard 129–Laxmi 108 (Palestine 133) (1979 5f² 5d 1980 8g 10g 8fg) lengthy, attractive filly; has shown little form since first outing at 2 yrs; not certain to stay 1¼m; ran poorly in blinkers final start; sold 19,000 gns Newmarket December Sales. *J. Hindley.* **–**

GRAY LOCH 2 b.f. Lochnager 132–Ensign Steel 57 (Majority Blue 126) (1980 5fg 6d 5s³ 5d⁴ 5d 5f) Mar 6; strong filly; first foal; dam, placed over 6f, is half-sister to very useful sprinters Red Track, Sovereign Set and Burwell; in frame in maiden races at Newcastle in August and Hamilton in September; beaten 4½ lengths by Mel's Choice in latter; probably stays 6f. *T. Fairhurst.* **63**

GREAGHLONE 2 gr.f. Young Emperor 133–Funny Face (Majority Blue 126) (1980 6s 7g⁴ 6fg) Mar 25; rather unfurnished filly; good walker; fourth foal; dam never ran; prominent in maiden and minor events in the autumn, finishing 4 lengths fourth of 17 to Golden Bowl at Salisbury and 2¾ lengths fifth of 19 behind Sea Aura at Lingfield; probably stays 7f; sold 2,500 gns Newmarket Autumn Sales. *J. Winter.* **76**

GREAT AUK 2 br.c. Auction Ring 123–King's Chase (King's Leap 111) (1980 5fg⁴ 5.1f 6g³ 6g⁴ 5d³ 5d² 5f⁴ 5d) Feb 16; 8,000Y; useful-looking colt; second foal; dam ran only twice; placed in varied company, on sixth outing failing by ½ length to catch Kent's Pride in nursery at Edinburgh in September; stays 6f; seems to act on any going; wears blinkers and finds little off the bridle; sweated up badly fifth start and isn't one to trust; sold to BBA 3,200 gns Newmarket Autumn Sales. *B. Hobbs.* **82**

GREAT CARE 3 br.f. Home Guard 129–Be Gyrful 89 (Gyr 131) (1979 6g 5.8g⁴ 5fg 1980 6fg² 6f) big filly; seems only plating class; stays 6f; yet to race on a soft surface; bandaged first outing in 1979; sweated up slightly final start. *J. Bethell.* **63**

GREAT DEVELOPER 3 br.g. Royalty 130–Spring Music (Silly Season 127) (1979 7g 1980 12.5v* 12.3f² 14fg⁴ 12g² 12d 15s³ 16d⁴) lengthy gelding; good walker; trounced 17 opponents in modest maiden race at Stockton in March; runner-up in handicaps subsequently; stays well; acts on any going but is particularly well suited by the mud. *M. Jarvis.* **83**

GREAT EASTERN 3 br.c. Jukebox 120–Miss Bangkok (Sovereign Path 125) (1979 6g⁴ 1980 6f* 6g* 6fg) leggy, lightly-built colt; good mover; quite a useful performer; won maiden race at Newmarket in April and £2,800 event at Newbury in July; led on line to beat Columnist a head in latter; will be suited by 7f; acts on firm going; sweated up final start. *J. Dunlop.* **98**

GREATER COLOMBO 3 b. or br.c. Tudor Melody 129–Crept In 106 (Crepello 136) (1979 6g² 7.3g³ 1980 8s⁴ 8f 10fg² 10fg* 10s 10g) quite attractive colt; won 14-runner maiden race at Leicester in May; had earlier run well when fourth to Master Willie in Easter Stakes at Kempton in April; stays 1¼m; probably acts on any going; blinkered nowadays. *F. J. Houghton.* **81**

GREATEST HITS 3 b.c. Derring-Do 131–Vallota 85 (Klairon 131) (1979 NR 1980 8fg 8d 8g 8g 8g 8s* 8.2s²) attractive, well-made colt; second foal; dam, half-sister to very smart Tudor Mill, won at 1¼m; showed improved form on last 2 starts in October, staying on strongly to win 24-runner maiden race at Sandown and finishing creditable second in handicap at Nottingham (apprentice ridden); will stay 1¼m; seems to need soft going; blinkered fourth start. *R. Laing.* **72**

GREAT EXPECTATIONS (USA) 5 b.h. Key To The Mint–Sweet Sue II (Sideral) (1979 7d³ 8fg 10f 10g³ 16.5g 15.5f 10f 8fg 12fg 1980 10d 10g 12d⁴ 10s) plater; stays 1¼m. *P. K. Mitchell.* **–**

GREAT GATSBY (USA) 2 b.c. Sir Gaylord–Sporting Flight (Ambehaving) (1980 7f 7fg 8d) Mar 21; $100,000Y; quite attractive, good sort; third foal; **78**

half-brother to a minor winner by Noble Decree; dam stakes-placed winner of 17 races at up to 1½m; 14/1, never in shake up when 7¾ lengths fifth of 6 to Baz Bombati in £5,500 event at Newmarket in August, second outing; off course nearly 2 months afterwards and didn't run up to that form in maiden race at Warwick on his return; should stay at least 1m; sold 13,500 gns Newmarket Autumn Sales. *M. Stoute.*

GREATHAM HOUSE 4 b.g. Run The Gantlet–Nyeri 104 (Saint Crespin III 132) (1979 11.7g* 13.3fg* 14g^2 14fg* 1980 12d 12d 11.7d) attractive gelding; poor mover; useful performer at 3 yrs when trained by H. Cecil; well beaten in 1980; subsequently gelded; stays well; acts on a firm surface; blinkered final outing; winner over hurdles. *B. Swift.* —

GREAT LIGHT 2 ch.g. Great Nephew 126–Failing Light 70 (Ballymoss 136) (1980 7fg) Feb 20; rangy gelding; brother to a minor winner in France; dam half-sister to dam of 1,000 Guineas winner Nocturnal Spree; 50/1, missed break when behind in 22-runner maiden race won by Clear Verdict at Newmarket in August. *A. Goodwill.* —

GREAT MOVE 2 br.f. Great Nephew 126–Manoeuvre 105 (Mountain Call 125) (1980 7g 6fg) Apr 17; 4,600F, 13,500Y; well-made, quite attractive filly; second produce; half-sister to a winner in Austria; dam won from 5f to 7f at 2 yrs; in rear in maiden race at Salisbury and 7-runner Blue Seal Stakes at Ascot in September. *P. Walwyn.* —

GREAT MYTH 3 ch.f. Sharpen Up 127–Leonora's Legend 83 (Rockefella) (1979 NR 1980 8f 9.4d 10s) 4,800Y; leggy filly; half-sister to 3 winners, including fair miler Living Legend (by Derring-Do); dam won at 1¼m; poor form, including in a seller; retained 580 gns Doncaster October Sales. *J. Fitzgerald.* —

GREAT RANGER 3 b.g. Private Walk 108–Sham Alarm (Chamier 128) (1979 8.5g 5.9g^3 6g* 1980 7fg^4 8g 8g 7.3fg 8d) compact ex-Irish gelding; won maiden race at Fairyhouse at 2 yrs; well beaten in 1980; should stay at least 1m. *H. Blagrave.* —

GREATS 4 b.c. Great Nephew 126–Grisbi 96 (Grey Sovereign 128§) (1979 12d^3 12s* 12fg* 12.3fg^2 12fg* 12f^2 12.2g 12d 1980 12d 12.2s) strong colt; had plenty of ability but went the wrong way temperamentally; stayed 1½m; acted on any going; was tried in blinkers (refused to race); dead. *B. Hobbs.* —

GREAT SUBSTENCE (USA) 2 br.c. Pretense–Gay Northerner (Northern Dancer) (1980 8g* 8d) Apr 28; $25,000Y; neat colt; half-brother to 2 minor winners; dam won 6f stakes race at 2 yrs in Canada; showed himself a smart performer, winning 6-runner Prix de Villebon at Longchamp in September by ¾ length from Troubetzkoy and fading only in last 100 yards when 2½ lengths fifth of 11 to Recitation in Grand Criterium on same course the following month; should stay 1¼m. *M. Saliba, France.* **121**

GREAT VERDICT (USA) 3 b.f. Le Fabuleux 133–Jury's Choice (Advocator) (1979 7g 8d^2 10v 1980 10fg 10.5fg^2 12d* 12d^2 12d* 13.5g 12.5d 15.5v) second foal; half-sister to Impartiality (by Jacinto), successful over 6f and 1m in USA; dam unraced half-sister to several winners, notably leading American staying 2-y-o of 1955 and successful sire Prince John; won maiden race at Chantilly in June and Prix de Minerve at Evry in July; held off Proustille (gave 6 lb) by a neck in latter; ran well in between to be beaten a length by Anifa in valuable race at Longchamp; well beaten in Prix de Pomone at Deauville and Prix de Royallieu and Prix Royal-Oak at Longchamp final 3 starts; suited by 1½m; acts on a firm and a soft surface. *G. Bridgland, France.* **110**

GRECIAN FIGHTER 8 ch.g. Fighting Ship 121–Arethusa 94 (Acropolis 132) (1979 NR 1980 18d) winner several times over long distances over hurdles but seems of little account on flat. *B. Richmond.* —

GRECIAN SEA (FR) 2 ch.f. Homeric 133–Sea Venture 98 (Diatome 132) (1980 5g^3 6d* 7g^4) Jan 15; first foal; dam, from same family as Reform, won over 6f at 2 yrs and stayed 1¼m; won 7-runner maiden event at Saint-Cloud in July in good style by 4 lengths from Zelda; wasn't disgraced in finishing 6¼ lengths fourth of 9 to Bernica when 9/1 for Group 3 Prix du Calvados at Deauville the following month; will stay at least 1¼m; to be trained by R. Hern. *J. Cunnington, jnr, France.* **99**

GREEK PRINCE 3 b.g. English Prince 129–Kaniz (Darius 129) (1979 7fg 7f^4 1980 8d^2 12f 10f 10s^3 10fg 10fg) deep-girthed gelding; placed in maiden race at Doncaster in March and minor event at Nottingham in June; should stay 1½m; probably acts on any going; blinkered last 2 starts. *C. Brittain.* **58**

GREEN DAWN (USA) 2 ch.c. Grey Dawn II 132–Boheme (Exbury 138) (1980 5.8f 7.2d) neat American-bred colt; good mover; dam, half-sister to high-class 1962 French 2-y-o Quiqui, won over middle distances in France; 50/1 when 7¼ lengths fifth of 10 to Steel Pass in maiden race at Bath in July; pulled hard and faded from 2f out when behind in similar race won by Craigour at Haydock in September; should be suited by 7f+. *B. Hills.* –

GREEN FIRE 2 ch.f. Hotfoot 126–Green Island 89 (St Paddy 133) (1980 5g 5f) Jan 27; 4,000F; robust, short-legged filly; third produce; dam won over 1¼m and is half-sister to very useful Escorial; behind in minor event at Goodwood in August (apprentice ridden and very backward indeed when last of 8) and in 18-runner maiden race at Folkestone in September; likely to need 7f+; sold 400 gns Newmarket Autumn Sales. *B. Swift.* –

GREEN HAZE (USA) 2 b.c. Irish Castle–Vanua 96 (Nashua) (1980 6f² 6g² 6d 6s* 7g³) Apr 2; $40,000Y; strong, good sort; excellent mover; second foal; dam, closely related to very smart middle-distance filly Fleet Wahine, stayed 13f; justified favouritism a shade cleverly by a neck from Priory Lane in 16-runner maiden race at Nottingham in August; moderate third of 7 to Royal Realm when odds on for minor event at Newcastle in August (sweated up a bit); should stay 1¼m; acts on any going. *M. Stoute.* 87

GREENLAND PARK 4 ch.f. Red God 128§–Centre Piece 73 (Tompion) (1979 5d³ 5fg 6f³ 5d⁴ 6g⁴ 5g* 5d³ 7s 1980 5fg³ 6fg³ 5fg 5g⁴ 6g) strong, most attractive filly; very smart performer at 2 yrs and 3 yrs; didn't run up to her best in 1980 (reportedly cut an eye badly early in season and is said to have suffered from a virus) but nevertheless ran respectably on occasions; in frame in Prix de Saint-Georges (5 lengths third to Adraan) at Longchamp, Leisure Stakes (odds on when over a length behind The Pug) at Lingfield and William Hill Sprint Championship at York; looked well and ran on strongly after getting outpaced early on when creditable fourth to Sharpo in last-named event in August; beaten 2f out when sixth of 8 behind Moorestyle in Vernons Sprint Cup at Haydock in September; best form at up to 6f; had an excellent smooth action and was ideally suited by a sound surface; visits Kris in 1981. *W. Hastings-Bass.* 109

GREEN MEMORY (USA) 2 ch.f. Forli–Memory Lane 100 (Never Bend) (1980 6f 9d⁴ 7d²) Feb 20; leggy, unfurnished filly; first foal; dam, sister to Mill Reef, won Princess Elizabeth Stakes; ran well in end-of-season maiden and minor events, on second occasion going down by a head to Button Top at Leicester in October; will stay 1¼m; sure to win a maiden race at 3 yrs. *I. Balding.* 86

GREEN SPRING 3 b.c. Green God 128–Saratoga Springs 92 (Worden II 129) (1979 5fg 7fg 1980 8fg 10.1g 10.6d) lengthy, light-framed colt; well beaten in varied company. *H. T. Jones.* –

GREENWAY (FR) 2 br.f. Targowice 130–Gracious (Habitat 134) (1980 5g 5d* 5g² 5g* 5f 5s*) 117

Those very smart French fillies Greenway and Gold River have more in common than their trainer and their owner-breeder Jacques Wertheimer. Both won important races in 1980 and both are descended from Glaneuse—she's the grandam of Greenway and the dam of Gold River. They differ though in one major respect; Gold River is a stayer, winner of the Prix Royal-Oak, whereas Greenway is a sprinter, winner of two of France's best five-furlong races, the Prix d'Arenberg at Chantilly and the all-aged Prix du Petit Couvert at Longchamp.

To win both the d'Arenberg and the Petit Couvert was a fine achievement on Greenway's behalf but in neither race did she meet high-class opposition. The field at Chantilly numbered only five. Three of these, Greenway, Affection and Sharmada had met five weeks earlier in the Prix des Reves d'Or at Vichy in August when Greenway, already winner of a maiden race at Maisons-Laffitte, failed by a neck to catch Affection, two of whose three previous successes had been gained in the Provinces, at Lyons. Greenway comfortably took her revenge on Affection in the d'Arenberg, drawing clear from the distance, despite drifting to her right, and scoring convincingly by two and a half lengths from Sharmada.

Before the Petit Couvert Greenway ran in the Prix de l'Abbaye de Longchamp. Although she finished only eighth of nine, nearly ten lengths behind Moorestyle, there was reason to believe she hadn't run up to her best, probably because she'd been involved in a collision with Just A Shadow at the start. The punters rightly chose to ignore her Abbaye running when she was one of six runners in the Petit Couvert, making her odds on. Her most serious

Prix d'Arenberg, Chantilly—Greenway outspeeds her four opponents. Sharmada is clear second best

challengers proved to be three animals who'd done most of their racing outside France; Blue Persian, the very speedy English filly who had accounted for Hanu and Runnett on her previous start; the ex-English Blue Courtier who had won twice in Norway; and the Prix de Seine-et-Oise fourth Realeza whose four wins in 1980 had all been gained in Spain. Surprisingly Realeza, whose successes had been over distances of seven to eleven furlongs, was able to lead to past halfway. Soon afterwards Greenway started to make smooth progress up the rails from fourth place, taking the lead with a furlong and a half to run, and she kept on well to win by one and a half lengths from Blue Persian.

Greenway (Fr) (br.f. Feb 10, 1978)	Targowice (b 1970)	Round Table (b 1954)	Princequillo
			Knight's Daughter
		Matriarch (br 1964)	Bold Ruler
			Lyceum
	Gracious (br 1972)	Habitat (b 1966)	Sir Gaylord
			Little Hut
		Glaneuse (b 1966)	Snob
			Glamour

Greenway, an attractive filly, is the second foal of Gold River's half-sister Gracious, a useful winner at up to seven furlongs both at two and three years. Gracious' first foal, the Kalamoun filly Gracious Lady, ran only as a two-year-old when a five-furlong winner. Although Greenway's grandam Glaneuse was a smart winner from a mile to a mile and a half and her sire Targowice stayed a mile well, Greenway's trainer regards her as a sprinter and Europe's top sprints are said to be her objectives in 1981. She hasn't yet done enough to convince us that she's capable of beating the very best sprinters but she's clearly very smart and should win more races, especially if she gets soft ground. *A. Head, France.*

GREENWOOD STAR 3 gr.c. No Mercy 126–Golden Palermo 70 (Dumbarnie 125) (1979 5s3 5v4 5g2 5fg3 5fg3 5fg3 5fg2 6fg* 6g2 1980 8fg 8.2f* 7f2 8.2fg* **102**

Cecil Frail Handicap, Haydock—Greenwood Star finishes well clear of Sunfield

10.5g 8d) small, compact colt; successful in valuable amateur riders event and Cecil Frail Handicap at Haydock in May; routed his field in latter, coming through strongly to lead inside last furlong and bursting clear to beat Sunfield by 5 lengths; ran well in valuable handicap at York in between; not certain to stay 1¼m; needs a sound surface; is sometimes rather slow into his stride; reportedly injured his back final outing. *G. Hunter.*

GREG 4 ch.g. My Swanee 122–Facade 99 (Double Jump 131) (1979 8s⁴ 8.5d⁴ 8g 10g 14f 1980 16fg) robust gelding; only plating class; best form at 1m, and is unlikely to stay long distances. *P. Mitchell.* —

GREGORIAN (USA) 4 br.c. Graustark–Natashka (Dedicate) (1979 10s³ 1980 7g 10f* 10f* 10g³ 12d³ 12g³ 10g*) **124**

Gregorian looked such an exciting prospect when a twelve-length winner of a maiden race at Leopardstown on his only start as a two-year-old that it was disappointing his three-year-old campaign amounted solely to a modest third behind Dickens Hill in the Ballymoss Stakes in the spring. However, it was decided to keep him in training alongside the huge number of potentially top-class younger animals in his stable and the move paid off handsomely. Gregorian turned out to be one of O'Brien's best horses in 1980. He won three pattern races, including the Joe McGrath Memorial Stakes at Leopardstown in September on his final outing, and was placed in the Coral Eclipse Stakes and the King George VI and Queen Elizabeth Diamond Stakes.

The Joe McGrath Memorial attracted a field of eleven, including runners from England and France; the stable, which had won with Inkerman in 1978 and Fordham in 1979, was represented by the three-year-olds Night Alert and Gonzales in addition to Gregorian. George McGrath proved an able deputy for Gregorian's intended rider Tommy Murphy who fractured an ankle pulling up on Critique after winning the previous race. He adopted forcing tactics

Joe McGrath Memorial Stakes, Leopardstown—Gregorian wins by a short head from Spence Bay (centre). Night Alert is behind the winner. Corvaro (left) is fourth

Mr D. Schwartz's "Gregorian"

similar to those which had proved so effective with Gregorian earlier in the season and took a definite lead three furlongs out. The horse was headed briefly in the final furlong by Spence Bay but rallied gamely and got home by a short head despite tending to hang. As Group 1 races go the Joe McGrath Memorial was far from outstanding: Spence Bay hadn't raced since June and had been hitherto regarded as a miler, third-placed Night Alert and fourth-placed Corvaro didn't have the best of runs, and fifth-placed Gonzales, who went on to an easy Irish St Leger win, almost certainly found the distance too short. Nevertheless, in winning it Gregorian added considerably to his value as a stallion, for which purpose he has been purchased by the Windfields Stud Farm and returned to the United States.

Gregorian had finally shown himself a very good colt when winning the Westbury Stakes at Sandown in April from Prince Rheingold and the Brigadier Gerard Stakes on the same course in May from Noelino in clear-cut fashion, but the horses in those races weren't quite from the top drawer and he was subsequently beaten by better opposition in the Eclipse and the King George. Not that he was disgraced in either; far from it. In the Eclipse he made a bold attempt to repeat the pillar-to-post tactics that had proved successful on the course earlier despite the presence of another front-runner in Sea Chimes. Piggott looked for a moment as though he might have stolen the race when he pushed Gregorian into a two-length lead on the home turn, but he was tackled by Ela-Mana-Mou a furlong and a half out and was thereafter fighting a losing battle. Hello Gorgeous also got the better of him before the line, and Gregorian finished third, a little over two lengths behind Ela-Mana-Mou. Gregorian also finished third to Ela-Mana-Mou in the King George, beaten over twice as far. Piggott switched to Mrs Penny following Gregorian's disappointing third to My Hollow in the Royal Whip Stakes at the Curragh a week earlier, a race in which waiting tactics were tried. Piggott proved right, of course, but Gregorian ran a lot better than many expected, keeping on stoutly though outpaced by the two principals and holding off the French challengers Dunette and Le Marmot for his valuable third place.

Gregorian (USA) (br.c. 1976)	Graustark (ch 1963)	Ribot (b 1952)	Tenerani
			Romanella
		Flower Bowl (b 1952)	Alibhai
			Flower Bed
	Natashka (b 1963)	Dedicate (b 1952)	Princequillo
			Dini
		Natasha (b 1952)	Nasrullah
			Vagrancy

Gregorian is an extremely well-bred colt. His sire Graustark has had such notable colts as Avatar, Jim French and Key To The Mint in the United States and in Europe he has been represented by Caracolero and Monseigneur in addition to Gregorian. The dam Natashka was a top-class filly and won eight races at up to a mile and a quarter, including the Monmouth Oaks and the Alabama Stakes; she was joint top-rated three-year-old filly in her year. Natashka is a granddaughter of another top-class filly Vagrancy who won the 1942 Coaching Club American Oaks and is the dam of Black Tarquin. Natashka has proved as successful in the paddocks as she was on the racetrack and she produced four winners before Gregorian, including Arkadina and Blood Royal (both by Ribot) who were also trained by O'Brien. Arkadina was placed in the Irish One Thousand Guineas, the Oaks and the Irish Guinness Oaks and is the dam of Forlene and Encyclopedia; Blood Royal was unbeaten in four races, gaining his most important wins in the Queen's Vase and the Jockey Club Cup. Natashka has produced another two winners since Gregorian, including the American-based Truly Bound (by In Reality), an outstanding two-year-old filly in 1980 who won all her three races and ended her season with a sensational eleven-length win in the Arlington-Washington Lassie Stakes.

Gregorian, an attractive, tall, lengthy colt who impressed us in appearance on more than one occasion, stayed a mile and a half and was best on a sound surface. A game and genuine sort, despite his habit of swishing his tail under pressure, he should do well in his new career. He will stand in Maryland alongside Northern Dancer and The Minstrel. *V. O'Brien, Ireland.*

GRESHAM ARMS 2 b.c. Royal Palace 131–Gresham Girl 99 (Right Tack — 131) (1980 6s 6g) May 11; neat colt; first foal; dam, daughter of very speedy Granville Greta, won 3 times over 6f; behind in 18-runner minor and maiden events at Nottingham and Yarmouth (tailed off) in July. *D. Ringer.*

GRESTEXPORT 3 ch.f. Porto Bello 118–Philanderess (Philemon 119) (1979 **60** 5g 5s 6s 5fg^3 5fg 6fg 8h 1980 8g 8d^2 7fg 8f 10fg 9s* 8.2s 8.2v) strong filly; plater; attracted no bid after winning at Hamilton in September; stays 9f; acts on soft going; inconsistent; trained by S. Wainwright first 3 starts; sold 500 gns Doncaster October Sales. *K. Stone.*

GREY AT LAST 2 gr.f. Copte–Marie Denise 68 (Dual 117) (1980 5f 6fg — 6d) Mar 25; compact filly; fourth foal; half-sister to 2 winners, including stayer Passerine (by My Swallow); dam a stayer and quite useful hurdler; unquoted when in rear in maiden and minor events; will need a test of stamina at 3 yrs. *B. Richmond.*

GREYBURN 3 gr.f. Saintly Song 128–Counter Coup (Busted 134) (1979 **85** 6fg* 6fg 6g 1980 8g 8f* 8s^2 10f^4 7.2g* 8g 7s) tall, useful sort; fair handicapper; successful at Beverley in July and Haydock in September; appears not to stay 1¼m; acts on any going. *W. Haigh.*

GREY EAGLE 4 gr.g. Warpath 113–Whisky Lima 82 (Midsummer Night — II 117) (1979 12f 14.7g 1980 13.8fg 16d 20.4g 14.7d^4) big, strong gelding; poor staying maiden; sold to T. Craig 4,900 gns Doncaster November Sales. *C. Thornton.*

GREY HAVEN 3 gr.g. Grey Thunder 106–Fulcrum Miss (Fulcrum) (1979 — 5v 5s 5d 5g 6g^2 7f 8h 8fg 1980 7fg) lightly-made gelding; bad plater; has worn blinkers. *A. Moore.*

GREY HUNTER 2 gr. or ro.c. Warpath 113–Janabelle 101 (Gentle Art 121) **77** (1980 5h 5fg 7s^3 7d^3 7g 7fg 6g 8d) Apr 9; 3,500Y; big, rather leggy colt; brother to 1978 2-y-o winner Vronsky, and closely related to winning sprinter Kelso Belle (by Town Crier); dam won at up to 7f; ran well when length third to Hollow Laughter in maiden race at Brighton on fourth outing; showed little worthwhile form on other outings; should stay 1m; acts on soft ground; blinkered second outing. *A. Demetriou.*

GREY MOUNTAIN 7 gr.g. Town Crier 119–Abernette 102 (Abernant 142) (1979 12v* 13s^2 12d^2 12s 12d^2 12s 12s 12fg 12fg^4 12f^2 12f^3 12fg^2 10fg 13s* 1980 12d^4 12s* 13s* 12d 13.3fg 12d^4 12s 13s^4 12v) moderate handicapper; successful in March at Leicester and Nottingham, leading in last 50 yds to beat Busting by ¾ length going away on latter; stays 13f; acts on any going, but revels in the mud; usually held up; good mount for an apprentice; off course for more than 5 months after fourth start. *P. Kelleway.* **79**

GREY SPACE 3 gr.g. Grey Mirage 128–Kathy King (Space King 115) (1979 6g 7f 8.2s 1980 10f 12fg) big gelding; poor maiden. *T. Fairhurst.* –

GREY SWAN 4 gr or ro.f. My Swanee 122–Suspense 83 (Anwar 120) (1979 8f 8h 8fg 12g 10s 1980 10g* 10g^2 12.2g 10f 12d) lightly-made ex-Irish filly; dropped in class when winning selling handicap at Nottingham in July (bought in 1,100 gns); stays 1½m; bandaged in front, second outing. *T. Kersey.* **41**

GREY VIXEN 2 gr.f. Habat 127–Altiora 100 (Taj Dewan 128) (1980 7g 7g 7f) Apr 1; leggy filly; third foal; dam won over 7f at 2 yrs; 6½ lengths fifth of 19 to Grand March in £2,600 event at Salisbury in August, second outing and best effort; will stay 1m; sold 470 gns Ascot November Sales. *C. Nelson.* **65**

GREY WATTY 2 gr.c. Runnymede 123–Lucy Jane (Palestine 133) (1980 6g 5d) Mar 25; workmanlike colt; half-brother to 2 winners, including useful jumper Vaguely Attractive (by Attractive); dam ran once; unquoted when behind in minor event at Brighton and maiden race at Sandown in October. *S. Matthews.* –

GRID 4 b. or br.g. Track Spare 125–Jacine 72 (Owen Tudor) (1979 8s^3 10g^4 8fg^3 8fg 10g 10.1g 10s^4 11.7g^4 12g* 12fg 13fg^4 16fg 1980 12f 18fg 12d) neat gelding; well beaten in 1980, including in a valuable seller; stays 1½m; acts on any going; blinkered once at 3 yrs. *M. H. Easterby.* –

GRIMA 3 b. or br.c. Rheingold 137–Ravie (Relko 136) (1979 NR 1980 10fg 10.5d^4 12g 10fg^3 12g) strong, lengthy colt; half-brother to useful middle-distance performer Ravel (by Levmoss); dam useful winner at up to 1m in France; quite a moderate maiden; will be suited by 1¾m; ran moderately third start. *W. Hastings-Bass.* **73**

GRINDSTONE 3 b.g. Grundy 137–Cursorial 115 (Crepello 136) (1979 NR 1980 11f^2 14fg^3 13.3fg 12g) big, strong gelding; half-brother to 4 winners, including very smart 1970 2-y-o Fine Blade (by Fortino II) and French 1,000 Guineas third Curtain Bow (by Jimmy Reppin); dam won Park Hill; promising second in maiden race at Newbury in May; ran moderately afterwards in similar events and an amateur riders race; should stay 1¾m. *M. Stoute.* **77** d

GRINGA 2 b.f. Morston 125–Teesdale 97 (Aggressor 130) (1980 7g) Mar 20; lightly-made filly; half-sister to several winners, including useful 1975 2-y-o Blue Cavalier (by Queen's Hussar); dam 1¼m winner, and half-sister to very smart Starry Halo; 20/1, ran on nicely over last 2f without being given a hard time to finish about 3½ lengths fifth of 26 to Full of Reason in maiden race at Newmarket in October; sure to improve over middle distances in 1981. *G. Harwood.* **76** p

GROOVY GIRL 3 b.f. Averof 123–Brass Finisher 93 (Cash and Courage 116) (1979 NR 1980 10s 7fg^2 7g 8fg 7g 10s 10.2v*) 6,000Y; strong filly; half-sister to very useful 1977 2-y-o 5f performer Emboss (by Tribal Chief); dam, sister to very smart Sol 'Argent, won at up to 1¼m and over hurdles; 33/1 and apprentice ridden, showed improved form to win handicap at Doncaster in November; stays 1¼m well; acts well on heavy going. *R. Boss.* **72**

GRUNDY'S DOWRY 3 ch.g. Grundy 137–Honey Portion 107 (Major Portion 129) (1979 6g 1980 10g 12fg 12g^4) small, quite attractive gelding; poor maiden; sold 825 gns Ascot August Sales. *R. Hollinshead.* –

GRUNELLA 2 ch.f. Grundy 137–Pollinella 108 (Charlottown 127) (1980 5f 6fg 6s) Apr 20; small, quite attractive filly; second living foal; dam stayed 1½m; soundly beaten in £2,500 race at Newbury and 2 maiden events at Lingfield; will stay 1½m; blinkered final start; sold to BBA 2,300 gns Newmarket Autumn Sales. *P. Walwyn* –

GRUNTLED 3 b.f. Grundy 137–Guillotina 118 (Busted 134) (1979 NR 1980 10fg 12g 16f^3 12s) strong, attractive filly; fourth foal; half-sister to 2 winners, –

including useful 1977 2-y-o 7f winner Shorthouse (by Habitat); dam smart middle-distance stayer; third in maiden race at York in September, easily best effort; possibly stays 2m; acts on firm going; sold 42,000 gns Newmarket December Sales. *P. Walwyn.*

GRYLOS 2 b.g. Dubassoff–Nevilles Cross 67 (Nodouble) (1980 6d 6g 10.2s) — Mar 26; 500Y; 1,300 2-y-o; useful sort; good walker; second foal; dam stayed 1m; unquoted when well behind in maiden and minor races at the back end. *O. Jorgensen.*

GULF PALM 2 ch.c. Gulf Pearl 117–Oriental Palm (Royal Palm 131) (1980 5d 74 6g^4 7d 8g 7fg 8d) Mar 15; 19,000Y; neat colt; half-brother to 3 winners by Pall Mall, including fairly useful sprinter Shot in the Dark and French stayer Pallorie; dam maiden Irish sprinter; quite moderate at best; not sure to stay 1m; blinkered fifth start. *R. Smyth.*

GUIDE MY SLEIGH 4 ch.f. Bonne Noel 115–Arctic Walk (Arctic Slave — 116) (1979 7s 8v 12d 11.2d^2 9g* 10g^2 8f 10d* 10d 10v 1980 8fg) neat ex-Irish filly; half-sister to several winners, notably smart performers Icelandic (by Rarity) and Snow (by Young Emperor); successful twice in 1979, including in handicap at Listowel; well beaten in apprentice race at Kempton in May on only outing of 1980; stays 11.2f; acts on a soft surface; blinkered at 3 yrs. *B. Palling.*

GUILSWAY 7 gr.m. Track Spare 125–Guilpath 77 (Sovereign Path 125) (1979 — 12s 8s 12g 9g 12f 12fg^3 12.2f 10f 10fg 1980 13g 8f 10.6fg 10.6fg 9f 10d 14g 8.2d) poor plater; stays 1½m; appears to act on any going; has been tried in blinkers; inconsistent. *R. Hollinshead.*

GULFPORT (FR) 3 b.c. Hard to Beat 132–Miss Sunshine (Mourne 126) (1979 — 7g^2 8g 1980 10.8s^2 12fg) well-made colt; second in maiden race at Warwick in April (hung left); well beaten only subsequent start in May; should stay 1½m; best form on an easy surface; sold 900 gns Newmarket Autumn Sales. *G. Harwood.*

GUNDI 4 b.f. Mummy's Pet 125–Little Bird 87 (Only for Life 126) (1979 — 5f 5fg 7g 5g 5fg 1980 5g 6g) neat filly; poor plater; blinkered at 3 yrs. *J. Hardy.*

GUNSMOKE 2 gr.g. Young Emperor 133–Tender Rose (Prince Tenderfoot — 126) (1980 7.6g 7f 8g) Apr 15; 1,500Y; lightly-made gelding; second foal; dam unraced half-sister to smart 1964 2-y-o sprinter Royal Garden; in rear in £4,300 event at Lingfield and maiden races at Newmarket in the autumn; sold 1,150 gns Ascot December Sales. *I. Walker.*

GUSTY'S GIFT 6 ch.g. Divine Gift 127–Gusty Girl 71 (Darling Boy 124) 81 (1979 6s 5s 6g 6g 6d 6fg 6f 5f 6g 7g^4 6g 7f 5.8fg 7.6fg 1980 5s 6g^2 6fg 7fg^4 7h 5.8fg^3 7d^4 6g 6g^3 6fg 7g* 7f^3 6g 7g) lengthy, good-topped gelding; good mover; fair handicapper; raced alone when scoring by 4 lengths from Intercraft Boy at Salisbury in August; ran well under a penalty next time; probably better suited by 7f than 6f and stays 1m; acts on any going but is well suited by top-of-the-ground; blinkered last 4 starts; goes well for an apprentice. *B. Swift.*

GUSTY WIND 3 ch.f. Windjammer (USA)–Moss Pink (Levmoss 133) (1979 59 5g 5g 7f^3 7g^2 6fg^3 7.2g* 8g* 1980 8.2d 10.6fg^4 8fg 8g 7fg 8.2d^4 8g 9s) neat, light-framed filly; plater; should stay 1¼m; acts on a firm and a soft surface; blinkered fifth and sixth outings at 2 yrs but does at least as well without; none too consistent; trained by T. Molony first 6 starts; sold 800 gns Newmarket Autumn Sales. *M. Cousins.*

GUYWOOD 2 b.g. Tudor Rhythm 112–Smokey Dawn 68 (March Past 124) — (1980 5g 8fg 7s) June 11; lengthy gelding; second reported foal; dam won over 1¼m as a 5-y-o; behind in maiden and minor events. *P. M. Taylor.*

GWYNDOLINE 3 ch.f. Sandford Lad 133–Come Aboard 82 (Whistler 129) — (1979 5d 5f 5f 1980 6fg 10.2fg 8s 10d) lengthy filly; poor form, including in a seller; trained by T. Gosling first start. *R. Laing.*

GWYNFI NI 4 b.c. Joshua 129–March Fairy (March Past 124) (1979 11d 7h — 1980 8s 10fg 12.2s 16.1d 10d 12fg 16f) useless. *K. Bridgwater.*

GYMER 2 ch.g. Crowned Prince 128–Anadyomene 101 (Sea Hawk II 131) — (1980 6d 6g 6g) Mar 9; 6,000Y; strong, workmanlike gelding; first foal; dam, daughter of Cheveley Park winner Lalibela, won over 11f and 13f; well beaten, including when badly drawn in a valuable seller; off course over 3 months before third start. *A. Bailey.*

GYPSY CASTLE 6 ch.h. Habitat 134–Romany 87 (King's Bench 132) (1979 8g4 8d 8v2 8f2 8f3 8fg 8f3 8f* 8d 8f3 8.2s 8s 1980 8fg2 8d* 8d3 8g3 8g) moderate handicapper; ridden by 7-lb claimer, led in final furlong when beating Seven Hearts by ½ length at Sandown in June; not disgraced afterwards; stays 1¼m; acts on any going; tends to get behind in early stages and is suited by an uphill finish. *J. Winter.* **80**

GYPSY DANCER (FR) 5 gr.g. Dancer's Image–La Tzigane (Barbare II 128) (1979 6g3 7s3 7.2s 6f 6g2 6g 6fg2 5d* 5s3 1980 6f* 6f2 5f* 6g 5fg3 6s3 6d 6v) strong useful-looking gelding; not a good mover in his slower paces; smart performer; won Ladbrokes Abernant Stakes at Newmarket in April (got up on line to beat Son of Shaka) and minor event at Beverley in June (beat Jebb Lane easily by 4 lengths); also placed in Duke of York Stakes in May (1½ lengths second to Flash N Thunder), handicap at Ascot in September (third to Oh Simmie) and Coral Racing Champion Sprint at York in October (3 lengths third to Runnett); stays 7f; acts on any going; game and genuine; off course for 3 months after fourth start. *W. O'Gorman.* **112**

GYVELD 2 ch.c. Manacle 123–Mow Meadow (Acropolis 132) (1980 5g 6fg3 7fg) Apr 14; 2,700Y; workmanlike colt; half-brother to Irish 1m winner Our David (by Great Nephew); dam sister to Craven Stakes winner Corifi; 5½ lengths third of 16 to Down The Hatch in maiden race at Salisbury in September, best effort; not sure to stay 7f. *T. Marshall.* **57**

H

HABADALE 3 b.c. Habat 127–Queen's Penny (Queen's Hussar 124) (1979 6d 1980 7s* 8.5g 8fg 8fg) good-bodied colt; won maiden race at Leicester in March; well beaten in minor event and handicaps afterwards; should have stayed 1m; acted on soft going; got very worked up in paddock when blinkered on final 2 outings; dead. *P. Cole.* **67**

HABALLOO 2 ch.c. Habat 127–Calloo 99 (Ballyciptic 122) (1980 6f 6d 7g 7fg2 8.2g) Feb 24; workmanlike colt; third foal; half-brother to 1977 2-y-o 5f **54**

Ladbrokes Abernant Stakes, Newmarket—Piggott's hard riding gets Gypsy Dancer home by a short head from Son of Shaka

winner Friendly Baker (by Be Friendly); dam won over 6f and 7f at 2 yrs; 5 lengths second of 8 to Sideline in seller at Newmarket in August, best effort; stays 7f but ran poorly over 1m. *M. Smyly.*

HABALOOK 3 gr.c. Habat 127–Private View 74 (Derring-Do 131) (1979 6s 76
1980 6s^3 6d 5f^4 7fg 6g 5g^3 5fg* 6s* 6s) big, strong colt; has been hobdayed; won maiden race at Warwick in August and handicap at Ayr in September; apprentice ridden, hung left in latter; disappointed from a moderate draw in seller at Ayr later same week (claimed by H. Bell afterwards); stays 6f; acts on any going; wears blinkers. *J. Bethell.*

HABATASHIE 2 gr.f. Habat 127–Shenachie 79 (Sheshoon 132) (1980 5fg^3 5g 62
6d 6d) Apr 15; strong, lengthy filly; third living foal; half-sister to 3-y-o 12.2f winner Strathdearn (by Saritamer); dam stayer; in frame in maiden races at Doncaster in May and Redcar in August; likely to stay 1¼m. *E. Carter.*

HAB DANCER 2 b.c. Habitat 134–Come Dancing 91 (Northern Dancer) (1980 –
7d 7d 8g) Apr 4; 82,000Y; strong, heavy-bodied colt; half-brother to very smart stayer General Ironside (by Sea Hawk II) and useful 7f to 1½m winner Welsh Dancer (by Welsh Pageant); dam stayed 1m; far from fully fit when down the field in end-of-season maiden and minor events at Newmarket (2) and Doncaster. *R. Armstrong.*

HABILLE 2 ch.f. On Your Mark 125–Lake Constance 85 (Star Gazer 123) –
(1980 6s 5fg) May 8; 2,200F, 3,400Y; half-sister to useful 1976 2-y-o sprinter Bodensee (by Wolver Hollow) and a winner in Denmark; dam best at sprint distances; behind in large fields of maidens at Chepstow in June and Windsor (last of 24) in August. *M. Masson.*

HABITO 3 br.c. Habitat 134–Saccato (Bagdad) (1979 6fg 6fg* 7f^2 7d 7f 7f 8s^4 83
1980 6s 6fg^2 6h* 6f^2 7f 7d 6fg 7g 6d 6s) dipped-backed colt; good mover; short-priced favourite, got up in final strides to win 5-runner handicap at Brighton in May; bred to stay 1m but is evidently best at 6f; suited by top-of-the-ground conditions; wears blinkers nowadays; sold 740 gns Newmarket Autumn Sales. *G. Hunter.*

HABITOR 2 ch.c. Habitat 134–Daphne 106 (Acropolis 132) (1980 5f 5f^2 7g^3 8g) 98
Apr 18; 40,000F; strong, well-made, quite attractive colt; brother to 3 winners, including fairly useful 1978 2-y-o 5f winner Hadon, and half-brother to another winner; dam, half-sister to numerous winners, stayed 1½m; placed in good-class maiden races, going down by 5 lengths to Motavato at Sandown in May and finishing 4 lengths third of 16 to To-Agori-Mou at Goodwood 2 months later; well-backed favourite for well-contested nursery at Doncaster in September but had very stiff task under top weight and finished only 7¾ lengths seventh of 10 to Sheer Grit; stays 1m and may get 1¼m; certain to win a maiden race. *R. Hern.*

HABITUATE 4 b.c. Habitat 134–Lalibela 123 (Honeyway 125) (1979 6d* 121
8fg^3 8fg* 8fg* 8d^2 1980 7.2f^2 8d) neat Irish colt; half-brother to several winners, notably useful middle-distance performer Anadyomene (by Sea Hawk II) and quite useful stayer Million (by Mill Reef); dam won Cheveley Park Stakes and showed form only at sprint distances; developed into a smart miler as a 3-y-o and won 3 races, including Irish Cambridgeshire Handicap at the Curragh; ran well on reappearance when length second to Kris (gave 8 lb) in Cold Shield Windows Trophy at Haydock in May; well-backed favourite, looked well but was beaten 2f out when eighth of 11 behind Blue Refrain in Queen Anne Stakes at Royal Ascot following month, only subsequent start; appeared to act on any going; wore blinkers once when successful; stud in Australia. *V. O'Brien, Ireland.*

HACKBRIDGE 5 gr.h. Levanter 121–Signal Melody 70 (Bleep-Bleep 134) 65
(1979 8d^4 7d* 7g^2 7s^3 7s 7fg^2 7f 8fg 7f 7f^3 7.3g 1980 7fg 7.6f 8d 7g 7.6d 8.3s 8g 10g^3 10g 8d) quite a moderate handicapper nowadays; stays 1¼m; acts on any going; occasionally sweats up; ran poorly second outing and didn't move well to post on third. *T. Gosling.*

HADAJAR 5 b.g. Royalty 130–Sea Gal (Sea Hawk II 131) (1979 NR 1980 61
12d 12d^2 12d) strong gelding; fair performer over hurdles; well backed when length second to Wonderful Surprise in handicap at Leicester in October, only worthwhile form on flat; stays 1½m. *M. Tate.*

HADDFAN 5 ch.h. Lorenzaccio 130–Golden Windlass 79 (Princely Gift 137) 75
(1979 10v 12.3v 8d 7fg 8fg^3 8g*·8g^2 8.3fg^4 8.3f^2 8f^2 8fg^4 8fg^2 1980 7g^3 7.6f^2 8f* 8d^4 8d* 8g^2 8g 8g 10f^4 8.3fg 8fg) won apprentice handicap at Sandown in

May (led last stride) and Brighton Mile Challenge Cup in June (made all and beat Reine Soleil 2½ lengths); stays 1¼m; acts on any going. *J. Dunlop.*

HADDIE'S LADDIE 2 b.c. Bigivor–Highland Jenny (Falls of Clyde 126) (1980 7s 7d 7fg) May 29; workmanlike colt; fifth foal; dam of no account; only poor form in maiden races. *A. W. Jones.* —

HADERA 5 ch.m. Northfields–Flat Impulse 75 (Meadow Court 129) (1979 8v 8s 8d 8fg^4 8g^3 8.3fg^2 8fg^4 8.3f 8fg 8fg 1980 8fg 8fg 7fg 8g^4 8d 9f 8.3fg^2 8.3f* 8.3fg 8d* 8.2s) quite a moderate handicapper; won at Windsor in August (apprentice ridden) and Leicester in October, beating Princess Pageant by a length on latter course; stays 1m; possibly not at her best on very soft ground but acts on any other; suitable mount for an apprentice. *B. Gubby.* **70**

HADJI BEY 2 b.f. Martinmas 128–Javelot's Dancer (Javelot 124) (1980 5fg 5fg* 6g 5f) Feb 20; 2,400F, 6,000Y; half-sister to a winner in Barbados; dam never ran; won 15-runner maiden race at Warwick in June in good style by 2 lengths from Mrs Palmer; eased once chance had gone when last of 7 to Chateau Dancer in £4,000 race at York the following month; well beaten in nursery final outing; bred to stay 1m. *N. Callaghan.* **75**

HADLEY RIFLE 3 br.g. Scottish Rifle 127–Dake (Floribunda 136) (1979 7fg 1980 11.7f 10fg 11.7fg) little worthwhile form in maiden races. *P. Cole.* —

HADLEY ROCKET 3 ro.c. Roan Rocket 128–Mockbridge 106 (Bleep-Bleep 134) (1979 6f^3 1980 8g 8s) lengthy colt; showed promise in maiden race at Salisbury at 2 yrs; well beaten in similar events in 1980; will stay 1¼m. *P. Cole.* —

HADRIAN'S WALL 3 br.g. Scottish Rifle 127–Roman Meeting (Quorum 126) (1979 7f 1980 10.1f 8.2f 10.1f) rather leggy gelding; well beaten in maiden and minor events. *W. Hastings-Bass.* —

HAILEBURY 2 ch.f. Ashmore 125–Serendip (Sing Sing 134) (1980 7s*) May 13; half-sister to very useful 7f and 1m performer Serencia (by Great Heron); dam never ran; 25/1, did very well for an inexperienced filly when winning 23-runner maiden race at the Curragh in November, leading inside final 2f to win by 3 lengths from odds-on Candle Hill; will probably stay 1¼m; bound to go on to better things. *S. Murless, Ireland.* **90** p

HALBA 4 ch.f. Habat 127–Marypark 93 (Charlottown 127) (1979 10d 11.5fg^4 12.3fg^3 13f^2 14.7g* 13.8d* 16s* 14.6fg 15.8s^2 14g 1980 16fg 16fg 20d^4 16d 14g 16g 16.1s^2 18d) fair sort; ridden by 7-lb claimer, ran well and finished long way clear of remainder when 3 lengths fourth of 12 to Heighlin in Ascot Stakes at Royal Ascot in June; disappointed on next 3 starts but finished very strongly after being well behind most of way when length second to Wild Rosie in 18-runner apprentice handicap at Haydock in October; stays very well; suited by some give in the ground. *M. Jarvis.* **74**

HALLEZ-LOUP 6 ch.m. Hallez 131–Miss Wolff 91 (Vilmorin) (1979 NR 1980 12d 12g^4 15.8d) poor performer; stays 1½m; acts on any going; blinkered once; has won over hurdles. *S. Wiles.* —

HALL HOUSE (USA) 2 b.f. Tisab–Minneapolitan (Minnesota Mac) (1980 5fg 5f 5fg 6g 5f) Feb 21; $8,000F; strong, sturdy filly; first produce; dam placed at 3 yrs; sire at his best at 2 yrs when winner from 3f to 6f; well beaten in maiden races; blinkered third start; trained by A. Hide first 3 outings; sold 600 gns Newmarket Autumn Sales. *R. Smyth.* —

HALLO CHEEKY 4 ch.f. Flatbush 95–Artlight (Articulate 121) (1979 8f^4 12f^2 9g* 8.2g^2 13.8fg^4 12fg 1980 10.6fg 10f 10g 10g 10d^2) plater; best form at up to 1¼m. *J. Fitzgerald.* **55**

HALL'S TREASURE 6 b.g. Quisling 117–Aggvus 86 (Aggressor 130) (1979 8s 1980 12d) lightly raced and little worthwhile form since 1977. *W. Marshall.* —

HALSTON 2 ch.g. Simbir 130–Yorkist (Crepello 136) (1980 7g 8d) Apr 7; 9,400Y; neat gelding; half-brother to 2 minor winners; dam unraced sister to very useful middle-distance performer Donello; never-dangerous eighth of 11 to King's General in £3,000 event at Goodwood in September; well-backed favourite when only ninth of 17 in maiden race won by Emblazon at Warwick the following month; should be suited by 1m. *P. Cundell.* —

HALYUDH (USA) 4 ch.c. Herbager 136–Swapsetta (Swaps) (1979 7s 8.5s 12v^2 12g 14s 12fg* 13.3fg 10f* 12s 1980 10g 13.3f 16f 12f* 16g 12d 10fg 11f) big, well-made colt; made all and held off Neparree by ¾ length in Northern Dancer Stakes (Handicap) at Epsom in June; ran well when fifth to Billion in Henry II Stakes at Sandown the previous month and when fifth again to Nicholas **103**

Bill in Princess of Wales's Stakes at Newmarket in July but was rather disappointing on his other starts; effective at $1\frac{1}{4}$m and stays well; acts on any going but is very well suited by top-of-the-ground. *A. Breasley.*

HAMMERING 2 b.g. Auction Ring 123–Etoile Doree (Aureole 132) (1980 5f 5f^{2} 6f^{2} 6fg^{2} 7d 6v) May 4; 3,600Y; lengthy gelding; second living foal; dam placed over 7.5f at 2 yrs in Ireland; second in maiden race at Naas, maiden auction event at Epsom (went down by a head to El Strad when favourite) and auction race at Phoenix Park ($\frac{1}{2}$ length behind The Neurologist), last-named in July; ran badly afterwards; should stay beyond sprint distances. *M. Kauntze, Ireland.* **79**

HAMMERTON PRIDE 4 b.g. Lineage 99–Claral Star 71 (Top Star 96) (1979 6g 8d 5f 8f 8h 5g 6fg 7d* 7f 6d 6g 5s 1980 7d 7f 7f 8g 7s^{4} 6d 6g 7f 7f 6g 6s 8f 7d) leggy gelding; plater; should stay 1m; appears to act on any going; sometimes wears blinkers; changed hands 420 gns after tenth outing. *S. Nesbitt.* **–**

HAMPSHIRE 6 b.g. Silly Season 127–Pirate Queen 77 (Pirate King 129) (1979 10d 10g 11.7g^{4} 10g 10g* 10fg^{3} 10fg 10d^{4} 10fg* 12f^{2} 12fg^{2} 12.2g^{3} 10fg^{3} 1980 12g^{3} 10f^{2} 12h^{3} 10fg 10f 10f 10fg 10g^{4} 10g^{3}) middle-distance handicapper; acts on any going but has done all his winning on a sound surface; wears blinkers; ran well for a lady once; bandaged in front. *A. Pitt.* **70**

HAND OF GOD 4 ch.g. Green God 128–Man's Hand 65 (Golden Cloud) (1979 8s 10d 9.4f* 8f 8d 12d 1980 12fg 17.1fg 12fg^{2} 15.8g* 12f 12f 16fg) won handicap at Catterick in August by length from Super Swallow; runner-up in seller on previous outing; suited by a test of stamina; acts on firm going; blinkered last 3 outings at 2 yrs; sometimes sweats up. *F. Yardley.* **52**

HAND OVER FIST 5 ch.g. Queen's Hussar 124–Grace Note 104 (Parthia 132) (1979 16.1v 16g^{2} 16s 1980 18s) staying maiden; acts on any going; wears blinkers; inconsistent. *R. Whitaker.* **–**

HANDSOME DAVE 3 br.g. Some Hand 119–Samia 73 (Galivanter 131) (1979 NR 1980 6f 6fg 6fg) 2,100F, 3,100Y; half-brother to a winner in Malaya; dam poor maiden; in rear in maiden and minor races, twice finishing last; sold 550 gns Doncaster August Sales. *C. Thornton.* **–**

HANDSOME HAZE 2 b.g. Some Hand 119–Noon Mist (Barbary Pirate 91) (1980 8d 7s) May 8: plain gelding; fourth living foal; dam poor maiden; tailed off in maiden and minor events at Warwick and Chepstow in October. *R. Blakeney.* **–**

HANDSOME KID 4 b.c. Polyfoto 124–Helen Maire (Queen's Hussar 124) (1979 7s* 8.2v^{4} 8d^{3} 7g* 7s^{4} 7v 7g* 1980 8d 10s 8g 7s 8.2s^{3} 8.2s) quite attractive colt; ran best race when close third to Kithairon in handicap at Haydock in October (blinkered first time, finished well); blinkered again next time; stays 1m; acts on soft going; suitable mount for an apprentice; usually held up; sold to S. Harris 5,600 gns Newmarket Autumn Sales. *E. Eldin.* **82**

HANDSOME TRAILBOSS 2 ch.c. Some Hand 119–Cedez Cela (Bleep-Bleep 134) (1980 5f^{3} 6d 7s) May 11; workmanlike colt; fifth produce; brother to a plating-class animal; dam of little account; $7\frac{1}{2}$ lengths third of 9 to Maltese Falcon in maiden race at Wolverhampton in May; subsequently off course until October when well beaten in maiden and minor events; not sure to stay 7f. *J. Douglas-Home.* **51**

HANDS TIED 2 ch.g. Manacle 123–Grass Skirt 77 (Native Prince) (1980 5fg 5g 7d) Mar 25; 2,000F, 3,500Y (privately); neat gelding; half-brother to 5f seller winner Minti Green (by Pieces of Eight); dam won over 5f; well behind in maiden races, final one at Catterick; sold 380 gns Doncaster November Sales. *C. Thornton.* **–**

HANDYCUFF 8 b.g. Manacle 123–Black Rage 91 (My Babu 136) (1979 10.2fg 8.2g 8d^{3} 11g^{4} 8d* 8s 1980 8d 8d 10d^{3} 8f 8.2d 10.2g 8g^{3} 8.2s 8d^{3} 8s^{3}) tall gelding; quite a moderate handicapper nowadays; stays $1\frac{1}{4}$m; acts on any going but is ideally suited by an easy surface; has worn blinkers. *A. Scott.* **67**

HANDY DANCER 3 ch.f. Green God 128–Miss Golightly 83 (Jimmy Reppin 131) (1979 5f 1980 7.6f 10d* 10s* 10.8fg^{2} 10f* 10g^{3} 10g) tall, rangy, attractive filly; successful in minor event at Brighton and amateur riders races at Folkestone and Lingfield; may well stay $1\frac{1}{2}$m; acts on any going; good mount for an inexperienced rider; ran moderately final start; sold 4,700 gns Newmarket December Sales. *G. Harwood.* **87**

HANDY SAINT 3 b.f. Some Hand 119–Pilicina (Milesian 125) (1979 6g 5.8g 5f 6s 1980 6s 7f 6h 7f 6f 6fg) poor plater; has been tried in blinkers; unreliable; sold 420 gns Newmarket July Sales *W. Musson.* **– §**

HANG-ON ELVIS 5 br.g. Right Tack 131–Prairie Princess (Sayajirao 132) (1979 10.2s* 10d 10g 12f 12f 12fg² 1980 12g 10fg 11f 10f 11.7d 12g 11.7f⁴ 10f 10g 12g³ 12v³ 15d⁴) disappointing handicapper nowadays; stays 15f; acts on any going; best in blinkers; suited by strong handling; trained until after fourth outing by N. Callaghan. *F. Durr.* **62**

HANGSENG 8 b.g. Sing Sing 134–Miss Charisma 104 (Ragusa 137) (1979 NR 1980 8d 13g 15h² 15f* 13.3g² 17.1fg 13.1h) poor handicapper; led close home when winning at Folkestone in June by ½ length from Down To Darkie; stays well; acts on hard going; has worn blinkers; needs to be held up. *W. Musson.* **40**

HANHAM ROAD 2 b.c. Shiny Tenth 120–Prompt Delivery (Catullus) (1980 5f² (dis) 5.8fg 6d 5d) Mar 15; 8,400Y; lengthy colt; half-brother to P. D. Quick (by Prince O'Morn), a winner at up to 1m in USA; dam won twice from 23 starts, over 5f and 6f in USA; 2½ lengths second of 3 finishers in minor event won by Quay Boy at Chepstow in May but hampered third horse and was disqualified; well beaten subsequently. *D. Marks.* –

HANLEY CASTLE 4 ch.g. Fischio–Vidi's First (Vidi Vici 112) (1979 7s 8g 7f 6fg 6g 1980 7.6g) unfurnished gelding; poor plater; stays 6f; acts on any going except perhaps heavy; has been tried in blinkers. *A. W. Jones.* –

HANNAH'S SONG 3 b.f. Saintly Song 128–Alice Springs 83 (Coronation Year 124) (1979 5fg 5f 1980 7f 7fg³ 9.4d 8g 8g 10s 10f³ 12.2d⁴) plating-class maiden; best run at 1¼m on firm going. *N. Crump.* **54**

HANNONBALL 2 ch.g. Patch 129–Tudorella 104 (Tudor Minstrel 144) (1980 6g) Apr 16; 1,000Y; half-brother to several winners, including 1m and 9f winner Dynastic (by Tamerlane), who also showed smart form over 1m in France; dam sprinter; 16/1 when eighth of 13 to Fath-El-Keir in maiden auction event at Folkestone in July. *R. Hannon.* –

HANOVER LAD 2 b.c. Continuation 120–Amber Anne (Amber X 133) (1980 5fg 5s 5f 8fg 6g 5d) Apr 22; leggy, fair sort; bad plater; blinkered third outing. *J. Hardy.* –

HANOVER'S MOONGIRL 8 b.m. Hanover–Flaming Wendy (Poaching 115) (1979 NR 1980 12g) second foal; dam ran once on flat and over hurdles; backward when tailed off in amateur riders race at Redcar in June, first outing. *M. James.* –

HANOVIA GOLD 4 ch.f. Yellow River 114–Muftet 75 (Matador 131) (1979 8d 7v 7s 5g 6g⁴ 5f* 5fg 6f³ 6g 1980 5g 6g 5.3d 6g³ 5g³ 6fg* 6fg 5g) sprint handicapper; made all and ran on very gamely when holding off Vorvados by ½ length at Goodwood in August; acts well on firm going. *M. Haynes.* **55**

HANOVIA HAUT GIRL 2 b.f. Roman Warrior 132–Last Report 96 (Democratic 124) (1980 6g 5fg 7g 7g 5d) Apr 28; tall filly; half-sister to 6f winner Jantu (by Deep Diver); dam 6f to 1m handicapper; showed a little ability on most of her outings, on penultimate one finishing only 5¼ lengths behind King's General when seventh of 11 in slowly-run £3,000 event at Goodwood in September; evidently stays 7f. *M. Haynes.* **70**

HANOVIA STAR 2 bl.f. Saritamer 130–Vilswitch 93 (Vilmorin) (1980 5d 5fg 5fg 6f) Mar 4; 4,700Y; quite a well-made filly; half-sister to smart sprinter Vilgora (by Raffingora) and useful 1978 2-y-o Ghazal (by Averof); dam sprinter; little worthwhile form in maiden and minor events; sold 400 gns Newmarket Autumn Sales. *M. Haynes.* –

HANS BRINKER 5 ch.g. Dike–Final Orders (Prince John) (1979 NR 1980 12s 12v) very useful performer (rated 111) at 3 yrs but pulled up lame (chipped a bone) on final outing; backward when tailed off behind Jam at Newmarket in October and Path of Peace at Doncaster in November on only subsequent outings; stays well; acts on a firm surface. *G. Harwood.* –

HANS CRESCENT 2 ch.c. Dragonara Palace 115–Hi Tess 65 (Supreme Court 135) (1980 5.8fg³ 6s⁴ 6fg 6fg 7d 8g³ 8.2s 8d 8s) Apr 14; 3,000Y; leggy, lightly-made colt; half-brother to 3 winners by Double-U-Jay; dam plating class; quite a moderate maiden; stays 1m; unsuited by really soft going; tailed off final start (blinkered). *J. Toller.* **74**

HANU 3 b.c. Hot Spark 126–Light Link 99 (Tudor Music 131) (1979 5g⁴ 6f* 5fg² 5g* 1980 7f 6f 5fg² 5g⁴ 5g* 6g 5fg² 5g 5v² 6v²) smallish colt; smart performer; beat Via Delta 2 lengths in handicap at Goodwood in July; also ran creditably when runner-up to same horse in valuable handicap at Ascot, to Blue Persian in 3-runner minor event at Newbury, to Valeriga in Group 3 **113**

Premio Omenoni at Milan and to Lightning Label in £4,000 race at Doncaster; best form at 5f and appears not to stay 7f; acts on any going. *A. Breasley.*

HAPPY BRIDE 2 b.f. Royal Match 117–Topping Girl (Sea Hawk II 131) (1980 6fg 6f4 6g* 7g4 7fg*) Apr 4; second foal; half-sister to Irish 1979 2-y-o 7.5f winner Thread of Gold (by Huntercombe); dam never ran; prominent throughout when winning maiden race at Navan in June and minor event at Naas the following month, in latter coming home 4 lengths clear of Kaffir Dance with 4 previous winners further behind; not disgraced in between when 2¾ lengths fourth of 14 to Sea of Echoes in well-contested race at Leopardstown; will stay 1¼m+; yet to race on a soft surface. *J. Bolger, Ireland.* **95**

HAPPY CALL 9 gr.g. Town Crier 119–French Laughter 96 (Gilles de Retz 132) (1979 NR 1980 12.2fg 16g) of little account; wears blinkers. *A. Potts.* –

HAPPY JUNGLE 2 br.g. Tarboosh–Holme Lacy 88 (March Past 124) (1980 8d) Mar 15; 8,600Y; half-brother to several winners, including very useful miler Silver Steel (by Double-U-Jay); dam sprinter; 25/1 when behind in 17-runner maiden race won by Emblazon at Warwick in October. *B. Hanbury.* –

HAPPY LANDING 2 b.f. Auction Ring 123–Lea Landing 81 (Meadow Court 129) (1980 7d 6g 6s) Apr 7; 1,500Y; leggy filly; fourth foal; half-sister to 3 winners, including fairly useful 1979 Irish 2-y-o 7.5f winner Tilbury (by Realm); dam placed from 5f to 7f; unquoted when behind in end-of-season maiden races. *I. Walker.* –

HAPPY VICTORIOUS 13 ch.g. Gratitude 130–Eastern Bloom (Full Bloom) (1979 7fg 1980 7fg 8d 6d) poor handicapper nowadays; stays 1m; acts on any going; wears blinkers; front runner. *A. Hide.* –

HAPPY WORKER 5 b.g. Workboy 123–Gypsy Refrain 86 (Romany Air 118) (1979 12fg2 16f* 15fg* 16f 15.8fg 19f* 16g 15.8d 16fg 1980 12fg 16f3 14.7f* 15.8fg 16g 13.8f 15.8f 12d 12fg 12.2fg 16fg) big gelding; landed the odds by 6 lengths in 4-runner handicap at Redcar in May; well beaten afterwards; suited by a test of stamina on a sound surface; does best when ridden up with pace. *M. W. Easterby.* –

HAPPY YAPPY 3 b.g. Pieces of Eight 128–Junipero Serra 85 (Sing Sing 134) (1979 5g 5g3 5g* 5d3 7fg 6fg 7f3 7g4 7fg 1980 5v2 6s 8f 7f 5d 5fg 12g) strong, good-bodied gelding; ran moderately after finishing creditable second in handicap at Salisbury in March; unlikely to stay 1½m; acts on any going; blinkered sixth start. *A. Demetriou.* **87** d

HARBOROUGH BOY 3 ch.g. Netherkelly 112–Piazza del Grillo 72 (Le Levanstell 122) (1979 6s 1980 8fg 10.2g 13s) poor maiden; blinkered final start; sold 410 gns Doncaster September Sales; dead. *A. Jarvis.* –

HARDBRIDGE 2 b.c. So Blessed 130–Mockbridge 106 (Bleep-Bleep 134) (1980 5d4) Jan 19; 12,500Y; attractive, well-made colt; half-brother to 3 winners, including quite useful 7f to 13f performer Bines Bridge (by Lorenzaccio); dam won over 5f and 7f at 2 yrs; well-backed favourite and easily pick of paddock, took too long to get going but made excellent progress in final 2f, until eased once cause was clearly lost, when 6½ lengths fourth to 20 to Little Starchy in maiden race at Sandown in October; will be suited by 6f+; should improve at 3 yrs. *R. Armstrong.* **72** p

HARD FOUGHT 3 ch.c. Habitat 134–Ambrosia 102 (Alcide 136) (1979 6f3 6d* 7d 6f2 1980 7f3 7.2fg* 7g* 6d 7.3d3 8g2 8fg4) **122**

The well-known Holliday colours of white, maroon hoop, armlets and cap have been less in evidence in the winner's circle in the past few years than they were from 1950 to 1970 when the late Major Holliday was leading owner on three occasions and such good horses as Neasham Belle, Narrator, Hethersett, Night Off, Vaguely Noble (as a two-year-old) and Highest Hopes represented him or his son on the track. Racing isn't undertaken nowadays on such a large scale as previously: many of the yearlings bred by Mr Holliday in the last decade (Relkino was one) have been sold at public auction rather than sent into training by their breeder. Occasionally an important runner still does appear carrying the colours. One of the yearlings retained in 1978 was Hard Fought, and his owner can have no regrets about keeping a colt who has shown very smart form from six furlongs to a mile.

As a two-year-old Hard Fought had hung badly in behind the leaders on his third start and as his career progressed in 1980 it became apparent that he is nervous and a far from easy ride. After a creditable pipe-opener under 9-3

Jersey Stakes, Ascot—Hard Fought beats Sunfield cleverly by a neck. Etoile de Paris is third

in a valuable handicap at York, Hard Fought proceeded to win two important races in June, the John of Gaunt Stakes at Haydock and the Jersey Stakes at Royal Ascot. In the former he pulled hard for his head early on but moved up smoothly to take command over a furlong out and, despite hanging quite badly left, went on to account for the Irish invader Gods Mark by two lengths. The Jersey Stakes presented Hard Fought with a stiffer task, especially since he was penalized for his earlier success. Starting a well-backed favourite despite sweating up a bit beforehand, he was ridden with artistry by Piggott, tracking the leaders on the outside, looking to have plenty to do a couple of furlongs out but being brought with a strong run to lead close home and beat Sunfield cleverly by a neck.

Hard Fought (ch.c. 1977)	Habitat (b 1966)	Sir Gaylord (b 1959)	Turn-to
			Somethingroyal
		Little Hut (b 1952)	Occupy
			Savage Beauty
	Ambrosia (ch 1965)	Alcide (b 1955)	Alycidon
			Chenille
		Bride Elect (br 1952)	Big Game
			Netherton Maid

Thereafter Hard Fought's lines were cast in choppier waters. He was very much on edge in the preliminaries for the William Hill July Cup at Newmarket but performed creditably against the specialist sprinters, running on to be fifth behind Moorestyle after being outpaced, and he did well to be third to Kampala in the Hungerford Stakes at Newbury after experiencing little luck in running. More than once Hard Fought had given the impression he would stay a mile, and the Waterford Crystal Mile at Goodwood late in August gave him a chance to prove it. He put up probably the best performance of his career. Receiving weight from Known Fact and Night Alert, he lay close up from the start, led over a furlong and a half out and stayed on extremely well, so well that it took all Carson's strength to force Known Fact past him in the dying strides to win by a neck with Night Alert half a length away third. A mile evidently suited Hard Fought, but unfortunately he didn't run up to his Goodwood form when tried over the trip again in the Queen Elizabeth II Stakes at Ascot the following month. Meeting Known Fact on better terms, he was a spent force halfway up the straight and came in a moderate fourth behind the Guineas winner.

There is a good chance that Hard Fought will stay beyond a mile. He is a half-brother to three winners, all of them by milers and all successful over at least a mile and a half, namely the stayer Lotus Eater (by Le Levanstell) and the useful middle-distance handicappers London God (by Pall Mall) and St Briavels (by Sovereign Path). The dam, Ambrosia, never fulfilled the promise of her first run at two years though she did manage to win a mile maiden race at Wolverhampton the following season when odds on. Her breeding is of more interest than her racecourse performances, for she is a half-sister to numerous winners, notably the St Leger winner Hethersett and Proud Chieftain, who showed good form at up to one and a half miles. Ambrosia's dam, Bride Elect, was the second-best two-year-old filly of 1954, winning the Queen Mary Stakes and finishing runner-up in the Cheveley Park. She failed to train on, unlike three of Netherton Maid's other good winners, Chatsworth, Pirate King and Pampered King. Netherton Maid ran second in the Oaks and was a sister to a winner of that race, Neasham Belle, and a Coronation Cup winner, Narrator.

Hard Fought is a strong, good sort who carries plenty of condition and has a nice, easy action. He has yet to race on very soft going but acts on any other. He requires strong handling. *M. Stoute.*

HARD FROST 4 br.c. Right Tack 131–Broken Blossoms (Breakspear II) (1979 6g 6g* 6fg 6g^{4} 8.2d* 8fg^{2} 8fg 10f^{4} 1980 8fg 9g 8g) strong, robust colt; poor walker; lightly raced and no worthwhile form in 1980 (apprentice ridden); stays 1$\frac{1}{4}$m; seems to act on any going; often wears blinkers. *B. Hobbs.* —

HARDGREEN (USA) 4 ch.c. Irish Castle–Colinear (Cohoes) (1979 7d 8g 10.5g^{2} 12g 12fg^{3} 10f* (dis) 10.5d 10f* 10.2fg* 10f^{2} 1980 10f 8f^{3} 8.5f* 8d^{4} 8g) lengthy, attractive colt; good walker; brother to Castle Green, a smart but **120**

Diomed Stakes, Epsom—Hardgreen makes all the running and wins from New Berry and Bonnie Isle

inconsistent 2-y-o in 1979, and to House of Erin, a stakes winner at up to 8.5f in USA; dam won a claiming race over 6f at 3 yrs in USA; very smart performer as a 2-y-o, runner-up to Kris in Horris Hill Stakes; ran over middle distances as a 3-y-o and was rather disappointing, gaining only wins in minor events at Sandown and Doncaster (also won at Newbury, but was disqualified); reverted to shorter distances in 1980 and did better, although only lightly raced; ran a fine race when less than a length third to Kris in Tote Lockinge Stakes at Newbury in May and beat New Berry by 1½ lengths after making nearly all in the Diomed Stakes at Epsom the following month; not disgraced afterwards when fourth to Blue Refrain in Queen Anne Stakes at Royal Ascot in June or when sixth to Posse in Sussex Stakes at Goodwood in July, beaten about 4 lengths in latter event; acted particularly well on firm going; well beaten when blinkered once as a 3-y-o (Benson & Hedges Gold Cup at York); standing at Rossenara Stud, Co. Kilkenny, at a fee of IR £1,500 (Oct 1st concession). *M. Stoute.*

HARD HELD 8 ch.h. Manacle 123–Ange d'Or (Golden Cloud) (1979 10.6s^4 **51**
10.6g 10fg^4 13g 7f* 8f* 12f* 8fg* 11d^2 8g^2 12s^2 12fg 8.2d^4 8.2s 12d 1980 12d 10v 8.2fg* 8f 12f 10.6fg 12fg^4 10.6fg 12d 8fg^2 8.2g 10g 8.2d) plater; attracted no bid after winning at Haydock in April; effective from 7f to 1½m; acts on any going; best in blinkers; good mount for an inexperienced rider; sometimes sweats up; usually held up. *G. Richards.*

HARDINVAST (FR) 3 b.c. Lyphard 132–Natively 95 (Native Prince) (1979 **82**
7g 7s 1980 6d^3 7f^2 8fg* 8fg^2 8fg^3 8fg 7.6g 8d^4 8g 8.3f 8d 7d) 250,000 francs Y (approx £30,000); well-made, attractive ex-French colt; good mover; second foal; dam won three 5f races at 2 yrs; made all to win 16-runner maiden race at Warwick in May; ran respectably in handicaps on several subsequent outings; has won over 1m but gives impression 7f suits him better; acts on firm going and is possibly unsuited by soft; blinkered ninth start; sold 7,200 gns Newmarket Autumn Sales. *J. Hindley.*

HARD TO SING (FR) 4 b.g. Hard to Beat 132–Concord Hymm 107 (Emerson) **120**
(1979 12s* 12g^2 12d^2 12v* 12g* 12g* 1980 12g* 12g* 12g* 15.5g* 15.5g* 12g^2) big French gelding; brother to smart 1977 French 2-y-o filly Praise, a winner over 1¼m at 3 yrs, and half-brother to 2 winners in France; dam won over 6f at 2 yrs; a very smart racehorse who had another very good season; met his only defeats when 2 lengths second to Shafaraz in Prix de Barbeville at Longchamp in April on fourth start (subsequently promoted to first after Shafaraz failed a routine dope test) and when beaten a head by Moulouki in Prix Jean de Chaudenay at Saint-Cloud in May on final outing; always going well and ran on strongly to repel Prove It Baby by a neck in Prix Jean Prat at Longchamp on fifth outing; had earlier won 3 times at Cagnes-sur-Mer, including 100,000 francs prize; stays well; acts on heavy going; wears blinkers; genuine and consistent. *C. Milbank, France.*

HARDWICK SUN 2 ch.f. Dieu Soleil 111–Hyper Rose 62 (Pinza 137) (1980 —
5f 5f 5f) Mar 28; narrow, leggy filly; half-sister to fairly useful River Petterill (by Another River), successful at up to 7f; dam, a plater, best at 1m; little better than plating-class form but needs further than 5f. *G. Richards.*

HARDY TURK 9 b.g. Hill Clown–Turkhan Law (Turkhan) (1979 13.8g 13g **63**
12f 13.8f^3 13fg* 12f^2 13g 13g 1980 12d 12f^3 12f^2 13f 13fg^4 15fg) neat gelding; has been fired; runner-up to Swagger Stick at Thirsk in April, best effort of 1980; tailed off final outing; stays well; acts on any going; sometimes wears blinkers; suitable mount for an apprentice; sometimes makes the running. *C. Thornton.*

HAREBELL 3 br.f. Firestreak 125–Blaeberry 100 (Hook Money 124) (1979 **71**
5v^3 5v^4 5s^2 5s^2 5d* 6f^3 6fg 5d^2 5fg 5g 1980 5fg^2 5.8f^2 5fg 5.8g^2 6d^4 5.8f 5f 5g* 5d 6d 6g) compact filly; quite a moderate handicapper; ridden by 7-lb claimer when winning at Chepstow in September; runs as though 6f is her limit; acts on any going. *P. Cundell.*

HARESCEUGH 2 b.c. Andrea Mantegna–Mertola (Tribal Chief 125) (1980 —
8d) May 30; workmanlike colt; second foal; half-brother to a winner in Hong Kong; dam ran only once; unquoted, dwelt when modest sixth of 9 to Akram in minor event at Leicester in October. *N. Vigors.*

HARFORD 3 br.g. Goldhill 125–Sage-Willow 69 (Mossborough 126) (1979 **71**
6s^2 7g^3 8g^2 1980 12fg^3 11.7f 8fg 10.2g 16fg) strong gelding; plating-class maiden; probably stays 1½m; acts on a firm surface and soft going; sweating final outing. *H. Candy.*

HARLEW 2 b.f. Fine Blade 121–Jillaroo 79 (Javelot 124) (1980 5f 6g 6fg 6fg 7g^{4} 8.2s 8d^{2} 7d^{3}) Mar 20; 2,000Y; neat filly; sister to Irish 1½m winner Jillette and 2 poor animals and half-sister to 3 winners; dam stayed 1½m; showed ability in maiden races, running best race when 2½ lengths second of 17 to Emblazon at Warwick in October; will stay 1½m; acts on a soft surface. *N. Guest.* **76**

HARLYN 3 b. or br.g. Mansingh 120–Harmony Thyme 73 (Sing Sing 134) (1979 5g 6g 6fg 5d* 6f 5s 1980 5s^{4} 7fg 5g 7fg 6s^{2} 6g 6s) tall gelding; plater; not certain to stay 7f; acts well on soft ground; sometimes blinkered; races with head high; exported to Malaysia. *P. Rohan.* **51**

HARMONY BAY 2 b.f. Jimmy Reppin 131–Even Song (Falcon 131) (1980 6g) Mar 9; 1,000F, 3,500Y; small filly; second living foal; half-sister to 6f to 1½m winner Winter Sunshine (by Crisp and Even); dam showed little sign of ability; 50/1, on backward side and apprentice ridden when in rear in 15-runner maiden race won by Kalaglow at Newmarket in August. *P. Haslam.* **–**

HARPERS FERRY (USA) 2 b.c. Angle Light–Flower Vase (Round Table) (1980 7g 7d) Feb 8; $20,500Y; strong, good-bodied colt; first foal; dam never ran; in rear in 11-runner minor event at Goodwood (burly and started slowly) and 14-runner maiden race at Leicester (made running for a long way) in the autumn. *J. Bethell.* **–**

HARP STRINGS (FR) 2 br.f. Luthier 126–Gilding 103 (Kauai King) (1980 5f^{3} 6g 6g* 7g^{4} 7d^{2}) Mar 12; lengthy filly; first foal; dam won Ascot 1,000 Guineas Trial; won 15-runner maiden race at Nottingham in July by 2 lengths from odds-on Wolverhants; very good head second to Supper's Ready in 14-runner nursery at Goodwood in September; will be suited by 1m, and may well get further; acts well on a soft surface; genuine. *I. Balding.* **109**

HARROW CROSS 2 b.f. Master Sing 109–Highland Night (Night Thought 83) (1980 6fg 6g 5d) useless plater. *D. Ringer.* **–**

HARRY LAWRENCE 2 b.c. Murrayfield 119–Hard to Catch 59 (Hardicanute 130) (1980 5fg 6g 6fg 5fg) Apr 9; 1,500Y; small colt; third foal; dam placed over 7f; plating-class maiden; bred to stay 1m; blinkered first outing; sold to L. Barratt 300 gns Doncaster October Sales. *R. Armstrong.* **54**

HARTSFIELD 3 ch.c Grundy 137–Omentello 91 (Elopement 125) (1979 NR 1980 11fg 12f* 12fg* 11fg^{3} 12fg 12d^{3} 12fg) big, strong colt with a lot of scope and a very long stride; half-brother to numerous winners, including very useful 1979 3-y-o Lyric Dance (by Lyphard) and smart 7f performer Tudor Mill (by Derring-Do); dam won over 13f; narrow winner of minor event and handicap at Kempton in May; suited by 1½m and will stay 1¾m; acts on firm going; seems to need strong handling; out of his depth fifth start. *R. Laing.* **86**

HARVESTER GLORY 2 b.g. Warpath 113–Pasdeux 107 (Ballyogan) (1980 8.2s 8g) Mar 23; 6,600Y; medium-sized, quite attractive gelding; brother to middle-distance winner Beau Geste, and half-brother to 4 other winners, including fairly useful 1973 5f winner Sunblessed (by So Blessed); dam won twice over 5f at 2 yrs; weak in market, always behind in end-of-season maiden and minor events. *M. Jarvis.* **–**

HARVESTER SOLAR 3 ch.g. Porto Bello 118–Netley (Major Portion 129) (1979 5s^{2} 6d 6fg 7g* 7f^{2} 7f^{4} 7g 1980 10f^{3} 10g 8d 8g^{2} 10f) quite well-made gelding; quite a moderate handicapper; stays 1¼m; acts on any going; below form final start. *M. Jarvis.* **82**

HARVEST FESTIVAL 3 ch.f. Silly Season 127–Calleva (Worden II 129) (1979 7fg^{4} 8f^{3} 1980 12fg^{3} 12fg^{3} 14g) quite a well-made filly; third in minor race at Salisbury in May and maiden event at Lingfield in June; stays 1½m (well beaten over further); acts on firm going; sold 3,800 gns Newmarket December Sales. *I. Balding.* **68**

HARVEST SUPPER 5 b.g. Silly Season 127–Royal Pancake 104 (Crepello 136) (1979 8d 16fg 10fg 1980 10.1g) poor handicapper; stays 1¼m; possibly needs a galloping track. *F. Muggeridge.* **–**

HASSI R'MEL 2 ch.c. Clear Run 109–Nuchiru (Chingnu 99) (1980 5fg 7d 7g 7g 8fg) Apr 8; third foal; dam never ran; bad plater. *F. Yardley.* **–**

HASTY ARAB 2 b.f. Hasty Word 84–Ol Arabel (Relic) (1980 5f 6g) compact filly; half-sister to several winners, including very useful 1967 sprint 2-y-o The Rift (by Major Portion); probably of little account. *G. Balding.* **–**

HASTY DAWN 3 br.f. Dawn Review 105–Welcome Sara 66 (Lucky Brief 128) (1979 7g^{3} 7fg^{4} 8f^{2} 1980 12fg^{2} 12h 11.7g^{2} 11.7s^{2} 13.1f^{2} 15.5fg^{3} 11.7fg^{4}) **71**

lightly-made filly; quite a moderate handicapper; possibly doesn't stay 2m; acts on any going with possible exception of hard. *H. Candy.*

HASTY'S GOLD 2 b.c. Gold Rod 129–Carina Janie 88 (Silver Cloud 121) (1980 5.8fg 7fg 6fg 8fg 8d^3 10d) sixth foal; dam 1¼m winner; plater; ¾-length third of 15 to Flying Dreamer in maiden race at Bath in October, easily best effort; suited by 1m but possibly doesn't stay 1¼m; best run on a soft surface; sold 400 gns Ascot November Sales. *J. Cann.* **57**

HATTAN 2 b.c. Rheingold 137–Bally's Gift 83 (So Blessed 130) (1980 7g 8fg 8d^3 7d) Apr 30; 37,000Y; good-looking colt; second foal; dam, winner over 1½m, is half-sister to very smart Mil's Bomb; showed first worthwhile form when 7 lengths third of 15 to King's College Boy in maiden race at Warwick in October; will stay 1½m. *P. M. Taylor.* **75**

HATTON LAD 4 b.g. Ben Novus 109–Cath 85 (Bewildered 102) (1979 10v 10.8s 13v 14f 16.1g 1980 16s) fair sort; seems of little account; often wears blinkers. *D. Ancil.* –

HAUL KNIGHT 4 ch.c. Firestreak 125–My Own II 96 (El Relicario 124) (1979 8v^4 11fg 10s^2 10v* 10fg* 10.5f^3 12g^3 10fg* 9f 10fg^3 10g^4 1980 9f^2 10f^3 10d^4 12fg^3 10.5d 11.1fg^4 9f 10d) well-made colt; good-class performer on his day; ran very well when neck second to Ela-Mana-Mou (gave 5 lb) in Earl of Sefton Stakes at Newmarket in April; ran best subsequent races on third and fourth outings, when 5½ lengths fourth to Ela-Mana-Mou in Prince of Wales's Stakes at Royal Ascot in June and when just over 4 lengths third behind Water Mill in Alycidon Stakes at Goodwood in August; stays 1½m; acts on any going but goes particularly well on top-of-the-ground; wears blinkers; suited by waiting tactics; sold 40,000 gns Newmarket December Sales, reportedly to race in Italy. *G. Harwood.* **114**

HAVA-NAGILA 3 br.g. Balliol 125–Lake Constance 85 (Star Gazer 123) (1979 6fg 6f 1980 6f 7f 8fg 10.1g) lengthy gelding; little worthwhile form in maiden and minor races; sold 640 gns Ascot October Sales. *R. Smyth.* –

HAVANEZA 2 b.f. Simbir 130–Lucindale (Ballyciptic 122) (1980 5fg 7d 7fg 8fg 7g) Mar 9; 2,200Y; leggy, workmanlike filly; half-sister to 2 winners here and abroad, including 1977 2-y-o 5f winner Sterling Lucy (by Sterling Bay); dam never ran; 2¼ lengths fifth of 13 to Martelli in modest 1m maiden race at Beverley in September, fourth start; probably needs a stiff test of stamina. *A. Demetriou.* **65**

HAVASU 3 ch.f. Porto Bello 118–Queen of Saba 105 (High Treason 126) (1979 5g 5f 5fg 5s 6s 5g^2 5d^2 1980 6d 5g 5s 8d 6s 7f 6s) fair sort; poor mover; plater; ran poorly at 3 yrs; should stay 6f; acts on a soft surface; wears blinkers. *W. Haigh.* –

HAVERHILL LAD 4 ch.g. Queen's Hussar 124–Court Sensation 73 (Appiani II 128) (1979 8d 8f 11.5fg 8fg 10fg 8fg^4 7fg^2 8g^3 8f^3 8fg 8f^3 1980 8fg^3 10f^3 10fg* 10fg 10d* 10g^4 11.7s 8g 10g* 11g^2 10fg^2 10.5s^3 10s^3) won maiden race at Leicester (made all) in May and handicaps at Yarmouth (gamely) in July and Ostend in August; ran creditably most other starts, including when close third to Telsmoss in valuable apprentice handicap at York in October; stays 11f; acts on any going; has worn blinkers but does better without. *G. Blum.* **70**

HAVERING HILL 2 b.c. So Blessed 130–Heaven and Earth (Midsummer Night II 117) (1980 7d^4) Mar 23; rangy colt; 3,600F, 10,000Y; third produce; half-brother to fairly useful 1979 2-y-o 5f winner Our Mother (by Bold Lad Ire); dam ran only twice; 6/1 and looking as though race would do him good, ran on well, after getting badly outpaced early on, to finish 4½ lengths fourth of 8 to Belloc in minor event at Leicester in November; should benefit from the experience. *P. Walwyn.* **80** p

HAVOC 2 br.c. Swing Easy 126–Bobelle 62 (Pirate King 129) (1980 6g) Mar 2; 8,600Y; big, rangy colt; has scope; half-brother to 2 winners, including 1979 2-y-o 1m winner Prince Warren (by Pieces of Eight); dam won in Holland; 10/1 and in need of race, broke none too well when remote fifth of 10 to Tinjar in maiden race at Newmarket in August, only outing. *C. Brittain.* –

HAVON AIR 2 ch.f. Celtic Cone 116–Mary's Date 60 (The Phoenix) (1980 7g 7g 8d) Mar 31; lightly-built filly; half-sister to winners here and abroad, including 1973 2-y-o sprint winner Lucky Affair (by Stephen George); dam stayed 1½m; in rear in minor and maiden events. *R. Hannon.* –

HAVON COOL 4 b.c. Celtic Cone 116–Lucky Affair 83 (Stephen George 102) (1979 12d 8d^4 8d^3 8f^3 10.1g^2 8.3g* 7g^4 8.2s 10d^3 10.2s 1980 8fg^3 10h 10.6g 8g^3 8fg 7.5g* 8fg* 8.3fg^3 8g^2 7.6d^4 7.2d 8d) neat, strong colt; won apprentice events at **79**

Chester (handicap) and Bath in July; stays 1¼m; seems to act on any going; wears blinkers nowadays; moved very poorly to post tenth outing. *F. Rimell.*

HAWA 2 b.c. Tumble Wind–Henco (High Hat 131) (1980 5fg 6s 7g 6s) Feb 24; 4,300F; close-coupled colt; half-brother to 3 winners, including Irish middle-distance stayer Sassafaction (by Sassafras); dam plating class; blinkered when 6¾ lengths sixth of 9 to Candaules in minor event at Brighton in October, third outing and only sign of ability; didn't wear blinkers when behind in Haydock seller next start; will stay at least 1m. *C. Nelson.* **64**

HAWALI 3 b.f. Gay Fandango 132–Gentle Way 74 (Gentle Art 121) (1979 NR 1980 7v 6fg* 6f^{4} 7.3f^{4} 7g 8g) 17,500Y; rangy, quite attractive filly; sixth foal; half-sister to good Belgian winner Arpad (by Connaught); dam half-sister to Sovereign Path; favourite, made virtually all and stayed on well to win maiden race at Folkestone in April; respectable fourth in handicap at Newbury in May on fourth outing; should stay 1m (ran moderately when tried at trip); acts on firm going. *J. Sutcliffe.* **69**

HA'WAY GEORDIE 5 b.g. Rarity 129–Apple Brandy 100 (Arctic Prince 135) (1979 13s^{3} 12d^{2} 12.3v^{4} 12d^{2} 10g 12v* 12g 15s 1980 12d 12.5s) well-made gelding; best form at up to 13f; has worn blinkers. *Denys Smith.* –

HAWKINS 5 b.h. Captain's Gig–Hadjella (Hardicanute 130) (1979 6s 6fg 5fg 5.3fg^{2} 6fg 5fg 8fg^{4} 7g 1980 5d^{4} 5s^{4} 6g 5f^{3} 5f^{3} 5g^{3} 5.1f^{4} 5fg 6g* 5f* 5d 6g 6f) won handicaps at Chester and Beverley in July (led close home both times) but is nothing like the force he was; best form at up to 6f; possibly unsuited by soft ground. *R. Sheather.* **73**

HAYATO 2 ch.c. Music Boy 124–Linden Lea 91 § (Hornbeam 130) (1980 6fg 5.1g^{2} 5d^{2}) Feb 3; 5,600F; small colt; good walker and mover; half-brother to 2 winning platers; dam at her best at 2 yrs; second in maiden races at Yarmouth and Sandown in the autumn, going down by 2 lengths to Little Starchy in 20-runner event on latter; gives impression 6f will suit him. *J. Winter.* **85**

HAY RIDE 7 br.h. Galivanter 131–Haytime (Alycidon 138) (1979 12g^{2} 11.7g 10f 10f^{3} 10fg^{3} 12fg 12.3s^{3} 16fg 10fg^{4} 1980 12f^{2} 12d* 12g^{2} 12f^{2} 13s* 10fg) middle-distance performer; ridden by 7-lb claimer when winning 2 handicaps at Hamilton in September; ran well in apprentice handicaps on his other starts, including when second at York, Salisbury and Wolverhampton; acts on any going; has been tried in blinkers; excellent mount for an inexperienced rider. *N. Guest.* **85**

HAYS FIRST 4 b.f. Birdbrook 110–Molvitesse 75 (Molvedo 137) (1979 8s 8fg 8.2g 8fg 8.2f 8g 8.2fg 8g 7g 7d) 1980 12.3s 13g 12f 12f 8.2fg 12g^{3} 12d 9d^{3} 8d 9s 12g 9v) plater; stays 1½m; seems suited by some give in the ground; sometimes wears blinkers; suitable mount for a boy. *W. H. H. Williams.* –

HAZARD CHASE 5 ch.h. Roi Soleil 125–Flying Goddess (Red God 128 §) (1979 5s^{3} 5s 5s 5.1g 5g^{4} 5fg 5g 1980 7f 7f 6fg 5g) sprint handicapper; didn't run up to his best in 1980 but was not disgraced over 7f on reappearance; dwelt penultimate outing; acts on any going; sold 800 gns Doncaster September Sales. *N. Callaghan.* –

HAZELDEAN 3 b.f. St Paddy 133–Royal Nutmeg (Entanglement 118) (1979 6g 7f^{4} 8.2g 10s* 1980 8d 10g 10.6fg^{3} 12f^{2} 12g 12g* 11g^{2} 12g 12f) rangy filly; fair handicapper; decisively beat York Cottage by 1½ lengths in slowly-run race at York in July; suited by 1½m; acts on any going; does best when ridden up with pace. *P. Rohan.* **90**

HAZING 2 b. or br.f. Home Guard 129–Amazing Maid 104 (Amazing) (1980 5f^{2} 5.1f 5s^{4}) Mar 8; 31,000Y; neat filly; second foal; closely related to 3-y-o 1¼m winner Astrantia (by Gay Fandango); dam second in Queen Mary Stakes; 2 lengths second of 9 to Unashamed in maiden race at Sandown in May; ran poorly next time out and had her tongue tied down when well-beaten fourth of 7 to Princess Gayle in maiden event at Newcastle in August; sold to BBA 3,000 gns Newmarket Autumn Sales. *J. Hindley.* **72**

HAZY LOVE 2 gr.f. Ardoon 124–Atonement 109 (Palestine 133) (1980 6d 7fg 8fg 8d) Apr 17; 1,600F, 2,100Y; compact filly; half-sister to 5 winners, including useful 1971 2-y-o 6f winner Fresh Start (by Busted); dam, speedy 2-y-o, is sister to Pall Mall; no sign of ability, including in sellers; wore a hood and blinkers on final start; sold 500 gns Ascot November Sales. *I. Walker.* –

HEAD OF STATE (FR) 2 b.c. Crowned Prince 128–Sweet and Gay (Sir Gaylord) (1980 8d) Mar 18; first foal; dam, half-sister to very smart middle- –

distance horse Anne's Pretender, won over 11.5f in French Provinces; 12/1 and fit, moved badly to start for 14-runner maiden race at Leicester in November and came back tailed off behind Sha'lan. *P. Cole.*

HEADSTONE 3 ch.g. Ragstone 128–Top Drawer 70 (High Hat 131) (1979 7f 7fg 7d 1980 12fg 16f 16g 16s^4 16fg^4 16s* 16fg^4) strong gelding; trotted up in 13-runner maiden race at Nottingham in August; stays well; probably acts on any going; often blinkered but wasn't when successful. *J. Dunlop.* **72**

HEARTBREAKER 2 gr.f. Steel Heart 128–Tetrazzini 70 (Sovereign Path 125) (1980 6g^4) Mar 6; 31,000Y; strong, compact filly; second foal; half-sister to useful 1979 2-y-o 5f to 7f winner Lady Downsview (by Prince Regent); dam placed over 6f; 20/1 and on burly side when promising 7 lengths fourth of 25 to Composer in maiden event at Newmarket in October, racing prominently throughout; not sure to stay beyond 6f. *Sir Mark Prescott.* **71** p

HEARTH 3 b.f. Home Guard 129–Fair Path (Javelot 124) (1979 7fg^4 1980 11fg* 12fg* 12h* 11.1f^3 11.5fg* 12g 11.7fg^3 12g^3 12fg^3) tall, leggy filly; fairly useful performer; successful in maiden race at Wolverhampton, minor events at Salisbury and Folkestone and handicap at Windsor; gamely beat Telsmoss by a neck in last-named in August; stays 1½m; yet to race on a soft surface; suitable mount for a boy; sold 14,500 gns Newmarket December Sales. *G. Harwood.* **94**

HEART N' SOUL 2 br.f. Bold Lad (Ire) 133–Relic Spirit (Relic) (1980 5f^2 5fg* 5f^4 5g* 5g^3 5g^2 5g^3 6s 5g^4 5g^3) Mar 20; 11,000Y; compact filly; second foal; half-sister to a winner in Austria; dam second 4 times over sprint distances in Ireland; winner twice at Leopardstown, making all in minor event in May and beating Creepin Suzie in nursery in July; also ran well on most of her other outings, finishing just over 2 lengths third of 10 to Swan Princess in Group 1 Gallaghouse Phoenix Stakes at Phoenix Park on seventh start and 4 lengths fifth of 14 to Arctique Royale in Group 2 Moyglare Stud Stakes at the Curragh on eighth; stays 6f; seems to act on any going. *J. Bolger, Ireland.* **101**

HEATED DEBATE 2 br.c. Politico 124–Lady Phoenix (Lorenzaccio 130) (1980 6g 6fg) Mar 25; 500Y; resold 520Y; big colt; first foal; dam unraced half-sister to very useful 1974 2-y-o Lady Rowley; behind in £2,700 event at Leicester (burly when tailed-off last of 8) in July and 14-runner maiden event at Yarmouth (never went pace) following month. *J. Gilbert.* –

HEATHEN PRINCE 2 ch.g. Sun Prince 128–Heather Grove (Hethersett 134) (1980 5d 6d 6f 6fg 5g 6d 6s) May 8; 7,200Y; small, strong gelding; good walker; half-brother to 3 winners, including very useful sprinter Meiwa King (by Sing Sing); dam French middle-distance maiden; blinkered, ran best race on fifth outing when 1¾ lengths fifth of 9 to Zoilo in modest maiden event at Nottingham in September; had stiffer task when again blinkered next time out; form only at 5f but is bred to stay at least 7f. *A. Breasley.* **70**

HEATH HOUSE 3 b.c. Jimmy Reppin 131–Bell Heather 66 (Langton Heath 97) (1979 5d 1980 7s 10.2fg 12f 12f) big, lengthy colt; has ability, but is very temperamental (unseated rider when swerving soon after start on first and final outings, wearing blinkers on latter); best left alone. *G. Beeson.* **§§**

HEARTS ARE TRUMPS 6 b.m. Knave To Play 79–Bilton Belle 88 (Star Gazer 123) (1979 NR 1980 14.7f 12.2fg 12g 16.1s) of no account. *A. Watson.* –

HEAVENLY CHOIR 6 ch.m. St Alphage 119–Tra-La-La (Penhurst) (1979 7s 6s 6g 6fg 6fg 6f 6f 6g^3 7fg 6g 7fg 1980 6s^4 6g 6h 7g 8g) robust mare; behind in sellers on last 2 outings; stays 6f well; acts on any going; has been tried in blinkers; suitable mount for an apprentice. *D. Weeden.* **41**

HEAVENLY CHORD 2 b.f. Hittite Glory 125–Dulcimer (Double Jump 131) (1980 5fg^2 6fg 6d* 7.2s^2 7f^3 7.2g^2 7s) May 27; 3,400 2-y-o; well-grown filly; second foal; dam unraced daughter of smart stayer Crotchet; made all to win maiden race at Ayr in June by 2 lengths from Joint Command; second twice at Haydock subsequently, going down by 3 lengths to Stats Emmar in Rose of Lancaster Stakes in July and by a length to Kareem in nursery 2 months later; will stay 1m; acts on any going. *M. H. Easterby.* **89**

HEAVENLY CHORUS 4 b.f. Green God 128–Lingay 99 (Sing Sing 134) (1979 10d 8d 8s 7g* 7fg 7f* 7f* 7f^4 7g 7f^3 7fg 7f^4 7fg^4 7fg* 7d 1980 7fg 7fg^3 7g 6g^4 7fg^2 7g^3 7g) strong, good-bodied filly; stays 7f; acts well on firm going and is not at her best on soft; suitable mount for an apprentice; front runner. *P. Cundell.* **73**

HEAVENLY RULER (CAN) 3 b.c. Riva Ridge–Heavenly Power (Bold Ruler) (1979 6fg^2 7f^2 7fg^2 7s 7f* 7fg* 7s^3 1980 8f 10f) good-bodied colt; fairly useful (rated 91) at 2 yrs; well beaten in handicaps at Thirsk (needed run) and Newmarket (moved very badly to post) early in 1980; should stay $1\frac{1}{4}$m; acts on firm going and is probably unsuited by soft; sold 2,000 gns Newmarket Autumn Sales. *M. Stoute.* 82

HEAVENLY VALLEY 2 b.f. Steel Heart 128–Focal 92 (Faubourg II 127) (1980 5f 5g* 5fg 5fg^2 6g 6g 7d) Apr 8; 22,000Y; powerful, deep-bodied filly; who carries plenty of condition; half-sister to numerous winners, including useful 1967 2-y-o The Industan (by El Gallo); dam won from 6f to 2m; made all when winning 7-runner maiden race at Epsom in April by 2 lengths from Jade Empress; ran best subsequent race when 5 lengths second to Stats Emmar, after leading 4f, in minor event at Kempton in May; runs as though 5f is her trip. *B. Swift.* 77

HEAVENS 2 gr. or ro.f. Sovereign Path 125–Kals Angel 68 (Kalydon 122) (1980 5f^3 5d 7g) Feb 22; 12,500F; leggy filly; closely related to a winner in Norway by Sovereign Gleam and half-sister to 3 winners, including useful Engage (by Whistling Wind), successful at up to 1m in Ireland, and 3-y-o 7f winner Bint Africa (by African Sky); dam won 7f seller; strong-finishing $1\frac{1}{2}$ lengths third of 17 to Sodina in maiden race at Lingfield in October; well beaten in large fields at Warwick and Newmarket (sweating, missed break and never recovered) afterwards; should be suited by 7f. *A. Breasley.* 67

HEAVY WEAPON 2 b.c. Bay Express 132–Autumn Double 72 (Double Jump 131) (1980 5f^3 6d 5d) Apr 30; 7,400Y; lightly-made colt; second foal; dam won over 9f; 6 lengths third of 11 to Goodbye Starter in maiden race at Newmarket in May; reportedly split a pastern and wasn't seen out again until October when soundly beaten in races won by Shark Song at Newmarket and Doncaster; should stay 6f. *W. Hastings-Bass.* 62

HEDGE SCHOOL 6 ch.h. Swinging Junior 118–Queen's Pet (Pall Mall 132) (1979 5s^2 6s^2 6d 5s^4 5d 5fg 5fg* 5f* 5fg 5fg^2 5f* 6fg* 5g 6fg* 6f^2 6g^2 1980 5d 6v 6g 6f 5f 5f^3 5f 6fg* 6fg 5f 6fg 5d 6g 6g 6g^2 5s 6d 6d) sprint handicapper; winner at Catterick in June but is inconsistent nowadays; acts on any going except perhaps heavy; used to wear blinkers; good mount for an apprentice. *Denys Smith.* 87

HEDINGHAM BOY 5 br.h. Amber Rama 133–Aberangell 96 (Abernant 142) (1979 10v 8d 7f 7s 8g 7fg 7f 7fg 7g 7f 8fg 5g 6g 6g^3 1980 8f 6f* 7f 6fg 7fg 6s^2 6g 6d^2 6g 7g* 7fg 6fg 6g 7g 7d 7s) former plater; won handicaps at Ripon in May and Catterick in August; stays 7f; acts on any going; has twice worn blinkers; often wears bandages; has worn a tongue strap. *A. Goodwill.* 63

HEDINGHAM LAD 4 ch.c. On Your Mark 125–Painter's Palate (Whistler 129) (1979 5s 5fg 5g 5g 5g 5f 5fg 1980 5d 6g) lengthy colt; fair sprint handicapper at his best, but hasn't won since his 2-y-o days and ran poorly in 1980 (tubed and bandaged); acts on firm going; usually wears blinkers. *W. O'Gorman.* –

HEGO'S HERO 2 b.c. L'Homme Arme 111–Shopping Centre (Miralgo 130) (1980 5f 5fg* 5g* 6fg^4 7f^4 8.2g^4 8f^2 8.2s^3 7g) Apr 29; 800F; neat colt; good walker and mover; half-brother to 1978 Irish 2-y-o 6f winner Kilteelagh Lady (by King's Leap); dam never ran; successful in sellers at Wolverhampton (bought in 1,050 gns) and Nottingham (no bid) in April; favourite, hung left final 100 yards when $\frac{1}{2}$-length second of 8 to Keelby Kavalier in nursery at Pontefract in September (sweated up a bit); likely to stay $1\frac{1}{4}$m; best form on a sound surface. *G. Richards.* 64

HEIGHLIN 4 b.g. High Line 125–Filiform 76 (Reform 132) (1979 11.7g 12s^3 11.7g* 12fg^4 13.1f* 13.1h* 12d^4 14f^4 13fg^3 1980 16s^2 18f* 18.4f 16fg^2 18.8fg* 20d* 16.1d^2 16g* 19g* 16.1fg 16d* 16.1g* 16fg* 16g^3 18d) 106

Trainer Elsworth has earned the reputation of having an eye for a bargain in his short career as a trainer; that reputation owes much to the exploits of Heighlin. Heighlin was bought out of Candy's stable for 14,000 guineas at the Newmarket Autumn Sales in 1979 after he had won three times in modest company at Bath. A lengthy, lightly-made gelding, he didn't look a particularly shrewd buy at the time, but within twelve months Elsworth had trained him to win the Daily Express Triumph Hurdle at Cheltenham and eight long-distance handicaps on the flat. Cheltenham alone virtually recouped Heighlin's purchase price and his subsequent efforts on the flat were so rewarding

Ascot Stakes—Heighlin beats Singing Amah and Taffy (rails)

that, after buying Grandiose for 31,000 guineas on behalf of Heighlin's owners at the 1980 Newmarket Autumn Sales, the trainer could tell the Press with some justification: 'You could say that Heighlin paid for this'.

Heighlin resumed flat racing only three weeks after winning at Cheltenham and he had fifteen races in the next six and a half months. He didn't run up to his best in his last race, the Tote Cesarewitch, and had probably had enough by then, but he won several other of the Calendar's most famous and long-established handicaps for stayers, including the Great Metropolitan at Epsom, the Ascot Stakes and the Goodwood Stakes; he was the first horse to win the last two races in the same year since Reynard Volant in 1946. Heighlin also won at Warwick (on a disqualification), Newbury, York, Haydock and Ascot again, putting up a particularly noteworthy performance in the Gordon Carter Handicap on the last-named course. Held up as usual and still last of the seven runners turning for home in that race, he was badly hampered when making smooth headway up the rails over a furlong out and had to be switched to the outside. He looked to be left with an impossible task, but he

*Goodwood Stakes—Heighlin races to the front,
beating Athford and Mountain Monarch*

quickened amazingly and in the end won rather comfortably by a length and a half from Jolimo.

Heighlin (b.g. 1976)	High Line (ch 1966)	High Hat (ch 1957)	Hyperion
			Madonna
		Time Call (b 1955)	Chanteur II
			Aleria
	Filiform (br 1970)	Reform (b 1964)	Pall Mall
			Country House
		Filigrana (b 1953)	Niccolo Dell 'Arca
			Gamble in Gold

Heighlin's turn of foot is probably his most telling weapon, for very few stayers can match it and he seems to be able to produce it on all types of going. His sire High Line also had an excellent turn of foot for a stayer and he too was a notably tough and genuine individual. High Line had an outstanding year in 1980, of course, and Heighlin was one of four winners sired by him in a memorable afternoon at York's Ebor meeting. The dam Filiform, a modest middle-distance winner, is from an excellent family. She is a half-sister to numerous winners, including the high-class filly Magic Flute and the very smart middle-distance performer Entanglement, and a granddaughter of the very speedy Gamble in Gold. Filiform has produced two other winners by High Line from only three foals to have raced, namely Fillaline, a winner at Lingfield as a two-year-old and subsequently successful in Hong Kong, and El Pais, winner of the Spanish St Leger in 1980. *D. Elsworth.*

HEIGHTEN 2 b.c. High Top 131–Curtains 113 (Busted 134) (1980 6fg^2 8d) **80**
Apr 14; well-made, good sort; second foal; half-brother to 1979 2-y-o 7f winner Cavalry Cut (by Queen's Hussar); dam, half-sister to Final Straw, won three 1½m races; finished in great style after being repeatedly baulked when promising 2½ lengths second of 16 to Priory Lane in maiden race at Salisbury in September; didn't look particularly well when second favourite for maiden race at Sandown in October and dropped out in straight, finishing out of first 9 of 21 behind Obrovac; bred to stay middle distances; possibly unsuited by a soft surface. *R. Hern.*

HEIRLINE 2 ch.f. Great Nephew 126–Cropfall 79 (Acropolis 132) (1980 7g^3 8g **60**
8fg 5g 6g) Mar 6; 4,200Y; quite a well-made filly; good walker and mover; second reported foal; dam 1¾m winner; last on home turn but ran on extremely well in straight to finish 13 lengths third of 10 behind Hunston in £3,000 maiden event at Sandown in July, only sign of ability; should be suited by 1m. *R. Smyth.*

HELANDY 3 br.g. Downstream 105–Steak House 68 (Road House II) (1979 **76**
5v^4 6g 1980 8f^3 8h* 9fg 8fg^2 8fg 8fg 8.2g 8fg) neat, strong gelding; not a particularly good mover; narrowly won 20-runner maiden race at Stockton in April; ran respectably in handicap on fourth start but was well beaten in seller on final outing, in July; stays 1m; acts on hard going; has run creditably for a 5-lb claimer. *J. Berry.*

HELEN'S SCEPTRE 4 ch.f. Gold Rod 129–Lady Helen 63 (Majority Blue 126) **47**
(1979 7s 6d 6s 6g 5d* (dis) 6g 5fg 6s* 6g 1980 6v 6f^4 7f 6fg^3 5g 6g 6g 7fg 5g 6g 6s) small filly; plater; stays 7f; acts on any going but goes well on soft; has won with and without blinkers; suitable mount for an apprentice; trained until after fourth outing by P. Asquith. *D. Dale.*

HELE STONE 4 gr.f. Ragstone 128–Daystar 91 (Major Portion 129) (1979 NR –
1980 16s) quite a moderate novice hurdler; dwelt when remote seventh in maiden race at Lingfield in June, first outing on flat. *D. Elsworth.*

HELEXIAN 3 b.c. Song 132–Permutation 79 (Pinza 137) (1979 5d 5g^3 5fg 5fg^2 **84**
6fg^4 7g 6f 5.3fg^4 6fg 1980 6s* 6fg^3 6fg^3 6f^4 6fg^3 6f^3 6fg 5.8fg 6g* 7d 7s^4 6fg 6fg^4 7fg^4 7g 8.3fg 8fg) compact, good sort; good mover; fair performer; won minor event at Warwick in April and handicap at Brighton in July; best at up to 7f; acts on any going; has worn blinkers but does at least as well without; suitable mount for a boy. *A. Ingham.*

HELIA 3 b.f. Song 132–Harriny 94 (Floribunda 136) (1979 5g 5s^2 5f 5fg^4 5fg –
1980 5fg 8fg 5d 5s 5fg 6g 5s) neat filly; has shown no form since 2 yrs; best at 5f; sometimes wears blinkers; unseated rider at halfway fourth start. *F. J. Houghton.*

HELLO GORGEOUS (USA) 3 ch.c. Mr Prospector–Bonny Jet (Jet Jewel) **128**
(1979 6f* 7fg^2 8f* 8g* 1980 7f 10fg^2 10.5f* 12f 10g^2)

Hello Gorgeous has been retired to stud. He didn't run again after the Coral Eclipse Stakes at Sandown in July and made only five appearances,

Mecca-Dante Stakes, York—Hello Gorgeous (left) wins by a neck from Master Willie, with Water Mill, Tyrnavos (spots) and Dukedom the next to finish

one more than in his first season. Although less successful a three-year-old than a two-year-old, he was by no stretch of the imagination a failure: he had fewer real chances and in terms of merit was clearly better than in 1979, only a little behind the best of his age. He beat Master Willie in the Mecca-Dante Stakes at York and finished a very good second to Ela-Mana-Mou in the Eclipse.

Hello Gorgeous was a good two-year-old. The only race he lost at that age was to Vielle at Yarmouth after a fairly lengthy absence from the course; he became the first horse (and only one so far) to win the Royal Lodge Stakes and the William Hill Futurity. He received 9-4 in the Free Handicap. Naturally, such form entitled him to very serious consideration for the classics but others had better claims, especially since as a two-year-old he ran as though a mile and a quarter would suit him better than a mile yet he had little in his pedigree to suggest he would get the Derby distance; his sire was a sprinter. The Guineas went by without Hello Gorgeous, as it did without any representative from his stable which had had nine of its two-year-old colts on 8-9 or more in the Free Handicap. Hello Gorgeous by then had already been moved up to a distance of a mile and a quarter following his fifth to Final Straw over seven furlongs in the Guineas trial at Newbury, the Clerical, Medical Greenham Stakes, tackling the Heathorn Stakes on the opening day of the Guineas meeting. He caught a tartar that day in Royal Fountain, the winner on his only previous appearance on the racecourse of what turned out to be a better Wood Ditton Stakes than usual, and went down by a neck after a close struggle over the last two furlongs.

What standing Hello Gorgeous lost as a Derby candidate through defeat in the Heathorn Stakes he recovered in the Mecca-Dante Stakes in May, two weeks later. The race is one of the leading Derby trials and had been won two years earlier by Shirley Heights. Besides Master Willie, Hello Gorgeous had up against him Dukedom, an impressive winner of the White Rose Stakes at Ascot; Water Mill, a highly-regarded stable-companion of Henbit, the latter of whom had beaten Master Willie at Sandown; three horses that had run in the Guineas, Star Way (fifth, promoted to fourth), Tyrnavos (seventh) and World Leader (last); and, finally, the 100/1-outsider Count Fernando. Dukedom and Water Mill started joint-favourites ahead of Hello Gorgeous. Misleadingly, Hello Gorgeous ran as though not only would he stay a longer distance than a mile and a quarter but would be well suited by one. He was flat out in the middle of the

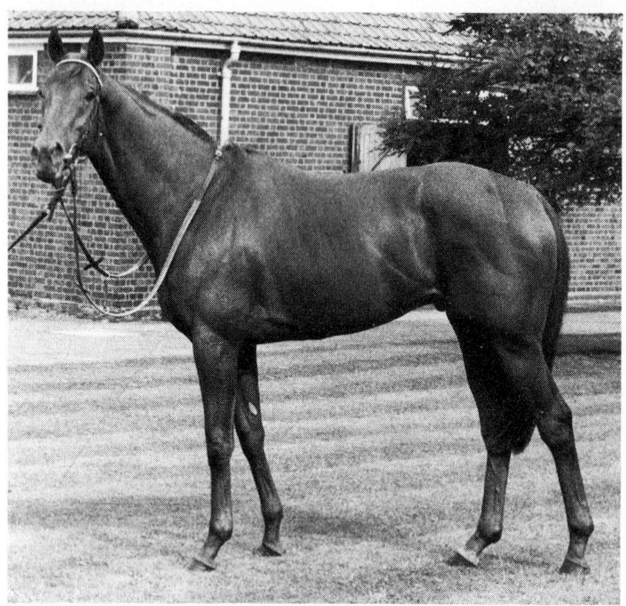

M D. Wildenstein's "Hello Gorgeous"

field with half a mile to go in a slowly-run affair, as Water Mill and Master Willie took over the lead from Dukedom and struck for home. He responded gamely and well to his jockey's urgings, so much so that he'd moved into a challenging position at the distance; and he kept up the good work right to the line, just getting the better of a hard fight with Master Willie over the last furlong. He won by a neck.

Hello Gorgeous (USA) (ch.c. 1977)	Mr Prospector (b 1970)	Raise A Native (ch 1961)	Native Dancer
			Raise You
		Gold Digger (b 1962)	Nashua
			Sequence
	Bonny Jet (b 1959)	Jet Jewel (b 1949)	Jet Pilot
			Crepe Myrtle
		Bonny Bush (ch 1953)	Mr Busher
			San Bonita

In the event the Derby proved Hello Gorgeous to be much closer so far as stamina was concerned to his former stable-companion Lyphard's Wish, the 1979 Mecca-Dante winner, than to Shirley Heights. He didn't get the trip. Looking as well as ever in the paddock, he ran a good race to put himself in with a chance upsides Henbit two furlongs out, and then weakened quickly into sixth place at the finish, just over five lengths behind the winner. There weren't five better horses than Hello Gorgeous in the Derby field even if there were five better stayers. Back at a mile and a quarter in the Eclipse, Hello Gorgeous ran probably the finest race of his career: Ela-Mana-Mou had to be driven right out to beat him by three parts of a length. Hello Gorgeous was held up this time, never far behind, and came past all the runners except Ela-Mana-Mou in the straight—Last

Fandango, Cracaval, Sea Chimes and then Gregorian—putting in a very strong challenge from distance to line. In this form he would have made them all go in the Benson and Hedges Gold Cup and the Champion Stakes had he been started.

Before the end of the summer it was rumoured that Hello Gorgeous would be going to race in the United States, where, incidentally, there are many opportunities for a horse of his type. By September, though, an announcement came that an offer for him reported in different places as four million dollars and five million dollars, had been taken up and he would be retired to stud in Ireland at Coolmore.

Hello Gorgeous should be an attraction for breeders. As detailed in the commentary on two-year-old Exclusively Raised, his sire belongs to one of the most vigorously flourishing families in the world. At the time of writing Mr Prospector is lying third in the sires' list in the United States, and in addition to Hello Gorgeous in Europe he had the French two-year-old Miswaki. The dam Bonny Jet, whom M Wildenstein now owns, had a good record as a broodmare in the States with five winners before Hello Gorgeous, among them the Noholme II colt Getajetholme, the winner of the W. L. McKnight Handicap (a race classed as a Group 3 pattern event). Bonny Jet was a winner herself, one of thirteen winners, in fact, for her dam.

Hello Gorgeous is an attractive colt. He was ideally suited by a mile and a quarter and well suited by top-of-the-ground conditions; he never raced on soft going. He was thoroughly genuine. *H. Cecil.*

HELLO SUSIE GREENE 2 ch.f. Shecky Greene–Speranza 89 (Hopeful Venture 125) (1980 5d² 5h⁴ 5g* 6d³ 5fg 5s² 5g* 5fg²) Feb 21; 13,000Y; neat filly; half-sister to a winner in USA by No Robbery; dam, half-sister to numerous winners, won twice over 7f at 2 yrs; goes well at Chester and won maiden race there in July and nursery in August, putting up a good effort in latter to win by 3 lengths from Salt; length second to comfortable winner Ashbrittle in minor event at Windsor in September; stays 6f but showed best form at 5f; seems to act on any going except hard. *R. Simpson.* **96**

HELSENA 2 b.f. Ellkar 86–Porec (I Say 125) (1980 5fg 6f 5fg 5.8fg 6d) compact, good-topped filly; of little account; swerved badly at start and refused to race third outing; blinkered final start. *B. Shaw.* **—**

HELVIC (USA) 2 b. or br.c. Angle Light–Red River (Diatome 132) (1980 6d 7fg⁴ 7g 7f) Feb 18; $23,000Y; small, useful sort; second foal; dam, plating-class French maiden, is granddaughter of high-class French filly Vamarie; quite moderate; 9 lengths sixth of 25 to Highland Range in maiden race at Redcar in September on fourth outing; will stay 1¼m. *W. O'Gorman.* **69**

HELVIC STORM (USA) 2 ch.g. T. V. Commercial–Signal Flag (Restless Wind) (1980 5fg* 6d⁴ 6fg² 7g² 6g* 6f³ 8g) Mar 24; $21,000Y; big, strong, workmanlike gelding; half-brother to several minor winners; dam won 2 small races at up to 5f at 2 yrs; winner of maiden race at Haydock in May and 3-runner event at Pontefract in August, latter by a neck from odds-on Steelinctive; second twice in between, failing by a short head to catch Salt in £2,400 event at Ripon and going down by 2½ lengths to odds-on Mushref in 4-runner Redcar Silver Salver; stays 1m; possibly unsuited by a soft surface; genuine and consistent; gelded after seventh start; sent to Hong Kong. *G. Richards* **102**

HENBIT (USA) 3 b.c. Hawaii–Chateaucreek (Chateaugay) (1979 6fg⁴ 8g* 7fg⁴ 1980 10f* 12.3f* 12f*) **130**

Illness and injury blighted the latest season. In all probability the incidence of 'the virus' (easily the most commonly-quoted sickness nowadays) and injury was little greater among the racehorse population than usual recently; it just seemed greater because of the importance of the issues affected. As a result of contracting 'the virus' the first past the post in a controversial Two Thousand Guineas never ran again after Newmarket; nor, because of injury, did the Derby and Oaks winners after Epsom. To the sport in general, and to those whose duty is to comment on racehorses in particular, this was a very sad fact. The second half of the season would have been considerably more interesting, more worthwhile, more informative with Nureyev, Henbit and Bireme, all unbeaten in 1980, in action. We shall never know now whether Nureyev was the great horse some claimed him to be or whether Bireme would have fulfilled her enormous potential: both have been retired to stud. They, and the Derby winner Henbit at present, must be judged on what they achieved in that all-too-short time before their careers had run their normal course.

Unlike the other two, Henbit hasn't yet formally been retired. The odds

Chester Vase—Henbit makes it all to win from Moomba Masquerade and Light Cavalry (partly hidden). Try Sandicliffe and Sweet Pretender complete the field

must be slightly on his departure from racing without providing anything further of significance to judge him upon, for he cracked his off-fore cannon at Epsom and was confined to his box in a light plaster during the next three months. If this should happen Henbit will go down as a tough but run-of-the-mill Derby winner who could well have achieved much more had circumstances allowed; he was just coming to himself when he beat an unexceptional field by classic standards in the Derby. His trainer, though, entertains high hopes that Henbit will return. The plaster was removed after X-rays showed the five-inch crack had healed satisfactorily, and the horse began work on the road towards the end of October with sights on two races he would normally be expected to go for as a four-year-old if not as a three-year-old, the King George VI and Queen Elizabeth Diamond Stakes and the Prix de l'Arc de Triomphe.

Henbit was the seventh American-bred Derby winner in the last twelve years, following Sir Ivor, Nijinsky, Mill Reef, Roberto, Empery and The Minstrel. At least four of that list possessed better pace than he, and all except Empery had superior records as two-year-olds. Henbit is more the staying type, probably better suited by a mile and a half than shorter distances. He ran three times as a two-year-old, finishing fourth in the Chesham Stakes at Ascot, winning a one-mile maiden at Newbury and then finishing fourth again, in the William Hill Dewhurst Stakes at Newmarket. It was his fourth to Monteverdi at Newmarket that first brought him into the classic picture; he set a good gallop and kept on steadily after being headed a quarter of a mile out to go down by less than five lengths to the horse who subsequently topped the Free Handicap. Henbit himself received 8-12.

Henbit wasn't in the Guineas. He made his reappearance as a three-year-old in the Classic Trial Stakes at Sandown, a ten-furlong race won the previous season by Troy. He looked extremely well if a little short of peak fitness, and started a well-backed favourite though appearing to have plenty on his plate in the small field, opposed principally by Huguenot (third-top weight in the Irish Free Handicap), Ginistrelli (9-1 in the Free Handicap) and Master Willie (8-9 Free Handicap, and already a winner during the season). All four ran encouragingly, even fourth-placed Master Willie for he had anything but a happy time of it; perhaps Monteverdi's stable-companion Huguenot came out best, going under by only half a length giving the others 5 lb; Ginistrelli finished a fairly close third in need of the outing while Henbit, who had certainly done well physically from two to three, gave the impression he would be seen to advantage over a longer distance, making all and holding on very gamely in the face of a sustained challenge from the second.

Henbit had the opportunity of tackling a longer distance in the Chester Vase less than a fortnight later, on a very tight, demanding course that is rightly regarded by the majority of trainers as providing excellent experience for Epsom candidates. The Chester Vase, which before 1959 used to be open also to four-year-olds, hadn't been won by any subsequent Derby winner since Windsor Lad though during the intervening period Taj Akbar, Fidalgo, Indiana, Linden Tree and Hot Grove had gone on to run second at Epsom, and Heliopolis and Swallow Tail third. Henbit ran an excellent trial, one of the best of the whole series in the spring and one whose significance increased almost daily in the succeeding weeks. He won in workmanlike fashion by four lengths from Moomba Masquerade; Light Cavalry, having his first race of the season, finished third, the Warren Stakes winner Try Sandicliffe fourth and the outsider Sweet Pretender a remote last of five. After providing evidence in the paddock of his continuing physical improvement, giving the impression at the same time that his trainer had left something to work on, Henbit went out to confirm in a race run in course-record time his toughness and resolution. He had to work to fulfil his jockey's strategy of dictating the pace throughout, especially in the last half mile or so, and took time to find top gear down the far side. Ridden along, Henbit really got down to business coming off the final bend and was galloping very strongly indeed in the straight, going away from the others towards the finish. This performance persuaded Henbit's connections that he

Derby Stakes, Epsom—rounding Tattenham Corner, Blast Off leads from Braughing, then come Rankin (rails) and Moomba Masquerade with Hello Gorgeous and Julius Caesar racing almost in line. Garrido is the third horse on the rails and Henbit is on his outside, with Pelerin immediately behind. The scrimmaging on the left concerns Tyrnavos (spots), Monteverdi (squeezed in the middle) and Master Willie (blaze)

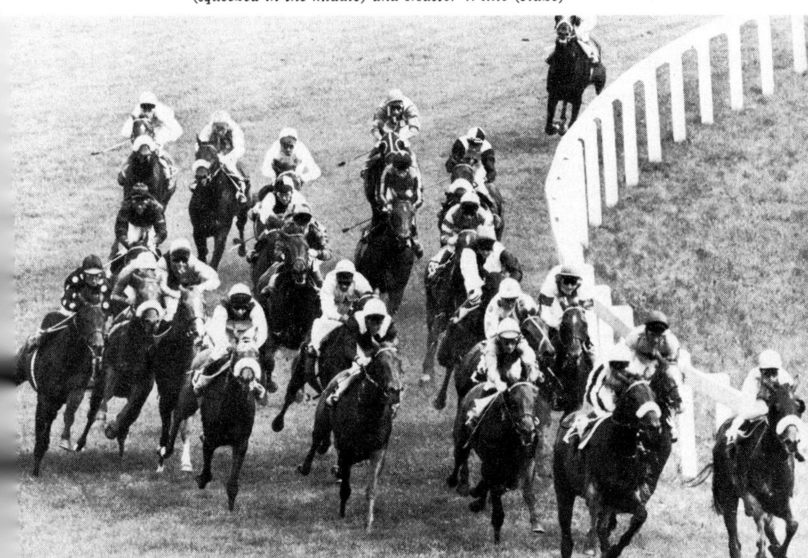

would handle Epsom satisfactorily, and they abandoned the alternative of running in the Prix du Jockey-Club.

Between Chester and Epsom the Derby market lay, for the most part, in an unusually confused state: four different favourites held call in less than a week in the middle of May. Nureyev, the obvious choice, vanished from the lists following reports of his sickness; his successor Monteverdi lasted on top only until the running of the Airlie/Coolmore Irish Two Thousand Guineas, whereupon Ginistrelli (for a day) and then Henbit, the last-named a definite starter unlike the Irish Guineas winner Nikoli at that time, took over. Henbit retained his position in the betting until a late run on Nikoli forced him out to 7/1, second favourite on the day, with Nikoli at 4/1. Proven over the distance and on firm going, Henbit had a good chance in the Derby, all the better for being preferred to the Mecca-Dante Stakes third Water Mill by stable-jockey Carson. Monteverdi had become disappointing; Hello Gorgeous' defeat of Master Willie at York, when the pair had beaten another fancied Derby runner Tyrnavos, hadn't been clear-cut; Master Willie himself had been held up for four days in his preparation by a throat infection and became a certain runner only at the overnight-declaration stage. Rankin, a good second to Prince Bee in the Predominate Stakes at Kempton, seemed to have the best credentials of the remainder. As more often than not nowadays the French sent over their second team, spearheaded by the Italian Derby winner Garrido, who started at 28/1, and backed up by Julius Caesar, Pimpont and Blast Off. Twenty-four runners went to post, making a field well up to standard in quantity but short, without much doubt, on quality. Only Master Willie and Tyrnavos of the number subsequently won a pattern race; Water Mill was subsequently placed in two over a longer distance.

That so many of the field still held a chance two furlongs out in the Derby is, we think, a fair pointer to the unexceptional standard of the latest race, as also is the fact that five, one of them Pelerin, stayed in serious contention to the end. At least nine horses were in the firing line passing the two-furlong pole, including Rankin who led, Henbit, Master Willie, Pelerin, Hello Gorgeous and Moomba Masquerade. Water Mill wasn't among their number, having been taken off his feet; nor was Monteverdi, whom Piggott reported never going; nor Tyrnavos; nor the heavily-supported Nikoli, only now closing slowly under pressure on the leading group from an always-unpromising position. With a lesser man in the saddle Henbit might not have been up there either. High among the assets which helped make Carson champion jockey in two of the last three seasons as well as in 1972 and 1973 are a shrewd tactical brain and seemingly boundless energy and perseverance. These he displayed to some effect on Henbit at Epsom. Henbit never looked completely at ease at any stage of the race. Carson bustled him along from the start to ensure a good place and kept pushing whenever necessary, which was quite often, to make certain of remaining in the first six or seven behind the front-runners Bozovici, Blast Off and Braughing. He kept to the rail until making his challenge, unhampered, through the bunch at around the two-furlong marker. Henbit was under strong pressure by now, and ground his way past Rankin into the lead over a furlong out; soon after, he faltered to the right, then straightened up and proceeded to hold on to his lead extremely gamely in the face of strenuous opposition from Master Willie, reaching the post three quarters of a length to the good. Rankin also kept on well for third, a length and a half further back, half a length in front of Pelerin on the inside, who beat Garrido by a short head. Hello Gorgeous didn't stay, but finished a clear sixth. Nikoli was eighth, Water Mill tenth, Tyrnavos twelfth and Monteverdi fourteenth. There is little doubt that Henbit sustained his injury at the point he hung right; how much it affected his performance is impossible to say, other than in the most general terms. He must have been hampered to some extent. Henbit provided a second Derby win in succession for his trainer and jockey, and a second win in the race for his owner whose Psidium never ran again after his success in 1961 because of injury. The owner's grandfather, incidentally, won the race in 1876 with Kisber.

Henbit's success should serve to encourage those owners with strictly limited resources: his sire has never really caught on in the United States and stood at 10,000 dollars in 1980, while Henbit sold as a yearling for 24,000 dollars, purchased by George Blackwell on behalf of Mme Plesch at the Kentucky Yearling Sales. By way of further encouragement, the Poule d'Essai des Poulains winner In Fijar (36,000 dollars) and the Kentucky Derby winner Genuine Risk (32,000 dollars) came from the same sale. Henbit's sire Hawaii was a top-class middle-distance horse on grass in South Africa and later in America; he won the Man o'War Stakes, among other races, and finished second to Karabas in the Washington International. He is the sire of horses placed in the Derby in Hawaiian Sound and the temperamental Hunza Dancer; he is also the latest of a remarkable number of animals descending from Signor Federico Tesio's bloodstock to have influenced the outcome of the Derby. Tesio held the Derby in the highest esteem: one of his deepest convictions, according to his partner Mario Incisa, was that the thoroughbred exists because its selection has depended, not on experts, technicians or zoologists but on a piece of wood—the winning post of the Derby. The point would make an interesting subject for debate!

Henbit (USA) (b.c. 1977)	Hawaii (b 1964)	Utrillo II (ch 1958)	Toulouse Lautrec
			Urbinella
		Ethane (br 1947)	Mehrali
			Ethyl
	Chateaucreek (ch 1970)	Chateaugay (ch 1960)	Swaps
			Banquet Bell
		Mooncreek (ch 1963)	Sailor
			Ouija

Henbit's dam has a relatively humble background. A daughter of the 1963 Kentucky Derby winner Chateaugay and the unraced Mooncreek, she

Derby Stakes, Epsom—gallant Henbit is strongly pressed throughout the last furlong by Master Willie (left). Rankin follows the winner with Pelerin on his inside and Garrido on his outside. Hello Gorgeous (extreme left) is sixth

was purchased privately early in life by eight Louisville businessmen and raced for them until claimed as a four-year-old for 25,000 dollars at Hialeah. She won six races at up to six furlongs as a three-year-old, including a small stakes event at River Downs, but had to be retired early by her new owners after fracturing a sesamoid bone. Her dam never raced; the dam of five minor winners in the States, she was sold to Venezuela for 18,000 dollars in 1976, four years after Chateaugay departed American shores for Japan. The third dam was a stakes winner, the winner of the nine-furlong Diana Handicap, and bred the very smart two-year-old Ouija Board. Henbit is Chateaucreek's second foal, following Lead Reek (by Mr Leader), sold for an even lower sum than he at Kentucky and a winner over jumps in France; her third foal, Airgator (by Dewan) fetched only 22,000 dollars as a yearling; her fourth, a yearling filly by Stop the Music, the sire of the latest Belmont Stakes winner Temperence Hill, brought 260,000 dollars at Saratoga in August.

Henbit is a lengthy colt, big enough to give rise to doubts about his ability to handle Epsom at one stage of his career. He went extremely well on firm going before his injury, never being called upon to race on anything softer than good. Whether firm ground will still suit him after his serious injury remains to be seen as does, unfortunately, whether he will come back at all. If he returns able to pick up where he left off he should win more good races at a mile and a half; he deserves to, at any rate, he's such a game horse. *R. Hern.*

HENCE 4 ch.g. Habat 127–Penitent 85 (Sing Sing 134) (1979 6g 8g 8s 1980 **46**
7d 6d 6f 6fg^{3} 5g 6f 6fg 6g 6s 6s 8.2d 7d^{2} 6s 8.2v^{3}) attractive gelding; plater; seems to stay 1m; probably acts on any going; blinkered eighth outing and wore a hood on tenth. *T. Craig.*

HENHAM GIRL 3 b.f. Saritamer 130–Tender Annie 122 (Tenerani 135) —
(1979 NR 1980 10fg) 7,000Y; half-sister to several minor winners here and in USA; dam third in 1962 Oaks; in rear in 13-runner maiden race won by Haverhill Lad at Leicester in May; dead. *P. Cole.*

HENLOW GAMBLE 5 b.g. Lineage 99–Keryl 106 (Infatuation 129) (1979 —
NR 1980 8fg 10.1fg) maiden plater; stays 1m; has been tried in blinkers. *O. O'Neill.*

HENRY BOOT 2 gr.g. Abwah 118–Double Bank 80 (Double Jump 131) —
(1980 5h 5f 5fg 6fg 7s 5.1fg 7f) Apr 1; fourth living foal; dam won twice over 5f at 2 yrs; plating-class maiden; blinkered sixth start. *M. Tompkins.*

HENRY GREEN 3 b.g. Brigadier Gerard 144–Bygone 105 (Busted 134) (1979 **76**
NR 1980 8f 8fg^{3} 10fg^{4} 10g^{3} 10.8s^{3} 8g^{2} 10s 8fg^{4}) big gelding; first foal; dam won from 7f to 2m; placed in maiden races and a handicap; should stay $1\frac{1}{2}$m; probably acts on any going. *B. Palling.*

HENRY MORGAN (USA) 2 b.c. Charles Elliott–Lost Earring (Craigwood) **95**
(1980 6g^{2} 7g^{2} 6g^{2} 7f^{4} 6g^{3} 7d^{3} 7fg^{3} 7f^{3} 7fg^{4} 7d^{2} 7s^{3}) Mar 20; 6,000Y; smallish, useful sort; second foal; dam won 6f claiming race; sire won 14 races from 5f to 9f; placed in varied races, finishing third in nurseries on fifth to eighth outings; will stay at least 1m; seems to act on any going; ran moderately in blinkers fourth outing and was below his best last 3 outings; suited by strong handling; sold to German International Bloodstock 6,800 gns Newmarket Autumn Sales. *R. Sheather.*

HENRY'S WISH 2 b.g. Wishing Star 117–Tudor Story 96 (Henry the Seventh **81**
125) (1980 6g^{4} 6g) Mar 10; 6,200F, 18,000Y; strong, good sort; half-brother to winners here and in Belgium, including Irish 3-y-o 5f winner Royal Express (by Bay Express); dam staying half-sister to very smart Sweet Story; outpaced after leading for $4\frac{1}{2}$f when 3 lengths fourth of 10 to Miss St Mawes in maiden race at Yarmouth in August, better effort; will be suited by middle distances. *H. Cecil.*

HERACLES 7 b.h. Breeders Dream 116–Papillon Rouge 60 (Klairon 131) **73**
(1979 7f 7g 7fg 6h^{3} 7d^{4} 6h* 7g 7g^{4} 7d 1980 7h 6h^{4} 7f 7.2d 7g) dipped-backed horse; creditable fourth to Caledonian in handicap at Pontefract in May; tailed off last 3 outings (off course 4 months after third start); stays 1m; appears to act on any going but goes extremely well on a sound surface; ran badly when tried in blinkers; excellent mount for an apprentice. *I. Walker.*

HERBIE HANCOCK 4 b.g. Souvran 98–Whitton Lane (Narrator 127) (1979 —
13v 1980 8g 10.1g 10d 10s 8fg 12g) strong gelding; of little account. *J. Benstead.*

HERBIE QUAYLE 2 b.c. Thatch 136–Bella Carlotta (Charlottesville 135) (1980 7f) Apr 27; big, strong colt; half-brother to 3 winners, notably very useful middle-distance colt Beauvallon (by Val de Loir); dam very useful sister to Sussex stakes winner Carlemont; unquoted, showed speed for over 5f when 14 lengths sixth of 11 to Glint of Gold in maiden race at Ascot in July, only outing. *B. Hills.* — p

HEREAS (FR) 3 b.c. Hard to Beat 132–Sarila (Snob 130) (1979 NR 1980 10.8s* 12d² 12fg* 12d² 12g³ 12g 11g* 15d*) workmanlike ex-English colt; third foal; half-brother to very useful but lightly-raced Rilasa (by St Paddy), a winner over 6f at 2 yrs; dam, from family of Crepellana, won over 12.5f; won 12-runner maiden event at Warwick and William Hill Southern Handicap at Goodwood, latter by a neck from Peppery, in July; sold privately out of F. J. Houghton's stable after fourth outing and won small race at Marseilles in October and handicap at Evry in November; stays well; probably acts on any going. *C. de Watrigant, France.* **103**

HERECOMES THEJUDGE 3 b.c. Shoolerville 121–Tree Paeony 86 (King Emperor) (1979 5.8g 6f³ 6fg 6g 6fg 6f³ 1980 7d 8.2d 8d 7g 7.2g 6d* 7g 6s 6fg 6d) useful-looking colt; won handicap at Hamilton in September; best at 6f; probably acts on any going; takes a good hold; sold 4,800 gns Newmarket Autumn Sales to race in Italy. *R. Hollinshead.* **67**

HER EXCELLENCY 3 b.f. Dragonara Palace 115–My Paddy 83 (St Paddy 133) (1979 5d 6g 1980 6f³ 5h⁴ 6g³) lightly-made filly; plater; will stay at least 7f; acts on firm going; has run respectably for a boy; sold 800 gns Ascot July Sales. *C. Nelson.* **30**

HER GRACE 2 ch.f. Great Nephew 126–Front Row 111 (Epaulette 125) (1980 6g* 6d⁴ 6g³) Apr 4; lightly-made filly; half-sister to several winners, including smart miler Long Row (by Linacre) and 3-y-o 7f winner Saville Row (by Habitat); dam won Irish 1,000 Guineas; odds on, could hardly have made a more impressive debut in maiden race at Doncaster in June, making all and drawing right away from the other 15 to win by 10 lengths from Miss St Mawes; subsequently beaten in much better company, finishing creditable 2½ lengths fourth of 11 to Nasseem in Cherry Hinton Stakes at Newmarket and 7½ lengths third of 7 to Tolmi in Princess Margaret Stakes at Ascot, both in July; will be suited by 1m; useful. *H. Cecil.* **101**

HERMIA 3 ch.f. Midsummer Night II 117–Cecilia Gallerani (Pinturischio 116) (1979 7g 7g 1980 8s⁴ 7f 8fg 10f 7d*) small, lengthy filly; won 15-runner maiden race at Salisbury in June; stays 1m; needs some give in the ground. *J. Winter.* **72**

HEROIC AIR 3 b.c. Song 132–So Valiant 80 (So Blessed 130) (1979 5d² 5g* 5f² 5s⁴ 5fg* 6f 1980 5f 5s 5g) quite attractive colt; fairly useful handicapper at his best; not certain to stay 6f; acts on any going; twice showed signs of temperament at 2 yrs, including when blinkered on fourth start; moved badly to post on reappearance; sold 700 gns Ascot October Sales. *A. Ingham.* **90**

HERONS HOLLOW 3 gr.c. Wolver Hollow 126–Sunbittern 112 (Sea Hawk II 131) (1979 6f 1980 8d* 8g* 10d³ 8fg 8d 8g* 8d³ 8d* 10g) neat, strong colt; has a round action; fairly useful performer; successful in maiden race at Doncaster and handicaps at Salisbury, Goodwood and Newbury; beat Malvan going away by 3 lengths on last-named course in October; stays 1¼m; suited by some give in the ground. *G. Harwood.* **101**

HERON'S MIRAGE 3 gr.f. Grey Mirage 128–Heron's Dolly (Combat 123) (1979 5g 5g 8f 5fg 1980 8fg 8f) strong, fair sort; in rear in maiden races and a handicap; refused to race from flag start second outing at 2 yrs. *J. H. Peacock.* —

HERR CAPITAN 4 ch.g. Lombard 126–Ista Jil 97 (Gratitude 130) (1979 8d² 10g⁴ 8d⁴ 10.2s* 10.6g 10fg 8g³ 10f 1980 12fg) leggy, narrow gelding; modest handicapper; stays 1¼m; acts on any going, but may be best served by a soft surface; blinkered final outing at 3 yrs. *J. Old.* —

HETHERMAI 3 b.f. Pee Mai 107–Hethersent 71 (Hethersett 134) (1979 5v 5s 5s 5g 1980 10h 12g 16g 16d 12s) small filly; bad maiden; sweated up second start; sometimes wears blinkers. *S. Kernick.* —

HEXGREAVE 3 ch.f. Mount Hagen 127–Granville Lady (High Hat 131) (1979 5g 5g 7s 8f 8h 9fg³ 1980 11f⁴ 12.2f) smallish, well-made filly; moderate (rated 81) at 2 yrs; well beaten in handicap at Ayr (had stiff task) and maiden race at Catterick in 1980; should stay 1½m; acts on a firm surface; wears blinkers nowadays; retained 1,000 gns Doncaster October Sales. *R. Hobson.* —

HEXGREAVE ELITE 3 gr.f. Home Guard 129–Femme Elite (Young Emperor 133) (1979 6f 6fg 7.2g³ 6s 7fg 7f 7g 1980 7f³ 7fg 7fg* 7g 6d⁴ 7fg 9d 7fg) leggy, lightly-made filly; stayed on to win 10-runner minor race at Catterick in June; should stay beyond 7f; acts on firm going; blinkered sixth start; sold 5,400 gns Doncaster October Sales. *R. Hobson.* **69**

HEXGREAVE FINESSE 2 br.f. Tower Walk 130–Finesse 87 (Miralgo 130) (1980 5fg 5g³ 5f) Feb 11; 9,400Y; leggy, quite useful sort; half-sister to 2 winners, including fair 6f to 1¼m winner Zarzaitine (by Murrayfield); dam won over 1½m; 2¼ lengths third of 7 to Jiva in Dick Turpin Stakes at York in June; off course 11 weeks subsequently and finished lame in maiden race at Beverley on return; should be suited by 6f+. *R. Hobson.* **78**

HEXGREAVE STAR 2 b. or br.c. Comedy Star 121–Double Grand (Coronation Year 124) (1980 5v² 5v* 5f² 5v² 5fg³ 6d 6g 6g*(dis) 6d 6g 6fg 6f³) Mar 17; 12,000Y; strong, compact colt; half-brother to 2 winners, including Nell Gwyn Stakes winner Angels Two (by Silver Cloud); dam poor hurdler; won minor event at Ayr in March and £4,000 nursery at Newmarket in August, staying on strongly under pressure in latter to win by ¾ length from Fee; disqualified after his Newmarket win because traces of Procaine were found in his system; good third of 12 to Scarrowmanwick in valuable nursery at Newmarket in October; stays 6f well and may get further; acts on any going; has worn bandages; lost chance at start ninth outing; genuine; sold 20,000 gns Doncaster October Sales. *R. Hobson.* **100**

HEYWOOD HARDY 4 b.c. Tribal Chief 125–Anna Barry 76 (Falls of Clyde 126) (1979 5d 5d 5s² 5f* 5g 5g* 5g⁴ 5f² 5fg 5fg* 5fg 5g* 5s² 1980 5d² 6f 5fg 5f) powerful colt; developed into a useful sprint handicapper in 1979; ran very well when second to Get Involved in handicap at Doncaster in March but was disappointing afterwards (not seen out after June); not certain to stay 6f; acts on any going; usually blinkered at 2 yrs; sold only 500 gns Newmarket Autumn Sales. *W. Wightman.* **91 d**

HIDE THE KEY (USA) 3 ch.f. Key To The Mint–Sno Where (Northern Dancer) (1979 6fg⁴ 7g³ 8f⁴ 8fg 1980 8.5g³ 12.3f 8d* 8g² 7fg 7g⁴ 8fg² 8v²) lengthy filly; short-priced favourite when cleverly winning maiden race at York in June; also ran well to be third to Bay Street in Princess Elizabeth Stakes at Epsom, and 1½ lengths second to Missed Blessing in £7,900 handicap at Ascot and to La Vreeland in Group 3 Premio Bagutta at Milan on last 2 starts; **87**

Vernons Fillies Plate, York—Hide the Key wins cleverly from Cavo Varka

appears not to stay 1½m; acts on any going; sweated up a bit sixth start; ran moderately fifth outing. *I. Balding.*

HI FRIDAY 4 ch.f. High Line 125–Decked Out 77 (Doutelle 128) (1979 8h^3 8fg^2 10f^4 10.1f 8.2fg 9g 10g 1980 7h 8fg 8fg) light-framed filly; plating-class maiden; should be suited by 1¼m; yet to race on a soft surface. *J. Powney.* —

HIGHAM GREY 4 gr.g. Warpath 113–Jackies Joy (Skymaster 126) (1979 10.5g 10.6g 10.5f^2 10.5f 14.6f 13g^2 12.3f 14.6f 12fg 1980 10.2d 12fg 10h 7f 12f 12f* 12fg* 12f^2 12d* 12g^3 10g^2 12g 8g 8fg^2 8g* 7s 15d) useful-looking gelding; none too reliable in the past but was reformed in 1980 and won handicaps at Pontefract, Carlisle (two) and Newcastle; made nearly all and seemed to catch his rivals napping when going clear 2f out on last-named course; behind in valuable seller at Doncaster on thirteenth outing; effective at 1m and stays at least 13f; seems to act on any going; wears blinkers. *D. Chapman.* **72**

HIGH ANNA 5 ch.m. Leander 119–Highway Jane (Royal Highway 117) (1979 8s 8f 20.4g 14fg 1980 10.1fg) of little account. *G. Wallace.* —

HIGH CIRCLES 2 b.c. High Line 125–Misnomer 85 (Milesian 131) (1980 10.2s) Mar 9; third foal; half-brother to 3-y-o 1½m winner York Cottage (by Royal Palace) and 1m winner Snow Chief (by Tribal Chief); dam, winner at up to 1½m, is daughter of St Leger third Cold Storage; 25/1, needed race and was always behind in 21-runner minor event won by Irish Heart at Doncaster in November. *W. Elsey.* —

HIGH CLASS BUILDER 2 ch.f. Flair Path 122–Holly (Chamossaire) (1980 6s* 7g^3 6g^3 7fg^4 7g 7g* 7g^3 8d) Apr 1; 900Y; compact filly; half-sister to Irish 3-y-o Karaberry (by Karabas), winner at up to 1½m; dam 7f winner in Ireland; attracted no bid when successful in sellers at Nottingham in June and Catterick in August, beating Amsam 1½ lengths in latter; will stay 1½m at 3 yrs (had little chance at weights over 1m on final start); seems to act on any going; blinkered fifth outing. *K. Stone.* **58**

HIGH COMMISSIONER 4 gr.g. Sahib 114–Right Beam 62 (Right Boy 137) (1979 NR 1980 12d 9s) brother to The Guvnor, successful at up to 1m; dam placed at 1m; tailed off in minor event at Edinburgh and seller at Hamilton in September; bolted before start on latter course. *B. McLean.* —

HIGHCROFT 2 b.f. Welsh Saint 126–Maryfield (Hul a Hul 124) (1980 5f 5fg^3 5g 6fg 6d 5fg 6g^3 5f* 5f^2 5fg 5g) Apr 1; 5,000Y; well-made, attractive filly; second foal; dam never ran; won 18-runner maiden event at Folkestone in September by 1½ lengths from Balatina; creditable second of 18 to Think Ahead in nursery at Redcar later in month; best form at 5f; acts well on firm going; ran poorly when ridden by very light apprentice on tenth outing; blinkered sixth and seventh outings. *G. Lewis.* **78**

HIGHDALGO 3 ch.c. Most Secret 119–Waltham Lady 78 (Highland Melody 112) (1979 NR 1980 8fg 8fg 9s 8f) compact colt; bad plater. *J. Mulhall.* —

HIGHEST BIDDER 3 b.c. Auction Ring 123–Bridle Path 82 (Pall Mall 132) (1979 7fg^3 6f^4 6f^4 7.3g^4 1980 8fg 7f^2 7.2fg 6fg) well-grown colt; none too good a mover; runner-up in minor race at Newmarket in May; not disgraced when 4½ lengths sixth to Hard Fought in John of Gaunt Stakes at Haydock in June, third start; stays 7f; acts on firm going; often blinkered; not seen out after June. *W. O'Gorman.* **102**

HIGHFIELD 3 b.g. Blue and Grey 93–Whistlewych 40 (Whistler 129) (1979 5g 5d 6fg 6g 6s 6g 8g^4 6g 1980 6fg 9g 7fg 6s 8f 7g) neat, strong gelding; poor plater; suited by 1m but ran as though 9f was too far for him on second start; has worn blinkers. *J. Carr.* —

HIGHFIELD JET 5 b.h. High Top 131–Cloudbreak 95 (Nimbus 130) (1979 10g 10f 8g* 11d* 10f 12.2fg^2 12.2d^3 13.8s 1980 10.2d 12f 8g) plater; effective at 1m to 1½m; acts on a firm and a soft surface; has run well in blinkers. *A. Smith.* —

HIGH GAIT 3 b.f. High Top 131–Gay Charlotte 95 (Charlottown 127) (1979 5s^3 6fg^3 6fg^4 1980 10fg^3 11.7f* 12.2fg* 12g^2 10d* 10fg 12g^4 12f) small, useful-looking filly; won 18-runner maiden race at Bath in May, minor event at Catterick in June and handicap at Brighton in July; long odds on when cantering home in last-named; ran creditably to be second to John O'Groats in King George V Stakes (Handicap) at Royal Ascot and fourth of 9 to Deadly Serious in Galtres Stakes at York in August; stays 1½m; acts on any going; ran abysmally final start; changed hands 12,000 gns Newmarket December Sales. *F. J. Houghton.* **90**

HIGH HILLS 6 gr.g. High Top 131–Charity Walk (Sovereign Path 125) (1979 13g 12d^2 13d* 12g^2 12f 12.5g 15s 1980 13v^3 11d 12f 13fg^2 12f^4 12d^2 12g^4 12g^2 12d **65**

13s^{4} 13s) quite a moderate middle-distance handicapper; goes well at Hamilton;
first past post there on sixth outing but was relegated to second by stewards
for bumping; acts on any going; used to wear blinkers; suitable mount for an
apprentice. *T. Craig.*

HIGHLAND BEAR 3 br.f. Scottish Rifle 127–Galoprise 88 (Tudor Music 131) –
(1979 6fg 6g^{4} 7fg* 7.3g 8fg^{2} 1980 9.6f 10f 8d 8d) small, quite well-made filly;
has shown no form since 1979; should stay beyond 1m; sold 3,800 gns Newmarket
December Sales. *J. Dunlop.*

HIGHLAND LIGHT 3 ch.f. Home Guard 129–Street Light 120 (St Chad 120) **99**
(1979 6g^{2} 5f* 6fg* 1980 7fg 6f* 7fg) big, rangy filly; lightly raced but is a
useful performer; battled on gamely to hold off Pavahra by a neck in £3,900
handicap at York in May; should stay 7f; acts on firm going and has yet to race on
a soft surface; genuine; not raced after July. *J. Hindley.*

HIGHLAND LINNET 3 b.c. Highland Melody 112–Golden Linnet 96 (Sing –
Sing 134) (1979 NR 1980 12f^{4} 16d 12g) leggy colt; half-brother to 3 winners
including fairly useful 5f performer Blue Linnet (by Habitat); dam won over 5f
and 6f and is half-sister to good sprinter Monet; little worthwhile form in minor
events; not certain to stay middle distances. *F. Durr.*

HIGHLAND LORD 4 br.g. Highland Melody 112–Dalton Lady (Sammy Davis –
129) (1979 NR 1980 10fg 10.6d) lengthy gelding; unquoted when tailed off
in maiden races at Redcar and Haydock in the summer. *J. Mulhall.*

HIGHLAND RANGE 2 ch.c. Crowned Prince 128–Caramel 93 (Crepello 136) **86**
(1980 7g 7g 7f*) Apr 10; 6,800F; tall, useful-looking colt; excellent mover; half-
brother to 4 winners, including Ribblesdale Stakes winner Northern Princess
(by Sir Ivor) and useful 1974 2-y-o 6f winner Marcela (by Reform); dam 1½m
winner; put up a fairly useful effort when making all to win 25-runner maiden race
at Redcar in September by 4 lengths from Hot Fire: will stay 1¼m; the type to
improve further at 3 yrs. *G. Lewis.*

HIGHLAND SONG 4 b.g. Highland Melody 112–My Song 85 (Songedor 116) **39**
(1979 8fg 6d 7d 5fg* 6s^{2} 1980 6d 6d 6g 5g 5g^{2}) sprint plater; acts on any
going. *W. A. Stephenson.*

HIGHLAND SPICE 6 br.g. Highland Melody 112–Sugar Sweet 87 (Zucchero –
133 §) (1979 NR 1980 10d) quite a useful hurdler; plater on flat; should
stay 1m; acts on firm going; sometimes wears blinkers; bandaged on only
outing of 1980. *K. Morgan.*

HIGH LIFT 2 ch.c. Sandford Lad 133–My Witty (My Babu 136) (1980 **70**
5f 5f 5fg 6d^{2} 6d 6d 7f 6g^{3}) Feb 5; 6,200F, 5,000Y; robust colt; third living
foal; dam won over 4.5f in French Provinces; placed in maiden race at Carlisle
in June and £2,700 seller at York (10½ lengths third of 21 to Supreme Show)
in October; in rear in nurseries in between; suited by 6f; acts on a soft surface;
wears blinkers; sold 2,000 gns Newmarket Autumn Sales. *J. W. Watts.*

HIGH LOADER 3 b.c. High Top 131–Terex (Khalkis 127) (1979 NR 1980 8fg –
10fg 10fg) workmanlike colt; half-brother to 2 winners, including fairly useful
stayer Ventrex (by Henry the Seventh); dam half-sister to 2 good animals; in rear
in maiden and minor races in the North; blinkered final start. *Hbt Jones.*

HIGH OLD TIME 4 ch.c. Mount Hagen 127–Witch of Endor 80 (Matador **79**
131) (1979 8d^{4} 9v^{3} 10s 10.2g 8g* 8.2fg* 8g^{2} 8.2g 1980 8s 8f 7h 7fg 12d*
10s^{2} 12fg^{2} 14d* 12g* 13g^{2} 12fg 12fg^{3} 10.6s* 18d) big colt; had a fine season;
beat Wise Man in good style by 6 lengths in amateur riders event at Haydock
in October; had earlier won similar events on same course and at Carlisle (trotted
up) and had also won easily at Folkestone; needs further than 1m and stays at
least 1¾m (behind in Tote Cesarewitch over further); acts on any going; used
to wear blinkers; lost ground at start twelfth outing. *S. Mellor.*

HIGH RAINBOW 3 b.g. High Line 125–Darwin Tulip (Campaign 106 or **78**
Pirate King 129) (1979 5g 6g 7g 8d^{4} 8g^{3} 1980 12fg 12g^{3} 12.2d^{3} 12g 12.2f^{2}
12g* 12.2g* 12g^{3} (dis) 12f) useful-looking gelding; won maiden race at
Hamilton and handicap at Catterick in the summer; will be suited by 1¾m;
probably acts on any going; sweated up badly first start and ran poorly on
final outing. *J. Etherington.*

HIGHWAY 3 br.c. High Top 131–Sacred Way 88 (Milesian 125) (1979 8f* **110**
1980 8.5f 10g 10.5g 12fg 12g^{2} 12fg* 14.6g) robust, well-made colt; odds on,
scrambled home by a head from Ditton Wood in £4,400 apprentice race at
Newmarket in August (pulled hard early on and drifted left in closing stages);
creditable second in £7,200 handicap on same course earlier in month; stays
1½m (ran badly when tried at 1¾m); acts on firm going. *J. Hindley.*

HIGHWAY ACE 2 b.f. Secret Ace 97–Highway Jane (Royal Highway 117) (1980 5fg 6g^{4} 5g 8.2d) Mar 15; useless plater. *G. Wallace.* —

HIKARI 5 b.h. Petingo 135–Without Reproach 102 (Above Suspicion 127) (1979 14g^{2} 14g 1980 16.1s) fairly useful handicapper; does little racing on flat nowadays; stays 1¾m; acts on firm going; genuine and consistent. *D. Kent.* —

HIKARUGENJI 3 ch.c. Nonoalco 131–Kinnerton Street (Accordant) (1979 7fg 1980 8h 11g 8f 8.2s) strong sort; poor maiden; sold to P. Mitchell 1,150 gns Ascot September Sales. *Sir Mark Prescott.* —

HILAL 4 ch.c. Royal and Regal–Whistling Rex (Whistling Wind 123) (1979 7.5s* 10.5fg 8g 7fg 8s* 7d^{3} 8v^{4} 1980 8v^{3} 8g^{4} 8d^{2} 8g^{2} 7s^{2} 8g^{3} 10s^{2} 8g 8g^{4} 8d* 8d*) **125**

Hilal was in splendid form in the autumn and reaped well-earned reward for a season's honest endeavour by winning the Prix du Rond-Point at Longchamp and the Prix Perth at Saint-Cloud. He showed marked improvement to beat the good Irish three-year-old Crofter in the latter event, for the balance of his previous form placed him some way behind the very best French milers. He had met most of the leading horses and hadn't managed to win before the Prix du Rond-Point, although he had been out of the frame only once. Hilal had been second to American Prince in the Prix du Muguet at Saint-Cloud, to Rostov in the Prix du Chemin de Fer du Nord at Chantilly and to Armistice Day in the Prix Gontaut-Biron at Deauville; he had also been moved up to second in the Prix de la Porte Maillot at Longchamp on the disqualification of Ya Zaman. Kilijaro, Nadjar and Katowice all beat him when he finished fourth in the Prix du Moulin, beaten about two lengths, on this outing before the Rond-Point.

Hilal won both his races in convincing fashion, finishing strongly after being waited with. He drew two and a half lengths clear of Safita in the last furlong of the Rond-Point, despite hanging left, and held off Crofter by three quarters of a length without being hard pressed in the Prix Perth. Crofter started a hot favourite in the latter event, having won three times and been second to Moorestyle in the Prix de la Foret on his only other start, and Hilal ran the race of his life giving 3 lb more than weight-for-age. The pair finished clear of Moon Ingraver, Speed Bus and thirteen others who included American Prince and Rostov.

Hilal (ch. c. 1976)	Royal and Regal (b 1970)	Vaguely Noble (b 1965)	Vienna
			Noble Lassie
		Native Street (gr 1963)	Native Dancer
			Beaver Street
	Whistling Rex (b 1969)	Whistling Wind (ch 1960)	Whistler
			Good As Gold
		Gallop On (gr 1960)	Grey Sovereign
			Tinted Venus

Hilal is the best colt produced so far by the Florida Derby winner Royal and Regal who in 1980 was also represented by the very promising Irish filly Arctique Royale. He is the third foal of the unraced Whistling Rex whose first foal Ballinavail (by Rarity) won a small race over a mile in Ireland. The next dam Gallop On was a useful performer as a two-year-old and a half-sister to the very speedy 1958 two-year-old Fortune's Darling. A tough and genuine colt Hilal stays a mile and a quarter although his best form is at a mile. He ran moderately when raced on firmish ground in 1979 and seems to need some give underfoot. *M. Saliba, France.*

Prix Perth, Saint-Cloud—Hilal beats the even-money favourite Crofter

HILL LAUGH (USA) 3 b.c. Hillary–She's Decided (Decidedly) (1979 NR **62**
1980 8f 12f 10f 10s 8fg^2 8f) big, good-bodied colt; good mover; brother to 2
winners in USA, including stakes-placed Hill Fox; dam, a stakes-placed winner,
is half-sister to smart filly Hill Shade (by Hillary), the dam of Mysterious and
J. O. Tobin; second in maiden race at Yarmouth in July but is only plating
class; one paced and should stay 1¼m+; sold 1,000 gns Doncaster October
Sales. *R. Armstrong.*

HILL OF BARRA 2 ch.c. Pieces of Eight 128–Red Sea 70 (Zimone) (1980 **–**
5d 5v 5f 7f 7d 6s) May 23; 1,200F, 3,000Y; leggy colt; half-brother to several
winners here and abroad; dam won 1¼m seller; in rear in varied company;
trained first 3 outings by C. Bewicke. *N. Vigors.*

HILLSDOWN GOLD 3 b.c. Goldhill 125–Dumana 96 (Dumbarnie 125) (1979 **81**
6g 1980 8g^3 8f^4 8fg* 8fg^2 8.2g^3) neat colt; won 17-runner maiden race at
Warwick in May; ran creditably afterwards; promises to stay 1¼m; yet to race
on a soft surface. *G. Huffer.*

HILLSDOWN LAD 2 b.c. Forlorn River 124–Alchorus 78 (Alcide 136) (1980 **92 p**
6d^3) Mar 31; 6,200Y; rangy colt; good mover; third foal; half-brother to
top-class Be Tuneful (by Be Friendly), a winner at 6f and 7f; dam won over
9f; third favourite, showed plenty of speed towards far side in 17-runner maiden
race at Newmarket but wandered quite badly under severe pressure and was
beaten ¾ length into third place behind Gabitat; will probably stay 7f; should win
races. *G. Huffer.*

HILL'S NORTHERN 3 ch.c. Northfields–Sovereign Court 87 (Sovereign Path **84**
125) (1979 6f 6fg 1980 8.2s^2 8fg* 8f* 8fg* 8g 8g 8h 8d) neat colt; won handicaps at Bath in April and at Pontefract and Doncaster in May; very confidently
ridden to beat State Trooper cleverly by ½ length on last-named; will stay 1¼m;
probably acts on any going; blinkered fourth and fifth starts; often hangs badly
and isn't an easy ride; ran poorly final start; sold to R. Turnell 8,200 gns Newmarket Autumn Sales. *P. Walwyn.*

HILL'S REALM (USA) 2 br.f. Key To The Kingdom–Princess Dare (Impres- **68**
sive) (1980 5f^4 5.1f^4 6g^4) Mar 10; 26,000Y; strong, good-quartered filly;
half-sister to French 3-y-o 1m winner Dare To (by Plenty Old); dam won at up
to 6f in USA; fourth in modest maiden company; stays 6f; sold 4,500 gns Newmarket Autumn Sales. *M. Stoute.*

HILL STATION 8 ch.g. Sheshoon 132–Space Suit 100 (Roan Rocket 128) **–**
(1979 18s 15.5d^3 16v^3 16.9s 16s^2 17.1g^4 16fg^2 20.4g* 16f 16f 1980 18f 16f 16g
16s 17.1fg 16.5g) poor handicapper; stays extremely well; acts on any going;
has been tried in blinkers. *M. Bolton.*

HILLS TREBLE 5 b.h. Blakeney 126–Pugnacity 117 (Pampered King 121) **–**
(1979 10d^4 10.2d 12s^2 14v 12.5fg^3 10.2fg* 10fg 10.5g 1980 9fg) useful performer
at his best, but ran badly last 2 starts in 1979 and was well beaten only outing
of 1980 (April); stays 1½m; acts on any going; has been tried in blinkers. *W.
Hastings-Bass.*

HILL VENTURE 5 ch.g. Goldhill 125–Sound Venture (Hopeful Venture 125) **–**
(1979 8g 12.2s 12.3s 10.4f 1980 12g 11.5fg 12.3g 10.4d 10fg 12.5s) of little
account; usually wears bandages. *R. E. Peacock.*

HIMALIA 3 ch.f. High Line 125–Season Ticket (Silly Season 127) (1979 7fg^2 **74**
1980 10fg^3 12d^3 8g^2 10.1f 8s 10g* 10.2v) lengthy filly; stayed on to win 22-
runner maiden race at Newmarket in November; needs further than 1m and
stays 1½m; acts on a firm and a soft surface; genuine. *G. Hunter.*

HIMAVAN 3 b.g. Sir Gaylord–Party Tricks (Tom Fool) (1979 NR 1980 **–**
10.2d 12s 12f 10fg 12g 14d 12s) well-made gelding; no sign of ability in varied
company; blinkered fifth and final starts; sold to R. Carter 1,500 gns Ascot July
Sales. *A. Breasley.*

HIMLEY PRINCE 3 b.g. Keren 100–Sinfi 75 (Pongee 106) (1979 5fg 7fg 6f **–**
8fg 8.2s 1980 8.3f 8d 10d) neat gelding; bad plater; has been tried in blinkers.
P. Kearney.

HIMY 2 b.f. High Top 131–Sacred Way 88 (Milesian 125) (1980 7g^4 7g) Mar **79 ?**
17; 50,000Y; small, lightly-made filly; sister to 3-y-o Highway, very useful at up
to 1½m, and half-sister to a winner; dam 2-y-o 5f winner; ran creditably for a
20/1-newcomer in slowly-run Somerville Tattersall Stakes at Newmarket in
October, finishing fourth of 8 to more-experienced Spark of Life, beaten little
more than 4 lengths; second favourite for 26-runner maiden event on same track
later in month but was most reluctant to go to post and was beaten over 2f out,

eventually finishing only tenth to Full of Reason; likely to stay $1\frac{1}{4}$m; one to be wary of. *J. Hindley.*

HINDI 2 b.f. Mummy's Pet 125–Sarong 97 (Taj Dewan 128) (1980 6f 5d* 5g) 83
Apr 11; quite attractive filly; first foal; dam 1m winner; put in a determined late challenge to win 23-runner maiden race at Haydock in October by short head from Middleton Lad; always struggling when about $3\frac{1}{2}$ lengths sixth of 16 to Fire Mountain in nursery at Newmarket later in month; $5\frac{1}{4}$ lengths sixth of 10 to Silken Knot in newcomers race at Ascot in July on only other start; runs as if a return to 6f will suit her. *M. Jarvis.*

HINDOO HAVEN 2 ch.g. Amber Rama 133–Tranquility Base 112 (Roan —
Rocket 128) (1980 6d 7d 7f) May 27; 3,600F, 4,200Y; neat gelding; half-brother to 5f and 7f winner Lady of Man (by So Blessed); dam stayed 6f well at 2 yrs but seemed not to stay $1\frac{1}{4}$m; well behind in varied races. *R. Armstrong.*

HINDOUSTAN 4 b.c. Blakeney 126–Elm Leaf 96 (Tudor Melody 129) (1979 51
8d 12d 11s 12d 1980 13f^3 12f 12g^4 15.8fg 15g 16g 20.4g^4 16f 16s) big, good sort; staying handicapper; probably unsuited by soft ground; sweating sixth outing; sold 2,600 gns Ascot September Sales. *T. Craig.*

HINDU HYMN 4 b.g. Saintly Song 128–Tigerlee 57 (Tiger 125) (1979 NR —
1980 7g 9.4g) of no account. *N. Chamberlain.*

HI NOON 4 b.f. Double-U-Jay 120–Hi Tess 65 (Supreme Court 135) (1979 8s 50
12.3v^3 13.8s 16fg 14f 13.8d* 12fg^4 12g^4 1980 12fg 12g^3 12d 13.8f 12fg* 12f 12.2fg 15.8d^3 12d 15d) leggy filly; plater; attracted no bid after scoring at Thirsk in August; stays 2m; acts on a firm and a soft surface; blinkered last 3 starts (ran creditably in non-seller first occasion). *Hbt Jones.*

HINTSBROOK 2 b.c. Upper Case–Leisure Hour (Persian Gulf) (1980 8d) —
May 22; big, good-looking colt; half-brother to 1m to 13f winner Simpson Jersey (by Highland Melody); dam never ran; unquoted and backward, started slowly when last of 16 to Jade and Diamond in maiden race at Warwick in October. *B. McMahon.*

HI RAMBI 3 b.c. Upper Case–Rambi (Ribot 142) (1979 5d 7.8g 7d 7d 7s —
1980 9g 9g 7g^3 6s 8d) ex-Irish colt; second living foal; half-brother to fairly useful 1m to $1\frac{3}{4}$m winner Thar She Blows (by Sea Hawk II); dam won over 1m and is sister to smart Riboprince; poor maiden; should stay middle distances; trained first 3 starts by B. Harrison Burcombe. *G. Beeson.*

HIRSUTE 3 ch.c. Blue Cashmere 129–Queen Flush (Twilight Alley 133) (1979 53
6g^4 6fg 7fg^4 6g 7fg^3 8fg 8d^3 8.2d 8fg 8g 8d^3 1980 10s 10f 8f 8g 8g^3 8g^2 8d^2 9g) lengthy colt; one-paced plater; stays 1m; acts on a firm and a soft surface; blinkered second start. *P. Asquith.*

HISLAND 2 ch.c. Roi Soleil 125–Parterre (Tudor Treasure 119) (1980 5f 6s 6fg) —
May 5; 940Y; first foal; dam never ran; well beaten in maiden auction events. *L. Barratt.*

HIS MASTER'S VOICE 2 ch.g. Brigadier Gerard 144–Heavenly Sound 115 —
(Sound Track 132) (1980 6fg 7f) Mar 1; strong, useful sort; half-brother to useful 3-y-o 6f and 7f winner Chant (by Habat) and very useful 1972 2-y-o Tranquility Base (by Roan Rocket); dam game 5f sprinter; behind in maiden races at Salisbury and Redcar in September (ridden by lad in paddock both starts); subsequently gelded. *Sir Mark Prescott.*

HISSING SID 2 gr. or ro.c. Royal Match 117–Serissa (Supreme Sovereign 119) 72
(1980 6g 6s 6d^3 8.2s 7.2d*) May 11; 2,600Y; robust colt; good mover; first foal; closely inbred to Sovereign Path; dam Irish $1\frac{3}{4}$m winner; attracted no bid after making all to win £2,400 seller at Haydock in October by $\frac{1}{2}$ length from Piping Queen; should stay at least 1m; yet to race on a firm surface. *R. Hollinshead.*

HI THERE 2 b.f. High Top 131–Thereby 99 (Star Moss 122) (1980 5fg 5f* 89
5f^4 5g 6g) Apr 12; 14,500Y; useful-looking filly; half-sister to several winners here and abroad, including very useful sprinter Captive Dream (by Sing Sing); dam won at up to 1m; made all when winning 12-runner maiden race at Wolverhampton in May unchallenged by 6 lengths from Spreading Sunset; also ran well under top weight when 4 lengths sixth of 20 to Salamina in 6f nursery at Lingfield in September; will stay 1m. *N. Gaselee.*

HIT ME AGAIN 2 ch.c. Quayside 124–Nell 76 (Gilles de Retz 132) (1980 5fg —
5.8fg 6g 8s 6g) Mar 21; 4,000Y; leggy, close-coupled colt; half-brother to 2 minor winners; dam showed little worthwhile form; bad maiden; trained by G. Hunter first 3 outings; blinkered fifth start. *C. Mackenzie.*

HIT RECORD 2 ch.c. Record Token 128–Silk Willoughby (Pirate King 129) (1980 5fg^4 7d^3 6g^4 5f 6d^2 6d^2) Mar 3; 8,200F, 14,000Y; quite an attractive, well-made colt; half-brother to fair 7f performer Marston (by Tribal Chief); dam unraced sister to smart stayer Avast; second in end-of-season maiden races, going down by 3 lengths to Shark Song in 17-runner race at Newmarket and by ½ length to Camisite in 18-runner event at Doncaster; finds 5f on sharp side and stays 7f; acts on a soft surface. *F. Durr.* **84**

HIT THE BUTTON 2 ch.f. Red Alert 127–Stand Off 61 (Murrayfield 119) (1980 5g 6fg 5.8g 6g) Apr 25; 2,700Y; leggy, rather unfurnished filly; first foal; dam won 5f seller at 2 yrs; no sign of ability, including under a low weight in a nursery. *J. Benstead.* –

HIT THE HAMMER 3 b.c. Blakeney 126–Guessing Game 87 (Doutelle 128) (1979 8g 1980 11f 10.2fg^4 16g^2 14g^3 14d 12d^2) strong, quite attractive colt; moderate maiden; suited by a test of stamina; suited by some give in the ground. *C. Brittain.* **74**

HIT THE ROAD (FR) 2 b.g. Sovereign Path 125–Hit It Off (Hardicanute 130) (1980 7.2d 8d^2 10s^2 8d) Apr 25; 13,000Y; strong, compact gelding; third foal; half-brother to 3-y-o 2m winner Red Toff (by Red God); dam won over 7.5f at 2 yrs in France; runner-up to easy winners King's College Boy and St Mawes in maiden races at Warwick and Nottingham in October; suited by 1¼m and will probably get further. *B. Hanbury.* **77**

HIYAGRIV 3 ch.c. Riverman 131–Bold Maiden 71 (Bold Lad USA) (1979 5fg 5f^4 6g 5g 5fg 7.3g 8f 1980 5f 8fg 6h^4 7fg 10f 8d 6d 6s 8fg^3 7f^4 10.1f 8d 8fg 10.1g) small colt; stays 1m; acts on a firm surface; sometimes blinkered; sold 1,500 gns Newmarket Autumn Sales. *A. Breasley.* **61**

HIZ 2 gr.c. Persian Plan–Miss Swift 79 (Canisbay 120) (1980 6s 7fg^4 6g 6s* 7d) Mar 16; 750F, 3,100Y; big, strong colt; second reported foal; dam won over 1m and 1¼m; showed improved form when winning 19-runner nursery at Nottingham in October by 1½ lengths from Welsh Noble, despite wandering badly when beginning his challenge; ran well next time out; will stay 1m; acts on a firm surface but is well suited by soft ground. *R. Price.* **96**

HOBA SUPREME 2 br.g. Sit In The Corner–Open Arms 77 (Dignitary 121) (1980 5f 5d 6s) Feb 21; 2,100Y; compact gelding; brother to successful sprinter Croft Close and 3-y-o 6f winner Young Croftie; dam 5f sprinter; behind in maiden and minor races but showed signs of ability on second start; should stay 6f. *R. E. Peacock.* –

HODAH 3 b.f. Blakeney 126–Try-Gun (Combat 123) (1979 5v 7fg 1980 12fg 16g 16fg 14fg) quite attractive well-made, robust filly; well beaten in varied company. *R. Boss.* –

HOD TIGHT 3 ch.f. Galivanter 131–Hod On 67 (Decoy Boy 129) (1979 5s 6d 5f 8g 5g 6g 1980 7f 6fg 5g 6d 8fg 12d) small filly; poor plater; best run at 5f; has worn blinkers; sometimes sweats up; sold 440 gns Doncaster Autumn Sales. *Hbt Jones.* –

HOGGLER 4 b.g. Murrayfield 119–Sky Songstress 72 (Sky Gipsy 117) (1979 NR 1980 10.1g 9d) small, compact gelding; first foal; dam poor sprint maiden; well beaten in minor event at Windsor and maiden race (burly) at Wolverhampton in summer. *J. Webber.* –

HO HAN WAI 4 b.f. Sassafras 135–Good Conduct (Sing Sing 134) (1979 12g 12g 12g* 12g 1980 12v* 10.5g* 12g 10.5d 12f 12d^2 12s 12g) French filly; third foal; half-sister to Canadian winner Do Good (by Derring-Do) and French winner Early Release (by Prince Regent); dam never ran; won Prix de Saint-Lo at Evry in 1979; successful twice at Saint-Cloud in the spring, in a handicap and in Group 3 Prix Corrida; beat Blinette by a short head in latter; ran best subsequent race when close second to La Ristonica in 19-runner handicap at Longchamp in September; stays 1½m; acts on heavy going. *A. Paus, France.* **106**

HO-LAC 2 gr.g. Brittany–Norma's Way 70 (Great White Way) (1980 6g 6f) May 23; 1,500Y; third foal; brother to plating-class animal, and half-brother to a winning plater; dam 2-y-o 5f winner; in rear in sellers at Lingfield. *P. K. Mitchell.* –

HOLDALL 2 ch.f. Manacle 123–Berostina 88 (Ribero 126) (1980 5g^3 5f^3 5f 5f 6g 6fg^4 6fg 6g* 6f^4 7fg) Apr 21; 1,100F; compact filly; first produce; dam, winner over hurdles, was at her best at 2 yrs on flat; beaten in sellers on fifth and sixth outings but improved radically to win £2,000 event at Ripon in August by 2 **80**

lengths from Train of Thought; creditable fourth of 13 to Star Pastures in good-class fillies' race at York in September; stays 6f but is by no means sure to stay 7f; acts on firm going; blinkered seventh outing; has often hung badly; goes very well for P. Robinson. *P. Asquith.*

HOLD FIRE 2 br.g. Rheingold 137–Little Firefly (Bold Ruler) (1980 8g 8fg) Mar 13; 2,500Y; lightly-made gelding; fifth foal; dam Irish 5f winner; in rear in 23-runner events at Goodwood and Newbury (last) in September. *R. Smyth.* —

HOLD OFF 3 b. or br.c. Red Alert 127–Wedding March (March Past 124) (1979 6s4 6fg 7g2 1980 10.1fg2 10fg2 9g4 11.7s 9g 8fg*) big, useful sort; blinkered when winning apprentice maiden race at Yarmouth in August; stays 1¼m (had stiff task when behind over further); acts on a firm surface. *M. Ryan.* 71

HOLIDAY CLUB 2 b.c. So Blessed 130–Gay Shadow 99 (Northfields) (1980 6g 6fg2 7d) Mar 15; 24,000Y; strong colt; first foal; dam, winner over 5f and 6f at 2 yrs, is half-sister to very smart sprinter Honeyblest (by So Blessed); 2 lengths second of 12 to Douschkina in minor event at Newmarket in August; not certain to stay 7f. *H. T. Jones.* 84

HOLLAND PARK 2 ch.c. Record Token 128–Pahaska 86 (Wolver Hollow 126) (1980 5fg 5fg 6f4 6d4 5d4 7g 7f3 7g4 7s 7d 8d) May 21; 3,700Y, resold 3,500Y; dipped-backed colt; first foal; dam stayed 1¼m; in frame in maiden company and in a nursery but finished in rear in selling nursery when blinkered on final outing; should stay 1m; seems to act on any going with exception of very soft; sold 1,200 gns Newmarket Autumn Sales. *G. Toft.* 70

HOLLOW LAUGH 2 b.c. Wolver Hollow 126–Catherine's Sister 96 (Petition 130) (1980 6g 6g2 7g) Mar 9; 5,000Y; rangy, good sort; half-brother to 3 winners, including middle-distance performer Mother Carey (by Sea Hawk II); dam won at 1m; ran very green for a long way but managed to finish 2 lengths second of 13 to Olympic Glory in minor event at Kempton in July; ridden along early in straight and didn't have much room 2f out when 4½ lengths sixth of 11 to King's General in slowly-run £3,000 event at Goodwood 2 months later; will be suited by 1m. *F. J. Houghton.* 81

HOLLOW LAUGHTER 2 br.c. Wolver Hollow 126–La Lola (Le Levanstell 122) (1980 5fg 5.8fg 7d* 7g4 7f4) Feb 3; 6,000Y; light-framed colt; fifth foal; dam won over 6f at 2 yrs in Ireland; won 15-runner maiden race at Brighton in July by ½ length from Shangarry; fair fourth under top weight in 8-runner nursery won by Shangarry on same course on next outing; will stay 1m; best form with some give in the ground. *G. Harwood.* 79

HOLLY PATCH 2 b.c. Realm 129–Sea Holly 93 (Larkspur 128) (1980 5fg3 5g* 5fg4 6d3 6d2 6g 6g 6d) Mar 7; 580 2-y-o; small, compact colt; half-brother to Italian 7f and 1¼m winner Piazza Navona (by Upper Case); dam stayed 1m; heavily-backed favourite, attracted no bid after winning 7-runner seller at Salisbury in June by 2½ lengths from Clarabelle; subsequently ran creditably when placed in valuable seller and a claiming race at Brighton; stays 6f; sold 2,200 gns Newmarket Autumn Sales. *E. Reavey.* 61

HOLMBURY LAD (USA) 2 gr.c. Al Hattab–Fairly Faithful 87 (Prove It) (1980 6g 5fg*(dis) 5d3) Apr 4; $28,000Y; tall, useful-looking colt; second foal; dam, daughter of very smart sprinter Krakenwake, won over 5f at 2 yrs; barged through to win 16-runner maiden race at Newbury in September by short head from Swinging Rhythm and was disqualified by stewards; made ground hand over fist in final 2f when ½-length third to 23 to Hindi in similar race at Haydock the following month, giving impression he'd have won if more favourably drawn; will be suited by a return to 6f; should gain compensation at 3 yrs. *G. Harwood.* 85

HOLY POWER 3 b.f. So Blessed 130–Double Vitesse (Double Jump 131) (1979 5d 5d4 5g3 5f2 1980 6f 8s 8.2d 6g 6g 6g) light-framed filly; plating-class maiden; best at sprint distances; sold 360 gns Ascot November Sales. *W. Elsey.* 43

HOLYWELL 3 br.f. Wolver Hollow 126–Santa Maria 103 (Tropique 128) (1979 5s 5g 6fg 6fg 1980 10fg 13.4g) leggy filly; well bred but is only plating class; should stay 1¼m; wore a hood and blinkers final start. *J. Bethell.* —

HOLY WRIT 3 ch.c. Dictus 126–The Nun 99 (Saint Crespin III 132) (1979 5s 5s3 5d 6f 7f 8fg4 1980 6s3 5fg 5f 6fg 6f4 5h 7d 7g 6s) neat colt; poor plater; probably acts on any going; sometimes blinkered; has run respectably for a boy. *S. Matthews.* —

HOMEFIELD 12 ch.g. El Cid 109–Part Exchange 78 (Faubourg II 127) (1979 12d 1980 17.1fg 16.5g) of little account nowadays. *W. Musson.* —

HOME GROUND 3 gr.g. No Mercy 126–Babble On 79 (Acropolis 132) (1979 6s^2 6fg^2 7g* 7g 6g* 7d^2 7f^2 8.2g* 8d^4 7fg^4 1980 7v 8v^2 10.6d^2 8.2f^2 8f^2 7f^2(dis) 7g 8fg 8d 8.2d) useful sort who carries plenty of condition; runner-up 5 times in varied company, putting up very good effort to be beaten ¾ length by Moorestyle in valuable handicap at York in May on sixth start (hung badly left in closing stages and was disqualified for hampering third horse); best at up to 1m and appears not to stay 1¼m; probably acts on any going; best in blinkers; ran creditably for an amateur on fourth outing but seems suited by strong handling; trained by G. Richards first 6 starts; ran atrociously final outing and was subsequently gelded. *B. Hills.* **101**

HOME ON THE RANGE 2 br.f. Habitat 134–Great Guns 109 (Busted 134) (1980 6s 7fg^4 7g^2) Mar 18; good sort; second foal; dam prolific winner from 1¼m to 2m; clear of remainder when going down by 2½ lengths to Investa in 18-runner maiden race at Leicester in August; will stay 1¼m; should win a race at 3 yrs. *H. Cecil.* **87**

HOMESON 3 b.c. Bustino 136–Reita 87 (Gilles de Retz 132) (1979 NR 1980 10s 14g* 12.3d^4) 15,000Y; rangy, good-bodied colt; half-brother to 3 winners, including very useful Homeboy (by King's Troop), successful at up to 1¼m; dam miler; dead-heated with Boost in maiden race at Sandown in July; suited by 1¾m; sold to J. Gifford 22,000 gns Newmarket Autumn Sales. *M. Jarvis.* **78**

HOME WIN 6 b.g. Habitat 134–Triumphantly (Bold Ruler) (1979 12d 16.1f 1980 8d 10.4d 12g 9s 12.5s) bad plater; sometimes wears blinkers; wears bandages *M. James.* **–**

HONEST EDGAR 5 br.h. Irish Love 117–Eutrippa 101 (Eudaemon 129) (1979 12s 9s 12.2g^3 16fg 12s 1980 10s* 10g^4) plater; dropped in class when winning at Nottingham in July (no bid); stays 1½m; acts on soft going. *D. Weeden.* **48**

HONEST KLAIRE 3 b.f. The Brianstan 128–Be Honest (Klairon 131) (1979 NR 1980 7g 8fg 9f^4 11.7g 8d) lengthy filly; third live foal; half-sister to 1½m seller winner Wealthy (by Gold Rod); dam won over 1m; little worthwhile form in varied company; not certain to stay middle distances; sold 440 gns Ascot August Sales. *P. Walwyn.* **–**

HONEY BARRON 3 b.c. Pitcairn 126–Rogan Honey (Abernant 142) (1979 6f* 7f* 1980 7fg 8.2fg 8g 7d^2 7g* 7d 7g^2 7g 7.3fg^3 7.2d^4 7d^2) neat, attractive colt; good mover; fairly useful handicapper; beat Triumphant a head at Sandown in July; best form at 7f; probably acts on any going; blinkered ninth and tenth starts; ran moderately sixth outing. *J. Dunlop.* **98**

HONORARIUM 3 br.f. The Brianstan 128–Honerone 85 (Sammy Davis 129) (1979 5s 6fg 1980 8.2fg 12.2fg 10.6d 10s) fair sort; in rear in minor and maiden events. *R. Hollinshead.* **–**

HONOURABLE MAN 7 b.g. Marcus Brutus 108–Woodland Maiden (Wood Cot) (1979 NR 1980 12fg 16g) sturdy gelding; winning point-to-pointer; behind in lady riders race at Ripon and maiden event at Beverley in June. *M. W. Easterby.* **–**

HONOURS EVEN (FR) 3 ch.g. Sweet Revenge 129–Monochrome 62 (Graustark) (1979 6fg 1980 10g 11.7f 12g 10d 12g 10f 16f 12g 15.5f 16fg) big gelding; well beaten in varied company and looks slow; sold out of I. Balding's stable 2,100 gns Ascot July Sales. *R. Armytage.* **–**

HOOD HILL 4 ch.g. Silly Season 127–Whatawind (Typhoon 125) (1979 6g 1980 6fg 7g 10g 12f 8d 10d^3 10s 6g) plater; stays 1¼m; best form in blinkers. *G. Fletcher.* **42**

HOODWINK 2 br.g. No Mercy 126–Rose Blanche 89 (French Beige 127) (1980 5fg 5fg 5.8fg 7fg^3 7fg^2 8d) Feb 3; quite a well-made gelding; brother to 3 minor winners; dam 2-y-o 7f winner; placed in maiden race at Warwick in July and nursery at Wolverhampton the following month; suited by 7f but didn't run up to his best over 1m; acts on a firm surface; wears blinkers. *R. Hern.* **71**

HOPE ETERNAL 6 b.g. Veiled Wonder–Yellow Streak (Shantung 132) (1979 7d^2 7v^3 5d^3 6d* 7g 6fg 5g 6d 1980 7f 8fg 11d^3 12d 12g 8.2s) poor handicapper; stays 9f; acts on any going; suitable mount for an apprentice. *W. H. H. Williams.* **–**

HOPEFUL 3 br.f. Spitsbergen 103–Obey 71 (Martial 131) (1979 NR 1980 9f 8f) small filly; third foal; dam won 5f seller at 2 yrs; behind in sellers at Wolverhampton (moved poorly to post) and Redcar in September. *J. Powney.* **–**

HOPEFUL COURAGE 5 br.g. Abwah 118–Mary Francis (Elopement 125) (1979 10.1fg 1980 12fg) plater; stays 9f; acts on any going; has worn blinkers; winning hurdler. *T. Hallett.* —

HOPEFUL PRINCESS 2 b.f. Astrapi 85–Southern Sun (Linacre 133) (1980 5fg 6f³ 6fg 6fg 7fg) May 9; 200Y; neat filly; fourth living foal; dam never ran; fairly close up in sellers at Yarmouth and Pontefract in the summer, second and fourth outings; should stay 7f. *H. Westbrook.* 42

HOPEFUL SHOT 3 ch.c. Wishing Star 117–Cannon Ball 91 (By Thunder! 122) (1979 5v 5s² 6f 6g* 7g 7d 8s 1980 10v⁴ 11.7g 16g 12s 11.7s*) strong, useful sort; won handicap at Windsor in July; stays 1½m (out of his depth over 2m); acts on soft going; suited by forcing tactics. *C. Bewicke.* 69

HORA ROYALE 6 b.m. Kibenka 119–Princess's Time (Arctic Time 127) (1979 NR 1980 8fg 7h 7h) poor handicapper at up to 1¼m in 1978; has since been to stud and produced a foal by My Swanee; not disgraced on second outing; reluctant to go to post and unseated rider leaving stalls on previous appearance; probably acts on any going; usually wears blinkers; has been taken down early to start. *S. Matthews.* —

HORKEY 3 ch.f. Shoolerville 121–Omnia Opera 83 (Major Portion 129) (1979 5h 6g² 6fg 7g 1980 8.2s 8g 8fg 8f 8fg 13.8fg 10s) leggy filly; of little account nowadays; best run at 6f; trained by N. Adam first 5 starts. *G. Wallace.* —

HORNCASTLE 2 b.g. So Blessed 130–Foxhorn (Hornbeam 130) (1980 5s² 5fg* 5fg* 5f* 5f⁴ 6g² 5g² 6g³ 7.2g⁴ 7g⁴ 6f) Apr 28; 5,000F, 8,400Y; leggy, rather narrow gelding; half-brother to 1½m winner Norton Cavalier (by Mon Fils); dam never ran; successful in minor events at Pontefract, Newmarket and Bath in the spring, making all to win by 1½ lengths from Miss Murton on last-named track; in frame on nearly all his other outings, running respectably when 5 lengths fourth of 10 to Kareem in 7.2f nursery at Haydock in September; will stay 1m; acts on any going; genuine and consistent. *W. O'Gorman.* 88

HORNET'S NEST 3 b.f. Realm 129–Ambuscade 77 (Relko 136) (1979 5f⁴ 5fg 8g² 1980 8v 8f* 8fg 8g 8fg⁴) lightly-made filly; won poor maiden race at Carlisle in May; will stay beyond 1m; acts on firm going and ran poorly only outing on heavy; sweated up a bit fourth start; didn't look a suitable mount for a boy final outing. *Sir Mark Prescott.* 57

HOROS (USA) 4 ch.c. Head of the River–Sound of Success (Successor) (1979 8s² 10s 8f² 8.3g* 8.5g² 10.2fg 8fg 1980 9fg 10.6f 12f 12d 8fg⁴ 12fg 10.6s) lengthy colt; quite a moderate handicapper; best form at up to 1m; acts on any going. *W. H. H. Williams.* —

HORTENSIA (FR) 3 b.f. Luthier 126–Helenouchka (Nijinsky 138) (1979 7.5s* 1980 11g³ 10.5g* 10.5g 10s³ 12d⁴ 9.2f*) 245,000 francs Y (approx £29,000); strong, well-made, attractive filly; first foal; dam won over 1¼m and comes from same family as Oaks winner Sicarelle; a smart filly who won Group 3 Prix Cleopatre at Saint-Cloud in May by ½ length from Laquiola and Group 2 Prix de l'Opera at Longchamp in October by a similar margin from stable-companion Moon Ingraver; good third of 8, nearly a length behind Luth de Saron, in Prix de Malleret at Longchamp in June; sweated up slightly, pulled hard early on and faded under pressure in straight when 5 lengths fourth to Shoot A Line in Yorkshire Oaks in August; best form at up to 10.5f; acts on any going. *O. Douieb, France.* 119

HOTBELOO 2 ch.f. Roi Soleil 125–Bleue Horizon II (Mourne 126) (1980 6g 5.8h 6f) Mar 14; half-sister to several minor winners here and abroad, including Irish 9f winner Chapeau Bleue (by High Hat); dam ran 3 times; well beaten in minor and maiden events; has worn bandages behind. *W. Wightman.* —

HOT CASE 3 gr.f. Upper Case–Chili Girl 112 (Skymaster 126) (1979 6g 5g² 6fg³ 6fg* 6g² 6g³ 1980 7f² 7fg* 7fg² 7.2g² 8fg 7g² 7g² 7fg⁴ 7fg 7s) neat filly; fair handicapper; beat Crockford Lad a short head at Warwick in May; ran creditably most starts afterwards; should stay 1m; acts well on firm ground; sweated up final start in 1979 (ran respectably); sold 41,000 gns Newmarket December Sales. *J. Dunlop.* 92

HOT EMBER 2 b.f. Hot Spark 126–Royal Rosette 66 (Pardao 120) (1980 5g 6fg⁴ 6fg) Apr 9; close-coupled filly; half-sister to 3-y-o Dragon's Head (by Star Appeal), successful over 7f and 1¼m, and to 2 minor winners; dam stayed 1¼m; 4¾ lengths fourth of 7 to Petroleuse in Blue Seal Stakes at Ascot in September; favourite for 19-runner minor event at Lingfield the following month but weakened in last 2f to finish 3 lengths sixth behind Sea Aura; may stay 1m. *R. Price.* 75

HOT FIRE 2 b.c. Hotfoot 126–Mischief 76 (Sassafras 135) (1980 7f^2 8g^3) **76**
Mar 26; 19,500Y; rangy, good sort; first foal; dam 1½m winner; 20/1 and just in need of race, came out best of far-side group when 4 lengths second of 25 to Highland Range in maiden race at Redcar in September; second favourite, had every chance when 3½ lengths third of 17 to Dragon Palace in similar race at Newmarket the following month; will be suited by 1¼m; should win a race. *J. Fitzgerald.*

HOT GUN 3 br.c. Hotfoot 126–Pop Gun 85 (King's Troop 118) (1979 5s **66**
5s 5g 5g 5d* 6g^2 6g 5fg^4 7f 7f 5fg 6fg 6fg 8fg 8g 1980 10s^2 5fg 5fg 8fg 12fg) sharp sort; plater; needs further than 5f and stays 1¼m; probably acts on any going; often blinkered; unseated rider ninth outing in 1979; claimed out of G. Beeson's stable after first start; sold 1,000 gns Newmarket July Sales. *K. Ivory.*

HOT HEART 2 ch.c. Hot Spark 126–Laxmi 108 (Palestine 133) (1980 6s) —
June 8; compact colt; 40,000Y; half-brother to 1,000 Guineas winner Enstone Spark (by Sparkler); dam best at 5f; 25/1 and in need of race, always behind in 22-runner maiden event at Doncaster in November won by Banbury Cross. *R. Armstrong.*

HOT LIPS MOLL 4 b.f. Firestreak 125–Saucy Moll 94 (Hard Sauce 131) —
(1979 8v^4 11s* 12s 12.3d^4 11fg^4 14f 12fg 1980 12s 16s) lightly-made filly; well beaten since winning maiden race early in 1979, including in seller; stays 11f; acts well on soft going; sometimes plays up in preliminaries and is said to be 'of a fractious nature'; blinkered final outing at 2 yrs; sold 900 gns Ascot August Sales. *W. Marshall.*

HOT MONEY 3 b.f. Mummy's Pet 125–Little Bird 87 (Only for Life 126) (1979 **50**
5s 5s 6g 1980 5s 6fg 8g 7g 6g* 6d) workmanlike filly; plater; showed improved form to win claiming handicap at Newmarket in October; stays 6f; blinkered last 2 starts. *W. Holden.*

HOT MORTAL 3 b.f. Hotfoot 126–Innovation 80 (Immortality) (1979 7fg —
7f^4 7f 6fg 1980 7fg 6f 6f) workmanlike filly; poor maiden; blinkered final start; sometimes wore bandages; dead. *M. Salaman.*

HOT PRESS 2 ch.f. Hotfoot 126–Star Story 117 (Red God 128§) (1980 **77**
5g* 6g 6g) Jan 31; smallish, stocky filly; half-sister to several winners, including 3-y-o Divetta, successful at up to 1m; dam prolific winner at 5f and 6f; favourite when getting up close home to win 17-runner maiden race at Wolverhampton in July by a short head from Trytravelscene; always struggling when seventh of 13 to Lord Clarence in minor event at Salisbury the following month and was well beaten in a nursery at Newmarket in October on only subsequent start; should be suited by 6f. *F. J. Houghton.*

HOT PRINCE 4 b.c. Sun Prince 128–Melodia 91 (Tudor Melody 129) (1979 —
7d 8g 11.7fg^4 13.4f 14fg^4 9g^2 7d 1980 10.1fg 17.1fg) quite a modest plater; seems to stay 1½m; often wears blinkers. *R. Keenor.*

HOT SILK 3 b.g. Hotfoot 126–China Girl 76 (Shantung 132) (1979 5.3fg **50**
6g^3 7s 1980 7s^3 7f 9f 10f 14g 8g^3 10f 10d 10d^3) lightly-built gelding; plater; stays 1¼m; suited by some give in the ground; blinkered third start (moved freely to post); ran poorly fourth outing; sold 460 gns Ascot November Sales. *W. Wightman.*

HOT SOVEREIGN 5 b.g. Hot Brandy 119–Serene Sovereign (Sovereign —
Lord 120) (1979 NR 1980 10h) novice hurdler; unquoted when last of 9 finishers in apprentice event won by Chukaroo at Brighton in May, first outing on flat; sold 470 gns Ascot August Sales. *D. Jermy.*

HOT TRAIL 3 ch.c. Hot Spark 126–Cathy Jane 86 (Lauso) (1979 5s 6g* **74**
6g* 7g 8.2g 8fg^2 8.2fg* 8.2s 1980 10d^2 10f 12fg 12h 10.2fg 10g^3 10.2g* 10fg* 10g*) robust colt; in good form in July, winning handicaps at Bath (apprentice race), Chepstow and Kempton; held off Glowing Tan by a neck on last-named; best at around 1¼m; acts on a firm and a soft surface; used to wear blinkers but didn't on last 4 outings; suitable mount for a boy; ran poorly fifth start. *P. M. Taylor.*

HOTWAVE 2 ch.f. Hotfoot 126–Pinwave 82 (Pinza 137) (1980 6f 7s 7g) Mar **67**
4; 2,100Y; compact, fair sort; good mover; closely related to useful 1¼m winner Wire Up (by Firestreak); dam won at up to 13f; quite moderate form in maiden and minor events, seeming to show promise on first outing when 14 lengths fifth of 13 to Star Pastures in £2,400 event at York in September (stayed on well after a slowish start); will be suited by 1¼m; sweating final start. *Miss. S. Hall.*

HOT WIND 2 ch.g. Hotfoot 126–Wind Goddess (Whistling Wind 123) (1980 **82**
5fg^4 5f 6d 6d^3 7g 7fg^2 7fg^4 7d^4) Mar 13; strong, good-looking gelding; half-brother to several winners, including smart 1974 2-y-o Windy Glen (by Wolver Hollow); dam Irish 5f winner; in frame in maiden races and nurseries; stays 7f; finds little off bridle and is untrustworthy. *B. Hobbs.*

HOUND SONG 2 b.f. Jukebox 120–Artemis 91 (King Emperor) (1980 5s **84**
5g^4 5fg^3 5f^4 5fg^3 5.3d 6g* 6fg* 6fg 6s) May 19; 8,600Y; lightly-made filly; third foal; half-sister to useful Italian 3-y-o Adolfina (by Gay Fandango); dam won over 7f at 2 yrs; showed improved form after changing stables, winning maiden race at Folkestone and nursery at Windsor within space of 5 days in August, latter under 7-lb penalty; will stay 7f; acts on firm going and is probably unsuited by a soft surface; blinkered fourth to sixth outings; trained by P. Feilden first 6 starts. *C. Nelson.*

HOURGLASS 3 br.f. Mansingh 120–Queen of Time (Roi Dagobert 128) (1979 –
NR 1980 8fg 9f) first foal; dam poor maiden; behind in maiden races at Warwick and Wolverhampton in May. *M. Jarvis.*

HOUSE GUARD 5 ch.h. Home Guard 129–Botany Bess (Right Royal V **118**
135) (1979 8d^3 7f* 7g 8fg 7f 8f* 8fg* 8fg* 8.2g* 7.6f^2 7f^2 7f* 8g 1980 8d 8f 7fg^4 8f*(dis) 8f* 8f 8g^4 7g 8g^2 8g) well-made horse; smart handicapper; first past post in Ultramar Jubilee Stakes at Kempton in May but hampered third-placed Piaffer and was relegated to last; gained compensation when beating Bradamante cleverly by $\frac{3}{4}$ length in valuable Hambleton Handicap at York later in month; ran well afterwards when close-up fifth of 7 behind Kris in Tote Lockinge Stakes at Newbury, about a length fourth to Rostov in Prix du Chemin de Fer du Nord at Chantilly and second to Crown Witness under 10-0 in handicap at Sandown; didn't race after injuring a tendon early in August; stayed 1m; appeared to act on any going, but was particularly well suited by firm; occasionally blinkered but was better without; usually held up and had a very good turn of foot; went well for L. Piggott; genuine and consistent; stud in South Africa. *R. Armstrong.*

HOUSEHOLDER 3 b.c. Home Guard 129–Palace of Medina 94 (Royal Palace **77**
131) (1979 NR 1980 11f 12g 11d^3 14g^3) big, lengthy colt; second foal; dam won over 1$\frac{1}{2}$m; close third in maiden race at Sandown in July, final start; stays 1$\frac{3}{4}$m; didn't stride out well to post first 2 starts; sold to W. Clay 2,600 gns Newmarket Autumn Sales. *G. Harwood.*

HOUSE MARTIN 5 ch.m. Quayside 124–Key of Laughter 67 (Merry Boy –
88) (1979 NR 1980 12fg) unquoted when last in maiden race won by Ankus at Haydock in April, first outing; sold 700 gns Ascot July Sales and resold 450 gns Doncaster November Sales. *C. Wildman.*

HOW SPLENDID 3 b.f. John Splendid 116–Double Grand (Coronation Year –
124) (1979 6d 1980 7.6f 8f 7.2d 8g 7.2d 7s 8.2g 8g) neat, lightly-made filly; only plating class; should stay 1m; blinkered nowadays; doesn't possess a great deal of scope. *W. Elsey.*

H. R. MICRO 2 br.f. High Award 119–Crusheen (Typhoon 125) (1980 5fg **77**
6g^4 6g 6s 5fg^3 6g 5fg^3 5g 5f 5d 5fg^4 5g^4 6d^4 5s^4 6g^2) Mar 15; small, lengthy filly; half-sister to 2 winners, including Dancing Partner (by Hul a Hul), a winner at up to 1m; dam ran twice at 2 yrs in Ireland; in frame in a variety of races, including several nurseries; beaten 3 lengths when second of 20 to Nello in maiden race at Leicester in November on final outing (apprentice ridden); stays 6f; probably acts on any going; blinkered sixth outing. *D. Dale.*

HUARALINO 5 br.h. Habitat 134–Lorna Doone (Tom Rolfe) (1979 16d **93**
18.4d 13.3g 16d 16fg* 16fg^3 1980 12f 16.1f 16fg^3 16fg 16g 16g^3 16.9f^2) big, strong-quartered horse; placed in handicaps at Kempton, Ascot and Wolverhampton, finishing 2$\frac{1}{2}$ lengths second to Shaab on last-named course in August; stays 2m; suited by a sound surface; has been tried in blinkers; sweated up sixth start. *G. Hunter.*

HUGUENOT (USA) 3 ch.c. Forli–Captain's Mate (Turn-to) (1979 7fg* **121**
6fg* 6.3d^2 8d* 1980 10f^2 8f 9d*) $190,000Y; attractive, lengthy colt; third living foal; half-brother to 2 winners, including Irish 5f and 7f winner Summer Fantasy (by Never Bend); dam unraced sister to high-class Captain's Gig; smart performer; smoothly beat Rhus by $\frac{3}{4}$ length in 8-runner Prix Daphnis at Evry in July; had earlier finished good $\frac{1}{2}$-length second of 6 to Henbit (rec 5 lb) in Classic Trial Stakes at Sandown in April and well-beaten eighth to

Mr R. E. Sangster's "Huguenot"

Nikoli in Airlie/Coolmore Irish 2,000 Guineas at the Curragh in May; stays 1¼m; seems to act on any going; to be trained by L. Barrera in USA in 1981. *V. O'Brien, Ireland.*

HULDA (FR) 5 ch.g. Linden Tree 127–Mapiona (Tompion) (1979 13g 13fg³ 12d 15fg) 1980 12.2v 17.1f) poor middle-distance handicapper; acts on a firm surface; blinkered final outing (tailed off). *O. O'Neill.* –

HUMBER CROSSING 2 b.f. Dragonara Palace 115–Bashi 73 (Zarathustra 131) (1980 5d 5d⁴ 5d⁴ 6d 6g 6fg² 5f² 7f* 6g) Feb 18; 4,000F; compact, lightly-made filly; sister to a winner in Belgium, and half-sister to several winners, including quite useful sprinter Attymon Place (by Mummy's Pet); held on by 4 lengths from Doubtful Friend after being long way clear in seller at Beverley in July (bought in 900 gns); not seen out again until October (didn't impress in paddock); needs further than 5f; best form on firm ground; usually wears blinkers. *A. Smith.* 63

HUMBER QUEEN 2 gr. or ro.f. Dragonara Palace 115–A-Prill (Manacle 123) (1980 6f 5d) May 30; 1,800F; second produce; sister to 1979 2-y-o 5f winner Norman's Way; dam broke down only start; well behind in minor race at Redcar in September and seller at Catterick in October. *T. Fairhurst.* –

HUMBILLIE 2 ch.f. Silly Season 127–Chumba (Cambremer 132) (1980 6d 7f) Apr 4; small, narrow filly; half-sister to fair sprinter Romany (by King's Bench); dam won 4 races at around 1m in France; well beaten in minor events at Windsor and Lingfield (last of 7) in the summer. *D. Whelan.* –

HUMBLE BLUE 2 ch.c. Some Hand 119–Papillon Rouge 60 (Klairon 131) (1980 5fg 5fg 5.1g⁴ 5s) Feb 12; 2,700F, 2,500Y; half-brother to 4 winners, including fairly useful 6f and 7f winner Heracles (by Breeders Dream); dam lightly raced; plating-class maiden; ran best race on third start (blinkered); off course 3 months before fourth outing. *G. Fletcher.* 52

HUNAN 7 b.g. Caliban 123–Moeru Bara 107 (Firestreak 125) (1979 7s 5g 6f 5fg^3 5fg 5f 8g 6d 6s 1980 5fg^4 6h 7h 5fg 7g 5fg 7f) plater; stays 7f; acts on any going; sometimes wears blinkers; inconsistent; sold 440 gns Ascot September Sales. *V. Soane.* —

HUNNY BUNNY 4 b.f. Streetfighter 120–Sweet Boronia 96 (Mandamus 120) (1979 5v^3 5s* 7s 6g 5s 7s 12fg 5h 5g 6d 1980 5v^3 5f 5fg^3 6h 5g 6s 6g 6s* 5g 6g 7f 5fg 6g 6g 6g) plater; attracted no bid after scoring at Newcastle in August; best form at up to 6f; well suited by some give in the ground; has run well for an apprentice; not particularly consistent. *D. Leslie.* **50**

HUNSTON 2 b.f. Blakeney 126–Catherine Wheel 116 (Roan Rocket 128) (1980 5f 5f^3 6fg^2 7g* 7.6g^3 10g^4) Jan 19; neat, well-made filly; half-sister to 1977 2-y-o 6f winner Azucena (by Queen's Hussar); dam, smart and tough, stayed at least 1¼m; made all and stayed on extremely well when winning 10-runner £3,000 maiden race at Sandown in July by 3 lengths from Star Pastures, pair well clear; excellent 2½ lengths third of 8 to Admiral's Heir when giving weight all round in £4,300 event at Lingfield in October and also ran respectably when 5½ lengths fourth of 9 to Krug in Zetland Stakes at Newmarket later in month; will stay 1½m+. *B. Hobbs.* **97**

HUNTERCOMBE LAD 7 b.g. Huntercombe 133–Lesson Two (Sheshoon 132) (1979 8s 8s 8.2g 10f 1980 8v^4 8fg^3 11f^2 9.6h) poor plater; stays 11f; acts on any going; has worn blinkers; wears bandages; sometimes sweats up; brought down final outing. *G. Wallace.* **34**

HUNTER'S GIFT 8 ch.g. Huntercombe 133–Mor'a Bai 80 (Sayajirao 132) (1979 NR 1980 10fg 12d^3 8g) ex-Irish gelding; finished lame when remote third in amateur riders handicap at Carlisle in July; out of his depth only subsequent outing; best form at middle distances; has been tried in blinkers; wears bandages. *D. H. Jones.* —

HUNTERS PARK 3 ch.f. Twilight Alley 133–Daisy Belle 114 (Abraxas 97) (1979 NR 1980 11.7f) half-sister to fair miler River Beau (by River Chanter); dam sprinter; ridden by 5-lb claimer when in rear in 18-runner maiden event at Bath in May. *H. Willis.* —

HUNTING CRY 6 b.g. Huntercombe 133–Rahat-Lakoum (Sayajirao 132) (1979 NR 1980 16f 16fg) poor maiden; stays 1½m; acts on any going; has been tried in blinkers; bandaged in 1980. *M. Salaman.* —

HUNTING HEIR 3 b.g. Huntercombe 133–Reddish Radish (Red God 128§) (1979 5fg 1980 8fg 10d) leggy gelding; well beaten in maiden and minor events. *P. Cole.* —

HURAKAN 5 b.g. Seaepic 100–Magical 95 (Aggressor 130) (1979 14d 12s 12s 1980 14fg) fair middle-distance performer at 3 yrs; seems to act on any going except heavy; heavily bandaged and on burly side only outing of 1980. *D. H. Jones.* —

HURLSTON HALL 2 b. or gr.g. Broxted 120–Silver Comb (Silver Cloud 121) (1980 6g) May 11; 1,150Y, resold 340Y; compact gelding; half-brother to a winner abroad; dam plater; unquoted and backward, started slowly when last of 9 behind Blessed Blue in seller at Ripon in August. *D. McCain.* —

HURRICANE HILL 3 b.g. Golden Dipper 119–High Corries (Soleil II 133) (1979 5v^2 5s^3 5g^3 5s^3 6fg 6g^4 5f* 5f 5fg 1980 5fg 6s^3 5fg^4 5g^3 6fg 6fg* 6s) workmanlike gelding; good mover; fair handicapper; dead-heated with En Avant in minor event at Brighton in August; not disgraced in Ladbrokes (Ayr) Gold Cup on final start; stays 6f; acts on any going; sometimes wears blinkers but didn't when successful. *W. Musson.* **83**

HURRICANE MORN 6 b.g. Typhoon 125–Dawn Reign 82 (Perfect Sovereign) (1979 NR 1980 15.4s) first foal; dam fair middle-distance handicapper; unquoted, tailed off when pulled up in minor event at Folkestone in July, first outing. *R. Hoad.* —

HURTWOOD LASS 2 ch.f. Realm 129–Abroad (Takawalk II 125) (1980 6s^4 6g 7g 5d 6g* 5fg 7g^4 6s) Feb 9; 5,000Y; leggy, rather lightly-made filly; half-sister to 1978 2-y-o 5f winner Nisma (by Green God) and to a winner in Norway and France; dam unplaced 4 times in Ireland; sold out of P. Kelleway's stable 3,400 gns after making all and running on strongly to win valuable 23-runner seller at Doncaster in September by ¾ length from Nanooka; creditable fifth of 21 to Doubtwash Girl in minor event at Catterick later in month; best form at up to 6f. *A. Balding.* **73**

HURWORTH HOUSE 4 ch.g. Habitat 134–Light Opera 101 (Vienna 127) (1979 6g3 6s* 5s2 6f 6g 6d 6s3 1980 6d* 6fg2 6fg 6d* 6fg 6g 6s 6d4 6s4) smallish, sturdy gelding; won twice at Nottingham, beating Overtrick by ½ length in valuable Home Ales Gold Tankard Handicap in June; ran best subsequent races when blinkered on last 2 starts, finishing fourth twice at Haydock in October; suited by 6f and should stay 1m; acts on a firm surface but is particularly well suited by some give in the ground; suitable mount for an apprentice. *H. T. Jones.* **84**

HYACINE 3 ch.f. High Line 125–Floradora Do 85 (Derring-Do 131) (1979 6g4 7fg 6g 1980 8s 11.7fg 11.7f 11.7f 12d3 10d 10s4 10f3 10g) small filly; plater; stays 1½m; acts any going. *Mrs R. Lomax.* **43**

HYDE 3 b.g. Royalty 130–Impatience (Kibenka 119) (1979 5f 7d4 7d 7fg 7g 7s 1980 6d 8fg 10f 9g2 12.2g 10f 10fg) second in maiden race at Hamilton in June; should stay 1¼m+; suited by some give in the ground; trained by S. Nesbitt first 4 starts. *M. W. Easterby.* **73**

HYJILL 3 br.f. No Mercy 126–Politesse 65 (Polic 126) (1979 5g4 5fg 5f* 5d 5g3 5h3 6g2 6s2 1980 6d 7.6g 6g 7.2d 8f2 7d 8d) neat, strong filly; quite moderate (rated 79) at 2 yrs; ran poorly, including in sellers, in 1980; stays 1m; acts on any going; has worn bandages. *J. Fitzgerald.* **41**

HYPER 4 ch.c. Allangrange 126–Dane Girl 78 (Hornbeam 130) (1979 10f 15.5g 15.5fg 1980 15f 15.5fg) poor maiden. *W. Stephenson.* **–**

HYPERION CHIEF 4 ch.c. Mansingh 120–Hyperion Lass (Punchinello 97) (1979 6g4 6s2 5s* 6d* 6s3 5d2 6d2 6g 6s 6g 1980 7d 6d 5f 6f 5f* 6s 6d 5fg2 5d 5d 6d 5.8g 6s) fair sort; won handicap at Thirsk in May; finished well when runner-up to Bri-Eden on same course in August; ran moderately afterwards; acts on any going. *W. Wharton.* **80**

HYPERMETRIC (USA) 4 ch.c. Vaguely Noble 140–Many Happy Returns (Sailor) (1979 13.5g* 14d3 1980 16fg3 13g 16f 16g 16g2 16v2 11.5d4 16v) workmanlike colt; placed in Saval Beg Stakes at Leopardstown in May (9 lengths third to Ardross) and amateur riders races at Tralee and Listowel in September; bit coltish in paddock, made running till weakening 2f out when seventh of 8 to Billion in Henry II Stakes at Sandown on third start; stays well; probably acts on any going. *T. Curtin, Ireland.* **82**

HYPIDION 5 gr.m. Sayfar 116–Monolyn (Happy Monarch 109) (1979 12d4 12s2 13g3 12.2fg4 12f4 16g4 14fg 14fg 12.2s* 13s4 1980 12f 12g 10fg 12d 12d 13s 18s) poor handicapper; stays well; acts on any going; good mount for an apprentice; has given us impression she is none too genuine in a finish. *D. Leslie.* **–**

HYPNOTHERAPIST 3 b.g. Forlorn River 124–Molly Flo (Paveh 126) (1979 5g 5s 5d 5f 6f 6fg4 7d 7fg 6g3 7g4 6g2 6d2 1980 7d3 6f3 7f 8g 8g 8d 7s 7s) leggy gelding; stays 7f but is probably better at 6f; suited by some give in the ground; blinkered eighth outing at 2 yrs. *J. Calvert.* **66** d

HYPODERMIC 3 b.c. Steel Heart 128–Narcotic (Narrator 127) (1979 NR 1980 7g4 8g* 8fg 8d 8fg 7g) 35,000Y, 650 2-y-o; lightly-made sort; half-brother to useful sprinter Fine Silver (by Silver Shark) and a winner abroad; dam, middle-distance winner in Ireland, is daughter of 1,000 Guineas winner Hypericum; won 17-runner maiden race at Ayr in July despite running green; not entirely disgraced on next outing; stays 1m; out of his depth fifth start and ran badly on final appearance; sold 820 gns Doncaster November Sales. *W. Stubbs.* **69**

I

ICATO (FR) 4 b.c. Cavo Doro 124–Cantatrice (Bold Ruler) (1979 8d 9v* 10g 10g3 8f2 10fg4 9g2 11g2 10s 1980 16g) good-looking, well-made colt; won minor event at Lingfield in 1979; last of 20 in handicap on same course in September on only outing of 1980; seems to stay 11f; acts on any going. *A. Moore.* **–**

I. C. DOLLAR (USA) 3 b.f. Icecapade–In Prosperity (Crimson Satan) (1979 6f 6fg 1980 6f 7d 10s4 10f 10.6d3 10fg2 10fg* 9g* 10s4) strong, good-bodied filly; successful in maiden race at Salisbury and minor event at Newcastle in the autumn; beat Marcello ¾ length in latter; will stay 1½m; probably acts on any going. *G. Pritchard-Gordon.* **80**

ICE 2 b.c. Northfields–Carmine City 104 (Charlottesville 135) (1980 6g 8d2 8g) Apr 9; 54,000Y; well-made, attractive colt; half-brother to 2 winners by Crowned **76**

Prince, including 7f to 1¼m winner Principality, and to successful 3-y-o Japanese filly Inter-Smash (by Derring-Do); dam stayed at least 2m; having first race for over 2 months, went down by ½ length to odds-on Nimblemoss in maiden race at Bath in October; every chance when 4½ lengths fifth of 15 to Riberetto in maiden race at Newmarket later in month; will stay 1½m. *I. Balding*

ICE HARBOUR (USA) 2 b. or br.c. Icecapade–Harbour Queen (Young Emperor 133) (1980 7fg 7g* 7g4) Apr 1; $50,000Y; tall, rather leggy colt; first foal; dam, half-sister to very smart 1976 French staying 2-y-o El Criollo, won over 1m; put up a useful effort when making all to win 13-runner minor event at Yarmouth in September by 2 lengths from odds-on Noalto; second favourite, faded very quickly after 5f when 7 lengths fourth of 11 to Junta in similar race at Goodwood later in month; will stay 1m. *J. Hindley.* **101 ?**

ICELANDIC 5 b.h. Rarity 129–Arctic Walk (Arctic Slave 116) (1979 10v2 12d* 12.5fg 10g 1980 10v* 12f 13.4f 12d4 14g 9fg4 11s2 11.5d3) neat, attractive horse; won John Porter Stakes at Newbury in 1979; ran well when second to Croghan Hill in Rank Cup at Phoenix Park in March and was later promoted to first (Croghan Hill disqualified after failing a routine dope test); put up best subsequent effort when length second to Sea Pigeon (gave 14 lb) in Doonside Cup at Ayr in September; fourth to My Hollow in Royal Whip Stakes at the Curragh and to Muscovite in Whitehall Stakes at Phoenix Park in between; stays 1½m; acts well in the mud; often wears blinkers but seems to do just as well without. *K. Prendergast, Ireland.* **107**

ICEN 2 b.c. Tycoon II–Pepstep 66 (Polic 126) (1980 6fg4 7fg3) Apr 16; 4,500Y; well-made, quite attractive colt; half-brother to several winners, including 7f winner Pepina (by Shoolerville); dam won over 5f and seemed to stay 1m; shaped well in maiden races on both starts, running on to finish 2¼ lengths fourth of 14 to Welham Green at Salisbury in September and 1¼ lengths third of 19 to Six Mile Bottom at Lingfield in October; runs as though he'll stay 1m. *M. Smyly.* **82**

The Exors of the late Mr P. J. Prendergast's "Icelandic"

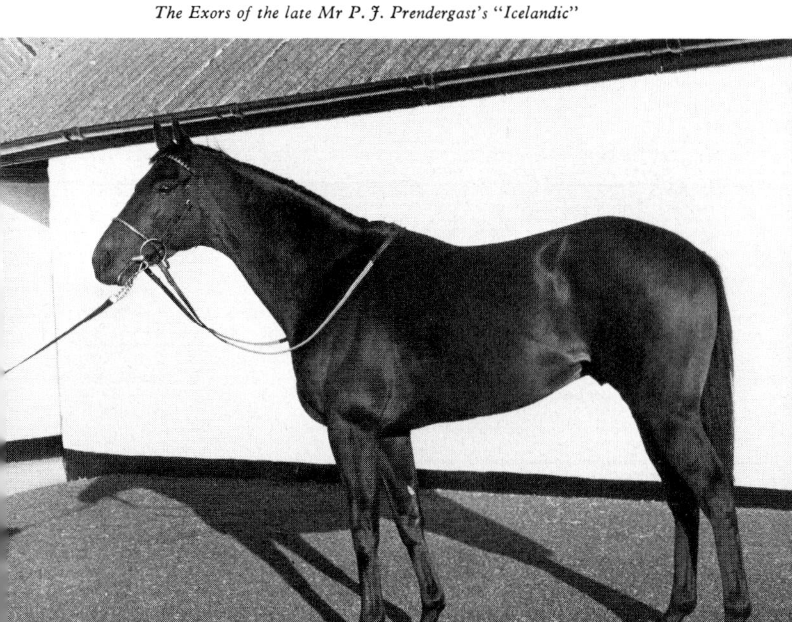

I-CHING 2 gr.f. No Mercy 126–China Girl 76 (Shantung 132) (1980 5fg 6s 5.8f 5.8h 8fg* 7g 8d 8d4 Apr 19; 2,300Y; unfurnished filly; half-sister to winners in Spain and Brazil; dam placed over 5f and 6f at 2 yrs; favourite and dropped in class when winning 16-runner seller at Leicester in September by 1½ lengths from Blue Garter; bought in 2,100 gns afterwards; well suited by 1m; blinkered sixth outing; sold 1,000 gns Ascot December Sales. *R. Laing.* **66**

ICKWORTH DAWN 3 b.f. Dawn Review 105–Ickworth Lady 69 (Fleece 114) (1979 5f 6g 6s 5.1g 1980 7s 6s 7fg 6fg) small, narrow filly; well behind in varied company, including selling; unseated rider second start. *A. Dalton.* –

IGLE 5 b.g. Run The Gantlet–Little Firefly (Bold Ruler) (1979 11d 13d 12fg 10.1fg 10f4 1980 11.7fg 12f 15.5fg) plater; stayed 1¼m; acted on any going; sometimes wore blinkers; dead. *P. Mitchell.* –

ILAKAN 2 b.f. Forlorn River 124–Nikali 89 (Siliconn 121) (1980 5f 5fg4 5fg 6g 8g 7fg 6s) Mar 28; first foal; dam second twice over sprint distances at 2 yrs; plating-class maiden; unlikely to stay 1m. *M. Bradley.* **61**

ILLEGAL LADY 2 b.f. Legal Eagle 126–Ravishing (Rage Royal 78) (1980 5g 7d) May 23; fair sort; third reported foal; half-sister to winning hurdler Drops O'Brandy (by Hot Brandy); dam won a point-to-point; behind in large fields of maidens at Lingfield in September (slowly away) and Leicester in October. *R. Hannon.* –

I'LL SEE YOU 2 b.c. Averof 123–Keeps (Roan Rocket 128) (1980 5f2 5fg2 6d 5.1g* 6g) Apr 6; 20,000Y; rangy colt; good mover; first foal; dam twice-raced half-sister to very useful stayer Caporello and very smart miler Buz Kashi; ran on to win 4-runner minor event at Yarmouth in July by 3 lengths from odds-on Pontin Lad; ran well on most of his other starts, particularly when just over 6 lengths fifth of 10 to Another Realm in Richmond Stakes at Goodwood later in July; will stay 1m; acts on firm going. *C. Brittain.* **95**

I'LL TAKE PARIS (USA) 2 ch.f. Vaguely Noble 140–Sailfast (Sailor) (1980 8d*) Feb 10; $170,000Y; leggy, lightly-built filly; half-sister to 3 minor winners in USA, one of them stakes placed; dam, winner at up to 1m, is half-sister to very versatile and high-class colt Ace of Aces (by Vaguely Noble); led halfway up straight and quickly drew clear to win 8-runner maiden race at Longchamp in October by 3 lengths from Carodan; an excellent first effort by a potentially smart middle-distance filly. *F. Boutin, France.* **103** p

ILMAZ 4 ch.c. Morston 125–Merisette (Phil Drake 132) (1979 12g 12g 12g 10.5g 12.5d 12s 14v4 10.5s2 1980 13v4 14s 12fg 13d 14g2 15.5fg* 12d 16fg4 15.8d) compact ex-French colt; won maiden race at Folkestone in August by 2 lengths from Nightwood; stays well; seems to act on any going; has been tried in blinkers; ran badly final start. *D. Morley.* **63**

ILSA KEMPINSKI 3 b.f. Right Tack 131–Allegretto (Preciptic 122) (1979 5d2 5s* 6g3 6g3 6g2 6s* 6s 1980 7d 7v 6d 10.2fg 10.6fg 7g 6s* 6g) unfurnished filly; 25/1 and apprentice ridden, returned to form when winning handicap at Chepstow in October; ran poorly most other starts, including in sellers; best at 6f on soft going; blinkered third start; sometimes sweats up; trained by S. Norton first 4 outings. *C. Nelson.* **55**

ILTCHI 5 br.g. Bold Lad (USA)–Hispanica 85 (Whistling Wind 123) (1979 8s 8fg 8fg 11d 8d 1980 7f 9fg 7g 7g) temperamental plater; best form at 7f; often wore blinkers; dead. *T. Craig.* –

I'M GRAND 3 b.f. Martinmas 128–Tarpon Springs (Grey Sovereign 128 §) (1979 5s 6f4 7fg* 7g 1980 8f 10g 10g 10fg 10.1g 8g) big, well-made filly; moderate handicapper at her best; probably stays 1¼m; acts on a firm surface. *G. Pritchard-Gordon.* **74**

IMPERIAL ACE 4 b.c. Derring-Do 131–Buss 102 (Busted 134) (1979 10v2 10f2 10f2 8g* 10d2 10g4 1980 8f* 10f) strong, attractive colt; looked extremely well and put up a fine performance when winning Whitsun Cup (Handicap) at Sandown in May, making all and quickening clear approaching final furlong to score by 2½ lengths from Northleach; respectable sixth of 8 to Sacrilege in Daily Mirror Handicap at Epsom in June on only subsequent outing; stays 1¼m; acts on any going; often sweats up. *M. Stoute.* **88**

IMPERIAL AMBER 4 br.g. Amber Rama 133–Pampered Angel 97 (Pampered King 121) (1979 9s 8fg 1980 8g 9g4 12f 12.2fg) attractive gelding; not disgraced in handicaps second and third starts; seems to stay 1½m; blinkered final start at 3 yrs. *J. Fitzgerald.* **42**

IMPERIAL DILEMMA (USA) 3 br.c. Damascus–Royal Dilemma (Buckpasser) (1979 6fg $7g^{*}$ $6g^{2}$ 1980 10d $7fg^{2}$ 7f) quite a well-made colt; good mover; creditable equal second to Salluzzo in handicap at Newmarket in May (apprentice ridden); bred to stay 1¼m but was well beaten at trip; best form on a sound surface; not raced after May. *H. T. Jones.* **77**

IMPERIAL MEASURE 2 b.c. Derring-Do 131–Buss 102 (Busted 134) (1980 $5f^{4}$ $6d^{*}$ $7d^{2}$ $7g^{2}$) May 2; small colt; very good walker; brother to useful 1m winner Imperial Ace, and half-brother to 11.5f winner Watch Out (by Blakeney); dam game performer at up to 11f; had to resist late challenge of Frome to win 19-runner maiden race at Salisbury in June by a short head; 4 lengths second subsequently behind Robellino in Donnington Castle Stakes at Newbury and behind Shangarry in £3,200 nursery at Brighton; will stay 1¼m; acts on a soft surface. *H. Candy.* **84**

IMPERIUM 3 ch.c. Mount Hagen 127–Idea (Ragusa 137) (1979 NR 1980 $10fg^{2}$ 10g 10.2g $7g^{2}$ 6fg 7f) well-made colt; fourth foal; half-brother to 2 winners in Italy; dam ran once in Italy at 2 yrs; runner-up in maiden race at Leicester and handicap at Newmarket; effective at 7f and stays 1¼m; blinkered final outing (had stiff task); ran badly fifth start; sold to J. Old 4,900 gns Newmarket Autumn Sales. *L. Cumani.* **70**

IMPISH EARS 2 ch.f. Import 127–Golden Ears 94 (Gratitude 131) (1980 5g 5g 7.2d $7s^{4}$ 8g) Apr 9; compact filly; half-sister to 4 winners, including smart 1977 2-y-o sprinter Fire Angel (by Sharpen Up) and useful 1979 2-y-o Earmark (by Hot Spark); dam best at 7f; ran on to finish 6 lengths fourth of 8 to Countess Olivia in maiden race at Ayr in September, only worthwhile form; stays 7f; evidently suited by soft going. *E. Weymes.* **65**

IMPISH SIOUX 2 ch.f. Import 127–Sioux 95 (Nimbus 130) (1980 5g 5fg 5fg 8d) May 14; 2,400Y; neat filly; no sign of ability, including in sellers. *R. Hobson.* **—**

IMPLICATOR 2 b.f. Imperial Crown 96–Sutania (Supreme Sovereign 119) (1980 8.2s) Mar 21; small, lightly-made filly; first foal; dam never ran; 33/1, when tailed off in 19-runner seller won by Dizzy Heights at Nottingham in October. *R. Hoad.* **—**

IMPLICIT 3 b.f. Grundy 137–Law and Impulse 104 (Roan Rocket 128) (1979 NR 1980 8s 7g 6g 6d 8g) strong, lengthy filly; good walker; half-sister to 2 winners, including useful 1974 2-y-o Cardinal Wolsey (by Henry the Seventh), subsequently successful in Spain and France; dam won over 5f at 2 yrs; well beaten in maiden races and a handicap; sold 4,100 gns Newmarket December Sales. *Sir Mark Prescott.* **—**

IMPORTANT 2 gr.g. Import 127–Donrae 106 (Don II 123) (1980 5f 5f) May 20; compact gelding; first foal; dam at her best at 2 yrs when winner twice over 5f; coltish in paddock prior to finishing behind in maiden races at York in May and Leicester (blinkered) in June and was subsequently gelded. *W. Wharton.* **—**

IMPORT EXPORT (FR) 2 b.c. Import 127–Lucy 83 (Sheshoon 132) (1980 8fg 8.2s $7.2d^{4}$) May 2; half-brother to 2 winners, including 1976 2-y-o 5f winner Hone (by Sharpen Up), subsequently very successful in Belgium; dam won over 1¼m; ran easily best race when just over 2 lengths fourth of 14 to Hissing Sid in £2,400 seller at Haydock in October; should stay 1m. *T. Fairhurst.* **67**

IMPORT LADY 2 ch.f. Import 127–Palfrey Jr (Yrrah Jr) (1980 6s 5d 5f 5d 5d 5g) May 13; fair sort; fourth foal; half-sister to 3-y-o 6f seller winner Palfrey's Supreme (by Native Bazaar); soundly beaten in maiden and minor races and in a seller; blinkered final start. *Denys Smith.* **—**

IMPRIMEUR 3 ro.f. Sandford Lad 133–Prancer 70 (Santa Claus 133) (1979 6f 7fg 6s 8h 10.6d 1980 $11v^{4}$ 12d 12h 12d 16d 12g 18f 13.8fg) dipped-backed filly; good mover; poor plater; brought down third start (bandaged in front). *R. Hobson.* **—**

INAKO (GER) 3 b. or br.c. Lombard 126–Indira II (Birkhahn) (1979 NR 1980 10fg 10s 13g $14.6fg^{3}$ 14fg) strong, workmanlike colt; half-brother to 1975 German Oaks winner Idrissa (by Tamerlane); dam, a winner 3 times including 6f Nereide-Rennen, is sister to 1965 German Oaks winner Indra; third in poor maiden race at Doncaster in July; would have stayed well; fell at halfway first start; broke a leg final outing and was destroyed. *H. Collingridge.* **61**

INCAS AWAY 4 ch.g. Sun Prince 128–Little Sunset (Canisbay 120) (1979 7fg 8g 12g $14fg^{*}$ $15.5f^{*}$ $12fg^{3}$ $14.6fg^{3}$ $14fg^{2}$ 18fg 14fg 1980 $12s^{2}$ 12.2s 16fg **—**

14.6fg 12d 11.7f 10s) useful-looking gelding; stays well; acts on any going; blinkered final start; suited by strong handling; sold 5,500 gns Doncaster September Sales. *S. Mellor.*

INCA WARRIOR 5 ch.g. Galivanter 131–Bight of Peru 100 (Denturius) **72** d
(1979 NR 1980 8d 8g* 8.2fg 8f 10f^4 10.6fg) rangy gelding; bought in 1,500 gns after winning seller at Ripon in April; stays 1m well; acts on any going; sometimes blinkered. *P. Rohan.*

INCHGOWER 3 b.g. Ribero 126–Lutine Bell 82 (Luthier 126) (1979 7d^4 —
8d 1980 11fg 8fg) well-made gelding; no sign of ability since first outing at 2 yrs. *A. Ingham.*

INDADO 2 b.c. Manado 130–Indian Beauty 93 (Indiana 129) (1980 6g) —
Apr 16; 14,000Y; half-brother to fairly useful 1979 2-y-o 6f winner Suncharmer (by Roi Soleil) and a winner in France; dam won over 1¼m; unquoted when tailed off in 21-runner maiden race won by Rahway at Newmarket in June. *I. Walker.*

INDECISIVE 3 b.f. Lombard 126–Saucy Kate 85 (March Past 124) (1979 —
5d 5f^3 5f 6fg 6s 5d 1980 5s 5g 5fg 7d 7g 8f^4 11fg 10fg 10f 10d) fair sort; poor walker; poor plater; sold 1,200 gns Ascot November Sales. *C. Austin.*

INDIAN BRAVE 4 gr.g. Warpath 113–Indian Error 64 (Seminole II) (1979 7g —
8g^4 9s^3 7fg 10.6g^3 12fg 11s 10f 1980 10fg) neat gelding; has ability but is none too consistent or enthusiastic; should be suited by 1½m; has been tried in blinkers; exported to Switzerland. *C. Thornton.*

INDIAN DANCER 2 ch.f. Streak 119–Crop (Acropolis 132) (1980 6v 5fg) —
Feb 22; 2,400F; small filly; third living produce; half-sister to 2 winners, including fair sprinter Spanish Issue (by Philip of Spain); dam of little account; in rear in maiden races at Warwick in March and May; blinkered second outing. *Peter Taylor.*

INDIAN KING (USA) 2 b.c. Raja Baba–Protest (Rash Prince) (1980 6fg^3(dis)) **84** p
Apr 11; $130,000Y; big, useful sort; third foal; half-brother to a winner by Nodouble; dam very useful stakes winner at 2 yrs and 3 yrs, winning at up to 1m; highly regarded but had an unhappy time when odds on and pick of paddock for 12-runner minor event at Newmarket in August, firstly missing break, then running into trouble when challenging at distance and finally being placed last by stewards after finishing 2 lengths third to Douschkina; subsequently found to have split a pastern; will stay 1m. *G. Harwood.*

INDIAN MARK 9 br.g. On Your Mark 125–Indian Music 82 (Dalesa 109) —
(1979 12.2s 16s 12f 1980 16fg 14fg 16.1d 16s 14g) poor handicapper; stays 2m; acts on any going; suitable mount for an apprentice; bandaged nowadays. *J. Cann.*

INDIAN POOL 4 br.g. Red Alert 127–Black Gnat (Typhoon 125) (1979 9f **59**
9f^4 8g^3 12.8fg^4 7g^2 8.5g 7g 9s 10s^4 1980 8fg^4 8g^4 8g 8fg) compact, well-made ex-Irish gelding; 50/1, ran very well when 5 lengths fourth of 17 to Cracking Form in ladies race at Ascot in July, staying on; ran better subsequent race on final start; best form at around 1m; has worn blinkers. *I. Wardle.*

INDIAN SPLASH 2 b. or br.f. Prince Tenderfoot 126–Raindrops (King's **94**
Troop 118) (1980 6fg^2 6f* 6s 6g* 5g) Feb 1; well-made, good-quartered filly; fourth foal; dam never ran; 5/4 favourite when winning 16-runner minor event at Naas in June and 5-runner Irish Chorus Stakes at Navan the following month, on latter course beating Foy Honey 4 lengths; second favourite when next seen out, in Cornwallis Stakes at Ascot in October, but was clearly held at distance and was allowed to ease up, coming home 8 lengths fifth of 7 to Pushy; will stay 7f. *K. Prendergast, Ireland.*

INDIAN TRAIL (USA) 2 b.c. Apalachee 137–Majestic Street (Majestic **79**
Prince) (1980 5.8f^3 6s^3 7d^4) Apr 25; small, lightly-made colt; good mover; second foal; dam, closely related to stakes winner Raise A Dancer and half-sister to 3 stakes winners, was stakes-placed winner of 2 races from 21 starts; going on at finish when in frame in maiden races at Bath and Nottingham in the summer and Leicester in October; 4½ lengths behind Norfolk Realm in 14-runner event on last-named; gives impression middle distances will suit him. *B. Hills.*

INDIA SONG (FR) 3 b.f. King of the Castle–Noix de Coco (Nuccio 133) **116**
(1979 5.5g* 5.5g* 5g^3 7fg* 8g^3 1980 8fg^4 8fg* 8s^2 10g^2 10d^3) half-sister to several winners, including miler Charlemagne (by Val de Loir); dam won over 4.5f and 5.5f and was third in French 1,000 Guineas; smart performer; won

9-runner Prix de Sandringham at Chantilly in June by a short neck from Teacher's Pet; placed subsequently in Prix d'Astarte and Prix de la Nonette at Deauville (beaten 4 lengths by Moon Ingraver (rec 7lb) in former and 2 lengths by Detroit in latter) and La Coupe de Maisons-Laffitte (¾-length third to Discretion); stays 1¼m; probably acts on any going; consistent. *F. Mathet, France.*

INDIOLA 2 br.f. Mansingh 120–Gambela 88 (Diplomat Way) (1980 5g 6g) **54**
Feb 17; 2,500Y; small filly; first foal; dam won over 1m; plating-class maiden *J. Winter.*

INDUNA 3 b.g. Starch Reduced 112–Bap 77 (Current Coin 118) (1979 7d 10d **—**
1980 8v 6v 8g 7f 9f^{3} 7fg 10v 10s) 520F, 1,450Y; third foal; half-brother to smart Baptism (by Northfields), successful at up to 1¼m; dam sprint plater; poor maiden; last of 7 in £1,500 race at Ayr on second start; not certain to stay 1¼m; unseated rider fourth outing; blinkered fifth and sixth starts. *P. Doyle, Ireland.*

INFANT PRODIGY 3 b.c. Mummy's Pet 125–Smash Hit (Roan Rocket 128) **103**
(1979 5.8h 1980 6d 6s^{4} 8fg^{2} 8fg* 8fg* 7f^{2} 8g* 8g*) strong, compact, good-bodied, useful sort; good mover; developed into a useful handicapper, winning three times at Ripon and once at Sandown; just held on to beat Prince Nonoalco a neck in £3,500 race on last-named in July; suited by 1m; acts on firm going; genuine; sent to race in USA. *B. Hills.*

IN FIJAR (USA) 3 b.c. Bold Commander–Apache Queen (Marshal At Arms **121**
114) (1979 7g^{3} 7.5d^{3} 8d* 8fg* 8s 8g 1980 8g 8g* 10.5fg^{3} 9fg^{4} 9.2s^{3} 10g 10d)

For the third time in nine years the Poule d'Essai des Poulains went to an American-bred colt, but the 1980 winner, In Fijar, cannot be regarded as the equal of the other two, Riverman and Green Dancer. The classic was the only race he won during the year and overall his record is a relatively modest one, showing him some way short of top class.

In Fijar had shown smart form at two years but was soundly beaten when taking on high-class opposition in the Grand Criterium and the William Hill Futurity. His second season started with a respectable fifth to Nice Havrais in the Prix de Fontainebleau, an acknowledged classic trial run at Longchamp early in April, and three of those that finished in front of him there were among the thirteen other runners for the Poule d'Essai des Poulains on the same course later in the month, Nice Havrais starting favourite. The remainder included the Tote Free Handicap winner Moorestyle, Argument, later to prove a top-notch performer over middle distances, and Dragon, in the same ownership as In Fijar and ridden by the stable's first jockey despite having run moderately in the Prix Noailles on his reappearance. In Fijar turned the form of the Prix de Fontainebleau upside-down and ran out a comfortable winner, taking over the lead from his stable companion early in the straight and never looking likely to be caught thereafter, being ridden a shade confidently in the closing stages to beat Moorestyle by a length with the subsequently-disqualified Ruscelli a head away third and Nice Havrais a moderate ninth. Allowing for the fact that there were some hard-luck stories—Argument was seriously impeded by Ruscelli and had in turn barged into Dragon—there is little doubt that In Fijar won on merit. Equally it must be said that the race did not take a great deal of winning. Moorestyle at a mile in April was not the horse he became over sprint distances from midsummer onwards, and none of the next three home, Ruscelli, Argument and Confetti, was anywhere near exceptional at a mile, though Ruscelli did subsequently win a pattern race over the trip.

In five races in good company after his win In Fijar's limitations were clearly revealed. Only fifth favourite for the Prix Lupin at Longchamp, he finished third to Belgio and Argument, beaten half a length; in the Prix Jean Prat

Poule d'Essai des Poulains, Longchamp—In Fijar is a comfortable winner from Moorestyle and the subsequently-disqualified Ruscelli (hidden). The first three home are followed by Argument and Confetti both of whom were moved up a place

Mr M. Fustok's "In Fijar" (G. Doleuze)

at Chantilly, Night Alert showed the strength in depth of the English and Irish three-year-olds, beating Ruscelli with In Fijar a respectable fourth. Third place behind the easy winner Nadjar in the Prix d'Ispahan at Longchamp was followed by a creditable run in La Coupe de Maisons-Laffitte, and In Fijar's season ended with his being unable to reach a challenging position in the Champion Stakes at Newmarket in October, coming home almost five lengths behind Cairn Rouge in fifth.

In Fijar (USA) (b.c. 1977)	Bold Commander (b 1960)	Bold Ruler (b 1954)	Nasrullah
			Miss Disco
		High Voltage (gr 1952)	Ambiorix
			Dynamo
	Apache Queen (b 1961)	Marshal At Arms (ch 1950)	Court Martial
			Sea Pride II
		Apache Love (b 1951)	Apache
			Love

Bold Commander, In Fijar's sire, won seven of his forty-one starts at up to nine furlongs, one of them a stakes race. Although not that well-known in Europe he has enjoyed a successful career as a stallion in his native country, siring some twenty stakes winners, most notably Dust Commander who won the 1970 Kentucky Derby by five lengths. Bold Commander's fee has stood at 5,000 dollars for over ten years—a rare example of stability in a period of fluctuating prices. Apache Queen picked up a meagre 260 dollars for being placed on her only start at two years but has done better at stud, producing seven winners besides In Fijar, including Nancy Be Good (by Burned Up) and Gin Jug and Jug O'Gin (both by Kentucky Jug), all successful in stakes races. Jug O'Gin was the best, notching up five stakes events out of fourteen wins at up to a mile. Considering that she hasn't been mated with fashionable stallions—her other winning progeny were by Social Climber Fulcrum and two by Te Vega—Apache Queen has a fine record, and her daughter by Social Climber, Social Queen, has also produced a stakes winner by Bold Commander. Apache Queen's dam, Apache Love, won twice from forty-eight outings in three seasons and at stud had three lesser American winners by Apache Queen's sire Marshal At Arms, a horse who was a very useful six-furlong handicapper in this country in the early 'fifties prior to going to the States where he continued racing until the age of eight. The third dam, Love, ran six times unplaced and produced winners in America, Europe and Peru, among them the useful French sprinter Carissimo and Loriga, successful in the Peruvian One Thousand Guineas. By the standards of the best American-bred performers in Europe the pedigree is unremarkable and In Fijar was bought for 36,000 dollars at the Fasig-Tipton Kentucky Sales in 1978. A big, strong colt, he stays a mile and a quarter well, appears to act on any going and is consistent. On occasions he has had his tongue tied down. *M. Saliba, France.*

INGLEMOTE SANDRA 3 b.f. Bronze Hill 96–Ambre d'Or (Golden Catch 87) (1979 7f 1980 9.4fg 8fg) light-framed filly; poor maiden; doesn't have much scope. *W. H. H. Williams.* —

INISHBOFIN 4 b.g. Bog Road 119–Cheena (Le Levanstell 122) (1979 10s 6g 12.8f 7.9f^{4} 7d 1980 7f 10fg) compact ex-Irish gelding; plating-class maiden; probably stays 1¼m; bandaged final outing. *G. Richards.* —

INKLING 3 gr.g. Sayfar 116–Inklet (Never Say Die 137) (1979 5s 8.2g 7f 10.6d 10s 1980 8d 10.1fg 14g) robust, workmanlike colt; in rear in varied company; trained by K. Ivory first 2 starts. *G. Huffer.* —

INKYBOO 4 gr.f. Sayfar 116–Inklet (Never Say Die 137) (1979 8fg 1980 8fg 8.3f 10d 10.1s 8.3f) poor plater; has been tried in blinkers. *Mrs N. Kennedy.* —

INLINE 2 ch.c. Import 127–Line of Defence (Persian Gulf) (1980 5fg 5.8g 5g) May 1; 1,200Y; half-brother to 2 winners, including fairly useful 1m and 1¼m winner Irresistible Miss (by High Hat); gambled on when ninth of 14 to Crosby Triangle in seller at Windsor in August, third outing; sold 420 gns Ascot September Sales. *M. Blanshard.* —

INNS OF COURT 2 gr.c. Malacate 131–Courting (Quorum 126) (1980 5d 5.8g 7g 6f) May 15; 4,800Y; compact colt; well bred but is only a poor plater; blinkered third outing; sold 520 gns Ascot September Sales. *Mrs R. Lomax.* —

IN RHYTHM 3 ch.c. Gay Fandango 132–Procession 118 (Sovereign Path 125) (1979 5fg 6fg* 1980 7fg 6g 6g^{4} 6g 5.8g 6fg 6d 6d) strong colt; sprint handicapper; ran his best races at Newmarket on third and seventh starts; stays 6f; acts on a firm and a soft surface; ran atrociously sixth outing. *P. Makin.* 77

INSIDE QUARTER 4 b.c. Tyrant–Forest Glen (Tarqogan 125) (1979 7v* 7v^{2} 7d* 7.2g* 7fg^{4} 7.2fg 8fg 6g 7fg 6s 7fg 1980 8d 7s^{3} 7g^{2} 7fg 7f 7d^{3} 7fg 7f^{3} 7f) tall colt; creditable second to R. J. Wallis in apprentice handicap at Epsom in April; third at Newcastle (twice) and Beverley; should stay 1m; acts on any going but is possibly best with some give in the ground; blinkered sixth and seventh outings; needs a strong gallop and is suited by front-running tactics. *Denys Smith.* 86

INSTANTER 2 b.f. Morston 125–Instant Justice 101 (Roan Rocket 128) (1980 7d) Apr 1; useful-looking filly; good walker; half-sister to 3-y-o 1¼m winner Winslow (by Busted); dam unbeaten in 3 starts over 6f and 7f at 2 yrs; 16/1 and in need of race when always behind in 21-runner maiden race won by Melissa Jane at Leicester in October; may do better over further at 3 yrs. *H. Candy.* —

INSTANT PRIME 4 ch.g. Simbir 130–Nanno (Busted 134) (1979 12fg* 12s 12fg^{2} 16f 1980 14g 12g) rangy gelding; bandaged and had stiff tasks when well beaten in 1980; stays 1½m; acts on a firm surface. *I. Wardle.* —

INSULINDE 2 b.c. Prince Tenderfoot 126–Miss Jones 61 (March Past 124) (1980 6fg 6f 8.2s) Feb 21; 20,000Y; neat, quite attractive colt; half-brother to several minor winners; dam ran only twice; behind in maiden races at Yarmouth and Haydock and minor race at Haydock in second half of season; well backed first time out. *E. Eldin.* —

INTAKE 3 b.g. Malicious–Skerne Glory 58 (Pinza 137) (1979 5s 6s 6g 6s 5f 7fg 8f^{3} 7f^{3} 8.2s 1980 8d 12s 12f^{3} 16f^{3} 14f 14f 16fg^{4} 12g^{3} 13g^{4} 16fg*) stocky gelding; plater at 2 yrs; raced in better company in 1980 and won maiden race at Newcastle in July; suited by 2m on firm ground; often wears blinkers; suitable mount for a claimer; sold 4,300 gns Newmarket Autumn Sales. *P. Kelleway.* 66

INTAN 2 gr.g. Thatch 136–Celestial Dawn 115 (Don II 123) (1980 5f) May 13; 2,000Y; second foal; dam very useful sprinter at 2 yrs and 3 yrs; 12/1, behind most of way when 11 lengths fifth of 6 to Loch Boyle in maiden race at Ayr in May. *Denys Smith.* —

INTEGRITY 2 gr.f. Reform 132–Cry of Truth 129 (Town Crier 119) (1980 6g* 6d 6fg* 6g⁴ 8fg) Feb 7; strong, good-bodied, short-legged filly; second foal; half-sister to 3-y-o 5f winner Truth Will Out (by Blakeney); dam best 2-y-o filly of 1974; made much of running when winning maiden race at Yarmouth in July and 4-runner Rous Memorial Stakes at Goodwood the following month, putting up a good effort in latter to win by 1½ lengths from odds-on Mattaboy (gave 6lb); beaten in pattern races on other outings, finishing 3 lengths sixth of 11 to Nasseem in Cherry Hinton Stakes at Newmarket and 4½ lengths fourth of 5 to Kittyhawk in Lowther Stakes at York; by no means sure to stay beyond 6f (never got in a blow after being held up when remote fifth to Leap Lively in Hoover Fillies Mile at Ascot in September). *B. Hobbs.* **100**

INTENSE (FR) 3 gr.f. Sassafras 135–Dancing Sher (Dancer's Image) (1979 6fg³ 9fg 1980 11.7fg 9d 14.7f 15.5g) neat filly; showed a little ability at 2 yrs; well beaten in 1980; should stay 1½m+; changed hands 1,900 gns Doncaster June Sales. *M. Salaman.* —

INTERCONTINENTAL 2 ch.c. Hot Spark 126–Raflex 72 (Skymaster 126) (1980 5f 6fg* 6d 7s⁴ 7d 8fg) Apr 23; 14,000Y; quite attractive, useful-looking colt; half-brother to 2 winners, including fairly useful 1976 2-y-o 5f winner Billie's Pal (by Breeders Dream); dam placed at 5f and 6f; won 15-runner maiden race at Newbury in June by a neck from newcomer Pellegrini; 5 lengths fifth of 11 to Bonnie Charlie in Piper Champagne Stakes at Salisbury next time out, best subsequent effort; by no means sure to stay 7f; acts on a firm and a soft surface; had stiff tasks in nurseries last 2 outings. *E. Eldin.* **90**

INTERCRAFT BOY 4 b.c. Virginia Boy 106–Winning Wave (Victory Morn) (1979 8d 8d 8s 7.6d² 7d 7f³ 8g⁴ 7g³ 7fg 7fg² 7g* 1980 8d² 7g 8f 7fg² 7d* 7d⁴ 7d 8g³ 7fg³ 7g² 8g 7.3fg 7g) neat, well-made colt; won Playboy Bookmakers Handicap at Epsom in June a shade comfortably from Touch Pirate and Grand Conde; ran creditably most other outings, although ran the odd bad race; stays 1m; acts on any going except perhaps soft; sold to Miss S. Morris 6,800 gns Newmarket Autumn Sales. *A. Pitt.* **97**

INTEREST 2 ch.g. Bold Lad (USA)–Katira 83 (Paveh 126) (1980 5fg 6d 7g 8g 8d) Apr 3; 10,500Y; strong, close-coupled gelding; third foal; half-brother to a winner in Belgium; dam, winner over 2m, is half-sister to high-class sprinter Royben; in rear in maiden and minor events; sometimes sweats up; blinkered second and fifth outings. *M. Francis.* —

INTERLUDE 2 gr.f. The Go-Between 129–Sheridans Daughter 75 (Majority Blue 126) (1980 5g) May 21; first foal; dam won over 1¼m; unquoted when behind in 18-runner maiden race won by Portogon at Bath in September. *D. Elsworth.* —

IN THE NEWS 3 ch.c. Green God 128–Disa 55 (Dike) (1979 6fg 1980 8fg 12fg 12g 16fg) little sign of ability in maiden races; not certain to stay 1½m; blinkered and sweated up final outing; sold 500 gns Newmarket Autumn Sales. *D. Kent.* —

INTINTO 3 gr.c. Connaught 130–Cranberry Sauce 119 (Crepello 136) (1979 7s* 1980 8f³ 10.6fg 10g 10fg 8fg⁴ 8g² 8fg² 10g² 8g³ 8s²) big, strong colt; good walker; runner-up 4 times in varied company but was unable to win; put up probably best effort on final outing, going down by a short head to Miss Raffles in handicap at Newmarket in October; stays 1¼m; probably acts on any going but goes well on soft; blinkered nowadays; sometimes sweats up; looked half-hearted about his effort seventh outing; sold to J. Old 14,000 gns Newmarket Autumn Sales. *H. Cecil.* **91**

IN TISSAR (USA) 2 b.c. Roberto 131–Strip Poker (Bold Bidder) (1980 8g* 9fg 10s³) Apr 30; $225,000Y; half-brother to 2 winners, including very useful stakes winner Clout (by Indian Chief), successful at up to 9f; dam half-sister to Prix de l'Arc de Triomphe winner Prince Royal II; won 5-runner new-comers race at Longchamp in September by ½ length from Glittertind; beaten in pattern races on same course subsequently but ran creditably, finishing 2½ lengths sixth of 8 to Mariacho in Prix Saint-Roman and being moved up to **114**

third place by stewards after finishing 1¾ lengths fourth of 8 to The Wonder in Prix de Conde; will stay 1½m; seems to act on any going. *M. Saliba, France.*

INTO ACTION (USA) 3 br.c. Never Bend–Swift Lady (Sailor) (1979 8fg 8fg* 1980 10f 7.6f^4 11d^4) strong, well-made colt; won 18-runner maiden race at Newmarket at 2 yrs; below form in 1980; should stay middle distances; acts on a firm surface; blinkered first start; not seen out after June. *J. Hindley.* **77**

INTREPID BOY 3 br.c. Realm 129–Nana's Girl 109 (Tin Whistle 128) (1979 5d 6f^4 5f* 5f^3 5g* 5s* 5fg^2 5f 1980 5f^4 5f^3 5g 5fg 6f 5f 5s 5d) strong, useful-looking colt; good mover; sprint handicapper; clearly best at 5f; acts on any going; sweated up slightly second start; trained by G. Pritchard-Gordon first 4 outings; ran badly last 3 starts. *W. Bentley.* **84** d

INVESTA 2 br.f. Lombard 126–Idrissa (Tamerlane 128) (1980 6g 6g 7g* 7g* 7g^2) Jan 4; compact, useful sort; first reported foal; dam won German Oaks; had something in hand when winning 18-runner maiden race at Leicester in August (by 2½ lengths from Home On The Range) and 6-runner nursery at Yarmouth the following month (by 1½ lengths from Rose of Raby); again ran very well when equal second of 17, 1½ lengths behind Remouleur, in £3,600 nursery at Ascot in October; will be suited by middle distances; useful. *M. Stoute.* **108**

INZERA 3 b.f. Decoy Boy 129–Pandomyne 71 (Pandofell 132) (1979 5s 5fg^2 6fg^2 6f 6fg^3 6fg 6d* 7g 6fg 5fg^4 1980 6d 7f 6f 6f^3 6g 7d 7fg 6fg 6s) small, good sort; good mover; sprint handicapper; stays 6f; probably acts on any going; blinkered seventh start; sold 2,700 gns Newmarket December Sales. *P. Kelleway.* **81**

IONIAN ISLE (FR) 4 br.f. Jim French–Itaria (Nearctic) (1979 10fg 12g 1980 8f 12h 10fg) smallish French-bred filly; plating-class maiden. *Miss A. Hill-Wood.* –

IONIAN RAJA (USA) 2 b.f. Raja Baba–Ionian Idol (Prince John) (1980 5.5fg^4 5.5d^3 7g* 8g^2 8f 8s^4) Mar 5; $75,000Y; leggy filly; second foal; half-sister to 3-y-o Stria (by Raise A Native); dam, winner at up to 6f in USA, is half-sister to useful 1968 staying Irish 2-y-o Mongolia II; improved with distance and proved herself one of the better staying 2-y-o fillies in France, winning maiden race at Chantilly in July and finishing close up in Group 3 Prix d'Aumale on same course in September (went down by ½ length to Ukraine Girl) and in Group 3 Prix des Reservoirs at Longchamp in October (1¼ lengths fourth of 10 behind Votre Altesse); made little show when ninth of 10 to Tropicaro in Prix Marcel Boussac at Longchamp on fifth start; will probably stay 1¼m; possibly unsuited by firm ground. *F. Boutin, France.* **111**

IQUACU 2 b.c. Porto Bello 118–Finest View 66 (Bold Lad, Ire 133) (1980 5g 5s 7g 7g^4 7fg^2 7d^3 8f) Apr 19; 4,000Y; robust, good sort; good walker; third foal; half-brother to prolific Italian winner Miss Vermont (by Sandford Lad); dam stayed 7f; ran well when placed in nurseries in August, going down by 2 lengths to Matilda Cave at Newmarket and finishing 3½ lengths third of 11 to Scintillating Air at York; suited by 7f but is by no means sure to stay 1m; acts on a firm and a soft surface. *R. Armstrong.* **90**

IRENE ADLER 2 br.f. Brigadier Gerard 144–Gingerale (Golden Horus 123) (1980 5.8h^4 8fg) Feb 10; unimpressive-looking filly; fourth foal; sister to 3-y-o 1m winner Countess Walewski; dam useful at up to 9.5f in France; prominent in maiden races, finishing 6½ lengths fourth of 10 to Tin Tessa at Bath in August and 4¾ lengths fifth of 24 to Allegretta at Leicester in September; will stay 1¼m. *H. Candy.* **73**

IRISH COMMANDMENT 3 ch.c. Shiny Tenth 120–Ritruda 95 (Roi Dagobert 128) (1979 6s^3 6s 5f^3 6g 1980 6f^2 7f* 7.3f 8fg 6g 6s^4 6d 7g) sturdy colt; good mover; won 13-runner maiden race at Epsom in April; not disgraced in handicaps on fifth and sixth starts; stays 7f; acts well on firm going; sweated up slightly on reappearance; bandaged in front seventh start. *F. Durr.* **84**

IRISH EMPEROR 3 br.c. Realm 129–Empress of Clare 73 (Persian Gulf or Premonition 130) (1979 5d* 5fg 5s 6g^4 5g^3 1980 7f 7g 5g 6g^4 6s 6f 6d^4) useful-looking colt; very useful (rated 114) at 2 yrs; didn't run up to his best in 1980; should stay 7f; suited by some give in the ground; sometimes sweats up; blinkered final start. *R. Sheather.* –

IRISH FONDUE 2 b.f. Pitskelly 122–Tenderness (Narrator 127) (1980 5s 5fg 6g) May 2; small, light-framed filly; well beaten, including in a seller; sold 1,400 gns Newmarket July Sales. *G. Blum.* –

IRISH GALA 5 br.g. Irish Love 117–Gala Tess (El Gallo 122) (1979 7.6v 7g 6g 1980 5fg) moderate sprinter in 1978; behind in 3 races in Ireland at 4 yrs and finished last in apprentice handicap on only outing of 1980 (April); stays 6f but best form at 5f; acts on any going. *G. Richards.* —

IRISH GRACE 3 b. or br.f. Home Guard 129–Terramar Lass (Tom Rolfe) (1979 5d 5d 6d 7g4 7d 7fg 1980 5g 5s2 5fg2 7.2g 5f 5d) fair sort; sixth in seller at Redcar prior to finishing second in maiden races at Nottingham and Warwick in the summer; bred to stay 1m; acts on soft going; blinkered fifth outing in 1979; ran moderately fifth start; sold out of P. Rohan's stable 1,300 gns Newmarket July Sales. *K. Ivory.* **60**

IRISH HEART 2 b.c. Steel Heart 128–Klairlone 116 (Klairon 131) (1980 8g 8g3 8.2s* 8s* 10.2s*) Apr 22; 11,000F, 25,000Y; good-topped colt; fourth foal; half-brother to French 1m winner Deep Image (by Dancer's Image) and quite useful 1¼m to 1½m winner Sandlone (by Sandford Lad); dam in frame in Irish 1,000 Guineas and Irish Guinness Oaks; defeated large fields for maiden and minor events at Haydock, Stockton and Doncaster in the autumn; gave a useful display on last-named, running on strongly to beat St Mawes in good style by 2 lengths; well suited by 1¼m and will probably get further; revels in the mud. *J. Dunlop.* **105**

IRISH MYTH 3 b.f. St Paddy 133–Uranda 93 (King's Troop 118) (1979 NR 1980 5f 7d 10g 8g) close-coupled filly; half-sister to several winners, including useful 1972 2-y-o Master Sing (by Sing Sing); dam sprinter; in rear in maiden and minor races; sold 820 gns Doncaster October Sales. *J. Douglas-Home.* —

IRISH PLAYBOY (USA) 2 b. or br.c. Irish Castle–Globetrotter (Globemaster) (1980 5.5g* 5.5g* 6fg 5f) **120**

When purchasing Irish Playboy for 51,000 dollars at Saratoga in August 1979, Sir Gordon White acquired what turned out to be his third good winner by the American stallion Irish Castle in as many years. Two years earlier he paid 40,000 dollars for Hardgreen, subsequently a winner four times, notably of the Diomed Stakes; the year in between he went to 77,000 dollars for Hardgreen's full brother Castle Green who, although something of a funny customer, won three races as a two-year-old, including the Richmond Stakes at Goodwood worth more than £21,000. Like Hardgreen and Castle Green, Irish Playboy wasn't long in showing ability. At Maisons-Laffitte in June he took a newcomers event over five and a half furlongs by two lengths, then repeated his success over the course and distance the following month, this time in the Prix Robert Papin, Europe's first Group 1 race of the season for two-year-olds. In Age Quod Agis and Penmarric, winners of the July Stakes and the National Stakes respectively, England fielded a seemingly strong challenge for the Papin. The main French hopes of keeping the prize at home lay with Ancient Regime, winner of a newcomers event at Evry and fourth to Pushy in the Queen Mary Stakes at Royal Ascot, Twig Prince, unbeaten in two outings, and Irish Playboy. Age Quod Agis started favourite and three furlongs from home had just about taken the lead. Shortly afterwards, when the pace quickened, he was forced to give way to Ancient Regime, who in turn began to struggle below the distance. Irish Playboy had never been far away, and it was he who proved to have the strongest finish in him: he took the lead a hundred and fifty yards out and put two lengths between himself and Ancient Regime by the post. Age Quod Agis came again to finish a close third. Although Irish Playboy won entirely on merit he didn't make the frame in either of his remaining races. In the Prix Morny at Deauville the following month he failed to produce anything like his form and finished fifth to Ancient Regime, beaten about four and a half lengths. He had considerably more on his plate in the Prix de l'Abbaye de Longchamp, and in the circumstances ran a good race to finish fifth of nine to Moorestyle, beaten just under five lengths.

Irish Playboy (USA) (b. or br.c. Mar 26, 1978)	Irish Castle (b 1967)	Bold Ruler (b 1954)	Nasrullah
			Miss Disco
		Castle Forbes (b 1961)	Tulyar
			Longford
	Globetrotter (b 1968)	Globemaster (b 1958)	Heliopolis
			No Strings
		Anadem (b 1954)	My Babu
			Anne of Essex

Irish Castle also showed good form as a two-year-old, winning four races and ending the 1969 season in America rated only 9 lb behind the leading juvenile

Prix Robert Papin, Maisons-Laffitte—Irish Playboy wins from Ancient Regime and English-trained Age Quod Agis. Valgo is fourth

Silent Screen. At three and four he was lightly raced and unsuccessful and was retired to stud at the end of 1971. He quickly made his mark as a stallion—his first crop included the Belmont Stakes and Kentucky Derby victor Bold Forbes—and other good winners by him in the States include Tiger Castle, who has earned more than 100,000 dollars. Irish Playboy is the second foal of Globetrotter to reach the racecourse; her first, Harlem Magician (by Kennedy Road) won a maiden race over six furlongs as a three-year-old. Globetrotter never ran but she is well related. Her dam is Anadem, a useful winner in England over five furlongs as a two-year-old and the dam of several winners in England and America, notably Tyrant, the winner of thirteen races at up to a mile and now a successful stallion. Anadem's dam, Anne of Essex, produced many winners, including Arietta, a smart filly at around a mile and herself the dam of Romulus. Irish Playboy's future is not easy to predict. From his pedigree it would be reasonable to anticipate his staying a mile but connections clearly regard him as a sprinter; with competition in the sprinting field in France so weak, perhaps that's where his best prospects lie. Irish Playboy is said by his stable to be nervous and, for this reason, has been blinkered in all his races. *O. Douieb, France.*

IRISH POET 6 ch.h. Allangrange 126–Christina Rosetti 102 (Monet 127) (1979 12s* 12v 14g^{4} 16s^{3} 12s^{2} 12s 14.6fg 14g^{3} 13g* 13g* 12.2d^{2} 12d^{2} 1980 12fg 12g 13g) moderate handicapper; lightly raced and well beaten in 1980; best form at distances short of 2m, and with some give in the ground; good mount for an apprentice. *G. Huffer.* —

IRISH PRINCE 7 b.g. Irish Ball 127–Miss Jessica 90 (Milesian 125) (1979 NR 1980 11f) plater nowadays; effective at 9f and stays 1½m; acts on any going; sometimes wears blinkers. *W. Wright.* —

IRISH RIFLE 3 b.c. Scottish Rifle 127–Sunsaly 75 (Sallymount 125) (1979 6fg 7g 8g 1980 11.7fg 11.7f^{3} 12d 10s) well-made colt; quite a moderate maiden at his best; off course 5 months after second start and was well beaten on his return (bandaged); stays 1½m; suited by firm going. *R. Laing.* **75**

IRISH SALT 2 b.c. Jukebox 120–Pendula 76 (Tamerlane 128) (1980 5fg 5.1f^{4} 5g 6g) Feb 2; 9,000Y; attractive, well-made colt; fourth foal; dam won at up to 1¾m; short-priced favourite, led 3f but weakened quickly when 6½ lengths fourth of 9 to Steelinctive in maiden race at Yarmouth in June; well beaten afterwards in small race at Bath and nursery at Windsor (blinkered, had stiff task); should stay 6f. *M. Stoute.* **70**

IRISH SOLITAIRE 3 ch.g. On Your Mark 125–Scarletta 103 (Red God 128 §) (1979 5s 5s^{2} 5fg* 5g^{2} 5f^{3} 5d 5g 1980 6h* 5fg 5fg^{3} 5fg^{2} 5fg 5d) leggy, light-framed gelding; narrowly won handicap at Stockton in April; stays 6f; best form on a sound surface and acts on hard going; ran moderately fifth start (off course over 3 months afterwards); sold 600 gns Doncaster November Sales. *Denys Smith* **63**

IRISH SPARKLE 2 ch.f. Sparkler 130–Limerick Queen (Whistling Wind 123) (1980 5g 5d 6d) Mar 31; 12,000Y; useful-looking filly; very good mover; third foal; half-sister to fairly useful 1979 2-y-o performer Charles Street (by Huntercombe); dam never ran; 11/1, beaten less than 1½ lengths when fifth of 23 to Hindi in maiden race at Haydock in October, second outing and best effort; should stay 6f. *B. Hills.* **79**

IRON LAD 4 b.c. Petingo 135–Maid of Iron (Crozier USA) (1979 8d* 8g 10v 8fg 8fg^{2} 8g^{4} 8.2g 8.3fg 8f 1980 8f 8g 8g 10s^{4} 8g 8.3s 8fg 8d) lengthy colt; good **84**

mover; fifth of 22 behind Tender Heart in Royal Hunt Cup at Royal Ascot in June on third outing, best effort of 1980; stays 1m and wasn't entirely disgraced over 1¼m fourth start; seems to act on any going; sometimes blinkered; not particularly reliable; sold 1,400 gns Newmarket Autumn Sales. *P. Cole.*

IRRAWADDY 3 br.f. Rapid River 127–Keyvala (Quisling 117) (1979 5s 5g^4 6g 1980 6f 5h 8f 8s^2 10g^3 9.4g 10d^2 10f 8g 10s) compact, lightly-made filly; stays 1¼m; needs some give in the ground; sweated up badly second appearance. *J. Carr.* **56**

ISHAMO (HOL) 2 b.c. Shamaraan–Ilse Kind (Orsini 124) (1980 7fg^3 7fg^2 6g 6s^4 8fg) May 10; big, strong, useful sort; dam daughter of German 1,000 Guineas and Oaks winner Ivresse; ran well when placed at Yarmouth in the summer, finishing 1¾ lengths third to Baz Bombati in maiden race and going down by 3 lengths to The Thatcher in minor event; beaten twice at Baden-Baden, putting up better effort there when 3¾ lengths fourth of 7 to Un Sprinter in Group 3 Zukunfts-Rennen in September on fourth start; ran moderately final start; bred to stay middle distances. *H. Collingridge.* **76**

ISKANNDAROUN 3 b.c. Kalamoun 129–Laparia (St Paddy 133) (1979 7s 1980 10fg* 12g* 10d^4 12g* 12g^4 12g 12fg) strong, good-topped colt; good mover; won maiden race at Leicester and handicaps at Pontefract and Brighton; trotted up by 7 lengths in 4-runner £4,100 race on last-named in August; stays 1½m; acts on a firm surface. *M. Stoute.* **92**

ISLAND BLOOM 4 b.f. The Brianstan 128–Dry Island 73 (Miralgo 130) (1979 8fg 1980 10g 10s 10g) fair sort; lightly raced and only poor form, including in sellers; sold 400 gns Doncaster November Sales. *A. Gillam.* –

ISLAND WALK 2 b.f. Palm Track 122–Ladyfold 60 (Never Dwell 89) (1980 5f) May 12; 350Y; small filly; fifth foal; dam 1½m winner; 25/1 and in need of race, didn't break well in 18-runner seller at Ripon in August but ran on to finish tenth to Crosby Triangle, only outing; bred to stay 1m. *W. Haigh.* –

ISLINGTON 3 b.g. Rarity 129–Angelaura (Le Levanstell 122) (1979 NR 1980 12f^3 12d 16.1s) 5,400F, 21,000Y; lengthy gelding; beaten a long way in varied company; didn't move to post well first start. *J. Hindley.* –

ISOMERIC 2 ch.c. Mount Hagen 127–Matrisse 89 (Matador 131) (1980 6g 6s^3 6f^3 (dis) 7fg 6g) Apr 3; 8,000Y; small, good-quartered colt; good mover; half-brother to several winners, including useful sprinter Spanish Gold (by Whistling Wind); dam 2-y-o 5f winner; third in maiden races in August, beaten 5¼ lengths by Green Haze at Nottingham and 2½ lengths by Top of the Mark at Epsom (disqualified for interfering with winner); well beaten subsequently; should stay 7f. *R. Price.* **73**

ITALIAN CONNECTION 5 ch.m. Communication 119–Ravenna (Celtic Ash) (1979 10.7g 10f 1980 16f 12s) poor maiden; bandaged on first outing. *M. Eckley.* –

ITSABONGO 3 b.g. Blue Cashmere 129–Ardent Belle (Buisson Ardent 129) (1979 5v 5s* 5d 6g^4 6f 5f^3 5.3d^3 5g^3 6fg* 1980 5v 7f 6fg 6h 5fg 6fg 7g 8.3s 6s 8g 10fg) big, strong gelding; plater; showed no form in 1980; stays 6f; acts on any going; blinkered seventh start; sold out of R. Smyth's stable 625 gns Ascot July Sales. *F. Yardley.* –

ITS MAGIC 4 b.f. Miracle 116–Tammy's Princess 78 (Tamerlane 128) (1979 7g 7g 8f^4 8f 7g 1980 7f 5f 7fg 6g^2 8d) plater; should stay 1m; blinkered third start; sweated up a bit final outing. *Denys Smith.* **36**

IVATAN (USA) 4 b.c. Sir Ivor 135–Tan Jane (Summer Tan) (1979 10s^2 10.5g^3 12g 12g* 11.7fg* 12fg^4 12d^2 18fg 1980 12d^4 14f) well-made colt; excellent mover; fairly useful performer at 3 yrs; ran well when 4½ lengths fourth of 16 to Beau Reef at Kempton in April; looked tremendously well but appeared not to get trip (dropped out quickly 2f from home) when behind in race won by Rowlandson at Newmarket later in month; stays 1½m; acts on any going; sent to race in Italy. *F. J. Houghton.* **92**

IVER 9 b.g. Tacitus 124–Goldella 60 (Golden Cloud) (1979 12s 11.7g 14s 12f 12fg^2 11.7f 12fg^2 12fg 13g 12.2d 1980 12f^3 12g^2 11.7s) middle-distance handicapper; acts on any going; good mount for an apprentice; usually blinkered in 1979; often sweats up. *D. Elsworth.* **49**

IVOR'S LADY 2 gr.f. Bigivor–Freehay-Lady (Vimadee 120) (1980 5fg) May 11; light-framed, unfurnished filly; poor mover; third reported foal; dam unraced; useless plater judged on her first effort. *S. Holland.* –

J

JACKALLA 6 b.g. David Jack 125–Candy Girl (Tutankhamen) (1979 13s* 12d 15g 12d 13.8g^4 12.3fg^2 10fg^3 10s 16s^2 12d 12.2fg 16.1g 1980 14.7f^3 11g) poor handicapper; stays well; seems to act on any going; sometimes sweats up; has won for an inexperienced rider; probably none too genuine. *I. Jordon.* —

JACK FOX 5 b.g. Porto Bello 118–Pertelot 63 (Falcon 131) (1979 6s 6fg 6f 5f* 5fg^4 5g^4 5fg 5g 1980 5f 5fg 5f^4 5.8g 5fg 5g 5s^4) strong gelding; poor mover; unplaced in 1980 but ran creditably on several occasions, on penultimate start finishing fifth of 17 to Ferryman in valuable Bovis Handicap at Ascot in October; best form at 5f; acts on any going; has given trouble at stalls; sold 1,500 gns Newmarket Autumn Sales. *P. Kelleway.* **80**

JACK RAT 3 b.g. Spanish Gold 101–Gambling Girl (Raise You Ten 125) (1979 NR 1980 9fg 6f 6f 6fg) plain sort; second foal; dam won over hurdles and fences; in rear in varied company, including selling; sold 680 gns Doncaster August Sales. *J. Wilson.* —

JACK SPLENDID 5 b.h. John Splendid 116–Grace (Gratitude 130) (1979 5s* 5v 5s 5fg 5f 5fg 5f 1980 5s 5fg 5g 5fg 5fg^3 5d 5f* 5d) big, strong horse; sprint handicapper; made all when scoring by $\frac{1}{2}$ length from Paul Diver at Chepstow in August; acts on any going; blinkered last 2 outings at 4 yrs; sometimes sweats up. *J. Holt.* **51**

JACQUI'S FOLLY 2 b.f. Mandamus 120–Archaic 65 (Relic) (1980 5g 5g 5f 5f 6g 7.2d) Feb 10; 11,500F; compact filly; poor mover; half-sister to very smart 1978 2-y-o 5f winner Schweppeshire Lad (by Decoy Boy); in rear in varied company, including selling; blinkered fifth and sixth outings. *A. Smith.* —

JADE AND DIAMOND 2 ch.c. Bold Lad (Ire) 133–Tegleaze 81 (Galivanter 131) (1980 5g 6g^4 6s 8.2s^2 8d*) Feb 26; compact colt; third foal; dam 2-y-o 5f winner; improved over 1m and rallied well to win 16-runner maiden race at Warwick in October by a neck from Princely Lad; acts on soft going and has yet to race on firm. *E. Eldin.* **78**

JADE EMPRESS 2 gr.f. Tower Walk 130–Daystar 91 (Major Portion 129) (1980 5fg^4 5g^2 5f^2 5f^3 5g^2 5f 5d) Apr 9; 2,200Y; close-coupled filly; half-sister to a winner in Italy by Royal Palace; dam disappointing daughter of smart Alborada; showed plenty of pace when second in 3 maiden races, coming closest to success when short headed by Swedish Rhapsody in auction event at Haydock in June on fifth start; not seen out again until October when seventh of 17 to Sodina in maiden event at Lingfield; runs as though 5f is her trip. *K. Ivory.* **66**

JADE GIRL (USA) 2 b.f. Bold Native–Ma Bloom (Bay Bloom) (1980 6s* 5g^2) Mar 7; \$13,000Y; \$27,000 2-y-o; rather unfurnished filly; sister to stakes-placed winner Bold Incentive, and half-sister to numerous winners, including minor stakes winner Future Session (by Whippleton); dam won several claiming races at up to 7f; favourite when winning weakly-contested maiden race at Stockton in June, soon recovering from a slowish start and coming through to beat Aruse by $\frac{1}{2}$ length; ridden along from halfway and stayed on well to finish 2 lengths second of 7 to Disco Dancing in minor event at Newcastle later in month; will be well suited by a return to 6f and will stay 7f; sold 12,000 gns Newmarket December Sales. *W. O'Gorman.* **77**

JADE'S DOUBLE 3 bl.g. Double-U-Jay 120–Hi Tess 65 (Supreme Court 135) (1979 NR 1980 11f 8fg) 860F, 2,300Y; tall, lengthy gelding; brother to 2 winners, including Irish 9f to 13f winner Hi Jay; dam plating class; behind in maiden races at Newbury in May and Warwick in June. *Mrs B. Waring.* —

JADE SEA 2 ch.f. Manado 130–Hataway (High Hat 131) (1980 5s 5g 5fg 5fg 5fg^3 6g* 6g 6g^3 7fg) Apr 17; 1,500F; dipped-backed filly; half-sister to two 2-y-o winners, including 1976 Irish 7f and 7.9f winner Pat's Swallow (by My Swallow); dam stayed 1$\frac{1}{2}$m; only a poor plater but managed to win at Warwick in June; should be very well suited by 7f (tailed off, wearing blinkers, when tried at trip); sold 800 gns Doncaster September Sales. *Denys Smith.* **47**

JAGATEK 4 ch.g. Jimmy Reppin 131–Erisca 88 (Doutelle 128) (1979 6.5v 8v* 7s^2 10v 7.3g^4 8s 8.2g 8d 8s 1980 10.6s 8d 7d) well-made gelding; suited by 1m but was well beaten over 1$\frac{1}{4}$m; acts on any going; ran poorly last 4 starts in 1979 and on all starts in 1980 (not seen out until October). *W. Hastings-Bass.* —

JAHIL 3 b.c. Song 132–Porto Novo (Sovereign Lord 120) (1979 5v 5g^3 5g^2 5s^2 5g 5fg 5d^3 1980 6d^3 6v^3 6s^2 6f^2 5f* 7f* 6fg* 8g 6d 7g 6d) compact colt; good walker; made all to win maiden race at Pontefract in April and minor events at Redcar and Hamilton in May; best at up to 7f; acts on any going; wears blinkers. *J. Hardy.* **82**

JAHODA 3 b.c. Deep Diver 134–Venette (Epaulette 125) (1979 5fg 5fg 5fg 5g –
1980 6s 8.2s 6d 7f 6fg 5g) close-coupled, useful-looking colt; in rear in varied
company, including selling, and is a short runner; sweated up second start;
pulled up third outing (reportedly broke blood vessel). *B. Richmond.*

JAIPUR ROSE 3 b.f. Mansingh 120–Tamerlante (Tiger 125) (1979 NR –
1980 5f 6f 6g 5g 5f 5g) good sort; good walker and mover; poor form in varied
company, including selling; trained by J. Winter first 4 starts. *W. Bentley.*

JALABAD 2 b.c. Kalamoun 129–Wenduyne 113 (Moutiers 127) (1980 7g^4 85
7fg* 7s^2) May 21; lengthy colt; good mover; fourth foal; dam won Irish 1,000
Guineas and stayed 1½m; ran on under pressure to win 19-runner maiden race at
Lingfield in October by a length from Casa Esquillina; would probably have won
18-runner minor event at Sandown next outing, instead of finishing head second
to Warily, had he not hung under pressure 1f out; will be suited by middle
distances; seems to act on any going. *J. Dunlop.*

JAM 6 ch.g. Fric 128–Still Room 84 (Major Portion 129) (1979 12fg^3 1980 94
16g 13g* 13g* 12fg^2 12s*) fairly useful handicapper; has been fired; successful
at Nottingham in July and September and at Newmarket in October, on latter
course beating Milloletta by ¾ length; went down by a short head to Admiral
Grenville after a good fight at Ascot; stays 13f; acts on any going; genuine and
consistent. *B. Hobbs.*

JAMAL 4 gr.g. Runnymede 123–No Halo 74 (Aureole 132) (1979 5fg^3 5f 5fg –
5g 5s 8.2g 8fg 10s 8s 1980 8s) fair sort; plater; best run at 5f and appears not
to stay 1m; has been tried in blinkers; sometimes bandaged; sold to J. Baker
1,000 gns Ascot May Sales. *W. Wharton.*

JAMANDA 2 b.f. Mummy's Pet 125–Lavender Royale (Royal Palace 131) 73
(1980 5fg 5fg 6s 5s) Apr 5; strong, well-made filly; second foal; dam unraced
daughter of very useful 6f and 7f winner Sea Lavender; only quite moderate form
in maiden and minor events; should stay 7f; sold 2,000 gns Newmarket December
Sales. *W. Hastings-Bass.*

JAMESTINO 2 ch.c. Bustino 136–Miss Wrekin 97 (Pardao 120) (1980 7fg* 104
7s^2 7f^2) Feb 3; 40,000Y; half-brother to several winners, including 3-y-o 1½m
winner Lakin and useful stayer Peter Wrekin (both by Lauso); dam 2-y-o 5f
winner; odds on, cruised into lead 1f out and was pushed right out with hands
and heels to win 16-runner minor event at Doncaster in July by 3 lengths from
Royal Realm; far from disgraced when 1½ lengths second of 5 to Robellino in
Group 3 Seaton Delaval Stakes at Newcastle the following month but ran well
below that form when going down by ½ length to Spindrifter when odds on for
4-runner minor event at Redcar in September; will stay 1½m; probably unsuited
by very firm ground. *M. H. Easterby.*

JAMES VALE 3 b.g. Auction Ring 123–Lady Gregory (Manacle 123) (1979 –
NR 1980 5f 8fg) 520Y; small gelding; second foal; dam ran twice; last in
maiden races at Sandown in April (blinkered) and Bath in June; sold 440 gns
Newmarket July Sales. *T. M. Jones.*

JAMIE SCOTT 3 b.c. Jimmy Reppin 131–Scottish Double (Dual 117) (1979 70
6fg^2 1980 8f^4 8fg 7g 8g^3 8g 10fg 11.1g 12d 10g^2 12fg^4) workmanlike colt;
quite a moderate maiden; stays 1¼m; blinkered fifth outing; none too consistent.
M. Masson.

JAMSHID 3 b.c. Dragonara Palace 115–Never Lonely (Never Say Die 137) 60
(1979 5fg^4 7fg 1980 9g 8h 10.6f^4 12.3f 9.4fg^4 12f 12g^4 10.2g^3 10.6d 12f^3 10.4d^2
10.6d^4 10.2g 10fg^4 10d^2 10.2v) compact colt; plating-class maiden; stays 1½m;
probably acts on any going; suitable mount for a boy. *R. Hollinshead.*

JANACEK (USA) 3 b.c. Mississipian 131–Klinchit's Girl (Everetts Pride) –
(1979 NR 1980 10.4f 10fg 10.8s) \$21,000Y; big, good sort; third foal; dam,
winner of 5f maiden race at 2 yrs, is half-sister to 2 stakes winners; behind in
minor race at Chester and maiden events at Kempton and Warwick; sold 2,100
gns Goffs August Sales. *B. Hills.*

JANE AUSTEN 3 b.f. Busted 134–Muffet 75 (Matador 131) (1979 7g 1980 56
10fg 10s^2 12d 10s 10g 10.1g) compact filly; best run at 1¼m on soft going;
sold 1,750 gns Newmarket December Sales. *R. Price.*

JANE AUSTEN (USA) 3 ch.f. Arts and Letters–Elegant Tern 102 (Sea-Bird II 65
145) (1979 7f 7g^2 8h 1980 10s 10.6f 10.2f 10fg^3 10.2fg^2 10.2g^4 10.1f^3 10.4d
8g^3 10g^3 9d 10g) neat filly; placed in varied company, including apprentice
handicap; will stay 1½m; acts on firm going and is possibly unsuited by soft; one
paced; sold 30,000 gns Newmarket December Sales. *I. Balding.*

JANES HARBOUR (USA) 3 gr. or ro.f. Raise A Native–Lexington Lark (Round Table) (1979 6fg 7g* 8f^{3} 1980 8.5g 12.3f 12f) compact, short-legged filly; good mover; fairly useful (rated 98) at 2 yrs; behind in good races at Epsom and Chester and handicap at Epsom again early in 1980; should stay middle distances; showed little interest final start; sent to USA. *B. Hills.* —

JAPES 4 ch.f. Galivanter 131–Port-le-Dor (Le Dieu d'Or 119) (1979 8fg 1980 8fg) workmanlike filly; poor plater; blinkered third outing at 2 yrs. *M. Hinchliffe.* —

JASMINE STAR 4 ch.c. Ridan–Gay Cloud 99 (Golden Cloud) (1979 7v^{2} 7s^{2} 6v^{3} 6s^{2} 5fg* 6f^{2} 6.3f* 6f^{4} 5g^{4} 6d^{2} 6d^{2} 1980 6fg* 6f* 6g 5fg 5fg^{2} 6fg^{4} 6f^{2} 5g^{3} 5g 5f) tall colt; winner of Castleknock Sprint Stakes at Phoenix Park and Greenlands Stakes at the Curragh, both in May; favourite when beating Kearney 2 lengths in latter; excellent third under 10-0 in valuable Philips Electrical Handicap won by Just A Shadow, again at the Curragh, in August; behind in Cork and Orrery Stakes and King's Stand Stakes at Royal Ascot on third and fourth starts, but wasn't disgraced when about 6 lengths sixth behind Moorestyle in Prix de l'Abbaye de Longchamp in October on final start; best at sprint distances; acts on any going; genuine and consistent. *M. Connolly, Ireland.* **113**

JASS 3 b.c. Mount Hagen 127–Pampered 109 (Abernant 142) (1979 7f 8g 1980 11fg 10.2g 10.1g) well-made colt; no sign of ability in varied company. *A. Pitt.* —

JASSIM (USA) 2 b.c. Cyane–Lady Bellaston (Tudor Minstrel 144) (1980 8g) Mar 11; \$27,000F, \$40,000Y; half-brother to several winners, including 2 stakes-placed animals; dam won at up to 1m, and is half-sister to Preakness Stakes winner Royal Orbit; 20/1 and very backward when behind in 17-runner minor race won by Video Tape at Newmarket in October. *J. Dunlop.* —

JAVA TIGER 2 gr.c. Saritamer 130–Country Music (Red God 128 §) (1980 6g 6v^{3}) Apr 4; 4,600F, 5,400Y; robust, short-backed colt; third live foal; half-brother to fair 1976 2-y-o 5f winner Willie Dobson (by Hul a Hul); dam won over 6f at 2 yrs in Ireland; never-dangerous 2¾ lengths fifth of 13 to Brummer in £3,200 maiden race at Doncaster in September; odds on for modest maiden event at Hamilton the following month but could finish only 4½ lengths third of 6 to Moonlight Sonata; probably not at his best on heavy going. *J. W. Watts.* **79**

JAWAD (USA) 3 ch.c. Raja Baba–Indovina (Mister Gus) (1979 5d^{3}(dis) 5fg^{2} 5f^{3} 5g* 5fg 1980 5g) well-made colt; very good mover; very useful at his best at 2 yrs but was none too consistent and ran poorly final start; well beaten in handicap at Goodwood in July, only outing in 1980 (gave trouble at start); has the type of action suited to a sound surface; wears blinkers; sometimes sweats up; doubtful temperamentally. *J. Tree.* —

JAYS GREY 2 gr.g. Pongee 106–September Fire (Firestreak 125) (1980 5h 5f 5g 8.2d 8fg 8.2s) Jan 19; 3,700F; small, robust gelding; brother to 5f to 15f winner Autumn Glow; poor plater; blinkered fourth outing. *T. Fairhurst.* **54**

JAZZMAN 4 ch.c. Jukebox 120–Chanyte's Rocket (Roan Rocket 128) (1979 8g 8g 7f 8.5g^{3} 10d 14g 1980 12.3s 12.2f 16fg 13s 8f* 8d) strong ex-Irish colt; lady-ridden and blinkered only time when winning seller (bought in 925 gns) at Beverley in August; stays 1m; acts on firm going. *M. Naughton.* **50**

JEAN MARJORIE 5 b.m. Sovereign Gleam 117–Anya (Alcide 136) (1979 8g 5s 8f 8g 9fg 6g 10g 1980 10d) plater; stays 1m; best form on a sound surface; often wears blinkers. *R. Ward.* —

JEANNE DU BARRY 4 ch.f. Dubassoff–Supreme Courtesan (Relic) (1979 10.2g 7s 6fg^{4} 6g 8fg^{4} 7s 1980 7.6d 9g^{4} 7g 7fg 8fg* 7g) tall, lengthy filly; plater; ridden by 7-lb claimer, attracted no bid after winning at Wolverhampton (made all) in August; stays 9f; seems to act on any going; sold 2,500 gns Doncaster September Sales. *P. Haslam.* **57**

JEAN'S DELIGHT 3 b.f. Biskrah 121–Raramie (Be Friendly 130) (1979 5v^{4} 5s 5g 7g 1980 8fg) neat filly; poor mover; little worthwhile form, including in a seller; blinkered only start at 3 yrs in June. *M. James.* —

JEAN'S GAMBLE 2 b.f. Shoolerville 121–Omnia Opera 83 (Major Portion 129) (1980 6g 6g 6s 6g 7g 7d 8s) May 14; 300Y; very short-backed filly; sister to 2 plating-class animals and half-sister to 2 minor winners; dam 6f winner; ran best race on final outing when seventh of 19 to Irish Heart in minor event at Stockton in October and is evidently suited by 1m; blinkered fifth outing; formerly trained by M. Ryan. *G. Lockerbie.* **69**

Thirsk Hall Stakes, Thirsk—Jebb Lane is a convincing winner from Al-Amal

JEBB LANE 3 b.c. The Brianstan 128–Trickster 92 (Major Portion 129) (1979 **104**
5s* 5s* 5f^{2} 5fg 5f^{3} 5fg* 5g 5g^{2} 1980 5d 6v 6fg 6f* 5f^{2} 6d 6fg 6g 7fg^{4} 7g^{2} 6g^{2} 5.6g 6fg) strong, fair sort; useful performer; returned to form when winning £4,600 race at Thirsk in April convincingly by 4 lengths from Al-Amal; ran creditably several times afterwards; stays 7f; acts on any going; sometimes sweats up; blinkered first and third starts; has run respectably for a boy; changed hands 18,000 gns Newmarket Autumn Sales. *S. Norton.*

JEBEL ALI 3 b.c. Lord Gayle 124–Itinerant 69 (Sky Gipsy 117) (1979 NR **64**
1980 8f 8fg 10.1fg 10g 8.2s 8g^{4} 8s 8s^{2} 10d^{3}) 9,400Y; small, robust colt; second foal; dam showed little worthwhile form; placed in handicap at Chepstow and minor event at Leicester in the autumn; stays $1\frac{1}{4}$m; suited by some give in the ground. *J. Benstead.*

J. E. B. STUART (USA) 5 b.h. Turn to Reason–Surfboard Betty (Bold **53** d
Commander) (1979 7s 6g 5fg 5fg 5f 6f^{3} 6fg 5fg 7.6fg^{2} 6g^{3} 7d 6s 1980 7v 7fg 7f 7f 8s 10d 7g) poor handicapper; behind in seller final outing; stays 1m; seems to act on any going; has been tried in blinkers; inconsistent; often wears bandages. *D. Ringer.*

JEFFS SONG 2 ch.f. Song 132–Ginger Puss (Worden II 129) (1980 5g 5d 6d) –
Apr 27; lengthy colt; poor mover; half-brother to 2 minor winners; dam never ran; in rear in maiden races. *G. Balding.*

JELLABIA 3 gr.f. Pals Passage 115–Silent Sail (Aglojo 119) (1979 6g^{4} 6g^{3} **68**
6d^{3} 1980 6fg^{2} 5.3d^{3} 5.3d* 6d) neat filly; won handicap at Brighton in July; ran moderately 3 days later and wasn't seen out again; stays 6f; acts on a firm and a soft surface. *R. Price.*

JELLY ROLL 2 b. or br.c. Prince Tenderfoot 126–Cake (Never Say Die 137) **56**
(1980 5h 5f 6d 5d 7g 7d) Apr 22; 18,000Y; small, compact colt; brother to very useful 1975 Irish 2-y-o 5f and 1m winner Icing, and half-brother to 2 winners; dam of little account; only poor form in maiden races and a nursery and looks expensive; should stay further than 5f. *Denys Smith.*

JEM JEN 3 b.f. Great Nephew 126–Io 112 (Tenerani 135) (1979 8d^{3} 1980 **85**
10fg* 10.5f 12f 12d 12s) big filly; half-sister to several winners, including useful middle-distance winner Shai (by Shantung); dam fourth in 1960 Oaks; confidently ridden to lead close home and beat Restful a neck in 10-runner Playboy Pretty Polly Stakes at Newmarket in May; well beaten in Musidora Stakes at York, Oaks, Ribblesdale Stakes at Royal Ascot and Lancashire Oaks at Haydock afterwards; should stay $1\frac{1}{2}$m; acts on a firm surface; sold 31,000 gns Newmarket December Sales. *P. Kelleway.*

JENARTH 3 b.g. Meldrum 112–French Joy (French Beige 127) (1979 7f 7s –
8g 1980 6f) small gelding; a twin; well beaten, including in sellers. *I. Vickers.*

JENNY BARCO 2 b.f. Arch Sculptor 123–True Time (Arctic Time 127) (1980 **52**
5f 5h* 5f^{4} 5.3fg^{4} 6s^{3} 5.1fg^{4}) May 11; 1,350Y; compact filly; eighth foal; half sister to a winner in Italy; dam Irish 1m and 9f winner; bought in 2,100 gns after winning seller at Stockton in April by $\frac{3}{4}$ length from Phoebegee; $4\frac{1}{2}$ lengths third of 20 to Allied Cardiff in similar race at Nottingham in August, best subsequent effort; will stay 7f; acts on any going; blinkered third outing; ran badly final start. *P. Haslam.*

JENNY SPLENDID 6 br.m. John Splendid 116–Gay Maria (Tacitus 124) –
(1979 6.5v 6.5s 8g^{4} 8s 8fg 7.6g 7g^{2} 7fg^{3} 7g^{4} 7g 7.2g* 7f* 7d* 7f^{2} 7g^{2} 1980 7s

7g 7fg) fairly useful handicapper; little worthwhile form in 1980 (not seen out after April); ideally suited by 7f; acts on any going; excellent mount for an apprentice. *J. Haine.*

JENNY'S ROCKET 4 ch.f. Roan Rocket 128–Debach Game 69 (Darius 129) (1979 7.2g 7f 8fg 1980 10g) strong filly; no form since winning over 6f at 2 yrs. *A. Goodwill.* —

JESTER'S BOY 3 b.c. John Splendid 116–Jester's Girl (Will Somers 114§) (1979 5s³ 5f* 5fg* 6fg³ 7fg 1980 6f 6f* 6d 7.2s² 8d³ 7fg 8s³) compact, good sort; useful handicapper; showed improved form to beat Anna Batic by 3 lengths at Windsor in May; placed subsequently at Haydock, Newcastle (3 lengths third to Atlantic Boy in Northern Goldsmiths' Handicap) and Ayr (ran below his best, blinkered first time); stays 1m; acts on any going. *P. Cole.* **100**

JET ROMANCE 2 ch.f. Roan Rocket 128–Romancing 82 (Romulus 129) (1980 5g 6g 8g³) Mar 9: 13,000Y; quite a well-made filly; good mover; half-sister to several winners here and abroad, including fairly useful 1975 2-y-o Stormy Affair (by Prevailing); dam won over 6f at 2 yrs; sweated up when 8 lengths third of 7 to Leap Lively in minor event at Goodwood in September, best effort; evidently suited by 1m. *F. Durr.* **90**

JET STAR 3 ch.c. Deep Diver 134–Islay 75 (Parthia 132) (1979 5fg 1980 6d 6d 5f 7fg⁴ 7.6f 10.1g 8d 7g 7fg 7fg⁴ 5g 6g 8g 8s 6g) strong, sprint type; plating-class maiden; best at 7f on a firm surface; often blinkered; sometimes sweats up. *A. Breasley.* **49**

JEWELLED TURBAN 6 ch.g. Mansingh 120–Chantry Pearl (Gulf Pearl 117) (1979 6fg⁴ 6h⁴ 7fg 1980 6fg 7g 6d) small gelding; behind in 1980; effective at 5f and stays 7f; acts on any going; bandaged in front at 5 yrs. *R. D. Peacock.* —

JEZREEL 3 b.f. Joshua 129–Falcon's Pride 65 (Falcon 131) (1979 6f 5g 1980 8.2g 7.2d⁴ 10.6d 10f 8f 13.8d*) unfurnished filly; plater; attracted no bid after winning at Catterick in October; stays 1¾m; acts on a soft surface; sold to P. Bevan 750 gns Doncaster October Sales. *Miss S. Hall.* **52**

JIG BORER 3 br.f. Royalty 130–Cabaret Star (Sing Sing 134) (1979 5d 5.1fg 7fg 7fg 1980 8fg 10.1s 9d 8.3f 6g 8g) narrow, unfurnished filly; poor plater; best run at 9f on a soft surface. *K. Ivory.* —

JIMS BID 2 ch.g. Communication 119–Bonnie Hellen 80 (Falls of Clyde 126) (1980 5fg⁴ 5fg² 5g⁴) May 4; 1,000Y; leggy, narrow gelding; in frame in Northern sellers in May and June; runs as though he'll stay 6f. *G. Richards.* **51**

JIM'S TRICKS 3 b.c. Jimsun 121–Floral Palm 69 (Floribunda 136) (1979 6fg* 6fg⁴ 1980 10fg² 10fg* 8g 10g⁴ 10g 10g⁴ 9g*) lengthy, good-looking colt; good mover; fairly useful handicapper; successful at Leicester in May and York in October; enterprisingly ridden to beat Our Birthday ½ length on latter; stays 1¼m; acts on a firm surface. *R. Laing.* **98**

JINJA 2 b.f. St Paddy 133–Feather Duster 80 (Tickler 106) (1980 6g 7d 7f²) May 6; 6,800Y; compact filly; third foal; half-sister to 1978 2-y-o 6f seller winner Dusty Brown (by Golden Mallard); dam won twice over 1m; flattered by proximity to winner when length second to Spindrifter in minor event at Catterick in July but had 5 others well beaten off; will probably stay 1¼m; possibly needs a firm surface. *K. Ivory.* **85**

JIVA 2 b.f. Mummy's Pet 125–Satina 83 (Pall Mall 132) (1980 5fg⁴ 5fg³ 5fg* 5g* 6d) Apr 7; compact filly; third foal; half-sister to 1¾m winner Chetinkaya (by Ragstone); dam, placed at up to 1m, is daughter of Irish 1,000 Guineas winner Black Satin; won maiden race at Doncaster in May and 7-runner Dick Turpin Stakes at York in June; always going well, quickened and ran on strongly to beat Wonderful 1½ lengths in good style on latter course; should stay 6f (had stiff task and looked a bit light when remote last of 11 to Nasseem in Cherry Hinton Stakes at Newmarket in July, first attempt at trip). *B. Hanbury.* **91**

JOB BAG 2 b.f. Streetfighter 120–Wood Anemone 83 (Tangle 121) (1980 5d 5f 5g 6g*) Mar 9; compact, fair sort; half-sister to several winners, including quite useful sprinter Model Soldier (by Military); dam sprinter; hacked up when tackling selling company for first time, winning easing up by 6 lengths from Gaythorn at Windsor in June; sold 3,400 gns afterwards and subsequently won in Belgium. *R. Hannon.* **71**

JODIK 4 ch.c. Mansingh 120–Datella (Floribunda 136) (1979 6fg 8fg 8fg 11.7h 1980 10fg 10g) poor plater; not bred to stay; usually wears blinkers —

nowadays; pulled up after saddle slipped on reappearance; sold out of W. Clay's stable 750 gns Doncaster May Sales. *H. Fleming.*

JOELLA 2 ch.f. Porto Bello 118–Jolisu 110 (Welsh Abbot 131) (1980 6g) —
Mar 17; 800F, 5,000Y; half-sister to fairly useful 1½m to 2¼m winner Jolimo (by Fortissimo) and successful stayer Kansu (by Caliban); dam miler; 20/1 and in need of race, behind in 21-runner maiden event won by Velvet Habit at Leicester in November. *M. Ryan.*

JOE POLES 3 b. or br.c. Sharpen Up 127–Caprice 90 (King's Leap 111) —
(1979 6fg 7f 7f 1980 7f 7f 6fg 5s 10f) leggy, attractive colt; headstrong and has shown little worthwhile form in maiden races and a handicap; sweated up badly and looked temperamental final outing at 2 yrs; trained by T. Molony first 4 starts. *W. Haigh.*

JOHN CHERRY (USA) 9 ch.g. Stage Door Johnny–Cerisette (My Babu **105**
136) (1979 18.4d 16.1v^2 22.2fg* 21d^4 15d^2 18fg^4 1980 18.4f 15s* 18d) high-class stayer at his best; won 13 races, including Ladbroke Chester Cup and SKF Cesarewitch in 1976, Prix Gladiateur in 1977 and Queen Alexandra Stakes in 1977 and 1979; gained his sole successs of 1980 when beating Majestic Maharaj in good style by 10 lengths in amateur riders race at Ayr in September; also a very useful hurdler on his day; appeared to act on any going, but was well suited by some give in the ground; usually held up; wore blinkers and wasn't entirely reliable; has been retired. *H. T. Jones.*

JOHN CLARE 2 b.c. Derring-Do 131–Madame Clare 66 (Ennis 128) (1980 **94**
6d 7d* 7f^4 7g) Feb 21; strong, shapely colt; good mover; half-brother to several winners, including Prix de la Salamandre winner John de Coombe (by Moulton); dam won two 6f sellers; clear-cut winner of 15-runner maiden race at Newbury in August, disputing lead from start and coming home 4 lengths clear of Blare; beaten in better company afterwards, finishing 6½ lengths fourth to Bustomi at York and 10 lengths fifth behind Junta at Goodwood; will stay 1m. *P. Cole.*

JOHNNY O'DAY (USA) 3 ch.c. Restless Wind–Lovely Shelia (Francis S) **105**
(1979 7g* 7d^3 7g* 6.3d^4 8d^2 1980 7g^3 8.5f^3 10fg^2 8f 12g 10.5f 11s) deep-bodied, attractive ex-Irish colt; placed in Gladness Stakes at the Curragh (creditable ½-length third to Night Alert), Ladbroke Blue Riband Trial at Epsom (4½ lengths third to Last Fandango) and BMW Nijinsky Stakes at Leopardstown (went down by ¾ length to Ramian) in first part of season; well beaten in Airlie/Coolmore Irish 2,000 Guineas at the Curragh (blinkered), King Edward VII Stakes at Royal Ascot, Garrowby Stakes (Limited Handicap) at York and Doonside Cup at Ayr afterwards; stays 1¼m; acts on firm going and a soft surface; genuine; sold out of A. Maxwell's stable 760,000 francs (approx £79,000) Chantilly June Sales after fifth start. *B. Hobbs.*

JOHN O'GROATS 3 b.c. Welsh Pageant 132–Romany 87 (King's Bench 132) **97**
(1979 5f 6g 7f^4 7fg^3 7fg^3 1980 8fg* 10.4f^2 10.6fg^3 12g* 12s^4 12g^2 10.5f 12fg) well-made colt; won maiden race at Pontefract in April and beat High Gait going away by 1½ lengths in 14-runner King George V Stakes (Handicap) at Royal Ascot; went down by a short head to Lorentino after a tremendous tussle in £3,000 handicap at Goodwood in August; suited by 1½m; acts on firm going and is probably unsuited by very soft; blinkered last 2 starts at 2 yrs; suited by strong handling; genuine; below form seventh start. *J. Winter.*

JOHN OLIVER 3 ch.c. Northfields–Pensodoro 71 (Roan Rocket 128) (1979 **86**
5d^2 7fg^2 7g^3 1980 7v 9s* 7g^3 10.4f 7fg^3 9f 8.5d^4 7s 10s^2 8.5v^3 10s^2) 7,000Y; small colt; third foal; half-brother to 1m winner Danny Bidder (by Mount Hagen); dam stayed 7f; narrowly won maiden race at Phoenix Park in April; placed in varied company afterwards, notably when creditable third in Madrid Handicap at the Curragh on third start; appeared not to act too well on course when remote seventh to Vaguely Tender in Grosvenor Stakes at Chester on fourth outing; stays 1¼m; probably acts on any going; blinkered eighth outing; has run creditably for a boy. *P. Prendergast, jnr, Ireland.*

JOHNS PRESENT 2 b.g. Gift Card 124–Kirmeen (Charlottesville 135) (1980 —
6s 7d) May 8; robust, hollow-backed gelding; fourth foal; dam unraced half-sister to smart French miler White Star; unquoted when behind in maiden races at Windsor in July and Newbury in August. *J. Benstead.*

JOHN WILDING 3 ch.g. Roi Soleil 125–Long Hill 91 (Vigo 130) (1979 **63**
5v 5d 5g 5fg 5.3fg 5f 1980 10fg^2 10fg) neat, strong gelding; poor mover; plating-class maiden; suited by 1¼m; acts on a firm surface. *Mrs D. Oughton.*

JOHN WILLOUGHBY 2 b.c. Run The Gantlet–Sensibility (Hail to Reason) (1980 7f 7d* 7s*) Apr 9; 6,000Y; rangy, attractive colt; good mover; third foal; half-brother to successful miler State Councellor (by Royal and Regal) and Irish 1979 2-y-o 9f winner Tree of Knowledge (by Sassafras); dam, winner over 9f in Ireland, stayed 13f and is half-sister to Prix de l'Arc de Triomphe winner Prince Royal II; won maiden race at Leicester and minor event at Chepstow inside a week in October, easily landing the odds from Ta Morgan and 11 others on latter; a taking individual who could well make a smart 3-y-o over middle distances. *J. Dunlop.* **97** p

JOINT COMMAND (USA) 2 ch.g. Mr Leader–Lady Sher (Sherluck) (1980 5fg^2 5f^4 5fg^3 6d^2 5g 7g* 7fg* 8g^2 7f^3) Mar 24; $25,000Y; neat gelding; excellent walker and mover; half-brother to several winners, including French 10.5f winner Dancing Sher (by Dancer's Image); dam won 2 small races at up to 6f; apprentice ridden when winning nurseries at Yarmouth (made all) and Wolverhampton in August; beat Hoodwink 3 lengths on latter course; placed subsequently in nurseries at Yarmouth and Redcar; suited by 7f and 1m and may get 1¼m; acts on a firm surface; gelded after last outing; sent to Singapore. *E. Eldin.* **91**

JOINT MERCY 2 gr.g. No Mercy 126–Legal Treasure 46 (Quorum 126) (1980 5f^4 5f^2 5f^4 6g 6fg 6g 5g^3 6g^2 7d^3 6g 7.2s^3 8d) May 4; 2,400Y; useful-looking gelding; has a round action; half-brother to 3 fairly useful winners, including sprinter Single Gal (by Mansingh); dam poor plater; in frame in varied company, including plating; caught close home by Mott the Hoople in seller at Newcastle in August; needs at least 6f but isn't sure to stay 1m; seems to act on any going; ran poorly in blinkers tenth outing; inconsistent. *G. Richards.* **65**

JOJA ROLY 4 b.c. Souvran 98–River Damsel (Forlorn River 124) (1979 10d 10s^4 10g 11.7d^3 14d 12fg^3 12fg 12fg* 13.1f^2 12f^2 12fg^4 12g 10f 1980 8fg 11.7fg^4 10fg 11.7fg^3 12fg^4 12d 11.7f 12f^4 10g^2 12f 10f 12f 10fg 12g^4) strong, compact colt; quite a moderate handicapper; stays 13f; acts on any going but goes well on firm; suitable mount for an apprentice; never dangerous when blinkered first time on thirteenth start; sold 4,800 gns Newmarket Autumn Sales. *J. Benstead.* **56**

JO-JO-SAN 2 b.f. Comedy Star 121–Geisha Girl (Soleil Levant 126) (1980 6fg 6f 7g^3 7g) Feb 5; strong filly; half-sister to winners in Italy, including prolific scorer Jap Fancy (by Espresso) and top 1967 2-y-o filly Juliet (by Jaddo); dam won once from 9 starts; ran easily best race when staying-on 3½ lengths third of 18 to Park Place in maiden race at Yarmouth in September; will probably stay 1¼m. *H. Wragg.* **76**

JOLEG 4 br.c. Targowice 130–Yavana (Milesian 125) (1979 8d^2 12d* 12v^3 7d^3 7fg 8g^3 8fg* 8s 10.2s^4 1980 10g^2 10fg^2 10f^2 10f^3 8f 10g^4 10.2g^4 10g^4 10d^2 10g) neat, strong-quartered colt; useful performer; runner-up in handicaps at Epsom (City and Suburban won by Sea Chimes) in April, Newmarket and Redcar in May and Newmarket (apprentices) again in October; also a very close third to Sacrilege in Daily Mirror Handicap at Epsom; may well be suited by a return to 1½m; acts on any going; genuine and consistent; suited by front-running tactics; often sweats up; changed hands 15,500 gns Newmarket Autumn Sales and raced once more here before being sent to USA. *B. Hills.* **97**

JOLIETTE 2 ch.f. Jimmy Reppin 131–Colonia (Colonist II 126) (1980 7f^3) May 27; strong filly; half-sister to winning hurdler Upton Grey (by Rugantino); dam poor N.H. performer; looked backward when 8/1-shot for maiden race at Newmarket in October but ran creditably to finish 5½ lengths third of 18 to Blackfoot; will be suited by 1¼m; should improve enough to win a race at 3 yrs. *W. Hastings-Bass.* **78** p

JOLIMO 4 ch.f. Fortissimo 111–Jolisu 110 (Welsh Abbot 131) (1979 8v 8.2s^4 8s^2 10.8s 9s 12g^3 9fg^3 12f^3 12fg* 12g^2 13g 12f* 13fg^2 11.7fg^3 12g* 12g^4 12d* 1980 13s^4 12fg 13g 12.3f* 12h^2 12fg^4 12f^3 12g 16s^4 16g^3 14fg* 18.1g* 16fg^2 16.1s^4 16g 18v^4 13s^3 18s) workmanlike filly; poor mover; successful in handicaps at Chester, Salisbury and Yarmouth, staying on strongly when scoring by 6 lengths from Mountain Monarch on last-named course in September; had no answer to winner's pace when 1½ lengths second to Heighlin at Ascot later in September; stays well; acts on any going; consistent; often bandaged in front; suitable mount for an apprentice; possibly needs a strongly-run race. *M. Ryan.* **79**

JOLLY GREEN GIANT 5 ch.g. Daring Display 129–Wish 106 (Whistler 129) (1979 NR 1980 8.2d^2 12f^4 12g 12d) compact gelding; runner-up in seller at **53**

Haydock in August; not entirely disgraced in better company next time; seems to stay 1½m; probably acts on any going; has worn blinkers and a hood. *F. Yardley.*

JOLLY MARJIM 3 ch.c. Jolly Me 114–Rose's Leader (Damremont 120) (1979 **70**
5d 6d 6s 6fg 1980 8v^2 9d^4 8h^3 8h^3 9fg^3 8g^2 8.2d^3 10fg^3 10s 10.6d) workmanlike colt; quite a moderate maiden; stays 1¼m; acts on any going; has run creditably for an apprentice. *J. Hardy.*

JOLLY TRIPPER 6 b.g. Tycoon II–Sunday Out 95 (Lord of Verona 120) —
(1979 17.1g 16fg 15.5f 16f^2 16f 17.1h^2 19f^4 1980 16.5g) poor staying handicapper; acts on any going; has been tried in blinkers; sometimes wears bandages. *D. Jermy.*

JONBEE 2 ch.c. Tickled Pink 114–Thundersquall 109 (Roi de Navarre II 123) —
(1980 5d 7s) June 6; half-brother to a winner in Malaya; dam stayer; unquoted when in rear in maiden and minor events at Warwick and Chepstow in October. *D. Elsworth.*

JONDALE 3 b.g. Le Johnstan 123–Levandale 102 (Le Levanstell 122) (1979 5f **97**
7g 6s^3 8fg^2 8s 8fg* 1980 8f 10g 10fg^4 8d 10s^2 10f 8g* 10.2d 8s*) workmanlike gelding; made all to win handicaps at York and Doncaster in the autumn; stays 1¼m; seems to act on any going; has run respectably for an apprentice; ran poorly sixth outing; inconsistent; trained by M. H. Easterby first 2 starts. *W. Elsey.*

JONDI 4 b.g. The Parson 119–Miss Sunblest 87 (Whistler 129) (1979 8d^4 10v **79§**
11.7d^2 10g* 10s^3 10v^3 8fg^4(dis) 10f* 8fg 10fg^3 12g^2 12g^2 12fg^3 10fg^4 10fg 1980 12d 12fg 14fg 12f 10g^3 12g^2 12g^2 12f^3 12f 14g^2 14fg 16fg) good-looking gelding; fairly useful middle-distance handicapper at his best but doesn't always go through with his effort; acts on any going; sometimes wears blinkers but does just as well without; sometimes sweats up; gelded at end of season. *P. Mitchell.*

JOSE COLLINS 3 b.f. Singing Bede 122–Piccadilly Etta 76 (Floribunda 136) **88**
(1979 5.1g* 5.1fg^2 1980 6fg 6fg 5s^4 5d^2 5fg 5g 5f 5g* 5g 5d^3 5v) sturdy filly; sprint handicapper; beat Springy by 4 lengths at Goodwood in September; best at 5f; probably acts on any going. *R. Armstrong.*

JOSMOLL 3 b.g. Golden Mallard 103–Peach Fair (Lord of Verona 120) (1979 **65**
6fg 7f 6s 8.2g^2 8d 8.2fg 1980 8.2g 10.2g 12g 8f 8f 7g) big, strong gelding; has shown no form since fourth start at 2 yrs; stays 1m well; sweated up and didn't impress particularly in paddock third outing. *E. Carter.*

JOSS-STICK 6 b.g. Frankincense 120–Pearl Barley 79 (Pinza 137) (1979 NR —
1980 11fg 8fg) poor maiden; lightly raced nowadays; stays 1½m; acts on any going; has been tried in blinkers. *J. Cann.*

JOSUVY 3 ch.f. Shoolerville 121–Severn Bridge 81 (Hornbeam 130) (1979 NR **79**
1980 6s 6f^2 8fg^3 8fg^2 8d^4 8s* 7s) 5,000Y; workmanlike filly; half-sister to very useful 1977 2-y-o 5f winner Swing Bridge (by Swing Easy) and a winner in Denmark; dam, half-sister to dam of Dibidale, won over 9f; placed in maiden races prior to winning handicap at Chepstow in October; stays 1m; acts on any going. *B. Hills.*

JOTA 4 gr.g. Dragonara Palace 115–Aspiration 53 (Roan Rocket 128) (1979 **58**
8fg 7fg 7fg 6f^3 8.2g 8h^4 8fg* 8h 7fg^2 8fg 1980 7fg 8fg 8fg^3 10g 10g^4 12f^4 10fg^3 10g* 10d) short-coupled gelding; poor walker; held up when winning apprentice handicap at Nottingham in September by a neck from Julip; seems to stay 1½m; has run well for an amateur and a claimer; yet to race on really soft ground; has won over hurdles. *W. Wharton.*

JOULOUVILLE 2 b.c. Reform 132–Queen of Twilight 107 (Off Key 121 or —
Twilight Alley 133) (1980 7s) Feb 27; half-brother to several winners, including smart stayer Antler (by Northfields); dam won at up to 1¾m, including Jockey Club Stakes; unquoted when 14 lengths sixth of 13 to John Willoughby in minor event at Chepstow in October; bred to stay 1½m. *P. M. Taylor.*

JOVENO 3 br.c. Blakeney 126–Miss Mandy 92 (Mandamus 120) (1979 8fg^4 —
7fg 8fg 1980 8.2s^3 10fg 16f^4 16f 16d 14fg 14fg^4 14.6d) neat, strong colt; in frame in maiden races and a handicap; should stay 2m; probably acts on any going; blinkered nowadays; sold 3,200 gns Newmarket Autumn Sales. *C. Brittain.*

JOYOUS 3 br.c. So Blessed 130–Syringa 98 (Set Fair 129) (1979 6fg^4 6s^3 7fg* **79**
1980 7d^2 7f^3 8fg^2 8fg* 8fg 10d^4 8s^3 8d* 8f^3 8g) lengthy, useful-looking colt; moderate handicapper; successful at Carlisle in June (apprentice event) and Ripon in August; had earlier run well when second in Northern Free Handicap

at Newcastle on first outing; stays 1m (ran moderately when tried at 1¼m); probably acts on any going; blinkered nowadays; doesn't find a great deal off bridle. *J. W. Watts.*

JUBILEE BILL 3 b.g. Sovereign Bill 105–Macera 85 (Acer 123) (1979 7d^3 1980 10g 12g 10d 10fg^4 10g* 10.1g* 10d* 10fg 10.5s 8s) leggy, lengthy gelding; improved once blinkers were fitted in second half of season and won minor events at Ripon and Windsor and a handicap at Brighton; stays 1¼m; suited by some give in the ground; bandaged second outing and didn't move too well to post at Ripon; sweated up a bit and dwelt eighth start; sold 6,200 gns Newmarket Autumn Sales. *P. Kelleway.* **94**

JUBILEE DANCER 4 br.f. Sahib 114–Qalibashi 77 (Master Rocky 106) (1979 9s 9g 10.1fg 10.8g 12fg 12fg 12fg 8g* 16s 10d 10s 1980 10fg 8fg 12d 10g 16.9f 16s^3 12g 16fg 12f 16g^3 17.1d 15s) plater; third in 2 handicaps at Nottingham; evidently stays well; seems suited by some give in the ground; blinkered final outing at 2 yrs. *K. Bridgwater.* **45**

JUBILEE DOLL 3 ch.f. Starch Reduced 112–Bella Doll 78 (Espresso 122) (1979 NR 1980 10f 9f) small filly; of no account. *G. Price.* –

JUBILEE EVE 3 b.f. Royalty 130–Little Rapide 90 (Rapace 130) (1979 NR 1980 10s 14.6d 15s) lightly-made filly; half-sister to fairly useful stayer Petit Pretendre (by Pretendre) and to a winner in USA; dam out-and-out stayer; behind in maiden races; sold 440 gns Doncaster November Sales. *M. Camacho.* –

JUBILEE IMP 4 gr.g. Rupert Bear 105–Grey Vision (Amber X 133) (1979 10d 1980 12fg 10f) light-framed gelding; poor maiden. *J. Holt.* –

JUBILEE JOY 3 b.f. Burglar 128–Quortina 88 (Quorum 126) (1979 5d 5g 5g 5g^4 1980 5fg 5f) neat filly; only plating class; not raced after April; will be suited by 6f. *J. Holt.* –

JUBILEE LADY 3 b.f. Cavo Doro 124–Argentina 115 (Nearco) (1979 5d 7fg 7s 1980 7fg^4 8fg 10fg^3 12.2fg 10.2g) well-made filly; plating-class form in maiden and minor races; best run at 1¼m on a firm surface. *T. Waugh.* **64**

JUBILEE LIGHTS 3 ch.g. Bustino 136–Lovely Light 105 (Henry the Seventh 125) (1979 7f 7d* 1980 10g*) big gelding; top weight and favourite, made all and ran on well to beat Kildanes cleverly by 2 lengths in handicap at Nottingham in April; gelded subsequently and wasn't seen out again; will stay 1½m+. *H. Cecil.* **96**

JUBILEE MEDAL 3 b.g. Sovereign Bill 105–Cash Award (Cash and Courage 116) (1979 6fg 6fg 8h 10s^4 8d 1980 13s 13g) short-backed gelding; showed ability on fourth outing at 2 yrs; well beaten in 1980; suited by 1¼m and should stay further. *H. Fleming.* –

JUBILEE PRINCE 5 ch.g. Sun Prince 128–Theban Queen (Pindari 124) (1979 14g 13v 9.4g 10g^2 10f^4 10f 10fg* 8fg 8g 10g^4 10f 8fg 14g 1980 8f* 10h* 10f* 10.5f* 10fg 10f^2 10s 10d^3 10fg^4 10g 10fg 8g* 10g 8s) moderate handicapper; successful at Pontefract and Stockton in April, Kempton and York in May and Yarmouth (apprentices) in September; dashed clear 3f out and came home unchallenged when scoring by 3 lengths from Vaigly Blue on last-named course; best at up to 1¼m; acts on any going but goes very well on top-of-the-ground; often starts slowly; ran moderately penultimate start. *F. Durr.* **74**

JUBILEE SAINT 4 ch.g. Saintly Song 128–Saint-Cyr 73 (Set Fair 129) (1979 8g^2 10s^2 12s^2 11d^4 10f 12f^3 10fg 14.6fg* 10s* 12.3s* 12g* 10.6g 1980 12.3d 14.7f^3 12fg^4 12g^2 12d^3) leggy gelding; in frame most starts and finished good third to Fascadale in handicap at Ripon in August on final start; effective from 1¼m to 1¾m; acts on any going but is well suited by some give in the ground; has won for an amateur. *Miss S. Hall.* **71**

JUDEAH 3 ch.f. Great Nephew 126–Jibuti 114 (Djebe) (1979 NR 1980 8d 7.2d^3 7g^4 7.2d 6g* 7d^3) tall filly; half-sister to several winners, including very useful middle-distance winner Cesarea (by Raeburn II); dam very useful from 1m to 1¼m; won 13-runner maiden race at Goodwood in September; ran creditably in handicap final outing; stays 7f well; sold 13,000 gns Newmarket December Sales. *P. Walwyn.* **69**

JUDY TWOSHOES 2 ch.f. My Swallow 134–Dame Judith 88 (Francis S) (1980 5d 6fg 6fg 6fg) Feb 19; 420F; lengthy filly; half-sister to 3 winners, including one in Austria; dam won over 5f at 2 yrs; well beaten, including in sellers; broke loose and had to be withdrawn when blinkered on intended second outing. *D. Thom.* –

JULARD 4 b.g. Golden Mallard 103–Jury 66 (Lucky Brief 128) (1979 NR 1980 12.5v^3 12f 12.5s) second foal; dam winning hurdler; modest third of 18 to Great Developer in maiden race at Stockton in March; never going next time (still looked in need of run) and was off course afterwards for 6 months; stays 1½m; possibly unsuited by firm ground. *J. Leigh.* —

JULESIAN 3 b.c. High Top 131–Bold Lass (Bold Lad, Ire 133) (1979 7f 1980 8fg 10fg 10s^2 10f^4 10s^2 10.1f* 11.7g^2 9.4fg^4) strong colt; won 9-runner maiden race at Windsor in August; stays 1½m; acts on any going; sold to D. Elsworth 9,400 gns Newmarket Autumn Sales. *P. Walwyn.* **79**

JULIE SIMONE 5 ch.m. Some Hand 119–Esquire Maid 86 (Aureole 132) (1979 8v 10fg 10g 10h 1980 10d 10g) bad plater. *T. Kersey.* —

JULIP 3 b.f. Track Spare 125—Jacine 72 (Owen Tudor) (1979 7fg 7g* 7g* 7d 7fg 7.3g^4 7f^2 7fg 1980 8.2d^4 8.2fg 8.5f^2 10d 10s 10g^2 10g^3 8fg^3 10g^2 11.7d 12s^3 12g) quite a well-made filly; moderate handicapper; good head second to Parlour Game in Ebbisham Stakes at Epsom in June on third outing; stays 1½m; acts on any going; blinkered eighth start; has run respectably for a boy. *J. Hindley.* **82**

JULIUS CAESAR (FR) 3 gr.c. Exbury 138—Queer Street (Busted 134) (1979 8g^4 1980 10g* 10g^2 11g* 12fg 12f) 36,000 francs Y (approx £4,300); leggy, light-framed colt; second foal; dam poor maiden; 46/1, won Group 2 Prix Noailles at Longchamp in April by neck from Dom Aldo; had earlier won 17-runner maiden race at Saint-Cloud by 5 lengths; not disgraced when sixth to Mot D'Or in Prix Hocquart at Longchamp and seventh to Henbit in Derby, beaten about 8¼ lengths, afterwards; not seen out after latter race; will stay beyond 1½m; yet to race on a soft surface. *S. Boullenger, France.* **115**

JULY THE FOURTH (USA) 3 b.f. Goose Creek 116—Firecracker Love (Crackpot) (1979 NR 1980 12d 16.9d^4 12f) American-bred filly; dam, placed 3 times in USA, is half-sister to 2 minor winners by Goose Creek; slow maiden. *I. Balding.* —

JUMPING BEAN 4 b.g. Double Jump 131—Windbag 109 (Borealis) (1979 10.2fg 8f 8f 10g 1980 12d) leggy gelding; plating-class maiden. *W. Wharton.* —

JUNE ROSE 4 ch.f. Ampney Prince 96—Wandering Rose (Tudor Minstrel 144) (1979 NR 1980 10fg) of no account. *Mrs N. Kennedy.* —

JUNGLE BUSTER 3 ch.g. Habitat 134—Riberta 89 (Ribot 142) (1979 NR 1980 12f 14f) big, lengthy gelding; half-brother to The Adrianstan (by Sparkler), a very useful performer at up to 1m, and 1978 2-y-o 7f winner Ribomil (by Petingo); dam, placed in Ribblesdale Stakes, is half-sister to top 1974 Irish 2-y-o Sea Break; in rear in minor race at Kempton and maiden race at Newmarket in May; sold to W. Clay 560 gns Ascot July Sales. *B. Hanbury.* —

JUNGLE JIM 2 b.c. Hotfoot 126—Jungle Queen (Twilight Alley 133) (1980 6d 7s 8g* 8fg^3 8g) Apr 13; 7,200F, 17,000Y; tall, rangy, long-striding colt; second living produce; half-brother to 3-y-o Sharp Deal (by Sharpen Up), successful over 1m; dam ran 3 times; having first race for over 2 months, showed improved form when making all and keeping on strongly to win 23-runner maiden race at Goodwood in September; confirmed his improvement when 2¾ lengths third of 23 to Shergar in minor event at Newbury later in month but ran moderately in nursery at Brighton in October; suited by 1m; acts on a firm surface. *G. Harwood.* **95**

JUNTA 2 b.c. Brigadier Gerard 144—Siliciana 113 (Silly Season 127) (1980 6g^2 7g^2 7g*) Mar 7; tall, narrow colt; fourth foal; half-brother to 2 winners, including 1979 2-y-o 7f winner Cabana (by Mill Reef); dam won 1973 Cambridgeshire; came through to lead in final furlong and kept on strongly to win well-contested minor event at Goodwood in September by 2 lengths from Dark Monarch; will stay 1¼m; useful. *I. Balding.* **100**

JUST ABROAD 3 b.f. Abwah 118—Seventh Bride 109 (Royal Record II) (1979 NR 1980 7f^2 8fg^3 7.6f^3 8fg 8f^2 8fg* 8g^3 7s* 8g^4) quite attractive, compact filly; half-sister to several winners, including Oaks winner Polygamy and Cheshire Oaks winner One Over Parr (both by Reform); dam won from 6f to 1½m; cleverly won maiden race at Warwick in August; finished well to force dead-heat with Some Bella in 10-runner minor event at Ayr following month; will be suited by 1¼m; acts on any going; sold 40,000 gns Newmarket December Sales. *P. Walwyn.* **73**

JUST AMBER 3 ch.c. Amber Rama 133—False Evidence 53 (Counsel 118) (1979 5s^3 5d* 6fg^4 6g 6fg^4 7fg^3 8s 1980 8.2d 8g 7fg* 8d 7d^2 7d 7fg 6s 7g 6fg) **107**

useful-looking colt; poor walker; useful handicapper; put up a fine effort under top weight to beat Hot Case a neck at Doncaster in May; again ran really well when $\frac{3}{4}$-length second to Lord Rochford at Newcastle in June; stays 7f but possibly not 1m; acts on a firm and a soft surface; blinkered final start; sold 12,500 gns Newmarket Autumn Sales. *T. Fairhurst.*

JUST ANDY 2 b.c. Furry Glen 121—Sequito Fortuna (Continuation 120) — (1980 6f) May 10; 3,000Y; fourth foal; dam Irish 9f winner; last of 18 to Scarrowmanwick in minor event at Lingfield in September; dead. *A. Demetriou.*

JUST ARCHY 2 br.g. Gold Form 108—Queen's Rose 85 (Queen's Hussar 124) **53** (1980 6fg 5fg 5g 6g^4 6fg*) Apr 19; 2,800F, 640Y; well-grown gelding; dam won over 7f at 2 yrs and appeared to stay 1$\frac{3}{4}$m; sold to Denys Smith 2,000 gns after winning 10-runner seller at Pontefract in July by a neck from Dollarerina, best effort; will probably stay 7f; hung left all way at Pontefract, proving a very difficult ride, and was subsequently gelded. *A. Smith.*

JUST GAYLE 4 ch.c. Lord Gayle 124—Golden Samantha 88 (Sammy Davis 129) — (1979 8.2v 6g* 6f 1980 6v^4 6d 6f 6f 6f 6g 6g 6g 7s 7.2d 8g^4) workmanlike colt; good walker; mainly disappointing in 1980; best form at 6f, although wasn't disgraced at 1m on final start; acts on any going but goes well on soft; a difficult ride (tends to hang and sometimes starts slowly); ran moderately in blinkers once; bandaged and didn't move well to post fourth start. *E. Weymes.*

JUST GEOFFREY 2 b.g. Comedy Star 121—Solvilium (Vilmorin) (1980 5s — 5f 5fg 7fg 7f 6f 6g) Feb 8; 4,000Y; quite attractive, rangy gelding; half-brother to 2 winners and to several winners over fences; dam of little account; little worthwhile form; blinkered seventh outing. *G. Lewis.*

JUSTICE PAO 2 b.g. Reform 132—Twill 89 (Crocket 130) (1980 7g) Feb 27; — 6,400Y; third foal; half-brother to 1m to 11f winner Corduroy (by Hotfoot); dam stayed 1$\frac{1}{2}$m; unquoted and very burly indeed, always behind in 15-runner maiden race won by McCarthy at Newmarket in August. *P. Haslam.*

JUST IN FUN (USA) 2 b.f. Buffalo Lark–Devilish Queen (Crimson Satan) — (1980 7g 6g 7d) Mar 20; $10,500Y; useful-looking, deep-girthed filly; good mover; fourth foal; closely related to T.V. Derby (by T.V. Commercial), winner of several small races in USA, and half-sister to another winner; dam unplaced 5 times; towards rear in maiden races at Sandown, Newbury and Leicester; showed up well for 5f, having been off course for 3 months, on last-named track in October; will stay 1$\frac{1}{4}$m; looks the type to do better at 3 yrs. *G. Hunter.*

JUST KILTON 2 ch.c. Jimmy Reppin 131–No Halo 74 (Aureole 132) (1980 — 7fg 7g 6s) Apr 13; 12,000Y; strong, compact colt; third foal; dam won over 1$\frac{1}{2}$m; behind in maiden races at Leicester and Doncaster on first and third outings and in Somerville Tattersall Stakes at Newmarket in between. *L. Cumani.*

JUST MARTIN 2 b.c. Martinmas 128–Just Alice (Worden II 129) (1980 **88** 5f 5f 7d 5d*) May 1; 1,800F, 4,700Y; leggy, lightly-built colt; half-brother to a winner in France and a winning hurdler; dam disappointing half-sister to good sprinter Tudor Grey; won 10-runner maiden auction race at Catterick in October with ease by 6 lengths from That's Magic; should stay 7f (took charge of jockey on way to start when tried at trip and finished last of 15); acts on a soft surface. *R. Price.*

JUST MIST 4 gr.g. Siliconn 121–Firmpostie (Goldhill 125) (1979 NR 1980 — 8fg) first living foal; dam ran only at 2 yrs; unquoted and bandaged on off-fore when well beaten in maiden race at Doncaster in July, first outing. *W. Wharton.*

JUST PASSING 2 ch.f. Most Secret 119–Roxanne (Sheshoon 132) (1980 8g) — May 6; fifth foal; dam well behind in maiden races; unquoted when last but one in 15-runner maiden race won by Scottish Dream in Edinburgh in October. *K. Morgan.*

JUST WHARTON 3 bl.g. Galivanter 131–Manor Pride 66 (Orbit 106) (1979 — NR 1980 8fg 7f 8fg 12g) leggy gelding; fourth foal; dam winning hurdler; in rear in maiden and minor events in the North; sold 960 gns Doncaster September Sales. *Denys Smith.*

JUST WISHING 2 b.f. Wishing Star 117–Lepe 65 (Exbury 138) (1980 6s — 7g 7fg) Mar 1; 900F, 2,300Y; small, workmanlike filly; half-sister to a winner in Italy and 2 winning jumpers; dam needed at least 1$\frac{1}{2}$m; well beaten in maiden races; likely to need a test of stamina. *J. Winter.*

K

KAHAILA 3 b. or br.f. Pitcairn 126–Chaldea (Tamerlane 128) (1979 6g 7fg 7fg^3 7g^4 1980 8f* 10f^2 12.3f 10fg 12s^2 12fg 12d^3 12d 10fg) compact filly; very useful performer; beat Souliotissa 1½ lengths in maiden race at Thirsk in April; placed afterwards in XYZ Handicap at Newcastle (7 lengths behind Fine Sun), Lancashire Oaks at Haydock (beaten 5 lengths by Vielle) and Yorkshire Oaks (4½ lengths third to Shoot A Line); well beaten in Princess Royal Stakes at Ascot and Yellow Ribbon Stakes at Santa Anita on her last 2 outings; stays 1½m; acts on any going; blinkered third start; trained most of season by R. Boss. *W. Hastings-Bass.* **103**

KAIMLAW 6 ch.g. Native Prince–Misty Morn 70 (Worden II 129) (1979 5s 6g 5f 5g 1980 5f* 6g 5s) sprint handicapper; has run tubed; 25/1 and ridden by 7-lb claimer when scoring narrowly at Ripon in August; well beaten afterwards; acts on firm going; used to wear blinkers. *H. Bell.* **55**

KAIROUAN 2 gr.g. No Mercy 126–Bouboulina (Hornbeam 130) (1980 7f 6d 6d) Apr 29; 3,000Y; leggy gelding; half-brother to 1¼m seller winner Andalucia (by Rheingold); dam reportedly won in Greece; unquoted when soundly beaten in maiden races in October. *R. Armstrong.* —

KALAGLOW 2 gr.c. Kalamoun 129–Aglow 78 (Crepello 136) (1980 6g* 7g* 7.3fg* 8g* 7.3d*) **126**

Guy Harwood and James Delahooke have together proved exceptional judges of yearlings. In 1977 they picked up two outstanding bargains at the sales, buying Ela-Mana-Mou for 4,500 guineas and Young Generation for 9,000 guineas, and at the 1979 sales they bettered even that. They acquired To-Agori-Mou, the best English two-year-old colt, for 20,000 guineas, Recitation, winner of the Grand Criterium, easily the most valuable race for two-year-olds in France, for 35,000 dollars, and Kalaglow, the unbeaten winner of the Horris Hill Stakes, for 11,500 guineas. Considering that the top-priced colts at the American and European sales fetched 1,600,000 dollars and 625,000 guineas respectively, it was a remarkable achievement to buy three of the very best two-year-olds in Europe for a total of around £50,000. What must the three be worth now?

The Horris Hill at Newbury in October was the last of Kalaglow's five

Horris Hill Stakes, Newbury—Kalaglow wins his fifth race in a row, beating Cut Above (rails)

Mr J. T. Vanner's "Kalaglow"

races and easily the most important. Kalaglow was one of eight winners among the ten runners, with the Laurent Perrier Champagne Stakes winner Gielgud, the Duke of Edinburgh Stakes winner Shasavaan and the impressive Champion Two Yrs Old Trophy winner Noalto best of the others. Kalaglow, who started second favourite to Gielgud, settled in the middle of the field as Noalto set a strong gallop ahead of Chief Speaker and Cut Above. After moving up steadily in the straight, he was at Cut Above's quarters as the latter headed the weakening Noalto below the distance. A stirring battle then developed between the two and it was only in the last fifty yards that Kalaglow, easily the more tenderly ridden, edged ahead to win going away by three quarters of a length.

Kalaglow gave the impression at Newbury that he's a lazy individual, the type who does little more than is necessary to win. Although this impression of his character isn't supported by his performance in a maiden race at Newmarket in August on his debut, when he sprinted six lengths clear in the final furlong, it is confirmed by his displays on his three other outings. In the Viewsport Stakes at Sandown later in August he came under pressure early in the straight and had to be very hard ridden to get in front close home for a two-length victory over the newcomers Centurius and Cut Above; under top weight of 9-7 in a nursery at Newbury the following month he lengthened his stride to win cleverly by a length and a half, but only after he'd been vigorously hand ridden; and, when giving weight to his eleven opponents in the Kinrara Stakes at Goodwood ten days later, he tended to idle after cruising into the lead two furlongs out and had to be kept up to his work with hands and heels to win by two lengths from Baz Bombati, with Irish Heart a further five lengths back in third. Kalaglow certainly learnt from his races and ended the season no longer the excitable colt who got a bit above himself in the paddock on his first two starts and who pulled very hard for his head on his third.

Kalaglow is a useful-looking colt, even though rather on the leg at two years, and he's an excellent mover. Although he has the smooth, flowing action normally associated with a top-of-the-ground performer, he wasn't troubled in the slightest by the sticky ground at Newbury and seems to act both on a firm and a soft surface. He's the first winner bred by Aglow, a winner of two small races who stayed two miles. Aglow is one of three winners, none of them out of the ordinary, bred by the fairly useful stayer Sun Palace, herself a daughter of the smart mile winner Sonsa. The dam's family is quite a stout one and Kalaglow is likely to need at least a mile and a quarter; indeed, of the three Harwood-trained colts, he seems the most likely to develop into a Derby horse. As yet he's a little short of Derby-winning standard but he was still improving at the end of his first season and may well make the necessary progress. Even if he fails to reach such great heights he has already accomplished enough to make Kalamoun's death in 1979 at the age of nine look even more regrettable.

Kalaglow (gr.c. Feb 19, 1978)	Kalamoun (gr 1970)	Zeddaan (gr 1965)	Grey Sovereign
			Vareta
		Khairunissa (gr 1960)	Prince Bio
			Palariva
	Aglow (ch 1970)	Crepello (ch 1954)	Donatello II
			Crepuscule
		Sun Palace (b 1964)	Charlottesville
			Sonsa

Kalamoun, a mile- to mile-and-a-quarter performer, has proved a top-class stallion despite developing fertility problems (Kalaglow is one of only fifteen reported foals by him in 1978). His other good winners in England include Kampala and Castle Keep while he has been represented on the Continent by Shakapour, second in the French Derby and runner of a dead heat in the Grand Prix de Saint-Cloud; Kenmare, winner of both the Prix Thomas Bryon and the Prix Jacques le Marois; Dom Racine, winner of the Prix Jean Prat; Tassmoun, successful in the Prix Messidor; Moon Ingraver, a good Italian filly who beat the French fillies in the Prix d'Astarte; and the Italian colts Frassino and Unoaprile, both winners of pattern races. *G. Harwood.*

KALI'S GLORY (USA) 2 ch.c. First Dawn–High Praise (Flag Raiser) (1980 6d 8.2s 8d) Mar 30; narrow colt; half-brother to 2 minor winners; dam never ran; sire, son of Bold Ruler, was a minor winner at up to 7f; in rear in maiden races, soon getting tailed off on third start. *S. Norton.* —

KAMARIDAAN 4 b.c. Djakao 124–Diamond Drop (Charlottesville 135) (1979 10.5v* 11d^3 15d^3 12d^3 12d 12.5v^2 1980 10s* 10g^4 11s^4 10s 12g) French colt; won Prix Mary at Maisons-Laffitte and was placed on several occasions, including when acting as pacemaker for Top Ville, as a 3-y-o; put up an excellent performance in Prix Exbury at Saint-Cloud in March on reappearance, leading halfway up straight and drawing away to beat Anifa easily by 6 lengths; ran creditably on his next 3 outings, when fourth to Three Troikas in Prix d'Harcourt at Longchamp in April and to Argument in Grand Prix Prince Rose at Ostend in July and when fifth to Armistice Day in Prix Gontaut-Biron at Deauville in August; effective at 1¼m and stays well; acts on heavy going; trained by F. Mathet until after second outing. *E. Chevalier du Fau, France.* **118**

KAMENCHA (CHI) 6 br.m. Kamen–Chanal (Azul Celeste) (1979 ? 1980 7fg 8fg 8g 9fg 8.3fg 8g^4) Chilean-bred mare; winner of 7 of her 8 races (at distances up to 7f) in native country; looked well and was gambled on when fourth of 23 to Belle Vue in valuable seller at Doncaster in September, staying on strongly towards finish after failing to go early pace and giving impression she'll be well suited by 1¼m. *D. Kent.* **65**

KAMENEV 3 b.g. Ribero 126–Welsh Mistress 113 (Abernant 142) (1979 7g 7fg 7fg^2 7d^3 1980 7fg^3 8g 8d) neat gelding; good mover; fairly useful at his best; below form in 1980; should stay 1m; best form on a firm surface; sold to D. Chapman 1,200 gns Doncaster September Sales. *R. Price.* —

KAMPALA 4 br.c. Kalamoun 129–State Pension 112 (Only for Life 126) (1979 8.2s* 8d^3 7d* 7.6d* 8.2s^2 7fg 8fg 7h^2 7d* 1980 6v* 7fg* 6f 6g 7d^2 7fg* 7.3d* 6g^2 6fg) **120**

At the end of Kampala's three-year-old days we expressed the opinion that he would be extremely well suited by a mile and a quarter. He had already won over a mile in testing conditions and had stayed on well when gaining his most important success in the seven-furlong City of York Stakes at York; and he was, after all, bred to be suited by middle distances. His sire had won the Prix

Lupin; his dam State Pension, second to Lupe in the 1970 Oaks, had already bred the good staying two-year-old State Occasion (by Roan Rocket) and the stayers Millionaire and Mill Street (both by Mill Reef). However, it was evident when Kampala reappeared in the six-furlong Unicheq Sprint Handicap at Salisbury in March that his trainer had other ideas, and in cruising home four lengths clear of Smoke Singer, Kampala virtually ensured that our opinion of his stamina wouldn't be put to the test. The longest distance he was raced over in his remaining eight starts was the seven furlongs and sixty yards of the Hungerford Stakes.

Kampala (br.c. 1976)	Kalamoun (gr 1970)	Zeddaan (gr 1965)	Grey Sovereign
			Vareta
		Khairunissa (gr 1960)	Prince Bio
			Palariva
	State Pension (b 1967)	Only for Life (b 1960)	Chanteur II
			Life Sentence
		Lorelei (b 1950)	Prince Chevalier
			Rock Goddess

Kampala continued to do really well after Salisbury although there's no doubt that he found six furlongs very much on the sharp side when the ground rode fast. He won three more good prizes, the Autobar Victoria Cup at Ascot in April, the Beeswing Stakes at Newcastle in July and the Hungerford Stakes at Newbury in August, gaining his first pattern-race success in the last-named event. At both Ascot and Newcastle, Kampala had stirring battles with Blue Refrain who won the Queen Anne Stakes at Royal Ascot in between. Kampala won by a neck in the Victoria Cup when receiving 2 lb and by half a length in the Beeswing Stakes when receiving 4 lb; the very useful Irish-trained three-year-old Muscovite was a soundly-beaten third in the latter event. In the Hungerford Stakes, Kampala was ideally suited by the conditions and had only seven opponents in a race postponed a day because of a waterlogged track. He started a short-priced favourite, with the three-year-old Hard Fought and the 1979 winner Skyliner his closest rivals in the betting, and he always looked like justifying his market position. Looking as well as ever, he was jumped straight out into the lead and for the first time he made all the running. He quickened impressively at the distance, getting so much on top that his jockey was able to drop his hands nearly fifty yards from the post. Neither Hard Fought, who finished third, nor Skyliner ever got in a serious challenge; it was the filly Missed Blessing who chased Kampala home, beaten three quarters of a length.

Kampala's two subsequent outings were over six furlongs; he ran by far his better race over the distance on the easier surface in the Vernons Sprint Cup at Haydock in September. He couldn't match Moorestyle's exceptional pace on that occasion, but he ran his usual game race and mastered the Hungerford fourth King of Spain close home to take second, two and a half lengths behind Moorestyle. On faster ground in the Diadem Stakes at Ascot later in the month

Hungerford Stakes, Newbury—Kampala makes all the running and wins from Missed Blessing (breastplate), Hard Fought (left) and King of Spain (blinkers)

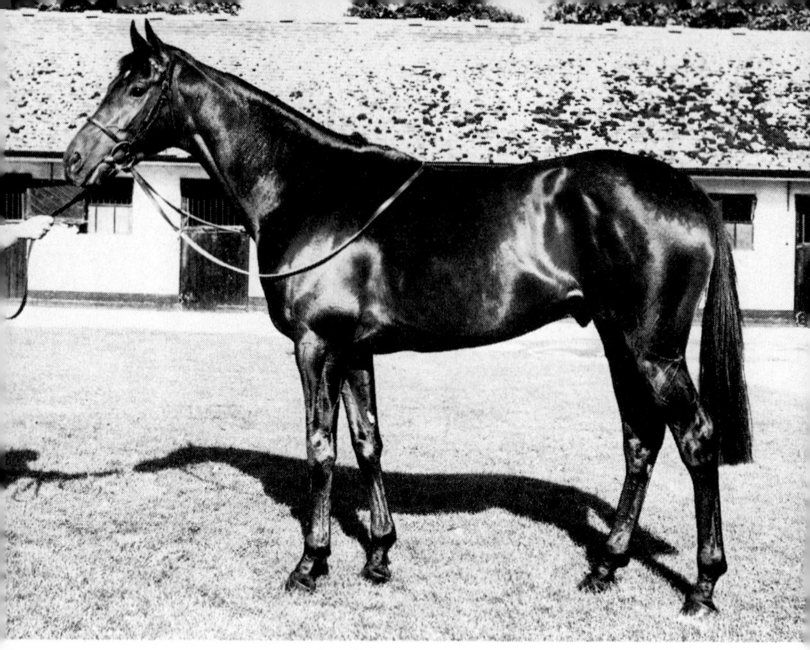

Mrs D. McCalmont's "Kampala"

he was outpaced all of the way—just as he had been earlier in the season over six in the Duke of York Stakes and the Cork and Orrery Stakes—and he finished a well-beaten seventh of nine behind Sovereign Rose.

Kampala takes up stallion duties in 1981 at the Rathbarry Stud, County Cork, at a fee of IR£2,200 with the live foal concession, and he begins his new career with the credentials to do well. An attractive, medium-sized colt who invariably impressed us with his well-being on the racecourse, Kampala has a pedigree to match his racing ability. His sire Kalamoun, a great success at stud, but now unfortunately dead, was also represented in 1980 by such as Castle Keep, Kalaglow and Shakapour. Kampala's dam State Pension, besides being a classic-placed mare, is from an excellent family and is half-sister to numerous winners including the good-class milers Honeymoor and Xerxes. *P. Walwyn.*

KANCHENJUNGA 2 b.f. Hotfoot 126–Climbing Rose 81 (Pirate King 129) **72** (1980 7fg 7fg 7g) Feb 4; smallish, well-made, attractive filly; half-sister to several winners, including smart 3-y-o Saint Jonathon (by Welsh Saint) and useful 6f to 1m winner Rocket Symphony (by Roan Rocket); dam 2-y-o 5f winner; showed some ability in large fields of maidens at Yarmouth in the summer on last 2 outings; will stay 1m. *F. Durr.*

KANDOSMAN 3 b. or br.g. Sweet Revenge 129–Rotondo (Royal Buck) **81** (1979 5.8s 5fg 1980 8v* 7v 10fg 12f* 13.5g 12s) 4,200F, 7,600Y; workmanlike gelding; won maiden race at Phoenix Park in March and handicap at Mallow in May; well beaten in Salisbury 2,000 Guineas Trial on second start; stays 1½m; acts on any going. *M. Kauntze, Ireland.*

KANGAROO ISLAND 2 gr.f. Murrayfield 119–Charter Island 88 (Runnymede — 123) (1980 6g) Feb 6; small, lightly-made filly; sister to very useful Watership Down, a winner at up to 1m in France; dam stayed 7f well; unquoted, broke smartly and showed speed for a long way before finishing in the mid-division behind stable-companion Composer in 25-runner maiden event at Newmarket in October. *W. Hastings-Bass.*

KARAJINSKA (USA) 2 b.f. Nijinsky 138–Karelina 115 (Sea-Bird II 145) – p
(1980 6d) Feb 20; big, rangy filly; good mover; second foal; half-sister to 3-y-o Karelia (by Sir Ivor), a very useful performer at up to $1\frac{1}{4}$m; dam won twice over $1\frac{1}{2}$m and is half-sister to high-class American sprinter Full Out; 20/1, with leaders to halfway when behind in 25-runner maiden race won by Little Wolf at Newbury in October; the type to do much better over middle distances at 3 yrs. *H. Candy.*

KARAMAZOV 4 b.g. High Top 131–Over The Water II (Doutelle 128) (1979 –
8g 1980 12f 10fg) probably of little account. *C. Crossley.*

KARAMITA 3 b.f. Shantung 132–Shahinaaz (Venture VII 129) (1979 NR **119**
1980 10f* 12d^2 10g* 10fg* 10g^2 10fg^2 12d*)

Being wise after the event, it has to be said that Karamita was one of the bets of the season in the valuable Extel Handicap at Goodwood in August. Carrying bottom weight after winning two of her three previous outings, a maiden race at Lingfield and a handicap at Newbury where she beat Bezique a length and a half, Karamita received at least 6 lb from her nine rivals and 21 lb from the top weights Lafontaine and Stanislavsky. Starting at 5/1, she made hacks of the opposition, travelling very easily throughout, fairly sprinting past Stanislavsky once shaken up around the distance and coming home a six-length winner. Karamita never ran in a handicap again. The Virginia Stakes at Newcastle saw her meeting all the other runners on unfavourable terms, and a concession of 6 lb to the Irish-trained Little Bonny would almost certainly have represented an impossible task for any English middle-distance filly in August. Karamita ran creditably to go down by four lengths to Little Bonny, finishing ahead of a couple of very useful fillies. In the Sean Graham Fillies Stakes at Kempton in September Karamita, giving weight all round, entered the straight in fourth place and didn't accelerate so quickly as anticipated when Dancing Shadow kicked on two furlongs out; she eventually began to run on strongly but was a neck behind at the post.

Karamita's running suggested she might be suited by a return to a mile and a half, the distance of the Princess Royal Stakes at Ascot. This race comes too late in the season for many of the best fillies and the quality of its fields varies a fair amount from year to year; in 1980 the most notable contestants apart from Karamita appeared to be Kahaila, the improving Broomstick Corner and two from the Dunlop stable, Astonished and the disappointing Bonnie Isle. Karamita looked remarkably well for a filly at this time of the year and her performance matched her appearance. Waited with as usual, she was pulled out approaching the final furlong and this time quickened in excellent style, soon going clear to account for Bonnie Isle very comfortably by three lengths. This success, following Nasseem's in the Cherry Hinton Stakes, gave the Aga Khan his second winner of a pattern race from his English-trained horses since he began patronizing English stables once again in 1979.

Karamita will probably be at stud in 1981. Her sire Shantung has made a reputation as a sire of good fillies, numbering La Bamba, Lacquer, Full Dress II, Saraca and Ginevra among his progeny. The dam, Shahinaaz, was very useful in France as a three-year-old, winning at a mile and thirteen furlongs

Extel Stakes, Goodwood—Karamita runs right away from Stanislavsky

H. H. Aga Khan's "Karamita" (J. Reid)

and finishing second in the Prix de Royallieu. Karamita is her fifth foal to win; best of the others were the smart middle-distance colt Kalidar (by Vienna) and the filly Khalida (by Tanerko), who showed useful form at up to thirteen furlongs. Shahinaaz is a half-sister to a French middle-distance winner, out of the useful Cherry who ran second in the Irish Oaks and gave the impression

Karamita (b.f. 1977)	Shantung (b 1956)	Sicambre (br 1948)	Prince Bio
			Sif
		Barley Corn (b 1950)	Hyperion
			Schiaparelli
	Shahinaaz (b 1965)	Venture VII (br 1957)	Relic
			Rose O'Lynn
		Cherry (b 1959)	Prince Bio
			Baghicheh

that she would have stayed well had she been given the chance. The third dam, Baghicheh, was placed in the Poule d'Essai des Pouliches and the Prix de Diane and came from the same family as Crepuscule, dam of Honeylight, Crepello and Twilight Alley. This is fairly stout breeding and Karamita may well have stayed beyond one and a half miles. A lengthy filly who wasn't a good mover in her slower paces, Karamita appeared to act on any going; she had a good turn of foot and was game and consistent. *M. Stoute.*

KAREEM 2 b.c. Northfields–Red Val 101 (Red God 128 §) (1980 5f* 6g 6d* 7d 7.2g* 7g) Mar 17; 25,000Y; neat, attractive colt; second foal; half-brother to useful 7f and 1m winner Carpet General (by Sallust); dam stayed 1½m; successful in maiden race at Chester in May and nurseries at Lingfield in July and Haydock in September; beat Heavenly Chord convincingly by a length when giving weight to his 9 rivals in last-named; will stay 1m; has won on firm going but has shown better form on an easy surface. *P. Walwyn.* **99**

KARELIA (USA) 3 b.f. Sir Ivor 135–Karelina 115 (Sea-Bird II 145) (1979 NR 1980 8g* 8g* 12f 12.5d³) $290,000Y; most attractive ex-English filly; first foal; dam won twice over 1½m and is half-sister to high-class American sprinter Full **111**

Out; favourite, won maiden race at Newbury (odds on) and 10-runner minor event at Sandown in the summer, making all to beat Intinto by 10 lengths in latter (outstanding in paddock); ran creditably in better company afterwards, being prominent until over 1f out when tenth of 12 to Mrs Penny in Prix Vermeille at Longchamp in September and keeping on well in straight to be 2¾ lengths third to Mariella in Prix de Royallieu on same course in October; stays 1½m well; possibly suited by some give in the ground; trained by R. Hern first 3 starts. *J. Cunnington jnr., France.*

KAREN'S STAR 3 b.g. Aglojo 119–Colate 59 (Como 120) (1979 5s 6d^2 5f 5g^2 **74**
5d^4 5d* 5f* 5fg* 5g^2 5g^2 1980 5g 5f* 5f 5g 6g 5fg^4 5f 6g^3) lightly-made gelding; bad mover; quite a moderate handicapper; gained his third success on course at Wolverhampton in May; ran creditably in apprentice race final outing (would have won with stronger handling); stays 6f; suited by top-of-the-ground; blinkered seventh start; sweated up fourth outing; ridden by apprentice A. Nesbitt when successful. *J. Doyle.*

KARIMA 2 ch.f. Song 132–Impregnable 66 (Never Say Die 137) (1980 5fg^4 6g^3 **79 ?**
6g^4) May 6; 3,100F; tall, unfurnished filly; half-sister to a winner in Norway; dam won over 1½m; in frame in maiden races, on last occasion beaten 4 lengths when fourth to Pieta at Brighton in August; will stay 7f. *N. Gaselee.*

KARIPIA 2 ch.f. Sharpen Up 127–Kalopia 80 (Kalydon 122) (1980 5fg) Jan **—**
20; 10,500Y; sister to 5f and 1m winner Cutler, and half-sister to a winner; dam won over 1¼m; 25/1 for 16-runner maiden race at Newmarket in May, picked up ground steadily in final furlong, without being knocked about unnecessarily, to finish 8¾ lengths fifth of 16 to Pushy; will stay 1m; looked promising here but wasn't seen out afterwards. *J. Winter.*

KARLINSKY (USA) 3 b.c. Rheingold 137–Sea Pay 64 (Sea-Bird II 145) (1979 **89**
7f 7fg* 8g* 1980 12fg 12fg^2 16fg 12g^4 12d) well-made, attractive colt; fair handicapper; stays 1½m but not 2m; acts on a firm surface and ran badly on soft final start; sold 1,500 gns Newmarket Autumn Sales. *H. Cecil.*

KARMINSKI 2 b.f. Pitskelly 122–Autumn Ballad 75 (Tudor Melody 129) (1980 **62**
7d 7g 8fg) Mar 1; well-grown filly; second foal; dam second twice over 6f; showed only a little ability in maiden company. *C. Brittain.*

KARRENE 6 b.m. Badedas 81–June Clare (Fairwell) (1979 NR 1980 8g 11.7f) **—**
neat, lightly-made mare; sister to winning plater Sadedab; dam of little account; well behind in maiden races at Beverley (started slowly) and Bath in July. *J. Edmunds.*

KARYOBINGA 2 b.f. So Blessed 130–Pine Ridge Gal (Arturo A) (1980 7f 8d 7g) **66**
Apr 12; 4,600F, 8,200Y; quite attractive filly; third foal; dam won 7 of her 73 races at up to 1m in USA; behind in maiden races at Chepstow in August and Warwick (missed break) and Newmarket (blinkered) in October; should stay 1m. *P. Makin.*

KASCINA 3 b.f. Midsummer Night II 117–Tavaro (Gustav 121) (1979 5d 5d 7g **—**
8f 7fg^4 1980 10.8s 12f 6fg 6g 8fg 8.3d) well-made filly; only plating class on balance of form; should stay beyond 1m; acts on firm going and is possibly unsuited by soft; blinkered fourth start. *H. O'Neill.*

KASHILL 2 b.c. Gulf Pearl 117–Wolver Hill (Wolver Hollow 126) (1980 7fg 8d) **—**
Apr 16; 2,300Y; strong, compact colt; first foal; dam won 2m bumpers race; last in maiden race at Warwick in July and minor event at Leicester in October. *H. O'Neill.*

KASHMIR BLUE 3 br.c. Blue Cashmere 129–Gay Donna (Tudor Jinks 121) **86**
(1979 5f 5.1g^3 6f^2 7fg^2 7g 7g* 7f^3 1980 6fg 6d^4 8.3d 8.2g^2 7g^3 8fg* 8fg^2) tall, lightly-made colt; fairly useful handicapper; beat Yorkshire Dancer 1½ lengths at Yarmouth in August; stays 1m; suited by a sound surface. *M. Stoute.*

KASHMIR LASS 3 ch.f. Kashmir II 125–Milly Moss 112 (Crepello 136) (1979 **118**
7g* 8f* 6s* 1980 10fg^4 8fg^3 8fg 8g* 10fg^3 10f^2) small, rather lightly-made filly; good mover; third foal; half-sister to 1978 2-y-o 7f winner Milly Lass (by Bold Lad USA); dam won Cheshire Oaks and is sister to Mil's Bomb; put up a smart display in Sun Chariot Stakes at Newmarket in October on final start, making running and keeping on well once challenged to be 1½ lengths second to Snow; had earlier raced alone on stand side to beat Africanos 3 lengths in handicap at Redcar in July and run respectably to be in frame in 3 races at Kempton, namely Lupe Stakes (fourth to Vielle), £7,100 event (2½ lengths third to Stumped) and Sean Graham Fillies Stakes (2¾ lengths third behind Dancing Shadow); stays 1¼m; acts on any going; takes a good hold. *H. Cecil.*

KASLAND 3 b.c. Shiny Tenth 120–Smokey's Sister (Forlorn River 124) (1979 **67**
5d 5d 6fg^3 7f^3 7fg^3 7s 1980 7fg^3 8.5g 7g^3 10g 10fg 8fg 8.2s 10g) fair sort; third in maiden race and handicap at Edinburgh; stays 7f (well beaten over further); acts on a firm surface. *H. O'Neill.*

KASSAK 4 gr.g. Dragonara Palace 115–Dauphiness 74 (Supreme Sovereign 119) **70**
(1979 5d 5s 6d 5d 5d^2 5.8g 5s^2 6fg^3 6fg 5g^3 7fg 1980 8g 7f 6g^4 5.8g 5v^3) leggy gelding; ran best races when in frame in handicaps at Goodwood in September and Doncaster (third to Covergirls Choice) in November; stays 6f; acts on any going; has worn blinkers but probably does as well without; has run well for an amateur rider; inconsistent. *H. O'Neill.*

KASSAMOTO 4 gr.g. My Swanee 122–Klondyke Fire (Klondyke Bill 125) **54**
(1979 7v 6f 5f 6d 8f 8.2g* 1980 7fg^2 8fg 7f 7fg 10d^3 10d^4 12fg 12fg 12fg^3) workmanlike sort; ran creditably in varied company, including selling; seems to stay 1½m; probably acts on any going; blinkered fifth start at 3 yrs; trained until after eighth outing by P. Makin; sent to Malaya. *J. Powney.*

KATE BUSH 3 ch.f. Goldhill 125–Sing High 85 (Sound Track 132) (1979 –
6g 7fg 7g 6d 1980 8s 8g) leggy, unfurnished filly; behind in maiden races. *K. Stone.*

KATHIES LAD 3 br.g. Forlorn River 124–Rollicking Rachael (Will Somers –
114§) (1979 NR 1980 6f 8fg) leggy, unfurnished gelding; second foal; dam never ran; in rear in maiden races at Newmarket in April and Yarmouth in July. *W. Stephenson.*

KATHRED 2 b.f. Starch Reduced 112–Kathy King (Space King 115) (1980 **79**
5g 6g^3 5g^2 6f* 6d) Feb 4; sister to a winner in Sweden; dam well beaten in maiden races; very useful in plating company and cost 5,200 gns to buy in after winning 18-runner seller at Newmarket in October in good style by 1½ lengths from Nun's Pride; took on better company next time out; stays 6f; acts on firm going. *R. Hollinshead.*

KATIE GREY 7 gr.m. Pongee 106–Spotless 89 (Tehran) (1979 NR 1980 –
8d^3 8fg) poor hurdler; lightly-raced maiden on flat (plating class); dwelt second outing. *W. Atkinson.*

KATMANDU 7 ch.g. Yellow God 129–Hunea (Hornbeam 130) (1979 NR –
1980 16.1s) quite a moderate stayer; acts on any going; has been tried in blinkers; sometimes wears bandages; quite a useful hurdler/chaser. *E. Carter.*

KATOWICE (FR) 4 gr.c. Targowice 130–Kaliopa (Zeddaan 130) (1979 7v^2 8d **115**
8g^2 8s^3 9d 8g 8fg 8d* 8d 8v^2 1980 8s 8g 8g^2 8g^3 7g 8d* 8s* 8g^3 8d^4) French colt; first foal; dam won twice at up to 1¼m; much improved in 1980 and ran race of his life when about 2 lengths third behind Kilijaro and Nadjar in Prix du Moulin at Longchamp in September; fourth to Hilal in Prix du Rond-Point on same course later in month; won handicaps at Longchamp and Saint-Cloud earlier, spreadeagling his 18 opponents and winning by 8 lengths from New Grandame on latter course in July; best at 1m; acts on heavy going; smart. *P. Biancone, France.*

KATUMBA 4 ch.g. Tower Walk 130–Independence 64 (Runnymede 123) **40**
(1979 6v 5d 9g 1980 8s 11fg 8f 8.3f^3 7fg 8g 8f 7fg* 7g 8.3f 8fg) plater; bought in 820 gns after scoring at Edinburgh in July; stays 1m; probably acts on any going. *D. Weeden.*

KATYANA 3 b.f. Reform 132–Greek Gift (Acropolis 132) (1979 8f 7fg^4 **56**
1980 10fg 12fg 10f^4 12g 10.1s^4 10.1d^3 10.1f 12g 10f 10fg^4 8g 14d) small, quite well-made filly; shows a lot of knee action; possibly stays 1½m; suited by some give in the ground; blinkered tenth start; dwelt and swerved left at start eighth outing; sold to D. Jermy 940 gns Newmarket Autumn Sales. *D. Whelan.*

KATY BELLE 3 br.f. Realm 129–Clear Belle (Klairon 131) (1979 5v 5g –
6f 6d 1980 6fg^4 6f 5f^2 5fg^4 5fg 5g^3 5.3d^3 5g 5.3fg 5g 5f 5s) well-made filly; poor handicapper; best form at 5f; acts on firm going; sold 4,300 gns Newmarket December Sales. *J. Benstead.*

KATY LIZ 2 b.f. Realm 129–Youee 66 (Buisson Ardent 129) (1980 5f 6fg –
5fg) Mar 14; 2,400Y; small, neat filly; bad plater; sold 400 gns Doncaster September Sales. *W. Wharton.*

KATYSUE 2 gr. or ro.f. King's Leap 111–Sweet Hostess (Candy Cane 125) **98**
(1980 5g^2 5f^2 6fg^2 5g* 5g* 5g^4 5fg* 5f* 5s*) Feb 23; 1,000F, 4,300Y; strong filly; good walker; second foal; dam never ran; had an excellent season, winning maiden race at Redcar, minor event and a nursery at Beverley, £5,100 nursery

Bloodstock and General Insurance Stakes Nursery Handicap, Newmarket—Katysue gets up to beat Brentex (No. 20)

at Newmarket in October and nursery at Haydock later in month; apprentice ridden at 3 lb overweight, came long way clear of stand-side group when beating Brentex ¾ length at Newmarket (scratched down to start); beat Water Of Life same margin at Haydock, almost losing her footing inside last furlong but being sufficiently on top at time to hold on nicely; best form at 5f but not disgraced over 6f; acts on any going; good mount for an apprentice; game, genuine and consistent. *W. Wharton.*

KEADEEN 3 b.g. Martinmas 128–Medaea 90 (Darius 129) (1979 5fg 5fg^2 5g 9.5g 7.5s^4 7s 1980 8g^4 8g 10d 8.2g 8g 9v* 10s) 15,000Y; sturdy ex-Irish gelding; won maiden race at Hamilton in October; should stay 1¼m; acts well on heavy going; blinkered fourth start. *J. Fitzgerald.* **68**

KEARNEY 3 b.c. Sandford Lad 133–Gilded Egg (Faberge II 121) (1979 5g^3 5s* 5fg^4 6g^3 7g 6.3d^3 6s* 1980 7s^4 6f^2 6fg 6g* 6d) compact, attractive Irish colt; second foal; dam won over 6f and 7f in Ireland; smart performer; 40/1, led below distance but was being caught towards finish when winning 20-runner Cork and Orrery Stakes at Royal Ascot by a neck from Sharpo; **120**

Cork and Orrery Stakes, Ascot—Kearney (left) beats Sharpo and Valeriga (rails). Flash N Thunder is fourth and Kampala fifth

well beaten in William Hill July Cup won by Moorestyle at Newmarket on his only subsequent start; ideally suited by 6f and some give in the ground. *W. Robinson, Ireland.*

KEELBY KAVALIER 2 b.c. Ardoon 124–Elegant Lady 69 (Round Table) 73
(1980 5fg 5s 7g^{3} 8f* 8fg^{3} 8fg^{2}) Mar 4; leggy colt; first foal; dam won over 1¼m in Ireland; won 8-runner nursery at Pontefract in September by ½ length from Hego's Hero; also placed in 3 sellers, wearing blinkers and starting favourite when going down by 1½ lengths to Cherry Corner at Redcar in October; will stay 1¼m; acts on firm going. *J. Etherington.*

KEEPS GOING RIGHT 3 b.c. Warpath 113–Sindo 91 (Derring-Do 131) 57
(1979 6fg^{4} 6s 8.2g 7f 6fg 1980 10v 9g 8f 6f 7.2g 8d^{4} 8d^{4} 8s^{4} 8g* 7fg^{3} 8fg^{2} 10g 9s 8fg^{2} 9f^{3} 8g 8.2s 8d^{2} 8d^{4} 10d) neat colt; plater; bought in 950 gns after winning at Leicester in July; stays 9f; probably acts on any going; sold 1,550 gns Doncaster October Sales. *R. Hollinshead.*

KELBOMEC (FR) 4 b.g. Direct Flight–Piqueuse (Piqu' arriere) (1979 10.5g^{3} 117
10fg 10g 13g* 15.5fg* 15g^{3} 1980 15.5g^{3} 15.5g^{3} 16.5fg 15s* 15g^{2} 13.5g 20d^{3} 12g*) French gelding; floored odds-on Soleil Noir by ½ length in Prix du Carrousel at Longchamp in June; ran best subsequent races when neck second to Marson in Prix Kergorlay at Deauville in August, 2 lengths third behind Anifa and Le Moss in Prix Gladiateur at Longchamp in September and head second to Proustille in Grand Prix de Nantes (promoted to first) in November; stays very well; probably acts on any going. *J. C. Cunnington, France.*

KELLET LANE 2 ch.f. Sandford Lad 133–Paduila (St Paddy 133) (1980 6d –
8fg) Feb 3; 1,300F, 2,000Y (privately); first produce; dam ran once in Italy; in rear in minor event at Ripon in August and seller at Carlisle in September; slowly away when blinkered first start; sold 370 gns Doncaster October Sales. *K. Stone.*

KELLORD 3 b.g. Lord Gayle 124–Flo Kelly (Florescence 120) (1979 5d 5g* 88
5d* 6g 6h^{2} 7d 1980 8v 7f^{3} 8h^{3} 7fg^{4} 7d*) neat gelding; fairly useful handicapper; dead-heated with Sipapu at Salisbury in June; stays 1m; probably acts on any going; exported to Hong Kong. *B. Hills.*

KELLY'S REP 3 bl. or br.c. Netherkelly 112–Cammy 75 (Sing Sing 134) (1979 –
8fg 1980 7s 12f 8g 10g 10.6d 12fg 13g 11d^{4} 10s 8d) compact, fair sort; plater; not certain to stay 1½m; sold 1,200 gns Doncaster November Sales. *R. Hollinshead.*

KELPIE 2 b.f. Import 127–River Moy (Niagara Falls 104) (1980 6g) Apr 16; –
well-grown, unfurnished filly; half-sister to 3 winners, including fair 6f winner Moybrook (by The Brianstan); dam chaser; 25/1, slowly into stride when remote ninth of 12 behind Ring of Quality in minor event at Carlisle in July; withdrawn at start next time out. *W. Haigh.*

KENMURRAY 2 gr.c. Dragonara Palace 115–Farida Jinks 106 (Tudor Jinks 72
121) (1980 5fg 5f^{3} 6f^{3} 7g^{4} 7g 7d) Mar 20; 4,700F, 6,000Y; strong, good-bodied colt; half-brother to several winners, including useful 5f performers Faridina (by Sky Gipsy) and Faridetta (by Good Bond); dam 5f sprinter; third in minor event at Bath in May (5½ lengths behind Horncastle) and £3,800 race at Epsom in June (beaten 4½ lengths by Poldhu); yet to show he stays 7f; off course over 2 months before final start (finished last, wearing blinkers); sold 1,700 gns Ascot November Sales. *G. Hunter.*

KENNY O'REILLY 2 b.c. Patch 129–Gracie Square 75 (Nelcius 133) (1980 71
5fg 6g 6g 7s 8d) Feb 17; neat colt; third foal; half-brother to a winning plater; dam middle-distance winner; prominent in maiden and minor events in Ireland when trained by L. Browne on first 3 outings, on third finishing 6 lengths sixth of 22 to Manaldo at Navan in September; always behind in minor event at Chepstow the following month and in maiden race at Leicester in November; bred to stay 1½m. *M. Blanshard.*

KENO HILL 5 b.g. Yukon Eric–Rock Me (Rockefella) (1979 NR 1980 –
10s 10g) of little account. *A. Davison.*

KENT'S PRIDE 2 gr.c. Runnymede 123–Monumental Moment 91 (St Paddy 65
133) (1980 5h 5fg 5fg 6fg 5f^{4} 5g^{4} 5f 5d* 5s 5s 5s) May 20; 1,050Y; small colt; moderate plater; apprentice ridden, made all under 7-2 to win nursery at Edinburgh in September by ½ length from Great Auk; had much stiffer tasks afterwards; form only at 5f; well suited by a soft surface. *S. Nesbitt.*

KENTUCKY 2 b.f. Warpath 113–Shenandoah 88 (Mossborough 126) (1980 – p
7g) May 25; well-made, useful-looking filly; good walker; third foal; sister to 1½m seller winner Rolling River; dam won over 14.7f, and is half-sister to very

useful Sovereign Edition; 20/1 when remote ninth of 14 to Golden Bowl in 14-runner minor event at York in October, being given a very easy time of it after having got well behind early on; has scope and should do better over middle distances in 1981. *C. Thornton.*

KEOLMORE 3 b.f. Ballymore 123–Rising Lark (Ballymoss 136) (1979 NR 1980 12g 13.3fg 12d 16d^{2} 16s^{2} 16fg 16s^{2} 14.6d) lengthy filly; half-sister to fairly useful stayer Francesco (by Royal and Regal); dam unraced half-sister to St Leger and Irish Sweeps Derby second Meadowville; runner-up in maiden races in the summer; suited by a test of stamina; suited by soft ground; ran poorly final start; sold 10,000 gns Newmarket December Sales. *P. Cole.* **66**

KERERA 3 b.f. Keren 100–Tudera (Primera 131) (1979 NR 1980 12d) half-sister to winning hurdler; dam never ran; tailed-off last in 13-runner maiden race at Carlisle in July (backward). *N. Chamberlain.* –

KERRYSDALE 3 br.f. Home Guard 129–Orchy 77 (Aureole 132) (1979 NR 1980 7f 9f 12d) rangy, robust filly; first foal; dam suited by a test of stamina; behind in maiden and minor races; sold 1,000 gns Newmarket December Sales. *P. Walwyn.* –

KESHOON 2 b.f. Sheshoon 132–Matt's Colleen 105 (Epaulette 125) (1980 8g 8d) Mar 5; 3,100Y; compact filly; half-sister to 3 winners abroad; dam won over 5f and 6f; in rear in minor event at Goodwood in September and maiden race at Bath in October. *D. Kent.* –

KEVIN KEEGAN (USA) 3 br.g. Big Spruce–Wageko (Jaipur) (1979 5d 6s 7fg* 7g^{2} 6g^{3} 7.3g 1980 8fg 10fg^{3} 11.7f 12fg^{4} 16s) big, well-made gelding; quite a moderate handicapper; stays 1¼m (well beaten over further); acts on a firm surface; blinkered last 2 outings at 2 yrs. *R. Smyth.* **70**

KEYNSHAM 5 b.g. Shiny Tenth 120–Humdinger 89 (Sammy Davis 129) (1979 7s 7fg 7.6f 1980 7h) leggy gelding; stays 1¼m; acts on a firm and a soft surface. *D. Marks.* –

KHAKI KATE 4 ch.f. Brigadier Gerard 144–Orapa 99 (Aureole 132) (1979 10d^{4} 12f^{2} 12f^{2} 12g^{3} 12d^{3} 1980 10.2d 12.3s^{4} 12fg^{2} 12.5h* 12fg 15f 11fg* 12f* 12g* 12f*) rangy filly; had an excellent season, winning maiden race at Stockton and handicaps at Redcar, Lingfield, Leicester and Beverley; led in final furlong when beating Another Move by 2 lengths going away on last-named course in August on final outing; probably stays 15f; acts on hard going; blinkered fourth to sixth outings; needs to be held up; sold 25,000 gns Newmarket December Sales. *H. Wragg.* **81**

KHALEEL 2 br.c. Lochnager 132–Vital Error 105 (Javelot 124) (1980 5d^{3} 5fg) Feb 26; 11,000Y; small, compact, good-topped colt; half-brother to numerous winners, including useful French middle-distance performer Major Busted (by Busted); dam best at up to 7f; 33/1 and very burly, nearest at finish when 4 lengths third of 13 to Supper's Ready in maiden race at Windsor in July; didn't fulfil promise of that run in similar race at Newcastle a week later, finishing last but one behind Chumwar; will stay 6f; possibly unsuited by a firm surface. *R. Boss.* **71**

KHEDIVE 3 b.c. Habat 127–Klairessa 88 (Klairon 131) (1979 5d* 5d 1980 6fg^{2} 6fg 5g* 6fg 6d^{2} 6s^{3} 6s) lengthy, attractive colt; won £3,800 event at Sandown in June by 2 lengths from Pert Lad; placed in handicaps afterwards, going down by 1½ lengths to Sovereign Rose at Newmarket in July and finishing 7½ lengths third to Flower in Northumberland Sprint Trophy at Newcastle in August; stays 6f; probably acts on any going; sold to D. Whelan 6,000 gns Newmarket Autumn Sales. *P. Walwyn.* **94**

KIBCOY 3 b.g. Kibenka 119–Coya 57 (Lauso) (1979 5s 6g 7fg 1980 12f 12fg) leggy, lengthy gelding; in rear in varied company. *W. Stephenson.* –

KIBER TRIX 2 br.g. Kibenka 119–Loose Trix 65 (Lauso) (1980 5s 7fg) Apr 30; leggy, narrow, unfurnished gelding; first reported living foal; dam 2-y-o 5f seller winner; never-dangerous sixth of 11 to Rollin Hand in maiden race at Leicester in March; in rear in another maiden race at Leicester 6 months later; trained by W. Stephenson first outing. *A. Jarvis.* –

KILBURN BOY 5 gr.h. No Mercy 126–Ruritania (Pampered King 121) (1979 6v^{2} 5s 6d 5g 5d 5f 5fg^{4} 5f 5h^{3} 6g 5d 1980 9g 8g) sprint plater; acts on any going; inconsistent; blinkered in 1979. *W. Haigh.* –

KILCOY CASTLE 2 b.g. On Your Mark 125–Primed (Primera 131) (1980 5s 5f 5fg 6d) Feb 18; 4,000F, 5,000Y; workmanlike gelding; seems of little account. *P. Rohan.* –

Prix de Meautry, Deauville—one of Kilijaro's many fine performances, beating Northjet five lengths. English challenger Standaan is third

KILDANES 3 b.c. Jimmy Reppin 131–Kermene 89 (Persian Gulf) (1979 6f 6g^4 7fg 1980 7s 10g^2 10.6f^3 11.7g* 12s^3 12d^3 11.7g 12g 10fg^2 12g) robust colt; won handicap at Windsor in June; suited by 1½m; acts on any going. *H. T. Jones.* **78**

KILIJARO 4 br.f. African Sky 124–Manfilia 95 (Mandamus 120) (1979 7s 8v 5fg 6f^3 5d 5d^2 7s^2 1980 7g* 5fg 7d^2 8g 7s^4 6.5d^3 6d* 8g* 8g* 6d* 7v^3 10fg*) **126**

Kilijaro, undoubtedly the best two-year-old filly in Ireland in 1978 (she was beaten only very narrowly in the William Hill Cheveley Park Stakes and the Queen Mary Stakes don't forget), went through her second season without a win and was offered for sale in France on the eve of the 1979 Prix de l'Arc de Triomphe. Kilijaro's owner must have been delighted when she realised top price of the day, knocked down for approximately £200,000, almost fifty times the sum she cost as a yearling. Her new owner has had no cause for regret, though. Less than twenty-four hours after the sale Kilijaro went a considerable way to justifying the confidence placed in her, failing by only a short head to cause an upset in the Prix de l'Abbaye behind Double Form. As a four-year-old Kilijaro emphasised time and again what a good buy she was: she enjoyed a memorable season, winning six races at distances ranging from six furlongs to a mile and a quarter worth more than £130,000.

Kilijaro (br.f. 1976)	African Sky (b 1970)	Sing Sing (b 1957)	Tudor Minstrel
			Agin the Law
		Sweet Caroline (b 1954)	Nimbus
			Lackaday
	Manfilia (b 1968)	Mandamus (br 1960)	Petition
			Great Fun
		Spare Filly (b 1961)	Beau Sabreur
			La Pucelle

Although she took a minor event over seven furlongs at Evry in April on her reappearance (where conditions favoured her greatly) Kilijaro didn't hit top form until the summer. At Deauville early in August she gave clear indications that a return to her best was imminent when finishing a very close third to Boitron and Moorestyle in the Prix Maurice de Gheest. Just over a fortnight later Kilijaro began a remarkable winning run that brought her four big races inside five weeks, the Prix de Meautry and the Prix Quincey at Deauville, the Prix du Moulin at Longchamp and the Prix de Seine-et-Oise at Maisons-Laffitte. In the Meautry, over six furlongs, she hacked up by five lengths from Northjet; stepping up in distance to a mile in the Prix Quincey she beat Tassmoun comfortably by three lengths. The Prix du Moulin though, one of the most

M S. Fradkoff's "Kilijaro"

important mile events in the Calendar, wasn't gained without a struggle. Nadjar, successful previously in the Prix d'Ispahan and the Prix Jacques le Marois, made her fight and it was only close home that Kilijaro, very hard ridden, got up by a neck. It must be said that in the absence of Kris, Posse, Known Fact and Nureyev the Moulin wasn't so competitive a race as it might have been or as it usually is.

Kilijaro's run was halted in the Prix de la Foret over seven furlongs at Longchamp in October when she had another attempt at beating Moorestyle, opposing him this time on terms considerably worse than in the Maurice de Gheest. Not surprisingly Moorestyle had far too many guns for her but nevertheless she ran creditably to finish third, one and a half lengths behind him. Kilijaro's powers of endurance were put fully to the test on her next start. Just two weeks after a hard race in the mud in the Foret she lined up for the Yellow Ribbon Stakes at Santa Anita. In spite of a busy season, a long journey across

Prix du Moulin de Longchamp—Kilijaro is a game winner from Nadjar

to the States with little time to acclimatise, and a jump up to a mile and a quarter, a new distance for her, Kilijaro managed to produce a spectacular performance, sprinting clean away in the closing stages to win by three and a quarter lengths from Ack's Secret.

It's not altogether surprising that Kilijaro stays a mile and a quarter looking at her breeding, although it is unusual for a racehorse to be so versatile. Her dam Manfilia won over the distance and her grandam, Spare Filly, stayed well. Moreover Kilijaro's older full brother African Hope is a smart middle-distance stayer in France. Manfilia's last two foals have sold very much better than either Kilijaro or African Hope did as yearlings. Noble Monk (also by African Sky) a winner over six furlongs in Ireland in 1980, was bought for 42,000 guineas at the 1979 Ballsbridge Yearling Sales, and at the most recent Goff's Select Yearling Sales her colt by Malinowski was sold to Barry Hills for 115,000 guineas. Kilijaro acts on any going and invariably wears blinkers. Her picture, taken late in the season, doesn't do her justice: at her best she's a useful-looking filly. *O. Douieb, France.*

KILLER SHARK 5 b.g. Tyrant–Aquaria (Double-U-Jay 120) (1979 10d 10g 10g^{2} 11s 1980 10s) well-made gelding; best form at 1¼m on soft ground, although has won on a firm surface; sometimes blinkered; broke blood vessel and slipped up 5f out on only outing of 1980. *G. Pritchard-Gordon* —

KILMARK 3 br.c. No Mercy 126–Celebrate 85 (Rockavon 120) (1979 5s 5s 6d 7f^{2} 7g^{2} 7g^{2} 7g^{2} 7.2g^{4} 8.2s 7d 1980 8.2g 8.2f^{4} 8.2d 8g 7g 8g) narrow colt; second in seller and 3 nurseries at 2 yrs; well beaten in 1980; should stay 1m; needs a sound surface; blinkered last 2 starts, running poorly on first occasion. *A. Jarvis.* —

KILROYALE 3 b.f. Rheingold 137–Witch of Endor 80 (Matador 131) (1979 6f^{3} 7d^{2} 6g* 5f 6g* 1980 7f 6f 7fg 7g 10g^{4} 10.8fg^{3} 10g 10s) small filly; fairly useful (rated 90) in 1979; didn't find her form in varied company at 3 yrs; possibly stays 1¼m; suited by some give in the ground; has run respectably for a claimer; ran poorly seventh start; sold 15,500 gns Newmarket December Sales. *L. Cumani.* —

KILROY HAWK (USA) 4 ch.c. Groshawk–Eastern Tale (Nasrullah) (1979 9fg^{4} 12fg 1980 10f 8g 8g 8g^{4} 10g* 12fg^{4} 10.2g* 10fg) quite attractive, strong colt; held up, put up a game effort to win slowly-run valuable Holsten Pils Handicap at Doncaster in September by 1½ lengths from Tolstoy; had been successful at Newmarket the previous month; best form at 1¼m; acts on firm going and has yet to race on soft; ran poorly final start (didn't go to post well and was scrubbed along early on); sent to race in USA. *L. Cumani.* **96**

KIM MARCHELLE 2 ch.c. Jim French–Karonde (Aureole 132) (1980 6d 6s) May 15; 5,400Y; neat colt; third foal; dam French 1¼m winner; 25/1 when seventh to General Breyfax in 25-runner maiden race at Windsor in July, second outing. *R. Laing.* —

KINDLY THOUGHT 2 br.f. Record Token 128–Crab Apple (Nelcius 133) (1980 5d 5fg) Apr 3; compact filly; second foal; dam unraced daughter of very useful 1962 2-y-o Tzigane; showed early speed when in rear in maiden races at Salibury in June and Newmarket in August. *Mrs R. Lomax.* —

KIND OF HUSH 2 b.c. Welsh Pageant 132–Sauceboat 120 (Connaught 130) (1980 6fg^{4}) May 19; 37,000Y; well-made, quite attractive colt; first foal; dam, very smart performer, won over 6f at 2 yrs and stayed 1¼m; outsider of party and on backward side, close up until weakening at distance when 9 lengths last of 4 to Integrity in Rous Memorial Stakes at Goodwood in August; will stay at least 1m; looked promising here but wasn't seen out again. *B. Hills.* — p

KINDRED 4 b.g. Thatch 136–Merry Mate 109 (Ballymoss 136) (1979 12g^{4} 12fg^{2} 12g* 12f 1980 8f 12g 12g 11fg 11g 8f 12s 12.5s^{4}) big, deep-girthed ex-Irish gelding; won maiden race at Mallow in 1979 when trained by V. O'Brien; poor form in 1980 in amateur riders race and handicaps; runs as though he will stay further than 1½m. *Miss S. Hall.* **43**

KINGCOOMBE 3 br.g. Supreme Sovereign 119–Madam Clare 66 (Ennis 128) (1979 NR 1980 10.1s 8d) tall, rangy gelding; half-brother to several winners, including Prix de la Salamandre winner John de Coombe (by Moulton); dam won two 6f sellers; behind in minor event at Windsor and maiden race at Salisbury in the summer. *P. Cole.* —

KINGDOM PRIZE (USA) 3 b.f. Key To The Kingdom–Libbet Cloud (Noble Jay) (1979 5g 7fg 7g 1980 7.2d 10d 8s) neat filly; little worthwhile form in maiden and minor events; trained by P. Read first start. *A. Breasley.* —

KINGFAST 3 b.g. Hotfoot 126–Tudor Top 104 (Tudor Minstrel 144) (1979 5s 5v3 5d 5s4 7f 6d 6g 1980 6v 6f 5g 5f) poor plater; will stay 1m; sometimes sweats up. *W. C. Watts.* —

KING HAGEN 3 b.c. Mount Hagen 127–Sea Queen (Le Fabuleux 133) (1979 5g 6d 7f 7d* 8fg 7fg3 7d2 7s3 8g3 1980 12f 10f 9f4 12f3 12g 12.2f2 13.8f2 13.8g 12fg 13.8d 10d2) workmanlike colt; runner-up in handicaps, including in selling event on final outing (claimed £2,500); stays 1¾m; acts on any going; wears blinkers; ran poorly eighth and tenth starts, sweating up on first occasion. *Hbt Jones.* **71**

KING HUSTLER 3 b.g. Supreme Sovereign 119–B. S. R. 68 (March Past 124) (1979 NR 1980 10.8s* 12.3f 9.6f* 10.1g2 11fg* 12d3 10g) big, workmanlike gelding; half-brother to several winners, including useful miler Florintina (by Floribunda); dam stayed 1m; won maiden race at Warwick (made all) and handicaps at Folkestone and Edinburgh; probably doesn't stay 1½m; acts on any going. *P. Cole.* **87**

KING JAMES 3 b.c. English Prince 129–Mary of Scots 84 (Relic) (1979 8f* 7s* 1980 12fg 8fg 8d2 8fg*) strong, workmanlike colt; good mover; very useful handicapper; creditable second to Atlantic Boy in Northern Goldsmiths' Handicap at Newcastle prior to beating Majestic Star in good style in £4,000 race at Kempton in September; should stay beyond 1m (had stiff task, sweated up and fought for his head when tried at 1½m); acts on any going but is well suited by top-of-the-ground; sold only 2,600 gns Newmarket Autumn Sales. *R. Price.* **109**

KING JAMIE 6 b.g. King Emperor–Effervescence II (Charlottesville 135) (1979 10d3 10.1g 16fg 1980 9.6fg) poor plater nowadays; stays 1¼m; acts on heavy going; blinkered second outing 1979 season; sold 600 gns Ascot July Sales. *A. Neaves.* —

KING LOREN 2 ch.c. Lorenzaccio 130–Queen Anne's Lace 103 (Mossborough 126) (1980 7f 6fg 6fg 7g 8fg3 8d2) Apr 30; 2,700F; neat colt; half-brother to 2 winners, including stayer Philigree (by Moulton); dam fourth in 1965 Oaks; ran best races when placed in sellers at Leicester and Warwick in the autumn, going down by 2½ lengths to Orkney Annie when favourite for latter; will be suited by 1¼m+; acts on a firm and a soft surface; sold 350 gns Doncaster October Sales. *M. Blanshard.* **63**

KING OF ACCORDA 5 b.g. Sassafras 135–Kinnerton Street (Accordant) (1979 NR 1980 11.7fg) poor maiden; stays 1½m; wears blinkers. *J. Old.* —

KING OF ITHAKA 3 ch.g. Blue Cashmere 129–Maya 86 (Nearula 132) (1979 5fg 7f 1980 7fg 8d) big, lengthy gelding; poor form in maiden events and a claiming race; sold 310 gns Ascot July Sales. *C. Nelson.* —

KING OF SPAIN 4 br.c. Philip of Spain 126–Sovereign Sails 94 (Sovereign Path 125) (1979 7s 7g 8.2s 6g2 6s2 6g 6fg3 1980 6v 6fg* 6f 6fg2 5f2 6s4 7.3d4 6g3 6fg2 6s2) strong colt; smart handicapper; beat Fast Colour in good style by 3 lengths in £4,700 handicap at Kempton in May; improved afterwards and was good second 3 times at Ascot, to Queen's Pride in Wokingham Stakes in June, to Via Delta in £3,400 event in July and to Sovereign Rose in Diadem Stakes in September; spoilt his chance by hanging right in closing stages on 2 of those occasions, in Diadem being caught close home after looking all over a winner when taking lead inside last furlong; also placed in Vernons Sprint Cup at Haydock (good third to Moorestyle) and Coral Racing Champion Sprint at York (1½ lengths second to Runnett); stays 7f; acts on any going; wears blinkers nowadays. *P. Cundell.* **117**

KING OF STRESS 2 ch.g. Galivanter 131–Belmont Girl 74 (Gelert 93) (1980 8.2d 8.2s 8fg 8.2s) May 29; 300Y; workmanlike gelding; second foal; dam in frame over sprint distances at 2 yrs; plater; probably stays 1m. *K. Stone.* —

KING OF TARA 4 b.c. King's Company 124–Hibernia III 120 (Masetto) (1979 NR 1980 12d 6f) of no account. *W. Wright.* —

KING OF THE HILL 2 b.c. Derring-Do 131–Hillsquaw (Hillary) (1980 7f) Feb 28; 10,000Y; neat colt; third foal; half-brother to 1979 2-y-o 7f winner Nahane (by Porto Bello); dam won over 7f in USA; 50/1 and in need of race, didn't move well to start prior to finishing behind in 19-runner maiden race won by King's Glory at Newmarket in October. *N. Vigors.* —

KING OF TROY 8 b.h. King's Troop 118–Clytemnestra 81 (Bullrush 106) (1979 ran 16 times, including 4.7g 6g* 7s 8g 6f 6.5d2 6g 1980 including 6d 4.7g ?

6g[4] 8g[4] 8g 6s[3]) useful-looking horse; successful in Norway, Germany and Denmark since 1975; not disgraced in high-class company in 1979, notably when runner-up to Boitron in Prix Maurice de Gheest at Deauville; ran mainly in Norway in 1980, winning handicap at Ovrevoll in May and making frame several times; length third to Old Dominion in Taby International Sprinters Stakes at Taby in September; showed speed to past halfway when ninth of 14 behind Moorestyle in William Hill July Cup at Newmarket 2 months earlier; effective at sprint distances and stays 1m; acts on any going. *T. Dahl, Norway.*

KING'S AGAIN 3 b.g. The Brianstan 128–Repel (Hardicanute 130) (1979 5d 5s 5g 5g 6s 7fg 7fg 6g 6s 1980 8g 5s 5f 5g 5fg) neat gelding; poor plater; form only at 5f; sometimes wears blinkers; refused to race fifth outing in 1979; sold 350 gns Doncaster November Sales. *J. Leigh.* —

KING'S AIM (USA) 3 b. or br.c. Quack–Spicy Living (Gallant Man) (1979 NR 1980 10g 13s 11.7h 12d 12.5s[2]) robust, deep-girthed colt; half-brother to several unraced animals; dam, second-best 3-y-o filly in USA in 1963, is daughter of Nasrullah's speedy sister Rivaz; second in modest maiden race at Stockton in October; will stay 1¾m; acts on soft going. *P. Walwyn.* 57

KINGSBERE 4 b.g. Dragonara Palace 115–Vahine 72 (Umberto 118) (1979 10d 10.5g 8g 8g[2] 8s 8.2s 1980 8f 8fg 8s 7s 7d) very useful in 1978 but seems a light of other days and is best left alone; gelded after second start; stays 1m; usually wears blinkers; sold to M. Cousins 1,500 gns Newmarket Autumn Sales. *I. Walker.* —

KING'S BIDDER 2 b.c. Lochnager 132–Ruling Class 92 (King Emperor) (1980 6g 5d 5d) May 16; 5,000Y; narrow, lightly-made colt; second foal; dam stayed 1¼m; showed a little ability in large fields of maidens in the autumn, best effort on final start; should stay 6f. *B. Gubby.* 72

KING'S COLLEGE BOY 2 b.g. Andrea Mantegna–The Guzzler 69 (Behistoun 131) (1980 7fg 8d*) Mar 22; big, rangy gelding; half-brother to winning 3-y-o stayer Champagne Charlie (by Charlottown) and 1m to 1½m winner La Piccolina (by Tudor Rhythm); dam won 6f seller; second favourite when quickening to lead 2f out and soon going clear of his field to beat Hit The Road impressively by 6 lengths in 15-runner maiden race at Warwick in October; will stay 1½m+. *N. Vigors.* 87

KINGS CROSS 2 gr.c. Sovereign Path 125–Some Dame 72 (Will Somers 114 §) (1980 5.8fg 6d 6fg) May 4; 20,000Y; leggy, fair sort; second foal; half-brother to French 3-y-o 7f seller winner Allerer (by Tower Walk); dam, winner over 1¼m, is half-sister to high-class middle-distance performer Record Run; put in best work from halfway when 5¼ lengths fifth of 18 to Wicked Will in maiden race at Bath in June, first outing and best effort; sold only 400 gns Newmarket Autumn Sales. *B. Hills.* —

KINGSFOLD FLASH 3 ch.f. Warpath 113–Piccadilly Rose 63 (Reform 132) (1979 5s 6fg 5f 7g 7fg 7f 1980 8h[3] 8fg[2]) small, compact filly; plater; will be suited by middle distances; acts on hard going. *J. Benstead.* 50

KINGS GENERAL 2 b.c. St Paddy 133–Babble On 79 (Acropolis 132) (1980 7g* 7fg[3]) Mar 27; 30,000Y; strong, quite attractive colt; half-brother to numerous winners, including very useful 1979 2-y-o 6f to 1m winner Home Ground (by No Mercy); dam, sister to Espresso, won at up to 11f; found a good turn of foot for so stoutly-bred a colt when winning slowly-run £3,000 event at Goodwood in September by 3 lengths from Junta; excellent third of 16 to Centurius in £3,900 race at Ascot later in month, running on very strongly after losing his place badly at halfway; will be well suited by middle distances; should develop into a very useful 3-y-o. *G. Harwood.* 104 p

KING'S GLORY 2 br.c. Royal and Regal–Dazzling Light 116 (Silly Season 127) (1980 6d 7g[4] 7f*) May 2; compact colt; second foal; dam, smart over 7f and 1m, is half-sister to Welsh Pageant; improved in the autumn and overcame difficulties in running to win 19-runner maiden race at Newmarket in October by a length from Standon Rock; will be suited by 1m; acts well on firm going; sweated up a bit at Newmarket; to be trained by H. Candy. *T. Waugh.* 95

KINGS LAKE (USA) 2 b.c. Nijinsky 138–Fish-Bar (Baldric II 131) (1980 6g[2] 6g* 7d*) May 14; half-brother to modest Irish 3-y-o Caitanya (by Roberto), top 1976 Irish 2-y-o Cloonlara (by Sir Ivor) and smart Irish sprinter Denizen (by Habitat); dam very useful French 1½m winner; evens favourite, put up a useful effort when winning 14-runner maiden race at the Curragh in August by 4 lengths 100 p

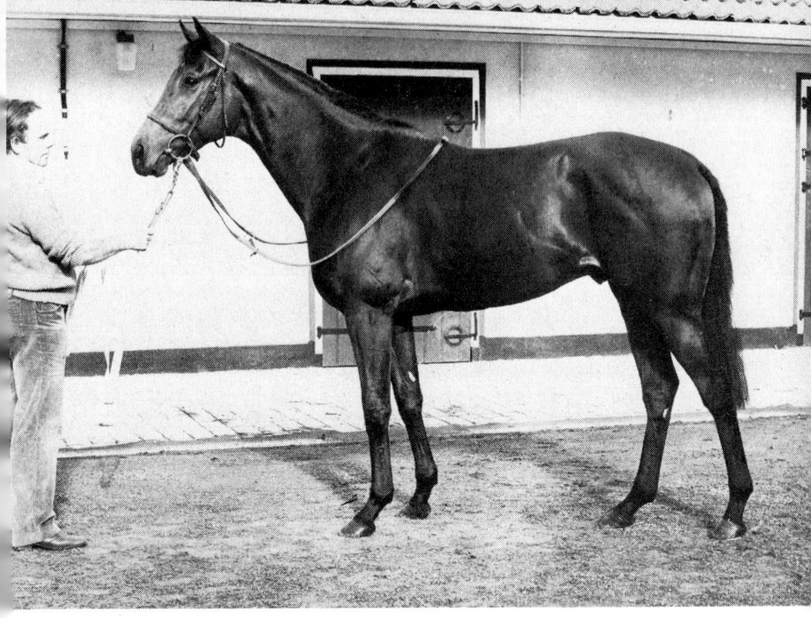

Mme J. P. Binet's "Kings Lake"

from Noble Monk; got home by only ½ length from Tellurano when 9/4 on for minor event at Naas in October but had 9 others well beaten off; will stay at least 1¼m. *V. O'Brien, Ireland.*

KINGSLEY HOUSE 2 b.g. Ancient Monro 89–Mi Lu 80 (Gilles de Retz 132) — (1980 8fg) leggy, narrow gelding with poor legs; third living foal; dam placed from 7f to 1¾m and won over hurdles; tenth of 11 in seller won by Cherry Corner at Redcar in October. *S. Nesbitt.*

KINGS OFFERING 5 b.g. Frankincense 120–Ribble Girl 96 (Trouville 125) 78 (1979 8s 6v 5d 5v* 6s^4 5s 6fg 6f^4 5f^2 5g^4 5g 6fg 6d 5g 5fg* 5s 1980 5s 5g 5fg 5f* 5f^2 6d 5g 6g^2 5fg^4 5fg 5d 5f 6g 6d 5d 5d) strong, good-topped gelding; made all when winning handicap at Chester in May by 6 lengths from St Terramar; ran poorly towards end of season; stays 7f; acts on any going; good mount for an apprentice; effective with or without blinkers; goes well on a sharp track. *R. Ward.*

KINGS PARADE 2 ch.c. Realm 129–La Lidia 78 (Matador 131) (1980 6g 6g 8g^4 90 8g 8d^4) Mar 29; strong, well-made colt; good walker and mover; closely related to 3-y-o Laodamia (by So Blessed), successful at up to 1m, and half-brother to several winners; dam, winner at up to 13f, is half-sister to Irish Derby winner Your Highness; 3½ lengths fourth of 23 to Jungle Jim in maiden race at Goodwood in September and ran creditably under top weight when 2¾ lengths fourth of 13 in nursery won by Piping Queen at Wolverhampton the following month; better suited by 1m than 6f *J. Dunlop.*

KING'S RIDE 4 b.c. Rarity 129–Ride 71 (Sovereign Path 125) (1979 8d^4 10s 88 10g 8g 7v^3 8g^4 8g^2 7g 8fg^2 9g^2 10d* 10s* 1980 8d* 10g 10.2fg^3 8g 10.6d* 10.5g 12f 12fg* 9f 10d 10g 12v^4) tall, attractive colt; got up near finish when winning valuable William Hill Lincoln Handicap at Doncaster in March by narrowest of margins from Blue Bridge; subsequently successful in handicaps at Haydock (beat Whitehall Bridge a length) and Kempton (got home by a head from Le Soleil); also ran well when staying-on fourth behind Path of Peace in William Hill Novem-

William Hill Lincoln Handicap, Doncaster—last-stride win for King's Ride who short heads Blue Bridge (left) with Be Better a close third

ber Handicap at Doncaster; better suited by 1½m than shorter distances when conditions aren't testing; acts on any going, but is very well suited by some give in the ground; has been tried in blinkers. *W. Wightman.*

KING'S SPY 2 b.c. Queen's Hussar 124–Shifty (Shantung 132) (1980 7f4 7fg2 8d 8d3) Apr 16; lengthy, lightly-made colt; first foal; dam never ran; in frame in maiden races in the autumn, going down by a length to Six Mile Bottom in 19-runner event at Lingfield; will stay 1¼m; best run on a firm surface. *B. Hobbs.* **83**

KINGSTON ROSE 3 ch.f. Tudor Music 131–Orient Queen (King's Troop 118) (1979 5v 5.9g 5fg 6d2 5d* 5d 5s 1980 5v2 5v3 6f4 5g3 6s 5s) 520Y; third foal; half-sister to Irish 7f winner Northern Shamrock (by Northfields); dam Irish 5f 3-y-o winner; placed in handicaps at Phoenix Park and Leopardstown and small race at Limerick Junction; out of her depth in £2,400 race at Haydock on final outing in October; stays 6f; acts on heavy going. *N. Chance, Ireland.* **–**

KING'S TOWN (FR) 3 b.g. Sir Ribot–Tatjana (Hornbeam 130) (1979 NR 1980 9fg 12s 11d4 10g 10fg3 9d) 45,000 francs Y (approx £5,300); quite attractive gelding; third foal; dam never ran; third in maiden race at Beverley in September; markedly one paced and should be suited by further than 1¼m; blinkered last 2 starts; sold to K. Ivory 4,000 gns Newmarket Autumn Sales. *P. Walwyn.* **75** d

KINKIO 3 b.g. Kibenka 119–Larcio (Lauso) (1979 5s 6f 7fg 1980 8d 7fg 10.8fg) leggy gelding; poor form in varied company; retained 1,300 gns Doncaster August Sales. *W. Stephenson.* **–**

KINNIGGER 2 b.g. Rapid River 127–Princess Gretel 97 (The Phoenix) (1980 5fg 6g3) May 7; 4,500Y; lengthy gelding; half-brother to several winners, including quite useful middle-distance winner Swallow Prince (by My Swallow); dam miler; 3 lengths third of 14 to Endless Moment in minor event at Brighton in October; stays 6f. *M. Francis.* **77**

KINTBURY 5 ch.g. Ballymoss 136–Brocette (Brocade Slipper 116) (1979 16s 1980 12f) plater; stays 9f; blinkered last 3 outings in 1978. *Mrs N. Kennedy.* **–**

KINTORE 8. b.g. Aberdeen 109–Dararole (Dara §§) (1979 6g3 7s 7fg3 6fg3 7f 7g 8g3 6s 7d 1980 7.2fg 6fg 8d 7d 7f 8g 6s) useful handicapper at his best; on the downgrade and was well beaten in 1980; best form at up to 7f; well suited by a sound surface; tried in blinkers at 3 yrs; acts on any track; suitable mount for an apprentice; usually held up; sometimes starts slowly; trained most of season by S. Wainwright. *W. A. Stephenson.* **–**

KIRTLING 2 b.c. Grundy 137–Silky 112 (Nijinsky 138) (1980 5f2 6g* 7g4 7s4) Apr 1; rather leggy colt; good mover; second foal; half-brother to 1979 2-y-o 6f winner Abington (by Jukebox); dam Irish 1,000 Guineas second and half-sister to Moulton and Freefoot; made up a deal of ground in final furlong, after being in rear early on, to win 8-runner Chesham Stakes at Royal Ascot in June by short head from Robellino; beaten in top company subsequently, staying on to finish 2¾ lengths fourth of 10 to Gielgud when co-favourite for Laurent Perrier Cham- **114**

pagne Stakes at Doncaster 3 months later and fading in final 2f when 11½ lengths fourth behind Storm Bird in 5-runner William Hill Dewhurst Stakes at Newmarket in October; will be suited by 1¼m+. *H. Wragg.*

KISSES FOR ME 4 b.f. Queen's Hussar 124–Fiery Kiss 82 (Floribunda 136) (1979 NR 1980 10v 8f) behind in maiden races; sold 1,100 gns Newmarket May Sales. *D. Ringer.* –

KISS THE CLOWNS (FR) 3 gr.f. Restless Native–Kate's Intent (Intentionally) (1979 4.5d4 7g 5g2 1980 7v 6.5d 5fg 5d4 5g 5fg3 5g2 5f* 5f) rangy ex-French filly; closely related to 2 winners by Dancer's Image, including top-class sprinter Godswalk, and half-sister to 2 other winners in France and USA; dam very useful stakes winner at up to 7f in USA; favourite, won 14-runner maiden race at Lingfield in September; best at 5f; probably acts on any going; blinkered third start (out of her depth); trained first 3 outings by R. Carver. *J. Dunlop.* 59

KISSUM 3 b.f. Kibenka 119–Miss Midsummer (Midsummer Night II 117) (1979 NR 1980 5s 10.8fg 8f) leggy filly; no sign of ability in maiden race and 2 sellers; trained by W. Stephenson first 2 starts. *A. Jarvis.* –

KITHAIRON 9 br.h. Klairon 131–Gin-Ginger 82 (Happy Monarch 109) (1979 8g 7s* 7.6d2 7.2s3 8d 8f 8fg2 8g2 8g3 8d3 8d 7d4 7.2g 8g3 8s 1980 8d 7v 7s 8f3 7.6f 8fg* 8d3 8d* 8fg3 8fg2 8fg2 8d 8fg2 8s 8.2s*) fair handicapper; a grand old horse; successful at Ayr in May, Carlisle in July (trotted up) and Haydock in October; best at around 1m; acts on any going but is possibly best with some give in the ground; excellent mount for an apprentice; used to wear blinkers; often gets well behind in early stages. *J. W. Watts.* 85

KITSON (USA) 2 b.c. Secretariat–Gunite (Crozier USA) (1980 7g) Jan 12; $205,000F, 50,000 gns Y; neat colt; half-brother to a winner in USA by Never Bend; dam, half-sister to CCA Oaks winner Lady Pitt, was very useful stakes winner at up to 6f; 6/1, weakened approaching final furlong and wasn't given at all a hard time when in rear in 10-runner Hyperion Stakes won by Sunley Builds at Ascot in October; should do better over further in 1981. *P. Walwyn.* – p

KITTASPEC GAL 3 br.f. Mandamus 120–Dior 80 (Dionisio 126) (1979 6s 6g 7g 8g 1980 8g3 8g 11g4 16f3 18f* 15d* 16.1s 15.8d4 16s2) unfurnished filly; has a round action; showed improved form once given a test of stamina, winning handicaps at Ripon in August and Edinburgh (apprentice ridden) in September; stays well; acts on any going. *M. H. Easterby.* 72

Chesham Stakes, Ascot—Kirtling (right) catches Robellino on the line

KITTYHAWK 2 b.f. Bustino 136–Sky Fever 108 (Skymaster 126) (1980 6fg^4 6g^2 6g*) **113**

When Kittyhawk provided Dick Hern with his only 1980 success in a two-year-old pattern race, her trainer had the wretched English weather to thank in a roundabout way; but for torrential rain which washed out the Newbury meeting on August 15th, Kittyhawk would have run there in the Sparsholt Maiden Fillies Stakes instead of in the prestigious Lowther Stakes at York five days later. Her connections subsequently had extra cause to be grateful that they had won an important race with her when they did, for she succumbed to a virus which affected many of the stable's two-year-olds in the autumn, missed the Cheveley Park Stakes and wasn't seen out again.

Although Kittyhawk's original objective had been a much less important race, it wasn't surprising that she started odds on for the Lowther. She had put up a first-rate effort in the Princess Margaret Stakes at Ascot the previous month, going down by only a length and a half to that excellent filly Tolmi with useful previous winners Her Grace, Oraston, Doobie Do and Lucaya well beaten off; and because she was still a maiden she received weight from three of her four opponents at York, getting 6 lb from the Curragh Stakes winner Crimson Heather and 3 lb from Integrity and Vocalist, winners respectively of the Rous Memorial Stakes and the Horn Blower Stakes. Whereas Kittyhawk had made the running for four furlongs at Ascot, she was held up at York. After travelling easily in behind Integrity and Crimson Heather for half a mile, she quickened smoothly to lead running into the final furlong and then kept on to win by a length and a half from Vocalist.

Kittyhawk (b.f. Apr 4, 1978)	Bustino (b 1971)	Busted (b 1963)	Crepello
			Sans le Sou
		Ship Yard (ch 1963)	Doutelle
			Paving Stone
	Sky Fever (b 1969)	Skymaster (ch 1958)	Golden Cloud
			Discipliner
		Harlequinade (br 1964)	Klairon
			Columbine

Kittyhawk, a lengthy, quite attractive filly, has the makings of a smart performer. It's not easy to say how far she will stay though—she's a daughter of a mating between a St Leger winner and a useful five-furlong sprinter. Little light is thrown on the matter by the performances of either of the previous foals produced by Sky Fever, a half-sister to the smart sprinter Matinee and the useful miler Rehearsal. The first, the Hotfoot filly Puss Moth, was of no account and

Lowther Stakes, York—Kittyhawk lands the odds from Vocalist

Lord Porchester's "Kittyhawk"

the second, the Queen's Hussar gelding Sky Rider, proved disappointing at up to a mile and a quarter on the flat although he has since won over hurdles.

Bustino's first foals won twenty races between them as three-year-olds in 1980 at an average distance of just over eleven furlongs. Kittyhawk, with a sprinter as her dam, is unlikely to stay that far and distances around a mile will probably suit her best. Incidentally, together with those promising animals Bustomi, Maiden's Blush, Overplay and Van Lingen, Kittyhawk is one of eight two year-old winners in Britain, Ireland, and France from Bustino's second crop—an excellent total for a stallion who didn't himself win as a two-year-old. *R. Hern.*

KLAVEN 3 br.g. Kalamoun 129–Ashavan 114 (Persian Gulf) (1979 NR 1980 8fg 10fg 8fg 7g 12g 10fg) leggy gelding; no sign of ability in maiden races and sellers; looked temperamental fourth start (blinkered); sold out of J. Hindley's stable 460 gns Newmarket July Sales after fourth outing. *P. Bevan.* —

KNIGHTHALL (USA) 2 b.c. King's Bishop–Midnight Hush (Sunrise Flight) (1980 6g 7d) Apr 3; $20,000Y; quite a useful sort; half-brother to 4 winners in USA, including Rip van Winkle (by Impressive), successful at up to 1¼m; dam won over 7f and 1m; backed from 10/1 to 5/1, finished 9½ lengths sixth of 20 to Soldan in 7f minor event at Doncaster in October; will stay 1¼m. *G. Hunter.* **62**

KNIGHT OF KASHMIR 3 ch.c. Blue Cashmere 129–Devon Night 100 (Midsummer Night II 117) (1979 5f 5fg 6g 1980 6v* 5f^2 7h^2 6fg^3 6d^2 6d^4 6g) neat colt; raced alone on far side and showed improved form to win £1,500 event at Ayr in March; placed in minor event and handicaps subsequently; suited by 6f and 7f; acts on any going; blinkered final outing at 2 yrs and in 1980. *J. W. Watts.* **74**

KNOT A WORD 2 b. or br.g. Most Secret 119–Viadao 87 (Pardao 120) (1980 7g) Apr 17; lightly-made gelding; third living foal; dam won twice over 5f at 2 yrs; 10/1 when always behind in 12-runner seller won by High Class Builder at Catterick in August; dead. *J. Fitzgerald.* —

KNOWN FACT (USA) 3 b.c. In Reality–Tamerett (Tim Tam) (1979 5fg* 6g² 6fg³ 6f* 1980 7f⁴ 8fg* 8d 8g* 7g* 8fg*) **135**

Seldom has a classic winner received so little attention or honour at the time of his success as did Known Fact. Known Fact was awarded the Two Thousand Guineas by the stewards and in the aftermath of the disqualification of Nureyev, who passed the post a neck ahead of him, the merit of Known Fact's performance tended to be overlooked. Illness kept Known Fact out of action for most of the summer but an impressive autumn campaign advertised his claims to be regarded as the best three-year-old miler of the year. On his final outing, in the Queen Elizabeth II Stakes at Ascot, he became only the second horse in sixteen races to defeat Kris, giving a performance that showed him to be an even better horse than he was on Guineas day. It is good news that he stays in training.

The leading two-year-olds of 1979 were a comparatively ordinary bunch but it usually pays to take the best two-year-old form as a guide to the Guineas; the race nearly always comes too soon and is run over too sharp a distance for most of those that have been unable to shine as youngsters. Known Fact was one of twenty-two two-year-olds, a staggeringly high number, that were rated within 7 lb of top weight Monteverdi in the Free Handicap (in our opinion, it was impossible for the leading two-year-olds to be so bad as the Free Handicap suggested). Monteverdi missed the Two Thousand Guineas after two defeats in the spring but Known Fact (9-5), Tyrnavos (9-2) and Final Straw (9-2) of the top twenty-three stood their ground. Nureyev, placed joint-second in the French Free Handicap and rated 1 lb higher than Known Fact in the International Classification, seemed a very worthy favourite. He had made only one appearance in his first season, winning the Prix Thomas Bryon, a Group 3 pattern race, by a wide margin, and his victory in the Prix Djebel in April on his reappearance was far and away the most impressive Guineas trial we had seen. There was one other unbeaten colt in the field, the highly regarded but largely untested Saint Jonathon who had been very

Two Thousand Guineas Stakes, Newmarket—Nureyev is a neck in front of Known Fact but is disqualified for interfering with Posse who finished third

Waterford Crystal Mile, Goodwood—Known Fact (noseband) catches Hard Fought (centre) in the last few strides. Night Alert (nearer rails) is a close third

impressive in his previous race, the Timeform Race Card Stakes at Thirsk which had been won twelve months earlier by the subsequent Two Thousand Guineas winner Tap On Wood. In the longer-established Guineas trials, Tyrnavos had just got the better of Star Way in the Ladbrokes Craven Stakes over the Guineas course and distance, and Taufan had run well enough under a big weight in the Tote Free Handicap at the Craven meeting to merit consideration. But the most competitive trial by far had been the Clerical, Medical Greenham Stakes at Newbury, a race which had attracted the winners of the previous season's three Group 1 two-year-old races in England open to colts: Monteverdi, winner of the William Hill Dewhurst; Hello Gorgeous, winner of the William Hill Futurity; and Known Fact, winner of the William Hill Middle Park. The Middle Park, once the most important race in England for two-year-olds, has lost a little ground over the years and is nowadays regarded as a less prestigious race to win than the Dewhurst. Known Fact's performance in the Middle Park, coming from behind to beat the Gimcrack winner Sonnen Gold by half a length, didn't convince that he was up to winning the Guineas in a normal year, but he clearly couldn't be ruled out altogether. Looking to have done well over the winter, he was a promising fourth in the Greenham to the tough and genuine Final Straw; Carson, Known Fact's regular rider, had forecast after the Middle Park that Known Fact would win the Guineas and he re-affirmed his conviction after the Greenham. Posse, having only his second race, had also taken the eye in the Greenham, finishing best of all into third place, just behind Monteverdi, whose performance led to his being replaced as his stable's representative at Newmarket by Night Alert, who had beaten Posse in the Houghton Stakes as a two-year-old and had won the Gladness Stakes at the Curragh on his reappearance.

But for the patrol camera, it is possible that Known Fact might not have been declared the Guineas winner. The incident which led to Nureyev's disqualification took place more than two furlongs from the finish near the back of the field; few racegoers—and not all the officials on duty—saw Nureyev barge his way out of a pocket, stopping Posse in his tracks and almost bringing him down. When the stewards reviewed the incident, they adjudged that Nureyev's jockey had been guilty of reckless riding, for which offence Nureyev was put down to last place and his jockey stood down for seven days. Nureyev, Posse, Known Fact and Night Alert were among those ridden from behind in the Guineas as the 66/1-outsider Highest Bidder cut out the donkey work until well past halfway, closely attended by Tyrnavos and Saint Jonathon. Running downhill into the Dip, Nureyev, racing towards the middle of the course, and Known Fact, next to the stand rails, both showed excellent acceleration to pass the leaders. Up the hill there was little to choose between them with first Known Fact then Nureyev, who was tending to drift over towards Known Fact, appearing the more likely to get to the post first. In

Kiveton Park Steel Stakes, Doncaster—an easy win for Known Fact

the end Nureyev just made it with the luckless Posse, who recovered a tremendous amount of ground in the last two furlongs, only three quarters of a length behind Known Fact; the first three finished clear of the remainder who were headed by Night Alert and Star Way.

There was never any question of Known Fact's getting the Derby distance as a three-year-old; the attack of bronchitis that laid him low soon after the Guineas therefore proved nowhere near so damaging to his career as it would have been had he been regarded as a potential Derby winner. He didn't run again until the middle of August when he finished fifth, three places behind Final Straw and one ahead of Star Way, in the Prix Jacques le Marois at Deauville. Within a week he was out again, contesting the Waterford Crystal Mile at Goodwood, a race in which he was due to meet Posse whose victories in the St James's Palace Stakes and the Sussex Stakes had helped to compensate for his wretched luck in the Guineas. Although Posse went down with the cough at the last minute and had to be withdrawn, it was still a good field that lined up against Known Fact: Night Alert had won the Prix Jean Prat at Chantilly on his only appearance since the Guineas, and both Hard Fought (Jersey Stakes) and the four-year-old Blue Refrain (Queen Anne Stakes) had put up good winning performances at Royal Ascot; Known Fact met each of his five rivals on terms worse than weight for age. Known Fact pulls hard and it is usually a struggle to restrain him through the early stages of his races; but if he can be covered up he usually settles down. Such riding tactics, essential to a horse like Known Fact, are not without their hazards; gaps don't always open up when they are wanted at the business end of the race. Known Fact had to overcome difficulties before getting home at Goodwood: finding no way through in the straight between the leaders Night Alert and Hard Fought, Carson had to drop Known Fact back and come round the outside. Known Fact didn't see daylight until inside the final furlong but he quickened well and ran on very gamely to beat Hard Fought and Night Alert by a neck and half a length. There were no alarms in his next race, the Kiveton Park Steel Stakes at Doncaster's St Leger meeting; they weren't bad horses that took him on—Captain Nick, Star Way and Alert—but Known Fact disposed of them with ease, again showing a good turn of foot.

Known Fact's period of convalescence after the Two Thousand Guineas, coupled with the training troubles that had kept the best four-year-old miler Kris off the track for four months in the middle of the season, served to cloud the issue of who was the leading miler. Nureyev, who wasn't raced after the Guineas, and Posse were others with sound claims. The issue seemed likely to be resolved to most people's satisfaction in the Queen Elizabeth II Stakes, a Group 2 pattern race run at Ascot at the end of September. Kris, Known Fact and Posse were all announced as runners and the early ante-post market suggested strongly that neither Known Fact nor Posse was expected to beat Kris. In the end, Posse wasn't risked because his trainer was unhappy with him. There's not much doubt, however, that both Kris and Known Fact were at their peak and they provided a superb contest, Known Fact gradually wearing down Kris in the last furlong and a half to win by a neck in a race run at a blistering pace throughout. Unlike Known Fact and Kris, the five other runners did not carry penalties but they were never in it in the straight, a testament to the excellence of the performances of both Known

Fact and Kris; the filly Gift Wrapped filled third place, six lengths behind Kris and two in front of Hard Fought. To use the Two Thousand Guineas result, as some did, to suggest that Nureyev and Posse would also have beaten Kris at Ascot is an example of the naive way some people use the form-book; a lot of water had flowed under the bridge since the Guineas and the way we interpret things Known Fact was a 5 lb better horse at Ascot at the end of September than he was at Newmarket at the beginning of May. In truth, there was precious little between Known Fact and Kris at Ascot; both showed themselves to be milers of the highest international class.

Known Fact (USA) (b.c. 1977)	In Reality (b 1964)	Intentionally (bl 1956)	Intent My Recipe
		My Dear Girl (ch 1957)	Rough'n Tumble Iltis
	Tamerett (b or br 1962)	Tim Tam (b 1955)	Tom Fool Two Lea
		Mixed Marriage (b 1952)	Tudor Minstrel Persian Maid

Had Known Fact met his engagement in the Champion Stakes, for which he was an intended runner until working disappointingly four days before the race, we should probably have been clearer about his prospects in 1981. He poses the same problem that Kris posed at the end of the previous season. Will he stay a mile and a quarter? As with Kris there are points for and against. Known Fact was bred in North America where his sire, who was by a champion sprinter, was a high-class racehorse in that vintage classic crop headed by Dr Fager and Damascus. In Reality won ten stakes races from six to nine furlongs and has been a highly successful stallion, siring a number of good-class performers that were effective at the North American classic distance of a mile and a quarter, or further. Known Fact's dam Tamerett won at up to a mile and bred four winners before Known Fact including two very good performers, Tentam (by Intentionally, the sire of In Reality) and Terete (by Boldnesian) who stayed beyond a mile and a quarter. If there were only breeding considerations to go on it would seem reasonable to expect Known Fact to get a mile and a quarter. But one can never be certain of these things and it's always important to refer to the horse himself. Known Fact's general

Queen Elizabeth II Stakes, Ascot—Known Fact beats Kris

Mr K. Abdulla's "Known Fact"

character as a racehorse is that of a horse with speed. His natural urge is to get on with it and such horses often fail to stay as far as their pedigrees might suggest. For the moment we prefer to put it as a possibility rather than a probability that Known Fact will be as effective over a mile and a quarter as he is over a mile. Much could depend on whether he becomes more tractable with another year on his back. Known Fact goes extremely well on top-of-the-ground; the only time he has encountered a soft surface was in the Prix Jacques le Marois in which his below-par run can just as easily be attributed to the fact that he had been off the course for more than three months as to the ground. Known Fact is a well-made, good-looking, medium-sized colt and a good mover; he is very genuine. Whatever the long-term plans for Known Fact it is probable that his first objective will be the Tote Lockinge Stakes over a mile at Newbury, a race which clashes with the Airlie/Coolmore Irish Two Thousand Guineas, a strong counter-attraction for the leading three-year-olds; the Lockinge should be tailor-made for Known Fact. Should he be kept to a mile he is certain to prove a very tough nut to crack. *J. Tree.*

KOCHIA 2 b.f. Firestreak 125–Lead Me On (King's Troop 118) (1980 7s 7g) Mar 28; small, stocky filly; second foal; dam never ran; unquoted when behind in minor event at Sandown (started slowly) and maiden race at Newmarket in October. *C. Read.* —

KOLME 3 b.c. Lord Gayle 124–Fille de Luxe (Le Levanstell 122) (1979 7[3] 7.5f* 8.5d 1980 12f* 10f[3] 13.5g* 14fg* 12s 12fg) 6,600Y; lengthy colt; first foal; dam won over 1m in Ireland; successful in handicaps at Naas (apprentice event), Dundalk and Gowran Park; staying-on fifth to No Bombs in valuable gentleman amateur riders race at Epsom on final start in August; suited by 1¾m; acts on firm going. *J. Oxx, Ireland.* **86**

KONOHANASAKUYA 3 br.f. Prince Regent 129–That's Better (Mourne 126) (1979 6s[2] 7f[3] 7fg 1980 8s 8f 8f 6fg) poor maiden; should stay at least 1m; blinkered third outing. *Sir Mark Prescott.* —

KRIS 4 ch.c. Sharpen Up 127–Doubly Sure 59 (Reliance II 137) (1979 7d* 8g^2 7d* 8g* 8g* 8g* 8f* 7fg* 1980 7.2f* 8f* 8g* 8fg^2) **134**

A horse of distinction who fell only a little way short of greatness: that's the ultimate verdict on Kris, a miler who in sixteen races was beaten only twice. There was no more thrilling prospect as the latest season opened than that of seeing Kris fulfil the ambitious programme planned for him. At the end of his three-year-old career he was being compared—prematurely in our view—to Brigadier Gerard. Not since the days of Brigadier Gerard had a horse so dominated racing at around a mile in England: only Tap On Wood in the Two Thousand Guineas managed to beat Kris in eight starts as a three-year-old and some of Kris's victories, including those in the Sussex Stakes and the Queen Elizabeth II Stakes, both of which he won by five lengths, were gained in the style typical of Brigadier Gerard, striding clear ridden out over the last two furlongs. In our book, the best performances of Kris as a three-year-old didn't compare with those of Brigadier Gerard who put up a great performance to beat Mill Reef and My Swallow in the Two Thousand Guineas and went unbeaten through six races, culminating in the Champion Stakes. If Kris wasn't in the Brigadier Gerard class as a three-year-old what chance had he got of matching that great horse's third-season record? In eight races as a four-year-old Brigadier Gerard put up top-class performances at a mile (Lockinge Stakes and Queen Elizabeth II Stakes), a mile and a quarter (Westbury Stakes, Prince of Wales's Stakes, Eclipse Stakes and Champion Stakes) and a mile and a half (King George VI and Queen Elizabeth Stakes); he was defeated for the only time in an eighteen-race career in the Benson and Hedges Gold Cup by the Derby winner Roberto.

Kris ended his second season without having been tried beyond a mile; the Champion Stakes was considered but in the end the attempt at the longer distance was postponed until another year. Kris's programme in 1980 was said to include a mixture of the best races at a mile and a mile and a quarter, races such as the Eclipse, the Sussex Stakes and the Champion Stakes. As readers of *Racehorses of 1979* will remember, we rated Kris's chances of staying a mile and a quarter in top company about fifty-fifty: his pedigree was a mixture of speed and stamina, and while some of his racecourse performances had suggested reserves of stamina, others raised a doubt, especially his victory in the seven-furlong Bisquit Cognac Challenge Stakes at Newmarket in October in which, against the high-class sprinter Absalom, he had gone the pace throughout. In the event, Kris's stamina was never put to the test: he raced only four times as a four-year-old and was off the course for almost four months in the middle of the season. His four-year-old career was something of an anti-climax but at least he was given the opportunity to add to his laurels. Not many three-year-olds of his outstanding ability are even given the chance to do that nowadays when huge sums are available to secure the best horses for stud.

The start of Kris's campaign as a four-year-old could hardly have been

Tote Lockinge Stakes, Newbury—Kris beats Foveros (on the rails) with Hardgreen third and Skyliner and House Guard in close attendance

bettered in so far as it maintained his image with the racing public and whetted the appetite for his big-race appearances in the summer. He was seen out twice in May, in the Cold Shield Windows Trophy at Haydock and the Tote Lockinge Stakes at Newbury, and his running attracted considerable publicity on each occasion, not least for the fact that he set a time record for the course and distance in both races. Some members of the racing Press seem to set great store by time records and often use them to promote good horses; Kris's record-breaking efforts received praise in some quarters out of all proportion to the actual merit that he displayed. As we have often said before, the fact that a horse beats a course record is, in itself, no indication to the layman one way or the other as to the merit of those engaged in the finish. A fast time usually means no more than that a race has been truly run and is nearly always an indication that the race has been run on ground at least on the firm side of good; both conditions obtained when Kris ran at Haydock and Newbury. The fact that the previous holders of the records were Son of Sequel and Great Uncle Fred—two consistent and reliable handicappers whom no-one would describe as better than useful racehorses—is a good illustration of the fact that a course-record shattering performance and an outstanding performance aren't necessarily the same thing. Kris made a satisfactory debut at Haydock, winning by a length from the Irish Cambridgeshire winner Habituate in a field of four, but he was made to work for his victory and it seemed pretty clear that he was in need of the run. A fortnight later, with most of the leading three-year-old milers at the Curragh for the same day's Airlie/Coolmore Irish Two Thousand Guineas, Kris had to concede 7 lb to four four-year-olds and two five-year-olds in the Tote Lockinge Stakes. Foveros, Hardgreen, Skyliner and Alert had all been beaten before by Kris and the Irish-trained challenger Gerald Martin was making his first appearance on a racecourse for a year; the good handicapper House Guard was the only one seriously backed to beat the odds-on Kris who looked magnificent, having clearly benefited from his outing at Haydock. As things turned out it was probably a good job for Kris that there wasn't another top-class horse in the field: Kris encountered considerable difficulty getting an opening to deliver his challenge and had to survive a stewards' inquiry after bursting through the middle of the field to get home by three quarters of a length

Lord Howard de Walden's "Kris"

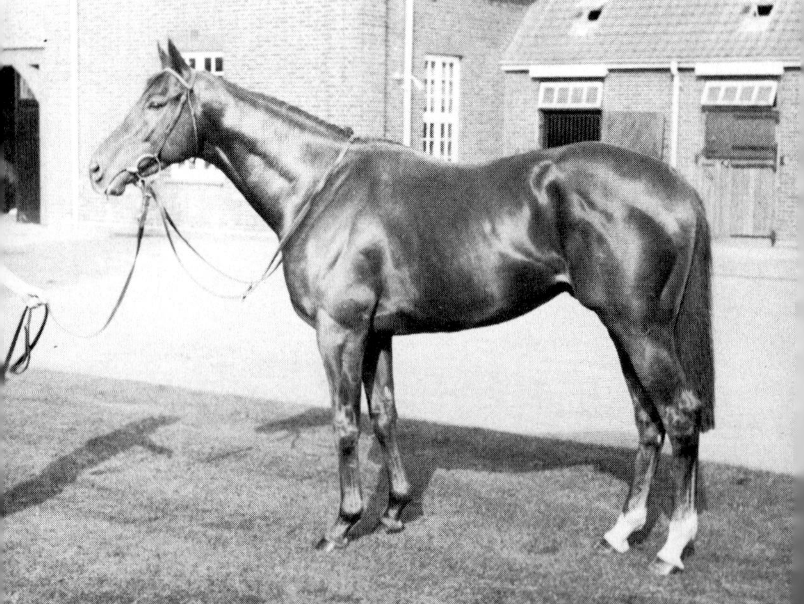

and a short head from Foveros and Hardgreen, with Skyliner and House Guard close behind.

Kris was to have run next in the Queen Anne Stakes at Royal Ascot but a pulled muscle in his quarters caused him to miss that race; nor could his trainer get him to his liking for the Eclipse Stakes, the Sussex Stakes or the Waterford Crystal Mile, each of which was named, successively, as his next objective. When Kris did reappear, in the middle of September, it was in the Crown of Crowns Stakes at Goodwood, a race of little importance in which he wasn't opposed by a miler that could stretch him. Mercer kept Kris going strongly all the way to the line, presumably feeling that he would benefit from a good work-out, and the winning margin over Millbank (USA) was twelve lengths. When ante-post betting opened on the Queen Elizabeth II Stakes, a Group 2 pattern race run at Ascot a fortnight later, Kris was installed 11/10 favourite with the top three-year-olds Posse and Known Fact at 3/1 and 4/1 respectively. The Queen Elizabeth II Stakes, for all that it was worth the relatively small sum of £14,740 to the winner, seemed likely to prove the most significant race of the season over a mile; Posse and Known Fact had almost equal claims at the time to be regarded as the best three-year-old miler in training in England. The withdrawal of Posse because his trainer considered he wasn't fully recovered from illness left Kris and Known Fact to do battle for the milers' championship. Kris, who had had to undergo an official stalls test after being reluctant to go behind the stalls at Goodwood, was a hot favourite at 2/1 on with Known Fact at 3/1. The race was a crackajack! The headlong gallop set by Star Way ensured that the race was truly run and when Kris quickened to take the lead—and a two-length advantage over Known Fact—rounding the final turn the stage seemed set for his fifteenth victory. But Known Fact came at him in the last furlong and a half and, after a tremendous battle, edged ahead in the last few strides to win by a neck with the others well beaten. The public reaction of Kris's connections to the defeat was a notably sporting one, considering the inevitable sense of frustration they must have felt through most of the season. 'That's what racing is all about. He was beaten by a very good horse,' said Kris's owner. No excuses were offered but it was announced that Kris would be retired without meeting his engagement in the Champion Stakes. The terms of his syndication valued him at four million pounds (forty shares at £100,000 each) and he will stand at the Thornton Stud, Thirsk, Yorkshire in 1981.

Kris (ch.c. 1976)	Sharpen Up (ch 1969)	Atan (ch 1961)	Native Dancer
			Mixed Marriage
		Rocchetta (ch 1961)	Rockefella
			Chambiges
	Doubly Sure (b 1971)	Reliance II (b 1962)	Tantieme
			Relance III
		Soft Angels (ch 1963)	Crepello
			Sweet Angel

Kris's sire Sharpen Up was also represented in the most recent season by the high-class sprinters Sharpo and Sovereign Rose and the smart two-year-olds Pushy and Cut Throat. Sharpen Up was a success as a stallion almost from the outset, siring fast-maturing animals, many of whom, like Kris, trained on; the sale of Sharpen Up to the United States could prove to be a significant loss to English breeders. Kris's dam Doubly Sure never won but was placed at a mile and a half as a three-year-old; the grandam Soft Angels won the 1965 Royal Lodge Stakes but became temperamental and never won again; the third dam Sweet Angel, a half-sister to the high-class middle-distance performers Faust, Young Lochinvar and Crepes d'Enfer, was also the dam of Sucaryl and Sweet Moss, two very good middle-distance colts. Kris is a strong, well-made, very attractive individual. He was an admirably genuine, reliable and enthusiastic racehorse who probably acted on any going, although he never raced on very soft ground. Among the impressive list of mares due to visit him in 1981 are the Oaks winner Bireme, the One Thousand Guineas winner One In A Million, the good sprinter Greenland Park, Oh So Fair (the dam of Roussalka), Fishermans Bridge (the dam of Connaught Bridge) and Hornton Grange (the dam of Swiss Maid). *H. Cecil.*

KRUG 2 br.c. Relko 136–Misplanted (Hul a Hul 124) (1980 8g 10g*) Mar 19; **102** p
5,200F, 10,500Y; compact, attractive colt; first foal; dam placed at around 1½m in Ireland; 33/1 but pick of paddock, ran on strongly up hill to win 9-runner Zetland Stakes at Newmarket in October by 1½ lengths from Allegretta; will be

suited by 1½m; impresses us as an individual and looks certain to improve further at 3 yrs. *M. Jarvis.*

KRUGERAMA 2 br.g. Amber Rama 133–Krugerrand 74 (Goldhill 125) (1980 5g4 5f2 5fg 5f* 5f 5f 5d 6s) June 9; 4,500Y; sturdy, compact, robust gelding; first foal; dam won over 9f; made much of running when winning 7-runner minor event at Beverley in August by ½ length from Think Ahead; subsequently in rear in nurseries; should stay 6f; acts on firm going; fell seventh outing; blinkered sixth start. *E. Weymes.* **83**

K-SERA 2 ch.f. Lord Gayle 124–Deirdre (Vimy 132) (1980 5f 5fg 7d2 7g3 7d* 6s) Mar 5; 8,200Y; well-made filly; half-sister to several winners, including smart sprinter Royal Captive (by High Treason) and very useful stayers Melody Rock (by Sayajirao) and Lawrence T (by Tamerlane); dam Irish 2m winner; put up easily best effort when winning £4,000 nursery at Chester in August by 8 lengths from Sunion; found 6f much too sharp when last of 7 to Star Pastures in £6,500 event at Ayr the following month; bred to stay middle distances; acts very well on a soft surface. *C. Brittain.* **95**

KUNUMA 5 b.m. Magnate 84–Rose Rogers (Rodgers II 101) (1979 NR 1980 9v 10s) novice hurdler; last of 11 in maiden race at Hamilton and apprentice event at Nottingham, both in October. *M. James.* **—**

KYOTO 2 b.c. Averof 123–Klondyke Fire (Klondyke Bill 125) (1980 6d4 7g4 7d2 7fg4) Mar 13; 5,000Y; half-brother to 6f and 1m winner Kassamoto (by My Swanee); dam unraced half-sister to very smart 1975 French 2-y-o French Swanee; in frame in maiden races prior to finishing 7 lengths fourth of 6 to Baz Bombati in £5,500 event at Newmarket in August; runs as though 1m will suit him; well capable of winning a maiden race at one of the minor meetings. *H. Collingridge.* **79**

L

LA-BELLA HENRIETTA 3 ch.f. Caliban 123–Wimosa 92 (Mossborough 126) (1979 NR 1980 7d 10.1g 9f) light-framed filly; poor form in varied company, including selling; trained part of season by S. Matthews. *P. Haslam.* **—**

LA BELLE SORCIERE 2 b.f. Sparkler 130–Singing Witch 71 (Sing Sing 134) (1980 5d 5g 5g2 5fg* 6fg3 5.3g2) Jan 27; 15,000Y; well-made filly; half-sister to 1978 2-y-o 5f and 6f winner Rose of Shenfield (by Upper Case); dam half-sister to smart sprinter Vilgora; made all to win 14-runner maiden race at Folkestone in August by 4 lengths from Penshiel; 2 lengths second to odds-on Blue Lass in minor event at Brighton in October; probably stays 6f; acts on a firm surface. *J. Sutcliffe.* **86**

LA BICHE 2 ch.f. Bold Lad (Ire) 133–Tudor Song (Tudor Minstrel 144) (1980 6fg 6s 7d2 6g3) Mar 25; 18,000Y; useful-looking filly; closely related to 1m winner Spring Heeled Jack (by Bold Lad USA), and half-sister to 3 winners, including quite useful 5f and 6f winner Inze Baba (by Huntercombe); dam won at up to 7f in USA; ran best race when 2 lengths second of 13 to Lambay in maiden race at Leicester in October, first outing for 4 months; suited by 7f. *H. T. Jones.* **83**

LABISTA 2 br.f. Crowned Prince 128–Balista 86 (Baldric II 131) (1980 5f* 5fg2 5g 5g3 5f* 5g*) **116**

Although she managed to win a maiden event at York in May on her first outing, Labista did not come into her own until the autumn, when she made light of 9-7 in a nursery at Wolverhampton, and strolled home, ten lengths clear, in the Bexley Stakes at Goodwood. Those behind her at Goodwood included Trina's Girl, a winner from twenty-three opponents, among them Red Gold, Man Of Song and Fire Mountain, in a maiden race at Windsor. If this last performance is to be believed, and we see no reason why it shouldn't be believed, Labista had improved into one of the fastest two-year-old fillies of the season.

Labista (br.f. Feb 17, 1978)	Crowned Prince (ch 1969)	Raise A Native (ch 1961)	Native Dancer
			Raise You
		Gay Hostess (ch 1957)	Royal Charger
			Your Hostess
	Balista (b 1970)	Baldric II (b 1961)	Round Table
			Two Cities
		Title Deed (br 1956)	Supreme Court
			Urshalim

By Crowned Prince out of a seven-furlong winner from the family of Sovereign and Lacquer, Labista is not bred to be a sprinter pure and simple, but that, we fancy, is what she is. Strong and shapely in appearance, she is tolerably certain to train on, and provided her Goodwood performance was no flash in the pan, seems sure to win more races. She has yet to race on a soft surface. *B. Hobbs.*

LA BORIE 2 ch.f. Son of Silver 123–Candid Queen 80 (Good Bond 122) (1980 5fg 6s 6g) Apr 1; quite attractive filly; first foal; dam won over 1¼m; little worthwhile form in maiden races. *P. Mitchell.* —

LACEBELL 2 b.f. Royal Palace 131–Corsley Bell 96 (Owen Tudor) (1980 6fg) Feb 7; half-sister to smart miler Town Crier (by Sovereign Path) and a winner abroad; dam 2-y-o 5f winner; 20/1 when behind in 19-runner minor event won by Sea Aura at Lingfield in October. *P. Walwyn.* —

LACEWORK (USA) 2 br.f. In Reality–Millicent (Cornish Prince) (1980 5.1fg* 5fg 5f) small, compact, attractive filly; sister to stakes-placed winner Marston's Mill, successful at up to 1m in USA, and half-sister to another winner; dam unraced half-sister to Mill Reef; ran on well to win 7-runner maiden race at Yarmouth in August by a length from Devon Bells; had stiffish task when third favourite for valuable nursery at Newbury the following month on next outing and wasn't disgraced in finishing 4¾ lengths ninth of 15 to Barnet Heir; will be much better suited by 6f+; sent to USA. *M. Stoute.* **80**

LA CHAUMIERE 2 gr.f. Thatch 136–Ruby of Iran (Cosmic Bomb) (1980 5g) May 25; 29,000Y; leggy filly; half-sister to several winners, including American stakes winner Star of Paducah (by Tudorka) and very useful 1971 French 2-y-o 5.5f winner Tamiran (by Tim Tam); dam, unplaced in seven starts in USA, is half-sister to Migoli and to Petite Etoile's dam; second favourite, never went pace when 6¼ lengths fifth of 7 to Jiva in Dick Turpin Stakes at York in June, only outing. *H. T. Jones.* — p

LADBROKES LEISURE 6 ch.g. St Chad 120–Lovely Sovereign 79 (Gustav 121) (1979 NR 1980 18d 16s 16fg 16fg) useful and improving stayer in 1978 but injured himself on final outing and showed no worthwhile form on his return in 1980; acts on any going; suitable mount for an apprentice; bandaged in front nowadays; sweated up third outing. *D. Kent.* —

LADOGA 3 b.g. Track Spare 125–Argitone (Aureole 132) (1979 8fg³ 1980 10.8s⁴ 13.3fg 14g) big gelding; quite a moderate maiden; best run at 10.8f on soft going. *J. Tree.* **73**

LA DOUVE (FR) 3 ch.f. Margouillat 133–Orangina (Mossborough 126) (1979 8fg 1980 16f 15.5fg) sturdy filly; good walker; behind in maiden races. *B. Hills.* —

LADY ABERNANT 5 b.m. Abwah 118–Paros 63 (Pardao 120) (1979 11.1v 10.8d 11.7g 15fg 10f⁴ 12f* 10g 10f 10g⁴ 11g 12.2d 12fg³ 11g 1980 12s 11fg 12f 12.2fg) poor middle-distance handicapper; acts any going; blinkered third start in 1979 and final outing; bandaged near-fore last 2 starts at 4 yrs. *D. Garraton.* —

LADY ACQUIESCE 2 br.f. Galivanter 131–Acquire 105 (Burglar 128) (1980 5fg² 5.1g* 5fg⁴ 5.3fg² 6fg 5d) May 8; 520Y; neat filly; first foal; dam won twice over 5f at 2 yrs; very strongly ridden when winning maiden auction event at Yarmouth in July by 2 lengths; 2½ lengths second of 8 to Miss Worth in claiming race at Brighton the following month; possibly doesn't stay 6f; acts on a firm surface; sweated up third outing (ran creditably). *P. Cole.* **67**

LADY ALINBA 5 b.m. Sharpen Up 127–Uproar 62 (Major Portion 129) (1979 8v⁴ 8s* 8s² 7d² 8f 7f 8.2fg 8f 7fg* 8.2s 6d 1980 7v 8f³ 9fg) plater; stays 1m; acts on any going; blinkered twice at 3 yrs; suitable mount for an apprentice. *J. Bingham.* —

LADY ANTONIA 2 br.f. Owen Anthony 102–Yasmin II 88 (Gilles de Retz 132) (1980 6g 7g) May 9; lightly-made filly; half-sister to 3-y-o miler Major Martin (by Decoy Boy), also successful in Italy, and to dam of good English and German colt Whip It Quick; dam, 2-y-o 7f winner, is half-sister to Lavant, the dam of So Blessed and Lucasland; behind in minor event at Windsor in August (25/1) and maiden race at Salisbury in September (20/1). *H. Candy.* —

LADY ARPEGE 2 b. or br.f. Swing Easy 126–Giglet (Frankincense 120) (1980 5g* 6d 5s²) Mar 14; lightly-made filly; second foal; dam showed no form; won minor event at Edinburgh in October, running on strongly to beat Christine's Folly by 3 lengths; beaten 1½ lengths when second in 14-runner minor **83**

event at Stockton in November won by Apapa Port; should stay 6f. *W. H. H. Williams.*

LADY ASTIR 2 b.f. Abwah 118–Ma Mitte (Faristan 123) (1980 6g 7f 7g 7fg 7d) Mar 3; fifth foal; dam of little account; only plating class. *M. McCormack.* –

LADY BLACKFOOT 2 b.f. Prince Tenderfoot 126–Indian Graduate (Chieftain) (1980 5v² 5f² 5fg* 5g³ 5g⁴ 5g² 5d* 5s²) Apr 7; 6,600Y; leggy, rather lightly-made filly; half-sister to Irish middle-distance winner Shaun Bawn (by Ballymore) and a winner in Malaya; dam won at up to 1½m; a genuine and consistent filly who won maiden auction event in May and valuable nursery in October, both at Phoenix Park, latter by 2½ lengths from Rhein Honey; also ran well in better races, when just over 3 lengths fourth of 10 to Swan Princess in Gallaghouse Phoenix Stakes at Phoenix Park in August, ½-length second to Cooleen Jack in Goffs Stakes at the Curragh the following month and ¾-length second to Martinova in Waterford Testimonial Stakes at the Curragh in October; will stay 6f; acts on any going; sold 50,000 gns Goffs November Sales. *K. Prendergast, Ireland.* **108**

LADY CYNARA 2 b.f. Starch Reduced 112–Golden Perch 79 (Sovereign Lord 120) (1980 5fg 5f 5.8h 6fg 7g 6f) Apr 8; small filly; second foal; dam placed over 1m and 11f, and also over hurdles; no worthwhile form, including in sellers; blinkered fifth outing; sold 400 gns Ascot December Sales. *J. Douglas-Home.* –

LADY DOWNSVIEW 3 b.f. Prince Regent 129–Tetrazzini 70 (Sovereign Path 125) (1979 5g* 5g 5d 6f 6f* 7g* 6f 6f 6fg² 6s 1980 8h 8fg 7.6g 8g 7g 8fg 6d) attractive, good-bodied filly; useful (rated 102) at 2 yrs; not disgraced on several outings in 1980 though failed to reach the frame; stays 1m; acts on firm going and is possibly not at her best on soft; blinkered fourth start at 2 yrs; suitable mount for an inexperienced rider; refused to enter stalls intended reappearance. *P. Feilden.* **81**

LADY ELECT 3 b.f. Veiled Wonder–Highview Jill 73 (Proud Chieftain 122) (1979 5s 6g 5s 5fg 5d⁴ 5fg 5f 5fg 6g 1980 6d 6f 6f³ 5f² 6fg 6fg 6d⁴ 5fg) bad mover; plater; stays 6f; acts on firm going; sometimes blinkered; wears bandages. *W. Bentley.* **44**

LADY EMBER 3 b.f. Hot Spark 126–Pladda (Reliance II 137) (1979 5g² 5g 5.3g 5g 6f 6fg² 5g* 1980 6fg 7fg² 8g² 7g 7g³ 8g) lightly-made filly; quite a moderate handicapper; stays 1m; yet to race on a soft surface; ran poorly final start; sold 5,800 gns Newmarket December Sales. *F. J. Houghton.* **76**

LADY EVER-SO-SURE 2 ch.f. Malicious–Time of Hope 98 (Matador 131) (1980 5g 5f 5fg 6g* 6d⁴ 6d* 7g² 7s² 7f⁴) Mar 6; 840F, 3,000Y; strong, compact filly; half-sister to a 2-y-o winner by Privy Councillor; dam sprinter; fairly useful plater; successful at Ripon (by 5 lengths) in June and Haydock (bought in 2,200 gns after beating Aunty May a length) the following month; second in nurseries at Redcar and Newcastle the following month, running particularly well when beaten a head by Salon Privee in former; stays 7f well; acts on soft going and isn't at her best on firm; wears blinkers. *J. Etherington.* **80**

LADY FOGGARTY 2 b.f. Windjammer (USA)–Tithe Barn (Zarathustra 131) (1980 6fg 6d 7g 6g 7g) Feb 18; 9,000Y; compact, quite attractive filly; half-sister to 3 winners, including fairly useful 6f and 7f winner Salinity (by Jukebox); dam, half-sister to top-class Bold Lad (Ire), won over 1m and 9f in Ireland; 5½ lengths fifth of 13 to Pieta in maiden race at Brighton in August, fourth outing and best effort; should stay 7f. *R. Smyth.* **67**

LADY GREENE 2 br.f. No Mercy 126–Sea Tycoon 80 (Tycoon II) (1980 6fg) Apr 24; second foal; half-sister to fairly useful 6f winner Davenport Boy (by Workboy); dam stayed 1½m; 10/1 when behind in 19-runner minor event won by Sea Aura at Lingfield in October. *A. Pitt.* –

LADY JASMINE 2 gr.f. Sun Prince 128–Jasminia 92 (Zeddaan 130) (1980 6g³) May 1; strong, compact filly; third foal; dam, half-sister to 1967 Derby third Dart Board, ran well over 1¼m on only start; third favourite, stayed on when 7¾ lengths third of 19 to Dancing Sally in newcomers race at Goodwood in September; should do better over middle distances at 3 yrs. *R. Hern.* – p

LADY LORELEI 2 b.f. Derring-Do 131–Friendly Sound 82 (Be Friendly 130) (1980 5s² 5g* 6s* 6s⁴) Apr 8; neat filly; first foal; dam won three 7f races; made all to justify favouritism by 2½ lengths from La Belle Sorciere in maiden race at Kempton in July and bettered that effort when winning 7-runner minor event at Newcastle the following month most convincingly by 2 lengths from Chief Admiral; respectable fourth of 7 to Star Pastures in valuable race at Ayr in September; will stay 7f; acts well on soft going. *B. Hobbs.* **92**

LADY LORENZA 3 b.f. Lorenzaccio 130–Lady Lowndes 97 (Tamerlane 128) (1979 5v 5v 5g 5.8g 1980 8.3s 9d 8.3g) bad plater. *M. Bradley.* —

LADY LOWERY 3 b.f. Communication 119–Vacation 102 (Remainder 106) (1979 5v4 5d 5f2 5fg 1980 5v 5s 5f) small, fair sort; poor form, including in a seller. *D. Sasse.* —

LADY MALA 2 b.f. So Blessed 130–Mala Mala (Crepello 136) (1980 5d) Apr 20; 21,000Y; good-topped filly; second foal; dam unraced sister to Derby fourth Great Wall; 10/1 and backward, made little show when 7 lengths sixth of 8 to Artistry in maiden race at Newbury in July. *D. Whelan.* —

LADY MANTEGNA 3 b.f. Andrea Mantegna–Grand Central 79 (Grand Roi 118) (1979 7g 7fg 8fg 10s 1980 11f 3 11.1f4 16f 12d 12d 10.1f 11.7h 12s4) leggy filly; plating-class maiden; not certain to stay 2m. *R. Laing.* **62**

LADY MENELAUS 2 b.f. Brigadier Gerard 144–Helen of Troy 83 (Grey Sovereign 128 §) (1980 6g 6fg) June 7; third foal; half-sister to a winner in Brazil; dam, half-sister to high-class 6f to 1m horse Joshua, won over 6f; 6¾ lengths seventh of 13 to Pieta in maiden race at Brighton in August; unquoted when behind in 19-runner minor event won by Sea Aura at Lingfield in October. *P. Makin.* —

LADY MIRAGE 2 ro.f. Grey Mirage 128–Lady Ace 66 (Space King 115) (1980 5f 5fg) Apr 7; lengthy, light-framed filly; fifth reported foal; dam won 5f seller at 2 yrs; in rear in seller and maiden race in the Midlands. *R. Whiston.* —

LADY NIGHTINGALE 2 b.f. Martinmas 128–Miss Anna (King's Company 124) (1980 5s 7g* 6s3) Mar 18; 1,000Y; first foal; dam showed no form in 5 races but is half-sister to French Derby third Providential; won minor event at Galway in August by ¾ length from Blue Wind when having first race for 4 months; second favourite, led for over 5f when 1¾ lengths third of 14 to Arctique Royale in Group 2 Moyglare Stud Stakes at the Curragh later in August; will stay 1m; yet to race on a firm surface. *L. Browne, Ireland.* **98**

LADY OAKLEY 3 ch.f. Gulf Pearl 117–Salima (Palestine 133) (1979 5d 5g* 5g 6f* 6f 1980 8fg* 7d 7fg3 7g3) robust, good sort; fairly useful handicapper; beat Bargain Line ½ length at Brighton in May; will stay 1¼m; acts on firm going and is probably unsuited by soft. *L. Cumani.* **94**

LADY OF THE ISLE 3 b.f. Pitskelly 122–Ribollina (Ribero 126) (1979 5d 5s3 5.1fg2 6f2 6fg2 6fg* 6fg2 6g4 6d 6f 5h 1980 7s 7f 7fg 8g 8fg 7g2 8g 7fg 8g3 8fg3 7f* 7g 7g3 7d) small filly; plater; won non-selling handicap at Ostend in August; stays 1m; acts on firm going; blinkered twice at 2 yrs; suitable mount for a boy; sold 1,250 gns Newmarket Autumn Sales. *G. Blum.* **62**

LADY OSBORNE 2 b.f. Royal Palace 131–Empress of England (Constable 119) (1980 9d) Apr 28; half-sister to a winner over hurdles; dam never ran; 20/1, started slowly when in rear in 11-runner minor event won by Cinderwench at Wolverhampton in October. *G. Balding.* —

LADY PROBUS 3 b.f. Shantung 132–Hunting Bee (Honeyway 125) (1979 8f 7fg 8d 1980 10f4 10.4g 8f 10.6d) lengthy filly; has some ability but is most unreliable and should be left alone; sometimes blinkered. *W. Elsey.* **§§**

LADY RAGSTONE 2 ch.f. Ragstone 128–Lady Advocate 116 (King's Bench 132) (1980 5fg 5h 5fg 6s 6g 7g 6fg 6g4) May 18; 3,000Y; short-backed filly; bad plater; sold 440 gns Doncaster September Sales. *M. W. Easterby.* **43**

LADY REVELLA 3 b.f. Sweet Revenge 129–Tavella 98 (Petingo 135) (1979 5s 5d 7f 7f 6f4 7g 6s4 7fg 8.2d* 8.2d 7f 1980 8s 8v 8f 10.1fg 10h 12.2fg 8d 10g 8fg) small filly; poor plater; stays 1m but is unlikely to stay 1½m; sometimes sweats up; sold 720 gns Doncaster August Sales. *G. Toft.* —

LADY ROMOHA 3 b.f. Sit In The Corner–Forthcoming 69 (New Brig 120) (1979 NR 1980 12.2f 10fg 10d 10f 13.8fg 13.8d) lightly-made filly; poor plater. *F. Wiles.* —

LADY SISTER 3 gr.f. Saritamer 130–Soft Chinook (Hitting Away) (1979 5.1g4 6fg* 5f4 1980 7f 6fg* 8fg4 6fg4 6fg 6f4 7g 7d* 6d) quite a useful-looking filly; quite a moderate handicapper; won at Pontefract in April and Catterick in October, stays 7f; acts on a firm and a soft surface; apprentice ridden at Catterick. *I. Walker.* **77**

LADY SULLIVAN 3 b.f. Pitcairn 126–Floragold 87 (Floribunda 136) (1979 NR 1980 7f 9.4d 8s 7g) third foal; dam stayed 6f; well beaten in maiden and minor events; blinkered final start. *M. W. Easterby.* —

LADYSWOOD 3 b.f. Great Nephew 126–Expo 80 (Sheshoon 132) (1979 5s 5g 6fg 7g 7fg 7fg 7.2g 1980 8.2s 8.2fg 8fg^3 7f 8d 8s^2 8g^3 11.7f 10.6d 12g 11.7h 10fg^4 9f 10fg) small filly; plater; probably stays $1\frac{1}{2}$m; seems to act on any going; often blinkered; reared up in stalls on second start; sold 450 gns Doncaster October Sales. *J. Haine.* **47**

LADY TIFFANY 2 b.f. Welsh Saint 126–Marla (Hul a Hul 124) (1980 5g 6g 6d 7.5fg* 7d* 6s^2 7fg^3 8g) May 20; 3,900Y; half-sister to 1977 French 2-y-o 5.5f winner Balian (by Green God); dam won at up to 9f in Ireland; won twice in July, beating Maryville Bick 2 lengths in maiden race at Gowran Park and Baladin 3 lengths in 15-runner nursery at Galway; performed with credit in pattern races on next two starts, running on to finish length second of 14 to Arctique Royale in Moyglare Stud Stakes at the Curragh in August and coming out best filly at weights when $\frac{3}{4}$-length third of 11 to Lone Bidder in Park Stakes at Phoenix Park the following month; stays 7f well but ran moderately over 1m; seems to act on any going. *N. Meade, Ireland.* **99**

LADY WESTLEIGH 2 b.f St Paddy 133–Beetroot 89 (Psidium 130) (1980 5d^3 5fg 6fg 7d* 7g 7d) Mar 31; 2,100F, 7,800Y; compact, good sort; good walker and mover; sister to a poor animal and half-sister to 2 minor winners; dam stayed well; landed a gamble in 12-runner maiden race at Brighton in July by $2\frac{1}{2}$ lengths from Aruse; will be suited by middle distances; possibly needs an easy surface; inconsistent. *R. Smyth.* **76**

LADY WHITEFOOT 5 b.m. Martinmas 128–Anneiv (Vienna 127) (1979 8s 8s 8g 10s 8s 8d* 8f^4 7fg^2 8fg 7fg^4 8fg^2 10g^4 7g 10g^3 1980 8f^4 8f 8g^4 7f 12d 10d) lengthy mare; has been hobdayed; won a seller in 1979; poor form in non sellers in 1980; stays $1\frac{1}{4}$m; seems to act on any going; suitable mount for an inexperienced rider; has worn bandages. *K. Ivory.* **–**

LADY WIMPY 2 ch.f. Mansingh 120–High Society 96 (So Blessed 130) (1980 5f) Apr 1; leggy, unfurnished filly; second foal; sister to a poor animal; dam 2-y-o 5f winner; unquoted, didn't move well on way to start and was always behind when eighth of 12 to Hi There in maiden race at Wolverhampton in May. *Mrs J. Reavey.* **–**

LA FEDHALA 2 ch.f. Swing Easy 126–Gay Amanda 75 (Counsel 118) (1980 5f 6g* 6s^2 6d^4) Mar 31; light-framed filly; good mover; third foal; half-sister to a winner in Malaya; dam stayed $1\frac{1}{4}$m; 33/1, attracted no bid after making all to win 19-runner seller at Goodwood in September by a length from Warwick Trailer; ran creditably in another big field of platers at Haydock and in £4,200 nursery at Newbury afterwards; may well stay 7f; acts on soft going. *N. Gaselee.* **73**

LA FILLE 4 b.f. Crooner 119–Drinka Pinta 101 (Court Feathers 120) (1979 8g 9s 8s 8f 10f^3 8f^3 10g^2 15.8d^2 8fg^3 12fg^3 10h^2 13.8s^3 11s* 1980 11d^4 12fg 12f 12fg 15.8fg^4 16fg 16.1d 20.4g^3 19f 16f^4) plater at 3 yrs; ran in better company in 1980; stays well; acts on any going; often wears blinkers nowadays; sweating penultimate start. *J. Berry.* **34**

LAFONTAINE (USA) 3 b.c. Sham–Valya (Vandale) (1979 NR 1980 8.2g* 8d 10g 10fg^3 10fg 10.5f 8s 8g) 14,000Y; big, strong colt; brother to smart American stakes winner Beau Sham, successful at up to 9f, and half-brother to useful Irish middle-distance filly Sassalya (by Sassafras); dam good French middle-distance performer; beat Moon Pad a length in 20-runner maiden event at Haydock in June; not disgraced in good company on second and fourth outings but ran poorly last 4 starts; stays $1\frac{1}{4}$m; possibly unsuited by very firm ground; sold 8,600 gns Newmarket Autumn Sales. *C. Brittain.* **83**

LA GLINETTE 2 ch.f. Hot Spark 126–Scarlet Woman (Red God 128 §) (1980 5fg) Mar 19; 8,200Y; fair sort; first foal; dam poor maiden; 50/1, started slowly and virtually took no part when last of 11 to Sybaris in maiden race at Sandown in April. *J. Winter.* **–**

LA GOULUE 2 br.f. Moulton 128–Pearl Wedding 83 (Gulf Pearl 117) (1980 7g 7fg 10s) May 4; 18,000Y; well-made filly; first foal; dam won over $1\frac{1}{4}$m and $1\frac{1}{2}$m; behind in maiden and minor events in second half of season. *J. Sutcliffe.* **–**

LAKI LADY 4 b.f. Frankincense 120–Cadera (Primera 131) (1979 6d 5s^4 6fg^3 6g^3 1980 5d 6s) plater; stays 6f. *K. Bridgwater.* **–**

LAKIN 3 br.c. Lauso–Miss Wrekin 97 (Pardao 120) (1979 7f^2 8fg^3 1980 12f* 12fg 12f^2) strong, workmanlike colt; useful performer; won maiden race at Newmarket in April very impressively from Mount Denali; ran moderately next **108**

time but returned to form to be creditable 2½ lengths second to Vaguely Tender in handicap at Epsom in June (flattered by proximity to winner but finished clear of remainder); subsequently had a set-back and wasn't seen out again; will stay 1¾m; yet to race on an easy surface. *B. Hobbs.*

LALDHEER 4 ch.g. Swing Easy 126–Hat Girl (High Hat 131) (1979 7g 5s 6fg 5g 5g^{2} 5.6fg 5fg 1980 5g 6fg 6fg 5f 6g^{2} 6d* 6g* 6fg 5f 5g 5d^{3}) leggy gelding; won handicaps at Brighton and Kempton in July convincingly; stays 6f but probably not 7f; acts on a firm and an easy surface; has worn blinkers. *R. Smyth.* **80**

LA LEGENDE (USA) 3 b.f. Reviewer–Lianga 133 (Dancer's Image) (1979 5f* 5f* 6f 6s* 1980 7.3fg^{4}) smallish, attractive filly; good mover; first foal; dam won 11 races from 4.5f to 1m, including Prix Robert Papin, Prix de l'Abbaye and Prix Jacques le Marois; won minor events at Newmarket and Salisbury and £3,800 race at Doncaster at 2 yrs; ran only once in 1980, finishing 4¼ lengths fourth of 11 to Millingdale Lillie in Fred Darling Stakes at Newbury in April (faded in final furlong due to lack of condition); will stay 1m; acts on any going; genuine. *H. Cecil.* **103**

LA LUCIA (USA) 2 ch.f. Forli–Wonderful Gal (The Axe 115) (1980 5g 6s 7g 6s 6fg) leggy, useful-looking filly; half-sister to minor stakes winner Hattab Voladora (by Dewan); dam, winner at up to 1m, is sister to very smart American colt Al Hattab; little better than plating class; should stay 1m. *H. Candy.* **67**

LA LUTINE 3 b.f. My Swallow 134–La Mome 109 (Princely Gift 137) (1979 5f* 6f 7g* 7d 8fg 1980 8fg^{2} 8h 10g 9g* 14g 10.2g* 10f 10.5s) leggy, lightly-made filly; fairly useful handicapper; successful at Ripon in August (enterprisingly ridden) and Doncaster in September; beat Snow Blessed a short head after a good tussle on latter course; unlikely to stay 1¾m; acts on firm going; blinkered final start at 2 yrs; suitable mount for an apprentice; genuine. *M. H. Easterby.* **95**

LA MASCOTTE 2 b.f. Hotfoot 126–Calling High 88 (Mountain Call 125) (1980 5f 6f) Mar 7; 16,000Y; lengthy, quite attractive colt; second foal; half-sister to 1m winner My Natalie (by Rheingold); dam 2-y-o 6f winner; 20/1 when towards rear in maiden races at Lingfield and Epsom in August. *J. Sutcliffe.* –

LAMBAY 2 ch.f. Lorenzaccio 130–Treasure Island 80 (Whistling Wind 123) (1980 5.3d 5g 7fg^{3} 8g^{2} 7d* 7d^{4}) Apr 17; close-coupled filly; half-sister to 3 winners, including Irish 1¾m winner Windward Isle (by Morston); dam, 2-y-o 5f winner, stayed 1m; kept on strongly to win 13-runner maiden race at Leicester in October decisively by 2 lengths from La Biche; creditable fourth under a 5-lb penalty in nursery won by Miss St James's at Doncaster later in month; will stay at least 1m; acts on a firm and a soft surface. *B. Hobbs.* **88**

LAMBRUSCA 3 b.f. Warpath 113–Lametta 94 (Alycidon 138) (1979 NR 1980 12fg^{4} 12f 14d 13.8d 15s) leggy, unfurnished filly; half-sister to several winners, including fairly useful stayer Lampardal (by Pardal); dam a stayer and half-sister to good staying handicapper Golden Fire; well beaten in varied company in the North. *C. Thornton.* –

LAMBS AT EIGHT 2 br.g. Pieces of Eight 128–Miss Tack (Right Tack 131) (1980 5s 5f 5f 6g 8.2g) Feb 4; 1,450Y; strong gelding; third foal; dam ran 3 times; blinkered, showed only sign of ability when 7 lengths sixth of 12 to Oratavo in 1m seller at Nottingham in September; trained by C. Bewicke first 3 outings. *N. Vigors.* **53**

LAMBWATH HALL 3 b.c. Caliban 123–Golden Dolly 76 (Golden Horus 123) (1979 5f 5fg 6g^{4} 8g 1980 8h 16g 9g* 10d 8d 7d) lengthy colt; has a round action; ridden by 5-lb claimer to win seller at Newcastle in June (bought in 2,300 gns); stays 9f; needs to be held up. *A. Smith.* **72** d

LAMYA 2 b.f. Hittite Glory 125–La Mome 109 (Princely Gift 137) (1980 5d 6g 7fg 7f 7fg) May 15; 10,000Y; unfurnished filly; half-sister to 3-y-o La Lutine (by My Swallow), successful at up to 1¼m, and a winner in Italy; dam stayed 1¼m; showed a little ability in maiden races on third and fourth outings; blinkered when in rear in seller at Newmarket in October on fifth. *W. O'Gorman.* **73**

LANA'S SECRET 4 br.f. Most Secret 119–Rosemarkie 75 (Goldhill 125) (1979 6v 5s 6s^{3} 7g 6f 5fg^{4} 5f^{2} 5f* 5g* 5h^{2} 5g 5g^{2} 5g 5g^{2} 1980 6h 5fg 5fg^{4} 5s^{3} 5g 5g^{4} 5fg* 5d 5f 5d^{2} 5d 5s 6f 6g^{4} 6fg^{3} 5d 6d 6s 5v) useful-looking filly; sprint handicapper; went down by ¾ length to Miss Redmarshall at Redcar in July, but was awarded race after winner was disqualified for bumping another runner, **72**

probably doesn't stay 7f; acts on any going; often wears blinkers; trained until seventh outing by M. H. Easterby. *G. Lockerbie.*

LANCAR 3 b.g. Lauso–Yolancar 65 (Kibenka 119) (1979 5f 5d 1980 8d^3 **52**
7f^4 8f 8fg^4 8fg^2) unimpressive gelding; plater; will stay 1¼m; acts on a firm and a soft surface; sometimes gives trouble at start; has run respectably for an apprentice. *W. Stephenson.*

LANCASTER MEWS 3 ch.c. Porto Bello 118–Tesco Maid (Tesco Boy 121) **75**
(1979 5s 5f^4 6g 5g^2 5d^2 5.1g* 5g^3 1980 5v^3 6fg 6fg 5fg* 5f^3 6d 5.1g 5g^3 5d^4 5.8g 5d) well-grown colt; quite a moderate handicapper; won at Stockton in June; form only at 5f; probably acts on any going; has worn a tongue strap. *B. Hanbury.*

LANCASTRIAN 3 b.c. Reform 132–Rosalie II 66 (Molvedo 137) (1979 **119**
NR 1980 10.5d^3 12.5g* 12g* 12.5d^4 12.5g* 14.6g 12s^2) shapely, attractive colt; has a round action; half-brother to 3 winners, notably good filly Cistus (by Sun Prince), a winner at up to 1¼m; dam won at 1¼m; successful in minor event at Saint-Cloud in May, Group 3 Prix du Lys at Chantilly the following month and Prix de Menneval at Deauville in August; beat Corvaro a neck at Chantilly and got home by a short head from Doux Lord at Deauville; also ran well to be in frame in Grand Prix de Saint-Cloud (strong-finishing fourth to dead-heaters Dunette and Shakapour) and Prix du Conseil de Paris at Longchamp (rec 8 lb less than w.f.a. when ½-length second to En Calcat); well-beaten fifth of 7 to Light Cavalry in St Leger at Doncaster in September; stays 1½m well; acts on soft going. *D. Smaga, France.*

LANCERBOSS 3 b.f. Lord Gayle 124–Late Spring 101 (Silly Season 127) **—**
(1979 NR 1980 9d) 4,400F, 10,000Y; closely related to Late Summer (by Habitat), successful over 5f in France, and half-sister to 3 winners, including prolific 2-y-o winner Spindrifter (by Sandford Lad); dam won twice over 5f at 2 yrs; very burly when eighth of 21 in maiden event at Wolverhampton in August; dead. *Sir Mark Prescott.*

L'ANCRESSE LODGE 2 ch.f. National Trust 89–Rosy Moll (Vermeil II **—**
104) (1980 5fg 5f 5g 5f 8d) June 10; 400Y; small, fair sort; fourth foal; dam point-to-point winner; in rear in maiden company. *J. Long.*

LAND AND SEA 3 ch.f. Realm 129–Paddle Boat 98 (St Paddy 133) (1979 **—**
6f 6f 7g^4 1980 8s^3 11fg 8f 8f 8fg 9.4d 10.4g 5g 7g) lengthy, attractive filly; poor maiden; best run at 1m on soft going. *R. Hollinshead.*

LANDA'S FRIEND 5 ch.g. Be Friendly 130–Amara (Sanctus II 132) (1979 **57**
11.7g 7.6v^4 7.6f^4 8f 1980 10fg 7fg 15fg* 12fg^3) big, rangy gelding; poor handicapper; 25/1 when scoring at Edinburgh in July; stayed well; probably acted on any going; sometimes wore blinkers; dead. *H. O'Neill.*

LANDED GENT 3 br.g. Pieces of Eight 128–Landed Lady 89 (Realm 129) **—**
(1979 8fg 1980 10f) tall, narrow gelding; in rear in maiden and minor events. *W. Hastings-Bass.*

LANDLADY 3 b.f. Busted 134–Freeholder 95 (Pinza 137) (1979 7.3s 1980 **60**
11fg* 12h^4 16g) leggy filly; made all and held on well to win moderate 7-runner maiden race at Wolverhampton in April; should stay at least 1½m; blinkered final start; sold 28,000 gns Newmarket December Sales. *R. Hern.*

LANGDALE'S BAZAAR 4 ch.f. Native Bazaar 122–Langdale Flyer (Hard **49**
Sauce 131) (1979 8.2g 5s 1980 8fg 10g 11d* 12fg 10s^2 10f 10d 10s 15d) fair sort of filly; dropped in class, showed first worthwhile form when winning selling handicap at Ayr (no bid) in July; stays 11f; suited by some give in the ground; blinkered last 2 outings (not disgraced first occasion). *J. Etherington.*

LAODAMIA 3 b.f. So Blessed 130–La Lidia 78 (Matador 131) (1979 5d 5s^3 **69**
5f 5g* 7f^2 6f* 7f 6d 6g 1980 7f 8f* 8fg 8g^4 8fg 8.2d 8d^4 10d^3 8s 8s) quite a moderate handicapper; awarded race at Ripon in May on relegation of winner to fourth; stays 1¼m; probably acts on any going; has run respectably for an apprentice; sold 4,000 gns Newmarket December Sales. *M. H. Easterby.*

LA PICCOLINA 4 b.f. Tudor Rhythm 112–The Guzzler 69 (Behistoun 131) **76**
(1979 8g^4 10s 10g 10.2g^2 10fg 9fg 10.8fg^2 8.3fg 10f 11.7f 12fg^2 1980 12.2s* 14fg 11.7fg 14g 12.2s^3 12fg 11.7d^3 11.7f 12fg^2 12g^4 12.2d* 12d 11d* 12d) small filly; won handicaps at Warwick (2) and Newbury, on latter course in October beating Divino Santi a shade comfortably by ¾ length; stays 1½m (well beaten over 1¾m); acts on any going; often apprentice ridden; genuine. *P. M. Taylor.*

LA PIMPERNELLE 2 b.f. The Go-Between 129–White Cliffs (Hill Rise 127) (1980 5.1f 6fg) May 28; 2,500Y; second foal; dam, daughter of very useful Victoria Quay, showed only poor form; seventh in maiden race at Yarmouth in June and seller at Doncaster (still on backward side) in July. *R. Boss.* —

LA PRINCIPESSA 3 b.f. Realm 129–Roman Twilight (Romulus 129) (1979 6g 6d 7f 1980 10s 8g 8f 10g 10g 10.4d 10f) useful-looking filly; has shown only a little ability in varied company; stays 1¼m; sweated up third outing and ran poorly on sixth (apprentice race); sold, covered by Royalty, 1,700 gns Newmarket December Sales. *R. Armstrong.* **62**

LAPSANG 3 b.c. Sweet Revenge 129–Tea Leaf (Cracksman NZ) (1979 5g 5s 6g 5fg 5f² 5f 5g 5s* 5g 1980 5f³ 5f³ 5fg 6g* 6f 6s 6d) strong colt; won handicap at Catterick in August: stays 6f; acts on any going but is particularly well suited by some give in the ground; blinkered sixth start; sold 4,500 gns Doncaster November Sales. *W. Haigh.* **70** d

LAPUKEI 2 ch.c. Tepukei 116–Lanata 64 (Charlottown 127) (1980 5fg 5fg 5f 5.3d 5.8fg 5.8f 6f) Mar 27; 3,000Y; neat, strong, attractive colt; only poor form in maiden races and sellers; bred to stay at least 1¼m; blinkered fifth outing. *A. Breasley.* **44**

LAQUIOLA (FR) 3 b.f. Lyphard 132–Kalila (Beau Prince II 131) (1979 8.5d* 1980 11g* 10.5g² 10.5g 9d) half-sister to several winners, notably French Derby winner Roi Lear (by Reform) and Prix Saint-Alary winner Lalika (by Le Fabuleux); dam winning half-sister to Val de Loir and Valoris; won 8-runner Prix de la Seine at Longchamp in April by ½ length from Belle de Caro; gave 4 lb away all round when keeping on strongly to be ½-length second to Hortensia in Prix Cleopatre at Saint-Cloud following month; seventh to Mrs Penny in Prix de Diane de Revlon at Chantilly in June and to Detroit in Prix Chloe at Evry in July; will stay 1½m; yet to race on a firm surface. *A. Head, France.* **113**

LA RUE ROYALE 3 b.f. Realm 129–Via Tritus 103 (Sovereign Path 125) (1979 6g 1980 7d 5h* 5d 6g) well-made filly; plater; won at Chepstow in May (no bid); best form at 5f; acts on hard going. *J. Sutcliffe.* **55**

LA SEINE 2 b.f. Blue Cashmere 129–Snap (Snob 130) (1980 6fg 5g 7g 7g 6f⁴ 6f) Feb 7; 4,000Y; workmanlike filly; half-sister to 2 winners in Italy; dam never ran; beaten only 1½ lengths when fourth of 18 to Scarrowmanwick in minor event at Lingfield in September; probably stays 7f. *S. Matthews.* **76**

LASER LADY 6 b.m. Laser Light 118–Miss Nesta (Conspirator 114) (1979 6s² 6fg 6s² 6s* 5.6fg³ 7.2g² 7fg* 1980 6fg 6fg 6d 6g 6f 6d* 7g 6d) useful handicapper at her best; 20/1, showed only form of 1980 when beating Ferriby Hall a length in valuable Joe Schofield Handicap at Haydock in October; stays 7f; acts on any going; blinkered twice at 2 yrs; good mount for an apprentice; showed a lot of knee action on way to post second start. *W. Haigh.* **98**

LASKA FLOKO 4 b.c. Thatch 136–Prima 75 (Alcide 136) (1979 8g 10.5g 12g 12f 10f* 12fg³ 10.5d 11.1f 8fg² 1980 7d 10.6fg* 10fg 10fg* 10.2fg 10fg 10f 12f³ 12g³ 12s 10.5g 12f 10fg⁴ 14g 12g⁴ 13.3fg⁴ 12s 10g 12v) strong, heavy-topped, good sort; very useful handicapper on his day; winner at Haydock in April and Newmarket in May, on latter beating Joleg 2 lengths; creditable third to Halyudh in Northern Dancer Stakes at Epsom in June and to Barley Hill in Bessborough Stakes at Royal Ascot later in month; probably stays 1¾m (not entirely disgraced in Tote-Ebor); acts well on firm going; often wears blinkers nowadays; has won for an apprentice; inconsistent. *C. Brittain.* **97**

LAST BUS 5 b.g. Tycoon II–Cloudy Day (Nimbus 130) (1979 NR 1980 6fg 7d 7g⁴ 8.3g 7g 8fg 7f³ 8f) plater; stays 1m; acts on firm going; blinkered fifth outing; has run well for a boy. *G. Lewis.* **42**

LAST DEVICE 3 b.g. Grey Mirage 128–Gorgeous Device 88 (Falls of Clyde 126) (1979 7.2g 7f 7s 1980 6fg 10.4f 7.2g 7.6g 7f² 7.2d* 7.6d 7g 7d) compact gelding; comfortably won handicap at Haydock in August; stays 7f well; probably acts on any going; blinkered final outing at 2 yrs and on fourth and fifth starts. *C. Crossley.* **62**

LAST FANDANGO 3 ch.c. Gay Fandango 132–Welsh Game (Pall Mall 132) (1979 NR 1980 8s 7f* 8.5f* 8f² 8d³ 10g) **125**

The influence of Forli on European racing, first brought to notice by the appearance of the versatile Home Guard and subsequently increased through

Ladbroke Blue Riband Trial Stakes, Epsom—Last Fandango wins well from Marathon Gold and Johnny O'Day

the top-class performers Thatch, Gay Fandango and Posse, looks certain to be continued through his best sons at stud. To date Home Guard, Thatch and Gay Fandango have sired the winners of races worth in excess of £750,000; while Gay Fandango's share is the smallest of the three he has had only two crops to represent him and can be regarded as having made a promising start to his stud career with several runners who are at least useful. Best of a list that also includes Spanish Dancer and Moomba Masquerade is Last Fandango who, in a season ending prematurely in July, nearly provided his sire with a classic success.

Unraced as a two-year-old, Last Fandango didn't take long to prove himself out of the ordinary. After a promising debut in the Easter Stakes at Kempton he won his next two starts, an eighteen-runner maiden event at Newmarket and the Ladbroke Blue Riband Trial at Epsom. If the opposition at Newmarket wasn't taxing, that at Epsom was fairly stiff, with Johnny O'Day, a close third in the Gladness Stakes on his reappearance, and Marathon Gold among Last Fandango's seven opponents. Waited with, Last Fandango made steady progress in the straight and, once pulled out approaching the distance, outpaced his rivals with a burst of acceleration that took him a length and a half clear of Marathon Gold at the post. With Saint Jonathon representing the Hills's stable in the Two Thousand Guineas, Last Fandango went to the Curragh in May for the Irish equivalent sponsored by the Airlie and Coolmore studs, and he ran a fine race. Prominent in the main group behind the tearaway leader Indian Lore in the early stages, he moved up in the straight and entered the final furlong disputing the lead with Nikoli, Final Straw and Posse. Under considerable pressure (he received a dozen cracks of the whip) Last Fandango galloped on with tremendous determination but in a driving finish he went down by a short head to Nikoli with Final Straw half a length away third.

His run at the Curragh was the highlight of Last Fandango's year. The St James's Palace Stakes at Royal Ascot saw him rematched with the colts that had finished third and fourth in Ireland, Final Straw and Posse, and it also saw his racing on a soft surface for the first time since his initial outing. The firm going at Newmarket, Epsom and the Curragh appeared to suit Last Fandango well—the zest and enthusiasm with which he strode out on it impressed us more than once—and he didn't look so comfortable at Royal Ascot. Even so in staying on strongly to finish just over two lengths third to Posse he ran creditably, particularly since his chances weren't helped by his having to be switched twice to get a clear run soon after turning for home. Last Fandango's final run in the Coral Eclipse Stakes at Sandown was a very disappointing one. The race proved nothing about his distance requirements for he wouldn't have been in the shake-up had the race been run over a mile. Despite looking very well and being decidedly on his toes in the paddock he ran as though something was wrong with him: he came under pressure three furlongs out, began to lose his action, dropped back rapidly and trailed in a dismal last of six to Ela-Mana-Mou. Significantly he wasn't seen out again.

Last Fandango (ch.c. 1977)	Gay Fandango (ch 1972)	Forli (ch 1963)	Aristophanes
			Trevisa
		Gay Violin (b 1964)	Sir Gaylord
			Blue Violin
	Welsh Game (b 1971)	Pall Mall (ch 1955)	Palestine
			Malapert
		Nantgarw (gr 1964)	Abernant
			Lynsted

Last Fandango is the first foal of a mare who showed very useful form in France, winning five races from a mile to a mile and a quarter, but the family is not a distinguished one on the whole and Last Fandango is the only good-class winner to have come from it in recent years. His grandam, the unraced Nant-

Mr A. D. Shead's "Last Fandango"

garw, has produced three minor winners in addition to Welsh Game and is a half-sister to a winner in England and to Prince Ted, a fair French middle-distance handicapper. A 15,000-guinea yearling, Last Fandango is a well-made, lengthy colt. We understand he will be in training with V. O'Brien in 1981. *B. Hills.*

LAST IDEA 2 b.c. Pitskelly 122–Madeira 104 (Combat 123) (1980 6d 6g) Apr 30; 13,500Y; half-brother to numerous winners, including smart 1968 2-y-o 5f and 7f winner Zarco (by Abernant), subsequently a stakes winner at up to 9f in USA; dam a useful miler; unquoted and blinkered when never-dangerous 6 lengths sixth of 11 to Norman Style in £5,900 event at Doncaster in September, second outing; will stay 1m. *Denys Smith.* **68**

LAST LIGHT (FR) 2 b.c. Round Table–Lighted Glory 118 (Nijinsky 138) (1980 7g*) Apr 25; 220,000Y; second foal; dam smart performer at up to 10.5f; 5/4 favourite, had a lot to do below distance in 6-runner maiden race at Leopardstown in August but came through strongly to win by 2 lengths from Ascending Star; will be suited by 1¼m; capable of winning in better company. *V. O'Brien, Ireland.* **90** p

LAST LOVE (FR) 2 b.f. Platonic Love–La Sagonaise (Prince Eric) (1980 7g 8g* 8f 8s) Mar 5; strong, compact filly; first foal; dam never ran; sire, son of Celtic Ash, won over middle distances in France and also won over jumps; an obscurely-bred filly but a very useful one; won maiden race at Chantilly in September prior to finishing close-up fifth in Prix Marcel Boussac at Longchamp (beaten 2½ lengths by Tropicaro) and Prix des Reservoirs on same course (1½ lengths behind Votre Altesse); will stay 1½m; acts on any going. *J. Laumain, France.* **110**

LAST MARCH PAST 3 b.c. March Past 124–Sapele 73 (Decoy Boy 129) (1979 5s 5g 6fg 7f 8fg 1980 10f 12g 16s 10g) compact colt; poor form, including in a seller. *M. Tompkins.* –

Mr R. E. Sangster's "Last Light"

LAST REQUEST 3 b.f. Dancer's Image–Torrefranca (Sicambre 135) (1979 7f 10s* 1980 12g 12f 12.3f) lightly-built filly; won maiden race at Nottingham at 2 yrs; didn't find her form in handicaps in 1980; should stay 1½m; suited by soft going; blinkered final start (May). *J. Hindley.* —

LATAKIA 3 b.f. Morston 125–Cigarette Case 89 (Faberge II 121) (1979 7g² 8fg 1980 10fg⁴ 12g 13.3fg 12fg* 11.7g³ 12fg² 12f³ 13.3d²) well-made, good sort; narrowly won 11-runner maiden race at Brighton in August; creditable second in handicaps at Leicester and Newbury subsequently; stays 13f; acts on a firm and a soft surface; sold 10,000 gns Newmarket December Sales. *J. Bethell.* **80**

LATE EVENT 3 ch.f. Appiani II 128–Frigateen 82 (Fighting Ship 121) (1979 5f 10s 6d 1980 10.8v 9g 10fg 10h 8fg 8fg 7g) of little account; has been tried in blinkers; sold 280 gns Ascot October Sales. *C. Austin.* —

LATE GEM (FR) 4 b.g. Luthier 126–Katopolis (Nelcius 133) (1979 12v 13v 16d 12s 11.7g 10fg 12f 13fg 12g 10.2d 12d³ 10s 1980 10.2d 13s 18f 12fg 12fg 22.2fg 10s 11d 12s 10g 9v) workmanlike gelding; unreliable maiden; had his last 5 races in France; often reluctant to race; sometimes wears blinkers; best left alone. *C. Austin.* **§§**

LATIN BOND 5 ch.h. Good Bond 122–Sans Peur (Nimbus 130) (1979 8fg 10.6s 1980 10v 11f 8g) only poor form, including in sellers last 2 starts; blinkered second outing; sold 800 gns Doncaster September Sales. *W. C. Watts.* —

LATIN ROCKET 3 ch.c. Touch Paper 113–Maria's Bisca 74 (Hook Money 124) (1979 5s 5fg 1980 7fg 6fg²) narrow, light-framed colt; plater; stays 6f; sweated up final start (June). *R. Hollinshead.* **47**

LA TROUVAILLE 4 br.f. Perdu 121–Cool Harmony 63 (Arctic Storm 134) (1979 10g 11g 11.7g 16s 8.3fg 10.1f³ 8.3fg² 10fg² 7g³ 10fg² 10f 1980 10.1fg 8.3f 8g³ 8f* 8g* 8fg 10g 12fg 10g 10d) deep-girthed filly; plater; bought in after winning at Yarmouth (1,100 gns) and Pontefract (2,000 gns) in June; behind in better company next 4 outings; stays 1¼m but no further; acts on firm going; suitable mount for a boy; blinkered final outing at 3 yrs and second start. *H. O'Neill.* **55**

LAUBALL 2 b.f. Lauso–Ballyputt (Ballymoss 136) (1980 5s⁴ 5f 6g) Mar 19; lengthy, light-framed filly; second foal; dam never ran; poor form in sellers; bred to stay 1½m+. *W. Stephenson.* —

LAUDON 5 b.h. African Sky 124–Stevia (Supreme Court 135) (1979 5d 5fg² 5fg 5fg 5fg 5.6fg 5fg 5fg 5g 1980 5d 6f 5fg 5f*) quite attractive, well-made horse; sprint handicapper; mainly disappointing since second outing in 1979, but returned to form when getting up on line (well outpaced early on) to beat Balvima by short head at Newmarket in May; probably stays 6f; goes well on top-of-the-ground and is possibly unsuited by soft; ridden by apprentice P. Bradwell at Newmarket; sold 5,000 gns Newmarket December Sales. *C. Brittain.* **95**

LAUGHING 2 b.c. Comedy Star 121–Lovely Laura (Lauso) (1980 5f 5h 5f* 5d*) Apr 25; compact, early sort; second foal; dam never ran; blinkered when winning sellers at Chepstow (made all) in May and Wolverhampton (sold 3,100 gns after beating Alison Nicola 2 lengths) in July; should stay 6f; seems to act on any going but goes well on a soft surface. *N. Gaselee.* **60**

LAUGHING LADY 2 br.f. Comedy Star 121–King's Fillet (King's Bench 132) (1980 5f 5g 6g 5.8f 5g) Feb 1; 3,000F, 2,000Y; small, plain filly; half-sister to winning sprinter My Raff (by Raffingora); behind in maiden races and sellers; blinkered fourth start; sold 400 gns Newmarket Autumn Sales. *Mrs J. Reavey.* —

LAUKING 3 ch.g. Lauso–Kingsbay (King's Leap 111) (1979 NR 1980 10s 10s 8fg 11.7g 12g 8.3g 8g 10g 9f 8.2v⁴ 10d⁴) leggy gelding; poor plater; stays 1¼m; acts on heavy going. *W. Holden.* **44**

LAUMINA 2 b.f. Lauso–Domina (Coronation Year 124) (1980 5g 6f) Apr 4; light-framed filly; seventh living foal; dam well beaten in 3 races on flat; blinkered when well beaten in maiden race and seller in June. *W. Stephenson.* —

LAURA'S PRIDE 3 ch.g. Midsummer Night II 117–Flashlight 88 (Firestreak 125) (1979 5g 5fg 6fg 6fg 6fg 1980 10s⁴ 8fg 10.1fg 8.3f 10.1s 12d 8.3f 10s) bad plater; has worn blinkers; sometimes sweats up. *T. M. Jones.* —

LAUREPPA 3 b.f. Jimmy Reppin 131–Lovely Laura (Lauso) (1979 NR 1980 8f⁴ 10g⁴ 12f) tall, lengthy filly; first foal; dam never ran; only plating class; should stay middle distances. *N. Gaselee.* —

LAURINA 3 ch.f. Lauso–Frustina (Alcide 136) (1979 NR 1980 9f 9.6f 10.1s^{2} **51**
10.1d* 12fg) unfurnished filly; plater; bought in 1,300 gns after winning easily at Windsor in July; should stay 1½m; acts well on soft ground; has worn bandages. *D. Ringer.*

LAURIUM 3 b. or br.c. Prince Regent 129–Grecian Palm 78 (Royal Palm 131) **76**
(1979 5.1f 6fg 5fg* 5f^{4} 5g^{3} 1980 6f^{2} 6f^{4} 6d 6g^{2} 6d 6d 6g 8fg 7g^{4} 6g 8f) compact, strong-topped colt; quite a moderate handicapper; not certain to stay 1m; best on a sound surface; blinkered fourth and fifth starts; has shown signs on occasions of being none too keen. *G. Pritchard-Gordon.*

LAURUS 8 b.g. Sassafras 135–Corbalton 103 (Milesian 125) (1979 NR 1980 **–**
12.2s 8g^{4}) quite a moderate hurdler/chaser; does little racing on flat; acts on firm going and is probably unsuited by soft; has worn blinkers. *R. Turnell.*

LAUTORB 2 b.f. Lauso–Torbay (Hill Prince) (1980 6s 6fg^{2} 6s 6d 8fg) Feb 14; **60**
smallish filly; sister to a poor animal and half-sister to winning jumper St Torbay (by St Paddy); dam winning Irish sprinter; made up a lot of ground from halfway and failed by only a length to catch Tumble Whirl in seller at Doncaster in July; respectable fifth to Wyn Miluv in selling nursery at Brighton in September on fourth start; should stay at least 1m; acts on a firm surface; trained first 3 starts by W. Stephenson. *A. Jarvis.*

LAUTREC 2 b.c. Wolver Hollow 126–Night Vision 100 (Yellow God 129) (1980 **86**
6g 7fg*) Apr 9; 36,000Y; good mover; first foal; dam, who won Duke of Edinburgh Stakes, is half-sister to high-class 1¼m performer Take a Reef; short-priced favourite for 18-runner maiden race at Lingfield in October but had to be very hard ridden to get the better of Monks Farm; will stay 1¼m; started slowly first outing. *R. Price.*

L'AVENIR 2 ro.f. Habat 127–Amanda Jane 75 (Rustam 127) (1980 5fg 6fg 8d **–**
6g) Feb 7; 4,400Y; smallish, lengthy filly; half-sister to 4 winners, including useful sprinter Major John (by Majority Blue); dam a plater, placed up to 7f; no worthwhile form in maiden races. *J. Hill.*

LAVINSKY 3 ch.c. Ridan–Solitude 129 (Nosca) (1979 6s* 6fg* 6d^{2} 6fg 1980 **–**
8.2fg 8.5f) big, attractive colt; shows a lot of knee action; gave a smart display on third start at 2 yrs, putting up a good fight against Sonnen Gold in Gimcrack Stakes at York before going down by 1½ lengths; below form all starts afterwards, including in Cecil Frail Handicap won by Greenwood Star at Haydock in May and Diomed Stakes won by Hardgreen at Epsom in June; should stay 1m+; best form on a soft surface; sent to USA. *R. Price.*

LAW BREAKER 3 br.c. Relko 136–Legal Error 94 (Mandamus 120) (1979 6d **69**
1980 8fg 10h 12f^{2}) big, rangy colt; second in maiden race at Folkestone in June; will be suited by 1¾m; sold to S. Pattemore 8,600 gns Ascot July Sales. *J. Winter.*

LAWMAKER (USA) 2 b.c. Round Table–Greek Victress (Victoria Park) **105**
(1980 6g^{2} 7g^{3} 6g* 5g 6.3g* 5s^{3}) Apr 20; $500,000Y; half-brother to several winners in North America, including high-class 1974 2-y-o Greek Answer (by Northern Answer), successful at up to 1m, and stakes winning filly Grecian Victory (by Dr Fager); dam 2-y-o 6f winner; 5-length winner from Personal Guard in maiden race at Phoenix Park in July and made all to justify favouritism by 2½ lengths from Lord Trendy in Group 3 Railway Stakes at the Curragh in September; only 5¼ lengths sixth of 10 to Swan Princess when second favourite for Gallaghouse Phoenix Stakes at Phoenix Park in between and finished only third, 2¾ lengths behind Martinova, when odds on for 7-runner Waterford Testimonial Stakes at the Curragh in October; needs further than 5f and should be suited by 1m. *V. O'Brien, Ireland.*

LAWNSWOOD MISS 2 b.f. Grey Mirage 128–Lor Darnie 65 (Dumbarnie 125) **–**
(1980 5g 5f 7g 8fg 9d 7d) May 21; narrow filly; third foal; sister to a poor animal and half-sister to a winning hurdler; dam won sellers over 7f and 1m; seems of little account. *R. Hollinshead.*

LAW OF THE LAND 3 b.g. Tyrant–Coralivia (Le Levanstell 122) (1979 NR **–**
1980 10s 10.1g) 34,000Y; rangy, good-looking gelding; has a round action; half-brother to 6f and 12.2f winner Bold Front (by Daring Display); dam won over 1½m in Ireland, and is half-sister to very smart Ballyhot; beaten a long way in maiden race at Nottingham in April and minor event at Windsor in September; sold to T. Hallett 2,100 gns Ascot October Sales. *J. Tree.*

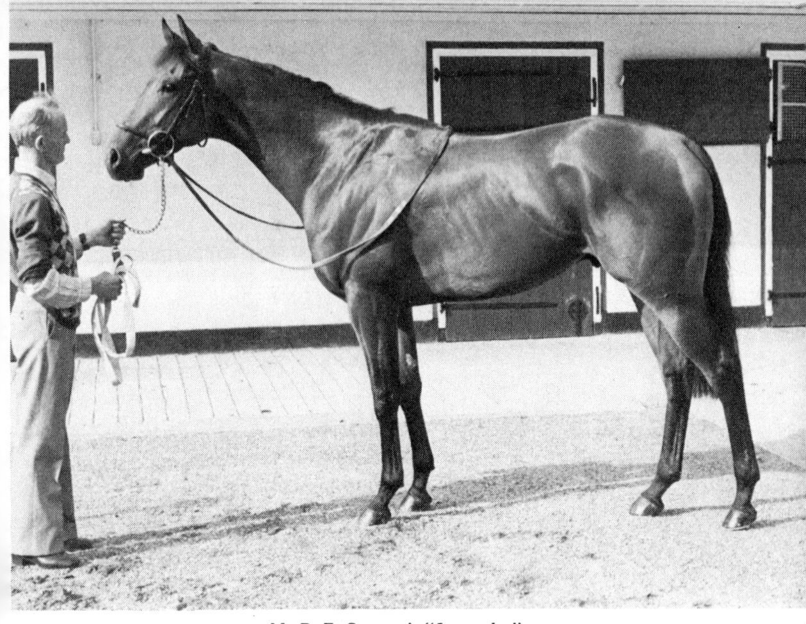

Mr R. E. Sangster's "Lawmaker"

LAWRENCE-LEE 3 ro.g. Grey Mirage 128–Mingwyn Wood (Pirate King 129) (1979 5v* 5fg 5s3 5v3 6g 7g 1980 8s3 10d 13s 12s2 16.9d 12s 16.5g) big gelding; has a round action; inconsistent handicapper; stays 1½m (well beaten over further); revels in the mud. *A. Davison.* **64**

LAW REPORT 2 b.f. Legal Eagle 126–Ravenna (Celtic Ash) (1980 5g 6fg 5fg 6d2 6d 6g 6g 6fg 7g) Apr 24; small, light-framed filly; half-sister to a winner in Norway; dam won over hurdles; showed only glimmer of ability when second to Tricky Rhythm in valuable seller at Brighton in June; should be well suited by 7f; suited by a soft surface; blinkered last 3 outings. *R. Hannon.* **59** d

LAWTON'S MEADOW 3 ch.g. Royben 125–Ember Grill 84 § (Indigenous 121) (1979 5fg 6fg 5f 5fg4 5d 5s 1980 8d 6v2 7d 6f 6f* 6fg 6fg 6g) leggy gelding; poor walker; quite a moderate plater in 1979; won modest maiden race at Haydock in May; better suited by 6f than longer distances; acts on any going; often wore blinkers at 2 yrs; sold out of Denys Smith's stable 590 gns Doncaster September Sales after seventh outing. *W. Stubbs.* **63**

LAYTH 3 b.c. Upper Case–Vilswitch 93 (Vilmorin) (1979 6f 6fg 7f 8g 1980 10s 10g 10fg4 10h3 10f3 12g4 12g) strong colt; plating-class maiden; probably stays 1½m; acts on hard going. *J. Hardy.* **67**

LAZZARO 3 b. or br.c. Levmoss 133–Maragay 65 (Match III 135) (1979 7g 7g 7fg4 8.2g 1980 14fg 16g 12g3 13s 16s 14fg* 14g 14.7f4) workmanlike colt; 25/1 winner of 13-runner maiden race at Yarmouth in August; will stay long distances; acts on a firm surface; blinkered fourth start. *A. Jarvis.* **58**

LEADER OF THE PACK (FR) 4 b.c. Sharpen Up 127–Highland Rocket (Paveh 126) (1979 5d4 5d3 6d 5fg2 5f3 6fg2 1980 6d 6f4 6f* 5f 6f2 6fg* 6fg 6fg 6g2 6g 6g 6g 6g 6fg 6d 7s 7g 7d 8s) good sort; won handicaps at Thirsk in April and Ripon in May, latter in good style from Turbo after being held up; best at up to 6f; acts on any going but probably finds 5f on fast ground too sharp. *R. Hollinshead.* **84**

LEAD THE FLOOR 3 gr.f. Dancer's Image–Virna (Coursing) (1979 7fg 7fg 8g 5.9g 7.5s2 8d* 1980 7v2 12.3f4 10fg 11.5d) workmanlike filly; first foal; dam won from 6f to 9f in France; in frame in Salisbury 1,000 Guineas Trial in March (8 lengths second to Battlewind) and Cheshire Oaks in May (led most of way and kept on to be 7½ lengths fourth to Shoot A Line); probably stays 1½m; acts on any going; wears blinkers; ran poorly last 2 starts (off course nearly 5 months before second one); sold 22,000 gns Newmarket December Sales. *N. Meade, Ireland.* **88**

LEAP BRIDGE 2 b.c. King's Leap 111–The Tower (High Treason 126) (1980 6g 6g 7f 6s4) May 4; 440Y; small colt; half-brother to several winners, including 1979 2-y-o 5f winner Calypso Queen (by Laser Light); dam showed little form; caught our eye in sellers at Wolverhampton and Nottingham in August on last 2 outings, particularly so at Nottingham when 5 lengths fourth of 20 behind Allied Cardiff (made significant late progress, without being given an unnecessarily hard time); promises to stay 7f. *J. Mulhall.* **58**

LEAP LIVELY (USA) 2 ch.f. Nijinsky 138–Quilloquick (Graustark) (1980 6f 7g 8g* 8fg*) **116**

If there was a prize for the most enterprising trainer of the year, the 1980 award would probably go to Ian Balding. He sent his horses far and wide, with excellent results. Glint of Gold picked up Italy's best race for two-year-olds, the Gran Criterium, while Wicked Will was prevented only by Beldale Flutter from gaining a similar success in Belgium's Grand Criterium International d'Ostende; Old Dominion collected over £7,000 in winning the Taby International Sprinters Stakes in Sweden; Be Better, Wicked Will and Mrs Penny ran well to be placed in pattern races in Ireland; and, most importantly, Mrs Penny established herself as a top-class filly by winning both the Prix de Diane and the Prix Vermeille in France. The stable didn't neglect the good meetings on its doorstep by any means, and at the Ascot September meeting it picked up two of the most important races for staying two-year-olds, the Royal Lodge Stakes with the colt Robellino and the Hoover Fillies Mile with Leap Lively.

Few, if any, could have predicted Leap Lively's Ascot success after her first two outings, on both of which she finished fifth. On her debut, in the Virginia Water Stakes at Ascot in July, the race was virtually over before

Hoover Fillies Mile, Ascot—Leap Lively draws away from Exclusively Raised and Fiesta Fun

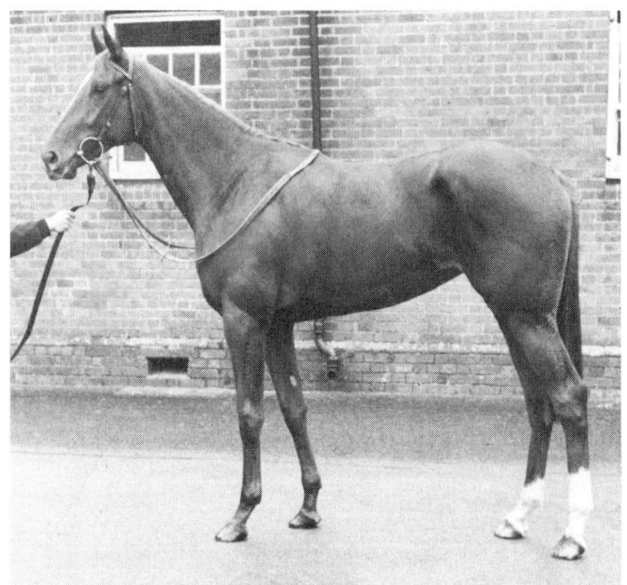

Mr Paul Mellon's "Leap Lively"

she realised what was required of her and her inexperience was again in evidence in the Waterford Candelabra Stakes at Goodwood a month later. There, after becoming unbalanced and losing a forward position when the pace quickened about two furlongs out, she ran on again to finish six lengths behind Fairy Footsteps. But slightly wiser, older and facing a stiffer test of stamina in the Goldener Oktober Stakes at Goodwood in September she gained her first success, but only after giving her rider a bit of a shock. Leap Lively looked as though she could leave Flighting standing whenever she wished as she tracked her on the bridle most of the way up the straight. However, when asked to quicken away coming to the final furlong, Leap Lively produced nothing like the expected response and Matthias had to use his whip to drive her into the lead. Only in the last hundred yards did she start to draw away; then she did so in good style and won by three lengths. The conclusions to be drawn from this performance were obvious—Leap Lively's long suit is stamina and, although she has sufficient speed to take a good early position, she doesn't possess instant acceleration.

Matthias' riding in the Hoover Fillies Mile showed that the lesson hadn't been lost on him. He quickly sent Leap Lively up into second place behind Shalwa who was setting far too fast a pace for her own good. As Shalwa dropped out on the turn into the straight Matthias immediately tried to send his filly clear. However, Leap Lively didn't succeed in shaking off the May Hill Stakes winner Exclusively Raised, who was giving her 4 lb, and it was the latter who looked the likely winner when she took over the lead at the distance. Leap Lively didn't give up, and as the fast early pace started to take its toll on Exclusively Raised she fought her way back into the lead to win going away by a length and a half, fractionally beating Ela-Mana-Mou's course record for two-year-olds. A smart effort and a game one!

In Leap Lively and Fairy Footsteps, England has two first-rate Oaks candidates. At the moment we prefer Fairy Footsteps but Leap Lively also has an excellent pedigree to back up her splendid racecourse performances. She's the best of the three winners bred by the minor mile winner Quilloquick who was sold, carrying to Honest Pleasure, for 185,000 dollars seven months after producing Leap Lively. Quilloquick comes from a very successful

Leap Lively (USA) (ch.f. Apr 11, 1978)	Nijinsky (b 1967)	Northern Dancer (b 1961)	Nearctic
			Natalma
		Flaming Page (b 1959)	Bull Page
			Flaring Top
	Quilloquick (ch 1969)	Graustark (ch 1963)	Ribot
			Flower Bowl
		Quillobelle (b 1961)	Princequillo
			Bellesoeur

American family: her half-brother Fifth Marine was one of the better three-year-olds of 1976, when his three stakes successes included the nine-furlong American Derby, and her grandam Bellesoeur has proved a very influential broodmare. Bellesoeur's sons included two stakes-winning stayers and the successful stallion Beau Gar, whose stock have won over 8,000,000 dollars, while she is found in the bottom line of the pedigrees of such high-class colts as Hawaiian Sound, Belle's Gold and Mr Leader, the last-named a highly successful stallion in the States. Leap Lively also has the appearance of a good filly. She's rangy and attractive, with the size and scope usually found in Nijinsky's stock, and certainly looks the type to train on. As yet she has raced only on a sound surface. *I. Balding.*

LEASONG 3 gr.g. Leander 119–Song of May 79 (Sing Sing 134) (1979 5s 5g 7f 1980 7f 8.2f 10d 8g* 9d^4) favourite, won seller at Carlisle in July (bought in 920 gns); stays 9f; acts on a soft surface; trained by W. Bentley first 2 starts and by S. Wainwright for third and fourth outings. *Denys Smith.* **55**

LE BEAU 2 b.c. Hot Spark 126–La Meme 90 (Pall Mall 132) (1980 7fg) Apr 7; 6,200Y; quite well-made, useful-looking colt; first foal; dam won 3 times over 2m and also won over hurdles; 33/1 when behind in 16-runner £3,900 event won by Centurius at Ascot in September; will stay at least 1m; looks capable of better. *P. Cole.* –

LE BOURSE 2 b.g. Native Bazaar 122–French Bond (Prince de Galles 125) (1980 5g 6g) Mar 8; 1,900Y; smallish, lengthy gelding; first foal; dam never ran; soundly beaten in sellers at Salisbury and Warwick (second favourite) in June. *P. Cole.* –

LE CHAMP TALOT (FR) 4 b.g. Our Mirage 123–Instantanee (Road House II) (1979 12g 11.7g* 12.3d^2 10.2s^2 10.6g 14d 10f 12g^3 10fg^2 1980 11fg 12.3f 12d 12d 13s) compact gelding; stays 1½m (well beaten over 1¾m); acts on any going; none too consistent. *R. Hollinshead.* –

LEDMIR (FR) 2 b.c. Platonic Love–Dragobra (Drago 120) (1980 7s 8g^2 9d* 10s^4 10v^4) Mar 10; first foal; dam, who never ran, is sister to a winning jumper and daughter of a winning jumper; won 15-runner maiden race at Evry in September by 5 lengths; subsequently put up excellent efforts in pattern races, being moved down to fourth place after running The Wonder to a short neck in Prix de Conde at Longchamp and being beaten little over a length when fourth to the same horse in Criterium de Saint-Cloud; stays very well; yet to race on a firm surface. *J. Laumain, France.* **117**

LEECREST PRINCESS 3 ch.f. Crowned Prince 128–High Day (High Hat 131) (1979 7fg 1980 7g) narrow filly; in rear in two races at Newmarket. *W. Hastings-Bass.* –

LEE PARK 2 b.c. Impecunious–Urschi (Fort Coulonge) (1980 6s) Apr 25; fifth reported foal; dam unraced sister to a winning stayer; unquoted and on burly side, moved badly to post when tailed off in 20-runner seller won by Allied Cardiff at Nottingham in August. *A. Davison.* –

LEFRAK CITY 3 ch.c. Saintly Song 128–Sweet Delphine 88 (Honeyway 125) (1979 5d 6fg 6fg 6fg 7fg^4 7g 7f 1980 10fg 8fg 10f 10fg 8g 7g) useful-looking colt; quite a moderate maiden at 2 yrs; well beaten, including in a seller, in 1980; should stay 1¼m; usually blinkered; sold 950 gns Ascot December Sales. *M. Haynes.* –

LEFRAK LADY 3 b.f. Starch Reduced 112–Misty Morn 70 (Worden II 129) (1979 6f^2 5f^4 5f 1980 9.6h 8.3s 7g 6fg 6g 6g) bad plater; has been tried in blinkers; unseated rider when saddle slipped fourth start. *A. Davison.* –

LEFT LONELY 3 gr.f. No Mercy 126–Ma Marie 104 (My Babu 136) (1979 NR 1980 6f 7f 8d^3 8g* 8g 7.2g) big, tall, rangy filly; half-sister to numerous winners, notably top 1975 2-y-o filly Pasty (by Raffingora); dam stayed 1¼m; won small 3-runner race at Ayr in July; stays 1m. *P. Walwyn.* **73**

LEGAL GAMBOL 2 ch.c. Double-U-Jay 120–Absuleno 78 (Above Suspicion 127) (1980 7f^4 7fg 10s) May 18; 900F, 3,600Y; half-brother to several winners, including 1979 2-y-o 5f winner Tommy Jack (by Tyrant); dam placed at up to 1½m; 9 lengths fourth of 7 to very easy winner To-Agori-Mou in minor event at Lingfield in August; well beaten in maiden races in the Midlands subsequently; should stay 1¼m. *J. Hudson.* **64**

LEGAL LAIRD 6 ch.h. Murrayfield 119–Legal Mistress (Counsel 118) (1979 8g 1980 10.6fg 8d^3 9g* 10g^2 8f 10g 8g 10g 10g) quite a moderate handicapper; won apprentice event at Kempton in July by 3 lengths from Pledge; stays 1¼m; suited by some give in the ground; wears blinkers; good mount for an inexperienced rider; dwelt seventh and eighth starts. *G. Balding.* **57**

LEGAL SESSION 3 ch.g. Sheshoon 132–Legal Treasure 46 (Quorum 126) (1979 NR 1980 11fg 16f 13d) 3,800Y; unfurnished gelding; well beaten in Northern maiden races. *J. W. Watts.* **–**

LE GARCON BLEUE 3 ch.g. Starch Reduced 112–Terre Bleue (Prince Bio) (1979 NR 1980 5fg) leggy gelding; half-brother to a winner in USA; dam placed over 9f in France; tailed-off last of 13 in maiden race at Wolverhampton in April. *G. Price.* **–**

LE GARCON GATE 3 b.c. Workboy 123–Pampered Lil 70 (Pampered King 121) (1979 5fg 1980 8fg 8.2g 7g) big, strong colt; poor form, including in a seller; sold 1,700 gns Ascot July Sales. *C. Nelson.* **–**

LEGENDRY KNIGHT 2 br.c. Mansingh 120–Lindy Ann (King's Leap 111) (1980 5fg 5fg 5d 5f 8d 8.2s 8g) Apr 17; 2,900Y; compact colt; first foal; dam unraced twin; plater; stays 1m. *M. Blanshard.* **57**

LEGIOUS 4 ch.g. Malicious–Leganter 79 (Galivanter 131) (1979 9v^4 8d 10d^3 11.5fg* 12fg* 12f* 12d* 12g^3 12g 1980 12f^3 12f^4 12.3g 12g^2 16.1d^3 12f^3 12fg^3) lengthy gelding; useful handicapper at his best; made winner fight quite hard when beaten ½ length by sole opponent Boon at Beverley in July; close third to Beggar's Bridge at Ascot later in month on penultimate outing, best subsequent effort; possibly doesn't stay 2m; seems to act on any going; sometimes sweats up; often makes the running; sold to R. York 5,200 gns Newmarket Autumn Sales. *G. Pritchard-Gordon.* **94**

LEGUARD 5 b.g. Derring-Do 131–Nun Neater 104 (Narrator 127) (1979 8g 8d 8d 1980 10s) rated 101 at 2 yrs; lightly raced and nothing like so good since; best form at up to 1m but should stay 1¼m; possibly unsuited by soft going. *G. Beeson.* **–**

LE HOPGROVE 2 ch.f. Le Johnstan 123–Last Sensation (Compensation 127) (1980 5fg 5f 5s 6s 5f 8fg) Mar 22; compact filly; useless plater. *R. Ward.* **–**

LEIKO 2 b. or br.c. Averof 123–My Conkers 70 (Aggressor 130) (1980 5v 5s^2 5g^4 5f^2 5fg^2 5fg^4 5f^4 5fg^4 5g 5.3g 5d) May 26; neat colt; third foal; dam 6f winner; plater; needs further than 5f and should stay at least 7f; acts on any going; has run well for an apprentice; sold 600 gns Newmarket Autumn Sales. *K. Ivory.* **54**

LEITH GLEAM 2 b.f. Shiny Tenth 120–Jane Escart (Escart III) (1980 5g^4 5f 6g^2 7.2g 7fg) Feb 17; lengthy non-thoroughbred filly; third living foal; half-sister to useful 1978 2-y-o 6f winner Leith Lady (by Joshua); dam poor N.H. performer; length second of 15 behind Hound Song in maiden race at Folkestone in August, easily best effort; should be suited by 7f. *M. Francis.* **77**

LEITH LADY 4 b.f. Joshua 129–Jane Escart (Escart III) (1979 7g 7fg 7f 7g 6fg 6d^3 6s^2 1980 6s 7fg 6fg 7f 7fg 7g 8.3f 6fg 6g* 6.7g) hollow-backed filly; good mover; useful performer (rated 106) at 3 yrs; showed first form of 1980 when beating Soustra by 2½ lengths in seller at Folkestone in October; sold out of M. Francis' stable 1,650 gns at subsequent auction; stays 7f; acts on any going; suitable mount for a boy; blinkered seventh outing. *J. P. Seguin, France.* **57**

LEITH PRINCE 5 b.g. Sun Prince 128–Fille de Fizz (Ragusa 137) (1979 12s 8g 8d 10.1fg^4 10f 10.8fg^2 10.8g^2 10fg 10s 1980 7.6g 10g 8.3g 16f 10.4d **–**

12g 10fg) poor plater; stays 11f; acts on a firm surface; tailed off when blinkered final start; trained by M. Cousins until after third outing. *M. James.*

LEITH PRINCESS 3 b.f. Joshua 129–Jane Escart (Escart III) (1979 6fg³ 7f 1980 10.8v 8fg 6g 7g 5g 6g) lengthy filly; poor plater nowadays; unlikely to stay middle distances; sometimes sweats up; blinkered final start; didn't look a suitable mount for a boy on second outing. *M. Francis.* —

LE MARMOT (FR) 4 b.c. Amarko–Molinka (Molvedo 137) (1979 10.5s* 12s* 12g² 12d* 12d² 12v³ 1980 10g³ 10.5d* 12g 12f* 12f) **128**

Le Marmot's season compares unfavourably with his previous one—when he won three good races and was second in both the Prix du Jockey-Club and the Prix de l'Arc de Triomphe. In 1980 he won the Prix Ganay and the Prix Foy but disappointed in his principal objectives, the King George VI and Queen Elizabeth Diamond Stakes and the Arc de Triomphe, and towards the end of his career began to give the impression that he had grown a little cunning and that a succession of hardish races had taken its toll. Reports that Le Marmot was showing increasingly little interest in his morning gallops would support such a view. Nevertheless, now he has been retired the point must be stressed that in his prime Le Marmot was a thoroughly dependable sort.

The season began well for Le Marmot. He made an encouraging reappearance when third to his old rival Three Troikas in the Prix d'Harcourt at Longchamp in April and showed the benefit of that race when turning the tables on her in the Prix Ganay over the same course and distance the following month. Three Troikas wasn't at her best in the Prix Ganay but Le Marmot put up a very good performance, especially as the distance of a mile and a quarter was hitherto considered on the short side for him. He was never going to be beaten after taking over from his stable-companion Northern Baby after the turn and won in clear-cut fashion by a length and a half. His win provided trainer Boutin with some compensation for Nureyev's disqualification in the Two Thousand Guineas the day before. Le Marmot's win in the Prix Foy at Longchamp in September was gained in very different style and it was there that we gained the impression that he had become wise to the game. With the late withdrawal of Dunette and Niniski, Le Marmot seemed to have a fairly simple task, provided that he could handle the going which was the firmest he had encountered. He started at long odds on in a field of five but with two furlongs to run his chance of winning seemed negligible. He was in third and under pressure, making little headway, and Anifa, receiving 9 lb, looked all set for victory. Then Le Marmot staged a terrific run, pulled off the rails, and just got up in a dramatic finish.

Le Marmot started favourite for the King George in between his wins, as he was entitled to on form. Not everyone knew at the time he had reportedly had a rather hurried preparation owing to a minor setback and had then struck the point of his off-hind hock travelling from France. Apparently Boutin instructed Paquet to ask permission to withdraw if he wasn't happy with the horse on the way down. Le Marmot went to post well, to Paquet's satisfaction evidently, and in the race held a good position until past halfway. With four furlongs to go he looked in some difficulty, lost his place quickly before the home turn and never got back on terms. The jockey reported that Le Marmot hung badly when asked to follow Ela-Mana-Mou at the four-furlong pole and that he couldn't ride him afterwards; although the horse made up a little ground in the straight and finished fifth, about seven lengths behind the winner, he was still hanging and his action was all wrong. Le Marmot was well fancied for the Arc and started favourite, coupled with Ela-Mana-Mou for betting purposes as both are part-owned by Tim Rogers. He went down tremendously

Prix Ganay, Longchamp—Le Marmot reverses previous form with Three Troikas

Mr R. Schafer's "Le Marmot" (P. Paquet)

well and was close up early on, but soon dropped back. He was never in the hunt afterwards, just staying on steadily in the straight to finish eighth, about five lengths behind Detroit. It was subsequently reported that he finished lame, and he wasn't seen out again.

Le Marmot (Fr) (b.c. 1976)	Amarko (b 1965)	Tanerko (br 1953)	Tantieme
			La Divine
		Thamar (ch 1958)	Mat de Cocagne
			Ines
	Molinka (b 1967)	Molvedo (br 1958)	Ribot
			Maggiolina
		Telstar (ch 1962)	Cambremer
			Sanelta

Despite the fact that there are plenty of stallions more fashionably bred than Le Marmot his excellent overall record should ensure that he is well patronised when he begins his new career at the Haras du Petit Tellier in 1981. His sire Amarko, now dead, was a tough and genuine sort who won eleven races during four seasons, including the Grand Prix de Bordeaux and the Derby de l'Ouest. Easily the best of Amarko's other runners is Le Marmot's sister Imogene, second to Vitiges in the 1975 Prix Morny and subsequently a stakes-placed winner in the USA. The dam Molinka won four times at up to a mile and a half in the French Provinces and is from the family of Sanctus II. Her only other previous foal to race, Kalimir (by Kashmir II), won over a mile and a quarter at Salisbury in 1978 and has since won several races in Italy. *F. Boutin, France.*

LE MONARC (NZ) 2 b.c. Sovereign Edition 109–Micheline (Le Filou 110) — (1980 7fg) neat colt; foaled in New Zealand to Northern Hemisphere time; syndicated as a foal, with 10 shares at NZ $10,000 each; brother to top-class Australian filly Surround, winner of numerous races at up to 12.5f including Victoria, Queensland and A.J.C. Oaks and half-brother to Purple Patch (by

Pakistan), a prolific winner at up to 11f in Australia; dam sister to **Fulmen**, winner of Brisbane Cup, Adelaide Cup and South Australian St Leger, and half-sister to Prix de l'Arc de Triomphe second Balmerino; 14/1 but fit, never threatened leaders and wasn't given an unnecessarily hard time when 15 lengths last of 6 to Baz Bombati in £5,500 event at Newmarket in August; likely to do better over further at 3 yrs. *J. Dunlop.*

LEMONTREE LAD 3 ch.g. King's Company 124–Frothy 83 (Watergate 117) (1979 6d 1980 7.2fg) seems useless; wears blinkers. *C. Crossley.* —

LE MOSS 5 ch.h. Le Levanstell 122–Feemoss (Ballymoss 136) (1979 16.1v* 20fg* 21d* 18fg* 16f 1980 20g* 21fg* 18g* 20d2) **135**

If the sprinter-miler Moorestyle had not ended the season with such a flourish, our vote for 'Horse of the Year' would have gone to Le Moss. Indeed, in the poll of leading racing journalists conducted by the Racegoers Club, some respected judges preferred Le Moss's claims to those of the likes of Moorestyle and the season's leading middle-distance performer Ela-Mana-Mou. Le Moss's achievement in winning the Gold Cup, the Goodwood Cup and the Doncaster Cup for the second year in succession and his three magnificent and memorable races with the Irish-trained Ardross lifted the series of Cup races to as great a prominence as they have enjoyed in any season since the 'forties, the days when the long-distance horse was king.

Le Moss is a phenomenon among racehorses: he's not the best long-distance horse we've ever seen, but if there is such a thing as a top-class racehorse that stays for ever Le Moss is probably the closest to him we have encountered since that great out-and-out stayer of the mid-'forties Marsyas II, and on the score of determination and courage precious few stayers of the post-war era rank with Le Moss. As a four-year-old he pulled off something of a surprise when beating his stable-mate Buckskin in the Gold Cup but his victories at Goodwood and Doncaster confirmed him as a rattling good horse over extreme distances. The Goodwood Cup, run over two miles five furlongs, provided a perfect illustration of the type of horse he is, genuine and resolute, and a real dyed-in-the-wool stayer who gets better the further he goes; his running at Doncaster and in the Jockey Club Cup, in which he was beaten, seemed to show that two miles

Gold Cup, Ascot—first of three memorable encounters, Le Moss beats Ardross

and a quarter was the minimum trip for him in good company.

We prefaced our remarks on Le Moss in *Racehorses of 1979* with the statement that it was unlikely that there would be a better Cup horse around in 1980. Our prediction was put to the test for the first time in the Gold Cup, which has in recent years regained from the Prix du Cadran the reputation of being Europe's premier long-distance race. Le Moss went to Royal Ascot unraced for eight months; a swollen hock and a virus infection kept him on the easy list for a time in the spring and he completed his preparation for the Gold Cup with racecourse gallops at Kempton and Yarmouth in the three-week period leading up to Royal Ascot. At one time it had seemed possible that Le Moss might not be able to take his place in the Gold Cup field but he certainly looked fit and well beforehand, belying any idea that he might be short of his peak. His seven rivals had each had the benefit of at least one previous outing in the current season. Four of them, Billion, Buttress, Noble Saint and Vincent, had run in the most important of the English trials for the Gold Cup, the Henry II Stakes at Sandown in May, when Billion had come out best in a very close finish which also involved Buttress and Noble Saint; Vincent lost his chance when badly hampered approaching halfway. Noble Saint, Buttress and Vincent had earlier finished first, second and third in the Yorkshire Cup. The five-year-old Arapahos, who had been in the frame behind Le Moss at Royal Ascot, Goodwood and Doncaster in 1979, had won the Ladbroke Chester Cup in May with 9-5 in the saddle. There was one challenger from France, the Prix du Cadran fourth Croque Monsieur, and one from Ireland, Ardross, a four-year-old who had had only five races in his life and had shown himself well suited by a distance of ground on his latest outing when slamming a useful field in the Saval Beg Stakes at Leopardstown. It was a highly competitive Gold Cup by present-day standards and the betting went: 3/1 Le Moss, 11/2 Arapahos, Noble Saint and Vincent, 6/1 Ardross, 15/2 Buttress, 10/1 Billion and 20/1 Croque Monsieur.

It is rare for a horse to make all the running over so long a distance as two and a half miles or more, but the tactics had been employed in the Goodwood Cup and the prospect held no fears for Le Moss's connections. Mercer set out to ensure that no horse would win the Gold Cup unless he stayed two and a half miles thoroughly at racing pace. They went a good clip from the start and, except for a few strides when Croque Monsieur showed in front about seven furlongs from home, Le Moss was never headed. The field was strung out a long way from home but Mercer took no chances and began to drive Le Moss along for all he was worth when there was still three quarters of a mile to be covered. Rounding the home turn, Vincent, Arapahos and Ardross were still in close touch but as soon as the field straightened out it became clear that Ardross was going to be the biggest danger. Ardross got on terms with Le Moss just inside the two-furlong marker and from that point the pair battled it out magnificently to the line. Many horses would have capitulated to the sustained challenge of Ardross. But not Le Moss. The more Ardross tried to pass, the more Le Moss seemed to be spurred on and at the winning post there was three quarters of a length between the pair; the third horse Vincent, who was six lengths behind Ardross, was the only one to finish within ten lengths of the first two. Le Moss's performance was one of the most stirring seen on a racecourse in many a year; it was an unforgettable display of endurance and courage. Ardross too came out of the race with enormous credit; seldom have we seen two horses galloping so resolutely at the end of a truly-run Cup race.

Six weeks elapsed before Le Moss and Ardross met for their second encounter, in the Goodwood Cup. None of those that had taken them on in the Gold Cup did so again and there were only three other runners. Le Moss and Ardross had met at level weights in the Gold Cup but Le Moss had to concede 2 lb at Goodwood. Again Le Moss led from start to finish, setting a good gallop all the way. Ardross pressed him strongly in the straight and the pair were almost level at the two-furlong marker, both jockeys having been hard at work from about half a mile out. Ardross challenged stoutly but he just couldn't get in front and Le Moss ran on with the utmost gameness to hold him off and beat him by a neck. Although never a threat to the first two, the three-year-old New Jerusalem ran very well to finish third, only three lengths behind Ardross.

The third meeting between Le Moss and Ardross was every bit as thrilling as the other two. The Doncaster Cup is run over a shorter course than the Gold Cup and the Goodwood Cup and we were not certain that Le Moss would beat Ardross this time; Arapahos had given Le Moss a much harder race in 1979 at Doncaster than at Royal Ascot or Goodwood. There were five runners but it was virtually a match, Le Moss starting at 6/4 on and Ardross at 13/8

Goodwood Cup—Le Moss again beats Ardross

against; the weight difference was the same as at Goodwood. The race unfolded much as the Gold Cup and the Goodwood Cup had done, with Le Moss setting out to make it a sound test of stamina and Ardross making his challenge over the final quarter of a mile or so. As usual, Le Moss was flat out a long way from home and with Ardross drawing nearer with every stride in the penultimate furlong there seemed a possibility that Ardross might take his revenge. But it was not to be: Le Moss battled on like a lion and Ardross, struggling manfully as usual, was still a neck behind at the post and no longer getting any closer. Le Moss thus completed an unparalleled sequence of victories in England's major Cup races: when he took the so-called stayers' triple crown as a four-year-old he became the first horse to do so for over twenty-five years, and no other horse has completed that notable treble two years in a row. And he achieved his second treble the hard way, making virtually every yard of the running in almost seven and a half miles of competition.

Le Moss made his final appearance in the two-and-a-half-mile Prix Gladiateur at Longchamp at the end of September. He seemed to have little to fear from any of the six French-trained stayers that took him on—provided the race was truly run. The success Le Moss enjoyed in a fine career was due in no small measure to the fine handling he received from his regular jockey Mercer but for once Mercer didn't ride a good race in the Gladiateur. The French probably knew that if they were to win the Gladiateur they would have to steal it. And that is precisely what Anifa did. The Gladiateur was allowed to degenerate into a slowly-run affair and Anifa, a good-class mare with finishing pace, came with a sharp run in the straight to pass Le Moss and take a good two lengths' lead. Le Moss couldn't respond immediately but he was going up again on Anifa in the closing stages and was beaten only half a length. If the pair had ever met again over the same distance we should have been surprised not to see Le Moss win. Anifa, who received 9 lb from Le Moss, went on to win the Turf Classic in North America in great style.

Le Moss's victories in the Gold Cup, the Goodwood Cup and the Doncaster Cup were worth £66,748 to his owner in 1980, compared to £55,338 a year earlier. All three races had their value increased again in 1980 and we very much hope to see this refreshing trend continued in future years. The Cup races can provide excellent entertainment, as we have seen on several occasions recently, and we trust that we have seen an end to the repressive measures that were taken against the stayers in previous decades. The turf authorities should have as a priority in the 'eighties the restoration of the status of long-distance racing in Britain to a proper level; the wide variety of distances over which racing takes place gives British racing an important advantage over its American cousin, which favours the miler to excess, and over its French cousin, which offers relatively few worthwhile opportunities for top-class sprinters or out-and-out stayers. We look forward to the day when races such as the Gold Cup are once again an automatic target for the best of the previous season's staying three-year-olds, some of whom are campaigned nowadays over distances which are too short for them to show their best, but over which it often pays better dividends to race them.

Le Moss (ch.h.1975)	Le Levanstell (b 1957)	Le Lavandou (b 1944)	Djebel
			Lavande
		Stella's Sister (ch 1950)	Ballyogan
			My Aid
	Feemoss (b 1960)	Ballymoss (ch 1954)	Mossborough
			Indian Call
		Feevagh (b 1951)	Solar Slipper
			Astrid Wood

The downgrading of the Cup races in the post-war era has contributed to a sharp decline in the stud prospects of the leading stayers. Two-year-old racing in Britain has always been weighted in favour of the sprint-bred animal and racing for three-year-olds and older horses now heavily favours the miler and the middle-distance performer. The racing programme places emphasis upon merit at two and three years. Many a true stayer is slow to mature and doesn't reach his best until after three years of age; any commercial breeder who persisted in trying to breed stayers today would be on his way to bankruptcy. Short of a wholesale change of emphasis in the pattern of racing, which is most unlikely, there will continue to be only limited demand for the stud services of a horse like Le Moss, unless he proves capable of siring horses good enough to win high-class races at middle distances, where all the prestige and big money is to be won. The stayer High Line, three times winner of the Jockey Club Cup, received only moderate support in his early years at stud but he has gradually proved himself an excellent sire; he was second in

Doncaster Cup—Le Moss and Ardross battle it out once more

Mr C. d'Alessio's "Le Moss"

the list of leading sires in 1980 when he was represented, along with others, by those tough performers Master Willie, Shoot A Line and Nicholas Bill, who between them won eight pattern races in 1980. We shall follow with interest the stud career of Le Moss and those other illustrious Cup horses of recent years Sagaro and Buckskin; all three were top-class racehorses, as good as any that have raced over extreme distances since Alycidon's day. Breeders shouldn't ignore them simply because they were stayers. Le Moss's fee for 1981 is a reasonable IR 1,500 guineas (Oct. 1st).

In terms of racing merit, we rate Le Moss slightly higher than his famous brother Levmoss. Levmoss, the only horse to win the Prix de l'Arc de Triomphe, the Gold Cup and the Prix du Cadran, died in 1977 after only a few seasons at stud; it couldn't be said that he was an outstanding success as a stallion but he was by no means a failure. Le Moss is also a brother to Sweet Mimosa, winner of the Prix de Diane, and a half-brother to three other winners including the useful Santamoss (by Santa Claus) who is at stud in East Germany. Le Moss is a member of the last crop of Le Levanstell, a very successful sprint-bred stallion who sired winners at all distances and included My Swallow, Allangrange and Sarah Siddons among his other notable winners. Le Moss's dam Feemoss, who is out of the Yorkshire Oaks winner Feevagh, was a useful stayer and a half-sister to Laurence O, winner of the Queen Alexandra Stakes and runner-up in the Doncaster Cup and the Cesarewitch. Le Moss was purchased during the season to stand at the McGraths' Brownstown Stud in Ireland; the McGraths sold Le Moss for 26,000 guineas as a yearling and are believed to have paid around ten times that amount to get him back, chicken-feed these days for a stallion with a good racing record. Le Moss is a lengthy, attractive horse and, although he was not a free mover in his slower paces, he was a powerful, relentless galloper. He acted on any going and was an extremely tough and genuine racehorse. As brave and willing as they come when racing, he wasn't always easy to deal with at home as a five-year-old and his success speaks volumes for the patience and skill of his trainer and those who handled him at Warren Place. *H. Cecil.*

L'EMPEREUR 3 b or br.g. Prince de Galles 125–Reine d'Etat 53 (High Hat 131) (1979 NR 1980 8g 10g 12fg 12.2g4 11.5fg 12fg 12f) fair sort; brother to 1¼m winner Le Pretendant; dam placed over 1½m; little worthwhile form in varied company; stays 1½m; blinkered second start. *F. Durr.* —

LEN ASHURST 4 br.g. Prince Regent 129–Telling 91 (High Treason 126) (1979 12d4 14f 11g2 12f* 12fg2 12d* 12f3 14fg 14.6g3 1980 12f* 12fg 13fg3 12fg 12g 12fg 13s3 12fg) tall gelding; won handicap at Edinburgh in April by 2½ lengths from Border Knight; third afterwards at Hamilton and Ayr, beaten over 8 lengths by Blakes Beacon in Royal Caledonian Hunt Cup on latter course in September; best form at 1½m; appears to act on any going; front runner; sold to T. Hallett 3,800 gns Doncaster October Sales. *J. W. Watts.* **87** d

LENDING (USA) 5 br.h. Buckpasser–Polly Girl (Prince Bio) (1979? 1980 9g) strong, good sort; ex-American horse; brother to a winner in USA and half-brother to several winners, including top-class Top Command (by Bold Ruler) and Straight and True (by Never Bend), also a stakes winner and a very good winner over jumps; dam very useful winner in France and daughter of Bella Paola; ran at least once in USA; 20/1 and in need of race when in rear in 22-runner minor event won by Sacrilege at Ripon in April. *I. Balding.* —

LE NORMAND 2 b.c. Ashmore 125–Haida (Astec 128) (1980 7f 8fg) Apr 13; 9,000F, 16,000Y; strong, compact colt; half-brother to Irish 5f winner Wind Shade (by Tumble Wind) and a winner in Denmark; dam poor half-sister to Lorenzaccio; made no show in £5,800 event at York (tailed off from halfway) and 23-runner minor race won by Shergar at Newbury in September; sold only 660 gns Newmarket Autumn Sales. *C. Brittain.* —

LENYGON 5 b.h. Le Levanstell 122–Nanette 100 (Worden II 129) (1979 12g3 9g3 11.7fg2 14.7g3 16d4 18fg 16f 14g2 1980 14f 14f4 12d* 16.1d* 13d2 12g3 10.6s 14s) fairly useful handicapper; looked very well when winning amateur riders races at Salisbury (trotted up) in June and Haydock (all out) in July; runner-up to easy winner Angelo Salvini in £2,500 event at Ayr later in July, best subsequent effort; one paced and stays well; acts on a firm surface but has done all his winning on a soft one; sold to G. Fletcher 6,000 gns Newmarket Autumn Sales. *H. T. Jones.* **84**

LEODEGRANCE (USA) 4 b.g. King's Bishop–Reasonably (Hail to Reason) (1979 10d 10s 12v 11.7d 12g 14fg* 16f2 16.1g3 14g2 12f* 14f3 12fg4 1980 11.7fg 13.3g 16fg2 16g 12g 16g 14g4 18d) well-made gelding; runner-up to Popsi's Joy in handicap at Ascot in June; mainly disappointing however; stays well; acts on firm going; blinkered and slowly away third start at 3 yrs. *G. Balding.* **69**

LEOPARD'S ROCK 6 b.g. Huntercombe 133–Reina Cristina 84 (Tamerlane 128) (1979 10s 10fg 10fg 12fg* 10.2fg* 12g 11.7fg2 10f2 10.2fg 10fg 10fg 12d 1980 10f 12h* 11.1fg4 12d 11.7d 12fg4 12g3 12fg4 10f4 10fg 10g) middle-distance handicapper; winner at Brighton in May; rather inconsistent afterwards; acts on any going but goes extremely well on top-of-the-ground; suitable mount for an inexperienced rider. *J. Dunlop.* **78**

LEO THE LION 3 b.g. Ragstone 128–Peteona 97 (Welsh Saint 126) (1979 NR 1980 12g4 16fg3 16.1s) first foal; dam won from 5f to 1m; quite a moderate maiden; stays well; unsuited by soft going; has run creditably for an amateur rider. *J. Dunlop.* **75**

LE PETITE VERT 7 ch.m. Green God 128–Mantua 80 (Ballyciptic 122) (1979 7g3 8g* 6fg 8f 10.8g 8fg 1980 5g 5d 8g) won seller at Warwick in 1979; behind in handicaps in 1980; stays 1m; used to wear blinkers. *P. Arthur.* —

LEPORELLO 3 b.g. Lombard 126–Zerbinetta 96 (Henry the Seventh 125) (1979 5s 5d 5f3 7f4 7g4 6f 1980 9.6f 10d2 10g*) lightly-made gelding; good walker; won maiden race at Brighton in July; will stay 1½m; probably acts on any going; exported to Hong Kong. *J. Dunlop.* **75**

LE SOLEIL 6 ch.h. Roi Soleil 125–Mayo Blues 73 (Abernant 142) (1979 11s* 12v 11s2 10g* 10.2s 10d3 10d2 10.2d 12s* 12s2 12fg2 12f4 12d* 12g3 12d2 12.5fg2 14g3 12s 1980 10s 12fg2 12fg3 12f 12g 12g4 12fg4 12fg2 12g2 13.3fg3 12fg4 14s4 12v) fairly useful performer at his best; didn't win in 1980, but was beaten narrowly when runner-up in 3 handicaps, on last occasion by Get Stoned in £3,200 event at Doncaster in September; also ran well when third to Castle Keep in Coral Autumn Cup at Newbury later in September (ridden by 7-lb claimer); best form at distances short of 1¾m; acts on any going; has been tried in blinkers; has won for a lady rider. *R. Price.* **81**

LETHE 2 b.f. Birdbrook 110–Enchanted 116 (Song 132) (1980 5d 6s 6d) Apr 23; first foal; dam smart sprinting 2-y-o; soundly beaten in maiden and minor events. *H. T. Jones.* —

LETITGO 4 ch.g. Shoolerville 121–Omnia Opera 83 (Major Portion 129) (1979 6v^2 6v^2 6v^2 7d 6g^4 5h 6fg 6s 1980 9g 8f^3 12d 10s^4 10d) strong gelding; quite a modest maiden; probably stays 1¼m (off course for 5 months before being tried over 1½m and needed race); acts on any going. *P. Felgate.* —

LET'S DANCE 6 b.m. Mansingh 120–Madame Birwood (Constable 119) (1979 10.2s 8v^3 7s^4 10g 9g 10f* 12f^3 10g* 11g* 10fg* 11g 12.3f* 12.2fg 11g^3 15.8s 1980 10h^3) fair handicapper; looked in need of race and wasn't disgraced when third of 10 to Jubilee Prince at Stockton in April on only outing of 1980; best form at up to 1½m; acts on any going but has done all her winning on a sound surface; has run well for an apprentice; genuine. *Miss S. Hall.* **61**

LEVANO 7 gr. or ro.h. Le Levanstell 122–Scargill 107 (Vilmorin) (1979 12d 1980 8fg 12d) seems of little account. *Dr. A. Jones.* —

LEVANTA LEE 2 b.g. Levanter 121–Metrolee (Metropolis 96) (1980 7g 8d 7d) rangy gelding; first known foal; dam well beaten on flat and over hurdles; moved badly on way to start but wasn't disgraced when about 11 lengths eighth of 19 to Grand March in £2,600 event at Salisbury in August, first outing and only sign of ability; should be suited by 1m. *Mrs J. Reavey.* —

LEVEL FLIGHT 4 b.g. Pitcairn 126–Skyway 76 (Skymaster 126) (1979 8d 8s^3 10d 10fg 12fg 10.1g 1980 12s) well-made gelding; stays 1m (well beaten over further); acts on soft going; blinkered final start in 1979 *M. Tompkins.* —

LEVOTESSE 2 b.f. Levmoss 133–Kaotesse (Djakao 124) (1980 7g 6fg 7g 8fg) Mar 14; first foal; dam placed at up to 11f in France; fairly prominent in maiden races in September on third and fourth outings, finishing fifth of 16 to More Stones at Chepstow and seventh of 24 to Allegretta at Leicester; will stay 1½m+. *G. Balding.* **63**

LEWESTON 4 b.g. Levmoss 133–Darrigle (Vilmoray 126) (1979 11d 16d 10s 11f 10.1fg 12g^3 12f^4 15.5fg^2 14f^2 12s 1980 14.6fg) lengthy gelding; plating-class maiden; stays well; acts on firm going; ran badly when blinkered final start at 3 yrs; sold 2,600 gns Ascot December Sales. *W. Wightman.* —

LEX (FR) 3 ch.c. Tarbes 125–Toranquine (Right Royal V 135) (1979 6d 8fg* 1980 12g^3 12g 16f^2 18.1g^3 19g^2 17.1d) big colt; moderate performer; stays well; suited by top-of-the-ground; has run creditably for an amateur rider. *N. Callaghan.* **77**

LEXBY LAD 3 gr.g. Be Friendly 130–Complex Girl 67 (Entanglement 118) (1979 8d 1980 6d 6fg 8fg 10.1f 10.1g 6g 7fg) tall gelding; poor maiden; has worn blinkers. *J. Davies.* —

LEXHAM VIEW 2 gr.f. Abwah 118–King's Caress 65 (King's Coup 108) (1980 6s 6g 7fg 7g^3 7.2g 7fg 8d) Apr 23; leggy filly; half-sister to 3 winners, including The Sampson Boys (by Most Secret), successful over 1¼m; dam, a plater, won over 6f and 1m; 3¾ lengths third of 11 to Free Forester in maiden race at Catterick in August, best effort; stays 7f, but isn't certain to get 1m (dwelt when blinkered and apprentice ridden seventh outing). *M. Tompkins.* **72**

LIBERATED 4 b.c. Busted 134–Parolee 88 (Sing Sing 134) (1979 10v 10g 8g 8d^2 8g 7fg* 1980 8fg 7.2fg 7fg^4 7d 8fg 10s* 10fg^3 12fg^2 12d^4) rangy colt; has a high knee action; short-priced favourite, overcame difficulties in running when winning handicap at Nottingham in August all out by ½ length from Sunburst; blinkered when in frame in similar races afterwards; stays 1½m; acts on any going except perhaps heavy. *J. Dunlop.* **78**

LIBERTA 3 ch.f. Mill Reef 141–L'Ecossaise (Dancer's Image) (1979 6fg^3 7f^4 1980 11fg 10fg 8f 14g) quite well-made filly; showed promise in minor event and £3,200 race at 2 yrs; well beaten in maiden races in 1980; should stay at least 1¼m; sold 9,600 gns Newmarket December Sales. *J. Dunlop.* —

LIBERTY CALLING 4 b.f. Caliban 123–Liberty Cry 89 (Democratic 124) (1979 NR 1980 8d 10.1s 10d) seems of little account. *G. Balding.* —

LIBOI (USA) 8 b.h. Tom Rolfe–Latin Walk (Roman Tread) (1979 12v^3 14d 11.7g 12.2g 12d 1980 17.1fg^4 22.2fg 16g^2 17.1fg 16g^4 18d 18s^4) poor staying handicapper; acts on any going; tried in blinkers at 2 yrs; suitable mount for an inexperienced rider. *Mrs R. Lomax.* **53**

LIBRAS SHININGSTAR (USA) 2 b.f. Gleaming–Libra 97 (Hyperion) (1980 6s 6s³ 6f 7g 8d) rather lightly-made filly; half-sister to numerous winners, including Irish Sweeps Derby and St Leger winners Ribocco and Ribero (both by Ribot), very smart middle-distance stayer Libra's Rib (also by Ribot) and Oaks second Roses for the Star (by Stage Door Johnny); dam 2-y-o 5f winner, is half-sister to 2 high-class animals; very well bred but is only a modest filly and was beaten under 7-11 in a nursery at Pontefract on final start; should be suited by middle distances. *F. J. Houghton.* **72**

LICARA (FR) 3 ch.f. Caro 133–Licata (Abdos 134) (1979 7g² 7.5g² 8g* 8v* 1980 8v 7d² 10.5g⁴ 10.5g 9d² 10d 10.5s² 10.5s) big filly; third foal; half-sister to Prix Lupin and Prix du Jockey-Club winner Acamas and Irish 13.5f winner Eupalinos (both by Mill Reef); dam good winner at up to 1¼m in France; runner-up in Prix Imprudence at Maisons-Laffitte in April (no match for 3-length winner Firyal), Prix Chloe at Evry in July (went down by 1½ lengths to Detroit) and minor race at Longchamp in October; ran creditably in Prix Cleopatre at Saint-Cloud in May (length fourth to Hortensia) and Prix de Diane at Chantilly in June (under 7 lengths sixth to Mrs Penny); stays 1¼m well; yet to race on a firm surface. *F. Mathet, France.* **112**

LICHEN GREEN 2 b.f. Welsh Saint 126–Lichen 93 (Tyrone 130) (1980 6g³ 6f 6g² 7d³) Apr 11; 920F, 3,100Y; rather unfurnished filly; poor mover; sixth foal; dam 2-y-o 5f winner; beaten only 1¼ lengths when third under a low weight in nursery won by Miss St James's at Doncaster in October on final start; will stay 1m. *J. W. Watts.* **85**

LIDGATE (USA) 4 b.c. Riva Ridge–Favoletta 115 (Baldric II 131) (1979 7fg⁴ 7.6d 1980 8g 7.3fg 6g⁴ 8.2s 7d) neat, strong, stocky colt; very lightly raced, best effort of 1980 when about 4 lengths fourth behind Chicken Again in apprentice handicap at Newcastle in October (still on burly side); should stay 1m+; possibly unsuited by soft going; sold 490 gns Ascot December Sales. *H. Wragg.* **—**

LIECHTENSTEIN 2 b.c. Sallust 134–Brilliant Gem 83 (Charlottown 127) (1980 6fg) Apr 7; 9,600Y; neat, strong colt; first foal; dam lightly-raced half-sister to smart staying filly Pink Gem; 20/1 and in need of race, scrubbed along throughout when 5½ lengths sixth of 16 to Priory Lane in maiden race at Salisbury in September; likely to stay 1¼m; sold 2,000 gns Newmarket Autumn Sales. *C. Brittain.* **—**

LIFE AT LAST 4 ch.f. Northfields–Royal News 74 (Sovereign Path 125) (1979 8f* 10fg* 10d³ 10fg 1980 10.5f 10fg*) tall, narrow filly; having first outing for over 3 months when getting up on post to beat Dawn Johnny in handicap at Yarmouth in August; stays 1¼m; seems to act on any going. *L. Cumani.* **79**

LIFE BEGAN 2 br.f. Home Guard 129–Eden Quay (King's Bench 132) (1980 5fg⁴ 6s*) Apr 13; 2,200Y; sister to fair 7f and 1m winner Alpine Meadow and half-sister to several winners; dam lightly-raced sister to speedy Victoria Quay; favourite when winning 14-runner maiden race at Fairyhouse in October in good style by 2½ lengths from Unreal; will stay 1m; likely to make further improvement. *E. O'Grady, Ireland.* **79 p**

LIFESTYLE 2 br.f. Jimmy Reppin 131–Cave Girl 67 (Pindari 124) (1980 5g 5f 6d² 6fg* 7d⁴ 7f² 8s*) May 17; 2,000Y; lightly-made filly; half-sister to 2 winners, including 1974 2-y-o 5f and 7f winner Cupids Cave (by Meldrum); dam plater on flat and over hurdles; favourite when winning 10-runner auction event at Newcastle in July and £3,800 nursery at Ayr in September, coming home ¾ length ahead of Lord Clewes after being eased about a length close home in latter; will stay 1¼m; acts on any going; genuine and consistent. *J. W. Watts.* **80**

LIGHT CAVALRY 3 b.c. Brigadier Gerard 144–Glass Slipper 100 (Relko 136) (1979 7fg* 1980 12.3f³ 12f* 12g* 12fg³ 12g² 14.6g*) **128**

Writing about the St Leger, the oldest of England's classics, frequently offers all the joy and satisfaction of preparing an obituary. Five times in the 'seventies the St Leger went to a horse 6 lb or 7lb below top classic standard at the time of his success and the race suffered another blow in 1980 when only seven colts, none of whom had shown top-class form, went to post to compete for a record first prize of £71,256. The St Leger is no longer an automatic target for the best of the classic horses bred to stay. In the opinion of some it needs a shot in the arm; but tradition dies hard and there is a powerful lobby that bitterly opposes any attempt to admit older horses to the race or to shorten its distance, the two

King Edward VII Stakes, Ascot—Light Cavalry wins from Saviour and Saint Jonathon

most often heard suggestions for reform. As far as we can judge, the St Leger is likely to continue in its present form in the foreseeable future; the five English classics seem sacrosanct in the eyes of the majority.

As regular readers will know we have long advocated the opening of the St Leger to four-year-olds and upwards, a move which in our view would intensify the competition most years and would make the St Leger the European championship for the true mile-and-three-quarter horses, many of whom are campaigned at middle distances as four-year-olds because of the absence of a really important and valuable race, a £50,000-plus event, for horses of their type. Far more often than should ever be so for a race of its importance the St Leger turns out to be little more than an inflated consolation prize for what might be termed the second division of the European staying three-year-olds. Take a look at the combined credentials of the seven runners for the most recent St Leger: between them the septet had won eleven of their thirty-four races in the current season, five of the victories coming in maiden races, minor events or handicaps and only three of them—Light Cavalry's success in the King Edward VII Stakes, Ramian's win in the BMW Nijinsky Stakes and Lancastrian's victory in the Prix du Lys—in pattern races; Ramian had finished third in the Irish Sweeps Derby and Water Mill joint third in the Grand Prix de Paris but none of the others had been placed in a Group 1 pattern race.

The Doncaster executive is deeply concerned about the loss of prestige of the St Leger relative to the other colts' classics; it sees the answer largely in terms of a sizeable injection of prize money (perhaps through sponsorship and changed entry conditions) which it thinks would make the St Leger a much more attractive alternative to the Prix de l'Arc de Triomphe, a race which always creams off some of the best three-year-olds who, in days gone by, would have been sent to Doncaster. But, even if its prize money matched or even exceeded that of the Arc, the St Leger is unlikely again to be so important as it used to be so long as it is confined to three-year-olds; the Prix de l'Arc brings top-class horses of all ages into battle and is firmly established as a race of enormous prestige, the race that counts most in the European racing year. Incidentally, we are strongly opposed to the idea, favoured in some influential quarters, of reducing the distance of the St Leger to a mile and a quarter. There are too few worthwhile opportunities for stayers in Europe: with the single exception of the St Leger all the really big stakes are at a mile, a mile and a quarter or a mile and a half. To cut the distance of the St Leger would be most unfair to what is already an underprivileged group.

The St Leger course, galloping in nature with a long run-in, is ideal for the powerful, long-striding horse who requires time and space to get opened out. The most recent St Leger winner Light Cavalry is just such a horse. On what had been seen of him before Doncaster it was plain that stamina was his strongest suit; he doesn't possess a first-class turn of finishing speed. His connections had him ridden for speed on his first two outings as a three-year-old but he showed no acceleration in the Chester Vase and made hard work of landing the odds in a handicap at Newbury in May. In his three other races before the St Leger, Light Cavalry was ridden for stamina to minimise the effectiveness of those of his rivals with a turn of foot. He won the King Edward VII Stakes at Royal Ascot, running on resolutely after being in the first two throughout to hold off Saviour and Saint Jonathon by three quarters of a length and a length, and was placed in the Gordon Stakes at Goodwood and the Great Voltigeur Stakes at York, which were both won by Prince Bee who received weight each time. The Voltigeur has often been a good guide to the St Leger and the race was a dress rehearsal for Doncaster so far as Light Cavalry was concerned. The tactics tried at York—Light Cavalry was sent to the front from the start, made a break for home on the final turn, and was strongly ridden all the way to the line—seemed to offer Light Cavalry a good chance of success at Doncaster. Although Prince Bee caught Light Cavalry halfway up the straight and beat him by two lengths at York, the extra distance of the St Leger seemed likely to be in Light Cavalry's favour and none of those he would run into at Doncaster had shown form so good as that of Prince Bee, the Irish Sweeps Derby runner-up.

Prince Bee's stable-companion Water Mill was a short-priced favourite for the St Leger; since being tried in blinkers he had won twice with ease at Goodwood, in the Alycidon Stakes and the March Stakes, and seemed likely to stay the trip, having already dead-heated for third place in very testing conditions in the fifteen-furlong Grand Prix de Paris in June. The St Leger field seemed in serious danger of being reduced to six, which would have made it the smallest since the war, when Lancastrian, one of the two French-trained challengers and the third favourite, unshipped his rider at the start and galloped back towards the stables. Fortunately, Lancastrian was soon caught and there was little delay. The race itself takes little describing. With no-one anxious to make the running, Mercer settled Light Cavalry in the lead, gradually warming up the pace until cracking Light Cavalry with the whip and going for home in earnest soon after entering the final straight. Flat out for the last half mile, pursued closely by Water Mill for some of the way, Light Cavalry stretched out magnificently and had the race in safe keeping with more than a furlong to go. At the line Light Cavalry was a most decisive winner, four lengths ahead of Water Mill with World Leader the same distance away third and the rest a dozen lengths and more behind the winner. Light Cavalry was the first horse to make all the running in the St Leger since Athens Wood in 1971.

Light Cavalry's St Leger win was a notable landmark in the career of his sire Brigadier Gerard whose achievements as a stallion have been overshadowed so far by those of his great contemporary Mill Reef. Brigadier Gerard has sired several good performers but Light Cavalry is his first classic winner. Light Cavalry is a big, rangy colt who always carries plenty of condition; he comes from one of the most successful families in the Stud Book, one which has been represented at the

St Leger Stakes, Doncaster—Light Cavalry is much too strong for Water Mill

Childwick Bury Stud for several generations. Light Cavalry's dam Glass Slipper, a staying half-sister to Royal Palace, Prince Consort and Selhurst, was placed in the Musidora Stakes and the Ribblesdale Stakes before gaining her only victory in a thirteen-furlong maiden race at Newbury. Light Cavalry is Glass Slipper's second foal; her first was the fairly useful stayer Crystal Coach (by Exbury) and her third is Fairy Footsteps (by Mill Reef) who won the Waterford Candelabra Stakes at Goodwood, one of the top races for two-year-old staying fillies. The owner of Childwick Bury, Mr Jim Joel, has owned and bred a succession of high-class horses over the past fifty years or so, with Light Cavalry, Royal Palace and Picture Play, winner of a war-time One Thousand Guineas and, incidentally, the fourth dam of Light Cavalry, providing him with victories in English classics as an owner.

Light Cavalry (b.c. 1977)	Brigadier Gerard (b 1968)	Queen's Hussar (b 1960)	March Past
			Jojo
		La Paiva (ch 1956)	Prince Chevalier
			Brazen Molly
	Glass Slipper (br 1969)	Relko (b 1960)	Tanerko
			Relance III
		Crystal Palace (b 1956)	Solar Slipper
			Queen of Light

Light Cavalry's prospects as a four-year-old seem to depend largely on two things. Firstly: has he got further improvement in him, enough to take him into the top class? Well, it's possible that he has: he was raced only once as a two-year-old, was brought along steadily at three, and his trainer reported that he was improving rapidly at the time of the St Leger. Secondly, assuming his improvement: will he be trained for the Cup races or will he be campaigned at middle distances, as happens with so many of his type nowadays? A really good middle-distance horse should always have the edge on Light Cavalry at a mile and a half; he is, of course, capable of winning at that distance but his lack of finishing pace seems likely to prove an insuperable handicap in the very best company.

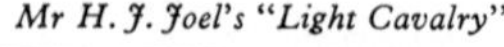
Mr H. J. Joel's "Light Cavalry"

Light Cavalry's trainer is a supporter of the Cup races and it's just possible that we shall see the genuine Light Cavalry in the Gold Cup line-up; his chance would have to be respected although, on breeding, he is not absolutely certain to stay two and a half miles in a truly-run race. He acts on firm going and has yet to race on a soft surface. *H. Cecil.*

LIGHT HEART 3 b.f. Laser Light 118–Hill Moss 87 (Priamos 123) (1979 **71** NR 1980 7f 7d^2 7.2d^2 8fg^4 10g^3) quite attractive, well-made filly; first foal; dam won over 1m, and is half-sister to top-class miler Sallust; narrowly-beaten second in maiden races at Salisbury in June and Haydock in July; best form at 7f on a soft surface; sold 3,800 gns Newmarket December Sales. *R. Hern.*

LIGHT HERE 2 ch.c. Touch Paper 113–Belle Josephine (Beau Sabreur 125) **102** (1980 5v* 5g^2 5f* 6d 6s 5d^4 7g^2 7g* 5g 6.3s^3 7g^3 8s) Mar 2; 5,600F, 6,600Y; lengthy, attractive colt; brother to a plating-class animal, and half-brother to several winners, including Ballycancan (by El Gallo), successful at up to 1½m in Ireland; dam won at 6f and 7f at 2 yrs; trained on very well after winning maiden race at Phoenix Park and minor event at Naas in first weeks of season and picked up a fairly valuable prize when beating Sea Of Echoes a length in Mullion Stakes at Leopardstown in August; also in frame in three Group 3 races, finishing 2 lengths fourth of 9 to Crimson Heather in Curragh Stakes, 6½ lengths third of 9 to Storm Bird in Anglesey Stakes, also at the Curragh, and 5 lengths third of 6 to Storm Bird in Larkspur Stakes at Leopardstown; better suited by 7f than 5f and stays 1m; acts on any going; blinkered sixth and seventh outings; genuine and consistent. *L. Browne, Ireland.*

LIGHT LAD 4 ch.g. Firestreak 125–Sophy 66 (Darius 129) (1979 9v 11g^3 **—** 11d^3 13g 12fg 12d 8.2g^3 1980 13g 11f 8g) poor plater; stayed 11f; dead. *Denys Smith.*

LIGHTNING BOY 2 b.g. Condorcet–Never So Late (Never Say Die 137) **63** (1980 5fg^3 6f 7g^4 7d^3 6g 7fg^3 7fg 8.2d^3) Mar 3; 720Y; lightly-made gelding; second foal; dam Irish 1½m winner; fair plater; will stay 1½m; best form on an easy surface; wears blinkers; sweated up profusely and ran poorly penultimate start. *P. Kelleway.*

LIGHTNING LABEL 4 br.c. African Sky 124–Soie Sauvage (Shantung **115** 132) (1979 7s 7.3g 8g^4 7fg 6fg^4 7fg^4 6s* 1980 9f 7fg^4 7.2f^4 5f 5fg^3 6fg^2 6g 7g 6d 5fg 5.3g^2 5g^4 8g* 5s* 6v*) leggy, rather lightly-made colt; in good form in the autumn and won minor events at Brighton, Haydock (impressively) and Doncaster, being pushed out to beat Hanu by 3 lengths in Remembrance Day Stakes on last-named course on final day of season; often faced stiff tasks, probably best previous efforts when runner-up in £4,700 event at Lingfield (beaten a length by The Pug) and £2,100 event at Brighton (beaten comfortably by Vaigly Great); stays 1m; probably acts on any going, but has done most of his winning on easy ground; blinkered third (ran very freely), ninth and tenth outings. *P. Kelleway.*

LIGHTNING LADY 3 ch.f. Green God 128–Soie Sauvage (Shantung 132) **62** (1979 NR 1980 8f 7f 8f 8s^2 10s) 2,900F, 9,600Y; lean, leggy, light-framed filly; half-sister to three winners, notably very smart 1978 2-y-o 6f winner Lightning Label (by African Sky), subsequently successful from 5f to 1m; dam won over 4.5f and 5.5f in France at 2 yrs; second in maiden race at Sandown in October, easily best effort; best run at 1m on soft going. *P. Kelleway.*

LIGHT OF REALM 3 b.f. Realm 129–Some Thing (Will Somers 114§) (1979 **101** 6d^2 6.5s* 7g^2 8g* 1980 7d^4 8g 8s 8d 8s 8s) 34,000Y; lightly-made filly; first foal; dam sister to 4 winners, notably very smart 1m to 1¾m filly La Troublerie; a leading French filly at 2 yrs, winning Group 3 Prix des Reservoirs at Longchamp on final outing; didn't run up to her best in 1980 though wasn't disgraced on first 2 starts, finishing fourth of 12 to Baptism in Prix du Palais Royal at Longchamp and 3½ lengths sixth to Cairn Rouge in Coronation Stakes at Royal Ascot; stays 1m well; acts on soft going. *J. Cunnington, jnr, France.*

LIGHT OF ZION 3 br.f. Pieces of Eight 128–Romardia 75 (Romulus 129) **48** (1979 6fg 5f 7fg 1980 8s 8f 8fg 7fg 8.5f 8d^2 10d 10g 10g^3) fair sort; plater; stays 1¼m; acts on a soft surface; sometimes sweats up. *J. Holt.*

LIGHT SENTENCE 2 bl.g. No Mercy 126–Injudicious 78 (Quorum 126) **66** (1980 5.8fg 5.3d 7g 7s) Mar 25; neat gelding; first foal; dam, half-sister to very useful stayer Cornuto, won over 1m; showed a little ability in maiden and minor events at Brighton on second and third outings but finished last of 18 on final appearance; stays 7f; sold 2,800 gns Doncaster November Sales. *R. Price.*

LIGHT SNACKS 3 b.g. Gulf Pearl 117–Mathilde 84 (Whistler 129) (1979 8g4 1980 8.2s4 10g 10fg 10fg4 10.2g 13.1g4 16.9d3 15.5fg 16s) narrow, lightly-made gelding; slow maiden; stays well; acts on a firm and a soft surface; sold 4,800 gns Newmarket Autumn Sales. *H. Candy.* **58**

LIKEABLE FELLA 3 br.c. Amber Rama 133–Pristina 84 (Petition 130) (1979 5g 1980 6d 8v 7fg 8fg 7.6d 7g 8f 7g 8d) strong colt; poor plater; has worn blinkers; pulled up fourth start. *S. Norton.* **–**

LIKI LIKI (USA) 4 b. or br.f Turn To Mars–Polyandry (Marino) (1979 9.3s 11fg 10.5g 9fg* 10.5g 10g* 10g2 10d* 10fg* 9.2d2 1980 10.5g3 12g 10d* 9.7d) French filly; favourite when fair third to Ho Han Wai in Prix Corrida at Saint-Cloud in April; won 6-runner minor event at Longchamp following month by 1½ lengths from Indoor; also ran respectably when about 5 lengths fifth to Northern Baby in Prix Dollar in June; best form at up to 1¼m; acts on a firm and a soft surface. *J. C. Cunnington, France.* **105**

LILAC STAR 4 br.f. Hard Man 102–Pink Star (Dunoon Star 110) (1979 NR 1980 6g 5f 5g* 5.1f* 5s2 5fg3 5.1g* 5d2 5fg3 5g2 5d* 5f 5d 5d 5v) tall filly; a speedy filly who improved and had a good season; won at Edinburgh (apprentice event), Yarmouth (twice, apprentice ridden and raced alone both times) and Wolverhampton (amateur riders) in the summer; beat Russian Winter comfortably by 2 lengths in last-named race; best at 5f; acts on any going; excellent mount for an inexperienced rider; game and genuine. *D. Leslie.* **69**

LILIAN CLARE 5 gr.m. Ribero 126–Pseudonym 110 (Acropolis 132) (1979 12fg 10.1f* 12.2d 13.8s4 12d 1980 13d 11f* 12f) plater; had poor run and did well to get up close home when winning at Edinburgh in April (bought in 3,600 gns); beaten a long way in better company only subsequent outing; stays 1¾m; acts on any going; has been tried in blinkers. *W. Bentley.* **38**

LILIAN MAY 3 bl.f. Blue Cashmere 129–Gail Time (Arctic Time 127) (1979 6f 1980 10.8s 10fg 10f 8g) quite attractive filly; well beaten in maiden races; pulled up first start; sold 850 gns Ascot July Sales. *J. Sutcliffe.* **–**

LILISEPIC 4 br.f. Seaepic 100–Lilian Langley 75 (Bleep-Bleep 134) (1979 NR 1980 10fg) neat filly; half-sister to a winning hurdler; dam a plater; 50/1, didn't impress in paddock and finished tailed off in minor event at Ripon in June, first outing. *B. McMahon.* **–**

LILLI PARKIN 3 ch.f. Crowned Prince 128–Rum Butter 94 (Hard Sauce 131) (1979 6fg 6fg3 8g* 1980 8fg) lengthy filly; good walker; won maiden race at Warwick in 1979; had stiff task only start at 3 yrs in May; will stay beyond 1m. *P. Cole.* **–**

LILTING STAR 3 b.f. Wishing Star 117–Darrigle (Vilmoray 126) (1979 5v 5d 5s 5g 5s2 5fg4 7g 7.2g 7g3 7f 7s2 7g 1980 8s 7f 7fg 8fg 10fg4 7fg 10fg) lightly-built filly; poor mover; has shown little form since 1979; should stay 1¼m; suited by some give in the ground; blinkered twice at 2 yrs; changed hands 6,400 gns Newmarket July Sales. *W. Marshall.* **–**

LILY THE GREY 3 gr.f. Towern 96–Fag Ash Lil 79 (Dumbarnie 125) (1979 5s 5f 7f4 7fg 8fg 1980 12.2fg 12g) compact filly; poor maiden; best run at 7f on firm going. *J. Fitzgerald.* **–**

LIMA CHARLIE (USA) 3 gr.c. Native Admiral–Sharp Babe (Amazing) (1979 NR 1980 5f 8.2g 10.6d 9v) poor form in maiden and minor races; trained by P. Read first start; sold 760 gns Newmarket Autumn Sales. *Mrs A. Cousins.* **–**

LIMOUSINE 3 b.f. Warpath 113–Whisky Lima 82 (Midsummer Night II 117) (1979 7s 1980 10fg 12g4 13d3 16f* 16s 16g 16g4 16d 15.8d 15d) leggy, quite well-made filly; won handicap at Thirsk in August; suited by test of stamina; goes well on firm ground and is unsuited by soft; blinkered ninth outing; sold 2,400 gns Newmarket December Sales. *C. Thornton.* **68**

LINAMAC 5 b.g. Linacre 133–Makura (Pampered King 121) (1979 NR 1980 12d 12h 12fg 16d 16fg 15.8g 12.5s) poor staying maiden. *B. Wilkinson.* **–**

LINDAG 5 ch.m. Crisp and Even 116–Most Precious (Matador 131) (1979 9s 8s 13.8s 12d 8f 8f2 9fg* 8g4 12fg 10h* 10h 1980 8f 12fg 8fg4 10g 9d 12fg 10fg 12g) plater; best form at up to 1¼m; acts on hard going; good mount for an apprentice. *R. Whitaker.* **–**

LINDORO 4 b.c. Sun Prince 128–Farce (Bon Mot III 132) (1979 11g4 12g* 12fg* 10f2 10s* 10.5fg4 1980 9f 10.2fg4 12g 12s 12f 10fg 10.6d2 12f 15.5v) attractive, small, shapely colt; developed into a very useful performer in 1979; didn't run up to his best in 1980, gaining only placing when 2½ lengths second to Side Track in Harvey Jones Handicap at Haydock in August; stays 1½m; acts on any going; effective with blinkers and without; acted as a pacemaker on reappearance and on last 2 outings; sold 15,000 gns Newmarket Autumn Sales, reportedly to race in Sweden. *R. Hern.* **98**

LINDRAMA 2 b.f. Amber Rama 133–Disa 55 (Dike) (1980 5fg 5fg 8d 8s) Mar 11; light-framed filly; second foal; dam of little account; emulating her dam; trained by M. Jarvis first 2 starts. *C. Booth.* —

LINDY BAY 3 br.g. Bay Express 132–Lindylee 99 (Grey Sovereign 128§) (1979 6s 5fg 5g2 5fg 6fg 5d2 1980 6s4 5fg 5f4 8f 8g 5g2 5.6fg* 5s4 5f 6g 5fg 5v) strong, good sort; sprint handicapper; successful at Doncaster in July; yet to show he stays 6f; goes well on top-of-the-ground; blinkered ninth outing; ran poorly third start; trained by W. Marshall part of season. *Hbt Jones.* **64**

LINEAL LAW 3 b.f. Lineage 99–Lady Friend (Be Friendly 130) (1979 NR 1980 8fg 9f) 320 2-y-o; first foal; dam never ran; tailed off in maiden races at Warwick and Wolverhampton in May. *M. Bradley.* —

LINGDALE 3 b.c. Crooner 119–Dream (Roan Rocket 128) (1979 5s 6f 6f2 6d* 7f3 6fg 6g4 1980 7d2 8.2d4 8.5f 9g 10.6d4 10.5g3 8d 8g 8s2 8g) strong, good sort; carries plenty of condition; quite useful handicapper; in frame in valuable races in the North; stays 1¼m; acts on firm going but is ideally suited by some give in the ground; blinkered sixth start; sometimes moves moderately to post; ran badly final outing. *W. Elsey.* **94**

LINGDALE LADY 2 ch.f. Sandford Lad 133–Amore Mare 80 (Varano) (1980 5d 6f 5g3 5d) Feb 26; 3,100Y; strong, useful-looking filly; first foal; dam showed form only at 5f; quite a moderate maiden; stays 6f. *W. Elsey.* **66**

LINGIA LIL 2 br.f. Mandamus 120–Tecllyn 97 (Technion 96) (1980 5f 5g4 5g 5g4 5f* 6g 5f) May 5; 2,500Y; strong, workmanlike filly; half-sister to winning sprinter Comtec (by Communication); dam sprinter; ran best race when winning 4-runner nursery at Lingfield in August by ½ length from Bohemian Rhapsody; well beaten in nurseries subsequently; should stay 6f; acts on firm going; inconsistent. *Mrs R. Lomax.* **83**

LINMILL 2 br.f. Amber Rama 133–Lady Millie 121 (Reneged) (1980 5g4 5fg2 5g3 6d4 6fg4 5f4 5fg2 5s) Apr 7; 6,400Y; lightly-made filly; half-sister to winners in Holland and France by Silver Shark; dam won Prix Thomas Bryon; in frame in varied races, including a valuable seller, prior to finishing creditable 2 lengths second of 16 to Katysue in nursery at Beverley in September; stays 6f but best form at 5f; best form on a sound surface; doesn't have a great deal of scope. *M. Jarvis.* **74**

LION IN WINTER 2 ch.c. Sun Prince 128–Place To Place (No Robbery) (1980 7s 6d3 6fg4 6f) May 22; 5,000Y; lengthy, light-framed colt; half-brother to Sosou Me (by Judgable), successful over 7f at 2 yrs in 1976 and subsequently a winner in USA, and to a winner abroad; dam won at up to 6f in USA; in frame in claiming race at Brighton (narrowly-beaten third to Welsh Folly) and seller at Goodwood in the summer; should stay 7f; possibly not at his best on a firm surface; blinkered second and fourth outings. *P. Cole.* **66**

LIQUIDATE 4 ch.g. Busted 134–St Pauli Girl 114 (St Paddy 133) (1979 11g 12.3fg* 12g 10.2fg 1980 12fg 10fg4 9g4 10.2g4 10g* 8.2g2 8f 8g 8g) big, rangy gelding; fair handicapper on his day; winner at Pontefract in July; bred to stay well; acts on a firm surface; well beaten when blinkered final outing (looked rather lean and light); has reputation of being none too honest; trained by G. Pritchard-Gordon until after eighth outing. *W. Elsey.* **81**

LIQUIDATION 6 ch.g. Yellow God 129–Taruni (Never Say Die 137) (1979 10.7g 10f 1980 10g) big gelding; said to be a whistler; plater; stays 1¼m; appears to act on any going; used to wear blinkers. *H. O'Neill.* —

LIR 3 b. or br.c. Lord Gayle 124–Mag (Noble Jay) (1979 5s 5d4 6s* 1980 7g 9f 12g2 12f4 10fg2 12f 6g 12g) 15,500Y; small ex-Irish colt; half-brother to several winners, including fairly useful 1978 Irish 2-y-o Chattahoochee (by Targowice) and useful 1976 Irish 2-y-o 6f winner Quick J (by Jim J); dam placed in USA; runner-up in handicaps at Killarney and the Curragh in first part of season; **82** d well beaten in varied company afterwards; stays 1½m; probably acts on any going; usually blinkered; trained by D. Weld first 6 starts. *A. Moore.*

LISANDRA 5 ch.m. Master Stephen 88–Lindie Leigh II (True Code 86) (1979 NR 1980 11.7f) non-thoroughbred mare; 100/1 when well beaten in maiden race at Bath in July, first outing. *T. Hallett.* –

LITTLE ATOM 3 gr. or ro.c. The Go-Between 129–Native Nymph 97 (Indigenous 121) (1979 5s4 5d4 5f 5f 5g 5f2 5fg2 6s 1980 5fg 5fg2 5fg 5h* 5fg2 5s 5s 5f2 5f* 5d 5d) robust colt; won 21-runner maiden race at Thirsk in May and minor event at Redcar in September; not sure to stay beyond 5f; acts on hard going and is unsuited by soft; trained by N. Adam first 6 starts. *D. Leslie.* **69**

LITTLE BIRDIE 2 gr.f. Town Crier 119–Sunningdale Sandy 53 (Sea Hawk II 131) (1980 6g 6fg 6g) Mar 17; 1,600Y; well-grown filly; half-sister to fair 1975 2-y-o 5f winner Balidale (by Balidar); dam daughter of very speedy Rose of Tralee; in rear in maiden auction event at Kempton in July, minor race at Lingfield in October and maiden race at Leicester in November. *D. Hanley.* –

LITTLE BOG (FR) 3 b.c. Bog Road 119–Hierapolis (Dapper Dan) (1979 8.2g 1980 10g 10.1fg 8f 10g 9f 8fg 10.8d 10s3 12d) workmanlike colt; best run at 1¼m on soft going. *G. Fletcher.* –

LITTLE BONNY 3 gr.f. Bonne Noel 115–Little Fuss (Sovereign Path 125) (1979 NR 1980 8g* 12.3f2 10fg3 8g* 10s3 8g2 12d2 10g* 12f2 12f 8.5g*) **126**

Little Bonny made up into a much better filly than her second behind Shoot A Line in the Cheshire Oaks promised: on that occasion she was well and truly outpointed by the winner, and appeared to lack the scope for significant improvement. She didn't improve straight away. By the time she was due to run in the Irish Guinness Oaks in July she had won two of her six races, a maiden event and a minor event at Leopardstown, and her form in better company made her

The Exors of the late Mr P. J. Prendergast's "Little Bonny" (C. Roche)

a 33/1-shot at the Curragh; she had already been beaten twice by Calandra. Little Bonny put up a tremendous performance in the Irish Oaks, going down by only two and a half lengths to Shoot A Line; she hung on extremely well in the straight to keep Racquette and Calandra out of second place, coming bang into the reckoning at last for the top fillies races still to be run.

Although her record now pointed to Little Bonny's being better suited by a mile and a half than shorter distances, the choice of her next race was a pretty shrewd one. She went for the Virginia Stakes over a mile and a quarter at Newcastle in August, receiving weight from all the other three-year-olds—Karamita, Dancing Shadow, Neenah, Star Chamber and Taverne de France—and meeting the older filly Bonnie Isle, the only other runner, on terms more favourable than weight-for-age. She won very impressively, by four lengths from Karamita who couldn't live with her in the last two furlongs. An even better performance, the performance of her career, followed in the Prix Vermeille at Longchamp in September. A mile and a half really does suit Little Bonny, for she succeeded in making the running to halfway up the straight and then fought back so well after seeming in danger of being swamped that she went under by only half a length to Mrs Penny. That Detroit would have beaten her with a clear run takes nothing away from Little Bonny: she accounted for a fair proportion of the top middle-distance three-year-olds of her sex in Europe on merit, one of them, of course, her compatriot Cairn Rouge. Little Bonny turned the tables on Mrs Penny in the Prix de l'Arc de Triomphe, her final race of the European season. She ran nearer her form in finishing eleventh than Mrs Penny did in finishing fifteenth, but wasn't good enough to challenge in the straight. Subsequently she was sent to the USA, and won an allowance race at Calder, Florida, in December.

Little Bonny (gr.f. 1977)	Bonne Noel (ch 1969)	Santa Claus (b 1961)	Chamossaire
			Aunt Clara
		Camilla Edge (ch 1963)	Alcide
			Carrozza
	Little Fuss (gr 1971)	Sovereign Path (gr 1956)	Grey Sovereign
			Mountain Path
		Ructions (bl 1965)	Rasper
			Rosie Redmond

Little Bonny's sire took time to come to himself as a racehorse; he won the Ebor Handicap as a four-year-old, and finished first in the Prix Kergorlay at the same age only to be relegated to second for bumping. He is one of the few sons of the Derby winner Santa Claus at stud (Reindeer and Santamoss are the only others we know of). Bonne Noel is also the sire of the second of the dam's two previous foals, the good four-year-old Noelino; another product of the same mating, a filly, fetched 88,000 guineas at Goffs Select Yearling Sales in October. The first foal of the dam, More Fuss (by Ballymore), won over nine furlongs at Ballinrobe in 1978. The female side of the family is American two generations back, though it has featured over here recently also through the exploits of Roscoe Blake and Jolly Good whose dam was a three-parts sister to Little Bonny's grandam. Ructions and Rosie Redmond both won in the USA, Ructions being stakes-placed too; the dam Little Fuss never ran.

Little Bonny, a smallish, compact filly, and a tough one, was very well bought as a yearling for 7,600 guineas. Though she has put up her best form at a mile and a half on firm ground she is certainly effective over shorter distances and probably acts on any going. *K. Prendergast, Ireland.*

LITTLE DARLING 2 ch.f. Paddy's Progress 113–Flying in Space (Bleep-Bleep 134) (1980 7d 7fg) Mar 25; half-sister to 1m seller winner Cornish Scot (by Rupert Bear); dam lightly-raced half-sister to very useful Secret Ray; behind in maiden races at Wolverhampton and Warwick (tailed off) in the summer. *M. Ryan.* —

LITTLE DEEP 2 ch.g. Galivanter 131–Skerne Springs 79 (Canadel II 126) (1980 5f 6g 5d 7fg 7d 7fg^3 7g 8.2d 8fg^3 8d) Mar 7; 1,300Y (privately); plain gelding; second foal; dam second over 7f and $1\frac{1}{2}$m; third in sellers at Redcar and Hamilton, being beaten only short head and a neck by Blue Garter on latter track in September; stays 1m; acts on a firm and a soft surface; sold 380 gns Doncaster October Sales. *H. Bell.* **60**

LITTLE HARP 3 ch.f. Communication 119–Tiny Tot 80 (Counsel 118) (1979 5g 5d 5fg* 5g 5f 1980 5.8f 6fg 5f 6g) very light-framed filly; plater; not certain to stay 6f; acts on a firm surface. *P. Haslam.* —

LITTLE IMP 3 br.g. Mummy's Pet 125–Cawkwell Beauty 61 (March Past 124) (1979 5v 5s 5s^4 5s^4 6f 1980 5h 5g 5.8g 6g 8g) poor plater; has worn blinkers. *M. Bradley.* –

LITTLE MISS ECHO 3 ch.f. Mountain Call 125–Ravenna (Celtic Ash) (1979 7.2g 7fg 8g 1980 10.8v) poor maiden. *A. W. Jones.* –

LITTLE NEWMARKET 5 b.g. Gold Rod 129–Sage Warbler (Le Sage 128) (1979 12.3s^4 10.4f 10.6g^4 10.5g 12s^3 13s^2 12d 1980 12d 12d* 16.1d^2 13g 14d^3 12d^4 15d^3 10.6s^4) staying handicapper; went down by neck to High Hills at Hamilton in June but was promoted to first by stewards; length second to Lenygon in amateur riders race at Haydock following month, best subsequent effort; seems to act on any going, except firm; suitable mount for a lady rider. *Mrs A. Cousins.* **52**

LITTLE PRINCE 4 br.c. Tribal Chief 125–Go Too 78 (Goldhill 125) (1979 5s 5s 5g 5fg^4 1980 5fg 5f 5g 5d) strong, compact colt; plating-class sprint maiden; blinkered final start. *N. Adam.* –

LITTLE STARCHY 2 b.c. Starch Reduced 112–Misty Morn 70 (Worden II 129) (1980 5s 5f 5fg 5h 5fg^2 5fg 5d^4 5d^2 5fg 5fg 5g^2 5f 5fg^2 5fg^2 5d*) Jan 14; fair sort; half-brother to 5f winner Kaimlaw (by Native Prince); dam stayed 11f; runner-up 4 times before gaining a well-deserved success in 20-runner maiden race at Sandown in October, beating Hayato 2 lengths after making all; unlikely to stay 6f; acts on a firm and a soft surface. *J. O'Donoghue.* **91 ?**

LITTLETON SONG 2 ch.f. Song 132–L'Aventura 65 (Elopement 125) (1980 5fg^4 5fg 5g 6s 7d^3 6fg* 6g^4 6fg 7d 6s^4) Apr 9; neat filly; closely related to quite useful sprinter Chin-Chin (by Sing Sing) and half-sister to 2 winners abroad; dam won at 1m and 1¼m, and is half-sister to Shirley Heights's dam; made all when winning 9-runner nursery at Folkestone in August by a head from Mexican Link; ran respectably in similar races on 2 occasions afterwards; stays 7f; probably acts on any going; wears blinkers nowadays and is best in them. *P. Cundell.* **73**

LITTLE TYRANT 3 br.g. Tyrant–Tadorna 82 (Sea-Bird II 145) (1979 5s* 5f 6f 7f 6f^2 6f 6g 7.2d 8g 6g 1980 8.2fg 6f 6fg 8g 8d) neat gelding; poor plater nowadays; should stay at least 7f; acts on any going; has worn blinkers. *R. Ward.* –

LITTLE ULLA 3 b.f. Forlorn River 124–Tarmandy (Black Tarquin 136) (1979 7s 1980 8g) tall filly; last in maiden races. *S. Harris.* –

LITTLE WOLF 2 ch.c. Grundy 137–Hiding Place 109 (Doutelle 128) (1980 6d*) Mar 23; close-coupled, quite attractive colt; brother to 3-y-o Major Gundry, a winner over 7f and 1¼m, and half-brother to numerous winners, including very smart 6f to 2m winner Smuggler (by Exbury); dam won at up to 1m; weak in market but fit, did particularly well to win 25-runner maiden race at Newbury in October by 1½ lengths from Casa Esquillina after starting rather slowly; stretched out really well in closing stages here and looks sure to make a good colt over middle distances; an interesting prospect. *R. Hern.* **88 P**

LIVE AMMO 3 ch.f. Home Guard 129–Molly Malone (Bold Lad, Ire 133) (1979 6fg^2 6g* 6fg 1980 7d) quite well-made filly; good mover; won maiden race at Newmarket in 1979; well beaten both subsequent starts, including in valuable handicap at Newmarket again in July; will stay 1m. *J. Hindley.* –

LIZ RAAPHORST (HOL) 3 b.f. Pantheon–Sica Girl S (Sica Boy 132) (1979 5g^3 5g^4 6.5fg^3 1980 8h 8f 12g) leggy, unfurnished ex-Dutch filly; well beaten in maiden race at Stockton and Dutch 1,000 Guineas and Dutch Derby, both at Duindigt; should stay at least 1m. *N. Guest.* –

LIZ WOLF 3 b.f. Sea Wolf 116–Ruedo Girl (El Ruedo 91) (1979 NR 1980 8f 12d 16fg) compact filly; first foal; dam well behind in 3 maiden races; seems of little account. *A. Jarvis.* –

LLARAE 3 b.f. Le Johnstan 123–Earall (Khalkis 127) (1979 5v^4 5v 5v 5s 5fg^2 5f 7f 7fg 1980 10.2g) compact filly; plating-class maiden; best run at 5f on a firm surface; blinkered fifth and sixth outings at 2 yrs. *K. Morgan.* –

LOAN CHARGE 4 b.g. Lombard 126–Something Else 66 (Paveh 126) (1979 8fg 8fg 1980 10s^3 8fg 9fg 12f* 10g^3 10g 10.2g) quite a moderate handicapper; made all in apprentice event at Chepstow in May; ran well next 2 starts but finished last on final start; stays 1½m; probably acts on any going. *R. Turnell.* **56**

LOCH BOISDALE 3 b.f. Saritamer 130–Hecla 117 (Henry the Seventh 125) (1979 6f 6g^4 6g 1980 8s) quite attractive filly; showed some ability at 2 yrs; well beaten only outing in 1980 (June); not sure to stay 1m; blinkered final start in 1979. *B. Hobbs.* –

LOCH BOYLE 2 b.c. Lochnager 132–Rise 68 (Fury Royal 108) (1980 5h^4 **74**
5f* 6fg^4 5fg 7g 7g 5d 5fg 7d) May 14; small colt; third foal; dam 7f winner and half-sister to smart sprinter Dutch Gold; won modest 6-runner maiden race at Ayr in May by ½ length from Noble Whin; creditable 2¼ lengths fourth of 17 to Sunny Smile in minor event at Ripon the following month but subsequently ran moderately; better suited by 6f than 5f but was well beaten over 7f. *C. Gray.*

LOCH ERROLL 2 b.f. Lochnager 132–Floragold 87 (Floribunda 136) (1980 —
5f 6g) Feb 13; fair sort; fourth foal; dam stayed 6f; unquoted and backward when behind in maiden race at Beverley in August and valuable seller at Doncaster in September. *M. W. Easterby.*

LOCH GATE 2 br.f. Lochnager 132–Nimble Gate 64 (Nimbus 130) (1980 —
5f 5f 5g 5fg) May 4; 7,400Y; compact, good-bodied filly; half-sister to 3 winners, including 3-y-o 1¼m winner Ceramic (by Cavo Doro) and very useful 1976 2-y-o 5f performer The Andrestan (by The Brianstan); dam won 5f seller at 2 yrs; behind in minor events in the North in first half of season; pulled hard early on and weakened quickly under pressure when blinkered final outing; dwelt second and third starts. *P. Asquith.*

LOCHRANZA 9 br.g. Highland Melody 112–Earall (Khalkis 127) (1979 **74**
12s^3 13s^2 12.3v 13g 13fg 12.2fg 12fg 13.8s 12.5g^3 1980 12d^3 13v* 13f* 12g^3 13d* 12g^3 11fg^4 14.7g^4 14d 12g^2 14f^3 13s^3 12g^3 12.5s) fairly useful and thoroughly genuine front-running handicapper at his best; not so good as he was but won 3 times at Ayr in 1980 and was gaining his tenth win on course when scoring by ½ length from Syncopate in June; ran a splendid race when runner-up to Dutch Treat in Great Yorkshire Handicap at York in August; best at up to 13f; ideally suited by some give in the ground nowadays; acts on any track: a grand battler; has worn blinkers; suitable mount for an inexperienced rider; occasionally sweats up; ran one of his rare bad races on final start. *J. Carr.*

LOCKER TARN 2 b.f. Hittite Glory 125–Miss Fenton 98 (Palestine 133) —
(1980 5d 5g 5f 5g) May 21; compact filly; half-sister to 3 winners, including Alanrod (by Gala Performance), a useful performer at up to 7f; dam 5f sprinter; behind in maiden and minor events; off course nearly 4 months before final outing (blinkered). *T. Fairhurst.*

LOCKINGTON LAD 2 ch.c. Song 132–Twin-Set (Double Jump 131) (1980 **63**
5fg^4 6g 6g) May 21; fair sort; fourth living foal; dam poor maiden; just over 4 lengths fourth of 7 to Miss Twiggy in maiden race at Catterick in May, best effort; should stay 6f; started slowly second outing and wore blinkers on third. *M. H. Easterby.*

LOCKSLEY (FR) 4 b.c. Tennyson 124–Telstop (Fine Top 125) (1979 10s —
12g 11.7g* 11s 13.1f 12f* 10g 12fg 1980 18f 12fg 16f^4 16g) shapely colt; won maiden race at Bath and ladies' race at Lingfield in 1979; stays 13f (well beaten over further); possibly unsuited by soft ground; pulled up final outing (blinkered). *P. Cundell.*

LOGAN 3 b.c. Biskrah 121–Amber Star (Amber Rama 133) (1979 6fg 6fg **65**
1980 10fg 7h^3 7s 8g* 10.1fg 10f) rather lightly-made colt; 25/1-winner of maiden race at Sandown in July; bred to stay 1¼m but was well beaten when tried at trip. *M. Masson.*

L. O. HARRY 5 b.g. Jan Ekels 122–Maesydd Mary (Nicolaus) (1979 12s —
13s 11.1v^3 12.3v^2 12g 12.3v^2 12.2s^2 1980 13s 12.3d^4 12f 12.2fg 12g 12g^4 12d) middle-distance handicapper; acts on any going; sold 400 gns Newmarket Autumn Sales. *R. Hollinshead.*

LOHENGRIN 4 b.g. Rheingold 137–Goosie 112 (Sea-Bird II 145) (1979 **95**
10s 10d* 12.3d* 11d^3 13.3fg 16f^4 14fg^2 1980 12fg^3 16g) rangy gelding; useful handicapper at 3 yrs; 4 lengths third of 5 to Bunce Boy under 10-0 at Lingfield in June; never on terms when behind in Queen's Vase at Royal Ascot later in month on only other outing; stays well; seems to act on any going. *J. Dunlop.*

LOLITO 3 b.f. Busted 134–My Witty (My Babu 136) (1979 NR 1980 12g^3 —
12fg 13g 10s) small, lightly-made filly; second living foal; dam won over 4.5f in French Provinces; well beaten in small races. *R. Boss.*

LOMBARDI (USA) 2 b.c. Northern Dancer–Julia B (Herbager 136) (1980 —
6fg^3) May 19; $375,000Y; big, useful sort; third foal; half-brother to a minor winner by Raja Baba; dam unraced half-sister to Observer Gold Cup winner Take Your Place and top-class American middle-distance mare Drumtop;

easy in market and not 100% wound up, missed break and was ridden along until eased in final furlong when 4 lengths last of 3 to Parkdale in Harry Peacock Challenge Cup at Newcastle in July; had previously had to be replated and moved poorly on way to start; not raced subsequently. *B. Hills.*

L'OMETTO 2 gr.g. Zeddaan 130–Rucellina (Clouet II 113) (1980 5fg 5f 6f 6s^3 6s^3 6g 6g 6f 6g 6s) Feb 11; 7,400F, 5,200Y; quite attractive, close-coupled gelding; second foal; dam lightly-raced half-sister to Italian Derby winner Appiani II; third in minor events at Windsor, beaten 10 lengths by Beulah Land in June and 5¾ lengths by Arndean in July; will stay at least 7f; form only on soft going. *G. Lewis.* **69**

LONARO 2 gr. or ch.f. Lorenzaccio 130–Path of Fortune (Sovereign Path 125) (1980 5f 6g) useless plater; sold 400 gns Newmarket Autumn Sales. *A. Bailey.* **—**

LONE BIDDER 2 b.f. Auction Ring 123–Seul 69 (Faberge II 121) (1980 6d^4 6fg* 6s 7fg*) Apr 12; 2,200Y; half-sister to Smokey Bear (by Gulf Pearl), a fairly useful winner at up to 15f; dam 2-y-o 7f winner; proved an excellent buy, winning 14-runner maiden race at Phoenix Park in July and Group 3 Park Stakes on same course in September; led close home to win latter by short head from Candle Hill; 25/1 when 6 lengths sixth of 14 to Arctique Royale in Moyglare Stud Stakes at the Curragh in between; will be suited by 1m; acts on a firm surface. *M. Kauntze, Ireland.* **97**

LONELY SIGNORITA 4 b.f. Hotfoot 126–Camusky 77 (Charlottown 127) (1979 7s 7v^3 8v 12f 12d 1980 including 10.6s*) won maiden race at Gowran Park in 1978 and finished third of 8 to Lady Segrave in Mulcahy Stakes at Phoenix Park in 1979 when trained in Ireland by L. Browne; having first outing in England when beating Rag Dancer decisively by 4 lengths in £2,400 event at Haydock in October; reportedly raced without success in Scandinavia earlier in year; stays 1¼m well; acts on heavy going; sold 8,200 gns Newmarket December Sales. *M. Stoute.* **85**

LONE RAIDER 3 b.c. Shantung 132–Love Resolved (Dan Cupid 132) (1979 7fg^4 1980 12f^3 16f^2 14f^2 16s 15fg* 12g* 14d^3 12.3g^4) big, workmanlike colt; won maiden race at Edinburgh (well-backed favourite) and amateur riders event at Newmarket in the summer; stays 2m; acts on firm going and is probably unsuited by very soft; ran moderately final start. *R. Boss.* **76**

LONESOME 3 b.f. Busted 134–Arvonia (Charlottesville 135) (1979 7g 1980 10g 14f^3 16d^3 16fg 14g 10g) staying maiden; acts on firm going; sold 6,200 gns Newmarket Autumn Sales. *T. Waugh.* **70**

LONGDON'S PRIDE 4 ch.c. Spanish Gold 101–Sunpas (The Bo'sun 114) (1979 NR 1980 10fg) of no account at 2 yrs; needed race on only outing since (September). *R. Hollinshead.* **—**

LONGGOE 2 ch.f. Lorenzaccio 130–Mey 78 (Canisbay 120) (1980 7fg 7d) Feb 3; half-sister to 3-y-o 1¼m winner Restful (by Ribero) and a winner in Italy; dam, best at 1¼m, is half-sister to smart Albany and Magna Carta; made late progress when 6½ lengths fifth of 20 in maiden race won by Queen's Mount at Brighton in August, first outing and better effort; will be suited by 1¼m. *W. Hastings-Bass.* **70**

LONGLANDS LADY 2 ro.f. Grey Mirage 128–Ursula 78 (Songedor 116) (1980 5fg 5d* 5g^3) Apr 10; 820 2-y-o; leggy filly; half-sister to fair sprinter Miss Anabella (by The Brianstan) and a winner in Belgium; dam placed over 5f at 2 yrs; bought in 2,000 gns after making all to win seller at Newcastle in June; ran well when length third of 7 to Merely Mozart in nursery at Hamilton the following month; should stay 6f; acts on a soft surface. *J. Berry.* **63**

LONG LEGEND (USA) 2 ch.f. Reviewer–Lianga 133 (Dancer's Image) (1980 6f*) Apr 26; well-made, attractive filly; second foal; sister to very useful 1979 2-y-o 5f and 6f winner La Legende; dam top-class winner from 4.5f to 1m; looked to have no chance after losing place at halfway in 19-runner maiden race at Newmarket in October but lengthened her stride in splendid style on meeting rising ground and got up close home to win by ½ length from Princess Dina; will stay 1m; likely to make a good 3-y-o. *H. Cecil.* **88 P**

LONGRIDGE 4 b.g. Derring-Do 131–Charlotteen 96 (Charlottown 127) (1979 8.2s 6v^3 7d 8d* 12g 12.2g^2 12fg 12.3fg^3 15.8f^3 14f^2 13.8fg^2 12.3fg 16g^4 13.8d 12h 12.2fg 12fg 1980 8d 10v 10fg 8f 8f 10h^4 12fg 8fg^4 10f 8g^2 9g^3 8fg^2 10g^3 8f^2 10f^3 12.2d) plater; stays fairly well; seems to act on any going; usually wears blinkers. *S. Nesbitt.* **47**

LOOSE MAID 3 b.f. Lauso–Spare Maid (Track Spare 125) (1979 5.1g 5fg 5g 5d 1980 5g) plain, light-framed filly; bad plater; was tried in blinkers; dead. *D. Yeoman.* —

LOPPYLUGS 4 ch.f. Amber Rama 133–Hitesca 110 (Tesco Boy 121) (1979 8d 7fg 6d^3 7fg 7s^3 8fg 9g^2 8g 1980 8v 7g 10f 7d 8d) neat filly; plater; stays 9f; best form on an easy surface; blinkered last 2 outings; sold 600 gns Doncaster October Sales. *C. Thornton.* 39

LOQUACITY 3 ch.f. On Your Mark 125–Macaw 85 (Narrator 127) (1979 6g 5fg 5g 5g 5fg 1980 6d 5s 5fg^2 5f 5fg^4 5f 5f^3 5fg 5s 5g^4 5g 5s 5fg^2 5d 5d 5s) compact filly; sprint handicapper; best at 5f on a firm surface; ran poorly fourth start; sold 3,200 gns Newmarket December Sales. *R. Hollinshead.* 59

LORALANE 3 b.f. Habitat 134–Lora (Lorenzaccio 130) (1979 6fg 6f 1980 7f* 8fg^4 9f^3 8g 8s 7d 8s) big, strong, rangy filly; won 23-runner maiden race at Newmarket in April; ran respectably next 2 starts but was off course 2 months afterwards and was well beaten in handicaps on her return; stays 1m; acts on firm going. *H. Wragg.* 86

LORD CLARENCE 2 b.c. Prince Tenderfoot 126–Lovely Clare 106 (Sing Sing 134) (1980 6f* 6g* 6g 6fg^4 7s) Feb 5; 3,000Y; rangy colt; fifth foal; brother to Irish 3-y-o $1\frac{1}{4}$m winner Well Pleased; dam 2-y-o 5f and 6f winner; looked a cut above a plater when winning seller at Lingfield in August by 4 lengths (bought in 3,600 gns) and quickly confirmed that he is, winning 13-runner minor event at Salisbury the following week by $1\frac{1}{2}$ lengths from Supper's Ready; put up easily best subsequent effort when strong-finishing $3\frac{1}{2}$ lengths fourth of 12 to Steelinctive in nursery at Ascot in September; promises to stay 7f; acts well on firm ground; sweated up second outing; sold to BBA 5,800 gns Newmarket Autumn Sales. *Mrs J. Reavey.* 91

LORD CLEWES 2 ch.c. Status Seeker–Calcine 75 (Roan Rocket 128) (1980 6g 7g* 7g^3 7fg^4 8f^3 8s^2 8fg) Apr 5; 2,030F, 3,600Y; workmanlike colt; half-brother to 2 minor winners; dam placed twice over 6f at 2 yrs; made all and held off unlucky-in-running Henry Morgan by a short head to win 7-runner maiden race at Chester in July; in frame in nurseries on fourth to sixth outings, running particularly well when $\frac{3}{4}$-length second of 6 to odds-on Lifestyle in £3,800 event at Ayr in September; suited by 1m; acts on any going but is possibly best on soft; genuine; bandaged near-hind at Ayr; well below form final start. *K. Stone.* 78

LORD EVER-SO-SURE 2 ch.c. Status Seeker–Scotch Polly 53 (Right Tack 131) (1980 6fg 6d^4 6g^4 7fg^2 8g 7d) Mar 16; 2,000F, 4,900Y; neat, strong, quite attractive colt; third foal; dam ran 4 times at 2 yrs; quite moderate form in maiden and minor events; stays 7f and should get 1m (had stiff task at weights when last in nursery over trip). *J. Etherington.* 75

LORD GALLANT 3 ch.c. Lord Gayle 124–Zerline 91 (Pandofell 132) (1979 6g 7fg 8.2g^4 8.2s*(dis) 7s 1980 8g 10g^2 8.5g^4 11fg^3 16g^3 16s^2 12d^2 12g^2 12f* 12d^2 12d 16d 16s) sturdy colt; won modest 9-runner maiden race at Beverley in August; stays well; acts on any going; blinkered nowadays; sold 5,400 gns Newmarket Autumn Sales. *B. Hanbury.* 69

LORD LAFF 2 b.c. Tumble Wind–You Never Can Tell (Never Say Die 137) (1980 6g 7fg) Mar 27; 5,200F, 6,000Y; strong, very attractive colt; half-brother to French 10.5f claiming race winner You Can Tell (by Tyrant); dam never ran; 50/1 and burly when well behind in minor event at Kempton and £6,200 event at Goodwood in July. *G. Lewis.* —

LORD LEIGHTON (USA) 4 ch.c. Vaguely Noble 140–Gentle Thoughts 118 (Bold Lad USA) (1979 10f 1980 12s 16.9d 13.1h) well-bred but has shown only poor form. *R. Boss.* —

LORD NEVER 2 b.c. Lord Gayle 124–Now or Never (Never Say Die 137) (1980 6s 7.9f^4 7fg^3 7g^4 6.3g^3 7s* 8s^2) Mar 16; half-brother to 2 winners, including Irish $1\frac{1}{2}$m winner All Ours (by Northfields), and to a bumpers winner; dam half-sister to some useful animals; improved with racing and won 19-runner maiden race at the Curragh in September in good style by 3 lengths from Roll of Drums; also in frame in National Stakes, Railway Stakes and Beresford Stakes on same course on fourth, fifth and seventh outings, putting up an excellent effort when going down by only a short head to Euclid in last-named in October; will be suited by middle distances; acts well on soft going; blinkered third start. *J. Bolger, Ireland.* 111

LORD OF HOSTS 6 ch.g. Jimmy Reppin 131–Eureka 78 (Major Portion 129) (1979 8g 8.3fg 8.2g 8fg 1980 9.6fg) plater; suited by 1m and give in the ground; has worn blinkers; probably needs strong handling. *C. James.* —

LORD OF MISRULE 6 gr.h. Supreme Sovereign 119–Mirth (Tamerlane 128) (1979 10v 11.1v^2 10g 10.7g 8s 10g 9fg^2 10g* 10fg 1980 12fg 11.7fg 10fg^4 12f 10fg^4 10s^2 11.7s^2 10g 8g 11.7f^2 8g 10fg^3 10g) quite a moderate handicapper; stays 1½m; acts on any going; usually wears blinkers; suitable mount for an inexperienced rider. *M. Haynes.* **59**

LORD OF THE REALM 2 ch.c. Realm 129–Suir-Delight (Precipitant 113) (1980 5s 5s 7d 6g) Apr 19; 9,200Y; small colt; half-brother to several winners, including useful French middle-distance winner Suirelko (by Relko); dam, half-sister to Golden Horus, won 2m bumpers race; sixth behind Beocan and fifth behind Endless Moment in minor events at Brighton in the autumn on last 2 outings; stays 7f. *G. Beeson.* **73**

LORD PERRYBAND 5 b.g. Hopeful Venture 125–Gay Natasha 105 (Prince Chevalier) (1979 12.2g 14f 1980 16fg 17.1f^4) poor staying handicapper. *J. Old.* **—**

LORD RAFFLES 4 b.g. Upper Case–Sonia 86 (Worden II 129) (1979 NR 1980 10fg 10h 9.6fg* 10f 8.3f^3 8g* 8g 8g) plater; made all when winning at Folkestone (bought in 800 gns) in June and Kempton (bought in 2,500 gns) in September; broke a leg and was destroyed at Goodwood later in September; acted on firm going. *W. Musson.* **59**

LORD ROCHFORD 5 ch.h. Tudor Music 131–Envy 98 (Princely Gift 137) (1979 6s 5s 6d 7s 7f 6d 6fg* 6g 6s* 6s 7f 7fg 1980 6v 8f 6fg 6f 7.6f* 8g^2 7d* 8f 8g) lengthy, quite attractive horse; developed into a smart performer and carried top weight when winning handicaps at Lingfield (Queen Elizabeth Stakes, from Northleach) and Newcastle (Sunday Sun Stakes, from Just Amber) in June; top weight and carrying penalty when excellent 3 lengths second of 22 behind Tender Heart in Royal Hunt Cup at Royal Ascot in between; beaten less than 3 lengths when fifth of 12 in Prix Messidor won by Tassmoun at Maisons-Laffitte in July but was never on terms when seventh of 12 under 10.0 in William Hill Gold Cup at Redcar in August; stays 1m; acts on any going; goes well for an apprentice. *B. Swift.* **118**

LORD SCRAP 4 ch.g. Tower Walk 130–La Concha (Le Levanstell 122) (1979 7f 6fg 6g* 6fg* 5f^2 6f 6fg* 6d 1980 5s 5g 6fg^3 6g 6g^2 6d^4 5.8f* 5f 6fg 6d) good-looking gelding; won handicap at Bath in July comfortably; bred to stay 1m, but is evidently regarded as a sprinter; acts on firm going and an easy surface; usually blinkered at 2 yrs; excellent mount for a boy. *B. Swift.* **73**

Sunday Sun Handicap, Newcastle—Lord Rochford takes the lead from Just Amber

LORD SEYMOUR 3 b.c. Habitat 134–Lady Seymour 109 (Tudor Melody 129) (1979 6fg* 6f2 6d4 6fg* 6f3 1980 6fg3 6g 7g3 7fg) neat, very good-looking colt; really good performer (rated 127) at 2 yrs when he won Mill Reef Stakes at Newbury; didn't grow much over the winter and failed to reproduce his 2-y-o form in Gus Demmy Memorial Stakes at Haydock (5¼ lengths third to Sayyaf), Cork and Orrery Stakes at Royal Ascot (6½ lengths seventh of 20 to Kearney) and £8,100 race at Newmarket in June (2 lengths third to Captain Nick); ran deplorably in blinkers in Beeswing Stakes at Newcastle in July on final start; stayed 7f; acted on firm going and probably wasn't at his best on soft; syndicated for A$693,000 to stand at Nook Stud, Victoria. *M. Stoute.* **111**

LORD TRENDY 2 b.c. Lord Gayle 124–Tenderly (Prince Tenderfoot 126) (1980 5fg* 7g 7g3 6g* 6.3s 6.3g2 8s 6d) Apr 8; 10,000Y; second foal; half-brother to Irish 3-y-o 7f and 9f winner Disco Dancer (by Gay Fandango); dam fairly useful winner from 5f to 9f in Ireland; awarded minor event at Leopardstown in May after winner failed its dope test; justified favouritism by a length from Bustineto in minor event at Phoenix Park 3 months later; also placed in 2 good-class races, finishing 2 lengths third to Light Here in Mullion Stakes at Leopardstown in August and going down by 2½ lengths to Lawmaker in Railway Stakes at the Curragh the following month; should stay at least 1m. *K. Prendergast, Ireland.* **98**

LORD WARWOOD 3 ch.g. Stan Flashman 72–Carnival Moon (Cave of Dracan 93) (1979 NR 1980 12f 11.7fg) second foal; dam never ran; behind in minor race at Wolverhampton and maiden race at Bath in first half of season. *M. Bradley.* –

LORD WESSCAM 2 b.c. Sassafras 135–Coral Lee (Le Levanstell 122) (1980 6fg 7g 8g) Jan 28; 4,600Y; small, compact colt; fourth foal; dam Irish 9f and 13f winner; well behind in maiden and minor events. *S. Matthews.* –

LORD WIMPY 2 gr.g. Dragonara Palace 115–My Worry 72 (March Past 124) (1980 5s3 5fg3 6f4 6d 7d 7d3 6g 7f3 7g 7d) Mar 16; robust gelding; seventh foal; half-brother to 3-y-o 6f winner Bokarah in Shallah (by Forlorn River); dam placed over 5f at 2 yrs; in frame in varied company, on sixth outing finishing respectable 6½ lengths third of 6 to Robellino in Donnington Castle Stakes at Newbury in July; stays 7f; seems to act on any going; often faced with stiff tasks, including when blinkered seventh outing. *R. Hannon.* **75**

LORENETTE 3 ch.f. Lorenzaccio 130–Crepinette 64 (Saint Crespin III 132) (1979 6f 6g 7g 8g 1980 8d 12g* 12g3 11d3 13g 12d 12d) won poor 4-runner event at Leicester in July; stays 1½m; acts on a soft surface; trained by A. Jarvis first 4 starts. *D. Gandolfo.* **60**

LORENTINO 3 b.g. Lorenzaccio 130–Timur's Daughter 103 (Tamerlane 128) (1979 8f3 1980 8f 10.4f 10.8s* 10s2 10d4 12g* 10g2) well-made gelding; has a long stride; won 12-runner maiden race at Warwick in July; just got home from John O'Groats after a tremendous tussle in £3,000 handicap at Goodwood in August; suited by 1½m; acts on soft going; looked totally unsuited by Chester track second start. *F. J. Houghton.* **86**

LORNA CRIQUE 3 b.f. Forlorn River 124–Martinique II (Relko 136) (1979 5d 5s2 6fg 5h3 6f* 5f 5d2 6g4 6g* 5g 1980 6fg 6s4 8fg 7fg 7g2 6f 6d 6s) narrow filly; quite a moderate handicapper; stays 7f; suited by some give in the ground. *J. Etherington.* **69**

LORRAINE GAY 2 ch.f. Continuation 120–Eve Darlin 50 (Arcticeelagh 119) (1980 5fg 5f) May 21; neat filly; fifth foal; dam poor plater; of little account; sold 280 gns Doncaster October Sales. *J. Hardy.* –

LOSANGES BLEU 2 ch.g. Dragonara Palace 115–St Gay 77 (St Chad 120) (1980 6g 6fg) May 1; 4,400Y; fair sort; second foal; dam won over 6f; behind in June in minor event at Haydock (slowly away) and maiden race at Newbury; gelded after second outing. *R. Hannon.* –

LOST CAUSE 2 br.f. Perdu 121–Silent Swindler 59 (Tacitus 124) (1980 6g 6s 7g 5f2 5g 5s 6d) Apr 28; robust filly; fourth foal; half-sister to 3-y-o 5f winner Fiddler (by Song); dam won 1¼m seller; improved greatly when blinkered, finishing length second of 17 to Sodina in maiden race at Lingfield in October; didn't reproduce that form, including in a Stockton seller; best run at 5f but should stay further; evidently suited by firm going; blinkered fourth to sixth outings; sold 440 gns Ascot December Sales. *C. Austin.* **68 ?**

LOST CONTACT 4 b.f. Communication 119–Lost Riches 75 (Forlorn River 124) (1979 5f 5f 6g 5g² 1980 5fg) plating-class maiden; should stay 6f; sold 600 gns Ascot November Sales. *M. Pipe.* —

LOST FOR WORDS 3 b.f. Firestreak 125–Sombrilla (Big Game) (1979 5s² 6g 5.8f 5g⁴ 8g 1980 8.2d 7f² 8fg 6fg* 6fg 7g 6g 6g 6d 6g) leggy, light-bodied filly; won handicap at Catterick in May; well beaten, including in a claiming handicap, afterwards; stays 1m but seems better at shorter distances; acts on any going; sometimes sweats up. *R. Boss.* 59

LOST LINE 3 b.g. High Line 125–Lost Riches 75 (Forlorn River 124) (1979 8fg⁴ 7d 8d 1980 10s 8s 11.7fg) lengthy gelding; only plating class; unseated rider first outing. *M. Pipe.* —

LOST VALLEY 3 b.f. Perdu 121–Long Valley 71 (Ribero 126) (1979 5fg* 5fg 1980 8g) plater; well beaten only start at 3 yrs in July; should stay 1m. *J. Hill.* —

LOTUS WATER BOY 3 br.c. Jukebox 120–Dusky Princess (Sayajirao 132) (1979 NR 1980 8fg 7f 5d 8f² 8fg 8g* 8d) 14,000Y; well-made colt; half-brother to 4 winners, including very useful Irish sprinters Excessive (by Experiment) and First Up (by Balidar); dam ran only twice; apprentice ridden, won modest maiden event at Edinburgh in October; stays 1m; acts on firm going; bandaged first outing; ran badly fifth start; sold 3,100 gns Newmarket Autumn Sales. *J. Hindley.* 75

LOUISE MOULTON 3 b.f. Moulton 128–Croomedale (Alcide 136) (1979 6f³ 6fg 7s⁴ 7fg³ 1980 10g² 12g² 12d 12d⁴ 10fg⁴ 9s* 10.2d 10d³) shapely filly; trotted up in 18-runner maiden event at York in October; stays 1½m; acts on any going; blinkered third, fourth and fifth outings; sometimes bandaged on near-hind; inconsistent and ran badly seventh start. *W. Elsey.* 78

LOUIS ROEDERER 3 b.g. Scottish Rifle 127–Fair Camilla 81 (Tiger 125) (1979 NR 1980 10fg 10fg 10fg 8.5f) strong, good sort; first foal; dam won over 1m and 1¼m; well beaten in maiden races and a valuable seller. *P. Cole.* —

LOU PIGUET (FR) 2 b.c. Habitat 134–Tuneria (Tanerko 134) (1980 5.5d* 7d² 8s* 9fg⁴ 7.5g³) Apr 3; 460,000 francs Y (approx £48,000); brother to successful Italian colt Hagg Hagg, and half-brother to a winner by Thatch; dam French middle-distance winner; a very smart colt who won maiden race at Evry in July and Prix des Ventes at Deauville in August, latter impressively by 3 lengths from Beau Danseur; also ran very well on his other starts, coming out best horse at weights when short-head second to Shoen in Prix des Yearlings at Deauville, finishing in good style when narrowly-beaten fourth of 8 to Mariacho in Prix Saint-Roman at Longchamp and being beaten little over 2 lengths by Big John (rec 3 lb) when third of 10 in Prix Thomas Bryon at Saint-Cloud; will stay 1¼m; seems to act on any going; consistent. *J. C. Cunnington, France.* 123

L'OUVERTURE 2 gr.f. Bustino 136–Key of the Kingdom 111 (Grey Sovereign 128 §) (1980 7fg 7g) Feb 22; 17,000Y; leggy, useful sort; first foal; dam speedy 2-y-o; 20/1 and looking fit and well, showed excellent speed till weakening quickly 1½f out when 8 lengths eighth of 17 behind Golden Bowl in maiden event at Salisbury in September; looked in need of race and missed break first outing; the type to do better at 3 yrs. *J. Sutcliffe.* — p

LOVE FOR MONEY 2 ch.f. Be Friendly 130–Rold Gold (Bold Combatant) (1980 5g 5g* 6g⁴ 5.1fg⁴) Jan 30; 2,000F, 11,500Y; small filly; first foal; dam won over 9f at 2 yrs in France; ran on strongly to win 10-runner maiden race at Redcar in July by 1½ lengths from Courreges; respectable fourth to Holdall in minor event at Ripon the following month, third outing; stays 6f. *L. Cumani.* 71

LOVELY TO LOOK AT 2 br.f. Comedy Star 121–Sonseeahray 67 (March Past 124) (1980 6g) Apr 5; second foal; dam seemed best at sprint distances; 25/1 when last of 13 to Pieta in maiden race at Brighton in August. *M. Masson.* —

LOVE ME TWO 6 b.m. Double Jump 131–Lilmi Love 82 (Miralgo 130) (1979 6g* 7d* 7f⁴ 6h 7f⁴ 6fg 7fg 6g 1980 6h 7f 7g 6d 7fg 6g) quite a moderate handicapper; well beaten in 1980; stays 7f; appears to act on any going; good mount for an apprentice. *B. Richmond.* —

LOVE SUPREME 3 ch.f. Sallust 134–Bordelaise 96 (Above Suspicion 127) (1979 5d⁴ 5d 5g² 5g⁴ 5g 6fg² 6d* 1980 8.5g⁴ 8fg⁴ 10d 8g² 8fg² 7g 8d 8d* 7d 8s) small, quite well-made filly; decisively beat Angor by a length in handicap at Pontefract in October; stays 1m (ran too freely when well beaten over 1¼m); acts on a firm and a soft surface; sometimes wears blinkers but is as effective without them; has run creditably for an apprentice. *G. Hunter.* 78

LOW MILEAGE 3 b.g. Royben 125–Ritz Bar 99 (Royal Palm 131) (1979 5.1g 6f 6f4 1980 6f 6fg 6fg 7f 5fg 7g 6g) leggy gelding; poor sprint handicapper; probably stays 6f. *N. Callaghan.* —

LOWNDES COURT 2 b.c. High Top 131–Queen's Grove 98 (Sing Sing 134) (1980 6g 7fg 7s) Apr 6; 5,200Y; rather lightly-made colt; third foal; half-brother to 1m and 9f winner Buckram (by Crepello); dam won over 5f at 2 yrs; behind in fairly useful company but showed signs of ability on final start; probably stays 7f. *D. Sasse.* —

LOWTHER STREET 2 gr.f. Grey Mirage 128–Sherbet (Zarathustra 131) (1980 6fg 7g) Mar 21; 600Y; half-sister to Talk of the Town (by Town Crier), a useful performer at up to 1m; dam, sister to useful stayer Le Pirate, won over 1m in Ireland; unquoted when in rear in newcomers event at Chepstow in August and 22-runner maiden race on same course following month. *D. Ancil.* —

LOYAL AND REGAL 4 b. or br.f. Royal and Regal–Meadows Alley (St Paddy 133) (1979 10v 8g 13fg 10fg 10fg 10d2 1980 11fg 10fg 10h 10fg 10d4 10s2 10g2 10g) plater; stays 1¼m; acts on soft going; sweating penultimate outing. *D. Leslie.* **39**

LUCAYA (FR) 2 b.f. Mill Reef 141–La Mirande (Le Fabuleux 133) (1980 5f4 5f2 5f* 5f3 5g* 6g 5fg2 6g) Apr 11; small filly; first foal; dam, sister to Oaks third La Manille, was very useful over middle distances in France; beat Rosy Cottage when successful in maiden race at Wolverhampton in June and minor event at Bath the following month, scoring by a neck and ¾ length respectively; creditable second to 6-length winner Queen of Prussia in £2,600 event at Salisbury in September; bred to stay middle distances but has shown best form over 5f; genuine. *H. Candy.* **86**

LUCCOMBE 2 b.g. Huntercombe 133–Azina (Canonero II) (1980 5d 5d2 6g) Apr 3; neat gelding; first foal; dam unraced half-sister to Swing Easy; didn't get a clear run until switched in final furlong and failed by a neck to get up and beat Longlands Lady in seller at Newcastle in June; ran well from a poor draw in similar event next time out; stays 6f. *M. H. Easterby.* **65**

LUCK OF THE DRAW 3 b.f. Auction Ring 123–La Fortune (Le Haar 126) (1979 6f* 6f* 6d 6f4 1980 7fg 8fg 7g4 7s* 7.3d 7f* 7v) **116**

The useful winner of two of her races in 1979, including the Princess Margaret Stakes, Luck Of The Draw continued the good work as a three-year-old and picked up important prizes at Longchamp and York. Before arriving at the former course for the Prix de la Porte Maillot at the end of June she had run three times, her best display coming in the One Thousand Guineas when, equipped with blinkers for the first time, she lay close up for a long way and eventually finished a creditable sixth to Quick As Lightning. Luck Of The Draw wore blinkers in all her subsequent races. Her nine opponents in the Porte Maillot included Baptism, Hilal and Kilijaro but it was Ya Zaman, having his first run in a pattern event, who gave the filly most trouble. Brought to challenge Ya Zaman a furlong out after following the leading group for much of the race, Luck Of The Draw put in a determined effort under very strong riding but despite making Ya Zaman fight hard she was always getting the worst of it and went down by half a length. Hilal was two and a half lengths away third.

By the time Luck Of The Draw ran in the Hungerford Stakes at Newbury in August she had been awarded the Porte Maillot by the French authorities who had no option but to disqualify the winner after traces of caffeine were found in him in a post-race test. Ya Zaman was the second French horse

Prix de la Porte Maillot, Longchamp—Luck Of The Draw has been hard ridden throughout the last furlong but fails by half a length to catch the subsequently-disqualified Ya Zaman

Strensall Stakes, York—Luck Of The Draw gets the better of Our Home by a head

to lose a pattern race in 1980 for having a prohibited substance in his system —Shafaraz in the Prix de Barbeville was the first. Luck Of The Draw carried a penalty at Newbury and ran rather lifelessly behind Kampala, perhaps because of her exertions at Longchamp. She returned to her best in the Strensall Stakes at York in September. Facing a stiff task conceding 10 lb to the Guineas second Our Home and 6 lb to Missed Blessing, who had finished ahead of her at Newbury, Luck Of The Draw put up a splendid performance, chasing the leader Miss Taymore from the start, gaining the upper hand a furlong and a half out and responding gamely to extreme pressure from her rider when challenged by Our Home inside the distance, finally getting home by a head with third-placed Missed Blessing three lengths further back. Her only subsequent start saw Luck Of The Draw returned to Longchamp in October for the Prix de la Foret; on this occasion she might as well have stayed at home. Prominent for five furlongs she dropped back very quickly thereafter and came in a well-beaten seventh of nine to Moorestyle. Possibly the heavy going was against her—it was her first outing on so testing a surface—though she had shown the ability to act on virtually any other type of ground.

Luck Of The Draw (b.f. 1977)	Auction Ring (b 1972)	Bold Bidder (b 1962)	Bold Ruler
			High Bid
		Hooplah (b 1965)	Hillary
			Beadah
	La Fortune (ch 1968)	Le Haar (ch 1954)	Vieux Manoir
			Mince Pie
		Fortunella (b 1959)	Pinza
			Respite

Before Luck Of The Draw, her dam La Fortune had produced the Homeric colt Latin Luck, who showed useful form in England as a three-year-old in 1978, winning over eleven furlongs, and has also won in Italy. La Fortune put up her best performance in a one-mile maiden race at Saint-Cloud as a two-year-old, finishing third. She was the only one of Fortunella's five living produce not to win. One of those winners had to go jumping in Italy before succeeding but the other three showed more ability and included the fair French middle-distance filly Silky Fortune and the useful Don Fortune, a winner from seven furlongs to one and a half miles. Fortunella was the second highest priced yearling of 1960 at 15,000 guineas, in the days when Pinza's stock were still in demand. She didn't recoup much of that expenditure on the racecourse, failing to train on after impressively winning her first start as a two-year-old. She was a half-sister to the Two Thousand Guineas winner Nearula, the top-class sprinter Drum Beat and the smart 1957 Irish two-year-old Talmud. Fortunella's dam, Respite, won over six furlongs as a four-year-old and was a half-sister to numerous winners, notably Oceana, dam of the outstanding Australian performers Todman and Noholme II.

Luck Of The Draw visits Alleged in 1981. A strong, attractive, full-quartered filly, she did particularly well physically from two years to three years and was a good walker and mover. She stayed a mile and was genuine, even though she wore blinkers. *R. Hern.*

LUCKY LOVE 2 b.f. Mummy's Pet 125–Gay Jennie 69 (Lord Gayle 124) **65**
(1980 5g 5g 5d) May 20; first foal; dam won over 1$\frac{1}{2}$m; never-dangerous seventh of 14 to Crosby Triangle in seller at Windsor in August; not disgraced when eighth in 19-runner maiden race won by Voting Day at Bath the following month; will be suited by 6f. *D. Elsworth.*

LUCKY MAN 4 b.g. Manacle 123–Quite Sweet 100 (Super Sam 124) (1979 **90**
6g^2 6g* 6d^4 6s 7f^2 8fg 7g* 7f^2 7fg* 7fg 1980 8f 7fg* 8f^3 7f^4 7g* 7d^2 8g^3 7g 6g 7.3fg^4 7fg^2 6d^3) workmanlike gelding; successful in handicaps at Salisbury in May (made all and held off Denmore by $\frac{3}{4}$ length) and Lingfield in June (ridden by 7-lb claimer, won readily from Flint); ran well most other starts, notably when short-head second to Tower Joy in valuable handicap at Ascot in September on penultimate outing (caught last strides after trying to make all); finds 6f on sharp side nowadays and stays 1m; acts on a soft surface but is suited by a sound one; tough and genuine. *P. M. Taylor.*

LUCKY MISTAKE 3 gr.f. Averof 123–Kingdom Come 77 (Klondyke Bill 125) **52**
(1979 5v 1980 8s 8s 6f 6h^3 6g 6s 6fg 6fg 6d 5d 7g* 8fg 8d 7s) strong filly; bought in 950 gns after winning seller at Yarmouth in September; stays 7f; acts on hard going; blinkered ninth and tenth outings; has worn bandages. *W. Marshall.*

LUCKY PROSPECT 3 b.f. Jimsun 121–Lucky Pigeon (The Mongoose 108) –
(1979 5s 6fg^2 1980 8s 10.2fg 6g) plater; best run at 6f on a firm surface; dead. *D. Gandolfo.*

LUCKY STORY 6 b.m. Lucky Sovereign–Frontier Legend (Border Legend –
119) (1979 NR 1980 8g) fourth foal; dam a point-to-pointer; 50/1 when well beaten in amateur riders race at Warwick in June, first outing. *J. Bosley.*

LUCKY TINA 2 br.f. Workboy 123–March Poulet (March Past 124) (1980 –
6d 6g) Mar 24; 5,100Y; sister to 1979 2-y-o 5f winner Spring Bird, and half-sister to 3 winners, including useful sprinter Golden Mallard (by Goldhill); dam of no account; unquoted when in rear in maiden races at Ayr in June and Carlisle in July. *J. Berry.*

LUCKY TONIGHT 2 br.f. So Blessed 130–Night Appeal 99 (Petition 130) **54**
(1980 5s* 5g) May 3; 1,100Y; narrow, unimpressive filly; half-sister to fair stayer Quiet (by Salvo); dam won Fred Darling Stakes; won 16-runner auction event at Leicester in March by a length from Miss Murton; moderate seventh in similar race at Ripon the following month, only subsequent start; sold 2,100 gns Newmarket December Sales. *G. Blum.*

LUCY LIMELIGHT 3 ch.f. Hot Spark 126–St Citrus 108 (Relic) (1979 **87**
5g^4 5s 5fg* 5fg^4 5d 5g^4 5fg^2 5fg^4 1980 6fg 6f 6fg 7fg 5.3g) strong, shapely filly; carries plenty of condition; fair handicapper at her best; ran creditably second start; well beaten afterwards; stays 6f; possibly needs a sound surface; sold 24,000 gns Newmarket December Sales. *J. Bethell.*

LUIGI'S GIRL 2 b.f. The Brianstan 128–Malton Hope 92 (High Treason 126) –
(1980 5g 5f) May 2; 4,000Y; half-sister to some minor winners; dam won over 6f and 7f at 2 yrs; seventh in maiden races at Wolverhampton in July (17-runner event) and Lingfield in August; will stay 6f. *J. Hudson.*

LULAV 2 br.c. Prince Regent 129–Scarletta 103 (Red God 128§) (1980 5fg –
6f 7d) Mar 8; 12,500Y; well-made colt; half-brother to fairly useful 5f and 7f winner Gerfalcon (by Falcon) and 3-y-o sprint winner Irish Solitaire (by On Your Mark); dam at her best at 2 yrs; unquoted when seventh of 15 behind Hollow Laughter in maiden race at Brighton in July, third outing; not fully wound up first 2 starts, moving badly to post second occasion; probably stays 7f. *R. Smyth.*

LULEW 2 b.f. African Sky 124–Welshpool 75 (Henry the Seventh 125) (1980 –
5fg 6d) Feb 6; 4,300Y; leggy, light-framed, narrow filly; sister to 3-y-o 7f

and 1m winner Africanos, and half-sister to a winning plater and a winner in Belgium; dam ran in England and Ireland; apprentice ridden when in rear in maiden race at Newmarket in May and valuable seller at Brighton in June. *P. Kelleway.*

LULU'S PET 2 b.f. Abwah 118–Oh Well 61 (Sahib 114) (1980 5s 5fg^4 5f 60
5fg^4 7g 5f) Mar 18; 3,200Y; small, lightly-made filly; first foal; dam stayed 1m; fourth in minor event at Folkestone and 17-runner maiden race at Catterick in first half of season; having first race for 3 months when tried over 7f (last of 18); sold 400 gns Newmarket Autumn Sales. *E. Eldin.*

LUMEN 5 br.g. Prince Tenderfoot 126–Bright Match 73 (Match III 135) (1979 86
10d 13.3s^4 12fg^3 12g^2 12g* 13.3fg 1980 16s 12g 12fg^2 13.3fg) compact, deep-girthed gelding; won Moet and Chandon Silver Magnum (gentleman riders) at Epsom in 1979; caught in last stride when short-head second to No Bombs (gave 4 lb) in same race in August; disappointing sixth behind Castle Keep in Coral Autumn Cup at Newbury in September; best form at up to 1½m; seems to act on any going but goes well on a sound surface; used to wear blinkers. *J. Gifford.*

LUNAR ECLIPSE 3 ch.f. Hot Spark 126–Wild Words 76 (Galivanter 131) 75
(1979 5fg* 5g^3 5fg^3 6f* 6f 6s 1980 5fg 6f 6fg 5fg 6fg 6g) small filly; quite a moderate handicapper; better suited by 6f than 5f and will stay further; acts on any going; sweated up fifth start; sold 3,500 gns Newmarket Autumn Sales. *J. Winter.*

LUNAR WIND 5 ch.g. Windjammer (USA)–Lunar Star (Star Gazer 123) 62
(1979 8v 6g 5.8g 6fg^2 6f 6f^4 8fg 6d^2 6g^3 6g^3 8.2s^3 1980 7d 8.2fg 8f 8f^2 8f^4 9fg* 8fg^3 9g^3 11g 8.2g^4 8.2g^4 8fg 8d) leggy, narrow gelding; poor handicapper; won at Hamilton in May; stays 9f (well beaten over 11f); acts on any going; has worn blinkers; suitable mount for an apprentice; sold out of G. Richards' stable 1,900 gns Doncaster March Sales after first outing; trained by M. Naughton second to eleventh outings. *N. Tinkler.*

LUSITANICA 3 b.f. Pieces of Eight 128–Auspice 84 (Aureole 132) (1979 –
NR 1980 10g 10.1fg 10s 10g) 500F; lengthy filly; fifth foal; dam 1¼m winner; no sign of ability in maiden and minor events. *M. Tompkins.*

LUSTROSO 5 b.g. Shiny Tenth 120–Lady Stone 67 (Zarathustra 131) (1979 8g –
10s 10f^4 8g* 1980 12fg 10s 8g^4) won minor event at Brighton in 1979; well beaten in handicaps in 1980; stays 1¼m. *P. K. Mitchell.*

LUTANIST 3 ch.c. Luthier 126–Escorial 110 (Royal Palace 131) (1979 8s 84
1980 13s^2 14g^4) lengthy colt; good second to North Buchan in maiden race at Nottingham in July; odds on, ran moderately in similar race at Salisbury later in month, only subsequent start; should stay 1¾m; sold to P. Makin 10,500 gns Newmarket December Sales. *R. Hern.*

LUTH DE SARON (FR) 3 b.f. Luthier 126–Rose de Saron 120 (Carvin 127) 118
(1979 6g* 7d* 8d 1980 9.5g* 10.5g^4 10s* 10g^3 12f) deep-bodied filly; half-sister to middle-distance winner Gay Saron (by Sir Gaylord) and useful 1978 2-y-o 7f winner Percussion (by Lyphard); dam smart winner from 5f to 1m; won Prix Vanteaux and Prix de Malleret at Longchamp in first half of year, beating Benicia a head each time; also ran creditably to be in frame in Prix de Diane at Chantilly (fourth to Mrs Penny) and Prix de la Nonette at Deauville (just over 2 lengths third to Detroit); ran moderately in Prix Vermeille at Longchamp final start; stays 1¼m well; possibly unsuited by firm going; smart. *J. Cunnington, jnr, France.*

LUTH MUSIC (FR) 3 b.f. Mon Fils 124–Music Lover (Luthier 126) (1979 111
N.R. 1980 10g^3 10.5g* 10.5fg* 10.5d 13.5g 9.2f) 100,000 francs Y (approx. £11,900); third foal; half-sister to useful French 1978 3-y-o 10.5f winner Loriquet (by Rheffic) and to Love Music (by Margouillat), successful over 1m in France at 2 yrs; dam ran twice at 2 yrs; won maiden race at Saint-Cloud in May and 10-runner Prix de Royaumont at Chantilly in June, beating As You Desire Me (gave 3lb) ½ length in latter; soundly beaten in Prix Fille de l'Air at Saint-Cloud and Prix de Pomone at Deauville on her next 2 starts but finished respectable sixth to Hortensia in Prix de l'Opera at Longchamp on final outing in October; stays 1¼m well; suited by top-of-the ground conditions. *E. Chevalier du Fau, France.*

LUTOMER L RIESLING 2 ch.c. Sun Prince 128–Golden Glimpse (Gallant –
Man) (1980 5f 5f 7fg 8g 8g) Feb 18; 18,000F, 20,000Y; lengthy colt; third produce; half-brother to useful 1978 French 2-y-o winner Silver Glimpse (by Petingo); dam, winner over 1m in USA, is daughter of sister to Habitat; well

beaten in maiden and minor races, twice sweating up; should stay 1m; wore a tongue strap on fourth and fifth starts, also wore blinkers on latter. *G. Pritchard-Gordon.*

LUXEMBOURG 2 b.g. Royal Palace 131–Karen 106 (Primera 131) (1980 7fg —
8g 7d) Mar 5; 480 2-y-o; workmanlike gelding; half-brother to 2 winners, including fairly useful 1m to 1½m winner African Star (by Taj Dewan); dam won at up to 13f; in mid-division in maiden races at Leicester in September and Edinburgh in October, first 2 outings; likely to need a test of stamina. *W. Stubbs.*

LUXULAM 2 b.c. Tower Walk 130–Immaculate (Sovereign Path 125) (1980 5fg **82**
6g 8d^3 7d^3 7d) Mar 12; 5,000F, 52,000Y; big, strong, good-looking colt; brother to a winner in Italy, and half-brother to several winners, including Spanish Oaks winner Delfica (by Hardicanute) and useful Irish 7f to 1½m winner Ball Night (by Gala Performance); dam lightly raced; close third in maiden race won by Jade and Diamond at Warwick in October; didn't find a great deal in closing stages when 2 lengths third of 14 to Norfolk Realm in similar event at Leicester later in month; stays 1m; ran freely in blinkers final start. *R. Armstrong.*

LUXURIATE (USA) 3 b.g. Tom Rolfe–Dee Dee Luxe (Cavan) (1979 7fg 8f **76**
1980 10.8s 16f 16f^2 14g^3 14g 16fg) lightly-made gelding; staying maiden; acts on firm going; blinkered nowadays; below form last 2 starts; sold out of N. Gaselee's stable 5,000 gns Doncaster August Sales after fourth outing. *I. Wardle.*

LUZ BAY 5 b.h. Mountain Call 125–Palmaressa 80 (Royal Palm 131) (1979 7v **58**
7.6v 8s 10g 10fg^2 10d^3 12g 10f 1980 11.7fg* 10h^2 11.1fg* 12f^4) strong, well-made horse; made virtually all in handicaps at Windsor and Kempton in May; stays 1½m; probably acts on any going; usually blinkered but not on last 2 starts. *T. Gosling.*

LYDIAN (FR) 2 ch.c. Lyphard 132–Miss Manon (Bon Mot III 132) (1980 8.5fg **99** p
8s^3 8g*) third foal; half-brother to 3-y-o Mot D'Or (by Rheingold), winner of 1½m Prix Hocquart, and to Sharpman (by Sharpen Up), a very smart performer at up to 1½m in France; dam smart French middle-distance performer; put up best effort when winning 12-runner maiden race at Maisons-Laffitte in November by 1½ lengths from Mourtazam; a very well-bred colt who is likely to leave this form behind over middle distances. *Mme C. Head, France.*

LYDIA ROSE 3 b.f. Mummy's Pet 125–Sprightly Sprite 80 (Babur 126) **68**
(1979 8f 7g 1980 8g^2 9d^4 8g 8g 10s^4 10s) small filly; in frame in maiden and minor events; suited by 1¼m; acts on soft going. *J. Winter.*

LYN AFFAIR 3 b.f. Royal Palace 131–True Dresden 58 (Vilmoray 126) (1979 **62**
6g 7f 7f 1980 8s^4 10g^4 11.7fg 10.6f 12.2fg^2 16g 12g^4 14.6fg 11d) workmanlike filly; poor maiden; stays 1½m; acts on a firm surface; wears blinkers; has had her tongue tied down; sold 2,600 gns Newmarket December Sales. *A. Bailey.*

LYNCONWISE 2 br.c. Tudor Music 131–Shopping Wise (Floribunda 136) **78**
(1980 6g 6fg 7d 5d 5d 6s^3) Apr 18; compact colt; half-brother to 3 winners, including useful Lynconlou (by Lord Gayle), a winner at up to 9f in Ireland; dam Irish 6f winner; showed a little ability in maiden races in England on first 5 outings when trained by D Morley; beaten 2 lengths and a short head when third of 21 to Mazzini in maiden event at Naas in November; best form at up to 6f. *J. Bolger, Ireland.*

LYNDALE 4 ch.f. The Go-Between 129–Word Perfect (Worden II 129) (1979 5f —
5f 6fg 5h 5fg 6s^4 1980 8fg 6fg 6d 6g) plater; stays 6f; best form on soft going. *J. Berry.*

LYNWOOD LADY 3 ch.f. Malicious–Maid of Kintail (Atlas 126) (1979 5f 5d 5fg **41**
6g 7fg 7f^3 6f 10g^2 1980 8f 8f^2 8f 7f^3 7f 8fg 9g 10g 12g 13.8f 8.2d^3 12g 9f 13.8fg^4) leggy filly; plater; needs further than 7f and stays 1¼m; acts on firm going; sometimes blinkered. *T. Fairhurst.*

M

MAB 3 b.f. Morston 125–Abbeyfield 109 (Abernant 142) (1979 NR 1980 —
7f 8f^3) lightly-made filly, fourth foal; half-sister to a winning stayer by French Beige; dam a sprinter; staying-on third of 18 to Sigh in maiden race at Thirsk in May; will be suited by 1¼m+. *W. Hastings-Bass.*

MACAROON 3 ch.f. Mount Hagen 127–Dusky Pearl 68 (Gulf Pearl 117) —
(1979 6g 1980 8f) no sign of ability in maiden race and seller. *J. Fitzgerald.*

MAC'S DELIGHT 3 ch.c. Scottish Rifle 127–Halkissimo 61 (Khalkis 127) (1979 6fg 7d^{4} 8d 8h^{3} 10.6d 1980 12.5g^{4} 10.4f^{4} 10.5f 10fg^{3} 9g* 8g^{2} 8d 8s 9fg^{3} 10.4d* 10.2g^{4} 10d 10s) strong colt; won maiden race at Hamilton in June and apprentice race at Chester in August; stays 1¼m well; best form on top-of-the-ground; often blinkered but is as effective without; suitable mount for a boy. *Denys Smith.* **81**

MAC'S TREASURE 3 ch.c. Pieces of Eight 128–Taurette (Major Portion 129) (1979 8fg 8g 7.2g^{3} 1980 8d 8v^{3} 10fg^{2} 12fg^{3} 12g 12g^{3} 12fg) small, strong colt; plater; stays 1½m; best form on a sound surface; blinkered second start; ran poorly final outing. *P. Haslam.* **55**

MADAM GAY 2 b.f. Star Appeal 133–Saucy Flirt 102 (King's Troop 118) (1980 6g 6d 7g^{2}) Feb 25; 8,000Y; tall, quite attractive filly; half-sister to a winning plater and a winner in Brazil; dam stayed 6f; improved with every race and put up a useful effort when taking second place close home, 4 lengths behind Fairy Footsteps, in 10-runner Waterford Candelabra Stakes at Goodwood in August; will stay 1m; sure to win when her sights are lowered. *P. Kelleway.* **107**

MADE MY DAY 4 b.f. Double Jump 131–Tartarbee 72 (Charlottesville 135) (1979 10fg 8.3fg^{3} 10g^{3} 8g^{2} 7d* 8g^{2} 1980 8f 8fg 8s^{4} 9g* 7f 8fg^{2} 10d* 12g* 12fg) unfurnished filly; won handicaps at Ripon (two, including an apprentice event) and Redcar; had stiffish task and didn't impress in paddock when well beaten final outing; stays 1½m; acts on a firm surface but seems suited by some give in the ground; blinkered sixth outing at 2 yrs; sometimes sweats up; goes well for apprentice K. Hodgson. *M. H. Easterby.* **68**

MADIGAN MILL 3 ch.f. Mill Reef 141–La Speroana 68 (Roan Rocket 128) (1979 6g^{2} 1980 10f 8d) lengthy, light-framed filly; good mover; good second in maiden race at Newmarket at 2 yrs; lightly raced in 1980, finishing well beaten in Sir Charles Clore Memorial Stakes at Newbury in May and maiden race at York following month; will be well suited by 1½m. *J. Winter.* **–**

MADISON STYLE 2 b.c. Crowned Prince 128–Monte Rosa (Crepello 136) (1980 5fg^{2} 5.8fg^{3} 6g^{2} 7f^{2}) Mar 2; 12,000Y; lightly-made colt; first foal; dam Irish 1m winner; second in newcomers race at Kempton in May, 28-runner minor event at Windsor in August and 18-runner maiden race at Newmarket in October, starting favourite when 2½ lengths second of 18 to Blackfoot in last-named; will be suited by 1m. *F. J. Houghton.* **88**

MAD MOMENTS 2 gr.c. Saritamer 130–Argent Soleil 68 (Silver Shark 129) (1980 5d 5f^{3} 5fg 5s 6fg 5f 6g) Apr 19; 1,300Y; neat colt; second foal; dam won over 6f; plating-class maiden. *G. Blum.* **52**

MAD TYCOON 2 b.g. Tycoon II–Polly Mead (Rasputin 83) (1980 5f 5s 5d 5d) strong gelding; fourth foal; brother to 7f seller winner Haldoon, subsequently successful over hurdles; dam of no account; burly when 5¼ lengths seventh of 18 to Welsh Noble in maiden race at Wolverhampton in June, third outing and only sign of ability; will be suited by 6f+. *A. Jarvis.* **49**

MAE MAE 3 ch.f. Communication 119–Vibel (Vienna 127) (1979 5v* 5g^{3} 5s 5d 5f 5fg 5g 1980 6s 5fg 5f 5fg^{4} 5fg 5fg 5s^{4} 5fg 5s) small, light-framed filly; poor sprint handicapper; best form at 5f; probably acts on any going; sweated up final start; didn't progress physically from 2 yrs to 3 yrs; seldom impresses in paddock; trained till seventh outing by N. Adam. *J. Spearing.* **–**

MAESGLAS 4 b.g. King Log 115–Fairy First 54 § (Fairey Fulmar 124) (1979 11s 12v 8s 8.2d 8v 8g 9.4f^{3} 9.4f 7.6f 8fg 8fg 1980 8v 8fg 8.2d 9g 8g 9fg 13s) plater; well beaten in 1980; stays 9f; best form on a sound surface; blinkered first 3 outings. *R. McDonald.* **–**

MA FOI 6 b.g. Most Secret 119–Rowin 71 (Sing Sing 134) (1979 5fg 6fg 5g 5d 1980 6d 5fg) poor plater; stays 6f; acts on any going; has run well for an apprentice. *W. Stubbs.* **–**

MAGADEN 2 b.f. Record Run 127–Messie (Linacre 133) (1980 5g 5fg 5f^{3} 5f* 6s^{3} 5d 6s) May 3; 860F, 1,600Y; fair sort; plater; short-priced favourite, attracted no bid after winning 7-runner event at Redcar in May by 2 lengths from Teslin; narrowly-beaten third to High Class Builder at Nottingham the following month; will stay 1m; acts on any going; blinkered sixth outing. *J. Hardy.* **51**

MAGDA RHEINHARD 3 ch.f. Busted 134–Chemise 75 (Shantung 132) (1979 NR 1980 9fg 12fg 16g 12d 12d 8f 10.2d 12s) 5,000Y, 4,000 3-y-o (privately); big filly; poor mover; third foal; half-sister to a winner in Malaya; dam won over 1¼m; behind in varied company. *R. Hollinshead.* –

MAGIC FORMULA 2 b.f. St Paddy 133–La Leventina (Le Levanstell 122) (1980 6fg 6g³ 7fg 10s) Feb 28; 3,700F, 12,000Y; quite well-made filly; first produce; dam won 6 times in Italy; 33/1, got behind early on but was running on strongly over last 2f when 1¾ lengths third of 14 to Musical Minx in maiden race at Nottingham in July, easily best effort; should be well suited by 7f+. *P. Rohan.* 70

MAGIC SOVEREIGN 2 gr.g. Young Emperor 133–Magic Lady (Gala Performance) (1980 5f² 5d 5s 5d 5.8f 5d⁴) Apr 29; 3,000Y; plater; failed by a neck to catch Laughing when second at Chepstow in May, only worthwhile form; should be suited by 6f; has worn blinkers; sold 760 gns Ascot August Sales. *M. Blanshard.* 46

MAGNETO 3 b.f. John Splendid 116–Magibbillibyte 77 (Constable 119) (1979 5s 5s⁴ 5s 1980 7d² 7g 8fg⁴ 7g 7g⁴ 6g 8d⁴) strong filly; plater; stays 1m; acts on a firm and a soft surface. *N. Callaghan.* 57

MAGNIFICENT LADY 3 ch.f. Nonoalco 131–Arenaria 102 (Aureole 132) (1979 NR 1980 8g 8fg² 8fg 10g 9.5g⁴ 7d² 10s) 170,000Y; rangy filly; half-sister to several winners, including very useful 1m to 1¼m performer Redesdale (by Bold Lad, Ire); dam, winner at 7f and 1m, is closely related to Miralgo and Parnell; runner-up in £4,400 race at Ascot in April and maiden event at Leopardstown in October; in rear in 18-runner Goffs Irish 1,000 Guineas at the Curragh on third start; should stay 1¼m; acts on a firm and a soft surface; usually blinkered. *D. Weld, Ireland.* 74

MAGNOLIA LAD 7 b.h. Mummy's Pet 125–Julita 87 (Rockavon 120) (1979 5s 5d 5f 5d 6fg 6f 5f⁴ 5f 6fg 6d² 6s 6fg 5fg³ 5.6fg 6s 6d³ 5fg⁴ 5d³ 6s² 6s 1980 6s 6d² 5g 6g 6h² 5g 6d 6fg 5d 6g 5d³ 5s 6f 5d 5d³ 6d³ 6d 6v⁴) sprint handicapper; acts on any going; suitable mount for an apprentice; has worn blinkers on several occasions; inconsistent; trained until after seventh start by N. Adam. *R. Hollinshead.* 80

MAHER 2 b.f. Simbir 130–High Dice 93 (High Hat 131) (1980 7g 9d) Mar 21; unfurnished filly; third foal; dam won at up to 14.7f; in rear in maiden race at Yarmouth in September and minor event at Wolverhampton in October; sold to T. Kersey 400 gns Newmarket Autumn Sales. *C. Brittain.* –

MAIDEN BEECH 3 b.f. Averof 123–Gloomy Portal 103 (Mossborough 126) (1979 7fg 7g 1980 7fg 7.2d) small filly; showed some ability on second start in 1979; well beaten at 3 yrs; will stay 1¼m. *P. Cole.* –

MAIDEN'S BLUSH (FR) 2 b.f. Bustino 136–Modeste (Hautain 128) (1980 8g*) Mar 29; 560,000 francs Y (approx £59,000); half-sister to 3 winners, including useful middle-distance winner Mon Zouzou (by Sicambre); dam won important races over 9f and 13f at 3 yrs after winning over hurdles; led inside final furlong to win 10-runner newcomers event at Maisons-Laffitte in September by 1½ lengths from Nasma; will make a very useful filly over 1¼m or more. *F. Boutin, France.* 92 p

MAIDEN'S WALK 3 b.f. Tower Walk 130–Rhine Maiden 106 (Crepello 136) (1979 5.8g 1980 6fg 7fg 7f² 6fg 7fg 8f² 8fg³ 8g²(dis) 8.2g 10s* 10.2d³ 10d⁴) small, light-framed filly; won 19-runner minor event at Newmarket in October; suited by 1¼m; acts on any going; blinkered sixth to ninth starts; has shown signs on occasions of being none too keen. *P. Walwyn.* 71

MAIN REEF 4 ch.c. Mill Reef 141–Lovely Light 105 (Henry the Seventh 125) (1979 8.5s² 10.4v² 8f* 12fg* 10fg 12s* 1980 10fg⁴ 12fg⁴ 12g 13.3d²(dis) 12fg⁴ 16g* (w.o.) 12d) well-made colt; good mover; half-brother to several winners, including smart middle-distance filly Moonlight Night (by Levmoss); dam twice-raced half-sister to successful broodmares Picture Light, Chandelier and Crystal Palace; high-class performer at his best, winner of Cumberland Lodge Stakes at Ascot and St Simon Stakes at Newbury as a 3-y-o; had rather a disappointing time in 1980; didn't have best of runs when close fourth to Scorpio in Hardwicke Stakes at Royal Ascot on second outing or when strong-finishing length second to Nicholas Bill in slowly-run Geoffrey Freer Stakes at Newbury in August; disqualified and placed last for hampering another runner on latter course; very disappointing in Cumberland Lodge Stakes at Ascot in September (seemed to show little desire to struggle and finished about 3½ lengths fourth 114

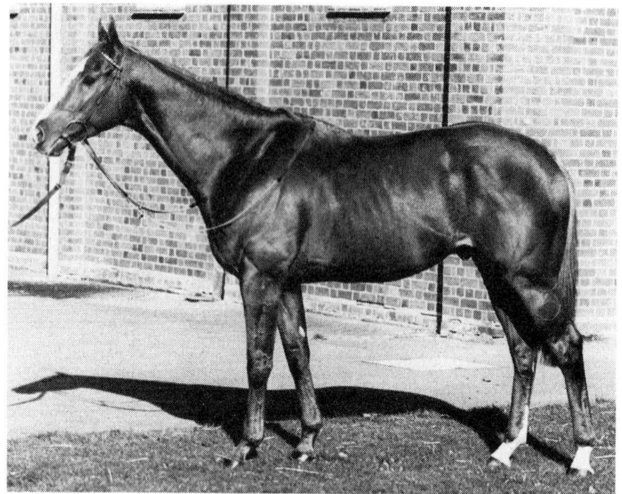

Mr H. J. Joel's "Main Reef"

of 5 behind impressive winner Fingal's Cave) and slowly-run St Simon Stakes at Newbury in October (poor eighth of 9 behind Shining Finish); walked over at Newmarket in between last 2 races; was well suited by 1½m; acted on any going; sometimes raced with his head on one side and was a difficult ride; standing at Greenmount Stud, Co. Limerick, at a fee of IR£6,000 with usual concession. *H. Cecil.*

MAIN ROYAL 3 b.g. Averof 123–Sovereign Sails 94 (Sovereign Path 125) (1979 6fg 6f 1980 7v 8fg 8fg² 8fg 8d 7g 7g 8d³ 7d) big, strong gelding; quite a moderate handicapper; stays 1m; acts on a firm and a soft surface; blinkered sixth start. *W. Wightman.* **77** d

MAINTOP 3 b.c. High Top 131–Jujube 102 (Ribero 126) (1979 NR 1980 8f 8f* 10.6s) strong, shapely colt; first foal; dam, a stayer, won 5 of her 6 races; favourite though having first outing for over 5 months, stayed on strongly to beat Braughing ¾ length in 13-runner minor event at Newmarket in October; ran moderately in £2,400 event at Haydock later in month; should stay 1¼m; possibly unsuited by very soft ground. *P. Walwyn.* **93**

MAISON D'OR 3 br.f. Goldhill 125–Open House 91 (Road House II) (1979 5g 5d 5g 5fg 6d³ 1980 6v⁴ 6d⁴ 6f) useful sort; quite a modest maiden at her best; below form in 1980; stays 6f. *W. H. H. Williams.* –

MAISON ROYALE 2 b.c. Home Guard 129–Vardan (Varano) (1980 7g 8d) Apr 19; 5,800Y; fair sort; second living foal; dam poor granddaughter of Irish 1,000 Guineas winner Royal Danseuse; in rear in 14-runner minor event at Kempton in September (backward) and 15-runner maiden race at Warwick in October (outpaced). *R. Armstrong.* –

MAJESTIC MAHARAJ 5 br.h. Taj Dewan 128–Canaan (Santa Claus 133) (1979 12d* 18.4d 12g² 10g 14.7f* 12f² 15g³ 12h² 12g* 14s 12h² 13s* 14g 15.8s 1980 12.3d³ 12f* 18.4f⁴ 12fg* 16d 18.4g* 12g 14g 18g⁴ 15s² 14s³) strong, useful-looking horse; good mover; won handicaps at Thirsk, Doncaster and Chester; put up a particularly good effort when beating Billion by 2 lengths on last-named course in July (made all); had stiff tasks on occasions afterwards; stays **105**

well; acts on any going; good mount for an amateur; ran very freely when tried in blinkers. *J. Hanson.*

MAJESTIC NURSE 5 br.m. On Your Mark 125–Bristol Milk 88 (Raise You Ten 125) (1979 9g* 8d* 8fg³ 10f 8.5f* 9g 8g 8.2g* 8fg 8.2s² 8s³ 1980 8d 8g 8.5fg³ 10d* 6fg 8g 8s) rather lightly-made mare; won 6-runner handicap at Phoenix Park in August; not disgraced when sixth of 24 behind I'm Ready in Irish Cambridgeshire at the Curragh in September on sixth outing, but was sweating when last of 8 behind Geoffrey's Sister in Royal Caledonian Hunt Handicap at Ayr 4 days later; probably finds 6f on sharp side and stays 1¼m; acts on any going; suitable mount for an apprentice; trained much of season by M. Cunningham in Ireland. *C. Nelson.* **70**

MAJESTIC STAR 3 b. or br.c. Star Appeal 133–Vivante 87 (Bold Lad, Ire 133) (1979 NR 1980 8fg 10.1f* 12f 10.1g⁴ 10g³ 9g* 8fg² 9f) 19,500Y; neat, strong, good sort; good walker; half-brother to 1977 2-y-o 6f winner Scotsman Ice (by Lombard); dam stayed 1m; successful in minor event at Windsor in June and handicap at Ripon in August; creditable ¾-length second to King James in £4,000 handicap at Kempton in September; stays 1¼m (tailed-off last in Derby only attempt at 1½m); yet to race on a soft surface; ran moderately final start. *G. Pritchard-Gordon.* **99**

MAJIEDA 2 ch.f. Kashmir II 125–Manushka (Sheshoon 132) (1980 6f³ 5g) Mar 30; quite attractive filly; second foal; half-sister to 1978 French 2-y-o 7.5f and 9f winner Grey Amber (by Amber Rama); dam, minor 11f winner, is sister to very useful French long-distance horse Croque Monsieur; favourite, stayed on without finding any extra pace when 2¼ lengths third of 10 to Silken Knot in Virginia Water Stakes at Ascot in July; found 5f much too sharp when co-favourite for minor event at Goodwood the following month and finished only fifth to Sanu; very stoutly bred on dam's side and will need at least 1m at 3 yrs. *F. J. Houghton.* **91**

MAJOR CRISP 4 ch.c. Frankincense 120–Golden Wonder (Golden Cloud) (1979 8v 10v 8.2g 8g 13.8f 1980 8g 6f) useless. *T. Kersey.* –

MAJOR DAY 3 br.g. Singing Bede 122–Penny Model (Pendragon) (1979 NR 1980 10f 12fg 11g 8.2g) non-thoroughbred gelding; dam never ran; no sign of ability in maiden and minor races in Scotland. *T. Craig.* –

MAJOR GUNDRY 3 ch.c. Grundy 137–Hiding Place 109 (Doutelle 128) (1979 6fg 7g⁴ 7g* 7fg 1980 10.6d* 12g² 12f⁴ 12g⁴ 13.3d 10.5g 10.2g 12d⁴) strong, compact colt; comfortably beat Home Ground 7 lengths in £2,700 race at Haydock in April; ran creditably next 3 starts to be in frame in Warren Stakes at Epsom, Ladbroke Derby Trial Stakes at Lingfield and Welsh Derby Stakes at Chepstow; well beaten afterwards; stays 1½m; acts on a soft surface; usually blinkered nowadays. *I. Balding.* **103** d

MAJORIAN 2 b.c. Majority Blue 126–Tinker Lass (Tin Whistle 128) (1980 5s 7fg 7d 8d*) Apr 26; 5,600Y; quite a useful-looking colt; half-brother to a winning plater and a winner abroad; dam lightly raced; backed from 10/1 to 9/2, showed improved form and made all when winning 14-runner maiden race at Leicester in November by 4 lengths from Commonty; suited by 1m; acts on a soft surface; off course nearly 4 months after second outing. *R. Price.* **96 ?**

MAJOR MARTIN 3 b.c. Decoy Boy 129–Yasmin II 88 (Gilles de Retz 132) (1979 5fg⁴ 5fg* 6g² 5g² 5f 6f³ 1980 8v 8fg⁴ 8fg³ 7.3f 8g³ 8fg 8g³ 8g² 8fg² 7.2d² 7g* 8g*) big, rangy ex-English colt; fairly useful handicapper in this country when trained by H. Candy, finishing creditable second at Kempton, Goodwood and Haydock in the summer; subsequently sent to Italy and won twice at Milan; stays 1m; probably acts on any going; sometimes sweats up; blinkered nowadays. *R. Brogi, Italy.* **94**

MAKBUBA'S GIRL 2 gr.f. Tycoon II–Makbuba 86 (Dumbarnie 125) (1980 7g 5g 5g 5g) June 9; small filly; half-sister to 3 winners, including Darling Bob (by Darling Boy), a winner from 5f to 1¼m; dam stayed 1m; last in maiden and minor events on second and third outings. *S. Mellor.* –

MAKER-MATCH 5 b.g. The Go-Between 129–Mrs Randy (Reneged) (1979 7s 6v 5s 6d 5.3fg 8fg 7f* 7fg³ 7g² 8g⁴ 1980 6g 6h 7h 6fg 5.3d* 6g 6d³ 5g² 5fg 5d 6g 8g) leggy gelding; won seller at Brighton in 1979; made all and raced alone in straight when winning handicap on same course in June by 2 lengths from General Wade; best at up to 7f; seems to act on any going; wears blinkers; shows traces of string-halt on near hind. *T. Gosling.* **56**

MAKIN MUSIC 2 b.f. Song 132–Makinlau 88 (Lauso) (1980 5fg 6s 6g 5g 5.1fg) Apr 1; small filly; first foal; dam won from 1m to 1½m; showed a little ability in maiden races; form only at 5f. *F. Dever.* 56

MAKRANEE 3 gr.f. Tycoon II–Makbuba 86 (Dumbarnie 125) (1979 6g 1980 8fg 7fg 12d 8g 9f) leggy filly; seems of little account; has sweated up; sold 550 gns Ascot October Sales; resold same venue 410 gns in November. *S. Mellor.* —

MAKSOUFA 3 ch.f. English Prince 129–Millmeadows (Indigenous 121) (1979 NR 1980 11.7fg 12fg 16fg 16s) 2,100Y; second reported foal; dam won bumpers race; slow maiden; sold 620 gns Newmarket Autumn Sales. *C. Nelson.* —

MALBORO (FR) 4 b.c. Satingo 129–Macana (Bold Lad USA) (1979 9v 10s* 10.1g 1980 13v) strong colt; won maiden race at Leicester early in 1979; stays 1¼m (well beaten over further on only outing of 1980); acts on soft going. *S. Leadbetter.* —

MALCOLMS PRIDE 6 br.g. Frankincense 120–Bruscar (Javelot 124) (1979 10.2s 1980 10f 12.2f) of little account. *A. Smith.* —

MALIA 2 b.f. Malacate 131–Lady Beck 104 (Sir Gaylord) (1980 5fg* 5f^3 6g 7s) Feb 24; first foal; compact, unfurnished filly; dam won over 1m at 2 yrs in France; made much of running to win 13-runner maiden race at Haydock in May by a length from Heavenly Chord; performed very well for so stoutly-bred a filly when 3¾ lengths third of 7 to Ashbrittle in Uplands Park Acorn Stakes at Epsom the following month; ran poorly on both outings over further than 5f but was off course nearly 4 months in between them. *F. J. Houghton.* 81

MALIC-A-SAN 4 ch.g. St Paddy 133–Parrullah (Valerullah 113) (1979 NR 1980 8g) seems of little account. *Hbt Jones.* —

MALICIOUS LOVE 3 b.f. Malicious–Larkspur's Love (Larkspur 128) (1979 7g 8g 8d 1980 12f 16d 16.9d 14g 14g^3 14fg^3 14g 16.1s^3 15s* 15d*) quite attractive filly; won modest maiden race and handicap at Stockton in the autumn; enterprisingly ridden in latter; stays well; acts well on soft going; suitable mount for an inexperienced rider. *H. Collingridge.* 79

MALICOURT 3 ch.c. Malicious–Sweet Councillor (Privy Councillor 125) (1979 7d 8d 1980 11v* 12fg 12d 15s 16g 16.1s) small, robust colt; won maiden race at Ayr in March; well beaten in handicaps and a minor event afterwards; should stay at least 1½m; acts on heavy going; blinkered last 3 starts, looking none too enthusiastic on first occasion; moved badly to start final outing. *J. W. Watts.* 61

MALISE 3 b.f. Royal Palace 131–Snap (Snob 130) (1979 NR 1980 12fg 10f) 6,000F, 7,000Y; smallish, lightly-made filly; half-sister to two winners in Italy; dam never ran; behind in minor event at Salisbury (moved poorly to post) and maiden race at Sandown in May; sold 560 gns Newmarket July Sales. *H. Candy.* —

MALITEVKA 2 b.f. Lombard 126–Faridina 100 (Sky Gipsy 117) (1980 5f) Mar 8; 3,000Y; first foal; dam soft-ground 5f performer; 10/1 and on burly side when 10 lengths sixth of 8 to Cleat in maiden race at Newcastle in April. *K. Stone.* —

MALMAISON 5 b.m. Royal Palace 131–Samanda (Alycidon 138) (1979 12d 1980 14.7f^4 12g 16.1d 14g) poor staying maiden on flat; winner over hurdles. *H. Wharton.* —

MALPASO 4 ch.c. Sun Prince 128–Tapia (Tanerko 134) (1979 10.2g 11.7g 11fg^4 15.5f^2 16fg^2 16fg* 14.7f^3 16d 1980 16s 16f^4 17.1f^3 16fg* 16g* 16g^4 19f* 16s 16g 16.1s) lightly-made colt; has been hobdayed; successful only at Beverley and won 3 handicaps there in summer; stays well; acts well on firm going; usually blinkered nowadays; genuine; sometimes sweats up; trained most of season by A. Johnson; sold to A. Smith 1,500 gns Newmarket Autumn Sales. *D. Francis.* 71

MALSEEDY 2 ch.f. Malicious–Ballyseedy 73 (Dicta Drake 126) (1980 5fg 5fg 6fg 6g 7g 6fg 6fg 7f^3 8.2d* 8fg^4 8.2s^4 8fg 10d^2 8d 8d) Mar 14; compact filly; half-sister to 3 minor winners; dam won early-season 5f seller; won 15-runner seller at Hamilton by 2½ lengths from Audit; bought in 2,100 gns afterwards; stays 1¼m; seems to act on any going except soft; blinkered seventh outing. *W. Stubbs.* 67

MALTESE FALCON 2 ch.g. Arch Sculptor 123–Dark Melody (Tudor Melody **73**
129) (1980 5f 5fg 5f*) Apr 1; 5,800Y; half-brother to Everlasting Song (by Continuation), a winner at up to 1m, and to a winner in Greece; dam never ran; well-backed second favourite, showed improved form when winning 9-runner maiden race at Wolverhampton in May by $\frac{1}{2}$ length from May Go Twice, the pair clear; exported to Hong Kong. *G. Huffer.*

MALVAN 4 b. or br.g. Decoy Boy 129–Khanum 81 (Soueida 111) (1979 5f **75**
6g 6g^2 8fg* 8fg 8d 7d* 1980 8fg 8.2s* 8g 8f 10g^4 7f 8fg 8fg 8d^4 8d^2 8.2s* 8s^2) moderate handicapper; apprentice ridden when winning at Nottingham in July (by a length from Willow Red) and October (decisively by 3 lengths from Greatest Hits); not certain to stay 1$\frac{1}{4}$m (pulled hard early on when tried at trip); acts on any going, but is well suited by soft; blinkered seventh and eighth outings, but is better without. *R. Turnell.*

MALZA 3 b.g. Malicious–Zagapu 72 (Supreme Sovereign 119) (1979 5s^4 7g **66**
7fg^4 7fg 8.2fg 7f^4 8.2s 8d^4 1980 10s 10.8s^4 12f^4 11.7fg^4 13s 11.7s 13.1g 12d^3 12g 12fg^2 14fg^3 12g* 12f) neat gelding; won amateur riders race at Kempton in September; in frame in varied company, including claiming, previously; stays 1$\frac{3}{4}$m; probably acts on any going; usually wears blinkers; unseated rider final start. *R. Hannon.*

MANALDO 2 b.c. Manado 130–Aldona 96 (Mossborough 126) (1980 5f^3 5g^4 **100**
7fg 5fg^2 6g* 5s*) Apr 17; 6,000Y; half-brother to fairly useful Irish 3-y-o middle-distance winner Haveaniceday (by Lord Gayle) and a winner in Germany; dam, half-sister to top-class 1960 2-y-o Kathy Too, won over 7f; improved in autumn and won 22-runner maiden race at Navan and nursery at the Curragh, latter by 2$\frac{1}{2}$ lengths under second-top weight; should stay 7f; acts very well on soft going and has run respectably on firm ground. *K. Prendergast, Ireland.*

MANDABOY 2 b.c. Weepers Boy 124–Grandmatty (John Splendid 116) (1980 **70**
5s 5f 5fg 5f 5d 6fg^2 6g*) Apr 23; 900Y; leggy, fair sort; first foal; dam never ran; driven clear to win 7-runner seller at Doncaster in June by 4 lengths from May Go Twice; sold 4,200 gns at subsequent auction, probably for export; well suited by 6f. *G. Toft.*

MANDALIA 3 b.f. Mansingh 120–Hay-Hay 62 (Hook Money 124) (1979 5d –
5f* 5f^2 6g 6fg^3 7fg^3 7fg 5fg* 1980 5fg 5d 5g 6fg) neat filly; successful in maiden race at Wolverhampton and nursery at Sandown in 1979; well beaten in handicaps at 3 yrs; has run respectably over 6f and 7f but is best at 5f; acts on firm going; bolted on way to start fourth outing in 1979; sold 560 gns Newmarket Autumn Sales. *J. Winter.*

MANDARRAY 3 ch.f. Mandao 51–First Array (Three Dons 91) (1979 7fg 7d 7g –
5f 1980 12g 15.5fg) useless. *Miss A. Sinclair.*

MANDAV 2 ch.c. Sallust 134–Robusta (Saint Crespin III 132) (1980 5f^4 5f 6fg^3 **97**
6fg^3 7fg^2 7f* 7f* 7s 7d) Mar 27; 39,000Y; smallish colt; brother to smart Irish 6f winner Roman Charger, and half-brother to several winners; dam never ran; ridden by apprentice M. Hills when successful in nurseries at Redcar and Lingfield in the autumn, making all on latter course to win £5,900 event by 2$\frac{1}{2}$ lengths from Remouleur; will stay 1m; acts well on firm going and is unsuited by soft. *J. Hindley.*

MANDINKA 3 ch.c. Roi Soleil 125–Anippe 102 (Aggressor 130) (1979 6fg –
1980 10s) lengthy colt; no sign of ability in minor and maiden races; bandaged only start at 2 yrs; sold 520 gns Doncaster May Sales. *J. Hardy.*

MANDY'S TIME 4 b.f. High Time 96–Mandy's Melody (Highland Melody 112) –
(1979 14g 14f^4 13f 16fg 1980 10fg) poor maiden. *J. Harris.*

MAN EN CO 2 b. or br.g. Shantung 132–J'Accuse (I Say 125) (1980 5f 5fg 6g) –
Apr 22; 2,600F, 2,900Y; lengthy gelding; half-brother to a winner in Switzerland; dam twice-raced half-sister to top miler The Creditor; last but one in 2 maiden races at Haydock and a minor event at Carlisle (blinkered) in first half of season; needs much further. *G. Richards.*

MANGAS 3 b.g. Sweet Revenge 129–Brilly 94 (Acropolis 132) (1979 6fg 1980 **69**
7f^3 7.6f 10.1g 8d^2 8g 8d^3 8g 7g^3 7d) strong gelding; placed in varied company; stays 1m; seems to act on any going; blinkered final start; often used to be coltish in paddock; sold 4,500 gns Newmarket Autumn Sales. *G. Harwood.*

MANGUIN (USA) 4 b. or br.c. Forli–Our Relation 83 (Ribot 142) (1979 8s^2 **117**
9s* 10fg* 12g^4 10g^2 10.5d 12d 1980 9.7g 9.2fg* 8g 10s* 12g^4 10s^4 10g 10s*) French colt; won Prix d' Argenteuil, Prix du Bois-Roussel and Prix du Point du

Jour, all at Longchamp; beat Strong Gale in good style by 4 lengths after making all in last-named event in October; stays 1¼m; seems to act on any going; sent to USA. *F. Boutin, France.*

MANHATTAN DANCER 2 b.f. Young Emperor 133–Hoberaute (Misti IV 132) **74** (1980 5f 5fg^3 6d* 6d 7f 7h) Apr 14; 1,500F; second foal; dam won over 9f and 10.7f in France; made all when winning 11-runner maiden race at Carlisle in June easing up by 1½ lengths from odds-on Ermac; beaten in nurseries afterwards; will stay 1m; probably unsuited by hard ground; pulled up after running very wide into straight sixth outing; sold 2,000 gns Ballsbridge December Sales. *C. Nelson.*

MANHATTAN STORY 2 b.c. Malacate 131–McCoy (Hillsdale) (1980 5.8fg^2 **76** 6g 7g^4) Feb 28; 13,000Y; strong colt; excellent mover; half-brother to several winners in France and USA; ran promisingly when 1½ lengths second of 18 to Wicked Will in maiden race at Bath in June; gave us impression he was going the wrong way temperamentally afterwards; ridden by a lad in paddock when in rear in Chesham Stakes at Royal Ascot and put up a headstrong display in blinkers at Catterick in August when 7¾ lengths fourth of 11 to Free Forester in maiden race; will stay middle distances; sold 3,100 gns Newmarket Autumn Sales. *B. Hills.*

MANIACE 3 b.f. Lorenzaccio 130–Ribotina (Ribot 142) (1979 5g 6f 5fg 6g **–** 1980 12h 11.7d 12f 15.5g 15.5g) compact, attractive filly; poor form, including in a seller; blinkered last 2 starts. *Miss A. Sinclair.*

MANILOW 3 ch.c. Singing Bede 122–Lease Lend 96 (Cash and Courage 116) **75** (1979 5g^4 5fg 5fg 5fg* 5g* 1980 5d 5v 5fg 5fg 5f^3) strong, good sort; sprint handicapper; best form on a sound surface; has run well for an apprentice; not raced after May. *B. Swift.*

MAN IN THE MIDDLE 4 ch.g. Good Bond 122–Sharp Work 110 (Beau **– §** Sabreur 125) (1979 8s 8.2s* 9v* 8.2v^2 8g* 8g^2 8.2s 7.6fg 1980 8d 10s 10f 10d 8.2g 8fg 8fg 9g^3 8.2s) big gelding; fair handicapper when in the mood; mainly disappointing in 1980; stays 9f; acts well in the mud; has won with and without blinkers; dwelt fourth and fifth starts and is not one to trust; sold 1,350 gns Newmarket Autumn Sales. *D. Sasse.*

MANITA 2 ch.f. Manacle 123–Conchita 113 (Matador 131) (1980 5h^3 5fg 5s* **88** 5fg* 6g 5f 5g 5g 6s) Apr 21; lengthy filly; half-sister to several winners, including quite useful sprinter Fish and Chips (by Major Portion); dam won 5 times at 6f; successful in 21-runner maiden race at Windsor in June and 10-runner minor event at Chepstow the following month, on latter course beating Salt 1½ lengths; creditable fifth of 20 when ridden by 7-lb claimer in 6f nursery won by Salamina at Lingfield in September; stays 6f; seems to act on any going; tailed off final start. *R. Hoad.*

MANITOBA 3 ch.f. Mansingh 120–Dauphiness 74 (Supreme Sovereign 119) **57** (1979 5v^3 5s^3 5fg 1980 7g 8g^4 7g* 10fg 8.2s) small filly; plater; sold out of G. Hunter's stable 1,700 gns after winning narrowly at Leicester in August; stays 7f; blinkered second start. *J. Gilbert.*

MANJAM 3 b. or br.c. Home Guard 129–Two Fast 78 (Dual 117) (1979 5g* 6g^2 **121** 5g* 5d^2 5d* 1980 5fg 5fg 6.5d^4 8d^3 8g) 6,000F, 6,200Y; half-brother to a winning plater and winners in South Africa and Trinidad; dam won 1m seller at 2 yrs; ran very well at Deauville in August on third and fourth starts, finishing ½-length fourth of 12 behind Boitron in Prix Maurice de Gheest and 3 lengths third to Nadjar and Final Straw in Prix Jacques le Marois; nearest finish when 5½ lengths sixth to African Song in King's Stand Stakes at Royal Ascot on second outing; ran moderately in Prix du Moulin de Longchamp on final start; well suited by further than 5f nowadays and stays 1m; acts well on a soft surface; very smart. *M. Saliba, France.*

MANNA GREEN 2 ch.f. Bustino 136–Marcela 107 (Reform 132) (1980 8d) **–** Mar 30; second foal; half-sister to 1979 2-y-o 6f claiming race winner Martinholme (by Saritamer); dam won three 6f races at 2 yrs; 12/1 when in rear in 15-runner maiden race won by Segos at Redcar in October. *Hbt Jones.*

MANNS BITTER 3 ch.f. Shiny Tenth 120–Candy Girl (Tutankhamen) (1979 **62** 5g 5g 5fg 1980 8.2s 8fg 7f 8d* 6d^2 8d^3 8fg 8fg^2 8.2d^2 9f* 9s^2 11d^2) unfurnished, leggy filly; plater; won at Wolverhampton in June (sold out of D. Marks's stable 1,800 gns) and September (bought in 1,550 gns); stays 11f; acts on any going; blinkered last 3 starts; has run creditably for an apprentice; often fails to impress in paddock. *A. Balding.*

MAN OF DESTINY 2 b. or br.c. High Top 131–Dame Foolish 121 (Silly — Season 127) (1980 6fg) Feb 10; shapely, attractive colt; first foal; dam at her best at 2 yrs when second in Cheveley Park Stakes; broke well but faded to finish last of 15 in maiden race won by Von Erlach at Salisbury in September; sold only 500 gns Ascot October Sales. *P. Walwyn.*

MAN OF SONG 2 br.g. Mansingh 120–Lindiana 84 (Indiana 129) (1980 5fg **89** 5s 5d^4 5fg^3 5fg 6g 6d* 6g) Apr 13; 7,200Y; strong, good-quartered gelding; fourth living foal; dam, half-sister to very useful miler Dalry, won twice over 6f; showed improved form when winning £4,200 nursery at Newbury in October, staying on strongly under pressure to win by 2 lengths from Praiselien; will probably stay 7f; has run respectably on a firm surface but seems well suited by some give in the ground; blinkered last 2 starts. *S. Mellor.*

MAN ON THE RUN 5 b.g. Mandamus 120–Cathy Jane 86 (Lauso) (1979 16v — 17.1g 16f^4 17.1h 16.9fg 16g^2 16f 16f 16fg^3 17.1fg* 16fg* 1980 12g 16g 17.1d) staying handicapper; not seen out until September in 1980 and had stiffish tasks; acts on any going; usually ridden up with leaders; genuine. *W. Wightman.*

MANOR FARM LEGACY 3 b.g. Royalty 130–Winklepicker (Hotfoot 126) **68** (1979 NR 1980 13g 15.5fg 11d* 10s*) plater; successful at Wolverhampton (no bid) and Nottingham (sold 3,000 gns) in October; stays 11f; acts well on soft going. *M. Tompkins.*

MANSIES GOLD 3 b. or br.f. Mansingh 120–Gold Ribbon 106 (Blast 125) **39** (1979 5v 5v 5s 5fg^4 5fg 5d 6fg 5fg 6g 1980 6s 6v 6d 5f 6g 8g 7fg 8f^3 7g 8.2v) small, light-framed filly; poor plater; stays 1m; acts on firm going; has worn blinkers. *W. Marshall.*

MANSTONE 3 ch.g. Ragstone 128–Roman Nose 95 (Nosca) (1979 6d 6g 7f **55** 7fg 8.2g 8h 7d 1980 12g 16d 16s^4 12f 14.6d^3 16f^4 15s 16g^4 16d) small gelding; plater at 2 yrs; in frame in maiden races and a handicap in the North in 1980; stays well; best form on soft ground; wears blinkers. *T. Fairhurst.*

MANSTON MARAUDER 4 b.c. Dubassoff–Smokey's Sister (Forlorn River — 124) (1979 6v^2 8.2s^3 7v 7g 12f^3 1980 13.1fg^4 16f^3 12fg) well-made colt; quite a moderate handicapper; seems to stay 2m; acts on any going; ran poorly in blinkers at 2 yrs; has run well for an apprentice. *R. Hannon.*

MANSTROVE 3 gr.c. Mansingh 120–Unclaimed Treasure 61 (Nice Guy 123) **76** (1979 5d 5g 7g 7fg* 7f^3 8fg^3 1980 8d 8.2d* 9fg* 10f* 8f^4 9f) small, useful-looking colt; in good form in April, making all to win handicaps at Nottingham, Wolverhampton and Pontefract; first past post at Ripon following month but hampered 2 other runners and was demoted to fourth by stewards; subsequently sent to Italy and won at Naples in July; stays 1¼m; acts well on firm ground. *C. Nelson.*

MANSURA 2 b.g. Mansingh 120–Kadsura (Klairon 131) (1980 6s) June 10; — 2,100Y; tall gelding; fourth foal; dam, from same family as Psidium, never ran; 50/1 and very backward when behind in 17-runner maiden race won by Cavalry Twill at Nottingham in August. *P. Asquith.*

MANUEL MEDINA 3 b.c. Levanter 121–Divine Heights (Divine Gift 127) — (1979 8f 10s 1980 12f 12fg 12g) poor form in maiden races. *N. Callaghan.*

MANX MILLENIUM 3 ch.f. Habitat 134–Daphne 106 (Acropolis 132) (1979 **66** NR 1980 8fg 7d 8d^2 7.2d) 48,000Y; quite well-made filly; sister to 3 winners, including 1978 2-y-o 5f winner Hadon, and half-sister to another winner; dam stayed 1½m and is half-sister to numerous winners; second in maiden race at Ayr in June, best effort; stays 1m. *J. Hindley.*

MANY MOONS (FR) 3 ch.c. Jim French–Mazawa (Kashmir II 125) (1979 **108** 7f* 8f* 7g^2 10g* 8s* 1980 8g 10d^3 10.5g^3 10.5f^3) strong, very attractive colt; third foal; half-brother to useful 6f to 1m winner Moyana (by Zeddaan); dam won over 5f at 2 yrs and over hurdles; very smart at 2 yrs; placed in varied company in 1980, running best race on third outing to be 2½ lengths third behind Bozovici in 9-runner Cordwainers Stakes at York in August; may stay 1½m; acts on any going; genuine; sent to USA. *H. Cecil.*

MARASALI (FR) 2 b.c. Tennyson 124–Monique (Tanerko 134) (1980 10s^4 **?** 10d*) Mar 18; half-brother to numerous winners in France, including very useful 1m to 1¼m filly Gayka (by Kalamoun), smart 1968 2-y-o Marrakech (by Le Haar) and French 1,000 Guineas fourth Ortanique (by Relic); dam won from 9f to 13f, including Prix de Royallieu; made all and won in the style of a very useful young stayer when winning 12-runner maiden race at Saint-Cloud in November by 4 lengths from Salute; sure to make a good 3-y-o. *F. Mathet, France.*

MARATHON GOLD 3 b.c. Derring-Do 131—Attica Meli 125 (Primera 131) (1979 6fg* 7d* 7fg2 7fg 1980 8.5f2 10.4f 8d 12g2) very attractive, shapely colt; very good mover; runner-up in Ladbroke Blue Riband Trial Stakes at Epsom in April (1½ lengths behind Last Fandango) and Welsh Derby Stakes at Chepstow in June (went down by ¾ length to Prince Roland); well beaten in between in Dee Stakes at Chester (found to be running a temperature afterwards) and St James's Palace Stakes at Royal Ascot; suited by middle distances; probably acted on any going; sold privately to stand at stud in South Africa. *H. Cecil.* **109**

MARCELLO (FR) 3 b.c. Sir Gaylord—Marlia (Crepello 136) (1979 7f2 7g 7d4 7fg2 7.6f3 1980 12f 12fg3 12f 10f3 10g 9g2 14s 12s) quite attractive colt; useful (rated 101) at 2 yrs; placed in maiden and minor races in 1980 but didn't look all that genuine on several occasions; should stay 1¾m; acts on firm going; blinkered third start (out of his depth); not one to trust. *C. Brittain.* **77 §**

MARCH HYWELL (USA) 3 ch.c. Pretense—Space Happy (Never Say Die 137) (1979 7fg 8fg2 8d4 1980 10g2 12f2 10g3 10f* 12fg4 12g3 12g3 10g2) $32,000Y; half-brother to numerous winners, including Vacation Lady (by Tatan), a smart stakes winner at up to 1m; dam stakes-placed daughter of 1,000 Guineas third Solar Myth; won minor event at the Curragh in May; ran creditably on several other occasions, notably when third of 10 to Noelino in Sean Graham Ballymoss Stakes at the Curragh on third start, fourth to Gonzales in Gallinule Stakes on same course and third to Prince Roland in Welsh Derby Stakes at Chepstow in June on seventh outing; stays 1½m; acts on firm going. *M. Kauntze, Ireland.* **105**

MARCHING ON 6 b.h. Tudor Melody 129—Procession 118 (Sovereign Path 125) (1979 6v* 5s2 6d 5fg* 6fg2 5fg* 6s3 5g* 5d* 5.6fg 6f4 5g* 5s 1980 6v 5g 6g2 5f 6fg 5g3 5fg4 5d 5f2 5fg 5g2 5d*) useful handicapper; gained a well-deserved success at Newbury in October, getting up close home to beat Go Total a head after being outpaced early on; second earlier at Rome (to Northjet in Premio Melton), Ostend (beaten short head by Song of Songs) and Ascot (just failed to catch Ferryman when attempting second win in valuable Bovis Handicap); stays 6f; acts on any going; has worn blinkers; consistent, but gave trouble at start on occasions in 1979. *Sir Mark Prescott.* **98**

MAR DEL PLATA 3 b.f. Crowned Prince 128—Copocabana 67 (Petingo 135) (1979 7g 6g 5f3 1980 6s 7f3 8f3 7f4 7fg4 7g 7g 8g* 7g) strong, robust, short-legged filly; won 17-runner maiden race at Salisbury in August by short head from Angor; stays 1m; acts on firm going; ran moderately in blinkers fourth start. *C. Brittain.* **73**

MARDY 2 b.g. Mummy's Pet 125—Tackard 87 (Hard Tack 111 §) (1980 5f 5f 6g 5d) Feb 15; fair sort; brother to useful 5f performer Petard, and half-brother to a winning plater; dam 2-y-o 6f winner; dwelt when 2¾ lengths fifth of 7 to Krugerama in minor event at Beverley in August, second outing and best effort; not sure to stay 6f. *W. C. Watts.* **75**

MARECHAL (FR) 3 b.c. Bolkonski 134—Miss Univers (Le Fabuleux 133) (1979 7f 8fg 10g3 1980 10s2 12s3 12fg* 12fg4 12g 13.1g2 13.3d 14fg2 16.5fg 12fg 16fg 16s 12g4) workmanlike colt; won maiden race at Haydock in April; went down by a head to Grandiose in handicap at Bath in July; stays 1¾m; probably acts on any going; blinkered last 3 starts, running moderately on first occasion. *S. Woodman.* **76**

MARGHELAN 3 br.f. Pretty Form 97—True Penny 67 (Relic) (1979 NR 1980 8fg 8f 8fg 10g) leggy, light-framed filly; of little account. *W. Whiston.* **—**

MARGUERITE GERARD 3 b.f. Rheingold 137—God Sent 75 (Red God 128 §) (1979 NR 1980 7f 8fg 12fg4 12d4 12d4 12f2 11fg 12f 10fg* 10f2 10g 10d) 15,000Y; workmanlike filly; second foal; dam placed over 5f at 2 yrs; very well ridden to win 19-runner amateur riders race at Leicester in September unchallenged from Kildanes; stays 1½m; probably acts on any going; suitable mount for an inexperienced rider; sold 3,700 gns Newmarket December Sales. *G. Harwood.* **78**

MARHILL BELL 8 ch.g. Gala Performance—Caracasana §§ (Whistler 129) (1979 NR 1980 12.5v) of little account. *D. Garraton.* **—**

MARIACHO 2 b.c. Mariacci 133—Sea Queen (Le Fabuleux 133) (1980 9g* 9fg*). **119**

One would think that as veterinary and medical knowledge grows over the years there would be a commensurate increase in the percentage of live foals

Prix Saint-Roman, Longchamp—about a length covers the first five. Mariacho (far side) wins from Arc d'Or with The Wonder (No. 3) third, Lou Piguet (No. 9) fourth, and Troubetzkoy (No. 5) fifth

produced each breeding season. Unfortunately, this doesn't seem to be happening. Live foals to the number of mares covered, as given in the Return of Mares, averaged 53.6% for the years 1961 to 1970 compared to an average of 52.1% for 1971 to 1980. One area where there seems to be great scope for improvement is in the efficiency of fertility testing carried out on the majority of colts being considered for stud purposes. The 1980 Return of Mares included some depressingly low fertility statistics for stallions which covered their first mares in 1979: Try My Best achieved only 37.50%, Gentilhombre 21.74%, Music Maestro 34.29% and Acamas a mere 16.67%. These figures may improve slightly as the late returns are received but even so they are extremely poor.

Acamas' part-owner, Captain Tim Rogers, has been unlucky enough to experience similar problems before. Although he has stood such outstandingly successful stallions as Petingo and Habitat at his stud complex he has also had his share of disappointments. D'Urberville, Lord David and Malacate all had a fertility deficiency to some degree and another stallion Rogers handled, the Grand Criterium winner Mariacci, proved such a failure that he was eventually gelded and sent to be trained for jump races in France. Mariacci sired only two reported foals. The exploits of one of them, the French colt Mariacho, have since made Mariacci's infertility disappointing in the extreme.

Mariacho ran only twice, winning both times. The ease with which he beat the Prix des Ventes runner-up Beau Danseur in a minor race at Evry in September stamped him as an excellent prospect, so much so that he started favourite for the Group 3 Prix Saint-Roman at Longchamp the following month. Next in the betting at Longchamp came the Deauville winner Arc d'Or, followed by the Prix de Fontenoy winner In Tissar, the Prix de Villebon runner-up Troubetzkoy who was the only maiden in the ten-strong field, and then Lou Piguet and The Wonder, winners respectively of the valuable Prix des Ventes and the Prix des Foals at Deauville. With no doubts about Mariacho's stamina, his rider sent him on, followed by In Tissar. Mariacho succeeded in shaking off In Tissar early in the straight only to be challenged immediately by Arc d'Or and Troubetzkoy, while The Wonder and Lou Piguet began to make progress. All four managed to draw alongside but Mariacho held on gamely to his narrow advantage to win by a short neck from Arc d'Or, with less than a length covering the first five. Although the value of the form looked questionable, especially when Arc d'Or ran poorly next time out, the other colts who finished close up went on to advertise the form. The Wonder followed up his win in the Group 3 Prix de Conde with a victory in the Group 2 Criterium de Saint-Cloud, Lou Piguet finished a very honourable third in the Prix Thomas Bryon and Troubetzkoy won his only subsequent start.

The leading French two-year-old colts were so much of a muchness that it's difficult to enthuse over any particular one of them. Mariacho though, who cost 50,000 francs, or approximately £5,300, as a yearling, certainly looks the type to make a good three-year-old. He should stay quite well too. Mariacci, from only five outings after winning all his three starts at two years, won two more races, including the Prix Greffulhe, and was second in the Prix Lupin and third in the French Derby. Mariacho's dam Sea Queen was only a very modest maiden in France but both her runners are winners, the other being the fair 1979

Mariacho (b.c. Apr 8, 1978)	Mariacci (b 1972)	Djakao (b 1966)	Tanerko
			Diagonale
		Marbrisa (b 1966)	Exbury
			Supremora
	Sea Queen (b 1968)	Le Fabuleux (ch 1961)	Wild Risk
			Anguar
		Sariegail (br 1956)	Hill Gail
			Sarie

two-year-old King Hagen (by Mount Hagen), and she is bred well enough for anything. She is the product of a mating between the French Derby winner Le Fabuleux and the middle-distance winner Sariegail, a half-sister to Sarcelle, the top two-year-old of 1956, to Prefect, a very smart handicapper who represented Canada in the Washington International, and to Samaria, who made her name as the dam of the top-class sprinter Sammy Davis and the good middle-distance colt Super Sam. *F. Palmer, France.*

MARIA MONK 2 b.f. Executioner–Opalina (Tudor Melody 129) (1980 5f **60**
5g^{3} 5g 5fg^{2} 5g 5g^{2} 5d) Apr 26; lightly-made, unfurnished filly; sixth foal; half-sister to American 3-y-o winner Another Role (by Droll Role); dam, unplaced twice in Ireland, is daughter of very useful 1m to 1½m winner Green Opal; placed in maiden races at Edinburgh (2) and Chester but is little better than a plater; bred to need considerably further than 5f; sold 2,700 gns Newmarket Autumn Sales. *Denys Smith.*

MARICEL OF PALMA 5 ch.m. Calpurnius 122–Dorothy Darling 76 (Red **—**
God 128§) (1979 7f 12fg 1980 9.6h 12f 12d) poor plater; sometimes blinkered. *P. Butler.*

MARIDAR 2 b.f. Balidar 133–Gracious Marie (Gratitude 130) (1980 5fg 6g **—**
6fg) Jan 31; useless. *M. W. Easterby.*

MARIE DU MONT (FR) 2 b.f. Go Marching–Grande Terre (Carvin 127) **110**
(1980 5d^{2} 5.5g* 5.5g* 5g^{2} 7g^{3} 8f) Apr 6; 27,000 francs Y (approx £2,800); neat filly: second foal; dam won twice at around a mile at 3 yrs in France; proved a very shrewd buy and ran consistently well, winning minor events at Maisons-Laffitte in May and June and subsequently putting up good efforts in better company; beaten 5¾ lengths when third of 9 behind Bernica and Phydilla in Group 3 Prix du Calvados at Deauville in August but was only about 2½ lengths behind Tropicaro when equal sixth of 10 in Prix Marcel Boussac at Longchamp in October; stays 1m well; acts on firm going: wears blinkers. *R. Touflan, France.*

MARIELLA 3 b.f. Sir Gaylord–Zambara 82 (Mossborough 126) (1979 8s^{3} **123**
1980 10fg* 10fg 10.5fg 12.5g 13.5g^{2} 12f 12.5d* 10.5g 14v*) sister to very smart 1½m performer Scorpio, and half-sister to outstanding stayer Sagaro (by Espresso); dam, half-sister to good stayer Chicago, won over 1m; won maiden race at Longchamp in April, Prix de Royallieu on same course in October (came from last to first in straight to beat Gold River (gave 3 lb) by ¼ length) and Premio Roma at Rome in November (beat Ataxerxes by 1¼ lengths); also ran well to be 3 lengths second to Gold River in Prix de Pomone at Deauville in August and 2½ lengths sixth of 12 to Mrs Penny in Prix Vermeille at Longchamp following month (nearest finish); suited by 1½m+; acts on any going; very smart. *F. Boutin, France.*

MARIE NOELLE (FR) 2 b.f. Brigadier Gerard 144–Marike (Nasram II 125) **114**
(1980 8g^{2} 7.5d* 8s^{2} 7.5g^{4}) Jan 26; 260,000 francs Y (approx £27,000); third foal; half-sister to 2 winners, notably 3-y-o Divin Marquis (by Devon III), a smart winner at up to 1m; dam, daughter of very smart French sprinter Vamarie, won over 7f; won 12-runner minor event at Saint-Cloud in September by ½ length; ran well on other outings, notably going down by only a short head to Votre Altesse in Group 3 Prix des Reservoirs at Longchamp in October and finishing just over 4 lengths fourth of 10 to Big John in Group 3 Prix Thomas Bryon at Saint-Cloud in November; stays 1m well; yet to race on a firm surface; very useful. *D. Smaga, France.*

MARINE 2 b.g. Hittite Glory 125–Seaside (Mossborough 126) (1980 6d 6g 8d 8d) May 31; well-made, quite attractive gelding; third living foal; half-brother to a winner in Italy; dam placed over 1½m; made very good late progress when seventh of 21 to Obrovac in maiden race at Sandown in October, fourth outing and best effort; will stay 1¼m. *I. Balding.* **73**

MARINE BALLAST 4 ch.f. Celtic Cone 116–Confectioner 71 (Kingsway) (1979 NR 1980 16s 15.4s) seems of little account. *R. Hoad.* —

MARINE VICTORY 4 gr.f. No Mercy 126–Wake Island 101 (Relic) (1979 NR 1980 5fg 7f) lengthy filly; plating-class maiden; wears bandages; started slowly second outing. *D. Ringer.* —

MARIS BARD 2 b.g. Bold Lad (Ire) 133–Lady Gaston 76 (Pall Mall 132) (1980 5d 5d) May 8; 3,900Y; rangy gelding; half-brother to fairly useful 1976 2-y-o 5f winner Sunny Spring (by Realm); dam, winner over 5f at 2 yrs, is half-sister to smart animals Cyrus and Right of the Line; remote fifth of 17 to Regency Prince in maiden race at Doncaster in March; not seen out again until June and was still backward when behind in similar event at Wolverhampton. *R. Hollinshead.* —

MARISCO 3 b.c. Habitat 134–Word From Lundy 93 (Worden II 129) (1979 NR 1980 8f 8fg) 60,000Y; attractive colt; half-brother to 3 winners, notably Derby winner Grundy (by Great Nephew); dam stayed 2m; showed ability when ninth of 19 in maiden race at Newmarket in May on second start; promises to stay beyond 1m; sent to Italy. *J. Dunlop.* —

MARIS QUEST 3 ch.f. Windjammer (USA)–Grandee Ann (Cyane) (1979 6f 7f 7fg^2 7d^2 7fg 7fg 8g^2 8g 8g 1980 7f 8fg^3 8g 8g 7fg 8fg* 8d* 9g 10.6d 8g) fair sort; plater; won at Redcar in July (bought in 1,650 gns); made all to win handicap at Pontefract following month; best form at 1m; acts on a firm and a soft surface; best in blinkers; suited by forcing tactics; ridden by 5-lb claimer K. Hodgson for her wins. *M. H. Easterby.* **70**

MARITA 3 b.f. Great Nephew 126–Divided 74 (Busted 134) (1979 5s 6fg 7g 7s* 8.2g 8.2d 1980 11fg 8d^4) small filly; has shown little form since fourth outing at 2 yrs; will stay 1½m; acts on soft going; sold 3,500 gns Newmarket December Sales. *T. Fairhurst.* —

MARK AUREL 2 br.c. Bustino 136–Amber Flyer 91 (Amber Rama 133) (1980 7fg 7g) Apr 5; 14,500Y; leggy, compact, good sort; first foal; dam 2-y-o 5f winner; 33/1, disputed lead 4f before finishing seventh of 8 to Spark Of Life in Somerville Tattersall Stakes at Newmarket in October, second outing; withdrawn at start from small race at Newcastle on intended second appearance; dead. *C. Brittain.* —

MARK EMPEROR 4 br.g. Young Emperor 133–Happy Evening 89 (Hethersett 134) (1979 8d 9v 11g 9s 10.1fg 10.1f^3 10g 10.1fg 10f 1980 10.1fg 9.6f^3 12d 10.1d 10fg 10f 8d) plater; stays 1¼m; acts on firm going; usually wears blinkers; sold 720 gns Newmarket Autumn Sales. *J. Benstead.* —

MARKET MELODY 3 b.f. Highland Melody 112–Sandalshoon 103 (Red God 128 §) (1979 5g^3 5d 5fg 1980 7g^3 8g^2 8f^4 8f 8g 7s) lengthy filly; good walker; runner-up in maiden race at Ayr in July; stays 1m; possibly needs some give in the ground; doesn't always impress in paddock. *J. Carr.* **65**

MARKHAM PRINCE 3 b.c. Prince Tenderfoot 126–Joyful 112 (Princely Gift 137) (1979 NR 1980 8fg 10fg 9d 12.2d 12d) 27,000Y; strong, good sort; half-brother to 3 winners, including smart miler Patris (by Petingo); dam won over 5f at 2 yrs; no sign of ability, including in selling company; not certain to stay 1¼m; sold to M. Pipe 880 gns Newmarket Autumn Sales. *J. Hindley.* —

MARK HENRY 9 ch.g. Henry the Seventh 125–Anglo Indian 86 (Alycidon 138) (1979 NR 1980 18.8g) lengthy gelding; lightly raced on flat nowadays; one paced and is suited by long distances; acts on any going; suitable mount for an apprentice. *W. Elsey.* —

MARKIE 4 br.g. On Your Mark 125–Jeannette (Whistler 129) (1979 7g 9g 8g^4 7fg* 9fg^4 7fg^3 7fg 7f^4 8g^4 7f 1980 7f 7f 8d 7.2d 8.2s 7d 8.2s 7s) well-made, attractive gelding; good walker; fairly useful performer at his best but showed little form in 1980 (rarely had ideal ground conditions); stays 1m; acts well on firm going; sometimes blinkered; sold out of M. Stoute's stable 1,800 gns Ascot July Sales after second outing. *R. E. Peacock.* —

MARKING TIME 2 b.c. On Your Mark 125–Cariole 84 (Pardao 120) (1980 5d^3 5d^3 5s* 6s*) Apr 30; 6,400Y; well-made colt; brother to winning sprinter X-Data, and half-brother to 2 other winners; dam won over 7.6f; won all-aged **92**

maiden race at Nottingham in October and 12-runner minor event at Stockton the following month; got the better of Bretton Park by $\frac{3}{4}$ length (pair clear) on latter; will stay 7f. *B. Hanbury.*

MARK THE LADY 3 ch.f. On Your Mark 125–Lady Tyrrel (Pall Mall 132) (1979 5s 5g 5fg 6fg 7g^4 8g^4 8.2fg 8g 7d 1980 7f 6f) smallish filly; quite a moderate maiden at her best; stays 1m. *R. Boss.* —

MARK YOUR CARD 3 b.c. On Your Mark 125–Lune Royale 77 (Sovereign Path 125) (1979 5s 1980 6f 5f 6fg^4 7d) quite attractive, good-quartered colt; quite moderate; should stay 7f; sold 2,700 gns Newmarket July Sales. *P. Walwyn.* **72**

MARLEESH 3 b.f. Netherkelly 112–Tidal Beacon (The Deacon 101) (1979 NR 1980 10s) small filly; fourth reported foal; dam never ran; unquoted and backward, tailed off from 4f out in maiden race at Nottingham in August. *D. Leslie.* —

MARMAGOA 2 br.c. Saritamer 130–Miss Argyle 92 (Mountain Call 125) (1980 5d 5d^2) June 7; third foal; half-brother to 7f seller winner Miss Supreme (by Supreme Gift); dam won over 5f at 2 yrs; clear of remainder when $\frac{1}{2}$-length second of 17 to Corn Street in maiden race at Wolverhampton late in season; will stay 6f. *N. Vigors.* **80**

MARMORERA (HOL) 2 gr.f. Amen II–Midgetina 88 (Silly Season 127) (1980 5g* 6.5g* 9g*) Dutch-bred filly; dam won over 5f at 2 yrs in England and 4 races at 3 yrs in Holland, including Sprintkampioenschap van Nederland; successful 3 times at Duindigt, Holland beating stable-companion Clo Clo $2\frac{1}{4}$ lengths in Van Brienens Memorial in July, Rober $1\frac{3}{4}$ lengths in Clingendaalren in August and Rober again, this time by 3 lengths, in Dutch Criterium in September; will stay $1\frac{1}{4}$m. *M. Ryan.* **75 ?**

MARQUIS BAY 3 br.g. Crowned Prince 128–Iron Maiden 87 (Klairon 131) (1979 6s 1980 10.1s 10s 10fg 10s) fair sort; bad plater; has worn bandages; trained by A. Davison first 3 starts. *C. Wildman.* —

MARRACCI 4 br.c. Sir Gaylord–Martine Boileau (Match III 135) (1979 10.5s^2 10.5d* 12fg* 12.5s 12.5s 11v^3 1980 12v^2 9.2d 10s^2 12g* 12g^2 12g^3 12d) French colt; seventh foal; half-brother to 6 winners in Italy, including high-class 1m to $1\frac{1}{4}$m winner Mannsfeld (by Crocket); dam unraced; won Derby Italiano at Rome in 1979; gained only success of 1980 in Group 1 Gran Premio di Milano at Milan in June, winning by 3 lengths and $2\frac{1}{2}$ lengths from 3-y-o's Pareo and Marmolada; had earlier gone down by a head to Stout Fellow in 60,000 francs event at Maisons-Laffitte and by $\frac{3}{4}$ length to Deauville in Premio Presidente della Repubblica at Rome; placed behind Nebos in Grosser Preis von Berlin at Dusseldorf in July ($3\frac{1}{2}$ lengths second) and Grosser Preis von Baden at Baden-Baden in September (third, beaten $1\frac{1}{2}$ lengths); suited by $1\frac{1}{2}$m; appears to act on any going. *F. Boutin, France.* **118**

MARSHALL BOLDELLA 2 b.g. Jimsun 121–Maella (Traffic) (1980 8d) rangy gelding; fourth foal; brother to a seemingly poor animal; dam won over hurdles in France; tailed-off eighth of 9 to Akram in minor event at Leicester in October. *R. Boss.* —

MARSHARLOT 5 b.g. Martinmas 128–Sharlotta 84 (Sheshoon 132) (1979 NR 1980 16s) 16/1 and having first outing on flat for two seasons when well beaten in handicap at Nottingham in April; stays well; acts on an easy surface; wore blinkers when successful at 3 yrs. *W. Wright.* —

MARSHGATE 2 b.c. Shiny Tenth 120–Tweetie Pie (Falcon 131) (1980 6fg 7g 6f) May 17; of no account. *D. Marks.* —

MARSON 5 ch.h. Jefferson 129–Damara 96 (Aggressor 130) (1979 10d 12s 11d 10g^3 10fg 15.5s^4 12d* 20fg* 12d 12.5g 1980 15.5g 16.5fg 15g* 13.5g^4 20d^4 14d) French horse; much improved in 1979, winning valuable handicap and Prix Gladiateur at Longchamp; one of the leading French stayers again in 1980 and beat Kelbomec by a neck in Prix Kergorlay at Deauville in August; 5 lengths fourth behind Anifa in Prix Gladiateur at Longchamp in September on penultimate outing; appears to act on any going. *R. Collet, France.* **121**

MARSTAIN 3 ch.g. Porto Bello 118–Florecilla 90 (Matador 131) (1979 5fg 6d 5g 5g 5fg^4 5fg^3 6fg^4 5f 1980 6d 5v* 6s 7fg 6fg^2 6g 5fg 5.3fg 7d 5f 7fg^3 7fg 7g^3 5d 6s^4 6d) quite attractive, lengthy gelding; quite a moderate handicapper; narrowly beat Happy Yappy at Salisbury in March; suited by 7f nowadays; **68**

probably acts on any going; sometimes blinkered but does at least as well without. *W. Wightman.*

MARSTON 5 br.g. Tribal Chief 125–Silk Willoughby (Pirate King 129) (1979 — 5s 7g 6d 8g 7f 6f 7g 6fg 1980 6f 8f 7f 7g 6g 6g) fair handicapper at 3 yrs; has run moderately since and finished well beaten in seller final outing; best form at 7f on top-of-the-ground; often blinkered nowadays; usually ridden up with the pace. *J. Carr.*

MARSTON MAGNA 2 ch.f. Morston 125–Coppice (Pardao 120) (1980 5f^{2} 6s 76 6g^{2}) May 5; 5,600Y; second foal; dam second in small 9f race in France; ran well when placed in maiden race at Windsor in May and £4,000 event at York in July but broke leg passing post in latter event and had to be put down; was probably unsuited by soft going. *J. Bethell.*

MARSTON MOOR 3 b.c. Ragstone 128–Mary Mars (Red God 128 §) (1979 — 7fg 7f 1980 12fg 12g 10g) strong colt; behind in varied company; blinkered final start; sweated up second outing. *R. D. Peacock.*

MARTELLI 2 b.f. Pitskelly 122–Martita 99 (Tacitus 124) (1980 6s 6fg 7g 7g 70 8fg* 8d^{4}) Mar 21; 6,000Y; useful sort; half-sister to Rendition (by Jukebox), 3 times a winner over 5f at 2 yrs in 1978; dam won over 1m at 2 yrs; proved very well suited by stiff mile when winning 13-runner maiden race at Beverley in September by a length from Same Date; blinkered when respectable fourth of 8 in minor event won by Akram at Leicester the following month; will stay 1¼m. *H. T. Jones.*

MARTIAL ARTS 4 ch.g. Gulf Pearl 117–Martial Air 113 (Court Martial) 81 (1979 10fg 8g 8f^{3} 9f 1980 10g 8fg 10d 8g^{3} 8g^{3} 8.3f^{2} 8fg) good-bodied gelding; rather disappointing since his 2-y-o days; placed 3 times in 1980, including when short-head second to Hadera in handicap at Windsor in August (ridden by 7-lb claimer); gives impression he'll be suited by a return to a longer distance than 1m and stays 1¼m; acts on firm going and an easy surface; sometimes sweats up (ran moderately when doing so on final start). *J. Tree.*

MARTIES BOY 3 b.g. Caliban 123–La Martinella (Mandamus 120) (1979 6g — 7g 6fg 7fg 1980 10s 8s^{4} 8fg 6d^{3} 8g 6g) workmanlike gelding; little worthwhile form in maiden and minor events; best run at 6f on a soft surface though is bred to stay further. *M. Haynes.*

MARTINOVA 2 b.f. Martinmas 128–Pavlova (Fidalgo 129) (1980 6d 6f* 5s*) 107 Apr 30; 29,000Y; half-sister to several winners, notably high-class 1¼m performer Lucky Wednesday (by Roi Soleil); dam, winner over 1½m in Ireland, is half-sister to good stayer Random Shot; apprentice ridden when winning 10-runner minor event at Phoenix Park in August by 2 lengths from Happy Reprieve and when coming from behind to win Waterford Testimonial Stakes at the Curragh in October by ¾ length from Lady Blackfoot, with useful animals Lawmaker and Cooleen Jack third and fourth; will stay 1m; seems to act on any going; should develop into a very useful 3-y-o. *C. Collins, Ireland.*

MARTIN PHILIP 2 br.c. Saulingo 122–Feenion (Technion 96) (1980 5.3d* 78 6fg 6g 5d) Apr 30; 1,700F; 6,000Y; compact colt; half-brother to 2 winners, including Irish 7f and 9f winner Feenion Bay (by Sterling Bay); dam placed at 2 yrs in Ireland; 33/1 and ridden by 5-lb claimer, made a successful debut in 8-runner maiden event at Brighton in June, beating Sitex a length; disputed lead 4f when 7¾ lengths fifth of 6 to Cut Throat in New Ham Stakes at Goodwood the following month, next outing and best subsequent effort; off course over 2 months before final start (poorly drawn). *R. Price.*

MARTIN'S CHOICE 3 ch.rig. Pals Passage 115–Rose Allana (Final Score 113) — (1979 NR 1980 6f) 500F, 1,500Y; half-brother to fairly useful 5f and 1m winner Stormy Summer (by Lord Gayle); dam sister to 6 winners; last in maiden race at Haydock in May; sold 400 gns Doncaster September Sales. *M. Cousins.*

MARTON BOY 2 br.c. Tycoon II–Marton Lady 103 (March Past 124) (1980 85 5fg* 5g* 6g^{4} 6g^{3} 6d^{4} 5f) Mar 15; neat colt; good mover; brother to very smart sprinter Haveroid, and half-brother to 2 winners; dam sprinter; successful in minor events at Ripon and Beverley in June, on latter course getting behind early on (reportedly tried to run out after 1½f) but staying on for a ½-length win over Horncastle; creditable fourth to Praiselien in nursery at Redcar in August on fifth outing; ran moderately when blinkered on final start. *M. H. Easterby.*

MARUBENI 3 ch.c. Kambalda 108–Remana (Remainder 106) (1979 7fg 49 1980 8fg 10.1fg 12fg^{2} 13s 11fg 12g^{4} 10s* 11.7fg 10g 12d^{3}) lengthy, lean sort; plater; bought in 2,000 gns after winning at Nottingham in August; will stay 1¾m; suited by some give in the ground. *W. Holden.*

MARWELL 2 b.f. Habitat 134–Lady Seymour 109 (Tudor Melody 129) (1980 5d* 5fg* 5g* 5g* 6fg*) **124**

Although the 1980 season had its highlights, such as the versatile Moorestyle's numerous top-class displays and the thrilling duels between Le Moss and Ardross, it would have been so much more exciting but for the prolonged absences from the course of several star performers. The middle-distance races could only have been enlivened by the presence of Henbit and Bireme; the mile races would have been worth travelling even further to see had Nureyev, Known Fact and Posse been fit enough to do battle again, the more so had Kris been able to take them all on; and among the two-year-olds almost everyone wanted a clash between those excellent fillies Marwell and Tolmi.

Unfortunately Tolmi wasn't able to race after July, by which time both she and Marwell had run and won twice. While Tolmi's sparkling win in the Princess Margaret Stakes in our view represented the better form, the way Marwell had slammed the opposition on both her starts made her equally promising. In Newmarket's Chesterfield Stakes she had quickened clear in effortless style to win by four lengths from Doc Marten and at Goodwood, in the Group 3 Molecomb Stakes, she had shown tremendous acceleration to cut down the subsequent Phoenix Stakes winner Swan Princess below the distance before going on to a two-and-a-half-length success. The Queen Mary winner Pushy, admittedly giving Marwell 8 lb, was beaten four lengths into third place in the Molecomb. When asked about his plans for Marwell her trainer said that if Piggott was satisfied that she would stay six furlongs she might take her chance in the Lowther Stakes, a race also said to be Tolmi's target. However, neither filly was to turn out for the Lowther, and after Marwell's next intended race, the St Hugh's Stakes at Newbury, had been rained off she reappeared in the Prince of Wales's Stakes at York, the day after the Lowther.

Marwell's performance in the Prince of Wales's Stakes made a future confrontation with Tolmi look even more intriguing. Although having to concede 7 lb to the very speedy Welshwyn, who had finished in front of Nasseem and Ancient Regime when second to Pushy at Royal Ascot, Marwell started at 9/4 on. She won as easily as the betting suggested she would. After travelling very easily just behind Welshwyn for three furlongs Marwell steadily drew alongside and, with her rider scarcely having to move a muscle, went clear to win by a length and a half, with Welshwyn holding on to second place. Mattaboy, who later won the William Hill Middle Park Stakes after finishing second in the Mill Reef, was four lengths behind Marwell in third place. To emphasize further the merit of this seemingly effortless display, the timefigure achieved by Marwell was 1.12 fast, equivalent to a rating of 128 and an exceptionally good one for a two-year-old; it beat Sharpo's highly respectable figure (0.82 fast) when winning the William Hill Sprint Championship over the same course and distance later in the afternoon.

The Flying Childers Stakes, another five-furlong event run at Doncaster on St Leger day, saw Marwell's next appearance. The strength of the opposition provided by her five opponents can be gauged from the fact that next after the 11/4-on Marwell in the market were the 8/1-shots Welshwyn, now taking on Marwell at level weights, and Crimson Heather, winner of the Curragh Stakes in Ireland but last of five in the Lowther Stakes on her previous visit to England. Nothing managed to extend Marwell. Starkey, taking the mount for the first time in place of the suspended Piggott, had no trouble in settling Marwell as the other Irish challenger, the Gimcrack fourth Brooklyn Prince, made the running to halfway where Doc Marten took over. A little over a furlong later the race was as good as over; Marwell, still hard held, produced a most impressive turn of foot to hit the front coming to the final furlong and then left the

Molecomb Stakes, Goodwood—Marwell looks and performs like a high-class filly, beating Swan Princess and Pushy

Flying Childers Stakes, Doncaster—another scintillating win by Marwell who is clear of Welshwyn and Tre Fontane

others standing to win easing up by three lengths, with Welshwyn again filling the runner-up position.

For her final outing of the season Marwell tackled six furlongs for the first time in the William Hill Cheveley Park Stakes at Newmarket in October. Two notable absentees were Tolmi, who had jarred a joint early in September, and the Lowther winner Kittyhawk, a victim of the virus, and with no challengers from either Ireland or France it seemed Marwell had only to stay the trip to win. She had already easily accounted for three of her four most serious rivals, Pushy, Ashbrittle and Welshwyn, and the form book suggested she would have little trouble with the second favourite, the Cherry Hinton winner Nasseem. The only chance Marwell's opponents seemed to have was to ensure a blistering gallop in an attempt both to blunt her finishing speed and to expose any lack of stamina. However, no-one was willing to go on, and they played right into Piggott's hands. Piggott held Marwell up in third place as long as possible, as Ashbrittle set a very modest gallop until giving way to Pushy who quickened the pace at halfway. Only running into the Dip did he ask Marwell to take the lead and although, as usual, she responded quickly, it was well inside the final furlong this time that she drew away for a length win over the willing Welshwyn, with Pushy just half a length further back in third place. Some observers thought Marwell won with plenty in hand but Piggott is a past master at giving the impression he has far more up his sleeve than he actually has. As we saw it, this was one such example and we doubt whether she could have found a lot more.

Marwell (b.f. May 21, 1978)	Habitat (b 1966)	Sir Gaylord (b 1959)	Turn-to
			Somethingroyal
		Little Hut (b 1952)	Occupy
			Savage Beauty
	Lady Seymour (b 1972)	Tudor Melody (br 1956)	Tudor Minstrel
			Matelda
		My Game (br 1957)	My Babu
			Flirting

So Marwell ended her first season unbeaten in five races, including the only Group 1 pattern race for two-year-old fillies in England, her rare ability to quicken virtually in a stride marking her as an extremely good filly. Marwell has other good points too: she's unusually placid for a filly and didn't give the slightest sign of temperament on any of her starts; she has shown form both on a firm and a soft surface; although only medium sized, she's a well-made, most attractive individual; she walks very well and is also a good mover; and, last but not least, her breeding is first class. She's the second foal, following the 1979 Mill Reef Stakes winner Lord Seymour, bred by Lady Seymour, a filly who was unbeaten in two starts including the Phoenix Stakes, the top sprint race for two-year-olds in Ireland. Marwell's grandam, the unraced My Game, was a half-sister to the Eclipse winner Arctic Explorer and a daughter of Flirting, herself a half-sister to the Two Thousand Guineas second The Cobbler. Habitat, Marwell's sire, enjoyed his customary highly successful season with the very good French two-year-old Lou Piguet, the good milers Crofter and Hard

William Hill Cheveley Park Stakes, Newmarket—Marwell's last-furlong run takes her to the front close home. Welshwyn is again second, and Pushy is third

Fought, the very smart sprinter Sayyaf and the One Thousand Guineas second Our Home among his other representatives.

Mention of the One Thousand Guineas brings us to the burning question of whether Marwell will win that race. We think not. Although she settles extremely well she can't be considered anything like sure to stay a mile. It must be of relevance that of the previous twelve two-year-old pattern race winners sired by Habitat—namely Bitty Girl, Habat, Hot Spark, Roussalka, Steel Heart, Diffusion, Hittite Glory, Petipa, Sigy, Lord Seymour, Smokey Lady and Suvero—only Roussalka went on to win over as great a distance as a mile at three years. Even more relevant is the three-year-old career of Lord Seymour, who like his sister was a most attractive, medium-sized individual with a first-rate turn of foot at two years. He failed to make normal progress, ran four times without success and never raced beyond seven furlongs. Only Waterloo, incidentally, of the last ten Cheveley Park winners has gone on to success in the Guineas.

What of Marwell's prospects should she fail to stay a mile? Excellent filly though she is she will have her work cut out to beat Moorestyle and there's

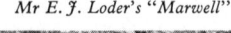

Mr E. J. Loder's "Marwell"

little encouragement to be found in the performances of other three-year-old fillies in the sprint pattern races. She will face very stiff tasks in the Group 3 sprints, most of which carry penalties of 10 lb to 12 lb for Group 1 winners, and you have to go a good way back to find the last successful three-year-old filly in the Group 1 and Group 2 events. Cassarate in 1962 was the last to win the King's Stand Stakes, Parsimony in 1972 the last to win the July Cup; no filly has won the William Hill Sprint Championship since Caterina in 1966 and the Vernons Sprint Cup has yet to fall to a three-year-old filly. Clearly the odds are stacked against her, but Marwell's acceleration makes her very much out of the ordinary and she may well prove capable of beating some of the colts, if not Moorestyle. *M. Stoute.*

MARYAM 3 gr. or ro.f. Rarity 129–Lost Angel 99 (Parthia 132) (1979 5f 1980 **67**
8v 8fg^3 8fg* 8s 10.2g 8.2s 8.2s* 7d) well-made, quite attractive filly; won maiden race at Bath in June and handicap at Hamilton in September; apprentice ridden when beating Bamp 1½ lengths in latter; should stay 1¼m; probably acts on any going; sold to D. Marks 5,200 gns Newmarket Autumn Sales. *B. Hills.*

MARY BROWNING 2 br.f. Grisaille 115–Virtuosity (Reliance II 137) (1980 —
5f 5g 6g 7g) Apr 9; 850F, 1,100Y; lightly-made filly; fourth foal; dam poor maiden; only plating class; backed from 20/1 to 11/2 when in rear in maiden auction event at Kempton on third start; sweated up and took strong hold on way to start final appearance. *D. Elsworth.*

MARYLAND COOKIE (USA) 2 b.f. Bold Hour–Efficiently (Dondeen 123) **97**
(1980 5f^4 5d^4 5.8fg* 5fg 6g* 6s^2 6s^2) Apr 5; $15,000Y; compact, good-bodied filly; good mover; third foal; dam won 6f claiming race; won maiden race at Bath in July and nursery at Salisbury in August, latter by ¾ length from Praiselien; well held by winner when second afterwards in Firth of Clyde Stakes at Ayr (went down by 4 lengths to Star Pastures) and 4-runner Marston Moor Stakes at York (beaten 5 lengths by Spark Of Life); will stay 1m; probably acts on any going; genuine and consistent. *J. Bethell.*

MARY LE BOW 3 b.f. Levmoss 133–Great Paul 117 (Great Nephew 126) **62**
(1979 NR 1980 12.2fg^4 12d^2 12.2f^3 16fg^3 14.7g^2 16f 14d 14.7d^4) lengthy filly; first foal; dam unbeaten in three 6f races at 2 yrs; placed in maiden races in the North; appears to stay 2m; probably acts on any going; ran badly last 3 starts. *M. W. Easterby.*

MARY MAGUIRE 3 b.f. Rapid River 127–Flicka (Balidar 133) (1979 NR **53**
1980 5f 6f^3 5h 5d^4 6g^3 6g 7g 8f 7g 5f 5s) 400 2-y-o; unfurnished filly; second foal; dam of little account; poor maiden; suited by 6f but isn't certain to stay 1m; acts on firm going; blinkered nowadays; sweated up tenth outing; saddle slipped sixth start. *S. Nesbitt.*

MARZOOK 4 gr.c. Blakeney 126–Abergrove 103 (Abernant 142) (1979 12g^2 —
11.7g^4 16d* 14d* 16fg^4 14d 18fg 1980 16s 16fg 16fg 16fg 16fg 16.1s 12d 12d) strong colt; fairly useful handicapper at his best; well beaten in 1980, including in a valuable seller; stays 2m; acts on a firm and a soft surface; possibly needs strong handling; blinkered fifth and eighth starts; often bandaged nowadays; sold out of J. Tree's stable 1,700 gns Ascot July Sales after fifth outing. *S. Holland.*

MASCARENHAS 5 b.g. Windjammer (USA)–Harvest Child 79 (Tamerlane 128) —
(1979 10s 10f 10fg 10f 15.5fg^2 15.5g^2 15.5fg 1980 14g 12fg) staying maiden; acts on firm going; usually wears blinkers. *T. Gosling.*

MASCARINA (USA) 2 b.f. Dewan–Manilata 115 (Dancer's Image) (1980 6fg **62**
5fg^2 5.1fg 5f 5fg 5d) Apr 16; 1,500Y; very small filly; first foal; dam won twice over 5f at 2 yrs in Germany and showed very useful form at up to 1m at 3 yrs in this country; beaten 3 lengths when second of 10 to Mummy's Treasure in maiden auction event at Folkestone; probably needs further than 5f; sold 800 gns Newmarket Autumn Sales. *D. Morley.*

MASHOOR 3 b.c. Prince Tenderfoot 126–Paper Sun 89 (Match III 135) (1979 **90**
6s^4 6fg 7g^4 7d* 1980 8fg 8f 8g 8g* 8g* 8g^2 8fg* 8.5fg^3 8fg 10fg^3 10f^3 10g) attractive, well-made colt; good mover; fairly useful handicapper; did well in the summer, winning at Salisbury, Kempton and Goodwood; ridden by 5-lb claimer, beat Major Martin 1½ lengths on last-named; ran respectably most subsequent starts; stays 1¼m; probably acts on any going. *J. Sutcliffe.*

MASKED MARVEL 4 b.c. Hard to Beat 132–Mosstown (Mossborough 126) **115**
(1979 11d^3 10g* 10.5g^4 10f^3 1980 8f^4 10.4f* 10f^4 10.5g^3 12fg^2 12f* 11.7g* 11.1fg^2 11s^3) well-made, deep-bodied colt; very useful middle-distance performer; won

M D. Wildenstein's "Masked Marvel"

Ladbroke Chester Handicap in May by 1½ lengths from Bradamante; made all when beating Cracaval by 2 lengths in £3,600 event at Lingfield in August and when landing odds in minor race at Windsor later in month; runner-up in Alycidon Stakes (no match for Water Mill) at Goodwood and in September Stakes (went down by 4 lengths to More Light) at Kempton and finished 5 lengths third to Sea Pigeon in Doonside Cup at Ayr on final outing; acts on any going but is probably best served by a sound surface; genuine and consistent; sent to race in USA. *H. Cecil.*

MASQUERADER 2 gr.c. Dancer's Image–Dash On 93 (Klairon 131) (1980 6g^4 6g) Mar 26; 23,000F, 47,000Y; compact colt; half-brother to 4 winners, including good Italian horse Le Michel (by Le Levanstell) and smart miler Alert (by Red Alert); dam won at 1¼m; nearest finish when 6 lengths fourth of 7 to New Years Day in Granville Stakes at Ascot in July; favourite for minor event at Salisbury the following month but was badly bumped as he began his challenge and had no chance afterwards, finishing 6¼ lengths sixth to Lord Clarence; will stay at least 1m. *P. Makin.* **71**

MASSENA 4 ch.g. Our Mirage 123–Barlassina (Taine 131) (1979 8v* 10v^4 11fg 13.1g^2 11g* 18.4f^4 12s 13.3g 13s 12s 1980 10.2g 12d 10.5s 12d) lengthy gelding; well beaten in 1980 (not seen out until September and had stiffish tasks); stays 13f well (tailed off over further); acts on any going. *D. Sasse.* –

MASTER CUTTER 7 b.g. Hard Tack 111§–Tailor Donore 83 (Donore 119) (1979 6d^2 6v 6g^2 7fg 6fg^4 5fg 1980 7f 8f 6fg 7g) robust gelding; stays 1m; appears to act on any going; sometimes wears blinkers and a hood; suited by forcing tactics; inconsistent. *W. H. H. Williams.* –

MASTER FARRIER 3 b.c. Singing Bede 122–Minor Chord 88 (Major Portion 129) (1979 5g 5g 5.3f 6f 5f 1980 6fg 6g 7g 8g 8g) neat, strong colt; poor plater. *D. Whelan.* –

MASTER GOLFER 2 ch.g. Swing Easy 126–Wimosa 92 (Mossborough 126) **85**
(1980 5d^3 5d 5g^4 7d 7fg^3 7.6f^3 7fg* 7s^2) May 9; well-made, good sort; second reported foal; dam suited by 1½m+; won 16-runner seller at Newmarket in October easily by 4 lengths from El Strad when well-backed favourite (bought in 3,200 gns); creditable second of 17 to 5-length winner Go Leasing in £3,800 nursery on same course later in month; will stay 1m; acts on any going; wears blinkers. *J. Sutcliffe.*

MASTER HOWARD 3 b.g. Forlorn River 124–Absent 66 (Abernant 142) (1979 **—**
5d 8d 1980 5f 7f 8d 7d) narrow gelding; poor maiden; sold 320 gns Ascot July Sales. *A. Breasley.*

MASTER MARTIN 2 b.c. Martinmas 128–Princess Irmgard 83 (Delirium 126) **71**
(1980 5fg 5f 5f^2 6d^4 7g^3 7d 8d 8.2s 7v) Apr 20; 6,400Y; neat colt; half-brother to numerous minor winners; dam winning sprint plater; in frame in maiden races in the North but is little better than plating class; seems to stay 1m. *R. Hollinshead.*

MASTER OAKLEA 2 br.c. Panama Canal 105–Quick Return (The Bo'sun 114) **—**
(1980 7f 7g 6fg 7fg) Apr 25; strong, compact colt; second reported foal; dam showed no ability at 2 yrs; 10½ lengths seventh of 19 to Grand March in £2,600 event at Salisbury in August, second outing and best effort; will stay 1m; will be more at home in sellers. *P. Mitchell.*

MASTER SHACKLES 3 ch.g. Manacle 123–Gedoparonija 88 (Right Boy 137) **—**
(1979 5g 6g* 1980 7s 9.6f^4 10.1g 8g 7g) narrow, unfurnished gelding; plater; unlikely to stay 1¼m; sold 400 gns Ascot August Sales. *T. Marshall.*

MASTER'S VOICE 2 b.c. Record Token 128–Hascombe Lady 70 (Galivanter 131) **67**
(1980 6d 7g 8d 8d 8s 8d) May 19; 3,000F, 4,000Y; smallish, lengthy colt; plater; stays 1m; acts on soft going. *J. Douglas-Home.*

MASTER TEMPLAR 3 b.g. Saintly Song 128–Sylphide 113 (Supreme Court **54**
135) (1979 5s 5v^2 5s 6fg 6g 6fg 7f 5g^2 6fg^4 7g 1980 8d 7d 12d 8f* 7f 8fg 9g 10d 12g^2 10g^3 12fg) workmanlike gelding; plater; successful at Thirsk in April (no bid); stays 1½m; seems to act on any going; blinkered nowadays; ran badly seventh start. *D. Thom.*

MASTER THATCH 2 ch.c. Thatch 136–Miss Sarah (The Axe 115) (1980 5f **107**
6fg 5g^2 6d 5g^3 6g* 6.3s^4 6f^3 7g^2 8s^2 8s) Feb 11; 34,000Y; strong colt; brother to disappointing Modella, and half-brother to 1m and 11.7f winner Rheinman (by Rheingold); dam, placed over 6f at 2 yrs in France, is sister to smart stakes winner Foggy Note; won 9-runner maiden race at Phoenix Park in August by ½ length from odds-on newcomer Kings Lake; also ran respectably when fifth to Recitation in Coventry Stakes at Royal Ascot on fourth outing and finished second in 2 pattern races at the Curragh, going down by 4 lengths to Storm Bird in National Stakes in August and by ¾ length to Benefice in Ashford Castle Stakes the following month; suited by 7f and 1m; acts well on soft going; blinkered last 3 outings; ran badly final start. *M. O'Toole, Ireland.*

MASTER THIEF 9 ch.g. Pieces of Eight 128–Tudor Song (Tudor Minstrel 144) **—**
(1979 16fg 16f^2 16f^4 16g^2 16f 16fg 1980 14fg 16g) poor stayer; acts on any going; suitable mount for an apprentice; used to wear blinkers. *P. Makin.*

MASTER TIMOTHY 4 ch.g. Malicious–Golden Tradition (Mossborough 126) **50**
(1979 6v^2 6v 9s^2 8fg^4 7fg^2 7fg 6fg^2 6f^4 8g 1980 6v^2 8f^2 7f^4 7h 8fg^4 8g^2 8g^4 7f^4 7f) neat, strong gelding; plater; not disgraced in better company in 1980 but is not one to rely on; effective at 6f and stays 9f well; acts on any going; has run well in blinkers but does just as well without. *I. Vickers.*

MASTER TONY 2 ch.c. Galivanter 131–Andromache 112 (Delirium 126) **—**
(1980 5f 5f 6g 6g 7fg 7g 5fg 7.2d) Mar 19; 2,600Y; compact colt; poor plater; blinkered seventh outing; sometimes ridden by lad in paddock. *W. Haigh.*

MASTER TOUCH 3 ch.c. Touch Paper 113–Adrienne (Democratic 124) **—**
(1979 5d^4 5g* 5fg^2 6fg 6fg 1980 5s 6s 5fg 5f 5g) plain, good-topped colt; moderate (rated 80) in 1979; ran poorly at 3 yrs; not certain to stay 6f; blinkered on last 3 starts; sold 700 gns Doncaster September Sales. *W. Wharton.*

MASTER WILLIE 3 ch.c. High Line 125–Fair Winter 111 (Set Fair 129) **129**
(1979 6fg^2 7fg* 7d^2 8fg* 1980 8s* 10f^4 10.5f^2 12f^2 12s 10.5d* 10d^2 10d^2)

No horse in training reached August more deserving of winning a good race than the outstandingly-determined Master Willie. Previously a close second in the Derby and the Mecca-Dante Stakes he finally gained his deserts

Benson and Hedges Gold Cup, York—Master Willie takes the lead close home from Cairn Rouge, with Cracaval third

in the Benson and Hedges Gold Cup at the big York meeting, at a time when a recent below-par run in the Irish Sweeps Derby gave rise to fears that he might just have missed the boat as a three-year-old.

There have been stronger fields for the Benson and Hedges Gold Cup than in the latest running of the event but Master Willie still needed a top-class performance to win it, opposed by two of the season's best fillies in Mrs Penny and Cairn Rouge supported by nine other runners, among whom the inconsistent Cracaval produced his best form for many a day blinkered for the first time. The two fillies were backed almost to the exclusion of the remainder, with Master Willie third favourite at 13/2 and the 1979 Champion Stakes winner Northern Baby at 7/1. Master Willie was tackling a shorter trip after two races at a mile and a half, and ran like it, seeming to find the pace uncomfortably hot almost from start to finish. Typically he showed true grit. He managed to hang on in the middle of the field round the bottom bend, pushed and chivvied; he got no respite as the other fancied horses began to chase after the front-running Royal Fountain and Prince Rheingold in the straight, and he came to the two-furlong pole only fourth or fifth, better placed than the unlucky Mrs Penny but looking certain to be beaten by Cairn Rouge at least. However, he stayed on so well under hard riding on the outside of Cairn Rouge that he gradually wore her down and in the end edged in front by half a length. Cracaval also stayed on for third place, ahead of Mrs Penny who found a way through too late. Northern Baby ran as disappointingly as on his previous outing in the Prix d'Ispahan and finished last but three, beaten also by World Leader, Royal Fountain, Buckpoint and the 1979 Champion Stakes third Haul Knight.

Master Willie stuck to a mile and a quarter for the rest of the season, and ran well in both his races. This, on top of his disappointing fifth to Tyrnavos when 7/4 favourite for the Irish Sweeps Derby, should not be taken as indicating he's not so effective at a mile and a half. He ran a cracking race at Epsom, going down by only three quarters of a length to Henbit: game as a pebble, he overcame jostling after half a mile, fought on when really stretched some way from home just as later he did at York, picked his way as best he could through the unusually crowded field in the straight and finished really strongly—slightly stronger than the winner, who admittedly suffered a serious leg injury. Master Willie had been off colour only a few days beforehand, unable to eat because of a throat infection, so there's a very good chance that he found the Irish Derby coming too soon for him after his exertions against Henbit.

The Derby was Master Willie's best race up to that point in his career, and he probably hasn't bettered that performance since, although he must have been pretty close on two or three occasions. Previously he'd shown more than useful form, soon improving from two to three years. He'd won the Easter Stakes at Kempton on his reappearance from the Salisbury Trial winner Poyle Crusher, and lost the Mecca-Dante at York by a neck, staying on, to Hello Gorgeous; in between he'd been ridden less enterprisingly than suits him when finishing fourth to Henbit in the Classic Trial at Sandown. Following the Benson and Hedges Gold Cup Master Willie was aimed for the Champion Stakes, missing the Prix de l'Arc de Triomphe in which his older stable-companion Nicholas Bill took sixth place. On the way there he put up another top-class performance in defeat in the Valdoe Stakes at Goodwood in September, a race ruined as a spectacle by a sea-fret. All we saw was the last furlong, through which Master Willie gave chase to the winner Welsh Chanter under strong riding, and was gamely pulling him back towards the finish. Welsh Chanter, a four-year-old receiving 8 lb more than weight-for-age, won by a length and a half; the third horse Fingal's Cave, a three-year-old, was receiving 12 lb. Master Willie beat Fingal's Cave a long way in the Champion Stakes; he beat everything in the race except for Cairn Rouge who was held up much longer than at York. He managed to take the lead surprisingly quickly when he made his effort two furlongs out, then had a good battle with Rankin which he won clearly, but he couldn't hold Cairn Rouge on the hill and was beaten the same distance as Henbit beat him in the Derby, three quarters of a length. He started favourite for the race at 7/2, looking as bright and well as at any stage of the season.

As was widely reported at the time, the stallion High Line, once difficult to fill at a modest fee, had his merit advertised in a big way the day Master Willie won the Benson and Hedges Gold Cup, through victories on the same card of three other runners of his, Shoot A Line (Yorkshire Oaks), Cocaine (Acomb Stakes) and Heighlin (Lonsdale Handicap). His fee for 1981 is £5,000 + £5,000 (live foal) compared with £750 (Oct. 1st) in 1979. Master Willie passed through the sale-ring twice, realizing a mere 2,200 guineas as a foal and a mere (in retrospect) 8,400 guineas when re-purchased by his breeder as a

Mr William Barnett's "Master Willie"

yearling. His dam was a very useful racemare who hadn't produced any important runners until Master Willie came along, her winners being Fair Cop (by Sing Sing), Fair Deed (by Derring-Do), Waveland (by Song) and two full sisters to Master Willie—Fair Head and Bumble-Bee, the former a two-year-old winner over a mile at Lingfield, the latter successful at two years and three in Austria. There are classic fillies in the pedigree: Red Winter finished third in the Irish Oaks and Winter Gleam is half-sister to Mor'a Bai, the dam of the Irish Oaks second Iskereen.

Master Willie (ch.c. 1977)	High Line (ch 1966)	High Hat (ch 1957)	Hyperion
			Madonna
		Time Call (b 1955)	Chanteur II
			Aleria
	Fair Winter (ch 1964)	Set Fair (ch 1949)	Denturius
			Ria Geno
		Winter Gleam (ch 1959)	Aureole
			Red Winter

Master Willie is not everyone's idea of a classic horse on looks: he's rather a plain, lengthy colt who does, however, walk well. One thing that impressed us about his appearance was the way he improved physically through a hard season, and his condition at Newmarket augurs well for his prospects as a four-year-old. We are confident he will do better than his dam did as a four-year-old and win races. Fair Winter had a remarkable career. She developed into one of the better three-year-old fillies of 1967 after beginning well down the weights in handicaps; she won six of her nine races that season, including the Nassau Stakes at Goodwood. At four years of age she was retired after four defeats. By a sprinter out of a mare who stayed two miles, she was never raced beyond a mile and a quarter. The way things went in the second half of the season it's possible that Master Willie won't be racing beyond a mile and a quarter for some time; nevertheless he will do at least as well at a mile and a half when the chance comes. As genuine and dependable as any in training, he acts on any going, and is altogether an excellent horse to go to the big meetings with. *H. Candy.*

MATAGOLD 3 b.f. Goldhill 125–Matala 65 (Misti IV 132) (1979 5f 1980 8fg 8fg 11.7fg) second foal; dam winning hurdler; in rear in maiden races; swerved left at start on second outing. *Mrs R. Lomax.* —

MATCHLESS DANCER 4 ch.c. Bold Lad (Ire) 133–Blue Butterfly 105 (Majority Blue 126) (1979 6s^{4} 6g 8.5s^{4} 8g 7d^{3} 8.5g 6f 1980 8fg 8fg 7h 10g 10.1g 10.1g 8g* 7f 8g^{3}) strong, good sort; favourite and dropped in class, attracted no bid after winning seller at Salisbury in September; stays 1m; acts on soft going and may be unsuited by firm; hooded last 3 starts. *J. Jenkins.* 63

MATILDA CAVE 2 b.f. King's Leap 111–Camilla Mary (Molvedo 137) (1980 5f^{4} 5g^{2} 6s 6g* 6fg^{2} 7fg*) Apr 5; 1,500Y; lightly-made filly; none too good a mover; sister to fairly useful miler Grove's Boy, and half-sister to a winner; dam of no account; won 17-runner maiden auction event at Kempton in July and was leniently weighted when winning 8-runner nursery at Newmarket the following month smoothly by 2 lengths from Iquacu; will stay 1m; acts on a firm surface. *M. Tompkins.* 80

MATNAT SABA 6 gr.h. Jukebox 120–Grandpa's Gift (Celtic Ash) (1979 10.2s 10s 13v^{3} 12d* 12s^{3} 13d^{3} 13.8g^{2} 12fg* 12fg 12fg 12s 12d 12d 1980 12d^{3} 13d^{3} 12h^{4} 12.2fg^{3} 12fg 12d 15fg 12.2fg) middle-distance performer; acts on any going; good mount for an inexperienced rider; sometimes gets behind in early stages. *D. Weeden.* 49

MATROSHKA (USA) 3 ch.f. Roberto 131–Lovelight 112 (Bleep-Bleep 134) (1979 5s^{3} 5g^{2} 1980 10.4d) small, light-framed filly; placed in maiden races at 2 yrs; didn't impress in paddock when behind in similar event at Chester in August, only start in 1980; not certain to stay 1¼m. *B. Hills.* —

MATTABOY 2 ch.c. Music Boy 124–Green Chartreuse 91 (French Beige 127) (1980 5g* 6fg^{2} 5g^{3} 6fg^{2} 6f*) 121

The William Hill Middle Park Stakes winner Mattaboy can't be considered anywhere near so good as many of the previous winners of the race—he's no Petingo or Brigadier Gerard that's for sure—but he has to be regarded as one of the best of a comparatively mediocre bunch of two-year-old colt sprinters in 1980. There was no clear-cut leader in this sphere, as is borne out by the fact that the Coventry, Norfolk, National, July, Richmond, Gimcrack, Mill Reef and

William Hill Middle Park Stakes, Newmarket—Mattaboy responds to Piggott's driving and wins from Bel Bolide and Poldhu

Middle Park Stakes all fell to different colts, while both the Flying Childers and the Cornwallis went to fillies.

Mattaboy's performance in the Middle Park at Newmarket early in October was his best. Although the field looked substandard it did include the Gimcrack winner Bel Bolide who was made favourite ahead of the Irish colt Cooliney Prince, having his first race since winning the Windsor Castle Stakes at Royal Ascot nearly four months earlier, the Cecil-trained Goodbye Starter, who hadn't been seen out since making an impressive debut in mid-May, and the other Irish challenger, the Phoenix Stakes and the Larkspur Stakes runner-up Band Practice. Mattaboy, a 7/1-shot, was preferred to the Gimcrack second and third, Parkdale and Poldhu, and the rank outsiders New Years Day and Von Erlach. After breaking well Mattaboy was settled towards the rear of the field as Bel Bolide strode along in the lead. At halfway, where he had only Von Erlach behind him, he still looked to have plenty to do but soon afterwards he burst through against the far rails and was challenging for the lead with two furlongs to run. From then on there was never much to choose between Mattaboy on the rails and Bel Bolide towards the centre of the course as both battled it out gamely, and it was only in the closing stages that Mattaboy forged ahead for a half-length win. Poldhu finished in good style to take third place, two lengths behind Bel Bolide.

Although it's possible to attribute Mattaboy's improved display to his rider's exercising more restraint than previously, another explanation is that he was simply very much on the upgrade; each of his earlier efforts had also bettered its predecessor. After landing the odds easily from just two opponents in the Star Stakes at Sandown in July he had run the useful filly Integrity to a length and a half when conceding 6 lb in the Rous Memorial Stakes at Goodwood's main meeting. From then on he tackled the best, finishing a respectable third behind Marwell and Welshwyn, beaten four lengths by the winner, in the Prince of Wales's Stakes at York and then going down by a length and a half to Sweet Monday, after leading, in the Mill Reef Stakes at Newbury.

Mattaboy (ch.c. Mar 3, 1978)	Music Boy (ch 1973)	Jukebox (b 1966)	Sing Sing
			Bibi Mah
		Veronique (b 1966)	Matador
			Narcisse
	Green Chartreuse (b 1970)	French Beige (b 1953)	Bois Roussel
			Nivea
		Green Velvet (ch 1965)	Epaulette
			Greenheart

Much improved though he was, Mattaboy still needs to make further progress if he's to reach the top at three years. Even so he's a fine advertisement for his young sire Music Boy who has made an encouraging start to his stud career. Despite standing his first years at stud at a bargain-basement £500 no foal, no fee, Music Boy topped the list of first-season sires in 1980, with Mattaboy, First Movement, Composer and four other winners representing him from only thirteen runners in Britain and Ireland. Mattaboy, a strong, compact colt, was the highest-priced yearling from his first crop at 10,500 guineas but his second crop was much better received, five fetching between 16,000 guineas and 46,000 guineas. Incidentally like those other top winners Moorestyle, Kilijaro, To-Agori-Mou and African Song, Mattaboy comes from the thriving Tudor Minstrel male line.

Music Boy had no pretensions to staying beyond six furlongs and the majority of the twelve races won by his stock in 1980 were over five furlongs. None of his seven winners has yet won over further than six furlongs but Mattaboy will probably stay seven furlongs and possibly a mile, especially if ridden with restraint. The mares on the bottom line of his pedigree, Green Chartreuse, Green Velvet and Greenheart, won at distances up to seven furlongs, nine furlongs and a mile and a half respectively. Mattaboy is the fourth foal and second winner bred by Green Chartreuse, a sister to Kunpuu, a useful winner at up to a mile and a quarter, and a half-sister to Stateff, one of the best Italian three-year-olds of 1977 when his most important success came in the Gran Premio del Jockey Club e Coppo d'Oro over a mile and a half. As yet Mattaboy has raced only on a sound surface and clearly acts very well on firm going. *R. Armstrong.*

MAURICE'S TIP 2 b.g. Jolly Me 114–Spaniard's Darling (Darling Boy 124) (1980 6s 6g 6g 7fg) Apr 25; 840F; compact gelding; only poor form, including in sellers. *M. Tompkins.* —

MAVRIS 2 br.c. Young Emperor 133–Hatu (Hornbeam 130) (1980 5d 5f 5fg 6f 7d 7fg) Mar 22; 760F, 1,800Y; tall, fair sort; no sign of ability, including in a valuable seller; blinkered fourth and sixth outings; sold 560 gns Doncaster September Sales. *A. Demetriou.* —

MAXINE 3 b.f. Maximilian 109–Swift Swallow (Hard Sauce 131) (1979 5d 6g 5f 6f 1980 8fg 7d) small, close-coupled filly; behind in varied company; sweated up badly third start at 2 yrs; sold 380 gns Ascot July Sales. *C. Bewicke.* —

MAXINE'S HERE 2 b.f. Copte–Consequently 101 (Con Brio 121) (1980 5d 5s* 5g 5g 6s^2 6g 7f 6g) Mar 24; small filly; fifth produce; dam stayed 1m; easily beat sole opponent in seller at Nottingham in March; head second to High Class Builder after having to be switched in another seller on same course in June; will stay 1m; appears to act on any going. *W. Wharton.* 52

MAYBEHANDY 2 b.f. Some Hand 119–Unpredictable 103 (Pardal 130) (1980 5g 5fg^3 6d^2 6g^2 6fg 8.2g^2) May 16; leggy filly; half-sister to 1¼m winner Gloom (by Sahib); dam useful 2-y-o 6f winner but became doubtful temperamentally; runner-up in valuable sellers and a nursery, finishing strongly when beaten 2 lengths by Show-A-Leg in last-named at Nottingham in September; suited by 1m. *P. Cole.* 66

MAYBE SO 3 b.f. So Blessed 130–Mayday Melody 117 (Highland Melody 112) (1979 5s^2 5g* 6fg^2 6d 1980 5fg^3 5fg 5g 6d* 6g 6s^3 6f) well-made, attractive filly; fair handicapper; beat Ravaduos a neck at Ayr in July; suited by 6f; probably acts on any going. *J. W. Watts.* 80

MAY DO 2 b.f. Foggy Bell 108–Rags and Tatters (Rugantino 97) (1980 5.8fg 7d 7g) lightly-made filly; first foal; dam unseated rider in a point-to-point, only outing; behind in maiden races and a £2,700 event. *G. Beeson.* —

MAYFIELD LASS 2 b.f. Rapid River 127–Molly Mayfield (Clear River 114) (1980 5fg 5g 5f 6g^4 5f 6f) May 2; compact filly; second foal; dam never ran; beaten about 7 lengths in maiden races at Catterick and Carlisle on third and fourth outings, both in July; stays 6f. *W. A. Stephenson.* 61

MAYGATE 2 gr.f. Malicious–Sovereign Gate 81 (Sovereign Path 125) (1980 7g) May 7; 1,900Y; compact filly; fourth foal; dam sprinter; 33/1 and in need of the outing, always tailed off in 26-runner maiden event won by Full Of Reason at Newmarket in October. *A. Hide.* —

MAYGOLD 4 ch.f. High Line 125–Empress of Britain 93 (Amber X 133) (1979 8.2d 8fg 1980 8v^4 8f 12f 12d 11s) leggy filly; poor maiden. *G. Wallace.* —

MAYGO-RED 2 ch.c. Communication 119–Pollastra (Punchinello 97) (1980 5f 5g 6s) Mar 30; tall colt; dam of little account; only poor form in maiden and minor events. *J. Spearing.* —

MAY GO TWICE 2 gr.c. The Go-Between 129–Mayflower Too 90 (Doutelle 128) (1980 5f 5h^2 5f^2 6g^2 5.8g 5f* 5s 5g^2 5d^2 5d^3) Mar 17; 3,600Y; compact colt; 72

half-brother to fairly useful sprinter Flashy Looker (by Good Bond) and 3 other winners; dam won at 1¼m; ridden by 5-lb claimer, made all to win 12-runner nursery at Wolverhampton in August by 3 lengths from Bellicosa; also runner-up in 2 maiden races, a seller and 2 nurseries; best form at 5f; possibly not at his best on very soft ground but acts on any other; genuine and consistent; trained by A. Johnson first 7 outings. *R. Baker.*

MAYSINA 2 ch.f. Sheshoon 132–Mirtala (Hauban 132) (1980 7fg² 8f³) Mar 7; fourth foal; half-sister to 3 winners, including 3-y-o Maysapour (by Hunter-combe), a winner at up to 9f in England and France; dam half-sister to high-class sprinter Moubariz; short-head second to Pearlaway in maiden race at Warwick in August; had every chance when 3½ lengths third of 10 to Cinderwench in similar race at Wolverhampton the following month; may well stay 1¼m. *M. Stoute.* **76**

MAZZINI 2 b.c. Auction Ring 123–How Much (Palestine 133) (1980 6s*) May 28; 11,500Y; half-brother to several winners, including Flower Man (by Floribunda), a fairly useful winner at up to 7f; dam of little account; put up a pleasing first effort when making most of running to win 21-runner maiden race at Naas in November by 2 lengths from Memories Call; will probably stay 1m; sure to improve. *L. Browne, Ireland.* **83** p

MCCARTHY 2 b.c. Steel Heart 128–Chevy Chase (Raise You Ten 125) (1980 5fg³ 6g² 6d³ 6d 7g 7g* 7s³ 7g⁴ 7g) Feb 7; 10,000Y; quite attractive colt; third foal; half-brother to Irish 3-y-o Ramian (by Mount Hagen), winner of 1¼m Nijinsky Stakes and third in Irish Sweeps Derby; dam successful Irish stayer; having second race in 3 days, came through to win 15-runner maiden race at Newmarket in August by 2½ lengths from The Dissident; subsequently acquitted himself very well in 3 important races, finishing 2½ lengths third of 5 to Robellino in Seaton Delaval Stakes at Newcastle in August, 9 lengths last of 4 to To-Agori-Mou in Intercraft Solario Stakes at Sandown later in month and about 3½ lengths sixth of 9 finishers behind Gielgud in Laurent Perrier Champagne Stakes at Doncaster the following month; will stay 1m; suited by waiting tactics; acts on soft going; ran poorly fourth start. *A. Bailey.* **113**

MCIVOR 2 b.f. McIndoe 97–Perky 47 (Three Wishes 114) (1980 5f 6fg 5g 5d) Feb 14; 580F, 240Y; lightly-made filly; bad plater; blinkered final outing. *Denys Smith.* –

MCMARTIM 3 b.g. Decoy Boy 129–Mossy 95 (Mossborough 126) (1979 5.1g 5fg* 6f³ 5d³ 5g⁴ 6f 1980 7s* 7fg³ 8h² 7fg 7fg) strong, attractive gelding; good mover; fair handicapper; won at Warwick in April; ran well on third start; stays 1m; acts on any going; exported to Hong Kong. *H. Westbrook.* **80**

MEAD LANE 3 ch.f. Ballymoss 136–Spring Parade (March Past 124) (1979 NR 1980 14d) 1,000 3-y-o; strong, good sort; third foal; dam never ran; tailed off in minor event at Sandown in October (apprentice ridden). *D. Gandolfo.* –

MECHANICAL LASS 2 b.f. Saritamer 130–Allanooka 94 (Be Friendly 130) (1980 5g 5.8f) May 14; 1,500Y; second live foal; half-sister to 1m winner French Charisma (by Young Emperor); dam won twice over 5f at 2 yrs, and is half-sister to very smart sprinter Royben; in rear in maiden race at Warwick and seller at Bath; sold 370 gns Doncaster September Sales. *P. Haslam.* –

MEDICI SOVEREIGN 2 br.f. Andrea Mantegna–Sovereign Maid 71 (Sovereign Lord 120) (1980 5g 6fg 7g 5d 8fg 8.2g 8fg) Mar 5; bad plater; blinkered fourth and fifth outings; has worn bandages. *J. Doyle.* –

MEGANTE 2 b.f. Tumble Wind–Negante 68 (Negotiation) (1980 5s 5f 5fg 5f) Apr 20; 1,500Y; third foal; dam won 7f seller at 2 yrs; no worthwhile form, including when favourite for a seller on debut; blinkered second and fourth outings; dwelt first and third appearances. *J. Hill.* –

MEGS GIRL 2 b.f. Wabash 99–Donbrilla (Donore 119) (1980 7fg 7g) Mar 13; compact, leggy filly; half-sister to a winning plater; dam of no account; tailed off in maiden races at Warwick and Chester in the summer. *A. W. Jones.* –

MEGS TOWN 5 ch.m. Charlottown 127–Meg Swerie (Whistler 129) (1979 7s 8s 10f 8f 7g 8fg 1980 10.1fg) poor plater; probably stays 1¼m; possibly unsuited by firm going; sometimes blinkered. *D. Ringer.* –

MEKAYLA 3 ch.f. Mountain Call 125–Dancing Class 75 (Compensation 127) (1979 5d 5h 1980 6fg³ 5fg³ 7f⁴ 7fg 8d 8g 7g 7g) robust filly; plater; stays 7f; acts on a firm surface; blinkered sixth start (ran poorly); sold 850 gns Ascot August Sales. *A. Johnson.* **67**

MELANIE JANE 3 b.f. Lord Gayle 124–Sapphire Spray (Floribunda 136) (1979 5d 7f 7d 8h 1980 12g 10g 13.8g) lightly-made filly; bad plater. *S. Wainwright.* —

MELATINA 2 br.f. Nero's Charger–Tina's Whistle 51 (Whistling Wind 123) (1980 5fg 7.2d 6s) of little account; blinkered first outing. *W. Clay.* —

MELBA TOAST 6 br.g. Meldrum 112–Ivory Coast 90 (Poaching 115) (1979 6s 5d⁴ 6d 5f 5f² 5g² 5f 5g 5f 5f³ 5f 5h* 6s 1980 5fg* 5fg 5fg 5g⁴ 5fg 5fg 6g² 5d 5d 5f) sprint handicapper; 4-length winner of apprentice event at Edinburgh in April; acts on hard going; suitable mount for an inexperienced rider; often wears blinkers. *T. Taylor.* **56** d

MELFIO LAD 3 b.g. Dawn Review 105–High Slipper (Solar Slipper 131) (1979 5g 6d 5g 5s³ 5fg 5f 5g 8f 6fg 1980 8fg 8.3f 10fg 8d 10.1s³ 10g 10.8fg 10f 8g) small, lightly-made gelding; bad plater; probably stays 1¼m; suited by soft ground; sometimes wears blinkers; usually apprentice ridden. *H. Candy.* —

MELFIO MISS 3 gr.f. Town Crier 119–Herods Palace 95 (Palestine 133) (1979 5d 6fg 7f 1980 6s 6d 7f 7f 8f 6g 8fg 7fg³ 7fg³ 10.4d 7g) lengthy filly; poor plater; stays 7f; acts on a firm surface; often blinkered; has worn bandages. *K. Ivory.* **40**

MELFORD MIST 2 gr. or ro.f. Grisaille 115–Crazy Slave (Arctic Slave 116) (1980 8fg 10d) Apr 11; leggy filly; half-sister to a winning point-to-pointer; dam won a point-to-point; well behind in sellers at Leicester in the autumn. *P. Cole.* —

MELINGO 2 b.c. Saulingo 122–White Legs (Preciptic 122) (1980 5g² 5f 6g⁴ 5d* 5g² 5f³ 5g 7fg 6s) Apr 9; 8,200Y; strong, robust colt; half-brother to numerous winners, including Musidora winner Princess of Man (by Green God), very useful sprinter Long Johns (by Whistling Wind) and very useful stayer Danton (by Gulf Pearl); dam placed in Ireland; held off Chief Admiral by a neck to win 11-runner maiden race at Hamilton in June; afterwards placed in minor event at Hamilton and 14-runner nursery at Beverley; form only 5f but was hampered at start when tried over 7f; seems to act on any going; in rear when blinkered ninth outing (had stiffish task). *J. Etherington.* **79**

MELISSA JANE 2 gr.f. No Mercy 126–Rich Harvest (Bounteous 125) (1980 7g 6f³ 7d*) May 17; lengthy filly; good mover; seventh living foal; dam never ran; confirmed promise of previous outing when winning 21-runner maiden race at Leicester in October by a length from Murmansk; may well stay 1m; seems to act on any going. *J. Dunlop.* **83**

MELODIC 3 b.f. Song 132–Petite Charlotte 74 (Charlottesville 135) (1979 6g³ 5.8g³ 6f* 5.8f³ 7.5g³ 6g⁴ 1980 7v 7g⁴ 7f* 7fg* 7.5f* 7g* 6.3s*) 3,700F, 7,800Y; third produce; half-sister to a minor winner; dam won over 1½m; unbeaten after being fitted with blinkers on third outing, winning handicaps at Naas, the Curragh (2), Gowran Park and Leopardstown; beat Indian Lore by a length in £7,700 Midsummer Scurry Handicap at the Curragh in June on final outing; stays 7f; acts on any going; genuine and consistent. *N. Meade, Ireland.* **97**

MELODRAMA 2 b.f. Busted 134–Matinee 119 (Zeddaan 130) (1980 7g⁴) Feb 20; second foal; half-sister to 1978 2-y-o 5f winner Safety Curtain (by Roan Rocket); dam won Portland Handicap; favourite for 26-runner maiden race at Newmarket in October, despite looking as though race would do her good, and came out best of runners on stand side, finishing about 2 lengths fourth to Full of Reason; will stay 1m; sure to win races at 3 yrs. *R. Hern.* **81** p

MELODY BOX 2 b.g. Jukebox 120–Diatomite 69 (Diatome 132) (1980 5v* 5f² 5f 5h 6fg⁴) May 26; 2,800Y, resold 7,000Y; compact gelding; half-brother to 2 winners, including useful 3-y-o Soaf (by Auction Ring), successful at up to 7f; dam placed twice over 1m; won maiden event at Stockton in March going away by 1½ lengths from Andy Lou; ran best race for some time when 3 lengths fourth of 9 to Salt in £2,400 event at Ripon in July; suited by 6f; acts on any going; exported to Hong Kong. *W. C. Watts.* **80**

MELON PATCH 2 b.c. Thatch 136–Melon Flower (Relko 136) (1980 5g³ 5f² 6g² 6fg² 6g* 6g) Feb 19; compact, well-grown ex-Irish colt; half-brother to fairly useful 6f and 7f winner Bolshevik (by Bold Lad Ire); dam, sister to top-class French colt Breton, won twice at up to 7.5f in France; second in £1,200 race at Phoenix Park and 2 maiden events at Yarmouth prior to making all to win 8-runner maiden race at Nottingham in September by 2½ lengths from Cabbage Man; ran creditably in a good nursery on only outing afterwards; will stay 1m; yet to race on a soft surface; trained first 2 outings by J. Bolger. *M. Stoute.* **93**

MEL'S CHOICE 2 b. or br.c. Birdbrook 110–Port Meadow 83 (Runnymede 123) (1980 5fg 5fg^{3} 5d* 5f) Mar 21; 2,100F, 10,000Y; strong, well-grown colt; fifth foal; half-brother to 1979 2-y-o 5f seller winner Bothwell Park (by John Splendid); dam probably stayed 1m; odds on when winning 12-runner maiden race at Hamilton in September easing up by 2 lengths from Middleton Lad; will be suited by 6f; best run on an easy surface. *J. Etherington.* **78**

MEMENTA MIA 2 ch.f. Music Boy 124–Young Mementa (Young Christopher 119) (1980 5s* 5f^{4} 5f^{2} 5fg^{4} 5g^{4} 5fg^{2} 6fg* 6g^{3} 6s^{3} 5g*) Feb 21; neat, strong-quartered filly; half-sister to several winners, including 1979 2-y-o 5.8f winner Akhter (by Manacle); dam never ran; successful in maiden race at Warwick in April and nurseries at Windsor in August (from Dear Jem) and Folkestone in October (from Pencil Point); stays 6f; acts on any going; consistent. *C. Nelson.* **100**

MEMPHIS FLYER 3 ch.f. Gay Fandango 132–Nas Dara (Aggressor 130) (1979 5g 1980 6f 7.2s 5fg 8.2g 8s) neat, robust filly; in rear in varied company; wears blinkers; sold 620 gns Newmarket Autumn Sales. *I. Walker.* —

MENALIST 4 ch.g. Traditionalist–Menu 85 (Tobrouk) (1979 NR 1980 8fg 11d 12.2f) compact gelding; plating-class maiden. *Denys Smith.* —

MENDALEAK 3 b.g. Hipster 101–Potter's Wheel 88 (Aureole 132) (1979 5s 5s^{2} 5v 6g 6s 6g 6f 7f 6g^{2} 1980 8f 7f^{3} 7fg^{2} 7s 13.8f 10g 8f 10f 9f^{2} 8f 8d 13.8d^{2} 11s^{4} 10d) light-framed gelding; plater; stays 1¾m; acts on any going; often blinkered. *P. Asquith.* **52**

MENDELITA 4 ch.f. King's Company 124–Ermine Beauty (Young Emperor 133) (1979 12s^{3} 12g^{2} 11d^{2} 11fg^{2} 16f^{3} 13g^{3} 15.5fg^{3} 16d^{2} 16fg^{3} 16fg 16.1s 1980 15.8fg^{2} 12d^{3} 15fg^{4} 16.1s) staying maiden; placed in handicaps in June at Catterick and Hamilton; acts on any going; unseated rider final start at 3 yrs. *J. Bingham.* **56**

MENDIP MINSTREL 3 b.c. Mon Fils 124–Angele 98 (Match III 135) (1979 5d 8g 8g 1980 10.8v 8fg 16g) big, rangy colt; showed some ability in maiden race on final start at 2 yrs; well beaten in similar event and handicaps in 1980; should stay 11f; trained part of year by R. Hannon; sold 725 gns Ascot July Sales. *J. Haine* —

MENDIP MONARCH 5 b.g. Mon Fils 124–Angele 98 (Match III 135) (1979 17.1fg 1980 8fg) poor maiden. *M. Pipe.* —

MEND IT 2 ch.c. Patch 129–Startop 72 (Divine Gift 127) (1980 7g 7fg 10s) May 21; 1,700Y; leggy, close-coupled colt; first foal; dam quite moderate; unquoted when behind in maiden and minor events. *D. Dale.* —

MEND YOUR WAYS 2 ch.g. Blackballed 64–Barbary Miss (Barbary Pirate 91) (1980 5fg 5f 6fg) Mar 5; good sort; useless plater. *P. Butler.* —

MENOTTE 3 ch.f. Manacle 123–Cordon Rouge 99 (Never Say Die 137) (1979 5fg 5f 1980 7f 8.5f 8s^{3} 7.2d) fair sort; poor maiden; will probably stay 1¼m; acts on soft going. *J. Winter.* **53**

MENT MORE 5 br.m. Sahib 114–Rural Poem (Zarathustra 131) (1979 NR 1980 14fg 17.1f) bad maiden. *H. Willis.* —

MEPHISTO WALTZ 3 gr.f. Dancer's Image–Mellifont (Hook Money 124) (1979 5s 6g* 6g^{3} 5f^{4} 6g^{2} 5fg* 6g^{2} 1980 6s^{4} 7.3fg 6g 6d 7g 5.8g) compact, good-quartered filly; ran respectably in handicap first outing but moderately most starts afterwards, including when blinkered on last 2 occasions; out of depth second outing; should stay 7f; acts on any going; trained first 5 outings by R. Hannon. *C. James.* —

MERCIFUL SUN 2 gr.f. No Mercy 118–Follow the Sun (Kythnos 126 or Saint Crespin III 132) (1980 6fg 7g) Apr 8; 1,000F, 1,100Y; compact filly; third foal; dam ran only once; unquoted when behind in maiden race at Windsor and minor event at Sandown in August. *M. Haynes.* —

MERCILESS KING 3 br.g. No Mercy 126–My Mary 93 (French Beige 127) (1979 NR 1980 9fg^{4} 12fg^{2} 11.5f* 14g^{2} 13g* 14g 12fg^{4}) quite useful-looking gelding; half-brother to several winners, including smart Bona-Mia (by Good Bond) successful at up to 1m; dam stayer; won maiden race at Yarmouth in June and handicap at Ayr in July; ran creditably in between; stays 1¾m; yet to race on a soft surface; pulled hard early on in apprentice race seventh start. *G. Pritchard-Gordon.* **89**

MERCURIAL 2 ch.f. Hotfoot 126–Mary Mars (Red God 128§) (1980 5f 5fg 5g 6d 6fg) Mar 26; fourth foal; dam twice-raced half-sister to smart middle-distance horse Marengo; only poor form in maiden and minor events; sold 1,200 gns Newmarket Autumn Sales. *R. D. Peacock.* **61**

MERCY CURE 4 gr.f. No Mercy 126–Sinecure (Parthia 132) (1979 5s 6f 6d 52
6fg 6f^3 5f* 5f^4 5g 1980 5.1fg 5.3d 5fg 5fg^3 5f 5g) neat filly; close third to
Ferryman in handicap at Windsor in August, easily best effort; sweating and
tailed off next time; stays 6f; acts on firm going; blinkered fourth outing at
3 yrs; retained by trainer 875 gns Ascot October Sales. *D. Dale.*

MERCY ME 3 gr.f. No Mercy 126–Scorton Green 84 (Above Suspicion 127) —
(1979 5s^2 5s^2 5g 5g 5f 6g 7g 1980 8f 5g 5d 5fg) leggy filly; has shown no form
since first 2 outings at 2 yrs; suited by soft going; blinkered final start at 2 yrs.
D. H. Jones.

MERE GAMBLER 3 b.c. Jimmy Reppin 131–Stormy Gal 71 (Rockavon 120) —
(1979 5v 5d^2 5g 5f 5f^3 5fg^2 5g^2 5g 5fg* 5f^3 1980 5d 5v 5fg 5fg 7.3f 5fg 5f 5fg
10fg) compact colt; moderate performer (rated 83) at 2 yrs; ran poorly in
handicaps and an amateur riders race in 1980; bred to stay at least 7f; probably
acts on any going; blinkered seventh start; trained by T. Marshall first 8 outings.
R. Sturdy.

MERELY MOZART 2 ch.c. Music Boy 124–Visitation 84 (Tarqogan 125) 84
(1980 5d 5v* 5v^2 5fg^3 5fg^3 6d 5g* 5f^4 5g^4 5d^4 5f) Feb 17; 6,000Y; small, chunky
sort; third foal; half-brother to 6f and 7f winner Masters (by Swing Easy); dam
stayed $1\frac{1}{2}$m; won maiden race at Ayr in March and nursery at Hamilton in
July, latter by a neck from Saulann; creditable fourth in nurseries subsequently;
form only at 5f; blinkered sixth and eleventh outings. *P. Haslam.*

MERITOUS 5 b.g. Decoy Boy 129–Welsh Huntress 106 (Big Game) 1979 84
6v* 6v^3 5f^3 6d 6d^4 6fg^2 6f 6d^2 5g^2 6fg^2 5.6fg 5fg 6d* 1980 5d 6v 6d 5g 6d 6g^4
6fg^2 6g* 6fg 6g 5f^3 6g* 6g 6s^3 6d 6d 6s* 5v) big, lengthy gelding; sprint handicapper; successful at Nottingham in July, Chester in August and Nottingham
again in October, in last-named event beating Tralee Falcon decisively by $\frac{1}{2}$ length;
effective at 5f but seems best at 6f; acts on any going, but is suited by some give
in the ground; has worn blinkers; suitable mount for an amateur; said to have
broken blood vessel once in 1979; trained by M. Haynes until after fourth start.
J. Bingham.

MEROKETTE 4 ch.f. Blast 125–Merok (Eastern Venture 107) (1979 10s^4 75
12fg* 12fg* 12f^2 12g^4 12fg^2 11.1fg 1980 12f 12fg 16fg^4 14d 14g^2 14g* 13.1h^2
14fg 16g^3 16g^4) rangy filly; fair handicapper; held up and confidently ridden
when scoring by neck from Broadsword at Salisbury in August; close second to
Successor at Bath later in month; stays 2m; acts well on firm going and is said
by trainer to be unsuited by soft. *N. Vigors.*

MERRYMEDE 2 gr.c. Runnymede 123–Fair Roxane (Acropolis 132) (1980 5f 65
6d 7g 7fg 7g^4 7fg 8.2g 7.2s) Jan 18; 3,400F, 6,000Y; rangy colt; third living
foal; dam poor maiden; plater; showed a little ability in better company in
mid-season; stays 7f; sometimes wears blinkers; sold 400 gns Newmarket Autumn
Sales. *S. Mellor.*

MERRY MUSKATEER 6 ch.g. Jimmy Reppin 131–Ranjita 84 (Ballylinan 118) 56
(1979 8g 10s 1980 10.6fg^3) big, strong gelding; on burly side when third to
Boltingo in selling handicap at Haydock in June, only outing of 1980; stays
10.6f; acts on any going; bandaged in front. *M. H. Easterby.*

MESNIL WARREN 3 ch.f. Connaught 130–Intrusion 101 (Aggressor 130) —
(1979 NR 1980 7f 10fg 10fg 14d 12.2f^4 13g 15.5g) strong filly; half-sister to 3
winners, including very smart stayer Mr Bigmore (by Mandamus) and useful
middle-distance performer Lily Langtry (by Prince de Galles); dam soft-ground
stayer; well beaten in maiden races and handicaps; blinkered fifth outing; sometimes sweats up; sold 3,400 gns Newmarket Autumn Sales. *W. Holden.*

MESSENGER OF PEACE 4 ch.c. Simbir 130–Pipeline 85 (Gulf Pearl 117) 91
(1979 10.5g 13.3g 12g^4 14fg 14.6f 1980 12f 18.4f 14f 16fg 16d) lengthy colt;
ran best race of season on third outing when fair fifth of 8 to Noble Saint in Yorkshire Cup at York in May; broke blood vessel next time; stays $1\frac{3}{4}$m (well beaten
over further); acts on firm going and has yet to race on really soft; ran respectably when blinkered once in 1978. *R. Boss.*

MEXICAN LINK 2 gr.c. The Go-Between 129–Tijuana 91 (Floribunda 136) 65
(1980 5s 5fg 6g 5d* 6fg^2 6g) Feb 18; 2,300Y; half-brother to a winning 2-y-o
plater; dam 2-y-o 5f winner; spreadeagled 5 opponents in seller at Lingfield in
July (no bid); didn't have a clear run 1f out and was probably unlucky to be
beaten a head by Littleton Song in nursery at Folkestone the following month;
stays 6f well; acts on a firm and a soft surface. *J. Holt.*

MIANACH OIR 2 b.f. Wolver Hollow 126–Regency Gold (Prince Regent 129) 80
(1980 5f 6fg 7.3d^3) Mar 9; big filly; second foal; dam won from 7f to 2m in

Ireland; ran easily best race when 1¾ lengths third of 12 to Boathouse in £5,000 event at Newbury in October; will be suited by 1¼m; trained by R. Hannon first outing. *F. J. Houghton.*

MICE BIRD 3 ch.f. Busted 134–Bird of Dawning (Sea-Bird II 145) (1979 7fg 97
8.5g^2 7.5s* 1980 8g 8fg^2 12d 11fg* 12g* 8g* 12d 12g 12g 8g) useful-looking filly; second living foal; dam, daughter of Argentinian 1,000 Guineas and Oaks winner Sweet Sue, won over 6f at 3 yrs in USA; successful in Bushy Park Race and a handicap at Galway and Cornelscourt Stakes at Leopardstown within space of 8 days in July and August; well beaten in better company on several other occasions, including when last in Irish Guinness Oaks at the Curragh on third start (blinkered) and fifth in Yorkshire Oaks and Galtres Stakes (7 lengths behind Deadly Serious) at York in August on seventh and eighth outings; stays 1½m; probably acts on any going. *L. Browne, Ireland.*

MICHAELMAS 3 b.f. Silly Season 127–Calvine 94 (Prince Chevalier) (1979 72
NR 1980 8fg 8f 10.6d) big, tall filly; good walker; sister to high-class 7f and 1m performer Martinmas and useful 6f to 1¼m winner Rowantree, and half-sister to smart 5f to 8.5f winner Quarryknowe (by Quorum); dam middle-distance winner; respectable fifth in £4,400 fillies race at Ascot in April; well beaten in £3,500 event at Sandown and maiden race at Haydock (moved poorly to post and was never going well) subsequently; should stay 1¼m. *I. Balding.*

MICHALA JANE 4 ch.f. Communication 119–Grandaire 65 (Grand Roi 118) –
(1979 5g 5fg 5g 1980 6f 5d 10d) bad plater. *K. Bridgwater.*

MICHELHAM LAD 4 ch.g. Double Jump 131–Sicilia 88 (Die Hard 127) (1979 –
12v^4 16s 12fg 16.9fg 1980 15fg^3) useful sort; poor stayer; probably acts on any going; often blinkered. *D. Weeden.*

MICKEY TIM 3 br.c. Gay Fandango 132–Amicable 73 (Bold Ruler) (1979 NR 87
1980 7f 8.2g^3 7g* 8g 10f^2 10fg^2 11.1g^3 10f) 15,000Y; tall, attractive colt; second foal; dam, placed over 1¼m, is half-sister to Sir Wimborne and Lady Capulet; landed odds all out by a neck from Souliotissa in 17-runner maiden race at Newcastle in June; placed in handicaps subsequently, not looking that keen when third at Kempton in September; suited by middle distances; acts on firm going; blinkered final start. *J. Dunlop.*

MICKLE FELL 3 b.c. Hill Clown–Fanny Farkel (Royal Palace 131) (1979 7fg –
6d 1980 9.4g 10g 12.2g) strong colt; poor maiden; sold 800 gns Ascot September Sales. *T. Barron.*

MICRO MAID 2 b.f. Owen Anthony 102–Paddygrino (St Paddy 133) (1980 55
5fg* 5fg^3 6d 7d) May 12; small, light-framed filly; half-sister to 2 minor winners; dam unraced; bought in 1,500 gns after winning 11-runner seller at Warwick in May by 1½ lengths from Babas Bally; ran respectably third outing; should stay 7f; blinkered fourth start. *P. Feilden.*

MI DAD 3 br.g. Undulate–Miss Alice 80 (High Hat 131) (1979 5d^2 6fg 6f 7d^4 71
7fg 8.2g^4 1980 9.4d 12g 11d 13.8f^3 14.7g^4 14.7d^3 12f 16.1s* 12d) workmanlike gelding; narrowly won amateur riders maiden race at Haydock in October; sixth in valuable selling handicap at Doncaster later in month; one paced and stays well; acts on any going but is particularly effective in the mud; often blinkered but wasn't when successful; pulled hard fourth start; sold 5,600 gns Newmarket Autumn Sales. *J. Etherington.*

MIDAS LADY 2 ch.f. Malicious–Golden Tradition (Mossborough 126) (1980 –
5g 5fg) Apr 26; strong filly; half-sister to a winner in Greece; dam never ran; behind in large fields of maidens at Windsor in July (very backward and sweating badly when tailed-off last) and August. *M. Salaman.*

MID DAY GUN 5 ch.g. Salvo 129–Ritournelle (Chanteur II 135) (1979 14fg –
1980 10d 12g) probably of little account on flat; winning jumper. *J. Webber.*

MIDDLEHAM 4 ch.g. Amber Rama 133–Mathilde 84 (Whistler 129) (1979 5s 72
5g 6f 7.2fg^3 6g 7fg^2 5.6fg 7.2g^2 8s 8fg 1980 7.2fg 6fg 7g 7f^3 7f 10fg^3 7g^3 7f* 8fg 7fg 8fg^3 7.2d) tall, useful-looking gelding; apprentice ridden and carrying 2 lb overweight when winning handicap by 2 lengths from Miss Cindy at Beverley in August; rather inconsistent subsequently; evidently stays 1¼m; seems to act on any going; blinkered fifth start at 3 yrs. *E. Weymes.*

MIDDLE-MOUNT 3 b.g. Yellow River 114–Miss Shrimpton (Cantab 94) –
(1979 8f 7fg 8f 1980 7fg 15.5g) small, well-made gelding; poor maiden. *R. Smyth.*

MIDDLETON LAD 2 b.c. Meldrum 112–Maid of Middleton (Clear River 114) 86
(1980 5d^2 5d^2 5s^2 5d) May 9; lengthy colt; good mover; second reported foal;

dam bad 5f plater; second in maiden and minor events in the autumn, going down by 2 lengths to Mel's Choice at Hamilton, by a short head to Hindi after being clear 2f out in 23-runner event at Haydock and by 3 lengths to Pettistree at York; speedy and may not stay 6f; ran moderately final outing. *C. Thornton.*

MIDDLIN THRANG 2 b.c. Farm Walk 111–Darling Do (Derring-Do 131) **89**
(1980 6g^2 8g^3) Apr 27; neat colt; brother to 1$\frac{1}{2}$m winner Another Move and very useful 1m to 1$\frac{3}{4}$m winner Move Off; dam unraced sister to high-class miler Quorum; looked in need of race when 33/1 for Convivial Stakes at York in August but ran an excellent first race, finishing neck second of 11 to Sweet Pleasure; didn't impress in paddock prior to finishing 5$\frac{1}{2}$ lengths third of 7 to Sula Bula in minor event at Newcastle in October; will be suited by middle distances. *Miss S. Hall.*

MIDNIGHT AFFAIR 4 br.f. Mandamus 120–Smokey Princess 83 (My Smokey —
125) (1979 NR 1980 10fg) compact filly; poor mover; probably useless. *J. Harris.*

MIDNIGHT MARY 5 b.m. Celtic Cone 116–Sweet Tyrolean (Tyrone 130) —
(1979 NR 1980 16g 12g 16fg 16.1s) second foal; dam winning hurdler; well beaten in poor maiden race and 3 amateur riders events. *R. Hollinshead.*

MIDRIDGE DRIFT 2 ch.f. Most Secret 119–Lyn's Pride 85 (Star Moss 122) **58**
(1980 5d 5s 5f 5fg^4 6g 6fg 6fg) Feb 20; 1,200Y; sturdy filly; half-sister to a winning plater by Aglojo; dam stayed 7f; only poor form, including in a valuable seller; blinkered third and seventh outings. *W. Stubbs.*

MIDSUMMER BOY 3 b.g. Midsummer Night II 117–Rosie Crucian (Polkemmet 91) **66**
(1979 6f 7g 7fg 1980 10f 13s 10s^4 10s 12d 13g^3 15.5g^4 16s) strong, shapely gelding; stays well; has run respectably for an apprentice. *P. Ashworth.*

MI FAVORITA 4 br.f. Mummy's Pet 125–Parlais 101 (Pardao 120) (1979 5v^3 **89**
5d 5h 6g 6d 5fg 5f^3 5h 5fg 5g 5g 6d 5s 1980 6h 7.2fg 6fg 5g^2 5s* 5g* 5fg 5fg) small, stocky filly; fairly useful handicapper; led 1f out and ran on strongly to win valuable Tilcon Trophy at York in July by 3 lengths from Balvima; made most when decisive winner at Haydock on previous outing; ran poorly final start (July); best form at 5f; acted on any going; wore blinkers; usually bandaged on off-hind; in foal to Lochnager. *M. H. Easterby.*

MIGELITTO (FR) 8 ch.g. Lorenzaccio 130–Vivien 66 (Nearco) (1979 16g^2 **67**
16d 18.8g 20g^2 22.2fg^4 16.1f^3 20.4g 18fg 17.4s^4 16fg^4 18fg 1980 18d 16.1d^4 16fg^4 15f^4 18fg^3 22.2fg 16.1d 20.4g* 19f^4 20g^3 16g^2 17.4s^3 18d) out-and-out staying handicapper; beat Bleu Nuit by 3 lengths at Ayr in July; acts on any going but is suited by firm; has worn blinkers (did so when running moderately on second start); suitable mount for an apprentice. *M. Naughton.*

MIGRATEUR (FR) 8 gr.g. Tiffauges 124–Mistoufle (Marino) (1979 NR —
1980 12g) lightly-made gelding; tailed off in amateur riders race at Beverley in July, first outing on flat for 3 seasons; stays well; has worn blinkers; novice hurdler. *W. Marshall.*

MIKADORA 3 b.f. Cavo Doro 124–Mimika 85 (Lorenzaccio 130) (1979 5s 8f —
1980 10h 12d) strong, compact filly; behind in varied company; sold 400 gns Newmarket Autumn Sales. *C. Brittain.*

MIKE CHANNON 4 b.g. Rheingold 137–Miss Match (Match III 135) (1979 10g **57**
11g 11d 12s^2 15v 1980 10f^3 10d 11.7f 16fg 16f* 16fg) quite well-made ex-Irish gelding; won amateur riders race at Lingfield in September by 2$\frac{1}{2}$ lengths from Crown Pageant; well beaten in similar race at Newbury shortly afterwards; stays well; acts on any going. *P. Makin.*

MIKE THE BIKE 3 b.g. Ascertain–Bassoon 78 (Sovereign Lord 120) (1979 7g —
10.6d 1980 8g 12fg) plain, leggy gelding; useless; has worn bandages. *J. Calvert.*

MILBIL 8 br.g. Mandamus 120–Quolanta 81 (Quorum 126) (1979 8s^4 11d 8s —
8d 10.6s 7fg 1980 8d) plater; stays 1m; well suited by heavy going; wears blinkers; suitable mount for an apprentice. *D. Chapman.*

MILIAR 3 b.c. Thatch 136–Countess Decima (Sir Gaylord) (1979 5v* 1980 **107**
5fg^2 5s^2 6d) third foal; half-brother to quite useful 1m to 1$\frac{1}{4}$m winner Countess Lor (by Lorenzaccio) and a winner in Italy; dam unraced half-sister to numerous winners in USA; twice runner-up to all-the-way winner Adraan when receiving weight, going down by 3 lengths in 7-runner Prix de Saint-Georges at Longchamp in May and by 4 lengths in 9-runner Prix du Gros Chene at Chantilly in June; 8$\frac{1}{2}$ lengths fifth to Kilijaro in Prix de Meautry at Deauville in August; bred to be well suited by 6f+; probably acts on any going. *M. Saliba, France.*

MILIBELLE 2 b.f. Military 112–Sunny Belle (Windsor Sun 116) (1980 7fg) — Apr 3; lightly-made filly; sister to 1m seller winner Captain Cheeko, and half-sister to a winning hurdler; dam won selling hurdle; unquoted and backward, started slowly when tailed-off last of 17 in maiden race won by Ardrox Pioneer at Warwick in July. *P. Allingham.*

MILK OF THE BARLEY 3 b.c. Mummy's Pet 125–Tots (Dual 117) (1979 **103** 5s^2 5.8s^2 5fg 5g* 5f 5.9g* 7.9g^3 7.5g^2 8d 6d* 1980 7g^4 6f 6.3s 5fg^4 6.3d 6fg^3 8d^3 5s^4) half-brother to 2 Irish winners, including Totalitarian (by Cavo Doro), successful at up to $1\frac{3}{4}$m; dam ran once; ran well to be in frame in Gladness Stakes at the Curragh ($2\frac{1}{2}$ lengths fourth to Night Alert) and 3 races at Phoenix Park, namely Stackallen Stakes, Matt Gallagher Sprint Stakes ($1\frac{1}{2}$ lengths third to Gods Mark) and Youghal Stakes (just over $\frac{3}{4}$-length third to Crofter); well beaten in valuable 5-runner event at York in October on final start (taken early to post); stays 1m; seems to act on any going. *A. Redmond, Ireland.*

MILLBANK 5 b.h. Mill Reef 141–Bold Desire 111 (Breakspear II) (1979 **66** 7.6v 10s^3 8s 8v* 8f^3 8d^2 7g 10fg^3 10f* 12f 12f 1980 10.6fg^3 9fg^3 10fg^3 10g 10d 10g^2) close-coupled, good sort; stays $1\frac{1}{4}$m; acts on any going; suitable mount for an apprentice; occasionally sweats up; exported to Trinidad. *D. Whelan.*

MILLBANK (USA) 3 b.g. Mill Reef 141–All Beautiful (Battlefield) (1979 **107** 6fg 7fg* 7s 7fg 7fg^2 1980 8s* 8s^3 8fg^4 7.6f^2 8g* 7g 8g^4 8g 8d 8g^2) neat, well-made, attractive gelding; really good mover; won minor event at Leicester in March and £2,800 race at Newbury in June; made all and stayed on well to beat Beldale Gunflint 4 lengths in latter; not disgraced though no match for winner when 12 lengths second of 5 to Kris in £2,400 event at Goodwood in September; stays 1m; acts on any going; has shown signs on occasions of being none too keen, including when blinkered on final start at 2 yrs. *I. Balding.*

MILLFIELD LAD 3 b.c. Jimmy Reppin 131–Alexa (Runnymede 123) (1979 **86** 5v* 5s* 6d^3 6fg^4 6fg^3 7g* 1980 7fg 8g 7.2s^4 7.6g^2 7f 6s 8d 7s^4 8g^2) useful-looking colt; good mover; moderate handicapper; stays 1m; needs some give in the ground; blinkered final start; has run creditably for a claimer. *M. H. Easterby.*

MILLFIELD ROYAL 3 b.f. Royalty 130–Most Precious (Matador 131) (1979 **71** 6f 6f^2 7g* 8h 8g 1980 10f 8fg 8.2d* 9s^3 8.2v*) leggy filly; plater; successful twice at Hamilton in the autumn, being bought in 1,550 gns on first occasion and sold 1,600 gns on second (blinkered); stays 9f; needs some give in the ground. *P. Rohan.*

MILLINGDALE 2 b.f. Tumble Wind–Narita 86 (Narrator 127) (1980 5g^2 **65** 6g 5fg 6fg^2 5s 5fg) Feb 26; 1,500F, 9,400Y; close-coupled filly; half-sister to 2 winners; dam won over 7f and 1m at 2 yrs; second in maiden race at Edinburgh in June and £1,800 seller at Goodwood in August, going down by 2 lengths to Spanish Tormenta at Goodwood; probably needs at least 6f nowadays; acts on a firm surface; sold 480 gns Ascot November Sales. *C. Nelson.*

MILLINGDALE LILLIE 3 ch.f. Tumble Wind–Zenoelg 84 (El Gallo 122) **113** (1979 5g^2 5g^2 5.8g^3 6f^2 7.2fg* 7fg^2 7d 6fg* 6f^2 1980 7.3fg* 8fg^4 8fg^2 7.2fg^4 8s 8g 8g)

No more than half a length separated Millingdale Lillie and Mrs Penny at the finish of their four encounters, beginning with the William Hill Cheveley Park Stakes and ending with the Goffs Irish One Thousand Guineas. Each finished in front of the other twice, and there would be great rejoicing among students of the form-book if all horses reproduced their running as consistently as this. Even so, we cannot rate Millingdale Lillie the equal of Mrs Penny as a three-year-old, for the latter was seen to much better advantage over middle distances than over the shorter trips at which the two fillies met.

The season wasn't very old when Millingdale Lillie avenged her short-head defeat in the Cheveley Park. Looking to have done very well over the winter she outshone Mrs Penny in the paddock before the Fred Darling Stakes at Newbury in April and won in sparkling style, coming through at the distance after being short of room for a long way in the straight and producing a good turn of foot to get her up near the post and account for Mrs Penny by half a length. Whereas five of the ten fillies that finished behind her at Newbury went on to win races, Millingdale Lillie failed to add to her tally. This wasn't for want of trying, since she raced consistently apart from on the day the soft going came against her in the Child Stakes at Newmarket. In the One Thousand Guineas, Millingdale Lillie ran on well in the closing stages to be fourth, a length behind the Fred Darling third Quick As Lightning and a neck behind Mrs Penny; in the Irish One Thousand at the Curragh she started favourite ahead

Fred Darling Stakes, Newbury—a sparkling performance by Millingdale Lillie who wrests the lead close home from Mrs Penny (*noseband*)

of Mrs Penny and beat her, but caught a tartar in Cairn Rouge and was decisively outpaced in the final furlong, going down by two and a half lengths. Millingdale Lillie reached the frame only once more, in the John of Gaunt Stakes at Haydock. She continued to be highly tried to the end, and was far from disgraced on her last two starts, in the Sussex Stakes and Waterford Crystal Mile at Goodwood. She didn't have much chance against some of the best milers in the country in these races, but was beaten only two and a half lengths on the first occasion and two on the second, finishing fifth both times.

Millingdale Lillie (ch.f. 1977)	Tumble Wind (b 1964)	Restless Wind (ch 1956)	Windy City
			Lump Sugar
		Easy Stages (b 1953)	Endeavour II
			Saturday Off
	Zenoelg (b 1966)	El Gallo (ch 1959)	Matador
			Discipliner
		Forget (br 1947)	Rockefella
			Roussette

Millingdale Lillie's breeding isn't that of a miler. Her sire Tumble Wind won at up to a mile and a half and the first two dams, Zenoelg and Forget, were each successful at one and a half miles and a mile and three quarters, Forget twice being placed in the Ebor. Zenoelg's three other runners have won, Nicko (by Whistling Wind) and Forget's Image (by Florescence) at a mile and Spiritus Veris (by Lord Gayle) at up to a mile and a quarter. By the end of the year it looked as if the latter trip wouldn't have been beyond Millingdale Lillie—she settled very well as a three-year-old—and since she will still be racing in 1981, in America with J. Gosden, it is to be hoped she'll be given a chance of running over the distance. Millingdale Lillie, bought for 4,100 guineas as a foal, 3,300 guineas a yearling, and subsequently privately by Robert Sangster, is a quite attractive, well-made individual. She acts particularly well on firm ground and is very tough and genuine. *C. Nelson.*

MILLOLETTA 3 b.f. Mill Reef 141–Aureoletta 118 (Aureole 132) (1979 NR 1980 10f4 10s* 10s 10s* 12.2f2 14g4 12f 12s2 14s) small, light-framed filly; second foal; half-sister to French 1½m seller winner Admiral Thatch (by Thatch); dam third in Oaks but became most disappointing; successful in minor event at Nottingham in June (odds on) and handicap at Newmarket following month; apprentice ridden, ran on strongly to beat Lorentino 1½ lengths in latter; ran creditably several subsequent outings; stays 1¾m; acts well on soft going and isn't at her best on firm; sweated up sixth start; game. *B. Hills.* **95**

MILLS AHEAD 3 b.c. Sallust 134–Tackaway 77 (Hard Tack 111 §) (1979 6f 6fg 6g 6g3 7fg* 7f 1980 8d3 7fg) strong, compact colt; fair third to Sterling Bank in handicap at Doncaster in March; stays 1m; often blinkered; not seen out after May. *C. Brittain.* **—**

MILLS HIGH 2 b.f. High Top 131–Iona 92 (Kalydon 122) (1980 6f 6fg3 7g) Jan 14; 7,400Y; small, fair sort; first foal; dam won twice over 1¾m; close up 5f when third of 14 behind 10-length winner Tina's Pet in maiden race at Yarmouth in August; moved badly to start and made little show in another maiden race at Yarmouth the following month; bred to stay 1¼m+. *C. Brittain.* **76**

MILTON DIVER 2 br.c. Runnymede 123–Premier Bond 90 (Good Bond 122) (1980 6g 6f) May 20; well-made, attractive colt; has bad hocks; first foal; dam stayed 1m well; behind in newcomers event at Goodwood and £2,000 seller at Newmarket in the autumn. *G. Lewis.* **—**

MINDBLOWING 3 br.f. Pongee 106–Forlorn Leap (Forlorn River 124) (1979 5s 5g 6fg3 5g2 5fg* 5fg2 5fg3 5g4 1980 5s3 5f 5fg 5f4 6fg 7fg4 7d3 7f 7.3fg) leggy, light-framed filly; quite a moderate handicapper; stays 7f; acts on any going; blinkered third start; sweated up on reappearance; trained by N. Adam first 6 outings. *R. Boss.* **67**

MINE OF GOLD 3 b.f. Gold Rod 129–Mary Mine 102 (Infatuation 129) (1979 6fg 1980 8f 8f2 8h 8fg2 8d2 9g2 8fg 8f3 10f) workmanlike filly; poor mover; plater; stays 9f; probably acts on any going; often wears bandages; has run respectably for a boy. *P. Asquith.* **50**

MINER'S LAMP 3 b.c. High Top 131–Coal Face 61 (Kalydon 122) (1979 6d 7fg 1980 8s* 8.5g* 9f* 10f3 8fg 8g2 8d* 8g*) strong, attractive colt; good **114**

Rose of York Handicap, York—Miner's Lamp (left) catches Darwood on the line. Behind are (left to right) Black Minstrel, Northleach, Be Better and Crown Witness

mover; had a very good year and developed into a smart performer, winning maiden race at Warwick, minor event at Epsom, 2 handicaps at York and Group 3 Oettingen-Rennen at Baden-Baden; led in last stride to beat Darwood in Rose of York Handicap on seventh start in August (hung quite badly left) and ran on gamely to lead well inside last furlong and account for Peloponnes by a neck at Baden-Baden following month; also ran well in William Hill Gold Cup (Handicap) at Redcar, going down by 1½ lengths to Carpet General; best form at up to 9f (apprentice ridden, pulled hard early on when tried at 1¼m); acts on any going; not the easiest of rides; sent to USA. *B. Hills.*

MINES BOY 3 ch.g. Gallo Gallante 96–Waterbeck (Weathercock 96) (1979 5s4 5d3 5v 5fg* 5fg4 6f* 5fg3 1980 8fg 7fg) strong gelding; plater; well beaten at 3 yrs; stays 6f; suited by a firm surface and ran badly only outing on heavy; sold 1,000 gns Doncaster August Sales. *J. Berry.* —

MINIBANK 2 b.c. Saritamer 130–Tilt Guard 75 (Crepello 136) (1980 5.1f 5g 6d2 6s 6g) Mar 3; 5,200Y; good-topped, workmanlike colt; half-brother to 2 winning sprinters, including Banking Coyne (by Deep Diver); dam ran only 3 times; 8 lengths second of 5 to odds-on Odin's Raven in minor event at Chester in August, best effort; stays 6f; dwelt when blinkered fourth outing. *C. Brittain.* 71

MINIGOLD 10 br.g. Goldhill 125–Minette 90 (Flush Royal 127) (1979 7g3 8g* 10f 10f 10f 1980 9.6fg 10g3 8fg2 7g4) plater; effective at 6f and stays 1¼m; acts on any going; often wears bandages; has worn blinkers. *A. Davison.* 40

MINMAX 2 b.c. Record Run 127–Paddy's Tickle (Shooting Chant) (1980 5fg 5f4 5fg 6g4 7fg2 7f2 7.6f2 7d4 7g2) Mar 25; 1,900F, 2,100Y; leggy, good-topped colt; second foal; dam unraced; didn't manage to win but made the frame in most races, including in nurseries; went down by a neck to Go Leasing in 17-runner nursery at Leicester in November on final start; will stay 1m; probably acts on any going; consistent; suitable mount for an apprentice. *P. K. Mitchell.* 84

MINSDEN'S IMAGE 2 gr.f. Dancer's Image–Ellida (Crepello 136) (1980 7g4 7s2 8d3) Apr 28; 26,000Y; useful-looking filly; half-sister to 3 winners, including very useful 1979 French 2-y-o 1m winner Elliodor (by Lyphard) and fairly useful middle-distance performer Ellidiana (by Great Nephew); dam, winner over 2m in Ireland, is sister to Busted; placed in maiden races, failing by only a short head to wear down Countess Olivia after losing a fair bit of ground at start at Ayr in September; will be suited by 1¼m; acts on soft going; blinkered third outing. *J. W. Watts.* 78

MINSTREL'S LODGE 3 gr.g. Habat 127–Forever 68 (Never Say Die 137) (1979 NR 1980 10s 10fg 8g) deep-girthed gelding; half-brother to 3 winners, notably Dante Stakes winner Hobnob (by Gyr); dam, half-sister to 2,000 Guineas third Balustrade, stayed 1m; in rear in maiden races; sold 1,200 gns Newmarket Autumn Sales. *L. Cumani.* —

MINTESSA 2 ch.f. Politico 124–Bovick 75 (Compensation 127) (1980 5f 5d 8fg) May 12; fair sort; first foal; dam won sellers from 6f to 1¼m; plater; will stay 1½m. *M. W. Easterby.* —

MINUS MAN 2 br.g. Firestreak 125–Cheb's Honour 70 (Chebs Lad 120) (1980 6s 6g 6s) Apr 16; lengthy gelding; fair sort; second foal; dam placed over 5f at 2 yrs; apprentice ridden when behind in large fields at Haydock (seller), Newmarket and Doncaster (maiden races) at the back end. *W. Holden.* —

MINWIN 5 ch.m. Murrayfield 119–Charlatana 75 (Dumbarnie 125) (1979 NR 1980 10.1fg 12f 8s3 8g 7.6g 8.2d 8fg 10.8d) compact mare; plater; suited by 1m; acts on soft ground; sweating fifth start (tailed off). *J. Spearing.* —

MIPURDU 3 br.c. Perdu 121–Mim-Joa 56 (Welsh Abbot 131) (1979 5f 5g 5fg 5g 5f 5s4 1980 5g 6s 5s 5g 8g 8fg 8s) fair sort; quite moderate (rated 74) at 2 yrs; well beaten in handicaps and maiden events in 1980; should stay 6f; possibly needs some give in the ground; trained by J. Haine first 3 starts. *Mrs J. Pitman.* —

MIRACLE BABY 2 b.f. Workboy 123–Ma's Baby 90 (Ashford Lea 95) (1980 5fg4 5g* 6fg) May 10; leggy, lightly-made filly; first foal; dam at her best at 2 yrs when winner twice over 5f; kept on gamely to win 11-runner maiden race at Pontefract in July by ½ length from Carnation; looked a bit lean when remote sixth to Solway Winds in minor event at Redcar later in month; not sure to stay 6f. *M. H. Easterby.* 65

MIRACLE BID 5 ch.g. Miracle 116–Sun Mat 99 (Matador 131) (1979 6s 6g 6g 5fg 7g 6g2 1980 5d 5fg) plater; stays 6f; acts on any going; best in blinkers. *J. H. Peacock.* —

Andy Capp Handicap, Redcar—Mirror Boy (left) challenges Fine Sun and quickly draws clear. The blinkered No Faith is third

MIRANDA ROCK 3 b.f. Andrea Mantegna–Petite Rock (Goldhill 125) (1979 NR 1980 10fg 10.6d 10s) 300F, 800Y; second foal; half-sister to winning hurdler Demi Rock (by Double-U-Jay); dam 9f winner; behind in maiden races. *S. Holland.* —

MIRROR BOY 3 ch.c. Pieces of Eight 128–Knocknashee 70 (Astec 128) (1979 6f 6g 7d^3 7fg^3 8.2g 8.2s^2 7d* 1980 8v 7f 10.2fg* 10g* 10g^2 12s* 13.3d^2 12g^2 13.3fg 12d^2 12v) well-made colt; useful handicapper; ridden by 5-lb claimer J. Blanks to win apprentice event at Bath, Andy Capp Handicap at Redcar (decisively beat Fine Sun $1\frac{1}{2}$ lengths) and £2,100 race at Lingfield; ran creditably most starts afterwards, notably when neck second to Castle Keep in Morland Brewery Trophy at Newbury on seventh outing; will stay $1\frac{3}{4}$m; suited by some give in the ground; consistent; ran as though something was wrong with him final outing; ran poorly in blinkers fifth start at 2 yrs. *R. Price.* **108**

MIRTHFUL 3 b or br.f. Will Somers 114 **§**–French Line 98 (Set Fair 129) (1979 6fg 6f^3 6fg 7g 7fg^2 8g^3 8g 1980 8g 10fg^4 9fg 10.6d 7.6d 7.2g^3 7g 6fg 8.2s 7s^2 6d) sturdy filly; best form at up to 1m; acts on any going; sometimes wears blinkers; suitable mount for a boy. *W. Elsey.* **61**

MISHOU L'AMOUR 2 b.c. Royal Palace 131–First Watch (Primera 131) (1980 8d 8d) May 18; workmanlike colt; half-brother to Irish 3-y-o 9f winner Cindy's Spec (by Shantung) and a winning hurdler; dam once-raced half-sister to dam of 1,000 Guineas winner Nocturnal Spree; showed ability in maiden races at Edinburgh (sixth of 11 to Savile Park) and Warwick (seventh of 16 to Rosie Black); will stay $1\frac{1}{4}$m; sold 5,400 gns Ascot December Sales. *R. Boss.* **66**

MISLED 2 b.f. Gilded Leader 75–Oaklands Miss (The Poacher) (1980 8f) Apr 26; light-framed non-thoroughbred filly; fourth known foal; dam never ran; moved poorly to start and came back tailed off in maiden race won by Cinderwench at Wolverhampton in September. *K. Bridgwater.* —

MISS ADMINGTON 4 gr.f. Double Jump 131–Solly Graham 82 (Romulus 129) (1979 6f 7.2fg 8f 8g 10.8g 8fg 7fg 10h 8.2fg 1980 7fg 10s^4 10.2g 10g 10g 11g^2 9d 12fg 12f 10fg^4 12d^4 12.5s) neat filly; plating-class maiden; probably stays $1\frac{1}{2}$m. *R. Hollinshead.* **37**

MISS AYTON 4 b.f. Firestreak 125–French Salute (Salvo 129) (1979 9g 1980 8.2fg 8g) of no account. *R. Allan.* —

MISS BARNABY 3 ch.f. Sun Prince 128–Meli (Acropolis 132) (1979 7.2fg 6g 7fg 8g^3 1980 8f^4 9.4fg^2 12g^3 12g 13g^2 12.3fg 12.2g* 12.2fg 12s) strong filly; favourite, won maiden race at Catterick in August; stays 13f; acts on a firm surface; has run creditably for an apprentice; ran very freely in blinkers eighth outing. *M. H. Easterby.* **67**

MISS BASSEY 2 b.f. Saritamer 130–Belinda Pocket 84 (Pampered King 121) (1980 5fg 5s 5.8f) Feb 20; half-sister to two 2-y-o winners; dam won over 5f at 2 yrs; blinkered when moderate sixth of 14 to E For Easy in seller at Bath in July, third outing; sold 440 gns Ascot August Sales. *A. Johnson.* —

MISS BEAMISH 2 ch.f. Hornet 116–My Sheroka (pedigree unknown) (1980 5g 5g) neat non-thoroughbred filly; in rear in maiden races in the Midlands in April and June. *D. Weeden.* —

MISS BURGLAR 3 ch.f. Burglar 128–Florabette (Floribunda 136) (1979 6fg 6g 7s 1980 7g) unimpressive-looking filly; bad maiden. *J. Mulhall.* —

MISS BUSHBY 4 b.f. King's Leap 111–Tommie (Final Score 113) (1979 5d 7g³ 5f* 5f⁴ 5f² 5f 5s 6s 1980 5g 5f* 5fg⁴ 6g 5f) leggy, fair sort; plater; attracted no bid after winning at Thirsk in April; creditable fourth to Bri-Eden in handicap at Edinburgh in July; best form at 5f; acts on hard going; blinkered final outing. *J. Fitzgerald.* **49**

MISS CHESSY 2 ch.f. Swing Easy 126–Tassel (Ragusa 137) (1980 5v² 5g³ 5g² 5f² 5f² 6g³ 6d 5d³ 5fg 6s⁴) May 10; 880Y; lightly-made filly; fourth foal; dam ran only at 3 yrs; placed in maiden and minor events; having first race for over 2 months when 3½ lengths third of 12 to Mel's Choice at Hamilton in September, eighth outing; runs as though 7f will suit her; acts on any going. *J. Berry.* **65**

MISS CINDY 5 br.m. Mansingh 120–Iridium 78 (Linacre 133) (1979 5s 7fg 7f 7f* 7f* 7fg 8g 7f* 7.2g⁴ 7f⁴ 8h² 7fg 7g 1980 6f 7g 7g 7fg 7f² 7f 7fg⁴) useful-looking mare; ran best races when in frame at Beverley in August and Catterick (started slowly) in September; stays 1m; needs a firm surface; has worn blinkers. *J. Etherington.* **65**

MISS CLOUDY 5 b.m. Saintly Song 128–Cloudy (Nyrcos 130) (1979 NR 1980 12.2fg 10f 16g) of no account. *W. Elsey.* —

MISS CORABELLE 2 b.f. Record Run 127–Farafa (Sing Sing 134) (1980 5d 6d 5d 5s) Mar 17; half-sister to Quarry Girl, successful in 5f seller in 1979, and to 6f and 7f winner Quarry Bank (both by Be Friendly); dam never ran; poor plater; sold 320 gns Doncaster November Sales. *S. Nesbitt.* —

MISS COUTURE 3 br.f. Tamerlane 128–Tragara (Buisson Ardent 129) (1979 NR 1980 7f 8fg 8fg 10.2g 16fg 16s 13.8fg* 13.8d) 1,500F, 4,000Y, resold 4,600Y; sister to fair sprinter Elton Abbess and half-sister to quite useful but temperamental 1973 2-y-o Bill The Black (by Levmoss); bought in 2,000 gns after winning 16-runner seller at Catterick in September by a wide margin; stays 1¾m; acts on a firm surface; blinkered fifth start; trained first 6 starts by T. Molony. *J. W. Watts.* **59**

MISS CYPRUS 2 b.f. Auction Ring 123–Skyway 76 (Skymaster 126) (1980 5fg 5h² 5.3d 5s³ 5g 5d 5g) Mar 15; 5,200Y; sturdy filly; sixth foal; sister to quite moderate Flying Bid; dam won over 1¼m; beaten a fair way when placed in 3-runner £2,100 event at Folkestone in May and 15-runner maiden race at Warwick in July and is only plating class; blinkered seventh start. *A. Demetriou.* **63**

MISS DAVENPORT 5 b.m. Shiny Tenth 120–Carina 98 (Tamerlane 128) (1979 14fg 8f 9g 1980 6d 8fg) of little account. *K. Ivory.* —

MISS DIAWARD 3 b.f. Supreme Sovereign 119–Gay Pretendre (Pretendre 126) (1979 NR 1980 8g 8g³ 10g⁴ 8.2g² 9s³ 9d³ 12d*) 1,900F, 5,800Y; quite attractive, lengthy filly; good walker; second foal; sister to a poor animal; dam never ran; placed in maiden races prior to winning valuable selling handicap at Doncaster in October (sold 2,600 gns afterwards); stays 1½m; yet to race on a firm surface; has run creditably for an apprentice. *B. Hills.* **75**

MISS DOULTON 3 ch.f. Weepers Boy 124–Fair Saint 79 (Bleep-Bleep 134) (1979 5fg 5fg³ 5s 1980 6fg 7g 8g 7fg 8g 6g) compact filly; poor plater; not certain to stay 7f; has been tried in blinkers. *C. James.* —

MISSED BLESSING 3 b.f. So Blessed 130–Miss By Miles 91 (Milesian 125) (1979 6g* 1980 7.3fg 8.5g² 8fg⁴ 8fg 7.3d² 7f³ 8fg* 7g³) lengthy filly; has a round action; second foal; dam genuine miler; smart performer; carrying 10-0 and outstandingly pick of paddock, beat Hide The Key in good style by 1½ lengths in £7,600 handicap at Ascot in September; had earlier run well to be runner-up in Princess Elizabeth Stakes at Epsom in April (went down by a neck to stable-companion Bay Street after hanging left in final furlong) and Hungerford Stakes at Newbury in August (kept on when beaten ¾ length by impressive winner Kampala); creditable length third to easy winner Moorestyle **115**

Tote Charity Stakes Handicap, Ascot—a fine weight-carrying performance by Missed Blessing who is clear of Hide The Key and Miss Raffles

in Bisquit Cognac Challenge Stakes at Newmarket in October; stays 1m well; acts on a firm and a soft surface; moved freely to start third outing; genuine. *F. J. Houghton.*

MISSELLY 2 gr. or ro.f. Linacre 133–Paddys Choice (Runnymede 123) (1980 7fg 5g 5f 7d 5s) May 19; 300Y; small, lengthy filly; first foal; dam won twice over 5f in Ireland; of no account. *T. Kersey.* –

MISS FALCON 4 br.f. King's Company 124–Grannie Boyd 67 (Linacre 133) (1979 8.2v³ 8g 8s⁴ 8.2d³ 6g 6d 1980 7v 6h 7f 6g 6f) lightly-made filly; stays 1m; probably acts on any going, but goes well in the mud; blinkered fourth start; sold to R. Cambidge 500 gns Doncaster October Sales. *M. Camacho.* –

MISS FRESHNESS 2 gr.f. Grey Mirage 128–Valiant Victress (Nulli Secundus 89) (1980 6f) Apr 7; eighth foal; dam never ran; unquoted when last but one in 17-runner minor event won by Flash 'N' Fire at Redcar in September. *E. Carter.* –

MISS FYLDE WASTE 2 b.f. Saulingo 122–Izbel 74 (Zeus Boy 121) (1980 5d) 260Y; half-sister to 1973 2-y-o 5f winner Dark Diver (by Golden Dipper) and a winner abroad; dam apparently of little account; behind in seller won by Sedona at Catterick in October; sold 290 gns Doncaster November Sales. *W. Wright.* –

MISS GAYLORD 3 b.f. Cavo Doro 124–Sea Pearl 75 (Sea Hawk II 131) (1979 5d 5g 7fg 8fg³ 1980 10g 11.7s 10.1d³ 16.9f) light-framed, narrow filly; plater; stays 1¼m; acts on a firm and a soft surface. *B. Gubby.* –

MISS GENEROUS 3 b.f. Bronze Hill 96–Generous Device 69 (Bounteous 125) (1979 NR 1980 10fg 10g 12f²) strong filly; fourth reported foal; dam best at 1m; kept on well to be second in modest 9-runner maiden event at Beverley in August, best effort; suited by 1½m; acts on firm going. *M. Camacho.* **57**

MISS GING 2 ch.f. Bay Express 132–Indolent 97 (Tyrone 130) (1980 5g) Mar 10; 10,500Y; big, strong filly; half-sister to 3 winners, including useful Irish 6f to 1¼m winner Slow March (by Queen's Hussar); dam won at up to 11f; 20/1 and in need of run, stayed on without being given a hard time when remote fourteenth of 26 to Nasseem in maiden race at Salisbury in June, only outing. *A. Breasley.* –

MISS GLANCY 2 gr. or ro.f. Wollow 132–Silecia (Sky Gipsy 117) (1980 6g 5g 5f 5g 6g) May 9; 8,600Y; small, light-framed filly; second living foal; half-sister to Irish 9f winner Maychild (by Swinging Junior), subsequently successful abroad; dam never ran; fifth in sizeable fields of maidens on second and third outings; subsequently well beaten in sellers, wearing blinkers on fifth start. *P. Haslam.* **63**

MISS HAGEN 2 ch.f. Mount Hagen 127–Laikipia 89 (St Paddy 133) (1980 5g 6g 7d 6f 5d) Mar 27; 5,800Y; short-backed filly; fifth foal; dam placed at up to 7f; well beaten in all races, including a Catterick seller; blinkered fifth outing. *S. Norton.* –

MISS HARTNELL 6 ch.m. Ballymoss 136–Guernavaca 46 (Klairon 131) 50
(1979 7d 7.6v 6d^3 6g 6fg 5fg 6d 1980 6f* 6h* 6fg 6s 6d* 7fg^3 5f 6s) quite a moderate handicapper; did well, winning seller (bought in 1,350 gns) at Pontefract and apprentice handicaps at Folkestone and Leicester; effective at 6f and stays 9f; appears to act on any going; has been tried in blinkers; off course 2 months before final start. *P. Makin.*

MISS HIPPOLYTA 3 b.f. High Line 125–Imperial Stake (Sovereign Lord 120) 65
(1979 7fg^4 8f^2 9fg^2 7g 1980 10fg 12fg 9f^3 8.5f 10.2fg^3 10.8fg* 7fg 10f 10.1g 10fg^3 12g 11.7d) neat filly; won 7-runner apprentice handicap at Warwick in July; stays 11f; acts on firm going. *G. Balding.*

MISS HONEYPENNY 4 ch.f. Good Bond 122–Maureen's Honey 93 (Taste of 53
Honey 92) (1979 8d 8s^3 10.2fg^2 10fg 10g^4 8.2g^4 12d* 10g 10.2s^2 1980 12s 12.2s 13g^3 16fg 16.1d 16.5g^4 16s) leggy, very lightly-made filly; stays 13f but not 2m; suited by some give in the ground. *D. Weeden.*

MISS IMPORT 2 ch.f. Import 127–Chinese Falcon 81 (Skymaster 126) (1980 58
5g 5f) May 20; workmanlike filly; first foal; dam 2-y-o 6f winner; fairly prominent in maiden races at Catterick and Beverley (6½ lengths fifth of 19 to Salamina) in August; should stay 6f. *T. Barron.*

MISSISSIPI SHUFFLE 3 b.f. Steel Heart 128–Merry Madcap 124 (Grey Sov- 78
ereign 128 §) (1979 6g^3 5.8g^3 7fg 1980 6f 5fg^4 5d 6s^2 5s* 5g^2 6fg* 5f 6s 6d) useful-looking filly; fair handicapper; successful at Windsor in July and Yarmouth in August (had very hard race); isn't bred to stay 7f; probably acts on any going but seems well suited by soft; blinkered third (hung left), fourth and eighth starts. *P. Cole.*

MISSIVE (FR) 3 ch.f. Bold Lad (USA)–Miss Monde (Cadmus 124) (1979 NR 55
1980 8f^3) 25,000 francs Y (approx £3,000), 600 2-y-o; third foal; half-sister to a French 1¼m seller winner (by Gift Card); dam, from very good family, won small 9.5f race; not seen out after finishing ½-length third of 12 to Hornet's Nest in moderate maiden race at Carlisle in May; stays 1m. *J. Fitzgerald.*

MISS KUWAIT 3 b.f. The Brianstan 128–Dry Island 73 (Miralgo 130) (1979 6d 46
6fg 6f^4 7d 7fg 8.2d 7.2d 1980 8v^3 8fg^4 10fg^2 9f* 8f 12fg 10g 13.8f^3 12d^3 8f^4 12g 13.8fg) plater; won at Ripon in May (no bid); possibly stays 1¾m; seems to act on any going; has worn blinkers. *J. Fitzgerald.*

MISS LAUSIENNE 4 b.f. Lauso–Tackienne (Hard Tack 111 §) (1979 8.2g 10s^4 56
1980 12.5v 10fg 10h^2 12.3d 13.8f* 13g^3 15.8g) plater; won handicap at Catterick in July by 3 lengths from Native Break; suited by a test of stamina; acts on hard going. *G. Lockerbie.*

MISS LIGHTENING 3 ch.f. Winden 109–Thundersquall 109 (Roi de Navarre –
II 123) (1979 NR 1980 11.7f) half-sister to a winner in Malaya; dam stayer; in rear in 18-runner maiden race at Bath in May. *D. Elsworth.*

MISS LOUISE 3 b.f. Virginia Boy 106–Chetim (Arctic Time 127) (1979 7s –
1980 8fg 8s 10.2g 9.4fg 13.8d^4 11s) big, strong filly; poor plater; has worn bandages; sold 550 gns Doncaster October Sales. *C. Thornton.*

MISS LOVE 3 ch.f. Ragstone 128–What's Left (Remainder 106) (1979 –
NR 1980 9f 12d 12d 16.9d 8f) leggy filly; fourth foal; dam won over 7f and 1m; no signs of ability in maiden and minor events. *M. Tate.*

MISS MATEY 2 b.f. Streetfighter 120–Carmoni Queen 71 (Quisling 117) –
(1980 5s 5f 5h) Apr 26; 500Y; bad plater; has worn blinkers; sold 390 gns Doncaster May Sales. *J. Berry.*

MISS MENTON 2 b.f. Brigadier Gerard 144–Miss Monaco 107 (Crepello 136) 88
(1980 6g 6s*) Apr 5; leggy filly; second foal; dam, a sprinter, at her best at 2 yrs; ran on strongly in last furlong and a half to win 12-runner minor event at Stockton in October by 2½ lengths from Perlesse; had previously finished 9 lengths sixth of 10 to Shasavaan in Duke of Edinburgh Stakes at Ascot in October; will stay 1m; struck us as immature at 2 yrs and may well improve further in 1981. *W. Hastings-Bass.*

MISS MERLIN 4 ch.f. Manacle 123–Pally Lass 90 (Palestine 133) (1979 51
7s 5s 6g 5fg 7fg 6g* 6g 5fg^3 5g 1980 5s 6g 6f^2 6g^4 5fg 5f^4 6g) quite a moderate sprint handicapper; best form at up to 6f; seems to act on any going. *J. Benstead.*

MISS METRO 3 b.f. Upper Case–Pilgrim Soul 89 (Tudor Melody 129) (1979 62
5d 6g 7fg 5fg 1980 5f 7f 8.5f^4 10.1g 8g^4 10fg 9s) big, well-made filly; only

plating class; should stay 1¼m; sold 1,050 gns Ascot November Sales. *W. Wightman.*

MISS MIDNIGHT 2 b.f. Brittany–Miss Pat (Pinturischio 116) (1980 8d 8d) May 18; 380 2-y-o; narrow filly; sixth foal; dam lightly-raced half-sister to Cesarewitch winner Mintmaster; soundly beaten in end-of-season maiden races at Warwick and Leicester. *G. Fletcher.* –

MISS MINEFIELD 3 b.f. Northfields–Bombshell 76 (Le Levanstell 122) (1979 6f 7.5f² 7f 7f 7fg 1980 8v 6d³ 6f 11g⁴ 9.4d⁴ 12d 10g 8.2g 12g⁴ 10d* 8.2d 11s) neat ex-Irish filly; won poor maiden race at Ayr in August (apprentice ridden); stays 1¼m; probably acts on any going; sold 12,000 gns Newmarket December Sales. *Denys Smith.* **50**

MISS MIRABELLE 4 br.f. Miracle 116–La Belle 118 (Vilmorin) (1979 8fg 7f 8fg 8fg³ 7f 7d² 7s* 7g* 6d 1980 7f 7g 7f 7g 7fg) sturdy filly; didn't run up to her best in 1980 and found little off bridle final start; stays 1m; acts on any going but seems well suited by some give in the ground. *G. Pritchard-Gordon.* –

MISS MOPS 4 br.f. Saulingo 122–Arcticanute 69 (Hardicanute 130) (1979 8g 8d 8fg 7fg 7d³ 8fg 8.2g 8d 1980 8s³ 8g 10fg³ 10f³ 10d 13.3f 10g² 10s) poor plater; hung left in final furlong when runner-up to Ravensbourne at Pontefract in August; stays 1¼m; seems to act on any going; blinkered final start at 3 yrs; sold 775 gns Ascot August Sales. *E. Carter.* **40**

MISS MURTON 2 b.f. Mummy's Pet 125–Murton Crags 81 (No Argument 107) (1980 5s² 5s³ 5s* 5f² 5h³ 7f 7g⁴ 7fg 6d² 6s) Apr 13; 3,000F, 2,500Y; neat filly; second foal; dam stayed 13f; bought in 3,400 gns after winning 8-runner seller at Newcastle in April; creditable second to Wyn Miluv in selling nursery at Brighton in September, ninth outing; stays 7f; seems to act on any going. *P. Haslam.* **67**

MISS NELSKI 3 ch.f. Most Secret 119–Nelski 83 (Skymaster 126) (1979 5g 5s 5g³ 5fg 5f⁴ 5g* 5fg* 5g² 5fg 5g 1980 5s 5d 5d³ 5v) small, strong filly; sprint handicapper; acts on a firm and a soft surface; usually wears blinkers; didn't impress in paddock final start; sold 520 gns Doncaster November Sales. *J. Etherington.* **75**

MISS NEUSTRIE 3 br.f. Roi Dagobert 128–Miss Segula (Nashua) (1979 6f 1980 8f² 10g² 12g 10fg* 10.1g² 10g² 12s) lengthy, very attractive filly; good mover; very easy winner of 13-runner maiden race at Yarmouth in August; runner-up on 4 of her other starts in varied company; appears not to stay 1½m; possibly unsuited by soft going; didn't act too well on sharp Thirsk track first outing. *M. Stoute.* **84**

MISS NINIAN 2 gr.f. The Go-Between 129–Sevantha 80 (Henry the Seventh 125) (1980 5fg 6fg³) Mar 3; 520F, 700Y; lightly-made, unfurnished filly; third foal; sister to a poor plater and half-sister to a winner in Norway by Sahib; dam ran only twice; nearest finish when 4½ lengths third of 6 to Friendly Falcon in auction seller at Pontefract in June; not seen out again. *W. Bentley.* **59**

MISS OAKLEA 3 b.f. Panama Canal 105–Quick Return (The Bo'sun 114) (1979 5f 1980 10.1fg) behind in maiden and minor events. *P. Mitchell.* –

MISS POINCIANA 3 b. or br.f. Averof 123–Miss Twomey (Will Somers 114§) (1979 5s 6fg 1980 7fg 7g 6g³ 5fg³ 6d² 5fg 5f³ 5d) strong filly; poor maiden; best form at 6f; probably acts on any going; often sweats up; sold 580 gns Doncaster November Sales. *M. Camacho.* **51**

MISS POLLY PECK 4 b.f. March Past 124–Headliner (Pampered King 121) (1979 7.6v 1980 10.1s 10.1d) leggy, light-framed filly; of little account. *A. Davison.* –

MISS POPPY 3 b.f. Lord Gayle 124–Linbel (Linacre 133) (1979 6g 6g 7g 7fg 7f 7d 1980 12h* 12.2fg² 12g) neat, lightly-made filly; plater; won at Thirsk in May (no bid); stays 1½m; acts on hard going. *J. Fitzgerald.* **52**

MISS PUCCI 2 br.f. So Blessed 130–Italian Idol (Sheshoon 132) (1980 5fg 7g 7g 7d) Apr 13; 6,500Y; strong, useful sort; has a round action; fourth foal; dam middle-distance winner in French Provinces; soundly beaten in maiden and minor races, final one at Catterick. *M. W. Easterby.* –

MISS PUDGE 5 b.m. Green God 128–Carnival Park (Carnival Dancer 113) (1979 5d 5s 6g* 6f 7.6f 6f 6h 8fg* 6fg⁴ 7.2g 6g* 6g* 6d 1980 6.3s⁴ 6.3d* 6fg) strong, compact, good-bodied mare; fairly useful sprinter at 4 yrs when trained by D. Francis; successful in 1980 in July Scurry Handicap at the Curragh, beating **81**

Nous by 3 lengths; behind in Spillers Stewards' Cup at Goodwood later in month on only subsequent outing; stayed 1m but was best at around 6f; probably acted on any going; sometimes sweated up; often gave trouble in preliminaries in England but won several times for apprentice N. Vaughan; sold in foal to Thatching, 42,000 gns Newmarket December Sales. *J. Hassett, Ireland.*

MISS QUAVER 2 b.f. Averof 123–Quick Burn 94 (Carnival Dancer 113) **85** (1980 5s^2 5d* 5fg* 5fg*) Apr 8; close-coupled, sharp sort; good mover; fourth foal; dam winning sister to smart sprinter Ubedizzy; in very good form early on and ran on well under pressure to win maiden race at Kempton and minor events at Folkestone and Brighton in April, all by less than a length, on last-named course getting home by a short head from Red Russet; seems to act on any going; genuine. *R. Hannon.*

MISS RAFFLES 3 br.f. Green God 128–Saint Mildred 89 (Saint Crespin III **82** 132) (1979 5s 5fg 7fg 6s 5f^4 5d 6g^3 1980 7d* 8.5g* 10.2f 8fg^3 8fg^4 8.3s^3 7f^2 7g* 7fg 8f^4 8fg^3 8.2d^2 8s*) compact filly; won valuable seller at Kempton in April (bought in 2,100 gns); subsequently showed herself better than a plater, winning handicaps at Epsom, Yarmouth and Newmarket; beat Intinto a short head in last-named in October; stays 1m but isn't certain to stay 1¼m; acts on any going; ran well in blinkers penultimate outing; genuine and consistent. *P. Haslam.*

MISS REDMARSHALL 3 ch.f. Most Secret 119–Miss Marvel 59 (Palestine 133) **76** (1979 5g 5f 6fg* 5f 6g^2 6d^2 6fg 6f^3 6s* 1980 5s^4 6d^2 5g^3 5g^2 5g^2(dis) 5d* 6g^2 5f^4 5d 5fg*) plater at 2 yrs; showed improved form in handicaps in 1980, winning apprentice events at Redcar and Beverley (made all) in the summer; also first past post at Redcar on fifth start but was disqualified for bumping second; stays 6f but gives impression she is better at 5f nowadays; probably acts on any going; often blinkered; suitable mount for a claimer. *J. Mason.*

MISS RELIANT 3 ch.f. Reliance II 137–Miss McLairon 96 (Klairon 131) **65** (1979 NR 1980 14.7g* 16.1g 15d 16g) leggy, unfurnished filly; half-sister to quite useful middle-distance performer Claironcita (by Don Carlos); dam won over 6f at 2 yrs; stayed on strongly to win modest maiden event at Redcar in August; well beaten in handicaps afterwards, looking most unimpressive in paddock and being pulled up on final occasion; stays well. *J. W. Watts.*

MISS SABRINA 2 b.f. Simbir 130–Mistrust (Rustam 127) (1980 7f 7g 7fg) – Mar 21; half-sister to several winners, including useful 1971 2-y-o 5f winner Pollster (by Majority Blue); dam raced only at 2 yrs; well behind in maiden races but was very backward on first 2 outings. *B. Swift.*

MISS SHIFTER 3 b.f. Realm 129–Sumintra 82 (El Gallo 122) (1979 NR – 1980 6s 7fg 6f 6s 5.3fg 6fg) 4,600F, 2,000Y; lengthy, lightly-made filly; sister to quite useful 1979 Irish sprinter Concordia, and half-sister to fairly useful 7f to 9f winner Aljo (by Status Seeker); dam sprint maiden; well beaten in maiden races and handicaps; trained by J. Sutcliffe first 3 starts. *P. K. Mitchell.*

MISS SMITH 4 b.f. Red Alert 127–Golden Pumpkin 86 (Monet 127) (1979 5s – 9g 1980 8g) ex-Irish filly; poor maiden. *R. Page.*

MISS SOLO POWER (USA) 3 b.f. Solo Landing–Fillypower (Chieftain) – (1979 5.1fg 5g 6g^2 5f 1980 5h 7f 6fg 5g) has shown no form since 2 yrs; better suited by 6f than 5f, and should stay 7f; sweated up second outing. *P. Read, Isle of Man.*

MISS SOMENAME 3 br.f. Swing Easy 126–Cavally (Major Portion 129) – (1979 NR 1980 8s 8f 8fg) 6,200Y; useful sort; half-sister to 2 winners, including 1¼m winner Caranx (by Double Jump); dam never ran; in rear in maiden and minor races; not raced after May. *J. Sutcliffe.*

MISS ST JAMES'S 2 b.f. Sovereign Path 125–Miss London 95 (Pall Mall 132) **92** (1980 6s 6g^2 6fg* 6d^3 7d*) Apr 18; well-grown filly; sister to 5f and 7f winner Miss Knightsbridge, closely related to 1979 2-y-o 5f winner Wolverina (by Wolver Hollow) and half-sister to 2 winners; dam stayed 1m; successful in maiden race at Carlisle in September and in nursery at Doncaster in October, latter by a neck from Supreme Fjord; may well stay 1m; acts on a firm and a soft surface. *M. Stoute.*

MISS ST MAWES 2 b.f. Derring-Do 131–Terre Promise (Soderini 123) (1980 **86** 6g^2 6g^4 6g* 6d^3) Feb 21; leggy filly; third living foal; half-sister to minor winners in France and USA; dam ran once; won 10-runner maiden race at Yarmouth in August by ½ length from odds-on Melon Patch; good 3½ lengths third of 14 to Piperhill in minor race at Ripon later in month; will stay 1m+. *B. Hobbs.*

MISS SUKI 3 b.f. Upper Case–La Garoupe 87 (Pirate King 129) (1979 5d 5g^4 7g 1980 11fg 12f 12g) good-looking filly; poor maiden; should stay middle distances; blinkered final start; sold to W. Clay 1,000 gns Doncaster September Sales. *C. Brittain.* —

MISS SUPREME 4 gr.f. Supreme Gift 121–Miss Argyle 92 (Mountain Call 125) (1979 8g 7g 6s 7g 7g* 8g 6d^3 6d 8f 7g 1980 7.6d 8g 6fg) leggy, narrow filly; plater; stays 7f; blinkered final outing in 1978; has run creditably for an apprentice. *A. W. Jones.* —

MISS TAYMORE (USA) 3 b. or br.f. Sham–Bend an Oar (Never Bend) (1979 5s^4 5f^2 5h^2 5fg^3 6fg^4 7fg* 7fg^2 1980 8d^3 8f^4 10.5f 10g 8g 7f^4 7s 6d 6fg* 6d*) fair sort; apprentice ridden when successful in handicaps at Redcar (awarded race by stewards) and Stockton in the autumn; beat Deputy $\frac{1}{2}$ length on latter; best form at up to 7f though ran respectably over 1m in Masaka Stakes at Kempton on reappearance; probably acts on any going; takes a good hold; didn't impress in paddock on second outing and ran moderately on fourth. *S. Norton.* **93**

MISS TEDCASTLE 3 ch.f. Hotfoot 126–Once For All (Quorum 126) (1979 6g 6s 7fg 1980 13g 12fg 12d 12g 10s 8d) strong, lengthy filly; useless plater; sold 1,350 gns Newmarket December Sales. *P. Rohan.* —

MISS TOMCA (DEN) 3 b.f. Hornbeam 130–Andalusia (Andalusier) (1979 7d^4 1980 9f) beaten some way in maiden races. *G. Fletcher.* —

MISS TROIA 3 ch.f. Cornuto 111–No Miss (Soueida 111) (1979 NR 1980 16fg) 900Y; second foal; dam of no account; remote tenth in 26-runner amateur riders maiden event at Ascot in September. *J. Old.* —

MISS TWIGGY 2 gr.f. Tycoon II–Golden Herb 80 (Goldhill 125) (1980 5fg 5fg 5fg^3 5fg* 5g^2 5d 5g^4 5f 5f) Mar 23; compact filly; third foal; sister to 1978 2-y-o 5f seller winner Zyppon; dam seemed to stay 1m; didn't stride out at all on way to start of maiden race at Catterick in May but came back much better, winning by $1\frac{1}{2}$ lengths from Texas Ranger; ran creditably in varied company afterwards; will stay 6f; trained by T. Molony first 7 outings. *D. Leslie.* **80**

MISS WOGAN 2 br.f. Sayfar 116–Miss Cornwall 69 (Brother 116) (1980 7g 6fg) Mar 21; small filly; fourth foal; dam poor half-sister to smart jumper Soloning; behind in maiden race at Leicester in August (last of 19) and 28-runner seller at Windsor in September. *D. Leslie.* —

MISS WORTH 2 ch.f. Streak 119–Bodicea (King's Troop 118) (1980 5fg 5fg* 5fg 5d^3 5g 5.3fg* 5fg^4 6g) Mar 7; small, narrow filly; first foal; dam never ran; a fair performer in plating company; won seller at Wolverhampton in April (bought in 1,500 gns) and claiming race at Brighton in August (by $2\frac{1}{2}$ lengths from Lady Acquiesce); should stay 6f (not well drawn when tried at trip); acts on a firm and a soft surface; good mount for an apprentice. *C. James.* **73**

MISTANGUET 2 b. or br.f. Comedy Star 121–Telouet 90 (Sing Sing 134) (1980 5d 5.8h) Mar 14; small filly; half-sister to 3 winners, including useful 1977 2-y-o 5f performer Edna's Choice (by So Blessed) and fairly useful sprinter Derringo (by Derring-Do); dam ran only 4 times; in rear in maiden races at Salisbury in June and Bath (last of 12) in August. *G. Balding.* —

MISTEREFF 3 b.g. Track Spare 125–Ring True 80 (Gulf Pearl 117) (1979 5f 5g 5d 5d 1980 7f 8g 8fg 8d^4 7fg 8g) very small gelding; poor plater; seems to stay 1m. *R. Mason* —

MISTER LUCKY 3 br.g. Royalty 130–Fair Songstress 100 (Compensation 127) (1979 7f 1980 8.2s^2 7f 10f 12f* 10.1g 11g^2 12g 10.2g^4 10fg^2 11.7d^4 10d 12s* 12g) useful sort; won maiden race at Folkestone in June and apprentice event at Chepstow in October; also ran well to go down by a neck to Spanish Dancer in £3,900 handicap at Ascot in September on ninth outing; stays $1\frac{1}{2}$m; acts on any going; suitable mount for a boy. *R. Hannon.* **81**

MISTRESS MAUDE 3 b.f. Welsh Pageant 132–Caer-Gai 103 (Royal Palace 131) (1979 NR 1980 10.2fg) 30,000Y; first foal; dam, a miler, is daughter of 1,000 Guineas winner Caergwrle; out of first 9 of 20 to Gilded Vanity in maiden race at Bath in July. *I. Balding.* —

MISTRESS MEDINA 3 b.f. Averof 123–Miss Robust (Busted 134) (1979 NR 1980 10v^4 8f^3 7f^4 8f^2 6fg 8fg 7fg 8fg* 8g^4 8d* 7g) 4,000Y; small, compact filly; dam never ran; won maiden race at Chepstow in August and handicap at Bath in October; needs further than 6f and should stay $1\frac{1}{4}$m; probably acts on any going; sold 5,200 gns Newmarket December Sales. *H. Candy.* **73**

MISTRESS MOIRA 3 b.f. Scottish Rifle 127–Credo's Daughter (Credo 123) (1979 7fg 8d 1980 10fg 10fg 12fg 12g 15.5fg) neat filly; poor form in maiden and minor races. *S. Woodman.* —

MISTRESS OF TURFAC 2 b.f. Averof 123–Tropical Fruit (Tropique 128) (1980 5fg 6fg 6g 6fg 7fg 8s) Feb 11; lengthy filly; half-sister to several winners here and abroad; poor plater. *J. Holt.* 47

MISTY FANTAN 4 ch.g. Habat 127–Misty Cat (Misty Flight) (1979 6v 6v 7d 7f^2 8fg* 8h 1980 8g) plater; tailed off on only outing of 1980; suited by 1m; acts on firm going. *M. Pipe.* —

MISWAKI (USA) 2 ch.c. Mr Prospector–Hopespringseternal (Buckpasser) (1980 5d* 6fg^2 7g* 7s^3) **124**

Trainer Boutin should have followed his first instincts not to run Miswaki in the William Hill Dewhurst Stakes at Newmarket in October. Having witnessed Storm Bird's highly impressive display in the Larkspur Stakes just a day before Miswaki's narrow win in the much more valuable Prix de la Salamandre, he said he had revised his original intention of sending Miswaki to Newmarket on learning that Storm Bird was a likely runner there. The Grand Criterium was said to be Miswaki's new objective. However, Boutin had another excellent candidate for that race in Cresta Rider, one likely to be better suited by the mile of the Criterium than Miswaki, and Miswaki eventually became one of Storm Bird's four challengers in the Dewhurst, rewarding his connections with the worthwhile third prize of £7,170 but doing nothing to enhance his reputation. Although he raced in behind Storm Bird and To-Agori-Mou for five furlongs, he hadn't helped his cause by pulling hard early on and he was completely unable to stay with them in the closing stages; at the line he was all of eight and a half lengths behind Storm Bird.

This was certainly not the Miswaki who had won one of France's top races for two-year-olds after finishing a close second in another. Possibly the very soft ground was against him at Newmarket but he hadn't been inconvenienced by dead going in the Prix Yacowlef at Deauville in August on his debut, when he left his opponents standing from halfway and won most impressively by six lengths. So favourable was the impression Miswaki created that he started favourite in the Prix Morny on his next appearance, three weeks later on the same course. The support looked likely to be justified when he moved smoothly into the lead two furlongs out, shaking off the Robert Papin winner Irish Playboy, but he was unable to match the filly Ancient Regime's strong late burst and went down by three quarters of a length. Miswaki and Ancient Regime renewed rivalry in the Prix de la Salamandre at Longchamp in September, but Ancient Regime failed to show her form because of injury, and Miswaki's most dangerous opponent turned out to be the blinkered Prince Mab, two lengths behind him in third place in the Morny. Miswaki looked set for a comfortable victory as he closed on the pacemaking Prince Mab coming to the final furlong but so dourly did Prince Mab hold on to his advantage that Miswaki had to battle all the way to the post to win by a head.

Miswaki (USA) (ch.c. Feb 22, 1978)	Mr Prospector (b 1970)	Raise A Native (ch 1961)	Native Dancer
			Raise You
		Gold Digger (b 1962)	Nashua
			Sequence
	Hopespringseternal (ch 1971)	Buckpasser (b 1963)	Tom Fool
			Busanda
		Rose Bower (ch 1958)	Princequillo
			Lea Lane

Miswaki provided Madame Plesch with her second 1980 Group 1 success, following Henbit's Derby win. Both were bought at auction in the USA with Miswaki easily the more expensive at 150,000 dollars. At the time of his sale neither of Hopespringseternal's previous runners had won a race but one of them, the Secretariat colt Lone Secretariat, broke his duck at four years in 1980 when he was also placed in the Seneca Handicap, a stakes race over thirteen furlongs. We should be surprised if Miswaki were to stay so well; a mile should prove to be his trip. Hopespringseternal is an unraced half-sister to a smart American colt, the grass-course miler True Colors, and a sister to a smart English colt, the Intercraft Solario Stakes winner Over to You who was at his best as a two-year-old. Several other good winners from the family also made their names at two; Miswaki's grandam Rose Bower was the second-highest filly in the Experimental Handicap in 1960 when she won two six-furlong stakes races; his great-

Prix de la Salamandre, Longchamp—Miswaki and Prince Mab are chased by Silver Express

grandam Lea Lane was the fifth highest-rated two-year-old filly in 1954 when she won the Pollyanna Stakes over five and a half furlongs; and Leallah, a sister to Lea Lane, was ranked second only to Alanesian in 1956. It's possible that the best has already been seen of Miswaki too. Although quite attractive and good-quartered he was on the small side at two years and may not make as much progress as some of his less precocious compatriots. *F. Boutin, France.*

MITIGATOR 4 br.g. Brigadier Gerard 144–Mitigation 91 (Milesian 125) (1979 **63**
8fg^3 10.1fg^4 9.4d* 10g* 10.6g 9d 12d 1980 10g 10d 10fg^2 9g 8d) useful-looking gelding; ran best race of season when neck second to Sirena in handicap at Leicester in September; slipped up on previous start; runs as though 1¼m is his limit; possibly unsuited by very soft ground. *W. Hastings-Bass.*

MITZI BELL 4 b.f. Shoolerville 121–Palacio 78 (Jock Scot 121) (1979 7d 6g —
5f 11d 9.4d 10h 12fg 10g 8s* 1980 8s 8v) plater; best form at 1m; acted on soft going; blinkered last 4 starts; dead. *S. Wainwright.*

MIZZENHEAD (USA) 5 br.g. Mill Reef 141–Black Satin 114 (Linacre 133) **48**
(1979 NR 1980 12.5v 13g^2 12.5s) a very well-bred gelding but is only a plating-class maiden; 1½ lengths second to Cantycroon at Hamilton in April; backward when well beaten only subsequent outing (October). *M. W. Easterby.*

M-LOLSHAN 5 br.h. Levmoss 133–Supreme Lady 86 (Grey Sovereign 128 §) —
(1979 13.3g^3 12s^4 12f^2 12f^4 12g* 13.3g^2 12g* 12g^3 11.2v 1980 12f) lengthy horse; good mover; a high-class performer at his best, winner of Irish St Leger at the Curragh in 1978 (rated 125) and Group 1 Grosser Preis von Baden at Baden-Baden in 1979; ran poorly final outing of 1979 and ran as though something was wrong with him on only outing of 1980, finishing tailed off in John Porter Stakes won by Niniski at Newbury in April; stayed well; acted on any going but was well suited by a sound surface; blinkered seventh and eighth outings at 4 yrs; trained most of his career by R. Price; stud in W. Germany. *H. Cecil.*

MMITAMUS 4 br.f. Mandamus 120–Golden Palermo 70 (Dumbarnie 125) —
(1979 5f 5f 7f* 9s 8fg* 8h^3 8fg* 7fg 8g 1980 7v 9fg^4 8f 8fg) strong, well-made filly; won seller at Beverley and handicaps at Ripon and Edinburgh in 1979; didn't recapture her form in 1980; stays 1m; suited by a firm surface. *M. W. Easterby.*

M-N-MS LASS 2 b.f. Workboy 123–Waterbeck (Weathercock 96) (1980 6g^4 **59**
5d^3 6d 6f 6g) May 26; strong, compact filly; second foal; half-sister to 5f and 6f sellers winner Mines Boy (by Gallo Gallante); dam successful hurdler; showed a little ability on first 2 outings but was well beaten when blinkered in valuable seller at Doncaster in September on fifth; stays 6f. *M. H. Easterby.*

MOBILE 3 ch.g. Bivouac 114–Moette 54 (Mossy Face 98) (1979 8g 1980 9.4g —
12.3s) strong gelding; seems of little account. *C. Booth.*

MOCK SUN 4 ch.g. Sharpen Up 127–Parhelia 84 § (Dante) (1979 8g^3 8g^3 10f —
8fg 1980 8fg 10.6fg 10g) useful-looking gelding; plater; stays 1m; dwelt second outing. *J. Mulhall.*

MODEL 3 b.f. Reform 132–Hitesca 110 (Tesco Boy 121) (1979 NR 1980 6f 7f —
7.2d 8g 9.4fg) compact filly; not the best of movers; third foal; sister to miler Referendum; dam, a very game filly, stayed 1m; little worthwhile form in maiden and minor races; bandaged in front third start. *C. Thornton.*

MODEL SOLDIER 6 ch.g. Military 112–Wood Anemone 83 (Tangle 121) —
(1979 5fg 6f 5g 5g^3 1980 7fg 7h) sprint handicapper; appears to act on any going; has twice been tried in blinkers; inconsistent. *I. Dudgeon.*

MODESTINE 2 b.f Welsh Pageant 132–Dauphine 102 (Pampered King 121) —
(1980 6g 6fg) Apr 30; small, lightly-made filly; sister to Free Handicap winner Man of Harlech, and half-sister to 2 winners, including fairly useful stayer Man

of France (by Crepello); dam genuine but rather one-paced stayer; 9 lengths eighth of 15 to Von Erlach after getting well behind in maiden race at Salisbury in September, second outing; likely to need at least 1m at 3 yrs; hasn't much scope. *J. Dunlop.*

MOHOCK 4 b.g. Streetfighter 120–Brighton Girl 96 (Right Boy 137) (1979 5f^2 5fg 5fg 6fg^2 5fg^4 5fg 6g 1980 7fg^2 5fg 6f^3 7f^2 8.3s 6g 7fg* 8g 8d) big, strong-quartered gelding; attracted no bid after winning seller at Folkestone in August; stays 7f; acts on firm going; often wears blinkers (didn't at Folkestone); sold 800 gns Ascot November Sales. *C. James.* 49

MOLLIFIED 4 b.f. Lombard 126–Molly Polly (Molvedo 137) (1979 8s 8s^4 10.1fg^2 10.1g 1980 10.8f 10fg 12d 10f* 10fg) compact filly; dropped in class, bought in 1,800 gns after winning seller at Chepstow in August; stays 1¼m; acts on any going; wears bandages. *J. Bethell.* 56

MOLLY'S LAD 6 ch.g. Chebs Lad 120–Lady Molly (King's Troop 118) (1979 NR 1980 7fg 8d 10s^3 8fg 10s 10g 8g) poor handicapper; stays 1¼m; probably acts on any going; sometimes blinkered. *B. Wise.* 45

MOLON LAVE 3 b.g. Welsh Pageant 132–Another Princess 83 (King Emperor) (1979 NR 1980 8f 8fg 8fg 7fg 7g^2 8d^4 7g) big, strong gelding; first foal; dam won over 1m; only plating class; should stay 1m; usually coltish in paddock early in year and sweated up badly when blinkered fourth start (subsequently gelded). *C. Brittain.* 66

MOMENT OF WEAKNESS 3 b.f. Pieces of Eight 128–Glimmer of Hope 90 (Never Say Die 137) (1979 5s 5g^4 6s* 7f^4 7g^2 7g^3 8fg* 1980 10.2fg* 10.2fg^4 10.6fg^4 10g 10g 10g^4 12g^2 10fg* 10g^2 12d^4) small, well-made filly; good walker; won handicap at Bath in May and seller at Leicester in September; changed hands 5,000 gns after easy win in latter; stays 1½m; acts on any going; suitable mount for an apprentice. *P. Cole.* 67

MOMENT'S PLEASURE (USA) 3 b.f. What A Pleasure–Plumfool (Tom Fool) (1979 5d^2 5g 6g^4 5f 7fg 6f 6fg^4 6f^4 5f 5f 1980 7.6f 10.2fg 8f 8g 7g 9.4g 7fg 7.6d^3 7.2g 8.2g 6d) unfurnished filly; good mover; shows traces of stringhalt; quite moderate (rated 72) at 2 yrs; showed only worthwhile form in 1980 on eighth start; stays 7f well; acts on a firm and a soft surface; blinkered fourth appearance in 1979. *R. Hollinshead.* –

MONACO GAMBLER 3 b.f. Royal Smoke 113–Petemoss (Bounteous 125) (1979 8d 1980 10.8v 11fg 8d) poor form in maiden races and a seller; sweating second start. *M. Francis.* –

MON ANN MILL 2 b.f. Tom Noddy 104–Kissing Grove (Midsummer Night II 117) (1980 5.1g^4 6g 6s 7g) Feb 23; compact, sturdy filly; bad mover; of little account. *J. Harris.* –

MONARCHY 3 b.g. Royalty 130–Cama 85 (Pardao 120) (1979 8fg 8g 1980 11fg 16d) strong, workmanlike gelding; poor maiden; off course 6 months before second start; sold out of D. Sasse's stable 3,800 gns Sandown May Sales. *W. Wightman.* –

MONARD 3 br.c. Pitcairn 126–Singing Blues 78 (Paveh 126) (1979 5d 6s 1980 8.2s 7fg 8d 8g) rangy colt; poor form in maiden races; sweated up badly final outing; unseated rider leaving stalls second start. *W. Wightman.* –

MON BEAUX 6 ch.g. Continuation 120–Affectionately 82 (Mark-Ye-Well) (1979 10.6s* 10.6g* 1980 12s) fair sort; winner of 2 sellers at Haydock in 1979; stays 1¼m well; acts on soft going; needed race and finished tailed off on only outing of 1980. *F. Yardley.* –

MONDAY NIGHT 4 b.f. Jukebox 120–Fair Halo (Nimbus 130) (1979 7s 6g 8f^4 8h 8f 8.2fg 8fg 10s 1980 7fg 8.3f^4 9.6f 8g) small filly; poor plater; stays 1m; sometimes wears blinkers; sold 500 gns Ascot August Sales. *S. Harris.* –

MONEVETTE 2 ch.f. Sweet Revenge 129–Nom de Plume 70 (Aureole 132) (1980 5f 5fg 6fg* 7f 7g*) Mar 17; 4,000Y; light-framed filly; second foal; dam ran only at 2 yrs when winner over 7f; successful in sellers at Stockton in June (bought in 1,700 gns) and Redcar in August (attracted no bid after staying on well to beat Tudorville 1½ lengths in 17-runner event); suited by 7f; yet to race on a soft surface; blinkered at Redcar. *G. Toft.* 67

MONEY TO SPARE 6 b.g. Track Spare 125–Lucre 76 (Privy Councillor 125) (1979 6s^3 6g 9s^2 12d 10f 9fg 1980 6g) workmanlike gelding; poor walker; quite a moderate handicapper nowadays; probably stays 1½m; needs some give in the ground; sold 350 gns Doncaster November Sales. *K. Stapleton.* –

Mr R. E. Sangster's "Monroe"

MONIEF 4 b.c. Mill Reef 141–Plotina 114 (Hugh Lupus 132) (1979 11fg 10fg³ 12fg 10.4f 1980 10s) tall, attractive colt; moderate handicapper; needed race and had stiff task when behind on only outing of 1980; should stay 1½m; possibly unsuited by soft ground; has worn a tongue strap; sold 1,600 gns Newmarket May Sales. *R. Sheather.* —

MONIVEA 3 b.f. Prince Regent 129–Zoom 97 (Zucchero 133§) (1979 7fg 7fg 7f 8g 1980 8f 7d³ 7d⁴ 8fg² 8g² 9s) close-coupled filly; quite a moderate maiden; will stay 1¼m; possibly unsuited by very soft ground; has run creditably for an apprentice; sold 6,400 gns Newmarket December Sales. *P. Cole.* **70**

MONKS FARM 2 b.c. So Blessed 130–Tomboy 95 (Sica Boy 132) (1980 7g 7fg² 7d²) Apr 28; smallish, workmanlike colt; half-brother to several winners, including very useful middle-distance winner Melantha (by Roan Rocket); dam stayed 1½m; second in sizeable fields for maiden races at Lingfield and Leicester in October, going down by a head to Lautrec on former and being caught close home by clever ½-length winner Norfolk Realm after leading 2½f out on latter; will be suited by 1m+; should win a race. *J. Dunlop.* **86**

MONMOUTH (FR) 2 ch.c. Welsh Pageant 132–Cockade 104 (Derring-Do 131) (1980 8g) Feb 27; 66,000Y; well-grown colt; first foal; dam, winner over 1m, is sister to High Top and Camden Town; 20/1, chased leaders for some way before finishing eighth of 16 to Uppety in minor event at Newmarket in October; will stay 1¼m. *A. Hide.* **73** p

MONPOLI (SPA) 3 ch.f. Ragstone 128–Katimba (Touragua) (1979 NR 1980 12g) Spanish-bred filly; apprentice ridden when behind in 19-runner maiden race won by Xarfina at Lingfield in June. *G. Harwood.* —

MONROE (USA) 3 b.f. Sir Ivor 135–Best in Show (Traffic Judge) (1979 5fg* 5f² 5f² 6g* 6f 1980 7s² 6f² 5g*) $300,000Y; small, quite attractive filly; didn't grow a lot over the winter; sister to 3 winners, including very smart Malinowski, a winner at up to 1m, and good 2-y-o Gielgud, and half-sister to 3 **102**

winners and to Sex Appeal, dam of Try My Best; dam very useful stakes winner at up to 7f; lightly raced but is a useful performer; evens favourite, in front rank throughout when winning Group 3 Ballyogan Stakes at Leopardstown in May by 4 lengths from Entre Fancy; second earlier at Phoenix Park in Mulcahy Stakes and Castleknock Sprint Stakes (went down by 2½ lengths to Jasmine Star); bred to be suited by 1m; acts on any going. *V. O'Brien, Ireland.*

MON'S BEAU 5 b.g. Mon Plaisir 121–Beauatire 86 (Beau Sabreur 125) (1979 **85**
16d^{4} 14d^{2} 16v* 14s^{2} 16d^{4} 20g* 16f^{3} 19g^{3} 16fg 1980 16s* 18.4f 20d 16d* 19g^{4} 18d 18s) out-and-out staying handicapper; ran on well to beat Russian George by ½ length in Coral Northumberland Plate at Newcastle in June; had earlier won Queen's Prize at Kempton by 1½ lengths from Heighlin; little other form, but was off course for nearly 3 months before sixth start (Tote Cesarewitch); best form with some give in the ground; suitable mount for a boy; game; occasionally sweats up. *G. Beeson.*

MONSIEUR MARCEL (FR) 4 br.c. Tiffauges 124–Cambrette (Cambremer **117**
132) (1979 10.5v 10v* 11d^{4} 10.5fg 10d^{4} 12.5d^{2} 13.5s 12g* 12v 10.5s 1980 10.5v^{2} 10s 10.5g 9.2d 10.5g 14d^{2} 15s^{3} 15g 12v^{4} 14d* 12.5g 15.5v^{2} 12d) leggy French colt; brother to Italian middle-distance winner Dom Perignon and a winner over jumps; dam, heavily raced, won 5 times; ran race of his life when 3 lengths second to Gold River in Prix Royal-Oak at Longchamp in October, keeping on gallantly up straight but having no chance with winner; had beaten Saint Fort a length at Evry the previous month and had run creditably in smart company on other occasions; evidently very well suited by a stiff test of stamina; acts well on heavy going; ran badly final start. *E. Bartholomew, France.*

MONTAZEM 3 ch.g. Sharpen Up 127–Sundream (Petingo 135) (1979 5g^{4} **45 §**
5g 5s 5f^{2} 6g 5f 5fg* 5f 5f 1980 5f 5f^{4} 7f 6fg^{2} 5g 6g^{2} 6d 8d) fair sort; inconsistent and unreliable plater; stays 6f; acts on firm going; usually wears blinkers; sold 380 gns Doncaster November Sales. *A. Balding.*

MONTCLAIR 2 b.c. Habitat 134–Artist and Model (Ribot 142) (1980 6fg^{3} **91**
6g^{2} 6d^{2}) May 30; good sort; third living produce; half-brother to Irish and American winner Le Militaire (by Le Levanstell); dam unraced half-sister to smart American middle-distance winner Landscaper; second twice, going down by a head to Brummer after a good battle in maiden race at Doncaster in September and by 2½ lengths to Cliff Bank, after finding little off bridle, when odds on for minor event at Leicester the following month; will be better suited by 7f+; well capable of winning a race. *M. Stoute.*

Coral Northumberland Plate, Newcastle—Mon's Beau beats Russian George (centre) and Vicomte (rails). Old Sea Pigeon (extreme left) is fourth, clear of the other runners

MONTE ACUTO 6 ch.g. Mountain Call 125–Island Woman 76 (King's Troop 118) (1979 8g $7g^4$ 8f* 1980 $8fg^3$ 8fg $8fg^3$ $8g^3$ 8d* 9g $8f^2$ 8.3fg $8fg^2$ $8g^4$ $8g^2$) strong, well-made, attractive gelding; ridden by 7-lb claimer when beating Grand Conde by ½ length in handicap at Brighton in July; second in 3 apprentice events at Ascot subsequently, being given too much to do on second occasion; best form at up to 1m; acts on any going; has twice run below form in blinkers; suitable mount for an apprentice. *G. Harwood.* **74**

MONTEVERDI 3 ch.c. Lyphard 132–Janina II (Match III 135) (1979 6fg* 7d* 8fg* 7fg* 1980 $7s^2$ $7f^2$ 8f 12f) **123**

For the third year in a row the horse that had topped the Two-Year-Old Free Handicap failed to make his mark on the classic scene. The high hopes entertained in the winter for unbeaten Monteverdi, after his clear-cut victories in the National Stakes at the Curragh and the William Hill Dewhurst Stakes at Newmarket, came to nothing; he made very little physical progress and didn't train on so well as expected. We excused his first defeat—by Nikoli in the McCairns Trial Stakes at Phoenix Park in April—because of the very soft ground and because he was known to be short of work; furthermore, his rider seemed to set him with a tremendous lot to do. A fortnight later Monteverdi was sent over for the Clerical, Medical Greenham Stakes at Newbury. Here there was no valid excuse for his defeat: Piggott rode him very hard indeed in the last furlong to get second place, half a length behind Final Straw, and although the form of the Greenham looked good there was just a suspicion that Monteverdi hadn't put his best foot forward. One picture, it is said, is often worth a thousand words and the facial expressions of Monteverdi's connections after the Greenham said it all: one journalist even wrote that salvaging Monteverdi's six-million dollar reputation was going to be the biggest job since the Amoco Cadiz!

Monteverdi deteriorated after Newbury, finishing fifth when tried in blinkers in the Airlie/Coolmore Irish Two Thousand Guineas and fourteenth, without blinkers, in the Derby; he started favourite at the Curragh and third favourite at Epsom. The support that Monteverdi received in the Derby betting was a remarkable tribute to the reputation of O'Brien and Piggott, a trainer-jockey partnership which had won the race with Sir Ivor, Nijinsky, Roberto and The Minstrel in the previous twelve-year period. The relationship between O'Brien and Piggott had reportedly been under strain for some time; O'Brien had been

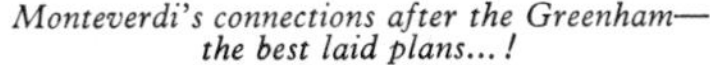

Monteverdi's connections after the Greenham— the best laid plans... !

quoted as saying that he would like Piggott to ride his horses in all the big races but in none of the trials or gallops for 'he rides them to find things out for himself and not to suit me'. A careless remark by Piggott in the unsaddling enclosure after the Irish Guineas must have contributed to the strain—Piggott called Monteverdi 'useless', hardly a tactful thing to do within earshot of Press correspondents. In early September it was announced that Eddery would replace Piggott in 1981 as the number-one rider for the Sangster-O'Brien team. Piggott took it in his stride, riding a hat-trick at Kempton on the day of the announcement and next day partnering Moorestyle to win the Vernons Sprint Cup. Within a week Piggott had arranged to ride for Henry Cecil in 1981; in the meantime, Cecil's stable-jockey Mercer was signed up by Peter Walwyn to replace Eddery.

Monteverdi (ch.c. 1977)	Lyphard (b 1969)	Northern Dancer (b 1961)	Nearctic
			Natalma
		Goofed (ch 1960)	Court Martial
			Barra II
	Janina II (br 1965)	Match III (br 1958)	Tantieme
			Relance III
		Jennifer (b 1948)	Hyperion
			Avena

Monteverdi is a neat, quite attractive colt and a good mover. He has been retired to Walmac Farm, Kentucky and should prove popular with American commercial breeders. His sire Lyphard is the height of fashion and his dam, the French mile-and-a-half winner Janina II, comes from a top-class family. Janina has bred four other winners, none of them anywhere near so good as Monteverdi, and she is a half-sister to Nagami, winner of the Coronation Cup and third in the Two Thousand Guineas, Derby and St Leger, and to the Irish One Thousand Guineas runner-up Young Empress, the dam of the champion 1965 two-year-old Young Emperor. The family has produced a number of classic winners over the years. Monteverdi stayed at least a mile and probably acted on any going. *V. O'Brien, Ireland.*

Mr R. E. Sangster's "Monteverdi"

Mr R. E. Sangster's "Moomba Masquerade" (L. Piggott)

MONT PELION (FR) 2 b.c. Luthier 126–Damaring (Saidam) (1980 5.5g^3 7g* 7d^3 8g^2 8d 10v^2) Apr 29; 215,000 francs Y (approx £23,000); half-brother to several winners, including fairly useful 6f to 1m winner King Pearl (by Gulf Pearl); dam 2-y-o 6f winner in USA; close-up second to The Wonder in two valuable races, going down by $\frac{3}{4}$ length in Prix des Foals at Deauville in August and by a length in Group 2 Criterium de Saint-Cloud in November; also put up some other good efforts and won a maiden race at Chantilly in July; stays well; acts on heavy going and has yet to race on a firm surface. *J. Laumain, France.* **117**

MONZA LADY 2 b.f. Balliol 125–Acceleration (On Your Mark 125) (1980 5fg 5fg 5fg^4 5fg* 5d^2 5g^4 6d* 6g^4 7fg 6s^2 6s*) May 4; 3,000F, 4,100Y; lengthy, rather leggy filly; first foal; dam never ran; won maiden race at Carlisle in May; subsequently ran well in nurseries, winning at Pontefract in August and Hamilton in October; stays 6f well but ran below her best over 7f; has won on a firm surface but has shown better form on soft ground; consistent. *E. Weymes.* **90**

MOOMBA MASQUERADE 3 b.c. Gay Fandango 132–Pampered Dancer (Pampered King 121) (1979 6f 6fg^3 7fg^4 7fg* 8fg* 8f^3 8g^3 8s^3 1980 9f^4 12.3f^2 10.1f* 12f 10d^2 10fg* 11d^2) attractive, good sort, moves well; half-brother to fairly useful sprinter Captain Irish (by Green God); dam once-raced half-sister to Irish 1,000 Guineas winner Royal Danseuse; smart performer; successful in 4-runner minor race at Windsor in May and 5-runner Land of Burns Stakes at Ayr in July (beat Te Kenawa a short head, pair clear); 1$\frac{1}{2}$ lengths second to Prince Roland in Mecca Bookmakers Scottish Derby on same course a week later; had earlier run well in Chester Vase (4 lengths second to Henbit after looking to be going well 2f out) and Prince of Wales's Stakes at Royal Ascot (stayed on steadily without threatening winner when going down by 2 lengths to Ela-Mana-Mou); gives impression 1$\frac{1}{4}$m suits him best; probably acts on any going. *J. Hindley.* **118**

MOON CRYSTAL 2 b.f. The Brianstan 128–Moon's Last 95 (Ballylinan 118) (1980 5f 5.3d 5f 5g) Mar 18; 6,400Y; lightly-made filly; half-sister to **62**

Ballymore Plate, York—Moores Miracle quickens in fine style and draws away from Chantry Bridge

5 winners, including very useful Irish sprinter Super (by Soueida); dam sprinter; 2¾ lengths sixth of 17 to Sodina in maiden race at Lingfield in October, third outing and only worthwhile form. *G. Beeson.*

MOON GOD 3 b.c. Green God 128–Chandravati (Hard Tack 111§) (1979 5g^3 5s^4 5f 6fg 7fg* 7f* 7f^3 1980 7f^3 7f 10fg 8g 7.6g 10.8fg 10fg 10f) close-coupled colt; quite a moderate handicapper at his best; possibly stays 1¼m; acts well on firm ground; usually wears blinkers and has worn a hood as well; often sweats up; ran moderately last 3 starts; sold 3,300 gns Newmarket Autumn Sales. *J. Bethell.* **70**

MOON INGRAVER 3 b.f. Kalamoun 129–Engraving (Crepello 136) (1979 won 4 races from 5 starts in Italy 1980 8g^2 7.5g* 8s* 8g 9.2f^2 8d^3) 9,000F; fifth foal; dam, a useful winner over 6f at 2 yrs in Ireland, stayed 1½m and is daughter of half-sister to Charlottown; put up an improved and smart performance to make all and win Group 3 Prix d'Astarte at Deauville in August by 4 lengths from India Song (gave 7 lb); had earlier finished ½-length second to Current Bay in Group 3 Premio Royal Mares at Turin and won Premio Stabio at Milan; ran on strongly in straight to go down by ½ length to stable-companion Hortensia in Group 2 Prix de l'Opera at Longchamp in October and finished creditable third to Hilal in Prix Perth at Saint-Cloud on final start in November; will stay 1¼m; acts on any going; trained by L. Brogi first 3 starts. *O. Douieb, France.* **118**

MOONLIGHT LOVE 2 b.c. My Swallow 134–Metaphorical (Pirate King 129) (1980 5d) May 24; 440F; fourth produce; brother to a winner in Italy; dam never ran; unquoted when last of 14 to Azaam in maiden race at Wolverhampton in October. *J. Harris.* —

MOONLIGHT SERENADE 2 b.f. Crooner 119–March Moonlight 86 (March Past 124) (1980 5d 5f^4 5.8h 5g 5fg 7g) May 26; neat filly; sister to smart sprinter Blackbird, and half-sister to several winners; dam miler; showed a little ability on first 3 outings but had stiff tasks in nurseries on last 2 appearances; probably stays 6f. *P. Walwyn.* **66**

MOONLIGHT SONATA 2 br.f. So Blessed 130–Midsummer Madness 66 (Silly Season 127) (1980 6d 6v*) Mar 18; useful-looking filly; first foal; dam won over 1½m; won 6-runner maiden race at Hamilton in October by 3 lengths from Fugacious; will be well suited by 1m; yet to race on a sound surface. *C. Thornton.* **78**

MOONLIT KNIGHT 3 ch.g. Silly Season 127–Thieves Honour (Hook Money 124) (1979 7f 1980 12fg) tall gelding; in rear in maiden and minor races. *D. Dale.* —

MOON MIRTH 4 br.f. Comedy Star 121–Moon's Last 95 (Ballylinan 118) (1979 5v 5s 5d^3 5s 6d 5s^3 5fg 6f 6g 5fg 5.8fg 1980 5s^2(dis) 5fg^2 5f 5g) quite well-made filly; inconsistent sprint handicapper; best form at 5f; acts on any going; wears blinkers; bolted before start on reappearance and refused to race final outing; one to leave alone. *R. Akehurst.* **56 §**

MOON PAD 3 b.c. Habitat 134–Moon Min (First Landing) (1979 7fg 1980 8.2g^2 8fg^2 9.4g^2 10g^4 10d* 10g^3 10.4d^3) small, robust colt; good walker; made all and stayed on strongly to beat Salthouse 3 lengths in maiden race at Pontefract in August; suited by 1¼m; acts on a firm and a soft surface; sold 12,000 gns Newmarket Autumn Sales. *P. Walwyn.* **81**

MOONVEIN 3 ch.f. New Member 119–Idyll-Liquor (Narrator 127) (1979 7fg 8f 1980 10g 8.5f4 10s 10.8fg 8fg3) leggy, unfurnished filly; poor plater; stays 1m; acts on firm going; sweated up first start. *W. Musson.* —

MOORES MIRACLE 2 ch.c. Manacle 123–Treasure Flower 67 (Donore 119) (1980 6d* 6g) Feb 9; 8,600Y; good mover; half-brother to several minor winners; dam stayed 1m; had to be ridden to lead over 1f out when favourite for 16-runner maiden race at York in June but then quickened in fine style to win fairly comfortably by 3 lengths from Chantry Bridge; well-backed favourite for 10-runner Richmond Stakes at Goodwood the following month but was beaten fully 2f out and finished remote seventh to Another Realm; will stay 7f; almost certainly a good deal better than his Goodwood running suggests. *R. Armstrong.* **96**

MOORESTYLE 3 b.c. Manacle 123–Guiding Star 70 (Reliance II 137) (1979 6fg3 6s* 6f2 5g* 1980 7f* 8g2 7f* 6d* 6.5d2 6g* 5f* 7g* 7v*) **137**

Moorestyle made history by winning the 'Horse of the Year' award, adjudged the horse to have done most for British racing during the season by a panel of thirty-one racing journalists. The award's main purpose is, worthily, to promote and sustain public interest in racing and has never taken itself, or been taken, so seriously as its counterparts in the United States; yet the outcome has always had significance as well as interest, never more than in 1980 when the recipient was the first in the sixteen-year-old series not to have won either the Derby or the King George VI and Queen Elizabeth Stakes. Moorestyle isn't a middle-distance horse at all. He's never been raced beyond a mile and is an exceptionally good sprinter, the best for many a year, nothing serving to illustrate his merit better, perhaps, than the fact that he gained his award by an overwhelming majority (he received twenty-three votes against two each for Ela-Mana-Mou, Le Moss and Nureyev, the runners-up) at a time when prejudice against sprinters (and stayers) still lives.

Moorestyle ran in nine races as a three-year-old without finishing worse than second; he won seven of them, improving consistently through an unusually long, hard season and establishing himself as easily the best sprinter in training through victories in pattern races on his last four outings, in the Vernons Sprint Cup (Group 2), the Prix de l'Abbaye de Longchamp (Group 1), the Bisquit Cognac Challenge Stakes (Group 3) and the Prix de la Foret (Group 1). He had already given a fair indication of his capabilities before that run of success with a magnificent win in another Group 1 contest, the William Hill July Cup, and a narrow defeat, on very unfavourable terms, in the Prix Maurice de Gheest. During the course of the season Moorestyle beat top sprinters with a decisiveness that bodes ill for those who will face him in 1981. Sharpo, Valeriga and Vaigly Great each fell to him twice, and no doubt the King's Stand Stakes winner African Song would have gone the same way as they, Sayyaf, Kampala, Kearney, Runnett, the good French horses Kilijaro and Adraan, and many others did, had he taken him on. Stronger opponents for Moorestyle may emerge from the current crop of two-year-olds, though it's impossible at present to see where they

Tote Free Handicap, Newmarket—Moorestyle is never in the slighest danger from the time he takes the lead. He is chased home by Taufan

William Hill July Cup, Newmarket—Moorestyle shows himself to be a fine sprinter, racing home from Vaigly Great (not in picture) and Sharpo (white cap)

may come from; if none should emerge, Moorestyle will carry all before him in the sprint races barring accidents.

The July Cup provided the first hard evidence that Moorestyle was an exceptional horse. The only time he'd taken on top-class opposition previously he'd been beaten a length by In Fijar in the Poule d'Essai des Poulains, the French Two Thousand Guineas, putting in a good run on the outside in the straight which took him from fifth place to second inside the last furlong and looked as though it might take him all the way until the winner held him comfortably over the last hundred and fifty yards. The race carries little of the prestige associated with its English equivalent; the best French milers are sometimes reserved for Newmarket, and our opinion then was that Moorestyle would not have got in the first three behind Nureyev had he been allowed to take his chance, as was mooted during Guineas week. Moorestyle's two other races, one on either side of his trip to Paris, were seven-furlong handicaps. Considered just above the minimum standard required for inclusion in the 1979 Tote Free Handicap after a promising first season containing impressive wins in the Convivial Maiden Stakes at York and the Doncaster Stakes from four starts, he decisively won the running of the race in April by a length from Taufan who was conceding 7 lb. In May he won the Norwest Holst Trophy at York with little or nothing in hand by three quarters of a length from Home Ground, subsequently disqualified for hampering the third horse Greenwood Star. The fourth horse Hard Fought carried 1 lb more than Moorestyle.

Hard Fought went on to win his next two races, including the Jersey Stakes. Moorestyle himself had to miss Royal Ascot because he became a little stumped up on the firm ground at York, but had an early opportunity of meeting Hard Fought again in the July Cup; he also had the opportunity of meeting other Royal Ascot runners at Newmarket, notably Kearney, Sharpo and Valeriga, the first three in the Cork and Orrery Stakes, and Runnett, second to African Song in the King's Stand Stakes. The last four runners mentioned, along with the previous year's July Cup second Vaigly Great, represented the main challenge to Moorestyle in the field of fourteen; Hard Fought wasn't likely to be suited by a return to six furlongs even on easy ground. The race was probably the best-contested sprint held at up to that stage of the season. Moorestyle, rather surprisingly favourite, led the group on the stand side (Sharpo, Runnett, Hard Fought, Swift Image and himself) from start to finish and was always in the first two, showing ahead once Standaan predictably ran out of steam after four furlongs. He never looked in the slightest danger of defeat, and had so much in hand through the last furlong that Piggott, who never had to go for his whip, could afford to look around four times on him. Moorestyle, lengthening his stride with a will up the hill, won by two and a half lengths and one and a half from Vaigly Great and Sharpo; it could have been more had his jockey wanted, and that the second was slightly hampered coming through two furlongs out had no bearing on the result.

Moorestyle was next sent to Deauville. As things turned out missing York (he hadn't been entered in the William Hill Sprint Championship) for the Prix Maurice de Gheest was a mistake; he would have had less to do in the Sprint Championship, won by Sharpo from Valeriga, and showed soon enough that there need have been no doubts about his effectiveness at five furlongs. At Deauville he had what might once have been considered his ideal—six and a half furlongs on a soft surface—yet he faced a task beyond any sprinter in training at the weights. He had to give 13 lb more than weight-for-age to the winner, the 1979 Two Thousand Guineas fourth Boitron; in addition he had to give 16 lb more than weight-for-age to the top-class four-year-old filly Kilijaro, who fortunately for him hadn't struck her very best form; on top of that he had to give weight to all the other runners, including 12 lb to the French One Thousand Guineas third Princesse Lida and 9 lb to the King's Stand sixth Manjam. Piggott was criticised most unfairly by some sections of the French Press for allegedly being caught napping after leading on Moorestyle. In fact he and his mount did exceptionally well almost to carry off the prize, just failing to hang on as Boitron won by a short neck. They beat Kilijaro and Manjam in a photo for second.

On the strength of this and his previous performance Moorestyle had an odds-on favourite's chance in his next race, the Vernons Sprint Cup at Haydock in September. One of the biggest dangers to him seemed the course, with its early bend; there seemed much less chance of a repeat of the upsets sometimes seen in this race now it has an earlier position in the Calendar and was being run, in this instance, on much truer ground than has sometimes been the case. He won convincingly by two and a half lengths from Kampala, a horse who like Hard Fought really needs further than six furlongs to be seen to best advantage in the top class. There were those in the race possessing better natural early pace than Kampala—King of Spain, Sayyaf, Vaigly Great, Greenland Park and Standaan to name them in order of finish—but with these, as with Kampala, Moorestyle had no difficulty in coping from the off. Whether he would be able to cope with a stronger field over five furlongs on firm going remained to be seen. The Prix de l'Abbaye de Longchamp the following month, Moorestyle's first race over the distance since his good performance at Doncaster as a two-year-old, provided the answer.

The Longchamp five-furlong course, as the Haydock six-furlong course, has been criticized for its apparent unfairness by some observers, including ourselves; there have been plenty of occasions when neither has seemed suitable for staging top-class sprint races, in that competitors were too much at the mercy of chance. Happily, Haydock is soon to have a new six-furlong course, courtesy of the Levy Board; at Longchamp, action has already been taken to remove the apparent bias of the draw (low numbers seemed very much favoured) by improving the drainage during the winter of 1979 and siting the stalls on the stand side instead of the far side. The effectiveness of the French authorities' move is properly judged in a year or two's time; the Abbaye result was encouraging, though.

Having made his Longchamp debut running honourably at a mile Moorestyle returned to the track, after dropping down gradually in distance and gaining two wins over six furlongs on easy ground, to take France's best sprint race in the manner of a great sprinter. Mistakenly, we thought the conditions would find him out, and expected to see him completely outpaced. Drawn eight of ten, he did appear to find the pace a little difficult early on but soon after halfway it was obvious he was going to peg back the home favourite Adraan (drawn 10). Once in the lead he had to meet a challenge from his old rival Sharpo (drawn 2); this he repelled very quickly, put the whole issue beyond doubt, and went away in the final furlong to win by a length and a half. Sharpo held on well by a neck from the fast-finishing Valeriga (drawn 4), as the first three places fell to foreign-

Vernons Sprint Cup, Haydock—Moorestyle is striding out well at the finish, clear of Kampala and King of Spain

Prix de l'Abbaye de Longchamp—Moorestyle wins from Sharpo and fast-finishing Valeriga. Adraan is the first of the French home

trained horses for the third time since England took them with Balidar, Huntercombe and Raffingora in 1970.

For the current season, at any rate, Moorestyle had become virtually unbeatable. It was difficult for him to add substantially to his reputation in the time remaining but he did so by illustrating his toughness and versatility as well as confirming his merit. Winning the Bisquit Cognac Challenge Stakes at Newmarket cost him no more effort than expected—he beat the fillies Sovereign Rose, Missed Blessing and Our Home virtually on a tight rein; nevertheless, it meant that when he was turned out for his final race of the season, in the Prix de la Foret, he was having his third outing in three weeks; this on top of making his second journey to Longchamp in the short period. The distance of the Foret was seven furlongs, the ground very testing and the opposition strong for the time of year. One of the opposition, Kilijaro, had struck form with a vengeance since their meeting at Deauville, winning four pattern races in four starts; Princesse Lida had lately shown a return to form; the Strensall Stakes winner Luck Of The Draw was in the field and so was Ya Zaman who had beaten her and Hilal in the Prix de la Porte Maillot; lesser-known quantities than these were the unbeaten Habitat colt from Ireland, Crofter, and Tropicaro, the winner of the important race for two-year-old fillies on Arc day, the Prix Marcel Boussac. Moorestyle led all the way for a clear-cut win from Crofter, Kilijaro (who subsequently did extremely well in the United States) and Ya Zaman. Tropicaro finished next to last.

Plans are that Moorestyle will go for the July Cup and the Sussex Stakes in 1981, a double decisively achieved by Thatch as a three-year-old. An offer of over a million pounds for him in the autumn was turned down by his owners who, like many in racing nowadays, are a limited company; Moorestyle remains in the same stable and will again be ridden by Piggott despite the jockey's retainer with Henry Cecil. To win the Sussex Stakes in a normal year will require of Moorestyle a better performance than his one in the French Guineas. We think he didn't quite get the mile that day but we shouldn't be completely surprised to see him get the distance as a four-year-old if he settles, although the chances are that

Prix de la Foret, Longchamp—seventh success of the season for Moorestyle who wins from Crofter and Kilijaro. The others in the picture are Ya Zaman, Safita and Princesse Lida

he'll still be at his most effective over sprint distances. If he runs at a mile he can almost certainly expect stiffer opposition than in the sprints.

Moorestyle (b.c. 1977)	Manacle (b 1964)	Sing Sing (b 1957)	Tudor Minstrel
			Agin the Law
		Hard and Fast (b 1957)	Hard Sauce
			Boodley
	Guiding Star (ch 1969)	Reliance II (b 1962)	Tantieme
			Relance III
		Star of Bethlehem (b 1959)	Arctic Star
			Merry Xmas

Moorestyle is by the five-furlong sprinter Manacle, who gets plenty of winners at a mile and gave us the Cesarewitch winner Sir Michael in 1979, out of a mare successful at two miles. Of his dam's two previous foals the first was unraced and the second no good. He shares with the previous Challenge Stakes winner Kris the distinction of having a Reliance II mare of modest racecourse achievements for a dam. Guiding Star was slightly better than Kris's dam and managed to get off the mark in a maiden race at Folkestone on the last of her five starts as a four-year-old. Reliance II, of course, was one of the best stayers seen since the war, beaten only once and that by Sea-Bird II in the Arc, and was covering some useful mares at the time Guiding Star was conceived. Star of Bethlehem developed into a successful staying handicapper at four years in Ireland after winning over six furlongs at two; she is a half-sister to the Eclipse winner Khalkis and several other winners. The third dam was a half-sister to the dam of the 1965 Doncaster Cup winner Prince Hansel.

Moorestyle in appearance is a tall, lengthy, quite attractive colt; what he looked like as a yearling we don't know, but he cost the Susan Piggott Bloodstock Agency only 4,000 guineas at the October Sales. The dam was sold in foal to Tachypous for 62,000 guineas at the latest December Sales. An excellent mover, Moorestyle acts on any going—a point very much in his favour, along with his consistency and generosity, as he prepares for what promises to be another long season. Such are his qualities he could be 'Horse of the Year' once again at the end of it. *R. Armstrong.*

Moores International Furnishing Ltd's "Moorestyle" (L. Piggott)

Basil Samuel Plate, York—Moor House wins from Sky Blue Pink (left)

MOOR HOUSE 3 b.g. Laxton 105–Asicion 89 (Above Suspicion 127) (1979 5d^2 1980 5h 5d* 6fg* 6s) strong gelding; successful in 17-runner maiden race at York in June and minor event at Ayr following month; landed odds by ¾ length from Swaying Tree in latter; stays 6f; acts on a firm and a soft surface; ran a bit freely in blinkers final outing. *M. H. Easterby.* **84**

MORAGOLD 3 gr.g. Goldhill 125–Belligerent 74 (Roan Rocket 128) (1979 NR 1980 8f 8fg 6g 9fg) strong gelding; brother to very speedy Goldhills Pride; dam half-sister to good French miler Kenmare; well beaten in maiden races; trained first 2 starts by W. Holden. *F. Durr.* —

MORALITY STONE 3 b.c. Ragstone 128–Miss Casanova 84 (Galivanter 131) (1979 7fg 1980 8fg 12f 12s* 12s^3 13.3d 10f 12g^3 11.1g* 12g^2 12g) robust, well-made colt; quite a moderate handicapper; successful at Lingfield in June and Kempton in September; quickened in good style to beat Franciscus 2 lengths on latter; will stay 1¾m; needs some give in the ground. *P. Mitchell.* **77**

MORASH 3 ch.f. Morston 125–Hepash 81 (Henry the Seventh 125) (1979 NR 1980 11.7fg 16f) small filly; third foal; closely related to a poor animal by Blakeney; dam best at 1m; blinkered when in rear in maiden races at Bath and Beverley in June; sold 310 gns Doncaster November Sales. *J. Bethell.* —

MORAYSHIRE 3 b.c. Royal Palace 131–Outward Bound 79 (Sing Sing 134) (1979 7g* 7g^2 8f* 7g^2 1980 8fg^3 10.2g 8fg*) lengthy colt; good mover; half-brother to several winners, including Boundless (by Queen's Hussar), successful at up to 7f; dam placed over 5f; very useful performer; set steady pace until quickening 2f out when winning £3,900 3-runner race at Newmarket in October readily by 1½ lengths from Etching (gave 4 lb); had earlier finished good third to Mashoor in handicap at Goodwood; gave impression 1¼m was too far for him in between; acts well on firm ground. *B. Hobbs.* **112**

MORDRED 3 ch.c. Morston 125–Red Sea 70 (Zimone) (1979 NR 1980 10.8s^3 9f^3 12fg^2) small colt; half-brother to several winners here and abroad; dam won 1¼m seller; placed in maiden and minor races, going down by a neck to Dumplino in maiden event at Haydock on final start in May; will stay 1¾m. *B. Hobbs.* **80**

MORE HARMONY 2 br.c. Morston 125–Melody Maid (Tudor Melody 129) (1980 6d 7f^3 7f^2 7v) Apr 20; quite attractive colt; closely related to very smart middle-distance horse Norfolk Air (by Blakeney), and half-brother to a winner in Holland; dam unraced sister to useful 5f to 1½m winner Bugle Boy; placed in 2 good-class races, being beaten only a neck and a short head by Glint of Gold in Sandwich Stakes at Ascot in July and going down by 2½ lengths to all-the-way winner Sula Bula in Gilbey Champion Racehorse Futurity at York the following month; bred to stay middle distances; acts on firm going and ran deplorably on heavy on final appearance. *J. Bethell.* **94**

MORE LAVENDER 3 b.c. Reliance II 137–Lavender Girl 92 (Petition 130) (1979 NR 1980 8v 12s^2 13g 12d^2) tall ex-Irish colt; brother to smart stayer Realistic, and half-brother to several winners; dam sprinter; only modest form; will be suited by 1¾m+; formerly trained by E. Harty. *H. Blagrave.* **60**

MORE LIGHT 4 b.c. Morston 125–Death Ray 100 (Tamerlane 128) (1979 9fg^2 10.5g^4 12g* 12g^3 12s 1980 12fg* 12fg^2 12d^3 12g 11.1fg* 16f^2) **124**

More Light has always been rather a difficult horse to weigh up and even now that he has been retired after three seasons one can't say with any certainty what his best distance was. He spent most of his three- and four-year-old days racing at around a mile and a half, a distance over which he was able to win his share of races when his opponents weren't quite out of the top drawer but over which he was sometimes found wanting for pace. He ran as though a longer distance would suit him well and was stoutly-enough bred, but when trying further for the first and only time he was stepped straight up to two miles for the Jockey Club Cup at Newmarket and was beaten by Ardross. In a race that wasn't particularly strongly run More Light was kicked on past Tin Soldier half a mile out and looked likely to win at least until the furlong-marker where Ardross was still struggling to get on terms. Ardross got on top in the closing stages and won by a length and a half, the pair finishing a long way clear. More Light certainly didn't see the trip out so well as the winner, but Ardross is, after all, a top-class stayer and More Light probably ran as well as in any race all season. However, he gave the impression that he wouldn't have made a Gold Cup horse had he been kept in training, and he might have proved best at around a mile and three quarters.

More Light had won the Jockey Club Stakes on the same course in the spring on his reappearance, beating Valour gamely by a neck when favoured by the weights, and the September Stakes at Kempton on his penultimate start, beating the good handicapper Masked Marvel by four lengths. He was also placed in two other good races, when second to Scorpio in the Hardwicke Stakes at Royal Ascot and when third behind Nicholas Bill and Son Fils in the Princess of Wales's Stakes at Newmarket. In the former race he couldn't quite find the pace to reach the winner but went down by only half a length in a thrilling finish. In the latter, on ground softer than ideal for him, he took a long time to get going but stayed on under pressure up the hill. On his only other start, in the King George VI and Queen Elizabeth Diamond Stakes won by his stable-companion Ela-Mana-Mou, he uncharacteristically dropped right out in the closing stages after helping to force the pace and he finished last of all. Still, he had little chance in the race, starting at 33/1.

More Light (b.c. 1976)	Morston (ch 1970)	Ragusa (b 1960)	Ribot
			Fantan II
		Windmill Girl (b 1961)	Hornbeam
			Chorus Beauty
	Death Ray (b 1959)	Tamerlane (br 1952)	Persian Gulf
			Eastern Empress
		Luminant (b 1951)	Nimbus
			Bardia

More Light's dam Death Ray bred four winners before him and has also done very well since with Shoot A Line (by High Line) and Sharp End (by Sharpen Up); the latter has yet to win but showed distinct promise on the first of his two outings as a two-year-old in 1980 and is sufficiently well thought of to have been entered for the Two Thousand Guineas. Death Ray herself won five times at around a mile and is a half-sister to several winners, including the very smart sprinter Daylight Robbery.

A big, rangy colt who wore blinkers in his last three races, More Light was ideally suited by top-of-the-ground conditions. He was sold privately at the end of the season and is to stand at stud in Argentina. *R. Hern.*

MORE OATS 2 b.c. Morston 125–Dashing Diana (Silver Shark 129) (1980 8fg 8g) Feb 27; 14,500Y; quite attractive, well-made colt; good mover; fourth foal; half-brother to 3-y-o 7f winner Bradette (by Great Nephew); dam won over 6f in Ireland; showed up in minor race at Newbury in September (fifth of 23 to Shergar) and maiden race at Newmarket in October (co-favourite when around 5 lengths sixth of 15 to Riberetto); looks capable of better over further at 3 yrs. *G. Harwood.* **74 p**

MORE STONES 2 ch.f. Morston 125–Astoria 92 (Derring-Do 131) (1980 7fg^2 7g* 9d^2) Mar 2; 30,000Y; small, narrow, unimpressive-looking filly; sister **95**

to quite moderate 1978 2-y-o All Is Great, and half-sister to fairly useful winners Rover's Day (by Shantung) and Shortbread (by Crisp and Even); dam stayed 1¼m, and is sister to Dominion; well-backed favourite, drew clear final furlong to win 16-runner maiden race at Chepstow in September by 5 lengths from Murmansk; went down by 3 lengths to Allegretta in minor event at Wolverhampton the following month; will stay 1½m. *J. Hindley.*

MORGAN'S CHOICE 3 ch.c. Reliance II 137–Piave (Alcide 136) (1979 6g 1980 8f 10.2fg 11f 12g 10.1g³ 11.7s* 13.1f³ 13.3d) small, well-made colt; beat Hasty Dawn 2½ lengths in handicap at Windsor in June; stays 1⅝m; suited by some give in the ground; usually wears blinkers. *H. Blagrave.* **74**

MORGAN'S PEARL 3 ch.c. Gulf Pearl 117–Morganette (Tudor Music 131) (1979 NR 1980 10.2d³ 10s 12.5h³ 11.7f 12fg² 11fg² 14d* 14g² 16fg³ 14g* 18d 14g²) 9,200Y; useful sort; not a good mover in his slower paces; second foal; dam half-sister to speedy 1967 2-y-o Canteen; fair handicapper; won at Yarmouth in July and Newmarket in October; beat Running Game in very good style by 5 lengths on latter; good second to Popsi's Joy at Newmarket again later in October; stays well; acts on any going with possible exception of very soft; retained 16,500 gns Newmarket Autumn Sales. *W. O'Gorman.* **88**

MORIAS 2 ch.c. Sallust 134–Purple Goddess 69 (Red God 128§) (1980 6fg 6s) Apr 21; 7,500Y; short-coupled colt; half-brother to 2 winners, including fairly useful 7f and 1¼m winner Celestial Gem (by Gulf Pearl); dam placed over 5f at 2 yrs; little worthwhile form in maiden race at Newmarket in August and minor event at Ayr in September. *C. Brittain.* **–**

MORILLE 3 ch.f. Malicious–Mange Tout 125 (Galivanter 131) (1979 6g 5.8g 5f 1980 10.2f) compact filly; little worthwhile form in maiden races and a handicap. *P. Cundell.* **–**

MORKULLA (SWE) 5 ch.m. Royal Park 114–Canary Bird 79 (Bleep-Bleep 134) (1979 8g 7g³ 7fg 8g⁴ 8g 10g 1980 10.1fg³ 8f 10g² 10s⁴ 10g* 10fg 10fg 12.5s³) inconsistent plater; bought in 1,850 gns after winning at Nottingham in July; stays at least 1¼m; seems to act on any going; usually blinkered nowadays. *G. Fletcher.* **44**

MORNING ENQUIRY 3 ro.f. Perhapsburg 112–Dawn Reign 82 (Perfect Sovereign) (1979 NR 1980 8g 10.1g 6g 12g) compact filly; second reported foal; dam won from 1¼m to 13f; tailed off all starts in varied company. *F. Muggeridge.* **–**

MORNING LINE 3 ch.g. Owen Anthony 102–Hill Cloud 60 (El Gallo 122) (1979 NR 1980 9fg 7fg³ 8fg 8fg 8fg⁴ 8d 7f 12f* 8fg) fair sort; long odds on, easily won match at Lingfield in August; in frame earlier in maiden races; probably stays 1½m; acts on firm going; didn't impress in paddock sixth outing. *P. M. Taylor.* **64**

MORSE CODE 5 ch.h. Morston 125–King's Mistress 102 (Rockefella) (1979 12fg 11.7g³ 12s⁴ 12fg* 14g 13.3fg² 12f* 12fg* 12s* 1980 12f² 13.4f⁴ 12d 12g⁴ 12g² 12s) rangy horse; useful handicapper; ran extremely well on reappearance when 3 lengths second of 16 to Niniski in John Porter Stakes at Newbury in April; about 4½ lengths fourth of 10 behind same horse in Ormonde Stakes at Chester following month; ran easily best subsequent race when length second to Broomstick Corner in £3,000 event at Lingfield in September; stays 13.3f; acts on any going but goes particularly well on firm; has a good turn of foot and is suited by waiting tactics; sold 8,400 gns Newmarket Autumn Sales, probably for export to Italy. *J. Dunlop.* **100**

MORSE PRINCESS 4 ch.f. Communication 119–Moss Princess (Star Moss 122) (1979 8fg 8g² 8fg³ 8.2g 1980 8s⁴ 8.2fg 7f⁴ 7f³ 8g⁴) poor plater; stays 1m; acts on any going. *M. Tate.* **33**

MORTADELLA 3 gr.f. Warpath 113–Piccalilli 78 (Klairon 131) (1979 7f 8d 10.6d 8g⁴ 1980 8v³ 8s² 9g³ 12f⁴ 10.2g 10.6d 13.8g* 12d²) lightly-built filly; won handicap at Catterick in August; will stay beyond 1¾m; suited by some give in the ground; sold to M. Masson 2,750 gns Newmarket Autumn Sales. *C. Thornton.* **66**

MORTAR 6 ch.g. Firestreak 125–Chance Shot 86 (Hornbeam 130) (1979 11v 10.6s³ 10.6g² 12fg² 12.3f 12g* 12g* 12.3f 12d 11d 12s 12d 1980 11d³ 12f 10.6fg 10.6fg 12f* 12g³ 12g³ 13g⁴ 12fg³ 15.8d 12fg 12d) plater; beat Higham Grey by ½ length in handicap at Hamilton in June; suited by 1½m; acts on any going; used to wears blinkers; sold out of C. Crossley's stable 1,300 gns Doncaster September Sales after eleventh start. *P. Bevan.* **50**

MORTON TERRACE 4 ch.f. Saintly Song 128–Goben (Neckar) (1979 7fg 6f^{3} 6g 5s 6s 5h 1980 6g 6f 7f 8f) poor sprint plater; acts on firm going; blinkered final start at 2 yrs. *J. Doyle.* —

MORVETTA 4 ch.c. Morston 125–Nevetta 108 (Never Say Die 137) (1979 12.3v^{2} 12g 10g^{2} 10.2s 12g 10.2fg* 9.4f* 12f^{3} 12f* 12f* 12g^{4} 16fg 18fg 1980 13v 14f 16.1f 12f^{2} 12g^{2} 16d 13d^{3} 12g* 14.7g^{4} 10d 12g^{3} 12f^{2}) big colt; enterprisingly ridden when winning amateur riders race at Redcar in August by 8 lengths from Virgin Soldier; beat Beau Reef a head in handicap at Newmarket in October when apprentice ridden at overweight, but hampered Beau Reef and placings were subsequently reversed (seemed a shade unlucky); in frame in between in Vaux Breweries Gold Tankard at Redcar (good fourth to Sea Pigeon) and £3,200 handicap at Doncaster; best form at up to 14.7f; acts well on firm going and is not at his best in the mud; often wears blinkers (didn't at Newmarket); probably needs a strong gallop. *Denys Smith.* **92**

MOSSAT 3 gr.c. Busted 134–Abettor 103 (Abernant 142) (1979 NR 1980 10fg 12g^{2} 10g* 10f^{3}) strong colt; half-brother to 1$\frac{1}{4}$m winner Honeybarrel (by Run The Gantlet) and a winner in Italy by Kalamoun; dam, winner over 1$\frac{1}{2}$m, is half-sister to good middle-distance horse Rehearsed; favourite, won 12-runner maiden race at Newmarket in August; will stay beyond 1$\frac{1}{2}$m; has run respectably for an apprentice; sold to B. Palling 8,000 gns Newmarket Autumn Sales. *H. Cecil.* **78**

MOTAVATO (USA) 2 br.c. Apalachee 137–Lovelight 112 (Bleep-Bleep 134) (1980 5f^{2} 5f* 6d^{2} 6f* 6g^{4}) Mar 21; rangy, long-striding colt; third foal; dam very game sprinter; impressive winner of maiden race at Sandown in May (lengthened stride in good style to beat Habitor 5 lengths) and 3-runner race at Catterick in July (looked to have run up rather light but came home 7 lengths clear of Donatella); also in frame in 2 pattern races, running on to finish 5 lengths second of 13 to Recitation in Coventry Stakes at Royal Ascot in June and finishing just over 6 lengths fourth of 10 behind Another Realm after having every chance 2f out in Richmond Stakes at Goodwood the following month; will stay 7f; seems to act on any going. *B. Hills.* **106**

MOT D'OR (FR) 3 b.c. Rheingold 137–Miss Manon (Bon Mot III 132) (1979 8.5d^{2} 8g^{3} 1980 10g^{2} 12g* 12fg* 12fg 15s^{3} 10d 13.5g) 25,000F; good-looking colt; second foal; half-brother to Sharpman (by Sharpen Up), very smart at up to 1$\frac{1}{2}$m in France; dam smart French middle-distance performer; won maiden race at Longchamp in April and Prix Hocquart on same course following month, latter by a short neck from Providential with Belgio 2 lengths away third; ran creditably next 2 starts, finishing equal sixth to Policeman in Prix du Jockey-Club at Chantilly and equal third, 3$\frac{1}{2}$ lengths behind Valiant Heart, in Grand Prix de Paris at Longchamp; well beaten behind Glenorum in 2 races at Deauville, Prix de la Cote Normande and Grand Prix, afterwards; stays well; probably acts on any going; very smart. *A. Head, France.* **119**

MOTHER EARTH 3 b.f. Jukebox 120–Demeter 83 (Silly Season 127) (1979 5s* 5fg* 6f^{4} 5g 1980 7f^{2} 6fg^{3} 5f 5fg) strong, rangy filly; good walker and mover; first foal; dam won over 7f at 2 yrs; ran well in Ladbrokes Nell Gwyn Stakes at Newmarket in April (went down by 1$\frac{1}{2}$ lengths to Evita after showing excellent speed) and handicap on same course in May (1$\frac{3}{4}$ lengths third to Bold Image); outpaced in Temple Stakes at Sandown and valuable handicap at Ascot subsequently; suited by 6f and 7f; acts on any going; not raced after June. *R. Hern.* **100**

MOTHER FLUTTER 3 ch.f. Gulf Pearl 117–Last Flutter (Stephen Paul 131) (1979 5d^{4} 5s 5v 5fg 5fg^{4} 7f 7g 1980 5s 5fg^{3} 6fg 6f 5fg 7fg 6g 5g) neat filly; poor maiden nowadays; gives impression 6f may be her trip; blinkered at 2 yrs. *W. Wightman.* **56**

MOTHER OF THE WIND 2 b.f. Tumble Wind–Navy Colors (Bupers) (1980 5f 5.8g 6d^{4} 7d 7fg* 7d 8.2g^{4} 7g) Mar 14; 3,100Y; quite attractive, well-made filly; half-sister to Irish 7f winner Reve d'Amour (by River Beauty); dam won 3 times at up to 6f from 75 starts in USA; put up easily best effort when making all to win 6-runner nursery at Epsom in August by $\frac{3}{4}$ length from Rathmoy's Sparkle; suited by 7f and should stay 1m; possibly needs a sound surface. *C. Nelson.* **82 ?**

MOTIVATE 3 b.c. Run The Gantlet–Motionless 109 (Midsummer Night II 117) (1979 NR 1980 11d^{4} 13d^{2} 13s^{4} 11d 14.6d) big, useful sort with plenty of scope; half-brother to 1m winner Speedy Tack (by Right Tack); dam third in English and Irish 1,000 Guineas; neck second to Glenvara (pair clear) in maiden race at Ayr in July, best effort; stays 13f; yet to race on a sound surface. *W. H. H. Williams.* **71** d

MOTO 2 br.f. Tudor Melody 129–Princely Maid 71 (King's Troop 118) (1980 5fg 5fg 5fg4 5g4 6d* 6d 7fg 6g 8g) Jan 11; small, lightly-made filly; good walker; half-sister to several winners, including Lady Constance (by Connaught), a very useful performer at up to 7f, and Pennina (by Great Nephew), a useful winner at up to 7.5f; dam 5f 2-y-o winner; retained 4,200 gns after winning 10-runner seller at Haydock in August by ½ length from Abwacadabwa; in rear in nurseries afterwards; needs further than 5f but isn't sure to stay 1m; acts on a soft surface; blinkered last 2 outings. *F. J. Houghton.* **65**

MOTORCENTRE 2 b.c. Abwah 118–Arctic Dream 75 (Arctic Slave 116) (1980 5s 5d 7d) Feb 13; 2,500F, 1,000Y; resold 500Y, 1,500 2-y-o; small, strong non-thoroughbred colt; third reported foal; dam best at sprint distances; no worthwhile form in maiden and minor events. *S. Holland.* –

MOTOR-PLAN SUPREME 2 b.c. Tudor Rhythm 112–Lady Amber Hope (Golden Surprise 65) (1980 5.1g 5d) useless. *D. Thom.* –

MOTT THE HOOPLE 2 gr.g. Goldhill 125–Belligerent 74 (Roan Rocket 128) (1980 5s 5s3 5s 7fg 6g 6g* 5f 6g 6f) Feb 21; 10,000Y (privately); neat gelding; brother to useful sprinter Goldhills Pride; dam half-sister to very good French miler Kenmare; very hard ridden to beat Joint Mercy a short head in 12-runner seller at Newcastle in August; attracted no bid afterwards; beaten in valuable sellers and a nursery subsequently; possibly needs further than 5f nowadays; blinkered last 4 outings. *P. Haslam.* **73**

MOUHANNED 2 b.c. Ashmore 125–French Bird (Guersant 129) (1980 7fg 7g 8g) Apr 2; 35,000Y; compact, good sort; half-brother to several winners, notably very smart 7f performer Pitskelly (by Petingo); dam sprinter; ran best race when about 8 lengths sixth of 17 to Dragon Palace in maiden event at Newmarket in October on third outing (faded steadily from 3f out); will probably stay 1¼m; missed break first outing. *C. Brittain.* **65**

MOULOUKI 3 ch.c. Sassafras 135–Senama (Sanctus II 132) (1979 NR 1980 8.5v* 12d* 12fg 12g* 10g 12f 12s) 9,400F, 20,000Y; second foal; dam French middle-distance winner; put up a good performance to win Group 2 Prix Jean de Chaudenay at Saint-Cloud in May, getting up close home to beat Hard To Sing a head with Buckpoint a short head away third; had earlier won newcomers race at Maisons-Laffitte and minor event at Saint-Cloud; respectable 5 lengths sixth of 7 to Dunette in Prix du Prince d'Orange at Longchamp in September but was subsequently well beaten in Prix de l'Arc de Triomphe and Prix du Conseil de Paris on same course in October; will stay beyond 1½m; possibly unsuited by firm ground. *M. Saliba, France.* **117**

MOUNTAINETTE 2 gr. or ro.f. Peter Wrekin 108–Young Florin (Aggressor 130) (1980 5fg 5d 7g) Feb 13; lengthy filly; half-sister to winning hurdler Quicksilver (by Espresso); dam lightly raced; twice last from 3 outings in maiden races; bred to need thorough test of stamina. *A. W. Jones.* –

MOUNTAIN GORGE 4 br.c. Joshua 129–Kergore (Hunsingore) (1979 6s 5s 7g3 8d* 9fg2 8fg 7d* 7g3 8g4 7.2g 8d2 7g 10g 1980 7f 8f 8fg 9g) big, strong colt; quite useful handicapper at 3 yrs; didn't find his best form in 1980 (not seen out after June); stays 9f; seems to act on any going; wears a tongue strap; usually makes running. *T. Barnes.* –

MOUNTAIN HAYS 5 b.g. Will Hays–Mountain Lark (Chamier 128) (1979 13g3 12v2 16f2 13g 1980 18d* 14.6g 16.1d 13s) quite a moderate handicapper; favourite when decisive winner from Fata Morgana at Doncaster in March, best effort; off course nearly 3 months before final start; stays well; acts on any going. *M. H. Easterby.* **73** d

MOUNTAIN MAN 4 b.g. Wolver Hollow 126–Beck 97 (St Paddy 133) (1979 NR 1980 9g 10fg 8f 10fg 12g2 16fg* 12d) tall, narrow gelding; finished clear of remainder when 2½ lengths second of 17 to Malza in amateur riders race at Kempton in September; beat My Saint Anne by 1½ lengths in similar race at Newbury later in month; stays 2m; acts on a firm surface; sold 5,800 gns Newmarket Autumn Sales. *W. Hastings-Bass.* **62**

MOUNTAIN MONARCH 3 b.g. Royal and Regal–Sally of the Hills 80 (Sallymount 125) (1979 5v 6s 7fg4 6f2 7g 7g 1980 10.8v* 12fg 16f3 17.1fg3 16g2 16fg* 19g3 16g3 18.1g2 19g3 16d) quite attractive, strong sort; won maiden race at Warwick in March and small event at Chepstow in July; ridden by 5-lb claimer when beating Broadsword 2 lengths in latter; stays well; appears to act on any going. *S. Woodman.* **79**

MOUNTAIN RECORD 2 ch.c. Jukebox 120–Grindlewald 76 (Le Levanstell 79
122) (1980 5f 5fg^4 6s 5f^2) Feb 17; 4,000Y; workmanlike colt; fourth foal; half-brother to 6f and 7f winner Movement (by Daring Display); dam won at up to 13f; showed much improved form when second favourite for valuable seller at York in September, disputing lead all way before going down by 2 lengths to Abrovian Rose; should stay at least 6f. *J. Hardy.*

MOUNTAIN THYME 2 b.f. Lochnager 132–Elspeth Ann 68 (Pardao 120) 54
(1980 5f 5g^4 5g) Jan 6; lengthy filly; fourth living foal; dam showed a little ability at 2 yrs; having second race in 4 days when 3¼ lengths fourth of 6 to Atilla the Hen in maiden race at Edinburgh in June; had stiff task when last of 12 in minor event at Beverley the following month (started slowly). *M. W. Easterby.*

MOUNT COLUM 3 b.f. Mountain Call 125–Royal Colum (Royal Levee) –
(1979 5f 5fg 1980 5s) in rear in maiden races. *W. Stephenson.*

MOUNT DENALI (USA) 3 b.c. Roberto 131–Maud Muller (Graustark) 80
(1979 7fg 7f^4 8g^3 1980 12f^2 14f^2 14fg^2 14d^2 13.4g* 15.5s^4 12g^2 13.8g^2 12g^3) lightly-made colt; gained well-deserved success in maiden race at Chester in July; stays well; probably acts on any going; blinkered last 3 starts; racing in USA, and won his first two starts there. *I. Balding.*

MOUNT ELIZA 2 b.f. Welsh Saint 126–Shantung Lassie (Shantung 132) 59
(1980 5s^4 5s 6fg^4 5.1fg^2 5.1fg^2 6g 6f) Mar 20; 500F, 2,600Y; compact filly; second foal; dam won at up to 1¼m in France; second in sellers won by Superb Music and Daphne's Favour at Yarmouth in August; should be suited by 6f; acts on a firm surface; sold 400 gns Newmarket Autumn Sales. *G. Blum.*

MOUNT HALA 3 b.f. Mount Hagen 127–Nantahala 84 (Nantallah) (1979 70
7d^3 1980 8s^4 7f^3 9s* 12.2d) lengthy, quite attractive filly; half-sister to Irish Guinness Oaks winner Olwyn (by Relko); dam won over 1m; stayed on to win minor event at Hamilton in September; should stay middle distances (ran moderately when tried over 1½m); acts on any going. *B. Hills.*

MOUNT IRVINE BAY 2 b.c. Targowice 130–L'Eaulne (Busted 134) (1980 –
5.8fg) Feb 2; 3,100F, 4,000Y; third reported foal; dam, useful performer in France, won over 1¼m; 25/1 when behind in 19-runner maiden race won by Ramwadash at Bath in June. *J. Bethell.*

MOUNT MAGIC 4 ch.g. Mount Hagen 127–Magical Music (Sing Sing 134) –
(1979 8v 8v 8s^3 7f 7g 6f 7fg 8g 7f 1980 12fg^3 12f 12h 12.2fg 12f 8.2d 15d 9s) ex-Irish gelding; poor maiden; stays 1½m. *R. Allan.*

MOUNT PARNASSUS 3 b.c. Mountain Call 125–Greek Serenade (Grey –
Sovereign 128§) (1979 5d 5g 6s 6fg 7f^4 1980 8.2s 8fg 10.1s 10fg 8f 8g 7g) workmanlike colt; plater; best run at 7f on firm going; often blinkered; trained by A. Johnson first 5 starts; sold to M. Pipe 760 gns Newmarket Autumn Sales. *J. W. Watts.*

MOUNT TEMPLE 4 b.g. Tudenham 118–Lady Bio (Prince Bio) (1979 10s^4 56
10s^2 10s 11d^3 1980 12.5v 13g^3 12f^2 12g 12d^4 14g) ex-Irish gelding; modest maiden; neck second to Gleaming Wave in handicap at Leicester in June, best effort of 1980; stays 13f; acts on any going. *D. Morley.*

MOURNDYKE 8 ch.g. Klondyke Bill 125–Moura (Mourne 126) (1979 –
14d 16s^4 14v^2 1980 14fg 14fg 16fg 11d) staying handicapper; goes well in the mud; bandaged nowadays. *R. Atkins.*

MOURTAZAM 2 gr.c. Kalamoun 129–Manush (Tanerko 134) (1980 8g^2 ?
8g^2 8v*) Mar 28; half-brother to several winners, including smart French miler Mannshour (by Kashmir II) and very useful French long-distance horse Croque Monsieur (by Sheshoon); dam won over 1¼m in France; ran well in useful company and had plenty in hand when winning 14-runner maiden race at Maisons-Laffitte in November by 4 lengths from Baron Tzigane; will be suited by 1¼m; a progressive type who'll make a smart 3-y-o. *F. Mathet, France.*

MOUSEHOLD 4 ch.c. Silly Season 127–Sedulous 96 (Restless Wind) (1979 66 d
7fg 8g 10.5g 8fg* 8s 8f 8.2g 1980 8f* 8f* 8f 8fg^3 7fg^4 8g) strong, lengthy colt; ridden by 7-lb claimer J. Fortune when successful in handicaps at Thirsk (apprentice event) in April and Ayr in May; beat Geoffrey's Sister by ½ length in latter; didn't run up to his best afterwards; suited by 1m; acts on firm going; often makes the running. *I. Walker.*

MOVE OFF 7 ch.h. Farm Walk 111–Darling Do (Derring-Do 131) (1979 12s 13.4v3 14d 12d2 12f 12f 10g2 14.7g2 14s3 14fg4 11d3 12.5g2 1980 12f2 13.4f 13fg3 14d2 12s2 15g4 11s) small, light-framed horse; poor mover; an admirably tough and genuine handicapper who has been retired after 6 busy seasons: was very useful at his best and won 10 races, including 1976 Zetland Gold Cup, 1977 Tote-Ebor Handicap and 1978 Old Newton Cup; second in 1980 in good handicaps at Thirsk (to Majestic Maharaj), York (to No Bombs) and Haydock (to Shady Nook), beaten only ½ length in last-named; stayed 15f; acted on any going; was a good mount for an apprentice; standing at Acrum Lodge Stud, West Auckland, £500 n.f.n.f. *J. Calvert.* **100**

MOVER (USA) 2 ro.f. Stage Door Johnny–Feet First (Native Dancer) (1980 8d2) Mar 22; $95,000Y; half-sister to fair Irish 1¼m winner Step Together (by Big Spruce) and to Silver Spook (by Tentam), a smart stakes-placed winner at 2 yrs in USA; dam 6f winner and daughter of Champion American filly Next Move; said to be highly regarded and showed promise when 5/4 favourite for 19-runner newcomers race at Maisons-Laffitte in October, finishing ¾-length second to Barbotte; will stay 1¼m; sure to win races. *M. Zilber, France.* **?**

MOYBROOK 4 br.c. The Brianstan 128–River Moy (Niagara Falls 104) (1979 6g* 6d 5g 6s4 6d* 6g 6d 6d 6s4 7fg 8g2 8d 8s 1980 5d 6v2 6g3 7f2 6f2 6f* 6d3 6fg2 6fg2 6d2 6d 6fg2 6s 7.2d 6fg4) strong, useful-looking colt; goes well at Ayr and was gaining his third win there when getting up to beat Primula Boy by a head in Ayr Sprint Handicap in May; ran well most other outings; stays 1m; acts on any going; suitable mount for an apprentice; has given trouble at start on occasions; blinkered last 3 outings; reportedly broke blood vessel final start. *G. Richards.* **76**

MR ARGENTINA 3 b.c. So Blessed 130–String Along 77 (Crepello 136) (1979 5s3 7f 5g 1980 7f 8fg 7f 8.2g 10g* 10.1fg2 10fg 10.1g4 10.2d2 8.2s4) neat colt; beat Brianka 2½ lengths in maiden race at Ripon in August; suited by 1¼m and may stay further; acts on a firm surface; trained first 3 outings by N. Callaghan; ran moderately seventh start; sold 7,200 gns Newmarket Autumn Sales. *F. Durr.* **70**

MR FASTBAC 5 br.g. Sahib 114–Goldelope (Elopement 125) (1979 12s 9.4g 1980 12fg2) plating-class maiden; stays 1½m; acts on a firm surface; usually wears blinkers; bandaged on only outing of 1980. *F. Yardley.* **—**

MR FRESHNESS 2 ch.g. Tumble Wind–Beba Saint (Welsh Saint 126) (1980 6g 6s4 5f 7g 7.2g 6s 6fg3 7d3 6s) May 26; 2,400F, 3,000Y; workmanlike gelding; first foal; dam won over 6f in Ireland; only quite moderate; stays 7f; blinkered final outing. *E. Carter.* **71**

MR GUS 2 b.g. Tower Walk 130–Chapeau Bleue (High Hat 131) (1980 5s 5f2 5fg2 5h4 5fg2 6fg* 7g* 7f2) Mar 29; 5,200F; compact, good-bodied gelding; carries plenty of condition; second produce; half-brother to 1m winner British Crown (by English Prince); dam won twice over 9f in Ireland; won minor events at Carlisle in June and Beverley in July, battling on most gamely to beat Sula Bula narrowly on latter course (pair 10 lengths clear); well suited by 7f and will stay 1m; sweated up badly but ran well final outing (July). *W. O'Gorman.* **92**

MR JERRY 5 ch.g. Roi Soleil 125–Bessborough (Mossborough 126) (1979 12d 12.2d4 12s 12.5g4 1980 14fg* 12h2 13.1fg* 14g 16.9f 14g3 13.1h) ex-Irish gelding; said to be a whistler; won handicaps at Salisbury in May and Bath in June; ran moderately final start; stays 1¾m; acts on any going; suitable mount for an apprentice. *M. Pipe.* **63**

MR MALLORY (USA) 2 b.g. Bold Hour–West Bramble (Krakatao 130) (1980 7fg 7d 7d2 8d) Apr 27; $22,000F; lengthy, lightly-made gelding; half-brother to numerous winners, including fairly useful 1975 5f and 6f winner Lei (by Hawaii); dam unraced sister to exceptionally speedy Krakenwake; blinkered, showed first form when 4 lengths second of 10 to Paltango in maiden race at Catterick in October (might have been closer but for being hampered turning for home); didn't wear blinkers when well beaten next time out; not sure to stay 1m; dwelt start first 2 outings. *J. Fitzgerald.* **71**

MR MATCH 4 b.g. Frankincense 120–Well Matched 79 (Niccolo Dell' Arca) (1979 7fg 7f 6s 1980 8v) poor plater; has worn blinkers. *Denys Smith.* **—**

MR MISCHIEF 2 ch.c. Sharp Edge 123–Talarea 76 (Takawalk II 125) (1980 6fg 5fg 5d) May 28; lightly-made colt; first foal; dam, 5f winner, stayed 7f; unquoted when behind in sizeable fields of maidens. *M. Masson.* **—**

MR MONEY BAGS 2 b.c. Pieces of Eight 128–My Sweet Afton 73 (Javelot 124) (1980 6g 7d 8.2s) Apr 23; 1,800Y; half-brother to several winners, including useful 1974 2-y-o 5f performer Hand Picked (by Tribal Chief); dam won 6f seller; well beaten, including in a seller; sold to R. Morris 380 gns Doncaster October Sales. *H. Bell.* –

MR MOONRAKER 3 b.g. Idiot's Delight 115–Burlington Belle (Galivanter 131) (1979 6g 7f 1980 8f 10.1fg 8fg* 8g^{4} 8.3d^{2} 8g 13.3d 10.2v) tall, narrow, unfurnished gelding; showed improved form to win maiden race at Bath in June; not certain to stay 13f; acts on a firm and a soft surface; sweated up on reappearance; didn't impress at all in paddock seventh outing; sold out of I. Balding's stable 5,000 gns Doncaster August Sales after fifth start. *Miss S. Morris.* **75**

MR NICE GUY 6 gr.g. Murrayfield 119–Mead 93 (Honeyway 125) (1979 8g^{2} 8g 8.2g 9fg^{3} 7f 10.2fg 8f^{4} 7g 12g^{3} 8d^{3} 11d^{3} 10h 12fg 1980 11d) quite a moderate handicapper; stayed 11f; acted on any going; sometimes wore blinkers; sold 1,600 gns Ascot May Sales; dead. *M. Naughton.* –

MR NOSEY PARKER 3 ch.g. Porto Bello 118–Doodle 87 (Doudance 99) (1979 5g 5g 5g 1980 8d 5g 10d 8s) of little account; wears blinkers; trained by Mrs R. Lomax first start. *M. Hinchliffe.* –

MR PETIT 3 gr. or ro.g. Zeddaan 130–Balholm 61 (Le Levanstell 122) (1979 5s 5d 6f 6f 7g 1980 10s* 8f 9f^{4} 10h 10g 13.8g^{3} 12fg^{4} 10fg* 13.8fg^{2}) narrow, lightly-made gelding; plater; successful at Nottingham in April (no bid) and September (bought in 2,100 gns); best at $1\frac{1}{4}$m; acts on soft going; has been tried in blinkers; races with head held high. *P. Asquith.* **53**

MR PRESIDENT WEAR 3 b.c. Welsh Saint 126–Rose Amber (Amber Rama 133) (1979 NR 1980 7d 8s 10fg 10.1f 10f) 2,300Y, resold 4,400Y; strong, compact colt; first foal; dam ran twice; well beaten in varied company; unlikely to stay $1\frac{1}{4}$m; blinkered last 2 starts. *B. Swift.* –

MR RAFFERTY 4 ch.g. Apollo Eight–Bebe Mine (Bleep-Bleep 134) (1979 6s 6v^{3} 6g* 7g^{4} 6s^{4} 7g^{4} 6fg* 7f 6fg 6s 6g 1980 6g 6d 6fg 6fg 7g 6d^{3}) strong, robust gelding; moderate handicapper; best form at 6f; acts on any going; suitable mount for an apprentice; blinkered fourth outing. *Denys Smith.* –

MRS CHIPS 3 b.f. Huntercombe 133–Moonlight Story (Narrator 127) (1979 5fg 6g 1980 8d 11d 10d) useless plater. *M. Salaman.* –

MRS HUBBARD 2 ch.f. Silly Season 127–Mrs Paddy 69 (Acropolis 132) (1980 7g 10.2s) Mar 25; fourth foal; sister to 3-y-o Madame Katrine, a winner at up to 11f in French Provinces, and half-sister to a winner; dam placed over $1\frac{1}{2}$m; 25/1 when behind in 26-runner maiden race at Newmarket in October and 21-runner minor event at Doncaster the following month. *W. Hastings-Bass.* **73**

MR SINCLAIR 2 b.g. Lochnager 132–Lively Lassie (Never Say Die 137) (1980 5d^{2} 5f^{3} 5fg 6s 6d) Mar 20; 6,000Y; rather unfurnished gelding; good walker; half-brother to a winning plater and a winner in Italy (both by Sweet Revenge); dam lightly-raced half-sister to Roan Rocket; placed in maiden races at Haydock and Chester in the spring, on latter course finishing $2\frac{1}{4}$ lengths third of 8 to Kareem; should stay 6f (ran moderately when tried over trip); possibly unsuited by soft ground. *M. H. Easterby.* **70**

MRS LEADBETTER 2 b.f. Birdbrook 110–Cricket Bat 87 (Indigenous 121) (1980 5g 5fg^{2} 5fg 5g 5s^{2}) Feb 26; 2,700Y; workmanlike filly; first foal; dam 2-y-o 6f winner; second in maiden races at Newmarket in August ($\frac{3}{4}$ length behind The Barons Lodge) and Hamilton in October (went down by a neck to Scottish Law); will stay 6f; probably acts on any going; hampered start third outing; often ridden by apprentice D. Brockbank. *G. Pritchard-Gordon.* **81**

MRS MUTTON 3 gr.f. Dancer's Image–Blonde Bomb 72 (Worden II 129) (1979 8f 8fg 1980 10fg 12.3f 10f 12d 8g 10s 12g 8g 12g 10.4d 12f^{3} 17.1d 14.6d) lightly-made filly; showed ability (rated 89) at 2 yrs; put up best effort in 1980 on eleventh outing; ran poorly all other starts; stays $1\frac{1}{2}$m; acts on firm going; sometimes wears blinkers; sold 8,800 gns Newmarket December Sales. *P. Kelleway.* **62**

MR SOLO 8 br.g. So Blessed 130–Zimbie 97 (Zimone) (1979 10f^{4} 1980 10d 14g 16f) poor maiden; behind in seller on first outing. *H. Wharton.* –

MRS PALMER 2 b.f. Martinmas 128–Harford Belle 97 (Track Spare 125) (1980 5g 5fg^{2} 5.8g* 5fg* 6fg^{3} 7.3fg^{4} 6d*) Mar 17; 3,400F, 4,000Y; lengthy, **88**

lightly-made filly; first produce; dam, out of half-sister to Oaks winner Ginevra, won over 5f at 2 yrs; winner of maiden auction event at Bath and of nurseries at Goodwood and Haydock, finishing very strongly in last-named in October to win by a length from Arndean; probably stays 7f; acts on a firm and a soft surface; genuine and consistent. *R. Hannon.*

MR SPENCER 3 b.c. Charlottown 127–Monk's Mistress (Rasputin 83) (1979 5g 6s 6fg 7fg 1980 13s 12s 14g 14g) light-framed colt; poor maiden; blinkered last 2 starts. *F. Durr.* —

MRS PENNY (USA) 3 ch.f. Great Nephew 126–Tananarive (Le Fabuleux 133) (1979 5g^{2} 5d^{2} 6f* 6d* 6fg^{4} 6f* 1980 7.3fg^{2} 8fg^{3} 8fg^{3} 10.5g* 12g^{2} 10.5d^{4} 12f* 12f) **127**

The French have had some exceptionally good fillies in the last ten years as the results of the Prix de l'Arc de Triomphe well illustrate. Most years during that period the best two middle-distance races in France confined to three-year-old fillies, the Prix de Diane (the French Oaks, now sponsored by Revlon) and the Prix Vermeille, have taken an enormous amount of winning and have been largely the preserve of the home side. From 1970, when Sweet Mimosa won the Diane and Highest Hopes the Vermeille, until the start of the latest season only Highclere kept a foreign flag flying; many top-class runners from abroad went down in the Vermeille, including the Oaks winners Ginevra, Fair Salinia and Scintillate as well as others just as good if not better. In 1980 both races fell to the English-trained Mrs Penny, who beat a representative field at Chantilly and a very strong one indeed at Longchamp.

Mrs Penny's record differed somewhat from Highclere's before she went to France. Highclere never showed top-class form until she won the One Thousand Guineas whereas Mrs Penny was the best two-year-old filly of her year: Mrs Penny won all three six-furlong pattern races in England in 1979 for two-year-old fillies, the Cherry Hinton Stakes, the Lowther Stakes and the William Hill Cheveley Park Stakes, receiving 9-5 in the Free Handicap against Highclere's 7-11 in 1973. Mrs Penny lost all three races as a three-year-old before Chantilly, whereas the Guineas was Highclere's only race. The point that needs to be made about Mrs Penny's performances in the spring is that she ran well, consistently well, over a distance short of her optimum at a time when she didn't look at her best. She finished second in the Fred Darling Stakes at Newbury, third in the One Thousand Guineas and third in the Goffs Irish One Thousand Guineas, running admirably close to her form with Fred Darling winner Millingdale Lillie when beaten just under a length behind Quick As Lightning and when beaten just under three behind Cairn Rouge.

By June, when the Prix de Diane de Revlon came to be decided, Mrs Penny had blossomed in condition. She needed to be on form to account for Aryenne, the best staying filly among the French two-year-olds of 1979; Aryenne had won the Poule d'Essai des Pouliches on her reappearance and had lost only once in her career, finishing a close fourth in the Prix Saint-Alary, the main Oaks trial in France. These two very game fillies produced a rousing finish to the Diane which resulted in victory by a short head for Mrs Penny. They made their efforts at about the same stage in the straight, Mrs Penny two or three places in front to begin with, and started to draw away from the others going into the final furlong where Mrs Penny had an advantage of half a length or so. Hard ridden by Piggott, Mrs Penny just held on. Apart from Aryenne, the leading French runners in the field of fourteen weren't from the very top drawer though they were good enough to make up what was, as we said, a representative field. Paranete who finished third, beaten about three lengths, had won the Saint-Alary; fourth-placed Luth de Saron had won the Prix Vanteaux from Benicia (third in

Prix de Diane de Revlon, Chantilly—the first of Mrs Penny's successes in France. This time she beats Aryenne in a tight finish. Paranete is third

Prix Vermeille, Longchamp—another game performance from Mrs Penny who wins from an outstanding field. Little Bonny is second, the unlucky Detroit third, Gold River fourth, Cairn Rouge fifth and Mariella sixth. Aryenne is only seventh this time

the Saint-Alary and fifth in the Diane) and Paranete. Surprisingly, this was Piggott's first win in the Prix de Diane.

Mrs Penny had two of her four subsequent races in France. The two in her home country she lost, leaving her without a win of any sort in England in 1980. Upon her return from Chantilly, Mrs Penny was aimed as highly as it was possible to aim, taking on the colts in the King George VI and Queen Elizabeth Diamond Stakes at Ascot and the Benson and Hedges Gold Cup at York; she came out of these tests with great credit, regarded even more highly than before. Mrs Penny went down by only three quarters of a length to Ela-Mana-Mou at Ascot, beating third-placed Gregorian, from whom Piggott had switched to ride her, by five lengths and the 1979 Prix de Diane winner Dunette by a little more. Mrs Penny looked very well again, staying cool, calm and collected in the parade; she is an excellent mover, and went beautifully to post. Held up towards the rear, she followed Ela-Mana-Mou when he went through to lead half a mile out and was on his heels in fourth place on the turn; at that stage and into the straight she was going strongly, and when she took second place on the bridle two furlongs out she looked as though she would beat the leader; she came off the bridle shortly after, though, and only her courage kept her going to the end. At York Mrs Penny didn't have the luck she deserved. Buckpoint trapped her on the rails in the straight and by the time she found enough room to work in, the leaders had gone; once she saw daylight below the distance she began to stay on under pressure, and she kept on for fourth, two and a half lengths behind Master Willie.

Any doubts that Mrs Penny hadn't stayed the mile and a half at Ascot were removed by her performance in the Prix Vermeille at Longchamp in September. If any of the leading contenders failed to stay it was Cairn Rouge, who faded slightly in the closing stages; Mrs Penny held on very well in the face of a strong challenge from a press of top-class European fillies. Close up in the first four of twelve from the start in the hands of stable-jockey Matthias, replacing the suspended Piggott, she was driven past Little Bonny into the lead halfway up the straight and had to fight all the way home for her half-length win. Only three and a half lengths covered the first seven, Aryenne finishing seventh, Mariella sixth, Cairn Rouge fifth, Gold River fourth, the unlucky Detroit third and Little Bonny second. Paranete finished eighth, Luth de Saron last.

What a very game, tough, consistent filly Mrs Penny is! To run so well after a long, hard season involving considerable travel was a marvellous achievement. She couldn't go on for ever, though, and had probably had enough when given a crack at the Prix de l'Arc de Triomphe the following month. She still looked well and she managed to obtain a very good position approaching the straight, but on this occasion Ela-Mana-Mou strode away from her and she soon dropped back through the field, eventually finishing fifteenth of twenty to Detroit who, as we anticipated, turned the tables on both Mrs Penny and Little Bonny. This was the first race in Mrs Penny's career in which she didn't draw prize money.

Mrs Penny, by Grundy's sire, is Great Nephew's best filly. Her dam was bred by M Wildenstein and won races at up to a mile and three quarters for him in France, before being passed on and eventually sold to America carrying Mrs

Mr E. N. Kronfeld's "Mrs Penny"

Penny; Mrs Penny was herself sold for 40,000 dollars at the Saratoga Yearling Sales. Thanks very largely to the exploits of Mrs Penny the dam, Tananarive, fetched 875,000 dollars in foal to Mr Prospector at the Keeneland November Sales in 1980. Tananarive produced two foals in France, one unraced the other unplaced, and has since had a second runner in England, the two-year-old filly Narnia's Princess (by Tentam). The second dam is the the dam of Wildenstein's Tahitian King (by Luthier) and of the good French staying two-year-old of 1968 Tuxpan (by French Beige). She was American bred, and very well bred too, out of a winning half-sister to the Belmont Stakes winner One Count.

Mrs Penny (USA) (ch.f. 1977)	Great Nephew (b 1963)	Honeyway (br 1941)	Fairway Honey Buzzard
		Sybil's Niece (ch 1951)	Admiral's Walk Sybil's Sister
	Tananarive (b 1970)	Le Fabuleux (ch 1961)	Wild Risk Anguar
		Ten Double (b 1961)	Decathlon Roodles

Mrs Penny is a lengthy filly. She seems to act on any going although she hasn't yet had the opportunity to race on really soft—the type of ground seen more often than not at Longchamp in the spring and autumn in recent years. She remains in training along with more of her contemporaries than one dares hope nowadays, so the middle-distance races should be very lively affairs in 1981. *I. Balding.*

MR WIMPY 3 b.g. Golden Mallard 103–Computer 69 (Chanteur II 135) (1979 7s^2 7fg 8.2g 7fg 1980 10s 10.2g 13s) compact gelding; has shown no form since first outing at 2 yrs; best run at 7f on soft going; sold 660 gns Doncaster October Sales. *K. Stone.* —

MT WHITNEY (USA) 3 b.c. Apalachee 137–Ole Liz (Double Jay) (1979 5d 5.8g* 1980 10f^2 8.2f 9fg^2 10f^2 10g 10g) strong, good sort; fair handicapper at his best; stays 1¼m; acts on firm going; none too consistent; sold 20,000 francs (approx £2,000) Chantilly October Sales. *B. Hills.* **88**

MUFF DIVER 5 bl.g. Deep Diver 134–Idiots Delight (USA) (Bold Ruler) (1979 5fg^3 5fg 5h^2 1980 5s 5fg 5f 5s 5f^4) moderate performer; winner of several races in Belgium; remote fourth to Song of Songs in £2,800 event at Ostend in August; stays 6f; looked ill at ease on hard ground on final outing in 1979. *W. Haigh.* **–**

MUI LINDA 5 b.m. Mon Fils 124–Maruka 70 (Abernant 142) (1979 10g^3 10g^3 10fg 12f 1980 16f 12d 12fg 10g 10fg) poor handicapper; stays 1¼m. *B. Wise.* **–**

MULL OF KINTYRE 2 ch.c. Murrayfield 119–Geordie Lass 58 (Bleep-Bleep 134) (1980 5d^3 5fg 5d* 6s 5g 5fg^3 5s^4 5d 5d 6g^2 6s 5d^4) Apr 7; 3,400Y; smallish, good-bodied colt; fourth foal; dam, who barely stayed 5f, is sister to smart sprinter Lazenby; sweating, quickened clear below distance when winning £1,700 seller at York in June by 1½ lengths from Anascend; cost 5,200 gns to buy in; subsequently in frame in nurseries and another valuable seller at York, finishing well clear of 9 others when 2½ lengths second to Supreme Show in last-named in October; stays 6f; seems to act on any going. *P. Haslam.* **77**

MUMMY'S PRIDE 2 b.f. Mummy's Pet 125–Wontell 80 (Buisson Ardent 129) (1980 5d 6g 6fg^4 6d 5g) Apr 9; compact filly; sister to very useful sprinter Mummy's Darling, and half-sister to a winner in Belgium; dam ran only at 2 yrs; 1¾ lengths fourth of 15 to Von Erlach in maiden race at Salisbury in September, best effort; unseated rider several times before finishing behind in nursery at Leicester the following month; blinkered fifth start; looks temperamental; sold 300 gns Ascot November Sales. *P. Cundell.* **66§**

MUMMY'S STAR 6 br.g. Mummy's Pet 125–Dycord 81 (Royal Record II) (1979 12g^3 16fg^2 16f^3 16f 16.1d 1980 22.2fg 16.1d) poor handicapper nowadays; stays 2m; best form on a sound surface; suitable mount for an amateur rider; usually wears blinkers. *S. Mellor.* **–**

MUMMY'S TREASURE 2 b.c. Mummy's Pet 125–Gold Bloom 72 (Klondyke Bill 125) (1980 6g 5fg* 5d 6s 5g) Apr 6; 2,800Y; compact colt; brother to modest 1979 2-y-o 5f winner Glasgows Pet, and half-brother to 5 winners, including tough 1976 2-y-o 5f and 6f winner Regency Bill (by Royalty); dam sprinter; made all to win 10-runner maiden auction event at Folkestone in August comfortably by 3 lengths from Mascarina; well beaten in nurseries last 2 starts; speedy and probably best suited by an easy 5f; acts on a firm surface. *P. Haslam.* **75**

MUMMY'S WHISTLER 3 b.f. Mummy's Pet 125–Clear Whistle 80 (Tin Whistle 128) (1979 5d 5g 5fg 1980 5fg 6f 7fg^4 7fg 7s 5f 6g) narrow, leggy **–**

Timeform Charity Day Selling Plate, York—easy for Mull of Kintyre

filly; has a round action; plater; possibly doesn't stay 7f; blinkered fifth start. *W. Haigh.*

MUNLOCHY 4 b.f. Allangrange 126–Bonne Surprise 105 (Grey Sovereign 128§) **36**
(1979 12g 10fg^3 10.1f 10fg 1980 10fg 10d^3) plater; stays 1¼m (out of her depth when tried over 1½m); sold 800 gns Ascot July Sales. *M. Smyly.*

MUPPET 4 br.g. Mummy's Pet 125–Cornflower 97 (Vilmorin) (1979 6d 5g^3 **61**
5fg^3 5fg^2 5g* 5.8fg 1980 6g 5fg 5fg 6f* 5fg 5f 7f* 5fg^2 6g) plater; successful at Windsor (made all and was bought in 1,450 gns) in May and Folkestone (bought in 1,050 gns) in September; ran poorly when short-priced favourite for similar race on final start; stayed 7f; acted on firm going; ran creditably when blinkered fourth outing at 3 yrs; refused to enter stalls and was withdrawn sixth appearance; dead. *M. Blanshard.*

MURILLO 4 b.g. Windjammer (USA)–Fuiseog (Eudaemon 129) (1979 7d^2 **88**
6g^2 6g* 7fg^4 8s^2 8g^2 10s^4 8.2g 1980 7d* 7.2d^2 8g^3 7fg 8g 7f^2 6s^2 7s^2 6d^2 7s^2) neat gelding; fairly useful handicapper; trotted up by 8 lengths from O. I. Oyston in 22-runner event at Doncaster in March; second 6 times subsequently, including to Sparkling Boy in Ladbrokes (Ayr) Gold Cup in September; probably stays 1¼m but is best at shorter distances; acts on any going but is very well suited by some give in the ground; wears blinkers, and a small bandage on his off-fore. *J. W. Watts.*

MURISCA 2 ch.f. Murrayfield 119–Court Victory 62 (Juvenile Court 112) **–**
(1980 5fg 5f 5fg) Apr 22; 300Y; short-coupled filly; poor plater. *J. Hill.*

MURMANSK 3 gr. or ro.f. Red God 128§–Portden (Worden II 129) (1979 **69**
5fg^2 5fg^3 5f 6fg 5fg^2 1980 6f 6f^2 8f^4 10.1f^4 10s 10f) fair sort; stays 1¼m; acts on firm going; wears blinkers. *F. J. Houghton.*

MURMANSK (USA) 2 b.f. Nijinsky 138–Mohmond (Jaipur) (1980 6g 7fg^2 **81**
7g^2 8fg^4 7d^2 7g^2) Mar 25; compact filly; good mover; half-sister to winners here and in USA, notably Deerslayer (by Tom Rolfe), a smart winner at up to 1¼m; dam never ran; second in maiden races at Brighton, Chepstow, Leicester and Newmarket; beat 24 others when going down by 1½ lengths to Full of Reason in October on last-named; will stay 1¼m; acts on a firm and a soft surface. *H. Cecil.*

MURRAY CLOSE 4 bl.f. Murrayfield 119–Close Your Eyes (Wrekin Rambler **–**
120) (1979 NR 1980 10.1s^4 10.1g) small, unimpressive filly; first foal; dam winning hurdler; fourth of 9 to Glasgow Central in minor event at Windsor in July; reluctant to enter stalls, started very slowly and was always behind when tailed off in similar event on same course later in month. *D. Nicholson.*

MURRFOLD 3 ch.f. Murrayfield 119–Starfold (Ratification 129) (1979 6fg 7f^4 **60**
8g^4 7s^3 1980 9g 8f 8.2d^3 9fg 10g^3 8.2s 8g 10d) workmanlike filly; plating-class maiden; possibly stays 1¼m; probably acts on any going. *Miss S. Hall.*

MURRMATCH 8 br.h. Murrayfield 119–Lobinstown Pilgrim (Tyrone 130) **–**
(1979 5s 6s^2 5s 5s^3 5s 6g^4 5.8g 5.8h 5fg 5d 1980 5fg 5d 10.4d) sprint handicapper; well beaten in 1980; acts on any going; has run moderately when blinkered; bandaged on reappearance. *J. Leigh.*

MUSCOVITE (USA) 3 b.c. Nijinsky 138–Alyne Que (Raise A Native) (1979 **105**
6g* 7d 1980 10g^3 10fg^3 7d 8g* 7fg^3 9fg* 8s^2) $285,000Y; second foal; dam, winner over 6f at 2 yrs, is sister to very useful sprinter L'Natural and closely related to champion sire Exclusive Native; won 4-runner Ballychorus Stakes at Leopardstown in July by 3 lengths from Little Bonny and Whitehall Stakes at Phoenix Park in September by similar margin from Phosphurian; creditable 3 lengths third to Kampala in Beeswing Stakes at Newcastle in between and went down by 2 lengths to My Hollow in Desmond Stakes at the Curragh on final start in September; said by jockey to have been unwilling to respond to pressure on third outing; stayed 1¼m; acted on any going but was well suited by top-of-the-ground; at Spendthrift Farm, Kentucky, fee $15,000 live foal. *V. O'Brien, Ireland.*

MUSHREF (USA) 2 b.c. Key To The Mint–Forever Amber (Bold Lad, Ire 133) **102**
(1980 6fg^2 7g* 6f^3) Apr 1; 110,000Y; compact, quite attractive colt; good mover; first living foal; dam, daughter of Irish Oaks winner Ambergris, won over 7.1f in Ireland; made all when 5/2 on for 4-runner Redcar Silver Salver in July and needed to be pushed out only with hands and heels to score by 2½ lengths from Helvic Storm; had run very well when short-headed by Pellegrini after an indifferent start in Fenwolf Stakes at Ascot the previous month; gave us impression he isn't completely genuine when odds on for Champion Two Yrs Old Trophy

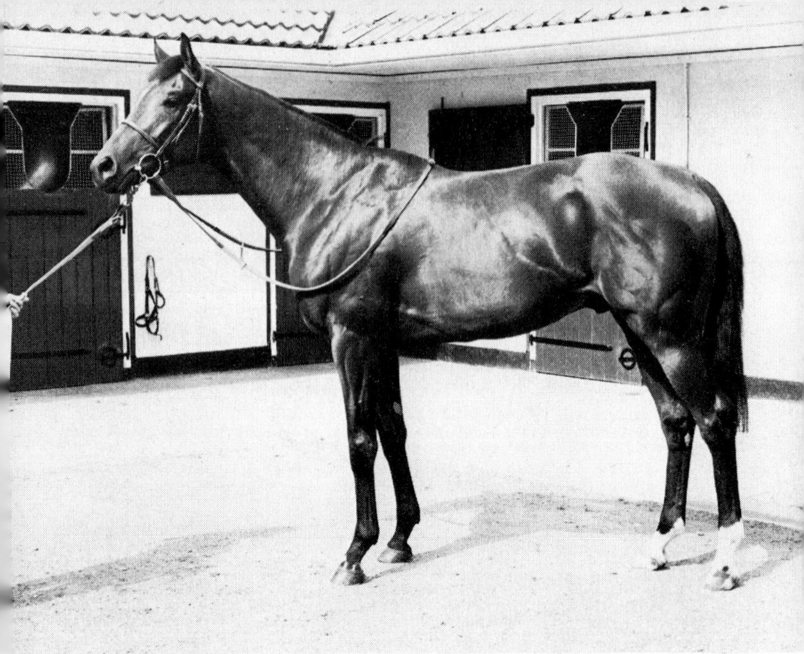

Mr D. Schwartz's "Muscovite"

at Ripon in August, finishing 8 lengths third of 6 to Noalto after racing with his head high; will be suited by a return to 7f or 1m. *H. T. Jones.*

MUSICAL BRIDGE 2 ch.g. Thatch 136–Sweet Sound 74 (Sound Track 132) — (1980 6fg 6s 6d) Feb 17; 74,000Y; attractive, well-made gelding; half-brother to several winners, notably high-class 1973 2-y-o The Blues (by Majority Blue); dam, who ran only at 2 yrs, is daughter of half-sister to Musidora; 12 lengths fifth of 14 behind Beulah Land in minor event at Windsor in June, second outing; tailed off in 25-runner maiden race at Newbury when next seen out, late in October, and was subsequently gelded. *J. Tree.*

MUSICAL KING 2 br.c. Tudor Rhythm 112–Sovereign Melody 89§ (Fortino II 75 120) (1980 5d 5s 5g 5.8f 6g 7d 7g 8.2s 7s) Apr 23; 2,100F, 3,000Y; third produce; dam 2-y-o 5f winner; ran best race when 11 lengths fifth of 13 to Ice Harbour in minor event at Yarmouth in September, seventh appearance; suited by 7f; blinkered second, fourth and fifth outings; trained by D. Elsworth first 5 starts; sold to Susan Piggott BA 1,500 gns Newmarket Autumn Sales. *R. Sheather.*

MUSICAL MINX 2 b.f. Jukebox 120–Battling Bessie (Typhoon 125) (1980 75 6g* 7fg 7fg^3 6fg) Apr 23; 2,500F, 6,000Y; useful sort; half-sister to 2 winners, including French miler Miss Bessie (by Pitskelly); dam, half-sister to Roman Warrior, placed over 6f at 2 yrs in Ireland; 20/1, won maiden race at Nottingham in July by a length from odds-on Miss St James's despite running green; not disgraced in nursery final outing; hung left throughout on second outing; not certain to stay 7f. *C. Nelson.*

MUSICAL PRINCESS 3 b. or br. f. Cavo Doro 124–Toccata (Kythnos 126) 53 (1979 NR 1980 10f^4 10.6d 10.6s 12s) compact filly; half-sister to several winners, including fairly useful 1m to 1¼m winner Abercata (by Aberdeen); dam never ran; showed some ability in maiden and minor races in the North; should be suited by 1½m; seems to act on any going. *E. Weymes.*

MUSICAL SON 2 ch.c. Music Boy 124–Cherio Honey (Macherio) (1980 6g 6f) Mar 17; 5,200F, 6,200Y; well-made, attractive colt; half-brother to a minor winner and to a winner in Malaya; dam half-sister to 1,000 Guineas runner-up Super Honey; in rear in small races at Newcastle and Pontefract; dead. *J. W. Watts.* —

MUSIC CITY 2 gr.c. Town Crier 119–Floating Melody 101 (Tudor Melody 129) (1980 7d²) Apr 12; 16,500Y; brother to Soie Grise, successful at up to 8.5f; dam useful at up to 1m; 20/1 and on burly side, kept on well without being knocked about unnecessarily when 2 lengths second of 20 to Soldan in minor event at Doncaster in October; will stay 1m; a pleasing first effort. *P. Walwyn.* **79** p

MUSIC NIGHT 3 ch.c. Jukebox 120–Directrice (Zank) (1979 5d 5g 5d 6h 7fg 7d² 6s 5fg² 5h* 5g⁴ 1980 6v⁴ 5g 5fg 6fg 6fg* 5g³ 5g 6s³ 5g⁴ 6d) sturdy colt; plater; won at Ripon in June (no bid); stays 7f; acts on any going; sweated up slightly fourth start; best in blinkers; has run respectably for an apprentice. *S. Wainwright.* **53**

MUSKETEER'S MOTTO (USA) 3 b.f. One For All–Duchess of Malfi (Prince John) (1979 NR 1980 10g 11g³ 11d² 12.2f* 13.8g³ 15.8d² 16fg²) $85,000F; compact filly; second produce; dam, winner over 9f at 4 yrs, is sister to Alleged's dam Princess Pout; won modest 16-runner maiden event at Catterick in July; creditable second to Cheka in handicap at Beverley in September on final outing; stays well; probably acts on any going. *J. W. Watts.* **69**

MUSTARDOR 4 ch.f. Relko 136–Skippon 93 (Supreme Court 135) (1979 12g 10d 12g 10.1d 10d 10s 8f 1980 12s 8f) big, rangy filly; poor maiden; blinkered final outing. *W. Musson.* —

MUSTER LANE 6 gr.g. Sovereign Path 125–Welsh Mistress 113 (Abernant 142) (1979 raced in USA 1980 6fg* 6fg³ 6g² 5d 6f* 6s 6f³ 7s³ 6d) big, useful sort of gelding; carries plenty of condition; fairly useful handicapper; successful at Pontefract in July (made all) and September (did well to overcome poor draw when beating Saint Motunde by 1½ lengths); also placed on same course (ridden by 5-lb claimer), at Redcar (twice) and at York; ran as though 7f was just too far for him, at least when conditions are testing, on last-named course; evidently acts on any going; used to wear blinkers. *M. H. Easterby.* **87**

MUSTIKA (USA) 2 b.c. Torsion–Bosuns Strike (Bosun) (1980 5f* 5g 5d 5g) Mar 25; $16,000F, $33,000Y; neat colt; third foal; half-brother to a winner in Puerto Rico by Proud Clarion; dam, very useful stakes winner at 2 yrs, won at up to 1m; disputed lead throughout when winning 11-runner minor event at Lingfield in June by ¾ length from subsequently-disqualified Lucaya; last subsequently in Norfolk Stakes at Royal Ascot, Chesterfield Stakes at Newmarket and Horn Blower Stakes at Ripon, on each occasion dropping right out after showing speed; should stay 6f if ridden with restraint; best run on firm ground; wore bandages final start (August). *E. Eldin.* **83**

MUSZAC 3 ch.c. Lorenzaccio 130–Tudor Madrigal (Tudor Melody 129) (1979 6fg 7f 5f 1980 10.1f 8g) lightly-made colt; in rear in varied company including selling; trained by N. Adam first start; sold 480 gns Ascot August Sales. *M. Blanshard.* —

MUTUAL INTEREST 3 ch.c. Queen's Hussar 124–Welsh Cape (Abernant 142) (1979 5s 5.8h² 5g² 5g³ 1980 6f⁴) well-made, robust colt; moderate (rated 82) at 2 yrs; well beaten only outing in 1980 (April); will stay 7f; acts on hard going. *J. Bethell.* —

MYAMY 3 ch.f. Tarboosh–Bullion (Quorum 126) (1979 5f 6fg 8.2g 1980 8g 8g⁴) leggy, unfurnished filly; poor plater; should stay 1m. *G. Lockerbie.* —

MY BABY LOVE 4 gr.f. Sovereign Path 125–Aucuparia 63 (Celtic Ash) (1979 8d 10f 12.2fg² 12.2d⁴ 12f* 12fg 14.7f 12g 1980 12g 12g 15.8g) big filly; should stay 1¾m; acts on firm going and is possibly unsuited by a soft surface; sometimes blinkered, and wore them when successful at 3 yrs. *K. Stone.* —

MY BALLY-ANNA 5 b.m. Another River 89–Balidium 69 (Psidium 130) (1979 NR 1980 12fg) probably of little account; has been tried in blinkers. *R. Atkins.* —

MY BIRTHDAY 4 b.g. Sun Prince 128–Winter Serenade (Whistling Wind 123) (1979 8s 7v 9s³ 7fg³ 7f 1980 7fg) quite well-made gelding; plater nowadays; best form at 7f; seems to act on any going; blinkered last 2 starts at 3 yrs. *M. Salaman.* —

MY BLUETTE 2 b.f. My Swallow 134–Bluets 74 (Hitting Away) (1980 8fg 8d) —
Jan 21; 3,500F; lengthy, unfurnished filly; third produce; dam won over 1¼m; tailed off in maiden races at Beverley and Redcar in the autumn. *J. Etherington.*

MY CHALLENGE 2 b.c. Copte–Wolfsburg (Neckar) (1980 5fg 5s 7g 5d 7fg —
8fg 8.2g 8d 8.2s) Mar 6; narrow, light-framed colt; in rear in maiden races and sellers; blinkered last 3 starts. *K. Bridgwater.*

MY CHANTAL 2 b.f. Targowice 130–Stipa (Silver Shark 129) (1980 5fg^{3} 5g^{2} **79**
5f* 5s) Apr 11; 9,000Y; small, sharp filly; poor mover in her slower paces; fourth foal; half-sister to 2 winners; dam won at up 6.5f in France; ran on to lead inside final furlong when landing the odds by 2½ lengths from Gloriama in 18-runner maiden race at Catterick in July; put up a poor effort in nursery next time out; should stay at least 6f if ridden with restraint; possibly unsuited by soft going and acts on firm; ran as Chantal first outing. *M. Stoute.*

MY DANNY BOY 3 ch.c. Malicious–Sinecure (Parthia 132) (1979 7fg 8d 1980 **48**
12s 10s 16f^{3} 13.8fg 14fg 13s 13g) strong, compact colt; poor maiden; suited by 2m; acts on firm going. *R. Hollinshead.*

MY GARDENIA 2 gr.f. Most Secret 119–White Gardenia (Right Boy 137) —
(1980 6fg) Mar 7; 1,150Y; big, lengthy filly; second foal; dam ran twice; unquoted and very backward, well behind most of way in 16-runner maiden race won by Priory Lane at Salisbury in September. *J. Hill.*

MY GENTIANA 3 b.f. Northfields–Grindlewald 76 (Le Levanstell 122) (1979 **63**
NR 1980 7fg^{3} 7g 8g 10.4d^{3} 10.1fg 8.2g 10s) 1,750Y; small filly; third foal; half-sister to 6f and 7f winner Movement (by Daring Display); dam won at up to 13f; third in maiden races at Chepstow and Chester in the summer; stays 1¼m; acts on a firm and a soft surface; blinkered sixth start; wears bandages. *R. Sheather.*

MY HOLLOW 5 b.m. Wolver Hollow 126–Saucy Mine 70 (Sheshoon 132) **111**
(1979 13.5g^{2} 12f* 12s* 7g* 10s^{3} 9v^{2} 1980 6fg 9f 13g* 10g^{4} 13.5g^{2} 12s 13.5f^{3} 12d* 12g^{4} 12s^{2} 12g* 9fg 8g^{2} 8s* 11.5d* 10d 12d) lightly-made Irish mare; second foal; dam placed over 1m at 2yrs; didn't race on flat until a 4-y-o (had several unsuccessful outings over hurdles) but developed into a smart performer; won 3 times in modest company from 6 starts late in 1979; improved dramatically in 1980 and won 5 times during a busy season; successful in 3 good races at the Curragh, winning by 3 lengths from Balu in Royal Whip Stakes in July, by 6 lengths from Katsura in Brownstown Fillies Stakes in August and by 2 lengths from Muscovite in Desmond Stakes in September; also won handicap at Leopardstown in June and Ulster Champion Stakes at Down Royal in October, latter by 8 lengths from Arminius; unplaced in Champion Stakes at Newmarket (ninth to Cairn Rouge) and St Simon Stakes at Newbury (respectable 4 lengths fifth to Shining Finish) on last 2 starts; effective at 1m and stays 13.5f; acts on any going; tough and genuine; sold 84,000 gns Newmarket December Sales; to race in USA. *J. Bolger, Ireland.*

MY JEM 2 b.f. My Swallow 134–Senna (Sica Boy 132) (1980 5fg^{3} 5fg* 5g* **82**
6fg^{3} 6g^{2} 5fg* 5s^{3} 6s) Mar 13; 2,000Y; sister to fairly useful 1¼m winner Sweet Swallow and half-sister to 2 winners here and one in Italy; dam won over 11f in France; winner of maiden auction event at Kempton and of nurseries at Folkestone and Warwick; got home by only a head from Ballylingo when short-priced favourite for last-named race in August; ran well next outing (giving impression a return to 6f would suit her), but moderately on final one; seems to act on any going; genuine. *S. Mellor.*

MY JOHN CHARLOTT 3 ch.c. Charlottown 127–My Queenie (Queen's **59**
Hussar 124) (1979 6d 8h 10.6d 10s 1980 12f 16f* 16f^{4} 12.5fg 16.9d 15.5f 18.1g 14.7f) big, strong colt; ridden by 5-lb claimer, won slowly-run maiden race at Thirsk in April; suited by a test of stamina; acts on firm going; blinkered nowadays; sold 4,300 gns Newmarket Autumn Sales. *F. Durr.*

MY LADY JANE 3 ch.f. Sweet Revenge 129–Hosanna (Honeyway 125) —
(1979 NR 1980 10g 10.1g 10.1g 8d) 8,200Y; sturdy filly; half-sister to 2 minor winners; dam poor half-sister to Aureole; well beaten in varied company; not sure to stay 1¼m. *R. Armstrong.*

MY MARTINA 3 b. or br.f. My Swallow 134–True Course II (Sea Charger —
129) (1979 5s 7f 8.2g 1980 10s 12fg 12fg) rangy filly; well beaten all outings in varied company. *P. Rohan.*

MY MORTON (USA) 2 ch.c. Groshawk–Wiltare (Petare) (1980 5s^{2} 5fg^{4} **85**
6f^{2} 6g* 7g^{2} 6g^{3} 6d^{3} 6g^{4} 7d^{2} 7d) Feb 21; $20,000Y; lightly-made, useful-looking colt; half-brother to 3 minor winners; dam, half-sister to high-class

Arbees Boy, won at up to 1m, including a claiming race; favourite when winning 10-runner maiden race at Chepstow in June by 2½ lengths from Fortified with rest quite well strung out; in frame in nurseries (3) and minor race on sixth to ninth outings, putting up a creditable show against Spindrifter at Catterick in October on last-named occasion; will stay 1m; sold to BBA 10,000 gns Newmarket Autumn Sales. *G. Hunter.*

MY MY 6 b.g. My Swanee 122–Particella (Parthia 132) (1979 6v 8f 7g 8g 1980 7.6f 8fg 7.6f) poor handicapper; stays 1m; acts on firm going; sometimes wears blinkers. *A. W. Jones.* —

MY PRETTY MUSIC 2 b.f. Jukebox 120–Pushpa Ji Rao (Sayajirao 132) (1980 5g 6g) well-grown filly; half-sister to numerous winners here and abroad, including fairly useful 5f performer Golden Dukat (by Golden Horus); dam fifth in Irish Oaks; well beaten in maiden race and seller (last of 19) in September; sold 350 gns Ascot November Sales. *J. Douglas-Home.* —

MY RAJAH 3 b.c. Martinmas 128–Gala Belle (Galivanter 131) (1979 6g 7fg 1980 6d 8g 10f^{2} 8g^{2} 8g 12g^{3} 12s*) quite attractive, lightly-built colt; won 24-runner maiden race at Doncaster in November; stays 1½m; acts well on soft going and didn't stride out too well to start on firm third outing. *R. Price.* 80

MYRA'S PET 2 b.f. Auction Ring 123–Blue Saree (Sayajirao 132) (1980 5s^{4} 5g 5d^{4} 6g) Mar 27; 9,200Y; small, narrow filly; half-sister to fairly useful 6f to 1m winner The Frummer (by Prince Tenderfoot) and a winner in Malaya; dam ran twice; put up easily best effort when 2 lengths fourth of 9 behind Trytravelscene in moderate maiden race at Pontefract in August, third outing (didn't have a clear run until well inside final furlong); likely to need at least 1m at 3 yrs. *M. Jarvis.* 64

MY REPPIN 4 ch.c. Jimmy Reppin 131–Knocknashee 70 (Astec 128) (1979 8s 8s^{4} 16s^{4} 12s^{2} 12fg 12f 10fg 1980 12.5v 13.8d 10d) unfurnished colt; best run at 1½m on soft ground (in 1979); has run creditably for an apprentice. *A. Smith.* —

MY SAINT ANNE 4 b.f. Saintly Song 128–My Queenie (Queen's Hussar 124) (1979 12g 11fg^{4} 12fg^{3} 12.3fg 12f^{4} 12f^{2} 12f^{2} 12g 15.8fg 12f 12.5g 10g 10s 1980 12f^{4} 14g 8fg 16fg^{2} 12f^{2} 16.1s) strong filly; plating-class maiden; stays 2m; acts on firm going; sometimes wears blinkers; sweated up third start; trained until after first outing by Hbt Jones; sold 660 gns Newmarket Autumn Sales. *F. Durr.* 60

MY SAINTED AUNT 3 b.f. Saintly Song 128–Deck (Le Dieu d'Or 119) (1979 5d 5d^{3} 5d 5f 5g 1980 8f 7fg 5g) neat filly; bad form, including in a seller; formerly trained by S. Nesbitt. *J. Doyle.* —

MYSTRIQUE 2 b.f. Streak 119–Abercourt 89 (Abernant 142) (1980 5g 5g 6s 5.8f) Mar 24; 4,000Y; half-sister to 5 winners, notably very useful 1979 sprinting 2-y-o Blue Courtier (by Blue Cashmere); dam won 4 times over 5f at 2 yrs; no worthwhile form, including in a seller. *T. Marshall.* —

MY SUSIE GIRL 3 ro.f. Roi Soleil 125–Oram Belle (Quorum 126) (1979 NR 1980 6fg 6f 9f) quite attractive, lightly-made filly; third reported foal; dam never ran; behind in maiden races in first part of season. *J. Dunlop.* —

MY SYLVIA 4 b.f. Shiny Tenth 120–Tweetie Pie (Falcon 131) (1979 6s^{4} 6s^{2} 6fg^{3} 6d 7v* 7f 7g 1980 7v 8.2g 10.8f 6h 7fg 6g 7d 6d 7f) neat, lightly-made filly; stays 7f well; acts on any going but seems well suited by the mud; blinkered nowadays. *D. Marks.* —

MY TIMMY 3 b.g. Lauso–Yanoula 79 (Nosca) (1979 6f 6fg 6fg 1980 10fg) big, rangy gelding; behind in Northern maiden races; will be suited by further; looks more a jumping type. *M. W. Easterby.* —

MY UNCLE SAM 4 b.g. Charlottown 127–My Audrey 100 (Pall Mall 132) (1979 NR 1980 13g 12f 16.1s) lengthy, good sort of gelding; half-brother to 3 winners here and abroad; dam useful 6f to 1m handicapper; won NH Flat race in March; little worthwhile form subsequently, although was off course nearly 5 months before second outing and still needed race final start. *C. Thornton.* —

MY WELLIE 7 b.g. Marcus Brutus 108–Snow Boots 62 (Marshal Pil 108) (1979 12d^{4} 13.8g 12f 12fg 10f 10s 12fg 12fg 1980 13g 12fg 12f 12.2fg* 12d 13.8f) poor middle-distance handicapper; all out when scoring by length from Coriace at Catterick in May, best effort; acts on any going; has been tried in blinkers; usually held up; often apprentice ridden. *W. C. Watts.* 41

N

NABAT 5 b.m. Targowice 130–Such Moor 77 (Santa Claus 133) (1979 NR 1980 8f) ex-Irish mare; winning hurdler; having first outing on flat for two seasons when eighth of 18 to State Councellor in amateur riders race at Thirsk in April (started slowly); stays 11f; acts on a firm surface. *Denys Smith.* —

NABILA (USA) 2 b.f. Foolish Pleasure–Opec (Bagdad) (1980 6fg 7g) Feb 17; $87,000Y; lengthy, slightly hollow-backed filly; good mover; second foal; half-sister to a winner by Key To The Mint; dam very useful winner at up to 1m; 2/1 for 8-runner Kingsclere Stakes at Newbury in June but was never going well and was eased right up from 1½f out, coming home seventh behind Chateau Dancer; not seen out again until August when seventh of 18 to Investa in maiden event at Leicester; bred to stay 1¼m; may be capable of better. *L. Cumani.* —

NADJA 3 b.f. Dancer's Image–Hariota 73 (Hook Money 124) (1979 6fg 7fg⁴ 8h* 1980 10g) neat, well-made filly; won maiden race at Pontefract in 1979; had stiff task and was well beaten in handicap only start at 3 yrs in July; should stay 1¼m. *M. Stoute.* —

NADJAR (FR) 4 gr.c. Zeddaan 130–Nuclea (Orsini 124) (1979 8v² 8fg³ 1980 8s⁴ 8g* 8d 9.2s* 8d* 8g² 10d³) **128**

Nadjar, who didn't race as a three-year-old after sustaining an injury to a cannon bone when finishing third to Irish River in the French Guineas, managed a full season in 1980 that brought excellent reward. With Irish River and Bellypha retired to stud at the end of 1979 and with the premature departure of Nureyev due to a lingering viral illness, Nadjar emerged as a much-needed replacement to defend the top French prizes at around a mile; he won three races, notably the Prix d'Ispahan at Longchamp in June and the Prix Jacques le Marois at Deauville in August.

Nadjar did enough in his first two races to confirm he had retained all his ability, and on his second start he won the Prix de Ris-Orangis at Evry in April by three quarters of a length from Boitron. However, after finishing only sixth of eight to American Prince in the Prix du Muguet at Saint-Cloud two weeks later he was rested for almost two months. Nadjar's lay-off clearly did him a power of good; when next seen out in the Ispahan, over an extended nine furlongs, he was better than ever and in devastating form. He lined up at Longchamp as joint-favourite due to his part-owner's also having a substantial share in the strongly-fancied Northern Baby, winner last time out of the Prix Dollar from Strong Gale and Three Troikas. The ten-runner Ispahan field also included In Fijar, Strong Gale, Foveros and Dragon. Nadjar routed the lot. Taking up the running after Northern Baby, who had set the pace from the off, started to weaken two furlongs from home Nadjar powered clear of his rivals up the straight and by the line had put five lengths between himself and his nearest pursuer, Foveros, who ran on to deprive In Fijar of second close home; this was a most impressive performance, particularly in a Group 1 contest. In August Nadjar defeated another strong field in the Prix Jacques le Marois, racing alone on the stand rails throughout and keeping on well to beat Final Straw a neck. Known Fact, not in top form after a lay-off, finished fifth, beaten about three lengths by Nadjar.

Nadjar continued to run extremely well. After the Marois he looked to have an excellent chance of landing the Prix du Moulin at Longchamp the following month but found the improving Kilijaro just too strong and went down by a neck after going on early in the straight. Nadjar didn't get the opportunity to take the lead in his final race, the Champion Stakes at Newmarket in October. Trapped on the inside rail two furlongs from home he was unable to get going until Cairn Rouge and Master Willie had gone clear entering the

Prix d'Ispahan, Longchamp—Nadjar is an impressive winner from Foveros and In Fijar

Prix Jacques le Marois, Deauville—a good performance by Nadjar who beats Final Straw a neck. Behind (left to right) come Boitron, Manjam, Star Way, Known Fact and Isopach

last furlong. Switched outside Rankin, who eventually finished fourth, Nadjar ran on strongly up the hill, but all too late. Third was the best—an excellent best in the circumstances—he could manage, one and a half lengths behind Cairn Rouge. Incidentally, here Nadjar had his tongue tied down.

An attractive colt Nadjar is a son of Zeddaan, a top-class racehorse from five furlongs to nine furlongs who also had that good sprinter Adraan representing him in 1980. Nuclea, Nadjar's dam, was bred in Germany but did her racing

Captain A. D. D. Rogers' "Nadjar"

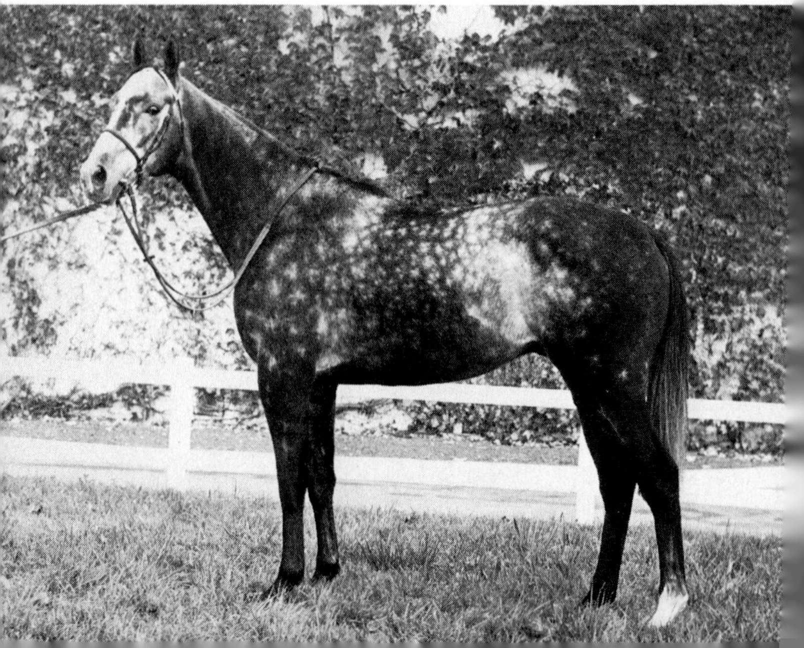

in France, winning three times at up to nine furlongs. She has produced two other winners, notably Nadjar's close relation No No Nanette (by Sovereign Path), a smart winner at up to ten and a half furlongs in France. Nuclea comes

Nadjar (Fr) (gr.c. 1976)	Zeddaan (gr 1965)	Grey Sovereign (gr 1948)	Nasrullah
			Kong
		Vareta (gr 1953)	Vilmorin
			Veronique
	Nuclea (br 1961)	Orsini (br 1954)	Ticino
			Oranien
		Nixe (b 1941)	Arjaman
			Nanon

from a family that has produced many good German horses, including Neckar and Nebos. Nadjar, who stayed a mile and a quarter and who appeared to act on any going, has been syndicated at 270,000 francs (approximately £25,000) a share to stand at the Haras du Thenney, Deauville. *A. Paus, France.*

NAHANE 3 b.f. Porto Bello 118–Hillsquaw (Hillary) (1979 5s 5fg 7g^{4} 7g* 7d 1980 10.2fg^{2} 10f^{4} 10g^{4} 8fg 9g) compact, quite attractive filly; quite a moderate handicapper; stays 1¼m; best form on a sound surface; wore small bandage on near hock final start; trained first 3 outings by B. Hobbs. *P. Bevan.* **69**

NAKHLI (USA) 3 b.c. Cougar–Glad (General Staff) (1979 5s 6g 7fg 7fg* 1980 10d^{4} 9fg^{2} 12fg* 12fg^{3} 11.7f^{4} 12f^{4} 12g 10fg 12f 10.2g) compact colt; quite a moderate handicapper; won at Wolverhampton in April despite not having a clear run; stays 1½m; acts on firm going and a soft surface; blinkered seventh and ninth outings. *F. J. Houghton.* **75**

NAMPARA COVE 5 ch.g. Fair Decision 93§–Aspida (Honeyway 125) (1979 NR 1980 7g) bad plater. *B. Wise.* **—**

NANCY BRIG 3 b.f. Brigadier Gerard 144–Montania 68 (Mourne 126) (1979 6g 7s 1980 9f^{3} 10f) neat filly; quite a moderate maiden; should stay 1¼m; off course 3 months before second start. *J. W. Watts.* **63**

NANKEEN 3 gr.f. Royal Smoke 113–Camlet 60 (Fleece 114) (1979 5s 5g 5s 5fg 1980 7f 8fg 6fg 6f 6fg 5.8g) small filly; little worthwhile form, including in sellers; blinkered third and fifth starts. *O. O'Neill.* **—**

NANNINA 5 b.m. Martinmas 128–Auriann (Aureole 132) (1979 9fg 10s 8d 1980 7d 6g 5.1g 6g 6g 6g 7fg 8f 8.2s^{4} 8s) lengthy, light-framed mare; ran best race for a long time when close fourth to Kithairon in handicap at Haydock in October; stays 1¼m; acts on any going. *I. Walker.* **61**

NANOOKA 2 b.f. Mansingh 120–Nootka (Dike) (1980 6fg 6g^{2} 7g 7fg) Jan 13; 1,500Y; rather lightly-made filly; second foal; dam never ran; 33/1, kept on strongly when ¾-length second of 23 to Hurtwood Lass in valuable seller at Doncaster in September; well beaten afterwards in maiden race and a £2,200 seller (last of 16 after moving badly to start); stays 6f; wears blinkers. *G. Pritchard-Gordon.* **68**

NAOMH ANTON 5 b.g. Bluerullah 115–Via Latina (Lauso) (1979 NR 1980 15.4s) ex-Irish gelding; runner-up in bumpers race in 1979; unquoted when behind in minor event at Folkestone in July. *R. Head.* **—**

NARIZ 4 ch.c. Brigadier Gerard 144–Luscinia 73 (Sing Sing 134) (1979 6v^{2} 5s^{2} 5d 6g^{4} 6g^{2} 6s^{2} 5f* 5f^{3} 7fg 7fg 6g* 6s^{4} 1980 6fg 6fg^{2} 5.8fg 6g 6fg 6fg 6f) strong, useful colt; poor mover; quite a moderate handicapper; best form at up to 6f; acts on any going; slowly away seventh outing. *G. Lewis.* **66**

NARNIA'S PRINCESS (USA) 2 b.f. Tentam–Tananarive (Le Fabuleux 133) (1980 5fg 6s^{3} 6fg^{3} 5f^{3} 8fg^{2}) Feb 28; $95,000Y; leggy filly; good walker; half-sister to leading 1979 2-y-o filly and top-class middle-distance 3-y-o Mrs Penny (by Great Nephew); dam won from 6f to 1¾m in France; placed in maiden races, final occasion finishing length second of 13 to Crystal Gael after running bit wide round bend at Beverley in September; will be well suited by 1¼m. *I. Balding.* **77**

NASH ROLLER (USA) 2 ch.c. Nashua–Gray Lawn Rabbit (Native Charger) (1980 7d 7fg 7fg) Mar 29; $20,000F; strong sort; second foal; half-brother to 1979 American 2-y-o winner Earlstone (by Dunfee); dam won over 1m; little worthwhile form in maiden races; looks slow. *A. Hide.* **—**

NASRUDIN (FR) 2 b.c. Filiberto 123–Niamara 110 (Emerson) (1980 6fg 7fg 7g) Feb 2; 1,000Y; 1,450 2-y-o; tall, lengthy colt; half-brother to Niara (by Appiani II), successful at up to 9f in France; dam second in Prix Saint-Alary and fourth in Oaks; no worthwhile form, including in a seller. *W. Bentley.* **—**

Cherry Hinton Stakes, Newmarket—Nasseem wins from Doobie Do and Chemin

H. H. Aga Khan's "Nasseem"

NASSEEM (FR) 2 gr.f. Zeddaan 130–Noureen (Astec 128) (1980 5g* 5g^3 6d* **108**
6fg^3 6fg^4) Feb 28; lengthy, attractive filly; excellent walker and good mover; first foal; dam unraced half-sister to Tajubena, a very smart winner at up to 1½m; successful in 26-runner maiden race at Salisbury in June and 11-runner Cherry Hinton Stakes at Newmarket the following month; always going well, led 1f out and ran on strongly when beating Doobie Do by ¾ length in latter event; behind Pushy when meeting her 3 defeats, finding 5f too sharp when 2¼ lengths third to her in Queen Mary Stakes at Royal Ascot, being beaten a length by her when 2½ lengths third to Cut Throat in Sirenia Stakes at Kempton and 1½ lengths by her when 3 lengths fourth of 8 to Marwell in William Hill Cheveley Park Stakes at Newmarket; a fine type of filly who will do much better when given stiffer tests of stamina at 3 yrs. *F. J. Houghton.*

NASSIB'S PRINCE 3 b.c. Red Alert 127–Lady Bio (Prince Bio) (1979 6fg **–**
5f 6d 1980 7v 8s 6f 8fg 6f 8d 7g) deep-bodied colt; poor maiden; best form at 6f on firm going; wears blinkers. *M. Haynes.*

NATHANIEL 3 b.g. Shantung 132–Pink Standard 81 (Tudor Melody 129) **–**
(1979 6fg 6g^3 7d 8fg* 8s 1980 10s^3 8f 8fg 8g 11d^4 10.6d 8fg 10s) sturdy gelding; quite a moderate handicapper; will stay 1½m; seems to act on any going. *M. W. Easterby.*

NATIONAL IMAGE 3 b.g. Sassafras 135–Pepi Image 111 (National) (1979 **83**
6.3f 6d^4 7.9g^2 7d^3 7.5d 1980 10s^4 10g* 11g* 12d) ex-Irish gelding; second foal; half-brother to Irish 6f winner President Elect (by Prince Regent); dam third in Irish 1,000 Guineas; successful in maiden race at Limerick and handicap at Galway in July; out of his depth in St Simon Stakes at Newbury in October; stays 11f; trained by N. Meade first 3 starts. *M. Tate.*

NATION WIDE 7 b.g. Irish Ball 127–Misylda 100 (Faubourg II 127) (1979 **76**
14g^3 18.4d^2 14f 16.1g^4 16d^3 15.8fg^3 14fg 17.4s^3 1980 14.6fg 16.1fg^4 16g^4 16.1g^3 17.4s^2 16.1s^3 16.1s* 14g^4 15d^3) modest handicapper; finished clear of remainder but refused to put his best foot forward when ½-length second to Angelo Salvini in Eglinton and Winton Memorial Handicap at Ayr in September; sympathetically handled when beating Tedham Moss by 1½ lengths at Haydock the following month; stays really well; acts on any going; blinkered twice at 3 yrs; has run well for an apprentice; often gets himself well behind in early stages; not resolute. *H. Wragg.*

NATIVE BREAK (USA) 3 b. or br.g. Native Charger–Commercial Break **70**
(Stevward) (1979 7f^3 7.2g^2 8.2g^4 8.2g 1980 8d 10v^4 12fg* 12.5fg^4 13.8fg* 12d 13.8f^2 15.8f^4 14.7f 16.1s 15.8d) compact gelding; has a round action; won maiden race at Edinburgh in April and handicap at Catterick in June; stays 1¾m (well beaten over 2m); acts on firm going and isn't at his best on soft; sometimes sweats up. *S. Norton.*

NATIVE HEATH 5 ch.g. Habitat 134–Rosolini 109 (Ragusa 137) (1979 8s^4 **–**
8s 9g 7f 7f 6s 12d 1980 10.2d) plater; best form at up to 1¼m; has worn blinkers; successful in Sweden. *W. Musson.*

NATIVE JEWEL 4 b.c. Native Prince–Somers Jewel (Will Somers 114 §) **53** d
(1979 6s^3 6s^4 6v^2 6s 6g 7g 7fg 8.2fg^4 8fg^4 8fg^3 8fg 9d^3 9d 1980 8fg^4 8fg* 8g 9d 10.8fg 10g) strong, compact, good-bodied colt; has been tubed; plater; retained 920 gns after winning at Carlisle in June; stays 1m; acts on any going except hard; sold 260 gns Doncaster October Sales. *W. Clay.*

NATIVE PROSPECTOR (USA) 3 b.c. Mr Prospector–French Blossom (Carlemont 132) **75**
(1979 5s 6f 7g 7g^3 6f 7.6f 6fg^2 1980 7f 8.2fg 7f 7g^2 8g 8d^4 8g* 8s^4) good sort; won 21-runner maiden race at Goodwood in September; twice ran creditably in handicaps, including when sweating up on fourth start; stays 1m; probably acts on any going; bandaged third outing; trained by P. Read first 5 starts. *A. Breasley.*

NATURE'S WAY 2 b.f. Zamindar–Free and Easy (Liberator III) (1980 5.8fg* **81**
6g) Apr 2; light-framed filly; half-sister to several winners, including smart 5f sprinter Bold and Free (by Bold Lad Ire) and good miler Watergate (by Sovereign Path); dam useful Irish miler; sire brother to high-class 1963 2-y-o Mesopotamia; 9/2, put up a pleasing first effort when winning 11-runner maiden race at Bath in July by a length from Sweet Monday; fair fifth of 10 to Maryland Cookie in nursery at Salisbury the following month; will be suited by 7f. *N. Vigors.*

NAUTIC STAR 2 b.c. Connaught 130–Starbright (Petingo 135) (1980 7d) **–**
Feb 27; first foal; dam, half-sister to useful 1979 3-y-o La Dolce (by Connaught),

ran once at 2 yrs; unquoted and in need of race when behind in 17-runner minor event won by Soldan at Doncaster in October. *C. Brittain.*

NAUTIQUE 2 ch.f. Windjammer (USA)–Porthole (Major Portion 129) (1980 **64**
5s 5f 6s^3 6d 6fg^4 8fg 7d) Mar 7; 5,000Y; leggy filly; sister to a modest plater and half-sister to 3 minor winners; dam ran only once; beaten 4 lengths when in frame in maiden races won by Jade Girl at Stockton in June and by Glenbank Lass at Redcar in July (auction event); best form at up to 6f but should stay 1m. *W. Wharton.*

NAVAJO BRAVE (USA) 2 gr.c. Navajo–Rosy Lark (T.V. Lark) (1980 7f 8d) —
Apr 5; $15,000Y; tall colt; half-brother to several minor winners; dam, 6f winner, is half-sister to smart filly Krislin; sire, son of Grey Dawn, won 22 races from 5f to 9.5f; behind in minor event at Lingfield and 21-runner maiden race at Sandown in October. *G. Hunter.*

NAVETTE 2 b.f. Ashmore 125–Diamond Spur (Preciptic 122) (1980 6g^3 6s^4 7fg **72**
8d 8d) June 5; 7,000F, 24,000Y; quite attractive, useful-looking filly; half-sister to 3 winners, notably top-class miler Sparkler (by Hard Tack); dam ran 4 times in Ireland; quite moderate; beaten less than 2 lengths when fifth in minor event at Newbury and maiden race at Warwick in the autumn, third and fourth outings; stays 1m; ran poorly in blinkers final outing. *J. Tree.*

NAVIGATIONAL AID 3 b.g. Blind Harbour 96–Tiny Clanger 73 (Sky Gipsy **94**
117) (1979 7fg 8h^2 8g* 1980 10v* 12g* 10f^3 12g 16g^2 16fg^3 18d 18s) big, rangy gelding; quite useful handicapper; won at Ayr in March and Ripon in April; ran creditably several times afterwards; stays 2m but not 2¼m; acts on any going; blinkered penultimate outing; possibly needs strong handling. *J. W. Watts.*

NAWAF (USA) 3 ch.c. Apalachee 137–Ideal Day (Buckpasser) (1979 6g^3 **94**
1980 10.5f^4 8fg^2 8.2g^4 10s^3 10g* 10d^2 8.2g* 8g*) big, strong, rangy colt; good mover; successful in maiden race at Ayr, minor event at Hamilton and ladies race at Newmarket in the summer; beat Tudor Chief 5 lengths in last-named; stays 1¼m; appears to act on any going; sweated up sixth start; gives impression he will always do best on a galloping track; suitable mount for an inexperienced rider; sold 8,000 gns Newmarket Autumn Sales. *M. Stoute.*

NEAT 2 ch.c. Wollow 132–Brilliantine 109 (Stage Door Johnny) (1980 7v) Mar — p
7; tall, lengthy colt; second foal; dam, winner over 7f and 1¼m, is half-sister to Bright Finish and Shining Finish; backed at long odds for 9-runner Steel Plate Autumn Stakes at Doncaster in November but started to struggle at halfway and finished only seventh to Sula Bula; not knocked about when chance had gone, has scope and is likely to do better over 1¼m+ at 3 yrs. *J. Tree.*

NEBOS (GER) 4 b.c. Caro 133–Nostrana (Botticelli 129) (1979 8.5g* 11f* **129**
12g^2 12s* 12g^2 12g* 1980 11g* 12g* 11g* 12g* 12g^2 12g* 12f 12d^3) German-bred colt; half-brother to numerous winners, including smart 1976 French 2-y-o 7f winner Numa Pompilius (by Dr Fager), subsequently a stakes winner at up to 11f in USA; dam won 2 races in Germany; an outstanding performer in Germany; gaining his fifth win of the season when beating Cherubin by a length in Group 1 Grosser Preis von Baden at Baden-Baden in September (had Nicholas Bill behind in fourth, Argument in fifth and Cracaval in eighth); successful earlier at Cologne, Dortmund and Dusseldorf (twice), including Grosser Preis von Dortmund (by 3 lengths from Windlauf), Grosser Preis von Dusseldorf (beat Konigsstuhl by 2½ lengths) and Group 1 Grosser Preis von Berlin (beat Marracci by 3½ lengths); made up a tremendous amount of ground in straight after being unable to go early pace and acquitted himself with great credit when less than 2 lengths fifth to Detroit in Prix de l'Arc de Triomphe at Longchamp in October; met only other defeats when beaten a nose by Wauthi in Group 1 Aral Pokal at Gelsenkirchen and when about 2 lengths third to Pawiment in Preis von Europa at Cologne; ran moderately in latter and was probably feeling effects of his Longchamp exertions; stayed 1½m; acted on any going; most genuine, although sometimes sweated up and gave trouble at start; syndicated for 3,000,000 DM (approx £650,000) before Arc and will stand at Gestut Erlenhof, near Frankfurt, at a fee of 15,000 DM. *H. Bollow, Germany.*

NEEDWOOD 2 b.c. Averof 123–The Doe 87 (Alcide 136) (1980 6fg 7.2d 8.2d) —
May 19; good-bodied colt with poor forelegs; in rear all outings, including in a seller; sold 700 gns Doncaster October Sales. *J. Fitzgerald.*

NEEDWOOD NAP 2 b.f. Some Hand 119–Suku 80 (Light Thrust 114) (1980 —
5f 5fg 5fg) Apr 8; compact, well-made filly; half-sister to sprint winner Tricia's

Treasure (by My Swanee); dam won over 1m; only poor form, including in a seller. *J. Fitzgerald.*

NEENAH 3 ch.f. Bold Lad (Ire) 133–Whitefoot 108 (Relko 136) (1979 6f* 6f^4 6f 7.3s^2 1980 7.3fg 10.5f 12f^2 10g 10s) rangy filly; good walker and mover; won Virginia Water Stakes at Ascot and finished 5 lengths second to Shoot A Line in £4,100 event at Newbury in 1979; didn't run up to her best at 3 yrs though wasn't disgraced when 7½ lengths sixth of 9 behind Bireme in Musidora Stakes at York in May on second start or 2½ lengths second of 3 to Beirut in small race at Beverley in July; stays 1½m; acts on any going; blinkered fourth start; sold 37,000 gns Newmarket December Sales. *H. Wragg.* **103**

NEEPROBLEM 5 b.m. Daring Display 129–Wolf Girl 89 (Romulus 129) (1979 NR 1980 18d) poor maiden. *B. Wilkinson.* —

NEFER 3 b.f. Mummy's Pet 125–Charming Thought (Stage Door Johnny) (1979 NR 1980 5fg) round-actioned filly; second foal; dam disappointing maiden; 20/1 and sweating, gave trouble at start and was always behind in minor race won by Sandra's Secret at Stockton in June; sold 550 gns Doncaster August Sales. *M. H. Easterby.* —

NELLO (USA) 2 b.f. Charles Elliott–Color Me Blonde (Craigwood) (1980 6fg^3 5f^4 6d 6g*) Mar 22; 12,000Y; plain filly; sister to Secret Visit, winner at up to 9f in USA, and half-sister to several minor winners; dam placed at 2 yrs in USA; 20/1, won 20-runner maiden race at Leicester in November by 3 lengths from H. R. Micro, quickening nicely in closing stages; will stay 1m. *G. Balding.* **85**

NELLY DO DA 3 gr.f. Derring-Do 131–Flying Nelly 107 (Nelcius 133) (1979 5.8g* 1980 7.3fg 8.5f 8g^4) small, lightly-made filly; won maiden race at Bath in 1979; had stiff tasks when well beaten in varied company at 3 yrs; should stay 1m+. *W. Wightman.* —

NELTINO 2 gr.c. Bustino 136–Flying Nelly 107 (Nelcius 133) (1980 7g^2 8fg 7g^3) Mar 5; 100,000Y; robust colt; second foal; half-brother to 1979 2-y-o 5.8f winner Nelly Do Da (by Derring-Do); dam stayed 13f but was best at 1m to 1¼m; short-priced favourite, kept on well under pressure after being headed 1½f out in 14-runner minor event at Kempton in September, finishing ½-length second to Rasa Penang; subsequently ran in much better races at Ascot (Royal Lodge Stakes) and Newmarket (Somerville Tattersall Stakes), better effort when about 4 lengths third of 8 to Spark Of Life on latter course in October; looks short of pace and will be suited by 1¼m+ at 3 yrs. *R. Hern.* **90**

NEMR 3 ch.c. Thatch 136–Grecian Craft 90 (Acropolis 132) (1979 8s 7.5g^2 8s 1980 9s* 9.2fg 8d^2 10fg* 9d 10s^3 10d 8d 8v*) 84,000Y; second foal; half-brother to 7f winner Meliora (by Crowned Prince); dam disappointing sister to smart stayer Mariner; won maiden race at Evry in March, Group 3 Prix la Force at Longchamp in May (beat Speed Bus ½ length) and 60,000 francs event at Saint-Cloud in December; creditable third of 11 to Corvaro in Prix Eugene Adam at Saint-Cloud in July; stays 1¼m; seems to act on any going; blinkered first outing at 2 yrs. *M. Saliba, France.* **116**

NEPARREE (USA) 5 b.h. Herbager 136–Clinkers 111 (Relic) (1979 12fg 12d 10.4d^2 12s^3 12s 12fg 1980 10.2s^2 10s^4 12fg 10f^4 12f* 12f^2 12g 12s 12.3g* 12fg^4 12fg^4 12.3d* 14.6g^3 13.3fg 14s) tall, useful-looking horse; held up when winning handicaps at York in May (beat Rafael Molina a neck) and at Chester in July and August; suited by 1½m and seems to stay 1¾m; acts on any going; suited by a strongly-run race; not the easiest of rides; to be trained by O. Douieb in 1981 and will probably act as a pacemaker for Detroit. *B. Hills.* **94**

NEPENTHA 2 br.f. Great Nephew 126–Opium 97 (Espresso 122) (1980 8f 8g^2) June 15; leggy, quite useful sort; half-brother to quite useful 1976 2-y-o winner Mecanopsis (by Major Portion); dam won at up to 1½m; well-backed 12/1 shot, prominent throughout and kept on strongly when length second of 17 to Dragon Palace in maiden race at Newmarket in October; missed break previous outing; will stay 1¼m+. *B. Hobbs.* **78**

NEPOTISM 3 b.c. Great Nephew 126–Lantana 74 (St Paddy 133) (1979 6f^4 1980 8fg 12g* 12g 12d^2 13.3d 11d 12g 11.1g 10g 8d) big, strong colt; showed much improved form to win 18-runner maiden race at Salisbury in June by 1½ lengths from Sir Eamon; ran respectably in handicaps on fourth and sixth starts; suited by 1½m (well beaten over further); suited by some give in the ground; blinkered last 2 outings. *G. Balding.* **90** d

NERVE 2 b.f. Daring Display 129–Bordelaise 96 (Above Suspicion 127) (1980 6g 6g 6g 5d) Apr 17; 1,500Y, resold 3,100Y; neat filly; poor mover; half-sister to 2 winners, including 3-y-o Love Supreme (by Sallust), a winner over 6f and 1m; no worthwhile form, including in sellers; blinkered fourth outing. *J. Doyle.* —

NETTLEFOLD 2 b.f. Netherkelly 112–Barlow Fold 99 (Monet 127) (1980 7fg) Feb 27; 2,500 Y; good-topped filly; half-sister to several winners here and abroad, including useful 1976 2-y-o sprinter Namara (by Pieces of Eight); dam won over 5f at 2 yrs; outsider of party and on backward side when tenth of 11 to Giannutri in minor event at Newbury in September. *J. Hudson.* —

NETT-RATE 5 b.m. Andrea Mantegna–Green Dale (Eudaemon 129) (1979 16s 16d 14d 12s4 11.1d 14g 12s 1980 12f 13.3g 16g) poor maiden; has been tried in blinkers. *P. Arthur.* —

NEVER ENOUGH 2 b.f. Sandford Lad 133–Suffice 84 (Faberge II 121) (1980 6g 6d) Apr 13; 6,600Y; well-made filly; good walker; third foal; dam won over 8.5f and 1½m; prominent most of way when eighth of 25 to Little Wolf in maiden race at Newbury in October, second outing; will stay 1m. *M. Smyly.* —

NEVER IN TROUBLE 2 ch.c. Nonoalco 131–Never In Need (Never Say Die 137) (1980 7g 7g 8fg 8d) Mar 4; 14,000Y; big, rangy colt; excellent mover; half-brother to 1½m winner Needless (by Petingo) and to a winner in Italy; dam twice-raced daughter of smart sprinter Patroness; a taking individual but seems not to have the ability to match his looks; blinkered fourth outing. *N. Vigors.* —

NEVER SAY WHEN 2 ch.f. Roman Warrior 132–Cordon Rouge 99 (Never Say Die 137) (1980 6g 5f 5.3g 6fg 7d) Apr 26; 6,600Y; big, strong filly; third living foal; dam suited by 1½m; in rear in maiden and minor events. *D. Whelan.* —

NEVER STOP (FR) 3 b.g. Go Marching–Telstop (Fine Top 125) (1979 5s 6g 1980 10f 12fg 12f 16fg 15s4) slow maiden; stays well; best run on soft going. *H. Bell.* —

NEVER SWEETER (USA) 4 b.c. Never Bend–Anne la Douce 123 (Silnet 131) (1979 10.5v 9d4 10.5d 7.5g3 8g 8d 1980 12.5v 13g4 12f4 12fg2 12d4 11g2 12g* 13g2 11fg4 13s2 12g 12fg) neat, attractive ex-French colt; ridden by 5-lb claimer, made all in handicap at Hamilton in July; stays 13f; probably unsuited by heavy ground; sweating ninth start. *T. Craig.* 59

NEWARK 5 br.g. Folkestone–Street Hawker 74 (Ben Hawke 94) (1979 8.2g 8.2fg 10f 7fg 1980 8s 8fg 12g2 14.6fg 16.5fg 12g) rangy gelding; ran best race for some time when second to Sakeena in handicap at Edinburgh in June; stays 1½m; acts on any going. *H. O'Neill.* —

NEW BERRY 4 br.c. Sir Gaylord–Red Berry 115 (Great Nephew 126) (1979 7fg2 8d* 10v* 10.5g* 12g 11.1f 11d4 1980 8d* 10f4 10fg2 8.5f2 8d2 10d) neat colt; good mover; very useful performer; beat Intercraft Boy a neck under 9-13 in Playboy Handicap at Kempton in April; runner-up subsequently in Clive Graham Stakes (4 lengths behind Sea Chimes) on same course, Diomed Stakes at Epsom (went down by 1½ lengths to Hardgreen) and Queen Anne Stakes (beaten 3 lengths by Blue Refrain) at Royal Ascot; disappointing eighth of 13 behind Mokka in Hessen-Pokal at Frankfurt in July on final outing; stays 10.5f; acts on any going, but has done all his winning on an easy surface; sent to race in USA. *P. Walwyn.* 111

NEW CONTINENT (USA) 2 ch.g. Son Ange–Clover Blossom (Green Ticket) (1980 6fg 8fg 10s) May 23; $30,000Y; rangy gelding; brother to Native Blossom, a very useful sprinting 2-y-o who later won over 1m, and half-brother to 3 winners; dam stakes-placed winner at up to 6f; unquoted and not fully fit when behind in large fields of maidens in second half of season. *E. Eldin.* —

NEW EMBASSY (USA) 3 b.g. Dynastic (USA)–Joys Will (Yes You Will) (1979 5fg3 6f 5g2 5d3 5f* 5s3 5fg3 6f 1980 6s 6fg4 6d 5fg 5g 8g4 8d) strong, well-made, good-quartered gelding; fairly useful handicapper at his best; ran creditably second start but moderately afterwards; best at sprint distances; acts on any going. *G. Balding.* 97

NEWGATE 7 b.g. Blakeney 126–Set Free 90 (Worden II 129) (1979 12s 12s2 13.8s 10f 12f* 12.2s 12.5g 1980 12.2g 12d 12fg4 12fg 12g 12fg4 15d) middle-distance performer; fourth to Gambling Wren in handicap at Carlisle in September, third and best effort; acts on any going; has been tried in blinkers. *A. Scott.* —

NEW JERUSALEM 3 b. or br.c. Reform 132–Desertville 92 (Charlottesville **112** 135) (1979 NR 1980 11fg^{3} 11.7fg 12g 14d* 12g^{2} 21fg^{3} 14g^{2} 17.4s^{4}) lengthy colt; has a round action; half-brother to several winners, including smart 1975 French staying 2-y-o Empty Jest (by Bon Mot III), subsequently a winner at up to 1¾m; dam, winner over 1m at 2 yrs, is half-sister to Tiger and Berber; wide-margin winner of maiden race at Sandown in June; ran well afterwards to be placed in small event at Kempton, Goodwood Cup (highly creditable 3¼ lengths third of 5 to Le Moss) and Tote-Ebor Handicap at York (4 lengths second to Shaftesbury); well suited by a test of stamina; possibly not at his best on very soft ground; best in blinkers; ran poorly second start; sold only 4,300 gns Newmarket Autumn Sales. *R. Hern.*

NEW JOURNALISM 2 br.g. London Gazette 117–October Rose (Hul a Hul **72** 124) (1980 5f 6g 5fg^{4} 6s 6g) Apr 18; 1,000F; small, lightly-made gelding; had a round action; second produce; dam never ran; ran best race when 3¾ lengths fourth of 11 to Chumwar in maiden race at Newcastle in July; badly drawn when distant eighth in £2,700 seller at York in October on final start (second favourite); should have been suited by 6f+; trained by Denys Smith first 3 outings; dead. *M. H. Easterby.*

NEWLIFE CONTRACTS 4 br.g. Warpath 113–Cashalaika (Cash and Courage **—** 116) (1979 12g 12g 16fg 12g 1980 8g 12.3d 9.4g 12.2f) of little account; dead. *W. A. Stephenson.*

NEW MODEL 2 b.c. Reform 132–Fashion Model 100 (Road House II) (1980 **—** 8g) Mar 9; 15,500Y; strong, workmanlike colt; brother to fairly useful 3-y-o 1m to 1¼m winner Pelayo, and half-brother to 2 winners, including very smart 1974 2-y-o 5f winner Desert Way (by Tribal Chief); dam sprinter; 50/1 and far from ready, started very slowly and was always in rear in 12-runner minor event won by Kalaglow at Goodwood in September. *B. Swift.*

NEW STRIKE (USA) 2 br.c. Dynastic (USA)–Latin Wave (Roman Line) **69** (1980 5f^{4} 5fg 5.8fg 6d^{3} 7g^{3} 7d^{4} 7h 8.2g 8d) Apr 12; $23,000Y; small, quite useful sort; brother to Gonzago, winner of 4 races at up to 6f, including claiming races; apprentice ridden when third in quite valuable nurseries at Lingfield and Brighton in the summer; stays 7f but has been well beaten over 1m, wearing blinkers on final outing; best form with some give in the ground; sweated up sixth start (ran respectably). *G. Balding.*

NEW THATCH 2 b.c. Thatch 136–Tinkling Sound 93 (Sound Track 132) **57** (1980 5fg 5fg) Mar 22; 9,800Y; good-bodied colt; half-brother to quite useful 1977 2-y-o sprinter Sounding Brass (by Philip of Spain); dam won over 6f at 2 yrs; backed from 20/1 to 8/1 when 8½ lengths sixth of 15 to Aridje in maiden race at Kempton in May, second outing; will stay 6f. *B. Hills.*

NEW TOP 4 b.f. New Brig 120–Peg Top 93 (Star Moss 122) (1979 10.8s^{2} **62** 10.8s^{3} 12fg 1980 16s^{3} 18s^{3}) staying maiden on flat; third in handicaps at Nottingham in April (hung off bridle) and Doncaster in November; acts on soft going and is probably unsuited by firm. *Miss A. Sinclair.*

NEW YEARS DAY (USA) 2 ch.c. Personality–Super Legend (Lucky Debon- **91** air) (1980 6g* 6fg^{2} 6f 7.3d) Mar 27; $33,000Y; strong, lengthy colt; first foal; dam won 3 times at up to 6f at 3 yrs; made all and held off Pavilion by ¾ length in 7-runner Granville Stakes at Ascot in July; went down by a head to No-U-Turn when 11/10 favourite for minor event at Windsor the following month; subsequently out of his depth in William Hill Middle Park Stakes and Horris Hill Stakes; should be suited by 7f; bolted at Ascot in September and had to be withdrawn. *P. Cole.*

NICE AND FRIENDLY 6 b.g. Be Friendly 130–Sidam 79 (Psidium 130) **—** (1979 NR 1980 12.2g 16f) strong gelding; plater; stayed 1½m; best form on an easy surface; wore bandages; dead. *T. Barron.*

NICE BOUNTY 5 ch.g. Dubassoff–Supreme Courtesan (Relic) (1979 10g **—** 12d 10g 10.1g 10f^{2} 10f* 11.7f 1980 10.6fg 10d 10g 10s) middle-distance handicapper; won amateur riders race at Folkestone in 1979; well beaten in 1980, including in seller; acts on firm going. *G. Balding.*

NICE VALUE 6 ch.g. Goldhill 125–Sinecure (Parthia 132) (1979 5s* 6s **85** 6g 5v 6fg 5fg^{4} 6f^{2} 6g^{3} 5fg^{2} 6s^{4} 6s 6fg 5g 6g 5f 6d 6s 1980 5d^{3} 6s 7.2d 5.8fg 6d^{4} 6d* 6g 6g 6g* 6fg 5.8g 7.2d 6s 7d 7s) sprint handicapper; winner at Carlisle in July and Pontefract in August; acts on any going but is well suited by some give in the ground; blinkered penultimate outing in 1979. *R. Hollinshead.*

NICHOLAS BILL 5 ch.h. High Line 125–Centro 86 (Vienna 127) (1979 16d2 16s* 14d3 16fg2 21d3 14fg* 16f* 1980 12d* 13.3d* 12g4 12f 12d2) **125**

Nicholas Bill continued on the upgrade in 1980 and developed into a fine five-year-old, probably an equal in merit to his sire High Line who at that age won the Jockey Club Cup and the Geoffrey Freer Stakes. His season, as High Line's, was shortened by injury—he threw a splint in the spring and missed the first part of the season—but he added two more good prizes to the five races he had already won and acquitted himself with credit on his other starts, most notably in the Prix de l'Arc de Triomphe.

Nicholas Bill won both his races in this country before the Arc, the Princess of Wales's Stakes at Newmarket in July and the Geoffrey Freer Stakes at Newbury in August. We were inclined to dismiss his chance at Newmarket because he hadn't had a previous run and he seemed likely to find the distance of a mile and a half on the sharp side, but he was always going nicely and looked the winner throughout the last two furlongs. He had to struggle to get the better of Son Fils but responded gamely to strong pressure and got home by a neck. In the Geoffrey Freer, over a slightly longer distance, Nicholas Bill again seemed to face a stiffish task conceding 5 lb to his principal rival Main Reef, but after sitting in last-of-five place most of the way, he was produced with a strong run to lead inside the last furlong and win by a length. Main Reef finished second after having a poor run and was subsequently disqualified.

At this stage of the season Nicholas Bill's trainer was undecided whether to aim him for a second win in the Jockey Club Cup, for the Arc or for Cologne's Preis von Europa in the autumn; eventually he decided to go for the Arc, with a run beforehand in the Grosser Preis von Baden at Baden-Baden. Nicholas Bill finished a fairly close fourth to the German champion Nebos at Baden-Baden, and he went to Longchamp one of the freshest in the field. He ran a cracking race in the Arc, far better than his Pari-Mutuel odds of 70/1 suggested he might, and turned into the finishing straight in an excellent position close behind the leaders on the rails. For a moment or two he looked as if he might well run into a place but he found the pace just a shade too hot in

Princess of Wales's Stakes, Newmarket—Nicholas Bill runs on gamely up the hill to catch Son Fils (rails)

Geoffrey Freer Stakes, Newbury—another genuine performance from Nicholas Bill. He beats Main Reef (blaze), Valour (hidden), Son Fils (right) and Noelino

the closing stages and finished sixth, about four lengths behind Detroit. Nicholas Bill's trainer was justifiably delighted and reported that he intended to come back and win in 1981. Probably Nicholas Bill would have a better chance in such a race on an easier surface, but he's not quite a good enough horse to win.

The St Simon Stakes at Newbury later in October provided Nicholas Bill with a chance to end his season on the high note he richly deserved and he started favourite, looking exceptionally well. However, Shining Finish was allowed to dictate matters at too slow a pace for some of the field, and Nicholas Bill found trouble making his run up the rails. He was squeezed by Snow just as he was beginning to get into top gear and was unable to get in a serious blow at the all-the-way winner. He finished about two and a half lengths behind Shining Finish in third, and was promoted to second by the stewards at the expense of Snow. We have little doubt that Nicholas Bill would have given Shining Finish a great deal more to do had he been ridden with any enterprise.

Nicholas Bill (ch.h. 1975)	High Line (ch 1966)	High Hat (ch 1957)	Hyperion
			Madonna
		Time Call (b 1955)	Chanteur II
			Aleria
	Centro (b 1966)	Vienna (ch 1957)	Aureole
			Turkish Blood
		Ocean Sailing (br 1950)	Big Game
			Kyanos

Much has been written about the success of High Line as a stallion in 1980; here it suffices to say that Nicholas Bill is a fine advertisement for High Line and he has inherited a great many of his qualities. The dam Centro, a half-sister to the prolific 1971 two-year-old filly Sea Music, won a seven-furlong nursery but failed to train on. Her three foals to race, all by High Line, are winners, the other two being the Lancashire Oaks winner Centrocon and the quite useful but one-paced stayer Athford. She has had two more foals by High Line, a colt in 1978 named Centroline, unraced as yet but entered in the classics, and a filly in 1979.

A big, rangy horse who acts on any going and has a good turn of foot for one who stays two miles, Nicholas Bill is an admirable racehorse and a credit to his trainer. We'll be surprised if he doesn't continue a tough nut to crack in 1981, and he may even improve on his sixth place in the Arc. *H. Candy.*

NICKADVENTURE 4 ch.g. On Your Mark 125–High Gloss (Super Sam 124) **65**
(1979 5v* 7s* 6d^2 6g^3 7s 8.3f^3 8.2g 7g^3 8.3fg^4 7f 7fg 8d^2 1980 8s 7fg 8fg 8h* 7h^4

8fg³ 8fg 8d³ 6d 8fg 8fg³) workmanlike gelding; attracted no bid after winning seller at Brighton in May; not disgraced in better company most subsequent outings; stays 1m; acts on any going; has run creditably for a boy; sold to N. Tinkler 3,100 gns Ascot August Sales. *R. Hannon.*

NIGHT ALERT (USA) 3 b.c. Nijinsky 138–Moment of Truth (Matador 131) **123**
(1979 7g³ 7fg* 1980 7g* 8fg³ 9fg* 8g³ 10g³)

Over the years the Houghton Stakes at Newmarket has been contested by a number of horses that have gone on to make a name for themselves as three-year-olds. Between 1968 and 1978 Blakeney, Prince de Galles, Levanter, Guillotina, Shebeen, Furioso, Quiet Fling, Valour, One In A Million and Milford either won or were placed in the race; and the subsequent records of those who filled all the first three places in 1979 bear the closest inspection. Posse and Bireme, second and third, were both top-notchers and the winner, Night Alert, wasn't that far behind; between them they won half a dozen races worth over £181,000, including two each in Group 1 and Group 2.

With Monteverdi in the same yard it can be assumed that Night Alert wasn't initially regarded as the stable's main Two Thousand Guineas candidate but the early-season classic trials changed the situation somewhat. Monteverdi's runs in the McCairns Trial and the Clerical, Medical Greenham Stakes, though neither was by any means a bad effort, put him under a cloud whereas Night Alert improved his standing by battling on courageously to beat Noelino and Johnny O'Day in a driving finish to the Gladness Stakes at the Curragh. Night Alert duly ran in the Guineas. In the rear to halfway, he worked his way through the field to reach a challenging position two furlongs out and stayed on without quickening appreciably to finish a four-length fourth to Nureyev, being moved up a place on the winner's disqualification.

The Group 2 Prix Jean Prat at Chantilly in June has attracted several colts from this side of the Channel in the past decade, and Night Alert followed two other Guineas thirds, Sharp Edge and Young Generation, in winning the race. His strongest opponents appeared to be the in-form In Fijar, successful in the Poule d'Essai des Poulains and a good third in the Prix Lupin, and Ruscelli, disqualified from third in the former race and recently a decisive winner of the Prix de la Jonchere. Night Alert was ridden with confidence, coming up smoothly to lead inside the distance and beat Ruscelli readily by a neck, breaking the course record in the process. The Expatriate was a close third, with In Fijar half a length further back in fourth. Night Alert ran only twice more, each time finishing third. In the Waterford Crystal Mile at Goodwood he made much of the running and kept on well once headed, going down by a neck and half a length to Known Fact and Hard Fought. He had to be snatched up in the last

Gladness Stakes, the Curragh—it takes all Piggott's driving to get Night Alert home in a tight finish with Noelino (right) and Johnny O'Day

Prix Jean Prat, Chantilly—Night Alert wins a shade comfortably from Ruscelli and The Expatriate. In Fijar is a close fourth

few strides but an objection by his rider to the second for boring and crossing near the finish was overruled. Night Alert didn't have too clear a run in the Joe McGrath Memorial Stakes at Leopardstown in September and came home a length and a half behind his stable-companion Gregorian and Spence Bay.

Night Alert (USA) (b.c. 1977)	Nijinsky (b 1967)	Northern Dancer (b 1961)	Nearctic
			Natalma
		Flaming Page (b 1959)	Bull Page
			Flaring Top
	Moment of Truth (ch 1959)	Matador (ch 1953)	Golden Cloud
			Spanish Galantry
		Kingsworthy (b 1953)	Kingstone
			Sotades

Moment of Truth died in the year Night Alert was foaled. She has left her mark at stud, producing seven winners besides Night Alert, including the

Mr R. E. Sangster's "Night Alert"

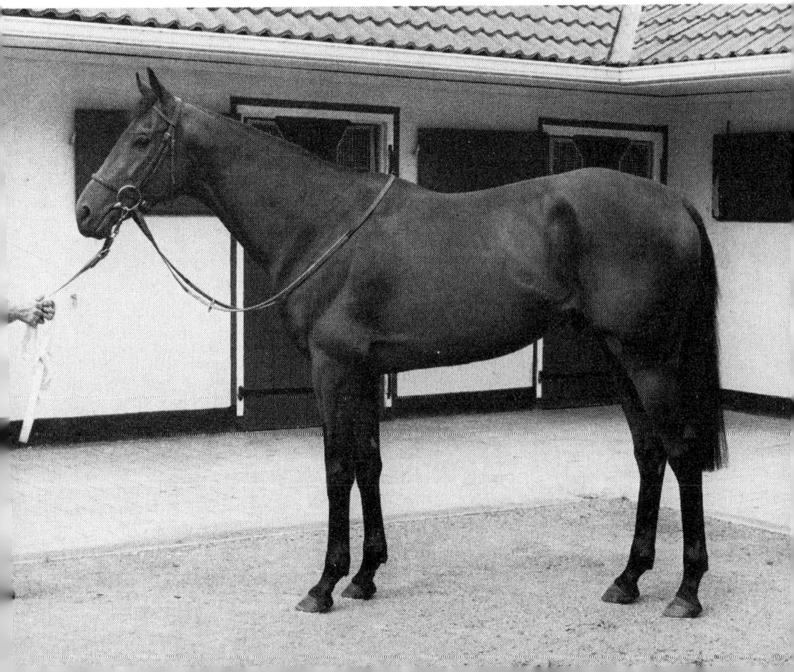

very good sprinter Indulto (by Royal Coinage), who won twenty-seven races, the high-class filly Convenience (by Fleet Nasrullah), successful at up to nine furlongs, and the very smart 1972 staying two-year-old Puntilla (by Never Bend). Moment of Truth was an unraced half-sister to Typhoon, rated the best colt in the 1960 Free Handicap after winning the Coventry and Richmond Stakes, and to Super Flower, dam of Faliraki and Thousandfold. An attractive if rather leggy colt, Night Alert was bought surprisingly cheaply as a yearling for 190,000 dollars. The two highest-priced Nijinsky colts sold in 1978, out of Shuvee and Crimson Saint, fetched 800,000 dollars and 525,000 dollars respectively; neither has done so well as Night Alert to date. Nijinsky's progeny remain popular, both to race and breed from, and Night Alert will stand in America after racing over there. Several ex-O'Brien runners, notably Caucasus, King Pellinore and Swingtime, have done well in the States, and success in a stakes race would make Night Alert an even more attractive proposition to American breeders. He has the right credentials to make a name for himself on the track over there; he is adaptable, equally effective at a mile and a mile and a quarter, distances around which half of the turf stakes races for which he will be eligible are run, and consistent. Night Alert acts on firm ground and has yet to race on soft. *V. O'Brien, Ireland.*

NIGHT AND DAY 3 b.c. Bustino 136–Verdun 82 (Relic) (1979 NR 1980 10fg 8g2 8g4 8g 9v4) 22,000Y; strong, very attractive colt; good mover; half-brother to a minor winner; dam half-sister to good stayer Rally; creditable second in maiden race at Kempton in July; didn't run up to that form afterwards and performed badly fourth start; will be suited by a return to 1¼m. *L. Cumani.* **84** d

NIGHT WATCH (USA) 6 br.g. Stage Door Johnny–Lucretia Bori (Bold Ruler) (1979 13s 14g 12s 14g 16d 13g2 12fg* 11.7g* 11g3 13.1g2 14f 12fg4 12d2 1980 14fg) strong, good-looking gelding; fairly useful staying handicapper at his best; behind at Salisbury in September on only outing of 1980; appears to act on any going; genuine; good mount for an apprentice. *I. Balding.* –

NIGHTWOOD 3 ch.f. Sparkler 130–Determination 74 (Never Say Die 137) (1979 7fg 7f 1980 10fg 12d 13g3 15.5fg2 14d 15.5g) staying maiden; acts on a firm surface; ran poorly final start. *J. Dunlop.* **60**

NIIGATO 2 b.g. Nonoalco 131–Merta (Jaipur) (1980 6g 6g) Apr 23; 30,000Y; close-coupled, attractive gelding; excellent mover; third foal; half-brother to 2 winners, including fairly useful 3-y-o sprinter Elegida (by Habitat); dam useful Irish 6f winner; drifted from 7/4 to 5/1 before finishing 5¾ lengths fifth of 13 to Lord Clarence in minor event at Salisbury in August; 6/1 for maiden race at Doncaster the following month but couldn't go early pace and finished eleventh of 13 to Brummer; bred to stay 7f; sold only 3,100 gns Newmarket Autumn Sales. *R. Hern.* **72**

NIJINSKY'S SECRET (USA) 2 ch.c. Nijinsky 138–Secret Beauty (Raise A Native) (1980 8g4 8d*) Feb 11; powerful, good-bodied colt; half-brother to 3 winners, including stakes-placed Secret Call (by Call Me Prince); dam second twice in USA; shot clear early in straight and wasn't troubled to win 8-runner maiden race at Longchamp in October by 1½ lengths from Russian Fox; will stay at least 1¼m; bound to go on to much better things at 3 yrs. *J. Cunnington, jnr, France.* **113** p

NIKEA 3 b.f. On Your Mark 125–Great Emerald 75 (Great Nephew 126) (1979 6g 5fg 5g 1980 5fg4 5fg 5fg 6g 5g 8fg 5g 5f) small, compact filly; looks a short runner; blinkered final start at 2 yrs; didn't move well to post fourth start; sold 560 gns Doncaster September Sales. *A. Demetriou.* –

NIKITINA 3 b.f. Nijinsky 138–Vela 123 (Sheshoon 132) (1979 6f2 8g2 1980 12g 10fg3 10g3 10g* 10s2 10s) attractive, well-made ex-English filly; won 11-runner maiden race at Navan in September; creditable second in apprentice event at the Curragh in November; should stay 1½m (last of 11 to Deadly Serious in Galtres Stakes at York when tried at trip); acts on any going; blinkered nowadays. *K. Prendergast, Ireland.* **80**

NIKOLI 3 b.c. Great Nephew 126–Aliceva (Alcide 136) (1979 7g* 1980 7s* 8f* 12f 12s) **125**

The first prize for the Airlie/Coolmore Irish Two Thousand Guineas was £86,878, easily a record for a Guineas in Europe and £30,000 more than was earned by the Guineas winner at Newmarket. The Irish One Thousand Guineas was worth slightly more than the English equivalent. The first two Irish

McCairns Trial Stakes, Phoenix Park—Nikoli wins from Monteverdi and Petringo

classics, which have a clause permitting later entry at a big fee, attract a much larger initial entry than their Newmarket counterparts because they close in March, fourteen months before the race; the Newmarket classics close in November when owners and trainers know much more about the merit of their classic prospects. Entry fees for the Irish Two Thousand Guineas were doubled for 1980, which accounted for the big increase in prize money, but it still cost less (except for a late entry) to run at the Curragh than it did at Newmarket, £300 as against £425. We doubt whether the British turf authorities will want to allow the prize money for the Two Thousand Guineas and the One Thousand Guineas to remain behind that for the Irish versions. A return to an early entry date with a late-entry clause would be one solution to the problem and an alternative to asking the Levy Board to increase its already substantial contribution.

Those connected with the Airlie Stud and the Coolmore/Castle Hyde Stud, which between them contributed £15,000 to the prize money for the Irish Two Thousand Guineas, must have been delighted with the field that turned out. Posse, Final Straw and Last Fandango made up a strong English challenge and the ten Irish-trained runners included Monteverdi, who had topped the English and Irish Free Handicaps, and two other colts, Huguenot and Johnny O'Day, who had figured in the top eight in the Irish Free Handicap. The only unbeaten horse in the field was Nikoli, a strong, most attractive colt who had won his only race at two and had beaten Monteverdi, who gave him 7 lb, by a length and a half in the McCairns Trial Stakes at Phoenix Park in April. We went to Phoenix Park to cast our eye over Monteverdi, who started at 3/1 on, and came away very impressed by Nikoli; every inch a top horse in appearance, he wasn't hard pressed to hold off Monteverdi and he looked a top-class colt in the making, our idea, even at this early stage, of a good Derby prospect. Nikoli's victory at the Curragh seemed to confirm that he had most of the credentials needed for a Derby candidate. He won the Irish Guineas by a short head from Last Fandango with Final Straw half a length away third and Posse a head behind Final Straw; entering the last furlong all four were in line abreast and it was a splendid battle to the line. We viewed Nikoli's performance at the Curragh as a triumph over specialist milers by a horse that seemed certain to be better suited by longer distances. Nikoli's pedigree suggested that he would not fail for want of stamina in the Derby. In fact he seemed a fair bet to follow in the footsteps of Grundy, another son of Great Nephew, who went on to success at Epsom after winning the Irish Two Thousand Guineas.

Nikoli's participation at Epsom was in some doubt for several days after the Irish Guineas. It was announced at first that he would not be sent to Epsom, his connections expressing reservations about whether he would act on the course and whether his temperament would stand up to the ordeal imposed

Airlie/Coolmore Irish Two Thousand Guineas, the Curragh—Nikoli is strongly pressed by three English-trained horses throughout the final furlong but holds on for a narrow win from Last Fandango (stripes), Final Straw (rails) and Posse (right)

by the protracted preliminaries. Whether the change of heart had anything to do with a desire to provide trainer Paddy Prendergast with a death-bed Derby winner, as some have said, we don't know, but Nikoli was sent over for the Derby and started 4/1 favourite. After a frustrating journey to Epsom on the Sunday before the Derby—there was a five-hour 'red tape' delay at Gatwick—Nikoli settled well in his temporary surroundings and seemed to handle the Epsom gradients without difficulty in his final workout. He remained cool and calm in the paddock before the race, but, as a precaution, was dismounted after the parade and led to the start; Nikoli's connections had a lad waiting to sponge him down before he was remounted. So far as we could see, Nikoli arrived at the start without really taking anything out of himself and his showing in the race—he was never a serious factor and came home eighth, nine lengths behind Henbit—was a big disappointment. Nikoli was saddled three and a half weeks later for the Irish Sweeps Derby but rumours that he had 'gone' were circulating before the race and this time the pre-race ordeal definitely got the better of him. He was lathered up by the time he arrived at the post and took some time to be persuaded to enter the stalls. Starting second favourite to the Derby runner-up Master Willie, he ran badly, never getting into the race and trailing home near the back of the field.

Nikoli (b.c. 1977)	Great Nephew (b 1963)	Honeyway (br 1941)	Fairway
			Honey Buzzard
		Sybil's Niece (ch 1951)	Admiral's Walk
			Sybil's Sister
	Aliceva (b 1966)	Alcide (b 1955)	Alycidon
			Chenille
		Feevagh (b 1951)	Solar Slipper
			Astrid Wood

Nikoli provided Paddy Prendergast with his final classic winner, although it was not, as many had hoped it would be, in the Derby, a race that eluded Prendergast throughout an illustrious career. Prendergast, who died on the Thursday of Royal Ascot after a long illness, was one of the great trainers of the post-war era and a notably colourful character. His success story had an undistinguished start: after serving his apprenticeship at the Curragh, he came to England to ride over hurdles, then tried his luck in Australia. On the outbreak of war he was back in Ireland where he clubbed together with three friends and paid £150 for a sprinter called Pelorus. Cleverly placed, Pelorus won a hatful of races and it was on this horse's success that the Prendergast empire was built. Before long Prendergast was embarking on ambitious raids on the best English prizes with top-class two-year-olds such as Windy City, The Pie King and Sixpence. There was hardly a major race in England and Ireland that he didn't win during his career. Prendergast-trained horses gained successes in all the Irish classics, and Martial (Two Thousand Guineas), Pourparler (One

Thousand Guineas), Noblesse (Oaks) and Ragusa (St Leger) were the stable's English classic winners. Prendergast's career was at its zenith in the early 'sixties: he topped the list of trainers in England three years in a row, a remarkable achievement for a foreign-based trainer, and won the King George VI and Queen Elizabeth Stakes with Ragusa and Meadow Court, both of whom won the Irish Sweeps Derby before going on to Ascot; in the same period he handled a brilliant sprinter in Floribunda and three two-year-olds who headed the Free Handicap, La Tendresse, Young Emperor and Bold Lad.

Nikoli comes from a well-established family of the McGraths' Brownstown Stud. His dam Aliceva is a half-sister to Feemoss—the dam of Levmoss, Sweet Mimosa and Le Moss—and to Laurence O, both of whom stayed well. Aliceva, a daughter of the top-class stayer Alcide and the Yorkshire Oaks winner Feevagh, was a moderate racemare whose only victory came in a mile-and-a-quarter maiden race but she would probably have stayed well given the chance. Aliceva's first two winners, Celtic Barge (by Faberge II) and Vivar (by Le Levanstell), both showed a fair amount of stamina but her next two foals, Captain James (by Captain's Gig) and Sutton Place (by Tyrant) showed their best form at a mile, the former winning the Waterford Crystal Mile and the latter Royal Ascot's Coronation Stakes. Nikoli is Aliceva's fifth winner and her best to date. In an all-too-short career he showed that he was a high-class racehorse at a mile and proved his ability to act on firm and soft going. Nothing could be settled about Nikoli's future as a stallion until a legal duel between John Doyle of the Baroda Stud, County Kildare, and the connections of the horse was over. An order was granted in August to Mr Doyle by the High Court in Dublin prohibiting the sale of Nikoli to a French bloodstock agency. Doyle claimed to have bought Nikoli, subject to a veterinary examination of the horse, for £650,000 at the end of July. The case was heard in November but

Lord Iveagh's "Nikoli"

was settled out of court. Nikoli has been exported to the United States; he will be joining the successful stallions Elocutionist (sire of Recitation), Accipiter (sire of Beldale Flutter) and Key To The Kingdom at Airdrie Stud in Kentucky. *K. Prendergast, Ireland.*

NIMBLE DOVE 4 b.f. Starch Reduced 112–Red Dove (All Red 110) (1979 8g 12f 1980 8d 12s) neat filly; very lightly raced and little form, although wasn't entirely disgraced in an apprentice event second start. *G. Price.* —

NIMBLEMOSS 2 br.c. Hotfoot 126–Milly Moss 112 (Crepello 136) (1980 6fg 7g² 8d* 8.2s²) Apr 20; shapely colt; excellent mover; fourth foal; half-brother to 2 winners, including very useful 3-y-o Kashmir Lass (by Kashmir II), a winner from 6f to 1m; dam won Cheshire Oaks and is sister to Mil's Bomb; odds on when winning 14-runner maiden event at Bath in October by ½ length from Ice; creditable second to Sharsha in nursery at Nottingham later in month; will be suited by 1¼m; should make a useful 3-y-o handicapper. *P. Walwyn.* 88

NIMBO 2 b.g. Mummy's Pet 125–Maureens Honey 93 (Taste of Honey 92) (1980 7g 7g 7fg) Apr 13; 7,000Y; good-topped gelding; half-brother to a winner in Austria; dam 2-y-o 6f winner; 13½ lengths sixth of 15 to Rasa Penang in minor event at Kempton in September; in rear in maiden and minor events at Yarmouth and Lingfield subsequently. *N. Callaghan.* —

NIMBOSTRATUS 3 br.f. Lorenzaccio 130–Cloudbreak 95 (Nimbus 130) (1979 6d 7g 1980 8f 14f 12g 9d) tall, unfurnished filly; poor form in maiden and minor races. *D. Weeden.* —

NINE OF DIAMONDS 2 b.g. Dragonara Palace 115–Shari (Rustam 127) (1980 6s) Mar 14; compact gelding; half-brother to 4 winners, including very smart 5f filly Harem (by Tribal Chief); dam, sister to Double Jump, won at 2 yrs in Italy on only start; 50/1 and on burly side, unseated rider on way to start and refused to race in maiden race at Nottingham in August; subsequently gelded; evidently temperamental and is one to leave severely alone. *R. Akehurst.* — §

NINEVEH 2 ch.f. Import 127–Catamaran 82 (Lauso) (1980 5f 5.8fg 6fg 7g 7f 7fg) May 31; neat, strong filly; first foal; dam won over 1½m; only poor form, including in a seller. *W. Wightman.* 57

NINGO 2 br.c. Saulingo 122–Swinging Nun (Tudor Melody 129) (1980 5f) Mar 18; 5,400Y; smallish colt; fourth living foal; half-brother to fair middle-distance handicapper Royal Coachman (by Supreme Sovereign); dam poor half-sister to high-class sprinter Tin Whistle; weak third favourite when behind in 15-runner maiden race won by Amorous at Newmarket in April, only outing. *R. Hannon.* —

NINIAN CENTRAL 2 ch.c. Lombard 126–Estructura 102 (Gulf Pearl 117) (1980 5fg² 5d 5.3d) Jan 29; 4,000Y; first foal; dam useful staying 2-y-o; 8 lengths second of 4 to Rikasso Beauty in minor race at Brighton in May; in rear the following month in £2,700 event at Sandown (tailed-off last of 7) and maiden race at Brighton; bred to stay middle distances. *G. Beeson.* 60

NINISKI (USA) 4 b.c. Nijinsky 138–Virginia Hills (Tom Rolfe) (1979 8g* 10.5g² 12g 12g² 13.3g* 14.6f³ 14d* 15.5s* 1980 12f* 13.4f* 12f² 12f 15.5v) 118

High hopes were held out for Niniski after his storming win in the John Porter Stakes at Newbury in April. It was his third win in succession—he had run away with the Irish St Leger and had beaten Anifa in the Prix Royal-Oak on his last two outings as a three-year-old—and the manner of his winning seemed to show a side to Niniski that hadn't been seen before. Very much a staying type in 1979, he showed an impressive turn of foot here to get out of trouble and win going away in a race at a mile and a half on firm going. After being badly boxed in on the rails he was switched round a wall of horses and must have had all of eight lengths to make up with two furlongs to go; however he quickened to such effect that he got to the front inside the last furlong and burst clear to win by three lengths from Morse Code.

Perhaps we became a little carried away with Niniski for he didn't fulfil his promise, and in retrospect the form of the John Porter didn't amount to a great deal by the best standards; only Beau Reef of those that occupied the next six places behind Niniski won during 1980. Niniski himself won his next race, the Ormonde Stakes at Chester in May, but he made very hard work of doing so and snatched the race only inside the last furlong from Two of Diamonds and Son Fils. Even so, he started favourite to beat the improving Sea Chimes, Soleil Noir and Valour in the Coronation Cup at Epsom in June, in which Niniski was held up and never promised to get on terms with the all-the-way winner Sea

Ormonde Stakes, Chester—Niniski (left) snatches the race from Two of Diamonds (centre) and Son Fils

Chimes in a slowly-run race. He finished a two-and-a-half-length second, and judging from the way he moved he was feeling the firm ground.

Niniski didn't turn out for a long time afterwards. He went straight into the Prix de l'Arc de Triomphe without another outing, having missed a preparatory race in the Prix Foy because of the firm ground. Niniski was turned out looking exceptionally well at Longchamp but didn't stride out at all well to post on going that was still firm, and didn't play much of a part. He lost a

Lady Beaverbrook's "Niniski"

prominent position for good at halfway and eventually finished thirteenth. The going had eased considerably when he attempted a second win in the Prix Royal-Oak at Longchamp later in October—in fact it was heavy—but Niniski fared little better than in the Arc. He flattered briefly after closing on the leaders running towards the straight then faded into sixth, about five lengths behind the winner Gold River. Carson reported that Niniski wasn't so good as in 1979 and could have been soured by too many races on firm ground.

Niniski (USA) (b.c. 1976)	Nijinsky (b 1967)	Northern Dancer (b 1961)	Nearctic
			Natalma
		Flaming Page (b 1959)	Bull Page
			Flaring Top
	Virginia Hills (b 1971)	Tom Rolfe (b 1962)	Ribot
			Pocahontas II
		Ridin' Easy (ch 1967)	Ridan
			Easy Eight

Niniski has been retired to the Lanwades Stud, Newmarket, having been syndicated. A good-looking American-bred colt, he is the best son of Nijinsky at stud in England apart from Ile de Bourbon and should appeal to breeders. He is the first foal of the nine-furlong winner Virginia Hills who is a daughter of the stakes-winning two-year-old Ridin' Easy and from the family of Cyane, Riboccare, Yelapa and Your Alibhai. A genuine sort who needed a strongly-run race to be seen to advantage over middle distances and stayed well, Niniski acted on any going but was ideally suited by an easy surface. His fee is £2,500 plus £2,500 (October 1st terms). *R. Hern.*

NINTH ADDITION 5 b.g. Henry the Seventh 125–Computer 69 (Chanteur II 135) (1979 NR 1980 16fg) novice staying hurdler; behind in amateur riders race won by Ribo Charter at Ascot in September, first outing on flat. *P. Felgate.* —

NISTERA 3 b.f. Nonoalco 131–Ruta (Ratification 129) (1979 NR 1980 10fg 10f 12f 11fg^4 10fg 9s) big, strong, rangy filly; half-sister to several winners, notably French Derby and Prix de l'Arc de Triomphe winner Sassafras (by Sheshoon); dam won at 2 yrs in Ireland and comes from same family as Roi Dagobert and Shantung; little worthwhile form in maiden races; seems to stay 11f; blinkered final outing. *P. Walwyn.* **62**

NOALTO 2 ch.c. Nonoalco 131–Lyrical 110 (Gratitude 130) (1980 6g 6g^4 6g* 7s^4 6f* 7g^2 7.3d^4) May 19; 26,000Y; well-made colt; good mover; half-brother to 3-y-o sprint maiden Blues (by Song) and 2 winners, notably smart 6f to 11f winner Rhyme Royal (by Crepello); dam very useful winner at 6f; successful in maiden race at Yarmouth in July and in 6-runner Champion Two Yrs Old Trophy at Ripon the following month; most impressive when winning by 5 lengths from Cut Throat in latter, travelling strongly on bridle at halfway and then quickening away in fine style in last 1½f; showed excellent speed to lead to below distance in Horris Hill Stakes at Newbury in October but then weakened quickly to finish 8¾ lengths fourth of 10 to Kalaglow; better at 6f than 7f at 2 yrs but is likely to be effective over 7f in 1981; acts well on firm going and is possibly not at his best on very soft; very useful. *F. Durr.* **114**

NOB 2 b.g. Mansingh 120–Fatherless 63 (Ragusa 137) (1980 6d 6g) Feb 26; strong, compact gelding; first foal; dam in frame both outings; 20/1 when behind in maiden races at Newmarket in October; subsequently gelded. *M. Jarvis.* —

NOBLE DRAGON 3 ch.g. Polacca 117–Penstemon (Pendragon) (1979 NR 1980 13g) half-brother to two winning jumpers; dam never ran; well behind in small race won by Noblissimo at Bath in September. *J. Thorne.* —

NOBLE DREAM 2 b.f. Noble Decree 127–Kayandjay 93 (Midsummer Night II 117) (1980 5.1f 5fg 5.1fg 7g 5g) Apr 14; small, compact filly; third foal; dam stayed 1m well; came from behind when sixth of 19 to Advertrack, beaten only about a length, at Folkestone in October, fifth outing and easily best effort in maiden races; should be suited by 7f; sold 480 gns Newmarket Autumn Sales. *R. Sheather.* **73**

NOBLE DUDLEY (USA) 3 ch.g. Giacometti 130–Noble Mark 120 (On Your Mark 125) (1979 5g 5s^2 5d 5s^2 8.2s 1980 8v 10f* 11fg* 9g* 9.4g^2 10fg^2 10s^3 12fg* 11fg^3) neat gelding; quite a moderate handicapper; had an excellent season and won at Redcar, Hamilton (twice) and Beverley; swerved violently **74**

under pressure when beating Liberated on last-named in September; effective at 9f and stays 1½m well; acts on any going; wears blinkers; suitable mount for a boy; sold 6,800 gns Newmarket Autumn Sales. *J. W. Watts.*

NOBLE HEIR 5 b.g. Duke of Ragusa 120–Starfold (Ratification 129) (1979 **74**
16d* 16g* 17.1g^2 16.9s 16d^2 20g^3 15.5f 18.8f^2 1980 16s^3 14fg^3 16.1f* 18fg 18.8g*(dis) 20d) fair handicapper; led on post when beating Rose Standish by short head at Haydock in May; got home by neck from Heighlin at Warwick following month but was disqualified for taking ground of runner-up; behind in Ascot Stakes at Royal Ascot on final outing; stays very well; acts on any going but is probably best suited by some give in the ground; genuine. *P. Cole.*

NOBLE LEGEND 2 b.c. Noble Decree 127–Novelista 101 (El Gallo 122) **85**
(1980 7g 8.2s 8s 10.2s^3) Feb 9; 6,800Y; useful-looking colt; fourth foal; half-brother to a winner in Australia; dam successful 2-y-o 5f performer; 25/1, showed improved form to finish 6 lengths third of 21 to Irish Heart in minor event at Doncaster in November; will stay 1½m; acts on soft going; the type to improve further at 3 yrs and looks sure to win a race or two in the North. *M. H. Easterby.*

NOBLE MISTRESS 4 ch.f. Lord Gayle 124–Light Diamond (Florescence —
120) (1979 7g 6d 6g^4 6s 8f 7fg 6d 6d 6s 6d 1980 5fg 7h 5d 5d) small filly; best form at 6f; seems to act on any going; sometimes wears blinkers but didn't when successful in 1978. *M. Bradley.*

NOBLE MONK 2 br.c. African Sky 124–Manfilia 95 (Mandamus 120) (1980 **96**
6g^3 6s^2 6g^2 6g* 8s) Feb 26; 42,000Y; third foal; brother to high-class 5f to 1¼m performer Kilijaro and smart French 9f to 13f winner African Hope; dam won at up to 1¼m; odds on and ridden by 5-lb claimer when winning 8-runner minor event at Navan in September by 3 lengths from Maiacourt; had previously finished second in maiden races at the Curragh in August, going down by a head to Ascending Star and by 4 lengths to Kings Lake; should stay beyond 6f (8/1 when well-beaten fifth behind Euclid in 1m Beresford Stakes at the Curragh); yet to race on a firm surface. *C. Collins, Ireland.*

NOBLE PERRY 2 b.f. Perdu 121–Noble Nugget (Klondyke Bill 125) (1980 **60**
5f 5fg 6g^2 7g^4 6g 6d 5d) May 2; 480Y, resold 720Y; leggy filly; fourth living foal; dam won at up to 10.7f at 4 yrs in French Provinces; length second of 14 to Southern Swanee in maiden auction event at Redcar in June; will stay 1m; trained by W. H. H. Williams first 5 outings. *J. Wilson.*

NOBLE PHILIP (USA) 3 br.c. Noble Decree 127–Quezette (Test Case 125) **69**
(1979 5.1g 6g^4 6fg 5g 7f* 6f^3 6fg 7f* 1980 7f 8.2fg 7f 10d 8g 8.2s 8fg 8d 7g 8g 7d^2 7s) compact colt; quite a moderate handicapper; best at 7f; probably acts on any going; blinkered final outing; sometimes bandaged; trained by P. Read first 6 starts. *A. Breasley.*

NOBLE SAINT (USA) 4 b.c. Vaguely Noble 140–Santa Paula (Santa Claus **118** d
133) (1979 12g 11f* 10.6g^2 12s* 10.5fg^2 12d 14v* 1980 12f 14f* 16f^4 20g 12.5d 14g 12f)

Noble Saint won the Yorkshire Cup in May in such good style that he looked set for a season at least as successful as in 1979 when his three wins included the Great Voltigeur Stakes on the same course and the Premio Roma. Conceding weight all round and racing on ground firmer than was considered ideal, he made steady headway to lead below the distance after being settled at the rear and needed only to be shaken up to go clear and win by a length and a half from Buttress who had also chased him home in the Voltigeur. However, Noble Saint showed worthwhile form only twice afterwards, when a very close fourth behind Billion in the Henry II Stakes at Sandown later in the month, in which he was brought through the field very quickly and perhaps a shade incautiously in the straight but couldn't last out, and when fifth to Dunette and Shakapour in the Grand Prix de Saint-Cloud in July; on both occasions he gave a good deal of trouble before the start. There were valid excuses for two of his other displays—he had been suffering from a virus before finishing last in the Tote-Ebor (reportedly he pulled a muscle in the race) and he couldn't reasonably have been expected to figure prominently in the Arc de Triomphe which was run on much faster ground than usual—but his record for the year after the Yorkshire Cup was nevertheless rather disappointing.

Noble Saint is a well-bred colt, by Vaguely Noble out of a half-sister to the leading American stallions Tom Rolfe and Chieftain who has bred two other winners. He was syndicated by Panorama Farms at the end of the season and in

Yorkshire Cup, York—Noble Saint beats Buttress and Vincent

1981 will stand alongside Super Asset in Florida at a fee of 7,500 dollars with the live-foal concession. Quite a well-made colt who spoilt his appearance by

Noble Saint (USA) (b.c. 1976)	Vaguely Noble (b 1965)	Vienna (ch 1957)	Aureole
			Turkish Blood
		Noble Lassie (b 1956)	Nearco
			Belle Sauvage
	Santa Paula (b 1967)	Santa Claus (b 1961)	Chamossaire
			Aunt Clara
		Pocahontas II (br 1955)	Roman
			How

sweating, he stayed two miles and evidently acted on any going; however he needed some give in the ground to show his best form when racing over middle distances. *R. Armstrong.*

NOBLE SHAMUS 3 b. or br.c. Royal and Regal–Spice Road (Gallant Man) (1979 6fg^{2} 7d^{3} 7g 6.3d* 8g^{4} 1980 7g 10fg 12fg 12f 12s 12d 9fg 10g) compact colt; showed very useful form at 2 yrs; ran probably best race in 1980 when 2½ lengths fifth of 8 to Ramian in BMW Nijinsky Stakes at Leopardstown in May on second outing (didn't have a clear run); well beaten in Derby and Irish Sweeps Derby at the Curragh on fourth and fifth starts; stays 1¼m; blinkered nowadays. *M. Fogarty, Ireland.* **103** d

NOBLE TASK 3 b.f. Star Appeal 133–Grand Slam 65 (Fidalgo 129) (1979 5fg 1980 8fg 12d 13.4g 12g 10fg 10.1fg^{4} 12s) lightly-made filly; fourth in minor event at Windsor in September, only sign of ability; should stay 1½m; best run on a firm surface; trained by C. Brittain first 6 starts. *C. Austin.* **61**

NOBLEU 3 ch.g. Blue Cashmere 129–Palanna 87 (Pall Mall 132) (1979 6fg 6f 6s 6fg 1980 8f 8fg 8f 8fg* 8d 8g^{3} 8s 8f* 8.2d) compact gelding; won handicaps at Pontefract in June and September; beat Swan Upping ½ length in latter; stays 1m; acts well on firm ground and is unsuited by soft; has run respectably for an apprentice. *P. Asquith.* **73**

NOBLE WHIN 2 ch.g. Flatbush 95–Noble Device (El Cid 109) (1980 5d^{4} 5f 5h^{4} 5f^{2} 5fg 5f 6g^{4} 5g 5d* 5d^{4} 5s) Apr 21; neat, strong gelding; apprentice ridden, **74§**

made all to win 4-runner nursery at Ayr in August by 4 lengths from Saulann; in frame in seller and maiden races previously; not disgraced over 6f but best form at 5f; acts on any going but seems particularly well suited by a soft surface; blinkered fourth and fifth outings; had to be withdrawn after bolting with inexperienced claiming rider at Ripon in late-August; unreliable. *H. Bell.*

NOBLISSIMO (FR) 3 ch.c. Sanctus II 132–Nobla (Dicta Drake 126) (1979 **83**
8v 1980 8d 10g^4 12d^4 13g* 10f^4 13.3d^4 12g 18s*) 24,000 francs Y (approx £2,850); close-coupled, good-looking ex-French colt; second foal; dam won twice at around 1¼m in France; won small race at Bath and handicap at Doncaster in the autumn; beat Padski by 4 lengths in latter; suited by a test of stamina; acts well on soft going. *A. Breasley.*

NO BOMBS 5 b.g. St Paddy 133–Land of Fire 99 (Buisson Ardent 129) (1979 **109**
10s^3 12f^2 16fg* 12f* 12f* 12f* 14.7f* 14s 12fg^4 12h^2 1980 12f* 13fg* 14d* 14.7g 14.7g^3 12fg*) big, useful sort; continued to improve in 1980 and had another fine season; looking particularly well, got up in last stride to win Moet and Chandon Silver Magnum (gentleman riders) at Epsom in August by short head from Lumen; successful earlier at York (apprentices), Ayr and York (beat Move Off by 2 lengths in valuable Troy Handicap) again; slipped up fourth outing; effective at 1½m to 2m; evidently acts on any going; tough and genuine and has a good turn of foot; has given trouble at start and was twice withdrawn not under orders in 1978; goes well for apprentice K. Hodgson; reportedly cracked a cannon bone after his final outing. *M. H. Easterby.*

NOCINO 3 br.c. Kaiseradler–Novara (Birkhahn) (1979 7fg^2 7f* 7fg* 7g* **110**
7fg* 8fg^2 7s* 1980 10f^2) neat, fair sort; good mover; successful in maiden race at Chester, minor event at Warwick, £2,500 race at Redcar, £4,100 nursery at Doncaster and small race at Catterick in 1979; in need of race and ridden by 7-lb claimer when good 3 lengths second to Easter Sun in handicap at Newmarket in May, only outing at 3 yrs; will stay 1½m; acts well on firm going and didn't run up to his best when successful on soft. *H. Cecil.*

NO CROWN 3 ch.f. Sovereign Path 125–No Halo 74 (Aureole 132) (1979 —
6f 5f 6d 1980 10.2fg 8f 6fg 6f) compact, stocky filly; poor form in varied company; blinkered final start; sold 1,000 gns Newmarket December Sales *R. Hannon.*

NOCTURNAL BOY 4 ch.c. Realm 129–Night Attire 77 (Shantung 132) (1979 **86**
7s^4 8.5s 7d^2 8fg^4 6s^4 7f 6g 6f 6f 6fg 6g^2 1980 6v 6fg^4 6f 6fg 6g^2 6g 6g^4 6g 6g 5d^4 6fg 6d*) quite a useful handicapper; held on by a length from Murillo, all out, after making running alone on far side in £6,700 Allendale Handicap at Doncaster in October (apprentice ridden and 33/1); ran creditably on several occasions earlier; races mainly at 6f but seems to stay 1m; probably not at his best on very soft ground. *N. Callaghan.*

NOELINO 4 gr.c. Bonne Noel 115–Little Fuss (Sovereign Path 125) (1979 **119**
10s* 12g 10.5d 14.6f 1980 7g^2 10g* 10f^2 12fg^3 13.3d^4 12f^4 12s) lengthy colt; smart middle-distance performer; conceding 3-y-o Night Alert several pounds more than w.f.a. when beaten a head by that horse in Gladness Stakes at the Curragh in April on reappearance; gained compensation in Sean Graham Ballymoss Stakes on same track later in month, beating Croghan Hill 2 lengths; ran well most subsequent outings, including when 3 lengths second to Gregorian in 3-runner Brigadier Gerard Stakes at Sandown, 1¼ lengths third to Scorpio in Hardwicke Stakes at Royal Ascot and very close fourth of 5 to Le Marmot in Prix Foy at Longchamp; beaten 2 lengths when last of 5 to Nicholas Bill in

Troy Stakes, York—it's easy for No Bombs who beats Move Off and Corral's Bond

slowly-run Geoffrey Freer Stakes at Newbury on fifth start but was hampered by second-placed Main Reef and promoted to fourth; acts on any going; trained by K. Prendergast in Ireland until before final outing. *C. Bartholomew, France.*

NO EXCUSES 3 b.c. Tamerlane 128–Lady Talisman (Continuation 120) — (1979 7f 7fg 1980 9f 12f 10f 10g 10g 10g) attractive, well-made colt; well beaten in varied company; by no means certain to stay 1½m; sold 2,500 gns Doncaster September Sales. *R. Price.*

NO FAITH (USA) 3 br.c. Noholme II–Be Ambitious (Ambiorix 130) (1979 **90** 5fg 6g* 7f* 7f 1980 8fg* 7f 8.2fg^{3} 10f 10g^{3} 10d^{2} 10fg 10g) small, useful-looking colt; fairly useful handicapper; ran on very gamely to lead again in last strides and beat dead-heaters Changabang and Tuthill Bond at Newbury in April; placed at Haydock, Redcar and Brighton subsequently; suited by 1¼m; probably acts on any going; best in blinkers. *I. Balding.*

NOMADIC PLEASURE 2 ch.f. Habitat 134–Petite Marmite 110 (Babur 126) **76** (1980 5s^{2} 5g^{2} 6d) Mar 7; 136,000Y; big, strong, good sort; half-sister to 3 winners, including Prix Vermeille winner Paulista (by Sea Hawk II) and smart French stayer Caribo (by Sassafras); dam very useful miler; close-up second in 21-runner maiden races at Windsor, going down by ¾ length to Manita in June and by a neck to Footshore when 13/8 on in July; didn't move well to start when next seen out at Newbury late in season, but ran respectably to finish 4¾ lengths sixth of 25 to Little Wolf, coming out second best of far-side group; will stay 7f+; should win a small race in 1981. *J. Tree.*

NONCHALANT 5 b.h. Wolver Hollow 126–Aspasie (Milesian 125) (1979 **81** 10d 8fg^{2} 10.5f 8d 8g 8.3fg 9fg 9f 1980 8fg 7g^{3} 7g 8d 10.5g 10fg 8g) rangy horse; good walker; mainly disappointing in 1980, easily best effort when third at Beverley in June; best form at up to 1¼m; acts on a firm and a soft surface; has worn a tongue strap; blinkered last 2 starts in 1979; sweating on reappearance. *A. Smith.*

NO NO HOLDINGS 4 b.g. Nonoalco 131–Marie Curie 96 (Exbury 138) (1979 **37** 8s 10v 8.2g 11f 11.5fg 12f 10fg 10g^{4} 1980 8s^{4} 8s* 9.6fg 7fg 8h 8f^{4} 10d 9d^{2} 8fg 8fg^{4} 8d 10d) lightly-made gelding; plater; attracted no bid after winning at Warwick in April; stays 9f; acts on soft going; has been tried in blinkers. *P. Feilden.*

NOOKIE BEAR 3 ch.g. Be Friendly 130–Marla (Hul a Hul 124) (1979 5v — 5d 6fg 6d 7fg 1980 10fg 10g 8g 11d 11.7g) tall, narrow gelding; plating-class maiden; best run at 7f on a firm surface. *P. Mitchell.*

NO PIRACY (USA) 2 ch.c. No Robbery–Navy Nymph (Raise A Native) **84** (1980 including 5f 5s^{4} 8s^{3} 8v) Feb 12; $38,000Y; lightly-built colt; half-brother to several winners in USA; dam never ran; 4 lengths fourth of 20 to Spanish Hind in maiden race at Nottingham in June; was subsequently sent to race in Italy, and did well when 6½ lengths third of 16 to English-trained Glint of Gold in Group 1 Gran Criterium at Milan; suited by 1m. *I. Balding.*

NO QUEENS 4 gr.f. No Mercy 126–Queens To Open 75 (Darius 129) (1979 — 8d 8.2g 8fg 8.2d 10.6g 1980 8d 12g 10s 12d 12d) strong filly; poor form in varied company; sold 2,800 gns Newmarket December Sales. *A. Bailey.*

NORBURY 4 b.c. Nonoalco 131–Kew 110 (Princely Gift 137) (1979 7.5d* **74** 8g 6s 1980 10g 8g 8g 8g 9f 8fg 7fg 7f 7f 7d 7g 7d 8g^{4} 7fg 6g^{3} 5.8g 6fg^{4} 6d) lengthy ex-French colt; in frame in handicaps at Brighton, Windsor (apprentices) and Lingfield; stays 1m; probably acts on any going; blinkered twelfth outing and ran poorly in a hood on fourteenth; sold 720 gns Newmarket Autumn Sales. *R. Akehurst.*

NORDAN ENTERPRISE 2 br.f. Rapid River 127–C'Est Bien (Gaily Mill 86) **69** (1980 5g 6g 6f^{3} 6f 6d 5s) Apr 10; compact filly; first foal; dam never ran; 100/1, showed plenty of speed till 1½f out when 8½ lengths third of 11 to Cavalry Twill in small race at Pontefract in September, only sign of ability. *M. Camacho.*

NORD HINDER 2 gr.g. Spitsbergen 103–Tipulidae (Game Rights 91) (1980 — 8d) Mar 25; non-thoroughbred gelding; sixth known foal; half-brother to successful hurdler Two Coppers (by St Gratien); dam staying hurdler; unquoted when last of 15 in maiden race won by Royal Heritage at Bath in October. *L. Kennard.*

NORDIC DANCER 3 ch.c. Northfields–Belinda (Ragusa 137) (1979 6fg 7f **77** d 8fg^{2} 1980 12f 11.7s 11.7f^{3} 10fg^{3} 9f^{2} 8d) strong colt; quite a moderate maiden;

stays 1½m; acts on any going; blinkered third and fourth starts; has run respectably for a boy. *J. Tree.*

NORFOLK ARROW 5 b.g. Blakeney 126–Cupids Delight 84 (St Paddy 133) (1979 16f 16f* 1980 18f) moderate performer; stays well; acts on firm going; suitable mount for an amateur. *J. Gifford.* —

NORFOLK FLIGHT 3 br.g. Blakeney 126–First Light 82 (Primera 131) (1979 NR 1980 10.2d4 10s 8s 8f* 10f* 11.7s 12g2 10fg4 10f* 8g 11fg* 12g 10.2v2) strong gelding; sixth foal; dam, effective from 5f to 1m, is half-sister to Laser Light; spreadeagled his field in seller at Newmarket in May (changed hands 4,000 gns); ran well in better company afterwards, winning handicaps at Yarmouth, Folkestone and Redcar (made all); needs further than 1m and stays 1½m; acts on any going; has run creditably for an apprentice. *W. Hastings-Bass.* **83**

NORFOLK GAL 3 b.f. Blakeney 126–Lucyrowe 125 (Crepello 136) (1979 NR 1980 10fg3 10fg2 10g* 12d 10fg) lengthy, quite attractive filly; good walker and mover; sister to 9f winner Edwinarowe, and half-sister to two winners, including fairly useful stayer Rowe Residence (by Royal Palace); dam won at up to 1¼m but was best at 1m; good ½-length second to Vielle (gave 5 lb) in Lupe Stakes at Kempton in May prior to beating Miss Neustrie 3 lengths in minor event at Newbury in June; well beaten afterwards in Ribblesdale Stakes at Royal Ascot and Nassau Stakes at Goodwood (poor last of 7); appears not to stay 1½m; acts on a firm surface. *P. Walwyn.* **100**

NORFOLK GOLD 3 b.f. Gilded Leader 75–Norfolk House (Cantab 94) (1979 5f 7g 7fg 8.2g 7f3 8.2fg3 1980 12g 11d 10g 12f 10fg 8d4 10.8d 10s3) lightly-built filly; poor mover; plater; stays 1¼m; acts on any going. *B. McMahon.* **51**

NORFOLK PRINCE 2 b.c. Sun Prince 128–Milveagh 92 (Milesian 125) (1980 6d4 8d2) Mar 30, 30,000Y; well-made, quite attractive colt; half-brother to several winners here and abroad, including fair 1975 2-y-o 6f winner Eagle Hill (by Tudor Music); dam won at up to 1m; 16/1 and looking well but in need of race, switched to outside 2f out and made up ground hand over fist when 8 lengths fourth of 19 to Oraston in maiden race at Salisbury in June; not seen out again until November when chasing home Sha'lan in similar event at Leicester (14 ran), the pair finishing clear; stays 1m. *J. Dunlop.* **85**

NORFOLK QUEEN 2 b.f. Blakeney 126–Eringa 101 (Saint Crespin III 132) (1980 6fg2 7f2 7g3) Mar 1; neat, attractive filly; sister to fairly useful 1½m winner Bewick and half-sister to a winner; dam disappointing half-sister to Huntercombe; placed in large fields of maidens at Windsor and Chepstow in August and Salisbury (soon pushed along but stayed on strongly in closing stages when 4 lengths third to Golden Bowl) in September; will be suited by 1½m. *J. Bethell.* **81**

NORFOLK REALM 2 b.c. Realm 129–Norfolk Light 86 (Blakeney 126) (1980 5fg 7fg 7d*) Mar 4; 29,000Y; rangy colt; first foal; dam, half-sister to Yanuka, won over 7f at 2 yrs and stayed 1½m; 20/1, ran on strongly to lead inside distance and beat Monks Farm a shade cleverly by ½ length in 14-runner maiden race at Leicester in October; will stay 1m; off course 4 months before second start (ran respectably). *C. Brittain.* **87**

NORFOLK STORM 2 b.c. Blakeney 126–Crystal Palace 121 (Solar Slipper 131) (1980 7d) Jan 16; good sort; half-brother to numerous winners, notably Royal Palace (by Ballymoss), Prince Consort (by Right Royal V) and Selhurst (by Charlottesville); dam smart at 7f to 1¼m; eased from 2/1 to 6/1 and looked in need of run prior to finishing 6½ lengths fifth of 20 to Soldan in minor event at Doncaster in October; should do better over 1¼m+ in 1981. *H. Cecil.* **69** p

NO RIFT 3 b.f. Be Friendly 130–Refifi 87 (Reform 132) (1979 NR 1980 6fg 7fg 6g 8d4) 1,500Y; first foal; dam won over 9f; little worthwhile form, including in a seller; blinkered last 2 outings; sold 520 gns Newmarket Autumn Sales. *J. Hudson.* —

NORMAN'S BOY 2 ch.g. Tarboosh–Flattery (Atan) (1980 5f 6fg 6d 7g2 7fg2) Mar 31; 1,750F, 4,700Y; fair sort; fourth produce; dam won over 5f at 2 yrs in Ireland; second in sellers at Beverley and Newcastle in July, in latter beaten a neck by Beechwood Seeker; will stay 1m; wears blinkers; sold to D. Hanley 1,850 gns Ascot July Sales. *J. W. Watts.* **63**

NORMAN STYLE 2 b.c. Malacate 131–Autocratic (Tyrant) (1980 6g* 8d) Feb 27; 10,000Y; lengthy, workmanlike colt; none too good a mover in his slower paces; first foal; dam fairly useful Irish 2-y-o 5f winner; ran on to catch Capstan in final furlong when winning 11-runner Ribero Stakes at Doncaster in September **80**

by a head, the pair 4 lengths clear; always in rear when 20/1-shot for William Hill Futurity on same course the following month, finishing last of 7 to Beldale Flutter; should stay 1m. *J. W. Watts.*

NORON 8 b.g. Shantung 132–Miss Peseta 95 (Sovereign Path 125) (1979 NR 1980 15.8g) quite a moderate hurdler; does little racing on flat nowadays; suited by a test of stamina; acts on any going. *R. Morris.* —

NORROY 3 ch.g. Northfields–Tzaritsa 113 (Young Emperor 133) (1979 NR 1980 8g 8g^{2} 8fg^{3} 8d^{2} 7fg* 8g 10s 8d 8d) well-made gelding; first foal; dam, at her best at 2 yrs, won at up to 1m; landed odds in 9-runner maiden race at Epsom in August; disappointed afterwards; stays 1m; acts on a firm and a soft surface; blinkered final outing; sold 4,600 gns Newmarket Autumn Sales. *P. Walwyn.* 78

NORSEMEN'S LADY 3 ch.f. Habat 127–Elizabeth Wales 95 (Abernant 142) (1979 NR 1980 8g 10.6d 10s 10s 12s) 5,400Y; workmanlike filly; third foal; half-sister to useful middle-distance performer Proven (by Tudor Melody); dam a sprinter; well beaten in maiden and minor races; blinkered last 3 outings; has given trouble at start; sold 420 gns Ascot November Sales. *I. Walker.* —

NORTH 3 b.g. Mount Hagen 127– Skippon 93 (Supreme Court 135) (1979 7f^{4} 8fg^{2} 1980 9d^{3} 12f^{2} 10f* 8h 10g 9g^{4}) strong, well-made gelding; good walker; made all to win 11-runner maiden race at Ayr in May; suited by middle distances; acts on firm going; blinkered nowadays; disappointing. *J. W. Watts.* 81

NORTHANGER 5 ch.g. Busted 134– Miss Klaire II 104 (Klairon 131) (1979 12.2s 10g 8s* 9fg 8.3fg 8f^{3} 8g 8g^{3} 8.3fg 8fg 1980 11g 10s^{2}) strong gelding; wasn't disgraced when runner-up to Ski Run in handicap at Newcastle in August, staying on well after being held up in slowly-run race; stays 1¼m; acts on any going but goes well on soft; has won over hurdles. *G. Richards.* 66

NORTH BUCHAN 3 ch.c. Lyphard 132–Spring Snow (Reliance II 137) (1979 NR 1980 11f^{4} 13s* 12fg^{2} 14g^{4} 14d^{2} 14g 13g^{2} 14g) neat colt; first foal; dam won over 15f in France; won 18-runner maiden race at Nottingham in July; narrowly beaten in minor event at Haydock on fifth start (blinkered when neck behind Xarfina) and handicap at Nottingham in September on seventh (short-headed by Teresilla); will stay 2m; suited by some give in the ground; game. *H. Cecil.* 91

NORTHERN BABY (CAN) 4 b.c. Northern Dancer–Two Rings (Round Table) (1979 10.5s* 10.5s^{2} 10fg^{2} 12g^{3} 10f^{3} 10g* 10fg^{3} 12d 10fg* 1980 10.5d^{3} 9.7d* 9.2s 10.5d 8g 10g^{3}) wiry colt; brother to a winner and half-brother to Bayford (by Foolish Pleasure), a leading 2-y-o in Canada in 1980; dam, a minor stakes winner, won 9 times at up to 1m from 31 starts; one of best middle-distance colts in 1979, winner of Champion Stakes at Newmarket; finished creditable third behind stable-companion Le Marmot in Prix Ganay at Longchamp before beating Strong Gale and Three Troikas by a length and 2½ lengths in Prix Dollar on same course in June; ran moderately next 3 starts, including in Benson and Hedges Gold Cup at York (didn't look particularly well and was given plenty to do when ninth to Master Willie), but returned to form when 2 lengths third to Dunette and Three Troikas in Prix du Prince d'Orange at Longchamp in September; acted on any going; retired to the Grangewilliam Stud, Maynooth, Co. Kildare. *F. Boutin, France.* 119

NORTHERNCOVERGIRL 3 ro.f. No Mercy 126–Skymistress 91 (Skymaster 126) (1979 5s 5g^{3} 5fg^{2} 5f^{3} 5g^{3} 5fg 5d 5d 5d 1980 5v 5f 5fg 5fg 5g 5g) rangy filly; plater nowadays; best form on a sound surface; has been tried in blinkers. *M. W. Easterby.* 49

NORTHERN ECHO 4 br.g. Scottish Rifle 127–Shine Bright 72 (Scintillant) (1979 11f^{3} 11d^{4} 15s^{2} 16d^{3} 16.1s 15g 1980 18d 12d) leggy gelding; poor maiden; stays well; acts on any going; best form in blinkers. *M. Naughton.* —

Prix Dollar, Longchamp—Northern Baby scores from Strong Gale and Three Troikas

NORTHERN ECLIPSE 3 b.c. Derring-Do 131–Haunting Melody 96 (Sing Sing 134) (1979 5g $5f^2$ 5f* $5g^2$ 1980 6fg 6d $6g^4$ 5d 5d) leggy, fair sort; very useful at 2 yrs; didn't find his form in handicaps in 1980; runs as though 5f is his trip; acts well on firm going; sold to G. Fletcher 6,600 gns Newmarket Autumn Sales. *J. Winter.* **79**

NORTHERN EMPRESS 3 ch.f. Northfields–Shahbanou 89 (Darius 129) (1979 7fg 1980 9f 8f) smallish filly; wasn't disgraced in maiden race at York at 2 yrs but was well beaten in similar events at Wolverhampton and Chepstow (blinkered) early in 1980; will stay 1¼m. *J. Tree.* –

NORTHERN GLORY 2 b.c. Northfields–Persian Pie (Tamerlane 128) (1980 $7d^3$) Jan 13; brother to very useful 6f and 7f winner Persepolis, and half-brother to numerous winners, including smart 1976 2-y-o Athlete's Foot (by Prince Tenderfoot) and smart sprinter Persian Breeze (by Whistling Wind); dam of little account; 14/1, put up a good first effort when 2½ lengths third of 19 to Dance Bid in maiden race at the Curragh in September; sure to win races. *M. O'Toole, Ireland.* **88** p

NORTHERN KING 3 gr.c. Northfields–Kathinka 79 (Sovereign Path 125) (1979 NR 1980 7f 10g 12g 8g 10.4g 8fg 8f) 26,000Y; compact colt; has shown a little ability in maiden races but is thoroughly unreliable nowadays (unseated rider after swerving left at start on sixth outing and refused to race when blinkered on final appearance); best left alone; sold 640 gns Newmarket Autumn Sales. *C. Brittain.* – §

NORTHERN MAGIC 5 b.h. Porto Bello 118–La Magicienne (Val de Loir 133) (1979 10.2s $10s^4$ 12d 8g 10s 10.2fg 8.2fg 10fg $9fg^3$ $12g^3$ $12fg^3$ $15.5f^2$ 18.1g 16f $12g^4$ 10.2d 12s 1980 $8f^3$ $8f^2$ $10fg^3$ 12fg) tall horse; placed in amateur riders race at Thirsk and apprentice handicaps at Newcastle and Goodwood; gives us impression 1m is on sharp side for him and stays 2m; acts on any going; used to wear blinkers. *M. Ryan.* **49**

NORTHERN MINSTREL (USA) 2 ch.c. Orbit Dancer–Old Tinker (Old Glendale) (1980 6d 8fg $8g^4$) $2,200F; dipped-backed colt; half-brother to **72**

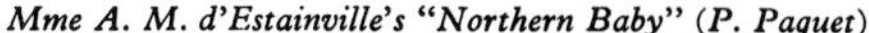

Mme A. M. d'Estainville's "Northern Baby" (P. Paquet)

several minor winners in USA; dam won 4 of her 44 starts; sire unraced son of Northern Dancer; about 2 lengths fourth of 15 behind Scottish Dream in maiden race at Edinburgh in October, best effort; stays 1m and will probably get 1¼m. *J. Fitzgerald.*

NORTHERN PRINCE 2 b.c. Northfields–Cecilia Q.C. 89 (Counsel 118) (1980 7d) May 21; 10,500F, 7,000Y; quite attractive, close-coupled, smallish colt; half-brother to 3 winners, including 1979 2-y-o 6f winner Queen's Counsellor (by Kalamoun); dam, best at up to 1m, is half-sister to high-class miler Saintly Song; very weak in market, nearest at finish when about 9 lengths sixth of 20 to John Willoughby in maiden race at Leicester in October; will be suited by 1m; should do better in 1981. *P. Walwyn.* **70 p**

NORTHERN SUPREMO (USA) 2 ch.c. Northern Dancer–Roussalka 123 (Habitat 134) (1980 6g) strong, deep-girthed colt; first foal; dam won 7 races at up to 1¼m from 2 yrs to 4 yrs, including Nassau Stakes twice, and is sister to 1,000 Guineas runner-up Our Home; 3/1 but not fully wound up, beaten soon after 4f when behind in 18-runner maiden race won by Noalto at Yarmouth in July, only outing. *H. Cecil.* –

NORTHERN VENTURE 5 b.m. St Alphage 119–Shopping Wise (Floribunda 136) (1979 6s 6g 7fg² 6f³ 7f 8g 8g 1980 6f) poor handicapper; stays 7f; acts on a firm surface; taken down early to start fourth outing of 1979 and was reluctant to go to post only outing of 1980 (came back tailed off). *J. Bingham.* –

NORTH FORLAND (FR) 3 ch.f. Northfields–Greenback II (Fric 128) (1979 NR 1980 10fg* 12d² 12s² 10fg 10fg 14.6g) 46,000Y; lengthy filly; half-sister to 2 winners, including very smart French middle-distance mare Infra Green (by Laser Light); dam never ran; beat Predominant ½ length in maiden race at Kempton in May; second in Ribblesdale Stakes at Royal Ascot (had no chance with 6-length winner Shoot A Line) and small race at Lingfield in June; well beaten in Nassau Stakes at Goodwood, Sean Graham Fillies Stakes at Kempton and Park Hill Stakes at Doncaster afterwards; stays 1½m; probably acts on any going; sold 580,000 francs (approx £57,000) Arc de Triomphe Sale. *B. Hills.* **99**

NORTHGATE LAD 4 b.g. Sterling Bay–Diriga (Track Spare 125) (1979 7v 8d 6d 5f³ 6f 7f³ 7f 8g 6s* 6d⁴ 6g 1980 6g 5fg 6f 5g 6fg) plater; best form at up to 7f; acts on any going; usually wears blinkers; often bandaged. *S. Nesbitt.* –

NORTHGATE LODGE 2 b.g. Warpath 113–Pall Nan 86 (Pall Mall 132) (1980 7g 8d) Apr 25; 3,000F, 5,400Y; leggy gelding; brother to 1m and 9f winner Dan Dare and half-brother to 3-y-o Appleby Park (by Bay Express), quite a useful winner over 7f in 1979, and to a winner in Malaya; dam best at 5f; unquoted and backward, always well behind in 12-runner minor event won by Sunion at Redcar in August and 14-runner maiden race won by Majorian at Leicester in November. *J. Etherington.* –

NORTH GREENWICH 3 br.g. Fireside Chat 122–Highland Rocket (Paveh 126) (1979 NR 1980 7fg 7f 5s³ 5g 5s 5fg⁴ 6f 5fg* 5d) 1,350F, 2,300Y; lengthy gelding; won all-aged seller at Beverley in September (no bid); form only at 5f; seems to act on any going; sweated up but ran respectably sixth start; sold 1,200 gns Newmarket Autumn Sales. *I. Walker.* **56**

NORTHJET 3 ch.c. Northfields–Jellatina (Fortino II 120) (1979 8s³ 5s* 7v² 1980 7s* 6d* 5g* 6g* 6g 6.5d 6d² 6s³ 5f) 24,000F; nice ex-Italian colt; closely related to very smart Italian sprinter Madang (by Habitat) and half-brother to winners in Hong Kong and Italy; dam won over 9f in Ireland; won 4 races in Italy early in year, 3 at Rome and one at Milan, putting up best effort on final occasion to beat Marching On 1½ lengths in Premio Melton at Rome (broke course record); well beaten in Cork and Orrery Stakes at Royal Ascot on fifth start but did well afterwards in France, finishing second to Kilijaro in Prix de Meautry at Deauville and third to same filly in Prix de Seine-et-Oise at Maisons-Laffitte, beaten 2½ lengths in latter; stays 7f; acts on soft going; trained in Italy by L. Brogi. *O. Douieb, France.* **120**

NORTHLEACH 5 ch.h. Northfields–Macaw 85 (Narrator 127) (1979 7g² 8s* 8v 10d 8g² 8fg* 7g* 8d* 8g 8g⁴ 9f 8d* 7.6fg* 8d⁴ 1980 8d⁴ 8f* 8f² 7.6f² 8g 8d 8fg 8d⁴ 8.2g 10fg 8g² 8d⁴ 8d) strong, attractive horse; useful handicapper on his day; favourite when winning Playboy Bookmakers Newbury Spring Cup in April by short head from strong-finishing Piaffer; runner-up subsequently **98**

Playboy Bookmakers Newbury Spring Cup—in a driving finish Northleach wins by a short head from Piaffer

in Whitsun Cup at Sandown in May (to Imperial Ace), Queen Elizabeth Stakes at Lingfield in June (to Lord Rochford) and handicap at Brighton in October (to Silley's Knight when ridden by 7-lb claimer); disappointed on several other occasions and isn't anywhere near so reliable as he used to be; best at around 1m; acts on any going and any track; suitable mount for an apprentice; usually held up and can produce good turn of foot. *J. Dunlop.*

NORTH LONDON 4 ch.g. Northfields–Flaring Angel (Nentego 119) (1979 11d 12g 9.4s 1980 10f 13fg) poor maiden; blinkered final start. *W. Stubbs.* —

NORTH MOOR 3 ch.f. Northfields–Ride 71 (Sovereign Path 125) (1979 5s 5g⁴ 7fg³ 1980 10v³ 12fg³ 12fg² 10.6fg² 13.8fg³ 16.9d 14.7g) quite attractive, small, compact filly; second in handicaps at Warwick and Haydock in May; stays 1½m but possibly not 1¾m; acts on a firm surface; blinkered nowadays; has shown signs of being none too keen on several occasions; sold 30,000 gns Newmarket December Sales. *B. Hills.* **65**

NORTH POLE (CAN) 3 ch.c. Northern Dancer–Canalu (Canadian Champ) (1979 6d² 1980 8g³ 8f* 7fg* 8g²) $100,000Y; half-brother to several winners in North America, including minor stakes winner Vickie's Champ (by Victorian Era), successful at up to 7f; dam, a stakes-placed winner at up to 1m, is half-sister to top-class Honest Pleasure and high-class For The Moment; landed odds in small events at Phoenix Park and the Curragh in May; blinkered, went down by 2 lengths to Combine Harvester in Kilruddery Stakes at Leopardstown later in month, only subsequent start; will stay 1¼m; acts on firm going; racing in USA. *V. O'Brien, Ireland.* **96**

NORTH SEA TIGER 3 ch.c. St Chad 120–Tudor Beauty (Tudor Melody 129) (1979 8h 10s 1980 8fg 8fg 7g 8fg 9f⁴ 10fg) leggy, lightly-made colt; plater; stays 9f; blinkered last 2 outings; sweated up badly on reappearance; trained by S. Norton first start. *J. Tierney.* —

NORTHSOUND 3 ch.g. Northfields–Tamarisk 93 (Rustam 127) (1979 7fg⁴ 7g³ 8f 6fg 1980 10h* 10.1f⁴ 12.2fg³ 10g) workmanlike gelding; good mover; made all to win 7-runner maiden race at Brighton in May; possibly stays 1½m; acts on hard going; exported to Hong Kong. *M. Jarvis.* **76**

NORTH TWO 7 b.g. Stupendous–Taking Silk (Shantung 132) (1979 NR 1980 9.6fg 9.6h⁴ 11.7d) unfurnished gelding; plater; very lightly raced since 1976; stays 9f; probably acts on any going; usually wears bandages. *B. Forsey.* —

NORTH WEST 5 ch.g. Welsh Pageant 132–Heather Grove (Hethersett 134) (1979 11.1v 10f 1980 12f 10fg 10fg) tall, short-backed gelding; well beaten since 1978; stays 1¼m; used to wear bandages. *M. Masson.* —

NORTH YARD 4 b.g. Realm 129–Campitello (Hornbeam 130) (1979 10g 9f* 8fg* 1980 10d) ex-Irish gelding; winner of 2 handicaps at Phoenix Park in 1979 —

when trained by J. M. Oxx; well beaten in minor event won by Spanish Dancer at Newbury in July; stays 9f; acts on firm going; winner over hurdles. *F. Rimell.*

NORTON CROSS 2 gr.c. Realm 129–Zameen (Armistice 131) (1980 5f^4 5f^4 6g* 6s 6f^4 8g^4) Apr 6; 11,000Y; sturdy colt; good mover; half-brother to winners in France and Algeria, including Azeem (by Le Haar), successful at up to 9f; dam won over 1½m in France; won 7-runner maiden race at Ayr in June by ¾ length from Prionsaa, first outing for 2 months; respectable fourth subsequently in £4,600 event at Ripon in August and 11-runner nursery at Thirsk in September; stays 1m. *M. H. Easterby.* **78**

NORWICH BOY 3 b.g. Averof 123–Teresa-Hernandez (Queen's Hussar 124) (1979 5s 5g^4 5fg 6h^3 6fg 1980 6d 5fg 5g 6g 6g^4 5g 6g) leggy gelding; plater; stays 6f; suited by some give in the ground; has worn blinkers; usually sweats up; looks ungenuine. *D. Weeden.* **— §**

NOSILLA 5 br.g. Irish Love 117–Julie's Gi-Gi (Brave Invader) (1979 NR 1980 10g 12fg 12g^4) strong gelding; poor maiden. *K. Tuer.* **—**

NOTICEABLE 4 ch.g. Amber Rama 133–Rave Notice (Princequillo) (1979 8fg 10f^2 12s 1980 10s 10.6d) tall, unfurnished gelding; stays 1¼m; probably unsuited by soft ground. *R. Armstrong.* **—**

NOTIKI 5 br.h. Town Crier 119–Zagora 95 (Tycoon II) (1979 7d* 7f^4 8fg^2 7g* 8fg 8fg 1980 8.2fg^3 8fg 8g 7g 10g^3 8g*) plater; well backed when beating Chapeau Vert by a head at Brighton in October (no bid); had run well in better company on previous start; stays 1¼m; probably acts on any going. *C. James.* **58**

NOTRE PLAISIR (HOL) 3 ch.c. Mon Plaisir 121–Crowd Pleaser 47 (Don II 123) (1979 7fg 6g 9g^3 6.5v* 1980 6fg 7.6f 8f* 9g 12g* 10g 14.5g^2) smallish, lengthy Dutch-bred colt; successful in Dutch 2,000 Guineas at Duindigt in May (awarded race on disqualification of winner) and Dutch Derby on same course in July (beat Go Go by 1½ lengths); second in Dutch St Leger at Duindigt again in August; has shown little form in this country; stays 1¾m; appears to act on any going. *M. Ryan.* **?**

NOUS 5 b.m. Le Johnstan 123–Nicola Jane 80 (River Chanter 121) (1979 5v 6g 5g^4 5f 5g 5g 9g 6s* 5.9g^3 7g 6d* 1980 5v* 6v 6f* 5fg* 6fg 6fg 6.3s 6.3d^2 5g^2 6fg 5g 6d 5v) sprint handicapper; winner at Naas in April on third start; promoted to first at Phoenix Park in March and Leopardstown in May on subsequent disqualification of both winners on technical grounds; ran creditably on other occasions, notably when length second to Just A Shadow in valuable Philips Electrical Handicap at the Curragh in August; stays 6f; acts on any going; trained by R. McCormick in Ireland until after tenth start. *T. Gosling.* **74**

NO-U-TURN 2 b.c. Nonoalco 131–Raffmarie 78 (Raffingora 130) (1980 7fg^4 6g^3 6fg* 6d^2 7v) Mar 18; 26,000Y; well-grown colt; first living foal; dam, sister to Cheveley Park winner Pasty, stayed 6f; hard ridden to catch New Years Day when winning 7-runner minor event at Windsor in August by head; creditable 1½ lengths second of 14 to Piperhill in similar race at Ripon later in month; should be suited by a return to 7f; probably unsuited by very soft ground. *F. Durr.* **95**

NOW HEAR THIS 6 br.g. Verbatim–Blackout 98 (Delirium 126) (1979 8g 1980 11.7fg) fair sort; stays 1½m; acts on any going; has been tried in blinkers; good mount for an amateur rider. *G. Balding.* **—**

NOXID 3 ch.g. Amber Rama 133–Gay Gadabout 91 (Galivanter 131) (1979 5g 5d 5d 5g 5fg^3 1980 5f^2 7fg 5f 6d 13.8fg) strong gelding; plater; best form at 5f on firm ground; has been tried in blinkers; retained 420 gns Doncaster August Sales. *Hbt Jones.* **39**

NUMAS 3 b.c. Porto Bello 118–Anjonic 56 (Le Levanstell 122) (1979 5v^2 5s 5s 6f^2 5g 7f^3 7f* 7g 1980 8.2d 7f 8g 7f* 7h^2 7.6g 8g 7g^3 7.6d^3 7fg 7g) rangy colt; good mover; fair handicapper; led close home to short-head Betsy Red at Chester in May; creditable second to Soaf at Thirsk later in month; suited by 7f and should stay 1m; acts on any going but goes particularly well on firm; ran moderately in blinkers third start at 2 yrs; out of his depth third outing and ran moderately on sixth; sold 13,000 gns Newmarket December Sales. *R. Sheather.* **89**

NUMBERS UP 3 b.g. So Blessed 130–River Severn 96 (Henry the Seventh 125) (1979 6s 5fg^3 6d^3 5g 6f 5fg 6s 1980 5fg^2 5d 5g 5s 7g^4 6g) rangy gelding; good walker and mover; plating-class maiden; promises to stay 7f; acts on a firm and a soft surface; ran badly in blinkers final start. *R. Turnell.* **62**

NUN 3 ch.f. Amber Rama 133–Virginia (Pirate King 129) (1979 NR 1980 8f 9.4d* 8s*) useful-looking filly; third foal; half-sister to 11f winner Californian (by Relko); dam lightly-raced sister to very useful stayer Avast; successful in maiden race at Carlisle in June and minor event at Stockton three days later (veered right in last furlong); will stay 1¼m; acts on soft going; sold 3,000 gns Newmarket December Sales. *C. Thornton.* **65**

NUNS LANE 3 b.f. Rapid River 127–Queen's Lane 107 (Tamerlane 128) (1979 NR 1980 6f 5f 5h) compact filly; half-sister to fairly useful 1975 2-y-o 6f winner Midnight Melody (by Linacre) and a winner in Malaya; dam stayed 9f; in rear in minor and maiden events; sold 670 gns Doncaster June Sales. *N. Chamberlain.* **–**

NUN'S PRIDE 2 ch.c. Manacle 123–Casona (Upper Case) (1980 5f 6f² 7d) neat colt; dam pulled up on one of her 3 outings; 7/1, finished strongly after having none too good a run when 1½ lengths second of 18 to Kathred in £2,000 seller at Newmarket in October; in rear in maiden race next time out; promises to stay 7f; acts on firm going; capable of winning a seller. *P. Cole.* **73**

NUNSWALK 3 ch.f. The Parson 119–Vital Error 105 (Javelot 124) (1979 7f 8fg⁴ 8f⁴ 1980 7f 8fg 7fg 10g 12g 14g 13.1f 12fg² 10fg⁴ 12fg⁴ 10f) short-coupled filly; plater; stays 1½m; acts on a firm surface; has worn blinkers; ran moderately last 2 starts, looking ungenerous on first occasion. *R. Hannon.* **59**

NUPPENCE 3 b.f. Reform 132–Money for Nothing 104 (Grey Sovereign 128§) (1979 5f 5f² 1980 5fg² 5f 6fg) compact, attractive filly; second in maiden race at Wolverhampton in April; should stay 6f; blinkered final outing; not seen out after April. *F. J. Houghton.* **65**

NUREYEV (USA) 3 b.c. Northern Dancer–Special (Forli) (1979 7.5s* 1980 7d* 8fg*(dis)). **131**

Disqualifications have occurred very infrequently in England's five classics. The most recent season saw the Two Thousand Guineas, which was established in 1809, provide its first instance of a horse's passing the post first and being disqualified: the French-trained Nureyev, 13/8 favourite for the Guineas, was the first horse to lose an English classic in the stewards' room for more than sixty years. The disqualification made headline news and was the subject of comment for several days but, outside Nureyev's connections, few could be found—after the patrol film was made available for public scrutiny—to disagree with the decision to take the race off Nureyev.

Although he was seen on a racecourse only twice before being sent to Newmarket, Nureyev provided regular copy for the newspapers from the day, in July 1978, when he was bought at the Keeneland Sales for 1,300,000 dollars on behalf of Stavros Niarchos. Transferred from Walwyn's yard, for reasons which weren't clear, in the summer of 1979, Nureyev won the Prix Thomas Bryon, a Group 3 pattern race run at Saint-Cloud in November, on his only appearance at two. His performance impressed everyone who saw it and

Prix Djebel, Maisons-Laffitte—one of the most impressive classic trials we have seen. Nureyev thrashes his opponents

only the Grand Criterium winner Dragon was rated higher in the French Free Handicap, in which Nureyev was allotted the equivalent of 9-8; Boutin thought Nureyev the equal of Nonoalco whom he had saddled to win the Two Thousand Guineas in 1974. Nureyev's pre-Guineas trial came in the Prix Djebel at Maisons-Laffitte in April, a race won in 1966 by the Guineas winner Kashmir II. The Prix Djebel has lost some prestige over the years although it did succeed in 1976 in attracting the two leading horses in the French Free Handicap, Manado and Vitiges, both of whom were afterwards sent over for the Guineas. Nureyev put up by far the most impressive public trial for the Guineas and immediately after the Prix Djebel was made a raging hot favourite for the Two Thousand Guineas, one leading firm of bookmakers reducing his odds to 5/4. And the major English trials were still to be run! We came away from Maisons-Laffitte convinced that Nureyev would win the Guineas; we hadn't seen a more impressive classic trial for many a long year. Ridden with supreme confidence, Nureyev easily disposed of Viteric (9-4 French Free Handicap) and four others; Paquet didn't make a move on Nureyev until approaching the final furlong but he went clean away to win by a long-looking six lengths, passing the post on the bridle with his ears pricked.

In the Guineas Paquet rode Nureyev in a manner which suggested almost complete disdain for the quality of the opposition. Restrained to such an extent that he was stone-cold last, ten lengths and more behind the leaders, until approaching halfway, Nureyev was set with an unnecessarily stiff task in the second part of the race. Making his way through the field, Paquet ran into trouble more than two furlongs from home where he found his way blocked by a wall of horses. With little prospect of finding a way through he elected to barge his way out—there probably wasn't time for him to pull back and switch round the outside of the field; Posse, the horse immediately on Nureyev's right, had to be snatched up and was very nearly brought down. Nureyev, showing fine acceleration to reach a challenging position, went on to win by a neck from Known Fact, in spite of drifting towards the stand rails in the final furlong. Posse recovered a tremendous amount of ground in the last two furlongs to finish third, only three quarters of a length behind Known Fact. The first three finished clear of the remainder. The patrol film showed clearly Nureyev's brush with Posse—and also a later incident when Posse collided with Taufan, putting paid to whatever chance that horse might have had of getting a place. The stewards deliberated for more than three quarters of an hour before announcing their decision. Acting according to the rules of racing, as they operate in Britain, the stewards had one matter to decide in each case. The interference caused by Nureyev to Posse was obvious, as was that caused by Posse to Taufan. What the stewards had to decide was whether the interference was accidental, in which case they would have available the options of allowing the result to stand or altering the placings, or whether the interference arose out of 'dangerous, reckless, carêless or improper riding' in which case they would have no option but to relegate the offenders to last place. The stewards made no mention in their announcement of Eddery's riding of Posse but they decided that Paquet had ridden recklessly. In our view they were completely justified in so deciding: Paquet rode in pursuit of his own chance with scant consideration for the chance of Posse or for the safety of his rider. Whether the hampering of Taufan by Posse was accidental or the result of careless riding by Eddery is a moot point.

We have consistently been among the critics of rule 153 of the Rules of Racing, which deals with improper riding. The nub of the argument against the rule as it stands is that the disciplining of jockeys for breaches of the rule, and consideration of the equity of the result of a race in which interference may have affected the result, are two quite different matters which should be dealt with separately. Towards the end of 1979, the Racehorse Owners Association submitted a paper on these lines, written by Phil Bull, to the Jockey Club; the paper later received the backing of the Horseracing Advisory Council, a newly-instituted body on which Mr Bull served as chairman for part of the year. The Disciplinary Committee of the Jockey Club examined the recommendations but rejected them for two main reasons: first, because it felt that the proposed changes would make racing less safe by bringing pressure on riders from owners and trainers to win at any price; and, secondly, because it considered it 'a matter of absolute prime importance for the integrity of racing that the owner, trainer, rider and horse must be considered as a team and not as separate individuals.' We have no wish to rake the embers of what is now a cold controversy, but it baffles comprehension how the Disciplinary Committee can describe the latter as being a matter of absolute prime

Mr S. S. Niarchos' "Nureyev" (P. Paquet)

importance for the integrity of racing in the face of actions taken by stewards under rule 153 regarding improper use of the whip and under rule 151 (ii), which deals with riders ensuring that their horses are given a full opportunity to win. As for the Disciplinary Committee's preoccupation with possible 'win-at-all-costs' conspiracies between owners, trainers and their riders, the infractions of rule 151 (ii) should be of particular interest to the committee. Here is a rule which, not to put too fine a point on it, relates to cases of possible 'non-triers'—precisely the area, one would imagine, where conspiracy between an owner, trainer and jockey is a presumptive possibility. Yet rule 151 is so framed as effectively to *separate* owner, trainer and jockey, rather than treat them as a team! As we said once before, the pronouncements of the Jockey Club are, on occasions, like the peace of God—they pass all understanding.

Nureyev's disqualification was a concrete instance of the injustice that many feel flows from rule 153. Nureyev was rightly disqualified. But we shouldn't think anybody—but we must be careful—would quarrel with the assertion that, as the race was run, Nureyev was, at worst, the second-best horse in the race. Known Fact, who was awarded the race, had an uninterrupted run all the way; although no two groups of stewards can be certain to read what has happened in a race in exactly the same way, it seems reasonable to assume that almost all would have decided that Nureyev should have been put back in the placings behind Posse. Had rules such as those favoured by the Racehorse Owners Association been in force, Known Fact would in all probability still have been awarded the race, with Posse second; Nureyev, however, would have been placed third. Paquet would have been deprived of his prize-money percentage and given a fine and/or a suspension, of severity appropriate to the seriousness of his offence. As the rule stands, the stewards at Newmarket couldn't discipline Paquet for reckless riding without disqualifying Nureyev to *last* place. Paquet was stood down for seven days. The maximum penalty that could have been imposed by the Newmarket stewards was a ten-day suspension and a £325 fine.

One more point before we leave the subject. There seems to have been some misunderstanding about the rules of racing that govern improper riding in France. Several commentators erroneously stated that Nureyev and his jockey would have been dealt with similarly in France. It's as well to get the facts straight. The French have more sense than to conduct this particular aspect of the game according to the Jockey Club's Rules of Racing. In fact, the stewards in France have the discretion, in a case like that involving Nureyev, to penalize the jockey without disqualifying the horse to last place; the French rules permit the stewards to alter the placings when a jockey has been guilty of an offence that requires suspension. Suspensions for improper riding are stiffer in France than in Britain. The French operate on the principle that jockeys should pay for their own mistakes and misdemeanours.

Nureyev (USA) (b.c. 1977)	Northern Dancer (b 1961)	Nearctic (br 1954)	Nearco
			Lady Angela
		Natalma (b 1957)	Native Dancer
			Almahmoud
	Special (b 1969)	Forli (ch 1963)	Aristophanes
			Trevisa
		Thong (b 1964)	Nantallah
			Rough Shod

The Two Thousand Guineas proved to be Nureyev's last race. The misfortune that attended his running at Newmarket dogged him for the rest of the season. He was ante-post favourite for the Derby until news broke in the middle of May that he had a viral chill, the effects of which lasted for some time. Ironically, one of the most likely reasons for his transfer to France as a two-year-old was to keep him away from the virus which was affecting some of the stables at Lambourn. It was clear long before the end of the year that we had seen the last of Nureyev on the racecourse. He is a smallish, lengthy, good-quartered colt and a good mover of very fashionable breeding; he has tremendous potential as a stallion. A son of Northern Dancer, the sire of Nijinsky, Lyphard, The Minstrel and a host of other top horses, Nureyev is the third foal and third winner of Special, a once-raced sister to Thatch, an outstanding colt, and Lisadell, a pretty good filly, and a half-sister to Marinsky and King Pellinore, both of whom were top-class animals. Nureyev's grandam Thong was a stakes-placed sister to the stallions Ridan and Lt Stevens and to Apalachee's dam Moccasin. Thatch, who won the July Cup, stayed a mile as also did Lisadell, winner of Ascot's Coronation Stakes; King Pellinore was second in the Irish Sweeps Derby and the St Leger and trained on into an even better horse in the States as a four-year-old; Marinsky was a sprinter who lost the July Cup in the stewards' room. On the limited evidence available it seems reasonable to conclude that Nureyev would have stayed a mile and a quarter; we didn't share the optimism of his trainer about Nureyev's ability to stay the Derby course. Nureyev probably acted on any going and he had a good turn of foot. He has been retired to his owner's stud, the Haras de Fresnay-le-Buffard; nominations available for his first season were quickly snapped up at 100,000 francs (about £10,000) plus a further 100,000 francs if the mare is in foal on October 1st. Nureyev was a top-class racehorse and it says a great deal for him that he was able to get to the post first in the Guineas after running into so much trouble. Had he been ridden more judiciously he might well have been a very impressive winner indeed. *F. Boutin, France.*

NUROSE 5 ch.g. Tobrouk–Gondolina (Aggressor 130) (1979 12fg 11.7fg 12.2d 10f 10f 10.6g 12d* 1980 12fg^4 12fg 12fg^3 10fg 12d^2 12g^4 12fg 12d 12d 12d) quite a modest middle-distance handicapper; seems to act on any going; has worn bandages; usually blinkered nowadays (ran creditably without on ninth start). *A. Hide.* **56**

NUTTY SLACK 2 gr.c. Saritamer 130–Mary Mullen 88 (Lorenzaccio 130) (1980 5fg 5fg 5s 5.8g 7fg 7g 7fg 8d 7fg 7d) Mar 31; 3,200Y; useful sort; second foal; brother to 1979 2-y-o 1m seller winner Mannerism; dam won over 5f at 2 yrs; improved a little late in season and finished sixth of 19 to Jalabad in maiden race at Lingfield in October on penultimate start; suited by 7f; blinkered seventh and eighth outings. *J. Haine.* **70**

N.Y. COMEX (USA) see Uncle Salty (USA)

NYONO (FR) 2 b.c. Caro 133–Nirvanita (Right Royal V 135) (1980 8g*) Mar 20; third foal; half-brother to 2 winners in France, including 3-y-o 1m winner Nager's Valley (by Jim French); dam unraced half-sister to high-class 1m to 1$\frac{1}{4}$m horse Nadjar; second favourite when winning 19-runner newcomers race at Maisons-Laffitte in September by $\frac{1}{2}$ length from Two Step; a well-bred colt who will make a very useful middle-distance performer. *M. Zilber, France.* **?**

O

OAK APPLE DAY 2 br.c. Firestreak 125–Umbertina (Umberto 118) (1980 8d 7s) Apr 6; 1,100F; leggy colt; half-brother to several winners, including fairly useful middle-distance handicapper Quortina (by Quorum); dam showed no form; unquoted when in rear in maiden race at Warwick and minor event at Chepstow in October. *D. Elsworth.* —

OATES REMOVALS 3 b. or br.f. Huntercombe 133–Debatable 84 (Counsel 118) (1979 5s 6f 6f 5fg 1980 8f 8s 8g 7fg^{4} 7g 7f^{3} 7g) small filly; plater; stays 7f; acts on firm going; blinkered fourth and fifth starts; has worn bandages; sold 1,750 gns Doncaster September Sales. *W. Wharton.* **48**

OBERGURGL 2 br.f. Warpath 113–Snow Goose (Santa Claus 133) (1980 8d 8d) Jan 22; fair sort; sister to Wild Goose Chase, successful at up to 2m, and half-sister to a winner; dam never ran; in mid-division in sizeable fields for maiden races at Redcar and Leicester at the back-end; likely to need 1½m+ at 3 yrs. *C. Thornton.* —

OBLIGATIONS 2 ch.f. Sun Prince 128–Crash Helmet 77 (Crocket 130) (1980 5g 5g) Mar 13; strong, quite useful sort; third living foal; closely related to winning sprinter Una Yappa and a winner in Italy (both by Realm); dam best at up to 1¼m; 12/1 when 8¾ lengths seventh to Doobie Do in 17-runner maiden event at Sandown in June, second appearance; needed race first outing; will be suited by 6f. *B. Hills.* —

OBORNE GIRL 3 b.f. Weepers Boy 124–Miss Emma (Round Up) (1979 7f 6fg 1980 8d 9d* 8.2d 10f^{4}) plater; won apprentice seller at Wolverhampton in July (bought in 1,450 gns); stayed 1¼m; seemed to act on any going; sweated up third start; dead. *J. Old.* **57**

OBROVAC (USA) 2 ch.c. Time Tested–Counterpart (Prince John) (1980 6g^{2} 8d*) Apr 10; $20,000Y; neat, attractive colt; good mover; third foal; half-brother to a winner by Tumiga; dam second twice in USA; looked to have done very well since first outing when short-priced favourite for 21-runner maiden race at Sandown in October and won with something in hand by 2 lengths from Soukab; had previously finished strongly when length second of 10 to Shasavaan in Duke of Edinburgh Stakes at Ascot; will stay 1¼m; likely to make a very useful 3-y-o. *R. Price.* **93** p

OBSERVE 4 b.g. Rheffic 129–Minorette (Miralgo 130) (1979 NR 1980 16fg) second foal; dam won over 1m at 3 yrs in France, and was also successful 6 times over jumps; modest sixth behind Mountain Man in amateur riders race at Newbury in September on first outing. *F. Winter.* —

OCEAN BELLE 2 ch.f. Deep Diver 134–Lady Player (Ballyciptic 122) (1980 5v 5g 5g 6v 6g) May 29; half-sister to Irish 3-y-o Baradorus (by Green God), successful at up to 1¼m, and to fair sprinter Ainsley Boy (by Virginia Boy); dam never ran; third favourite when 13½ lengths fifth of 10 to Merely Mozart in maiden race at Ayr in March; in rear in maiden and minor events in Ireland subsequently. *P. Doyle, Ireland.* —

OCEAN VICTORY 5 b.m. Seaepic 100–Gold Case 74 (Petition 130) (1979 10s 1980 8s) poor plater; blinkered on only outing of 1980. *Mrs R. Lomax.* —

OCH AYE 2 br.f. Lochnager 132–Daisy Knot 81 (Acer 123) (1980 7g^{4}) May 11; big filly; third foal; dam 2-y-o 1m winner; unquoted and in need of race, shaped quite well when staying on over final 2f to finish 6½ lengths fourth of 19 to Canaille in maiden event at Leicester in August, only outing. *J. Bethell.* **69** p

OCHIL HILLS STAR 7 b.g. Chebs Lad 120–Turkish Maid 58 (Menelek 114) (1979 8s^{2} 10g* 10fg^{3} 9.4g 8.2d 11d 10.6g 1980 8.2g 7f^{2} 9fg^{2} 7g* 9f 8fg 8.2g 8d 8d 8.2s) poor handicapper; winner at Edinburgh in June; stays 1¼m; acts on any going; has been tried in blinkers; good mount for an inexperienced rider. *J. Wilson.* **45**

OCTAVIA 3 ch.f. Sallust 134–Exmoor Lass 86 (Exbury 138) (1979 5g^{4} 5g 5f^{4} 6f 6g^{3} 7g^{3} 7d 8fg 1980 8s 8f^{3} 7.6f 9f 8fg 7d 7g 8.2g 9s 7d) small ex-Irish filly; third in maiden race at Thirsk in April, only worthwhile form; best run at 1m on firm going. *R. Hollinshead.* —

ODIN'S RAVEN 2 br.c. Jukebox 120–Bare Costs (Petition 130) (1980 6g^{3} 6g^{4} 6d* 6s* 7d 7d^{2}) Feb 8; 39,000Y; strong, good sort; none too good a mover; brother to high-class 6f to 1m winner Record Token, and half-brother to 3 **99** ?

winners; dam unraced sister to dam of very smart Delmora; successful twice, landing the odds by 8 lengths from Minibank in minor event at Chester in August and winning £2,900 race at Ayr the following month by ½ length from newcomer Church Mountain; good second (apprentice ridden) to Belloc in minor event at Leicester in November; may well get 1m; acts well on soft ground. *J. Hindley.*

OFFA'S DYKE 7 b.g. Adropejo 114–Nichucath (Nimbus 130) (1979 NR 1980 12d) of little account on flat but is a winner over hurdles. *R. E. Peacock.* —

OFFA'S MEAD 11 ch.g. Rathlin–Eridantini (Indigenous 121) (1979 5d4 5s2 5fg 5fg4 5fg 5g 5d* 5fg 5fg 5fg 5g 1980 5s 5g 5.8fg 5d 5g 5fg 5d 6g) sprint handicapper; had stiffish tasks in 1980 and showed little form; acts on any going; sometimes wears bandages; suitable mount for an amateur rider; does best when brought wide to race alone. *M. Bradley.* —

OFFERING 2 b.f. Dubassoff–Ready And Willing 82 (Reliance II 137) (1980 7g) Apr 29; rangy filly; third foal; half-sister to a winner in Italy; dam won over 12.2f and comes from a good family; 33/1 and on burly side when behind in 26-runner maiden race at Newmarket in October won by Full of Reason. *Sir Mark Prescott.* —

OFF SHORE 3 b.f. Grundy 137–No Relation 94 (Klairon 131) (1979 5g 7g* 7fg 1980 12.3f3 12d 12g* 14.6g) lengthy, rather unfurnished filly; pushed clear to beat Ripcorn (gave 12 lb) by 4 lengths in minor event at Newmarket in August; had earlier finished 7½ lengths third of 13 to Shoot A Line in Cheshire Oaks in May; well beaten in Ribblesdale Stakes at Royal Ascot and Park Hill Stakes at Doncaster on her other starts; stays 1½m; acts on firm going; sold 36,000 gns Newmarket December Sales. *H. Wragg.* **88**

OFF THE RED 2 b.c. Red God 128§–Off The Mark (On Your Mark 125) (1980 5s 5s 5fg 5fg 5h* 6fg 5fg 5g) Mar 18; 6,000Y; neat, quite attractive colt; first foal; dam won over 1m in France; backed from 33/1 to 8/1, showed only worthwhile form when winning 13-runner maiden race at Folkestone in May by 2 lengths from May Go Twice; should stay 6f; acts well on hard ground; started none too well last 3 outings; best left alone until showing a return to form. *A. Bailey.* **76** d

OH SIMMIE 5 b.m. African Sky 124–Trusian (Milesian 125) (1979 5d 5fg3 5.8g 5f4 5fg* 5f3 5f3 6g2 5d3 6fg 5.6fg* 5fg* 5g 6g 5s 1980 5g 5f4 5f 5g 5g* 5g 5f4 5d 5d4 5.6g 5fg* 5g 5s 5v) compact mare; fairly useful sprinter on her day; quickened clear in closing stages when beating Cottam Rocket by 2 lengths in Gosforth Park Cup at Newcastle in June; beat Westburg by a neck in £4,000 handicap at Ascot in September; virtually refused to race eighth outing; best form at up to 5.6f; acts on any going; excellent mount for an apprentice. *R. Hollinshead.* **88**

O. I. OYSTON 4 b.g. Martinmas 128–Last Lap 75 (Immortality) (1979 8g* 5s 8s2 8fg4 8s 8fg 10fg 8.2g 8.2g 8d* 1980 7d2 7v* 7f 7.6f 8fg 8d2 7g 7.6g3 7f4 7.6d* 6fg* 7fg2 7s4 6d) leggy gelding; did well in 1980 and put up a particularly good effort when beating Moybrook by 1½ lengths in handicap at Carlisle in September; had earlier made all at Stockton and Chester; stays 1m; acts on any going; has worn blinkers (not when successful). *J. Berry.* **74**

OKAVAMBA 2 ch.f. Wollow 132–Orapa 88 (Aureole 132) (1980 6s 6fg* 6g) Apr 8; neat filly; third foal; half-sister to middle-distance winner Khaki Kate (by Brigadier Gerard); dam won at up to 1m and is half-sister to smart African Dancer; third favourite, made all to win 22-runner maiden race at Windsor in August by a neck from Norfolk Queen, the pair clear; had very stiff task when outpaced throughout in nursery won by Amorous at Newmarket in October; likely to need 1¼m at 3 yrs. *H. Wragg.* **82**

OKLAHOMA STAR 2 gr.f. Hotfoot 126–America 112 (Buisson Ardent 129) (1980 6s 7fg 7fg* 7d 7g) Mar 13; neat filly; half-sister to a winner in Norway and useful hurdler Mount Harvard (by High Top); dam, very useful at 2 yrs, stayed 1m; won 19-runner maiden race at Warwick in August by ½ length from Crackaway; ran well, although unplaced, in nursery on final appearance; will stay 1m; possibly unsuited by a soft surface. *M. Jarvis.* **85**

OLBAS 3 ch.f. Mountain Call 125–Aurelia 68 (Aureole 132) (1979 5s 7fg 1980 11fg) behind in maiden races; very unruly in paddock and reared over backwards at start when withdrawn before intended second outing. *P. Feilden.* —

OLD BIRD 3 gr.g. Birdbrook 110–Elfin Smile (Be Friendly 130) (1979 6f 1980 6f 8h 6fg2 6g4) fair sort; quite moderate; should stay beyond 6f; yet to race on a soft surface; sold to J. Bingham 940 gns Newmarket Autumn Sales. *J. W. Watts.* **66**

OLD DOMINION (USA) 3 b.g. In Reality–Virginia Green 83 (Nashua) (1979 5s 5g³ 5fg* 5f³ 6fg² 5d² 5f⁴ 1980 5s⁴ 6s³ 5fg³ 6f* 6f³ 6f* 6fg 6g⁴ 6g² 6g 6s 6g 6s* 5g 6d) strong, good sort; good mover; fairly useful handicapper; successful at Kempton (by 2½ lengths from Laurium) and Chepstow (beat Habito 2 lengths) in May and at Taby (Sweden) in September; beat ex-English Song of Songs and King of Troy in Taby International Sprinters' Stakes on last-named; suited by 6f and may stay further; seems to act on any going; genuine and consistent. *I. Balding.* **92**

OLD HOLLOW 2 b.g. Wolver Hollow 126–Red Madonna 84 (Red God 128§) (1980 6s 7fg 7s) May 10; 5,000Y; fifth foal; half-brother to a winner in Ireland; dam, half-sister to Crozier, won over 5f at 2 yrs; behind in maiden and minor events at Windsor, Lingfield and Chepstow. *J. Bethell.* –

OLD KATE 3 ch.f. Busted 134–Country Path 101 (Mossborough 126) (1979 NR 1980 10fg 10f 12.2fg³ 9fg* 12g² 10g² 10.2g*) well-made filly; sister to very smart soft-ground stayer Old Bill, and half-sister to 3 winners, including middle-distance winner Dogwalk (by Ribero); dam won at 1½m and 13f; very useful performer; successful in maiden race at Newcastle in July and 11-runner Fitzwilliam Stakes at Doncaster in September; beat Etching a neck in latter despite hanging left; runner-up in between in Galtres Stakes at York (looked sure to win leading over 1f out but faded in last 100 yards, going down by 1½ lengths to Deadly Serious) and 6-runner handicap at Sandown (beaten ½ length by One Fleet Street); stays 1½m; yet to race on a soft surface; difficult ride. *H. Wragg.* **110**

OLD KNOCKER 4 b.c. Mummy's Pet 125–The Keys 71 (Major Portion 129) (1979 6fg⁴ 7d 8h 7h 7g 6fg² 6g 6d⁴ 1980 7v 7fg 8fg 10fg² 10f* 10.1g 11.7s 9f 8g 10fg 10g* 12d³ 12s 12d) attractive colt; won handicaps at Leicester in June and Brighton in October, latter by a length from Sunset Ray when apprentice ridden; suited by middle distances nowadays; acts on any going, except perhaps very soft; usually wears blinkers nowadays; often sweats up; well beaten last 2 starts (bandaged final one). *R. Laing.* **78**

OLD PAL 3 b.f. Roan Rocket 128–Nascar 81 (King's Bench 132) (1979 NR 1980 9.4d 8d 8.2d 8fg 10g 8.2d 11d 9.4fg) useless; pulled up first and sixth starts. *T. Craig.* –

OLD STAGER (USA) 2 ch.c. Forli–Queen of the Stage (Bold Ruler) (1980 8g) tall, narrow colt; half-brother to minor winners in USA by Buckpasser and Round Table; dam best 2-y-o filly in USA in 1967 when winner of 7 races at up to 1m, and is sister to high-class Reviewer; unquoted but looking quite fit and moving down to start really well, ran a pleasing race under sympathetic handling on his debut when eighth of 15 to Riberetto in maiden race at Newmarket in October; should improve at 3 yrs. *J. Dunlop.* – p

OLDSTOCK 4 b.c. Sovereign Path 125–Rosemarin (Mossborough 126) (1979 7g 8fg 7.2fg* 6g 7f³ 7f⁴ 7fg 1980 7fg³ 7f 8g 7d 8fg 7g 7f* 7fg 7s 7g) rangy, good sort; good walker; has been hobdayed; useful performer at his best; led well inside final furlong when winning handicap at Lingfield in September by ½ length from Sipapu; had earlier finished 3 lengths third to Kampala in Autobar Victoria Cup at Ascot; inconsistent nowadays however and ran poorly on several occasions; best at up to 7f; acts on firm going; moved short to post and dwelt fourth start; sold 8,000 gns Newmarket Autumn Sales. *G. Harwood.* **97**

OLIVE OYLE 3 b.f. Sassafras 135–Never Never Land (Habitat 134) (1979 NR 1980 12d 8g 8g) quite attractive, compact filly; first foal; dam unraced half-sister to Bombazine, dam of Bruni; in rear in maiden races at Brighton, Salisbury and Goodwood in the summer, twice finishing last; sold 925 gns Ascot August Sales. *B. Swift.* –

OLRO'S FOLLY 4 br.g. African Sky 124–Shlanta 85 (St Paddy 133) (1979 8g 7g² 7fg 6fg 7f 7d* 7s 1980 10fg⁴ 8f 7g 6fg³ 7fg 6fg) fair sort; 2 lengths third of 6 behind dead-heaters Hurricane Hill and En Avant in minor event at Brighton in August; well beaten afterwards; evidently effective at 6f and wasn't disgraced over 1¼m on reappearance; appears to act on any going. *G. Huffer.* –

OLYMPIC GLORY 2 ch.c. Hittite Glory 125–Nalindele 78 (Miralgo 130) (1980 5d 5g* 6g* 6fg² 6s³ 5f 6g⁴) May 21; 9,800F, 14,500Y; strong, lengthy, useful sort; good mover; second foal; half-brother to winning hurdler Dampsulate (by Shiny Tenth); dam stayed 1½m; successful in minor events in July, beating Court Queen impressively by 5 lengths at Salisbury but being all out to win by 2 lengths from Hollow Laugh in 13-runner race at Kempton; favourite when **94**

creditable 1½ lengths second of 6 to Cut Throat in New Ham Stakes at Goodwood later in month; also ran well when fourth to Amorous in 6f nursery at Newmarket in October; suited by 6f and may well get further as a 3-y-o; best form on a sound surface. *G. Harwood.*

OLYMPIC VICTORY (USA) 2 b.c. Nijinsky 138–Shama (Bold Ruler) (1980 7g 8g) lengthy colt; good mover; half-brother to several winners, 3 of them stakes winners, including good American filly Sea Saga (by Sea-Bird II), successful at up to 1¼m; dam stakes-placed winner and closely related to good fillies Lea Lane and Leallah; behind in Hyperion Stakes at Ascot and in minor event at Newmarket (showed up for a long way) in October; will be suited by middle distances; may do better at 3 yrs. *I. Balding.* —

OLYMPIOS 5 b.h. Busted 134–Bacchanalia 94 (Nearco) (1979 12d² 12s³ 14d 16fg² 16fg 1980 16s⁴ 16fg²) strong, good-bodied horse; useful performer; placed 3 times in smart company in 1979; still on backward side when proving no match for Arapahos in 3-runner Newmarket Challenge Whip in May; not seen out again; suited by 2m; acts on any going but is suited by some give in the ground. *B. Hobbs.* **96**

OMAR KHAYYAMS SON 3 b.c. Furry Glen 121–Sara Tal (Cagire II 122) (1979 7g 7g 1980 12s⁴ 16f 13g 16fg³ 14fg 15.5g² 16f³ 14d 16fg 16d 14.6d⁴ 12s) robust, useful-looking colt; staying maiden; probably acts on any going; trained by N. Callaghan first 2 starts. *F. Durr.* **68**

OMER 2 b.c. Thatch 136–Saccato (Bagdad) (1980 5f⁴ 5g³ 6fg*) Feb 21; neat colt; second foal; half-brother to 3-y-o 6f winner Habito (by Habitat); dam won at up to 1½m in Ireland; odds on on all 3 outings but didn't get off the mark until last of them when beating Maiacourt a neck in 12-runner maiden race at Naas in July, the pair a long way clear; will be suited by 1m+; sent to USA. *V. O'Brien, Ireland.* **98**

Mrs G. Charalambous' "Olympic Glory"

Mr Louis Freedman's "One Fleet Street"

ON A CLOUD (USA) 2 b.c. Val de l'Orne 130–Pleasant Flight (Bold Ruler) (1980 8d 8g^2) well-made colt; half-brother to very useful Flitalong (by Herbager), successful at up to 1½m; dam, 2-y-o 6f winner, is sister to smart fillies Bold Princess, Bold Queen and Great Era and to leading American stallion What A Pleasure; well-backed favourite, didn't get best of starts for 16-runner minor event at Newmarket in October but weaved his way through field to hold every chance 1f out only to catch a tartar in Uppety, who beat him 1½ lengths; will be suited by 1¼m; sure to win a race in 1981. *J. Dunlop.* **84** p

ONAPROMISE 4 ch.g. Sharp Edge 123–Halkissimo 61 (Khalkis 127) (1979 8g 8d^2 9g 10.2s^3 8fg^2 8fg 1980 10.2d) fair handicapper; probably stays 1¼m; seems to act on any going; needed race on only outing of 1980. *Denys Smith.* —

ONE DAY 3 ch.g. Pompous 118–Stevie 79 (The Phoenix) (1979 5v 5s 6f^3 5g 6fg 1980 7f 8f) workmanlike gelding; has shown no form since third start at 2 yrs; should stay 7f; sold 500 gns Doncaster October Sales. *J. Hardy.* —

ON EDGE 5 gr.g. Sharp Edge 123–The Country Lane 90 (Red God 128 **§**) (1979 7d^2 8f 7fg* 8f 8g 8fg^4 8.2g^3 8fg^3 8g^4 1980 8s^3 8fg^2 9fg* 8fg^2 8fg* 9g^2 8d^4 9f^4 8d^4 9fg^2 8g 9g) plater in 1979; improved in 1980 and won handicaps at Wolverhampton in April and Thirsk in May; ran well most other outings; stays 9f; acts on any going; blinkered once at 2 yrs; consistent. *J. Spearing.* **66**

ONE FLEET STREET 3 b.c. Habitat 134–The Creditor 127 (Crepello 136) (1979 NR 1980 8f 8fg* 10f* 10.2fg^3 8fg 8g^2 10g^4 10f* 10g* 9f) strong, well-made, good-looking colt; good mover; half-brother to several winners, including smart 1m to 1¼m performer Owen Dudley (by Tudor Melody), and speedy Abwah and A-Bye (both by Abernant); dam top-class miler; made all to win handicaps at Lingfield (blinkered) and Sandown in August, scoring by ½ length from Old Kate in £3,100 event on latter; had earlier won maiden race at Sandown and £2,900 event at Lingfield; stays 1¼m; goes well on firm ground and has yet to race on soft; didn't act on track at Beverley sixth start; genuine. *P. Walwyn.* **97**

ONE FOR ALL 2 b.f. Continuation 120–Final Girl (Dadda Bert 95) (1980 5v **53**
5s* 5f* 6g 5f) Apr 12; light-framed filly; first foal; dam poor plater; bought in
750 gns after winning 9-runner sellers at Warwick in April, beating Leikö by less
than a length on both occasions; stays 6f; acts on any going; sold 1,000 gns
Newmarket Autumn Sales. *J. Hardy.*

ONE NO TRUMP 3 b.c. Auction Ring 123–One Only 77 (Sicambre 135) (1979 –
6s* 7.2fg* 7d^{2} 7fg 1980 8g 10d) attractive colt; good walker and mover; has
been hobdayed; won maiden race at Newbury and Cock of the North Stakes at
Haydock and finished good 2½ lengths second to Marathon Gold in Lanson
Champagne Stakes at Goodwood at 2 yrs; lightly raced in 1980, finishing well
beaten in handicaps at Sandown in August and October (had very stiff tasks);
should stay 1¼m; probably acts on any going; blinkered final start in 1979; sold
5,800 gns Newmarket Autumn Sales. *R. Hern.*

ON HER OWN 2 b.f. Busted 134–Turiana (Citation) (1980 7g 9d^{2}) Mar 18; **71**
47,000Y; second living foal; dam, winner at up to 7f, is half-sister to Kentucky
Derby and Preakness Stakes winner Forward Pass; caught only well inside final
furlong when length second of 11 to Cinderwench in minor event at Wolverhampton in October; will stay 1½m+. *G. Harwood.*

ON LEAVE 3 br.g. Queen's Hussar 124–Bound Over (Taj Dewan 128) (1979 **73**
6f 8g 1980 6h^{2} 7.6f 10f^{2} 10g* 12d) workmanlike gelding; plater; won non-
selling apprentice handicap at Folkestone in October; stays 1¼m; probably acts
on any going; sold 3,800 gns Doncaster November Sales. *R. Price.*

ONLY A SHANTY 2 ch.c. Busted 134–The Bungalow 81 (Habitat 134) (1980 –
8g) May 26; 30,000Y; useful sort; second living foal; dam won over 1m, and is
half-sister to good stayer Crozier; backward and weak in market, moved short on
way down and never went pace when in rear in 17-runner maiden race won by
Dragon Palace at Newmarket in October. *B. Hills.*

ON RECORD 2 ch.c. Record Token 128–Whitestake 74 (Compensation 127) –
(1980 5f 5fg) Apr 10; 9,700Y; quite well-made colt; half-brother to useful
sprinter Palmvinnia (by Royal Palm); dam won 5f seller at 2 yrs; behind in sizeable fields of maidens at Newmarket (12/1, moved poorly to post) and Sandown
(20/1) in April. *N. Callaghan.*

ON SHOW 2 br.f. Welsh Pageant 132–African Dancer 116 (Nijinsky 138) –
(1980 5g) Apr 18; first foal; dam won Cheshire Oaks and Park Hill Stakes; 16/1
when behind in 21-runner maiden race won by Footshore at Windsor in July;
will need much further as a 3-y-o. *H. Wragg.*

ON SONG 2 b.f. Ardoon 124–Champion Jay (Double-U-Jay 120) (1980 5g 5f **79 ?**
6g^{3}) Apr 16; 1,050F, 5,100Y, 3,000 2-y-o; third produce; half-sister to a winner
in Belgium by Jukebox; dam never ran; prominent in sizeable fields of maidens
in the autumn; beaten 4 lengths when third of 21 to Velvet Habit at Leicester in
November, staying on well after struggling to go early pace; will be suited by
7f and 1m; sold 2,200 gns Doncaster November Sales; resubmitted same venue 2
days later and made only 320 gns. *R. Price.*

ON THE BEACH 2 ch.c. Sandford Lad 133–Curragha (Le Levanstell 122) **78**
(1980 6fg 7fg 7s) Mar 14; 3,100F, 12,000Y; robust, good sort; good mover;
second known foal; dam third over 9f and 1½m in Ireland; improved physically
and ran best race on final outing, finishing 3¼ lengths fifth of 17 to Warily in
minor event at Sandown in October after disputing lead to distance; will stay at
least 1m; should win a race at 3 yrs. *G. Hunter.*

ONWARD GAL 2 b.f. Continuation 120–Hillset (Hill Clown) 1980 5s 5fg* 5d **47**
6g 7.2d 7.2s) Mar 30; rather a leggy filly; half-sister to fair 2-y-o winner Pom-
pously (by Pompous); sold out of J. Hardy's stable 1,400 gns after winning 20-
runner seller at Ripon in May by 1½ lengths from Cilla's Secret; should stay 6f+;
ran poorly last 3 starts, wearing blinkers on final one; sold 460 gns Doncaster
October Sales *M. Camacho.*

OOLYWIG 2 b.f. Copte–Dotonlok (Quadrangle) (1980 6g 8g 8fg) Apr 19; –
compact non-thoroughbred filly; fourth known foal; dam never ran; in rear in
maiden races; trained by M. Smyly first 2 outings. *S. Norton.*

OOPLA 4 ch.g. Some Hand 119–Lebanon 87 (Palestine 133) (1979 5s 5d 5g* 5s^{4} –
5.3fg 5f 5fg 9f 1980 8s 8.3f 6f) sprint plater; best run at 5f; ran badly in
blinkers final outing. *B. Forsey.*

OPAL LADY 2 b.f. Averof 123–Hum 69 (Crooner 119) (1980 5fg) Mar 6; –
4,600Y; first foal; dam stayed 1¼m; 33/1, never in race when seventh of 11 to
Ashbrittle in minor event at Windsor in September; needs further. *G. Lewis.*

William Hill Trophy, York—the most valuable event on Timeform Charity Day which raised £63,269 for Cancer Charities. Optimate wins from Westacombe (near side)

OPERATION CYRIL 2 ch.c. Jimmy Reppin 131–Western Vale (Milesian 125) (1980 6g $6g^4$ 7f) Feb 11; 2,000F, 12,000Y; fair sort; half-brother to 3 winners, including fairly useful 1979 5f performer Westburg (by Burglar); dam ran only at 2 yrs; unquoted and short of peak fitness when 8 lengths fourth of 15 to Kalaglow in maiden race at Newmarket in August; sixth to Beldale Flutter in 12-runner Grand Criterium International d'Ostende later in month; should stay 7f. *N. Guest.* **73**

OPIUM QUEEN 6 b.m. King's Troop 118–Poppy Time 77 (Hook Money 124) (1979 9fg $10f^2$ 8.2fg 10f $10h^2$ 10.6g 1980 8g 8.2fg 10h $10.6fg^3$ 10.6fg 10f) plater; stays 1¼m; probably acts on any going; has worn bandages; sold 540 gns Ascot September Sales. *I. Vickers.* **36**

OPTIMATE 3 b.c. Great Nephew 126–Queen of Arisai 73 (Persian Gulf) (1979 5f 7fg $6g^4$ 7fg $5fg^2$ $5f^2$ 1980 $6d^2$ 6d* 6fg 6g 8g 6s 6d 5s) strong, good-bodied, quite attractive colt; stayed on well to lead inside last furlong and beat Westacombe a neck in £10,000 William Hill Trophy (Handicap) at York in June; well beaten in handicaps afterwards; bred to stay at least 1m but is evidently best at sprint distances; seems to act on any going; ran particularly moderately fourth and sixth starts, wearing blinkers on latter. *C. Brittain.* **88**

ORANGE LEAF 3 ch.f. Thatch 136–Jaffa 103 (Right Royal V 135) (1979 NR 1980 $8f^4$ 8.5f* 8g 10.2g) strong, good sort; half-sister to 4 winners, including top-class 2-y-o and miler Jacinth (by Red God); dam consistent stayer; won maiden race at Epsom in June by 5 lengths from Spring Is Grey despite seeming ill at ease coming down hill; respectable seventh to Cairn Rouge, beaten about 6 lengths, in Coronation Stakes at Royal Ascot later in month (hampered 1f out); off course 3 months afterwards and was well beaten on her return; stays 1m well; yet to race on a soft surface. *B. Hills.* **100**

ORANGE VALLEY 2 br.f. Alto Volante 109–Noaxe To Grind (The Axe 115) (1980 7f 10s) Apr 18; second foal; dam plating-class novice hurdler; unquoted when behind in maiden races at Newmarket and Nottingham in October. *G. Pritchard-Gordon.* **–**

ORANMORE 10 b.g. Le Prince 98–La Pucelle (Prince Chevalier) (1979 NR 1980 11d) lightly-raced stayer on flat; better known as a hurdler nowadays; acts on any going. *R. Atkins.* —

ORASTON 2 ch.f. Morston 125–Orange Cap (Red God 128§) (1980 6d* 6g4 8g4) Mar 4; 18,000,000 lire Y (approx £11,000); half-sister to smart French 1m and 1¼m performer The Abbot (by Sea Hawk II) and a winner in Italy by Connaught; dam useful winner at up to 1m in France; kept on strongly to beat Sharp End by 2½ lengths, pair clear, in 19-runner maiden race at Salisbury in June; fourth in Princess Margaret Stakes at Ascot (11½ lengths behind Tolmi) and May Hill Stakes at Doncaster (never promised to get on terms when beaten 8½ lengths by Exclusively Raised), only subsequent starts; will stay 1¼m. *F. J. Houghton.* **98**

ORATAVO 2 br.g. The Brianstan 128–Nimble Star (Space King 115) (1980 5fg 5f 6d 5.8f 7fg 7d 8.2g* 8d*) Apr 17; 5,200Y; well-made gelding; first foal; dam never ran; well-backed favourite when winning sellers in the autumn, being bought in 1,550 gns after beating Billie Gibb 2 lengths at Nottingham and attracting no bid after scoring by ½ length from Radical Rethink in nursery at Doncaster; suited by 1m; seems to act on any going. *J. Sutcliffe.* **76**

ORE 2 ch.c. Ballymore 123–Minatonka (Linacre 133) (1980 8s*) Mar 8; third foal; half-brother to bumpers race winner Karatonka (by Karabas); dam Irish 1m winner; backed from 7/2 to 6/4 favourite, created a highly favourable impression when winning 13-runner maiden race at Leopardstown in October, drawing clear early in straight to win by 5 lengths from Keep Your Money despite having missed break; will probably stay 1½m; very promising. *K. Prendergast, Ireland.* **90** p

ORESTO 4 b.g. King Emperor–Autella (Aureole 132) (1979 12s 12.2g 12f 9fg 9fg3 10f2 13.8d 12d 13.8fg2 10fg 13.8d3 1980 13v 13g 11f) compact gelding; inconsistent plater; stays 1¾m; acts on firm going; usually blinkered. *W. Stubbs.* —

ORIENT BOY 6 br.g. Realm 129–Flapperette 92 (Hardicanute 130) (1979 NR 1980 7.6f 6fg 7fg2 8d 7g) quite a moderate handicapper; stayed 1m; acted well on firm going; was an excellent mount for an apprentice; dead. *M. Masson.* **63**

ORKNEY ANNIE 2 br.f. Scottish Rifle 127–Mother Brown 103 (Candy Cane 125) (1980 6g 6g 6fg4 7f 8d*) Mar 2; small filly; first foal; dam, genuine and consistent handicapper, stayed 1¼m; bought in 1,350 gns after running easily best race to win 16-runner seller at Warwick in October by 2½ lengths from King Loren; will stay 1¼m+; acts well on a soft surface and is possibly unsuited by firm going; sold 1,600 gns Newmarket Autumn Sales. *J. Dunlop.* **65**

ORPHELINE 3 ch.f. Thatch 136–Ouda 111 (Traffic) (1979 NR 1980 10f4 7d 10s* 10.1g4 10f3 10.6d) big, rangy filly; third living foal; half-sister to useful 6f winner Oudalia (by Gala Performance); dam 1m to 1¼m handicapper; made all and ran on well to beat Foolish Pet 1½ lengths in 11-runner maiden race at Lingfield in June; respectable third in minor event at Chepstow in August; suited by 1¼m; acts on any going; ran poorly in blinkers final start. *P. Walwyn.* **76**

OSCAR WILDE (USA) 3 b.c. Creme de la Creme–Bunch of Daisies (Sir Gaylord) (1979 7.5s 9s2 1980 8v2 10s 12f 12g* 12g 12f3 12g* 16g 12g* 12d3 12g 14d2 12d 12v* 12g2) $50,000Y; shapely colt; brother to Sixty Sails, a very useful stakes winner at up to 9f, and half-brother to a winner; dam won 7 races at up to 6f; successful in maiden race at Clonmel and 3 handicaps at Roscommon; stays 1½m well (in rear in Queen's Vase at Royal Ascot over 2m); appears to act on any going. *A. Maxwell, Ireland.* **80**

OSWIN 3 b.c. Silly Season 127–Angello 87 (Crepello 136) (1979 NR 1980 9fg 10d 8f4 8g 8.2s) big, good-bodied colt; brother to Royal Lodge Stakes winner Adios and 1m winner Caelidh, and half-brother to other winners; dam won at 1m; didn't seem suited by track when fourth in 14-runner maiden race at Beverley in August, easily best effort; should stay 1¼m. *Denys Smith.* **69**

OUI MONSIEUR 6 b.g. Levanter 121–Melody Call 55 (Tudor Melody 129) (1979 12v 15.5g* 12d* 13.3s* 16fg3 15.5f2 16f 12fg4 14g 12g 12fg3 12f 16fg 1980 12fg2 12f4 12fg* 12f4 13.3g 12d 12g 16.5fg 12g) quite a moderate handicapper; ran on gamely to beat Le Soleil by a head at Kempton in May; didn't reproduce that form and ran badly last 2 starts; stays 2m; acts on any going; suitable mount for an inexperienced rider. *M. Haynes.* **62** d

OUR BARA BOY 3 b.g. Baragoi 115–Primeapple (Primera 131) (1979 5f 7g 7fg 8fg^3 1980 10s 10s 12fg 12fg^3 10fg^4 12f 13s^4 14d^2 16.9d* 14fg* 16f 16s^2 14g 17.1d 16s) narrow, light-framed gelding; quite a moderate handicapper; won at Wolverhampton and Yarmouth in July, making all to beat Marechal by 3 lengths on latter; suited by a test of stamina; acts on any going with possible exception of very firm; blinkered nowadays; suitable mount for a boy. *M. Ryan.* 76

OUR BIRTHDAY 4 b.c. Great Nephew 126–Renoir Picture 90 (Relko 136) (1979 9v^2 10g 8g 8s 8g 10.2s 1980 10s 9s 8fg 8fg^4 8g* 8fg 9g 9fg 8g^2 8g* 9g^2 8d 8s) neat colt; won handicaps at Chepstow in June (from Camacho) and September (comfortably from Queen's Niece); runner-up to Lord Raffles in seller at Kempton in between and to Jim's Tricks at York in October; should stay 1¼m; acts on any going; wears blinkers nowadays. *J. Benstead.* 69

OUR DENISE 4 ch.f. Bend A Bow–Dainty 74 (Epaulette 125) (1979 8g 7f^3 8fg^3 7g 8fg 1980 8.3s 8.3g) plater; probably stays 1m; bandaged nowadays and broke down final outing. *J. O'Donoghue.* —

OUR FOXBAR 5 ch.m. Swinging Junior 118–Shepherd's Crook 81 (Current Coin 118) (1979 6s^4 5s^4 5g* 8fg 8fg 7f^3 6s 8d 5d^3 6s 1980 5v 6g^4 6d^4 6f 6h 6fg 5g* 6g^3 5s 5g^2 5g^3 6g 5d* 5s 6s 5d 6d^4 7d) plater; bought in 1,000 gns after winning at Edinburgh in June; successful in better company at Hamilton in September; stays 7f; seems to act on any going but is suited by soft; suitable mount for an apprentice. *M. Naughton.* 53

OUR HOBBY HORSE 3 b.c. Saulingo 122–Magnanimous 65 (Runnymede 123) (1979 5fg 5g^3 5fg 1980 5fg 5.8f 5fg 6g) lightly-made colt; quite moderate (rated 73) at 2 yrs; well beaten in 1980; not certain to have stayed beyond 5f; blinkered last 2 starts; dead. *A. Johnson.* —

OUR HOME 3 b.f. Habitat 134–Oh So Fair (Graustark) (1979 5s^2 6f^3 1980 8fg^2 10.5f^3 8g^3 8s^2 7fg^3 8g* 7f^2 8g^2 8g* 7g^4) 115

Since 1950 four maidens have been placed in the One Thousand Guineas. Petite Gina dead-heated for third, three lengths behind Pourparler, in 1964; Gleam was a seven-length runner-up to Humble Duty in 1970; Marisela went down by a couple of lengths to Waterloo in 1972. In 1980 the final member of the quartet, Our Home, came closer to success than the others, being beaten a neck by Quick As Lightning, yet for a filly good enough to be involved in a photo-finish to a classic she didn't have a notably successful season.

Few who saw this big, rangy, attractive individual's performance in the Guineas would have been prepared to bet on her still being a maiden by mid-August. Well backed ante-post on the strength of good reports of her gallops, Our Home started joint-third favourite at Newmarket despite not having raced since the previous July. She put up an excellent display, taking over from Mrs Penny at the foot of the hill and keeping on well only to be run out of it close home by the strong-finishing Quick As Lightning. At this stage of her career Our Home looked to have a bright future; by the end of the year she was generally classified as disappointing and her courage had been questioned in some quarters. Certainly the balance sheet was not that impressive for a Guineas second, the chief credits being a facile success in a Goodwood maiden race in August and a smooth length win over Premier Rose, who was conceding 6 lb, in the Marlborough House Stakes at Ascot in October. However, Our Home didn't once run a bad race and her record of never being out of the frame in twelve starts, frequently in good company and on all types of going, is meritorious. In fact it was probably relative lack of pace rather than lack of courage that was her undoing. After appearing to show that she stayed a mile and a quarter by finishing a creditable third to Bireme in the Musidora Stakes at York, Our Home was raced exclusively at shorter trips. She was invariably outpaced at some stage of the proceedings, putting up her best efforts to be third to Cairn Rouge and Quick As Lightning in the Coronation Stakes at Royal Ascot and a staying-on second in the Child Stakes at Newmarket and the seven-furlong Strensall Stakes at York. In the former, her fourth race, she was beaten three quarters of a length by Stumped, and at York Luck Of The Draw, giving her 10 lb, held on by a head after a good battle. It is conceivable that Our Home would have done better kept at around one and a quarter miles; be that as it may, her achievement in finishing in the first three in four pattern races at three years was matched by just Gift Wrapped, Mrs Penny, Shoot A Line and Vielle among the English fillies.

Our Home has an attractive pedigree as well as smart form, and she will be at stud in 1981. Her dam, Oh So Fair, has produced three other winners, notably Our Home's sister Roussalka, who was a good-class performer at up to a mile and a quarter, winning the Nassau Stakes twice, and Etienne Gerard (by Brigadier Gerard), successful in the 1977 Jersey Stakes. Oh So Fair, a winner

Our Home (b.f. 1977)	Habitat (b 1966)	Sir Gaylord (b 1959)	Turn-to
			Somethingroyal
		Little Hut (b 1952)	Occupy
			Savage Beauty
	Oh So Fair (b 1967)	Graustark (ch 1963)	Ribot
			Flower Bowl
		Chandelle (b 1959)	Swaps
			Malindi

over one and a quarter miles in Ireland, is a half-sister to four winners in America and Ireland, the best of them the stakes-placed Name and Fame. Chandelle, her dam, was a lightly-raced half-sister to the very smart Prince Taj, leading sire in France in 1967 and 1968, out of Nasrullah's sister Malindi. *M. Stoute.*

OUR JIMMY (USA) 6 br.h. Tom Rolfe–Flitter Flutter (Cohoes) (1979 NR 1980 7v 8s) half-brother to Beldale Flutter (by Accipiter); smart sprinter at his best, when trained by G. Harwood; was well suited by some give in the ground; standing at Semley Stud, Dorset, at £500 n.f.n.f. *S. Pattemore.* —

OUR LAL 4 b.f. Levmoss 133–Oola Rose (Breakspear II) (1979 10g 12d^{2} 12.5g^{4} 12s 1980 16d 16s 12s^{4} 12d) leggy filly; in frame in varied company; springer in market when behind in valuable seller on final start; should stay 2m; sold 1,250 gns Newmarket Autumn Sales. *I. Walker.* —

OUR LUCKY JIM 2 b.c. Jimsun 121–Ruby's Chance 71 (Charlottesville 135) (1980 7g 7f 8s 10.2s) Jan 17; fair sort; third foal; half-brother to 2 winners abroad; dam won over 1½m but was disqualified; in rear in minor events in the North in second half of season; sweating third start; should be suited by 1¼m. *Hbt Jones.* 69

OUR LUCY 3 ch.f. Porto Bello 118–My Conkers 70 (Aggressor 130) (1979 5g 5d 5f 6s 6g 5g 5fg 5fg^{2} 5fg 1980 6h 6f 6fg 5s 5f 6g) small, short-legged filly; bad plater; usually wears blinkers. *K. Ivory.* —

OUR MANDY 3 b.f. Mansingh 120–All Love 83 (No Argument 107) (1979 8f 9fg 1980 8s 11v) neat filly; no worthwhile form in maiden and minor events. *W. Stubbs.* —

OUR SYMBOL 3 b.g. Status Seeker–Hop Step (Double Jump 131) (1979 5g 5.8g^{3} 6fg^{3} 6fg 6g^{2} 6fg 1980 7fg^{2} 8fg 8fg 6s 10.1f 9d) well-made gelding; second in maiden event at Leicester in April; ran poorly afterwards; should stay at least 1m; ran moderately in blinkers final start at 2 yrs; sold out of J. Bethell's stable 4,000 gns Doncaster August Sales after fifth start. *M. Delahooke.* 62 d

OUT OF THIS WORLD 3 b.f. High Top 131–Be Merry 104 (Charlottown 127) (1979 6g 7fg 6f 1980 10fg 12d 10.6d^{2} 12s^{2} 10d) well-made filly; good walker; suited by 1½m; acts on soft going; trained by R. Hannon first 2 outings; sold 14,500 gns Newmarket December Sales. *N. Henderson.* 64

OVERHOLT 3 b.g. Highland Melody 112–Gigi 85 (Acropolis 132) (1979 5g^{3} 5s 5g 7fg^{3} 7f 8d 1980 10s) neat gelding; showed some ability in 1979 but ran abysmally in seller on fifth start; behind in handicap only start at 3 yrs, in October; best run at 7f on a firm surface; wore blinkers at 2 yrs; best left alone. *R. Hannon.* §§

OVERPLAY 2 b.f. Bustino 136–Melodramatic 112 (Tudor Melody 129) (1980 8.5d* 8g^{2}) Apr 9; 62,000Y; half-sister to fairly useful miler Crown Witness (by Crowned Prince) and successful Irish 3-y-o stayer Public Opinion (by Run The Gantlet); dam very useful winner over 7f and 9f at 3 yrs; a very promising filly who ran well to win 13-runner maiden race at Galway in September by 4 lengths from Tripping the Light and to finish 2½ lengths second of 11 to Blue Wind in Group 3 Silken Glider Stakes at Leopardstown later in month; will be suited by middle distances; likely to make a good 3-y-o. *D. Weld, Ireland.* 105

OVERSEAS ADMIRER 6 b.g. High Top 131–Villa Marina 96 (Tudor Melody 129) (1979 6g 5f 6d 6fg 5f 6f^{3} 7fg 7g 7fg* 7g 7g 6s 1980 6g^{3} 7h* 6fg 7d 7f 6fg 6g 7f) quite a moderate handicapper; held off Prince of Spain by short head when successful at Brighton in May; stays 7f; appears to act on any going but goes well on a firm surface; sometimes wears blinkers; inconsistent. *J. Winter.* 75 d

OVERSHOE 2 ch.g. Import 127–Snow Boots 62 (Marshal Pil 108) (1980 5g 5f 7g) May 5; leggy gelding; half-brother to 3 minor winners; dam won long-distance seller; plating-class maiden; should stay 7f. *W. C. Watts.* **64**

OVER THE PEAK 2 br.f. High Top 131–Self Satisfied 100 (Great Nephew 126) (1980 6g 5f) Apr 8; first foal; dam a sprinter; unquoted when behind in newcomers race at Goodwood and maiden race at Lingfield in the autumn. *W. Wightman.* —

OVER THE RAINBOW 3 b.g. Song 132–Lady Matador 108 (Matador 131) (1979 5fg* 5f* 5d² 1980 5d 5f² 5fg³ 5s⁴ 5g 6fg 5f) strong, compact, sprint type; fairly useful handicapper; good 1¾ lengths third to Via Delta in valuable race at Ascot in June; best at 5f; acts on any going; blinkered final start; sometimes sweats up. *A. Hide.* **93**

OVER THE TOP 2 b.g. Upper Case–Shelby (Pall Mall 132) (1980 8g³ 8s 8d³) Apr 10; neat, well-made gelding; half-brother to 2 winners, including middle-distance 3-y-o Beirut (by Northfields); dam won at up to 1¾m in Ireland; third in maiden races at Newmarket and Leicester in the autumn, staying on well both times; beaten 5½ lengths behind Majorian on latter; will be suited by 1¼m+; possibly not at his best on soft going. *W. O'Gorman.* **81**

OVERTRICK 5 b.h. Great Nephew 126–Jackyda 71 (Royal Palm 131) (1979 6v* 6s² 6s* 6d² 6fg 6g 6g 6d* 6s 6s 6g³ 1980 7d⁴ 7s⁴ 7fg 6fg 6d² 6fg 6s² 6g 6d) useful handicapper on his day; runner-up at Nottingham in valuable Home Ales Gold Tankard in June and Nottingham Stewards Cup in August; went down by short head to Emperor's Shadow in latter event; didn't find much eighth start; stays 7f; needs some give in the ground and revels in the mud; usually held up. *J. Dunlop.* **101**

OXTON ANNE 2 br.f. Workboy 123–Oxton Lady 81 (Chebs Lad 120) (1980 5fg 5fg⁴ 5fg² 5g 5f) Mar 1; neat, sturdy non-thoroughbred filly; second foal; dam useful sprint plater; went down by only a neck to Gold Breeze in 17-runner maiden event at Catterick in June but is only plating-class. *M. W. Easterby.* **62**

OYSTON ESTATES 4 gr.g. Goldhill 125–Port Relic 90 (Relic) (1979 7s 6d 6s 6d* 6fg 6fg* 6fg 7g 6d* 6d* 6d⁴ 6d 6d* 1980 6v³ 6d³ 6fg 7h 6f³ 6g⁴ 6d 6d⁴ 5g 7g⁴ 7fg 6s* 6d 6s) strong gelding; gaining his fifth win on the course when beating Ravaduos by ¾ length in handicap at Hamilton in September; seems to stay 7f; probably acts on any going; has won with and without blinkers; good mount for an apprentice; sold 3,800 gns Newmarket Autumn Sales. *P. Haslam.* **68**

OYSTON IDOL 4 b.f. Continuation 120–Lissome Lisa (Sir Ribot) (1979 7.6d 5s³ 5d² 5g 5fg 6fg 6d 6s 1980 5f 5f 5f) plater; best form at up to 6f but should stay further; sometimes wears blinkers; sold 420 gns Newmarket July Sales. *J. Berry.* —

OYSTON'S AGENCY 2 ch.c. Goldhill 125–Va Beni (Infatuation 129) (1980 5f 5f 5fg² 6fg⁴ 6d 5f) Mar 27; compact colt; brother to 1975 2-y-o 5f seller winner Va-Presto and half-brother to several winners; dam Irish 1¼m winner; ½-length second of 7 to Rathmoy's Sparkle in maiden race at Carlisle in May, easily best effort; off course 2 months after fifth start; possibly better at 5f than 6f; gave trouble at start first 2 outings; sold 420 gns Doncaster September Sales. *J. Berry.* **68**

P

PACE JEAN 3 br.c. Tudor Melody 129–Elected 74 (Red God 128§) (1979 6fg³ 5fg* 6g³ 6fg* 6fg* 6f* 1980 7f⁴ 6d 6fg 6s 6g³ 6d* 6fg³ 6d 6d) well-made, very good-looking colt; good walker; very useful performer; landed the odds by an easy 2 lengths from Alert in 6-runner £2,100 race at Brighton in September; ran best race of season in Diadem Stakes at Ascot later in month, finishing very strongly to take close third behind Sovereign Rose and King of Spain after being outpaced; in frame earlier in Tote Free Handicap at Newmarket in April (fourth to Moorestyle) and Top Rank Club Handicap at Newcastle in August (½-length third behind Denmore); stays 7f; acts well on firm going and isn't at his best on soft; sold privately to race in USA. *G. Harwood.* **114**

PACIFIC DREAM 3 ch.f. Meldrum 112–Bon Feu 75 (Blason 109) (1979 5s 5g 7f 1980 8.2fg 8fg 8d 10g 12g* 10d 12fg 12d⁴ 13.8g⁴ 12fg 12fg 13.8d³) neat filly; plater; won at Pontefract in July (bought in 1,000 gns); stays 1½m; usually sweats up. *K. Stone.* **43**

PADDLE WHEEL 4 b.f. Huntercombe 133–Paddle Boat 98 (St Paddy 133) (1979 8f 10fg 8fg 8g 7.6f4 6f 8fg 1980 6g 8fg 7g 6g2 6d 7.6g2 5fg 6g3 6g 6s) smallish filly; placed in 3 handicaps, one an apprentice event; best form at distances short of 1m. *D. H. Jones.* **50**

PADDY-ONE-ROW 5 b.h. St Paddy 133–Hilia 67 (Hill Gail) (1979 11v* 12d 16f 1980 10v 11fg2 12f 12d) plater; stays 11f; goes well in the mud; blinkered once at 2 yrs; wears bandages; suitable mount for an apprentice. *I. Vickers.* **41**

PADDY'S GLEN 3 br.g. Furry Glen 121–Tricia (St Paddy 133) (1979 5g 7g 7s 8.2s3 6g 1980 8h 8fg 8g 12.2f 10d 8g3 8g 9v 8d3) leggy, rather narrow gelding; third in a minor event and a selling handicap in the North; best form at around 1m on an easy surface; often blinkered; ran badly seventh start. *J. Calvert.* **53**

PADSKI 7 ch.g. St Paddy 133–No Relation 94 (Klairon 131) (1979 16.9s4 18s2 15s 1980 18d4 16s4 16fg 16.1s4 18s2) poor handicapper; stays well; probably acts on any going; none too enthusiastic. *R. Hollinshead.* **53**

PADUCAH 4 b.c. Swing Easy 126–Hunting Bee (Honeyway 125) (1979 7d* 7g 6f 8fg 6g 6s 1980 7f 6f 6h 6s3 6g 6d 6g2 5fg3 6fg4 5d4 6s3 6g 5f3 6s) strong, compact gelding; probably finds 5f on sharp side nowadays and stays 7f well; seems to act on any going, although has done all his winning when there has been give in the ground; sometimes wears blinkers. *T. Fairhurst.* **82**

PAGAPAS BAY 3 br.c. Welsh Saint 126–Cherry Plum (Primera 131) (1979 5g 5s 5d 5.1g 1980 6fg 5fg 5d 5s 6g 5g* 5d3 6s3) lengthy colt; not a good mover in his slower paces; plater; backed down to favouritism, showed improved form to win at Edinburgh in October (bought in 1,700 gns); third in better company afterwards; stays 6f; acts well on soft ground; blinkered fourth outing; sometimes sweats up; has run creditably for a boy. *A. Jarvis.* **46**

PAGINA 3 b.f. Welsh Pageant 132–Pot Pourri 97 (Busted 134) (1979 NR 1980 8d 10.2fg 12d 11fg 12d3) strong, attractive, deep-girthed filly; third foal; half-sister to 1½m winner Potshot (by Roan Rocket); dam a stayer and half-sister to very smart Almiranta; remote third in maiden race at Brighton in September, best effort; will stay beyond 1½m; sold 7,400 gns Newmarket December Sales. *P. Walwyn.* **59**

PAGOS SON (USA) 2 ch.c. Pago Pago–Pappa's Toy (Crimson Satan) (1980 6fg 5d 5fg 5d 5fg 5g 6s) Apr 17; $3,000F; neat, strong colt; half-brother to 3 minor winners; dam won claiming races at 4f and 6f; showed a little ability in maiden race at Wolverhampton on third outing; beaten in sellers subsequently; should stay 6f; has worn blinkers; sweating third start. *J. Fitzgerald.* **63**

PAILLE (USA) 3 b.f. Bold Bidder–Paulista 130 (Sea Hawk II 131) (1979 NR 1980 10g 10fg 10.1fg* 10g3) compact, workmanlike filly; first foal; dam won Prix Vermeille; beat odds-on Cymbal by 2½ lengths in 12-runner minor event at Windsor in September; will stay 1½m; yet to race on a soft surface; sold 78,000 gns Newmarket December Sales. *H. Cecil.* **77**

PAINTBOX 3 b.f. Jukebox 120–Schull (Yorick II 127) (1979 5d4 5s 5g2 5g 6g4 5d2 5fg4 7fg 6f2 1980 7f 7fg4 7g 7g 6fg3 6g 8f 7g4 6d4 10.6d 8g 6s3 7g 6g 6d) compact filly; plater; unlikely to stay 1¼m; acts on any going; often blinkered; sold 480 gns Doncaster November Sales. *J. Etherington.* **–**

PAINTBRUSH 5 br.g. Lorenzaccio 130–Golden Ivy 97 (Sir Ivor 135) (1979 NR 1980 8fg 10fg) strong gelding; useful and promising 2-y-o (rated 106p) when trained by R. Hern; well behind in handicap at Wolverhampton and minor event at Leicester in April, only outings since. *P. M. Taylor.* **–**

PAINTED SAINT 3 ch.g. Owen Anthony 102–Tinternell 96 (Tenerani 135) (1979 5d 6fg 7fg 7d 7s 1980 6d 10.8s 10g 13.3fg 8d3 8g) narrow gelding; plater; stays 1m; blinkered final start. *D. Ancil.* **54**

PAINT MY WAY 2 ro.c. The Go-Between 129–Warmheart (Arctic Storm 134) (1980 5.8fg 5d 5s 5.8fg 5d 5fg) robust colt; seems of little account. *M. Bradley.* **–**

PAIS DE GALES 2 b. or br.c. Mummy's Pet 125–Regal Artist 72 (Breakspear II) (1980 5f 5fg 7d 7d 8fg) Feb 23; lightly-made colt; fourth foal; half-brother to 2 winners; dam stayed 7f; no worthwhile form in maiden and minor events. *J. Etherington.* **–**

PALACE GOLD (FR) 2 b.c. Empery 128–Pallakis (Narrator 127) (1980 8d*) Mar 4; 1,190,000 francs yearling (approx £125,000); half-brother to several winners in France, including smart 1978 staying 2-y-o Polynikis and smart middle-distance winner Pale Ale (both by Shantung); dam, a twice-raced twin, is sister to 1,000 Guineas winner Night Off; put up an encouraging display when winning **?**

18-runner newcomers event at Maisons-Laffitte in October by 1½ lengths from Marinko; the type to make a smart middle-distance 3-y-o. *B. Secly, France.*

PALATINATE 2 b.c. Rheingold 137–Cloudbreak 95 (Nimbus 130) (1980 7f) Mar 30; 12,500Y; half-brother to several winners, including useful 1976 2-y-o 5f and 7f winner Beriosova (by Lorenzaccio); dam 2-y-o 5f winner; 8/1 and in need of race, showed up 5f when about 11 lengths ninth of 18 to Blackfoot in maiden race at Newmarket in October; should do better over further at 3 yrs. *B. Hills.* — p

PALEMON 5 b.h. Busted 134–Seaswan 104 (Sea-Bird II 145) (1979 10.5d* 10d 12f 10d 10fg 1980 11f 10g 8s) tall, good-bodied horse; good mover; useful handicapper in 1979; had stiff tasks and showed no worthwhile form in 1980; stays 1½m; appears to act on any going; has been tried in blinkers; formerly trained by M. Jarvis. *S. Harris.* —

PALE MOON 2 ch.f. Jukebox 120–Rose of Tralee 114 (Buisson Ardent 129) (1980 7g) Mar 20; 6,500Y; lengthy filly; half-sister to several minor winners; dam very speedy at 2 yrs; backward when behind in 26-runner maiden race at Newmarket in October won by Full Of Reason. *B. Hills.* —

PALEOR 3 ch.c. Ortis 127–Paleen (Queen's Hussar 124) (1979 6fg 8fg^{3} 1980 11f 10f 10fg^{3} 10fg^{2} 10g^{2} 11.5g* 10f* 12fg^{2} 10.6s) strong, well-made colt; favourite, won modest maiden race at Yarmouth (landed odds very easily) and minor event at Lingfield in the autumn; beat Marguerite Gerard ¾ length in latter; suited by 1½m; possibly unsuited by very soft going; sold 10,500 gns Newmarket Autumn Sales. *L. Cumani.* **82**

PALESTINES GOLD 3 gr.c. Gold Form 108–Palmural 111 (Palestine 133) (1979 5g 1980 8d 9.4g 12g 12.3d) neat colt; no sign of ability in maiden and minor races. *I. Jordon.* —

PALETTE KNIFE 2 b.g. Bay Express 132–My Bushbaby 100 (Hul a Hul 124) (1980 5d) June 14; 5,800Y; third foal; half-brother to 2 winners, including fairly useful 1978 2-y-o 6f winner Bushwhacker (by No Mercy); dam won over 5f at 2 yrs, and is half-sister to smart Panomark; unquoted and apprentice ridden when in rear in 14-runner maiden race won by Azaam at Wolverhampton in October. *Peter Taylor.* —

PALFREY'S SURPRISE 3 ch.f. Native Bazaar 122–Palfrey Jr (Yrrah Jr) (1979 5d 5d 5fg 7d 6g 1980 8v 6f 8h 8f 7fg 9g 7fg 6g*) narrow filly; plater; attracted no bid after winning at Hamilton in July (apprentice ridden); best run at 6f; blinkered fourth and fifth starts; sold 580 gns Doncaster August Sales. *Denys Smith.* **41**

PALMABELLA 3 ch.f. Palm Track 122–Lady Amabel (I Say 125) (1979 5g 5fg* 5f^{3} 5fg 1980 7.2fg 6d 7fg 8fg^{3} 8d^{3} 7g 7f 8d) leggy, unfurnished filly; plater; stays 1m; acts on a firm and a soft surface; sold out of W. Haigh's stable 610 gns Doncaster September Sales. *A. Potts.* **47**

PALMAYA 2 b.f. Palm Track 122–Ommaya (Ommeyad 120) (1980 5g 6fg^{3}) Mar 18; 770Y; leggy filly; half-sister to a winning hurdler; dam won at up to 1¾m; kept on under very strong pressure when length third of 11 to Glenbank Lass in maiden auction event at Redcar in July; will be suited by 1m; sold 420 gns Doncaster October Sales. *W. Haigh.* **60**

PALM COURT JOE 7 b.g. Welsh Saint 126–Cis (Eudaemon 129) (1979 NR 1980 6d 5fg) temperamental sprint handicapper; tailed off in 1980; acts on any going; used to sweat up. *M. Naughton.* —

PALM CROSS 3 ch.f. Palm Track 122–Sea Cross (Sea Moss) (1979 NR 1980 15s) big, strong filly; second reported foal; half-sister to winning hurdler Parklands (by Royal Park); dam refused to race in 2 novice hurdles; backward when in rear in 17-runner maiden race at Stockton in October. *Mrs A. Cousins.* —

PALMEIN 4 ch.g. Pall Mall 132–Ma Reine 89 (Grand Roi 118) (1979 9fg 11d^{4} 12g^{3} 16fg^{4} 1980 14g 14.6g 20.4g) poor plater; appears to stay 2m; blinkered final start. *C. Crossley.* —

PALMELLA (USA) 3 ch.f. Grundy 137–Furioso 116 (Ballymoss 136) (1979 5s^{4} 6f^{3} 6g^{2} 1980 10g^{3} 12g^{2} 10s* 10g^{3} 10f^{2} 10g 10d* 12v) strong, well-made filly; won maiden race at Lingfield in July and handicap at Redcar in October; beat Teresilla in good style by 2 lengths in latter; stays 1½m; acts on any going but is well suited by some give in the ground. *H. Wragg.* **89**

PALM THE ACE 2 b.c. Palm Track 122–Aces High 62 (Acer 123) (1980 5f 5d 5.1g^{4} 7g 5d) May 7; small colt; of little account. *W. Charles.* —

Mrs E. Holland-Martin's "Palumba"

PALS GEM 3 ch.f. Pals Passage 115–Shangara (Credo 123) (1979 NR 1980 9fg 8fg 9f 12d 10.1s 9d) 2,600Y; big, strong filly; sister to useful middle-distance stayer Pal's Bambino; dam won twice over 5f at 2 yrs; well beaten in varied company, including selling. *D. Wintle.* –

PALTANGO 2 ch.g. Royal Palace 131–Orange Sensation 69 (Floribunda 136) (1980 6d3 7g2 7.2d 5d 7d* 7d) Feb 14; 3,100Y; strong, quite useful sort; half-brother to several winners here and abroad, including 3-y-o 6f winner Anglo Greek (by English Prince) and useful 1976 2-y-o Swift Sensation (by My Swallow); dam placed at up to 7f at 2 yrs; favourite, won 10-runner maiden race at Catterick in October by 4 lengths from Mr Mallory, leading throughout; had stiffish task under a penalty next time out; much better suited by 7f than 5f; acts on a soft surface. *M. W. Easterby.* 80

PALUMBA 2 b.f. Derring-Do 131–Dove 92 (Sea Hawk II 131) (1980 5g3 5g* 6g3 5fg 6f4) Apr 12; neat filly; first foal; dam 2-y-o 6f winner; quickened in good style after disputing lead from start when winning 14-runner maiden race at Newbury in June quite comfortably by 4 lengths from Shalwa; subsequently ran well in strongly-contested nurseries; will be suited by 7f and 1m. *H. Candy.* 100

PAMANJO 4 b.g. Royalty 130–Alkaline (Alcide 136) (1979 12s 16f2 14fg3 16d* 16fg* 1980 16g) leggy gelding; winner of maiden race at Nottingham and handicap at Warwick in 1979 (rated 79); bandaged in front and pulled up lame on only outing of 1980 (June); suited by a test of stamina; acts on any going except perhaps very soft; sweated up badly third outing at 3 yrs. *D. Ringer.* –

PAMPAS SUE 3 b.f. Ampney Prince 96–Sue's Last (Como 120) (1979 5s 1980 6fg 12d 5fg) neat, lightly-made filly; useless. *H. Fleming.* –

PAMPERED ISLE 2 b.f. Mummy's Pet 125–Barnie's Isle (Dumbarnie 125) (1980 5v4 5f 5fg 5fg 5d3 5f4 5d 5s) May 13; 2,400Y; unfurnished filly; sixth foal; sister to a plating-class animal; dam never ran; ran best races when in frame in maiden races at Pontefract and Beverley in the summer, fifth and sixth starts; 67

well beaten in a Stockton seller on final appearance; blinkered fourth outing. *W. C. Watts.*

PAM'S SONG 3 b.f. Song 132–Pamagilan 89 (Pall Mall 132) (1979 6fg 5s* 5d —
6f 5fg 1980 5v^3 6s 5f 7fg 6s 6s 6g) workmanlike filly; ran respectably in handicaps on first 2 starts; well beaten subsequently, running badly on final outing; stays 6f; suited by some give in the ground; dwelt fifth start; sold 5,200 gns Newmarket December Sales. *N. Guest.*

PANAMAN 4 ch.c. Red Man 75–Panalady 83 (Panaslipper 130) (1979 12g 12g^2 —
16s^3 12g 16s^4 13f^2 12g 1980 12d 16g 16s) compact colt; possibly doesn't quite stay 2m; seems to act on any going. *P. Mitchell.*

PANAVISE 3 b.g. Silly Season 127–Field Daisy (White Fire III) (1979 NR **73**
1980 8g 8g^3) 2,400Y; short-backed gelding; fourth foal; dam never ran; not seen out after finishing respectable 2½ lengths third to Karelia in maiden race at Newbury in July; will stay 1¼m. *P. Cundell.*

PANAY 2 b.f. Arch Sculptor 123–Sundalgo 82 (Fidalgo 129) (1980 5v^3 5s* 5fg^3 **77**
5f^3 5f^3 5g^3 5f) Feb 19; half-sister to 2 winning platers; dam won over 7f at 2 yrs and probably stayed 2m; won 14-runner maiden race at Nottingham in April by short head from Miss Quaver; third subsequently in minor events, final occasion when finishing 2 lengths behind Disco Dancing at Newcastle in June; not seen out again until September (looked in need of race and moved badly to start) when in rear in valuable seller at York; acts on any going. *T. Fairhurst.*

PANDIT 3 ch.c. Porto Bello 118–Dwindle 81 (Major Portion 129) (1979 6fg **51**
7fg 6g 5g 1980 5fg 6f 5f 6d 6g^3 5g^3 6g^4 6s 5d 5f 5fg 5d) workmanlike colt; plater; stays 6f; acts on firm going and is possibly unsuited by soft; sometimes blinkered; ran moderately third and eleventh starts; sold 400 gns Newmarket Autumn Sales. *T. Fairhurst.*

PANGKOR 4 b.f. Tribal Chief 125–Casually 78 (Cash and Courage 116) (1979 **46**
6v^3 6s 5fg 5g 6f 5f 6d 5s 1980 6s^4 5g 5.8fg^4 5d^4 5.1g^4 5d 5g^2 6g 5d) leggy filly; sprint handicapper; runner-up at Catterick (apprentices) in August; stays 7f; seems to act on any going; has worn blinkers. *A. Goodwill.*

PANJANDRUM (USA) 2 b.c. His Majesty–Muriel's Dream (Blue Prince 123) **117**
(1980 7s* 7d^3 8v*) May 11; $50,000Y; fifth foal; half-brother to 3 winners in USA; dam, winner over 5f and 6f, is half-sister to smart 6f to 9f winner Double Edge Sword; odds on, put up a good first effort to win 13-runner maiden race at Warwick in July by 6 lengths from Violino Fandango with rest well strung out; showed himself a smart animal at Rome in November, beating Belviale 4 lengths in Premio Tevere with English-trained colts Golden Flak and Wicked Will well behind in fourth and sixth; odds on for minor race at Wolverhampton in between but could finish only 3 lengths third of 12 to Admiral's Heir after having every chance; will stay 1¼m; clearly revels in the mud. *H. Cecil.*

PANSING 2 br.c. Crooner 119–Petploy 82 (Faberge II 121) (1980 5s 5f 5f 5.8fg **78**
7s 7g 7g 8.2d 8fg^4 10d^3 10d^3 8d^2) neat colt; has a round action; plater; stays 1¼m; usually wears blinkers; consistent. *A. Goodwill.*

PANTO ISLAND 2 ch.g. Silly Season 127–Wrekinianne 96 (Reform 132) (1980 **60**
5d 5f^3 5f 6fg 6d 8.2g 6g) Mar 6; 12,500Y; leggy, quite useful-looking gelding; poor maiden; blinkered when ninth of 23 to Hurtwood Lass in valuable seller at Doncaster in September, seventh outing; should stay 1m. *T. Fairhurst.*

PANTOMIME KING 2 b.g. Moulton 128–Miss Jessica 90 (Milesian 125) (1980 —
6g 7f) Jan 21; 4,100Y; rangy gelding; brother to modest 11.7f winner High Wycombe, and half-brother to a winner; dam probably best at sprint distances; in rear in newcomers race at Goodwood and maiden race at Redcar in September. *Peter Taylor.*

PAPAFINGO 3 ch.g. Simbir 130–Asail (Atan) (1979 NR 1980 12d 16.9d^3 **56**
14.7g 11.5g^4) 13,000Y; tall, narrow gelding; half-brother to 5f winner Land of Point (by Pontifex); dam sister to prolific 1971 2-y-o Sea Music; in frame in modest maiden races; stays well; ran poorly third start (didn't move to post particularly well). *C. Brittain.*

PAPAROUNA 3 ch.f. Red Alert 127–Trusian (Milesian 125) (1979 5g^2 5d 5g^3 **64**
5fg 6f^2 6g 6g^3 6g 8.2d^3 7f 1980 6f^2(dis) 6fg^4 7g 7g 7g 6d) leggy filly; inconsistent plater nowadays; stays 1m; seems to act on any going; sometimes blinkered; sweated up badly third start; has run creditably for an apprentice; sold 400 gns Newmarket Autumn Sales. *C. Nelson.*

PAPER LAD 3 b.g. Touch Paper 113–Church Bay 76 (Reliance II 137) (1979 **73** d
6fg 6f* 5f^2 5f^2 6g^4 6g 7s^4 6g 1980 5f 5h^2 5fg 5fg 6g 6s 6s 5f) neat gelding; poor

handicapper; stays 6f; needs a sound surface and goes well on firm ground; retained 400 gns Newmarket Autumn Sales. *R. D. Peacock.*

PAPER MOON 3 b.c. Touch Paper 113–Tin Tina 72 (Tin Whistle 128) (1979 NR 1980 8v 8f 12g 10g2 12fg 10d) 12,000Y; compact colt; plater; stays 1¼m; blinkered second start; trained by B. Hanbury first 4 outings. *D. Wintle.* **44**

PARADISE BAY 3 b.c. Mill Reef 141–Light Duty 113 (Queen's Hussar 124) (1979 6fg3 7f* 7s 7fg 1980 12g3 12g3) attractive, well-made colt; has reportedly been operated on for soft palate; most impressive winner of 7-runner Limekilns Stakes at Newmarket at 2 yrs; hasn't really fulfilled promise of that run, although did nothing wrong under top weight in King George V Stakes (Handicap) at Royal Ascot on second outing in 1980, having every chance 1f out before finishing 2¼ lengths third of 14 to John O'Groats; reluctant to struggle when 10 lengths third of 6 to Try Sandicliffe in Warren Stakes at Epsom on reappearance; should stay beyond 1½m; acts well on firm going; blinkered final start at 2 yrs; sold 34,000 gns Newmarket December Sales. *R. Hern.* **110**

PARADISE BIRD 2 ch.f. Sallust 134–Fair Darling 93 (Darling Boy 124) (1980 5g 6d 6d* 6g3 6s*) Feb 27; 11,000Y; small filly; sister to a disappointing animal, and half-sister to several winners, including 7f and 1¼m winner Tudor Lord (by Tudor Music); dam best at up to 1m; won 11-runner maiden race at Redcar in August and £4,000 nursery at Ayr the following month, putting up her best effort in latter when making much of running to win by 1½ lengths from odds-on Ponchielli; will stay 1m; yet to race on firm ground and goes very well on soft. *P. Calver.* **94**

PARANETE (FR) 3 b.f. King of the Castle–Parthenia (Sea Hawk II 131) (1979 7.5fg* 8g 1980 8v2 10.5v 9.5g3 10.5g3 10fg* 10.5g3 12f) robust filly; fourth foal; half-sister to 2 minor French winners, middle-distance performer Le Rayonnant (by Ribero) and Orthenix (by Ortis), successful over 1¼m at 2 yrs; dam French 1¼m winner; showed much improved form to win 8-runner Prix Saint-Alary at Longchamp in May by ¾ length from Safita; creditable 3 lengths third to Mrs Penny in 14-runner Prix de Diane de Revlon at Chantilly following month; 5¼ lengths eighth of 12 behind same filly in Prix Vermeille at Longchamp in September; probably stays 1½m; seems to act on any going but is suited by a firm surface; ran moderately second outing; sent to USA. *M. Saliba, France.* **119**

PARBEAU 4 ch.g. Parnell 130–Belle Reine 109 (Red Slipper 126 or King's Leap 111) (1979 13s2 12s3 10g 10g 10d 14g 14s 12d4 1980 12g) ex-Irish gelding; plating-class maiden when trained by D. Weld at 3 yrs; had stiff task on only outing of 1980 (bandaged in front); blinkered last 3 starts in 1979. *A. Moore.* **—**

PARCHED 4 ch.c. Busted 134–Parsimony 121 (Parthia 132) (1979 5f 8fg 1980 7fg 7fg) big, rangy colt; has been tubed; in frame in good-class races at Ascot at 2 yrs; lightly raced since and finished behind in handicaps in 1980; should stay 1m; yet to race on a soft surface. *N. Vigors.* **—**

PARISCENE 2 gr.f. Dragonara Palace 115–Rennett 109 (King's Bench 132) (1980 5g 5g4 5f2 5fg* 5fg 6f 5d) Feb 24; leggy filly; half-sister to several winners, including very smart 3-y-o sprinter Runnett and 1977 2-y-o 5f performer Cala-Vadella (both by Mummy's Pet); dam stayed 1¼m; favourite, made all and was clear below distance when winning 17-runner maiden race at Wolverhampton in August comfortably by 3 lengths from Wollingo; not disgraced in valuable nurseries subsequently; probably stays 6f; acts on firm going; hampered in early stages final outing. *N. Callaghan.* **86**

PARK BRIDGE 3 ch.g. Park Lawn 111–Asa-Bridge 77 (Como 120) (1979 5g 1980 10.8v 6f* 7f 5h2 8g* 7d 7g3 8g 8g2 8g) compact gelding; plater; successful **62**

Prix Saint-Alary, Longchamp—Paranete wins from Safita, Benicia and Aryenne. Firyal is fifth

Mrs N. Nuttall's "Parkdale"

at Pontefract in April (bought in 2,000 gns) and Bath in July (no bid); stays 1m; acts on hard going; has worn bandages; ran poorly final start. *D. H. Jones.*

PARKDALE 2 ch.c. Swing Easy 126–Miss McWorden 75 (Worden II 129) (1980 5d 5f* 5fg² 6d² 6fg* 6g² 7g 6f) Feb 28; 25,000Y; big, strong, well-made colt; excellent mover; half-brother to 4 winners, including fairly useful stayer Mr McMandy (by Mandamus); dam a stayer; improved physically and proved himself a very useful performer when length second of 9 to Bel Bolide in Gimcrack Stakes at York in August; successful earlier in good-class events at York in May and Newcastle in July; also prominent in 2 other valuable races, finishing 3 lengths second of 13 to Cooliney Prince in Windsor Castle Stakes at Royal Ascot in June on third outing and being beaten about the same distance, after leading for 5½f, when fifth to Gielgud in 7f Laurent Perrier Champagne Stakes at Doncaster in September; will stay 1m; seems to act on any going; genuine; trained by M. W. Easterby first outing. *P. Rohan.* **113**

PARK JET 4 b.g. Lear Jet 123–Parallelogram 63 (Pardal 130) (1979 8fg 10.4f 8f 7fg 7.6f 9.4d⁴ 8.2g 1980 10f 10g 10f) poor plater; evidently stays 9f; acts on a firm and a soft surface; blinkered once at 2 yrs and last 2 starts. *L. Barratt.* **—**

PARK PLACE 2 b.f. Royal and Regal–Tanndara (Venture VII 129) (1980 7g* 7g) Feb 27; 5,000Y (privately); neat filly; half-sister to winning stayer Let 'Em Have It (by Le Levanstell); dam, French middle-distance winner, is half-sister to outstanding New Zealand stallion Pakistan II; always front rank when winning 18-runner maiden race at Yarmouth in September by ½ length from Devon Bells; well-backed favourite when respectable sixth of 17 to Remouleur in £3,600 nursery at Ascot the following month; will be suited by middle distances. *H. T. Jones.* **86**

PARKSTONE QUAY 3 b.g. Ragstone 128–Palmyrrha 98 (Palestine 133) (1979 6fg 1980 12s 15s) lengthy gelding; behind in maiden and minor races. *J. W. Watts.* **—**

PARLOUR GAME 3 gr.f. Birdbrook 110–Dairy Queen 76 (Queen's Hussar 124) **108**
(1979 5fg 5.3f* 6fg* 7g^3 6f 8f 1980 7f* 7.3f* 8.5f* 10g^4 7d* 8d^2 7fg* 8fg 8fg^4 8s) rangy, useful-looking filly; useful handicapper; had a good year, winning 3 times at Epsom and once each at Newbury and Newmarket; beat Julip a head in Ebbisham Stakes at Epsom on third start, Premier Rose by 2 lengths in Duchess of Montrose Handicap at Newmarket on fifth and carried 10-0 when holding off Protectress by a neck at Epsom on seventh outing in August; best at up to 8.5f; possibly unsuited by very soft going but acts on any other; genuine and consistent *R. Smyth.*

PARSLEY JACK 5 b.g. Upper Case–Graceful 83 (Grey Sovereign 128§) (1979 **44**
10.2s 8s^2 8d^2 8g 9g 11.5fg 8g 8fg 1980 8.2g 8f^3 9d^4 8.2d 8fg 7g) plater nowadays; best form at 1m; acts on any going; sometimes wears blinkers. *B. Richmond.*

PARSON'S PRIDE 5 ch.g. The Parson 119–Ankole 85 (Crepello 136) (1979 —
15.5f 1980 13g 12f) of little account. *W. Stubbs.*

PARTI-PRISM 5 bl.m. West Partisan 101–Prism 69 (Primera 131) (1979 NR —
1980 10.1g 10fg) compact mare; first foal; dam won over 1m; tailed off in minor event at Windsor (needed race and wore bandages) and apprentice event at Leicester, both in September. *R. Atkins.*

PARTNERPLAN 5 b.g. Green God 128–Pladda (Reliance II 137) (1979 10g —
10f^2 10fg^4 15.5fg^3 10.1fg 1980 9.6fg 12d 10g 10f) plater; stays 2m; acts on firm going; often sweats up. *P. K. Mitchell.*

PARTNERPLAN TOO 2 b.g. Young Emperor 133–Hi Jay (Double-U-Jay 120) —
(1980 6s 6f) Feb 17; 1,750Y; second foal; dam won 5 times from 9f to 1¾m in Ireland; unquoted when behind in maiden and minor events at Windsor in July and Lingfield in September. *M. Masson.*

PARTON GOLD 2 ch.f. The Go-Between 129–Golden April 71 (Sovereign **74§**
Lord 120) (1980 5f^2 5g 5fg 5d^3 5d 5d) Mar 1; 560Y; close-coupled, fair sort; third reported live foal; half-sister to 2 winners, including Valdee (by Philip of Spain), successful over 1¼m; dam won two 1¼m sellers; put up easily best effort when fast-finishing 2¾ lengths third of 19 to Voting Day in maiden race at Bath in October; will stay 6f; evidently suited by a soft surface; unseated rider at start fifth outing and refused to start on sixth; one to be wary of. *D. Wintle.*

PARTON PRINCE 2 b.c. Andrea Mantegna–Greek Bazaar 49 (Philemon 119) —
(1980 6g 6fg 6g 7f) Mar 14; 500Y; compact colt; brother to 3-y-o 10.8f seller winner Taika Chancery; bad plater. *Mrs R. Lomax.*

PASHA'S DREAM 3 b.f. Tarboosh–Grandma 101 (Gilles de Retz 132) (1979 **70**
5s 5g^2 1980 6fg^3 7d^4 8fg) strong, compact filly; good mover; quite a moderate maiden; will be suited by 1¼m; acts on a firm and a soft surface. *R. Price.*

PASS-A-DEANEY 4 ch.f. Connaught 130–China Girl 76 (Shantung 132) (1979 —
7d 8g 7f 7fg 8.3fg 7g 7fg 7fg 1980 7h 8g 8.3s 6g) poor plater; should be suited by 1m+; blinkered final start at 3 yrs. *D. Jermy.*

PASSERINE 6 b.m. My Swallow 134–Marie Denise 68 (Dual 117) (1979 16s **50**
14.6s^3 16f 1980 16f 15.8fg 15g^3) poor staying handicapper; acts on any going but is well suited by some give in the ground; suited by forcing tactics; has run well for an apprentice. *B. Richmond.*

PASSIONATE 3 br.f. Dragonara Palace 115–Old Scandal 72 (Elopement 125) —
(1979 5.8h^3 6g 1980 6fg 7f 8g 7.2g 8d 9d) poor maiden; often blinkered. *D. Sasse.*

PASSION WAGON 2 b.f. Bay Express 132–Belitis 109 (Tudor Melody 129) **94**
(1980 6f 6d* 6s^4 8g) Mar 2; half-sister to winners in Ireland and France, including Bizantus (by Sassafras), successful from 9f to 11f; dam, winner from 5f to 1m, is daughter of top 1963 2-y-o filly Mesopotamia; won 13-runner maiden race at the Curragh in July by a short head from Chat Up; 20/1 when creditable 3½ lengths fourth of 14 to Arctique Royale in Group 2 Moyglare Stud Stakes on same course the following month; stays 6f but is by no means sure to stay 1m; acts on soft going. *A. Maxwell, Ireland.*

PASTURES NEW 2 b.c. Broxted 120–Wispy Vision 70 (Gulf Pearl 117) (1980 —
6fg 8fg 7.2d 7d^4) Apr 12; first foal; dam won over 1m; in rear on all outings, including in a seller. *D. Francis.*

PATAS BLANCAS 2 br.f. Tumble Wind–Vivungi (Exbury 138) (1980 5g) —
May 6; 700F (privately), 2,200Y; leggy filly; third produce; dam placed at around 7f in France and Ireland; 20/1 and bit backward, moved moderately to

Ebbisham Stakes, Epsom—Parlour Game comes with a strong run on the outside and beats Julip (rails) a head. Twice Noble (centre of picture) beats Bezique a short head for third place but the placings are reversed

start and dwelt when ninth of 10 to Goody Goody in minor event at Goodwood in September; likely to need considerably further. *G. Lewis.*

PATCHINIA 2 b.f. Patch 129–Tapia (Tanerko 134) (1980 6s 7d* 7f 8d) Mar 16; 3,000F, 3,500Y; tall, leggy filly; half-sister to 2 winners, including stayer Malpaso (by Sun Prince); dam closely related to disqualified French Gold Cup winner Tulip II; 25/1, behind for long way but finished very strongly to win 12-runner maiden race at Chester in August by a length from Wrong Page; in rear in nurseries subsequently, on final outing running very wide on bend after 2f at Pontefract; bred to stay at least 1½m; acts on a soft surface; is taken down early to start. *S. Norton.* **77**

PATHIAN 2 b.f. Abwah 118–Pilamenon 90 (Parthia 132) (1980 7s) Apr 23; 6,800F, 5,000Y; well-grown filly; half-sister to 3 winners, including My Habibi (by Habitat), a useful winner over 5f at 2 yrs in 1977; dam won over 1m and 1¼m; 20/1 and in need of race, never on terms when 11½ lengths sixth of 8 to Countess Olivia in maiden race at Ayr in September. *J. W. Watts.* **–**

PATH OF PEACE 4 br.g. Warpath 113–Turtle Dove (Gyr 131) (1979 10.2fg 12f² 13g* 13s* 13.8d² 13d* 14.7f² 14fg³ 1980 12d² 13v² 12.3d* 12f⁴ 12f 12f **95**

William Hill November Handicap, Doncaster—Path of Peace ploughs through the mud to beat Rhyme Royal and Russian George (rails)

13fg[2] 13g 12g 13s* 14s[2] 14s[2] 12v*) small gelding; fairly useful handicapper; well suited by plenty of give in the ground and revelled in the muddy conditions when beating Rhyme Royal gamely by ½ length in William Hill November Handicap at Doncaster; had won impressively by 20 lengths from Rafael Molina at Newcastle in April and most decisively by 5 lengths from Smokey Bear in 3-runner Bogside Cup (Handicap) at Ayr in September; second on 5 other occasions, including to Beau Reef at York on eleventh start after swerving to avoid a spectator; stays 1¾m well; changed hands privately 10,000 gns Newmarket Autumn Sales before final start. *C. Thornton.*

PATMORE 3 ch.g. Panco 91–Nicky's Vulgan (Vulgan 123) (1979 7fg 8d 1980 10.1d[4]) small, close-coupled gelding; little worthwhile form in varied company; will stay 1½m. *G. Balding.* —

PATOUCHE 2 ro.f. Shiny Tenth 120–Shallot (Sheshoon 132) (1980 8d) Apr 1; 5,400Y; half-sister to 2 winners in this country and a winner abroad; dam of little account; 20/1 and in need of race when in rear in 15-runner maiden event won by Segos at Redcar in October. *J. Etherington.* —

PATRICK'S FAIR 4 br.g. Tudenham 118–Little Squaw (Proud Chieftain 122) (1979 8s 10.1fg 1980 10fg 7h 8d 9.4g 10f) leggy gelding; plater; sometimes wears blinkers. *D. H. Jones.* —

PAT'S SONG 2 b.f. Song 132–Marsajac 74§ (Zucchero 133§) (1980 5g 5d 6g) Apr 9; 4,500Y; good-topped filly; poor mover; half-sister to 3 winners, including useful middle-distance handicapper Silver Doctor (by Salvo); dam, temperamental middle-distance winner, is daughter of Oaks third Reel In; in rear in maiden race and sellers; sold 600 gns Newmarket Autumn Sales. *B. Swift.* —

PAT'S STREAK 2 b.c. Streak 119–Pat's Best (Star Moss 122) (1980 5h 5fg[4] 6g 5g 6fg) May 8; big, strong colt; no sign of ability, including in a seller; sold 340 gns Ascot November Sales. *D. Jermy.* —

PAUILLAC 5 b.g. Martinmas 128–Silver Wonder 77 (Delirium 126) (1979 NR 1980 7v 6d) poor handicapper; blinkered second start. *J. Davies.* —

PAULAGER 2 b.c. Lochnager 132–Hopeful Subject 82 (Mandamus 120) (1980 5h[4] 5fg* 6d[3] 7.2d*) Mar 28; strong colt; first live foal; dam, half-sister to useful animals Blind Harbour and Delayed Tip, won over 1m at 2 yrs; stayed on well to win 7-runner maiden race at Thirsk in May and 4-runner Cock of the North Stakes at Haydock in July, in latter event beating Akram, who was racing on opposite side of course, by 1½ lengths; creditable 3½ lengths third of 5 to Another Realm in Chesters Stakes at Newcastle in between; will stay at least 1m. *M. H. Easterby.* 87

PAUL DIVER 6 ch.g. Deep Diver 134–Pink Foot 97 (Wilwyn 129) (1979 5s 5s 5.8g 5.8g[2] 5f[3] 5fg[3] 5.8h* 5g* 5fg[2] 5fg[3] 5g 5g 1980 5.8fg 5.8fg 5g 6g 5f 5f[2] 5g[4] 5.8g 5fg 5d) sprint handicapper; ran well under top weight when ½-length second of 18 to Jack Splendid at Chepstow in August; dwelt and wasn't disgraced next time; probably acts on any going; blinkered last 3 starts in 1978; sold 1,350 gns Ascot November Sales. *G. Cottrell.* 76

PAUSE FOR THOUGHT 3 ch.g. Jukebox 120–Madlin 102 (Sovereign Path 125) (1979 5g[2] 5s[3] 5g 5s 6fg 6d[3] 5f[4] 5g 1980 7d 8h[2] 8fg[4]) useful-looking gelding; quite a moderate maiden; stays 1m; acts on any going; blinkered last 2 starts in 1979; sweated up first start. *Denys Smith.* 76

PAVAHRA 3 b.f. Mummy's Pet 125–Avahra 108 (Sahib 114) (1979 5s[4] 5f* 5f* 6g* 6fg 1980 5g 6f[2] 6fg 6g[3] 7fg 6g* 7f 6fg) lengthy, sparely-made filly; fairly useful handicapper; held on well to beat Rabdan a neck in £4,000 race at York in August; had earlier run well to be second of 9 to Highland Light on same course in May; stays 6f; acts on firm going; sweated up final start at 2 yrs. *P. Rohan.* 93

PAVARICO 2 gr.c. Record Token 128–Dark Dolores 83 (I Say 125) (1980 5f[4]) Apr 20; 5,600F; lengthy colt; half-brother to 3 minor winners; dam won over 5f at 2 yrs; 9/2, dwelt, ran very green and swerved violently left 3f out when distant last of 4 to Akram in minor event at Newmarket in April. *F. Durr.* —

PAVILION 2 gr.c. Habitat 134–Game All 109 (Alcide 136) (1980 6g[2] 7d 5d[4]) Mar 21; 90,000Y; shapely, attractive colt; good mover; half-brother to several winners, including very smart French 1m and 1¼m winner Bally Game (by Ballymoss); dam, half-sister to Birdbrook, was game performer at up to 84

11f; went down by ¾ length to New Years Day when favourite for 7-runner Granville Stakes at Ascot in July; dwelt and had a lot to do at halfway in 23-runner maiden race at Haydock in October but ran on strongly to finish length fourth to Hindi; will be suited by a return to 6f and should stay 7f. *H. T. Jones.*

PAWIMENT (POL) 6 b.h. Mehari 123–Pytia (De Corte) (1979 one win **118**
from 9 starts 1980 3 wins from at least 14 starts, including 12g^4 12g 12d* 12v* 12f 12fg) Polish-bred horse; a much-travelled performer who won 16 races, in Poland, Czechoslovakia, Italy and Germany; champion juvenile in his native country in 1976 and won 2,000 Guineas and was second in Derby there in 1977 (also ran respectably in England as a 3-y-o, although last behind Alleged in Great Voltigeur); successful 3 times in 1980, twice in Group 1 events; won Preis von Europa at Cologne in October, starting at 120/1 and winning by 2 lengths and a neck from Dhausli and Nebos; had field well strung out when beating Lotar by 8 lengths in Gran Premio del Jockey Club at Milan later in month; retired to Polish National Stud after running unplaced at Santa Anita and Buenos Aires; stayed at least 1½m; seemed to act well on soft going. *C. Seiffert, Germany.*

PAWNBROKER 2 ch.g. Lombard 126–Italian Sky 94 (Skymaster 126) (1980 —
8g 10s) Mar 26; tall, rangy, narrow gelding; well beaten in maiden races at Newmarket (dwelt) and Nottingham at the back-end; looks a plater; sold 500 gns Newmarket Autumn Sales. *W. Hastings-Bass.*

PAXTON PIRATE 3 b.g. Morston 125–Nylon Pirate (Derring-Do 131) (1979 —
8d 7s 1980 10.6d) fair sort; behind in large fields of maidens; sold 460 gns Newmarket Autumn Sales. *D. Thom.*

PEACE CALL 3 b.f. Martinmas 128–Awaken (Narrator 127) (1979 5v 6s —
6fg 7g 1980 10.8s 8g) lightly-made filly; behind in varied company. *M. Blanshard.*

PEACEFUL RIVER 5 ch.m. Meldrum 112–Rippling Water 80 (Star Moss —
122) (1979 8d 7s^4 6g 10f 1980 6s) big mare; plater; seems to stay 1m although is possibly better at shorter distances; acts on any going. *J. Hill.*

PEACOCK CHARM 4 ch.g. Crisp and Even 116–Besselsleigh Lass (Quorum —
126) (1979 11.7g 12s^4 12g 7fg 8d 1980 12.2f) of little account. *J. Mason.*

PEARLAWAY 2 b.c. Derring-Do 131–Pearlesque 88 (Gulf Pearl 117) (1980 **92**
6g^4 5.8f 7fg* 7d^2 7g) Jan 14; small, strong colt; fourth foal; half-brother to 2 winners, including smart Pearlescent (by My Swallow), successful at up to 1m; dam won over 5f and is sister to numerous winners; proved well suited by 7f when winning 19-runner maiden race at Warwick in August by short head from Maysina; good second, a neck behind Beocan, in 10-runner minor event at Brighton the following month; will stay 1m; acts on a firm and a soft surface; had stiffish task in nursery final outing. *P. Walwyn.*

PEARL OF PRICE 3 ch.f. Hotfoot 126–Gift Token 107 (Firestreak 125) —
(1979 5g 7fg^3 8fg 1980 10fg 10.6f 12.5fg 12d 10d 10s 10fg 10fg 10s) lengthy filly; plating-class maiden; appeared not to stay 1m on final start at 2 yrs; blinkered fourth and fifth starts; sweated up sixth outing. *A. Hide.*

PEARL'S FANTASY 4 ch.f. Gulf Pearl 117–Queen's Fantasy 97 (Pampered —
King 121) (1979 8s 10.6g 9g 12.2s 10.2d 10s 1980 10fg 10g 12d) neat, strong filly; little worthwhile form, including in a valuable seller. *P. Asquith.*

PEARSON 2 gr.c. Runnymede 123–Constance Spry (Gentle Art 121) (1980 **51**
5.1g 6g 6fg 5fg 5.1fg 6fg 6g) May 16; 1,800Y; small, narrow colt; only poor form, including in sellers; has worn blinkers; sold 300 gns Doncaster November Sales. *M. Tompkins.*

PEDANG 2 b.c. Sharpen Up 127–Carcosa 103 (Sovereign Lord 120) (1980 **72**
5g 6g^4) Feb 17; lengthy colt; half-brother to 3-y-o Flash Connection (by Hot Spark), a winner over 5f in France; dam won over 6f and 7f at 2 yrs; 13/2, had no sort of run until finding a gap inside final furlong and ran on strongly to finish 2½ lengths fourth of 15 behind Sipestro in maiden race at Doncaster in June; will stay 7f. *W. Hastings-Bass.*

PEECO PENCO 3 b.g. Green God 128–Tin Saint 99 (Tin Whistle 128) (1979 —
5f 5g^2 1980 7s 8.2f 6f 6g 10g 8g 12.5s) fair sort; has shown no form since second outing at 2 yrs; not certain to stay 7f; didn't appear to handle track too well at Pontefract on third start. *D. Weeden.*

PEEK-A-BOO 3 b.f. Bustino 136–True Love 89 (Princely Gift 137) (1979 **91**
8g 1980 7.2d* 8g^2 8.2g^2 9g 7.2g 7s* 7d* 7s 7s) lengthy, rather dipped-backed

filly; good walker; won maiden race at Haydock in July and handicaps at Ayr and Wolverhampton in the autumn; beat Rabdan by $1\frac{1}{2}$ lengths in £5,300 race at Ayr (swished her tail under pressure); best at up to 1m; acts well on soft going. *C. Thornton.*

PEERLESS KNIGHT 5 ch.g. Midsummer Night II 117–Trenora 89 (Ballymoss 136) (1979 8fg 10.6s 1980 14g) of little account. *P. Arthur.* —

PEERLESS PRINCESS 3 b.f. Averof 123–Trenora 89 (Ballymoss 136) (1979 7g 6g 1980 8f 7.6f) compact filly; behind in maiden races. *J. Dunlop.* —

PEGASOS 3 b.g. Martinmas 128–L'Alouette (Aureole 132) (1979 NR 1980 8fg 10.1f 10fg) 8,800Y; good sort; half-brother to 3 winners here and abroad; dam half-sister to 1,000 Guineas and Oaks runner-up Spree and to dam of Juliette Marny, Julio Mariner and Scintillate; in rear in 2 maiden races at Kempton and minor event at Windsor in May; sold 950 gns Ascot September Sales. *D. Elsworth.* —

PEGASSE 2 ch.f. Arts and Letters–Walk In The Sun (Walker's) (1980 6fg) Mar 23; 25,000Y; attractive, rangy filly; first foal; dam one of best 2-y-o fillies in the USA in 1975 when winner of 3 of her 5 starts at up to 6f; 12/1 and very backward, always trailing when last of 7 to Petroleuse in Blue Seal Stakes at Ascot in September. *G. Hunter.* —

PEKOES TAIL 3 b.f. Tumble Wind–Cariba 78 (Fidalgo 129) (1979 5f 5g 5f^{3} 5fg^{2} 6fg^{4} 6fg 7fg^{2} 7fg 1980 6fg 7fg 6f^{3} 6fg* 5d 7g 7fg 7.2g 6g^{4} 6d) rangy filly; beat Fairmile Lad a head in apprentice handicap at Folkestone in June; stays 7f; acts on firm going; sometimes wears blinkers; suitable mount for a boy; sold 4,300 gns Newmarket December Sales. *F. Durr.* **65**

PELAYO 3 b.c. Reform 132-Fashion Model 100 (Road House II) (1979 6fg^{4} 7fg^{3} 8f 1980 8.5g^{4} 9f* 10f* 12g 10d^{4} 8.3d* 10fg^{3} 8fg 9f 8s*) well-made colt; showed improved form in 1980, winning minor event at Lingfield and handicaps at Epsom, Windsor and Sandown; beat Seven Hearts $\frac{1}{2}$ length (pair well clear) on last-named in October despite swerving violently right; stays $1\frac{1}{4}$m; acts on any going. *R. Smyth.* **96**

PELEKE 3 b.c. Communication 119–Pollastra (Punchinello 97) (1979 5g 6fg 6s 5fg^{2} 1980 6f 5h^{3} 5d 5fg) strong colt; evidently better at 5f than 6f; acts on hard going and is possibly unsuited by soft; sold 500 gns Newmarket Autumn Sales. *T. Fairhurst.* —

PELERIN (FR) 3 b. or br.c. Sir Gaylord–Padrona 103 (St Paddy 133) (1979 7fg^{4} 7fg^{2} 7fg^{4} 1980 9f 10fg 10.5f* 12f^{4} 12s 12g 12g^{4}) **125** d

Nothing Pelerin achieved before or after the Derby matched his performance in that race. He came to Epsom the winner of the eight-runner Glasgow Stakes at York in May in which, blinkered for the first time, he showed improved form to win by a length and a half and five lengths from Winslow and the odds-on Royal Fountain, receiving weight from both. Pelerin wore blinkers on all his subsequent starts. Ridden by Eddery and starting at 18/1 he ran a fine race at Epsom, lying towards the rear in the early stages, moving up from halfway and going on better than anything in the straight to finish fourth to Henbit, beaten about three lengths. Pelerin ran as though longer trips would suit him well, but he raced only at a mile and a half afterwards and proved disappointing. His sixth place in the Irish Sweeps Derby was by no means a bad run, especially as the soft ground might have been against him, but in the King George VI and Queen Elizabeth Diamond Stakes and the Great Voltigeur Stakes he ran poorly, being ridden some way out and beating only one home each time. There might have been something wrong with him physically, though it's equally possible that the deterioration was due to temperament. Whatever the reason, Pelerin in August was a pale shadow of the colt that finished fourth in the Derby and he is one to be wary of until showing signs of a return to form.

Pelerin (Fr) (b. or br.c. 1977)	Sir Gaylord (b 1959)	Turn-to (b 1951)	Royal Charger
			Source Sucree
		Somethingroyal (b 1952)	Princequillo
			Imperatrice
	Padrona (gr 1969)	St Paddy (b 1957)	Aureole
			Edie Kelly
		Donna (gr 1956)	Donore
			Bashful

Pelerin's dam, Padrona, won over five furlongs and six furlongs at two years and from just two starts the following year showed she stayed one and

Glasgow Stakes, York—blinkers on Pelerin do the trick and he wins from Winslow

a quarter miles. Her two foals prior to Pelerin included Fair Melys (by Welsh Pageant), successful at seven furlongs and a mile; she has a two-year-old colt by Green Dancer called Al Nasr and a colt foal by Habitat. Padrona was one of eleven winners out of Donna, a very speedy two-year-old who stayed seven furlongs at three. The most notable of her offspring were the One Thousand Guineas second Gwen, dam of the smart 1968 two-year-old Timon, and the useful miler Eldo. Donna was a half-sister to Diffidence, a better-than-average performer at up to one mile, and to Stage Fright, the dam of the Cheshire Oaks and Prix de Malleret winner Hardiesse and grandam of Final Straw. Pelerin is a strong, attractive colt, a good walker and mover who acts well on firm ground. He will stay a mile and three quarters. *H. Wragg.*

PELLEGRINI (USA) 2 ch.c. Snow Knight 125–Solometeor (Victoria Park) **104**
(1980 6fg² 6fg* 6d² 8.2g* 7g) May 16; $55,000Y; quite well-made colt; half-brother to several winners, including good Canadian 3-y-o stakes winner Solartic (by Briartic), smart French 1½m winner Nuclear Pulse (by Nijinsky) and very useful American filly Meteor Dancer (by Northern Dancer); dam won Canadian Oaks; successful in 2 good-class races, running on gamely to beat Mushref a short head in Fenwolf Stakes at Ascot in June and putting up a workmanlike display when beating Grand March 1½ lengths in £4,100 event at Haydock in September; tended to hang when 2 lengths second of 4 to Poldhu in Washington Singer Stakes at Newbury in between; will be suited by 1¼m; acts on a firm and a soft surface. *R. Price.*

PELTON SON 2 gr.c. Spanish Gold 101–Raffinrula 75 (Raffingora 130) (1980 **66**
5f 5f 5fg 6g 7f 7g³ 8.2d 8f 7.2s) Apr 24; well-grown colt; second reported foal; dam won twice over 5f at 2 yrs; 1¾ lengths third of 12 to Silver Leo in poor maiden race at Catterick in August, best effort; well beaten subsequently, including in a seller; stays 7f; possibly unsuited by soft ground; blinkered last 4 outings; sold 660 gns Doncaster November Sales. *S. Nesbitt.*

PENCIL POINT 2 ch.c Sharpen Up 127–Miss Carefree 99 (Hill Clown) (1980 **81**
6d 6g³ 5d² 5fg³ 5d 5g² 6g²) Mar 26; 8,800Y; lengthy colt; second reported foal; brother to a poor animal; dam 2-y-o 7f winner; placed in maiden races and nurseries, running particularly well when 2½ lengths second of 14 to Steel Pass in £3,500 nursery at Newmarket in October on final outing; will stay 7f; acts on a firm and a soft surface; consistent. *P. Haslam.*

PENDLE ROYAL 4 ch.g. Royal Duet–Pennis Pearl (Pendragon) (1979 10.6g 1980 8g) of little account. *A. Watson.* –

PENDLE'S SECRET 4 ch.f. Le Johnstan 123–Secret Folly 83 (Infatuation 129) (1979 7.2fg 9.4f^{4} 10fg^{3} 12g^{4} 10g* 9.4d 10d^{2} 10fg 8g 10g 10.2s 1980 9fg 10d 12fg 10fg^{3}) quite a moderate handicapper; ran best race of season when third behind Be My Sweet at Beverley in September; should stay 1½m; acts on firm going and a soft surface. *E. Weymes.* **54**

PENMARRIC (USA) 2 b.c. Cornish Prince–Hello Teddy Bear (Court Martial) (1980 5fg* 5g* 5.5g 6g) Jan 20; $43,000Y; lengthy, good sort; brother to a minor winner, and half-brother to several winners, including a minor stakes winner by Nashua; dam placed at 3 yrs; heavily-backed favourite when winning Erroll Stakes at Ascot in June impressively by 4 lengths from Appaloosa and 5-runner National Stakes at Sandown the following month, in latter event quickening really well to lead inside final furlong and staying on strongly to beat Swan Princess by 3 lengths; disappointed on both subsequent starts, finishing 12 lengths eighth of 10 to Irish Playboy in Prix Robert Papin at Maisons-Laffitte in July and poor eighth of 9 to Bel Bolide, after moving badly to start, when 11/2 for Gimcrack Stakes at York in August; should stay 6f; one to be wary of until showing a return to form. *G. Hunter.* **111 ?**

PENNY SNOW 3 b.f. Jukebox 120–Efficiency (Pardao 120) (1979 6f 6g 1980 6s) leggy filly; little worthwhile form in maiden races. *J. Winter.* –

PEN PUSHAR 3 ch.f. Sharpen Up 127–Miss Kaly 92 (Kalydon 122) (1979 NR 1980 6f 5f 6f 9g 6d) strong filly; poor plater; has been tried in blinkers. *W. Haigh.* –

PENSHIEL 2 b.c. Comedy Star 121–Cereum 84 (Tudor Grey 119) (1980 5g^{4} 5s^{3} 5fg^{2} 6g 6fg^{4} 6fg* 6s) Mar 15; 15,000F, 11,000Y; neat colt; second foal; dam won over 5f at 2 yrs; in frame on most of his outings and won 6-runner maiden race at Redcar in October by 2 lengths from Badsworth Girl; stays 6f; probably not at his best on soft going; sold to BBA 4,300 gns Newmarket Autumn Sales. *J. Dunlop.* **79**

National Stakes, Sandown—Penmarric forges clear of Swan Princess

Mrs George F. Getty II's "Pentaquod"

PENTAQUOD (USA) 3 gr.c. London Company–Enamor (Drone) (1979 ran once unplaced in USA 1980 8f^2 8fg* 8.2fg* 7f*) $32,000Y; narrow, lightly-made colt; second foal; dam never ran; developed into a useful performer, winning 19-runner maiden race at Newmarket and 8-runner minor event at Haydock (odds on) in May and 11-runner handicap at Epsom following month; won in good style on last-named, cruising up to lead 2f out and going on to beat Rapid Class 2 lengths despite idling in front and hanging slightly left; stays 1m; yet to race on a soft surface; returned to USA. *H. Cecil.* **109**

PENWITH 4 b.c. Welsh Saint 126–Sweet Meadow 67 (Meadow Court 129) (1979 13v* 14d^4 16s^2 1980 16fg) tall, slightly hollow-backed colt; last at Newbury in April on only outing of 1980; stays 2m; acts on any going but goes well in the mud. *P. Cole.* –

PENWOOD 5 b.m. Precipice Wood 123–Penview 73 (Pendragon) (1979 NR 1980 16s* 16s* 16g^4 12d 13s) staying handicapper; apprentice ridden when trotting up in April at Nottingham (by 10 lengths) and Warwick (by 5 lengths); lightly raced afterwards (heavily backed but well beaten final start); revels in the mud. *N. Hall.* **62**

PEPINA 4 ch.f. Shoolerville 121–Pepstep 88 (Polic 126) (1979 6g 6g^4 6d 7fg* 7g^3 7f* 8fg 7fg^2 8d 7fg 1980 6f^4 7.2fg 7f 7fg 7fg 7f* 7fg) small, stocky filly; 25/1 when scoring by $\frac{1}{2}$ length from Murillo in £4,200 handicap at York in September; suited by 7f (ran moderately over 1m); acts on firm going and is possibly not at her best on a soft surface; sweated up badly last 2 starts at 3 yrs; trained by J. Bingham third to fifth outings. *M. Haynes.* **69**

PEPPER WINE 3 b.g. Tudor Harmony 104–Melba Sauce (Sing Sing 134) (1979 NR 1980 8f 8f) first foal in Ireland; dam, sister to very smart sprinter Saulingo and closely related to smart 5f colt Music Maestro, ran twice at 2 yrs in England –

and reportedly won in Jamaica; well beaten in Northern maiden races. *Denys Smith.*

PEPPERY 3 b.c. Red God 128 § –Powder Box (Faberge II 121) (1979 6fg 6f 7fg 7fg 8g* 1980 8fg 10.1g* 10d* 10d* 10g* 12fg² 10.5f⁴) neat, attractive colt; good mover; fairly useful handicapper; in good form in the summer, scoring at Windsor, Newcastle, Brighton and Sandown; beat Glowing Tan ½ length on last-named; went down by a neck to Hereas in valuable event at Goodwood on next start; stays 1½m; acts on a firm and a soft surface; consistent; sold privately, reportedly to race in Belgium. *G. Pritchard-Gordon.* **93**

PERDICCAS 2 br.g. Perdu 121–Requisition 101 (Petition 130) (1980 5fg 5f 6fg 6g 7fg 6s 7d³) May 16; compact gelding; poor mover; half-brother to smart 1977 2-y-o 6f winner Labienus (by Brigadier Gerard); 50/1, appeared to show vastly improved form (worth a rating of 85) when running on well to finish 2½ lengths third of 8 to Belloc in minor event at Leicester in November; had previously been well beaten, including in sellers; will stay 1m; has often worn blinkers but didn't do so at Leicester; wears bandages behind. *C. Austin.* **?**

PERFECT SAINT 3 b.f. St Paddy 133–Love-Lies-Bleeding 74 (Javelot 124) (1979 5g 6fg 6g 1980 8.5g 10.2f 12f 11.7g 8g) leggy filly; poor maiden; has been tried in blinkers. *A. Ingham.* **–**

PERGODA 2 b.c. High Top 131–Saint Joan 63 (Grey Sovereign 128 §) (1980 5f 5f² 5fg 6g 5f* 5fg 5d³ 5d 5f 5s) Feb 21; 8,000Y; useful-looking colt; fourth foal; dam showed a little ability over sprint distances; looked fully fit for first time when winning 16-runner maiden race at Catterick in July by 1½ lengths from Krugerama; good third of 10 to Southern Swanee in nursery at Newcastle in August; should stay 6f; seems to act on any going, except perhaps very soft; doesn't find much off the bridle. *M. W. Easterby.* **87**

PERGOLA (USA) 2 b.f. Thatch 136–Regent Queen (Buckpasser) (1980 7d² 6v*) Mar 23; second foal; dam, out of a sister to top American stallion What A Pleasure, won over 6f in USA; landed the odds in fine style in 14-runner maiden race at the Curragh in November, drawing clear in final furlong to win by 6 lengths from Tutti Frutti; should stay 1m; should make a useful 3-y-o. *V. O'Brien, Ireland.* **93** p

PERICULO LUDUS (FR) 4 ch.c. Timmy My Boy 125–La Beuvriere (Right Royal V 135) (1979 10s⁴ 10s 9g* 10g 10fg* 8g 1980 8fg 13.4f 9fg³ 12f 9g 10d² 10g 11.5g⁴ 7g 10s 9g) workmanlike ex-French colt; stays 1¼m; seems to act on any going; sometimes wears blinkers; looked none too keen eighth start; sweating ninth outing and didn't impress in paddock last 2 starts; has string-halt. *J. Harris.* **–**

PERLESSE 2 gr.f. Bold Lad (USA)–Perle Grise (Zeddaan 130) (1980 6g² 6f 6d* 6s²) Jan 14; 6,000F; quite well-made, good-quartered filly; first foal; dam won over 1¼m in France on only start at 3 yrs; overcame a high draw when winning 18-runner minor event at Pontefract in October by ½ length from Princess Dina; creditable second to Miss Menton in minor event at Stockton later in month; will stay 1¼m; acts on soft going and is unsuited by firm. *M. Stoute.* **88**

PERMA FINA 2 b.f. Nonoalco 131–Ginger 90 (Red God 128 §) (1980 6f 7d) Mar 6; 31,000Y; neat, attractive filly; good mover; first foal; dam, granddaughter of 2,000 Guineas winner Garden Path, won over 5f at 2 yrs; co-favourite, never looked like justifying the support when 6 lengths fifth of 21 behind Melissa Jane in maiden event at Leicester in October, second outing; probably stays 7f. *M. Stoute.* **69**

PEROUGES (FR) 5 b.h. Tiffauges 124–Petula II (Vieux Chateau) (1979 11g* 11g* 11g* 13.5g* 12.5s 12g* 12.5g* 12g³ 1980 12g 12g* 13.5g 10g³ 12d* 12s* 12fg) French horse; second foal; half-brother to a winning jumper; dam, placed once on flat in France, won 9 times over jumps; one of the top performers in the French Provinces, winner 6 times in 1979 and 3 times in 1980; gained his 1980 wins in Grand Prix de Vichy (for second time, beating Perrault a neck), Grand Prix de Bordeaux (won by 1½ lengths from Roymel) and Prix Max Sicard at Toulouse (beat P'Tite Tete by 1½ lengths); gained last 2 wins in November, scoring in good style both times; stays 13.5f; probably acts on any going; reportedly broke blood vessel first outing and was off course 3½ months afterwards. *A. Lyon, France.* **116**

PERRAULT 3 ch.c. Djakao 124–Innocent Air 75 (Court Martial) (1979 7g⁴ 8d³ 9v⁴ 1980 10.5g* 12g* 12.5s³ 12g² 13.5g² 12s) 14,500 gns F, 260,000 francs Y (approx. £30,900); half-brother to 2 winners, including Black Minstrel (by **113**

Luthier), a fairly useful winner from 7f to 1m; dam won 3 small races at up to 10.5f in France; won maiden race at Longchamp in May and Prix Sica Boy at Saint-Cloud in June; beat Maiymad 2 lengths in latter; ran well on all subsequent starts, finishing third to Buckpoint in Prix Maurice de Nieuil at Saint-Cloud, runner-up to Perouges, beaten a neck, in Grand Prix de Vichy, 3 lengths second to Glenorum in Grand Prix de Deauville and fifth to En Calcat in Prix du Conseil de Paris at Longchamp; stays 1$\frac{3}{4}$m; acts on soft going and has yet to race on a firm surface; blinkered last 2 starts; consistent. *P. Pelat, France.*

PERSIAN BEAU 2 ch.c. Persian Breeze 121–Lacemaker (Astec 128) (1980 5v 5f 5d) Apr 1; 2,000Y; first foal; dam twice-raced half-sister to good 1964 2-y-o Leonardo; in rear in maiden races at Warwick, Lingfield and Salisbury, twice finishing last; trained first outing by M. McCormack. *D. Elsworth.* –

PERSIAN BRONZE 4 ch.f. Crozier 117–Bronze Foliage (Bois Le Roi) (1979 NR 1980 15.5g) half-sister to a winner over jumps; dam never ran; lightly-raced novice hurdler; started slowly when tailed off in maiden race at Folkestone in August, first outing on flat. *R. Atkins.* –

PERSIAN PACT 2 br.c. Persian Breeze 121–Bridge of Stories 80 (Appian Bridge 111) (1980 6s 5fg 6s 5fg^{4} 5g^{2} 5d) Apr 15; 2,500Y; compact, good-quartered colt; eighth foal; half-brother to a minor sprint winner by The Brianstan; dam 2-y-o 5f winner; in frame in maiden races in the Midlands, at Nottingham in September going down by 3 lengths to Shasavaan; best form at 5f on a sound surface. *W. Wharton.* **74**

PERSIAN PRINCESS 3 ch.f. Palm Track 122–Persian Silver 61 (Cash and Courage 116) (1979 5fg 6d^{4} 7g 1980 8f 8.2f^{2} 8.2d^{2} 8.2g* 8g^{4} 8.2d* 7.2g 8.2s^{3} 10s^{3}) robust filly; successful in modest maiden race and a handicap at Hamilton in the summer; stays 1$\frac{1}{4}$m; acts on any going; has run creditably for an apprentice. *C. Crossley.* **67**

PERSIAN RIVER 2 ro.g. Rapid River 127–Empress Donna 48 (Don II 123) (1980 5f 5fg 6g 6d 6s 5f) May 10; dipped-backed, lightly-made gelding; fifth in maiden race on second outing and in seller on fifth, in latter beaten 5$\frac{1}{2}$ lengths by Allied Cardiff in 20-runner race at Nottingham in August; has twice given a lot of trouble at start and put up a headstrong display when blinkered on fourth appearance; one to be wary of; sold 300 gns Doncaster November Sales. *K. Stone.* **58 §**

PERSISTENCE 3 ch.f. Owen Anthony 102–Pertinacity 106 (Aggressor 130) (1979 7fg 1980 8f 10fg 10fg^{4} 10.8s 13d^{4} 12f 10fg) well-made filly; poor maiden; appears not to stay 1$\frac{1}{2}$m; blinkered final start. *J. Bethell.* **61**

PERSONAL GUARD 2 ch.c. Home Guard 129–Fairly Flattered 73 (Pall Mall 132) (1980 5fg 6s^{2} 6g^{2}) Jan 18; 21,000Y; half-brother to 3 winners here and abroad, including quite useful 1974 Irish 2-y-o Kogiku (by Lord Gayle), successful at up to 7.5f; dam won at up to 1$\frac{1}{4}$m; 16/1, ran very well when going down by $\frac{3}{4}$ length to Prince Echo in 18-runner Tyros Stakes at the Curragh in June; evens favourite for maiden event at Phoenix Park the following month but started slowly and went down by 5 lengths to Lawmaker; wasn't seen out again; will stay 1m. *M. Kauntze, Ireland.* **96**

PERT LAD 3 ch.c. Bold Lad (Ire) 133–Painted Glen (Pall Mall 132) (1979 NR 1980 6f 5fg* 5g^{3} 5g* 6g) 20,000Y; well-made colt; brother to very useful 1971 2-y-o 5f performer Pert Lassie and half-brother to 2 winners; dam never ran; favourite, won maiden race at Bath and minor event at Chepstow in June; beat Eaglesfield a neck in latter; not disgraced in between; best at 5f; yet to race on a soft surface; moved very badly to post final start; sold 1,100 gns Newmarket Autumn Sales. *M. Stoute.* **82**

PERTON STAINLESS 2 ch.c. Golden Dipper 119–Maud 87 (Vilmorin) (1980 5.1g 8fg) Apr 16: 2,300Y; compact colt; half-brother to 2 winners, including fair 1972 2-y-o 5f winner Marleyvous (by Bleep-Bleep); dam won over 6f; backward when behind in maiden race at Yarmouth and seller at Leicester in September. *P. Haslam.* –

PETER CULTER 8 br.h. Sky Gipsy 117–Gloaming 94 (High Treason 126) (1979 NR 1980 6g 5g 6d 5fg) poor sprinter nowadays; last in a seller on final start; acts on any going; sometimes wears blinkers. *J. Mulhall.* –

PETER HUTT 2 b.c. Streak 119–Jamuna (Canisbay 120) (1980 5s 5g 5fg 5f 5d 6f 7fg) May 16; lightly-made colt; half-brother to 1978 2-y-o 5f and 6f winner Royal Connection (by Royalty); dam placed over 1m in France; put up easily best effort when 4$\frac{1}{2}$ lengths fifth of 19 to Universal Penny in valuable seller at Sandown in August, fifth start; should stay 6f; acts on a soft surface. *D. Jermy.* **58**

PETER'S PLEASURE 3 gr. or ro.f. Jimsun 121–Kamariya (Zeddaan 130) (1979 5fg 5fg^2 5fg^4 6s 1980 7f 8fg 6g 6d 10.1fg) fair sort; has shown no form since 2 yrs; should stay at least 1m; took a strong hold going down third start. *Peter Taylor.* –

PETER THE BUTCHER 3 br.g. Autre Prince 125–Circumstance 72 (Bleep-Bleep 134) (1979 5d 5g 5g 6g 6s 6f 6fg 7fg 7g^2 8h* 8s^3 8.2fg^2 8fg* 8g 1980 8d 8.2d 10f^3 12fg 12fg^4 11fg 9g^3 8fg 8g^4 9g^3 8d^3 9g 8.2d^4 8f) poor handicapper; ran best race on ninth start; seems to stay 1¼m but not 1½m; acts on any going; blinkered eighth outing. *S. Nesbitt.* **64**

PETHAM BELLE 2 ch.f. Red Alert 127–Glen Devon (Klairon 131) (1980 5f 5g 5.3d^3 6fg 7g) Jan 26; 12,500Y; well-made filly; half-sister to 2 minor winners in France; dam won small races over 7f and 8.5f in France; narrowly-beaten third of 11 to Court Queen in maiden race at Brighton in June; had stiffish tasks subsequently; should stay at least 6f. *J. Winter.* **73**

PETITE FLECHE 2 b.f. Tower Walk 130–Little Bird 87 (Only for Life 126) (1980 5fg^2 5fg 5fg* 5g 5fg) Apr 12; 6,200Y; compact, rather lightly-made filly; half-sister to several winners, including very useful sprinter Geopelia (by Raffingora); dam 2-y-o 5f winner; won 6-runner maiden race at Edinburgh in July by 5 lengths from Maria Monk; well beaten afterwards; sold 2,000 gns Newmarket Autumn Sales. *Sir Mark Prescott.* **75**

PETITE HESTER 2 b.f. Wollow 132–Lady Hester (Native Prince) (1980 7g 7d^3) Feb 20; 39,000Y; small, quite attractive filly; first foal; dam, grand-daughter of Zanzara, won over 5f and 6f in Ireland; ran on when 2½ lengths third of 21 to Melissa Jane in maiden race at Leicester in October; will stay 1m; has little scope. *I. Balding.* **77**

PET MILER 2 b.g. Mummy's Pet 125–Mile by Mile 92 (Milesian 125) (1980 6fg 5g) Mar 23; 6,000Y; well-grown gelding; half-brother to fairly useful 1977 2-y-o 5f winner Speedometer (by Sharp Edge); dam won over 6f at 2 yrs; showed early speed when in rear in maiden races at Salisbury and Nottingham in September; blinkered second outing. *P. Cole.* –

PETONA 2 b. or br.f. Mummy's Pet 125–Princess of Verona 95 (King's Leap 111) (1980 6g) Apr 20; neat, short-backed filly; first foal; dam, half-sister to Music Boy, was best at 5f; unquoted when behind in 25-runner maiden race won by Composer at Newmarket in October. *M. Jarvis.* –

PETRINELLA 2 br.f. Mummy's Pet 125–Tinella 87 (Nelcius 133) (1980 6fg 6s* 7.2s^3 7g 7d^3) June 5; lightly-made filly; third foal; dam, half-sister to Alverton, won over 1m and 11.2f; won 10-runner maiden race at Stockton in June going away by 1½ lengths from subsequently-disqualified Wrightway Blues; creditable third to Stats Emmar in Rose of Lancaster Stakes at Haydock the following month and in £2,500 event at Newcastle (3 lengths behind Cifonelli) in August; runs as though she'll stay 1m; seems suited by a soft surface; unseated rider at start and had to be withdrawn on final appearance (September). *K. Stone.* **79**

PETROLEUSE 2 b.f. Habitat 134–Plencia (Le Haar 126) (1980 6fg*) **101** p

When winning the Blue Seal Stakes at Ascot in September Petroleuse became the third successive filly her stable had sent out to make a successful debut in the race, following One In A Million and Evita. One In A Million went on to win the One Thousand Guineas but Evita was lightly raced and comparatively disappointing after taking the Nell Gwyn Stakes on her first outing as a three-year-old. Which of the pair Petroleuse is the more likely to take after is impossible to say: she could be anything.

Like her two predecessors Petroleuse, a lengthy, attractive sort who impressed in her paces on the way to the start, was rumoured to be one of her stable's best two-year-old fillies and she started at odds on. For much of the race though it seemed unlikely that Petroleuse would justify the support: after breaking smartly she appeared to run green and dropped back, so that with two furlongs to race she had plenty to do. Petroleuse eventually began to get the hang of things, and running on very well in the last furlong she caught the long-time leader Shark Song and won going away by half a length. The time for the Blue Seal Stakes compares very favourably with that recorded by Steelinctive in a competitive nursery over the course and distance earlier in the afternoon. However, the proximity of fourth-placed Hot Ember, beaten beforehand in a minor event at Goodwood and subsequently out of the frame in a moderate maiden race at Lingfield, makes us just a little suspicious of the form and at this stage we can't rate Petroleuse so good as either Evita or One In A

Blue Seal Stakes, Ascot—highly-regarded Petroleuse about to take the lead from the grey Shark Song

Million. That's not to say though that she won't turn out better than either in time.

Petroleuse (b.f. May 13, 1978)	Habitat (b 1966)	Sir Gaylord (b 1959)	Turn-to
			Somethingroyal
		Little Hut (b 1952)	Occupy
			Savage Beauty
	Plencia (ch 1968)	Le Haar (ch 1954)	Vieux Manoir
			Mince Pie
		Petite Saguenay (ch 1961)	Nordiste
			Ballynash

Petroleuse, who is engaged in the One Thousand Guineas and the Oaks, has a fine pedigree. Her dam Plencia, a useful winner at around a mile and a half in France, is out of Petite Saguenay, an unraced half-sister to four very good horses in Montaval, Paimpont, Mourne and Moutiers. Plencia produced three foals before Petroleuse, all of them middle-distance winners and the first of them no less than Pawneese, outstanding among the fillies of her generation in Europe in 1976 when she won six races off the reel, including the Oaks, the French Oaks and the King George VI and Queen Elizabeth Diamond Stakes. Neither One In A Million nor Evita attempted a distance beyond a mile, and if Petroleuse is to make a name it will almost certainly be at up to a mile or a mile and a quarter; it's doubtful whether she'll stay a mile and a half. Her sire Habitat was a miler and has yet to get a pattern-race winner at further than a mile and a quarter. *H. Cecil.*

PETRUS 2 b.g. Mummy's Pet 125–Super Nova 86 (Raise You Ten 125) (1980 6s 6g) Mar 28; 4,200Y; lightly-made gelding; first foal; dam won Chester Cup and showed very smart form over hurdles; behind in July in maiden race at Windsor and minor event (last of 13) at Kempton. *D. Morley.* —

PETTISTREE 2 ch.c. Sallust 134–Kokuwa (Klairon 131) (1980 6d 6g 5s* $5d^2$) Apr 6; 16,500Y; neat, fair sort; half-brother to 2 minor 2-y-o winners; dam never ran; showed much improved form when winning 11-runner minor event at York in October going away by 3 lengths from Middleton Lad; confirmed his improvement when $\frac{1}{2}$-length second of 5 to Shark Song in similar event at Doncaster later in month; withdrawn, after breaking out of stall, when favourite for nursery at Newmarket the following week; should stay 6f; acts well on soft going. *N. Callaghan.* **105**

PETULENGRA 3 br.f. Mummy's Pet 125–Magic Maiden 97 (Magic Red) (1979 $5g^3$ 5s* 5fg $5g^3$ 6g 6d* 6g 1980 6f 5g) tall filly; has a high knee action; won maiden race at Doncaster and valuable nursery at Ayr in 1979; well beaten in handicaps at 3 yrs; suited by 6f; seems to need a soft surface. *T. Fairhurst.* —

PEYTON PLACE 3 b.c. Pitcairn 126–Modern Millie 95 (Milesian 125) (1979 —
6fg 6f 6d 1980 5fg^{4} 6g 5g) full-quartered, good sort; creditable fourth of 15 to Via Delta in valuable handicap at Ascot in June (saddle slipped some way out); ran moderately both subsequent starts; should be suited by 6f; sold 680 gns Newmarket Autumn Sales. *C. Brittain.*

PHIDEM 3 ch.c. Pieces of Eight 128–Maratea II 69 (Sedan II) (1979 7g —
1980 10s 11v 10fg) poor form in maiden races and a seller. *P. Haslam.*

PHILANMATTIE 2 ch.c. Bolkonski 134–Aromata (Hallez 131) (1980 6g^{4} **47**
7d 8.2d 8fg 7f) May 6; 4,200F, 2,600Y; very small, narrow colt; bad plater; blinkered fifth outing. *Mrs J. Reavey.*

PHILANTHROPIST 2 br.g. Saulingo 122–Lane House 68 (Bounteous 125) **82**
(1980 6s 5.8f* 6fg) Apr 8; 5,800Y; brother to 1979 French 2-y-o winner Lane Speed, and half-brother to a winner; dam best at around 1m; won 11-runner maiden race at Bath in July by 2 lengths from Beggar's Bush; poor sixth of 7 to Hound Song in nursery at Windsor the following month; will stay 7f; sent to Hong Kong. *P. Haslam.*

PHIL BENNETT 3 b. or br.c. Mountain Call 125–Gold Pension 76 (Compensa- **67**
tion 127) (1979 5s 5g 5f 5s 5g 6s 1980 6f^{2} 6f 5h^{2} 6fg* 5f 5g^{2} 5d 5g^{3} 6g^{2} 5d 6g 7g 6s) neat colt; made all to beat Old Bird a head in 9-runner maiden race at Hamilton in May; ran respectably on several other occasions; appears not to stay 7f; suited by a sound surface; usually blinkered nowadays; bandaged near-hind on reappearance; suitable mount for a boy; sold 1,600 gns Doncaster November Sales. *Denys Smith.*

PHILNORM 3 b.g. Sit In The Corner–Birdcage 78 (Manacle 123) (1979 —
6g 5g 1980 10fg 10.1f) strong gelding; little worthwhile form in minor and maiden races. *D. Gandolfo.*

PHILORN 2 b.g. Brittany–Whiphand 83 (Supreme Court 135) (1980 5fg —
5fg 7g) Apr 19; 1,000F, 2,300Y; half-brother to several minor winners; dam disappointing half-sister to Connaught; behind in maiden races and a seller. *J. Hill.*

PHOEBEGEE 2 b.f. Comedy Star 121–Burdigala (Above Suspicion 127) **79**
(1980 5d 5s 5g^{2} 5h^{2} 6fg^{3} 5fg^{2} 5g* 5f 6g 6f 5g^{3} 5g) Apr 27; 550F; neat filly; first living produce; dam poor maiden; bought in 1,000 gns after winning seller at Hamilton in June by 1½ lengths from Sparkler's Star; ran creditably on occasions afterwards, particularly on final outing when about 2½ lengths fifth of 16 to Fire Mountain in nursery at Newmarket in October; will stay 7f; acts on hard going; often blinkered, and usually runs creditably in them; sold out of P. Rohan's stable 2,500 gns Newmarket July Sales after seventh outing. *B. Hanbury.*

PHOEBE'S GAMBLE 2 b.c. Native Bazaar 122–Norian (Normandy 103) —
(1980 6s 7fg) May 5; leggy, compact colt; tailed off in maiden races at Windsor and Warwick in July; sold 320 gns Ascot October Sales. *J. Holt.*

PHOTOGRAPH 9 b.g. St Paddy 133–Photo Flash 119 (Match III 135) (1979 —
NR 1980 9.6h 15f) of no account. *J. Long.*

PHRED 7 ch.g. Continuation 120–Phrygia (Mossborough 126) (1979 11d^{4} —
10d^{4} 10.6s 10f 8fg^{3} 10f 1980 8g) plater; stays 11f; acts on any going; has worn blinkers. *Dr A. Jones.*

PHRYNE 2 ch.f. Jimmy Reppin 131–Phaedima 76 (Darius 129) (1980 5g —
6g 7g 6d) May 5; compact, good-bodied filly; fourth living foal; dam winner at up to 2m and half-sister to Coup de Feu and Peleid; in rear in varied company, finishing last of 18 in maiden race on fourth start. *W. Elsey.*

Prix Eclipse, Saint-Cloud—Phydilla wins from Silver Express

PHYDILLA (FR) 2 b.f. Lyphard 132–Godzilla 106 (Gyr 131) (1980 6g* 7g² 7d* 6.5s*) Feb 13; second foal; half-sister to French 3-y-o Aristarque (by Rheingold), placed numerous times at up to 1½m; dam, granddaughter of Gimcrack Stakes and Champagne Stakes winner Be Careful, won 5 times at up to 7.5f at 2 yrs in Italy and showed form over 6f at 3 yrs in England; justified favouritism in Group 3 Prix Eclipse at Saint-Cloud in October, coming through in final furlong without being touched with the whip to win by 1½ lengths from Silver Express; had previously won a newcomers race at Deauville in August by 4 lengths from Godille and fairly valuable 7-runner Prix de l'Obelisque at Longchamp in September comfortably by 1½ lengths from Tysfjsa; met her only defeat when 5/4 on for Group 3 Prix du Calvados at Deauville in August, finishing 5 lengths clear of third-placed Marie du Mont when failing by ¾ length to hold off fast-finishing Bernica; will stay 1m; acts on soft going and has yet to race on a firm surface; looks sure to develop into a leading 3-y-o filly. *O. Douieb, France.* **113** p

PHYLLIRA (FR) 2 b.f. Sea Break 129–Armoricana (Bel Baraka 120) (1980 7g 8fg) Apr 30; half-sister to 2 winners, including very useful French and Canadian 1¼m winner Adieu (by Tompion); dam smart French middle-distance winner; little worthwhile form in maiden races at Leicester in August and September. *P. Kelleway.* —

PHYLLISIA 4 b.f. Philip of Spain 126–Paladore (St Paddy 133) (1979 12v³ 11.7g 8s 5f 6fg 10fg⁴ 6fg 6d 1980 7fg 7f 8.3s 12g 8g) plain filly; poor plater; not certain to stay 1¼m; sometimes blinkered. *Dr A. Jones.* —

PIAFFER (USA) 5 b.h. Nijinsky 138–Strong Drink (Sound Track 132) (1979 8s* 7f⁴ 8f* 8g⁴ 8d* 1980 8f² 8f² 8f 8g*) strong, well-made, attractive ex- **113**

Mrs Peter E. Burrell's "Piaffer"

American horse; third foal; half-brother to Moss Pink (by Levmoss), placed over 5f at 3 yrs in Ireland; dam useful Irish 5f performer; raced only once at 2 and 3 yrs due to a broken bone in a knee; developed into a very useful handicapper; won Crocker Bulteel Handicap at Ascot in July for second time, beating Royaber by a neck with rest well behind; had run well when strong-finishing short-head second to Northleach in Playboy Bookmakers Newbury Spring Cup and third behind subsequently-disqualified House Guard and Blue Refrain in Ultramar Jubilee Stakes at Kempton (badly hampered); stayed 1m; acted on any going; game, genuine and consistent; was suited by waiting tactics; standing at Hart Hill Stud, Shaftesbury, fee £200 + £400 (October 1st terms). *H. Cecil.*

PIANOSO (FR) 3 b.g. Appiani II 128–Cosa Nostra (Bel Baraka 120) (1979 NR 1980 12g 11f) 35,000 francs Y (privately) (approx £4,200); powerful gelding; half-brother to winners in France, including successful jumper Hard Cash (by Hardicanute) and 4.5f to 10.7f winner Our Enchantment (by Luthier); dam, middle-distance maiden, is half-sister to French St Leger winner Vasco da Gama; in rear in Warren Stakes at Epsom and 22-runner maiden race at Newbury (moved poorly to post) in first part of season. *C. Austin.* —

PIBROCH LASS 3 br.f. Highland Melody 112–Quite Safe 74 (Quorum 126) (1979 5.3g 5f 5.3f 5g 5fg* 5fg^2 6f 5.3fg 5fg^4 1980 6fg 5.8f^4 5g 5.3d^4 5.3d^2 5fg 5.3fg 5d) compact, attractive filly; sprint handicapper; not certain to stay 6f; seems to act on any going; suitable mount for a claimer; ran moderately last 3 starts. *B. Wise.* **53**

PICASSO PAINT 3 ch.g. Shiny Tenth 120–Bernina (Prudent II 133) (1979 NR 1980 5f^3 6f 5h^3 7fg^3 8s 8.3g 6fg 6g 6g) small gelding; plater; stays 7f; possibly unsuited by soft going. *D. Marks.* —

PICKERING BROOK 3 ch.f. Royal Smoke 113–Bonny Legend 66 (Border Legend 119) (1979 NR 1980 11.7fg 8fg 8fg 10.8s 10.2fg) small, compact filly; half-sister to a winning stayer and a winner over hurdles; dam showed fair form over hurdles; little sign of ability in maiden races; dead. *D. Nicholson.* —

PICKET POST 3 ch.g. Supreme Red 93–Dracula's Daughter (Hook Money 124) (1979 5f 5g 6fg 1980 8d 10g) no sign of ability in maiden and minor events. *J. Old.* —

PICKLED 3 b.f. Pitcairn 126–Honeysuckle 96 (Darius 129) (1979 6g 6fg 1980 8s 10s^4 10.1g 10fg^2 10fg* 10f 10.2d) lightly-made filly; stayed on to win weakly-contested maiden race at Beverley in September; gives strong impression she'll get 1½m; probably acts on any going; sold 23,000 gns Newmarket December Sales. *M. Smyly.* **70**

PICKLED TINK 3 b.f. Tickled Pink 114–Brown Jockeen 75 (Jock Scot 121) (1979 NR 1980 8f 8fg 12d 10.8s) small filly; first reported foal by a thoroughbred sire; dam won over 1m; behind in maiden and minor races. *G. Price.* —

PICKMERE 3 b.g. No Mercy 126–Sugar Sweet 87 (Zucchero 133§) (1979 5s 5s 5g 6d^3 1980 8g 9.4g) big gelding; poor form, including in a seller; will stay 1¼m; blinkered final start in 1979. *G. Richards.* —

PICK O'THE CATCH 3 b.f. Laser Light 118–Jane Shaw (Galivanter 131) (1979 5g 5g^3 5fg 6fg^4 6g^3 6fg 5g 5d 1980 6fg^4 6h 8d 7g^2 7g 7g 8h^3 8g 8g 7g*) compact filly; good mover; plater; attracted no bid after winning at Brighton in October; stays 1m; suited by top-of-the-ground; has been tried in blinkers; pulled very hard on way to start eighth outing; has looked none too genuine on occasions. *M. McCourt.* **48**

PIECE OF LUNDY 5 b.h. Pieces of Eight 128–Word From Lundy 93 (Worden II 129) (1979 9g* 10.5d 1980 12f 16fg^4 16.1fg^3 16g 16.1d^4 14g **12fg**) ex-French horse; half-brother to Grundy; won minor event at Evry in 1979 when trained by F. Mathet (sold 22,000 gns at end of year); 3¾ lengths last of 4 finishers behind Pragmatic in Sagaro Stakes at Ascot in April; weakened final furlong, having gone clear 3f out, when 3 lengths third to Balinger in Lymm Stakes at Haydock following month; not disgraced on sixth start (had been off course for 2 months) but was well beaten on last; gives impression he finds 2m shade too far; probably acts on any going. *G. Harwood.* **102**

PIECE OF THE REALM 2 ch.f. Realm 129–Fall to Pieces 101 (Forli) (1980 6fg* 6f^3 7g) Feb 17; 12,500Y; first foal; dam won over 7f and 1m; favourite when winning 14-runner newcomers event at Chepstow in August in good style **80**

by 4 lengths from Still Free; creditable third, 1¼ lengths behind Scarrowmanwick, in 18-runner minor race at Lingfield the following month; stays 6f and may get further (had stiffish task when tried at 7f). *H. Candy.*

PIECES OF GOLD 3 b.f. Pieces of Eight 128–Reproach Me Not (Connaught 130) (1979 5v 5d* 5d^3 6d^4 8fg* 8f 1980 8v^2 8fg 12f 12d 12s^4 10fg 10fg 8g) fair, lightly-made sort; second in handicap at Salisbury in March; out of her depth on most other starts but wasn't disgraced when sixth to Bireme in Oaks on third outing or just over 6 lengths fifth of 7 to Vielle in Nassau Stakes at Goodwood in August on sixth; stays 1½m; acts on any going. *G. Beeson.* **102**

PIEL CANELA (SPA) 3 b.f. Sallust 134–Padella (St Paddy 133) (1979 NR 1980 7d^3 7.6f^4 8g^4 10fg 8fg) 7,200Y; strong filly; half-sister to winners in France and Spain; dam won over 7.5f and is sister to smart miler St Padarn; seems only plating class; should stay beyond 1m. *J. Winter.* **67**

PIENCOURT 2 br.c. Averof 123–French Bugle 71 (Bleep-Bleep 134) (1980 5d 5d^3 6s) Feb 11; half-brother to several winners, including French 3-y-o 7.5f winner Grand Wazir and sprinter Friendly Neighbour (both by Mansingh); dam won over 1m; 6½ lengths third of 17 to Corn Street in maiden race at Wolverhampton in October, best effort; should be suited by 6f. *D. Hanley.* **62+**

PIERCING NOTE 8 b.g. Bleep-Bleep 134–Brief Note 92 (Counsel 118) (1979 7g 5fg 6fg 6f^4 7g 1980 5fg^4 6h^2 6fg 6g 5fg 6g 5.8f) plater; ran in better company in 1980, best effort on second outing; stays 7f but has done all his winning over 6f; appears to act on any going; often blinkered; good mount for a boy. *N. Vigors.* **41**

PIERRE NOIR 2 br.c. Dragonara Palace 115–Ventrella (Wolver Hollow 126) (1980 5fg 5f 5f) June 6; 2,800Y; light-framed colt; towards rear in maiden races and a Catterick seller (co-favourite); sold 300 gns Ascot August Sales. *M. Blanshard.* **—**

PIETA 2 br.f. No Mercy 126–Mantua 80 (Ballyciptic 122) (1980 5d 6g* 6fg* 7fg) May 2; lightly-made filly; half-sister to 2 winners, including useful middle-distance performer Amber Town (by Amber Rama); dam stayer; won maiden race at Brighton and minor event at Epsom in August, latter very gamely by a head from Golden Bowl; ridden along throughout but wasn't disgraced when giving plenty of weight all round in £2,900 nursery at Catterick the following month, finishing about 7 lengths fifth of 13 to Stormy Jim; will probably stay 1m; acts on a firm surface. *M. Stoute.* **95**

PILLAR TO POST 2 b.f. Decoy Boy 129–Rose Red 95 (Ballymoss 136) (1980 5fg 5fg 5.8fg 5g*) Apr 22; small filly; half-sister to a winner in Italy by Swing Easy; dam won over 7f at 2 yrs and stayed well; favourite and dropped in class, attracted no bid after making all to win 6-runner seller at Folkestone in August easily by 5 lengths from Sparkler's Star; should stay 6f. *W. Wightman.* **67**

PILTON 2 ch.g. Record Token 128–Wordless 74 (Worden II 129) (1980 8g) Apr 28; 26,000Y; half-brother to several winners, including smart French 4-y-o Discretion (by Bold Lad, USA), successful at up to 10.5f; dam won over 1¼m and half-sister to good staying filly Sunny Cove; 33/1 and in need of the outing when behind in 17-runner minor event at Newmarket in October. *A. Hide.* **—**

PIMAR (DEN) 3 b.c. Pieces of Eight 128–Miss Mary (Bounteous 125) (1979 5s^4 6d 7f^3 7g 6fg 8.2g 8h^4 8.2g^3 8.2d 1980 10fg) lengthy, plain colt; quite a moderate maiden at his best; ran moderately only start at 3 yrs in May; will stay beyond 1¼m; probably acts on any going; usually blinkered. *G. Fletcher.* **—**

PIMETOR (AUS) 5 b.g. Agricultore 108–Golden Pine (Duccio) (1980 10d) Australian-bred gelding; seems of no account over hurdles; 33/1 when tailed off in minor event won by Handy Dancer at Brighton in June, first outing over here. *J. Powney.* **—**

PIMPERNELS TUNE 3 br.c. Blakeney 126–Melody Maid (Tudor Melody 129) (1979 NR 1980 9fg^2 12f) neat colt; brother to very smart middle-distance horse Norfolk Air and half-brother to a winner in Holland; dam unraced sister to useful 5f to 1½m winner Bugle Sound; showed ability in newcomers race at Wolverhampton (second to Claudius Secundus) and minor event at Kempton early in year; will be suited by long distances. *J. Bethell.* **73**

PIMPONT (FR) 3 b.c. Green Dancer 132–Panpryl (Bon Mot II 132) (1979 NR 1980 10g* 12f 8d^2 8g^3 8s 10fg^2) 260,000 francs Y (approx £30,900); third foal; half-brother to Providence (by Caracolero), successful twice at around 1¼m in France; dam very useful winner over 1m in France; drew clear to win 6-runner **106**

maiden race at Longchamp in May; placed in small races at Saint-Cloud, Evry and Deauville afterwards; never a factor when twenty-second in Derby on second outing; best at up to 1¼m; wears blinkers; sold 300,000 francs (approx £30,000) Vermeille Sale at Longchamp in September. *C. Milbank, France.*

PINCENTS 6 ch.g. Queen's Hussar 124–Piave (Alcide 136) (1979 11.7g⁴ 14g³ 13.1g* 13.1g* 14f 12.2g 1980 11.7fg 14fg² 13.1fg 17.1fg 14g 13.1h 14fg²) middle-distance handicapper; second at Salisbury in May (didn't have best of runs) and September; well suited by top-of-the-ground conditions; wears blinkers; goes well for S. Raymont; has won 5 times at Bath. *H. Blagrave.* **73**

PINE FIELD 3 ch.f. Murrayfield 119–Jacobean Spirit 76 (Ben Novus 109) (1979 NR 1980 11.7fg) second foal; dam won over 5f at 2 yrs; in rear in 18-runner maiden event at Bath in June. *D. Gandolfo.* —

PINEY LAKE 4 b.f. Sassafras 135–Cafe au Lait 97 (Espresso 122) (1979 11.7g 13fg 8.2d³ 8.3fg 10.1fg³ 10fg⁴ 1980 12d 12fg⁴ 16f 11.7fg 11.7g) well-made filly; poor maiden; should stay 1½m; acts on a firm and an easy surface; started very slowly first outing. *D. Marks.* —

PINGALONG 3 gr. or ro.f. The Go-Between 129–Intolerable Burden 91 (Palestine 133) (1979 5v 5s² 5s³ 5g 5fg³ 5h² 5g 1980 5s 5f 6fg 5g 5fg) light-framed filly; plater; best form at 5f; acts on any going; sold 460 gns Doncaster October Sales. *J. Hardy.* —

PINK BLUES 3 b.f. Tickled Pink 114–Rhythm 64 (Bleep-Bleep 134) (1979 5fg³ 5g* 6g* 6fg* 6f⁴ 6d* 6g³ 1980 7v 7f 6f² 6g 6fg 6s 6d 5s 6v) lightly-made non-thoroughbred filly; sprint handicapper; suited by 6f; appears to act on any going; has run well for a boy; didn't move to post too well but ran creditably third start. *F. Durr.* **91**

PINKERSUN 3 br.g. Tickled Pink 114–Sun Queen 76 (Lucky Sovereign) (1979 6g 6fg 7fg 1980 10.1s 6fg 6g 5g 6f⁴ 5d 6d 5s) light-framed, dipped-backed gelding; plating-class maiden; best run at 6f on firm going; blinkered sixth and seventh starts; sold 400 gns Newmarket Autumn Sales. *F. Durr.* —

PINKERTON'S MAN 4 br. or bl.c. Will Hays–Miss Pinkerton (Above Suspicion 127) (1979 8.2v⁴ 8s⁴ 7s 7d 7v 6g 10f 8d⁴ 1980 8d³ 7v 8f³ 8fg² 8d* 8d² 8d² 8g 8.2g³ 8d² 8g 8d 7f) neat, well-made colt; won handicap at Carlisle in June; ran moderately last 3 starts; stays 1m; acts on any going. *G. Richards.* **74**

PINK PRISM (USA) 2 b.f. Explodent–Bay of Persia 91 (Hafiz II 136) (1980 7d* 8d 8s) Mar 5; $60,000 2-y-o; workmanlike filly; half-sister to several winners, including minor stakes winner Shifty Gypsy (by Better Bee); dam 1¼m winner; won 12-runner newcomers race at Maisons-Laffitte in September by a length from Kazadancoa; subsequently put up bold shows in pattern races at Longchamp, finishing about 9½ lengths seventh of 11 to Recitation after showing up well below distance in Grand Criterium and 3 lengths sixth of 10 to Votre Altesse in Prix des Reservoirs; may stay 1¼m. *M. Zilber, France.* **107**

PINK TANK 7 b.h. Wolver Hollow 126–Pinks (Pink Flower) (1979 10s³ 11d* 11.7g* 10g* 12g² 11.1d³ 10f² 10.2fg* 10fg³ 10.7d* 11.7g* 11d 12fg* 12.5fg* 12f 12fg³ 12fg 1980 13s 12f 12fg 12fg 14f³ 12g 14g 12fg² 14fg 14fg³ 12.5g 12d 10.8d) middle-distance handicapper; useful performer in 1979 (won 8 times) but was rather disappointing in 1980; acts on any going but seems well suited by a sound surface; acts on any track; blinkered twice at 3 yrs; usually held up and has a good turn of foot; suitable mount for an apprentice; sometimes wears bandages. *M. Ryan.* **82**

PIORA 5 b.m. Winden 109–Pisces 115 (Polic 126) (1979 5g 7d 5f 5g 8fg 1980 8fg) sprint plater; sold 470 gns Ascot September Sales; dead. *D. Elsworth.* —

PIPERHILL 2 ch.c. Red God 128 §–Parthian Song (Parthia 132) (1980 5d* 6d* 6g*) Apr 3; 20,000Y; lightly-made colt; third foal; half-brother to a winner in Brazil by Royal and Regal; dam unraced half-sister to Porto Bello; ridden by apprentice N. Day when successful in minor events at Wolverhampton and Ripon in August and in £3,600 nursery at Doncaster the following month; impressive at Doncaster, making up ground in excellent style 2f out after a slowish start and drawing clear on bridle to win by 6 lengths from Sipestro; will stay 1m; yet to race on a firm surface; useful. *H. Cecil.* **106**

PIPES (USA) 3 ch.g. Singh–Milestrina 84 (Milesian 125) (1979 NR 1980 8fg 8fg 10fg) 11,500Y; small gelding; half-brother to 3 minor winners; dam, who stayed 7f, is half-sister to Matatina, Showdown, etc; behind in maiden and minor events in the North. *J. W. Watts.* —

Rous Nursery Handicap, Doncaster—third win in a row for Piperhill who wins in fine style and retains his unbeaten record

PIPING QUEEN 2 b.f. Tudor Music 131–Harambee 64 (Doutelle 128) (1980 5s 6g 6g 6g 8fg³ 7.2d² 8s² 8d* 10.2s) Mar 14; 3,000F, 5,600Y; compact filly; half-sister to several winners, including Irish 5f to 1½m winner Poquito (by Major Portion); dam won over 1¼m; second in good-class sellers prior to winning 13-runner nursery at Wolverhampton in October by 2 lengths from Beggar's Bush; will probably stay 1¼m (had stiffish task when tried over trip); seems to act on any going; blinkered fourth outing; consistent. *D. Morley.* **81**

PIPPERETTA 2 b.f. Tarboosh–Whistling Goddess (Yellow God 129) (1980 5g 5d³ 5fg² 5f* 5g 5fg 5g) Mar 25; 2,000F, 3,500Y; neat filly; first produce; dam won over 9f at 4 yrs in Ireland; fought back in good style to win 12-runner maiden race at Lingfield in August by a neck from Pariscene; not disgraced in valuable nursery sixth outing; should be suited by 6f+; seems to act on any going. *R. Smyth.* **81**

PIPPIN GILL 5 gr.m. Ribston 104–Gill Breeze (Farm Walk 111) (1979 9g³ 6v² 7fg 7.6f 6d 8.2g 1980 8v 5g 5g 6fg) plater; stays 7f; acts on any going; has run well for an amateur rider; ran moderately when tried in blinkers. *J. Wilson.* **–**

PIPUL 3 b.f. Pitskelly 122–Kay's Hour 93 (Bleep-Bleep 134) (1979 5d 5d 6g 7fg 6f⁴ 7d³ 8.2g* 8h³ 7fg 8.2fg 8g 1980 10s⁴ 10g 8f 10.6fg 8g 8d 10.4d 10fg 10d) tall, leggy unfurnished filly; modest performer (rated 82) at 2 yrs; showed no form in 1980, including in sellers; better suited by 1m than shorter distances but isn't bred to stay 1¼m; sometimes blinkered. *T. Fairhurst.* **–**

PITILESS PANTHER 3 b.f. No Mercy 126–Maltese Cat 58 (Pall Mall 132) (1979 5d⁴ 6s* 7.2fg³ 6g⁴ 6d 1980 7.3f³ 8.5f 8fg 7g 8.3g 7g) lengthy, lightly-made filly; good mover; creditable third to Parlour Game in handicap at Newbury in April; ran moderately afterwards; should stay 1m; acts on any going; blinkered final start; sold 37,000 gns Newmarket December Sales. *I. Balding.* **78**

PITLOCHRY 3 b.g. Pitcairn 126–Nicias 94 (Acropolis 132) (1979 7fg 7fg 8g⁴ 1980 10.8s 7fg 7s³ 8.3d 7f 12d⁴ 12d⁴) lengthy gelding; plating-class maiden; should stay middle distances; acts on soft going; ran moderately in blinkers on first, second and fifth starts; has run respectably for an apprentice. *S. Woodman.* **58**

PITMARIE 3 b.f. Pitskelly 122–Mary's Dream (Midsummer Night II 117) (1979 5g² 5g² 5g* 5f 5f* 5g⁴ 5f³ 5fg² 5d 1980 5fg 5fg* 5fg 5g 6f* 5g 6d) 1,000F; small, compact, full-quartered filly; half-sister to 1978 2-y-o 7f winner Mrs **108**

McNicholas (by Tudor Music); dam won over 1m in Ireland; winner of 2 good races at Phoenix Park, Stackallen Stakes in July and Herbertstown Stakes in August; beat Jasmine Star in both events, by a short head on first occasion and by 1½ lengths on second; 4½ lengths sixth to Valeriga in King George Stakes at Goodwood on third start; stays 6f; acts on firm going. *J. Bolger, Ireland.*

PITSBIRD 2 br.c. Pitskelly 122–Reelin Bridge (New Day) (1980 6fg 5g 6g 7f **57**
6fg^4 7fg) Feb 14; 7,800F, 22,000Y; lightly-made colt; half-brother to 3 winners by Jukebox, including very useful sprinter Reelin Jig; dam won over 1½m in Ireland; little better than plating class; stays 7f. *T. Gosling.*

PITSKELLY BLUES 3 b.f. Pitskelly 122–Hilltop Chimes (Mountain Call 125) **–**
(1979 NR 1980 7f 10fg 12g) 1,800F, 3,100Y; big, strong filly; first foal; dam poor Irish maiden; in rear in maiden races; unlikely to stay 1½m; sold 700 gns Newmarket July Sales. *B. Swift.*

PITSPOLLY 3 b. or br.f. Pitskelly 122–Talkative Polly 76 (Takawalk II 125) **60**
(1979 5f 1980 5fg 7fg 6fg* 7g^3) tall filly; plater; sold out of H. T. Jones's stable 950 gns after winning apprentice seller at Windsor in August; stays 7f; acts on a firm surface; moved poorly to post first start. *W. Musson.*

PIT STOP 4 b.g. Pitskelly 122–Mrs Moss 81 (Reform 132) (1979 5v 5s* 5v* 6v **–**
5d^2 5d* 5d^4 5s^2 5d* 5s^3 5fg^4 5fg^4 5fg 5f 5d 5g 1980 5g 5d 5g 5fg 5fg 5fg 5g) narrow, leggy gelding; best form at 5f but probably stays 6f; acts on any going, but is particularly well suited by soft; effective with or without blinkers; suitable mount for an apprentice. *W. Stubbs.*

PITSVILLE 4 b.c. Pitskelly 122–Villa Primavera (Primera 131) (1979 7v* 8v **95**
6f 9d^3 8fg 8g^3 8d 1980 9v* 10v 16.3d 7s^3 8g 10g 8s) attractive colt; won Burmah Castrol Trophy at Phoenix Park early in 1979 and Burmah Lincolnshire Trial Handicap on same course in March (well-backed favourite, beat Gambling Sam 1½ lengths); ran creditably in handicaps on fourth and fifth starts, notably when fifth of 24 behind I'm Ready under 10.0 in Irish Cambridgeshire at the Curragh in September; stays 9f (always well behind in amateur riders race when tried at 2m); acts on heavy going. *J. Bolger, Ireland.*

PITSYLVAN 2 b.f. Pitskelly 122–Hill Time (Hill Gail) (1980 7g 8.2s 8d) **–**
Apr 28; 4,100F, 8,200Y; half-sister to 3 winners, including 1¼m winner Larryr (by Capistrano); dam won over 6f at 2 yrs in Ireland; well beaten in maiden races in second half of season. *Sir Mark Prescott.*

PITTANCE 3 b. or br.f. Great Nephew 126–Sans le Sou (Vimy 132) (1979 NR **58**
1980 7f 8d 7g 8g 10.6d 10s) 25,000Y; lengthy filly; half-sister to numerous winners, notably top-class middle-distance horse Busted (by Crepello); dam Irish 9f winner; soundly beaten in maiden and minor races. *H. T. Jones.*

PITTENCRIEFF 5 ch.g. Manacle 123–Anatevka (Privy Councillor 125) (1979 **82**
11d 11g 10g^2 11g^2 11d^3 10s^2 12.2d* 1980 11fg^2 12f^4 10s^2 11d^2 11fg 10d^3 12g 10d 12d^4 12.2fg* 12g^2 12.2d^2 13.8d* 12d) workmanlike gelding; led inside final furlong when winning handicaps at Catterick in September and October, on latter occasion beating Field Day a short head; stays 1¾m; acts on any going; ran moderately when tried in blinkers. *E. Weymes.*

PITTI DONNA 2 ch.f. Hot Spark 126–Juvenescence 87 (Golden Horus 123) **62**
(1980 5f 6g 8d) Feb 8; 6,000F; third produce; half-sister to fair sprinter Sweet Zest (by Sweet Revenge); dam won over 5f at 2 yrs; poor form in maiden races. *C. Brittain.*

PLACE IN THE SUN 3 ch.f. Sun Prince 128–Place to Place (No Robbery) **48**
(1979 5fg 5.8g 7g 1980 7d 7f 7fg 8d 8g^2 8g 7g 8h 6g 7g) small, fair sort; poor mover; plater; stays 1m; has worn blinkers; sometimes sweats up. *P. M. Taylor.*

PLAGE (FR) 3 b.f. Sir Gaylord–Gone With The Wind (Snob 130) (1979 NR **–**
1980 7f 7fg^3 8g 8fg 11.7g 8g^4 11.5g 8.2g) 200,000 francs Y (approx. £23,800); lightly-made filly; second foal; dam won twice at around 1½m in France; in frame in maiden and minor races but is only plating class; best at up to 1m; yet to race on a soft surface; ran badly seventh start; sold 15,000 gns Newmarket December Sales. *R. Sheather.*

PLAIN STALKER 2 b.f. Warpath 113–Painter's Bay (Monet 127) (1980 8.2d **53**
8fg 8.2s^2 10d 8.2s) May 2; compact filly; eighth reported foal; dam, placed over 1m here, won in Scandinavia; plater; ran best race when 2¾ lengths second of 13 to Audit at Hamilton in September; ran badly over 1¼m; suited by soft going; blinkered second and fifth starts; sold to Mrs G. Forbes 1,200 gns Doncaster November Sales. *K. Stone.*

PLAINT 3 b.f. Weepers Boy 124–Twite (Chanteur II 135) (1979 5fg 1980 5h 7g) bad plater. *C. James.* —

PLAIN TREE 3 br.f. Wolver Hollow 126–Diagonale II (Ribot 142) (1979 NR 1980 6f^{3} 8f 8d^{4} 7fg* 7f) lengthy filly; half-sister to several winners, including good French stayer Djakao (by Tanerko); dam useful middle-distance filly and half-sister to Shantung; beat Groovy Girl 3 lengths in 12-runner maiden race at Chepstow in July; bred to stay 1½m; probably acts on any going; blinkered last 2 starts: doesn't always impress in paddock. *P. Walwyn.* **71**

PLANTAGENET 4 b.g. English Prince 129–Paddyflower 88 (St Paddy 133) (1979 11d^{2} 12s 12g^{2} 1980 10fg 12d^{3} 12.3d^{4} 12.2f^{4} 12fg) quite a moderate maiden; stays 1½m; blinkered penultimate start (found little off bridle); suited by some give in the ground. *J. Mason.* —

PLASTIC CUP 6 b.g. Jukebox 120–Miss Melanie (Hard Ridden 131) (1979 NR 1980 7fg 7fg^{3}) winning jumper; has been fired; third in seller at Edinburgh in July, best effort on flat. *H. O'Neill.* **42**

PLATINUM GIRL 3 b. or gr.f. Rugantino 97–Santina 67 (Sanctum 116) (1979 NR 1980 6f 6f 7.6f 8d 6s) big filly; well beaten in varied company, including selling. *G. Balding.* —

PLATTS PIECE 3 b.f. Super Slip 86–Crisp Star (Star Moss 122) (1979 7g 7fg 7g 8fg 1980 12g 8g 12f 11.7h 10fg 12fg^{3}) sturdy, fair sort; poor maiden; may stay beyond 1½m. *P. M. Taylor.* **50**

PLAYBOY BUNNY 2 b.f. African Sky 124–Spa Track (Track Spare 125) (1980 5f 6fg 6s 6f) May 2; 9,000Y; leggy filly; first foal; dam placed over 5f at 3 yrs in Ireland; soundly beaten in maiden races. *F. Durr.* —

PLAYBOY CASINO 3 b.c. Thatch 136–Miss Slip 107 (Coursing) (1979 NR 1980 8g 8fg 5f) 24,000F, 15,000Y; lengthy colt; second foal; dam won Molecomb Stakes; poor form in maiden and minor events; pulled up lame final start; sold 400 gns Newmarket Autumn Sales. *F. Durr.* —

PLAYBOY JUBILEE 3 b.c. Connaught 130–Paphos 99 (Vilmorin) (1979 6fg^{3} 6fg^{3} 7g 1980 10fg^{3} 10.4f* 10.6fg^{2} 10d 10.5d) good-looking, rangy colt; ridden by 3-lb claimer unable to claim his allowance, put up a useful performance when quickening well to lead 1f out and beat Prince Bee ¾ length in 9-runner Dee Stakes at Chester in May; creditable 2½ lengths second to Stanislavsky in valuable handicap at Haydock following month; well beaten in Prince of Wales's Stakes at Royal Ascot and Benson and Hedges Gold Cup at York subsequently; stays 1¼m well; acts well on firm ground. *F. Durr.* **102**

PLAYFUL PADDY 4 br.g. St Paddy 133–Toccata (Kythnos 126) (1979 8fg 8fg 8.2g 1980 10fg* 11.7fg^{2} 10g 10g 10g* 8fg 10f* 10g^{4} 10.2d) middle-distance performer; won minor event at Leicester (comfortably) and handicaps at Nottingham and Beverley; looked tremendously well when beating Be My Sweet by ¾ length on last-named course in August; acts on firm going (well beaten first outing on softish ground). *J. Bethell.* **60**

PLAY ME 2 b. or br.f. Murrayfield 119–Dinamarsh (Nelcius 133) (1980 5s 5fg 5g 5f 5d) Feb 17; fair sort; second foal; dam probably of no account; only poor form, including in a valuable seller. *D. Leslie.* —

PLAY WITH FIRE 3 ch.c. Gay Fandango 132–High Density 66 (Pall Mall 132) (1979 NR 1980 6s 8fg 8fg^{4}) 4,700F, 4,400Y; strong, well-made colt; first foal; dam won 1m seller; little worthwhile form in maiden races; gives impression he'll be suited by 1¼m. *L. Cumani.* **54**

PLAZA SUITE 4 b.c. Tudor Melody 129–Casual (Solar Slipper 131) (1979 6s 10.1g 10s 10.2fg 12fg^{2} 15.5fg* 16fg^{3} 18.1g^{2} 16f^{3} 16fg 16s 1980 15fg 18f 18.1g) quite a useful-looking colt; good mover; quite a moderate handicapper; bandaged and having first outing for nearly 5 months when running badly on final outing; stays well; best form on a sound surface; suitable mount for an amateur rider. *A. Davison.* —

PLEDGE 7 br.g. Rarity 129–Boucle 86 (Princely Gift 137) (1979 11.1v^{4} 12.2s* 12s 11.7g 12s^{3} 10.2fg* 10.5g 11s 12d 1980 12.2v 12.2s 8fg 8fg 10s 11.7s 8g^{2} 11.7g 10s^{4} 13.1h 12f 10.2g) quite a moderate handicapper nowadays; seems to stay 1¾m; appears to act on any going but is possibly best with some give in the ground; below his best when tried in blinkers; good mount for an apprentice; often makes the running; well beaten last 3 starts. *H. Candy.* **60**

PLENTY SPIRIT 7 ch.h. Jimmy Reppin 131–Holiday Spirit 99 (Live Spirit 121) (1979 12g 1980 12fg 12g4 12g 12g) one-time useful handicapper; tailed off last 2 outings; seems to stay 15f; unsuited by soft ground but acts on any other; wears bandages nowadays. *K. Stapleton.* —

PLUM LANE 2 br.c. Thatch 136–Plum Fool (Silly Season 127) (1980 5fg3 5.2fg* 6d 6g) Apr 27; 36,000Y; big, workmanlike colt; good mover; second foal; dam half-sister to top-class French 1969 2-y-o Breton; produced a fine turn of foot when winning 4-runner minor event at Bath in June by 4 lengths from Violino Fandango; also ran well in nursery on final start; will stay 1m; acts on a firm surface. *I. Balding.* **91**

POACHERS PINE 5 ch.g. Knotty Pine 113–Deirdre (Vimy 132) (1979 NR 1980 12f 16fg) won maiden race at 3 yrs; well beaten in 1980; stays well; acts on a firm surface; wears bandages. *R. Whitaker.* —

PODZOLA 4 b.f. Royal Prerogative 119–Sharivari 81 (Hugh Lupus 132) (1979 10g 8.2s 8f 8fg 8f2 8.2f4 7f 7g 10.6g 1980 8v*) won minor event at Ayr in March on only outing of 1980; stays 1m well (below form at 1¼m); acts on any going; blinkered eighth start and refused to enter stalls once at 3 yrs. *M. W. Easterby.* **48**

POETIC SMILE 4 ch.f. Calpurnius 122–Teersaway 74 (Weepers Boy 124) (1979 5f 1980 10fg 7fg3 8g 7.6g 7fg 8.3fg 8g 8.2s 8d 6s 6g) plater; stays 1m; wears bandages nowadays. *C. Wildman.* —

POINT NORTH 2 b. or br.c. Lorenzaccio 130–Off Scent 92 (Faberge II 121) (1980 7g 7d 8.2g 8.2s 7v) Apr 16; strong colt; third foal; half-brother to 1979 2-y-o winner What-A-Case (by Upper Case); dam stayed 11f; quite moderate form in varied company; will probably stay 1¼m. *W. H. H. Williams.* **73**

POLAR CALL 3 ch.f. Northfields–Anxious Call (Whistler 129) (1979 7s 1980 9g) good-topped filly; in rear in maiden races. *Sir Mark Prescott.* —

POLCUTA 3 b.f. John Splendid 116–Miss Merida 64 (Midsummer Night II 117) (1979 5d 1980 10fg 12fg 10.1f4 7f) quite well-made filly; well behind in varied company, including selling; not certain to stay 1¼m. *R. Atkins.* —

POLDHU 2 b.c. Manado 130–First Bleep (Bleep-Bleep 134) (1980 5fg2 6f* 6g3 6d* 6g3 6fg3 6f3) Mar 31; 5,800Y; lengthy, lightly-made colt; second living foal; dam Irish 2-y-o 5f winner; came through smoothly to win quite valuable races at Epsom in June and Newbury in August, in latter (4-runner Washington Singer Stakes) needing only to be hand ridden to score by 2 lengths from Pellegrini; subsequently ran well to be third in Gimcrack Stakes at York (beaten 1½ lengths by Bel Bolide but would have gone close had he not had to be checked 1f out), Mill Reef Stakes at Newbury (3½ lengths behind Sweet Monday) and William Hill **114**

Washington Singer Stakes, Newbury—Poldhu is a comfortable winner from Pellegrini

Prix du Jockey-Club, Chantilly—another classic for Willie Carson who drives Policeman clear of Shakapour

Middle Park Stakes at Newmarket (again had none too good a run when 2½ lengths behind Mattaboy); stays 6f well; seems to act on any going; usually held up; consistent. *M. Jarvis.*

POLES APART 3 ch.c. Northfields–Coquette (St Paddy 133) (1979 6s 6fg^4 77
6fg^2 1980 8fg^4 8fg* 8fg 8g^4 8g^2 7f* 7.2d^4 7g^3 7g) lengthy, unfurnished colt; successful in maiden race at Stockton in June (trotted up from Tudor Claire) and handicap at Thirsk in August (held off Last Device by a short head); should stay middle distances; goes well on firm going; good mount for a boy; ran poorly third start; sent to Italy. *H. Cecil.*

POLICEMAN (FR) 3 b.c. Riverman 131–Indianapolis (Barbare II 128) (1979 124
NR 1980 8.5g 8g* 10g^3 10g* 10g^4 9.7g^3 9g^3 12fg* 12.5d^3 12f 12f)

Policeman was a surprise winner from a weak field in the Prix du Jockey-Club, the French Derby, at Chantilly in June. He started the 54/1-outsider of fourteen, having done barely enough in seven outings as a three-year-old to earn a place in the line-up for such an important race. Policeman had begun his career at the end of the winter at Cagnes-sur-Mer, winning the second and fourth of his four races for minor prize-money there. Returned north when the Parisian flat season opened, he ran three times on the major tracks without a win; he was placed in two of the lesser classic trials, the Prix de Guiche at Longchamp (behind Shakapour) and the Prix Matchem at Evry (behind Axius), beaten around two lengths on each occasion.

Policeman won the Prix du Jockey-Club on merit, decisively, by one and a half lengths from Shakapour; the third horse Providential was beaten a further three lengths, and the Irish-trained favourite Gonzales finished only fifth. The best horse in the race, Argument, ran unaccountably moderately and came in nearly last. There seem to be two very good reasons why Policeman showed considerably improved form: number one, he was running over a mile and a half for the first time (a very strongly-run mile and a half as it turned out); number two, he was ridden for the first time by Carson, who rode him very enterprisingly indeed. Carson, fresh from his wins in the Derby and Oaks, came in as a replacement for Cauthen who was originally offered the mount. Policeman's previous riders had been Doleuze (now on the stable-companion Dom Aldo) and Badel. Carson had Policeman in the first three behind Tom's Serenade's pacemaker Hybrid, decided to press on six furlongs out and then, in his own words, 'waited for the others to attack'. No really substantial challenge materialized. The others appeared to appreciate the threat of the leader, rank outsider though he was; they just couldn't do much about it the way Policeman kept going up the straight. Shakapour came out of the pack as if he meant business with approaching two furlongs left, but almost as soon as he got within two lengths he ran out of steam and the winner never looked like being beaten in the last furlong. Policeman, had he not been qualified for the owner's premium of 50% of the first prize and breeder's premium of 25%, would have earned significantly less for his victory than Henbit's at Epsom (£93,264 against £166,820). Five years ago the French Derby was worth a minimum £141,183 to the winner compared with Epsom's £106,465: a sign of the times?

Policeman only once reproduced his form in three outings. That was next time out when Carson finished third on him in the more competitive Grand Prix de Saint-Cloud in July, beaten three lengths by the dead-heaters Dunette and Shakapour. Although Shakapour turned the tables, Policeman gave a thoroughly satisfactory account of himself, taking the lead six furlongs out once again and defying the others to catch him. An excellent race ensued in the straight, in the course of which Dunette and Shakapour gradually wore him down. Policeman's trainer regretted not having a pacemaker to call on for the Grand Prix, but judging by the good time for the race he need have no regrets on that score. Policeman then had a rest until the autumn in preparation for the Prix de l'Arc de Triomphe. As Carson wasn't available Saint-Martin rode him in the Prix Niel, and when Saint-Martin switched to Aryenne in the Arc the horse acquired his fifth jockey of the season, Dubroeucq. Saint-Martin's tactics in the Niel were puzzling, for he seemed content to ride a waiting race, the upshot being that he never got in a blow and finished last of nine to Prince Bee, beaten about four lengths. The more-enterprising Dubroeucq hit the front halfway down the hill in the Arc, only to be swallowed up quickly after Ela-Mana-Mou went by; Policeman beat only four home eventually, finishing alongside Mrs Penny.

Policeman was retired after the Arc and has followed his sire to the United States. Report has it that he was syndicated for 4.4 million dollars and will stand at a nomination fee of 25,000 dollars, at Clermont Farm, Germantown, New York State. The last French Derby winner to be retired to the States, Youth, is 40,000 dollars a nomination in 1981; Riverman is 50,000 dollars + 50,000 dollars.

Policeman (Fr) (b.c. 1977)	Riverman (b 1969)	Never Bend (b 1960)	Nasrullah
			Lalun
		River Lady (b 1963)	Prince John
			Nile Lily
	Indianapolis (ch 1969)	Barbare II (b 1963)	Sicambre
			Barbara
		Iberide (ch 1962)	Charlottesville
			Candytuft

Policeman comes from one of the National Stud's old-established families. His great grandam Candytuft was a half-sister to Big Game; she won over sprint distances as a two-year-old at Brighton and Birmingham. His grandam, exported to France as a yearling, won three middle-distance races in the Provinces there but she would have been a failure at stud without Indianapolis, a lightly-raced and modest maiden sired by the 1966 French Two Thousand Guineas runner-up Barbare II. Policeman's owner bought Indianapolis carrying Police-

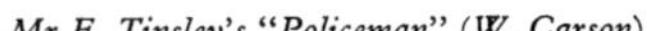

Mr F. Tinsley's "Policeman" (W. Carson)

man for 55,000 francs at the Deauville Sales. Neither of her two foals of racing age had achieved anything at that time; subsequently her second, Iverny (by Satingo), won small races in the States. The foal she produced the year of her sale, Fleur de Pierre (by Lyphard), won twice over a mile in France in 1979.

Policeman is a lengthy, good sort of colt. He was clearly well suited by a strongly-run race at a mile and a half, and also by strong, enterprising jockeyship. Very firm ground might have been against him, though he won on good to firm at Chantilly. *C. Milbank, France.*

POLISH PRIDE (FR) 3 b.f. Amen–Orendona (Palestine 133) (1979 5s 5s 5fg 5.1g 5.8g 7g 8g 10s 8d 1980 7.2fg 6fg 5g⁴ 6g 6fg) neat filly; plater; best run at 5f; blinkered final 2 outings in 1979. *A. Jarvis.* —

POLISTEPPIN 2 ch.f. Jimmy Reppin 131–Polistina 106 (Acropolis 132) (1980 6g 5.8h 6d) June 6; 1,700F, 5,600Y; smallish filly; half-sister to fairly useful 1974 2-y-o 6f winner Creptina (by Crepello) and a winner in USA; dam stayed 7f; fifth in maiden races at Bath and Newmarket on last 2 starts; beaten 10¾ lengths by Gabitat in 17-runner event on latter course in October; will stay 1m. *G. Beeson.* **63**

POLLARDSTOWN 5 b.g. Lord Gayle 124–Mear-Aille (Hard Ridden 131) (1979 10.6s* 1980 18.4f² 20d 16d 12fg 14g) high-class performer over hurdles; has plenty of ability on flat too and ran an excellent race when 1½ lengths second to Arapahos in Ladbroke Chester Cup (Handicap) in May, making running till headed in final furlong and keeping on well; remote fifth to Mon's Beau in Coral Northumberland Plate at Newcastle in June on third outing, probably best subsequent effort; effective at middle distances and stays well; acts on any going; suitable mount for an apprentice; tough and genuine; usually wears blinkers, but didn't on last two starts. *S. Mellor.* **96**

POLLIFORM 3 b.g. Reform 132–Pollinella 108 (Charlottown 127) (1979 5s⁴ 5d⁴ 5g 1980 7fg⁴ 8f 8.2f 6f 12h 11fg⁴ 11g² 9f 12g 12d 11fg² 12fg³ 11g³ 13d 11d³ 12.3s² 10g³ 12.3g 11d³ 12d³) neat, attractive gelding; placed in varied company; stays 1½m; probably acts on any going; has run creditably for a claimer; doesn't always impress in paddock. *H. Bell.* **57**

POLLY QUINN 2 gr.f. Birdbrook 110–Roman Dawn 87 (Neron 121) (1980 6g 6fg 7g 8fg) May 10; 1,800Y; sister to 6f winner Sweet As A Nut and half-sister to a winner; dam won at up to 1¼m; in rear in sellers, twice starting none too well. *D. Garraton.* —

POLLY ROYAL 2 ch.f. Music Boy 124–Royal Tactic 62 (Right Tack 131) (1980 5d² 5.8h³ 5fg 5g³ 5s) May 5; 2,800Y; neat filly; first foal; dam third once over 1m; placed in maiden and minor events, best effort when finishing head behind Piperhill at Wolverhampton in August on debut; should stay 6f; best form on an easy surface; lacks scope and may not train on. *G. Huffer.* **75**

POLLY'S BROTHER 2 ch.c. Roi Soleil 125–Polairia 66 (Polic 126) (1980 6g 6s) May 26; strong, compact colt; brother to 3-y-o Polly Soleil, and half-brother to several other winners; dam, successful selling handicapper at 7f, stayed 1¼m; showed a little ability in large fields for maiden races at Newmarket and Doncaster late in season; will stay 1m. *B. Hills.* **70**

POLLY SOLEIL 3 br.f. Roi Soleil 125–Polairia 66 (Polic 126) (1979 NR 1980 8g 8.2g 8.2s³ 8s 10g² 10d*) lengthy filly; half-sister to several winners, including speedy Avon Valley (by Galivanter); dam, winning plater, stayed 1¼m; won minor event at Stockton in November; suited by 1¼m; acts well on soft ground; has run creditably for an apprentice. *B. Hills.* **72**

POLLY WOLLY DOODLE 3 br.f. Warpath 113–Bolton Girl 87 (Blue Lightning 114) (1979 NR 1980 10.2g 10g) lightly-made filly; half-sister to very smart sprinter Polly Peachum (by Singing Strand) and to a winner in Austria; dam won at up to 1½m; well beaten in maiden races at Doncaster and Ayr in the summer. *C. Thornton.* —

POLWICK 3 b.g. Red Alert 127–Gay Sylvia (Sayajirao 132) (1979 5g⁴ 5g 1980 9g 7fg⁴ 6fg 6fg 7g* 7f⁴ 7g 7g 8g) well-made gelding; dropped in class when making virtually all to win valuable seller at Newmarket in June (bought in 3,200 gns); best form at 7f; sometimes blinkered; sold 3,600 gns Newmarket Autumn Sales. *J. Hindley.* **60**

POLYGON 4 b.f. Tarboosh–Polar Polly 88 (Arctic Storm 134) (1979 9v 11d 8s 7f 1980 17.1fg 11.7f) narrow filly; poor form in varied company, including handicap; blinkered second and third starts at 3 yrs; winner over hurdles; sold, covered by Kala Shikari, 1,500 gns Newmarket December Sales. *N. Gaselee.* —

POM POES (DEN) 3 ch.f. Belmont–Wilhelmina (Pall Mall 132) (1979 including 6g* 6.5g* 5.5g* 7g* 6g* 8d^{2} 1980 8fg^{3} 8fg 8fg 5s 9.2f) approx £2,900Y; small, unimpressive-looking filly; an outstanding performer in Denmark and Sweden in 1979, winning all her 7 races; proved herself well up to international competition when failing by 1½ lengths to hold off Aryenne in Criterium des Pouliches at Longchamp on final outing; 2¾ lengths third to same filly in Prix de la Grotte at Longchamp in April, best effort at 3 yrs, though wasn't disgraced when fifth to Hortensia in Group 2 Prix de l'Opera at Longchamp on final outing in October; well-beaten thirteenth of 23 to Quick As Lightning in 1,000 Guineas at Newmarket on second start; needs further than 5f and stays 9f well; probably acts on any going; sold for a figure rumoured to be around £135,000 after Criterium des Pouliches; sent to USA. *M. Saliba, France.* **112**

POMPOSITY 3 ch.g. Pompous 118–Brave Heart 90 (Never Give In 97) (1979 5s^{3} 5f 6d^{3} 7fg 8.2g 8.2fg 1980 10s 10g 10fg) tall, leggy gelding; has shown little form since third start at 2 yrs; should stay at least 1m; seems to need a soft surface. *J. Hardy.* —

PONCHIELLI 2 b.c. Pitskelly 122–Pennycress 99 (Florescence 120) (1980 6g 6d^{4} 6g 6d* 6s^{2} 6d^{4} 6s) Mar 4; 10,500Y; smallish, sturdy colt; third living foal; half-brother to a winning plater; dam won twice over 5f at 2 yrs; well-backed second favourite, showed much improved form when winning 16-runner nursery at Haydock in September, bursting into lead 2f out and being ridden clear to score by 6 lengths from Fee; in frame in 2 more nurseries subsequently, running well when just over a length fourth of 17 to Mrs Palmer at Haydock in October; not sure to stay beyond 6f; yet to race on a firm surface; ran moderately final start. *R. Armstrong.* **94**

PONGO PONGO 3 b.g. African Sky 124–Sniff 81 (Espresso 122) (1979 6fg 8d 1980 12fg^{4} 12.5h 13.8fg 13s) rangy gelding; slow maiden; blinkered third start; sold 500 gns Ascot November Sales. *J. W. Watts.* —

PONTET 2 b.f. Ballynockan 112–Cissac (Indian Ruler 89) (1980 5s 5s 5g 6s 7g 6g 8fg) Apr 27; neat filly; half-sister to 5f winner Tou Fou (by Royben); no sign of ability, including in a seller; blinkered sixth outing. *D. Ancil.* —

PONTIN LAD 2 br.g. Mansingh 120–Mildura 98 (Vilmorin) (1980 5f* 5f* 5g^{3} 5.1g^{2}) Mar 19; 11,000Y; neat, strong, attractive gelding; good mover; half-brother to fairly useful sprinters Gourmet (by Grey Sovereign) and Gauleiter (by Mummy's Pet); dam 5f sprinter; never came off bridle when making all to win minor event at Lingfield in May and had more in hand than length margin over Remouleur suggests when winning 5-runner Great Surrey Stakes at Epsom the following month; unfortunately seemed to go the wrong way temperamentally, unseating jockey on way to start of Norfolk Stakes at Royal Ascot in June and having to be led to start after unseating rider several times, and plunging through paddock rails, at Yarmouth the following month; still managed to finish 3 lengths third to Chummy's Special at Royal Ascot and 3 lengths runner-up to I'll See You at Yarmouth; unlikely to stay beyond 5f; yet to race on a soft surface; gelded after final outing. *H. T. Jones.* **96**

PONTOON 2 b.g. Grey Mirage 128–Penview 73 (Pendragon) (1980 6g 7.2d) Feb 23; compact gelding; half-brother to winning stayer Penwood (by Precipice Wood); dam, a stayer, won on flat and over hurdles; last in £2,000 event at Leicester in August (unseated rider on way to start) and 19-runner maiden race at Haydock in September. *N. Hall.* —

PONTYLAY 6 b.g. Pontifex (USA)–Lay Lady Lay (Celtic Ash) (1979 NR 1980 11.7g 12g 15.5f) of little account; blinkered once; bandaged on first outing. *J. O'Donoghue.* —

POOLE BAY 4 ch.g. Rugantino 97–Poole Park 83 (Fairey Fulmar 124) (1979 8s^{4} 12s^{4} 11.7fg 10.1g^{4} 8g 11.1fg 12f^{4} 1980 11.7fg 10g 12fg 16.9d 8g) strong, good-bodied gelding; plating-class maiden; stays 1½m; probably acts on any going; blinkered first 2 outings. *J. Cann.* —

POP A LONG (USA) 6 b.h. Baldric II 131–Popkins 120 (Romulus 129) (1979 11.1d 9fg^{2} 1980 8fg 6g 8s) poor handicapper; stays 1¼m; often wears bandages; blinkered second outing in 1978; apprentice ridden. *H. Wragg.* —

POPAWAY 3 b.f. Run The Gantlet–Feather Bed 111 (Gratitude 130) (1979 NR 1980 10g 12g^{4} 12d^{3} 12f* 12f* 18d^{2}) big, strong filly; half-sister to several winners, including smart middle-distance filly Cheveley Princess (by Busted); dam second in Irish 1,000 Guineas; successful in maiden race at Ripon in August and minor event at Pontefract in September; improved on those efforts when **102**

good 2½ lengths second to Popsi's Joy in Tote Cesarewitch Handicap at Newmarket in October, leading 3f out and keeping on well; suited by a test of stamina; probably acts on any going; ridden by 5-lb claimer at Newmarket; sold 43,000 gns Newmarket December Sales and reportedly visits Kris in 1981. *H. Wragg.*

POP IN ZIPPER 3 b.c. Pompous 118–Zip Flip (Bleep-Bleep 134) (1979 NR 1980 7.6f 5g 8g 5g 5s 6g) leggy colt; little sign of ability in varied company, including selling; blinkered last 2 starts, sweating up badly on latter. *W. Charles.* —

POPPIN GILL 4 gr.f. Most Secret 119–Gill Breeze (Farm Walk 111) (1979 6s 6s 6f* 5f3 6fg 5d 6d2 6d 7s 1980 5v 6f 7g 8fg4 8.2d 7d) neat, strong filly; well beaten in 1980, including in sellers last 2 outings; stays 6f; seems to act on any going; blinkered occasionally at 3 yrs; sold 520 gns Doncaster October Sales. *Miss S. Hall.* —

POPSI'S JOY 5 b.g. Hill Clown–Popsie's Pride (Border Legend 119) (1979 14d* 14g* 14f* 14v 16fg4 16.9fg 16.5g4 14f3 14f 16d3 14g* 1980 14f 14fg* 16fg 16f* 16fg* 16g* 16g3 14g* 16.1fg2 14g3 14g* 18d* 14g*) **110**

Hats off to Popsi's Joy! What a magnificent season he enjoyed, winning eight races worth more than £44,000—an outstanding return by a handicapper —and improving by upwards of two stones on the best of his 1979 form. For a horse that as a three-year-old was close to death after contracting tetanus, his achievements are remarkable.

Without doubt winning the Tote Cesarewitch at Newmarket in October on his twelfth outing was the highlight of Popsi's Joy's campaign. At £26,677 the Cesarewitch was the most valuable handicap of the season, and for that race and the Coral Northumberland Plate at Newcastle the Jockey Club opened the entry to all-comers instead of sticking to the previous year's damaging and futile minimum qualifying rating of 35. As a result the race attracted eighty entries, seventeen more than the year before, of which twenty-seven went to post including a sizeable number who wouldn't have qualified in 1979. The new conditions made for a much more interesting race, although the closing stages were dominated by just two horses Popaway and Popsi's Joy. Popsi's Joy was settled at the back early on as the field went a good gallop from the outset. A mile from home he steadily began to improve his position and three furlongs out, where Popaway kicked on, it could be seen he was going particularly well. Running down into the Dip, Piggott, who has struck up a fine partnership with the horse, asked Popsi's Joy to quicken and quicken he did, passing Popaway up the hill to win comfortably by two and a half lengths. The performances of Popaway (originally handicapped at 6-9), fifth-placed Migelitto (6-12) and the sixth horse, Morgan's Pearl (6-4), were good enough in themselves to justify the shelving of this silly idea of having a qualifying rating for the race. Furthermore, the large field that the Cesarewitch produced made it a very popular race with the punters: William Hill reported that they took twice as many bets as they did on what looked an open and competitive race for the Champion Stakes thirty-five minutes earlier.

Two weeks later Popsi's Joy ended his season with an equally smooth performance on the same course in the Haddenham Handicap, beating Morgan's

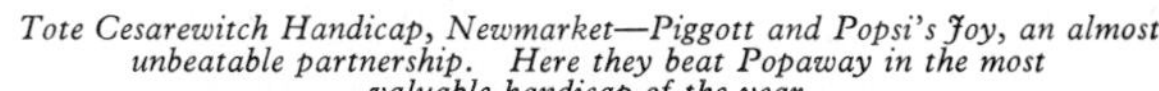

Tote Cesarewitch Handicap, Newmarket—Piggott and Popsi's Joy, an almost unbeatable partnership. Here they beat Popaway in the most valuable handicap of the year

Pearl by a length. His wins at Newmarket followed four at Sandown and one each at Lingfield and Ascot; creditable performances in defeat included a third to Shaftesbury in the Tote-Ebor at York.

Popsi's Joy (b.g. 1975)	Hill Clown (b 1963)	Hillary (br 1952)	Khaled Snow Bunny
		Mary Machree (b 1951)	Moonlight Run Jessie-O-Doon
	Popsie's Pride (b 1965)	Border Legend (b 1948)	King Legend Sweet Repose
		Miss Popsi-Wopsi (ch 1952)	Nomellini Shell Transit

Popsi's Joy, who impressed in the paddock on almost every occasion we saw him, was bred by his owner Mr Victor Morley Lawson, who also owned the 1974 Cesarewitch winner Ocean King. Popsi's Joy is the fourth foal produced by the unraced Popsie's Pride, a daughter of a useful staying chaser called Miss Popsi-Wopsi. Popsi's Poppet, a full sister to Popsi's Joy, won twice over two miles as a three-year-old in 1976. Hill Clown, their sire, was a tough and very useful winner in the States at up to a mile and a half; his best winner before Popsi's Joy was May Hill, who took the Yorkshire Oaks and the Park Hill Stakes in 1975. Popsi's Joy, who is invariably held up, stays extremely well and acts on any going except, possibly, very soft. He possesses a useful turn of foot and, added to that, is most genuine and consistent. *M. Haynes.*

PORKERS 2 ch.c. Porto Bello 118–Diamond Wedding (Never Say Die 137) **62**
(1980 5fg 6s 6g 5g 6fg^2) May 14; 2,400Y; half-brother to Tudor Jewel (by Henry the Seventh), a winner at up to 9f; dam unraced half-sister to Major Portion; plater; showed first worthwhile form when 1½ lengths second of 28 to Tricky Rhythm at Windsor in September; will stay 1m; acts on a firm surface. *T. M. Jones.*

PORTAL PRINCE 6 b.g. Crowned Prince 128–Torrefranca (Sicambre 135) **45**
(1979 10v 11d^2 8f* 10f 8g 10f 8fg 10f^3 1980 9fg 8.2fg 10f^4 8fg^3) big gelding; plater; stays 11f; appears to act on any going; front runner; often bandaged in front; withdrawn fourth intended outing after giving lot of trouble in preliminaries and stewards subsequently declared that they didn't consider the horse a suitable mount for an apprentice; sold 670 gns Doncaster August Sales. *J. Bingham.*

PORT ARANSAS (USA) 3 gr.f. Quack–Colombe (Grey Dawn II 132) (1979 **80**
NR 1980 10v^2 12f^2 12fg 16s 12g^2 15.5g* 15.5f* 14g* 16.1s 14g^4 14g) big, strong filly; good mover; third foal; half-sister to a winner in USA by Delta Judge; dam, winner of 4 of her 8 starts in USA, is half-sister to stakes winner Princess Papulee; successful in maiden race and amateur riders event at Folkestone and apprentice race at Goodwood; ran well on second start when 3 lengths second to Gift Wrapped in Johnnie Walker Oaks Trial at Lingfield; stays well; acts well on firm going and isn't at her best on soft. *G. Harwood.*

PORTENCROSS 3 b.f. Porto Bello 118–Sybilla (Relic) (1979 5s 5fg 5fg^4 7g 6s –
1980 11fg 8fg 8.3d 8.2s) big, useful-looking filly; good mover; poor maiden; not certain to stay 7f; blinkered third outing in 1979. *R. Price.*

PORTERHOUSE 3 ch.c. Red Alert 127–Yatagirl (Yatasto) (1979 NR 1980 –
6g 5g) workmanlike colt; half-brother to 4 winners by Silky Sullivan in Ireland and USA; dam won in USA; 3 lengths fifth of 23 behind Sharp Celeste in maiden race at Kempton in September, second outing and better effort; will stay 7f. *D. H. Jones.*

PORTHOS 6 b.g. Run The Gantlet–First Light 82 (Primera 131) (1979 NR –
1980 10fg) poor plater at 4 yrs; tailed off in lady riders race at Lingfield in June; has worn blinkers. *R. Atkins.*

PORTIA'S MAID 3 ch.f. Mill Reef 141–Nerissa 117 (Court Martial) (1979 NR –
1980 6f 10fg) quite well-made, useful-looking filly; half-sister to several winners, including very speedy 1968 2-y-o Red Rose Prince (by Henry the Seventh); dam 5f performer; behind in maiden races at Kempton (sweated up slightly) and Brighton in May. *P. Walwyn.*

PORTIMAO (USA) 5 b.h. Exclusive Native–Strange Times (Nearctic) (1979 –
12f 1980 14.7f 12fg 9f) strong ex-Irish horse; won 3 races at up to 1¼m at 3 yrs; well beaten in amateur riders events and a lady riders race in 1980; acts on firm going. *Denys Smith.*

PORTINAIX 5 ch.m. Pontifex (USA)–St Pet (St Chad 120) (1979 5f3 6fg 5f3 5f 5d 6s 1980 5v 5f 6fg) poor sprint handicapper; behind in seller final start; best at 5f; appears to act on any going. *C. Booth.* —

PORTIQUE 2 b.f. Porto Bello 118–Mystique 71 (French Beige 127) (1980 5fg 6d 5g4 6g 6g 5d2 5f 5d4 5fg4) Apr 23; 1,200F, 2,100Y; compact, well-made filly; dam poor sister to useful middle-distance performer French Vine; in frame in maiden race and sellers; possibly unlucky in all-aged seller at Beverley in September on final start, being beaten only 2¾ lengths into fourth place behind Wanchai Lass after being badly hampered when making progress 2f out; promises to stay 6f; acts on a firm and a soft surface; wears blinkers; sold, probably for export, 380 gns Doncaster November Sales. *J. Etherington.* 60

PORTOGON 2 gr.c. Porto Bello 118–Helgonet (Soueida 111) (1980 5fg 5f2 5g*) May 4; 4,800Y; big, workmanlike colt; half-brother to 1978 2-y-o 6f winner Mantle (by Manacle); dam won in Sweden and Denmark; made all to win 18-runner maiden race at Bath in September by ¾ length from Kathred; will probably stay 6f. *T. Marshall.* 84

PORTRAYAL 7 ch.g. Porto Bello 118–Zimbie 97 (Zimone) (1979 5fg* 5fg 5d 5s 1980 6fg 5g 7fg 5fg) plater; stays 7f; acts on firm going and is unsuited by heavy; has been tried in blinkers; suitable mount for an apprentice. *D. Chapman.* —

PORTULACA 2 ch.f. Porto Bello 118–Sea Daisy 90 (Mossborough 126) (1980 5g4 5d 5.8g3 7g 6fg 7g4) Apr 30; lightly-made, useful-looking filly; good walker; second foal; dam won over 10.4f; fairly prominent in maiden races and a nursery; seems to stay 7f. *I. Balding.* 69

POSSE (USA) 3 ch.c. Forli–In Hot Pursuit (Bold Ruler) (1979 7fg2 1980 7f3 8fg2 8f4 8d* 8g*) 130

With Known Fact and Kris on the easy list, Posse was the dominant figure among the English-trained milers from midsummer to the end of July. His victories in the St James's Palace Stakes at Royal Ascot and the Sussex Stakes at Goodwood were achieved in breathtaking style and there was a sense of anti-climax when the cough and its after-effects kept him out of the Waterford Crystal Mile and the Queen Elizabeth II Stakes in which he would have met other leading contenders for the milers' championship. Posse's absence from the field for the Queen Elizabeth II Stakes at Ascot in September was the bigger disappointment because the race attracted both Kris and Known Fact. Posse's connections rightly declined to risk him when he was not one hundred per cent but his retirement left unanswered the question: just how good was Posse? The pressures on Posse's owners to retire the horse to stud were obvious, and their action understandable; but if he had been kept in training we should surely have had a better idea of him.

Posse arrived at Royal Ascot still a maiden after four races. But he was no ordinary maiden: a half-share in him was bought the day before the St James's Palace Stakes by the Derisley Wood Stud for a million dollars (about £425,000 at prevailing exchange rates). Raced only once as a two-year-old Posse put himself in the classic picture when finishing strongly into third place

St James's Palace Stakes, Ascot—Posse wins easily from Final Straw, Last Fandango (not shown), Dalsaan and Lafontaine

in the Clerical, Medical Greenham Stakes at Newbury on his reappearance. Starting at 12/1 for the Two Thousand Guineas, Posse suffered wretched luck in the race, being almost brought down by Nureyev more than two furlongs out; Posse recovered an enormous amount of ground—bumping Taufan when squeezing through just after the Bushes—to finish third, a neck and three quarters of a length behind Nureyev and Known Fact. On Nureyev's disqualification Posse was promoted to second. Posse took time to get over his arduous race in the Two Thousand Guineas and he was slightly disappointing in his final gallop before the Airlie/Coolmore Irish Two Thousand Guineas a fortnight later. He finished a very close fourth at the Curragh, after looking to be going best of all two furlongs out, and some observers were heard to suggest that Posse had shirked the issue. One should always be wary of accepting an explanation for a defeat which reflects upon a horse's honesty: by and large the racehorse is a genuine animal and should always be regarded as such unless there is convincing evidence to the contrary. Those who labelled Posse a coward after the Irish Guineas were subsequently made to look very foolish.

Posse was transformed in the month between the Irish Guineas and Royal Ascot: he won the St James's Palace Stakes like a champion. It was good to see the St James's Palace moved from its old place at the end of the first-day programme to a much more suitable position as the third race and the race certainly lived up to its higher billing. Last Fandango and Final Straw, who had finished second and third in the Irish Two Thousand Guineas, took the field but Final Straw's stable-companion Dalsaan, who had won most impressively at Kempton at the end of May, started odds on. There were eight runners and Posse was third favourite at 11/2. It was decided to ride Posse with more restraint than previously and Eddery held him up near the back of the field for much of the race. Brought up on a tight rein in the straight, Posse was clearly going much the best from about two furlongs out but it was not until well inside the final furlong that Eddery let him go. The response was immediate and, showing a dazzling turn of speed, Posse won very easily by a length and a half and three quarters of a length from Final Straw and Last Fandango. The margin by which Posse won the Sussex Stakes at Goodwood

Sussex Stakes, Goodwood—Pat Eddery rides Posse with supreme confidence to beat Final Straw

Mr Ogden Mills Phipps' "Posse" (P. Eddery)

six weeks later was much narrower but responsibility for that must rest with the remarkably confident and audacious manner in which he was ridden. Posse was 13/8 on in a field of nine—five three-year-olds, two four-year-olds and two five-year-olds—and Final Straw was generally thought to be his most serious rival. Eddery gave Posse's supporters a few palpitations before landing the odds by a head. Dropped to the rear as soon as the stalls opened, Posse made ground on the inside in the straight, drawing up smoothly to the heels of the leaders. Eddery left his challenge very late indeed but his faith in Posse was vindicated as, switched to the outside, he unleashed another devastating finishing burst to catch Final Straw a stride before the post. Star Way, Skyliner, Millingdale Lillie and Hardgreen were also within four lengths of Posse at the line.

Posse (USA) (ch. c. 1977)	Forli (ch 1963)	Aristophanes (ch 1948)	Hyperion
			Commotion
		Trevisa (ch 1951)	Advocate
			Veneta
	In Hot Pursuit (b 1971)	Bold Ruler (b 1954)	Nasrullah
			Miss Disco
		Lady Be Good (b 1956)	Better Self
			Past Eight

The Argentinian Triple Crown winner Forli, who raced with success afterwards in the United States, has certainly made his mark at stud, siring top-class horses on both sides of the Atlantic; Thatch, Home Guard, Gay Fandango and Boone's Cabin are among his best winners in Britain. Most of Forli's best stock have shown more speed than stamina. Posse is the second foal of In Hot Pursuit, one of the leading two-year-olds in North America in 1973; In Hot Pursuit, who won three of her five races at two (her only season to race), was rated 118, 8 lb below the top, in the Experimental Handicap. Posse's grandam Lady Be Good, a winner four times as a two-year-old, has bred ten winners, including the fillies Discipline and Full Of Hope, and the colt Disciplinarian, each of whom won well over 100,000 dollars in stakes. Discipline is the dam of Squander, winner of the six-furlong Sorority Stakes, a Grade 1 two-year-old race. Posse, a medium-sized, lengthy colt and a good mover in all his paces, acted on firm going and on a soft surface. He was syndicated at £55,000 per share, placing a valuation on him of £2,200,000. The Derisley Wood Stud, Newmarket, retained eleven shares, and a few nominations were available for 1981 at £7,500 plus £7,500 if the mare is in foal on October 1st. Posse has a lot to recommend him as a stallion. *J. Dunlop.*

POUNENTES 3 b.g. Tumble Wind–La Chanteuse 81 (Hethersett 134) (1979 **78**
5d 6fg 6fg^{2} 6f^{3} 7d^{2} 7d 8fg^{4} 7fg 1980 7v 7fg 8f* 8f^{2} 11f^{2}) shapely gelding; won maiden race at Edinburgh in April; respectable second in handicaps at Carlisle and Ayr following month; stays 11f; seems to act on any going; best in blinkers; has run well for an apprentice; not raced after May. *G. Richards.*

POWDER HORN 3 b.f. Scottish Rifle 127–Ticking Hill 93 (Hillary) (1979 **66**
5s 5f 7fg 1980 10g^{3} 12fg^{4} 12g 12d 10fg 10g^{4} 10s) leggy filly; in frame in varied company, including selling; should stay 1½m; sometimes blinkered; doesn't always impress in paddock; ran moderately third and fourth outings. *W. Elsey.*

POWERFUL SNORT 3 b.c. So Blessed 130–Sticky Green 91 (Herbager 136) **73** d
(1979 5d 5d^{3} 5s 5f 7fg^{4} 7.2g 8.2fg^{4} 8g* 1980 10v 12f^{4} 12h^{4} 8.5f* 10fg 11.7s 8.2g 9g 10f 8g^{3} 10f) small colt; plater; won valuable seller at Epsom in June (bought in 3,500 gns); stays 1½m; best form on a sound surface; sometimes wears blinkers but is just as effective without them; has run respectably for a boy. *P. Haslam.*

POWER LOVE 3 b. or br.c. High Top 131–Goddess 69 (Immortality) (1979 –
NR 1980 10g 8fg 8h 16f 16g^{3} 16d 16.9d 16f 16f 14g 13g) small colt; slow maiden; stays well; blinkered fifth and sixth starts; sold 950 gns Ascot December Sales. *B. Hanbury.*

POWERSCOURT (USA) 3 b.g. Buckpasser–Irish Manor (Bold Ruler) (1979 –
7g 7g 7fg^{2} 1980 7f 8f 8h) most attractive gelding; showed ability in Southern maiden and minor races at 2 yrs; didn't find his form in handicaps in 1980; will be suited by middle distances. *J. Dunlop.*

POWERS OF DARKNESS 6 br.g. Falcon 131–Charley's Aunt 80 (Will Somers –
114§) (1979 NR 1980 8f) ungenerous selling hurdler; finished lame at Thirsk in May, first outing on flat since 1977. *D. Yeoman.*

POYLE CRUSHER 3 ch.c. Sweet Revenge 129–Swan Ann 84 (My Swanee **102**
122) (1979 5fg^{2} 5d^{2} 6g^{4} 6fg* 1980 7v* 8s^{2} 7f 7g 8g 8d^{4} 8fg^{4} 8g) rangy colt; showed improved form on first 2 starts, putting up useful performances in Salisbury 2,000 Guineas Trial in March (beat Cyprus Sky 2 lengths) and Easter Stakes at Kempton in April (length second to Master Willie, giving him 7 lb); not disgraced when fourth in handicaps won by Belmont Bay at Newmarket and Mashoor at Goodwood in July; stays 1m; suited by some give in the ground; sweated up badly but ran well on third outing at 2 yrs; sold 26,000 gns Newmarket Autumn Sales. *Mrs J. Reavey.*

PRAED STREET 3 gr.c. Habitat 134–West Two 104 (Connaught 130) (1979 **57**
5s 1980 8g 8g 8fg^{2} 13g 8g 10f) small, strong colt; poor maiden; best run at 1m on a firm surface; often blinkered; sold out of P. Walwyn's stable 2,000 gns Ascot August Sales after third start. *R. Atkins.*

PRAETORIAN 3 gr.g. Home Guard 129–Song In The Air 83 (Tudor Melody –
129) (1979 5f 1980 7fg 10.1f) behind in varied company, twice finishing last; blinkered in 1980. *D. Whelan.*

PRAETORIAN GUARD 2 b.c. Home Guard 129–Prinia 77 (On Your Mark **81** p
125) (1980 6fg^{4}) May 15; 12,500Y; first foal; dam, 1¼m winner, is closely related to Mandrake Major; 14/1 and in need of race, looked dangerous 2f out but ran very green under pressure, drifting badly left, and was beaten 2¾ lengths into fourth-of-11 position behind Chantry Bridge in maiden race at Doncaster in July; would have finished second had he kept straight; will stay 7f; looked promising here but didn't race again. *Denys Smith.*

PRAGMATIC 5 gr.h. Relko 136–Paracelle (Vimy 132) (1979 12d* 16s* 14d* **109**
16s^{2} 12fg^{4} 13.5s 12fg 1980 16fg* 14f 16f) big, rangy horse; improved in 1979 and won 3 races, including Yorkshire Cup; stayed on well under quite

Sagaro Stakes, Ascot—Pragmatic (centre) wins from Vincent and Buttress (right)

hard driving when beating Vincent by ¾ length in Sagaro Stakes at Ascot in April; never going particularly well when behind in Yorkshire Cup won by Noble Saint in May and lost all chance when slipping badly in Henry II Stakes at Sandown later in month on his only other starts; stays 2m; acts on a firm surface but is better suited by some give in the ground. *F. J. Houghton.*

PRAISELIEN 2 b.c. So Blessed 130–Collateral 99 (Compensation 127) (1980 5fg 5fg 6g* 6g* 6d* 6g² 6g 6d² 6g) May 29; 4,000Y; lightly-made colt; half-brother to 2 winners; dam effective at 6f to 1m; failed to attract a bid after winning seller at Lingfield in June but showed himself a cut above a plater when winning nurseries at Windsor following month and Redcar in August, on latter course beating Regency Prince ½ length; creditable second in 2 more nurseries later on; will stay 1m; acts on a soft surface. *T. Marshall.* **83**

PREACHER MAN 3 b.c. Gulf Pearl 117–Miss Etta (King's Troop 118) (1979 8d 7f 1980 10.5d 12g² 10.2g 15s⁴ 12.2d 12d 15s⁴) strong, good sort; in frame in maiden and minor races; beaten some way in valuable seller on sixth start; stays well; blinkered last 2 outings; sweated up fourth appearance; sold to B. Lunness 2,700 gns Doncaster November Sales. *J. Hanson.* **69**

PRECIOUS JADE 3 ch.f. Northfields–Love Letter 91 (Gratitude 130) (1979 6f 6g 8d 1980 7s 7fg 7.2d² 8g³ 8g² 7d³ 8.2s) compact filly; quite a moderate maiden; stays 1m; acts on a soft surface; has run creditably for a boy. *W. Hastings-Bass.* **68**

PRECIOUS MOMENTS 2 b.c. Furry Glen 121–Contourno (Continuation 120) (1980 5f³ 5f³ 6d) Mar 22; 2,800F, 7,200Y; attractive, rangy colt; very good mover; half-brother to fairly useful 1975 2-y-o 5f to 1m winner Shukran (by Illa Laudo); dam unraced half-sister to Queen's Vase winner Tara Brooch; third in maiden races at Lingfield and Newbury in May; not seen out again until end of season when creditable 4 lengths fifth of 25 behind Little Wolf in maiden event at Newbury; will be suited by 1m. *R. Price.* **78**

PRECIOUS VIEW 3 b.f. Sit In The Corner–Sicalaine 52 (Sica Boy 132) (1979 5s 6g 6s* 6g* 7f² 1980 8g 6g 7fg* 7fg) leggy, narrow filly; plater; won at Newcastle in July (bought in 3,300 gns); runs as if 7f is a minimum trip and will stay 1¼m; fell second start; sold 1,100 gns Doncaster November Sales. *J. Etherington.* **61**

PREDOMINANT 3 br.c. Busted 134–Saulisa 108 (Hard Sauce 131) (1979 6d 1980 10fg² 12g* 14g 10g⁴ 10fg 10s) neat, strong, good sort; landed odds all out by 1½ lengths from Count Fernando in 13-runner maiden race at Redcar in June; not disgraced in handicap at Newmarket in August on fourth start; stays 1½m (well beaten over further); blinkered fifth outing; sold to Denys Smith 11,000 gns Newmarket Autumn Sales. *M. Stoute.* **82**

PRELKO 5 br.h. Relko 136–Pretty Cage 110 (Cagire II 122) (1979 12.2s 12.5g² 12s* 1980 16f* 15.8fg 16s³ 16d⁴) strong, compact horse; has been **66**

fired; battled on gamely to beat Ribble Rouser ½ length in handicap at Ripon in May; ran best subsequent race on third start; stays well; acts on any going; wears bandages. *J. Fitzgerald.*

PREMIER ROSE 3 b.f. Sharp Edge 123–Florintina 104 (Floribunda 136) (1979 5fg³ 6f 6f* 7g⁴ 6fg* 1980 7.3fg 6f² 6d⁴ 7g² 7d² 7fg² 7g² 7g* 8g²) attractive, rather leggy filly; very useful performer; gained a well-deserved success when beating Betsy Red by 8 lengths in 5-runner £2,900 race at Goodwood in September; finished runner-up in 6 good races, namely Great Eastern Handicap (head behind Sayyaf), Sir Noel Murless Stakes (beaten ½ length by Captain Nick) and Duchess of Montrose Handicap (went down by 2 lengths to Parlour Game), all at Newmarket, New Stand Stakes at Goodwood (¾ length behind Trevita), City of York Stakes (beaten 4 lengths by Sunfield) and Marlborough House Stakes at Ascot (beaten a length by Our Home, who rec 6 lb); stays 1m; probably acts on any going; very tough and genuine. *P. Cole.* **115**

PREMIER STATE 2 b.c. Thatch 136–Lotka (Welsh Pageant 132) (1980 7f 6f 8s) Mar 13; 6,200Y; small colt; first foal; dam never ran; gave signs of ability in maiden race on first outing but subsequently finished behind in sellers at Newmarket; sold 400 gns Newmarket Autumn Sales. *P. Haslam.* **–**

PRESENT COMPANY 2 b.g. Morston 125–Crisalgo 83 (Miralgo 130) (1980 7g 7g 8fg 8d) Feb 24; 3,500F, 3,400Y; attractive, good-looking gelding; second foal; dam won Chester Cup; little worthwhile form but finished eighth in 23-runner minor event won by Shergar at Newbury in September on third outing; will be suited by 1½m+ as a 3-y-o. *A. Ingham.* **–**

PRESUMPTUOUS 2 b.f. Gay Fandango 132–Paracelle (Vimy 132) (1980 8.2s) Apr 11; half-sister to smart stayer Pragmatic (by Relko) and 2 winners in France; dam, half-sister to Silver Shark, won over 1m in France; very weak 10/1-shot, always behind in 20-runner maiden race won by Irish Heart at Haydock in October; wasn't knocked about and may improve over further at 3 yrs. *F. J. Houghton.* **–**

PRETTY GOOD 5 ch.g. Pretty Form 97–Jolie 64 (Jolly Jet 111) (1979 7s 6s⁴ 6v 6g⁴ 1980 7.6f 6h 7.2fg 5fg³ 6g 6g 5g⁴ 6g 8d 6fg 6f⁴) quite a moderate handicapper; best form at sprint distances; seems to act on any going but goes well on firm; good mount for an inexperienced rider; blinkered final outing in 1977. *A. W. Jones.* **60**

PRETTY LASS 3 br.f. Workboy 123–Pretty Cage 110 (Cagire II 122) (1979 6d 6g 5d 7fg 7g 1980 12.2fg 12g 12.2f 12fg 12d) leggy, quite useful sort; poor maiden; blinkered fourth start. *J. Fitzgerald.* **–**

PRETTY MUSIC 2 ch.f. Music Boy 124–Pritillor 93 (Privy Councillor 125) (1980 5d 5fg³ 6g⁴ 5s) Mar 3; workmanlike filly; third foal; half-sister to 1m and 1½m winner Robert Adam (by Mansingh); dam best at up to 1¼m; beaten 5 lengths when in frame in minor event won by Ashbrittle at Windsor and 12-runner maiden race won by Spark of Life at Yarmouth, both in September; stays 6f; possibly not at her best on soft ground. *D. Weeden.* **76**

PRETTY SHARP 3 ch.c. Sharpen Up 127–Sara's Star 70 (Sheshoon 132) (1979 5f 6g 6fg 7f 1980 8.2s 8fg⁴ 10fg 11.5f 10d 10g 8fg 9f) leggy colt; has a round action; poor form, including in a seller; sometimes blinkered; sold 560 gns Newmarket Autumn Sales. *G. Blum.* **–**

PRETTY TOUGH 2 b.c. Firestreak 125–Idyll-Liquor (Narrator 127) (1980 5d 5v 5f 5.8fg) Mar 29; rangy colt; brother to 9f winner Pretty Useful, and half-brother to a bumpers winner; dam ran over hurdles; only plating class; should be suited by 7f. *P. Arthur.* **60**

PRETTY USEFUL 6 ch.m. Firestreak 125–Idyll-Liquor (Narrator 127) (1979 8v³ 10.8d⁴ 9s* 7g 8s² 8d 8s² 8f 8d 8.2s 1980 8d² 10s 8fg 8g 8g 12.5s 8s) quite a moderate handicapper; second of 23 to Royal Obligation in apprentice handicap at Doncaster in March; best form at around 1m; needs some give in the ground; trained by P. Arthur until after fifth start. *N. Tinkler.* **69** d

PRICE FAIRLY 4 b.g. Sallust 134–Santa Chiara 79 (Astec 128) (1979 8g 12fg 12f 13g 12f³ 12f⁴ 12fg 12g⁴ 15g 10s 1980 12fg 8g 10g 6s⁴ 6s 9g* 7d) neat, strong gelding; plater; successful in £240 race in Jersey in August; stays 1½m; sometimes wears blinkers. *M. Naughton.* **–**

PRICE OF PEACE 2 gr.c. Averof 123–Kingdom Come 77 (Klondyke Bill 125) (1980 5.8fg⁴ 5fg 7g* 7d 6fg 6d) Apr 1; 4,300Y; big colt; half-brother to **79**

3 winning platers; dam won over 6f; justified favouritism by 1½ lengths from Aldenham, despite having been badly hampered soon after halfway, in 18-runner maiden race at Salisbury in July; ran well next 2 starts; stays 7f. *J. Hill.*

PRIDDY BLUE 3 b.f. Blue Cashmere 129–Priddy Fair 108 (Preciptic 122) (1979 5d 8g 7s 1980 8f 7fg 8g 9fg^{4} 8f 10g 15.8fg 10.6d 12.2d 10s) leggy filly; little worthwhile form in varied company; best run at 9f on firm ground. *P. Asquith.* —

PRIDE AND FAITH (USA) 3 ch.c. Blood Royal 129 or Angle Light–Tomboy Tamele (Verbatim) (1979 5s 5f* 6fg^{2} 6fg^{3} 6d^{2} 6fg* 7s* 7s^{3} 1980 7f 7fg 7fg) lengthy colt; fairly useful (rated 97) at 2 yrs; didn't run up to his best in handicaps in 1980; will be suited by 1m; acts on any going; usually wears a bandage or boot on near-hind. *E. Eldin.* —

PRIESTCROFT BOY 7 b.g. Chebs Lad 120–Alfreda 78 (Fidalgo 129) (1979 8g* 8g^{4} 8d^{2} 8.2g^{3} 8s^{2} 9fg^{3} 8f 8h^{2} 8fg^{2} 8g* 8.2g^{4} 8g* 8d* 8f* 8d 1980 8fg^{4} 10.6g^{3} 8d 8d^{2} 8d^{4} 8fg^{2} 8fg^{4} 8g^{4} 8f 8fg) moderate handicapper; second at Newcastle in June and Pontefract in July; stays 1¼m; acts on any going; sometimes wears blinkers; good mount for an inexperienced rider. *M. W. Easterby.* **80**

PRIESTCROFT STAR 6 ch.m. Saintly Song 128–Queen Mab (Twilight Alley 133) (1979 10fg 1980 15h) of little account on flat but is a winner over hurdles. *M. Haynes.* —

PRIME CAPTIVE 3 br.c. Royal Captive 116–Fadmoor (Primera 131) (1979 5d 5s^{4} 5d 5g^{3} 7.2d 1980 10s 7fg 8fg 8d 7g 9g) well-made colt; poor plater; sometimes wears blinkers; has worn bandages; trained by R. Hannon first 3 starts. *A. Moore.* —

PRIMERVILLE 3 b.g. Shoolerville 121–Prim Dot (Primera 131) (1979 5v^{2} 5g^{3} 5s^{4} 6g 6f 5fg^{4} 5fg 1980 6fg 6fg^{3} 8f 6g 5g 6g 5f) workmanlike gelding; plater nowadays; stays 6f (ran as though 1m was too far for him third start); probably acts on any going; wears blinkers; ran badly fifth and final starts. *M. H. Easterby.* **49**

PRIME TIME 2 ch.f. Sharpen Up 127–Primage 99 (Primera 131) (1980 6d 7g) May 19; 31,000Y; half-sister to several winners, including very useful 1979 2-y-o 7f winner Swift Image (by Bay Express) and very useful Irish 1m to 1¼m winner Mitchelstown (by Sweet Revenge); dam won over 6f at 2 yrs; 33/1, chased leaders when seventh of 26 to Full Of Reason in maiden race at Newmarket in October, second outing; will be suited by 1m. *W. Hastings-Bass.* — p

PRIMSIDE 4 b.g. Connaught 130–Never Alone 86 (Never Say Die 137) (1979 10fg 12fg^{4} 12fg 16g^{2} 11.7f 16f* 16f*(dis) 16fg^{2} 17.1fg^{4} 16fg^{3} 1980 16g 16g 16s 16fg 13g 16fg 17.1d^{3}) small gelding; ran best race on final outing; suited by a test of stamina; acts on firm going and a soft surface; wore blinkers in 1978. *C. Wildman.* **43**

PRIMULA BOY 5 ch.g. Sallust 134–Catriona 96 (Sing Sing 134) (1979 5d 5d 6g 5f 8g 7d 6fg 6fg^{2} 6s* 6fg^{3} 6g^{4} 6g* 1980 6f 6f^{2} 6fg^{2} 5g^{4} 6fg* 6fg 6g 6d 6s^{4} 6f^{2} 6d 6d^{4} 6v) useful handicapper; made all when comfortable winner of valuable Tote Sprint Trophy (Handicap) at Ayr in July, beating Moybrook by 2½ lengths; in frame subsequently on same course (Ladbrokes Ayr Gold Cup) and at Redcar and Doncaster; best form at sprint distances; acts on any going; blinkered twice in 1978 and once in 1979; started slowly sixth start; goes well for W. Higgins. *W. Bentley.* **100**

PRINCE 6 br.g. Prince de Galles 125–Regal Artist 72 (Breakspear II) (1979 9s 8g^{2} 9g 8f* 8f* 8f 8h^{3} 7f 8h* 8d^{4} 8fg* 1980 8f 8f 8f^{3} 8fg 8fg^{4} 10.2g^{3} 9g^{3} 10fg 10fg^{2} 11d* 12.2g 12.3d 8fg* 8f^{3} 9g 8.2s) moderate handicapper; held up when winning narrowly at Ayr in August (from Doogali) and Beverley in September (from Higham Grey); stays 11f; possibly unsuited by very soft or heavy ground; successful with blinkers and without. *K. Stone.* **59**

PRINCE ALLANDER 5 b.g. Breeders Dream 116–Darlingka 77 (Darling Boy 124) (1979 NR 1980 10g^{3} 10g^{4}) plater; stayed 1¼m; dead. *R. Hobson.* **36**

PRINCE BEAU 5 b.g. Crowned Prince 128–Belgian Bullet (Vimy 132) (1979 11d 1980 9f 12g 12d) big, strong, rangy gelding; lightly raced and well beaten since 1978; stays 1½m; acts on a firm surface. *V. Thompson.* —

Great Voltigeur Stakes, York—tough and resolute Prince Bee wins from Light Cavalry, with Saviour a modest third

PRINCE BEE 3 b.c. Sun Prince 128–Honerko 112 (Tanerko 134) (1979 NR **128**
1980 8f² 10fg 10.4f² 12fg* 12s² 12fg* 12g* 12f*)

Henbit's stable will have a strong team of older horses in 1981, with or without the Derby winner, for Prince Bee and that fine filly Shoot A Line remain in training. Prince Bee is a particularly interesting prospect. Later developing than the majority of leading three-year-olds, unraced at two and away to an uncertain start at three, he enjoyed a very fine second half of the season, winning three pattern races in succession, the Gordon Stakes, Great Voltigeur Stakes and Prix Niel, after taking second place in the Irish Sweeps Derby. He wasn't far behind the best when last seen out, and may have a shade more than the normal improvement in him.

Apparently Prince Bee was a very slow learner. Running him at Chester in the Dee Stakes probably did him a lot of good, for he was a different horse afterwards; previously he'd gone very promisingly against other backward animals in the Wood Ditton Stakes for newcomers at Newmarket (he finished second to Royal Fountain) and then very disappointingly, never in the hunt, when favourite for the White Rose Stakes at Ascot. The Chester track certainly gave Prince Bee plenty to think about: he was last of nine and off the bridle most of the way, labouring round the turns in a strongly-run race, but he really picked up in the last two furlongs and nearly overhauled Playboy Jubilee. Two weeks later Prince Bee was well placed from the start against Derby probables in the Predominate Stakes at Kempton and battled on up the straight like an old hand to hold Rankin by three parts of a length.

In the five weeks or so between Kempton and the Curragh, Prince Bee improved substantially: he'd been receiving weight from the leading contenders in the Predominate Stakes, 5 lb from Rankin. Except for Tyrnavos he beat all those in the Irish Derby who'd run at Epsom, including the four who chased Henbit home—Master Willie, Rankin, Pelerin and Garrido—and he would have gone close to giving his trainer and jockey yet another classic success but for being hampered as the field prepared to make the turn into the straight. Neither in this race nor in any of his others did Prince Bee show any great powers of acceleration. He's essentially a horse who needs to be kept right up to his work to be seen to advantage and he nearly always runs as though a mile and three quarters would suit him. Bustled along as early as halfway to hold on to a good position, he almost lost his footing in the incident before the turn but came into the straight in fourth place; from that point he ran on steadily to pass Master Willie and Ramian for second, challenging Tyrnavos over the last two furlongs without threatening to reduce the gap between them to less than a length and a half.

Although Prince Bee runs like a stayer he isn't regarded as one by his stable and wasn't trained for the St Leger: two of the objectives considered for him at around that period were the Grosser Preis von Baden and the Benson and Hedges Gold Cup. Had he been in the Leger his runs in the Gordon Stakes at Goodwood in July and the Great Voltigeur Stakes at York in August would have been looked upon as among the best of the trials for that race. At Goodwood he came from behind Light Cavalry to outstay the threatening Fingal's Cave by two and a half lengths, pushed out; at York, ridden by Piggott deputising for Carson, he beat Light Cavalry by two lengths, having to be rousted along in the lead over the last two furlongs after seeming about to enjoy one of his easier races a furlong or so earlier. Light Cavalry was conceding 6 lb on the first occasion and 4 lb on the second.

The day after Light Cavalry beat Water Mill in the Leger, Prince Bee put up another high-class performance in the Prix Niel at Longchamp, accounting for eight opponents including some Prix de l'Arc de Triomphe probables. Favourite, he won by a length and a half and a neck from the filly Satilla and Ruscelli, who took tenth and ninth places respectively in the Arc; Garrido was fourth, Bozovici eighth and the French Derby winner Policeman a fairly close-up last. There seemed to be no pace in the early stages, Prince Bee the reluctant leader until settling down third or fourth. He moved up strongly on the bridle rounding the turn (showing at least as much pace as he'd ever shown, which may be significant for the future) and soon went ahead. From then on Carson punched away and Prince Bee never seemed likely to be caught, going clear in the last furlong. He looked a picture in the paddock; he had improved steadily in appearance and condition through the season.

Prince Bee (b.c. 1977)	Sun Prince (ch 1969)	Princely Gift (b 1951)	Nasrullah
			Blue Gem
		Costa Sola (ch 1963)	Worden II
			Sunny Cove
	Honerko (b 1968)	Tanerko (br 1953)	Tantieme
			La Divine
		Be a Honey (b 1959)	Honeys Alibi
			Neola

Prince Bee and his sire were bred by the Ballymacoll Stud. His sire Sun Prince, now in Japan, sired another good racehorse for the Stud in the French Oaks runner-up Cistus. Sun Prince remained in training as a four-year-old after having his three-year-old season cut short by injury; he won the Queen Anne Stakes from Sparkler and was twice tried at around a mile and a quarter at four, finishing a good third in the Eclipse but barely staying the trip in the Benson and Hedges Gold Cup. He was a strong, attractive individual, as also is Prince Bee. The dam Honerko stayed at least a mile and a half, showing improved, very useful, form over the distance in France at the back-end of her three-year-old season; she had raced in England for part of her career and won a maiden at Bath. She is a granddaughter of the top-class 1944 two-year-old Neola, the latter a full sister to the One Thousand Guineas second Neolight and half-sister to Tudor Minstrel. Honerko's grandsire Honeys Alibi was a high-class American horse who stayed fairly well. Honerko produced one foal before

Prix Niel, Longchamp—Prince Bee is chased home by Satilla, Ruscelli and Garrido

Sir Michael Sobell's "Prince Bee"

Prince Bee, the Baldric II colt Balteus who showed smart staying form in France as a two-year-old and later ran on the flat and over hurdles in England.

Sun Prince and Honerko acted on any going, though the latter seemed at her very best on soft; Prince Bee, a good mover, acts on any. As for Prince Bee's distance, we have no doubt he would stay a mile and three quarters and little doubt he would be suited by such a trip; but it seems on the cards he will be kept at no further than a mile and a half as long as he does well. Stolidly genuine, he should do well as a four-year-old. *R. Hern.*

PRINCE BEOWULF 2 gr.c. Young Emperor 133–Aibrean (Amber Light 114) (1980 5fg³ 5fg⁴ 5fg 6fg 6d 5d 6d) Apr 21; 2,600Y, resold 4,800Y; fair sort; half-brother to a winner in Hungary; dam won from 6f to 1¼m in Ireland; in frame in maiden races at Wolverhampton and Leicester in April but is little better than a plater; should stay 6f. *R. Hollinshead.* **67**

PRINCE BUSTINO 3 b.g. Bustino 136–Karenina 95 (Silver Shark 129) (1979 NR 1980 10.1fg 12fg² 14d) 36,000Y; tall, lightly-made gelding; half-brother to 2 winners, including smart 1976 staying 2-y-o Sultan's Ruby (by Royal Palace); dam won twice from 4 starts at 2 yrs; went down by ¾ length to stable-companion Aswad in 9-runner maiden race at Brighton in May; stays 1½m (weakened in last 2f over 1¾m). *J. Dunlop.* **78**

PRINCE CARL 6 b.g. Connaught 130–Maladie d'Amour 98 (Fidalgo 129) (1979 10g 12g 12d* 14.7f 12f² 1980 12h 12fg 15g⁴) well-made, good-bodied gelding; won lady riders race at Ripon in 1979; well beaten in 1980 (not raced after June); stays 1½m; seems to act on any going. *Mrs A. Cousins.* **—**

PRINCE CARUSO 3 ch.g. Caruso 112–Vidi's Zulema (Vidi Vici 112) (1979 NR 1980 10.1f 8g 8fg 12fg) leggy gelding; of little account. *M. McCormack.* **—**

PRINCE COPPER 2 ch.c. Ampney Prince 96–Rose of Ennis 78 (Ennis 128) (1980 5s 5fg 5d 5f 5g² 6f 6s 6s) Apr 17; small, close-coupled colt; half-brother to **68**

5f and 1m seller winner Hallah (by Halation); dam ran only at 2 yrs when best at 5f; apprentice ridden at 4-lb overweight, showed only sign of ability when ¾-length second of 17 to Super Smile in maiden race at Bath in September; behind in sellers on third, sixth and seventh outings, wearing blinkers on last occasion; should stay 6f. *S. Mellor.*

PRINCE DIAMOND 2 b.c. Prince Tenderfoot 126–Spare Filly 95 (Beau Sabreur 125) (1980 5fg² 5fg 6d 6g) Feb 13; 48,000Y; strong, quite attractive colt; half-brother to numerous winners, including fairly useful 1m to 1¼m performer Manfilia (by Mandamus), herself dam of African Hope and Kilijaro, and good Italian winner Van Houten (by Northfields); dam soft-ground stayer; disputed lead most of way when going down by ½ length to Grain Race in 17-runner maiden event at Newbury in April; finished only sixth when odds on for similar race at Bath later in month and wasn't seen out again until end of season, better effort on fourth start when sixth of 25 to Composer at Newmarket; should be suited by 7f and 1m. *B. Hills.* **72**

PRINCE DILIGENCE 3 b.c. Prince Tenderfoot 126–Cariole 84 (Pardao 120) (1979 5f³ 5g³ 1980 7fg² 8g² 8g 8fg* 8.2s³ 8fg 8d² 8fg*) attractive colt; has been tubed; beat Hill Laugh in maiden race at Yarmouth in July and short-headed Vagabond King in handicap at Redcar in October; stays 1m; acts on any going; sometimes sweats up; has worn a tongue strap; ran moderately sixth start. *M. Stoute.* **70**

PRINCE ECHO 2 ch.c. Crowned Prince 128–Dawn Echo (Don II 123) (1980 6g 6s* 6.3s² 7g²) **120**

Although the Irish sent twelve individual two-year-olds, two of which ran twice, to challenge for the English pattern races in 1980 it was only with the last of them that they gained their first success, when Storm Bird took the William Hill Dewhurst Stakes. They had gone very close to taking another major prize when Prince Echo failed by only a neck to win the Laurent Perrier Champagne Stakes at the St Leger meeting. He put up a good effort in defeat. After wearing down the pacemaking Parkdale to lead at the distance he battled on well, although challenged on either side by Church Parade and Gielgud, and only close home did he knuckle under to Gielgud. Prince Echo was to have tried to go one better the following month in the William Hill Middle Park

Tyros Stakes, the Curragh—apprentice-ridden Prince Echo (left) springs a surprise, winning from Personal Guard and British Gunner

Stakes, for which he was co-favourite in the sponsor's ante-post betting, but he worked poorly the day before the race and was withdrawn.

Prince Echo started 4/1 co-favourite at Doncaster on the strength of two excellent efforts in his home country. He first showed himself above average when 25/1 and ridden by a 7-lb claimer in the Tyros Stakes at the Curragh on Irish Sweeps Derby Day, a race won over the previous ten years by such good animals as Abergwaun, Thatch, It's Freezing, Roman Charger and Miami Springs. He accounted for his seventeen rivals, who included seven previous winners, in good style, running on under pressure to win by three quarters of a length from Personal Guard after leading inside the final furlong. He followed this performance with an even better one in the Group 3 Anglesey Stakes on the same course eight weeks later, when he went down by only half a length to Storm Bird who was receiving 6 lb. He was no doubt flattered by his proximity to Storm Bird, since the latter had tended to idle in the lead, but even so he put up an excellent effort to finish six lengths clear of the three-times successful Light Here, eleven lengths clear of the useful Master Thatch and fifteen lengths clear of the dual winner Severiano, the next three horses home.

Prince Echo (ch.c. May 4, 1978)	Crowned Prince (ch 1969)	Raise A Native (ch 1961)	Native Dancer
			Raise You
		Gay Hostess (ch 1957)	Royal Charger
			Your Hostess
	Dawn Echo (gr 1973)	Don II (gr 1966)	Grey Sovereign
			Diviana II
		Solar Echo (b 1957)	Solar Slipper
			Eastern Echo

A useful-looking colt, Prince Echo was sold for the comparatively low figure of 7,000 guineas as a yearling. Like Labista he belongs to the last Irish crop sired by the disappointing Crowned Prince, who has been sent to Japan by way of Australia. He's the first foal of Dawn Echo, a well-bred filly who showed no sign of ability in three outings in England and Ireland. Her sister Seminar was a much more able filly, winner of three five-furlong races as a two-year-old when also fourth in both the Queen Mary and the Lowther Stakes, and her three-parts brother Sovereign Slipper put up a very smart performance to win the 1966 Beresford Stakes. Even better than these was one of Dawn Echo's half-brothers, that wonderful old gelding Boldboy. Dawn Echo is a granddaughter of the versatile Eastern Echo, who finished second in the Park Hill Stakes in between winning two good races over a mile; the next dam was a sister to the St Leger winner Singapore.

Prince Echo may not stay much beyond a mile and it's significant that his only English classic engagement is in the Two Thousand Guineas. Although he doesn't seem up to classic-winning standard he showed himself superior at two years to all bar Storm Bird and Critique of the Irish colts and should win a worthwhile race or two. He acts well on soft ground and has yet to race on a firm surface. *L. Browne, Ireland.*

PRINCE JUDGER (USA) 3 b.c. Judger–Bett's Mandy (Beau Gar) (1979 NR 1980 8fg 8fg 8d^4 10d 8g*) rangy colt; plater; sold 2,600 gns after winning at Newmarket in August; stays 1m; ran badly fourth start; blinkered last 2 outings; sold to Denys Smith 1,900 gns Newmarket Autumn Sales. *M. Stoute.* **77**

PRINCE LIGHTNING 2 ch.c. Royal Match 117–Up In Arms (Breakspear II) (1980 6g 7d) Mar 12; 1,700F, 4,800Y; third live foal; half-brother to a winning hurdler; dam Irish 2-y-o 5f winner; well beaten in maiden and minor races at Brighton in July, starting slowly on debut. *R. Price.* —

PRINCELY CHIEF (USA) 8 br.g. Chieftain–Corner Garth 102 (Solonaway 128) (1979 12g 12g^4 12fg 12g* 12fg^3 13g^3 12.2d 1980 11fg 13g^4 12f) strong, well-made gelding; quite a moderate handicapper; stays 13f; suited by top-of-the-ground. *D. Ringer.* **46**

PRINCELY DANCER 3 ch.g. Connaught 130–Italian Idol (Sheshoon 132) (1979 7f 1980 8g 8.5g^2 12f 10f) strong, fair sort; has ability but is thoroughly temperamental and has twice swerved left at the start and unseated his rider; should stay 1½m; trained by R. Akehurst first 3 starts; best left alone. *J. Etherington.* **§§**

PRINCELY FOOL 5 ch.g. Run The Gantlet–Crepello Gift 75 (Crepello 136) (1979 17.1g 1980 16fg) good-bodied gelding; stays 1¾m; acts on a soft surface; has been tried in blinkers; lightly raced. *B. Palling.* —

PRINCELY GUY 5 b.h. Lorenzaccio 130–Cranberry Sauce 119 (Crepello 136) **57**
(1979 14fg 10.1fg 12g 10g* 10fg 1980 10d 12d*) leggy horse; attracted no bid after winning seller at Brighton in July; stays 1½m; seems suited by some give in the ground; blinkered last 2 starts in 1979 and at Brighton. *A. Pitt.*

PRINCELY LAD 2 ch.g. Sun Prince 128–Edissa 66 (Honeyway 125) (1980 **77**
8d $8d^2$ 8s) Apr 14; 25,000Y; small, unimpressive gelding; half-brother to several winners, including very smart French 1¼m performer Odisea (by Majority Blue): dam 1½m winner; neck second of 16 to Jade and Diamond in maiden race at Warwick in October; blinkered and sweating when well beaten in minor event at Stockton later in month; will stay 1¼m+; sold 4,700 gns Newmarket Autumn Sales. *J. Hindley.*

PRINCELY REALM 2 b.c. Realm 129–Clear Belle (Klairon 131) (1980 5d –
5f 6f) Apr 8; 5,000Y; 1,600 2-y-o; fair sort; half-brother to 2 winners, including useful Italian winner Laser Belle (by Laser Light); behind all outings, including in a seller. *P. K. Mitchell.*

PRINCELY RULER (USA) 2 ch.c. Foolish Pleasure–Sun Valley Linda **97** p
(Prince John) (1980 7g 8g*) Feb 26; half-brother to a minor winner by Pat McGroder; dam never ran; created a favourable impression when winning 13-runner maiden race at Maisons-Laffitte in October by 2½ lengths from world-record priced yearling Hoist The King, leading early in straight and not being hard pressed afterwards; will stay 1¼m; sure to make further progress. *J. Cunnington, jnr, France.*

PRINCE MAB (FR) 2 ch.c. Targowice 130–Princess Mab (Turn-to) (1980 **124**
$5d^3$ $5.5fg^3$ 5.5d* 6g* 6s* $6fg^3$ $7g^2$)

Although it's some considerable time since the Japanese managed to get their hands on a Derby winner the export of European-based stallions to Japan continues on a large scale. Since the beginning of 1978 about twenty stallions have been sent there, among them Bold Lad (USA), Dancer's Image, Pitcairn, Rheingold and Zeddaan, between them sires of Sirlad, Godswalk, Lianga, Saritamer, Ela-Mana-Mou, Cairn Rouge, Noir Et Or, Kalamoun and Nadjar, all top-class winners in recent seasons. It's easy to be wise after the event but of the above Bold Lad, Dancer's Image and Zeddaan were all well established at the time of their sale, Rheingold, whose first runners didn't appear until 1977, was given little chance to prove himself and Pitcairn, who was sold before his first crop completed their first full season, virtually none at all. Their loss is to be regretted as, so it seems, is that of Targowice, sold to Japan early in 1980. Before the latest season began Targowice had had three crops to represent him, and though they contained nothing outstanding he was far from a failure. Alas, all too late, his fourth crop had very good two-year-olds in Ukraine Girl, Greenway and Prince Mab, all of them trained in France.

Ukraine Girl (Prix d'Aumale) and Greenway (Prix d'Arenberg and Prix du Petit Couvert) took important events, but the best of the three is Prince Mab who came very close to landing the Prix de la Salamandre over seven furlongs at Longchamp in September on his final outing. Prince Mab, quickly into his stride, made the running at a good gallop and went clear early in the straight; soon afterwards he was joined by Miswaki and the pair of them fought out a terrific battle to the line where Miswaki prevailed by a head. The three other runners Silver Express, Travolta and Ancient Regime, finished upwards of five lengths behind, the last-named running way below her form. Four weeks earlier Prince Mab, fresh from a hat-trick of wins in good-class maiden and minor events at Evry, Maisons-Laffitte and Deauville, had finished two lengths behind Miswaki when the pair had been beaten by Ancient Regime in the Prix Morny. Once again Prince Mab showed up with the leaders from the start.

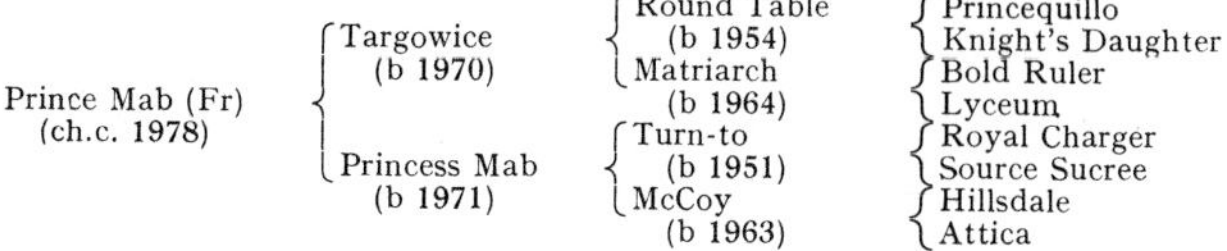

Prince Mab (Fr) (ch.c. 1978)	Targowice (b 1970)	Round Table (b 1954)	Princequillo
			Knight's Daughter
		Matriarch (b 1964)	Bold Ruler
			Lyceum
	Princess Mab (b 1971)	Turn-to (b 1951)	Royal Charger
			Source Sucree
		McCoy (b 1963)	Hillsdale
			Attica

Clearly the distance of the Salamandre suited Prince Mab, but stamina won't be his forte as a three-year-old. A free-running sort who wears blinkers, Prince Mab seems likely to prove best at around a mile. His pedigree supports this view. Targowice, the outstanding French two-year-old of 1972, only once attempted a distance longer than a mile and didn't run up to his best. Princess Mab, the dam, successful in a nine-furlong handicap at Compiegne as a three-year-old, is a daughter of McCoy, the winner of three races at up to six furlongs in America. Her first foal, a full sister to Prince Mab named Princesse Margo, is a sprinter. McCoy, a half-sister to Sir Ivor, is the grandam of the very smart French three-year-old Ruscelli. In general the French two-year-olds look below average and Prince Mab will have to improve considerably to upset Storm Bird or To-Agori-Mou in the Guineas in the unlikely event of his coming over. However, we shouldn't be at all surprised to see him run well in the French Guineas. He appears to act on any going. *A. Head, France.*

PRINCE MAJ (USA) 2 b.c. His Majesty–Lady Rosse (Hail to Reason) (1980 6g) Mar 4; $160,000Y; unfurnished colt; second foal; dam, winner over 1m, is half-sister to very smart stakes winner Prince Dantan and Stage Door Betty; unquoted, didn't move very well to post and appeared to swerve at start when behind in 21-runner maiden race won by Rahway at Newmarket in June. *M. Stoute.* –

PRINCE MOULTON 2 b.c. Moulton 128–Every Blessing 110 (Parthia 132) (1980 6g 7g 7fg 7fg 8fg4 8.2v) May 5; 27,000Y; compact colt; half-brother to 2 winners, including fairly useful 1½m winner Pine Tree Hill (by Sir Ivor); dam, winner at up to 8.5f, is half-sister to high-class stayer Die Hard; quite a moderate maiden; will stay 1¼m+; acts on a firm surface and was well beaten on heavy going (had little chance at weights); blinkered third and fourth outings; sold 5,600 gns Newmarket Autumn Sales. *J. Dunlop.* **72**

PRINCE NONO 2 br.c. Nonoalco 131–Kissing 98 (Sing Sing 134) (1980 7f) Mar 13; 54,000Y; third foal; half-brother to 1¼m winner Bustedaway (by Busted) and a winner in Italy; dam won twice over 5f at 2 yrs; 25/1 and in need of race when 9½ lengths ninth of 19 to King's Glory in maiden race at Newmarket in October. *M. Stoute.* **72** p

PRINCE NONOALCO (USA) 3 gr.c. Nonoalco 131–Ileana 113 (Abernant 142) (1979 7fg3 1980 10fg* 10fg 12f 8g 8fg 8g2 8g) big, strong colt; landed odds in maiden race at Brighton in April; ran best subsequent race to be neck second to Infant Prodigy in £3,500 handicap at Sandown in July; stays 1¼m but isn't bred to stay further; yet to race on a soft surface. *J. Dunlop.* **95**

PRINCE NORTHFIELDS 3 b.c. Northfields–The Game 80 (Petition 130) (1979 7f 7fg* 1980 10d4 10g) attractive, lengthy colt; easily won minor event at Lingfield at 2 yrs; lightly raced in 1980, putting up better effort when fourth of 7 to Dragon's Head in valuable handicap at Sandown in June; will stay 1½m; acts on a firm surface. *J. Dunlop.* –

PRINCE OF ARABIA 4 b.c. Amber Rama 133–Singing Girl 96 (Sing Sing 134) (1979 6fg 5f 1980 8fg 6f) neat colt; plater; stays 6f; sometimes wears blinkers; sold 480 gns Doncaster June Sales. *W. Clay.* –

PRINCE OF BLADES 3 b. or br.g. Fine Blade 121–Princess Irmgard 83 (Delirium 126) (1979 5d 6f 1980 6f 7fg4 8fg 8g 8g 7fg2 8g2 7f* 8g 7g2) fair sort; plater; attracted no bid after winning at Beverley in August; will stay beyond 1m; acts on firm going; best in blinkers. *P. Rohan.* **57**

PRINCE OF CROFT 2 br.c. Badedas 81–Photogenic 74 (Polic 126) (1980 6s 7g) Mar 28; fifth foal; dam showed a little ability at 2 yrs; unquoted when behind in minor event at Nottingham and maiden race at Leicester in July. *J. Edmunds.* –

PRINCE OF LIGHT 8 b.g. Laser Light 118–Royal Escape 94 (King's Bench 132) (1979 8.2f4 7fg 1980 10v 8f 10.6fg* 8fg4 8fg 9g 8d 8fg* 8f 8s) quite a moderate handicapper; beat Priestcroft Boy by 2½ lengths at Pontefract in July; had earlier won seller (no bid) at Haydock; best form at up to 1¼m; acts on any going except heavy; good mount for an apprentice; suited by an uphill finish and has won 5 times at Carlisle. *Denys Smith.* **63**

PRINCE OF PADUA 3 b.c. Wolver Hollow 126–Polonaise (Takawalk II 125) (1979 7s* 1980 7f4 10f* 11fg* 10g 10g 8.2d) well-made, attractive colt; fairly useful handicapper; narrow winner at Lingfield in May (from Comedy Croft) and Newbury in June (held off Champagne Charlie by a head, pair clear); not **96**

disgraced final start (apprentice ridden); stays 11f; acts on any going; sold 9,600 gns Newmarket Autumn Sales. *H. Cecil.*

PRINCE OF PLEASURE 7 b.g. Saintly Song 128–Counsel's Opinion 83 (Counsel 118) (1979 12s2 13s 14g 12d 12.3f3 15.8fg* 1980 17.1d) fair handicapper on his day; last of 23 behind Botanist at Bath in October on only outing of 1980; stays well; acts on any going; has been tried in blinkers; seems well suited by strong handling; quite a useful hurdler. *M. Tate.* —

PRINCE OF SHEBA (USA) 4 b.g. Raja Baba–Miss Glamour Gal (Ambiorix 130) (1979 7d2 6s2 6fg 6g3 6s 5.8fg 5fg2 1980 5s 6g 6h 7fg 5.1g2 5g*) lightly-made gelding; good mover; finished strongly when neck winner from Winsor Boy in handicap at Leicester in July; behind in seller on fourth outing; stays 7f; probably acts on any going; sometimes wears blinkers and did so last 3 starts; sold to N. Callaghan 860 gns Newmarket December Sales. *J. Sutcliffe.* **68**

PRINCE OF SPAIN 5 b.h. Philip of Spain 126–Miss Meryl 80 (River Chanter 121) (1979 7d3 8d 6g4 7s* 6g 6g 7fg* 7f 7fg 7g3 8g2 8f4 7f 1980 7v3 7fg4 7g 8fg2 7h2 7fg4 7h* 8d4 8fg 7d3 7fg 7f4 7fg4 7s4) won handicap at Chepstow in May by short head from Chads Gamble; stays 1m; acts on any going; suitable mount for an apprentice; blinkered thirteenth start. *P. M. Taylor.* **72**

PRINCE OF STEEL 3 b.c. Prince Regent 129–Autumn Ballad 75 (Tudor Melody 129) (1979 5s 6fg 6f 6g 6fg 1980 7d 12g 12fg 10s 10fg 12fg 12g4 11d2 15.8fg 12s 12d) leggy, rather hollow-backed colt; only plating class; stays 11f; acts on a soft surface. *R. Hollinshead.* **61**

PRINCE RHEINGOLD 4 br.c. Rheingold 137–Hail to Vail (Hail to Reason) (1979 10s2 10fg3 12g 12g3 11.5s 10.5s4 1980 10f2 12fg 10f* 12fg* 12fg 10.5f 11.1fg 10d4) rangy, good-looking ex-French colt; favourite when winning minor event at Pontefract in May (hacked up) and Watt Memorial Stakes at Beverley in June, latter very cheekily by ½ length from Golden River (gave 7 lb); also ran well when 3 lengths second to Gregorian in Westbury Stakes at Sandown in April and when 3½ lengths fourth of 6 behind Welsh Chanter in Valdoe Stakes at Goodwood in September but was tailed off on all his other starts; stays 1½m; acts on any going; has worn bandages; blinkered final start at 3 yrs and at Goodwood; none too reliable. *J. Dunlop.* **103 ?**

PRINCE ROLAND 3 b.c. Prince Regent 129–Aunt Audrey 111 (Aureole 132) (1979 8fg4 1980 10.5f 10f* 10.5d* 12fg2 12g* 11d*) attractive, well-made colt; third foal; half-brother to fairly useful middle-distance winner Uncle Ivor (by Sir Ivor); dam, very useful over 5f and 6f at 2 yrs, is half-sister to Queen's Hussar; developed into a smart performer, winning maiden event at Epsom, £2,500 race at York, Welsh Derby at Chepstow (by ¾ length from Marathon Gold) and Mecca Bookmakers Scottish Derby at Ayr; made all and ran on strongly to beat Moomba Masquerade 1½ lengths (pair clear) in last- **119**

Daniel Prenn Plate, York—a two-length win for Prince Roland

Mr Richard Swift's "Prince Roland"

named in July; stays 1½m; seems well suited by some give in the ground; game and consistent; sent to Oman. *B. Hills.*

PRINCE RUNNYMEDE 3 br.c. Great Nephew 126–Princess Runnymede 108 (Runnymede 123) (1979 6fg 7g 6g 1980 9f 10.2d 12s 10s) neat, quite attractive colt; no sign of ability in varied company and gave distinct impression on third outing at 2 yrs that his mind wasn't on racing. *J. Douglas-Home.* —

PRINCE SANDRO 3 br.c. Hotfoot 126–Otra 88 (Sayajirao 132) (1979 6g 1980 8fg[4] 10g[4] 8fg* 8g 10.1d[2] 11d* 10fg[4] 12g 13s[2] 12d) big, well-made colt; fair performer; won 22-runner maiden race at Warwick in June and handicap at Wolverhampton in August; beat Tenoria 2 lengths in latter under 10-0; stays 13f; suited by some give in the ground; game. *F. J. Houghton.* **88**

PRINCES ARCADE 7 b.g. Prince Regent 129–Valley Farm 88 (Red God 128§) (1979 NR 1980 13.3f 10.1g) winning hurdler; poor maiden on flat. *G. Kindersley.* —

PRINCE'S DRIVE 2 b.g. Sovereign Path 125–Fille de Fizz (Ragusa 137) (1980 5fg 6g 7g 7fg 8g) Apr 2; 12,000Y; half-brother to modest 7f winner Sparta (by Averof); dam unraced daughter of Oaks fourth Taittinger; poor maiden; blinkered fifth outing. *S. Woodman.* —

PRINCES GATE 3 br.c. Realm 129–Consensus (Majority Blue 126) (1979 NR 1980 6f 8fg 8d* 10d* 8g* 8d[4] 8g* 9f 8s) strong, workmanlike colt; third foal; half-brother to good Italian winner Mispy (by Pall Mall); dam, winner over 6f at 2 yrs, is half-sister to very smart miler Pally; successful in maiden race at Salisbury, amateur riders event at Newmarket, ladies race at Salisbury (odds on) and gentleman riders event at Goodwood; stays 1¼m; suited by some give in the ground; good mount for an inexperienced rider. *H. T. Jones.* **95**

PRINCE'S LILLIE 3 b.f. Some Hand 119–Saucy Queen 110 (Hard Sauce 131) (1979 7fg 5.8g 8.2fg 1980 11.7f 12h 8s) bad plater; sold 460 gns Ascot July Sales. *J. Bethell.* —

PRINCE SPRUCE (USA) 3 b.c. Big Spruce–Matoa (Tom Rolfe) (1979 7f 8f^4 7g 1980 8.5f^3 8fg* 10f^2 10.2fg^2 12f 10g 10g 13.1f* 12f* 14fg^3 16g 11.2g^2) neat, strong colt; very good mover; successful in maiden race at Kempton and handicaps at Bath (from Hasty Dawn) and Lingfield (made all to beat Ceramic hard held in 3-runner event); stays 1¾m; genuine; sold 16,000 gns Newmarket Autumn Sales, and ran well in Italy final start. *J. Dunlop.* **94**

PRINCESS ADELINE 3 ch.f. Mount Hagen 127–Theban Queen (Pindari 124) (1979 5d^4 6fg 5g 1980 10fg 12s 10.2d) of little account. *R. Hollinshead.* **—**

PRINCESS CHARYBDIS 3 b.f. Ballymoss 136–Pictynna (Polic 126) (1979 NR 1980 7.6f) sixth foal; dam ran only at 2 yrs; distant ninth of 12 behind Salt Of The Earth in maiden race at Lingfield in June. *G. Balding.* **—**

PRINCESS DINA 2 b.f. Huntercombe 133–Russian Princess 99 (Henry the Seventh 125) (1980 7g 7fg 6f^2 6d^2) Mar 11; 40,000Y; good-bodied, useful-looking, rangy filly; good mover; sister to fairly useful 1m and 1¼m winner Lady Mason, and half-sister to numerous winners, including good French middle-distance stayer Paddy's Princess (by St Paddy); dam, half-sister to Connaught, won over 6f at 2 yrs; ½-length second in 19-runner maiden race won by Long Legend at Newmarket and in 18-runner minor event won by Perlesse at Pontefract, both in October; didn't seem suited by track at Pontefract and put in all her best work in closing stages; will stay 1m as a 3-y-o; looks the type to train on. *J. Dunlop.* **87**

PRINCESSE LIDA (USA) 3 b.f. Nijinsky 138–Princesse Lee 125 (Habitat 134) (1979 5g* 6fg* 7g* 8s^3 1980 8fg^2 8d^3 7s 6.5d 7d* 7v) attractive filly; first foal; dam very speedy French 2-y-o in 1974; won Prix du Pin at Longchamp in October by short head from Safita (gave 6 lb); ran best other races on same course when neck second to Aryenne in Prix de la Grotte, 1½ lengths third to same filly in Poule d'Essai des Pouliches and almost 3 lengths sixth of 9 to Moorestyle in Prix de la Foret on final start; stays 1m; probably acts on any going; blinkered fourth start; smart. *A. Head, France.* **114**

PRINCESS GALICIA 2 b.f. Welsh Pageant 132–Galicia 105 (Great Nephew 126) (1980 6g 6g^4 7g 6d^4 6g^2) Mar 28; 38,000Y; well-made filly; sister to minor French 1¼m and 13f winner Mazouz, and half-sister to 2 winners, including fairly useful 1979 2-y-o Galatch (by Thatch); dam won at up to 1m; in frame in maiden and minor races late in season; went down by 2½ lengths to Velvet Habit in 21-runner event at Leicester on final outing; took on better company on first 3 outings; will stay 1¼m. *J. Dunlop.* **82**

PRINCESS GAYLE 2 b.f. Lord Gayle 124–Ermyn Lass 64 (Ennis 128) (1980 5s* 5g* 5s^3 5g) Mar 10; 33,000Y; rather leggy filly; poor mover; half-sister to 3 winners by Carnival Dancer, notably smart sprinter Ubedizzy; dam 5f winner; landed the odds by 2½ lengths in modest maiden race at Newcastle in August and ran on gamely to win by a head and the same from First Movement and Amorous in Highflyer Stakes at Thirsk the following month; faced stiffish tasks subsequently, finishing last of 3 to Tina's Pet in Harry Rosebery Challenge Trophy at Ayr later in September and ninth of 16 to Fire Mountain in nursery at Newmarket in October; will stay 6f. *M. Stoute.* **94**

PRINCESS GIFT (HOL) 3 ch.f. Uncanny–Pequeno (Divine Gift 127) (1979 5 times unplaced in Holland 1980 6fg 8f^3 12d 12g 12.5g) ex-Dutch filly; third of 12 in Dutch 1,000 Guineas at Duindigt in May; well beaten in varied company on her other starts; best run at 1m on firm going. *M. Ryan.* **—**

PRINCESS KARIMA 2 gr.f. Young Emperor 133–Salima (Palestine 133) (1980 7fg 7g 8s 8.2s) Mar 29; 7,500Y; small, light-framed filly; sister to 1978 2-y-o 7f winner Marmourah, and half-sister to 3 winners, including fairly useful 3-y-o Lady Oakley (by Gulf Pearl), successful from 5f to 1m; poor plater; sold to BBA 700 gns Newmarket Autumn Sales. *I. Walker.* **—**

PRINCESS KOFIYAH 3 b.f. High Line 125–Kofiyah 95 (Petition 130) (1979 6f^3 7fg 6f 1980 8.2g 8g^2 8g 9.4fg^2 8f*) leggy, light-framed filly; beat Vagabond King by ¾ length in handicap at Wolverhampton in September; will stay 1¼m+; acts well on firm going; bandaged off-hind first outing. *N. Guest.* **72**

PRINCESS MATILDA 3 br.f. Habitat 134–Bombazine 110 (Shantung 132) (1979 5f^4 6f^2 1980 7f^3 8fg 8fg^3 7d^2 7g* 7g* 8g^4) lengthy, good sort; good walker; successful in maiden race at Leicester in July (beat Scigueta ¾ length) and minor event at Redcar following month (clever neck winner from Souliotissa); will stay 1¼m; probably acts on any going; blinkered nowadays. *F. J. Houghton.* **82**

PRINCESS MOURN 2 br.f. Royal and Regal–Bella Fino (Major Portion 129) (1980 7.2d 8.2g 7g 10s) Apr 20; 3,500Y; fair sort; half-sister to a winner abroad; dam Irish 2-y-o 5f winner; little worthwhile form in maiden and minor events. *R. Hollinshead.* —

PRINCESS NAMNAN 4 gr.f. Namnan 102–Seasail 63 (Hard Tack 111§) (1979 8d 8g 1980 12f) poor maiden. *P. Cundell.* —

PRINCESS PAGEANT 3 br.f. Welsh Pageant 132–Too Much 100 (Major Portion 129) (1979 NR 1980 7f³ 7f* 8.5f 8d² 10f* 8d² 12g* 12v) 13,000Y; narrow, light-framed filly; half-sister to several winners in France; dam won at up to 1m; won maiden race at Ayr in May (odds on) and 2 handicaps at Newmarket in the autumn, beating Cowdenbeath smoothly by 2 lengths for final success; suited by middle distances; probably acts on any going. *B. Hills.* **95**

PRINCESS SCYLLA 3 ch.f. Ballymoss 136–Treasury (Henry the Seventh 125) (1979 NR 1980 7d 7fg 10.2fg) small filly; fourth foal; dam of little account; no sign of ability in maiden races in the South. *G. Balding.* —

PRINCESS VRONSKI 2 b.f. The Brianstan 128–Vron 91 (Anwar 120) (1980 5fg 5f 6f 5g 5s) Mar 29; 1,500Y; workmanlike filly; half-sister to several winners, including fair 1m to 2¼m winner Voie Unique (by Takawalk II); dam won at 1m and 1¼m; seventh of 19 to Wonderful in maiden race at Windsor in May, second outing; well beaten afterwards, final race a Stockton seller. *J. Toller.* —

PRINCESS WILHEMINA 3 b.f. Royalty 130–Miss Wilhemina 84 (Quorum 126) (1979 5fg 1980 11d) workmanlike filly; broke her back in maiden race at Newbury in July; dead. *Miss A. Sinclair.* —

PRINCES TOWER 2 gr.c. Saritamer 130–Lady Anne Neville 92 (Right Boy 137) (1980 6d 6fg 7g) Mar 26; strong colt; half-brother to a winning plater; dam won all her 4 starts, each at 5f; not fully wound up when in rear in maiden races; sold 760 gns Newmarket Autumn Sales. *R. D. Peacock.* —

PRINCETON 3 gr.g. Sun Prince 128–Queen's Castle 98 (Sovereign Path 125) (1979 6g 6fg³ 8fg 1980 7f 8.2fg² 8d² 8g 8d 8fg*) rangy gelding; good mover; won handicap at Leicester in September all out by ½ length from Vagabond King; will be suited by 1¼m; sometimes blinkered but wasn't at Leicester; ran poorly fourth start; sold 10,000 gns Newmarket Autumn Sales. *R. Hern.* **77**

PRINCE WARREN 3 b.g. Pieces of Eight 128–Bobelle 62 (Pirate King 129) (1979 5f 6fg 6fg 7f² 8fg 8s* 1980 8.2d 8.5f 8fg 10g² 8g⁴ 12s² 10g 12g⁴) good-bodied gelding; good mover; fairly useful handicapper; suited by middle distances; acts on any going but is particularly well suited by soft; sometimes sweats up; out of his depth second outing and ran badly on final appearance; sold to W. Stubbs 2,400 gns Newmarket Autumn Sales. *P. Kelleway.* **88**

PRINCIBAL 2 b.c. Balliol 125–Dusky Princess (Sayajirao 132) (1980 6g 5.8fg 6g 7fg 8.2d 7g) Apr 8; 5,200Y; closely related to very useful Irish sprinter First Up (by Balidar); no worthwhile form, including in a seller; blinkered sixth outing; sold 270 gns Ascot October Sales. *D. Hanley.* —

PRINCIPAL DANCER 2 b.c. Prince Tenderfoot 126–Gay Bird 111 (Birdbrook 110) (1980 7s* 7g* 8.2g² 8g⁴ 7.3fg² 7g⁴ 7v) Mar 22; 5,200Y; strong, lengthy, short-legged colt; first foal; dam best at up to 1¼m; won 15-runner maiden race at Warwick in July by short head and minor event at Sandown later in month by a neck, fighting back extremely gamely to beat Campton in latter; subsequently ran well when in frame in nurseries, going down by 1½ lengths to Kalaglow when apprentice ridden at Newbury in September on fifth outing; stays 1m well; seems to act on any going, except perhaps heavy; very genuine. *P. Cole.* **103**

PRINCIPALITY 4 b.g. Crowned Prince 128–Carmine City 104 (Charlottesville 135) (1979 10d 8.2s 8fg² 10f 10f* 10fg⁴ 1980 12.3f 12h) strong, good sort; has reportedly had a wind operation; should stay 1½m; acts well on firm going; seen to best advantage when ridden up with the pace; sold 2,800 gns Ascot November Sales. *S. Mellor.* —

PRIONSAA 2 ch.c. Crowned Prince 128–Frame Up (Alycidon 138) (1980 6g²) May 8; 11,000Y; well-grown colt; half-brother to several winners, including fair Irish 1¼m Swift Verdict (by My Swallow); dam ran only twice; easy in market and in need of race, shaped well when ¾-length second of 7 to Norton Cross in maiden race at Ayr in July, challenging strongly from 2f out until eased close home when clearly held; will be suited by 7f and 1m. *W. H. H. Williams.* **76** p

PRIORY GIRL 7 b.m. Rugantino 97–Colonia (Colonist II 126) (1979 15.5g 16f 10g 12fg 1980 9.6fg 9.6h 12fg 12d 10f 12g) of no account. *J. O'Donoghue.* —

PRIORY LANE 2 b.c. Martinmas 128–Jane Shaw (Galivanter 131) (1980 7fg 6s^2 6fg* 7fg^4 6g) May 26; 7,600Y; tall, lightly-built colt; half-brother to 4 winners, including fair middle-distance winner Visconti (by Lord Gayle); dam poor maiden; won 16-runner maiden race at Salisbury in September by 2½ lengths from unlucky-in-running Heighten; excellent fourth of 16, 2¾ lengths behind Centurius, in £3,900 event at Ascot later in month; needs further than 6f to be seen to best advantage nowadays, and will be suited by 1m; seems to act on any going. *S. Mellor.* **98**

PRISON PAYMENT 2 ch.g. Song 132–Miss Filbert 95 (Compensation 127) (1980 5fg 5d^4 5g^2 5g^3 5.8fg 5g 6g 6g^3 6g 5d^3) May 25; 6,000Y; neat, strong gelding; first foal; dam quite useful 7f to 1m handicapper; none too consistent but gained a place in maiden and minor events and a nursery; stays 6f; acts on a soft surface. *R. Hannon.* **78**

PRIVATE AUDIENCE 4 b.c. So Blessed 130–Private View 74 (Derring-Do 131) (1979 7fg 8g 7f 8f^4 8g^3 8fg^4 8fg* 1980 10g 14.6g^4 16g 11.5g) tall, rather narrow colt; fourth of 12 to Super Swallow in handicap at Doncaster in June, easily best effort of 1980; evidently stays 1¾m; yet to race on soft ground. *G. Beeson.* **60**

PRIVATE LIVES 2 b.f. So Blessed 130–Private View 74 (Derring-Do 131) (1980 5fg) May 1; 15,000Y; sister to 1m winner Private Audience and half-sister to 3 winners; dam stayed 1m; third favourite, never threatened leaders when seventh of 16 to Dressedtokill in maiden race at Leicester in May, only outing. *A. Hide.* **–**

PRIVATE LOVE 4 ch.g. Most Secret 119–Its-A-Match 72 (Compensation 127) (1979 6v 6s 8g 8s^4 5g 8g 7f 6s^2 6g^2 6d 6fg 1980 10d 8g 7g) narrow gelding; plater; unlikely to stay beyond sprint distances; best form in blinkers; sometimes sweats up. *A. Moore.* **–**

PROCLAIMER 2 gr.f. Town Crier 119–Deck (Le Dieu d'Or 119) (1980 5fg 5d^3 6fg^4 7f 5d 6d 6g) May 29; lightly-made filly; second foal; dam ran twice; plater; stays 6f; wears blinkers. *J. Mulhall.* **43**

PRODIGALITY 3 ch.f. Mount Hagen 127–Solviliana (Vilmorin) (1979 5d 5g 6f 1980 8d^2 9fg 10fg 12g 11d) small filly; second in seller at Doncaster in March; stays 1m; blinkered final start; sold 2,000 gns Newmarket July Sales. *P. Rohan.* **–**

PROMENADE CONCERT 2 b.f. Tower Walk 130–Music Mistress 83 (Guide 118) (1980 5f 5fg 7f 5g) May 15; leggy, rather sparely-made filly; good mover; only poor form, including when blinkered in seller on fourth start. *M. H. Easterby.* **–**

PROPER GENTLEMAN 2 b.c. Manacle 123–Molly Morgan 91 (Pirate King 129) (1980 5fg^3 5h 6g 6d^3 7fg 7d) Feb 10; 2,300Y; leggy colt; sixth living foal; dam 6f 2-y-o winner; modest third in maiden races at Kempton in May (auction event) and Chester in August; stays 6f but was well beaten over 7f; sold to BBA 1,600 gns Doncaster November Sales. *J. Douglas-Home.* **70**

PROPER MADAM 4 b.f. Mummy's Pet 125–Old Scandal 72 (Elopement 125) (1979 6d 5d^2 6d 6g 5fg 5f* 5g 5fg* 5d 6fg 5g 6s 5h* 5f^2 6g^4 5s 1980 6f 5f 5f 5f 5g 5g 5fg 5fg 5d 7f 7f 6f 5d 5d) strong, useful-looking filly; useful performer on her day in 1979; little worthwhile form in 1980; stays 6f; seems to act on any going except perhaps heavy; unruly in paddock when blinkered once as a 2-y-o; not an easy ride. *P. Asquith.* **–**

PROSERPINE 3 ch.f. Proverb 127–Aucuba 98 (Hornbeam 130) (1979 10s 1980 10g^4 12s 12d) rangy filly; has shown some ability in maiden races; will stay 1¾m. *W. Hastings-Bass.* **–**

PROSETT 2 br.c. Heres 81–Native Verse (Indigenous 121) (1980 6fg 6fg 8d^4 10d) Mar 22; leggy, narrow colt; fourth live foal; dam of little account; plater; suited by 1m but was well beaten over 1¼m. *C. Wildman.* **59**

PROSPECTOR'S SECRET (USA) 3 ch.f. Mr Prospector–Secret Veil (Royal Union) (1979 5d^4 6g 5fg^2 7fg* 7g 1980 6f 8.5f 5.3fg 7g 7fg 6fg^3 7g) leggy filly; quite a moderate handicapper at her best; stays 7f; acts on a firm surface; sometimes sweats up; bandaged second start; trained by P. Read first 2 outings. *A. Breasley.* **74**

PROTECTION RACKET (USA) 2 b.c. Graustark–Protectora (Prologo) (1980 7fg 7d 8g^3) strong, rangy colt; has a round action; dam top filly in Chile, winning 9 races from 6f to 1½m, and subsequently showed very useful form in USA, winning at up to 1¼m; favourite for Houghton Stakes and minor race at **84**

Newmarket in October on second and third outings, finishing fifth to Sunley Builds and third to Video Tape; beaten 2½ lengths and a head in latter and looks rather one paced; will probably stay well. *J. Hindley.*

PROTECTRESS 3 b.f. Auction Ring 123–Blue Plover (Majority Blue 126) (1979 6fg 5fg 6fg4 6s2 5fg 1980 7f* 7f* 7fg* 7g* 7d4 7g* 7fg2 7f4) big, rangy filly; had a fine season, winning maiden race at Lingfield (made all), minor event at Catterick and handicaps at Wolverhampton, Sandown and Brighton; carried 10-0 when beating Swing The Axe by ½ length on last-named in August; will stay 1m; acts on any going; genuine and consistent; sold 32,000 gns Newmarket December Sales, reportedly for export to South Africa. *G. Pritchard-Gordon.* **94**

PROUD BREED 2 b.f. Nonoalco 131–Ruta (Ratification 129) (1980 6d) Apr 3; 31,000Y; light-framed filly; half-sister to several winners, notably French Derby and Prix de l'Arc de Triomphe winner Sassafras (by Sheshoon) and smart French 1m to 1¼m winner Sorbi (by Stupendous); dam won at 2 yrs in Ireland and comes from family of Roi Dagobert and Shantung; unquoted but reasonably fit, never showed with chance when behind in 25-runner maiden race won by Little Wolf at Newbury at the back-end. *J. Dunlop.* **—**

PROUD QUEEN 5 ch.m. Florescence 120–Betsy Cluppins 68 (Soueida 111) (1979 8s 12g 8fg 1980 10.1g 10.1g 7f) leggy, light-framed mare; of no account. *J. Jenkins.* **—**

PROUSTILLE (FR) 3 b.f. Armos–Chinoise (Kurun 127) (1979 8s2 10v* 10v4 1980 8v4 10.5v2 9.5g 10fg 12g* 10.5g 12.5s2 12d2 13.5g 13.5g 12f 12.5d4 12s 12g4) rangy filly; sixth foal by a thoroughbred stallion; half-sister to a winning stayer by Whippoorwill; dam never ran; had a very busy season, but ran a number of good races; won Prix des Tuileries at Longchamp in May; moved down to fourth after beating Kelbomec a neck in Grand Prix de Nantes in November; creditable second in Prix Penelope at Saint-Cloud (½ length behind Good To Beat), Prix Maurice de Nieuil on same course (beaten 3 lengths by Buckpoint) and Prix de Minerve at Evry (went down by a neck to Great Verdict, rec 6 lb); not disgraced when fourth to Mariella in Prix de Royallieu at Longchamp in October; stays 1½m well; needs some give in the ground; sometimes bandaged; has had her tongue tied down. *P. Biancone, France.* **113**

PROVE IT BABY (USA) 4 b.c. Prove Out–Mail Rush (Prince John) (1979 10g* 15s2 15d* 15fg4 15g4 15g* 15.5s 1980 15.5g 15.5g2 20fg2 12g* 12.5s 12.5d) leggy colt; won Group 3 La Coupe at Chantilly in June by 3 lengths from Boucicault; second previously in Prix Jean Prat at Longchamp (ran on gamely but was beaten a neck by Hard To Sing) and Prix du Cadran on same course (went down by 6 lengths to Shafaraz); effective at 1½m and stays very well; appears to act on any going; wears blinkers; sent to race in USA. *F. Boutin, France.* **119**

PROVIDENTIAL 3 b.c. Run The Gantlet–Prudent Girl 92 (Primera 131) (1979 7.5s* 10v* 1980 10.5fg* 12fg2 12fg3 10g 12f 12s4 14v3 12fg) third foal; half-brother to Irish 7.5f to 11.5f winner Miller's Lass (by Mill Reef); dam, half-sister to Hethersett, Proud Chieftain and Royal Prerogative, won over middle distances; smart performer; won Prix Greffulhe at Longchamp in April **118**

Prix Greffulhe, Longchamp—Providential wins from Blast Off and Bobiffic

by 1½ lengths from Blast Off; in frame subsequently in Prix Hocquart on same course (short-neck second to Mot D'Or), Prix du Jockey-Club at Chantilly (4½ lengths third to Policeman), Prix du Conseil de Paris at Longchamp (met winner on terms 12 lb worse than w.f.a. when 3 lengths fourth to En Calcat) and Premio Roma at Rome (7½ lengths third behind Mariella); best form at up to 1½m; probably acts on any going; trained first 3 outings by F. Boutin. *O. Douieb, France.*

PROW 3 ch.c. Hotfoot 126–Bedeni 100 (Parthia 132) (1979 6g 1980 11fg 12g 10s 11.7g* 13.3d) good-topped, good-looking colt; awarded minor event at Windsor in September after being interfered with by ½-length winner Crispin; should stay beyond 1½m; blinkered last 2 starts; sold to S. Nesbitt 10,000 gns Newmarket Autumn Sales. *R. Hern.* **74**

PRUNHECO 2 b.c. Bustino 136–I'll Be Here (Ambiopoise) (1980 8.5g* 10v) Feb 11; 43,000Y; third foal; half-brother to 2 minor winners, including stayer Royal Resident (by Prince Regent); dam, winner of claiming races at up to 1m in USA, is half-sister to successful broodmare Peace; won 18-runner maiden race at Maisons-Laffitte in October by ¾ length from Montsegur; started 2/1 favourite for Group 2 Criterium de Saint-Cloud the following month but was beaten early in straight and faded to finish remote eighth of 10 to The Wonder; said to be very highly regarded and must be given a chance to show his form on the heavy ground at Saint-Cloud is all wrong. *F. Mathet, France.* **?**

PULCINI 5 b.m. Quartette 106–Pulchra 107 (Celtic Ash) (1979 NR 1980 12s² 16.5g³ 15.5fg³ 16fg 16fg 18s) staying maiden; seems to act on any going. *J. Benstead.* **41**

PULHAM VENTURE 3 b.g. Tudor Music 131–Mille Fleurs (Floribunda 136) (1979 6fg² 6fg 7fg⁴ 8g³ 1980 10s⁴ 10g³ 8.2g 8fg 8.2g⁴ 8g 8fg 10fg⁴ 8.2s) small gelding; plater; stays 1¼m; blinkered sixth start. *D. Weeden.* **—**

PULL THE CRACKER 3 ch.f. Habat 127–Cracker 103 (Court Harwell 130) (1979 5f 7g 1980 7h 10g 7g 8.2g 8s) lightly-made filly; poor form in varied company; sold 2,400 gns Newmarket December Sales. *J. Winter.* **—**

PULSE RATE 4 b.g. Prince Tenderfoot 126–Florence Nightingale 78 (Above Suspicion 127) (1979 8s² 10d* 8fg* 12g² 1980 10d 8g 11s* 9f³) quite an attractive gelding; ridden by 5-lb claimer and looking extremely well, fulfilled promise of his previous run and put up an excellent performance when winning valuable Ladbroke Ayrshire Handicap at Ayr in September by 1½ lengths from Amber Vale, leading 2f out and holding on well under pressure; ran another fine race in William Hill Cambridgeshire at Newmarket the following month, finishing length behind Baronet and Dromefs in third after racing prominently throughout; probably stays 1½m; acts on any going; genuine. *M. H. Easterby.* **108**

PUNCTILIOUS 2 b.c. Prince Tenderfoot 126–Heure de Pointe (Le Fabuleux 133) (1980 5f 6s 6g 7fg 7fg³) Mar 28; 6,800F; narrow colt; third produce; dam half-sister to Grand Prix de Paris runner-up Point de Riz; ran on well to finish 6 lengths third of 16 to Master Golfer in seller at Newmarket in October, best effort: will be suited by middle distances; blinkered second to fourth outings. *M. Stoute.* **69**

PUNDY 3 b.f. Grundy 137–Palatch 120 (Match III 135) (1979 NR 1980 7f 12d) good-looking, rangy filly; eighth foal; half-sister to top-class middle-distance performer Patch (by St Paddy); dam won Musidora Stakes and Yorkshire Oaks; behind in newcomers race at Newbury in April and maiden race at Brighton in June. *P. Walwyn.* **—**

PURE SPEED 2 b.c. Speedy Dakota 124–Purissima (Walhalla) (1980 5g 6g 7f) Apr 30; 1,800Y; leggy colt; fourth living foal; dam unraced half-sister to Worden II; little sign of ability in maiden races, two of them auction events. *A. Jarvis.* **—**

PURPLE FLAG 3 ch.g. Reform 132–Windflower 77 (Crepello 136) (1979 7f² 7f⁴ 7fg² 1980 9fg 8fg³ 10.1g* 10.1s 10s 10d) quite attractive, well-made gelding; made virtually all and ran on gamely to beat Spanish Dancer ½ length all out in minor race at Windsor in June, easily best effort; will stay 1½m; acts on firm going and is unsuited by soft; usually blinkered; sold out of R. Hern's stable 2,700 gns Ascot July Sales after fourth start. *O. O'Neill.* **83**

PUSEY STREET 3 ch.f. Native Bazaar 122–Diamond Talk (Counsel 118) (1979 5fg³ 5f 5fg* 5fg² 5g³(dis) 6s⁴ 1980 5fg³ 6f 6f⁴ 5f 5.8fg³ 5d² 5fg³ 5f³ 6s 8h 5f 5.8g 6fg⁴ 6fg³ 6d) leggy, light-framed filly; fair handicapper; best **86**

at sprint distances; probably acts on any going; suitable mount for a boy; ran moderately ninth start. *J. Bosley.*

PUSHY 2 ch.f. Sharpen Up 127–Mrs Moss 81 (Reform 132) (1980 5fg* 5fg* 5g* 6d 5fg³ 6fg² 6fg³ 5g*) **112**

The splendidly courageous and consistent Pushy has run her last race. She retires to stud with an admirable record, the winner of four races including the Group 2 Queen Mary Stakes and the Group 3 Cornwallis Stakes and only once unplaced in eight starts, most of them against smart opposition.

Pushy's performance in the Queen Mary at Royal Ascot in June was one of her best. The race was one of the most strongly-contested two-year-old events of the season, attracting no less than fourteen previous winners who'd been successful collectively in twenty-two of their thirty-one starts. The unbeaten Pushy, second favourite at 7/1, had already won twice at Newmarket, getting the better of Queen of Prussia by a neck in a maiden race before making all for a comfortable three-length victory in the George Lambton Stakes. Favourite at 5/2 was Nasseem, most impressive when slamming her twenty-five opponents on her debut at Salisbury, while next in the betting after Pushy were Welshwyn, a smooth winner of both her starts, the French filly Ancient Regime who had also shown a deal of promise when winning her only race, Ashbrittle, winner of the valuable Uplands Park Acorn Stakes, and Stats Emmar, a five-length winner first time out. With the field spread halfway across the course early on it wasn't easy to distinguish the leaders but by halfway Vienna Miss definitely held the lead with Welshwyn, Pushy, Nasseem, Stats Emmar and Ashbrittle also prominent. As Welshwyn came to take it up towards the middle of the course inside the final two furlongs, with Pushy on her heels, Ancient Regime looked to be coming with a dangerous run against the rails. The French filly didn't help her cause though by edging to her right and it was the game Pushy who ran on the strongest, leading inside the final furlong to win by a length and a half from Welshwyn. Nasseem kept on to deprive Ancient Regime of third place by a neck, three quarters of a length behind Welshwyn.

Pushy went on to confirm her standing as one of the best two-year-old fillies despite four successive defeats. Her Group 2 success brought her the maximum penalty in each of her next three races and in the circumstances she was far from disgraced. When giving weight to all ten of her opponents in the Cherry Hinton Stakes at Newmarket in July she was beaten less than three lengths into fifth place behind Nasseem, who received 6 lb, even though Piggott wasn't hard on her once her chance had gone; in the Molecomb Stakes she did as well as could be expected conceding 8 lb to the odds-on Marwell and the exceptionally speedy Swan Princess, running on to finish a four-length third to Marwell; and in the Sirenia Stakes at Kempton in September she once more proved superior to Nasseem after a prolonged battle, only to find the colt Cut Throat too strong in the final furlong. The last of her defeats came in the William Hill Cheveley Park Stakes at Newmarket in October. She put up a bold show, quickening into the lead at halfway, but Welshwyn had her measure with a furlong to run and neither could find an answer to Marwell's finishing burst. At the line Pushy was third, beaten a length and half a length, with Nasseem again behind her.

Just ten days after the Cheveley Park Pushy made her final appearance in the Cornwallis Stakes at Ascot. Of her six opponents the best supported

Queen Mary Stakes, Ascot—the game Pushy runs on strongly to beat Welshwyn. Nasseem, fourth at this stage, beats Ancient Regime for third place

Lord Tavistock's "Pushy"

were the Irish filly Indian Splash, an impressive winner of the Irish Chorus Stakes three months earlier on her last appearance, and Red Russet, a creditable fourth in the Mill Reef Stakes, but none looked a threat to Pushy on weight-for-sex terms. So it proved and Pushy ran on with all her customary zest, after leading soon after halfway, to win by a length and a half from The Quiet Bidder.

	Sharpen Up (ch 1969)	Atan (ch 1961)	Native Dancer
			Mixed Marriage
Pushy (ch.f. Mar 2, 1978)		Rocchetta (ch 1961)	Rockefella
			Chambiges
	Mrs Moss (ch 1969)	Reform (b 1964)	Pall Mall
			Country House
		Golden Plate (ch 1964)	Whistler
			Good as Gold

The £37,000 Pushy collected in prize money went further to showing what a bargain the Marchioness of Tavistock secured when she purchased the then six-year-old Mrs Moss for 2,100 guineas at the 1975 December Sales. Mrs Moss had won a five-furlong maiden race at two years from only four starts; her sire Reform was an established success, with nominations selling for an average of nearly 5,000 guineas at the time; her dam Golden Plate was a sister to the unbeaten Whistling Wind, who topped the Irish Two-Year-Old Free Handicap in 1962; her great-grandam was Gamble in Gold, the speediest two-year-old filly in England in 1950; and Mrs Moss's fecundity was established since she was carrying her third foal in as many years at stud. Since her sale in 1975 all five of Mrs Moss's foals of racing age have won, although one had to be sent to Malaysia to do so. None was so good as Pushy but the Pitskelly colt Pitstop has won five times over five furlongs and Pushy's brother Socks Up is a fairly useful sprinter.

Pushy has been sent to Kentucky to be covered by a leading stallion. Her sire Sharpen Up will also be at stud in Kentucky in 1981, standing his first season in America at a fee of 50,000 dollars, a substantial increase on the 10,500 guineas paid at auction for one of his 1980 nominations. Although Pushy's connections came in for some criticism in the Press over their decision to retire her after only one season they have, in our opinion, done the right thing. Pushy was most unlikely to stay beyond sprint distances and, as we have detailed at the end of Marwell's commentary, three-year-old fillies face an uphill struggle in the top sprint races. We also concur with connections' opinion that Pushy didn't have the size and scope to be confident of her training on satisfactorily—she was a useful-looking filly but definitely neat and on the small side. However, we cannot agree with part of a letter from Pushy's part-breeder which was published in *The Sporting Life*. The Marchioness expressed the view that 'if (a filly) has a hard racing career I believe that this is not in the best interest of her progeny'. The Americans would certainly disagree too. A look at the racing record of the dams of some of the most outstanding American breds of recent years shows that the theory doesn't hold water. Certainly the dams of Secretariat and Mill Reef ran only once each but what harm did a hard racing career do the dams of Seattle Slew (32 races), Affirmed (23), Alleged (31), Dahlia (71), The Minstrel (22), Sir Ivor (34), Roberto (38) and Exceller (24)? *H. Cecil.*

PUY-DE-VENT 3 b.c. Tumble Wind–Puya (Psidium 130) (1979 NR 1980 7f 6f 5fg^3 5d 5g 5g 5fg 5g 6f^2) 5,500Y; strong, attractive colt; half-brother to a winner; dam Irish 1m winner; blinkered first time when second in all-aged race at Folkestone in September; stays 6f; acts on firm going; displayed signs of temperament fourth start, giving a lot of trouble at start and swerving once put under pressure; sold 1,500 gns Newmarket Autumn Sales. *B. Swift.* **61**

PYJAMA GAME 3 b.f. Cavo Doro 124–Noddy Time 97 (Gratitude 130) (1979 7g 1980 10g 12f 11.5g^3 13g 16g^2 16d 14.6d^3 14g) plating-class maiden; stays well. *H. Collingridge.* **56**

PYKESTAFF 3 b.c. Giacometti 130–Miss Melanie (Hard Ridden 131) (1979 7fg 7f^3 7fg^4 1980 7s^4 6f^4 8h 7fg 6f^2 7g 8g 10f 6g^3 6g 7g 7g 6d 6d) leggy colt; best at 6f on firm going; often wears blinkers; sometimes sweats up; out of his depth sixth outing. *C. Austin.* **66**

PYMOOR PET 2 b.f. Mummy's Pet 125–Gold Ribbon 106 (Blast 125) (1980 5d) Apr 11; 4,200F, 5, 400Y; neat filly; half-sister to 2 winners, including fairly useful 1976 2-y-o 6f winner Sarasingh (by Mansingh); dam won over 7f and 1m at 2 yrs; 14/1 when tenth of 20 in maiden race won by Little Starchy at Sandown in October. *P. Cole.* –

PYTCHLEY MOSS 3 ch.f. Shiny Tenth 120–Pink Moss 82 (Ballymoss 136) (1979 5g 6f 5f 1980 12g) small filly; in rear in maiden and minor events. *R. Smyth.* –

Q

QUACK SHOT (USA) 3 b.f. Quack–Bombycid (Shantung 132) (1979 6g 1980 8g 10fg) narrow filly; showed a little ability in minor event at Newmarket in August, first start; should stay 1¼m; sold 940 gns Newmarket Autumn Sales. *J. Hindley.* –

QUAESTOR 2 b.c. Track Spare 125–Syltung (Shantung 132) (1980 5d 5s 7g^4 7g) Feb 21; 3,400Y; fair sort; first foal; dam won 3 small races over 11f in France; 2¼ lengths fourth of 18 to Price of Peace in maiden race at Salisbury in July, best effort; will be suited by 1m. *D. Elsworth.* **70**

QUAE SUPRA 3 ch.f. On Your Mark 125–Lunar Star (Star Gazer 123) (1979 5g 5s^3 5fg^2 5f^3 5d^4 5fg^4 1980 6f 5fg 5d^4 5d* 5g^4 5fg^4 5fg) big, quite well-made filly; won maiden race at Lingfield in July; not disgraced in handicaps next 2 starts; best at 5f; acts on a firm and a soft surface; usually wears blinkers. *P. Cundell.* **67**

QUAI D'OR 3 b.f. Joshua 129–Cropfall 79 (Acropolis 132) (1979 5fg 5f 1980 8fg 9f 10fg) well beaten in maiden races; sold 500 gns Ascot July Sales. *A. Breasley.* –

QUAI HAIS (USA) 3 b. or br.c. Arts and Letters–Rosewater (Sir Ivor 135) (1979 6fg 6f 7d* 8fg^4 8s^3 1980 8g) compact, good sort; won maiden race at Brighton in 1979; ran deplorably in seller only start at 3 yrs, in September; stays 7f. *P. Cole.* –

QUAINT 2 b.f. St Paddy 133–Quine 91 (Counsel 118) (1980 5d 7d 7g^4 7fg 9d) Apr 13; quite an attractive filly; half-sister to several winners here and abroad, **69**

including very useful 6f and 7f winner Miss Tweedie (by Aberdeen); dam won over 5f at 2 yrs; put up easily best effort when 1¾ lengths fourth of 16 to Skytrain Hostess in maiden race at Salisbury in September and would have gone very close to winning had she not been very short of room when challenging at distance; stays 7f but was well beaten over 9f. *R. Hannon.*

QUAKER STAR 4 b.g. Blast 125–Star of Bethlehem 77 (Arctic Star) (1979 10s4 8.2d* 8g* 9.4f* 9fg2 8s 8.2g 8g2 10g4 1980 8f 8fg2 9g 9g2 8fg3 10s3 8f 8fg4 8fg 8g 8s3) neat gelding; runner-up at Stockton in June and Hamilton in July; seems to stay 1¼m; acts on any going; ran poorly in blinkers seventh outing; has shown a tendency to hang; ridden by apprentice N. Connorton when successful; fell third start; sold to B. Lunness 2,700 gns Doncaster November Sales. *J. W. Watts* **61**

QUALITAIR QUEEN 3 b.f. Mummy's Pet 125–Great Blue White 73 (Great Nephew 126) (1979 5s 7fg 8.2g 1980 8.2s 8s 9f2 10.1fg 8f3 7f 7s 8d 8.3s* 8fg) leggy filly; plater; won at Windsor in July (bought in 1,600 gns); stays 9f; acts on any going; often wears blinkers; sometimes sweats up. *M. Ryan.* **44**

QUALITY ROAD 2 b.c. Roman Warrior 132–Llynian 81 (Ballylinan 118) (1980 5v 5g4 5f2 5h2 5f3 6d 5d3 6g 5f 5g* 5fg 6d 5d 5f2 5f 5d) Apr 29; 6,600Y; neat, strong colt; half-brother to a minor 2-y-o winner; dam won 6 races in Belgium and once over 5.5f in France; plater; ridden along all way when winning 6-runner event at Ayr in July by a neck from Awel-Haf; returned to form when 2 lengths second of 18 to Crosby Triangle at Ripon the following month and ran creditably in nursery on next start; form only at 5f; seems to act on any going; wears blinkers; none too consistent. *G. Richards.* **71**

QUAM CELERRIME 2 gr.f. Hasty Word 84–Hasty Decision 85 (Elopement 125) (1980 5g 5f 6g 6fg 7fg 6d4 7g 8.2d 8fg 8fg) Apr 12; 550F, 1,100Y; workmanlike filly; bad plater; usually blinkered. *W. Bentley.* **41**

QUANTUM MAJOR 4 b.c. Thatch 136–Smart Sheila 113 (King's Leap 111) (1979 5d 6v 5fg 5.3fg4 5h2 6fg2 5g* 5g 5f2 5g 1980 5g 5f4 5f 5fg 5.3g4) big, well-made colt; 4 lengths fourth of 12 to Crews Hill in Northern Sprint Handicap at Redcar in May on second outing, best effort of 1980; stays 6f; acts on hard going. *D. Whelan.* **68**

QUARRY BANK 5 b.g. Be Friendly 130–Farafa (Sing Sing 134) (1979 5v 5d 5d 5f 7f 7f 6g* 7d 7f 8.2g 7g* 1980 5d 6g4 6g 7fg 5g 8.2d* 6s 6s 7s) plater; attracted no bid after winning at Haydock in August; stays 1m; acts well on soft going; blinkered fifth start. *S. Nesbitt.* **52**

QUARRY BOY 3 br.g. Workboy 123–Goldwyn 107 (Goldhill 125) (1979 5g 5s 5fg 5f 1980 5h4 5fg4 5d 5fg) strong gelding; sprint maiden; will stay 6f; suited by fast ground. *M. W. Easterby.* **–**

QUARRY GIRL 3 b.f. Be Friendly 130–Farafa (Sing Sing 134) (1979 5d 5g 5s3 5f2 5fg 6g 5d 5g* 5d 1980 6fg 6d 7d 6d) neat filly; plater; well beaten in 1980; best form at 5f; probably acts on any going; went down and ran very freely third start. *S. Nesbitt.* **–**

QUAY BOY 2 b.c. Sandford Lad 133–Princess Quay (Babur 126) (1980 5fg 5f* 5f* 6g 6g) Mar 4; 2,000Y, resold 8,600Y; good-quartered colt; half-brother to several winners, including very useful 5f to 1¾m winner Netherkelly (by Le Levanstell); dam won over 7f in Ireland; favourite when winning maiden race at Windsor and weakly-contested minor event at Chepstow in May, making all in latter to beat subsequently-disqualified Hanham Road 2½ lengths; should stay 6f (had stiff tasks when in rear in nurseries over that distance); yet to race on a soft surface. *R. Laing.* **68**

QUAZAR LIGHT 3 ch.g. Hot Spark 126–Wrong Call 63 (High Perch 126) (1979 5f 6s3 5fg 5f 5fg3 5d 5s3 5g3 5g 6fg 8f 8g3 1980 8fg 11.7h) neat gelding; modest (rated 80) in 1979; in rear in maiden races at 3 yrs; not certain to stay middle distances; seems to act on any going; blinkered sixth start at 2 yrs; none too consistent. *L. Kennard.* **–**

QUEEN ADRIANA (ITY) 4 b. or br.f. King of the Castle–Adriana Lecouvreur (Nasram II 125) (1979 7g 11.1g 10g 1980 11.7fg 14.6g) very lightly-made filly; ran promisingly only start at 2 yrs but has been lightly raced and well beaten since; should be suited by middle distances. *J. Toller.* **–**

QUEEN BERENGARIA (CYP) 2 ch.f. Esperos–Turnbeam (Hornbeam 130) (1980 7d) tall, useful-looking filly; half-sister to several winners, including very useful sprinter Oscilight (by Swing Easy); dam won at 2 yrs in Sweden; 16/1 but **–**

fit when always behind in 13-runner maiden race won by Lambay at Leicester in October. *J. Dunlop.*

QUEEN GUINEVERE 2 b.f. Mansingh 120–Glencora (Ribero 126) (1980 5fg 5fg 5g3) Mar 21; small, lengthy filly; first foal; dam unraced twin; 4 lengths third of 17 to Hot Press in maiden race at Wolverhampton in July; will stay 6f; sold 400 gns Newmarket Autumn Sales. *J. Winter.* **65**

QUEEN KATE 3 b.f. Queen's Hussar 124–Krafty Kate 73 (Klairon 131) (1979 5s 5.3g 6f4 6g 6fg 1980 8.3g2 8.3f* 8h2 8g) compact filly; plater; attracted no bid after winning at Windsor in August; stays 1m well; acts on hard going; good mount for a boy. *N. Vigors.* **52**

QUEEN OF CORNWALL (USA) 3 br.f. Cornish Prince–Sweety Kid (Olympia) (1979 5s2 5d* 5fg* 5f3 6f 1980 5f 5fg4 5fg3) $69,000Y; neat, strong filly; poor mover in her slower paces; half-sister to numerous winners, including smart 1975 American 2-y-o Favorite Beau (by Beau Brummel) and useful stakes winner Bridewell (by Majestic Prince or Roberto); dam stakes winner at up to 6f; ran creditably to be in frame in King's Stand Stakes at Royal Ascot (3 lengths fourth to African Song) and King George Stakes at Goodwood (beaten 4 lengths into third behind Valeriga); should stay 6f; acts on any going. *M. Stoute.* **109**

QUEEN OF PRUSSIA 2 b.f. Bay Express 132–Julie Be Quick (Selari) (1980 5fg2 5g 5fg* 5fg*) Apr 2; neat, compact filly; excellent mover; second foal; dam won at up to 1m in USA; having first race for 3 months and ridden by 5-lb claimer, quickened away to win 6-runner minor event at Salisbury in September most impressively by 6 lengths from Lucaya; 11/4 on for 5-runner race at Ascot later in month but found nothing when let down in final furlong and finished 1½ lengths second to Dollar Pocket (subsequently promoted to first when Dollar Pocket failed a dope test); not sure to stay 6f. *W. Hastings-Bass.* **94**

QUEEN OF THE KOP 2 b.f. Queen's Hussar 124–Bound Over (Taj Dewan 128) (1980 6g 8f 8fg) Mar 21; 4,000Y; small filly; second foal; sister to 3-y-o 1¼m winner On Leave; dam never ran; little worthwhile form in maiden races. *F. Durr.* **—**

QUEEN OF VICTORY (USA) 2 ch.f. Apalachee 137–Ian Maid (Determine) (1980 8g 10d*) Feb 28; $220,000Y; half-sister to 3 winners, including Sans Critique (by Reviewer), a very useful stakes winner at up to 9f; dam, from same family as Atan and Known Fact, ran 8 times unplaced; beat subsequent winners Princesse Bea and Samata into second and third places when narrowly winning 16-runner minor event at Saint-Cloud in October; will stay 1½m; promising. *M. Saliba, France.* **?**

QUEEN'S AGLO 3 gr.f. Aglojo 119–Mountain Queen 58 (Sovereign Path 125) (1979 5fg 7.2g 1980 7fg 8g 10g 10g 10g 8f 7g) useless plater. *Mrs A. Harvey.* **—**

QUEEN'S BIDDER 3 br.f. Auction Ring 123–Stormy Queen 64 (Typhoon 125) (1979 5fg 5s 5g* 5fg* 1980 5g 5.8f* 5f4 5fg 5fg 6s 5.8g) small, full-quartered filly; won handicap at Bath in May; stays 6f; acts on firm going and is possibly unsuited by soft; ran poorly first start. *B. Gubby.* **78**

QUEENSBURY BOY 2 ch.c. Manacle 123–Lynn Regis (Ballymoss 136) (1980 5d4 5s 5.1f3 6d 7d3 6d 6g 6g 6d4 6g 6g 6g 8.2s) Mar 13; leggy colt; third foal; dam ran only once; quite moderate; stays 7f; acts on firm going and a soft surface; sweated up very badly sixth outing. *D. Dale.* **71**

QUEENSBURY GIRL 2 b.f. Whiffenpoof 97 §–Samataj (Taj Dewan 128) (1980 5d 5h 5fg 6f) Mar 22; leggy, very lightly-made filly; well beaten, including in sellers. *D. Dale.* **—**

QUEENSBURY LADY 3 b.f. Undulate–Dream Shared (Majority Blue 126) (1979 6g 8fg 10s3 1980 10s2 12f 12f 12h 12g 14g) plain, light-framed filly; poor maiden; best run at 1¼m on soft going. *D. Dale.* **—**

QUEEN'S CLUB 2 ch.f. Roman Warrior 132–Passing Shot 72 (Salvo 129) (1980 7fg 7d) Apr 10; small filly; second foal; dam, useful hurdler, won 1½m seller on flat; tailed off in maiden races at Lingfield (last of 19) and Leicester (missed break and always struggling) in October; sold 480 gns Ascot December Sales. *S. Woodman.* **—**

QUEEN'S COUNSELLOR 3 gr.f. Kalamoun 129–Cecilia Q.C. 89 (Counsel 118) (1979 6fg* 1980 8f2 8.5f 8g 8s 8g3 8fg) close-coupled filly; fair performer; creditable 2 lengths second of 9 to Dancing Shadow (rec 9 lb) in £3,500 fillies race at Sandown in May; ran respectably penultimate outing; stays 1m; acts on firm going and is probably unsuited by soft; bandaged off-hind fourth start; sold 50,000 gns Newmarket December Sales. *M. Stoute.* **85**

QUEEN'S COUP 2 ch.f. Dragonara Palace 115–Kumon Lass 92 (King's —
Coup 108) (1980 5fg 5fg 5fg 5fg 5g 7d 5f 7g 5g 8d 8.2s) Apr 18; 580Y; narrow,
leggy filly; half-sister to 1m winner Most Jubilant (by Most Secret); dam won
twice over 5f at 2 yrs; only poor form, including in sellers. *K. Bridgwater.*

QUEEN'S EQUERRY 3 b.g. Hotfoot 126–Queendom 109 (Quorum 126) 72
(1979 5d 5g 5g^{2} 1980 7.6f^{4} 8g 8g 8.3g^{4} 10f* 10.6d^{2} 8d^{3} 10d) small, useful-
looking gelding; good mover; won maiden race at Epsom in August; fair second
in handicap at Haydock following month; needs further than 1m and will
stay 1¼m; probably acts on any going; sweated up third start. *W. Wightman.*

QUEEN'S GALLERY 3 ch.f. King's Company 124–Private Collection 70 50
(Whistling Wind 123) (1979 5v 5d 5g 5.8g 5g^{4} 6g 6f 6fg^{2} 1980 7s 5fg 6g
7g 6g^{3} 10g) strong sort; plater; stays 6f and wasn't disgraced over 7f on fourth
start; suited by top-of-the-ground; has run respectably for a boy; sold to Mrs
R. Lomax 450 gns Ascot November Sales. *W. Wightman.*

QUEEN'S GARDEN 4 ch.f. Mill Reef 141–Meadow Pipit 103 (Worden II —
129) (1979 10s 11g 12g^{3} 1980 12fg 13.3g 12d^{4}) small, well-made filly;
plating-class maiden; should stay further than 1½m; moved poorly to post
on reappearance. *I. Balding.*

QUEEN'S MAGIC 3 ch.f. King's Company 124–Magic Lady (Gala Performance) —
(1979 5g 5d^{3} 6fg 6fg 6fg^{2} 7g 8fg 1980 9d 8.3f 8.3f) plater; best run at 6f
on a firm surface. *J. Hill.*

QUEEN'S MEAD 3 gr.f. Runnymede 123–Dorothy Darling 76 (Red God —
128 §) (1979 5g^{3} 5fg^{2} 5f 1980 6d 6f 7f 5d 6s 6fg 6g) small filly; quite moderate
(rated 76) at 2 yrs; ran poorly in 1980, including in a seller; should stay beyond
5f; sold 330 gns Ascot October Sales. *P. Kelleway.*

QUEEN'S MERCY 2 ch.c. No Mercy 126–Garrison Girl 67 (Queen's Hussar 43
124) (1980 5fg 5f 5fg 5f^{4} 6fg) Mar 5; workmanlike colt; plater; should stay
6f (ran wide on bend when tried at trip). *M. W. Easterby.*

QUEEN'S MOUNT 2 ch.g. Gay Fandango 132–Mountain Lark (Chamier 128) 89
(1980 5fg^{3} 5g^{3} 7fg* 7f^{3}) Apr 17; 5,000F, 6,800Y; well-made, attractive gelding;
good walker and mover; half-brother to several winners, including Irish 9f
winner Ballywackmacroo (by Ballymore); dam ran only twice; proved well
suited by the longer distance when winning 20-runner maiden race at Brighton
in August easily by 2 lengths from Castelnau; creditable third of 8 to comfortable
winner Cavalry Twill in minor event at Epsom later in month; will stay 1m;
yet to race on a soft surface; gelded and sent to Hong Kong. *J. Tree.*

QUEEN'S MUSIC 4 b.g. Queen's Hussar 124–Zither 72 (Vienna 127) (1979 —
10g 10s* 12fg^{4} 1980 16g 12fg) useful-looking gelding; won maiden race at
Leicester in 1979; had stiffish tasks when well behind in 2 races late in 1980;
probably stays 1½m; acts well on soft ground; wears blinkers; looked none
too genuine final outing of 1979. *J. Jenkins.*

QUEEN'S NIECE 4 b.f. Great Nephew 126–Queendom 109 (Quorum 126) 65
(1979 8d 8g 12d 8fg 8g 7g 8f 8fg 8fg^{3} 8.2s* 1980 7f 8fg 7fg 8d 8fg 8.3fg^{4} 8g^{2} 8d
7d) quite attractive, rangy filly; well-backed favourite, led till final furlong
when runner-up to Our Birthday in handicap at Chepstow in September, probably best effort; stays 1m; acts on any going; blinkered fourth start at 3 yrs.
W. Wightman.

QUEEN'S PATTERN 3 ro.c. Perhapsburg 112–Annamanda (Tycoon II) 64
(1979 6s^{4} 7f 7f 1980 8fg^{3} 10f 12.2fg 9.4d 12g 12g^{3} 10d^{4} 12d 12.5s) fair sort;
only plating class; will stay beyond 1½m; usually wears blinkers. *P. Asquith.*

QUEEN'S PRIDE 4 b.g. Royben 125–Queen's Penny (Queen's Hussar 124) 91
(1979 6v* 5d* 6g 7g^{2} 7.3g^{2} 7d^{3} 6f^{3} 1980 6v* 7f^{4} 6f 6fg* 6fg 6s 6s 6s 5s) compact,

Wokingham Stakes, Ascot—Queen's Pride, racing down the centre of the course, beats the blinkered King of Spain (rails)

useful sort; poor mover; made all and kept on well to win Wokingham Stakes at Royal Ascot in June by a length from King of Spain; had earlier scored by 4 lengths at Ayr; fair sixth of 28 to Repetitious in Spillers Stewards' Cup at Goodwood on penultimate outing in July, best subsequent effort; stays 7f; acts on any going; suitable mount for an apprentice; genuine. *P. Cole.*

QUEENS ROAD 2 br.f. Ballymore 123–Hailing Distance 94 (Hail to Reason) (1980 7fg 8fg 8.2s) May 1; 1,400Y, resold 7,600Y; good sort; second foal; half-sister to 3-y-o Irish 7f winner Good Cheer (by Bonne Noel); dam, placed over 6f at 2 yrs, is half-sister to very smart 1975 American 2-y-o Old Goat; behind in maiden and minor races at Doncaster, Leicester and Haydock. *K. Stone.* —

QUEEN'S ROYALE 5 b.m. Tobrouk–Fibula (King's Bench 132) (1979 7d 8d^4 7s 7fg 7f 8.3fg 8f 6g^4 5f 7.6fg 6s 1980 9.6fg 7g 6s^4 7g* 8.3g* 10g^2 8.3fg^2 12f) plater; won at Folkestone (no bid) and Windsor (bought in 1,800 gns) in July; ran well in better company next 2 starts; stays 1¼m; seems to act on any going; has worn blinkers. *M. Bolton.* **58**

QUEEN'S TOKEN 2 ch.f. Record Token 128–Queen Of Saba 105 (High Treason 126) (1980 5fg 5fg* 5g^2 5f^2 6g) Apr 7; lightly-built, leggy filly; half-sister to a winner; dam 5f sprinter; ran on strongly to win minor event at Ripon in May by a length from Bella Travaille; close-up second in nurseries won by Southern Swanee at Leicester and by Donatella at Beverley in July, in latter running well from a low draw; apprentice ridden, ran as though she didn't stay when tried over 6f; acted on firm going; dead. *W. Hastings-Bass.* **81**

QUEEN'S TRAVELLER 3 ch.g. St Columbus 98–Crafty Ann (Wily Trout 115) (1979 6s 6fg 6f* 7f^2 7fg^4 8g 1980 13.8f) lengthy gelding; plater; last in better company only start at 3 yrs, in July; should be suited by middle distances; acts on firm going; sold 1,750 gns Ascot October Sales. *P. Wigham.* —

QUES ANY 3 gr.f. Brittany–Endless Questions (Never Say Die 137) (1979 5g 5.3g 7fg 6g 5.8g 6f^3 7f 5fg 6g^4 1980 8fg^4 5.8f) neat filly; plater; should stay 1m; yet to race on a soft surface; often blinkered. *L. Carrod.* —

QUEST 2 br.f. Welsh Pageant 132–Round Eye (Round Table) (1980 5fg 5d 7d* 7h) Feb 20; small, useful-looking filly; half-sister to fairly useful middle-distance performer Old Cosimos (by Dike), subsequently successful in USA, and to 2 winners abroad; dam unraced daughter of half-sister to Mossborough; won maiden race at Wolverhampton in July by ½ length from K-Sera; had none too clear a run when favourite for nursery at Bath the following month and finished modest fifth to Violino Fandango; will stay 1¼m; possibly needs a soft surface. *R. Hern.* **72**

QUESTURNIUS 5 b.g. Calpurnius 122–Donquest (Don Carlos) (1979 NR 1980 13d) probably of little account. *H. Willis.* —

QUICK AS LIGHTNING (USA) 3 b.f. Buckpasser–Clear Ceiling (Bold Ruler) (1979 6fg* 7g^3 8fg* 1980 7.3fg^3 8fg* 12f^4 8g^2 12d 8.5g^2) **123**

Quick As Lightning won a close race for the One Thousand Guineas, just getting up from the second-largest field since 1927; a good-sized table-cloth would have covered the first five of the twenty-three runners. The winner's victory turned out to be her only one of the year and, like some of her recent predecessors, she failed to play a major role in the remainder of the season. Even so, she confirmed herself a good filly at a mile by finishing a close second to Cairn Rouge in the Coronation Stakes at Royal Ascot; she ran well below her best at a mile and a half in the Oaks and Irish Guinness Oaks, her only other races before her departure to Florida where she finished second in an allowance race at Calder in December.

Two-year-old form is usually the best guide to the early classics and certainly was in the latest One Thousand Guineas, when the very inexperienced favourite Saison, unraced at two, finished only thirteenth. Three of the first four, Quick As Lightning, Mrs Penny and Millingdale Lillie, had been leading two-year-old fillies; they had been, without much doubt, the best of the English-trained runners in the Guineas as youngsters. Whereas Mrs Penny and Millingdale Lillie had shown their best form over six furlongs, Quick As Lightning had shown hers beating Vielle a neck in the Hoover Fillies Mile at Ascot. At that stage Quick As Lightning seemed to need at least a mile and whether she would be speedy enough for the Guineas seemed in doubt, but she did well against Millingdale Lillie and Mrs Penny over seven furlongs on fast ground in the Fred Darling

One Thousand Guineas Stakes, Newmarket—Quick As Lightning (nearest camera) beats Our Home (centre) and Mrs Penny in a driving finish

Stakes at Newbury in April on her seasonal reappearance, finishing strongly for third place after being badly baulked on her way through around the two-furlong mark.

The following day, Saison trounced a field of maidens at Newbury and became a fairly firm favourite for the Guineas on this and reports of her gallops against Evita, the Ladbrokes Nell Gwyn Stakes winner and a horse with much better public form than she. The runners so far mentioned, plus Our Home (who hadn't been out since finishing third to Mrs Penny in the Cherry Hinton Stakes in July), formed the mainstay of the English defence against the French-trained Firyal, a half-sister to Comtesse de Loir who had won the Prix Imprudence; Pom Poes, formerly a Danish-trained filly who had been bought for a French stable after running second to Aryenne in the Criterium des Pouliches in the autumn; Dellear, third to Firyal in the Prix Imprudence; and the Irish-trained Etoile de Paris, winner of the Group 3 Athasi Stakes the previous week. Saison started favourite at 4/1; Evita was 15/2, Millingdale Lillie, Mrs Penny and Our Home 8/1, Firyal 10/1, and next came Quick As Lightning at 12/1.

Except to say that the three highest-drawn runners, Princess Matilda, Battlewind and Grandola, raced forlornly by themselves on the far side and Mrs Penny's stable-companion Shere Beauty hardly raced at all, nothing needs recounting of the race until it reached a little over two furlongs out. At that point the long-time leader Etoile de Paris was weakening, Saison and the disappointing Evita were already beaten and Firyal was getting nowhere under pressure, but plenty of the others still had a good chance. Mrs Penny had gone on, on the rails, chased by Our Home, Ararat, Quick As Lightning on the wide outside, Luck Of The Draw, Rapids and Millingdale Lillie. At the foot of the hill Our Home just got the lead and hung on very well considering her lengthy absence from the racecourse, but in the last hundred yards she was joined and then finally passed near the line by Quick As Lightning. Unusually for this event, the first five all stayed on really well. Quick As Lightning had a neck to spare; Our Home beat Mrs Penny half a length; Mrs Penny beat Millingdale Lillie a neck, and the latter had half a length in hand of Rapids.

On the strength of this performance and the probability that she'd be suited by middle distances Quick As Lightning started favourite for the Oaks. She was beaten eight lengths into fourth place behind Bireme. She looked well in the paddock and moved down well but she never threatened the leaders, ridden from behind by the free-lance Rouse who had made the most of a chance mount on her in the Guineas. Disappointingly, she didn't quicken with the others early in the straight. This run taken on its own wasn't sufficient evidence of her not staying the distance, but when added to that in the Irish Guinness Oaks and compared with her run in between over a mile at Royal Ascot it makes a pretty convincing case. Quick As Lightning, given every opportunity of staying in the Irish Oaks, was beaten after a mile and a quarter, trailing in fifth of nine, almost nine lengths behind Shoot A Line. She cut a contrasting figure in the Coronation Stakes, in which she went down only by a neck to the Irish One Thousand Guineas winner Cairn Rouge at level weights and decisively accounted for Our Home, giving her 4 lb. Quick As Lightning wore blinkers at Ascot and the Curragh.

Quick As Lightning (USA) (b.f. 1977)	Buckpasser (b 1963)	Tom Fool (b 1949)	Menow
			Gaga
		Busanda (bl 1947)	War Admiral
			Businesslike
	Clear Ceiling (b 1968)	Bold Ruler (b 1954)	Nasrullah
			Miss Disco
		Grey Flight (gr 1945)	Mahmoud
			Planetoid

More than half the field for the One Thousand Guineas were wholly or partly of American origin. In the first five, Quick As Lightning, Mrs Penny and Rapids carry the (USA) suffix, Our Home is by the American-bred Habitat out of a Graustark mare and Millingdale Lillie is by the American racehorse Tumble Wind. Quick As Lightning has an illustrious American pedigree. Her grandam Grey Flight was one of the best-ever broodmares over there, producing fourteen winners, nine of them stakes winners, from fifteen foals. The odd one out wasn't Quick As Lightning's dam Clear Ceiling—she won five of her seventeen races—but a Princequillo colt called Daylight Flight who was second once from six

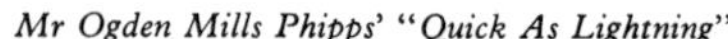

Mr Ogden Mills Phipps' "Quick As Lightning"

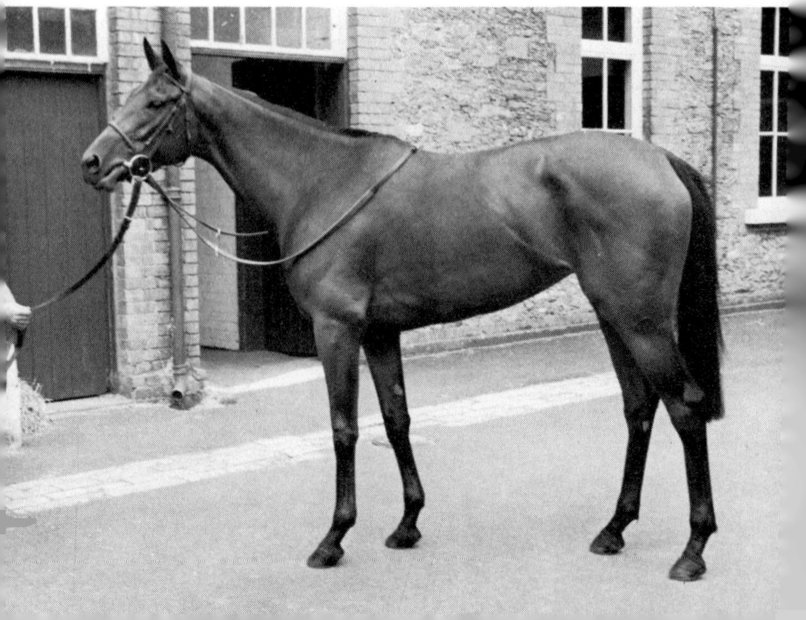

starts in a single season's racing. Clear Ceiling, a winner at up to six furlongs, didn't win a stakes; two of her sisters did though (Bold Princess and Bold Queen), and also one of her brothers (What A Pleasure, twice leading American sire and sire of the outstanding first-season stallion in the States in 1980, Foolish Pleasure). Another of Grey Flight's foals by Princequillo, the stakes winner Misty Morn, is the dam of the stallion Bold Lad (USA). One of Clear Ceiling's two previous foals ran; indeed, we saw her running in this country for Barry Hills's stable as a three-year-old in 1978. Gilt (by Majestic Prince), as she was called, was placed in one-mile maiden events at Haydock and Sandown.

Quick As Lightning enhanced Buckpasser's reputation as a sire of good fillies, but there won't be many more of his stock racing as he died in 1978. Buckpasser was an outstanding racehorse at distances up to two miles, and it came as something of a surprise that Quick As Lightning stays no better than she does. An attractive, well-made filly, Quick As Lightning is very well suited by a firm surface. *J. Dunlop.*

QUICKBEAM 2 ch.f. Roan Rocket 128–Ostrya 116 (Hornbeam 130) (1980 8d) May 23; narrow, very lightly-made filly; half-sister to several winners, including Ribblesdale Stakes winner Catalpa (by Reform); dam won 1963 Ribblesdale Stakes; 25/1, started slowly when tailed-off last of 15 to Segos in maiden race at Redcar in October. *E. Weymes.* —

QUICKTHORN LADY 2 ch.f. Hotfoot 126–Donnarose (Fighting Don) (1980 5f^4 5fg^4 7d 6g) Mar 18; rather light-framed filly; half-sister to several winners, including fairly useful 7f and 1m winner Summer Madness (by Silly Season) and useful 7f performer Fighting Lady (by Chebs Lad); dam of little account; showed promise when fourth in maiden races at Newmarket and Salisbury in the spring but was then off course 2 months and was soundly beaten on return; should be suited by 6f+; sold 700 gns Newmarket Autumn Sales. *G. Harwood.* **66**

QUIET CANNON 3 b.c. Connaught 130–Green Chiffon 83 (Crepello 136) (1979 6g 7fg^2 8f^4 1980 12g* 12s* 11.7s* 12g 12g* 12fg) good-bodied colt; developed into a useful performer in the summer, winning maiden race at Salisbury, minor event at Lingfield and handicaps at Windsor and Kempton; held off Lord of Misrule by a length under 10-4 at Windsor and short-headed Jondi at Kempton; below form fourth start; may well stay beyond 1½m; acts well on soft going; game. *G. Harwood.* **107**

QUIET COVE 2 ch.c. Import 127–Corcyra Beach 60 (Behistoun 131) (1980 5g 6g^3 6g 6g) Apr 27; 3,000Y; rangy colt; good mover; second foal; dam of little account; in rear on all starts, final one a valuable seller when badly drawn. *P. Asquith.* —

QUIET TOUCH 3 b.g. Decoy Boy 129–Coup 106 (Hook Money 124) (1979 5fg 5h 5fg^3 6s 1980 6s 5fg^2 6fg^2 6fg^2 6s 6d*) lengthy gelding; got home by a short head in 12-runner maiden race at Brighton in July; stays 6f; acts on a firm surface and isn't at his best on soft; blinkered nowadays. *J. Tree.* **70**

QUILPEE MAI 3 b.f. Pee Mai 107–Boyden Memory 80 (Combat 123) (1979 5g 5s 6g 5f^4 5.1f^2 7fg^2 6fg 7fg^4 7g 8.2g 7g 6d 7s 1980 7f 7fg 8f 10fg^4 10f^3 14d 13.4g 14g^4 10g 12g 12.2g^2 11.5fg* 8fg 10g 10fg 13g 11.7d) well-made filly; won ladies race at Yarmouth in August; ran moderately most starts afterwards; suited by 1½m but appears not to stay 1¾m; suited by fast ground; blinkered twice at 2 yrs; suitable mount for an inexperienced rider. *A. Goodwill.* **61**

QUISTADOR 4 ch.c. Le Johnstan 123–Little Bo Bleep 71 (Bleep-Bleep 134) (1979 5fg* 5.6fg 6d* 6g 1980 6h 5.1f 5.1g 6fg 6fg 5f 5fg^4) strong colt; mainly disappointing in 1980 (blinkered sixth start); stays 6f; acts on a firm and soft surface: sold to M. Chapman 620 gns Newmarket Autumn Sales. *G. Huffer.* **54**

QUITE LUCKY 3 ch.f. Precipice Wood 123–Quite Sweet 100 (Super Sam 124) (1979 7g 8fg 6g 1980 10fg 10g 12g 10.2fg 10.1fg 11.7h^2 12f 16fg^2) strong filly; quite a moderate maiden; stays well; acts on hard going; has run creditably for an amateur rider. *P. M. Taylor.* **69**

QUITE RIGHT 4 b.g. Ribero 126–Sheer Bliss 76 (St Paddy 133) (1979 12s^3 10v^3 12g 12s^4 14g^3 16fg^3 16fg* 16g^3 16f 18fg^4 16f 16fg^4 1980 14fg 16fg 16g 16fg 14fg 16g 17.1d 16.1s) robust, good-bodied gelding; no worthwhile form in 1980; stays very well; acts on any going; blinkered once at 3 yrs; sold to W. Clay 1,800 gns Newmarket Autumn Sales. *W. Wightman.* —

R

RABALA 3 b.g. The Diddler 99–Gairney (Our Babu 131) (1979 6g 6d 6s 8g 1980 7d 9.4d 7d^2 8.2d^4 8fg 8d* 12fg 9d 12fg 8f 9s 8.2v) unfurnished gelding; plater; won at Ayr in July (no bid); stays 1m; suited by some give in the ground. *W. H. H. Williams.* **55**

RABDAN 3 b.c. Bold Lad (Ire) 133–Bualim (Khalkis 127) (1979 5g 6fg 1980 6.5g^3 6.5g* 8g^2 7.6f 8g^2 8g^3 7g* 7g^3 6g^2 7g* 6s^4 7s^2 7g^2 6d^3) neat, attractive colt; useful handicapper; won small race at Cagnes-sur-Mer early in year and handicaps at Leicester in July and Kempton in September; beat Varuna quite comfortably by ¾ length on last-named; stays 1m but seems better at shorter distances; acts on soft going; genuine and consistent. *R. Armstrong.* **104**

RABDAN (USA) 3 br.c. Sham–Jolly Boat (Jester) (1979 6fg 6d^2 6s 7fg^3 6d 1980 8fg 8fg 10fg 10f 6g 7fg^2 6g^2 6f* 7g) compact colt; landed odds in all-aged race at Folkestone in September; stays 7f; possibly not at his best on very soft going; best in blinkers; has run creditably for an apprentice. *J. Dunlop.* **65**

RABHA 4 gr.f. Parnell 130–Margo's Pal 91 § (Palestine 133) (1979 8.2v 10v^2 10.6s 8s^2 8fg^3 8f 10.6g 9f 8g^4 1980 10v 8f^4 8fg 7g^4 9g^3 7f 8fg) light-framed filly; inconsistent handicapper; stays 1¼m; acts on any going; usually blinkered nowadays; sold 3,100 gns Newmarket Autumn Sales. *J. Hardy.* –

RACEAWAY 2 b.c. Lauso–Kingsbay (King's Leap 111) (1980 7fg) Feb 13; 2,000Y; second foal; dam ran only twice; unquoted when behind in 19-runner maiden race won by Six Mile Bottom at Lingfield in October. *C. James.* –

RACHEL STREET 4 gr.f. Precipice Wood 123–Stolen Kiss 75 (Lord of Verona 120) (1979 10fg 12d 1980 12f 10fg) compact filly; fifth foal; dam won on flat and over hurdles; in rear in minor and maiden events. *G. Vergette.* –

RACING BLONDE 3 ch.f. On Your Mark 125–Strawberry Blonde II (Red God 128 §) (1979 5g 5d* 1980 8v^3 6s 6f) strong, attractive ex-Irish filly; has shown no form since 1979; should stay at least 6f; acts on a soft surface. *M. W. Easterby.* –

RACONTEUR 3 b.c. Rarity 129–Festive Diplomat (Diplomat Way) (1979 5f^4 6fg^2 7fg^2 1980 8.2s* 10g^4 8fg 8d^3 8g* 8.3g^2) smallish, useful-looking colt; won maiden race at Nottingham in March and gamely held off Poles Apart by ½ length in handicap at Yarmouth in July; best at around 1m; probably acts on any going; sold 9,200 gns Newmarket Autumn Sales. *B. Hobbs.* **81**

RACQUETTE 3 b.f. Ballymore 123–Arctic Melody 113 (Arctic Slave 116) (1979 6s^2 1980 7g* 10f* 8fg 10s^2 12d^3 10g 8s) sister to 1m and 1¼m winner Ballybannon, closely related to Irish 7f and 1m winner Lagosta (by Ragusa) and half-sister to promising 2-y-o Arctique Royale (by Royal and Regal) and useful Nilie (by Relko) and Le Melody (by Levmoss); dam won Musidora Stakes; successful in April Fillies Stakes at the Curragh (beat Etoile de Paris a length) and Azalea Fillies Stakes at Phoenix Park (landed odds by 1½ lengths from Tree of Knowledge) in May; placed afterwards in Pretty Polly Stakes and Irish Guinness Oaks at the Curragh, in latter finishing 3¼ lengths third to Shoot A Line; suited by middle distances; acts on any going. *K. Prendergast, Ireland.* **120**

RADELLA 2 b.f. Phaeton 123–Admiralita (War Admiral) (1980 5s 5fg^4 5g^4 7d 6g 8d 10d) Apr 27; 700Y; leggy filly; poor mover; half-sister to several winners in USA and Europe, including Norwegian 1,000 Guineas winner Diagona (by Alcibiades), but is a bad plater herself; sold 410 gns Ascot December Sales. *R. Hannon.* **42**

RADIANT PEARL 5 ch.m. Gulf Pearl 117–Miss Maverick 76 (Vilmorin) (1979 7g 7s^3 7fg 8g 8.3fg* 7fg 10.2fg 10fg^3 10fg 1980 8d 8fg 10.8f 8.3s 8g) workmanlike mare; stays 1¼m; probably acts on any going; blinkered final start (ran poorly); retained 2,000 gns Newmarket December Sales. *T. Marshall.* –

RADICAL RETHINK 2 b.g. Owen Anthony 102–Press Button 58 (Precipice Wood 123) (1980 5f^3 5fg^3 5g 5d 5g 6d^3 7fg^4 8d^2) Mar 6; leggy, light-framed gelding; second foal; dam ran only at 2 yrs; plater; spoilt his chance by hanging left close home when ½-length second of 18 to Oratavo in selling nursery at Doncaster in October; will probably stay 1¼m+; seems to act on any going; sold out of R. Smyth's stable 550 gns Ascot July Sales after fourth start. *W. Musson.* **68**

RADIGO 4 b.f. Ragstone 128–Dinner Gong 99 (Major Portion 129) (1979 7d^2 10.2g* 11.1s^3 12d^4 11.7g^2 13.1f^3 16f^4 12g 10.1fg^2 8.2g^3 8f 10d 1980 12.2v^2 15fg 11.7fg 10s* 10g 10fg 10f^3 10d 10s^2 12d) light-framed, leggy filly; made all in **51**

handicap at Lingfield in June; probably finds 1m on sharp side and stays well; acts on any going; blinkered last 4 starts at 3 yrs and second outing; good mount for an apprentice. *P. Mitchell.*

RADNORCLIFFE 4 b.f. Mountain Call 125–Tinella 87 (Nelcius 133) (1979 10d 7v2 8s 8fg 10f 10.2h 8fg 12f 15.5fg 1980 7fg) poor plater; unlikely to stay 2m; has been tried in blinkers. *A. Moore.* —

RAFAEL MOLINA (USA) 4 b.g. Ace of Aces 126–Rainbow Rose (Ambiorix 130) (1979 9fg 11.7g2 12f* 13fg2 14fg 1980 12.3d2 12f3 12fg2 12f2 12fg3 13d3 10.6d 11fg* 10d2 11d 10.5g4 10d) big, strong gelding; won handicap at Ayr in July; went down by ½ length to Tolstoy on same course later in month; well beaten after; suited by middle distances (had very stiff task when well beaten over 1¾m in 1979); acts well on firm going. *Denys Smith.* **75**

RAFFIA SET 7 b.g. Raffingora 130–Sue Set 99 (Set Fair 129) (1979 6s* 5s3 5d* 6g3 5fg 6g3 6fg4 5fg3 5f 6g 5g4 5g3 5s 1980 6g4 6fg 6fg 5s3 5g 5g 6g 5d 6s) sprint handicapper; creditable third to The Pug at Lingfield in June, best effort of 1980; acts on any going; wears blinkers and is bandaged behind. *C. Wildman.* **84** d

RAGAFAN 3 ch.g. Ragstone 128–Hi-Baby 102 (High Treason 126) (1979 5d 5d 6g 1980 11.7fg 16g) compact gelding; behind in maiden races and handicaps; blinkered second start at 2 yrs. *R. Smyth.* —

RAGATAT 3 b.c. Habitat 134–Bella Ragusa (Ragusa 137) (1979 NR 1980 8.2fg 8fg 9.4g) 14,000Y; strong colt; poor mover; first foal; dam, closely related to Irish Sweeps Derby runner-up Exdirectory, won over 1½m in Ireland; well bred but seems only plating class on form so far. *M. Jarvis.* —

RAG DANCER 3 br.c. Ragstone 128–May Day Follies 80 (Bleep-Bleep 134) (1979 6d 5fg 7fg 1980 10s* 9g2 12.3f 10.6fg 10.6d 10fg 10s2 12g 9f 10.6s2 8.2s* 8.2s 10.2v) lightly-made colt; won maiden race at Nottingham in April and handicap at Hamilton in October; ran creditably several times in between; stays 1¼m; needs some give in the ground; ran as though something was wrong with him when tailed off eighth start. *W. Elsey.* **81**

RAGE GLEN 3 gr.f. Grey Mirage 128–Septieme Ciel (Welsh Abbot 131) (1979 NR 1980 8.2g 9s 10.2d2) compact filly; sister to 9f seller winner Gris Ciel and half-sister to 2 winners; dam lightly raced; showed first worthwhile form when second in minor event at Doncaster in October; evidently suited by 1¼m; yet to race on a firm surface. *J. Leigh.* **67**

RAG GIRL 3 br.f. Virginia Boy 106–Sum Toy (Chieftain) (1979 5g 5g4 5f 5.8f 7fg* 7.2g2 7.3g 7f 1980 8fg 6fg4 6d2 5.8g 7d) neat filly; quite a moderate handicapper; stays 7f well; acts on a firm and a soft surface; has run creditably for a boy; suited by forcing tactics; sold 9,000 gns Newmarket December Sales. *J. Bethell.* **68**

RAGNAR 4 b.c. Welsh Pageant 132–Saucy Flirt 102 (King's Troop 118) (1979 NR 1980 14.7f 12fg) workmanlike colt; lightly raced and little worthwhile form; blinkered final start (still needed race). *H. Wharton.* —

RAGONDA 3 b.f. Ragstone 128–Dodone 98 (March Past 124) (1979 8.2d3 8d2 7d2 8g3 1980 8d 8v* 9g 12h 9g) compact filly; plater; won at Ayr in March (no bid); should stay at least 9f; acts on heavy going; brought down fourth outing; ran poorly final start. *J. Berry.* **58**

RAGS AND BAGS 3 b.f. Ragstone 128–Tashkin 103 (Red God 128§) (1979 NR 1980 9f 10fg 12g 12g 12f3 15.5g3 12f* 12.2d* 12s4) attractive, robust filly; third foal; dam sprinter; won modest maiden race at Redcar and minor event at Catterick in the autumn; stays well; probably acts on any going; brought down second start; sold 5,200 gns Newmarket December Sales. *J. Dunlop.* **74**

RAG TIME BAND 5 br.g. Polyfoto 124–Chanfrin 88 (Chamossaire) (1979 8g 8fg4 8f 9f3 10g 10f 8fg 1980 10.6fg) plater nowadays; stays 9f; acts on firm going; often starts slowly; wore a tongue strap last 2 starts at 4 yrs and was blinkered on final outing. *G. Balding.* —

RAHOTEP (FR) 2 b.c. Matahawk 127–La Masure (Net 116) (1980 7.5g* 8d4 10s) Mar 21; 115,000 francs Y (approx. £12,100); fifth reported foal; half-brother to useful miler Bois Mineau (by Franc Luron); dam won several small races from 6f to 1¼m in France; ran in pattern races at Longchamp after winning 12-runner newcomers event at Deauville in August, finishing just over 3 lengths fourth to Dunphy in Prix des Chenes and 2 lengths fifth to The Wonder (gave 2lb) in Prix de Conde; will stay 1½m; very useful. *B. Secly, France.* **116**

RAHWAY 2 gr.c. Sovereign Path 125–Rhodie Blake 101 (Blakeney 126) (1980 **101**
6fg^3 6g* 7s* 7fg^4 7g^3 7s 7.3d) Feb 16; good-topped, useful-looking colt; good mover; first foal; dam ran only twice, winning over 7f at 2 yrs, and is sister to very smart Roscoe Blake, successful at up to 11f here and in USA, and half-sister to very smart middle-distance performer Jolly Good; won 21-runner maiden race at Newmarket in June gamely by ½ length from Green Haze and £4,500 event on same course the following month by 2 lengths from Golden Brigadier; had mainly stiff tasks afterwards, running creditably when 2½ lengths fourth of 6 to Church Parade in Lanson Champagne Stakes at Goodwood but being beaten nearly 15 lengths when fifth of 10 behind Kalaglow in Horris Hill Stakes at Newbury on seventh start; will stay 1¼m; seems to act on any going. *B. Hobbs.*

RAINA 3 b.f. Connaught 130–Relza 91 (Relko 136) (1979 7.2fg 7f^4 7f 8fg 1980 —
10f 13.8fg 8g 10g 8f 10fg 7g) neat filly; bad plater. *T. Kersey.*

RAINBOW HILL 2 ch.g. Royalty 130–Hill Cloud 60 (El Gallo 122) (1980 6fg **67**
7fg 7s) May 14; big, strong gelding; second foal; half-brother to 3-y-o Morning Line (by Owen Anthony), winner of a 1½m match; dam stayed 7f; about 8 lengths sixth of 18 to Warily in minor event at Sandown in October, third outing and first sign of ability; will stay 1¼m. *P. M. Taylor.*

RAINFALL 4 ch.f. Relko 136–Aries (Acropolis 132) (1979 12s^2 12g* 12fg^3 12f* **94**
16.1d^2 14g^3 1980 12fg^2 16fg 14g^3 16g^2 16g^2 16.1fg*) big, rangy filly; led 5f out and soon went clear when winning handicap at Newmarket in August by 7 lengths from Popsi's Joy; second 3 times earlier, on previous outing to Barley Hill in Brown Jack Stakes at Ascot; stays 2m; acts on any going. *J. Dunlop.*

RAISE YOU 6 ch.g. Saintly Song 128–Queen Flush (Twilight Alley 133) —
(1979 NR 1980 16fg) poor handicapper on flat nowadays; yet to show he stays 2m; acts on any going; has worn blinkers; winning hurdler. *P. Asquith.*

RAJA SCULPTOR 2 b.c. Arch Sculptor 123–Bertona (Darius 129) (1980 5d **63**
5s^4 5f 6g 6f 7fg 5fg 7g* 8fg^2 7fg 7.2s 8s 8d^3) Mar 11; 3,000F, 8,600Y; small, strong colt; fair plater; bought in 1,500 gns after winning 19-runner seller at Chepstow in September by a neck from Chenstone; placed in 2 selling nurseries subsequently; suited by 7f and 1m; probably acts on any going; blinkered fourth start; sold to Susan Piggott BA 2,200 gns Newmarket Autumn Sales. *P Haslam.*

RAJWA 3 b.f. Scottish Rifle 127–Birthday Present 80 (Bleep-Bleep 134) (1979 —
NR 1980 9fg 10g 10f) 3,000Y; lightly-made filly; fifth foal; half-sister to a winner in Hungary; dam, winner over 5f at 2 yrs, is sister to smart sprinter Lazenby; well beaten in newcomers race and maiden events early in year; pulled very hard last 2 starts. *R. Boss.*

RALPHY 3 br.g. Alto Volante 109–Dibby's Cousin (Be Friendly 130) (1979 5d —
5s 5g 6s 8f 1980 11.7fg 15h 12g) leggy gelding; of no account; has worn blinkers. *D. Jermy.*

RAMADA 3 ch.c. St Alphage 119–Strathclair (Klairon 131) (1979 5s 6fg 5g 7f 7g **35**
1980 8d 10s 5f^4 6f* 6fg 5g 6g^4 6g^4 6s^4 7g) strong, compact colt; plater; won at Carlisle in May (bought in 1,100 gns); stays 6f; acts on any going; often wears blinkers. *B. Richmond.*

RAMANNOLIE (FR) 2 b.c. Caro 133–Manoline (Vieux Manoir 132) (1980 7f^3 **81**
7g) Apr 1; 43,000Y; tall colt; fifth foal; dam unraced half-sister to Prix Morny winner Princeline; 7/1, acquitted himself well against 2 useful animals when 1½ lengths third of 4 to Spindrifter in minor event at Redcar in September; second favourite, showed a round action on way down and never promised to get on terms in race when around 9 lengths sixth of 8 to Spark of Life in Somerville Tattersall Stakes at Newmarket in October; will stay 1¼m. *H. T. Jones.*

RAMAS SILK 2 gr.f. Amber Rama 133–Guiletta 63 (Runnymede 123) (1980 **73**
5fg 5g 5g) Mar 11; third foal; half-sister to 1979 2-y-o 5f winner Rapid Spring (by Forlorn River); dam ran only 3 times; 33/1 when never-dangerous fifth of 19 to Advertrack, beaten only about a length, in maiden race at Folkestone in October, third outing and first sign of ability. *P. Ashworth.*

RAMA TIBODI 3 br.g. Amber Rama 133–Warrior Queen 95 (King's Bench **97**
132) (1979 5.8g^4 6f 5.8h* 6g^4 6f^4 1980 6v 7fg^4 5.8fg* 5.8fg 6fg* 7d^2 7.6g*) strong, well-made gelding; fairly useful handicapper; won at Bath, Pontefract and Chester in the summer; beat Millfield Lad a head on last-named; stays 7.6f; probably acts on any going; blinkered nowadays; consistent; exported to Hong Kong. *I. Balding.*

RAMBERT 2 b.f. Mandamus 120–Liliberto (Umberto 118) (1980 7g) May 9; —
half-sister to 2 winners; dam ran only once; unquoted when last of 22 in maiden race won by Ring Moylan at Chepstow in September. *P. Makin.*

Mr M. Soudavar's "Ramian"

RAMBLING DAN 6 b.h. Ridan–Kings Rose 71 (Pampered King 121) (1979 — NR 1980 12.2fg) ex-Irish horse; won maiden race at 3 yrs; very lightly raced on flat since; suited by middle distances; acts on firm going; used to wear blinkers; sold 700 gns Doncaster June Sales. *P. Bevan.*

RAMBLING RIVER 3 b.c. Forlorn River 124–Who-Done-It 98 (Lucero 124) **96** d (1979 5fg* 6fg^2 5d* 5f^2 5d 5fg 5g 5g* 5g* 1980 5f 6fg 6fg^4 6d 5g 6d 5.6g 6f 6d 5v) strong, useful sort; very useful (rated 111) at 2 yrs; ran best race in 1980 when fourth of 5 to Taufan in £4,900 event at Thirsk in May; well beaten in handicaps subsequently; best form at 5f; has won on a soft surface but is better on a sound one. *W. A. Stephenson.*

RAMBORO AGAIN 3 gr.c. Runnymede 123–Balisland's Queen 93 (Abernant **77** 142) (1979 7fg 7f 1980 6d 6s^2 6v^2 6d* 5f* 6f 5f* 5s 5fg^4 5g 5.3fg^4 5d 5d) compact colt; won maiden race and handicap at Hamilton and minor event at Edinburgh in first half of season; best form at sprint distances; acts on any going; suitable mount for an inexperienced rider. *P. Haslam.*

RAMESES 2 ch.c. Le Johnstan 123–Athanna (Athenien II 126) (1980 5fg — 6fg 5f 6f 5f 8d 10d 8d) June 2; 240Y; lengthy, fair sort; useless plater; formerly trained by D. Chapman; sold 340 gns Doncaster November Sales. *M. Tate.*

RAMETTA 2 ch.f. Amber Rama 133–Nevetta 108 (Never Say Die 137) (1980 **59** 5g 5f^3 6fg 7d 7g 7s 6f 7g) Feb 19; 5,000Y; fair sort; half-sister to 5 winners, including Morvetta (by Morston), successful at up to 1$\frac{3}{4}$m; dam won at up to 9f; only plating class; stays 7f; form only on a sound surface; blinkered third and fifth outings; dwelt final start. *T. Fairhurst.*

RAMIAN 3 b.c. Mount Hagen 127–Chevy Chase (Raise You Ten 125) (1979 **119** d NR 1980 8f 12f*(dis) 12fg* 12s^3 14.6g 14s) 23,000Y; lengthy, workmanlike colt; second foal; dam successful Irish stayer; put up a good performance in

Irish Sweeps Derby at the Curragh in June, keeping on well in straight to finish 4 lengths third of 13 to Tyrnavos; had earlier been first past post in maiden race at Naas (disqualified for hampering third horse) and BMW Nijinsky Stakes at Leopardstown; led inside last furlong to account for Johnny O'Day (gave 5 lb) by ¾ length in latter; ran poorly in St Leger at Doncaster and Irish St Leger at the Curragh (blinkered) on his last 2 starts; should stay 1¾m; acts on any going. *D. Weld, Ireland.*

RAMSHACKLE 2 b.f. Manacle 123–Private Collection 70 (Whistling Wind 123) (1980 7g 6fg 7g) Feb 12; well-grown filly; third foal; dam stayed 1m; little worthwhile form in maiden races at Salisbury and Newmarket and in minor event at Lingfield in the autumn. *W. Wightman.* —

RAMWADASH 2 ch.c. Jukebox 120–Country Court 81 (Meadow Court 129) (1980 5s4 5f3 5f 5.8fg* 5g 5g3 6fg 6fg 6f 6d2) Apr 5; 2,800F, 5,600Y; neat colt; brother to a winning plater; dam, daughter of 1,000 Guineas winner Abermaid, won over 5f at 2 yrs; won 19-runner maiden race at Bath in June by ½ length from Candaules; returned to form when blinkered in nursery at Leicester in October, finishing 2½ lengths second of 20 to Faiz; stays 6f and may get 7f as a 3-y-o; probably acts on any going. *G. Lewis.* **75**

RANKIN (FR) 3 ch.c. Owen Dudley 121–Cup Cake (Dan Cupid 132) (1979 6fg2 7g* 7g* 7f* 1980 8s 12fg2 12f3 12s 12fg4 10d4) **126**

For a colt of his ability Rankin had a frustrating season. He improved on his useful two-year-old form by more than a stone but became only the second colt in over twenty years to be placed in the Derby and go through the year without a win. The pity is, he's such a genuine sort, far more deserving of a win on that account than his irresolute predecessor Freefoot.

On the day Rankin was the best-backed colt in the Derby, coming down from 20/1 to 14/1. In his favour it could be said that he was certain to see

Mr Ron Fennell's "Rankin"

the trip out—in the Predominate Stakes run over the distance at Kempton he had given Prince Bee 5 lb and stayed on gamely to go down by three quarters of a length, the pair seven lengths clear of a representative field. Moreover, firm going was known to suit him particularly well, and with Starkey on board there were no doubts about jockeyship. Rankin, who sweated up in the preliminaries, put up a fine display, finishing third. Well placed from the start, he led halfway up the straight and battled on courageously without finding any extra acceleration when Henbit and Master Willie challenged him. He was beaten three quarters of a length and a length and a half.

Things didn't go right for Rankin in his next two races, the Irish Sweeps Derby at the Curragh and the Gordon Stakes at Goodwood. Soft going at the Curragh wasn't to his advantage; on top of this, down at the start he managed to put a leg over one of the stalls, and had to be taken out and trotted round to check that he was sound. Though walking none too freely Rankin was allowed to run and in finishing seventh to Tyrnavos he failed to do himself justice. At Goodwood he hurt his back in running and trailed in a distant fourth to Prince Bee. The injury was serious enough to keep him off the track for three months and on his return he faced Cairn Rouge, Master Willie, Nadjar and nine others in the Champion Stakes at Newmarket. Rankin ran right up to his Derby form, making much of the running on the stand rail until inside the final furlong. He came in fourth, just over two lengths behind Cairn Rouge; second-placed Master Willie beat him by one and a half lengths and he lost third to Nadjar on the line.

Rankin (Fr) (ch.c. 1977)	Owen Dudley (b 1970)	Tudor Melody (br 1956)	Tudor Minstrel
			Matelda
		The Creditor (ch 1960)	Crepello
			The Accused
	Cup Cake (b 1968)	Dan Cupid (ch 1956)	Native Dancer
			Vixenette
		Thiamine (b 1958)	Vandale
			Tallulah

As things turned out Rankin was very well bought as a yearling for 9,000 guineas but at the time he barely looked a bargain, with an unproven sire and a distaff side to his pedigree that would do credit to a jumper. Owen Dudley, a well-bred, good-class, genuine and consistent performer at up to a mile and a quarter, stood in France for three years but was sent back to England in 1978 after receiving only modest patronage. Whilst Rankin is easily Owen Dudley's best runner, the two-year-old Goodbye Starter showed useful form in 1980 and Owen Dudley has also sired the winners of over twenty races in France from his limited opportunities there. Cup Cake, Rankin's dam, won a one-mile nursery, an eleven-furlong handicap and a hurdle race in three seasons' racing in France. She visited King Emperor, Pontifex and Will Hays before going to Owen Dudley and had no live produce to show for it; her 1979 foal, a colt by Rose Laurel named Ransom, fetched 23,000 guineas as a yearling and is to be trained by Peter Walwyn in 1981. Cup Cake is a half-sister to three winners on the flat and over jumps in France and Belgium. Her dam, Thiamine, won a thirteen-furlong event from three starts as a three-year-old and was a daughter of Tallulah, dam of numerous winners in France and Italy including a winner of the Gran Steeplechase di Milano.

Rankin, who was reportedly sold for £200,000 after the season ended, stays in training. Although he is at a disadvantage with some of the other good horses in that he needs a strong gallop to show to advantage there are races to be won with him, and it will be interesting to see his running in either the John Porter Stakes or the Jockey Club Stakes, the conditions of which favour horses that haven't won pattern events. A quite attractive, lightly-made colt, he stays a mile and a half and is a good mover, possessing the type of action associated with the top-of-the-ground performer. *G. Harwood.*

RAPERON 2 b.f. Rapid River 127–Reignon 74 (Lucky Brief 128) (1980 5g* 5g4 7g4) Apr 29; workmanlike filly; third foal; dam, useful hurdler, stayed 1½m; dwelt but finished strongly to head My Chantal close home in 10-runner maiden race at Pontefract in July; respectable fourth in nursery and £2,600 event within space of 5 days at Redcar the following month; gives impression 6f may be her trip. *M. H. Easterby.* **81**

RAPID CLASS (USA) 3 b.c. Cannonade–Seminar 113 (Don II 123) (1979 NR 1980 8f4 10fg 8f* 7f2 8d 7.3fg 8s) good sort; first foal; dam, half-sister to Boldboy, was very useful over 5f at 2 yrs and won over 1m in USA at 3 yrs; **96**

landed odds by a head from Home Ground in very slowly-run 4-runner £4,400 race at Ayr in May; creditable second to Pentaquod in handicap at Epsom following month; stays 1m but not 1¼m; acts on firm going and is possibly unsuited by soft; sweated up but ran respectably sixth start; sold 6,800 gns Newmarket Autumn Sales. *B. Hills.*

RAPIDE 6 ch.g. Gulf Pearl 117–Donine (Soleil II 133) (1979 18d 1980 17.1fg) — poor handicapper; bandaged and well beaten since 1977; evidently stays 13f; acts on any going; has been tried in blinkers. *T. Hallett.*

RAPID LAD 2 b.c. Rapid River 127–Seacona (Espresso 122) (1980 5fg 5d **75** 5d 6g 6g 7.2s 5s*) May 11; compact colt; third foal; dam well behind on both outings; gambled on, showed improved form when returned to 5f on final start, beating Apapa Port ½ length in 24-runner seller at Stockton in October (no bid); acts on soft going. *A. Gillam.*

RAPIDS (USA) 3 ch.f. Head of the River–Sound of Success (Successor) (1979 **112** 7fg^4 7g^2 1980 8fg 10.5f^4 8fg^2 12.2fg* 12g^3 14.6g^3) rather leggy filly; landed odds comfortably by 4 lengths from Crazyfoot in Warwick Oaks in June; ran creditably in much better company on several occasions, finishing 1½ lengths fifth of 23 to Quick As Lightning in 1,000 Guineas at Newmarket, 6 lengths fourth to Bireme in Musidora Stakes at York and 2½ lengths second to Stumped in £7,100 race at Kempton; third to Deadly Serious in Galtres Stakes at York in August and to Shoot A Line in Park Hill Stakes at Doncaster in September; stays 1¾m; yet to race on a soft surface (didn't stride out too well on very firm second start); blinkered last 3 starts. *B. Hills.*

RAPID SPRING 3 gr.f. Forlorn River 124–Guiletta 63 (Runnymede 123) **48** (1979 5g 5g 5fg 5f* 5.3d* 6fg 5fg 1980 6fg 6g 6g 7g 6s 7g 7g 7fg^2 8g 7g^3 7g 6g) sparely-made filly; plater; stays 7f; seems to act on any going; sometimes blinkered; has run respectably for a boy; sold 2,000 gns Newmarket December Sales. *A. Davison.*

RAPIDUS 3 b.f. Sharpen Up 127–Sea Magic (Hardicanute 130) (1979 7fg — 1980 7f 8s) unfurnished filly; behind in maiden races. *M. Ryan.*

RARE DATE 3 b.f. Rarity 129–First Date 117 (Royal Palm 131) (1979 6fg — 7s 1980 7f 8f 10g 10g) small filly; well beaten in maiden races; sweated up last 2 starts; sold 1,700 gns Newmarket Autumn Sales. *G. Pritchard-Gordon.*

RASA PENANG 2 ch.c. Gay Fandango 132–Lancette (Double Jump 131) **91** (1980 7g* 7g^3) Apr 2; 16,000Y; rangy, attractive colt; second foal; half-brother to fairly useful 1979 Irish 2-y-o 7f winner Lagolette (by Green God); dam, half-sister to Gimcrack winner Golden Horus, placed at up to 1½m in France; disputed lead throughout when winning 14-runner minor event at Kempton in September a shade cleverly by ½ length from Neltino; 5/4 favourite for £3,000 race at Goodwood later in month but was given an indifferent ride, getting completely boxed in early in straight, and could finish only 3½ lengths third of 11 to King's General; will stay 1m; better than his Goodwood running suggests. *R. Armstrong.*

RASA SAYANG 3 b.f. Green Dancer 132–Silly Symphony 100 (Silly Season — 127) (1979 6f^4 7fg^4 1980 7d 6g 6fg) compact, quite attractive filly; has shown only a little ability in maiden races; needs further than 6f and will stay 1¼m; sold 140,000 francs (approx £13,700) Deauville December Sales. *P. Walwyn.*

RASHERCAP 2 br.c. Home Guard 129–Ciotog (Varano) (1980 10g) May **83** p 9; 5,800F; rangy colt; third foal; dam won over 7.5f at 3 yrs in Ireland; 11/1 and backward, running on steadily in closing stages when well-beaten sixth of 9 to Krug in Zetland Stakes at Newmarket in October; wasn't knocked about here and should improve in 1981. *B. Hobbs.*

RATAMATAZ 6 b.g. Shiny Tenth 120–Water Rat 83 (Hard Tack 111 §) (1979 **73** d 5s^2 6v^2 7g 6d 5g^3 6fg^3 6g* 6fg* 6fg 7g 6g^2 6s 6s^4 1980 5d 6s* 6d^3 6g 6d 6fg 6g 5fg 6fg 5d^3 5d 6g 6g 7d) sprint handicapper; easy winner from Carpet General at Nottingham in March; didn't reproduce that form; acts on any going; blinkered tenth and eleventh outings; goes well for a boy. *D. Marks.*

RATAN BOY 4 br.g. Workboy 123–Rubbish (Major Portion 129) (1979 **50** 6d^3 6g 5fg 5.3fg 8.2g 7g^4 6g 7f^4 6g* 1980 6g 5fg 5f 6fg 6d 5.8f^2 7fg^3) useful sort; won seller at Newmarket at 3 yrs; placed in handicaps at Bath and Yarmouth in 1980; stays 7f; acts on hard going and has yet to race on really soft; best in blinkers. *J. Sutcliffe.*

RA TAPU 3 ch.c. Sun Prince 128–Bracey Bridge 115 (Chanteur II 135) (1979 **70** NR 1980 8d 10s^4 12s^3 15s^2 12d*) 17,500Y; tall colt; half-brother to 1½m winner Smiddly Hill (by Crepello) and smart but lightly-raced The Parson (by Aureole); dam won Ribblesdale Stakes and Park Hill Stakes; won handicap at Leicester in November; stays well; acts on soft going; has worn bandages; sold out of H. T. Jones's stable 5,000 gns Newmarket Autumn Sales. *P. Mitchell.*

RATHER EASY 3 b.f. Swing Easy 126–Golden Storm 95 (Golden Cloud) **64**
(1979 6g 1980 5fg 7d 7d^2 7.2d^3 8.3d 8f 8g^4 8g) big, useful-looking filly; good mover; in frame in maiden races; seems to stay 1m; evidently needs some give in the ground; pulled hard fourth and fifth starts; sweated up but ran creditably third outing. *P. Cole.*

RATHMOY'S SPARKLE 2 b.g. Sparkler 130–Trigamy 112 (Tribal Chief 125) **84**
(1980 5v^3 5v^3 5fg* 6fg^3 6g^4 6g^2 6d^2 7fg^2 6fg^3 7d) May 19; compact gelding; first foal; dam 5f performer; showed improved form when winning maiden race at Carlisle in May cleverly by ½ length from Oyston's Agency; second in nurseries at Windsor, Haydock and Epsom subsequently, going down by ¾ length to Mother of the Wind when favourite on last-named in August; stays 7f; possibly not at his best on heavy going; genuine and consistent; looked to be beginning to feel the effects of his hard season on final appearance (ran moderately). *N. Callaghan.*

RAVADUOS 3 ch.c. Mansingh 120–Cawston Tower 112 (Maharaj Kumar 124) **78**
(1979 5g 5fg^3 5fg^4 6s* 6f^3 1980 7f 7f 6f 6d 6d^2 5.6fg 6s^2 6s^2 6g^4) big, shapely, attractive, good-quartered colt; moderate handicapper; suited by 6f but isn't certain to stay 7f; acts on any going but is well suited by some give in the ground; blinkered nowadays; has shown signs on occasions of being none too genuine; sold 7,600 gns Newmarket Autumn Sales. *Denys Smith.*

RAVENSBOURNE 7 br.h. Siliconn 121–Suzy Wong II 71 (Mincio 127) (1979 **53**
NR 1980 10s 8s 10d* 8fg 10g* 8g) plater; has been fired; successful at Nottingham (bought in 1,150 gns) in June and Pontefract (retained 1,100 gns) in August; stays 1¼m; acts on heavy going; has worn blinkers; wears bandages. *R. Akehurst.*

RAVENS TOWER 3 gr.c. Tower Walk 130–Grey Mink 86 (Double Jump 131) **76**
(1979 5d 5d 5d 5f 5s^3 6g 5fg 5f 6d* 7d 6fg 6fg 1980 7v^2 7s^3 7f 8h^4 8fg 8g^3 7g 8.2s^4 8.3g 8fg^3 8.2d^3 8f 11s^3 9g 10d) lengthy colt; quite a moderate handicapper; not certain to stay middle distances; suited by some give in the ground. *W. Marshall.*

RAWALPINDI 2 b.c. Hotfoot 126–Rotisserie 106 (Tesco Boy 121) (1980 7f^3 **71**
7d) Apr 4; 8,600Y; fifth foal; half-brother to useful Rowlandson (by Blakeney), successful at up to 1¾m; dam won Fred Darling Stakes; 40/1, no threat to first 2 when 6¾ lengths third of 6 to Belloc in minor event at Lingfield in October; had every chance below distance in Houghton Stakes at Newmarket later in month but ran better than his final placing (7¾ lengths eighth of 14 to Sunley Builds) suggests; will be suited by 1¼m. *G. Harwood.*

RAWLINSON END 2 b.c. Song 132–Wong Way Girl 99 (Kibenka 119) (1980 **79**
6g 5d^2 5d 5d^4) Mar 8; 10,000Y; neat, strong colt; good walker; first foal; dam successful at up to 7f; in frame in maiden races at Wolverhampton in October, better effort when short-head second of 14 to Corn Street; should stay 6f. *R. Laing.*

RAY CHARLES 2 gr.c. Sun Prince 128–Ivory Gull 70 (Sea Hawk II 131) —
(1980 7g 7s) Apr 3; 11,500Y; tall, narrow, leggy colt; none too good a walker or mover; dam lightly-raced half-sister to smart sprinter Broxted; prominent 2f out in minor events at Goodwood in September and Sandown (eighth of 18 to Warily) in October; may do better over 1¼m+. *G. Harwood.*

RAY'S BELLE 2 gr.f. Fleece 114–Sovereign Comment (Sovereign Path 125) —
(1980 5f 6fg 6d) Apr 24; 1,100Y; leggy, narrow, unfurnished filly; half-sister to fairly useful 7f to 1½m winner Fiery Copper (by Lord Gayle); dam won over 1m in Ireland; behind in maiden auction and maiden events. *J. Berry.*

RAZORBACK (FR) 5 b.g. Ridan–Charmaine Gift 86 (Galivanter 131) (1979 6v —
8d 6s 7s 5g^2 5s^2 6fg 5fg^2 5fg^3 5d^2 5g^4 6d* 6s 5fg 5fg 8s 5s 1980 8d 6s 5g^4 7fg 5fg 6fg 6f 6fg 5g 5d 10d 6fg 10g 10fg 10g 5d) small gelding; races mainly over sprint distances but stays 1m; acts on any going; sometimes wears blinkers; not particularly consistent and was withdrawn after being unruly going to post on one occasion in 1980 (had tongue tied down). *C. Austin.*

R. B. CHESNE 4 b.c. Brigadier Gerard 144–Vive la Reine (Vienna 127) (1979 **112**
7fg^2 1980 10f^3 10d) attractive, well-made colt; very smart at 2 yrs; raced only once in 1979 due to a lung infection, finishing length second to Tap On Wood (gave 10lb) in Kiveton Park Steel Stakes at Doncaster; favourite but looking in need of race when 3¾ lengths third to Gregorian in 9-runner Westbury Stakes at

Sandown in April, weakening in final stages; looked hard and fit but ran as though something was wrong with him when well beaten in Prince of Wales's Stakes won by Ela-Mana-Mou at Royal Ascot in June on only subsequent start; bred to stay 1½m; appeared to act on any going; stud in France. *H. Cecil.*

READ 'N' RITE 3 ch.f. High Line 125–Night Lark (Larkspur 128) (1979 6s 6fg^3 8.2d 1980 11fg) lightly-made filly; poor plater. *W. Wharton.* —

REAL CASH 3 b.c. Realm 129–Moneycashen 72 (Hook Money 124) (1979 5g^2 5s 6s 6fg^4 7g^3 7f^2 1980 8.2g 10.1g 10s^3 12s 9d) narrow colt; quite a moderate maiden at his best; unlikely to stay 1½m; acts on any going; sold 2,700 gns Ascot December Sales. *P. Cole.* **66**

REALERT 4 ch.g. Red Alert 127–Persian Mourne (Mourne 126) (1979 6fg^3 7d 7f^3 8f^3 7fg* 8g^4 8fg^2 1980 7fg) attractive gelding; won handicap at Yarmouth in 1979; behind at Salisbury in May on only outing of 1980; stays 1m; acts on firm going and ran badly on only outing on a soft surface; usually wears blinkers but didn't at Salisbury; sold to R. Turnell 520 gns Newmarket Autumn Sales. *J. Winter.* —

REALM GIFT 2 ch.f. Realm 129–Anxious Call (Whistler 129) (1980 5f^3 6fg^4 5g^4 5g^3 5d^2) May 5; 9,200Y; rangy filly; half-sister to 2 winners, including fairly useful sprinter Katricia (by Skymaster), herself dam of Roland Gardens; dam half-sister to good 1962 2-y-o Daybreak; in frame in maiden and minor events, going closest to winning when just over length equal third of 22 to Copt Hall Realm at Lingfield in September on fourth outing; will be suited by a return to 6f. *A. Breasley.* **75**

REALMINA 3 b. or br.f. Realm 129–Bee Keeper 90 (Honeyway 125) (1979 6f 1980 7d 5d 8g) lightly-made filly; poor maiden; sold 470 gns Ascot August Sales. *E. Reavey.* —

REALMIO (FR) 3 b.c. Realm 129–Djaseelia (Djakao 124) (1979 5s 6f^4 1980 6f^3 7f) attractive, lengthy colt; quite a moderate maiden; looks short of pace and will probably stay 1m+; not raced after May. *R. Hern.* **72**

REBECCA MAID 5 gr.m. My Swanee 122–Prize Penny 97 (Pampered King 121) (1979 10f 10h 8fg* 7fg 8g 10s 1980 8f 7fg 9d 8fg) plater; stays 1m; probably acts on any going; has been tried in blinkers. *B. Richmond.* —

REBECK 2 b.g. Hittite Glory 125–Mattinata 90 (Matador 131) (1980 5f^4 5.8fg 5g 5f^3 5d 5f^4 5d 6fg^4 6g) May 2; good-bodied gelding; carries plenty of condition; half-brother to several winners, including useful 1978 2-y-o 7f winner Chalumeau (by Relko); dam 5f sprinter; in frame in varied races, final occasion when 4½ lengths fourth of 12 to The Quiet Bidder in £6,000 nursery at Newmarket in August; stays 6f; blinkered fifth outing; sold 2,100 gns Newmarket Autumn Sales. *W. Hastings-Bass.* **74**

REBEL YELL 3 b.c. Connaught 130–Heavenly Music 93 (Tudor Melody 129) (1979 6d 1980 10.8v^4 10g^2 10.1fg^3 11.5f^4 10s 12g^3 10s 8f) strong, good-bodied, rather plain colt; quite a moderate maiden; stays 1½m; best form on a sound surface; sometimes sweats up; blinkered final start; has run respectably for an amateur rider. *D. Ringer.* **72**

REBID 3 b.f. Jimmy Reppin 131–Gallant Bid 109 (Galivanter 131) (1979 7s 1980 8s* 8f* 10g 10d 11fg 11g 8f 8fg^4 8.2d 9g) well-grown filly; won maiden race at Newcastle in April and handicap at York in May; ran moderately most subsequent outings; best at around 1m; acts on any going; blinkered fifth start. *W. Elsey.* **69**

RECITATION (USA) 2 b.c. Elocutionist–Irish Party (Irish Lancer) (1980 5f^3 5f* 6d* 6s^2 8g^2 8fg^2 8d* 8d^4) **126**

Recitation's career so far has been something of a curate's egg. The good parts include a runaway success in the Coventry Stakes at Royal Ascot and a win in France's most valuable and prestigious race for two-year-olds, the Grand Criterium at Longchamp; between these first-class displays are three defeats, and at the end is a modest display in the William Hill Futurity Stakes. Although never out of the frame in eight starts Recitation didn't show the consistency one hopes to see in a top colt.

The fluctuations in Recitation's form are reflected in his starting price both at Royal Ascot and at Longchamp. There had been nothing extraordinary about his half-length defeat of I'll See You in a Newbury maiden race on the second of his two outings before Ascot and no less than six of his twelve opponents were preferred to him in the Coventry Stakes betting. His performance there was a revelation. Only Motavato managed to offer any

Coventry Stakes, Ascot—Recitation relishes the easy ground and is a decisive winner from Motavato and Bel Bolide

sort of resistance once Recitation hit the front inside the final quarter mile and even he was easily shaken off in the last furlong as Recitation strode powerfully clear for a five-length success. Back in third and fourth places, a further three lengths and two and a half lengths behind, came the subsequent Gimcrack Stakes and Richmond Stakes winners Bel Bolide and Another Realm. An even better performance came from Recitation in the Grand Criterium four months later, when three intervening defeats had taken some of the shine off him and he started at 14/1 after opening at 19/1. Co-favourites at 7/4, together with the pacemaker Gilgit, were the unbeaten French colts Cresta Rider and Dunphy, respectively impressive winners on their last appearances of the Group 2 Criterium de Maisons-Laffitte and the Group 3 Prix des Chenes. Also preferred to Recitation were the Irish challenger Critique, a ten-length winner last time out, the Prix des Chenes runner-up Watchdog and the Prix la Rochette second Shoen. Recitation's chances of winning looked none too bright as he rounded the final turn only ninth of the eleven runners but the picture changed quickly in the straight. As the lead passed rapidly from Gilgit to the filly Pink Prism and then to the Prix de Villebon winner Great Substence, Recitation could be seen coming with a determined run on the outside. Cresta Rider and Critique were simultaneously making excellent headway and the three came to vie for the lead running into the final furlong. From then on it was touch-and-go between the English and Irish challengers as they edged ahead. Although neither flinched under his rider's strongest urgings, Recitation kept on fractionally the better to win by a short head. Dunphy, who had lain even further back than the winner, came through to snatch third place from Cresta Rider, a length behind Critique.

Recitation thereby became only the third foreign-trained winner of the Grand Criterium since the war, following Sir Ivor in 1967 and My Swallow in 1970. A splendid achievement. It's doubtful whether Recitation accomplished as much as his predecessors, though, both of whom were exceptional two-year-olds. He didn't have to contend with the placed horses, let alone the winners, from the Prix Robert Papin, Morny and the Salamandre, whereas Sir Ivor slammed the winners of both the Morny and the Salamandre and My Swallow became the first horse ever to land France's four top juvenile events. Recita-

Grand Criterium, Longchamp—this important prize goes to Recitation who beats Critique in a photo finish. Dunphy is third, just in front of Cresta Rider (No 8). The other horses in the photograph are Great Substence and Watchdog

tion's trainer put matters in perspective with his post-race comment: 'A very nice horse, but I've one much better!'.

Now to Recitation's defeats. It's easy enough to excuse his lifeless display when only fourth, seven lengths behind Beldale Flutter, in the William Hill Futurity at Doncaster. The race probably came too soon after Longchamp (just thirteen days before). And his performance in the Royal Lodge Stakes at Ascot late in September on his outing before Longchamp needs no excusing: he ran very well to go down by only half a length to Robellino, finishing just ahead of both the Laurent Perrier Champagne Stakes winner Gielgud and Beldale Flutter. But what explanation is there for his two other defeats after Royal Ascot? When 5/2 on for the three-runner July Stakes at Newmarket he failed by two and a half lengths to cope with Age Quod Agis, few people's idea of a top-class colt. Although his rider attributed his defeat to the distance, it seems improbable that he was no longer effective over a distance which had brought about such marked improvement in him only three weeks earlier. Possibly the soft ground was against him but it wasn't so very different from that at Ascot. It literally wasn't easy to see what went wrong with the odds-on Recitation in the Westhampnett Stakes on a foggy day at Goodwood in September. After emerging from the murk in a length lead a furlong out he failed by a neck to hold off Clear Verdict. There are three feasible excuses here: firstly that he wasn't fully fit after an absence of over two months; secondly he was said to have run too freely; thirdly, the undulating Goodwood course might not have suited him.

Recitation seemed surprisingly precocious for such a big, well-made colt. He probably favours his sire Elocutionist, one of the best American three-year-olds of 1976 when winner of the nine-and-a-half furlong Preakness Stakes. Elocutionist won all four of his starts as a two-year-old and he has quickly proved his ability to produce fast-maturing animals, siring three American two-year-old winners in April 1980 from his first four runners. Recitation's

Mr A. Bodie's "Recitation"

dam Irish Party didn't run as a two-year-old but she later won nine of her forty starts, including two stakes at around a mile, and a total of over 100,000 dollars. Recitation is her fourth winner from as many foals. Best of the others is the three-year-old Icecapade colt Irish Escapade, the winner of three minor stakes races at up to a mile. None of the next three mares on the bottom line of Recitation's pedigree won a stakes race and Irish Party is the only stakes winner produced by any of them. Consequently, it's not surprising that Recitation fetched only 35,000 dollars as a yearling, a comparatively modest sum by American standards.

Recitation (USA) (b.c. Feb 20, 1978)	Elocutionist (b 1973)	Gallant Romeo (b 1961)	Gallant Man
			Juliets Nurse
		Strictly Speaking (b 1967)	Fleet Nasrullah
			Believe Me
	Irish Party (br 1968)	Irish Lancer (b 1957)	Royal Charger
			Tige O'Myheart
		Party Favor (b 1960)	Tim Tam
			Beaukiss

A mile and a quarter or more will suit Recitation well at three years. Although he has been entered for the Derby, the Epsom gradients are likely to be against him and his objectives are said to be the Prix du Jockey-Club followed by the Irish Sweeps Derby. Unless the French colts already seen improve a good deal over the winter or some better ones come along he looks sure to figure prominently at Chantilly. He has run well enough on firm going but is best suited by an easy surface. Let's hope he's more consistent as a three-year-old. *G. Harwood.*

RECONQUEST 2 ch.c. Red Alert 127–La Concha (Le Levanstell 122) (1980 5f* 5g 6fg^4 6g 6fg 6d 6s* 6g) Mar 17; 4,200Y; small colt; half-brother to several winners, including sprinter Lord Scrap (by Tower Walk); dam never ran; came through to win 12-runner maiden race at Leicester in June by a length from Texas Ranger; well-backed favourite, always going like a winner in 23-runner seller at Haydock in October, and beat La Fedhala by 4 lengths (no bid); beaten in nurseries on most of his other starts but ran respectably in one on final start; will stay 7f; acts on any going. *D. Kent.* **89**

RECORD BREAKER 4 b.c. Jukebox 120–Bare Costs (Petition 130) (1979 7s 1980 7v 7g 5f 5f 6f 6fg) useful-looking colt; poor maiden; should stay 7f; possibly unsuited by heavy ground; blinkered third outing (never going pace); sold out of P. Walwyn's stable 1,150 gns Doncaster June Sales after third start. *B. McMahon.* **59**

RECORD CHOICE 5 b.m. Jukebox 120–Debatable 84 (Counsel 118) (1979 10.2s 12s^3 13v 8g^4 13.8s 12.2g 8f 10h 10f 12g^2 12s 12.5g 12s 1980 11fg 10h 10f 12f^3 10f 10s) poor plater; stays $1\frac{1}{2}$m; probably acts on any going; usually wears blinkers and wore a hood second outing; none too generous in a finish. *K. Stone.* **30**

RECORDED 2 ch.c. Record Token 128–Jukay (Galivanter 131) (1980 6f 6d) May 15; 4,000Y; neat colt; fourth foal; half-brother to a winner in Isle of Man by The Go-Between; dam last both outings; in rear in minor events at Lingfield and Leicester (last of 9) in the autumn; sold 380 gns Ascot November Sales. *P. Walwyn.* **—**

RECORD ROYALE 2 br.g. Record Token 128–Mahal 101 (Tutankhamen) (1980 5s 5s 6s 6fg 7fg 6g) Mar 26; 5,800Y; small, rather narrow gelding; fifth living foal; dam, winner from 1m to $1\frac{1}{4}$m, is half-sister to very smart Tesco Boy; only poor form in maiden and minor events; went down to start very badly on sixth start. *G. Balding.* **58**

RECORD STAR 2 ch.g. Jukebox 120–St Rosalie (Aureole 132) (1980 5f 5f 5.3d 7g 5fg 6g 6g) Apr 28; 5,400Y; compact gelding; half-brother to 2 winners, including 1m and $1\frac{1}{2}$m winner Mount Grace (by Mountain Call); above himself in paddock prior to finishing $4\frac{3}{4}$ lengths fifth of 19 to La Fedhala in seller at Goodwood in September, seventh outing; should stay 7f; blinkered fifth outing; gelded at end of season. *G. Lewis.* **64**

RECORD SURPRISE 2 b.f. Record Run 127–Bonne Surprise 105 (Grey Sovereign 128§) (1980 6d 6s 8d 8d 6g^4 6s^2) Apr 4; 8,000Y; neat filly; half-sister to 3 winners, including fair 6f winner Galoprise (by Tudor Music); dam ran only at 2 yrs when winner twice over 6f; showed improved form when blinkered on last 2 appearances, running well in large fields for maiden races **78**

at Leicester and Doncaster in November, on both occasions showing good speed from outset and at Doncaster being caught only close home by Banbury Cross; best form at 6f. *N. Callaghan.*

RECORD WING 2 b.c. Record Run 127–O'Flynn (Prince Regent 129) (1980 **52**
7d 6fg 6f 10d 8.2s) Feb 24; 2,000F, 6,400Y; neat colt; plater; should stay 1m. *P. Haslam.*

RED AMBION 8 ch.g. Hotfoot 126–Cherry Traces (Escart III) (1979 12f –
1980 12d) of little account on flat; has been tried in blinkers. *A. Davison.*

RED ARTIST 4 ch.g. Red Alert 127–Lane House 68 (Bounteous 125) (1979 –
7v^4 7fg^3 6fg 7f^2 8.2g^2 8.2d 9g^3 7g^3 10.2s 1980 12.5h 10fg 10f 10d 12d) neat, fair sort; plating-class maiden; best form at up to 1m; acts on firm going but is possibly unsuited by hard; sold out of J. Winter's stable 1,350 gns Doncaster August Sales after fourth outing. *J. Perrett.*

RED CLIP 6 b.g. Double Red 122–Barnstables 72 (Pay Up) (1979 NR 1980 –
9fg) poor novice hurdler/chaser; 100/1 when well beaten in maiden race at Newcastle in July, first outing on flat. *J. Gilbert.*

RED CREST 3 ch.f. Red God 128§–Crested Egret (Great Heron 127) (1979 **64**
5g 6fg 1980 5d 6f^3 8f^3 8g^4 8f 8f 8d) neat, strong filly; third in maiden races; stays 1m; acts on firm going; blinkered fourth start. *R. Boss.*

RED CURRENT 3 b.f. My Swallow 134–Red Ribbons II (Red God 128§) –
(1979 5g 5f 6fg 1980 11fg 10f) poor form in maiden races and a handicap; not sure to stay middle distances; blinkered final start. *H. Wragg.*

REDDEN 2 ch.c. Red God 128§–Portden (Worden II 129) (1980 5s 5fg^2 **80**
6f*) Apr 3; 19,000Y; well-made colt; half-brother to 2 winners, including middle-distance performer Azd (by Be Friendly); dam won over 9f in Ireland; favourite, made virtually all and never looked like being beaten when winning 8-runner Woodcote Stakes at Epsom in June by 1½ lengths from Royal Bid; had previously made running until caught in last 100 yards when ½-length second of 16 to Bel Bolide in maiden race at Kempton; should stay 7f; acts on firm going. *B. Swift.*

REDENHAM 4 b.g. Brigadier Gerard 144–Secret Ray 114 (Privy Councillor **72**
125) (1979 7fg^3 7s 7d 7d* 7.2g^4 7v 6fg^2 7fg^3 7f 7fg^3 7fg^4 1980 7f 8f 8fg 11d* 12.3g^4 8d 10s 10d 8fg* 12.2fg^2 8g^2 10.2d) big gelding; won handicaps at Ayr in June and Carlisle (apprentices) in September; effective at 7f and barely stays 1½m; acts on a firm and a soft surface; often blinkered at 3 yrs; has looked ungenuine on occasions. *W. A. Stephenson.*

REDESIGN 2 ch.c. Red Alert 127–Miss Remont 89 (Damremont 120) (1980 **67**
6fg 6fg 6fg) Apr 10; 8,200Y; quite well-made colt; closely related to winning Irish middle-distance stayer and useful hurdler Yellow Dean (by Yellow God) and half-brother to 3 winners here and abroad; showed ability in maiden races at Goodwood (2) and Newmarket; will be suited by 7f and 1m. *T. Marshall.*

RED FIELD 2 b.c. Tudor Rhythm 112–Glebe 83 (Tacitus 124) (1980 7g^3 **65**
7d 7fg 7fg 7g 6g 6d) June 4; narrow, unfurnished colt; half-brother to winners here and in Austria, including 7f and 1¼m winner Chennel Lane (by Caerdeon); dam, winner over 2m, is half-sister to top-class staying filly Bringley; little better than plating class; will stay 1¼m. *H. Westbrook.*

REDFORD 2 ch.c. Red God 128§–Ashton Jane 86 (Gratitude 130) (1980 5fg^3 **79**
5fg^3 5d^4 6d 6fg) Mar 20; 68,000Y; strong, quite attractive, good sort; brother to Red Alert, a high-class performer at up to 7f, and useful 5f sprinter Martianess; dam 2-y-o 5f winner; in frame in maiden race at Kempton in May, Erroll Stakes at Ascot (6 lengths third to Penmarric) the following month and Chesterfield Stakes at Newmarket (respectable 7½ lengths fourth behind Marwell) in July; yet to show he stays 6f (had stiff task on second attempt at trip); sweated up when blinkered on fourth intended outing and had to be withdrawn after rearing up and throwing jockey. *F. J. Houghton.*

RED GENIE 4 ch.f. Swinging Junior 118–Dunderry Class (Dusky Boy 112) –
(1979 NR 1980 8g 14g) sparely-made filly; probably of no account; unseated rider second outing. *J. Powney.*

RED GLOVES 2 b.f. Red God 128§–Nighty Night (Sassafras 135) (1980 **83**
6g^2 7g^2 8fg) May 4; 17,000Y; compact filly; first foal; dam unraced half-sister to 1969 Criterium des Pouliches winner Vela; good second on first 2 outings, going down by 1½ lengths to Glyndebourne in £2,700 event at Leicester in July and by 2 lengths to Seasurf in 16-runner maiden race at Sandown later

in month; ran moderately over 1m on final appearance but should stay trip. *B. Hobbs.*

RED GOLD 2 ch.c. Red Alert 127–Golden Samantha 88 (Sammy Davis 129) **97** (1980 5fg^{3} 6fg 6d 6d 5fg^{2} 5g* 5g^{3} 5d* 5g^{2}) May 17; 9,200F; well-made, quite attractive colt; half-brother to 3 winners, including useful sprinter Just Gayle (by Lord Gayle); dam 2-y-o 5f winner; made all to win nurseries at Goodwood in August and Sandown in October, latter an apprentice event; also ran well final start; best at 5f; acts on a firm and a soft surface; genuine and consistent. *P. Cundell.*

RED HABIT 3 b.f. Habitat 134–Red Berry 115 (Great Nephew 126) (1979 — NR 1980 7d) big, well-made, attractive filly; second foal; half-sister to smart 4-y-o New Berry (by Sir Gaylord), successful at up to 10.5f; dam at her best at 2 yrs when runner-up in Cheveley Park Stakes; very burly, behind throughout in 15-runner maiden race won by Bint Africa at Salisbury in June. *P. Walwyn.*

RED JANE 3 b.f. Red Alert 127–Brother John (Will Somers 114 §) (1979 — 5s 5s 5s 5f^{2} 5fg^{3} 5fg* 5d 5f 5fg 1980 5fg 6s 8g 8d) workmanlike filly; poor plater nowadays; should stay beyond 5f; acts on firm going; often sweats up; sold 660 gns Newmarket Autumn Sales. *W. Wharton.*

RED JAY 4 ch.f. Redundant 120–Jayberne § (Double-U-Jay 120) (1979 **64** 10v 8f^{4} 8d^{4} 10.1fg^{2} 10.1fg 10f^{3} 12fg 1980 8s 10fg 11.7f* 10g 10s 12g* 11.7d* 12fg 11.7fg^{3} 13.1h^{3} 12fg 14g 12.2d) fair sort; did well in 1980 and won handicaps at Windsor (2, trotting up on second occasion) and Salisbury; behind in a seller on first outing; stays 1$\frac{1}{2}$m; acts on any going except soft or heavy; sometimes sweats up badly. *S. Matthews.*

RED JENNY 3 b.f. Red God 128 §–Corbara II (Marino) (1979 5d^{4} 5v^{4} 1980 — 5s 5g) neat filly; poor maiden. *C. Brittain.*

RED LADY 2 gr.f. Warpath 113–Whisky Lima 82 (Midsummer Night II 117) **78** (1980 7g^{3} 8d^{2}) May 28; narrow, lightly-made filly; fourth foal; sister to winning stayer Gin and Lime; dam placed at up to 1$\frac{1}{4}$m; stayed on well when remote third of 14 to Golden Bowl in 14-runner minor event at York in October and when 1$\frac{1}{2}$ lengths second of 15 to Segos in maiden race at Redcar later in month; will stay 1$\frac{1}{2}$m. *C. Thornton.*

REDOUBTABLE (FR) 2 b.c. Tyrant–Alvina (Snob 130) (1980 7.5g 7.5d* **111** 8g*) Apr 10; 145,000 francs Y (approx £15,300); half-brother to three minor French winners; dam French 1$\frac{1}{4}$m winner; a promising colt who won a minor event at Saint-Cloud in September by 2 lengths and 50,000 francs race at Maisons-Laffitte the following month, latter by 1$\frac{1}{2}$ lengths from Mondino; stays 1m well. *F. Palmer, France.*

RED PETAL 2 ch.f. Red Alert 127–Petal (Whistler 129) (1980 6f 7f 7d 7fg **65** 6g 6d 6v^{4} 6s) Apr 27; 4,500Y; compact filly; half-sister to a winner in Ireland and 2 winners abroad; dam fourth in Irish 1,000 Guineas; 5$\frac{1}{4}$ lengths fourth of 6 to Moonlight Sonata in maiden race at Hamilton in October, best effort; not sure to stay 7f; evidently suited by heavy going. *W. Marshall.*

RED REPORT 2 ch.g. Red Alert 127–No Fooling 83 (Narrator 127) (1980 — 6g 6g) Mar 28; 8,400Y; strong, useful sort; good walker; half-brother to a winning plater by Fleece and to 3 winners abroad; dam probably best at middle distances; made no show in maiden races at Yarmouth and Newmarket (5/1) in the summer. *F. Durr.*

RED RUFUS 4 b.c. Busted 134–Red Velvet 114 (Red God 128 §) (1979 **99** 8s^{3} 12s^{2} 10v* 10f^{2} 10s^{2} 10.6g^{3} 10fg* 10s*(dis) 10.5fg^{3} 10f* 10fg^{2} 1980 10s 10g^{3} 10.1fg^{2} 10f^{3} 10g 10fg 10g^{2} 10d) lengthy, good-looking colt; useful handicapper on his day; placed in valuable events at Epsom, Doncaster, Redcar and Ascot, on last-named course in October finishing $\frac{1}{2}$-length second to Funny Spring (possibly hit front earlier than was intended and could find no more when headed by winner); seems best at 1$\frac{1}{4}$m; acts on any going; sometimes taken early to post; usually held up; slowly away and never on terms final start; sold 37,000 gns Newmarket December Sales. *P. Walwyn.*

RED RUSSET 2 b.c. Huntercombe 133–Little Apple (Sovereign Lord 120) **109** (1980 5s* 5fg^{2} 5f* 5f* 5g^{4} 6fg^{4} 5g^{4} 5d^{3}) Mar 7; 5,200Y; sharp, useful sort; half-brother to Eve (by Quisling), a winner at up to 1m, and to a winner in Scandinavia; dam disappointing plater; successful at Warwick, Ripon and Kempton in the spring, gaining his last 2 successes within space of 3 days; off course 3 months afterwards and finished fourth in 3 good-class races on his return, beaten

6½ lengths by Marwell in Prince of Wales's Stakes at York, 5 lengths behind Sweet Monday in Mill Reef Stakes at Newbury and 2 lengths behind Pushy in Cornwallis Stakes at Ascot; stays 6f; acts on any going; genuine and consistent. *I. Balding.*

RED SPARK 3 ch.f. Hot Spark 126–Rosie Bacardi (Ballymoss 136) (1979 **49**
NR 1980 6fg 6f^3 6f^2 6fg^4 6fg) 5,000Y; small filly; half-sister to 2 winners; dam French 1¼m winner; little worthwhile form in varied company; will stay 7f; sold 3,100 gns Newmarket Autumn Sales. *G. Huffer.*

RED TAPIS 3 ch.g. Red Alert 127–Squirrel 91 (White Fire III) (1979 5s^3 **69** d
5v^3 5g* 5fg 6h^4 7f^4 6g^2 6g 6fg 6d 5d^4 6fg 1980 7v 8f^2(dis) 7f^3 7f 7f 7g 6g 7fg 6f) neat gelding; stays 1m; probably acts on any going; sometimes wears blinkers; disappointing; sold 920 gns Doncaster November Sales. *Denys Smith.*

RED TOFF 3 b.g. Red God 128§–Hit It Off (Hardicanute 130) (1979 5s 5g **68**
6s 5fg 6fg^3 7f 6g 7f 6f^4 7g 1980 6f 7.3f 10f 8fg 10.8s 10.1f 10fg 16f*) strong, good-looking gelding; good mover; just held on from Brontolino in moderate maiden event at York in September; stays 2m; suited by top-of-the-ground; sometimes blinkered but wasn't when successful. *C. Brittain.*

RED TREASURE 2 ch.f. Red Alert 127–Persian Mourne (Mourne 126) (1980 **61**
5d 6fg 6d^3 5f 6d 6g^4 7fg) Jan 28; 5,000Y; lengthy filly; sister to Realert, fairly useful winner at up to 7f, and half-sister to a winner in USA; dam half-sister to Gimcrack winner Golden Horus; in frame in sellers at Newcastle in June and August; seems to stay 7f. *P. Rohan.*

RED WOLVER 3 b.c. Wolver Hollow 126–Kentucky Robin 73 (Falcon 131) **83**
(1979 NR 1980 8fg 8fg^4 8.2g 10s^2 10.2g^3 10.4g* 10g 10g^4 10d) big, strong sort; third foal; half-brother to 1m winner Elysee Palace (by Royal Palace), and 1977 2-y-o 6f winner Red Letter (by Major Portion); dam won at up to 11f; favourite, made all and readily beat Spectacular Belle by 2½ lengths in 8-runner maiden event at Chester in July; stays 1¼m well; appears to act on any going; sometimes wears a boot on his near-fore; sold 4,500 gns Newmarket Autumn Sales. *H. Cecil.*

REDWOOD LODGE 2 b. or br.f. On Your Mark 125–Lost Horizon (Narrator 127) **59**
(1980 5s 5fg 5s 5d 5.8g 5g 5.8f 5fg^4 6fg 7.2d 8d^3 8g) Mar 4; 2,300Y; compact filly who carries plenty of condition; sister to very useful 1975 French 2-y-o winner Fiddlers Dream; only quite a moderate plater; stays 1m; acts on a firm and a soft surface; has worn blinkers; sold 300 gns Doncaster November Sales. *J. Haine.*

REEL KEEN 4 ch.f. Firestreak 125–Gleaming Horn 97 (Hornbeam 130) (1979 –
6f 8f 6s 6s 8s 1980 10g 8.2v) compact filly; poor plater; should stay 1m. *I. Jordon.*

REFERENDUM 7 b.g. Reform 132–Hitesca 110 (Tesco Boy 121) (1979 8s –
8.2v 9g^4 8fg* 8f* 8.2fg^4 8f* 8h 8f 8f^4 1980 8s 12fg) moderate handicapper; best at around 1m; acts on any going; often makes the running; used to wear a tongue strap. *Miss S. Morris.*

REFINED LAD 3 br.g. Master Sing 109–Polite 79 (Polic 126) (1979 5d –
5g 5fg 6f 7f^3 8g 1980 12fg 7f 6d) tall gelding; plater; unlikely to stay 1½m. *P. Cundell.*

REFRESH 2 b.c. Reform 132–Jujube 102 (Ribero 126) (1980 7g 7fg^4 8g^4) **73**
Mar 30; good-bodied colt; good mover; second foal; half-brother to 3-y-o 1m winner Maintop (by High Top); dam, a stayer, won 5 of her 6 races; made up a tremendous amount of ground under pressure from halfway when 1¼ lengths fourth of 19 to Toe Tapper in maiden race at Leicester in September; favourite, never going comfortably and looked one paced when 5 lengths fourth of 17 to Dragon Palace in maiden race at Newmarket the following month; looks as though he needs a test of stamina. *P. Walwyn.*

REGAL FLEECE 4 b.f. Run The Gantlet–Knightside (Graustark) (1979 –
9s 14.6fg 12g 10g 13.8d 1980 12f 10fg) leggy, unfurnished filly; of little account. *M. Jarvis.*

REGAL RITA 3 b.f. Take a Reef 127–Regal Winnie 88 (Royal Avenue 123) **60**
(1979 NR 1980 12d^3 12d 12s^3) half-sister to 1976 2-y-o 5f winner Daring Dan (by Run The Gantlet); dam, half-sister to smart sprinter Hard Water, won at up to 1¼m; third in minor and maiden races at Hamilton in the autumn; stays 1½m; yet to race on a sound surface. *W. H. H. Williams.*

REGAL STEEL 2 ch.c. Welsh Pageant 132–All Souls 96 (Saint Crespin III **84**
132) (1980 7g^3 7.2d^4 8.2s^4 7v) Mar 7; 9,400Y; compact colt; half-brother to winners in Ireland and Italy, including 3-y-o sprinter When the Saints (by

Bay Express); dam won twice at around 1¼m; in frame in maiden and minor races, final occasion when 6 lengths fourth of 20 to Irish Heart at Haydock in October; will probably stay 1½m; gave trouble at start at Haydock; should win small race in North. *R. Hollinshead.*

REGAL TIME 2 br.c. Royal and Regal–Rathcoffey Duchy (Faberge II 121) (1980 6s*) Apr 14; 5,400Y; half-brother to 2 winners in Ireland by Jukebox, including useful 1977 2-y-o sprinter Rathcoffey Dodo; dam won 5 times from 7f to 11f in Ireland; put up an encouraging display when putting in a strong late run to win 13-runner minor event at Fairyhouse in October by a length from Sales Ring, the pair finishing clear; quite stoutly bred and should make a useful colt over a mile or more. *M. Fogarty, Ireland.* **90** p

REGAL TOUCH 2 b.c. Royal Match 117–Msida (Majority Blue 126) (1980 7f 6g4) May 1; 7,000Y; big, strong colt; half-brother to a winner in Belgium; dam, placed over 9f in Ireland, is half-sister to numerous winners; 20/1, always front rank when 5¾ lengths fourth of 11 to Norman Style in £5,900 event at Doncaster in September; will be suited by 7f and 1m. *M. H. Easterby.* **69**

REGALUS 6 br.g. Dike–March the First 90 (Martial 131) (1979 12d 16g 12f 12fg 12f4 12fg3 12g* 12fg 14g4 12fg3 13.3fg 12fg4 1980 12d 13v4 12d 14f 12fg 12f 12fg3 12.3g3 12g4 12fg 16.1fg3) middle-distance performer; didn't run up to his best; acts on any going; blinkered final start in 1979 and fifth outing; sold 5,500 gns Doncaster August Sales. *N. Callaghan.* **54**

REGAL VILLAGE 4 b.g. Royal and Regal–Chitterne (Ommeyad 120) (1979 NR 1980 8fg 8g) of little account; sold 500 gns Doncaster August Sales. *D. McCain.* –

REGENCY BRIGHTON 2 ch.f. Royal Palace 131–Gay City 99 (Forlorn River 124) (1980 7d 6g) May 8; 4,000F; fourth reported foal; half-sister to 1978 2-y-o 5f winner Blessingtonia (by So Blessed); dam sprinter; unquoted when behind in maiden races at Leicester at the back-end. *M. Tate.* –

REGENCY ELITE 5 br.g. Prince Regent 129–Leit Motif 95 (Fortino II 120) (1979 7d3 10s 8fg* 9fg* 8f 8d3 9fg3 8g3 10s4 8.2d* 8f3 1980 7f* 7g4 8d 7g 6d2 8fg* 8.2g2 8fg* 8f2 8fg 7.2d 8s) robust gelding; won handicaps at Edinburgh (2) and Thirsk, beating Kithairon by 5 lengths in apprentice event on latter course in August; didn't run up to his best last 3 starts; best form at up to 9f; acts on any going except very soft; blinkered final outing at 2 yrs; suitable mount for an apprentice. *Denys Smith.* **74**

REGENCY PRINCE 2 b.c. or br.c. Furry Glen 121–Lyonata (Atan) (1980 5d* 5v2(dis) 5h 5g 6d2 7d 6s) May 4; 1,300F, 1,300Y; leggy, narrow sort; good walker; fourth produce; dam Irish 6f winner; stayed on to win maiden race at Doncaster in March by ½ length from Sovereign Landing; second in minor event at Ayr later in month (subsequently disqualified when theobromine was found in his system) and in nursery at Redcar in August (ran well when ½ length behind Praiselien); suited by 6f but ran poorly when tried over 7f; seems to act on any going; has a tendency to hang under pressure. *P. Rohan.* **83**

REGENCY WOOD 5 b.m. Prince Regent 129–Whitewood 74 (Worden II 129) (1979 16s 1980 10d) of little account. *T. Craig.* –

REGENT'S BOY 3 b.g. Prince Regent 129–Whitewood 74 (Worden II 129) (1979 5d 5d2 5g 5g4 6fg2 6fg3 7.2fg4 7g2 7f3 7g 8.2g4 6d2 1980 8h 8fg3 8f2 8fg 9.4fg3 6g 14g) workmanlike gelding; best form at 1m; probably acted on any going; effective with or without blinkers; bandaged final outing (didn't impress in paddock); trained by S. Wainwright first 6 starts; dead. *M. Ryan.* **62**

REGON CLIPPER 4 ch.f. Cavo Doro 124–Pamabella (Pardao 120) (1979 5s 6s3 7d4 6s 7.6v 6d 8s 9f3 8fg 1980 8s 9fg 11.1fg 10f 10s 10fg 10.2d 8d) plater; stays 9f; acts on any going; often blinkered at 3 yrs. *V. Soane.* –

REHOBOAM 2 b.c. Mummy's Pet 125–La Mirabelle 92 (Princely Gift 137) (1980 5f2 5fg 5fg2 5fg3 5.1g3 5g2) Apr 5; lengthy, narrow colt; good mover; half-brother to 3 winners, including Jeroboam (by Sharpen Up), a smart winner at up to 7f; dam won over 6f; beaten favourite on second, third, fourth and sixth outings, on final occasion giving impression something is wrong with him when going down by 2 lengths to Bold Scuffle in maiden race at York in October; one to leave alone; sold to T. Craig 2,600 gns Newmarket Autumn Sales. *H. Wragg.* **76 §**

REIDOR 2 br.c. Roi Soleil 125–Bella Musica (Sing Sing 134) (1980 5f 5fg*) May 7; 1,250Y; half-brother to winning miler Sir Pelleas (by Sahib); dam ran 3 times; won 16-runner maiden race at Catterick in June by a length from Tough an Rough; will stay 6f. *W. Haigh.* **79**

REINE SOLEIL 4 ch.f. Roi Soleil 125–Rosslea (Klairon 131) (1979 7s 7s 7s* **86**
7d 7.6f^{2} 7g 8s^{2} 8f 8fg 1980 8d 8d 8f 8d^{2} 8fg 8fg 8fg 8g^{2} 7d) lengthy filly; second in handicap at Brighton in June and minor event on same course in October, beaten 2 lengths by clever winner Lightning Label in latter event; well beaten in between, and was also disappointing on final start; stays 1m; acts on any going, but is ideally suited by some give in the ground; blinkered third outing; sold 7,600 gns Newmarket December Sales. *N. Vigors.*

REIN STOPPED PLAY 4 bl.g. Linacre 133–Galona (El Gallo 122) (1979 8f^{4} —
10.4f 10g^{4} 10.6g* 10.6g 16d 1980 12.2v) smallish gelding; stayed 1¼m; seemed suited by some give in the ground; blinkered final outing at 2 yrs; dead. *D. Gandolfo.*

REJUVENATOR 4 bl. or br.g. Reliance II 137–Juvenescence 87 (Golden Horus —
123) (1979 11.7g 1980 8f 12.3f 12f) poor maiden; blinkered final outing. *G. Richards.*

REKAL 2 gr.c. Busted 134–Idover 95 (Fortino II 120) (1980 6fg 6g 6g 8s^{4}) **77**
Feb 17; 27,000F, 12,500Y; quite well-made colt; half-brother to several winners, including 5f to 7f winner Hamdani (by Welsh Pageant); dam sprinter; 33/1, ran easily best race when about 5 lengths fourth to Irish Heart in 19-runner minor event at Stockton in October; evidently suited by 1m and soft ground. *C. Brittain.*

RELATIVE EASE 9 ch.g. Great Nephew 126–Glider 82 (Buisson Ardent 129) **69**
(1979 5fg^{3} 5f^{3} 6fg^{4} 5f^{3} 5g 1980 5fg 5f^{4} 5fg^{4} 5d^{2} 5g* 5f^{2} 5f 6g^{2} 5s^{4} 6f 6g 5v) sprint handicapper; made all at Catterick (apprentices) in August and ran well most other outings; acts on any going but is particularly well suited by top-of-the-ground conditions; has worn blinkers; splendid mount for an inexperienced rider; sometimes sweats up; has worn a tongue strap; best on an easy course. *D. Chapman.*

RELEVANCE 5 br.h. Reliance II 137–Julieta 108 (Ratification 129) (1979 9s —
10s^{3} 10f 10g 8g^{3} 1980 10.2d 10.6fg) compact horse; has deteriorated, and is a plater nowadays; stays 1¼m; acts on soft going and is not at his best on firm; usually wears blinkers; suitable mount for an apprentice. *P. Ransom.*

RELIANCE NEWS 2 b.f. English Prince 129–Mink Fur (Victoria Park) (1980 **74**
7g 7g 7g 8fg 10d* 8s) Mar 21; 5,700Y; quite a well-made filly; first foal; dam unplaced once in France; second favourite and dropped in class, put up best effort when winning 14-runner seller at Pontefract in October a shade cleverly by a neck from Billie Gibb, the pair clear; bought in 1,300 gns afterwards; will probably stay 1½m; sold 600 gns Ascot November Sales. *N. Callaghan.*

RELKO BOY 3 br.g. Relko 136–Woodland Nymph (Hornbeam 130) (1979 5d —
7g 1980 8.5g 11.7f 14f 16s) rangy gelding; poor maiden. *A. Ingham.*

RELKOZINI 4 ch.c. Relko 136–Discernment 66 (Pan II 130) (1979 7fg 12.2f —
14.7g^{4} 12.3s^{2} 12.3s 15.8fg 16d^{4} 15g^{3} 1980 15fg) narrow colt; tailed off only outing of 1980; stays well; suited by soft going; sweating last 2 starts at 3 yrs. *I. Jordon.*

REMA 5 b.m. Will Hays–Miss Wolff 91 (Vilmorin) (1979 7d^{4} 7g* 7g 7s 7fg 7f 7g **41**
7g^{4} 6fg 1980 9.6f^{4} 9.6h^{3} 7fg 7d 7g^{3} 8.3g 7fg^{2} 8.3f^{2} 7f^{2} 8fg 8g 8g) plater; stays 9.6f; seems to act on any going; has worn blinkers. *J. O'Donoghue.*

REMAINDER IMP 3 ch.g. Jimmy Reppin 131–Romany Girl 103 (Worden II **73**
129) (1979 NR 1980 7d* 10d 7fg 8d 7.6d^{2} 8.3d^{3} 8g 7d 8s^{4}) close-coupled, useful-looking gelding; half-brother to a winner in Brazil by Right Tack; dam won at up to 13f in Ireland; made virtually all to win newcomers race at Doncaster in March; creditable second in apprentice handicap at Lingfield in July; stays 1m; suited by some give in the ground; sometimes gives trouble at start; ran moderately seventh and eighth starts, wearing blinkers on second occasion. *G. Harwood.*

REMEZZO 6 ch.h. Ribero 126–Camina Bay 109 (Whistling Wind 123) (1979 **88**
12s^{4} 11fg 12s 12g^{4} 12fg^{3} 12g 14s 12g 12fg 1980 18d 12.2s 12g^{4} 15g 14g^{4}) fair handicapper nowadays; best form at up to 15f (did not stay when well beaten over further on reappearance); acts on any going; blinkered fifth and last 3 starts 1979. *D. Elsworth.*

REMNOS 3 b.c. Blue Cashmere 129–Silleys Maid 100 (Continuation 120) (1979 —
NR 1980 5d 7g 6s^{4} 6g) good sort; second foal; half-brother to 4-y-o Silley's

Knight (by Derring-Do), successful at up to 1m; dam sprinter; little sign of ability in minor and maiden races; blinkered final start; sold 1,100 gns Ascot August Sales. *M. Stoute.*

REMOULEUR 2 ch.c. Sharpen Up 127–Coulter Belle 80 (Quorum 126) (1980 5f² 5fg 6g 6fg 7.3fg³ 7f² 7g*) Feb 9; 14,000Y; rangy colt; good walker and excellent mover; half-brother to 4 winners here and abroad; dam miler; ran creditably in nurseries in the autumn and stayed on really well to win 17-runner event at Ascot in October by 1½ lengths from dead-heaters Investa and Emphasis; will stay 1m; sometimes takes a long time to find his stride; yet to race on a soft surface. *R. Price.* **100**

RENCONTRE (FR) 3 b.f. Reform 132–Belle Melodie (Tudor Melody 129) (1979 NR 1980 7fg 8g 12f 10.1f² 10fg*) 58,000Y; quite attractive, lightly-made filly; first foal; dam, winner over 11f in France, is daughter of French Oaks winner Belle Sicambre; favourite, narrowly won maiden race at Beverley in September; stays 1¼m; yet to race on a soft surface. *J. Dunlop.* **73**

RENDEZVOUS 4 br.f. Lorenzaccio 130–Seam 100 (Nearula 132) (1979 7v 9s 8.3f 7g 9g 8fg 1980 8d 12d 10d 12g) plating-class maiden; looked temperamental penultimate start; sold 1,000 gns Newmarket Autumn Sales. *N. Guest.* **–**

RENOVATE 3 ro.c. The Go-Between 129–Touch It Up (Trojan Monarch) (1979 5s 5s 5d* 5f⁴ 5fg² 5f² 5f³ 5f* 6g* 6s³ 5d² 1980 5d* 6fg 6fg 6f* 5fg 5fg 5g 6g⁴ 6g 5.6g 6d) sturdy colt; poor mover in his slower paces; successful in handicaps at Doncaster in March and Redcar in May, on latter making all to beat Westacombe 1½ lengths; creditable fifth to Swelter in William Hill Portland Handicap at Doncaster in September on tenth outing; suited by 6f; probably acts on any going; blinkered sixth start; ran badly final appearance; goes well for P. Eddery. *J. Hardy.* **93**

REPENTANCE 3 ch.f. Tower Walk 130–Penitent 85 (Sing Sing 134) (1979 NR 1980 6fg 5f 8d 5d 6s) useful-looking filly; half-sister to 3 winners, including sprinters Pennycress (by Florescence) and Penumbra (by Wolver Hollow); dam closely related to top sprinter Song; in rear in maiden races and handicaps. *P. Mitchell.* **–**

REPETITIOUS 3 b.f. Northfields–Nanette 100 (Worden II 129) (1979 7f* 7fg 6g² 7d 6fg³ 1980 7s⁴ 6f 8fg* 6f* 6fg 6d² 6fg* 6fg³) 32,000Y; lengthy, fair ex- **103**

Spillers Stewards' Cup, Goodwood—Repetitious (far side) wins from Eagle Boy

Irish filly; sister to 9f winner Norette and smart middle-distance filly Nanticious, closely related to useful sprinter Tanella (by Habitat) and half-sister to another winner; dam stayed 1¼m; gained an important success when apprentice ridden in Spillers Stewards' Cup at Goodwood in July, holding on by a short head from Eagle Boy; had earlier won apprentice race at Kempton and 4-runner £2,100 event at Lingfield (made all); effective from 6f to 1m; appears to act on any going; good mount for a boy; trained until after second outing by M. Kauntze; sent to USA and has been placed there. *G. Harwood.*

REPIQUE 6 b.g. Jimmy Reppin 131–Winning Bid 93 (Great Captain) (1979 — 13g^2 12s 12d 1980 16.1s) disappointing middle-distance handicapper; best form with some give in the ground; has been tried in blinkers; needed race only outing of 1980. *E. Jones.*

REPPIN CASTLE 6 ch.h. Jimmy Reppin 131–Castle Rough 96 (Counsel 118) — (1979 8d 8s 1980 7f 7.6f 8fg 8fg) one-time fair handicapper; tailed off since 1978; stays 1m; acts on any going; blinkered penultimate outing; sold 1,000 gns Doncaster August Sales. *J. Bingham.*

RESEDA PALACE 2 ch.f. Dragonara Palace 115–Judolyn 87 (Canisbay 120) — (1980 8fg 6f 8g 8.2s) Apr 24; half-sister to 2 sprint winners; dam won at up to 1m; little sign of ability in maiden and minor races; blinkered fourth outing. *K. Stone.*

RESIDE 4 ch.c. Quayside 124–Resurgence (Runnymede 123) (1979 12s* 10v **95** 10f 10fg^2 8f* 10.6g* 8d 10s 1980 8d 10fg^4 8d^3 12fg^4 8g 8f) strong colt; useful handicapper at his best; ran quite well when fifth to Doogali under top weight at Newcastle in April on reappearance but was off course subsequently until July and didn't run up to his best on his return (found nothing when let down on last 2 starts); has won over 1½m but has shown best form at shorter distances; probably best served by a sound surface; suitable mount for an apprentice. *G. Toft.*

RESTFUL 3 ch.f. Ribero 126–Mey 78 (Canisbay 120) (1979 7.2fg^2 1980 **84** 7f^2 10fg^2 10fg 8fg^2 10.2fg^2 10d* 10.1g^3 8g) well-made, quite attractive filly; good mover; landed odds very easily in modest 5-runner £1,700 event at Salisbury in August; runner-up in varied company earlier, putting up best efforts when going down by a neck to Jem Jen in Playboy Pretty Polly Stakes at Newmarket in May on second start and by ¾ length to Trevita in £4,000 handicap at Ascot in June on fourth outing; will be suited by 1½m; probably acts on any going; blinkered third start. *R. Hern.*

RESTLESS CAPTAIN 2 ch.g. Sandford Lad 133–Kirkwall 74 (Sheshoon **81** 132) (1980 6g 6g^3 7d^2 8.2g^4) Mar 27; 5,000Y; workmanlike gelding; good mover; third foal; dam stayed at least 1½m; ran best races when short-head second of 11 to odds-on Cifonelli in £2,500 event at Newcastle in August and when 3¼ lengths fourth of 7 to Pellegrini in £4,100 race at Haydock the following month; may well stay 1¼m; acts on a soft surface. *G. Richards.*

RESTLESS IMP (USA) 3 ch.f. Tom Rolfe–War Khal (Khaled) (1979 NR — 1980 10fg 10fg 11.7fg) strong, compact filly; sister to a moderate animal in USA, and half-sister to 3 winners, including smart 7f and 1½m winner Corby (by Round Table); dam won over 1m in USA; little worthwhile form in maiden races; should stay 1½m; not raced after June. *P. Walwyn.*

RESTLESS LADY 3 ch.f. Sandford Lad 133–Super Restless (Restless Wind) — (1979 NR 1980 6fg 8.5f 10s 10g) 19,000Y; rangy filly; second foal; dam, sister to On Your Mark, won over 5f in Ireland; modest form in maiden races; stays 1¼m; got very upset and tried to rear over backwards in stalls on second start (off course 4 months afterwards). *R. Price.*

RESTLESS MORN 4 ch.f. Morston 125–Restive 96 (Relic) (1979 7.2fg — 8fg 7f 8.2fg 1980 12f 12d) poor maiden. *J. Hudson.*

RETAINER 6 ch.g. Gay Pilot 92–Most Precious (Matador 131) (1979 NR — 1980 16g 12.3d) poor maiden; blinkered final start. *H. Wharton.*

RETIRED EARLY 6 b.m. Miracle 116–Growing Leisure 81 (Constable 119) — (1979 NR 1980 13.8g^4 12f) small, compact mare; of no account. *W. C. Watts.*

RETZA 5 ch.g. Richboy 117–Shari (Rustam 127) (1979 6s^3 7d 6d 7d 6f 7fg — 6g^4 6g 5g^2 6g^4 5fg 6fg 6d^2 6d* 6d 1980 6s 7d) won handicap at Catterick in 1979; well beaten in 1980 (not raced until October); stays 7f; probably acts on any going; often blinkered but wasn't at Catterick; good mount for an apprentice. *A. Davison.*

REVLOW 6 br.h. Wolver Hollow 126–Velvet Sheen 92 (Linacre 133) (1979 12d⁴ 12d⁴ 12fg² 12f 10.5f 1980 10fg) useful handicapper at his best, but seems to have deteriorated; stays 1½m; suited by forcing tactics. *J. Mason.* —

REVNANT 3 ch.g. Sweet Revenge 129–One Extra 85 (Abernant 142) (1979 5g 5v 6fg 10.6d 1980 8h 8fg) big, strong gelding; poor mover; poor form in maiden and minor races; sold 360 gns Doncaster October Sales. *J. Hardy.* —

REVOCATION (USA) 3 ch.c. Reviewer–Recall (Reneged) (1979 NR 1980 10.1fg* 12f³ 10.1g⁴ 8d* 8fg 8g³ 8g³) $75,000Y; good sort; half-brother to several minor winners; dam smart stakes winner at up to 1m; successful in maiden race at Windsor in May and handicap at Wolverhampton in July; good third to Herons Hollow in handicap at Goodwood in September but ran moderately final start (reportedly jockey thought horse had broken down); best at up to 1¼m; acts on a firm and a soft surface. *P. Walwyn.* **86**

REVOLUTIONARY (USA) 3 ch.c. Vaguely Noble 140–Night Staker (Claim Staker) (1979 NR 1980 12fg 12g) $150,000Y; strong, well-made colt; third foal; half-brother to a winner in USA by Boldnesian; dam smart stakes winner at up to 1m at 3 yrs but ended up in claiming races; behind in maiden events at Doncaster in May (tailed-off last) and Salisbury in June. *J. Dunlop.* —

REVOLVER 3 br.g. Scottish Rifle 127–Passing Shot 72 (Salvo 129) (1979 NR 1980 15.5g 15.5g) first foal; dam, useful hurdler, won 1½m seller on flat; beaten a long way in maiden races at Folkestone. *S. Woodman.* —

RHEIN BRIDGE 2 b.f. Rheingold 137–Fishermans Bridge 113 (Crepello 136) (1980 7d⁴ 8s*) Mar 5; 26,000Y; useful-looking filly; sister to moderate 1m winner Freia, and half-sister to very smart middle-distance filly Connaught Bridge (by Connaught); dam stayed 1¼m; had a lot to do 2f out, as a result of having a very poor run, when odds on for 8-runner maiden race at Ayr in September, but made up ground in good style to win cleverly by ¾ length from Ring Bidder; creditable 3¾ lengths fourth of 11 to Cocaine in Acomb Stakes at York previous month; will be suited by 1¼m; yet to race on a sound surface; better than her Ayr running suggests. *J. W. Watts.* **88** p

RHEINFORD 4 gr.g. Rheingold 137–Florrie Ford 79 (Kelly 122) (1979 8.2v² 8g³ 12.3d⁴ 8.2s 8fg 8fg⁴ 8f 8fg⁴(dis) 8g 8s 1980 10fg 12h⁴ 10fg 10d 10.2g 10g 10fg) attractive gelding; quite a moderate handicapper nowadays; stays 1¼m; has won on a firm surface but needs soft ground to show his best form; blinkered eighth and ninth starts at 3 yrs. *J. Old.* —

RHEINGOLD'S GIFT 2 b.c. Rheingold 137–Love Story 79 (Aureole 132) (1980 7fg 8fg 10s) Apr 13; 15,000Y; small, narrow colt; first foal; dam won twice over 1m; quite moderate form in maiden races, best effort on final start; will be suited by 1½m. *C. Brittain.* **71**

RHEINMAN 4 gr.c. Rheingold 137–Miss Sarah (The Axe 115) (1979 10.2g 12v 13.3f³ 13.1h² 14g 1980 11.7fg* 12f² 11f 12fg⁴ 12fg² 12d 12fg 12fg) middle-distance handicapper; winner at Bath in April; twice runner-up to Russian George afterwards, on second occasion going down by 2½ lengths in Newbury Summer Cup in June; ran poorly last 3 outings; stays 13f; acts on hard going and is not at his best on soft; ran badly in blinkers final outing in 1979; unruly at start and parted company with rider leaving stalls third outing; not the easiest of rides. *C. Nelson.* **81**

RHEINSPARKLE 4 br.f. Rheingold 137–Happy II (Rockefella) (1979 12v³ 12d 12fg³ 13d* 12f 1980 12h* 20d 12g³) good mover; useful performer as a 3-y-o; beat Jolimo a length in 19-runner amateur riders event at Thirsk in May; 4 lengths third to Broomstick Corner in £3,000 event at Lingfield in September; almost certainly didn't stay trip when tailed off in Ascot Stakes (Handicap) at Royal Ascot in between; stays 13f; acts on any going; genuine. *B. Hills.* **91**

RHIANNON 2 b.f. Welsh Pageant 132–Lady Lowndes 97 (Tamerlane 128) (1980 8d³ 8d) Mar 21; neat filly; fourth foal; half-sister to a winner in Cyprus; dam won from 1¼m to 13.8f; 25/1 when 4½ lengths third of 14 to Nimblemoss in maiden race at Bath in October, better effort; will stay 1¼m+. *P. Cundell.* **65**

RHUS (USA) 3 b.c. Riva Ridge–Bold Pink (Bold Bidder) (1979 NR 1980 10v* 10g* 9d² 11s) $85,000Y; fourth foal; half-brother to very useful French 1977 2-y-o 6f and 7f winner Lady Jane Grey (by Zeddaan) and to a minor winner in USA by Key To The Mint; dam won over 5f at 2 yrs in Ireland; won newcomers race at Evry in March and Group 3 Premio Lazio at Rome in May, **116**

latter by 3 lengths from Barbaccio; good ¾-length second to Huguenot in Prix Daphnis at Evry in July; stays 1¼m (poor last in Grand Prix Prince Rose at Ostend over further); yet to race on a firm surface; to be trained by M. Stoute in 1981. *F. Boutin, France.*

RHYME ROYAL 5 ch.g. Crepello 136–Lyrical 110 (Gratitude 130) (1979 **116**
10d* 11fg* 10d^{2} 12d 12s^{3} 1980 12g^{3} 11s^{4} 12v^{2}) rangy gelding, who carries a lot of condition; smart handicapper; won Sandown Cup and London Gold Cup at Newbury in 1979; ran only 3 times in 1980, following a short spell over hurdles (won once), but showed that he retained his ability; ran best race on last day of season when well-backed favourite for William Hill November Handicap at Doncaster, racing prominently throughout and going down by only ½ length to Path of Peace under 9-13; ran easily better previous race when third to Dutch Treat in Great Yorkshire Handicap at York in August; reportedly not himself when disappointing fourth behind Sea Pigeon in Doonside Cup at Ayr in between; stays 1¾m; appears to act on any going but goes well in the mud; usually ridden up with the leaders; thoroughly genuine and consistent. *R. Hern.*

RHYTHM STICK 3 ch.g. Pieces of Eight 128–My Audrey 100 (Pall Mall 132) –
(1979 NR 1980 10fg 8fg) 2,000Y, resold 2,300Y; brother to a winner in Brazil and half-brother to 2 winners; dam stayed 1m; well beaten in maiden races in first half of season. *P. Cole.*

RIBBLE ROUSER 7 ch.g. Marcus Brutus 108–Ribble Reed 75 (Bullrush **63**
106) (1979 16.1v^{4} 16d^{4} 16s 18s 15.8g* 16f 16f^{2} 15.8fg* 19f^{3} 15.8d^{3} 18g^{2} 15fg^{2} 16fg 1980 18d 16f^{2} 15f* 18fg^{4} 15.8fg* 16fg 15.8f* 15.8g 15.8d) quite a moderate handicapper; winner at Ayr in May and Catterick in June and July; beaten 3 lengths by Wild Rosie on last occasion but was crossed by that horse 1½f out and was promoted to first after a stewards inquiry (unquestionably second best on merit); stays well; acts on any going; has worn blinkers; suitable mount for an apprentice; often makes the running; inconsistent. *W. C. Watts.*

RIBELLARO 8 b.g. Riboccare 118–Dianella (Aureole 132) (1979 12s 12d –
12g 12d^{3} 1980 16s 12g^{4}) fairly useful handicapper at his best; suited by 1½m or more; usually wears blinkers (didn't in 1980); wears bandages. *M. Haynes.*

RIBERETTO 2 b.c. Ribero 126–Love Resolved (Dan Cupid 132) (1980 **85**
7f 8g* 7.3d) Apr 22; strong colt; good mover; half-brother to 3-y-o 1½m and 15f winner Lone Raider (by Shantung) and useful 5f and 7f winner Tribal Warrior (by Tribal Chief); dam placed over 13f in France; confirmed promise of his previous run by winning 15-runner maiden race at Newmarket in October by a head from Fandangle, fighting back well under very strong riding to get back in front on line; 14/1 when last of 10 to Kalaglow in Horris Hill Stakes at Newbury later in month; will be suited by a test of stamina. *R. Boss.*

RIBO CHARTER 3 b.g. Ribero 126–Grecian Charter (Runnymede 123) **85**
(1979 6g^{3} 6fg^{3} 7f^{4} 7d^{2} 7g^{2} 8fg^{2} 10d^{3} 10v 1980 8s 10f 12f^{2} 12f 10.5d^{3} 12fg^{3} 12g 12d 16fg* 12g^{3} 14d^{2}) lengthy gelding; readily won amateur riders maiden race at Ascot in September; had earlier shown very useful form on occasions, including when length second to Ginistrelli (USA) (gave 5 lb) in Ladbroke Derby Trial Stakes at Lingfield in May, but ran badly on seventh start, has twice seemed unwilling to exert himself in a finish and is none too consistent; stays well; seems to act on any going; sometimes sweats up. *P. Kelleway.*

RIBODEN 2 b.g. Ribero 126–True Dresden 58 (Vilmoray 126) (1980 5f 6f –
6g 7fg) Apr 21; 2,200Y; half-brother to several minor winners; dam sprint maiden; well beaten in maiden races, once finishing last in a Folkestone auction event. *G. Fletcher.*

RIBOLANE 5 b.g. Ribero 126–Mamzelle 85 (King's Troop 118) (1979 12.2s^{4} –
1980 8g 12g 16fg) middle-distance staying handicapper; seems to act on any going; inconsistent; often bandaged. *H. Willis.*

RIBONNY (FR) 4 b.f. Fast Hilarious–Ribbon Candy (Ribot 142) (1979 9.4d –
10h 12s 1980 10v^{3} 12.3s^{3} 15g 13s^{4} 12g 12.5s) small filly; plating-class maiden; probably stays 13f; acts on heavy going. *W. Elsey.*

RIBOT FAIR 3 b.f. Andrea Mantegna–Fair Exchange (Port Frere 108) (1979 **55**
NR 1980 11fg 10fg 12fg 8d^{2} 10.1s* 11d) workmanlike filly; plater; won at Windsor in June (sold out of P. Cole's stable 2,300 gns); stays 1¼m; suited by some give in the ground; virtually refused to race first outing. *D. Ringer.*

RIBOT MANTEGNA 5 b.g. Andrea Mantegna–Djemm (Djakao 124) (1979 16s 15.5d 1980 16.5g) poor maiden. *T. M. Jones.* –

RIBSTON PIPPIN 4 ch.g. Ribston 104–Cuddly Toy (Sovereign Lord 120) (1979 NR 1980 12.2f) sturdy gelding; tailed off in maiden race at Catterick in July, first outing. *N. Chamberlain.* –

RICHESSE (FR) 4 b.f. Faraway Son 130–Rosalin (Tissot 131) (1979 NR 1980 12.5h) third reported foal; dam placed at up to 10.5f in French Provinces; unquoted and in need of race when last of 13 finishers behind Khaki Kate in maiden race at Stockton in April, first outing. *W. Bentley.* –

RICH VISION 6 gr.m. Richboy 117–Grey Vision (Amber X 133) (1979 10v2 10.8d* 10g 12v2 10s3 10s2 10g 10s3 11s 12d 1980 12s3 12fg 10g 11.7s) poor handicapper; stays 1½m; acts on any going, but goes well in the mud. *J. Holt.* –

RICKFORD CHOICE 3 ch.g. Henry the Seventh 125–Rao Ash (Celtic Ash) (1979 7fg 8.2g 8f 1980 9.6h 9.6f 7f 12d) lightly-made gelding; bad plater; often blinkered; slipped up first start. *R. Hoad.* –

RICKFORD PRIDE 3 ch.c. St Paddy 133–Garnette Rose 74 (Floribunda 136) (1979 5s 5v 5g 7g 7fg 6f 7f 1980 7f 12fg 11.7f 16g3 10fg 16.5g 16s) plating-class maiden; suited by a test of stamina; dead. *C. Wildman.* –

RIDAN FLIGHT 4 b.g. Ridan–Irish Flight (Ballymoss 136) (1979 12v 10v 12fg 1980 10s 8.3f) wiry gelding; plater; should stay 1m; changed hands 370 gns Ascot May Sales. *H. O'Neill.* –

RIDARRAGH 6 b.g. Ridan–Relegere (Relic) (1979 NR 1980 12.5v 9g 12fg 10fg 16.1s 12.5s) big gelding; slow maiden; wears bandages; pulled up on reappearance. *F. Yardley.* –

RIDGEFIELD 2 br.c. Firestreak 125–Chebs Lass 84 (Chebs Lad 120) (1980 8g) May 1; 8,600Y; brother to 1979 2-y-o 6f winner Awahnee Lady; dam won twice over 7f at 2 yrs; easy in market and very backward, ran on steadily to finish promising seventh of 16 to Uppety in minor event at Newmarket in October. *G. Harwood.* **74** p

RIDGMONT 2 gr.g. Saulingo 122–Chrysolite 93 (Dante) (1980 6fg) Apr 1; 2,500F, 1,000Y; compact gelding; half-brother to 3 winners, including 5f to 7f winner Lusty Len (by Faberge II); dam placed at 2 yrs and 3 yrs; 12/1, never showed when remote sixth of 14 behind wide-margin winner Tina's Pet in maiden race at Yarmouth in August. *B. Hobbs.* –

RIFLEFIRE 4 bl.g. Warpath 113–Sunflower 96 (Paveh 126) (1979 10g 12s 13g 1980 16f 16s 15.4s) useful sort; slow maiden. *P. K. Mitchell.* –

RIGHT DIAMOND 3 b.c. Right Tack 131–Garzoni (Ribot 142) (1979 7fg 7g 7fg3 8fg3 8f 1980 10s* 12g2 12fg3 13s* 12g* 12.2s* 13.3d3 14g2) good-bodied colt; developed into a fairly useful handicapper after winning maiden race at Leicester in the spring, scoring at Nottingham, Ripon and Warwick; ran well last 2 starts to be third to Castle Keep in Morland Brewery Trophy at Newbury and neck second to Another Generation at Goodwood (ridden by 5-lb claimer); stays 1¾m; suited by some give in the ground; game and consistent. *R. Akehurst.* **92**

RIGHT OF LIGHT 6 ch.h. Tyrant–Daisy June (Epaulette 125) (1979 6g* 6d 7fg*(dis) 6fg 7f 8g 8f 7f2 7.3g 1980 6fg 6f2 7.2fg3 6fg 7d3 7fg4 6fg3 7f3 7fg2 6fg2 7g) neat horse; second in handicaps at Newbury, Salisbury and Newmarket, beaten ½ length by Welsh Blossom on last-named course in October; best form at up to 7f; probably acts on any going; often blinkered nowadays; usually held up; needs strong handling; finds little off bridle. *P. Makin.* **95**

RIGHT REGENT 2 ch.c. Kambalda 108–Vetsera (Hopeful Venture 125) (1980 6fg 8d 8d) compact colt; second foal; dam never ran; behind in newcomers race at Chepstow in August and maiden events at Bath and Warwick in October; likely to need a thorough test of stamina. *D. Elsworth.* –

RIGHT SHADY 3 b.f. Right Tack 131–Shady 101 (Royal Palm 131) (1979 NR 1980 8fg 10.1s 6g) second living foal; half-sister to very smart 7f filly Green Girl (by Petingo); dam won from 6f to 1m; no sign of ability in maiden and minor races. *D. Marks.* –

RIGHT SO 7 ch.g. Falcon 131–Nectis (Honeyway 125) (1979 8g 8g4 8d2 8f3 8s4 1980 10.2d3 10s4 8fg 10fg* 10.5f3 10.2g 10.2d) useful sort; carries his head high; 2-length winner of minor event at Leicester in April, beating Smokey Bear; third of 8 to Jubilee Prince at York following month; ran moderately on his return in the autumn; stays 1¼m; acts on any going; well beaten when blinkered; sold 1,300 gns Ascot November Sales. *I. Walker.* **76** d

RIGHTS OF MAN 2 ch.c. Morston 125–Proper True (Right Tack 131) (1980 7fg 7g^3) Feb 12; 13,000F, 32,000Y; lengthy colt; second foal; dam ran only once; showed promise in 2 good-class races at Ascot in the autumn, running on well to finish 2½ lengths third of 10 to Sunley Builds when favourite for Hyperion Stakes; will stay 1¼m. *G. Pritchard-Gordon.* **91**

RIKASSO BEAUTY 2 ch.f. Double-U-Jay 120–Mary Bold (Hard Ridden 131) (1980 5s 5s 5g^4 5fg^2 5h 5fg* 6fg^3 7g* 6d 7g 7fg 6g 6fg^2 6s 5f) Apr 29; 1,000F, 3,400Y; leggy, light-framed filly; half-sister to 1979 Irish 2-y-o 5f winner Browne Eclipse (by Tudor Music) and a winner in Malaya; dam never ran; made all to win weakly-contested minor events at Brighton (by 8 lengths) in May and Yarmouth in July; ran very well when 1½ lengths second of 12 to The Quiet Bidder in £6,000 nursery at Newmarket in August and put up another good effort when 6 lengths fifth of 7 to Star Pastures in well-contested race at Ayr in September on next start; needs 6f+; probably acts on any going. *A. Demetriou.* **82**

RINGAL 2 br.c. Auction Ring 123–Jeannette (Whistler 129) (1980 5fg^2 6fg 6fg^2 5fg^3 5.3g^3 5fg) Jan 21; 27,000Y; strong, well-made colt; half-brother to several winners, including fairly useful 7f and 1m winner Markie (by On Your Mark); dam once-raced half-sister to Irish 1,000 Guineas winner Shandon Belle; second in maiden races at Salisbury in May and September, going down by 1½ lengths to Welham Green on latter occasion; stays 6f; yet to race on a soft surface; blinkered sixth outing (had stiffish task in nursery). *A. Breasley.* **79**

RINGAWOODY 3 b.f. Auction Ring 123–New One 77 (Tyrone 130) (1979 5g* 5fg 5g* 1980 7v 7s 7g* 8fg 7g 6.3s 5g 8g^3) 7,200Y; quite attractive filly; third foal; dam won over 1¼m; won 21-runner Madrid Handicap at the Curragh in April by ¾ length from Snapper Point; good 5½ lengths fifth of 18 to Cairn Rouge in Goffs Irish 1,000 Guineas on same course following month and finished creditable 3½ lengths third to Calandra in Gilltown Stud Stakes at the Curragh again in September; remote eighth to Hard Fought in Jersey Stakes at Royal Ascot on fifth start; suited by 1m; best form on top-of-the-ground. *P. Prendergast, jnr, Ireland.* **102**

RING BIDDER 2 b.c. Auction Ring 123–Miss Holborn (Pall Mall 132) (1980 6g 6g^2 8s^2 7d*) Jan 17; 8,000Y; useful sort; half-brother to several winners, including useful 1m and 1¼m winner Saffron Hill (by Gulf Pearl); dam sister to very smart sprinter Holborn; second in maiden races at Newcastle and Ayr prior to winning 4-runner maiden event at Redcar in October by 1½ lengths from odds-on Henry Morgan; stays 1m; acts on soft going. *C. Brittain.* **88**

RING FINGER 2 b.f. Auction Ring 123–Fianna 99 (Royal Palm 131) (1980 5f 5g) May 23; 8,000Y; compact filly; half-sister to 5 winners by Pall Mall, including useful 6f and 7f winner Giselle, and to another winner; dam half-sister to smart sprinter High Flying; in rear in maiden races at Sandown in May (8/1) and Salisbury in June (33/1). *B. Hills.* **—**

RINGGIT 4 b.c. Targowice 130–Torrefranca (Sicambre 135) (1979 7g 8fg 7fg 8.3fg 8fg 7f 7f 8fg 8f^3 7fg^3 8f* 8s^3 1980 8g 6.5g^4 8g 10g* 10s* 10s^2 10fg* 10fg 10fg* 10f* 8g 8g) neat, attractive colt; good mover; won 30,000 francs race at Cagnes-sur-Mer in February and handicaps at Leicester in March, Sandown in April, Kempton in May and Yarmouth in June; put up an excellent performance under 10-5 on last-named course when beating Jubilee Prince gamely by a head; well beaten last 2 starts and wasn't seen out after July; suited by 1¼m nowadays; acts on any going; used to wear blinkers; suited by enterprising riding tactics. *R. Armstrong.* **97**

RING MOYLAN 2 b.f. Auction Ring 123–Moneycashen 72 (Hook Money 124) (1980 5fg^3 5f^3 5g^2 6g^2 6s^3 7g* 7s) Feb 19; 9,400Y; neat, well-made filly; good mover; third foal; dam stayed 1m; placed in varied company prior to winning 22-runner maiden race at Chepstow in September by ¾ length from Same Date; stays 7f; acts on any going. *M. Jarvis.* **83**

RING OF QUALITY 2 b.c. Auction Ring 123–Metrovision (Golden Vision 105) (1980 6d^3 6g* 6g^2 7fg^3 6fg) May 19; 9,000Y; strong, good-topped colt; half-brother to 4 winners by Gulf Pearl, including Ebor winner Anji; dam poor middle-distance maiden; stayed on strongly to win 12-runner minor event at Carlisle in July by ½ length from Alex Flyer; placed subsequently in 3-runner event at Hamilton (went down by a head to Easterly Wind) and nursery at Newmarket; stays 7f; below his best final start. *Sir Mark Prescott.* **83**

RING OF STEEL 2 b.c. Steel Heart 128–Woo 72 (Stage Door Johnny) (1980 5v 5v* 5g* 6.3g) third foal; dam middle-distance maiden; successful twice early in season, coming through to win 15-runner maiden race at Phoenix Park **93**

by 2 lengths from Pinch of Comfort and getting the better of another previous winner, Light Here, by short head in minor event at the Curragh; not seen out again until September when only sixth of 7 to Lawmaker in Railway Stakes at the Curragh; should be suited by 6f; ridden to successes by apprentice J. Deegan. *D. Weld, Ireland.*

RING OUT 2 b.g. Auction Ring 123–Miss Etta (King's Troop 118) (1980 **75**
6g^4 7f^3) Apr 16; 8,000Y; sturdy gelding; good mover; half-brother to several winners, including useful sprinter Maccaboy (by Will Somers); dam unraced half-sister to very useful 3-y-o Etching (by Auction Ring); in frame in maiden races in September, beaten 3 lengths when fourth to Sones at Yarmouth and 4½ lengths when third of 25 to Highland Range at Redcar; stays 7f. *W. O'Gorman.*

RING THE NURSE 3 ch.f. Mon Fils 124–Aroosha (Le Haar 126) (1979 —
NR 1980 10s 8f 8fg 12d) third reported foal; dam placed over 1¼m in French Provinces on only outing; in rear in maiden and minor races in the Midlands; sold 400 gns Ascot July Sales. *J. Haine.*

RIO DEVA 2 b.c. Spanish Gold 101–Deva Rose 80 (Chestergate 111) (1980 **74**
7fg 6g 8fg^4 8s 8g) May 22; first foal; dam won 4 times over 5f; put up easily best effort when strong-finishing 1¾ lengths fourth of 13 to Cliphome in maiden race at Beverley in September; eighth of 21 to Santella Ascot in well-contested seller at Newmarket the following month; evidently needs 1m; acts on a firm surface. *R. Hollinshead.*

RIONORE 5 b.h. Ribero 126–True Course 124 (Hill Gail) (1979 NR 1980 **81**
8f 12h 12fg* 12g^4 15g^2 11g* 10.4d^2 12.5g^4 12s 12v) well-made ex-Irish horse; led in final furlong and ran on well, despite swerving violently left on two occasions, when winning lady riders race at Ripon in June by 3 lengths from Francesco; also won handicap at Ostend in August; stays well; acts on a firm and a soft surface; said by trainer to be prone to breaking blood vessels and isn't particularly reliable. *M. Ryan.*

RIPCORN (USA) 3 b.c. Cornish Prince–Ripit (Relko 136) (1979 NR 1980 **88**
10.1s^2 12s* 12g^2 14d^4) 150,000Y; most attractive colt; good mover; second foal; dam won at up to 1½m and half-sister to St Leger and Irish Sweeps Derby second Meadowville; beat Crispin by 2½ lengths in 9-runner maiden race at Lingfield in July; stays 1½m (well beaten over further); acts on soft going. *P. Walwyn.*

RIPOLIN 2 b.c. Sweet Revenge 129–Gilda 65 (Connaught 130) (1980 5s **69**
5fg 7s^3 7g 6g 7d 6fg 7.3fg) May 2; 3,600Y; useful-looking colt; first foal; dam won 1m seller; quite a moderate maiden; stays 7f; blinkered eighth outing. *R. Hannon.*

RISGOLD 3 b.g. Rheingold 137–Quismina 62 (Quisling 117) (1979 7f 1980 —
10f) strong gelding; behind in minor and maiden races. *J. Mason.*

RISING FAST 3 b.g. High Line 125–Sunny Sovereign 85 (Lucky Sovereign) —
(1979 5d 8fg 1980 10.8v^3 10.8s 10.1fg 12.3g 11.1g 12d) lengthy, good sort; poor maiden; should stay 1½m; best run on heavy going; blinkered final start; sold to D. Elsworth 1,250 gns Newmarket Autumn Sales. *D. Sasse.*

RISING TIDE 2 ch.f. Red Alert 127–Naiad Queen (Pampered King 121) **101**
(1980 5fg 5f^2 5g 5g* 5g 5g* 5g^4) Feb 19; 14,000Y; strong, rangy filly; third foal; closely related to useful 1977 Irish 2-y-o 6f winner Inishannagh (by St Alphage); dam fairly useful at up to 7f in Ireland; impressive winner of well-contested minor event at Phoenix Park in July, coming home 5 lengths clear of Arch Melody, and won small race at Down Royal the following month by 6 lengths from Picture Lady when 4/1 on; put up her best other effort in Uplands Park Acorn Stakes at Epsom in June when beaten ¾ length by Ashbrittle after looking likely winner when on bridle at halfway; should stay 6f. *M. Kauntze, Ireland.*

RISQUONS TOUT (FR) 3 ch.c. Jim French–Riverina (Snob 130) (1979 **61**
NR 1980 10.2d 10fg^4 12f 13.4g 16fg^2 14.7g 14.6d 14d) 200,000 francs Y (approx £24,000), 6,200 2-y-o; workmanlike colt; half-brother to smart 1978 French 3-y-o Lys River (by Lyphard), successful at up to 10.5f; dam, placed over 1½m in France, is half-sister to good staying 2-y-o's Riverton and Robertino; second in maiden race at Newcastle in July, best effort; evidently suited by 2m; acts on a firm surface; blinkered last 2 starts. *R. Hollinshead.*

RIVA BE GOOD (USA) 3 ch.g. Riva Ridge–Best Go (Mongo) (1979 7g **56**
7s^3 1980 12fg^3 16f^4 13.8fg^3 16g 10d^3 16f) leggy, narrow gelding; in frame

in varied company, including selling; stays well; ran moderately in blinkers fourth start; didn't handle Catterick track too well third outing; trained by J. Hindley first 5 starts. *O. O'Neill.*

RIVADON (USA) 4 b.g. Riva Ridge–Sarah Bernhardt (Buckpasser) (1979 — 8.5s 8s 12f $8f^2$ $8d^3$ 7g 12d 1980 10.2d) leggy gelding; moderate maiden; tailed off only outing of 1980 (March); should be suited by 1¼m+ (out of his depth when tried at 1½m); possibly unsuited by soft ground; sold to W. Clay 600 gns Newmarket Autumn Sales. *A. Bailey.*

RIVAL 2 b.c. Forlorn River 124–La Magna 104 (Runnymede 123) (1980 **64** 5f 5d 6g 6fg 8d 8.2s $8g^3$) Mar 12; 2,700F, 5,800Y; compact colt; first produce; dam won twice over 5f at 2 yrs; plater; stays 1m. *T. Marshall.*

RIVALRY 2 b.g. Murrayfield 119–Collina 88 (Matador 131) (1980 6g 6g 6s) **64** June 19; half-brother to fair sprinter Pircol (by Pirate King); dam sprinter; 5½ lengths sixth of 15 behind Sipestro in maiden race at Doncaster in June, first outing and best effort. *K. Stone.*

RIVER BREEZE 2 b.f. Rapid River 127–Groovy 86 (Sound Track 132) **75** (1980 5f 5g* 5g $5f^3$ 5s) May 16; 700Y; rather leggy filly; half-sister to a winning plater and a winning hurdler; dam 2-y-o 5f winner; made all and held on by a neck from Doubtwash Girl to win 16-runner maiden race at Catterick in August; gambled on from 20/1 to 4/1 when creditable third of 17 to Labista in nursery at Wolverhampton the following month; running on at Wolverhampton and may stay 6f; probably unsuited by soft ground. *J. Doyle.*

RIVERDINA 2 b.f. Riverman 131–Madina 119 (Beau Prince II 131) (1980 **113** p 8g* $8s^3$) Apr 12; 80,000Y; half-sister to 2 winners, notably very smart French miler Nonoalca (by Nonoalco), and to leading French hurdler Mazel Tov (by Sigebert); dam won Prix Morny; showed a deal of promise on both starts, winning 9-runner newcomers event at Evry in September by 1½ lengths and finishing ½-length third of 10 to Votre Altesse in Group 3 Prix des Reservoirs at Longchamp the following month; will probably stay 1¼m; sure to win good races. *Mme C. Head, France.*

RIVERHILL LAD 2 ch.g. Streak 119–Fleur de Sol 64 (Vilmorin) (1980 — 5f 5f 5d 5d 5s) Mar 10; 3,200Y; useful-looking gelding; closely related to winning sprinter Fishy Tale, and half-brother to fairly useful sprinter Luke Splendid (by John Splendid); dam placed over 7f at 2 yrs; behind in maiden races and sellers; blinkered third outing; formerly trained by T. M. Jones. *G. Hunter.*

RIVER JORDAN 5 b.g. Crowned Prince 128–Pantoufle 86 (Panaslipper — 130) (1979 NR 1980 13g) has been pin-fired on near-hind; lightly-raced maiden; stays 1½m; blinkered only outing of 1980. *I. Walker.*

RIVER PETTERILL 7 b.m. Another River 89–Hyper Rose 62 (Pinza 137) — (1979 $7v^4$ $7s^2$ 7d $9.4g^2$ 8f 8s 8f 7fg 7fg 7g 1980 8f 8fg) fair sort; stays 9f; acts on any going; has been tried in blinkers. *T. Barnes.*

RIVER REED 4 b.f. Forlorn River 124–Ribble Reed 75 (Bullrush 106) (1979 — NR 1980 12.3s 8f 10f) lengthy filly; plating-class maiden; stays 1m; acts on any going; suitable mount for an apprentice. *W. C. Watts.*

RIVER RIVER (FR) 4 b.c. Riverman 131–Riverside (Sheshoon 132) (1979 NR **117** 1980 $9.7g^3$ 10.5fg* $12g^4$ 10d 12d* 12.5d* 13.5g) strong, very handsome colt; good mover; blinkered when winning Prix de Villebon at Longchamp on only start at 2 yrs (rated 111p); didn't race at 3 yrs due to a leg injury; won minor event at Evry in May, Grand Prix de Compiegne in July and Prix de Reux at Deauville in August, beating Gain by 3 lengths in last-named event; always behind when last of 10 behind Ela-Mana-Mou in Prince of Wales's Stakes at Royal Ascot on fourth start; broke down ½m out when favourite for Grand Prix de Deauville on final outing; stayed 1½m well; acted on a soft surface; stud. *F. Boutin, France.*

RIVER ROMANCE 3 b.g. Yellow River 114–Invisible Romance 79 (Romancero — 100) (1979 NR 1980 16s 12g) first foal; dam won over 1m at 2 yrs; in rear in maiden races at Lingfield and Folkestone in the summer. *M. Bolton.*

RIVERS EDGE 2 b.g. Sharpen Up 127–Ebb and Flo 82 (Forlorn River 124) **84** (1980 5.1f $6g^2$ $6g^2$ 6g 6s) Apr 2; neat gelding; first foal; dam 2-y-o 6f winner and stayed 1½m; failed by a short head to get up and beat Admiral's Heir in 8-runner maiden race at Brighton in July; didn't fulfil promise of that run, going down by 5 lengths to Ermac when odds on for maiden race at Carlisle, finishing in rear in similar event at Brighton (odds on) and in a nursery (blinkered); will be suited by 7f; sometimes wears a muzzle; sold to W. Stubbs 1,200 gns Newmarket Autumn Sales. *M. Stoute.*

RIVERS MAID 3 b.f. Rarity 129–Takette (Takawalk II 125) (1979 7g^4 7fg* 1980 10fg 10.6fg 7fg) lengthy filly; won maiden race at Chepstow in 1979; well beaten in handicaps at 3 yrs; should stay 1¼m. *G. Balding.* —

RIVER SNAIL 3 gr.f. My Swanee 122–Conch 92 (Vimy 132) (1979 NR 1980 9.4g 12d) 775 2-y-o; big filly; half-sister to 3 winners over jumps; dam won at 1¼m and is half-sister to very speedy Kerrabee; in rear in maiden races at Carlisle and Haydock in the summer. *G. Richards.* —

RIVER VIEW 3 br.f. Mountain Call 125–Mystic Halo (Aureole 132) (1979 5s 5v 5d^4 5s^4 5g^3 5s^2 6g 5fg 1980 5f 5h 7f) small filly; poor plater; best form at 5f; needs some give in the ground. *D. Wintle.* —

RIVER WARRIOR 2 b.g. Forlorn River 124–Wounded Knee 78 (Busted 134) (1980 6g 6g 6d) Mar 28; 1,350F, 2,500Y; small, narrow gelding; first produce; dam won over 1½m and 1¾m; plating-class maiden. *C. James.* —

R. J. WALLIS 5 b.g. David Jack 125–Josuelind 78 (Nimbus 130) (1979 10.1g^4 10f 10f^3 1980 8s 8fg 7g* 8fg* 7fg 7d 8fg^3 7fg 7f^4) quite a moderate handicapper; ridden by 7-lb claimer and carrying overweight when comfortable winner at Epsom (apprentice event) in April and Salisbury in May and when creditable fourth to Oldstock at Lingfield in September; stays 1¼m; probably acts on any going. *A. Pitt.* 64

ROAD TO MANDALAY 3 gr.g. Warpath 113–Turtle Dove (Gyr 131) (1979 NR 1980 10.2d 11v^2 12d^2 16f^2 12g^2 12g^4 13.4g^4 16f^2 14.6d* 15d^2) fair sort; good walker; second foal; brother to fair 4-y-o Path of Peace, successful at 1½m and 13f; dam ran only once; gained a well-deserved success in 10-runner maiden race at Ripon in August; runner-up in varied company on 6 of his other starts; stays well; acts on any going; consistent; sold to D. Barons 5,200 gns Newmarket Autumn Sales. *C. Thornton.* 79

ROAD TO RIO (FR) 2 b.c. Riverman 131–Boulevard 114 (Pall Mall 132) (1980 8fg 10v*) Apr 1; fourth foal; brother to very useful French miler Waterway, and half-brother to 2 useful winners, including middle-distance filly Silken Way (by Shantung); dam, half-sister to Sun Prince, won Princess Margaret Stakes at 2 yrs and showed useful form at up to 1m at 3 yrs in France; showed plenty of promise when winning 14-runner maiden race at Saint-Cloud in November by ¾ length from Midnight Cowboy; runs as though he'll stay 1½m; likely to go on to better things. *J. Cunnington, jnr, France.* ?

ROANDER 3 b.g. Leander 119–Superbum 69 (Super Sam 124) (1979 5d 5d 5fg^4 5d 5g 6d 7f 8.2d^2 1980 8d 8d 7d 7g 10d) small, lengthy gelding; poor plater; probably needs further than 1m nowadays and will stay 1½m; acts on a soft surface; wears blinkers. *W. Marshall.* —

ROAN MELODY 4 b.c. Roan Rocket 128–Harvest Melody 103 (Tudor Minstrel 144) (1979 7fg 8d 8.2d^4 7d^4 5g 6f^2 7.6f^2 7g 8g^2 1980 7fg* 8d 8fg^3) strong, fair sort; dropped in class and well backed despite being burly, won seller at Kempton in May by ½ length from Wise Man (bought in 5,100 gns); stays 1m; acts on firm going; has run creditably in blinkers; bandaged in 1980; good mount for an apprentice; trained by P. Haslam until after second outing. *G. Lockerbie.* 60

ROAN MIST 2 b.c. Roan Rocket 128–Barchessa 67 (Prince Chevalier) (1980 6fg 7d^4) Feb 21; 11,000Y; big, strong colt; good mover; half-brother to winners here, in USA and in France, including 3-y-o Vouchessa (by Gift Card), successful over 7f; dam won at 1¼m; prominent in 15-runner maiden races at Newbury in June and August, in latter finishing just over 4 lengths fourth to John Clare; will be suited by 1m. *D. Kent.* 84

ROAN SONG 3 ro.g. Song 132–Creolina 72 (Quorum 126) (1979 6fg 6f 6fg 1980 7f 5g 7g 6d* 6s* 6d 6fg 6s 7g) fair sort; plater; won at Carlisle in July (bought in 900 gns) and Ayr in August (bought in 3,800 gns); stays 6f; acts on soft going; blinkered nowadays; has had his tongue tied down. *M. H. Easterby.* 58

ROBANON 3 ch.f. Burglar 128–Priddy Soon (Behistoun 131) (1979 5d 5g 5fg 5f 6f 1980 6fg) compact filly; poor maiden; blinkered final outing at 2 yrs. *R. Smyth.* —

ROBARD 2 ch.c. Brigadier Gerard 144–Kentucky Robin 73 (Falcon 131) (1980 6g 7g 7f^4 7s) Apr 28; 6,400Y; big, compact colt; half-brother to 3-y-o middle-distance winner Red Wolver (by Wolver Hollow) and 2 other winners, 76 including 1m winner Elysee Palace (by Royal Palace); dam won at up to 11f; last 2f out but ran on strongly without being unduly hard ridden to finish 4½ lengths fifth of 11 to King's General in slowly-run £3,000 event at Goodwood in September, second outing; outsider of party when 4½ lengths last of 4 to Spindrifter in minor event at Redcar later in month; will stay 1¼m; possibly not at his best on soft going. *G. Lewis.*

ROBBIE LAD (USA) 5 b.h. Roberto 131–Alyce Clover (Needles) (1979 12.2s 12.2s 8g³ 10f² 9fg 8.2fg 10f² 11.5fg² 12g 14g 12fg⁴ 12.2g 14f³ 1980 13g 12f 11.7g) quite a moderate handicapper; stayed 1¾m; suited by a sound surface; was good mount for an inexperienced rider; dead. *D. H. Jones.* —

ROBELLINO (USA) 2 b.c. Roberto 131–Isobelline (Pronto) (1980 6fg* 6g² 7d* 7s* 8fg* 8d) **127**

It's ironic that of the eleven yearlings sold by Comte Roland de Chambure at the 1979 Houghton Sales for the record-breaking aggregate of 1,697,000 guineas, easily the most successful so far has been the cheapest of the bunch, Robellino, whose price of 36,000 guineas was nearly 120,000 guineas below the consignment's average. Robellino has already more than recouped his purchase price and went into winter quarters, after wins in the Group 3 Seaton Delaval Stakes and the Group 2 Royal Lodge Stakes, as one of the leading English-trained candidates for the Two Thousand Guineas and Derby.

He would, however, have been much more strongly fancied for the classics had he not put up a deplorable display when favourite for the William Hill Futurity Stakes at Doncaster late in October; he was one of the first under pressure and trailed in over ten lengths behind Beldale Flutter, a colt he had beaten on his previous outing. Probably he was past his best for the season—he had looked to be going in his coat beforehand—and certainly this display cannot be reconciled with his earlier performances. He had been beaten only once in five starts, when pipped on the post by Kirtling after looking all over the winner in the Chesham Stakes at Royal Ascot, and had shown himself a consistently progressive colt.

Royal Lodge Stakes, Ascot—Robellino is a convincing winner from Recitation and Gielgud. Beldale Flutter is fourth

Mrs John A. McDougald's "Robellino"

The form of Robellino's first two wins, both at Newbury, amounted to nothing out of the ordinary but he had shown a good turn of foot, winning a maiden race going away from Bonnie Charlie and then drawing four lengths clear in the final furlong of the Donnington Castle Stakes. He looked capable of much better things and started a short-priced favourite when tackling pattern-race company for the first time in the Seaton Delaval Stakes at Newcastle in August. Although only four took him on, all were winners and Robellino had to give 3 lb to three of them, including the highly regarded Northern colt Jamestino. He won well, quickening past the early leaders Grain Race and Noalto over two furlongs out and then staying on strongly in the testing conditions to hold Jamestino's challenge by a length and a half.

Robellino had a much stiffer task in the Royal Lodge Stakes at Ascot nearly seven weeks later, the distance of which seemed sure to bring out further improvement in him. Among his seven opponents were: Gielgud, favourite on the strength of his encouraging win in the Laurent Perrier Champagne Stakes; Recitation, so impressive when winning the Coventry Stakes but beaten twice since; Cocaine, an easy winner of the Acomb Stakes; and Beldale Flutter who had taken the valuable Criterium International d'Ostende a month before. Robellino put up an extremely game display to win. He was still only fifth as Beldale Flutter took over the lead from the weakening Cocaine turning into the straight, where Recitation in third place and Gielgud in sixth also started to make progress. No sooner had he made progress to reach the heels of the leaders than Beldale Flutter began to drift to his right, leaving Robellino very little room to challenge along the rails at the furlong pole. However, Robellino went for the small gap without hesitation, battled his way alongside Recitation and Gielgud as Beldale Flutter cracked with a hundred yards to race, and then produced the best finishing speed to win by half a length. Recitation, the subsequent winner of the Grand Criterium, was second, half a length in front of Gielgud with Beldale Flutter a further three quarters of a length back fourth.

The last three winners of the Royal Lodge were Hello Gorgeous, Ela-Mana-Mou (who beat Troy into second place) and Shirley Heights so Robellino has plenty to live up to at three. He's a deep-girthed, good sort of colt who moves well and he looks the sort to make a fine three-year-old. He's the second foal and first winner bred by Isobelline whose third foal, a yearling colt by The Minstrel, fetched nearly ten times as much as Robellino at the 1980 Houghton Sales. Isobelline herself was sold for 19,000 guineas at the end of her three-year old days, having won a seven-furlong maiden race in Ireland at two from a total of only four starts. Her appeal lay in her pedigree rather than her racing record. Her sire, the unbeaten Argentinian horse Pronto, didn't meet with the same success at stud in the USA as he'd done in his native country, where three of his sons took the Horse of the Year title, but Isobelline's dam is extremely well related. Isobella is a daughter of one of the best American two-year-old fillies of 1959 in Monarchy, who was a sister to that exceptional racehorse and first-rate stallion Round Table. Isobella is also a sister to the very useful sprint stakes winner Title and to the successful stallions Blade and Envoy, and a half-sister to the smart American colt Fabled Monarch and to Lord of the Dance, a very smart winner at up to a mile and three quarters in Ireland.

Robellino (USA) (b.c. Jan 29, 1978)	Roberto (b 1969)	Hail to Reason (br 1958)	Turn-to
			Nothirdchance
		Bramalea (br 1959)	Nashua
			Rarelea
	Isobelline (b 1971)	Pronto (b 1958)	Timor
			Prosperina
		Isobella (ch 1963)	Bold Ruler
			Monarchy

Roberto, Robellino's sire, made a magnificent start to his stud career with Sookera, Octavo, Duke of Normandy and several American stakes winners among his first crop. He hasn't quite maintained that rate of success but he had stakes winners representing him in North America in 1980, including the top Canadian three-year-old Driving Home, while in Europe he had the Grand Criterium runner-up Critique in addition to Robellino. Many of his offspring stay fairly well and Robellino is likely to need a mile and a quarter or more at three. He has yet to race on really firm ground but seems to act on any other. *I. Balding.*

ROBERT ADAM 5 ch.g. Mansingh 120–Pritillor 93 (Privy Councillor 125) (1979 8s^3 8d^4 8.3fg^4(dis) 8f^4 8f 8g 8h 8fg^3 8fg^4 8.2s^4 1980 12s 13d 12fg* 12fg^4 12fg 12f 12fg^4 10fg) quite a moderate handicapper; beat Al Kuwait by short head at Folkestone in April; stays 1½m; acts on any going; sometimes wears blinkers; suitable mount for an inexperienced rider. *M. McCormack.* **59**

ROBERTA'S JEANS (USA) 3 b.f. Roberto 131–Pink Bluejeans (Roi Dagobert 128) (1979 NR 1980 10.6d* 10.2d^4) small American-bred filly; not a good mover; dam placed once from 7 starts in France; pushed out to beat Out Of This World with a little in hand by 2½ lengths in 19-runner maiden race at Haydock in October; fourth in minor event at Doncaster later in month; will stay 1½m; sold 21,000 gns Newmarket December Sales. *L. Cumani.* **69**

ROBERTA STAR (USA) 2 b.f. Roberto 131–Starmount Belle 110 (Nantallah) (1980 6fg 7g 7g^3 8fg^4) Feb 12: $38,000F; leggy, fair sort; half-sister to winners in USA by Semi-Pro and Advocate; dam second in Queen Mary Stakes; in frame in 19-runner maiden race at Leicester in August and 10-runner nursery at Newmarket in October, beaten 4¾ lengths by Coal Bunker on latter after moving badly to start; will stay 1¼m. *R. Akehurst.* **74**

ROBERT BRUCE 3 ch.g. Take a Reef 127–Adamay (Florescence 120) (1979 6g 6g 6fg 6fg^4 1980 10.1d) neat, attractive gelding; poor plater; sold 750 gns Ascot October Sales; dead. *J. Sutcliffe.* **—**

ROBIN HOOD 5 br.g. Tudor Melody 129–Hirondelle 86 (Falcon 131) (1979 NR 1980 16f^2 17.1f) poor handicapper nowadays; stays well; acts on any going; blinkered second outing. *B. Palling.* **—**

ROBIN RED BREAST 2 ch.f. Red Alert 127–Trusian (Milesian 125) (1980 5f* 5f^4 5fg^3 5d^4 5f) Mar 11; lightly-made, sharp sort; sister to modest 1979 2-y-o Paparouna, and half-sister to several winners, including quite useful sprinter Oh Simmie (by African Sky); dam daughter of Irish 1,000 Guineas winner Princess Trudy; won maiden race at Edinburgh in April by a short head **74**

from Quality Road; looked a big danger inside last 2f in nursery at Redcar in July but edged away from whip and was beaten just over a length into third-of-14 position behind Force of Action; will stay 6f; acts on firm going; slowly away fourth outing and ran poorly on fifth (sweated up, pulled hard on way to start and again ducked away from whip). *J. W. Watts.*

ROBIN WONDER 2 b.g. Dawn Review 105–Rainbow Wonder (Runnymede 123) (1980 6s) Apr 5; third reported foal; half-brother to 1½m winner Sunset Wonder (by Tickled Pink); dam apparently of little account; unquoted when behind in 25-runner maiden race won by General Breyfax at Windsor in July. *D. Elsworth.* —

ROBOLIN 5 b.h. Master Sing 109–Charlies Double (Fighting Charlie 127) (1979 6s 6v 6d 6s 7s 6fg 7.6f 7g³ 7fg² 8g 7.6f 8d 8fg* 7fg⁴ 8d 8s 1980 8d) strong horse; won valuable seller at Doncaster in 1979; not disgraced in apprentice handicap on same course in March; stays 1m; seems to act on any going; good mount for an apprentice; blinkered fourth and fifth starts in 1979. *R. Hollinshead.* —

ROCHE GIRL 2 ch.f. Mujon 103–Quiet Sailing (Dumbarnie 125) (1980 9d 6g) third foal; dam winning hurdler; well beaten in end-of-season maiden races in the Midlands. *W. Wharton.* —

ROCK ANGEL 3 gr.f. Ribero 126–Rockney 84 (Roan Rocket 128) (1979 6s 7fg 6f 6fg 7g 10s 7s 1980 8f³ 8f² 8.2f 8g) unfurnished filly; poor maiden; stays 1m; suited by firm going; ran moderately last 2 starts. *N. Adam.* 56

ROCK CONCERT 3 br.f. Star Appeal 133–Plumtree Plain (Primera 131) (1979 6f⁴ 1980 11.7f 11fg* 12fg⁴) small, useful-looking filly; won 14-runner maiden race at Wolverhampton in August; looked short of pace only subsequent start (sweated up a little); will stay beyond 1½m; sold 2,600 gns Newmarket December Sales. *R. Hern.* 76

ROCKER 2 ch.c. Habitat 134–Treacle 85 (Hornbeam 130) (1980 6fg 6d 7s 8d) Mar 22; small, hollow-backed colt; half-brother to several winners, including useful Ivory Girl (by Sir Ivor), a winner at up to 1½m; dam, half-sister to Darling Boy, won twice at 1¼m; soundly beaten in maiden and minor races. *J. Douglas-Home.* —

ROCKET LANCER 6 ch.h. Roan Rocket 128–Colony 93 (Constable 119) (1979 NR 1980 8fg) poor handicapper; finished lame when last in seller in August; stays 6f; probably needs a sound surface; has been tried in blinkers. *S. Holland.* —

ROCKETONE 2 gr.c. Roan Rocket 128–Sweetstone (Honeyway 125) (1980 6d) Feb 24; 8,200Y; big, robust colt; half-brother to 2 winners in Italy, notably Italian 1,000 Guineas winner Sinthesis (by Court Fool); dam, a twin, never ran; unquoted and very backward when behind in 25-runner maiden race won by Little Wolf at Newbury in October. *J. Benstead.* —

ROCKET SONG 2 gr.c. Roan Rocket 128–Our Song 70 (Song 132) (1980 6g* 6fg⁴ 8d² 7g⁴) Apr 30; 12,000Y; strong colt; good walker and mover; first foal; dam, half-sister to Swiss Maid, won over 6f and 7f; led close home to win 10-runner maiden event at Hamilton in June by short head from Romoss; ran well in nurseries on last 2 starts; suited by 7f and 1m. *Sir Mark Prescott.* 81

ROCKETTE (HOL) 3 gr.f. Roan Rocket 128–Facette (Swe) (Fastnet Rock 123) (1979 6d 1980 8h 8f) small, strong-quartered, lengthy filly; showed a little ability in maiden race at Stockton on first outing in April (moved poorly to post); stays 1m. *G. Huffer.* —

ROCKET VENTURE 2 gr. or ro.c. Roan Rocket 128–Evening Venture 111 (Hopeful Venture 125) (1980 7d 7f*) Feb 14; 2,500Y; workmanlike colt; none too good a mover; first foal; dam won Galtres Stakes; landed a gamble when getting up close home to win 18-runner seller at Redcar in September by short head from Sun Diver; will stay 1¼m+. *C. James.* 67

ROCK GODDESS 3 ch.f. Green God 128–Rocelle 101 (Sodium 128) (1979 6f 6f³ 6s 6f² 1980 6s 7f 7f 6f* 6f⁴ 6f⁴ 5fg 5.8g 6g 5.3fg³ 7g³ 10.1g³ 10.2g) strong, rangy filly; won 19-runner maiden race at Kempton in May unchallenged by 7 lengths from Shady Spring; in frame in handicaps afterwards; stays 1¼m; acts well on firm going; usually sweats up; sometimes blinkered, but seems to do just as well without them; sold 10,500 gns Newmarket December Sales. *B. Swift.* 81

ROCKON TOMMIE 2 ch.c. Malicious–Larkspur's Love (Larkspur 128) (1980 **54**
5g^2 5fg^4 6f 7d 6g 6f 6d 6g) Apr 4; 2,500Y; neat colt; soundly beaten when in frame in maiden races at Epsom in April and Kempton in May; blinkered when eighth of 9 in selling nursery at Brighton in September, seventh start; should be suited by 6f+; missed break third outing. *A. Pitt.*

ROCK PSALM 3 b.f. Saintly Song 128–Rock Snake 76 (Rockefella) (1979 –
6f 7fg 1980 10f 8f 8s 12d 8g) neat filly; of no account; has worn blinkers; sold 450 gns Doncaster September Sales. *C. Thornton.*

RODEO 2 ch.c. Bustino 136–Hitesca 110 (Tesco Boy 121) (1980 6s 6g 8.2s) **72**
Mar 1; compact colt; half-brother to miler Referendum (by Reform); dam, very game filly, stayed 1m; 7 lengths fifth of 15 to Sage King in 1m maiden race at Hamilton in September, third outing and best effort; will be suited by 1¼m+. *C. Thornton.*

RODIN 4 b.c. High Top 131–Hazy Idea 118 (Hethersett 134) (1979 8g^3 10.2g^2 **98** d
10g* 10.5f^3 8h^3 1980 8s* 8f 8fg 8d 8fg) useful sort; has a round action; put up a good performance under top weight when beating Blue Patrol 2½ lengths in 23-runner handicap at Warwick in April; didn't reproduce that form and looked none too enthusiastic fourth start; stays 1¼m; acts on any going, but is evidently well suited by soft; inconsistent. *P. Walwyn.*

RODSHOT 5 gr.g. Abwah 118–Warning Shot (Premonition 130) (1979 8s –
8d 8g 7s 8f^3 8f^4 7fg^4 8f^2 10f 10g 8g 8.2d^3 8fg 7fg^4 7g 1980 7g 8fg^4 8.2g^3 12g^3 12.2g^4 10g^4 12.3d 12f 12.2fg) poor handicapper; stays 1½m; acts on any going; has run creditably in blinkers; started slowly fourth outing; sold to D. Grissell 2,300 gns Ascot October Sales. *C. Booth.*

ROGAIRIO 4 b.g. Royal Prerogative 119–Polairia 66 (Polic 126) (1979 –
8g^2 7g^3 8s 8g^3 8.2f* 1980 11.7f 10f^4) lightly-built gelding; stays 1m and should get further; acts on firm going and is possibly not at his best on soft. *P. Bailey.*

ROGER BACON 5 gr.g. Comedy Star 121–Tinsel 95 (Right Boy 137) (1979 –
6s 5d 5s 5d* 5fg 5.8g 5fg 5fg^2 5f^3 5f^2 5g* 5d^2 5.6fg 5f 5g 1980 5s 5fg 5fg 5d 5.6g 5fg 5g 5g 5s 5s) strong, compact gelding; carries plenty of condition; poor mover; quite useful at best but showed little worthwhile form in 1980; stays 6f, but has done all his winning at 5f; acts on any going; usually wears blinkers; dwelt fourth outing. *J. Haine.*

ROLLAHEAD 3 ch.c. Tower Walk 130–First Round 97 (Primera 131) (1979 **105**
5g^2 5f* 5g^2 5fg* 5f* 5.5fg 5f^4 1980 6fg^4 5f^4 5fg) strong, compact colt; useful performer; made a lot of headway in last 2f after being outpaced early on when 6½ lengths fourth of 10 to Sharpo in Temple Stakes at Sandown in May, second start; well beaten in King's Stand Stakes at Royal Ascot following month and wasn't seen out again; will be suited by a return to 6f; acts well on firm going. *R. Price.*

ROLLING RIVER 4 b.f. Warpath 113–Shenandoah 88 (Mossborough 126) **50**
(1979 10g 11d 1980 12.3s 12fg 12f* 12fg* 12d^4 13.8f^4 13g 12fg^4 12fg 10g) lightly-made filly; dropped in class when winning sellers at Wolverhampton (no bid) and Thirsk (bought in 2,100 gns) in May; will stay 1¾m; acts on firm going; gave trouble at stalls and finished well beaten when blinkered final start; sold out of C. Thornton's stable 1,900 gns Doncaster August Sales after ninth outing. *K. Morgan.*

ROLLIN HAND 2 b.c. Some Hand 119–Josilu (Caliban 123) (1980 5s* 5f^2 **82**
5fg^4 5f^3 6d^2 6g 6g^4 7d) May 13; useful-looking colt; good walker; second foal; half-brother to 1979 2-y-o seller winner Lottie Boy (by Weepers Boy); dam of no account; impressive 5-length winner from Cyclonic in maiden race at Leicester in March; second twice afterwards, on final occasion going down by ¾ length to Kareem in £4,000 nursery at Lingfield in July (apprentice ridden); best form at up to 6f but wasn't disgraced over 7f; seems to act on any going; ran poorly sixth start. *P. Cole.*

ROLL ME OVER 6 br.g. Hopeful Venture 125–Elaine 90 (Mossborough –
126) (1979 14v 1980 8g 12fg) lightly raced nowadays and was well beaten in 1980, including in a seller; stays 2m; acts on any going; wears blinkers. *J. Harris.*

ROLL OF DRUMS 4 ch.g. Royal Prerogative 119–Tantara (Pakistan II –
84) (1979 7d 10.5g 10.6g 10d^3 10g^2 10h 1980 18f^2 16f 18.8g 17.1fg) rangy gelding; made much of running when 7 lengths second to Heighlin in Great Metropolitan Handicap at Epsom in April; well beaten subsequently, wearing blinkers on final outing; stayed well; seemed to act on any going; dead. *J. Haine.*

ROLL OF DRUMS (USA) 2 b.c. Hoist the Flag–Recall (Reneged) (1980 7s²) May 4; $375,000Y; sixth foal; half-brother to 3-y-o 1m and 1¼m winner Revocation (by Reviewer) and 4 minor winners; dam smart stakes winner at up to 1m; led for long way when 5/4 favourite for 19-runner maiden race at the Curragh in September but veered right across course over 2f out and went down by 3 lengths to Lord Never; will probably stay 1½m; very promising and should win good races. *V. O'Brien, Ireland.* **90** p

ROLLRIGHTS 2 ch.f. Ragstone 128–Skiboule (Boulou) (1980 7s² 8d*) small, quite attractive filly; has a round action; first foal in this country; dam Belgian; favourite, following an eyecatching debut when very sympathetically ridden by an apprentice, ran on strongly under hand riding to win 15-runner maiden race at Leicester in November in good style by 4 lengths from Double Sharp; sure to improve further over 1¼m+ at 3 yrs. *J. Dunlop.* **91** p

ROMANETTE 3 ch.f. Copper Man–Young Rowette 99 (Delirium 126) (1979 NR 1980 9fg 8f) half-sister to several winners here and abroad, including 1974 2-y-o 7f winner King Solomon (by Mandamus); dam sprinting half-sister to smart miler Young Christopher; well behind in newcomers event and maiden race. *D. Leslie.* —

ROMAN SCRIBE 5 ch.h. Sallust 134–Souza Rose 80 (Songedor 116) (1979 6s 6d 7s 6g 7s 6g 6g³ 6f 5.8h² 6s* 6g² 6fg 5.8fg 7.6fg 6s³ 7d³ 1980 6v 7fg 6h 6fg 6g 6g 6g² 5.8f 6fg 6g 6fg 6d) quite a moderate handicapper nowadays; stays 7f well; seems to act on any going but is suited by some give in the ground; occasionally sweats up; sold 1,700 gns Newmarket Autumn Sales. *S. Woodman.* **73** d

ROMAN SMILE 5 ch.g. Calpurnius 122–Teersaway 74 (Weepers Boy 124) (1979 NR 1980 10g 8fg⁴ 8g 7s 10d) of little account. *C. Wildman.* —

ROMANTIC AFFAIR 2 ch.f. Weepers Boy 124–Dawn Affair 77 (Entanglement 118) (1980 5v) Mar 26; first foal; dam ran 49 times on Flat and over hurdles but failed to win; ran wide into straight when tailed-off last in seller won by Swynford's Miss at Warwick in March. *Mrs I. Cross.* —

ROMAN TREASURE 2 ch.c. Roman Warrior 132–Most Precious (Matador 131) (1980 5d 6d 6d 6g 6fg 6f 7g 6g 7f) Apr 5; 3,300Y; well-grown colt; bad plater; has worn blinkers. *J. Mulhall.* —

ROMEO ROMANI (USA) 3 br.c. Jacinto–Harbor Wine (Herbager 136) (1979 5fg* 7fg³ 1980 8f 12fg) $95,000Y; lengthy, good sort; good walker and mover; second foal; brother to American winner Little Lady Luck; dam won 3 times at up to 1m; very smart at 2 yrs, beating Jawad 1½ lengths in Norfolk Stakes at Royal Ascot and finishing creditable 3½ lengths third of 6 to Monteverdi in William Hill Dewhurst Stakes at Newmarket; lightly raced in 1980, finishing 5¼ lengths sixth of 9 to Tyrnavos in Ladbrokes Craven Stakes at Newmarket in April and remote last of 6 to Prince Bee in Gordon Stakes at Goodwood 3 months later; should stay middle distances; yet to race on an easy surface; sent to USA. *R. Price.* **108**

ROMOSS 2 ch.g. Royal Match 117–Pamela Rose 107 (Vilmorin) (1980 5f 5f³ 6fg³ 5fg 6g² 5f⁴ 5s 5d⁴) Apr 27; 4,000F, 6,800Y; strong, rangy gelding; half-brother to 2 winners; dam at her best at 2 yrs when winner over 5f and 6f; placed in maiden and minor events, coming closest to success when short-headed by Rocket Song at Hamilton in June; finds 5f on sharp side and will stay 7f; acts on any going. *S. Wainwright.* **76**

RONDAROSA 2 b.f. Mummy's Pet 125–Stockingful (Santa Claus 133) (1980 6d 6g) May 14; neat filly; fifth foal; half-sister to useful stayer Wesley (by High Top) and to 3-y-o Mansell (by Habat), a winner at up to 8.5f in England and France; dam half-sister to smart miler Richboy; showed early speed in maiden races at Doncaster in October (11 lengths sixth of 18 to Camisite) and Leicester (tenth of 20 to Nello) the following month. *J. W. Watts.* —

RONTINO 3 b.c. Bustino 136–Tudoron 108 (Tudor Melody 129) (1979 6fg* 7d* 8f³ 1980 9f³ 12f³ 12g 12d) attractive, robust colt; useful performer at his best; third in Heath Stakes at Newmarket in April (slightly hampered when beaten 4 lengths by Running Mill, who rec 10 lb) and Ladbroke Derby Trial Stakes at Lingfield in May (5 lengths behind Ginistrelli (USA)); ran moderately afterwards in King Edward VII Stakes at Royal Ascot and handicap at Salisbury (blinkered) in June; stays 1½m; appears to act on any going; best left alone until showing signs of returning to form. *R. Hern.* **107**

ROOFER 2 gr.c. Brittany–Piccadilly Rose 63 (Reform 132) (1980 5fg 6fg 7d 7fg 7fg 8d 7d 6s⁴) Mar 19; 1,650F; robust colt; not a good mover; second foal; **70**

dam stayed 1½m; beaten 5¼ lengths when fourth of 22 to Banbury Cross in maiden race at Doncaster in November, easily best effort; should stay 1m; wears blinkers nowadays. *M. Ryan.*

ROOK WOOD 4 b.c. Pall Mall 132–Bonnie Bird 73 (Aureole 132) (1979 7s3 8g 8fg 8fg 12s 1980 16f) big, robust colt; disappointing maiden on flat; should stay at least 1m; acts on any going. *R. Hannon.* —

ROOM SERVICE 6 b.h. Silly Season 127–Tabulator (Never Say Die 137) (1979 7.6v 8s 7s 7fg 8fg 8.3fg2 7fg2 8.3fg 8f 8fg2 8fg 1980 6fg 7fg 7d 11.5g 12g 7d) quite a moderate handicapper; best form at up to 9f; acts on any going; ran badly when tried in blinkers; inconsistent; sold out of R. Smyth's stable 1,000 gns Ascot July Sales after third outing. *M. Chapman.* —

ROOSTER COGBURN 6 br.g. Bing II–True Grit 65 (Klairon 131) (1979 NR 1980 9g 12f) plating-class maiden; should stay well. *J. Dodds.* —

ROSALIE'S STAR 3 ch.f. St Paddy 133–Skyey 70 (Skymaster 126) (1979 7fg 7f 1980 8s 7fg) probably of little account; sold 580 gns Ascot July Sales. *R. Akehurst.* —

ROSARI 3 b.f. Saritamer 130–Roanello 102 (Roan Rocket 128) (1979 5f3 6d 1980 8fg 8f 8g 8fg 6g) small, quite well-made filly; has shown no form since first outing at 2 yrs; should stay at least 6f; acts on firm going; blinkered last 2 starts. *R. Laing.* —

ROSE CHARTER 3 gr.c. Runnymede 123–Tavel (Tabriz 111) (1979 5s 5.8f 5g 5fg 5fg2 5s3 5d* 1980 5d 5v3 6f 5fg2 5d 5d) compact colt; quite a moderate handicapper; not sure to stay 6f; probably acts on any going; ran moderately last 2 starts, wearing blinkers on first occasion. *R. Price.* 69

ROSEFOX 3 ch.f. Owen Anthony 102–Sovereign Bracelet (Manacle 123) (1979 5d 5s2 1980 8f 7fg 8fg 7f 7f 8f) small, quite well-made filly; fair second in maiden race at Goodwood in 1979; ran moderately most starts at 3 yrs; should stay 1m; blinkered final start; sold 460 gns Newmarket Autumn Sales. *Mrs J. Reavey.* —

ROSE IGNITION 2 ch.f. Hot Spark 126–Rodi (Le Dieu d'Or 119) (1980 5d) May 1; neat filly; half-sister to 3 winners in Italy; dam never ran; 20/1 when behind in 20-runner maiden race won by Little Starchy at Sandown in October. *H. Wragg.* —

ROSELINGO 2 b.f. Saulingo 122–Rose Marullah 104 (Valerullah 113) (1980 5s4) Apr 9; 2,000Y; neat filly; half-sister to several winners, including fair sprinter Whistling Fool (by Whistling Wind); dam won over 5f in Ireland at 2 yrs; co-second favourite but in need of race, had none too clear a run in final furlong when just over 2 lengths fourth of 16 to Lucky Tonight in auction event at Leicester in March, only outing. *P. Haslam.* 54

ROSE MUSIC 2 ch.f. Luthier 126–Rambling Rose 118 (Silly Season 127) (1980 6s 7g4) Apr 24; leggy filly; third foal; half-sister to fairly useful 1976 2-y-o 7f winner Rose Melody (by Tudor Melody); dam sprinter; 10/1 and having first race for 3 months, weakened from 2f out and finished well-beaten fourth behind Golden Bowl in 14-runner minor event at York in October. *R. Armstrong.* 63

ROSE OF DAVEEN 3 ch.f. Proverb 127–Cayton Rose (Aggressor 130) (1979 6fg 9fg 1980 14f 16d 16.9d4) tall filly; slow maiden; stays well. *F. Durr.* —

ROSE OF LANCASTER 3 br.f. No Mercy 126–Rose Blanche 89 (French Beige 127) (1979 5s 6fg 5fg2 5f3 5fg* 1980 5fg 7fg) fair sort; won seller at 2 yrs; well beaten in non-selling handicaps early in 1980; should stay beyond 5f; sold, covered by Jellaby, 1,300 gns Newmarket December Sales. *N. Vigors.* —

ROSE OF LORRAINE 4 b.f. Blast 125–Chiana (Compensation 127) (1979 8g 7g 7f 7fg 9f 9g3 11g3 1980 11fg 10h 10fg4 11d4) bad plater; seems to stay 11f; blinkered final start. *C. Crossley.* —

ROSE OF RABY 2 b.f. Averof 123–Softly Glowing 90 (Tutankhamen) (1980 5fg 5.1f* 5g2 7g 7g2 7fg2) May 10; leggy, narrow filly; good mover; half-sister to 1½m winner King Ashoka (by Relko); dam won over 6f at 2 yrs; quickened clear from 2f out when winning maiden race at Yarmouth in June by 5 lengths from Star Issue; creditable second in minor event at Beverley in July and nurseries at Yarmouth and Leicester in September subsequently; will stay at least 1m; yet to race on a soft surface; ran poorly fourth outing. *T. Waugh.* 85

ROSE OF SHENFIELD 4 b.f. Upper Case–Singing Witch 71 (Sing Sing 134) (1979 5v2 6d4 6g4 6g 6g 6fg 6fg 6fg 1980 8f 8fg 8d 8g 7fg) small filly; —

quite a moderate handicapper; suited by 6f (didn't run up to her best over further in 1980); acts on any going; suitable mount for a boy. *M. Haynes.*

ROSE STANDISH 4 b. or br.f. Gulf Pearl 117–Wild Bee (Hill Gail) (1979 9s 10.1d 12f3 13.4f* 13g 13s3 1980 14f 16.1f2 18.8g4 16fg 14.6fg 16s) good mover; kept on when short-head second to Noble Heir in handicap at Haydock in May; well beaten afterwards; stays well; acts on firm going; sold 4,700 gns Newmarket December Sales. *A. Johnson.* **71**

ROSE STUART 3 b. or br.f. Scottish Rifle 127–Early Rose (Will Somers 114 §) (1979 NR 1980 8fg 6d) lightly-made filly; half-sister to 3 winners, including useful sprinter Briarvanter (by Galivanter); dam of little account; tailed-off last of 12 in maiden races at Sandown in April and Brighton in July; sold 440 gns Ascot November Sales. *A. Ingham.* **–**

ROSE TRACK 8 b.g. Track Spare 125–Camp Follower 90 (Darius 129) (1979 8g2 1980 10s) strong, sturdy gelding; very lightly raced nowadays; stays 1¼m: seems to act on any going; wore blinkers at 2 yrs; suitable mount for an inexperienced rider. *J. Toller.* **–**

ROSETTA STONE 2 ch.f. Guillaume Tell 121–Lady Clodagh 113 (Tyrone 130) (1980 7g 7g 8fg) Mar 11; 5,000Y (privately); lengthy filly; has a rather round action; half-sister to 2 winners, including very useful Irish 6f and 7f winner Columbanus (by So Blessed); dam third in Irish 1,000 Guineas on only start; unquoted, never far behind when 5¼ lengths fifth of 15 to Kalaglow in minor event at Sandown in August, second outing; never going well when remote sixth of 7 to Leap Lively in Hoover Fillies Mile at Ascot the following month; should be suited by 1m. *G. Pritchard-Gordon.* **77**

ROSETTE 3 ch.f. Red Alert 127–Star Set (Sunny Way 120) (1979 5d* 5g3 5s3 5g 6f* 6fg4 1980 6fg 6g 6s) useful-looking filly; fairly useful (rated 91) in 1979; didn't find her form in handicaps at 3 yrs; better suited by 6f than 5f and will stay 1m; probably acts on any going. *G. Hunter.* **–**

ROSEWING 2 b.g. Swing Easy 126–Rosetown 84 (Charlottown 127) (1980 5s 5fg* 5h2 6f 5g 5g3) Feb 28; 6,800Y; lightly-built gelding; second living foal; half-brother to fairly useful 1m winner Sombreuil (by Bold Lad, Ire); dam, winner over 1m, is daughter of 1,000 Guineas runner-up Rosalba; made all to win 8-runner maiden race at Leicester in April by ¾ length from Texas Ranger; creditable third of 8 under top weight in nursery won by My Jem at Folkestone in July; should stay 6f (pushed onto rails by a rival in early stages when tried at trip); acts on hard going; gelded after final outing; sent to Hong Kong. *B. Hobbs.* **97**

ROSEY COVERT 4 b.f. Sahib 114–Quelle Pas (Kelling 122) (1979 8s 11.7g 9.4f 8g 1980 17.1fg 16.5g) plating-class maiden; blinkered final start; winning hurdler. *D. Gandolfo.* **–**

ROSIA BAY 3 b.f. High Top 131–Ouija 104 (Silly Season 127) (1979 6d4 7.6f* 7.3s4 1980 10g 8g 8fg 8g* 8s4) rather lightly-made filly; blinkered, stayed on well to beat Schweppes Forever 2 lengths despite hanging right in 4-runner £3,600 event at Sandown in August; again blinkered when running poorly only subsequent start; should stay 1¼m; possibly best on a sound surface; retained 6,200 gns Newmarket December Sales. *W. Hastings-Bass.* **96**

ROSIE BLACK 2 gr.f. Roan Rocket 128–Maltese Cat 58 (Pall Mall 132) (1980 5f4 7g 7fg4 7g3 8d* 8d4) Feb 26; 18,000Y; lengthy filly; half-sister to 3 winners, including fairly useful 2-y-o fillies Franca (by Frankincense) and Pitiless Panther (by No Mercy); dam poor performer; ran on gamely under pressure to lead on post and beat Go My Love a short head in 16-runner maiden event at Warwick in October; didn't move well and ran moderately at Newbury later in month; stays 1m. *P. Cole.* **80**

ROSIE'S PONY 2 b.f. Wishing Star 117–Audition (Tower Walk 130) (1980 5.8f) Feb 6; 210F, 3,200Y; first foal; dam never ran; unquoted when tenth of 11 to Philanthropist in maiden race at Bath in July; sold 300 gns Doncaster October Sales. *J. Hudson.* **–**

ROSIE'S SECRET 3 b. or br.g. Most Secret 119–Rose Palm 73 (Bleep-Bleep 134) (1979 6fg3 5s4 6s3 5d3 5f 6g4 7g 1980 5g 8d* 8f 8d3 8fg 10d 8d*) fair sort; plater; attracted no bid after winning at Redcar in August and Stockton in November; stays 1m; suited by some give in the ground; has run respectably for a boy; sometimes has his tongue tied down. *M. H. Easterby.* **63**

ROSINA COPPER 3 ch.f. Song 132–Jane Somers 64 (Will Somers 114§) **52**
(1979 5f 1980 8fg 5g 6g 5f^3 5d 6d) leggy, lightly-made filly; best run at 5f on firm going. *R. Price.*

ROSINANTE (FR) 3 ch.f. Busted 134–Rambling Rose 118 (Silly Season 127) **65**
(1979 NR 1980 7f 6f 10.1d 7s^3 7d) big filly; second foal; half-sister to fairly useful 1976 2-y-o 7f winner Rose Melody (by Tudor Melody); dam sprinter; third in minor event at Ayr in September; best run at 7f on soft going; possibly needs a galloping track; ran moderately final start. *H. T. Jones.*

ROSTON 2 ch.c. Morston 125–Rose Mullion 82 (Tudor Melody 129) (1980 –
7f 8.2s) Apr 17; leggy, close-coupled colt; third foal; closely related to 1978 2-y-o 5f winner Regina Magna (by Blakeney); dam won over 5f at 2 yrs; 25/1 when ninth of 25 to Highland Range in maiden race at Redcar in September; well behind in 20-runner similar race at Haydock in October. *M. Camacho.*

ROSTOV 6 b.g. Charlottown 127–Plotina 114 (Hugh Lupus 132) (1979 NR –
1980 18f 16f) unreliable stayer; best form on a sound surface; has worn blinkers; bandaged in front in 1980. *D. Jermy.*

ROSTOV (USA) 6 b.h. Advocator–Pertly (First Landing) (1979 8s 9.2s^4 **118**
8g^2 8g 8fg 1980 8d* 7.5g* 8g* 8g* 8d^3 8d 8d) French horse; smart at his best; won minor races at Saint-Cloud and Maisons-Laffitte (two) and Prix du Chemin de Fer du Nord at Chantilly in first half of year, beating Hilal a neck in last-named event in June; having first outing for more than 3 months when 3 lengths third to Hilal in Prix du Rond-Point at Longchamp in September, best subsequent effort; stays 1¼m but usually races at around 1m; appears to acts on any going; has worn blinkers; sent to Australia. *A. Paus, France.*

ROSY COTTAGE 2 b.f. Thatch 136–Rose Noir (Floribunda 136) (1980 5fg^2 **85**
5f^2 5fg* 5g^2 6g^2) May 23; 25,000Y; leggy, lightly-made filly; fourth foal; half-sister to 2 winners, including Irish 1,000 Guineas runner-up Clover Princess (by Right Tack); dam lightly-raced sister to Florescence; favourite, made all to win 14-runner maiden race at Warwick in June by 2½ lengths from Dragonist; second on all other outings, on final occasion going down by a length to Spindrifter in 3-runner race at Hamilton in July; stays 6f; yet to race on a soft surface. *B. Hills.*

ROSY TIMES 3 b.f. Reform 132–Midsummertime (Midsummer Night II –
117) (1979 NR 1980 10g) small, fair sort; third foal; half-sister to Park Hill winner Idle Waters (by Mill Reef); dam never ran; behind in 17-runner maiden race won by Chevington at Sandown in June (moved badly to post). *F. J. Houghton.*

ROTINGO 5 b.h. Petingo 135–Sea Lichen 106 (Ballymoss 136) (1979 7s –
8s^2 7d 7d 7f^4 8.2fg 7f^4 7fg^3 7g^3 7f^3 8fg 1980 12s 8fg 7fg 7f^4) poor handicapper; stays 1¼m; acts on any going; sometimes wears blinkers. *A. Dalton.*

ROUND DANCE 2 b.f. Auction Ring 123–Dance Away (Red God 128§) –
(1980 5f) Feb 14; 5,200F, 7,600Y; half-sister to 3 winners, including Irish 7f and 1¼m winner Maculata (by Right Tack); dam fairly useful 2-y-o 5f winner; 16/1, started none too well when eighth of 12 to Pipperetta in maiden race at Lingfield in August. *J. Winter.*

ROUNDWAY MILL 3 b.f. Mill Reef 141–Spring Maiden 90 (Silly Season 127) –
(1979 NR 1980 7fg 10d^2 10fg 8g) small filly; fourth foal; dam 7f winner; little worthwhile form in varied company; will be suited by 1½m; best run on soft ground. *H. Blagrave.*

ROUSSLANA 3 b.f. Queen's Hussar 124–High Rise (Ballymoss 136) (1979 –
NR 1980 10s 12d 13s) half-sister to winning French stayer Rise and Fight (by St Paddy) and a winner in Hong Kong; dam half-sister to very smart performers Favorita and I Titan; well beaten in maiden and minor races; sold 420 gns Newmarket Autumn Sales. *N. Vigors.*

ROWANIA 2 br.f. Workboy 123–Ruritania (Pampered King 121) (1980 –
5s 5fg 5fg) Apr 18; 2,600Y; strong filly; half-sister to 3 winners, including 3-y-o Go Martell (by Golden Mallard), successful over 1m and 1¼m; dam unraced half-sister to high-class 1964 staying 2-y-o Leonardo; behind in maiden races in the spring; missed break first and third outings. *J. Hill.*

ROWLANDSON 4 b.c. Blakeney 126–Rotisserie 106 (Tesco Boy 121) (1979 **96**
10fg^2 12f* 12g 12g* 14g^2 13.3fg 14fg^4 1980 12d 16s 14f* 16fg^3) most attractive colt; good mover; useful handicapper; did well physically from 3 yrs to

4 yrs and looked very well when scoring by 2½ lengths from Taffy at Newmarket in April; favourite and again looking very well, seemed to find trip beyond him when 6½ lengths third to Balinger on same course the following month, only subsequent outing; stays 1¾m; extremely well suited by top-of-the-ground conditions; genuine; sold to D. Elsworth 7,400 gns Newmarket Autumn Sales. *G. Harwood.*

ROYABER 4 ch.g. Sandford Lad 133–Honeymoon II (Ballymoss 136) (1979 6fg 6fg^4 5g 6g^4 6g 7g^2 7fg* 7fg^2 7f 7fg* 8fg* 1980 8d 7g 8fg 7d 8d 8g^3 8g^2 8g^2 8.3fg 8h 8g 8d^2 8d^4 7d) big, strong gelding; ran well and finished clear of remainder when close second in handicaps at Ascot in July (to Piaffer) and October (to Golden Elder); sweated up slightly when beaten a length by Dromefs at Newmarket in between; ran moderately most other starts; stays 1m; yet to race on really soft going, but probably acts on any other. *J. Benstead.* **82**

ROYAL ABBOTT 2 b.c. Most Secret 119–Royal Abbess 74 (Fury Royal 108) (1980 6g 6f 5g) Mar 24; turns his off-fore out; bad mover; in rear in maiden race and sellers; sold 290 gns Doncaster September Sales. *J. Carr.* **—**

ROYAL BAT 4 gr.f. Crowned Prince 128–Die Fledermaus (Palestine 133) (1979 7v 7s^3 8d 8g^3 10s 1980 7d 7.2d^4 6s^4 6g 6g 6d 5s^3) useful-looking filly; quite a moderate maiden; stays 1m; acts on soft going; suitable mount for an apprentice; blinkered and wore a hood fifth and sixth starts; retained 500 gns Newmarket Autumn Sales. *I. Walker.* **—**

ROYAL BEACON 3 b.g. Manacle 123–Vicomtesse 97 (Relko 136) (1979 5f 6g 8f 8g^4 8fg^4 7f 1980 8fg 10fg 8fg 12s 12d) big, well-made gelding; has shown no form since 1979; best run at 1m on a firm surface; usually blinkered. *J. Cann.* **—**

ROYAL BID 2 b.c. Auction Ring 123–Palgal (Le Prince 98) (1980 5s 5fg* 5fg^2 6f^2 6fg 6g^2 7d) Apr 25; 5,000Y; useful-looking colt; half-brother to 7f winner Adirondack (by Wolver Hollow) and to winners in Belgium and Italy; dam won at up to 1½m in Ireland; won 17-runner maiden event at Bath in April by 1½ lengths from Mr Gus; second subsequently in minor event at Redcar, 8-runner Woodcote Stakes at Epsom and in minor event at Leicester (ran well when beaten behind Spindrifter in slowly-run race); suited by 6f and should stay 7f; acts on firm going and is possibly not at his best on soft ground. *N. Vigors.* **77**

ROYAL BIRTHDAY 4 b.f. St Paddy 133–Laroyso 87 (Lauso) (1979 NR 1980 12fg 10fg) unfurnished filly; plating-class maiden. *P. Arthur.* **—**

ROYAL BLAST 7 b.m. Royal Palm 131–Balandra Star 92 (Blast 125) (1979 NR 1980 10f 10d 12d) of little account. *H. O'Neill.* **—**

ROYAL BLOOD 2 gr.c. Bay Express 132–Porsanger (Zeddaan 130) (1980 5fg^2 5fg^3 5fg^2 5.3d^3 5s* 5fg^3 5g 5g) Feb 26; compact colt; second foal; dam from family of Grey Dawn II; made all when winning 15-runner maiden race at Warwick in July by 5 lengths from Bold Scuffle; acts on a firm surface but evidently goes well on soft ground; nowhere near so consistent as his record suggests. *C. Nelson.* **85**

ROYAL BOUNTY 2 b. or br.c. English Prince 129–Royal Levi (Levmoss 133) (1980 7fg 7f 8d 10s) Apr 29; 13,000Y; strong, lengthy colt; second living foal; half-brother to Irish 9f winner Hypersonic (by Roan Rocket); dam, half-sister to smart Bog Road, won over 1½m in Ireland; behind in maiden races in the autumn, including one at Warwick; blinkered third start. *N. Vigors.* **—**

ROYAL BOXER 6 b.h. Royal Palace 131–Pugnacity 117 (Pampered King 121) (1979 NR 1980 16fg) very useful handicapper (rated 112) at 3 yrs when trained by P. Walwyn; raced twice on flat in France in 1978; behind under 10-0 at Kempton in May on only outing of 1980; stays 1½m; acts on any going; useful hurdler. *M. Bradley.* **—**

ROYAL CAPITAL 2 ch.c. Royal Match 117–Sunday's Child (Nice Guy 123) (1980 6d^3 6d 6d^4 6g 7fg^4 7d) Mar 23; 5,000Y; strong, compact colt; carries plenty of condition; half-brother to Irish 3-y-o 1½m winner Sunday Saint (by Welsh Saint), to a winner in this country and a prolific winner in Italy; dam won over 6f at 3 yrs in Ireland; 6¾ lengths sixth of 9 to Bel Bolide in Gimcrack Stakes at York in August on fourth outing but is only moderate on the balance of his form; appears not to stay 7f; trained by S. Wainwright first 4 outings. *A. Pitt.* **81**

ROYAL CASINO 3 ch.c. Gambling Debt 98–Pickled Walnut 88 (Hornbeam 130) (1979 NR 1980 8d 13g) strong colt; brother to Military Debt, quite **—**

a useful winner over hurdles, and half-brother to another winner over jumps; dam disappointing maiden; behind in maiden race at Salisbury and small race at Bath in summer. *I. Wardle.*

ROYAL CHARTER (HOL) 2 b.c. Cadmus 124–Gratissa (Psidium 130) (1980 8d) half-brother to Dutch winners Boxberger David (by Balbo) and Boxberger Olymp (by Ishan); dam daughter of fairly useful 6f and 7f filly Ever Grateful; 9/1 when tenth of 11 to Blue Garter in seller at Warwick in October. *D. Ringer.* –

ROYAL CHORUS 2 br.f. Jukebox 120–Route Royale (Roi Soleil 125) (1980 5f 5d) Feb 13; 1,850Y; leggy, narrow filly; second foal; half-sister to 1979 2-y-o 6f winner Another Signcentre (by Pitskelly); dam never ran; in rear in maiden race at Catterick and seller at Ripon in the summer; sold 310 gns Doncaster October Sales. *R. D. Peacock.* –

ROYAL CLASSIC 3 b.f. Lauso–Princess's Time (Arctic Time 127) (1979 5g 5fg 7fg 1980 12s4 12fg 16s 13g 16d) leggy, unfurnished filly; poor maiden; best run at 1½m on soft going. *D. Wintle.* –

ROYAL COACHMAN 6 br.h. Supreme Sovereign 119–Swinging Nun (Tudor Melody 129) (1979 10fg 1980 18f3 10d 14g) good sort; looked very well when third to comfortable winner Heighlin in Great Metropolitan Handicap at Epsom in April; off course afterwards until October; stays well; acts on any going; reportedly once broke a blood vessel when hurdling. *Miss A. Sinclair.* –

ROYAL CONNECTION 4 b.g. Royalty 130–Jamuna (Canisbay 120) (1979 7s 8.5s 7d4 11.7g 8.5g3 10.1fg 1980 7fg 9fg4 12g 10g) lengthy gelding; quite a modest handicapper; best form at up to 8.5f but should stay further; acts on firm going; bandaged and sweating on reappearance. *M. Bradley.* –

ROYAL DIPLOMAT 3 ch.g. The Go-Between 129–Grace (Gratitude 130) (1979 5.8g 5fg4 6f* 6g 6s 1980 7s 6f 6g 6g* 6g4 6g3 5.8g4) attractive gelding; won seller at Newmarket in August (no bid); not certain to stay 7f; acts on firm going; suitable mount for an apprentice; trained by T. Marshall first 2 starts. *J. Holt.* **65**

ROYAL DRAGOON 2 gr. or ro.c. Dragonara Palace 115–Royal Line 51 (Henry the Seventh 125) (1980 7g) Apr 23; 4,000Y; big, strong colt; first foal; dam, half-sister to Ebor winner Alignment, ran 4 times at 2 yrs; unquoted and very much in need of race, dropped right out after 4f when last of 11 to Sheer Grit in maiden race at Kempton in July. *A. Demetriou.* –

ROYAL DUTY 2 b.g. Import 127–Lunar Queen 96 (Queen's Hussar 124) (1980 6fg 5g3 5g* 5d2 5d 6d 6g 5d2) Feb 2; lengthy, useful sort; good mover; second living foal; dam won three 5f races at 2 yrs; ridden by 7-lb claimer, ran on to win well-contested minor event at Beverley in July by ½ length from Steel Garrison; second afterwards in small race at Ayr and 17-runner nursery at Wolverhampton, going down by 4 lengths to Ardoony in latter in October; form only at 5f; acts on a soft surface; blinkered fifth outing and reared as stalls opened on seventh. *E. Weymes.* **81**

ROYAL ESTATE 6 ch.h. Realm 129–Cayenne (Hornbeam 130) (1979 7.2v 6v 7fg4 8.2fg 6g 7g 7fg2 8fg 8fg2 1980 7h 7fg 8d4 8fg 7.6d 8g) strong, good sort; stays 1m; best form on a sound surface; sometimes wears blinkers. *P. Makin.* –

ROYAL FOUNTAIN 3 br.c. Royalty 130–Fountain 90 (Reform 132) (1979 NR 1980 8f* 10fg* 10.5f3 10.5d) 2,000F, 10,500Y; strong, good sort; has rather a pounding action; half-brother to a winner in USA by Appiani II; dam, winner over 5f at 2 yrs, is half-sister to high-class French sprinter King of Macedon; only lightly raced but is smart; won Wood Ditton Stakes at Newmarket in April (beat Prince Bee 1½ lengths) and 4-runner Heathorn Stakes on same course in May (put up a good performance when keeping on resolutely to beat Hello Gorgeous by a neck, pair clear); ran better subsequent race to be creditable 5½ lengths sixth of 12 to Master Willie in Benson and Hedges Gold Cup at York in August (led until 2f out and kept on well); will stay 1½m; acts on firm going though his action suggests he will always be suited by some give in the ground; to be trained by P. Walwyn. *L. Cumani.* **119**

ROYAL GALA 2 b.f. Royal Palace 131–Sweet Alyssum (Gala Performance) (1980 5d) May 12; 860F, 820Y; neat filly; second produce; dam of no account; behind in 17-runner maiden race won by Regency Prince at Doncaster in March; fifth to Blackmanship in void maiden race at Wolverhampton the following month and was withdrawn from re-run. *L. Barratt.* –

Heathorn Stakes, Newmarket—a narrow win for Royal Fountain who beats Hello Gorgeous (right) by a neck

ROYAL GENERATION (USA) 2 b.c. Native Royalty–Daredevilly (Reflected Glory) (1980 6d 7d) Feb 1; $15,000F, $48,000Y; smallish, quite attractive colt; first foal; dam won claiming races at up to 1m; sire won from 6f to 9f; made no show in October in maiden race at Newmarket (20/1) and minor event at Doncaster (11/1); sold 1,400 gns Newmarket Autumn Sales. *G. Harwood.* —

ROYAL HERITAGE (FR) 2 b.g. Welsh Pageant 132–Escorial 110 (Royal Palace 131) (1980 7d 7f² 8d* 7s*) Mar 19; lengthy gelding; third foal; half-brother to 3-y-o Lutanist (by Luthier) and English and French 7f to 1¼m winner Herrera (by Zeddaan); dam very useful at up to 10.5f; landed the odds in maiden race at Bath and minor event at Chepstow, both in October, beating Whittington 4 lengths on latter; had earlier finished 3 lengths second of 11 to Bustomi in Sancton Stakes at York in September; will be suited by middle distances; acts on any going; gelded at end of season. *I. Balding.* 98

ROYAL IDOL 6 b.g. Royal Captive 116–Lesanne (Faberge II 121) (1979 NR 1980 10.1g 16g 14fg) quite a moderate hurdler; of little account on flat. *R. Atkins.* —

ROYAL KINGDOM 3 b.c. Saritamer 130–Derring May (Derring-Do 131) (1979 5.8h 6f 1980 6fg 5fg⁴ 5.8g* 5g 6g⁴ 6g³ 6g² 5.8g*) small, strong colt; sprint handicapper; won at Bath in July (from Harebell) and September (from subsequently-disqualified Belfort); stays 6f; suited by some give in the ground. *M. Smyly.* 77

ROYAL MANTLE 3 b.c. Royal Palace 131–Do Something 77 (Pardao 120) (1979 NR 1980 10.1d 12g) 6,200Y; third foal; half-brother to 1977 2-y-o 7f winner Harwood (by Great Nephew); dam ran only twice; well beaten in minor event at Windsor in July and amateur riders race at Kempton in September. *A. Pitt.* —

ROYAL MANX 3 b.g. Prince de Galles 125–Tender Song (Pretendre 126) (1979 NR 1980 12fg² 14f⁴ 13d 10f 12g) 15,000Y, $47,000 2-y-o; fair sort; second living foal; half-brother to 1m winner Mr Juicy (by The Brianstan); dam unraced half-sister to high-class Noble Dancer (by Prince de Galles); in —

frame in maiden races at Hamilton in May and Yarmouth in June but is only plating class; needs further than 1¼m and stays 1¾m; possibly unsuited by a soft surface; sold 3,700 gns Doncaster September Sales. *B. Hanbury.*

ROYAL MARCIA 4 b.f. Pitskelly 122–Warbug (Anwar 120) (1979 5.8f⁴ 10g³ 9g³ 10s³ 8g 9g² 12d³ 12s³ 12v 9s 1980 10fg 12.2fg 16g 14g) small, neat ex-Irish filly; middle-distance maiden; well beaten in 1980; acts on soft going. *G. Huffer.* —

ROYAL MEATH 2 b.f. Realm 129–Hill of Tara (Royal Palace 131) (1980 6g* 7.3d) Jan 19; first foal; dam twice-raced half-sister to very smart middle-distance performer Knockroe; put up a good first effort when drawing away in final furlong to win 21-runner maiden race at Navan in September by 4 lengths from Birdspeed; sweated up when second favourite for £5,000 event at Newbury the following month and dropped out very quickly to finish eleventh of 12 to Boathouse after leading to past halfway; should stay 7f. *R. Lister, Ireland.* **83**

ROYAL OBLIGATION 4 ch.g. Busted 134–Lady of Chalon (Young Emperor 133) (1979 10f 8.3g² 8fg* 8f 8f⁴ 1980 8d* 8d* 7g³ 8f* 8d) attractive, lengthy gelding; good mover; improved and won handicaps at Doncaster (apprentices), Salisbury and Ascot (apprentices again); ridden out when scoring by 1½ lengths from Monte Acuto on last-named course in July; off course afterwards until October and ran disappointingly on his return (looked well and was heavily backed); suited by 1m; acts on any going. *J. Tree.* **83**

ROYAL ORLEANS 2 br.c. Crowned Prince 128–Hispanica 85 (Whistling Wind 123) (1980 7g⁴ 7d) Mar 16; 8,200F; strong colt; half-brother to 3 winners, including sprinter Amiga Mia (by Be Friendly); dam 2-y-o 5f winner; ran very green when about 15 lengths last of 4 to Mushref in Redcar Silver Salver in July; unquoted and still on burly side when tenth to Cocaine in 11-runner Acomb Stakes at York the following month; to be trained by J. Carr. *S. Wainwright.* **66**

ROYAL POWER 3 b.c. Runnymede 123–Alangia 101 (Shantung 132) (1979 5s 6f 6g 1980 7f 8fg 8fg 10fg 8.3d) neat colt; well beaten in varied company; sold 4,500 gns Newmarket Autumn Sales. *H. T. Jones.* —

ROYAL RAMPAGE 2 ch.f. Fury Royal 108–Flare Square (Red God 128§) (1980 6s 5d) May 2; first foal; dam ran only 3 times; behind in sellers at Nottingham and Ripon in August; dead. *W. Wharton.* —

ROYAL RASCAL 2 gr.c. Scallywag 127–Sea Queen (Ribomar 108) (1980 6fg 8d) May 8; robust, useful-looking colt; has a high knee action; first foal; dam ran once at 2 yrs; behind in minor event at Newmarket in August and 21-runner maiden race at Sandown in October. *J. Winter.* —

ROYAL REALM (USA) 2 ch.f. Blood Royal 129–Tomboy Tamele (Verbatim) (1980 7fg² 7g³ 7g* 8s³) May 4; strong, fair sort; second foal; half-sister to fairly useful 1979 2-y-o 5f to 7f winner Pride and Faith (by Blood Royal or Angle Light); dam ,winner at up to 6f, is half-sister to very useful Star of Kuwait, successful at up to 9f; kept on under strong pressure to win 7-runner minor event at Newcastle in August by ¾ length from Ermac; stayed on through beaten horses to finish 4¾ lengths third of 6 to Lifestyle in £3,800 nursery at Ayr the following month; runs as though 1¼m+ will suit her; seems to act on any going; genuine. *S. Norton.* **84**

ROYAL REX 4 b.c. Royal Prerogative 119–Ballynulta 91 (Djebel) (1979 10v 8d 8d 9g* 10.2s⁴ 11s⁴ 10fg 12fg 12.3fg⁴ 10fg 10.6g 1980 10.2d⁴ 10s 9fg² 10g* 9g² 10g³ 10d² 10g² 10g³ 9g 10.2d⁴ 10s) small colt; quite moderate handicapper; game winner from Burleigh at Chepstow in June; ran well afterwards and looked a shade unlucky when third to Crowning Moment at Goodwood in September on ninth start; yet to show he stays 1½m; seems to act on any going; blinkered final start at 3 yrs. *J. Tierney.* **69**

ROYAL SCENE 4 b.f. Royal Prerogative 119–Nicassine 90 (Nicolaus) (1979 NR 1980 11g 8g 13s 12d 9s 8g 12d) compact filly; seems of little account; sold 500 gns Doncaster November Sales. *T. Craig.* —

ROYAL SEAM 4 b.g. Royalty 130–Slip Stitch 120 (Parthia 132) (1979 11.7g⁴ 11.7g 12s 12s 1980 13d²) big, good-bodied gelding; on burly side when creditable second of 20 to Russian George in amateur riders race at Nottingham in April, giving impression he would be suited by further; not seen out again; acts on a soft surface; sold to A. Scott 2,500 gns Doncaster November Sales. *J. Bethell.* **51**

ROYAL SIGNAL 4 gr.g. Royal Park 114–Miss Langley (Hard Tack 111§) (1979 7f 8f 10s 1980 10v 8f 8g 10g 8f) of no account; blinkered last 2 starts. *P. Wigham.* –

ROYAL SMILE 2 ch.c. Royal Palace 131–Pollster 101 (Majority Blue 126) (1980 5.8fg 6d) Apr 29; 11,000Y; unfurnished colt; third foal; half-brother to Irish 9f winner Really Proud (by Silly Season) and to Speed Bonnie Boat (by Swing Easy), successful at up to 1m; dam won 3 races over 5f at 2 yrs; 12/1 when remote tenth of 19 behind Oraston in maiden race at Salisbury in June (eased when chance had gone), second outing. *R. Boss.* –

ROYAL SWAN 2 b.c. Souvran 98–May Britt 62 (Sammy Davis 129) (1980 8d) Mar 17; rangy colt; third reported living foal; dam stayed fairly well; unquoted when behind in 21-runner maiden race won by Obrovac at Sandown in October. *M. Haynes.* –

ROYAL VULCAN 2 ch.c. Royal Match 117–Acropolita Mia 75 (Acropolis 132) (1980 7fg 7.2d) Apr 11; 6,800Y; useful sort; half-brother to Mia Saint (by St Alphage), successful 4 times over 5f at 2 yrs in 1976, and a winner in Austria; dam won over 11.7f; stayed on well when 3¾ lengths sixth of 19 to Craigour in maiden race at Haydock in September, second outing; will stay 1¼m. *N. Callaghan.* 75

ROYBIRDIE 3 gr.f. Mansingh 120–Donna Julia 79 (Don II 123) (1979 5d 5fg2 6fg 5.8g2 6f3 6f 6fg3 1980 6f4 7f 7fg 7.6f 6g 6s4 6f 7g2 8s 6d) leggy filly; in frame in varied company, including selling; stays 7f; acts on any going; often blinkered; ran badly fifth start. *G. Balding.* 53

ROYSIA 3 b.c. Tumble Wind–Beautician (Barron's Court) (1979 5f3 6fg4 7g3 7fg3 7g* 7g 1980 7fg 7fg 7g 8d 10g4 10g2 10g* 10.6d 10g* 10fg) small, sturdy colt; moderate handicapper; beat Denston a neck at Leicester in August and Miss Neustrie by ½ length at Yarmouth in September; suited by 1¼m and may stay further; best form on a sound surface; had his tongue tied down third start. *G. Pritchard-Gordon.* 81

R. T. DEEP 3 ch.f. Deep Diver 134–Hayrake 98 (Galivanter 131) (1979 5g 6s 5fg 6g 5.8g 1980 6d 5fg 10f 7.6f) leggy, light-framed filly; little worthwhile form; unlikely to stay 1¼m; sometimes blinkered; has sweated up on occasions. *Mrs J. Reavey.* –

RUBINA PARK 2 b.f. Ashmore 125–Keep Going 113 (Hard Sauce 131) (1980 7d) Apr 3; 8,000F, 19,000Y; rangy filly; half-sister to 3 winners, including smart 6f and 7f winner Skyliner (by African Sky) and useful filly Slip the Ferret (by Klairon); dam won 6 times over 5f at 2 yrs; 16/1 and backward when always behind in 13-runner maiden race won by Lambay at Leicester in October. *P. Cole.* –

RUBY RAY 2 ch.f. Laser Light 118–Witty (Will Somers 114§) (1980 5d 5.8h 6fg 5d 6s) Apr 7; sturdy filly; sister to a winning hurdler and half-sister to another; dam poor sister to Ayr Gold Cup winners Kamundu and Somersway; behind in maiden races and a seller; sweated up third outing. *W. Wightman.* –

RUBY RED DRESS 3 b.f. Sparkler 130–Red Cape 84 (Matador 131) (1979 6g 6fg 6g 1980 8s 10fg 12.3d 10.6d 10s3 10g 10.2v) big, well-made filly; best run at 1¼m on soft going. *M. Camacho.* 69

RUDRY GRANGE 2 br.c. Stype Grange 92–Pearl Bailey (Sing Sing 134) (1980 5g 5d 8d) Mar 20; small colt; fifth foal; dam never ran; no sign of ability in maiden races. *D. H. Jones.* –

RUGBY EXCAVATION 2 b.f. Lord Nelson 107–Misty Belle (Foggy Bell 108) (1980 8fg) May 16; second foal; dam of no account; unimpressive in paddock when last of 24 in maiden race won by Allegretta at Leicester in September. *J. Czerpak.* –

RULE BRITANNIA 3 ch.f. English Prince 129–Sea Music 108 (Atan) (1979 6f4 1980 8d 9f* 12f 8s4 8g4 8fg 8g3) well-made, strong-quartered filly; good mover; quickened clear to beat Broomstick Corner 5 lengths in 14-runner maiden event at Wolverhampton in May; in frame afterwards in Child Stakes at Newmarket (just over 6 lengths fourth to Stumped), £3,200 race at Doncaster and Marlborough House Stakes at Ascot; blinkered when 3½ lengths third to Our Home in last-named in October; not certain to stay 1½m (well beaten in Oaks 102

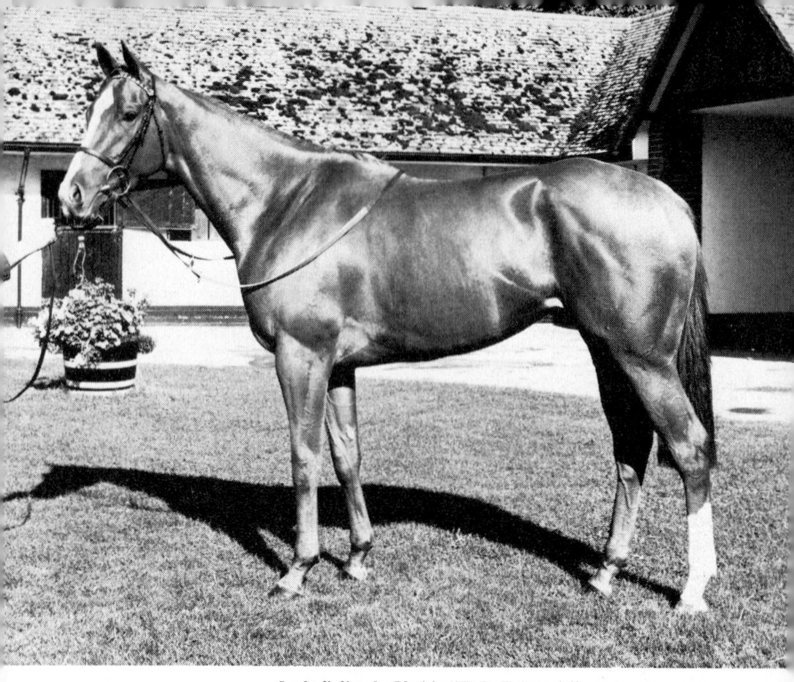

Lady Juliet de Chair's "Rule Britannia"

when tried at trip); seems to act on any going; sold 37,000 gns Newmarket December Sales. *P. Walwyn.*

RULE OF THUMB 3 ch.f. Young Emperor 133–Tom's Delight (Tom Rolfe) (1979 5fg 6g 7g 1980 6d 5d) strong filly; showed only a little ability in varied company; best run at 6f; dead. *G. Hunter.* —

RUMANDA 5 b.g. Quadriga 97–Stephela (Young Stratford 92) (1979 8d 12d 8s 10fg 7f 1980 8fg 10f 10g) useless. *D. Chapman.* —

RUMASA 2 b.c. Lochnager 132–Sparkling Jewel (Faberge II 121) (1980 5fg 6g) Feb 8; 6,000Y; big colt; half-brother to Champagne Willie (by The Brianstan), a useful winner at up to 9f, and to a winner over hurdles; dam of little account; 4/1, didn't recover from a slow start when 9½ lengths fifth of 7 to Rathmoy's Sparkle in maiden race at Carlisle in May; behind in 9-runner Eagle Development Stakes won by Beulah Land at York the following month. *M. H. Easterby.* —

RUM GIRL 2 br.f. Le Johnstan 123–Rum Year (Quorum 126) (1980 8.2d 8fg 8fg 8.2g3 8d) May 18; small filly; first foal; dam placed over hurdles; plater; 4½ lengths third of 12 to Oratavo at Nottingham in September; runs as though 1¼m will suit her; sold 780 gns Doncaster November Sales. *K. Stone.* 56

RUM PUNCH 4 gr.g. Warpath 113–Brandy (Busted 134) (1979 12fg 1980 10.2g 12.2f 12g 12.2g3 12f3 12d2) workmanlike gelding; made running and kept on well when ½-length second to Hay Ride in handicap at Hamilton in September; will be suited by 1¾m+. *C. Thornton.* 44

RUN FOR HER LIFE 2 b.f. Runnymede 123–Gallows Gal 107 (High Treason 126) (1980 5g 5g3 6g) Mar 23; 4,000Y; neat, lightly-made fully; sister to fairly useful 1974 2-y-o 7f winner Chelwood Lady, and half-sister to 3 other winners; dam very speedy at 2 yrs; co-favourite, beaten by Advertrack and 75

Welsh Cygnet in blanket finish to 19-runner maiden race at Folkestone in October, being well there throughout. *R. Price.*

RUN HARD 5 b.g. Run The Gantlet–Isola D'Asti 106 (Court Harwell 130) (1979 12d^3 16s 14fg* 14.6fg^2 13g^4 14g^2 14fg^3 1980 18f) fairly useful handicapper on flat at his best, but is better known as a hurdler nowadays; stays well; acts on any going; bandaged in front on only outing of 1980 (Great Metropolitan). *R. Turnell.* –

RUNNELA 2 gr.f. Runnymede 123–River Palace (Royal Palace 131) (1980 5f 6fg 7g) Mar 10; light-framed, narrow filly; second live foal; half-sister to 1½m winner Bazz's Boy (by Dragonara Palace); dam ran only twice; 10½ lengths fifth of 16 to Go Leasing in maiden race at Lingfield in June, second outing; subsequently off course over 2 months and needed run on her return. *P. Ashworth.* –

RUNNETT 3 b.c. Mummy's Pet 125–Rennett 109 (King's Bench 132) (1979 5g* 5d* 5fg* 5f^3 5s^3 5g^2 1980 6fg* 6fg^2 5fg^2 6d 5g 5fg^3 5fg* 5s*) big, lengthy colt; brother to very useful 1977 2-y-o 5f winner Cala-Vadella and 1m winner Placid Pet, and half-brother to 2 sprint winners by Tribal Chief; dam stayed 1¼m; smart performer; won minor race at Folkestone in April and Raffingora Sprint at Beverley and valuable 5-runner Coral Racing Champion Sprint at York in the autumn; led below distance and kept on well to beat King of Spain 1½ lengths in last-named; placed in between in Gus Demmy Memorial Stakes at Haydock (beaten a neck by Sayyaf, gave 3 lb), King's Stand Stakes at Royal Ascot (sweated up slightly when going down by 1½ lengths to African Song) and minor event at Newbury (favourite and blinkered, went very freely to post when 1½ lengths last of 3 to Blue Persian, rec 3 lb); beaten some way in William Hill July Cup at Newmarket and William Hill Sprint Championship at York on other starts; stays 6f; seems to act on any going. *J. Dunlop.* **120**

RUNNING GAME 3 b.f. Run The Gantlet–Game All 109 (Alcide 136) (1979 6d 1980 10s 12d^4 16f* 15s^2 14g^2) lengthy filly; narrowly won 10-runner maiden race at Beverley in August; ran creditably both subsequent starts, sweating up on second occasion; suited by a test of stamina; acts on any going. *H. T. Jones.* **81**

RUNNING JUMP 8 ch.g. Runnymede 123–High Acres (High Perch 126) (1979 NR 1980 8d 7s) fairly useful handicapper (rated 99) in 1978; didn't race in 1979 due to a knee injury sustained when winning at Ayr on his final appearance as a 6-y-o (also missed 1977 season with a knee injury); unimpressive in paddock when unplaced in valuable handicaps early in 1980 (not disgraced when sweating and still in need of race on second outing); stays 1m; acts on any going but has done nearly all his winning on an easy surface; suited by forcing tactics; suitable mount for an apprentice, although gave trouble going to, and at, start on first outing. *J. W. Watts.* –

RUNNING MILL 3 b.c. Mill Reef 141–Running Blue 115 (Blue Peter) (1979 7f^3 8f^2 1980 9f* 12fg 12f 12d 8fg^3) neat, attractive colt; forged clear of his rivals in last furlong, despite going right near finish, to win Heath Stakes at Newmarket in April by 2½ lengths from Fingal's Cave; fair third to Morayshire **105**

Coral Racing Champion Sprint, York—another for Willie Carson as he drives Runnett home from King of Spain and Gypsy Dancer

(rec 4 lb) in £3,900 3-runner race on same course in October; well beaten in between in Predominate Stakes at Kempton (fifth to Prince Bee), Derby (twenty-first to Henbit) and Princess of Wales's Stakes at Newmarket (seventh to Nicholas Bill); should stay at least 1$\frac{1}{2}$m; acts on firm going; sold 41,000 gns Newmarket December Sales, reportedly for export to Italy. *M. Stoute.*

RUNNING ROCKET 3 gr.c. Runnymede 123–Rosy Morn (Roan Rocket 128) (1979 5s 5g 6fg 6g 6fg^4 6fg^2 6d^4 7f^2 6g* 6g 1980 6v^2 7f 7h^4 6f 8.2d* 8g^3 10s* 9g^3 8.2d 8.2g 10s^3 8d) light-framed colt; fair handicapper; successful at Hamilton in June and Ayr in August; stays 1$\frac{1}{4}$m; appears to act on any going; suitable mount for a boy; below form last 4 outings. *T. Craig.* **91**

RUN RABBIT RUN 3 b.g. Caliban 123–Flapperette 92 (Hardicanute 130) (1979 5g 6fg 6g 7fg 8.2d* 7f 10g 1980 10s 8s 11fg 6d) small, light-framed gelding; plater; ran poorly in 1980; should stay at least 1$\frac{1}{4}$m; acts on a soft surface; sold out of W. Marshall's stable 1,000 gns Doncaster May Sales. *D. McCain.* –

RUN RECORD RUN 2 ch.f. Record Run 127–Firecrest 58 (Firestreak 125) (1980 6f 7fg 7g^2 7g 7d) Apr 8; 4,000F, 5,000Y; lengthy filly; half-sister to several minor winners; dam of little account; 3 lengths second of 19 behind Canaille in maiden race at Leicester in August, best effort; will stay 1m; blinkered final outing. *G. Pritchard-Gordon.* **77**

RUSCELLI (FR) 3 b.c. Val de l'Orne 130–Coy Maid (Habitat 134) (1979 6.5d^2 7fg* 1980 8g 8g^3(dis) 8fg* 9fg^2 10s 12f^3 12f) 160,000 francs Y (approx £19,000); neat colt; first foal; dam, from same family as Sir Ivor, won small race over 9f in France; very smart performer; won 5-runner Prix de la Jonchere at Longchamp in May by 1$\frac{1}{2}$ lengths from Joberan; ran well to be placed in Poule d'Essai des Poulains on same course (disqualified after finishing just over a length third to In Fijar), Prix Jean Prat at Chantilly (went down by a neck to clever winner Night Alert) and Prix Niel at Longchamp; bandaged behind when finishing strongly to be 1$\frac{3}{4}$ lengths third to Prince Bee in last-named in September; not disgraced in Prix de l'Arc de Triomphe, at Longchamp again, in October, running on well to be ninth of 20 to Detroit; stays 1$\frac{1}{2}$m; probably unsuited by very soft going. *F. Palmer, France.* **122**

RUSHMERE 7 br.h. Blakeney 126–Omentello 91 (Elopement 125) (1979 16s* 14v* 16fg 14f^4 21d 16d 1980 14fg 12fg^4 15f 14g 22.2fg 16g 16s^3 16g 14g 16g) staying handicapper; acts on any going but revels in the mud; used to wear blinkers; bandaged on reappearance. *R. Atkins.* **46**

RUSHMOOR 2 br.g. Queen's Hussar 124–Heathfield 99 (Hethersett 134) (1980 6fg 6g^2 6d^3) May 5; strong, useful-looking gelding; brother to very useful 1976 2-y-o 6f winner Fife and Drum, and half-brother to 3 winners, all at least fairly useful; dam won from 6f to 1m; drifted left in final furlong when neck second to The Quiet Bidder in maiden race at York in July, pair clear; blinkered first time and short-priced favourite for similar event at Haydock in August, had every chance 1$\frac{1}{2}$f out but could finish only third, 1$\frac{1}{2}$ lengths behind Foresters Lad; will stay 1m; possibly not at his best on a soft surface; gelded after final outing. *R. Hern.* **88**

RUSHOCK 5 b.g. Comedy Star 121–Miss Blade (Skymaster 126) (1979 5d 5g^2 5fg 6g 5g 1980 5g 5fg^3 6g^2 6f^3 5fg 6h 6fg^4 6s 5d 6s* 7g^2 8.3g^3 7g^2) compact gelding; plater; bought in 920 gns after winning at Windsor in July; stays 1m; acts on any going; suitable mount for an apprentice. *D. Marks.* **46**

RUSPER GEM 3 ch.f. Amber Rama 133–Coppice (Pardao 120) (1979 6f 7fg 1980 6d 8d 8.3s 8.3f 10f) of no account; sold 330 gns Ascot November Sales. *M. Francis.* –

RUSSIAN GEORGE (FR) 4 ch.c. Hard to Beat 132–Kirmidian (Bold Bidder) (1979 11d 11g 11fg* 14f 11g^4 1980 13d* 12f* 11f^2 12fg* 12fg* 16d^2 15g^2 12.5d 16f^4 12v^3) lengthy colt; improved considerably and developed into a useful handicapper; won amateur riders race at Nottingham, £3,700 event at Haydock, handicap at Leicester and Newbury Summer Cup in first half of season, beating Rheinman smoothly by 1$\frac{1}{2}$ lengths in last-named event; placed in 3 valuable handicaps afterwards, finishing close second to Mon's Beau in Coral Northumberland Plate at Newcastle and to Smokey Bear in Tennent Trophy at Ayr and 1$\frac{1}{2}$ lengths third to Path of Peace in William Hill November Handicap at Doncaster; sweated up when unplaced in amateur riders event at Deauville on eighth start and was out of his depth on ninth outing; stays 2m; appears to act on any going; genuine and consistent. *G. Hunter.* **102**

RUSSIAN ROMANCE 2 ch.g. Red Alert 127–Wild Romance 96 (Pirate King 129) (1980 5f^3 5fg 5fg 6g^2 6s^4 6fg) Apr 8; 4,200F, 33,000Y; well-made, good-looking gelding; half-brother to 1979 2-y-o 5f and 6f winner Tremiti (by Sun Prince) and a winner in Malaya; dam won at up to 7f; quite moderate form in maiden and minor races; suited by 6f nowadays; blinkered third start; gelded after final outing. *C. Brittain.* **75**

RUSSIAN WINTER 5 b.h. King Emperor–Am Stretchin (Ambiorix 130) (1979 7.2v 8g 8g 6g* 6f 6fg 6h 6f^3 7g 8.2g 1980 6d 6d* 7f 6f^4 5fg* 5fg* 6f^2 6d* 6d* 5s^3 5g* 6fg^2 5d^2 6g 5d* 6s 5d) lengthy horse; much improved and had a very successful season; won handicaps at Hamilton (4), Ayr (an amateur riders event and an apprentice event) and Haydock; put up a particularly good effort when beating Friendly Fun by a neck on last-named course in September; stays 1m but has done all his winning over shorter distances; probably unsuited by very soft going; wears blinkers; genuine and consistent; excellent mount for an inexperienced rider; possibly best on a galloping track. *A. W. Jones.* **73**

RUSTIC CHARM 2 br.g. Palm Track 122–Polly-Ann Tanja (Cletus) (1980 6g) Apr 12; workmanlike gelding; second foal; half-brother to 3-y-o 1m seller winner Zanveatic (by Beatic); dam never ran; 100/1 when twelfth of 13 to Brummer in £3,200 maiden race at Doncaster in September. *J. Carr.* –

RUSWARP 2 b.c. Gold Form 108–Lady Cortina 80 (Cortachy 107) (1980 5f* 5fg^3 5fg 6fg) Mar 31; 1,800F; strong colt; half-brother to winning sprinter Queensway (by Typhoon); dam won at up to 1m; led 1f out when winning 15-runner event at Beverley in April by 1½ lengths from Hexgreave Star; creditable 1¾ lengths third of 13 to Sunny Smile in well-contested race on same course in June, best subsequent effort; ran poorly when tried over 6f. *D. Garraton.* **83**

RUTHELEN 3 ro.f. Pongee 106–Stephela (Young Stratford 92) (1979 NR 1980 8f 10d) second foal; dam won over hurdles and fences; looks useless. *D. Chapman.* –

RUTHERTON 3 br.c. Singing Bede 122–Pat's Best (Star Moss 122) (1979 6fg 5f 1980 7g 7g) small colt; poor plater; possibly stays 7f. *R. Simpson.* –

RYECROFT 2 b.c. Condorcet–Moonlight Story (Narrator 127) (1980 7g 7fg) Apr 29; 640Y, resold 3,100Y; useful-looking colt; half-brother to Irish middle-distance winner Carraig Isle (by Status Seeker) and a winner in Trinidad; dam never ran; unquoted when behind in sizeable fields of maidens at Newmarket in the summer. *R. Armstrong.* –

RYEMAN 3 b.g. Andrea Mantegna–Enniris (Ennis 128) (1979 NR 1980 14.7f 16.1s 15s 12s) 760Y, 1,200 3-y-o; leggy gelding; well beaten in maiden and minor races in the North. *M. H. Easterby.* –

RYE MOSS 3 ch.g. Ballymoss 136–Preston Sue 73 (Sicilian Prince 126) (1979 5f 7f 7f 1980 13.8fg^2 16g 15fg^3 16fg) leggy gelding; staying maiden; acts on a firm surface; blinkered fourth start; bandaged off-hind second outing; didn't handle Catterick track too well on reappearance. *J. Fitzgerald.* **57**

S

SABA NEJD 2 b.c. Malacate 131–Padova (Forli) (1980 6g^3 6g* 8fg) Mar 27; 22,000F, 26,000Y; neat, strong, attractive colt; good walker and mover; third foal; half-brother to winning American 3-y-o Mister Parrot (by Nonoalco); dam placed over 1¼m; ran on gamely to win 5-runner minor event at Windsor in September by short head from Buffavento; never dangerous when modest sixth of 23 to Shergar in similar race at Newbury later in month; should be well suited by 1m+. *P. Walwyn.* **85**

SABEK 2 ch.c. Virginia Boy 106–Diamonds For Ever (Ionian 128) (1980 5.1g 5g 7d) Apr 25; 6,200Y; strong, compact colt; half-brother to very useful 1979 2-y-o 6f and 7f winner Schweppes Forever (by Lord Gayle) and to a bumpers winner; dam Irish 2-y-o 6f winner; not fully wound up when behind in maiden races. *R. Boss.* –

SABIR 4 ch.c. Sallust 134–Mrs Binks (Whistling Wind 123) (1979 9v 9g^4 8d^2 8h^2 7h* 8h^2 8s* 7.6f 7fg 7fg 1980 7s^2 8f 8f^3 8f^3 8d 8g) useful-looking colt; placed in good handicaps at Newcastle, York and Sandown; ran moderately last 2 starts and wasn't seen out after July; best form at up to 1m; acts on any going; good mount for an apprentice; sweated up second outing; sold to W. Stubbs 740 gns Newmarket Autumn Sales. *B. Hills.* **86**

SACHA'S SONG 2 ch.g. Crooner 119–Bouleversee (Napoleon Bonaparte 114) (1980 7fg 7fg 6fg 8d 7fg) Apr 30; well-grown gelding; half-brother to a winning plater; dam never ran; moderate sixth of 16 to Down The Hatch in maiden race at Salisbury in September, third outing and only glimmer of ability. *R. Hannon.* —

SACRILEGE 4 b.c. St Paddy 133–Rebuke (Princely Gift 137) (1979 8d 12g^{2} 10.1g^{2} 10s^{2} 10v 1980 10v* 9g* 8f 10g* 10.5g^{4} 10fg 10f^{2} 9f 10g) attractive colt; won Daily Mirror Handicap at Epsom in June by head from Dasman; successful earlier in maiden race at Stockton and minor event at Ripon; stuck on well when fourth to Fine Sun in John Smith's Magnet Cup at York in July and went down by a length to Norfolk Flight under top weight in handicap at Folkestone in September; probably finds 1m on sharp side nowadays and stays 1½m; acts on any going but seems suited by some give in the ground; genuine; sold 30,000 gns Newmarket December Sales and is to be trained by H. Cecil in 1981. *P. Walwyn.* 95

SADEDAB 7 br.h. Badedas 81–June Clare (Fairwell) (1979 11.1v 18s 12f 10f 11.5fg 16.9fg 11.7g 16g 12fg 12s 13s 1980 10.2d 13s 12fg 12fg 12f 16g 17.1fg 13g 17.1d 18s) poor handicapper; stays 2m; acts on any going; sometimes wears blinkers; suitable mount for an apprentice. *J. Edmunds.* —

SAFEGUARD 4 b.f. Wolver Hollow 126–Queen's Keys 84 (Right Royal V 135) (1979 8d 9.4s 12g^{3} 16.1g^{3} 15.8fg^{2} 12f 1980 18f 17.1f) narrow, lengthy filly; plating-class staying maiden; acts on a firm surface. *D. Elsworth.* —

SAFE SEAT 3 ch.c. Majority Blue 126–Tabankulu (Selko) (1979 6f 8.2s^{2} 1980 10s) second in seller at 2 yrs; well beaten in maiden race only start in 1980 (March); stays 1m well. *J. Hudson.* —

SAFIDAR 3 gr.f. Roan Rocket 128–Nigretta (Ribot 142) (1979 5s 5f 5fg^{2} 7d 6f^{4} 7.2g 7fg 7g 7d^{2} 1980 8g 8f* 8s) neat filly; narrowly won maiden race at Thirsk in April; off course 6 months afterwards and was tailed off on return; stays 1m well; probably acts on any going. *R. Hollinshead.* 72

SA FILLE 4 ch.f. Mon Fils 124–Crespinall 110 (Saint Crespin III 132) (1979 8d 8s 9d 10.5g* 10.5d 10.5s 1980 7fg 11.1fg) tall filly; sister to very useful middle-distance winner Son Fils; dam won Princess Elizabeth Stakes and Nassau Stakes; won minor event at Le Croise-Laroche in 1979; well beaten in Philip Cornes Trophy at Leicester in April and handicap at Kempton in May; stays 1¼m well. *R. Hannon.* —

SAFITA 3 gr.f. Habitat 134–Safaya (Zeddaan 130) (1979 NR 1980 7.5d^{2} 7v* 8d^{2} 10fg^{2} 10s 8fg* 8d^{2} 7d^{2} 7v) lightly-built filly; first foal; dam won twice over 5f at 2 yrs in France; smart performer; won maiden race at Maisons-Laffitte in March and Prix de la Calonne at Deauville in August; beat Exactly So 1½ lengths in latter; ran well most other starts, notably at Longchamp when short-headed by Aryenne in Poule d'Essai des Pouliches, beaten ¾ length by Paranete in Prix Saint-Alary and going down by 2½ lengths to Hilal in Prix du Rond-Point on seventh start; stays 1¼m; seems to act on any going; genuine and consistent. *F. Mathet, France.* 117

SAGE KING 2 b.c. Shantung 132–Lady Gaylord (Double Jump 131) (1980 8d^{2} 8.2s* 8.2s^{2}) Apr 20; 3,800Y; half-brother to 1977 2-y-o 7f winner Winter Queen (by Calpurnius); dam unraced half-sister to smart colt Romper; won 15-runner maiden race at Hamilton in September easing up by 4 lengths from Jade and Diamond; odds on when beaten 2 lengths by Emblazon in minor event on same course the following month; will be suited by 1¼m; yet to race on a sound surface. *J. W. Watts.* 90

SAGITTA ROCKET 3 b.f. Roan Rocket 128–Salonica II (Ocarina 131) (1979 7f 7f 8f 8h^{4} 8g 1980 10g^{4} 12h^{3} 12.2fg^{3} 12g) well-made, deep-girthed filly; one-paced maiden; stays 1½m; yet to race on a soft surface. *J. Winter.* 61

SAHER 4 b.c. Great Nephew 126–Another Chance 75 (Romulus 129) (1979 7s^{2} 7g 8g 6g^{3} 8s^{4} 10.4f^{2} 10.2fg^{2} 8fg* 8fg^{3} 1980 8d^{4} 10s 7fg 7.6f* 7.2fg 7g* 8d^{4} 8g^{3} 8g* 8d* 8f 7g^{4} 8g^{2} 8d^{3}) useful-looking colt; had an excellent season and put up a fine performance to win handicap at Wolverhampton in August by 2 lengths from Willow Red; successful earlier in similar events at Chester, York and Pontefract; in frame in handicaps at Doncaster and Sandown and in £2,500 event at York on last 3 starts, beaten a head by Anglepoise on last-named course on penultimate outing; stays 1¼m but races mainly at shorter distances; acts on any going; blinkered fourth start at 3 yrs; consistent; has a good turn of foot. *R. Sheather.* 102

SAILORD 4 b.g. Gold Rod 129–Sailanna 97 (Sailing Light 119) (1979 6g 6fg 7fg 12fg 8fg* 1980 9.6fg 9fg 7g 7g2 8fg* 7fg* 8.3fg 8.3f 8fg 8fg3 8d 8d) plater at 3 yrs; showed improved form when winning apprentice handicaps at Redcar in July and Folkestone in August; slipped up seventh outing and ran poorly next time; stays 1m; acts on a firm surface; wears blinkers nowadays; often sweats up; usually bandaged nowadays. *P. Mitchell.* **54**

SAILOR KING (USA) 2 ch.c. Nijinsky 138–Syrian Sea (Bold Ruler) (1980 6s4) Mar 22; $1,400,000Y; fifth foal; half-brother to Alada (by Riva Ridge), a very useful stakes winner at up to 8.5f; dam, sister to Secretariat and half-sister to Sir Gaylord, was third best 2-y-o filly in USA in 1967 when winner at up to 1m; had difficulty going the early pace when odds on for 14-runner maiden race at the Curragh in August but kept on to finish 2¼ lengths fourth to Ascending Star; will be well suited by 1¼m or more; bound to do a lot better at 3 yrs. *V. O'Brien, Ireland.* **83** P

SAILOR'S HAZE (USA) 2 b.f. Pat McGroder–Grand Ma Julia (Prince Taj 123) (1980 8g) Mar 1; $15,000Y; half-sister to a winner by Riva Ridge; dam, half-sister to high-class grass horse London Company, won 3 times at up to 11f including claiming races; sire, son of Graustark, won once over 8.5f; 25/1 when eleventh of 15 behind Scottish Dream in maiden race at Edinburgh in October. *G. Richards.* –

SAILOR'S PRAYER 2 gr.c. Martinmas 128–Coral Mermaid (Silver Shark 129) (1980 5s2 5fg* 5f 5f3 5f) Apr 23; leggy colt; half-brother to 2 minor winners in Ireland; dam never ran; clear approaching final furlong but held on by only a short head from Chief Admiral in 6-runner minor event at Edinburgh in July; creditable third to Krugerama in small race at Beverley the following month; will stay 6f; sweated up when never going well third outing and had stiffish task in nursery on fifth. *J. Powney.* **83**

SAILORS REVENGE 2 ch.c. Sweet Revenge 129–Admiral's Bird 61 (Sea Hawk II 131) (1980 7d 7g 8g) May 8; tall colt; first foal; dam poor 1½m performer; in mid-division in maiden races won by Hollow Laughter at Brighton and by To-Agori-Mou at Goodwood in July, first 2 outings; looks sort likely to need time. *G. Beeson.* –

SAINERA (USA) 2 b.f. Stop The Music–Summer Hill (Sir Gaylord) (1980 6g3 7fg* 8g) Mar 12; $47,000Y; leggy, lightly-made filly; half-sister to several winners, including stakes-placed Lean To (by Silent Screen); dam never ran; won 17-runner maiden race at Yarmouth in August comfortably by ½ length from More Stones; 14/1 and unimpressive in paddock, disputed lead 5f when remote sixth of 8 to Exclusively Raised in May Hill Stakes at Doncaster in September; promises to stay 1m. *L. Cumani.* **89**

SAINT CRISPIAN 2 ch.c. Rouser 118–Celestial Star 108 (So Blessed 130) (1980 7d 10s) Mar 22; useful sort; third foal; dam won both her starts at 2 yrs, over 5f and 6f; unquoted when always behind in maiden races at Leicester and Nottingham in October; sold 775 gns Ascot November Sales. *N. Vigors.* –

SAINT GERAN 4 ch.g. Red Alert 127–Blue Shark (Silver Shark 129) (1979 8s3 8.5s 10.1g4 10fg3 10fg* 11.7fg3 10.1g* 10.2fg 1980 11fg4 10f 10.6g 9f3 12g 12fg) well-made gelding; quite a moderate handicapper; stays 1½m; acts on any going; blinkered final start at 2 yrs; suited by forcing tactics; owner ridden at around 11-11 last 4 starts. *W. Charles.* –

SAINTINGO 3 b.f. Saulingo 122–Saint Veronica (Saint Crespin III 132) (1979 5g4 6g 1980 8f4 8fg 7g 8g2 8.3f 12s) fair sort; plater; stays 1m; blinkered fourth and fifth starts; sold out of N. Vigors' stable 600 gns Ascot August Sales after fifth outing. *S. Kernick.* **51**

SAINT JONATHON 3 b.c. Welsh Saint 126–Climbing Rose 81 (Pirate King 129) (1979 7fg* 1980 8v* 8f* 8fg 10.5f4 12f 12g3 12d 8g3) **116**

Nureyev and Saint Jonathon were the only unbeaten colts in the Two Thousand Guineas field. Compared to Nureyev, who was a celebrity before he set foot on a racecourse, Saint Jonathon was almost unknown until the start of his three-year-old career. His performance in a big field at Kempton in September on his only outing at two earned him 8-6 in the Free Handicap, only 15 lb behind Monteverdi but joint-seventy-first in the order of merit! Saint Jonathon's trainer, who stood to win a very substantial sum from ante-post bets if Saint Jonathon won the Guineas, gave him two races before Newmarket, sending him North for the Roseberry Stakes at Stockton in March and the Timeform Race Card Stakes at Thirsk two weeks before Newmarket. He

Timeform Race Card Stakes, Thirsk—Saint Jonathon striding out in great style

was impressive in both races, showing himself to be a powerful, relentless galloper, and went to Newmarket one of England's best hopes of keeping the Two Thousand Guineas at home. Incidentally, the Timeform Race Card Stakes, conceived as a preparatory race for the Newmarket classics, has so far served its purpose admirably; in 1979 the race was won by the subsequent Two Thousand Guineas winner Tap On Wood from Abbeydale, who went on to finish second in the One Thousand Guineas. The movable feast of Easter often creates problems with

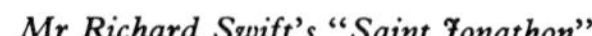

Mr Richard Swift's "Saint Jonathon"

racing fixtures and, unfortunately, Thirsk's traditional April fixture has been lost in 1981. But the Timeform Race Card Stakes will be resumed in 1982. Saint Jonathon finished well down the field in the Guineas and was afterwards reported to have been suffering from a foot infection. Put over longer distances after Newmarket, he ran creditably to finish fourth in the Prix Lupin, beaten two lengths by the winner Belgio, and third in the King Edward VII Stakes, a length and three quarters behind Light Cavalry. In between Longchamp and Royal Ascot, Saint Jonathon took his chance in the Derby, in which he finished thirteenth. Four tough races in a little over six weeks may have knocked some of the stuffing out of him and he was seen out only twice more during the season, running below his best on each occasion.

Saint Jonathon (b.c. 1977)	Welsh Saint (b 1966)	St Paddy (b 1957)	Aureole
			Edie Kelly
		Welsh Way (gr 1954)	Abernant
			Winning Ways
	Climbing Rose (b 1967)	Pirate King (b 1953)	Prince Chevalier
			Netherton Maid
		La Colline (ch 1962)	Acropolis
			Star of France

Time will tell whether Saint Jonathon can justify his trainer's very high opinion of him. It will be interesting to see the policy adopted with Saint Jonathon at four. Although he stays a mile and a half, he may revert to shorter distances. Saint Jonathon's sire Welsh Saint was a six-furlong performer and the average winning distance of his progeny is eight and a half furlongs; Saint Jonathon's dam raced only at sprint distances, although she was bred to get further, and her best offspring before Saint Jonathon was Rocket Symphony (by Roan Rocket), a useful performer at around a mile. Saint Jonathon, a lengthy, quite attractive colt and a good mover, acts on any going. *B. Hills.*

SAINTLY LADY 5 b.m. Saintly Song 128–Melody Lady 74 (Highland Melody 112) (1979 10s 8g 8d^3 8fg 7f 7fg 8.2g^4 8g^2 8fg 1980 7f 6fg 8f 6g) plater; stays 1¼m; seems to act on any going; has run creditably for an apprentice; has worn bandages; sold 650 gns Doncaster August Sales. *A. Balding.* —

SAINTLY SOVEREIGN 4 b.g. Saintly Song 128–Golden Alice 93 (Alycidon 138) (1979 6v 8d 8s 11.5fg 8fg 8g 8fg 7fg 1980 6f^4 6h 7f) poor maiden; best runs at 6f on firm ground and in blinkers. *A. Dalton.* —

SAINT MIA 2 ch.f. Arch Sculptor 123–Blue Bleep (Bleep-Bleep 134) (1980 5s^3 5f 5fg^3 5fg^4 5f) Feb 3; 2,100F, 6,100Y; well-made filly; third produce; dam won over 5f at 2 yrs in Ireland; third in April in maiden races at Warwick (2½ lengths behind Mementa Mia) and Wolverhampton (3½ lengths behind Etesian); runs as though she'll stay 6f; blinkered fourth and fifth outings. *J. Hill.* **63**

SAINT MOTUNDE 7 ch.m. Tyrant–Saint Veronica (Saint Crespin III 132) (1979 7s 7.6d 7.2g^3 6fg 7f^3 7fg 8h^3 7f 7.2g 8f 8h 1980 8fg 8g 7g* 6g 6fg^3(dis) 7fg 6g 7g 7f^4 6f^2 8fg^4) plater at 6 yrs; won handicap at Beverley in June by 1½ lengths from Swizzle; stays 1m; appears to act on any going; sometimes blinkered in 1979. *B. McMahon.* **57**

SAINT OSYTH 3 b.f. Blakeney 126–Vaunt (Hill Rise 127) (1979 NR 1980 7f^4 10f^2 12f* 12d^3) very attractive filly; half-sister to Oyster Catcher (by Gulf Pearl), a winner at up to 1½m, and to a winner in Brazil; dam won 3 races at up to 6f; landed odds by 5 lengths in 15-runner maiden race at Folkestone in September; ran well when second to The Dancer in Sir Charles Clore Memorial Stakes at Newbury in May and 3½ lengths third to Karamita in Princess Royal Stakes at Ascot in October; will be suited by 1¾m; probably acts on any going. *P. Walwyn.* **105**

SAINT ROSE 2 b.f. Welsh Saint 126–Bawn Rose (Menelek 114) (1980 5f 5fg 6s 7fg 7g) Apr 2; lightly-made filly; first foal; dam won 3 times on flat and 6 times over jumps in Belgium; poor plater. *P. Rohan.* —

SAISON (USA) 3 b.f. L'Enjoleur–Singing Bird (T. V. Lark) (1979 NR 1980 including 7f* 8fg 8f 8.5g* 9g*) lightly-made, attractive ex-English filly; not a particularly good mover; half-sister to very useful 1972 French 2-y-o 5.5f and 1m winner Stanleyville (by Val de Loir); dam unraced half-sister to brilliant 1m and 1¼m filly Hula Dancer; trained by H. Cecil first 3 starts; won 15-runner newcomers race at Newbury (odds on, made virtually all to beat Just Abroad 5 lengths); favourite, weakened after having every chance 2f out in 1,000 Guineas at Newmarket (thirteenth to Quick As Lightning) and £3,500 race at Sandown (sixth to Dancing Shadow); subsequently sent to USA and won first 3 starts there, **90**

M D. Wildenstein's "Saison"

including races at Belmont Park and Aqueduct; stays 9f; acts on firm going. *A. Penna, U.S.A.*

SAKANOONO 2 gr.c. Sovereign Path 125–Sage Green (Pampered King 121) (1980 7fg 6g 6d) Apr 19; 6,600F, 3,400Y; leggy, short-backed colt; third foal; half-brother to a winner in Italy; dam won over 1m and 1¼m in Ireland; only plating-class form so far; should be suited by 1m; sold to Denys Smith 1,500 gns Newmarket Autumn Sales. *W. Wharton.* –

SAKEENA 4 b.f. Moulton 128–High Order 102 (Hugh Lupus 132) (1979 10.6g 9g 10fg² 14g 12s 1980 10.2d 12h* 11.7f³ 12g* 12fg 11.5g* 11.7g 12g²) strong, leggy filly; won minor event at Pontefract in May (by ½ length from Angelo Salvini) and handicaps at Edinburgh in June and Yarmouth in July; made virtually all when beating Comedy Croft by 4 lengths on last-named course; looked bit light final outing (August); stays 1½m; acts on any going except perhaps soft; usually wears bandages. *R. Boss.* **76**

SALADO (ITY) 9 b.g. Molvedo 137– Gallura (Sedan II) (1979 12s 1980 12.2v 16s 16f) one-time smart performer on flat; temperamental nowadays and refused to race final outing; best left severely alone; sold 600 gns Ascot May Sales. *G. Price.* –

SALAMINA 2 ch.f. Welsh Pageant 132–Femme Elite (Young Emperor 133) (1980 5fg 5f* 6g* 6fg) May 9; leggy filly; half-sister to 3-y-o 7f winner Hexgreave Elite (by Home Guard) and Irish 9.5f winner Virginia Chat (by Welsh Saint); dam, winner at up to 5f at 2 yrs in USA, is daughter of high-class sprinter Fairy Flax; a progressive filly who won 19-runner maiden race at Beverley in August and 20-runner nursery at Lingfield the following month, latter by ¾ length from Cumulus; never dangerous but was far from disgraced when 4 lengths fifth of 8 to Marwell in William Hill Cheveley Park Stakes at Newmarket in October; better suited by 6f than 5f and will stay further. *G. Pritchard-Gordon.* **106**

SALDATORE 3 ch.g. Sallust 134–Chaduaille (St Chad 120) (1979 6g 6fg 8fg 1980 10d 8fg 8fg 7.6f³ 8fg⁴ 8g) tall, useful-looking gelding; stays 1m; acts on firm going; sweated up third start; blinkered nowadays. *H. Candy.* **65**

SALFORD SUPREME 3 ch.c. On Your Mark 125–Lady Midge 120 (Nearco) (1979 5d 7s 1980 8d 6fg 6h⁴ 6fg 6s 8d 6g) small colt; poor maiden; stays 6f; off course 5 months before fifth start and ran badly on return. *R. Hollinshead.* —

SALLACHY 3 ch.f. Hot Spark 126–Brush's Choice (Robson's Choice 105) (1979 NR 1980 6f 8f 12fg) 3,100Y; lightly-made filly; half-sister to 2 winners, including fairly useful miler Town Farm (by Tycoon II); seems of little account. *J. Hudson.* —

SALLAMETTI (USA) 2 b.f. Giacometti 130–Gay Sally (Sir Gaylord) (1980 6s 7fg 8d⁴ 8.2v⁴) lengthy filly; half-sister to 2 winners in USA, including Native Sir (by Exclusive Native), successful at up to 1m; dam, second once from 7 starts, comes from same family as champion American 2-y-o filly Evening Out; quite a modest maiden; will be suited by 1¼m. *J. Hindley.* **69**

SALLUSTENO 4 ch.f. Sallust 134–Absuleno 78 (Above Suspicion 127) (1979 7g 8d 8f 8f 7g² 8s 7f 7s 8.2g 12.2s 1980 8d 8f 10g 8d²) small filly; stays 1m; often wears blinkers. *J. Calvert.* **49**

SALLUTAY 3 b.g. Sallust 134–Stevia (Supreme Court 135) (1979 7f 6g 7fg 1980 7f 8fg 7d 6d 7g 6g²) small, sturdy gelding; poor walker; second in seller at Newmarket in August; runs as if he will be suited by a return to 7f; blinkered last 2 starts. *C. Brittain.* **58**

SALLY JON JEAN 2 ch.f. Lord Gayle 124–Mecara 90 (Gulf Pearl 117) (1980 6fg³) Feb 19; 8,000Y; well-made filly; good mover; third foal; dam, half-sister to smart Majetta, won twice over 5f at 2 yrs; third favourite, showed good speed most of way when 4½ lengths third of 7 to Petroleuse in Blue Seal Stakes at Ascot in September; will stay 1m; should improve. *C. Nelson.* **71** p

SALLY ROSE 2 b.f. Sallust 134–Desert Flower 93 (Ballymoss 136) (1980 6f³) neat filly; good mover; third foal; sister to useful 1977 2-y-o 1m winner Demetrius and half-sister to a winner; dam, winner at up to 13f, is half-sister to very smart performers Tiger and Berber; 6/1, completely outpaced by first 2 but stuck on well to finish 10½ lengths third of 13 to Star Pastures in £2,400 event at York in September; will stay 1¼m; will improve at 3 yrs. *R. Hern.* **77** p

SALLY'S SILVER 4 gr.f. No Mercy 126–Pin Worker (Pindari 124) (1979 5d 6g 6d 7g 6f⁴ 6f 6fg³ 6d⁴ 6d³ 6d* 6h 6fg⁴ 6fg 1980 5fg 6h 6fg 6g 6g 5.8f 5f 6g⁴ 6g³) light-framed filly; 33/1 and apprentice ridden when creditable third of 30 to Hot Money in claiming handicap at Newmarket in October; best form at 6f; appears to act on any going, except perhaps hard. *J. Benstead.* **42**

SALMAGUNDI 3 b.f. Shoolerville 121–Soulier 101 (Sheshoon 132) (1979 10.6d 10s 1980 10.4f 12fg 13.8fg 14.6fg 16s) small filly; poor maiden. *T. Molony.* —

SALMAN 2 gr.c. Comedy Star 121–Lovely Beak (Counsel 118) (1980 5fg 5f 5fg) Feb 6; 3,800F, 5,200Y; tall colt; brother to useful 1m to 1¼m winner Starfen, and half-brother to a winner; dam ran only once; unquoted when behind in sizeable fields of maidens in the spring. *P. M. Taylor.* —

SALMANA (FR) 2 ch.f. Manado 130–Salto Mortale (Hul a Hul 124) (1980 5.5d 7s³ 6d* 6fg 8g⁴ 8f³) Feb 8; 80,000 francs Y (approx. £8,500); lightly-built filly; second foal; half-sister to minor French 6.5f winner Salvavida (by Sallust); dam showed useful form at up to 1¼m in Ireland, winning over 6f and 7f; ran in pattern races after winning maiden race at Deauville in August by 4 lengths and put up 2 good efforts, being beaten only 1¼ lengths when fourth of 9 to Ukraine Girl in Group 3 Prix d'Aumale at Chantilly and closing fast on leaders in final stages when just over 2 lengths third of 10 to Tropicaro in Prix Marcel Boussac at Longchamp; suited by 1m and may stay further; seems to act on any going. *P. Biancone, France.* **111**

SALMON BERRY 2 b.f. Sassafras 135–Lady Sykes 76 (Sovereign Lord 120) (1980 7d* 7g 8g) Apr 19; strong, workmanlike filly; half-sister to several winners here and abroad, including good Italian winners Guido Lord (by Linacre) and Giadolino (by Skymaster); dam placed over 1m at 2 yrs; looked backward at Newmarket in July but came through to beat sole opponent Stars In Your Eyes by 1½ lengths in Limekilns Stakes; not disgraced subsequently; will probably stay 1¼m; sold 16,500 gns Newmarket December Sales. *W. Hastings-Bass.* **83**

SALON PRIVEE 2 b.g. Dragonara Palace 115–Pied A Terre (Ribocco 129) (1980 5fg⁴ 7s 7g² 7g* 7f² 8g⁴) Mar 4; 6,800F, 19,000Y; neat, attractive gelding; **84**

good mover; third living foal; half-brother to fair 1977 2-y-o 5f winner Sharp Pad (by Sharp Edge), subsequently successful in Trinidad; dam daughter of sister to Reform; odds on for 8-runner nursery at Redcar in August but got home by only a head from Lady Ever-So-Sure; failed by only a short head to catch Stormy Jim when second in nursery at Beverley later in month, better subsequent effort; suited by 7f but didn't run up to his best over 1m (blinkered first time); acts on firm going; exported to Hong Kong. *H. T. Jones.*

SALORA LADY 2 b.f. Sassafras 135–Rocaserena 104 (Jimmy Reppin 131) (1980 7g 8d 10.2s) Mar 13; 4,200Y; neat filly; second foal; dam won over 6f and 7f; little worthwhile form in maiden and minor races in the North. *E. Weymes.* —

SALT 2 ch.f. Sallust 134–Albercaro 88 (Hard Tack 111§) (1980 5g² 5d* 5fg² 6fg* 5d² 5fg) Feb 19; light-framed filly; half-sister to several winners, including useful 6f to 1m winner Alber Run (by Run The Gantlet) and very useful sprinter Bold Tack (by Bold Lad, Ire); dam 5f sprinter; made all to win maiden race at Wolverhampton in June and £2,400 event at Ripon in July, holding off Helvic Storm by a short head in latter; gives impression 6f suits her better than 5f; acts on a firm and a soft surface; genuine and consistent but ran moderately on final outing. *H. T. Jones.* **90**

SALTHOUSE 3 b.g. Blakeney 126–Grilse Run 94 (Stupendous) (1979 NR 1980 10fg 10.8s⁴ 10.1d 10d² 9d) 10,000Y; attractive, neat, strong gelding; second live foal; dam won over 5f at 2 yrs; second in maiden race at Pontefract in August; needs further than 9f and will stay 1½m; acts on a soft surface; sold to N. Callaghan 7,000 gns Newmarket Autumn Sales. *H. Cecil.* **74**

SALT OF THE EARTH 3 b.f. Sterling Bay–Pinch of Salt 78 (Super Sam 124) (1979 5fg 1980 7.6f* 8g* 7fg⁴ 6g³) neat filly; successful in maiden race at Lingfield in June and small event at Bath in July; good fourth to Trevita, beaten 3¾ lengths, in valuable race at Goodwood later in month; may well stay beyond 1m; yet to race on a soft surface; sweated up quite badly final start. *M. Smyly.* **85**

Mr David Kerr's "Salt of the Earth"

SALTY SUSIE 3 b.f. Nonoalco 131–Arctic Lace 106 (Arctic Chevalier) (1979 **79**
NR 1980 10.2g 9fg² 10d³ 10fg* 10g² 10fg⁴ 12s* 12d³) 47,000Y; big, rangy filly; half-sister to 3 winners, notably high-class 7f to 13.4f winner Oats (by Northfields); dam third in Irish 1000 Guineas; successful in maiden race at Yarmouth in August (odds on) and handicap at Haydock in October; beat Dame Sue ¾ length in latter; suited by 1½m; probably acts on any going. *M. Stoute.*

SALUBRE 3 ch.c. Sallust 134–Orange Grove 81 (Aggressor 130) (1979 NR **90**
1980 10.1g³ 10.2g* 10.1s* 12g³ 10.5g) small, sturdy colt; half-brother to Derby second Hot Grove (by Hotfoot); dam won over 1¼m and was a very useful hurdler; successful in 26-runner maiden race at Doncaster in June and minor event at Windsor following month; landed odds by 2 lengths from Silmira in latter; hung under pressure but ran creditably next time; stays 1½m; acts on soft going; blinkered and pulled hard early on final start. *F. J. Houghton.*

SALUD (GER) 2 br.c. Lombard 126–Shantou (Charlottown 127) (1980 8g) **84** p
first foal; dam, half-sister to several good winners in Germany, was one of best German 3-y-o fillies of 1976 when second in German 1,000 Guineas and Oaks; unquoted and in need of race, shaped encouragingly in 16-runner minor event at Newmarket in October, going on very nicely over last 2f to finish 3½ lengths fifth to Uppety and not being knocked about; certain to do much better over middle distances in 1981. *M. Stoute.*

SALUT 3 ch.f. Sallust 134–Ballynanty (King's Bench 132) (1979 NR 1980 –
7d 7g 8g 8g 10.6d 8d) 15,000Y; compact filly; half-sister to very smart 1972 2-y-o 5f and 7f winner Silver Birch (by Silver Shark) and 2 winners abroad; dam unraced half-sister to smart filly Pugnacity; fifth of 15 to Bint Africa in maiden race at Salisbury in June, first start and best effort; should stay 1m; retained 9,200 gns Newmarket Autumn Sales. *B. Hills.*

SALUZZO (FR) 3 b.c. Sallust 134–Siraf 85 (Alcide 136) (1979 6d* 6f² 6g **102**
1980 7fg* 8fg) lengthy, good sort; good walker and mover; beat dead-heaters Goldliner Game and Imperial Dilemma by a neck in handicap at Newmarket in May; well beaten in Britannia Stakes (Handicap) at Royal Ascot, only subsequent start; should be suited by 1m; acts on firm going and a soft surface; sold only 3,000 gns Newmarket Autumn Sales. *H. Cecil.*

SAMANTHA DANE 3 b.f. Brittany–Norma's Way 70 (Great White Way) **45**
(1979 6f 6f 6g 1980 10g 7fg³ 7fg 7f² 7f 8fg 7g 7g⁴ 7f) fair sort; plater; probably stays 1m; acts on firm going; has been tried in blinkers. *W. Bentley.*

SAMASHA 2 gr.f. Sharp Edge 123–Yofi (Articulate 121) (1980 5fg 5s 6fg) –
May 8; first foal; dam poor novice hurdler; beaten some way in maiden races. *S. Harris.*

SAMBISTA 3 b.c. The Brianstan 128–Premiette 87 (Con Brio 121) (1979 **73**
5d 5g 5fg³ 6fg⁴ 7fg² 7d² 1980 7f³ 10f 8fg² 6f 7.6f* 7d) strong colt; turns his off-hind out; beat Summer Soldier 2 lengths in maiden race at Lingfield in June; best form at up to 1m; seems to act on any going; sold 7,000 gns Ascot July Sales. *R. Laing.*

SAM CARMEDY 3 b.g. My Swallow 134–Watch Em Go (Hidden Treasure) **64**
(1979 6d⁴ 6f 5f 7fg 1980 9d² 8fg 8d 9.4g 8.2g³ 7g 10f 11d) robust gelding; quite a moderate maiden at his best; seems to stay 9f; acts on a soft surface; ran a bit freely in blinkers seventh start. *Denys Smith.*

SAME DATE 2 b.f. Mandamus 120–Catherine Rose 59 (Floribunda 136) (1980 **?**
6g 6fg 6fg 7g² 8fg² 6d 7d 6g) Mar 18; workmanlike filly; fifth reported foal; dam won over hurdles; ridden at overweight by apprentice J. Rowe on first 5 outings but for which she would have won a race; carried 7 lb over when beaten ¾ length by Ring Moylan in maiden race at Chepstow in September and 8 lb over when length second to Martelli in similar race at Beverley later in month; will stay 1¼m; acts on a firm surface and is possibly unsuited by a soft one; inconsistent and ran badly last 3 outings. *S. Mellor.*

SAMEDI 3 ch.c. Mon Fils 124–Crespinall 110 (Saint Crespin III 132) (1979 –
7f 6g 1980 8d 10.1s 8.2s) very tall, rangy colt; only plating class; should stay at least 1m. *R. Hannon.*

SAMI 2 b. or br.c. So Blessed 130–Slipperty 99 (Hardicanute 130) (1980 5f³) **65** p
Feb 11; 29,000Y; second foal; half-brother to 3-y-o middle-distance winner York Terrace (by Derring-Do); dam won over 5f at 2 yrs; favourite, started slowly and in circumstances ran creditable first race when 5½ lengths third of 18 to Highcroft in maiden event at Folkestone in September; will stay 1m. *P. M. Taylor.*

SAMMY BEAR 2 gr.f. Rupert Bear 105–Samba 69 (Sammy Davis 129) (1980 5fg 5d 6fg) May 7; 1,600Y; compact filly; second foal; dam won over 5f; behind in maiden races, 2 of them auction events; retained 480 gns Doncaster September Sales. *W. Bentley.* –

SAMMY SOUZA 6 b.g. Double-U-Jay 120–Robert's Carol 69 (Sing Sing 134) (1979 10.8fg 10fg 1980 6g) of little account. *Mrs R. Lomax.* –

SAN BENITO 3 ch.g. Spitsbergen 103–Pollytooky (Polic 126) (1979 5g 6fg^4 7fg 7f 8fg 1980 8fg 16g 8g) plain gelding; poor plater; has worn blinkers. *W. R. Williams.* –

SANDALAY 2 ch.c. Sandford Lad 133–No Delay 72 (Never Say Die 137) (1980 5f 6d 7g^2 7d 8fg 10s) Apr 23; 2,600Y; well-grown, rangy colt; brother to Sandford Lass, a fair performer at up to 1m, and half-brother to French 3-y-o middle-distance winner Sandina (by Sovereign Path); dam, suited by a distance of ground, is daughter of Nassau Stakes winner Cracker; 5 lengths second of 7 to Sula Bula in maiden race at York in July, best effort; will probably stay 1¼m (easy in market, got a long way behind early on but then ran on steadily to finish respectable sixth when tried over trip). *P. Rohan.* **80 ?**

SANDFORD BOY 4 ch.c. Sandford Lad 133–Shelby (Pall Mall 132) (1979 6s* 5d^2 5s^2 5fg 6fg^3 7g 7d 8f 8fg* 8g^3 6s 1980 6v^4 6f^4 8f 6f^3 7g 7d^4 6fg 7fg^2 7g* 8g^3 8g) lengthy, good sort; useful handicapper; made all when beating Hot Case by 2 lengths at Folkestone in August; creditable third to Seven Hearts in Playtex Trophy at Sandown later in month, better subsequent effort; stays 1m; acts on any going; blinkered fourth start (ran a bit freely); suitable mount for an amateur. *R. Price.* **100**

SANDFORD ROSE 3 ch.f. Sandford Lad 133–Montmartre Rose (Forli) (1979 5fg 6f^3 6s^3 6g^2 7g^3 7fg 8h^2 8fg* 1980 7f 8fg 10.2g 10g 8fg 10g) unfurnished filly; won seller at Warwick at 2 yrs; behind in handicaps in 1980; suited by 1m; acts on any going; blinkered fifth start; trained by W. Wightman first 2 outings. *J. Priday.* –

SANDHAVEN 3 ch.c. Sandford Lad 133–Phobos 65 (Relko 136) (1979 5s^4 5fg^2 6fg* 6g* 1980 7d 7fg 6g 6g 6fg 6d^3 6s) smallish colt; moderate handicapper; stays 6f; acts on a firm and a soft surface; blinkered nowadays; sold 4,000 gns Newmarket Autumn Sales. *J. Dunlop.* **83**

SAND HAWK 3 ch.c. Grundy 137–Parsimony 121 (Parthia 132) (1979 NR 1980 8fg 12g^2 10f^2 7g*) 264,000Y (the most expensive yearling sold at public auction in Great Britain or Ireland up to end of 1978); strong, quite attractive colt; has an enlarged near-hind fetlock joint; fourth foal; half-brother to two winners, namely very useful Petty Purse (by Petingo), successful at up to 7f, and smart sprinter Scarcely Blessed (by So Blessed); dam won July Cup and half-sister to Mummy's Pet and Arch Sculptor; kept on well to beat Alpaga (gave 6 lb) by 3 lengths in 8-runner minor event over 7f at Goodwood in August; seems to stay 1½m; acts on firm going; sweated up first start. *J. Tree.* **88**

SANDIA 3 gr.f. Saritamer 130–Graceful 83 (Grey Sovereign 128§) (1979 5d^3 5fg^2 5fg^4 6d 5fg* 1980 5h 6f^3 5f^4 6g*) quite attractive, leggy, good-bodied filly; beat Alpine Rocket a head in handicap at York in July; suited by 6f; blinkered final outing at 2 yrs and on third start; sold, covered by Lochnager, 3,700 gns Newmarket December Sales. *J. Etherington.* **79**

SANDICLIFFE 5 b.g. Frankincense 120–Pagan Princess (Primera 131) (1979 12.2fg 1980 12h) quite a moderate middle-distance performer in 1978; behind in amateur riders event at Thirsk in May, only second start since; acts on firm going. *V. Thompson.* –

SANDIVER 2 br.f. Deep Diver 134–Miss Sandman 86 (Manacle 123) (1980 5fg 5fg 6g 5f 6g) Mar 20; 3,500Y; lightly-made filly; first foal; dam 2-y-o 5f winner; bad plater; wears blinkers. *R. Hobson.* –

SANDIWOOD 2 b.f. Saritamer 130–Tamergene 100 (Tamerlane 128) (1980 5fg 5g 6f) Apr 16; half-sister to 2 winners, including 3-y-o sprinter Tarvie (by Swing Easy); dam won at up to 1¼m; in rear in maiden races and a seller. *D. Marks.* –

SANDOLI 2 gr.f. Sandford Lad 133–Greytino 91 (Fortino II 120) (1980 5.1g) Mar 13; 1,300F; small filly; half-sister to 1975 Irish 2-y-o 5f winner Fort Etna (by Be Friendly); dam won over 7f at 2 yrs; 20/1 when last of 11 to Garnish Island in maiden race at Yarmouth in August. *J. Winter.* –

SANDON BUOY 2 b.g. Windjammer (USA)–Kay's Hour 93 (Bleep-Bleep 134) (1980 5s 5g* 5fg 6g^3 6g^4) Apr 11; 5,000Y; lightly-made gelding who doesn't **97**

Harewood Handicap, York—Sandra's Secret (nearer camera) beats Firbeck a head

usually impress in paddock; half-brother to 1979 2-y-o 1m winner Pipul (by Pitskelly); dam won twice over 5f; always going very smoothly and had race won from 1½f out when winning 8-runner maiden event at Sandown in July by 5 lengths from Banoco; also ran well when in frame in nurseries at Newmarket in October; stays 6f. *R. Armstrong.*

SANDRA'S SECRET 3 b.f. Most Secret 119–Grovenka (Kibenka 119) (1979 **88**
5s 5s 5g 5d^4 5v^4 5fg^4 5fg 5fg 5h 5g^3 6g^3 1980 6f 6f^3 6f 5fg* 5fg^2 5s* 5g* 5g 5g 5fg 5d* 5f 5.6g 5g^2 5d* 5v) leggy, narrow filly; moderate plater at 2 yrs; showed much improved form in 1980, winning minor race at Stockton and handicaps at Stockton again, Doncaster, York (Harewood Handicap) and Warwick; best at 5f; probably acts on any going; blinkered twice at 2 yrs; ridden for 4 successes by apprentice N. Connorton. *R. Whitaker.*

SANHEDRIN (FR) 3 ch.g. Satingo 129–India (Hautain 128) (1979 5.8g 6f **59**
7fg^3 7d 8fg^3 8s^4 1980 10.1d 12d^3 12s) fair sort; poor maiden; possibly stays 1½m; probably acts on any going; sweated up on fifth start at 2 yrs; pulled hard early on second outing. *G. Balding.*

SAN JOSE 2 b.f. Netherkelly 112–Settebello (Hul a Hul 124) (1980 5g^2 5g^4 7fg **55**
6d 6s) May 14; very small, light-framed filly; first foal; dam never ran; 2 lengths second of 5 to Sir Jester in poor seller at Hamilton in July and will be hard pressed to win; tailed off over 7f. *Peter Taylor.*

SANSKRITIK (USA) 4 b.g. Dynastic (USA)–Say Grace (Round Table) (1979 **—**
10d 11.7g 16d 14fg^4 14fg 12fg 11.7h^4 15.5g^4 16f^3 15.5fg 12s 1980 16fg) quite attractive, rangy gelding; stays 2m; acts on firm going; sometimes blinkered; sometimes sweats up; not one to trust; sold 1,600gns Newmarket Autumn Sales. *J. Benstead.*

SANT ANGELO 10 ch.g. Twilight Alley 133–Snap 106 (Big Game) (1979 18d **—**
12g 15s 1980 18d 12f) poor plater; stayed well; dead. *P. Rohan.*

SANTELLA ASCOT 2 b.c. Furry Glen 121–Good Court (Takawalk II 125) **80**
(1980 6d 7g^4 7g 7fg 8d 8s* 10v) Mar 26; 4,500F, 4,000Y; strong, well-made colt;

first produce; dam poor Irish maiden; ran best race for some time when well-backed 7/1-shot for 21-runner seller at Newmarket in October, winning by a length from Piping Queen; sold out of G. Harwood's stable 4,400 gns afterwards; subsequently finished last of 10 in Criterium de Saint-Cloud in November behind The Wonder but wasn't disgraced and probably stays 1¼m; revels in the mud. *E. Lellouche, France.*

SANTELLAS 2 b.c. Arch Sculptor 123–Stop Thinking (Divine Gift 127) (1980 7g4) Mar 23; 9,200Y; well-grown, attractive colt; second foal; half-brother to 1979 2-y-o 5f winner Andyjon (by Virginia Boy); dam never ran; 20/1 and backward, shaped promisingly when 5½ lengths fourth of 9 to Button Top in £2,300 race at Newmarket in October, making good progress to join leaders 2f out but then running green and not being knocked about when his chance had gone; has scope and looks sure to do better at 3 yrs. *G. Harwood.* **70** p

SANU 2 b.c. Steel Heart 128–Light Link 99 (Tudor Music 131) (1980 5d 5g 5d 6g2 5g* 5g* 5g* 6fg4 5fg) Feb 26; neat colt; second foal; closely related to very useful 3-y-o sprinter Hanu (by Hot Spark); dam won over 5f and 6f at 2 yrs; improved rapidly in August, winning maiden race at Salisbury, minor event at Goodwood and nursery at Sandown; gave weight all round when gaining last 2 wins, at Sandown quickening nicely in final furlong to score by 1½ lengths from Little Starchy; carried 8-lb penalty when creditable 2½ lengths fourth of 13 to Airship in £3,700 nursery at Kempton in September; stays 6f; acts on a firm surface. *A. Breasley.* **101**

SARACEN PRINCE 4 b.g. Crowned Prince 128–Carcharus 80 (Silver Shark 129) (1979 8d3 10.5s 8d 12g 1980 10fg 12g) small gelding; good mover; stays 1m; blinkered and refused to race once at 3 yrs. *P. Kelleway.* **— §**

SARAGUSA 8 ch.g. Aggressor 130–Sugar Sugar (Midsummer Night II 117) (1979 NR 1980 16f) poor staying handicapper on flat; sometimes wears blinkers; bandaged only outing of 1980. *H. Westbrook.* **—**

SARAH BERNHARDT 2 ch.f. Ballymore 123–Song of Westmeath (Golden Horus 123) (1980 7g) May 6; 5,200F; second living produce; dam useful 5f and 6f winner at 2 yrs in Ireland; 33/1 when down the field behind stable-companion Full of Reason in 26-runner maiden race at Newmarket in October. *L. Cumani.* **—**

SARAH PAUL 5 b.m. Crooner 119–Cadera (Primera 131) (1979 NR 1980 10d 12g) seems useless. *P. Kearney.* **—**

SARATOGA CHIP (USA) 2 b.f. Plenty Old–Saratoga Gal (Royal Orbit) (1980 7g) neat, lightly-made filly; first foal; dam won claiming races over 6f and 1m in USA; 50/1 when in rear in 18-runner maiden race won by Park Place at Yarmouth in September. *R. Sheather.* **—**

SARDINE 2 br.f. Saritamer 130–Rose Arbour 106 (Pall Mall 132) (1980 5g2 5f 6f 6s 6g 7g 6fg 5g4 6g) Feb 15; 8,200Y; lengthy filly; not a good mover in her slower paces; half-sister to 3 winners, including fairly useful 1979 staying 2-y-o Ben Elid (by Upper Case); dam stayed 1m; blinkered for only time, showed improved form to finish very close fourth of 19 to Advertrack in maiden race at Folkestone in October; seems not to stay 6f; swerved violently at start on second outing and was slowly away on third. *A. Ingham.* **74**

SARI DANCER 3 b.g. Saritamer 130–Latin Verses (Appiani II 128) (1979 5g 5s 5f 5fg 5f 5g 7f 1980 9.4g 10.1f) lightly-made gelding; bad plater; sometimes wore blinkers; dead. *M. Bradley.* **—**

SARIFFE 3 gr.c. Saritamer 130–Ma Griffe (Indian Ruler 89) (1979 5d* 1980 6v* 6fg 6d 6d* 7g 7s 7.2d 6s) tall, well-made colt; fair handicapper; ½-length winner at Stockton in March (from Running Rocket) and Newcastle in June (beat Swizzle); has won only at up to 6f but gave impression on sixth start that he will be well suited by 1m; needs some give in the ground; blinkered final start; sold 2,100 gns Newmarket Autumn Sales. *J. W. Watts.* **89**

SARIGUE 3 gr.f. Saritamer 130–Gwendoline 76 (Crepello 136) (1979 5d 5g2 5f2 5s4 5g* 1980 5fg* 5fg 5f 5fg 5s2 5fg) useful-looking, slightly hollow-backed filly; quite a moderate handicapper; won at Newbury in April by 2 lengths from Copper Beeches; will be suited by 6f; acts on any going; ran moderately final start. *P. Walwyn.* **75**

SARMENTUM 3 b.f. Porto Bello 118–Sonseeahray 67 (March Past 124) (1979 NR 1980 11d 12f) light-framed filly; first foal; dam seemed best at sprint distances; behind in maiden races at Newbury and Lingfield in the summer; unlikely to stay middle distances. *M. Masson.* **—**

SARUS 4 b.f. Amber Rama 133–Life Story 65 (Only for Life 126) (1979 6g 7f2 5f2 6g 6g4 7g 1980 7d 7v 7.2d 9fg 10h* 10g 10g 12fg4) big, strong filly; won handicap at Chepstow in May by a head from Luz Bay; stays 1½m; acts on hard going; has run creditably in blinkers. *D. H. Jones.* **59**

SASHKA 3 b.f. Levmoss 133–Sayraf (Ragusa 137) (1979 NR 1980 10.2g2 10s2 10fg* 10g2 8g 8d2) small, unfurnished filly; first living foal; dam won over 1m in France; beat a modest collection of animals with exceptional ease in 10-runner maiden race at Yarmouth in August; runner-up in similar events and minor races on 4 other occasions; will stay 1½m; probably acts on any going; hung violently left second start. *M. Stoute.* **84**

SASH OF GOLD 4 ch.g. Sheshoon 132–More Sunshine (Continuation 120) (1979 11.7g 12g 12f 11.7fg 1980 12.2s 12fg 10.1g 10g3) plating-class maiden; third in claiming race at Brighton in August; will probably stay beyond 1½m; sometimes wears blinkers; sold 2,600 gns Ascot September Sales. *I. Wardle.* **54**

SASS 2 ch.c. Sassafras 135–Sister Agnes 90 (St Paddy 133) (1980 7g 8fg) Apr 30; 5,800F, 8,400Y; rangy colt; half-brother to 3 minor winners; dam sprinter and daughter of very smart sprinter Seph; 20/1, stayed on when remote eighth of 23 to Shergar in minor event at Newbury in September; dwelt first outing. *P. Kelleway.* **–**

SATILLA (FR) 3 br.f. Targowice 130–Saratoga (Snob 130) (1979 5.5g* 1980 9g* 10fg* 12g4 10g4 13g3 12.5g* 12f2 12f 12s3 12s) light-framed French filly; half-sister to 6 winners; dam won at up to 1½m in France; began her 3-y-o career in modest company and won at Rouen in April and Longchamp in May; claimed out of Mme C. Head's stable for 83,360 francs (approx £8,300) after winning a claiming race on latter course; much improved in second half of season, winning handicap at Deauville in August and finishing excellent 1½ lengths second to Prince Bee (gave 7 lb) in Group 3 Prix Niel at Longchamp in September; not disgraced on next 2 outings at Longchamp in October, finishing tenth of 20 to Detroit in Prix de l'Arc de Triomphe and 3 lengths third of 14 to En Calcat in Prix du Conseil de Paris; stays 13f; acts on any going; moved moderately to post eighth start. *J. Gobel, France.* **118**

SATINANDA 2 ch.f. Leander 119–Super Satin (Lord of Verona 120) (1980 5v 5fg* 5f 5fg 5g) Apr 28; strong, workmanlike filly; second foal; dam placed over hurdles; won 5-runner minor event at Edinburgh in April by a head from Consent, in rear on other outings and is no better than a plater; blinkered final start. *Denys Smith.* **56**

SATIN BOX 3 ch.f. Jukebox 120–Satina 83 (Pall Mall 132) (1979 NR 1980 11fg2 8.5f3 8s 10fg2 9s 9d) plain, workmanlike filly; second foal; half-sister to 1¾m winner Chetinkaya (by Ragstone); dam, placed at up to 1m, is daughter of Irish 1,000 Guineas winner Black Satin; placed in maiden races; needs further than 1m and stays 11f; needs top-of-the-ground conditions; blinkered final start. *B. Hanbury.* **73**

SATIN GRANGE 2 br.c. Satingo 129–Court Circular (Ambiorix 130) (1980 5fg 5d3 6d2 6g3 6g3 6d 6d) Apr 22; 5,800Y; quite attractive colt who carries plenty of condition; half-brother to winners in France and Belgium; dam won at up to 7f in USA; placed in maiden races, on final occasion finishing 2½ lengths third of 8 to Melon Patch at Nottingham in September; blinkered when seventh of 17 to Mrs Palmer in nursery at Haydock on next outing; needs further than 6f and will stay at least 1m; trained by C. Bewicke first 3 outings. *B. Hobbs.* **84**

SATURNUS 7 ch.h. Dike–Shoofly 83 (Skymaster 126) (1979 NR 1980 11.7fg 10h 10f 12fg 12d) poor middle-distance handicapper nowadays; probably acts on any going; has been tried in blinkers. *Mrs N. Kennedy.* **–**

SAUCEY DEVIL 2 br.c. Ampney Prince 96–Sing Saucey (Hard Sauce 131) (1980 5fg) Mar 15; fourth foal; dam of little account; carried wide at start when always behind in 15-runner maiden race won by Arndean at Leicester in May; dead. *A. Jarvis.* **–**

SAUCY DOVE 8 b.m. Saucy Kit 76–Red Dove (All Red 110) (1979 NR 1980 14.7f) useful hurdler; tailed off in amateur riders race at Redcar in May, first outing on flat. *G. Price.* **–**

SAUCY PRINCE 8 gr.g. Prince Hansel 118–Kali Maere (Rise 'N Shine II) (1979 NR 1980 12.3d 12.2f) strong gelding; of little account. *C. Booth.* **–**

SAUCY SERGENT 3 b.g. Home Guard 129–Kiss Me 82 (Tamerlane 128) (1979 7f 7.2g 1980 6s 6f 7fg 8fg 6fg* 8f 8d 7.6g 9g 10g 10fg* 8f3 10g3 8.2d 8fg3 10d4 10.2v3) compact gelding; won seller at Leicester in May (bought in 1,100 gns) **63**

and handicap at Newmarket in August (apprentice ridden); stays 1¼m; goes well on firm ground; sometimes blinkered but is just as effective without; unruly in paddock on reappearance. *R. Hollinshead.*

SAULANN 2 b. or br.c. Saulingo 122–Lucerne 76 (Gun Shot) (1980 5d⁴ 5fg⁴ 5f² 5g* 5g² 5d² 6g⁴ 6s⁴ 6s 6s) Mar 17; 5,400F; compact colt; half-brother to 3 winners, including Irish 1m winner Captain Birdseye (by Windjammer); dam won at up to 11f; won 5-runner minor event at Hamilton in July by a length from Melingo; ran creditably in several nurseries afterwards but was below best final start; stays 6f; suited by some give in the ground *W. H. H. Williams.* **82**

SAULINGDALE 2 b.c. Saulingo 122–Hibernia III 120 (Masetto) (1980 6f 7f 8g 7g 7v³) July 4; 1,600Y; small colt; half-brother to 2 winners, notably very useful 6f to 1½m winner Hibernian (by Hethersett); dam won 1963 Irish Guinness Oaks; ran well in nurseries on last 2 starts, final occasion when 6 lengths third of 20 to Supreme Fjord at Doncaster in November; not sure to stay 1m; well suited by the mud. *W. Elsey.* **78**

SAULONIKA 3 b.f. Saulingo 122–Lauso Girl 67 (Lauso) (1979 5g* 5fg 6f 6g 6s 1980 7.2g 8d 7.6g) neat, compact filly; has shown no form since 1979; should stay at least 6f. *C. Booth.* **–**

SAUL'S SON 4 b.g. Saulingo 122–Buggles 66 (Kelly 122) (1979 5v⁴ 5g 5h⁴ 5d 1980 5f 5fg 5fg) leggy gelding; has been tubed; poor sprint handicapper; probably acts on any going; has been tried in blinkers; has run respectably for an apprentice. *W. C. Watts.* **–**

SAUNA 3 br.f. Saulingo 122–Samosata 75 (Super Sam 124) (1979 5v 5d 5d³ 5g 7g 8g 6s 1980 6fg 8d 10.1s) big filly; plater; form only at 5f; blinkered last 2 outings in 1979; sold 800 gns Ascot July Sales. *P. Cundell.* **–**

SAUNA TIME (USA) 4 b.f. Cougar II–Tea Time (Court Martial) (1979 8s 11fg 12f 12f 12.2fg³ 10h² 12.2s² 10g* 1980 12fg 12fg 12.2fg) lightly-made filly; won poor seller at Redcar in 1979; well beaten in handicaps in 1980; stays 1½m; acts on any going. *W. Haigh.* **–**

SAUNDERTON 2 b.f. Saulingo 122–Anya (Alcide 136) (1980 6g 6d⁴ 7fg) May 5; 2,000F; strong filly; half-sister to a winning plater; dam well behind in maiden races; ran respectably in sellers at Warwick and Brighton in June, beaten 3½ lengths by Tricky Rhythm in £2,100 race on latter track; runs as though 7f will suit her (had stiff task when tried at trip). *J. Holt.* **51**

SAUSOLITO 2 br.c. Relko 136–Rosia Steps 98 (Red Pins 114) (1980 5f 6d⁴ 6d² 7fg* 7s³ 8g 7d) Mar 29; 4,000Y; well-grown, useful sort; half-brother to a winning plater; dam won over 5f and 7f at 2 yrs; favourite when winning 8-runner maiden race at Ayr in July by 3 lengths from Lord Ever-So-Sure; had previously battled on gamely when going down by a neck to Another Realm in 5-runner Chesters Stakes at Newcastle but was soundly beaten when third of 4 to Engulf in Heronslea Stakes at Ayr in August; should be well suited by 1m; seems to act on any going; had stiff tasks when last on last 2 outings, finishing tailed off on final one. *M. H. Easterby.* **86**

SAUVAGE 2 b.c. Wolver Hollow 126–Belle Affaire 96 (Elopement 125) (1980 7fg² 7f³ 7g) Apr 1; strong, good-bodied colt; good mover; closely related to very useful 6f to 1m filly Miss Paris, and half-brother to several winners, including useful 6f to 1m winner Casino Royale (by Petingo); dam a miler; looked likely winner until lack of experience and peak fitness told in final furlong when excellent 1½ lengths second of 22 to Clear Verdict in maiden race at Newmarket in August; beaten favourite on both outings afterwards, finishing 6½ lengths third of 5 to Sula Bula when odds on for valuable race at York and running badly when in rear behind Junta in minor event at Goodwood; should stay 1m; disappointing. *M. Stoute.* **91**

SAVAGE SALLY 2 br.f. Owen Anthony 102–Buttonback 73 (Fleece 114) (1980 5g) Mar 11; rangy filly; third foal; dam won 7.2f seller at 2 yrs; unquoted, close up 3f when last of 14 to Palumba in maiden race at Newbury in June; sold 500 gns Ascot July Sales. *R. Smyth.* **–**

SAVILE PARK 2 b.g. Reformed Character 107–Angel's Halo (Aureole 132) (1980 6fg 8d*) Apr 15; 2,000F; neat gelding; fourth living foal; half-brother to Wollop (by Wolver Hollow), successful over 1¼m, and to a winning plater; dam fairly useful winner over 6f in Ireland at 2 yrs; 20/1 and having first race for 2 months, got up close home to win 11-runner maiden event at Edinburgh in September by short head from Sage King; will be suited by middle distances; trained by Denys Smith first outing. *M. H. Easterby.* **75**

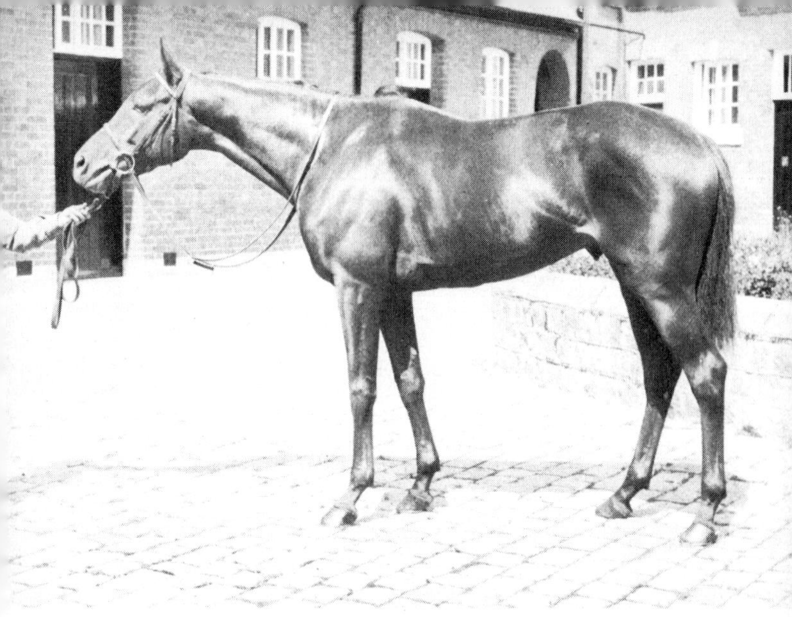

Mr J. I. Morrison's "Saviour"

SAVILLE ROW 3 b.c. Habitat 134–Front Row 111 (Epaulette 125) (1979 NR 1980 8fg 7f* 8g) rangy colt with plenty of scope; half-brother to several winners, including smart miler Long Row (by Linacre); dam won Irish 1,000 Guineas; ran on strongly to beat Highest Bidder 4 lengths in minor race at Newmarket in May; not seen out after running moderately in £2,800 race at Newbury following month; stays 1m; acts on firm going. *H. Cecil.* **90**

SAVIOUR 3 b.c. Blakeney 126–Set Free 90 (Worden II 129) (1979 NR 1980 11fg* 12g² 12d⁴ 12g³ 14.6g⁴) attractive, rather lightly-built colt; good mover; brother to St Leger winner Julio Mariner and Oaks and Irish Guinness Oaks winner Juliette Marny, and half-brother to Oaks winner Scintillate (by Sparkler); dam, half-sister to 1963 1,000 Guineas and Oaks runner-up Spree, won at 1m; comfortably beat Sentry Duty 2 lengths in 20-runner maiden race at Newbury in April; in frame afterwards in King Edward VII Stakes at Royal Ascot (¾-length second to Light Cavalry), Princess of Wales's Stakes at Newmarket, Great Voltigeur Stakes at York (7 lengths third of 5 to Prince Bee) and St Leger at Doncaster (blinkered when 12 lengths fourth of 7 to Light Cavalry); should stay 1¾m; best form on a sound surface; sent to Far East. *J. Tree.* **118**

SAXON DAWN 3 b.f. Mins Baby 81–Honey Gift (Heswall Honey 120) (1979 6s 7fg 1980 10s) big filly; in rear in varied company. *G. Beeson.* —

SAYFARI 2 b.g. Sayfar 116–Flying Nun 66 (Welsh Abbot 131) (1980 7g 7fg 7fg) Jan 30; compact, good-topped gelding; half-brother to 6f and 1m winner Welch Soldier (by Easter Island); dam won over 5f at 2 yrs; prominent 5f when 6½ lengths fifth of 9 to The Thatcher in minor event at Yarmouth in August, second outing; will be suited by 1¼m. *Sir Mark Prescott.* **68**

SAYFAR'S GREY 2 gr. or ro.c. Sayfar 116–Antigua III (Worden II 129) (1980 5fg) May 10; half-brother to a winning chaser; dam won 3 minor races at around 1½m in France; 14/1, started slowly when tailed-off last of 8 to Steel Garrison in minor event at Leicester in May. *D. Leslie.* —

SAY PRIMULA 2 ch.c. Hotfoot 126–Renoir Picture 90 (Relko 136) (1980 8s²) Apr 6; 16,000Y; lengthy colt; half-brother to 2 minor winners; dam stayed **84** p

1¼m; 16/1 and not fully wound up, not given an unnecessarily hard time when it was clear he couldn't win and went down by 2 lengths to Irish Heart in 19-runner minor event at Stockton in October; will be suited by 1¼m+; a promising first effort by a colt who should win races in the North at 3 yrs. *J. W. Watts.*

SAYYAF 3 b.c. Habitat 134–Pavello 94 (Crepello 136) (1979 6f $7g^2$ $6g^3$ 6fg* **121**
$6fg^4$ 1980 7d $5fg^4$ $5fg^2$ 6f* 6fg* $6fg^2$ 6d $5fg^4$ $6g^4$ 5g* $6fg^4$)
Scarcely a year goes by without trainer O'Gorman's producing a tough, genuine three-year-old sprinter, and in 1980 Sayyaf was as good a servant to his stable as Manor Farm Boy and Abdu had been before him. Sayyaf is similar to Abdu, about 10 lb below top class but lacking nothing in consistency. A useful handicapper early in the year, he developed into a colt capable of running with credit against the leading sprinters and in an arduous season he ran his only disappointing race when the ground came up soft in the William Hill July Cup.

Sayyaf (b.c. 1977)	Habitat (b 1966)	Sir Gaylord (b 1959)	Turn-to
			Somethingroyal
		Little Hut (b 1952)	Occupy
			Savage Beauty
	Pavello (ch 1972)	Crepello (ch 1954)	Donatello II
			Crepuscule
		Piave (b 1965)	Alcide
			Peseta II

Prior to the five-furlong Scarbrough Stakes at Doncaster in September, Sayyaf had run his best races at six furlongs, winning the Great Eastern Handicap at Newmarket by a head from Premier Rose, making virtually all to account for Runnett, who received 3 lb, by a neck in the Gus Demmy Memorial Stakes at Haydock, going down by three quarters of a length to Taufan, giving him 10 lb, in the Asda Trophy at Thirsk and coming in a creditable fourth to Moorestyle in the Vernons Sprint Cup at Haydock. The manner in which he was outpaced in the closing stages of the King George Stakes at Goodwood, finishing fourth, suggested that the minimum trip was too sharp for him and his prospects of beating Sharpo at levels at Doncaster didn't appear bright. With Sharpo odds on, Sayyaf was an easy-to-back third favourite in the five-runner field that was completed by the useful handicapper Epsom Imp, Lightning Label and Tissue

Gus Demmy Memorial Stakes, Haydock—Sayyaf is driven out to hold Runnett

Mr Moufid F. Dabaghi's "Sayyaf"

Paper. For some unknown reason Sharpo ran below form, but even so Sayyaf's performance was a revelation and it conclusively proved that on a galloping track he is as effective at five furlongs as six. Breaking smartly, he soon gained a clear lead which enabled him to cross over to the stand rail; running on strongly, he was in no danger from halfway and won, ridden right out, by four lengths from Sharpo with Epsom Imp a head away third. On his only subsequent start Sayyaf was beaten a length and a half into fourth behind Sovereign Rose in the Diadem Stakes at Ascot after being close up all the way.

Sayyaf is the first foal of the lightly-raced one-mile winner Pavello; he is small, though quite attractive. Pavello is one of five winners out of Piave, the best of them Rymer who showed plenty of ability over middle distances but managed to win no more than two of his thirty races, including the Brigadier Gerard Stakes. Piave won at a mile and a quarter in France and is a half-sister to numerous winners in England, France and Germany, notably the 1967 Oaks winner Pia. Though his breeding suggests he could stay further than seven furlongs, a trip that wasn't beyond him at two, Sayyaf is evidently best at sprint distances nowadays. A 21,000-guinea yearling, he acts particularly well on top-of-the-ground. *W. O'Gorman.*

SCAMPER 4 b.f. Abwah 118–Miss Rocket 88 (Roan Rocket 128) (1979 10.1d^4 11.7g^3 12fg^3 14f^2 14g* 13g 1980 16f 11.7g) strong filly; won amateur riders event at Haydock as a 3-y-o; well beaten in 1980; stays $1\frac{3}{4}$m; acts on firm going. *G. Kindersley.* —

SCARCITY 4 gr.f. Rarity 129–Lindera 71 (Linacre 133) (1979 NR 1980 10.8f 8fg 7h 8g 14.6fg 9d 8h^4 8g) poor plater; blinkered once at 2 yrs. *S. Mellor.* —

SCARLET TOWN 2 b.c. Town Crier 119–Sindo 91 (Derring-Do 131) (1980 5d* (dis) 5f 5fg^4 6s^2 6g^3 5g 6d 5s^4 6g 6s) Feb 19; lightly-made, quite attractive colt; **76**

Mrs Archie Kidd's "Scarrowmanwick"

good mover; second foal; closely related to 3-y-o 1m seller winner Keeps Going Right (by Warpath); dam won over 5f at 2 yrs; hampered 2 opponents before drawing away to win maiden race at Haydock in April by 4 lengths from Cyclonic and was disqualified; in frame subsequently in similar events, and in nursery won by Katysue at Haydock in October; needs further than 5f; not at his best on a firm surface and acts well on soft ground; possibly needs a galloping course. *R. Hollinshead.*

SCARROWMANWICK 2 b.c. Tickled Pink 114–Almadena 73 (Dairialatan 111) **99**
(1980 5.8f 5g^3 6g^4 6fg^2 6f* 6f* 6d) May 7; quite a useful sort; good walker; second foal; dam placed at 2 yrs; gained a well-deserved victory when getting up close home to win 18-runner minor event at Lingfield in September by a neck from Charm To Spare; picked up a valuable prize when putting in a strong late run to beat Amorous $\frac{3}{4}$ length in Martini Trophy (Nursery) at Newmarket the following month; will stay 7f; acts well on firm going (hampered at start on only outing on a soft surface); genuine and consistent. *N. Vigors.*

SCHAPINGEN 3 gr.f. Sharp Edge 123–Lucy Jane (Palestine 133) (1979 7fg 7g —
8f 1980 10fg) neat filly; little worthwhile form in varied company, including selling; sold to D. Ringer 680 gns Newmarket Autumn Sales. *G. Pritchard-Gordon.*

SCHILLER 2 b.g. Lorenzaccio 130–Pahlavi Line 65 (Young Emperor 133) **89**
(1980 6fg 7g* 7g^3 8f) Mar 14; 8,400Y; good-looking gelding; second foal; dam placed at 1$\frac{1}{4}$m; made all and held on very gamely under hard riding when beating Nimblemoss a neck in 9-runner maiden event at Sandown in July; put up better subsequent effort when length third of 7 to Principal Dancer at odds on in minor race at Sandown in August; will stay 1$\frac{1}{4}$m; suited by some give in the ground; gelded after final outing; sent to Hong Kong. *R. Price.*

SCHOLAR'S RING 4 b.g. Continuation 120–Schull (Yorick II 127) (1979 7g^2 **70**
8g^4 7.6v 7f 5g^4 8.2g^4 8fg 8f 1980 8d 7v 12h 14.7f* 9f 12g 10f 8d) strong gelding;

beaten 1½ lengths by Cisto (pair clear) in amateur riders race at Redcar in May; subsequently promoted to first when it was found Cisto was not qualified; ran poorly afterwards; seems to stay well; probably acts on any going except heavy; has worn blinkers; ran away with his jockey on one occasion. *P. Haslam.*

SCHUMANN 5 gr.g. Hotfoot 126–Tanara 93 (Romulus 129) (1979 10s 10s 10.5f 12g4 12fg 12fg 1980 12d) useful-looking gelding; good walker; middle-distance handicapper; possibly needs some give in the ground; wears blinkers nowadays; disappointing. *M. H. Easterby.* —

SCHWARZENBERG 2 ch.c. Redundant 120–Authors Correction 68 (Narrator 127) (1980 7fg) May 5; strong, compact, good-bodied colt; half-brother to middle-distance winner Grade Well (by Derring-Do); dam won 17f amateur riders event; 12/1, in need of race and coltish in paddock, always in rear when eleventh of 12 to Smuggle in seller at Redcar in July. *C. Brittain.* —

SCHWEPPES FOREVER 3 b.f. Lord Gayle 124—Diamonds For Ever (Ionian 128) (1979 6fg 6fg* 7g* 8f2 1980 7fg 8g2 7g3) lengthy filly; excellent mover; very useful at 2 yrs when winning 2 good-class races, St Catherine's Stakes at Newbury and Waterford Candelabra Stakes at Ascot; didn't run up to her best in 1980, finishing fifth in £7,300 race at Goodwood in July, 2 lengths second to Rosia Bay in 4-runner £3,600 event at Sandown in August and over 10 lengths third to Premier Rose in 5-runner £2,900 race at Goodwood in September; stays 1m; yet to race on a soft surface. *R. Price.* **94**

SCIGUETA 3 b.f. Prince Tenderfoot 126–Coming-Of-Age 93 (Majority Blue 126) (1979 6fg 1980 7f3 8fg 7g2 8g) attractive, shapely filly; good mover; ran on very strongly in last 2f when just over 1½ lengths third of 11 to Evita in Ladbrokes Nell Gwyn Stakes at Newmarket in April; ¾-length second to Princess Matilda in maiden race at Leicester in July; in rear in 1,000 Guineas at Newmarket in between; will stay 1¼m; broke blood vessel and was pulled up final start. *L. Cumani.* **100**

SCINTILLATING AIR 2 b.c. Sparkler 130–Chantal 74 (Charlottesville 135) (1980 5f 5fg3 6f4 6fg 7d* 7fg3 7d*) Apr 13; 4,700F, 16,000Y; strong, burly sort; third foal; dam placed twice over 1¼m; showed improved form when ridden with more restraint, winning maiden race at Newmarket in July and getting up close home to beat Sula Bula ½ length in £4,200 nursery at York the following month; acquitted himself well in 6-runner Lanson Champagne Stakes at Goodwood in between, staying on steadily to finish 1¾ lengths third to Church Parade; will stay 1¼m; acts on a firm and a soft surface. *B. Hobbs.* **106**

SCIROCCO 2 b.c. Welsh Saint 126–Till 85 (Hook Money 124) (1980 5fg 5f4(dis) 6fg 5fg4) Mar 3; 2,000F, 3,000Y; useful-looking colt; brother to winning sprinter Imari, and half-brother to a winner in Norway; dam won at 1m; prominent most of way on first 2 outings, on second being disqualified because rider failed to weigh in after finishing 10 lengths fourth of 8 to Red Russet in £2,100 event at Kempton in May; not seen out again until September when in rear at Salisbury and Ascot; should stay 6f. *D. Sasse.* **56**

SCORE 7 b.g. Dike–Opening Chorus 81 (Tudor Minstrel 144) (1979 15.5d* 16v2 15.5g2 1980 17.1fg 15d) staying handicapper; acts on any going; used to wear blinkers. *G. Blum.* —

SCORPIO (FR) 4 b.c. Sir Gaylord–Zambara 82 (Mossborough 126) (1979 12d* 12fg* 12g2 12f4 12.5d* 14.6f 12v* 1980 12g* 12g* 12fg* 12.5d) **127**

It was no surprise that Scorpio improved on his good record as a three-year-old. A big, handsome, late-developing sort who didn't race as a two-year-old, he had won four races as a three-year-old, showing he could act on any going, and romping home in the Group 1 Gran Premio del Jockey Club at San Siro on his final outing. His wins as a four-year-old weren't, however, gained over the longer distances that we thought might well have suited him; his trainer evidently felt that Scorpio found the distance too far for him when fifth in the St Leger and all his races in 1980 were at around a mile and a half.

Scorpio had a very short season—he wasn't seen out after disappointing when favourite for the Grand Prix de Saint-Cloud early in July—but it was nevertheless a most productive one. He won the Prix d'Hedouville at Longchamp in April on his reappearance in good style by four lengths from Monsieur Dagobert (the St Leger first and second, Son Of Love and Soleil Noir, finished behind him); and the following month he won the Grand Prix d'Evry a shade comfortably by a short neck from Gain with the good filly Dunette a further

Grand Prix d'Evry—Scorpio wins from Gain with Dunette third

two lengths away in third. Scorpio reportedly suffered from a minor liver problem afterwards but had recovered by Royal Ascot where he won his third successive race, the Hardwicke Stakes. Scorpio was always going well in the Hardwicke and moved past Son Fils into the lead soon after the turn. He couldn't shake off his opponents in the straight but held on gamely under strong riding by half a length from More Light, with Noelino and the unlucky-in-running Main Reef right behind in third and fourth. His win was the first by a French-trained runner at Royal Ascot for two years and only the second since his half-brother Sagaro won his last Gold Cup in 1977.

Scorpio was in such good form at this point that his poor showing in the Grand Prix de Saint-Cloud is hard to account for. He reportedly stumbled leaving the stalls but, unless he injured himself, this in itself doesn't excuse him, for he was able to move smoothly up to challenge on the home turn before dropping back to last behind the dead-heaters Dunette and Shakapour. Possibly the explanation is that Scorpio didn't get over his hardish race in the Hardwicke Stakes in the sixteen days between the two events. Whatever the reason, Scorpio wasn't persevered with and shortly afterwards he was syndicated for stud by the BBA.

Scorpio (Fr) (b.c. 1976)	Sir Gaylord (b 1959)	Turn-to (b 1951)	Royal Charger
			Source Sucree
		Somethingroyal (b 1952)	Princequillo
			Imperatrice
	Zambara (b 1966)	Mossborough (ch 1947)	Nearco
			All Moonshine
		Grischuna (b 1959)	Ratification
			Mountain Path

Scorpio will stand alongside Jaazeiro at the Ballylinch Stud, County Kilkenny, where his fee will be £4,500 with the October 1st concession. His sire, the much-travelled Sir Gaylord, has been an important influence on European racing and has been represented by such notable colts as Sir Ivor, Habitat and Lord Gayle, all successful stallions themselves. The dam Zambara, who produced only four living foals before her death in 1980, had a much better record as a broodmare than most of those with twice as many offspring. Sagaro (by Espresso) won three consecutive Gold Cups and was also successful in the Prix du Cadran and the Grand Prix de Paris; her second foal Amarena (by Aureole) won a nine-furlong race in Ireland; her fourth foal Mariella, a full sister to Scorpio, was a very smart three-year-old filly in 1980, winner of three races including the Prix de Royallieu and the Premio Roma. Zambara herself won the Wood Ditton Stakes and was a half-sister to the good stayer Chicago and the very smart 1977 French two-year-old Tarona. The next dam Grischuna, useful at her best, was a half-sister to Sovereign Path. *F. Boutin, France.*

SCOT BENNETT 2 b.c. Tarboosh–Hell's Mistress (Skymaster 126) (1980 6s 7fg) Mar 2; 6,800Y; second foal; dam once-raced half-sister to 2,000 Guineas third Thieving Demon; behind in large fields of maidens at Nottingham and Warwick in August. *C. Brittain.* –

SCOTSEZO 3 br.c. Scottish Rifle 127–Spice Berry 63 (Tutankhamen) (1979 NR 1980 10s 8fg 8fg 7f^4 8g* 8fg 8d^4 8fg 7.6d 8g) 7,200F, 7,800Y; well-made colt; good mover; sixth foal; dam half-sister to smart animals Red Berry and Big Bead; brought wide in straight when staying on well to win maiden race at Pontefract in June; well beaten in valuable seller final outing; should stay beyond 1m; usually blinkered; ran moderately sixth start and looked ungenuine on eighth; sold 4,600 gns Newmarket Autumn Sales. *C. Brittain.* **69** d

SCOTTISH BELLE 3 br.f. Scottish Rifle 127–Persian Belle 77 (Darius 129) (1979 5v 5s 6s^2 6fg^2 6f^2 6f 6fg^3 6g^3 8fg 7fg^2 8g^4 7g^2 7g 1980 7f 12g 10fg 14d) leggy filly; runner-up 5 times in varied company at 2 yrs; ran moderately in 1980; should stay middle distances; probably acts on any going; usually blinkered and has worn a hood as well; trained by P. Feilden until after second start. *A. Moore.* —

SCOTTISH DREAM 2 ch.c. Palm Track 122–Captain Frances (Captain's Gig) (1980 6f 6f 8s^3 8g* 8d 8s 6s) Feb 27; lengthy colt; first foal; dam last on only start; improved over 1m and at Edinburgh in October beat Lambay by a neck in 15-runner maiden race; well beaten subsequently, including in nurseries; acts on a soft surface. *J. Calvert.* **76**

SCOTTISH GREEN 2 ch.c. Scottish Rifle 127–Nuque (Suceso) (1980 5.8fg 7fg 7g 8.2g 8d^4 8.2s) May 23; neat colt; sixth reported foal; dam won Chilean 1,000 Guineas and one of her 32 starts in USA; moderate plater; will stay 1$\frac{1}{4}$m; sweated up fourth outing. *P. Makin.* **54**

SCOTTISH LAW 2 b. or br.f. Scottish Rifle 127–Gallic Law 91 (Galivanter 131) (1980 6fg 6s^3 5g 5s* 5s^3) Mar 25; compact filly; second foal; half-sister to fairly useful 3-y-o sprinter Ferriby Hall (by Malicious); dam won twice over 7f at 2 yrs; blinkered following a poor effort, rallied to win 8-runner maiden race at Hamilton in October by $\frac{1}{2}$ length from Mrs Leadbetter; again blinkered when running creditably next time out; will stay 7f; form only on soft going; sold 2,800 gns Newmarket December Sales. *J. W. Watts.* **82**

SCRAPPIT 2 b.g. Laser Light 118–Ballydell (Pall Mall 132) (1980 6fg 6d 8s 8.2s^4 8d) Feb 21; 1,000F, 4,800Y; big gelding; brother to 1m and 11f winner **73**

Hardwicke Stakes, Ascot—Scorpio keeps on well to win from More Light (right). Noelino (rails) keeps Main Reef out of third place

Dismantler; dam never ran; little better than plating class; will stay 1¼m; best run on soft going. *S. Norton.*

SCULPTRESS 2 b.f. Arch Sculptor 123–Jaquetta (Amerigo 116§) (1980 6g* 6s*) Apr 6; half-sister to Irish 1½m winner Prominetto (by Prominer); dam won 6f maiden race at 3 yrs in USA; won both her starts, beating Hawthorn Arch ¾ length in 11-runner newcomers event at Navan in September and putting up a fairly useful effort to beat Bridewell Belle 2½ lengths in 15-runner minor event at Punchestown the following month; will probably stay 7f; yet to race on a firm surface. *A. Maxwell, Ireland.* **96**

S. D. DEMO 2 b.c. Mansingh 120–Blickling 64 (Blakeney 126) (1980 5fg² 6d³ 5.8fg² 6g³ 6fg³ 6s 6g³) Apr 12; 4,400Y; compact colt; first foal; dam needed long distances; ran consistently without winning, coming closest to success when narrowly-beaten third of 20 to Doc Marten in maiden race at Nottingham in July on fourth outing; will be suited by 7f and 1m; best form on a sound surface; wears blinkers; looked a bit light last 2 outings. *Mrs J. Reavey.* **84**

SDENKA PRINCESS 2 b.f. Prince de Galles 125–Sdenka 79 (Habitat 134) (1980 6d 6fg) Mar 19; plain, lengthy filly; first foal; dam placed over 7f; unquoted when in rear in maiden races at Windsor in the summer. *Mrs R. Lomax.* –

SEA AURA 2 b.f. Roi Soleil 125–Sinkit (Sing Sing 134) (1980 6fg⁴ 6fg*) Apr 24; 4,000Y; sturdy, good sort; fourth foal; dam never ran; put up a pleasing effort when winning 19-runner minor event at Lingfield in October by 1½ lengths from Flash 'N' Fire; will stay 7f; likely to improve further. *G. Pritchard-Gordon.* **83** p

SEA BOAT 6 b.h. Royal Palace 131–Anchor 106 (Major Portion 129) (1979 16d 1980 14g) fairly useful handicapper at his best; stays 2m; best form on a sound surface; wears blinkers; sometimes sweats up; backward, bandaged in front and tailed off on only outing in 1980 (October). *C. Mackenzie.* –

SEABUTY 3 b.f. Bustino 136–Seaswan 104 (Sea-Bird II 145) (1979 6g 8fg 1980 8fg 7d 10g) tall, lengthy filly; showed promise second start at 2 yrs; well beaten in 1980; should be suited by middle distances (pulled hard and ran moderately in blinkers when tried at 1¼m); sold 1,600 gns Newmarket December Sales. *R. Hern.* –

SEA CHIMES 4 ch.c. Gulf Pearl 117–Canterbury Belle (St Alphage 119) (1979 8.2v³ 10g* 10f* 10s* 12fg* 1980 10g* 10.2fg* 10fg* 12f* 10g⁴) **123**

Such was the rate of Sea Chimes's improvement and the skill with which his trainer placed him that he won eight consecutive races as a three- and four-year-old, the first an apprentice handicap under a low weight at Newmarket and the last the Coronation Cup. The Coronation Cup has been won by such as Mill Reef,

Sporting Chronicle Spring Handicap, Doncaster—Sea Chimes gallops on resolutely to beat Red Rufus and King's Ride

Coronation Cup, Epsom—another all-the-way win for Sea Chimes. Niniski takes second place from Soleil Noir. Valour completes the field

Roberto, Bustino and Ile de Bourbon in recent years; although Sea Chimes isn't in their class, he's a very smart colt and a notably genuine one too.

Sea Chimes caught a virus after gaining his fourth consecutive win as a three-year-old in very good style in the King George V Stakes at Royal Ascot and didn't race again that season. He looked in good shape however when reappearing in the City and Suburban Handicap at Epsom in April and put up an impressive performance under ten stone to win pushed out by three lengths from Joleg. He followed up with all-the-way wins in the Sporting Chronicle Spring Handicap at Doncaster and the Clive Graham Stakes at Kempton in May, impressing us no end in the latter with the way he went about his work and the acceleration he showed in the closing stages to draw four lengths clear of New Berry.

Conditions were very much in Sea Chimes's favour in the Coronation Cup at Epsom in June. The small field and fast going were tailor-made for a front runner with a turn of foot, and counted against the favourite Niniski; the St Leger second Soleil Noir and Valour who made up the field, would, like Niniski, have been suited by a stiffer test of stamina. Sea Chimes dictated the pace at a steady gallop from the start and had the race in his pocket from the moment Piggott kicked him into a clear lead as the field straightened up for home. None of his opponents could get in a serious blow and Sea Chimes passed the post two and a half lengths ahead of Niniski who just got up to deprive Soleil Noir of second.

Sea Chimes had a much harder task in the Coral Eclipse Stakes at Sandown in July, opposed by Ela-Mana-Mou, Gregorian and Cracaval as well as the three-year-olds Hello Gorgeous and Last Fandango. Piggott was claimed to ride Gregorian and Carson, who had won several times on Sea Chimes, rode Ela-Mana-Mou, so Sea Chimes was partnered for the first time by Eddery. Piggott was so

Mr J. H. Thursby's "Sea Chimes"

determined to make the running on Gregorian—another free-running sort—that Sea Chimes, who got rather stirred up beforehand, never had the chance to run his usual race. Taking on Gregorian for the lead drained a lot out of him, and when Gregorian quickened turning for home Sea Chimes couldn't keep up. Sea Chimes was passed by Ela-Mana-Mou and Hello Gorgeous before the post and finished about four lengths behind the winner. It subsequently transpired that Sea Chimes had wrenched a joint in the race; although he made a complete recovery he wasn't seen out again.

Sea Chimes (ch.c. 1976)	Gulf Pearl (ch 1962)	Persian Gulf (b 1940)	Bahram
			Double Life
		Nan (ch 1955)	Nearco
			Marsyaka
	Canterbury Belle (ch 1971)	St Alphage (ch 1963)	Red God
			Sally Deans
		Palamina (ch 1962)	Pall Mall
			Miss Stephen

Sea Chimes is the first foal of the once-raced St Alphage mare Canterbury Belle whose only subsequent foal Deep Blue Sea, a sister to Sea Chimes, is a poor maiden. The grandam Palamina won over five furlongs as a two-year-old and is a half-sister to the Irish Two Thousand Guineas winner King's Company and the outstanding sprinter Deep Diver. Sea Chimes is bred on fairly similar lines to Deep Diver, both being by Gulf Pearl, but has turned out a very different sort of racehorse. Gulf Pearl has produced few high-class racehorses and Sea Chimes is easily his best since Deep Diver.

A half-share in Sea Chimes was sold to Dogwood Farm shortly before the Eclipse for a sum believed to be around a quarter of a million pounds. Dogwood is an American-based racing concern but we understand that Sea Chimes is to continue his racing career over here and will be with Dunlop again in 1981. A tall, lengthy sort in appearance and a good mover, Sea Chimes acts on any going. He is an admirable racehorse, a credit to his trainer, and is likely to continue a force to reckon with in the top middle-distance races. *J. Dunlop.*

SEAJAN 4 gr.f. Mandamus 120–Sea Empress (Perhapsburg 112) (1979 NR 1980 12d 13d 13.8fg 12fg^3 16g 16.1d^4 14g* 12.3g^2 12g) won poorly-contested amateur riders maiden race at Yarmouth in July; stays well; acts on a firm and a soft surface. *F. Durr.* **54**

SEA LAD 5 gr.g. Dalesa 109–Miss Sleep (Olein's Grace 127) (1979 NR 1980 12g 13d) strong gelding; won bumpers race at Limerick at 4 yrs; tailed off in amateur riders event at Beverley and £2,500 race at Ayr, both in July; winning hurdler. *T. Craig.* —

SEAMARK 6 ch.g. On Your Mark 125–Nicest (Sheshoon 132) (1979 16s 15g 14v* 16.1g 16.1d^4 14f 14g 1980 18d 16s 16f 16fg 16.1d 16s^2 17.1fg* 19f^3 16s* 14fg 15.8d 18.1g^4 16.1s) quite a moderate handicapper; successful at Bath in July and Newcastle in August; possibly doesn't stay extreme distances; acts on any going but seems particularly well suited by the mud; used to wear blinkers; often wears bandages; suitable mount for an apprentice; finished lame final start. *A. Goodwill.* **52**

SEA MINSTREL 6 b.g. Seaepic 100–Lunar Hornpipe 75 (Mossborough 126) (1979 NR 1980 12d 6g^3 8f 8fg 10.6g 7.6g) plater; stays 1¼m; acts on a firm surface; has worn a hood and blinkers. *M. James.* —

SEA MISS 2 b.f. Matahawk 127–Lillima 73 (Crooner 119) (1980 7fg^3 8g 9d^3) Apr 6; 1,700Y; close-coupled, good sort; second foal; dam 6f winner; third twice in the Midlands, on third outing finishing 5 lengths behind Allegretta in minor event at Wolverhampton; 33/1, stayed on without troubling leaders when 8¾ lengths fifth of 8 to Exclusively Raised in May Hill Stakes at Doncaster in between; stays 9f and will probably get further. *P. Kelleway.* **93**

SEA OF ECHOES 2 b.c. Wolver Hollow 126–Sea of Moyle 111 (Skymaster 126) (1980 5f^2 6fg* 6f^3 6s^4 7g* 7f^2 7g 7g 8s) Apr 7; second foal; dam at her best at 2 yrs; apprentice ridden when successful in maiden race at Phoenix Park in May and 14-runner Hennessy VSOP Stakes at Leopardstown in July, showing improved form in latter race when coming through to win by ¾ length from Light Here; again ran well when going down by a length to Light Here in 10-runner Mullion Stakes, again at Leopardstown, in August but was subsequently out of his depth in pattern races; should stay 1m; seems to act on any going. *S. McGrath, Ireland.* **101**

SEAPARK 3 ch.c. Murrayfield 119–Last Summer 66 (Will Somers 114 §) (1979 5v 5d 6s 5.3fg 7fg 1980 10.8s 8g) tall, lengthy colt; turns his near-fore out badly; plating-class maiden; has worn boots in front. *G. Beeson.* —

SEA PIGEON (USA) 10 br.g. Sea-Bird II 145–Around The Roses (Round Table) (1979 18.4d^3 14d^4 12f^4 16fg^4 15g* 14.7g 14s* 15d* 16f 14g* 1980 18.4f 9f* 16d^4 12g^2 15g^3 14.7g* 14f^2 11s* 12fg^3 14s) **123**

The story so far . . . Starting his racing life in Jeremy Tree's flat-racing stable in 1972, Sea Pigeon was prepared for the Derby after winning the Duke of Edinburgh Stakes on his only outing at two. Had he won the Derby instead of finishing seventh to Morston, no student of bloodstock breeding would have been much surprised. His sire Sea-Bird II was one of the best racehorses of all time and his dam, Around The Roses, who was by the American champion Round Table, won four times at up to seven furlongs in the States, and finished second in the one-mile Acorn Stakes, the first leg of the American triple crown for fillies. Sea Pigeon was bought privately, reportedly for around £10,000, out of Tree's stable at the end of his ultimately disappointing three-year-old career. He had already been gelded and was given two outings in amateur riders events as a four-year-old before having his attentions turned to hurdling. Gordon Richards guided Sea Pigeon's early jumping career, taking him almost to the top of the hurdling tree. In his third season as a hurdler Sea Pigeon was transferred to his present trainer who has turned him into something of a sporting legend. After a fourth place and two seconds in the Champion Hurdle, Sea Pigeon finally became Champion Hurdler in 1980; by the end of the 1979/80 jumping season Sea Pigeon had won eighteen of his thirty-four races over jumps, earning £83,905 in first-prize money. He made a comeback to flat-racing in 1977 and over three seasons added twelve races to his tally, including the Tote-Ebor Handicap, the Ladbroke Chester Cup, which he won in successive years, and several other good trophy races. In both 1978 and 1979 Sea Pigeon was the outstanding staying handicapper in training; by the end of 1979 he had

Vaux Breweries Gold Tankard, Redcar—Sea Pigeon wins this race for the third time and beats subsequent Ebor winner Shaftesbury and stable-companion No Bombs

moved into second place in the list of money-winning geldings trained in Britain on the flat. *Now read on . . .*

Sea Pigeon had two important targets in 1980: to pass Boldboy's record earnings for an English-trained gelding on the flat and to provide the owner's son with a winning ride on Saints and Sinners Day at Hamilton in June, the latter being regarded as much the more important by Sea Pigeon's owner! Sea Pigeon had seventeen opponents in the Bull and Bear Amateur Riders Stakes at Hamilton. Most of them couldn't run fast enough to keep warm but the combination of the big field, the distance of the race—nine furlongs—and the relative inexperience of Sea Pigeon's rider, led to Sea Pigeon's being allowed to start at even money. Those who took advantage of such generosity never had a moment's anxiety: Sea Pigeon skated in by six lengths. Except for an attempt to provide young Mr Muldoon with another victory at Beverley in July—the less said about Sea Pigeon's defeat on this occasion the better—Sea Pigeon's campaign followed a familiar pattern, with his performing creditably under big weights in some of the season's best long-distance handicaps and making an occasional sortie into higher company. He gave a vintage performance in the Vaux Breweries Gold Tankard at Redcar in August, toying with the opposition to win the race for the third time; Shaftesbury, in receipt of 20 lb, finished second, a length and a half behind Sea Pigeon. Sea Pigeon's entry form for the Tote-Ebor, one of his main objectives, was mislaid and his connections had all the more reason to regret his enforced absence from the race when Shaftesbury went on to win the Ebor by four lengths.

Except for two occasions when he has slipped and fallen—the most recent of them on his final appearance as a ten-year-old when looking to have a third successive Sam Hall Memorial Trophy at York at his mercy—Sea Pigeon has been out of the frame only twice in handicap company in the past four seasons. His finishing speed has helped to make him a very formidable opponent in handicap company; few staying handicappers have any pretensions to matching the acceleration Sea Pigeon can call upon. The top races, however, are usually run at a faster pace than lesser races over the same distance and Sea Pigeon's ventures into pattern-race company have failed to meet with success, even when he has appeared very favourably treated by the weights. Sea Pigeon did win a listed race (a race just below pattern status) in 1980. Giving weight all round to a good-class field in the Doonside Cup at Ayr in September, Sea Pigeon won by a length and four lengths from Icelandic and Masked Marvel; he was always going easily in a race run at a moderate gallop on soft ground and his turn of foot proved decisive.

Sea Pigeon (USA) (br.g. 1970)	Sea-Bird II (ch 1962)	Dan Cupid (ch 1956)	Native Dancer
			Vixenette
		Sicalade (b 1956)	Sicambre
			Marmelade
	Around The Roses (br 1963)	Round Table (b 1954)	Princequillo
			Knight's Daughter
		Rose Coral (br 1950)	Rockefella
			Lady Mary Rose

Sea Pigeon's victory in the Doonside Cup took his first-place earnings on the flat to £96,985; Boldboy's fourteen victories were worth £95,392. Much was made in the Press of Sea Pigeon's achievement in passing Boldboy's total, although one correspondent wrote that Sea Pigeon's victory at two (worth £2,890) should not be counted because that prize was earned before he was gelded. The same writer raised the question of whether place money should also be taken into consideration—by his calculations Boldboy was still ahead using such a formula. Both points have some validity but, for our part, we mention prize-money statistics as a point of interest rather than importance. The level of prize money rises steadily over the years as the value of money falls and comparisons are meaningless unless the extent to which prizes have increased is taken into account. The argument about Sea Pigeon's earnings is of little relevance: his record is good enough to stand up for itself without recourse to such a dubious prop. His story is one of the most extraordinary sports stories ever told. He has been a magnificent ambassador for the sport; his achievements have transcended the confines of racing in a similar way to those of Brown Jack, Golden Miller, Arkle and Red Rum, probably the most famous geldings to race in Britain in living memory.

Mr P. L. Muldoon's "Sea Pigeon" (J. Mercer)

Sea Pigeon is a good-looking gelding and a good walker. He is effective at middle distances and stays extremely well. He acts on any going although there is a possibility—and we wouldn't put it any stronger—that nowadays he may not be at his best on very firm going (Shaftesbury turned the tables on him most decisively when the pair met, on terms similar to those at Redcar, on very firm going at York in September). Sea Pigeon is a genuine and dependable racehorse but his tendency to idle in front makes him a tricky ride: he has to be nursed very carefully and his challenge delayed, desirably, until the last possible moment. Sea Pigeon's usual rider over jumps, O'Neill, partnered him more often than anyone else on the flat in 1980 and he handles him very well. The passing years seem to have made little impression on Sea Pigeon: if anything, he was better than ever on the flat in the most recent season. We wish him well in 1981. *M. H. Easterby.*

SEAQUIN 2 b.f. Shiny Tenth 120–Sea Magic (Hardicanute 130) (1980 5fg4 5f 6g 6fg 7d 8fg* 9d3 8d) Feb 23; 2.900Y; neat filly; half-sister to 1½m seller winner Sea Mystery (by Nice Music); dam never ran; attracted no bid after showing first worthwhile form to win 18-runner seller at Leicester in September with plenty in hand by 1½ lengths from Venja; creditable third to Cinderwench in minor event at Wolverhampton the following month, easily better subsequent effort; runs as though she'll stay 1¼m; acts on a firm and a soft surface; trained by A. Johnson first 5 outings; retained 900 gns Ascot December Sales. *R. Baker.* **64**

SEARCH FOR GOLD 3 ch.f. Lord Gayle 124–Laconia 58 (Great Nephew 126) (1979 NR 1980 10.6d) 3,400Y; 440 2-y-o; third foal; half-sister to Spartan Call (by Realm), successful at up to 7f; dam half-sister to very useful stayer Tudor Tale; dwelt and always behind in 19-runner maiden race won by Roberta's Jeans at Haydock in October. *D. H. Jones.* **–**

SEA ROCKET 2 b.f. Saucy Kit 76–Another Wave (Haris II 93) (1980 7.2d 8d) smallish filly; seventh known foal; dam fair staying hurdler; behind in sellers at Haydock and Warwick in October. *S. Norton.* **–**

SEASPY 3 b.f. Silly Season 127–Spytra 64 (Spy Well 126) (1979 8fg 7g 1980 8v 8f 9.4fg 8f3 8s 7f 7g 7f4 5f 6g) lightly-made filly; poor form, including in a seller; probably stays 1m; acts on firm going and is possibly unsuited by very soft; sweating first start; sold 520 gns Doncaster November Sales. *G. Toft.* **–**

SEASURF 2 b.f. Seaepic 100–On Demand 80 (Mandamus 120) (1980 7g* 7g 7.3d2) Feb 28; lengthy, useful-looking filly; third foal; sister to disqualified 1977 2-y-o 6f winner Salacia; dam stayed 1½m; quickened clear below distance when winning 16-runner maiden race at Sandown in July by 2 lengths from Red Gloves; beaten in good-class fillies races subsequently, running well when 1½ lengths second of 11 to Boathouse in Radley Stakes at Newbury in October; will be suited by middle distances; yet to race on firm ground but action suggests she'll be suited by it. *M. Jarvis.* **89**

SEAWAVE LAD 2 ro.c. Be Friendly 130–Haunting 79 (Lord Gayle 124) (1980 5fg 6s) Feb 28; 2,700Y; leggy colt; first foal; dam placed at up to 9f; tailed off in minor event at Leicester (dwelt) in May and maiden auction race at Nottingham (still in need of run when last of 18) in June. *G. Huffer.* **–**

SEAWAY 3 br.g. Kalamoun 129–Sea Dog (Sea Hawk II 131) (1979 7fg 8g* 7d2 1980 8v 8g 10f 10.1g 11.7fg 10f*) strong, attractive gelding; dropped in class when winning seller at Lingfield in October (sold 4,100 gns); stays 1¼m; seems to act on any going. *J. Sutcliffe.* **78**

SECOND EVENT 3 b.f. Fine Blade 121–Gala Tess (El Gallo 122) (1979 6fg 5f* 7g 7fg3 7g 1980 8fg3 10.8g3 8.3fg 8.3f 8.3fg*) rangy filly; won handicap at Windsor in September; stays 1m well; acts on firm going. *D. Kent.* **86**

SECRET ALLIANCE 3 b. or br.f. Chelanda 71–Qalibashi 77 (Master Rocky 106) (1979 NR 1980 8f 10s 8.2d) of no account. *G. Wallace.* **–**

SECRET ARMY 2 b.g. Record Run 127–Gatecrasher (Will Somers 114 §) (1980 5f 5f 7f 6g) Apr 26; 3,100Y; compact gelding; half-brother to a winner in USA by Allangrange; dam bad Irish maiden; 20/1, blinkered and sweating, wasn't disgraced when 8¼ lengths fifth of 23 to Hurtwood Lass in valuable seller at Doncaster in September, final outing; should stay 7f; possibly needs some give in the ground. *Miss S. Hall.* **52**

SECRET CHARITY 3 ch.f. Ribston 104–Fox Covert 82 (Gigantic 102) (1979 5g 5h 6d 8h³ 7d 10g⁴ 1980 8h 12.2fg 12g 10g) small filly; poor plater; best run at 1m on hard going; has worn blinkers; sold 290 gns Doncaster October Sales. *E. Weymes.* —

SECRET EXPRESS 4 gr.c. Most Secret 119–Empress Donna 48 (Don II 123) (1979 8v 6s* 7s 5g 6d² 6s³ 5g³ 6d 6f 6f² 6fg 6g* 6g⁴ 6fg 6s² 6s³ 6d² 6d 1980 6.5g 5g 5v 6v³ 6g* 6f² 6h 6f 6fg 6fg² 6d² 6fg 6fg 5f 6g 5d 6g⁴ 6v) lightly-made colt; bought in 980 gns after winning seller at Hamilton in April; not disgraced in better company in the autumn; best form at 6f; acts on any going; wears blinkers and sometimes bandages; has been ridden in spurs. *W. Stubbs.* **53**

SECRET GILL 3 gr.f. Most Secret 119–Gill Breeze (Farm Walk 111) (1979 NR 1980 8s² 8g 8f³ 8g² 7s 8d³ 7d³ 7s*) lengthy, rather unfurnished filly; sister to 6f winner Poppin Gill and half-sister to 2 winning platers; dam never ran; 25/1 and apprentice ridden when winning handicap at Doncaster in November; stays 1m; acts well on soft going; sometimes wears boots in front; doesn't always find a great deal off bridle. *Miss S. Hall.* **68**

SECRET HARBOUR 2 ch.c. Home Guard 129–Summer Day 117 (Golden Cloud) (1980 5g⁴ 6g 7f 6d) Apr 11; 25,000Y; strong, well-made colt; half-brother to several winners, including useful 7f performer Heave To (by Pirate King); dam won six 5f races at 2 yrs; showed only a little ability, best run over 7f. *C. Brittain.* **67**

SECRET LADY 2 gr. or ro.f. The Go-Between 129–Keravnos 64 (Ionian 128) (1980 5fg 5g 5g 5fg 5d 5d) May 1; small, light-framed filly; sister to fairly useful 1979 2-y-o 6f winner Vorvados; dam won over 6f; in rear in maiden races. *J. Spearing.* —

SEDONA 2 b.f. On Your Mark 125–Spadilla 59 (Javelot 124) (1980 5f* 5f⁴ 5f 6g³ 5d 5fg 5d 5d*) Mar 22; 3,600F, 2,000Y (privately); neat, strong filly; half-sister to Wyn-Bank (by Green God), successful at up to 1¼m; dam Irish 1½m winner; won 6-runner maiden race at Chester in May and 20-runner seller at Catterick in October; apprentice-ridden favourite when beating Case History ¾ length on latter (no bid); stays 6f; appears to act on any going; acts well on sharp tracks; sold, reportedly for export to Trinidad, 3,200 gns Doncaster October Sales. *J. Fitzgerald.* **75**

SEE ANDY 3 b.f. Redundant 120–Elia (Narrator 127) (1979 5v 5s 5s 5g 7fg⁴ 7fg 7fg 6s 8d⁴ 7s 1980 8h 10h 8g 10g³ 8fg³ 10g⁴ 8f 10g) lengthy, unfurnished filly; poor plater; stays 1¼m; sometimes wears boots; has been tried in blinkers; sold 400 gns Doncaster November Sales. *M. Camacho.* **33**

SEEK HIM HERE 3 b.c. Status Seeker–Nice One Jackie (Prince Tenderfoot 126) (1979 7.5f 1980 8v 12f 10g 8.2g 10g 8d) leggy, lightly-made ex-Irish colt; first foal; dam ran once; poor form in maiden races and sellers; blinkered nowadays; trained by Mrs A. Riddell Martin first 2 starts. *W. Wright.* —

SEEMS A NICE BOY 3 ch.g. Fair Decision 93§–Jevington 102 (Fairey Fulmar 124) (1979 NR 1980 10.1fg 10f) 220Y; in rear in Southern maiden races. *B. Wise.* —

SEGOS 2 b.f. Runnymede 123–Eastwood Bounty 87 (Bounteous 125) (1980 6s 7fg³ 7g 7g⁴ 8d* 8s) Feb 28; unfurnished filly; sister to smart Woodsome, a winner at up to 8.5f in England and USA, and half-sister to fairly useful sprinter Woodchat (by Song); dam effective from 5f to 1¼m; proved well suited by trip when tried over 1m, winning 15-runner maiden race at Redcar in October a shade comfortably by 1½ lengths from Red Lady; had stiffish task next time out; acts well on a soft surface. *G. Harwood.* **81**

SEKAM 2 ch.g. Lorenzaccio 130–Wold Lass 77 (Vilmorin) (1980 6g⁴ 7fg⁴ 7g* 7f 8s 8fg) May 11; 16,000Y; useful sort; half-brother to 2 winners, notably smart 5f to 7f winner Mofida (by Right Tack); dam, a sprinter, is half-sister to very smart Chebs Lad; well on top at finish when winning 5-runner minor event at Newmarket in August by 1½ lengths from Buffavento; didn't show anything like that form in nurseries afterwards, dwelling at start and wearing blinkers when tailed off final appearance; should stay 1m; form only on good ground; gelded at end of season; one to leave alone. *J. Hindley.* **81 §**

SELBORNE RECORD 2 ch.g. Record Run 127–Flatter Me (Palestine 133) (1980 7g 8s 8s) Mar 28; 3,800Y; well-grown, rather leggy gelding; half-brother to French middle-distance winner Fujikawa (by Pampered King) and to a winner in Venezuela; dam ran only 3 times; in rear in minor events in the North in second half of season. *J. Etherington.* **69**

SELECTION TRUST 4 ch.g. Sassafras 135–Lady Hazel (Hornbeam 130) (1979 10s 1980 12s 14g 16f^4 16.1s) big, rangy gelding; plating-class staying maiden. *H.T. Jones.* —

SELECTOR 2 b. or br.c. Jukebox 120–Passage Hawk (Falcon 131) (1980 5s 5g^2) Apr 22; fair sort; third foal; brother to Irish 3-y-o 9.5f winner Beechlawn Flyer; nearest at finish after starting none too well when 5 lengths second of 19 to Creamy in seller at Beverley in April; sold 300 gns Newmarket July Sales. *P. Rohan.* **44**

SELOCHROME 6 ch.m. Blast 125–Resurgence (Runnymede 123) (1979 NR 1980 8.2fg) of no account. *S. Wiles.* —

SELSDON PARK 3 b.c. Morston 125–Teesdale 97 (Aggressor 130) (1979 NR 1980 9fg 12.3f 13s^3 15.5s^3 14g^4 12fg^3 16fg) 5,200F, 25,000Y; good-bodied colt; half-brother to several winners, including useful 1975 2-y-o Blue Cavalier (by Queen's Hussar); dam 1¼m winner and half-sister to Starry Halo; quite moderate; suited by test of stamina; probably acts on any going; blinkered last 3 starts, sweating up on final occasion; sold 1,500 gns Newmarket Autumn Sales. *C. Brittain.* **68**

SEMIBREVE 2 br.f. Relko 136–Band Call (Don II 123) (1980 5f^3 5f 6g 6fg 7f 8fg) May 18; 1,500Y; small, light-framed filly; showed a little ability in sellers; will stay 1¼m+; sold 480 gns Doncaster September Sales. *P. Haslam.* **41**

SEMPER NOVA 7 gr.h. Right Boy 137–Blue Queen 54 (Majority Blue 126) (1979 8g^3 8g 8g 8fg 8g 10fg 9fg^3 8d 1980 7d 8.2fg 10h 10.4f 8s 8fg) fair handicapper when in the mood; on the downgrade and finished last in seller second outing; stays 9f well; best form on a sound surface; has been tried in blinkers; sometimes wears bandages; has twice bolted to start, but has nonetheless run well for an apprentice; sold 2,100 gns Doncaster August Sales. *J. Bingham.* —

SENATOR MURPHY 4 b.c. Reform 132–Belle Sicambre 120 (Sicambre 135) (1979 10.2s^3 14g^2 13fg^2 16d 14g 14.6fg* 15.5f* 14f* 1980 14d) lengthy colt; has a round action; winner of maiden race at Ripon, amateurs event at Folkestone and minor race at Sandown in 1979 when trained by F. Durr (rated 89); tailed off when pulled up 3f out on only outing of 1980 (August); stays well; probably acts on any going. *R. Cambidge.* —

SENATOR SAM 7 gr.g. Meldrum 112–Pinnacle 70 (High Perch 126) (1979 10.5d 10fg^4 9fg* 10.2fg 9f 10fg^4 10s^4 10s 10.2fg^3 10fg 1980 12g) quite a moderate handicapper; needed race when well beaten only outing of 1980 (August); stays 11f; acts on any going; has been tried in blinkers; good mount for an apprentice. *P. Bevan.* —

SENTA'S GIRL 2 br.f. Averof 123–Senta 103 (Chanteur II 135) (1980 5f) Feb 9; half-sister to several winners here and abroad, including Wishing Star (by Reform), winner of 1971 Gimcrack Stakes and subsequently successful at up to 1½m; dam won at up to 2m; gambled on although looking in need of race, always struggling to go pace when about 10 lengths fifth of 10 to Lucaya in maiden race at Wolverhampton in May, only outing; likely to need at least 1¼m at 3 yrs. *G. Huffer.* —

SENTIMENTAL ME 5 b.m. Precipice Wood 123–Lady C (Princely Gift 137) (1979 NR 1980 13.8fg) novice hurdler; unquoted when well behind in maiden race at Catterick in May, first outing on flat. *R. Morris.* —

SENTRY DUTY 3 b.c. Sparkler 130–Noble Duty (Reliance II 137) (1979 8fg 10g^2 1980 11fg^2 14f* 12f*) big, strong colt; won maiden race at Newmarket and handicap at Thirsk in May; beat Teresilla 1½ lengths in latter; looked like developing into a very useful staying handicapper but wasn't seen out again; suited by 1¾m; yet to race on a soft surface. *B. Hobbs.* **105**

SEPARATE BID 2 b.c. Auction Ring 123–Fellow's Eyot (Roan Rocket 128) (1980 6g^3 7fg) Apr 29; 37,000Y; third foal; dam unraced half-sister to smart performers Piccadilly and Fast Colour; unquoted, never got in a blow at Norman Style and Capstan when about 4 lengths third of 11 in £5,900 event at Doncaster in September; only seventh of 19 to Jalabad in maiden race at Lingfield the following month; possibly better suited by 6f than 7f. *I. Walker.* **69**

SEPT ETOILE 2 b.c. Auction Ring 123–Musical Watch (Tudor Melody 129) (1980 6d 6g 6g 8.5s* 8s^4) Mar 29; 9,000Y; brother to useful Irish 3-y-o 7f and 9f winner Ozone, and half-brother to several winners; dam ran only at 2 yrs; showed improved form when tried over 1m, winning 12-runner maiden race at Galway in September by 4 lengths from United Stand; third favourite when 5¼ lengths fourth of 8 to Benefice in Group 3 Ashford Castle Stakes at the Curragh later in month; yet to race on a firm surface. *D. Weld, Ireland.* **99**

SERAMUS 3 b.f. Mandamus 120–Serein (Prince Chevalier) (1979 6f 7fg 7d 45
8.2d^2 8d* 8fg^3 1980 12g 10f 10f 12h^3 12fg^4 8g 9g 8fg 9s^4 8.2d^4) neat filly; plater; suited by 1$\frac{1}{2}$m; appears to act on any going; often blinkered; sold 680 gns Doncaster September Sales. *E. Weymes.*

SERENE PEARL 3 ch.f. Gulf Pearl 117–Damascus Sky (Skymaster 126) —
(1979 NR 1980 6d 6s 6f 6fg 7d 7g) 6,200Y; attractive, rangy filly; half-sister to 2 winners, including Sky Jump (by Double Jump), successful at up to 7.5f; dam ran four times unplaced; in rear in varied company, including selling. *B. Swift.*

SERGEI 4 br.c. Sir Gaylord–Cover Girl (Edellic 124) (1979 8d 10s 10v* 8fg^3 12f^2 87
12g 1980 12d 12fg* 12fg^3 12fg) lengthy colt; fair handicapper; neck winner from Rainfall at Kempton in May; stayed 1$\frac{1}{2}$m; acted on any going; blinkered second and final outings; dead. *H. Candy.*

SERPICO 2 br.g. Drumbeg 94–Porringer (Vigo 130) (1980 5v^2 5s^4 5fg^4 5f) 45
Apr 16; leggy, narrow gelding; poor plater; not raced after May; sold 520 gns Newmarket July Sales. *J. Berry.*

SERPINA 2 b.f. Saritamer 130–A Deux 80 (Crepello 136) (1980 6fg^2 5g) 62
Apr 15; neat filly; good walker and mover; half-sister to 2 winners, including fairly useful 6f to 1$\frac{1}{2}$m winner Dasman (by Tower Walk); dam placed from 6f to 1$\frac{1}{2}$m; badly outpaced early on but ran on to finish 2$\frac{1}{2}$ lengths second of 16 to Down The Hatch in maiden race at Salisbury in September; favourite for similar event at Bath later in month but found 5f too sharp and finished modest sixth of 18 to Portogon; will be suited by 7f+. *F. J. Houghton.*

SETMARK 5 gr.m. Sharpen Up 127–Aberside (Abernant 142) (1979 5s^4 —
5s* 5v^3 5s 5f 5f 5g^4 5d 5g* 5g 5d 5g 5s 1980 5s 5g 5f 5.1f 6g) compact mare; stays 6f; needs some give in the ground; wears blinkers; good mount for an apprentice; sold 2,500 gns Newmarket July Sales. *G. Toft.*

SETTA SPRATT 2 b.f. Firestreak 125–Meg Swerie (Whistler 129) (1980 —
5g) May 29; sister to fairly useful 1976 2-y-o 5f and 6f winner Home Fire; dam second 3 times from 6f to 1m in Ireland; unquoted when behind in 22-runner maiden race won by Copt Hall Realm at Lingfield in September. *S. Matthews.*

SETTIMINO (USA) 2 b.c. Exclusive Native–Lucretia Bori (Bold Ruler) — p
(1980 7g 8fg) Feb 14; $160,000Y; strong, short-legged colt; half-brother to 3 winners, including fairly useful 1$\frac{1}{4}$m to 1$\frac{3}{4}$m winner Night Watch (by Stage Door Johnny) and Draw the Line (by Prove It), a very useful winner at up to 1$\frac{1}{4}$m; dam, half-sister to Romulus and Sostenuto, was very useful stakes winner at up to 6f; showed up well from a low draw when ninth of 23 to Shergar in minor race at Newbury in September, second outing; the type to make a useful staying 3-y-o. *F. J. Houghton.*

SETTING TRICK (USA) 3 b.f. Tom Rolfe–Winning Trick (Damascus) 81
(1979 6fg^4 6fg^3 5.8g^3 7f^3 8g* 1980 10.8f 10.2f^3 10.2fg^4 10fg^2 8.2g* 8.5fg 8f 8fg^4) lightly-made filly; moderate handicapper; beat Kashmir Blue $\frac{1}{2}$ length at Nottingham in July; stays 1$\frac{1}{4}$m; acts on firm going; sometimes sweats up; ran moderately seventh start; sold 41,000 gns Newmarket December Sales. *J. Dunlop.*

SEVEN COMM 3 ch.c. Communication 119–Severndale (Bounteous 125) —
(1979 5g 5d 1980 8g) small colt; looks useless. *K. Bridgwater.*

SEVEN HEARTS 4 ch.c. Some Hand 119–Vienna Love 68 (Vienna 127) (1979 98
7g 7d 7g^4 7f 8fg^2 1980 8f 8d^2 8d^3 8g^2 8g^4 8g* 8fg^2 10fg^3 8s^2) strong colt; good mover; led 3f out and was soon clear when winning Playtex Trophy at Sandown in August by 4 lengths from Darwood; in frame on nearly all his other starts and was runner-up on same course (twice) and at York (beaten neck by Geoffrey's Sister in Harp Lager Handicap) and Salisbury; respectable third to Etching in valuable 1$\frac{1}{4}$m handicap at Newbury and probably stayed the distance; probably acts on any going; wore a blinker last 4 starts; suitable mount for an apprentice; sometimes wears a boot on off-fore. *W. Hastings-Bass.*

SEVEN SPADES 3 b.g. Red Alert 127–Spadilla 59 (Javelot 124) (1979 5d^4 —
5g 1980 8.2g 10.2g 10g) sturdy gelding; seems of little account; has worn blinkers; sold 200 gns Doncaster October Sales. *K. Morgan.*

SEVEN YEAR ITCH 3 b.f. Jimsun 121–Quelle Pas (Kelling 122) (1979 53
5g* 6f 6fg^3 6g^4 6g 7fg 6f 1980 11.7s 8g 8g 9f 10g*) small filly; plater; sold 1,100 gns after winning at Nottingham in September; stays 1$\frac{1}{4}$m. *D. Gandolfo.*

SEVERIANO (USA) 2 ro. or gr.c. Native Royalty–Erin O'Connell (Dondeen **103**
123) (1980 5f 5g* 5g* 5g^4 5d^3 6.3s 5g^3) Mar 30; $20,000Y; lengthy, quite attractive colt; second foal; dam won claiming races at up to 1m at 3 yrs; successful twice within space of 3 days at Leopardstown, beating Dawn is Breaking 2½ lengths in maiden race in May and Master Thatch 4 lengths in 4-runner event in June; in frame in Norfolk Stakes at Royal Ascot and Curragh Stakes on next 2 outings, beaten 7 lengths by Chummy's Special in former, and ran very well under top weight when 2½ lengths third of 11 to Brooklyn Prince in nursery at the Curragh in August; form only at 5f; acts on a soft surface. *M. Kauntze, Ireland.*

SEYMOUR LADY 2 b.f. Malicious–Asheldham Lady (Typhoon 125) (1980 **62**
5s 5s^2 5s^3 5fg 6g^2 6fg 6g^4 7f 6s^2 6fg 6g 8d 8.2s^4) Mar 7; 500Y; leggy filly; first foal; dam well behind in 5 races; second in sellers, on final occasion going down by 2 lengths to Allied Cardiff in 20-runner event at Nottingham in August; should stay 1m; best form with some give in the ground; sweated up and ran moderately eleventh outing. *D. Weeden.*

SHAAB 5 b.h. Busted 134–Chieftain Girl (Chieftain) (1979 12.2s* 16s^2 18s **85**
14g^2 14s 13.1g 16fg^2 16f* 16f^3 16.9fg* 16f^3 16fg* 18fg 1980 16s 16fg^3 14fg^4 16f* 16fg^2 16fg 16fg^3 16g^4 16g 16.9f* 16f* 16g 17.1d 18d) fair staying handicapper; led 2f out and ran on well to beat Another Generation by 5 lengths at Lingfield in August; successful earlier on same course and at Wolverhampton; acts on any going but is particularly well suited by firm; one paced and is suited by a strong gallop. *J. Benstead.*

SHAARID 3 gr.c. Supreme Sovereign 119–Maxie's Melody (Tudor Melody 129) **94**
(1979 6g* 6fg* 6fg^2 7s^3 6f 6f* 6g 1980 6s^2 6f* 6f 7g 6d) compact colt; not a good mover in his slower paces; fairly useful handicapper; creditable ¾-length second to Gambler's Dream at Kempton prior to beating same horse by a head at Newmarket in April (wandered under pressure and only just held on); best form at 6f; acts on any going; ran moderately third and final starts. *W. O'Gorman.*

SHADY DRIVE 2 b.f. Warpath 113–Counter Coup (Busted 134) (1980 7g) –
Apr 15; 1,500Y; third foal; half-sister to 3-y-o Greyburn (by Saintly Song), winner at up to 1m; dam lightly-raced daughter of smart filly Alborada; unquoted when in rear in 16-runner maiden event won by More Stones at Chepstow in September. *J. Hill.*

SHADY NOOK 5 b.g. Green God 128–Pilica's Melody (Tudor Melody 125) **102**
(1979 8d 11fg^3 12s* 10fg^3 12f^3 12f* 12g^3 11.7fg* 10fg 11s^2 1980 11f* 12fg^3 12s* 12f^4 14g^4 11.7f^3 13.3fg^2) useful handicapper; ½-length winner of London Gold Cup at Newbury in May (from Russian George) and Old Newton Cup at Haydock in July (from Move Off); in frame on all his other starts, running particularly well on last occasion when 1½ lengths second to Castle Keep in Coral Autumn Cup at Newbury in September; stays 13f; acts on any going; often sweats up; has a good turn of foot; goes well for S. Raymont. *H. Blagrave.*

Old Newton Cup, Haydock—Shady Nook (extreme right) and Move Off (extreme left) finish first and second in this valuable handicap

M Y. Skalka's "Shafaraz"

SHADY PALM 2 b.c. Palm Track 122–Singing In The Rain 83 (Tudor Melody 129) (1980 5fg 6s) Feb 5; 2,500Y; well-made colt; half-brother to 2 winners by Crooner, including fairly useful 1974 2-y-o 5f winner Falsetto; behind in maiden races at Kempton (last of 16 to Bel Bolide) in May and Nottingham (auction event) the following month; retained 370 gns Ascot August Sales. *A. Johnson.* —

SHADY SPRING 3 b.f. Dancer's Image–Go Friendly (Be Friendly 130) (1979 NR 1980 6f^2 6f^2 7fg 6g^4 5f 6d^4) 13,500F, 14,500Y; strong filly; second foal; sister to useful Italian performer Garozzo, successful at up to 1m; dam poor half-sister to useful stayer Attivo; in frame in maiden races and a handicap; best at sprint distances; probably acts on any going; sold 12,500 gns Newmarket December Sales. *L. Cumani.* **71**

SHAFARAZ (FR) 7 b.h. Levmoss 133–Asharaz (Sicambre 135) (1979 15.5v^4 15.5fg^4 20fg^2 15g^3 13.5s^5 15.5s* 20fg^3 1980 15.5g*(dis) 15.5g^3 20fg* 15g^3 15.5v^4) French horse; a tough performer who maintained his form very well over the years; came from behind when beating Prove It Baby in good style by 6 lengths in Prix du Cadran at Longchamp in May; had failed a dope test and **124**

Prix du Cadran, Longchamp—the veteran Shafaraz is clear of Prove It Baby. Marriageable is third

Tote-Ebor Handicap, York—the second most valuable handicap of the year goes to Shaftesbury who is clear of New Jerusalem and Popsi's Joy (left)

been disqualified after beating Hard to Sing by 2 lengths in Prix de Barbeville on same course the previous month; also in frame in Prix Jean Prat and Prix Royal-Oak, also at Longchamp, and in Prix Kergorlay at Deauville; stayed extremely well; probably acted on any going; wore bandages; consistent; retired to Haras du Bois Roussel. *P. Biancone, France.*

SHAFIYA (FR) 2 b.f. Zeddaan 130–Safiah (St Paddy 133) (1980 8d*) May 6; **93** p
fifth foal; half-sister to 3 winners, including very useful French 6.5f to 10.5f winner Shelina (by Mill Reef); dam won at up to 11f and comes from same family as Blushing Groom; won her only start, an 11-runner maiden race at Maisons-Laffitte in November, in promising style by 2 lengths from El Dancerina; will probably stay 1¼m; bound to improve a good deal. *F. Mathet, France.*

SHAFTESBURY 4 b.c. Prince de Galles 125–Belle-Dame 92 (Primera 131) **113**
(1979 10v* 10d^3 10s^2 10g^3 12g* 12d^2 11d* 14g* 14s^4 1980 14f^3 16fg 14d^4 12f^2 12fg* 14.7g^2 14g* 14f* 14.6g^4) well-made, useful sort; not the best of movers in his slower paces; developed into a very useful handicapper; scored a resounding win in £25,000 Tote-Ebor Handicap at York in August, beating New Jerusalem unchallenged by 4 lengths after going clear 3f out; beat Sea Pigeon by 10 lengths (value nearer 6 lengths) in 3-runner Harrison Drape Stayers Handicap on same course in September; had also trotted up in £3,600 handicap at Thirsk on fifth start; never going particularly well and was eased when beaten when fourth of 5 behind Castle Keep at Doncaster on final outing; stays 1¾m; acts on any going; genuine and consistent; suited by a strong gallop. *M. Stoute.*

SHAHABAD 5 b.g. Mummy's Pet 125–Lady Anne Neville 92 (Right Boy —
137) (1979 NR 1980 10s) poor plater; stays 9f; acts on firm going. *D. Weeden.*

SHAKAPOUR 3 gr.c. Kalamoun 129–Shamim (Le Haar 126) (1979 7g^3 8d^2 **125**
7s* 1980 9.7g* 12fg^4 12fg^2 12.5d*)

The runnings of the Grand Prix de Saint-Cloud and the King George VI and Queen Elizabeth Diamond Stakes in July showed the current crop of three-year-olds in a better light than was generally anticipated. The two races usually provide the earliest opportunities for the top three-year-olds

Grand Prix de Saint-Cloud—a dead-heat between Dunette (far side) and Shakapour who are three lengths in front of Policeman

to meet their elders over a mile and a half, and did so in 1980. The younger generation came out of the Grand Prix de Saint-Cloud even better than it did at Ascot, with the French Derby second Shakapour's dead-heating with the year-older Dunette while three-year-olds Policeman and Lancastrian took the rest of the prize-money; following on were Noble Saint, three-year-old Belgio, Two of Diamonds and the French older horses Gain and Scorpio. The race provided a fine spectacle as well as a significant result, there being little or nothing between the dead-heaters from the time they wore down Policeman at the distance.

Saint-Martin felt he could have won outright on Shakapour had he not dropped his whip a furlong out, but that might be disputed on the grounds that Dunette's rider passed the post with arm raised in premature celebration of victory and that Shakapour ran on much more sweetly than on his previous outing in the French Derby, the Prix du Jockey-Club at Chantilly. Shakapour is a horse who carries his head high in a finish, and probably tender handling suits him ideally. He went down by a length and a half to Policeman at Chantilly (he beat him three lengths at Saint-Cloud), finding little over the last furlong after quickening nicely away from the pack chasing the winner in the straight. The result of the French Derby said nothing for the consistency of the majority of those who had contested the series of classic trials in France in the spring. Shakapour himself had run twice previously during the season. First time out he had shown great promise in winning the Prix de Guiche at Longchamp by two lengths and a neck from Corvaro and Policeman. Then he had finished a rather disappointing fourth behind Mot D'Or, Providential and Belgio, all three of whom he beat decisively in the French Derby, in the Prix Hocquart at Longchamp. Any opportunity for Shakapour to establish himself further after Saint-Cloud was denied him by injury; regrettably he had to miss the big races in the autumn, including his main objective, the Prix de l'Arc de Triomphe.

Shakapour (gr.c. 1977)	Kalamoun (gr 1970)	Zeddaan (gr 1965)	Grey Sovereign
			Vareta
		Khairunissa (gr 1960)	Prince Bio
			Palariva
	Shamim (ch 1968)	Le Haar (ch 1954)	Vieux Manoir
			Mince Pie
		Diamond Drop (ch 1963)	Charlottesville
			Martine

Shakapour could make an adequate replacement at stud for his sire Kalamoun who died young in 1979. The dam's family is a good one of the Aga Khan's. Shakapour's great grandam Martine just lost the Irish One Thousand Guineas, and finished third to Darius in the Eclipse. She is a half-sister to the King Edward VII Stakes winner Skyraider and to Amante, the Irish Oaks winner and second in the One Thousand Guineas. The grandam Diamond Drop was a good winner over a mile at two years and ran in useful company at three; she was a half-sister to that good filly Opaline II, the top weight in the Two-Year-Old Free Handicap of 1960. The dam Shamim also won over a mile in France at two years; she is a half-sister to two French pattern-race winners in Kamaraan and Kamaridaan, the former a high-class horse at distances of a mile and a quarter to two miles who ran well in the Arc two years in succession. Shamim produced one previous foal—an African Sky filly called Sharma, winner over a mile and a quarter at Le Croise–Laroche in 1979. Her next produce Shademah (by Thatch), a late foal, was in training with Stoute in 1980 but hasn't run.

Kalamoun didn't quite last out the trip in testing conditions in the French Derby, and for a time it seemed as though Shakapour might have similar limitations. However, Shakapour's run in the Grand Prix de Saint-Cloud showed that he stays a mile and a half really well. He seems to act on any going. *F. Mathet, France.*

SHA'LAN 2 b.c. Arch Sculptor 123–Aurelie (Aureole 132) (1980 6fg 7fg 7s 8d*) Mar 18; 7,200Y; well-made colt; half-brother to 3 winners, including Irish middle-distance performer Rarely (by Rarity); dam won over 7f at 2 yrs in Ireland; 33/1, made all to beat Norfolk Prince ½ length in maiden race at Leicester in November; suited by 1m. *G. Hunter.* **86**

SHALLOT BOY 2 ro.g. Workboy 123–Shall Do (Passenger 122 or Derring-Do 131) (1980 5f 5h 6d 6f 5g 5f) Mar 14; lengthy, unfurnished gelding; no worthwhile form in sellers. *J. Carr.* –

SHALL WE TELL 2 b.g. Guillaume Tell 121–Muraka (Off Key 121) (1980 7g) Mar 14; 3,500Y; well-made, quite attractive gelding; third foal; half-brother to 2 winners, including Irish 3-y-o 1½m performer Whisper Gently (by Pitskelly); dam won bumpers race; unquoted and on backward side when last of 15 to Kalaglow in minor event at Sandown in August. *D. Kent.* –

SHALWA 2 b.f. Broxted 120–Hopeful Gift 95 (Bounteous 125) (1980 5g^2 5.8f^2 5.8h* 7fg^3 8fg 6d) Mar 22; 2,200Y; quite well-made filly; fourth foal; half-sister to winning jumpers Murray's Gift (by Murrayfield) and Mandy's Gift (by Mandamus); dam won over 9f; won 12-runner maiden race at Bath in August by 4 lengths from Barbara Allen despite having hung badly 1f out; excellent third of 11, a length behind Giannutri, in better race at Newbury the following month; suited by 7f (out of her depth when tried over 1m); acts on hard going; unseated rider leaving paddock on fifth outing and galloped riderless to start. *P. M. Taylor.* **79**

SHAMSTAR (USA) 2 b.c. Sham–Campus Star (Raise A Native) (1980 7.5d*) Apr 25; $30,000Y, $87,000 2-y-o; second foal; dam unraced sister to very useful sprinter L'Natural and is closely related to champion sire Exclusive Native; not seen out after winning 7-runner maiden race at Deauville in August by a length from Kamara; will probably stay 1¼m; entered in 2,000 Guineas and Derby and is evidently well thought of. *F. Boutin, France.* **?**

SHANGARRY 2 br.c. Pitskelly 122–Jean Amour 88 (Delirium 126) (1980 5s 7d^2 7g^4 7g* 7f^2 8g) May 7; 6,900F, 15,000Y; well-made colt; half-brother to 3 winners here and abroad, including Sovereign's Escort (by Supreme Sovereign), successful at up to 1¼m; dam middle-distance winner; ran out a smooth 4-length winner from Imperial Measure when ridden by 5-lb claimer in £3,200 nursery at Brighton in August; again ran well when ½-length second to comfortable winner Cavalry Twill in minor event at Epsom later in month but never got into race when looking to have good chance in nursery won by Sheer Grit at Doncaster in September; should stay 1m; acts on firm going and a soft surface. *R. Price.* **94**

SHANKLY 3 ch.g. Brittany–Golden Crusader (King's Scholarship 107) (1979 5s 5d 7d 1980 12.5v) plain gelding; in rear in moderate maiden company; sold 500 gns Doncaster May Sales. *J. Berry.* –

SHANVEAN 4 ch.g. Shantung 132–Miss Budock Vean (Never Say Die 137) (1979 11d 14f 1980 12fg 11g 16fg) leggy gelding; poor maiden. *M. Camacho.* –

SHAOLIN WARRIOR 2 br.c. Balidar 133–Braeval (Quorum 126) (1980 7f^4) Apr 23; 2,800Y; lightly-made colt; second foal; dam unraced sister to high-class 1969 2-y-o Quarryknowe; claimed after finishing 4 lengths fourth to Rocket Venture in 18-runner seller at Redcar in September (needed race); stays 7f. *P. Haslam.* **57**

SHARALEE 2 b.f. Saritamer 130–Sharivari 81 (Hugh Lupus 132) (1980 5v 5g 5f 5fg^3 5fg 6fg 5g) May 20; 2,100Y; workmanlike filly; half-sister to 1m winner Podzola (by Royal Prerogative); dam half-sister to very smart 5f filly Harem; plater; ran best race when 1½ lengths third of 20 to Onward Gal at Ripon in May; should stay 6f; wears blinkers. *M. W. Easterby.* **43**

SHARAVOGUE 3 gr.f. Silly Season 127–Charter Island 88 (Runnymede 123) (1979 NR 1980 7g 6g 7fg 6g 7d 6g) useful sort; third foal; half-sister to very useful Watership Down (by Murrayfield), a winner at up to 1m in France; dam stayed 7f well; well beaten in varied company, including claiming; bolted before start fifth outing and was taken early to post when blinkered on final appearance; trained part of season by W. Hastings-Bass. *P. Calver.* –

SHARELLE 2 b.f. Relko 136–Damiana 84 (Mourne 126) (1980 8g 8d 10s) Mar 21; big, strong filly; second live foal; dam 1m winner; ran on steadily over last 3f **67** p when eighth of 17 to Spin of a Coin in maiden race at Nottingham in October, third outing and best effort; will be suited by 1½m; the type to do better at 3 yrs. *P. Cundell.*

SHARK SONG 2 gr.f. Song 132–Sylvanecte 70 (Silver Shark 129) (1980 $6g^{4}$ $6fg^{2}$ 6d* 5d*) Apr 16; 40,000Y; strong, good sort; third foal; sister to modest 5f winner Jubilee Song, and half-sister to Silver Lord (by Abwah), a useful winner at up to 7f; dam won over 1¼m; eased 2 or 3 lengths when landing the odds by 3 lengths from Hit Record in 17-runner maiden race at Newmarket in October; tended to hang when 7/4 on for minor event at Doncaster later in month but finally won in fairly good style by ½ length from Pettistree; had run very well on previous starts, looking sure to win when 3 lengths clear 1f out in Blue Seal Stakes at Ascot only to fail by ½ length to hold off Petroleuse; not sure to stay beyond 6f; useful. *J. Hindley.* **103**

SHARMADA (FR) 2 ch.f. Zeddaan 130–Shireen (Prince Taj 123) (1980 5d* $5s^{4}$ 5g* 5g $5d^{2}$ $5g^{2}$) sister to very useful French miler Shariyar, closely related to a minor winner by Kalamoun, and half-sister to a winner; dam won twice over 1¼m in France; a speedy filly who won a newcomers race at Longchamp in May and 50,000 franc Prix des Jouvencelles at Vichy in July, latter by 2 lengths from Marie du Mont; also second in 2 good races, going down by only ½ length to Enigma (rec 4 lb) in Prix de la Vallee d'Auge at Deauville in August and by 2½ lengths to Greenway in Group 3 Prix d'Arenberg at Chantilly in September; bred to stay at least 1m but is evidently regarded as a sprinter; yet to race on a firm surface. *F. Mathet, France.* **113**

SHARP CASTAN 3 ch.f. Sharpen Up 127–Sultry One (Tropique 128) (1979 6d 5g* $6fg^{3}$ $8fg^{3}$ 1980 7v 7v $6f^{3}$) tall, lightly-made filly; useful (rated 101) in 1979; well beaten at 3 yrs; needs further than 6f and stays 1m; acts on a firm surface; blinkered final start. *C. Brittain.* **89**

SHARP CELESTE 3 ch.f. Sharpen Up 127–Celeste 83 (Sing Sing 134) (1979 5fg $5fg^{4}$ 5g 6fg 1980 6fg 6fg 6d $7g^{3}$ $5.8g^{4}$ $7fg^{2}$ $6fg^{4}$ $8g^{3}$ 5g* 8g 7g* 7g*) small filly; in good form in September, winning 23-runner maiden race at Kempton and handicaps at Lingfield (from Star Flare) and Goodwood (rather comfortably by 2 lengths from Rabdan); stays 1m; acts on a firm surface; sweated up at Kempton; swerved badly left at start first outing; has run creditably for an apprentice; sold 16,500 gns Newmarket December Sales. *S. Matthews.* **81**

SHARP CHRISTMAS 3 b.g. Sharpen Up 127–Christmas Pageant (March Past 124) (1979 6d 6f 1980 6v 5f $5f^{2}$ 6f $6f^{4}$ 7f 6fg 5g 5f 6g 6g 6d) robust gelding; poor mover; sprint plater; sometimes blinkered; has run respectably for a boy; sold 670 gns Doncaster September Sales. *G. Toft.* **—**

SHARP DANCER 2 ch.f. Sharpen Up 127–Georgia (Hopeful Venture 125) (1980 5g 5.1fg 5g 5f) Mar 2; 3,200F, 6,000Y; compact filly; first produce; dam, in rear twice in France, is daughter of very useful 1965 2-y-o America; 5¾ lengths sixth of 22 to Copt Hall Realm in maiden race at Lingfield in September, third outing and best effort; will be suited by 7f+. *A. Demetriou.* **61**

SHARP DEAL 3 ch.c. Sharpen Up 127–Jungle Queen (Twilight Alley 133) (1979 8.2g* 1980 10.2fg 8fg* 8g 8fg $8d^{4}$ 8g $8fg^{4}$ 8g) compact colt; ran on gamely to win trainers race at Kempton in May; well beaten afterwards; stays 1m well; acts on a firm surface; pulled very hard when blinkered in apprentice race on sixth outing. *C. Nelson.* **79**

SHARP END 2 b.c. Sharpen Up 127–Death Ray 100 (Tamerlane 128) (1980 $6d^{2}$ 7f) Apr 10; well-made, attractive colt; half-brother to 6 winners, including Irish Guinness Oaks winner Shoot A Line (by High Line) and good 7f to 1½m winner More Light (by Morston); dam miler; looked extremely well when weak 15/2 shot for maiden race at Salisbury in June but dwelt at start and ran very green when taking up the running 1½f out, eventually going down by 1½ lengths to Oraston; again looked very well when favourite for Sandwich Stakes at Ascot the following month but was beaten over 2f out and finished ninth of 11 behind Glint of Gold; should be well suited by 7f; possibly not at his best on firm going. *R. Hern.* **86**

SHARPENER 3 ch.f. Sharpen Up 127–Cansanta 96 (Canisbay 120) (1979 5.1fg 5f 7g 7g 8g 8g* $8g^{3}$ 1980 10f $8g^{3}$ 8g 8s* $8.2d^{4}$ 8d) small filly; beat Greyburn a length in handicap at Newcastle in August; stays 1m well; acts well on soft going; ran moderately final outing; sold 12,500 gns Newmarket December Sales. *G. Pritchard-Gordon.* **80**

William Hill Sprint Championship, York—a most impressive performance from Sharpo, who wins from Valeriga

SHARP ENOUGH 3 ro.g. Sharp Edge 123–Quite Enough (Quorum 126) **50**
(1979 5g 5v 5g 6d^2 5s 7f^3 7f^2 7fg^2 7g^3 7d^3 8fg 7fg^4 8.2fg 7fg 7d 1980 8.2s 7f 7fg 8f^2) compact gelding; second in seller at Newmarket in May; not seen out again; will probably stay beyond 1m; seems to act on any going; often blinkered. *P. Kelleway.*

SHARP FIDDLE 5 b.g. Sharpen Up 127–Second Fiddle (Fair Trial) (1979 **73** d
15.5g 14fg^2 12g^2 16fg 12f^2 12f^2 1980 17.1f* 12f* 14g^2 22.2fg 16g) quite a moderate handicapper; successful in May at Bath and Wolverhampton (made all); well beaten in Queen Alexandra Stakes at Royal Ascot in June and doesn't get extreme distances; probably needs a sound surface; tried in blinkers at 3 yrs; goes well for an amateur rider; sold 540 gns Newmarket Autumn Sales. *R. Boss.*

SHARPO 3 ch.c. Sharpen Up 127–Moiety Bird (Falcon 131) (1979 5fg 1980 **128**
5f* 6g^2 6d^3 5g* 5g^2 5f^2)

Sharpo recovered from his previous year's hip injury to put up two of the most impressive performances of the season over five furlongs, in the Temple Stakes at Sandown and the William Hill Sprint Championship at York. He was probably good enough to have been champion sprinter in some seasons. Unluckily for him, though, he was foaled in the same year as Moorestyle who has beaten him at five furlongs and six furlongs on the two occasions they have met. Sharpo is bound to win more good races, but those two defeats were decisive enough to show that his opportunities will be limited as long as Moorestyle is kept to sprinting.

Sharpo's performance in the Temple Stakes in May, on only the second outing in his life, held out the promise of the arrival of one of the top-class sprinters racing urgently needed. He wasn't well placed in the early stages but soon after halfway he started to run, and he produced an electrifying turn of speed to pass the field with considerable ease and go clear in the last furlong. He won by two and a half lengths from the one-time leader Abdu, the Palace House Stakes third; the Palace House runner-up Vaigly Great was outpaced. Next time out Sharpo beat the Palace House winner Valeriga into third place when second to Kearney in the Cork and Orrery Stakes at Royal Ascot. The 11/4 favourite on this occasion (he'd been 33/1 at Sandown), he stayed six furlongs well, coming back so strongly after looking done with that he would have won with a little further to travel. Kearney, receiving 4 lb, beat him a neck.

Sharpo ran only once at six furlongs afterwards, confirming on that occasion he stays the trip. The occasion was the William Hill July Cup at Newmarket, astoundingly the only Group 1 race at the distance in Europe not restricted to two-year-olds. Moorestyle won the race like an exceptionally good horse by two and a half lengths from Vaigly Great. Sharpo was one of four that raced with Moorestyle on the stand side and had no excuses; he tracked the winner, never going quite so well, and ran on under pressure up the hill for third place four lengths behind.

Moorestyle wasn't entered in the William Hill Sprint Championship, nor was Vaigly Great; and the King's Stand Stakes winner African Song appeared to go lame in the race. That left Sharpo with Valeriga, who had in the meantime won the King George Stakes at Goodwood, to contend with—plus Abdu, Runnett, Flash N Thunder, Greenland Park, the two-year-olds Chummy's Special and Swan Princess, and the handicappers Cree Song and Crews Hill. Sharpo raced towards the stand side of the course again, the side at York which if anything had seemed the slower during the previous two days of the meeting, while Valeriga stuck to the far side. Sharpo trounced them all. Held up (riding him this way seems to suit him well), he was pushed past Swan Princess to take the lead from Valeriga one and a half furlongs out; once in front there was no danger and he steadily increased his advantage to two and a half lengths ridden along with hands and heels. Abdu was beaten as far again. The William Hill Sprint Championship continues, by the way, to be classed as Group 2 in the so-called Pattern of Racing. Such a low classification, indefensible right from the start, becomes a bigger nonsense than ever in 1981 with £50,000 added to the stakes.

Sharpo (ch.c. 1977)	Sharpen Up (ch 1969)	Atan (ch 1961)	Native Dancer
			Mixed Marriage
		Rocchetta (ch 1961)	Rockefella
			Chambiges
	Moiety Bird (ch 1971)	Falcon (b 1964)	Milesian
			Pretty Swift
		Gaska (ch 1961)	Gilles de Retz
			Sally Deans

Almost as baffling as why the William Hill Sprint Championship isn't Group 1 is why Sharpo should follow the best display of his career with his first and only disappointing one. 11/4 on for the Scarbrough Stakes at Doncaster in September, he could make no impression on the fast-starting Sayyaf and went down by four lengths, only just holding off old Epsom Imp. If anything ailed him it didn't last long, for a month later he ran a cracking race against Moorestyle in the Prix de l'Abbaye de Longchamp. As always, he looked very well in himself in the paddock. Drawn two—a highly-favoured position before the course was drained during the winter and the stalls were re-sited—he moved up with Moorestyle (drawn eight of ten) to challenge Adraan around halfway, and having passed Adraan with a measure of ease he gave Moorestyle a good fight until well held in the last furlong. He tired quickly near the end, barely hanging on to second place from Valeriga. Moorestyle beat him by a length and a half.

Sharpo's dam never ran; his grandam Gaska was a speedy two-year-old who didn't train on; his great grandam Sally Deans was a miler, the daughter of

Miss M. Sheriffe's "Sharpo"

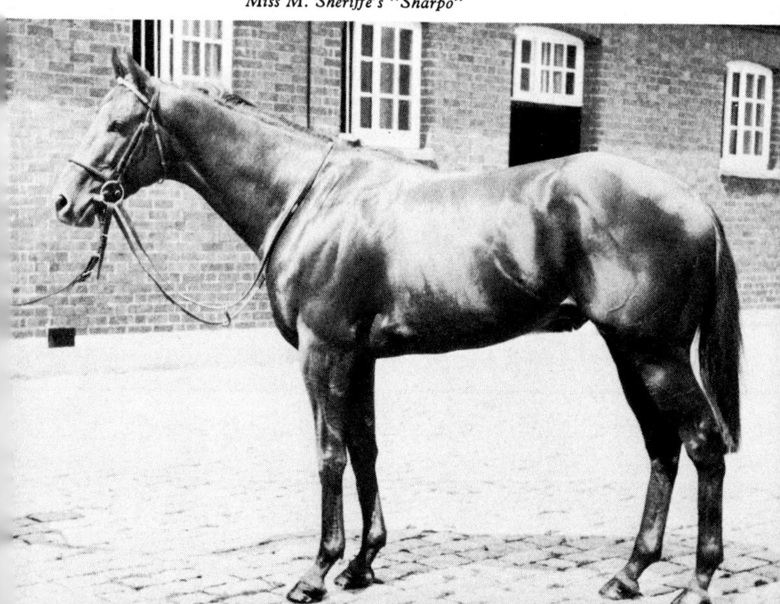

a Wokingham winner. There has been another important sprinter in the family in recent years—the tip-top handicapper St Alphage—and another top-class horse, Yellow God. Both were half-brothers, by Red God, to Gaska. Sharpo is a half-brother to the four-year-old Demi Feu (by Firestreak), a winner at up to a mile and a quarter who has gone the wrong way temperamentally.

Sharpo appears to have a very even temperament, and certainly has a relaxed style of racing for a sprinter. He goes particularly well for Eddery though he has also won for Rouse; so far, Carson's bustling and driving has seemed less effective on him than on most horses. Sharpo, an attractive, close-coupled colt and a good mover, acts well on firm going; the only time he ran on anything softer than good was on dead in the July Cup. He has the advantage over some of the sprinters in that he's effective at both five furlongs and six furlongs. *J. Tree.*

SHARP STAR 2 ch.g. Sharpen Up 127–Sara's Star 70 (Sheshoon 132) (1980 5f 5f3 6f4 6g 6fg 6g 8.2g 6g4 7d) Apr 7; 1,700Y; leggy gelding; half-brother to several winners, including useful and very tough 5f to 1m winner Venus of Stretham (by Tower Walk); in frame in maiden auction events and a £2,700 seller; should stay 7f+; suited by some give in the ground; blinkered sixth to eighth outings. *G. Blum.* **64**

SHARPSUN 2 ch.c. Sunyboy 110–Sharpie 72 (Roan Rocket 128) (1980 5fg 5f 7s 7fg 7fg 7.2d 8d4 8d 7d 10s) Mar 13; small colt; first foal; dam placed over 1m and 1¼m; 8¾ lengths fourth of 15 to Royal Heritage in maiden race at Bath in October, best effort; should be suited by 1¼m; ran badly eighth start. *J. Haine.* **61**

SHARP TALKER 4 b.g. Sharpen Up 127–Ethne (I Say 125) (1979 8s 10.1g 8g 8fg3 7f 1980 8fg 8.3f 7fg) plater; stays 1m; tailed off final start. *J. Douglas-Home.* **—**

SHARP VENITA 2 b.f. Sharp Edge 123–Miss Venus (Comedy Star 121) (1980 5f* 5f2 6fg 5g 5fg2 5f3 5fg 5f 6g) Feb 21; good sort; walks and moves well; first foal; dam never ran; won 19-runner maiden race at Newbury in April by 4 lengths from Fair Rosalind; second afterwards in £2,900 event at York and 11-runner nursery at Goodwood, in latter going down by 1½ lengths to Mrs Palmer; should stay 6f; acts on firm going. *P. Cole.* **84**

SHARSHA (FR) 2 b. or br.f. Labus–Semnica (Bon Mot III 132) (1980 7fg 7g3 8fg3 8.2s*) Mar 9; neat filly; good mover; fourth foal; dam second 4 times at around 1½m in France; showed improved form when winning 8-runner nursery at Nottingham in October by a length from Nimblemoss; will stay 1½m; evidently well suited by soft going. *M. Stoute.* **84**

SHASAVAAN 2 b.c. Red God 128§–Shaara (Sanctus II 132) (1980 5g* 6g* 7.3d3) **117**

Shasavaan is probably the best representative from the penultimate crop of Red God, who died in April, 1979. Red God's influence at stud has been considerable: Blushing Groom, Yellow God, Green God, St Alphage, Red Alert, Red Lord, Silver God and Stanford are among the good colts he sired, and Folle Rousse, Jacinth and Greenland Park are the pick of his good fillies. Red God

Duke of Edinburgh Stakes, Ascot—Shasavaan beats newcomers Obrovac (centre), Ghadeer (left) and Spectacular Sky

even managed to make his mark on National Hunt racing—through Kelanne, winner of the Irish Sweeps Hurdle in 1971. As a potential stallion Shasavaan is unlikely to be the attraction that Blushing Groom (syndicated for six million dollars before he ran in the Derby) was, but if he can win a good race or two as a three-year-old his future at stud should be assured: there are few Red God horses apart from Stanford and Red Alert standing in Europe.

Shasavaan's stiffest and most important test came on his third outing, in the Horris Hill Stakes at Newbury in October. He started joint-third favourite with Cut Above in a field of ten runners behind Gielgud and Kalaglow, both with much better form to their credit than Shasavaan and the latter unbeaten in four races. Shasavaan took the eye in the paddock—he's an attractive, quality-looking colt—and ran well for third place, three and three quarter lengths behind Kalaglow after having to be switched passing the two-furlong marker. Cut Above, receiving the 5-lb maiden allowance from the others, took second. Shasavaan had made his debut only four weeks earlier, in a moderate maiden race at Nottingham; he won easily there, and eleven days later went on to take the Duke of Edinburgh Stakes at Ascot by a length from Obrovac, running on strongly in the last two furlongs after starting slowly.

Shasavaan (b.c. May 10, 1978)	Red God (ch 1954)	Nasrullah (b 1940)	Nearco
			Mumtaz Begum
		Spring Run (b 1948)	Menow
			Boola Brook
	Shaara (b 1972)	Sanctus II (b 1960)	Fine Top
			Sanelta
		Shiraza (b 1966)	Twilight Alley
			But Lovely

Shaara, the dam, had a brief and distinctly moderate career on the racecourse, gaining places in three maiden races at up to eleven furlongs in the French Provinces as a three-year-old from four outings. Shaara's dam, though, was a very useful racemare in France at up to thirteen furlongs; she is also the dam of five winners, two of them, Shimnar (by Baldric II) and Sharazar (by Silver Shark), good ones in France. Few of Red God's progeny show their best form beyond a mile and we don't anticipate Shasavaan's doing so either. After such a short career to date, it's most unlikely that we've seen the best of Shasavaan. *M. Stoute.*

SHAYBOOB 3 ch.g. The Go-Between 129–Pepin (Midsummer Night II 117) (1979 6d* 1980 6s* 6fg^{4} 6d^{3} 6g* 6g* 6fg 6d 6s^{4} 6d^{4}) big gelding; successful in minor event at Nottingham and handicaps at Ripon and Yarmouth, making all on 2 occasions; ran creditably when blinkered last 2 starts; will stay 7f; needs some give in the ground; genuine and consistent. *W. O'Gorman.* **98**

SHEBA'S GLORY 2 br.c. Averof 123–Little Miss 92 (Aggressor 130) (1980 5g 5fg^{2} 5f* 5g^{3} 6g^{2} 6fg 6d 6g 6g) Apr 9; 4,300F, 8,000Y; small, compact colt; brother to Irish 3-y-o 1½m winner Queen of the Brush, and half-brother to 2 middle-distance winners; dam, half-sister to Favoletta and Furioso, won over middle distances; sweated up badly prior to winning 9-runner maiden race at Epsom in June by a neck from Chanson du Nuit; again didn't impress in paddock when good second to Borisov in minor event at Newcastle later in month; will be suited by 7f; beaten in nurseries last 4 outings, wearing blinkers on eighth appearance. *F. Durr.* **90**

SHEDAR 2 b.f. Owen Anthony 102–Saratoga Maid (Saratoga Skiddy 113) (1980 5.3fg 5g 6fg 5f 5g) first foal; dam of no account; only poor form, including in sellers. *R. Hoad.* **–**

SHEER DELIGHT 2 ch.f. Gay Fandango 132–Sheer Joy (Major Portion 129) (1980 5g 6s^{3} 6d 7g^{4}) Feb 19; 25,000Y; well-made, robust filly; doesn't impress in her slower paces; half-sister to 3 winners, including smart 1m and 1¼m handicapper Jumpabout (by Double Jump); dam never ran; quite moderate form in maiden races; seems to stay 7f. *A. Johnson.* **78**

SHEER GRIT 2 b.c. Busted 134–Abettor 103 (Abernant 142) (1980 6g 7g* 8g* 8d^{3}) **117**

1980 must be a year that trainer Brittain would rather forget. If it wasn't bad enough that his recently-appointed jockey Lynch was critically injured in a road accident in June, most of his horses were so badly out of form that the stable ended the season with a total of only twenty-five wins from a complement

Prince of Wales' Nursery, Doncaster—a smooth win for Sheer Grit who makes it all and beats Wicked Will

of over a hundred. There was, however, at least one ray of hope in the performances of the two-year-old Sheer Grit.

This rangy, attractive Busted colt proved more precocious than either his breeding or his physique would have led one to expect: he won two of his four starts and ended his first season with a sterling effort in the William Hill Futurity Stakes at Doncaster in October. Sheer Grit started at 16/1 at Doncaster, only fifth choice in the seven-strong field, despite his two wins. It was obvious that he was both useful and improving but neither his length defeat of Cima in the Wren Stakes at Kempton in July nor his smooth defeat of Wicked Will under 7-13 in the Prince of Wales' Nursery at the St Leger meeting suggested he would prove a serious threat to the favourites. He adopted the same tactics he'd used when successful, quickly taking up the running at a strong gallop. The pace proved too much for Robellino and Recitation, both of whom were below par, and it was the 14/1-shot Beldale Flutter who loomed alongside with two furlongs to run. Sheer Grit hung on grimly when headed, living up to his name, and it was only from the distance that Beldale Flutter and then Shergar started to leave him behind. He held on to third place easily enough, four and a half lengths behind Beldale Flutter.

Sheer Grit (b.c. Jan 21, 1978)	Busted (b 1963)	Crepello (ch 1954)	Donatello II
			Crepuscule
		Sans le Sou (b 1957)	Vimy
			Martial Loan
	Abettor (gr 1967)	Abernant (gr 1946)	Owen Tudor
			Rustom Mahal
		Diction (b 1954)	Precipitation
			Dickneos

Sheer Grit was originally knocked down to his trainer for 45,000 guineas at the Newmarket October Sales but after he'd been found to be a crib-biter his owner was able to negotiate a new price of 30,000 guineas, a modest amount to pay for an attractive, classically-bred colt. There's no doubt that Sheer Grit will need a test of stamina and he should make a very smart performer over a mile and a half or more. His dam Abettor was a useful winner over a mile and a half, and her two previous winners in England are the mile-and-a-quarter winners Mossat (a brother to Sheer Grit) and Honeybarrel (by Run The Gantlet). Abettor is a half-sister to the smart Rehearsed, who won the Solario Stakes as well as finishing in the frame in such good races as the Royal Lodge, Eclipse and

Hardwicke Stakes. Their dam, the stayer Diction, was also useful but nowhere near so good as her brother Dickens, a versatile colt who won both the Dante Stakes and the Goodwood Cup as a three-year-old and the Yorkshire Cup the following season. *C. Brittain.*

SHELFORD LAD 3 b. or br.g. Mansingh 120–Enlighten (Twilight Alley 133) (1979 6f 5h^2 6s^3 5g^4 5.1f 1980 7fg 6f 6fg 5fg) leggy, unfurnished gelding; only plating class nowadays; best form at 6f; probably acts on any going; sold 1,050 gns Newmarket July Sales. *W. O'Gorman.* —

SHELLEY LOUISE 2 ch.f. Sweet Revenge 129–Jailhouse Rock (Gulf Pearl 117) (1980 5fg 5.8h 5g 6f) Mar 8; 1,500Y; strong filly; half-sister to a winning hurdler; dam ran only twice; in mid-division in maiden and minor events (backed from 10/1 to 7/2 on third outing). *Mrs J. Reavey.* **61**

SHELTON GIRL 3 b.f. Mummy's Pet 125–Under Cover (Bleep-Bleep 134) (1979 5fg 5s 5g 5f 1980 6f) big, workmanlike filly; poor form in maiden races; blinkered final start at 2 yrs. *C. Bewicke.* —

SHENOULA 2 ch.f. Sheshoon 132–Yanoula 79 (Nosca) (1980 5d 5s 6s) May 13; 1,600Y; neat filly; half-sister to several minor winners; dam best at 2 yrs; well beaten at Catterick (seller) and Stockton (seller and minor event) in October. *W. Haigh.* —

SHEPERION 3 ch.c. Sheshoon 132–Hyperion Lass (Punchinello 97) (1979 NR 1980 10s 16d) big colt; fourth foal; half-brother to winning sprinter Hyperion Chief (by Mansingh); dam a point-to-pointer; in rear in minor and maiden events at Nottingham in June, once finishing last. *W. Wharton.* —

SHEPHERD'S GLASS 4 b.c. Blakeney 126–Pampas Flower 80 (Pampered King 121) (1979 10v^2 11.7g 16d^4 10fg^2 12g 12s 1980 12fg 8f* 7fg 8fg^4 8g^2 8fg 8g^2 8g 8h) attractive colt; won amateur riders event at Ripon in May by 2½ lengths from Terry Paine; best form at up to 1¼m and probably doesn't stay 2m; acts on any going; trained by J. Haine until after sixth outing. *Mrs J. Pitman.* **65**

SHERBET DIP 3 ch.g. Golden Dipper 119–Sherbet (Zarathustra 131) (1979 6f 8fg 1980 8g 8d) of no account; sold 320 gns Ascot November Sales. *T. Marshall.* —

SHERE BEAUTY 3 b.f. Mummy's Pet 125–Mossgo 106 (Vigo 130) (1979 5d^4 5d* 6g 6s^2 6fg 7.3s 1980 7.2fg 8fg) tall, sparely-made filly; moderate (rated 83) at 2 yrs; tailed-off last in Fred Darling Stakes at Newbury in April; refused to race in 1,000 Guineas at Newmarket following month and appears to have gone the wrong way temperamentally; stays 6f; acts on soft going and is possibly not at her best on a firm surface; best left alone; sold privately 2,000 gns Doncaster August Sales. *I. Balding.* §§

SHERELCO 2 ro.c. Relko 136–Mary D 99 (Vigo 130) (1980 5g 6g 6fg 6g) May 24; 2,500Y; big colt; half-brother to 3 winners, including very useful 1971 Irish 2-y-o 5f winner Supercede (by Super Sam); dam 5f sprinter; little worthwhile form in maiden and minor events; blinkered fourth outing. *S. Matthews.* —

SHERGAR 2 b.c. Great Nephew 126–Sharmeen (Val de Loir 133) (1980 8fg* 8d^2) **122**

At the end of September, the Stoute stable looked to contain two first-rate classic hopes in the Great Nephew colts Centurius and Shergar. Grundy's younger brother Centurius had looked worthy of his 270,000-guinea purchase price when sauntering home a very smooth winner of the Mornington Stakes at Ascot and Shergar had made a highly impressive debut when favourite for the twenty-three-runner Kris Plate at Newbury, coming to the final one and a half furlongs with his head still tucked in his chest then quickening away in excellent style to win by four lengths from Chief Speaker. By the end of October, though, both had been beaten in pattern races. Centurius' effort when last of five to Storm Bird in the Dewhurst was bad, too bad to be true, but Shergar ran extremely well for an inexperienced colt when defeated in the William Hill Futurity at Doncaster.

Shergar seemed to have a stiff task at Doncaster against Robellino and Recitation, already the winners of Europe's two other top mile races for two-year-old colts, the Royal Lodge Stakes and the Grand Criterium. He'd created such a favourable impression at Newbury though that he vied for favouritism, eventually starting third choice at 5/2 behind Robellino at 2/1 and Recitation

Kris Plate, Newbury—favourite Shergar makes a winning debut, beating Chief Speaker and Jungle Jim (rails)

at 9/4. He ran a good deal better than either but still found one too good for him. After being well placed from the start Shergar was driven up to look a real threat as Beldale Flutter finally shook off the front-running Sheer Grit coming to the final furlong. A length was as close as he got. He couldn't find any extra pace and Beldale Flutter forged away to beat him two and a half lengths.

Shergar (b.c. Mar 3, 1978)	Great Nephew (b 1963)	Honeyway (br 1941)	Fairway
			Honey Buzzard
		Sybil's Niece (ch 1951)	Admiral's Walk
			Sybil's Sister
	Sharmeen (b 1972)	Val de Loir (b 1959)	Vieux Manoir
			Vali
		Nasreen (b 1964)	Charlottesville
			Ginetta

It seems that the Derby is to be Shergar's main objective, for he hasn't even been entered for the Two Thousand Guineas. His performance at Doncaster suggests that stamina will prove his long suit, and he has the makings of a very good colt over middle distances. He's a deep-girthed, good sort, with scope, and his pedigree is first-class. Together with Tolmi, Mrs Penny, Nikoli and Vaigly Great he was one of Great Nephew's wide variety of high-class runners in 1980. He comes from one of the most influential families in the Stud Book, having as his sixth dam Mumtaz Begum, the dam of Nasrullah and herself a daughter of Mumtaz Mahal. Shergar's dam Sharmeen was no Mumtaz Mahal, just a fairly useful French middle-distance winner, but both her first two foals are winners. Sharmeen is a half-sister to the very smart Naasiri, winner of the Prix Greffulhe, a granddaughter of the French One Thousand Guineas and Prix du Moulin de Longchamp winner Ginetta, and a great-granddaughter of the outstanding Diableretta, whose seven successes as a two-year-old include the Queen Mary, July, Cherry Hinton and Molecomb Stakes. *M. Stoute.*

SHERKIN ISLAND 3 gr.f. Dragonara Palace 115–Judolyn 87 (Canisbay 120) (1979 NR 1980 7f 7.6f 5d 5s 7g 8g 8g) 4,600Y; rangy filly; half-sister to 2 sprint winners; dam won at up to 1m; little worthwhile form in varied company, including selling; sold 390 gns Ascot October Sales. *P. Kelleway.* —

SHERRYMAN 2 b.c. Manacle 123–Sherry Girl 81 (Appiani II 128) (1980 5d 6g 7g 10d) Mar 22; neat colt; cost 10,000 gns as a yearling but is only a bad plater; blinkered third outing; sold out of J. Dunlop's stable 800 gns Ascot September Sales after third start. *I. Vickers.* —

SHERRY SPICE 3 ch.g. Sheshoon 132–Latin Spice (Frankincense 120) (1979 NR 1980 11fg 11.7fg 11.7f 11f 10g 10.8s) compact gelding; behind in maiden races; blinkered fourth and fifth starts; sold 625 gns Ascot July Sales. *P. M. Taylor.* —

SHINING FINISH 3 b.c. Nijinsky 138–Lacquer 118 (Shantung 132) (1979 8g 8s4 1980 12fg* 16g 13.3d 12d* 12g* 12d* 12d*) **124**

This most attractive colt is due to join his brother Bright Finish at stud in Australia in 1981. As his services won't be needed until into the second half of the year, and as he was in such magnificent form in the autumn, it has been decided to let him race on for a while in England. Like his brother, Shining Finish improved enormously as a three-year-old, ending up by winning a pattern event; he won his last four races on the trot, the last of them the St Simon Stakes at Newbury.

Shining Finish couldn't equal Bright Finish's unbeaten record at three. He was unplaced in the Queen's Vase and the Morland Brewery Handicap, supplying pretty convincing evidence that he doesn't stay two miles when finishing tailed off in the former. If it's true that he has stamina limitations we have an interesting example here of two horses bred the same way exhibiting a significant difference in character. Bright Finish was extremely well suited by a mile and three quarters and two miles (his best performances were in winning the Yorkshire Cup and the Jockey Club Cup); on the evidence we have before us, Shining Finish is unquestionably best at a mile and a half.

Shining Finish, who had run in races won by Henbit and Many Moons as a two-year-old, began his second season by winning the Culford Stakes at Newmarket in May. The form didn't make him a world-beater; an interesting point, though, was that he was ridden from behind and brought with a strong run to lead near the post. He next won in August, from four opponents in a limited handicap, the A.T.S. Trophy, at Newbury; then he won further handicaps at Goodwood and Ascot from fields of the same size. He made all when beating Mirror Boy at Goodwood and Ascot, Piggott treating us to one of his best exhibitions of waiting in front as he won a shade comfortably by half a length on the latter occasion.

Shining Finish was conceding only 5 lb to Mirror Boy at Ascot, and that had been his best performance; in contrast, most of his eight opponents in the St Simon Stakes had won or run well in pattern races. But he was bang in form whereas some of the others weren't and in addition he got the run of the race, shrewdly ridden by Cauthen who set a very steady pace until quickening it up considerably on the turn. From three furlongs out Shining Finish never looked in any danger, and he won by two lengths from another rapidly improving horse Snow. Quite a rough race developed behind him in the straight as the opposition fought for openings. Nicholas Bill had a particularly poor run, and was subsequently promoted from third to second because Snow crossed him. Given a clear run, there wouldn't have been much in it between Nicholas Bill and Shining Finish, the latter of whom was receiving 5 lb more than weight-for-age.

Stayers haven't been much in evidence in Shining Finish's family in recent times; on the contrary Horama's descendants have been noted for their speed.

St Simon Stakes, Newbury—the improving Shining Finish wins from Snow (subsequently relegated to third) and Nicholas Bill

Lacquer won the Cambridgeshire and Irish One Thousand Guineas, never being tried beyond nine furlongs. However, the other flat-race winner she has produced, Brilliantine (by Stage Door Johnny), finished a good third in the Cheshire Oaks. Brilliantine also ran creditably over the Morland Brewery course in the Geoffrey Freer Stakes; she ran too freely when tried in blinkers in the longer Park Hill Stakes. Shining Finish's performance in the Morland Brewery wasn't such as to rule him out of future races at thirteen furlongs or so, but it does raise doubts

Shining Finish (b.c. 1977)	Nijinsky (b 1967)	Northern Dancer (b 1961)	Nearctic
			Natalma
		Flaming Page (b 1959)	Bull Page
			Flaring Top
	Lacquer (b 1964)	Shantung (b 1956)	Sicambre
			Barley Corn
		Urshalim (b 1951)	Nasrullah
			Horama

about his prospects of staying the trip in the Yorkshire Cup, which may well be on his programme. For our money, we'd much prefer to see him at a mile and a half. Bright Finish was very well suited by soft going. Shining Finish hasn't raced on extremes since he came to himself; he has won on good to firm and good to soft, showing easily his best form on the latter. He probably has more improvement in him. *J. Tree.*

SHINING GRACE 3 gr.f. Supreme Sovereign 119–Codicil 95 (Prince Chevalier) —
(1979 6g 5.8g 1980 10fg 11f) lengthy filly; little worthwhile form in maiden races. *N. Vigors.*

SHINING PRINCE 6 ch.h. Prince des Loges 73–Polish Polish (Clairefontaine —
74) (1979 NR 1980 6d 8g) first foal; dam poor plater; last in minor events at Brighton in September (behind Pace Jean) and October (behind Lightning Label). *R. Sturdy.*

SHINING TOR 3 b.c. High Top 131–Wolverene 114 (Relko 136) (1979 7d **112**
1980 10fg^{2} 11f* 12g^{4} 11d^{4}) tall, lengthy colt; good mover; kept on strongly to beat Grindstone 1½ lengths in 22-runner maiden race at Newbury in May; fourth subsequently in King Edward VII Stakes at Royal Ascot (3¾ lengths behind Light Cavalry) and Mecca Bookmakers Scottish Derby at Ayr in July (well beaten by Prince Roland); had earlier run well when 6 lengths second to Dukedom in White Rose Stakes at Ascot; suited by 1½m; acts on firm going and is possibly unsuited by a soft surface. *J. Winter.*

SHINY COPPER 2 b.g. Shiny Tenth 120–Comprella 54 (Compensation 127) —
(1980 5f 5fg^{4}) Mar 1; half-brother to 1m winner First Vote (by Royal Prerogative), subsequently a very good winner over hurdles in France; dam won 11f seller; 9 lengths fourth of 7 to Rathmoy's Sparkle in maiden race at Carlisle in May. *Denys Smith.*

SHINY FUTURE 3 ch.f. Shiny Tenth 120–Pemba (Sodium 128) (1979 NR —
1980 8fg 10.2fg 8d 12s) first reported foal; dam won over 11f in France; no worthwhile form in varied company. *S. Kernick.*

SHIRLEY GROVE 2 b.f. Vulgan Slave–Maidensgrove 61 (Canadel II 126) —
(1980 8f 9d 7d 8d) Apr 30; neat filly; first foal; dam won 1m seller; well beaten in maiden and minor events at Wolverhampton (2) and Leicester (2) in the autumn. *R. Hollinshead.*

SHIRLEY RAAPHORST (HOL) 2 ch.f. Go Marching–Reedy 81 (Klairon 131) —
(1980 5d 6s 5g 6.5g) half-sister to a winner in Holland by Sun Prince; dam, half-sister to very useful Tiber, won over 7f at 2 yrs; unquoted when behind in maiden race at Wolverhampton (backward and went down poorly) in June and 18-runner minor event at Nottingham the following month; unplaced twice behind Marmorera in Holland subsequently. *N. Guest.*

SHOEN (FR) 2 ch.c. Viceregal–Kalinia (Puissant Chef 132) (1980 7s^{2} 7d* 8g^{2} **116**
7g^{3} 8d) Mar 6; 115,000 francs Y (approx £12,100); half-brother to 2 minor French winners; dam very useful French middle-distance winner and also won over jumps; a very useful colt who won valuable Prix des Yearlings at Deauville in August by a short head from Lou Piguet (gave 3lb); put up good efforts on next 2 starts, going down by only ½ length to Vorias (rec 3lb) in Group 3 Prix la Rochette at Longchamp in September and finishing 2½ lengths third of 5 to Cresta Rider (rec 4lb) in Group 2 Criterium de Maisons-Laffitte; will stay 1¼m; yet to race on a firm surface; sent to USA. *G. Bonnaventure, France.*

SHOESHINE LAD 3 br.c. The Brianstan 128–Bridge of Stories 80 (Appian Bridge 111) (1979 5s 5fg 6fg 1980 5s* 5fg 6g 5f) leggy, quite useful sort; has been hobdayed; won handicap at Leicester in March by 3 lengths from Tokata; best at 5f; needs some give in the ground; sold 460 gns Newmarket Autumn Sales. *P. Cole.* **73**

SHOOLERBOY 4 b.c. Shoolerville 121–Lovely Lady II 81 (My Love 133) (1979 NR 1980 10fg 10f 12fg 16d) compact colt; poor maiden. *K. Stapleton.* —

SHOOT A LINE 3 b.f. High Line 125–Death Ray 100 (Tamerlane 128) (1979 7.3s* 1980 12.3f* 12f 12d* 12d* 12d* 14.6g*) **127**

We wonder how many of our readers recollect the exploits of a filly called Ark Royal. The fact that Meld was her contemporary deprived Ark Royal of victory in a classic—she was a comfortable second to Meld in the Oaks—but she won her six other races at three, including the Lingfield Oaks Trial, the Ribblesdale Stakes, the Yorkshire Oaks, the Park Hill Stakes and the Newmarket Oaks. Felsetta, the grandam of Ark Royal, is the fourth dam of Shoot A Line whose record as a three-year-old bore a striking resemblance to that of Ark Royal a quarter of a century earlier. Shoot A Line also suffered her only defeat in the Oaks and won three of the races—the Ribblesdale, the Yorkshire Oaks and the Park Hill—that Ark Royal won; Shoot A Line's record, however, boasted a classic success, in the Irish Guinness Oaks. There is also a physical similarity between Ark Royal and Shoot A Line: like Ark Royal, Shoot A Line is wiry and light of build, and not at all an impressive filly to look at.

The best of the middle-distance fillies in training in England in 1980 were a near-vintage bunch. None was so good as Meld, an outstanding filly who won the One Thousand Guineas, the Oaks and the St Leger, but whereas Meld was far and away the best of the three-year-old fillies of 1955, Mrs Penny and the stable-companions Bireme and Shoot A Line each had sound claims to be regarded as the best of her age and sex in training in England in 1980. Mrs Penny, who won the Prix de Diane de Revlon and the Prix Vermeille and was second in the King George VI and Queen Elizabeth Diamond Stakes, didn't meet Bireme or Shoot A Line in racecourse competition; when Bireme and Shoot A Line met for the only time in the Oaks, Shoot A Line seemed clearly out of sorts, playing up at the start and running no sort of race at all. It's our verdict that there was probably little to choose between Mrs Penny, Bireme and Shoot A Line at their best; not for many a year have there been three classic middle-distance fillies of such merit in training in the same year in England.

When the season opened it was common knowledge that the West Ilsley Stables had a very strong team of three-year-old fillies, headed by The Dancer, the top staying filly in the Free Handicap. Shoot A Line had shown immense promise on her only outing at two, winning the Radley Stakes at Newbury in late-October by five lengths from her stable-companion Dancing Shadow, who had started favourite. Shoot A Line earned her place in the Oaks line-up with a five-length victory over the Irish-trained Little Bonny in the Cheshire Oaks; it was a very good performance, considering that Shoot A Line was in need of the race and looked ill at ease on the tight, turning track. After her disappointing run at Epsom, Shoot A Line was sent to Royal Ascot where she was most impressive when joint-favourite for the Ribblesdale Stakes, winning by five lengths from North Forland after being in front, forcing the pace, for most of the way; Shoot A Line ran on with great resolution when tackled by the other joint-favourite Norfolk Gal early in the straight. On the morning of the Ribblesdale Stakes, Bireme got loose at exercise and cut herself. Plans to run Bireme in the

Ribblesdale Stakes, Ascot—Shoot A Line runs away from North Forland

Irish Guinness Oaks, the Curragh—Shoot A Line beats Little Bonny (almost hidden) and Racquette

Irish Guinness Oaks in July had to be shelved and Shoot A Line was sent over in her stead. It's doubtful whether Bireme could have bettered Shoot A Line's display at the Curragh: Carson again had her in front early and she kept on in very determined fashion when the Prendergast-trained pair Little Bonny and Racquette tried to get to her in the straight. Shoot A Line won most decisively by two and a half lengths and three quarters of a length from Little Bonny and Racquette. Shoot A Line's success enabled her trainer to equal Vincent O'Brien's hitherto-unique achievement of having saddled a winner in each of the English and Irish classics.

By the middle of July it had become apparent that West Ilsley was also harbouring a very fine collection of middle-distance colts; the chance of Shoot A Line's stepping up to tackle races such as the King George VI and Queen Elizabeth Diamond Stakes and the St Leger therefore looked remote. She went next to York in August where six opposed her in the Yorkshire Oaks, including the Oaks runner-up Vielle who had been unbeaten since Epsom, easily winning the Lancashire Oaks and the Nassau Stakes. Shoot A Line looked outclassed in the paddock and was completely overshadowed by the strong, shapely Vielle; Yorkshire racegoers, seeing Shoot A Line for the first time, could have been excused for thinking that she had strayed in from an adjacent field—she looked a bag of bones. There may not be much of Shoot A Line but what there is is the right stuff, as the York crowd, who made Vielle favourite, were to see for themselves. Shoot A Line made every yard of the running, setting a good gallop from the start and increasing the tempo in the straight; Vielle looked very dangerous two furlongs out but Shoot A Line is an extremely tough nut to crack and Shoot A Line's tenacity won the day, Vielle ducking to the left soon after being put under strong pressure and Shoot A Line keeping on under the whip to win by a length and a half. The Yorkshire crowd were not taken in by Shoot A Line's appearance when she was returned North for the Park Hill Stakes at the

Yorkshire Oaks, York—an all-the-way win for Shoot A Line who beats the odds-on Vielle

Doncaster St Leger meeting. Starting at 2/1 on, she galloped her five opponents into the ground, coming home an easy winner by eight lengths from Broomstick Corner. In this sort of form, Shoot A Line would have given the colts plenty to do in the St Leger, in which her stable was represented by Water Mill.

Although Shoot A Line was not tested on the racecourse against the best colts we have little doubt that she would have performed creditably against them; she will, however, get her chance in 1981. When a filly reaches the age

Park Hill Stakes, Doncaster—fifth pattern-race win for Shoot A Line, who is well clear of Broomstick Corner and Rapids

of four her connections have a narrower choice of top-class objectives to aim at. The European racing programme offers very few opportunities for a high-class filly above the age of three; in England, four-year-olds and upwards are barred from most of the important fillies' races, including some, such as the Yorkshire Oaks and the Park Hill Stakes, which take place in the second half of the season. Is there a good case for having any pattern race confined to three-year-olds after the first part of the season? Unless there's a better reason for the existing state of affairs than any we have thought of, we'd like to see *all* pattern races for three-year-olds opened up to four year-olds and upwards after midsummer. At present a filly has to beat the colts on weight-for-sex terms to win a top race once she is over the age of three, and, with the regulation sex allowance at only 3 lb, the odds are stacked against her. With races such as the Yorkshire Oaks and the Park Hill Stakes to aim at, owners would have a greater incentive to keep high-class staying fillies in training after the end of their three-year-old careers. And wouldn't the presence in the Yorkshire Oaks field of a four-year-old filly of Shoot A Line's calibre enrich that race and make it more significant?

Shoot A Line (b.f. 1977)	High Line (ch 1966)	High Hat (ch 1957)	Hyperion
			Madonna
		Time Call (b 1955)	Chanteur II
			Aleria
	Death Ray (b 1959)	Tamerlane (br 1952)	Persian Gulf
			Eastern Empress
		Luminant (b 1951)	Nimbus
			Bardia

Plans for Shoot A Line's four-year-old career have not been finalised at the time of writing, although we know her trainer favours a tilt at the Gold Cup. Whether or not Shoot A Line is trained for long-distance races depends, one supposes, on what happens in the interim to Prince Bee, Henbit and one or two of the other colts in the stable. Shoot A Line is effective at a mile and a half

Mr R. A. Budgett's "Shoot A Line" (W. Carson)

but stamina is her strong suit and she is certain to stay at least two miles. Her sire High Line, the only horse this century to win the Jockey Club Cup three years in a row, missed the 1970 Gold Cup because of hard ground and the 1971 Gold Cup because of injury; he never raced beyond two miles but would probably have stayed the Gold Cup trip. Shoot A Line's dam Death Ray was a miler and a half-sister to three horses who made their mark as sprinters—the July Cup winner Daylight Robbery and those very useful two-year-olds Hell's Angels and Winkie. Death Ray often imparts more stamina to her offspring than she herself showed on the racecourse: four of her five previous winners, Hired Assassin (by the sprinter Hook Money), Open Fire (by Aggressor), Sizzler (by Blakeney) and More Light (by Morston) won at around a mile and a half. The very smart four-year-old More Light was second in the Jockey Club Cup to Ardross. We'd put Shoot A Line's chances of staying the Gold Cup course in a truly-run race at better than fifty-fifty; her appearance and her style of racing is very much that of a stayer. If she makes normal progress from three to four—and many fillies don't—she could well prove a live contender for the Cup races. She acts on firm going but is very well suited by some give in the ground. *R. Hern.*

SHOOTING MATCH 2 gr.g. Home Guard 129–Bundling (Petingo 135) (1980 5d 5s3 5f 5f 5s 5s 7f 7fg) Mar 31; 5,400Y; strong, compact gelding; ¾-length third of 10 to Tallishire Abode in maiden race at Nottingham in March, only worthwhile form; should stay 7f; acts on soft going; blinkered sixth outing. *A. Goodwill.* **66**

SHOOT THE SUN 3 b.g. Right Tack 131–Arriva (Disciplinarian) (1979 6fg 6fg2 6s4 1980 7s 10fg 8.5f 10fg 10d*) leggy gelding; won seller at Newmarket in July (sold 3,400 gns afterwards, probably for export to Belgium); stays 1¼m; acts on a firm and a soft surface; sometimes wears blinkers (did when successful). *J. Sutcliffe.* **62**

SHORESWOOD GIRL 3 b.f. Bing II–Tishoorona (Lord of Verona 120) (1979 NR 1980 11d) non-thoroughbred filly; second foal; dam never ran; dwelt and soon tailed-off last in maiden race at Hamilton in June. *H. Bell.* **–**

SHORT OF GOLD 3 b.f. Goldhill 125–Shortino 71 (Fortino II 120) (1979 5d 5fg 1980 6d 6v 6d) neat filly; in rear in minor and maiden races. *R. Hollinshead.* **–**

SHORTSTEP 2 b.c. Tudor Rhythm 112–Shortigal (Galivanter 131) (1980 5f 5f 6g 5f) May 5; second foal; dam unraced half-sister to smart middle-distance handicapper Royal Match; bad maiden. *R. Ward.* **–**

SHOTGUN 2 gr.c. Warpath 113–Brief Flight 108 (Counsel 118) (1980 6g3 7d* 8f*) Feb 12; strong colt; brother to Arrow, successful over 9f and 1½m here and subsequently a good winner in Spain, and half-brother to several winners, including smart Aviator (by Frankincense), a winner at up 1¼m; dam won Northern Free Handicap; a progressive colt who won maiden race at Ayr in August and £3,800 nursery at York the following month, in latter coming with good run in straight to win by a length from Lifestyle despite hanging badly left; will stay 1½m; seems to act on any going; useful and is certain to win more races providing he is not tried too highly. *C. Thornton.* **102** p

SHOUTITOUT 3 gr.g. Town Crier 119–Desert Moss 111 (Mossborough 126) (1979 6fg 5fg 7d 1980 8d) behind in varied company, including selling. *J. Cann.* **–**

SHOW-A-LEG 2 b.c. Tumble Wind–Lovely Woman 81 (Primera 131) (1980 5fg3 5f 6f2 7g* 7d* 8g3 8.2g* 7s) May 8; 1,500F, 9,500Y; strong, shapely colt; half-brother to winning sprinter Argumental P (by Green God) and a winner in Italy; dam won 5 times at up to 9f; improved with distance, winning 21-runner maiden race at Leicester in July and carrying top weight to victory in nurseries at Wolverhampton in August and Nottingham in September; landed the odds by 2 lengths from Maybehandy in last-named; suited by 1m; possibly not at his best on very soft going; consistent. *B. Hobbs.* **106**

SHOW BUSINESS 3 b.f. Auction Ring 123–Modern Miracle (St Chad 120) (1979 5d 5d2 5d 5g 6fg 5f 5f 5f3 1980 5fg 5d3 5.3d 5s 5d 6g) attractive, lengthy filly; has shown no form since 1979 and finished well beaten in seller on final outing; should stay 6f; seems to act on any going; blinkered fifth start; sold 480 gns Ascot August Sales. *A. Ingham.* **46**

SHOW OF HANDS 4 b.g. Royal Prerogative 119–Lindylee 99 (Grey Sovereign 128§) (1979 6g2 5f3 7fg 6g4 1980 8f* 8fg 7fg3 7f* 7f 7g) tall gelding; made all **76**

when winning handicaps at Newcastle (apprentice event) in April and Thirsk (beat Azerila ¾ length) in May; ran moderately last 2 starts and wasn't seen out after June; stays 1m; acts well on firm going; blinkered third start in 1979. *J. Hindley.*

SHOWPIECE 6 b.g. Daring Display 129–Magic Thrust 102 (Zarathustra 131) **64**
(1979 7d 6fg^{3} 6fg 7f 6g^{3} 7g 1980 7d 6g*) dipped-backed gelding; plater in 1979; 20/1 when winning apprentice handicap at Lingfield in June by ½ length from Lord Scrap; seems to stay 7f; acts on any going; excellent mount for a boy; has worn blinkers; sold to D. Wilson only 380 gns Ascot August Sales. *T. Gosling.*

SHRED 3 b.f. Shoolerville 121–Red Barrel 95 (Aureole 132) (1979 5s 6g^{4} 5.8g^{2} –
6f 6s 1980 7.6f 7d 5s^{3} 5fg 5g) rangy filly; good walker; sprint handicapper; acts on soft going; blinkered nowadays. *F. J. Houghton.*

SHREE 2 b.f. Moulton 128–Garnette Rose 74 (St Paddy 133) (1980 5g 5g 5f 6f **49**
5d) Feb 26; rather lightly-made filly; third living foal; half-sister to 1977 2-y-o 5f winner Superior Class (by Decoy Boy); dam seemed to stay 1m; showed a little ability in maiden races, on third outing finishing 9½ lengths seventh of 19 to Salamina at Beverley in August; will stay 1m. *G. Toft.*

SHUFFLING 9 ch.g. St Chad 120–Shoofly 83 (Skymaster 126) (1979 6v^{2} 6g^{4} **74**
7f 7.2s 6s 6g^{2} 6fg 6f^{3} 6f^{4} 7fg^{2} 6g^{4} 7d 1980 6fg 7f 6fg 6fg 7g 6fg^{2} 6f) useful handicapper at his best but is on the downgrade; ran best race of 1980 when second to Welsh Blossom at Newmarket in August; stays 7f; acts on any going; has been tried in blinkers; sometimes wears bandages; excellent mount for an apprentice; started slowly third outing. *W. Hastings-Bass.*

SHURLAND 4 br.g. Mandamus 120–Prattler 68 (Narrator 127) (1979 NR –
1980 10.6s 12.5s 10d) strong, good sort; fifth foal; dam lightly-raced maiden; well beaten in minor events and an amateur riders race in the autumn; still needed race second outing. *M. W. Easterby.*

SHUTTLE D'OR 2 ch.g. Goldhill 125–Northern Flight (Borealis) (1980 –
6g) Feb 26; 6,400Y; brother to Gold Flight, a prolific winner from 7f to 13f, and half-brother to several winners, including useful sprinter Tashkin (by Red God); dam ran once; 50/1 when last of 28 to Cavalry Twill in minor event at Windsor in August. *D. Elsworth.*

SHY TALK 4 ch.f. Sharpen Up 127–Skymistress 91 (Skymaster 126) (1979 –
5d 5s 6d^{2} 5d 6s 6g^{4} 6s 6f 1980 6h 6fg 5g 5s^{4} 6fg^{3} 5f 6g 6d 6f 6fg 6d) leggy, unfurnished filly; quite a moderate handicapper; suited by 6f nowadays; seems to act on any going except very soft; ran moderately when blinkered once at 3 yrs; sometimes bandaged off-hind; trained by W. Haigh until after ninth start. *A. W. Jones.*

SIANORA 2 b.f. Dragonara Palace 115–Sari (Taj Dewan 128) (1980 5f 5f **60**
5fg 6s^{4} 6g 6d 6g 5s) Mar 14; leggy filly; second foal; dam ran only 4 times; plater; suited by 6f and some give in the ground; blinkered penultimate start. *E. Weymes.*

SIBONETTE 2 ch.f. Roman Warrior 132–Golden Mary 71 (Bounteous 125) **68**
(1980 5fg 5.1f 6s 5fg 5.1fg^{3} 5fg 6g) May 4; 2,900Y; good-topped, strong-quartered filly; half-sister to 1979 2-y-o 5f winner Woolcana (by Some Hand); dam placed from 6f to 2m; ran easily best race when 1½ lengths third of 11 to Garnish Island in maiden event at Yarmouth in August; should stay 6f. *A. Demetriou.*

SICASANTA 8 ch.g. Sica Dan 116–Christmas Rush (Klondyke Bill 125) –
(1979 5s 5s 5s 5.8g 5fg 5fg 5f 6fg 5g 7g^{2} 6fg 8fg 5fg 1980 6f 5fg 5fg 5g 5fg 7g 5g 5g 5d) sprint plater; acts on any going but has done all his winning on an easy surface; sometimes wears blinkers; suitable mount for an apprentice; often sweats up. *P. Cundell.*

SIDE BY STEP (USA) 3 br.f. Cougar–Side by Side 77 (Nantallah) (1979 –
NR 1980 10fg 9.4d) $25,000Y; half-sister to winners here and in USA, including fairly useful 1972 2-y-o 6f winner Mile by Mile (by Milesian); dam, half-sister to very smart Twin Time, stayed 13f; beaten some way in maiden races at Brighton in May and Carlisle in June. *L. Cumani.*

SIDE HILL STAR 2 b.f. Comedy Star 121–Outcry (Alcide 136) (1980 –
7fg 7fg 6g) Apr 12; 8,600Y; smallish, compact filly; first foal; dam, behind in 4 races, is sister to good staying filly Outback and daughter of best staying filly of 1963 Outcrop; behind in maiden and minor events. *D. Morley.*

SIDELINE 2 b.f. Ardoon 124–Royal Train (Aureole 132) (1980 5fg 6g 7d^2 7fg* 74
8.2g 8g 7fg* 7f 7d 7g) Mar 27; 1,200Y; leggy filly; none too good a mover; half-sister to winners over jumps here and in Italy; dam left at start on second of only 2 outings; bought out of P. Rohan's stable 3,800 gns after winning seller at Newmarket in August by 5 lengths from Haballoo; won nursery at Leicester under bottom weight the following month, beating Rose of Raby 1½ lengths; has run respectably over 1m but seems better suited by 7f; acts on a firm and a soft surface. *K. Ivory.*

SIDE TRACK 4 br.c. Track Spare 125–Bench Game (King's Bench 132) 84
(1979 7fg 8d^4 9d* 9s^2 10f* 10fg^2 10s 10fg^4 10fg 1980 10.6fg 10fg^2 10.4f^3 11f 10f* 10fg* 10fg 10.6d* 10.2g^3 11s^4 10.5s^2) well-made colt; fair handicapper; successful at Redcar in May (beat Joleg by ½ length in Zetland Gold Cup), Ripon in July and Haydock in August (won Harvey Jones Handicap easily by 2½ lengths from Lindoro); in frame several other times, finishing close second to Telsmoss in valuable apprentice handicap at York in October on final start; best form at up to 1¼m; acts on any going; usually held up. *G. Pritchard-Gordon.*

SIGH 3 br.f. Highland Melody 112–Sioux 95 (Nimbus 130) (1979 5d 5f 5d 72
7g^3 7g 1980 8fg 9f 8f* 8f 8d^2 8fg 10g 8f) workmanlike filly; 25/1 and apprentice ridden when winning 18-runner maiden race at Thirsk in May; respectable second in handicap at Wolverhampton in July; stays 1m; seems to act on any going; often bandaged behind. *W. Marshall.*

SIGIR 2 ch.c. Simbir 130–La Girouette (Double Jump 131) (1980 8g 8g) 77
tall, useful-looking colt; first foal; dam minor French 6f to 1m winner; running on when fairly close-up fifth of 17 to Video Tape in minor event at Newmarket, second outing; will be suited by 1¼m. *L. Cumani.*

SIGNA 2 b.f. On Your Mark 125–Tumblova (Karabas 132) (1980 5.1f 5g) –
Apr 10; 500F, 460Y; small filly; first produce; dam ran only twice; behind in maiden races at Yarmouth and Pontefract (auction event) in June; looks a plater. *I. Walker.*

SIGNAL RAAPHORST (HOL) 3 b.c. Mon Plaisir 121–Hand Signal (For ?
the Road) (1979 NR 1980 8.2s 7.6f^3 8f*(dis) 12g 12g 8fg 9.5s 10.7g) useful sort; good walker; narrowly won Dutch 2,000 Guineas at Duindigt in May but was disqualified after hampering 2 other runners; third of 7 to Verduret in minor race at Chester earlier in month, best effort in this country; not certain to stay 1½m; acts on firm going. *M. Ryan.*

SIGN CENTRE AGAIN 3 ch.g. Jupiter Pluvius 119–Amy's Choice (Whistling –
Wind 123) (1979 NR 1980 10.1f) second living foal; dam of no account; well beaten in 24-runner maiden race at Windsor in August. *A. Pitt.*

SIGNMAKER 3 ch.c. Laser Light 118–Doin Foine 65 **§** (Quorum 126) (1979 55
5s 5d^4 6f 6f 5fg 6fg 1980 7d^4 10fg^3 8fg^3 10fg 10h^4 11fg 10d^4 10.1s 12fg) sturdy colt; in frame in varied company, including selling; seems to stay 1¼m; acts on a firm and a soft surface; blinkered final start. *R. Hannon.*

SILARI 6 gr.g. Birdbrook 110–Ciao Ciao Bambina (Welsh Abbot 131) (1979 8d^4 –
8g 8fg* 7g^4 8g 8g* 8fg^2 8fg 8fg^2 1980 8s^3 8.2fg 9.6h 7fg^4 8g 8f^4 8g 8fg 7.6d 7g 8fg^3 8g) plater; stays 1m; appears to act on any going; good mount for an apprentice. *C. Wildman.*

SILCAKEY 3 b.f. High Line 125–Resurgence (Runnymede 123) (1979 NR 69
1980 10g 12g 10.1f 10f^3 10fg^3 8g^2 10f^3 9s 10g) 2,500Y; lengthy, light-framed filly; half-sister to 2 winners, including very useful 1979 3-y-o Reside (by Quayside), successful at up to 1½m; dam lightly raced and showed no sign of ability; placed in maiden and minor races; stays 1¼m; suited by top-of-the-ground; sweated up eighth start; has run respectably for a boy; sold 3,800 gns Newmarket December Sales. *G. Harwood.*

SILCA STAR KEY (USA) 2 b.c. Majestic Prince–Who's to Know (Fleet – p
Nasrullah) (1980 6d) May 1; \$70,000Y; well-made, quite attractive colt; fourth foal; half-brother to 2 winners, including Angel Island (by Cougar), a leading 2-y-o filly in 1978; dam, minor stakes winner at up to 6f, is half-sister to very smart 1974 French 2-y-o sprinter Raise A Lady; favourite for 17-runner maiden race at Newmarket in October but never got into contention and finished only eighth to Gabitat; evidently quite well thought of and should improve over 7f+ at 3 yrs. *G. Harwood.*

SILENCER 3 br.g. Pinsun 108–Roychateau (Royal Record II) (1979 5g 5d 5g^3 49
6g 7g 6s 8h 8fg 1980 9g 12h 13.8fg^4 10g 12g^4 13.8f^2 11d^3 10g 12d 15s) neat

gelding; plater; stays 1$\frac{3}{4}$m; acts on firm going; has worn blinkers; sometimes sweats up; brought down second outing; trained part of season by W. Bentley. *R. Allan.*

SILENT MISSILE 5 b.g. Silent Spring 102–Fair Missile (Fairford) (1979 8v 12d 1980 8f) little worthwhile form in varied company, including selling; sold 410 gns Ascot August Sales. *M. Tompkins.* —

SILENT PRAYER 4 ch.f. Queen's Hussar 124–Mecca II 90 (Exbury 138) (1979 12g^4 12g 12f^4 12d^3 15.5fg^4 1980 15f^4 13s) plating-class staying maiden; seems to act on any going; used to wear a hood. *D. Gandolfo.* **58**

SILENT TEARS 3 br.f. Weepers Boy 124–Skilla (Mexico III) (1979 5g 5f 5fg 5g^3 6d^3 7fg 1980 6v 6d 7fg 7f 6fg 6fg 6g 6g^3 6d* 6d 6fg) small filly; plater; attracted no bid after making virtually all to win at Newcastle in August; stays 6f; suited by some give in the ground; blinkered nowadays; ran poorly fourth outing. *M. Cousins.* **53**

SILIGIFT 4 ch.c. Siliconn 121–Coral Flower (Quorum 126) (1979 8fg^2 8fg 10g 10f 1980 7fg 10fg^3) plater; stays 1m (well beaten over further). *W. Stephenson.* —

SILK 3 ch.f. Shantung 132–Tactless 91 (Romulus 129) (1979 NR 1980 12s 8fg 8fg^3 8g^4 8g 10g^2 10fg 11d*) lengthy filly; half-sister to Padro (by Runnymede), a very useful performer at up to 1m; dam 1$\frac{1}{4}$m winner; won 9-runner maiden race at Hamilton in September; stays 11f; suited by some give in the ground. *B. Hobbs.* **68**

SILKEN ANNA 3 br.f. Scottish Rifle 127–Bar Gold 80 (Lucky Brief 128) (1979 NR 1980 10fg 7.6f 7g 8g^4 8.3f 10s) poor plater; will stay 1$\frac{1}{2}$m; possibly unsuited by soft going; blinkered fourth and fifth starts; sold 520 gns Ascot September Sales. *P. Cole.* **47**

SILKEN EASE 2 br.f. Swing Easy 126–Twice Shy (Lord of Verona 120) (1980 5f^2 6g 5fg^3 6g^4) May 22; rather leggy filly; half-sister to 2 winning platers; dam of little account; soundly beaten when placed in maiden races at Carlisle in May and Edinburgh in July, beaten 5$\frac{3}{4}$ lengths by Petite Fleche in latter; should stay 6f. *G. Richards.* **58**

SILKEN KNOT 2 ch.f. Nonoalco 131–Silken Way 103 (Shantung 132) (1980 6f* 7g^3 8g^2) **113**

Up to September hardly a big meeting went by without notable success for the powerful Hern string. Royal Ascot and York's Ebor meeting brought as many as four winners, Chester in May and Goodwood in the summer three. Things didn't go with quite the same swing in the autumn, and the St Leger meeting at Doncaster proved a very frustrating one for the stable. It had its winner—Shoot A Line took the Park Hill Stakes on the second day—but Hern's chances of passing the £1,000,000 mark in prize money were virtually ended by the defeat of the stable's ten other runners, four of which started well-backed favourites. Three of that quartet, Water Mill, Silken Knot and Capstan, went down one after the other on the final afternoon in races worth a total of £88,503.

Silken Knot (ch.f. Feb 25, 1978)	Nonoalco (b 1971)	Nearctic (br 1954)	Nearco
			Lady Angela
		Seximee (ch 1956)	Hasty Road
			Jambo
	Silken Way (ch 1973)	Shantung (b 1956)	Sicambre
			Barley Corn
		Boulevard (ch 1968)	Pall Mall
			Costa Sola

Silken Knot, who was beaten one and a half lengths by Exclusively Raised in the May Hill Stakes, ran very well and showed form as good as any two-year-old filly that Hern introduced during the season. Exclusively Raised is a smart filly and had the better turn of foot on the day, cutting down Silken Knot in the last furlong after the latter had looked sure to win when establishing a two-length advantage early in the straight. The pair finished upwards of four lengths clear of the remainder led by Chateau Dancer. This was Silken Knot's third outing and her second defeat: the previous month she had started favourite for the Waterford Candelabra Stakes at Goodwood, having made a successful debut in the Virginia Water Stakes at Ascot in July from Will of Victory. At Goodwood, Silken Knot never looked like winning, running on in the closing stages to take third place behind Fairy Footsteps and Madam Gay, both receiving 8 lb, beaten four lengths and a length. Exclusively Raised was just behind Silken Knot in fourth that day.

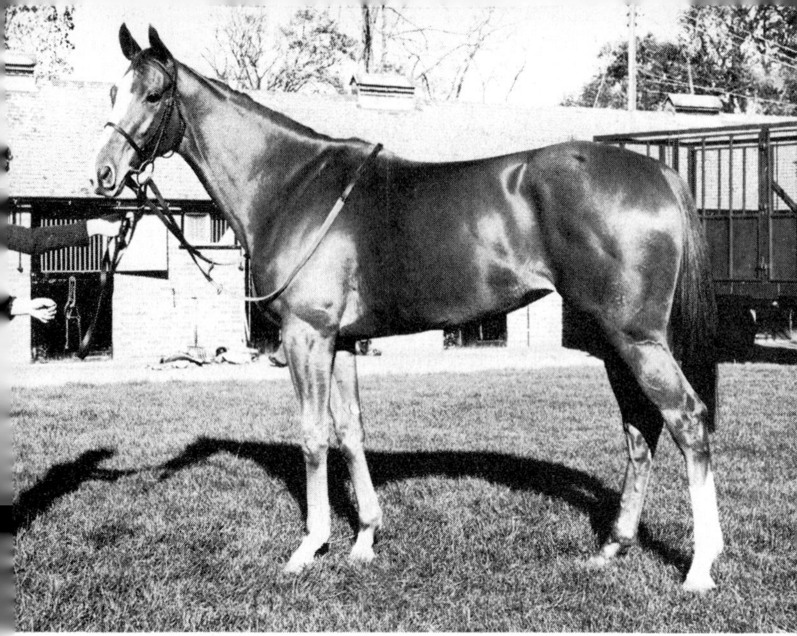

Sir Michael Sobell's "Silken Knot"

There's no reason why Silken Knot, a lengthy filly with an excellent action, shouldn't train on and play a part in the good fillies races at up to a mile and a quarter. She comes from a good family. Her dam, Silken Way, ran only three times as a three-year-old, winning once over a mile and a quarter and finishing third to Roussalka in the Nassau Stakes at Goodwood over the same distance. Silken Way's dam, Boulevard, was a very useful two-year-old winner who stayed a mile at three years. Boulevard is a half-sister to Sun Prince and their grandam is the Park Hill winner Sunny Cove. Silken Knot's sire Nonoalco was one of the best milers of 1974, winning the Two Thousand Guineas and the Prix Jacques le Marois. He has made a reasonable start to his stud career, having sired a handful of good winners, including Un Reitre and Nonoalca in France and Mesange Bleue in Italy, from three crops. *R. Hern.*

SILKEN SHEBA 3 b.f. Royalty 130–Strawberry Ice (Arctic Storm 134) (1979 6g 8g 10s4 1980 10.8s 11.5f 12d 15.5g) leggy, narrow filly; poor maiden; should stay at least 1½m; acts on soft going; sold 390 gns Ascot November Sales. *D. Weeden.* —

SILK FASHION 6 b.m. Breeders Dream 116–Maud 87 (Vilmorin) (1979 13v 15.5d 10.1g3 12s 10.8g3 10.1fg 10f2 1980 12s 12fg 10fg 10g* 12d2 12f) small, light-framed mare; plater; attracted no bid after winning at Yarmouth in July; stays 1½m; seems to act on any going; suitable mount for an apprentice; blinkered third outing. *A. Pitt.* **48**

SILKY BABY (USA) 2 b.c. What A Pleasure–Gazala 124 (Dark Star) (1980 7d2 7.5d*) Feb 22; $680,000Y; half-brother to 4 winners, notably 3-y-o Irish St Leger winner Gonzales, top-class Mississipian (both by Vaguely Noble) and tip-top 1976 3-y-o Youth (by Ack Ack); dam won French 1,000 Guineas and Oaks; an exceptionally well-related colt who looked a very good prospect when justifying favouritism by 2 lengths from Russian Fox in 11-runner maiden race at Saint-Cloud in October; will stay at least 1¼m; bound to win good races. *J. Cunnington, jnr, France.* **111** p

SILLEY'S KNIGHT 4 b.c. Derring-Do 131–Silley's Maid 100 (Continuation 120) (1979 8d 8.2s^3 7d* 7v^2 8fg* 8f* 8fg 8s^4 8f^4 7f 1980 8d 7.6f 7f* 7.6f 8d 7g 8g 8g 8g*) strong, good-bodied, attractive colt; fairly useful handicapper; made all to beat Terry Paine by 1½ lengths at Newmarket in May: disappointing afterwards until tried in blinkers at Brighton in October, when beating Northleach by a length; stays 1m; acts on any going; sold to J. Hanson 15,500 gns Newmarket Autumn Sales. *M. Stoute.* **93**

SILLY ABDULL 4 ch.c. St Alphage 119–Hirsova (Gulf Pearl 117) (1979 8g^2 7d^4 5fg^2 6f^3 6fg 8d^3 6s 1980 7d 8fg^3 7.6f^3 7f* 7fg 7fg) strong, compact, short-legged colt; won apprentice handicap at Newbury in May by neck from Denmore; ran moderately afterwards, including in a seller on final start; stays 1m; probably acts on any going but seems suited by firm; blinkered fourth start at 3 yrs (missed break) and last 3 outings; inconsistent; sold 650 gns Ascot July Sales. *R. Price.* **70**

SILLY MONEY 2 b.g. Silly Season 127–Royal Bliss 90 (King's Bench 132) (1980 5f 5g^3 6g 7fg 7g 7f 7.2d^3) May 4; 1,350Y; leggy, narrow gelding; third foal; half-brother to a winner in Singapore; dam best at up to 1¼m; third in maiden auction event and a £2,400 seller at Haydock, staying on under hard driving when beaten 2 lengths by Hissing Sid in latter in October; will stay 1¼m; possibly needs some give in the ground; blinkered last 2 outings. *M. H. Easterby.* **68**

SILLY MOO 2 b.f. Silly Season 127–Rikis (Town Crier 119) (1980 7fg 7fg 5d) May 17; 1,200Y; narrow, compact filly; first foal; dam ran only 3 times; well beaten in maiden races. *D. Morley.* **–**

SILLY PRICES 3 b.c. Silly Season 127–Galosh 86 (Pandofell 132) (1979 5g* 6d* 6fg^3 6fg* 6f^3 7s^2 6d^3 7fg 8d^2 1980 8.2fg 8g 8g 8s 8f) strong, compact, good-bodied colt; good mover; very useful (rated 110) at 2 yrs; well beaten in varied company in 1980; should stay 1¼m; probably acts on any going; blinkered final outing. *M. H. Easterby.* **–**

SILLY TWIST 3 b.c. Silly Season 127–Twist of Lemon 80 (Northfields) (1979 7.5f 7fg^4 7.9g^4 6d 6s^2 5g 7.5s^4 1980 10s 8g 12g 9f^4 9f^4 9f* 9g 10g^4 8d 10g 12g 12.2d*) good sort; ex-Irish; first foal; dam 11.1f winner and half-sister to Oaks winner Ginevra; won handicap at Waterford and Tramore in May and apprentice race at Catterick in October; stays 1½m; probably acts on any going; trained first 9 outings by L. Greene. *J. Fitzgerald.* **73**

SILMIRA 3 gr.f. Grey Mirage 128–Silent Post 70 (Dumbarnie 125) (1979 5g 5g 7fg 6fg 7fg 1980 8f 8fg^2 10.1s^2 10.1d 11.7f 10fg^4 10fg^2 10g 10s) plain filly; stays 1¼m; probably acts on any going; has run respectably for an apprentice. *Mrs R. Lomax.* **65**

SILVER BAY 5 b.m. Sterling Bay–Akola (Hard Tack 111 §) (1979 10.2s 10g^4 8g 8fg^4 10.8fg 12h 12g 8g 1980 12d 13d 8f) neat mare; seems to stay 1¼m, but has yet to prove she gets further; acts on a firm surface; has worn blinkers; suitable mount for an amateur. *D. Weeden.* **–**

SILVER BILL 2 b.g. Young Emperor 133–Cashmere Shawl (Ballyciptic 122) (1980 5v 5d 5f 5fg^2 5fg 5d 5fg 6fg) May 4; 2,500F, 5,000Y; strong, compact gelding; half-brother to several winners, including fairly useful 1979 Irish 2-y-o 7f winner Castlemara (by Virginia Boy); dam poor Irish maiden; neck second of 7 to Boganach in maiden race at Hamilton in May but was well beaten in most of his other races; usually blinkered; will be more at home in sellers. *W. O'Gorman.* **58**

SILVER BONNET 4 gr.f. Sun Prince 128–Tiara III (Persian Gulf) (1979 10v 1980 6fg 7g 8g 12g 16f) ex-Irish filly; plating-class maiden. *G. Fletcher.* **–**

SILVER CHAIN 3 b.c. Manacle 123–Silver Comb (Silver Cloud 121) (1979 5v 5g 1980 6d 5f 5h 7f 7fg 7s 5f 8d) light-framed colt; bad plater; often sweats up; sold 410 gns Doncaster August Sales. *S. Wainwright.* **–**

SILVER CHORD 2 gr.c. Swing Easy 126–Piana (Supreme Sovereign 119) (1980 6g 8fg 6f) Mar 25; 2,900F, 8,000Y; workmanlike colt; first live foal; dam placed twice from 6 starts in France; well behind in maiden race and sellers; blinkered third outing; sold 400 gns Newmarket Autumn Sales. *P. Haslam.* **–**

SILVER CITY 3 gr.f. No Mercy 126–City Carriage 88 (Counsel 118) (1979 5s 5d^2 5v 5g 6g 1980 8g 8g 7g 7fg 6g 7f 7g) tall filly; poor plater; best run at 5f on a soft surface; has been tried in blinkers; sold 480 gns Ascot November Sales. *J. O'Donoghue.* **–**

SILVER CREEK 2 b.c. English Prince 129–Corbalton 103 (Milesian 125) **97**
(1980 7g 7fg^{4} 7g^{3} 8g^{3}) Feb 27; 20,000F, 37,000Y; brother to Irish 1¼m winner Royal Priority, and half-brother to numerous winners, including very smart middle-distance performer Knockroe (by Fortino II); dam won at up to 11f; twice third to very good colts, finishing 8 lengths behind Storm Bird in Group 2 National Stakes at the Curragh in August and 12½ lengths behind Critique in 16-runner maiden event at Leopardstown the following month; will be suited by 1¼m+. *C. Collins, Ireland.*

SILVER DANCER 2 b.g. Tarboosh–Dark Dam (Linacre 133) (1980 7d 7fg 7fg^{4} **71**
8g) Mar 11; 3,000Y; 2,500 2-y-o; lightly-made gelding; fourth foal; half-brother to a winner in Italy by Supreme Sovereign; dam never ran; 4¼ lengths fourth of 19 to Pearlaway in maiden race at Warwick in August, best effort; should stay 1m. *N. Gaselee.*

SILVER EXPRESS (USA) 2 b.c. Key To The Kingdom–Vickie's Lady (Don **112**
Poggio) (1980 5d* 5.5g* 7d^{2} 7g^{3} 6.5s^{2}) Mar 10; $45,000Y; half-brother to several winners, including minor stakes winner Troll By (by Military Plume); dam, sister to a stakes winner, won a 5f claiming race; made all to win 10-runner newcomers event and 6-runner Prix Fast Fox at Maisons-Laffitte in May and June; 2/1 on when beating Valgo a length in latter event; not disgraced when just over 5 lengths third of 5 to Miswaki in Prix de la Salamandre at Longchamp in September and ran well when 1½ lengths second of 9 behind Phydilla in Group 3 Prix Eclipse at Saint-Cloud the following month; will stay 1m; racing in USA. *M. Saliba, France.*

SILVER GATES 2 ch.f. Pieces of Eight 128–Seven Gates 77 (Henry the Seventh –
125) (1980 5fg 5fg 6g 7g 8s) Mar 25; 900Y; workmanlike filly; plater; stays 1m; trained by W. Bentley first 4 outings. *G. Lockerbie.*

SILVER KETTLE 2 gr.c. Habat 127–The Maid (Milesian 125) (1980 6g) –
Apr 19; useful-looking colt; half-brother to 2 minor winners and a winner in Norway; dam won over 6f at 2 yrs in Ireland; 50/1 and bandaged in front when twelfth of 13 to Olympic Glory in minor event at Kempton in July. *G. Balding.*

SILVER LASER 3 ch.g. Laser Light 118–Silver Perch 58 (High Perch 126) –
(1979 7f 7d 7f 7d 1980 10h) in rear in maiden races and sellers; blinkered final 2 starts at 2 yrs; sometimes sweats up. *J. Fitzgerald.*

SILVER LEO 2 br.c. Dubassoff–Fingerofortune 100 (Fortino II 120) (1980 6d **70**
6d 7g 7g* 8g^{2} 7fg 8g 8d 8.2s) Mar 2; 2,300F, 3,000Y, 5,000 2-y-o; strong, useful sort; brother to 1978 2-y-o 1m seller winner Wind-O-Fortune, and half-brother to a winner; dam won at up to 7f; 100/1 when winning poor maiden race at Catterick in August by a length from Tamdown Flyer; 2¾ lengths second of 11 to Glenbank Lass in nursery at Thirsk the following month, easily best subsequent effort; suited by 7f and 1m; possibly needs a sound surface; blinkered final start. *J. Harris.*

SILVER MELODY 3 b.f. Highland Melody 112–Silver Cherry 69 (Silver Cloud **50**
121) (1979 5s 5f 5f 5f 6g 6s 7s 6d 1980 7fg 8s 7g 8fg 7fg 7f^{2} 8f 8.2v) unfurnished filly; plater; stays 7f; acts on firm going; best in blinkers; fell final start. *P. Asquith.*

SILVER RULER 2 b.c. Sovereign Path 125–Argentessa 80 (Sing Sing 134) –
(1980 7d) May 5; 48,000Y; strong, attractive colt; half-brother to 2 winners, including fairly useful 5f to 7.6f winner Nantucket (by Pall Mall); dam placed at 2 yrs; 12/1, didn't move particularly well to start and made little show when behind in 14-runner Houghton Stakes won by Sunley Builds at Newmarket in October. *P. Walwyn.*

SILVER SAL 3 gr.f. Saritamer 130–Little Alice (Djefou) (1979 6fg 1980 11fg –
11.7fg 11.7f 12g) fair sort; poor form in varied company. *Mrs A. Finch.*

SILVER SAMANTHA 2 gr.f. Zeddaan 130–Pontresina 70 (Ballymoss 136) **56**
(1980 5f 5fg 5.1g* 5f 5fg) Apr 30; 7,200Y; very light-framed filly; first foal; dam needed a test of stamina; bought in 4,200 gns after easily landing the odds in 4-runner seller at Yarmouth in July by 3 lengths from Superb Music; last in nurseries subsequently; not bred to be a 5f performer; blinkered third and fourth starts. *P. Haslam.*

SILVER SEASON 2 b.c. Martinmas 128–Silver Ray 70 (Skymaster 126) **82**
(1980 5fg 6g 7f 7fg 7s^{4}) Mar 31; 3,600Y; lengthy colt; has a rather round action; second living foal; dam poor handicapper; improved late in season and was beaten little more than a length when fourth of 18 to Warily in minor event at Sandown; will probably stay 1m; best run on soft going. *C. Brittain.*

SILVER SNOW 2 gr.f. Abwah 118–Silver Yarn (Peter's Yarn 106) (1980 6fg 8fg² 8d⁴) Apr 14; well-grown, rather leggy filly; half-sister to Silver Seal (by Privy Seal), a fairly useful winner at up to 1m; dam point-to-pointer; very weak in market when 2½ lengths second of 24 to stable-companion Allegretta in maiden race at Leicester in September; favourite for similar race at Redcar the following month but finished only fourth, 3¼ lengths behind Segos, after having every chance; stays 1m. *M. Stoute.* **78**

SILVER TACK 3 b.g. Right Tack 131–Colour Bar (Majority Blue 126) (1979 6fg 6fg 7fg 8.2s⁴ 1980 6f 6f⁴ 6fg 8d 10g) plating-class maiden; should stay 1m; retained 700 gns Doncaster August Sales. *W. H. H. Williams.* –

SILVER TIPS 4 gr.f. High Top 131–Silver Birch 122 (Silver Shark 129) (1979 6g 7f³ 8g* 8fg² 1980 7f 7g³ 8.3s* 8g⁴ 8.3f⁴ 7.2d* 7g³ 8.2s) very lightly-made filly; won handicaps at Windsor in July (ridden out, by 2½ lengths from Crown Witness) and Haydock in October (held on well under pressure and beat Willow Red a short head); stays 1m; acts on any going. *T. Waugh.* **81**

SILVER WINDMILL 3 b.f. Morston 125–Silver Birch 122 (Silver Shark 129) (1979 NR 1980 10.2d 8f 10fg) 11,000Y; lengthy, plain filly; third foal; half-sister to 4-y-o Silver Tips, winner at up to 8.3f, and useful Golden Elder (both by High Top), successful from 6f to 1m; dam, unbeaten at 2 yrs, stayed 1m; well beaten in newcomers race and maiden events in first part of season; sold 2,900 gns Newmarket December Sales. *W. Wightman.* –

SILVERY MOON 3 ch.f. Lorenzaccio 130–Aunt Jobiska 71 (Grey Sovereign 128 § or Aureole 132) (1979 NR 1980 6f) quite attractive filly; fourth living foal; half-sister to a winner in Trinidad; dam, who stayed 1¾m, is half-sister to Queen's Hussar; going on nicely at finish when nearly 7 lengths seventh of 15 to Great Eastern in maiden race at Newmarket in April; not seen out again. *W. Hastings-Bass.* –

SIMETTE 3 ch.g. Simbir 130–Machete (Macherio) (1979 5d 6f 1980 10s* 10d³ 12fg² 16g³ 12d⁴ 12s 17.4s 16.1s 14g³ 13s) quite well-made, useful-looking gelding; stayed on to win maiden race at Leicester in March; first past post in handicap on same course in April but was moved down a place after stewards enquiry; ran creditably subsequently to be third in Queen's Vase at Royal Ascot (behind Toondra) and handicap at Newmarket in October; stays well; appears to act on any going. *J. Bethell.* **91** d

SIMITIKA 2 ch.f. Cavo Doro 124–Kamitisi (Worden II 129) (1980 9d 8d 10d 8d) Mar 14; half-sister to two minor 2-y-o winners; dam never ran; well beaten in minor event, a maiden race and sellers in the Midlands; wore a tongue strap final start; sold 480 gns Ascot December Sales. *C. Austin.* –

SIMLA 4 ch.c. Simbir 130–Persian Gal 68 (Persian Gulf) (1979 10g³ 12d* 15.8g² 1980 12d 12fg⁴ 14f² 12f 12g* 12fg³ 12g³ 12f² 12g 12fg² 12g) lightly-built colt; apprentice ridden when 5-length winner of handicap at Brighton in July; ran best subsequent races when second in apprentice handicaps won by Telsmoss at Epsom in August and Sir Michael at Ascot in September, on latter course being hampered when challenging strongly in last furlong and subsequently moved up from his original third place; stays well; probably acts on any going; ran moderately in blinkers seventh outing. *P. Walwyn.* **82**

SIMPLICITY 3 b.g. The Brianstan 128–Sovereign Help 98 (Sovereign Lord 120) (1979 5d³ 5g* 5s³ 6fg⁴ 5fg* 5f 1980 5h 5f 5g 6g 6s) lightly-made gelding; plater; stays 6f; probably acts on any going; sometimes sweats up; blinkered last two starts; retained 1,300 gns Ascot July Sales. *T. Fairhurst.* –

SIMPSON JERSEY 6 br.h. Highland Melody 112–Leisure Hour (Persian Gulf) (1979 7v 8s* 10s 9s 8g 10d 12f 14.6fg⁴ 12h² 12fg 10f³ 10f 10fg³ 10.6s⁴ 1980 12f³ 13.3g* 12d² 14.6g 11.7f* 10s³ 12g) modest middle-distance handicapper; successful at Newbury in June and Windsor in August; acts on any going; has worn blinkers. *B. McMahon.* **68**

SINCERELY MILLS 2 ch.f. Ardoon 124–Coastal Rocket 74 (Roan Rocket 128) (1980 5fg⁴ 5f 6g³ 6s 7fg³ 8g³ 8fg) Feb 5; 3,000F, 11,000Y; neat filly; third foal; half-sister to 1m winner Emerald Rocket (by Green God); dam showed a little ability at 2 yrs; third in maiden race and nurseries; suited by 1m. *C. Brittain.* **74**

SINGADEE 3 b.g. Master Sing 109–Sugadee 69 (Vimadee 120) (1979 5s 5v 1980 12.2f) neat gelding; behind in maiden races; dead. *W. Wharton.* –

SING-A-LING 3 br.f. Mansingh 120–Dawn Songster (Primera 131) (1979 5g4 5fg4 6f 6g3 7g3 6s4 1980 7s 7f 8d4 7g4 6fg4) plater; suited by 7f; possibly not at her best on soft ground; blinkered fourth start; sold 700 gns Ascot September Sales. *G. Hunter.* **47**

SINGALONG JOE 2 ch.c. Sharpen Up 127–Captive Flower 99 (Manacle 123) (1980 6d 6g4 5.1g 7s3 7v) May 18; 3,000Y; leggy, light-framed colt; half-brother to useful 1m to 1¼m winner Tesoro Mio (by Cavo Doro); dam won twice over 5f at 2 yrs; ran easily best race when 5 lengths third of 17 to Go Leasing in nursery at Newmarket in October; well beaten next time out; better suited by 7f than shorter distances; acts on soft going and has yet to race on firm. *I. Walker.* **80**

SINGALONG SAM 3 b.g. Master Sing 109–Sam's Song 99 (Narrator 127) (1979 6s 6f 1980 12g) tall gelding; behind in maiden races and an amateur riders event. *P. Cundell.* –

SINGAPORE RIVER (USA) 2 b.c. Buckpasser–Satin (Forli) (1980 6d2 8g* 8d) Apr 14; $77,000Y; third foal; half-brother to 2 winners, including Sateen (by Round Table), a smart winner at up to 6f; dam stakes-placed winner from 4f to 6f; got home by a head from Ledmir in maiden event at Chantilly in September; just over 4 lengths sixth of 8 to Dunphy when second favourite for Group 3 Prix des Chenes at Longchamp later in month; will stay 1¼m. *A. Paus, France.* **114**

SINGAPORE SUE 2 ch.f. Carnival Dancer 113–Coatham 81 (Divine Gift 127) (1980 5fg 5f 5f 5g) May 23; small filly; headstrong plater; took charge of rider on way to start on second and intended fourth outings, on latter occasion wearing blinkers and unseating jockey before being withdrawn; dwelt third start. *Denys Smith.* – §

SING BABY SING 2 b.f. Caruso 112–Triarder 43 (Hard Ridden 131) (1980 5d 5d4 5f 5f 6g2 5g4 6f) Mar 4; leggy filly; bad plater; blinkered fourth outing. *J. Berry.* **44**

SINGH SPRITE 4 b. or br.f. Mansingh 120–Sprightly Sprite 80 (Babur 126) (1979 6v 6d 9s 6d 5f 7fg 8.3fg4 8.3g 7g2 7d 8g 1980 10fg 10.8fg4 8fg 10s) poor plater; stays 10.8f; has worn blinkers. *D. Leslie.* **35**

SINGING AMAH 5 ch.g. Tudor Melody 129–Amorella 106 (Crepello 136) (1979 13v 12g 9s 12f 16.3fg 12f2 12g 12d 16d* 16s* 1980 12g 20d2 12s 16.3d 16g4 16s 18d) shapely gelding; kept on well when 1½ lengths second to Heighlin in Ascot Stakes at Royal Ascot in June (well backed); fourth to Diomedes at Leopardstown in September; well suited by a test of stamina; acts on any going but goes well in the mud; often used to wear blinkers. *M. O'Toole, Ireland.* **73**

SINGING FOOL 4 gr.g. Singing Bede 122–Dilwyn 84 (Immortality) (1979 6s 7s 8s 10h 8h 1980 12s 10g) poor maiden; blinkered final start. *D. Jermy.* –

SINGING OATS 3 ch.f. Tudor Music 131–Regal Cloud (Golden Cloud) (1979 NR 1980 10fg 12d) 2,500Y; third foal; dam won at up to 7f in Ireland; well beaten in maiden races at Brighton; sold 470 gns Ascot July Sales. *G. Harwood.* –

SINGING TUDOR 4 br.f. Crooner 119–Tudor Top 104 (Tudor Minstrel 144) (1979 8g3 7.6d 7d 6d4 8fg2 5f 1980 8s 8fg) poor plater; suited by 1m. *D. Garraton.* –

SINGLE SWINGER 3 b.f. Saritamer 130–Attuned (Faberge II 121) (1979 5s3 5fg2 7f* 7f* 6fg 7g 8g4 7d 1980 8v* 8.2d 8fg 9g4 8d 8g 8s 7s) fair sort; won handicap at Salisbury in March; stays 1m; acts on any going; sold 3,700 gns Newmarket December Sales. *G. Hunter.* **74**

SINGWARA 2 br.f. Blue Cashmere 129–Exeat (Quartette 106) (1980 5g 5f4 5g 6d) May 1; first foal; dam well beaten on flat and over hurdles; showed a little ability in maiden races late in season (well backed in 2); will be much better suited by 7f+. *J. Benstead.* **71**

SIN NO MORE 5 b.g. So Blessed 130–Moghari 78 (Djebe) (1979 NR 1980 8g) lightly raced and only poor form, including in seller. *M. Reddan.* –

SIPAPU 3 b.f. Targowice 130–Nakomis (Sky High) (1979 6s4 6f4 6fg* 1980 7f 7.3f 8fg 7d* 8.3d 7g 7f2 7g) good-looking, well-made filly; moderate handicapper; just held on to dead-heat with Kellord at Salisbury in June; best form at up to 7f; probably acts on any going; needs to be ridden up with pace; blinkered last 2 starts; ran poorly fifth outing. *J. Dunlop.* **80**

SIPESTRO 2 ro.c. Crowned Prince 128–Boule de Suif 88 (Major Portion 129) **86**
(1980 5f 6g* 7g^4 7f^3 7d 6g^2 6f) Mar 22; 5,200Y; lengthy colt; good walker; half-brother to 3-y-o 1½m winner Dumplino (by Bustino) and 2 winners in Italy; dam stayed 1m and is half-sister to 3 good animals; won 15-runner maiden race at Doncaster in June by 1½ lengths from Russian Romance; placed afterwards in nurseries at Thirsk and Doncaster, going down by 6 lengths to Piperhill after having none too clear a run in 12-runner event on latter in September; will stay 1m; acts on firm going; sometimes sweats up; sold 6,600 gns Newmarket Autumn Sales. *P. Rohan.*

SIR BILLY (USA) 3 b.c. Sir Ivor 135–Shellshock 110 (Salvo 129) (1979 **78**
6g 8g 1980 8v 12d* 12.3f^4 12.5fg^3 14.6g 12.2f* 13.8f* 14d^4 12g 12.3g^3 12d^3 13.8d^4 16s^3 18s) small, strong, shapely colt; successful in maiden race at Hamilton in April and two handicaps at Catterick in July; stays 2m; acts on any going; suitable mount for an inexperienced rider; sold out of J. Watts's stable 10,200 gns Ascot July Sales after seventh start; resold 5,000 gns Ascot December Sales. *N. Tinkler.*

SIR DESTRIER 7 br.g. Sir Gaylord–Ruby of Iran (Cosmic Bomb) (1979 –
8s 6s 8f 8f 9fg 7f^2 7f^3 8f^4 7g^2 7f 1980 6g 7.6d 9g) poor handicapper; stays 9f; well suited by top-of-the-ground conditions; used to wear blinkers; good mount for an apprentice; sold 1,900 gns Ascot October Sales. *P. Butler.*

SIR DOMINO 2 ch.g. Morston 125–Dominant 86 (Behistoun 131) (1980 **69**
7g 8g 7g) Apr 20; 6,400Y; well-made gelding; second foal; half-brother to a winner in USA by Derring-Do; dam, winner at 1½m, is half-sister to very smart English and American horse Dominion; always outpaced when 9¼ lengths sixth of 15 to McCarthy in maiden race at Newmarket in August; in rear subsequently in 23-runner maiden race at Goodwood (favourite) and 10-runner Hyperion Stakes at Ascot; will be suited by middle distances. *F. Durr.*

SIR DORO 3 b.c. Cavo Doro 124–Privas (Preciptic 122) (1979 NR 1980 **77**
10.2d^2 12fg^3 10.5f 13.3fg 12g 14g^2 12d^2 14.7d* 17.4s) 6,200Y; strong, good-bodied colt; landed odds in 5-runner maiden race at Redcar in August; runner-up in varied company earlier; stays well; acts on a firm and a soft surface; blinkered fourth and fifth starts. *C. Brittain.*

SIR EAMON 3 b.c. Martinmas 128–La Viola (Guersant 129) (1979 7f^2 1980 **87**
8f 12fg 12fg^2 16g^4 12d^3 13.1g 10d^3 8fg* 8.3g 10.1g) useful-looking colt; moderate handicapper; gamely held off Love Supreme by ¾ length at Warwick in July; effective from 1m to 1½m (seemed to find 2m too far on fourth start); probably acts on any going; inconsistent; sold 8,200 gns Ascot December Sales. *P. Cole.*

SIRENA 3 ch.f. Red Alert 127–Buenaventura II (Celtic Ash) (1979 6f 7fg 1980 **84**
7f 8fg 10f^2 10s^3 12s^4 11.5g* 12g^3 10.1g* 10fg* 10g^3) rangy, good-bodied filly; improved in second half of season and won minor event at Yarmouth and handicaps at Windsor (beat Stonehenge) and Leicester (from Mitigator); stays 1½m; acts on any going; best in blinkers; has run well for a claimer; genuine. *T. Waugh.*

SIR GORDON 3 ch.c. Bustino 136–Wrekinianne 96 (Reform 132) (1979 **86**
7s 1980 10f 10g 8g 14fg 14d^2 15.5g* 14d*) big, strong colt; won maiden race at Folkestone and minor event at Sandown in October; suited by a test of stamina; acts on a soft surface; one paced; sold to D. Nicholson 21,000 gns Newmarket Autumn Sales. *M. Jarvis.*

SIR HUSSAR 3 ch.c. Queen's Hussar 124–Campagna (Romulus 129) (1979 –
6s 7fg 7f 7fg 1980 10.8s 10fg^4 10.1f^3 12g 10.1d 10g 13g 14d^3 12d) quite attractive, short-legged, good-bodied colt; possibly stays 1¾m; acts on any going except perhaps very soft; sometimes blinkered; didn't move well to post sixth start. *R. Laing.*

SIR JESTER 2 br.c. Bronze Hill 96–Jet Maiden (Star Gazer 123) (1980 **59**
5fg 5fg 5d 5g* 6g^3 8.2d^4 8fg 8.2s) Mar 29; small colt; not a good mover; bought in 1,350 gns after winning poor seller at Hamilton in July by 2 lengths from San Jose; stays 1m. *R. Johnson.*

SIR MICHAEL 4 b.c. Manacle 123–Ragirl (Ragusa 137) (1979 8g* 10f **100**
10fg^4 8f^3 12fg^2 12fg* 12g 12.2fg 13fg* 18fg* 1980 12g^2 13g^4 12fg* 14g 16g^4 12fg* 18d 12v) big colt; useful handicapper; won at Folkestone in August (made all and held on by a neck from Fine Tale) and Ascot in September (beat subsequently-disqualified Hearth by a head in apprentice event); had every chance when sixth of 16 behind Shaftesbury in Tote-Ebor at York, better effort in between; unsuited by the soft ground when behind in Tote Cesarewitch (attempting a second win) and William Hill November Handicap on last 2 outings; stays well; ideally suited by firm going; genuine; sweated up badly second start. *G. Huffer.*

SIR OPTIMIST (USA) 3 br.c. Sir Ivor 135–Seigniorage (Royal Coinage) (1979 NR 1980 10f 12.3d 12g 8g 9v³ 10d²) $90,000F; big, rangy colt; half-brother to 3 minor winners; dam, minor winner over 6f at 2 yrs, is half-sister to several very good performers, including top filly Convenience; placed in maiden and minor races in the autumn; stays 1¼m; acts well on soft ground. *P. Walwyn.* **66**

SIR SAMUEL (USA) 3 ch.c. L'Enjoleur–Amber Fields (Ambiorix 130) (1979 5d 5g* 6fg² 6f 6fg² 6d³ 5g* 5fg² 5f³ 5g 5g 1980 5fg 5fg 5fg 8h 6f 5g 5fg 5g 5.3fg 5fg* 5f 5g) big, well-made, good sort; very useful (rated 111) at 2 yrs; blinkered, showed first form in 1980 when making all to beat Loquacity 1½ lengths in 8-runner handicap at Wolverhampton in August; well beaten when blinkered again subsequently; has form over 6f but is better at 5f; acts on firm going; inconsistent nowadays. *S. Woodman.* **90**

SIR TRISTAN 3 br.c. Brigadier Gerard 144–Ysolda 100 (Elopement 125) (1979 5f³ 6g* 1980 8g⁴ 8fg 10s 11d³ 10fg⁴) compact colt; fairly useful performer; in frame in handicap at Salisbury, Mecca Bookmakers Scottish Derby at Ayr (respectable third of 5 to Prince Roland) and Extel Stakes (Handicap) at Goodwood (staying-on fourth to Karamita); appears to stay 11f; acts on a firm and a soft surface; didn't impress in paddock or on way to start second outing. *R. Sheather.* **91**

SISTER KITTY 2 b.f. Lochnager 132–Anneiv (Vienna 127) (1980 5g 6s² 8d⁴ 7g) Apr 20; 7,000Y; small filly; half-sister to a minor winner; dam of little account; prominent in large fields of maidens at Windsor, Nottingham and Warwick, on last-named finishing 6 lengths fourth of 17 to Emblazon; behind in nursery final appearance; seems to stay 1m. *B. Hills.* **72**

SITEX 2 b.c. Record Run 127–Glorious Light 53 (Alcide 136) (1980 5f 5fg 5.3d² 6s² 6g² 6g³ 6fg) May 19; 980Y; useful-looking colt; poor walker; half-brother to a bumpers winner and a winner in Belgium; dam slow maiden; runner-up in maiden races at Brighton, Windsor (beaten 4 lengths by General Breyfax in 25-runner event) and Kempton (went down by a head to Matilda Cave) in the summer; quite stoutly bred and will probably stay 1¼m; suited by some give in the ground. *M. Bolton.* **63**

SITICA 3 b.c. Siliconn 121–Time Call (Chanteur II 135) (1979 5s 6fg⁴ 5fg* 6g* 5d⁴ 6d² 6f 6d² 1980 7d⁴ 6fg 7f 6fg) narrow, fair sort; very useful at 2 yrs; below form in 1980, putting up best effort when fourth to Bonol in Northern Free Handicap at Newcastle in April; better suited by 6f than 5f and should stay 7f; goes well on a soft surface and is unsuited by really firm going; usually ridden by apprentice S. Lawes; sweated up third start. *G. Toft.* **—**

SIX MILE BOTTOM 2 b.c. Brigadier Gerard 144–Bamba 76 (Busted 134) (1980 6g³ 6g 7fg 7fg* 7d*) May 10; strong, attractive colt; first foal; dam, second 3 times at around 1m, is daughter of high-class Sovereign; improved late in season and won 19-runner maiden race at Lingfield and 11-runner nursery at Sandown, quickening in excellent style in last furlong to win latter by a length from Standon Rock; will be suited by 1m; acts on a firm and a soft surface; should make a very useful 3-y-o. *H. Wragg.* **106**

SKAT 3 b.f. Sharpen Up 127–Heart of Gold 72 (Infatuation 129) (1979 6d 5f 7g 8g 8d* 1980 8h 8.3f* 8fg 10f⁴ 8s) compact filly; won seller at Windsor in May (bought in 2,800 gns); stays 1m well; probably acts on any going. *M. Pipe.* **59**

SKATEBOARD 4 b.g. Tower Walk 130–Palgal (Le Prince 98) (1979 6fg 7d 7fg 1980 10s 8s 11.7f 8fg 12fg 8g² 8d 12d) lengthy, good sort; ran on strongly in last 3f when beaten ¾ length by Matchless Dancer in seller at Salisbury in September; best form at up to 1m; sold to R. Carter 1,050 gns Ascot December Sales. *W. Wightman.* **60**

SKELBROOKE 3 b.f. Mummy's Pet 125–Deep Freeze 75 (Varano) (1979 5g 6g 6fg 6g 1980 7.2d 7g 9.4fg* 10s³ 9g³ 10s² 10d) unfurnished filly; 33/1, showed much improved form to win minor event at Carlisle in September; good second in handicap at Stockton following month; stays 1¼m; seems to act on any going; didn't look too genuine fifth start and ran poorly final appearance. *E. Weymes.* **77**

SKERRY DANCE 3 br.f. Ragstone 128–Sea Tune (Klairon 131) (1979 NR 1980 8fg 7.6f 8g² 10fg² 10f) quite attractive, lightly-made filly; good mover; half-sister to fairly useful Melanesta (by Estaminet), successful at up to 7.3f; dam won over 6f at 2 yrs in Ireland; quite a moderate maiden; will stay 1½m; yet to race on a soft surface; below form final start. *R. Price.* **71**

SKEWSBY 4 b.c. Andrea Mantegna–Rogali 80 (Royal Avenue 123) (1979 8fg 10.6g 12d^2(dis) 16.1g* 16d* 16.1d* 14.6g^4 1980 16s 16g 12g 12fg 15.8d 18s) big, useful sort; good walker; staying handicapper; well beaten in 1980 (off course 5 months after first outing) but was not entirely disgraced when well backed final start; acts on firm going and a soft surface. *M. W. Easterby.* —

SKI LIFT 3 ch.f. Mount Hagen 127–Single Line (Rash Prince) (1979 8fg^4 1980 10fg^3 10f^2 10g* 10.1fg* 10.1g^3 10f^2 10.6d 10fg 12d^4) lengthy, smallish filly; successful in maiden race at Nottingham and minor event at Windsor in the summer; in frame in varied company on most of her other starts, running well to be third in Playboy Pretty Polly Stakes at Newmarket on reappearance and 3¾ lengths fourth to Karamita in Princess Royal Stakes at Ascot in October; suited by 1½m; probably acts on any going. *B. Hills.* **81**

SKIN DEEP 7 b.m. Prevailing–Vanity Case 77 (Counsel 118) (1979 6g 6fg 6s^2 6g^3 6d^3 6d 6s 1980 5d 6v 7f^3 7.6f 7fg* 8g 7g 7d 6g 7s 7d) well-made, attractive mare; fair handicapper; kept on strongly when scoring by 2 lengths from Intercraft Boy at Kempton in May; not disgraced next start but became rather disappointing; suited by 7f nowadays and probably stays 1m; acts on any going; blinkered once in 1979; suitable mount for an apprentice; trained most of season by A. Johnson. *W. Musson.* **87** d

SKIPAWAY BLUES 2 b.f. Blue Cashmere 129–Ardent Belle (Buisson Ardent 129) (1980 5s 5g 5f 5fg^4 5f 6fg 5d 5.1g 5d 5g 5d) Apr 30; 2,000Y; lightly-made filly; of no account; sold out of K. Ivory's stable 540 gns Newmarket July Sales after fifth start; resold 400 gns Ascot November Sales. *W. Charles.* —

SKI RUN 5 b.g. Workboy 123–Snow Rum (Quorum 126) (1979 8s 8g^2 9fg 7f* 8fg^3 8h 8fg^2 8.2g^2 8g 1980 7v 8.2fg^2 10f 8s^2 10g^3 8fg^2 10fg^2 10fg* 11g* 10s*) plater in 1979; improved in 1980 and was gaining second win in 4 days when winning handicap at Newcastle in August by a length (value 3 lengths) from Northanger; successful earlier in similar events on same course and at Redcar; stays 11f; acts on any going; usually races with tongue tied down nowadays; ridden by apprentice N. Connorton when successful in 1980. *P. Wigham.* **74**

SKI'S DOUBLE 4 br.g. Double-U-Jay 120–Some Poser (Will Somers 114 §) (1979 14.6fg 12f 12f 12d 12s^2 1980 12d 13d 11fg^3 12.3f 12f 10.6g 12d 12d 12.3g 12g^3 15.8d^3 12fg^2 12.2fg^3 12d^3 12d* 12s^2(dis) 10.2d^2 12d^2) won handicap at Wolverhampton in October when ridden by 5-lb claimer, beating Grade Well a neck despite hanging left; also ridden by claimer when second at Haydock, Doncaster and Leicester subsequently, on first-named course being disqualified after hanging again; stays 1½m; acts on any going; finds little off the bridle. *R. Hollinshead.* **64**

SKI WAX 3 b.g. Upper Case–Sealing-Wax (Crepello 136) (1979 NR 1980 10.1f 10fg) 2,300Y; in rear in minor races at Windsor in May and Ripon in June. *E. Eldin.* —

SKUKUZA (FR) 3 b. or br.f. Rheingold 137–Labold (Bold Lad, Ire 133) (1979 6f^3 5g^3 1980 9f 8fg* 7g 10g) strong, useful-looking filly; made all to win modest maiden event at Yarmouth in August; should stay 1¼m; acts on a firm surface; sold 1,600 gns Newmarket Autumn Sales. *J. Winter.* **63**

SKY BLUE PINK 3 gr.f. Singing Bede 122–Farida Jinks 106 (Tudor Jinks 121) (1979 5fg 1980 5f 5d^2 5d 5d 5g 5f 5g 5fg 5d 5d*) sturdy filly; narrowly won handicap at Catterick in October; suited by some give in the ground; usually wears blinkers; behaved very badly only outing at 2 yrs and is none too consistent. *G. Fletcher.* **67**

SKYBRIGHT 2 b.f. The Brianstan 128–Sky Hostess 72 (Skymaster 126) (1980 5fg 5.1g 6fg 9d 8d 7d 6g) Apr 8; 2,600Y; strong filly; third foal; dam tough performer at around 1m; only plating class; beaten 8½ lengths when fifth of 21 to Velvet Habit in maiden race at Leicester in November; best run at 6f. *G. Blum.* **67**

SKY JUMP 6 ch.g. Double Jump 131–Damascus Sky (Skymaster 126) (1979 7s^3 7s 7v^4 7d 7g 7s^2 6fg^2 6fg* 7fg^4 7fg 6g^2 7fg^4 5f^4 1980 7d 7v^4 7g 6h 6d 7g* 6g* 7fg* 7f 7d) quite a moderate handicapper; top weight and dropped in class when winning selling handicap at Brighton in August (no bid); successful in better company at Windsor (apprentice event) and Salisbury (ridden by 7-lb claimer when beating Right of Light 2 lengths) the following month; stays 7f well; appears to act on any going; has been tried in blinkers; suitable mount for a boy. *B. Swift.* **70**

SKY LARKER 3 b.g. Roi Soleil 125–Juicy Lucy 80 (King's Troop 118) (1979 6g 6fg 7f^3 1980 8v 8.2s) lengthy gelding; showed ability on final start at 2 yrs; —

Mr D. A. R. Rowland's "Skyliner"

lightly raced and well beaten in 1980, including when blinkered in a seller on final start; best run at 7f on firm going; sold to G. Lewis 925 gns Ascot October Sales. *P. Cundell.*

SKYLINE DRIVE 6 ch.g. High Line 125–Picture Palace 83 (Princely Gift 137) (1979 16s* 18s* 17.1g* 14f 16s^3 17.1g* 22.2fg 1980 16fg 14fg 18.8g^3 17.1fg*) staying handicapper; beat Chain of Reasoning by 4 lengths in handicap at Bath in June; acts on a firm surface, but is ideally suited by plenty of give in the ground; has twice been tried in blinkers. *C. James.* **60**

SKYLINER 5 b.h. African Sky 124–Keep Going 113 (Hard Sauce 131) (1979 7s^2 8fg^2 8g 7.3g* 8f 7s 1980 7fg^2 8f^4 8.5f^4 8g^4 7.3d 8g 8g) quite attractive, well-made horse; half-brother to 2 winners, including Slip The Ferret (by Klairon) a very useful filly at up to 1m; dam won six 5f races at 2 yrs; smart performer at his best, winner of 1979 Hungerford Stakes at Newbury; good fourth in Tote Lockinge Stakes at Newbury in May on second start (1¼ lengths behind Kris) and Sussex Stakes at Goodwood in July on fourth outing (beaten nearly 2½ lengths by Posse); also ran well when 1½ lengths second to Foveros in Philip Cornes Trophy at Leicester early in year, but ran moderately third and final starts; stayed 1m; acted on any going; sometimes sweated up; standing at Athassel House Stud, Golden, Co. Tipperary, at IR£1,000 n.f.n.f. *P. Cole.* **114**

SKY MARTIN 2 br.g. Martinmas 128–Faa Paa (Skymaster 126) (1980 5.1g 8.2s) May 18; 15,000Y; smallish, compact gelding; half-brother to several winners, including useful 7f performer The Yellow Girl (by Yellow God); dam 2-y-o 7f winner in Ireland; tailed off in maiden race and a seller in September; sold 240 gns Ascot November Sales. *P. Haslam.* **–**

SKYTRAIN HOSTESS 2 ch.f. Roan Rocket 128–Djenarelle (Djefou) (1980 5d 7g 6g 7g* 7g) Feb 27; 10,000F; lengthy filly; half-sister to 3 winners, including 3-y-o 1m and 1¼m winner Tryton Lines (by Wolver Hollow) and good 1976 Italian 2-y-o Chinacci (by Bold Lad USA); dam very useful French middle-distance performer; rallied well to win 16-runner maiden race at Salisbury in **73**

September by a short head from Toe Tapper; had stiff task in nursery next time out and wasn't disgraced in finishing seventh of 17; will stay at least 1m. *R. Smyth.*

SKY WALK 3 b. or br.f. Tower Walk 130–Nuageuse (Prince Regent 129) (1979 6g 5fg 1980 6d 6h³ 6fg² 6d⁴ 6fg 6s 6g) small, strong filly; good walker; sprint handicapper; stays 6f; seems to act on any going; ran moderately last 3 starts (off course nearly 4 months beforehand); sold 560 gns Newmarket Autumn Sales. *B. Hills.* **66**

SLADELANDS 2 b.g. Owen Anthony 102–Lavant 101 (Le Lavandou 111) (1980 6g 6d) May 19; lightly-made, useful-looking gelding; brother to 3-y-o middle-distance winner Dunderave, and half-brother to several winners, notably top-class sprinters So Blessed (by Princely Gift) and Lucasland (by Lucero); dam 5f sprinter; unquoted when behind in 19-runner newcomers event at Goodwood in September and 25-runner maiden race (speed 4f) at Newbury in October. *W. Wightman.* **–**

SLANEY IDOL 5 b.g. Simbir 130–Pastina 92 (March Past 124) (1979 10s⁴ 10d² 16s 1980 10v² 8g²) Irish gelding; showed himself a very smart middle-distance racehorse as a 3-y-o (rated 116), when first past post in all but one of his 7 starts; fairly lightly raced on flat since (a good hurdler nowadays), but retains much of his ability; promoted to second on winner's disqualification when 1¾ lengths third to Croghan Hill in Rank Cup at Phoenix Park in March; ½-length second of 23 to Folk Hero under 10.0 in Irish Lincolnshire Handicap at the Curragh in April; stays 1½m; seems to act on any going; blinkered first start at 4 yrs. *L. Browne, Ireland.* **98**

SLEEPLINE GOLD 3 br.f. Goldhill 125–Camerons Counsel (Jolly Jet 111) (1979 5d 5s⁴ 6d 6fg³ 6fg³ 7f 6fg 6s 6g 1980 8fg 7g 7f 8fg 7.2g 5d 6g) workmanlike filly; plating-class maiden; stays 6f; acts on a firm surface; blinkered fourth start; has worn bandages; trained part of season by R. Armstrong. *P. Cundell.* **–**

SLEEPLINE PRINCESS 2 ch.f. Royal Palace 131–Tin Mary 96 (Tin King 126) (1980 5fg 5g 5g³ 5fg 6g* 7d⁴(dis) 7fg 6g³) Mar 15; 3,700Y; close-coupled filly; half-sister to 3-y-o 6f winner Widd (by Derring-Do) and useful 1m to 1¾m winner Gallant Welsh (by Welsh Pageant); dam stayed 1m; favourite, made all to win 12-runner maiden race at Chepstow in June by 12 lengths from Welsh Diamond; ran best race afterwards when 2¾ lengths third of 10 to Maryland Cookie in nursery at Salisbury in August (sweated up and looked light); best form at 6f but should stay further; to be trained by R. Armstrong. *D. Elsworth.* **86**

SLEIGH QUEEN 2 b. or br.f. Comedy Star 121–Snow Rum (Quorum 126) (1980 5d 7g) Apr 20; compact filly; half-sister to 3 winners, including fairly useful 1973 2-y-o 5f winner Skijump (by King's Leap) and fair 1978 2-y-o 6f winner Golden Leicester (by Workboy); dam last in seller on only start; unquoted when in rear in maiden races at Newbury (backward, didn't stride out at all well to post) in July and Chepstow in September. *R. Akehurst.* **–**

SLIGO 3 b.f. Shantung 132–Manzanilla 88 (Major Portion 129) (1979 NR 1980 10s 10g) 8,600F; small, lightly-made filly; half-sister to several winners here and abroad, notably smart Spanish Warrior (by Tamerlane), successful at up to 1¼m; dam won at 1m and 1¼m; soundly beaten in minor event and maiden race at Newmarket in the autumn. *L. Cumani.* **–**

SLIGO BAY 3 b.c. Sassafras 135–Sleat 112 (Santa Claus 133) (1979 7s 1980 11fg 14f³ 16f* 16.9d² 15.5s* 16f³ 16.1g²) strong colt; good walker; fairly useful performer; successful in maiden race at Beverley in June (didn't seem suited by track) and small event at Folkestone in July (made all); went down by a short head to Heighlin in handicap at Haydock in September; suited by a test of stamina; acts on any going; genuine and consistent. *F. J. Houghton.* **96**

SLIM BOY 3 b.g. Starch Reduced 112–Astec Ann 66 (Astec 128) (1979 NR 1980 8fg 10d 12g⁴ 15.5g 15.5f) small, narrow gelding; first foal; dam of little account; poor maiden; not certain to stay 2m; sweated up third start. *M. Haynes.* **–**

SLITHERUM 5 ch.h. Frankincense 120–Scorton Green 84 (Above Suspicion 127) (1979 7s 7g* 7s 6g 6g 7fg 6d 6d 1980 12.2v* 12fg 12fg 13.3g 12d) quite a moderate handicapper; won easily at Warwick in March; stays 1½m; acts on any going; has worn blinkers (didn't first 4 starts). *R. Hannon.* **58**

SLOANE STREET 3 b.g. Pitcairn 126–Pleaseme 100 (Javelot 124) (1979 8fg 8d 1980 10g 10.1fg⁴ 10fg 12g 12d 12s) workmanlike gelding; best run at 1¼m **–**

on a firm surface; blinkered nowadays; unseated rider going to post on reappearance. *A. Hide.*

SMACKOVER 5 ch.h. Pontifex (USA)–Atanya (Atan) (1979 8g 7.6g3 8fg 8g 8fg2 7g2 8s 1980 7fg3 8f 7fg 8g4 8fg 8d 7d 8s) strong, good-bodied horse; useful handicapper at his best, but hasn't won since 1978; creditable third to Foveros in Philip Cornes Trophy at Leicester in April; didn't seem to put heart into his effort when fourth to Grand Conde at Kempton in July; stays 1m; acts on any going but has done all his winning on a sound surface; blinkered fifth and last 2 starts; usually held up and is not the easiest of rides. *I. Walker.* **83**

SMALL HOPE BAY 2 b.f. The Brianstan 128–Great Hope (Great Nephew 126) (1980 5g 5f 5fg 6s) May 7; small, strong, lengthy filly; first foal; dam never ran; sweating when remote seventh of 17 behind Pariscene in maiden race at Wolverhampton in August, third outing; well beaten in seller final appearance; refused to enter stalls when withdrawn at Salisbury and Leicester in between. *S. Holland.* –

SMALL PARADISE 3 ch.f. Habat 127–Howrytuar 90 (Sound Track 132) (1979 5fg 5fg 6g 1980 7.6f 7d 5.3d 6g 5fg 5g 5d 10d) small, attractive filly; poor form, including in a selling handicap; blinkered fifth outing. *R. Laing.* –

SMART GUARD 3 b.g. Shiny Tenth 120–Smartie Pants 69 (Galivanter 131) (1979 6fg 1980 6d 6d2 7fg 6g 7d 7fg 7g 8f 8fg 7d) big, rangy gelding; little worthwhile form in varied company; best run at 6f on a soft surface; sweated up badly third and fifth starts; blinkered seventh outing; has been bandaged in front. *W. Holden.* –

SMARTSET 5 b.h. Martinmas 128–Tess 90 (Road House II) (1979 8g* 8d2 8fg3 8fg2 8f 8d 9f* 1980 8d 8f 8g3 8d 8g* 8g) useful handicapper; sweating, made all when beating Mashoor shade cleverly by a length at Sandown in July; had earlier run well when third of 22 to Tender Heart in Royal Hunt Cup at Royal Ascot; had stiffish task when behind final outing; stays 1¼m; probably acts on any going but seems well suited by firm; has run well for an apprentice; suited by forcing tactics; sent to race in USA. *F. J. Houghton.* **100**

SMASHING FELLOW 3 gr.g. Dragonara Palace 115–Singing (Petingo 135) (1979 5d4 5d3 5g 5v 6f 5fg 5fg4 8fg3 8d* 1080 10d 8f2 8fg* 7.3f 7f 7d 8g3 7g4 7f3 7g 7fg) robust, compact gelding; good mover; moderate handicapper; won at Salisbury in May; suited by 1m; acts on any going; blinkered fourth start in 1979; ran moderately fifth and final outings. *R. Hannon.* **81**

SMILE FOR ME 2 br.c. Song 132–Teersaway 74 (Weepers Boy 124) (1980 5d 5fg 5d4) Apr 17; robust, well-made colt; good mover; fifth foal; half-brother to very useful 1979 2-y-o 5f and 6f winner Try To Smile (by Murrayfield); dam sprinter; prominent in 2 races in the Midlands, at Warwick in October finishing 4¾ lengths fourth of 19 to Brentex in maiden race. *F. J. Houghton.* **73**

SMILING CAVALIER 4 b.g. Cavo Doro 124–Politely 61 (Polic 126) (1979 10s 1980 10d 14g) compact gelding; probably of no account; sold out of G. Richards' stable 780 gns Doncaster March Sales. *D. Thom.* –

SMILING EYES 2 b.f. Connaught 130–Perfect Picture 78 (Hopeful Venture 125) (1980 7fg) Apr 17; lengthy filly; first foal; dam lightly-raced daughter of 1,000 Guineas second Photo Flash, herself a half-sister to Welsh Pageant; 50/1, made no show when behind in 17-runner maiden race won by Sainera at Yarmouth in August. *T. Waugh.* –

SMILING PRINCESS 2 b.f. Prince de Galles 125–Golden Giggle (Golden Dipper 119) (1980 7d 8g) Apr 28; plain filly; first foal; dam of little account; unquoted when well beaten maiden races at Leicester at the back-end. *I. Dudgeon.* –

SMITH SEAL 5 b.h. Royal Palace 131–Dilly 89 (Princely Gift 137) (1979 8s 8g 8s4 8fg2 8.2fg3 8h* 8g2 8g4 8fg 1980 8fg* 8fg 8fg* 8fg 8fg 8fg* 8fg2(dis) 9f 8.3fg 8fg 8.2s) won handicaps at Wolverhampton, Stockton and Bath; beat Can Run by 2 lengths on last-named course in July; best form at 1m but stays 1¼m; seems to act on any going but goes very well on top-of-the-ground; usually wears blinkers but didn't at Wolverhampton; trained most of season by A. Johnson. *R. Baker.* **63**

SMITHY LANE 2 b.c. Pitskelly 122–Seamstress (Sea Hawk II 131) (1980 5fg 5d 7s) May 11; 3,800Y; compact colt; half-brother to fairly useful 6f –

performer Classy Dame (by Jukebox); dam ran only twice; behind in maiden races at Leicester in May and Wolverhampton in June and in minor event at Chepstow in October; sold 625 gns Ascot November Sales. *G. Hunter.*

SMOKE BABY 2 ch.f. Royal Smoke 113–Ginger Jane 69 (Hornbeam 130) **43** (1980 5f 5f^4 6g^4 6g 6fg^3 6g) Mar 7; very small filly; fifth living foal; dam placed over sprint distances at 2 yrs; plater; suited by 6f and will probably stay further. *P. Calver.*

SMOKE SCREEN 4 b.c. Blakeney 126–Cigarette Case 89 (Faberge II 121) **70** (1979 10f^4 11f^4 12d* 12.3s^2 11.7f 12g 1980 11fg 12fg 14f*) good sort; moves well; not seen out after beating Simla by ¾ length in handicap at Newmarket in May; suited by 1¾m when conditions aren't testing; acts on any going; blinkered fourth and fifth starts at 3 yrs. *S. Mellor.*

SMOKE SINGER 5 b.h. Crooner 119–Smokey Dawn 78 (March Past 124) **94** (1979 5d^2 6d^2 5s* 6fg 6g 6s 6s 7f 1980 6v^2 5fg 5f 6fg^3 5fg 5s 6d 5g 6fg 7g 11.1fg^3 10d 9f 10g 7s) neat, strong horse; useful performer; placed in handicaps at Salisbury and Doncaster and in September Stakes at Kempton; had very stiff task and was beaten long way by More Light in last-named event, but was by no means disgraced; effective at 5f and 6f and evidently stays 11f; acts on any going; blinkered fifth outing. *P. Kelleway.*

SMOKEY BEAR 5 b.h. Gulf Pearl 117–Seul 69 (Faberge II 121) (1979 **92** 10.5d 8.2g^4 7f 10h^4 10f^3 11g^2 10.5s^2 10.4f 10.2fg^2 10h* 10.6g 1980 10fg^2 12f^4 10.5f^2 10fg* 12g* 12.3g* 12g 15g* 12fg 13s^2 18d) fair handicapper; sometimes doesn't impress in his slower paces; improved and had a good season; put up a game performance when tackling a long distance for the first time in Tennent Trophy at Ayr in July, making most of running and holding off Russian George by ½ length; had earlier won at Ripon, York and Newcastle; made most of the running and ran a fine race when seventh of 27 to Popsi's Joy in Tote Cesarewitch at Newmarket in October; stays well; acts on any going; has run creditably for an amateur. *J. Hanson.*

SMOKEY SHADOW 3 gr.g. Dragonara Palace 115–Camdamus 83 (Mandamus **81** 120) (1979 NR 1980 8fg 8fg* 8.2g^4 8f 8f^2 10.8d^3) 5,100F, 12,000Y; fair sort; second foal; dam best at up to 1¼m; stayed on to win maiden race at Stockton in June despite showing signs of inexperience; not disgraced on third and fifth (apprentice handicap) starts; stays 1m well; acts well on firm ground and is possibly unsuited by soft. *E. Eldin.*

SMOKEY STAR 4 gr.f. Smokey Rockett 107–Sheba's Lass (Sheshoon 132) **—** (1979 5fg 6s 7g^4 8f^4 8g 6g^3 6s 1980 8s 10fg 8h 10fg 8fg 8f 8g 6g) bad plater; probably stays 1m; acts on firm going; sometimes wears blinkers. *G. Wallace.*

SMUGGLE 2 b.f. Import 127–Manipulation 90 (Appiani II 128) (1980 6s **59** 6g 7fg* 7h) May 14; small, light-framed filly; third foal; half-sister to middle-distance winner Syncopate (by Highland Melody); dam won over 6f at 2 yrs and stayed well; dropped in class, showed first sign of ability when staying on gamely to win 12-runner seller at Redcar in July by short head from Goldliner Abbey; attracted no bid; moderate sixth in nursery at Bath next time out; will be suited by 1m; sold to Mrs G. Forbes 1,400 gns Newmarket Autumn Sales. *Sir Mark Prescott.*

SNAPPER POINT 3 br.c. Right Tack 131–Xanadu 86 (Zimone) (1979 **100** 6.3f* 6.3g* 6f 1980 7s 7g^2 8f^4 7g 8g* 6.5d 6d) strong, shapely, attractive ex-Irish colt; won Premio Caronno at Milan in July; top weight when going down by ¾ length to Ringawoody in 21-runner Madrid Handicap at the Curragh earlier in season; well beaten in Jersey Stakes at Royal Ascot (blinkered) on fourth outing; stays 1m; acts on firm going; sold out of A. Maxwell's stable 300,000 francs (approx £31,200) Chantilly June Sales. *J. Audon, France.*

SNAP TIN 2 ch.f. Jimmy Reppin 131–Hunu (Hul a Hul 124) (1980 5v 5d **35** 5g 5f 5f^4 6s 5f 5fg 8fg 6d 5s) Apr 26; 400F; leggy filly; bad plater; sometimes wears blinkers. *R. Ward.*

SNOOZY TIME 2 b.f. Cavo Doro 124–Noddy Time 97 (Gratitude 130) (1980 **65** 5fg 5fg 5f* 5f 6g 6d^4 8g 6d) Mar 19; strong, good sort; half-sister to smart 1¼m performer The Dunce (by High Hat) and a winner in Italy; dam stayed 1m; won 9-runner minor event at Ayr in May by a neck from Cleat; blinkered when 11 lengths equal fourth of 16 to Ponchielli in nursery at Haydock in September; should be suited by 7f+ (out of her depth when well beaten over 1m). *D. Thom.*

Sun Chariot Stakes, Newmarket—Snow puts up a smart performance to win this pattern race from Kashmir Lass and Gift Wrapped (not in picture)

SNOW 3 gr.f. Young Emperor 133–Arctic Walk (Arctic Slave 116) (1979 7f 1980 6f* 10f4 7fg 7.5f4 7f 8fg* 12g2 10g* 8g4 10f* 12d3) **123**

As a rule the better horses in Europe race less often than their American counterparts. The reasons for this vary, with climate, a lack of suitable opportunities within the pattern of racing, financial considerations and simply custom among them. Perhaps we pamper our horses too much. It's unusual, and refreshing, to come across a filly like Snow in Europe, whose two best efforts came at the end of a strenuous campaign that saw her out eleven times in varied company from April to October. None of the other leading three-year-old fillies was kept as busy. Nevertheless, Snow's form for most of the year was some way below that of the autumn and had she been retired before the Sun Chariot Stakes we could not have regarded her as better than useful. Her achievements to the end of September were limited to successes in a maiden race at Naas and handicaps at Phoenix Park (the CBA Cup) and the Curragh; on the occasions she ran in listed events Snow finished only fourth, to Racquette in the mile-and-a-quarter Azalea Stakes at Phoenix Park and to Calandra in the one-mile Gilltown Stud Stakes at the Curragh. Consequently, when Prendergast sent Snow to Newmarket with his Jockey Club Cup contender Ardross most observers viewed the latter as much more likely to win and he started at odds on while Snow, carrying 3 lb overweight for Piggott's services, attracted little support in the Sun Chariot market at 12/1. In the race Snow seemed outpaced as the leaders quickened two furlongs out but once put under pressure she began to run on strongly, collared Kashmir Lass inside the distance and went on to win going away by a length and a half with Gift Wrapped two and a half lengths back in third. Although her cause was helped by the moderate showing of the short-priced favourite Vielle, Snow had put up a much improved performance. She confirmed her improvement in the St Simon Stakes at Newbury later in October. Having tracked the leaders throughout, she came under quite strong pressure again a couple of furlongs from home, and wandered about, interfering with Nicholas Bill who was trying to get through on the rails; nevertheless she ran on well to go down by two lengths to Shining Finish, giving him 3 lb, with Nicholas Bill half a length behind third. Almost inevitably an objection and a stewards' enquiry followed, resulting in Snow's being moved down a place.

Young Emperor, Snow's sire, headed the 1965 Free Handicap after runaway wins in the Coventry Stakes and Gimcrack Stakes. He spent seven years at stud in America prior to being returned to Ireland but enjoyed only modest

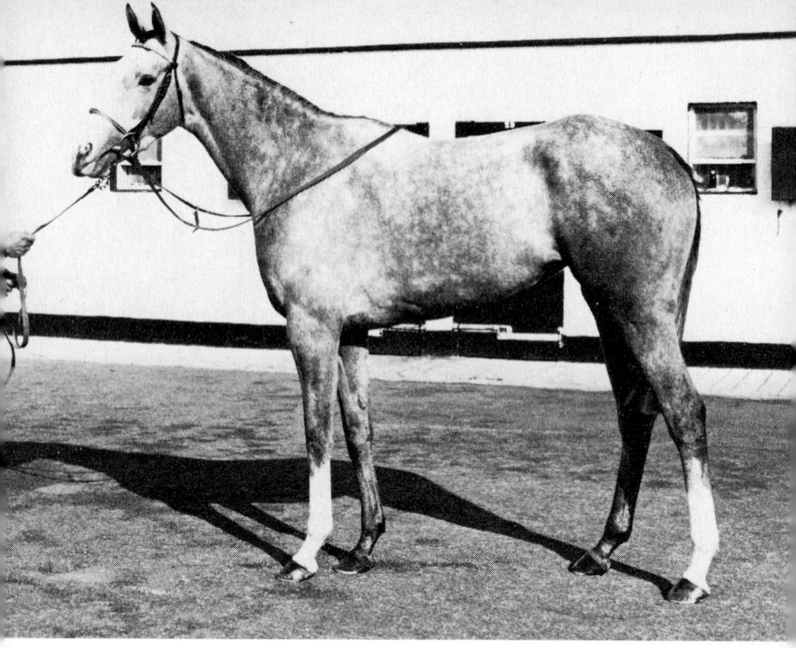

Mr M. Fraser's "Snow"

success in each country and was exported to Italy in 1979. Snow is his best runner to date, ahead of Dragonara Palace. The breeding of Snow's dam is far from fashionable from a flat-racing angle but that hasn't stopped her producing three other winners, notably Icelandic (by Rarity), a smart performer at up to one and a half miles. She visited Mill Reef in 1979, and now has a filly foal by him. Arctic Walk, who won over a mile and a half and two miles in Ireland, is

Snow (gr.f. 1977)	Young Emperor (gr 1963)	Grey Sovereign (gr 1948)	Nasrullah
			Kong
		Young Empress (b 1957)	Petition
			Jennifer
	Arctic Walk (b or br 1967)	Arctic Slave (b 1950)	Arctic Star
			Roman Galley
		Walking High (br 1962)	Court Harwell
			Solitaire

one of three foals, all successful, out of the unraced Walking High, a half-sister to numerous winners, including the good sprinter Lady Midge, dam of the smart but unreliable miler Prince Midge. Snow, a 15,000-guinea yearling, is suited by middle distances; she seems to act on any going. A tall filly, she is very tough and game. *K. Prendergast, Ireland.*

SNOW BLESSED 3 br.c. So Blessed 130–Snow Tribe 94 (Great Nephew 126) (1979 6fg 6f^{2} 6d 7fg 7fg^{2} 8g^{2} 1980 8d^{4} 10g 10f^{4} 8fg 12g* 12d 12.2f* 12.3fg^{3} 12.2g 10d^{4} 10.2g^{2} 10s* 10g 10.5s 10s) big, strong colt; successful in maiden race at Edinburgh and minor event at Catterick in the summer and handicap at Ayr in September; stays 1½m well; acts on any going; blinkered nowadays; sweated up final start; sold privately at end of year and is to be trained by R. Johnson. *W. Elsey.* **84**

SNOWFLAME 2 b. or br.f. Sassafras 135–Snow Damsel (Mandamus 120) (1980 8.2s) May 6; 7,600Y; first foal; dam, unplaced twice at 3 yrs, is half-sister to —

Snow Knight; 6/1 when eighth of 15 in maiden race won by Sage King at Hamilton in September. *C. Nelson.*

SOAF 3 b.c. Auction Ring 123–Diatomite 69 (Diatome 132) (1979 5v^3 5d* 5d* 99
5d* 5g^4 6fg* 6d 7d 1980 6s 7f 6fg^4 7h* 6fg 6d 6fg 7g 5s*) strong, attractive, good-quartered colt; excellent mover; useful handicapper; successful at Thirsk in May (odds on) and Sandown in October; beat Gamblers Dream ¾ length in latter; stays 7f; acts on any going; sold 8,800 gns Newmarket Autumn Sales to race in USA. *B. Hills.*

SOBIESKI 4 b. or br.g. Swing Easy 126–Sparkle in the Sky (Sky Gipsy 117) —
(1979 8s^3 6v* 6s^2 8d 7g 6s 5fg 5fg 6g 1980 5.8f 5fg) won maiden race at Leicester early in 1979; well beaten in 1980; best form at 6f with some give in the ground; blinkered fourth start in 1978. *J. Hill.*

SOBRINO GRANDE 3 b.c. Great Nephew 126–Sharondor 84 (Matador 131) —
(1979 NR 1980 10.1g 12s 10s) 6,600F, 10,500Y; strong-topped, useful sort; half-brother to 4 winners, including useful 1972 2-y-o Altiora (by Taj Dewan); dam 6f sprinter; behind in minor and maiden events, once finishing last; sold 1,750 gns Ascot August Sales. *B. Swift.*

SOCCIA (FR) 3 br.f. Realm 129–Goldena (Relko 136) (1979 6f 6g^2 6d 7g^2 6f^4 64
6g 1980 8f^4 7fg 8.2g^2 8f^3) shapely, good-bodied filly; quite a moderate maiden at her best; stays 1m; yet to race on a soft surface; ran moderately second start; sold 4,000 gns Goffs November Sales. *M. Stoute.*

SOCKBURN 5 b.g. My Swallow 134–Blue Bird 84 (Majority Blue 126) (1979 78
12g 12g 13fg* 14g* 1980 12.3g 14.6fg 12g^3 12g 12g 16.1s) big, strong gelding; fair handicapper; didn't run up to his best in 1980 but showed signs that he retained his ability when easy in market on fourth and fifth outings and was gambled on at Haydock on final start (raced on unfavourable side of course and had no chance with those on stand side in closing stages); suited by a test of stamina; seems to act on any going but goes well on a sound surface; suitable mount for an apprentice; game and genuine. *M. Camacho.*

SOCKS UP 3 ch.g. Sharpen Up 127–Mrs Moss 81 (Reform 132) (1979 5v* 5d* 84
5s* 6g^2 6g 6f 6fg^4 1980 6s 7f 7d 7s 7.2d^3 7d 6g* 6fg 5s) leggy, somewhat lightly-made gelding; good mover; won handicap at Goodwood in September; stays 7f; acts on any going with possible exception of very firm; blinkered fifth and sixth starts (played up in paddock on latter); has hung badly on occasions and isn't an easy ride. *F. J. Houghton.*

Chivas Regal Sprint, Sandown—first blood to the visitors as Shoemaker on Soaf beats Mercer on Gamblers Dream. The United States went on to beat Great Britain in the Chivas Regal Trophy between teams of jockeys from the two countries

SO DEAR 2 b.f. St Paddy 133–Sooner or Later (Sheshoon 132) (1980 8g 8d^{4}) **73 p** Apr 3; robust, attractive filly; half-sister to middle-distance winners Solatia (by Kalydon) and Salian (by Salvo); dam lightly-raced half-sister to Oaks third Suni; 12/1, led far side to halfway before finishing 7½ lengths fourth of 15 to Rollrights in maiden race at Leicester in November; has scope and will do better over longer distances in 1981. *J. Hindley.*

SODINA 2 b.f. Saulingo 122–Red Rag (Ragusa 137) (1980 5fg^{2} 5f 5.3d 5f 5g^{2} **75** 5f* 5d) Feb 20; 3,500Y; lightly-made filly; half-sister to 2 winners, including quite useful Irish middle-distance stayer Negrada (by Nelcius); dam half-sister to Irish 1,000 Guineas winner Gazpacho; returned to form in the autumn and won 17-runner maiden race at Lingfield in October by a length from Lost Cause after making all; made no show under a 10-lb penalty later same month; will stay 6f. *B. Hanbury.*

SOFRONOFF 5 br.g. Dubassoff–My Dream 119 (King of the Tudors 129) **–** (1979 16v* 16d* 18.8g 14f 17.4s 1980 16s 12g) staying handicapper; well beaten in 1980; acts on any going. *J. Old.*

SOFT VOICE 3 b.f. Simbir 130–Tuscan Tune 75 (Tudor Melody 129) (1979 6g **61** 5.8g^{4} 1980 8f^{3} 13s 13g^{2} 15.5g^{4} 11fg 14fg^{4}) lengthy filly; placed in maiden races at Chepstow in May and Nottingham in July; suited by a test of stamina; possibly unsuited by soft going. *H. Candy.*

SOHEIR 3 ch.f. Track Spare 125–My Dearest Sarah 79 (Anwar 120) (1979 6g **74** 6d 1980 7f 7fg 8fg 11.1f^{2} 10.2fg* 9.6f^{3} 10.5d 9g^{2} 10.1g 11.7d 10g 10.2d 10.2v) small filly; quite a moderate handicapper; won at Doncaster in May; suited by middle distances; acts on firm going and is unsuited by soft; blinkered final start; retained 2,300 gns Newmarket Autumn Sales. *M. Ryan.*

SOIE GRISE 4 gr.c Town Crier 119–Floating Melody 101 (Tudor Melody 129) **71** (1979 8s* 8d^{2} 10v^{2} 8d* 8.5d* 8g 8g 10g 1980 10.2d 7v 7.2d 10.6fg^{2} 8.2s 10s) tall, rangy colt; not a good mover; top weight when beaten short head by Boltingo in selling handicap at Haydock in June, best effort; finds 7f on sharp side and stays 10.6f; seems to act on any going. *A. Smith.*

SOLAIRE PRINCE 2 b.g. Jimsun 121–Demta (Astec 128) (1980 5fg 8d 7s) **–** Apr 18; 900Y; first live foal; dam won from 6f to 1¼m in France; unquoted when in rear in maiden and minor events. *T. M. Jones.*

SOLAR EMPEROR 4 ch.g. Tyrant–Luna 85 (Milesian 125) (1979 8s 8s 5f **§§** 7f 10g^{3} 10h^{4} 7d^{3} 12fg 10.2d 10s 1980 12h^{2} 12f) well-grown gelding; poor maiden; stays 1½m; used to wear blinkers; refused to race final outing. *C. Gray.*

SOLAR GIFT 4 b.g. Frankincense 120–Sunsaly 75 (Sallymount 125) (1979 **–** 10s^{3} 10fg 10d 10.1fg 1980 10fg) poor maiden; stays 1¼m; probably acts on any going; has been tried in blinkers. *J. Powney.*

SOLAR GRASS 5 b.g. Veiled Wonder–Fair Marilyn (Macherio) (1979 8v **70** 13v 8s 10g 8.2g 9g^{4} 5f^{3} 10f 8.2g 5g 12g 6f 10.6g 1980 8f 8f 5fg 8g 5d 5d 5fg^{2} 5fg* 5d^{4} 6d* 5d^{2} 6fg* 6s^{2} 6d^{4} 6v^{3}) strong, fair sort; won handicaps at Warwick in July, Ripon in August and Leicester in September, making virtually all on last 2 occasions; had stiff task and ran well when third to Lightning Label in minor event at Doncaster in November on final start; evidently best at sprint distances; probably acts on any going; suitable mount for an inexperienced rider. *W. Charles.*

SOLAR HONEY 3 b.f. Roi Soleil 125–Sailor's Honey 83 (Poker) (1979 5.3g^{3} **61** 5f* 1980 6f 6s^{2} 6g 6d) useful sort; good walker; won maiden race at Nottingham in 1979 but is only plating class nowadays; stays 6f; acts on any going; sold 650 gns Doncaster November Sales. *R. Price.*

SOLARIUM 2 br.g. Scottish Rifle 127–Daydreamer 78 (Star Gazer 123) (1980 **50** 6d 7d 6g 7fg^{4} 8.2g 8fg) May 9; 800Y; compact gelding; brother to winning stayer Barnbougle, and half-brother to 2 winners abroad; dam won 1m seller; poor plater; stays 7f and should be suited by 1m; blinkered second outing. *W. Musson.*

SOLAR LOVE 4 ch.c. Thatch 136–Solar Echo (Solar Slipper 131) (1979 **49** 5fg 1980 8v^{2} 8fg 7g 8fg) lightly-made colt; plating-class maiden; stays 1m; best form with some give in the ground; moved very badly to post only start at 3 yrs; sold 390 gns Ascot December Sales. *B. Hanbury.*

SOLDAN 2 br.c. Royalty 130–Mercilla 94 (Welsh Abbot 131) (1980 7d* **106** 7v^{2}) May 30; half-brother to 2 winners, including fairly useful miler Computercall (by Good Bond); dam 2-y-o 5f winner; 16/1 but well drawn, led inside final furlong when winning 20-runner minor event at Doncaster in October by 2 lengths from Music City; head second of 9 to Sula Bula in 9-runner Steel Plate Autumn Stakes on same course the following month; will stay 1¼m; useful. *J. W. Watts.*

SOLDIER 3 ch.c. Sun Prince 128–Militello 71 (Habitat 134) (1979 6g 1980 7f 8d* 8g³ 8fg 10g 11fg) lengthy colt; good mover; won 13-runner maiden race at Salisbury in June; should stay beyond 1m; possibly needs some give in the ground; sold 1,650 gns Ascot December Sales. *J. Dunlop.* **73**

SOLE BIDDER 2 b. or br.g. Touch Paper 113–Mariola 93 (Royal Hamlet 115) (1980 6d 5g 6g 6s) Apr 11; 1,500Y, resold 1,300Y; half-brother to winners in Spain and Malaya; dam won at up to 1m; well behind in maiden races and a minor event; blinkered third and fourth outings. *E. Carter.* **–**

SOLEIL NOIR (FR) 4 gr.c. Exbury 138–Skelda 117 (La Varende 125) (1979 12v* 10.5s³ 15s* 15fg* 12.5fg 14.6f² 1980 12g³ 12g⁴ 12f³ 15s² 12fg) French colt; useful sort; good walker; won 3 races at 3 yrs, including Grand Prix de Paris at Longchamp, and was a very close second to Son Of Love in St Leger at Doncaster; came closest to success in 1980 when ½-length second to Kelbomec (rec 8 lb) in Prix du Carrousel at Longchamp in June (3/1 on, tried to make all); in frame earlier in Prix d'Hedouville on same course and Grand Prix d'Evry, both won by Scorpio, and in Coronation Cup at Epsom won by Sea Chimes (2¾ lengths third of 4); stays well; acts on any going but may be best suited by a sound surface; racing in Argentina. *F. Mathet, France.* **116**

SOLEROF 2 b.c. Averof 123–Solhoon 74 (Tycoon II) (1980 7fg 6g 7fg² 7fg) Apr 29; 3,000Y; lengthy, unfurnished colt; second foal; dam won sellers over 6f and 7f; short-head second of 19 to Toe Tapper in maiden race at Leicester in September, best effort; not disgraced next time out; will stay 1m. *P. Cole.* **76**

SOLEURE 5 b.g. Sun Prince 128–Kiyofuji 98 (Grey Sovereign 128 §) (1979 12s 8d 10d⁴ 7fg 8f 8f 1980 13d 12f) plating-class maiden; stays 1¼m. *M. Tate.* **–**

SOLOMON'S LAMP 3 ch.g. Pall Mall 132–Spring Blossom 85 (Queen's Hussar 124) (1979 5g 7fg 1980 9d 8g* 8d) lengthy gelding; has rather a round action; 50/1 when short-heading Secret Gill in minor event at Thirsk in September; stays 1m. *I. Walker.* **71**

SO LONG LILLY 3 br.f. Saulingo 122–Silly Song (Silly Season 127) (1979 5s² 5g 6fg 5g 5g 5f 1980 5s 8fg 7fg 8f) light-framed filly; has shown little worthwhile form since first outing at 2 yrs; well beaten in seller final outing (May); not certain to stay 1m; has been tried in blinkers. *M. Salaman.* **–**

SOLO STAR 2 br.c. Jukebox 120–Ansedonia (Captain's Gig) (1980 6.3d* 6.3g 6s² 6d*) May 5; 8,400Y; first living foal; dam 2-y-o 5f winner in Ireland; apprentice ridden when successful in maiden race at the Curragh in July and Birdcatcher Nursery at Naas in October, leading at distance to win latter by 3 lengths from Jasmine Prince; stays 6f well; yet to race on a firm surface. *T. Burns, Ireland.* **106**

SOLO THE JACK 2 ch.c. Amber Rama 133–Maroukh (Kashmir II 125) (1980 7g) Mar 23; 2,300Y; first foal; dam ran only twice; unquoted and apprentice ridden when behind in 18-runner maiden race won by Price of Peace at Salisbury in July. *R. Akehurst.* **–**

SOLTARA 2 b.f. The Go-Between 129–Dear Sol (Dear Gazelle 113) (1980 6s 5s) May 26; neat, lightly-made filly; half-sister to 1976 2-y-o 5f seller winner Solchella (by Welham); dam of little account; well behind in minor events in second half of season. *W. Stubbs.* **–**

SOLWAY WINDS 2 b.g. Windjammer (USA)–Maggie Mine 85 (Native Prince) (1980 5f 5fg³ 6d³ 6d* 6fg* 6d 6d) Apr 26; 3,500F, 4,500Y; leggy gelding; half-brother to Irish 1m to 9f winner Godspenny (by Martinmas); dam 2-y-o 5f winner; came to himself in the summer, winning maiden auction event at Newcastle in June by 3 lengths and staying on strongly to beat Border Spoil a short head in minor race at Redcar the following month; ran moderately in nurseries on next 2 outings and was subsequently gelded; will stay 7f; acts on a firm and a soft surface. *N. Crump.* **88**

SOMBRERO 4 ch.c. Warpath 113–Poncho 80 (Ragusa 137) (1979 10v 12g⁴ 12d 12.2g⁴ 11f 10g⁴ 11d⁴ 13fg⁴ 1980 12.2v⁴ 11.7fg) neat colt; stays 13f and is likely to get further; seems to act on any going. *S. Pattemore.* **–**

SOME BABY 3 b.f. Some Hand 119–Scottish Lullaby 92 (Aberdeen 109) (1979 5s 5.8g 6fg² 5.1f 7fg 1980 8s 8fg 6h 5h) compact filly; bad plater; **– §**

best run at 6f on a firm surface; has worn blinkers; gives impression of being ungenuine. *S. Kernick.*

SOME BELLA 3 ch.f. Some Hand 119–Bella Lisa (River Chanter 121) (1979 NR 1980 6f 5s 7g 7g² 6g² 7s* 7d⁴ 7d) lengthy, good-quartered filly; third foal; half-sister to fairly useful sprinter Kingsfold Trooper (by King's Troop) and stayer Kingsfold Lad (by Tobrouk); dam ran only 3 times; second in seller and maiden race prior to dead-heating with Just Abroad in 10-runner minor event at Ayr in September; will stay 1m; acts on soft going; sweated up a bit fifth outing. *P. Kelleway.* **67**

SOME CHERRY 4 br.f. Some Hand 119–Cherry Brandy (Tenerani 135) (1979 9s 16fg 10s 1980 8s 8.2d* 10fg 8.2fg 8g³ 7fg² 8d 8fg 8.2s) unfurnished filly; plater; bought in 1,100 gns after winning at Hamilton in April; seems best at around 1m; acts on a firm and a soft surface. *T. Taylor.* **40**

SOME JET 2 ch.c. Some Hand 119–Jetador 73 (Queen's Hussar 124) (1980 5d 6s) Mar 3; neat colt; first foal; dam won from 1¼m to 2m; 16/1 and sweating when behind in 23-runner maiden race won by Hindi at Haydock in October; 20/1 and blinkered, finished in rear in well-contested seller on same course later in month. *C. Crossley.* **–**

SOMERS BRIDGE 2 br.c. Realm 129–Gwen Somers (Will Somers 114§) (1980 6s) Apr 20; 1,350Y; neat colt; good mover; second foal; dam unraced half-sister to smart animals Cyrus and Right of the Line; 50/1 when last of 17 in maiden race at Nottingham in August. *J. Mulhall.* **–**

SOMERS HEIR 5 b.g. Will Somers 114§–Treatisan 67 (Milesian 125) (1979 7s⁴ 7.2v² 7d² 7.6v 7g 7fg 6g 7fg 7.2g 6d 7g* 7d 1980 7d³ 7v 7fg 7d) quite a moderate handicapper; suited by 7f and 1m; goes well in the mud; occasionally wears blinkers; has done all his winning on a round course; has won for an apprentice; trained until after third start by W. Wightman (off course for 6 months afterwards). *D. Wintle.* **58**

SOMERTON PRINCESS 3 b.f. My Swanee 122–Mia Samantha 60 (Welsh Abbot 131 or Don Carlos) (1979 5g 1980 8d 10.1s 10.2fg 10fg) tall filly; well beaten in maiden and minor events. *S. Pattemore.* **–**

SOMETHING SPECIAL 3 b.c. Queen's Hussar 124–Calling The Tune 84 (Tudor Melody 129) (1979 6fg 7g³ 7fg 7f 7.3g 1980 11.7fg⁴ 12fg* 12f² 12f 12g 11.7s 12.3fg) well-made, good-looking colt; enterprisingly ridden to win handicap at Doncaster in May; not disgraced next start but was well beaten subsequently, including when blinkered final appearance; stays 1½m; acts on firm going. *R. Boss.* **75**

SOMETIME SOON 2 gr.f. No Mercy 126–Cansanta 96 (Canisbay 120) (1980 5fg 5g³ 6g 6g 8.2g 8g 7d³) May 19; compact filly; sister to fair 1978 2-y-o 6f winner Santaclair and half-sister to winning 3-y-o miler Sharpener (by Sharpen Up); dam won twice over 5f at 2 yrs; quite moderate form in varied company; stays 1m; acts on a soft surface. *H. Collingridge.* **68**

SONANT 3 ch.g. Master Sing 109–Mutchkin 65 (Espresso 122) (1979 5fg 1980 6d⁴ 6d 6f² 6f) leggy gelding; quite a moderate maiden; stays 6f; acts on firm going; not raced after May. *P. Rohan.* **60**

SONES (USA) 2 ch.c. Full Pocket–Irish Sunrise (Amber Morn) (1980 6g* 7s) Apr 7; $47,000Y; half-brother to 3 winners, including minor stakes winner Too Much Irish (by Flit-To); dam won at up to 1m; landed the odds comfortably by a length from Fontana di Trevi in 9-runner maiden race at Yarmouth in September; well-backed favourite for 17-runner nursery at Newmarket the following month but was struggling 3f out and wasn't persevered with, finishing out of first 9 behind Go Leasing; should stay at least 7f. *H. Cecil.* **78**

SON FILS 5 ch.h. Mon Fils 124–Crespinall 110 (Saint Crespin III 132) (1979 12s* 10.5d⁴ 1980 10s² 12g* 13.4f³ 12fg 12d² 12fg 13.3d³) tall, narrow horse; really good mover; very useful middle-distance performer; ran well when second to Baronet in handicap at Kempton in April and made all and held off Ambler narrowly in similar race at Epsom later in month; ran in better company afterwards and was placed in Ormonde Stakes (close third to Niniski) at Chester, Princess of Wales's Stakes (went down by neck to Nicholas Bill) at Newmarket and slowly-run Geoffrey Freer Stakes at Newbury; 2 lengths fourth to Nicholas Bill (promoted to third) in last-named event in August; acts on any going but is best with some give in the ground; game and genuine; ideally suited by front-running tactics. *R. Hannon.* **111**

SONG BEAM 4 b.f. Song 132–Beamless 73 (Hornbeam 130) (1979 6v 5s 6s³ 6d* 6s* 6fg⁴ 6f⁴ 7g 6g⁴ 7g 1980 6v 6g 7fg 7f 7fg 7f) strong, compact **–**

filly; fair handicapper at her best; didn't find her form in 1980; stays 6f and ran respectably on first outing over 7f; acts on any going except perhaps heavy; suitable mount for an apprentice. *J. Holt.*

SONG MAIDEN 3 b.f. Forlorn River 124–Maiden d'Or 87 (Songedor 116) — (1979 5f 5h 5fg^3 5f^4 5g^2 5fg 1980 5f 7f 10s 8d) smallish filly; plater; best form at 5f on an easy surface; sometimes blinkered. *T. Kersey.*

SONG MINSTREL 2 b.c. Song 132–Tribal Festival 65 (Tribal Chief 125) — (1980 5fg 5s 5s) Apr 22; compact, sprint type; first foal; dam 6f winner, is half-sister to very useful sprinters Cala-Vadella and Runnett; in rear in maiden and minor events. *M. Camacho.*

SONG SUNG BLUE 4 b.f. Song 132–Green Velvet (Epaulette 125) (1979 **50** 6g^3 1980 8f 8f^2 5d^3 6f 5f^2 5d) attractive filly; placed in amateur riders races at Ripon and Wolverhampton and a maiden race at Redcar; probably stays 1m; sold 15,500 gns Newmarket December Sales. *L. Cumani.*

SONG TO REMEMBER 2 b.f. Song 132–Darya 104 (Darius 129) (1980 6d **73** 6g^4) May 4; 4,300F, 8,000Y; well-made, attractive filly; half-sister to 1m winner Bernice Clare (by Skymaster) and 2 winners abroad; dam best at 6f; 8/1, chased along throughout when $4\frac{3}{4}$ lengths fourth of 20 to Nello in maiden race at Leicester in November; may stay 7f. *J. Dunlop.*

SONNEN GOLD 3 br.c. Home Guard 129–Mulattin (Henry the Seventh 125) — (1979 5d* 5g* 5f* 5g* 7.2fg^3 6d* 6g* 6d* 6f^2 1980 8f^4) 1,700F; strong, useful sort; third living foal; half-brother to middle-distance winner Cooks Corner (by Martinmas); dam never ran; a very smart and thoroughly game colt at 2 yrs, who won 7 races including Gimcrack Stakes at York (beat Lavinsky $1\frac{1}{2}$ lengths after good tussle) and finished very good $\frac{1}{2}$-length second to Known Fact in William Hill Middle Park Stakes at Newmarket on final start; ran only once in 1980, finishing modest fourth of 5 to Saint Jonathon in £3,000 event at Thirsk in April; might have stayed 1m; probably acted on any going; standing at Norton Grove Stud, Malton at £1,500 with Oct 1st concession. *M. H. Easterby.*

SON OF LOVE (FR) 4 ch.c. Jefferson 129–Mot d'Amour (Bon Mot III 132) **116** (1979 10.5v^4 10v^3 11d^2 12s^4 12g 15fg^2 12d 12.5s^2 15g^2 13.5s^4 14.6f* 12g 12v^4 1980 10s^3 10g 12g 12.5s^4 15g) French colt; had a busy time of it in 1979 but showed himself a high-class horse when given a test of stamina, winning St Leger at Doncaster by a short head from Soleil Noir; not disgraced first 4 outings in 1980 over distances on sharp side for him, including when third behind Kamari-daan and Anifa in Prix Exbury at Saint-Cloud in March and fourth to Buckpoint in Prix Maurice de Nieuil at Saint-Cloud in July, but ran poorly when last of 7 behind Marson in Prix Kergorlay at Deauville in August and wasn't seen out again; acts on any going; led out unsold at 580,000 francs (approx £58,000) at Vermeille Sale in September. *R. Collet, France.*

SON OF SHAKA 4 b.c. Tribal Chief 125–Pink Garter (Henry the Seventh 125) — (1979 6d 6fg* 6f* 6s^2 6fg 6g^4 5d 5fg^4 1980 6f^2 6f 6g 5g 5s^4) big, strong, sprint type; smart performer at his best; winner of 2 handicaps at Newmarket and also in frame in better company as a 3-y-o; looked very well when short-head second to Gypsy Dancer in Ladbrokes Abernant Stakes at Newmarket in April; disappointing afterwards (blinkered third and last starts), but was off course for nearly 4 months before fourth outing; better suited by 6f than 5f; acts on any going but goes particularly well on top-of-the-ground; suited by front-running tactics. *R. Price.*

SON OF THE TUDORS 3 b.c. Royal Palace 131–Madge (Tudor Melody 129) — (1979 7s 1980 14g^4 12d) leggy, quite attractive colt; fourth in maiden race at Sandown in July; well beaten in similar event at Goodwood in September, giving impression a return to $1\frac{3}{4}$m would suit him. *R. Price.*

SONOMA (FR) 2 ch.f. Habitat 134–Satu (Primera 131) (1980 5d 6d 5s* 6.5g*) **111** Apr 8; sister to brilliantly speedy French filly Sigy; dam smart French middle-distance winner; won twice late in the year, coming home 4 lengths clear in maiden race at Maisons-Laffitte in October and coming out comfortably best at weights when beating Wicked Lady a short head in all-aged Prix Contessina at Evry in November; should stay 1m; acts on soft going; pulled up soon after start on debut. *Mme C. Head, France.*

SOPHIA WESTERN 2 ch.f. Steel Heart 128–La Grisette (Fortino II 120) — (1980 5s) Jan 13; 6,200F, 19,000Y; half-sister to fairly useful 1979 2-y-o 6f winner Viva L'Armour (by Gay Fandango) and a winner in Malaya; dam won at up to $1\frac{3}{4}$m in Ireland; 8/1 and in need of race, made no show when eighth of 14 to Apapa Port in minor event at Stockton in November. *A. Gillam.*

SOROCHINSKY FAIR 2 b.g. Legal Eagle 126–Sarasail 58 (Hitting Away) –
(1980 7f 7d) Feb 15; 1,200F, 3,000Y; workmanlike gelding; half-brother to a
winning jumper and a winner abroad; dam placed at up to 1¼m; unquoted when
behind in maiden and minor events at Redcar and Doncaster in the autumn. *W. Bentley.*

SOSPIRAE 2 ch.f. Sandford Lad 133–Jewel Tower 91 (Double-U-Jay 120) **90**
(1980 5fg 6g 6d^2 7g 6d* 7fg^3 7s 7d) Feb 13; 2,000F; smallish filly; half-sister to
a winning plater; dam won over 6f at 2 yrs; won small race at Hamilton in September by 1½ lengths from odds-on Faiz; subsequently ran well in nurseries;
stays 7f; seems to act on any going. *N. Guest.*

SO SPLENDID 3 b.f. John Splendid 116–Lady Maggie (Distinctive 118) (1979 –
NR 1980 8fg 9f 8g 8f 6fg 8fg 6g 8g 6d) compact filly; poor plater; best run at 6f.
Mrs B. Waring.

SO SWIFTLY 2 br.f. So Blessed 130–Hirondelle 86 (Falcon 131) (1980 5g 6d) –
Mar 5; strong, useful sort; half-sister to 2 winners, including useful 1¼m winner
April (by Silly Season); dam won at 1m; didn't look ready and started none too
well when behind in maiden races at Doncaster in October; will probably do
better at around 1m in 1981. *C. Thornton.*

SOUKAB 2 ch.c. Good Counsel–Colonial Cousin (Tom Rolfe) (1980 7g 7.6g^4 **84**
7fg 8d^2 7g) Apr 20; strong, well-made, quite attractive colt; first foal; dam
never ran; sire won from 7f to 1¼m, including Widener Handicap; ran well when
2 lengths second of 21 to Obrovac in maiden race at Sandown in October and
when fifth to Go Leasing in 17-runner nursery at Leicester in November; will stay
1½m; possibly needs some give in the ground. *G. Lewis.*

SOULIOTISSA (USA) 3 ch.f. What A Pleasure–Such Nobility (Vaguely Noble **71**
140) (1979 6fg 1980 8f^2 8h 10.2fg^3 8fg^2 7g^2 8g^4 7g^2 7.2g^4 7s^4 8g^3) sparely-made filly; runner-up in Northern maiden and minor events; probably stays 1¼m;
possibly unsuited by hard going; blinkered nowadays; tends to hang under
pressure and is probably ungenuine. *J. W. Watts.*

SOUL SINGER 5 b. or br.h. Saulingo 122–Ribocana (Molvedo 137) (1979 6d **89**
6d 7s 6d 6fg 7f^2 6g* 6g 6d^3 6g^3 8f 7f 1980 6s 6d 6g^3 7fg 6fg^3 7f 6d 7d 6fg 6fg* 7g
7.3fg 6fg 7g) quite a useful handicapper on his day; won Brighton Sprint
Handicap in August by a length from Denmore; didn't get best of runs next
time; stays 7f well and wasn't disgraced over 1m; appears to act on any going
but is well suited by a sound surface; acts on any track. *B. Swift.*

SOUSTRA 3 b.f. Souvran 98–Moonstream 62 (Forlorn River 124) (1979 5fg **51**
6g 7fg 1980 8fg 10g 7fg 7g 6g^2 6d) tall, lightly-made filly; plater; best run at 6f.
J. Benstead.

SOUTHERN BREEZE (FR) 3 b.c. Caro 133–Snow Castle (Snow Cat 120) **80**
(1979 NR 1980 11.5f^3 12g*) tall, rangy, useful-looking colt; second living foal;
dam won in Argentina and Prix Foy in France; didn't act too well on course
when landing odds all out by 1½ lengths from Welsh Display in 15-runner maiden
race at Beverley in June; will stay 1¾m. *H. Cecil.*

SOUTHERN FRONTIER 2 b.c. Derring-Do 131–Sage Willow 69 (Moss- **100**
borough 126) (1980 5d* 5s* 6d^3 6fg) Mar 16; 9,000Y; compact, good-quartered
colt; sixth foal; half-brother to moderate 1979 2-y-o maiden Harford (by Goldhill); dam won over 1¼m; won 18-runner maiden race at Salisbury in June in
good style by 3 lengths from Faiz and 9-runner minor event at Windsor the
following month by 2 lengths from Another Rumbo; beaten afterwards in better
company at Newbury, finishing 4 lengths third of 4 to Poldhu when odds on for
Washington Singer Stakes in August and 8¼ lengths sixth of 7 behind Sweet
Monday in Mill Reef Stakes in September; will stay at least 1m; seems to act on
any going. *F. J. Houghton.*

SOUTHERN SWANEE 2 ch.f. My Swanee 122–Buggles 66 (Kelly 122) (1980 **86**
6f^3 6g* 5g* 5g^2 5fg^2 5d* 6s^3 6fg 7.3d) Mar 30; 1,500Y; rangy filly; half-sister
to some minor winners; dam won 6f seller at 2 yrs and stayed 1¼m; successful in
maiden auction event at Redcar in July and nurseries at Leicester in July and
Newcastle in August; made headway on bridle but had to be pushed right out
when beating Bohemian Rhapsody a length on last-named; again ran very well
when 5½ lengths third of 7 to Star Pastures in Firth of Clyde Stakes at Ayr in
September, best subsequent effort; not sure to stay 7f; seems to act on any
going; genuine and consistent. *D. Dale.*

SOUTHERN WIND 2 b.c. Tumble Wind–Eternity (Never Say Die 137) –
(1980 5fg 6fg 7d) Mar 11; 6,400Y; workmanlike colt; half-brother to Al Burak
(by Silver Shark), a useful winner at up to 1¼m, and winners in Belgium and

Italy; dam never ran; out of first 6 in varied races, final start Acomb Stakes at York in August; dead. *Hbt Jones.*

SOUTHOE BELL 2 gr.f. Saritamer 130–Nylon Pirate (Derring-Do 131) (1980 5d 5f 5g³ 5h⁴ 5d 5s³ 5g³ 5g 5g³ 5s* 5d) Feb 21; 1,550F; neat filly; half-sister to 15f winner Your Love (by Blakeney); dam of little account; improved after finishing sixth in seller on fifth outing; came through to win nursery at Nottingham in August by ¾ length from Hello Susie Greene despite having stumbled at start; off course 2 months afterwards and finished last on return; should stay 6f; acts well on soft going; wears blinkers. *D. Thom.* **72**

SOVEREIGN CASTLE 2 ch.f. Habat 127–Track Music 74 (Track Spare 125) (1980 6g 6fg 5fg³ 5.1fg 5.1fg⁴) Apr 6; 1,200Y; big, strong filly; fourth foal; half-sister to a winner in Austria by Town Crier; dam won over 5f at 2 yrs; showed a little ability in maiden races and sellers; apprentice ridden and bandaged, gave impression she'd be suited by stronger handling when 2 lengths fourth to Daphne's Favour at Yarmouth in August; seems better suited by 5f than 6f. *K. Ivory.* **57**

SOVEREIGN CELLAR 2 gr.c. Sovereign Path 125–Kessella (Le Levanstell 122) (1980 7f) May 30; 3,300Y; closely related to Irish middle-distance winner Rathconrath (by Wolver Hollow) and half-brother to 3 other winners; dam never ran; unquoted and in need of race when last of 25 in maiden race won by Highland Range at Redcar in September. *J. Mulhall.* —

SOVEREIGN DONA 3 b.f. Sovereign Path 125–Dogana (Zank) (1979 7fg 6g* 1980 7fg 7g² 8g* 8d* 8g⁴ 10d* 8g 9.2f) half-sister to 3 winners, including very good milers Don (by Yellow God) and 4-y-o American Prince (by Prince Tenderfoot); dam won over 9.5f in Ireland; showed improved form to win Group 3 Prix de Psyche at Deauville in August by a head from Trevita; successful earlier in fillies race at Navan and handicap at the Curragh; fair fifth to Calandra in Gilltown Stud Stakes at the Curragh in September but was well beaten in Prix de l'Opera at Longchamp following month; very well suited by 1¼m; needs some give in the ground. *S. Murless, Ireland.* **117**

SOVEREIGN ELLA 5 ch.m. Sovereign Bill 105–Hardella 60 (Hard Ridden 131) (1979 NR 1980 10.1g 12g 16fg 16fg) fourth foal; dam won 1m amateur riders race; behind in minor event at Windsor and amateur riders races at Kempton, Newbury and Ascot. *R. Blakeney.* —

SOVEREIGN FLAME 2 ch.f. Supreme Sovereign 119–Flaming Peace 104 (Queen's Hussar 124) (1980 6f 6s*) May 11; 3,000Y; useful-looking filly; first foal; dam won twice over 7f at 2 yrs; ridden by 5-lb claimer when winning 6-runner maiden race at Ayr in August by ½ length from Star Heading; will stay 7f; acts on soft going. *M. McCormack.* **75**

SOVEREIGN JIM 4 br.g. Sovereign Bill 105–Counten (Counsel 118) (1979 6s 5g⁴ 6d 5f 8g 9.4f 8g 10f 10g 8fg³ 1980 7f 6h 8fg 10f) plater; stays 1m (well beaten over further); best form on a sound surface. *W. Bentley.* —

SOVEREIGN JOE 3 ch.c. Sovereign Bill 105–Trixie Dean (Drumbeg 94) (1979 5fg 5fg 1980 6d 8h 10fg 12f 10fg 10.2g) neat, strong colt; poor maiden; blinkered fourth and fifth starts; sweated up first outing. *T. Molony.* —

SOVEREIGN LANDING 2 gr.c. Sovereign Path 125–Pearl Harbour 83 (Martial 131) (1980 5d² 5fg³ 5f² 6g³ 6fg³ 7f³ 7fg⁴ 6s* 8s) Mar 12; 6,600Y; leggy colt; half-brother to 2 winners, including fairly useful 1976 2-y-o winner Pearl Haven (by Raffingora); dam won over 6f at 3 yrs; finally got his head in front when blinkered in 14-runner nursery at Hamilton in September, winning by ½ length from Monza Lady; stays 7f but ran as though 1m was too far for him on final start (again blinkered); seems to act on any going but goes particularly well on soft; consistent. *M. H. Easterby.* **88**

SOVEREIGN MERCY 5 ch.g. No Mercy 126–Inn (Welsh Rake 118) (1979 5s 5d 5s 5fg 5g 5f 5f 1980 5fg 5fg 5f 5fg 8fg) poor sprinter; seems to act on any going; blinkered penultimate start. *M. Bradley.* —

SOVEREIGN MUSTAPHA 2 b.c. Track Spare 125–Sovereign Game 60 (Sovereign Path 125) (1980 5s 5f 5f 6f 6g² 7d 6fg³ 6f⁴ 8g) Apr 25; 3,100Y; neat colt; half-brother to a minor winner; dam, maiden sprint handicapper, is half-sister to very smart 1m to 1¼m performer Record Run (by Track Spare); placed behind useful platers at Lingfield and Goodwood in the summer; ran particularly well on final start when seventh in 23-runner 1m maiden race won by Jungle Jim at Goodwood in September; acts on a firm surface; wears blinkers. *M. Haynes.* **68**

Diadem Stakes, Ascot—Sovereign Rose wins from King of Spain (not in picture). Pace Jean is third, just in front of Sayyaf

SOVEREIGN ROSE 3 ch.f. Sharpen Up 127–Sovereign Flower 86 (Sovereign Path 125) (1979 5s^2 5fg* 6fg^4 6fg* 6g^4 6f 5fg* 5s^2 1980 6f* 6fg* 6d* 6fg^3 6g 6fg* 7g^2) **116**

It says a great deal for Moorestyle that he should beat Sovereign Rose as easily as he did in the Bisquit Cognac Challenge Stakes at Newmarket in the autumn. Sovereign Rose ran well that day, and had developed into a smart filly by then; only three weeks before, she had won the Diadem Stakes.

Sovereign Rose spent the greater part of her season in handicaps, faring so well in them that in the end she earned promotion to pattern company. She wasn't beaten as a three-year-old until her fourth race, the Spillers Stewards' Cup at Goodwood, for which she started favourite with a penalty. By that time she had won from horses of her own age over six furlongs at Lingfield, Kempton and Newmarket; oddly enough, her form at two years had suggested she might be better at five than six. Sovereign Rose went close in the Stewards' Cup, carrying more weight than any in the big field except the older Standaan and Gold Song, finishing strongly for third place, less than a length behind the winner Repetitious. Re-handicapped, she ran well enough behind Enchantment on the same course the following month to be allowed her chance against Valeriga, Sayyaf and company in the Diadem Stakes at Ascot in September.

Neither Valeriga nor Sayyaf ran so well in the Diadem as he can; the strongest challenge to Sovereign Rose came from King of Spain and Pace Jean. Sovereign Rose for long enough seemed unlikely to be concerned in the finish of the race; she put up a remarkable performance. Last of nine at halfway, she began to get going on the stand side below the distance and made up a tremendous amount of ground under strong driving to win fairly comfortably by a margin of three quarters of a length. King of Spain, having looked all over a winner, hung away to the right as he had in similar circumstances in the Wokingham.

Sovereign Rose (ch.f. 1977)	Sharpen Up (ch 1969)	Atan (ch 1961)	Native Dancer Mixed Marriage
		Rocchetta (ch 1961)	Rockefella Chambiges
	Sovereign Flower (ch 1966)	Sovereign Path (gr 1956)	Grey Sovereign Mountain Path
		Sunflower (b 1960)	Pardal Helianthe

Sovereign Rose was a far better racemare than her dam or her grandam, the former of whom ran over hurdles as well as on the flat; her great grandam was useful at a mile to a mile and a quarter though, and was by Hyperion out of the dam of King's Troop and King Chesnut. Neither Sovereign Rose nor her dam moved well in her slower paces and Sovereign Rose was, for a sprinter, slow to warm up in a race. The only previous reported foal of the dam is Colonel's Boy (by Siliconn), a fair winner over seven furlongs.

A close-coupled, leggy filly, Sovereign Rose stayed seven furlongs and acted on any going except perhaps very soft. She was very genuine. She has been retired, and in 1981 visits Homing. *R. Hern.*

SOVEREIGN SAGE 2 b.f. Sovereign Path 125–Hot Spot (Vienna 127) (1980 7d 9d) May 21; sister to disappointing 7.6f winner Greezo, and half-sister to a winner; dam poor half-sister to Middle Park winner Spanish Express (by Sovereign Path); well behind in maiden race at Brighton in July and minor event at Wolverhampton in October. *R. Akehurst.* —

SOVEREIGN SHOT 2 ch.f. Supreme Sovereign 119–Shot (I Say 125) (1980 7g 8fg 7d) Apr 28; lengthy filly; fourth reported living foal; dam poor maiden; little better than plating-class on form so far but was backed from 20/1 to 6/1 in maiden race on third outing; will stay 1¼m. *N. Vigors.* **65**

SOVEREIGN STEED 2 gr.c. Royalty 130–Green Sovereign (Sovereign Path 125) (1980 7d) June 15; 760F, 4,400Y; small, lightly-made colt; fifth reported foal; dam won over 8.5f in France; 25/1 and bandaged when behind in 20-runner minor event won by Soldan at Doncaster in October. *E. Eldin.* —

SOVEREIGN TOWER 3 b.g. Tower Walk 130–Field Mouse 108 (Grey Sovereign 128 §) (1979 6f 7f 8g 1980 8s 8fg 8f) lengthy gelding; little worthwhile form in varied company, including selling. *J. Hardy.* —

SOVRETTO 3 b.c. Cerreto–Sovereign Maid 71 (Sovereign Lord 120) (1979 6g 6g 7fg^2 6fg^2 6fg* 1980 8.2d 6h^2 7fg^2 7d 6g 6fg 6g 6fg* 6fg^3 6fg^3 6g 5d) lengthy colt; moderate handicapper; beat Blues Swinger a neck at Yarmouth in August; stays 7f; suited by fast ground and acts on hard going; blinkered nowadays; sweated up ninth start; has run creditably for an apprentice; doesn't always go through with his effort; sold 3,000 gns Newmarket Autumn Sales. *N. Guest.* **75**

SPACE SPECIAL 5 b.g. Space King 115–Pip's Princess (Border Chief 101) (1979 NR 1980 12f 14g) fair but inconsistent handicapper at 3 yrs; not disgraced on reappearance; finished lame only subsequent start; best form from 1¼m to 1½m; suited by some give in the ground; good mount for an apprentice; bandaged in front nowadays. *S. Holland.* —

SPANISH ARMADA 6 b.g. Levmoss 133–Plymouth Sound 89 (Tudor Melody 129) (1979 18d 13s 16d 16.1g 16d 16f 18fg 18.1g 1980 16s 18.1g) one-time fair handicapper; poor performer nowadays; stays very well; acts on any going; has been tried in blinkers. *W. Marshall.* —

SPANISH BAY 2 b.c. Roan Rocket 128–Spanish Sail 113 (Matador 131) (1980 6g^3 7f^3 7g^2) Feb 24; 12,500Y; well-grown, good sort; half-brother to fairly useful 1977 2-y-o 5f winner Artiste Management (by Some Hand); dam a sprinter; third in £3,200 maiden races, finishing strongly when narrowly beaten by Brummer at Doncaster in September and having a very poor run from 2f out when 4 lengths behind King's Glory in 19-runner event at Newmarket in October; went down by only a short head to Spark of Life in slowly-run Somerville Tattersall Stakes at Newmarket later in October; runs as though he'll stay 1m; possibly better than we are able to rate him; sure to win a maiden race in 1981. *G. Pritchard-Gordon.* **91+**

SPANISH DANCER 3 b.c. Gay Fandango 132–Come True (Nasram II 125) (1979 NR 1980 7f 8fg* 10.1g^2 10g* 9.4g* 10d* 10fg^3 10.5f^2 10fg* 10g*) 7,000Y; strong, good-bodied, attractive colt; second foal; half-brother to 1m winner True Target (by Targowice); dam won over 1½m in Ireland; had a splendid season and developed into a useful performer, winning minor event at Leicester, small race at Newbury and handicaps at Lingfield, Carlisle, Ascot and Newmarket; put up a very genuine display when beating Fine Sun a short head in Irish Sweeps Autumn Handicap on last-named course; will stay 1½m; acts on any going; game and consistent. *P. Walwyn.* **102**

SPANISH FASNET (USA) 2 b.c. Master Derby–Glen Cova (Hill Rise 127) (1980 6fg^3 7g 6fg^3 6g) Feb 27; $42,000Y; quite attractive, well-made colt; excellent mover; third foal; half-brother to 1979 USA 2-y-o winner Fortunate Glenna (by What Luck); dam ran once; third twice at Ascot, finishing length behind Pellegrini in Fenwolf Stakes in June and 6½ lengths behind Doc Marten in Clarence House Stakes in September; should be suited by 7f+. *G. Hunter.* **81**

SPANISH FLUTE 5 b.m. Philip of Spain 126–Cute 75 (Hardicanute 130) (1979 6g 6g 7f 1980 5d 7f 7g) poor plater; blinkered second start. *J. Mulhall.* —

SPANISH GREY 3 gr.f. Spanish Gold 101–Vila Real 76 (Town Crier 119) (1979 NR 1980 5fg 5h 5g 7.2d 7g) small filly; poor form, including in a seller. *R. Hollinshead.* —

SPANISH HANDFUL 5 br.g. Philip of Spain 126–Double Handful 96 (Major Portion 129) (1979 8s 10s 8.2v* 9s 8d 8g 8s^3 9g 8d 8.2fg 12.2d 8g 1980 10v^3 —

10v^4 8f 8f 8.2d 8fg 7g^3 6fg 8s) poor handicapper; probably stays 1¼m; revels in the mud; blinkered sometimes in 1979 (not when successful); suitable mount for an apprentice. *W. Stubbs.*

SPANISH HAT 2 gr.f. Gay Fandango 132–Dancing Hat 73 (High Hat 131) (1980 5g 5d) Mar 27; 18,000Y; half-sister to 3-y-o 1m winner Spring is Grey (by Steel Heart) and to winners in Italy, Holland and Trinidad; dam, half-sister to very useful stayer Dancing Moss, was second twice over 1¼m; in mid-division in maiden races at Bath and Warwick in the autumn; needs further. *B. Hills.* —

SPANISH HIND 2 ch.c. On Your Mark 125–Desist 92 (Supreme Court 135) (1980 5fg 5fg^4 5f^3 5s* 5g* 5g 6g) May 5; 4,700F, 8,000Y; neat colt; half-brother to 2 winners in France; dam miler; improved to win 20-runner maiden race at Nottingham and 8-runner minor event at Lingfield; beat Final Call 2½ lengths on latter course in June; beaten subsequently in minor event and a nursery; should be suited by 6f; seems to act on any going; sometimes taken down early to start. *J. Sutcliffe.* 86

SPANISH ISSUE 5 b.g. Philip of Spain 126–Crop (Acropolis 132) (1979 6s 6d 7g^2 7s 5.8g^2 5.8g 6f^2 6fg^2 6fg 6fg^3 7.3g 6g 1980 6d 7f^3 6fg 6g 7g* 8fg) moderate handicapper; favourite and dropped in class, sold out of P. Cundell's stable 900 gns after winning seller at Folkestone in July; stayed 7f; acted on any going; blinkered final outing at 3 yrs; was a suitable mount for a boy; dead. *A. Ingham.* 69

SPANISH LAMP 6 br.m. Don Carlos–Lantern (Relic) (1979 NR 1980 10g 6fg) compact mare; of little account. *M. Reddan.* —

SPANISH TORMENTA 2 b.f. Furry Glen 121–Bold Aroon (Bold Lad, Ire 133) (1980 5fg 5fg^3 5s 5g^2 6fg*) Mar 16; lengthy, light-framed filly; first foal; dam never ran; favourite but sweating, won 11-runner seller at Goodwood in August by 2 lengths from Millingdale; stays 6f well; blinkered fourth and fifth starts; sold 4,000 gns at Goodwood to race in Belgium. *G. Hunter.* 70

SPANISH WAR 4 br.f. Warpath 113–Corrida 96 (Matador 131) (1979 10g 12f 13.8d^4 1980 10fg) poor plater. *R. Hoad.* —

SPANNERLEE 2 b.g. Swing Easy 126–Volley (Ratification 129) (1980 5fg 5.8fg 6s 6s 6f 7fg) Mar 21; 3,200Y; tall gelding; half-brother to 3 winners; dam once-raced half-sister to good stayer Rally; fifth in sizeable fields on fourth and fifth outings, on latter being beaten only 2½ lengths by Scarrowmanwick in minor event at Lingfield in September; ran badly in nursery at Leicester later in September; should be suited by 7f. *G. Balding.* 76

SPARE THE ROD 2 br.f. Sweet Revenge 129–Grilse Run 94 (Stupendous) (1980 6d^3 6g) Apr 29; 2,000Y; narrow filly; third live foal; dam 2-y-o 5f winner; unquoted, stayed on strongly to be nearest at finish when 3 lengths third of 25 to Little Wolf in maiden race at Newbury in October; always struggling in similar event at Leicester the following month; will stay 7f. *T. Marshall.* 77

SPARKLER AGAIN 3 ch.f. Midsummer Night II 117–Panto 71 (Ben Novus 109) (1979 5d 5d 5g 5.3g 5f 5s 1980 6fg 8g 8g 8fg) neat filly; bad plater; has worn blinkers; sold 410 gns Ascot September Sales. *H. O'Neill.* —

SPARKLER BRIGHT 2 b.f. Dubassoff–Hotazur 52 (Hotfoot 126) (1980 5d 5fg 6fg 7fg) Mar 6; workmanlike filly; first foal; dam, poor plater, comes from good family; in rear in maiden races; blinkered fourth outing. *P. Ashworth.* —

SPARKLER CLEAR 2 b.g. Double Jump 131–Fiery Flo 78 (Firestreak 125) (1980 5s 5f 6f 6s 7g 6f 7f^3 6fg 7.6f 7fg 10s) May 22; 3,300Y; rangy gelding; half-brother to several winners, including Dad (by Constable), a fairly useful winner from 5f to 1¼m; dam sprint maiden; flattered by proximity to very easy winner To-Agori-Mou when 5 lengths third of 7 in minor event at Lingfield in August but nevertheless ran his best race; soundly beaten afterwards; not sure to stay 1¼m; has worn blinkers; formerly trained by P. Ashworth. *T. Gosling.* 64

SPARKLER'S STAR 2 b.f. Sparkler 130–Miss Poker Face (Raise You Ten 125) (1980 5f 6g^3 5g^2 5d^2 7fg 5g^2) Mar 9; 4,000Y; very small filly; first foal; dam fairly useful hurdler; plater; second 3 times in the summer; should be suited by 7f; blinkered fourth outing. *P. Haslam.* 52

SPARKLER SUPERB 3 b.f. Grisaille 115–Fiery Flo 78 (Firestreak 125) (1979 5d 5d^4 5s 6f 6s 6fg^4 6f 6fg 1980 7g 8d 10d 10d) close-coupled filly; poor plater. *H. O'Neill.* —

SPARKLING BARRON 3 b.g. Sparkler 130–Little Miss Muffet 102 (Tourment 132) (1979 8fg 1980 12s 11fg 10fg) strong, good-looking gelding; lightly raced, but has shown signs of a little ability in maiden events; probably stays 1½m. *B. Swift.* —

Ladbrokes (Ayr) Gold Cup Handicap—Sparkling Boy wins from Murillo (not shown) and Eagle Boy

SPARKLING BOY 3 br.c. Comedy Star 121–Tinsel 95 (Right Boy 137) (1979 **110**
6f^{2} 1980 6f* 6f^{2} 7f 5f* 6fg* 6d 5fg 6d 6fg^{4} 6g 6g 5.6g^{2} 6s* 6fg 6d) useful sort; good mover; very useful performer; won minor race at Thirsk in April and handicaps at Sandown and Kempton following month and Ayr in September; came with a strong run to beat Murillo going away by 2 lengths in £18,400 Ladbrokes (Ayr) Gold Cup on last-named course; had earlier finished good fourth to Repetitious in Spillers Stewards' Cup (Handicap) at Goodwood and gone down by a neck to Swelter in William Hill Portland Handicap at Doncaster; stays 6f; acts on any going; sometimes wears blinkers but is as effective without them. *P. Kelleway.*

SPARKLING EARS 3 ch.f. Sparkler 130–Burning Ears 87 (Firestreak 125) **61**
(1979 NR 1980 8f 9.4d^{3} 9.4g 8.2g^{3} 10g 10fg 9g) deep-girthed filly; first foal; dam won over 1m and 1$\frac{1}{4}$m, and is half-sister to smart 1977 2-y-o Fire Angel; only plating class; stays 1$\frac{1}{4}$m; acts on a firm and a soft surface; sweated up sixth outing. *E. Weymes.*

SPARKLING LADY 2 ch.f. Hot Spark 126–Eilan Aigas 93 (Counsel 118) (1980 **74**
5fg^{3} 5fg^{2} 5f^{4} 5g^{3} 5g 5fg) Feb 21; 4,600F, 9,400Y; neat filly; half-sister to several winners, including prolific 1m and 9f winner Geoffrey's Sister (by Sparkler); dam won at 1m and 11f; in frame in maiden and minor events, on fourth outing finishing 1$\frac{1}{2}$ lengths third of 6 to Lucaya at Bath in July; speedy and isn't certain to stay beyond 5f; sold 5,600 gns Newmarket Autumn Sales. *B. Swift.*

SPARK OFF 4 b.g. Sparkler 130–Mossinella 69 (Ballymoss 136) (1979 8g 8f^{4} —
10s^{3} 11.5fg^{4} 12.3s^{3} 12d^{4} 16.1g^{2} 12f^{3} 16.1s* 1980 16f) compact gelding; stays well; acts on any going; blinkered once at 3 yrs. *J. Baker.*

SPARK OF LIFE 2 br.c. Home Guard 129–Tokara (Hard Tack 111 §) (1980 **112**
6g* 6s* 7g*)

Spark of Life ended his first season unbeaten, having landed the odds in a maiden race at Yarmouth, the Marston Moor Stakes at York and the Somerville Tattersall Stakes at Newmarket. All three wins were gained in the space of a month and in his first two races, over six furlongs, he won easily and impressively, at York needing only a little rein to sprint away and beat the useful Maryland Cookie by four lengths. Things were different in the Somerville Tattersall Stakes: Spark of Life scrambled home by the narrowest of margins from Spanish Bay, who was receiving 12 lb, and then only after a superb piece of riding from Piggott who nursed him cleverly through the last furlong when it appeared certain that he would be caught.

Spark of Life (br.c. May 16, 1978)	Home Guard (bl 1969)	Forli (ch 1963)	Aristophanes
			Trevisa
		Stay at Home (b 1961)	Bold Ruler
			Alanesian
	Tokara (b 1973)	Hard Tack (b 1955)	Hard Sauce
			Cowes
		Diamond Spur (ch 1961)	Preciptic
			Diamond Princess

Spark of Life gave us the impression at Newmarket that seven furlongs, and a slowly-run seven furlongs at that, was a shade too far for him but it's quite

Marston Moor Stakes, York—an easy win for Spark of Life

possible that the race came too soon after York, as his trainer believes. There were only five days between the two, and Spark of Life is only lightly made. The trainer expects him to get a mile as a three-year-old. We should like to reserve judgement on whether he will get that far but, looking at his pedigree, there's no reason why seven furlongs should have found him wanting. His sire Home Guard was a top-class racehorse at distances from five furlongs to a mile and a quarter and most of his progeny stay at least seven furlongs. Tokara, the dam, is an unraced sister to the top-class miler Sparkler. Incidentally, both Home Guard and Sparkler are doing well at stud, the latter already the sire of classic winners Enstone Spark and Scintillate. Whatever his best distance Spark of Life is unlikely to turn out so good a three-year-old as either Home Guard or Sparkler, but it's in his favour that he begins his second season on a handy mark and he is sure to win a decent prize or two. He acts on soft going and has yet to race on firm. *M. Stoute.*

SPARK TOP 2 b.f. Red Lord 124–Rearmed 79 (Relko 136) (1980 5fg 6f 5fg) — Apr 28; 600Y; lightly-made filly; bad mover; useless plater. *J. O'Donoghue.*

SPARKY'S MELODY 4 b.f. Songedor 116–Avonteous 60 (Rockavon 120) — (1979 8d 6g 10.1fg 10f^4 10fg^3 1980 8s 9.6fg 10.1fg 8.3s 7g 7fg 6g) bad plater; has been tried in blinkers. *A. Davison.*

SPARTA 4 b.g. Averof 123–Fille de Fizz (Ragusa 137) (1979 8.2s^3 7v* 8d 7fg — 12fg 10g 1980 7f 6d 8fg) strong, well-made gelding; won maiden race at Newcastle in 1979; behind in handicaps in 1980; should stay middle distances; acts on heavy going; blinkered last 4 outings; sold 2,000 gns Doncaster September Sales. *S. Leadbetter.*

SPARTAN CALL 5 b.h. Realm 129–Laconia 58 (Great Nephew 126) (1979 7g **55** 7d* 8f 8.3fg^3 8f 7fg* 6g* 7f 8fg^2 8g 1980 7g 7fg* 8fg 7fg 7g) won apprentice handicap at Leicester in May; stayed 1m; acted on any going; trained by M. Haynes until after second outing; dead. *J. Bingham.*

SPEARGUN 6 ch.h. Deep Diver 134–Annie Oakley 106 (Big Game) (1979 10s **51** 12d 1980 12s^4 10fg^2 11f 12f 10s) big horse; poor maiden; gambled on when runner-up to Playful Paddy at Leicester in April, best effort; had stifter tasks afterwards; seems to stay $1\frac{1}{2}$m, probably acts on any going; has been tried in blinkers; sweating final outing. *P. Arthur.*

SPECTACULAR BELLE (USA) 3 gr.f. Crimson Satan–Spectacular (Promised **70** Land) (1979 NR 1980 10.4g^2 9fg^3 10s^2 10g) workmanlike filly; half-sister to brilliant American 4-y-o Spectacular Bid (by Bold Bidder); dam stakes-placed winner at up to 1m; runner-up in maiden event at Chester in July and minor event at Newmarket in October, hanging quite badly under pressure in latter; stays $1\frac{1}{4}$m; acts on soft going. *B. Hills.*

SPECTACULAR SKY 2 b.c. African Sky 124–Orient Queen (King's Troop 118) **93** p (1980 6g^4) Feb 17; 12,500Y; fourth foal; half-brother to Irish 7f winner Northern Shamrock (by Northfields); dam Irish 5f 3-y-o winner; ran with a deal of promise when well-backed favourite for 10-runner Duke of Edinburgh Stakes at Ascot in October, showing excellent speed to lead the field until weakening quickly back into fourth place, $1\frac{3}{4}$ lengths behind Shasavaan, in closing stages; handled very sympathetically here and should improve and make a useful sprinter in 1981. *R. Armstrong.*

SPECTINA 4 ch.f. White Speck 98–Tacitina (Tacitus 124) (1979 NR 1980 9d) — non-thoroughbred filly; half-sister to several winning jumpers; unquoted, dwelt and was tailed off in apprentice event at Ripon in August, first outing. *R. Johnson.*

SPEEDAWAY 3 gr.f. Hotfoot 126–Sovereign Gate 81 (Sovereign Path 125) — (1979 6fg^3 6g 7s 7fg 7g^3 1980 7fg^2 8f 8f 7.2g 7s 8g 11s) third foal; dam sprinter; runner-up in maiden event at Edinburgh in April; well beaten afterwards, including in a seller; should stay at least 1m; acts on a firm surface. *W. H. H. Williams.*

SPEED BONNIE BOAT 4 b.g. Swing Easy 126–Pollster 101 (Majority Blue — 126) (1979 8s 6.5v* 8v* 10g 6d^3 8.2v* 7s 8s^2 7d^2 8s 1980 8g 8.2s 7d 8s) rangy gelding; finds 6f on sharp side but probably does not stay 1¼m; acts well on heavy ground; effective with or without blinkers; sold out of S. Mellor's stable 900 gns Doncaster May Sales and was well beaten all outings for new connections. *D. Wilson.*

SPEED OF LIGHT 5 ch.g. Laser Light 118–Herality (Immortality) (1979 10g — 15.5fg 1980 16fg) poor middle-distance maiden on flat; acts on any going. *G. Balding.*

SPEKES VALLEY 4 ch.f. Green God 128–Winbeam (Hornbeam 130) (1979 — 5s^2 5f 5f 6g^4 10f 1980 7fg 10.1fg) quite a moderate plater; not certain to stay 1¼m; sometimes wears blinkers; has run creditably for an apprentice. *S. Kernick.*

SPENCE BAY 5 ch.h. Sterling Bay–Lestrimache (Le Levanstell 122) (1979 8g^4 **124** 7.2fg^2 8fg* 8g^4 8d* 7s 1980 6f^4 7.2fg 10g^2) useful-looking Irish horse; very smart performer; won Ballychorus Stakes at Leopardstown and Desmond Stakes at the Curragh in 1979; having first race for 3½ months, put up an excellent performance when short-headed by Gregorian in Joe McGrath Memorial Stakes at Leopardstown in September with Night Alert 1½ lengths away third; ran only twice earlier, finishing about 3 lengths fourth of 6 to Jasmine Star in Greenlands Stakes at the Curragh and last of 8 (didn't impress in paddock) behind Hard Fought in John of Gaunt Stakes at Haydock; evidently suited by 1¼m nowadays; appears to act on any going except very soft; sold 550,000 francs (approx £54,500) at Arc de Triomphe Sales and sent to USA. *S. McGrath, Ireland.*

SPIC AND SPAN 3 ch.f. Crisp and Even 116–Cedar Valley (High Perch 126) **39** (1979 7fg 1980 10fg 11f 11.7g 7fg 8f 5g^4 8d 10d) short-backed filly; poor plater; bred to stay middle distances; sometimes sweats up. *P. Calver.*

SPIKEY BILL 3 ch.c. Souvran 98–Whitton Lane (Narrator 127) (1979 8d **56** 1980 8f 10.1s 8.3g 8g 8s 10s^2 10d) tall colt; plater; stays 1¼m; acts on soft going. *J. Benstead.*

SPINDRIFTER 2 ch.c. Sandford Lad 133–Late Spring 101 (Silly Season 127) **102** (1980 5d* 5fg^2 5f* 5h* 5fg* 6fg* 6g* 6g* 7f* 6g* 6fg* 6g* 6f^2 6f^2 7g* 8d^2 7d* 5s^2 7v)

The closing weeks of the season, when the emphasis so often seems to be on the tedious and the mediocre, were greatly enlivened in 1980 by Spindrifter's exploits. Already the winner of thirteen races, he was attempting to better Nagwa's record number of wins for a two-year-old this century. His presence in the Carrs Stakes made it an intriguing contest although worth less than £1,000 to the winner and run at Stockton late in October. Spindrifter looked to have his work cut out against Doc Marten, the easy winner of the Clarence House Stakes and fourth to Marwell in the Flying Childers Stakes, particularly since he was returning to five furlongs after a dozen races over longer distances, but he very nearly pulled it off with a typically dogged performance. As the field turned into the straight with four furlongs to run Spindrifter was being scrubbed along in the rear as Doc Marten disputed the lead. Despite responding magnificently to his rider's urgings he still looked held a furlong out but kept battling so well that he narrowed Doc Marten's advantage to a head by the line. So near to the record and yet so far! Perhaps this hard race temporarily knocked the stuffing out of Spindrifter since he ran his only poor race on his subsequent appearance, his nineteenth of the season. When favourite for the last two-year-old race of the year, the Amoco Jockeys' Trophy Nursery at Doncaster, he was never going particularly well on almost indescribably bad ground and finished towards the rear.

So Spindrifter narrowly missed taking Nagwa's place in the record books.

He nonetheless achieved the amazing feat of winning thirteen races as well as finishing second in five more. Needless to say the neat, robust Spindrifter possesses an iron constitution, and a lion-heart too, but even so his trainer earned great credit for his placing and training of the colt. He kept him both sound and keen throughout a long, hard season which never saw Spindrifter off the course for so long as three weeks. While in no way wishing to detract from Nagwa's wonderful achievement, Spindrifter's bettered it in three respects: it took him only seventeen outings to reach the record which had taken Nagwa twenty races to establish; he won no less than ten races in a row; and, because he wasn't nearly so talented a two-year-old as Nagwa, his task was that much more difficult.

No distance was too far for Spindrifter to travel for a suitable target. He made two trips to Hamilton, both victorious, five to Pontefract, where he won three times, four to Catterick, all successful, two to Redcar for two more wins and single journeys with reward to Thirsk and Leicester. Perhaps the most meritorious of his winning performances was his twelfth, when he made all to beat the Seaton Delaval runner-up Jamestino by three quarters of a length in the Tally-Ho Stakes at Redcar. Spindrifter also ran at Ripon in August where the very speedy Tina's Pet brought his winning streak to an end with a bang, routing him by eight lengths, and at Newcastle where over a mile he never looked like overhauling the very useful Sula Bula who beat him four lengths.

Spindrifter (ch.c. Mar 31, 1978)	Sandford Lad (ch 1970)	St Alphage (ch 1963)	Red God
			Sally Deans
		Hill Queen (b 1958)	Djebe
			Home Rule
	Late Spring (b 1968)	Silly Season (br 1962)	Tom Fool
			Double Deal
		Viburnum (br 1958)	Guersant
			Aralia

Spindrifter's versatility knows few bounds. He has won on all sorts of courses and has run well on all types of ground except that he found at Doncaster; he's been ridden to success both from the front and coming from behind; and he seems effective at distances from five furlongs to a mile. It's a little surprising that he stays so well. His sire Sandford Lad never raced beyond five

Crathorne Stakes, Thirsk—tough and genuine Spindrifter recording the tenth of his record-sharing thirteen wins as a two-year-old. He beats Standon Rock

furlongs and his dam, Late Spring, grandam Viburnum and great-grandam Aralia gained all their wins over sprint distances. Two of Late Spring's three previous winners, the Irish gelding Seasonal Blues (by King's Troop) and the French filly Late Summer (by Habitat), were also sprint winners while the third is the prolific French seven-furlong and mile winner Springo (by Petingo).

What of Spindrifter's future? He's been entered in the Two Thousand Guineas but he's nowhere near classic standard and he'll have to take his chance in second-class races and handicaps. He can expect little mercy from the handicapper, though. Probably he'll manage another success or two, but even if he doesn't he has already won twice as much as his cost of 10,000 guineas as a yearling (he was also sold for 7,600 guineas as a foal) and few horses can have given their owners more fun. *Sir Mark Prescott.*

SPIN OF A COIN 2 bl.c. Boreen (Fr) 123–Lovely Linan (Ballylinan 118) (1980 6g 7g^4 10s* 10.2s^4) Mar 13; 3,300F, 11,000Y; strong, attractive colt; half-brother to several winners, including fairly useful 1m and 1¼m winner Sweet Accord (by Balidar); dam never ran; 20/1, ran on well when 5 lengths fourth of 16 to To-Agori-Mou in £3,900 maiden race at Goodwood in July; not seen out again until late-October, when landing the odds comfortably in 17-runner maiden race at Nottingham; beaten 10 lengths behind Irish Heart in minor event at Doncaster in November; will be suited by 1½m. *R. Price.* **85**

SPINOLA 2 gr.f. Sweet Revenge 129–Manche 82 (Palestine 133) (1980 7g 5g) May 5; 7,200Y; third foal; half-sister to 2 bad animals; dam second in three 5f races at 2 yrs; tailed off in maiden race at Chepstow in September (last of 16) and minor event at Edinburgh in October. *K. Morgan.* –

SPITHEAD REVIEW 4 br.g. Daring Display 129–First Sail 74 (Vilmorin) (1979 7g 7s 10fg^2 10fg 1980 7v) rangy gelding; good walker; stays 1¼m; acts on firm going; blinkered second outing at 3 yrs; had stiff task only outing of 1980. *K. Bailey.* –

SPLENDID AGAIN 5 b.g. John Splendid 116–Maella (Traffic) (1979 NR 1980 8fg) plater; stays 1m; acts on any going. *C. James.* –

SPLENDID GIRLIE 4 b.f. John Splendid 116–Tracemma (Pandofell 132) (1979 NR 1980 5fg 6f^2 7fg 5d 6s 8g) compact, unfurnished filly; plater; second of 24 to easy winner Muppet at Windsor in May; stays 6f; probably acts on any going. *D. Wintle.* **38**

SPLENDID SUMMER 6 gr.h. John Splendid 116–Rue Talma § (Vigo 130) (1979 12d 16s 12fg^4 12f^3 8f^3 7g^3 12fg 8fg 8fg 7.6fg 1980 6fg 7fg) poor handicapper; effective at 1m and stays 1½m; probably acts on any going; usually wears blinkers. *P. Ashworth.* –

SPLENDID SURPRISE 3 b.f. Status Seeker–Gig (Dionisio 126) (1979 5g^3 5g* 5f^4 7f 7d 5g^4 6g^4 1980 6v 5g^3 5fg^2 5fg^4 5f 6d 6d^4 5d 6s) small filly; poor sprint handicapper; stays 6f; acts on a firm and a soft surface; has run respectably for a boy. *W. H. H. Williams.* **50**

SPOILT FOR CHOICE 2 b.g. The Brianstan 128–Song of May 79 (Sing Sing 134) (1980 5fg 5fg^4 6g 5fg 7d 6g 6d 5g^4 5d^4 6s) Mar 28; 800Y (privately); neat gelding; half-brother to 7f winner Song of Gold (by Goldhill); dam 5f sprinter; quite moderate; didn't have clear run when fourth in maiden race at Nottingham and 17-runner nursery at Wolverhampton on eighth and ninth outings; not sure to stay beyond 6f; possibly unsuited by really soft going. *K. Stone.* **73**

SPOLETO 2 b.c. Nonoalco 131–Antrona 126 (Royal Palace 131) (1980 6g* 6.5s) Feb 3; first foal; dam, one of the best of her sex at 2 yrs and 3 yrs, won from 6f to 1¼m; had a hard race when justifying favouritism by ½ length from Arock in valuable 8-runner newcomers event at Chantilly in September; 5 lengths sixth of 9 to Phydilla in Group 3 Prix Eclipse at Saint-Cloud the following month; may do better over 1m+ at 3 yrs. *F. Boutin, France.* **104**

SPONSORSHIP 3 b.f. Sparkler 130–Petingalyn (Petingo 135) (1979 5d 6fg 7g 6g^4 6fg* 6fg 7fg 7f 1980 8f 8f 12f 12.5fg 8g 12f^3 9g 8f 8f) fair sort; poor plater; has worn blinkers. *S. Nesbitt.* –

SPORTING BOY 4 b.g. Prince Tenderfoot 126–Primrose 86 (Primera 131) (1979 8d 7fg^3 1980 8f 10h^4 10fg 7.6d 8fg 8g 8fg*) quite well-made gelding; ridden by 7-lb claimer and dropped in class, bought in 1,050 gns after winning selling handicap at Warwick in August; probably stayed 1¼m; acted on hard going; dead. *M. Salaman.* **69**

SPORTING COVERGIRL 3 b. or br.f. Luthier 126–Dance All Night 106 (Double-U-Jay 120) (1979 NR 1980 8v³ 8s³ 9.4fg* 9g 10g 8.5fg 10g) 15,000Y; quite useful sort; first foal; dam won from 5f to 9f; won 11-runner maiden race at Carlisle in May; well beaten in handicaps afterwards; should stay 1¼m; probably acts on any going; sold 15,000 gns Newmarket December Sales. *N. Callaghan.* **73**

SPORTING EMPRESS 3 ch.f. Busted 134–Austria 93 (Henry the Seventh 125) (1979 NR 1980 12fg) neat filly; third living foal; half-sister to a winner in Malaya; dam stayed 1½m; backward, moved badly to post when distant eighth of 13 to Broken Flight in maiden race at Doncaster in May. *J. W. Watts.* –

SPORTOLA 3 ch.c. Hot Spark 126–Tortola § (Narrator 127) (1979 NR 1980 6s 6s) 24,000F, 50,000Y; small colt; half-brother to 3 winners, including quite useful miler Peace Symbol and 6f and 7f winner Avenged (both by Sweet Revenge); dam half-sister to high-class stayer Almeria; well beaten in minor races at Nottingham and Warwick in April. *B. Hills.* –

SPREADING SUNSET 2 ch.f. Amber Rama 133–Lantana 74 (St Paddy 133) (1980 5f 5fg 5f² 6fg⁴) Feb 9; 8,200Y; useful sort; second foal; half-sister to 3-y-o Nepotism (by Great Nephew); dam won over 1½m; blinkered when in frame in maiden races at Wolverhampton in May and Haydock (5½ lengths fourth of 16 to Blue Singh) in June; sold 1,750 gns Newmarket Autumn Sales, but stays in training. *I. Balding.* **68**

SPRING BIRD 3 b. or br.f. Workboy 123–March Poulet (March Past 124) (1979 5s³ 5s* 5v³ 5d* 5d³ 5d⁴ 5g 5fg³ 5fg 5d³ 6s³ 1980 8d 6d 8f 6g 6g³ 6g 6f 7d 6s) leggy filly; used to have ability, but ran badly at 3 yrs, including in sellers (blinkered last two outings); best at 6f; acts on soft going; trained by W. H. H. Williams first 3 starts; sold 460 gns Newmarket Autumn Sales. *Denys Smith.* –

SPRING BOX 2 gr.c. Pongee 106–Drifting Along (Farm Walk 111) (1980 5fg 5f 7f) May 23; 1,200Y; lightly-made colt; second foal; half-brother to 1m winner Carried Along (by Mansingh); dam never ran; in rear in maiden races and a seller; unseated rider several times and refused to go to start when withdrawn at Thirsk in August. *W. Bentley.* –

SPRING BRIDE 2 b.f. Auction Ring 123–Bridle Path 82 (Pall Mall 132) (1980 5f 5fg 5f 5fg 5f) May 15; small filly; sister to very useful 1979 2-y-o Highest Bidder, and half-sister to numerous winners, including good American horse Peregrinator (by Upper Case) and smart sprinter Royal Ride (by Native Prince); dam half-sister to top-class sprinter Sound Track; only poor form so far. *W. Wightman.* **57**

SPRING GALA 3 b. or br.f. Ancient Monro 89–Gala Queen 90 (Darius 129) (1979 NR 1980 14.7g) lengthy filly; half-sister to 3 winners, including Carlton's Girl (by Hotfoot), a fair winner over 11f and 1½m; dam won over 11f; backward, moved poorly to start and was soon tailed-off last in maiden race at Redcar in August. *Denys Smith.* –

SPRING IS GREY 3 gr.f. Steel Heart 128–Dancing Hat 73 (High Hat 131) (1979 NR 1980 7fg³ 8f³ 8.5f² 8g* 10.1s³ 8.2d* 8g⁴ 8v) 1,900Y, resold 16,500Y; lengthy, good sort; half-sister to several winners abroad; dam, half-sister to very useful stayer Dancing Moss, was second twice over 1¼m; landed odds very easily in modest 8-runner maiden race at Yarmouth in July; beat Miss Raffles 3 lengths in handicap at Haydock in October; ran creditably to be fourth to Our Home in Marlborough House Stakes at Ascot later in month; possibly doesn't stay 1¼m; probably acts on any going. *L. Cumani.* **96**

SPRING MOON 4 gr.g. Kalamoun 129–Ring Time II 100 (Pardal 130) (1979 11fg 12f⁴ 12s* 1980 12.2fg² 12d³ 13g* 16s 15d⁴ 13s) big, useful sort of gelding; disappointed after winning handicap at Hamilton in July by 2 lengths from Never Sweeter; placed earlier in amateur riders events at Catterick and Salisbury; stays 13f; seems to act on any going. *Sir Mark Prescott.* **70**

SPRING SURPRISE 3 b.g. Saritamer 130–A Deux 80 (Crepello 136) (1979 6f 6f 6fg 7f 8g 7fg² 8g⁴ 1980 8.2s 10f 8fg³ 8fg 11d) strong gelding; quite moderate; stays 1m (well beaten over further); suited by a sound surface; blinkered nowadays. *J. Hardy.* **75**

SPRINGY 5 ch.h. Realm 129–Wandoo 79 (Hard Sauce 131) (1979 6g² 6s³ 6s 7f 6s³ 6s 1980 6d 6g 6g 5d³ 6g⁴ 6g² 5g² 6fg² 6d) sprint handicapper; second at Goodwood (twice, including in apprentice event) and Lingfield, beaten 1½ **82**

lengths by Cast Pearls on latter course in October; seems to act on any going except firm; started slowly seventh start. *L. Cumani.*

SPRITELY 3 ch.f. Charlottown 127–Datella (Floribunda 136) (1979 NR 1980 10s 10.1s 9.4g^{4} 9d 12f 8.2s) small, light-framed filly; sister to fair 1977 2-y-o 7f winner Charles James; dam unraced half-sister to smart fillies Weeber and Amicable; only plating class; should stay middle distances; blinkered final start. *M. Jarvis.* —

SPURSTOW 2 b.g. Saulingo 122–Dian (Dike) (1980 5d 5f 5f^{2} 5d^{3} 6fg 6fg^{3} 6d^{4} 5d^{2} 8fg 6f) Mar 20; 3,000Y; resold 5,100Y; lightly-made, compact gelding; in frame in maiden races and sellers; went down by a length to Disco Fever in 20-runner seller at Ripon in August, eighth outing; blinkered, showed early speed when in rear in £2,000 seller won by Kathred at Newmarket in October on final start and could have finished a great deal closer had jockey not eased right back once chance had gone; seems to stay 1m; probably acts on any going; consistent. *J. Hardy.* **65**

STAFFORDSHIRE KNOT 5 ch.g. Welsh Pageant 132–Wrekinianne 96 (Reform 132) (1979 8d 8s^{3} 7.6d 8g 7.2s 8.2g 7fg 7f 8s 8g 7.2g 8fg 8fg 8d 8.2s^{3} 8f 7d 8s 1980 8fg 8f 7.6f^{2} 7.2fg 9g 7g 8d 7.6g 8f^{3}) fairly useful handicapper at his best; ridden by 7-lb claimer when placed at Chester in May and Ripon in August; stays 1m well; acts on any going; used to wears blinkers; often ridden up with the pace; inconsistent. *R. Hollinshead.* **59**

STALSUNO 3 b.f. Bay Express 132–Lancashire Lass 73 (King's Troop 118) (1979 5g 5f 5fg 6f^{2} 6fg^{4} 8.2d 8d^{4} 10g* 10g 1980 12g 13.8f 10g 8f 10f 13.8fg) small, lightly-made filly; plater; well beaten in 1980; suited by 1¼m; trained by T. Kersey first 2 starts. *W. Wright.* —

STALY BELL 2 b.f. Porto Bello 118–Stalybridge 88 (The Brianstan 128) (1980 5f) Mar 18; fair sort; first foal; dam won twice over 7f at 2 yrs and stayed 1¼m; unquoted and in need of race, nearest at finish when 8 lengths sixth of 19 to Salamina in maiden race at Beverley in August, only start; will stay 6f+. *C. Thornton.* — p

STAMEN 3 ch.f. Ballymore 123–Flower Centre 98 (Jaipur) (1979 5fg* 6fg^{2} 6g 1980 8fg^{4} 8g 8.3g*) small, stocky filly; ridden by 5-lb claimer when trotting up by 8 lengths from Raconteur in handicap at Windsor in August; will stay 1¼m; acts on a firm surface. *R. Armstrong.* **89**

STANDAAN (FR) 4 gr.c. Zeddaan 130–Castania (Orsini 124) (1979 7d^{3} 6g* 8g 6d^{3} 6s^{3} 6f 6fg* 6f* 6g* 6g^{2} 5d 5d^{2} 1980 5fg^{4} 6f^{4} 5f 5f^{3} 5fg 6d 6fg 6d^{3} 6g 5.6g 5fg) strong, quite useful sort; possesses very good early speed; won 4 races in 1979, including Spillers Stewards' Cup at Goodwood; often had stiff tasks in 1980 but finished in frame several times, including when close fourth to Valeriga in Palace House Stakes at Newmarket on reappearance and about 7 lengths third of 8 to Kilijaro in Prix de Meautry at Deauville in August on eighth start; also ran creditably when fifth of 28 to Repetitious under top weight in Spillers Stewards' Cup on seventh outing; stays 6f; seems to act on any going; below his best in blinkers fourth start. *C. Brittain.* **109**

STAND EASY 3 b.g. Connaught 130–Paresseuse 114 (Relko 136) (1979 7d 7s 1980 10g* 10g^{2} 6fg 11.7g^{4} 10s) big, strong gelding; successful once from 2 starts at Cagnes-sur-Mer in spring (made all); not entirely disgraced in handicap at Windsor on fourth start; will stay beyond 1½m; possibly unsuited by very soft going. *W. Hastings-Bass.* **71**

STANDON ROCK 2 ch.c. Mansingh 120–Teenager 71 (Never Say Die 137) (1980 5d 5g^{3} 6fg^{2} 6g 6fg 7f^{2} 7g 7d^{2}) Apr 28; shapely colt; first foal; dam second over 6f at 2 yrs; ran best races over 7f, finishing length second of 19 to King's Glory in maiden race at Newmarket in October and going down by same margin to Six Mile Bottom in nursery at Sandown later in month; may well get 1m; seems to act on any going; blinkered fourth outing. *P. Kelleway.* **93**

STANISLAVSKY (USA) 3 b.c. Sir Ivor 135–Delray Dancer (Chateaugay) (1979 7g^{2} 7g^{2} 7f 7s^{2} 1980 10f* 10.6fg* 12g^{4} 10.5g 10g 10fg^{2} 10.5f* 10fg 10f) compact, good-bodied colt; successful in 15-runner maiden race at Sandown in May and valuable handicaps at Haydock in June and York in September; routed his field in Stones Best Bitter Handicap at Haydock, beating Playboy Jubilee 2½ lengths, and made much of running to score by 3 lengths from Spanish Dancer in Garrowby Stakes at York; also ran creditably though no match for **108**

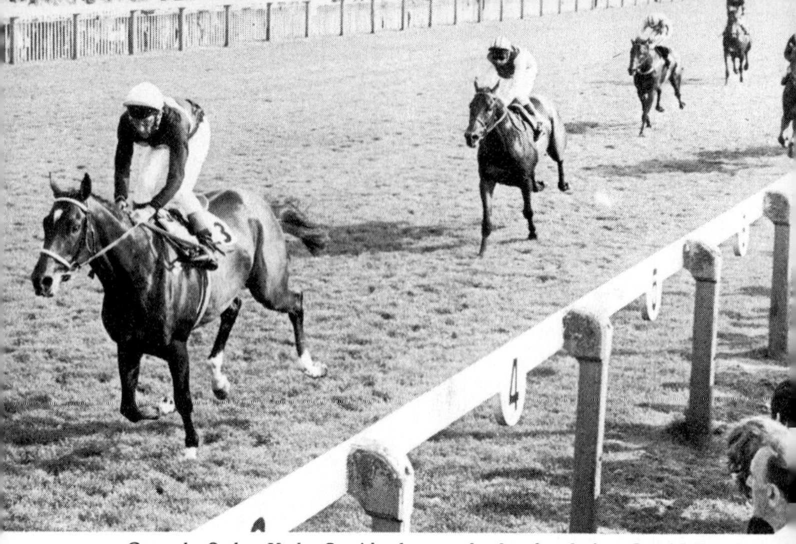

Garrowby Stakes, York—Stanislavsky scores by three lengths from Spanish Dancer

winner when 6 lengths second to Karamita in Extel Stakes (Handicap) at Goodwood in August; best at $1\frac{1}{4}$m; acts on any going but goes well on firm ground; below form fourth start; useful. *R. Price.*

STANSTED 3 ch.c. Gay Fandango 132–Sweet Almond 83 (Busted 134) (1979 — 6f 1980 8v 10g) well-grown, rangy colt; poor form in £4,800 race and maiden events; sold to W. Clay 900 gns Doncaster June Sales. *N. Callaghan.*

STAR ALERT 3 b.f. Red Alert 127–Breide's Wood (Le Levanstell 122) (1979 — 5fg 1980 8d^3 8g 10s) has shown only a little ability in varied company; best run at 1m on a soft surface; sold 480 gns Newmarket Autumn Sales. *I. Walker.*

STAR ATTENTION 6 b.m. Northfields–Star Relation (Star Gazer 123) — (1979 8g 1980 6f 6g 8.2s) small, unfurnished mare; well beaten since 1977; seems to stay 7f although is probably better at shorter distances; acts on any going but is suited by softish ground; has worn blinkers. *M. Reddan.*

STAR BAIRN 2 ch.f. Wishing Star 117–Judiths Bairn (Double-U-Jay 120) **66** (1980 5s 5g 5fg^4 5f* 5fg* 5f 5s 5fg^4 5d) Apr 27; 800Y; workmanlike filly; fifth foal; half-sister to a winner abroad; dam of little account; won sellers at Wolverhampton and Doncaster in May, costing 5,200 gns to buy in after making all for a 2-length win over Anascend on latter; ran moderately afterwards; probably needs further than 5f nowadays; acts well on firm going and possibly isn't at her best on soft; blinkered seventh start (well beaten); sold 2,700 gns Newmarket Autumn Sales. *W. Wharton.*

STARBLOOM 3 b.f. Lorenzaccio 130–Star of Bagdad 95 (Bagdad) (1979 6fg **57** 1980 11fg^2 11.7fg 12.3f) unfurnished filly; second in modest maiden race at Wolverhampton in April; stays 11f; yet to race on an easy surface; blinkered final start. *N. Gaselee.*

STAR BURST 3 b.g. Busted 134–Pearl Star 110 (Gulf Pearl 117) (1979 NR **73** 1980 8.2g 11d* 11g^2 10.6d) fourth foal; half-brother to Startingo (by Petingo), successful at up to 13f; dam, game performer at up to 7f, is sister to very useful Seadiver; won maiden race at Hamilton in June; will stay $1\frac{1}{2}$m+; yet to race on a firm surface; good mount for a boy. *D. Francis.*

STAR CHAMBER (FR) 3 b.f. Tower Walk 130–Wig and Gown (Mandamus **102** 120) (1979 NR 1980 8s* 8fg 8fg 8fg 10g^4 10fg 8fg 12d) 13,000Y; lengthy, lightly-made filly; half-sister to useful Freight Forwarder (by Calpurnius), a winner on flat and over hurdles, and to a winner in Austria; dam never ran; beat Bay Street virtually unchallenged by 3 lengths in 6-runner Masaka Stakes at Kempton in April; ran best subsequent race when respectable 6 lengths fourth to Little Bonny in 7-runner Virginia Stakes at Newcastle in August; appears to stay $1\frac{1}{4}$m; needs some give in the ground; often bandaged off-hind; changed hands 10,000 gns Newmarket December Sales. *P. Kelleway.*

STARFEN 4 b. or br.g. Comedy Star 121–Lovely Beak (Counsel 118) (1979 9g^2 8s* 8d^3 10f^4 8f 10s^2 9s* 8s^3 10s* 10.5g 1980 8fg 12d) leggy gelding; useful handicapper in 1979; not seen out until September in 1980 and still didn't look ready second start; suited by $1\frac{1}{4}$m and should stay $1\frac{1}{2}$m; acts on any going; genuine and consistent; very useful hurdler. *M. H. Easterby.* –

STARFINDER 3 b.c. Comedy Star 121–Delfina (Salvo 129) (1979 5s 5f 1980 8v 10g 10fg* 8.2fg^{4}10fg 8f^2 8fg 9g* 8f 9g) compact colt; won 12-runner maiden race at Redcar in May and handicap at Hamilton in July (ridden by 5-lb claimer); stays $1\frac{1}{4}$m; best form on a sound surface; sweated up badly sixth start. *E. Weymes.* **74**

STAR FLARE (USA) 3 ch.f. On The Warpath–Hour of Parting (Native Dancer) (1979 5v^3 5g^2 5.8g^2 6d^3 5.8g* 5f^2 1980 7d^4 7v 7s 6fg 6d 8fg^2 7f* 8g 7g^4 7.2g^2 7g^2 7g^2 7d) neat filly; moderate handicapper; beat Miss Raffles a neck at Bath in July; stays 1m; needs top-of-the-ground; suitable mount for a boy. *I. Balding.* **85**

STAR FLECK 3 gr.f. Sallust 134–Grey Fleck (Sing Sing 134) (1979 5fg 5g 1980 7f 6fg 7g) well beaten in varied company; blinkered final start. *B. Hanbury.* –

STAR FLEET 2 ch.c. Record Token 128–New Way 103 (Klairon 131) (1980 6f 7g 8fg) Mar 20; 51,000Y; compact, attractive colt; third foal; half-brother to smart 3-y-o Star Way (by Star Appeal) and a winner in Cyprus; dam won at up to 6f at 2 yrs; showed ability when 50/1-shot for Laurent Perrier Champagne Stakes at Doncaster and Royal Lodge Stakes at Ascot on second and third outings, finishing 9 lengths behind Gielgud when last of 9 in former and $9\frac{3}{4}$ lengths fifth of 8 to Robellino in latter; probably stays 1m; has the ability to win virtually any maiden race. *P. Kelleway.* **106**

STAR HEADING 2 ch.f. Upper Case–Star Deal (Red God 128§) (1980 5fg^4 5fg^3 5g^2 6d^3 7g^2 6s^2 6d 8s 5s^3) Mar 8; 2,600F, 3,200Y; half-sister to 1973 2-y-o 5f winner London By Night (by Pall Mall) and 3 winners abroad; dam Irish 2-y-o 5f winner; second in 3 Scottish maiden races, last 2 at Ayr when beaten neck by Crimson Advocate in July and $\frac{1}{2}$ length by Sovereign Flame in August; stays 7f; best form with some give in the ground; wears blinkers; well beaten last 3 starts. *W. H. H. Williams.* **74**

STAR ISSUE 2 br.f. Comedy Star 121–Top Secret 90 (Manacle 123) (1980 5f 5.1f^2 5.1g^2 6g 5.1fg^4 5f 6g) Apr 14; 2,500Y; neat filly; second foal; dam won over 5f and 1m; in frame in maiden races at Yarmouth, one of them an auction event; should stay 6f. *J. Winter.* **66**

STAR KID 5 ch.h. Stardao 83–Babulass (Babu 117) (1979 5s* 5g^4 5g 6fg 5f 5d 5f 5g^4 5s* 5d 6s 1980 5f 5f 5fg 5g* 5fg 5f 5d 5d 5d^2) quite a moderate handicapper; well backed when scoring at Carlisle in July; best form at 5f; acts on soft going. *V. Mitchell.* **65**

STARLIGHT PEAKS (USA) 3 b.f. Stop The Music–Mistypano (Misty Flight) (1979 5s^4 5.1fg^3 5f 8fg 7fg 1980 12h^2 12fg 13.8fg 12.2f 14fg^2 12f 15.8fg) neat filly; poor walker; poor maiden nowadays; stays $1\frac{3}{4}$m; acts on hard going; blinkered fourth and sixth starts. *R. Sheather.* **60**

STARLITPATH 3 br.f. Warpath 113–Starsilk 83 (Counsel 118) (1979 6fg 6g 7fg* 6f 7fg^4 8.2s 1980 12f 10fg 12d 8g) leggy filly; has shown no form since 1979; should stay at least 1m; acts on a firm surface; blinkered fifth outing at 2 yrs; didn't impress in paddock on reappearance; sold 560 gns Doncaster October Sales. *R. Hollinshead.* –

STAR OF ENZO 2 b.c. Comedy Star 121–Cry Help 94 (Martial 131) (1980 5fg 5fg 5f^4 5f 6g 5fg* 5d 5d 5d) Mar 22; small, fair sort; half-brother to useful sprinter Alarm Call (by Bleep-Bleep); dam a sprinter and half-sister to top-class sprinters So Blessed and Lucasland; 20/1, soon clear when showing much improved form to win 8-runner nursery at Chepstow in August by 5 lengths from Artistry; fair fifth of 17 to Ardoony in another nursery at Wolverhampton in October on penultimate start; suited by a sharp 5f and doesn't stay 6f; best form on a firm surface although has run respectably on a soft one; blinkered fifth outing. *T. Marshall.* **79**

STAR OF ISIS 3 br.g. The Brianstan 128–Isis Rapide (I Say 125) (1979 7fg 7fg 7d 7g 8.2g^4 8g 8.2s 1980 8f^4) strong, attractive gelding; fourth in seller at Thirsk in April; stays 1m; wears blinkers; sold 1,000 gns Newmarket May Sales and subsequently won in Austria. *K. Ivory.* —

STAR OF JOLLEES 3 b.f. Saucy Kit 76–Straight Avenue 62 (Royal Avenue 123) (1979 5v 5s 5d^4 5d^4 5d 5g 5.1f^2 5fg 8h 1980 8s 8f) lengthy, unfurnished filly; plater; bred to be suited by 1$\frac{1}{4}$m+. *M. Reddan.* —

STAR OF SALFORD 2 gr.c. Town Crier 119–False Evidence 53 (Counsel 118) (1980 5f^3 5fg^3 6g 5f 5d 5d^4 5g) Mar 31; 30,000Y; tall, quite well-made colt; good walker and mover; brother to top-class 1974 2-y-o Cry of Truth and very useful sprinter Pascualete, and half-brother to several winners, including very useful 3-y-o Just Amber (by Amber Rama), successful at up to 7f; dam placed over 1$\frac{1}{2}$m; only quite moderate; possibly needs further than 5f nowadays. *R. Hollinshead.* 75

STAR OF SPRING 3 gr.f. Silly Season 127–Daystar 91 (Major Portion 129) (1979 NR 1980 7.6d 8g 12fg^3 10.6d) 550 3-y-o; of no account. *J. Gilbert.* —

STAR PASTURES 2 b.f. Northfields–Spirit in the Sky 106 (Tudor Melody 129) (1980 7g^2 7g^3 7g^3 6f* 6s*) Apr 24; 24,000Y; quite an attractive filly; good mover; half-sister to 2 winners here and in France, including fair 1977 2-y-o 7f winner Fine Wine (by Petingo); dam won from 6f to 1$\frac{1}{2}$m; put up very useful efforts when winning 13-runner Crathorne Stakes at York and 7-runner Firth of Clyde Stakes at Ayr in September, having rest of field well strung out when beating Cardie Girl 2$\frac{1}{2}$ lengths at York and being eased a couple of lengths when coming home 4 lengths clear of Maryland Cookie at Ayr; had previously been placed in good-class fillies races, on third outing finishing 1$\frac{3}{4}$ lengths third of 7 to Exclusively Raised in Sweet Solera Stakes at Newmarket in August; best form at 6f; acts on any going; started slowly second outing. *J. Hindley.* **110**

STAR PERFORMANCE 9 ch.g. Gala Performance–Immaculate (Sovereign Path 125) (1979 12d^3 1980 12fg 10s 12fg^3 10f^4 12g 10fg) middle-distance performer; best form on a sound surface; often wears blinkers; good mount for an inexperienced rider; started slowly fourth outing. *M. Masson.* 57

STAR RHYTHM 2 b.c. Tudor Rhythm 112–Maryland Star 76 (I Say 125) (1980 5s 5s 5f^3 5fg 6g^3 6g^2 6g^2 6f 6g 8fg^4 8d^2) Feb 23; 1,350F; compact, lightly-made colt; third foal; dam won at up to 11f; plater; second at Ripon, Leicester and Warwick, going down by 2$\frac{1}{2}$ lengths to Blue Garter on last-named in October; will probably stay 1$\frac{1}{4}$m; yet to show he acts on really soft ground but acts on any other; missed break first 2 outings and wore blinkers on next 2. *J. Hardy.* 65

STARSHOT 5 gr.g. Roan Rocket 128–Tiara II (Sunny Boy III) (1979 10s 11.7g 12d 10s 10.7g 10fg 8f 10d* 10s 10g^4 10.2fg^4 1980 12f 15f) poor handicapper; probably stays 1$\frac{1}{2}$m; appears to act on any going; good mount for an inexperienced rider; sold 850 gns Ascot July Sales. *R. Atkins.* —

STAR SING 3 b.g. Master Sing 109–Eastern Promise 62 (Eastern Lyric 114) (1979 5s 6f 6g 5d 1980 8h 8d) narrow gelding; of little account. *S. Wiles.* —

STARS IN YOUR EYES 2 br.c. Royalty 130–Pink Sky 86 (Midsummer Night II 117) (1980 6g 7d^2 7d^2 8g 7s) Feb 8; 12,500Y; unfurnished, light-framed colt; half-brother to useful 1$\frac{1}{2}$m winner Night Sky (by Star Moss) and useful Town Sky (by Town Crier), winner at up to 7f at 2 yrs in 1978; dam won over 6f at 2 yrs; made up a huge amount of ground in final 2f when 2 lengths second to Scintillating Air in 14-runner maiden race at Newmarket in July; never 73

Firth of Clyde Stakes, Ayr—Star Pastures slaughters the opposition which is headed by Maryland Cookie

looked happy in lead when 11/4 on for 2-runner event on same course later in month and failed by 1½ lengths to hold off Salmon Berry; should be suited by 1m; had stiff tasks in nurseries last 2 outings. *R. Armstrong.*

STAR VENTURE 4 br.g. Swing Easy 126–Street Vendor 60 (High Perch 126) **66**
(1979 6v 6v* 6g* 6g 6f $6d^3$ 7fg 7fg $6d^2$ 1980 $7v^2$ $6d^4$ $7fg^3$ $7f^3$ $7f^3$ 7f 7g 10d $7fg^4$ $7fg^4$ 7fg $6fg^2$ $6s^4$) strong gelding; quite a moderate handicapper; gives impression he may stay 1m but was well beaten over 1¼m; acts on any going; has worn blinkers but is better without; suitable mount for an apprentice; has had tongue tied down. *G. Huffer.*

STAR WAY 3 ch.c. Star Appeal 133–New Way 103 (Klairon 131) (1979 $5d^2$ **119**
6fg* $6f^4$ $7s^3$ $7fg^4$ $8f^2$ 8s 1980 $8f^2$ $8fg^4$ 10.5f 12f 12g 12d $8d^2$ $8g^3$ 8d $7g^3$ 8fg 10d) 16,500Y; quite well-made colt; good mover; second foal; half-brother to a winner in Cyprus; dam won at up to 6f at 2 yrs; smart performer; excellent third to Posse, beaten just over 1½ lengths, in Sussex Stakes at Goodwood in July, making running and keeping on well once headed; had earlier run 3 good races at Newmarket, finishing neck second to Tyrnavos in Ladbrokes Craven Stakes, 4¾ lengths fifth (promoted to fourth) behind subsequently-disqualified Nureyev in 2,000 Guineas and equal second to Belmont Bay, beaten 1½ lengths, in £7,400 handicap; best at 1m; acts on any going; blinkered final start at 2 yrs and on fifth outing; didn't run up to his best last 3 starts. *P. Kelleway.*

STARYLLIS GIRL 7 ch.m. Star Moss 122–Double Handful 96 (Major Portion —
129) (1979 NR 1980 11.7g) lightly raced and of little account. *M. Bradley.*

STATE COUNCELLOR 4 b.g. Royal and Regal–Sensibility (Hail to Reason) **73**
(1979 10s $13.6g^2$ $9d^4$ $9.2g^2$ 9s 8s* 1980 8f* 12f 8f* $8f^2$ $8fg^2$ 9g* 8g $9g^3$ $9fg^3$ $8s^3$ 8.2d* 8f* $9g^4$) ex-Irish gelding; had a very good year and won amateur riders events at Thirsk (made all) and Ripon and handicaps at York, Hamilton and Redcar; beat Smokey Shadow decisively by 3 lengths in apprentice event on last-named course in September; best form at up to 9f; acts on any going; blinkered final outing at 3 yrs and ninth start. *Denys Smith.*

STATE TROOPER 3 ch.c. Status Seeker–Sarah Pipellini (French Beige 127) **90**
(1979 6fg* $6d^4$ 7f* $7s^4$ 7d $8.2g^2$ 8g 1980 $8.2d^3$ 7f $8fg^2$ 7.2g* $8f^4$ 8d* $8fg^4$ 9g* $7fg^2$ 7f $8.2d^3$ $8s^3$ $8d^4$) fair sort; fairly useful handicapper; successful at Haydock, Ayr and York; beat Royal Rex ¾ length on last-named in July; stays 9f; acts on any going; genuine and consistent; moved poorly to post tenth start. *B. Hanbury.*

STATFOLD CHARLIE 3 b.g. Sayfar 116–Pride of Statfold (Compensation 127) —
(1979 NR 1980 10g 10d 14.6d) workmanlike gelding; behind in maiden races; didn't move well to post second start. *W. Wharton.*

ST ATHAN'S BOY 2 ch.c. Imperial Crown 96–Moneywise (Hook Money 124) —
(1980 7g) Apr 5; compact colt; fourth reported foal; dam never ran; 50/1 and in need of run when tailed-off last of 7 in minor race won by Principal Dancer at Sandown in July. *M. Haynes.*

STATS EMMAR 2 br.f. Steel Heart 128–Lavendula Rose 108 (Le Levanstell **102**
122) (1980 5fg* 5g 7.2s* 6g* 7g) Feb 2; rangy, attractive filly; good mover with a long stride; half-sister to several winners, including Torenaga (by Bold Lad, Ire), a winner over 1m and 1½m in Ireland and a good young hurdler; dam, third in Irish Guinness Oaks, is half-sister to Wrekin Rambler; picked up 2 good prizes after winning minor event at Kempton in May, quickening well to beat Heavenly Chord 3 lengths in Rose of Lancaster Stakes at Haydock in July and landing the odds by 1½ lengths from Supine in St Catherine's Stakes at Newbury later in month despite having hung left most of way; beaten when taking on very useful fillies, finishing 3¾ lengths fifth of 17 to Pushy in Queen Mary Stakes at Royal Ascot and modest seventh of 10 to Fairy Footsteps in Waterford Candelabra Stakes at Goodwood; will be suited by 1m; appears to act on any going; useful. *R. Price.*

STAYING ALIVE (USA) 3 ch.c. Vitriolic–Back in Paris (Carry Back) (1979 **86**
NR 1980 $8fg^3$ 8g* $8fg^2$ 7g $8g^2$ 8g) $35,000Y; tall, strong colt; has a round action; half-brother to stakes-placed Film Festival (by Spring Double), a winner at up to 7f; dam, half-sister to very smart 1974 2-y-o 5f performer Paris Review, was smart winner of 23 races at up to 1m; landed odds in 14-runner maiden race at Pontefract in July; creditable second in races won by Astonished and Herons Hollow at Goodwood afterwards; will be suited by 1¼m; yet to race on a soft surface though his action suggests he'll be suited by one; ran moderately final start. *L. Cumani.*

STAY SECRET 3 b.g. Most Secret 119–Sayvanter (Galivanter 131) (1979 5g 5d 5f* 6fg^2 5fg^2 5f^2 5g^3 5d 5g* 5h 1980 5h 5fg 5f 5g 5f* 5g 5.6fg 6g 6d^3 6d 5s^3 6s* 6s) plater; won at Catterick in July and Ayr in September (no bid on either occasion); stays 6f; acts on any going; best in blinkers. *W. Bentley.* **59**

ST BENEDICT 3 br.c. So Blessed 130–Catalonia 97 (Abernant 142) (1979 5g* 5d^4 1980 5f 5fg 5f 5g 5g 5s 5d) strong, good sort; sprint handicapper; promises to stay 6f; didn't move to post too well final start; sold 760 gns Newmarket Autumn Sales. *Sir Mark Prescott.* **—**

ST BRIDE 2 b.f. St Paddy 133–Season Ticket (Silly Season 127) (1980 6fg 8d) May 11; half-sister to 3-y-o 1¼m winner Himalia (by High Line) and quite useful sprinter Union Card (by Good Bond); dam never ran; 25/1 when eighth of 15 to Flying Dreamer in maiden race at Bath in October, second outing. *G. Hunter.* **—**

STEADY HAND 4 ch.g. Some Hand 119–Can't Wait (Eudaemon 129) (1979 5s 6g 6g 6g 7f* 8.3f 6fg* 7g 7fg 7f 7fg 6fg 1980 7fg 7f 6g 6g 6g) quite a moderate handicapper; best form at up to 7f; suited by a firm surface; usually wears blinkers. *G. Balding.* **—**

STEEL CHARGER 3 b.c. Steel Heart 128–Belaying Pin (Iron Peg **§§**) (1979 NR 1980 8f 7fg 5g^4 5s 5fg 5g* 5.3fg^2) 5,400Y; half-brother to winning stayer Ernel (by Sassafras); dam won at up to 7f in USA; showed improved form to win 18-runner maiden race at Nottingham in July; ran creditably in handicap only subsequent start; best at around 5f on top-of-the-ground; blinkered fifth start (had very stiff task). *R. Boss.* **70**

STEEL CITY 6 ch.h. Sharpen Up 127–Tantau's Delight 77 (Tantieme 136) (1979 10.5d 8d 9fg 8g^4 8.2f^3 8h^4 8h^2 12fg^3 13g 8fg 1980 8f^3 8fg 8d^2 8g^4 8fg^3 8d 8g^3) quite a moderate 1m handicapper nowadays; acts well on firm going and is not at his best on soft; suited by waiting tactics; suitable mount for an inexperienced rider; has been tried in blinkers; none too genuine. *G. Huffer.* **60**

STEEL GARRISON 2 br.c. Steel Heart 128–Party Tricks (Tom Fool) (1980 5d 5d* 5fg^3 5fg* 5g^2 5fg 5g^2 6d 5f 5g 5g) Apr 11; neat, strong colt; second foal; dam never ran; successful in maiden race at Nottingham in April and minor event at Leicester the following month, in latter winning by 1½ lengths from Mr Gus; ran well when second in Berkshire Stakes at Newbury (1½ lengths behind Cut Throat) in June and in well-contested minor event at Beverley (went down by ½ length to Royal Duty, giving winner 7 lb) the following month; should stay 6f but was well beaten when tried at trip; acts on a firm and a soft surface; off course for almost 3 months after eighth outing, and was blinkered in his subsequent races (sweated up first occasion). *G. Hunter.* **83**

STEELINCTIVE 2 br.c. Steel Heart 128–Distinctiveness (Distinctive) (1980 5.1f* 6g* 6fg^3 6g^2 5g 6fg* 5d) Feb 13; small, attractive colt; second foal; dam lightly-raced half-sister to American Derby winner Determined King; narrow winner of maiden race at Yarmouth, minor event at Chester and nursery at Ascot, holding on by a head from unlucky-in-running Airship in last-named in September; will stay 7f; acts well on firm going; genuine but didn't run up to his best when apprentice ridden on fifth and seventh outings; sold 15,500 gns to BBA, reportedly for export to California, Newmarket Autumn Sales. *J. Hindley.* **101**

STEEL LADY 2 ch.f. Continuation 120–Betony 76 (Sovereign Path 125) (1980 5f 5g* 6g^4 6fg^3) Apr 8; 400F; leggy filly; first produce; dam 2-y-o 5f winner; apprentice ridden, attracted no bid after winning 10-runner seller at Beverley in June by 1½ lengths from Good Sweep; subsequently ran creditably in sellers at York and Ripon, being beaten only a length by Aunty May after being hampered on latter track; suited by 6f; sold 1,500 gns Newmarket Autumn Sales. *J. Hardy.* **60**

STEEL LINK 3 gr.f. The Go-Between 129–Copper Gold (Democratic 124) (1979 5s 5d 5v 6g 6fg 5f 5f 5fg 1980 6g) sturdy filly; temperamental plater; refused to race from flag start on third outing at 2 yrs; has been tried in blinkers. *M. Bolton.* **— §**

STEEL MAIDEN 2 b.f. Steel Heart 128–Bold Maiden 71 (Bold Lad USA) (1980 8fg 6d) May 2; compact, attractive filly; second foal; dam ran only at 2 yrs when best at 5f; well beaten in maiden and minor events at Leicester and Pontefract in the autumn; evidently nowhere near so good as she looks; sold 1,000 gns Newmarket Autumn Sales. *J. Hindley.* **—**

STEEL PART 2 ch.g. Steel Heart 128–Dalriada (Ribot 142) (1980 5s 5f^3 5fg) Apr 11; 2,600Y; small gelding; first foal; dam won over 1½m in Ireland at 4 yrs; only plating class; likely to need 1m as a 3-y-o. *D. Gandolfo.* **—**

Ward Hill Bunbury Cup Handicap, Newmarket—Steeple Bell beats Kampala and the blinkered Right of Light

STEEL PASS 2 b.c. Steel Heart 128–Senorita Rugby 86 (Forward Pass) (1980 5fg^2 6fg^4 6d^2 6s^2 5.8f* 6fg 6fg 6d 6g*) Jan 29; good-bodied colt; first foal; dam won twice over 7f; won maiden race at Bath in July and £3,500 nursery at Newmarket in October; showed markedly improved form in latter, cruising through on bridle to win by $2\frac{1}{2}$ lengths from Pencil Point; will stay 7f; acts on any going; wears blinkers; well suited by waiting tactics. *G. Hunter.* **101**

STEEL SON 2 ch.c. Steel Heart 128–Aspara 58 (Crimson Satan) (1980 6f 6fg 6g 6s) Mar 25; strong, well-made colt; second foal; half-brother to fairly useful 3-y-o 7f winner Varuna (by Luthier); dam placed over 5f in Ireland and England; showed signs of ability in large fields for maiden races. *A. Breasley.* **–**

STEEL TRADE 4 ch.g. Great Nephew 126–Lioba 80 (Alcide 136) (1979 6g^3 6f^3 6s 7fg 6g 8.5g 7f 1980 9fg) fair sort; suited by 6f (below form over further); acts well on firm going; blinkered final start at 3 yrs. *M. Bradley.* **–**

STEELWORKS 2 ch.c. Steel Heart 128–Hariota 73 (Hook Money 124) (1980 6g 5g) May 19; 24,000Y; compact, sturdy colt; half-brother to several winners, including 1979 2-y-o 1m winner Nadja (by Dancer's Image); dam middle-distance winner; behind in September in £5,900 event at Doncaster (moved poorly to start) and 17-runner maiden race at Bath (second favourite). *B. Hills.* **–**

STEEPLE BELL 4 b.g. Tower Walk 130–Nine Lessons 101 (Santa Claus 133) (1979 8g^2 8s^3 7fg 8fg* 8f^2 8g* 8f^2 1980 8fg 8d 7g^2 7d* 7fg^2 7g* 7fg 7g*) useful handicapper; made all in valuable events at Newmarket (beat Kampala by a length in Ward Hill Bunbury Cup) in July and Doncaster (got home by short head from Tugoflove in Battle of Britain Handicap) in September; prominent throughout and was in command 3f from home when beating Tugoflove in good style by $1\frac{1}{2}$ lengths at Newmarket in October; stays 1m; probably not at his best on very soft ground; genuine and consistent. *M. Stoute.* **101**

STEFANIA 2 br.f. Mansingh 120–Scarlet Thread 80 (Joshua 129) (1980 5d) Apr 28; 2,000Y; first foal; dam won over 9f and $1\frac{1}{4}$m; 20/1 when behind in 16-runner maiden race won by Salt at Wolverhampton in June. *J. Dunlop.* **–**

STEPHEN'S DAY 3 b.c. Bonne Noel 115–Fulfilment (David Jack 125) (1979 5g 7fg 7g^4 8s 7g 8g* 1980 12g^4 12f* 12fg* 14f 12d 12d) sturdy, good-bodied colt; fair handicapper; won apprentice event at Newmarket and handicap at Leicester (awarded race) in April; stayed $1\frac{1}{2}$m; needed top-of-the-ground conditions; blinkered final outing at 2 yrs; sold 2,000 gns Newmarket Autumn Sales; dead. *F. Durr.* **94**

STEPHOUETTE 4 ch.f. Stephen George 102–Sweet Silhouette 79 (Setay 105) (1979 9s 7f 8s^2 8fg^2 9fg 10s 8g 8g 1980 8d) plater; best form at 1m; has worn blinkers; sold 440 gns Ascot November Sales. *R. Morris.* **–**

STEPPING GAILY 3 b.f. Gay Fandango 132–Quantas 91 (Roan Rocket 128) (1979 6f 1980 5fg* 6f 6f^3 6fg 6fg* 5g) leggy filly; won 10-runner maiden race at Wolverhampton in April and handicap at Haydock in June; beat Depict 2 **79**

lengths going away in latter; stays 6f; acts on firm going; sweated up slightly and ran poorly second and final starts. *R. Hollinshead.*

STERLING BANK 3 br.g. Sterling Bay–Gavotte (Queen's Hussar 124) (1979 5f^4 6f* 1980 8d* 10v^2 10s* 10f^2 11d^3 10d) leggy gelding; successful in handicaps at Doncaster in March and Newcastle in April; probably stays 11f; acts on any going; suited by strong handling; didn't move well to post final start (blinkered), in June. *Denys Smith.* 71

STERLING GIFT 6 b.h. Sterling Bay–Shivers (Arctic Storm 134) (1979 NR 1980 12d 13d 9f 10d 12g) strong horse; seems of little account. *W. Marshall.* –

STERLONIA 4 b. or br.f. Sterling Bay–Milonia (Tambourine II 133) (1979 7fg 8g 10.5d 8.5d 7g 7g 8fg 7f 8fg 10fg^2 8fg^4 1980 8s 8f 8fg^2 9g 7g^4 8fg 8f 8fg 10g 8.2d^2 8g 8.2s) compact filly; quite a moderate handicapper; stays 1¼m; acts on a firm and a soft surface; not particularly consistent. *W. Marshall.* 60

STERN 4 br.g. No Mercy 126–Rudder (Reliance II 137) (1979 11d 10s 12d 1980 7g^3 7f 7f* 8.3fg 8g^4 7d) won handicap at Chepstow in August by ¾ length from Chads Gamble; ran creditably under a penalty next time; stays 1m; acts on firm going; blinkered final outing at 3 yrs. *I. Walker.* 70

STERRIDGE VALLEY 2 gr.f. Dragonara Palace 115–Standoffish (Be Friendly 130) (1980 5f 5f 6fg 5g 5.8g^4 5s 5g 5g) Mar 12; 2,600Y; strong, compact filly; third foal; sister to a poor animal; dam never ran; 3½ lengths fourth of 16 to Mrs Palmer in maiden auction race at Bath in July; ran out soon after start on second outing and wore blinkers on seventh; will do better in sellers. *J. Hill.* 66

STETCHWORTH (USA) 4 ch.c. Nijinsky 138–Grenadiere 111 (Right Royal V 135) (1979 10s* 12s* 12.3d^2 11fg^2 14f* 14.6f^4 1980 15.5g 12g*) lengthy, very attractive colt; good mover; half-brother to Battlecry (by Bold Lad, Ire), a very useful performer at up to 15f; dam, very useful stayer, is half-sister to some good winners; won handicaps at Ayr, Ripon and York and finished good fourth to Son of Love in St Leger as a 3-y-o, when rated 120 (sold out of H. Wragg's stable 74,000 gns at end of year); bandaged in front when well behind in Prix de Barbeville won by Shafaraz at Longchamp in April; blinkered when beating Maraffic very easily by 3 lengths in 35,000 francs event at Evry later in month on only subsequent start; stayed well; acted on any going; standing at Lodge Stud, Co. Waterford. *M. Zilber, France.* ?

STEWART'S RISE 3 ch.f. Good Bond 122–Devadara 73 (Royal Levee) (1979 NR 1980 6fg 7s^2 6g 7g 10g^2 10f 10fg^2 10g^2 8d*) leggy, light-framed filly; plater; bought in 1,050 gns after winning at Warwick in October; stays 1¼m; seems to act on any going except very firm. *B. McMahon.* 52

STIFFKEY GIRL 7 b.m. Remainder 106–Forest Maiden (Woodcut 114) (1979 NR 1980 10v) third foal; dam never ran; unquoted when tailed off in maiden race won by Sacrilege at Stockton in March, first outing. *K. Bridgwater.* –

STILEBRIDGE MISS 3 b.f. Amber Light 114–Joan Pil (Marshal Pil 108) (1979 5fg 1980 6fg 6f 8d 10.1s 10fg^4 12f) quite well-made filly; bad plater; has worn blinkers. *P. Mitchell.* –

STILL FREE 2 ch.g. Manacle 123–Shilly Shally 89 (Sallymount 125) (1980 6fg^2 6fg) May 10; lightly-made gelding; half-brother to 2 winners, including fair middle-distance winner Equivocal (by I Say); dam ran only 3 times; 4 lengths second of 14 to Piece of the Realm in newcomers event at Chepstow in August, better effort; will stay 7f. *R. Turnell.* 63

STILL HOPE 4 gr.g. No Mercy 126–Shilly Shally 89 (Sallymount 125) (1979 6s 6s 5.8f^3 8fg^3 7h 7g 7fg 8f^2 8f 10d 1980 8fg^3 10fg^2 10h^4 8d 8fg^3 8fg^4 8g 8g 8fg* 8h 8g^2) workmanlike gelding; won apprentice handicap at Chepstow in August; good second to Coral Leisure in amateur riders event at Goodwood the following month; stays 1¼m; acts on firm going; sometimes wears blinkers and did so at Chepstow and Goodwood. *R. Turnell.* 60

STIMLER 3 b.c. Charlottown 127–Pardalina 69 (Pardal 130) (1979 6f 6g 7g 7fg 1980 7d 7fg 8fg^2 8d 7g* 7.6d^4 7s 10g 7g 8fg* 8g^4 7f) lightly-made colt; plater; won at Brighton in July (bought in 2,000 gns) and August (bought in 1,800 gns); should stay beyond 1m; acts on a firm and a soft surface; blinkered nowadays; suitable mount for a boy. *M. Bolton.* 52

ST LOUIS SUE (FR) 4 ch.f. Nonoalco 131–Noble Native 98 (Indigenous 121) (1979 8v^3 10s 7s^2 8d^2 7v^4 8fg 6f 7d^4 8d^4 10.1f^4 8f 8d 7s 8g* 10s^3 8s 1980 8s 8fg 10f 7h^3 6fg^4 8fg 6g 8s 8d 6fg^4 8g 7fg^4 8fg^4 8g^3 8g 8.2s) compact filly; ran well when 58

4 lengths third to clever winner Lightning Label in minor event at Brighton in October; in frame in varied company earlier, including at Deauville; out of her depth third, seventh and eighth outings; stays 1¼m; acts on any going; often blinkered in first half of season. *C. Austin.*

ST MALO 2 b.g. Martinmas 128–Tomelilla (High Hat 131) (1980 8d^4) Apr 27; 1,600F, 10,000Y; fair sort; brother to French 10.5f winner Sabzawar and half-brother to a winner in Ireland; dam poor Irish maiden; 14/1, stayed on when 6½ lengths fourth of 14 to Majorian in maiden race at Leicester in November; subsequently gelded; will be suited by middle distances. *J. Hindley.* **82** p

ST MARY BOURNE 2 br.f. St Paddy 133–Ulador (Sovereign Lord 120) (1980 7d 7g 7g 7f) Apr 28; of no account; broke leg and was destroyed at Redcar in September. *A. Jarvis.* —

ST MAWES 2 b.c. Relko 136–Asturia 104 (The Phoenix) (1980 7g 8fg 10s* 10.2s^2) Mar 16; 10,000F, 14,000Y; big, strong colt; half-brother to several winners, including very useful 7f to 1¼m winner Escorial (by Royal Palace); dam 2-y-o 5f winner; looking particularly well, justified favouritism for 16-runner maiden race at Nottingham in October in good style, drawing clear under hand riding in last 2f to beat Hit The Road 6 lengths; beaten 2 lengths by Irish Heart in 21-runner minor event at Doncaster the following month; will be very well suited by 1½m; acts on soft going. *B. Hobbs.* **95**

STOKE CITY 3 ch.g. Habat 127–Wind Break 81 (Borealis) (1979 6fg 6g 7s 1980 12fg^3 10.4f 10fg 10fg 12g 16d) strong gelding; poor maiden; stays 1½m. *R. Hollinshead.* —

STOLEN HALO 3 b.f. Manacle 123–Street Vendor 60 (High Perch 126) (1979 5g 5v 5g 5fg 5f 5fg 8.2g 10.6d 8g 1980 8f 8fg 7d 6d) sturdy filly; of little account; has worn blinkers. *J. Berry.* —

STONEHENGE 3 gr.c. Great Nephew 126–Fairy Ring 91 (Quorum 126) (1979 6fg 7g 6f 1980 7f^3 10fg* 10.2fg* 10.6fg 10d 8g 10.1g^2 10.2g^3 10.2g) good-bodied, attractive colt; good mover; successful in maiden race at Salisbury and £3,100 event at Doncaster in May; beat Prince Spruce ½ length in latter; apprentice ridden when good second in handicap at Windsor in September; suited by 1¼m on top-of-the-ground. *I. Balding.* **86**

ST OONA 2 ch.f. Ardoon 124–I'm No Saint (St Chad 120) (1980 5d 5.8f 5d) Feb 5; 4,000Y; second foal; half-sister to French 3-y-o Lust for Life (by Sallust), winner of 1m claiming race; dam poor Irish maiden; unquoted when behind in maiden races. *G. Hunter.* **61**

STORMAHEAD 3 ch.g. Red Alert 127–Windy Breeze 77 (Pindari 124) (1979 7fg 7fg 7fg 8.2g 8f 1980 10.8s 16f 12f) good-topped gelding; no sign of ability in maiden and minor events; blinkered fourth start in 1979; sold 650 gns Ascot July Sales. *C. Dingwall.* —

STORM BIRD (CAN) 2 b.c. Northern Dancer–South Ocean (New Providence) (1980 6d* 6.3s* 7g* 7g* 7s*) **134**

As the William Hill Dewhurst Stakes at Newmarket increasingly takes on the role of Britain's most important race for two-year-olds, so too do trainer Vincent O'Brien and owner Robert Sangster increase their grip on it. Storm Bird's win in 1980 provided O'Brien with his sixth Dewhurst winner, all unbeaten, in the last twelve years and Sangster with his fourth winner in a five-year period. It almost goes without saying that Storm Bird is an extremely good colt—he headed the International Classification—but how does he compare as a two-year-old with O'Brien's previous winners? According to our assessment of the form the answer is that he compares very favourably. The best four of the six—Storm Bird, Nijinsky, The Minstrel and Try My Best—are all sons of Northern Dancer, and of these we rate Storm Bird the highest.

Storm Bird's career at two bears a marked resemblance to those of the other Northern Dancer colts. Like The Minstrel and Try My Best he came to the Dewhurst Stakes in October fresh from a win in the Larkspur Stakes, and the similarity between his record and Nijinsky's is even more striking. Both won the Erne Maiden Plate first time out, then three races in Ireland which are now classed as pattern races, including the Anglesey Stakes, before starting odds on at Newmarket. However, the strength of the opposition faced by Nijinsky and Storm Bird was very different. Whereas Nijinsky's competition consisted only of Sayes, the Gimcrack sixth who had subsequently won a nursery, Sandal, a very useful colt from the North, and the maidens Cumbernauld, Recalled and Thundergay, Storm Bird was confronted by To-Agori-Mou, a highly-impressive winner of

National Stakes, the Curragh—Ireland's most valuable two-year-old race falls to Storm Bird on whom Master Thatch can make no impression

three of his four races including the Intercraft Solario Stakes, Centurius, a very expensive brother to the 1974 Dewhurst winner Grundy and a most promising winner at Ascot, Miswaki, second in the Prix Morny before winning the Prix de la Salamandre, and Kirtling who had beaten Robellino in the Chesham Stakes. In view of the stiffer opposition, coupled with the prevailing testing ground and severe weather conditions, Storm Bird couldn't be expected to win so impressively as Nijinsky; he didn't, but nonetheless put up an excellent performance. After racing in second place at To-Agori-Mou's quarters for a while Storm Bird took over the lead fully five furlongs from home. The field stayed closely grouped until Centurius started to flounder two furlongs out and then the whole complexion of the race changed in a matter of strides. Storm Bird and his close rival To-Agori-Mou suddenly quickened coming to the Dip, shaking off Miswaki and Kirtling as though they were third-raters, and from then on the pair engaged in a prolonged duel. Although Storm Bird tended to veer right under pressure in the final furlong, laying grounds for the subsequent lengthy stewards' inquiry, he always seemed in control of the situation and kept on strongly to win by half a length. The superiority of the first two over the rest of the field was overwhelming; Miswaki took third place a long-looking eight lengths behind To-Agori-Mou with Kirtling a further three lengths back in fourth.

Storm Bird's reputation in his home country had been such that on his four outings there he'd been returned respectively at 5/2 on, 9/4 on, 5/2 on and 2/1 on. Only once had he given his supporters the slightest cause for concern. Even a rival's cannoning into him soon after the start on his debut, in a nineteen-runner maiden race at the Curragh in July, hadn't prevented him from strolling home by six lengths. It was in his second race, the Anglesey Stakes on the same course the following month, that Storm Bird seemed to take things too easily for comfort; after moving into the lead over a quarter of a mile out he tended to idle and got home by only half a length from the subsequent Laurent Perrier Champagne Stakes runner-up Prince Echo, who was giving him 6 lb. Any thoughts that this performance revealed the limits of Storm Bird's ability were quickly dispelled by his next two runs, both over the slightly longer trip of seven furlongs. Only a fortnight later he made his nine opponents in the valuable National Stakes at the Curragh look like platers, coming home unchallenged four lengths ahead of Master Thatch after cruising quickly into a clear lead coming to the final quarter mile. And when faced with a stiffer task in the Larkspur Stakes at Leopardstown in September he won in similar style. He had to give weight to each of his five opponents, four of them winners, including 7 lb to the highly-regarded Band Practice who had run out a ten-length winner on his first appearance and then failed by only a head to land the Group 1 Phoenix Stakes on his next. Neither Band Practice nor any of the others got in a blow once they turned into the straight. Cauthen, a late replacement for the injured Murphy, had only to give Storm Bird a few light taps down the shoulder to make him quicken clear and the pair crossed the line easing up, four lengths ahead of Band Practice.

Storm Bird (Can) (b.c. April 19, 1978)	Northern Dancer (b 1961)	Nearctic (br 1954)	Nearco
			Lady Angela
		Natalma (b 1957)	Native Dancer
			Almahmoud
	South Ocean (b 1967)	New Providence (b 1956)	Bull Page
			Fair Colleen
		Shining Sun (b 1962)	Chop Chop
			Solar Display

Interestingly the similarities between Nijinsky, The Minstrel and Storm Bird also extend to their breeding. Nijinsky's dam was a daughter of Bull Page, The Minstrel's dam is by a son of Chop Chop out of a daughter of Bull Page, and Storm Bird's dam is by a son of Bull Page out of a daughter of Chop Chop. With such a pedigree it's no wonder it took 1,000,000 dollars to buy him as a yearling.

Storm Bird was foaled in Canada where many of his relatives made their names on the racecourse. His great-grandam Solar Display, an unraced half-sister to the top-class American horse Battlefield, bred eight winners including the Canadian Oaks winner Solometeor and one of the best Canadian three-year-olds of 1958 Dr Em Jay, winner of the Breeders' Stakes over a mile and a quarter and fourth in Canada's top race, the Queen's Plate. Shining Sun, successful three times at up to a mile at three years and a sister to Dr Em Jay, bred four winners from as many foals. Easily best of the four was Storm Bird's dam South Ocean who numbered the Yearling Sales Stakes at two and the nine-furlong Canadian Oaks at three among her four successes. She was rated the third-best three-year-old filly in Canada behind the top-class Fanfreluche whom she'd beaten in the Oaks.

Storm Bird is South Ocean's fifth foal and her second by Northern Dancer, following the very good filly Northernette. Northernette was the highest-weighted filly in the Canadian Free Handicap at two years. She landed the odds by eleven lengths in the 1977 Canadian Oaks and failed by only half a length to become the first filly since Flaming Page, the dam of Nijinsky and grandam of The Minstrel, to complete the Canadian Oaks-Queen's Plate double; and when sold to race in the USA she proved only a few pounds behind the very best American fillies, winning the Chrysanthemum Handicap at three and both the 75,000-dollar Top Flight Handicap and the 100,000-dollar Apple Blossom

William Hill Dewhurst Stakes, Newmarket—Storm Bird and To-Agori-Mou place themselves top two in the two-year-old Free Handicap. French challenger Miswaki is a well-beaten third

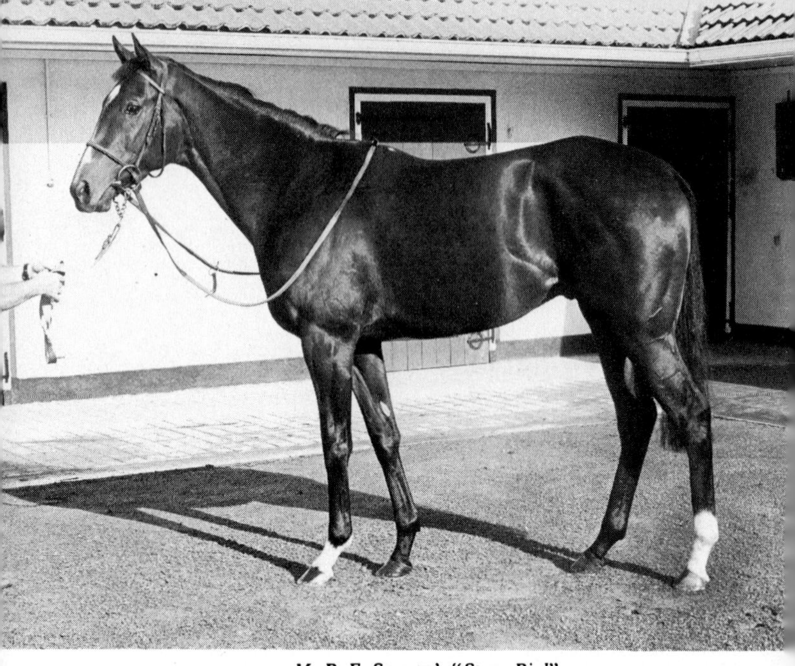

Mr R. E. Sangster's "Storm Bird"

Handicap at four. Northernette ended her career the winner of thirteen of her thirty-three starts with earnings of over 400,000 dollars. All of South Ocean's three other foals of racing age were by sons of Northern Dancer. Two were good performers in Canada, including the Northern Answer filly Ocean's Answer who won the Natalma Stakes over a mile at two, and the third, the Nijinsky colt Sevastopol, was considered such an excellent prospect, although he never made it to the races, that he was retired to stud at the Windfields Farm in Ontario.

How will Storm Bird compare with O'Brien's other Dewhurst winners as a three-year-old? We'll be very surprised and disappointed if he doesn't compare very favourably with Cellini, Try My Best and Monteverdi, and in our opinion he's a very worthy favourite to emulate the victories of Nijinsky in the Two Thousand Guineas and of Nijinsky and The Minstrel in the Derby. The major obstacle he has to overcome to win the Guineas seems at the moment to be To-Agori-Mou, and a lot will depend on how they progress through the winter. Though To-Agori-Mou is the bigger, more imposing individual, both have the scope to train on. For his part, tall, quite attractive Storm Bird is more substantially-made than another son of Northern Dancer, Nureyev, who passed the post first in the latest Guineas. A tricky problem faces O'Brien in that he needs to have Storm Bird at or near his best to take on To-Agori-Mou on May 2nd when the Derby, the more valuable of the two races and the one which virtually guarantees a sky-high valuation as a stallion, is still over four weeks away. However, no trainer alive is better equipped to solve such a dilemma: he's faced similar problems many times, and he has done the double with Sir Ivor and Nijinsky followed by near misses with Roberto and The Minstrel, and at present we see no reason why he shouldn't win both races again with Storm Bird. As yet Storm Bird has raced only on an easy surface, conditions which suit him well and which he might well meet in the Guineas, but he's such a good-actioned colt it's probable that he'll act on the firm going so often prevalent on Derby Day. *V. O'Brien, Ireland.*

STORM DANCER 3 b.f. Carnival Dancer 117–Stormkhamen (Tutankhamen) (1979 NR 1980 7fg 8f 5fg 5g 5g 7g 8d 10s 10d) 300 2-y-o; compact filly; of no account. *B. Shaw.* —

STORM LADY 2 b.f. Realm 129–Storm Lass 65 (Typhoon 125) (1980 5g 5s 5s 8d 6g) Mar 27; 6,800Y; quite an attractive, neat filly; good mover; third foal; dam placed at up to 9f in Ireland; evidently of little account. *P. Kelleway.* —

STORM ROCK 2 br.g. Swing Easy 126–Golden Storm 95 (Golden Cloud) (1980 5fg 5fg 5d^2 5d) Apr 17; 8,600Y; big, strong-quartered gelding; brother to 1m winner Stormalong and half-brother to several winners, including very useful 7f and 1m performer Apple King (by Birdbrook); dam sprinter; disputed lead most of way when 4 lengths second of 7 to Tax Haven in £2,700 event at Sandown in June; should stay 6f; acts on a soft surface; gelded after final start. *H. Candy.* **71**

STORM TROOPER 3 b.c. Saulingo 122–Party Love (Parthia 132) (1979 7fg 1980 6d 8fg 8.2g 8d 12g 7fg 7d*) big, strong colt; plater; sold 1,600 gns after winning at Edinburgh in September; unlikely to stay 1½m; acts on a soft surface; blinkered fourth start. *B. Hanbury.* **47**

STORMY CLOUD 2 b.c. Import 127–Clouds of Gold (Goldhill 125) (1980 5s 7s) Apr 20; 4,300Y; half-brother to 1m and 1½m winner Farthing (by Maystreak); dam never ran; behind in maiden races at Warwick in April and July; sold 390 gns Ascot August Sales. *T. Marshall.* —

STORMY JIM 2 ch.c. Jimmy Reppin 131–Stormy Gal 71 (Rockavon 120) (1980 5f^3 5f 5f^4 6g 7f* 8g^3 7fg* 8g* 7d 7v^2) Apr 30; 4,000Y; fair sort; brother to 1979 2-y-o 5f winner Mere Gambler, and half-brother to a winner; dam stayed 1m; ran well in nurseries in second half of season, winning at Beverley, Catterick and York; beat Beechwood Seeker a shade comfortably by 2½ lengths when carrying a 10-lb penalty at York in October; suited by 7f and 1m; acts on any going; game, genuine and consistent. *Hbt Jones.* **92**

STOTFIELD MAJOR 2 ch.g. Queen's Hussar 124–Guiding Light 78 (Crepello 136) (1980 7g 8.2s) Apr 14; 2,000Y; well-grown gelding; half-brother to 4 winners, including useful 1m to 1½m filly La Dolce (by Connaught); dam middle-distance maiden; in rear in maiden race at Catterick and seller at Hamilton. *J. Berry.* —

STOUT 3 b.c. Bold Lad (Ire) 133–Vendemmia (Silly Season 127) (1979 5d 5d* 5s* 5v 6g 6g 5d 5g^2 5g 5f 7.6f 1980 7v^3 8s 7f 7f^4 7f 8d 6g 5fg) small, well-made colt; excellent mover; in frame in Salisbury 2,000 Guineas Trial in March (7 lengths third of 12 to Poyle Crusher) and handicap at Chester in May (fourth to Numas); best at up to 7f; probably acts on any going; sometimes sweats up; blinkered sixth start at 2 yrs; ran badly seventh start; inconsistent. *G. Beeson.* **86**

STOWMARKET 2 b.c. Realm 129–Sovereign 129 (Pardao 120) (1980 6g 6d 6fg 6g^2) Apr 1; attractive colt; half-brother to 4 winners, including Irish Sweeps Derby second Lucky Sovereign (by Nijinsky), very useful miler Flashy (by Sir Ivor) and 1979 2-y-o 5f winner Annabella (by Habitat); dam fastest 2-y-o filly of 1967 and stayed 1m; ran best race when 3 lengths second of 12 to odds-on Spark of Life in maiden race at Yarmouth in September; not fully fit in his earlier races; should win a race. *H. Wragg.* **84**

ST PEDRO 2 b.c. St Paddy 133–Jinkin (King's Troop 118) (1980 8g) Feb 27; fourth foal; dam never ran; 33/1 and in need of race when last of 16 in minor event won by Uppety at Newmarket in October. *E. Eldin.* —

STRAIGHTAWAY (USA) 3 b.c. Never Bend–Which Away (Tom Fool) (1979 NR 1980 8f 9.4fg 10f 6s 6fg) strong colt; poor form in varied company; blinkered last 2 starts. *F. Durr.* —

STRAIGHT TURN 7 ch.h. Straight King 98–Star Turn (Anton 106) (1979 NR 1980 12g) novice hurdler; tailed off in amateur riders race at Redcar in June, first outing on flat. *J. Mulhall.* —

STRAITS 3 b.g. Busted 134–Smeralda 105 (Grey Sovereign 128§) (1979 NR 1980 10fg 12f^2 12fg 12g^2 14d^3 10.6d 13g^3) 45,000Y; tall, attractive, well-made gelding; good mover; brother to French 1¼m winner Swing Is Back, closely related to Belgian winner Brussels Night (by Crepello) and half-brother to a winner in France; dam a sprinter; placed in maiden and minor races but is disappointing; **79** d stays 1½m; acts on firm going; usually makes the running; sweated up and ran deplorably when blinkered on sixth start; sold 6,000 gns Newmarket Autumn Sales. *P. Walwyn.*

STRALOCH 3 ch.c. Lombard 126–Jabelina (Alcide 136) (1979 5d 6fg 7f 7g 7f 1980 11v^3 13s 14g 10g 10s) neat colt; plater; should stay at least 1½m; trained by C. Bewicke first 3 outings. *R. Hartop.* —

STRATHDEARN 3 gr.f. Saritamer 130–Shenachie 79 (Sheshoon 132) (1979 6f 6fg 6d 7g^4 7s^2 1980 8fg^4 7.6f 12.2fg* 12d 12g 12g^3 11g^3 8g 8fg^4 10.4d^3 12f^3 16d 12.2d^3 12s^2 12d) big, strong filly; not a good mover in her slower paces; won 13-runner maiden race at Catterick in June; suited by 1½m; acts on any going; suitable mount for a boy. *D. Francis* **67**

STRATHFILLAN 3 br.c. Hotfoot 126–Ista Jil 97 (Gratitude 130) (1979 5s^2 5f 6fg 6fg^4 7fg 7fg^2 7f^4 8g^4 8fg* 1980 8fg* 7d* 8g* 7g 8fg 8fg) smallish, useful-looking colt; in good form in handicaps in first half of season, winning at Leicester (twice) and Wolverhampton; stays 1m; probably acts on any going; does best when held up; below form last 3 starts; sold to Denys Smith 4,200 gns Newmarket Autumn Sales. *B. Hobbs.* **91**

STRAVARNEY 3 ch.f. The Go-Between 129–Riotous 97 (Silver Cloud 121) (1979 5g 5g 6f 8fg 8.2s 1980 8fg 8fg 8d 8s 8.3f 6fg 8fg 6g) small filly; bad plater. *M. Bradley.* —

STRAW KING 4 b.c. Thatch 136–Kiyofuji 98 (Grey Sovereign 128§) (1979 7d 8fg 6f 7fg^4 6d^2 6d^2 7.6f 6fg^3 5fg 1980 7f^3 12h 7fg 8g 5d) robust, good-topped colt; has been tubed; plater; stays 7f but is most unlikely to get 1½m; acts on a firm and a soft surface; often wears blinkers; sometimes sweats up. *P. Bailey.* —

STRAWMAN 3 ch.c. Thatch 136–Purple Goddess 69 (Red God 128§) (1979 5fg 1980 5fg* 6f 5d 5g) strong, good-bodied colt; won 13-runner maiden race at Wolverhampton in April; not disgraced next start; stays 6f; blinkered final outing; sold 330 gns Ascot November Sales. *N. Gaselee.* **72**

STREET CRIER 2 ch.c. Town Crier 119–Decatullus (Catullus) (1980 6d 5d) Mar 31; strong, workmanlike colt; good mover; second live foal; half-brother to 9f winner Wesscam (by Scottish Rifle); dam won claiming races at up to 9f in USA; rather slow into stride when ninth of 20 to Little Starchy in 5f maiden race at Sandown in October. *S. Matthews.* —

STREGGA 2 b.f. Roman Warrior 132–Mehir 59 (King's Company 124) (1980 5g 5g^3 5fg 5g 5f 5g) Apr 22; 4,100Y; small filly; second foal; half-sister to a winning 2-y-o plater by Appiani II; dam poor maiden; 5½ lengths third of 12 to Lady Lorelei in maiden race at Kempton in July, best effort; will stay 6f. *M. Masson.* **71**

STRIA (USA) 3 ch.f. Raise A Native–Ionian Idol (Prince John) (1979 NR 1980 5h 5fg) $47,000Y; lengthy filly; first foal; dam, winner at up to 6f in USA, is half-sister to useful 1968 staying Irish 2-y-o Mongolia II; showed a little ability in maiden race at Thirsk in May on first outing; well beaten in similar event at Bath in June, only subsequent start; will be suited by 6f. *L. Cumani.* —

STRICTLY CASH 3 br.c. Lock And Load 72–Golden Dream (Golden Surprise 65) (1979 NR 1980 10.1f) second reported foal; dam never ran; soon behind and pulled up after 1m in maiden race at Windsor in August. *W. Charles.* —

STRICTLY SWING 4 ch.f. Swing Easy 126–Arrangement 72 (Floribunda 136) (1979 5d 5d 5f 5fg^2 5fg^3 6f^3 5fg^3 5fg* 5g^4 5g* 5.6fg 5f 1980 6g 6fg 5f 6g^2 5g 5g* 5d) big, rangy filly; ridden by 7-lb claimer, held up when beating Ferryman by short head in handicap at Salisbury in September; stays 6f; acts on a firm and a soft surface; blinkered sixth start in 1979 and last 2 outings; sold 5,600 gns Newmarket Autumn Sales. *J. Sutcliffe.* **75**

STRIGIDA 2 b.f. Habitat 134–Catalpa 115 (Reform 132) (1980 7g) Apr 7; lengthy filly; first foal; dam won Ribblesdale Stakes; weakened from 3/1 to 12/1 and didn't impress particularly as an individual before finishing never-dangerous seventh of 18 to Park Place in maiden race at Yarmouth in September, only outing; should do better. *H. Cecil.* — p

STRIKE ACTION 3 b.g. Tyrant–Corte (Alcide 136) (1979 NR 1980 8d^3 9.4g 10g 8g 8.2s) 1,700Y; poor walker; little worthwhile form in maiden and minor events; should stay 1¼m; acts on a soft surface; blinkered final start. *C. Booth.* —

STRIKE AGAIN 2 ch.c. Redundant 120–Kimolina (Ki Myth 96) (1980 5g 5f 5d^3 7fg^4 6fg 7d) Mar 27; 2,000Y; big, strong colt; half-brother to a winning plater; dam never ran; in frame in maiden events at Carlisle (auction race) and Warwick in July; stays 7f. *M. Tate.* **70**

STRIP FAST 7 ch.m. Virginia Boy 106–Light Gail (Hill Gail) (1979 10f 10f^{3} **66**
8h* 10f^{4} 9fg^{3} 10.4f^{3} 10.2fg^{3} 10.2fg* 10.8g 1980 8g 8fg^{2} 8fg 11.7g^{3} 10fg 10.4d^{4} 8.3fg 10.2d^{3}) neat mare; stays 1½m; probably needs a sound surface; game; excellent mount for a boy. *D. H. Jones.*

STRONG GALE 5 br.h. Lord Gayle 124–Sterntau (Tamerlane 128) (1979 10v^{4} **107**
9.7s 9.2fg^{2} 10.5d* 11f^{2} 10g^{3} 10fg 1980 10s 10.5g^{3} 9.7d^{2} 9.2s 11s^{3} 10g^{2} 10g 12d 10s^{2}) smart middle-distance horse; second in Prix Dollar at Longchamp (beaten length by Northern Baby), Prix Ridgway at Deauville (went down by 1½ lengths to Dom D'Albignac) and Prix du Point du Jour at Longchamp again (beaten 4 lengths by Manguin); ran well when 2 lengths third to Argument in Grand Prix Prince Rose at Ostend on fifth start; probably acts on any going; genuine and consistent. *A. Paus, France.*

ST SEVERIN 8 b.g. Manacle 123–Crag Bay 77 (Road House II) (1979 10.8fg **–**
1980 10v) plater; stays 1¼m; acts on any going; often wears blinkers; suitable mount for an apprentice; sold out of P. Allingham's stable 750 gns Doncaster January Sales. *R. Ward.*

ST TERRAMAR 5 b.h. St Alphage 119–Terramar Lass (Tom Rolfe) (1979 5s **84**
5v 6v 5s 5.1g 5fg 6f^{3} 6f^{2} 5f* 6fg 5d^{2} 5fg* 5.6fg^{2} 5fg^{4} 5g 5g 1980 5g 5f^{2} 5f 5f 5f^{4} 5g* 5g^{3} 5g 5d 5d 5f 5.6g^{4} 5fg 5g 5g^{4} 5s) sprint handicapper; got home by ½ length from Mi Favorita at Beverley in June; fourth subsequently in William Hill Portland Handicap at Doncaster (to Swelter) and Bovis Handicap at Ascot (to Ferryman); appears to act on any going but is particularly well suited by a sound surface; acts on any track; suitable mount for a boy; best in blinkers; sometimes wears a bandage on his off-fore; usually held up; dwelt ninth outing. *N. Guest.*

STUART KING 3 ch.g. Sassafras 135–Miss Scotland 111 (Henry the Seventh 125) **79**
(1979 5s 6f^{2} 6fg 6fg 7g^{3} 6g 7f 6fg 7d 1980 10fg* 12g^{2} 12d^{4} 12g) neat gelding; won maiden race at Redcar in July; ran creditably next start but moderately on last 2; stays 1½m; acts well on firm ground; showed signs of temperament at 2 yrs and was blinkered final 3 outings. *R. Hollinshead.*

STUBBINGTON GREEN 3 br.g. Swing Easy 126–Lake Victoria 94 (Stupen- **–**
dous) (1979 5g^{2} 5.8g 6f* 6fg 6s* 6g 1980 6s 7fg 6g 6g 6g 7g^{3} 8d) leggy gelding; plater; stays 7f; acts on any going; sweated up fourth start. *G. Balding.*

STUCK FOR WORDS 3 ch.f. Some Hand 119–Clear Speech (Articulate 121) **43**
(1979 5f 5f 1980 7h 6fg 10f 10.1s 10s 10fg* 8fg^{2} 11.7fg 10f) quite well-made filly; plater; bought in 1,500 gns after comfortably winning at Folkestone in August; stays 1¼m; acts on a firm surface; suitable mount for a boy. *A. Moore.*

STUDIO COPY (FR) 3 b.c. Habitat 134–Artists Proof (Ribot 142) (1979 NR **–**
1980 8.2g 8d^{3} 8g 8g) big, rangy colt; half-brother to 3 winners, including William Hill Futurity winner Dactylographer (by Secretariat); dam very useful stakes winner, successful at up to 1m; third in maiden race at Salisbury in June, best effort; stays 1m; sweated up final start; one paced; sold 6,600 gns Newmarket December Sales. *P. Walwyn.*

STUMPED 3 b.f. Owen Anthony 102–Luckhurst (Busted 134) (1979 6fg* 6f^{3} **117**
7fg* 6s^{2} 1980 7f 8fg* 8g^{4} 8s* 7fg) 7,000Y; quite attractive, well-made filly; second foal; sister to 5f winner Torbay Express; dam unraced daughter of good sprinter Lucasland; smart performer; readily beat Rapids in UBM Merchants International Fillies Stakes at Kempton in May and put up a game performance when holding off Our Home by ¾ length in 9-runner Child Stakes at Newmarket in July; 3¼ lengths fourth to Cairn Rouge in Coronation Stakes at Royal Ascot in between; below form final outing; stays 1m; acts on any going; genuine; sold 110,000 gns Newmarket December Sales, for export to USA. *B. Hobbs.*

STUN ON 4 ch.g. Lombard 126–Hasta (Skymaster 126) (1979 9.4v 10fg 12.3s **–**
1980 10v) poor maiden; dead. *B. Wilkinson.*

ST WILLIAM 3 b.c. St Paddy 133–Lower Slade (Solar Duke 103) (1979 7d 7g **67**
8g 7d 1980 10fg 10fg^{3} 10f^{3} 16s^{4} 14g 10.1f 16fg) big, tall colt; best form at 1¼m though is bred to stay well; acts on firm going. *Mrs R. Lomax.*

SUAVITY (USA) 3 b.c. Personality–Smooth 114 (Sound Track 132) (1979 6fg* **103**
6fg* 6d* 6fg* 6f 1980 6fg 7g 7g^{4} 8d^{3}) strong, well-made, attractive colt; good mover; went on well near finish when 2 lengths fourth to Captain Nick in £8,100 event at Newmarket in June; appeared to find 1m too far for him in handicap on same course in July, finishing third to Belmont Bay; stays 7f; best form on an easy surface and ran poorly on really firm going on final outing at 2 yrs; useful; sold 7,400 gns Newmarket Autumn Sales. *H. Cecil.*

SUBRIQUETTE 2 b.f. English Prince 129–Lady Mickey (Swaps) (1980 6f 6f) Mar 14; 8,600Y; big, workmanlike filly; half-sister to two 2-y-o winners, including 1979 5f winner Ivoronica (by Targowice); dam won 6f maiden race at 3 yrs in USA; 25/1, showed up well to below distance when seventh of 18 to Scarrowmanwick in minor event at Lingfield in September, first outing and better effort; will be suited by further; gave trouble at start and was withdrawn after dislodging and injuring her rider on third intended outing. *M. Smyly.* **66**

SUBURBAN SUE 2 ch.f. Native Bazaar 122–Susanella 83 (Eborneezer 105) (1980 5fg 5f² 5.8fg 6g³ 6g 5.8h³) Jan 31; leggy filly; third foal; dam needed long distances; hampered Annie Panny before winning seller at Bath in May by ¾ length and was moved down to second by stewards; ran respectably in better company afterwards; stays 6f; acts on hard going. *G. Cottrell.* **57**

SUCCESSOR 11 ch.g. Great Nephew 126–Loidien 95 (Ribot 142) (1979 12s* 10.7g 12f³ 10f 12d 1980 12f² 10g 12fg³ 13g 12fg 13.1h* 10g) a grand old middle-distance handicapper; led near finish when scoring by ½ length from Merokette at Bath in August; acts on any going; has worn blinkers; good mount for an inexperienced rider; has won 7 times at Chepstow. *R. Turnell.* **52**

SUCH BLISS 5 b.m. So Blessed 130–Paddle Boat 98 (St Paddy 133) (1979 10.7g 7f 10.8fg 8g² 8fg 6f 7g 1980 8d³ 9fg 10g 8d 7s) lengthy mare; ridden by 7-lb claimer when creditable third to Saher in handicap at Wolverhampton in August, best effort; stays 1¼m; sometimes wears blinkers; winning hurdler. *M. Tate.* **55**

SUCHONG 2 b.f. No Mercy 126–Tea Leaf (Cracksman NZ) (1980 7f 7g) Apr 20; well-grown filly; half-sister to 2 winners by Sweet Revenge, including 3-y-o sprinter Lapsang; dam apparently of little account; behind in large fields of maidens at Chepstow in August and Salisbury (still on backward side) following month. *P. Makin.* **–**

SUCH STYLE 3 b.f. Sassafras 135–Regal Lady 93 (Relko 136) (1979 NR 1980 12g³) third foal; half-sister to Oaks third Britannia's Rule (by Blakeney); dam, winner at up to 13f, is half-sister to Vaguely Noble; not seen out after finishing promising third to Nepotism in maiden race at Salisbury in June; will stay 1¾m; sold 16,000 gns Newmarket December Sales. *H. Candy.* **80**

Gilbey Champion Racehorse Futurity, York—Sula Bula has no trouble beating the better-fancied More Harmony and Sauvage

SUE'S PRINCE 2 b.c. King Log 115–Fairy First 54§ (Fairey Fulmar 124) (1980 5d 6g 7d 6g3 7f 8d 8d) Mar 30; well-grown, useful sort; brother to very useful 7f to 1¼m winner King Frog; dam ran only at 2 yrs; 4 lengths third to Mott The Hoople in 12-runner seller at Newcastle in August; had stiffish tasks in nurseries subsequently, one of them a seller; will be suited by middle distances. *W. H. H. Williams.* **66**

SUFFIELD PARK 2 b.f. Wolver Hollow 126–Jungle Princess (Native Prince) (1980 6fg 8d 8d) June 5; 1,200Y; well-made, attractive filly; sister to Wolf Trap, placed at around 7f in Ireland, and half-sister to 1977 2-y-o 1m winner Jungle Trial (by Run The Gantlet); dam fairly useful winner over 5f at 2 yrs in Ireland; modest fifth in 1m maiden races at Bath and Warwick in October. *F. J. Houghton.* **66**

SUGAR COATED 2 b.f. Track Spare 125–Star Abbess 86 (Welsh Abbot 131) (1980 5d4 5fg 6fg) May 9; leggy, light-framed filly; half-sister to a minor 2-y-o winner and 2 winners abroad; dam won 5f seller at 2 yrs; ran on when 1¾ lengths fourth of 8 to Artistry in maiden race at Newbury in July; well beaten in similar events subsequently; possibly unsuited by a firm surface. *M. Masson.* **72**

SUKATA (FR) 2 b.f. Sukawa 124–Catalogne (Mourne 126) (1980 8d*) Mar 2; half-sister to a minor 2-y-o winner in France by Shoemaker; dam modest half-sister to French colt Mincio, a high-class winner at up to 9f; made all to win valuable Prix de la Cascade, a newcomers race at Longchamp in September, by 1½ lengths from El Dancerina; should make a smart middle-distance filly. *D. Smaga, France.* **96** p

SULA BULA 2 b.c. Midsummer Night II 117–Blue Ann 60 (Road House II) (1980 5g2 5f3 6d* 7g2 7g* 7s2 7d2 7f* 8g* 7v*) **109**

Success is all the sweeter when it is the result of hard work and determination. This eager beaver began his career on almost the lowest rung of racing's ladder and climbed to the top in the North, improving with almost every race and showing himself to be one of the toughest and gamest horses in training. Between his initial outing in a maiden auction event at Ripon in the second week of April and his tenth and final outing in the Steel Plate Autumn Stakes at Doncaster on the last day of the season, Sula Bula improved by some three stones. He rarely enjoyed the luxury of an easy race and most of his victories —he also won a maiden race at Carlisle in June, a minor event at York in July, the Gilbey Champion Racehorse Futurity at York in September and a small race at Newcastle in October (in which he gave weight and a beating to Spindrifter)—were gained the hard way. His performance in the Steel Plate Autumn Stakes, in which he beat Soldan by a head in a driving finish, was typical of him: out in front forcing the pace from some way out, he battled on most courageously, showing tremendous zest for the job. Sula Bula's performances earned him joint-top weight in the Northern Free Handicap, a position he shared with Engulf and Parkdale. Of the three, Sula Bula is the one we fancy to make most progress at three; he has a lot of improvement to make before we can regard him as a live contender for the Two Thousand Guineas, his first important target, but, whatever his fate at Newmarket, Sula Bula should win more good races. He is a grand racehorse.

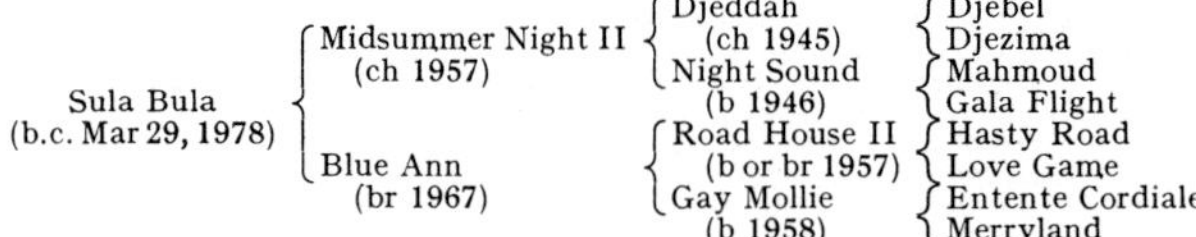

Sula Bula (b.c. Mar 29, 1978)	Midsummer Night II (ch 1957)	Djeddah (ch 1945)	Djebel
			Djezima
		Night Sound (b 1946)	Mahmoud
			Gala Flight
	Blue Ann (br 1967)	Road House II (b or br 1957)	Hasty Road
			Love Game
		Gay Mollie (b 1958)	Entente Cordiale
			Merryland

Sula Bula was a bargain-basement yearling: his trainer picked him up for 2,200 guineas at the Doncaster September Sales. Sula Bula's dam Blue Ann was plating class and ran eight times over five furlongs as a two-year-old, gaining a place only once. Blue Ann's record as a broodmare was unimpressive before Sula Bula came along: her only other winner is Bloomsbury Girl (by Weepers Boy), winner of a five-furlong seller at Ayr as a three-year-old. Sula Bula's improved form went hand in hand with physical improvement through the season; on the leg when we first saw him, he developed into quite a useful-looking colt. He is well suited by seven furlongs and a

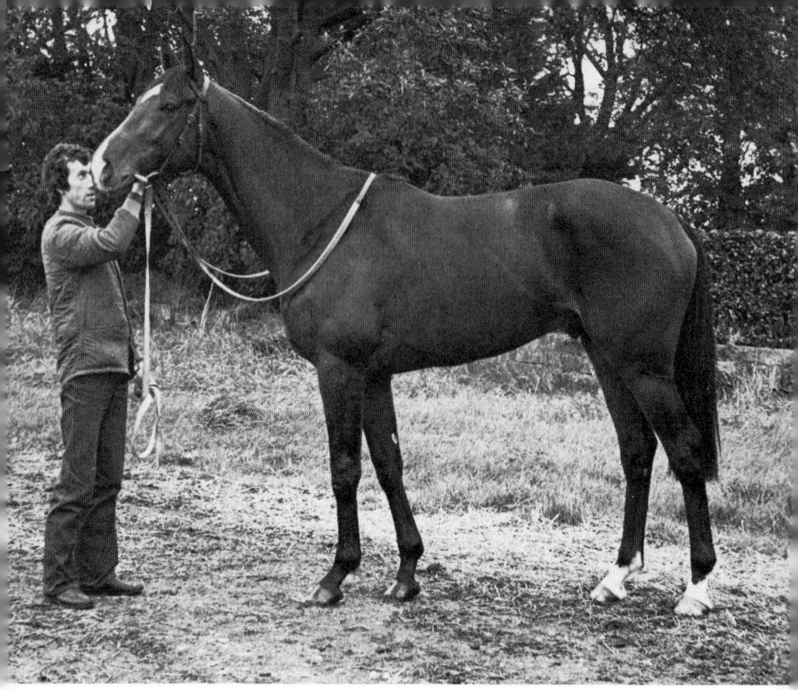

Mr G. W. Pratt's "Sula Bula"

mile and may stay a little further at three; and he acts on any going. *M. H. Easterby.*

SULE SKERRY 3 b.f. Scottish Rifle 127–Ruddy Duck 84 (Dicta Drake 126) (1979 7g 7f 1980 10fg 12fg 12d 12d* 10.1d 12g 11.7fg^2 12f^4 12g^4 11.7d 12v* 12g) attractive, lengthy filly; good mover; 3-length winner of maiden race at Brighton in July and 4-runner handicap at Hamilton in October; will stay 1¾m; probably acts on any going but is well suited by the mud; wears blinkers. *J. Dunlop.* **78**

SULPHUR 2 ch.c. Simbir 130–Dazzling Hue (Double Jump 131) (1980 8g) Mar 18; 8,200Y; medium-sized, active individual; good walker and mover; third foal; half-brother to Irish 1½m winner Northern Queen (by Northfields); dam unraced half-sister to Cambridgeshire winner King Midas; 14/1, finished well down the field behind Video Tape in 17-runner minor event at Newmarket in October but ran much better than finishing position suggests, showing up with leaders for more than 5f and not being persevered with when chance had gone; will do better over middle distances at 3 yrs. *P. Walwyn.* — p

SULZANO 2 b.c. Rheingold 137–Ribasha (Ribot 142) (1980 7g 6g 7g) May 12; 12,000F, 20,000Y; well-made colt; half-brother to fairly useful stayer Ribarbaro (by Charlottown) and to a winner in Italy; dam, slow maiden, is closely related to high-class animals Blood Royal, Arkadina and Gregorian; showed little worthwhile form in maiden and minor events but looks capable of better in time; will be suited by 1½m. *W. Hastings-Bass.* —

SUMMARY 3 b.c. Mandamus 120–Abstract 73 (French Beige 127) (1979 7g* 7.6f 7fg* 1980 10d^3 8f^4 10f^4 9.6f^2 10s 10s^3 10fg 10fg^3 10.1g 10fg) well-made colt; fair handicapper; stays 1¼m; acts on any going; blinkered last 2 starts; sold 10,000 gns Newmarket Autumn Sales. *B. Hobbs.* **89**

SUMMERFIELD 5 ch.g. Jukebox 120–Ballyelegant (Ballylinan 118) (1979 —
16.9s 12f^{2} 12s^{3} 12f 13.4f^{3} 16.9fg 16s 12d 13.8s 1980 16f^{3}) poor handicapper; probably stays 2m; acts on any going; usually blinkered; suitable mount for an inexperienced rider; whipped round start (flag) on fourth outing at 4 yrs; sold 1,300 gns Ascot July Sales. *R. Morris.*

SUMMER FROLIC 3 ch.c. Relko 136–Miss Wolff 91 (Vilmorin) (1979 6g —
1980 10fg 13.3fg 12s 11.7f 10g^{4}) big, strong colt; little worthwhile form in varied company; seems to stay $1\frac{1}{4}$m; blinkered nowadays. *M. Smyly.*

SUMMER PATH 3 gr.f. Warpath 113–Summersoon 89 (Sheshoon 132) (1979 53
5s 5s 5v 1980 8f 7fg 16g 10g^{2} 9s* 10.6d 14.7f^{3} 12fg^{2} 15d) compact filly; plater; attracted no bid after winning at Newcastle in August; twice placed in better company subsequently; stays $1\frac{3}{4}$m; acts on any going. *T. Fairhurst.*

SUMMER SAINT 6 b.g. Welsh Saint 126–Summer's Lease (Soderini 123) —
(1979 NR 1980 10d) lightly raced and little sign of ability on flat (showed some temperament on only outing of 1980); winner over hurdles. *A. Gillam.*

SUMMER SOLDIER 3 b. or br.g. Home Guard 129–Crepe Myrtle 80 (Crepello 80
136) (1979 NR 1980 8.2s^{4} 8s^{3} 7.6f^{2} 8d* 8g^{3}) half-brother to useful 1976 2-y-o 5f winner Ground Cover (by Huntercombe), subsequently a stakes winner in North America; dam won over 1m; beat Clarendon a neck in maiden race at Salisbury in June; stays 1m; appears to act on any going; blinkered third start; has run creditably for an apprentice; sold 6,800 gns Ascot July Sales and is in training with F. Walwyn. *J. Tree.*

SUM STAR 5 br.m. Comedy Star 121–Quotient 91 (Quorum 126) (1979 8.3fg 67
10f 8fg 6s 1980 8fg* 6h^{2} 6fg* 6f* 7g* 6g^{2} 5fg 5g* 6d^{3} 6f) won seller at Edinburgh in April (sold out of H. O'Neill's stable 1,600 gns) and non-selling handicaps at Carlisle, Hamilton (made all), Edinburgh and Hamilton again; beat Lilac Star a length on last-named course in July; effective at 5f to 1m; acts on hard going; blinkered second outing at 4 yrs. *J. Berry.*

SUN BLOSSOM 2 b.f. Blakeney 126–Penumbra 99 (Wolver Hollow 126) 74
(1980 6fg^{3} 6d) Feb 24; 10,000Y; neat, attractive filly; third foal; dam a sprinter; 20/1, showed promise when strong-finishing $1\frac{3}{4}$ lengths third of 19 to Sea Aura in minor event at Lingfield in October; possibly had too much use made of her when out of first 9 of 25 in maiden race won by Little Wolf at Newbury later in month; will be better suited by 7f and 1m. *M. Smyly.*

SUNBURST (FR) 4 b.c. Sassafras 135–Miss Sunshine (Mourne 126) (1979 69
12fg^{3} 10.5g 12g 10.5fg^{3} 12.5g 11d* 12.5fg^{2} 12g 1980 6f 8fg 13.4f 12g* 10f^{3} 10s 12g^{4} 12g 12d 13g 10s^{2} 16fg 10g 13s) big ex-French colt; won handicap at Thirsk in May by neck from Syncopate; ran best subsequent race when strong-finishing $\frac{1}{2}$-length second to Liberated in similar event at Nottingham in August; stays $1\frac{1}{2}$m; probably acts on any going but seems well suited by some give in the ground; sweated up on reappearance; trained most of season by K. Bridgwater. *A. Jarvis.*

SUN DIVER 2 ch.g. Sun Prince 128–Sea Swallow 90 (Dan Cupid 132) (1980 5f 67
6g 7g 7d 7fg 7f^{2} 7d^{3} 7d^{4}) May 20; 3,000Y; neat, strong gelding; half-brother to 3 winners, including 1979 2-y-o 7f winner Good Companions (by Lorenzaccio); dam won over $1\frac{1}{4}$m; dropped in class, ran easily best race in 18-runner seller at Redcar in September, failing by only a short head to hold off Rocket Venture after having nothing to race with in final 2f on stand side; did as well as could be expected when out of his depth on next 2 outings; will stay $1\frac{1}{4}$m; blinkered last 3 appearances; sold 1,100 gns Doncaster November Sales. *Denys Smith.*

SUNFIELD 3 b.c. Northfields–Boucle 86 (Princely Gift 137) (1979 NR 1980 114
8f* 9f^{2} 8.2fg^{2} 7g^{2} 7g 8g 7g*) 26,000Y; well-made colt; good mover; half-brother to 3 winners, including fair performers Tenochca (by Astec) and Pledge (by Rarity); dam sprinter; very useful performer; beat Pentaquod a short head in 25-runner maiden race at Newbury in April and skated in by 4 lengths from Premier Rose in City of York Stakes in August; ran creditably on third and fourth starts in Cecil Frail Handicap at Haydock (5 lengths second to Greenwood Star) and Jersey Stakes at Royal Ascot (went down by a neck to Hard Fought (gave 6 lb)); stays 9f but is better at shorter distances; acts on firm going; genuine; sent to USA. *F. J. Houghton.*

SUNILAWS 3 ch.f. Sandford Lad 133–Cressonnette (Saint Crespin III 132) —
(1979 5g 5fg 5f 1980 8g^{3} 8f) leggy filly; poor maiden; blinkered final outing at 2 yrs. *W. A. Stephenson.*

SUNION (GER) 2 b.c. Lombard 126–Shura (Birkhahn) (1980 6s^{3} 6fg^{2} 7fg* 93
7g* 7d^{2} 7.3fg) small, narrow, compact colt; brother to useful Sharifa, and half-

Timeform Race Card Stakes, Redcar—it takes strong Piggott riding to land Sunion a narrow winner from blinkered newcomer Canton Lightning

brother to several winners in Germany, including top 1973 3-y-o filly Sheba (by Dschingis Khan), smart middle-distance horse Schiwago (by Masetto) and German 1,000 Guineas and Oaks second Shantoo (by Charlottown); dam won at up to 10.5f in Germany; favourite when winning maiden race at Warwick in July and £2,600 event at Redcar the following month, putting up best effort in latter when staying on under strong pressure to win by a short head from Canton Lightning; 8 lengths second of 7 to K-Sera in nursery at Chester later in August; will stay 1¼m+; seems to act on any going; genuine. *M. Stoute.*

SUNITI 2 b.f. Derring-Do 131–Sounion 69 (Vimy 132) (1980 5g 7g) Mar 5; quite an attractive, lightly-made filly; half-sister to numerous winners, including Oaks third Suni (by Crepello) and very useful middle-distance performer Honorius (by Hornbeam); dam won at 1½m; 13/2, wasn't given an unnecessarily hard race once chance had gone when ninth of 19 behind Canaille in 7f maiden event at Leicester in August; should do better over further at 3 yrs. *P. Walwyn.* — p

SUNIUM 4 b.f. Roi Soleil 125–Pouponne 118 (Owen Tudor or Prince Chevalier) (1979 NR 1980 12.3d 12fg) rangy filly; unquoted when behind in maiden race at Newcastle in June and minor event at Pontefract in July. *B. McMahon.* —

SUNLEY BUILDS 2 ch.c. Patch 129–Dance Mistress (Javelot 124) (1980 7fg 7g* 7d* 10g) Mar 7; 12,000Y; quite attractive, rangy colt; third foal; dam from same family as Roan Rocket; made all to win 2 prestigious races in October, beating Western Knight 1½ lengths in Hyperion Stakes at Ascot and holding on by ¾ length from Bedford in 14-runner Houghton Stakes at Newmarket; struggling from 2½f out when 7 lengths fifth of 9 to Krug in Zetland Stakes on same course later in month; will stay 1½m; acts on a soft surface. *G. Hunter.* **97**

SUNLEY SPECIAL (USA) 2 b.f. Proud Clarion or Triple Bend–Ancora (Ribot 142) (1980 6g 7d) Apr 21; $25,000Y; third reported foal; dam sister to high-class French 7.7f to 1¼m winner Corpora; 8/1, swerved at start and was always struggling when 4¾ lengths equal fifth of 7 to Chateau Dancer in £4,000 event at York in July; 9/4, never there with a chance when eighth of 10 to Supreme Fjord in small race at Catterick three months later; bred to stay 1¼m. *G. Hunter.* **58**

SUNLIT MEMORY 3 b.f. Jimsun 121–Amore (Kashmir II 125) (1979 NR 1980 7fg 8d) neat filly; third foal; dam ran only once; in rear in maiden races at Chepstow and Salisbury (last of 14) in the summer. *R. Turnell.* —

SUNLIT RIVER 3 br.f. Roi Soleil 125–River Moy (Niagara Falls 104) (1979 5fg 5g 7s 1980 8f 10fg 9.4fg 9.4d^2 8g^3 12d 9.4g 10f 9.4fg 9s 9v) well-made filly; poor maiden; stays 9f well; suited by some give in the ground; blinkered final start. *W. Haigh.* **47**

SUNNINGDALE QUEEN 2 ch.f. Gay Fandango 132–Lisabella (Right Royal V 135) (1980 5g 7d^3 7.2d 7fg) Apr 13; 3,100F, 20,000Y; lengthy, quite attractive filly; fourth reported foal; half-sister to Irish 3-y-o Bellagold (by Rheingold), a winner at around 9f; dam, daughter of Irish Guinness Oaks winner Aurabella, won over 9f and 1¼m in France; 33/1, always in touch when creditable 3¾ lengths third of 11 to Cocaine in Acomb Stakes at York in August; didn't reproduce that form but was beaten little more than 3 lengths when sixth of 11 to Giannutri in minor event at Newbury in September on final start; will probably stay 1¼m. *B. Hills.* **88** d

SUNNYBANKS ANGEL 4 b.f. Scottish Rifle 127–Playtime (Primera 131) (1979 8fg 10.1fg 8fg^4 8fg* 8fg 8fg* 7fg 1980 7g 8fg^3 8fg 7g^4 8.3f* 8g 8g^3) leggy, lightly-built filly; plater; sold out of R. Simpson's stable 1,350 gns after making all at Windsor in August; should stay middle distances; acts on firm going; wears blinkers nowadays. *A. Pitt.* **55**

SUNNY PRINCESS 3 ch.f. Sun Prince 128–Cayenne (Hornbeam 130) (1979 7g^3 1980 12fg^4 12g 10g 12f 11.7h) tall, lengthy filly; seems only plating class; stays 1½m; acts on firm going. *R. Boss.* **64**

SUNNY SMILE 2 b.g. Mummy's Pet 125–Magic Maiden 97 (Magic Red) (1980 5f* 6fg* 5fg* 6d 6f 7g^3 6f) Apr 6; 7,400F, 21,000Y; good-looking gelding; brother to Hey Presto, 4 times a winner over 5f at 2 yrs, and fairly useful 1979 2-y-o 5f and 6f winner Petulengra, and half-brother to 2 winners; dam won over 7f; followed up wins in maiden and minor events at Lingfield and Ripon with a useful performance in well-contested race at Beverley in June, coming through strongly to win with something in hand by 1½ lengths from Tre Fontane; returned to form when 4½ lengths third of 6 to Investa under top weight in nursery at Yarmouth in September; stays 7f; acts on firm going; ran poorly final outing; exported to Singapore. *E. Eldin.* **95**

SUN OF SCHWEPPES 3 b.c. Roi Soleil 125–March Malona 88 (Derring-Do 131) (1979 7f 7fg* 6g* 1980 7v 7f 6f 7g^2 6g^3 6s 6g^3 6s) small, strong colt; poor mover; fair handicapper; suited by 7f and will stay 1m; suited by top-of-the-ground; often blinkered; ran moderately sixth start. *W. O'Gorman.* **86**

SUNSET RAY 4 br.f. Hotfoot 126–Queen of Twilight 107 (Off Key 121 or Twilight Alley 133) (1979 8g 10f 8fg^2 10.1f 10g* 1980 11f 14f^2 12g 12s^3 8g* 10g^2 8s) well-made filly; won handicap at Yarmouth in September by **69**

Houghton Stakes, Newmarket—Sunley Builds is a game winner from the strong-finishing Bedford (behind winner) and Blackfoot (rails)

neck from Coral Leisure; effective at 1m and stays 1¾m; acts on any going but is possibly best on a sound surface. *J. Winter.*

SUNSET VALUE 8 br.g. Current Coin 118–Elected 74 (Red God 128§) (1979 6d 7g 7s 7g⁴ 7fg 7g 7f 7f 7fg 1980 6d 7fg 6g 7fg 7h 7f 7g 6fg 7d 6s) one-time useful handicapper; on the downgrade; best form at up to 1m; acts on any going and on any track; ran very freely when blinkered sixth outing; good mount for an inexperienced rider. *V. Soane.* —

SUNSET WONDER 4 ch.g. Tickled Pink 114–Rainbow Wonder (Runnymede 123) (1979 8g 8f³ 12fg⁴ 8fg 8fg 1980 17.1fg⁴ 11.7f² 12fg* 13.1h⁴ 10.2g) lightly-made gelding; plater at 3 yrs; showed improved form when winning handicap at Chepstow in August by 2 lengths from La Piccolina; ran creditably afterwards; stays well; acts on firm going. *L. Kennard.* **70**

SUNSHINE GAL 2 br.f. Alto Volante 109–Chinese Princess (Sunny Way 120) (1980 8fg 8d 7d) 570Y; neat filly; third foal; half-sister to 1978 2-y-o 1m seller winner Magic Kit (by Namnan); dam unraced half-sister to very smart Streetfighter; fairly prominent in modest maiden company on first 2 outings; will be suited by 1¼m+. *N. Guest.* **63**

SUNSHINE LIE 6 b.g. Shiny Tenth 120–Liebeslust (Mangon) (1979 10v 10fg* 9.4g⁴ 11g 10g³ 10fg* 11d⁴ 10s* 10.5g 1980 10.2d 11fg* 10h² 12.3f⁴ 12.2fg⁴ 10.6g 10.2g 10fg) middle-distance handicapper; beat Pittencrieff ¾ length at Edinburgh in April; acts on any going; has been tried in blinkers; suitable mount for an apprentice. *Denys Smith.* **61**

SUNSPEED 2 b.c. Warpath 113–Croisette 95 (Sunny Way 120) (1980 7f) May 1; neat colt; first foal; dam won 9 times from 6f to 11f; 20/1, in touch to halfway when in rear in 25-runner maiden race won by Highland Range at Redcar in September; may improve over middle distances in 1981. *C. Thornton.* —

SUNWILLOW 3 gr.f. So Blessed 130–Tranquility Base 112 (Roan Rocket 128) (1979 5fg 1980 5g 8d) small, close-coupled filly; seems of no account; sold 430 gns Ascot August Sales. *P. Calver.* —

SUPER ASSET (USA) 3 b.c. Sir Ivor 135–Sunday Purchase (T. V. Lark) (1979 7f² 7fg* 7g* 7.3g* 1980 10.4f 10.1f² 12g) good-looking colt; second foal; half-brother to a winner in USA by Hawaii; dam, winner of 1m maiden **113**

Mr Michael Doyle Riordan's "Super Asset"

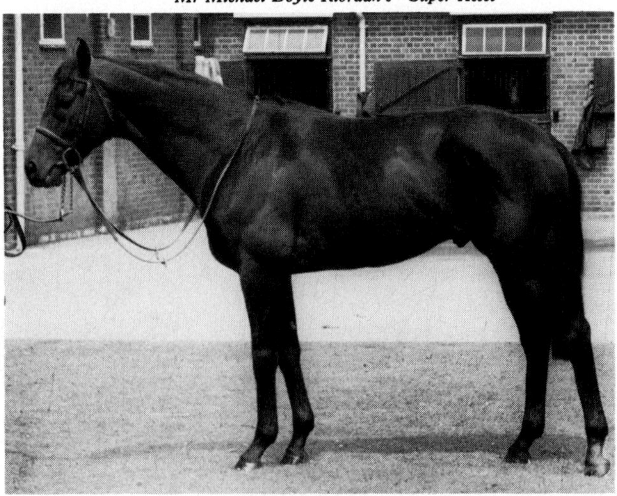

race, is half-sister to high-class 1971 2-y-o Rest Your Case and very smart filly Charming Story, and to the dam of top-class filly Optimistic Gal (by Sir Ivor); very smart at 2 yrs, when he won 3 races, notably 4-runner Horris Hill Stakes at Newbury; length second to Moomba Masquerade in 4-runner minor race at Windsor in May, easily best effort in 1980; burly first outing and finished last of 9 in King Edward VII Stakes at Royal Ascot on final start; should have stayed 1½m; acted on firm going; genuine; standing at Panorama Farm, Ocala, Florida at a fee of $7,500. *H. Cecil.*

SUPERB LADY 4 b.f. Marcus Superbus 100–Nasca 81 (King's Bench 132) (1979 5d4 5s2 5v* 5g* 5d3 5d2 5fg4 1980 5g 5fg 5f 5f 5f 5.8fg 5d 5g 5fg 6s) compact filly; useful performer at her best; didn't run up to her best in 1980 (tried in blinkers sixth outing); best form at 5f; acts on any going; sold 8,200 gns Newmarket December Sales. *K. Ivory.* —

SUPERB MUSIC 2 b.f. Music Boy 124–Prefer (Preciptic 122) (1980 5v4 5fg3 5f2 5fg 5h2 5fg4 5fg* 5.1g2 5f 5.3fg 5d3 5.1fg* 5fg 6g) May 22; 1,800F, 1,200Y; small filly; half-sister to several minor winners; dam placed at 3 yrs and 4 yrs in Ireland; made all to win 6-runner sellers at Lingfield in June and Yarmouth in August; sold out of K. Ivory's stable 2,000 gns after holding off Mount Eliza gamely by ½ length on latter course; had stiff task in nursery and was tailed off when tried over 6f; seems to act on any going. *M. Ryan.* 60

SUPER EAGLE 2 b.g. Legal Eagle 126–Superbum 69 (Super Sam 124) (1980 5v 5d 5f3 6g 7g 5s 8.2g 8s 5s) Feb 24; 5,000Y; small, strong gelding; bad plater; should stay 1m; blinkered sixth outing. *W. Marshall.* 48

SUPER FELLA 3 ch.c. Touch Paper 113–Joanart (Atan) (1979 5fg 5f 1980 7fg 10fg 8g) well-made, good sort; behind in maiden races; sold 625 gns Ascot November Sales. *G. Hunter.* —

SUPER FIT 3 b.c. Communication 119–Smoke Room (Road House II) (1979 5v 5s 5s 5f 7f 1980 8.2s 5h 7f 6fg 7fg4 8s 7g 10fg) lengthy colt; plater; best run at 7f on a firm surface; wears blinkers; sold 480 gns Doncaster September Sales. *W. Clay.* —

SUPER HOSTESS 2 ch.f. Red Alert 127–Saint Veronica (Saint Crespin III 132) (1980 5f 5f 6fg 7g 6fg) May 6; 4,400Y; robust filly; closely related to a winner in Italy by St Alphage and half-sister to 2 winners; no worthwhile form, including in a seller; sold 460 gns Ascot August Sales. *R. Hannon.* —

SUPERIOR SAINT 2 b.c. Welsh Saint 126–Superina 62 (Super Sam 124) (1980 5f 5fg 6g 6g3 7d 7d 8g 7s 7s4) Jan 31; 4,500F, 7,200Y; strong, compact, short-legged colt; third produce; dam won 5f seller at 2 yrs; quite a moderate colt; stays 1m; blinkered sixth outing. *R. Hannon.* 78

SUPERNACULUM 6 gr.g. Supreme Sovereign 119–Perpelia (Red God 128§) (1979 NR 1980 8g 12d 10d 10g 16f) quite a moderate handicapper: stays 1¼m; acts on a firm and a soft surface; used to wear blinkers; slowly away first 2 outings. *M. Tate.* —

SUPER RUN 2 b.c. Run The Gantlet–Super Honey 118 (Tesco Boy 121) (1980 6s 7d 7.2d) May 5; 5,600Y; rangy colt; brother to poor animal, and half-brother to unraced stallion Energist (by Graustark); dam second in 1,000 Guineas; fairly prominent in maiden races at Windsor on first outing (fifth of 25) and Haydock on third (seventh of 19); will be suited by 1¼m. *F. J. Houghton.* —

SUPER SEASON 2 ch.g. Silly Season 127–Floral Gift 84 (Princely Gift 137) (1980 6g 7fg) Feb 18; 5,800Y; strong, good sort; brother to useful 3-y-o miler April Bouquet, and half-brother to 7f and 1m winner Best Offer (by Crepello) and a winner in Malaya; dam won over 5f at 2 yrs; in rear in £5,900 event at Doncaster and 19-runner maiden race at Leicester in September, finishing tailed off in latter; subsequently gelded. *R. Hollinshead.* —

SUPER SERVICE 2 b.c. Rheingold 137–Ensnarer (Bold Ruler) (1980 6d 7f2 8d 8d) June 28; 16,000F; lengthy, attractive colt; good mover; brother to winning Italian 3-y-o Starring and half-brother to 1976 2-y-o 1m winner Catchword (by Mountain Call); dam unraced daughter of top 1967 Brazilian filly Embuche; neck second of 11 to Glint of Gold in Sandwich Stakes at Ascot in July after disputing lead all way; not seen out again until late-October and ran moderately; should stay at least 1m; possibly needs a firm surface. *P. Walwyn.* 94 ?

SUPER SMILE 2 b. or br.c. High Top 131–Hedge Warbler 89 (Sing Sing 134) (1980 5f 6d3 6g 5f3 5g* 5f 6g 5d) Jan 25; 14,500Y; compact, rather lightly-made colt; second produce; half-brother to a winner in Italy by Blakeney; 83

dam won over 6f and 1m; favourite when winning 17-runner maiden race at Bath in September by ¾ length from Prince Copper; creditable fifth in good nurseries won by Katysue and Amorous respectively at Newmarket on next 2 outings, apprentice ridden on first occasion; stays 6f; acts on firm going and a soft surface; badly drawn final start. *N. Callaghan.*

SUPER SPARTAN 2 ch.c. Roi Soleil 125–Last Summer 66 (Will Somers 114 §) (1980 5fg 6d 7fg 6f* 6g 8f³ 7f 8.2s 8d⁴) Feb 18; 5,000F, 5,200Y; strong, lengthy colt; half-brother to 3 winning platers and a winner in Spain; dam fair plater at 2 yrs; sold out of T. Fairhurst's stable 3,500 gns after winning 14-runner seller at Thirsk in August by 2 lengths from Georgina Girl; stays 1m; seems to act on any going; blinkered sixth to eighth outings but does as well without. *J. Etherington.* **68**

SUPER SWALLOW 5 ch.m. My Swallow 134–Blue Bird 84 (Majority Blue 126) (1979 12s 16g* 15f 15.8fg⁴ 16g* 16g⁴ 16fg 15fg⁴ 14.6g² 1980 12f 15.8fg 14.6fg* 16g³ 19f 15.8g² 16g 16g⁴ 16fg 15d) staying handicapper; held on bravely when beating Wild Rosie and 3 others in a driving finish at Doncaster in June; probably wasn't at her best on very firm ground; was good mount for an apprentice; dead. *M. Camacho.* **51**

SUPERTRAMP 2 b.g. Mummy's Pet 125–Babanina (Bleep-Bleep 134) (1980 5fg⁴ 5g* 5g 5g 5d 6f 5s) Mar 9; 1,200F, 7,200Y; useful sort; fourth living foal; dam unraced sister to useful sprinter Charicles; landed the odds in good style in small race at Ripon in June, beating Miss Twiggy 3 lengths; beaten favourite on 2 of his subsequent outings, sweating up a lot and going to post very freely at Beverley on third start and finishing seventh of 11 when apprentice ridden in nursery at Edinburgh on fifth; not sure to stay 6f. *J. Fitzgerald.* **82**

SUPINE 2 b.f. Supreme Sovereign 119–Twilight Lady (Shantung 132) (1980 5d* 6g² 6fg) May 1; well-made filly; third reported foal; dam unraced sister to dam of 1,000 Guineas winner Nocturnal Spree (by Supreme Sovereign); 33/1 and burly when winning 23-runner maiden race at Salisbury in June by 1½ lengths from Bright Landing; looked very dangerous 1f out in St Catherine's Stakes at Newbury the following month but couldn't sustain challenge and went down by 1½ lengths to odds-on Stats Emmar, better subsequent effort; will stay 1m; fairly useful. *R. Hern.* **95**

SUPPER'S READY (USA) 2 br.c. Nalees Man–Irish Wedding (Advocator) (1980 5d 6g³ 5d* 6g² 7d*) Apr 2; $25,000Y; lightly-made colt; second foal; half-brother to a winner; dam stakes-placed winner at up to 6f; sire, stakes winner, won over 6f and 8.5f; came through to win 13-runner maiden race at Windsor in July and 14-runner nursery at Goodwood 2 months later, latter by a head from Harp Strings when ridden by 5-lb claimer; will stay at least 1m; yet to race on a firm surface. *H. Candy.* **98**

SUPREME COIN 3 br.c. Great Nephew 126–Pennycuick 101 (Celtic Ash) (1979 6fg 1980 10f 10f² 10.8s² 11.7f* 12g 11.7fg) neat, useful sort; favourite, won maiden race at Bath in July; stays 1½m; acts well on firm going; ran moderately last 2 starts, wearing blinkers on second occasion; sold 4,000 gns Newmarket Autumn Sales. *P. Walwyn.* **75**

SUPREME FJORD 2 ch.f. Targowice 130–Macaw 85 (Narrator 127) (1980 6fg 7g³ 8fg 7d* 7d² 7v*) Apr 11; 15,000Y; small, lightly-made filly; half-sister to 2 winners, including prolific 6f to 1m winner Northleach (by Northfields); dam won over 1m; won small race at Catterick in October by a neck from Zambo and well-contested nursery at Doncaster in November by 4 lengths from Stormy Jim; better at 7f than 1m; very well suited by some give in the ground; good mount for an apprentice. *M. Jarvis.* **92**

SUPREME FOLLY 3 br.f. Supreme Sovereign 119–Past Folly 90 (Narrator 127) (1979 NR 1980 10.1g) half-sister to several minor winners; dam middle-distance performer; tailed-off last in minor event at Windsor in August. *R. Simpson.* **—**

SUPREME RULER 3 ch.g. Sovereign Path 125–Marble Cloud (Hard Tack 111 §) (1979 5s 6s 6fg 1980 6d 8s 10f² 12fg⁴ 11.7f² 12f⁴ 16f² 16d 16.9d) good-looking gelding; runner-up in handicaps and a maiden race; stays 2m; needs top-of-the-ground conditions; has run respectably for an apprentice. *A. Goodwill.* **60**

SUPREME SHOW 2 gr. rig. Supreme Sovereign 119–Drury Lane 83 (Gala Performance) (1980 5d 5f 6fg 6g*) May 20; 1,500Y; quite a useful sort; bad mover; second foal; dam won over 1m; made all from a favourable draw when winning £2,700 seller at York in October by 2½ lengths from Mull of **77 ?**

Kintyre with 19 others well beaten off; sold 5,200 gns afterwards, probably for export; will stay 7f. *Hbt Jones.*

SURFER 3 ch.g. Gulf Pearl 117–Land Ho (Primera 131) (1979 NR 1980 8g 10.1g^2) attractive gelding; third live foal; half-brother to 2 winners by Swing Easy, including very useful 1976 5f winner Easy Landing; dam daughter of very smart sprinter Lucasland; staying-on second of 15 to Ballytop in minor event at Windsor in July; not seen out again and was gelded; may stay 1½m. *J. Tree.* **68**

SUSAN GREGORY 3 ch.f. Good Bond 122–Miss Vanadium (Helmar) (1979 5g 1980 5h 6fg 7g 8s) small, light-framed filly; well beaten in varied company. *J. Toller.* **–**

SUSANNA (USA) 2 b.f. Nijinsky 138–Full Dress II 115 (Shantung 132) (1980 6f 7g) big, strong, attractive filly; half-sister to useful 1m winner Fairly Hot (by Sir Ivor); dam won 1969 1,000 Guineas; backward when last in good-class fillies races at Ascot and Newmarket, showing up well until lack of fitness told 2f out in race won by Exclusively Raised on latter course in August; a very taking, well-bred filly who is likely to do very much better over 1m+ at 3 yrs. *H. Wragg.* **–** p

SUSAN'S SUNSET 2 br.f. Welsh Saint 126–Honi Soit (Above Suspicion 127) (1980 5fg 5fg 5g 6g 7g 8d) Feb 25; 4,500Y; neat filly; sister to Clanrickard, winner twice over 5f at 2 yrs in Ireland in 1977, and half-sister to another 2-y-o winner; dam poor Irish maiden; only plating class; ran best races over 7f and 1m. *S. Woodman.* **61**

SUSARMA (USA) 4 gr.c. Tudor Grey 119–Maui Moon (Swoon's Son) (1979 5s* 5s* 5s 5fg 5g^2 5g 5fg^3 5.6fg 5fg* 5s* 1980 5g* 5f^3 5f^2 5f^3 6fg^4 5f* 5fg 5fg 5f^3) strong, short-legged colt; good mover; useful handicapper; won at Epsom in April (narrowly from Ferryman) and June (smoothly from Gold Song); in frame on most of his other starts, on fourth outing finishing 4½ lengths third to Sharpo in Temple Stakes at Sandown; best form at 5f but may be worth another chance over 6f (given plenty to do and wasn't knocked about on only attempt so far); acts on any going; blinkered eighth outing at 3 yrs; consistent. *A. Breasley.* **107**

SUZANNE'S PRINCE 3 ch.g. Shiny Tenth 120–Ballyceltic (Balidar 133) (1979 6g 8fg 1980 10.8v 12fg 16g 10fg 12d) compact gelding; poor maiden. *M. Eckley.* **–**

SWAGGER STICK 5 br.g. Brigadier Gerard 144–Lupulin 68 (Romulus 129) (1979 10f 10.2fg 10h 11g 12fg^3 15fg^3 12.2fg* 12g^2 1980 13g^2 12f* 12fg^4 10.6g* 12.3g) won handicaps at Thirsk in May and Haydock (amateur riders) in June, latter by ½ length from Wickwell; stays 15f; needs a sound surface; suited by a strong gallop; joined I. Wardle after final outing. *E. Weymes.* **79**

SWALLANGA 2 ch.c. My Swallow 134–Vanga (Rockavon 120) (1980 6d^2) brother to very useful Command Freddy, successful at up to 1m in France, and half-brother to 2 winners, including very useful 6f to 1¼m performer Ridaness (by Ridan); dam won at up to 1½m in France; 33/1, prominent throughout when 6 lengths second of 19 to impressive winner Storm Bird in maiden race at the Curragh in July; looked promising but wasn't seen out again; will stay at least 1m. *L. Browne, Ireland.* **84** p

SWAN PRINCESS 2 br.f. So Blessed 130–Swan Ann 84 (My Swanee 122) (1980 5d* 5f^3 5h* 5f^2 5fg^4 5g^2 5fg^2 5g* 5g) **106**

Swan Princess is a filly with tremendous nervous energy. She's like a coiled spring and unfortunately the spring occasionally unwinds far faster than intended. At Newmarket in April she put up a deplorable effort after tearing down to the start, a performance we excused on the grounds that she was found to be running a temperature, but at Epsom in June no less a jockey than Piggott was unable to hold her on the way to post. She virtually bolted, cracked Piggott's knee against the running rail and had to be withdrawn at the start. Thereafter she was always taken down very quietly, often well in advance of the others, and was much more controllable.

At her best Swan Princess is an exceptionally speedy filly. She made all for each of her three successes, the first of which came on the third day of the season at Doncaster when she slammed fourteen other fillies despite careering about. Two opponents failed to get her off the bit in the Metropole Challenge Cup at Folkestone in May, and in August she became the eleventh filly in the last twelve years to win the valuable Gallaghouse Phoenix Stakes. She shot out of the stalls at Phoenix Park, quickly establishing a clear lead that was to last until the final furlong, and then held on gamely as her stamina began to run out. She held off the favourite Band Practice by a head. Incidentally while on the subject of the Phoenix Stakes, we are at a loss to understand why the Pattern Race Committee promoted the race from Group 2 to Group 1 in 1979. Of the last dozen Phoenix Stakes winners only Noble Mark and Kilijaro went on to win a pattern race in following seasons and surely the Irish have another race more worthy of Group 1 status in the National Stakes, a race won over the same period by such as Decies, King's Company and Pampapaul, all subsequent winners of the Irish Two Thousand Guineas, and by Tap On Wood and Roberto, winners of the Two Thousand Guineas and Derby respectively.

To return to Swan Princess, she failed to last out the trip on her other outings in valuable races. In both the Windsor Castle Stakes at Royal Ascot and the National Stakes at Sandown she maintained her lead until inside the final furlong before finishing respectively a three-and-half-length fourth to Cooliney Prince and a three-length second to Penmarric; in the Molecomb Stakes at Goodwood she led Marwell to below the distance and then hung on to finish second, beaten two and a half lengths; and in the William Hill Sprint Championship at York in August on her last appearance she matched strides for a long way with several of the leading older sprinters before fading to finish a respectable sixth of eleven to Sharpo.

Swan Princess (br.f. Mar 8, 1978)	So Blessed (br 1965)	Princely Gift (b 1951)	Nasrullah
			Blue Gem
		Lavant (b 1955)	Le Lavandou
			Firle
	Swan Ann (ch 1971)	My Swanee (gr 1963)	Petition
			Grey Rhythm
		Anna Barry (ch 1964)	Falls of Clyde
			Anagram

It was to be expected that Swan Princess, a good sort of filly who cost 13,000 guineas as a yearling, would turn out a sprinter. Although she's a half-sister to Poyle Crusher, a useful three-year-old by Sweet Revenge who stays a mile, very few from her female line have stayed so far. Swan Ann, a half-sister to the useful five-furlong performer Heywood Hardy, gained her sole success over six furlongs and both Anna Barry and Anagram were best at the minimum distance. Only one of Anagram's seven winners won over further than six furlongs and among her best performers were the fast 1974 two-year-old Strictly Private and the prolific sprint winner Kiyoswanee, who like Swan Ann was by My Swanee.

Swan Princess' owner has paid £140 to enter her for the One Thousand Guineas. He should have saved his money as she has no prospects of staying beyond five furlongs. In theory a sound surface should suit her best since it should make fewer demands on her stamina, but in practice she seems to act on any going. *B. Swift.*

SWAN RIVER 2 ch.f. Roan Rocket 128–Parmelia 118 (Ballymoss 136) (1980 6s^4 6g) June 6; compact filly; half-sister to 3 winners, including very useful miler Rebec (by Tudor Melody) and useful stayer Ormeley (by Crepello); dam, half-sister to St Paddy, won Park Hill Stakes; ran respectably for a newcomer when 1¾ lengths fourth of 6 to Sovereign Flame in maiden race at Ayr in August; favourite, spoilt chance by hanging badly right when 7 lengths fifth to Holdall in 9-runner minor event at Ripon later in month; will be suited by 1¼m. *E. Weymes.* **70**

SWAN UPPING 3 ch.f. Lord Gayle 124–The Swan (My Swanee 122) (1979 6s^2 6fg 6s^4 1980 7fg* 10.4f 8f^3 11fg^3 11g^4 9g 9d* 8f^2 8d* 8fg 8d 7s) neat, well-made filly; won maiden race at Edinburgh in April, apprentice event at Ripon in August and handicap at Edinburgh in September; stays 11f but is better at shorter distances; probably acts on any going; suitable mount for a boy. *W. Elsey.* **71**

SWAYING TREE 3 ch.g. Swing Easy 126–My Bushbaby 100 (Hul a Hul 124) (1979 6fg 1980 7g 6fg^2 6g* 7g* 6f) strong gelding; carries plenty of condition; successful in handicaps at Ripon and Redcar in August, holding off Lorna Crique by a neck on latter; suited by 7f; yet to race on a soft surface; has worn bandages; ridden by 5-lb claimer at Redcar. *R. D. Peacock.* **76**

SWEATER GIRL 3 ch.f. Blue Cashmere 129–Dick's Yarn 80 (Peter's Yarn 106) (1979 5f 5f 7g 1980 7f 7d 10.1f 12d 14.6d^2 12f^4 14.7f^4 12s*) light-framed filly; good mover; won modest maiden race at Hamilton in October; stays 1¾m; acts well on soft ground; apprentice ridden when successful; sold 3,000 gns Newmarket December Sales. *F. Durr.* **70**

SWEDISH RHAPSODY 2 br.f. Targowice 130–Tuola (High Flown 117) (1980 5f4 5g* 6d4 7g2 7fg4) Apr 22; 2,600Y; useful-looking filly; good mover; second reported foal; dam won 3 races in Scandinavia, and finished fifth in Swedish 1,000 Guineas and Oaks; hard ridden to win 12-runner maiden auction event at Haydock in June by short head from Jade Empress; creditable second to Joint Command in nursery at Yarmouth in August; will probably stay 1m. *G. Pritchard-Gordon.* **81**

SWEET AND SOUR 3 ch.f. Sharpen Up 127–First Delight 80 (Primera 131) (1979 5g 5fg2 5s 5g4 6f2 5fg* 1980 7f2 7fg 7.3f 8.5f) useful-looking filly; close second in 21-runner handicap at Newmarket in April; put up a temperamental display in similar event on same course next start, refusing to race after being very troublesome leaving paddock; should be suited by 1m; acts on firm going; one to be wary of. *J. Bethell.* **79 §**

SWEET AS A NUT 4 b.f. Birdbrook 110–Roman Dawn 87 (Neron 121) (1979 6g 7s2 7fg 6g* 7fg 1980 6fg 6g 6g 6s2 7d) tall, lengthy filly; beaten a head by Ilsa Kempinski in handicap at Chepstow in October; stays 7f; best form with some give in the ground; suitable mount for an apprentice. *W. Wightman.* **53**

SWEET BISCUIT 3 br.f. Biskrah 121–Perfume Ali (Baba Ali 111) (1979 NR 1980 12h 16s 16s) second foal; half-sister to a winning hurdler; dam ran once in Ireland; behind in maiden and minor races; sold 420 gns Ascot July Sales. *Miss A. Sinclair.* **–**

SWEET COMPENSATION 3 b.g. Sweet Revenge 129–Sweet Slavery 88 (Manacle 123) (1979 5d 5s 5d* 5d4 5s3 5g 5fg 5f 6fg 1980 5s 7f 7f 8fg 6g 7g 7fg 8fg* 8fg) stocky gelding; fair (rated 85) at 2 yrs; plater nowadays; attracted no bid after winning at Yarmouth in August; stays 1m; probably acts on any going; retained 1,600 gns Newmarket July Sales. *W. Marshall.* **62**

SWEET DIPPER 3 br.c. Golden Dipper 119–Sharp and Sweet (Javelot 124) (1979 5v2 5s* 6fg3 1980 7s4 7fg4 6fg 7fg*) quite a moderate handicapper; ran on courageously to win at Warwick in June by a length from Lady Ember; stays 7f; probably acts on any going; has run creditably for an apprentice. *P. Cole.* **74**

SWEET ENCHANTMENT 3 br.f. Birdbrook 110–Star Abbess 86 (Welsh Abbot 131) (1979 5f 1980 7d 10f 11.7g 12f) lengthy filly; well beaten in Southern maiden and minor races. *M. Masson.* **–**

SWEET FORTUNE 3 ch.f. Dubassoff–Fingerofortune 100 (Fortino II 120) (1979 5s 5d 5f4 6fg 5g 8h 1980 6f 6f 7f) leggy filly; bad plater; has worn blinkers; sold 500 gns Doncaster August Sales. *A. Balding.* **–**

SWEET HIGHNESS 2 ch.f. Sweet Revenge 129–Her Worship 61 (Privy Councillor 125) (1980 5fg) Jan 15; 3,500Y; well-grown filly; half-sister to 7.6f winner Unexpected (by Laser Light) and a winner in Malaya; dam placed over 9f; 50/1 and apprentice ridden when behind in 18-runner maiden race won by Another Realm at Windsor in May; unseated rider at start, bolted and was withdrawn on one occasion. *M. Ryan.* **–**

SWEETHILL 2 gr.f. Runnymede 123–Clouded Lamp 99 (Nimbus 130) (1980 5f 5fg 5.8fg 5.8fg 7d4 7f 6g 7g) Apr 6; 6,100F, 9,000Y; strong, useful sort; sister to useful 5f performer Canton Silk, and half-sister to several winners, including very useful sprinter Irma Flintstone (by Compensation); dam miler; only plating class; best form at 7f; blinkered fifth and sixth outings. *M. McCormack.* **60**

SWEET JANE 3 b.f. Furry Glen 121–Red Sunrise (Red God 128 §) (1979 5f 1980 6fg 6f 5fg3 5d2 5d3 6s 5g 5f 7g) rangy filly; sprint handicapper; best form at 5f; acts on a firm and a soft surface. *R. Smyth.* **59**

SWEET JASMINE 2 b.f. Jimmy Reppin 131–Flora Day 92 (Floribunda 136) (1980 5g 7f 6g4) Jan 22; compact filly; good walker; fourth foal; dam stayed 1m; blinkered and dropped in class, ran best race when just over 4 lengths fourth of 19 to La Fedhala in seller at Goodwood in September; should stay 7f; sold 700 gns Newmarket Autumn Sales. *H. Candy.* **62**

SWEET LOUISE 3 b.f. Sweet Revenge 129–Tropical Fruit (Tropique 128) (1979 5d 5d 5v2 5s 5fg 5fg 5s 6d 7s 1980 8s 8s) tall, workmanlike filly; plating-class maiden; best run at 5f on heavy going; wears blinkers. *P. Feilden.* **–**

SWEET MARK BOY 4 ch.c. Decoy Boy 129–Sweet Reason (Elopement 125) (1979 5v2 5v2 7s2 7d* 6g 8s 7fg4 8f 8fg 1980 7v 8fg 7g 7d 8d) strong colt; quite a moderate handicapper; best form at 7f; seems to act on any going; **–**

ran poorly when tried in blinkers; sold to J. Jenkins 520 gns Newmarket Autumn Sales. *J. Benstead.*

SWEET MONDAY 2 b.c. Sweet Revenge 129–Solly Graham 82 (Romulus 129) **122**
(1980 5f 5.8fg[2] 6fg* 6fg[4] 6fg*)

In these days of the million-dollar yearling it's heartening for the ordinary owner to see that high-class horses can still be picked up relatively cheaply: Ela-Mana-Mou, Moorestyle and Cairn Rouge were each purchased for less than 5,000 guineas as yearlings. Even cheaper than those as a yearling was the Mill Reef Stakes winner Sweet Monday, who changed hands in a private transaction at the Doncaster Sales for the bargain price of 2,100 guineas, 1,200 guineas less than he'd cost as a foal.

Sweet Monday's performance in the Mill Reef at Newbury established him as one of the best of the juvenile sprinters and marked a considerable advance on his previous form. He had won one of his four races, the Selsey Maiden Stakes at Goodwood in July in which he'd beaten Bracadale a length and a half in fast time, but he had subsequently been beaten over five lengths into fourth place behind Cut Throat in the Sirenia Stakes at Kempton, just a fortnight before Newbury. His running at Kempton was better than it might have seemed: he had held a good position until losing several lengths jumping a path at around halfway and his jockey wasn't at all hard on him once the leaders clearly had his measure. Sweet Monday made no such mistake in the Mill Reef. After disputing the lead with Mattaboy from the start he took a definite advantage at the distance and gradually drew away to win by a length and a half, Mattaboy holding on to second place by two lengths from Poldhu. The form was made to look better twelve days later when Mattaboy and Poldhu took first and third places in the William Hill Middle Park Stakes.

It is evidently the intention of Sweet Monday's trainer to run him in the Two Thousand Guineas. However, it's questionable whether Sweet Monday will be good enough or have the stamina to win the race. In our opinion six or seven furlongs will be his trip: his sire Sweet Revenge, although a winner over seven furlongs, was undoubtedly best at sprint distances and his dam Solly Graham, who was placed several times at up to a mile, is a daughter of the useful sprinter Solensister, herself a sister to the very useful Solennis who did all her winning over five and six furlongs.

Mill Reef Stakes, Newbury—Sweet Monday wins from Mattaboy

Sweet Monday (b.c. Mar 17, 1978)	Sweet Revenge (ch 1967)	Compensation (ch 1959)	Gratitude Shillelagh
		Too Much Honey (ch 1952)	Honeyway Honey Hill
	Solly Graham (br 1968)	Romulus (b 1959)	Ribot Arietta
		Solensister (b 1963)	Ennis Soloneire

As is to be expected of a 2,100-guinea yearling, Sweet Monday, a lengthy, good-bodied colt, comes from a family which is nothing out of the ordinary. None of Solly Graham's four previous foals managed to win in Britain, although one won twice in Barbados, and Solensister's only successful offspring have been Summer Serenade, a minor winner on the flat who later won selling hurdles, and the winning hurdler Solentown. No matter how moderate his relatives, Sweet Monday is a good-class colt and he'll figure prominently in more top races if not in the Guineas. As yet he has raced only on a firm surface which clearly suits him well but it's worth remembering that he comes from a male line noted for producing soft-ground performers. He races with enthusiasm, and racegoers shouldn't be put off by his habit of sweating up profusely in the preliminaries. *J. Holt.*

SWEET MUSIC 2 br.f. More Music 61–Brass (Sovereign Path 125) (1980 5fg 5f 6g) Feb 27; 620Y; unfurnished filly; half-sister to several winners; in rear in maiden and minor events and a seller; blinkered first and third outings; sold 360 gns Ascot August Sales. *B. Gubby.* —

SWEET PLEASURE 2 b.f. Sweet Revenge 129–Arrangement 72 (Floribunda 136) (1980 7g 6g* 6s 6fg) Mar 29; 12,000Y; strong, good sort; half-sister to fair 5f winner Strictly Swing (by Swing Easy); dam stayed 7f; 25/1, ran on strongly to win 11-runner Convivial Stakes at York in August by a neck from Middlin Thrang; well-beaten sixth of 7 to Star Pastures in £6,500 race at Ayr the following month and moved badly to start prior to finishing tailed-off last of 8 to Marwell in William Hill Cheveley Park Stakes at Newmarket in October; not sure to stay 7f. *C. Nelson.* 83

SWEET PRETENDER (USA) 3 b.c. Pretense–Anne la Douce 123 (Silnet 131) (1979 7s 8g* 7.5g 10s^{2} 1980 8.5f 12.3f 12g^{3} 8.2d 8g^{4} 8s) neat, quite attractive colt; won 12-runner maiden race at Chantilly in 1979; showed no ability in varied company at 3 yrs; should stay 1½m; blinkered fifth start; out of his depth first 3 outings; sold 7,000 gns Newmarket December Sales. *D. Sasse.* —

SWEET RIDE 4 b.f. Sweet Revenge 129–Margaret's Ruby (Tesco Boy 121) (1979 8d 6g 6f 8d 10g 7fg* 1980 8s 7fg 7f 7fg 7fg 6g* 8g 6g^{3} 5.8g) lengthy filly; won 25-runner handicap at Windsor in June; best form at up to 7f; acts on a firm surface; wears blinkers; sold 3,500 gns Newmarket December Sales. *S. Matthews.* 64

SWEET SCULPTRESS 2 br.f. Arch Sculptor 123–Sweet Gem 102 (Hard Sauce 131) (1980 5s 5fg^{2} 5h^{3}(dis)) Feb 13; 600F, 560Y; compact filly; fifth foal; half-sister to a winner in Trinidad; dam stayed 1¼m; placed in sellers at Wolverhampton and Stockton in April but was disqualified on latter course after finishing 1½ lengths third to Jenny Barco; will stay 6f; didn't keep a straight course when apprentice ridden on third outing; claimed at Stockton. *W. Musson.* 48

SWEET SPARK 2 b.f. Hot Spark 126–Sweet Serenade 93 (High Perch 126) (1980 5f* 6g 6d^{3}) Apr 29; 10,000Y; lightly-made filly; half-sister to 3 winners, including 3-y-o 1½m winner El Kabir (by Green God); dam won over 6f at 2 yrs; always close up when winning 16-runner maiden race at Wolverhampton in August by a comfortable neck from odds-on Faiz; not disgraced subsequently in minor event at Windsor and nursery at Haydock (10 lengths third of 16 to Ponchielli); stays 6f; seems to act on any going. *B. Hills.* 77

SWEET STEAL 3 br.g. Steel Heart 128–Gay Baby 101 (Galivanter 131) (1979 5s* 5v 5d^{3} 5fg* 5fg 5fg^{2} 5fg^{4} 5g 5d^{3} 6d 1980 5v 6v* 6f 6f* 6f 5g^{3} 6g 6fg) 4,000Y; robust gelding; half-brother to 2 winners, including fairly useful sprinter Laughing Goddess (by Green God); dam speedy 2-y-o; useful performer; successful in 2 handicaps at Phoenix Park and also ran creditably on fifth and sixth starts, finishing 3½ lengths fifth of 6 to Jasmine Star in Greenlands Stakes at the Curragh and third, beaten 6 lengths, to Monroe in Ballyogan Stakes at Leopardstown; in rear in 20-runner Cork and Orrery 90

Stakes at Royal Ascot on seventh outing; stays 6f; acts on any going. *A. Maxwell, Ireland.*

SWEET TANGO 2 b.f. Gay Fandango 132–Rogan Honey (Abernant 142) (1980 5f) Apr 30; 6,400F, 24,000Y; half-sister to 3 winners, including fairly useful 3-y-o Honey Barron (by Pitcairn), successful at up to 7f; dam placed over sprint distances at 2 yrs in Ireland; 12/1 when behind in 18-runner maiden event won by Blue Lass at Folkestone in September. *F. Durr.* –

SWELTER 4 br.f. Tickled Pink 114–Sun Queen 76 (Lucky Sovereign) (1979 5s 5s* 5d⁴ 5g* 5fg 5g³ 5s 5g² 5fg 1980 5d* 5d* 5d* 5.6g* 5g) slightly hollow-backed filly; developed into a useful handicapper; put up a good performance to win William Hill Portland Handicap at Doncaster in September, making all on stand side and running on gamely to hold off Sparkling Boy by a neck; reportedly had a setback afterwards and finished last of 11 behind Walter Osborne at York the following month; successful earlier at Wolverhampton, Newmarket (made all) and Haydock; speedy and is best at around 5f; probably acts on any going but seems suited by some give in the ground. *F. Durr.* **99**

SWIFT ACRE 2 ch.f. Bay Express 132–Misacre 66 (St Alphage 119) (1980 5g) Apr 28; first reported foal; dam only plating class; very weak in market, never showed behind Advertrack in 19-runner maiden race at Folkestone in October. *A. Breasley.* –

SWIFT IMAGE 3 b.c. Bay Express 132–Primage 99 (Primera 131) (1979 6g² 7f* 7f* 1980 7f 8fg 7.2fg 6d) strong, rangy, attractive colt; ran creditably on first 2 starts when sixth to Final Straw in Clerical, Medical Greenham Stakes at Newbury in April and to subsequently-disqualified Nureyev (beaten just over 7 lengths) in 2,000 Guineas at Newmarket following month; well beaten subsequently in John of Gaunt Stakes at Haydock and William Hill July Cup at Newmarket (last of 14); stays 1m; acts well on firm going; very useful. *J. Winter.* **113**

SWIFT KISS 3 b.c. Sparkler 130–Fiery Kiss 82 (Floribunda 136) (1979 5d² 5s³ 6fg 8fg*(dis) 8g* 8fg³ 1980 8f 8fg 10fg³ 10s 10fg 11.7d 10.8d 12.5s) neat colt; moderate handicapper; stays 1½m; acts on a firm and a soft surface: ran moderately fifth and final starts; sold 3,600 gns Newmarket Autumn Sales. *B. Hills.* **82**

SWIFT PALM 3 b.g. Some Hand 119–March Stone 84 (March Past 124) (1979 5g³ 5fg 6s 6s 1980 8d 8.2d² 10.6f* 12fg) lengthy gelding; won handicap at Haydock in May; ran poorly 2 days later and wasn't seen out again; stays 1¼m; appears to act on any going. *P. Cundell.* **66**

SWIFT SAINT 2 br.c. Welsh Saint 126–Ciao (Mandamus 120) (1980 7f) Feb 21; 4,700Y; first living foal; dam Irish 5f winner; unquoted and in need of race, moved poorly to start and was soon tailed off when last of 18 to Blackfoot in maiden race at Newmarket in October; sold 410 gns Ascot November Sales. *A. Goodwill.* –

SWIFT STEP (USA) 2 b.g. Shecky Greene–Fur Boots 94 (Northern Dancer) (1980 5f 6d 7g 7g 7g) Apr 13; $57,000Y; robust, good sort; fourth foal; half-brother to 2 winners; dam, closely related to very useful middle-distance colt Stoned, won over 1¼m; ran easily best race when making progress to finish 6½ lengths sixth of 18 to Price of Peace in maiden race at Salisbury in July, third outing; will stay 1m; sweated up and ran badly final start; subsequently gelded. *G. Balding.* **61**

SWINGAGAIN 2 b. or br.f. Swing Easy 126–Jeldi 58 (Tribal Chief 125) (1980 5d 5f* 5f 5fg 6g) Feb 28; small, lightly-made filly; good mover; third foal; half-sister to a winner in Malaya; dam ran only at 2 yrs; bought in 1,000 gns after making all to win seller at Beverley in April by 3 lengths from Alison Nicola; subsequently had stiffish tasks in nurseries and a valuable seller. *P. Rohan.* **46**

SWING ALONE 5 gr.g. Swinging Junior 118–Independence 64 (Runnymede 123) (1979 6s 5g 6d 6s 5.8g 5fg 5fg 5fg 5f 5fg 5g 1980 6s 6g 6f 6fg) sprint handicapper; acts on any going; often wears blinkers. *P. M. Taylor.* –

SWING BACK 3 br.f. Great Nephew 126–Well Rowed (Delta Judge) (1979 NR 1980 8g 8g 7s 6d) lengthy filly; second foal; dam lightly-raced sister to high-class sprinter Swing Easy; behind in varied company. *R. Hollinshead.* –

SWING BY 3 ch.g. Swing Easy 126–Twice Shy (Lord of Verona 120) (1979 NR 1980 10.1s 8g 8.3g 10s 10g) leggy gelding; bad plater; sold 500 gns Ascot October Sales. *K. Ivory.* –

SWING GENTLY 3 br.f. Swing Easy 126–Native Soil 71 (Herbager 136) (1979 6d 1980 10fg³ 8h 10fg 10.4g⁴ 10g 10fg 10.4d) lengthy filly; poor maiden; not certain to stay 1¼m; blinkered nowadays. *P. Feilden.* –

William Hill Portland Handicap, Doncaster—fourth win in succession for Swelter who holds strong-finishing Sparkling Boy by a neck

SWINGING BELLE 6 br.m. Swinging Junior 118–Belle Sauntea (Little Buskins 119) (1979 12.2g 12fg 1980 9g 5f 5f 5fg 6s 5d 5fg 6s) of little account. *W. Clay.* —

SWINGING JUDGE 3 ch.g. Swing Easy 126–La Miranda 80 (Miralgo 130) (1979 6fg 6fg 1980 6h 5fg 5d 6s) fair sort; no worthwhile form in varied company, including selling. *G. Lewis.* —

SWINGING REBEL 2 br.c. Swing Easy 126–Rebecca (Quorum 126) (1980 6d) Feb 26; 3,500Y; lengthy colt; half-brother to a winner in Barbados by Club House; dam poor half-sister to Irish Sweeps Derby winner Steel Pulse; unquoted when behind in 17-runner maiden race won by Shark Song at Newmarket in October. *P. Haslam.* —

SWINGING RHYTHM 2 ch.c. Swing Easy 126–Soft Chinook (Hitting Away) (1980 5fg 6g 5g^{2} 5fg*) Mar 9; 7,200Y; lengthy colt; good mover; third reported foal; half-brother to 3-y-o 6f winner Lady Sister (by Saritamer) and a winner in Norway; dam French plater; finished strongly when close-up second in minor event won by Sanu at Goodwood in August and 16-runner maiden race won by Holmbury Lad at Newbury the following month (awarded latter race by stewards); should be suited by 6f. *J. Holt.* **89**

SWINGING SOVEREIGN 2 ch.f. Swing Easy 126–Ten Sovereigns (Sovereign Path 125) (1980 6fg) Apr 27; well-grown filly; third reported foal; dam of little account; unquoted and backward when behind in 16-runner maiden race won by Priory Lane at Salisbury in September. *M. McCormack.* —

SWINGING SWANEE 2 gr.g. My Swanee 122–Spin Out 97 (Pall Mall 132) (1980 5d 5s 6fg 6f 7d 8fg 10d 10d) Jan 20; 2,500F, 3,100Y; leggy gelding with poor forelegs; no worthwhile form, including in sellers. *W. Marshall.* **45**

SWINGING TRIO 4 ch.g. Swing Easy 126–Algarve 94 (Alcide 136) (1979 5d 6d^{3} 6s 6fg^{3} 6fg^{4} 7f 6d* 6g* 6g 6s 1980 6f 6fg 6fg 6g 6fg 6fg 8d) well-made gelding; good mover; fairly useful handicapper at 3 yrs; ran poorly in 1980, including when blinkered sixth start; stays 7f; acts on any going; sold out of J. Sutcliffe's stable 5,000 gns Ascot September Sales after sixth outing. *R. Atkins.* —

SWING ME 6 ch.m. Swing Easy 126–Hi Baby (High Treason 126) (1979 NR 1980 12.5h 9fg) unfurnished mare; virtually refused to race in maiden event at Stockton in March and was tailed off in minor contest at Ripon in May (blinkered); one to leave alone. *J. Calvert.* — §

SWING THE AXE 3 gr.f. No Mercy 126–Beech Tree 67 (Fighting Ship 121) (1979 6d 5fg^{4} 7fg 7g^{3} 7fg* 8fg^{4}(dis) 8.2s^{3} 1980 8.2d 10.6f 9.4g 8g 8.3d^{4} 7fg 7g^{2} 8g 7fg* 7d 7s) workmanlike filly; won handicap at Catterick in September; stays 1m; probably acts on any going. *D. Weeden.* **71**

SWING TO AND FRO 5 br.g. Swing Easy 126–Everlasting Song 88 (Continuation 120) (1979 6s 6d 8.2g 7fg 5fg 5.8h 5g^{3} 5fg 5fg 1980 8f 7f 5fg* 6g^{3} 5d) plater; short-head winner of amateur riders handicap at Edinburgh in July; stays 6f; acts on any going; used to wear blinkers. *C. Nelson.* **57**

SWIZZLE 4 ch.g. Firestreak 125–Arak 74 (Rustam 127) (1979 6s 7v 6g^{3} 6d^{4} 8g 6f* 6g^{3} 5f^{4} 6fg 6d^{4} 6g^{2} 8h^{2} 7s 7g 1980 7f^{2} 7.2fg* 8fg^{4} 7g^{2} 6d^{2} 5fg 7g 6d^{4} 7fg 6g) strong gelding; hung left in final furlong when narrowly beating Can Run in handicap at Haydock in May; effective at 6f and stays 1m; acts on any going; occasionally blinkered; sold 3,600 gns Newmarket Autumn Sales. *Denys Smith.* **71**

SWORD EDGE 3 ch.g. Sharpen Up 127–Coulter Belle 80 (Quorum 126) (1979 5v 5d^{4} 5d 5f 6fg 1980 8d 8v^{4} 10g 12fg) workmanlike gelding; poor —

form, including in a seller; stays 1m; suited by some give in the ground. *W. C. Watts.*

SWORD PRINCE 3 ch.g. Sun Prince 128–Cutlass Bay 68 (King's Bench 132) (1979 NR 1980 12.3d 16f 14d) 22,000Y; half-brother to 3 winners, including very useful sprinter Sonnenblick (by Song); dam won at 1m; no sign of ability in maiden and minor races; pulled up second start; sold 700 gns Newmarket Autumn Sales. *D. Sasse.* –

SWYNFORD'S MISS 2 gr.f. Grey Mirage 128–Altarnum (Alcide 136) (1980 5d 5v* 5s³ 5fg 7d 8.2d 8f 6g) Feb 3; 1,000F, 1,500Y; neat filly; half-sister to 1977 2-y-o 1m winner Enby Arco (by Streetfighter); dam slow maiden; attracted no bid after slamming her 4 opponents in seller at Warwick in March; should be suited by 7f+; acts well on heavy going; virtually pulled up in final 2f in nursery on seventh start and wore blinkers on eighth; sold 800 gns Newmarket Autumn Sales. *W. Marshall.* **53**

SWYNFORD'S PRIDE 3 b.f. Rapid River 127–Wroth Silver 79 (Tenterhooks 128) (1979 5v 5g 5s* 5g* 5s² 5fg 7g⁴ 1980 7d 6f 5fg) lengthy, plain filly; fairly useful (rated 95) at 2 yrs; didn't find her form in handicaps in 1980; not certain to stay 7f; acted on soft going; stud. *W. Marshall.* –

SYBARIS 2 ch.f. Crowned Prince 128–Sacred Ibis (Red God 128§) (1980 5f² 5fg* 5f* 5g 6s) Feb 25; 23,000Y; well-grown, attractive filly; good mover; first foal; dam, sister to very useful 1969 2-y-o Red Velvet, looked a short runner; made all when successful twice in the spring, holding off Brassy by a head in maiden race at Sandown and coming home 2½ lengths clear of Sharp Venita in 4-runner Wilkinson Memorial Stakes at York; 20/1 when 12½ lengths eighth of 17 to Pushy in Queen Mary Stakes at Royal Ascot in June; should stays 6f; acts very well on fast ground and is possibly unsuited by soft going; sent to race in California. *B. Hills.* **91**

SYLVAN GIRL 3 b.f. Saulingo 122–Hardihood (Hard Ridden 131) (1979 6g 6g⁴ 7fg 5f 5fg* 1980 6f 6f⁴ 5fg 6s) rangy filly; quite a moderate handicapper at her best; stays 6f; acts on firm going; wears blinkers. *R. Hannon.* –

SYLVIA'S DREAM 6 b.m. Sahib 114–Point of View (Vilmorin) (1979 8g* 8d 10.8fg 7.6f* 8f 7fg 10g 8g 1980 7h 8g 10fg 8g) poor handicapper; winner of seller at Brighton and apprentice handicap at Lingfield in 1979; stays 1m; acts on any going; often wears blinkers; good mount for an inexperienced rider. *D. Gandolfo.* –

SYMBOLROSE 3 ch.f. Status Seeker–Rose of Damascus (Ommeyad 120) (1979 6f 5f* 1980 6h³ 6fg) well-built filly; won 22-runner maiden race at Lingfield in 1979; moderate third in handicap at Stockton in April, better run at 3 yrs; will be suited by 7f+. *J. Winter.* **65**

SYMPATIQUE 2 ch.c. Simbir 130–Fun of the Fair (Skymaster 126) (1980 6d 7g³ 7fg⁴ 8.2g³ 7d 7f) Feb 22; 21,000Y; strong, good sort; moves well; second foal; dam poor sister to dam of Roland Gardens; in frame in maiden races prior to finishing 1¾ lengths third of 7 to Pellegrini in £4,100 event at Haydock in September; ran moderately when favourite for nursery later in September; had very stiff task in another nursery on final outing; better suited by 1m than 7f. *C. Brittain.* **82**

SYNCOPATE 4 br.f. Highland Melody 112–Manipulation 90 (Appiani II 128) (1979 9.4s* 9.4f³ 10f* 11.5f* 10fg³ 11.7fg 10fg 1980 10.2d 10v* 10s* 12fg² 12f 12f³ 12fg² 12d 11g³ 13d² 12.3g² 13g² 16.9f⁴ 12g 12.2fg 12fg 13s³ 12d 12s) neat filly; quite moderate handicapper; won at Stockton (apprentice event, by 10 lengths) and Nottingham in March; ran creditably most subsequent outings, but looked as though she was past her best on final start; stays 13f; acts on any going; good mount for an apprentice. *K. Stone.* **63**

SYNDROME 2 b.c. Connaught 130–Lilybelle 78 (Appiani II 128) (1980 6d 7d) Feb 15; 5,600F, 14,000Y; strong, compact, useful sort; third foal; dam won over 6f at 2 yrs; in rear in maiden race and Acomb Stakes, both at York; went to post very freely when blinkered in latter in August and finished last of 11 to Cocaine; sold 400 gns Ascot August Sales. *M. H. Easterby.* –

SYSTEMS ANALYSIS 4 b.c. Rheingold 137–Maragay 65 (Match III 135) (1979 14.7g² 14.7g 14g 16.1g* 17.1fg² 16s 1980 18d 16s 16f 12.3f 16fg² 16g* 16g 16f² 16s 18f⁴ 16g 16g² 17.1d) leggy, light-framed colt; has a round action; won handicap at Lingfield in June; stays well; acts on any going except soft; suitable mount for an apprentice; often makes the running; sold to G. Huffer 3,400 gns Newmarket Autumn Sales. *A. Goodwill.* **59**

T

TABERNACLE 7 b.g. Manacle 123–Tabarka (Dicta Drake 126) (1979 10.2s 8v 10v3 8.2g 8.3fg 8g4 10.8g 10s4 1980 12d 8s 10g 10fg) plater; stays 1¼m; seems to act on any going. *K. Bridgwater.* —

TACAMA 3 b.f. Daring Display 129–Nice Child 77 (Narrator 127) (1979 6f4 5f2 6g4 6f 1980 7fg 6fg 7s 6d3) compact filly; plater; best form at sprint distances; probably acts on any going; has been tried in blinkers; races with head held high; sold 1,050 gns Newmarket July Sales. *P. Rohan.* **44**

TAFFY 5 b.g. Prince de Galles 125–Bird In The Hand 82 (Major Portion 129) (1979 NR 1980 14f2 18.4f3 16fg* 18fg* 20d3 16d 16fg) lengthy gelding; quite a useful staying handicapper; won at Kempton (beat Shaab comfortably by 2 lengths) and Doncaster (made all and trotted up by 7 lengths from Wesley) in May; dashed clear 4f out and stayed on after being headed 1½f out when 2¼ lengths third of 12 to Heighlin in Ascot Stakes at Royal Ascot in June, best subsequent effort (off course nearly 3 months before final start); acts on any going; genuine and consistent. *J. Hindley.* **96**

TAHER (FR) 2 b.c. Weavers' Hall 122–Lotties Charm (Charlottesville 135) (1980 7g 8g) Apr 10; 10,500Y; tall, close-coupled colt; third foal; half-brother to French 9f and 10.5f winner Campeador (by Tarqogan); dam showed little worthwhile form in Ireland; 25/1 when running promisingly to finish 11½ lengths fifth of 10 to Sunley Builds in Hyperion Stakes at Ascot in October; second favourite for minor event at Newmarket later in month but never got into contest and wasn't knocked about; looked immature at 2 yrs and should do better over long distances in 1981. *G. Harwood.* — p

TAHITIAN KING 4 b.c. Luthier 126–Ten Double (Decathlon) (1979 8fg* 8d* 9g* 8fg* 10.2s2 1980 8fg3 9fg* 8g*) lengthy, attractive colt; smart performer; ridden by 7-lb claimer when landing odds by 2½ lengths from Mt Whitney in minor event at Ripon in May; led over 1f out and ran on strongly **116**

M D. Wildenstein's "Tahitian King"

to beat Cracking Form a length in quite well-contested Monkgate Stakes at York in July on only subsequent start; stays 1¼m; acts on any going; genuine and consistent; reportedly sent to France. *H. Cecil.*

TAIKA CHANCERY 3 b.g. Andrea Mantegna–Greek Bazaar 49 (Philemon 119) 42
(1979 NR 1980 10.8s 10g 12f 12h 10.8fg* 10fg^2 10f) lightly-made gelding; plater; successful at Warwick in July (bought in 1,200 gns); should stay 1½m; acts on a firm surface; fell fourth appearance; sold 1,350 gns Doncaster October Sales. *P. Cole.*

TAJARAMA 3 b.g. Amber Rama 133–Town House 91 (Pall Mall 132) (1979 –
7d 7fg 8fg^4 1980 11.7f 11.7f 8g^4 12fg 10g) leggy gelding; plater; not certain to stay 1½m; often blinkered. *P. Cole.*

TAKACHIHO 8 b.h. Don II 123–Face Lift (Herbager 136) (1979 11d 10g 9g –
10fg^2 9.4g* 8s 11fg^2 11g* 10.2fg 8.2f* 11fg* 11g 10fg^3 10s^3 10.5s 8.2d 8f 1980 8fg 11g 8.2d 8fg 8d 8.2s 12g 11fg 10.2d) moderate handicapper; not seen out until July in 1980 and didn't find his form; effective at 1m to 11f; well suited by top-of-the-ground conditions; sometimes wears blinkers; suitable mount for an apprentice; started slowly fourth outing. *T. Craig.*

TAKE-A-CHOICE 2 ch.f. Take a Reef 127–Quandary 80 (Aureole 132) (1980 –
5g 5g 5f 6d 6fg) Jan 31; 400F, 2,300Y, 800 2-y-o; neat filly; second foal; sister to a plater; dam won on flat and over hurdles; no sign of ability in maiden and minor events. *R. Whitaker.*

TAKEAFENCE 2 ch.g. My Swallow 134–Set Piece 69 (Firestreak 125) (1980 –
5f 5f 6fg) Mar 28; 3,000Y; quite well-made, useful-looking gelding; second foal in this country; dam prolific winner in Norway; in rear in maiden and minor events but showed speed 4f on final start. *M. McCormack.*

TAKE AIM 7 ch.g. Firestreak 125–Take a Chance 107 (Rockefella) (1979 10fg –
8f^3 8f 9fg^4 1980 8fg^4 13.8f 9g^4 10g) plater; has been tubed; effective from 1m to 13f; probably acts on any going; often wears blinkers; inconsistent but is a suitable mount for an apprentice. *M. Naughton.*

TAKEN FOR GRANTED 2 b.c. Martinmas 128–Romanee Conti (Will Somers 78
114§) (1980 7f 7fg^3) Mar 30; 9,800Y; rather lightly-made colt; second foal; half-brother to useful 1979 2-y-o 7f and 1m winner Schwepperusschian (by Take a Reef); dam placed at up to 1¼m in Ireland; prominent in large fields of maidens at Newmarket and Lingfield in October, on latter course finishing 3 lengths third to Jalabad when co-favourite; will be suited by 1m. *P. Walwyn.*

TAKE REVENGE 2 ch.c. Sweet Revenge 129–Ciel d'Or 71 (Sky Gipsy 117) –
(1980 6g 6s) compact colt; first foal; dam placed over 5f at 2 yrs; of little account. *S. Wiles.*

TAKE SHELTER 2 ch.c. Red Alert 127–Libonia (Le Haar 126) (1980 5f 62
6g 6d^3 5s 6v) Mar 17; 4,400Y; lightly-made colt; second foal; brother to 3-y-o Bionial Scramble, successful over 5f in 1979; dam never ran; close-up third of 6, after hanging left at halfway, in seller won by Consent at Ayr in August; beaten in non-sellers afterwards; will be suited by 7f; sold 1,050 gns Newmarket Autumn Sales. *W. H. H. Williams.*

TAKE TO HEART 2 b.f. Steel Heart 128–Tackaway 77 (Hard Tack 111§) 72
(1980 5f^3 5g 5d 6g^4 6g^4) Apr 23; 7,000F, 40,000Y; well-made, attractive filly; good walker; half-sister to 4 winners, including useful middle-distance performer Noble Bay (by Lord Gayle); dam won at 1m; looked on backward side and distinctly green when promising 3 lengths third of 9 to Unashamed in maiden race at Sandown in May; not disgraced in similar events afterwards, on fourth outing wearing blinkers but finding little under pressure when 2 lengths fourth of 14 to Musical Minx at Nottingham in July; should stay 7f. *H. Candy.*

TALLISHIRE ABODE 2 b.c. Crooner 119–Tudor Cream 73§ (Tudor Melody 87
129) (1980 5s* 5f 5f 5d 6s^3) May 18; 4,000Y; lengthy colt; good walker but doesn't move well in his slower paces; half-brother to several winners here and abroad; dam disappointing; won maiden race at Nottingham in March by ½ length from Horncastle; ran easily best race afterwards on same track in October, finishing about 1½ lengths third of 19 to Hiz in nursery; stays 6f; acts on soft going; trained by G. Toft first 3 outings. *F. Durr.*

TALLISHIRE HOMES 2 b.c. Lombard 126–Maladie d'Amour 98 (Fidalgo 81
129) (1980 6fg 7g^3 7fg^3 7d^4 8d 10s^3) Mar 15; 2,000F, 4,000Y; tall, quite attractive colt; half-brother to several winners, including fairly useful Prince Carl (by Connaught), successful at up to 1½m; dam stayer; in frame in maiden and minor events; kept on strongly in closing stages when about 2 lengths

third of 17 to Spin of a Coin at Nottingham in October on final start; will be suited by 1½m; trained by G. Toft first 4 starts. *F. Durr.*

TALLISHIRE TOMMY 4 gr.g. Song 132–Djenina 87 (Djebe) (1979 8s 7v^{2} 8d 7d 5f 7d 8f 8fg^{4} 8f^{3} 10g 7.6f 8h 1980 12.5v 8g^{3} 8.2fg 7f 8f^{2} 8fg^{3} 8g^{2} 8fg^{2} 8f) lengthy gelding; plater; stays 1m but no further; acts on any going; has been tried in blinkers; often wears bandages. *G. Toft.* **50**

TALLON 7 b.g. Falcon 131–Tulita 73 (Tudor Melody 129) (1979 6v 7g 7s 12s^{4} 8s 10f 1980 8g) poor handicapper; stays 1½m; acts on any going; sometimes sweats up; sometimes wears bandages; has won for an apprentice. *D. Elsworth.* –

TAMANGO 2 gr.f. Murrayfield 119–Relax 73 (Seminole II) (1980 7fg 8fg 7g) Mar 27; lightly-made filly; third living foal; half-sister to a winning plater; dam stayed well; little worthwhile form in maiden and minor events in the North; will stay 1¼m; will do better in sellers; sweating final appearance. *K. Stone.* –

TAMARIND GEM 4 ch.f. Salvo 129–Twisette (Alcide 136) (1979 10s 11d 10g^{4} 12s 12fg 14fg^{3} 14f^{4} 14f^{4} 15.5fg 1980 12fg) inconsistent maiden; should stay 2m+; has been tried in blinkers; sold 2,000 gns Doncaster November Sales. *M. Francis.* –

TAMARIN FALLS 4 ch.c. Mount Hagen 127–Taggs Island 76 (Silly Season 127) (1979 8d 8d 8g 10f^{2} 10f* 12fg^{3} 10f 10fg 1980 12fg^{3} 12fg* 12fg 12.3f^{2} 12f^{4} 12d^{3} 12g^{4} 12.3g^{3} 12f^{4} 12d) quite attractive colt; enterprisingly ridden when winning handicap at Pontefract in April; neck second to Jolimo at Chester following month, best subsequent effort (behind in a valuable seller on final start); stays 1½m well; best form on a sound surface; sold 2,800 gns Newmarket Autumn Sales. *G. Hunter.* **63**

TAMBOUR 2 ch.f. Tudor Music 131–Vaguely Related (Pall Mall 132) (1980 5g^{3} 5f 5f 5s^{4}) May 5; 3,500Y; small filly; half-sister to 2 winners, including fairly useful 5f and 7f winner Primonato (by Native Prince); dam poor maiden; plater; probably needs further than 5f; blinkered final start. *A. Pitt.* **51**

TAMDOWN FLYER 2 b.c. Hotfoot 126–Swing The Cat (Swing Easy 126) (1980 5f 7g^{2} 7fg 8g^{4} 8d) Apr 3; leggy, light-framed colt; first foal; dam never ran; in frame in maiden race at Catterick in August and £4,800 nursery at Brighton in October, running creditably when fourth of 11 to Aperitivo in latter; suited by 1m. *W. Holden.* **68**

TAMERCO 3 b. or br.g. Saritamer 130–Congola (Bold Lad, Ire 133) (1979 6f 6g^{4} 1980 8fg 12fg 14f) narrow gelding; showed promise second start at 2 yrs; well beaten in 1980; unlikely to stay 1½m; sold 1,600 gns Ascot July Sales. *J. Winter.* –

TAMIAMI 3 b.f. Rapid River 127–Super Chick (John Splendid 116) (1979 6f 5g 5g 5d 5fg 5fg^{4} 1980 5fg 5g^{4} 5fg 6g) only plating class; appeared not to stay 6f; dead. *W. A. Stephenson.* –

TAMMYRA 4 b. or br.f. Home Guard 129–Tammy (Kaiseradler) (1979 8g^{3} 12d 10s* 10s^{3} 1980 11.7fg) sturdy, short-legged filly; last of 15 in handicap at Windsor in May, only outing of 1980; stays 1¼m; acts on soft going. *G. Huffer.* –

TA MORGAN 2 b.c. Targowice 130–Sericana (Petingo 135) (1980 7fg 7s^{2}) Mar 20; 1,000Y; second foal; dam won four races over 1m in Ireland; 5 lengths second of 13 to odds-on John Willoughby in minor event at Chepstow in October; will stay 1m. *G. Lewis.* **79**

TAMPA BAY 4 b.c. Ickford 101–Tide and Time (Easter Island 101) (1979 6s 6v^{4} 6v^{4} 7d 8s 5fg* 6fg^{3} 6fg 5s^{4} 5g 5f^{3} 10f 1980 8fg 10g 10g 8g 10fg 6g) tall, attractive colt; best form at sprint distances but wasn't entirely disgraced over 1m on fourth start; seems to act on any going; blinkered once at 2 yrs. *D. Leslie.* –

TANAKLI 2 b.c. Hittite Glory 125–Crescent Dart 103 (Sing Sing 134) (1980 5d 5d 6g 8d) Feb 6; small, sturdy colt; poor mover; half-brother to 3 winners, including smart 1974 2-y-o sprinter Double Dart (by Songedor); dam sprinter; well behind in maiden races and sellers; sold 320 gns Ascot November Sales. *J. Douglas-Home.* –

TANGAROA 3 b.f. Lord Gayle 124–Yavana (Milesian 125) (1979 5v 5fg 7g 1980 8fg 10fg 8fg 8g 8g) lengthy filly; poor maiden. *A. Ingham.* –

TANGLO 3 b.g. Busted 134–Moon Stone (Misti IV 132) (1979 NR 1980 8fg 12g 12d 13g 8s) 1,500Y, 2,600 2-y-o; lengthy, rather plain gelding; behind in varied company; blinkered fourth start. *D. H. Jones.* –

TANGO SIERRA 3 b.f. Andrea Mantegna–Rashina (Pal O'Mine 96) (1979 NR 1980 14.6d) compact filly; third foal; dam never ran; in need of race when tailed-off last of 14 in maiden race at Doncaster in October. *J. Bethell.* –

TANGSEN 5 b.g. The Brianstan 128–Lovely Sensation 65 (Compensation 127) (1979 6s 6v 1980 11f^4 12fg 6h 10.6fg 6fg* 7fg^4 6g) leggy gelding; plater; sold out of W. Wright's stable 800 gns after winning at Hamilton in May; not certain to stay middle distances; probably unsuited by soft ground; often wears blinkers (didn't last 3 starts). *T. Taylor.* **40**

TANSANA 4 b.f. Ridan–Kildare Honey 79 (Khalkis 127) (1979 10g 10fg 14fg^4 12d^4 12.5g^3 12s 1980 12.5v 12.5h 12g) rangy filly; poor maiden; best form at 1½m. *T. Molony.* –

TANSOR 4 b.f. Royalty 130–Dust Sheet (Silly Season 127) (1979 9v 8s^4 8.2g^3 10f 10.1g^3 10.1f^3 10h 10f 1980 9g 7g 10g^4 8d*) light-framed, leggy filly; sold 1,600 gns after beating Keeps Going Right narrowly in seller at Wolverhampton in October (apprentice ridden); stays 1¼m; probably acts on any going; ran badly in blinkers second outing. *R. Carter.* **49**

TANTOT 4 ch.f. Charlottown 127–Now What 109 (Premonition 130) (1979 8g^4 10f 10f^2 10f^2 10.8g^3 13.3g 1980 12.2s^2 15fg^4 11.7fg) small, attractive filly; apprentice ridden when ½-length second to La Piccolina in handicap at Warwick in April, best effort; stays 1½m; acts on any going. *R. Hannon.* **55**

TAPDANCER 2 b.g. Hotfoot 126–Giselle 104 (Pall Mall 132) (1980 5fg 5d) May 20; quite well-made gelding; second foal; dam stayed 1¼m; unquoted and very much in need of race, made late progress to finish 4 lengths sixth in 16-runner maiden event awarded to Swinging Rhythm at Newbury in September; favourite for similar race at Wolverhampton the following month but finished only tenth behind Azaam; bred to stay at least 1m. *M. Smyly.* **73**

TARA'S CHIEFTAIN 2 b.g. African Sky 124–Hillberry Corner 70 (Atan) (1980 6g) Mar 20; 4,500Y; compact gelding; brother to very useful 1978 French 2-y-o 5f and 7f winner Chrisfranol, and half-brother to a winner; dam won over 5f at 2 yrs; 25/1 and on backward side when well behind in 25-runner maiden race won by Composer at Newmarket in October. *G. Huffer.* –

TARDOT 5 br.g. Targowice 130–Red Dot 100 (Red God 128§) (1979 7g^2 7s^3 7.6d 6s 6fg 7fg 7fg^4 7d 7f 7f 1980 8fg) fairly useful performer on his day; behind on only outing of 1980 (May); stays 1m; seems to act on any going but is possibly best suited by an easy surface; sometimes wears blinkers; sold 860 gns Newmarket Autumn Sales. *D. Kent.* –

TARISMA 4 b.f. Most Secret 119–Tarik 54 (Even Money 121) (1979 NR 1980 8fg 12.3d) unquoted and burly when tailed off in maiden races at Stockton and Newcastle in June. *I. Jordon.* –

TARLETON 3 b. or br.c. Workboy 123–Lady Jester 108 (Bleep-Bleep 134) (1979 5fg 5g 6f 1980 8g 8g^4 6g^4 7.6d 8g) poor performer; well beaten in valuable seller on final start; stays 1m. *P. Rohan.* **59**

TARNISHED IMAGE 3 b.f. Targowice 130–Jolie Madame (Bald Eagle 119) (1979 5f 6f 5g* 5f 1980 6fg 6fg 5fg) lengthy filly; won maiden race at Wolverhampton in 1979; well beaten in handicaps at 3 yrs; will be suited by 7f+; possibly needs some give in the ground. *W. Hastings-Bass.* –

TARROPEKE 6 gr.g. Good Bond 122–Pen Friend 90 (Vigo 130) (1979 NR 1980 10.2d 8.2g) poor performer nowadays; stays 1m; acts on firm going; sold to D. McCain 1,800 gns Doncaster August Sales. *A. Gillam.* –

TARROUNA 2 b.c. Manacle 123–Copthorne Polly (Double-U-Jay 120) (1980 6fg 5f 6g) Mar 25; 3,100Y; neat, strong colt; first foal; dam showed no worthwhile form; well beaten in maiden races and a £2,700 seller; sold 300 gns Doncaster November Sales. *R. Armstrong.* –

TARTAN BOY 3 gr.g. Sovereign Path 125–Tantara (Pakistan II 84) (1979 NR 1980 8g 8s 5s) rangy gelding; no sign of ability in maiden races. *R. Turnell.* –

TARTE AUX POMMES 3 b.f. Song 132–King's Mistress 102 (Rockefella) (1979 5s 5f^3 5f^4 1980 8fg 5d^4 6s^3 6g 6fg 5f^2 6fg) good-bodied filly; runner-up in maiden race at Lingfield in September; not certain to stay 1m; appears to act on any going; blinkered fifth outing. *W. Wightman.* **53**

Avon and Airlie Sporting Ltd's "Tarvie"

TARVIE 3 ch.f. Swing Easy 126–Tamergene 100 (Tamerlane 128) (1979 5g 5s 6g* 6f2 7g 1980 6fg3 6g2 6d 6d3 6g* 6g 6s 6g* 6d4) neat, attractive filly; useful sprinter; won handicap at Windsor in July (from Westburg) and minor event at York in October (made virtually all to beat Another Venture); stays 6f (had stiffish task when tried at 7f); best form on a sound surface; game. *P. Walwyn.* **101**

TARYN 4 ch.f. Crooner 119–Young Mementa (Young Christopher 119) (1979 8g 7g 6s* 6g3 6g 5f2 6d 1980 5fg) quite a moderate handicapper; best at up to 6f; acts on any going; suitable mount for a boy. *C. Nelson.* **–**

TASSMOUN 4 b.g. Kalamoun 129–Tremogia (Silver Shark 129) (1979 7.5d3 7g* 6.5s* 8s3 1980 9fg4 8g* 10d* 8g* 8d2 8g2) French gelding; first foal; dam unraced half-sister to very smart middle-distance stayer Sauvage, is daughter of Prix Saint-Alary winner Tonnera; won at Evry (twice) and Maisons-Laffitte, beating Discretion (gave 5 lb) and Hilal by a neck and ¾ length in Prix Messidor on latter course in July; second in a handicap and in Prix Quincey at Deauville in August, beaten 3 lengths by Kilijaro when favourite in latter event on final outing; stays 1¼m; acts on soft going; has run creditably in blinkers but is better without. *F. Mathet, France.* **118**

TAT SAT 3 gr.g. Young Emperor 133–Raise the Roof (Raise You Ten 125) (1979 NR 1980 8f 8fg) 6,600Y; third living foal; half-brother to 6f and 1m winner Roi-des-Toits (by Roi Soleil); dam won at up to 17f in Ireland; in rear in newcomers race and maiden event at Newmarket early in year; sold to R. Hollinshead 640 gns Newmarket Autumn Sales. *I. Balding.* **–**

TAUFAN (USA) 3 b.c. Stop the Music–Stolen Date (Sadair) (1979 6d2 6fg2 5g* 1980 7f2 8fg 6fg* 6g) $102,000Y; strong, attractive colt; excellent mover with a long stride; didn't seem ideally suited by sharp track and had to be kept up to his work to beat Sayyaf (gave 10 lb) ¾ length in 5-runner Asda **113**

Sheikh Mohammed's "Taufan"

Sprint Trophy at Thirsk in May; had earlier finished good length second to Moorestyle in Tote Free Handicap at Newmarket and been prominent a long way before being hampered when eighth of 14 to Nureyev in 2,000 Guineas; blinkered when behind in Cork and Orrery Stakes won by Kearney at Royal Ascot in June (reportedly injured back); gives impression 7f is his optimum trip; probably acts on any going; had his tongue tied down at Royal Ascot; very useful. *F. J. Houghton.*

TAVADORA 3 ch.f. Cavo Doro 124–Plunder 77 (Tamerlane 128) (1979 8f 1980 12d) plain filly; well beaten in maiden and minor races; sold 720 gns Newmarket Autumn Sales. *C. Brittain.* —

TAVERNE DE FRANCE (FR) 3 ch.f. Caracolero 131–Northern Tavern (Charlottesville 135) (1979 8f* 7f⁴ 7g 1980 10.2f² 11.1f* 10.6fg* 10g 11.7s 9g 10f⁴ 10g 10.2g³ 10f) big, strong filly; successful in handicaps at Wolverhampton and Haydock in May; decisively beat North Moor 2 lengths on latter; stays 11f; acts on firm going and is possibly not at her best on soft; ran moderately sixth start and was out of depth on eighth. *R. Boss.* **92** d

TAX HAVEN (USA) 2 ch.c. No Robbery–Little Jen (Time Tested) (1980 5d* 5g² 5g 7g) Mar 31; $35,000Y; lengthy, quite attractive colt; excellent mover; second foal; dam, from same family as Gay Fandango, won at up to 1m; quickened in good style to win £2,700 event at Sandown in June by 4 lengths from Storm Rock; again put in best work in closing stages when failing by ½ length to catch Chummy's Special in 6-runner Norfolk Stakes at Royal Ascot the following week; disappointing last of 5 behind Penmarric in National Stakes at Sandown in July and wasn't seen out again until October when last of 17 to Remouleur in nursery at Ascot; should be suited by 7f. *R. Armstrong.* **100**

TAXI STAR 3 b.f. Comedy Star 121–Roving Eye 63 (Galivanter 131) (1979 5f 6f 6h⁴ 1980 6v 6f 6f⁴ 7f 6fg) bad plater; probably stays 6f; has been tried in blinkers. *J. Berry.* —

TEACHER'S PET 3 b.f. Mummy's Pet 125–Moben 73 (Counsel 118) (1979 5v* 5d^2 5d* 5fg^2 6f 5g 5g^2 6d^2 7g^4 8d^3 1980 7d 8d^4 8fg^2 8s 8s 8s* 8d 7d^3 7d) rangy ex-English filly; excellent mover; second reported living foal; dam, half-sister to high-class stayer Grey Baron, stayed 7f; won 10-runner 50,000 francs event at Clairefontaine in August; ran creditably to be in frame in Poule d'Essai des Pouliches at Longchamp (just over 1½ lengths fourth of 6 to Aryenne), Prix de Sandringham at Chantilly (short-headed by India Song) and Prix du Pin at Longchamp (close third to Princesse Lida); stays 1m; acts on any going except perhaps very firm; blinkered nowadays; ran moderately fourth outing. *O. Douieb, France.* **110**

TEAGARDEN 3 b. or br.g. Home Guard 129–Rose Princess (Princely Gift 137) (1979 7g 7f 8g 1980 7fg 8fg 12.3d 10g 11.7fg 16fg) useful sort; poor maiden; pulled up lame final start; sold 820 gns Newmarket Autumn Sales. *D. Sasse.* —

TEAL EYE 4 b.f. Mon Fils 124–Bunny Club 66 (Astec 128) (1979 8v 12v 16d 12fg 12h^4 12fg 12s 1980 16g) of little account. *J. Leigh.* —

TEAMWORK 3 br.c. Workboy 123–Affirmative 96 (Derring-Do 131) (1979 6fg 6d^4 1980 6s 8g 8g* 8fg 8fg* 8fg^3) strong, good-bodied colt: won 12-runner maiden race at Kempton and handicap at Newmarket in the summer; did well to get up and beat Circuit Judge ½ length after losing many lengths at start in latter; ran creditably final appearance; runs as if he'll stay 1¼m; acts on a firm surface; reared up as stalls opened first start. *G. Harwood.* **91**

TEA-POT 4 ch.f. Ragstone 128–Desert Ash (Celtic Ash) (1979 7v 10s 16fg^2 14g 16.1g 16f 1980 16fg 15.5g 16f^4 15.5f^3 17.1d) workmanlike filly; quite a moderate maiden; stays well; seems to act on any going. *M. Blanshard.* —

TEARS OF GOLD 2 ch.f. Grisaille 115–Jenhill (Continuation 120) (1980 5fg 5f 5d^4 6f 6g 8g) Mar 16; 520Y; small filly; well beaten, including in sellers. *P. K. Mitchell.* —

TECAMUS 3 b.f. Mandamus 120–Tecllyn 97 (Technion 96) (1979 5d 5s 6g 5f 8f 1980 8.3f 10fg 9.6f) small filly; poor plater. *A. Davison.* —

TECHMATIC 5 b.g. Fine Blade 121–Description (Queen's Hussar 124) (1979 NR 1980 8d 10g 8.3g) selling hurdler; of no account on flat; headstrong. *F. Muggeridge.* —

TEDHAM MOSS 3 b.g. Ballymore 123–Madelon 112 (Saint Crespin III 132) (1979 7fg 7g^3 1980 9.4g^3 12g^3 12fg* 13s* 12.3d^3 15s^3 16.1s^2 15d^2) fair sort; has a round action; won maiden race at Redcar and minor event at Ayr in the summer; ran creditably in varied company afterwards; stays well; acts well on soft going, although has won on fast; seldom impresses in paddock. *W. Elsey.* **86**

TEESPORT BOY 3 b.g. Huntercombe 133–Zaza 85 (Pinza 137) (1979 5v 5d 5d^3 6d 6fg 6f 5f 6f 7g 5d^2 5g 6g 7g 1980 6v 7d^2 6d 6f^4 7g 5fg 6s) robust, good-bodied gelding; second in maiden event at Newcastle in April; well beaten in seller on final start (August); suited by 7f; seems to act on any going; often blinkered. *S. Wainwright.* **52**

TE KENAWA (USA) 3 b.c. Wajima–Karmana (Abernant 142) (1979 NR 1980 7f^2 8fg* 8f* 8fg^4 10fg^2 10.2g^4) $105,000Y; tall, rather leggy colt; not a good mover in his slower paces; third foal; half-brother to Balkayn (by Ribero), winner of 11f claiming race in France; dam unraced sister to Prix de l'Abbaye winner Farhana; useful performer; odds on when 4-length winner of 24-runner maiden race at Doncaster in May and £2,700 race at York later in month (didn't seem at home on very firm ground); ran well next 2 starts to be fourth to April Bouquet under top weight in Britannia Stakes (Handicap) at Royal Ascot and short-head second to Moomba Masquerade (pair clear) in Land of Burns Stakes at Ayr in July; pulled hard early on when fourth to Old Kate in Fitzwilliam Stakes at Doncaster in September; stays 1¼m; yet to race on a soft surface. *H. Cecil.* **109**

TEK RIBA 2 b.f. Palm Track 122–Kindling 80 (Psidium 130) (1980 5f 5g 8fg 8.2s 7d 8d) Feb 21; strong filly; has rather a round action; sister to 3-y-o 1¼m to 13f winner Timber Track and half-sister to 2 winners; dam ran only 3 times; poor form in maiden races, best effort on fifth outing when about 6 lengths fifth of 10 to Paltango at Catterick in October; should stay 1m; formerly trained by J. Berry. *E. Weymes.* **63**

TELECOMMUNICATION 5 b.h. Communication 119–Cavan 82 (Anwar 120) (1979 10v 8.2v^4 8f 1980 8g 8g) one-time fair handicapper; lightly raced and no form on flat since 1978; stays 1m; seems to act on any going. *O. Jorgensen.* —

TEL EL AMARNA 2 ch.g. Native Bazaar 122–Star Royal (Royal Tara 123) (1980 5fg 5fg 5f 6fg 7fg) compact gelding; bad plater; wears blinkers; sold 400 gns Ascot October Sales. *M. Scudamore.* —

TELEMON LAD 4 br.g. Furry Glen 121–Maggie Mine 85 (Native Prince) (1979 8.2s 11fg 8.2g 6g 5g² 5s 5g 5g 5f⁴ 5d 6s⁴ 6d⁴ 1980 8g 7fg 9s⁴) strong gelding; stays 6f (well beaten over further); acts on any going; suitable mount for an apprentice; has worn a tongue strap; sold 500 gns Ascot October Sales. *G. Richards.* —

TELEPRITY 2 b.f. Welsh Pageant 132–Ankole 85 (Crepello 136) (1980 5d 6fg³ 8.2d) Mar 16; 5,000Y; lengthy filly; good mover; half-sister to several winners, including 3-y-o 11f winner Count Fernando (by Connaught) and useful miler Horbury (by Sing Sing); dam won at up to 13f; no match for Integrity and Mattaboy in 4-runner Rous Memorial Stakes at Goodwood in August but ran on very nicely to finish 4 lengths third; weakened after leading 2½f out when 4 lengths fifth of 7 to Pellegrini in £4,100 event at Haydock the following month; bred to stay middle distances; possibly unsuited by a soft surface. *F. Durr.* 82

TELESTAR 6 b.g. Irish Ball 127–Fair Rosamond (Owen Tudor) (1979 NR 1980 12.2fg) plating-class maiden on flat; should stay 1½m; blinkered final outing. *M. Chapman.* —

TELLINGO 2 gr.f. Rustingo 94–Teller 64 (Quorum 126) (1980 5d 6g) Mar 21; fifth foal; dam poor performer; unquoted when 4 lengths sixth of 11 to Laughing in seller at Wolverhampton in July, first outing and easily better effort; should stay 6f+. *G. Price.* —

TELL ME A STORY 3 ro.f. Roan Rocket 128–Novelista 101 (El Gallo 122) (1979 5d³ 5d² 5g 5s 5.1g 5f² 5fg³ 1980 5d 5fg² 6g 5g 5g 5f) small, sturdy filly; second in apprentice race at Edinburgh in July; well beaten subsequently and ran badly in blinkers final start; should stay 6f; suited by fast ground. *P. Cole.* 48

TELLURANO 2 ch.c. Guillaume Tell 121–Uranus (Manacle 123) (1980 8g 7d²) Apr 29; 4,200F, 9,000Y; brother to Belgian winner Beldale Guillaume, and half-brother to 5f winner Tralee Falcon (by Falcon); dam won twice over 5f at 2 yrs in Ireland; well-backed second favourite, finished long way clear of 90

Crown Plus Two Apprentice Championship Final, York—Shaun Payne clinches the series on Telsmoss. Side Track is second by a short head from Haverhill Lad (rails)

remainder when going down by only ½ length to odds-on Kings Lake in 11-runner minor event at Naas in October; will stay 1m; sure to win races. *K. Prendergast, Ireland.*

TELLYWOG 5 b.g. Communication 119–Poliwog (Polic 126) (1979 7.6d 7f 8.3fg 8.3fg 1980 8s 8g 10s 8fg 7g) poor plater; seems to stay 1m; acts on hard going and is possibly not at his best on soft; has worn bandages; sometimes sweats up; changed hands 1,250 gns Doncaster May Sales and was sold to N. Waggott 460 gns Newmarket Autumn Sales. *W. Marshall.* —

TELSMOSS 4 b.c. Levmoss 133–Elakonee Wind 110 (Restless Wind) (1979 8v^2 10v 7s 7fg 7f^3 8.3f* 8f^2 8.3fg^3 10.1fg^4 8.3f 10f^4 10fg^3 9f 1980 8d 10g^4 8fg 10d^4 8g 10fg* 11fg^3 11.7fg^2 11.7f* 12f* 12g^3 12f^2 10fg^2 10.5s* 10g) small colt; fairly useful middle-distance handicapper; ran consistently well and was gaining his fourth win when beating Side Track gamely by ¾ length in valuable apprentice handicap at York in October; successful earlier at Redcar, Windsor and Epsom (apprentices), making all on last 2 tracks; also ran extremely well when short-head second to very leniently-handicapped Etching in Peter Hastings Stakes at Newbury (pair clear); acts on any going; suitable mount for an inexperienced rider. *P. Mitchell.* **91**

TEN BEARS 4 ch.g. Salvo 129–Lunar Bug (Master Rocky 106) (1979 NR 1980 16f) novice hurdler; unquoted when well behind in amateur riders race at Lingfield in September, first outing on flat. *T. M. Jones.* —

TENDER ANGUS (USA) 2 ch.c. Grey Dawn II 132–Colfax Miss (Raise A Native) (1980 7g 7d) Mar 7; $25,000Y; strong, well-made, good sort; has a grand, long stride; brother to 1979 American 2-y-o winner Gloomy and to Spring Up, a promising 2-y-o of 1977 who ran only once afterwards, and half-brother to 2 winners; dam unraced half-sister to very smart American stakes winner Captain Cee Jay; in mid-division in 15-runner maiden races at Newmarket and Newbury in August; will stay 1m; looks capable of better. *G. Harwood.* **74** p

TENDER HEART 4 br.g. Prince Tenderfoot 126–Pirana (High Hat 131) (1979 7g 7s^3 8g 8fg^2 8fg^2 8fg* 8fg^4 8.5g* 8f 8d* 9f 1980 8d 8f 8f^3 8g* 10.5g^2 **115**

Royal Hunt Cup Handicap, Ascot—Joe Mercer on Tender Heart glances round for non-existent dangers. They are followed by Lord Rochford (noseband), Smartset and Baronet (hooped sleeves)

8fg^2 9f) good-looking gelding; good mover; very useful handicapper; heavily backed, fulfilled promise of his earlier runs when winning Royal Hunt Cup at Royal Ascot in June by 3 lengths from Lord Rochford; started clear favourite for William Hill Cambridgeshire at Newmarket in October but lost several lengths when having to be snatched up running down the hill and in circumstances did well to finish less than 2 lengths fifth behind Baronet (would probably have won with a clear run); ran very well when ½-length second to Fine Sun in John Smith's Magnet Cup at York and rallied well and just failed when beaten a short head by sole opponent Baronet in handicap at Ascot in between; stays 10.5f; acts on any going; blinkered last 2 outings at 2 yrs. *J. Sutcliffe.*

TENDERMEAT 2 br.c. Daring Display 129–Posh 80 (Migoli 132) (1980 5f 5fg 5fg 5fg 7g 5g) Mar 29; 3,300Y; resold 7,000Y; smallish colt; half-brother to several winners here and abroad, including 1969 2-y-o 6f winner L'Anguissola (by Soderini); only plating class; put up best effort when seventh of 18 to Portogon in maiden race at Bath in September on sixth outing; should stay at least 6f; wears blinkers. *G. Huffer.* —

TENNIS TRACK 2 br.f. Track Spare 125–Get Set 65 (Stupendous) (1980 6s 7s 7d 6s 6g 7d 8d) Feb 19; lightly-made filly; fourth foal; dam won over 1¼m; 11 lengths sixth of 23 to Hurtwood Lass in valuable seller at Doncaster in September, fifth outing; should stay 1m. *R. Mason.* **58**

TENORIA 3 ch.f. Mansingh 120–Ibozia 73 (Mossborough 126) (1979 5d 5g 7fg^4 7g* 7g 1980 8h 8fg 11.7s^4 11.7s^2 11.7g 11d^2 10.6d* 12fg^3) small filly; beat Queen's Equerry decisively by 1½ lengths in handicap at Haydock in September; stays 1½m; suited by some give in the ground. *M. Jarvis.* **73**

TENTH HUSSAR 2 ch.f. Shiny Tenth 120–Floral Palm 69 (Floribunda 136) (1980 5fg 6s 5fg 6f 5fg^4 5g) May 18; tall, lengthy filly; half-sister to 3 winners, including very useful Italian sprinter Dublin Taxi (by Sharpen Up); dam won 5f seller at 2 yrs; 6 lengths fourth of 11 to Ashbrittle in minor event at Windsor in September, only sign of ability. *Peter Taylor.* **73**

TENTH LADY 3 b.f. Shiny Tenth 120–Lucky Number (River Chanter 121) (1979 6g 7d 1980 8fg 9.4d 9g 12d^2 13.8g) tall, leggy filly; plater; suited by 1½m; acts on a soft surface; unseated rider on way to start fourth outing. *J. Etherington.* —

TENTWORT 3 ch.f. Shiny Tenth 120–Pinguicula (Pinza 137) (1979 NR 1980 8h 13s 12g^2 14.6d*) lengthy filly; first foal; dam never ran; showed improved form on last 2 starts, winning 14-runner maiden race at Doncaster in October on second occasion; stays 1¾m; acts on a soft surface. *W. Elsey.* **79**

TERESILLA (FR) 3 gr.f. High Echelon–Tarakanova (Bold Lad, USA) (1979 6d^2 6g* 6g^2 8f^4 9fg* 10g 1980 12f 12.3f 12h^2 12f^2 12.2fg^4 12d^4 12g 12.3d^3 11.7fg* 12.2fg 13g* 10d^2 16s) lightly-made filly; fair handicapper; successful at Windsor and Nottingham in September, beating North Buchan a short head on latter (apprentice ridden); stays 13f; seems to act on any going; flashed tail under pressure fifth start. *R. Sheather.* **88**

TERRY PAINE 5 b.g. Red God 128§–Distant Horizon 92 (Nimbus 130) (1979 8g^3 10g^2 8s^3 8fg^2 10f^2 8g 8g* 8f 8s^4 1980 8f 8f^2 7f^2 8f 8fg 10fg 8.3fg 8g) strong gelding; stays 1¼m; acts on any going; usually wears blinkers; suitable mount for an inexperienced rider. *D. Ringer.* **63**

TESLIN 2 br.g. Yukon Eric–La Martinella (Mandamus 120) (1980 5s 5f 5f^2 6g 6d) Mar 28; 1,050Y; leggy gelding; bad plater; should be suited by 6f+. *M. Cousins.* **44**

TESORO MIO 5 b.h. Cavo Doro 124–Captive Flower 99 (Manacle 123) (1979 10.4d* 10g^4 10.5f* 10f^2 12g 1980 10.6fg^2 10f^4 12g 10.5g 10fg^3 10fg 10.6d^3 10d) fair sort; retained most of his ability and was placed at Haydock (twice) and Ripon; suited by 1¼m and wasn't disgraced over 1½m on third outing (Bessborough Stakes at Royal Ascot); seems to act on any going but goes well on top-of-the-ground; suited by a strong gallop; usually held up and has a good turn of foot; looked hard trained when well beaten final outing. *J. Etherington.* **90**

TESSIE'S GIRL 4 ch.f. Midsummer Night II 117–Queen Plum (Pampered King 121) (1979 13.8fg 1980 8fg 9f) of no account. *A. W. Jones.* —

TESTING TIMES (USA) 2 br.c. Olden Times–Fierce Ruffian (What A Pleasure) (1980 6g^4 6d 5g^4 6fg 6g^4 5g) Feb 23; $50,000Y; strong, compact colt; first foal; dam stakes-placed winner at up to 6f, including 4 races at 2 yrs; ran a good first race when 3¼ lengths fourth of 8 to Kirtling in Chesham Stakes **79§**

at Royal Ascot in June; didn't fulfil the promise of that performance and wore blinkers on his last 2 outings; one to leave severely alone. *P. Cole.*

TESTON LAD 3 b.g. Blast 125–Right On Time 78 (Right Boy 137) (1979 65
5.3fg 5f^2 6f 6fg 1980 9f 6d^4 6s^2 7g 6fg 6f^3 7f^3 8s 6d) lengthy, fair sort; quite moderate; best at 6f or 7f; acts on any going. *P. K. Mitchell.*

TESTWOOD PARK 3 ro.f. John Splendid 116–Carli Coote (El Gaucho 107) –
(1979 NR 1980 7fg 8g) light-framed filly; fourth foal; half-sister to a winning plater; dam placed over hurdles; in mid-division in maiden races at Chepstow and Salisbury in the summer. *G. Balding.*

TEXAS RANGER 2 b.g. Tumble Wind–Game Laura (Relic) (1980 5f 5fg^2 74
5fg^2 5fg^2 5f^2 5d 5d) Mar 25; 11,000F, 18,000Y; leggy gelding; half-brother to 2 winners, including useful Caven Mill (by Clever Fella), successful here and in Belgium; dam half-sister to The Go-Between; runner-up in 4 maiden and minor events, on final occasion going down by a length to Reconquest at Leicester in June (broke out of stalls beforehand); not seen out again until October when sixth of 19 at Warwick; will be suited by 6f; acts on firm going; exported to Singapore. *E. Eldin.*

TEYE 3 b.f. Mummy's Pet 125–Monagram 77 (Mon Fetiche 120) (1979 5f 5fg –
1980 8f) behind in maiden and minor events; sold 480 gns Ascot July Sales. *C. Wildman.*

THAHUL (USA) 3 b.c. Nijinsky 138–Queen City Miss (Royal Union) (1979 76
NR 1980 13.3fg 12s 14g^2 16f^3 13g^4 12s) $50,000Y; deep-girthed, rangy colt; good walker; half-brother to several winners, including Tinajero (by Decidedly), a high-class winner at up to $1\frac{1}{4}$m; dam stakes-placed winner at up to 1m; placed in maiden races at Salisbury and Beverley (didn't seem suited by track) in the summer; needs a test of stamina; acts on firm going. *F. J. Houghton.*

THAI ANNA 2 b.f. Amber Rama 133–Brevity 76 (Pindari 124) (1980 5h 65
5d 5f*) Mar 18; 2,500Y; half-sister to 3 winners, including prolific 1975 2-y-o sprint winner Short Reign (by Tribal Chief); dam won over 7f at 2 yrs; bought in 1,100 gns after running out convincing $2\frac{1}{2}$-length winner from Humber Crossing in seller at Catterick in July (50/1 and bandaged, made all); started none too well first 2 outings and was taken down early at Catterick. *I. Vickers.*

THATCHING TIME 3 b.c. Thatch 136–Boscage 104 (Queen's Hussar 124) 77
(1979 6fg^3 6fg^2 7fg* 1980 8f 7fg 8g 7d^4 7d* 7g 7d) strong, well-made colt; beat Rama Tibodi a head in handicap at Brighton in July; ran moderately afterwards; should stay 1m; acts on a firm and a soft surface; blinkered nowadays; sweated up final start; highly-strung; retained 2,300 gns Newmarket Autumn Sales. *P. Cole.*

THAT'S MAGIC 2 ch.f. Bay Express 132–Alumina 86 (Fortino II 120) (1980 82
5fg^2 5g 5fg 5s^2 5d 5d^3 6g^2 6s^2 5d^2) May 20; 2,000F, 2,800Y; neat filly; second living produce; dam miler; second in a variety of races at Catterick (two), Newcastle, Salisbury and Hamilton, coming closest to success when beaten $\frac{1}{2}$ length by Church Mountain on last-named in September; stays 6f; seems to act on any going. *J. Etherington.*

THAULING 4 b.f. Saulingo 122–Moth 73 (Midsummer Night II 117) (1979 –
11.1s 10.6g 7fg 8f 12fg^2 12g 10g 7s 1980 10.2d 10.8f 10h 10fg) modest plater; stays $1\frac{1}{2}$m; probably acts on any going; blinkered fourth outing at 2 yrs. *P. Arthur.*

THAUMATURGE 2 b.c. Thatch 136–Grecian Craft 90 (Acropolis 132) (1980 –
7f 8fg) Mar 20; 120,000Y; strong colt; third foal; brother to very useful French 3-y-o 1m to $1\frac{1}{4}$m winner Nemr, and half-brother to 7f winner Meliora (by Crowned Prince); dam disappointing sister to smart stayer Mariner; made little show in maiden race at Ascot in July and 23-runner minor event at Newbury in September; looked very nervous on first outing and wore blinkers on second. *J. Tree.*

THE ADRIANSTAN 5 ch.g. Sparkler 130–Riberta 89 (Ribot 142) (1979 8d –
8d 7s* 8g 7g 8fg 8d 10d^3 8s 1980 8d 8d 8d) useful handicapper on his day; completely unreliable however and showed no worthwhile form in 1980; stays $1\frac{1}{4}$m; acts on any going; has been tried in blinkers; sometimes starts slowly; not an easy ride; sold to D. Hanley 1,800 gns Ascot August Sales. *J. Sutcliffe.*

THE ARKESDEN AXE 3 ch.c. Redundant 120–Brocette (Brocade Slipper 45
116) (1979 7f 7fg 7g 10s 8d 1980 12s 12fg 10h^3 12.2fg^3) big colt; plater; stays $1\frac{1}{2}$m; blinkered final start at 2 yrs; sold 4,600 gns Doncaster November Sales. *N. Callaghan.*

THE ASPEL 2 b.g. Pongee 106–Stephela (Young Stratford 92) (1980 5f 6d 7fg) May 12; workmanlike gelding; well behind in maiden races and a seller. *D. Chapman.* —

THE BARONS LODGE 2 b.c. The Brianstan 128–Villa Vera (Gilles de Retz 132) (1980 6g 5fg* 5.1fg 6f 6g) Feb 12; 5,200Y; compact colt; brother to quite moderate 1976 2-y-o maiden Briareus; dam won 3 times over 1½m in Ireland; 25/1, made all to win 6-runner maiden race at Newmarket in August by ¾ length from Mrs Leadbetter; in rear subsequently in minor event at Yarmouth (saddle slipped) and valuable nurseries at Newmarket; should stay 6f. *P. Haslam.* **80**

THE BEDFORD 4 b.c. English Prince 129–Grass Emerald (Alcide 136) (1979 8g 11fg^2 16f* 13d^2 14g^4 16.1g^2 12fg* 14f* 16fg* 1980 14f) strong, attractive colt; fairly useful performer (rated 93) at 3 yrs; favourite, raced with his head on one side and failed to respond when shaken up 2f out when behind at Newmarket in May on only outing of 1980; stays well; seems suited by top-of-the-ground; genuine and consistent in 1979. *F. Durr.* —

THE BLINDFOLD 2 b.f. More Music 61–Queen's Rifles (Queen's Hussar 124) (1980 5g 5f 7d) Apr 8; sturdy filly; second foal; dam ran only twice; unquoted when in rear in maiden races. *W. Wharton.* —

THE BRITISHER 3 b.c. English Prince 129–Obelisk 122 (Abernant 142) (1979 6fg 7fg 7.2g 7f 7fg^4 8d^4 1980 12fg 10s^4 10g 8.2d* 9.4g 8g^2 8.2s 8s 10.2v) big, strong colt; not the best of movers; won apprentice maiden race at Hamilton in June; probably stays 1¼m; acts on a soft surface; suitable mount for a boy. *A. Jarvis.* **70**

THE CEIRIOG 5 ch.m. Deep Diver 134–La Foire II 90 (Arabian) (1979 12s 8s^3 12g^3 16.9fg^2 14fg 1980 12fg 13.4g^3) fair sort; 5 lengths third to Mount Denali in maiden race at Chester in July; stays well; acts on any going; blinkered final outing at 2 yrs; winning hurdler. *F. Yardley.* —

THE CENTAUR (FR) 5 br.g. Reliance II 137–Celine (El Centauro) (1979 NR 1980 10v^3 10g 12fg 12s^4 12d 14d^3 12fg) useful performer at around 10f in France at 3 yrs when trained by F. Boutin; ran creditably when fourth in Rank Cup (beaten 4¾ lengths by subsequently-disqualified Croghan Hill) at Phoenix Park in March and in handicap at the Curragh in June; bandaged in front when behind in Moet and Chandon Silver Magnum (gentleman riders) won by No Bombs at Epsom in August on final outing; useful hurdler in France in 1979 and was successful over hurdles at Galway in July; suited by middle distances; acts on any going. *C. Magnier, Ireland.* **93**

THE CLIFTONIAN 2 b.c. Firestreak 125–Ile de France 84 (French Beige 127) (1980 5.8fg^3 6s^2 6s 6g 8.2g^3 8g) Apr 18; 4,200F, 6,800Y; 5,000 2-y-o; half-brother to 1¼m winner Village Idol (by Blakeney); dam won at up to 7f; returned to form when tried over 1m, finishing good third of 10 to Show-A-Leg in nursery at Nottingham in September; stays 1m; none too consistent. *R. Hannon.* **76**

THE DANCER (FR) 3 b.f. Green Dancer 132–Khazaeen (Charlottesville 135) (1979 5g* 6f 8f* 8d 1980 10f* 12f^3 12s^3) **122**

The periodic ophthalmia which affected The Dancer as a two-year-old took a turn for the worse over the winter and by the time she reappeared this strong, attractive filly was blind in her left eye. This handicap didn't impair her ability, any more than a similar one prevented Del Sarto and Gain from showing above-average form in 1980, but it did force her trainer to run her solely on left-handed tracks. From only three starts The Dancer twice put up good, game displays of front running.

The Sir Charles Clore Memorial Stakes at Newbury, previously the Sandleford Priory Stakes, presented The Dancer with a fairly easy task for a filly with classic pretensions and she was a short-priced favourite to beat eight opponents. The outside draw proved no problem since Carson quickly took her into the lead and crossed over to the rails. She was always going easily and quickened right away in the closing stages to win by seven lengths from Saint Osyth whose jockey accepted the situation inside the distance. Impressive as this display was, The Dancer started at 14/1 for the Oaks, the least fancied of her trainer's three runners. A belief persists in some quarters that there is an intrinsic disadvantage in making the running, despite proof to the contrary. Admittedly certain horses need to be held up, but coming from behind can present a jockey with more problems than lying up with the pace, especially in a slowly-run race

Sir Charles Clore Memorial Stakes, Newbury—The Dancer finishes clear of Saint Osyth and Good Lassie (rails)

as was shown by Nicholas Bill's unlucky run in the St Simon Stakes. The jockey in front is usually allowed to set a gallop to suit his mount, he is in a good position to exploit any weaknesses his opponents have and can sometimes virtually steal a race, in the way Buoy's rider did in the 1974 Coronation Cup. In fact Epsom, with its pronounced gradients including the steep downhill turn at Tattenham Corner, is a good course for front-running tactics and Johnson rode a copybook race on The Dancer. Soon at the head of affairs on the rails, she took them along at a strong pace that had several in trouble entering the straight. To all intents and purposes there were only three in it from two furlongs out and once challenged The Dancer kept on with great courage, going down by two lengths and a short head to her stable-companion Bireme and Vielle, losing second place only in the last few strides. Her front running had been so effective that the remainder were well strung out. The firm ground at Epsom suited The Dancer very well. She hadn't run up to her best on soft in the 1979 Criterium des Pouliches and she ran a long way below form on soft in the Lancashire Oaks at Haydock in July, losing the lead three furlongs out and staying on at one pace to be third, beaten seven lengths by Vielle and two by Kahaila. There were few suitable opportunities subsequently for a filly with The Dancer's specialised requirements and Haydock was the last we saw of her.

The Dancer (Fr) (b.f. 1977)	Green Dancer (b 1972)	Nijinsky (b 1967)	Northern Dancer Flaming Page
		Green Valley (br 1967)	Val de Loir Sly Pola
	Khazaeen (b 1968)	Charlottesville (b 1957)	Prince Chevalier Noorani
		Aimee (b 1957)	Tudor Minstrel Emali

The Dancer comes from a fine family. She is a half-sister to The Dundass (by Amber Rama), a fair winner over five furlongs at two years, and Beaming Bride (by King Emperor), successful twice in America. Her two-year-old sister Kazadancoa showed ability in 1980, finishing second at Maisons-Laffitte and

Longchamp from three starts. The dam, Khazaeen, sold for a mere 1,250 guineas at Goffs November Sales in 1975, is an unraced daughter of Aimee. The latter didn't win but produced the very smart miler Afayoon and the dams of Blushing Groom, the Italian Oaks winner Zabarella and Maroun, successful in the nine-furlong Prix Jean Prat. Flaming Heart, Maroun's dam, was closely related to Khazaeen, being by Charlottesville's half-brother Sheshoon. Aimee's dam, a half-sister to Khaled, was out of a sister to Infra Red, the fourth dam of Mill Reef and third dam of Wollow.

Because of her blindness The Dancer wore a hood with a cup over the left eye on every outing at three years. A rather nervous filly, not surprisingly, who didn't always look at ease in the paddock, sweating up at Newbury and Epsom, she was suited by a mile and a half. She visits Homing in 1981. *R. Hern.*

THE DISSIDENT 2 b.c. Lyphard 132–Siraf 85 (Alcide 136) (1980 7g2) Mar 9; useful-looking colt; half-brother to useful 6f and 7f winner Saluzzo (by Sallust) and 3 winners in France; dam staying half-sister to smart Harmony Hall; favourite but looking as though run would do him good, couldn't match more-experienced McCarthy's speed in final furlong of 15-runner maiden race at Newmarket in August and went down by 2½ lengths; will stay 1¼m; a promising debut. *H. Cecil.* **85** p

THE DOWNS 4 b.g. Blast 125–Princess Lorna 63 (Royal Palm 131) (1979 7f 7d 7.5s4 1980 9.5f 7g 8g2 9g2 8d2 8g 8g*) ex-Irish gelding; runner-up in handicaps at Phoenix Park in July and Mallow and Phoenix Park in August; also won over hurdles in July; reportedly landed a substantial off-course gamble when beating Park Bridge decisively by 3 lengths in seller at Bath in September on first outing over here; bought in 2,000 gns afterwards; stays 9f; acts on soft going; blinkered first 2 outings; trained in Ireland by A. Geraghty. *H. O'Neill.* **67**

THE DUPECATER 3 b.f. Le Johnstan 123–The Dupecat 75 (Javelot 124) (1979 NR 1980 7f 10fg 7fg 8g) quite a well-made filly; no sign of ability in maiden races and a seller; sold 600 gns Ascot July Sales. *J. Sutcliffe.* –

THE ESCAPER (USA) 4 b.g. Ack Ack–Psychedelic Dream (Carry Back) (1979 8d 10s 10fg3 14fg 1980 8s 10s) big, rangy gelding; quite a moderate maiden; stays 1¼m (well beaten when tried at 1¾m). *J. Sutcliffe.* –

THE EXPATRIATE 3 ch.c. Exbury 138–Mintika (Prince Bio) (1979 6.5d2 7s3 1980 8v* 8g 8.5d* 10fg4 9fg3 9.2s 10g) half-brother to several winners in France, including smart 1¼m to 13f winner Karoon (by Saint Crespin III); dam won twice at around 9f; won minor events at Saint-Cloud in March and Maisons-Laffitte in May; in frame in Prix la Force at Longchamp (¾-length fourth to Nemr) and Prix Jean Prat at Chantilly (excellent third to Night Alert and Ruscelli, beaten a neck and a short neck) on next 2 starts; ran moderately in Prix d'Ispahan at Longchamp and La Coupe de Maisons-Laffitte subsequently; will probably stay 1½m; seems to act on any going. *N. Pelat, France.* **121**

THE FALLEN KNIGHT 4 b.g. Ribero 126–Brown Braids (Turn-to) (1979 12v 10v3 10v3 1980 13s 13g 14.7f4 12fg) plating-class maiden; should stay further than 1¼m; has been tried in blinkers; sold 1,650 gns Newmarket July Sales. *N. Adam.* –

THE FLOORLAYER 2 b.g. Import 127–Lonely Nymph 60 (Forlorn River 124) (1980 5g 5d 7s) Apr 8; 1,200 2-y-o (privately); third foal; half-brother to 1979 2-y-o 6f winner Vana (by Mummy's Pet); dam placed over 1¼m; unquoted when behind in maiden and minor events in the autumn. *D. Elsworth.* –

THE FRIEND 2 ch.c. Run The Gantlet–Loose Cover 106 (Venture VII 129) (1980 8g) Mar 23; 16,000F; lightly-made colt; brother to Smoggy, a smart winner at up to 9f in France and USA, and half-brother to several winners; dam miler; 16/1 but looking fit, chased leaders before finishing seventh of 15 to Riberetto in maiden race at Newmarket in October; will be suited by 1¼m. *H. T. Jones.* –

THE GASCON 5 br.g. Brigadier Gerard 144–Iron Maiden 87 (Klairon 131) (1979 NR 1980 10g 11d) won over 1¼m as a 3-y-o but was well beaten on flat subsequently; wasn't the easiest of rides; dead. *Dr A. Jones.* –

THE GOLDSTONE 8 ch.g. Murrayfield 119–Delph 89 (Final Score 113) (1979 8d 7d 7g 7s 7g3 7.6s4 8fg 8fg 7fg3 8f4 8d3 8g2 8fg 7.3g 7d 8s 1980 10.2d –

8s4 8fg 11d4) moderate handicapper nowadays; made very good late progress when fairly close fourth behind La Piccolina at Newbury in October (had been off course 5 months before previous start and still looked burly); evidently stays 11f; acts on any going; has been tried in blinkers; suitable mount for an inexperienced rider. *W. Wightman.*

THE GREAT 4 b.c. Tamerlane 128–Maud 87 (Vilmorin) (1979 6s 5s 5f4 5f2 6f 5h 7d 1980 5f 6f 6h 6fg 5g4 5g) stocky colt; moderate plater at his best; should be suited by 6f+; possibly unsuited by soft going; wears blinkers; suitable mount for an apprentice; sold 340 gns Doncaster September Sales. *D. Yeoman.* **41**

THE GROCKALL 2 ch.f. Balidar 133–Laarne (Le Haar 126) (1980 7g 8d 8d) Apr 28; quite well-made filly; half-sister to La Marsa (by Royalty), a winner at up to 1½m; dam ran only twice; showed a little ability in maiden races in the autumn; probably stays 1m. *R. Laing.* **72**

THE HAGUE 4 ch.g. Mount Hagen 127–Vraiment (Relko 136) (1979 12s 10g 11d2 12g3 12fg2 12.2f2 13g 1980 16s 13.1fg 12f 11.7g) quite a moderate maiden; stayed 1½m; acted on firm going and a soft surface; sometimes blinkered; none too genuine; dead. *B. Palling.* **–**

THE HERTFORD 9 b.g. Supreme Sovereign 119–Emerald Velvet 76 (Sheshoon 132) (1979 10v 10v 10g 10.2s3 8d3 10g* 10s 8g 10s* 10d 10g* 10fg4 10fg 8fg 9f 10g 1980 10.2d 10s 10fg 12s 11.7d) poor handicapper nowadays; stays 1¼m; probably best with some give in the ground; has often spoiled his chance by starting slowly; usually blinkered; unreliable. *B. Swift.* **–**

THE HIT MAN 5 gr.h. Capistrano 120–Spring Bonnet (Cash and Courage 116) (1979 8v 11.1v 7d 10d 8g 8.3d 6g 8fg 8.3fg3 10.1f 8.3g4 1980 10d 12g 8fg) plater; stays 7f; seems to act on any going; usually blinkered in 1979; has worn bandages. *J. Jenkins.* **–**

THE HOOD 3 b.g. Busted 134–King's Gem 88 (King's Troop 118) (1979 NR 1980 9fg 11f 11.7fg3 12.2d 11.7f 16.1s) strong, sturdy gelding; third of 18 in maiden event at Bath in June, best effort; stays 1½m; acts on firm ground and is possibly unsuited by soft; sold out of J. Dunlop's stable 3,100 gns Ascot August Sales after fifth start. *F. Yardley.* **70**

THE HOOLEE 2 ch.f. Four Burrow 91–Primasilia 76 (Romulus 129) (1980 6fg 7g) Apr 26; leggy filly; fourth foal; dam stayed 1m at 2 yrs but showed little form afterwards; in rear in large fields of maidens at Windsor and Leicester in August. *S. Mellor.* **–**

THE HUYTON GIRLS 2 ch.f. Master Sing 109–Artway 82 (Articulate 121) (1980 5d 5d 5d 5s 5s 6g) Jan 21; 500F, 1,100Y; plain filly; half-sister to some minor winners and a winner in Hungary; dam won at 5f and 6f; 25/1, ran best race on fifth start when 3¾ lengths fifth of 20 to Marking Time in maiden event at Nottingham in October; may stay 6f; slowly away fourth appearance; formerly trained by M. Cousins. *M. James.* **58**

THE IMMIGRANT 3 b.g. Martinmas 128–Seul 69 (Faberge II 121) (1979 7f 1980 8d 10.1f 10fg 12g 8d 11d) leggy, narrow gelding; poor plater; best run at 1m on a soft surface; has been tried in blinkers; retained 800 gns Newmarket Autumn Sales. *K. Ivory.* **–**

THE KAFFIR 5 b.g. Hotfoot 126–Davina 71 (Darius 129) (1979 8fg 7fg 13fg 15d 1980 12f) of little account. *K. Oliver.* **–**

THE KNIFE 2 b.c. Fine Blade 121–Mary Kanga 67 (Charlottesville 135) (1980 5.8fg 5f 7s 7d 7fg 8fg 7fg) Mar 21; 2,200Y, 3,500 2-y-o; useful-looking colt; first foal; dam placed over 1¾m; little sign of ability in maiden and minor events; should stay well; blinkered sixth outing. *J. Bosley.* **–**

THE LOWER DECK 2 b.f. Sallust 134–Beatrice Frost 78 (Princely Gift 137) (1980 5f3 5f 5f4 5fg 5d) Jan 30; 3,200Y; leggy, rather light-framed filly; half-sister to winners in Italy by Queen's Hussar and Daring Display; dam winning stayer; in frame in maiden races in the spring; only seventh of 14 to Mull of Kintyre in £1,700 seller at York in June on fifth start; almost certainly finds 5f too sharp; blinkered fourth appearance. *N. Callaghan.* **–**

THE MARIESTAN 2 b.f. The Brianstan 128–Columba (Star Gazer 123) (1980 5d 7g 8fg3 8d 8g) Apr 2; neat filly; second reported foal; dam ran at 2 yrs; 20/1 when 5½ lengths third of 16 to I-Ching in seller at Leicester in September, best effort; evidently stays 1m. *P. Cundell.* **54**

THE MIXER 3 b.c. Biskrah 121–Full Swing 71 (Ballyciptic 122) (1979 8fg 8g 1980 16s 12g 10.1f 10fg 15.5g 8s) strong, good sort; poor maiden; often blinkered; trained by D. Kent first outing. *J. Long.* —

THE MO 4 ch.g. Some Hand 119–Wonderful One 90 (Princely Gift 137) (1979 6s 7s 8.2v 5g 6d 8s 6fg 6fg 8g^2 7g* 7fg 9f* 10fg 1980 8.3fg) plater; stays 9f; acts on firm going; often wears blinkers (did when successful); bandaged last 3 starts in 1979; sold out of K. Ivory's stable 1,000 gns Ascot March Sales. *S. Cole.* —

THE NIP 4 ch.c. Malicious–Queen Maya (Epaulette 125) (1979 9s 8s 16f 12h^4 1980 10g 10g 16f) lengthy colt; of little account nowadays; used to wear blinkers. *Mrs A. Harvey.* —

THE OLD FELLER 4 gr.g. Starch Reduced 112–Spanish Gal (El Gallo 122) (1979 8v 8s 6d 5d 5fg 5f 6fg 6fg* 6fg* 7g 7f 6fg 6d 8fg 7fg^2 1980 8s 8g 7fg 7f* 6s* 6g 6g 7g 6g 7fg 6s 6s) plater; attracted no bid after making all at Leicester in June; won handicap at Nottingham later in month; best at 6f or 7f and doesn't stay 1m; acts on any going; usually wears blinkers; suited by strong handling. *K. Ivory.* **57** d

THE OLD PRETENDER 9 ch.g. King's Leap 111–Angelique (Hill Gail) (1979 7s 7fg 6fg 1980 8f) tubed gelding; of little account in his later days; had been tried in blinkers; dead. *K. Morgan.* —

THEONLIWON 2 ch.c. Rarity 129–Quiet Colleen (Be Friendly 130) (1980 5f 5fg 5f^4) Mar 24; 1,000F, 4,000Y; leggy colt; first produce; dam placed over 6f at 3 yrs in Ireland; dropped in class and second favourite when 4¾ lengths fourth of 18 to Crosby Triangle in seller at Ripon in August; will be suited by 6f+; trained by J. Carr first 2 outings; sold 390 gns Doncaster October Sales. *D. Chapman.* **56**

THEO'S BABY 2 ch.f. Lombard 126–Anatevka (Privy Councillor 125) (1980 5s 5g^4 5fg 8.2g) Apr 2; 4,200Y; rather narrow, leggy filly; half-sister to several winners, including useful Pittencrieff (by Manacle), winner from 7f to 1¾m, but is only a poor maiden herself. *A. Demetriou.* —

THE PINGER 4 br.c. Town Crier 119–Hurly Burly (Sing Sing 134) (1979 7d 1980 10v 6f 7s) seems of no account. *D. Ringer.* —

THE POLCHAR 2 b.g. Tudor Rhythm 112–Mary Newall 69 (Coronation Year 124) (1980 6g^4 6g) Feb 27; 2,450F; lengthy, fair sort; closely related to winning sprinter Hei'land Mary and very useful sprinter Hei'land Jamie (both by Highland Melody); dam won sellers over 6f and 1m; moved poorly to start but showed ability when staying-on 4¾ lengths fourth of 16 to Floridian Dawn in seller at Yarmouth in September; favourite for £2,700 seller at York the following month but never got into contest and finished well behind Supreme Show; will stay 1m; wears bandages. *G. Pritchard-Gordon.* **55**

THE PROFESSOR 3 br.g. Welsh Pageant 132–Pulchra 107 (Celtic Ash) (1979 NR 1980 9g^3 10fg^2 10fg^2 10d^3 12g 12.3s^3 12f^2(dis) 15.8fg^2 14.7f*) tall gelding; half-brother to winning stayers Orcis and Glen Orcis (both by Quartette); dam won Nassau Stakes; well-backed favourite when winning minor event at Redcar in September; stays well; probably acts on any going; gives impression he needs strong handling. *J. W. Watts.* **73**

THE PUG 3 b.c. Mummy's Pet 125–Veronique 96 (Matador 131) (1979 5fg^3 5d^3 5s^2 5.3fg* 5f 5f^2 6f* 6f* 6fg^3 6g^2 1980 6f 5fg 6fg* 5s* 5fg 6g 6fg) good-bodied, quite attractive colt; good mover; returned to form when leading inside last furlong to beat Lightning Label readily by a length in 6-runner £4,700 race at Lingfield in June; comfortably beat Go Total 2 lengths in handicap on same course later in month; ran best subsequent race to be nearly 4½ lengths fifth to Valeriga in King George Stakes at Goodwood in July on fifth start; stayed 6f; acted on any going; sometimes sweated up; blinkered final outing; sold 37,000 gns Newmarket December Sales; stud in Australia. *J. Dunlop.* **113**

THE QUIET BIDDER 2 b.c. Auction Ring 123–Capule (Middleground) (1980 6g* 6fg* 6s^3 5f^3 5g^2) Apr 25; 6,000Y; quite useful sort; half-brother to 3 winners, including fairly useful 1975 2-y-o 6f and 7f winner El Capitan (by Captain's Gig), subsequently successful in Belgium and France; dam minor 2-y-o 5f winner in USA; successful in maiden race at York in July and in Philip Cornes Nickel Alloys Nursery at Newmarket the following month, putting up a useful effort under 9-7 when winning latter by 1½ lengths from Rikasso Beauty; third under top weight in valuable nurseries on next 2 starts and ran very well when 1½ lengths second of 7 to Pushy in Cornwallis Stakes **110**

at Ascot in October; effective at 5f and 6f, and will probably stay 7f; acts on any going but is well suited by a sound surface; consistent. *R. Hollinshead.*

THE RAGGED ROBBER 4 b.g. Ragstone 128–Burglars Moll 94 (Burglar 128) (1979 NR 1980 10.1d 10.8fg) useless; sold 350 gns Ascot September Sales. *H. O'Neill.* –

THE SANDFORD 5 b.h. Sandford Lad 133–Sovereign Whistle 67 (Sovereign Path 125) (1979 6s 7s 6s 6d* 7.6s^2 6fg 6g^4 6g^2 6d 6s 6s 1980 6fg 7.6f 6fg 6g 6fg 6s 6fg 7s 6d 7s) attractive, well-made horse; useful performer at his best; disappointing in 1980, best effort when seventh of 24 behind Sparkling Boy in Ladbrokes (Ayr) Gold Cup in September on sixth start; stays 7.6f; acts on any going, but is suited by some give in the ground; wears blinkers; sold to P. Brookshaw 5,400 gns Newmarket December Sales. *C. Brittain.* –

THE SERGEANT 8 br.g. King's Troop 118–Sincerity 91 (Soderini 123) (1979 NR 1980 8g) rangy gelding; lightly raced nowadays and finished behind in seller (very burly) on only outing of 1980; stays 1¼m; acts on a firm surface but is particularly well suited by a soft one; wears bandages. *J. Carr.* –

THE SMALL MIRACLE 2 gr.c. Most Secret 119–Grey Aglow 89 (Aglojo 119) (1980 5f 5fg 7f 6g 8.2v* 8s* 7v) Mar 10; workmanlike colt; first foal; dam won from 5f to 2m; off course most of the summer; much improved after his return and won nurseries at Hamilton and Stockton in October; stayed on strongly when beating Andrea's Pet ¾ length (pair clear) on latter; will probably stay 1¼m; revels in the mud; formerly trained by M. W. Easterby. *W. Elsey* **77**

THE SOLENT 4 ch.g. Exbury 138–West Side Story 127 (Rockefella) (1979 12g^3 14f* 16s* 16.9fg* 19g* 16d^2 1980 14s^4) narrow, unfurnished gelding; very useful stayer as a 3-y-o when trained by H. Cecil, winner of 4 races, including Goodwood Stakes; successful over hurdles early in 1980 but became temperamental and was sold out of R. Turnell's stable 3,100 gns Ascot June Sales; virtually refused to race on only subsequent outing on flat (October) and is best left alone. *M. Naughton.* – §

THE SON 3 br.g. Roi Soleil 125–Memento 101 (Relic) (1979 NR 1980 10s) 3,400Y; quite useful-looking gelding; half-brother to several winners, including fairly useful sprinter Bosun's Whistle (by Whistler); dam, half-sister to Credo, won at up to 11f; started slowly when last of 17 in maiden race at Nottingham in April; sold 460 gns Ascot July Sales. *J. Douglas-Home.* –

THE SOUK 4 ch.c. Native Bazaar 122–Sister Willow 95 (Premonition 130) (1979 6g^4 6d 7fg 8fg^4 8h 6fg 1980 8d 10v 8fg 8g 8d) well-made colt; stayed 1m; acted on any going; was often blinkered; gave impression he was none too genuine; dead. *B. Richmond.* –

THE SPROUT 3 b.f. Flatbush 95–Artlight (Articulate 121) (1979 NR 1980 12.2g 11d) second foal; sister to a winning plater; dam never ran; tailed off in maiden races at Catterick and Hamilton. *J. Fitzgerald.* –

THE STIRRER 4 gr.c. Capistrano 120–Josephine (Tamerlane 128) (1979 8fg 10.8fg^3 10fg* 10.8g 10d^3 10fg* 1980 14fg) workmanlike colt; plater; stays 1¼m; acts on a firm surface. *S. Pattemore.* –

THE SUN HOTEL 2 b.f. Owen Anthony 102–Any Cloud 47 (Golden Cloud) (1980 6g 5g 6g 8g) Mar 21; 500Y; 1,000 2-y-o; small filly; sister to a winner in Malaya, and half-sister to 2 other winners abroad; dam of little account; emulating her dam. *Mrs A. Harvey.* –

THE SURVEYOR 4 br.g. Goldhill 125–Shortino 71 (Fortino II 120) (1979 6v 6s 7f 8f 10s 10s 1980 10s 8f 8f^4 8g 7g 9d 12d) poor maiden; stays 1m (tailed-off last in valuable seller over 1½m); acts on firm going. *R. Hollinshead.* –

THETCHU 2 b.c. Averof 123–Cavalier's Blush 75 (King's Troop 118) (1980 7d 8d) Apr 17; 5,000Y; fair sort; first foal; dam needed a test of stamina; unquoted and in need of race when behind in 20-runner minor event won by Soldan at Doncaster in October; brought down in similar event at Leicester the following month. *A. Hide.* –

THE THATCHER 2 b.c. Thatch 136–Jolie Fleur 111 (Exbury 138) (1980 7fg* 7fg^2) Feb 13; big, strong, good sort; third foal; half-brother to 1¼m winner Welsh Carnival (by Welsh Pageant); dam, half-sister to Connaught, showed very useful form at 1m to 1¼m; impressed us when winning 9-runner minor event at Yarmouth in August, leading at distance and then striding out in splendid style to draw 3 lengths clear of Ishamo; 2/1 on for 6-runner Fitzroy House Stakes at Newmarket later in month but was being niggled at when in **100** p lead 2f out and went down by a short head to Baz Bombati; will stay 1¼m. *H. Cecil.*

THE TON MACHINE 3 ch.f. Mountain Call 125–My Nan 65 (Pampered King 121) (1979 5d 1980 13s 8g) of little account. *J. Bingham.* —

THE TRADER 3 b.c. The Brianstan 128–Romancing 82 (Romulus 129) (1979 NR 1980 6f 7fg* 7f 7g 7g) 10,500Y; lengthy, good sort; half-brother to several winners here and abroad, including fairly useful Stormy Affair (by Prevailing); dam won over 6f at 2 yrs; won 15-runner maiden race at Leicester in April; last in handicaps subsequently; stays 7f; acts on a firm surface; blinkered final 2 outings, swerving badly at start on first occasion. *J. Sutcliffe.* **67**

THE TRUCK PEOPLE 3 b.f. Some Hand 119–Rock Me (Rockefella) (1979 5fg 6g 7g 1980 8v 6f) in rear in varied company, including selling; sold 600 gns Newmarket May Sales. *J. Berry.* —

THE TURNED REVENGE 3 ch.g. Sweet Revenge 129–Turnstone 83 (Sea Hawk II 131) (1979 6g 6fg² 5f 6f⁴ 6f 8f 7d 1980 6h 6fg 8d 10fg) poor form, including in sellers; best run at 6f on a firm surface. *T. Gosling.* —

THE VAGRANT 2 ch.c. Sandford Lad 133–Battlemaid (Captain's Gig) (1980 5fg 5d) May 18; lengthy colt; second foal; half-brother to moderate 1979 2-y-o Henham Lodge (by Tyrant); dam third over 6f and 7.5f in Ireland at 2 yrs; looked extremely well in paddock at Sandown in June on second outing and showed very good speed until weakening at distance, coming home 12 lengths fifth of 7 to Tax Haven in £2,700 event; not seen out again. *G. Lewis.* —

THE VIC 4 gr.g. Saritamer 130–Blue Sash 107 (Djebe) (1979 8.2s 6fg 7g² 8fg⁴ 9.4f* 12f 9fg 1980 8.2s 12.5s) poor performer; behind in a seller and an amateur event (last) in October; best form at up to 9.4f and does not stay 1½m. *S. Nesbitt.* —

THE WONDER (FR) 2 br.c. Wittgenstein 123–The Lark (Lanark 123) (1980 5.5d⁴ 7d* 8g* 9fg³ 10s* 10v*) **123**

If the President of the Societe des Steeple-Chases intended the mating between his only thoroughbred mare The Lark and the little-used stallion Wittgenstein to produce a jumper, he has received an unexpected bonus. The resultant foal, The Wonder, was one of the best French two-year-olds of 1980, with the Group 3 Prix de Conde and the Group 2 Criterium de Saint-Cloud among his four successes, and earned over 800,000 francs in prize money and premiums.

The Wonder's record very nearly read five wins, not four, from six starts. On his first appearance in pattern-race company in the Prix Saint-Roman at Longchamp in October, when already a winner at Evry and of the valuable

Criterium de Saint-Cloud—The Wonder gives weight all round, beating Mont Pelion (white cap), Brinkbero (blaze) and Ledmir

Prix des Foals at Deauville, he failed by only a short neck and a head to overhaul the all-the-way winner Mariacho. He finished best of all over the nine furlongs, giving the strong impression he'd be better suited by an even stiffer test of stamina; and so it proved. Over another furlong on soft ground in the Prix de Conde at Longchamp later in the month he burst through against the rails, after coming to the final hundred and fifty yards still in only fifth place, to win by a short neck from the subsequently-demoted Ledmir. Brinkbero finished third, a length and a half back. And on even softer ground in the Criterium de Saint-Cloud in November he won again, when 2 lb worse off with both Ledmir and Brinkbero and 4 lb worse off with Mont Pelion, whom he'd beaten by only three quarters of a length at Deauville. Favourite was the Bustino colt Prunheco, said to be one of the most promising two-year-olds in the huge Mathet stable, but he was already back-pedalling as they entered the straight with less than three furlongs to run. Although The Wonder was still towards the rear at this stage he moved up quickly to challenge the long-time leader Mont Pelion one and a half furlongs out, soon took command and battled on courageously to win by a length. Mont Pelion held on to second place by only a short head from the fast-finishing Brinkbero, whom many thought had been given too much to do.

The Wonder (Fr) (br.c. Mar 15, 1978)	Wittgenstein (br 1971)	Roi Dagobert (b 1964)	Sicambre
			Dame d'Atour
		Stavroula (b 1956)	Nasrullah
			Segula
	The Lark (gr 1972)	Lanark (gr 1963)	Grey Sovereign
			Vermilion O'Toole
		Norman Lass (b 1968)	Timmy Lad
			Golden Glory

Wittgenstein stood his first season at stud as a five-year-old, having won the Criterium de Maisons-Laffitte at two and La Coupe de Maisons-Laffitte at three from a total of only ten starts. If he wasn't raced hard The Lark certainly was. She ran thirty times on the flat, winning over nine, ten and fourteen furlongs in the Provinces, as well as finishing second in a hurdle race at Rouen. The Wonder is The Lark's first foal and she in turn is the only reported produce of Norman Lass, a half-sister to the French Two Thousand Guineas winner Moulines.

The stiffer the test of stamina the better it suited The Wonder at two years and he's sure to need at least a mile and a quarter at three. Although he's a stayer he's not without a turn of foot and he should again give a good account of himself in the top French races. He hasn't yet raced on really firm ground but acts on any other. *J. de Chevigny, France.*

THEYDON PRINCE 4 ch.g. Morston 125–Maiden Erlegh 100 (Never Say — Die 137) (1979 11g 12g^2 13.3s^2 12f 10fg* 10d^3 1980 12h) strong gelding; won maiden race at Brighton in 1979; well beaten in handicap on same course in May; stays 13f; possibly unsuited by very firm ground; hung left second and fourth starts at 3 yrs. *C. Read.*

THINK AHEAD 2 b.f. Sharpen Up 127–Regal Splendour 76 (Sovereign Path **101** 125) (1980 5fg* 5h* 5g 6d^2 5f^2 5f* 5fg* 5s) Apr 10; leggy filly; third foal; half-sister to 2 winners, including Collector's Item (by Run The Gantlet), successful over 5f and 1m in Ireland; dam 6f winner; successful in minor events at Windsor and Chepstow in May and put up fairly useful efforts to win nurseries at Redcar and Lingfield in the autumn; carried 6-lb penalty when winning going away by 2½ lengths from Little Starchy at Lingfield; stays 6f; acts well on very firm ground and has run creditably on a soft surface; put up a moderate effort when ridden by very light apprentice on fifth start but is genuine and consistent. *H. T. Jones.*

THIRD GENERATION 2 b.f. Decoy Boy 129–Once Removed (Great Nephew **58** 126) (1980 5fg 5.1f 5s) Feb 27; 4,100Y; big, leggy filly; second foal; sister to fair sprinter Second Generation; dam unraced daughter of very useful sprinter Tumbrel; 7¾ lengths fifth of 10 to Rose of Raby in maiden race at Yarmouth in June, second outing; off course afterwards until November and was reluctant to go to post on her return. *H. Collingridge.*

THISTLETON 2 br.f. Comedy Star 121–Halma (Hallez 131) (1980 6g) — Mar 30; 1,500Y; first foal; dam showed no worthwhile form; unquoted when tenth of 12 to Spark of Life in maiden race at Yarmouth in September; sold 400 gns Newmarket Autumn Sales. *D. Ringer.*

THOLT E WILL (USA) 3 ch.c. Giacometti 130–Italian Belle (Tom Rolfe) **79** (1979 7fg 7g 7.2g* 8fg^{3} 8s 8s 1980 10d 14f 11fg 12s 12.2f^{3} 16g^{2} 16d) attractive colt; good mover; moderate handicapper at his best; stays well; seems unsuited by soft ground; sometimes sweats up; virtually pulled up second start, ran badly on seventh and is not one to trust implicitly; sold 5,600 gns Newmarket Autumn Sales. *B. Hills.*

THOMSON'S MELODY 3 br.f. Derring-Do 131–Elm Leaf 96 (Tudor Melody — 129) (1979 5fg 5f* 1980 5fg) small filly; won maiden race at Lingfield at 2 yrs; fell only outing in 1980 (April); would have been suited by 6f+; dead. *J. Sutcliffe.*

THOMSON'S POLICY 6 b.g. Jukebox 120–Reelin Bridge (New Day) (1979 — NR 1980 12.2v^{3}) middle-distance handicapper; joint-favourite and having first outing on flat since winning on only start in 1978 when third of 10 to easy winner Slitherum at Warwick in March; suited by 1½m: revels in the mud; has worn blinkers. *J. Edwards.*

THORGANBY MIRACLE 3 b.g. Porto Bello 118–Miracle Girl 75 (Sing Sing **46** 134) (1979 5g 5s 5.1g 6g 6fg* 7s 7fg 1980 8v 7fg 7fg^{2} 6g 8d 6g 7g 7g) tall gelding; plater; best at up to 7f; acts well on a firm surface and is possibly unsuited by soft; often blinkered; ran badly final start; sold 600 gns Doncaster October Sales. *R. Hobson.*

THOUSANDFOLD (USA) 3 b. or br.c. Forli–Super Flower 64 (Super Sam **107** 124) (1979 6g^{2} 6f* 5d* 1980 6fg^{2} 6f) $185,000Y; big, rangy, good-looking colt; half-brother to very smart Faliraki (by Prince Tenderfoot), a winner at up to 9f here and in USA; dam, half-sister to Typhoon, stayed 7f; smart (rated 119) at 2 yrs; didn't make his reappearance until July and put up easily better effort when failing by short head to hold off Gods Mark in 10-runner Matt Gallagher Sprint Stakes at Phoenix Park; 2/1 on for 11-runner Herbertstown Stakes on same course the following month but could finish only fifth behind Pitmarie; will stay 7f; appears to act on any going; racing in USA. *V. O'Brien, Ireland.*

THREEPWOOD 3 b.g. Jimsun 121–Mountain Child 70 (Mountain Call 125) — (1979 5d 5fg^{4} 5fg* 6d 1980 5f 6s 6d) small gelding; plater; should stay 6f; acts on a firm surface. *C. Booth.*

THREE SHOES 4 b.c. Decoy Boy 129–Huna 84 (Doutelle 128) (1979 7d — 8v 10d 7g 7s^{4} 7s 7v* 7d 8fg 7f 8.2g 12g 1980 7v 8g) small, sturdy colt; stayed 7f; suited by some give in the ground; inconsistent; dead. *W. Marshall.*

THREE TROIKAS (FR) 4 b.f. Lyphard 132–Three Roses (Dual 117) (1979 **128** 9.5d* 8s* 10fg* 10.5g^{2} 12fg* 12d* 1980 10g* 10.5d^{2} 9.7d^{3} 10g^{2} 12f^{4} 12v)

The serious injury that struck Three Troikas in June provided some of the season's saddest news. In a year of comparative mediocrity for European middle-distance racing there emerged no successors of the quality of Troy and Three Troikas, the leading middle-distance performers of 1979. The injury to Three Troikas, a broken bone in her off-fore foot sustained in the Prix Dollar in June, kept her off the course for three and a half months and might well have cost her a second successive victory in the Prix de l'Arc de Triomphe, Europe's most prestigious middle-distance event. Three Troikas would have brought off something remarkable had she managed to win the Arc: immediately after her injury she was confined to her box for five weeks and went to post for the Arc short of peak fitness, having done very little serious work before her only outing in the interim—in the Prix du Prince d'Orange at Longchamp in late-September in which she was beaten half a length by Dunette who conceded her 2 lb. Three Troikas ran very well in the Arc: making up ground smoothly on the downhill stretch before the entrance to the final straight, she was soon challenging strongly for the lead and, after looking likely to win about two furlongs out, she passed the post in fourth place, less than a length behind Detroit. Three Troikas blew hard afterwards and her trainer expressed the view that she would have won with another week's preparation.

Three Troikas began the season in brilliant form. We were most impressed by her in the Prix d'Harcourt at Longchamp in April. She was opposed by six good colts, including the Prix de l'Arc runner-up Le Marmot, and she outclassed them in the paddock and in the race, winning easily by a length and a half and a head from Gain and Le Marmot; it seemed that she was headed for another fine season. On her only other outing before the Prix Dollar, Three Troikas was beaten by Le Marmot in the Prix Ganay, the most valuable race in Europe in the first part of the season for horses above the age of three;

Prix d'Harcourt, Longchamp—Three Troikas wins readily from Gain and Le Marmot (hidden)

Le Marmot beat Three Troikas by a length and a half, Head easing up on Three Troikas near the post when it was clear that Le Marmot had the upper hand. Had Three Troikas produced her best form she would have won the Ganay comfortably; her performance was very disappointing in the light of her sparkling reappearance. Three Troikas was sent to race in the United States after the Prix de l'Arc: by all accounts she travelled badly and was retired after running poorly in the Turf Classic at Aqueduct. She will visit Exclusive Native in 1981.

Three Troikas (Fr) (b.f. 1976)	Lyphard (b 1969)	Northern Dancer (b 1961)	Nearctic
			Natalma
		Goofed (ch 1960)	Court Martial
			Barra II
	Three Roses (b 1968)	Dual (b 1958)	Chanteur II
			Duplicity
		Always Loyal (ch 1963)	King's Troop
			Constant Worry

Three Troikas enjoyed a magnificent season as a three-year-old, winning five of her six races, notably the Poule d'Essai des Pouliches (the French One Thousand Guineas), the Prix Vermeille and the Prix de l'Arc. She was a resounding three-length winner of the Arc, showing easily the best turn of finishing speed in a big field that included the Derby winners of England and France, the third in the Derby, the runner-up in the French Derby and the winner of the Coronation Cup. Three Troikas headed the International Classification at the end of her three-year-old career, being allotted a rating of 97 (she was rated 87 at the end of the most recent season). As a daughter of Lyphard, a stallion whose stock are in great demand these days, Three Troikas is worth her weight in gold as a broodmare; her dam Three Roses, whose second foal and second winner she is, showed useful form as a two-year-old in Ireland, winning a six-furlong maiden race and the Park Stakes over a mile at Phoenix Park, but failed to add to her laurels when raced at three and four in France. The dam's family isn't particularly distinguished. A most attractive individual, Three Troikas stayed a mile and a half and probably acted on any going. She was a genuine performer. *Mme C. Head, France.*

THREE WAYS 4 gr.g. Grey Mirage 128–Siciliana 77 (Sicilian Prince 126) — (1979 8s 8f 10f 8f^3 12d^2 9fg^2 10h 12d 10g 1980 10.2d 10v^2 10v^3 10h 12.5s) robust gelding; stays 1½m; acts on any going; suitable mount for an apprentice. *M. W. Easterby.*

THRIFTY MISSTRESS 3 ch.f. Sovereign Bill 105–Saving Season (Silly — Season 127) (1979 6fg 6fg 5f 6g 5fg^3 6f 1980 8fg 10.1s 10g 10.1d 7f) lengthy filly; poor form, including in sellers; best run at 5f on a firm surface; blinkered last 2 starts; has worn bandages. *J. Davies.*

THRILLING 4 b.f. So Blessed 130–Loop the Loop 81 (Hopeful Venture 125) **49** (1979 8fg 10.6s 1980 10v^2 12fg 12fg 8fg 8s 10g 9fg 10fg 10s^4 8.2s^4 8s 10d) workmanlike filly; in frame in varied company, including in a seller on tenth start; blinkered seventh outing; stays 1¼m; acts on heavy going. *C. Thornton.*

THROUGH GREEN 3 b.f. Manacle 123–Douane 87 (Runnymede 123) (1979 **59** 5d 5g 5fg^3 5g^3 5fg 5fg 5fg^4 1980 5v 5f 5fg 10.1g 8g^3 8g 8s 6g) neat filly; in frame in maiden races at 2 yrs; third in seller at Kempton in September, easily best effort in 1980; unlikely to stay 1¼m; best form on top-of-the-ground; blinkered final 2 starts in 1979; one paced; sold 850 gns Ascot December Sales. *W. Wightman.*

THROUGH THE VALLEY 2 b.g. Furry Glen 121–Best Way (Great White Way) (1980 5v* 5g 5f^3 5h^3 7g 7.2g 7.6f) May 3; 800F, 5,000Y; small, close-coupled gelding; good mover; second foal; dam ran twice; won 13-runner maiden race at Warwick in March by a head from Gemsbok; showed worthwhile form on two subsequent occasions; stays 7f; needs a straight course; exported to Hong Kong. *R. Hannon.* **76**

THUNDER WONDER 2 b.g. Winden 109–Saffron Princess (Thriller 77) (1980 6fg 6fg 7d 7fg 7fg) Apr 7; small, lightly-made gelding; first foal; dam placed in a selling hurdle; twice showed ability in sellers, on third outing finishing about 11 lengths sixth of 16 to Friendly Falcon at Newmarket in July; will stay well; has shown a tendency to hang. *D. Elsworth.* **51**

TICKETS 7 b.g. Yellow God 129–La Gamberge 87 (Vieux Manoir 132) (1979 8s* 10s 8fg 1980 8fg 9.6h 8f 10d 8fg) poor plater; stays 1m; acts on soft going; sold to G. Ripley 410 gns Ascot September Sales. *H. O'Neill.* **–**

TIDDLEY 2 ch.f. Filiberto 123–Neater (Double Jump 131) (1980 5.8h 7d) Mar 23; first foal; dam won over 7.5f in France; ninth of 10 in maiden race at Bath in August (10/1) and minor event at Brighton the following month (20/1). *J. Dunlop.* **–**

TIE ANCHOR 3 ch.c. Quayside 124–Charming Girl 75 (Sound Track 132) (1979 5fg^3 5.8fg^2 6f 7f* 7fg* 7fg^3 7s* 7f^2 8fg^3 1980 7v 7s 10g^2 10.4f^3 12f* 12fg 8d 9g 11.5g 12d 7s) lengthy colt; won £2,700 event at Limerick Junction in May; placed earlier in The Minstrel Stakes at Leopardstown (2½ lengths second to Del Sarto) and Dee Stakes at Chester (finished well when 1½ lengths third to Playboy Jubilee); well beaten in Queen Anne Stakes at Royal Ascot on seventh start; suited by middle distances; acts on any going; blinkered nowadays; very promising hurdler. *P. Prendergast, jnr, Ireland.* **95** d

TIEBREAKER 4 b.g. Cavo Doro 124–Desist 92 (Supreme Court 135) (1979 12s 1980 10.1g) probably of little account; sold 2,200 gns Ascot September Sales. *S. James.* **–**

TILBURY 3 b.c. Realm 129–Lea Landing 81 (Meadow Court 129) (1979 5s 5s^2 5fg 6s 7g^4 6d^2 7.5s* 1980 6v 6v 7f 12f 10fg 9f^3 10g^4) very attractive colt; won maiden race at Gowran Park in 1979; showed little form in varied company at 3 yrs; stays 7f well; acts on soft going; sometimes blinkered; trained by B. H. Burcombe in Ireland first 6 starts. *G. Beeson.* **–**

TILLYMORGAN 2 b.f. Lochnager 132–Hodhard 101 (Hard Sauce 131) (1980 5f 5fg) June 4; strong, compact, sturdy filly; third reported living foal; dam speedy 2-y-o; well behind in maiden race at Beverley in August and minor event at Catterick in September. *M. W. Easterby.* **–**

TILTING 4 ch.f. Galivanter 131–Swordblade 84 (Pall Mall 132) (1979 7d^3 7s^4 7fg 5g^4 5.3d^3 1980 5s 5g 5f 6h) small, useful-looking filly; good mover; needs further than 5f and stays 7f; seems to act on any going. *P. Feilden.* **–**

TIMARACK 4 ch.c. Double Act 94–Gondook 97 (Chamier 128) (1979 7v 8fg 7f 8f 8f 1980 10.6fg 8fg 6g 8.2d 10f^2 8d 7fg 8f^4 8.2s^2 11fg) plater; stays 1¼m; acts on any going; blinkered fourth start at 3 yrs; has worn bandages. *S. Nesbitt.* **55**

TIMBER LINE 3 b.f. High Line 125–Dolan's Bay (Hard Ridden 131) (1979 NR 1980 12d 11fg 14d) wiry filly; second reported foal; dam showed no form in bumpers and hurdle races but was lightly raced; well beaten in maiden events at Haydock (2) and Wolverhampton. *H. Candy.* **–**

TIMBER TRACK 3 b.g. Palm Track 122–Kindling 80 (Psidium 130) (1979 NR 1980 12fg^4 10g^2 10f* 12d* 13.3d*) big gelding; has a round action; third live foal; half-brother to 1977 2-y-o 5f winner Vascar (by Roi Soleil), subsequently a fairly useful winner over hurdles, and to a winner in Brazil; dam ran only 3 times; a progressive individual who won maiden race at Ripon, minor event at Edinburgh and handicap at Newbury in second half of season; comfortably beat Latakia by 3 lengths in last-named; will stay 1¾m; probably acts on any going; sweated up slightly second start (ran creditably). *E. Weymes.* **90**

TIME FOR THOUGHT 2 b.f. Crooner 119–Time Call (Chanteur II 135) (1980 5fg^2 6fg^3 5d^3 7d^3) May 2; lightly-made filly; good mover; half-sister **75**

to numerous winners, including very useful 1979 2-y-o sprinter Sitica (by Siliconn) and high-class stayer High Line (by High Hat); dam fair 5f sprinter; placed in maiden races, on final occasion finishing 1¼ lengths third of 12 to Patchinia at Chester in August; suited by 7f. *H. Candy.*

TIME GENTS 5 b.g. Polyfoto 124–Blue Mistress (Skymaster 126) (1979 11g 16g 7d 1980 12g² 12d 5g 10g³ 12.5s) ex-Irish gelding; second foal; dam placed in France; placed in bumpers race at Sligo and ladies race at Tralee in August; stays 1½m; formerly trained by B. H. Burcombe. *C. Mackenzie.* —

TIME-TABLE 2 b.f. Mansingh 120–Queen of Time (Roi Dagobert 128) (1980 6f 6v²) Mar 29; 9,000Y; second foal; dam poor maiden; 5 lengths second of 5 to Bretton Park in maiden race at Hamilton in October. *J. W. Watts.* **66**

TIMONEL 4 ch.c. Sallust 134–Pamette (Pampered King 121) (1979 NR 1980 10fg 8f 8fg) useful (rated 101) at 2 yrs; didn't regain his form in 1980 and dropped himself out leaving stalls and came back tailed off on penultimate appearance; stays 1m; yet to race on a soft surface; retained 720 gns Newmarket Autumn Sales. *G. Hunter.* —

TIMONIER (FR) 3 b. or br.g. Satingo 129–Trelex (Exbury 138) (1979 6g 7f 1980 11.7fg 14g 12fg⁴ 10.1g⁴) tall gelding; plating-class maiden; stays 1½m; has run respectably for an apprentice; sold to Denys Smith 3,700 gns Newmarket Autumn Sales. *J. Tree.* **66**

TIMONISE 2 br.f. Saulingo 122–Castletimon (Tudor Music 131) (1980 6fg 6fg) Mar 19; 4,000Y; second living foal; half-sister to 3-y-o Italian winner Solbiati (by Sandford Lad); dam lightly-raced half-sister to very useful middle-distance performer Shamsan; behind in newcomers race at Chepstow in August and 28-runner seller at Windsor (9/1) in September. *N. Vigors.* —

TIM WHISKY 2 br.c. Home Guard 129–Song God 96 (Red God 128 §) (1980 6d) Mar 26; strong, deep-girthed colt; first foal; dam 2-y-o 5f winner; unquoted, apprentice ridden and looking as though race would do him good, showed promise when seventh of 25 to Little Wolf in maiden race at Newbury in October, chasing leaders throughout and not being punished unnecessarily; sure to do better. *P. Cole.* **76** p

TINAGARY 3 ch.f. Lauso–Torbay (Hill Prince) (1979 5s 5s 5s 6d 5f 1980 8v 8.2d 10fg) small, plain filly; of little account; sold 500 gns Doncaster May Sales. *J. Berry.* —

TINA'S PET 2 b.c. Mummy's Pet 125–Merry Weather 69 (Will Somers 114 §) (1980 6fg 6s² 6fg* 6f* 5s*) **121**

The name of Tina's Pet will not be uppermost in the minds of many when it comes to selecting horses to follow in the best races in 1981. He hasn't been tried in pattern-race company but, judging by his runaway victories at Yarmouth, Ripon and Ayr on his last three appearances, he will surely be aimed higher as a three-year-old—and he could well make a name for himself. Spindrifter and Tre Fontane were the best horses Tina's Pet came across as a two-year-old; Tina's Pet trounced Spindrifter by eight lengths at Ripon in August, becoming only the second to beat that horse in thirteen races, and on his next appearance Tina's Pet beat Tre Fontane by five lengths in the Harry Rosebery Challenge Trophy at Ayr in September (on his previous outing Tre Fontane had finished a five-length third to Marwell in the Flying Childers Stakes at Doncaster). These two performances convinced us that Tina's Pet was one of the best of the season's sprinting two-year-olds; we have a higher opinion of him than the Jockey Club's handicapper who gave him 8-8 in the Tote European Free Handicap which was published on December 4th.

As its new name implies, the Tote European Free Handicap, which will have £20,000 added in 1981, has a wider scope than its predecessors. The 1980 Free Handicap includes all forty-five two-year-olds listed in the International Classification, a move which the sponsors hope will result in some of the best of the French and Irish coming over for the race. We can't see the idea resulting in any significant change in the type of field that turns out for the Free Handicap. Most of the top French two-year-olds in a normal year are staying types—the Free Handicap is run over seven furlongs—and, in any case, we couldn't envisage the race's proving a counter-attraction to the traditional early-season classic trials in France. As for the Irish, in a normal season there won't be enough of them in the Classification to ensure a runner on the day. Perhaps another year the qualification could be extended to include all the two-year-olds in the French and Irish Free Handicaps; that would be a better way to give an international flavour to the race. Whilst on

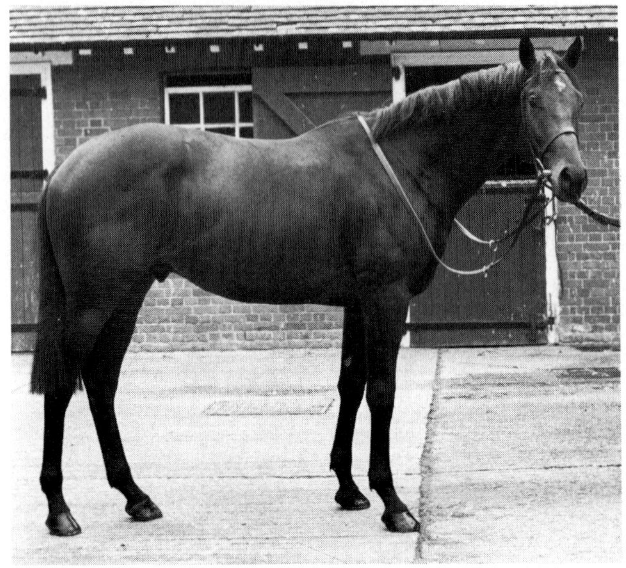

Mr M. Mouskos' "Tina's Pet"

the subject of the Free Handicap, the framing of the weights makes much more sense than it did in 1979 when the official handicapper's work brought a hornet's nest about his ears; in marked contrast to 1979 when there were sixty-seven horses—a ridiculous number—in the top 14 lb weight range, there were forty-five in the same weight range in 1980. Taking into account the presence of sixteen or seventeen French and Irish who wouldn't formerly have been included, the top of the 1980 Free Handicap has a much more familiar look about it; between 1969 and 1978 the average number of horses in the top 14 lb weight range in the Free Handicaps was about twenty-one.

Tina's Pet (b.c. Mar 4, 1978)	Mummy's Pet (b 1968)	Sing Sing (b 1957)	Tudor Minstrel
			Agin the Law
		Money for Nothing (br 1962)	Grey Sovereign
			Sweet Nothings
	Merry Weather (br 1971)	Will Somers (br 1955)	Tudor Minstrel
			Queen's Jest
		Copper Sky (b 1964)	Hook Money
			Eternal Goddess

We have already said that we regard Tina's Pet as favourably treated in the Free Handicap. We also think he's the right type for the race—sharp enough for the test of speed that the race usually entails. On breeding he is unlikely to stay much beyond sprint distances—by Mummy's Pet out of a Will Somers mare he has a pedigree with speed written all over it. The average distance of races won at three years and upwards by the progeny of Mummy's Pet is only six and a half furlongs; that for Will Somers is just under a mile. Tina's Pet's dam Merry Weather, whose dam and grandam were sprinters, gained her only success in a nine-furlong maiden race at Carlisle as a three-year-old; her only previous foal, the plater Indian Spring (by the sprinter

Mansingh), won over seven furlongs and stayed a mile. Tina's Pet, a well-made, quite attractive colt who was well bought as a yearling for 5,900 guineas, acts on any going. *G. Huffer.*

TINDER RIDGE 4 gr.c. Mountain Call 125–Grey Gal (Grey Sovereign 128§) (1979 NR 1980 8f 12h 14.7f) of little account; blinkered first start; sold 380 gns Ascot July Sales. *M. Naughton.* —

TINJAR 2 ch.c. Brittany–Sweet Minuet (Setay 105) (1980 6s 6d 6g* 6g² 6fg 5g³) Apr 16; 4,200Y; strong colt; half-brother to 2 winners in this country, one of them subsequently successful in Belgium, and a winner abroad; dam ran once each on flat and over hurdles; quickened right away in final furlong to win 10-runner maiden race at Newmarket in August by 6 lengths from Wurli; placed afterwards in nursery at Goodwood and in Cornwallis Stakes at Ascot, excelling himself in latter when 2 lengths third of 7 to Pushy; effective at 5f and 6f; evidently suited by a sound surface; sweated up fifth outing. *J. Holt.* **109**

TINSAUL 2 b.f. Saulingo 122–Itinerant 69 (Sky Gipsy 117) (1980 5f 5d 6g) Apr 30; 2,000Y; small, compact filly; well beaten in maiden race and sellers; sold 340 gns Ascot October Sales. *M. Blanshard.* —

TIN SOLDIER 4 br.c. Petingo 135–War Maiden (Aggressor 130) (1979 10s 10.5g 10.5d 10g 10.5fg² 12g² 13g 10.5d 10.5s 1980 11g* 16.5fg⁴ 16d* 14d 15g* 15.5g* 16f³) French colt; won handicaps at Evry in April, Longchamp in June, Ostend in July and Longchamp again in September; beat Rionore by 4 lengths at Ostend; had no chance with first 2 in last half mile but wasn't disgraced when about 12 lengths third of 5 behind Ardross in Jockey Club Cup at Newmarket in October; stays well; probably acts on any going. *P. Head, France.* **100**

TIN TESSA 2 b.f. Martinmas 128–Gala Tess (El Gallo 122) (1980 5fg³ 5.8h* 5g² 6f⁴) Mar 3; 13,500Y; rangy, somewhat unfurnished filly; good walker and mover; third foal; half-sister to 2 winners, including 3-y-o Second Event (by Fine Blade), a winner at up to 1m; dam half-sister to Irish 2,000 Guineas winner Furry Glen; made all to win 10-runner maiden race at Bath in August by a length from Fair Rosalind; put up better subsequent effort when going down by 1½ lengths to Goody Goody in £2,800 race at Goodwood the following month; will stay 7f; yet to race on a soft surface; sold 5,400 gns Newmarket Autumn Sales. *I. Balding.* **87**

TIPO 3 gr.g. Silly Season 127–Gay Life 72 (Zeus Boy 121) (1979 5fg 7fg² 7d² 8.2g² 1980 10.8s 11f³ 12f³ 10g² 10s) strong, compact gelding; excellent mover; quite a moderate maiden; stays 1½m; suited by top-of-the-ground conditions; blinkered nowadays. *I. Balding.* **74**

TIP TOOL 3 ch.g. Redundant 120–Liliberto (Umberto 118) (1979 5fg 8.2g 7fg⁴ 8.2g 7f 8g 1980 10g 10s 10.8s 10d) big, good-looking gelding; poor maiden; blinkered final start; virtually took no part first outing in 1979. *W. Marshall.* —

TIRAN (HUN) 7 b.h. Imperial–Troja (Swashbuckler 112) (1979 10.7g⁴ 10f 11.7f³ 10.1g² 12g 11.1f 10f 8fg⁴ 8g 1980 11.7f 10.7g 8g 12g 10s) poor handicapper; stays 1½m; acts on firm going; suitable mount for an inexperienced rider; sometimes wears blinkers; trained until after third start by P. Calver. *N. Vigors.* —

TISDALL'S GROVE 3 b.c. Martinmas 128–Land 62 (Baldric II 131) (1979 5v 5v² 5.8s* 5fg² 6f³ 7fg⁴ 6.3f³ 6fg 5d 6d³ 1980 10s* 10g³ 10.4f 12f² 10g 12s³ 10g⁴ 12v³) 2,500F; half-brother to Gala Lad (by Gala Performance), a winner from 6f to 1½m, and a winner in Italy; dam of little account; made all to win £1,000 event at Navan in April by 12 lengths; placed in The Minstrel Stakes at Leopardstown (4½ lengths third to Del Sarto), £2,700 event at Limerick Junction and two handicaps afterwards; fifth of 9 to Playboy Jubilee in Dee Stakes at Chester on third start; stays 1½m; acts on any going. *N. Meade, Ireland.* **94**

TISSUE PAPER 3 ch.f. Touch Paper 113–Tacora (Cernobbio 123) (1979 5v* 5g² 5s* 5v² 5d* 5fg 5f 5f 1980 7g 7f 5g) 520F, 640Y; leggy ex-Irish filly; half-sister to 3 winners in France; dam, half-sister to top-class stayer Taine, won Spanish Derby; proved a bargain at 2 yrs, winning maiden race at Phoenix Park and minor events at Leopardstown and Phoenix Park; had very stiff tasks in 1980 though wasn't entirely disgraced when remote sixth to Sunfield in City of York Stakes in August, first outing; may stay 7f; acts on heavy going. *Denys Smith.* —

TIVOLI (FR) 2 gr.c. Caro 133–Take Off (Nasram II 125) (1980 7f) Mar 1; 570,000 francs Y (approx £60,000); well-grown, quite attractive colt; half-brother to a winner in Spain by Bourbon; dam unraced half-sister to dam of **80** p

Grand Prix de Paris winner Galiani; 9/1 and fairly straight, pushed along from halfway but wasn't knocked about unnecessarily when 6¼ lengths seventh of 19 to King's Glory in maiden race at Newmarket in October; will stay 1¼m; should do better. *H. Cecil.*

T. J. CUNNIFFE 2 ch.g. Communication 119–Miss Helen (Only for Life 126) (1980 5d3 5fg 5fg3 5f2 5f4 5f2 6s 5f 5fg 8d) Apr 12; 720F, 900Y; leggy, unfurnished gelding; placed in maiden race and sellers in the spring; barely stays 5f let alone 1m; trained by N. Adam first 7 outings. *A. W. Jones.* **49**

TO-AGORI-MOU 2 br.c. Tudor Music 131–Sarah Van Fleet (Cracksman 111) (1980 6d2 7g* 7f* 7g* 7s2) **133**

There can be few more galling experiences in racing than selling a horse and then seeing it improve into just about the best middle-distance performer in Europe the following season, with earnings of over a quarter of a million pounds and a syndication valuation of £3,200,000. This befell Mrs Andry Muinos, but at least she can console herself with the knowledge that Ela-Mana-Mou, the horse in question, had won her over £100,000 before his sale for £500,000—not a bad return on the 4,500 guineas she paid for him—and that she now owns the best English-trained two-year-old of 1980 in To-Agori-Mou, for whom an offer of £2,000,000 for a half-share is already said to have been rejected.

It wasn't until running in the William Hill Dewhurst Stakes at Newmarket in October on the last of his five outings that To-Agori-Mou definitely established what had always seemed likely—that he was a top-class colt. He and Storm Bird made the Dewhurst a race to remember, with never more than a length separating them throughout the seven furlongs. To-Agori-Mou, after setting a steady gallop for the first two furlongs, settled in second place and was only about a neck behind when Storm Bird quickened impressively coming to the Dip. He too found a first-rate turn of foot, although perhaps not quite so effortlessly, and maintained a most determined effort up the hill until cracking in the last fifty yards. He went down by only half a length with the three other runners, including the Prix de la Salamandre winner Miswaki and the Laurent Perrier Champagne Stakes fourth Kirtling, trailing well behind.

The Dewhurst marked the first occasion To-Agori-Mou came under strong pressure. Under typically sympathetic handling from Starkey he had impressed us enormously in defeat in a maiden race at Newmarket in July on his debut, when he went down by three quarters of a length to the much more strongly-ridden Church Parade. And he was never fully extended in winning his next three races, all before the end of August. In the Foxhall Maiden Stakes at Goodwood he was up disputing the lead after little more than a furlong, had the race sewn up below the distance and won by two lengths from the newcomer Clear Verdict; in the Crawley Stakes at Lingfield six third-raters were barely able to get him out of a canter; and in the valuable Intercraft Solario Stakes at Sandown he won easing up by two lengths from the strong-finishing Bold Raider after quickening away in splendid style from Chirk Castle and McCarthy

Foxhall Maiden Stakes, Goodwood—To-Agori-Mou beats Clear Verdict

Intercraft Solario Stakes, Sandown—To-Agori-Mou is very impressive, winning from Bold Raider

one and a half furlongs out. Incidentally he seemed equally at home on firm ground at Lingfield as he did on soft at Newmarket.

To-Agori-Mou impressed us just as much in the paddock before his races. He's a big, rangy, attractive colt, altogether a grand individual, and he moves well too. His trainer must have been influenced more by his appearance than by his immediate family when be bought him for 20,000 guineas as a yearling, a figure nearly four times that paid for the next most expensive of Tudor Music's ten other yearlings sold in 1979. Although Tudor Music was a top-class racehorse and as handsome a colt as one could wish to see, he hasn't done particularly well at stud. By the time of To-Agori-Mou's sale, when he'd had runners for nearly seven seasons, Tudor Music had been represented by only one pattern-race winner, Orchestra, and in the year preceding his death in 1979 he attracted a book of only twenty-seven mares. Nor are the records of To-Agori-Mou's dam Sarah Van Fleet and grandam La Rage those of high-class broodmares. The unraced La Rage, although still at stud at the age of twenty-five, produced only three other winners besides Sarah Van Fleet and one of those was in Peru. Sarah Van Fleet, a daughter of the unexceptional racehorse and indifferent sire Cracksman, was most successful over hurdles, winning five times. She also managed to win bumpers races at Powerstown Park and Baldoyle from twenty-seven starts on the flat but that she was of no great account is obvious from the fact she carried only 6-11 when down the back in the Irish Cesarewitch as a six-year-old. To-Agori-Mou, her second winner from her first three foals, is by far her best produce.

To-Agori-Mou (br.c. Apr 22, 1978)	Tudor Music (br 1966)	Tudor Melody (br 1956)	Tudor Minstrel
			Matelda
		Fran (ch 1959)	Acropolis
			Madrilene
	Sarah Van Fleet (b 1966)	Cracksman (ch 1958)	Chamossaire
			Nearly
		La Rage (br 1954)	Mieuxce
			Hell's Fury

The achievements of To-Agori-Mou's third and fourth dams make much better reading. His great-grandam, the five-furlong winner Hell's Fury, produced the smart middle-distance horse Si Furieux and the very useful two-year-old Satan's Slide from only five foals. Even so she didn't do nearly so well as her dam, the highly influential broodmare Sister Sarah, whose other foals included Lady Sybil, winner of the Cheveley Park Stakes, Welsh Abbot, a top-class sprinter, Black Peter, winner of the Jockey Club Stakes, Lady Angela,

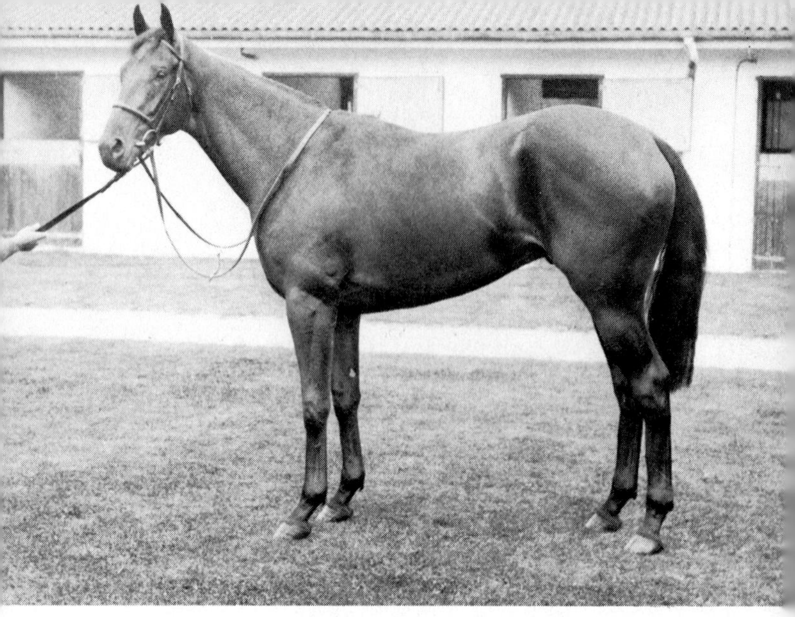

Mrs Andry Muinos' "To-Agori-Mou"

the dam of Nearctic, Caerlissa, the grandam of St Paddy, and Sybil's Sister, the grandam of Great Nephew. Sister Sarah is also the ancestress of such good horses as Klondyke Bill, Lucyrowe and Lord David.

We're confident To-Agori-Mou will become another major winner from the family. He retired for the winter as second favourite to Storm Bird for the Two Thousand Guineas and Derby. While we think he's bound to go very close in the Guineas it's a moot point whether he'll stay well enough for the Derby. He can't be discounted though simply because his sire never won beyond six furlongs. Tudor Music was by a grandson of the Gold Cup winner Owen Tudor out of a mare by Acropolis, a brother to another Gold Cup winner Alycidon, and many of his progeny stay much better than he did; the average winning distance of his stock is over nine furlongs and he has sired ten individual winners over a mile and a half or more. Theoretically, none of his offspring should be more certain to stay a mile and a half than To-Agori-Mou, whose dam won at up to seventeen furlongs and whose maternal grandsire needed at least two miles. On the other hand we feel that To-Agori-Mou races too freely and shows too much pace to be expected to be fully effective beyond a mile and a quarter. It's also significant that when Sarah Van Fleet was mated to Laser Light, another sprinter who was bred to stay a good deal further, she produced Van Laser, a fairly useful filly who gained all her five successes over the minimum trip. *G. Harwood.*

TOBERJOVIC 2 b.g. Tudor Rhythm 112–Decked Out 77 (Doutelle 128) (1980 6f 10d) Apr 11; 660Y; last in sellers, once wearing blinkers, and is useless. *A. Davison.* —

TOBERMORY BOY 3 b.g. Mummy's Pet 125–Penny Pincher 95 (Constable 119) (1979 6h^4 5fg* 1980 6s^2 6f 5fg* 5fg 5g* 5fg^4 5s 5fg^4 5g) neat gelding; fairly useful handicapper; successful at Redcar in May (from Wynburry) and Chester in July (apprentice ridden when beating Willowbrook Flyer); stays 6f; probably acts on any going. *J. Hardy.* **93**

TOE TAPPER 2 ch.f. Record Run 127–Cobblers Daughter 84 (Right Boy 137) (1980 6g 7fg 7g^2 7fg*) Mar 18; 5,000Y; compact filly; half-sister to 3 **73**

minor winners; dam stayed 1m; gained a well-deserved success when battling on gamely to win 19-runner maiden race at Leicester in September by a short head from Solerof; will stay 1m. *G. Pritchard-Gordon.*

TOFIQUE 2 ch.c. Patch 129–Tra-La-La (Penhurst) (1980 8d) Apr 10; 6,800F, 12,500Y; rangy colt; half-brother to 3 winners, including sprinter Heavenly Choir (by St Alphage); dam never ran; 25/1 and very much on toes, made little show when behind in 21-runner maiden race won by Obrovac at Sandown in October. *R. Boss.* —

TOGETHER 7 b.m. Grand Roi 118–Glide 86 (Quorum 126) (1979 NR 1980 6f 8g 13.4g) of little account. *D. H. Jones.* —

TOGG (FR) 2 ch.c. Carvin 127–Pachuca (Pan II 130) (1980 6fg² 6s⁴ 7d 8.2s) Mar 12; 200,000 francs Y (approx £21,100); neat colt; half-brother to minor French middle-distance winner Vanchuka (by Cavan) and a winner in West Indies; dam unraced half-sister to dam of outstanding filly Pawneese (by Carvin); 1½ lengths second of 17 to Sunny Smile in minor event at Ripon in June; had stiff tasks when soundly beaten on next 2 starts and made no show in maiden race at Hamilton in September; should be suited by 1m. *A. W. Jones.* **70**

TOKATA 3 b.f. Sharp Edge 123–Liberation 63 (Native Prince) (1979 5s 5d 5s* 5g 5d⁴ 5s⁴ 5fg 5g* 5fg² 5d 5fg 5f 5d² 5g³ 5fg⁴ 1980 5s² 5v 5fg⁴ 6fg 5f 5h 5s 5g³ 6fg 7fg 8.3fg) small, light-framed filly; has a round action; poor handicapper; not certain to stay 7f; probably acts on any going; has run respectably for a boy. *K. Ivory.* **50**

TOLLERS GOLD 2 ch.g. Roan Rocket 128–Hurly Burly (Sing Sing 134) (1980 5fg 5f 5h) Feb 2; 920Y; small, sturdy gelding; second living foal; dam showed no worthwhile form; well beaten in maiden races, twice finishing last. *A. Davison.* —

TOLLERS ROSE 4 b.f. Some Hand 119–Boston Sunshine (Beau Sabreur 125) (1979 10v 8.3d 8d 8.5d 10.1fg* 8f 10fg 8.3fg* 10.1fg 1980 10.1fg 8.3f 10fg 9.6f 10.1s 8.3g 8.3f⁴ 10g) plater; stays 1¼m; acts on a firm surface; usually wears blinkers; often bandaged. *A. Davison.* —

TOLMI 2 b.f. Great Nephew 126–Stilvi 126 (Derring-Do 131) (1980 6s* 6g*) **122**

'I had hoped she would win in Britain so I could breed from her in Greece. In the end she proved a little too good to be brought there.' This quote from George Cambanis about his purchase in 1970 of a yearling filly by Derring-Do shows that the English aren't the only masters of the understatement. The filly, subsequently named Stilvi, did more than just win—she collected the National Stakes at two, both the Duke of York Stakes and the King George Stakes at three, beating that outstanding sprinter Deep Diver in the King George, and was officially rated the second-best three-year-old filly of 1972. What a loss to British racing and breeding she would have been had she gone to Greece! Stilvi's name translates from the Greek as 'glitter of the stars'—it should have been 'mother of the stars' since she has proved an outstandingly

Princess Margaret Stakes, Ascot—two good fillies, Tolmi and Kittyhawk, finish clear of their rivals

successful broodmare. In 1974 Stilvi foaled the Hotfoot colt Tachypous, winner of the Middle Park Stakes, second in the Two Thousand Guineas and now at stud; her foal of 1975 was the Brigadier Gerard colt Taxiarchos who was retired to stud in South Africa the winner of three races, including the Land of Burns Stakes in which he beat the Two Thousand Guineas runner-up and Derby third Remainder Man; her 1976 produce, the Busted colt Tromos, topped the International Classification as a two-year-old after a scintillating win in the Dewhurst Stakes and has now been retired to stud in the USA after bowing a tendon in the second of his two races there; and Tyrnavos, her 1977 colt by Blakeney, has also gone to stud, having provided Stilvi with her first classic winner by taking the 1980 Irish Sweeps Derby.

Tolmi (b.f. Mar 23, 1978)	Great Nephew (b 1963)	Honeyway (br 1941)	Fairway
			Honey Buzzard
		Sybil's Niece (ch 1951)	Admiral's Walk
			Sybil's Sister
	Stilvi (b 1969)	Derring-Do (br 1961)	Darius
			Sipsey Bridge
		Djerella (ch 1960)	Guersant
			Djeretta

As if these achievements weren't enough, just eleven days after Tyrnavos' win in Ireland Stilvi's fifth foal, Tolmi, ran out an impressive winner of the Princess Maiden Stakes at Newmarket on her first appearance, leaving no doubts that she would add even more to her dam's marvellous record. She outclassed her twenty opponents, quickening right away in the final one and a half furlongs to win easily by four lengths from Exclusively Raised, the subsequent May Hill Stakes winner. Later in July Tolmi put up the performance of a very smart filly when successful in the Princess Margaret Stakes at Ascot. Although the opposition included the Cherry Hinton Stakes second, Doobie Do, and the fourth, Her Grace, as well as the promising Salisbury winner Oraston and the twice-successful Lucaya, Tolmi started odds on. Her bridle broke and had to be mended down at the start, and perhaps because of this unsettling incident she was a bit slow leaving the stalls. Soon after halfway she started to recover the lost ground, making steady headway to challenge the long-time leader Kittyhawk approaching the final furlong. Tolmi soon took Kittyhawk's measure, although she was giving her 4 lb, and lengthened her stride to win by a length

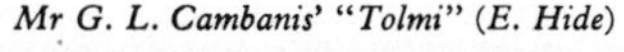

Mr G. L. Cambanis' "Tolmi" (E. Hide)

and a half despite tending to hang. The others were left toiling at least a further six lengths behind.

This splendid effort established Tolmi as potentially the best of the two-year-old fillies, and an intriguing clash looked in prospect when just three days later Marwell put up a similarly impressive display in the Molecomb Stakes. Unfortunately Tolmi was unable to race again. A low blood count prevented her running in the Lowther Stakes, a race won in style by Kittyhawk, and all chance of her meeting Marwell in the Cheveley Park disappeared when Tolmi jarred the joint at the head of her off-fore cannon bone early in September.

So Tolmi ended her short first season unbeaten and also winter favourite for the One Thousand Guineas, a race due to be run fully nine months after her last appearance. Since such a lot can happen in nine months it seems questionable whether it's wise to back her yet for the Guineas—far better to see first how she performs on her reappearance. Nevertheless we regard Tolmi as an extremely promising filly, well up to classic winning standard, and unlike Marwell it's hard to envisage her failing to stay the Guineas trip; although Stilvi was a sprinter, all her sons have stayed at least a mile and Tolmi's sire stayed a mile and a quarter well. She has also shown she acts on soft ground. Besides first-class form and an excellent pedigree Tolmi has good looks to recommend her—she's an attractive filly, strong, compact and well-made, and the image of Stilvi according to her trainer. It will be fascinating to see how she fares in 1981 and also to see if Stilvi can extend her influence even further through her next foal, the two-year-old Reform filly Tenea, and through her first grandchildren from Tachypous' first crop. *B. Hobbs.*

TOLSTOY 4 b.c. Reform 132–Stardom 75 (Hornbeam 130) (1979 12s^{2} 11s^{2} **91**
11d* 10fg* 10.1g* 11g* 10s^{2} 11d^{3} 11s^{4} 1980 10fg 10f 10g* 12g 10.6d^{3} 10d* 10.5g^{2} 10.2g^{2} 10g^{2} 10g) lightly-made, attractive colt; useful handicapper; winner at Salisbury in June and Ayr in July; second afterwards at York (to Beggar's Bridge), Doncaster (to Kilroy Hawk) and Rome (to Ladislao di Oppelm in Group 3 Premio Roma Vecchia); didn't seem to find much off bridle at Doncaster; best form at up to 11f; acts on any going; blinkered third and fourth outings. *M. Jarvis.*

TOM DOWDESWELL 4 br.c. Balidar 133–Georgian Princess 75 (Tamerlane **56**
128) (1979 8.2s 6s 6g 5g 5f 5f^{4} 6f^{4} 5g* 5s 5g 6fg 5f^{4} 1980 5.8fg 5fg* 5d 5d) strong, good sort; beat Wedding Vows by a length in handicap at Beverley in June; stays 6f; seems to act on any going; usually blinkered but didn't wear them first 2 starts. *J. Bethell.*

TOM HORN 3 br.g. Warpath 113–Creek Alley 91 (Klairon 131) (1979 8h 7.2g —
10g^{3} 8.2s 1980 9.4g 10fg) big gelding; poor form, including in a seller; will stay 1½m; blinkered third start in 1979; changed hands 850 gns Doncaster May Sales. *J. Berry.*

TOMMY'S GOLD 2 b.f. Goldhill 125–Golden Palermo 70 (Dumbarnie 125) **58**
(1980 5f 5fg 5fg 6g 5d^{2} 5fg 5fg 5s) Feb 23; 1,800Y; small filly; sister to 2 minor winners, and half-sister to 4 winners, including useful 3-y-o Greenwood Star (by No Mercy), successful at up to 1m; dam won 5f seller; 2½ lengths second of 11 to Tudor Dream in maiden auction race at Carlisle in July, easily best effort; fifth in a seller previous start; speedy and is better at 5f than 6f. *M. Tompkins.*

TOMMY'S HOPE 7 b.h. Military 112–Shropshire Lyric (Eastern Lyric 114) —
(1979 NR 1980 10.6fg 10f 18s) plater nowadays; bandaged when behind in 1980; stays 1m; acts on firm going. *J. Wilson.*

TOMMY'S TREASURE 3 b.g. Tudor Rhythm 112–Liza Goblin 83 (King —
Legend) (1979 NR 1980 10.2d) half-brother to three minor winners and a good winner in Norway; dam best at around 1m; backward when last of 11 in newcomers race at Doncaster in March; sold 1,000 gns Newmarket May Sales. *K. Ivory.*

TOMMY TUCKER 3 b.g. Singing Bede 122–Fashion Wear (Hard Tack 111 **§**) **48**
(1979 5s 5g^{3} 5f* 5f^{3} 6fg^{3} 5g^{3} 6f^{3} 6d^{4} 6g 5h 5d 1980 6v 6h 6fg 5g 5f^{4} 6g^{4} 5g^{2}) strong, compact gelding; plater; stays 6f but gives impression 5f suits him better; acts on firm going; blinkered penultimate appearance in 1979; has worn bandages. *S. Norton.*

TOM'S SERENADE (USA) 3 b.c. Tom Rolfe–Gay Serenade (Royal Serenade **114**
132) (1979 NR 1980 10.5d* 12d* 12fg 15s 15g^{2} 13f 16f) $210,000Y; half-brother to several winners in USA, notably Gulls Cry (by Sea Bird II), a very smart stakes winner at up to 1¼m; dam won 2 stakes races at around 9f; won newcomers event

and Prix de l'Avre at Longchamp in May, latter by ½ length from Zambrano; ran creditably subsequently in Prix du Jockey-Club at Chantilly (6 lengths equal sixth of 14 to Policeman), Grand Prix at Longchamp (5 lengths fifth of 14 to Valiant Heart), Prix de Lutece at Longchamp (close third, promoted to second, to What A Joy) and 13f Canadian International at Woodbine (strong-finishing fifth to Great Neck); stays well; probably acts on any going. *M. Zilber, France.*

TOM'S STAR 2 bl. or br.f. Comedy Star 121–Fleet Street Fifty 51 (I Say 125) (1980 5g 5g) May 26; compact filly; fourth foal; dam poor plater; in rear in maiden races at Wolverhampton (last of 17) in July and Salisbury (blinkered) in August. *W. R. Williams.* —

TOM STRAUSS 5 ch.h. Tompion–Ortica (Alcaeus 127) (1979 10s 10d 6g 7g 6s* 1980 5d 6s 6g 6f³ 8g 8d 6g 7f 7f) useful sort; has been fired; quite a moderate handicapper; good third to Galaxy Leo in minor event at York in May; out of his depth next 2 outings; evidently best at sprint distances; acts on any going; usually wears blinkers. *M. McCormack.* —

TOM THE TRAVELLER (USA) 2 b.c. Cougar–I'm On Purpose (Intentionally) (1980 6f³ 6d 7s⁴ 7f) Mar 31; $20,000Y; neat colt; half-brother to winners by Hail to Reason and Graustark; dam won at up to 6f at 3 yrs; seemed to run a promising race when 2½ lengths third of 8 to Redden in Woodcote Stakes at Epsom in June but didn't fulfil that promise, on final start finishing seventh of 9 in a nursery at Thirsk; should stay at least 1m; best run on firm ground. *N. Callaghan.* **75**

TONGSUNIAN 3 gr.c. Moulton 128–Queen's Message 93 (Town Crier 119) (1979 7f² 1980 7f³ 8.2g 8fg² 8fg 10f) lightly-made colt; quite a moderate maiden; should stay 1¼m; acts on firm going. *W. Hastings-Bass.* **69**

TONY 8 br.g. Pongee 106–Lilt 52 (Drumbeg 94) (1979 12g³ 12.2s 12d 12s⁴ 13.8s² 12.5g 15s³ 1980 12fg 12.2fg³ 12.2fg 12d⁴) quite a moderate handicapper; finished well when in frame at Catterick (amateur riders) and Haydock; stays well; particularly well suited by an easy surface; has been tried in blinkers; sometimes sweats up; suitable mount for an apprentice. *E. Weymes.* **64**

TOO BRIGHT 2 b.f. Laser Light 118–Too Much 100 (Major Portion 129) (1980 5d⁴ 5fg² 7fg) Apr 4; doesn't walk well; half-sister to several winners in France and to 3-y-o 7f to 1½m winner Princess Pageant (by Welsh Pageant); dam won at up to 1m; 7 lengths second of 18 to Gandoorah in maiden race at Haydock in April; nearest at finish when 4¾ lengths fifth of 19 to Pearlaway in similar race at Warwick over 4 months later; stays 7f; refused to enter stalls on intended third start and ran from a flag start at Warwick. *W. Elsey.* **65**

TOOTENS 2 ch.f. Northfields–Night Attire 77 (Shantung 132) (1980 8g 7.5g*) Mar 27; half-sister to several winners, notably 1,000 Guineas winner Nocturnal Spree (by Supreme Sovereign); dam sister to smart 1972 staying 2-y-o filly Setsu; won 14-runner maiden race at Saint-Cloud in November in promising style by 2 lengths from Jark; will be suited by 1¼m+; engaged in 1,000 Guineas and Oaks. *E. Bartholomew, France.* **112**

TOONDRA 3 ch.c. Northfields–Aucuparia (Celtic Ash) (1979 6f³ 7g³ 8g 1980 12fg* 16g* 12s 14g³ 14g 18g) shapely colt; good mover; came from last to first in space of 2f to beat Good Thyne a length in Queen's Vase at Royal Ascot; had earlier won 15-runner maiden race at Haydock in May; close third to Another Generation in handicap at Goodwood in July; well beaten in Tote-Ebor Handicap at York in August and Doncaster Cup (blinkered) following month; suited by a test of stamina; probably acts on any going; hurdling with D. Nicholson. *M. Jarvis.* **103**

TOPA INCA (FR) 3 b.f. Lyphard 132–Native Smoke (Raise A Native) (1979 NR 1980 8fg 14d 12g) 320,000 francs Y (approx £38,000), 38,000 gns 2-y-o, small, quite attractive filly; half-sister to winners in USA, France and Italy, including Her Love (by Herbager), successful twice at around 9f; dam half-sister to Stewards Cup winner Royal Smoke; well beaten in Southern maiden races; unlikely to stay 1¾m. *G. Harwood.* —

TOP AWARD 2 b.c. High Award 119–Swing Right 69 (Swing Easy 126) (1980 5f) Mar 31; small colt; first foal; dam won twice over sprint distances; tailed-off last of 16 to Pergoda in maiden race at Catterick in July; sold 280 gns Doncaster August Sales. *A. Potts.* —

TOP DANCER (FR) 2 b.c. Green Dancer 131–Toffee (Shantung 132) (1980 8g 10s*) May 15; 420,000 francs Y (approx £44,000); half-brother to several winners in France, including Tabatiere (by Val d'Aoste), a very useful winner at up to 13f, and to very smart middle-distance performer and top French **?**

Queen's Vase, Ascot—Toondra (right) gets to the front

hurdler Top Gear (by Yelapa); dam won over 7.5f at 2 yrs; accounted for his 16 opponents in good style in maiden race at Saint-Cloud in November, winning by 2½ lengths; will be suited by 1½m; should make a very useful 3-y-o. *B. Secly, France.*

TOPHILL JENNY 3 b. or br.f. Sayfar 116–Tide and Time (Easter Island 101) (1979 5s 5g 6f 6fg² 7g⁴ 6fg 8h⁴ 8d 1980 8v 8f 9f 9f 8g 8d) bad plater; stays 1m; best form on a sound surface; has been tried in blinkers; sold 410 gns Doncaster August Sales. *D. Yeoman.* —

TOPICALITY 3 b.c. High Top 131–Tyronera 82 (Tyrone 130) (1979 NR 1980 10fg 11f 9d) 11,000 2-y-o; strong, compact colt; closely related to fairly useful middle-distance winner Tyrondero (by Derring-Do) and half-brother to 2 winners in France; dam won over 1⅛m; well beaten in maiden races; usually gives trouble at start; sold to M. Bradley 1,550 gns Ascot October Sales. *P. Walwyn.* —

TOP OF THE MARK 2 ch.c. On Your Mark 125–None-So-Pretty (Never Say Die 137) (1980 5f 5s⁴ 5d³ 6g 6s⁴ 6f* 6fg 5g) Apr 4; 940F, 11,500Y; strong colt; fourth living produce; dam ran 3 times at 2 yrs; stayed on strongly when winning 13-runner maiden race at Epsom in August by ½ length from Endless Moment; had stiffish tasks in nurseries afterwards; finds 5f on sharp side and will be suited by 7f; acts on any going but goes well on firm. *C. Brittain.* **80**

TOP OF THE TABLE 4 b.c. Royal Prerogative 119–Fenland Queen (King's Troop 118) (1979 10v 8s 10f 8fg 8f* 8s 8f⁴ 8fg 8f 1980 10f 8fg 12f 16g) useful sort of colt; inconsistent in 1979 and showed no form in 1980; should stay 1¼m; acts on firm going and is possibly unsuited by soft; has been tried in blinkers; not one to trust. *D. Marks.* — §

TOP O' TH' LANE 3 b.g. Palm Track 122–Poachings Folly (Poaching 115) (1979 6g⁴ 5g³ 6g² 1980 8f* 8h² 10g 8g⁴ 7fg³ 9g⁴ 8d 7s) lengthy gelding; quite a moderate handicapper; narrowly won at Thirsk in April; suited by 1m on top-of-the-ground. *W. Haigh.* **76**

TOP REEF 2 br.c. Take a Reef 127–Bienvenida 75 (Sheshoon 132) (1980 6g 6fg 6s 5.1fg 8.2d⁴ 7.2s 8d 8g 10.2s) Apr 10; small, neat colt; fourth live foal; dam a stayer; prominent in large fields of platers at Nottingham and Haydock on third and fifth outings, in latter finishing 10¾ lengths fourth of 19 to Tudorville in September; bred to stay at least 1¼m (had very stiff task when tried at trip). *D. Leslie.* **55**

TOPS 3 ch.f. Club House 110–Peg Top 93 (Star Moss 122) (1979 5d 7g* 8.2g 8s 8f 8g⁴ 1980 12s³ 12g 11.7g³ 12.2fg 11.7s 8d 10g) won seller at Newmarket at 2 yrs; showed little worthwhile form in better company in 1980; will stay 1¾m; acts on soft going; ran moderately second start. *D. Dale.* **56**

TOPSIN (FR) 5 ch.h. Dictus 126–Top Twig (High Perch 126) (1979 8s 10fg 8fg 8fg* 10fg 8d 12d 1980 12fg 11.7fg³ 10f⁴ 12fg 10g 12fg 10d 8fg 10fg² 11.7f 10g 13.1h 10.2g 12g 10d) good-looking French-bred horse; led until close home when length second to Galaxy Capricorn in handicap at Yarmouth in July; best form at distances short of 1½m; acts on firm going; ran moderately when **62**

blinkered fifth to eighth outings; sometimes starts slowly; sold 3,200 gns Newmarket Autumn Sales. *A. Breasley.*

TOP STREAM 4 b.f. Highland Melody 112–Aquanimba (Acropolis 132) (1979 10.5d 10.2s 12d 12f^3 10f 12fg 10s 12fg^4 10.5g 1980 10.2d 10fg^4 10fg 9f 8s^3 8f 10.2g 8d) useful-looking filly; seems to stay 1½m; acts on any going; blinkered ninth outing at 2 yrs and final start (ran poorly). *P. Asquith.* –

TOP SWORD 3 ch.g. High Line 125–Swordblade 84 (Pall Mall 132) (1979 5d 5s 5v 7fg 8.2g 8f 1980 10s 10g 8g 16d 13.8f) useless; has worn blinkers; sold out of W. Marshall's stable 700 gns Doncaster May Sales. *R. Ward.* –

TOPTOOL 2 b.g. The Brianstan 128–Grecian Cloud 76 (Galivanter 131) (1980 5.8fg 6fg 6d 5.8g^3 6g) Apr 23; 3,000Y, 4,400 2-y-o; close-coupled, useful-looking gelding; first foal; dam won 7f seller at 2 yrs and stayed 13f; 1½ lengths third of 16 to Mrs Palmer in maiden auction event at Bath in July, best effort; will probably stay 7f; blinkered last 2 outings. *P. Cundell.* **74**

TORBAY EXPRESS 4 b.g. Owen Anthony 102–Luckhurst (Busted 134) (1979 8d 7.3g 8g 6fg 6fg 5s^2 5fg^2 5fg* 5f* 5.8fg^4 1980 5s 5g 6f 5f 5.8fg 5s 5g 5.8f 5fg 5d 5f) sturdy gelding; didn't run up to his best; placed over 6f and 7f but is best at 5f; acts on any going; blinkered seventh outing at 2 yrs; suitable mount for an apprentice. *Mrs R. Lomax.* **64**

TORBOLE 3 ch.g. Reliance II 137–Buss 102 (Busted 134) (1979 NR 1980 15.5g 15s) 17,000Y; big, rangy gelding; third foal; half-brother to two winners, including useful 1977 2-y-o Watch Out (by Blakeney), subsequently a winner over 11.5f; dam game performer at up to 11f; soundly beaten in maiden races at Folkestone and Stockton in October. *W. Hastings-Bass.* –

TORREMODO 2 gr.g. Grey Mirage 128–Smiling 62 (Silly Season 127) (1980 6g 7.2d 8fg) Mar 8; 2,000Y; lightly-made gelding; first foal; dam, placed at up to 13.8f, won over hurdles; behind in maiden races. *A. W. Jones.* –

TORUS 4 b.c. Ribero 126–Lighted Lamp (Sir Gaylord) (1979 9fg^3 10.2g^4 10.5g 10.6g^2 12fg 12g* 14.6f 12fg^2 14d^2 12s^4 1980 12f^3 12fg 11g 12d) strong colt; smart performer at his best; ran well when 4½ lengths third of 16 to Niniski in John Porter Stakes at Newbury in April; well-beaten sixth of 8 behind More Light in Jockey Club Stakes at Newmarket in May on next outing and was subsequently sold to race abroad; well behind in Grosser Preis von Dusseldorf in June (last of 9 to Nebos) and in Preis von Europa at Cologne in October; stays 1¾m; acts on any going; probably needs a galloping track. *F. J. Houghton.* **101**

TO THE MANOR BORN 2 b.c. Furry Glen 121–Willow Grove (Irish Ball 127) (1980 6s 7fg 7g) Apr 21; 500F, 1,350Y; neat colt; first foal; dam never ran; showed a little ability in maiden auction event at Doncaster and seller at Redcar, last 2 outings; will stay 1¼m. *T. Molony.* **53**

TOTOWAH 6 b.h. Biskrah 121–Scotts (Orthodox) (1979 12d^3 12d^2 16fg* 14.7g 14s 18fg^3 16f^4 1980 16.1fg) strong, robust horse; won 6 races, including Tote-Ebor at York in 1978 and Coral Northumberland Plate at Newcastle in 1979; also in frame in Doncaster Cup and Jockey Club Cup at Newmarket in latter year; backward when fifth of 6 behind Balinger in Lymm Stakes at Haydock in May on only outing of 1980; stayed well; was extremely well suited by top-of-the-ground conditions; genuine; standing at Manor House Farm Stud, Tring, Hertfordshire, fee £50 straight plus £250 (October 1st terms). *M. Jarvis.* –

TOTTERIDGE 3 b.f. Huntercombe 133–Catherine's Plea 95 (Petition 130) (1979 NR 1980 8fg 7g 8g) 2,700Y; fair sort; behind in a maiden race and 2 sellers; sold 540 gns Ascot August Sales. *R. Hannon.* –

TOUCH BOY 4 b.c. Touch Paper 113–Hello Amy 70 (Forlorn River 124) (1979 7.2s 6s^4 7fg^3 6fg^2 7fg^3 6h^4 6s^3 6fg^4 5d^2 6g 1980 6fg 6fg 6d 5g 5fg 6s 6g 5.6g^3 6s 6d) compact, robust colt; useful performer; often faced with stiff tasks and hasn't won since his 2-y-o days; third to Swelter in 20-runner William Hill Portland Handicap at Doncaster in September; best form at up to 6f; acts on any going; blinkered last 3 outings. *R. D. Peacock.* **95**

TOUCH OF CLASS (FR) 3 ch.f. Luthier 126–La Theve (Red God 128§) (1979 NR 1980 10.1s 10.2fg 14g 17.1d 10g) second foal; dam won twice over 1m in France; poor maiden; blinkered last 3 starts. *R. Simpson.* –

TOUCH OF FROST 3 b.c. Habat 127–Nip in the Air 114 (Northern Dancer) (1979 6fg 7f 7fg 1980 7f 8f 8fg^3 8fg^3 8g 10g^3 12d^2 10v^4 11.2g) strong, well-made, attractive colt; has a round action; only plating class; stays 1½m; suited by some give in the ground; blinkered fifth start; winner in Italy. *I. Balding.* **67**

TOUCH PIRATE 5 ch.h. Touch Paper 113–Pirate Gal (Pirate King 129) (1979 **84**
5d 7g 6g^3 6fg^2 6fg* 6f^2 6g^4 6s 1980 7f 7f 7f^2 7g 6g* 6fg 7fg 7g 7d 7d 7s) fair handicapper; well-backed favourite when scoring by a head from Paducah at Pontefract in July; stays 7f; acts well on firm going; blinkered last 2 outings, running respectably on first occasion; trained until after eighth start by W. Stephenson. *A. Jarvis.*

TOU FOU 4 b.g. Royben 125–Cissac (Indian Ruler 89) (1979 10s 10d 8g 8fg –
5g 6g 5g^4 5fg 5fg^4 5g* 6d* 6s^3 1980 5fg 5fg^2 5f 7fg 6fg) compact, strong-quartered gelding; sprint handicapper; 7 lengths second of 19 to Winsor Boy at Warwick in May, best effort; acts on any going; wears blinkers; good mount for an apprentice; didn't impress in paddock fourth start. *D. Ancil.*

TOUGH AN ROUGH 2 b.g. Saulingo 122–Frensham 67 (Floribunda 136) **79**
(1980 5d^3 5f^3 5h^2 5fg^2 5g* 5g 5fg^3) Apr 12; 1,250Y; small, sharp sort; second reported foal; dam only plating class; apprentice ridden when making much of running to win 10-runner maiden race at Edinburgh in June by 3 lengths from Star Heading; not disgraced in nursery and £2,600 event afterwards; unlikely to stay 6f; probably acts on any going; sold 2,500 gns Newmarket Autumn Sales. *J. Hardy.*

TOUGH BABU 2 br.g. No Mercy 126–Lily Elsie 74 (Our Babu 131) (1980 –
8fg 8.2s) Mar 18; 3,200F, 10,000Y; half-brother to minor winners here and in France; dam 1½m winner; in rear in maiden races at Beverley and Hamilton in September; sold 880 gns Doncaster November Sales. *W. Marshall.*

TOUGH GUY 5 ch.g. Burglar 128–Robust Lady (Gunflint) (1979 6s 6v^3 5v 6v **53**
5s 6g^4 7d 5g^4 6g^4 7d 8fg 8.2g^3 7fg 7g 7d^2 1980 7v^4 8g^4 6f^4 8f 7f 7g^4 6d 7f 9g^2 9d^2 8.2d^4 8fg 8d) plater; ran creditably in better company on several occasions in 1980; stays 9f; acts on any going but is suited by some give in the ground; sometimes wears blinkers; suitable mount for an apprentice; sweating third start; claimed out of P. Asquith's stable after ninth start. *J. S. Wilson.*

TOUGH LADY 3 ch.f. Bay Express 132–Nevetta 108 (Never Say Die 137) **73**
(1979 5d 6fg^4 6g* 6fg 6d^3 1980 7d 6fg 7h 8s) big, strong filly; fairly useful (rated 91) at 2 yrs; below form in handicaps in 1980 and ran poorly last 2 starts; suited by 6f and should stay 7f; sold 2,100 gns Newmarket December Sales. *R. D. Peacock.*

TOUGH SHOW 2 b.g. No Mercy 126–Vanity (Vimy 132) (1980 5d 5v 5f^4 –
7s 6fg 5.1fg 6g) Mar 1; 1,300F, 3,700Y; lengthy gelding; brother to several winners but is only a bad plater himself. *W. Marshall.*

TOWER JOY 6 b.h. Tower Walk 130–Great Joy (Kythnos 126) (1979 7v^3 **92**
7d 7f 1980 7fg* 8fg^2 7f^4 8fg^2 7g* 7d 7fg^2 7fg* 7.3fg^2 7fg* 7g) strong, good-looking ex-Italian horse; had a very good season and was gaining his fourth success when getting up close home to beat Lucky Man by a short head in Cavendish Cape South African Sherry Stakes (Handicap) at Ascot in September; ran disappointingly under a penalty only subsequent outing; had won handicaps at Wolverhampton and Yarmouth (2) earlier and had also run well on most other starts; stays 1m; acts on any going; consistent; suitable mount for an apprentice. *L. Cumani.*

TOWER WIN 3 ch.c. Tower Walk 130–Takawin 109 (Takawalk II 125) (1979 **51**
5fg 7fg 7d 1980 5v^4 5fg 5.8f^3 6f 6fg 7g 7f 6g 8s^3 6d) quite attractive colt; poor handicapper; stays 1m; acts on any going; blinkered sixth to eighth starts; sometimes sweats up. *J. Benstead.*

TOWN FARM 8 b.g. Tycoon II–Brush's Choice (Robson's Choice 105) (1979 –
12.2g 12d 1980 12h 10.6g) compact gelding; lightly raced and well beaten after 1977; stayed 1¼m; acted on any going; used to wear blinkers; dead. *M. Tate.*

TOWN JENNY 2 b.f. Town Crier 119–Just Jenny 88 (Ennis 128) (1980 5d 6s) –
Apr 17; sister to 5f sprinter Just Fred and a winner in Barbados, and half-sister to 2 winners; dam sprinter; behind in sizeable fields for maiden races at Wolverhampton and Doncaster in November. *R. Hollinshead.*

TOWN LINE 3 b.f. High Line 125–Arodstown Alice (Sahib 114) (1979 NR –
1980 8d 10s) 400F, 500Y; second foal; dam ran only 3 times; behind in minor event at Warwick and maiden race at Nottingham (dwelt) in October. *M. Bradley.*

TOWN MASTER 2 b.c. Town Crier 119–Anjonic 56 (Le Levanstell 122) –
(1980 8fg 6d) May 13; 6,400Y; leggy colt; half-brother to 4 winners, including

3-y-o 7f winner Numas (by Porto Bello) and speedy 1977 early-season 2-y-o Silk Lady (by Tribal Chief); dam of little account; unquoted when behind in minor event at Newbury and maiden race at Newmarket in the autumn. *B. Hanbury.*

TOWN SKY 4 gr.c. Town Crier 119–Pink Sky 86 (Midsummer Night II 117) **70**
(1979 7v 7v^3 8g 6s^3 6f 5.6fg^4 6s 6f 7fg 1980 8g 8s^4 8d 7.6d 6f 6g 5d^3 6d^2 7s^4) strong colt; good mover; has been hobdayed and has had a soft palate operation; useful handicapper at 3 yrs; ran best races of 1980 in the autumn, when in frame in handicaps at Catterick, Redcar and Doncaster; best form at up to 7f; appears to act on any going, except perhaps very firm; has shown a tendency to hang; best in blinkers nowadays. *S. Norton.*

TOWN STORY 4 gr.f. Town Crier 119–Golden Legend 87 (Gratitude 130) –
(1979 6f 8.3fg 8fg 6fg 6g 1980 7fg) worthless plater; has been tried in blinkers. *C. Wildman.*

TRACE OF GOLD 3 ch.g. Golden Dipper 119–Thracia 83 (Pindari 124) –
(1979 7g 1980 8fg 10.8s) behind in maiden races. *J. Bosley.*

TRACK BELLE 6 b.m. Track Spare 125–Ring True 80 (Gulf Pearl 117) (1979 **58**
8g 7.6d 8s 8f 7f^4 7.6f* 8f 8g 7g 7fg 7.6f 8fg^3 8fg 1980 8fg^4 8fg 7f 8fg 8g 8g 7.6g 8g 8fg^2 10fg 8g) poor handicapper; stays 1m; acts on any going but is suited by a sound surface; good mount for an apprentice; trained by R. Mason until after seventh start. *P. M. Taylor.*

TRACK DOWN 4 b.f. Take a Reef 127–Dandy Brush 82 (Will Somers 114 §) –
(1979 5v^4 7d^3 6g* 5.8g* 6g^4 7s^4 7f 8fg 5fg 1980 6g 5.8f) fair sort; well beaten in 1980; should stay 1m; seems to act on any going. *J. Hill.*

TRACY'S BROTHER 5 gr.g. Roan Rocket 128–Valiant Heart (Reform 132) **50**
(1979 6s^2 6d^2 6g 7d 8s 6f^4 6fg 1980 6d 6g 8.2fg* 8f 10g^4 10g 8.3g) poor handicapper; dropped in class when winning seller at Hamilton (bought in 1,200 gns) in May; stays 1m; acts on any going; used to wear blinkers; suitable mount for an apprentice; often sweats up; sold 1,700 gns Ascot September Sales. *D. Ringer.*

TRACY'S SPECIAL 3 b.g. High Top 131–Devastating 103 (Honeyway 125) –
(1979 7d^4 1980 12s 12g 13.3fg 14g 15.5g) big, strong gelding; well beaten in maiden and minor races; blinkered final start. *R. Hannon.*

TRADEWINDS 3 ch.c. Bay Express 132–Tamilian 89 (Tamerlane 128) (1979 –
NR 1980 7g) 9,000Y; strong, well-made colt; good walker; second foal; dam won at up to 1¼m; slowly away and always trailing in 8-runner minor event at Goodwood in August; dead. *B. Swift.*

TRADITIONAL MISS 5 ch.m. Traditionalist–Starboard Mist 81 (Right Boy **71**
137) (1979 10.1fg 8g* 10.2fg^4 10fg* 1980 10.8f 10g^3 8.2s 8fg* 9f^3 8.3fg^4 8g* 8h*) plater at 4 yrs; improved in 1980 and won handicaps at Chepstow, Salisbury (apprentices) and Bath; squeezed through in final furlong when getting home by a head from Albert Hall on last-named course in August; stays 1¼m; acts on hard going; good mount for an apprentice. *J. Hill.*

TRAIN OF THOUGHT 2 b.f. Bay Express 132–Kirkby 85 (Midsummer Night **75**
II 117) (1980 6g^2 6g^2 7fg^2 7g) Apr 9; 17,000Y; leggy filly; first foal; dam won twice over 1¼m; second in maiden race at Newmarket and minor events at Ripon and Newbury in second half of season; favourite when going down by a neck to Giannutri at Newbury in September; stays 7f. *R. Armstrong.*

TRALEE FALCON 4 ch.f. Falcon 131–Uranus (Manacle 123) (1979 5g* 5fg* **75**
6g^2 5f* 5g^3 5g 1980 5f^3 5g^4 6d 5fg^2 6g 5g 5d 5f 5fg^2 6g^2 6fg^2 6s^2 5v) small filly; ridden by 7-lb claimer when getting home narrowly in handicap at Redcar in October on eleventh start, but edged right in closing stages and was relegated to second; second on 4 other occasions, including in 2 apprentice events; stays 6f; acts on any going; blinkered fourth to seventh outings; slowly away last 2 starts at 2 yrs; doesn't find much off the bridle these days. *J. Fitzgerald.*

TRAMPLER 3 br.c. Bustino 136–Chieftain Girl (Chieftain) (1979 7g 1980 12fg^4 **79**
12fg^4 12g^3 16d* 12g* 13.8g^2 18f 12g) neat, well-made colt; won modest maiden race at Nottingham in June and 4-runner handicap at Hamilton following month (odds on); suited by a test of stamina; acts on a firm and soft surface; ran poorly last 2 starts, sweating up badly and pulling hard on first occasion; trained by J. Hindley first 7 outings. *M. Masson.*

TRAPEZEY 2 ch.g. Red Alert 127–Floatingonair (Whistling Wind 123) (1980 –
5d 8g) Mar 13; 4,800F, 8,200Y, 620 2-y-o; third produce; half-brother to Irish

13f winner Could It Happen (by Double-U-Jay); dam placed over 6f and 7.9f in Ireland at 2 yrs; unquoted, apprentice ridden and blinkered when well beaten in maiden race at Wolverhampton in October and seller at Leicester the following month. *R. Morris.*

TRAQUAIR 11 b.g. Klairon 131–Brandina (Never Say Die 137) (1979 10fg 8f 8g* 8f² 10.2fg² 8g* 8.2s 1980 8fg 7f⁴ 10fg* 10d² 9g³ 8g 10fg 10g* 12g 12fg 10g 10d*) fair handicapper still, and has kept his form remarkably well; won apprentice events at Goodwood (made all) in August and Newmarket (held up, beat Joleg by 1½ lengths) in October; ridden by 7-lb claimer when winning at Brighton earlier; stays 11f; acts on any going; excellent mount for a boy. *J. Dunlop.* **82**

TRAVEL 3 b.f. Saritamer 130–Prima 75 (Alcide 136) (1979 NR 1980 8g 8g 10s 10s) tall filly; half-sister to several winners, including 4-y-o Laska Floko (by Thatch), successful at around 1¼m, and good Italian performers King Jay (by King Emperor) and My Royal Prima (by Captain's Gig); dam half-sister to very useful stayer Saraceno; in rear in maiden and minor races in the autumn. *P. Walwyn.* **–**

TREAD A MEASURE 2 b.c. Tudor Rhythm 112–Lady Jewel (Kibenka 119) (1980 6g 6d) May 20; 3,000Y; first foal; dam never ran; still backward when 12 lengths fifth of 17 to Shark Song in maiden race at Newmarket in October; will be suited by 7f+. *J. Douglas-Home.* **–**

TREAD SOFTLY 6 br.m. High Flown 117–Two Slippers (Solstice 118) (1979 NR 1980 12g) Swedish-bred mare; of no account. *S. Nesbitt.* **–**

TREE FELLA 3 br.g. King Log 115–Gold Reid (Le Dieu d'Or 119) (1979 6fg³ 6g 6g 5g 5s* 5f 1980 6fg 5f³ 5h* 5f² 5g⁴ 5g 6g⁴ 6g² 6s³ 6g⁴ 6g) leggy gelding; sprint handicapper; won at Pontefract in May; stays 6f; acts on any going; suitable mount for a boy. *C. Crossley.* **62**

TREE MALLOW 2 b.f. Malicious–Potentilla 89 (Nearula 132) (1980 7fg 7d) Apr 27; lightly-made filly; half-sister to several winners, including fairly useful stayers Potent Councillor (by Privy Councillor) and Junella (by Midsummer Night II); dam won over 13f; modest fifth of 13 to Lambay in maiden race at Leicester in October, second outing. *M. Smyly.* **–**

TREE TOPS 4 b.f. Moulton 128–Gambling Girl (Raise You Ten 125) (1979 10.6g 1980 10v 11fg 10fg 10h 12fg 10f 8.3f) leggy filly; poor plater; often sweats up. *M. Cousins.* **–**

TRE FONTANE 2 b.c. Windjammer (USA)–St Tropez 99 (Princely Gift 137) (1980 5f 5fg* 5fg² 5d* 5g⁴ 6d⁴ 5g⁴ 5g⁴ 5g³ 5s² 5g) Mar 28; 12,000Y; good sort; half-brother to numerous winners, including Madrid Free Handicap winner Market Square and useful 1971 2-y-o Parbleu (both by Pardao); dam ran only at 2 yrs when winner at 5f; won maiden race at Doncaster in May and £3,100 event at Ayr in June, making all in latter to beat Black Charmer easily by 4 lengths; not disgraced on most of his other outings, putting up an excellent effort to finish 5 lengths third of 6 to Marwell in Flying Childers Stakes at Doncaster in September and finishing same distance behind Tina's Pet in 3-runner Harry Rosebery Challenge Trophy at Ayr soon afterwards; probably better at 5f than 6f; seems to act on any going; consistent until running below form final start. *J. Etherington.* **104**

TRES BARRAS 3 ch.f. St Paddy 133–Marbella II 64 (Match III 135) (1979 NR 1980 10fg 14g 13g 10g² 12d 10.1g 10s 12s) compact filly; half-sister to 1972 5f winner Guethary (by Manacle); dam from same family as Miralgo and Parnell; quite a moderate maiden at her best; will stay 1¾m; saddle slipped second and third starts; ran abysmally seventh outing. *B. Hobbs.* **72**

TREVITA 3 b.f. Tyrant–Tack 88 (Tacitus 124) (1979 6f³ 6fg* 7g* 8fg⁴ 1980 8fg* 8s³ 7fg* 10d² 10g⁴ 10f) small filly; half-sister to several winners, including fairly useful 6f to 1m winner Chum-Chum (by On Your Mark) and 1978 2-y-o 5f winner On The Wind (by Windjammer); dam stayer; put up good performances to win £4,000 handicap at Ascot from Restful and New Stand Stakes at Goodwood from Premier Rose in the summer, on each occasion quickening well to lead inside last furlong and win rather cleverly by ¾ length; also ran creditably to finish in frame in Child Stakes at Newmarket (3¼ lengths third of 9 to Stumped) and 2 races at Deauville in August, Prix de Psyche (good head second to Sovereign Dona) and Prix de la Nonette (just over 4 lengths fourth to Detroit); didn't impress in paddock when fifth to Snow in Sun Chariot Stakes at Newmarket in **117**

New Stand Stakes, Goodwood—Trevita's late run on the outside takes her past Premier Rose and Our Home (rails)

October; stays 1$\frac{1}{4}$m; seems to act on any going; smart; sold privately and has been sent to USA. *H. T. Jones.*

TREVS WAY 3 b.g. Gilded Leader 75–Mererit (Fort Coulonge) (1979 NR 1980 12f) fourth foal; half-brother to winning plater Sea Mermaid (by Seaepic); dam of no account; backward when in rear in 9-runner maiden race at Redcar in September. *A. Jarvis.* —

TRIAL SHOT 3 ch.f. Scottish Rifle 127–Her Worship 61 (Privy Councillor 125) (1979 7g 1980 11f 12g 10s) big filly; poor maiden. *M. Francis.* —

TRIBAL EYE 5 b.m. Tribal Chief 125–Nocturnal (Combat 123) (1979 6s^{2} 5.8g 6fg* 6f* 6f* 6f* 6d* 6g^{4} 6h^{3} 1980 6fg 6g 6fg 6fg 6fg^{3} 6g 6d^{3} 6fg^{4} 8d) rangy mare; blind in one eye; fairly useful handicapper in 1979; ran creditably fifth, seventh and eighth outings but was mainly disappointing; best at 6f; acts on any going, but goes well on firm; usually held up; has run well for an apprentice; has won 3 times at Brighton; sold 15,000 gns Newmarket December Sales. *P. Cole.* 87

TRIBAL PATH 3 ch.g. Warpath 113–Tuesday Eve 98 (Silnet 131) (1979 7fg 7g 7g 1980 10.1s 12d) robust gelding; plating-class maiden; should stay at least 1$\frac{1}{2}$m; blinkered second start; sold 2,100 gns Ascot September Sales. *N. Vigors.* —

TRIBAL WARLORD 4 ch.g. Scottish Rifle 127–Callidice 77 (Worden II 129) (1979 12.3fg 12f^{4} 10h 13.8d^{2} 12fg 10g 12.5g 1980 13g) strong, compact gelding; plater; probably stays 1$\frac{3}{4}$m. *M. Naughton.* —

TRIBAL WARRIOR 4 b. or br.c. Tribal Chief 125–Love Resolved (Dan Cupid 132) (1979 7s^{3} 7g 8v 6s 7fg^{4} 9g 1980 7.2fg 5.8fg^{4} 7g* 7d 6g^{3} 7fg 7.3d) strong, stocky colt; chipped a bone in his knee at 2 yrs and reportedly suffers from arthritis; quite a useful handicapper nevertheless; led in final furlong when scoring by 1$\frac{1}{2}$ lengths from Sun of Schweppes at Redcar in June; ran badly sixth start (sweating) and was out of his depth final outing; gives impression that 6f is on sharp side for him nowadays and is suited by 7f (well beaten over further); best form on a sound surface; blinkered last two starts at 3 yrs. *R. Boss.* 93

TRICHORIA 2 b.f. Saritamer 130–Thermopylae 91 (Firestreak 125) (1980 5f 5fg 5g 7g 5g 5d^{2} 6g^{4} 8s) Apr 18; quite attractive filly; half-sister to 2 winners in Brazil, including prolific scorer Headband (by Henry the Seventh); dam 2-y-o 5f winner; in frame in valuable 19-runner seller at Sandown in August (1$\frac{1}{2}$ lengths second to Universal Penny) and 20-runner nursery at Lingfield in September (3$\frac{1}{2}$ lengths behind Salamina under a low weight); best form at up to 6f but wasn't disgraced over 1m. *R. Smyth.* 66

TRICKY RHYTHM 2 b.f. Touch Paper 113–St Music (Sovereign Lord 120) (1980 5f^{4} 5fg* 6d* 6g 6fg 5.1fg^{3} 6fg* 7f^{4}) Mar 23; 500Y; small, light-framed 70 filly; fourth living produce; dam poor Irish maiden; won maiden auction event and a valuable seller at Brighton in first half of season and returned to form in September when winning 28-runner seller at Windsor by 1½ lengths from Porkers; bought in 2,850 gns and 2,100 gns after her seller wins; not sure to stay 7f; acts on a firm and a soft surface; wears blinkers nowadays. *P. Haslam.*

TRICKY VICTORIA 5 br.m. Baragoi 115–Eirlys 90 (Elopement 125) (1979 12.2g 12.2f 1980 10v) poor maiden; probably stays 1½m. *N. Callaghan.* —

TRIGOWEN 2 ch.g. Owen Anthony 102–Salvo of Conkers 79 (Salvo 129) (1980 6g 5s 5.8fg 6s 5g^{3} 5g) May 29; 620F, 900Y; second produce; dam won twice over 1½m; 2¼ lengths third of 17 to Super Smile in maiden race at Bath in September, best effort; hampered when challenging 1f out on next appearance; should stay at least 6f. *B. Palling.* 60

TRINA'S GIRL 2 b.f. Nonoalco 131–Chit Chat (Baldric II 131) (1980 5g 5fg* 5g 5fg 5g^{3}) Apr 6; 40,000Y; robust, well-made, strong-quartered filly; good mover; first foal; dam, daughter of smart French filly Chatter Box, won over 7.5f at 2 yrs from 2 starts in France; well-backed favourite when making all and holding off Red Gold by a head to win 24-runner maiden race at Windsor in August; soundly beaten afterwards, finishing 12 lengths third of 6 to Labista in small race at Goodwood in September; should stay further if ridden with more restraint; sent to France. *B. Swift.* 78

TRIOLOGY 2 b.c. Hot Spark 126–Playtime (Primera 131) (1980 5s 5d 6s 7g^{3} 8d) May 5; 3,600Y; half-brother to several winners here and abroad; dam poor half-sister to good 1½m horse Auroy; 3½ lengths third of 9 to Candaules in minor event at Brighton in August, best effort; should stay 1m. *D. Weeden.* 72

TRIPLE BAR 3 ch.f. Jimmy Reppin 131–Dismantle 77 (Aureole 132) (1979 5fg 7fg 1980 8fg 7.2d* 8fg 8g^{4} 10fg^{4} 11s^{4} 10d) small, compact filly; ridden by 5-lb claimer, won 12-runner maiden race at Haydock in July; stays 1¼m; acts on a firm and a soft surface; sweated up badly third outing; probably needs a galloping track; sold 6,800 gns Newmarket December Sales. *G. Pritchard-Gordon.* 71

TRIPLE SECRET 2 b.c. Relko 136–Secret Isle (Voluntario III) (1980 7d 7f 8s) Mar 29; 13,500Y; lengthy colt; first foal; dam, placed in Norway at 3 yrs, is half-sister to the dam of Noble Decree; showed promise when not fully fit on first 2 outings but was well beaten on final start; bred to stay at least 1¼m. *Denys Smith.* —

TRITON 3 ch.c. Simbir 130–Milosun 79 (Milesian 125) (1979 5fg 6f 6s 6f 1980 12fg 14d 8g 8g) strong, good-bodied colt; well behind in minor and maiden races; blinkered second and final starts; sold 520 gns Ascot August Sales; resold 460 gns same venue in December. *C. Bewicke.* —

TRIUMPHANT 3 b.f. Track Spare 125–Pugnacity 117 (Pampered King 121) (1979 NR 1980 7fg^{2} 7.6f* 7f 8.5f 8fg 7d 7g^{2} 7fg) quite attractive filly; seventh foal; half-sister to 6 winners, all at least useful, notably top-class middle-distance performer Relkino (by Relko); dam smart from 5f to 1¼m; beat Broomstick Corner 2½ lengths in 10-runner maiden race at Chester in May; creditable second in handicap at Sandown in July; gives impression 1m may be limit of her stamina; acts on firm going; blinkered nowadays. *H. Candy.* 90

TROLL LADY 3 b.f. Crisp and Even 116–Fire Hawk 70 (Firestreak 125) (1979 NR 1980 8s^{2} 8fg 8g 9f) leggy filly; second foal; dam, placed over 6f at 2 yrs, is daughter of smart 1959 2-y-o Laminate; second in maiden race at Warwick in April; well beaten afterwards, including in a seller on final outing; will stay 1¼m; probably needs some give in the ground; sweated up third start. *P. Feilden.* 69

TROPICAL LOVE 2 ch.g. Red Alert 127–Luluna (Pinza 137) (1980 5fg 7g 8fg 8d 6s 8d) Apr 20; 8,000Y; neat, strong gelding; half-brother to fairly useful middle-distance handicapper Fir's Hill (by Jukebox) and closely related to 1978 2-y-o 7f winner Spanish General (by Green God); dam won over 1½m in Ireland; modest sixth of 13 to Gifford in maiden race at Beverley in September, third start and best effort; had his tongue tied down fifth start. *B. Hanbury.* 62

TROPICAL PARK 5 b.m. My Swallow 134–Hialeah (Snob II 130) (1979 NR 1980 12g 16fg) lengthy mare; probably of little account. *J. Mason.* —

TROPICARO (FR) 2 b.f. Caro 133–Tropical Cream (Creme dela Creme) (1980 8g* 8f* 7v) 115

The mediocrity of the 1980 crop of two-year-olds in France was such that the top nine positions in the International Classification were filled by animals trained in England or Ireland. Numerically the French just about held their own in the Classification where colts were concerned, with fourteen included as opposed to fifteen from England and three from Ireland, but it was a different matter with the fillies. Whereas England had eleven considered worthy of inclusion, France surprisingly mustered only two, the Prix Morny winner Ancient Regime and the Prix Marcel Boussac winner Tropicaro.

Tropicaro was gaining her second success from as many starts when she won the Prix Marcel Boussac at Longchamp in October, a Group 1 race more recognisable under its previous name, the Criterium des Pouliches. She started second favourite to the unbeaten Bernica on the strength of a particularly taking display in the Prix de Toutevoie over the same course and distance a month earlier, when she'd burst through a gap halfway up the straight to win easily by two and a half lengths from Marie Noelle. Making up the field were: Ukraine Girl, Ionian Raja, Coral Dance and Salmana, the first four home in the Group 3 Prix d'Aumale at Chantilly in September; Marie du Mont, a soundly-beaten third behind Bernica in the Group 3 Prix du Calvados; the Irish challenger Blue Wind, a comfortable winner of the Group 3 Silken Glider Stakes; Last Love, a winner at Chantilly; and the once-raced Kazadancoa, a sister to The Dancer. On fast ground it took the leaders more than thirty seconds to cover the first two furlongs and Tropicaro's rider wisely had her up towards the front, nearly always the best place to be in a slowly-run race. Coral Dance temporarily took over the lead, setting a much stronger pace, but Tropicaro made a break for home early in the straight and galloped on far too strongly for her opponents to pull her back; she covered the last two furlongs in twenty-three seconds, and crossed the line two lengths clear of Coral Dance. There was a scramble for the places with only a head, a nose, a short neck and a head separating Coral Dance from the dead-heaters for sixth place, Blue Wind and Marie du Mont.

There was talk of Tropicaro's turning out for the Grand Criterium the following Sunday. Instead she was held in reserve for the Prix de la Foret at Longchamp three weeks later when, the only two-year-old in the nine-horse field, she started third favourite behind Moorestyle and Kilijaro. Probably she simply wasn't good enough in such high-class company but she didn't seem suited by the heavy ground either and trailed in eighth behind Moorestyle, never getting into the race.

Tropicaro (Fr) (b.f. Apr 6, 1978)	Caro (gr 1967)	Fortino II (gr 1959)	Grey Sovereign
			Ranavalo
		Chambord (ch 1955)	Chamossaire
			Life Hill
	Tropical Cream (b 1971)	Creme dela Creme (b 1963)	Olympia
			Judy Rullah
		Tropic Star (ch 1959)	Tropique
			Patricia's Star

Tropicaro doesn't take the eye as an individual—she's leggy and lightly-built—but she's clearly a smart filly and is a well-bred one too. Both her grandam Tropic Star and her dam Tropical Cream were well above average on the racecourse; Tropic Star was at her best as a three-year-old, when she picked up the Cheshire Oaks and the Pretty Polly Stakes at the Curragh, while Tropical Cream was a smart performer both at two, when she won the Prix d'Aumale over a mile, and at three, when she took the Prix Cleopatre over ten and a half furlongs. Although Tropic Star is also the dam of five winners in the USA her most notable offspring apart from Tropical Cream is an unraced filly, Dusk, who produced the 1977 Washington International winner Johnny D. Tropical Cream's only previous runner, the useful French three-year-old Tropical Lightning (by Lyphard), is a winner over a mile and a quarter.

It's doubtful whether Tropicaro is as good as many of the past Criterium des Pouliches winners but she's a match for nearly all the other leading French fillies and should again do well at three. She seems to have inherited a measure of both speed and stamina from her fairly versatile parents and she's likely to go close in the French One Thousand Guineas before making her mark over middle distances. *M. Zilber, France.*

TROUBETZKOY (ITY) 2 b.c. Lyphard 132–Therese Landier (Ribero 126) **116** (1980 $8g^2$ 9fg 10s*) Apr 16; second foal; dam useful Italian 2-y-o; 2/1 on when winning 10-runner maiden race at Saint-Cloud in October by 2½ lengths from Palikaraki; had previously run well when ¾-length second to Great Substence in Prix de Villebon at Longchamp in September and when close-up fifth of 8 to Mariacho in Group 3 Prix Saint-Roman on same course the follow-

Prix Marcel Boussac, Longchamp—Tropicaro gets the mile well and wins from Coral Dance (No 8), strong-finishing Salmana (rails) and Bernica (No 9).

ing month; will be suited by 1½m: seems to act on any going; should make a smart 3-y-o. *F. Boutin, France.*

TROUVAILLE 6 b.h. Tratteggio 123–Helen Allingham (Busted 134) (1979 8f³ 9fg³ 1980 7fg 10f* 9g 12d² 12fg 8.2d) plater; attracted no bid after winning apprentice handicap at Beverley in June; runner-up to easy winner High Old Time in amateur riders handicap at Carlisle following month; seems to stay 1½m; appears to act on any going; blinkered on reappearance; usually wears bandages; good mount for an inexperienced rider. *R. E. Peacock.* **37**

TRUDY'S BOY 4 ch.g. Doeskin 105–Cash Deal 71 (Hook Money 124) (1979 10.8s⁴ 8s 8g² 8f 10.1fg² 1980 8fg⁴ 8.3fg 10.1f 16f 12g² 12d) lightly-made gelding; plating-class maiden; second to comfortable winner Ambler in amateur riders race at Brighton in October; stays 1½m. *R. Akehurst.* **55**

TRUESIGN 2 b.c. Upper Case–Corneater (Skymaster 126) (1980 5f 6g 5d 6v³ 6s) 7,000Y; first foal; dam ran once; only plating class. *R. Hollinshead.* **66**

TRUE VIEW (USA) 3 b.c. Reviewer–Actual (Round Table) (1979 NR 1980 12g³ 11.7h*) $85,000Y; strong, good-bodied, attractive colt; third foal; brother to a minor winner in USA and half-brother to a winner by Damascus; dam, sister to smart stakes winner Bicker and half-sister to high-class performer Judger, won 3 races at up to 1m; favourite, fulfilled promise of first outing when beating Quite Lucky by 1½ lengths in 12-runner maiden event at Bath in August; will stay 1¾m; acts on hard going; wears a tongue strap; sold to M. Pipe only 3,600 gns Newmarket Autumn Sales. *R. Hern.* **75**

TRU MAR 4 ch.c. Northfields–High Corinda 85 (High Treason 126) (1979 11.7g 14f 14f* 16f* 14d 16f 1980 14f 14fg² 16f³ 18fg 12d 14g⁴ 16g² 14g³ 12g²) big, rangy colt; placed 5 times, on last occasion being caught on line by York Cottage at York in October; has won over 2m but gives impression shorter distances suit him better; acts on firm going and is possibly unsuited by a soft surface. *R. Armstrong.* **76**

TRUPER GEE 2 b.g. Rheingold 137–Cappuccilli 111 (Lorenzaccio 130) (1980 7d) Feb 8; 4,100Y; small gelding; first foal; dam very useful staying 2-y-o but failed to train on; unquoted when behind in 20-runner minor event won by Soldan at Doncaster in October. *R. Whitaker.* **—**

TRUSTY CATCHER (USA) 2 ch.g. Pass Catcher–In Trust (Buckpasser) (1980 7d) Apr 10; $29,000Y; rangy gelding; third foal; dam, placed at 3 yrs, is half-sister to dam of Cesarewitch winner John Cherry; unquoted when always in rear behind Sunley Builds in 14-runner Houghton Stakes at Newmarket in October. *H. T. Jones.* **—**

TRUTH WILL OUT 3 b.f. Blakeney 126–Cry of Truth 129 (Town Crier 119) (1979 6f⁴ 5g³ 7g 5fg⁴ 1980 6f 5fg* 5fg* 5d³ 7.2g) small, quite attractive filly; moderate handicapper; won at Warwick in June and Bath in July; evidently best at 5f; acts on a firm and a soft surface; game. *D. Ancil.* **82**

TRY SANDICLIFFE 3 ch.c. Star Appeal 133–Peral Five 72 (Will Somers 114§) (1979 7g 1980 9d* 12g* 12.3f⁴ 11f* 16g 14.7g* 14g) narrow colt; **113**

Sandicliffe Motor Group's "Try Sandicliffe"

good mover; had a fine year and gained fourth success when accounting for Francesco in really good style by 2½ lengths in £3,700 handicap at Redcar in July; had earlier beaten small fields in maiden race at Newcastle, Warren Stakes at Epsom and handicap at Ayr; well-beaten favourite for Tote-Ebor Handicap at York in August (made no headway in last 3f and was eased when beaten); stays well; appears to act on any going; very useful; sent to Oman. *B. Hills.*

TRYTON LINES 3 b.c. Wolver Hollow 126–Djenarelle (Djefou) (1979 NR 1980 7d² 7d 8f² 8h* 8fg⁴ 10d⁴ 10fg* 8f³) 8,400Y; good sort; good mover; half-brother to 2 winners, including good Italian 1976 2-y-o Chinacci (by Bold Lad, USA); dam very useful French middle-distance performer; successful in maiden race and slowly-run handicap at Pontefract; stays 1¼m; suited by fast ground. *M. H. Easterby.* **72**

TRYTRAVELSCENE 2 gr.f. Dragonara Palace 115–Ash Fell 83 (Bleep-Bleep 134) (1980 5g² 5d* 5g² 5f) May 7; strong filly; half-sister to 2 winners, including very useful 1974 2-y-o 5f and 6f winner Lady Rowley (by Royal Levee); dam 5f sprinter; all out when landing the odds in moderate maiden race at Pontefract in August by ½ length from Gloriama; creditable 1½ lengths second to Dalegarth in nursery at Windsor the following month; may stay 6f. *P. Makin.* **87**

TSAR'S BRIDE 2 b.f. Song 132–Empress of Russia 79 (Royal Palace 131) (1980 6s⁴ 5g 6f) Mar 6; big, rangy filly; first foal; dam, half-sister to Connaught, won over 1½m at 4 yrs; unquoted, running on in closing stages when 4 lengths fourth to Chilblains in 20-runner maiden event at Lingfield in June, only worthwhile form; will stay 7f; sold to D. Whelan 2,200 gns Newmarket Autumn Sales. *A. Ingham.* **69**

TSHAINIK (USA) 6 b.h. Vaguely Noble 140–Anonymous (Buckpasser) (1979 16f 1980 14.7f 16fg³ 16g*) poor performer; got home by ½ length **39**

from Elizabeth Jane when winning maiden race at Beverley in June; stays well. *P. Felgate.*

TTOKKOS 2 ch.c. Royal Match 117–Parmassia (Pampered King 121) (1980 5g 6g 8s 10s) May 28; 1,650Y; third foal; half-brother to 3-y-o Bucklow Hill (by Rheingold); dam French 2-y-o 1m winner; in rear in maiden auction events, a valuable seller and a maiden race; sold 1,050 gns Doncaster November Sales. *A. Demetriou.* —

TUCSON 4 b.g. Lear Jet 123–Clean Verdict 109 (Whistler 129) (1979 6g 5d 6fg 6fg 7fg² 7f³ 7fg² 1980 8d 8d 6g) lightly-made gelding; plater; stays 1m; probably acts on any going; ran creditably in blinkers last 2 starts. *D. Underwood.* —

TUDENORS PLACE 3 b.g. St Paddy 133–Matia's 77 (Klairon 131 or Runnymede 123) (1979 NR 1980 9d) 2,500F, 720Y; first foal; dam, placed at up to 5.8f at 2 yrs, is half-sister to good middle-distance stayer Marquis De Sade; tailed-off last of 21 in maiden race at Wolverhampton in August. *J. Edwards.* —

TUDOR BENKA 3 br.f. Kibenka 119–Tudor Yan 72 (Tudor Bar 91) (1979 5f 5fg 5f 5d 5d⁴ 5h⁴ 6g 7s⁴ 1980 6d² 5d 7fg 6fg³ 7d³) lightly-made filly; plater; will be suited by 1m; acts on a firm and a soft surface; suitable mount for a boy. *T. Fairhurst.* **47**

TUDOR BOB 2 b.g. Tudor Rhythm 112–La Belle 118 (Vilmorin) (1980 5s 6d 7fg 7f⁴ 8d³) May 15; well-grown gelding; half-brother to several winners, including fairly useful 7f and 1m winner Sorebelle (by Prince Tenderfoot); dam, best at 6f, won Diadem Stakes; quite moderate; in frame in sizeable fields of maidens at Newmarket and Warwick in October; stays 1m; the type to do better at 3 yrs. *G. Pritchard-Gordon.* **76**

TUDOR CHIEF 4 b.g. Tudenham 118–Bally Girl (Ballyciptic 122) (1979 7s 7f* 8f⁴ 8.5g⁴ 8g* 8g* 8g 1980 10f 8fg³ 9f² 7d 8g² 8f) neat ex-Irish gelding; runner-up to easy winners Sea Pigeon in amateur riders event at Hamilton in June and Nawaf in lady riders race at Newmarket in August; reluctant to go to post and finished well beaten final start; stays 9f; probably acts on any going; good mount for an inexperienced rider. *A. W. Jones.* **69**

TUDOR CLAIRE 3 b.f. Tudor Music 131–Traffic Offence 61 (Traffic Judge) (1979 6g 7g⁴ 1980 11fg⁴ 8fg² 8g³ 8g 10g 10.6d 10g 12.5s 12s) fair sort; seems only plating class; best form at 1m; probably acts on any going; doesn't always impress in paddock. *H. Collingridge.* **61**

TUDOR DREAM 2 b. or br.f. Averof 123–So Smooth (Pall Mall 132) (1980 5g⁴ 5d* 6fg³ 5f 5d 6s⁴) Mar 20; 1,200Y; leggy, lengthy filly; half-sister to Jolly Smooth (by Jolly Jet), successful over 1m and 13f; dam ran three times at 2 yrs; apprentice ridden when landing the odds in maiden auction race at Carlisle in July by 2½ lengths from Tommy's Gold; respectable 4 lengths third of 10 to Lifestyle in auction event at Newcastle later in month but was subsequently beaten in nurseries; finds 5f on sharp side nowadays and will stay 7f. *W. H. H. Williams.* **70**

TUDOR FOLLY 4 br.g. Mummy's Pet 125–Anna Boleyna 84 (Right Royal V 135) (1979 9.4f 10s 10g 9.4d³ 9d⁴ 12.5g* 1980 12fg) well-grown gelding; stays 1½m well; acts on a soft surface. *W. A. Stephenson.* —

TUDOR JUDGE 2 b.g. Tudor Rhythm 112–Jedburgh Justice (Mossborough 126) (1980 5fg* 5fg² 5h* 5fg²) Mar 27; 2,700Y; lightly-made gelding; half-brother to 3 minor winners; dam never ran; bought in for 2,100 gns after winning seller at Leicester in April by 5 lengths from Veeya and won claiming race at Brighton the following month by 1½ lengths from Superb Music; odds on when beaten on other outings; will be suited by 6f; acts on hard going; exported to Hong Kong. *N. Vigors.* **57**

TUDOR LINK 6 b.m. Manacle 123–Royal Tucson 87 (Henry the Seventh 125) (1979 NR 1980 10v) quite moderate (rated 77) at 2 yrs; subsequently successful several times in Norway; 20/1 when tailed-off last in apprentice handicap at Stockton in March. *P. Haslam.* —

TUDOR LYRIC 3 gr.g. Tudor Melody 129–Bolting 108 (King's Bench 132) (1979 6fg 7fg 1980 6d 7f 9f 10.1f 8.5f 8d 12f² 12d) poor form in varied company, including selling; has been tried in blinkers; trained by B. Swift first 6 starts; sold 500 gns Ascot December Sales. *M. Bolton.* —

TUDOR REGENT 2 b.c. Prince Regent 129–Small Size (My Babu 136) (1980 6d 7g) May 23; 17,500Y; big, strong, rangy colt; half-brother to 2 winners, —

including fair 1974 2-y-o 6f winner Sir Expedier (by Ribero); dam won over 6f at 3 yrs in USA; behind in maiden race at Newmarket in July and minor event at Yarmouth (50/1) in September. *B. Hobbs.*

TUDOR'S DILEMMA 3 b.f. Tudor Rhythm 112–Horn's Dilemma (Quadriga 97) (1979 6f 6g^3 6g 7.2g 7g 1980 8s 8f 10.8s^4 10s 9.4g* 8.2s 10f 8fg) lengthy filly; won modest maiden race at Carlisle in July; should stay 1¼m; suited by some give in the ground; sold 2,000 gns Newmarket Autumn Sales. *J. Powney.* **56**

TUDOR TWAIN 3 b.f. Shoolerville 121–Tumbrel 113 (Djebe) (1979 5fg 1980 8f 7f) in rear in maiden and minor races. *J. Winter.* **–**

TUDORVILLE 2 br.c. Shoolerville 121–Razia 97 (Martial 131) (1980 5fg 5f 6fg 6fg 6fg 7g^2 8.2d* 8s^4 8.2s* 8s^3 7v) Mar 12; 2,200Y; leggy, close-coupled colt; has rather a round action; half-brother to winners in Ireland, France and Belgium; dam won over 5f at 2 yrs; successful in September in 19-runner seller at Haydock and nursery at Hamilton, showing improved form when winning latter by 4 lengths from Beechwood Seeker; suited by 1m; acts very well on soft going; blinkered fifth outing. *K. Stone.* **80**

TUDOR WYDDIAL 3 b.g. Tudor Rhythm 112–Chung May (Blarney Stone 121) (1979 8fg 10s^3 1980 10s^4 12fg 13s 16s^3 14g^2 14.6fg^4 14fg^2 14g^4 16fg^4 15s) leggy, narrow gelding; one paced and needs a test of stamina; probably acts on any going; suitable mount for an inexperienced rider. *A. Hide.* **56**

TUDOR WYNK 7 br.g. Wynkell 88–Wandering Rose (Tudor Minstrel 144) (1979 12f 12fg^4 11.7f^4 11.7fg* 11.7g^2 12fg^2 12f 14f* 12f^4 16d 14f 14g 1980 13.3g^4) quite a moderate handicapper; stays 1¾m but possibly not 2m; acts on any going; has been tried in blinkers; good mount for an apprentice; consistent. *S. Mellor.* **–**

TUGOFLOVE 4 b.c. Tudor Rhythm 112–Speyside 84 (Live Spirit 121) (1979 6g 7d^3 7v 6fg 6f 7g^4 6fg^4 7d 1980 6f^3 6fg^3 8g 7g^4 7d 7g* 7g^2 7g^2 6d 7s) quite well-made colt; fair handicapper; looked well when scoring by a length from Imperium at Newmarket in August; finished very strongly when runner-up to Steeple Bell in valuable Battle of Britain Handicap at Doncaster in September (just failed) and in handicap at Newmarket in October; suited by 7f and should stay 1m (hampered when tried at trip); probably acts on any going. *R. Laing.* **86**

TULA SINGH 4 gr.f. Mansingh 120–Iridium 78 (Linacre 133) (1979 5g* 6fg 8fg 5h 6fg 6fg^2 6fg 6fg 1980 6s^3 7fg 6g^2 6h 6d) workmanlike filly; best form at sprint distances; seems to act on any going; blinkered final outing at 2 yrs; sold 1,025 gns Ascot August Sales. *N. Vigors.* **50**

TULCHAN LODGE 3 b.f. Pitcairn 126–Scattering 69 (Busted 134) (1979 6fg 6fg^3 6d 1980 6fg^2 8.2f 6fg^4 6s 6d^3 6s 5g) plater; best form at 6f though is bred to stay at least 1m; acts on a firm and a soft surface; sold to R. Hollinshead 700 gns Doncaster November Sales. *Denys Smith.* **45**

TULLIA 2 ch.f. Mount Hagen 127–Tribal Lass (Tribal Chief 125) (1980 5f 6g 5g^4) Mar 23; 9,200F, 7,000Y; leggy filly; second foal; dam Irish 1m winner; second favourite, ridden along most of way when 5 lengths fourth to River Breeze in 16-runner maiden race at Catterick in August; will be suited by a return to 6f; possesses little scope. *L. Cumani.* **61**

TUMBLE DANCER 2 b.c. Tumble Wind–Sea of Gems (Princely Gift 137) (1980 5f 5f 5s 5fg 5fg) Apr 13; 5,000F, 9,400Y; strong, neat, good sort; half-brother to several winners in Ireland and to 2 winners abroad; dam of little account; behind in maiden and minor events; blinkered fourth start. *B. Swift.* **–**

TUMBLEDOWN DICK 3 b.g. Tumble Wind–Semper Fi (Above Suspicion 127) (1979 5g 5fg 6g^4 6fg 7g 1980 7v 10fg 6fg 6g 7g 7g) neat gelding; quite moderate (rated 73) in 1979; ran badly in varied company, including selling, at 3 yrs; often blinkered; sold 925 gns Ascot August Sales; dead. *C. Dingwall.* **–**

TUMBLEDOWNHILL 2 ch.c. Tumble Wind–Little Hills (Candy Cane 125) (1980 5f^3 5f^3 5f^4 6g* 7.2d^3 6fg^2 6d^3 7d 7.2g 7fg) Mar 24; 3,000F, 6,000Y; workmanlike colt; second produce; half-brother to top-class 3-y-o filly Cairn Rouge (by Pitcairn); dam, winner over 1½m in Ireland, also won over hurdles; won 9-runner minor event at Haydock in June by ½ length from Horncastle; far from disgraced when placed in quite valuable events on next 2 outings but ran below his best on 2 of his last 3 starts; will be suited by 1m+; never going well when blinkered eighth outing and looked to be feeling the effects of his races on ninth (moved moderately to start). *W. Wright.* **77**

TUMBLE HOME 2 b.f. Tumble Wind–Rudder (Reliance II 137) (1980 6f^4 **72**
6d^4) Mar 24; 300Y; narrow, very lightly-made filly; fourth foal; half-sister to 7f winner Stern (by No Mercy); dam unraced daughter of Coronation Stakes winner Ocean; showed up well throughout when 6 lengths fourth of 18 to Long Legend in maiden race at Newmarket in October; raced alone when respectable 7 lengths fourth of 17 in similar event won by Shark Song on same course later in month; will stay at least 1m. *I. Walker.*

TUMBLELLA 2 b.f. Tumble Wind–Pavella (Palestine 133) (1980 5s 5g^4 **101**
6f^3 6g^3 7.9f* 7fg 7.9f^2 7.9g* 8g^3) Mar 12; half-sister to numerous winners, including useful middle-distance stayer Dowdall (by Dike); dam won Madrid Free Handicap and was fourth in Irish 1,000 Guineas: improved when given a test of stamina, winning maiden and minor events at Dundalk in July and September, latter by 4 lengths from Lohunda Lady; also ran well in another race at Dundalk, going down by only a head to Callixena (rec 7 lb), and in Group 3 Silken Glider Stakes at Leopardstown, when 4 lengths third to Blue Wind; will stay $1\frac{1}{4}$m; acts on firm going; useful. *K. Kerr, Ireland.*

TUMBLE PUPA (USA) 3 br.f. Pretense–Unhurried (Restless Wind) (1979 —
NR 1980 7f 8fg 8.2g) $33,000Y; well-made filly; first foal; dam, unplaced 4 times, is sister to Tumble Wind, a very smart winner at up to $1\frac{1}{2}$m; beaten some way in newcomers and maiden events; will be suited by $1\frac{1}{4}$m. *L. Cumani.*

TUMBLER 5 b.g. Tumble Wind–La Roquette (Sammy Davis 129) (1979 —
8s 8v* 8d 10g 10d 10f 8fg 9fg 8fg^2 8d 8f 1980 8fg) moderate handicapper; poor mover; stays $1\frac{1}{4}$m; acts on any going; wears blinkers; sometimes sweats up; inconsistent. *A. Pitt.*

TUMBLE WHIRL 2 b.g. Tumble Wind–Mary Money (Hook Money 124) **65**
(1980 5fg 5fg 6fg 6g 6fg* 7f 6g 6g) Apr 19; 3,200F, 1,500Y; compact gelding; fourth foal; dam poor plater; bought in 2,700 gns after winning 11-runner seller at Doncaster in July by a length from Lautorb; should stay 7f; yet to race on a soft surface. *P. Rohan.*

TUNE UP 3 ch.f. On Your Mark 125–Sing Along (Nasram II 125) (1979 **60**
5v^2 5d 5fg 1980 5fg 5s 6g^3 8.3g 7fg^3 8.2g^4 7g^2 7g 7d 7s) lightly-made filly: placed in handicaps and a maiden race, stays 1m; probably acts on any going; blinkered nowadays. *F. J. Houghton.*

TUNG SING 3 b.f. Averof 123–Kentucky Blues 83 (Royal Record II) (1979 —
NR 1980 12g 16fg 13.8g) leggy filly; behind in maiden races and a seller in the North. *C. Booth.*

TURBO 5 gr.g. Song 132–Field Mouse 108 (Grey Sovereign 128 §) (1979 6s 5d **51**
5fg 5fg 5g 5f 6d 8.2g 6s 1980 6g* 5fg 6f^3 6f^4 6fg^2 5fg^2 6g^4 5fg^3 7g^2 7fg^3 6f 6s 6d) strong gelding; won apprentice handicap at Ripon in April; ran creditably most subsequent outings; best at sprint distances; acts on any going; has worn blinkers; has tongue tied down; good mount for an inexperienced rider. *A. W. Jones.*

TURBOT ISLAND 3 ch.g. Communication 119–Vilna 81 (Vilmorin) (1979 5f **58**
5.1g 1980 6fg^3 5fg^3) third in seller and minor race in first half of year (taken down early both times); appears not to stay 6f. *P. Felgate.*

TURENNE'S LAST 7 b.g. Turenne–Damneris (Damascus 86) (1979 NR —
1980 16fg) quite a moderate novice hurdler; behind in amateur riders race won by Ribo Charter at Ascot in September on first outing on flat. *J. Scallan.*

TURN BACK THE TIME (USA) 2 b.c. Youth 135–Topolly (Turn-to) **80** p
(1980 7g^4 8fg^4) Mar 5; tall, lengthy, quite attractive colt; good mover; half-brother to French $1\frac{1}{2}$m winner Meg's Pride (by Sparkler); dam, French 9f winner, is granddaughter of top-class filly Bella Paola; fourth in minor events at Kempton and Newbury in September, in latter running on steadily without being knocked about to finish $6\frac{3}{4}$ lengths behind Shergar in 23-runner race; will stay middle distances; likely to do much better at 3 yrs. *B. Hills.*

TURNER 9 gr.g. Typhoon 125–Palmural 111 (Palestine 133) (1979 10.6g —
16.1f^4 13.4f^4 16f* 16.9fg^4 1980 16.1s) staying handicapper; acts on firm going; suitable mount for an inexperienced rider; has run creditably in blinkers. *R. Murphy.*

TURQUEY TERRI 2 ch.f. Ardoon 124–Mayfield Girl (Le Prince 98) (1980 5g **41**
5fg 5fg) Feb 5; 450Y; small, compact filly; bad plater; sold 300 gns Doncaster August Sales. *F. Dever.*

TURTLETON 3 b.g. Le Coq d'Or 101–Buzz About (Dara §§) (1979 NR 1980 —
13s 12.3s) no sign of ability in minor event at Ayr and maiden race at Newcastle in August. *R. McDonald.*

TUTHILL BELLO 2 ch.f. Porto Bello 118–Grill Room 79 (Connaught 130) (1980 5h 5g 6g^3 6g 6d 8g) Apr 14; plain filly; second foal; dam ran only twice; made good late headway when 4½ lengths third of 18 to Noalto in maiden race at Yarmouth in July, best effort; well-beaten fifth in 24-runner Leicester seller on final outing; not sure to stay 1m; had stiff task in nursery fourth outing. *P. Allingham.* **59**

TUTHILL BOND 3 ch.c. Good Bond 122–Whirlibird 78 (The Pelican) (1979 5s* 5d^2 5d 7f 7f* 7g 1980 8.2d* 8fg^2 8.2fg 10g 8g 8fg 8g) leggy, narrow colt; fair handicapper at his best; won £5,500 race at Haydock in April by 1½ lengths from Galatch; good equal second, short head behind No Faith, at Newbury later in month; below form subsequently; stays 1m; acts on any going; sweated up sixth start; none too consistent. *N. Callaghan.* **93 d**

TUTHILL WARRIOR 2 ch.c. Roman Warrior 132–Tiny Tot 80 (Counsel 118) (1980 6g 6f 5s) Feb 6; 2,800Y; good-topped individual; half-brother to several winners here and abroad; dam 2-y-o 5f winner; little worthwhile form in a maiden race and 2 sellers. *N. Callaghan.* **–**

TUXEDO PARK 4 b.g. Club House 110–Grosvenor Square 101 (Hugh Lupus 132) (1979 10.6g 10.2fg 10fg^3 10g* 8g* 12.3s* 10.6g^2 12fg 12d^4 1980 12d 13d 10.5f 8fg 10.6g^4 12g^3 12f 10g^3 12fg 12g 10s 12.3g) useful sort; often owner ridden in amateur riders races; didn't run up to his best in 1980, including when blinkered final start; stays 1½m but gives impression he's better at shorter distances; acts well on soft going; tends to hang. *P. Rohan.* **–**

TUYENU 4 ch.f. Welsh Pageant 132–Attuned (Faberge II 121) (1979 8s 8d^3 8g* 8g* 8.2g 10s 8g 1980 10s 8f^4 10fg 7.2d 9g 7d) big filly; weak in market when creditable fourth to Carpet General in handicap at Redcar in May; off course for 4 months after next start and looked burly on her return; best form at 1m and appears not to stay 1¼m; possibly not at her best on very soft ground. *M. Camacho.* **–**

T.V. STAR 3 ch.f. St Columbus 98–Bloomsbury Girl 63 (Weepers Boy 124) (1979 5f 5h 6d 8f 1980 6d 6s^4 5f^4 6f 7f^2 7g 7g 8f^3 8fg 7.6d^2 8g* 8d 8f) sparely-made filly; won minor event at Thirsk in September; stays 1m; probably acts on any going. *N. Guest.* **71**

TWEEL 4 b.f. Owen Dudley 121–Miss Tweedie 114 (Aberdeen 109) (1979 6g 7v 5fg 10.1f 15.5fg^4 12s 1980 14fg 12fg 15f 16f 14g 12d 12.2d 12d) robust filly; plating-class staying maiden; often blinkered nowadays. *D. Elsworth.* **–**

TWELFTH NIGHT 3 b.c. Martinmas 128–Joyful Scene 104 (Vilmorin) (1979 NR 1980 8f 8fg 7.6f 8g^4 8g^2 8d^2 7.6f 8g 9d^4) 4,500F, 8,400Y; useful sort; half-brother to several winners, including useful Irish 5f performer Catch (by Burglar); dam sprinter; second in maiden race and handicap at Pontefract; runs as if he'll stay 1¼m; suited by some give in the ground; ran poorly seventh and eighth starts, looking ungenuine on first occasion and wearing blinkers on second. *I. Balding.* **66**

TWENTY FOUR CARAT 2 b.g. Fine Blade 121–Goldeneye 91 (Aureole 132) (1980 7d 6s 7fg 8s 8.2s^3) May 6; 2,800Y; resold 3,800Y; compact gelding; fourth reported foal; half-brother to Irish 3-y-o 1½m and 1¾m winner Miss Golden Eye (by Simbir); dam won at up to 1½m; blinkered when 3 lengths third of 19 to Dizzy Heights in seller at Nottingham in October; will stay 1½m; sweating third start and at Nottingham. *E. Eldin.* **62**

TWENTY TWO (FR) 3 b.f. Busted 134–Bally's Mil 98 (Ballymoss 136) (1979 NR 1980 12g* 11.5g^2 12g) narrow, leggy, unfurnished filly; closely related to very smart 1¼m to 1¾m filly Mil's Bomb and Cheshire Oaks winner Milly Moss (both by Crepello) and half-sister to 2 winners; dam won twice at 1¼m; stayed on well to beat Sand Hawk 3 lengths in 9-runner maiden race at York in July; long odds on when easily beaten by Sirena in slowly-run 3-runner event at Yarmouth following month; behind in Galtres Stakes at York later in August (didn't impress in paddock); will be suited by 1¾m. *H. Cecil.* **90**

TWICE NICE 3 b.f. Double Jump 131–Marie Denise 68 (Dual 117) (1979 6fg 7d 1980 12g 12.2f^4 13.8g^2 16f^4 14d^3 15.8fg 14.6d) leggy filly; in frame in varied company, including selling; probably acts on any going; sweated up first start. *J. Fitzgerald.* **58**

TWICE NOBLE (USA) 3 ch.f. Targowice 130–Fleet Noble (Vaguely Noble 140) (1979 6fg 6fg 1980 8fg^3 9f* 8.5f^4 8fg 10g 8g 8g 10.2d^3 10d^4 10.2v) small filly; favourite when making most to win maiden race at Wolverhampton in May; in **74**

frame in handicaps and a minor event subsequently; stays 1¼m; probably acts on any going; has run respectably for an apprentice. *B. Hanbury.*

TWICKENHAM 4 b.g. Martinmas 128–Ember Grill 84 § (Indigenous 121) (1979 8s^2 8s^3 8g 7g 8f 8fg^4 1980 7g 7fg 10g^4 10s* 10d 8g* 8g^3 9fg 10d^3) leggy gelding; poor walker; won handicaps at Nottingham in June and Sandown in July, making all and holding on by ¾ length from Fettered in apprentice event on latter course; didn't impress in paddock seventh outing; stays 1¼m; acts on any going but goes well on soft. *I. Balding.* **82**

TWIDALE 7 ch.g. Twilight Alley 133–Leadendale Lady 90 (Damremont 120) (1979 16f^3 16f 1980 16f) fairly useful jumper; poor staying maiden on flat. *J. Wilson.* **—**

TWIXT' TWEEN 3 ch.f. The Go-Between 129–Che Bella (Beau Sabreur 125) (1979 5v^3 5g* 5g^2 5d 5d^3 5d^4 5d 5g 1980 6d 8f^4 8f^4 8d^3 8.2d 7d 7fg 6f* 5d 5s 6f 5d*) small, lightly-made filly; successful in handicaps at Ripon in August (beat Westburg) and Pontefract in October (from Wynburry); best at sprint distances; seems to act on any going; suitable mount for a boy. *W. H. H. Williams.* **77**

TWO DIAMONDS 2 ch.f. Double Jump 131–Aleta 71 (Montaval 129) (1980 5g 5fg 5g 5fg) Apr 8; small, sturdy filly; in rear all outings, including in sellers. *P. Ashworth.* **—**

TWO OF DIAMONDS 4 b.c. Blakeney 126–Santa Maria 103 (Tropique 128) (1979 10s^2 10.4v* 12g 10g^2 12d 1980 12f^4 13.4f^2 14f 12.5d) well-made colt; smart performer; ran well on first 2 outings, when fourth of 16 to Niniski in John Porter Stakes at Newbury and when going down by a neck to same horse in Ormonde Stakes at Chester; seventh to Noble Saint in Yorkshire Cup at York in May and to Dunette and Shakapour in Grand Prix de Saint-Cloud in July on only subsequent outings; stayed 13f; acted on firm going but was well suited by soft; dead. *B. Hills.* **109**

TWO ROCK 3 b.f. Mill Reef 141–St Pauli Girl 114 (St Paddy 133) (1979 NR 1980 10fg^4 13g*) 44,000Y; attractive, well-made filly; half-sister to several winners, including useful 1¼m performer and smart hurdler Major Thompson (by Brigadier Gerard); dam runner-up in 1,000 Guineas and Oaks; pushed out to win 18-runner maiden event at Nottingham in July by 2½ lengths from Soft Voice; not seen out again; will stay 1¾m. *H. Cecil.* **70**

TWO STROKE 3 ch.f. Malicious–Palouci 59 (Palestine 133) (1979 6f 6fg 1980 6f 7d 8g) small, lightly-made filly; little worthwhile form in maiden races; bandaged behind last 2 starts. *J. Winter.* **—**

TWO SWALLOWS 7 gr.g. My Swallow 134–Two Blues 95 (Kingsway) (1979 18d 1980 18d) fairly useful chaser; of little account on flat nowadays; blinkered on only outing of 1980. *K. Ivory.* **—**

TY-AR-EEN 4 b.g. St Paddy 133–Hover 75 (Double Jump 131) (1979 8d^4 8d 8g 7g 10f* 8fg* 10.8g^4 12d^4 1980 12fg 10d^4 10g 11.7g) small, quite well-made gelding; plater; behind in better company in 1980; seems to stay 1½m; acts on firm going and a soft surface; has worn blinkers, but didn't when successful. *A. Ingham.* **—**

TYEJEST 2 b. or br.f. Tycoon II–Fair Jest 79 (Dumbarnie 125) (1980 5d 6fg 7fg 5fg) Jan 25; 720F, 180Y; sixth produce; dam won twice over 5f; 7¾ lengths fifth of 13 finishers behind Aunty May in seller at Ripon in July, second outing; beaten in non-sellers afterwards. *Miss S. Hall.* **—**

TYPE EDITION 3 b.c. Saulingo 122–Gracie Square 75 (Nelcius 133) (1979 5g^2 5s 6g 5g 1980 5d 5.8g 8f 7fg) compact colt; has shown some ability in varied company but finished well beaten in seller on final start; best form at sprint distances; sometimes sweats up; sold 400 gns Ascot September Sales. *E. Reavey.* **—**

TYRAN 4 b.f. Tyrant–Parthian Song (Parthia 132) (1979 7fg^2 7h^3 7g^3 8g^4 7.6f 1980 8f 8fg 8g 9f 10d 12d 9s^3) lightly-made filly; plating-class maiden; should stay 1m; yet to race on a soft surface; blinkered final outing at 3 yrs; trained by N. Adam first 2 outings. *J. Berry.* **—**

TYRNAVOS 3 b.c. Blakeney 126–Stilvi 126 (Derring-Do 131) (1979 6f^3 7fg* 7fg^2 1980 8f* 8fg 10.5f^4 12f 12s* 12g) **129**

In 1969 the Derby winner Blakeney was defeated in the Irish Sweeps Derby behind Prince Regent, who had had a very unlucky run at Epsom; eleven years later Blakeney's son Tyrnavos, a bad sufferer in the usual first-mile scrimmaging in the Derby and never in the hunt behind Henbit, turned the Epsom form round to some tune at the Curragh. In our opinion Tyrnavos wouldn't have been placed at Epsom given a smoother run, and for an Irish Sweeps Derby winner he had a modest record as a three-year-old. He was well beaten in the Two Thousand Guineas and the King George VI and Queen Elizabeth Diamond Stakes, and finished fourth in the Mecca-Dante Stakes; the only other race he won was the Ladbrokes Craven Stakes first time out. Nevertheless he might have done better had it been discovered sooner that he was very well suited by a mile and a half and front-running tactics; and also had he enjoyed more opportunities of racing on soft ground.

Tyrnavos was a good two-year-old, a very impressive-looking one, too. The big question with him was whether he had the turn of foot to put him right in the top class at three. He won the Roberre Trophy over seven furlongs at the Ascot September meeting and subsequently ran second to Monteverdi in the William Hill Dewhurst Stakes; on the latter occasion he proved fast enough to go second to Henbit from the start but was the first of the six runners to be ridden along (three furlongs out), then plugged along gamely to stay ahead of Romeo Romani, Marathon Gold and Final Straw. Tyrnavos clearly wasn't so dashing an individual as his half-brother Tromos who had won the Dewhurst the year before—it wasn't to be expected with Blakeney his sire—but he kept himself in the Guineas picture with his victory in the Craven Stakes at Newmarket in April, gained very gamely from Star Way and World Leader.

Tyrnavos finished seventh in the Guineas, about eight lengths behind Nureyev. He had every chance, showing up all the way on the stand side but failing to quicken over the last furlong. Then, when Hello Gorgeous, Master Willie and Water Mill beat him in the Mecca-Dante Stakes at York, Water Mill having his first run of the season, it began to seem as if Tyrnavos might not be so good as he looked, though he was well supported for the Derby on the grounds that a longer distance would suit him better, which was how he ran at York. Beaten about two lengths by Hello Gorgeous, he stayed on as well as anything once his jockey managed to pull him outside to make his run; the horse hung in behind the leaders when first asked for an effort. Although Tyrnavos promised to be suited by a mile and a half, his dam was a sprinter, so one could understand his being ridden with restraint in the Derby: it seemed the best thing to do. However, he was bumped and cut off several times before reaching Tattenham Hill and held an unpromising position on the wide outside making the descent. Rounding the Corner, at the point shown on the photograph in Henbit's commentary on page 347, he almost lost his footing. He made only a little progress thereafter, really rousted along early in the straight, and eventually he finished twelfth of the twenty-four runners, again beaten by Hello Gorgeous, Master Willie and Water Mill.

The ground came up soft at the Curragh. Tyrnavos had never been raced

Ladbrokes Craven Stakes, Newmarket—at the post there's only a neck between Tyrnavos and Star Way

Irish Sweeps Derby, the Curragh—enterprisingly-ridden Tyrnavos wins from Prince Bee

on soft nor, among those with good form, had Pelerin, Prince Bee, Fingal's Cave and Ramian. The possibility existed that Rankin was unsuited by soft, but both Master Willie and Nikoli were proven on it and Garrido was proven on good to soft. With the first five in the Derby except the injured Henbit in the field, plus Nikoli who had beaten Tyrnavos when himself disappointing, there seemed reason enough for anticipating another defeat for Tyrnavos however well he handled the ground; on top of that he wasn't sure to get the trip in the conditions, and he started at 25/1, Master Willie being the substantially-supported favourite at 7/4.

Murray stood in for Hide on Tyrnavos. He risked making the running when the field dawdled out of the stalls and reaped handsome if generally unexpected reward for his enterprise. They were never headed. Tyrnavos kept on extremely well in the straight and won on merit by a length and a half from Prince Bee. The winner was in no real danger from two furlongs out. There was no question of Tyrnavos' stealing what was, admittedly, a very slowly-run race. The other jockeys were alive to his threat a long way from home (Prince Bee, for one, was being pushed along hard to keep in touch at halfway) but they were powerless to prevent his quickening clear soon after the turn. A below-par Master Willie chased him until fading below the distance, Ramian and Garrido chased a little longer before weakening to leave Prince Bee, who'd been hampered on the turn, to stay on for a clear second place. If Tyrnavos enjoyed any obvious stroke of good fortune it was that neither Master Willie nor Rankin showed its form; they would have given him a hard race otherwise. Rankin finished only seventh, a place behind Pelerin.

Tyrnavos seldom enjoyed conspicuous good fortune as a three-year-old. His luck was out on two counts on his only subsequent appearance after the Irish Sweeps Derby in the King George VI and Queen Elizabeth Diamond Stakes at Ascot in July: the ground was good, not soft, and he received a bump at a critical point in the race. Ridden by Hide, Tyrnavos made the running to two and a half furlongs out; approaching the straight, that is. Then Ela-Mana-Mou passed him quickly enough to convince us which was the better horse but Tyrnavos, who had gone quite well and seemed far from done with, was cannoned into by More Light as he, More Light, fought for second position. Tyrnavos, definitely hampered though not so severely that many noticed or, at any rate, saw fit to comment at the time, gradually weakened afterwards into eighth-of-ten spot, beating just Pelerin and More Light. As in the Derby in similar circumstances he found very little when hard ridden.

Tyrnavos (b.c. 1977)	Blakeney (b 1966)	Hethersett (b 1959)	Hugh Lupus
			Bride Elect
		Windmill Girl (b 1961)	Hornbeam
			Chorus Beauty
	Stilvi (b 1969)	Derring-Do (br 1961)	Darius
			Sipsey Bridge
		Djerella (ch 1960)	Guersant
			Djeretta

The race on the Ascot card immediately preceding the King George, the Princess Margaret Stakes for two-year-old fillies, had been won in very useful style by Tyrnavos' half-sister Tolmi (by Great Nephew). That made five important winners for Stilvi, the dam, from her first five foals. The Middle

Mr G. L. Cambanis' "Tyrnavos"

Park winner and Two Thousand Guineas runner-up Tachypous (by Hotfoot) was her first, followed by the mile -to mile-and-a-quarter horse Taxiarchos (by Brigadier Gerard) and the champion two-year-old Tromos (by Busted), all of them standing as stallions now. The brilliantly speedy Stilvi, rated in her own narrow sphere of racing activity the equal of Blakeney in his very different one, cost 6,200 guineas as a yearling in 1970. She beat Sallust and Workboy in the National Stakes at two years and progressed to do well in top sprints at three, winning the Duke of York Stakes at York and the King George Stakes at Goodwood. Her dam Djerella, bred by Phil Bull, didn't race; she met with an accident as a yearling and was given away. The third dam Djeretta, a winner, was out of the good broodmare Candida who bred such good winners as Dionisio, Mozart and Charicles besides the dam of the Ayr Gold Cup winner Swinging Junior.

All Stilvi's runners have been good looking. Tyrnavos, a nice, strong, good-bodied colt, is the equal in appearance of any of the others, the pick of whom to our mind was the magnificent Tachypous, and he never failed to stand out in the paddock. He also walked well and moved well. Of this outstanding collection of racehorses, Tyrnavos has proved beyond question the stoutest stayer; he was, as we said, very well suited by a mile and a half. He acted on any going but put up his best, easily his most memorable, performance on soft. Soon after Ascot he was advertised for syndication at £20,000 a share, and will begin his new career at the Gazeley Stud at Newmarket in 1981. *B. Hobbs.*

U

UBERLIEFERUNG (ATA) 4 ch.f. Stante Pede–Uberlegenheit (Nu-Or) (1980 11d) Austrian-bred filly; eighth of 9 behind Manor Farm Legacy in seller at Wolverhampton in October; changed hands 440 gns Ascot August Sales. *J. Edmunds.* —

UKRAINE GIRL 2 ch.f. Targowice 130–Paddy's Flair (Alcide 136) (1980 6g 7.5d* 8g* 8f) Apr 19; useful sort; half-sister to Irish 2,000 Guineas and French Derby third Flair Path (by Ragusa) and a winner in France; dam unraced half-sister to Irish 2,000 Guineas winner Ballymore and daughter of high-class 1959 2-y-o Paddy's Sister; won maiden race at Deauville in August and Group 3 Prix d'Aumale at Chantilly the following month, justifying favouritism in latter by ½ length from Ionian Raja; beaten 1f out and was eased up in Prix Marcel Boussac at Longchamp in October, coming home last behind Tropicaro; will probably stay 1¼m; better than her Longchamp running suggests. *R. Collet, France.* **112**

ULLEY OAK 4 b.f. Sit In The Corner–Koko Nor 56 (Crocket 130) (1979 12f3 11g 12fg 12f 10fg 13.8s 1980 5v 8f 10fg 12g 11d2 9g 10g) plater; not certain to stay 1¾m; bandaged behind fourth start (unseated apprentice rider and bolted). *G. Wallace.* **36**

ULTRA VIRES 3 b.f. High Line 125–Ultra Violet 84 (Sunny Brae 121) (1979 8d2(dis) 1980 10g 14g4 15.5s2 15.5fg* 16g* 14fg 14g) leggy, rather narrow filly; won maiden race at Folkestone and handicap at Sandown in August; beat Tru Mar 7 lengths in latter; stays well; probably acts on any going; ran poorly last 2 starts. *Sir Mark Prescott.* **87**

UNASHAMED (USA) 2 b. or br.f. Torsion–Crumb Snatcher (Kentucky Pride) (1980 5f2 5f* 5g 6d 7d) Mar 11; $29,000F, $26,000Y; rather leggy, unfurnished filly; good mover; first produce; dam won at up to 1m; very much the fittest of 9-strong field for maiden race at Sandown in May and made all to win by 2 lengths from Hazing; modest sixth of 11 to Kareem in £4,000 nursery at Lingfield in July, 2 outings later; bred to stay at least 7f. *L. Cumani.* **78**

UNA YAPPA 4 b.c. Realm 129–Crash Helmet 77 (Crocket 130) (1979 6g4 6d 5g 5fg2 5f* 5f 5g 5f3 6d2 6d2 6d2 1980 5s* 5g 5f 5g* 5.8fg* 6d 6g 5fg 5g 5s 6d) neat, strong colt; sprint handicapper; won at Warwick (twice) and Bath, making most of running on 2 occasions and beating Winsor Boy a neck on latter course in June; ran moderately in second half of season; stays 6f; acts on any going; usually wears blinkers; suitable mount for an apprentice; sold 4,000 gns Ascot October Sales. *J. Bethell.* **83** d

UNBIASED (USA) 2 b.f. Foolish Pleasure–Unfurled (Hoist the Flag) (1980 6s) Feb 16; $77,000Y; lengthy, useful sort; first foal; dam, 2-y-o 6f winner, is half-sister to very useful stakes winner Wageko; unquoted and in need of race, outpaced halfway but stayed on well final furlong when 6 lengths fifth of 21 to Tolmi in maiden event at Newmarket in July; will stay at least 1m; should do better in 1981. *L. Cumani.* **81** p

UNCLE BARRON 2 b. or br.c. Manado 130–Aspasie (Milesian 125) (1980 6s 7fg) May 15; 22,000Y; half-brother to several winners, including fairly useful 1m to 1¼m winner Nonchalant (by Wolver Hollow); dam won over 1m in Ireland; behind in large fields of maidens at Windsor in July (25/1) and Brighton in August (20/1); sold 1,650 gns Newmarket Autumn Sales. *B. Swift.* –

UNCLE DICK 3 b.c. Right Tack 131–Golly Green (Super Sam 124) (1979 5g 6s 7fg 7g 8f 1980 10fg4 11.7fg* 14f3 12d 13.1f4 12d) workmanlike colt; stayed on well to win 18-runner maiden race at Bath in April; appears not to stay 13f; acts on firm ground and is possibly unsuited by soft. *J. Hudson.* **70**

UNCLE SALTY (USA) 2 ch.c. Nodouble–So Vain (Drone) (1980 6g4 7s) Mar 4; $72,000 2-y-o; lengthy, useful sort; second foal; half-brother to a winner by Raise A Bid; dam unraced half-sister to stakes winner Dr Knighton; made progress at halfway in 9-runner Eagle Development Stakes at York in June, but couldn't get into race and was eased, finishing 6¾ lengths fourth behind Beulah Land; not seen out again until late-October when seventh of 18 behind Warily in minor event at Sandown; should stay 1m; ran under the name N.Y. Comex (USA) on first start. *L. Cumani.* –

UNDER-RATED 2 b.g. Undulate–Ruffino 99 (Como 120) (1980 7fg 7g 7g) Apr 30; leggy gelding; half-brother to several winners, 4 at least useful, including smart sprinter Bream (by Hornbeam); dam a sprinter; in rear in minor events and a poor miaden race *M. W. Easterby.* –

UNDER THE COUNTER 3 b. or br.g. Pieces of Eight 128–Lady Spy 80 (Spy Well 126) (1979 7d 7s 7f 10.6d 1980 8v 9g 7f) poor maiden; sold 750 gns Doncaster June Sales. *W. H. H. Williams.* –

UNDISMAYED 2 ch.g. Supreme Sovereign 119–Intrusion 101 (Aggressor 130) (1980 6s) May 30; half-brother to 3 winners, including very smart stayer Mr Bigmore (by Mandamus) and useful middle-distance performer Lily Langtry (by Prince de Galles); dam soft-ground stayer; 33/1 when last of 22 in maiden race won by Banbury Cross at Doncaster in November; subsequently gelded. *W. Holden.* —

UNIQUE LADY 2 br.f. Lord David 121–Westerlands Prism (Primera 131) (1980 7g 7fg 7fg) Feb 26; 2,000Y; half-sister to a winning plater; dam showed only poor form; no worthwhile form in maiden and minor events. *S. Matthews.* —

UNIT TENT 2 bl.g. Double-U-Jay 120–Signal Melody 70 (Bleep-Bleep 134) (1980 5f 5s 6g³ 6g² 5g 7.6f 7f) May 5; 1,500Y; neat, quite attractive gelding; fourth foal; half-brother to 2 winners by Levanter, including useful 1977 2-y-o Hackbridge; dam placed three times from 4 starts; placed in maiden auction events at Kempton and Folkestone in July, going down by a neck to Fath-El-Keir in latter; form only at 6f. *G. Lewis.* **68**

UNIVERSAL PENNY 2 ch.f. Royal Match 117–Rose of Damascus (Ommeyad 120) (1980 5v 5s 5f 6s 7d 6f² 5d* 6g) Feb 21; 7,800Y; half-sister to several winners, including useful 1973 Irish 2-y-o 5f winner Tonegawa (by Be Friendly) and 1979 2-y-o 5f winner Symbolrose (by Status Seeker); dam won over 5f and 7f in Ireland; made all when favourably drawn in valuable seller at Sandown in August, keeping on well to win by 1½ lengths from Trichoria; cost 5,400 gns to buy in; poorly drawn in nursery next time out; stays 6f; acts on any going; blinkered last 3 outings; sold to W. Marshall 4,600 gns Newmarket Autumn Sales. *B. Swift.* **68**

UN POUR TOUS (USA) 5 b.h. One For All–Beaufix (Weather Chart) (1979 10.2s² 10s² 9s² 10fg⁴ 10fg² 1980 10h² 10fg³ 8d 10d²) quite a moderate handicapper; stays 1¼m; acts on any going; blinkered in 1980; suitable mount for an inexperienced rider; sold 440 gns Ascot August Sales. *A. Pitt.* —

UNSUNG HERO 3 gr. or ro.g. Song 132–Sue's Dolly (Quorum 126) (1979 NR 1980 6d 6f 9.4fg 8.2f 7g 8.2d 8g) 2,000F; strong, sprint type; bad maiden; unlikely to stay beyond sprint distances; trained by T. Craig first 6 starts. *R. Cross.* —

UP COUNTRY 2 br.g. Upper Case–The Country Lane 90 (Red God 128§) (1980 6s 7fg 7.6g) Mar 10; 6,200Y; half-brother to several winners, including fairly useful 1979 Irish 2-y-o 7.5f winner Trouncer (by Saritamer); dam won 4 times over 6f; fairly prominent in minor event at Nottingham in July (eighth of 18) and maiden race at Warwick the following month (seventh of 19 to Oklahoma Star), first 2 outings; stays 7f. *H. Candy.* **64**

UPPERFIELD 2 b.f. Upper Case–Snowfield 69 (Meadow Court 129) (1980 6g) Apr 17; half-sister to fair 1978 2-y-o Gouldswood (by Averof); dam half-sister to very useful Polish Warrior; unquoted and in need of race when last but one in 14-runner seller won by Lady Ever-So-Sure at Ripon in June. *M. W. Easterby.* —

UPPETY 2 b.c. Rouser 118–Pavillon 88 (French Beige 127) (1980 8g*) Feb 6; useful sort; half-brother to 3 winners, including 3-y-o Boon (by Great Nephew), successful at up to 1½m, and useful stayer Elusive (by Blakeney); dam 1¼m winner; backed at long odds and looking to have done plenty of work, gave a pleasing display to win 16-runner minor event at Newmarket in October, lengthening his stride in good style up the hill to beat On A Cloud 2 lengths; will stay well; should make a useful 3-y-o. *B. Hobbs.* **88** p

V

VAGABOND KING 3 ch.c. Realm 129–Alley Cat 100 (Alycidon 138) (1979 6fg 5fg 5f² 6d 1980 6fg* 7g² 7d 6g⁴ 7.2d 8f² 8fg² 8d⁴ 8fg²) strong, useful sort; won minor race at Folkestone in June; ran creditably several times afterwards; spoilt his chance by hanging quite badly right final start; stays 1m; seems to act on any going; sold 6,000 gns Newmarket Autumn Sales. *M. Jarvis.* **78**

VAGUELY DIVINE (USA) 2 b.f. Master Derby–Louisianan (Vaguely Noble 140) (1980 5f 5d 6s) Mar 31; $33,000Y; quite well-made filly; second foal; dam won over 1m in France; sire won from 4.5f to 8.5f, including Preakness Stakes; showed promise when sixth of 9 to Vienna Miss in £2,500 minor event at Newbury in May; subsequently off course until October; tailed-off last in minor event at Stockton in November on final start; bred to stay at least 1m. *G. Hunter.* —

VAGUELY JAMES 6 ch.g. Jimmy Reppin 131–Vaguely Hopeful 65 (Fortino II 120) (1979 16f 16d2 1980 16fg 15f 16.5fg4 14g 16g 17.1d4 18d) quite a moderate stayer; needs some give in the ground; sometimes blinkered. *G. Beeson.* —

VAGUELY TENDER (USA) 3 b.c. Vaguely Noble 140–Tender Camilla 115 (Prince Tenderfoot 126) (1979 NR 1980 8s 10.2fg* 10.4f* 10.1f3 12f* 12g 12fg) $380,000Y; attractive, well-made colt; first foal; dam, smart 2-y-o sprinter, seemed to stay 1¼m and is half-sister to smart stayer Bonne Noel; successful in minor races at Bath and Chester in May and 6-runner handicap at Epsom in June; impressive on last-named, cruising up to leader in straight and quickening clear to beat Lakin very comfortably by 2½ lengths; sweated up when sixth to Light Cavalry in King Edward VII Stakes at Royal Ascot and fifth to Water Mill in Alycidon Stakes at Goodwood subsequently; stays 1½m; acts on firm going; racing in USA. *P. Walwyn.* **113**

VAIGLY BLUE 3 b.f. Blue Cashmere 129–Dervaig 90 (Derring-Do 131) (1979 NR 1980 7f4 7fg3 7d 5g 8fg4 8g2 8.2g* 8s2 7s) nice, lengthy filly; second foal; half-sister to high-class sprinter Vaigly Great (by Great Nephew); dam won over 5f at 2 yrs and subsequently became a leading sprinter in Trinidad; won maiden race at Nottingham in September; ran creditably in apprentice handicap next time; stays 1m; probably acts on any going; suitable mount for a boy; didn't look too keen fifth start; sold 12,000 gns Newmarket December Sales. *M. Stoute.* **64**

VAIGLY GREAT 5 ch.h. Great Nephew 126–Dervaig 90 (Derring-Do 131) (1979 6g* 5g* 6d3 5fg 6f2 5d4 6fg 1980 5fg2 5f 6d2 5.3g* 6g) **127**

One could have been excused for thinking that the best had been seen of Vaigly Great when he trailed in fifth of six behind Absalom in the Diadem Stakes at Ascot at the end of his four-year-old season, wearing blinkers. Hailed as the champion sprinter-elect after winning the Ladbrokes Abernant Stakes and the Palace House Stakes at Newmarket in great style in the spring, he had only once reproduced anything like that in five starts, and serious doubts were expressed concerning his enthusiasm. However, he recovered his form completely as a five-year-old, although he remained somewhat enigmatic, and his second to Moorestyle in the William Hill July Cup at Newmarket was probably the performance of his life.

There are good grounds for concluding that Vaigly Great came to reserve his best for his home course, after winning on tracks as far afield as Goodwood, Newcastle and Ayr (the Burmah-Castrol Ayr Gold Cup) in his younger days. The evidence suggested as much in 1979 and his form in 1980 virtually confirmed it. He ran his best two races in 1980 at Newmarket and ran far better in the Palace House Stakes on his reappearance in May than in the Temple Stakes over the same distance at Sandown later in the month; he had the Palace House at his mercy until Valeriga, receiving 4 lb, came with a strong late burst to snatch victory near the line. After heavy rain, conditions were ideal for him when he was returned to Newmarket for the July Cup, and he turned in an excellent effort despite being in a muck sweat by the time he cantered down to the start. He burst through from the back of the field when an opening appeared and was clear second best from the furlong marker. He kept on strongly in the closing stages and finished clear of Sharpo and Valeriga who were third and fourth, but he couldn't get to grips with the impressive winner Moorestyle and was beaten two and a half lengths.

Vaigly Great (ch.h. 1975)	Great Nephew (b 1963)	Honeyway (br 1941)	Fairway
			Honey Buzzard
		Sybil's Niece (ch 1951)	Admiral's Walk
			Sybil's Sister
	Dervaig (b 1967)	Derring-Do (br 1961)	Darius
			Sipsey Bridge
		Babucon (ch 1956)	My Babu
			Conkers

Vaigly Great ran only twice after the July Cup. He had a simple task in a minor event at Brighton in August on the first occasion and easily landed the odds from Lightning Label and Go Total. At Haydock the following month he clashed with Moorestyle again in the Vernons Sprint Cup and failed to reproduce his Newmarket running. He moved up alongside Kampala with a fairly dangerous-looking challenge two furlongs out, then folded up tamely under pressure and finished only fifth of eight, over seven lengths behind Moorestyle.

Vaigly Great is by Mrs Penny's sire Great Nephew out of the prolific West Indian sprint winner Dervaig who won at Thirsk as a two-year-old. His best distance was six furlongs, but his half-sister Vaigly Blue, by the sprinter Blue Cashmere, won over a mile. A useful sort, he acted on any going although he did nearly all his winning on an easy surface. He will stand at the Waverton Stud, Moreton-in-Marsh, in 1981 at the reasonable fee of £750 plus £750 (October 1st terms). *M. Stoute.*

VALANTER 3 ch.f. Galivanter 131–Valansarah 65 (Fighting Ship 121) (1979 5f 6f 1980 12d) workmanlike filly; in rear in maiden races. *K. Morgan.* —

VALDEE 5 b. or br.h. Philip of Spain 126–Golden April 71 (Sovereign Lord 120) (1979 12.2s² 12.3s³ 12v 10s⁴ 10fg⁴ 10d 1980 10s³ 12.2s⁴ 11fg) middle-distance handicapper; suited by some give in the ground; sold to M. Pipe 1,400 gns Ascot July Sales. *R. Akehurst.* —

VAL DE GLOIRE (FR) 3 b.c. Bolkonski 134–Vali (Sunny Boy III) (1979 6fg² 7fg* 7d* 7s² 1980 9f 10f) strong colt; won maiden and minor events at Yarmouth very easily prior to finishing creditable second in small race at Newcastle in 1979; lightly raced at 3 yrs, putting up better effort when fifth to Running Mill in Heath Stakes at Newmarket in April on reappearance; possibly doesn't stay 1¼m; probably acts on any going. *H. Cecil.* **95**

VAL D'ERICA 2 ch.f. Ashmore 125–Laconia 58 (Great Nephew 126) (1980 including 8v*) Mar 15; 5,000F, 4,000Y; half-sister to 6f and 7f winner Spartan Call (by Realm); dam half-sister to numerous winners, including very useful stayer Tudor Tale; one of the best Italian 2-y-o's and beat useful French filly Tysfjsa 4 lengths when winning Group 2 Premio Dormello at Milan in October; had earlier won Premio Ceriano and finished second to All Silk in Premio Novello, both at Milan; will be suited by 1¼m+; acts on heavy going; engaged in 1,000 Guineas and Oaks. *A. Botti, Italy.* **?**

VALENTINIAN 2 ch.c. Morston 125–Appian Way 89 (Romulus 129) (1980 8g⁴) Feb 27; strong, good sort; brother to a winner in Hungary and closely related to 1½m winner By-Way (by Blakeney); dam won over middle distances; 11/1 and very much in need of race when about 13 lengths fourth of 6 to Clear Verdict in minor event at Goodwood in September; has scope and will do better over middle distances at 3 yrs. *R. Hern.* **78** p

VALENTINO 4 b.g. Sun Prince 128–Ardent Range 73 (Buisson Ardent 129) (1979 10.6v³ 12g² 12s 12s 11.7g 8.2g 9fg 8fg 8fg 1980 10s 8fg 11.7fg 12.3f³ 10h 12s) inconsistent handicapper; stays 1½m; probably unsuited by soft ground; sometimes wears blinkers; sold 920 gns Newmarket Autumn Sales. *D. Sasse.* —

VALERIGA 4 b.c. Polyfoto 124–Bag of Bones (Relic) (1979 6fg⁴ 6f³ 6g³ 6g* 6s² 7s⁴ 1980 5fg* 6f 6g³ 6g⁴ 5fg* 5g² 6fg 5f³ 5v* 7s² 6v) **126**

Valeriga made the improvement that we predicted he might from three to four and there were very few sprinters better than he at the end of the year. He made the transition from handicap company without much difficulty and stood up well to a hard season, particularly for one so highly-strung. His racing performance clearly wasn't adversely affected by his increasing tendency to sweat up and misbehave during the preliminaries; if anything the more he played up the better he ran.

Rather surprisingly, perhaps, Valeriga showed his best form in 1980 over five furlongs, a distance over which he hadn't raced since his two-year-old days. His wins in the Palace House Stakes at Newmarket, the King George Stakes at Goodwood and the Premio Omenoni in Milan, were all gained over five, as were his second to Sharpo in the William Hill Sprint Championship at York and his third to Moorestyle in the Prix de l'Abbaye at Longchamp. Five furlongs seemed barely far enough when he got home narrowly from Vaigly Great after producing a terrific late burst at Newmarket but his other wins were gained more comfortably. He was always going well and quickened clear in good style to win by two lengths from Flash N Thunder at Goodwood, while in Milan he won by a slightly wider margin from the smart English handicapper Hanu after reportedly delaying the start by twenty minutes. His best effort at this distance, however, came at Longchamp where he finished so strongly from eighth-of-nine position a furlong and a half out that he failed by only a neck to overhaul Sharpo in second place; he'd been outpaced for a long way.

The remainder of Valeriga's races were over six furlongs or more. Although he ran pretty well when third behind Kearney and Sharpo from a poor draw

Palace House Stakes, Newmarket—a strong late run gets Valeriga in front of Vaigly Great (blaze) close home. Abdu keeps the grey Standaan out of third place

in the Cork and Orrery Stakes at Royal Ascot and when fourth to Moorestyle in the William Hill July Cup at Newmarket, his form in these two races didn't match his five-furlong form; nor did his second to Esclavo in the seven-furlong Premio Chiusura at Milan on his penultimate start. In the last-named, he reportedly finished strongly after being held up but was beaten comfortably by the German-trained winner.

Valeriga (b.c. 1976)	Polyfoto (br 1962)	Polic (br 1953)	Relic
			Polaire
		Brabantia (br 1953)	Honeyway
			Porthaven
	Bag of Bones (ch 1962)	Relic (bl 1945)	War Relic
			Bridal Colors
		Ouranna (gr 1945)	Khosro or Owenstown
			Ouresse

Valeriga probably inherits his temperament from his sire, the Nunthorpe winner Polyfoto, who was so unco-operative at the start in his early days that he had to be sent to race in France to get the benefit of starting stalls. Polyfoto, however, became more tractable as time went by, and was no trouble as a four-year-old. The dam Bag of Bones didn't race but had a good record as a brood-mare. She produced six winners in all before her death in 1978, four of them by Polyfoto. The best winners besides Valeriga were his sisters Dacani, a smart French sprinter, and Tuesday Night, a winner of both her starts as a two-year-old and subsequently successful five times in Brazil. The grandam Ouranna won at up to a mile and three quarters on the flat and was also successful over hurdles. She produced several winners, including the Irish St Leger second Our Charger.

A strong colt who acts on any going, Valeriga will continue a force to reckon with provided his temperament doesn't get the better of him. However, he's likely to clash with Sharpo in most of the top five-furlong races and it's worth noting that Sharpo has come out on top on each of the four occasions they have met, albeit very narrowly at Longchamp. Valeriga races particularly sweetly for Piggott and Starkey nowadays, although in 1980 he managed to unseat each of them on at least one occasion before the start. *L. Cumani.*

VALIANT HEART (FR) 3 b.c. Matahawk 127–La Vigerie (Buisson d'Or 126) **125** (1979 NR 1980 10.5v^4 12d* 12d^3 15d^3 15s* 15.5v) French colt; half-brother to French 4-y-o Coral Dawn (by Bel Baraka), successful at 7.5f and 1½m, and to a winner in Belgium by Kimberley; dam, half-sister to several winners, won 3 times over 1½m; won maiden race at Saint-Cloud in April and 14-runner Grand Prix de Paris at Longchamp in June; showed himself a good young stayer when leading over 1f out and running on stoutly to win latter event by 1½ lengths from stable-companion What A Joy with Water Mill and Mot D'Or 2 lengths away

Grand Prix de Paris, Longchamp—Valiant Heart shows himself to be a very stout stayer, beating What A Joy and the dead-heaters Water Mill (far side) and Mot D'Or

equal third; well beaten in Prix Royal-Oak at Longchamp only subsequent start; stays well; yet to race on a sound surface. *B. Secly, France.*

VALLEY-ANN 2 ro.f. Runnymede 123–Right Abella 74 (Right Boy 137) (1980 5g 5fg) May 18; 1,850Y; small filly; third foal; dam sprinter; outsider of party and backward when remote sixth of 7 to Holly Patch in seller at Salisbury in June; behind in 24-runner maiden event at Windsor 2 months later. *J. Hill.* —

VALLEY MAID 3 ch.f. Welsh Pageant 132–Sealskerry (Worden II 129) (1979 5f 6f 7s 1980 7v4 8.5f 10fg 12f3 10fg 8f 9s 10s 10.2d*) lengthy filly; made all and stayed on well to beat Rage Glen 4 lengths in 10-runner minor event at Doncaster in October; had earlier faced stiff tasks on several occasions and ran respectably more than once; seems to stay 1¼m; probably acts on any going; blinkered fifth, eighth and final starts; sold 17,000 gns Newmarket December Sales. *P. Kelleway.* **75**

VALOUR (USA) 5 b.h. Vaguely Noble 140–Louisador (Indian Hemp 124) (1979 12d 12s 13.3g2 12g* 12.5fg 10f4 12f3 12d 1980 12fg2 12g 12f4 12fg 13.3d2) well-made horse; smart middle-distance performer; ran a cracking race on reappearance, finishing neck second of 8 to More Light (rec 8 lb) in Jockey Club Stakes at Newmarket in May; put up best subsequent effort when 1½ lengths third (promoted to second) to Nicholas Bill in slowly-run Geoffrey Freer Stakes at Newbury in August; ran poorly in Grand Prix d'Evry on second outing; acts on any going; often has his tongue tied down; genuine; said to have injured his nose after forcing his way out of stall (which failed to open) at Newmarket; sent to USA. *F. J. Houghton.* **116**

VAL'S MILL 3 b.c. Mill Reef 141–Val's Girl 113 (Sir Ivor 135) (1979 7f 8g2 1980 10.5g 10g3 12d 8s 12s) neat colt; didn't grow at all from 2 yrs to 3 yrs; showed promise both outings in 1979; didn't run up to his best in 1980, though wasn't disgraced in maiden race at Sandown on second start; should have stayed 1½m; broke a leg final outing and was destroyed. *M. Stoute.* **81**

VANA 3 b.f. Mummy's Pet 125–Lonely Nymph 60 (Forlorn River 124) (1979 5d 5g 6f 5f 6fg* 5.1fg3 5g 5d 6d 5d 5fg 5fg 5g4 5g 1980 5s 7s 6fg 6h 5f 5fg 6g 8g 5g2 6g3 5d) leggy, light-framed filly; plater; unlikely to stay beyond sprint distances; possibly unsuited by soft ground; blinkered final 2 outings at 2 yrs; sometimes sweats up. *A. Demetriou.* **42**

VAN LINGEN 2 ch.f. Bustino 136–Idiot's Delight (USA) (Bold Ruler) (1980 7d2 7d*) Feb 11; third foal; half-sister to successful Belgian horse Muff Diver (by Deep Diver); dam unraced daughter of Musidora Stakes winner Fool's Gold; always in first 2 when winning 13-runner maiden race at Phoenix Park in October by 2 lengths from favourite Fireplace; had earlier put up a pleasing first effort when failing by only ¾ length to overhaul all-the-way winner Condessa in 20-runner maiden race at the Curragh in September; will stay 1½m; sure to win more races and should make a very useful filly. *A. Maxwell, Ireland.* **95** p

VANRENOS 2 b.f. Gold Rod 129–Supafrag 55 (Track Spare 125) (1980 6s 5d 6d 5d 7f* 8.2d) Mar 17; small filly; first foal; dam poor juvenile hurdler; backed from 14/1 to 8/1 when showing improved form to win 14-runner seller at Wolverhampton in August by 1½ lengths from Cristina Times; bought in 1,150 gns afterwards; last of 19 in another seller at Haydock the following month; suited by 7f and should stay 1m; form only on firm going. *W. Clay.* **53**

VANTAGE 2 b.f. Bay Express 132–Valdesta 106 (Persian Gulf) (1980 8g 7d) May 4; good-bodied filly; half-sister to French 9f winner Valiant Cry —

(by Town Crier) and 1¼m winner Ben Donachan (by Reform); dam, closely related to Rustam and Zabara, won 3 times over 7f; behind in October in maiden race at Newmarket and minor event at Doncaster (speed 5f). *J. Hindley.*

VARINGO 3 br.c. Saulingo 122–Vraiment (Relko 136) (1979 5d* 5s* 6g* 6g^2 6fg^2 5f^2 1980 7v 7f) strong, rangy colt; smart and genuine at 2 yrs when he won newcomers race at Goodwood, Berkshire Stakes at Newbury and Coventry Stakes at Royal Ascot and finished second in 3 important races, Richmond Stakes at Goodwood, Prix Morny at Deauville and Flying Childers Stakes at Doncaster; well beaten in Salisbury 2,000 Guineas Trial and Clerical, Medical Greenham Stakes at Newbury early in 1980; appeared not to stay 7f; probably acted on any going; dead. *R. Price.* —

VARTKEZ (FR) 3 b.g. A Tempo 127–Caecilia 76 (Skymaster 126) (1979 NR 1980 10.1s 13g 10s* 10.1g^2 12f^4 10fg^4) strong gelding; brother to French 1m and 1¼m winner Briefing and to a winning jumper; dam placed from 5f to 1m; 33/1, stayed on well to win 18-runner maiden race at Nottingham in August; good second in minor event at Windsor later in month; should stay 1½m; acts on soft going and is possibly unsuited by firm. *D. Morley.* **82**

VARUNA 3 ch.c. Luthier 126–Aspara 58 (Crimson Satan) (1979 5d 5s 5f^3 6fg 6g^3 6fg^2 1980 7f 7h* 7fg* 7f^3 8g 8fg 8.5fg^4 7g^2 7.3fg 8g^4 8s) neat colt; good mover; successful in two £1,800 events at Brighton in May; good second in handicap at Kempton in September; probably stays 1m; acts on hard going and is probably unsuited by soft; sweated up badly fourth start; ran poorly fifth outing; sold 6,800 gns Newmarket Autumn Sales. *A. Breasley.* **79**

VASCAR 5 ch.g. Roi Soleil 125–Kindling 80 (Psidium 130) (1979 11g^4 1980 10.6s) poor handicapper on flat; useful hurdler however; acts well on soft going. *J. Berry.* —

VAUDEVILLE QUEEN 3 b.f. Saulingo 122–Fiddle Myree 69 (Frankincense 120) (1979 5v 5d 5d^4 5.3g 5fg 5g^4 6f^2 6fg 5g 1980 12g 9f 10.6s 12g) well-made filly; poor plater; not certain to stay beyond 6f; has been tried in blinkers; changed hands 400 gns Doncaster January Sales. *M. Eckley.* —

VEEYA 2 gr.g. Deep Diver 134–Ginkgo (Green God 128) (1980 5f 5fg^2 5fg* 5d 5fg 5d) Apr 26; 2,300F; fairly useful-looking gelding; good walker; first produce; dam never ran; cost 4,500 gns to buy in after winning 4-runner seller at Kempton in May by 4 lengths from Tudor Judge, easily best effort; ran too freely when blinkered next time out; acts on a firm surface. *A. Bailey.* **68**

VELESO 2 b.g. Jimsun 121–Dracaena 62 (Double Jump 131) (1980 5f 6d 6d* 7g^4 6g^4) Apr 1; useful sort; second foal; brother to 3-y-o 7f winner Charlie's Sunshine; dam won 7f seller at 2 yrs; showed improved form when making all to win 8-runner maiden race at Lingfield in July by 2½ lengths from Beggar's Bush; fourth subsequently in minor event at Newmarket (sweated up badly) and nursery at Salisbury (ran well behind Maryland Cookie); probably stays 7f; acts on a soft surface. *R. Hannon.* **94**

VELVET BOY 6 b.g. Shantung 132–Amara (Sanctus II 132) (1979 10.2s 10s 1980 8f) plater; should stay middle distances; has worn blinkers; refused to leave stalls and virtually took no part on only outing of 1980. *A. Smith.* —

VELVETEEN SLIPPER 3 b.f. Shiny Tenth 120–Las Ventas (Breton 130) (1979 5f 6fg 1980 8g^3 8fg 8fg 7g) unfurnished filly; showed some ability in maiden race on reappearance but was well beaten afterwards, including in a seller; appears to stay 1m; sold 625 gns Ascot November Sales. *G. Pritchard-Gordon.* —

VELVET GREEN 3 ch.f. Legal Tender 94–Gretel Green (Prince Hansel 118) (1979 NR 1980 8fg) lengthy filly; first foal; dam poor N.H. performer; behind in maiden race at Doncaster in July; dead. *J. Webber.* —

VELVET HABIT 2 ch.f. Habitat 134–Red Velvet 114 (Red God 128**§**) (1980 7d^4 6g*) Mar 24; strong filly; good walker; half-sister to 3 winners, including very useful 1974 2-y-o Red Cross (by Crepello) and useful 1¼m winner Red Rufus (by Busted); dam, half-sister to Lord David, at her best at 2 yrs; well-backed favourite and pick of paddock for 21-runner maiden race at Leicester in November and justified the support, always going well and being pushed clear to beat Princess Galicia 2½ lengths; will probably stay 1m; a useful 3-y-o in the making. *P. Walwyn.* **89** p

VENDIBILITY 2 b.c. Auction Ring 123–Wiener City (Chief) (1980 5f 5f 6g 5d^4 5s 6s) Mar 15; 5,000Y; lightly-made colt; poor mover; half-brother **66**

to 2 winners in Ireland, including 3-y-o 1m winner Vienna Girl (by Ballymore), and to winners in Germany and France; dam won 3 times in Germany; only plating class; ran moderately over 6f final outing, but should stay trip. *G. Toft.*

VENJA 2 ch.c. Native Bazaar 122–Avengeress 73 (Aggressor 130) (1980 8fg^2 **67**
8s) May 16; 1,800Y; tall, light-framed, lengthy colt; third reported foal; dam won at up to 13.8f; well-backed favourite when 1½ lengths second of 18 to Seaquin in seller at Leicester in September; respectable 6 lengths fifth to Santella Ascot in 21-runner seller at Newmarket the following month; stays 1m; should win a seller. *P. Cole.*

VERBALISM (USA) 3 br.c. Verbatim–Sandy Nichols (Baffle) (1979 5f **58**
5h^3 6g 6s 7fg 8h^4 7fg^3 8g 1980 8v 7fg 8f* 10.6f 7.2fg^2 8fg* 7g) quite a useful-looking colt; plater; attracted no bid when winning at Newcastle in April and Ayr in May; stays 1m; suited by firm ground; blinkered fourth start at 2 yrs. *G. Richards.*

VERDURET (FR) 3 b.c. Green Dancer 132–Tarmac (Takawalk II 125) (1979 **103**
6g* 1980 7.6f* 7f 7g) good-looking colt; pushed clear to beat Millbank (USA) in good style by 7 lengths in minor race at Chester in May; ran better subsequent race when just over 2 lengths fifth to Captain Nick in £8,100 race at Newmarket in June, third start; will stay 1m+; acts on firm going. *H. Cecil.*

VEROWEN 2 ch.g. Owen Anthony 102–Sovereign Bracelet (Manacle 123) **67**
(1980 5f 5h^3 5fg^4 5fg 5f 6fg^4 5s) Apr 6; lightly-made gelding; second foal; dam poor maiden; only plating class; better suited by 6f than 5f and should stay further; blinkered fifth outing. *W. Stubbs.*

VERSAILLES PRINCE 7 br.g. Versailles–Villarrica (Dan Cupid 132) (1979 **63**
8s 8v^4 8g* 7g* 8s* 8s 8s^3 8fg 8g 8fg^4 1980 8fg 7d* 7g 7.6d 8g 8fg 10g^4 7s) won handicap at Brighton in June; probably best at 7f or 1m, but wasn't disgraced at 1¼m; acts on any going but is well suited by soft; best in blinkers; excellent mount for an inexperienced rider. *A. Ingham.*

VERY FRIENDLY 4 b.g. Be Friendly 130–Little Hexa (Exar 130) (1979 **38**
8s 7.6f 6f 8fg 15.8d 1980 8s 8s 8fg 8.2d^2 8fg 10.4d 8d) poor plater; stays 1m; acts on soft going. *M. James.*

VIA DELTA 3 ch.f. Red Alert 127–Vi 90 (Vilmorin) (1979 5v* 5d^2 5d 5g^3 5d* **104**
1980 5fg 5f* 5fg* 5fg* 5s 5f* 5g^2 5fg*) small filly; developed into a useful performer, winning handicaps at Chester, Haydock (apprentice event) and Ascot (2) and all-aged race at Chepstow; made all on both occasions at Ascot, beating Hanu by 1½ lengths in Fortnum and Mason Stakes in June on fourth start; races only at 5f; acts on any going but is well suited by firm; suitable mount for a claimer; consistent. *G. Balding.*

VICARAGE LAD 3 b.c. Military 112–Erisca 88 (Doutelle 128) (1979 6fg **65**
5fg^2 5g^3 5g 5.1g^4 5fg^4 1980 7f 8fg 8fg 6s 6g* 5d 6d) neat colt; 20/1 when showing much improved form to win handicap at Yarmouth in September; stays 6f; unsuited by soft ground; blinkered fifth start at 2 yrs. *F. Durr.*

VICOLS LAD 2 ch.g. Sandford Lad 133–Lady Exbury 111 (Exbury 138) **52**
(1980 5fg 6s 6fg 6g) Apr 5; 6,600Y; smallish, fair sort; first foal; dam stayed 1½m well, and is half-sister to very smart Boreen; modest sixth in maiden races at Nottingham and Salisbury on second and third outings but made no show in seller on fourth; will be suited by 7f+. *G. Balding.*

Fortnum & Mason Handicap, Ascot—Via Delta has too much speed for Hanu and Over the Rainbow

VICOMTE 4 ch.c. Firestreak 125–Vicomtesse 97 (Relko 136) (1979 10s4 12.3v* 12.3s* 12s 16fg 13g3 14.7g* 14.6f 14g4 1980 16.1d* 16.1f3 16f3 16d3 21fg 18g3 16f 18d) big, strong colt; has enlarged near-fore fetlock joint; won handicap at Haydock in April by ¾ length from Wesley; ran very well on third and fourth starts when close third to Billion in Henry II Stakes at Sandown and to Mon's Beau in Coral Northumberland Plate at Newcastle; not disgraced when 15 lengths third of 5 behind Le Moss in Doncaster Cup in September on sixth outing; stays well; acts on any going but is particularly well suited by some give in the ground; blinkered final start (well beaten in Tote Cesarewitch). *J. Fitzgerald.* **104**

VICTOR HUGO 3 b. or br.c. Vaguely Noble 140–Anna Karenina (Princely Gift 137) (1979 NR 1980 8s 8f 6h 5fg) 40,000Y, 800 2-y-o; compact colt; last on all outings in varied company; blinkered first 2 starts. *P. Arthur.* –

VICTORIA SPIRIT 3 ch.f. Henry the Seventh 125–Golf Ball (Persian Gulf) (1979 5s 5s 6g 7f 6f 7fg* 8h 8.2d4 8g 1980 10s) neat filly; won 4-runner seller at Catterick in 1979; tailed off in better company only start at 3 yrs in April; should stay 1¼m; probably acts on any going; seems best in blinkers; has worn bandages. *W. Bentley.* –

VICTORIA STATION 3 b.c. Run The Gantlet–Headin' Home 105 (Habitat 134) (1979 6f 1980 10s 12fg 12f 12g4 10d4 10g 12f*) neat, well-made colt; plater; won at Ostend in August; will probably stay beyond 1½m; acts on firm going; blinkered fourth and fifth outings. *M. Jarvis.* –

VICTOR'S BOAST (USA) 2 ch.c. Roberto 131–Noble Mark 120 (On Your Mark 125) (1980 5s3 5f3 5f4 7fg3 7.2g3) Mar 22; small, compact colt; half-brother to 3-y-o middle-distance winner Noble Dudley (by Giacometti); dam very smart sprinter at 2 yrs and 3 yrs; in frame in maiden races and a nursery; ridden by 7-lb claimer when fair 5 lengths third of 10 to Kareem in last-named race at Haydock in September, fifth start; will stay 1m. *B. Hills.* **83**

VICTORY CORNER 3 b.f. Sit In The Corner–La Vickstan 72 (El Gallo 122) (1979 5f 5f 5f 6fg 1980 5fg 7f 6h 5fg 6fg 6g3 7g 7fg 6g 6g) light-framed filly; plater; stays 6f; has been tried in blinkers. *P. Butler.* –

VICTORY HYMN 4 gr.c. Seaepic 100–Decorators Ditty (Sing Sing 134) (1979 7s2 10.1g3 10s 10fg3 1980 10fg 8fg) quite well-made colt; plating-class maiden; stays 1¼m; probably acts on any going. *N. Henderson.* –

VIDEO BOY 3 b.g. Laser Light 118–Somers Jewel (Will Somers 114§) (1979 5fg 5f3 6f3 5fg4 6g4 6s* 6g 5fg3 6g 6s4 6g 1980 5fg 5s 5g 7d) strong gelding; made all to win maiden race at Newcastle in 1979; well beaten in handicaps at 3 yrs; stays 6f; suited by some give in the ground. *S. Wainwright.* –

VIDEO TAPE (USA) 2 br.c. Cannonade–Virunga 115 (Sodium 128) (1980 7d 8g*) Apr 5; strong, rangy, most attractive colt; dam smart middle-distance performer, third in French Oaks; 25/1 and apprentice ridden at overweight, burst through to lead in Dip and beat stable-companion Beaux Arts 2½ lengths in 17-runner minor event at Newmarket in October; sure to improve further over middle distances in 1981. *H. Cecil.* **90** p

VIELLE 3 b.f. Ribero 126–Hurdy-Gurdy 90 (Espresso 122) (1979 7f* 6f2 7g2 7g2 7fg* 8fg2 1980 7f 10fg* 12f2 12s* 10fg* 12d2 10f) **123**

The race for the Sun Chariot Stakes at Newmarket in October produced a typical back-end result, with the much improved Snow and Kashmir Lass fighting out the finish while the short-priced favourite Vielle trailed in a jaded sixth of seven. The first two were only just approaching their peak whereas Vielle was well past hers. At her best Vielle had very few superiors among the three-year-old fillies over middle distances. She won the Lupe Stakes, the Lancashire Oaks and the Nassau Stakes, the last two very decisively, and finished a good second in the Oaks and the Yorkshire Oaks. Her main strength lay in her finishing speed, her main weakness in her tendency to hang when fully extended.

Vielle almost beat Quick As Lightning in the Hoover Fillies Mile at Ascot as a two-year-old, and would have done so ridden more conservatively; she went clear in the second-last furlong but hung badly in the last and was caught on the post. Her speed had been used both too soon and too quickly. Bred as she is, Vielle's prospects of staying middle distances as a three-year-old were never really in doubt (her grandam was a sprinter, true enough, but had produced an Irish St Leger third Torano, and Hurdy-Gurdy herself stayed at least a mile and a quarter). Her performance behind Evita in the Ladbrokes Nell Gwyn Stakes in April showed straight away that seven furlongs had become far too sharp for her,

Lancashire Oaks, Haydock—Vielle is an easy winner

and we marked her down there and then for the Musidora Stakes. But Vielle apparently had a throat infection after Newmarket; instead of running at York she turned out later in May in the Lupe Stakes, a race transferred to Kempton because of rebuilding at Goodwood. Although the Lupe Stakes attracted a field inferior to the Musidora's it was hard not to be impressed with Vielle as an Oaks candidate after seeing her beat Norfolk Gal much more emphatically than the half-length margin might suggest. She started joint-second favourite with the Musidora winner Bireme behind the Guineas winner Quick As Lightning at Epsom.

Vielle went down by two lengths to Bireme in the Oaks. She hung badly left when making her challenge, but for which she would surely have been closer. The way she made her ground from over two furlongs out would have done credit to an Oaks winner, but once she reached The Dancer and Bireme a furlong from home she ducked in; her jockey had to stop riding to straighten her, and when

Nassau Stakes, Goodwood—Vielle comes home clear of Bonnie Isle

straightened the winner was as good as home. Many's the horse who has hung towards the rail in the last furlong at Epsom: the course's camber positively encourages it, yet on this occasion the blame must rest largely on Vielle and on the jockey, the latter of whom, after all, had ridden her and the course before. Once straightened, Vielle plugged on, her speed now blunted, to beat The Dancer by a short head for second.

Vielle (b.f. 1977)	Ribero (b 1965)	Ribot (b 1952)	Tenerani
			Romanella
		Libra (ch 1956)	Hyperion
			Weighbridge
	Hurdy-Gurdy (b 1970)	Espresso (ch 1958)	Acropolis
			Babylon
		Street Singer (br 1954)	Kingsway
			Record Serenade

Although The Dancer had finished so close to Vielle at Epsom, Vielle started odds on to beat her in the Lancashire Oaks at Haydock in July and beat her very easily. The Dancer didn't run up to her best that day and wasn't seen out again; apart from The Dancer, Vielle had little of note against her and she won by five lengths from Kahaila despite drifting towards the middle of the track after striking the front almost two furlongs out. Vielle started an even firmer favourite (15/8 on) against the 1979 Oaks runner-up Bonnie Isle and five three-year-old fillies, including Norfolk Gal, in the ten-furlong Nassau Stakes at Goodwood the following month. She made Bonnie Isle seem desperately one paced as she came by her on the bridle at the distance and quickened stylishly away for an easy two-length win. We thought Vielle might do the same in the Yorkshire Oaks to The Dancer's stable-companion Shoot A Line, who had finished only fifth at Epsom; there was only a small field, nothing except Shoot A Line seemed to have a chance against her on the form-book, and things seemed tailor-made for Vielle to pounce on the stouter stayer late in the race. Vielle was ridden from behind as expected, coming through from fourth place on the bridle looking as though she would smother the front-running Shoot A Line two furlongs out. Once given the office she hung left onto the rails, failed to do more than draw level with Shoot A Line,

Mr T. F. Blackwell's "Vielle"

began to run on at one pace under pressure and was finally outstayed by a length and a half.

Vielle's dam won the first ladies race at Ascot, the Cullinan Diamond Stakes in 1973: she was quite useful at up to a mile and a quarter and ran as though she would have had no difficulty staying further. Vielle is her third foal and second winner, following Sideshow (by Welsh Pageant) who won four races at up to a mile and also ran as though she'd stay further; her two-year-old Organist (by Jupiter Pluvius) was in training in 1980. The grandam Street Singer, by Kingsway out of a Straight Deal mare, turned out to be a high-class sprinter much to everyone's surprise after hopes had been entertained of her developing into a Guineas or even an Oaks filly. Most of her dam's stock stayed quite well, though there was one other notable exception—Cameo, the dam of Raffingora. Both Record Serenade and Street Singer proved excellent producers, and Street Singer is the dam of eight winners all told, the best of them probably Torano and the useful miler Glitter Song.

Vielle is a strong, shapely, good sort of filly, a good walker and mover. She stays a mile and a half and acts on any going. She is not an easy ride. *B. Hobbs.*

VIENNA MISS 2 b.f. Thatch 136–Light Opera 101 (Vienna 127) (1980 **101**
5fg 5f* 5g $6d^3$ $5g^2$ 5.1fg* 6fg) Feb 1; 28,000Y; small, strong, good-bodied filly; half-sister to several winners, including fairly useful 5f and 1m winner Little Tern (by Sea Hawk II); dam, closely related to Laser Light, stayed 7f; winner of £2,500 event at Newbury in May (got up to beat Chateau Dancer a neck) and minor race at Yarmouth in August (landed the odds by 3 lengths from Dalegarth); beaten in more valuable races on most of her other starts, running well when neck second to Vocalist in Horn Blower Stakes at Ripon in August and not being disgraced when 6 lengths seventh of 8 to Marwell in William Hill Cheveley Park Stakes at Newmarket in October; seems barely to stay 6f; probably acts on any going. *H. T. Jones.*

VIENNA WALTZ 2 ch.f. Town Crier 119–Melodor 103 (Songedor 116) (1980 —
5fg) Apr 23; 875F, 1,300Y; tall filly; fifth produce; dam miler; 14/1 and bit backward, started slowly but stayed on well from below distance when remote tenth of 17 behind Pariscene in maiden event at Wolverhampton in August; refused to enter stalls on intended debut. *S. Woodman.*

VIGEZZINA 2 br.f. Averof 123–Peta's Bay 67 (I Say 125) (1980 5.8fg 5.8f **76**
$7f^4$ 7g) Feb 13; 5,000Y; half-sister to 1979 2-y-o 5f winner Repeat Performance (by Targowice) and to a winner in South Africa by Petingo; dam, half-sister to high-class Gold Rod, won over 7f; put up best effort when 4¼ lengths fourth of 20 to Briar in maiden race at Chepstow in August; suited by 7f and will probably stay 1m. *J. Dunlop.*

VILAMOURA 2 ch.f. Swing Easy 126–Algarve 94 (Alcide 136) (1980 6d) —
May 16; lengthy filly; sister to fairly useful sprinter Swinging Trio; dam won over 1¼m and 1½m, and is daughter of 1,000 Guineas and Oaks runner-up Spree; unquoted and apprentice ridden when behind in 25-runner maiden race won by Little Wolf at Newbury in October. *J. Tree.*

VILLAGE VOICE 4 gr.f. Town Crier 119–Wrong Direction 90 (Young Emperor —
133) (1979 7fg 7fg 8fg 1980 7fg 7f) big filly; good mover; lightly raced and little worthwhile form since 1978; should stay 1m; yet to race on a soft surface; sold 5,200 gns Newmarket December Sales. *W. Hastings-Bass.*

VILLAJOYOSA (FR) 2 b. or br.f. Satingo 129–La Ramee (White Label II **73**
126) (1980 6d 6d 7.5d $5d^3$ 6.5g $5g^3$ 6fg 7d 4.2g* 8v) May 18; 30,000 francs Y (approx £3,200); leggy filly; poor walker; sister to French 3-y-o 1¼m claiming race winner Fiordiligi and useful 1978 French 2-y-o 5.5f winner Vox Dei, and half-sister to a winner in Belgium; dam French middle-distance winner; nearest at finish when 3½ lengths third of 10 to Goody Goody in minor event at Goodwood in September, sixth start; won claimer at Amiens in November; should be suited by 6f+; best in blinkers; trained until last outing by C. Austin. *J. P. Pelat, France.*

VILLA MILL 5 b.g. Porto Bello 118–Amante 121 § (Tehran) (1979 8s* 8s **62**
12g 10.5d 8s 8d 8fg 10g 8g 8.2d 1980 8d $8v^2$ 8f 9fg 8d 8g* 8g 8s) well-made gelding; sold out of T. Fairhurst's stable 1,500 gns after winning apprentice seller at Carlisle in July; stays 1¼m but not 1½m; suited by some give in the ground; has been tried in blinkers; inconsistent. *C. Crossley.*

VILLA SET 3 b.g. Track Spare 125–Get Set 65 (Stupendous) (1979 7d 1980 —
10s 10.8s 10d 7.6d) leggy gelding; poor maiden; blinkered second start. *R. Mason.*

VINCCI 3 br.g. Saulingo 122–Kazannka (Wild Risk) (1979 6s 7f 7g 7fg 7s 1980 8d 7fg 8h 8d) strong gelding; bad plater; sometimes wears blinkers; has had his tongue tied down. *G. Hunter.* —

VINCENT 4 b.c. Busted 134–Lady Vincent 75 (High Hat 131) (1979 10f* 12d² 12g* 12fg² 16f² 14fg* 1980 16fg² 14f³ 16f 20g³ 13.5g³ 15.5v) strong, good sort; ex-English; poor mover with a rather round action; very smart stayer as a 3-y-o (rated 121); didn't win in 1980, best effort when about 7 lengths third behind Le Moss and Ardross in Gold Cup at Royal Ascot in June, appearing to run out of stamina after looking to be going better than winner on home turn; also placed in Sagaro Stakes at Ascot (¾-length second to Pragmatic), Yorkshire Cup at York (third to Noble Saint) and Grand Prix de Deauville (third to Glenorum) and was far from disgraced when fifth to Gold River in Prix Royal-Oak at Longchamp on final outing; acts on any going; hampered third start; trained by J. Hindley until after fourth start and by F. Palmer fifth start. *J. C. Lebrun, France.* **108**

VINEPARK PARADE 6 b.m. Impecunious–Fernhill Melody 88 (Golden Cloud) (1979 NR 1980 16d) of little account. *J. Hardy.* —

VINOVIA 4 ro.f. Ribston 104–Bluest 96 (Infatuation 129) (1979 NR 1980 8f 8f 8fg 7g 8g 7f 6g 8.2v) workmanlike filly; poor plater; sometimes wears blinkers. *N. Chamberlain.* —

VIOLINO FANDANGO 2 b.c. Gay Fandango 132–Parkhurst (Sing Sing 134) (1980 5s 5.8fg² 7s² 7f* 7h* 8f) Feb 4; 5,000Y (privately); tall colt; half-brother to 2 winners here and abroad; dam never ran; won maiden race at Catterick in July and nursery at Bath in August, holding on by a neck from Coal Bunker in latter; soundly beaten under a 6-lb penalty in nursery at York in September; stays 7f well; acts on any going. *B. Hills.* **82**

VIRGINIA HEIGHTS 3 ch.f. Virginia Boy 106–Weirdi 76 (Yrrah Jr) (1979 6g 1980 8fg 8f 9.4fg 8f 7g) narrow, sparely-made filly; poor plater; sometimes sweats up. *W. A. Stephenson.* —

VIRGIN SOLDIER 4 b.g. Queen's Hussar 124–Saintly Miss 63 (St Paddy 133) (1979 10.1fg* 10fg* 1980 10fg* 10g 12g² 12fg² 10d) leggy gelding; led close home when beating Eyelight by a neck in lady riders race at Lingfield in June; runner-up in amateur riders event at Redcar and handicap at Epsom afterwards; probably stays 1½m; acts on a firm surface and ran moderately on dead ground final outing; sold to J. Old 7,000 gns Newmarket Autumn Sales. *W. Hastings-Bass.* **76**

VIRIBUS (FR) 4 b.c. Sir Gaylord–Vasveliya (Saint Crespin III 132) (1979 8d³ 10g 10.1g* 10.1fg² 10fg⁴ 9g 8.3f 8g 8.2g 1980 10.6fg 12f 10.6s³ 10s²) tall, attractive colt; good mover; ran best races when placed in £2,400 event at Haydock (first outing for 5 months) and apprentice event at Nottingham, both in October; should stay 1½m. *R. Hollinshead.* **74**

VISALA (FR) 3 b.f. Labus–Evisa (Dan Cupid 132) (1979 NR 1980 9f) fourth foal; half-sister to very useful French 1m and 10.5f winner Demia (by Abdos); dam never ran; eighth of 14 to Rule Britannia in maiden race at Wolverhampton in May; sold 950 gns Goffs November Sales. *M. Stoute.* —

VISCONTI 4 b.g. Lord Gayle 124–Jane Shaw (Galivanter 131) (1979 8v³ 10v² 10s* 12f 11f* 11fg* 10d 1980 8g 12fg³ 10s*) ex-Irish gelding; well-backed favourite when winning apprentice event at Nottingham in October in good style by 4 lengths from Viribus; needed race both previous starts; stays 11f; acts on any going; useful young hurdler. *M. Dickinson.* **79**

VISCOUNT 6 b.g. Realm 129–Sunflower 96 (Paveh 126) (1979 NR 1980 12f 14.7f) poor middle-distance handicapper (rated 67) at 4 yrs; lightly raced and well beaten since; acts on hard going. *V. Thompson.* —

VITAL SEASON 6 ch.h. Silly Season 127–Vital Match 113 (Match III 135) (1979 12d 18.4d 13.3g* 16s 12s² 13.3g 12g⁴ 1980 12f 13.3f⁴ 12g) useful performer; made all when winning Aston Park Stakes at Newbury in 1979; 5 lengths fourth of 8 behind Balinger in same race in May, best effort of 1980; stayed 2m but was possibly best at up to 1¾m; acted on any going; suitable mount for an amateur rider; stud. *H. Blagrave.* **98**

VIVA L'ARMOUR 3 ch.c. Gay Fandango 132–La Grisette (Fortino II 120) (1979 5fg 5fg 6fg² 6g* 7g 6f 1980 6g 5f⁴) big, good-looking colt; respectable fourth of 17 to Crews Hill in valuable handicap at York in May; needed further than 5f and would have stayed 1m; acted on firm going; dead. *A. Breasley.* **90**

VIVARIO 3 ch.g. Reliance II 137–Parrullah (Valerullah 113) (1979 NR 1980 15.8fg 12g 14.7d³ 15s³ 12s) strong, workmanlike gelding; sixth reported foal by a thoroughbred stallion; dam ran at 2 yrs in Ireland; staying maiden; acts on soft going; sweated up third start. *Hbt Jones.* **63**

VIVA SINGAPURA 2 b.g. Town Crier 119–Magibbilibyte 77 (Constable 119) (1980 5f 6fg 6d) Mar 12; 13,000Y; compact gelding; half-brother to several winners, including fairly useful 1977 2-y-o 5f performer Maggydamus (by Mandamus); dam 7f to 1¼m selling handicapper; burly and showed no worthwhile form in varied company in the North in first half of season (moved extremely well to start on last 2 outings). *M. W. Easterby.* **–**

VIVRE L'AMOUR 2 b.c. Song 132–Ribot's Affair 100 (Ribot 142) (1980 6d 6fg) Apr 12; 6,600F, 5,800Y; third foal; half-brother to a winner in France by Bold Lad, Ire; dam Irish 2-y-o 6f winner; unquoted and backward when behind in maiden races at Salisbury in June and September. *R. Hannon.* **–**

VOCALIST 2 b.f. Crooner 119–Rhythm 64 (Bleep-Bleep 134) (1980 6g 5s* 5g* 6g²) Apr 15; compact, narrow non-thoroughbred filly; half-sister to useful 1979 2-y-o 5f and 6f winner Pink Blues (by Tickled Pink); dam seemed to stay 1½m; romped home by 10 lengths in 14-runner maiden race at Windsor in July and beat Vienna Miss a neck in 6-runner Horn Blower Stakes at Ripon the following month; made odds-on Kittyhawk knuckle down to her task when excellent 1½ lengths second of 5 in Group 3 Lowther Stakes at York later in August; stays 6f well; acts very well on soft going; useful. *F. Durr.* **102**

VON ERLACH 2 b. or br.c. Huntercombe 133–Fulcrum Miss (Fulcrum) (1980 6fg* 6fg 6f 7.3d) Mar 26; well-made, quite attractive colt; good mover; fifth foal; dam won 4 times at up to 6f in USA, including claiming events; began to tire in final furlong after making running in 16-runner maiden race at Salisbury in September but held on to win by ½ length from Charlie's Song; subsequently had very stiff tasks in pattern races and ran well in William Hill Middle Park Stakes at Newmarket on third start, although 11 lengths last of 9 to Mattaboy; not sure to stay 7f; sold to F. Durr 13,500 gns Newmarket Autumn Sales. *C. Brittain.* **90**

VORIAS (USA) 2 b. or br.c. Cannonade–Via Venise (Shoemaker 121) (1980 6d* 7g* 8g* 10s) Feb 4; first foal; dam useful winner at up to 1½m in France and comes from same family as Val de Loir; unbeaten in first 3 races, namely newcomers race at Saint-Cloud in July, valuable Criterium de Bernay at Deauville the following month (had 6 other previous winners behind when scoring by ½ length) and 4-runner Group 3 Prix la Rochette at Longchamp in September (odds on, kept on gamely under strong driving to hold off Shoen by ½ length); beaten 5 lengths when sixth of 8 behind The Wonder in Group 3 Prix de Conde at Longchamp in October; will stay 1½m. *F. Boutin, France.* **114**

VORVADOS 3 gr.c. The Go-Between 129–Keravnos 64 (Ionian 128) (1979 5f³ 6f* 7f⁴ 6fg 6s² 1980 5fg 6f³ 6f² 6f³ 6g⁴ 6fg² 6g 6g 5f 7fg) lightly-built colt; fair handicapper; runner-up at Kempton in May and Goodwood in August; best form at 6f; acts on any going; wore a small bandage on off-hind last 2 starts; dwelt ninth outing. *D. Elsworth.* **88**

VOTING DAY 2 b.f. Swing Easy 126–Miss Wolff 91 (Vilmorin) (1980 5fg 5f 5.8h 6fg 5d*) Apr 30; 1,400Y; rangy filly; half-sister to 3 minor winners here and abroad; dam genuine sprinter; showed first worthwhile form when winning 19-runner maiden race at Bath in October by 2½ lengths from Realm Gift; clearly suited by 5f and a soft surface. *J. Hill.* **82**

VOTRE ALTESSE (FR) 2 b.f. Riverman 131–Vahinee (Mourne 126) (1980 7d* 8s*) May 13; half-sister to several winners in France, including very smart but short-lived Dragoon (by Le Fabuleux) and very useful 5f to 1m winner Virgin (by Zeddaan); dam won at 2 yrs; in front rank throughout when successful twice in October, winning newcomers race at Saint-Cloud by 2 lengths and Group 3 Prix des Reservoirs at Longchamp by short head from Marie Noelle; will stay 1¼m; yet to race on a sound surface; has the makings of a good 3-y-o. *M. Saliba, France.* **114**

VOUCHESSA 3 b.f. Gift Card 124–Barchessa 67 (Prince Chevalier) (1979 7fg 7g² 1980 10.8s³ 10fg 8.2fg³ 7fg³ 7fg* 7fg 7.2g 8d⁴ 7d) deep-girthed, useful-looking filly; won 11-runner maiden race at Chepstow in July; stays 1¼m; probably acts on any going; blinkered final start; sold 6,200 gns Newmarket December Sales. *B. Hobbs.* **71**

VRONSKY 4 gr.g. Warpath 113–Janabelle 101 (Gentle Art 121) (1979 7d^2 7v 8g 8s 5f 6g^3 6fg 5f 6d 6d 10.6g 8fg 7fg 6d 1980 5g 7f 5f^3 6h 7g^2 7g 7f 6s 5fg) strong, compact gelding; plater; not certain to stay 1¼m; seems to act on any going; sometimes wears blinkers; taken to post early fourth start. *C. Gray.* **50**

W

WADI ALI 3 ch.c. Red Alert 127–The Star of Sharon 73 (Midsummer Night II 117) (1979 6g^4 6s* 6fg^4 7.3g 1980 7g 8fg 7d 10.2g 10fg) big, rangy colt; good walker and mover; moderate handicapper; not certain to stay 1¼m; suited by some give in the ground; blinkered third and fourth starts; ran badly second outing. *R. Price.* **80**

WAGNERIEN (FR) 3 b.g. Rheingold 137–Tia Bella (Le Fabuleux 133) (1979 NR 1980 12f 16d^4 15.8fg 10fg) 400,000 francs Y (approx £47,000); fine, big gelding but has shown only poor form; probably needs long distances and some give in the ground; ran badly in blinkers final outing; trained by J. Hindley first 2 starts. *M. Chapman.* **—**

WAGON MASTER 7 ch.g. Birdbrook 110–Covered Wagon 74 (Klondyke Bill 125) (1979 10s 10.6s 10f 8.2g 6d 1980 5f 7h 8g^4 8.2d 8.3f^3 8fg 7d^4) plater; ran well in non-seller final outing; stays 1¼m; acts on any going, except possibly very soft; has been tried in blinkers; has worn bandages. *D. H. Jones.* **47**

WAHED 5 gr.g. Red God 128§–Welsh Crest 86 (Abernant 142) (1979 8s 7g 7s^3 7fg^4 8fg 8h 8g 8g 1980 8f^4 8f 9fg^4 8fg 8s 6d 7f* 5g 7g 8f* 8d) quite a moderate handicapper nowadays; won narrowly at Catterick and Ripon in summer; seems to stay 1m but not 1¼m; probably unsuited by soft ground; blinkered third outing at 3 yrs and fourth start (ran moderately); does best when brought wide to race alone. *Denys Smith.* **61**

WAKKAD 4 ch.c. Northfields–Gold Pollen 110 (Klondyke Bill 125) (1979 7f* 9s^4 8fg 8fg 7fg 1980 8f 8f^2 8f 8fg 8fg) compact, useful sort; backed from 12/1 to 6/1, caught on post by Jubilee Prince in handicap at Pontefract in April; lightly raced and well beaten afterwards; stays 1m; acts on firm going and is possibly unsuited by soft; sold out of R. Sheather's stable 12,000 gns Newmarket May Sales after second start and was trained by T. Molony next two starts. *W. Haigh.* **84**

WALADAH 3 b.f. Thatch 136–Treacle 86 (Hornbeam 130) (1979 NR 1980 10fg 7d) 30,000Y; lengthy filly; half-sister to several winners, including useful Ivory Girl (by Sir Ivor), a winner at up to 1½m; dam, half-sister to Darling Boy, won twice at 1¼m; in rear in maiden races at Kempton in May and Salisbury in June. *R. Boss.* **—**

WALK MARCH 2 b.c. Sharpen Up 127–Walk By 113 (Tower Walk 130) (1980 6fg 5fg 5d) Mar 23; lengthy, useful sort; good walker and mover; first foal; dam, very useful sprinter, is half-sister to smart sprinter Smarten Up (by Sharpen Up); behind in maiden races in the autumn; will stay 7f; very much takes the eye and should do better at 3 yrs. *W. Wightman.* **— p**

WALK ON WATER 2 ch.c. Astrapi 85–Kinca 55 (King of the Tudors 129) (1980 5fg) May 9; 380Y; half-brother to minor winners in France and West Indies; dam second over 7f; slowly away when last of 11 in seller won by Micro Maid at Warwick in May. *D. Leslie.* **—**

WALLAWALLA 3 ch.f. Amber Rama 133–Ardneasken 84 (Right Royal V 135) (1979 7s* 7fg 10.6d* 1980 10f 12f 10.6d 13g^4 12.3fg) rather light-framed filly; fair (rated 85) at 2 yrs; didn't run up to her best in 1980; will probably stay 1¾m; acts on soft going and is possibly unsuited by firm; blinkered last 2 starts, running badly on second occasion. *C. Thornton.* **71**

WALLSWALK 4 b.c. Pals Passage 115–Terre Bleue (Prince Bio) (1979 5s 1980 12d) probably of little account. *G. Price.* **—**

WALLYFRED 2 ch.f. Manado 130–Javatina 87 (Javelot 124) (1980 5g 5g 8.2d^3 7f) Feb 13; 3,800Y; light-framed filly; half-sister to 2 minor winners; dam, sister to smart miler Presto, won at up to 1½m; plater; 4½ lengths third of 15 to Malseedy at Hamilton in September; will stay 1¼m; possibly needs a soft surface. *J. Fitzgerald.* **52**

WALLY WOMBAT 2 b.c. Abwah 118–Enlighten (Twilight Alley 133) (1980 5fg 7fg 7fg 8g 7fg) Apr 19; 2,600Y; quite a well-made, burly sort; half-brother to fairly useful 1¼m winner Godoliero (by Green God); dam poor maiden; 100/1 **—**

when remote fifth of 12 to Kalaglow in £3,100 event over 1m at Goodwood in September, only sign of ability; will probably stay 1¼m. *J. Holt.*

WALMARI 4 b.f. Communication 119–Angillian (Your Fancy 106) (1979 5s 6s 5g 5fg 6fg 5fg 6fg 8fg 8fg^4 8g^2 10fg^4 10s 10d* 1980 10s 8.3fg 10fg 8d) small filly; plater; stays 1¼m; acts on a firm and a soft surface; sometimes blinkered (not when successful); sold 520 gns Ascot December Sales. *J. Spearing.* —

WALNUT CREEK 2 br.c. Saulingo 122–Laburnum Grove 70 (Pall Mall 132) (1980 5fg 5fg 5d 6fg 5.1fg) Apr 20; neat colt; of no account; blinkered third outing; unseated rider by swerving at start on fourth appearance and is temperamental. *C. Brittain.* —

WALTER OSBORNE 3 ch.c. Welsh Pageant 132–Island Princess (Raise A Native) (1979 5v* 5v^3 5f^2 5f 6fg 6g 5g 1980 8d^4 5g^2 6fg^2 5f^2 7fg 6d^3 5g^2 5g* 5s* 5d 5s* 5g*) lengthy, attractive ex-Irish colt; useful handicapper; successful at Beverley, Nottingham, Ayr and York; ridden by 5-lb claimer, had best of draw when making virtually all to beat Sandra's Secret by 4 lengths on last-named in October; best at 5f; acts on any going. *M. W. Easterby.* **104**

WANCHAI LASS 3 b.f Balliol 125–Fairy Goddess (Yellow God 129) (1979 5s 5f 6fg^3 5d^3 5s 5h 1980 6v 6d^4 5h 6fg 5g^2 5f^2 6g 6s 5fg*) neat filly; plater; won all-aged race at Beverley in September (no bid); stays 6f; isn't at her best on very soft going; sometimes blinkered (wasn't at Beverley); sold 900 gns Doncaster October Sales. *M. Camacho.* **49**

WANDERING (USA) 3 b. or br.f. Forli–Big Advance (Bold Ruler) (1979 6s 1980 8fg 7d) strong, well-made filly; in rear in maiden races; sold 22,000 gns Newmarket December Sales. *J. Dunlop.* —

WANDERING ABOUT 2 b.c. Farm Walk 111–Wandering On (Klairon 131) (1980 5g 8d 7f 7d^3 6s 10.2s) May 31; 650Y; neat colt; third foal; dam of little account; apprentice ridden, just over 4 lengths third of 10 to Paltango in maiden race at Catterick in October, first sign of ability; should be suited by 1m. *J. Calvert.* **70**

WANGLE 2 ch.f. Great Nephew 126–Criminelle (Crepello 136) (1980 6g) Feb 23; compact filly; third foal; dam lightly-raced sister to 2 winners; unquoted and looking as though run would do her good when remote seventh of 19 to stable-companion Dancing Sally in newcomers race at Goodwood in September; should do better over further at 3 yrs. *J. Dunlop.* — p

WARDSOFF 3 b.g. Dubassoff–Greensward II (Count Turf) (1979 5v 6fg 7fg 8d 1980 8fg 8h 10f 16f 9g 8fg^4 7fg 8f 8f^4) leggy, narrow gelding; poor plater; best at 1m on a firm surface; has worn blinkers. *C. Gray.* —

WARESLEY 2 gr.c. Town Crier 119–Nasca 81 (King's Bench 132) (1980 6g 6g 5f 5f 6f) May 14; 6,600Y; neat colt; half-brother to 3 winners, including useful 5f performer Superb Lady (by Marcus Superbus); dam won 5.8f seller at 2 yrs; fifth in £2,000 event at Leicester in August on second outing (1½ lengths behind Spindrifter but was probably flattered in a slowly-run race) and 18-runner maiden event at Folkestone in September on fourth appearance (beaten 6½ lengths by Blue Lass); stays 6f. *G. Huffer.* **74**

WARILY 2 ro.c. Balidar 133–Admonish 101 (Palestine 133) (1980 6g 7s*) Feb 12; 50,000Y; useful-looking colt; good walker; half-brother to several winners, notably high-class performer Remand (by Alcide); dam stayed 1½m and is sister to high-class 1961 2-y-o Escort; always going well and quickened to lead in final furlong when winning 18-runner minor event at Sandown in October by a head from Jalabad; will stay 1m; probably has further improvement in him. *J. Tree.* **83** p

WAROOKA 3 gr.g. Veiled Wonder–Grey Parrot (Abernant 142) (1979 5fg 5fg 1980 8g 6s 6g 6d^3) leggy gelding; has a round action; best form at 6f on soft ground. *A. Breasley.* **62**

WARREN ROAD 2 br.g. Murrayfield 119–Maggie Gore (Dilawarji) (1980 5d 6g 8fg 8d) May 5; 4,600Y; neat gelding; bad plater. *A. Bailey.* —

WARRIOR BOLD 3 b. or br.g. Levmoss 133–Bravour II (Birkhahn) (1979 NR 1980 12f 14.6d 10g 12s) 2,500 3-y-o; lightly-made gelding; beaten a long way in maiden and minor events. *P. Felgate.* —

WAR SIGNAL 2 gr.c. Warpath 113–Lindy Light (Borealis) (1980 5fg) May 29; 2,800Y; half-brother to 2 winners, including fairly useful 1973 2-y-o 6f and 7f winner Enpeadee (by Le Dieu d'Or); dam never ran; unquoted and apprentice ridden when behind in 17-runner maiden race won by Royal Bid at Bath in April. *A. Bailey.* —

WARSOP BOY 3 b.g. Netherkelly 112–Derry Willow (Sunny Way 120) **65** (1979 6f 1980 12fg 12fg 12g^2 14.7g^3 16s 14d) strong, compact gelding; staying maiden; possibly unsuited by very soft ground; sweated up second start. *J. Hardy.*

WARWICK TRAILER 2 ro.c. Sharp Edge 123–Grace (Gratitude 130) (1980 **73** 5v^3 5s^4 5f^3 5g 5f^3 5fg 6d^4 6g^2) Apr 22; lightly-made colt; half-brother to 5f performer Jack Splendid (by John Splendid) and 3-y-o 6f winner Royal Diplomat (by The Go-Between); dam apparently of little account; in frame in varied company, on final occasion running on to finish length second of 19 to La Fedhala in seller at Goodwood in September; will stay 7f; probably acts on any going. *T. Marshall.*

WATAWONDER 4 ch.c. Deep Diver 134–March Wonder 99 (March Past 124) **–** (1979 6d 6f 5fg* 6f^2 5f^2 6g 6fg^3 5.6fg 6h^2 7g 6d^4 1980 5f 6fg) rangy colt; good walker; fairly useful sprint handicapper; acted on hard going; dead. *M. Camacho.*

WATCHDOG 2 br.c. Home Guard 129–Miss Olga (Le Leyanstell 122) (1980 5.5d **119** 6d* 6fg^4 8d^2 8d 7.5g^2) Apr 29; 8,000Y; useful-looking colt; second foal; dam, sister to Irish St Leger winner Allangrange, won over 9.5f and 2m in Ireland; ran very well in top company after winning maiden race at Deauville in August by 3 lengths, finishing 2¾ lengths fourth to Ancient Regime in Prix Morny on same course, 1½ lengths second of 8 to Dunphy in Prix des Chenes at Longchamp, 3¼ lengths sixth of 11 to Recitation in Grand Criterium again at Longchamp and 2 lengths second of 10 to Big John in Prix Thomas Bryon at Saint-Cloud; will stay at least 1¼m; acts on a firm and a soft surface. *R. Collet, France.*

WATER DANCE (USA) 3 ch.f. Nijinsky 138–Luiana (My Babu 136) (1979 **76** 7f^2 7g 1980 10fg^2 12f 12g^3 8f* 7g^3) big, rangy filly; poor walker; beat Just Abroad ¾ length in maiden race at Wolverhampton in August; probably stays 1½m; acts on firm going. *I. Balding.*

WATER GUARD 2 br.c. Tower Walk 130–Move Over (Galivanter 131) (1980 **–** 5fg) May 6; 880Y; second foal; dam won over 7f at 2 yrs in Ireland; 10/1, dwelt when eighth of 9 to Another Rumbo in maiden race at Wolverhampton in April; sold 2,500 gns Doncaster June Sales. *C. Bewicke.*

WATER MILL 3 b.c. Mill Reef 141–Heavenly Thought 110 (St Paddy 133) **124** (1979 7g* 7fg* 7.3g^2 1980 10.5f^3 12f 15s^3 12fg* 12g* 14.6g^2)

This well-bred, good-looking colt has been sold to Australia as a stallion and will stand in Victoria, at the Stockwell Stud, in 1981. He fell just short of the top class as a three-year-old and didn't manage to win a pattern race, but he ran second to Light Cavalry in the St Leger, for which he started an 11/8 favourite in a field of seven.

For a brief period less than two weeks before the event Water Mill was also second favourite for the Derby behind his stable-companion Henbit, whom Carson chose to ride. Water Mill had given a good staying performance against Super Asset in the Horris Hill Stakes as a two-year-old (he received 9-5 in the Free Handicap) and had run an excellent Derby trial behind Hello Gorgeous and Master Willie on his reappearance in the Mecca-Dante Stakes. However, he wasn't fast enough to take a hand in the Derby: after experiencing a pretty

Alycidon Stakes, Goodwood—Water Mill stays on strongly to win from Masked Marvel and Haul Knight (rails)

Lord Rotherwick's "Water Mill"

rough passage early on, he stayed on steadily from the back of the field to take tenth place. Prince Bee represented the stable in the Irish Sweeps Derby, while Water Mill went for the much longer Grand Prix de Paris at Longchamp and ran a dead-heat with the French Derby sixth Mot D'Or for third place, three and a half lengths behind Valiant Heart.

We saw Water Mill run in Paris and thought maybe he hadn't quite seen the trip out: he tired in the last furlong after a battle with the second horse What A Joy. His trainer, we read, was a shade disappointed with his apparent lack of sparkle. Subsequently Water Mill always ran in blinkers and, like his half-brother Homing, showed good form in them. Considering the strenuous race he had in Paris, and that he was brought back to run a fast mile and a half against relatively sharp animals, Water Mill's performance in winning the Alycidon Stakes at the big Goodwood meeting next time out was a particularly impressive one. He was held up almost to the distance, then he quickened to the outside in style and went right away, giving none of the opposition a chance, to beat Masked Marvel four lengths. The Alycidon Stakes virtually completed Water Mill's preparation for the St Leger. The finishing touches, so far as his public work was concerned, were applied by a very easy, richly rewarding workout against Ballytop and Sweet Pretender in a three-runner March Stakes at Goodwood later in August. He accomplished all required very smoothly indeed.

Water Mill seemed a worthy favourite for the Leger in a weak field. But Light Cavalry, who had never before tackled the trip, proved far too good for him, making all the running and increasing his pace as Water Mill began to challenge early in the straight. The contest was virtually decided by the time they passed the two-furlong pole; Water Mill, hard ridden, could do nothing about closing the three- or four-length gap that had opened up between them and he went down by four lengths in the end. He stayed the trip well enough. Water Mill would have run in the St Simon Stakes over a mile and a half at Newbury subsequently had he not bruised a foot; as it was, the Leger turned out to be his last race.

To say that Water Mill is well bred might be an understatement. His great grandam won the One Thousand Guineas and Oaks in 1949; his grandam was a useful middle-distance performer who finished second in the Nassau Stakes in 1963; his dam was more than useful at middle distances and won four of her seven races, including the Princess Royal Stakes at Ascot. Mill Reef's merit as a racehorse and sire is well enough appreciated not to require anything further written of him here, while nothing needs telling of Water Mill's half-brother Homing (by Habitat) except that he was probably the best miler in Europe in 1978.

Water Mill (b.c. 1977)	Mill Reef (b 1968)	Never Bend (b 1960)	Nasrullah
			Lalun
		Milan Mill (b 1962)	Princequillo
			Virginia Water
	Heavenly Thought (b 1967)	St Paddy (b 1957)	Aureole
			Edie Kelly
		Wishful Thinking (ch 1960)	Petition
			Musidora

Water Mill, a strong and shapely individual typical of his sire, a good mover too, stayed a mile and three quarters and acted on any going. He occasionally sweated up. *R. Hern.*

WATER OF LIFE 2 b.g. Mummy's Pet 125–Leger Bar 63 (French Beige 127) (1980 5f 5fg 6g 6fg^4 6g^2 5g* 5f* 5fg^4 5s^2 5g) Jan 26; compact gelding; brother to quite a moderate animal, and half-brother to middle-distance winner Walk Around (by Farm Walk); much improved in August and won twice at Ripon, costing 4,000 gns to buy in after winning seller by 5 lengths and beating Bracken Gill 2 lengths under a 10-lb penalty when apprentice ridden in nursery; very good second to Katysue in nursery at Haydock in October, going down by only ¾ length when ridden by apprentice at 5 lb overweight; gives us impression a return to 6f will suit him; acts on any going but put up his best effort on soft. *W. Haigh.* **85**

WAVING CORN 3 b.f. Undulate–Gold Spangle 97 (Klondyke Bill 125) (1979 6f 6g 6fg 6f 8g 1980 6fg^4 8fg 6s 6g* 6g^3 6g^3 6fg^4 6g 6fg 6g) strong filly; won apprentice maiden race at Pontefract in June; appears not to stay 1m; bandaged behind nowadays. *H. Collingridge.* **60**

WAY AHEAD 3 b.f. Sovereign Path 125–Emma Canute 93 (Hardicanute 130) (1979 6f^4 1980 8f*) lightly-made filly; landed odds by 2 lengths from Arwa in 18-runner maiden race at Leicester in June; not seen out again; will stay 1¼m. *H. Cecil.* **81**

WAY OF THE WOLD 2 b.c. Sandford Lad 133–Tatty Kay (Tarqogan 125) (1980 5g 5d 6fg^4 6fg^2 7g 8d^3 8fg) May 27; 1,000Y; small, rather lightly-made colt; first foal; dam placed at up to 1¼m in Ireland; in frame in maiden races, 2 of them auction events, being beaten only ½ length on last 2 occasions; stays 1m; didn't run up to his best when blinkered seventh outing. *S. Norton.* **74**

WAZIR 4 ch.c. Roan Rocket 128–Procession 118 (Sovereign Path 125) (1979 8s 6d 7f^2 1980 6fg 8g 10d^3 8g) lengthy colt; plating-class maiden; seems to stay 1¼m; appears to act on any going. *M. Masson.* **–**

WEARMOUTH 4 b.g. Pitcairn 126–Pyracantha 68 (Firestreak 125) (1979 8d 12g^3 10.5g 12g^4 11s^3 8f^3 12g^2 10f* 13.3g^3 1980 10fg^4 11f 10d* 10g 12g 10fg 10g^2 12s) well-made gelding; middle-distance handicapper; showed improved form when beating Galaxy Capricorn by 2 lengths in Gwen Blagrave Stakes at Salisbury in June; ran easily best subsequent race when ½-length second to Crowning Moment at Goodwood in September (well-backed favourite); acts on any going but is possibly best with some give in the ground nowadays. *W. Wightman.* **83**

WEATHERPROOF 3 b.f. Thatch 136–Rustling Waters 72 (Ballymoss 136) (1979 NR 1980 12d 10f 10g 12s) compact, good sort; half-sister to fairly useful stayer Croagh Patrick (by Connaught) and useful middle-distance performers Shallow Stream (by Reliance II) and Danish King (by Hardicanute); dam half-sister to St Leger winner Cantelo; in rear in maiden and minor events in the autumn; sold 6,000 gns Newmarket December Sales. *J. Dunlop.* **–**

WEAVERHAM BOY 3 b.g. Shoolerville 121–Mercilla 94 (Welsh Abbot 131) (1979 7f 7fg* 7.2g^4 7g 8.2g 8g^2 1980 9fg^4 12fg^4 12.3f 10.8g 12.3g) unfurnished gelding; has shown no form since 2 yrs; unlikely to stay 1½m; sometimes blinkered. *R. Murphy.* **–**

WEDDED BLISS 4 b.f. Relko 136–True Love 89 (Princely Gift 137) (1979 —
9.4f 9fg^4 10d 7d 1980 9fg 8fg 7s 8g 12.2g 10f 12fg 13.8d 12d) neat filly; plater; should be suited by 1½m; sometimes sweats up; sold out of C. Thornton's stable 480 gns Doncaster June Sales after fourth start; has given trouble on way to post and was taken down early sixth outing. *D. Chapman.*

WEDDERBURN 3 br.f. Royalty 130–Ocean Legend (Eborneezer 105) (1979 —
NR 1980 9fg 10d) poor mover; seems useless. *R. McDonald.*

WEDDING VOWS 4 b.f. Traditionalist–Sealed Contract 76 (Runnymede **70**
123) (1979 5s^4 5g^3 5fg 6s 5f^2 5g* 1980 5f^2 5f^2 5fg^2 6g 5fg 5fg^2 5d^3 5f^2 5d 5fg 5d^4) useful sort; didn't find a great deal off bridle when runner-up to Yoohoo at Beverley in August on eighth outing; best form at 5f; probably acts on any going but is well suited by firm; ran creditably in blinkers final start. *W. Haigh.*

WEE GEEFAYE 2 b.f. Crooner 119–Wee Geenova 78 (Gallup Poll or Blast —
125) (1980 5f 5fg 7g 8fg 8d) Apr 24; lengthy filly; second reported foal; dam 2-y-o 5f winner; behind in maiden races. *Mrs R. Lomax.*

WEE GEEVAL 3 b.f. Murrayfield 119–Wee Geenova 78 (Gallup Poll or Blast —
125) (1979 5.8g 1980 11.7f) no sign of ability in maiden races. *Mrs R. Lomax.*

WEE WILLIAM 3 b.g. Workboy 123–Obedience (Reliance II 137) (1979 —
5d 5g 5s 5g 5f 1980 9d) stocky gelding; behind in maiden races; blinkered final outing at 2 yrs. *M. Bradley.*

WEIGHHOUSE GALLERY 2 ro.f. Town Crier 119–Miss Golightly 83 (Jimmy —
Reppin 131) (1980 6fg 7s 7d 6fg 8g 6g) Feb 3; quite well-made filly; half-sister to 1¼m winner Handy Dancer (by Green God); dam 5f 2-y-o winner; only poor form, including in a seller; blinkered fourth outing; sold 390 gns Ascot October Sales. *W. Musson.*

WELCOMBE 3 b.c. Mountain Call 125–Angel Row 96 (Prince Regent 129) **87**
(1979 5s 5v* 5fg* 1980 7f 6d 6g 7g 8f) strong, well-made colt; good mover; fair handicapper; didn't reach frame but ran respectably on several occasions; stays 7f; seems to act on any going; sold to R. Hobson 5,000 gns Newmarket Autumn Sales. *H. Cecil.*

WELHAM GREEN (USA) 2 b.c. Tom Rolfe–Near Lyn (Nearctic) (1980 **94**
6fg* 7.6g^2 7f^4 7d) Feb 4; $82,000F; well-made, quite attractive colt; half-brother to 2 winners, including 1976 Irish 2-y-o 5f winner Raise A Princess (by Raise A Native); dam unraced half-sister to very smart Filiberto and White Star Line; put up a very pleasing first effort when second favourite for 14-runner maiden race at Salisbury in September, coming through to win with something in hand by 1½ lengths from Ringal; in frame subsequently at Lingfield, going down by 2 lengths to Admiral's Heir in £4,300 event later in September and finishing fair fourth of 6 to Mandav when favourite for valuable nursery the following month; will stay 1¼m; acts on firm going. *G. Harwood.*

WELL APPRAISED 2 br.f. Wolver Hollow 126–Emma Canute 93 (Hardi- **68**
canute 130) (1980 6s 6g 8fg) Mar 4; 39,000Y; closely related to 3-y-o 1m winner Way Ahead and very useful 5f to 10.5f winner Everything Nice (both by Sovereign Path); dam stayed 1¾m; showed speed 3½f when over 2 lengths fifth of 14 to Musical Minx in maiden race at Nottingham in July, second outing; should be suited by 1m. *P. Cole.*

WELL BREAD 3 gr. or ro.f. Birdbrook 110–Debra C 72 (Combat 123) (1979 —
5s 6fg 7g 1980 8.5g 6fg 6f) lightly-made filly; in rear in varied company, including selling. *R. Smyth.*

WELL DONE 2 br.c. Nonoalco 131–Aurambre (Sicambre 135) (1980 7s **79** p
8g^4) Apr 14; 22,000Y; sturdy, good-topped, attractive colt; fifth living foal: half-brother to 2m winner and winning chaser Ambremont (by Bon Mot III); dam minor French 9f winner; 33/1, improved considerably on his first effort (slowly away) when finishing fourth, beaten just over 4 lengths, to Video Tape in 17-runner maiden race at Newmarket in October; ran on very nicely under hand riding over last 3f here, having been well behind, and should do better over middle distances as a 3-y-o. *J. Dunlop.*

WELL GREASED 3 b. or br.f. Workboy 123–Jolly Smooth 84 (Jolly Jet **60**
111) (1979 5d 5g 6fg 1980 7f 7f^2 7f^2 7fg* 6fg^4 7g^3 7g 8.2g* 8d) lengthy filly; plater; won at Doncaster in May (no bid); ran creditably in better company

afterwards and won handicap at Nottingham in September; stays 1m well; acts on firm going; good mount for a boy. *W. Holden.*

WE'LL MEET AGAIN 3 b.c. Song 132–Coaster 61 (Right Tack 131) (1979 **68**
NR 1980 6s 5f 6f 6fg^2 7fg^4 7g 6fg 7d 6d^2) 5,600Y; compact colt; first foal; dam, half-sister to top-class sprinter Roman Warrior, won over 1m; runner-up in minor race at Folkestone and apprentice handicap at Leicester; stays 7f; acts on a firm and a soft surface. *J. Benstead.*

WELSH BALLET 3 b.f. Owen Anthony 102–Graceful Scot (Aberdeen 109) —
(1979 NR 1980 8f 12g 12g 11.5fg^4 8g) sturdy, compact filly; third foal; half-sister to winning sprinter Isthatchew (by Burglar); dam never ran; plating-class maiden; possibly stays 1½m; wears blinkers. *P. Feilden.*

WELSH BAZAAR 3 ch.c. Native Bazaar 122–Antigua III (Worden II 129) —
(1979 6fg 1980 8g 8fg) poor maiden. *M. Bradley.*

WELSH BLOSSOM 5 b.m. Welsh Saint 126–Riding High (Hard Ridden **88**
131) (1979 7g^4 7.6d 6s 6f* 6f 6f 6fg^2 6g* 6g* 6fg^4 5fg 6f 1980 5f 6fg^4 6fg^2 5g 6g 5g 6g* 6s 6fg* 5.6g 6fg* 7g 6d 6v) leggy mare; won 3 handicaps at Newmarket, on last occasion in October beating Right of Light by ½ length (disputed lead throughout and showed much more resolution than the runner-up); best at 6f; not at her best on soft ground; suitable mount for an apprentice. *W. Wharton.*

WELSH CARNIVAL 4 ch.f. Welsh Pageant 132–Jolie Fleur 111 (Exbury **62**
138) (1979 10g* 10g^3 10d^3 1980 10.8f* 12fg^4 12f 14f 10g) big, rangy filly; won handicap at Warwick in April; fair fourth to Sergei in similar event at Kempton following month, best subsequent effort; stays 1½m (well beaten over 1¾m); probably acts on any going; sold 12,500 gns Newmarket Autumn Sales. *T. Waugh.*

WELSH CHANTER 4 b.c. Welsh Pageant 132–Miss Ryvita 75 (St Paddy 133) **124**
(1979 8g* 10s^4 8fg* 1980 9f^4 8d 10d*)

Because of training difficulties Welsh Chanter's career has been tantalisingly brief, restricted to just six races. Unluckily he has suffered from a cracked cannon bone which prevented his running at two, recurring lameness—he is stiff after most races—and the virus. What little has been seen of him has made it plain that Welsh Chanter is a colt of well above average ability, one capable of troubling the best on his day.

The Earl of Sefton Stakes at Newmarket in April was Welsh Chanter's first race since he won the Britannia Stakes at Royal Ascot in fine style ten months previously, and not surprisingly he looked as though he needed the outing. He ran most creditably, being prominent all the way and keeping on well to finish fourth, two necks and a short head behind Ela-Mana-Mou. Two months elapsed before Welsh Chanter ran again and another three before his final appearance. At Royal Ascot he never promised to take a hand in the Queen Anne Stakes, coming in a well-beaten seventh, but the Valdoe Stakes at Goodwood in September showed him in a very different light. He looked in tremendous shape beforehand, a real credit to his trainer, and put up the best performance of his career. There were glowing reports of his work on the gallops with Kris and this, plus the fact that he was meeting Master Willie on terms 8 lb better than weight-for-age, saw his starting a firm third favourite to the latter and Fingal's Cave. Visibility was extremely poor, but when the runners came into view about a furlong out Welsh Chanter was taking over in front from Prince Rheingold; running on stoutly he held off the strong-finishing Master Willie by a length and a half with Fingal's Cave half a length away third. The Champion Stakes was mentioned as a possible target for Welsh Chanter following his win, but he was withdrawn at the first forfeit stage a fortnight after the Valdoe and didn't run again.

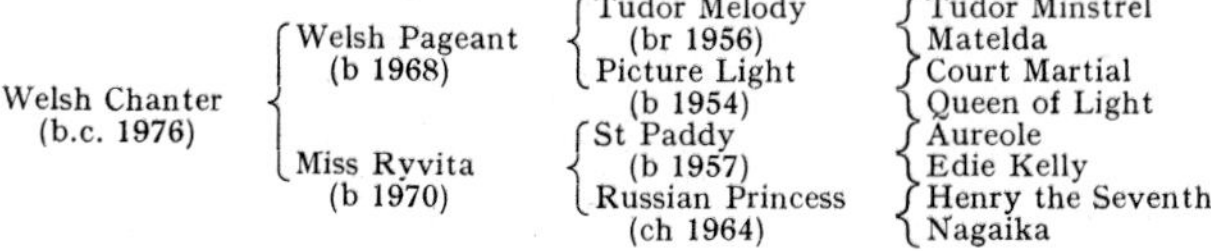

Welsh Chanter (b.c. 1976)	Welsh Pageant (b 1968)	Tudor Melody (br 1956)	Tudor Minstrel
			Matelda
		Picture Light (b 1954)	Court Martial
			Queen of Light
	Miss Ryvita (b 1970)	St Paddy (b 1957)	Aureole
			Edie Kelly
		Russian Princess (ch 1964)	Henry the Seventh
			Nagaika

Welsh Chanter is the first foal of Miss Ryvita, who won over eleven furlongs in the French Provinces and was sent to Australia in 1976, having fetched

16,000 guineas at the Newmarket December Sales. Russian Princess, successful over six furlongs at two years, her only season to race, has produced several winners besides Miss Ryvita, two of them by the latter's sire St Paddy, notably the very useful French middle-distance stayer Paddy's Princess. Russian Princess is out of that grand broodmare Nagaika, not far short of classic standard and the dam of the top-class middle-distance horse Connaught (by St Paddy), the smart miler Court Sentence and Honoured Guest, successful in the Dante Stakes.

Welsh Chanter impresses us greatly as an individual, being big and attractive with none of the coarseness often associated with substantially-built horses. However, his commanding size is almost certainly a doubled-edged weapon since it must place a great strain on his legs. Should he stay sound it will be surprising if Welsh Chanter doesn't win a good race as a five-year-old, and the conditions of the Westbury Stakes at Sandown would make it an ideal target for him early in the year. He is suited by a mile and a quarter, acts on any going with the probable exception of very soft, and is genuine. *H. Cecil.*

WELSH CYGNET 2 b.f. Prince de Galles 125–Oca (O'Grady) (1980 5d^3 5g^3 6s 5d^4 5g^2 6d) May 1; well-made filly; half-sister to a winning plater and a winner in Trinidad; dam moderate plater; in frame in maiden races, on final occasion finishing neck second of 19 to Advertrack at Folkestone in October; ran poorly both outings over 6f but should stay that far; possibly not at her best on very soft ground. *M. Smyly.* **76**

WELSH DAI 3 gr.g. Royal Palace 131–Sister Agnes 90 (St Paddy 133) (1979 NR 1980 10.2d 13g 12fg 16f 16g) 2,000Y; tall, lengthy gelding; slow maiden; trained by J. Bingham second and third starts. *M. Haynes.* **—**

WELSH DIAMOND 2 b.f. High Top 131–Camarina 62 (Aureole 132) (1980 5g 6g^2 7f 6d 8.2g^3 8.2s 8s) Apr 5; second foal; half-sister to 1979 2-y-o French 1m winner Great Dictator (by No Mercy); dam won over 1½m; placed in maiden race at Chepstow and nursery at Nottingham, running very well when 1½ lengths third of 15 to Baas in latter in September; one paced and will stay 1½m; probably unsuited by soft going. *P. Calver.* **66**

WELSH DISPLAY 3 b.c. Welsh Pageant 132–Born Free 105 (Alycidon 138) (1979 NR 1980 7f 10f 12g^2 12g* 10.1fg^3 11.5fg^2 12g^4 10fg 11.7d^3 12d) lengthy, very attractive colt; half-brother to several winners, notably high-class miler Free State (by Hotfoot); dam won at up to 1m; short-priced favourite when winning maiden race at Folkestone in July; twice ran respectably afterwards; suited by 1½m; acts on a firm and a soft surface; ran moderately final start; sold 5,400 gns Newmarket Autumn Sales. *P. Walwyn.* **77**

WELSH FOLLY 2 b.f. Welsh Saint 126–By Mistake 64 (Miralgo 130) (1980 6d* 6d) Mar 27; 2,000F, 4,600Y; half-sister to a winner in Germany by Tyrant; dam won 11f seller; came out best in tight finish to claiming race at Brighton in July, winning by a neck from Holly Patch; third favourite when last of 9 in selling nursery won by Wyn Miluv at Brighton in September; will be suited by 7f and 1m. *P. Makin.* **65**

WELSH FUSILIER 4 b.g. Welsh Pageant 132–Nagaika 117 (Goyama 127) (1979 10.6g 10s 10g 12g 1980 12fg 12fg 10g) bad maiden; wears blinkers. *S. Wiles.* **—**

WELSH HERO 6 br.g. Welsh Advocate 86–Tibbee (Nulli Secundus 89) (1979 NR 1980 8.2d) of little account; was tried in blinkers; dead. *S. Holland.* **—**

WELSH NOBLE 2 b.c. Welsh Saint 126–Just A Glimmer 75 (Dumbarnie 125) (1980 5d^4 5d^3 5f^4 5d* 6g 6d 6g 5f 5d 6s^2) Mar 26; 4,700Y; good-topped colt; second foal; dam won over 5f and 6f, and stayed 1m; won 18-runner maiden event at Wolverhampton in June by short head from Beggar's Bush; not disgraced on most of his subsequent outings, finishing creditable second to Hiz in 19-runner nursery at Nottingham in October on final appearance; will probably stay 7f; needs some give in the ground. *W. Wharton.* **81**

WELSH PIPER 5 b.h. Stephen George 102–Wild Duck 94 (Amour Drake 129) (1979 8s 7v 7f^2 7fg 8g 1980 7d 6d 7f 8f 6h 8.2fg^3 6fg^4 7g 7g^3 6g 6d 8g^2 8fg* 7f 8.2g 8fg^3 8.3d 10s) plater; favourite when winning easily at Edinburgh in July (changed hands 500 gns); pulled up final outing; stays 1m; acts on firm going; sometimes wears bandages; suitable mount for a boy; sold 420 gns Doncaster November Sales. *A. Scott.* **57**

WELSH PRIDE 3 b.f. Welsh Saint 126–Relko's Pride (Relko 136) (1979 5d 5d* 5f^4 5s^2 5d 6f 5fg^3 6fg^2 6fg^3 7g 1980 6h 6s^4 5.3d^4 7g 8.2s 8fg 8d 10s) neat filly; **—**

didn't run up to her best at 3 yrs; seems to stay 7f (well beaten over further); probably acts on any going; blinkered fifth start. *A. Ingham.*

WELSH SONATA 3 gr.f. Young Emperor 133–Welsh Rhythm (Abernant 142) (1979 6d* 6g* 7g^{2} 1980 8f 8f^{4} 9fg^{2} 8d 10fg^{3} 9g 8g) useful sort of filly; in frame in varied company; probably stays 1¼m; acts on a firm and a soft surface; blinkered last 3 starts; ran poorly fourth outing. *Sir Mark Prescott.* **63**

WELSH VALLEY 4 b.f. Welsh Saint 126–Ebvale (Relic) (1979 8d 9s 12g 14fg 13f 12g 1980 12.5h 14.7f 12g 10d 10s^{3} 10g 10g 12fg 10s) fair sort; plater; stays 1½m; acts on soft going; sometimes wears blinkers. *P. Felgate.* —

WELSHWYN 2 b.f. Welsh Saint 126–Takawin 109 (Takawalk II 125) (1980 5fg* 5fg* 5g^{2} 5g^{2} 5g^{2} 6fg^{2}) **113**

Welsh Garden and Welshwyn, arguably the best two animals by Welsh Saint, have more in common than their sire and the fact that both were among the best two-year-old fillies of their year—they also share a marked dislike of starting stalls. Welsh Garden, the top-ranked filly in the 1975 Irish Free Handicap, simply refused to have anything to do with stalls and had to spend her time taking on lesser opposition from tape-starts on the Irish provincial tracks. Thankfully Welshwyn's aversion didn't prevent her contesting several important races but it gave her connections many an anxious moment and twice brought about her withdrawal; when odds on for the Cucumber Stakes at Kempton in May she burst out of her stall while the others were being loaded, surprisingly doing more damage to the apparatus than to herself; and, when second favourite to Marwell in the Molecomb Stakes at Goodwood in July, she reared and lashed out as the handlers tried to push her in, giving one of her forelegs such a crack against the stalls that she briefly looked to have seriously injured herself.

Once her ordeal in the stalls is over Welshwyn races as genuinely and consistently as any filly one could wish to see and she was never out of the first two in six starts. Her two successes were gained at Kempton in May. After taking a maiden race by a wide margin she wasn't at all hard pressed to beat the subsequent Norfolk Stakes winner Chummy's Special by a couple of lengths in the Manor Stakes—performances which caused her to start third favourite for the seventeen-runner Queen Mary Stakes at Royal Ascot. She gave one of her best displays there, coming to take the lead inside the final quarter mile and keeping on well, although passed by Pushy, to hold on to second place in front of Nasseem and Ancient Regime, the subsequent winners of the Cherry Hinton Stakes and the Prix Morny.

Welshwyn subsequently had the misfortune constantly to come up against the exceptionally speedy Marwell. Although she once missed taking her on because of her antics at the start and on another occasion because the St Hugh's Stakes was rained off, she still met her on each of her last three outings. When in receipt of 7lb in the Prince of Wales's Stakes at York in August she had no answer to Marwell's turn of foot, after trying to make all, and went down by a length and a half; different tactics proved of no avail in the Flying Childers Stakes at Doncaster the following month when she failed to get Marwell off the bit and was beaten three lengths; and in the William Hill Cheveley Park Stakes at Newmarket in October she went down by a length. Marwell didn't run up to her very best at Newmarket but even so Welshwyn's performance there was a particularly admirable one. She was never far off the lead, came to take Pushy's measure at the distance and kept on so strongly that it was only well inside the final furlong that Marwell passed her.

Welshwyn (b.f. Mar 1, 1978)	Welsh Saint (b 1966)	St Paddy (b 1957)	Aureole
			Edie Kelly
		Welsh Way (gr 1954)	Abernant
			Winning Ways
	Takawin (ro 1969)	Takawalk II (b 1961)	Native Dancer
			Ampola
		Colloquy (gr 1964)	Quorum
			Comfort

It's hard to envisage Welshwyn as a serious contender for the One Thousand Guineas, for which she was quoted at 33/1 in the ante-post lists: she's not good enough to win the race and she isn't certain to stay the distance. She seemed to be running on well at the end of six furlongs at Newmarket but both her parents were tried over a mile without success and reverted to sprinting. Takawin, a useful filly who won three times over five furlongs and once over six, has produced two winners by stallions who stayed a good deal further than Welsh Saint. Her filly by Prince Regent, Careless Princess, was a sprinter and her gelding by Dike,

Dyk-A-Tak, has won twice over a mile and a quarter. The next dam Colloquy, no good on the racecourse, is out of the mile winner Comfort, a half-sister to the brilliantly speedy Careless Nora and to the dam of the outstanding broodmare Review.

Even if Welshwyn falls short of classic standard she's a lengthy, useful-looking filly with the scope to train on and she should win another race or two. As yet she has raced only on a sound surface. *J. Benstead.*

WEMBLEY MARKET 2 ch.c. Malicious–Perfect Lady 85 (Sovereign Lord **62**
120) (1980 5fg^2 5g^3 5.8g 5f 6fg 6g) May 7; 1,550Y; narrow, leggy colt; half-brother to fair 1979 2-y-o maiden Bobo Major (by The Brianstan); dam won over 5f at 2 yrs; placed in maiden auction events in May and June but was well beaten in a seller on final start; should be suited by 6f; wears blinkers. *R. Akehurst.*

WENSUM GIRL 3 ch.f. Ballymoss 136–Lady Colonist 67 (Colonist II 126) –
(1979 NR 1980 12.2fg) first reported foal; dam won over 1m and also over hurdles; in rear in 13-runner maiden race at Catterick in June. *C. Brittain.*

WESLEY 4 b.c. High Top 131–Stockingful (Santa Claus 133) (1979 10g* **102**
10.2s^4 12g* 12fg 13g^4 14.7g 14s 17.4s* 16fg^2 1980 12d 16.1d^2 18.4f 18fg^2) rangy colt; did well from 3 yrs to 4 yrs; useful handicapper; runner-up at Haydock (went down by ¾ length to Vicomte) in April and Doncaster (not given an unnecessarily hard time when beaten 7 lengths by Taffy) in May; not raced after latter event; stays well; acts on any going but seems best suited by some give in the ground; usually blinkered. *J. W. Watts.*

WESLEY BOAT 6 b.m. Forlorn River 124–Ever Grateful 95 (King's Bench **38**
132) (1979 7g 7s 6d 8fg 1980 8s^2) plater; runner-up at Warwick in April; stays 1m; acts on any going. *M. Bradley.*

WESSCAM 4 ch.f. Scottish Rifle 127–Decatullus (Catullus) (1979 7s^3 8g^4 **49**
8.2fg^3 9g* 10s^4 1980 11fg 10.8f^2 8fg 10d 11.7s^4 11.7s^3 11.7f^4 14g 10g 12fg) small, close-coupled filly; stays 11.7f; probably acts on any going; weak finisher. *S. Matthews.*

WESTACOMBE 3 br.f. Huntercombe 133–Ambient 68 (Amber Rama 133) **102**
(1979 6g^3 1980 6d^2 5fg* 6f* 6f^2 6d^2 6fg^2 5g* 5fg* 6s^2 5f* 5fg^3 5g) fair sort; useful performer; successful in maiden race at Pontefract, minor event at Thirsk and handicaps at Carlisle, Newcastle (made all on last 2) and York; beat Willowbrook Flyer by 1½ lengths in Playboy Bookmakers Sprint Handicap on last-named in September; also ran well to be runner-up in William Hill Handicap at York on fifth start (neck behind Optimate) and Northumberland Sprint Trophy (Handicap) at Newcastle on ninth (went down by ½ length to Flower, pair 7 lengths clear); stays 6f; acts on any going; genuine and very consistent. *M. Camacho.*

WESTBURG 3 ch.c. Burglar 128–Western Vale (Milesian 125) (1979 5s **83**
5d 5s 5g^2 5.1g^4 6f 5f 5fg 5fg* 5fg^3 5fg^3 1980 5d 5f^4 5f 5f 5fg 6d^3 5g 6g^2 6f^2 6g^3 6fg 5fg^2 6d 5g 6d) small colt; sprint handicapper; runner-up at Windsor, Ripon and Ascot; finished strongly when beaten a neck by Oh Simmie in £4,000 race on last-named in September; stays 6f; best on top-of-the-ground; blinkered eighth outing in 1979; suitable mount for a boy. *N. Guest.*

WEST END BOY 2 ch.g. Tarboosh–Smiling Diplomat (Dual 117) (1980 –
5fg 5f 7fg 8fg 8d) May 14; 620Y; third foal; dam Irish 9f winner; in rear in maiden races and sellers; none too well away last 2 starts, wearing blinkers on final one; trained by L. Carrod first 2 outings. *J. Hudson.*

WESTERN KNIGHT 2 ch.c. Grundy 137–Western Air 101 (Sound Track **93** p
132) (1980 7f 7g^2) Apr 10; big, strong, rangy colt; half-brother to 3 winners, including very smart 1975 2-y-o 5f performer Western Jewel (by Tower Walk); dam best at 5f; looked on backward side but showed promise in 2 races in October, finishing 8¾ lengths eighth of 19 to King's Glory, after holding every chance 1f out, in maiden race at Newmarket and 1½ lengths second of 10 to Sunley Builds in Hyperion Stakes at Ascot; will stay 1¼m; should make a useful 3-y-o. *P. Walwyn.*

WESTERN RIVER 7 b.g. Yellow River 114–Westerlands Rosebud (Combat –
123) (1979 NR 1980 14g) probably of no account; blinkered only outing of 1980 (sweated up badly). *K. Ivory.*

WESTERPAYNE 2 b.c. Mummy's Pet 125–Hay-Hay 62 (Hook Money **61**
124) (1980 5v^4 5f 5g^3) Feb 27; 3,000Y; half-brother to 2 winners by Mansingh,

including fairly useful 1979 2-y-o 5f winner Mandalia; dam stayed 1¼m; favourite although having first race for 4 months, weakened in final furlong when 5½ lengths third of 14 to Crosby Triangle in seller at Windsor in August; should win in similar company at 3 yrs. *J. Hill.*

WESTER ROSS 3 b.g. Shoolerville 121–Huna 84 (Doutelle 128) (1979 —
5v 5s 5g 5.8g 7fg 8fg 7d 8d 1980 16.9d 12g) small, light-framed, unimpressive gelding; little sign of ability in maiden and minor events; blinkered fifth start in 1979. *W. R. Williams.*

WESTGATE DANCER 3 br.c. So Blessed 130–Flame Dancer 72 (Hop Bridge 56
87) (1979 5s 5fg 5fg 1980 5s 5v^2 5f 5f) compact colt; poor performer; best run at 5f on heavy going. *W. Stubbs.*

WESTGATE OPERA 3 ch.c. Bold Lad (Ire) 133–Light Opera 101 (Vienna —
127) (1979 6fg 6s 5g 5f 1980 6v 6f 8fg 8.2g 9.4g) strong colt; no worthwhile form in varied company; has worn blinkers; trained by W. Stubbs first 3 starts; sold 300 gns Doncaster September Sales. *J. Berry.*

WEST MEON 2 b.c. Derring-Do 131–Sweet Reason (Elopement 125) (1980 67
5f 5f 6g 7d 6fg 5d 6v^4) Mar 31; 16,500Y; small, sturdy colt; half-brother to 4 winners, including 7f winner Sweet Mark Boy (by Decoy Boy) and useful fillies Exemplary (by Sovereign Lord) and Brightelmstone (by Prince Regent); dam unraced half-sister to 2 very useful stayers; quite moderate at best; should stay 7f+; blinkered sixth start. *D. Sasse.*

WEST MON 4 ch.g. Manacle 123–Scorton Gold 101 (Reverse Charge 115) 59
(1979 10g 12s 8fg* 11f 1980 12d* 12g^2 12g 8.5g*) ex-English gelding; won seller at Edinburgh in 1979; 33/1, looked very fit and showed improved form when making all to beat Falkelly by short head (pair clear) in 24-runner amateur riders race at Doncaster in March; subsequently transferred out of W. Marshall's stable and won similar event at Divonne-les-Bains in French Provinces in August; stays 1½m; acts on a firm and a soft surface; suitable mount for an inexperienced rider. *H. Woop, France.*

WESTON BAY 3 b.g. Mon Fils 124–Mineral 67 (Tarqogan 125) (1979 5.8g 58
6f^3 5.8h^2 7g 7f^2 8fg^2 8.2s* 1980 8.2fg 8fg* 8h^2 8d) compact gelding; plater; won at Bath in April (retained 1,550 gns); will stay 1¼m; acts on any going; wears blinkers nowadays. *M. Pipe.*

WEST PARADE 2 gr. or ro.f. No Mercy 126–Rush Green (Bullrush 106) —
(1980 5s) May 5; 360Y, 440 2-y-o; lightly-made filly; second reported foal; dam never ran; unquoted when tailed off in 24-runner seller won by Rapid Lad at Stockton in October. *C. Booth.*

WESTPORT BAY 2 b.c. Realm 129–Modern Millie 95 (Milesian 125) (1980 55
5h^4 5d 5.1g 5d 5s^4) Mar 4; 6,600F; neat colt; half-brother to 2 winners by Deep Diver; dam won twice over 5f at 2 yrs; fourth in maiden race at Thirsk in May and in 24-runner seller at Stockton in October; not certain to stay further than 5f; moved badly to start at Stockton. *Sir Mark Prescott.*

WESTWARD LEADING 9 b.g. Frankincense 120–Teflon 80 (Pan II 130) —
(1979 NR 1980 8.2s 10g 8fg) poor plater; stays 1¼m; probably acts on any going; sometimes wears blinkers. *H. Fleming.*

WESTWOOD LADY 3 gr.f. No Mercy 126–Port Relic 90 (Relic) (1979 —
5s 5v 5s 5g 5f^2 5f* 5g 5d 7d 5fg 1980 5fg 5f 5fg 5fg) lengthy, strong filly; has shown no form since 1979; should stay beyond 5f; suited by firm ground; blinkered once at 2 yrs and on fourth start; twice raced wide of others in 1979; sold to Mrs A. Finch 1,800 gns Ascot July Sales. *T. Fairhurst.*

W. G. GREYS 5 gr.g. Grey Mirage 128–Santa Marta 51 (Lavandin 128) (1979 54
7s 7v 7g 8d 7g 7s 7d^3 8.2g 8s 7.6f 8f 8g 1980 8s 8.2fg^4 6f^3 8g 6fg) moderate plater; stayed 1m; acted on any going but was suited by some give in the ground; none too genuine; dead. *M. Tate.*

WHANGAREI 2 b.f. Gold Rod 129–Vilmainder 78 (Remainder 106) (1980 58
7g 7fg 7f 6fg^3 7g^4) Mar 1; plain filly; second foal; dam won over 5f at 2 yrs; plater; ran best race when 2 lengths third of 28 to Tricky Rhythm at Windsor in September; probably better at 6f than 7f. *S. Holland.*

WHAT-A-CASE 3 b. or br.f. Upper Case–Off Scent 92 (Faberge II 121) —
(1979 6fg 6g^2 7g 6d* 6s 6f 1980 8f 8fg 9.4g 8.2d 8.2d 6d) leggy, narrow filly; won maiden race at Carlisle at 2 yrs; well beaten in handicaps in 1980; should stay at least 1m; pulled hard third start. *W. H. H. Williams.*

WHAT A COUP 5 gr.m. Malicious–Counter Coup (Busted 134) (1979 8g —
12.2g^4 16f 18g^4 18fg 1980 15f 13fg 12.2fg 9f 16d 20.4g) poor staying maiden;

gives impression she needs soft ground; sold 1,900 gns Doncaster November Sales. *T. Craig.*

WHAT A JOY (FR) 3 br.c. Exbury 138–Joyfully (Dilettante II 121) (1979 8g 9g 8g 1980 10.5d² 12d* 15s² 13.5g 15g* 15.5v) good-bodied French colt; second foal; dam successful over 1¼m in Ireland; narrowly won maiden race at Saint-Cloud in June prior to putting up a good performance in 14-runner Grand Prix de Paris at Longchamp later in month, going down by 1½ lengths to stable-companion Valiant Heart with Water Mill and Mot D'Or 2 lengths away equal third; won Group 3 Prix de Lutece at Longchamp in September by short neck from subsequently-disqualified Dhaubix (gave 3 lb); ran badly in Prix Royal-Oak at Longchamp in October on final outing; very well suited by a test of stamina; acts well on soft going; twice successful over hurdles earlier in year. *B. Secly, France.* **122**

WHAT-A-PRINCE 7 b.g. Mummy's Pet 125–Evendo 83 (Derring-Do 131) (1979 10.6g 1980 10.6fg) of little account. *R. Morris.* –

WHAT A SHAM (USA) 3 br.g. Sham–Royal Suspicion (Bagdad) (1979 NR 1980 6d 7f⁴ 6f 7fg) $130,000F, $160,000Y; useful sort; first foal; dam, stakes-placed winner at up to 7f, is sister to smart filly Unknown Heiress; fourth of 13 to Irish Commandment in maiden race at Epsom in April, easily best effort; will be suited by 1m; sold 3,100 gns Doncaster August Sales. *P. Walwyn.* **76** d

WHATATIPOFF 3 b.c. Jimmy Reppin 131–Stately Gala (Gala Performance) (1979 5g 6fg 1980 7f 8fg² 7f 8g⁴ 8g) compact, good-topped colt; plating-class maiden; evidently suited by 1m; acts on a firm surface. *A. Pitt.* **78** d

WHAT HEAVEN 2 b.f. So Blessed 130–Stolen Love 85 (Alcide 136) (1980 6s⁴ 5fg 6g³ 5s⁴) Mar 23; 6,000Y; lightly-made, quite attractive filly; half-sister to a winning hurdler; dam placed at up to 1½m; came up against very useful fillies on first 3 outings and wasn't at all disgraced when 3 lengths third of 15 to Kittyhawk in Group 3 Lowther Stakes at York in August; favourite for minor event on same course in October but was soon struggling and finished 9 lengths fourth of 11 to Pettistree; finds 5f inadequate and is bred to stay at least 1m. *P. Kelleway.* **90**

WHENBY 6 br.g. Prevailing–Sea Music 108 (Atan) (1979 5d 6g 5s 5d 5f⁴ 5fg⁴ 5f³ 5fg 6s 5d 5.6fg 1980 6v 5fg 5f 5f 5g 5g 6g 5fg³ 6g 7s) fairly useful handicapper at his best; third to North Greenwich in seller at Beverley in September, only placing of 1980; best at 5f; suited by a sound surface; best in blinkers; inconsistent; started slowly sixth outing. *J. Mason.* **57**

WHERE'S HENRY 5 ch.g. Hotfoot 126–Long Days 92 (Bleep-Bleep 134) (1979 8g² 8.3d³ 8d 6g 8fg⁴ 8.3fg* 7g 6g 8fg 10fg 1980 9.6fg³ 10.1fg 7f 8g) plater; best form at up to 9.6f; acts on a firm and a soft surface. *A. Neaves.* **31**

WHERE'S MY PRESENT 2 ch.c. Gift Card 124–Morwena (Masetto) (1980 6d 8fg 7fg) May 14; 4,400F, 1,900Y; strong, good sort; half-brother to 2 winners in France; dam won twice over middle distances; ran best race when 5¼ lengths sixth of 19 to Toe Tapper in 7f maiden race at Leicester in September; bred to stay middle distances. *H. Candy.* **63**

WHETSTONE 3 ch.g. Porto Bello 118–Algarve 94 (Alcide 136) (1979 NR 1980 7f 8fg 10f 10f⁴) 4,000Y; fair sort; little worthwhile form in maiden races; not certain to stay 1¼m; moved poorly to post final start (June); sold 1,550 gns Ascot December Sales. *J. Sutcliffe.* –

WHIMBREL WADER 3 ch.g. Starch Reduced 112–Cunard Eagle (Parthia 132) (1979 5s 5g 6f 5f⁴ 6fg² 7fg³ 7.2g⁴ 6s³ 8g 1980 8v 8.2fg 6fg⁴ 7d 8g) robust gelding; inconsistent plater; stays 7f; probably acts on any going; blinkered nowadays. *Mrs A. Cousins.* **53**

WHISKEY SKID 2 ch.g. Northfields–Shot Silk 110 (High Treason 126) (1980 5v 5f² 5f* 5fg 5fg⁴ 6fg⁴ 6f 7g 6f 8g) Mar 21; 3,300Y; sturdy gelding; half-brother to several winners, including very speedy 1966 2-y-o Rose of Tralee (by Buisson Ardent); dam won Queen Mary Stakes; in frame in maiden and minor events, coming nearest to success when 1½ lengths second of 11 to Arch Melody in maiden race at Naas in April on third outing (awarded race some time later after winner failed a dope test); not sure to stay beyond 6f; trained by W. Fennin in Ireland first 7 outings (off course over 2 months afterwards and was burly in his races over here). *G. Richards.* **81**

WHISKY GO GO 4 ch.g. Grey Mirage 128–My Nan 65 (Pampered King 121) (1979 8v 8.2s 7s 7s 5g 1980 11d² 12s) compact gelding; plating-class maiden; should stay 1¼m (off course 6 months before trying trip). *R. Morris.* **38**

WHISPER A WORD 3 ch.c. Most Secret 119–Wordrone (Worden II 129) (1979 6fg 6s 1980 7d 6f 8fg 8f3 7f 8fg 10.2g 9.4g3 10fg 12f2 11d4 15.8fg 12f) rangy colt; poor maiden; stays 1½m; acts on firm going; usually blinkered. *E. Weymes.* **55**

WHISPER GENTLY 3 b.f. Pitskelly 122–Muraka (Off Key 121) (1979 6f 5d 9g2 9.5g* 7s 1980 9f4 10f 12f2 12g* 12g 10s 8g 12d* 12d* 12g 12g 12d 16g) 2,200F, 7,000Y; lightly-made filly; second foal; half-sister to a winning plater; dam won bumpers race; won handicaps at the Curragh in June and Killarney and Galway following month; well-beaten seventh to Deadly Serious in Galtres Stakes at York in August on eleventh start; stays 1½m; probably acts on any going; blinkered seventh outing; ran poorly fifth start. *N. Meade, Ireland.* **91**

WHISPER TO ME 2 br.f. Cavo Doro 124–Myna Tyna 85 (Blast 125) (1980 5g 5d 5d 5d) Jan 24; half-sister to 2 winners, including 3-y-o Another Venture (by Roan Rocket), successful over 5f in 1979; dam won over 5f at 2 yrs, and is half-sister to good stayer Lomond; unquoted when behind in sizeable fields of maidens in the autumn. *R. Hollinshead.* –

WHISTLER'S IMAGE 4 br.g. Dancer's Image–Spring Azure 98 (Mountain Call 125) (1979 6g 6s 6g2 6d 7.6f 8f2 7.2g 8.2g 1980 9g) neat, strong, good sort; stays 1m; acts on firm going; wears blinkers; needed race only outing of 1980. *J. Hardy.* –

WHISTLER'S LANE 10 b.g. Whistling Wind 123–Scarlet Sash 75 (Umidwar) (1979 NR 1980 17.1fg 17.1fg) of little account nowadays. *I. Wardle.* –

WHISTLING JET 4 b.g. Blue and Grey 93–Whistlewych 40 (Whistler 129) (1979 7g 8s 6d* 7fg 6g2 6s 6s 1980 6v4 8f 6g) compact gelding; plater; best form at up to 6f and in blinkers; probably acts on any going; moved badly to post penultimate outing. *J. Carr.* –

WHISTLING JIM 2 b.g. Jimsun 121–Metis 55 (Be Friendly 130) (1980 6g 7g 6fg 7f) Mar 26; 1,250Y; third foal; dam a plater; poor form in sellers. *Hbt Jones.* **44**

WHISTLING TOWER 2 b.c. Tower Walk 130–Whistling Gold (Whistling Wind 123) (1980 7s 8fg3 8d2 8d2) Apr 24; 6,400Y; short-backed colt; third foal; half-brother to a winner in Malaya; dam ran only twice; close-up second in maiden and minor events in the autumn, on third outing failing by a head to overhaul Akram at Leicester; suited by 1m; acts on a firm and a soft surface. *C. Brittain.* **80**

WHITE DOMINO 5 b.m. Sharpen Up 127–Chiltern Miss 85 (Hook Money 124) (1979 8s 7f 8g 7fg 8fg 8fg 8g3 1980 7f 7fg 8fg 8g 8fg 8fg 7fg 8f) workmanlike mare; poor handicapper; suited by 1m; acts well on a firm surface; suitable mount for a lady rider; retained 2,100 gns Newmarket December Sales. *R. Hollinshead.* –

WHITEHALL BRIDGE 3 b.c. Auction Ring 123–Farce (Bon Mot III 132) (1979 6s2 6fg2 7f2 1980 8g 10.6d2 10fg 10.5g4 10.2g3 12d*) attractive, well-made colt; good mover; landed odds very easily by a wide margin from modest opposition in 10-runner maiden race at Newbury in October; in frame earlier in handicap at Haydock (length second to King's Ride), Cordwainers Stakes at York (2½ lengths fourth to Bozovici) and Fitzwilliam Stakes at Doncaster (2¾ lengths third to Old Kate); stays 1½m; seems to act on any going; blinkered last 2 outings; ran atrociously third start (Extel Stakes (Handicap) at Goodwood); sent to race in France. *R. Hern.* **103**

WHITE SAINT 2 b.f. Welsh Saint 126–Whitewood 74 (Worden II 129) (1980 5fg 5d) Mar 30; neat filly; half-sister to 3 winners, including quite useful out-and-out stayer Amberwood (by Amber Light); dam ran only at 2 yrs; 20/1 when eighth of 16 to subsequently-disqualified Holmbury Lad in maiden race at Newbury in September, first outing; probably needs further. *B. Hills.* **70**

WHITE'S UMBRELLA 3 ch.c. Siliconn 121–Lurex (Golden Cloud) (1979 7f 6f* 1980 10g 8.5g 10g 8f4 7.2fg) sturdy, compact colt; plater; not certain to stay 1¼m; sweated up badly final start; sold 2,100 gns Doncaster June Sales. *N. Callaghan.* –

WHITE WATER 2 br.f. Rapid River 127–Weirdi 76 (Yrrah Jr) (1980 5g) May 30; lightly-made filly; third foal; dam placed over 1m at 2 yrs; 14/1 when in rear in 14-runner seller won by Water of Life at Ripon in August; unruly at start when withdrawn on same course later in month. *W. A. Stephenson.* –

Mr Paul Mellon's "Wicked Will"

WHITTINGTON (USA) 2 b.c. Best Turn–Novee (Judgable) (1980 5f 6fg 7g 8g 7s² 7g) Apr 26; $31,000Y; workmanlike colt; first foal; dam, unplaced 4 times, is half-sister to very useful 1964 USA 2-y-o Mr B's Sister; 25/1 when 4 lengths second of 14 to Royal Heritage in minor event at Chepstow in October, best effort; will stay 1¼m; possibly needs the mud. *G. Balding.* **73**

WHITWORTH 2 ch.g. Hot Spark 126–Clarity 98 (Panaslipper 130) (1980 7f 8d⁴ 10s⁴) Mar 10; 24,000Y; rangy gelding; half-brother to several winners, including quite useful 1979 2-y-o 5f winner Loyal Manacle (by Manacle), and fairly useful stayer Amity (by Amber Rama); dam, winner at up to 1½m, is half-sister to Santa Claus; quite a moderate maiden; stays 1¼m; sold to D. Morley 4,100 gns Newmarket December Sales. *J. Hindley.* **74**

WHY BIRD 6 gr.m. Birdbrook 110–Freddie Why (Primera 131) (1979 NR 1980 8fg 12g) unreliable plater; best form at 1m; acts on firm going; has been tried in blinkers. *M. Bradley.* **—**

WICKED WILL 2 b.c. Mill Reef 141–Green Glade (Correspondent) (1980 5fg 5.8fg* 5d⁴ 6g⁴ 7d² 7f* 7f² 8g² 8s³ 8g² 8v) Apr 21; compact colt; half-brother to 3 minor winners in USA; dam smart stakes winner at up to 9f in USA, and is half-sister to very useful Morris Dancer and Kew Gardens; won 18-runner maiden race at Bath in June and quickened in good style to win £2,500 event at Beverley the following month; second subsequently in Grand Criterium International d'Ostende (went down by ¾ length to Beldale Flutter) and fairly valuable nurseries at Doncaster and Brighton, running well under 9-7 when beaten ¾ length by Aperitivo in last-named in October; also ran creditably when 2¼ lengths third of 8 to Benefice in Ashford Castle Stakes at the Curragh in September; will be suited by middle distances; thoroughly genuine and consistent but ran moderately behind Panjandrum in Premio Tevere at Rome in November; acts on any going except, perhaps, heavy; has run well for an apprentice. *I. Balding.* **108**

WICKWELL 7 b.h. Wolver Hollow 126–Wise Counsel (Counsel 118) (1979 10.2s 8d 10.4d 10g 8g 10.8fg³ 11g 11.5g² 9g³ 10.4f⁴ 10.6g 1980 10v 11fg 9fg 12h³ 10.6g² 12.3g 11.5g 12fg 11.5fg³ 12.3g 10g 10.6s 11g) poor handicapper; stays 1½m; acts on any going except soft; good mount for an inexperienced rider; inconsistent and doesn't find much off bridle. *A. W. Jones.* –

WIDD 3 b.c. Derring-Do 131–Tin Mary 96 (Tin King 126) (1979 5s² 5fg³ 1980 7f 8fg 7g 7s* 6fg⁴ 6fg 6g⁴ 6fg⁴ 8fg) workmanlike colt; comfortably won 17-runner maiden race at Folkestone in July; ran respectably most starts afterwards; suited by 7f; seems to act on any going; out of his depth second and third starts (blinkered on latter). *M. Masson.* **81**

WILD FANDANGO (USA) 3 ch.f. Forli–Cellist (Bagdad) (1979 NR 1980 9fg*) small, lightly-made American-bred filly; dam, smart stakes winner at up to 1m, is half-sister to top-class Gay Fandango (by Forli); made all and kept on well to beat Falkland Palace ½ length in newcomers race at Wolverhampton in April (pair clear); stays 9f; sent to USA. *B. Hills.* **72**

WILD IDEA 3 ch.f. Silly Season 127–Generous Thought 81 (Compensation 127) (1979 5.5d² 6g² 6g³ 7s 7g* 6fg³ 8g² 7.5s² 1980 8v 8g* 9g² 8fg² 8fg³ 9.2s⁴ 9d⁴ 10d³ 10g 9.2f³) first foal; dam at her best at 2 yrs; favourite when winning fillies handicap at Saint-Cloud in April; ran well afterwards to be fourth to Nadjar in Prix d'Ispahan at Longchamp in June on sixth outing and third to Sovereign Dona in Prix de Psyche at Deauville and to Hortensia in Prix de l'Opera at Longchamp; beaten 1½ lengths after making running and keeping on well in last-named in October; stays 1¼m; appears to act on any going; consistent. *P. Lallie, France.* **116**

WILD OATS (FR) 5 b.h. Sir Gaylord–Sybarite (Royal Record II) (1979 12s* 12s² 12g* 12g* 13.5s 10g 12d 12v 1980 10s 10.5g⁴ 12fg 10.5g⁴ 10s³ 12f 10f 12s³ 12d³ 12s³) strong, compact, well-made French horse; useful performer; in frame 6 times, notably when 4 lengths third to Armistice Day in Prix Gontaut-Biron at Deauville in August; 5½ lengths fifth of 8 behind More Light in Jockey Club Stakes at Newmarket on third start; stays 1½m; appears to act on any going but is well suited by some give in the ground. *P. Head, France.* **106**

WILD PUMPKIN 3 b.f. Auction Ring 123–Wild Thyme 63 (Galivanter 131) (1979 6fg 6f 5f 1980 12d 12s 8.2g 7g 12d) lengthy, narrow filly; poor form in varied company; unseated rider second start. *Peter Taylor.* –

WILD ROSIE 4 gr.f. Warpath 113–Rosie Wings 102 (Telegram II 130) (1979 9.4d 12fg 12.2s³ 15g* 1980 13s 15f 15.8g 15g² 14.6g² 15.8f² 16f* 16s² 16fg* 16fg³ 16.1s* 16.1s³ 15.8d) staying handicapper; won at Thirsk and Warwick in August and at Haydock in October, beating Halba by a length in apprentice event on last-named course; beat Ribble Rouser on merit at Catterick on sixth outing but crossed that horse and was relegated to second after a stewards inquiry; acts on any going; game and genuine. *C. Thornton.* **59**

WILJA 3 b.f. Ribero 126–Lovely One 65 (Ballymoss 136) (1979 9fg 10g 1980 11fg 11.7f 11.1f) small, unimpressive filly; poor form in varied company. *R. Hollinshead.* –

WILLAWAY 2 b.f. Willipeg 112–Pontesbury (Falls of Clyde 126) (1980 6g) May 6; 410Y; half-sister to 2 winners, including quite useful sprinter Mino Boy (by Decoy Boy); dam ran only at 2 yrs when of little account; 25/1 when behind in 20-runner maiden race at Leicester in November won by Nello. *D. Ancil.* –

WILLERBY 3 b.g. Great Nephew 126–Sera Sera 88 (Hill Clown) (1979 6d 6fg 5fg 1980 8g 8g³ 8.2d) neat gelding; poor maiden; will stay 1¼m. *J. Fitzgerald.* –

WILL GULF 3 ch.g. Gulf Pearl 117–Gwen Somers (Will Somers 114 §) (1979 7f 7g 8fg 8fg 1980 10.8v 10g 7f 8.5f² 7d 8f 8g) strong gelding; plater; stays 1m well; acts on firm going; blinkered nowadays; ran abysmally final start; sold to J. Bingham 760 gns Newmarket Autumn Sales. *R. Akehurst.* –

WILLIAM THE FIRST (USA) 5 b.g. Fleet Nasrullah–Minorstone (Ribot 142) (1979 16s 1980 11fg³ 12.5s) plater nowadays; stays middle distances; probably best on a sound surface; has been tried in blinkers. *A. W. Jones.* **37**

WILLICRESS 6 b.g. Willipeg 112–Cressida Queen 84 (Troilus 101) (1979 11g³ 9g⁴ 8s⁴ 10fg 12d³ 12d 1980 11.7d) poor middle-distance handicapper; acts on any going; suitable mount for an apprentice. *T. Hallett.* –

WILLIE GAN 2 ch.g. McIndoe 97–Queen's Bay 73 (King's Troop 118) (1980 5d 6d 5fg³ 5fg³ 6s 5d 5d⁴ 5s) Apr 15; 800F; third produce; brother to 1979 2-y-o **73**

6f seller winner McQueen; dam stayed 6f; in frame in varied races, including a nursery; form only at 5f; not well served by very soft ground. *Denys Smith.*

WILLIE WEDGE 2 ro.g. Sharp Edge 123–Primrose Day 64 (The Brianstan 128) (1980 5h) May 1; 1,000Y; first foal; dam in frame in early-season events at 2 yrs; last of 7 in claiming race at Brighton in May; sold 330 gns Ascot October Sales. *D. Thom.* –

WILL OF IRON (FR) 2 gr.c. Dancer's Image–Wow 106 (Baldric II 131) (1980 5fg 5.1f) Mar 16; neat colt; brother to useful 1979 2-y-o 5f and 6f winner Why Not; dam won over 1¼m; always outpaced when in rear in maiden races at Doncaster in May and Yarmouth (apprentice ridden) in June; has reportedly been sent to France. *H. Cecil.* –

WILL OF VICTORY 2 gr.f. Dancer's Image–Warsaw (Bon Mot III 132) (1980 6f^2 6s*) Apr 12; strong, well-made filly; second foal; dam, smart winner over 11f and 13f on only starts, is half-sister to top American mare Waya; didn't have much to beat when odds on for 18-runner maiden race at Nottingham in August but couldn't have won more impressively, drawing right away in final 2f to win by 12 lengths from Sister Kitty; had previously shown plenty of of promise when 1½ lengths second of 10 to Silken Knot in Virginia Water Stakes at Ascot; will stay at least 1m; a smart filly in the making. *H. Cecil.* **102** p

WILLOWBROOK FLYER 3 b.c. Saulingo 122–Golden Pumpkin 86 (Monet 127) (1979 5s^4 5s* 5d^2 5s^4 5f 5f^4 5g^2 6g 5f 1980 5d 5s^2 5f* 5fg 5fg^4 5g 5g^2 5.6fg 5f^2 5f 5g 6d) compact colt; moderate handicapper; made all to win at Thirsk in April despite hanging left; good 1½ lengths second to Westacombe in valuable race at York in September on ninth start; speedy and almost certainly doesn't stay 6f; acts on any going; sometimes wears blinkers; bandaged off-fore tenth outing; sold 3,000 gns Newmarket Autumn Sales. *W. Wharton.* **82**

WILLOW HERB 2 gr.f. Habat 127–Windflower 77 (Crepello 136) (1980 8g 7s 6g) Apr 8; neat filly; half-sister to useful 1978 2-y-o 6f and 7.3f winner Bluebell (by Town Crier) and 3-y-o 1¼m winner Purple Flag (by Reform); dam, half-sister to Queen's Hussar, seemed to stay 1¾m; prominent long way when behind in end-of-season maiden and minor events at Newmarket (2) and Sandown, best effort on third start; should stay 1m. *W. Hastings-Bass.* **68**

WILLOW PATH 4 ch.f. Farm Walk 111–Market Fortune (Fortina) (1979 NR 1980 12.5v^2 12f) poor maiden; stays 1½m well; possibly needs the mud. *Miss S. Hall.* –

WILLOW RED 4 ch.g. Red Alert 127–Willow Bird 74 (Weepers Boy 124) (1979 8s 8.2g^2 8f* 10fg 8s^2 9s^3 8.2g 8g^3 7g^3 1980 7.2d^3 8fg 7.2fg 8fg 8d^4 8.2s^2 7f 7fg^4 6d* 8d^2 7f^3 (dis) 7.3fg 7.2d^2 8.2s 7d* 7s*) workmanlike gelding; held up when winning handicaps at Ayr in August and Doncaster and Nottingham in October, quickening well to beat Mirthful by 2 lengths on last-named course; effective at 6f and stays 1m; acts on any going but is very well suited by some give in the ground; wears blinkers; sweated up eighth outing; often hangs and is not the easiest of rides. *J. Etherington.* **86**

WILLSPAL 2 ch.c. Firestreak 125–Beauklairon (Klairon 131) (1980 7f 8g) Mar 30; half-brother to several winners, including Irish 3-y-o 1½m and 1¾m winner Castleshane Pat (by Caliban); dam poor maiden; in need of race when soundly beaten in maiden race at Redcar and minor event at Newcastle in the autumn. *J. Etherington.* –

WILTON BEACON 4 br.g. Goldhill 125–Daylight 92 (Princely Gift 137) (1979 NR 1980 9g 8fg^4 8g^2 8g 10g 10fg 12.2d 13s 10d) strong, compact gelding; close second to Dawn Johnny in maiden race at Beverley in July; subsequently sold out of W. Hastings-Bass's stable 7,600 gns Newmarket July Sales and was well beaten afterwards (blinkered final start). *J. Harris.* –

WIMSEY 3 b.c. Run The Gantlet–Bell Song 101 (Tudor Melody 129) (1979 NR 1980 12g 12d 16fg 15.5g^3) 21,000Y; tall, lengthy colt; half-brother to 3 winners, including smart 1974 2-y-o Great Paul (by Great Nephew); dam stayed 1¼m; showed first worthwhile form when staying-on third in maiden race at Folkestone in October; stays well; sold 7,400 gns Newmarket Autumn Sales. *P. Walwyn.* **67**

WINART 2 br.c. Scottish Rifle 127–Alice (Parthia 132) (1980 6f 6g^3 7g^3 7f 6g^4 6fg 8d) Apr 21; 4,100F, 5,800Y; neat colt; half-brother to 3 winners, including fairly useful 1979 Irish 2-y-o 6f winner Surface Heat (by Hot Spark); dam never ran; in frame in maiden and minor events; probably flattered by proximity to winner when 5½ lengths fourth of 5 to Saba Nejd at Windsor in **70**

September; bred to stay middle distances; form only on an easy surface and moved badly to post on firm ground on fourth start. *K. Ivory.*

WINCHESTER RIFLE 4 bl. or br.g. Scottish Rifle 127–Hughbilu 85 (Hugh Lupus 132) (1979 9.4f 13g 1980 10g) leggy, rather narrow gelding; poor maiden; took strong hold early on when behind in seller on only outing of 1980 (September); sold 370 gns Ascot October Sales. *G. Richards.* —

WIND AND REIGN 2 b.f. Tumble Wind–Tyrant Gleam (Tyrant) (1980 5fg 5f 5f 5fg 5f 5d4(dis) 6fg 5d 5s) Mar 16; 1,700F, 6,400Y; small filly; first foal; dam unraced half-sister to several winners; quite a moderate plater; probably stays 6f; blinkered seventh start; sold out of P. Haslam's stable 430 gns Doncaster September Sales after seventh outing. *D. Chapman.* **55**

WIND CATCHER (FR) 3 b.c. Busted 134–Wadi (Snob 130) (1979 NR 1980 10g* 12f*) useful sort; third foal; half-brother to useful middle-distance performer War Legend (by Caro); dam won at up to 10.5f in France; successful in 19-runner maiden race at Nottingham in April and 8-runner minor event at Wolverhampton following month; kept up to his work to draw steadily clear and beat Something Special by 6 lengths on latter course; not seen out again; will stay 1¾m+. *H. Cecil.* **89**

WINDE UP 4 b.c. Vilmoray 126–Sibilant 106 (Whistler 129) (1979 6s 1980 8fg 7fg 6fg 6g4 5g 6g3 6d 6g 5.8f 8.3f4 6g) small, lengthy colt; in frame in handicaps at Salisbury in June and Brighton (ridden by 7-lb claimer) in July; fourth in seller at Windsor in August; best form at 6f; blinkered eighth, ninth and eleventh outings. *S. Matthews.* —

WINDLE 3 b. or br.f. Windjammer–Crimson Velvet 89 (Above Suspicion 127) (1979 NR 1980 8f* 10f2 10fg4) 3,800Y; big, strong filly; sister to useful 2-y-o Grain Race and half-sister to 2 winners, including Redfern (by Red God), quite a useful performer at up to 1¼m; dam stayer; sweated up when beating Maiden's Walk 2 lengths despite hanging left in 13-runner maiden event at Wolverhampton in August; not disgraced on next start; stays 1¼m; yet to race on an easy surface. *C. James.* **77**

WINDPIPE 2 ch.g. Leander 119–Whiffle 105 (King's Troop 118) (1980 5g 7d) Mar 7; fourth living foal; dam stayed 1m; 5 lengths fifth of 10 to Shotgun in 7f maiden race at Ayr in August; started slowly first outing and took some time to find his stride at Ayr; should stay 1m. *J. W. Watts.* **74**

WINDS OF MARCH 3 br.f. Tyrant–March Brown 90 (March Past 124) (1979 NR 1980 8fg 9f 14f 11.7fg 16f4 12.2fg 12.2f3 11.7h) 8,200Y; 4,000 2-y-o; rangy, good sort; plating-class maiden; possibly stays 1½m; acts on firm going; usually wears blinkers. *M. McCormack.* —

WINDS OF WINTER (USA) 3 b.c. Prince John–Stiff Breeze (Never Bend) (1979 5v* 5fg3 5fg 6f 5f 7d 7.9g* 7g2 1980 7v2 7v 8f) attractive colt; creditable length second to Skinflint (rec 9 lb) in Burmah-Castrol Trophy at Phoenix Park in March; ran poorly afterwards in Salisbury 2,000 Guineas Trial and Airlie/Coolmore Irish 2,000 Guineas at the Curragh; will stay at least 1¼m; acts on heavy going; blinkered fifth outing in 1979; sent to USA. *D. Weld, Ireland.* **91**

WINDSOR BROOK 3 ch.f. Deep Diver 134–Cherry Pie 81 (Rockavon 120) (1979 5g 5.3g 6fg 5fg 6g 5fg 1980 6f 5h 5s) lightly-made filly; poor sprint plater; has been tried in blinkers. *C. Dingwall.* —

WINDSOR WARRIOR 3 gr.g. Supreme Sovereign 119–Coleen's Peep (Don't Look 107) (1979 7f 1980 10.1g 12g 12fg3 14fg 12fg 11s) lengthy gelding; poor maiden; best run at 1½m on a firm surface; blinkered final start. *Peter Taylor.* —

WIND SPRAY 2 b.f. Mill Reef 141–Lacquer 118 (Shantung 132) (1980 6d 7g 7f) Jan 29; lightly-made filly; half-sister to good 3-y-o 1½m winner Shining Finish, very smart stayer Bright Finish (both by Nijinsky) and very useful Brilliantine (by Stage Door Johnny); dam won Cambridgeshire and Irish 1,000 Guineas; showed some promise in maiden events at Salisbury and Sandown on first 2 outings but made no show in a Chepstow maiden race on third; will be suited by middle distances; possibly unsuited by firm ground. *J. Tree.* **69**

WINDY HILL (FR) 3 ch.c. Royal and Regal–Where's Alice 95 (Raise A Native) (1979 5f 6fg 7g* 7g* 8fg* 7fg2 1980 7fg 7f3 8fg2 8d4 8fg) robust, deep-girthed colt; good mover; placed in handicaps at Epsom and Royal Ascot; led 1f out but couldn't match winner when 4 lengths second to April Bouquet **91**

in Britannia Stakes on latter; stays 1m; acts well on fast ground; ran poorly final start; sold 14,000 gns Newmarket Autumn Sales. *M. Stoute.*

WINDY SPOT 6 br.g. Silly Season 127–Lonely Leopardess 80 (Pardal 130) – (1979 NR 1980 11.7f) poor maiden. *G. Cottrell.*

WINDY WILLOW 2 ch.c. Windjammer (USA)–Morning Glow (Grey Dawn – II 132) (1980 5fg) May 27; 800F, 1,000Y; compact colt; half-brother to fairly useful 1979 2-y-o 6f winner Hurtwood Lad (by Realm); dam placed in USA; weak 6/1 shot, dwelt and was never dangerous when 9½ lengths fifth of 9 to Bellicosa in maiden auction event at Salisbury in May. *J. Hudson.*

WINGED BEAUTY 3 b.f. Dubassoff–Dissipation 83 (Disciplinarian) (1979 68 6fg 6d 1980 10d 6fg^{3} 5g^{4} 6fg^{2} 7fg* 6s* 7fg^{3} 7g 7g^{4} 6d^{2} 6d) lengthy filly; won handicap at Doncaster in July and apprentice race at Nottingham in August; stays 7f; probably acts on any going; suitable mount for a boy. *A. Hide.*

WINGED DAGGER 11 b.g. Falcon 131–Gay Natasha 105 (Prince Chevalier) 56 (1979 11.7g 12g^{4} 12s^{3} 12d^{2} 13.3s 12fg^{3} 12fg^{2} 12fg 12fg 12fg^{4} 12f 12fg 12fg^{4} 1980 12fg* 11.7fg^{2} 12f^{3} 12fg^{2} 12g^{3} 12g^{4} 12f^{3} 12g^{3}) middle-distance handicapper; beat Oui Monsieur by 1½ lengths at Brighton in April; ran creditably afterwards; acts on any going but is suited by a sound surface; has worn blinkers; suitable mount for an apprentice. *J. Old.*

WINGS GROUND 3 ch.f. Murrayfield 119–Oca (O'Grady) (1979 6g^{3} 7fg 67 1980 8fg 10.2fg 10.4d^{2} 10fg 10f^{3} 10s^{4}) workmanlike filly; placed in maiden race at Chester in August and seller at Lingfield in October; runs as if she'll stay 1½m; suited by some give in the ground. *M. Smyly.*

WING VELVET 2 b.c. Sayfar 116–Tide and Time (Easter Island 101) (1980 – 6g 5d) May 7; third foal; half-brother to 5f winner Tampa Bay (by Ickford); dam never ran; little sign of ability in newcomers race at Goodwood and maiden event at Wolverhampton in the autumn. *D. Leslie.*

WINKING FIELDS 4 ch.g. Northfields–Winky Joe (Eudaemon 129) (1979 – 10.8s 13v 10.2fg 10fg 14.6fg 14g 14f 1980 8s 11fg 12f^{4} 11.5fg 12g) poor plater; has worn blinkers; wears a tongue strap. *D. Weeden.*

WINMARIE 2 b.c. Windjammer (USA)–Mary's Dream (Midsummer Night – II 117) (1980 5f 6g) Mar 9; 3,600F; half-brother to two winners, including useful Irish 3-y-o sprinter Pitmarie (by Pitskelly); dam Irish 1m winner; in rear in maiden races at Wolverhampton in May and Chepstow (last of 12) in June. *J. Hill.*

WINNER TAKES ALL 3 b.c. Singing Bede 122–Julita 87 (Rockavon 120) 53 (1979 5fg 5s 5.8g 5fg^{2} 5fg^{4} 5fg^{3} 5g^{3} 6g* 6f 5g 6s^{2} 1980 7f 6fg 6f 5fg 5s^{3} 6g 5.6fg^{4} 6g 6d 6d^{4}) compact colt; poor sprint handicapper; suited by 6f; suited by some give in the ground; blinkered ninth start. *D. Marks.*

WINNING HABIT 2 ch.f. Sassafras 135–Victorian Habit 101 (Habitat 134) – (1980 7d 6d) Mar 14; lightly-made filly; first foal; dam 2-y-o 5f winner; in rear in small race at Catterick and maiden event at Doncaster in October. *W. Hastings-Bass.*

WINNINGS THE GAME 2 b.f. Workboy 123–Pams Choice 87 (Mandamus 72 120) (1980 5.1f^{3} 5g 5d 7d) Apr 11; 1,500F, 1,700Y; light-framed filly; second reported produce; dam won over 1m; prominent in 2 maiden races, being beaten only 3½ lengths when sixth of 19 to Voting Day at Bath in October on third outing; not sure to stay 7f. *J. Powney.*

WINSLOW 3 ch.c. Busted 134–Instant Justice 101 (Roan Rocket 128) (1979 109 7d^{3} 7f^{2} 8g 7f^{2} 7fg^{3} 1980 10d^{2} 10g* 10.5f^{2}) big, rangy colt; landed odds by 2½ lengths from Golden Reef in 18-runner maiden race at Nottingham in April; ran well when going down by 1½ lengths to Pelerin (pair clear) in 8-runner Glasgow Stakes at York following month; not seen out again; will stay 1½m; best form on a sound surface. *B. Hobbs.*

WINSOR BOY 4 br.c. Comedy Star 121–Spatula (Epaulette 125) (1979 82 6v 5fg 5fg^{4} 5f^{3} 5g^{4} 5s* 6d^{4} 1980 5fg* 5fg* 6h 5.8fg 5.8fg^{2} 5g^{2} 5g* 5d^{2} 5fg^{2} 5g^{3} 5g^{4} 5d^{4}) close-coupled colt; a speedy colt who trotted up in handicaps at Wolverhampton in April, Warwick (apprentice event) in May and Sandown in July; ran well most other outings too; best form at up to 5.8f; probably acts on any going; blinkered once at 2 yrs; got bit warm in paddock at Sandown; broke out of stalls and was withdrawn on one occasion late in season. *R. Turnell.*

WINTERREISE 2 b.g. Fine Blade 121–Pouilly Fuse (Tudor Music 131) (1980 – 6d) Apr 5; 2,900Y; strong gelding; third foal; half-brother to 2 winners in

Malaya; dam never ran; unquoted and looking backward, didn't move to post particularly well when tailed-off last of 14 behind Solway Winds in maiden auction event at Newcastle in June. *W. Bentley.*

WINTER SUNSHINE 4 b.f. Crisp and Even 116–Even Song (Falcon 131) (1979 12d* 12s 11.1s² 11fg* 10.2g³ 11.7fg³ 10.2f 10d 10.4f⁴ 11.7f⁴ 11g* 10fg² 12fg 1980 10v² 16s² 12f 16fg 12fg 11.7s 11g 12g³ 12.2fg 13s²) neat filly; effective at 1¼m and stays well; acts on any going; sometimes wears blinkers; goes well for apprentice D. McKeown. *P. Haslam.* **60**

WINTER WIND 4 b.c. Tumble Wind–Northern Beauty (Borealis) (1979 7v 8f 7f 7g⁴ 5f 6s 1980 5d 5g³ 5f³ 6fg* 6g³ 6g 5d* 6g 5g 6s³ 6d* 7d) very attractive colt; good mover with a nice, easy action; won handicaps at Kempton in May and Newbury in August and October; quickened to lead inside final furlong when scoring by 1½ lengths from Broon's Secret in last-named event; best form at up to 6f; acts on any going; usually held up; blinkered fifth outing at 3 yrs; badly hampered ninth outing. *D. Kent.* **80**

WIPYER SAPER 2 ch.f. Gold Rod 129–Track Mary (Tracker 95) (1980 5d 7d 5g 7f) Mar 7; 500Y; plain filly; third foal; dam never ran; in rear in maiden races and a seller. *R. Cambidge.* **—**

WISE MAN 4 ch.g. Frankincense 120–Sans Gene 77 (Songedor 116) (1979 8d* 8g 7g 8fg 8fg³ 8h³ 7fg 1980 7fg² 9g 10g⁴ 9fg 9fg 8g² 10.6s² 8.2s² 8.2s⁴) light-framed gelding; runner-up at Kempton, Doncaster, Haydock (amateur riders) and Hamilton, on first 2 occasions in sellers; stays 1¼m; acts on any going; trained until after Kempton by W. Hastings-Bass. *J. Fitzgerald.* **61**

WISH UPON A STAR 2 br.c. Wishing Star 117–San Estrella (Star Gazer 123) (1980 5f 5f 5g 5fg 5f 7g⁴ 5s³ 5fg 6g 6s 6s) Apr 20; 2,700Y; neat colt; has a round action; half-brother to fair 1970 2-y-o 6f performer Star of Levant (by Le Levanstell); dam maiden Irish sprinter; in frame in seller at Redcar in August and apprentice nursery at Ayr the following month; finds 5f too sharp and will be suited by a return to 7f; often wears blinkers nowadays; sold 500 gns Doncaster November Sales. *S. Nesbitt.* **59**

WISSINGTON JOY 3 br.f. Pirate Cloud 75–Cream Tea 59 (Seafront) (1979 NR 1980 6fg 8.3g) compact filly; tailed off in sellers; reluctant to race first start. *M. Tompkins.* **—**

WISTANWICK 7 b.g. Salvo 129–Miss Peseta 95 (Sovereign Path 125) (1979 NR 1980 11f³ 13fg 8g 14g) bad plater; probably stays 1¾m; acts on firm going; sometimes wears blinkers. *A. W. Jones.* **34**

WITCHINGHAM LASS 3 ch.f. Sweet Revenge 129–Callidice 77 (Worden II 129) (1979 6fg 5g 7g 6fg 6fg 6s² 6g* 1980 7f 6fg³ 7fg 7g 6fg³ 6fg³ 6fg 6fg 7g* 6fg 6fg 6s 6d) strong filly; won apprentice handicap at Doncaster in September; stays 7f; seems to act on any going; often blinkered but wasn't when successful; sweated up on reappearance; suitable mount for an apprentice. *R. Hannon.* **60**

WITHY COPSE 3 b.c. Blakeney 126–Chiltern Lass 100 (High Hat 131) (1979 NR 1980 10.1fg 11.5f 13d* 16s 14.6fg* 14fg³ 14fg² 14g⁴ 13s*) neat colt; second foal; dam game middle-distance performer; won 6-runner maiden race at Ayr in June and handicaps at Doncaster in July (from Argive) and Nottingham in October (beat Prince Sandro in good style by a length); stays well; probably acts on any going. *M. Stoute.* **93**

WIVETON 2 br.c. Blakeney 126–Wolverene 114 (Relko 136) (1980 7fg³) Mar 4; useful-looking colt; half-brother to useful 3-y-o middle-distance winner Shining Tor (by High Top) and fairly useful 1½m and 1¾m winner Coyote (by Welsh Pageant); dam game stayer; outsider of party and short of peak fitness, didn't move particularly well on way to start of Fitzroy House Stakes at Newmarket in August but ran with plenty of promise, finishing 3 lengths third of 6 to Baz Bombati after disputing lead 6f; very stoutly bred and should make a useful 3-y-o over a distance of ground. *W. Hastings-Bass.* **89 p**

WOLF CUB (USA) 3 b.c. Apalachee 137–Wolverida (Wolver Hollow 126) (1979 6fg 6fg 1980 6f 5d 5d 5d) neat colt; sprint maiden; should stay 6f; trained by C. Brittain first 2 starts. *C. Austin.* **—**

WOLLINGO 2 b.f. Wollow 132–Sabrewing 105 (Petingo 135) (1980 5fg² 5f 6g) Mar 28; 21,000Y; neat, unfurnished filly; second foal; half-sister to Borisgodunov (by Home Guard), successful at up to 1¼m in Ireland; dam won over 6f at 2 yrs; quite a moderate maiden; should be well suited by 6f+. *H. Candy.* **71**

WOLVER BAY 2 b.c. Bay Express 132–Wolver Valley 72 (Wolver Hollow 126) (1980 5.1g 7d 7d) Feb 7; neat colt; first foal; dam won 5 middle-distance races; 12/1 and backward, put in best work in closing stages when remote sixth of 11 to Directorate in maiden race at Yarmouth in September, first outing and best effort; should be suited by 7f. *T. Waugh.* –

WOLVERHANTS 2 b.f. Wolver Hollow 126–Hants 111 (Exbury 138) (1980 6g² 6g²) Mar 21; lengthy, rather unfurnished filly; half-sister to 2 winners, including very useful 1978 2-y-o 6f to 1m winner Potemkin (by Sir Gaylord), subsequently a stakes winner in USA; dam won 4 times at around 1¼m; 11/10 favourite for 12-runner maiden race at Yarmouth in July and looked sure to win when leading 1½f out but ran green and was caught close home by Integrity; odds on, led till 1f out when 2 lengths second to Harp Strings in similar event at Nottingham later in month; will stay 1¼m; should win a little race. *H. Cecil.* **79**

WOLVER HEIGHTS 2 b.c. Wolver Hollow 126–Mariska (Tanerko 134) (1980 7s 8s*) Mar 19; second living foal; dam twice-raced sister to Relko; won 4-runner minor event at Leopardstown in October by ¾ length from Top Pac; will do better over 1¼m+. *M. O'Toole, Ireland.* **95** p

WOLVER LEGEND 2 b.c. Wolver Hollow 126–Miss Legend (Bold Legend) (1980 6d⁴) Apr 13; 40,000Y; tall, quite attractive colt; good mover; half-brother to useful 1978 Irish 2-y-o 5f winner Devilish (by Red God); dam won twice over 6f in USA; 7/1 and very awkward at stalls, dwelt and was always trailing when distant last of 4 to Poldhu in Washington Singer Stakes at Newbury in August; given a very easy time once chance had gone and has the scope to do a lot better in time. *J. Dunlop.* – p

WOLVERTON 4 b.c. Wolver Hollow 126–Mary Murphy 85 (Aureole 132) (1979 10.5s² 10.5s* 10.5fg⁵ 10g 10d* 10g⁴ 8d* 8fg 1980 8v* 8g) big, strong, good-looking colt; won 3 races in 1979, notably Prix du Rond-Point at Longchamp; made a successful reappearance in Prix Edmond Blanc at Saint-Cloud in March, beating Kaldoun by ½ length; about 3 lengths fifth of 7 behind Nadjar in Prix de Ris-Orangis at Evry in April on only other start; bred to stay 1½m; probably acts on any going but seems suited by some give in the ground. *A. Head, France.* **116**

WONDERFUL 2 b.f. Martinmas 128–Wonder Star (Royal Palm 131) (1980 5fg² 5f* 5g² 6g³ 5fg 6d) Apr 15; 6,200Y; neat, quite attractive filly; half-sister to useful 1968 2-y-o winner Chellice (by Proud Chieftain); dam won over 5f at 2 yrs; dwelt when odds on for 19-runner maiden race at Windsor in May but recovered to win by a length from Marston Magna; placed afterwards in £2,600 race at York in June and £2,700 event at Leicester the following month but finished in rear on last 2 starts (off course 11 weeks before final outing); stays 6f; acts on firm going; sold 2,700 gns, reportedly for export to Belgium, Newmarket December Sales. *H. Candy.* **87**

WONDERFUL SURPRISE 3 b.c. Run The Gantlet–Ashling's Lass 89 (Levmoss 133) (1979 7s 1980 12fg 10fg⁴ 11s² 12s* 12d*) compact, quite attractive colt; bandaged in front when winning maiden race at Haydock by a wide margin and handicap at Leicester a shade cleverly by a length from Hadajar in October; will stay beyond 1½m; acts well on soft going; blinkered second start. *E. Eldin.* **88**

WOODCHAT 5 b.g. Song 132–Eastwood Bounty 87 (Bounteous 125) (1979 5s 6s³ 7s 5s 6g 6fg 1980 6fg 5fg 8g) sprint handicapper; has become most disappointing and was well beaten in seller final outing; appears to act on any going. *T. Fairhurst.* –

WOODHALL 2 b.f. Shiny Tenth 120–Stella Roma (Le Levanstell 122) (1980 6fg⁴ 5s*) Mar 5; 2,000Y; small filly; fourth foal; half-sister to a winner abroad; dam ran three times at 2 yrs; sold to race in Belgium for 3,600 gns after landing the odds by 4 lengths in seller at Folkestone in July. *M. Blanshard.* **60**

WOODRUSH 3 b.f. Mummy's Pet 125–Regal Silk (Henry the Seventh 125) (1979 5g 5s³ 5g³ 5s³ 5d³ 1980 5fg 5d 5g 5f 5.6fg 7d 5fg⁴ 5g) sprint plater; acts on soft going; has worn blinkers; sold 300 gns Doncaster October Sales. *J. Etherington.* **43**

WOODVALE 10 ch.g. Astec 128–Petronella 97 (Petition 130) (1979 NR 1980 18.4g) poor staying handicapper; probably acts on any going; usually wears blinkers; winning hurdler. *R. Murphy.* –

WOOLCANA 3 ch.f. Some Hand 119–Golden Mary 71 (Bounteous 125) (1979 5fg 5fg² 5.3d² 5g³ 7fg 5fg² 6fg⁴ 5fg* 1980 5fg 6fg 6f 6fg 5d* 5s 5.8g 6d⁴ 5fg 5.3fg 6g 5f 5g 5d 6d) neat filly; sprint handicapper; won at Salisbury in June; best at 5f; acts on a firm and a soft surface; blinkered fourth outing at 2 yrs and on final start; ran moderately towards end of season. *R. Hannon.* 68

WOOLY WONG 2 gr.f. Lorenzaccio 130–Wimbledon 105 (Abernant 142) (1980 5g⁴ 6fg³ 6g) Feb 25; neat filly; half-sister to several winners, including fairly useful sprinter Young and Foolish (by Crocket); dam won over 5f at 2 yrs; prominent in 11-runner maiden races in July, finishing length fourth to Miracle Baby at Pontefract and 2¼ lengths third behind Chantry Bridge at Doncaster; off course 2 months subsequently; runs as though 7f will suit her. *Miss A. Hill-Wood.* 79

WORKRIGHT 2 br.c. Workboy 123–Right Beauty 66 (Right Boy 137) (1980 5fg 5f⁴ 5d³ 5d⁴ 6g³ 5f 5s 8g 8g) Mar 13; 3,500Y; strong colt; first foal; dam, a plater, is half-sister to top-class sprinter Lochnager; in frame in maiden and minor events, running best race on third start when close-up third of 18 to Welsh Noble at Wolverhampton in June; appears not to stay 6f, let alone 1m; blinkered third and fourth outings. *A. Jarvis.* 63

WORKSHY 3 br.g. Workboy 123–Firmpostie (Goldhill 125) (1979 5s 6f*(w.o.) 6fg⁴ 6fg 6g* 6h 1980 7fg 7fg³ 7f⁴ 7g³ 6g 7fg*) neat gelding; plater; bought in 7,200 gns after winning at Newmarket in August; stays 7f; acts on firm going; blinkered fifth start; has worn bandages. *W. Wharton.* 51

WORLD AFFAIR (USA) 3 ch.c. Secretariat–Northern Gem 121 (Northern Dancer) (1979 raced 4 times in USA, finishing third once 1980 6d⁴ 8f* 8.2f⁴ 8f⁴ 9fg² 10g 10s 8g* 8.5fg* 8d*) strong, useful-looking ex-American colt; first foal; dam won Fred Darling Stakes, finished second in Champion Stakes and is daughter of smart Bamboozle; developed into a useful performer, winning minor events at Warwick and Brighton and handicaps at Epsom and Brighton; put up a fine effort to beat Prince Diligence a head under 10-0 on last-named in September; best at up to 9f; acts on any going with possible exception of very soft; good mount for a boy though pulled hard in amateur riders race third start; genuine. *H. T. Jones.* 105

WORLD LEADER (FR) 3 ch.c. Bolkonski 134–Worlica (Bon Mot III 132) (1979 6g* 7fg 1980 8f³ 8fg 10.5f 10.6fg⁴ 10g* 10.5d 14.6g³) 120

Once his regular work rider Guest was given the opportunity of riding him in races World Leader developed into a very smart performer, ending the year with a creditable third in the St Leger. That he had a lot of ability was evident from the Ladbrokes Craven Stakes at Newmarket in the spring, when he finished strongly after pursuing a serpentine path to be third to Tyrnavos, but his temperament threatened to get the better of him. At Newmarket he threw his head about and fought his jockey for a long way, while his perform-

Daniel Prenn Handicap, Newmarket—a finish of heads between World Leader (right), Easter Sun (rails) and Fine Sun (centre)

ances in the Two Thousand Guineas and Mecca-Dante Stakes were very much open to criticism. In the Guineas he sweated up slightly and ran deplorably, trailing in last, and at York he pulled extremely hard early on and found little when asked in the straight, finishing a well-beaten sixth to Hello Gorgeous. At this stage World Leader's future looked in the balance but on his next appearance, with Guest up, he ran less freely and kept on to be fourth in a valuable handicap at Haydock. This was a distinct improvement, and in the Daniel Prenn Handicap at Newmarket in June World Leader put up one of the best handicap performances of the year. Sweating up quite badly, he again settled better than usual, made progress from three furlongs out and though swishing his tail under pressure ran on in good style to lead close home, winning by two heads from Easter Sun and Fine Sun who were receiving 18 lb and 10 lb respectively. World Leader acquitted himself well in much better company on his last two starts. In the Benson and Hedges Gold Cup he went on strongly in the closing stages to be fifth, four lengths behind Master Willie; in the St Leger, despite reverting to his bad habit of pulling violently, he came through to take third place at the two-furlong pole and stayed on well without threatening Light Cavalry or Water Mill, going down by four lengths and the same.

World Leader (Fr) (ch.c. 1977)	Bolkonski (ch 1972)	Balidar (br 1966)	Will Somers
			Violet Bank
		Perennial (ch 1955)	Dante
			Cypher
	Worlica (ch 1970)	Bon Mot III (ch 1963)	Worden II
			Djebel Idra
		Dentrelic (ch 1965)	Prudent II
			Relict

Worlica, World Leader's dam, won over a mile and a quarter in the French Provinces on the last of her twelve starts. Her first two produce, both by New Chapter, are winners in France and the 1978 foal, War Whisper (by My Swallow), fetched 230,000 francs at Deauville as a yearling and has won in Italy. The second dam, Dentrelic, won at eleven furlongs and in addition to Worlica produced the good-class miler Dandy Lute and Trelex, dam of the 1980 Prix Thomas Bryon winner Big John.

World Leader comes from the first crop of Bolkonski, a crop that also included the useful Stella Matutina and the 1979 Premio Tevere winner Mister Ski. Bolkonski was highly strung; he often battled with his jockey, sweated up profusely before winning the Sussex Stakes and ran miserably on his final appearance. World Leader has obviously inherited one or two of the worst elements in Bolkonski's make-up along with a fair measure of his ability: while putting Guest on board has helped enormously it hasn't solved the problem. He has the ability to win more races but his prospects of doing so depend largely on his disposition. A strong, rangy colt, a 14,500-guinea yearling, World Leader stays a mile and three quarters, though he is probably better at shorter distances; he seems to act on any going. *L. Cumani.*

WORLD'S FAIR (USA) 2 ch.f. Our Hero–Sunday Purchase (T. V. Lark) — p
(1980 6g) neat, attractive filly; third foal; half-sister to 2 winners, including 3-y-o Super Asset (by Sir Ivor), a very smart winner at up to 7.3f at 2 yrs; dam, 1m winner, is half-sister to high-class 1971 USA 2-y-o Rest Your Case; sire, son of Bold Ruler and champion Argentinian filly Dorine, was smart winner from 6f to 7f; 25/1, apprentice ridden and looking as though race would do her good, never got out of mid-division in 16-runner maiden race won impressively by stable-companion Her Grace at Doncaster in June; bred to stay at least 1m; looks capable of better. *H. Cecil.*

WORTH AVENUE 4 ch.c. Busted 134–Lavenham Rose 85 (Floribunda 136) **57**
(1979 12g^4 12s 11.5fg^2 10.2fg 11.5fg* 10fg 12g 1980 12f^4 15h^4 12d^3) poor handicapper; stays 1½m; acts on firm going and a soft surface; well beaten second start. *I. Walker.*

WOT THE DICKINS 2 gr.g. Runnymede 123–Gardenia (Cagire II 122) **71**
(1980 7s^4 7g^3) Mar 30; 2,000F, 3,300Y; brother to fair 1978 2-y-o 7f winner James Ward, and half-brother to several minor winners; dam Irish 1¼m winner; 1¾ lengths third of 18 to Price of Peace in maiden race at Salisbury in July; stays 7f. *S. Mellor.*

WREN ROCKET 3 gr.f. Roan Rocket 128–Chick 106 (My Swanee 122) (1979 **84**
5d 5s* 5fg^3 5fg^3 6f^2 5fg 5fg^3 1980 6f 6fg^4 6f 6d 5d^4 6fg 5f) light-framed filly;

sprint handicapper; stays 6f; acts on any going; blinkered fifth and sixth starts (ran a bit freely on latter); ran moderately final outing; sold 13,500 gns Newmarket December Sales. *M. Jarvis.*

WRIGHTWAY BLUES 2 b.f. Majority Blue 126–Kitty Wake (Milesian 125) (1980 6fg³ 6s³ 5d* 6d 5s) Apr 8; 2,200Y; sturdy filly; sister to a poor filly and half-sister to winners here and abroad, including fairly useful 6f to 1¼m winner Czarist (by Faberge II); dam Irish maiden; apprentice ridden, made all to win 3-runner minor event at Ayr in June by 1½ lengths from Monza Lady; unplaced in nurseries subsequently; stays 6f; probably acts on any going. *B. Hanbury.* **75**

WRONG PAGE (USA) 2 br.c. Sir Ivor 135–Kateri (Pretense) (1980 6g 7g 7d² 8g) Mar 18; $57,000Y; fair sort; first foal; dam, unplaced 6 times, is closely related to Santa Anita Derby winner Sham; caught close home when length second of 12 to Patchinia in maiden race at Chester in September, best effort; should stay at least 1m. *P. Cole.* **78**

WURLI 2 b.f. Wolver Hollow 126–Tanella 103 (Habitat 134) (1980 6g² 5g 7g 7g 6s³) Mar 16; 36,000Y; small, lightly-made filly; first foal; dam, closely related to smart 1½m filly Nanticious, won over 5f and 6f at 2 yrs; placed in maiden race at Newmarket in August and nursery at Hamilton in October; needs further than 5f and should be suited by 7f; yet to race on a firm surface; possesses little scope. *J. Hindley.* **70**

WYDDIAL PARK 3 br.f. Tarboosh–Clearing Mist 62 (Double Jump 131) (1979 5fg³ 5g* 5g 5f³ 5fg 6fg 1980 6f 6fg 6d* 6fg* 6g 6s) wiry sort; won handicaps at Lingfield (backed from 14/1 to 13/2 when making all to beat Repetitious 2 lengths) and Yarmouth (by a head from Winged Beauty) in July; stays 6f; probably acts on any going; ran poorly fifth start. *P. Cole.* **86**

WYKE 2 b.g. No Mercy 126–Harvest Melody 103 (Tudor Minstrel 144) (1980 6g) Apr 23; half-brother to several winners, including smart stayer Flagon (by Alcide); dam won over 1½m; easy in market and in need of race when remote eighth of 19 to Dancing Sally in maiden race at Goodwood in September. *P. Cole.* **–**

WYN-BANK 4 b.f. Green God 128–Spadilla 59 (Javelot 124) (1979 8g 8fg 8f³ 8f² 10f² 9fg* 8s 8fg 10s* 10.6g³ 12g⁴ 1980 12g 11g 12.3d⁴ 10.6s) fair handicapper when in the mood; reluctant to enter stalls nowadays (withdrawn third outing) and often starts slowly; stays 1¼m but possibly not 1½m; acts on any going; suited by a strong gallop. *J. Fitzgerald.* **–**

WYNBURRY 3 br.f. No Mercy 126–Lucinda Anne (Abernant 142) (1979 5s 5s* 5d² 5d 5f 5g 5fg 5d 6fg 5fg² 5f 5g 1980 5f² 5f⁴ 5fg² 6f⁴ 5g² 5g 7g⁴ 6g 6g³ 6g⁴ 6f³ 6g 5f³ 5fg 5d² 5d) useful-looking filly; sprint handicapper; stays 6f; acts on any going; often blinkered; suitable mount for a boy. *M. W. Easterby.* **69**

WYN MILUV 2 gr.f. Young Emperor 133–Bargy Music (Tudor Music 131) (1980 6d 6g 6fg* 7fg 6d* 6g 5d 6s) Apr 27; neat filly; fourth foal; half-sister to winning Irish hurdler This Song For You (by Simbir); dam never ran; bought in 4,000 gns after winning seller at Yarmouth in July and for 1,650 gns after beating Miss Murton by 4 lengths in selling nursery at Brighton 2 months later; suited by 6f but probably doesn't get 7f; acts on a firm surface but put up best efforts on a soft one. *R. Hannon.* **73**

WYNNWITH 3 b.g. Klairon 131–Pinchbeck (Chanteur II 135) (1979 5g 5.8g* 6fg³ 7s³ 8fg 1980 10fg 12fg 10f) useful-looking gelding; good walker; won minor event at Bath in 1979; didn't find his form in handicaps at 3 yrs; bred to stay middle distances; probably acts on any going; blinkered once at 2 yrs and on final start; exported to Hong Kong. *N. Vigors.* **–**

WYNNWITH SOVEREIGN 2 br.c. Sovereign Path 125–Sheer Bliss 76 (St Paddy 133) (1980 6d) Feb 3; 32,000Y; leggy colt; brother to speedy 1976 Italian 2-y-o Sleeping, and half-brother to 3 winners, including Irish 3-y-o middle-distance winner Sheringham (by Blakeney); dam possessed only a little ability; 14/1 when behind in 25-runner maiden race won by Little Wolf at Newbury in October. *N. Vigors.* **–**

WYTON BAR 2 b.g. Royal Palace 131–Swordblade 84 (Pall Mall 132) (1980 5d 5v 5g 5f³ 5g 6g 7g 5d 5f 8fg) Apr 7; 1,900Y; unfurnished gelding; bad plater; has worn blinkers. *A. Smith.* **–**

X

XARFINA 3 b.f. High Line 125–Zugela 90 (Zucchero 133 §) (1979 7fg 7fg **89**
1980 12fg 11f 13.3fg 12g* 13.1g^{3} 13.3d^{4} 14d*) strong, good-topped filly; successful in maiden race at Lingfield in June (from Palmella) and minor event at Haydock in August; ran on gamely to beat North Buchan a neck (pair clear) in latter despite hanging left; will stay beyond 1$\frac{3}{4}$m; suited by some give in the ground; has run well for an apprentice. *W. Wightman.*

XENIA 2 b.f. High Line 125–Zugela 90 (Zucchero 133 §) (1980 6d 7g 7g 8g) **—**
May 19; lengthy filly; sister to 3-y-o 1$\frac{1}{2}$m and 1$\frac{3}{4}$m winner Xarfina, and half-sister to several winners here and abroad; dam stayer; unquoted when in rear in maiden and minor events; will be suited by middle distances. *W. Wightman.*

XIAN 3 ch.f. Sallust 134–Tuna 63 (Silver Shark 129) (1979 6g^{3} 7.3s 1980 **74**
8s* 8.5g 12.3f 11fg 12g) tall, narrow filly; stayed on to win maiden race at Leicester in March; out of her depth next 2 starts and finished last in handicaps subsequently; stays 1m; acts on soft going. *G. Hunter.*

Y

YAT DING YAN 2 gr.f. Birdbrook 110–Edict 51 (Privy Councillor 125) (1980 **—**
5fg 5f 5d 7f 5d 6s) May 19; 1,350Y; neat filly; sister to 2 winners, including 11f winner Jean D'Argent, and half-sister to a winner; dam won 2 sellers at up to 1$\frac{1}{2}$m; probably of little account; formerly trained by A. Davison. *R. Ward.*

YA ZAMAN (FR) 3 b.c. Gallant Man–Irish Exchange (Swaps) (1979 6d **120**
9v 1980 8s* 8s 6.5s* 7g* 7s*(dis) 7d 7v^{4}) $20,000Y; big colt; half-brother to 3 winners, including very useful French middle-distance performer Zabriskie Point (by Sword Dancer); dam daughter of Irish Oaks and Irish St Leger winner Lynchris; smart performer; led over 2$\frac{1}{2}$f out and kept on to beat Luck Of The Draw $\frac{1}{2}$ length in 9-runner Prix de la Porte Maillot at Longchamp in June (subsequently disqualified after traces of caffeine were found in his system); had earlier won maiden race at Saint-Cloud, minor event at Evry and 49,000 francs handicap at Longchamp; creditable 1$\frac{3}{4}$ lengths fourth of 9 to Moorestyle in Prix de la Foret at Longchamp again in October; stays 1m; acts on heavy going. *M. Saliba, France.*

YEALM OYSTER 4 b.g. Cornuto 111–Daring Liz (Dairialatan 111) (1979 **—**
NR 1980 16s 16.9d) first foal; dam never ran; tailed off in maiden races in July at Lingfield and Wolverhampton. *D. Morley.*

YEARS AHEAD 4 b.c. Sweet Revenge 129–Warrior Queen 95 (King's Bench **45**
132) (1979 8s 6.5v 8v 6v* 6s* 6d 6v 7g 7f 6s 6d 1980 5s 7f 10fg 7.6d^{3} 9g 8fg) neat colt; reportedly finished lame when tailed off in seller final outing; best form at up to 7.6f; acts on heavy going; often wears blinkers; trained by S. Woodman until after fifth outing. *J. Jenkins.*

YEDDAAN (FR) 3 ch.c. Zeddaan 130–Yetta (Ragusa 137) (1979 NR 1980 **—**
6f 8h 7f 10g) 4,000 2-y-o; compact colt; third foal; half-brother to a winner in France by Bold Lad (USA); dam won over 7.5f and 1m in France; behind in minor and maiden events in the North; blinkered last 2 starts. *J. Carr.*

YELED 2 br.c. Youth 135–Lalibela 123 (Honeyway 125) (1980 7f^{4} 7g) Feb **71**
18; 8,400Y; big, lengthy colt; half-brother to several winners, including smart Irish miler Habituate (by Habitat) and useful Anadyomene (by Sea Hawk II), successful over 11f and 13f; dam won Cheveley Park Stakes and showed form only at sprint distances; in touch 5f when 9$\frac{1}{2}$ lengths fourth of 5 to Sula Bula in valuable race at York in September; third favourite for Hyperion Stakes at Ascot the following month but was beaten and eased from distance, finishing 12$\frac{1}{2}$ lengths sixth to Sunley Builds; will stay 1$\frac{1}{4}$m+. *P. Kelleway.*

YELLOW CHARTREUSE 3 ch.g. Charlottown 127–Meadow Wood (Meadow **—**
Court 129) (1979 6f 7f 8.2fg 1980 8fg 10.1fg 8d) compact gelding; of little account; has been tried in blinkers; sold 740 gns Ascot July Sales. *P. Makin.*

YELLOW JERSEY 4 ch.g. Levmoss 133–Merta (Jaipur) (1979 10.8s* 12g **84**
16s^{2} 1980 16s^{3} 14fg^{3} 16fg 14g* 16fg 16g^{2} 14g 14s* 14g) lengthy gelding; won handicaps at Sandown in June (by a head from Al Kuwait) and October (by $\frac{3}{4}$ length from Path of Peace); 2 lengths second to Heighlin at Newbury, best effort in between; stays well; very well suited by some give in the ground; suitable mount for an apprentice; game. *P. Cole.*

YIGDAL 3 b.g. Saulingo 122–Flaring Angel (Nentego 119) (1979 NR 1980 10s 12s) workmanlike gelding; well beaten in maiden races at Leicester and Kempton early in year; sold 610 gns Doncaster June Sales. *N. Callaghan.* —

YIORGAKIS 3 ch.g. Amber Rama 133–Malpractice (Pall Mall 132) (1979 5fg 5fg 5d 6d 1980 6d 5v2 8s 5fg 5h 6fg 5fg 5s) fair sort; poor handicapper; not certain to stay 1m; acts on heavy going; blinkered nowadays; sweated up seventh start; has run respectably for an apprentice; sold 520 gns Doncaster September Sales. *A. Demetriou.* **59** d

YLVA 3 b.f. Bay Express 132–Berga (Baldric II 131) (1979 5g2 5.1g2 5f 6g* 6g4 5g 1980 6f 7fg 7.2g 6s 6f 5f4 6fg 8d 7s) big filly; sprint handicapper; stays 6f; acts on firm going; blinkered nowadays and has worn a hood as well; sold 3,100 gns Newmarket Autumn Sales. *N. Guest.* **75**

YONDER HE GOES 5 b.g. Gulf Pearl 117–Hark Hark 75 (Sing Sing 134) (1979 9.4g 9fg 10f 10f4 10f3 9fg 12fg 12.2fg 10h3 11g2 15s 1980 13d 12f 12h4 10.6fg 10.6fg 10f2 10g 10g 15.8g 12fg) plater; seems to stay 1½m; acts on firm going; sometimes wears blinkers; occasionally sweats up; sold 900 gns Doncaster September Sales. *J. Etherington.* **35**

YOOHOO 6 ch.g. Mountain Call 125–Dreamy Idea 68 (Double Jump 131) (1979 6s* 6v 6d 6fg 5f4 5g3 6g4 5f2 6fg 5d2 6g 1980 6fg 5fg 5fg 5d4 7g 5f* 6g4 5s2 6f 6fg) sprint handicapper; held up when beating Wedding Vows by 1½ lengths at Beverley in August; acts on any going; usually wears blinkers; didn't have a clear run final start. *C. Booth.* **65**

YORK COTTAGE 3 b.c. Royal Palace 131–Misnomer 85 (Milesian 131) (1979 7f 8d 8d 8fg 1980 12f* 12fg3 12d* 12g2 14.6fg4 12g* 14g 12f4 12fg2 11s2 12g* 12v2 12.5s*) quite attractive colt; had a splendid season, winning maiden race at Carlisle (made all), minor event at Pontefract (enterprisingly ridden) and handicaps at Newcastle, York and Stockton; beat Entebbe all out by a neck on last-named in October; stays 1¾m; acts on any going; usually blinkered; consistent; sold 12,000 gns Newmarket Autumn Sales. *W. Elsey.* **91**

YORKSHIRE DANCER (USA) 3 b.c. Northern Fling–Spiral On (On-And-On) (1979 5s 6s4 6d* 6fg* 7g3 6s 1980 7d 6v3 7d 6fg 6fg 6g 8fg2 8.2g2 8f 8fg3 8d 8d 7s 7s) small, robust colt; stays 1m well; probably acts on any going; blinkered eighth and ninth starts; trained by S. Norton first 5 outings. *F. Durr.* **65**

YORK TERRACE 3 b.c. Derring-Do 131–Slipperty 99 (Hardicanute 130) (1979 6fg2 1980 8g4 8fg4 10.8s2 10.1f* 10f* 10.1g 10f) small, good sort; won 24-runner maiden race at Windsor and small 3-runner event at Ripon in August; will stay 1½m; acts on any going; sold to D. Elsworth 5,200 gns Newmarket Autumn Sales. *P. Walwyn.* **80**

YOUNG ATHENA 2 br.f. Young Emperor 133–Alea-Yacta (Javelot 124) (1980 6d 6d 6f 7g) Jan 20; 1,200F, 2,000Y; small filly; half-sister to useful Rio Alta (by My Swanee), successful from 5f to 1¼m; dam unplaced 4 times in Ireland; little worthwhile form, including in an auction event. *C. Booth.* **59**

YOUNG COUSIN 2 ro.c. Streetfighter 120–Happiness (Right Boy 137) (1980 5.8fg 5s 5.8fg 5fg 6fg 5g4 5d) Mar 4; workmanlike colt; fourth foal; dam poor plater; prominent in large fields of maidens on fourth and sixth outings, finishing 4 lengths fourth of 18 to Portogon at Bath in September; form only at 5f. *M. Bradley.* **72**

YOUNG CROFTIE 3 b.g. Sit In The Corner–Open Arms 77 (Dignitary 121) (1979 5g 6fg 6g4 7fg 6g 1980 7s 7f 8f 7f3 6fg4 7fg 7.6g4 6g3 6g* 6g 6f4 7.6d) compact gelding; apprentice ridden when winning handicap at Carlisle in July; stays 7f; acts on firm going; blinkered nowadays. *R. Morris.* **65**

YOUNG DAI 3 b.g. Streetfighter 120–Happiness (Right Boy 137) (1979 5fg 1980 5s 5fg 5fg 5g 5s 5fg2 5g) small gelding; second in handicap at Bath in July; not disgraced in maiden event on final start; well beaten in seller on fourth appearance; acts on a firm surface; usually blinkered nowadays; sweated up second outing. *M. Bradley.* **62**

YOUNG DANIEL 2 b.c. Dragonara Palace 115–Pepperita 79 (Nelcius 133) (1980 6s) Mar 29; 5,400Y; second foal; half-brother to 1½m winner Economy Pep (by Jimmy Reppin); dam won over 7.6f at 2 yrs; 33/1 when eighth of 22 to Banbury Cross in maiden race at Doncaster in November. *R. Armstrong.* —

YOUNG FERRANTI 3 b.c. Pitcairn 126–Annatown 68 (Charlottown 127) (1979 5g 5s 6g 7f 1980 9h 8h2 12.2d2 12g3) robust ex-Irish colt; quite a modest **70**

maiden; stays 1½m; probably acts on any going; hurdling with F. Rimell. *G. Pritchard-Gordon.*

YOUNG GEOFF 7 b.g. Prevailing–Scandale 117 (Vilmorin) (1979 NR 1980 10.4d) poor novice hurdler; unquoted when tailed off in ladies race at Chester in August, first outing on flat. *J. Priday.* —

YOUNG IMPORT 2 ch.c. Import 127–Bishop's Song 67 (Bishop's Move 92) (1980 5g 7f 7d) Mar 16; sturdy colt; third foal; dam 1¼m winner; close up 5½f when seventh of 10 to Paltango at Catterick in October, final outing; probably stays 7f. *G. Lockerbie.* —

YOUNG INCA 2 gr.g. Young Emperor 133–Sunny Eyes (Reliance II 137) (1980 5d) Apr 29; compact gelding; 6,700Y; third foal; half-brother to 7f winner Sun Lamp (by Pall Mall); dam never ran; 50/1 and very backward when distant sixth of 7 to Tax Haven in £2,700 event at Sandown in June. *R. Smyth.* —

YOUNG ROBIN 3 ch.g. High Line 125–Goldilocks II (Pinza 137) (1979 NR 1980 7f 8fg 12g⁴ 12.2f 12g) leggy, non-thoroughbred gelding; only plating class; will stay long distances. *N. Crump.* —

YOUNG ROYALIST (USA) 2 br.c. Youth 135–My Great Aunt (Bold Ruler) (1980 8d) Mar 8; $50,000Y; lightly-made colt; third foal; half-brother to 3-y-o American winner Guinness (by Grundy); dam smart French middle-distance performer and daughter of top filly Aunt Edith; second favourite, beaten and eased over 2f out when seventh of 9 to Akram in small race at Leicester in October; will need at least 1¼m; looks immature at present. *P. Cole.* —

YOUNG SAINT 3 b.f. Saintly Song 128–Young Romance (King's Troop 118) (1979 6f 1980 7.2fg 8s 10g) neat, strong filly; poor form, including in sellers; sold 400 gns Doncaster August Sales. *M. H. Easterby.* —

YOUNG STAN 5 b.h. Bold and Free 118–Merry Madrigal (Sing Sing 134) (1979 6g 5d 6g² 5g 5fg² 6s 5d 1980 5v 6f) poor plater nowadays; best at 5f; probably unsuited by very firm ground; usually wears blinkers. *Hbt Jones.* —

Z

ZACCIO 2 ch.c. Lorenzaccio 130–Hepash 81 (Henry the Seventh 125) (1980 5.8g 7fg⁴ 7g⁴ 8d³ 10.2s) May 14; 4,000Y; small colt; good mover; fourth foal; dam best at 1m; in frame in maiden and minor events; looked very well despite an absence of over 2 months when 2¼ lengths third of 9 to Akram at Leicester in October; stays 1m. *J. Bethell.* 75

ZAHAROFF 5 b.h. Wolver Hollow 126–Morinda 87 (Matador 131) (1979 7s 7d 6fg 6fg* 7fg² 6h 7fg 6g 6fg 5f 1980 6g 5fg 6fg³ 6h³ 6g 5.8f³ 6fg 5f 7fg 8g 5d 6fg) strong, useful sort; quite a moderate handicapper; stays 1m; acts on hard going; occasionally wears blinkers; inconsistent. *M. Bradley.* 64

ZAHIAH 3 b.f. So Blessed 130–St Padina 91 (St Paddy 133) (1979 5g² 6g* 6d 6g* 6fg 1980 8h 7.2s 6g 6fg 7fg 6g 5.8g) small, lightly-made filly; good mover; won maiden race at Redcar and minor event at Epsom in 1979; didn't train on at 3 yrs; blinkered 3 times in 1980. *R. Boss.* —

ZAKUSHKI 3 br.f. Royal Palace 131–Kushi 65 (Paridel 112) (1979 NR 1980 12d) small, lightly-made filly; half-sister to several winners, including fair sprinter Friendly Annie (by Be Friendly); dam a miler; tailed-off last in 14-runner maiden race at Goodwood in September. *G. Lewis.* —

ZAMBO (HOL) 2 b.f. Shamaraan–Zauberie (Soderini 123) (1980 7fg 6g 7g 7d² 6g) well-made, workmanlike Dutch-bred filly; 20/1 when neck second of 10 to Supreme Fjord in small race at Catterick in October, best effort; ran at Baden-Baden on previous outing; finds 6f on sharp side and will be suited by middle distances. *H. Collingridge.* 76

ZANVEATIC 3 bl.g. Beatic–Polly-Ann Tanja (Cletus) (1979 5s 5g 6g 7g 6g 8.2d 8d 1980 8f⁴ 6f² 8f* 8d 8g 8g 12g) lightly-made gelding; plater; won at Pontefract in May (bought in 950 gns); stays 1m; suited by firm going; has worn boots; good mount for an apprentice. *T. Barnes.* 48

ZEBRA CROSSING 5 br.g. Pals Passage 115–Jungle Law 67 (Martial 131) (1979 6s 8.2v 11d 6d 1980 9f) bad plater. *G. Wallace.* —

ZEBRA GRASS 3 b.f. Run The Gantlet–Ash Lawn 94 (Charlottesville 135) (1979 6g 6f* 6fg 7g* 7fg 7d 1980 10f³ 13s) leggy filly; fair but inconsistent —

performer at 2 yrs; ran poorly in handicaps in 1980; should stay well; acts on firm going and is possibly unsuited by soft. *T. Waugh.*

ZEDATIVE (FR) 3 gr.f. Zeddaan 130–Noble Native 98 (Indigenous 121) (1979 **74**
5g^{2} 5d^{2} 5s 5fg 5s 5g 1980 5fg^{3} 5fg* 5g^{3} 5s^{3} 5fg 5d 5d) useful-looking filly; won handicap at Brighton in May; only just stays 5f; probably acts on any going. *C. Brittain.*

ZELDABEC 3 b.f. Saulingo 122–African Dawn 72 (Chanteur II 135) (1979 **—**
5d 5d 5fg 5fg 6fg 1980 7f 8fg 7fg 8g) neat filly; bad plater; has worn blinkers. *J. Fitzgerald.*

ZELKOVA 2 ch.c. Sassafras 135–Ruffled Bird 79 (Relko 136) (1980 7d 7g) **—**
Apr 30; useful sort; fourth foal; half-brother to a winner in Italy; dam won at up to 13f; 16/1, close up 4f when eleventh of 13 to Buffavento in maiden race at Newbury in July; left in stalls and took no part at Newmarket earlier in month; will stay middle distances; sold 2,000 gns Newmarket Autumn Sales. *B. Hills.*

ZEP 3 b.f. Thatch 136–Beck 97 (St Paddy 133) (1979 NR 1980 6f 5fg 5d) **—**
8,200Y, 3,800 2-y-o; good sort; second living foal; dam won over 6f and 7f at 2 yrs; well beaten in maiden races; will stay 7f. *N. Vigors.*

ZEPHYROS 3 b.c. Auction Ring 123–Miss Stephen (Stephen Paul 131) (1979 **88**
NR 1980 5f^{2} 6f* 6fg^{2} 5g^{2} 6g 7g) 15,000Y; small, quite well-made colt; half-brother to numerous winners, including top sprinter Deep Diver (by Gulf Pearl) and Irish 2,000 Guineas winner King's Company (by King's Troop); dam never ran; long odds on when comfortably winning 9-runner maiden event at Ayr in May; ran creditably in handicap at Kempton and £3,800 race at Sandown on next 2 starts; best at sprint distances; yet to race on a soft surface. *G. Pritchard-Gordon.*

ERXES 2 b.c. Targowice 130–High Command (High Hat 131) (1980 5f 5fg **77**
6g^{4} 6f^{3} 7g) Mar 2; 5,000Y; neat colt; half-brother to 2 winners in Ireland, including 1½m and 2m winner High Simbir (by Simbir); dam placed over 6f at 2 yrs in Ireland; 3¾ lengths sixth of 13 to Cooliney Prince in Windsor Castle Stakes at Royal Ascot in June, second outing; beaten favourite in maiden races on next 2 outings, better effort when 3 lengths fourth of 13 to Top of the Mark at Epsom in August (moved up to third by stewards); should be suited by 7f (had stiffish task in nursery when tried at trip). *R. Armstrong.*

IPARIB 2 ch.c. Ribston 104–Zaraspar 70 (Zarathustra 131) (1980 5v^{3} 5f^{2} **76**
5f* 6fg^{2} 6g 7g 7g) Mar 16; 1,000Y; small, sturdy colt; half-brother to fairly useful 1¼m to 13f winner Sunlit Spar (by Lauso); dam sister to useful stayer Arc of Fire; led close home to win 7-runner maiden auction event at Haydock in May by ½ length from Joint Mercy; good second to Mr Gus in minor race at Carlisle the following month; ran moderately last 2 starts; bred to stay at least 1¼m. *W. Elsey.*

OBO 3 ch.c. Welsh Pageant 132–Babanina (Bleep-Bleep 134) (1979 6s 6s **—**
1980 7s 7fg 7fg 12fg 8g^{3} 8d 9.4fg 8.2s) workmanlike colt; plating-class maiden; best run at 1m. *R. Hollinshead.*

OILO 2 b.c. Workboy 123–L'Elita 83 (Porto Bello 118) (1980 5f 5g 5f^{4} 5g* **76**
5s) Apr 13; big, strong colt; second foal; half-brother to a winning 2-y-o plater; dam 2-y-o 5f winner; won maiden race at Nottingham in September, holding on by a neck from Bretton Park after making all; 12/1 when in rear in 11-runner minor event won by Pettistree at York the following month; unlikely to stay 6f; probably not at his best on soft going. *M. W. Easterby.*

ORO 5 ch.g. Cavo Doro 124–Camina Bay 109 (Whistling Wind 123) (1979 **70**
10.2s^{2} 10d^{3} 10.2d 10s 10g 10.5f 10g 10fg 9f^{2} 10fg 10g^{4} 10.5s 10.2fg 10f 10fg 1980 12fg 11.1fg 10f^{4} 10s 10g* 10g^{2} 11.7g* 12fg 10g 12fg 12g) moody middle-distance handicapper; narrow winner at Beverley (apprentice ridden) in June and Windsor in July; acts on any going; used to wear blinkers; inclined to put head in air under pressure and is not an easy ride; sold to A. Ingham 740 gns Newmarket Autumn Sales. *G. Balding.*

HUR 2 b. or br.f. Reform 132–Vivante 87 (Bold Lad Ire 133) (1980 5g) **—**
May 15; 8,000F; neat filly; half-sister to 3-y-o 9f and 1¼m winner Majestic Star (by Star Appeal) and 1977 2-y-o 6f winner Scotsman Ice (by Lombard); dam stayed 1m; third favourite but in need of race, showed up until lack of fitness told in final 2f when seventh of 11 to Katysue in maiden race at Redcar in June, only outing; will stay 1m. *R. Boss.*

MOORESTYLE

TIMEFORM
HORSE OF THE YEAR 1980

TIMEFORM CHAMPIONS OF 1980

HORSE OF THE YEAR (RATED AT 137)

MOORESTYLE

3 b.c. Manacle-Guiding Star (Reliance II)
Owner Moores Furnishings Ltd ***Trainer*** R. Armstrong

BEST TWO-YEAR-OLD COLT (RATED AT 134)

STORM BIRD (CAN)

2 b.c. Northern Dancer-South Ocean (New Providence)
Owner Mr R. E. Sangster ***Trainer*** V. O'Brien

BEST TWO-YEAR-OLD FILLY (RATED AT 124)

MARWELL

2 b.f. Habitat-Lady Seymour (Tudor Melody)
Owner Mr E. Loder ***Trainer*** M. Stoute

BEST SPRINTER (RATED AT 137)

MOORESTYLE

3 b.c. Manacle-Guiding Star (Reliance II)
Owner Moores Furnishings Ltd ***Trainer*** R. Armstrong

BEST MILER (RATED AT 135)

KNOWN FACT (USA)

3 b.c. In Reality-Tamerett (Tim Tam)
Owner Mr K. Abdulla ***Trainer*** J. Tree

BEST MIDDLE-DISTANCE HORSE (RATED AT 133)

ARGUMENT (FR)

3 b.c. Kautokeino-Arantelle (Tapioca)
Owners Mr B. McNall and Mr B. Gordy ***Trainer*** M. Zilber

BEST STAYER (RATED AT 135)

LE MOSS

5 ch.h. Le Levanstell-Feemoss (Ballymoss)
Owner Mr C. d'Alessio ***Trainer*** H. Cecil

1980 STATISTICS

The following tables show the leading owners, trainers, breeders, jockeys, horses and the sires of winners during the 1980 season. Except for the list of sires, which relates to racing in both England and Ireland, these statistics refer only to racing under Jockey Club Rules. The tables are reproduced by permission of *The Sporting Life*.

OWNERS	Horses	Races Won	Stakes £
1. S. Weinstock	1	4	236,332
2. Mrs A. Plesch	1	3	186,198
3. K. Abdulla	10	20	161,442
4. R. Sangster	25	42	151,474
5. W. Barnett	3	6	137,304
6. O. Phipps	4	5	118,536
7. H. J. Joel	9	11	117,272
8. R. Hollingsworth	5	11	112,160
9. C. d'Alessio	8	14	111,148
10. R. Budgett	2	6	105,046
11. Moores International Furnishings Ltd	2	6	100,144
12. C. St George	14	21	99,623

TRAINERS	Horses	Races Won	Stakes £
1. W. Hern	38	65	831,964
2. H. Cecil	57	84	461,036
3. J. Dunlop	54	91	384,434
4. M. Stoute	54	101	372,679
5. J. Tree	15	30	225,558
6. R. Armstrong	18	29	206,751
7. P. Walwyn	43	78	203,175
8. G. Harwood	33	69	198,341
9. B. Hobbs	34	60	194,879
10. H. Candy	18	28	180,494
11. B. Hills	33	61	171,193
12. F. Durr	26	51	161,299

BREEDERS	Horses	Races Won	Stakes £
1. P. Clarke	2	5	237,435
2. Mrs J. G. Jones	1	3	186,198
3. W. and R. Barnett Ltd	5	15	170,644
4. O. Phipps	4	5	118,536
5. R. Hollingsworth	6	12	114,273
6. H. J. Joel	8	10	110,629
7. Dr Wm O. Reed	3	7	107,029
8. R. Budgett	2	6	105,046
9. J. Parker	1	5	97,584
10. E. J. Loder	6	14	87,903
11. Mrs Janet Brady	2	3	83,559
12. Ballymacoll Stud	10	13	78,787

JOCKEYS

		1st	2nd	3rd	Unpl	Total Mts	Per Cent
1.	W. Carson ..	166	135	109	442	852	19·48
2.	L. Piggott ..	156	96	65	318	635	24·56
3.	P. Eddery	130	118	114	492	854	15·22
4.	E. Hide	106	92	102	407	707	14·99
5.	J. Mercer	103	74	67	335	579	17·78
6.	P. Cook	90	95	57	466	708	12·71
7.	G. Starkey ..	82	67	78	384	611	13·42
8.	J. Reid	79	84	69	467	699	11·30
9.	G. Duffield ..	78	54	55	416	603	12·93
10.	M. Birch	71	62	61	382	576	12·32
11.	B. Raymond ..	62	52	47	395	520	11·92
12.	S. Cauthen ..	61	46	45	283	435	14·02

HORSES

		Races Won	Stakes £
1.	Ela-Mana-Mou (4 yrs) b.c. by Pitcairn—Rose Bertin	4	236,332
2.	Henbit (USA) (3 yrs) b.c. by Hawaii—Chateaucreek	3	186,198
3.	Moorestyle (3 yrs) b.c. by Manacle—Guiding Star	5	97,584
4.	Known Fact (USA) (3 yrs) b.c. by In Reality—Tamerett	4	96,263
5.	Light Cavalry (3 yrs) b.c. by Brigadier Gerard—Glass Slipper	3	95,673
6.	Master Willie (3 yrs) ch.c. by High Line—Fair Winter	2	89,285
7.	Bireme (3 yrs) ch.f. by Grundy—Ripeck ..	2	84,056
8.	Cairn Rouge (3 yrs) b.f. by Pitcairn—Little Hills	2	81,510
9.	Shoot A Line (3 yrs) b.f. by High Line—Death Ray	4	80,778
10.	Le Moss (5 yrs) ch.h. Le Levanstell—Feemoss ..	3	66,748
11.	Posse (USA) (3 yrs) ch.c. Forli—In Hot Pursuit ..	2	65,709
12.	Marwell (2 yrs) b.f. by Habitat—Lady Seymour ..	4	62,551

SIRES OF WINNERS

		Horses	Races Won	Stakes £
1.	Pitcairn (1971), by Petingo ..	10	16	391,651
2.	High Line (1966), by High Hat ..	14	32	324,753
3.	Blakeney (1966), by Hethersett ..	18	28	203,489
4.	Habitat (1966), by Sir Gaylord ..	29	52	203,119
5.	Sharpen Up (1969), by Atan ..	21	46	195,742
6.	Hawaii (1964), by Utrillo	1	3	186,198
7.	Great Nephew (1963), by Honeyway	23	35	176,743
8.	Grundy (1972), by Great Nephew	10	15	132,684
9.	Brigadier Gerard (1968), by Queen's Hussar	15	25	132,604
10.	Manacle (1964), by Sing Sing ..	12	21	130,847
11.	Mummy's Pet (1968), by Sing Sing	32	50	126,942
12.	In Reality (1964), by Intentionally	5	11	115,731

THE FREE HANDICAPS

TWO-YEAR-OLDS OF 1980

The following are the weights allotted in the Tote European Free Handicap published on 4th December. The race is to be run over seven furlongs at Newmarket on 15th April, 1981.

Horse	st	lb
Storm Bird	9	7
To-Agori-Mou	9	6
Robellino	9	2
Critique	9	1
Marwell	9	1
Recitation	9	1
Tolmi	9	1
Beldale Flutter	9	0
Gielgud	9	0
Cresta Rider	8	13
Cut Throat	8	13
Dunphy	8	13
Clear Verdict	8	12
Miswaki	8	12
Prince Mab	8	12
Sweet Monday	8	12
The Wonder	8	12
Ancient Regime	8	11
Exclusively Raised	8	11
Irish Playboy	8	11
Prince Echo	8	11
Welshwyn	8	11
Big John	8	10
Church Parade	8	10
Fairy Footsteps	8	10
Great Substence	8	10
Kalaglow	8	10
Leap Lively	8	10
Mariacho	8	10
Pushy	8	10
Arc d'Or	8	9
Lou Piguet	8	9
Mattaboy	8	9
Shergar	8	9
Shoen	8	9
Tropicaro	8	9
Another Realm	8	8
Bel Bolide	8	8
Chemin	8	8
Kittyhawk	8	8
Nasseem	8	8
Silken Knot	8	8
Tinas Pet	8	8
Troubetzkoy	8	8
Watchdog	8	8
Penmarric	8	7
Age Quod Agis	8	6
Kirtling	8	6
Swan Princess	8	6
Engulf	8	5
Parkdale	8	5
Poldhu	8	5
Salamina	8	5
Sheer Grit	8	5
Sula Bula	8	5
Will of Victory	8	5
McCarthy	8	4
Panjandrum	8	4
Star Pastures	8	4
Stats Emmar	8	4
Centurius	8	3
Chummy's Special	8	3
Flighting	8	3
Her Grace	8	3
Integrity	8	2
Noalto	8	2
Shasavaan	8	2
Vocalist	8	2
Ashbrittle	8	1
Bonnie Charlie	8	1
Cooliney Prince	8	1
Motavato	8	1
Soldan	8	1
Spark of Life	8	1
Vienna Miss	8	1
Chateau Dancer	8	0
Golden Bowl	8	0
Goodbye Starter	8	0
Madam Gay	8	0
Baz Bombati	7	13
Go Leasing	7	13
I'll See You	7	13
Sunley Builds	7	13
The Thatcher	7	13

	st	lb		st	lb
Tre Fontane	7	13	Rasa Penang	7	11
Wicked Will	7	13	Spindrifter	7	11
Admiral's Heir ..	7	12	The Quiet Bidder ..	7	11
Amorous	7	12	Allegretta	7	10
Cocaine	7	12	Belloc	7	10
Doc Marten	7	12	Blackfoot	7	10
Glyndebourne ..	7	12	Bold Raider	7	10
Krug	7	12	Chirk Castle	7	10
Moores Miracle ..	7	12	Doobie Do	7	10
Petroleuse	7	12	Glint of Gold ..	7	10
Appaloosa	7	11	Harp Strings	7	10
Bustomi	7	11	Ice Harbour	7	10
Fiesta Fun	7	11	Piperhill	7	10
Jamestino	7	11	Red Russet	7	10
King's General ..	7	11	Scintillating Air ..	7	10
Oraston	7	11	Tinjar	7	10
Pontin Lad	7	11	What Heaven	7	10

THREE-YEAR-OLDS OF 1980

The following handicap, published on 4th December, is for information only. The figures shown against each horse represent the official assessment of its merit against a norm of 100.

		st	lb			st	lb
Moorestyle ..	91	10	0	Water Mill ..	81	9	4
Known Fact ..	89	9	12	Dalsaan	80	9	3
Henbit	88	9	11	Huguenot ..	80	9	3
Posse	88	9	11	Quick As Lightning	80	9	3
Light Cavalry ..	87	9	10	Castle Keep ..	79	9	2
Hello Gorgeous ..	86	9	9	Shining Finish ..	79	9	2
Master Willie ..	86	9	9	Snow	79	9	2
Mrs Penny ..	86	9	9	Karamita ..	78	9	1
Sharpo	86	9	9	Runnett	78	9	1
Shoot A Line ..	86	9	9	Flash N Thunder	77	9	0
Tyrnavos	86	9	9	Dancing Shadow	76	8	13
Bireme	85	9	8	Lord Seymour ..	76	8	13
Cairn Rouge ..	85	9	8	Millingdale Lillie	76	8	13
Final Straw ..	85	9	8	World Leader ..	76	8	13
Last Fandango ..	84	9	7	Etoile De Paris ..	75	8	12
Little Bonny ..	84	9	7	Ginistrelli (USA) ..	75	8	12
African Song ..	83	9	6	Star Way	75	8	12
Monteverdi ..	83	9	6	Fingal's Cave ..	74	8	11
Prince Bee ..	83	9	6	Kashmir Lass ..	74	8	11
Rankin	83	9	6	Luck of the Draw	74	8	11
Kearney	82	9	5	Nocino	74	8	11
Night Alert ..	82	9	5	Sovereign Rose ..	74	8	11
Vielle	82	9	5	Sunfield	74	8	11
Hard Fought ..	81	9	4	Dukedom ..	73	8	10
Pelerin	81	9	4	Prince Roland ..	73	8	10
The Dancer ..	81	9	4	Saviour	73	8	10

Sayyaf	73	8	10	Evita	66	8	3
Bozovici	72	8	9	Johnny O'Day ..	66	8	3
Royal Fountain ..	72	8	9	Sentry Duty ..	66	8	3
Saint Jonathon ..	72	8	9	Try Sandicliffe ..	66	8	3
The Pug	72	8	9	Bay Street ..	65	8	2
Gift Wrapped ..	71	8	8	Durandal	65	8	2
Marathon Gold ..	71	8	8	Mother Earth ..	65	8	2
Etching	70	8	7	Muscovite ..	65	8	2
Hanu	70	8	7	Our Home ..	65	8	2
Moomba Masquerade ..	70	8	7	Pentaquod ..	65	8	2
Morayshire ..	70	8	7	Saint Osyth ..	65	8	2
Old Kate ..	70	8	7	Saville Row ..	65	8	2
Pace Jean ..	70	8	7	Artipiar	64	8	1
Premier Rose ..	70	8	7	Deadly Serious ..	64	8	1
Taufan	70	8	7	Missed Blessing ..	64	8	1
Te Kenawa ..	70	8	7	Paradise Bay ..	64	8	1
Battlewind ..	69	8	6	Playboy Jubilee ..	64	8	1
Blue Persian ..	69	8	6	Whitehall Bridge	64	8	1
Queen of Cornwall	69	8	6	Fine Sun ..	63	8	0
Winslow	69	8	6	New Jerusalem ..	63	8	0
Belmont Bay ..	68	8	5	Sparkling Boy ..	63	8	0
Bonol	68	8	5	Via Delta	63	8	0
Many Moons ..	68	8	5	April Bouquet ..	62	7	13
March Hywell ..	68	8	5	Braughing ..	62	7	13
Running Mill ..	68	8	5	Columnist ..	62	7	13
Shining Tor ..	68	8	5	Conbrian ..	62	7	13
Super Asset ..	68	8	5	Miner's Lamp ..	62	7	13
Astonished ..	67	8	4	Repetitious ..	62	7	13
Cracking Form ..	67	8	4	Suavity	62	7	13
Rontino	67	8	4	Westacombe ..	62	7	13
Stumped	67	8	4	King James ..	61	7	12
Trevita	67	8	4	Salubre	61	7	12
Vaguely Tender ..	67	8	4	Gillson	60	7	11
Verduret	67	8	4	Poyle Crusher ..	60	7	11
				Stanislavsky ..	60	7	11

FOUR-YEAR-OLDS AND UPWARDS, 1980

The following handicap, published on 4th December, is for information only. The figures shown against each horse represent the official assessment of its merit against a norm of 100.

Ela-Mana-Mou ..	90	10	0	Gregorian ..	83	9	7
Kris	89	9	13	Sea Chimes ..	82	9	6
Le Moss	89	9	13	Noelino	81	9	5
Nadjar	87	9	11	Cracaval ..	80	9	4
Ardross	86	9	10	More Light ..	80	9	4
Scorpio	86	9	10	Niniski	80	9	4
Nicholas Bill ..	84	9	8	Vaigly Great ..	80	9	4
Valeriga	84	9	8	Valour	80	9	4

Foveros	79	9	3	Bonnie Isle ..	70	8	8
Habituate ..	79	9	3	Greenland Park ..	70	8	8
Hardgreen ..	79	9	3	Haul Knight ..	70	8	8
Soleil Noir ..	79	9	3	Lightning Label ..	70	8	8
Welsh Chanter ..	79	9	3	Pragmatic ..	70	8	8
Abdu	78	9	2	Beggar's Bridge ..	69	8	7
Blue Refrain ..	78	9	2	Prince Rheingold	69	8	7
Gods Mark ..	76	9	0	Barley Hill ..	68	8	6
Son Fils ..	76	9	0	Billion	68	8	6
House Guard ..	75	8	13	Buttress	68	8	6
Kampala	75	8	13	Crews Hill ..	68	8	6
New Berry ..	75	8	13	Baronet	67	8	5
Sea Pigeon ..	75	8	13	Epsom Imp ..	67	8	5
Skyliner	75	8	13	Piaffer	67	8	5
King of Spain ..	74	8	12	Rhyme Royal ..	67	8	5
Lord Rochford ..	74	8	12	Standaan ..	67	8	5
Noble Saint ..	74	8	12	Heighlin	66	8	4
Arapahos ..	73	8	11	Torus	66	8	4
Beau Reef ..	73	8	11	Escovitch	65	8	3
Icelandic	73	8	11	Alert	64	8	2
Masked Marvel ..	73	8	11	Popsi's Joy ..	63	8	1
Balinger	72	8	10	Shady Nook ..	63	8	1
Captain Nick ..	72	8	10	Tender Heart ..	63	8	1
Gypsy Dancer ..	72	8	10	Vicomte	63	8	1
Susarma ..	72	8	10	Halyudh	62	8	0
Tahitian King ..	72	8	10	No Bombs ..	62	8	0
Golden River ..	71	8	9	Shaftesbury ..	62	8	0
R. B. Chesne ..	71	8	9	Cunard	60	7	12
Two of Diamonds	71	8	9	Majestic Maharaj	60	7	12
Vincent	71	8	9	Tin Soldier ..	60	7	12

ROBIN McENERY

M.V.B., M.R.C.V.S.

BLOODSTOCK AGENT

PURCHASING
INSURANCE — **COMPETITIVE RATES**
STALLION SHARES
NOMINATIONS
MANAGEMENT
MATING SELECTIONS
OVERSEAS INSPECTION
HORSES IN TRAINING

Managing:
IRISH STAR
by Relko—Chanter

$\frac{7}{8}$ths brother to French champion Breton

4th	Gr. I	Gran Premio di Milano
4th	Gr. III	Furstenberg Rennen
WON	Gr. III	Grosser Preis der Stadt Gelsenkirchen
2nd	Gr. I	Preis von Europa

Standing at Haggardstown Stud, Ireland.
Tel: Dundalk (042) 4390

THE ORCHARD, CROCKFORDS ROAD,
NEWMARKET, SUFFOLK CB8 9BG
Tel: NEWMARKET (0638) 3260 or **4838 (office)**
Telex: 817666 THI BGI

AN IRISH CLASSIFICATION 1980

THE TWO-YEAR-OLDS

Published on 4th December, for information only.

	st	lb
Storm Bird	9	7
Critique	9	1
Prince Echo	8	11
Kings Lake	8	8
Band Practice	8	7
Swan Princess	8	6
Cooliney Prince	8	5
Lawmaker	8	5
Lady Blackfoot	8	4
Rising Tide	8	4
Blue Wind	8	3
Martinova	8	3
Cooleen Jack	8	2
Euclid	8	2
Light Here	8	2
Sea of Echoes	8	2
Solo Star	8	2
Arctique Royale	8	1
Benefice	8	1
Clandestina	8	1
Crimson Heather	8	1
Brooklyn Prince	8	0
Lord Never	8	0
Personal Guard	8	0
British Gunner	7	13
Last Light	7	13
Wicked Will	7	13
Heart 'N Soul	7	12
Lady Tiffany	7	12
Lord Trendy	7	12
Master Thatch	7	12
Omer	7	12
Severiano	7	12
Cloonawillin	7	11
Singari	7	11
Tellurano	7	11
Arch Melody	7	10
Happy Bride	7	10
Lady Nightingale	7	10
Manaldo	7	10
Pergola	7	10
Red Nanda	7	10
Ring of Steel	7	10
What A Riot	7	10
Candle Hill	7	9
Happy Reprieve	7	9
Lone Bidder	7	9
Noble Monk	7	9
Condessa	7	8
Klewraye	7	8
Overplay	7	8
Swallanga	7	8
Van Lingen	7	8
Ascending Star	7	7
Bustineto	7	7
Corkstone Ace	7	7
Harveysfield	7	7
Indian Splash	7	7
Likely Sort	7	7
Maiacourt	7	7
Miltown Eagle	7	7
Passion Wagon	7	7
Top Pac	7	7
William Ashford	7	7
Wolver Heights	7	7

THREE-YEARS-OLDS OF 1980

The following ratings were published on 4th December for information only. The rating given to each horse represents the official assessment of its merit against a norm of 100.

Master Willie	86
Mrs Penny	86
Shoot A Line	86
Tyrnavos	86
Cairn Rouge	85
Final Straw	85
Nikoli	85
Last Fandango	84
Little Bonny	84
Monteverdi	83
Prince Bee	83
Rankin	83

Crofter	82	Etoile De Paris	75
Garrido	82	Gonzales	75
Kearney	82	Cobblers Cove	71
Night Alert	82	Opachisco	71
Corvaro	81	Sovereign Dona	71
Pelerin	81	Thousandfold	71
Huguenot	80	Galland	70
Quick As Lightning	80	Muscovite	69
Racquette	80	Milk of the Barley	67
Snow	79	Pitmarie	66
Ramian	76	Mice Bird	65
Calandra	75	Monroe	65
		Ringawoody	65

FOUR-YEAR-OLDS AND UPWARDS, 1980

The following ratings were published on 4th December for information only. The rating given to each horse represents the official assessment of its merit against a norm of 100.

Ardross	86	Habituate	79
Gregorian	83	Gods Mark	71
Spence Bay	82	Icelandic	68
Noelino	81	Jasmine Star	68
American Prince	80	My Hollow	68

THE FRENCH FREE HANDICAPS

TWO-YEAR-OLDS, 1980

The following are the weights allotted in the Handicap Libre, published on 11th December.

	st	lb
Critique	9	8
Recitation	9	8
Cresta Rider	9	6
Dunphy	9	6
Miswaki	9	5
Prince Mab	9	5
The Wonder	9	5
Ancient Regime ..	9	4
Irish Playboy	9	4
Big John	9	3
Great Substence ..	9	3
Mariacho	9	3
Arc d'Or	9	2
Lou Piguet	9	2
Shoen	9	2
Tropicaro	9	2
Troubetzkoy	9	1
Watchdog	9	1
Bernica	9	0
Diamond Prospect ..	9	0
Greenway	9	0
Ledmir	9	0
Vorias	9	0
Brinkbero	8	13
Mont Pelion	8	13
Phydilla	8	13
Silver Express ..	8	13
Votre Altesse	8	13
Ayaan	8	11
Bardenac	8	11
Coral Dance	8	11
In Tissar	8	11
Marie Noelle ..	8	11
Redoubtable	8	11
Riverdina	8	11
Salmana	8	11
Sharmada	8	11
Ukraine Girl	8	11
Age Quod Agis ..	8	10
Blue Wind	8	10
Dare You	8	10
Gilgit	8	10
Ionian Raja	8	10
Last Love	8	10
Marasali	8	10
Marie du Mont ..	8	10
Nijinsky's Secret ..	8	10
Rahotep	8	10
Running Back	8	10
Sun Row	8	10
Affection	8	9
Asania	8	9
Daumont	8	9
Godille	8	9
Lalaria	8	9
Maxim's Fair	8	9
Mourtazam	8	9
Silky Baby	8	9
Sonoma	8	9
Twig Prince	8	9
Tysfjsa	8	9

THREE-YEAR-OLDS, 1980

The following are the weights allotted in the Handicap Libre, published on 11th December.

	st	lb
Moorestyle	10	3
Argument	10	2
Nureyev	10	1
Detroit	10	0
Shakapour	10	0
Policeman	9	13
Mrs Penny	9	12
Sharpo	9	12
Adraan	9	11
Aryenne	9	11
Final Straw	9	11
Gold River	9	11

Horse	st	lb
Little Bonny	9	11
Valiant Heart	9	11
Glenorum	9	10
Prince Bee	9	10
Crofter	9	8
Garrido	9	8
In Fijar	9	8
Night Alert	9	8
Belgio	9	7
Corvaro	9	7
Manjam	9	7
Ruscelli	9	7
The Expatriate	9	7
What a Joy	9	7
Hortensia	9	6
Huguenot	9	6
Lancastrian	9	6
Mariella	9	6
Paranete	9	6
Ya Zaman	9	6
Luth de Saron	9	5
Moon Ingraver	9	5
Northjet	9	5
Sovereign Dona	9	5
Trevita	9	5
As You Desire Me	9	4
Benicia	9	4
Dhaubix	9	4
Dom d'Albignac	9	4
Good to Beat	9	4
Providential	9	4
Wild Idea	9	4
India Song	9	3
Joberan	9	3
Mot d'Or	9	3
Moulouki	9	3
Princesse Lida	9	3
Safita	9	3
Saint Jonathon	9	3
Torsom	9	3
Water Mill	9	3
Chicbury	9	2
Julius Caesar	9	2
Laquiola	9	2
Licara	9	2
Luck of the Draw	9	2
Luth Music	9	2
Nemr	9	2
Rhus	9	2
Axius	9	1
Blast Off	9	1

Horse	st	lb
Falamoun	9	1
La Toulzanie	9	1
Nice Havrais	9	1
Perrault	9	1
Suvero	9	1
Battlewind	9	0
Confetti	9	0
Deliballe	9	0
Divin Marquis	9	0
Firyal	9	0
Goldiko	9	0
Karelia	9	0
Pom Poes	9	0
Realeza	9	0
Rivermaid	9	0
Roymel	9	0
Saint Sever	9	0
Sea Boy	9	0
Speed Bus	9	0
Teacher's Pet	9	0
Tom's Serenade	9	0
Un Reitre	9	0
Zaramann	9	0
Alfalfa	8	13
Bobiffic	8	13
Dhausli	8	13
Dip	8	13
Doux Lord	8	13
Exactly So	8	13
Great Verdict	8	13
Indigene	8	13
Kareliaan	8	13
Maiymad	8	13
Multicolore	8	13
Noalcoholic	8	13
Proustille	8	13
Satilla	8	13
Viteric	8	13
Ayila	8	11
Balibest	8	11
Cavo Staras	8	11
Chatelain	8	11
Clodion	8	11
Dragon	8	11
First of the Line	8	11
Hortensio	8	11
Shannfara	8	11
Sir Raleigh	8	11
This Man	8	11
Trephine	8	11

FOUR-YEAR-OLDS AND UPWARDS, 1980

The following are the weights allotted in the Handicap Libre, published on 11th December.

Horse	st	lb
Ela-Mana-Mou	10	2
Le Marmot	10	1
Le Moss	10	1
Nebos	10	0
Nadjar	9	13
Three Troikas	9	13
Scorpio	9	12
Dunette	9	11
Kilijaro	9	11
Nicholas Bill	9	11
Shafaraz	9	11
Valeriga	9	11
Hard to Sing	9	10
Hilal	9	10
Northern Baby	9	10
Buckpoint	9	8
Prove it Baby	9	8
Boitron	9	7
High Sierra	9	7
Noelino	9	7
American Prince	9	6
Anifa	9	6
Baptism	9	6
Kamaridaan	9	6
Perouges	9	6
Son of Love	9	6
Tassmoun	9	6
Wolverton	9	6
Ardross	9	5
Discretion	9	5
Kaldoun	9	5
Katowice	9	5
Kelbomec	9	5
Monsieur Marcel	9	5
Foveros	9	4
Rostov	9	4

Horse	st	lb
Gain	9	3
House Guard	9	3
Marson	9	3
River River	9	3
African Hope	9	2
Cherubin	9	2
En Calcat	9	2
Manguin	9	2
Marracci	9	2
Vincent	9	2
Dernier Violon	9	1
Soleil Noir	9	1
Arnol	9	0
Boucicault	9	0
Narablue	9	0
Natchitoches	9	0
Rolling Bowl	9	0
Sheikdom	9	0
Jeune Loup	8	13
King Crimson	8	13
Liki Liki	8	13
Monsieur Dagobert	8	13
Prince Melchior	8	13
San Rosario	8	13
Standaan	8	13
Strong Gale	8	13
Callio	8	11
Dauphin du Roi	8	11
Gosport	8	11
Indoor	8	11
Iseo	8	11
Planing	8	11
Prince Thatch	8	11
Stout Fellow	8	11
Yvonand	8	11

AN INTERNATIONAL CLASSIFICATION, 1980

The following ratings for horses which ran in France, Great Britain or Ireland were allotted jointly by the official Handicappers concerned and published on 4th December. The rating given to each horse represents the official assessment of its merit against a norm of 100.

TWO-YEAR-OLDS, 1980

Storm Bird	88
To-Agori-Mou	87
Robellino	83
Critique	82
Marwell	82
Recitation	82
Tolmi	82
Beldale Flutter	81
Gielgud	81
Cresta Rider	80
Cut Throat	80
Dunphy	80
Clear Verdict	79
Miswaki	79
Prince Mab	79
Sweet Monday	79
The Wonder	79
Ancient Regime	78
Exclusively Raised	78
Irish Playboy	78
Prince Echo	78
Welshwyn	78
Big John	77
Church Parade	77
Fairy Footsteps	77
Great Substence	77
Kalaglow	77
Leap Lively	77
Mariacho	77
Pushy	77
Arc D'Or	76
Lou Piguet	76
Mattaboy	76
Shergar	76
Shoen	76
Tropicaro	76
Another Realm	75
Bel Bolide	75
Chemin	75
Kittyhawk	75
Nasseem	75
Silken Knot	75
Tina's Pet	75
Troubetzkoy	75
Watchdog	75

THREE-YEAR-OLDS, 1980

Moorestyle	91
Argument	90
Known Fact	89
Nureyev	89
Detroit	88
Henbit	88
Posse	88
Shakapour	88
Light Cavalry	87
Policeman	87
Hello Gorgeous	86
Master Willie	86
Mrs Penny	86
Sharpo	86
Shoot A Line	86
Tyrnavos	86
Adraan	85
Aryenne	85
Bireme	85
Cairn Rouge	85
Final Straw	85
Gold River	85
Nikoli	85
Valiant Heart	85
Last Fandango	84
Little Bonny	84
African Song	83
Glenorum	83
Monteverdi	83
Prince Bee	83
Rankin	83
Crofter	82

Garrido	82	The Expatriate	81
In Fijar	82	Water Mill	81
Kearney	82	What A Joy	81
Night Alert	82	Dalsaan	80
Vielle	82	Hortensia	80
Belgio	81	Huguenot	80
Corvaro	81	Lancastrian	80
Hard Fought	81	Mariella	80
Manjam	81	Quick As Lightning	80
Pelerin	81	Paranete	80
Ruscelli	81	Racquette	80
The Dancer	81	Ya Zaman	80

FOUR-YEAR-OLDS AND UPWARDS, 1980

Ela-Mana-Mou	90	Prove It Baby	82
Kris	89	Sea Chimes	82
Le Marmot	89	Spence Bay	82
Le Moss	89	Boitron	81
Nebos	88	High Sierra	81
Nadjar	87	Noelino	81
Three Troikas	87	American Prince	80
Ardross	86	Anifa	80
Scorpio	86	Baptism	80
Dunette	85	Cracaval	80
Kilijaro	85	Kamaridaan	80
Nicholas Bill	84	More Light	80
Shafaraz	84	Niniski	80
Valeriga	84	Perouges	80
Gregorian	83	Son Of Love	80
Hard To Sing	83	Tassmoun	80
Hilal	83	Vaigly Great	80
Northern Baby	83	Valour	80
Buckpoint	82	Wolverton	80

ERRATA & ADDENDA "RACEHORSES OF 1979"

Choucri (**Can**)	beaten 2½ lengths in Prix de la Salamandre
Eastern Wind	Windy Glen (by Wolver Hollow)
J.E.B. Stuart (**USA**)	was a colt
Kris	p377 grandam is Rocchetta
Last Request	dam won twice over 1¼m
Many Moons (**Fr**)	foaled Apr 9
Moor House	dam is Asicion
Noble Saint (**USA**)	line 7 maiden race at Newbury
Prince of Padua	dam won over 5f
Sea Pigeon (**USA**)	line 10 for the race this century,
Shakapour	dam is Shamim
Valdee	sold 2,800 gns

RACING ABROAD

1 PRIX EDMOND BLANC 1m
£14,629 Saint-Cloud 13 March

Wolverton 4-9-0 F Head....**1**
Kaldoun 5-9-0 JHeloury..½.**2**
Hilal 4-9-0 A Gibert.....2½.**3**
Gosport 4-9-0 J-CDesaint.5.4
Blinette 4-8-11 ALequeux.2.5
Planing 4-9-0 J-P-AGodard 6.6
Darling Dale 4-8-11 HSamani 2.7
Miss Bessie 4-8-11 ABadel ¾.8

6/4 Kaldoun, 17/10 WOLVERTON, 4/1 Hilal, 6/1 Blinette, 12/1 Planing, 35/1 Darling Dale, 40/1 Miss Bessie, 43/1 Gosport.
J. Wertheimer (A. Head) 8rn 1m 56.2 (Heavy).

2 PRIX EXBURY 1¼m
£14,629 Saint-Cloud 22 March

Kamaridaan 4-8-12 HSamani **1**
Anifa 4-8-13 AGibert.....6.**2**
Son of Love 4-9-6 GDubroeucq nk.**3**
Cherubin 5-9-0 JDupin....½.4
Monsieur Marcel 4-9-0 M-LDureuil ½.5
Monsieur Dagobert 4-9-0 MPhilipperon 1½.6
Strong Gale 5-8-12 FHead.6.7
Yvonand 4-9-0 MJerome...¾.8
Wild Oats 5-9-0 JTaillard..5.9
Louksor 5-9-0 J-CDesaint.8.10
Telescopico 5-9-0 ALequeux 11
1 Gosport 4-9-4 APerrotta...12

2/1 Anifa and Telescopico, 46/10 KAMARIDAAN, 5/1 Cherubin, 17/2 Strong Gale, 35/4 Louksor, 9/1 Son of Love, 10/1 Monsieur Marcel, 15/1 Monsieur Dagobert, 17/1 Yvonand, 27/1 Gosport, 34/1 Wild Oats.
H.H. Aga Khan (F. Mathet) 12rn 2m 23.6 (Soft).

3 PRIX PENELOPE 3y 1m 2½f
£14,629 Saint-Cloud 29 March

Good to Beat 8-11 RJallu...**1**
Proustille 8-11 MPhilipperon ½.**2**
Akinoa 8-11 APerrotta....1.**3**
Lorelta 8-11 J-LKessas....4.4
Paranete 8-11 AGibert.....3.5
Belle d'Avril 8-11 FHead 2½.6
La Grande Coudre 8-11 YSaint-Martin ¾.7
Tarsiere 8-11 MJerome....**4**.8
Bev Bev 8-11 J-CDesaint..5.9
Deliballe 8-11 ABadel...1½.10
Indigene 8-11 J-PLefevre....0
Forbidden Fruit 8-11 JHeloury 0
Spoilt Miss 8-11 PPaquet....0
Tudor Diamond 8-11 FPegurri 0

7/2 Paranete, 9/2 Bev Bev, 6/1 La Grande Coudre, 13/2 Proustille, 15/2 Indigene, 8/1 Belle d'Avril, 13/1 Spoilt Miss, 16/1 Tarsiere, 17/1 GOOD TO BEAT, 19/1 Akinoa, 30/1 Tudor Diamond, 33/1 Deliballe, 41/1 Lorelta, 50/1 Forbidden Fruit.
H. d'Aillieres (H. d'Aillieres) 14rn 2m 35.4 (Heavy).

4 PRIX DE FONTAINEBLEAU 3y 1m
£15,512 Longchamp 7 April

Nice Havrais 9-2 FHead....**1**
Confetti 9-2 HSamani...nk.**2**
Un Reitre 9-2 PPaquet...nk.**3**
Koboko 9-2 MPhilipperon.½.4
In Fijar 9-2 A Gibert.....1½.5
The Expatriate 9-2 JDupin 1½.6
Adraan 9-2 YSaint-Martin 1.7
Choucri 9-2 ALequeux....1.8
Ruscelli 9-2 ABadel......10.9

14/10 NICE HAVRAIS, 7/2 Un Reitre, 6/1 Confetti, 9/1 Choucri, In Fijar, 10/1 Adraan, 15/1 Koboko, 21/1 Ruscelli, 39/1 The Expatriate.
A. Clore (F. Boutin) 9rn 1m 45 (Good).

5 PRIX D'HARCOURT 1¼m
£20,683 Longchamp 7 April

Three Troikas 4-9-1 FHead.**1**
Gain 4-8-12 ALequeux...1½.**2**
Le Marmot 4-9-2 PPaquet hd.**3**
2* Kamaridaan 4-9-0 YSaint-Martin hd.4
High Sierra 4-9-2 MJerome s.hd.5
2³ Son of Love 4-9-4 GDubroeucq 4.6
2 Louksor 5-8-12 J-CDesaint hd.7

7/10 THREE TROIKAS, 5/2 Le Marmot, 9/2 Kamaridaan, 14/1 Son of Love, 17/1 High Sierra, 26/1 Gain, 41/1 Louksor.
Mme A. Head (Mme C. Head) 7 rn 2m 10.6 (Good).

6 PRIX DE BARBEVILLE 1m 7½f
£15,512 Longchamp 7 April

Hard To Sing 4-8-11 GDoleuze **1**
Marlion 6-8-11 FHead 5.**2**
Kelbomec 4-8-11 J-CDesaint 4.**3**
2 Monsieur Dagobert 4-8-11 APerrotta 2½.4
Prove It Baby 4-8-13 PPaquet nk.6
2[2] Anifa 4-8-10 AGibert . . . s.nk.7
Stout Fellow 4-8-11 J-LKessas 5.8
Stetchworth (USA) 4-8-11 ALequeux 6.9
Marson 5-8-13 YSaint-Martin 1½.10
Slimy 6-8-11 JDupin 0
San Rosario 7-8-11 HSamani 0
Croque Monsieur 6-8-11 J-PLefevre 0
Shafaraz 7-8-11 MPhilipperon . . . . disq.

11/4 Anifa, 17/4 HARD TO SING, 11/2 Stout Fellow, 13/2 Stetchworth, 67/10 Shafaraz, 11/1 Kelbomec, 13/1 Prove It Baby, 17/1 Marson, 20/1 Marlion, 22/1 Croque Monsieur, 33/1 Monsieur Dagobert, 39/1 San Rosario, 40/1 Slimy.

Shafaraz finished first, 2 lengths in front of Hard To Sing, but was subsequently disqualified for failing a dope test.

N. Lathom-Sharp (C. Milbank) 13rn 3m 28 (Good).

7 PRIX IMPRUDENCE 3y 7f
£6,205 Maisons-Laffitte 8 April

Firyal 9-2 PPaquet **1**
Licara 9-2 YSaint-Martin 3.**2**
Dellear 9-2 J-PLefevre . . nk.**3**
Inner Pearl 9-2 GDoleuze . . ¾.4
Teacher's Pet 9-2 HSamani s.nk.5
Bold Green 9-2 PLagoutte s.hd.6
Souristane 9-2 JHeloury . . hd.7
Selerina 9-2 FHead 6.8

Evens FIRYAL and Bold Green, 7/2 Teacher's Pet, 15/4 Licara, 25/4 Selerina, 12/1 Dellear, 13/1 Inner Pearl, 22/1 Souristane.

S. Niarchos (F. Boutin) 8 rn 1m 28 (Dead).

8 PRIX DJEBEL 3y 7f
£6,205 Maisons-Laffitte 8 April

Nureyev 9-2 PPaquet **1**
Viteric 9-2 AGibert 6.**2**
Royal Pleasure 9-2 YSaint-Martin 3.**3**
Prince Dias 9-2 GDoleuze 1½.4
Timely Bidder 9-2 PLagoutte 10.5
Clodion 9-2 MPhilipperon 2½.6

2/10 NUREYEV and Timely Bidder, 13/4 Viteric, 11/1 Prince Dias, Royal Pleasure, 17/1 Clodion.

S. Niarchos (F. Boutin) 6rn 1m 27.5 (Dead).

9 PREMIO PARIOLI 3y 1m
£15,488 Rome 7 April

Red Rocket 9-2 SDettori . . . **1**
Manet 9-2 GPucciatti 1¼.**2**
Sea's Valley 9-2 SFancera hd.**3**
Levanto 9-2 LBietolini . s.nk.4
Royal Brook 9-2 GDettori . . ¾.5
Godot 9-2 ADiNardo 3.6
Berruguete 9-2 OPessi 5.7
Avilov 9-2 VPanici 1.8
Akedoro 9-2 PPerlanti 1.9

6/4 Sea's Valley, 2/1 Godot, 7/2 Royal Brook, 9/2 Berruguete, 5/1 RED ROCKET, 12/1 Avilov, 20/1 Levanto, 22/1 Manet, 33/1 Akedoro.

Scuderia El-Vi (A. Pandolfi) 9rn 1m 43 (Good).

10 PRIX DE LA GROTTE 3y 1m
£15,674 Longchamp 13 April

Aryenne 9-2 MPhilipperon . . **1**
Princesse Lida 9-2 FHead nk.**2**
Pom Poes 9-2 AGibert . . 2½.**3**
Shannfara 9-2 YSaint-Martin 1.4
La Vreeland 9-2 PPaquet . . 2½.5
La Nobleza 9-2 HSamani . 2½.6
Charles Bridge 9-2 GDoleuze 8.7
Etoile d'Orient 9-2 RJallu . . 1.8

8/10 Princess Lida and Etoile d'Orient, 28/10 ARYENNE, 23/4 Shannfara, 9/1 Pom Poes, 15/1 La Nobleza, La Vreeland, 36/1 Charles Bridge.

D. G. Volkert (J. Fellows) 8rn 1m 39.7 (Good to Firm).

11 PRIX GREFFULHE 3y 1m 2½f
£26,123 Longchamp 13 April

Providential 9-2 PPaquet . . . **1**
Blast Off 9-2 MPhilipperon 1½.**2**
Bobiffic 9-2 GDubroeucq s.hd.**3**
First of the Line 9-2 FHead . ¾.4
Garrido 9-2 ALequeux . . s.hd.5
Dhausli 9-2 J-LKessas ¾.6
Goldiko 9-2 YSaint-Martin . ¾.7
Duncen Grant 9-2 HSamani 2.8
Jurisconsulte 9-2 AGibert . 1½.9
Pharnace 9-2 J-PLefevre . 2.10

9/10 PROVIDENTIAL, 3/1 First

of the Line, 9/2 Goldiko, 11/1 Bobiffic, 20/1 Dhausli, 22/1 Blast Off, Jurisconsulte, 33/1 Garrido, 48/1 Duncen Grant, 54/1 Pharnace.
S. Fradkoff (F. Boutin) 10rn 2m 13.1 (Good to Firm).

12 PRIX DE RIS-ORANGIS 1m
£12,539 Evry 17 April

Nadjar 4-8-12 YSaint-Martin **1**
Boitron 4-9-0 PPaquet....¾.**2**
1 **Planing** 4-9-2 J-P-AGodard s.hd.**3**
1[3] Hilal 4-8-12 AGibert....s.hd.4
1* Wolverton 4-9-0 FHead...2.5
Flying Ace 4-8-12 ALequeux ½.6
Player 4-8-12 GDoleuze....5 7

7/4 Boitron, Wolverton, 57/10 NADJAR, 15/2 Hilal, 16/1 Planing, 20/1 Flying Ace, Player.
G. Schjelderup (A. Paus) 7rn 1m 36.7 (Good).

13 PRIX D'HEDOUVILLE 1½m
£11,458 Longchamp 20 April

Scorpio 4-9-2 PPaquet.....**1**
6 **Monsieur Dagobert** 4-8-10 MPhilipperon....4.**2**
Soleil Noir 4-9-2 YSaint-Martin 1½.**3**
African Hope 5-8-12 ALequeux.............½.4
Son of Love 4-9-2 GDubroeucq 1½.5
Atilla the Hun 5-8-7 AGibert 8.6
Perouges 5-8-12 JLeDeunf 2.7

16/10 SCORPIO, 5/2 Soleil Noir, 4/1 Son of Love, 15/2 Perouges, 9/1 African Hope, 15/1 Atilla the Hun, 19/1 Monsieur Dagobert.
G. A. Oldham (F. Boutin) 7rn 2m 33.4 (Good).

14 PRIX VANTEAUX 3y 1m 1½f
£15,625 Longchamp 20 April

Luth de Saron 9-2 MPhilipperon **1**
Benicia 9-2 FHead......hd.**2**
3 **Paranete** 9-2 AGibert....1.**3**
3* Good To Beat 9-2 RJallu..............s.hd.4
Deep Music 9-2 PPaquet..½.5
3[2] Proustille 9-2 APerrotta....½.6
3[3] Akinoa 9-2 J-CDesaint....1.7
La Vedrelle 9-2 JHeloury.ns.8
3 Lorelta 9-2 J-LKessas...s.nk.9
3 Indigene 9-2 J-PLefevre.1½.10
3 Belle d'Avril 9-2 ABadel.....0
3 La Grande Coudre 9-2 YSaint-Martin 0
Zolinana 9-2 FPegurri.......0

5/4 Benicia, 49/10 LUTH DE SARON, 11/2 Good To Beat, 10/1 La Grande Coudre, 14/1 Deep Music, 17/1 Indigene, Paranete, Zolinana, 19/1 Proustille, 21/1 Akinoa, 23/1 Belle d'Avril, 39/1 Lorelta, 97/1 La Vedrelle.
P. de Moussac (J. Cunnington, jnr) 13 rn 2m 3.7 (Good).

15 PRIX NOAILLES 3y 1m 3f
£26,042 Longchamp 20 April

Julius Caesar 9-2 HSamani **1**
Dom Aldo 9-2 GDoleuze nk.**2**
Grandak 9-2 JDupin.......**3**
Kareliaan 9-2 YSaint-Martin 4
Belgio 9-2 MPhilipperon.s.hd.5
Saint Sever 9-2 FHead....2.6
Bardamu 9-2 J-CDesaint.1½.7
Dragon 9-2 AGibert......1.8
4[3] Un Reitre 9-2 PPaquet.....2.9
Tropical Lightning 9-2 ALequeux...........10.10
Good Laugh 9-2 FPegurri 11

6/4 Un Reitre, 2/1 Kareliaan, 13/2 Dragon, 11/1 Dom Aldo, 12/1 Saint Sever, 19/1 Belgio, 20/1 Tropical Lightning, 28/1 Grandak, 34/1 Bardamu, 46/1 JULIUS CAESAR, 81/1 Good Laugh.
Kareliaan finished third, a head behind Dom Aldo and 1½ lengths in front of Grandak, but after an objection for interference was placed fourth and Grandak promoted to third.
R. W. Dilley (S. Boullenger) 11rn 2m 19.9 (Good).

16 PRIX DE GUICHE 3y 1m 1¾f
£15,625 Longchamp 20 April

Shakapour 9-2 YSaint-Martin...........**1**
Corvaro 9-2 PPaquet.....2.**2**
Policeman 9-2 GDoleuze nk.**3**
Dip 9-2 FHead...........½.4
Shape 9-2 J-CDesaint....¾.5
Popset 9-2 AGibert.......6.6
Jacinbar 9-2 ABadel.......5.7

7/4 Corvaro 9/4 Shape, 7/2 Dip, 37/10 SHAKAPOUR, 9/1 Policeman, 30/1 Jacinbar, 35/1 Popset.
H.H. Aga Khan (F. Mathet) 7rn 2m 5.6 (Good).

17 POULE D'ESSAI DES POULAINS 3y 1m
£36,496 Longchamp 27 April

4 **In Fijar** 9-2 GDoleuze.....**1**
Moorestyle 9-2 LPiggott..1.**2**
Argument 9-2 J-CDesaint..**3**

4^2 Confetti 9-2 J-LKessas....1.4
Joberan 9-2 JDupin.......2.6
15 Dragon 9-2 AGibert....s.nk.7
Norwegian 9-2 HSamani.s.nk.8
4* Nice Havrais 9-2 FHead...¾.9
Ice Plant 9-2 PPaquet...nk.10
4 Koboko 9-2 MPhilipperon 11
4 Choucri 9-2 ALequeux.....12
Numas 9-2 RCochrane.....13
4 Ruscelli 9-2 YSaint-Martin ....disq.

7/4 Nice Havrais, 19/4 Moorestyle, 52/10 Dragon and IN FIJAR, 19/2 Koboko, 9/1 Confetti, 37/4 Ruscelli, 12/1 Choucri, 13/1 Argument, 21/1 Norwegian, 23/1 Joberan, 28/1 Ice Plant, 99/1 Numas.

Ruscelli finished third, a head behind Moorestyle and 1½ lengths in front of Argument, but after a stewards inquiry was disqualified and placed last for interference. Argument was promoted to third.

M. Fustok (M. Saliba) 13rn 1m 38.4 (Good).

18 PRIX JEAN PRAT 1m 7½f
£20,855 Longchamp 27 April

6* **Hard To Sing** 4-9-0 GDoleuze **1**
6 **Prove It Baby** 4-9-0 PPaquet nk.**2**
6*(dis) **Shafaraz** 7-8-12 MPhilipperon ½.**3**
Marriageable 6-8-12 J-P-AGodard 1.4
13 African Hope 5-9-0 ALequeux ¾.5
6 Stout Fellow 4-8-12 J-LKessas 2.6
6^2 Marlion 6-8-12 FHead....½.7
6 Croque Monsieur 6-8-12 J-PLefevre 6.8
Montjardin 4-8-12 GDubroeucq 6.9

2/1 Shafaraz, 3/1 African Hope, 32/10 HARD TO SING, 27/4 Prove It Baby, 37/4 Marlion, 16/1 Stout Fellow, 19/1 Croque Monsieur, 28/1 Marriageable, 36/1 Montjardin.

N. Lathom-Sharp (C. Milbank) 9rn 3m 24.9 (Good).

19 PRIX CORRIDA 1m 2½f
£14,599 Saint-Cloud 28 April

Ho Han Wai 4-9-0 ALequeux **1**
Blinette 4-9-0 YSaint-Martin.s.hd.**2**
Liki Liki 4-9-0 J-CDesaint.2.**3**
New Grandame 5-9-0 PPaquet......s.nk.4
Indoor 4-9-2 MJerome..ns.5
Miss Mouse 4-9-0 MPhilipperon 1.6
Give Off 4-9-0 J-LKessas..4.7
Rouchiza 4-8-12 HSamani..6.8
Sealy 4-9-2 FHead........4.9
Yamba 4-9-0 MGentile.dist.10
6 Anifa 4-9-2 AGibert......u.r

2/1 Liki Liki, 3/1 Anifa, 5/1 Sealy, 9/1 Give Off, Indoor, 10/1 Blinette, 14/1 Miss Mouse, 18/1 HO HAN WAI, 30/1 New Grandame, Yamba, 40/1 Rouchiza.

Sir D. Clague (A. Paus) 11rn 2m 21.1 (Good).

20 PRIX DU MUGUET 1m
£14,599 Saint-Cloud 1 May

American Prince 4-8-12 CRoche **1**
12 **Hilal** 4-8-8 GDoleuze....½.**2**
1^2 **Kaldoun** 5-8-8 JHeloury..3.**3**
Callio 4-9-2 ALequeux.s.nk.4
5 Louksor 5-8-8 J-CDesaint..1.5
12* Nadjar 4-8-12 FHead.....2.6
Trio Boy 4-8-8 MJerome..1.7
12^2 Boitron 4-8-12 GDubroeucq 8.8

9/4 Nadjar, 13/4 Boitron, 7/2 Kaldoun, 13/2 AMERICAN PRINCE, 15/2 Hilal, 11/1 Callio, Louksor, 17/1 Trio Boy.

B. F. Bacharach (S. Murless, Ireland) 8rn 1m 37.2 (Dead).

21 POULE D'ESSAI DES POULICHES 3y 1m
£36,649 Longchamp 4 May

10* **Aryenne** 9-2 MPhilipperon.**1**
Safita 9-2 YSaint-Martin s.hd.**2**
10^2 **Princesse Lida** 9-2 FHead 1½.**3**
7 Teacher's Pet 9-2 HSamani s.hd.4
14 La Grande Coudre 9-2 GDubroeucq 2.5
Kifissia 9-2 J-CDesaint....4.6

9/10 Princesse Lida, 13/10 ARYENNE and Kifissia, 17/4 Safita, 16/1 Teacher's Pet, 21/1 La Grande Coudre.

D. G. Volkert (J. Fellows) 6rn 1m 43.6 (Dead).

22 PRIX GANAY 1m 2½f
£41,885 Longchamp 4 May

5^3 **Le Marmot** 4-9-2 PPaquet..**1**
5* **Three Troikas** 4-8-13 FHead 1½.**2**
Northern Baby 4-9-2 PEddery **3**.**3**
5^2 Gain 4-9-2 ALequeux.....2.4
5 High Sierra 4-9-2 MJerome.5.5
12^3 Planing 4-9-2 J-P-AGodard 6.6

3/10 Three Troikas, 46/10 LE MARMOT, 35/4 Northern Baby,

19/2 Gain, 12/1 High Sierra, 28/1 Planing.
R. Schafer (F. Boutin) 6rn 2m 15.0 (Dead).

23 PRIX MATCHEM 3y 1m 1f
£8,337 Evry 10 May

Axius 9-0 J-LKessas.......**1**
16 **Dip** 8-12 HSamani.........1.**2**
16[3] **Policeman** 8-12 GDoleuze 1.**3**
Aliyoun 9-0 YSaint-Martin.½.4
16 Shape 9-0 J-CDesaint....1½.5
17 Ice Plant 9-0 PPaquet...ns.6
11 Jurisconsulte 9-0 MPhilipperon ¾.7
Divin Marquis 9-2 JTaillard s.nk.8
Clericy 9-0 FHead........4.9
Spaten 9-0 ALequeux....4.10

15/4 Dip, Shape, 17/4 Policeman, 5/1 Aliyoun, 15/2 Clericy, 9/1 AXIUS, 10/1 Ice Plant, 13/1 Jurisconsulte, 14/1 Divin Marquis, 17/1 Spaten.
Mlle E. de Waldner (J. M. de Choubersky) 10rn 1m 49.3 (Good).

24 GRAND PRIX D'EVRY 1½m
£20,942 Evry 10 May

13* **Scorpio** 4-9-5 PPaquet.....**1**
22 **Gain** 4-8-9 ALequeux..s.nk.**2**
Dunette 4-9-2 GDoleuze..2.**3**
13[3] Soleil Noir 4-9-5 YSaint-Martin 3.4
Jeune Loup 5-8-9 FHead..½.5
19[3] Liki Liki 4-8-7 J-CDesaint 1½.6
Valour 5-9-5 JReid........3.7
6 San Rosario 7-8-9 EBarelli 15.8

17/10 SCORPIO, 13/4 Gain, 11/2 Soleil Noir, 7/1 Dunette, 31/4 Jeune Loup. 9/1 San Rosario, 10/1 Valour, 19/1 Liki Liki.
G. A. Oldham (F. Boutin) 8rn 2m 27.0 (Good).

25 PRIX HOCQUART 3y 1½m
£31,381 Longchamp 11 May

Mot D'Or 9-2 FHead......**1**
11* **Providential** 9-2 PPaquet s.nk.**2**
15 **Belgio** 9-2 MPhilipperon.2.**3**
16* Shakapour 9-2 YSaint-Martin ns.4
11[3] Bobiffic 9-2 GDubroeucq.3.5
15* Julius Caesar 9-2 HSamani.2.6
Moulouki 9-2 AGibert.s.nk.7
Fabulous Prince 9-2 GDoleuze 2.8
Daroda 9-2 ABredillet....8.9
Lord Jack 9-2 J-PLefevre ½.10
Dom Savary 9-2 PLagoutte..0
Na Fer 9-2 AGoldsztejn.....0

5/4 Providential and Dom Savary, 3/1 Shakapour, 6/1 Moulouki and Na Fer 83/10 MOT D'OR, 17/2 Julius Caesar, 12/1 Belgio, 22/1 Bobiffic, 28/1 Fabulous Prince, 35/1 Lord Jack, 47/1 Daroda.
J. Wertheimer (A. Head) **12rn** 2m 32.0 (Good to Firm).

26 PRIX DE SAINT-GEORGES 5f
£15,690 Longchamp 11 May

4 **Adraan** 3-8-13 YSaint-Martin **1**
Miliar 3-8-9 GDoleuze....3.**2**
Greenland Park 4-8-13 JReid 2.**3**
20 Trio Boy 4-9-4 MJerome..1½.4
Manjam 3-8-13 AGibert...¾.5
Kilijaro 4-8-13 HSamani..2.6
Kiss The Clowns 3-8-6 MPhilipperon 2.7

6/4 Kilijaro, 11/4 Manjam and Miliar, 28/10 ADRAAN, 21/4 Greenland Park, 15/1 Trio Boy, 16/1 Kiss The Clowns.
H. H. Aga Khan (F. Mathet) 7rn 55.5 sec (Good to Firm).

27 PREMIO EMANUELE FILIBERTO 3y 1¼m
£10,320 Milan 20 April

Lotar 9-2 PPerlanti........**1**
Pareo 9-2 GDettori hd.**2**
Pian del Lupo 9-2 SAtzori.8.**3**
9 Royal Brook 9-2 GStarkey..6.4
Spirit of Crow 9-2 VPanici.3.5
Ober 9-2 ADiNardo......6.6

1/10 Pareo, 4/1 LOTAR, 10/1 Ober, 20/1 Royal Brook, 30/1 Pian del Lupo, 40/1 Spirit of Crow.
Scuderia dell'Abete Blu (A. Botti) 6rn 2m 04.4 (Good).

28 PREMIO REGINA ELENA 3y 1m
£15,480 Rome 25 April

Tibalda 8-11 OPessi.......**1**
Cos Display 8-11 GDettori 1.**2**
Katalina Girl 8-11 MMassimi 7.**3**
Adolfina 8-11 PPerlanti....3.4
Sandford Linda 8-11 MDepalmas nk.5
Alcana 8-11 LBietolini...1½.6
Uliana di Trer 8-11 PWray 2½.7
Tourinfore 8-11 GPucciatti 3.8
Opera Italiana 8-11 SFancera 1.9
Gentle Age 8-11 LFicuciello 2.10
Love Me Tight 8-11 GDoleuze 4.11

4/5 TIBALDA, 6/4 Cos Display, 9/2 Opera Italiana and Tourinfore,

8/1 Love Me Tight, 20/1 Sandford Linda, 22/1 Adolfina, 33/1 Katalina Girl, 50/1 Alcana, 80/1 Uliana di Trer, 100/1 Gentle Age.

Razza Dormello-Olgiata (U. Pandolfi) 11rn 1m 43.4 (Heavy).

29 PREMIO ELLINGTON 1½m
£6,753 Rome 9 May

Sifounas 4-9-2 MDepalmas . **1**

Mazzanti 4-9-2 GDettori . . 3.**2**

Van der Linden 4-9-2 SAtzori 1¾.**3**

Quadrupler 4-8-13 VPanici . 2.4

Be Regal 4-9-2 LFicuciello 10.5

5/6 Mazzanti and Be Regal, 7/4 SIFOUNAS, 2/1 Quadrupler, 5/1 Van der linden.

W. Sommer (F. Boutin) 5 rn 2m 32.4 (Good).

30 DERBY ITALIANO 3y 1½m
£36,232 Rome 11 May

11 **Garrido** 9-2 MDepalmas . . . **1**

27^{3} **Pian del Lupo** 9-2 PPerlanti 2½.**2**

9^{3} **Sea's Valley** 9-2 SFancera nk.**3**

9★ Red Rocket 9-2 WCarson . 2½.4

Deauville 9-2 GDettori ½.5

Scouting Miller 9-2 JMercer 6.6

Lanai 9-2 MMassimi nk.7

9^{2} Manet 9-2 GPucciatti ½.8

Narvaez 9-2 OPessi 5.9

Lucumone 9-2 ADiNardo 5.10

Trash 9-2 LPiggott 4.11

Arnhem 9-2 VPanici 1.12

Albert Tota 9-2 CCastaldi 10.13

4/6 GARRIDO and Narvaez, 2/1 Deauville, 6/1 Sea's Valley and Scouting Miller, 13/2 Red Rocket, 7/1 Trash, 8/1 Manet, 10/1 Pian del Lupo, 28/1 Lucumone, 30/1 Albert Tota, 33/1 Arnhem, 40/1 Lanai.

Razza Dormello - Olgiata (F. Boutin) 13rn 2m 30 (Good).

31 PREMIO MELTON 6f
£10,352 Rome 11 May

Northjet 3-8-8 SFancera **1**

Marching On 6-9-3 GDuffield 1½.**2**

Rissoso 4-9-3 MDepalmas 1¼.**3**

Tres Gate 3-8-8 SAtzori . . hd.4

Hagg Hagg 4-9-3 LBietolini ½.5

Rent and Fly 4-9-3 CPeraino 1½.6

Silver Lord 5-9-3 JMercer . 1½.7

Super Sky 3-8-8 GDettori . . 2.8

Face of Love 4-9-3 LPiggott 2.9

6/5 Tres Gate, 7/2 NORTHJET, 4/1 Super Sky, 11/2 Rissoso, 9/1 Face of Love, 10/1 Marching On, 15/1 Hagg Hagg, 20/1 Rent and Fly, 33/1 Silver Lord.

Razza Spineta (L. Brogi) 9rn 1m 08.8 (record) (Good).

32 PRIX CLEOPATRE 3y 1m 2½f
£14,644 Saint-Cloud 12 May

Hortensia 8-7 ALequeux . . . **1**

Laquiola 8-11 FHead ½.**2**

14^{3} **Paranete** 8 7 AGibert ½.**3**

7^{2} Licara 8-7 YSaint-Martin s.hd.4

Exactly So 8-7 GRivases . . . 2.5

3 Bev Bev 8-7 J-CDesaint . . ns.6

Belle de Caro 8-7 HSamani s.hd.7

Belle Rieuse 8-7 PBruneau ¾.8

Adam's Rib 8-7 MPhilipperon 1½.9

Golden Vale 8-7 J-LKessas ¾.10

14 Akinoa 8-7 APerrotta 0

14 Deep Music 8-7 JTaillard 0

10 La Nobleza 8-7 GDoleuze . . . 0

32 La Vedrelle 8-7 JHeloury 0

3/1 Laquiola, 5/1 Paranete, 7/1 Licara, 74/10 HORTENSIA, 9/1 Adam's Rib, Belle de Caro, Bev Bev, Deep Music, 18/1 Golden Vale, 29/1 Exactly So, 31/1 La Nobleza, 32/1 Akinoa, Belle Rieuse, 64/1 La Vedrelle.

R. Sangster (O. Douieb) 14rn 2m 13.6 (Good).

33 PRIX DE LA JONCHERE 3y 1m
£15,690 Longchamp 15 May

17^{3}(dis)**Ruscelli** 8-8 YSaint-Martin **1**

17 **Joberan** 8-8 JDupin 1½.**2**

Saratoga Game 8-8 MPhilipperon 1½.**3**

15 Un Reitre 8-12 FHead nk.4

8^{2} Viteric 9-2 AGibert ½.5

12/10 RUSCELLI, 5/4 Un Reitre, 11/2 Viteric, 13/2 Joberan, 11/1 Saratoga Game.

A. Tomita (F. Palmer) 5rn 1m 43.9 (Good to Firm).

34 AIRLIE/COOLMORE IRISH 2,000 GUINEAS 3y 1m
£86,878 The Curragh 17 May

Nikoli 9-0 CRoche **1**

Last Fandango 9-0 SCauthen s.hd.**2**

Final Straw 9-0 GStarkey . ½.**3**

Posse 9-0 PEddery hd.4

Monteverdi 9-0 LPiggott . . . 4.5

Galland 9-0 RCarroll 1.6

Johnny O'Day 9-0 AMurray ¾.7
Huguenot 9-0 TMurphy...2.8
Current Charge 9-0 DHogan.............. 1½.9
Winds of Winter 9-0 WSwinburn............4.10
Swan's Rock 9-0 MJKinane 4.11
Skinflint 9-0 GCurran...10.12
Indian Lore 9-0 PMatthews 4.13

11/4 Monteverdi, 7/2 Posse, 5/1 NIKOLI, 7/1 Final Straw, Huguenot, 10/1 Last Fandango, 25/1 Current Charge. 33/1 Johnny O'Day, 50/1 Galland, 100/1 Indian Lore, Skinflint, Swan's Rock, Winds of Winter.

Lord Iveagh (P. Prendergast) 13rn 1m 40.0 (Firm).

35 PRIX LUPIN 3y 1m 2½f
£52,083 Longchamp 18 May

25[3] **Belgio** 9-2 MPhilipperon....**1**
17[3] **Argument** 9-2 J-CDesaint. ½.**2**
17* **In Fijar** 9-2 AGibert...s.hd.**3**
Saint Jonathon 9-2 SCauthen.............1½.4
16[2] Corvaro 9-2 LPiggott......½.5
11[2] Blast Off 9-2GDoleuze......¾.6
11 First of the Line 9-2 FHead 1½.7
15[3] Grandak 9-2 ALequeux.s.nk.8
17 Confetti 9-2 J-LKessas...nk.9
17 Nice Havrais 9-2 JMercer.............1½.10
15 Kareliaan 9-2 YSaint-Martin.0
Maiymad 9-2 JHeloury......0
Boulad 9-2 AGoldsztejn.....0

6/4 Kareliaan and Maiymad, 5/1 Corvaro, 25/4 First of the Line, 29/4 Grandak, 31/4 In Fijar and Boulad, 14/1 Nice Havrais, 16/1 BELGIO, Saint Jonathon, 19/1 Confetti, 21/1 Argument, 25/1 Blast Off.

H. Boccara (J. Cunnington, jnr) 13rn 2m 9.0 (Good to Firm).

36 GOFFS IRISH 1,000 GUINEAS 3y 1m
£52,742 The Curragh 24 May

Cairn Rouge 9-0 AMurray..**1**
Millingdale Lillie 9-0 LPiggott 2½.**2**
Mrs Penny 9-0 JMatthias hd.**3**
Ararat 9-0 JLowe.........1.4
Ringawoody 9-0 GMcGrath 2.5
Etoile de Paris 9-0 MJKinane 1.6
Coneenford 9-0 YSaint-Martin 1½.7
Timarina 9-0 DGillespie...½.8
Goldora 9-0 RCarroll......1.9
Glenardina 9-0 DHogan..¾.10
Racquette 9-0 CRoche...nk.11
Island Time 9-0 TCarberry............4.12
Nazwa 9-0 TMurphy....nk.13
Welsh Daylight 9-0 PVGilson hd.14
Prominent Rose 9-0 JVSmith 2½.15
Magnificent Lady 9-0 WSwinburn..........1½.16
Olinda 9-0 GCurran......2.17
Palmalina 9-0 SCraine....5.18

100/30 Millingdale Lillie, 5/1 CAIRN ROUGE, Mrs Penny, Racquette, 10/1 Etoile de Paris, 12/1 Olinda, 20/1 Ararat, Coneenford, Goldora, 25/1 Magnificent Lady, Ringawoody, 33/1 Glenardina, 40/1 Nazwa, 100/1 Island Time, Palmalina, Prominent Rose, Timarina, Welsh Daylight.

D. Brady (M. Cunningham) 18rn 1m 39.1 (Good to Firm).

37 PRIX SAINT-ALARY 3y 1¼m
£35,934 Longchamp 25 May

32[3] **Paranete** 9-2 AGibert......**1**
21[2] **Safita** 9-2 YSaint-Martin..¾.**2**
14[2] **Benicia** 9-2 FHead......nk.**3**
21* Aryenne 9-2 MPhilipperon s.nk.4
7* Firyal 9-2 ALequeux......2.5
Mariella 9-2 PPaquet......8.6
14 Proustille 9-2 APerrotta....6.7
Militante 9-2 PBruneau....3.8

6/4 Aryenne, 11/4 Benicia and Militante, 7/2 Mariella, Safita, 21/1 PARANETE, 30/1 Firyal, 37/1 Proustille.

M. Fustok (M. Saliba) 8rn 2m 4.8 (Good to Firm).

38 PRIX DU CADRAN 2½m
£30,801 Longchamp 25 May

18[3] **Shafaraz** 7-9-2 MPhilipperon............**1**
18[2] **Prove It Baby** 4-9-2 PPaquet 6.**2**
18 **Marriageable** 6-9-2 J-P-AGodard 2.**3**
18 Croque Monsieur 6-9-2 J-PLefevre nk.4
18 African Hope 5-9-2 ALequeux nk.5
24 San Rosario 7-9-2 ABredillet dist.6

14/10 SHAFARAZ, 9/4 Prove It Baby, 3/1 African Hope, 9/1 Croque Monsieur, 37/4 San Rosario, 12/1 Marriageable.

Y. Skalka (P. Biancone) 6rn 4m 17.4 (Good to Firm).

39 PRIX LA FORCE 3y 1¼m
£15,400 Longchamp 25 May

Nemr 8-10 AGibert........**1**
Speed Bus 8-10 GDoleuze.½.**2**
Glenorum 8-13 FHead..hd.**3**
4 The Expatriate 8-13
YSaint-Martin........hd.4
23* Axius 8-13 MPhilipperon.1½.5
23 Shape 8-10 DVincent......5.6
Grechetto 8-13 PPaquet....4.7
Schwepperusschian 8-13
J-LKessas.............2.8
Black Angel 8-10
ALequeux.............5.9

3/1 Axius, 9/2 Speed Bus, The Expatriate, 49/10 NEMR, 21/4 Shape, 25/4 Glenorum, 13/1 Schwepperusschian, 20/1 Black Angel, Grechetto.

M. Fustok (M. Saliba) 9rn 2m 6.0 (Good to Firm).

40 PRIX JEAN DE CHAUDENAY 1½m
£25,667 Saint-Cloud 26 May

25 **Moulouki** 3-8-0 AGibert....**1**
18* **Hard To Sing** 4-9-8
GDoleuze.............hd.**2**
Buckpoint 4-9-2
J-LKessas..........s.hd.**3**
River River 4-9-2
PPaquet.............nk.4
24[2] Jeune Loup 5-9-2 FHead...2.5
24 Gain 4-9-2 ALequeux...s.hd.6
19* Ho Han Wai 4-9-1
YSaint-Martin.........5.7
13[2] Monsieur Dagobert 4-9-2
APerrotta.............4.8

Evens Gain, 7/2 Hard To Sing, 48/10 MOULOUKI, 17/2 Jeune Loup, 11/1 Ho Han Wai, 13/1 River River, 14/1 Buckpoint, 19/1 Monsieur Dagobert.

M. Fustok (M. Saliba) 8rn 2m 32.1 (Good).

41 OAKS D'ITALIA 3y 1m 3f
£18,605 Milan 18 May

Marmolada 8-11 GDettori..**1**
28[2] **Cos Display** 8-11
SFancera............10.**2**
28 **Adolfina** 8-11 EHide.....3.**3**
28* Tibalda 8-11 OPessi......1½.4
Novesia 8-11 ADiNardo...8.5
Giulia Alberti 8-11 SAtzori.½.6
Panthere Rouge 8-11
NMulas..............2.7
Geppina Umbra 8-11
MDepalmas..........1½.8
Ginetta 8-11 CPeraino...1½.9
28[3] Katalina Girl 8-11
MMassimi...........3.10
Miss Waterloo 8-11
PPerlanti............4.11
Fabrizia 8-11 PAgus......6.12
Mirza 8-11 CCastaldi.....6.13

4/5 MARMOLADA and Mirza, 2/1 Tibalda, 5/1 Geppina Umbra and Ginetta, 7/1 Cos Display, 15/1 Adolfina and Miss Waterloo, 20/1 Giulia Alberti, 33/1 Panthere Rouge, 40/1 Katalina Girl, 50/1 Novesia, 100/1 Fabrizia.

Scuderia Gabriella (E. Camici) 13rn 2m 18.8 (Soft).

42 PREMIO PRESIDENTE DELLA REPUBBLICA 1m 2f
£16,506 Rome 25 May

30 **Deauville** 3-8-6 GDettori...**1**
Marracci 4-9-6
MDepalmas...........¾.**2**
Auxiliante 6-9-6 SFancera..**3**
30 Red Rocket 3-8-6 WCarson..4
30 Manet 3-8-6 GPucciatti....4.5
30[3] Sea's Valley 3-8-6 JMercer.8.6
Nebbia sul Bradano 4-9-3
BJovine...............6.7
Fatusael 5-9-6 SCauthen...3.8
Hultar Pacha 3-8-6
ATortorella...........4.9

6/4 Red Rocket, 7/4 Marracci, 9/2 Fatusael, 6/1 DEAUVILLE and Hultar Pacha, 8/1 Sea's Valley, 9/1 Auxiliante, 33/1 Nebbia sul Bradano 66/1 Manet.

Red Rocket finished third, ¾-length behind Marracci and 3 lengths in front of Auxiliante, but after a stewards inquiry Red Rocket was adjudged to have interferred with Auziliante and was placed fourth and Auxiliante promoted to third.

Scuderia Cieffedi (S. Cumani) 9rn 2m 03 (Soft).

43 PRIX DU PALAIS ROYAL 7f
£15,496 Longchamp 1 June

Baptism 4-9-7 PEddery....**1**
26 **Kilijaro** 4-9-1 HSamani. 3.**2**
Vox Populi 4-9-1
LHassine.............1½.**3**
Light of Realm 3-8-9
MPhilipperon.........3.4
White Pleasure 3-8-9
FHead...............2.5
33 Viteric 3-9-2 AGibert......5.6
Current Bay 4-9-1
J-LTheault...........¾.7
Massalia 3-8-6 ALequeux..3.8
Muscovite 3-8-9 LPiggott..5.9
Suvero 3-8-13 PPaquet..1½.10
23 Divin Marquis 3-8-9
JTaillard...............0
21 La Grande Coudre 3-8-6
GDubroeucq...........0

5/2 Kilijaro, 23/4 Muscovite, 13/2 Suvero, 7/1 Light of Realm, Viteric, 9/1 BAPTISM, 10/1 White Pleasure, 13/1 Divin Marquis, 14/1 La Grande Coudre, 17/1 Massalia, 22/1

Current Bay, 33/1 Vox Populi.
J. Whitney (J. Tree) 12rn 1m 25.6 (Dead).

44 PRIX DOLLAR 1m 1¾f
£25,826 Longchamp 1 June

22[3] **Northern Baby** 4-9-6 PPaquet **1**
2 **Strong Gale** 5-8-11 AGibert 1.**2**
22[2] **Three Troikas** 4-9-3 FHead 2½.**3**
Rolling Bowl 4-8-11 J-LKessas nk.4
24 Liki Liki 4-8-8 J-CDesaint.1.5
20 Callio 4-8-11 ALequeux...½.6
Star's Salute 6-8-11 LHassine 6.7
Sheikdom 5-8-11 MPhilipperon 4.8

4/10 Three Troikas, 53/10 NORTHERN BABY, 29/4 Sheikdom, 10/1 Strong Gale and Star's Salute, 15/1 Liki Liki, 19/1 Rolling Bowl, 20/1 Callio.
Mme A. M. d'Estainville (F. Boutin) 2m 7.7 (Dead).

45 PRIX DE L'ESPERANCE 3y 1m 7f
£15,496 Longchamp 1 June

Chicbury 8-11 GDoleuze...**1**
Hortensio 8-11 AGibert...2.**2**
Valiant Heart 8-11 J-LKessas s.hd.**3**
Intrigant 8-11 MPhilipperon nk.4
Vezzani 8-11 FPegurri..d-ht.4
Koreillo 8-11 GDubroeucq 5.6
Cumuls 8-11 FSauret......1.7
Balibest 8-11 YSaint-Martin 6.8
11 Dhausli 8-11 FHead.......4.9
Cesarion 8-11 HSamani...8.10
16 Popset 8-11 AGoldsztejn....0
Zambrano 8-11 PPaquet.....0

13/4 Balibest, 17/4 Hortensio, 9/2 Koreillo, 21/4 Dhausli, 8/1 Zambrano, 39/4 Vezzani, 12/1 Valiant Heart, 29/2 CHICBURY, 16/1 Intrigant, 30/1 Cumuls, 49/1 Popset, 53/1 Cesarion.
A.D.S. Mangnall (C. Milbank) 12rn 3m 24.9 (Dead).

46 PRIX DE SANDRINGHAM 3y 1m
£15,496 Chantilly 5 June

India Song 9-0 FHead.....**1**
21 **Teacher's Pet** 9-2 ALequeux s.nk.**2**
Wild Idea 9-0 J-PLefevre s.nk.**3**
10 La Vreeland 8-12 PPaquet.2.4
10[3] Pom Poes 9-2 AGibert....2.5
Dare To 8-8 MPhilipperon nk.6
14 Zolinana 9-2 FPegurri....hd.7
3 Spoilt Miss 8-8 PLagoutte nk.8
Powder 'N Patch 8-10 GDoleuze 4.9

3/1 INDIA SONG, Pom Poes, 4/1 Teacher's Pet, 6/1 Wild Idea, 8/1 La Vreeland, 9/1 Dare To, 13/1 Powder 'N Patch, 15/1 Zolinana, 51/1 Spoilt Miss.
P. Bensussan (F. Mathet) 9rn 1m 38.2 (Good to Firm).

47 PRIX JEAN PRAT 3y 1m 1f
£25,907 Chantilly 8 June

Night Alert 9-2 LPiggott...**1**
33* **Ruscelli** 9-2 YSaint-Martin nk.**2**
39 **The Expatriate** 9-2 MPhilipperon s.nk.**3**
35[3] In Fijar 9-2 AGibert......½.4
33[2] Joberan 9-2 JDupin.....1½.5
Falamoun 9-2 J-CDesaint nk.6
23[2] Dip 9-2 FHead..........¾.7
17 Norwegian 9-2 GDoleuze..2.8
Pharnace 9-2 J-PLefevre.1½.9
Never Cry 9-2 ALequeux s.nk.10
35 Boulad 9-2 AGoldsztejn.....0
Rolling Star 9-2 PPaquet....0

5/4 In Fijar and Boulad, 36/10 NIGHT ALERT, 15/4 Ruscelli, 17/2 Never Cry, 18/1 The Expatriate, Dip, 22/1 Joberan, 24/1 Norwegian, 27/1 Falamoun, 29/1 Rolling Star, 37/1 Pharnace.
R. Sangster (V. O'Brien) 12rn 1m 48.2 (Good to Firm).

48 PRIX DU JOCKEY-CLUB 3y 1½m
£93,264 Chantilly 8 June

23[3] **Policeman** 9-2 WCarson...**1**
25 **Shakapour** 9-2 YSaint-Martin 1½.**2**
25[2] **Providential** 9-2 PPaquet.3.**3**
15[2] Dom Aldo 9-2 GDoleuze.1½.4
Gonzales 9-2 LPiggott..s.nk.5
Tom's Serenade 9-2 ALequeux hd.6
25* Mot D'Or 9-2 FHead..d-ht.6
39[2] Speed Bus 9-2 PEddery...4.8
35 Grandak 9-2 ABadel.....hd.9
17 Dragon 9-2 AGibert....1½.10
35* Belgio 9-2 MPhilipperon....0
25 Dom Savary 9-2 PLagoutte..0
Hybrid 9-2 J-PLefevre......0
35[2] Argument 9-2 J-CDesaint...0

9/4 Gonzales, 4/1 Providential and Dom Savary, 19/4 Mot D'Or, 6/1 Shakapour, 17/2 Tom's Serenade and Hybrid, 9/1 Argument, 15/1 Belgio, 20/1 Dragon, 23/1 Dom Aldo, 38/1 Speed Bus, 46/1 Grandak, 54/1 POLICEMAN.
F. Tinsley (C. Milbank) 14rn 2m 27.7 (Good to Firm).

49 PRIX DE ROYAUMONT 3y 1m 2½f
£15,544 Chantilly 8 June

Luth Music 8-10 MJerome **1**
As You Desire Me 8-13 YSaint-Martin ½.**2**
32 **Exactly So** 8-10 PEddery 1½.**3**
14 Indigene 8-10 J-PLefevre s.hd.4
37 Mariella 8-10 PPaquet.....2.5
Free Dance 8-10 FHead...½.6
14 Lorelta 8-10 AGibert......1.7
Riverbird 8-10 GDoleuze 5.8
32 Golden Vale 8-10 J-LKessas hd.9
La Carmagnole 8-10 MGentile hd.10

6/4 As You Desire Me, 15/4 Mariella, 5/1 Free Dance, 9/1 Exactly So, 93/10 LUTH MUSIC 11/1 Indigene, 15/1 Lorelta, 18/1 La Carmagnole, 20/1 Riverbird, 26/1 Golden Vale.
J. Dorise (E. Chevalier du Fau) 10rn 2m 8.4 (Good to Firm).

50 PRIX DU CHEMIN DE FER DU NORD 1m
£15,544 Chantilly 11 June

Rostov 6-9-2 FHead.......**1**
20[2] **Hilal** 4-8-12 AGibert....nk.**2**
Discretion 4-9-2 MPhilipperon ¾.**3**
House Guard 5-9-2 LPiggott nk.4
43[2] Kilijaro 4-8-9 ALequeux..¾.5
44 Callio 4-9-0 YSaint-Martin.5.6
Manguin 4-8-12 PPaquet.1½.7
Marquis du Loir 4-8-12 MGentile 4.8

2/1 House Guard, 3/1 Hilal, 6/1 Callio, 61/10 ROSTOV, 13/2 Kilijaro, 10/1 Manguin, 11/1 Discretion, 15/1 Marquis du Loir.
R. J. Lipman (A. Paus) 8rn 1m 37.4 (Good).

51 LA COUPE 1½m
£15,593 Chantilly 15 June

38[2] **Prove It Baby** 4-9-0 PPaquet **1**
Boucicault 4-8-12 YSaint-Martin 3 **2**
40 **Monsieur Dagobert** 4-8-12 MPhilipperon ½.**3**
40[3] Buckpoint 4-8-12 J-LKessas s.nk.4
24[3] Dunette 4-9-1 GDoleuze.1½.5
40 Gain 4-8-12 ALequeux...2.6
40 Jeune Loup 5-8-12 FHead.½.7

9/10 Dunette, 15/4 Gain, 21/4 Boucicault, 7/1 Buckpoint, 79/10 PROVE IT BABY, 10/1 Jeune Loup, 25/1 Monsieur Dagobert.
W. Haefner (F. Boutin) 7rn 2m 31.9 (Good).

52 PRIX DE DIANE DE REVLON 3y 1m 2½f
£72,765 Chantilly 15 June

36[3] **Mrs Penny** 9-2 LPiggott....**1**
37 **Aryenne** 9-2 GDoleuze.s.hd.**2**
37* **Paranete** 9-2 AGibert....3.**3**
14* Luth de Saron 9-2 MPhilipperon ¾.4
37[3] Benicia 9-2 PPaquet.......2.5
32 Licara 9-2 YSaint-Martin..1.6
32[2] Laquiola 9-2 FHead.....1½.7
32 Bev Bev 9-2 J-CDesaint...4.8
Dancing Shadow 9-2 WCarson ¾.9
32 Belle Rieuse 9-2 PBruneau s.nk.10
32* Hortensia 9-2 ALequeux d-ht.10
14 Belle d'Avril 9-2 J-P-AGodard 0
Lyphard's Bonnet 9-2 AGoldsztejn 0
37 Proustille 9-2 MPlanard.....0

4/1 Benicia and Laquiola, 19/4 Licara, 21/4 Hortensia, 11/2 Paranete and Lyphard's Bonnet, 13/2 Aryenne, 82/10 MRS PENNY, 9/1 Luth de Saron, 15/1 Bev Bev, Dancing Shadow, 22/1 Proustille, 34/1 Belle d'Avril, 43/1 Belle Rieuse.
E. N. Kronfeld (I. Balding) 14rn 2m 10.1 (Good).

53 PRIX DU LYS 3y 1½m
£15,593 Chantilly 15 June

Lancastrian 8-9 ALequeux **1**
35 **Corvaro** 8-9 PPaquet....nk.**2**
35 **First of the Line** 8-9 FHead **4.3**
25 Fabulous Prince 8-9 AGibert nk.4
Sabzawar 8-9 LPiggott....6.5

5/4 Corvaro, 5/2 First of the Line, 28/10 LANCASTRIAN, 8/1 Fabulous Prince, 10/1 Sabzawar.
Sir M. Sobell (D. Smaga) 5rn 2m 35.2 (Good).

54 PRIX BERTEUX 3y 1m 7f
£15,593 Chantilly 17 June

Dhaubix 8-9 FHead.......**1**
45 **Balibest** 8-9 YSaint-Martin 2½.**2**
45 **Zambrano** 8-9 ALequeux.1.**3**
45 Vezzani 8-9 FPegurri......2.4
Lochiel 8-9 J-CDesaint..hd.5
Pointe Rousse 8-6 J-PLefevre 5.6

22/10 DHAUBIX, 9/4 Vezzani, 7/2 Balibest, 5/1 Lochiel, 23/4 Zambrano, 15/1 Pointe Rousse.
D. G. Courtois (R. Corme) 6rn 3m 16.9 (Dead).

55 GRAN PREMIO D'ITALIA 3y 1½m
£18,936 Milan 1 June

27² **Pareo** 9-2 GDettori........1
27* **Lotar** 9-2 PPerlanti.......3.2
30² **Pian del Lupo** 9-2 SFancera.............4½.3
Choco Air 9-2 MDepalmas.........dist.4
42 Hultar Pacha 9-2 DSantoni............dist.5

3/5 PAREO and Hultar Pacha, 6/4 Lotar, 5/1 Pian del Lupo, 10/1 Choco Air.
Scuderia Cieffedi (S. Cumani) 5rn 2m 30 (Dead).

56 CRITERIUM DI ROMA 2y 6f
£7,677 Rome 7 June

Travolta (GB) 8-11 CWigham...............1
Lover Prince 8-11 GPucciatti............nk.2
Warden Key 8-11 GDettori..............6.3
El Adem 8-11 LBietolini...2.4
Belviale 8-11 RFestinesi...3.5
Roman Top 8-11 LFicuciello............2.6

1/10 Warden Key and Lover Prince, 5/2 TRAVOLTA, 11/2 El Adem, 40/1 Roman Top, 100/1 Belviale.
G. Gilardoni (B. Agriformi) 6rn 1m 10.4 (Good).

57 PREMIO EMILIO TURATI 1m
£17,921 Milan 8 June

Isopach 3-8-7 MDepalmas..1
Good Times 4-9-3 GPucciatti............1½.2
Savingrant 4-9-3 GDettori..............5.3
Ladislao di Oppelm 4-9-3 SFancera.............3½.4
9 Godot 3-8-7 ADiNardo...1½.5
20* American Prince 4-9-3 CRoche...............8.6
42³ Auxiliante 6-9-3 LLizarazo.............4.7

4/5 ISOPACH, 5/2 American Prince, 4/1 Good Times and Savingrant, 6/1 Auxiliante, 12/1 Godot, 16/1 Ladislao di Oppelm.
N. B. Hunt (L. Turner) 7rn 1m 43 (Heavy).

58 GRAN PREMIO DI MILANO 1½m
£38,462 Milan 15 June

42² **Marracci** 4-9-6 MDepalmas.1
55* **Pareo** 3-8-6 GDettori.....3.2
41* **Marmolada** 3-8-3 SCauthen.............2½.3
29² Mazzanti 4-9-6 PPerlanti...¾.4
42* Deauville 3-8-6 GPucciatti.1.5
57² Good Times 4-9-6 DSantoni.............10.6
Roberto Bellarmino 4-9-6 CPanici.............dist.7
Black Marlin 7-9-6 VPanici.............dist.8

3/5 Pareo, Good Times and Deauville, 5/4 Marmolada, 6/1 MARRACCI, 50/1 Mazzanti, 200/1 Black Marlin and Roberto Bellarmino.
Razza Dormello-Olgiata (F. Boutin) 8rn No time taken (Good).

59 PREMIO PRIMI PASSI 2y 6f
£7,692 Milan 15 June

Erodoto 8-11 GDettori.....1
Seiorlando 8-11 CForte..nk.2
Richard Sorge 8-11 MMassimi............nk.3
All Silk 8-8 PPerlanti.....¾.4
Roman Black 8-11 SFancera..............1.5
Pizzocorno 8-11 VPanici...4.6
Willard 8-11 SAtzori......4.7

4/6 ERODOTO, 6/1 Richard Sorge, 7/1 Seiorlando, 8/1 Roman Black, 9/1 Pizzocorno, 10/1 All Silk, 25/1 Willard.
Scuderia Cieffedi (S. Cumani) 7rn 1m 13.3 (Good).

60 PRIX FILLE DE L'AIR 1m 2½f
£14,553 Saint-Cloud 21 June

Detroit 3-8-3 ALequeux....1
Gold River 3-8-3 PBruneau.............2½.2
49 **Indigene** 3-8-7 J-PLefevre...........1½.3
49³ Exactly So 3-8-6 GDoleuze.3.4
40 Ho Han Wai 4-9-6 AGibert.¾.5
Turnablade 3-8-3 PLagoutte...........s.hd.6
49* Luth Music 3-8-7 MJerome..............1.7
Mill Princess 3-8-3 JDupin.¾.8
32 Deep Music 3-8-4 PPaquet.............2½.9
Matcha 3-8-5 MPapoin...6.10

21/10 DETROIT, 7/2 Luth Music, 9/2 Gold River, 7/1 Deep Music, 8/1 Ho Han Wai, 9/1 Exactly So, 10/1 Indigene, 23/1 Mill Princess, 28/1 Matcha, 54/1 Turnablade.
R. Sangster (O. Douieb) 10rn 2m 12.7 (Dead).

61 PRIX DU GROS CHENE 5f
£15,609 Chantilly 24 June

26* **Adraan** 3-9-5 YSaint-Martin...........1
26² **Miliar** 3-8-10 GDoleuze.............4.2
26 **Trio Boy** 4-9-5 MJerome..¾.3

46 Powder 'N Patch 3-8-7
ALequeux ½.4
Wicked Lady 3-8-7
MPhilipperon 2.5
7 Selerina 3-9-0 FHead.....1½.6
Concordia 4-9-5 HSamani.ns.7
46 Pom Poes 3-9-2 AGibert..1½.8
Windelia 3-8-7 PPaquet....3.9

6/10 ADRAAN, 9/2 Miliar, 11/2 Pom Poes, 10/1 Selerina, 14/1 Trio Boy, 16/1 Concordia, 32/1 Wicked Lady, 41/1 Powder 'N Patch, 57/1 Windelia.

H. H. Aga Khan (F. Mathet) 9rn 1m 0.7 (Soft).

62 IRISH SWEEPS DERBY 3y 1½m
£143,045 The Curragh 28 June

Tyrnavos 9-0 AMurray.....**1**
Prince Bee 9-0 WCarson.1½.**2**
Ramian 9-0 WSwinburn.2½.**3**
30* Garrido 9-0 PPaquet.....1½.4
Master Willie 9-0
PWaldron..........s.hd.5
Pelerin 9-0 LPiggott......2½.6
Rankin 9-0 GStarkey.....1½.7
Noble Shamus 9-0
TCarberry.............2.8
Cobblers Cove 9-0 SCraine.½.9
Graben 9-0 DGillespie..hd.10
34* Nikoli 9-0 CRoche.......½.11
Fingal's Cave 9-0
TMurphy 2½.12
34 Current Charge 9-0
SCauthen.............8.13

7/4 Master Willie, 4/1 Nikoli, 13/2 Pelerin, 10/1 Garrido, 11/1 Fingal's Cave, Prince Bee, 12/1 Rankin, 25/1 TYRNAVOS, 33/1 Ramian, 66/1 Cobblers Cove, 100/1 Current Charge, Graben, Noble Shamus.

G. L. Cambanis (B. Hobbs) 13rn 2m 43.8 (Soft).

63 PRIX DU CARROUSEL 1m 7f
£10,363 Longchamp 29 June

6[3] **Kelbomec** 4-9-1 J-CDesaint.**1**
24 **Soleil Noir** 4-8-8
YSaint-Martin ½.**2**
2 **Monsieur Marcel** 4-8-9
GDoleuze 2.**3**
51[3] Monsieur Dagobert 4-9-1
MPhilipperon 1½.4
38[3] Marriageable 6-8-12
J-P-AGodard..........p.u.

3/10 Soleil Noir, 6/1 KELBOMEC, 27/4 Monsieur Marcel, 9/1 Marriageable, Monsieur Dagobert.

Mme J. Barker (J. C. Cunnington) 5rn 3m 26 (Soft).

64 PRIX DE MALLERET 3y 1¼m
£20,725 Longchamp 29 June

52 **Luth de Saron** 8-11
MPhilipperon............**1**
52 **Benicia** 8-11 FHead.....hd.**2**
52 **Hortensia** 8-11 ALequeux.¾.**3**
Battlewind 8-11 LPiggott.1½.4
Evgenia 8-11 ABadel....s.hd.5
60 Deep Music 8-11 PPaquet..2.6
37[2] Safita 8-11 YSaint-Martin.nk.7
52 Belle d'Avril 8-11
J-P-AGodard 4.8

18/10 LUTH DE SARON, 9/4 Safita, 5/2 Hortensia, 19/4 Benicia, 16/1 Battlewind, 28/1 Evgenia, 32/1 Deep Music, 38/1 Belle d'Avril.

P. de Moussac (J. Cunnington, jnr) 8rn 2m 14.4 (Soft).

65 GRAND PRIX DE PARIS 3y 1m 7f
£41,451 Longchamp 29 June

45[3] **Valiant Heart** 8-11 AGibert.**1**
What A Joy 8-11
J-LKessas 1½.**2**
Water Mill 8-11 WCarson.2.**3**
48 Mot D'Or 8-11 FHead..d-ht.**3**
48 Tom's Serenade 8-11
ALequeux 1½.5
54[2] Balibest 8-11
YSaint-Martin ½.6
45[2] Hortensio 8-11 GDoleuze..½.7
45 Intrigant 8-11
MPhilipperon s.hd.8
54 Vezzani 8-11 FPegurri.....2.9
Abisko 8-11 JDupin......6.10
54* Dhaubix 8-11 PPaquet......0
Good Thyne 8-11
WSwinburn 0
L'Octroi 8-11 HSamani.....0
Vaneau 8-11 APerrotta......0

11/4 Dhaubix, 3/1 Mot D'Or, 5/1 Tom's Serenade, 25/4 Water Mill, 11/1 VALIANT HEART, 12/1 Balibest, Hortensio, 22/1 Good Thyne, 26/1 What A Joy, 31/1 Vezzani, 32/1 Intrigant, 40/1 L'Octroi, 41/1 Vaneau, 99/1 Abisko.

A. Michel (B. Secly) 14rn 3m 25.1 (Soft).

66 PRIX D'ISPAHAN 1m 1¼f
£41,451 Longchamp 29 June

20 **Nadjar** 4-9-6 ALequeux....**1**
Foveros 4-9-6 WCarson...5.**2**
47 **In Fijar** 3-8-9 AGibert....¾.**3**
46[3] Wild Idea 3-8-6
J-PLefevre s.nk.4
44* Northern Baby 4-9-6
PPaquet 1½.5
35 Kareliaan 3-8-9
YSaint-Martin 1½.6
47[3] The Expatriate 3-8-9
MPhilipperon 1½.7
48 Dragon 3-8-9 GDoleuze..10.8
44[2] Strong Gale 5-9-6 FHead..¾.9
57 Ladislao di Oppelm 4-9-6
MDepalmas 6.10

6/10 NADJAR and Northern Baby, 19/4 Kareliaan, 5/1 Dragon and In

Fijar, 33/4 The Expatriate, 10/1 Strong Gale, 13/1 Foveros, 29/1 Wild Idea, 40/1 Ladislao di Oppelm.
G. Schjelderup (A. Paus) 10rn 1m 57.4 (Soft).

67 PRIX DE LA PORTE MAILLOT 7f
£15,544 Longchamp 29 June

Luck of the Draw 3-8-6 WCarson **1**
50² **Hilal** 4-9-2 GDoleuze....2½.**2**
43 **Suvero** 3-8-11 PPaquet.s.nk.**3**
50 Kilijaro 4-8 13 HSamani..1½.4
43³ Vox Populi 4-8-13 LHassine 1½.5
47 Joberan 3-8-9 JDupin.....2.7
34* Baptism 4-9-4 LPiggott...nk.8
21³ Princesse Lida 3-9-0 FHead 8.9
Ya Zaman 3-8-9 AGibert..disq

2/1 Baptism, 13/4 Princesse Lida, 39/10 Hilal and Ya Zaman, 13/2 Joberan, 15/2 Kilijaro, 33/4 LUCK OF THE DRAW, 17/1 Suvero, Vox Populi.
Sir M. Sobell (R. Hern) 9rn 1m 24.5 (Soft).
Ya Zaman finished first, ½ length in front of Luck of the Draw, but was subsequently disqualified after traces of caffeine had been found in his system.

68 PRIX DAPHNIS 3y 1m 1f
£12,435 Evry 5 July

34 **Huguenot** 9-2 YSaint-Martin **1**
Rhus 9-2 PPaquet........¾.**2**
Sea Boy 9-2 FHead.......¾.**3**
47 Dip 9-2 J-CDesaint.......½.4
Some Lute 9-2 GDoleuze..½.5
39* Nemr 9-2 AGibert........¾.6
Cesario 9-2 MPhilipperon.1½.7
Coquet 9-2 CHeroult.....1½.8

13/10 HUGUENOT, 11/4 Nemr, 6/1 Dip, 29/4 Sea Boy, 17/2 Cesario, 11/1 Rhus, 18/1 Some Lute, 47/1 Coquet.
R. Sangster (V. O'Brien) 8rn 1m 54.6 (Dead).

69 GRAND PRIX DE SAINT-CLOUD 1m 4½f
£62,370 Saint-Cloud 6 July

51 **Dunette** 4-9-5 GDoleuze....**1**
48 **Shakapour** 3-8-9 YSaint-Martin.......d-ht.**1**
48* **Policeman** 3-8-9 WCarson 3.**3**
53* Lancastrian 3-8-9 ALequeux 1½.4
Noble Saint 4-9-8 LPiggott.2.5
48 Belgio 3-8-9 MPhilipperon 1½.6
Two of Diamonds 4-9-8 SCauthen 2.7
51 Gain 4-9-8 FHead.......hd.8
24* Scorpio 4-9-8 PPaquet.....3.9

6/4 Scorpio, 3/1 SHAKAPOUR, 19/4 Policeman, 6/1 DUNETTE, 9/1 Lancastrian, 12/1 Gain, 13/1 Belgio, Noble Saint, 34/1 Two of Diamonds.
DUNETTE, Mme H. A. Love (E. Chevalier du Fau). SHAKAPOUR, H.H. Aga Khan (F. Mathet) 9rn 2m 39.8 (Dead)

70 PRIX MAURICE DE NIEUIL 1m 4½f
£20,833 Saint-Cloud 14 July

51 **Buckpoint** 4-9-2 J-LKessas.**1**
52 **Proustille** 3-8-2 MPhilipperon 3.**2**
Perrault 3-8-3 ABadel....¾.**3**
13 Son of Love 4-9-8 ALequeux s.hd.4
2 Cherubin 5-9-2 JDupin...hd.5
19 Indoor 4-9-1 MJerome....3 6
51² Boucicault 4-9-2 YSaint-Martin 4.7
48 Dom Aldo 3-8-3 GDoleuze 1½.8
19 Anifa 4-9-1 AGibert.......¾.9
Pappagallo 7-9-2 GDubroeucq 10.10
51* Prove It Baby 4-9-6 PPaquet 11

7/4 Dom Aldo, 11/2 Anifa, 13/2 Prove It Baby, 17/2 Boucicault, 10/1 BUCKPOINT, Proustille, 12/1 Perrault, 15/1 Son of Love, 17/1 Pappagallo, 19/1 Indoor, 21/1 Cherubin.
Mme J. P. Binet (B. Secly) 11rn 2m 47.0 (Soft).

71 IRISH GUINNESS 3y OAKS 1½m
£56,125 The Curragh 19 July

Shoot A Line 9 0 WCarson..**1**
Little Bonny 9-0 GCurran 2½.**2**
36 **Racquette** 9-0 CRoche....¾.**3**
Calandra 9-0 LPiggott.....4.4
Quick As Lightning 9-0 AMurray 1½.5
Audmore 9-0 DGillespie..12.6
Wedgewood Blue 9-0 TMurphy ¾.7
Mice Bird 9-0 SCraine....nk.8

6/4 SHOOT A LINE, 3/1 Calandra, 9/2 Quick As Lightning, 7/1 Racquette, 9/1 Mice Bird, 20/1 Audmore, 33/1 Little Bonny, 66/1 Wedgewood Blue.
R. A. Budgett (R. Hern) 8rn 2m 39.4 (Dead).

72 PRIX CHLOE 3y 1m 1f
£12,500 Evry 19 July

60* **Detroit** 9-2 ALequeux......**1**
52 **Licara** 9-2

YSaint-Martin 1½.**2**
3 **Deliballe** 9-2 ABadel....½.**3**
66 Wild Idea 9-2 J-PLefevre..½.4
7 Inner Pearl 9-2 MPhilipperon nk.5
60 Exactly So 9-2 AGibert....½.6
52 Laquiola 9-2 FHead.......¾.7
Sunny Time 9-2 JLe Deunf............1½.8
46 Zolinana 9-2 FPegurri.....2.9
46 La Vreeland 9-2 PPaquet..¾.10

14/10 DETROIT, 4/1 Licara, 5/1 Laquiola, 27/4 Wild Idea, 11/1 Exactly So, La Vreeland, 15/1 Deliballe, 23/1 Zolinana, 26/1 Sunny Time, 30/1 Inner Pearl.
R. Sangster (O. Douieb) 10rn 1m 56.1 (Dead).

73 PRIX EUGENE ADAM 3y 1¼m
£25,961 Saint-Cloud 20 July

53[2] **Corvaro** 8-10 PPaquet......**1**
Dom D'Albignac 9-0 ALequeux 5.**2**
68 **Nemr** 9-0 AGibert......hd.**3**
66 Kareliaan 8-12 YSaint-Martin s.nk.4
60[3] Indigene 8-7 J-PLefevre....2.5
47[2] Ruscelli 9-0 HSamani.....nk.6
Tajtal 8-10 GDubroeucq...2.7
55[3] Pian del Lupo 8-10 GDettori 2½.8
47 Falamoun 8-12 J-CDesaint 2½.9
35 Blast Off 8-12 MPhilipperon 4.10
Beyond Recall 8-10 DDehard 11

29/10 CORVARO, 3/1 Kareliaan, 7/2 Ruscelli, 33/4 Blast Off and Beyond Recall, 9/1 Nemr, 10/1 Falamoun, 11/1 Dom D'Albignac, 15/1 Tajtal, 16/1 Indigene, 20/1 Pian del Lupo.
G. A. Oldham (F. Boutin) 11rn 2m 17.3 (Soft).

74 GRAND PRIX PRINCE ROSE 1m 3f
£48,208 Ostend 21 July

48 **Argument** 3-8-6 J-CDesaint.**1**
45 **Dhausli** 3-8-5 ALequeux..2.**2**
66 **Strong Gale** 5-9-4 AGibert ns.**3**
5 Kamaridaan 4-9-6 GDoleuze 1½.4
Konigsstuhl 4-9-11PAlafi..8.5
Duke of Normandy 5-8-11 DVanOost 6
Epsiba 3-7-6 SVanPee.......7
Boden's Ride 4-8-4 KDavies.8
68[2] Rhus 3-8-7 PPaquet........9

Mme P. Ribes (J. Cunnington, nr) 9rn 2m 21.9 (Soft).

75 PRIX MESSIDOR 1m
£14,538 Maisons-Laffitte 24 July

Tassmoun 4-8-9 YSaint-Martin **1**
50[3] **Discretion** 4-9-0 MPhilipperon nk.**2**
67[2] **Hilal** 4-8-9 AGibert......¾.**3**
50 Callio 4-9-4 ALequeux....¾.4
Lord Rochford 5-9-0 WSwinburn 1.5
35 Confetti 3-8-0 J-LKessas.hd.6
Torsom 3-8-0 ABadel....nk.7
8 Clodion 3-8-0 J-PLefevre.1½.8
Fabi Si 6-8-9 GDubroeucq.3.9
Shamra 3-7-11 PBruneau.¾.10
67[3] Suvero 3-8-5 PPaquet.......0
68 Some Lute 3-8-0 J-P-AGodard 0

3/1 Hilal, 4/1 Lord Rochford, 48/10 TASSMOUN, 29/4 Confetti, 31/4 Discretion, 11/1 Fabi Si, 12/1 Torsom, 14/1 Callio, 15/1 Shamra, 19/1 Suvero, 28/1 Clodion, 29/1 Some Lute.
H.H. Aga Khan (F. Mathet) 12rn 1m 36.2 (Good).

76 PRIX DE MINERVE 3y 1½m
£12,461 Evry 26 July

Great Verdict 8-10 HSamani **1**
70[2] **Proustille** 9-2 MPhilipperon nk.**2**
60[2] **Gold River** 8-13 FHead...1.**3**
Ayila 8-13 YSaint-Martin..½.4
54 Pointe Rousse 8-10 J-PLefevre 1½.5
Polemia 8-10 G-WMoore..3.6
Blithe Spirit 8-10 ALequeux 2.7

6/4 Gold River, 3/1 Proustille, 7/2 Ayila, 51/10 GREAT VERDICT, 11/1 Blithe Spirit, 15/1 Polemia, 30/1 Pointe Rousse.
Mme P. L. Hexter (G. Bridgland) 7rn 2m 35.9 (Dead).

77 PRIX ROBERT PAPIN 2y 5½f
£20,790 Maisons-Laffitte 27 July

Irish Playboy 8-11 ALequeux **1**
Ancient Regime 8-9 MPhilipperon 2.**2**
Age Quod Agis 8-11 JMercer ½.**3**
Valgo 8-11 J-LKessas......4.4
Diamond Prospect 8-11 AGibert 2.5
Twig Prince 8-11 MPlanard 2.6
Yourki 8-11 APerrotta.....1.7
Penmarric 8-11 GStarkey.hd.8
Goldorak 8-11 PPaquet....4.9
Swift Song 8-11 YSaint-Martin 2.10

5/2 Age Quod Agis, 38/10 IRISH PLAYBOY, 5/1 Ancient Regime,

23/4 Twig Prince and Valgo, 13/2 Penmarric, 7/1 Swift Song, 10/1 Diamond Prospect, 23/1 Goldorak, 25/1 Yourki.
Sir G. White (O. Douieb) 10rn 1m 5.4 (Good).

78 PRIX D'ASTARTE 1m
£15,593 Deauville 2 August

Moon Ingraver 3-8-7 GDettori **1**
46* **India Song** 3-9-0 FHead . . 4.**2**
72^3 **Deliballe** 3-8-9 ABadel . . . ½.**3**
49^2 As You Desire Me 3-8-11 YSaint-Martin 1½.4
46^2 Teacher's Pet 3-8-7 ALequeux 1.5
43 Light of Realm 3-8-7 MPhilipperon ¾.6
19 New Grandame 5-9-0 MJerome hd.7
37 Firyal 3-8-9 PPaquet 1½.8
72 Inner Pearl 3-8-7 MDepalmas 3.9
43 Current Bay 4-9-6 AGibert 1.10
Lignee Grise 4-9-2 GDoleuze 0
St Louis Sue 4-9-0 GDubroeucq 0
61 Windelia 3-8-7 GWMoore . . 0

13/4 As You Desire Me, 7/2 Light of Realm, 6/1 Firyal, 29/4 Teacher's Pet, 8/1 New Grandame, 9/1 India Song, 10/1 Deliballe, 15/1 Lignee Grise, 25/1 Current Bay, 27/1 Inner Pearl, 28/1 MOON INGRAVER, 47/1 Windelia, 52/1 St Louis Sue.
Razza Spineta (L. Brogi, Italy) 13rn 1m 42.6 (Soft).

79 PRIX MAURICE DE GHEEST 6½f
£20,640 Deauville 3 August

20 **Boitron** 4-8-12 PPaquet **1**
17^2 **Moorestyle** 3-9-3 LPiggott s.nk.**2**
67 **Kilijaro** 4-8-9 ALequeux s.nk.**3**
26 Manjam 3-8-8 GDoleuze . hd.4
Red Coral 5-8-9 GWMoore . 6.5
31* Northjet 3-9-0 SFancera . . ½.6
7^3 Dellear 3-8-5 JPLefevre . . . 4.7
61 Wicked Lady 3-8-5 HSamani ½.8
Snapper Point 3-8-8 YSaint-Martin hd.9
2 Gosport 4-8-12 J-CDesaint 4.10
67 Vox Populi 4-8-9 LHassine . . 0
67 Princesse Lida 3-8-5 FHead . . 0

6/4 Moorestyle, 4/1 Princesse Lida, 13/2 Kilijaro, 15/2 Gosport, 10/1 BOITRON, Manjam, 17/1 Snapper Point, 23/1 Wicked Lady, 24/1 Dellear, 25/1 Northjet, Vox Populi, 31/1 Red Coral.
S. Niarchos (F. Boutin) 12rn 1m 20.2 (Dead).

80 PRIX DE LA VILLE 3y 1¼m DE TROUVILLE
£10,320 Deauville 3 August

Noalcoholic 8-12 ALequeux **1**
73 **Falamoun** 9-4 J-CDesaint ½.**2**
53 **Fabulous Prince** 8-12 AGibert 1.**3**
65 Hortensio 8-12 GDoleuze . . ¾.4
75 Confetti 9-1 J-LKessas 4.5
48 Speed Bus 8-12 LPiggott . . ¾.6
73 Tajtal 8-12 MPhilipperon . nk.7
72^2 Licara 8-8 YSaint-Martin . 1½.8
45 Koreillo 9-1 GDubroeucq . . 6.9
68^3 Sea Boy 9-4 FHead ½.10
Ballet Royal 8-12 PPaquet . . 11

2/1 Licara, 21/4 Speed Bus, 13/2 NOALCOHOLIC, 8/1 Confetti, 9/1 Sea Boy, 10/1 Koreillo, 12/1 Fabulous Prince, 13/1 Tajtal, 14/1 Falamoun, 18/1 Hortensio, 30/1 Ballet Royal.
W. du Pont (O. Douieb) 11rn 2m 6.2 (Dead).

81 GRAND PRIX DE VICHY 1½m
£20,640 Vichy 4 August

13 **Perouges** 5-9-6 JLeDeunf . . **1**
70^3 **Perrault** 3-8-3 ABadel . . . nk.**2**
Brousoy 3-8-5 RLaplanche 1½.**3**
50 Manguin 4-9-2 PPaquet 1.4
70 Boucicault 4-9-2 YSaint-Martin 3.5
Montorselli 6-9-0 J-PRoman nk.6
Armistice Day 4-9-4 HRossi ½.7
Marittimo 3-8-7 FHead . . . 3.8
63 Monsieur Dagobert 4-9 0 MPhilipperon 5.9
Mac Flipper 4-9-2 FFlachi 2½.10

3/1 Perrault, 13/4 Boucicault, 21/4 Monsieur Dagobert, 33/4 Armistice Day, 86/10 PEROUGES, 35/4 Manguin, 10/1 Marittimo, 14/1 Montorselli, 15/1 Brousoy, 18/1 Mac Flipper.
A. Riviere (A. Lyon) 10rn 2m 36.0 (Good).

82 PRIX DE MENNEVAL 3y 1m 4½f
£10,320 Deauville 9 August

69 **Lancastrian** 9-4 ALequeux . **1**
Doux Lord 9-0 FHead . s.hd.**2**
25 **Bobiffic** 9-0 GDubroeucq . 1½.**3**
Vermillon Chine 8-12 G-WMoore 2½.4
65 Vezzani 9-0 FPegurri 2.5

7/10 LANCASTRIAN, 9/4 Doux

Lord, 5/1 Bobiffic, 14/1 Vermillon Chine, 15/1 Vezzani.
Sir M. Sobell (D. Smaga) 5rn 2m 44.5 (Good).

83 PRIX KERGORLAY 1m 7f
£20,408 Deauville 10 August
6 **Marson** 5-9-8 YSaint-Martin **1**
63* **Kelbomec** 4-9-4 J-CDesaint nk.**2**
38* **Shafaraz** 7-9-13 MPhilipperon ½.**3**
70 Anifa 4-9-5 AGibert......¾.4
63³ Monsieur Marcel 4-9-4 GDoleuze s.hd.5
Ferragu 3-8-7 ABadel......1.6
70 Son of Love 4-9-13 ALequeux 5.7
2/1 Shafaraz, 11/4 Kelbomec, 7/2 Son of Love, 9/2 Anifa, 15/2 MARSON, 11/1 Monsieur Marcel, 22/1 Ferragu.
M. Engel (R. Collet) 7rn 3m 14.4 (Good).

84 PRIX GONTAUT-BIRON 1¼m
£15,306 Deauville 15 August
81 **Armistice Day** 4-8-12 YSaint-Martin...........**1**
75³ **Hilal** 4-8-12 AGibert.....1.**2**
2 **Wild Oats** 5-8-12 JTaillard 3.**3**
81 Manguin 4-8-12 PPaquet..1.4
74 Kamaridaan 4-9-2 GDoleuze 1.5
75² Discretion 4-8-12 MPhilipperon 2½.6
75 Callio 4-8-12 ALequeux...3.7
2/1 Kamaridaan, 9/4 Discretion, 4/1 Hilal, 9/2 Manguin, 17/2 Callio, 10/1 ARMISTICE DAY, 25/1 Wild Oats.
L. U. Sanabria (C. de Watrigant) 7rn 2m 9.1 (Soft).

85 PRIX DE LA COTE NORMANDE 3y 1¼m
£15,306 Deauville 16 August
39³ **Glenorum** 8-9 ABadel......**1**
74* **Argument** 9-4 J-CDesaint hd.**2**
33 **Un Reitre** 8-9 PPaquet...nk.**3**
73² Dom d'Albignac 8-9 ALequeux...........s.nk.4
Opachisco 8-9 HSamani..1½.5
80³ Fabulous Prince 8-9 GDubroeucq..........1½.6
65³ Mot D'Or 9-2 FHead......¾.7
68 Dip 8-9 MJerome.........½.8
73 Indigene 8-6 J-PLefevre...½.9
73 Kareliaan 8-9 YSaint-Martin 1.10
73³ Nemr 9-0 AGibert..........0
Sarrad 8-9 GWMoore......0
4/1 Kareliaan, 19/4 Dom d'Albignac Mot D'Or, 11/2 Argument, 25/4 Opachisco, 11/1 Nemr, 14/1 GLENORUM, 15/1 Un Reitre, 19/1 Dip, 20/1 Fabulous Prince, Indigene, 23/1 Sarrad.
Mme A. W. Stollery (D. Smaga) 12rn 2m 6.9 (Dead).

86 PRIX JACQUES LE MAROIS 1m
£30,426 Deauville 17 August
66* **Nadjar** 4-9-2 ALequeux....**1**
34³ **Final Straw** 3-8-10 GStarkey.............nk.**2**
79 **Manjam** 3-8-10 GDoleuze 2½.**3**
79* Boitron 4-9-2 PPaquet..s.nk.4
Known Fact 3-8-10 PEddery nk.5
Star Way 3-8-10 LPiggott s.nk.6
57* Isopach 3-8-10 MDepalmas nk.7
75 Clodion 3-8-10 GWMoore 4.8
78 Light of Realm 3-8-7 MPhilipperon 1.9
14/10 NADJAR, 9/2 Final Straw, 11/2 Known Fact, 25/4 Boitron, 17/2 Isopach, 10/1 Light of Realm, 12/1 Star Way, 17/1 Manjam, 26/1 Clodion.
A. D. D. Rogers (A. Paus) 9rn 1m 38.4 (Dead).

87 PRIX DE PSYCHE 3y 1¼m
£15,213 Deauville 17 August
Sovereign Dona 8-13 PEddery **1**
Trevita 8-13 PCook.....hd.**2**
72 **Wild Idea** 8-13 J-PLefevre.½.**3**
64² Benicia 8-10 FHead.......2.4
78 As You Desire Me 8-13 ALequeux s.hd.5
32 Akinoa 8-13 J-CDesaint....8.6
6/10 Benicia, 15/4 As You Desire Me, 25/4 Akinoa, 17/2 Wild Idea, 9/1 Trevita, 15/1 SOVEREIGN DONA.
W. Vischer (S. Murless, Ireland) 6rn 2m 8.9 (Dead).

88 PRIX DE MEAUTRY 6f
£15,213 Deauville 20 August
79³ **Kilijaro** 4-8-8 ALequeux....**1**
79 **Northjet** 3-9-2 ABadel....5.**2**
Standaan 4-9-1 YSaint-Martin 2½.**3**
78 Lignee Grise 4-8-11 MPhilipperon 1.4
61² Miliar 3-8-7 GDoleuze...hd.5
79 Red Coral 5-9-1 PPaquet..1½.6
Try To Smile 3-8-7 RJallu.5.7
Come On Steve 8-9-4 JTaillard ½.8

6/10 KILIJARO and Try To Smile, 3/1 Miliar, 9/2 Standaan, 12/1 Lignee Grise, 13/1 Red Coral, 28/1 Northjet, 30/1 Come On Steve.
S. Fradkoff (O. Douieb) 8rn 1m 11.7 (Dead).

89 PRIX DE POMONE 1m 5½f
£15,213 Deauville 23 August

76² **Gold River** 3-8-7 FHead...**1**
49 **Mariella** 3-8-7 PPaquet....3.**2**
Larkland 3-8-7 ALequeux.1.**3**
83 Anifa 4-9-6 AGibert.......½.4
Saintonge 4-9-4 GWMoore 2.5
60 Luth Music 3-8-11 YSaint-Martin 1½.6
76² Proustille 3-8-9 MPhilipperon ½.7
76* Great Verdict 3-8-11 HSamani............s.hd.8
Benoite 4-9-4 SProu......2½.9
Kalinski 3-8-8 GDoleuze 2½.10

11/4 Proustille, 28/10 GOLD RIVER, 3/1 Anifa, 6/1 Luth Music, 12/1 Great Verdict, 15/1 Kalinski, 18/1 Larkland, Saintonge, 24/1 Mariella, 34/1 Benoite.
J. Wertheimer (A. Head) 10rn 3m 0.8 (Good).

90 PRIX MORNY 2y 6f
£25,100 Deauville 24 August

77² **Ancient Regime** 8-8 MPhilipperon............**1**
Miswaki 8-11 PPaquet....¾.**2**
Prince Mab 8-11 FHead..2.**3**
Watchdog 8-11 HSamani..ns.4
77* Irish Playboy 8-11 ALequeux............1½.5
Salmana 8-8 GWMoore....1.6
Noble Defi 8-11 YSaint-Martin 2.7

9/4 Miswaki, 5/2 Irish Playboy, Prince Mab, 57/10 ANCIENT REGIME, 9/1 Noble Defi, 12/1 Salmana, 23/1 Watchdog.
R. Scully (J. Fellows) 7rn 1m 10.1 (Good to Firm).

91 PRIX DE LA CALONNE 3y 1m
£10,040 Deauville 24 August

64 **Safita** 8-10 YSaint-Martin..**1**
72 **Exactly So** 8-10 GDubroeucq..........1½.**2**
87 **Benicia** 8-13 FHead......½.**3**
Trephine 8-13 PPaquet....¾.4
Lastline 8-10 GDoleuze...........s.hd.5
52 Bev Bev 8-13 J-CDesaint...1.6
3 Forbidden Fruit 8-13 HSamani..............2.7
Exegese 8-10 AGibert.....½.8

11/10 SAFITA, 3/1 Benicia, 9/2 Trephine, 10/1 Bev Bev, Lastline, 14/1 Exactly So, 19/1 Exegese, 20/1 Forbidden Fruit.
H.H. Aga Khan (F. Mathet) 8rn 1m 40.8 (Good to Firm).

92 PRIX QUINCEY 1m
£15,060 Deauville 28 August

88* **Kilijaro** 4-9-1 FHead......**1**
75* **Tassmoun** 4-9-4 YSaint-Martin 3.**2**
84 **Callio** 4-9-0 J-CDesaint...½.**3**
86 Boitron 4-9-6 PPaquet....nk.4
84² Hilal 4-9-0 AGibert.......½.5
80 Confetti 3-8-11 GWMoore.1.6
22 Planing 4-9-0 JPAGodard...........1½.7
78* Moon Ingraver 3-8-8 ABadel................1.8
17 Koboko 3-8-7 MPhilipperon 1½.9
88 Red Coral 5-9-1 GDubroeucq..........3.10

2/1 Tassmoun, 17/4 Moon Ingraver, 19/4 Hilal, 13/2 Boitron, 19/2 Confetti, 11/1 KILIJARO, Planing, 13/1 Callio, 18/1 Koboko, 37/1 Red Coral.
S. Fradkoff (O. Douieb) 10rn 1m 40.4 (Good).

93 PRIX DE LA NONETTE 3y 1¼m
£15,000 Deauville 31 August

72* **Detroit** 8-12 FHead........**1**
78² **India Song** 8-12 YSaint-Martin 2.**2**
64* **Luth de Saron** 9-0 MPhilipperon........s.nk.**3**
87² Trevita 8-10 PCook.......2.4
87³ Wild Idea 8-10 J-PLefevre.½.5
91 Trephine 8-10 PPaquet....3.6
Gamalat 8-10 AGibert.....¾.7
64 Evgenia 8-10 ABadel......2.8
85 Indigene 8-10 J-LKessas...½.9

9/10 DETROIT, 15/4 Luth de Saron, 6/1 India Song, 7/1 Wild Idea, 8/1 Trevita, 14/1 Trephine, 21/1 Indigene, 31/1 Gamalat, 32/1 Evgenia.
R. Sangster (O. Douieb) 9rn 2m 6.0 (Good).

94 GRAND PRIX DE DEAUVILLE 1m 5½f
£25,000 Deauville 31 August

85* **Glenorum** 3-8-7 LPiggott..**1**
81² **Perrault** 3-8-5 ABadel....3.**2**
Vincent 4-9-0 WCarson..nk.**3**
83* Marson 5-9-5 YSaint-Martin ¾.4
82² Doux Lord 3-8-5 GWMoore 1½.5
Akifool 4-9-0 DVincent...nk.6
81* Perouges 5-9-5 JLeDeunf..5.7

85 Mot D'Or 3-8-10 FHead . . 2½.8
48 Grandak 3-8-5 HSamani . . 2½.9
83[2] Kelbomec 4-9-0 J-CDesaint ½.10
40 River River 4-9-0 PPaquet . . . 0
65[2] What A Joy 3-8-5 J-LKessas . 0
89 Proustille 3-8-4 MPhilipperon 0

7/4 River River, 6/1 Doux Lord and Mot D'Or, 25/4 Perouges, 8/1 Marson, 37/4 Kelbomec, 10/1 Perrault, 13/1 What A Joy, 15/1 GLENORUM, 16/1 Vincent, 19/1 Grandak, 21/1 Proustille, 39/1 Akifool.

Mme. A. W. Stollery (D. Smaga) 13rn 2m 56.1 (Good).

95 PRIX DU CALVADOS 2y 7f

£15,000 Deauville 31 August

Bernica 8-10 PPaquet **1**
Phydilla 8-10 FHead ¾.**2**
Marie du Mont 9-0 APerrotta 5.**3**
Grecian Sea 8-10 MPhilipperon . ½.4
Libergold 8-10 HSamani . . . ¾.5
Nawazich 8-10 YSaint-Martin ½.6
Leandra 8-10 ABadel 2.7
Amberina 8-10 GWMoore . 6.8
Kouklita 8-10 J-LKessas . . . 1.9

5/4 Phydilla, 17/4 Leandra, 11/2 Nawazich, 25/4 Libergold, 9/1 Grecian Sea, 12/1 BERNICA, 16/1 Amberina, 27/1 Kouklita, 28/1 Marie du Mont.

J. Ternynck (F. Boutin) 9rn 1m 24.7 (Good).

96 GROSSER PREIS VON BADEN 1½m

£45,692 Baden-Baden 7 September

Nebos 4-9-6 LMader **1**
70 **Cherubin** 5-9-2 JDupin . . . 1.**2**
58* **Marracci** 4-9-6 MDepalmas ½.**3**
Nicholas Bill 5-9-4 PWaldron ¾.4
85[2] Argument 3-8-9 J-CDesaint ns.5
Toscarimus 3-8-7 GBocskai . 5.6
Navarino 3-8-9 DKRichardson ½.7
Cracaval 4-9-2 SCauthen 8
Jabo 5-9-2 MissFPflunger . . . 9
Pawiment 6-9-2 OGervai . . . 10

Countess M. Batthyany (H. Bollow) 10rn 2m 37.6 (Good).

97 PRIX LA ROCHETTE 2y 1m

£15,015 Longchamp 7 September

Vorias 8-13 PPaquet **1**
Shoen 9-2 GDubroeucq . . . ½.**2**
Padirac 8-10 FHead ¾.**3**
Proudfoot 8-10 GDoleuze . . 6.4

7/10 VORIAS, 5/2 Padirac, 3/1 Shoen, 5/1 Proudfoot.

P. Goulandris (F. Boutin) 4rn 1m 41.8 (Good).

98 PRIX DU MOULIN DE LONGCHAMP 1m

£35,035 Longchamp 7 September

92* **Kilijaro** 4-8-13 FHead **1**
86* **Nadjar** 4-9-2 YSaint-Martin nk.**2**
Katowice 4-9-2 J-LKessas . 2.**3**
92 Hilal 4-9-2 AGibert nk.4
66 Northern Baby 4-9-2 PPaquet 4.5
66[2] Foveros 4-9-2 EJohnson 7
86 Final Straw 3-8-12 GStarkey 2.8
86 Isopach 3-8-12 LPiggott . . . 4.9
78[3] Deliballe 3-8-9 ABadel . . . 2½.10
86[3] Manjam 3-8-12GDoleuze . . . 11
92[3] Callio 4-9-2 MPhilipperon . disq

Evens Nadjar and Northern Baby, 3/1 Final Straw, 61/10 KILIJARO, 19/2 Katowice, 12/1 Isopach, 16/1 Hilal, 21/1 Callio, 28/1 Manjam, 30/1 Foveros, 33/1 Deliballe.

Callio finished sixth, a neck behind Northern Baby and 2 lengths in front of Foveros, but was subsequently disqualified.

S. Fradkoff (O. Douieb) 11rn 1m 36.9 (Good).

99 PRIX D'ARENBERG 2y 5f

£15,015 Chantilly 9 September

Greenway 8-7 FHead **1**
Sharmada 8-10 YSaint-Martin 2½.**2**
Monday Morning 8-10 AGibert 2.**3**
77 Twig Prince 8-13 MPhilipperon ½.4
Affection 8-13 APerrotta . d-ht.4

13/10 GREENWAY, 2/1 Sharmada, 4/1 Twig Prince, 23/4 Affection, 9/1 Monday Morning.

J. Wertheimer (A. Head) 4rn 59.4 sec (Good).

100 PRIX NIEL 3y 1½m

£15,106 Longchamp 14 September

62[2] **Prince Bee** 9-2 WCarson . . . **1**
Satilla 8-9 AGibert 1½.**2**
73 **Ruscelli** 9-0 GDoleuze . . . nk.**3**
62 Garrido 9-4 PPaquet s.hd.4
85 Dom D'Albignac 8-12 FHead 1.5
74[2] Dhausli 8-12 J-LKessas . . . nk.6
Platinum 8-12 ABadel . . . s.nk.7
Bozovici 8-12 BTaylor . . s.hd.8
69[3] Policeman 9-4 YSaint-Martin 1.9

12/10 PRINCE BEE, 2/1 Policeman, 19/4 Dom D'Albignac, 17/1 Gar-

rido, 18/1 Ruscelli, 19/1 Platinum, 23/1 Dhausli, 24/1 Bozovici, 31/1 Satilla.
Sir M. Sobell (R. Hern) 9rn 2m 32.3 (Firm).

101 PRIX VERMEILLE 3y 1½m
£60,423 Longchamp 14 September

$52^{\star}$ **Mrs Penny** 9-2 JMatthias . . . **1**
71^{2} **Little Bonny** 9-2 CRoche . . ½.**2**
$93^{\star}$ **Detroit** 9-2 PEddery ¾.**3**
$89^{\star}$ Gold River 9-2 FHead ½.4
$36^{\star}$ Cairn Rouge 9-2 AMurray . ¾.5
89^{2} Mariella 9-2 PPaquet ns.6
52^{2} Aryenne 9-2 YSaint-Martin ¾.7
52^{3} Paranete 9-2 AGibert 2.8
36 Coneenford 9-2 SCauthen . . 3.9
Karelia 9-2 WCarson ½.10
94 Proustille 9-2 J-CDesaint . . . 11
93^{3} Luth de Saron 9-2 MPhilipperon 12

11/4 Detroit, 7/2 Aryenne, 17/4 Cairn Rouge, 13/2 Gold River, 88/10 MRS PENNY, 9/1 Luth de Saron, 16/1 Karelia, 17/1 Paranete, 29/1 Little Bonny, 35/1 Mariella, 37/1 Proustille, 55/1 Coneenford.
E. N. Kronfeld (I. Balding) 12rn 2m 34.9 (Firm).

102 PRIX FOY 1½m
£15,106 Longchamp 14 September

$22^{\star}$ **Le Marmot** 4-9-4 PPaquet . . **1**
89 **Anifa** 4-8-9 AGibert s.nk.**2**
69 **Gain** 4-8-12 FHead ½.**3**
Noelino 4-9-2 CRoche . . s.hd.4
81 Monsieur Dagobert 4-8-12 MPhilipperon 5.5

4/10 LE MARMOT, 19/4 Noelino, 5/1 Anifa, 27/4 Gain, 12/1 Monsieur Dagobert.
R. Schafer (F. Boutin) 5rn 2m 32.8 (Firm).

103 PRIX D'AUMALE 2y 1m
£15,106 Chantilly 16 September

Ukraine Girl 8-10 YSaint-Martin **1**
Ionian Raja 8-12 PPaquet . ½.**2**
Coral Dance 8-10 GDubroeucq ¾.**3**
90 Salmana 8-10 FHead ns.4
99 Affection 9-0 APerrotta . . . 1½.5
Lalaria 9-0 J-PLefevre . . s.hd.6
Marenga 8-10 ABadel ½.7
Black Pearl 8-10 J-CDesaint ½.8
Shangrila 8-10 JTaillard . s.hd.9

16/10 UKRAINE GIRL, 5/1 Ionian Raja, 6/1 Salmana, 7/1 Coral Dance, 8/1 Lalaria, 11/1 Marenga, Shangrila, 14/1 Affection, 20/1 Black Pearl.
Mrs. J. R. Mullion (R. Collet) 9rn 1m 41.6 (Good).

104 JOE MCGRATH MEMORIAL STAKES 1¼m
£20,484 Leopardstown 20 September

Gregorian (USA) 4-9-5 GMcGrath **1**
Spence Bay 5-9-5 AMurray s.hd.**2**
$47^{\star}$ **Night Alert** 3-8-11 WSwinburn 1½.**3**
$73^{\star}$ Corvaro 3-8-11 PPaquet s.hd.4
48 Gonzales 3-8-11 RCarroll . . 2.5
Pitsville 4-9-5 DGillespie . . 6.6
Phosphurian 4-9-5 PGilson 8.7
71^{3} Racquette 3-8-8 CRoche . . . 2.8
96 Cracaval 4-9-5 SCauthen . 1½.9
Sheringham 3-8-11 JDeegan 5.10
Combine Harvester 4-9-5 TCarberry . . . . p.u

11/4 GREGORIAN, 3/1 Corvaro, 11/2 Gonzales, 6/1 Cracaval, 7/1 Night Alert, 8/1 Racquette, 40/1 Pitsville, Spence Bay, 50/1 Combine Harvester, 100/1 Phosphurian, Sheringham.
D. Schwartz (V. O'Brien) 11rn 2m 7.8 (Good).

105 PRIX DE LA SALAMANDRE 2y 7f
£24,802 Longchamp 21 September

90^{2} **Miswaki** 8-11 PPaquet **1**
90^{3} **Prince Mab** 8-11 FHead . hd.**2**
Silver Express 8-11 AGibert 5.**3**
Travolta 8-11 YSaint-Martin 1½.4
$90^{\star}$ Ancient Regime 8-8 MPhilipperon ½.5

5/4 Ancient Regime, 21/10 MISWAKI, 11/4 Prince Mab, 13/2 Travolta, 19/2 Silver Express.
Mme A. Plesch (F. Boutin) 5rn 1m 22.7 (Good).

106 PRIX DE LUTECE 3y 1m 7f
£14,881 Longchamp 21 September

94 **What A Joy** 8-12 J-LKessas . **1**
65 **Tom's Serenade** 8-12 ABadel **2**
11 **Goldiko** 8-12 YSaint-Martin hd.**3**
65 Dhaubix 9-1 FHead 4
Mainland 8-12 PPaquet 4.5
65 Balibest 8-12 GDubroeucq . 5.6
Imperial Eagle 8-12 J-CDesaint 6.7

2/1 Tom's Serenade, 5/2 Goldiko, 13/4 Dhaubix, 34/10 WHAT A JOY, 14/1 Mainland, 17/1 Balibest, 28/1 Imperial Eagle.

Dhaubix finished second, a short neck behind What A Joy and ½ length in front of Tom's Serenade, but was subsequently disqualified and placed fourth. Tom's Serenade and Goldiko were promoted to second and third places respectively.

L. M. Gelb (B. Secly) 7rn 3m 24.2 (Good).

107 PRIX DU PRINCE D'ORANGE 1¼m
£14,881 Longchamp 21 September

69* **Dunette** 4-9-3 GDoleuze...**1**
44 **Three Troikas** 4-9-1 FHead ½.**2**
98 **Northern Baby** 4-9-4 PPaquet 1½.**3**
43 Viteric 3-8-10 AGibert...2½.4
48 Providential 3-9-0 RJallu..½.5
40* Moulouki 3-9-0 HSamani s.nk.6
74 Strong Gale 5-9-0 YSaint-Martin s.nk.7

7/10 Three Troikas, 49/10 DUNETTE, 11/2 Providential, 27/4 Moulouki and Viteric, 29/4 Northern Baby, 37/4 Strong Gale.

Mme H. A. Love (E. Chevalier du Fau) 7rn 2m 9.8 (Good).

108 PRIX DE SEINE-ET-OISE 6f
£13,889 Maisons-Laffitte 22 September

98* **Kilijaro** 4-9-5 ALequeux...**1**
92 **Boitron** 4-9-8 PPaquet..1½.**2**
88 **Northjet** 3-9-6 FHead....1.**3**
Realeza 3-9-6 JDupin.....2.4
88 Lignee Grise 4-9-5 MPhilipperon 4.5
79 Snapper Point 3-9-6 YSaint-Martin 2.6
88 Come On Steve 8-9-8 MJerome 1½.7
Avricourt 2-7-12 GGuignard 5.8

6/10 KILIJARO, 3/1 Boitron, 7/1 Northjet, 18/1 Lignee Grise, Snapper Point, 26/1 Avricourt, 33/1 Come On Steve, 40/1 Realeza.

S. Fradkoff (O. Douieb) 8rn 1m 11.3 (Dead).

109 CRITERIUM DE MAISONS-LAFFITTE 2y 7f
£14,881 Maisons-Laffitte 25 September

Cresta Rider 8-7 PPaquet..**1**
77 **Diamond Prospect** 8-7 AGibert 1½.**2**
97 **Shoen** 8-11 YSaint-Martin.1.**3**
Sun Row 8-7 FHead......¾.4
99 Twig Prince 8-11 MPhilipperon 3.5

4/10 CRESTA RIDER, 13/4 Shoen, 33/4 Sun Row, 35/4 Diamond Prospect, 46/1 Twig Prince.

S. Niarchos (F. Boutin) 5rn 1m 32.3 (Good).

110 PRIX DES CHENES 2y 1m
£14,925 Longchamp 28 September

Dunphy 8-9 FHead........**1**
90 **Watchdog** 8-9 YSaint-Martin 1½.**2**
Big John 8-9 GDoleuze..hd.**3**
Rahotep 8-9 J-LKessas..1½.4
Brinkbero 8-9 PPaquet...½.5
Singapore River 8-9 ALequeux ½.6
Mont Pelion 8-9 MPhilipperon 2.7
Delta Fox 8-9 AGibert..1½.8

9/4 Watchdog, 3/1 Singapore River, 34/10 DUNPHY, 15/2 Brinkbero, Rahotep, 9/1 Mont Pelion, 16/1 Big John, 24/1 Delta Fox.

Mme A. Head (Mme C. Head) 8rn 1m 44.5 (Dead).

111 PRIX DU ROND-POINT 1m
£14,925 Longchamp 28 September

98 **Hilal** 4-9-0 AGibert........**1**
91* **Safita** 3-8-8 YSaint-Martin 2½.**2**
50* **Rostov** 6-9-2 FHead.....½.**3**
98[3] Katowice 4-9-0 J-LKessas..½.4
79 Gosport 4-9-0 J-CDesaint.1½.5
66 Dragon 3-8-11 HSamani..1½.6
86 Clodion 3-8-11 MPhilipperon s.hd.7
75 Suvero 3-8-11 PPaquet..s.hd.8
78 Teacher's Pet 3-8-8 ALequeux 4.9
Springfield House 7-9-0 APerrotta 6.10

2/1 Safita, 3/1 HILAL and Dragon, 13/4 Katowice, 5/1 Rostov, 11/1 Gosport, 12/1 Teacher's Pet, 26/1 Suvero, 33/1 Clodion, 54/1 Springfield House.

M. Fustok (M. Saliba) 10rn 1m 42.6 (Dead).

112 PRIX GLADIATEUR 2½m
£14,925 Longchamp 28 September

102[2] **Anifa** 4-8-9 AGibert **1**
Le Moss 5-9-4 JMercer...½.**2**
94 **Kelbomec** 4-8-12 J-CDesaint 1½.**3**
94 Marson 5-9-2 YSaint-Martin 3.4
38 Croque Monsieur 6-8-12 J-PLefevre ½.5
Challal 4-8-12 HSamani ..10.6
63 Marriageable 6-8-12 J-P-AGodard 20.7

7/10 Le Moss, 3/1 Marson, 42/10 ANIFA and Challal, 15/2

Kelbomec, 19/1 Croque Monsieur, 21/1 Marriageable.

M. Fustok (M. Saliba) 7rn 4m 32.0 (Dead).

113 LA COUPE DE MAISONS-LAFFITTE 1¼m

£13,930 Maisons-Laffitte 29 September

84 **Discretion** 4-9-2 MPhilipperon **1**
80 **Speed Bus** 3-8-6 GDubroeucq ½.**2**
93[2] **India Song** 3-8-9 YSaint-Martin nk.**3**
Arnol 4-9-2 FHead.......¾.4
100 Dom d'Albignac 3-8-12 ALequeux ns.5
66[3] In Fijar 3-9-2 AGibert...hd.6
80[2] Falamoun 3-8-10 J-CDesaint ¾.7
80 Tajtal 3-8-6 J-LKessas....2.8
Dauphin du Roi 7-9-2 HSamani 6.9
98 Callio 4-8-12 ABadel.....2.10
Dernier Violon 5-9-4 SProu..0
81 Montorselli 6-9-2 J-PRoman 0
84 Manguin 4-9-2 PPaquet.....0
102 Monsieur Dagobert 4-9-2 APerrotta 0
66 The Expatriate 3-8-10 JDupin 0

3/1 India Song, 9/2 In Fijar, 5/1 Dom D'Albignac, 67/10 DISCRETION, 9/1 Callio, 10/1 Dernier Violon, 17/1 Arnol, Tajtal, 21/1 Manguin, 22/1 Speed Bus, 23/1 Falamoun, 26/1 Dauphin du Roi, 34/1 The Expatriate, 57/1 Montorselli, 64/1 Monsieur Dagobert.

Sir M. Sobell (J. Cunnington, jnr) 15rn 2m 3.0 (Good).

114 PRIX SAINT-ROMAN 2y 1m 1f

£14,925 Longchamp 4 October

Mariacho 8-11 GDoleuze...**1**
Arc d'Or 8-11 MPhilipperon........s.nk.**2**
The Wonder 8-11 ALequeux............hd.**3**
Lou Piguet 8-11 J-CDesaint..........s.nk.4
Troubetzkoy 8-11 PPaquet.½.5
In Tissar 8-11 AGibert...1½.6
Lyllos 8-11 FHead........½.7
Kebir Khan 8-11 YSaint-Martin 4.8

5/2 MARIACHO, 7/2 Arc d'Or, 15/4 In Tissar, 9/2 Troubetzkoy, 5/1 Lou Piguet, 31/4 The Wonder, 9/1 Lyllos, 18/1 Kebir Khan.

Mme A. Savin (F. Palmer) 8rn 1m 57.4 (Good to Firm).

115 PRIX MARCEL BOUSSAC 2y 1m

(formerly Criterium des Pouliches)

£24,975 Longchamp 5 October

Tropicaro 8-9 ALequeux...**1**
103[3] **Coral Dance** 8-9 GDubroeucq...........**2.2**
103 **Salmana** 8-9 FHead.....hd.**3**
95* Bernica 8-9 PPaquet......ns.4
Last Love 8-9 HSamani............s.nk.5
95[3] Marie du Mont 8-9 APerrotta hd.6
Blue Wind 8-9 CRoche..d.ht.6
Kazadancoa 8-9 J-CDesaint 2.8
103[2] Ionian Raja 8-9 LPiggott............s.hd.9
103*Ukraine Girl 8-9 YSaint-Martin ½.10

6/4 Bernica, 26/10 TROPICARO 4/1 Ukraine Girl, 9/1 Ionian Raja, 11/1 Blue Wind, 20/1 Coral Dance, 21/1 Kazadancoa, 28/1 Last Love, 32/1 Salmana, 33/1 Marie du Mont.

B. Coates (M. Zilber) 10rn 1m 43.4 (Firm).

116 PRIX DE L'ABBAYE DE LONGCHAMP 5f

£24,975 Longchamp 5 October

79[2] **Moorestyle** 3-9-11 LPiggott.**1**
Sharpo 3-9-11 PEddery..1½.**2**
Valeriga 4-9-11 GStarkey.............nk.**3**
61* Adraan 3-9-11 YSaint-Martin 2½.4
90 Irish Playboy 2-8-8 ALequeux.............¾.5
Jasmine Star 4-9-11 WCarson..............1.6
108[3] Northjet 3-9-11 PPaquet...2.7
99* Greenway 2-8-6 FHead...1½.8
36 Nazwa 3-9-7 JMercer 1½.9

5/4 Adraan, 17/10 MOORESTYLE, 33/4 Sharpo, 9/1 Greenway, 11/1 Irish Playboy, 32/1 Jasmine Star, Valeriga, 34/1 Northjet, 69/1 Nazwa.

Moores International Furnishings Limited (R. Armstrong) 9rn 56.3s (Firm).

117 PRIX DE L'ARC DE TRIOMPHE 1½m

£119,880 Longchamp 5 October

101[3] **Detroit** 3-8-8 PEddery.....**1**
96 **Argument** 3-8-11 J-CDesaint ½.**2**
Ela-Mana-Mou 4-9-4 WCarson s.hd.**3**
107[2] Three Troikas 4-9-1 FHead nk.4
96* Nebos 4-9-4 LMader......1.5
96 Nicholas Bill 5-9-4 PWaldron 2.6
107*Dunette 4-9-1 GDoleuze...........s.nk.7

102* Le Marmot 4-9-4 PPaquet . ½.8
100^{3} Ruscelli 3-8-11 MPhilipperon ¾.9
100^{2} Satilla 3-8-8 APerrotta . . . 2.10
101^{2} Little Bonny 3-8-8 CRoche 3.11
107 Moulouki 3-8-11 AGibert hd.12
Niniski 4-9-4 JMercer ½.13
107 Providential 3-8-11 ALequeux s.hd.14
101* Mrs Penny 3-8-8 JMatthias ½.15
100 Policeman 3-8-11 GDubroeucq s.hd.16
69 Noble Saint 4-9-4 GStarkey 5.17
94* Glenorum 3-8-11 LPiggott 4.18
Lindoro 4-9-4 MLThomas t.o.19
Iseo 5-9-4 JHeloury t.o.20

2/1 Ela-Mana-Mou and Le Marmot, 4/1 Three Troikas, 67/10 DETROIT, 7/1 Nebos, 12/1 Policeman and Iseo, Glenorum, Mrs Penny, 15/1 Dunette, 21/1 Niniski and Lindoro, 32/1 Providential, 41/1 Little Bonny, 70/1 Nicholas Bill, 74/1 Argument, 76/1 Moulouki, 80/1 Ruscellli, 99/1 Noble Saint, Satilla.

R. Sangster (O. Douieb) 20rn 2m 28.0 (Firm).

118 PRIX DE L'OPERA 1m 1¼f
£19,980 Longchamp 5 October

64^{3} **Hortensia** 3-8-10 ALequeux **1**
92 **Moon Ingraver** 3-8-10 YSaint-Martin ½.**2**
93 **Wild Idea** 3-8-10 J-PLefevre ¾.**3**
91^{3} Benicia 3-8-10 FHead . . . s.nk.4
61 Pom Poes 3-8-10 AGibert . . 2.5
89 Luth Music 3-8-10 MJerome ¾.6
Fair Davina 4-9-0 J-CDesaint ½.7
87* Sovereign Dona 3-8-10 JMercer 5.8
Kalliope 3-8-10 LMader . . . 2.9
Fast Bird 3-8-10 ABadel . 15.10

5/4 Benicia, 36/10 HORTENSIA, 11/2 Wild Idea and Fast Bird, 27/4 Moon Ingraver, 8/1 Sovereign Dona, 15/1 Pom Poes, 18/1 Luth Music, 21/1 Kalliope, 32/1 Fair Davina.

R. Sangster (O. Douieb) 10rn 1m 52.2 (Firm).

119 CRITERIUM NAZIONALE 2y 6f
£9,723 Milan 21 September

Jeanne Iron 8-8 GDettori . . . **1**
Alvar Major 8-11 ADi Nardo 1½.**2**
Bal Ami 8-11 CForte 1.**3**
59 Pizzocorno 8-11 VPanici . . 2.4
Arctic Walker 8-11 MSacco 3.5
59^{2} Seiorlando 8-11 SAtzori . . 1.6

4/5 JEANNE IRON, 6/4 Bal Ami, 4/1 Seiorlando, 16/1 Alvar Major, 25/1 Arctic Walker, 40/1 Pizzocorno.

Scuderia Cieffedi (M. Andreucci) 6rn 1m 13.1 (Good).

120 PREMIO FEDERICO TESIO 1m 3f
£9,723 Milan 21 September

58^{3} **Marmolada** 3-8-6 CForte . . **1**
73 **Pian Del Lupo** 3-8-9 PPerlanti 2.**2**
84* **Armistice Day** 4-9-2 HRossi 2½.**3**
66 Ladislao di Oppelm 4-9-2 SFancera sh.4
Van Houten 5-9-2 SDettori 1.5
29 Quadrupler 4-8-13 MDepalmas 3.6
Brenneville 4-9-2 ADi Nardo 3.7
58 Black Marlin 7-9-2 VPanici. pu

2/5 MARMOLADA, 2/1 Armistice Day, 6/1 Van Houten, 8/1 Pian del Lupo, 15/1 Ladislao di Oppelm, 25/1 Quadrupler, 30/1 Brenneville, 200 Black Marlin.

Scuderia Gabriella (E. Camici) 8rn 2m 16 (Good).

121 ST LEGER ITALIANO 3y 1¾m
£8,491 Milan 28 September

55^{2} **Lotar** 9-2 PPerlanti **1**
Barbaccio 9-2 SDettori . . . ½.**2**
54^{3} **Zambrano** 9-2 MDepalmas 1½.**3**
30 Narvaez 9-2 OPessi 2.4
Rapanello 9-2 ADi Nardo . . 6.5
Blakes Beacon 9-2 PEddery 2.6

Evens LOTAR, 16/10 Blakes Beacon, 5/2 Zambrano and Narvaez, 20/1 Barbaccio, 50/1 Rapanello.

Scuderia dell'Abete Blu (A. Botti) 6rn 3m 03.9 (Good).

122 MAN O'WAR STAKES 1m 3f
£35,125 Belmont 3 October

French Colonial 5-9-0 JVasquez **1**
Just A Game 4-8-11 DBrumfield 1½.**2**
Golden Act 4-9-0 LPincay, jnr 3¾.**3**
70* Buckpoint 4-9-0 CJMcCarron ns.4
Morold 5-9-0 EMaple ½.5

9/10 Just A Game, 29/10 Golden Act, 41/10 Buckpoint, 56/10 Morold,

107/10 FRENCH COLONIAL.
Lazy F. Ranch (D. Whiteley) 5rn 2m 15.4 (Firm).

123 PREMIO LYDIA TESIO 1¼m
£15,769 Rome 4 October

120* **Marmolada** 3-8-10 CForte . **1**
41 **Tibalda** 3-8-10 OPessi 6.**2**
Incantada 4-9-0 RSannino 4.**3**
41^{2} Cos Display 3-8-10 GDettori 4.4
Risacca 3-8-10 MMassimi . . 4.5
Black Star 4-9-0 RFestinesi 6.6
120 Quadrupler 4-9-0 SFancera 3.7

1/4 MARMOLADA, 5/2 Tibalda, 10/1 Cos Display, 16/1 Risacca, 20/1 Quadrupler, 33/1 Incantada, 200/1 Black Star.
Scuderia Gabriella (E. Camici) 7rn 2m 2.8 (Good).

124 IRISH ST LEGER 3y 1¾m
£21,578 The Curragh 11 October

104 **Gonzales** 9-0 RCarroll **1**
65 **Good Thyne** 9-0 AMurray . 5.**2**
El Cito 9-0 Joanna Morgan . 3.**3**
Sir Mordred 9-0 PShanahan ¾.4
62^{3} Ramian 9-0 WSwinburn . . 2½.5
Prancing Prince 9-0 DJMurphy 1.6
104 Sheringham 9-0 JDeegan 7
Capitano 9-0 GCurran 8

4/7 GONZALES, 7/2 Ramian, 13/2 Good Thyne, 16/1 Capitano, 25/1 Sheringham, 33/1 Prancing Prince, 50/1 El Cito, Sir Mordred.
R. Sangster (V. O'Brien) 8rn 3m 23.6 (Soft).

125 GRAND CRITERIUM 2y 1m
£49,505 Longchamp 12 October

Recitation 8-11 GStarkey . . **1**
Critique 8-11 PEddery . s.hd.**2**
110* **Dunphy** 8-11 FHead 1.**3**
109* Cresta Rider 8-11 PPaquet s.hd.4
Great Substence 8-11 AGibert 1½.5
110^{2} Watchdog 8-11 LPiggott . . ¾.6
Pink Prism 8-8 ALequeux . . 6.7
109^{3} Shoen 8-11 YSaint-Martin s.hd.8
105 Travolta 8-11 MPhilipperon 8.9
Music Streak 8-11 JTandari 5.10
Gilgit 8-11 ABadel 11

7/4 Cresta Rider and Gilgit, Dunphy, 25/4 Critique, 12/1 Shoen, Watchdog, 14/1 RECITATION, 18/1 Music Streak, 20/1 Pink Prism, 24/1 Great Substence, 27/1 Travolta.
A Bodie (G. Harwood) 11rn 1m 44.2 (Dead).

126 PRIX DE ROYALLIEU 1m 4½f
£14,851 Longchamp 12 October

101 **Mariella** 3-8-8 PPaquet **1**
101 **Gold River** 3-8-11 FHead . ¾.**2**
101 **Karelia** 3-8-8 MPhilipperon 2.**3**
101 Proustille 3-8-8 J-CDesaint . ¾.4
La Toulzanie 3-8-8 YSaint-Martin ns.5
Nanthilde 3-8-8 DVincent . 2½.6
89 Great Verdict 3-8-11 HSamani ¾.7
93 Indigene 3-8-11 J-PLefevre 5.8
89^{3} Larkland 3-8-8 ALequeux . 6.9
Riverlily 3-8-8 LPiggott . . 3.10

Evens Gold River, 57/10 MARIELLA, 29/4 La Toulzanie, 8/1 Karelia, 11/1 Proustille, 12/1 Larkland, 15/1 Nanthilde, 16/1 Great Verdict, 18/1 Riverlily, 20/1 Indigene.
G. A. Oldham (F. Boutin) 10rn 2m 49.3 (Dead).

127 GRAN CRITERIUM 2y 1m
£15,685 Milan 12 October

Glint of Gold 8-11 JMatthias **1**
Bold Brigadier 8-11 PPerlanti 3½.**2**
No Piracy 8-11 GSorrentino 3.**3**
119^{2} Alvar Major 8-11 ADiNardo s.nk.4
Rilo 8-11 SDettori hd.5
Semipalatinsk 8-11 GDettori 1½.6
Guest Day 8-11 GFois 2.7
119 Pizzocorno 8-11 CCastaldi 1.8
103 Affection 8-8 APerrotta 2.9
The Daan 8-11 LBietolini . 2.10
Maratoneta 8-11 NMulas 11
Champoluc 8-11 SAtzori 12
Princely Unfair 8-11 WCarson 13
119 Seiorlando 8-11 CForte 14
Scapricciatello 8-11 PAgus 15
59* Erodoto 8-11 GPucciatti 16

6/4 GLINT OF GOLD, 6/1 Semipalatinsk and Erodoto, 13/2 Princely Unfair and The Daan, 15/2 Affection, 8/1 Champoluc and Scapricciatello, 9/1 Bold Brigadier, 10/1 No Piracy, 12/1 Rilo, 13/1 Maratoneta, 14/1 Alvar Major, 25/1 Seiorlando, 33/1 Guest Day, 100/1 Pizzocorno.
P. Mellon (I. Balding) 16rn 1m 44.1 (Soft).

128 CANADIAN INTERNATIONAL CHAMPIONSHIP 1m 5f
£42,857 Woodbine 13 October

Great Neck 4-9-0 MVenezia.**1**
122 **Buckpoint** 4-9-0 RPlatts.2½.**2**
Ben Fab 3-8-6 GStahlbaum 1¼.**3**
122[3] Golden Act 4-9-0 SHawley 1¼.4
106[2] Tom's Serenade 3-8-6 LPincay, jun...........½.5
Lobsang 4-9-0 DClark.....¾.6
Proctor 3-8-6 VBracciale, jnr........2½.7
Rossi Gold 4-9-0 PDay....½.8
122 Morold 5-9-0 EMaple....2½.9
102[3] Gain 4-9-0 LDuffy.....7½.10

19/10 Ben Fab, 28/10 Rossi Gold, 44/10 Golden Act, 8/1 Gain, 93/10 Tom's Serenade, 132/10 Buckpoint, 15/1 Proctor, 196/10 GREAT NECK, 42/1 Morold, 128/1 Lobsang.

Tartan Stable (Jan H. Nerud) 10rn 2m 42.6 (Firm).

129 PRIX ECLIPSE 2y 6½f
£13,861 Saint-Cloud 13 October

95[2] **Phydilla** 8-8 ALequeux.....**1**
105[3] **Silver Express** 8-11 AGibert 1½.**2**
77 **Valgo** 8-7 MPhilipperon.ns.**3**
Matho 8-7 MJerome......1.4
Singing Boy 8-7 YSaint-Martin 2½.5
Spoleto 8-11 PPaquet...s.hd.6
95 Amberina 8-4 SGorli......½.7
103 Lalaria 8-8 J-PLefevre...2½.8
Arock 8-7 HSamani.......6.9

Evens PHYDILLA, 3/1 Spoleto, 6/1 Silver Express, 9/1 Singing Boy, Valgo, 11/1 Arock, 17/1 Lalaria, 38/1 Matho, 50/1 Amberina.

R. Sangster (O. Douieb) 9rn 1m 26/1 (Soft).

130 PRIX DE CONDE 2y 1¼m
£14,368 Longchamp 19 October

114[3] **The Wonder** 9-0 YSaint-Martin **1**
110 **Brinkbero** 8-12 ALequeux..**2**
114 **In Tissar** 8-12 AGibert...nk.**3**
Ledmir 8-12 HSamani......4
110 Rahotep 8-12 J-LKessas.s.hd.5
97* Vorias 9-2 PPaquet.......3.6
114[2] Arc d'Or 8-12 MPhilipperon 2.7
97[3] Padirac 8-12 FHead.......1.8

7/4 Arc d'Or, 38/10 THE WONDER, 9/2 Brinkbero, 11/2 Vorias, 29/4 Ledmir, 12/1 Rahotep, 14/1 In Tissar, 16/1 Padirac.

Ledmir finished second, a short neck behind The Wonder and 1½ lengths in front of Brinkbero, but, after an objection by the riders of Brinkbero and In Tissar, was disqualified and placed fourth.

Mme A. du Breil (J. de Chevigny) 8rn 2m 16.9 (Soft).

131 PRIX DU PETIT COUVERT 5f
£14,368 Longchamp 19 October

116 **Greenway** 2-8-5 FHead....**1**
Blue Persian 3-9-7 BRaymond 1½.**2**
108 **Realeza** 3-9-11 JDupin...1½.**3**
Blue Courtier 3-9-11 AGibert 2½.4
61 Selerina 3-9-7 PBruneau..3.5
129 Matho 2-8-8 MJerome....¾.6

9/10 GREENWAY and Selerina, 3/1 Blue Persian, 4/1 Realeza, 11/2 Blue Courtier, 25/4 Matho.

J. Wertheimer (A. Head) 6rn 1m 0.5 (Soft).

132 PRIX DU CONSEIL DE PARIS 1½m
£28,736 Longchamp 19 October

En Calcat 4-9-0 MPhilipperon **1**
82* **Lancastrian** 3-8-13 LPiggott ½.**2**
117 **Satilla** 3-8-5 APerrotta..2½.**3**
117 Providential 3-9-3 PPaquet..............ns.4
94[2] Perrault 3-8-10 ABadel..s.nk.5
126 Proustille 3-8-7 J-CDesaint.5.6
117 Moulouki 3-9-1 AGibert...2.7
106 Dhaubix 3-8-13 YSaint-Martin 2.8
113[2] Speed Bus 3-8-8 GDubroeucq 6.9
94 Doux Lord 3-8-8 PBruneau 1.10
102 Noelino 4-9-6 HSamani.....0
60 Ho Han Wai 4-9-1 GDoleuze.0
100 Platinum 3-8-8 ALequeux...0
Sir Raleigh 3-8-8 FHead.....0

7/2 Doux Lord and Sir Raleigh, 4/1 Lancastrian, 21/4 Providential, 7/1 Perrault, 17/2 Dhaubix, 37/4 Satilla, 14/1 Noelino, 17/1 Proustille, 18/1 Platinum, 39/2 EN CALCAT, 20/1 Moulouki, 25/1 Speed Bus, 26/1 Ho Han Wai.

P. Barthe (J. Cunnington, jnr) 14rn 2m 41.3 (Soft).

133 PRIX DE FLORE 3y 1m 2½f
£13,410 Saint-Cloud 20 October

118 **Benicia** 8-13 FHead.........**1**
14 **Good to Beat** 9-2 RJallu.1½.**2**
126 **Indigene** 9-2 J-PLefevre.2½.**3**
93 Evgenia 8-10 ABadel.....hd.4
126* Mariella 9-2 PPaquet....hd.5

Dramatic Lady 8-10 YSaint-Martin 1½.6
Liane de Pougy 8-10 ALequeux 2.7
32 La Nobleza 8-10 GDubroeucq 6.8
87 Akinoa 8-13 J-CDesaint....6.9

14/10 BENICIA, 3/1 Mariella, 6/1 Dramatic Lady, Liane de Pougy, 7/1 Good To Beat, 29/1 Akinoa, Indigene, 31/1 Evgenia, 52/1 La Nobleza.

Mme A. Head (Mme C. Head) 9rn 2m 21.2 (Good).

134 PRIX DES RESERVOIRS 2y 1m
£14,368 Longchamp 21 October

Votre Altesse 8-9 GDoleuze.**1**
Marie Noelle 8-9 YSaint-Martin s.hd.**2**
Riverdina 8-9 FHead.....½.**3**
115 Ionian Raja 8-9 ABadel...¾.4
115 Last Love 8-9 HSamani..nk.5
125 Pink Prism 8-9 ALequeux.1½.6
Layalina 8-9 AGibert.....¾.7
La Margalaise 8-9 MPhilipperon 4.8
Ska 8-9 GDubroeucq.....nk.9
Godille 8-9 PPaquet......4.10

9/4 Riverdina, 3/1 Marie Noelle, 5/1 Pink Prism, 59/10 VOTRE ALTESSE and Layalina, 7/1 Last Love, 8/1 Godille, 12/1 La Margalaise, 29/1 Ionian Raja, 35/1 Ska.

M. Fustok (M. Saliba) 10rn 1m 48.5 (Soft).

135 TURF CLASSIC 1½m
£74,074 Aqueduct 25 October

112***Anifa** 4-8-11 AGibert......**1**
128 **Golden Act** 4-9-0 JFell...3.**2**
John Henry 5-9-0 LPincay, jnr...........5.**3**
Match The Hatch 4-9-0 CJMcCarron nk.4
100 Garrido 3-8-9 PPaquet....1¾.5
128[2] Buckpoint 4-9-0 JVelasquez 1¾.6
Temperence Hill 3-8-9 EMaple 4¼.7
117 Three Troikas 4-8-11 FHead 6¼.8

2/1 John Henry, 24/10 Temperence Hill, Three Troikas, 9/1 Buckpoint, 103/10 Match The Hatch, 171/10 Golden Act, 418/10 Garrido, 443/10 ANIFA.

M. Fustok (M. Saliba) 8rn 2m 43.7 (Heavy).

136 PREMIO VITTORIO DI CAPUA 1m
£11,699 Rome 25 October

98 **Isopach** 3-8-9 MDepalmas..**1**
120[2] **Pian Del Lupo** 3-8-9 PPerlanti 1¼.**2**
58 **Good Times** 4-8-11 GDettori nk.**3**
Geoffrey's Sister 4-8-8 JBleasdale 3.4
120 Van Houten 5-8-11 SDettori nk.5
Orbiolo 5-8-11 VPanici....½.6
57 Godot 3-8-9 ADiNardo....4.7
Brilli Peri 3-8-9 RSannino..2.8

13/10 ISOPACH, 7/2 Pian del Lupo, 4/1 Good Times, 9/2 Geoffrey's Sister, 10/1 Van Houten, 45/1 Godot, 50/1 Orbiolo, 100/1 Brilli Peri.

N. B. Hunt (L. Turner) 8rn 1m 44.5 (Heavy).

137 PREMIO DORMELLO 2y 1m
£9,221 Milan 26 October

Val D'Erica 8-11 PPerlanti..**1**
Tysfjsa 8-11 MDepalmas..4.**2**
59 **All Silk** 8-11 SAtzori.....1.**3**
Yang Tze 8-11 GDettori...1.4
127 Affection 8-11 APerrotta s.hd.5
Don Furia 8-11 CForte....2.6
Genisbay 8-11 GPucciatti..2.7
Dabat 8-11 SFancera......2.8

5/6 Tysfjsa, 7/2 All Silk, 7/1 Yang Tze, 8/1 Don Furia, 9/1 VAL D'ERICA, 10/1 Affection, 14/1 Genisbay, 22/1 Dabat.

Scud. dell'Abete Blu (A. Botti) 8rn 1m 43.5 (Heavy).

138 GRAN PREMIO DEL JOCKEY CLUB 1½m
£34,578 Milan 26 October

96 **Pawiment** 6-9-3 CGervai...**1**
121***Lotar** 3-8-11 PPerlanti....8.**2**
123***Marmolada** 3-8-8 CForte.8.**3**
Dahomey 4-9-3 UCavalleri.............7.4
Dukedom 3-8-11 JMatthias.............½.5
Iskenderun 4-9-3 GDettori 8.6

6/4 Marmolada and Iskenderun, 2/1 Lotar and Dahomey, 5/2 PAWIMENT, 3/1 Dukedom.

Gestut Moritzberg (C. Seiffert) 6rn 2m 26.4 (Heavy).

139 PRIX DE LA FORET 7f
£28,436 Longchamp 26 October

116***Moorestyle** 3-9-11 LPiggott.**1**
Crofter 3-9-11 PEddery...1.**2**
108***Kilijaro** 4-9-9 ALequeux..½.**3**
67*(dis)Ya Zaman 3-9-11 AGibert.............nk.4
111[2] Safita 3-9-8 YSaint-Martin 1.5
79 Princesse Lida 3-9-8 FHead.............s.nk.6
67* Luck of the Draw 3-9-8 WCarson 5.7

115^{*}Tropicaro 2-8-2 J-LKessas . 5.8
Gods Mark 4-9-12 DHogan dist.9

18/10 MOORESTYLE, 5/2 Kilijaro, 11/2 Tropicaro, 31/2 Safita, 11/1 Luck of the Draw, 13/1 Crofter, Princesse Lida, 24/1 Ya Zaman, 49/1 Gods Mark.

Moores International Furnishings Limited (R. Armstrong) 9rn 1m 25.8 (Heavy).

140 PRIX ROYAL-OAK 1m 7½f
£28,436 Longchamp 26 October

126^{2} **Gold River** 3-8-9 FHead . . . **1**
83 **Monsieur Marcel** 4-9-3 GDoleuze 3.**2**
Ardross 4-9-3 LPiggott . s.hd.**3**
83^{3} Shafaraz 7-9-3 MPhilipperon hd.4
94^{3} Vincent 4-9-3 ALequeux . . 1½.5
117 Niniski 4-9-3 WCarson . . . hd.6
106^{*}What A Joy 3-8-12 J-LKessas 6.7
126 Great Verdict 3-8-9 HSamani 6.8
65^{*} Valiant Heart 3-8-12 AGibert 2.9
106^{3} Goldiko 3-8-12 YSaint-Martin s.hd.10
117 Lindoro 4-9-3 MLThomas . . . 0
18 Montjardin 4-9-3 JTaillard . . 0
132 Dhaubix 3-8-12 GDubroeucq 0

11/4 Ardross, 15/4 Shafaraz, 4/1 Niniski and Lindoro, 7/1 GOLD RIVER, 37/4 Goldiko, 10/1 Valiant Heart, 16/1 Vincent, What A Joy, 24/1 Montjardin, 25/1 Dhaubix, 33/1 Monsieur Marcel, 65/1 Great Verdict.

J. Wertheimer (A. Head) 13rn 3m 39.5 (Heavy).

141 PREMIO CHIUSURA 7f
£20,520 Milan 3 November

Esclavo 4-9-6 RSuerland . . . **1**
116^{2} **Valeriga** 4-9-6 GDettori . 1½.**2**
136^{*}**Isopach** 3-9-6 MDepalmas nk.**3**
42 Red Rocket 3-9-6 SDettori nk.4
Vargas Llosa 4-9-6 GFois . 1½.5
Garozzo 4-9-6 SAtzori 1.6
127 Alvar Major 2-8-0 ADiNardo ½.7
41^{3} Adolfina 3-9-3 PPerlanti . . . 1.8
27 Royal Brook 3-9-6 AMarcialis 3.9
136 Godot 3-9-6 CForte 10
Steel Dancer 3-9-6 GFontini 11
111 Teacher's Pet 3-9-3 RJallu 12
Conrad 2-8-0 VPanici 13

6/4 Valeriga, 9/4 Isopach, 4/1 ESCLAVO, 7/1 Teacher's Pet, 12/1 Red Rocket, 15/1 Alvar Major, 18/1 Adolfina, 20/1 Conrad, 50/1 Garozzo, 100/1 Vargas Llosa, Royal Brook, Godot, Steel Dancer.

Gestut Bona (H. Jentzsch) 13rn 1m 27.1 (Soft).

142 PRIX THOMAS BRYON 2y 7½f
£13,011 Saint-Cloud 3 November

110^{3} **Big John** 8-8 GDoleuze **1**
125 **Watchdog** 8-7 LPiggott . . . 2.**2**
114 **Lou Piguet** 8-11 J-CDesaint s.nk.**3**
134^{2} Marie Noelle 8-4 ALequeux 2.4
Bardenac 8-11 PPaquet . . s.nk.5
Glittertind 8-7 GDubroeucq ½.6
Blackfoot 8-8 YSaint-Martin 2½.7
Samer 8-7 AGibert s.hd.8
Red Paradise 8-7 ABadel . . 2.9
Kisty 8-11 FHead s.hd.10

6/1 Lou Piguet, 4/1 Watchdog, 5/1 Bardenac, 7/1 Black Foot, 15/2 Marie Noelle, 13/1 BIG JOHN, 17/1 Red Paradise, 22/1 Samer, 36/1 Glittertind, 38/1 Kisty.

J. Michael (E. Chevalier du Fau) 10rn 1m 38 (Good).

143 WASHINGTON D.C. INTERNATIONAL 1½m
£61,475 Laurel 8 November

117^{2} **Argument** 3-8-8 LPiggott . . **1**
The Very One 5-8-12 JVelasquez 1.**2**
2 **Yvonand** 4-9-1 VBracciale, jnr 1¾.**3**
It's True 4-9-1 EMaple . . . 1¼.4
128^{3} Ben Fab 3-8-8 GStahlbaum ns.5
135 Buckpoint 4-9-1 WShoemaker 9.6
128^{*}Great Neck 4-9-1 MVenezia nk.7
Hashi Kurantsu 4-9-1 MShibata 31.8
135^{*}Anifa 4-8-12 AGibert . . . . p.u.

24/10 ARGUMENT, 36/10 The Very One, 44/10 Great Neck, 56/10 Anifa, 105/10 It's True, 121/10 Yvonand, 127/10 Ben Fab, 138/10 Buckpoint, 31/1 Hashi Kurantsu.

B. Gordy and B. McNall (M. Zilber) 9rn 2m 30.2 (Firm).

144 PREMIO TEVERE 2y 1m
£23,712 Rome 9 November

Panjandrum 8-11 GDettori . **1**
56 **Belviale** 8-11 RFestinesi . . 4.**2**
Terrific Jim 8-11 PPaquet . 4.**3**

Golden Flak 8-11
BRaymond 4.4
War Whisper 8-11
LBietolini ½.5
Wicked Will 8-11
JMatthias 2.6
127[3] No Piracy 8-11
GSorrentino 2.7
59[3] Richard Sorge 8-11
SFancera 4.8
Pedang 8-11 CWigham.....6.9

Evens Wicked Will, 9/4 Terrific Jim, 4/1 PANJANDRUM, 9/2 Golden Flak, 8/1 Belviale, 12/1 No Piracy, 25/1 War Whisper, 28/1 Richard Sorge, 66/1 Pedang.

C. D'Alessio (H. Cecil) 9rn 1m 47.8 (Heavy).

145 PRIX PERTH 1m
£13,245 Saint-Cloud 11 November

111*__Hilal__ 4-9-2 AGibert.........**1**
139[2] **Crofter** 3-8-10
YSaint-Martin ¾.**2**
118[2] **Moon Ingraver** 3-8-11
ALequeux 2½.**3**
132 Speed Bus 3-8-10
MPhilipperon ½.4
80 Sea Boy 3-8-12 PBruneau.nk.5
85 Nemr 3-9-0 GDoleuze......½.6
118 Fair Davina 4-8-11
APerrotta nk.7
92 Confetti 3-8-12 HSamani..2.8
113 Falamoun 3-8-12
J-CDesaint 2.9
111 Suvero 3-8-10 PPaquet...5.10
57 American Prince 4-9-2
JHeloury 0
111[3] Rostov 6-9-2 GDubroeucq...0
92 Planing 4-8-12 J-PLefevre...0
Verdier de Vaux 3-8-10
AGaston 0
Etinceleur 3-8-10
J-P-AGodard 0
Rivermaid 3-8-8 FHead......0
Rosalka 3-8-7 RJallu.........0

Evens Crofter, 8/1 HILAL and Nemr, Sea Boy and Rivermaid, 17/2 Moon Ingraver and Rosalka, 9/1 Etinceleur, 14/1 Rostov, 15/1 Falamoun, 16/1 American Prince, 23/1 Confetti, Suvero, 25/1 Speed Bus, 47/1 Verdier de Vaux, 49/1 Planing, 62/1 Fair Davina.

M. Fustok (M. Saliba) 17rn 1m 40.8 (Dead).

146 PREMIO RIBOT 1m
£22,800 Rome 16 November

Peloponnes 5-8-11
DRichardson **1**
141[3] **Isopach** 3-8-11
MDepalmas sh.**2**
136[3] **Good Times** 4-8-11
GPucciatti 3½.**3**
123 Cos Display 3-8-9
SFancera nk.4
57 Auxiliante 6-8-11
GDoleuze 1.5
123[2] Tibalda 3-8-8 OPessi......3.6
23 Ice Plant 3-8-11 PPaquet...4.7

6/5 Isopach, 7/2 PELOPONNES, 11/2 Tibalda, 6/1 Auxiliante, 7/1 Good Times, 8/1 Ice Plant. 20/1 Cos Display.

Stall Mazel-Tov (H. Degner) 7rn 1m 45.9 (Heavy).

147 PREMIO ROMA 1m 6f
£45,600 Rome 16 November

133 **Mariella** 3-8-7 PPaquet.....**1**
Ataxerxes 3-8-9
DRichardson 1¼.**2**
132 **Providential** 3-8-9
ALequeux 6.**3**
30 Scouting Miller 3-8-9
LFicuciello 3.4
42 Nebbia sul Bradano 4-8-10
BJovine 2.5
Giannino Umbro 3-8-9
CForte 5.6
138[2] Lotar 3-8-9 PPerlanti......4.7

Evens MARIELLA, 2/1 Ataxerxes, 9/4 Lotar, 5/2 Providential, 30/1 Nebbia sul Bradano, 40/1 Scouting Miller, 100/1 Giannino Umbro.

G. A. Oldham (F. Boutin) 7rn 3m 13.1 (Heavy).

148 CRITERIUM DE SAINT-CLOUD 2y 1¼m
£13,993 Saint-Cloud 17 November

130*__The Wonder__ 9-0 AGibert...**1**
110 **Mont Pelion** 8-10 FHead..1.**2**
130[2] **Brinkbero** 8-10
PPaquet s.hd.**3**
130 Ledmir 8-10 J-CDesaint.s.hd.4
130 Padirac 8-10 HSamani.....6.5
Rians 8-12 JDupin.......1½.6
Aliberta 8-7 JHeloury.....4.7
Prunheco 8-10
YSaint-Martin 3.8
Princess Pirate 8-11 ABadel.8.9
Santella Ascot 8-10
ALequeux hd.10

2/1 Prunheco, 22/10 THE WONDER, 4/1 Ledmir, 6/1 Brinkbero, 11/1 Mont Pelion, 23/1 Princess Pirate, 38/1 Padirac, Santella Ascot, 59/1 Rians, 90/1 Aliberta.

Mme A. du Breil (J. de Chevigny) 10rn 2m 18.7 (Heavy).

Note: Prize money for racing abroad has been converted to £ Sterling at the exchange rate current at the time of the race. The figures are correct to the nearest £.

INDEX TO RACING ABROAD

Abisko 65
Adam's Rib .. 32
Adolfina 28 41^3 141
Adraan 4 26* 61* 116
Affection 99 103 127 137
African Hope 13 18 38
Age Quod Agis .. 77^3
Akedoro 9
Akifool 94
Akinoa 3^3 14 32 87 133
Albert Tota .. 30
Alcana 28
Aliberta 148
Aliyoun 23
All Silk .. 59 137^3
Alvar Major 119^2 127
Amberina .. 95 129
American Prince 20* 57 145
Ancient Regime 77^2 90* 105
Anifa 2^2 6 19 70 83 89 102^2 112* 135* 143
Ararat 36
Arc d'Or .. 114^2 130
Arctic Walker .. 119
Ardross .. .. 140^3
Argument 17^3 35^2 48 74* 85^2 96 117^2 143*
Armistice Day 81 84* 119^3
Arnhem 30
Arnol 113
Arock 129
Aryenne 10* 21* 37 52^2 101
As You Desire Me 49^2 78 87
Ataxerxes .. .. 147^2
Atilla The Hun .. 13
Audmore 71
Auxiliante 42^3 57 146
Avilov 9
Avricourt .. 108
Axius . 23* 39
Ayila 76

Bal Ami .. .. 119^3
Balibest 45 54^2 65 106
Ballet Royal .. 80
Baptism .. 43* 67
Barbaccio .. .. 121^2
Bardamu 15
Bardenac 142
Battlewind .. 64
Belgio 15 25^3 35* 48 69
Belle d'Avril 3 14 52 64
Belle de Caro .. 32
Belle Rieuse 32 52
Belviale .. 56 144^2
Ben Fab .. 128^3 143
Benicia 14^2 37^3 52 64^2 87 91^3 118 133*
Benoite 89
Be Regal .. 29
Bernica .. 95* 115
Berruguete .. 9
Bev Bev 3 32 52 91
Beyond Recall .. 73
Big John 110^3 142*
Black Angel .. 39
Blackfoot .. 142
Black Marlin 58 120
Black Pearl .. 103
Black Star .. 123
Blakes Beacon .. 121
Blast Off 11^2 35 73
Blinette 1 19^2
Blithe Spirit .. 76
Blue Courtier .. 131
Blue Persian .. 131^2
Blue Wind .. 115
Bobiffic 11^3 25 82^3
Boden's Ride .. 74
Boitron 12^2 20 79* 86 92 108^2
Bold Brigadier .. 127^2
Bold Green .. 7
Boucicault 51^2 70 81
Boulad .. 35 47
Bozovici 100
Brenneville .. 120
Brilli Peri .. 136
Brinkbero 110 130^2 148^3
Brousoy .. .. 81^3
Buckpoint 40^3 51 70* 122 128^2 135 143

Cairn Rouge 36* 101
Calandra .. 71
Callio 20 44 50 75 84 92^3 98 113
Capitano .. 124
Cesario 68
Cesarion 45
Challal 112
Champoluc .. 127
Charles Bridge .. 10
Cherubin 2 70 96^2
Chicbury 45*
Choco Air .. 55
Choucri .. 4 17
Clericy 23
Clodion 8 75 86 111
Cobblers Cove .. 62
Combine Harvester 104
Come on Steve 88 108
Concordia .. 61
Coneenford 36 101
Confetti 4^2 17 35 75 80 92 145
Conrad 141
Coquet 68
Coral Dance 103^3 115^2
Corvaro 16^2 35 53^2 73* 104
Cos Display 28^2 41^2 123 146
Cracaval .. 96 104
Cresta Rider 109* 125
Critique .. 125^2
Crofter 139^2 145^2
Croque Monsieur 6 18 38 112
Cumuls 45
Current Bay 43 78
Current Charge 34 62

Dabat 137
Dahomey .. 138
Dancing Shadow 52
Dare To 46
Darling Dale .. 1
Daroda 25
Dauphin du Roi .. 113
Deauville 30 42* 58
Deep Music 14 32 60 64
Deliballe 3 72^3 78^3 98
Dellear .. 7^3 79
Delta Fox .. 110
Dernier Violon .. 113
Detroit 60* 72* 93* 101^3 117*
Dhaubix 54* 65 106 132 140
Dhausli 11 45 74^2 100
Diamond Prospect 77 109^2
Dip 16 23^2 47 68 85
Discretion 50^3 75^2 84 113*
Divin Marquis 23 43
Dom Aldo 15^2 48 70
Dom D'Albignac 73^2 85 100 113
Dom Savary 25 48
Don Furia .. 137
Doux Lord 82^2 94 132
Dragon 15 17 48 66 111
Dramatic Lady .. 133
Dukedom .. 138
Duke of Normandy 74
Duncen Grant .. 11
Dunette 24^3 51 69* 107* 117
Dunphy 110* 125^3

El Adem 56
Ela-Mana-Mou .. 117^3
El Cito .. .. 124^3
En Calcat 132*
Epsiba 74
Erodoto .. 59* 127

Esclavo .. 141*
Etinceleur .. 145
Etoile de Paris .. 36
Etoile d'Orient .. 10
Evgenia .. 64 93 133
Exactly So 32 49^3 60 72 91^2
Exegese 91

Fabi Si 75
Fabrizia 41
Fabulous Prince 25 53 80^3 85
Face of Love .. 31
Fair Davina 118 145
Falamoun 47 73 80^2 113 145
Fast Bird 118
Fatusael 42
Ferragu 83
Final Straw 34^3 86^2 98
Fingal's Cave .. 62
First of the Line 11 35 53^3
Firyal .. 7* 37 78
Flying Ace .. 12
Forbidden Fruit 3 91
Foveros .. 66^2 98
Free Dance .. 49
French Colonial 122*

Gain 5^2 22 24^2 40 51 69 102^3 128
Galland 34
Gamalat 93
Garozzo 141
Garrido 11 30* 62 100 135
Genisbay 137
Gentle Age .. 28
Geoffrey's Sister 136
Geppina Umbra .. 41
Giannino Umbro 147
Gilgit 125
Ginetta 41
Giulia Alberti .. 41
Give Off 19
Glenardina .. 36
Glenorum 39^3 85* 94* 117
Glint of Gold 127*
Glittertind .. 142
Godille 134
Godot 9 57 136 141
God's Mark .. 139
Golden Act 122^3 128 135^2
Golden Flak .. 144
Golden Vale 32 49
Goldiko 11 106^3 140
Goldora 36
Goldorak 77
Gold River 60^2 76^3 89* 101 126^2 140*
Gonzales 48 104 124*
Good Laugh .. 15
Good Thyne 65 124^2
Good Times 57^2 58 136^3 146^3
Good To Beat 3* 14 133^2
Gosport 1 2 79 111
Graben 62
Grandak 15^3 35 48 94
Great Neck 128* 143
Great Substence 125
Great Verdict 76* 89 126 140
Grechetto 39
Grecian Sea .. 95
Greenland Park .. 26^3
Greenway 99* 116 131*
Gregorian (USA) 104*
Guest Day .. 127

Hagg Hagg .. 31
Hard To Sing 6* 18* 40^2
Hashi Kurantsu 143
High Sierra 5 22
Hilal 1^3 12 20^2 50^2 67^2 75^3 84^2 92 98 111* 145*
Ho Han Wai 19* 40 60 132
Hortensia 32* 52 64^3 118*
Hortensio 45^2 65 80
House Guard .. 50
Huguenot .. 34 68*
Hultar Pacha 42 55
Hybrid 48

Ice Plant 17 23 146
Imperial Eagle .. 106
Incantada .. 123^3
Indian Lore .. 34
India Song 46* 78^2 93^2 113^3
Indigene 3 14 49 60^3 73 85 93 126 133^3
Indoor .. 19 70
In Fijar 4 17* 35^3 47 66^3 113
Inner Pearl 7 72 78
In Tissar .. 114 130
Intrigant .. 45 65
Ionian Raja 103^2 115 134
Irish Playboy 77* 90 116
Iseo 117
Iskenderun .. 138
Island Time .. 36
Isopach 57* 86 98 136* 141^3 146^2
It's True 143

Jabo 96
Jacinbar 16
Jasmine Star .. 116
Jeanne Iron 119*
Jeune Loup 24 40 51
Joberan 17 33^2 47 67
John Henry .. 135^3
Johnny O'Day .. 34
Julius Caesar 15* 25
Jurisconsulte 11 23
Just A Game .. 122^2

Kaldoun .. 1^2 20^3
Kalinski 89
Kalliope 118
Kamaridaan 2* 5 74 84
Karelia .. 101 126^3
Kareliaan 15 35 66 73 85
Katalina Girl 28^3 41
Katowice .. 98^3 111
Kazadancoa .. 115
Kebir Khan .. 114
Kelbomec 6^3 63* 83^2 94 112^3
Kifissia 21
Kilijaro 26 43^2 50 67 79^3 88* 92* 98* 108* 139^3
Kiss The Clowns 26
Kisty 142
Known Fact .. 86
Koboko .. 4 17 92
Konigsstuhl .. 74
Koreillo .. 45 80
Kouklita 95

La Carmagnole .. 49
Ladislao di Oppelm 57 66 120
La Grande Coudre 3 14 21 43
Lalaria .. 103 129
La Margalaise .. 134
Lanai 30
Lancastrian 53* 69 82* 132^2
La Nobleza 10 32 133
Laquiola 32^2 52 72
Larkland 89^3 126
Last Fandango .. 34^2
Lastline 91
Last Love 115 134
La Toulzanie .. 126
La Vedrelle 14 32
La Vreeland 10 46 72
Layalina 134
Leandra 95
Ledmir .. 130 148
Le Marmot 5^3 22* 102* 117
Le Moss .. .. 112^2
Levanto 9
Liane de Pougy .. 133
Libergold .. 95
Licara 7^2 32 52 72^2 80
Light of Realm 43 78 86
Lignee Grise 78 88 108
Liki Liki 19^3 24 44
Lindoro .. 117 140
Little Bonny 71^2 101^2 117
Lobsang 128
Lochiel 54

L'Octroi 65
Lord Jack .. 25
Lord Rochford .. 75
Lorelta .. 3 14 49
Lotar 27* 55^2 121* 138^2 147
Louksor .. 2 5 20
Lou Piguet 114 142^3
Love Me Tight .. 28
Lover Prince .. 56^2
Luck of the Draw 67* 139
Lucumone .. 30
Luth de Saron 14* 52 64* 93^3 101
Luth Music 49* 60 89 118
Lyllos 114
Lyphard's Bonnet 52

Mac Flipper .. 81
Magnificent Lady 36
Mainland .. 106
Maiymad 35
Manet .. 9^2 30 42
Manguin 50 81 84 113
Manjam 26 79 86^3 98
Maratoneta .. 127
Marching On .. 31^2
Marenga 103
Mariacho .. 114*
Marie du Mont 95^3 115
Mariella 37 49 89^2 101 126* 133 147*
Marie Noelle 134^2 142
Marittimo .. 81
Marlion .. 6^2 18
Marmolada 41* 58^3 120* 123* 138^3
Marquis du Loir .. 50
Marracci 42^2 58* 96^3
Marriageable 18 38^3 63 112
Marson 6 83* 94 112
Massalia 43
Master Willie .. 62
Matcha 60
Match The Hatch 135
Matho .. 129 131
Mazzanti .. 29^2 58
Mice Bird .. 71
Miliar .. 26^2 61^2 88
Militante 37
Millingdale Lillie 36^2
Mill Princess .. 60
Mirza 41
Miss Bessie .. 1
Miss Mouse .. 19
Miss Waterloo .. 41
Miswaki .. 90^2 105*
Monday Morning 99^3
Monsieur Dagobert 2 6 13^2 40 51^3 63 81 102 113
Monsieur Marcel 2 63^3 83 140^2
Monteverdi .. 34
Montjardin 18 140
Montorselli 81 113
Mont Pelion 110 148^2
Moon Ingraver 78* 92 118^2 145^3
Moorestyle 17^2 79^2 116* 139*
Morold .. 122 128
Mot D'Or 25* 48 65^3 85 94
Moulouki 25 40* 107 117 132
Mrs Penny 36^3 52* 101* 117
Muscovite .. 43
Music Streak .. 125

Nadjar 12* 20 66* 86* 98^2
Na Fer 25
Nanthilde.. .. 126
Narvaez .. 30 121
Navarino 96
Nawazich .. 95
Nazwa .. 36 116
Nebbia sul Bradano 42 147
Nebos .. 96* 117
Nemr 39* 68 73^3 85 145
Never Cry .. 47
New Grandame 19 78
Nice Havrais 4* 17 35
Nicholas Bill 96 117
Night Alert 47* 104^3
Nikoli .. 34* 62
Niniski .. 117 140
Noalcoholic .. 80*
Noble Defi .. 90
Noble Saint 69 117
Noble Shamus .. 62
Noelino .. 102 132
No Piracy 127^3 144
Northern Baby 22^3 44* 66 98 107^3
Northjet 31* 79 88^2 108^3 116
Norwegian 17 47
Novesia 41
Numas 17
Nureyev 8*

Ober 27
Olinda 36
Opachisco .. 85
Opera Italiana .. 28
Orbiolo 136

Padirac 97^3 130 148
Palmalina .. 36
Panjandrum 144*
Panthere Rouge .. 41
Pappagallo .. 70
Paranete 3 14^3 32^3 37* 52^3 101
Pareo 27^2 55* 58^2
Pawiment 96 138*
Pedang 144
Pelerin 62
Peloponnes 146*
Penmarric .. 77
Perouges 13 81* 94
Perrault 70^3 81^2 94^2 132
Pharnace 11 47
Phosphurian .. 104
Phydilla .. 95^2 129*
Pian del Lupo 27^3 30^2 55^3 73 120^2 136^2
Pink Prism 125 134
Pitsville 104
Pizzocorno 59 119 127
Planing 1 12^3 22 92 145
Platinum 100 132
Player 12
Pointe Rousse 54 76
Polemia 76
Policeman 16^3 23^3 48* 69^3 100 117
Pom Poes 10^3 46 61 118
Popset .. 16 45
Posse 34
Powder 'N Patch 46 61
Prancing Prince 124
Prince Bee 62^2 100*
Prince Dias .. 8
Princely Unfair .. 127
Prince Mab 90^3 105^2
Princesse Lida 10^2 21^3 67 79 139
Princess Pirate .. 148
Proctor 128
Prominent Rose 36
Proudfoot.. .. 97
Proustille 3^2 14 37 52 70^2 76^2 89 94 101 126 132
Prove It Baby 6 18^2 38^2 51* 70
Providential 11* 25^2 48^3 107 117 132 147
Prunheco 148

Quadrupler 29 120 123
Quick As Lightning 71

Racquette 36 71^3 104
Rahotep .. 110 130
Ramian .. 62^3 124
Rankin 62
Rapanello .. 121
Realeza .. 108 131^3
Recitation 125*
Red Coral 79 88 92
Red Paradise .. 142
Red Rocket 9* 30 42 141
Rent And Fly .. 31
Rhus .. 68^2 74
Rians 148
Richard Sorge 59^3 144
Rilo 127
Ringawoody .. 36
Risacca 123
Rissoso .. .. 31^3

Riverbird .. 49
Riverdina .. 134
Riverlily 126
Rivermaid .. 145
River River 40 94
Roberto Bellarmino 58
Rolling Bowl .. 44
Rolling Star .. 47
Roman Black .. 59
Roman Top .. 56
Rosalka 145
Rossi Gold .. 128
Rostov 50* 111³ 145
Rouchiza 19
Royal Brook 9 27 141
Royal Pleasure .. 8³
Ruscelli 4 17³(dis) 33* 47² 73 100³ 117

Sabzawar 53
Safita .. 21² 37² 64 91* 111² 139
Saint Jonathon .. 35
Saintonge .. 89
Saint Sever .. 15
Salmana 90 103 115³
Samer 142
Sandford Linda .. 28
San Rosario 6 24 38
Santella Ascot .. 148
Saratoga Game .. 33³
Sarrad 85
Satilla 100² 117 132³
Savingrant .. 57³
Scapricciatello .. 127
Schwepperusschian 39
Scorpio .. 13* 24* 69
Scouting Miller 30 147
Sea Boy 68³ 80 145
Sealy 19
Sea's Valley 9³ 30³ 42
Seiorlando 59² 119 127
Selerina .. 7 61 131
Semipalatinsk .. 127
Shafaraz 6*(dis) 18³ 38* 83³ 140
Shakapour 16* 25 48² 69*
Shamra 75
Shangrila .. 103
Shannfara .. 10
Shape .. 16 23 39
Sharmada 99²
Sharpo 116²
Sheikdom 44
Sheringham 104 124
Shoen 97² 109³ 125
Shoot A Line .. 71*
Sifounas 29*
Silver Express 105³ 129²
Silver Lord .. 31
Singapore River .. 110
Singing Boy .. 129
Sir Mordred .. 124
Sir Raleigh .. 132
Ska 134
Skinflint 34
Slimy 6
Snapper Point 79 108
Soleil Noir 13³ 24 63²
Some Lute 68 75
Son of Love 2³ 5 13 70 83
Souristane .. 7
Sovereign Dona 87* 118
Spaten 23
Speed Bus 39² 48 80 113² 132 145
Spence Bay 104²
Spirit of Crow .. 27
Spoilt Miss 3 46
Spoleto 129
Springfield House 111
Standaan 88³
Star's Salute .. 44
Star Way 86
Steel Dancer .. 141
Stetchworth (USA) 6
St Louis Sue .. 78
Stout Fellow 6 18
Strong Gale 2 44² 66 74³ 107
Sunny Time .. 72
Sun Row 109
Super Sky .. 31
Suvero 43 67³ 75 111 145
Swan's Rock .. 34
Swift Song .. 77

Tajtal 73 80 113
Tarsiere 3
Tassmoun 75* 92²
Teacher's Pet 7 21 46² 78 111 141
Telescopico .. 2
The Daan .. 127
Temperence Hill .. 135
Terrific Jim 144³
The Expatriate 4 39 47³ 66 113
The Very One 143²
The Wonder 114³ 130* 148*
Three Troikas 5* 22² 44³ 107² 117 135
Tibalda 28* 41 123² 146
Timarina 36
Timely Bidder .. 8
Tom's Serenade 48 65 106² 128
Torsom 75
Toscarimus .. 96
Tourinfore .. 28
Trash 30
Travolta .. 105 125
Travolta (GB) .. 56*
Trephine .. 91 93
Tres Gate .. 31
Trevita .. 87² 93
Trio Boy 20 26 61³
Tropical Lightning 15
Tropicaro .. 115* 139
Troubetzkoy .. 114
Try To Smile .. 88
Tudor Diamond 3
Turnablade .. 60
Twig Prince 77 99 109
Two of Diamonds 69
Tyrnavos .. 62*
Tysfjsa .. 137²

Ukraine Girl 103* 115
Uliana di Trer .. 28
Un Reitre 4³ 15 33 85³

Val D'Erica 137*
Valgo .. 77 129
Valeriga .. 116³ 141²
Valiant Heart 45³ 65* 140
Valour 24
Van der Linden 29³
Vaneau 65
Van Houten 120 136
Vargas Llosa .. 141
Verdier de Vaux .. 145
Vermillon Chine 82
Vezzani 45 54 65 82
Vincent .. 94³ 140
Viteric 8² 33 43 107
Vorias .. 97* 130
Votre Altesse 134*
Vox Populi 43³ 67 79

Warden Key .. 56³
War Whisper .. 144
Watchdog 90 110² 125 142²
Water Mill .. 65³
Wedgewood Blue 71
Welsh Daylight .. 36
What A Joy 65² 94 106* 140
White Pleasure .. 43
Wicked Lady 61 79
Wicked Will .. 144
Wild Idea 46³ 66 72 87³ 93 118³
Wild Oats 2 84³
Willard 59
Windelia .. 61 78
Winds of Winter .. 34
Wolverton 1* 12

Yamba 19
Yang Tze .. 137
Ya Zaman 67*(dis) 139
Yourki 77
Yvonand .. 2 143³

Zambrano 45 54³ 121³
Zolinana 14 46 72

Complete your library and your knowledge of performances of British Bloodstock with

PUBLISHED BY WEATHERBYS

4 UP-TO-DATE EDITIONS EVERY YEAR+RETURN OF MARES+SIRES.
2,000 PAGES CONTAINING ALL THE FACTS. SEE THE SIRES THAT GET EARLY 2-Y-O WINNERS.
GET TO KNOW THE BEST TRIP FOR 3-Y-O's. MAKE MONEY BY USING THE RECORD.

The Statistical Record, Weatherbys, Sanders Road, Wellingborough, Northants. NN8 4BX.
Telephone: Wellingborough (0933) 76241. Telex: 311582

TRAINERS

The figures in brackets are the number of winners each trainer has had over the past five seasons, from 1976 to 1980 inclusive. Quarters and telephone numbers are given beneath the trainer's name.

Akehurst, R. P. J. (23:13:15:14:9)
Lambourn Lambourn (0488) 71850
Albina, M. H. (—:—:—:—:0)
Allan, A. R. (—:—:0:1:0)
Roxburghshire
St Boswells (083 52) 2403
Allingham, P. B. (1:3:0:0:0)
Luton Offley (046 276) 337
Ancil, D. I. (0:3:2:2:2)
Banbury Banbury (0295) 711006
Armstrong, R. W. (30:19:30:38:29)
Newmarket
Newmarket (0638) 3333/4
Armytage, R. C. (0:0:0:0:0)
East Ilsley
East Ilsley (063 528) 203
Arnold, A. T. (—:—:0:0:0)
Bridgnorth Quatt (0746) 780400
Arthur, P. J. (0:7:4:4:0)
Didcot Blewbury (0235) 850338
Ashworth, P. H. (3:6:6:0:1)
Epsom Epsom (037 27) 20336
Home—Burgh Heath 54550
Asquith, P. (—:—:12:9:6)
Wetherby Wetherby (0937) 62122
Atkins, R. A. L. (—:0:1:2:0)
Elstead Elstead (0252) 702028
Atkinson, W. (0:0:0:0:0)
Carlisle Carlisle (0228) 25649
Austin, C. A. (—:—:2:2:4)
Wokingham
Wokingham (0734) 786 425
Bailey, A. (—:—:—:—:6)
Newmarket
Newmarket (0638) 750847
Bailey, K. C. (—:—:0:0:0)
Brackley Brackley (0280) 703486
Bailey, P. G. (0:0:0:0:0)
Wantage Childrey (023 559) 288
Baker, J. H. (—:—:0:1:0)
Tiverton Tiverton (088 42) 56618
Baker, R. J. (—:—:—:—:1)
Balding, A. (4:0:2:5:4)
Doncaster Doncaster (0302) 710221
Balding, G. B. (18:22:16:17:26)
Weyhill Weyhill (026 477) 2278
Balding, I. A. (36:33:39:39:49)
Kingsclere
Kingsclere (0635) 298210
Barnes, T. A. (—:0:5:3:1)
Ousby Langwathby (076 881) 379
Barons, D. H. (0:0:0:0:0)
Kingsbridge
Loddiswell (054 855) 326
Barratt, L. J. (0:2:3:2:1)
Oswestry
Queenshead (069 188) 209
Barron, T. D. (—:—:—:0:0)
Northallerton
Northallerton (0609) 2331

Beeson, E. E. G. (0:0:2:8:6)
Lewes
Lewes (079 16) 4581 and 5654
Bell, C. H. (5:0:0:0:6)
Hawick Denholm (045 087) 278
Benstead, C. J. (16:16:18:17:17)
Epsom Ashtead (037 22) 73152
Bentley, W. (—:—:—:7:6)
Middleham
Wensleydale (0969) 22289
Berry, J. (3:6:20:11:15)
Lancaster Forton (0524) 791179
Bethell, J. D. W. (17:25:14:15:19)
Fordingbridge
Rockbourne (072 53) 220
Bevan, P. J. (0:0:0:0:0)
Kingstone
Dapple Heath (088 921) 647 and 670
Bingham, J. D. (—:—:5:6:3)
Doncaster Haxey (0427) 7522
Blagrave, H. H. G. C. (3:3:11:8:4)
Beckhampton Avebury (067 23) 345
Home—Avebury (067 23) 218
Blakeney, R. E. (0:0:0:0:0)
Ashford Charing (023 371) 2667
Blanshard, M. T. W. (—:—:—:0:4)
Lambourn Lambourn (0488) 71091
Blum, G. (10:9:5:7:6)
Newmarket Newmarket (0638) 2734
Bolton, M. J. (1:2:2:1:5)
Felcourt
Dormans Park (034 287) 403
Booth, C. B. B. (—:2:1:5:1)
Flaxton
Whitwell-on-the-Hill (065 381) 586
Bosley, J. R. (—:—:—:2:1)
Bampton
Bampton Castle (0993) 850212
Boss, R. (14:15:18:14:21)
Newmarket
Newmarket (0638) 61335 and 2880
Bradley, J. M. (9:8:7:4:2)
Chepstow Chepstow (029 12) 2486
Breasley, A. E. (—:—:3:19:19)
Epsom Epsom (03727) 23204
Brennan, O. (—:0:0:0:0)
Kelham Caunton (063 686) 332
Bridgwater, K. S. (1:0:4:2:1)
Solihull Knowle (056 45) 77026
Brittain, C. E. (53:31:52:34:25)
Newmarket
Newmarket (0638) 3739 and 4347
Brookshaw, S. J. (0:0:0:0:0)
Ternhill Ternhill (063 083) 272
Butler, P. (—:0:0:0:0)
Lewes Plumpton (0273) 890124
Callaghan, N. A. (24:24:40:34:14)
Newmarket
Newmarket (0638) 4040

Calver, P. (5:0:2:7:2)
Ripon Ripon (0765) 700313
Calvert, J. B. (12:9:3:0:5)
Hambleton Sutton (084 56) 373
Camacho, M. J. C. (5:20:17:13:7)
Towton Tadcaster (0937) 833294
Cambidge, B. R. (1:0:0:0:0)
Shifnal
Weston-under-Lizard (095 276) 249
Candy, H. D. N. B.
(26:32:35:39:28)
Wantage Uffington (036 782) 276
Cann, J. F. (0:0:1:0:0)
Cullompton
Kentisbeare (088 46) 356
Carr, E. J. (13:13:11:4:3)
Hambleton Sutton (084 56) 288
Carrod, L. N. L. (—:0:0:0:0)
Wragby Wragby (067 34) 285
Carter, E. (—:2:2:2:0)
Malton Malton (0653) 3522
Carter, R. (1:3:0:0:2)
Swaffham
Gooderstone (036 621) 226
Cecil, H. R. A. (52:74:108:128:84)
Newmarket
Newmarket (0638) 2192
Home—(0638) 2387
Chamberlain, N. (—:—:—:—:0)
West Auckland
Bishop Auckland (0388) 832 465
Chapman, D. W. (2:2:2:2:5)
Stillington
Easingwold (0347) 21683
Chapman, M. C. (—:0:0:0:0)
Clipston Clipston (085 886) 255
Charles, W. (0:0:0:1:3)
Warwick Warwick (0926) 43878
Chesmore, Mrs S. M. P.
(0:0:—:—:0)
Melrose Melrose (089682) 2715
Clay, W. (1:0:0:0:2)
Uttoxeter Uttoxeter (088 93) 2068
Cole, P. F. I. (51:47:56:61:48)
Lambourn Lambourn (0488) 71632
Cole, S. N. (0:0:0:0:0)
Newport Pagnell
Northampton (0604) 870330
Collingridge, H. J. (2:1:3:9:3)
Newmarket Newmarket (0638) 5454
Cottrell, L. G. (1:0:0:2:2)
Cullompton
Kentisbeare (088 46) 320
Cousins, Mrs S. A. (—:—:—:—:1)
Carnforth
Carnforth (052 473) 3058
Cousins, M. A. (—:—:1:0:1)
Tarporley
Little Budworth (082 921) 316
Craig, T. (19:24:16:10:5)
Dunbar Dunbar (0368) 62583
Cross, R. F. (0:0:0:0:0)
Alnwick Chattan (066 85) 247
Crossley, C. C. (2:6:8:7:12)
Wirral Neston (051 336) 2382
Crump, N. F. (1:0:4:3:2)
Middleham
Wensleydale (0969) 23269
Cumani, L. M. (12:30:53:19:26)
Newmarket
Newmarket (0638) 61569 and 5432
Cundell, P. D. (18:12:10:10:10)
Compton Compton (063 522) 267
Cuthbert, T. A. (—:—:—:—:0)
Carlisle Wetheral (0228) 60822
Czerpak, J. D. (—:—:—:—:0)
Kenilworth
Coventry (0203) 304724
Dale, D. (0:0:0:4:4)
Newmarket
Newmarket (0638) 61586
Dalton, A. (4:5:2:2:3)
Newmarket
Newmarket (0638) 3741
Davies, J. D. J. (—:—:—:—:0)
Billinghurst
Billinghurst (040381) 2678
Davison, A. R. (2:0:2:6:0)
Caterham Caterham (0883) 43857
Delahooke, M. C. (—:0:0:0:0)
Cheltenham
Bishops Cleeve (024 267) 2162
Demetriou, A. (—:—:—:4:2)
Newmarket
Newmarket (0638) 77459
Dever, F. (0:2:1:0:0)
Newark Mansfield (0623) 870276
Dickinson, M. W. (—:—:—:—:1)
Harewood
Office: Harewood (0532) 886536
Home: Harewood (0532) 886346
Dingwall, C. B. J. (2:3:0:1:0)
East Ilsley East Ilsely (063 528) 253
Dingwall, Mrs L. E. (0:3:2:0:0)
Poole Canford Cliffs (0202) 708165
Docker, L. O. J. (0:1:0:1:0)
Dodds, J. P. (—:0:0:0:0)
Alnwick Chatton (066 85) 216
Douglas-Home, J. T. A.
(—:—:—:0:0)
East Hendred (023588) 247
Doyle, J. C. M. (—:—:—:—:5)
Wetherby Wetherby (0937) 62420
Dudgeon, I. M. (0:0:1:0:0)
Warminster
Codford St Mary (09855) 477
Dunlop, J. L. (48:42:73:96:91)
Arundel Arundel (0903) 882194
Home—Arundel (0903) 882106
Durr, F. (—:—:—:38:51)
Newmarket
Newmarket (0638) 2090
Easterby, M. H.
(50:46:50:74:63)
Malton
Kirby Misperton (065 386) 600
Easterby, M. W.
(53:24:12:31:17)
Sheriff Hutton
Sheriff Hutton (03477) 368
Eckley, M. W. (—:—:—:—:0)
Ludlow Brumfield 372
Edmunds, J. (0:2:1:0:0)
Wythall Wythall (0564) 822334

Edwards, J. A. C. (0:1:0:0:0)
Ross-on-Wye
Harewood End (098987) 259
Eldin, E. (—:—:—:0:11)
Newmarket
Newmarket (0638) 2036 or 3217
Elsey, C. W. C. (14:21:18:12:26)
Malton Malton (0653) 3149
Elsworth, D. R. C.
(—:—:—:10:12)
Durrington
Durrington Walls (0980) 52706
Etherington, J. (26:29:22:24:20)
Malton Malton (0653) 2842
Fairbairn, G. B. (—:—:—:0:0)
Hallington
Great Whittington (043 472) 215
Fairhurst, T. (33:18:34:20:11)
Middleham
Wensleydale (0969) 23362
Feilden, P. J. (—:—:—:3:3)
Newmarket Exning (063877) 637
Felgate, P. S. (0:0:0:0:1)
Aslockton Whatton (0949) 50335
Finch, Mrs A. (0:0:0:0:0)
Shaftesbury
East Knoyle (074 783) 305
Fisher, A. L. (—:0:0:0:0)
Gaddesby
Gaddesby (066 472) 3306
Fisher, W. E. (0:0:0:0:0)
Chewton Mendip
Chewton Mendip (076 21) 283
Fitzgerald, J. G. (5:15:9:15:13)
Malton Malton (0653) 2718
Fleming, H. (—:0:0:0:1)
Cleethorpes
Cleethorpes (0472) 65215
Fletcher, G. G. (—:—:—:2:3)
Newmarket
Newmarket (0638) 61081
Forsey, B. (—:—:—:—:0)
Warminster
Codford St Mary (09855) 491
Forster, T. A. (0:0:0:0:0)
Letcombe Bassett
Wantage (023 57) 3092
Francis, M. E. D. (5:7:2:3:3)
Lambourn Lambourn (0488) 71700
Francis, W. D. (0:0:2:4:2)
Malpas Tilston (082 98) 208
Gandolfo, D. R. (0:6:3:4:2)
Wantage Wantage (023 57) 3242
Garraton, D. T. (—:—:—:—:1)
Malton Rillington (094 42) 506
Gaselee, N. A. D. C. (—:0:3:2:5)
Lambourn
Lambourn (0488) 71503
Gifford, J. T. (0:1:0:3:1)
Findon Findon (090 671) 2226
Winchcombe (0242) 602194
Gilbert, J. A. (—:—:—:—:1)
Oakham Somerby (066 477) 614
Gillam, T. A. (0:0:0:0:1)
Boroughbridge
Boroughbridge (09012) 2592

Goodwill, A. W. (6:6:5:2:7)
Newmarket
Newmarket (0638) 3218
Gosling, T. (4:6:4:2:4)
Epsom Epsom (037 27) 22080
Gray, C. W. (—:—:—:—:1)
Beverley Beverley (0482) 882490
Gubby, B. (—:—:—:2:4)
Bagshot Bagshot (0273) 63282
Guest, W. N. (1:6:5:14:11)
Newmarket
Newmarket (0638) 61680
Haigh, W. W. (10:8:10:6:9)
Malton Malton (0653) 4428
Haine, J. (4:7:1:7:2)
Haresfield
Hardwicke, Glos. (045 272) 256
Hall, N. (0:0:0:0:2)
Burton-on-Trent
Barton-U-Needwood (028 371) 2279
Hall, Miss S. E. (12:9:7:15:7)
Middleham
Wensleydale (0969) 40223
Hallett, T. B. (—:—:0:0:0)
Saltash Saltash (075 55) 2064
Hanbury, B. (23:21:18:8:25)
Newmarket
Newmarket (0638) 3193
Home—Wickhambrook (044 082) 396
Hanley, D. L. (7:5:2:0:0)
Lambourn
Lambourn (0488) 72169 and 72219
Hannon, R. M. (46:37:47:30:37)
Marlborough
Collingbourne Ducis (026 485) 254
Hanson, J. (10:9:12:8:13)
Wetherby Wetherby (0937) 62841
Hardy, J. (15:22:31:14:17)
Staunton
Long Bennington (040 05) 212
Harris, J. L. (1:2:0:2:1)
Melton Mowbray
Harby (0949) 60671
Harris, S. T. (—:—:—:0:1)
Amersham
Amersham (02403) 21718 or 22239
Hartop, R. W. (—:—:—:—:0)
Cheltenham
Andoversford (024 282) 418
Harvey, Mrs A. (—:—:—:0:0)
Doncaster Doncaster (0302) 49787
Harwood, G. (48:50:59:48:69)
Pulborough
Pulborough (079 82) 2335
Haslam, P. C. (12:7:10:25:38)
Newmarket
Newmarket (0638) 4525 and 4523
Hastings-Bass, W. E. R. H.
(—:26:27:27:26)
Newmarket
Newmarket (0638) 2024
Haynes, M. J. (5:6:12:16:12)
Epsom
Burgh Heath (073 73) 51140
Head, R. A. (0:0:0:0:0)
Lambourn
Lambourn (0488) 71411

Henderson, N. J. (—:—:0:0:0)
Lambourn Lambourn (0488) 72259
Hern, W. R. (69:74:74:61:65)
West Ilsley
East Ilsley (063 528) 219 and 251
Hide, A. G. (—:2:4:5:4)
Newmarket
Newmarket (0638) 2063
Hill, C. J. (20:13:12:13:7)
Barnstaple Barnstaple (0271) 2048
Hills, B. W. (60:76:86:56:61)
Lambourn Lambourn (0488) 71548
Hill-Wood, Miss A. K.
(—:—:—:—:0)
Grantham Knipton (047 682) 226
Hinchliffe, M. J. (—:—:—:—:0)
Lambourn
Marlborough (0672) 40755
and Chaddleworth (04882) 586
Hindley, J. J. (49:41:42:41:46)
Newmarket
Newmarket (0638) 4141
Hoad, R. P. C. (—:—:—:—:2)
Lewes
(07916) 77124 or Alfriston (0323) 870720
Hobbs, B. R. (55:65:43:42:60)
Newmarket
Newmarket (0638) 2129
Hobson, R. (—:—:13:5:4)
Worksop Worksop (0909) 5962
Holden, W. (6:11:15:8:4)
Newmarket
Newmarket (0638) 2771
Holland, S. F. (0:1:6:2:0)
Shrewsbury Cressage (095 289) 392
Hollinshead, R. (48:49:50:25:26)
Upper Longdon
Armitage (0543) 490298
Holt, L. J. (5:6:6:12:9)
Tunworth
Long Sutton (025 681) 376
Houghton, R. F. J. (40:54:47:39:42)
Blewbury Blewbury (0235) 850480
Hudson J. P. (—:—:—:2:1)
Lambourn Lambourn (0488) 71784
Huffer, G. A. (—:—:—:23:11)
Newmarket
Newmarket (0638) 730391
Hunter, G. H. (25:25:24:22:30)
East Ilsley East Ilsley (063 528) 250
Ingham, A. P. (—:19:16:9:3)
Headley Ashtead (037 22) 72859
Ivory, K. T. (3:11:11:15:9)
Radlett Radlett (092 76) 6081
James, C. J. (0:3:5:3:10)
Newbury
Great Shefford (048 839) 280
James, M. B. C. (1:—:—:—:0)
Whitchurch
Whitchurch (0948) 3155
James, S. S. (2:0:0:0:0)
East Ilsley
East Ilsley (063 528) 248
Jarvis, A. P. (3:3:13:5:6)
Royston
Royston, Herts (0763) 46611
Jarvis, M. A. (31:27:31:39:30)
Newmarket
Newmarket (0638) 61702 and 2519
Jenkins, J. R. (—:—:—:—:1)
Horsham
Lower Beeding (040 376) 606
Jermy, D. C. (0:2:2:0:0)
Carshalton
01-668 3765 and 01-668 8814
Johnson, J. A. T. (3:11:9:12:10)
Lambourn Lambourn (0488) 71368
Johnson, R. (—:—:—:0:1)
Crook Crook (038 882) 2113
Jones, A. W. (1:2:5:3:8)
Oswestry Oswestry (0691) 59720
Jones, Dr A. (3:2:0:0:0)
Swansea Clydach (0792) 3504
Jones, D. H. (2:2:0:3:4)
Pontypridd
Newtown-Llantwit (044 362) 2515
Jones, E. (0:0:0:0:0)
Hednesford
Hednesford (054 38) 2721
Jones, Hbt (6:7:2:5:9)
Malton Malton (0653) 2630
Jones, H. T. (6:15:20:13:41)
Newmarket
Newmarket (0638) 4884
Home—Exning (063 877) 260
Jones, T. M. (2:0:0:1:0)
Guildford Shere (048 641) 2604
Jordon, I. D. (0:1:2:2:0)
Newcastle-on-Tyne
Newcastle-on-Tyne (0632) 869143
Jorgensen, O. (—:—:—:—:0)
Kearney, P. J. (—:—:—:—:0)
Cheltenham
Withington (024 289) 253
Keenor, R. F. (0:0:0:0:0)
Chulmleigh
Chulmleigh (076 98) 432
Kelleway, P. A. (—:6:26:21:23)
Newmarket
Newmarket (0638) 61461
Kennard, L. G. (0:1:0:0:2)
Bishops Lydeard
Bishops Lydeard (0823) 432550
Kennedy, Mrs K. A. A.
(—:—:—:0:0)
Lambourn
Lambourn (0488) 71636
Kent, D. W. J. (0:8:17:5:10)
Chichester
West Ashling (024 358) 231
Kernick, S. G. (—:0:0:0:0)
Kingsteignton
Newton Abbot (0626) 5899
Kersey, T. (0:0:2:0:2)
West Melton
Rotherham (0709) 873166
Kinderlsey, G. (0:1:0:0:0)
Newbury
Great Shefford (048 839) 301
Laing, D. R. (—:—:8:7:17)
Lambourn
Lambourn (0488) 71825
Lamb, C. R. (0:0:0:0:0)
Seahouses Seahouses (0665) 260

Leadbetter, S. J. (—:—:1:0:0)
Denholm Denholm (045 087) 260
Leigh, J. P. (1:0:0:0:1)
Willoughton
Hemswell (042 773) 210
Leslie, D. M. (—:—:1:7:7)
Leicester Tugby (053756) 257/357
Lewis, E. R. K. (—:—:—:—:0)
Carmarthen
St Clears (0994) 230383
Lewis, G. (—:—:—:0:5)
Epsom
Ashtead (037 22) 77662 or 77366
Lockerbie, G. (—:—:—:—:1)
Middleham
Wensleydale (0969) 22736
Lomax, Mrs R. A. (4:3:3:5:2)
Marlborough
Marlborough (0672) 40288
Long, J. E. (0:0:0:0:0)
Elham Elham (030 384) 229
Mackenzie, C. (—:—:—:—:0)
Makin, P. J. (10:12:6:10:7)
Ogbourne Maisey
Marlborough (0672) 52973
Marks, D. (6:4:13:8:4)
Lambourn
Lambourn (0488) 71767
Marshall, T. C. (4:10:6:12:6)
Lambourn Lambourn (0488) 71025
Marshall, W. C. (30:35:26:16:6)
Newmarket
Newmarket (0638) 61574
Mason, J. (—:—:—:—:4)
Stockton
Mason, R. E. G. (5:9:5:3:2)
Guilsborough
Guilsborough (060 122) 381
Masson, M. J. (18:15:4:3:3)
Lewes Lewes (079 16) 4984
Matthews, S. G. (0:1:0:2:7)
Winchester
Winchester (0962) 880808
McCain, D. (0:1:0:0:0)
Birkdale
Southport (0704) 66007 and 69677
McCormack, M. (—:—:—:—:3)
Wantage Childrey (023 559) 433
McCourt, M. (2:6:4:2:3)
Letcombe Regis
Wantage (023 57) 4456
McDonald, R. (—:—:—:—:0)
McLean, D. B. (—:—:0:0:0)
Morpeth Felton (067087) 478
McMahon, B. A. (1:0:1:2:6)
Tamworth
Tamworth (0827) 62901
Mellor, S. T. E. (0:8:4:4:10)
Lambourn Lambourn (0488) 71485
Miller, C. J. V. (0:2:0:0:0)
Stratford-on-Avon
Alderminster (078 987) 296 and 232
Mitchell, P. (2:3:6:7:11)
Epsom Ashtead (037 22) 73729
Mitchell, P. K. (—:—:0:0:0)
Folkington Polegate (032 12) 2437
Mitchell, V. J. (0:4:2:2:1)
Bishopsthorpe York (0904) 36099

Molony, T. (7:5:6:8:6)
Melton Mowbray
Wymondham (057 284) 273
Moore, A. (—:0:0:0:1)
Woodingdean
Brighton (0273) 681679
Morgan, K. A. (—:—:—:—:0)
Sandiway Sandiway (0606) 781907
Morley, M. F. D. (1:1:3:0:5)
Bury St Edmunds
Culford (028 484) 278
Morris, R. W. (—:—:—:1:1)
Welshpool Trewern (093874) 355
Morris, Miss S. O. (0:0:0:0:0)
Chard
Chard (046 06) 3187 and 3379
Muggeridge, F. M. (0:0:0:0:0)
Romsey
West Wellow (0794) 22430
Mulhall, J. (2:4:4:0:0)
York York (0904) 706321
Murphy, R. G. R. (2:5:1:5:0)
Wellington Telford (0952) 42209
Musson, W. J. (—:0:1:2:4)
Bramley
Bramley, Surrey (048 647) 8100
Naughton, M. P. (1:8:3:0:5)
Richmond Richmond (0748) 2803
Neaves, A. S. (0:1:3:1:0)
Eastling Eastling (079 589) 274
Nelson, C. R. (—:4:16:16:31)
Lambourn
Lambourn (0488) 71391
Nesbitt, S. (20:7:11:16:3)
Middleham
Wensleydale (0969) 23645
Nicholson, D. (0:2:0:0:3)
Stow-on-the-Wold
Stow-on-the-Wold (0451) 30417
Norton, S. G. (2:2:5:14:14)
Barnsley Bretton (092 485) 450
O'Donoghue, J. (0:0:0:1:1)
Reigate Reigate (073 72) 45241
O'Gorman, W. A. (7:16:32:25:30)
Newmarket
Newmarket (0638) 3330
Old, J. A. B. (2:2:2:3:3)
Salisbury
Fontmell Magna (074 781) 648
Oliver, J. K. M. (0:0:0:0:0)
Hawick Denholm (045 087) 216
O'Neill, H. (0:0:0:2:5)
Coldharbour Dorking (0306) 6223
O'Neill, O. (2:1:0:0:0)
Cheltenham
Bishops Cleeve (024 267) 3275
Oughton, Mrs D. R. (0:0:0:0:0)
Findon Findon (090 617) 2113
Owen, E. H. jnr (—:0:0:0:0)
Denbigh Llandyrnog (082 44) 264
Page, W. R. (—:—:—:1:0)
Billinghay Billinghay (05266) 365
Palling, B. (—:—:0:0:0)
Cowbridge
Cowbridge (04463) 2089
Pattemore, S. P. (—:0:0:0:0)
Somerton Somerton (0458) 73112

Peacock, J. H. (0:0:0:0:0)
Ludlow Seifton (058 473) 217
Peacock, R. D. (16:8:9:3:3)
Middleham
Wensleydale (0969) 23291
Peacock, R. E. (0:0:0:2:1)
Tarporley Tarporley (082 93) 2716
Perrett, A. C. J. (—:0:0:0:0)
Cheltenham
Andoversford (024 282) 244
Pipe, M. C. (—:0:0:3:4)
Wellington, Somerset
Craddock (0884) 40715
Pitman, Mrs J. S. (0:1:1:1:1)
Lambourn Lambourn (0488) 71714
Pitt, A. J. (5:7:9:9:9)
Epsom Epsom (037 27) 25034
Potts, A. W. (0:1:0:0:0)
Barton-on-Humber
Saxby All Saints (065 261) 750
Powney, J. (7:14:3:1:2)
Newmarket
Newmarket (0638) 3343
Prescott, Sir Mark
(27:26:28:30:34)
Newmarket
Newmarket (0638) 2117
Price, G. H. (—:—:—:0:0)
Leominster
Steens Bridge (056 882) 235
Price, H. R. (83:73:61:60:48)
Findon Findon (090 671) 2388
Priday, J. (—:—:—:0:0)
Kington Lyonshall (054 48) 230
Pritchard-Gordon, G. A.
(30:41:39:58:47)
Newmarket
Newmarket (0638) 2824
Ransom, P. B. (0:0:0:0:0)
Wigmore Wigmore (056 886) 253
Read, C. P. (—:—:—:—:1)
West Chiltington
West Chiltington (079 83) 3489
Reavey, Mrs C. J. (—:—:—:—:—)
East Hendred
East Hendred (023 588) 297
Reddan, M. T. (—:—:—:0:0)
Houghton-Le-Spring
Houghton-Le-Spring (0783) 844639
Richards G. (9:11:10:14:19)
Penrith Greystoke (085 33) 392
Richmond, B. A. (2:6:3:1:1)
Wellingore Lincoln (0522) 810578
Rimell, T. F. (0:4:7:1:2)
Kinnersley
Severn Stoke (090 567) 233
Ringer, D. S. (3:3:5:5:3)
Newmarket
Newmarket (0638) 2653
Rohan, H. P. (22:19:18:28:28)
Malton Malton (0653) 2337/8
Ryan, M. J. (2:5:6:23:11)
Newmarket
Newmarket (0638) 4172
Salaman, M. (2:4:6:3:1)
Lambourn Lambourn (0488) 72121
Sasse, D. J. G. (7:6:11:14:2)
Lambourn Lambourn (0488) 71902

Scallan, J. J. (—:—:—:0:0)
Nayland, Nr. Colchester
Nayland (0206) 262238
Scott, A. (—:—:0:2:1)
Northumbria
Wooperton (066 87) 252
Scudamore, M. J. (0:0:0:0:0)
Hoarwithy Carey (043 270) 253
Shaw, B. (—:—:0:0:0)
Cheltenham
Cheltenham (0242) 25705
Sheather, R. (—:—:6:10:15)
Newmarket
Newmarket (0638) 4687
Home—Newmarket (0638) 2468
Simpson, R. (0:—:—:5:3)
Abingdon
Sutton Courtney (023 582) 609
Sinclair, Miss A. V. (9:3:3:1:0)
Lewes Lewes (079 16) 6619
Home—Lewes (079 16) 3851
Smith, A. (4:5:8:1:4)
Beverley Hull (0482) 882520
Smith, Denys (44:30:28:53:35)
Bishop Auckland
Bishop Auckland (0388) 603317
Smyly, R. M. (12:9:8:5:12)
Lambourn Lambourn (0488) 71408
Smyth, R. V. (19:19:12:9:17)
Epsom Epsom (037 27) 20053
Soane, V. St. John (—:—:—:—:0)
Spearing, J. L. (3:1:0:4:3)
Alcester
Bidford-on-Avon (078 988) 2639
Stapleton, K. G. (1:0:0:0:0)
Skipton Skipton (0756) 2703
Stephenson, W. A. (15:6:5:9:3)
Bishop Auckland
Rushyford (0388) 720213
Stone, K. (—:—:0:9:17)
Malton Malton (0653) 4597
Stoute, M. R. (62:62:69:80:101)
Newmarket
Newmarket (0638) 3801
Stubbs, R. W. (1:0:2:7:4)
Northallerton
Kirkby Fleetham (060 984) 318
Sturdy, R. C. (2:4:1:—:1)
Shrewton Shrewton (098 062) 472
Sutcliffe, J. R. E. (24:18:24:21:19)
Epsom Ashtead (037 22) 72825
Swift, B. C. (16:23:22:24:22)
Headley
Leatherhead (037 23) 77209 and 77308
Tate, F. M. (7:3:1:1:2)
Kidderminster
Chaddesley Corbett (056 283) 243
Taylor, Peter (—:0:0:0:3)
Swindon Swindon (079379) 683
Taylor, P. M. (3:3:8:8:12)
Upper Lambourn
Lambourn (0488) 71667
Taylor, T. (—:0:0:0:2)
Ashbourne, Derbyshire
Rochester (0889) 590334
Thom, D. T. (4:3:4:5:7)
Newmarket Exning (063 877) 288

Thompson, V. (0:0:0:0:0)
Alnwick Embleton (066 576) 272
Thorne, J. (0:0:0:0:0)
Bridgwater Holford (027 874) 216
Thornton, C. W. (—:34:35:33:32)
Middleham
Wensleydale (0969) 23350
Tierney, J. (—:—:4:1:1)
Stafford
Wheaton Ashton (0785) 840225
Tinkler, N. D. (—:—:—:—:0)
Toft, G. (11:10:9:11:8)
Malton Malton (0653) 5039
Toller, J. R. (—:—:—:—:0)
Newmarket
Newmarket (0638) 68503
Tompkins, M. H. (—:—:—:—:4)
Newmarket
Newmarket (0638) 61434
Tree, A. J. (17:17:24:30:30)
Beckhampton
Avebury (067 23) 204
Home—Avebury (067 23) 244
Tuer, K. H. (—:—:0:0:0)
Penrith
Pooley Bridge (085 36) 238
Turnell, A. R. (7:4:1:4:9)
Ogbourne Maisey
Marlborough (0672) 52542
Turner, W. G. M. (—:—:0:1:0)
Tavistock Marytavy (082281) 237
Underhill, S. (0:0:—:—:0)
Alcester
Bidford-on-Avon (078 988) 3714
Underwood, D. B. (5:0:0:1:0)
Bramley
Bramley, Surrey (048 647) 3147
Vergette, G. M. (1:0:0:0:0)
Market Deeping
Market Deeping (0778) 342226
Vickers, I. (—:—:—:2:1)
Darlington Dinsdale (032573) 2450
Vigors, N. A. C. (8:12:15:13:13)
Lambourn Lambourn (0488) 71657
Walker, I. S. (11:15:17:14:16)
Newmarket
Exning (063 877) 219 and
Newmarket (0638) 2457
Walwyn, F. T. T. (0:0:1:1:0)
Lambourn Lambourn (0488) 71555
Walwyn, P. T. (110:110:70:44:78)
Lambourn Lambourn (0488) 71347
Ward, R. C. (1:2:1:2:2)
Doncaster Doncaster (0302) 700574
Wardle, I. P. (0:0:0:0:0)
East Horrington
Wells, Somerset (0749) 73167
Waring, Mrs B. H. (—:—:—:0:0)
Wellington
Wellington (082 347) 3418
Watson, Alf (—:0:0:0:0)
Skipton-in-Craven
Earby (923 84) 2228
Watts, J. W. (45:57:50:46:47)
Richmond Richmond (0748) 2287
Watts, W. C. (7:12:8:3:7)
Bridlington Bridlington (0262) 3719
Waugh, T. A. (17:9:11:12:11)
Newmarket
Newmarket (0638) 2233
Webber, J. H. 0:0:1:2:0)
Mollington
Cropredy (029 575) 226
Weeden, D. E. (7:8:16:5:4)
Newmarket
Newmarket (0638) 5050
Westbrook, H. C. (7:1:3:3:2)
Newmarket
Newmarket (0638) 3657
Weymes, E. (14:17:24:9:19)
Leyburn Wensleydale (0969) 40229
Wharton, H. (1:0:0:0:1)
Doncaster Doncaster (0302) 54126
Wharton, W. (7:12:15:15:24)
Melton Mowbray
Waltham-on-the-Wolds (066 478) 258
Home—Melton Mowbray (0664) 5225
Whelan, D. (7:8:6:3:1)
Epsom Epsom (037 27) 22763
Home—Epsom (037 27) 21482
Whiston, W. R. (0:0:0:0:0)
Market Drayton
Hodnet (063 084) 203
Whitaker, R. M. (—:—:0:0:5)
Leeds Leeds (0532) 892265
Wigham, P. (2:7:2:1:4)
Malton Rillington (094 42) 332
Wightman, W. G. R.
(18:29:27:17:14)
Upham
Bishops Waltham (048 93) 2565
Wildman, C. P. (—:—:—:—:2)
Larkhill
Durrington Walls (0980) 52226
Wiles, S. J. (—:—:—:0:0)
Wakefield Flockton (0924) 848468
Wilkinson, B. E. (0:0:0:0:0)
Middleham
Wensleydale (0969) 23385
Williams, C. N. (—:—:—:—:0)
Williams, R. J. R. (—:—:—:—:0)
Williams, W. H. H.
(—:—:26:19:15)
Ayr Ayr (0292) 66232
Williams, W. R. (0:0:0:0:0)
Buckfastleigh
Buckfastleigh (036 44) 3590
Willis, H. (—:—:—:0:0)
Winchester
Twyford (0962) 713483
Wilson, J. H. (—:—:—:1:2)
Tarleton
Hesketh Bank (077 473) 2780
Wilson, D. A. (—:—:—:—:0)
Epsom
Business: Ashtead (037 22) 77645
Home: Ashtead (037 22) 73839
Wilson, J. S. (—:—:—:—:0)
Motherwell
Motherwell (0698) 62653
Winter, F. T. (1:1:0:5:0)
Lambourn Lambourn (0488) 71438

Winter, J. R. (26:22:23:31:13)
Newmarket
Newmarket (0638) 3898

Wintle, D. J. (—:1:1:0:0)
Westbury-on-Severn
Westbury-on-Severn (045 276) 459

Wise, B. J. (2:5:1:1:0)
Polegate
Polegate (032 12) 3331 and 2505

Woodman, S. (9:8:10:4:4)
Chichester
Chichester (0243) 527136

Wragg, H. (30:39:34:30:33)
Newmarket
Newmarket (0638) 2328

Wright, W. (—:—:—:—:2)
Preston Cleveleys (0253) 700279

Yardley, F. (0:1:0:2:1)
Droitwich
Worcester (0905) 620477

Yeoman, D. (1:0:1:0:0)
Richmond
Richmond (0748) 811756

The following also held a licence for part of the year:
Bewicke, C.
Blackshaw, H. F.
Cross, Mrs I.
Dickinson, A. E.
Reavey, E., The late
Stephenson, W.
Wainwright, S.
Wallace, G., The late

JOCKEYS

The figures in brackets show the number of winners each jockey has ridden in this country during the past five seasons, from 1976 to 1980 inclusive. The telephone numbers and riding weights are added, where known.

Appleton, D. N. (0:—:—:0:0) 8 4
Dinsdale (032573) 2450
Apter, E. R. (19:20:29:20:6).. 8 0
c/o Beverley (0482) 885041
Armstrong, J. (—:0:0:—:0).. 8 7
Astbury, C. F.
(—:—:—:—:0)............ 8 11
Rugeley (088 94) 77038
Atkinson, D. J. (0:1:0:5:3)... 8 0
Wantage (023 57) 3164
Balding, J. (0:0:0:0:1)....... 8 9
Doncaster (0302) 710096
Ballantine, H.
(19:19:—:—:1)............ 7 10
Balmer, W. N. (—:0:—:—:0) 8 7
Barker, R. S. (5:2:2:0:0)..... 8 4
c/o Malton (0653) 2842
Barnes, M. A. (—:0:—:—:0). 9 0
c/o Langwathby (067 881) 379
Baxter, G. E. (44:62:63:64:52) 7 13
Lambourn (0488) 71320
Bentley, W. (5:0:0:0:0)...... 7 10
Wensleydale (0969) 22289
Birch, M. (48:62:65:77:71)... 8 0
Malton (0653) 3885
Blanks, J. (0:2:11:6:11)...... 7 7
Bleasdale, J. (17:67:90:41:41) 8 0
Bedale (0677) 22222
Bond, A. M. (46:25:19:16:16). 7 12
Stetchworth (063 876) 681
Butler, K. R. (0:0:0:0:0)..... 7 7
Winchester (0962) 880310
Cadwaladr, G. E. (6:0:—:0:0) 8 6
Chester (0244) 679898
Carmody, T. M. (—:—:0:0:0) 9 7
Harrogate (0423) 66429
Carroll, D. (—:—:0:—:0).... 7 9
Carson, W. F. H.
(138:160:182:142:166)...... 7 10
Newmarket (0638) 3623 and East Ilsley (063 528) 348
Cauthen, S. (—:—:—:52:61). 8 0
Kingsclere (0635) 40834
Charlton, S. F. (4:0:0:0:1)... 8 12
c/o York (0904) 28693
Charnock, L. (12:25:15:25:15) 7 7
Malton (0653) 5703
Cheese, P. (1:0:1:2:0)....... 7 12
Clotworthy, B. J. (2:2:0:0:0). 7 13
Wensleydale (0969) 22289
Cochrane, Mrs Anne
(—:—:—:0:0)............ 7 9
Colquhoun, P. R. (0:3:7:12:7) 7 13
Exning (063877) 219
Cook, P. A. (66:72:90:80:90). 8 0
Wanborough (079 379) 552
Cousins, A. M. (5:—:5:1:0).. 8 4
Cheltenham (0242) 23393
Cressy, A. (8:1:—:—:0)..... 7 8
Crook, A. (5:2:—:—:1)...... 7 12

Crowther, N. (22:9:13:15:5).. 8 4
Barnsley (0226) 384677
Curant, R. D. (10:15:25:31:18) 7 13
Hungerford (048 86) 3216
and Boxford (048 838) 433
D'Arcy, P. W. (2:0:9:11:3)... 7 12
Lambourn (0488) 72153
Darley, K. P. (—:11:70:14:19) 7 7
Wolverhampton (0902) 337195
and 724541
Davies, N. (0:—:—:0:0)..... 8 4
Newmarket (0628) 4524
Dineley, D. D. (54:0:0:2:4)... 8 3
Lambourn (0488) 71025
Duffield, G. P.
(50:60:75:76:78)........... 7 12
Stetchworth (063 876) 544
Dwyer, C. A. (17:9:16:20:23). 8 3
Malton (0653) 3471
Eccles, S. (21:9:25:23:12).... 8 1
Hungerford (04886) 3096
Eccleston, C. H.
(29:19:29:4:2)............. 7 7
York (0904) 21374
Eddery, P. J. J.
(162:176:148:123:130)...... 8 3
Cheltenham (0242) 28763
Elder, B. (—:—:—:—:0)..... 7 8
Elliot, R. S. (1:1:1:0:0)...... 8 0
Avebury (06723) 204 and 244
Ellison, B. (—:—:—:0:0).... 8 11
Emes, I. M. (0:0:—:0:0)..... 8 5
East Ilsley (063 528) 253
Enright, G. P. (—:—:—:—:0) 9 5
Worthing (0903) 6117
Ferguson, R. J. (3:8:1:2:2)... 7 9
Newmarket (0638) 2004
Flint, A. W. (—:0:0:—:0).... 8 7
c/o Malton (0653) 3149
Fox, R. D. S. (31:29:14:17:26) 7 9
(0285) 61344
Francois, G. G. A. (0:0:0:0:0) 8 0
c/o Winchester (0962) 880808
Gibson, Dominic J.
(1:1:0:0:0)................ 7 13
Giles, M. S. (0:1:2:0:0)...... 8 4
c/o Newmarket (0638) 3801
Gosney, G. (2:7:7:5:1)....... 8 0
c/o Tadcaster (0937) 833294
Gray, O. J. (13:9:11:10:8).... 8 0
Coverdale (0969) 22403
Guest, R. (0:—:—:1:7)...... 8 5
Newmarket (0638) 61508
Gwilliam, C. K.
(—:—:—:—:0)............ 8 2
c/o Findon (090 671) 2388
Hedley, B. F. (1:0:0:0:0)..... 8 3
Malton (0653) 3749 or 2511
Henry, B. (4:2:11:0:0)....... 8 2

Hide, E. W. G. (103:111:88:53:106)........ 8 3
Malton (0653) 2132 and Newmarket (0638) 750155
Higgins, J. J. (2:1:0:10:9)..... 8 2
Newmarket (0638) 61537
Higgins, W. F. (6:6:2:11:13).. 7 8
c/o Newmarket (0638) 2090
Hood, B. (4:5:0:0:0)......... 7 12
Malton (0653) 2842
Hunt, Mrs L. I.(—:—:—:—:0) 8 7
Hutchinson, Richard (1:11:0:3:5)............... 7 12
Ayr (0292) 66232
Ives, T. A. (48:41:29:38:53)... 8 4
Newmarket (0638) 79414
Jago, B. (10:9:11:16:30)...... 8 0
Epsom (037 27) 21025
Jenkinson, I. P. (7:4:2:4:1)... 7 7
Epsom (037 27) 24484
Johnson, E. (65:72:86:61:49).. 7 10
(099 38) 7332
Johnson, I. E. (22:13:0:3:19).. 8 3
Kintbury (04885) 749 or Boxford (048838) 433
Kelleher, P (—:—:4:2:3).... 8 0
c/o Carlisle (0228) 25649
Kettle, M. (10:10:5:1:4)...... 8 0
Newmarket (0638) 712428
Kimberley, A. A. (35:39:44:27:15)........... 8 3
Newmarket (0638) 3267
Knight, S. G. (—:—:—:—:0). 8 11
Launchbury, A. T. (—:—:—:—:0)............ 7 12
Lawes, S. D. (—:2:2:8:0).... 7 11
Leason, K. M. (18:24:20:14:10)........... 7 9
(0709) 815252
Leonard, C. S. (1:3:5:3:2)... 7 0
Newmarket (0638) 751048
Logie, J. (0:—:1:0:1)........ 8 0
c/o East Hendred (023 588) 247
Lowe, J. J. (47:86:57:49:54)... 7 7
York (0904) 489040
Lucas, T. G. (—:—:—:10:14). 8 1
Sheriff Hutton (03477) 368 or 327
Lynch, J. (46:26:36:65:12).... 7 12
Wantage (023 57) 3682
Madden, P. J. (9:10:26:8:8).. 8 5
Newmarket (0638) 750603
Maitland, D. (7:6:4:3:0)..... 7 7
Newmarket (0638) 61615
Marshall, E. T. (0:0:—:—:0). 7 7
Marshall, R. C. (22:30:10:9:1) 8 2
Newmarket (0638) 61374
Matthias, J. J. (21:21:25:23:41) 8 3
c/o Kingsclere (0635) 298210 and 297205
McGhin, R. (—:—:0:0:2).... 8 0
c/o Ashtead (03722) 73729
McGregor, J. P. (—:—:—:—:0)............ 8 2
McGuffie, Miss E. M. (—:—:—:2:0)............. 8 0
Newmarket (0638) 4485

McIntosh, N. (0:0:1:0:0)..... 7 0
c/o Dunbar (0368) 62583
McKay, D. J. (18:24:17:23:11) 7 7
Lambourn (0488) 71735 and Box (022 121) 2777
McNamee, C. J. (0:0:0:0:0).. 8 0
Lambourn (0488) 71956
Mercer, A. (—:2:30:18:14)... 7 6
Mercer, J. (98:102:115:164:103)....... 8 4
Hermitage (0635) 200 306
Miller, M. M. (19:5:0:19:14).. 7 10
Newmarket (0638) 730374
Mills, A. E. (—:—:—:—:0).. 8 0
Moore, G. M. (1:0:0:0:0).... 8 4
Boroughbridge (090 12) 2037
Morby, F. (30:18:20:19:19)... 8 2
Newbury (0635) 42610
Moss, C. J. T. (18:15:14:9:2).. 8 2
Daventry (032 72) 5906
Muddle, R. J. (9:4:24:17:9)... 7 12
Passfield (042877) 316
Naughton, Mrs A. M. (0:0:—:0:1)............... 8 4
Richmond (0748) 2803
Nicholls, D. (6:22:8:0:4)..... 8 0
Wetherby (0937) 61291
Nicholson, W. J. C. (0:—:0:2:0)............... 7 12
Nutter, C. (4:11:8:6:0)....... 7 9
Newmarket (0638) 68153
Oldroyd, G. R. (9:11:4:7:4).. 8 3
Malton (0653) 5991
O'Leary P. (0:0:1:1:1)....... 7 9
01-979 6046
O'Neill, J. J. (0:0:0:7:3)...... 9 0
Plumpton (076 884) 270
Oxland, R. (0:0:0:0:0)....... 8 0
c/o Newmarket (0638) 3286
Parkes, L. C. (6:6:4:0:0)..... 7 5
Malton (0653) 2845
Perkins, P. (1:0:7:0:1)....... 8 0
Ely (0353) 720895
Perks, S. J. (16:14:15:8:5).... 8 1
Hednesford (054 38) 4836
Piggott, L. K. (87:103:97:77:156)......... 8 6
Newmarket (0638) 2584
Procter, B. T. (1:0:1:3:3).... 8 3
East Ilsley (063 528) 367 and 219
Ramshaw, G. (14:15:5:6:4).. 8 3
Burgh Heath (073 73) 53611
Rawlinson, A. C. (—:—:—:—:3)............ 8 4
Lambourn (0488) 72205
Raymond, B. H. (58:56:48:58:62)........... 8 4
Newmarket (0638) 730387
Reid, J. A. (14:33:54:72:79).. 8 2
Boxford (048 838) 433 and Chieveley (063521) 8801
Reilly, B. A. (3:3:0:—:0).... 9 0
Robinson, C. E. (—:—:—:—:0)............ 8 3
Rodrigues, C. (7:10:8:0:0)... 7 3
Newmarket (0638) 61443

Rogers, T. (4:3:11:16:39).... 8 2
Thatcham (0635) 63047
Rouse, B. A. (34:48:60:42:43) 7 11
Epsom (037 27) 2140
Salmon, S. E. W.
(22:12:10:2:8)............. 7 8
Malton (0653) 4285
Seagrave, J. (50:43:15:25:24). 8 4
Malton (0653) 2692
Sexton, G. C. (12:16:11:16:9). 8 0
Newmarket (0638) 4367
Shrimpton, P. R. E.
(0:1:2:0:0)................ 7 8
Skilling, J. F. (2:—:—:—:1).. 8 2
Smith, Dennis (—:—:—:—:0) 8 5
Sozzi, Miss T. L.
(—:—:—:—:0)............ 8 2
Starkey, G. M. W.
(73:76:107:98:82).......... 8 5
Mildenhall (0638) 714672
Street, R. (10:25:17:13:3).... 7 7
Lambourn (0488) 71412 and
71548
Stroud, M. R. H. (—:—:0:0:1) 8 0
Sturrock, T. T. (—:—:0:2:0). 8 4
Abingdon (0235) 831730
Taylor, B. (108:83:59:56:32).. 8 4
Stetchworth (063 876) 515 or
530
Taylor, K. (—:—:—:—:0).... 7 7
Thomas, M. L.
(90:98:52:48:27)........... 7 9
Mildenhall (0638) 713916
Tinkler, C. H. (0:0:0:0:0).... 9 4
Hovingham (065 382) 492
Treanor, A. (—:—:—:—:1).. 7 9
Tucker, K. J. (—:—:0:1:0)... 8 0
c/o Cannings (038 086) 245
Tulk, P. F. (24:10:2:14:10)... 8 2
Newmarket (0638) 3209

Waldron, P. (33:44:42:53:53). 8 2
Newbury (0635) 43620
Weaver, R. I. (0:10:11:13:10). 8 3
Chieveley (063521) 519 or
Weyhill (026477) 2278
Webb, A. (0:—:—:—:0)...... 9 0
c/o Stow-on-the-Wold (9451)
30417
Webster, S. G.
(25:18:23:10:13)........... 7 11
Wensleydale (0969) 23576
Welsh, G. (0:0:—:0:0)....... 7 10
Wensleydale (0969) 23350
Wharton, W. J.
(10:18:25:18:15)........... 8 2
Melton Mowbray (0664) 5225
Wigham, M. (10:32:56:25:37) 8 2
Rillington (09442) 332
Wilkins, L. F. (0:0:0:0:0)..... 8 0
Bagshot (0276) 71030
Wilkinson, W. P.
(—:—:—:0:1)............. 8 1
Epsom (037 27) 28788
Williams, C. N. (3:3:1:0:0).. 8 3
Goring (049 14) 2843
Williams, J. A. N. (0:0:0:0:0) 8 6
Clydach (044 15) 3407
Woolley, S. J. (0:4:5:1:3).... 8 3
Yates, D. I. (0:1:3:5:2)....... 8 0
Yeoman, Mrs M. M.
(0:0:0:0:0)................ 8 7
York (0904) 28693
Young, P. J. (9:26:13:15:22).. 8 4
Newmarket (0638) 730371
and 5050

The following relinquished his licence during the season:
Losh, P.

APPRENTICES

The following list shows the employer and riding weight of every apprentice who held a licence at the ena of the 1980 season, and the number of winners he or she has ridden in this country up to the end of the 1980 season, wins in apprentice races being recorded separately.

Apprentices under 24 years of age may claim 7 lb until they have won 10 races, 5 lb until they have won 50 races and 3 lb until they have won 75 races. Apprentice races are excepted in all these cases. The claim may be exercised in all handicaps and selling races, and all other races with guaranteed prize money of not more than £3,500. The allowance each apprentice is entitled to claim is shown in brackets.

Adams, N. M. (7) 7 2
(F. J. Houghton)
Alcock, G. (7) 7 12
(H. T. Jones)
Alderman, A. A. (7) 1 ap 7 13
(J. Jenkins)
Alford, P. G. (7) 7 0
(R. Price)
Anderson, P. J. O. (7) 7 0
(R. Hollinshead)
Atkinson, C. B. (7) 7 7
(I. Walker)
Atkinson, Miss S. J. (7) 7 2
(W. Hastings-Bass)
Banner, M. (7) 6+5 ap 8 3
(H. T. Jones)
Barker, M. G. (7) 8 0
(B. Swift)
Bates, D. W. (7) 7 12
(P. Cole)
Beecroft, M. C. (7) 1 ap 7 11
(T. Fairhurst)
Bell, C. J. (7) 8 0
(A. Davison)
Bell, K. (7) 1 ap 7 2
(R. Hollinshead)
Bell, P. (7) 7 2
(J. Etherington)
Billingham, M. A. (7) 7 10
(M. Tate)
Black, J. (7) 1+3 ap 7 11
(G. Huffer)
Blackburn, P. J. (7) 7 0
(J. Leigh)
Blackett, G. R. (7) 8 0
(R. Hern)
Blake, J. W. (7) 6 7
(H. Wragg)
Bloomfield, P. S. (7) 3+9 ap ... 7 12
(G. Harwood)
Bond K. J. (7) 8 0
(D. Elsworth)
Bourton, D. D. (7) 7 7
(R. Atkins)
Bowmer, S. J. (7) 7 7
(M. Jarvis)
Bradley, Miss S. I. (7) 8 4
(M. Bradley)
Bradwell, P. (5) 18+7 ap 7 6
(C. Brittain)
Brockbank, D. (7) 1+1 ap 7 7
(G. Pritchard-Gordon)
Brough, J. H. (7) 8 0
(R. Hollinshead)

Brown, D. (7) 7 0
(M. Masson)
Brown, G. (7) 2 ap 7 2
(R. Hollinshead)
Brown, W. J. (7) 8 0
(M. Ryan)
Bryan, T. (7) 5 ap 7 13
(G. Balding)
Buckton, S. (7) 1 .... 7 7
(J. Calvert)
Burke, K. R. (7) 1 ap 8 2
(A. Jarvis)
Burnham, M. J. (7) 7 7
(G. Balding)
Byles, J. M. (7) 8 13
(J. Tree)
Campbell, C. R. (7) 1+1 ap ... 7 2
(K. Ivory)
Campbell, R. (7) 6+6 ap 7 11
(Denys Smith)
Carcary, D. R. (7) 7 9
(R. Hollinshead)
Carlisle, N. (5) 11+2 ap 7 0
(R. Hollinshead)
Carter, C. A. (7) 7 0
(P. Cundell)
Cartmill, R. A. (7) 7 8
(V. Soane)
Chilton, M. J. (7) 1+2 ap 9 7
(G. Balding)
Christopher P. (7) 8 0
(B. Palling)
Clark, A. S. (5) 20+3 ap 7 1
(G. Harwood)
Cochrane, R. (5) 38+4 ap 8 3
(R. Sheather)
Cockburn, A. D. (7) 7 7
(G. Richards)
Coleman, N. F. (7) 8 11
(D. Nicholson)
Connorton, N. B. (5) 24+7 ap .. 7 7
(J. W. Watts)
Cooper, Miss S. J. (7) 6 10
(F. J. Houghton)
Coughlin, C. (7) 7 6
(Mrs R. Lomax)
Cox, J. D. (7) 6 9
(J. Tree)
Crossley, B. G. (5) 24+3 ap ... 7 4
(G. Huffer)
Davies, S. P. (7) 1 ap 7 9
(I. Balding)
Dawe, N. J. (7) 1+6 ap 7 2
(J. Dunlop)

Dawson, S. (7) 1 . . . . 8 7
(N. Vigors)
Day, N. P. (5) 10 + 5 ap 8 0
(H. Cecil)
Dennison, S. (7) 2 ap 7 12
(N. Callaghan)
Dickie, G. (7) 7 1
Dicks, A. C. (7) 7 0
(M. Bradley)
Docwra, P. (7) 7 6
(A. Moore)
Dodd, D. (7) 4 ap 8 4
(G. Richards)
Donkin, S. (7) 7 5
(M. H. Easterby)
Doyle, A. J. P. (7) 8 7
(M. Smyly)
Durr, S. P. (7) 9 0
(F. Durr)
Earp, D. F. I. (7) 7 12
(B. Richmond)
Eatwell, M. (7) 1 . . . . 7 5
(P. Cole)
Eddery, C. R. (7) 8 5
(I. Jordon)
Eddery, P. A. (5) 13 + 6 ap 6 9
(R. Hollinshead)
Eddington, P. V. (7) 7 10
(G. Pritchard-Gordon)
Edwards, S. (7) 1 ap 7 10
(D. Dale)
Evans, C. (7) 7 12
(B. Palling)
Fairburn, D. (7) 7 4
(C. Thornton)
Fayle, A. R. (7) 6 7
(P.Rohan)
Fenlon, S. (7) 8 0
(P. Taylor)
Fielden, Miss J. L. (7) 7 12
(P. Fielden)
Finlayson, J. (7) 2 + 1 ap 8 0
(H. Candy)
Finneran, K. (7) 7 7
(H. Candy)
Ford, D. A. P. (7) 7 4
(M. Jarvis)
Ford, D. K. (7) 7 10
(C. Nelson)
Ford, P. A. (7) 7 7
(B. Palling)
Fortune, J. (7) 2 + 1 ap 7 2
(I. Walker)
Fotheringham, R. (7) 7 0
(J. W. Watts)
Fowler-Wright, J. D. (7) 6 2
(R. Smyth)
Fox, D. (7) 1 ap 6 7
(A. Hide)
Fozzard, M. G. (7) 1 ap 7 0
(R. Hannon)
Freer, S. (7) 7 0
(R. Hollinshead)
Fretwell, K. (7) 4 + 4 ap 7 5
(B. Swift)
Fry, M. J. (7) 1 . . . . 7 6
(R. Stubbs)

Garstang, Miss Mary (7) 8 7
(R.Hannon)
Geran, M. P. (7) 7 6
(J. Berry)
Gibbons, A. J. (7) 8 5
(G. Balding)
Gibson, A. (7) 7 10
(P. Haslam)
Gillingham, W. (7) 8 0
(M. Blanshard)
Goldsborough, W. (7) 7 9
(C. Brittain)
Goswell, P. W. (7) 7 12
(R. Simpson)
Green, M. S. (7) 2 . . . . 7 9
(M. Haynes)
Gregg, J. (7) 1 . . . . 7 0
(N. Vigors)
Griffin, D. A. (7) 7 7
(Mrs J. Pitman)
Griffin, J. P. (7) 7 7
(J. Hill)
Grimes, F. P. (7) 1 ap 8 7
(A. Ingham)
Guest, E. J. (7) 2 . . . . 7 7
(W. Guest)
Guest, Miss Sally (7) 7 12
(N. Guest)
Gunn, P. G. (5) 23 + 3 ap 8 1
(W. Holden)
Hadley, S. R. (7) 1 + 1 ap 7 5
(R. Hern)
Hall, S. (7) 7 10
(J. Berry)
Hamm, M. A. (7) 7 3
(J. Hindley)
Hamilton, G. (7) 8 0
(B. Hills)
Hansen, J. M. (7) 8 7
(J. Berry)
Harding, T J (7) 7 6
(M. Haynes)
Harmer, D. (7) 8 4
(I. Jordon)
Harris, J. A. (7) 8 0
(J. Harris)
Harrison, M. J. (7) 7 5
(A. Ingham)
Harwood, G. A. (7) 8 0
(R. Price)
Haworth, N. (7) 7 9
(P. Taylor)
Hickey, C. M. (7) 7 12
(K. Morgan)
Hill, P. D. (7) 1 ap 6 7
(W. Wharton)
Hills, M. P. (5) 11 + 6 ap 6 3
(J. Hindley)
Hills, R. J. (7) 6 + 2 ap 5 9
(H. T. Jones)
Hodgson, K. (5) 22 + 9 ap 7 4
(M. H. Easterby)
Hodgson, R. (7) 1 ap 7 4
(P. Haslam)
Holgate, C. S. (7) 7 0
(W. Musson)
Houlker, A. D. (7) 8 10
(R. Hollinshead)

Homewood, S. (7) 7 10
(L. Cumani)
Honeywill, B. G. (7) 7 7
(B. Hobbs)
Hood, S. (7) 7 12
(N. Vigors)
Howe, N. J. (5) 32 + 10 ap 7 8
(P. Walwyn)
Hughes, G. (7) 1 ap 7 13
(P. Rohan)
Humphreys, G. M. (7) 7 9
(I. Walker)
Hurd, P. A. (7) 7 11
(S. Norton)
Hurst, Miss D. E. (7) 7 10
(D. Leslie)
Imrie, S. T. (7) 7 12
(W. Bentley)
Jarvis, S. J. (5) 30 + 3 ap 8 3
(A. Jarvis)
Jarvis, T. O. (7) 7 0
(A. Jarvis)
Jenkins, C. V. (7) 7 7
(G. Huffer)
Jewell, S. (7) 7 6
(S. Matthews)
Johnson, Miss D. S. (7) 7 0
(Miss S. Hall)
Jones, B. (7) 9 + 4 ap 6 10
(R. Hollinshead)
Jones, G. P. (7) 1 + 2 ap 8 7
(J. Hindley)
Jones, K. (7) 8 0
(W. A. Stephenson)
Jones, M. (7) 6 7
(A. Goodwill)
Jones, N. S. (7) 7 4
(O. O'Neill)
Kell, J. T. K. (7) 7 10
(T. Fairhurst)
Kelly, S. A. C. S. (7) 6 10
(J. Hindley)
Kennedy, J. B. (7) 7 0
(H. Candy)
Keogh, M. A. (7) 8 0
(B. Hanbury)
Kerr, R. (7) 7 0
(M. Tompkins)
Knox, W. D. R. (7) 7 7
(P. Cundell)
Lake, P. M. (7) 8 5
(N. Adam)
Langfrey, P. (7) 8 0
(A. Ingham)
Latter, D. (7) 7 9
(P. Haslam)
Lawson, R. (7) 8 0
(P. Taylor)
Lingham, J. J. (7) 2 ap 8 4
(B. Hobbs)
Lloyd, M. (7) 7 0
(W. Holden)
Longair, C. (7) 7 7
(W. Williams)
MacKay, A. (5) 13 + 8 ap 7 5
(N. Callaghan)
Maith, M. B. (7) 7 7
(A. Potts)
Malham, M. S. T. (7) 7 + 7 ap . . 7 9
(P. Cole)
Martin, J. S. (7) 6 12
(P. Mitchell)
Mason, P. (7) 7 3
(P. Cole)
Matthews, B. (7) 1 . . . . 7 10
(H. T. Jones)
Matthews, S. (7) 7 7
(F. Durr)
McAndrew, M. A. (7) 7 9
(R. Ward)
McCready, C. (7) 7 7
(A. Davison)
McCrystal, S. (7) 6 7
(R. Armstrong)
McDermott, G. S. (7) 7 12
(K. Stone)
McElroy, F. S. (7) 8 0
(J. Jenkins)
McFeeters, D. M. (7) 7 0
(J. O'Donoghue)
McGlone, A. D. (7) 4 + 7 ap 7 0
(R. Hannon)
McIlfatrick, C. (7) 1 + 7 ap 8 11
(J. Old)
McKeon, W. A. P. (7) 4 + 2 ap . . 7 13
(F. Durr)
McKeown, D. R. (5) 13 + 5 ap . . 7 5
(W. Hastings-Bass)
McLaughlin, J. F. S. (7) 1 ap . . . 8 6
(G. Huffer)
McLean, J. A. (7) 1 . . . . 6 8
(K. Ivory)
Mills, G. (7) 2 ap 7 12
(R. Hollinshead)
Mitchell, J. A. (7) 8 0
(H. Jones)
Mitchell, J. O. F. (7) 7 7
(V. Mitchell)
Mitchell, S. (7) 8 4
(J. Fitzgerald)
Moore, P. (7) 7 9
(R. Morris)
Morris, A. P. (7) 7 7
(W. Marshall)
Morris, W. A. F. F. (7) 8 2
(F. Yardley)
Moseley, M. F. (7) 7 3
(P. Walwyn)
Muggeridge, R. J. (7) 8 10
(F. Muggeridge)
Murray, D. (7) 7 7
(T. Craig)
Mutton, Miss K. D. (7) 7 0
(T. Hallett)
Nesbitt, H. A. (5) 24 + 3 ap 7 2
(S. Nesbitt)
Newman, Miss K. E. (7) 7 6
(W. Wightman)
Newman, R. J. (7) 5 ap 7 9
(W. Wightman)
Newnes, W. A. P. (3) 54 + 5 ap . . 7 4
(H. Candy)
Nicholson, S. (7) 7 7
(B. Hanbury)
Nolan, P. M. (7) 8 0
(K. Bridgewater)

Ollivier, C. G. (5) 12+3 ap....7 12
(Denys Smith)
Osborne, S. (7)..............7 7
(J. Holt)
O'Sullivan, P. (7)............7 7
(H. Wragg)
Palmer, M. (7)...............9 0
(R. Hern)
Park, A. (7)..................7 7
(G. Lewis)
Parr, S. (5) 17+9 ap..........7 13
(H. Wragg)
Payne, S. M. (5) 12+7 ap......7 7
(I. Balding)
Pearson, B. (7)..............7 7
(D. Jermy)
Pearson, J. T. (7)............7 7
(N. Guest)
Peckham, M. A. (7) 1 ap......7 7
(P. Asquith)
Perrett, M. E. (7)............9 0
(G. Harwood)
Phillips, G. B. (7)............7 7
(R. Armstrong)
Pinto, L. J. (7)..............7 10
(W. Wharton)
Plows, N. J. (7)...............8 3
(I. Balding)
Pope, M. J. (7)...............7 0
(J. Benstead)
Postill, F. G. M. (7)...........8 0
(W. C. Watts)
Potel, S. A. (7)...............7 10
(R. Hoad)
Pott, S. T. (7)................7 7
(W. Marshall)
Powdrell, K. (7)..............7 3
(P. Cole)
Price, D. J. (7)...............7 0
(F. J. Houghton)
Proud, A. (5) 15+2 ap........7 4
(J. Hardy)
Quinn, T. R. (7)..............7 0
(Hbt Jones)
Radcliffe, K. (7).............7 0
(H. Candy)
Rawlinson, A. (7).............7 2
(F. Durr)
Raymont, K. N. (7) 3+6 ap....7 12
(J. Tree)
Raymont, S. J. (3) 58+5 ap....7 12
(J. Tree)
Rayner, C. T. (7).............8 7
(W. C. Watts)
Read, K. M. (7)..............8 9
(D. Marks)
Richards, S. D. (7)...........8 4
(T. Craig)
Richardson, S. (7)...........7 7
(A. Bailey)
Ridge, N. P. (7)..............8 2
(W. C. Watts)
Rimmer, M. E. (5) 43+8 ap...7 11
(G. Pritchard-Gordon)
Rimmer, M. T. (7)...........8 4
(G. Pritchard-Gordon)
Roberts, S. (7)...............7 9
(J. Dunlop)

Robinson, P. P. 116+5 ap.....7 8
(F. Durr)
Rogers, P. A. (7).............7 12
(N. Vigors)
Rowe, J. (5) 14+7 ap..........8 13
(S. Mellor)
Russell, D. H. (7) 1...........7 12
(R. Armstrong)
Russell, G. J. N. I. (7) 1 ap.....7 12
(J. Holt)
Ryan, M. J. (7)...............8 0
(G. Lewis)
Sadler, S. (7)................8 0
(N. Vigors)
Salmon, I. P. A. (7) 1 ap.......7 12
(R. Price)
Saunders, M. G. (7) 1+2 ap...7 5
(A. Pitt)
Shaw, H. (7)..................7 7
(B. Shaw)
Shelton, R. L. (7) 1 ap.........7 9
(J. Benstead)
Sheridan, F. (7) 1 ap..........8 7
(C. Crossley)
Sherren, Miss Y-S (7)........8 11
(D. Morley)
Sidebottom, R. (5) 35+9 ap...7 12
(Denys Smith)
Sims, D. J. (7) 3+3 ap.........8 0
(P. Cundell)
Smith, D. (7).................9 0
(G. Richards)
Smith, G. R. L. (7) 1 ap.......8 5
(W. Elsey)
Smith, I. J. (7)...............8 0
(P. Asquith)
Smith, J. J. (7)...............7 8
(B. Hobbs)
Smith, R. J. (7)..............8 0
(I. Balding)
Smith, Miss S. R. (7).........8 0
(P. Wigham)
Spiller, G. V. (7) 2 ap.........7 10
(G. Huffer)
Spink, Miss K. A. (7).........7 2
(Mrs A. Harvey)
Springer, P. M. (7)...........8 10
(I. Balding)
Stockton, J. (7)..............8 0
(R. Whitaker)
Storey, C. V. (7) 4+2 ap.......8 0
(M. W. Easterby)
Storrie, G. (7)...............7 6
(B. Gubby)
Sweetapple, I. R. (7)..........7 2
(C. Austin)
Swinburn, W. R. J. 104+5 ap..7 12
(R. Hollinshead)
Tanner, W. G. (7) 2 ap........7 5
(W. Hastings-Bass)
Tasker, P. (7) 3+3 ap.........7 4
(P. Haslam)
Taylor, Miss J. (7)............8 7
(H. T. Jones)
Telford, W. (7)...............7 8
(M. Reddan)
Thorpe, Miss G. M. (7).......7 0
(R. Hollinshead)

Thomas, G. (7) 7 4
(G. Pritchard-Gordon)
Thompson, D. W. (7) 8 0
(Denys Smith)
Tootell, J. (7) 6 7
(C. Thornton)
Tudor, P. (7) 7 0
(E. Weymes)
Tyldesley, J. S. (7) 1 . . . . 7 12
(J. Etherington)
Varnham, R. W. (7) 1 . . . . 7 8
(C. James)
Vaughan, N. J. (7) 5 + 4 ap 7 12
(D. Francis)
Walsh, S. (7) 8 7
(I. Walker)
Wathen, J. Q. (7) 8 5
(D. Wintle)
Webb, Miss S. J. (7) 7 10
(P. K. Mitchell)
Welling, T. (7) 1 ap 7 12
(R. Akehurst)
Welsh, A. (7) 7 0
(G. Harwood)
Whitworth, S. J. (7) 7 0
(M. Stoute)
Willey, K. M. (7) 1 . . . . 7 9
(B. Hills)
Williams, Miss J. H. (7) 7 7
(J. W. Watts)
Williams, K. E. J. (7) 7 7
(Sir Mark Prescott)
Williams, S. J. (7) 7 7
(G. Lewis)
Williams, T. J. (7) 7 10
(M. Salaman)
Winter, P. D. (5) 18 + 6 ap 7 11
(G. Hunter)
Wood, M. (5) 36 + 3 ap 7 9
(G. Richards)
Woods, W. E. (7) 6 8
(R. Smyth)
Wollard, R. G. (7) 4 + 5 ap 7 12
(P. M. Taylor)
Woolnough, K. L. (7) 7 0
(R. Smyth)
Wright, A. M. (7) 3 ap 7 9
(M. Haynes)
Young, D. (7) 7 10
(W. Hastings-Bass)
Young, P. W. (7) 1 ap 8 0
(P. Asquith)
Young, W. A. (7) 1 ap 7 7
(D. Marks)

CHARACTERISTICS OF RACECOURSES

ASCOT (Group 1).—The Ascot round course is a right-handed, triangular circuit of 1m 6f 34yds, with a run-in of 2½f. There is a straight mile course, over which the Royal Hunt Cup is run, and the Old mile course which joins the round course in Swinley Bottom. All races shorter than a mile are decided on the straight course. From the 1½-mile starting gate the round course runs downhill to the bend in Swinley Bottom, where it is level, then rises steadily to the turn into the straight, from where it is uphill until less than a furlong from the winning post, the last hundred yards being more or less level. The straight mile is slightly downhill from the start and then rises to the 5f gate, after which there is a slight fall before the junction with the round course. Despite the downhill run into Swinley Bottom and the relatively short run-in from the final turn, the Ascot course is galloping in character; the turns are easy, there are no minor surface undulations to throw a long-striding horse off balance, and all races are very much against the collar over the last half-mile. The course is, in fact, quite a testing one, and very much so in soft going, when there is a heavy premium on stamina. In such circumstances races over 2 miles to 2¾ miles are very severe tests.
DRAW: On occasions it has seemed that high numbers have had a considerable advantage on the straight course and on other occasions it has seemed that low numbers have had a considerable advantage. An analysis of results since the course was reconstructed in 1954 *disclosed that slightly more than half the winners have come from the high numbers.*

AYR (Group 1).—The Ayr round course is a left-handed, oval track, about twelve furlongs in extent, with a run-in of half a mile. Eleven-furlong races start on a chute which joins the round course after about a furlong. There is a straight six-furlong course of considerable width. The course is relatively flat, but there are gentle undulations throughout, perhaps more marked in the straight. It has a good surface and well-graded turns, and is a fine and very fair track, on the whole galloping in character.
DRAW: In races over seven furlongs and a mile a low number is desirable. On the straight course the draw is ordinarily of little consequence.

BATH (Group 3).—The Bath round course is a left-handed, oval track, just over a mile and a half in extent, with a run-in of nearly half a mile. There is an extension for races over five furlongs and five furlongs and 167 yards. The run-in bends to the left, and is on the rise all the way. The mile and the mile-and-a-quarter courses have been designed to give over a quarter of a mile straight at the start, and the track generally is galloping rather than sharp. The course consists of old downland turf.
DRAW: The draw seems of little consequence nowadays.

BEVERLEY (Group 3).—The Beverley round course is a right-handed, oval track, just over a mile and three furlongs in extent, with a run-in of two and a half furlongs. The five-furlong track bends right at halfway. The general galloping nature of the track is modified by the downhill turn into the straight and the relatively short run-in. The five-furlong course is on the rise throughout, and so is rather testing even in normal conditions; in soft going it takes some getting, particularly for two-year-olds early in the season.
DRAW: High numbers have an advantage over the five-furlong course.

BRIGHTON (Group 2).—The Brighton course takes the shape of an extended 'U' and is 1½ miles in length. The first three furlongs are uphill, after which there is a slight descent followed by a slight rise to about four furlongs from home; the track then runs more sharply downhill until a quarter of a mile out, from where it rises to the last hundred yards, the finish being level. The run-in is about 3½ furlongs, and there is no straight course. This is essentially a sharp track. While the turns are easy enough, the pronounced gradients make Brighton an unsuitable course for big, long-striding horses, resolute gallopers or round-actioned horses. Handy, medium-sized, fluent-movers, and quick-actioned horses are much more at home on the

CHESTER RACES

1981

MAY MEETING

Tuesday, May 5th	CHESTER VASE
Wednesday, May 6th	THE LADBROKE CHESTER CUP
Thursday, May 7th	168th DEE STAKES

SUMMER MEETING

Friday (Evening), July 10th
(probable time of first race 6.30 p.m.)

Saturday, July 11th

AUGUST MEETING

Friday, August 21st

Saturday, August 22nd

For further particulars please apply to Secretaries, Chester Race Company Ltd., 27, Newgate Street, Chester (Tel. 48976).

course. There are no opportunities for long-distance plodders at Brighton. *DRAW: In sprint races a low number is advantageous, and speed out of the gate even more so.*

CARLISLE (Group 4).—Carlisle is a right-handed, pear-shaped course, just over a mile and a half in extent, with a run-in of a little more than three furlongs. The six-furlong course, of which the five-furlong course is a part, the mile course, and the mile and a half course start on three separate off-shoot extensions. For the first three furlongs or so the course runs downhill, then rises for a short distance, levelling out just beyond the mile post. From there until the turn into the straight the course is flat, apart from minor undulations. The six-furlong course, which bears right soon after the start, and again at the turn into the straight, is level for two furlongs, then rises fairly steeply until the distance, from which point it is practically level. The track is galloping in character, and the six-furlong course is a stiff test of stamina for a two-year-old.
DRAW: High numbers have an advantage which is more marked in the shorter races.

CATTERICK (Group 4).—The Catterick round course is a left-handed, oval track, measuring one mile and 180 yards, with a run-in of three furlongs. The five-furlong course bears left before and at the junction with the round course. From the seven-furlong starting gate the round course is downhill almost all the way, and there is a sharp turn on the falling gradient into the straight. The five-furlong course is downhill throughout, quite steeply to start with, and less so thereafter. Catterick is an exceedingly sharp track with pronounced undulations of surface, and it is therefore an impossible course for a big, long-striding animal. Experience of the track counts for a great deal, and jockeyship is of the utmost importance.
DRAW: A low number gives a slight advantage over five furlongs, and a much more definite one in the six and seven-furlong course but a quick start is essential whatever the draw. A slow beginner on the inside is almost certain to be cut off.

CHEPSTOW (Group 3).—The Chepstow round course is a left-handed, oval track, about two miles in extent, with a run-in of five furlongs. There is a straight mile course, over which all races up to a mile are run. The round course has well-marked undulations, and the straight course is generally downhill and level alternately as far as the run-in, thereafter rising sharply for over two furlongs, and then gradually levelling out to the winning post. Notwithstanding the long run-in and general rise over the last five furlongs, this is not an ideal galloping track because of the changing gradients.
DRAW: High numbers have a slight advantage on the straight course.

CHESTER (Group 2).—Chester is a left-handed, circular course, only a few yards over a mile round, the smallest circuit of any flat-race course in Great Britain. It is quite flat and on the turn almost throughout, and although the run-in is nearly straight, it is less than two furlongs in length. The Chester Cup which is invariably run at a very strong gallop all the way, is a testing race demanding exceptional stamina and is always won by an out-and-out stayer. Apart from extreme distance events, such as the Cup and other 2¼m races, the course is against the long-striding, resolute galloper and greatly favours the handy, medium-sized, sharp-actioned horse.
DRAW: A low number is of great importance in races at up to seven and a half furlongs and a quick beginning is essential. It is virtually impossible to overcome a slow start over sprint distances.

DONCASTER (Group 1).—Doncaster is a left-handed, pear-shaped course, over 15 furlongs round and quite flat, except for a slight hill about 1½ miles from the finish. There is a perfectly straight mile, and a round mile starting on an off-shoot of the round course. The run-in from the turn is about 4½ furlongs. This is one of the fairest courses in the country, but its flat surface and great width, its sweeping turn into the straight, and long run-in, make it galloping in character, and ideal for the big, long-striding stayer.
DRAW: The draw is of no importance on the round course. On the straight course high numbers used to have a considerable advantage, but nowadays low numbers are usually favoured.

EDINBURGH (Group 4).—The Edinburgh round course is a right-handed oval track, nearly a mile and a quarter in extent, with a run-in of half a mile. There is a straight five-furlong course. The track is flat, with slight undulations and a gentle rise from the distance to the winning post. The turns at the top end of the course and into the straight are very sharp, and handiness and adaptability to negotiate the bends is of the utmost importance. The big, long-striding, cumbersome horse is at a distinct disadvantage on the round track, especially in races at up to a mile and three furlongs, but to a lesser extent in races over longer distances.
DRAW: High numbers have an advantage in seven-furlong and mile races.

EPSOM (Group 1).—Epsom is a left-handed, U-shaped course, 1½ miles in extent, with an interior unfenced track, known as the Metropolitan course, used only in 2¼-mile races. In these races the horses start at the winning post and proceed the reverse way of the course, branching off to the right just before reaching Tattenham Corner and rejoining the course proper just over 8½ furlongs from the winning post. The Derby course is decidedly uphill for the first half-mile, level for nearly two furlongs and then quite sharply downhill round the bend to Tattenham Corner and all the way up the straight until approaching the final furlong, from where there is a fairish rise to the winning post. The run-in is less than four furlongs. The 7f and 6f courses start on tangential extensions. The 5f course is quite straight and sharply downhill to the junction with the round course. Races over 2¼ miles are, of course, true tests of stamina, and races over 1½ miles can also be testing if the pace over the first uphill four furlongs is strong, as it frequently is in the Derby. Otherwise the track is not really testing in itself, and races up to 8½ furlongs are very sharp indeed, the sprint courses being the fastest in the world. Owing to its bends and pronounced downhill gradients, Epsom favours the handy, fluent-actioned, medium-sized horse: big horses sometimes handle the course well enough, but cumbersome horses, long-striding gallopers, or those with pronounced 'knee-action' are not suited by it and are frequently quite unable to act upon it, especially when the going is firm or hard. Any hesitation at the start or slowness into stride results in considerable loss of ground over the first furlong in sprint races. For this reason Epsom is no course for a green and inexperienced two-year-old, slow to realise what is required.
DRAW: In races up to eight and a half furlongs a low number is advantageous, but quickness out of the gate is of far greater importance, particularly in five-furlong, six-furlong and seven-furlong races.

FOLKESTONE (Group 4).—The Folkestone round course is a right-handed, pear-shaped track, about ten and a half furlongs in extent, with a run-in of two and a half furlongs. There is a straight six-furlong course. The course is undulating, with the last part slightly on the rise, but notwithstanding its width, the easy turns and the uphill finish, it is by no means a galloping track.
DRAW: Low numbers have a slight advantage on the straight course.

GOODWOOD (Group 1).—The Goodwood track consists of a nearly straight 6f course, with a triangular right-handed loop circuit. The Goodwood Cup, about 2m 5f, is started by flag in front of the stands: the horses run the reverse way of the straight, branch left at the first or lower bend, go right-handed round the loop and return to the straight course via the top bend. Races over 2m 3f, 1¾m, 1½m and 1¼m are also run on this course, but 1m races rejoin the straight course via the lower bend. Although there is a 5f run-in for races of 1¼m and upwards, the turns and, more specially, the pronounced downhill gradients from the turn make Goodwood essentially a sharp track, favouring the active, handy, fluent mover rather than the big, long-striding horse. This is of lesser importance in 2m 3f and 2m 5f races, where the emphasis is on sound stamina, and of greater importance in the shorter distance races, particularly in sprints and especially when the going is on top. The 5f course is one of the fastest in the country.
DRAW: A high number is regarded as advantageous in sprint races, but the advantage is not great. Alacrity out of the gate is certainly of importance in five-furlong races.

HAMILTON (Group 3).—The Hamilton track is a perfectly straight six-furlong course, with a pear-shaped, right-handed loop, the whole being a mile and five furlongs in extent from a start in front of the stands, round the loop and back to the winning post. The run-in is five furlongs. The turns are very easy, and the course is undulating for the most part, but just over three furlongs from the winning post there are steep gradients into and out of a pronounced hollow, followed by a severe hill to the finish.
DRAW: Middle to high numbers are thought to have a slight advantage in races over the straight course.

HAYDOCK (Group 1).—Haydock is a left-handed, oval-shaped course, about 13 furlongs round, with a run-in of 4½ furlongs, and a straight 5-furlong course. Races of 6 furlongs and 1½ miles start on tangential extensions to the round course. This course is rather galloping in character, with a rise of twenty-one feet throughout the straight.
DRAW: Horses drawn in the low numbers are regarded as having an advantage in races of six, seven and eight furlongs. On the straight course the draw is of no consequence when the going is sound, but when it is soft, horses racing under the stand rails (high numbers) seem to be favoured.

KEMPTON (Group 1).—Kempton is a right-handed, triangular course, just over 13 furlongs round. The ten-furlong Jubilee course starts on an extension to the round course. Sprint races are run over a separate diagonal course. The Kempton track is perfectly flat with normal characteristics, being neither a sharp track nor a galloping one.
DRAW: The draw is of no particular consequence.

LEICESTER (Group 3).—The Leicester round course is a right-handed, oval track, about a mile and three quarters in extent, with a run-in of four and a half furlongs. The straight mile course, on which all races of up to a mile are run, is mainly downhill to halfway, then rises gradually for over two furlongs, finishing on the level. The course is well-drained, the bends into the straight and beyond the winning post have been eased and cambered, and the track is galloping. For two-year-olds early in the season it poses quite a test of stamina.
DRAW: High numbers have an advantage in races at up to a mile and the advantage seems to be more marked when the going is on the soft side.

LINGFIELD (Group 2).—The Lingfield round course is a left-handed loop, which intersects the straight course of seven furlongs and 140 yards nearly half a mile out and again less than two furlongs from the winning post. The run-in is not much more than three furlongs. For nearly half its length the round course is quite flat, then rises with easy gradients to the summit of a slight hill, after which there is a downhill turn to the straight. The straight course has a considerable downhill gradient to halfway, and is slightly downhill for the rest of the way. The straight course is very easy, and the track as a whole is sharp, putting a premium on speed and adaptability, and making relatively small demands upon stamina, though this does not, of course, apply to races over two miles. The mile and a half course, over which the Derby Trial is run, bears quite close resemblance to the Epsom Derby course.
DRAW: On the straight course high numbers have a slight advantage in normal conditions but when the going is heavy low numbers are favoured.

NEWBURY (Group 1).—The Newbury round course is a left-handed, oval track, about a mile and seven furlongs in extent, with a run-in of nearly five furlongs. There is a straight mile course, which is slightly undulating throughout. Races on the round mile and over the extended seven furlongs start on an extension from the round course. Notwithstanding the undulations this is a good galloping track, and excellent arrangements have been made for watering the course.
DRAW: A high number used to be a fairly considerable advantage over the straight course, but since the narrowing of the track the advantage seems to have disappeared

RACING FIXTURES 1981
HAYDOCK PARK

JANUARY
9th & 10th Fri. & Sat.*
Gamekeepers' Chase (£3,000); Vaux Breweries Novice Chase (Qualifier) £1,500 (Friday); Tote Northern Hurdle (£10,000); Lancashire Handicap Chase (£3,000); Philip Cornes Hurdle (Qualifier) (£1,500) (Saturday).

24th Sat.*
Peter Marsh Chase (£16,000); Premier Long Distance Hurdle (£5,000); Haydock Park Champion Hurdle Trial (£8,000).

FEBRUARY
4th & 5th Wed. & Thurs.*
Haydock Park National Trial Chase (£4,000) (Wednesday); Boston Pit Handicap Chase (£3,000); Haig Novices Hurdle (Qualifier) (£1,500) (Thursday).

MARCH
6th & 7th Fri. & Sat*
White Rabbit Chase (£3,000); Hattons Hunters' Chase (£1,000) (Friday); Greenall Whitley Breweries Chase (£12,000); Timeform Chase (£12,000); Victor Ludorum Hurdle (£9,000) (Saturday).

APRIL
15th Wed.
Field Marshal Stakes (£5,000); Freddy Fox Handicap (£4,000).

18th Sat.
Valspar Paints Handicap (£10,000); PTS Racing Stakes (£5,000); Philip Cornes Nickel Alloys (Qualifier) (£2,000); Danny Maher Handicap (£5,000).

MAY
2nd & 4th Sat. & Mon.
Cold Shield Windows Trophy (£15,000); Ordsall Lane Handicap (£5,000); Cold Shield Windows Handicap (£3,000); Cold Shield Windows 4,000 Guineas (£4,200) (Saturday); Royal Doulton Handicap Hurdle (£35,000); Minton Chase (£3,500); Royal Crown Derby Stakes (£2,000) (Monday).

22nd & 23rd Fri. & Sat.
John Davies Handicap (£3,500) (Friday); Gus Demmy Stakes (£11,000); Cecil Frail Handicap (£17,500); Lymm Stakes (£5,000) (Saturday).

JUNE
5th & 6th Fri. (Evening) & Sat.
Blackburn Handicap (£3,500); Burtonwood Brewery Handicap (£3,000) (Friday); Stones Best Bitter Handicap (£12,000); John of Gaunt Stakes (£17,500) (Saturday).

JULY
3rd & 4th Fri. & Sat.
Cock of the North Stakes (£5,000) (Friday); Lancashire Oaks (£21,000); Old Newton Cup (£17,500); Sporting Chronicle Handicap (£8,000); Rose of Lancaster Stakes (£5,000) (Saturday).

AUGUST
7th & 8th Fri. (Evening) & Sat.
Matthew Peacock Handicap (£3,500) (Friday); Better Bet Coral Handicap (£8,000); Tia Maria Handicap (£10,000); Harvey Jones Handicap (£7,500) (Saturday).

SEPTEMBER
4th & 5th Fri. & Sat.
Claude Harrison Trophy (£4,000); Lytham Stakes (£4,000) (Friday); Vernon's Sprint Cup (£40,000); Morecambe Handicap (£5,000); Liverpool Handicap (£4,000) (Saturday).

OCTOBER
2nd & 3rd Fri. & Sat.
Cutland Handicap (£3,500) (Friday); Brooke Bond Oxo Final (£4,000); Crown Plus Two Apprentice Handicap (£2,500); Buggins Farm Nursery Handicap (£5,000) (Saturday).

14th & 15th Wed. & Thurs.
Oak Handicap (£3,500) (Wedesday); Beech Handicap (£3,500) (Thursday).

NOVEMBER
25th & 26th Wed. & Thurs.*
Edward Hanmer Memorial Chase (£10,000); Sporting Chronicle Handicap Book Northern Hurdle (£4,000) (Wednesday); Garswood Pattern Hurdle (£3,000); Hollowburn Handicap Chase (£5,000) (Thursday).

All enquiries to:
J. K. PYE
HAYDOCK PARK RACECOURSE
NEWTON-LE-WILLOWS WA12 0HQ
MERSEYSIDE
Phone: Ashton-in-Makerfield 77345

N.B. The details given above are correct at time of going to press, but factors outside the control of the Haydock Park Executive may result in alterations having to be made.

* National Hunt

NEWCASTLE (Group 1).—Newcastle is a left-handed, oval-shaped course of 1m 6f in circumference. There is also a straight course, over which all races of seven furlongs or less are run. The course is decidedly galloping in character, and a steady climb from the turn into the straight makes Newcastle a testing track, particularly for two-year-olds early in the season. Ability to see the journey out thoroughly is most important.
DRAW: The draw is of no particular consequence.

NEWMARKET ROWLEY MILE COURSE (Group 1).—The Cesarewitch course is two and a quarter miles in extent, with a right-handed bend after a mile, the last mile and a quarter being the straight Across the Flat. From the Cesarewitch start the course runs generally downhill to a sharp rise just before the turn. There are undulations throughout the first mile of the straight, then the course runs downhill for a furlong to the Dip, and uphill for the last furlong to the winning post. This is an exceedingly wide, galloping track, without minor irregularities of surfaces, so it is ideal for the big, long-striding horse, except for the descent into the Dip, which is more than counterbalanced by the final hill. Ability to see the trip out thoroughly is absolutely essential.
DRAW: There is no material advantage.

NEWMARKET SUMMER COURSE (Group 1).—The Newmarket Summer course is two miles and twenty-four yards in extent, with a right-handed bend at halfway, the first mile being part of the Cesarewitch course, and the last the straight Bunbury Mile. The course runs generally downhill to a sharp rise just before the turn. There are undulations for the first three-quarters of a mile of the straight, then the course runs downhill for a furlong to a dip, and uphill for the last furlong to the winning post. This is an exceedingly wide, galloping track, ideal for the big, long-striding horse, except for the descent into the dip which is more than counterbalanced by the final hill. Ability to see the trip out thoroughly is essential.
DRAW: The draw confers little advantage.

NOTTINGHAM (Group 3).—The Nottingham round course is a left-handed, oval track, about a mile and a half in extent, with a run-in of four and a half furlongs. There is a straight 6f course but no longer a straight mile. The course is flat and the turns are easy.
DRAW: High numbers are slightly preferred over the straight course.

PONTEFRACT (Group 3).—Pontefract is a left-handed track, a mile and a half in extent occupying three-parts of an oval. There is no straight course, and the run-in is only just over two furlongs. There are considerable gradients and a testing hill over the last three furlongs. The undulations, the sharp bend into the straight, and the short run-in disqualify it from being described as a galloping track, but there is a premium on stamina.
DRAW: A low number is advantageous particularly over five furlongs but it becomes a decided disadvantage if a horse fails to jump off well.

REDCAR (Group 2).—Redcar is a narrow, left-handed, oval track, about a mile and threequarters in extent, with a run-in of five furlongs, which is part of the straight mile course. The course is perfectly flat with normal characteristics, and provides an excellent gallop.
DRAW: The draw confers no advantage.

RIPON (Group 2).—The Ripon course is a right-handed, oval circuit of 13 furlongs, with a run-in of 5f, and a straight 6f course. Owing to the rather cramped bends and the surface undulations in the straight, the Ripon track is rather sharp in character.
DRAW: On the straight course the draw is of no importance but in races on the mile course, horses drawn in the high numbers seem to have an advantage.

SALISBURY (Group 2).—The Salisbury track is a right-handed loop course, with a run-in of seven furlongs, which, however, is not straight, for the mile course, of which it is a part, has a right-handed elbow after three furlongs. For races over a mile and threequarters horses start opposite the Club Enclosure, and running away from the stands, bear to the left, and go round the loop. The course, which is uphill throughout the last half-mile is galloping and rather testing.
DRAW: Low numbers are favoured in sprints when the going is soft.

SANDOWN (Group 1).—Sandown is a right-handed, oval-shaped course of 13 furlongs, with a straight run-in of 4f. There is a separate straight course which runs across the main circuit and over which all 5f races are decided. From the 1¼m starting gate, the Eclipse Stakes course, the track is level to the turn into the straight, from where it is uphill until less than a furlong from the winning post, the last hundred yards being more or less level. The 5f track is perfectly straight and rises steadily throughout. Apart from the minor gradients between the main winning post and the 1¼m starting gate, there are no undulations to throw a long-striding horse off balance, and all races over the round course are very much against the collar from the turn into the straight. The course is, in fact, a testing one, and over all distances the ability to see the trip out well is of the utmost importance.
DRAW: On the five-furlong course high numbers have a considerable advantage in big fields when the ground is soft.

STOCKTON (Group 4).—The Stockton track is a left-handed course, nearly a mile and three quarters in extent, with a run-in of half a mile. The five- and six-furlong courses start on separate tangential extensions, the five-furlong track joining the round course on a left incline after a furlong, and the six-furlong track being so laid out as to give a straight start of two furlongs before the bend to the run-in. The turns are sweeping and easy, and the course is perfectly flat, but it is rather a sharp track, and for a flat course it is very fast indeed when the going is firm. The premium is always upon speed.
DRAW: A low number is a fairly considerable advantage in five- and six-furlong races, and is also advantageous in seven-furlong and mile races.

THIRSK (Group 2).—The Thirsk round course is a left-handed, oval track, just over a mile and a quarter in extent, with a run-in of half a mile. There is a straight six-furlong course, which is slightly undulating throughout. The round course itself is almost perfectly flat, but though the turns are relatively easy and the ground well levelled all round, the track is on the sharp side, and by no means ideal for a horse that requires time to settle down, and time and space to get down to work in the straight.
DRAW: High numbers have an advantage on the straight course.

WARWICK (Group 4).—Warwick is a broad, left-handed, oval track, just over a mile and threequarters in extent, with a run-in of about three and a half furlongs. There is no straight course, the five-furlong course having a left-hand elbow at the junction with the round course. Mile races start on an extension from the round course, the first four and a half furlongs being perfectly straight. This is a sharp track, with the emphasis on speed and adaptability rather than stamina. The laboured galloper is at a disadvantage, especially in races at up to a mile.
DRAW: The draw seems to confer little advantage nowadays, but a quick beginning is important in the shorter races.

WINDSOR (Group 3).—Windsor racecourse, laid out in the form of a figure eight, is 12½ furlongs in extent. In races of around 1½ miles both left-handed and right-handed turns are encountered, but in races over 1m 70 yds only right handed turns are met. The last five furlongs of the course are straight, except for a slight bend to the right three furlongs from the finish. The six-furlong start is now on an extension of this straight. Although perfectly flat throughout, the bends make this track rather sharp in character. However, as there is a nearly straight 5f run-in the relative sharpness of the track is of no consequence in the longer races. Big, long-striding horses which normally require a more galloping course are at little or no disadvantage over these trips. The course gives spectators a very good view of the racing, since the runners are broadside on to the stands for all but about 20 yards of the circuit, and all starts are in sight of the stands.
DRAW: In five- and six-furlong races horses drawn in the high numbers have an advantage provided they start well enough to be able to avoid being squeezed out or impeded at the slight right-hand elbow in the straight.

WOLVERHAMPTON (Group 4).—The Wolverhampton round course is a left-handed, pear-shaped or triangular track, just over a mile and a half in extent, with a run-in of five furlongs. There is a straight course of five furlongs. The course is level throughout, with normal characteristics.
DRAW: The draw confers no advantage.

YARMOUTH (Group 3).—The Yarmouth round course is a narrow, left-handed, oval track, about thirteen furlongs in extent, with a run-in of five furlongs. There is a straight mile course. Apart from a slight fall just before the run-in, the track is perfectly flat, with normal characteristics.
DRAW: High numbers have a slight advantage on the straight course.

YORK (Group 1).—York is a left-handed, U-shaped course, 2 miles in extent, and quite flat throughout. There is also a perfectly flat straight course, over which all 5f and 6f races are run. 7f races start on a spur which joins the round course after about two furlongs. The run-in from the turn is nearly 5 furlongs. This is one of the best courses in the country, of great width throughout and with a sweeping turn into the long straight. The entire absence of surface undulations makes it ideal for a long-striding, resolute galloper, but it is really a splendid track, bestowing no great favour on any type of horse.
DRAW: The draw used to be of no consequence, but recently low numbers have had a marked advantage, particularly when the ground has been on the soft side.

Note: Racecourse groupings are as in 1980. The system will not be used in 1981.

Stallion Section

Timeform Ratings quoted in the Stallion Section are those which appeared in the 'Racehorses' annuals except where otherwise stated.

Standing at the Sandley Stud, Gillingham, Dorset

AIR TROOPER

ch 1973 King's Troop - Aries (Acropolis)

AIR TROOPER won 7 races (8-10½f), £29,959 including Rosebery Handicap (by 4 lengths), Newbury Spring Cup (by 3 lengths, see above), Sandown Cup (by 6 lengths), Hong Kong Handicap (by 4 lengths) and John Smith's Magnet Cup (carried 9-6). He was **second (beaten head)** in **Group 2 Queen Elizabeth II Stakes** (beating **Radetzky, Don, Duke Ellington,** etc.).

Racehorses of 1977: 'won five good handicaps besides going close in one of the most prestigious mile races of the season, the Queen Elizabeth II Stakes at Ascot . . . on each occasion when successful Air Trooper was held up and produced a fine turn of foot in the closing stages . . . a strong colt . . . seems to act on any going . . . thoroughly dependable.'

Sire KING'S TROOP is sire of the winners of 255 races, £286,530, in the British Isles including **King's Company** (Irish 2,000 Guineas Gr 1) and **Majetta,** both successful sires.

Dam ARIES is half-sister to 6 winners including the dam of leading sire **Double-U-Jay** and grandam of **Riverqueen** (French 1,000 Guineas Gr 1, Prix Saint Alary Gr 1 and Grand Prix de Saint-Cloud Gr 1).

Fee for 1981 £500 straight or
£650 NFNF (concessions)
First runners 1981
All enquiries: Sandley Stud, Gillingham, Dorset.
Tel: Sherborne (093581) 3182

BUSTED

Bay, 1963, by CREPELLO out of SANS LE SOU, by VIMY

European Champion of 1967
Unbeaten 'Horse of the Year'
LEADING SIRE (Races Won) in **1974**
2nd LEADING SIRE (Races Won) in **1975 & 1977**
LEADING SIRE (58 Races Won) in **1976**
LEADING SIRE (35 Individual Winners) in **1976**
Sire of **European 2-y-o Champion** in **1978**
LEADING SIRE (Races Won) in **1979**
Sire of 38 winners of 61 races value £187,695 in 1980

With ten crops of runners, Busted has sired the winners of 529 races value £1,519,905 including **BUSTINO** (St. Leger, Coronation Cup, Great Voltigeur, 2nd King George and Queen Elizabeth Stakes), **WEAVERS' HALL** (Irish Sweeps Derby and £67,757), **TROMOS** (Champion 2-y-o in International Classification 1978, Dewhurst Stakes Gr 1), **VALUTA** (Prix Kergorlay, Prix Maurice de Nieuil and over £30,000), **GUILLOTINA** (Prix de Royallieu), **BOG ROAD** (Gallinule Stakes, Ballymoss Stakes, 2nd Prix Ganay, total £37,419), **BUSACA** (Yorkshire Oaks, Lancashire Oaks), **PEVERO** (Prix de Conde, a leading 2-y-o in France, 1977, Prix Foy, placed Ganay & Arc 1979), **CHEVELEY PRINCESS** (Ascot 1,000 Guineas Trial, Nassau Stakes, Sun Chariot Stakes), **CRASH COURSE** (Doncaster Cup, 1975, March Stakes, Goodwood, Ascot Stakes, Top Rank Club Stakes), **BUTTRESS** (Queen's Vase), **FOOL'S MATE** (PTS Laurels Stakes, Bessborough Stakes, Old Newton Cup), **OLD BILL** (Chester Vase), **BUSS**, also **SORBUS** (Irish Oaks, Gr 1, but disqualified), etc.

Full 1968—1981. Over 80% fertility in 1980 At SNAILWELL STUD, NEWMARKET, The property of Snailwell Stud Co. Ltd.

Apply: **ANTHONY W. EARL, The Manager, Moulton Paddocks, Newmarket. Telephone: (0638) 2867**

Snailwell Stud will be offering ALL their yearling colts in the October and Houghton Sales from 1981.

Standing at BROWNSTOWN STUD, Curragh, Co. Kildare

Condorcet

Bay, 1972 by LUTHIER-PAN AMERICAN, by Pan II

Group Winner and Classic Placed

Winner of 5 races and £114,750, from 2-4 years, including Prix Maurice de Nieuil (Gp II). PLACED in 8 other GROUP RACES, including 2nd Poule d'Essai des Poulains (Gp. I), beaten 1 length by GREEN DANCER (European Champion 1st Season Sire 1979), also 2nd Prix Exbury (Gp. III), 3rd Prix Jean de Chaudenay (Gp. II), Prix de la Cote Normande (Gp. III), La Coupe de Maisons-Laffitte (Gp. III), 4th Prix Lupin (Gp. I), etc.

By Europe's Record Breaking Sire of 1976

His sire, **LUTHIER,** Prix Lupin, Prix Jacques Le Marois, etc., and Fr. 953,285, is also sire of RIVERQUEEN, ASHMORE, TWIG MOSS, MONTCONTOUR, GUADANINI, RED GIRL, GALIANI, etc.

Family of Prince Rose

His dam, **PAN AMERICAN,** has bred four winners from her first four runners. She is half-sister to the dam of SUPER HONEY and closely related to FULL OF HOPE. His third dam, FRAGRANT VIEW, is half-sister to the Derby winner AIRBORNE. His fourth dam is own sister to the dam of PRINCE ROSE, an influential stallion sire. CONDORCET is completely free of PHALARIS blood for four generations.

CONDORCET's first two crops of yearlings have produced VERY GOOD LOOKING PROGENY and his only YEARLING sold at the 1979 HOUGHTON SALES fetched 20,000 Guineas.

Sire of stakes winner CONDESSA (Waterford Glass Nursery Stakes, Gowran Park and Seven Springs Plate, Curragh, total £5,874) and others of high promise with his first crop in 1980.

All Enquiries to:

JOSEPH McGRATH, Brownstown Stud, Curragh, Co. Kildare

Tel: Curragh 41303

CHAMPION CANADIAN THREE-YEAR-OLD

DANCE IN TIME

Bay 1974, 16 h., by NORTHERN DANCER, out of ALLEGRO, by CHOP CHOP
WINNER OF SEVEN RACES $122,100 AT 2 AND 3 YEARS INCLUDING THE SECOND TWO LEGS OF THE CANADIAN TRIPLE CROWN

TWO races at 2 years over 6 furlongs. **FIVE** races at 3 years. Stakes Winner at 6½f. to 1½m., including: Prince of Wales Stakes, Fort Erie, 1⅛m. Gr 1 Can. Breeders Stakes, Woodbine, 1½m. Gr 1 Can. (beating his three parts brother GIBOULEE on both occasions), and Friar Rock Stakes, Woodbine 6½f. (beating Champion 2-year-old and Queens Plate winner SOUND REASON).

NORTHERN DANCER—Champion Racehorse and Sire of 71 Stakes winners, 12 Champions, including: NIJINSKY, LYPHARD, NORTHFIELDS, THE MINSTREL, NORTHERN BABY, NORTHERN TASTE, FANFRELUCHE, ONE FOR ALL, WHITE STAR LINE, NORTHERNETTE, STORM BIRD, NUREYEV.

1st dam **Allegro,** by Chop Chop. 5 wins at 2 and 3, 3rd Boniface S. Dam of 6 foals to race, 5 winners, including **DANCE IN TIME, SWINGING APACHE** (c. by Northern Dancer). 6 wins at $35,898, Canadian Derby, Ascot Sophamore S., Harbour H. **ICY NOTE** (c. by Nearctic). 7 wins, $22,412, Journal H. Sire.

2nd dam ***ORCHESTRA,** (by *Menetrier). 7 wins at 2 and 3, $25,390, Woodstock S. Friar Rock S., etc. Sister to **Matassin,** half-sister to **HOLARCTIC, MOSKOVA.** Produced 8 foals, all winners, including—**TWO VIOLINS** 6 wins at 3 and 5, $21,240 Marine S. Also grandam of **GIBOULEE** (by Northern Dancer). 13 wins, 2 to 4, $358,578, champion handicap horse in Canada Manitoba Derby-C II, Dominion Day H.-C III, etc.

FULL 1978, 1979, 1980 and 1981
With an estimated average fertility of 82%
FEE: £1,500 plus £2,000 on 1st October (unless mare is certified barren).
Approved mares.

All enquiries to: Leslie Harrison, Plantation Stud, Exning, Newmarket. Tel: Exning (063877) 341 *or* the Secretaries to the Syndicate: London Thoroughbred Services Ltd., 21 Embankment Gardens, Chelsea SW3. Tel: (01-351 2181). Telex: 916950.

At Aston Park Stud, Aston Rowant, Oxfordshire

The HIGHEST STAKES WINNER
sired by DERRING-DO

DOMINION

Bay 1972 by DERRING-DO out of PICTURE PALACE (PRINCELY GIFT)

Dominion won 14 races (8-9f) and over £145,289 including **Prix** Perth, St-Cloud, Gr 3 and Bernard Baruch H'cap, Saratoga, Gr 3; also placed in eight other pattern races including 2,000 Guineas (third to **Bolkonski** and **Grundy**). Retired to stud perfectly sound after 46 races. He holds the $8\frac{1}{2}$f record at Gulfstream Park.
Derring-Do is the sire of classic winners **HIGH TOP,** a leading sire, **ROLAND GARDENS** and **PELEID.** His pattern winners include CAMDEN TOWN, DERRYLIN, VARISHKINA, JAN EKELS and STILVI etc. His progeny also include HUNTERCOMBE, a leading sire.
Picture Palace won 2 races and bred eight winners of 57 races including PROMINENT, 19 races, Prix Foy Gr 3, etc.; she is also a half-sister to 5 other winners.

First Season 1979: FULL in 1979, 1980 and 1981

The property of a syndicate

Syndicate Chairman: **R. J. McCreery,** Stowell Hill, Templecombe, Somerset. Tel: (0963) 70212. Syndicate Secretary: **Penny Willder,** Aston Park House, Aston Rowant, Oxford. Tel: (0844) 51433. Stud Manager: **R. E. Baskerville,** B.V.Sc., M.R.C.V.S. Tel: (0844) 52090 or 51492 (office).

FINAL STRAW

A LEADING MILER

Ch. 1977, 15h. 3 in. by THATCH, out of LAST CALL, by KLAIRON

Winner of FIVE races and placed SIX times at 2 and 3 years (5-8f); total earnings £116,708.
At 2 years won 4 races including: Gr 2, Laurent Perrier Champagne Stakes (7 furlongs), Gr 3, Seaton Delaval Stakes (7 furlongs), Gr 3, July Stakes (6 furlongs); also 3rd Gr 2, Coventry Stakes (6 furlongs).

At 3 years won Gr 3, Clerical Medical Greenham Stakes (7 furlongs); also 2nd Gr 1, Sussex Stakes (1 mile), beaten a head, 2nd Gr 1, Prix Jacques le Marois (1 mile), beaten a neck, 2nd Gr 2, St. James's Palace Stakes (1 mile), 3rd Airlie/Coolmore Irish 2,000 Guineas (1 mile), beaten ½ length.

Sire **THATCH (USA)** Champion Irish 2-Year-Old of 1972 and Champion 3-Year-Old Colt of 1973. Won 7 races, £40,277, at 2 and 3 years, 6-8 furlongs, including Gr 1, Sussex Stakes, Gr 2, St. James's Palace Stakes, Gr 2, July Cup and Gr 3, Vauxhall Trial Stakes; placed fourth in Gr 1, 2,000 Guineas and Gr 1, Prix Morny. Retired to stud in 1974 and sire of the winners of 98 races and £481,421 to August 23rd, 1980, including: FINAL STRAW, THATCHING, TANNENBERG, GOLDEN THATCH, NEMR PULL THE LATCH, etc.

1st dam **Last Call**—Winner at 3 years, dam of 5 winners, including **FINAL STRAW, FINAL CHORD** (3 races, including Britannia Stakes, Royal Ascot) and **Curtains** (3 races, at 3 years, also placed 2nd in Galtres Stakes, York).

2nd dam **Stage Fright**—Winner at 3 years, dam of 4 winners, including **HARDIESSE** (4 races, at 2 and 3 years, including Gr 3 Cheshire Oaks, and Gr 3, Prix de Malleret, Longchamp, also 3rd in Gr 1, Yorkshire Oaks and 4th in Gr 1, Epsom Oaks); also Opening Chorus (placed at 3 years, herself dam of 8 winners, including Italian Stakes winner **TERRY**). Half-sister to 7 winners, including Stakes winner **DIFFIDENCE** and Donna, herself the dam of 11 winners, including **GWEN, PADRONA,** and **DON COMISO.** Family of **HERBAGER, LAUSO, DURTAL, DETROIT,** etc.

FULL FIRST SEASON 1981
FEE: On application

All enquiries to: The Director, National Stud, Newmarket. Tel: Newmarket (0638) 3464. *or:* **the Secretaries to the Syndicate: London Thoroughbred Services Ltd., 21 Embankment Gardens, Chelsea SW3. Tel: (01) 351 2181. Telex: 916950.**

Standing at Brownstown Stud, Curragh, Co. Kildare.

THE CLASSIC-WINNING SON OF WOLVER HOLLOW

Furry Glen

Bay 1971 **Wolver Hollow—Cleftess (Hill Gail)**

Furry Glen wins the Irish 2,000 Guineas from Pitcairn (the champion sire of 1980, sire of Ela-Mana-Mou, Cairn Rouge etc). Cellini is third, then comes Red Alert (a leading sire of two-year-olds in 1980).

Furry Glen won five races £31,757, from 5 to 9 furlongs, at 2 and 3 years, including Gr I Irish Two Thousand Guineas, beating PITCAIRN, CELLINI, RED ALERT, etc. Gr 3 Whitehall Stakes, Marble Hill Stakes, Mullion Stakes; also placed 2nd in Gr 2 Gallinule Stakes (btn sh hd), and Gr 3 Vauxhall Trial Stakes (btn hd), and 3rd in Gr 2 Coventry Stakes, Royal Ascot, and Gr 3 Larkspur Stakes.

By the Champion Sire of 1976; also sire of **WOLLOW,** etc. **FURRY GLEN** is half-brother to 3 winners; his dam is own-sister to CARTIER (16 races). Gran-dam won 4 races, and comes from the family of DELIRIUM (leading sprinter and successful sire).

STAKES SIRE IN 1980

Sire of 7 individual winners in 1980, £27,511 including **ALL SILK** (Premio Novella & Premio Delleana, Milan both stakes races—total £14,355). With just 3 crops of runners **FURRY GLEN** is sire of **GLENHAWK** (March Stakes, Doncaster, 3rd Houghton Stakes, to One in a Million and Milford), **COOL DECISION, AMMUNITION, GLEN DANCER, KUDU KING** etc. and the winners of 44 races, **£93,932.**

Full 1975-1980

His Yearlings have made up to 28,000 guineas.

Enquiries to: **Joseph McGrath (as above). Tel.: Curragh 41303**

AT THE BEECH HOUSE STUD, NEWMARKET

HABAT

Grey, 1971

by HABITAT out of ATREVIDA by SUNNY BOY III

HABAT was the leading English two-year-old of 1973 when winning the Berkshire Stakes, Newbury by five lengths, the Norfolk Stakes, Royal Ascot (Group III), by six lengths, the Mill Reef Stakes, Newbury (Group II) by five lengths and the Middle Park Stakes, Newmarket (Group I), by two-and-a-half lengths. As a three-year-old he won the 2,000 Guineas Trial Stakes, Ascot (Group III) by one-and-a-half lengths and second in the Sussex Stakes, Goodwood (Group I). Total earnings, £49,636.

HABAT traces through Kalamoun's grandam Palariva, and NASRULLAH'S sister Rivaz, to MUMTAZ MAHAL.

HABAT has sired 12 individual winners in 1980 including VARGAS LLOSA, Gran Premio Citta di Torino, Group III. Chant, placed fourth in Salisbury 2,000 Guineas Trial, Group III.

Some nominations available at £1,000 +£1,000 mare in foal 1st October.

Enquiries to: **Rustons & Lloyd, Newmarket (0638) 61221,**
or: **Beech House Stud, Newmarket (0638) 730335**
or **Keith Freeman (Bloodstock) Ltd., Pettus House, Elm Hill, Norwich, Norfolk NR3 1HS. Telephone: Norwich (0603) 21307, 27773 or 27747**

AT THE BEECH HOUSE STUD, NEWMARKET

IMPERIAL FLING

Bay, 1976, by NORTHERN DANCER out of ROYAL DILEMMA by BUCKPASSER

THE ONLY GROUP WINNING SON OF NORTHERN DANCER AT STUD IN ENGLAND

Winner of two races and £31,097 at two and three years:

At Two Years

WON Erroll Stakes, Ascot, 5f, by three lengths

3rd Champagne Stakes, Doncaster, Group II, 7f

3rd Champion Two Year Old Trophy, Ripon (Stakes race), 6f

At Three Years

WON Bayerisches Zuchtrennen, Munich, Group III, 12f

2nd Grosser Hertie-Preis, Munich, Group II, 11f

4th Classic Trial, Sandown, Group III, 10f, to TROY

First foal of a winning daughter of the champion U.S.A. Two Year Old QUEEN EMPRESS (15 races and $431,428) herself a full sister to KING EMPEROR (13 races and $453,918).

NORTHERN DANCER has sired LYPHARD, NIJINSKY, THE MINSTREL, NORTHFIELDS, TRY MY BEST, NORTHERN BABY, and in 1980 NUREYEV and STORM BIRD. He is the most influential living sire of sires with his sons and grandsons responsible for the Group I winners GREEN DANCER, ILE DE BOURBON, NINISKI, THREE TROIKAS, MONTEVERDI, PRINCESSE LIDA and ARYENNE.

Those covered in his first season included three Group winners of two Group I races, four Group II races, and four Group III races; eighteen winners; fifteen dams of winners; seven half sisters to Group winners and two daughters of classic winners.

FEE £1,500 straight for strictly approved mares.

Enquiries to: Rustons & Lloyd, Newmarket (0638) 61221, or Beech House Stud, Newmarket (0638) 730335, or Keith Freeman (Bloodstock) Ltd., Pettus House, Elm Hill, Norwich, Norfolk NR3 1HS. Telephone: Norwich (0603) 21307, 27773 or 27747.

ASHLEY HEATH STUD

JULIO MARINER

Bay 1975 BLAKENEY-SET FREE (WORDEN II)

Winner of 1978 St. Leger Stakes, Gr I, in Record Time
Own Brother to dual Oaks winner JULIETTE MARNY
Half brother to 1979 Epsom Oaks, Gr I, winner SCINTILLATE

His excellent first crop of foals in 1980 averaged 9,620 gns at the December Sales.
JULIO MARINER was again fully booked with 51 mares of which 46 were tested in foal.

FULL 1981

Enquiries for JULIO MARINER to: British Bloodstock Agency, 11a Albemarle Street, London, W1X 4DB. 01-493 9402 Telex: 27403 or Alton House, Newmarket (5021) Telex: 817157 or R. E. Waugh, Ashley Heath Stud, Newmarket (730102).

CHAMPION EUROPEAN MILER

KRIS

Chesnut 1976, 16h. 0½ in. by SHARPEN UP, out of DOUBLY SURE, by RELIANCE II
CURRENT HOLDER OF THREE COURSE RECORDS

WINNER OF 14 OF HIS 16 STARTS INCLUDING 8 PATTERN RACES: Sussex Stakes, Lockinge Stakes, Queen Elizabeth II Stakes, St. James's Palace Stakes, Waterford Crystal Mile, Clerical Medical Greenham Stakes, Bisquit Cognac Challenge Stakes, Horris Hill Stakes and 2nd The 2,000 Guineas, Queen Elizabeth II Stakes.

SHARPEN UP—Leading first season sire in 1976. Leading sire of 2-year-olds (races won) in 1978. Leading sire standing in England in 1979. Unbeaten winner of 5 races £19,888, at 2 years, including Gr 1 Middle Park Stakes, Gr 3 Seaton Delaval Stakes also placed second in Gr 2 July Cup and Gr 3 Greenham Stakes, at 3 years. Sire of the winners of 306 races and £997,807 to August 23rd, 1980, including KRIS, SHARPMAN, SHARPO, SMARTEN UP, SOVEREIGN ROSE, DUBLIN TAXI, EYELET, CUT THROAT, PUSHY, etc.

1st dam **Doubly Sure**—Placed at 3 years. KRIS is her first foal. 2nd dam **SOFT ANGELS**—Won Gr 2 Royal Lodge Stakes, and Princess Margaret Stakes, Ascot Three-parts sister in blood to **MIL'S BOMB** (4 races, including Gr 2 Park Hill Stakes Gr 3 Lancashire Oaks and Cheshire Oaks, etc.) and **MILLY MOSS** (Gr 3 Cheshire Oaks), Half-sister to **SWEET MOSS, SUCARYL**. Family of **YOUNG LOCHINVAR MARCHE PERSAN**, etc.

FULL FIRST SEASON 1981 FEE: ON APPLICATION

All enquiries to: J. F. Day (Manager), Thornton Stud, Thornton-le-Street, Thirsk
Tel: Thirsk (0845) 22522. *or:* **the Secretaries to the Syndicate:**
London Thoroughbred Services Ltd., 21 Embankment Gardens, Chelsea SW3
Tel: (01-351 2181). Telex: 916950.

Standing in 1981 at Brownstown Stud, Curragh, Co. Kildare.

LE MOSS

Ch 1975, LE LEVANSTELL—FEEMOSS (BALLYMOSS)

The only horse ever to win
THE ASCOT GOLD CUP
THE GOODWOOD CUP &
THE DONCASTER CUP
two years in succession

Own brother to LEVMOSS (the only horse ever to win the Prix de l'Arc de Triomphe, the Ascot Gold Cup and the Prix du Cadran) and SWEET MIMOSA winner of French Oaks, 1970.

'A phenomenon among racehorses'
—see pages 440-444 of this volume

Enquiries: **Joseph McGrath, Brownstown Stud, Curragh, Co. Kildare. (Tel: Curragh 41303)**
or: **BBA (Ireland) Ltd, 51 Lansdowne Road, Ballsbridge, Dublin 4. (Tel: Dublin 686222. Telex: 25599).**

Standing at Beech House Stud, Cheveley, Newmarket

ORANGE BAY

Bay 1972, by CANISBAY out of ORANGE TRIUMPH by MOLVEDO

Arguably the best older horse in training in 1977, **ORANGE BAY** won 9 races from two to five years including:

Italian Derby, Rome, Group I
Hardwicke Stakes, Royal Ascot, Group II
Premio Emanuele Filiberto, Milan, Group II
Cumberland Lodge Stakes, Ascot, Group III
Jockey Club Stakes, Newmarket, Group III

Also placed in six Group I races including *twice* in King George VI and Queen Elizabeth Diamond Stakes, Ascot.

"*. . . a tremendous effort to run The Minstrel to a short head . . . rallied splendidly after looking likely to be beaten comfortably . . .*"

TIMEFORM
Annual Rating 131

TOTAL EARNINGS approx £135,500

Some shareholders nominations available at **£1,500 straight**

Apply: KEITH FREEMAN (BLOODSTOCK) LTD., PETTUS HOUSE, ELM HILL, NORWICH, NORFOLK NR3 1HS
(Telephone: Norwich 27773 or 21307)

POSSE

Ch. 1977 **FORLI**—IN HOT PURSUIT (**BOLD RULER**)

St James's Palace Stakes 1980: Posse easily beats Final Straw

At 2 years: placed 2nd Houghton Stakes, Newmarket (to Night Alert, with Bireme (Oaks) 3rd) on his only start.

At 3 years: won Sussex Stakes, Gr 1, St James's Palace Stakes, Gr 2; 2nd 2,000 Guineas, Gr 1; 3rd Clerical Medical Greenham Stakes, Gr 3; 4th Airlie/Coolmore Irish 2,000 Guineas, Gr 1, all his starts. Total earnings £96,652.

His sire FORLI was undefeated classic winner in Argentine. Horse of the Year at 3, Argentine Triple Crown, also a good winner in the United States. Sire of over 30 stakes winners including FOREGO, THATCH, INTREPID HERO, HOME GUARD, BOONE'S CABIN, FORMIDABLE, GAY FANDANGO. Also a leading broodmare sire (sire of the dams of NUREYEV and JAAZEIRO).

His dam IN HOT PURSUIT was only raced at 2 and won 3 races from 5 starts including Fashion Stakes Gr 3. Full sister to FULL OF HOPE, DISCIPLINARIAN, BOLD SULTAN, etc., and half-sister to DISCIPLINE.

See pages 619-622 of this volume.

The Property of a Syndicate.

Standing at Derisley Wood Stud Farm, Woodditton Road, Newmarket, Suffolk CB8 9HF.

Apply to A. W. Johnson, The Manager, as above. Tel: Newmarket (0638) 730055 or 730100. Telex: 817886.

or: **Secretaries to the Syndicate, Rustons and Lloyd, High Street Newmarket. Tel: Newmarket (0638) 61221. Telex: 817970.**

YOUNG GENERATION

AN OUTSTANDING EUROPEAN MILER

Bay 1976, 16h 2ins, by BALIDAR out of BRIG O'DOON by SHANTUNG

Amongst the 40 mares that visited Young Generation in his first season at stud, 1980 have been:
AMBUSCADE (winning half-sister to 7 winners, including CAMOUFLAGE, DISGUISE, SMUGGLER and ELUSIVE PIMPERNEL); **BLUE QUEEN** (dam of 5 winners, including REPROCOLOR); **CURTAINS** (Stakes placed winning half-sister to FINAL STRAW); **HARDIRONDO** (winner of 7 races and daughter of a half-sister to IRISH MINSTREL); **MADINA** (winner of Gr 1 Prix Morny and dam of NONOALCA); **MIDNIGHT LADY** (daughter of MIA POLA, herself a half-sister to GREY DAWN II); **NICHOLAS GREY** (winner of 8 races in England and Italy and Classic placed); **RIDE** (dam of COURT CHAD and KING'S RIDE); **TEJADA** (winner of Gr. 3 Premio Legnano and Classic placed dam of TANDINA); **WOLD LASS** (dam of 2 winners, including MOFIDA).

Winner of 4 races, £110,880, at 2 and 3 years (5-9f) including: Gr 2, Lockinge Stakes, beating Skyliner, Formidable, Spence Bay, Roland Gardens, Camden Town. Gr 2, Prix Jean Prat, beating Pitasia, Boitron. Gr 2, Richmond Stakes, by 3 lengths.

Second 4 times, including: Gr 1, Middle Park Stakes, beaten 1 length in course record time. Gr 2, St. James's Palace Stakes, to Kris. Gr 3, Greenham Stakes, to Kris.

Third 3 times, including: Gr 1, 2,000 Guineas, beaten ½ length, short head, beating Lyphard's Wish, Boitron, etc. Gr 1, Prix Morny.

Fourth: Gr 2, Mill Reef Stakes. **ALL HIS STARTS.**

Sire **BALIDAR**, Champion European Sprinter, Gr 1, Prix de l'Abbaye, etc. Sire of BOLKONSKI (Champion Miler, Gr 1, 2,000 Guineas, Gr1, Sussex Stakes, a leading European first crop sire, 1979), ABDU, YOUNG GENERATION, etc.

FULL 1980 with 40 mares (fertility over 90%) **FEE: £3,500 straight**

All enquiries to: London Thoroughbred Services Ltd., 21 Embankment Gardens, Chelsea SW3. Tel: (01) 351 2181. Telex: 916950. *or:* **C. J. Harper, Whitsbury Manor Stud, Nr. Fordingbridge, Hants. Tel: Rockbourne (07253) 283.**

AIRLIE STALLIONS 1981

1980:	**Champion Sire**	**(PITCAIRN)**
	Champion Broodmare Sire	**(HIGH HAT)**
1979:	**Champion Sire**	**(PETINGO)**
	Champion Sire of 2-Y-O's	**(HABITAT)**
1978:	**Champion Sire (Races Won)**	**(PETINGO)**

For the stallions listed in
the following pages apply to:

Captain A. D. D. Rogers,
Airlie Stud,
Lucan,
County Dublin,
Irish Republic.
Tel: Dublin 280267 or 281548
Telex: 31049 TROG E.1

ARTAIUS

CHAMPION OF EUROPE AT A MILE & A MILE AND A QUARTER IN 1977 when winner of Sussex Stakes, Gr 1 (beating Relkino, Nebbiolo, Mrs McArdy, etc.), Eclipse Stakes Gr 1 (in course record time) and Classic Trial Stakes Gr 3. Also 2nd in Prix du Jockey Club, Gr 1, (beaten ½ l by Crystal Palace with Pharly, Funny Hobby, etc. behind), Benson & Hedges Gold Cup, Gr 1, (beating Malacate, Lightning, etc.) and Beresford Stakes, Gr 2 (only start at 2).
Timeform 129.

Stud Record
Artaius retired to stud in 1978. Book Full 1978-1980. Fertility 96%.
24 yearlings sold in 1980 averaged 31,792 gns.

ARTAIUS (bay 1974)	Round Table (b 1954)	Princequillo	Prince Rose
			Cosquilla
		Knight's Daughter	Sir Cosmo
			Feola
	Stylish Pattern (b 1961)	My Babu	Djebel
			Perfume II
		Sunset Gun II	Hyperion
			Ace of Spades

By ROUND TABLE, winner of 43 races, $1,749,869, Champion North American Sire 1972. Sire of over 70 stakes winners incl. ARTAIUS, TARGOWICE (a leading sire), BALDRIC, KING PELLINORE, APALACHEE, FLIRTING AROUND etc.
Out of STYLISH PATTERN, dam of 6 winners, including ARTAIUS, EMBROIDERY (Ascot 1,000 Guineas Trial Gr III), STYLISH GENIE (Fairway Fun Stakes and $49,195; dam of world-record yearling $1,700,000). Her dam won at 3 years in England and bred 5 winners including SPRING DOUBLE (22 wins, $438,317, Pimlico Futurity, etc.; stakes sire in USA) and ARTHURIAN (Churchill Stakes, Ascot). Traces to PRETTY POLLY.

Stands at: Airlie Stud, Lucan, Co. Dublin.
Apply: Capt A.D.D. Rogers, Airlie Stud, Lucan, Co. Dublin (tel: Dublin 280267; telex 31049 TROG E. I.)

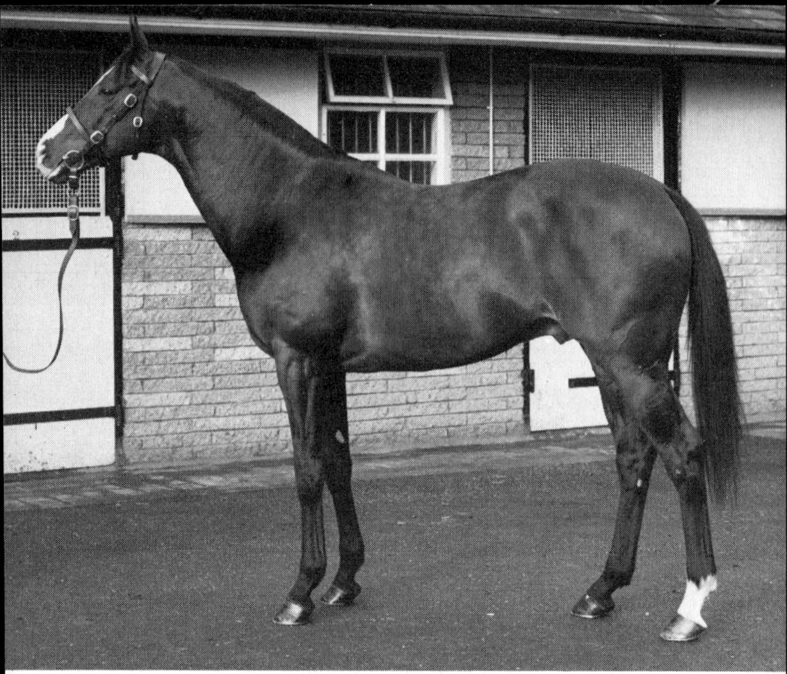

ASHMORE

Winner of 6 races, £164,848, including Grand Prix de Deauville, Gr 2, twice, and Prix Jean de Chaudenay, Gr 2. Also 2nd in Grand Prix de Saint-Cloud, Gr I, twice, and Coronation Cup, Gr I (beaten by 1 l. by Bustino in course-record time) and 3rd in Prix Royal-Oak, Gr I, and Prix Maurice de Nieuil, Gr 2.

Racehorses of 1976: 'A really good sort of horse . . . in point of merit he is about as good a racehorse as was his sire Luthier.' **Timeform 125.**

Stud Record. Sire in his first crop of VAL d'ERICA (Premio Dormello, Gr 2, and leading 2-y-o filly in Italy), EL BALISTA, HAILEBURY etc.

Yearlings have fetched 40,000 gns., 35,000 gns., 25,000 gns., 24,000 gns., etc.. Fertility 88%.

ASHMORE (bay 1971)	Luthier (br 1965)	Klairon	Clarion
			Kalmia
		Flute Enchantee	Cranach
			Montagnana
	Almyre (b 1964)	Wild Risk	Rialto
			Wild Violet
		Ad Gloriam	Alizier
			Ad Altiora

OUTSTANDING CROSS FOR MOST MARES. NO PHALARIS, NO HYPERION for 5 generations.

By LUTHIER, winner of Prix Jacques le Marois, Gr 1, and Prix Lupin, Gr 1, and European Record-Breaking Sire in 1976 (RIVERQUEEN, ASHMORE, CONDORCET etc.).

Out of ALMYRE, 3 wins including Prix Omnium and 2nd Prix de Pomone, Gr 3. Her first six foals are winners including ASHMORE and ACOMA (Prix de Minerve, Gr III). Broodmare sire WILD RISK is also the broodmare sire of BLUSHING GROOM and sire of WORDEN etc.

Stands at: Grangewilliam Stud, Maynooth, Co. Kildare

Apply: Capt. A. D. D. Rogers, Airlie Stud, Lucan, Co. Dublin (tel: Dublin 280267; telex 31049 TROG E.I.)

DOUBLE FORM

Europe's record-breaking sprinter 1979. The only horse ever to win the King's Stand Stakes, Gr. 1, and the Prix de l'Abbaye, Gr. 1, in the same year; and winner of £94,000 in first-place money, record earnings for a sprinter trained in England or Ireland. Also won Vernons Sprint Cup, Gr. 2, Temple Stakes, Gr. 3, Great Eastern Handicap (top-weight), Thirsk Hall Stakes and £127,154.
Racehorses of 1979: 'He defeated every leading contender on both sides of the Channel . . . Double Form's record as a four-year-old is that of a top-class racehorse, and for consistency he beats Thatching'. **Timeform 130.**

Stud Record
Double Form retired to stud in 1980. Estimated fertility for 1980 covering season 96%.

DOUBLE FORM (b. 1975)	Habitat (b. 1966)	Sir Gaylord	Turn-to
			Somethingroyal
		Little Hut	Occupy
			Savage Beauty
	Fanghorn (ch. 1966)	Crocket	King of the Tudors
			Chandelier
		Honeymoon House	Honeyway
			Primavera

By **HABITAT,** 5 races, £40,751, European Champion Miler, Gr. 1 Prix du Moulin, etc. Champion sire of 2-y-o's four times. A leading sire of Group-winners, including Flying Water, Rose Bowl, Habat, Homing, Sigy, Steel Heart, Hittite Glory, Marwell etc.
Out of **FANGHORN,** winner of 2 races at 2 years; 3rd Gr. 1 French 1,000 Guineas, Her grandam Primavera won Gr. 2 Queen Mary Stakes, and traces to Pretty Polly, ancestress of Great Nephew, Nearctic, Don, Donatello II, St. Paddy, Brigadier Gerard, etc.

Stands at: Airlie Stud, Lucan, Co. Dublin
Appy: Capt. A. D. D. Rogers, Airlie Stud, Lucan, Co. Dublin (tel. Dublin 280267; telex 31049 TROG E.I.)

Ela-Mana-Mou winning England's most prestigious weight-for-age race, the King George VI and Queen Elizabeth Diamond Stakes

ELA - MANA - MOU

Europe's record-breaking middle-distance champion 1980. In 1980 Ela-Mana-Mou won the King George VI and Queen Elizabeth Diamond Stakes, Gr 1, Coral Eclipse Stakes, Gr 1, Prince of Wales's Stakes, Gr 2, and Earl of Sefton Stakes, Gr 3, earning £236,332 in first-prize money, a record for a 4-y-o trained in England. In a splendid career he also won Royal Lodge Stakes, Gr 2 (allotted 9-2 2-y-o Free Handicap, ahead of Troy), King Edward VII Stakes, Gr 2, and was also 2nd Grand Prix de Saint-Cloud, Gr 1, 3rd Prix de l'Arc de Triomphe, Gr 1, 3rd King George VI and Queen Elizabeth Diamond Stakes, Gr 1, 4th Derby, Gr 1.

See pages 242-249 of this volume

Stud Record
Ela-Mana-Mou retires to stud in 1981

ELA-MANA-MOU (b.c. 1976)	Pitcairn (b 1971)	Petingo (b 1965)	Petition
			Alcazar
		Border Bounty (b 1965)	Bounteous
			B Flat
	Rose Bertin (ch 1970)	High Hat (ch 1957)	Hyperion
			Madonna
		Wide Awake (b 1964)	Major Portion
			Wake Island

By **PITCAIRN**, Champion Sire in 1980—also sire of CAIRN ROUGE (Champion Stakes, Gr 1, Goffs Irish 1,000 Guineas, Gr 1) and pattern-placed KAHAILA, PETRINGO and BONNIE ISLE.

Out of **ROSE BERTIN**, winner at 3 years. Her dam WIDE AWAKE won the Ebbisham Stakes and was 3rd Nell Gwyn Stakes, Gr 3, traces to BELLE OF ALL, champion filly of 1950 and 1951, 1,000 Guineas, Gr 1, Cheveley Park Stakes, Gr 1, etc.

Stands at: Simmonstown Stud, Celbridge, Co. Kildare, Ireland.
Apply to Captain A. D. D. Rogers, Airlie Stud, Lucan, Co. Dublin, Ireland. Tel: Dublin 280267 or 281548. Telex: 31049. Trog E.I.

HABITAT

CHAMPION EUROPEAN MILER OF 1969 when winner of Prix du Moulin de Long champ, Gr 1, Lockinge S . Gr 2 Prix Quincey, Gr 3 and Wills Mile, Gr 3. **Timeform 134**
Stud Record First Runners 1973. Sire of winners of 460 races, £2,073,188
Champion sire of 2-y-o's in the British Isles 1973, 74, 75 & 79
Principal winners: FLYING WATER (1,000 Guineas, Gr 1, Champion Stakes, Gr 1, Prix Jacques le Marois, Gr 1), ROSE BOWL (Champion Stakes, Gr 1), DOUBLE FORM (King's Stand Gr 1, Prix de l'Abbaye Gr 1, Vernons Sprint Gr 2) HOMING (Queen Elizabeth II Stakes, Gr 2), SIGY (Prix de l'Abbaye de Longchamp Gr 1), HABITONY (Santa Anita Derby, Gr 1), HABAT (Middle Park Stakes, Gr 1), STEEL HEART (Middle Park Stakes, Gr 1), HITTITE GLORY (Middle Park Stakes, Gr 1, Flying Childers Stakes, Gr 1), HOT SPARK (Flying Childers Stakes, Gr 1), BITTY GIRL (Queen Mary Stakes, Gr 2), ROUSSALKA (Coronation Stakes, Gr 2, Nassau Stakes, Gr 2 (twice). MADANG, MARWELL (Cheveley Park Gr 1), HARD FOUGHT, TOPSY, etc. Fertility 93%. Yearlings have made up to 252,000 gns and in 1979 a yearling out of a daughter of Habitat made 625,000 gns.

HABITAT (bay 1966)	Sir Gaylord (b 1959)	Turn-to	Royal Charger
			Source Sucree
		Somethingroyal	Princequillo
			Imperatrice
	Little Hut (b 1952)	Occupy	Bull Dog
			Miss Bunting
		Savage Beauty	Challenger II
			Khara

By SIR GAYLORD winner of 10 races, Sire of SIR IVOR (Champion at 2 and 3 years, winning Epsom Derby, Washington International, etc., a leading sire). Out of LITTLE HUT also dam of NORTHFIELDS (Louisiana Derby classic sire with his first crop) and GUEST ROOM (SW of $172,954).

Stands at: Grangewilliam Stud, Maynooth, Co. Kildare.
Apply: Capt. A. D. D. Rogers, Airlie Stud, Lucan, Co. Dublin. (tel. Dublin 280267; telex 31049 TROG E.I.)

KALA SHIKARI

Top European Sprinter by Huntercombe. Winner of 6 races and £36,814 including Prix du Gros-Chene, Chantilly, Gr 3 (beating Arch Sculptor, Polly Peachum and Mendip Man), Prix de Seine-et-Oise, Maisons Laffitte, Gr 3 (beating Raga Navarro, Mendip Man, Vitiges, Girl Friend, Polyponder, Hittite Glory, etc.), 2nd Prix du Petit Couvert, Longchamp, Gr 3, 3rd Palace House Stakes, Newmarket, Gr 3, 3rd Duke of York Stakes, Gr 3. **Timeform 125.**
Stud Record: First crop are yearlings of 1981. Estimated fertility 87·76% for 1980 covering season.

KALA SHIKARI (b/br 1973)	**Huntercombe** (b 1967)	**Derring-Do**	**Darius**
			Sipsey Bridge
		Ergina	**Fair Trial**
			Ballechin
	Vigour (gr 1961)	**Vilmorin**	**Gold Bridge**
			Queen of the Meadows
		Pompeienne	**Eble**
			Pomelane

By HUNTERCOMBE, won 6 races and £39,415 incl. Middle Park Stakes, Gr I, July Cup, Gr 2, Nunthorpe Stakes, Gr 2, etc., sire of winners of £739,493 incl. PYJAMA HUNT, RADETZKY, KALA SHIKARI, GROUND COVER, ABBEYDALE—all stakes winners. Out of VIGOUR, won at 2 yrs: dam of 5 winners and out of own sister to Pomare (winner of Poule d'Essai des Pouliches).

Stands at: Blackmore Vale Stud, Sandley, Gillingham, Dorset (07476) 3396.
Apply: C. R. C. Watkins at the stud or Capt. A. D. D. Rogers, Airlie Stud, Lucan, Co. Dublin (tel: Dublin 280267 or 281548; telex 31049 TROG E.I.).

Airlie..

MANADO

CHAMPION EUROPEAN 2-y-o OF 1975. Winner of Grand Criterium, Gr I, Prix de la Salamandre, Gr I, Prix Yacowlef (by 8 lengths), third Prix du Moulin, Gr I, Prix de la Foret, Gr I, Prix du Rond-Point, Gr 3 and fourth Prix Jacques le Marois, Gr I (beaten two heads). Total earnings £100,545. Timeform considered his form to be 'the best of any 2-y-o colt who raced in England, France or Ireland in 1975' and he was their HIGHEST RATED 2-y-o OF 1975. **Timeform 130.**

Stud Record: First winners (1980) included POLDHU (Washington Singer Stakes, also 3rd Middle Park, 3rd Mill Reef), SALMANA, AIRSHIP, ISLES BAY, JADE SEA, MISS HEBBRONVILLE and MANALDO. His yearlings averaged 13,665 gns in 1980 (20 sold). Fertility 89%.

MANADO (bay 1973)	Captain's Gig (b/br 1965)	Turn-to	Royal Charger
			Source Sucree
		Make Sail	Ambiorix II
			Anchors Aweigh
	Slipstream (ITY) (gr 1967)	Sing Sing	Tudor Minstrel
			Agin the Law
		Palestream	Palestine
			Millstream

By CAPTAIN'S GIG winner of 8 races, $205,312 including Jim Dandy S, Gr 3, second rated 2-y-o of his year. Sire of stakes winners in North America and Europe. His 6 crops included 44 individual 2-y-o winners.

Out of SLIPSTREAM a winner who is out of a winning half-sister to MEDWAY (Goodwood Cup, Gr 3), REEL IN (Nassau S, Gr 2, third Oaks), MILADY (Ribblesdale S, Gr 2), etc.

Stands at: Simmonstown Stud, Celbridge, Co. Kildare.

Apply: Capt. A. D. D. Rogers, Airlie Stud, Lucan, Co. Dublin (tel. Dublin 280267; telex 31049 TROG E.I).

NONOALCO

Winner of 7 races from 10 starts including Prix Morny, Gr 1 (in record time from LIANGA) Prix de la Salamandre, Gr I, Prix Yacowlef (by 8 lengths in record time) at 2 years and 2,000 Guineas, Gr I (beating GIACOMETTI, Champion S, etc.), Prix Jacques le Marois, Gr I and Prix du Rond-Point, Gr 3 (beating LIANGA) at 3 years. Total earnings £148,255. Timeform said of him 'an exceptionally brilliant 2-y-o' and 'a top class miler. He lacks none of the qualities to be found in the better class North American bred colts, which breeders are rightly attracted to in increasing numbers nowadays.' **Timeform 131.**

Stud Record

Sire of NONOALCA (Prix des Reservoirs, Gr 3, Prix de la Grotte, Gr 3, 2nd Poule d'Essai des Pouliches, Gr 1), UN REITRE (Prix la Rochette, Gr 3), FIRYAL (Prix Imprudence, 3rd Prix Morny, Gr 1), DELANEIGE, MESANGE BLEUE (Premio Dormello, Gr 2), LALARIA (Prix La Fleche), NOALCOHOLIC (Prix de la Ville de Trouville), SPOLETO NOALTO, SILKEN KNOT, etc.

Fertility 96%. Yearlings averaged 34,600 gns in 1980 (17 sold).

NONOALCO (bay 1971)	Nearctic (br 1954)	Nearco	Pharos
			Nogara
		Lady Angela	Hyperion
			Sister Sarah
	Seximee (ch 1966)	Hasty Road	Roman
			Traffic Court
		Jambo	Crafty Admiral
			Bank Account

Sire, NEARCTIC winner of 21 races, $152,384 and Canadian Horse of the Year. Sire of the winners of over $7,000,000 including NORTHERN DANCER (Kentucky Derby, Champion at 2 and 3 years and sire of NIJINSKY, THE MINSTREL, BE MY GUEST, NORTHERN BABY, NUREYEV, STORM BIRD etc.), Champion 2-y-o COOL RECEPTION, ICECAPADE (Saranac S, Gr II, $256,400), etc.

Dam, SEXIMEE a winner out of a winning half-sister to NANCY JR (Kentucky Oaks). Family of SECRETARIAT, SIR GAYLORD, ALLEGED, EMPERY, etc.

Stands at: Airlie Stud, Lucan, Co. Dublin
Apply: Capt. A. D. D. Rogers,
Airlie Stud, Lucan, Co. Dublin (tel. Dublin 280267; telex 31049 TROG E.I.)

Airlie..

Northern Baby winning Group 1 Champion Stakes

NORTHERN BABY

Northern Baby won 5 races, £165,715, including Champion Stakes, Gr 1, Prix Dollar, Gr 2, Prix de la Cote Normande, Gr 3, Prix Mieuxce (at 2); also 3rd Derby, Gr 1, Prix Ganay, Gr 1, and Coral Eclipse Stakes, Gr 1.

Racehorses of 1979: 'He's an exceptionally tough and genuine little horse . . . he should certainly make a fine stallion in due course.' **Timeform 127.**

Stud Record
Northern Baby retires to stud in 1981

Northern Baby (Can) (bay 1976)	Northern Dancer (b 1961)	Nearctic (br 1954)	Nearco
			Lady Angela
		Natalma (b 1957)	Native Dancer
			Almahmoud
	Two Rings (b 1970)	Round Table (b 1954)	Princequillo
			Knight's Daughter
		Allofthem (ch 1964)	Bagdad
			Gal I Love

By **NORTHERN DANCER,** 14 races, $580,647 including Kentucky Derby, Gr 1 and Preakness Stakes, Gr 1, Champion at 2 and 3 years and sire of NIJINSKY, (Triple Crown; sire of champions), THE MINSTREL (Derby, Gr 1, Irish Derby, Gr 1, King George VI and Queen Elizabeth Diamond Stakes, Gr 1), LYPHARD (leading sire), NORTHFIELDS (leading sire), NUREYEV (2,000 Guineas, Gr 1, disq), STORM BIRD (Champion 2-y-o of Europe 1980), etc.

Out of **TWO RINGS** 9 races 2-4 years, Nassau Stakes, Fort Erie, 2nd Nettie Stakes, Gr 3; dam of 3 winners (her first three foals) including BAYFORD, the leading 2-y-o in Canada in 1980. Her grandam GAL I LOVE was a full-sister to NADIR (Champion 2-y-o of 1957 in USA and winner of American Derby, Gr 2) and dam of 5 winners including three pattern-race winners.

Stands at: Grangewilliam, Maynooth, Co. Kildare. Apply to Capt. A. D. D. Rogers, Airlie Stud, Lucan, Co. Dublin. Tel: Dublin 280267 or 281548. Telex: 31049 TROG E.I.

TUMBLE WIND

Winner of 9 races (5½f-12f), $249,175 including Haggin and Westchester S, Gr 2 (at 2 years), Hollywood Derby, Gr 1, Argonaut S, Gr 2, San Vincente S, Gr 3, etc. Second Hollywood Juvenile Championship, Gr 2 and Santa Anita Derby, Gr 1. Course record breaker for 1⅛m at Santa Anita.

Stud Record

Tumble Wind has sired the winners of 210 races and £568,519 including MILLINGDALE LILLIE (Fred Darling Stakes, Gr 3, 2nd Goffs Irish 1,000 Guineas, Gr 1, 4th 1,000 Guineas, Gr 1), TUMBLEDOWNWIND (Gimcrack Stakes, Gr 2, Rous Memorial Stakes, 4th 2,000 Guineas, Gr 1), PEPPONE (Criterium di Roma, Gr 3), WINDY CHEYENNE (Hollywood Nursery), DRIFTIN' ALONG (La Habra Stakes), COOLINEY PRINCE (Windsor Castle Stakes), LYON BAY (Grand Prix du Chasse de Princes), TARZAN, WINDY SUNSET, ISONDA, MOULIN ROUGE, DOGS BAY, WINTER WIND and TUMBLER. Fertility 82%.

TUMBLE WIND (bay 1964)	Restless Wind (ch 1956)	Windy City II	Wyndham
			Staunton
		Lump Sugar	Bull Lea
			Sugar Run
	Easy Stages (b 1953)	Endeavour II	British Empire
			Himalaya
		Saturday Off	Kiev
			Mexican Tea

His sire RESTLESS WIND has sired the winners of over $6,000,000 including PROCESS SHOT (Champion 2-y-o filly, $463,200), WINDJAMMER (Keeneland Breeders Futurity, Kentucky Jockey Club S) and ON YOUR MARK (a noted sire of fast 2-y-o's). This is a male line renowned for speed and precocity.

His dam EASY STAGES is own-sister to the dam of HUL A HUL, sire of record breaking 2-y-o Chamozzle. Third dam Mexican Tea is also third dam of classic filly FLYING RYTHM (Hollywood Oaks) and grandam of FLYING LILL (Kentucky Oaks).

Stands at: Ongar Stud, Clonsilla, Co. Dublin
Apply: Capt. A. D. D. Rogers, Airlie Stud, Lucan, Co. Dublin (tel. Dublin 280267; telex 31049 TROG E.I.)

N.B. All sales prices are quoted in Irish guineas at 1·20 to the English pound.

BE MY GUEST

Ch. 1974 by Northern Dancer ex What a Treat by Tudor Minstrel

Won 4 races and £28,814 at two and three years. His wins included Waterford Crystal Mile (Gr 2), *(beating Jellaby, Don, Duke Ellington etc.)*, **Blue Riband Trial Stakes (Gr 3), Epsom.** *(". . . a scintillating performance." Timeform)*, **and Desmond Stakes (Gr 3) beating Poacher's Moon by 4 lengths. Also placed second in Nijinsky Stakes (Gr 2). Timeform 126.**
Dam won 11 races and $321,608 including Alabama Stakes (Gr 1) First crop yearlings averaged 43,297 gns. A colt out of Street Light made 154,000 gns at Goffs Invitational Yearling Sales and a filly out of Oh So Fair made 192,000 gns at Houghton Yearling Sales.

	Nearctic	Nearco
Northern Dancer		Lady Angela
	Natalma	Native Dancer
BE MY GUEST		Almahmoud
	Tudor Minstrel	Owen Tudor
What A Treat		Sansonnet
	Rare Treat	Stymie
		Rare Perfume

COOLMORE
AND ASSOCIATED STUD FARMS

Stands at COOLMORE-Bob Lanigan
Tel: Clonmel 31298 Telex: 8695

CAPTAIN JAMES

Bay 1974 by Captain's Gig ex Aliceva by Alcide

Won 3 races and £31,346 at two, three and four years.
His wins included 1978 Waterford Crystal Mile (Gr 2), *defeating Group 1 winners Formidable and Jaazeiro.*
Timeform 123.
Half-brother to Nikoli (Irish 2,000 Guineas Gr 1) and Sutton Place (Coronation Stakes Gr 2).
His dam is half-sister to Feemoss, dam of Levmoss, Le Moss and Sweet Mimosa.
A half-brother to Captain James realised a record 300,000 gns at Goffs 1980.

CAPTAIN JAMES	Captain's Gig	Turn-to	Royal Charger
			Source Sucree
		Make Sail	Ambiorix
			Anchors Aweigh
	Aliceva	Alcide	Alycidon
			Chenille
		Feevagh	Solar Slipper
			Astrid Wood

COOLMORE
AND ASSOCIATED STUD FARMS

Stands at CASTLE HYDE STUD - Gay O'Callaghan
Tel: Fermoy (025) 31689. Telex: 8470

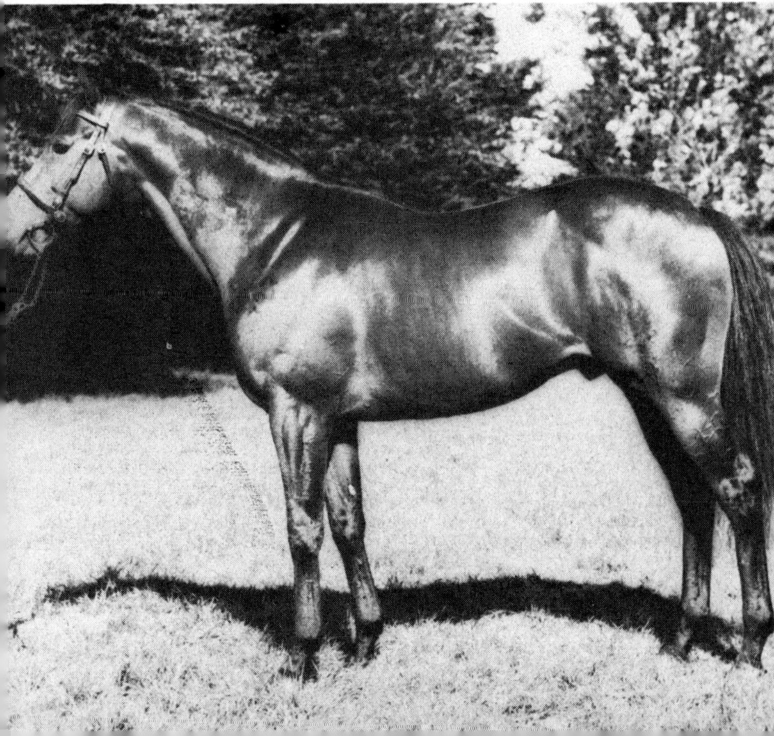

CROFTER

Ch. 1977 by Habitat ex Marie Curie by Exbury

Winner of 3 races and second twice from 5 starts. Crofter won his first 3 starts (7-8f) including the Youghal Stakes (listed race). He was also second in the Prix de la Foret (Gr. 1), (beaten 1 length by Horse of the Year Moorestyle and beating triple champion Kilijaro) and the Prix Perth (Gr. 3).
Champion Miler **Habitat** is one of Europe's outstanding sires, his winners including **Marwell, Flying Water, Rose Bowl, Steel Heart, Hot Spark, Homing,** etc.
Marie Curie, a winner and group-placed, has produced 3 winners from her first 3 foals. She is half-sister to **Mariel** (Gr. 2 Pretty Polly Stakes, second Gr. 1 Irish 1,000 Guineas; dam of **Sarah Siddons,** Gr. 1 Irish 1,000 Guineas). Her dam won Gr. 3 Fred Darling Stakes, Gr. 3 Musidora Stakes and is half-sister to **Ragusa** (Gr. 1 Irish Derby, Gr. 1 St. Leger, outstanding sire).

CROFTER (USA)	Habitat	Sir Gaylord	Turn-To
			Somethingroyal
		Little Hut	Occupy
			Savage Beauty
	Marie Curie	Exbury	Le Haar
			Greensward
		Ela Marita	Red God
			Fantan II

COOLMORE
AND ASSOCIATED STUD FARMS

Stands at CASTLE HYDE STUD — Gay O'Callaghan
Tel: Fermoy (025) 31689. Telex: 8470

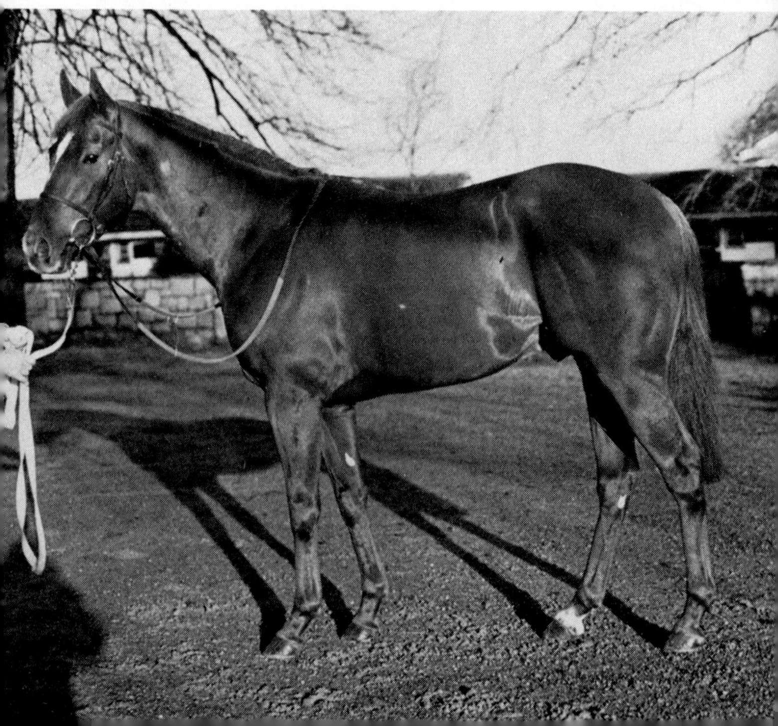

FORDHAM

B. 1975 by Forli ex Bold Enchantress by Bold Ruler

Won 4 races, £30,761, at 3 and 4 years, including Joe McGrath Memorial Stakes (Gr 1) *(beating Dickens Hill, Two of Diamonds, Orchestra, Icelandic)*, **and Cumberland Lodge Stakes (Gr 3)** *(beating Idle Waters, Town and Country)*.
Very closely related to leading sire Home Guard and to Boone's Cabin (Stakes winner, stakes sire); being by their sire Forli (also responsible for Forego, Thatch, Posse Intrepid Hero, etc), out of Bold Enchantress, three-parts-sister to their dam Stay at Home, and to Boldnesian (Santa Anita Derby, a leading sire). Grandam Princessnesian (Hollywood Gold Cup Gr 1) dam of $1,050,000 yearling at Keeneland 1980.

FORDHAM (U.S.A.)	Forli	Aristophanes	Hyperion
			Commotion
		Trevisa	Advocate
			Veneta
	Bold Enchantress	Bold Ruler	Nasrullah
			Miss Disco
		Princessnesian	Princequillo
			Alanesian

COOLMORE
AND ASSOCIATED STUD FARMS

Stands at GRANGE STUD - David Magnier
Tel: Fermoy (025) 31465. Telex: 8470.

GAY FANDANGO

Ch. 1972, by Forli ex Gay Violin by Sir Gaylord

Won 2 races and £15,443 at three years, his only season to race. Won Waterford Crystal Mile (Gr 2) *(beating Rose Bowl, Roussalka, Mark Anthony etc)*, **and Jersey Stakes, (Gr 3), Royal Ascot. Also second in Queen Elizabeth II Stakes (Gr 2), Ascot** *(to Rose Bowl and beating Anne's Pretender, Bolkonski, etc.)*. **Timeform 132.**

Sire of the winners of 45 races, £171,986, including Last Fandango (Blue Riband Trial, 2nd Irish 2,000 Guineas Gr 1, *btn sh. hd*), **Adolfina (stakes winner, placed Italian Oaks and 1,000 Guineas), Moomba Masquerade (Land of Burns Stakes), Spanish Dancer (Irish Sweeps Autumn Handicap) etc.**

GAY FANDANGO	Forli	Aristophanes	Hyperion
			Commotion
		Trevisa	Advocate
			Veneta
	Gay Violin	Sir Gaylord	Turn-To
			Somethingroyal
		Blue Violin	First Fiddle
			Blue Lu

COOLMORE
AND ASSOCIATED STUD FARMS

Stands at GRANGE STUD
—David Magnier
Tel: Fermoy (025) 31465 Telex: 8470

GODSWALK

Grey 1974 by Dancer's Image ex Kate's Intent by Intentionally

**Won 8 races and £55,760 over 5 and 6 furlongs.
His wins included King's Stand Stakes (Gr 1) and Norfolk Stakes (Gr 3), Royal Ascot, Ballyogan Stakes, Leopardstown (Gr 3), Airlie Coolmore Castle Hyde Stakes, Waterford Testimonial Stakes and Marble Hill Stakes, Curragh.
Top 2-y-o colt on 1976 Irish Free Handicap rated superior to The Minstrel, Pampapaul, Nebbiolo and Captain James.
Timeform 130.
Dam stakes winner of 8 races.**

Dancer's Image	Native Dancer	Polynesian
		Geisha
	Noors Image	Noor
		Little Sphinx
GODSWALK		
Kate's Intent	Intentionally	Intent
		My Recipe
	Julie Kate	Hill Price
		Doggin' It

COOLMORE
AND ASSOCIATED STUD FARMS

First crop yearlings averaged 14,414 gns (colt out of Wilhelmina and filly out of Apple Peel both made 48,000 gns at Houghton Sales).

**Stands at CASTLE HYDE STUD - Gay O'Callaghan
Tel: Fermoy (025) 31689. Telex: 8470**

HELLO GORGEOUS

Ch. 1977 by Mr. Prospector—Bonny Jet by Jet Jewel

Won 4 races, £129,647 at 2 and 3 years, (6-10½f), including William Hill Futurity, (Gr 1), *(beating In Fijar, Choucri)*; **Royal Lodge Stakes, (Gr 2),** *(beating Star Way)*; **Mecca-Dante Stakes (Gr 2),** *(beating Master Willie, Water Mill, Tyrnavos)* **and Ballymore Stakes,** *(beating Millingdale Lillie)*. **Also placed second in the Eclipse Stakes, (Gr 1),** *(beaten ¾ length by Ela Mana Mou, beating Gregorian, Sea Chimes)*, **and Heathorn Stakes. Rated 9—4 on Free Handicap, above Henbit, Shoot A Line, Quick as Lightning, Tyrnavos Master Willie, Night Alert, Moorestyle, etc. Timeform 128. MR. PROSPECTOR, Champion in U.S.A. Champion first crop sire in 1978. Champion sire of 2-year-olds in 1979. Sire of It's In The Air (Champion 2 and 3-year-old filly), Hello Gorgeous, Antique Gold, Gold Stage, Miswaki, etc. Re-syndicated in 1980 for $24,000,000. FULL 1981.**

HELLO GORGEOUS	Mr. Prospector	Raise a Native: Native Dancer, Raise You
		Gold Digger: Nashua, Sequence
	Bonny Jet	Jet Jewel: Jet Pilot, Crepe Myrtle
		Bonny Bush: Mr. Busher, San Bonita

COOLMORE
AND ASSOCIATED STUD FARMS

Stands at COOLMORE-Bob Lanigan
Tel: Clonmel 31298. Telex: 8695.

HOME GUARD

Brown 1969 by Forli ex Stay at Home by Bold Ruler

Won 7 races and £30,357.
His wins included Tetrarch Stakes (Gr 3) (*7 f*), **Diadem Stakes (Gr 3)** (*6 f*) **and Philips Electrical Rockingham Stakes** (*5 f*).
Also second in Prix de L'Abbaye (Gr 1) and third in Eclipse Stakes (*to Brigadier Gerard*). **Timeform 129.**
From his first 4 crops, sire of the winners of 106 races, £440,315, including MARQUEE UNIVERSAL (Dixie Handicap Gr 2, Edgemere Handicap Gr 3, 1980), SONNEN GOLD (7 races, including Gimcrack Gr 2), MANJAM (3 races, including Prix du Petit Couvert Gr 3), HOUSE GUARD, WATCHDOG, WARMINGTON, SPARK OF LIFE, etc.

HOME GUARD	Forli	Aristophanes	Hyperion
			Commotion
		Trevisa	Advocate
			Veneta
	Stay at Home	Bold Ruler	Nasrullah
			Miss Disco
		Alanesian	Polynesian
			Alablue

COOLMORE
AND ASSOCIATED STUD FARMS

Stands at LONGFIELD STUD - Tommy Stack
Tel: Thurles (0504) 42234

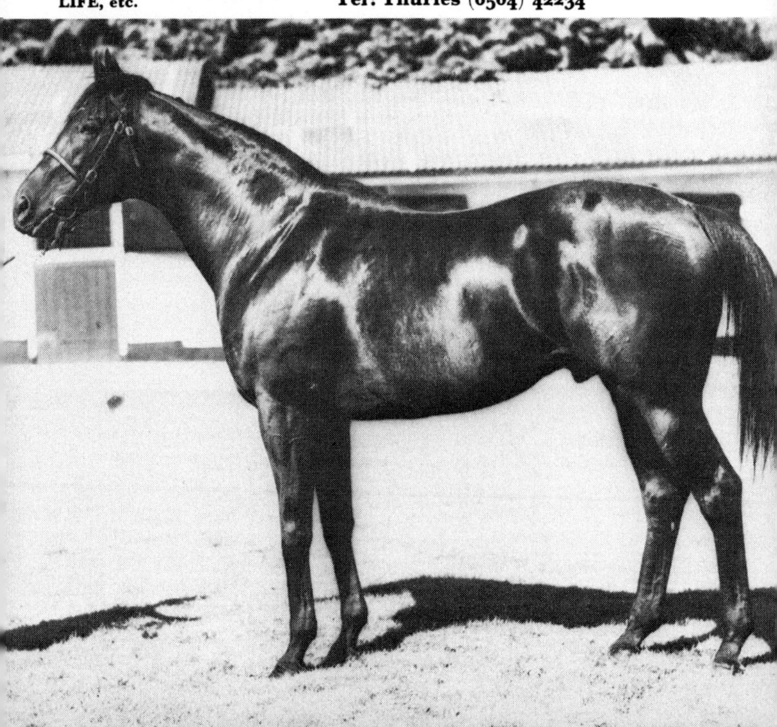

LONDON BELLS

Bay 1977 by Nijinsky—Shake A Leg by Raise A Native

Won 4 races in Ireland and U.S.A., £35,749 at 2 and 3 years, Holder of track record over 6 furlongs at The Curragh, previously held by Nijinsky and The Minstrel; second in Coventry Stakes, Royal Ascot (Gr 2), (*beating Final Straw by* 3 *lengths*) **and Rochester Cup; fourth in Lanson Champagne Stakes. Rated 8—11 on Irish Free Handicap, above Smokey Lady, Night Alert, Nikoli, etc. Timeform** "*big, strong, good-bodied, attractive colt.*"

NIJINSKY, Champion at 2 and 3 years, sire of over 40 Stakes winners, including dual European Champion Ile de Bourbon, Green Dancer, (*leading European First Crop Sire,* 1979) **Czaravich, Upper Nile, Terpsichorist, Princesse Lida, Night Alert, etc.**

SHAKE A LEG, a Group winner of 9 races and also dam of Vaguely Modest (Selene Stakes, (Gr 3)), is by RAISE A NATIVE, sire and grandsire of champions Exclusive Native, Affirmed, Alydar, Genuine Risk, Mr Prospector, etc.

LONDON BELLS	Nijinsky	Northern Dancer	Nearctic
			Natalma
		Flaming Page	Bull Page
			Flaring Top
	Shake A Leg	Raise A Native	Native Dancer
			Raise You
		Fleeting Doll	Fleet Nasrullah
			Chinese Doll

COOLMORE

AND ASSOCIATED STUD FARMS

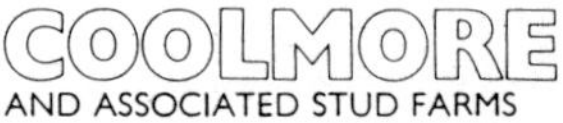

Stands at CASTLE HYDE STUD - Gay O'Callaghan

Tel: Fermoy (025) 31689. Telex: 8470

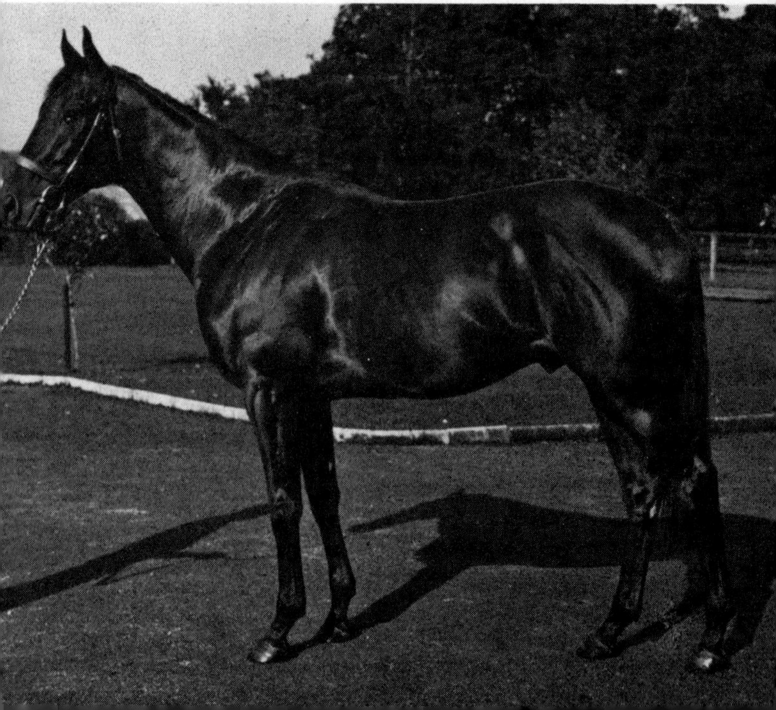

NORTHFIELDS

Ch. 1968 by Northern Dancer ex Little Hut by Occupy

Won 7 races and $195,071 at two and three years. His wins included Louisiana Derby (Gr 2), Hawthorne Derby (Gr 3), and Kent Stakes (Gr 3).
Also group placed 4 times. Sire of the winners of 296 races, £928,388, from his first six crops, including NORTHERN TREASURE (Irish 2,000 Guineas (Gr 1), Blandford Stakes (Gr 2), OATS (Blue Riband Trial (Gr 3), Jockey Club Stakes (Gr 3), NANTICIOUS (Ribblesdale Stakes (Gr 2), Silken Glider Stakes (Gr 3), NORTH STOKE (Joe McGrath Memorial Stakes (Gr 1), BAPTISM, NORTHERN VIEW, MIAMI SPRINGS, REPETITIOUS, TOONDRA, etc. NORTHFIELDS is half-brother to HABITAT. His yearlings averaged 71,907 gns and made up to 300,000 gns in 1980.

NORTHFIELDS	Northern Dancer	Nearctic	Nearco
			Lady Angela
		Natalma	Native Dancer
			Almahmoud
	Little Hut	Occupy	Bull Dog
			Miss Bunting
		Savage Beauty	Challenger II
			Khara

COOLMORE
AND ASSOCIATED STUD FARMS

Stands at COOLMORE - Bob Lanigan
Tel: Clonmel 31298. Telex: 8695

RED ALERT

Ch. 1971 by Red God ex Ashton Jane by Gratitude

Won 5 races and £19,413 at two and three years.
His wins included Jersey Stakes (Gr 3), Royal Ascot, Spillers Stewards Cup and Enniskillen Stakes.
Also placed four times, including Norfolk Stakes (Gr 3), Anglesey Stakes (Gr 3) and Tetrarch Stakes (Gr 3).
Also placed fourth in Irish Two Thousand Guineas (Gr 1)
Timeform 127.
Sire from his first three crops of the winners of 98 races, £254,568, including CRIMSON HEATHER (Curragh Stakes Gr 3), ALERT, VIA DELTA, I'M READY (Irish Cambridgeshire) and 13 2-y-o winners in 1980.

N.B. TOOVERPRIME, by Red Alert, stakes winner of his first 3 starts in California, 1980.

RED ALERT	Red God	Nasrullah	Nearco
			Mumtaz Begum
		Spring Run	Menow
			Boola Brook
	Ashton Jane	Gratitude	Golden Cloud
			Verdura
		Rye Girl	Blue Water
			Brosna

COOLMORE
AND ASSOCIATED STUD FARMS

Stands at GRANGE STUD - David Magnier
Tel: Fermoy (025) 31465. Telex: 8470

SANDY CREEK

Ch. 1976 by Petingo ex Keep Right by Klairon

Champion two-year-old and a Group 1 winning son of Petingo. Won 2 races and £43,836 at two years from only five starts. He won the William Hill Futurity (Gr 1) *(beating Lyphard's Wish, Two of Diamonds, Northern Baby, etc., in a course record time)*; **and the Larkspur Stakes (Gr 3). Also placed second in the Beresford Stakes (Gr 2) and third in the National Stakes (Gr 2)** *(beaten a length behind Tap on Wood and Dickens Hill)*. **Rated equal with TROY and KRIS in Timeform's Racehorses of 1978. Top rated two-year-old in Irish Free Handicap, and rated second in the English Free Handicap. Second dam is half-sister to Pushful (by Petition), winner of Timeform Gold Cup (Gr 1). Family of Ambiorix, Turn-to, My Babu, English Prince (by Petingo), Bustino, Irish River, etc.**

SANDY CREEK	Petingo	Petition	Fair Trial
			Art Paper
		Alcazar	Alycidon
			Quarterdeck
	Keep Right	Klairon	Clarion III
			Kalmia
		Narrow Escape	Narrator
			Press Forward

Stands at CASTLE HYDE STUD - Gay O'Callaghan
Tel: Fermoy (025) 31689. Telex: 8470

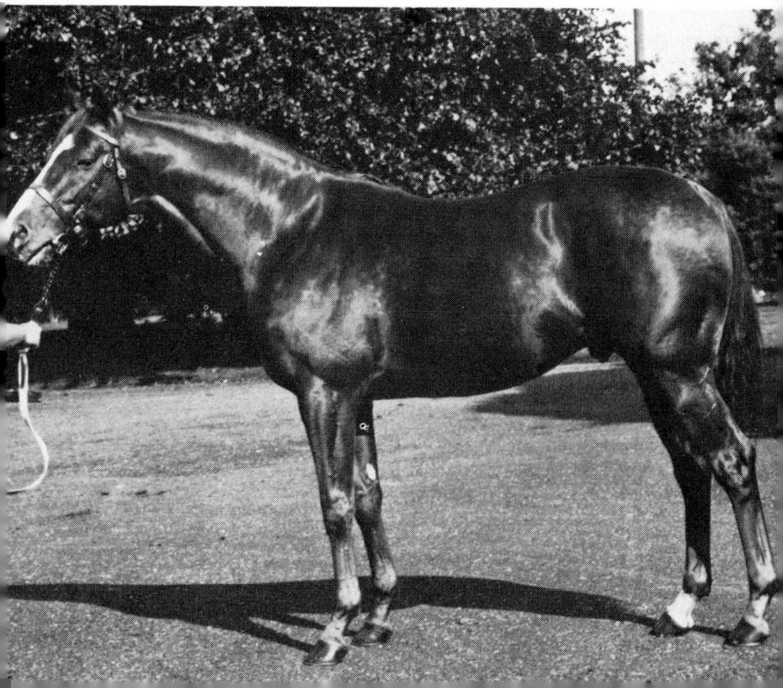

THATCH

Bay 1970 by Forli ex Thong by Nantallah

Champion two-and-three-year-old. Won 7 races and £40,277 at two and three years. His wins included July Cup (Gr 1), Sussex Stakes (Gr 1) *(by 3 lengths from Jacinth)*, **and St James' Palace Stakes (Gr 2)** *(by 15 lengths)*. **Also placed fourth in Prix Morny (Gr 1) and 2,000 Guineas (Gr 1). Timeform 136. From his first 4 crops, sire of the winners of 108 races, £515,872, incl FINAL STRAW (Laurent Perrier Champagne Gr 2, July Stakes Gr 3, Greenham Stakes Gr 3, Seaton Delaval Stakes Gr 3), THATCHING (Wm Hill July Cup, Gr 1, Cork and Orrery Gr 3, Duke of York Gr 3), GOLDEN THATCH, NEMR, TANNENBERG, etc. His yearlings averaged 49,655 gns and made up to 194,400 gns in 1980.**

	Aristophanes	Hyperion Commotion
Forli	Trevisa	Advocate Veneta
THATCH		
Thong	Nantallah	Nasrullah Shimmer
	Rough Shod	Gold Bridge Dalmary

COOLMORE

AND ASSOCIATED STUD FARMS

Stands at COOLMORE-Bob Lanigan
Tel: Clonmel 31298. Telex: 8695

THATCHING

Bay 1975 by Thatch ex Abella by Abernant

CHAMPION EUROPEAN SPRINTER
Won 4 races and £50,606 at three and four years.
His wins included William Hill July Cup (Gr 1), by 5 lengths, *(beating Vaigly Great, Greenland Park, Devon Ditty, King of Troy, Absalom, One in a Million. Sigy, etc)*, **Cork and Orrery Stakes (Gr 3) by 4 lengths, and Duke of York Stakes (Gr 3). Also won William Hill Sprint Championship (Gr 2) by 2½ lengths** *(beating Ahoonora, Double Form, etc.)* **but disqualified.**
Timeform 131.
Dam won three races and placed second Challenge Stakes (Gr 3). (Timeform 121). Full brother to Golden Thatch (Greenlands Stakes (Gr 3), Ballyogan Stakes (Gr 3)). Half brother to Ashford Castle (won over $100,000 in U.S.A.). Family of Reform, Val de Loir, Ridan, Apalachee, King Pellinore, Nureyev, etc.

THATCHING	Thatch	Forli	Aristophanes
			Trevisa
		Thong	Nantallah
			Rough Shod
	Abella	Abernant	Owen Tudor
			Rustom Mahal
		Darrica	Darius
			Erica Fragrans

COOLMORE
AND ASSOCIATED STUD FARMS

Stands at LONGFIELD STUD - Tommy Stack
Tel: Thurles (0504) 42234

TRY MY BEST

Bay 1975 by Northern Dancer ex Sex Appeal by Buckpasser

Champion European two-year-old. Won 4 races and £48,239 at two and three years from 5 starts. His wins included the William Hill Dewhurst Stakes (Gr 1), Larkspur Stakes (Gr 3) and Vauxhall Trial Stakes (Gr 3). Timeform 130.
Try My Best cost $185,000 as a yearling and is half-brother to the unbeaten two-year-old, Solar. His dam is half-sister to champion two-year-old Malinowski, Gielgud (Laurent Perrier Champagne Stakes, Gr 2) and Monroe (Ballyogan Stakes, Gr 3).

TRY MY BEST (USA)	Northern Dancer	Nearctic	Nearco
			Lady Angela
		Natalma	Native Dancer
			Almahmoud
	Sex Appeal	Buckpasser	Tom Fool
			Busanda
		Best In Show	Traffic Judge
			Stolen Hour

COOLMORE
AND ASSOCIATED STUD FARMS

Fee private and nominations available from shareholders only.

Stands at COOLMORE - Bob Lanigan
Tel: Clonmel 31298. Telex: 8695.

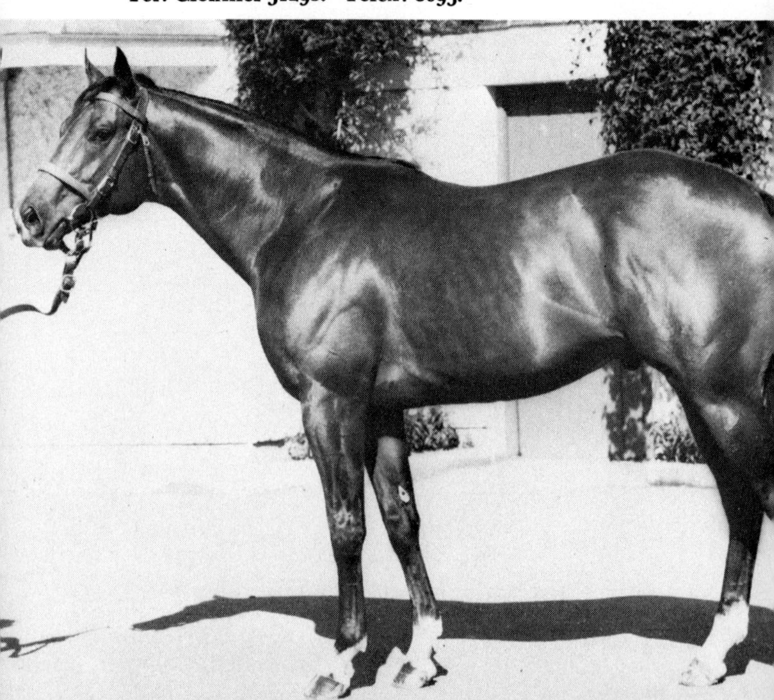

NATIONAL STUD STALLIONS 1981

MILL REEF
Standing at The National Stud, Newmarket, Suffolk.

GRUNDY
Standing at The National Stud, Newmarket, Suffolk.

BLAKENEY
Standing at The National Stud, Newmarket, Suffolk.

STAR APPEAL
Standing at The National Stud, Newmarket, Suffolk.

FINAL STRAW
Standing at Egerton Stud, Newmarket, Suffolk.

HOMING
Standing at Highclere Stud, Newbury, Berkshire

SAGARO
Standing at Limestone Stud, Willoughton, Gainsborough, Lincolnshire.

ROYAL PALACE
Standing at Chesters Stud, Humshaugh, Hexham, Northumberland.

Enquiries for 1982 to Mr. Michael Bramwell, Director, The National Stud, Newmarket, Suffolk CB8 0XE.

B. B. A. STALLIONS 1981

ANAX
BACTON STUD,
BACTON, HEREFORDSHIRE.

BALIDAR
MEDDLER STUD,
NEWMARKET, SUFFOLK.

BUSTINO
WOLFERTON STUD,
SANDRINGHAM, NORFOLK.

CORVARO
ARDENODE STUD,
NAAS, IRELAND.

DRAGONARA PALACE
BARLEYTHORPE STUD,
OAKHAM, LEICESTER.

FAIR SEASON
LITTLETON STUD,
WINCHESTER, HAMPSHIRE.

FREE STATE
BARLEYTHORPE STUD,
OAKHAM, LEICESTER.

GREAT NEPHEW
DALHAM HALL STUD,
NEWMARKET, SUFFOLK.

GUNNER B
LIMESTONE STUD,
WILLOUGHTON,
GAINSBOROUGH, LINCOLNSHIRE.

HIGH TOP
WOODLAND STUD,
NEWMARKET, SUFFOLK.

HITTITE GLORY
NEW ENGLAND STUD,
NEWMARKET, SUFFOLK.

HOT GROVE
NEW ENGLAND STUD,
NEWMARKET, SUFFOLK.

ILE DE BOURBON
BANSTEAD MANOR STUD
NEWMARKET, SUFFOLK.

JULIO MARINER
ASHLEY HEATH STUD,
NEWMARKET, SUFFOLK.

LOMBARD
FAWLEY STUD,
WANTAGE, OXON.

LUCKY WEDNESDAY
HARNESS GROVE STUD,
WORKSOP, NOTTS.

MANSINGH
RED HOUSE STUD, EXNING
NEWMARKET, SUFFOLK.

MILL REEF
NATIONAL STUD,
NEWMARKET, SUFFOLK.

MUMMYS PET
BARLEYTHORPE STUD,
OAKHAM, LEICESTER.

MUSIC MAESTRO
LAVINGTON STUD,
GRAFFHAM, SUSSEX.

NINISKI
LANWADES STUD,
NEWMARKET, SUFFOLK.

NUREYEV
HARAS FRESNAY-LE-BUFFARD,
NORMANDY, FRANCE.

PORTO BELLO
HERRIDGE STUD,
COLLINGBOURNE
DUCIS, WILTS.

B. B. A. STALLIONS 1981

PYJAMA HUNT
SHADWELL STUD,
THETFORD, NORFOLK.

RADETZKY
LONGHOLES STUD.
CHEVELEY, NEWMARKET.

RECORD TOKEN
LIMESTONE STUD,
WILLOUGHTON,
GAINSBOROUGH, LINCS.

REFORM
SHADWELL STUD, THETFORD,
NORFOLK.

RELKINO
BARTON STUD, BURY ST.
EDMUNDS, SUFFOLK.

RIBOBOY
LAVINGTON STUD,
GRAFFHAM, SUSSEX.

ROYALTY
BARTON STUD, BURY ST.
EDMUNDS, SUFFOLK.

SARITAMER
SOUTHCOURT STUD,
LEIGHTON BUZZARD, BEDS.

SCORPIO
BALLYLINCH STUD,
THOMASTOWN,
CO. KILKENNY, IRELAND.

SHIRLEY HEIGHTS
SANDRINGHAM STUD,
KINGS LYNN, NORFOLK.

STAR APPEAL
NATIONAL STUD, NEWMARKET
SUFFOLK.

SWING EASY
BUTTERSTOCKS STUD,
HORSHAM, SUSSEX.

TOWER WALK
LIMESTONE STUD,
WILLOUGHTON,
GAINSBOROUGH, LINCS.

TOWN CRIER
SOUTHCOURT STUD, LEIGHTON
BUZZARD, BEDS.

WHITSTEAD
SIDE HILL STUD,
NEWMARKET, SUFFOLK.

WINDJAMMER
BUTTERSTOCKS STUD,
HORSHAM, SUSSEX.

British Bloodstock Agency

11A ALBEMARLE STREET, LONDON W1X 4JB
Telephone: 01-493 9402 Telex: 27403

or ALTON HOUSE, NEWMARKET CB8 9AF
Telephone: Newmarket (0638) 5021 Telex: 817157

AHONOORA (Ch. 1975)
Lorenzaccio Klairon
Phoenissa
Helen Nichols Martial
Quaker Girl

Winner of 7 races including Steward's Cup Goodwood; King George Stakes (Gr. III); William Hill Sprint Championship York (Gr. II); 2nd King's Stand Stakes (Gr. I) Ascot.
Total Stakes £86,300.

Fee: £2,250 - Special Live Foal.

LORD GAYLE (B. 1965)
Sir Gaylord Turn-To
Somethingroyal
Sticky Case Court Martial
Run Honey

Winner of eight races once unplaced including William Hill Gold Cup, Mitre Stakes, Ripon Rowels, Prix Perth.

Fee: £2,500 - Special Live Foal.

CRASH COURSE (B. 1971)
Busted Crepello
Sans le Sou
Lucky Stream Persian Gulf
Kypris

Winner of five races, and placed, including Wheatsheaf Maiden Plate, March Stakes, Ascot Stakes, Top Rank Club and Doncaster Cup.

Fee: £500 - Special Live Foal.

SWEET REVENGE (Ch. 1967)
Compensation Gratitude
Shillelagh
Too Much Honey Honeyway
Honey Hill

Winner of ten races from 2 to 5 including King's Stand Stakes, Prix de l'Abbaye de Longchamp; Prix Maurice de Gheest; Champion 2 y.o. Trophy etc. and placed nine times.
Total Stakes £24,557 in England and 210,230 francs in France.

Fee: £700 - Special Live Foal.

ROYAL MATCH (Ch. 1971)
Sovereign Path Grey Sovereign
Mountain Path
Shortwood Skymaster
Go Honey

Winner of 13 races and placed 14 times out of 37 starts, including Littlewoods Spring Cup, Sandown Cup, Bessborough Stakes, London Gold Cup, Ultramar Jubilee Stakes, Great Yorkshire Handicap and Quortina Challenge Cup.
Total Stakes £44,000.

Fee: £750 - Special Live Foal.

Terms and Conditions:

The terms for all stallions include a special live foal concession. The service fee becomes payable on 15th October, 1981, unless a veterinary certificate of barrenness is produced on or before that date.

For further information and application forms APPLY The Manager
Irish National Stud Co.Ltd., Tully Kildare Telephone 045/21251/21301/21377 Telex 31770

Brindley

INDEX TO ADVERTISEMENTS

	Page
African Sky	1032
Agence Flying Fox ..	23
Ahonoora	1033
Airlie Stud ..	15, 999-1009
Air Trooper	982
Anax	1030
Artaius	1000
Ashley Heath Stud ..	993
Ashmore	1001
Ayr Racecourse	968
Balidar	1030
Ballsbridge Tattersalls Bloodstock Sales ..	36
Ray Barnes (Bloodstock) Ltd.	33
B.B.A. (Ireland) Ltd. ..	1010
Be My Guest	1012
Blakeney	1028
Bloodstock Breeders' Review 1979 ..	24
Bloodstock & General Insurance	35
Bloodstock Publications	967
British Bloodstock Agency	14, 1029-31
Brownstown Stud ..	22
Busted	983
Bustino	1030
Captain James	1013
Catoctin/Gilltown	I/Front Cover
Chester Racecourse ..	970
Condorcet	984
Connaught	1027
Coolmore ..	1011-1026
Coral Racing	5
Corvaro	1030
Crash Course	1033
Crofter	1014
Curragh Bloodstock Agency	3
Dance In Time	985
Dominion	986
Double Form	1002
Dragonara Palace ..	1030
Ela-Mana-Mou	1003
The European Racehorse	10
Fair Season	1030
P. T. Fawcett Ltd. ..	973
Final Straw ..	987, 1028
Dan Flynn Ltd.	1036
Fordham	1015
Formidable	988
Keith Freeman & Partners	20
Free State	1030
Furry Glen	989
Gay Fandango	1016
Gilbey Racing Ltd. ..	904
Gilltown Stud	I/Front Cover
Giolla Mear	1032
Godswalk	1017
Goffs Bloodstock Sales ..	42
Great Nephew	1030
Grundy	990, 1028
Gunner B	1030
Habat	991
Habitat	1004
Haydock Park Racecourse	975
Heathorns	11
Hello Gorgeous	1018
High Top	1030
William Hill Organization	O/Back Cover
Hittite Glory	1030
Home Guard	1019
Homing	1028
Hot Grove	1030
Ile de Bourbon	1030
Imperial Fling	992
The Irish Field	950
Irish National Stud	1032-3
Julio Mariner ..	993, 1030
Junius	1010
Kala Shikari	1005

	Page
Kerr & Co. Ltd. ..	912
Kris	994
Ladbrokes	I/Back Cover
Le Moss	995, 1010
Lombard	1030
London Bells	1020
Lord Gayle	1033
Lucky Wednesday ..	1030
Malinowski	1032
Manado	1006
Mansingh	1030
Robin McEnery	909
Mecca Bookmakers ..	6
Mill Reef	1028, 1030
Mummys Pet	1030
Music Maestro	1030
The National Stud ..	1028
New Zealand Blood-Horse	13
Niniski	1030
Nonoalco	1007
Northern Baby	1008
Northfields	1021
Nureyev	1030
Octavo	1010
On Your Mark ..	1010
Orange Bay	996
Owners Magazine ..	34
Pacemaker	8
Penfold Bloodstock ..	911
Philip Cornes	977
Pitskelly	1010
Porto Bello	1030
Posse	997
PTS Racing Ltd.	7
Pyjama Hunt	1031
Racehorses of 1981 ..	959
Radetzky	1031
Raise You Ten	1010

	Page
Record Token	1031
Red Alert	1022
Reform	1031
Relkino	1031
Riboboy	1031
Royal Match	1332
Royal Palace	1028
Royalty	1031
Sagaro	1028
Sallust	1032
Sandy Creek	1023
Saritamer	1031
Scorpio	1031
Shirley Heights	1031
Societe d'Encouragement	918
Sporting Chronicle ..	4
Sporting Life	2
Stallion Review ..	24
Star Appeal ..	1028, 1031
Statistical Record ..	951
Sweet Revenge	1033
Swing Easy	1031
Tattersalls	9
Tepukei	1032
Thatch	1024
Thatching	1025
Tote	16
Tower Walk	1031
Town Crier	1031
Try My Best	1026
Tug of War	1032
Tumble Wind	1009
Ward Hill	12
Welsh Pageant ..	1027
Whitstead	1031
Windjammer	1031
Wolverlife	1010
Woodditton Stud ..	1027
York Racecourse ..	979
Young Generation ..	998

Whatever your betting requirements, you can always count on, Immediate acceptance, Courtesy, Promptness of payment. Plus the privacy you expect from your Banker

Open a Credit Account now

Speak to
Alf Johnstone,
"Tattersall's Rails"
or 'phone . . .

041-332 2861

Dan Flynn

1 Lynedoch Street, Glasgow, G3.